» » *The American Literary Record* « «

» » « «

THE AMERICAN LITERARY RECORD

Edited by

WILLARD THORP, professor of english, princeton university

CARLOS BAKER, professor of english, princeton university

JAMES K. FOLSOM, instructor of english, yale university

MERLE CURTI, professor of history, university of wisconsin

J. B. LIPPINCOTT COMPANY
CHICAGO PHILADELPHIA NEW YORK

FOREWORD

FOR JUST TWENTY years, this anthology, in a different form and under another title,[1] has been used by hundreds of teachers and thousands of college students. When it appeared in 1941 it was linked to a companion volume,[2] the compiling and editing of which was largely the work of Professor Merle Curti. At the time it seemed to the editors of both volumes that American literature was being taught in a too narrowly belletristic fashion, disconnected from the issues which had helped to shape it. The success of the twin anthologies suggests that there was a need for them and that the editors' diagnosis of the situation was correct.

But methods of instruction have changed under the pressure of the times. Teachers of American literature pay more attention to American history than they once did. And American historians take account of literary as well as political and economic "documents." Since both anthologies needed to be revised again, the time seemed propitious for separating them and permitting each to make its way by itself.

The revisions required in the present volume after twenty years (some revisions were made in 1954) were considerable. In two instances new texts were needed, and permission to use them was granted: the Max Farrand text of Franklin's *Autobiography* and the Thomas H. Johnson text of the Emily Dickinson poems. The selections from the poetry of Ezra Pound, T. S. Eliot, and Wallace Stevens have been increased. Short stories by Willa Cather, F. Scott Fitzgerald, Katherine Anne Porter, and Flannery O'Connor have been added. The readings in criticism have been expanded by the addition of essays by Edmund Wilson, H. L. Mencken, and Lionel Trilling. A group of selections which attempt to define the American character has been included. The volume now concludes with a "Supplementary Reading List," supplementary, that is, to the bibliographies attached to the biographical introductions. The bibliographies have been revised and brought up to date. In the older introductions changes have been made in places where error had crept in or where new information has come to light.

[1] *American Issues: The Literary Record*, J. B. Lippincott Company, Chicago, 1941, 1954. THE EDITORS
[2] *American Issues: The Social Record*, J. B. Lippincott Company, Chicago, 1941, 1944, & 1955.

ACKNOWLEDGMENTS

THE EDITORS gratefully acknowledge the kind permission of the following publishers and individuals to reprint material in this book:

Allen Tate: for "Seasons of the Soul," from *The Winter Sea*, published by the Cummington Press, 1944.
American Book Company: for "Mike Fink Beats Davy Crockett at a Shooting Match," from *Native American Humor*, edited by Walter Blair.
R. P. Blackmur: for "The Enabling Act of Criticism."
Albert & Charles Boni: for "Chickamauga," from *In the Midst of Life*, by Ambrose Bierce.
Brandt & Brandt: for selections from *U.S.A.*, published by Harcourt, Brace and Company, copyright, 1930, 1932, 1933, 1934, 1935, 1936, 1937 by John Dos Passos.
L. W. Chappell: for "John Henry," from *John Henry: A Folklore Study*.
Columbia University Press: for "Barbary Ellen," from *A Song Catcher in Southern Mountains*, by Dorothy Scarborough.

v

ACKNOWLEDGMENTS

Constable & Company, Limited: for "Materialism and Idealism in The United States," from *Character and Opinion in The United States*, by George Santayana.

Doubleday, Doran and Company: for selections from *A Deal in Wheat*, by Frank Norris, copyright, 1903, 1931, and from *Leaves of Grass*, by Walt Whitman, copyright, 1924, by Doubleday, Doran and Company, Inc.

Farrar & Rinehart, Inc.: for "Speech to Those Who Say Comrade," "The Lost Speakers," " 'Dover Beach'—A Note to That Poem," and two selections from "The Woman on the Stair," from *Public Speech*, Poems by Archibald MacLeish, copyright 1936.

Hamlin Garland: for "Mrs. Ripley's Trip," from *Main Travelled Roads*, published by Harper & Brothers.

Harcourt, Brace and Company: for "The Love Song of J. Alfred Prufrock," "Gerontion," "The Hollow Men," from *Collected Poems of T. S. Eliot;* for "Tradition and the Individual Talent," and "Second Thoughts about Humanism," from *Selected Essays of T. S. Eliot;* for a selection from "Religion and Literature," *Essays, Ancient and Modern*, by T. S. Eliot; and for a selection from *The People, Yes*, by Carl Sandburg.

Harper & Brothers: for "The Man That Corrupted Hadleyburg," from *The Man That Corrupted Hadleyburg*, by Mark Twain; and for "Whittier Birthday Speech," from Appendix O of *Mark Twain, A Biography*, by A. B. Paine.

Lucien Harris: for "Death and the Negro Man" and "Brother Rabbit's Money Mint," from *Uncle Remus and His Friends*, by Joel Chandler Harris.

The Belknap Press of Harvard University Press: for "There's a certain Slant of light," "Wild Nights—Wild Nights," "I cannot live with You," "Of all the Souls that stand create," "Not with a Club, the Heart," "The Soul selects her own Society," "Let me not mar that perfect Dream," "My life closed twice before its close," "I hav'nt told my garden yet," "Because I could not stop for Death," "Safe in their Alabaster Chambers," "A Bird came down the Walk," "The Spider as an Artist," "Lightly stepped a yellow star," "A Route of Evanescence," "He preached upon 'Breadth'," "Elysium is as far as to," "It was not Death," from *The Poems of Emily Dickinson*, edited by Thomas H. Johnson, Copyright 1951, 1955, by The President and Fellows of Harvard College.

Henry Holt and Company: for "My November Guest," "A Late Walk," "Storm Fear," "The Code," "The Woodpile," "An Old Man's Winter Night," "Birches," "The Cow in Apple Time," "Out, Out—," "The Need of Being Versed in Country Things," "The Runaway," "Stopping by Woods on a Snowy Evening," "A Soldier," "A Lone Striker," and "A Blue Ribbon at Amesbury," from *Collected Poems, 1939*, by Robert Frost; and for "Graves," from *Chicago Poems*, and "Three Pieces on the Smoke of Autumn," "Memoir of a Proud Boy," and "Cool Tombs," from *Cornhuskers*, by Carl Sandburg.

Houghton Mifflin Company: for "The Only Rose," from *The Life of Nancy*, by Sarah Orne Jewett; for "You, Andrew Marvell," "Invocation to the Social Muse," and "Lines for an Interment," from *Poems, 1924–1933*, and a selection from "American Letter," by Archibald MacLeish; and for selections from William Bradford's *History of the Plimmoth Plantation*.

Miss Mildred Howells: for chapters 2 and 3 from *A Traveller from Altruria*, by William Dean Howells, copyright 1894 by Harper & Brothers, copyright 1921 by Mildred Howells and John Mead Howells.

Alfred A. Knopf, Inc.: for "The Open Boat," reprinted from *The Open Boat and Other Tales of Adventure*, by Stephen Crane, by permission of and special arrangement with Alfred A. Knopf, Inc., authorized publishers; for "Dead Boy," "Judith of Bethulia," "Two in August," and "Man Without a Sense of Direction," from *Selected Poems*, by John Crowe Ransom; for "The Emperor of Ice Cream," from *Harmonium*, by Wallace Stevens; for "Mrs. Alfred Uruguay," from *Parts of a World*, by Wallace Stevens; for "On the Trip Around the World," "The Poem Goes From the Poets Gibberish," from *Notes Toward A Supreme Fiction*, by Wallace Stevens; for "Bantams in Pine-Woods," "Anglais Mort a Florence," "A Postcard from The Volcano," "Study of Two Pears," "Girl in a Nightgown," "Of Hartford in A Purple Light," "This Solitude of Cataracts," and "The River of Rivers in Connecticut," by Wallace Stevens; for Neighbor Rosicky," from *Obscure Destinies*, by Willa Cather; and for Footnote on Criticism, from *Prejudices*, Third Series, by H. L. Mencken.

Liveright Publishing Corporation: for "Sea Poppies," "Helen," "Fragment 113," and "Oread," and "Orion Dead," from *Collected Poems of H. D. (Hilda Doolittle)*; and for "Ave Maria," "To Brooklyn Bridge," "The Dance," "The Broken Tower," and "Modern Poetry," from *Collected Poems of Hart Crane*.

John A. Lomax: for "Jesse James," from *Cowboy Songs*, 1910.

The Macmillan Company: for "Flammonde" and "The Dark House," from *Man Against the Sky*, "The Dark Hills" and "Demos," from *The Three Taverns*, and "Mr. Flood's Party," from *Avon's Harvest*, by Edwin Arlington Robinson; for "The Eagle That Is Forgotten," "General William Booth," and "The Congo," from *Collected Poems*, by Vachel Lindsay; and for "Part of a Novel, Part of a Poem, Part of a Play" and "Black Earth," from *Selected Poems*, by Marianne Moore; "What are Years?" from *What Are Years?* by Marianne Moore; and "In Distrust of Merits," from *Nevertheless*, by Marianne Moore.

Edgar Lee Masters: for "Ollie McGee," "Fletcher McGee," "Hare Drummer," "Conrad Siever," "A. D. Blood," "The Circuit Judge," "Editor Whedon," "Anne Rutledge," "Magrady Graham," "Archibald Higbie," and "Jennie M'Grew," from *Spoon River Anthology*, by Edgar Lee Masters. New Directions: for "Canto 45," from *The Cantos*, by Ezra Pound; and a selection from *Hugh Selwyn Mauberley*, by Ezra Pound.

W. W. Norton and Company; for a quotation from *Hart Crane*, by Philip Horton.

James B. Pinker & Son, London: for *The Pupil*, by Henry James.

Princeton University Press: for "A Note on Poe's Method," from *The Demon of the Absolute*, by Paul Elmer More.

G. P. Putnam's Sons: for "Tension in Poetry," from *Reason in Madness*, by Allen Tate.

Random House, Inc.: for *The Hound*, by William Faulkner, and *Emperor Jones*, by Eugene O'Neill.

The Religious Society of Friends: for certain passages from the Gummere edition of *The Journal of John Woolman*.

Random House, Inc.: for "My Grandmother," "Drug Store," and "Poet," from *Person, Place and Thing*, by Karl Shapiro; and for "Troop Train," from *V-Letter*, by Karl Shapiro.

Rockland Editions: for poems from *The Poetical Works of Edward Taylor*.

Charles Scribner's Sons: for "Haircut," from *Round Up*, by Ring Lardner; for "The Killers," from *The Fifth Column and the First Forty-nine Stories*, by Ernest Hemingway; for "The Marshes of Glynn," "Uncle Jim's Baptist Revival Hymn," and "The Symphony," from *The Poems of Sidney Lanier;* for " 'Tite Poulette," from *Old Creole Days*, by George Washington Cable; for "Two Men" and "Richard Cory," from *Children of the Night*, and "The Master," "Pasa Thalassa Thalassa," "Miniver Cheevy," and "For a Dead Lady," from *The Town Down the River*, by Edwin Arlington Robinson; for "The Mediterranean" and "To the Lacedemonians," from *Selected Poems*, by Allen Tate, and for "The Rich Boy," by F. Scott Fitzgerald. Copyright 1925, 1926 Consolidated Magazine Corporation; renewal copyright 1953, 1954 By Frances Scott Fitzgerald Lanahan. Reprinted from *All the Sad Young Men*, by F. Scott Fitzgerald with the permission of Charles Scribner's Sons.

Shapiro, Bernstein & Company: for "Casey Jones," by Eddie Newton and T. Lawrence Seibert, copyright 1909 by Eddie Newton and T. Lawrence Seibert, copyright renewed and assigned to Shapiro, Bernstein & Company, Inc.; used by permission.

Simon and Schuster: for a quotation from *Sister Carrie*, and for "Free" from *Free and Other Stories*, by Theodore Dreiser.

The Spiral Press: for selections from Michael Wigglesworth's *The Day of Doom*, edited by Professor Kenneth B. Murdock.

University of California Press: for a selection from *The Autobiography of Benjamin Franklin*, edited by Max Farrand.

University of North Carolina Press: for "Bear Cat Down in Georgia," from *Workaday Songs*, by Odum and Johnson.

viii]   ACKNOWLEDGMENTS

The Viking Press, Inc.: for "Go Down Moses" and "All God's Chillun," from *Book of American Spirituals*, by James Weldon and J. Rosamond Johnson, copyright 1925; for "The Raid," from *The Long Valley*, by John Steinbeck, copyright 1938; for "Mother," from *Winesburg, Ohio*, by Sherwood Anderson, copyright 1919 by B. W. Huebsch; and for "Freud and Literature," from *The Liberal Imagination*, by Lionel Trilling. Edmund Wilson: for "The Historical Interpretation of Literature," from *The Triple Thinkers*, revised edition published by Oxford University Press.

CONTENTS

ix

» » *The American Literary Record* « «

» »   « «

JOHN SMITH

1580–1631

CAPTAIN JOHN SMITH'S name is so thoroughly identified with Virginia that it is difficult to realize that only two years and a half of his active life were spent in the infant colony. Through his services in exploring and mapping the New England coast, he was, as one historian says, "as much a 'founder' of New England as he was of Virginia."

A Lincolnshire orphan, at nineteen Smith was a veteran fighter who had seen three years of service in the Low Countries. Before he was twenty-six, when he embarked on the Virginia voyage, he had killed Turks in Transylvania, escaped from slavery by braining his master, and sought adventure in North Africa and Ireland. These early deeds of valor he related, with a hero's proper pride but with doubtful accuracy, in the *True Travels, Adventures, and Observations of Captaine John Smith*, published in 1630.

Among the indolent gentlemen who arrived in Virginia in May, 1607, Captain Smith was conspicious for his courage, his curiosity about the new country, and his resourcefulness in meeting the difficulties of the ill-prepared expedition. Shortly after his arrival he sent to England *A True Relation of such occurences and accidents of noate as hath hapned in Virginia since the first planting of that Collony* (1608)—the first of his eight books. He left Virginia in October, 1609. Subsequently he explored New England and in 1616 published the results of his observations.

The rest of Smith's life was spent in London. In 1624 he gathered together and expanded the accounts of his voyages in *The Generall Historie of Virginia, New-England and the Summer Isles*. The famous incident of his rescue by Pocahontas is told here for the first time, sixteen years after the alleged event and ten after her marriage to John Rolfe. Many historians have questioned the story, but the best opinion now holds that it is possibly true, even though Smith does not set it down in his earlier *True Relation*.

Travels and Works of Captain John Smith, Edward Arber, ed., 2 vols., Edinburgh, 1910. (A new edition, with a biographical and critical introduction by A. G. Bradley.)

Henry Adams, "Captaine John Smith," *Historical Essays*, New York, 1891, pp. 42–79.

A. G. Bradley, *Captain John Smith*, London, 1905.

J. M. Morse, "John Smith and His Critics: A Chapter in Colonial Historiography," *Journal of Southern History*, I (May, 1935), 123–137.

Bradford Smith, *Captain John Smith, His Life and Legend*, Philadelphia, 1953.

From: THE GENERALL HISTORIE OF VIRGINIA, NEW-ENGLAND AND THE SUMMER ISLES

BOOK III, CHAPTER II

[CAPTIVITY]

. . . But our *Comædies* never endured long without a *Tragedie*; some idle exceptions being muttered against Captaine *Smith*, for not discovering the head of *Chickahamania* river, and [being] taxed by the Councell, to be too slow in so worthy an attempt. The next voyage hee proceeded so farre that with much labour by cutting of trees insunder he made his passage; but when his Barge could passe no farther, he left her in a broad bay out of danger of shot, commanding none should goe a shore till his returne: himselfe with two English and two Salvages went up higher in a Canowe; but hee was not long absent, but his men went a shore, whose want of government gave both occasion and opportunity to the Salvages to surprise one *George Cassen,* whom they slew, and much failed not to have cut of[f] the boat and all the rest.

Smith little dreaming of that accident, being got to the marshes at the rivers head, twentie myles in the desert, had his two men slaine (as is supposed) sleeping by the Canowe, whilst himselfe by fowling sought them victuall: who finding he was beset with 200. Salvages, two of them hee slew, still defending himselfe with the ayd of a Salvage his guid, whom he bound to his arme with his garters, and used him as a buckler, yet he was shot in his thigh a little, and had many arrowes that stucke in his cloathes but no great hurt, till at last they tooke him prisoner.

When this newes came to *Iames* towne, much was their sorrow for his losse, fewe expecting what ensued.

Six or seven weekes those Barbarians kept him prisoner, many strange triumphes and coniurations they made of him, yet hee so demeaned himselfe amongst them, as he not onely diverted them from surprising the Fort, but procured his owne libertie, and got himselfe and his company such estimation amongst them, that those Salvages admired him more than their owne *Quiyouckosucks.*

The manner how they used and delivered him, is as followeth.

The Salvages having drawne from *George Cassen* whether Captaine *Smith* was gone, prosecuting that opportunity they followed him with 300. bowmen, conducted by the King of *Pamaunkee,* who in divisions searching the turnings of the river, found *Robinson* and *Emry* by the fire side: those they shot full of arrowes and slew. Then finding the Captaine, as is said, that used the Salvage that was his guide as his shield (three of them being slaine and divers other so gauld) all the rest would not come neere him. Thinking thus to have returned to his boat, regarding them, as he marched, more then his way, [he] slipped up to the middle in an oasie creeke and his Salvage with him; yet durst they not come to him til being neere dead with cold, he threw away his armes. Then according to their composition they drew him

forth and led him to the fire, where his men were slaine. Diligently they chafed his benummed limbs.

He demanding for their Captaine, they shewed him *Opechankanough,* King of *Pamaunkee,* to whom he gave a round Ivory double compass Dyall. Much they marvailed at the playing of the Fly and Needle, which they could see so plainely, and yet not touch it, because of the glasse that covered them. But when he demonstrated by that Globe-like Iewell, the roundnesse of the earth, and skies, the spheare of the Sunne, Moone, and Starres, and how the Sunne did chase the night round about the world continually; the greatnesse of the Land and Sea, the diversitie of Nations, varietie of complexions, and how we were to them *Antipodes,* and many other such like matters, they all stood as amazed with admiration.

Notwithstanding, within an houre after they tyed him to a tree, and as many as could stand about him prepared to shoot him: but the King holding up the Compass in his hand, they all laid downe their Bowes and Arrowes, and in a triumphant manner led him to *Orapaks,* where he was after their manner kindly feasted, and well used.

Their order in conducting him was thus; Drawing themselves all in fyle, the King in the middest had all their Peeces and Swords borne before him. Captaine *Smith* was led after him by three great Salvages, holding him fast by each arme: and on each side six went in fyle with their Arrowes nocked.[1] But arriving at the Towne (which was but onely thirtie or fortie hunting houses made of Mats, which they remove as they please, as we our tents) all the women and children staring to behold him, the souldiers first all in fyle performed the forme of a *Bissone* [2] so well as could be; and on each flanke, officers as Serieants to see them keepe their orders. A good time they continued this exercise, and then cast themselves in a ring, dauncing in such severall Postures, and singing and yelling out such hellish notes and screeches; being strangely painted, every one his quiver of Arrowes, and at his backe a club; on his arme a Fox or an Otters skinne, or some such matter for his umbrace;[3] their heads and shoulders painted red, with Oyle and *Pocones* [4] mingled together, which Scarlet-like colour made

---

1 Fitted to the bowstring.
2 Bishion—a military formation.
3 Shield.
4 Bloodroot.

an exceeding handsome shew; his Bow in his hand, and the skinne of a Bird with her wings abroad dryed, tyed on his head, a peece of copper, a white shell, a long feather, with a small rattle growing at the tayles of their snak[e]s tyed to it, or some such like toy. All this while *Smith* and the King stood in the middest guarded, as before is said: and after three dances they all departed. *Smith* they conducted to a long house, where thirtie or fortie tall fellowes did guard him; and ere long more bread and venison was brought him then would have served twentie men. I thinke his stomacke at that time was not very good; what he left they put in baskets and tyed over his head. About midnight they set the meate againe before him, all this time not one of them would eate a bit with him, till the next morning they brought him as much more; and then did they eate all the old, and reserved the new as they had done the other, which made him thinke they would fat him to eate him. Yet in this desperate estate to defend him from the cold, one *Maocassater* brought him his gowne, in requitall of some beads and toyes *Smith* had given him at his first arrivall in *Virginia.*

Two dayes after a man would have slaine him (but that the guard prevented it) for the death of his sonne, to whom they conducted him to recover the poore man then breathing his last. *Smith* told them that at *Iames* towne he had a water would doe it, if they would let him fetch it, but they would not permit that: but made all the preparations they could to assault *Iames* towne, craving his advice; and for recompence he should have life, libertie, land, and women. In part of a Table booke he writ his minde to them at the Fort, what was intended, how they should follow that direction to affright the messengers, and without fayle send him such things as he writ for. And an Inventory with them. The difficultie and danger, he told the Salvages, of the Mines, great gunnes, and other Engins exceedingly affrighted them, yet according to his request they went to *Iames* towne, in as bitter weather as could be of frost and snow, and within three dayes returned with an answer.

But when they came to *Iame[s]* towne, seeing men sally out as he had told them they would, they fled; yet in the night they came againe to the same place where he had told them they should receive an answer, and such things as he had promised them: which they

found accordingly, and with which they returned with no small expedition, to the wonder of them all that heard it, that he could either divine, or the paper could speake.

Then they led him to the *Youthtanunds,* the *Mattapanients,* the *Payankatanks,* the *Nantaughtacunds,* and *Onawmanients* upon the rivers of *Rapahanock,* and *Patawomek;* over all those rivers, and backe againe by divers other severall Nations, to the Kings habitation at *Pamaunkee:* where they entertained him with most strange and fearefull Coniurations;

> As if neare led to hell,
> Amongst the Devils to dwell.

Not long after, early in a morning a great fire was made in a long house, and a mat spread on the one side, as on the other; on the one they caused him to sit, and all the guard went out of the house, and presently came skipping in a great grim fellow, all painted over with coale, mingled with oyle; and many Snakes and Wesels skins stuffed with mosse, and all their tayles tyed together, so as they met on the crowne of his head in a tassell; and round about the tassell was as a Coronet of feathers, the skins hanging round about his head, backe, and shoulders, and in a manner covered his face; with a hellish voyce, and a rattle in his hand. With most strange gestures and passions he began his invocation, and environed the fire with a circle of meale; which done, three more such like devils came rushing in with the like antique tricks, painted halfe blacke, halfe red: but all their eyes were painted white, and some red stroakes like Mutchato's,[5] along their cheekes: round about him those fiends daunced a pretty while, and then came in three more as ugly as the rest; with red eyes, and white stroakes over their blacke faces, at last they all sat downe right against him; three of them on the one hand of the chiefe Priest, and three on the other. Then all with their rattles began a song, which ended, the chiefe Priest layd downe five wheat cornes: then strayning his armes and hands with such violence that he sweat, and his veynes swelled, he began a short Oration: at the conclusion they all gave a short groane; and then layd down three graines more. After that, began their song againe, and then another Oration, ever laying downe so many cornes as before, till they had twice incirculed the fire; that done, they tooke a bunch of little stickes

---
[5] Moustaches.

10

20

30

40

50

prepared for that purpose, continuing still their devotion, and at the end of every song and Oration, they layd downe a sticke betwixt the divisions of Corne. Till night, neither he nor they did either eate or drinke; and then they feasted merrily, with the best provisions they could make. Three dayes they used this Ceremony; the meaning whereof they told him, was to know if he intended them well or no.

10 The circle of meale signified their Country, the circles of corne the bounds of the Sea, and the stickes his Country. They imagined the world to be flat and round, like a trencher; and they in the middest.

After this they brought him a bagge of gunpowder, which they carefully preserved till the next spring, to plant as they did their corne; because they would be acquainted with the nature of that seede.

20 *Opitchapam* the Kings brother invited him to his house, where, with as many platters of bread, foule, and wild beasts, as did environ him, he bid him wellcome; but not any of them would eate a bit with him, but put up all the remainder in Baskets.

At his returne to *Opechancanoughs,* all the Kings women, and their children, flocked about him for their parts; as a due by Custome, to be

29 merry with such fragments.

But his waking mind in hydeous dreames did oft
    see wondrous shapes,
Of bodies strange, and huge in growth, and of
    stupendious makes.

At last they brought him to *Meronocomoco,* where was *Powhatan* their Emperor. Here more than two hundred of those grim Courtiers stood wondering at him, as he had beene a monster; till *Powhatan* and his trayne had put them-

40 selves in their greatest braveries. Before a fire upon a seat like a bedsted, he sat covered with a great robe, made of *Rarowcun* skinnes, and all the tayles hanging by. On either hand did sit a young wench of 16 or 18 yeares, and along on each side the house, two rowes of men, and behind them as many women, with all their heads and shoulders painted red: many of their heads bedecked with the white downe of Birds; but every one with something:

50 and a great chayne of white beads about their necks.

At his entrance before the King, all the people gave a great shout. The Queene of *Appamatuck* was appointed to bring him water to

wash his hands, and another brought him a bunch of feathers, in stead of a Towell to dry them: having feasted him after their best barbarous manner they could, a long consultation was held, but the conclusion was, two great stones were brought before *Powhatan:* then as many as could layd hands on him, dragged him to them, and thereon laid his head, and being ready with their clubs, to beate out his braines, *Pocahontas* the Kings dearest daughter, when no intreaty could prevaile, got his head in her armes, and laid her owne upon his to save him from death: whereat the Emperour was contented he should live to make him hatchets, and her bells, beads, and copper; for they thought him aswell of all occupations as themselves. For the King himselfe will make his owne robes, shooes, bowes, arrows, pots; plant, hunt, or doe any thing so well as the rest.

They say he bore a pleasant shew,
But sure his heart was sad.
For who can pleasant be, and rest,
That lives in feare and dread:
And having life suspected, doth
It still suspected lead.

Two days after, *Powhatan* having disguised himselfe in the most fearefullest manner he could, caused Captain *Smith* to be brought forth to a great house in the woods, and there upon a mat by the fire to be left alone. Not long after from behinde a mat that divided the house, was made the most dolefullest noyse he ever heard; then *Powhatan* more like a devil then a man, with some two hundred more as blacke as himselfe, came unto him and told him now they were friends, and presently he should goe to *Iames* towne, to send him two great gunnes, and a gryndstone, for which he would give him the Country of *Capahowosick,* and for ever esteeme him as his sonne *Nantaquoud.*

So to *Iames* towne with 12 guides *Powhatan* sent him. That night they quarterd in the woods, he still expecting (as he had done all this long time of his imprisonment) every houre to be put to one death or other: for all their feasting. But almightie God (by his divine providence) had mollified the hearts of those sterne *Barbarians* with compassion. The next morning betimes they came to the Fort, where *Smith* having used the Salvages with what kindnesse he could, he shewed *Rawhunt, Powhatans* trusty servant, two demi-Culverings and a millstone to carry *Powhatan:* they found them somewhat too heavie; but when they did see him discharge them, being loaded with stones, among the boughs of a great tree loaded with Isickles, the yce and branches came so tumbling downe, that the poore Salvages ran away halfe dead with feare. But at last we regained some conference with them, and gave them such toyes; and sent to *Powhatan,* his women, and children such presents, as gave them in generall full content. . . .   1624

WILLIAM BRADFORD

1590–1657

THE SON of a prosperous Yorkshire farmer, William Bradford was at eighteen already a leader in the group of Separatists in Scrooby. He assisted them in their desperate removal to Holland in 1609, where he earned his living as a weaver. The esteem in which he was held by the Pilgrims is shown by their having elected him governor when John Carver died at Plymouth in 1621. This office he held for thirty of his thirty-six years in New England.

Bradford possessed all the qualities necessary to a pioneering effort. Capable of triumphing over unexpected difficulties in Indian relations and in the business and administrative affairs of the plantation, he had also the learning—largely self-acquired—and the piety expected of a puritan Moses. His journal shows him to have been a more tolerant man and a more skillful writer than Governor Winthrop of Massachusetts Bay. It is by far the most interesting and moving of the seventeenth-century narratives of the New England migration.

Of Plimouth Plantation, the journal, was begun shortly after Bradford's arrival in America and was finished about 1650. Though preserved in the family, it was used by the historians Morton, Hubbard, and Cotton Mather. For a time Judge Samuel Sewall had it in his charge. At the time of the Revolution it was in the Prince library of New England material lodged in the Old South Church. Apparently carried off by a British soldier in 1776, it was discovered eighty years later in the archives of the Bishop of London. After prolonged negotiations the manuscript was returned, in 1897, to the state of Massachusetts.

Of Plymouth Plantation, S. E. Morison, ed., New York, 1952.
E. F. Bradford, "Conscious Art in Bradford's History," *NEQ,* I (April, 1928), 133–157.
Bradford Smith, *Bradford of Plymouth,* Philadelphia, 1951.

» » *From:* OF PLIMMOTH PLANTATION « «

And first of the occasion and Indusments ther unto; the which that I may truly unfould, I must begine at the very roote and rise of the same. The which I shall endevor to manefest in a plaine stile; with singuler regard unto the simple trueth in all things, at least as near as my slender Judgmente can attaine the same.

THE ·4· CHAPTER [BOOK I]

Showing the reasons, and causes of their remooval

After they had lived in this citie [1] about some ·11· or ·12· years, (which is the more ob-

[1] Leyden, Holland.

servable being the whole time of that famose truce between that state and the Spaniards,) and sundrie of them were taken away by death; and many others begane to be well striken in years (the grave mistris Experience haveing taught them many things) those prudent governours with sundrie of the sagest members begane both deeply to apprehend their present dangers, and wisely to foresee the future; and thinke of timly remedy. In the agitation of their thoughts, and much discours of things hear aboute, at length they began to incline to this conclusion, of remoovall to some other place. Not out of any new fanglednes, or other shuch like giddie humor, by which men are oftentimes transported to their great hurt and danger, but for sundrie weightie and solid reasons; some of the cheefe of which I will hear breefly touch.

And first, they saw and found by experience the hardnes of the place and countrie to be shuch, as few in comparison would come to them; and fewer that would bide it out, and continew with them. For many that came to them, and many more that desired to be with them, could not endure that great labor and hard fare, with other inconveniences which they underwent and were contented with. But though they loved their persons, approved their cause, and honoured their sufferings, yet they left them, as it were weeping, as Orpah did her mother in law Naomie; or as those Romans did Cato in Utica, who desired to be excused and borne with, though they could not all be Catoes. For many, though they desired to injoye the ordinances of God in their puritie, and the libertie of the gospell with them, yet (alass) they admitted of bondage—with deanger of conscience, rather than to indure these hardships; yea, some preferred, and chose the prisons in England, rather than this libertie in Holland, with these afflictions. But it was thought that if a better, and easier place of living, could be had, it would draw many, and take away these discouragements. Yea, their pastor [2] would often say, that many of those that both wrote and preached now against them, if they were in a place, wher they might have libertie and live comfortably, they would then practise as they did.

2ly. They saw, that though the people generally, bore all these difficulties very cherfully, and with a resolute courage, being in the best, and strength of their years, yet old age began

[2] John Robinson.

to steal on many of them, (and their great and continuall labours, with other crosses, and sorrows, hastened it before the time) so as it was not only probably thought, but apparently seen, that within a few years more, they would be in danger to scatter (by necessities pressing them) or sinke under their burdens, or both. And therfore according to the devine proverb, that a wise man seeth the plague when it cometh, and hideth him selfe, Pro. 22. 3. so they like skillfull and beaten souldiers were fearfull, either to be intrapped or surrounded by their enimies, so as they should neither be able to fight nor flie. And therfor thought it better to dislodge betimes to some place of better advantage and less danger, if any shuch could be found.

3ly. Thirdly; As necessitie was a taskmaster over them, so they were forced to be shuch, not only to their servants (but in a sorte) to their dearest chilldren; the which as it did not a litle wound the tender harts of many a loving father, and mother; so it produced likwise sundrie sad and sorowfull effects. For many of their children, that were of best dispositions and gracious Inclinations; (haveing lernde to bear the yoake in their youth) and willing to bear parte of their parents burden, were (often times) so oppressed with their hevie labours, that though their minds were free and willing, yet their bodies bowed under the weight of the same, and became decreped in their early youth; the vigor of nature being consumed in the very budd as it were. But that which was more lamentable, and of all sorowes most heavie to be borne, was that many of their children, by these occasions, and the great licentiousnes of youth in that countrie, and the manifold temptations of the place, were drawne away by evill examples into extravagante and dangerous courses, getting the raines off their neks, and departing from their parents. Some became souldiers, others tooke upon them farr viages by sea; and other some worse courses, tending to dissolutnes and the danger of their soules, to the great greefe of their parents and dishonour of God. So that they saw their posteritie would be in danger to degenerate and be corrupted.

Lastly, (and which was not least) a great hope, and inward zeall they had of laying some good foundation, (or at least to make some way therunto) for the propagating, and advancing the gospell of the kingdom of Christ in those remote parts of the world; yea, though they should be but even as stepping-stones unto others for the performing of so great a work.

These, and some other like reasons, moved them to undertake this resolution of their removall; the which they afterward prosecuted with so great difficulties, as by the sequell will appeare. . . .

THE 2. BOOKE

The remainder of Anno 1620

I shall a litle returne backe and begine with a combination made by them before they came a shore, being the first foundation of their governermente in this place; occasioned partly by the discontented and mutinous speeches that some of the strangers amongst them had let fall from them in the ship; That when they came a shore they would use their owne libertie; for none had power to command them, the patente they had being for Virginia, and not for New england, which belonged to an other Government, with which the Virginia Company had nothing to doe. And partly that shuch an acte by them done (this their condition considered) might be as firme as any patent, and in some respects more sure.

The forme was as followeth.

In the name of God, Amen. We whose names are underwriten, the loyall subjects of our dread soveraigne Lord, King James, by the grace of God, of Great Britaine, Franc, and Ireland king, defender of the faith, etc.

Haveing undertaken, for the glorie of God, and advancemente of the Christian faith, and honour of our king and countrie, a voyage to plant the first colonie in the Northerne parts of Virginia, doe by these presents solemnly and mutualy in the presence of God, and one of another, covenant and combine our selves togeather into a civill body politick, for our better ordering and preservation and furtherance of the ends aforesaid; and by vertue hereof to enacte, constitute, and frame shuch just and equall lawes, ordinances, acts, constitutions, and offices, from time to time, as shall be thought most meete and convenient for the generall good of the Colonie, unto which we promise all due submission and obedience. In witnes wherof we have hereunder subscribed our names at Cap-Codd the ·11· of November, in the year of the raigne of our soveraigne lord, King James, of England, France, and Ireland, the eighteenth, and of Scotland the fiftie fourth. Anno Dom. 1620.

After this they chose, or rather confirmed, Mr. John Carver (a man godly and well approved amongst them) their Governour for that year. And after they had provided a place for their goods, or comone store, (which were long in unlading for want of boats, foulnes of the winter weather, and sickness of divers,) and begune some small cottages for their habitation, as time would admitte, they mette and consulted of lawes and orders, both for their 10 civill and military Govermente, as the necessitie of their condition did require, still adding thereunto as urgent occasion in severall times, and as cases did require.

In these hard and difficulte beginings they found some discontents and murmurings arise amongst some, and mutinous speeches and carriages in other; but they were soone quelled and overcome by the wisdome, patience, and just and equall carrage of things by the Gov- 20 [erno]r and better part, which clave faithfully togeather in the maine. But that which was most sadd and lamentable was, that in ·2· or ·3· moneths time halfe of their company dyed, espetialy in Jan: and February, being the depth of winter, and wanting houses and other comforts; being infected with the scurvie and other diseases, which this long voiage and their inacomodate condition had brought upon them; so as ther dyed some times ·2· or ·3· of a day, 30 in the aforesaid time; that of ·100· and odd persons, scarce ·50· remained. And of these in the time of most distres, ther was but ·6· or ·7· sound persons, who, to their great comendations be it spoken, spared no pains, night nor day, but with abundance of toyle and hazard of their owne health, fetched them woode, made them fires, drest them meat, made their beads, washed their lothsome cloaths, cloathed and uncloathed them; in a word, did all the 40 homly and necessarie offices for them which dainty and quesie stomacks cannot endure to hear named; and all this willingly and cherfully, without any grudging in the least, shewing herein their true love unto their freinds and bretheren. A rare example and worthy to be remembered. Tow of these ·7· were Mr. William Brewster, ther reverend Elder, and Myles Standish, ther Captein and Military comander, unto whom my selfe, and many others, were 50 much beholden in our low and sicke condition. And yet the Lord so upheld these persons, as in this generall calamity they were not at all infected either with sicknes, or lamnes. And what I have said of these, I may say of **many** others who dyed in this generall visitation, and others yet living, that whilst they had health, yea, or any strength continuing, they were not wanting to any that had need of them. And I doute not but their recompence is with the Lord. . . .

All this while the Indians came skulking about them, and would sometimes show them selves aloofe of, but when any aproached near them, they would rune away. And once they stoale away their tools wher they had been at worke, and were gone to diner. But about the ·16· of March a certaine Indian came bouldly amongst them, and spoke to them in broken English, which they could well understand, but marvelled at it. At length they understood by discourse with him, that he was not of these parts, but belonged to the eastrene parts, wher some English-ships came to fhish, with whom he was acquainted, and could name sundrie of them by their names, amongst whom he had gott his language. He became prof[i]table to them in aquainting them with many things concerning the state of the cuntry in the east-parts wher he lived, which was afterwards profitable unto them; as also of the people hear, of their names, number, and strength; of their situation and distance from this place, and who was cheefe amongst them. His name was *Samasett;* he tould them also of another Indian whose name was *Squanto,* a native of this place, who had been in England and could speake better English then him selfe. Being, after some time of entertainmente and gifts, dismist, a while after he came againe, and ·5· more with him, and they brought againe all the tooles that were stolen away before, and made way for the coming of their great Sachem, called *Massasoyt;* who, about ·4· or ·5· *days after,* came with the cheefe of his freinds and other attendance, with the aforesaid *Squanto.* With whom, after frendly entertainment, and some gifts given him, they made a peace with him (which hath now continued this ·24· years) in these terms.

·1· That neither he nor any of his, should injurie or doe hurte to any of their peopl[e].

·2· That if any of his did any hurte to any of theirs, he should send the offender, that they might punish him.

·3· That if any thing were taken away from any of theirs, he should cause it to be restored; and they should doe the like to his.

·4· If any did unjustly warr against him,

they would aide him; if any did warr against them, he should aide them.

·5· He should send to his neighbours confederates, to certifie them of this, that they might not wrong them, but might be likewise comprised in the conditions of peace.

·6· That when ther men came to them, they should leave their bows and arrows behind them. . . .

Anno Dom: ·1624·

. . . With the former letter write by Mr. Sherley,[1] there were sente sundrie objections concerning which he thus writeth. "These are the cheefe objections which they that are now returned make against you and the countrie. I pray you consider them, and answer them by the first conveniencie." These objections were made by some of those that came over on their perticuler and were returned home, as is before mentioned, and were of the same suite with those that this other letter mentions.

I shall here set them downe, with the answers then made unto them, and sent over at the returne of this ship; which did so confound the objectors, as some confessed their falte, and others deneyed what they had said, and eate their words, and some others of them have since come over againe and heere lived to convince them selves sufficiently, both in their owne and other mens judgments.

1. obj. was diversitie aboute Religion. Ans: We know no shuch matter, for here was never any controversie or opposition, either publicke or private, (to our knowledg,) since we came.

2. ob: Neglecte of familie duties, on the Lords day.

Ans. We allow no such thing, but blame it in our selves and others; and they that thus reporte it, should have shewed their Christian love the more if they had in love tould the offenders of it, rather then thus to reproach them behind their baks. But (to say no more) we wish them selves had given better example. . . .

5. obj: Many of the perticuler members of the plantation will not work for the generall.

Ans: This also is not wholy true; for though some doe it not willingly, and other not honestly, yet all doe it; and he that doth worst gets his owne foode and something besides.

---

[1] James Sherley of London was in 1623 treasurer of the New Plymouth Adventurers.

But we will not excuse them, but labour to reforme them the best we cane, or else to quitte the plantation of them.

6. ob: The water is not wholsome.

Ans: If they mean, not so wholsome as the good beere and wine in London, (which they so dearly love,) we will not dispute with them; but els, for water, it is as good as any in the world, (for ought we knowe,) and it is wholsome enough to us that can be contente therwith.

7. ob: The ground is barren and doth bear no grasse.

Ans: It is hear (as in all places) some better and some worse; and if they well consider their woods, in England they shall not find shuch grasse in them, as in their feelds and meadows. The catle find grasse, for they are as fatt as need be; we wish we had but one for every hundred that hear is grase to keep. Indeed, this objection, as some other, are ridiculous to all here which see and know the contrary.

8. ob: The fish will not take salt to keepe sweete.

Ans: This is as true as that which was written, that ther is scarce a foule to be seene or a fish to be taken. Things likly to be true in a cuntrie wher so many sayle of ships come yearly a fishing; they might as well say, there can no aile or beere in London be kept from sowering.

9. ob: Many of them are theevish and steale one from an other.

Ans: Would London had been free from that crime, then we should not have been trobled with these here; it is well knowne sundrie have smarted well for it, and so are the rest like to doe, if they be taken.

10. ob: The countrie is anoyed with foxes and wolves.

Ans: So are many other good cuntries too; but poyson, traps, and other shuch means will help to destroy them.

11. ob: The Dutch are planted nere Hudsons Bay, and are likely to overthrow the trade.

Ans: They will come and plante in these parts, also, if we and others doe not, but goe home and leave it to them. We rather commend them, then condemne them for it.

12. ob: The people are much anoyed with muskeetoes.

Ans: They are too delicate and unfitte to begine new-plantations and collonies, that cannot enduer the biting of a muskeeto; we would wish shuch to keepe at home till at least they be muskeeto proofe. Yet this place is as free as any, and experience teacheth that the more the land is tild and the woods cut downe, the fewer ther will be, and in the end scarse any at all. . . .

Anno Dom: ·1633·

. . . Mr. Roger Williams (a man godly and zealous, having many precious parts, but very unsettled in judgmente) came over first to the Massachusets, but upon some discontente left that place, and came hither, (wher he was friendly entertained, according to their poore abilitie,) and exercised his gifts amongst them, and after some time was admitted a member of the church; and his teaching well approved, for the benefite wherof I still blese God, and am thankfull to him, even for his sharpest admonitions and reproufs, so farr as they agreed with truth. He this year begane to fall into some strang opinions, and from opinion to practise; which caused some controversie betweene the church and him, and in the end some discontente on his parte, by occasion wherof he left them some thing abruptly. Yet after wards sued for his dismission to the church of Salem, which was granted, with some caution to them concerning him, and what care they ought to have of him. But he soone fell into more things ther, both to their and the goverments troble and disturbance. I shall not need to name perticulers, they are too well knowen now to all, though for a time the church here wente under some hard scensure by his occassion, from some that afterwards smarted them selves. But he is to be pitied, and prayed for, and so I shall leave the matter, and desire the Lord to shew him his errors, and reduce him into the way of truth, and give him a setled judgment and constancie in the same; for I hope he belongs to the Lord, and that he will shew him mercie. . . .

1856

THOMAS MORTON

?1575–1646

IN 1627 a burst of bacchanalian revelry at Thomas Morton's "Merry Mount," near the present Quincy, Massachusetts, scandalized the pious, hard-working settlers in the vicinity. They were perturbed not merely because "mine host" and his companions in mischief "set up a May-pole, drinking and dancing aboute it many days togeather, inviting the Indean women, for their conforts, dancing and shriking togither, (like so many fairies, or furies rather,) and worse practises." This was bad enough, but Morton had been a trouble-maker since he first arrived in New England in 1622 and he would continue to vex the godly there until he died, old and half crazy, in York, Maine, twenty years later. His neighbors were disturbed in 1627 chiefly because he traded firearms to the Indians and taught the savages their use.

Soon he would have a monopoly of the fur trade if his influence with the Indians continued. Captain Miles Standish, under orders, arrested Morton, and he was shipped to England for trial. He was soon back in New England, but this time he had to reckon with Governor Endecott of the Massachusetts Bay Colony. His house was burned and again he was sent prisoner to England. Henceforth he worked unceasingly with members of the High Church party to bring the affairs of the settlers under the direct rule of Archbishop Laud and Charles I. At the moment when he thought his schemes most likely to succeed, he published *The New English Canaan* (1637). A confused but amusing account of the resources of the region and its settlement, the book was obviously written to convict the Puritans there of contempt of the King and so accomplish their undoing.

The New English Canaan, C. F. Adams, Jr., ed., Boston, Publications of the Prince Society, 1883.

» » *From:* THE NEW ENGLISH CANAAN « «

BOOK III, CHAPTER XIV

Of the Revells of New Canaan

The Inhabitants of Pasonagessit,[1] (having translated the name of their habitation from that ancient Salvage name to Ma-re Mount, and being resolved to have the new name confirmed for a memorial to after ages,) did devise amongst themselves to have it performed in a solemne manner, with Revels and merriment after the old English custome; [they] prepared to sett up a Maypole upon the festivall day of Philip and Iacob, and therefore brewed a barrell of excellent beare and provided a case of bottles, to be spent, with other good cheare,

for all commers of that day. And because they would have it in a compleat forme, they had prepared a song fitting to the time and present occasion. And upon Mayday they brought the Maypole to the place appointed, with drumes, gunnes, pistols and other fitting instruments, for that purpose; and there erected it with the help of Salvages, that came thether of purpose to see the manner of our Revels. A goodly pine tree of 80. foote longe was reared up, with a peare of buckshorns nayled one somewhat neare unto the top of it: where it stood, as a faire sea marke for directions how to finde out the way to mine Hoste of Ma-re Mount.

And because it should more fully appeare to what end it was placed there, they had a poem in readines made, which was fixed to the Maypole, to shew the new name confirmed

[1] Mount Wollaston was named by the captain who settled the company on the shores of Quincy Bay.

upon that plantation; which, allthough it were made according to the occurrents of the time, it, being Enigmattically composed, pussilled the Seperatists most pittifully to expound it, which, (for the better information of the reader,) I have here inserted.

Rise Oedipeus, and, if thou canst, unfould
What meanes Caribdis underneath the mould,
When Scilla sollitary on the ground
(Sitting in forme of Niobe,) was found,
Till Amphitrites Darling did acquaint
Grim Neptune with the Tenor of her plaint,
And causd him send forth Triton with the sound
Of Trumpet lowd, at which the Seas were found
So full of Protean formes that the bold shore
Presented Scilla a new parramore
So stronge as Sampson and so patient
As Job himselfe, directed thus, by fate,
To comfort Scilla so unfortunate.
I doe professe, by Cupids beautious mother,
Heres Scogans choise for Scilla, and none other;
Though Scilla's sick with greife, because no signe
Can there be found of vertue masculine.
Esculapius come; I know right well
His laboure's lost when you may ring her Knell.
The fatall sisters doome none can withstand,
Nor Cithareas powre, who poynts to land
With proclamation that the first of May
At Ma-re Mount shall be kept hollyday.

The setting up of this Maypole was a lamentable spectacle to the precise seperatists, that lived at new Plimmouth. They termed it an Idoll; yea, they called it the Calfe of Horeb, and stood at defiance with the place, naming it Mount Dagon,[2] threatning to make it a woefull mount and not a merry mount.

. . . . .

CHAPTER XV

Of a great Monster supposed to be at Ma-re Mount; and the preparation made to destroy it

The Seperatists, envying the prosperity and hope of the Plantation at Ma-re Mount, (which they perceaved beganne to come forward, and to be in a good way for gaine in the Beaver trade,) conspired together against mine Host especially, (who was the owner of that Plantation,) and made up a party against him; and mustred up what aide they could, accounting of him as of a great Monster.

[2] Dagon was a god of the Philistines.

Many threatening speeches were given out both against his person and his Habitation, which they divulged should be consumed with fire: And taking advantage of the time when his company, (which seemed little to regard theire threats,) were gone up into the Inlands to trade with the Salvages for Beaver, they set upon my honest host at a place called Wessaguscus, where, by accident, they found him. The inhabitants there were in good hope of the subvertion of the plantation at Mare Mount, (which they principally aymed at;) and the rather because mine host was a man that indeavoured to advaunce the dignity of the Church of England; which they, (on the contrary part,) would laboure to vilifie with uncivile termes: enveying against the sacred booke of common prayer, and mine host that used it in a laudable manner amongst his family, as a practise of piety.

There hee would be a meanes to bring sacks to their mill, (such is the thirst after Beaver,) and helped the conspiratores to surprise mine host, (who was there all alone;) and they chardged him, (because they would seeme to have some reasonable cause against him to sett a glosse upon their mallice,) with criminall things; which indeede had beene done by such a person, but was of their conspiracy; mine host demaunded of the conspirators who it was that was author of that information, that seemed to be their ground for what they now intended. And because they answered they would not tell him, hee as peremptorily replyed, that hee would not say whether he had, or he had not done as they had bin informed.

The answere made no matter, (as it seemed,) whether it had bin negatively or affirmatively made; for they had resolved that hee should suffer, because, (as they boasted,) they were now become the greater number: they had shaked of their shackles of servitude, and were become Masters, and masterles people.

It appeares they were like beares whelpes in former time, when mine hosts plantation was of as much strength as theirs, but now, (theirs being stronger,) they, (like overgrowne beares,) seemed monsterous. In breife, mine host must indure to be their prisoner untill they could contrive it so that they might send him for England, (as they said,) there to suffer according to the merrit of the fact which they intended to father upon him; supposing, (belike,) it would proove a hainous crime.

Much rejoycing was made that they had gotten their capitall enemy, (as they concluded him;) whome they purposed to hamper in such sort that hee should not be able to uphold his plantation at Ma-re Mount.

The Conspirators sported themselves at my honest host, that meant them no hurt, and were so joccund that they feasted their bodies, and fell to tippeling as if they had obtained a
10   great prize; like the Trojans when they had the custody of Hippeus pinetree horse.

Mine host fained greefe, and could not be perswaded either to eate or drinke; because hee knew emptines would be a meanes to make him as watchfull as the Geese kept in the Roman Cappitall: whereon, the contrary part, the conspirators would be so drowsy that hee might have an opportunity to give them a slip, insteade of a tester. Six persons of the
20   conspiracy were set to watch him at Wessagus-cus: But hee kept waking; and in the dead of night, (one lying on the bed for further suerty,) up gets mine Host and got to the second dore that hee was to passe, which, not-withstanding the lock, hee got open, and shut it after him with such violence that it affrighted some of the conspirators.

The word, which was given with an alarme, was, ô he's gon, he's gon, what shall wee doe,
30   he's gon! The rest, (halfe a sleepe,) start up in a maze, and, like rames, ran theire heads one at another full butt in the darke.

Theire grande leader, Captaine Shrimp,[3] tooke on most furiously and tore his clothes for anger, to see the empty nest, and their bird gone.

The rest were eager to have torne theire haire from theire heads; but it was so short that it would give them no hold. Now Cap-
40   taine Shrimp thought in the losse of this prize, (which hee accoumpted his Master peece,) all his honor would be lost for ever.

In the meane time mine Host was got home to Ma-re Mount through the woods, eight miles round about the head of the river Monatoquit that parted the two Plantations, finding his way by the helpe of the lightening, (for it thundred as hee went terribly;) and there hee prepared powther, three pounds dried, for his
50   present imployement, and foure good gunnes for him and the two assistants left at his howse, with bullets of severall sizes, three hounderd or thereabouts, to be used if the conspirators should pursue him thether: and these two per-

sons promised theire aides in the quarrell, and confirmed that promise with health in good rosa solis.[4]

Now Captaine Shrimp, the first Captaine in the Land, (as hee supposed,) must doe some new act to repaire this losse, and, to vindicate his reputation, who had sustained blemish by this oversight, begins now to study, how to repaire or survive his honor: in this manner, callinge of Councell, they conclude.

Hee takes eight persons more to him, and, (like the nine Worthies of New Canaan,) they imbarque with preparation against Ma-re Mount, where this Monster of a man, as theire phrase was, had his denne; the whole number, had the rest not bin from home, being but seaven, would have given Captain Shrimpe, (a quondam Drummer,) such a wellcome as would have made him wish for a Drume as bigg as Diogenes tubb, that hee might have crept into it out of sight.

Now the nine Worthies are approached, and mine Host prepared: having intelligence by a Salvage, that hastened in love from Wessagus-cus to give him notice of their intent.

One of mine Hosts men prooved a craven: the other had prooved his wits to purchase a little valoure, before mine Host had observed his posture.

The nine worthies comming before the Denne of this supposed Monster, (this seaven headed hydra, as they termed him,) and began, like Don Quixote against the Windmill, to beate a parly, and to offer quarter, if mine Host would yeald; for they resolved to send him for England; and bad him lay by his armes.

But hee, (who was the Sonne of a Souldier,) having taken up armes in his just defence, re-plyed that hee would not lay by those armes, because they were so needefull at Sea, if hee should be sent over. Yet, to save the effusion of so much worthy bloud, as would have issued out of the vaynes of these 9. worthies of New Canaan, if mine Host should have played upon them out at his port holes, (for they came within danger like a flocke of wild geese, as if they had bin tayled one to another, as coults to be sold at a faier,) mine Host was content to yeelde upon quarter; and did capitulate with them in what manner it should be for more certainety, because hee knew what Captaine Shrimpe was.

Hee expressed that no violence should be offered to his person, none to his goods, nor

---

[3] Miles Standish.   [4] A cordial.

any of his Howsehold: but that hee should have his armes, and what els was requisit for the voyage: which theire Herald retornes, it was agreed upon, and should be performed.

But mine Host no sooner had set open the dore, and issued out, but instantly Captaine Shrimpe and the rest of the worthies stepped to him, layd hold of his armes, and had him downe: and so eagerly was every man bent against him, (not regarding any agreement made with such a carnall man,) that they fell upon him as if they would have eaten him: some of them were so violent that they would have a slice with scabbert, and all for haste; until an old Souldier, (of the Queenes, as the

Proverbe is,) that was there by accident, clapt his gunne under the weapons, and sharply rebuked these worthies for their unworthy practises. So the matter was taken into more deliberate consideration.

Captaine Shrimp, and the rest of the nine worthies, made themselves, (by this outragious riot,) Masters of mine Host of Ma-re Mount, and disposed of what hee had at his plantation.

This they knew, (in the eye of the Salvages,) would add to their glory, and diminish the reputation of mine honest Host; whome they practised to be ridd of upon any termes, as willingly as if hee had bin the very Hidra of the time.   1637

ANNE BRADSTREET

1612–1672

A MEMBER of the first group to come to the new Massachusetts Bay Colony, Anne Bradstreet disembarked from the *Arabella* in 1630 with her father and her husband Simon Bradstreet, who later became the Colony's governor. "I changed my condition and was marryed, and came into this country, where I found a new world and new manners, at which my heart rose," she wrote long afterwards in a literary legacy to her children. Gently born and brought up genteelly at Tattershall Castle, where her father was the Earl of Lincoln's steward, she experienced in the new land the trials of all pioneer women. In the midst of a busy life as the wife of a colonial magistrate and the mother of eight children, all of whom did her proud, she found solace in the writers she had been taught to admire as a girl.

Like many other Puritans with a literary bent, she was especially fond of Du Bartas' *La Semaine*, in the translation of Joshua Sylvester. It was unfortunate that she took the tedious Sylvester as her literary model, but even Dryden, as a boy, "thought inimitable Spenser a mean poet in comparison of Sylvester's Du Bartas." Mrs. Bradstreet's verses, which had circulated in private, were given to the public by her brother-in-law when he was in England in 1650. He acted without her knowledge; she would hardly have consented to the reference to herself on the title page as "The Tenth Muse lately sprung up in America." The bulk of the volume consists of long and very dull poems, patterned after Du Bartas, on the Four Elements, the Four Ages, the Four Seasons, the Four Monarchies. As Professor C. E. Norton remarked, "their reader readily accepts her assertion concerning them:

> And for the same I hours not few did spend,
> And weary lines, though lank, I many penn'd."

These ambitious works give little evidence of the tender and witty Anne Bradstreet of the later lyrical poems, by which she is chiefly represented here.

No other volume appeared in her lifetime, but six years after her death a second edition of the *Tenth Muse* (with a more modest title-page) was issued in Boston (1678). It contained many additional poems, notably her "Contemplations." The remainder of her work was first printed in Ellis' edition of 1867.

Oscar Wegelin, "A Checklist of Editions of the Poems of Anne Bradstreet," *American Book Collector*, IV, 15–16.
The Works of Anne Bradstreet, in Prose and Verse, J. H. Ellis, ed., Charlestown, 1867; New York, 1932.
Helen Campbell, *Anne Bradstreet and her Time*, Boston, 1891.
S. E. Morison, "Mistress Anne Bradstreet," *Builders of the Bay Colony*, Boston, 1930, pp. 320–336.

PROLOGUE

1

To sing of Wars, of Captains, and of Kings,
Of Cities founded, Common-wealths begun,
For my mean pen are too superiour things:
Or how they all, or each their dates have run
Let Poets and Historians set these forth,
My obscure Lines shall not so dim their worth.

2

But when my wondring eyes and envious heart
Great *Bartas* sugar'd lines, do but read o're
Fool I do grudg the Muses did not part
'Twixt him and me that overfluent store;   10
A *Bartas* can, do what a *Bartas* will
But simple I according to my skill.

3

From school-boyes tongue no rhet'rick we
   expect
Nor yet a sweet Consort from broken strings,
Nor perfect beauty, where's a main defect:
My foolish, broken, blemish'd Muse so sings
And this to mend, alas, no Art is able,
'Cause nature, made it so irreparable.

4

Nor can I, like that fluent sweet tongu'd Greek,
Who lisp'd at first, in future times speak plain
By Art he gladly found what he did seek   21
A full requital of his, striving pain
Art can do much, but this maxime's most sure
A weak or wounded brain admits no cure.

5

I am obnoxious to each carping tongue
Who says my hand a needle better fits,
A Poets pen all scorn I should thus wrong,
For such despite they cast on Female wits:
If what I do prove well, it won't advance,
They'l say it's stoln, or else it was by chance.   30

6

But sure the Antique Greeks were far more
   mild

Else of our Sexe, why feigned they those Nine
And poesy made, *Calliope's* own Child;
So 'mongst the rest they placed the Arts Divine,
But this weak knot, they will full soon untie,
The Greeks did nought, but play the fools and
   lye.

7

Let Greeks be Greeks, and women what they
   are
Men have precedency and still excell,
It is but vain unjustly to wage warre;
Men can do best, and women know it well
Preheminence in all and each is yours;   41
Yet grant some small acknowledgement of ours.

8

And oh ye high flown quills that soar the Skies,
And ever with your prey still catch your praise,
If e're you daigne these lowly lines your eyes
Give Thyme or Parsley wreath, I ask no bayes,
This mean and unrefined ure of mine
Will make you glistring gold, but more to shine.
   1650

CONTEMPLATIONS

1

Some time now past in the Autumnal Tide,
When *Phœbus* wanted but one hour to bed,
The trees all richly clad, yet void of pride,
Where gilded o're by his rich golden head.
Their leaves and fruits seem'd painted, but
   was true
Of green, of red, of yellow, mixed hew,
Rapt were my sences at this delectable view.

2

I wist not what to wish, yet sure thought I,
If so much excellence abide below;
How excellent is he that dwells on high?   10
Whose power and beauty by his works we
   know.
Sure he is goodness, wisdome, glory, light,
That hath this under world so richly dight:

More Heaven then Earth was here no winter
  and no night.

3

Then on a stately Oak I cast mine Eye,
Whose ruffling top the Clouds seem'd to aspire;
How long since thou wast in thine Infancy?
Thy strength, and stature, more thy years
  admire,
Hath hundred winters past since thou wast
  born?
Or thousand since thou brakest thy shell of
  horn,   20
If so, all these as nought, Eternity doth scorn.

4

Then higher on the glistering Sun I gaz'd,
Whose beams was shaded by the leavie Tree,
The more I look'd, the more I grew amaz'd,
And softly said, what glory's like to thee?
Soul of this world, this Universes Eye,
No wonder, some made thee a Deity:
Had I not better known, (alas) the same had I.

5

Thou as a Bridegroom from thy Chamber
  rushes,
And as a strong man, joyes to run a race,   30
The morn doth usher thee, with smiles and
  blushes,
The Earth reflects her glances in thy face.
Birds, insects, Animals with Vegative,
Thy heart from death and dulness doth revive:
And in the darksome womb of fruitful nature
  dive.

6

Thy swift Annual, and diurnal Course,
Thy daily streight, and yearly oblique path,
Thy pleasing fervor, and thy scorching force,
All mortals here the feeling knowledg hath.
Thy presence makes it day, thy absence
  night,   40
Quaternal Seasons caused by thy might:
Hail Creature, full of sweetness, beauty and
  delight.

7

Art thou so full of glory, that no Eye
Hath strength, thy shining Rayes once to
  behold?
And is thy splendid Throne erect so high?
As to approach it, can no earthly mould.
How full of glory then must thy Creator be?
Who gave this bright light luster unto thee:
Admir'd, ador'd for ever, be that Majesty.

8

Silent alone, where none or saw, or heard,   50
In pathless paths I lead my wandring feet,
My humble Eyes to lofty Skyes I rear'd
To sing some Song, my mazed Muse thought
  meet.
My great Creator I would magnifie,
That nature had, thus decked liberally:
But Ah, and Ah, again, my imbecility!

9

I heard the merry grashopper then sing,
The black clad Cricket, bear a second part,
They kept one tune, and plaid on the same
  string,
Seeming to glory in their little Art.   60
Shall Creatures abject, thus their voices raise?
And in their kind resound their makers praise:
Whilst I as mute, can warble forth no higher
  layes.

10

When present times look back to Ages past,
And men in being fancy those are dead,
It makes things gone perpetually to last,
And calls back moneths and years that long
  since fled
It makes a man more aged in conceit,
Then was *Methuselah,* or's grand-sire great:
While of their persons and their acts his mind
  doth treat.   70

11

Sometimes in *Eden* fair, he seems to be,
Sees glorious *Adam* there made Lord of all,
Fancyes the Apple, dangle on the Tree,
That turn'd his Sovereign to a naked thral.
Who like a miscreant's driven from that place,
To get his bread with pain, and sweat of face:
A penalty impos'd on his backsliding Race.

12

Here sits our Grandame in retired place,
And in her lap, her bloody *Cain* new born,
The weeping Imp oft looks her in the face,   80
Bewails his unknown hap, and fate forlorn;
His Mother sighs, to think of Paradise,
And how she lost her bliss, to be more wise,
Believing him that was, and is, Father of lyes.

13

Here *Cain* and *Abel* come to sacrifice,
Fruits of the Earth, and Fatlings each do bring,
On *Abels* gift the fire descends from Skies,

But no such sign on false *Cain's* offering;
With sullen hateful looks he goes his wayes.
Hath thousand thoughts to end his brothers
dayes,   90
Upon whose blood his future good he hopes
to raise.

14

There *Abel* keeps his sheep, no ill he thinks,
His brother comes, then acts his fratricide,
The Virgin Earth, of blood her first draught
drinks
But since that time she often hath been cloy'd;
The wretch with gastly face and dreadful
mind,
Thinks each he sees will serve him in his kind,
Though none on Earth but kindred near then
could he find.

15

Who fancyes not his looks now at the Barr,
His face like death, his heart with horror
fraught,   100
Nor Male-factor ever felt like warr,
When deep dispair, with wish of life hath
fought.
Branded with guilt, and crusht with treble
woes,
A Vagabond to Land of *Nod* he goes.
A City builds, that wals might him secure from
foes.

16

Who thinks not oft upon the Fathers ages.
Their long descent, how nephews sons they
saw,
The starry observations of those Sages,
And how their precepts to their sons were law,
How Adam sigh'd to see his Progeny,   110
Cloath'd all in his black sinfull Livery,
Who neither guilt, nor yet the punishment
could fly.

17

Our Life compare we with their length of
dayes
Who to the tenth of theirs doth now arrive?
And though thus short, we shorten many
wayes,
Living so little while we are alive;
In eating, drinking, sleeping, vain delight
So unawares comes on perpetual night,
And puts all pleasures vain unto eternal flight.

18

When I behold the heavens as in their
prime,   120
And then the earth (though old) stil clad in
green,
The stones and trees, insensible to time,
Nor age nor wrinkle on their front are seen;
If winter come, and greeness then do fade,
A Spring returns, and they more youthfull
made;
But Man grows old, lies down, remains where
once he's laid.

19

By birth more noble then those creatures all,
Yet seems by nature and by custome curs'd,
No sooner born, but grief and care makes fall
That state obliterate he had at first: 130
Nor youth, nor strength, nor wisdom spring
again
Nor habitations long their names retain,
But in oblivion to the final day remain.

20

Shall I then praise the heavens, the trees, the
earth
Because their beauty and their strength last
longer
Shall I wish there, or never to had birth,
Because they're bigger, and their bodyes
stronger?
Nay, they shall darken, perish, fade and dye,
And when unmade, so ever shall they lye,
But man was made for endless immor-
tality.   140

21

Under the cooling shadow of a stately Elm
Close sate I by a goodly Rivers side,
Where gliding streams the Rocks did over-
whelm;
A lonely place, with pleasures dignifi'd.
I once that lov'd the shady woods so well,
Now thought the rivers did the trees excel,
And if the sun would ever shine, there would
I dwell.

22

While on the stealing stream I fixt mine eye,
Which to the long'd for Ocean held its course,
I markt, nor crooks, nor rubs that there did
lye   150
Could hinder ought, but still augment its force:
O happy Flood, quoth I, that holds thy race

Till thou arrive at thy beloved place,
Nor is it rocks or shoals that can obstruct thy
pace

23

Nor is't enough, that thou alone may'st slide,
But hundred brooks in thy cleer waves do
meet,
So hand in hand along with thee they glide
To *Thetis* house, where all imbrace and greet:
Thou Emblem true, of what I count the best,
O could I lead my Rivolets to rest,   160
So may we press to that vast mansion, ever
blest.

24

Ye Fish which in this liquid Region 'bide,
That for each season, have your habitation,
Now salt, now fresh where you think best to
glide
To unknown coasts to give a visitation,
In Lakes and ponds, you leave your numerous
fry,
So nature taught, and yet you know not why,
You watry folk that know not your felicity.

25

Look how the wantons frisk to tast the air,
Then to the colder bottome streight they
dive,   170
Eftsoon to *Neptun's* glassie Hall repair
To see what trade they great ones there do
drive,
Who forrage o're the spacious sea-green field,
And take the trembling prey before it yield,
Whose armour is their scales, their spreading
fins their shield.

26

While musing thus with contemplation fed,
And thousand fancies buzzing in my brain,
The sweet-tongu'd Philomel percht ore my
head,
And chanted forth a most melodious strain
Which rapt me so with wonder and de-
light,   180
I judg'd my hearing better then my sight,
And wisht me wings with her a while to take
my flight.

27

O merry Bird (said I) that fears no snares,
That neither toyles nor hoards up in thy barn,
Feels no sad thoughts, nor cruciating cares

To gain more good, or shun what might thee
harm
Thy cloaths ne're wear, thy meat is every
where,
Thy bed a bough, thy drink the water cleer,
Reminds not what is past, nor whats to come
dost fear.

28

The dawning morn with songs thou dost
prevent,   190
Sets hundred notes unto thy feathered crew,
So each one tunes his pretty instrument,
And warbling out the old, begin anew,
And thus they pass their youth in summer
season,
Then follow thee into a better Region,
Where winter's never felt by that sweet airy
legion.

29

Man at the best a creature frail and vain,
In knowledg ignorant, in strength but weak,
Subject to sorrows, losses, sickness, pain,
Each storm his state, his mind, his body
break,   200
From some of these he never finds cessation,
But day or night, within, without, vexation,
Troubles from foes, from friends, from dearest,
near'st Relation.

30

And yet this sinfull creature, frail and vain,
This lump of wretchedness, of sin and sorrow,
This weather-beaten vessel wrackt with pain,
Joyes not in hope of an eternal morrow;
Nor all his losses, crosses, and vexation,
In weight, in frequency and long duration
Can make him deeply groan for that divine
Translation.   210

31

The Mariner that on smooth waves doth glide,
Sings merrily, and steers his Barque with ease,
As if he had command of wind and tide,
And now become great Master of the seas;
But suddenly a storm spoiles all the sport,
And makes him long for a more quiet port,
Which 'gainst all adverse winds may serve for
fort.

32

So he that saileth in this world of pleasure,
Feeding on sweets, that never bit of th' sowre,

That's full of friends, of honour and of
    treasure,   220
Fond fool, he takes this earth ev'n for heav'ns
    bower.
But sad affliction comes and makes him see
Here's neither honour, wealth, nor safety;
Only above is found all with security.

33

O Time the fatal wrack of mortal things,
That draws oblivions curtains over kings,
Their sumptuous monuments, men know them
    not,
Their names without a Record are forgot,
Their parts, their ports, their pomp's all laid
    in th'dust
Nor wit nor gold, nor buildings scape times
    rust;   230
But he whose name is graved in the white
    stone
Shall last and shine when all of these are
    gone.   1678

A LETTER TO HER HUSBAND, AB-SENT UPON PUBLIC EMPLOYMENT

Phœbus, make haste: the day's too long; be
    gone;
The silent night's the fittest time for moan
But stay this once, unto my suit give ear,
And tell my griefs in either Hemisphere;
And if the whirling of thy wheels don't drown'd
The woful accents of my doleful sound,
If in thy swift Carrier thou canst make stay,
I crave this boon, this Errand by the way:
Commend me to the man more lov'd than life;
Shew him the sorrows of his widdowed
    wife,   10
My dumpish thoughts, my groans, my brakish
    tears,
My sobs, my longing hopes, my doubting fears;
And if he love, how can he there abide?
My interest's more than all the world beside.
He that can tell the starrs or Ocean sand,
Or all the grass that in the Meads do stand,
The leaves in th' woods, the hail or drops of
    rain,
Or in a corn-field number every grain,
Or every mote that in the sun-shine hops,
May count my sighs and number all my
    drops.   20
Tell him the countless steps that thou dost
    trace

That once a day thy Spouse thou mayst im-
    brace;
And when thou canst not treat by loving mouth,
Thy rayes afar salute her from the south.
But for one moneth I see no day, poor soul,
Like those far scituate under the pole,
Which day by day long wait for thy arise:
O how they joy when thou dost light the skyes.
O *Phœbus*, hadst thou but thus long from
    thine
Restrain'd the beams of thy beloved shine,   30
At thy return, if so thou could'st or durst,
Behold a Chaos blacker than the first.
Tell him here's worse than a confused matter—
His little world's a fathom under water;
Nought but the fervor of his ardent beams
Hath power to dry the torrent of these streams.
Tell him I would say more, but cannot well:
Oppressed minds abruptest tales do tell.
Now post with double speed, mark what I say;
By all our loves conjure him not to stay.   40
                                            1678

TO MY DEAR AND LOVING HUSBAND

If ever two were one, then surely we.
If ever man were lov'd by wife, then thee;
If ever wife was happy in a man,
Compare with me ye women if you can.
I prize thy love more than whole Mines of
    gold,
Or all the riches that the East doth hold.
My love is such that Rivers cannot quench,
Nor ought but love from thee, give recom-
    pence.
Thy love is such I can no way repay,
The heavens reward thee manifold I pray.   10
Then while we live, in love lets so persever,
That when we live no more, we may live ever.
                                            1678

THE AUTHOR TO HER BOOK

Thou ill-form'd offspring of my feeble brain,
Who after birth did'st by my side remain,
Till snatcht from thence by friends, less wise
    then true
Who thee abroad, expos'd to publick view,
Made thee in raggs, halting to th' press to
    trudg,
Where errors were not lessened (all may judg)

At thy return my blushing was not small,
My rambling brat (in print) should mother call,
I cast thee by as one unfit for light,
Thy Visage was so irksome in my sight; 10
Yet being mine own, at length affection would
Thy blemishes amend, if so I could:
I wash'd thy face, but more defects I saw,
And rubbing off a spot, still made a flaw.
I stretcht thy joynts to make thee even feet,
Yet still thou run'st more hobling than is meet;
In better dress to trim thee was my mind,
But nought save home-spun Cloth, i' th' house I find.
In this array, 'mongst Vulgars mayst thou roam
In Criticks hands, beware thou dost not come; 20
And take thy way where yet thou art not known,
If for thy Father askt, say, thou hadst none:
And for thy Mother, she alas is poor,
Which caus'd her thus to send thee out of door.

1678

MICHAEL WIGGLESWORTH

1631-1705

WHEN HE WAS NOT "full seven years old" Michael Wigglesworth came to Massachusetts with his parents. A graduate of Harvard and a tutor there, he was settled in 1656 as minister at Malden. Though he was plagued with ill health "for some whole sevens of years" and could not preach, he carried on the Lord's work by writing a terrifying poem, intended to justify God's ways to man, which became at once a best seller. One person in twenty in New England possessed a copy of *The Day of Doom* soon after its first appearance in 1662, and edition followed edition in England and America down through the eighteenth century. Cotton Mather, preaching Wigglesworth's funeral sermon, prophesied that the poem would be read by the descendants of the Puritans "till the day itself arrive."

Wigglesworth exhibited more than the usual Puritan anxiety lest he and those committed to his care deserve the wrath to come. "Let me rather live a melancholy life all my days," he once wrote, "than by merriment run into a course of provoking my God." He had long meditated the subject of his poem—the terrors of the Judgment and the answers with which Christ will confound the presumptuous arguments of the sinner—for he records that in October, 1653, he dreamed "of the approach of that great and dreadful day of judgment; and was thereby exceedingly awakened in spirit . . . to follow God with teares and cries until he gave me some hopes of his gracious good will toward me." His imagination had dwelt so long on the subject that his poem was, for his readers, satisfyingly explicit about the order of events on the *Dies Iræ*. It possessed the further charm of being in the popular seven-stress ballad measure which had no profane or courtly connotations.

In 1662 Wigglesworth wrote "God's Controversy with New England" in which the Creator upbraids and warns the backsliders in that declining and threatened country. This poem was not printed in his lifetime. In 1670 appeared his *Meat out of the Eater, or Meditations concerning the Necessity, End, and Usefulness of Affliction unto God's Children*, a poem "tending to prepare them for, and comfort them under the Cross."

The Day of Doom, K. B. Murdock, ed., New York, 1929.
Richard Crowder, "Meat Out of the Eater," *Boston Pub. Lib. Quarterly*, XI (October, 1959), 179–192.
J. W. Dean, *Memoir of Rev. Michael Wigglesworth*, 2d. edition, Albany, 1871.
F. O. Matthiessen, "Michael Wigglesworth, a Puritan Artist," *NEQ*, I (October, 1928), 491–504.

» » *From:* THE DAY OF DOOM « «

A Prayer unto Christ
The Judge of the World

O Dearest Dread, most glorious King,
I'le of thy justest Judgments sing:
Do thou my head and heart inspire,
To Sing aright, as I desire.
Thee, thee alone I'le invocate,
For I do much abominate
To call the *Muses* to mine aid:
Which is th' Unchristian use, and trade
Of some that Christians would be thought,
And yet they worship worse than nought.   10
Oh! what a deal of Blasphemy,
And Heathenish Impiety,
In Christian Poets may be found,
Where Heathen gods with praise are Crown'd,
They make *Jehovah* to stand by,
Till *Juno, Venus, Mercury,*
With frowning *Mars,* and thundering *Jove*
Rule Earth below, and Heaven above.
But I have learnt to pray to none,
Save unto God in Christ alone.   20
Nor will I laud, no, not in jest,
That which I know God doth detest.
I reckon it a damning evil
To give Gods Praises to the Devil.
Thou, *Christ,* art he to whom I pray,
Thy Glory fain I would display.
Oh! guide me by thy sacred Sprite
So to indite, and so to write,
That I thine holy Name may praise,
And teach the Sons of men thy wayes.   30

. . .

10

No heart so bold, but now grows cold
  and almost dead with fear:
No eye so dry, but now can cry,
  and pour out many a tear.
Earths Potentates and pow'rful States,
  Captains and Men of Might
Are quite abasht, their courage dasht
  at this most dreadful sight.

11

Mean men lament, great men do rent
  their Robes, and tear their hair: 40
They do not spare their flesh to tear
  through horrible despair.

All Kindreds wail: all hearts do fail:
  horror the world doth fill
With weeping eyes, and loud out-cries,
  yet knows not how to kill.

12

Some hide themselves in Caves and Delves,
  in places under ground:
Some rashly leap into the Deap
  to scape by being drown'd: 50
Some to the Rocks (O sensless blocks!)
  And woody Mountains run,
That there they might this fearful sight,
  and dreaded Presence shun.

13

In vain do they to Mountains say,
  Fall on us, and us hide
From Judges ire, more hot than fire,
  for who may it abide?
No hiding place can from his Face,
  sinners at all conceal,   60
Whose flaming Eyes hid things doth 'spy,
  and darkest things reveal.

14

The Judge draws nigh, exalted high
  upon a lofty Throne,
Amidst the throng of Angels strong,
  lo, Israel's Holy One!
The excellence of whose Presence
  and awful Majesty,
Amazeth Nature, and every Creature,
  doth more than terrify.   70

15

The Mountains smoak, and Hills are shook,
  the Earth is rent and torn,
As if she should be clear dissolv'd,
  or from her Center born.
The Sea doth roar, forsakes the shore,
  and shrinks away for fear;
The wild Beasts flee into the Sea,
  so soon as he draws near.

. . .

17

Before his Throne a Trump is blown,
  Proclaiming th' Day of Doom: 80

Forthwith he cries, *Ye Dead arise,*
   and unto Judgment come.
No sooner said, but 'tis obey'd;
   Sepulchers open'd are:
Dead Bodies all rise at his call,
   and's mighty power declare.

. . . .

166

Then to the Bar, all they drew near
   Who dy'd in Infancy,
And never had or good or bad
   effected pers'nally,   90
But from the womb unto the tomb
   were straightway carried,
(Or at the last e're they transgrest)
   who thus began to plead:

167

If for our own transgression,
   or disobedience,
We here did stand at thy left-hand
   just were the Recompence:
But *Adam's* guilt our souls hath spilt,
   his fault is charg'd on us;   100
And that alone hath overthrown
   and utterly undone us.

168

Not we, but he, ate of the Tree,
   whose fruit was interdicted:
Yet on us all of his sad Fall,
   the punishment's inflicted.
How could we sin that had not been,
   or how is his sin our,
Without consent, which to prevent,
   we never had a pow'r?   110

169

O great Creator, why was our Nature
   depraved and forlorn?
Why so defil'd and made so vild
   whilst we were yet unborn?
If it be just, and needs we must
   transgressors reck'ned be,
Thy Mercy, Lord, to us afford,
   which sinners hath set free.

170

Behold we see *Adam* set free,
   and sav'd from his trespass,   120
Whose sinful Fall hath spilt us all,
   and brought us to this pass.

Canst thou deny us once to try,
   or Grace to us to tender,
When he finds grace before thy face,
   that was the chief offender?

171

Then answered the Judge most dread,
   God doth such doom forbid,
That men should die eternally
   for what they never did.   130
But what you call old *Adam's* Fall,
   and only his Trespass,
You call amiss to call it his,
   both his and yours it was.

172

He was design'd of all Mankind
   to be a publick Head,
A common Root, whence all should shoot,
   and stood in all their stead.
He stood and fell, did ill or well,
   not for himself alone,   140
But for you all, who now his Fall
   and trespass would disown.

173

If he had stood, then all his brood
   had been established
In Gods true love, never to move,
   nor once awry to tread:
Then all his Race, my Father's Grace,
   should have enjoy'd for ever,
And wicked Sprights by subtile sleights
   could them have harmed never.   150

174

Would you have griev'd to have receiv'd
   through *Adam* so much good,
As had been your for evermore,
   if he at first had stood?
Would you have said, we ne'r obey'd,
   nor did thy Laws regard;
It ill befits with benefits,
   us, Lord, to so reward?

175

Since then to share in his welfare,
   you could have been content,   160
You may with reason share in his treason,
   and in the punishment.
Hence you were born in state forlorn,
   with Natures so depraved;
Death was your due, because that you
   had thus your selves behaved.

176

You think if we had been as he,
  whom God did so betrust,
We to our cost would ne'er have lost
  all for a paltry Lust.   170
Had you been made in *Adam's* stead,
  you would like things have wrought,
And so into the self-same wo,
  yourselves and yours have brought.

177

I may deny you once to try,
  or Grace to you to tender,
Though he finds Grace before my face
  who was the chief offender;
Else should my Grace cease to be Grace;
  for it would not be free,   180
If to release whom I should please
  I have no libertee.

178

If upon one what's due to none
  I frankly shall bestow,
And on the rest shall not think best
  compassions skirt to throw,
Whom injure I? will you envy
  and grudge at others' weal?
Or me accuse, who do refuse
  your selves to help and heal?   190

179

Am I alone of what's my own,
  no Master or no Lord?
And if I am, how can you claim
  what I to some afford?
Will you demand Grace at my hand,
  and challenge what is mine?
Will you teach me whom to set free,
  and thus my Grace confine?

180

You sinners are, and such a share
  as sinners may expect,   200
Such you shall have; for I do save
  none but mine own Elect.
Yet to compare your sin with their,
  who liv'd a longer time,
I do confess yours is much less,
  though every sin's a crime.

181

A crime it is, therefore in bliss
  you may not hope to dwell;
But unto you I shall allow
  the easiest room in Hell.   210
The glorious King thus answering,
  they cease, and plead no longer:
Their Consciences must needs confess
  his Reasons are the stronger.

182

Thus all mens Pleas the Judge with ease
  doth answer and confute,
Until that all, both great and small,
  are silenced and mute.
Vain hopes are cropt, all mouths are stopt,
  sinners have nought to say,   220
But that 'tis just, and equal most
  they should be damn'd for ay.

183

Now what remains, but that to pains
  and everlasting smart,
Christ should condemn the Sons of men,
  which is their just desert;
Oh, rueful plights of sinful wights!
  Oh wretches all forlorn:
'T had happy been they ne're had seen
  the Sun, or not been born. . . .   230
                                        1662

EDWARD TAYLOR

?1642–1729

WHEN the Rev. Edward Taylor, first pastor of the church in Westfield, Massachusetts, died in 1729 he left to his son-in-law a four-hundred-page manuscript volume of his poetry, with the injunction that the poems were never to be published. Not until 1937 were any of them printed. Two years later Dr. T. H. Johnson brought out a carefully annotated volume of selections. Those who have read his verses are certain that Taylor is without question the finest poet of colonial America.

Born in Leicestershire, he had come to Boston in 1668, bringing with him letters to eminent New Englanders. The Rev. Increase Mather and John Hull, the wealthy mint-master, entertained him. President Chauncy of Harvard kept him for the night when he called. As he and Elnathan, the president's son were going to bed, a "white-[s]peckled dove pigeon" flew into the room and sat on the casement of the window. "The President, when he heard it, said he would not (of any good) he should be hurt, for one should not hear of the like; it was ominous surely." Possibly the President had a premonition that this was the Spirit, invoked by Milton in writing *Paradise Lost*, which "dove-like sat, and brooding on the vast Abyss," at the Creation. At any rate he promptly admitted the charming young Englishman to the college the next day. When the congregation at Westfield called Taylor soon after his graduation, President Chauncy reluctantly let him leave.

Almost all of the poems of Taylor are contained in two groups. The first is a long poem on election, reprobation, free grace, and church fellowship, bearing the title *Gods Determinations Touching His Elect: and the Elects Combat in their Conversion, and Coming up to God in Christ: Together with the Comfortable Effects Thereof*. Through a series of lyrics and dialogues which present the soul's effort to escape from the taunts of Satan, the poem rises, in the last seven lyrics, to a controlled ecstasy surpassed by few English religious poets. The other group of poems consists of two hundred and seventeen "Sacramental Meditations." These show many of the characteristics of the metaphysical poets. Personal and intense, making use of shocking images and homely words, they are also logical in structure, in some instances even syllogistic. Taylor has the power, possessed by the best metaphysical poets, of establishing a tension within his poem by compelling incongruities to merge with the argument and the dominant image.

How did it happen that this ministerial poet, living on the Massachusetts frontier from 1671 to 1729, wrote like a Puritan Donne? The only volume of verse in his library was Anne Bradstreet's *Several Poems* of 1678. Probably, as has been suggested, his taste was already formed when he came to Boston. Herbert he had almost certainly read, for the "Meditations" show striking metrical similarities to the poems of *The Temple*. But is there any need to seek for masters and influences? Given his passionate, direct way of speaking to God, his logical mind, and his Elizabethan love of sense-striking words, how could he have been anything but a metaphysical poet?

The Poems of Edward Taylor, Donald E. Stanford, ed., New Haven, 1960.
"Diary of Edward Taylor," *Proceedings of the Massachusetts Historical Society*, XVIII, pp. 4–18.
T. H. Johnson, "Edward Taylor: A Puritan 'Sacred Poet,' " *New England Quarterly*, X (June, 1937), 290–322.

» » UPON WEDLOCK AND DEATH OF CHILDREN [1] « «

A Curious Knot God made in Paradise,
  And drew it out inamled neatly Fresh.
It was the True-Love Knot, more sweet than spice,
  And set with all the flowres of Graces dress.
Its Weddens [2] Knot, that ne're can be un-ti'de:
No Alexanders Sword can it divide.

The slips here planted, gay and glorious grow:

Unless an Hellish breath do sindge their Plumes.
Here Primrose, Cowslips, Roses, Lilies blow,
  With Violets and Pinkes that voide perfumes: 10
Whose beautious leaves are lac'd with Hony Dew,
And Chanting birds Chirp out Sweet Musick true.

When in this Knot I planted was, my Stock
Soon knotted, and a manly flower out brake.

[1] The poem was apparently written in the 1680's when two of his children died.
[2] Weddings.

And after it my branch again did knot:
Brought out another Flowre: its sweet
breath'd mate.
One knot gave tother and tothers place;
Thence Checkling ³ Smiles fought in each
others face.

But oh! a glorious hand from glory came,
Guarded with Angells, soon did Crop this
flowre,   20
Which almost tore the root up of the same,
At that unlookt for, Dolesome, darksome
houre.
In Pray're to Christ perfum'de it did ascend,
And Angells bright did it to heaven tend.

But pausing on't this Sweet perfum'd my
thought,
Christ would in Glory have a Flowre,
Choice, Prime.
And having Choice, chose this my branch
forth brought.

³ Chuckling.

Lord, take! I thanke thee, thou takst ought
of mine;
It is my pledg in glory; part of mee
Is now in it, Lord, glorifi'de with thee.   30

But praying o're my branch, my branch did
sprout,
And bore another manly flower, and gay,
And after that another, sweet brake out,
The which the former hand soon got away.
But oh! the torture, Vomit, screechings,
groans:
And six weeks fever would pierce hearts like
stones.

Griefe o're doth flow: and nature fault would
finde
Were not thy Will my Spell, Charm, Joy, and
Gem:
That as I said, I say, take, Lord, they're thine:
I piecemeale pass to Glory bright in them.
I joy, may I sweet Flowers for Glory breed,
Whether thou getst them green, or lets them
seed.   42
1937

» » From: SACRAMENTAL MEDITATIONS « «

MEDITATION ONE

What Love is this of thine, that Cannot bee
In thine Infinity, O Lord, Confide,
Unless it in thy very Person see
Infinity and Finity Conjoyn'd?
What! hath thy Godhead, as not satisfi'de,
Marri'de our Manhood, making it its Bride?

Oh, Matchless Love! Filling Heaven to the
brim!
O'rerunning it: all running o're beside
This World! Nay, Overflowing Hell, wherein
For thine Elect, there rose a mighty Tide!
That there our Veans might through thy
Person bleed,   11
To quench those flames, that else would on
us feed.

Oh! that thy love might overflow my Heart!
To fire the same with Love: for Love I
would.
But oh! my streight'ned Breast! my Lifeless
Sparke!
My Fireless Flame! What Chilly Love, and
Cold?

In measure small! In Manner Chilly! See!
Lord, blow the Coal: Thy Love Enflame in
mee.
1682   1937

THE EXPERIENCE

Canticles I:3: . . . thy name is as ointment poured forth.

Oh! that I always breath'd in such an aire
As I suck't in, feeding on sweet Content!
Disht up unto my Soul ev'n in that pray're
Pour'de out to God over last Sacrament.
What Beam of Light wrapt up my sight to
finde
Me neerer God than ere Came in my minde?

Most strange it was! But yet more strange that
shine
Which fill'd my Soul then to the brim to spy
My nature with thy Nature all Divine
Together joyn'd in Him that's Thou, and I.
Flesh of my Flesh, Bone of my Bone: there's
run   11
Thy Godhead and my Manhood in thy Son.

Oh! that that Flame which thou didst on me
    Cast
Might me enflame, and Lighten ery where.
Then Heaven to me would be less at last,
    So much of heaven I should have while here.
Oh! Sweet though Short! I'le not forget the
    same.
My neerness, Lord, to thee did me Enflame.

I'le Claim my Right: Give place ye Angells
    Bright.
Ye further from the Godhead stande than I.
My Nature is your Lord; and doth Unite   21
    Better than Yours unto the Deity.
Gods Throne is first and mine is next: to
    you
Onely the place of Waiting-men is due.

Oh! that my Heart, thy Golden Harp might bee
    Well tun'd by Glorious Grace, that e'ry
        string
Screw'd to the highest pitch, might unto thee
    All Praises wrapt in sweetest Musick bring.
I praise thee, Lord, and better praise thee
    would,
    If what I had, my heart might ever hold. 30
1682/3   1937

MEDITATION THIRTY-EIGHT

1 John 11:1: And if any man sin, we have an advocate
with the Father.

Oh! What a thing is Man? Lord, Who am I?
    That thou shouldst give him Law (Oh!
        golden Line)
To regulate his Thoughts, Words, Life thereby:
    And judge him wilt thereby too in thy time.
    A Court of Justice thou in heaven holdst,
    To try his Case while he's here housd on
        mould.

How do thy Angells lay before thine eye
    My Deeds both White and Black I dayly
        doe?
How doth thy Court thou Pannellst there them
    try?
    But flesh complains. What right for this? let's
        know!   10
    For right or wrong, I can't appeare unto't.
    And shall a sentence Pass on such a suite?

Soft; blemish not this golden Bench, or place.
    There is no Bribe, nor Colourings to hide,
Nor Pettifogger to befog the Case;
    But Justice hath her Glory here well tri'de:

Her spotless Law all spotted Cases tends;
    Without Respect or Disrespect them ends.
God's Judge himselfe, and Christ Atturny is;
    The Holy Ghost Regesterer is founde.   20
Angells the sergeants are, all Creatures kiss
    The booke, and doe as Evidence abounde.
    All Cases pass according to pure Law,
    And in the sentence is no Fret nor flaw.

What saith, my soule? Here all thy Deeds are
    tri'de.
    Is Christ thy Advocate to pleade thy Cause?
Art thou his Client? Such shall never slide.
    He never lost his Case: he pleads such Laws
    As Carry do the same, nor doth refuse
    The Vilest sinners Case that doth him
        Choose.   30

This is his Honour, not Dishonour: nay,
    No Habeas-Corpus 'gainst his Clients came;
For all their Fines his Purse doth make down
    pay.
    He Non-Suites Satan's suite or Casts the
        same.
    He'l plead thy Case, and not accept a Fee.
    He'l plead Sub Forma Pauperis for thee.

My Case is bad. Lord, be my Advocate.
    My sin is red: I'me under Gods Arrest.   38
Thou hast the Hit of Pleading; plead my state.
    Although it's bad, thy Plea will make it best.
    If thou wilt plead my Case before the King,
    I'le Waggon Loads of Love and Glory bring.
1690   1937

MEDITATION FORTY-NINE

Matthew XXV:21: Enter thou into the joy of thy lord.

Lord, do away my Motes and Mountains great.
    My nut is vitiate. Its kirnell rots.
Come, kill the Worm that doth its kirnell eate.
    And strike thy sparkes within my tinderbox.
    Drill through my metall heart an hole,
        wherein
    With graces Cotters to thyselfe it pin.

A Lock of Steel upon my Soule, whose key
    The serpent keeps, I feare, doth lock my
        doore:
O pick't: and through the key-hole make thy
    way,
    And enter in, and let thy joyes run o're. 10
    My Wards are rusty, Oyle them till they trig
    Before thy golden key: thy Oyle makes glib.

Take out the Splinters of the World that stick
   Do in my heart. Friends, Honours, Riches,
   and
The Shivers in't of Hell whose venoms quick
   And firy, make it swoln and ranckling stand.
     These wound and kill: those shackle strongly
     to
     Poore knobs of Clay, my heart: hence sor-
     rows grow.

Cleanse and enlarge my kask: it is too small:
   And tartariz'd with worldly dregs dri'de
   in't.   20
It's bad mouth'd too: and though thy joyes do
   Call
     That boundless are, it ever doth them stint.
     Make me thy Chrystall Caske: those wines
     in't tun
     That in the Rivers of thy joyes do run.

Lord, make me, though suck't through a straw
   or Quill,
   Tast of the Rivers of thy joyes, some drop.
'Twill sweeten me: and all my Love distill
   Into thy glass; and me for joy make hop.
     'Twill turn my water into wine, and fill
     My Harp with Songs my Masters joyes dis-
     till.   30
1692/93   1939

MEDITATION THIRTY-THREE

Second Series

John XV:13: Greater love hath no man than this, that
a man lay down his life for his friends.

Walking, my Lord, within thy Paradise,
   I finde a Fruite, whose Beauty smites mine
   Eye,
And Taste my Tooth, that had no Core nor
   Vice:
     An Hony Sweet, that's never rotting, ly
     Under a Tree, which view'd, I knew to bee
     The Tree of Life, whose bulk's Thean-
     thropie.[4]

And looking up, I saw its boughs all bow
   With Clusters of this Fruit that it doth bring,
Nam'de Greatest Love, and well. For bulk and
   brow
     Thereof, of th' sap of Godhood-Manhood
     spring.   10
     What Love is here for kinde? What sort?
     How much?

[4] Mr. Johnson notes: "Theanthropy or theanthropism: the
union or combination of the divine and human natures."

None ever, but the Tree of Life, bore such.

Who is the Object of this Love? and in
   Whose mouth doth fall the Apple of this
   tree?
Is Man? A Sinner? Such a Wormhole thing?
     Oh! matchless Love, laid out on such as
     Hee!
     Should Gold wed Dung, should Stars wooe
     Lobster Claws,
     It would no wonder, like this Wonder, cause.

Is sinfull Man the object of this Love?
   What then doth it for this its Object doe? 20
It doth require a purging far above
     The whiteness Sope and Nitre can bestow:
     (Else Justice will its Object take away,
     Out of its bosome, and to hell't convay.)

Hence in it steps; to justice saith, I'll make
   Thee satisfaction, and my Object shine.
I'l slay my humane Nature for thy sake,
   Fil[l']d with the Worthiness of thy Divine.
     Make pay therewith. The Fruite doth sacri-
     fice   29
     The tree that bore't. This for its object dies.

An Higher round upon this golden scale
   Love cannot Climbe, than to lay down the
   Life
Of him that loves, for him belov'd to bail;
     Thereby to satisfy, and end all strife.
     Thou lay'st, my Lord, thy life down for thy
     Friend,
     And greater Love than this none can out
     send.

Then make me, Lord, thy Friend, I humbly
   pray,
   Though I thereby should be deare bought by
   thee:
Not dearer yet than others, for the pay
     Is but the same for others as for mee. 40
     If I be in thy booke, my Life shall proove
     My Love to thee; an Offering to thy Love.
1699   1939

MEDITATION ONE HUNDRED AND TWELVE

Second Series

2 Corinthians V:14: For the love of Christ constraineth us; because we thus judge, that if one died for all, then were all dead.

Oh! Good, Good, Good, my Lord. What, more
   Love yet!

Thou dy for mee! What, am I dead in thee:
What, did Deaths arrow shot at me thee hit?
  Didst slip between that flying shaft and mee?
  Didst make thyselfe Deaths marke shot at
    for mee?
  So that her Shaft shall fly no far than thee?

Didst dy for mee indeed, and in thy Death
  Take in thy Dying thus my death the Cause.
And lay I dying in thy Dying breath,
  According unto Graces Redemption Laws?
  If one did dy for all, it needs must bee   11
  That all did dy in one, and from death free.

Infinities fierce firy arrow red
  Shot from the splendid Bow of Justice bright
Did smite thee down, for thine. Thou art their
    head.
  They di'de in thee. Their death did on thee
    light.
  They di'de their Death in thee; thy Death is
    theirs;
  Hence thine is mine; thy death my trespass
    cleares.

How sweet is this: my Death lies buried
  Within thy Grave, my Lord, deep under
    ground.   20
It is unskin'd, as Carrion rotten Dead.
  For Grace's hand gave Death its deadly
    wound.

Deaths no such terrour in th' Saints blesst
    Coast,
  Its but a harmless Shade: No walking Ghost.

The Painter lies: the Bellfrey Pillars weare
  A false Effigies now of Death alas.
With empty Eyeholes, Butter teeth, bones bare
  And spraggling arms, having an Hour Glass
  In one grim paw. Th'other a Spade doth
    hold,
  To shew deaths frightfull region under
    mould.   30

Whereas its Sting is gone: its life is lost.
  Though unto Christless ones it is most Grim,
Its but a Shade to Saints whose path it Crosst:
  Or Shell or Washen face, in which she sing
  Their Bodies in her lap a Lollaboy
  And sends their Souls to sing their Masters
    joy.

Lord, let me finde Sin, Curse, and Death that
    doe
  Belong to me by [thee] slain in thy Grave.
And let thy law my clearing hence bestow,
  And from these things let me acquittance
    have.   40
  The Law suffic'de: and I discharg'd, Hence
    Sing
  Thy praise I will, over Deaths Death and
    Sin.
1712/13   1937

COTTON MATHER

1663–1728

TO HIS ENEMIES, and he had many, from royal governors and liberal ministers down to humble sinners, Cotton Mather seemed a Zeal-of-the-Land-Busy. From 1680, when he became his father's assistant at the Second Church in Boston, until his death in 1728, he battled unceasingly against the foes of orthodoxy. By the turn of the century Mather probably knew the fight would be lost, but he never gave up.

The twelve-year-old freshman at Harvard, grandson of the Rev. Richard Mather and the Rev. John Cotton and son of the Rev. Increase Mather, was destined for the pulpit. An impediment in his speech seemed likely to divert him to medicine, but he procured a happy delivery from his affliction by practicing a "dilated deliberation in speaking." During the absence of his father on a diplomatic mission to England in 1688, the young minister rose to the leadership of the Boston clergy. Henceforth the two Mathers stood together as champions of the declining theocracy.

Cotton Mather faced the world as a preacher whose mere improvised sermons were worthy to be printed, as a polemist to be feared, and as an author whose nearly five hundred works are a library in themselves. But he bore more than his share of sorrow. In his attack on the judges and the clergy for their determination to carry through the witchcraft trials, Robert Calef laid the heaviest calumnies on Mather. The office he most coveted, the presidency of Harvard College, went to an opponent. In his old age only four of his fifteen children were living, and the dearest of these, Cressy (Increase), disgraced the Mather name when "an Harlot, big with a bastard," charged him with her condition. Mather's third wife went insane. For his farsighted practice of inoculation for smallpox, he received a "fired granado" through the window, with a paper containing these words: "Cotton Mather, you Dog; Dam you; I'l enoculate you with this with a pox to you."

Five of Mather's works are remembered today: *Wonders of the Invisible World,* published in 1693 as a defense of the witchcraft trials; *Magnalia Christi Americana; or, the Ecclesiastical History of New-England* (1702); the *Essays to do Good* (1710); *The Christian Philosopher* (1721); and *Manuductio ad Ministerium* (1726). Something of their author's vigor, forthrightness, and learning entered into each of these, but the *Magnalia* is his best work. Written in a little over two years, during hours which he "might have taken use for less profitable recreations," this history proposed "to preserve and secure the Interest of Religion in the Churches of that little Country New-England . . . but also to offer the Churches of the Reformation, abroad in the World, some small Memorials, that may be serviceable unto the designs of Reformation, whereto, I believe, they are quickly to be awakened." Its seven books cover the settlement, the lives of the leaders, the "faith and order" of the New England churches, the illustrious demonstrations which Providence vouchsafed them, and the wonderful methods whereby they were delivered from their enemies.

T. J. Holmes, *Cotton Mather: A Bibliography of His Works,* Cambridge, 1940.
Magnalia Christi Americana, 2 vols., Hartford, Connecticut, 1853.
Selections from Cotton Mather (American Authors Series), K. B. Murdock, ed., New York, 1926.
The Diary of Cotton Mather, W. C. Ford, ed., *Mass. Hist. Soc.,* ser. 7, vols. VII–VIII, Boston, 1921–1922.
O. T. Beall and R. H. Shryock, *Cotton Mather, First Significant Figure in American Medicine,* Baltimore, 1954.
N. R. and L. Boas, *Cotton Mather, Keeper of the Puritan Conscience,* New York, 1928.
Perry Miller, *The New England Mind: From Colony to Province,* Cambridge, 1953.
Barrett Wendell, *Cotton Mather, the Puritan Priest,* New York (1891), 1926.

» » *From:* MAGNALIA CHRISTI AMERICANA « «

THE SECOND BOOK

CHAPTER I

Galeacius Secundus [1]

The Life of William Bradford, Esq., Governour of Plymouth Colony

§ 1. It has been a Matter of some Observation, that although *Yorkshire* be one of the largest Shires in *England,* yet, for all the *Fires*

[1] The Second Shield-bearer.

of Martyrdom which were kindled in the Days of Queen *Mary,* it afforded no more *Fuel* than one poor *Leaf;* namely, *John Leaf,* an Apprentice, who suffered for the *Doctrine* of the *Reformation* at the same Time and Stake with the Famous *John Bradford.* But when the Reign of Queen *Elizabeth* would not admit the *Reformation* of *Worship* to proceed unto those Degrees, which were proposed and pursued by no small number of the Faithful in those Days, *Yorkshire* was not the least of the Shires in *England* that afforded Suffering *Witnesses* thereunto. The *Churches* there *gathered* were quickly molested with such a raging *Persecution,* that if the Spirit of *Separation* in them did carry them unto a further *Extream* than it should have done, one blameable Cause thereof will be found in the *Extremity* of that *Persecution.* Their *Troubles* made that *Cold* Country too *Hot* for them, so that they were under a necessity to *seek* a Retreat in the *Low Countries;* and yet the watchful Malice and Fury of their Adversaries rendred it almost impossible for them to *find* what they sought. For them to leave their *Native Soil,* their *Lands* and their *Friends,* and go into a *Strange Place,* where they must hear *Forreign Language,* and live *meanly* and *hardly,* and in other Imployments than that of *Husbandry,* wherein they had been Educated, *these* must needs have been such *Discouragements* as could have been Conquered by none, save those who *sought first the Kingdom of God, and the Righteousness thereof.* But that which would have made these Discouragements the more Unconquerable unto an ordinary Faith, was the terrible Zeal of their Enemies to Guard all *Ports,* and Search all *Ships,* that none of them should be carried off. I will not relate the *sad things* of this kind, then *seen* and *felt* by this People of God; but only exemplifie those *Trials* with one short Story. Divers of this People having Hired a *Dutchman* then lying at *Hull,* to carry them over to *Holland,* he promised faithfully to take them in between *Grimsby* and *Hull;* but *they* coming to the Place a Day or Two too soon, the appearance of such a Multitude alarmed the *Officers* of the Town adjoining, who came with a great Body of *Soldiers* to seize upon them. Now it happened that one Boat full of *Men* had been carried Aboard, while the *Women* were yet in a *Bark* that lay Aground in a Creek at Low-Water. The *Dutchman* perceiving the *Storm* that was thus beginning *Ashore,* swore by the *Sacrament* that he would stay no longer for any of them; and so taking the Advantage of a Fair Wind then Blowing, he put out to *Sea* for *Zealand.* The Women thus left near *Grimsby-Common,* bereaved of their Husbands, who had been hurried from them, and forsaken of their Neighbours, of whom none durst in this Fright stay with them, were a very rueful Spectacle; some crying for *Fear,* some shaking for *Cold,* all dragg'd by Troops of *Armed* and *Angry* Men from one Justice to another, till not knowing what to do with them, they e'en dismiss'd them to shift as well as they could for themselves. But by their singular *Af-*

flictions, and by their Christian *Behaviours,* the *Cause* for which they exposed themselves did gain considerably. In the mean time, the Men at Sea found Reason to be glad that their Families were not with them, for they were surprized with an *horrible Tempest,* which held them for Fourteen Days together, in Seven whereof they saw not *Sun, Moon,* or *Star,* but were driven upon the Coast of *Norway.* The *Mariners* often despaired of Life, and once with doleful shrieks gave over all, as thinking the Vessel was Foundred: But the Vessel rose again, and when the *Mariners* with sunk Hearts often cried out, *We Sink! We Sink!* The Passengers without such Distraction of Mind, even while the Water was running into their Mouths and Ears, would chearfully Shout, *Yet Lord, thou canst save! Yet Lord, thou canst save!* And the Lord accordingly brought them at last safe unto their *Desired Haven:* And not long after helped their Distressed Relations thither after them, where indeed they found upon almost all Accounts *a new World,* but a World in which they found that they must live like *Strangers* and *Pilgrims.*

§ 2. Among those Devout People was our *William Bradford,* who was Born *Anno* 1588. in an obscure Village call'd *Austerfield,* where the People were as unacquainted with the *Bible,* as the *Jews* do seem to have been with *part* of it in the Days of *Josiah;* a most Ignorant and Licentious *People,* and *like unto their Priest.* Here, and in some other Places, he had a Comfortable *Inheritance* left him of his Honest Parents, who died while he was yet a Child, and cast him on the Education, first of his *Grand Parents,* and then of his *Uncles,* who devoted him, like his Ancestors, unto the Affairs of *Husbandry.* Soon and long Sickness kept him, as he would afterwards thankfully say, from the *Vanities of Youth,* and made him the fitter for what he was afterwards to undergo. When he was about a Dozen Years Old, the Reading of the *Scriptures* began to cause great Impressions upon him; and those Impressions were much assisted and improved, when he came to enjoy Mr. *Richard Clifton's* Illuminating Ministry, not far from his Abode; he was then also further befriended, by being brought into the Company and Fellowship of such as were then called *Professors;* though the Young Man that brought him into it, did after become a Prophane and Wicked *Apostate.* Nor could the *Wrath* of his *Uncles,* nor the *Scoff* of his *Neighbours* now turn'd upon him, as one of the

10

20

30

40

50

Puritans, divert him from his Pious Inclinations.

§ 3. At last beholding how fearfully the Evangelical and Apostolical *Church-Form,* whereinto the Churches of the *Primitive Times* were cast by the good Spirit of God, had been *Deformed* by the *Apostacy* of the *Succeeding Times;* and what little Progress the *Reformation* had yet made in many Parts of *Christendom* towards its Recovery, he set himself by Reading, by Discourse, by Prayer, to learn whether it was not his Duty to *withdraw* from the Communion of the *Parish-Assemblies,* and *engage* with some *Society* of the Faithful, that should keep close unto the *Written Word* of God, as the *Rule* of their *Worship.* And after many Distresses of Mind concerning it, he took up a very Deliberate and Understanding *Resolution* of doing so; which *Resolution* he chearfully Prosecuted, although the provoked *Rage* of his Friends tried all the ways imaginable to reclaim him from it, unto all whom his Answer was, *Were I like to endanger my Life, or consume my Estate by any ungodly Courses, your Counsels to me were very seasonable: But you know that I have been Diligent and Provident in my Calling, and not only desirous to augment what I have, but also to enjoy it in your Company; to part from which will be as great a Cross as can befal me. Nevertheless, to keep a good Conscience, and walk in such a Way as God has prescribed in his Word, is a thing which I must prefer before you all, and above Life it self. Wherefore, since 'tis for a good Cause that I am like to suffer the Disasters which you lay before me, you have no Cause to be either angry with me, or sorry for me; yea, I am not only willing to part with every thing that is dear to me in this World for this Cause, but I am also thankful that God has given me an Heart so to do, and will accept me so to suffer for him.* Some lamented him, *some* derided him, *all* disswaded him: Nevertheless the more they did it, the more fixed he was in his Purpose to seek the Ordinances of the Gospel, where they should be dispensed with most of the *Commanded Purity;* and the *sudden Deaths* of the chief Relations which thus lay at him, quickly after convinced him what a Folly it had been to have quitted his *Profession,* in Expectation of any Satisfaction from them. So to *Holland* he attempted a removal.

§ 4. Having with a great Company of Christians Hired a Ship to Transport them for *Holland,* the Master perfidiously betrayed them into the Hands of those *Persecutors,* who Rifled and Ransack'd their Goods, and clapp'd their Persons into Prison at *Boston,* where they lay for a Month together. But Mr. *Bradford* being a Young Man of about *Eighteen,* was dismissed sooner than the rest, so that within a while he had Opportunity with some others to get over to *Zealand,* through *Perils* both by *Land* and *Sea* not inconsiderable; where he was not long Ashore e're a *Viper* seized on his Hand, that is, an Officer, who carried him unto the Magistrates, unto whom an envious Passenger had accused him as having *fled* out of *England.* When the Magistrates understood the True Cause of his coming thither, they were well satisfied with him; and so he repaired joyfully unto his Brethren at *Amsterdam,* where the Difficulties to which he afterwards stooped in Learning and Serving of a *Frenchman* at the Working of *Silks,* were abundantly Compensated by the *Delight* wherewith he sat under the *Shadow* of our Lord in his purely dispensed Ordinances. At the end of Two Years, he did, being of Age to do it, convert his Estate in *England* into Money; but Setting up for himself, he found some of his Designs by the *Providence* of God frowned upon, which he judged a *Correction* bestowed by God upon him for certain Decays of *Internal Piety,* whereinto he had fallen; the *Consumption* of his *Estate* he thought came to prevent a *Consumption* in his *Virtue.* But after he had resided in *Holland* about half a Score Years, he was one of those who bore a part in that Hazardous and Generous Enterprize of removing into *New-England,* with part of the *English* Church at *Leyden,* where at their first Landing, his dearest Consort accidentally falling Overboard, was drowned in the *Harbour;* and the rest of his Days were spent in the Services, and the Temptations, of that *American Wilderness.*

§ 5. Here was Mr. *Bradford* in the Year 1621. Unanimously chosen the *Governour* of the Plantation: The Difficulties whereof were such, that if he had not been a Person of more than Ordinary Piety, Wisdom and Courage, he must have sunk under them. He had with a Laudable Industry been laying up a Treasure of *Experiences,* and he had now occasion to use it: Indeed nothing but an *Experienced* Man could have been suitable to the Necessities of the People. The Potent Nations of the *Indians,* into whose Country they were come, would have cut them off, if the Blessing of God upon *his* Conduct had not quell'd them; and if his Prudence, Justice and Moderation had not over-ruled them, they had been ruined by their own *Distempers.* One *Specimen* of his Demeanour is to this Day particularly spoken of. A Company of Young Fellows that were newly arrived, were very unwilling to comply with the Governour's Order for *Working* abroad on the Publick Account; and therefore on *Christmas-Day,* when he had called upon them, they excused themselves, with a pretence that it was against their *Conscience* to *Work* such a Day. The Governour gave them no Answer, only that he would spare them till they were better informed; but by and by he found them all at *Play* in the Street, sporting themselves with various Diversions; whereupon Commanding the Instruments of their Games to be taken from them, he effectually gave them to understand, *That it was against his Conscience that they should play whilst others were at Work; and that if they had any Devotion to the Day, they should show it at Home in the Exercises of Religion, and not in the Streets with Pastime and Frolicks;* and this gentle Reproof put a final stop to all such Disorders for the future.

§ 6. For Two Years together after the beginning of the Colony, whereof he was now Governour, the poor People had a great Experiment of *Man's not living by Bread alone;* for when they were left all together without one Morsel of *Bread* for many Months one after another, still the good Providence of God relieved them, and supplied them, and this for the most part out of the *Sea.* In this low Condition of Affairs, there was no little Exercise for the *Prudence* and *Patience* of the Governour, who chearfully bore his part in all: And that *Industry* might not flag, he quickly set himself to settle *Propriety* [2] among the New-Planters; foreseeing that while the whole Country labour'd upon a *Common Stock,* the *Husbandry* and *Business* of the Plantation could not *flourish,* as *Plato* and others long since dream'd that it would, if a *Community* were established. Certainly, if the Spirit which dwelt in the *Old Puritans,* had not inspired these *New-Planters,* they had sunk under the Burden of these Difficulties; but our *Bradford* had a *double Portion* of that Spirit.

§ 7. The Plantation was quickly thrown into a *Storm* that almost overwhelmed it, by the unhappy Actions of a Minister sent over from *England* by the *Adventurers* concerned for the Plantation; but by the Blessing of Heaven on

[2] Property.

the Conduct of the Governour, they Weathered out that *Storm.* Only the *Adventurers* hereupon breaking to pieces, threw up all their Concernments with the *Infant Colony;* whereof they gave this as one Reason, *That the Planters dissembled with His Majesty, and their Friends in their Petition, wherein they declared for a Church-Discipline, agreeing with the* French *and others of the Reforming Churches in* Europe. Whereas 'twas now urged, that they had admitted into their Communion a Person, who at his Admission utterly *renounced* the Churches of *England,* (which Person by the way, was *that* very Man who had made the Complaints against them) and therefore though they denied the *Name* of *Brownists,* yet they were the *Thing.* In Answer hereunto, the very Words written by the Governour were these; *Whereas you Tax us with dissembling about the* French *Discipline, you do us wrong, for we both hold and practice the* Discipline of the French *and other* Reformed *Churches (as they have published the same in the* Harmony of Confessions) *according to our Means, in Effect and Substance. But whereas you would tie us up to the* French Discipline *in every Circumstance, you derogate from the* Liberty *we have in Christ Jesus. The* French *may err, we may err, and other Churches may err, and doubtless do in many* Circumstances. *That Honour therefore belongs only to the* Infallible Word of God, *and* pure Testament of Christ, *to be propounded and followed as the only Rule and Pattern for Direction herein to all Churches and Christians. And it is too great Arrogancy for any Men or Church to think, that he or they have so sounded the Word of God unto the bottom, as precisely to set down the Churches Discipline without Error in Substance or Circumstance, that no other without blame may digress or differ in any thing from the same. And it is not difficult to shew that the* Reformed Churches *differ in many* Circumstances *among themselves.* By which Words it appears how far he was free from that *Rigid Spirit of Separation,* which broke to pieces the *Separatists* themselves in the *Low Countries,* unto the great Scandal of the *Reforming Churches.* He was indeed a Person of a *well-temper'd Spirit,* or else it had been scarce possible for him to have kept the Affairs of *Plymouth* in so good a

Temper for *Thirty Seven* Years together; in every one of which he was chosen their Governour, except the *Three Years,* wherein Mr. *Winslow,* and the *Two Years,* wherein Mr. *Prince,* at the choice of the People, took a *turn* with him.

§ 8. The *Leader* of a People in a *Wilderness* had need to be a *Moses;* and if a *Moses* had not led the People of *Plymouth-Colony,* when this Worthy Person was their Governour, the People had never with so much Unanimity and Importunity still called *him* to lead them. Among many Instances thereof, let this one piece of *Self denial be told for a Memorial of him, wheresoever this History shall be considered.* The Patent of the Colony was taken in *his* Name, running in these Terms, *To* William Bradford, *his Heirs, Associates and Assigns:* But when the number of the *Freemen* was much Increased, and many New *Townships* Erected, the *General Court* there desired of Mr. *Bradford,* that he would make a Surrender of the same into *their Hands,* which *he* willingly and presently assented unto, and confirmed it according to their Desire by his *Hand* and *Seal,* reserving no more for himself than was his *Proportion,* with others, by *Agreement.* But as he found the Providence of Heaven many ways *Recompencing* his many Acts of *Self-denial,* so he gave this Testimony to the Faithfulness of the Divine Promises; *That he had forsaken Friends, Houses and Lands for the sake of the Gospel, and the Lord gave them him again. Here* he prospered in his *Estate;* and besides a Worthy *Son* which he had by a former Wife, he had also Two Sons and a Daughter by another, whom he Married in this Land.

§ 9. He was a Person for *Study* as well as *Action;* and hence, notwithstanding the Difficulties through which he passed in his Youth, he attained unto a notable Skill in *Languages;* the *Dutch* Tongue was become almost as Vernacular to him as the *English;* the *French* Tongue he could also manage; the *Latin* and

the *Greek* he had Mastered; but the *Hebrew* he most of all studied, *Because,* he said, *he would see with his own Eyes the Ancient Oracles of God in their Native Beauty.* He was also well skill'd in *History,* in *Antiquity,* and in *Philosophy;* and for *Theology* he became so versed in it, that he was an *Irrefragable Disputant* against the *Errors,* especially those of *Anabaptism,* which with Trouble he saw rising in his Colony; wherefore he wrote some Significant things for the Confutation of those Errors. But the *Crown* of all was his Holy, Prayerful, Watchful and Fruitful *Walk with God,* wherein he was very Exemplary.

§ 10. At length he fell into an Indisposition of Body, which rendred him unhealthy for a whole *Winter;* and as the *Spring* advanced, his Health yet more declined; yet he felt himself not what he counted *Sick,* till one *Day;* in the *Night* after which, the God of Heaven so fill'd his Mind with *Ineffable Consolations,* that he seemed little short of *Paul,* rapt up unto the *Unutterable* Entertainments of *Paradise.* The next Morning he told his Friends, *That the good Spirit of God had given him a Pledge of his Happiness in another World, and the First-fruits of his Eternal Glory:* And on the Day following he died, *May* 9. 1657. in the 69th Year of his Age. Lamented by all the Colonies of *New-England,* as a Common Blessing and Father to them all.

O mihi si Similis Contingat Clausula Vitæ! [3]

Plato's brief Description of a *Governour,* is all that I will now leave as his Character, in an

EPITAPH

Νομεὺς Τροφός ἀγέλης ἀνθρωπίνης. [4]

MEN *are but* FLOCKS: BRADFORD *beheld their Need,*
And long did them at once both Rule and Feed.

1702

---

[3] If only a similar end of life befall me!
[4] Herdsman—feeder of his human flock.

» »   « «

SAMUEL SEWALL

1652–1730

THERE IS no other record surviving from colonial days so full of details future generations would care to know about as Samuel Sewall's diary, which he kept from December 3, 1673, until October 13, 1729. A member of the Royal Council of the Province, Judge of
the Superior Court, and from 1718 to 1728 Chief Justice, by virtue of his prestige, his wealth,
and his Puritan rectitude, he was at the center of life in Boston. Little escaped his notice, and
much that he saw he set down.

It is scarcely fair to the worthy judge to print here only the entries from his diary which
concern his autumnal courtship of Madame Winthrop, who jilted him when she was fifty-six
and he was sixty-nine—apparently because he tried to drive too hard a bargain and would not
agree to keep a coach and wear a periwig. Yet the story discloses many of his traits. Lack of
space prevents reprinting other absorbing passages which show the gradual secularization of
the colony or others which reveal Sewall's tenderness toward his children, his humane concern
for Negroes and Indians, and his constant anxiety over the state of his own soul.

Diary of Samuel Sewall, Mass. Hist. Soc. Collections, ser. 5, vols. V–VII, Boston, 1878–1882.
N. H. Chamberlain, Samuel Sewall and the World He Lived In, Boston, 1897.
H. W. Lawrence, "Samuel Sewall," So. Atlantic Quarterly, XXXIII (January, 1934), 20–37.

» » From: THE DIARY OF SAMUEL SEWALL « «

Tuesday, May, 31. [1720] Buried my dear
Wife.[1] Bearers, Col. Tailer, Bromfield; Stoddard, Davenport; Dudley, Mr. Dan[1] Oliver.
Gov[r] and L[t] Gov[r] had Scarvs and Rings. Bro[r]
heard the Funeral was not over, by the Post,
came away after 2. and was timely at the Funeral: had a Comfortable day; though threatened with Rain. Laus Deo. I went into the
Tomb: The good Lord prepare for me a House
not made with Hands, eternal in the Heavens,
and the Consideration of that will make the
Grave a Lightsom place. My Son prays in his
Sister's Chamber very pertinently, affection-
atly.

. . .

Sept[r]. 5. Mary Hirst goes to Board with
Madam Oliver and her Mother Loyd. Going
to Son Sewall's I there meet with Madam
Winthrop,[2] told her I was glad to meet her
there, had not seen her a great while; gave
her Mr. Homes's Sermon.

. . .

8[r] 1. Satterday, I dine at Mr. Stoddard's:
from thence I went to Madam Winthrop's just
at 3. Spake to her, saying, my loving wife died
so soon and suddenly, 'twas hardly convenient
for me to think of Marrying again; however I
came to this Resolution, that I would not make
my Court to any person without first Consulting with her. Had a pleasant discourse about
7 Single persons sitting in the Fore-seat 7[r]
29th, viz. Mad[m] Rebekah Dudley, Catharine
Winthrop, Bridget Usher, Deliverance Legg,
Rebekah Loyd, Lydia Colman, Elizabeth Bel-
lingham. She propounded one and another for
me; but none would do, said Mrs. Loyd was
about her Age.

Octob[r] 3. 2. Waited on Madam Winthrop
again; 'twas a little while before she came in.
Her daughter Noyes being there alone with
me, I said, I hoped my Waiting on her Mother
would not be disagreeable to her. She answer'd
she should not be against that that might be
for her Comfort. I Saluted her, and told her
I perceiv'd I must shortly wish her a good
Time; (her mother had told me, she was with
Child, and within a Moneth or two of her

1 Sewall married Hannah Hull, daughter of mint-master John
Hull, in 1678. She died in 1717. He married his second wife in 1719.
It is her death which is here referred to.
2 Madam Winthrop had been twice widowed. She never married
again.

Time). By and by in came Mr. Airs, Chaplain of the Castle, and hang'd up his Hat, which I was a little startled at, it seeming as if he was to lodge there. At last Madam Winthrop came too. After a considerable time, I went up to her and said, if it might not be inconvenient I desired to speak with her. She assented, and spake of going into another Room; but Mr. Airs and Mrs. Noyes presently rose up, and
10 went out, leaving us there alone. Then I usher'd in Discourse from the names in the Fore-seat; at last I pray'd that Katharine [Mrs. Winthrop] might be the person assign'd for me. She instantly took it up in the way of Denyal, as if she had catch'd at an Opportunity to do it, saying she could not do it before she was asked. Said that was her mind unless she should Change it, which she believed she should not; could not leave her Children. I
20 express'd my Sorrow that she should do it so Speedily, pray'd her Consideration, and ask'd her when I should wait on her agen. She setting no time, I mention'd that day Sennight. Gave her Mr. Willard's Fountain [3] open'd with the little print and verses; saying, I hop'd if we did well read that book, we should meet together hereafter, if we did not now. She took the Book, and put it in her Pocket. Took
29 Leave.

. . .

8ʳ. 6ᵗʰ. . . . A little after 6. p. m. I went to Madam Winthrop's. She was not within. I gave Sarah Chickering the Maid 2ˢ, Juno, who brought in wood, 1ˢ. Afterward the Nurse came in, I gave her 18ᵈ, having no other small Bill. After awhile Dr. Noyes came in with his Mother; and quickly after his wife came in:
40 They sat talking, I think, till eight a-clock. I said I fear'd I might be some Interruption to their Business: Dr. Noyes reply'd pleasantly: He fear'd they might be an Interruption to me, and went away. Madam seem'd to harp upon the same string. Must take care of her Children; could not leave that House and Neighbourhood where she had dwelt so long. I told her she might doe her children as much or more good by bestowing what she laid out in
50 Hous-keeping, upon them. Said her Son would be of Age the 7ᵗʰ of August. I said it might be inconvenient for her to dwell with her Daughter-in-law, who must be Mistress of the

House. I gave her a piece of Mr. Belcher's Cake and Ginger-Bread wrapped up in a clean sheet of Paper; told her of her Father's kindness to me when Treasurer, and I Constable. My Daughter Judith was gon from me and I was more lonesom—might help to forward one another in our Journey to Canaan.—Mr. Eyre came within the door; I saluted him, ask'd how Mr. Clark did, and he went away. I took leave about 9 aclock. I told [her] I came now to refresh her Memory as to Monday-night; said she had not forgot it. In discourse with her, I ask'd leave to speak with her Sister; I meant to gain Madᵐ Mico's [4] favour to persuade her Sister. She seem'd surpris'd and displeas'd, and said she was in the same condition!

. . .

8ʳ. 10ᵗʰ. . . . In the Evening I visited Madam Winthrop, who treated me with a great deal of Curtesy; Wine, Marmalade. I gave her a News-Letter about the Thanksgiving; Proposals, for sale of the verses for David Jeffries. She tells me Dr. Increase Mather visited her this day, in Mr. Hutchinson's Coach. . . .

8ʳ 11ᵗʰ I writ a few Lines to Madam Winthrop to this purpose: "Madam, These wait on you with Mr. Mayhew's Sermon,[5] and Account of the state of the Indians on Martha's Vinyard. I thank you for your Unmerited Favours of yesterday; and hope to have the Hapiness of Waiting on you to-morrow before Eight a-clock after Noon. I pray GOD to keep you, and give you a joyfull entrance upon the Two Hundred and twenty ninth year of Christopher Columbus his Discovery; and take Leave, who am, Madam, your humble Servᵗ.

S. S"

. . .

8ʳ. 12. . . . Mrs. Anne Cotton came to door (twas before 8.) said Madam Winthrop was within, directed me into the little Room, where she was full of work behind a Stand; Mrs. Cotton came in and stood. Madam Winthrop pointed to her to set me a Chair. Madam Winthrop's Countenance was much changed from what 'twas on Monday, look'd dark and lowering. At last, the work, (black stuff or Silk) was taken away, I got my Chair in place, had some Converse, but very Cold and indifferent to what 'twas before. Ask'd her to acquit me

---

[3] Samuel Willard (1640–1707), pastor of the Old South Church, and Increase Mather were at the time the two leading ministers in Boston.

[4] Mary (Brattle) Mico, widow of John Mico.
[5] Experience Mayhew was missionary to the Indians on Martha's Vineyard.

of Rudeness if I drew off her Glove. Enquiring the reason, I told her twas great odds between handling a dead Goat, and a living Lady. Got it off. I told her I had one Petition to ask of her, that was, that she would take off the Negative she laid on me the third of October; She readily answer'd she could not, and enlarg'd upon it; She told me of it so soon as she could; could not leave her house, children, neighbours, business. I told her she might do som Good to help and suport me. Mentioning Mrs. Gookin, Nath, the widow Weld was spoken of; said I had visited Mrs. Denison. I told her Yes! Afterward I said, If after a first and second Vagary she would Accept of me returning, Her Victorious Kindness and Good Will would be very Obliging. She thank'd me for my Book, (Mr. Mayhew's Sermon), But said not a word of the Letter. When she insisted on the Negative, I pray'd there might be no more Thunder and Lightening, I should not sleep all night. I gave her Dr. Preston, The Church's Marriage and the Church's Carriage, which cost me 6ˢ at the Sale. The door standing open, Mr. Airs came in, hung up his Hat, and sat down. After awhile, Madam Winthrop moving, he went out. Jnᵒ Eyre look'd in, I said How do ye, or, your servant Mr. Eyre: but heard no word from him. Sarah fill'd a Glass of Wine, she drank to me, I to her, She sent Juno home with me with a good Lantern, I gave her 6ᵈ and bid her thank her Mistress. In some of our Discourse, I told her I had rather go to the Stone-House adjoining to her, than to come to her against her mind. Told her the reason why I came every other night was lest I should drink too deep draughts of Pleasure. She had talk'd of Canary, her Kisses were to me better than the best Canary. Explain'd the expression Concerning Columbus. . . .

. . .

8ʳ. 17. . . . In the Evening I visited Madam Winthrop, who Treated me Courteously, but not in Clean Linen as sometimes. She said, she did not know whether I would come again, or no. I ask'd her how she could so impute inconstancy to me. (I had not visited her since Wednesday night being unable to get over the Indisposition received by the Treatment received that night, and *I must* in it seem'd to sound like a made piece of Formality.) Gave her this day's Gazett. . . .

8ʳ 18. Visited Madam Mico, who came to me in a splendid Dress. I said, It may be you

have heard of my Visiting Madam Winthrop, her Sister. She answered, Her Sister had told her of it. I ask'd her good Will in the Affair. She answer'd, If her Sister were for it, she should not hinder it. I gave her Mr. Homes's Sermon. She gave me a Glass of Canary, entertain'd me with good Discourse, and a Respectfull Remembrance of my first Wife. I took Leave.

8ʳ 19. Midweek, Visited Madam Winthrop; Sarah told me she was at Mr. Walley's, would not come home till late. I gave her Hañah 3 oranges with her Duty, not knowing whether I should find her or no. Was ready to go home: but said if I knew she was there, I would go thither. Sarah seem'd to speak with pretty good Courage, She would be there. I went and found her there, with Mr. Walley and his wife in the little Room below. At 7 a-clock I mentioned going home; at 8. I put on my Coat, and quickly waited on her home. She found occasion to speak loud to the servant, as if she had a mind to be known. Was Courteous to me; but took occasion to speak pretty earnestly about my keeping a Coach: I said 'twould cost £100. per añum: she said 'twould cost but £40. Spake much against John Winthrop, his false-heartedness. Mr. Eyre came in and sat awhile; I offer'd him Dr. Incr. Mather's Sermons, whereof Mr. Apleton's Ordination Sermon was one; said he had them already. I said I would give him another. Exit. Came away somewhat late.

8ʳ. 20. Mr. Colman preaches from Luke 15.10. Joy among the Angels: made an Excellent Discourse. At Council, Col. Townsend spake to me of my Hood: Should get a Wigg. I said twas my chief ornament: I wore it for sake of the Day. Broʳ Odlin, and Sam, Mary, and Jane Hirst dine with us. Promis'd to wait on the Govʳ about 7. Madam Winthrop not being at Lecture, I went thither first; found her very Serene with her dâter Noyes, Mrs. Dering, and the widow Shipreev sitting at a little Table, she in her arm'd Chair. She drank to me, and I to Mrs. Noyes. After awhile pray'd the favour to speak with her. She took one of the Candles, and went into the best Room, clos'd the shutters, sat down upon the Couch. She told me Madam Usher had been there, and said the Coach must be set on Wheels, and not by Rusting. She spake somthing of my needing a Wigg. Ask'd me what her Sister said to me. I told her, She said, If her Sister were for it, She would not hinder it. But I told her,

she did not say she would be glad to have me for her Brother. Said, I shall keep you in the Cold, and asked her if she would be within to morrow night, for we had had but a running Feat. She said she could not tell whether she should, or no. I took Leave. As were drinking at the Governour's, he said: In England the Ladies minded little more than that they might have Money, and Coaches to ride in. I said, And
10 New-England brooks its Name. At which Mr. Dudley smiled. Govr said they were not quite so bad here.

8^r. 21. Friday, My Son, the Minister, came to me p. m by ap̄ointment and we pray one for another in the Old Chamber; more especially respecting my Courtship. About 6. a-clock I go to Madam Winthrop's; Sarah told me her Mistress was gon out, but did not tell me whither she went. She presently order'd me a Fire; so
20 I went in, having Dr. Sibb's Bowels [6] with me to read. I read the two first Sermons, still no body came in: at last about 9. a-clock Mr. Jn° Eyre came in; I took the op̄ortunity to say to him as I had done to Mrs. Noyes before, that I hoped my Visiting his Mother would not be disagreeable to him; He answered me with much Respect. When twas after 9. a-clock He of himself said he would go and call her, she was but at one of his Brothers: A while after
30 I heard Madam Winthrop's voice, enquiring somthing about John. After a good while and Clap̄ing the Garden door twice or thrice, she came in. I mention'd somthing of the lateness; she banter'd me, and said I was later. She receiv'd me Courteously. I ask'd when our proceedings should be made publick: She said They were like to be no more publick than they were already. Offer'd me no Wine that I remember. I rose up at 11 a-clock to come
40 away, saying I would put on my Coat. She offer'd not to help me. I pray'd her that Juno might light me home, she open'd the Shutter, and said twas pretty light abroad; Juno was weary and gon to bed. So I came hôm by Starlight as well as I could. At my first coming in, I gave Sarah five Shillings. I writ Mr. Eyre his Name in his book with the date Octob^r 21. 1720. It cost me 8^s. Jehovah jireh! Madam told me she had visited M. Mico, Wendell, and W^m
50 Clark of the South [Church].

Octob^r. 22. Dâter Cooper visited me before my going out of Town, staid till about Sun set. I brought her going near as far as the

[6] *Bowels opened; or, a discovery of the Union betwixt Christ and the Church* (1639), by Richard Sibbes. an English Puritan.

Orange Tree. Coming back, near Leg's Corner, Little David Jeffries saw me, and looking upon me very lovingly, ask'd me if I was going to see his Grandmother? I said, Not to-night. Gave him a peny, and bid him present my Service to his Grandmother.

Octob^r. 24. I went in the Hackny Coach through the Cōmon, stop'd at Madam Winthrop's (had told her I would take my departure from thence). Sarah came to the door with Katee in her Arms: but I did not think to take notice of the Child. Call'd her Mistress. I told her, being encourag'd by David Jeffries loving eyes, and sweet Words, I was come to enquire whether she could find in her heart to leave that House and Neighbourhood, and go and dwell with me at the South-end; I think she said softly, Not yet. I told her It did not ly in my Lands to keep a Coach. If I should, I should be in danger to be brought to keep company with her Neighbour Brooker, (he was a little before sent to prison for Debt). Told her I had an Antipathy against those who would pretend to give themselves; but nothing of their Estate. I would a proportion of my Estate with my self. And I sup̄os'd she would do so. As to a Perriwig, My best and greatest Friend, I could not possibly have a greater, began to find me with Hair before I was born, and had continued to do so ever since; and I could not find in my heart to go to another. She cōmended the book I gave her, Dr. Preston, the Church Marriage; quoted him saying 'twas inconvenient keeping out of a Fashion cōmonly used. I said the Time and Tide did circumscribe my Visit. She gave me a Dram of Black-Cherry Brandy, and gave me a lump of the Sugar that was in it. She wish'd me a good Journy. I pray'd God to keep her, and came away. Had a very pleasant Journy to Salem.

. . .

Novr 2. Midweek, went again, and found Mrs. Alden there, who quickly went out. Gave her about ½ pound of Sugar Almonds, cost 3^s per £. Carried them on Monday. She seem'd pleas'd with them, ask'd what they cost. Spake of giving her a Hundred pounds per añum if I dy'd before her. Ask'd her what sum she would give me, if she should dy first? Said I would give her time to Consider of it. She said she heard as if I had given all to my Children by Deeds of Gift. I told her 'twas a mistake, Point-Judith was mine &c. That in England, I own'd, my Father's desire was that it should go to my eldest Son; 'twas 20 £ per añum; she thought 'twas forty. I think when I seem'd to excuse pressing this, she seem'd to think twas best to speak of it; a long winter was coming on. Gave me a Glass or two of Canary.

Novr. 4th. Friday, Went again about 7. a-clock; found there Mr. John Walley and his wife: sat discoursing pleasantly. I shew'd them Isaac Moses's [an Indian] Writing. Madam W. serv'd Comfeits to us. After a-while a Table was spread, and Super was set. I urg'd Mr. Walley to Crave a Blessing; but he put it upon me. About 9. they went away. I ask'd Madam what fashioned Neck-lace I should present her with, She said, None at all. I ask'd her Whereabout we left off last time; mention'd what I had offer'd to give her; Ask'd her what she would give me; She said she could not Change her Condition: She had said so from the beginning; could not be so far from her Children, the Lecture. Quoted the Apostle Paul affirming that a single Life was better than a Married. I answer'd That was for the present Distress. Said she had not pleasure in things of that nature as formerly: I said, you are the fitter to make me a Wife. If she held in that mind, I must go home and bewail my Rashness in making more haste than good Speed. However, considering the Super, I desired her to be within next Monday night, if we liv'd so long. Assented. She charg'd me with saying, that she must put away Juno, if she came to me: I utterly deny'd it, it never came in my heart; yet she insisted upon it; saying it came in upon Discourse about the Indian woman that obtained her Freedom this Court. About 10. I said I would not disturb the good orders of her House, and came away. She not seeming pleas'd with my Coming away. Spake to her about David Jeffries, had not seen him.

Monday, Novr. 7th. My Son pray'd in the Old Chamber. Our time had been taken up by Son and Daughter Cooper's Visit; so that I only read the 130th and 143. Psalm. Twas on the Account of my Courtship. I went to Mad. Winthrop; found her rocking her little Katee in the Cradle. I excus'd my Coming so late (near Eight). She set me an arm'd Chair and Cusheon; and so the Cradle was between her arm'd Chair and mine. Gave her the remnant of my Almonds; She did not eat of them as before; but laid them away; I said I came to enquire whether she had alter'd her mind since Friday, or remained of the same mind still. She said,

Thereabouts. I told her I loved her, and was so fond as to think that she loved me: She said had a great respect for me. I told her, I had made her an offer, without asking any advice; she had so many to advise with, that twas a hindrance. The Fire was come to one short Brand besides the Block, which Brand was set up in end; at last it fell to pieces, and no Recruit was made: She gave me a Glass of Wine. I think I repeated again that I would go home and bewail my Rashness in making more haste than good Speed. I would endeavour to contain myself, and not go on to sollicit her to do that which she could not Consent to. Took leave of her. As came down the steps she bid me have a Care. Treated me Courteously. Told her she had enter'd the 4th year of her Widowhood. I had given her the News-Letter before: I did not bid her draw off her Glove as sometime I had done. Her Dress was not so clean as sometime it had been. Jehovah jireh!

Midweek, 9^r. 9th. Dine at Bro^r Stoddard's: were so kind as to enquire of me if they should invite M^{rm} Winthrop; I answer'd No.

. . .

Novr 11th. Went not to M^m. Winthrop's. This is the 2^d Withdraw. . . .

[Samuel Sewall marries in 1722, but not Madam Winthrop]

Friday, Jan^r. 26. I rode to Newtown in the Coach, and visited Mrs. Gibbs. Spake of the proposals I had intimated per Mr. H. Gibbs; for her Sons to be bound to save me harmless as to her Administration; and to pay me £ 100. provided their Mother died before me: I to pay her £ 50. per añum during her Life, if I left her a Widow. She said 'twas hard, she knew not how to have her children bound to pay that Sum; she might dye in a little time. Mr. Cotton, whom she call'd, spake to the same purpose, spake of a Joynture. I said I was peremptory as to the indemnifying Bond; Offer'd to take up with that alone, and allow her £ 40. per añum; Scolly's Tenement yielded but £ 33., and then I made no question but that there must be a Deduction for Repairs. She said she would consider of it: I said, I would also Consider. Afterward she excus'd her speaking to me. I supose she meant the word Hard. Carried her a pound of Glaz'd Almonds, and a Duz. Meers Cakes; Two bottles of Canary. Visited Mrs. Cotton, wish'd her Joy of her young Daughter Elizabeth. Gave little Mary 2ˢ. Had a very good Legge of Pork, and a Turkey for Diñer. Mrs. Gibbs help'd me on with my Coat at Coming away; and stood in the Front door till the Coach mov'd, then I pull'd off my Hat, and she Curtesied. I had moved to be published next Thorsday; to carry in our names to Col. Checkley. . . .

March, 29th. Samuel Sewall, and Mrs. Mary Gibbs were joined in Marriage by the Revᵈ. Mr. William Cooper, Mr. Sewall pray'd once . . .

Lord's day, April, 1. Sat with my wife in her Pue.

April 2. Brought her home to my House.

April, 8. introduc'd her into my Pue, and sat with her there.

April, 15. Conducted my wife to the Fore-Seat; having been invited by David Jeffries esqr, Danˡ Oliver esqr, and Mr. Ezekiel Lewis, March 31. as overseers.   1878

SARAH KEMBLE KNIGHT

1666–1727

MADAM KNIGHT, as she was deferentially called in her lifetime, was a spirited and enterprising citizen of Boston. Left a widow, apparently about 1706, she supported her family by copying legal documents and by keeping a shop and a boarding house near North Square. Benjamin Franklin is said to have been a pupil at the writing-school which she conducted. From 1714 until her death she lived in Connecticut, where she managed several farms, kept a shop and tavern, and speculated in Indian lands. She left her heirs a substantial property worth £1800.

To settle the estate of a kinsman Madam Knight undertook, in 1704, the then fairly hazardous journey to New Haven and New York. She made shorthand notes of the exciting and amusing events of her seven days on the road. Transcribed into a small book, now lost, these notes were first published in 1825. No document exists which brings before us so clearly the life of ordinary folk in the years just midway between the settlement of America and the Revolution.

The Journals of Madam Knight and Reverend Mr. Buckingham, Theodore Dwight, ed., New York, 1825.
The Journal of Madam Knight, G. P. Winship, ed., Boston, 1920.
Sidney Gunn, "Sarah Kemble Knight," *Dictionary of American Biography*, X, 468–469.

» » *From:* THE PRIVATE JOURNAL ON A JOURNEY FROM BOSTON TO NEW-YORK « «

Monday, Octb'r. yᵉ second, 1704.

About three o'clock afternoon, I begun my Journey from Boston to New-Haven; being about two Hundred Mile. My Kinsman, Capt. Robert Luist, waited on me as farr as Dedham, where I was to meet yᵉ Western post.

. . . .

Tuesday, October yᵉ third,

about 8 in the morning, I with the Post proceeded forward without observing any thing remarkable; And about two, afternoon, Arrived at the Post's second stage, where the western Post mett him and exchanged Letters. Here, having called for something to eat, yᵉ woman bro't in a Twisted thing like a cable, but something whiter; and laying it on the bord, tugg'd for life to bring it into a capacity to spread; wᶜʰ having wᵗʰ great pains accomplished, she serv'd in a dish of Pork and Cabage, I suppose the remains of Dinner. The sause was of a deep Purple, wᶜʰ I tho't was boil'd in her dye

Kettle; the bread was Indian, and every thing on the Table service Agreeable to these. I, being hungry, gott a little down; but my stomach was soon cloy'd, and what cabbage I swallowed serv'd me for a Cudd the whole day after.

Having here discharged the Ordnary[1] for self and Guide, (as I understood was the custom,) About Three, afternoon, went on with my Third Guide, who Rode very hard; and having crossed Providence Ferry, we come to a River wch they Generally Ride thro'. But I dare not venture; so the Post got a Ladd and Cannoo to carry me to tother side, and hee rid thro' and Led my hors. The Cannoo was very small and shallow, so that when we were in she seem'd redy to take in water, which greatly terrified mee, and caused me to be very circumspect, sitting with my hands fast on each side, my eyes stedy, not daring so much as to lodg my tongue a hair's breadth more on one side of my mouth than tother, nor so much as think on Lott's wife, for a wry thought would have oversett our wherey: But was soon put out of this pain, by feeling the Cannoo on shore, wch I as soon almost saluted with my feet; and Rewarding my sculler, again mounted and made the best of our way forwards. The Rode here was very even and ye day pleasant, it being now near Sunsett. But the Post told mee we had neer 14 miles to Ride to the next Stage, (where we were to Lodg.) I askt him of the rest of the Rode, foreseeing we must travail in the night. Hee told mee there was a bad River we were to Ride thro', wch was so very firce a hors could sometimes hardly stem it: But it was but narrow, and wee should soon be over. I cannot express the concern of mind this relation sett me in: no thoughts but those of the dang'ros River could entertain my Imagination, and they were as formidable as varios, still Tormenting me with blackest Ideas of my Approching fate—Sometimes seeing my self drowning, otherwhiles drowned, and at the best like a holy Sister Just come out of a Spiritual Bath in dripping Garments.

Now was the Glorious Luminary, wth his swift Coursers arrived at his Stage, leaving poor me wth the rest of this part of the lower world in darkness, with which wee were soon Surrounded. The only Glimering we now had was from the spangled Skies, Whose Imperfect Reflections rendered every Object formidable. Each lifeless Trunk, with its shatter'd Limbs, appear'd an Armed Enymie; and every little

stump like a Ravenous devourer. Nor could I so much as discern my Guide, when at any distance, which added to the terror.

Thus, absolutely lost in Thought, and dying with the very thoughts of drowning, I come up with the Post, who I did not see till even with his Hors: he told mee he stopt for mee; and wee Rode on Very deliberately a few paces, when we entred a Thickett of Trees and Shrubs, and I perceived by the Hors's going, we were on the descent of a Hill, w^ch, as wee come neerer the bottom, 'twas totaly dark wth the Trees that surrounded it. But I knew by the Going of the Hors wee had entred the water, wch my Guide told mee was the hazzardos River he had told me off; and hee, Riding up close to my Side, Bid me not fear—we should be over Imediatly. I now ralyed all the Courage I was mistriss of, Knowing that I must either Venture my fate of drowning, or be left like ye Children in the wood. So, as the Post bid me, I gave Reins to my Nagg; and sitting as Stedy as Just before in the Cannoo, in a few minutes got safe to the other side, which hee told mee was the Narragansett country.

• • •

Wedensday, Octob^r 4th.

About four in the morning, we set out for Kingston[2] (for so was the Town called) with a french Docter in our company. Hee and ye Post put on very furiously, so that I could not keep up with them, only as now and then they'd stop till they see mee. This Rode was poorly furnished wth accommodations for Travellers, so that we were forced to ride 22 miles by the post's account, but neerer thirty by mine, before wee could bait so much as our Horses, wch I exceedingly complained of. But the post encourag'd mee, by saying wee should be well accommodated anon at mr. Devills, a few miles further. But I questioned whether we ought to go to the Devil to be helpt out of affliction. However, like the rest of Deluded souls that post to ye Infernal denn, Wee made all posible speed to this Devil's Habitation; where alliting, in full assurance of good accommodation, wee were going in. But meeting his two daughters, as I suposed twins, they so neerly resembled each other, both in features and habit, and look't as old as the Divel himselfe, and quite as Ugly, We desired entertainm't, but could hardly get a word out of 'um, till with our Importunity, telling them our necesity, &c. they call'd the old Sophister, who was as spar-

---

[1] Paid for the meal at the tavern (or ordinary).

[2] In Rhode Island.

ing of his words as his daughters had bin, and no, or none, was the reply's hee made us to our demands. Hee differed only in this from the old fellow in to'ther Country: hee let us depart. However, I thought it proper to warn poor Travailers to endeavor to Avoid falling into circumstances like ours, wch at our next Stage I sat down and did as followeth:

10   May all that dread the cruel feind of night
  Keep on, and not at this curs't Mansion light.
  'Tis Hell; 'tis Hell! and Devills here do dwell:
  Here dwells the Devill—surely this's Hell.
  Nothing but Wants: a drop to cool yo'r Tongue
  Cant be procur'd these cruel Feinds among.
  Plenty of horrid Grins and looks sevear,
  Hunger and thirst, But pitty's bannish'd here—
  The Right hand keep, if Hell on Earth you fear!

20 Thus leaving this habitation of cruelty, we went forward; and arriving at an Ordinary about two mile further, found tollerable accommodation. But our Hostes, being a pretty full mouth'd old creature, entertain'd our fellow travailer, ye french Docter wth Inumirable complaints of her bodily infirmities; and whispered to him so lou'd, that all ye House had as full a hearing as hee: which was very divirting to ye company, (of which there was a great many,) as one might see by their sneering. But poor 30 weary I slipt out to enter my mind in my Jornal, and left my Great Landly with her Talkative Guests to themselves.

From hence we proceeded (about ten forenoon) through the Narragansett country, pretty Leisurely; and about one afternoon come to Paukataug River, wch was about two hundred paces over, and now very high, and no way over to to'ther side but this. I darid not venture to Ride thro, my courage at best in such cases 40 but small, And now at the Lowest Ebb, by reason of my weary, very weary, hungry and uneasy Circumstances. So takeing leave of my company, tho' wth no little Reluctance, that I could not proceed wth them on my Jorny, Stop at a little cottage Just by the River, to wait the Waters falling, wch the old man that lived there said would be in a little time, and he would conduct me safe over. This little Hutt was one of the wretchedest I ever saw a habitation for 50 human creatures. It was suported with shores enclosed with Clapbords, laid on Lengthways, and so much asunder, that the Light come throu' every where; the doore tyed on wth a cord in ye place of hinges; The floor the bear earth; no windows but such as the thin cover-

ing afforded, nor any furniture but a Bedd wth a glass Bottle hanging at ye head on't; an earthan cupp, a small pewter Bason, A Bord wth sticks to stand on, instead of a table, and a block or two in ye corner instead of chairs. The family were the old man, his wife and two Children; all and every part being the picture of poverty. Notwithstanding both the Hutt and its Inhabitance were very clean and tydee: to the crossing the Old Proverb, that bare walls make giddy hows-wifes.

· · ·

Saturday, Oct. 7th.
. . . About two a clock afternoon we arrived at New Haven, where I was received with all Possible Respects and civility. Here I discharged Mr. Wheeler with a reward to his satisfaction, and took some time to rest after so long and toilsome a Journey; and Inform'd myselfe of the manners and customs of the place, and at the same time employed myselfe in the afair I went there upon.

They are Govern'd by the same Laws as wee in Boston, (or little differing,) thr'out this whole Colony of Connecticot, And much the same way of Church Government, and many of them good, Sociable people, and I hope Religious too: but a little too much Independent in their principalls, and, as I have been told, were formerly in their Zeal very Riggid in their Administrations towards such as their Lawes made Offenders, even to a harmless Kiss or Innocent merriment among Young people. Whipping being a frequent and counted an easy Punishment, about wch as other Crimes, the Judges were absolute in their Sentances. They told mee a pleasant story about a pair of Justices in those parts, wch I may not omit the relation of.

A negro Slave belonging to a man in ye Town, stole a hogs head from his master, and gave or sold it to an Indian, native of the place. The Indian sold it in the neighbourhood, and so the theft was found out. Thereupon the Heathen was Seized, and carried to the Justices House to be Examined. But his worship (it seems) was gone into the feild, with a Brother in office, to gather in his Pompions.[3] Whither the malefactor is hurried, And Complaint made, and satisfaction in the name of Justice demanded. Their Worships cann't proceed in form without a Bench: whereupon they Order one to be Imediately erected, which, for want of fitter materials, they made with pompions—

---

³ Pumpkins.

which being finished, down setts their Worships, and the Malefactor call'd, and by the Senior Justice Interrogated after the following manner. You Indian why did You steal from this man? You sho'dn't do so—it's a Grandy wicked thing to steal. Hol't Hol't cryes Justice Junr. Brother, You speak negro to him. I'le ask him. You sirrah, why did You steal this man's Hoggshead? Hoggshead? (replys the Indian,) me no stomany. No? says his Worship; and pulling off his hatt, Patted his own head with his hand, sais, Tatapa—You, Tatapa—you; all one this. Hoggshead all one this. Hah! says Netop, now me stomany that. Whereupon the Company fell into a great fitt of Laughter, even to Roreing. Silence is comanded, but to no effect: for they continued perfectly Shouting. Nay, sais his worship, in an angry tone, if it be so, *take mee off the Bench.*

Their Diversions in this part of the Country are on Lecture days and Training days[4] mostly: on the former there is Riding from town to town.

And on training dayes The Youth divert themselves by Shooting at the Target, as they call it, (but it very much resembles a pillory,) where hee that hitts neerest the white has some yards of Red Ribbin presented him wch being tied to his hattband, the two ends streeming down his back, he is Led away in Triumph, wth great applause, as the winners of the Olympiack Games. They generally marry very young: the males oftener as I am told under twentie than above; they generally make public wedings, and have a way something singular (as they say) in some of them, *viz.* Just before Joyning hands the Bridegroom quitts the place, who is soon followed by the Bridesmen, and as it were, dragg'd back to duty—being the reverse to ye former practice among us, to steal the Bride.

There are great plenty of Oysters all along by the sea side, as farr as I Rode in the Collony, and those very good. And they Generally lived very well and comfortably in their famelies. But too Indulgent (especially ye farmers) to their slaves: sufering too great familiarity from them, permitting y^m to sit at Table and eat with them, (as they say to save time,) and into the dish goes the black hoof as freely as the white hand. They told me there was a farmer lived nere the Town where I lodgd who had some difference wth his slave, concerning something the master had promised him and did not punctualy perform; wch caused some hard words between them; But at length they put the matter to Arbitration and Bound themselves to stand to the award of such as they named—wch done, the Arbitrators Having heard the Allegations of both parties, Order the master to pay 40^s to black face, and acknowledge his fault. And so the matter ended: the poor master very honestly standing to the award.

There are every where in the Towns as I passed, a Number of Indians the Natives of the Country, and are the most salvage of all the salvages of that kind that I had ever Seen: little or no care taken (as I heard upon enquiry) to make them otherwise. They have in some places Landes of their owne, and Govern'd by Law's of their own making;—they marry many wives and at pleasure put them away, and on the least dislike or fickle humour, on either side, saying *stand away* to one another is a sufficient Divorce. And indeed those uncomely *Stand aways* are too much in Vougue among the English in this (Indulgent Colony) as their Records plentifully prove, and that on very trivial matters, of which some have been told me, but are not proper to be Related by a Female pen, tho some of that foolish sex have had too large a share in the story.

If the natives committ any crime on their own precincts among themselves, ye English takes no Cognezens of. But if on the English ground, they are punishable by our Laws. They mourn for their Dead by blacking their faces, and cutting their hair, after an Awkerd and frightfull manner; But can't bear You should mention the names of their dead Relations to them: they trade most for Rum, for wch they^d hazzard their very lives; and the English fit them Generally as well, by seasoning it plentifully with water.

. . .

Decr 6th . . . The Cittie of New York is a pleasant, well compacted place, situated on a Commodius River wch is a fine harbour for shipping. The Buildings Brick Generaly, very stately and high, though not altogether like ours in Boston. The Bricks in some of the Houses are of divers Coullers and laid in Checkers, being glazed look very agreeable. The inside of them are neat to admiration, the wooden work, for only the walls are plasterd, and the Sumers and Gist[5] are plained and kept very white scowr'd as so is all the partitions if made of Bords. The fire places have no Jambs (as ours have) But the Backs run flush with the walls,

---

[4] Days appointed for religious lectures and for militia drill.

[5] Beams and joists.

and the Hearth is of Tyles and is as farr out into the Room at the Ends as before the fire, wch is Generally Five foot in the Low'r rooms, and the peice over where the mantel tree should be is made as ours with Joyners work, and as I suppose is fasten'd to iron rodds inside. The House where the Vendue [6] was, had Chimney Corners like ours, and they and the hearths were laid wth the finest tile that I ever see, and the stair cases laid all with white tile which is ever clean, and so are the walls of the Kitchen wch had a Brick floor. They were making Great preparations to Receive their Governor, Lord Cornbury from the Jerseys, and for that End raised the militia to Gard him on shore to the fort.

They are Generaly of the Church of England and have a New England Gentleman for their minister, and a very fine church set out with all Customary requisites. There are also a Dutch and Divers Conventicles as they call them, *viz.* Baptist, Quakers, &c. They are not strict in keeping the Sabbath as in Boston and other places where I had bin, But seem to deal with great exactness as farr as I see or Deall with. They are sociable to one another and Curteos and Civill to strangers and fare well in their houses. The English go very fasheonable in their dress. But the Dutch, especially the middling sort, differ from our women, in their habitt go loose, were French muches wch are like a Capp and a head band in one, leaving their ears bare, which are sett out wth Jewells of a large size and many in number. And their fingers hoop't with Rings, some with large stones in

[6] Auction.

them of many Coullers as were their pendants in their ears, which You should see very old women wear as well as Young.

They have Vendues very frequently and make their Earnings very well by them, for they treat with good Liquor Liberally, and the Customers Drink as Liberally and Generally pay for't as well, by paying for that which they Bidd up Briskly for, after the sack has gone plentifully about, tho' sometimes good penny worths are got there. Their Diversions in the Winter is Riding Sleys about three or four Miles out of Town, where they have Houses of entertainment at a place called the Bowery, and some go to friends Houses who handsomely treat them. Mr. Burroughs cary'd his spouse and Daughter and myself out to one Madame Dowes, a Gentlewoman that lived at a farm House, who gave us a handsome Entertainment of five or six Dishes and choice Beer and metheglin,[7] Cyder, &c. all which she said was the produce of her farm. I believe we mett 50 or 60 slays that day—they fly with great swiftness and some are so furious that they'le turn out of the path for none except a Loaden Cart. Nor do they spare for any diversion the place affords, and sociable to a degree, they'r Tables being as free to their Naybours as to themselves.

Having here transacted the affair I went upon and some other that fell in the way, after about a fortnight's stay there I left New-York with no Little regrett. . . .
1704   1825

[7] Spiced mead.

WILLIAM BYRD

1674–1744

THE GRANDSON of a London goldsmith and the son of the first William Byrd who died a Virginia gentleman in 1704, the second William was born into the aristocracy of the colony. From 1681 until 1696 he lived most of the time in England, where he was educated to the law at the Middle Temple. He became so fond of London society that he probably never quite relinquished the hope of settling in England. On his return to Virginia he entered political life as a Burgess. He represented the colony in London, and in 1708 he became a member of the Council. Lucrative offices came his way, such as the Receiver-Generalship of Quit Rents. As a public servant Byrd was jealous of the rights of the aristocratic Council and opposed Governor Spotswood in quarrels over the prerogatives of that body. In these quarrels can be seen adumbrations of the revolution to come.

Like other men of his class Byrd was land hungry. By shrewd purchases he increased the family holdings from 26,231 to 179,440 acres. In spite of the richness of these properties and the magnificence of his principal estate, Westover, on the banks of the James, he was seldom free from debt and constantly sought some speedy way of producing wealth.

As a cultivated eighteenth-century gentleman, a member of the Royal Society, and the possessor of the finest library in the colonies, Byrd naturally kept a record of his varied activities and observations, as well as a private journal, large portions of which have now been edited. In 1728 he was one of the Virginia commissioners who determined, by a survey, the dividing line between Virginia and North Carolina. Byrd wrote, possibly for the amusement of his friends, a "Secret History" of this survey, full of lively comments on the conduct of his fellow commissioners.

Subsequently he enlarged and revised this account, perhaps with a view to publication. This *History of the Dividing Line* contains more information about the region covered and is particularly amusing at the expense of the North Carolinians, for whom Byrd had an aristocrat's humorous contempt. Ever on the lookout for profitable investments, Byrd made, in 1732, a trip to the Rappahannock to inspect iron mines. This expedition he described in *A Progress to the Mines*. In the following year he traveled to the North Carolina border to explore a tract of land he had acquired. One event of the journey is memorable in Virginia history. "When we got home," Byrd remarks on the ninth day of the journey, "we laid the foundations of two large cities. One at Shacco's to be called Richmond, and the other at the point of Appomattox river, to be named Petersburg." The trip was recorded by Byrd in his *A Journey to the Land of Eden*.

These three works of Byrd were not published until 1841, when the manuscripts passed from the possession of the family. The *Secret History* was not in print until 1929.

The Writings of "Colonel William Byrd of Westover in Virginia Esqr.," J. S. Bassett, ed., New York, 1901.

William Byrd's Histories of the Dividing Line, W. K. Boyd, ed., Raleigh, N. C., 1929.

The Secret Diary of William Byrd of Westover, 1709–1712, Richmond, 1941; *The London Diary (1717–1721) and Other Writings*, N. Y., 1958; *Another Secret Diary of William Byrd of Westover, 1739–1741*, Richmond, 1942.

R. C. Beatty, *William Byrd of Westover*, Boston, 1932.

J. B. Hubbell, *The South in American Literature, 1607–1900*, Durham, N. C., 1954, pp. 40–51.

L. B. Wright, "William Byrd: Citizen of the Enlightenment," in L. Howard and L. B. Wright, *Anglo-American, Cultural Relations in the Seventeenth and Eighteenth Centuries*, Los Angeles, 1959, pp. 26–40.

» » *From:* HISTORY OF THE DIVIDING LINE « «

[THE DISMAL SWAMP]

14 March, [1728]. Before nine of the Clock this Morning, the Provisions, Bedding and other Necessaries, were made up into Packs for the Men to carry on their Shoulders into the Dismal. They were victuall'd for 8 days at full Allowance, Nobody doubting but that wou'd be abundantly Sufficient to carry them thro' that Inhospitable Place; nor Indeed was it possible for the Poor Fellows to Stagger under more. As it was, their Loads weigh'd from 60 to 70 Pounds, in just Proportion to the Strength of those who were to bear them.

Twou'd have been unconscionable to have Saddled them with Burthens heavier than that, when they were to lugg them thro' a filthy Bogg, which was hardly practicable with no Burthen at all.

Besides this Luggage at their Backs, they were oblig'd to measure the distance, mark the Trees, and clear the way for the Surveyors every Step they went. It was really a Pleasure to see with how much Cheerfulness they undertook, and with how much Spirit they went thro' all this Drudgery. For their Greater Safety, the Commissioners took care to furnish them with Peruvian-Bark, Rhubarb and Hipocoacanah,[1]

---

1 Ipecacuanha (ipecac), a plant with emetic properties.

in case they might happen, in that wet Journey, to be taken with fevers or Fluxes.

Altho' there was no need of Example to inflame Persons already so cheerful, yet to enter the People with better grace, the Author and two more of the Commissioners accompanied them half a Mile into the Dismal. The Skirts of it were thinly Planted with Dwarf Reeds and Gall-Bushes, but when we got into the Dismal
10 itself, we found the Reeds grew there much taller and closer, and, to mend the matter was so interlac'd with bamboe-briars, that there was no scuffling thro' them without the help of Pioneers. At the same time, we found the Ground moist and trembling under our feet like a Quagmire, insomuch that it was an easy Matter to run a Ten-Foot-Pole up to the Head in it, without exerting any uncommon Strength to do it.

Two of the Men, whose Burthens were the
20 least cumbersome, had orders to march before, with their Tomahawks, and clear the way, in order to make an Opening for the Surveyors. By their Assistance we made a Shift to push the Line half a Mile in 3 Hours, and then reacht a small piece of firm Land, about 100 Yards wide, Standing up above the rest like an Island. Here the people were glad to lay down their Loads and take a little refreshment, while the happy man, whose lot it was to carry the Jugg
30 of Rum, began already, like Aesop's Bread-Carriers, to find it grow a good deal lighter.

After reposing about an Hour, the Commissioners recommended Vigour and Constancy to their Fellow-Travellers, by whom they were answer'd with 3 Cheerful Huzzas, in Token of Obedience. This Ceremony was no sooner over but they took up their Burthens and attended the Motion of the Surveyors, who, tho' they workt with all their might, could reach but one
40 Mile farther, the same obstacles still attending them which they had met with in the Morning.

However small this distance may seem to such as are us'd to travel at their Ease, yet our Poor Men, who were oblig'd to work with an unwieldy Load at their Backs, had reason to think it a long way; Especially in a Bogg where they had no firm Footing, but every Step made a deep Impression, which was instantly fill'd with Water. At the same time they were la-
50 bouring with their Hands to cut down the Reeds, which were Ten-feet high, their Legs were hampered with the Bryars. Besides, the Weather happen'd to be very warm, and the tallness of the Reeds kept off every Friendly Breeze from coming to refresh them. And, in-

deed, it was a little provoking to hear the Wind whistling among the Branches of the White Cedars, which grew here and there amongst the Reeds, and at the same time not have the Comfort to feel the least Breath of it.

In the mean time the 3 Commissioners return'd out of the Dismal the same way they went in, and, having join'd their Brethren, proceeded that Night as far as Mr. Wilson's.

This worthy Person lives within sight of the Dismal, in the Skirts whereof his Stocks range and Maintain themselves all the Winter, and yet he knew as little of it as he did of Terra Australis Incognita. He told us a Canterbury Tale of a North Briton, whose Curiosity Spurr'd him a long way into this great Desart, as he call'd it, near 20 Years ago, but he having no Compass, nor seeing the Sun for several Days Together, wander'd about till he was almost famisht; but at last he bethought himself of a Secret his Countrymen make use of to Pilot themselves in a Dark day.

He took a fat Louse out of his Collar, and expos'd it to the open day on a Piece of White Paper, which he brought along with him for his Journal. The poor Insect having no Eye-lids, turn'd himself about till he found the Darkest Part of the Heavens, and so made the best of his way towards the North. By this Direction he Steer'd himself Safe out, and gave such a frightful account of the Monsters he saw, and the Distresses he underwent, that no mortall Since has been hardy enough to go upon the like dangerous Discovery.

15.   The Surveyors pursued their work with all Diligence, but Still found the Soil of the Dismal so Spongy that the Water ouzed up into every footstep they took. To their Sorrow, too, they found the Reeds and Bryars more firmly interwoven than they did the day before. But the greatest Grievance was from large Cypresses, which the Wind had blown down and heap'd upon one another. On the Limbs of most of them grew Sharp Snags, Pointing every way like so many Pikes, that requir'd much Pains and Caution to avoid.

. . .

While the Surveyors were thus painfully employ'd, the Commissioners discharged the long Score they had with Mr. Wilson, for the Men and Horses which had been quarter'd upon him during our Expedition to Coratuck. From thence we march'd in good Order along the East Side of the Dismal, and passt the long Bridge that lies over the South Branch of Elizabeth River. At the End of 18 Miles we reacht Timothy Ivy's Plantation, where we pitcht our Tent for the first Time, and were furnisht with every thing the Place afforded.

We perceiv'd the happy Effects of Industry in this Family, in which every one lookt tidy and clean, and carri'd in their countenances the chearful Marks of Plenty. We saw no Drones there, which are but too Common, alas, in that Part of the World. Tho', in truth, the Distemper of Laziness seizes the Men oftener much than the Women. These last Spin, weave and knit, all with their own Hands, while their Husbands, depending on the Bounty of the Climate, are Sloathfull in every thing but getting of Children, and in that only Instance make themselves useful Members of an Infant-Colony.

There is but little Wool in that Province, tho' Cotton grows very kindly, and, so far South, is Seldom nippt by the Frost. The Good Women mix this with their Wool for their outer Garments; tho', for want of Fulling, that kind of Manufacture is Open and Sleazy. Flax likewise thrives there extreamly, being perhaps as fine as any in the World, and I question not might, with a little care, and pains, be brought to rival that of Egypt; and yet the Men are here so intolerable Lazy, they seldom take the trouble to propagate it.

16. The Line was this day carry'd one Mile and half and 16 Poles. The Soil continued soft and Miry, but fuller of Trees, especially White cedars. Many of these too were thrown down and piled in Heaps, high enough for a good Muscovite Fortification. The worst of it was, the Poor Fellows began now to be troubled with Fluxes, occasion'd by bad Water and moist Lodgings: but chewing of Rhubarb kept that Malady within Bounds.

In the mean time the Commissioners decampt early in the Morning, and made a March of 25 Miles, as far as Mr. Andrew Mead's, who lives upon Nansimond River. They were no sooner got under the Shelter of that Hospitable Roof, but it began to rain hard, and continued so to do great part of the Night. This gave them much Pain for their Friends in the Dismal, whose sufferings spoilt their Taste for the good Chear, wherewith they were entertain'd themselves.

However, late that Evening, these poor Men had the Fortune to come upon another Terra-firma, which was the Luckyer for them, because the Lower ground, by the rain that fell, was made a fitter Lodging for Tadpoles than men.

In our Journey we remarkt that the North Side of this great Swamp lies higher than either the East or the West, nor were the approaches to it so full of Sunken Grounds. We passt by no less than two Quaker Meeting Houses, one of which had an Awkward Ornament on the West End of it, that seem'd to Ape a Steeple. I must own I expected no such Piece of Foppery from a Sect of so much outside Simplicity.

That persuasion prevails much in the lower end of Nansimond county, for want of Ministers to Pilot the People a decenter way to Heaven.

The ill Reputation of Tobacco planted in those lower Parishes makes the Clergy unwilling to accept of them, unless it be such whose abilities are as mean as their Pay. Thus, whether the Churches be quite void or but indifferently filled, the Quakers will have an Opportunity of gaining Proselytes. Tis a wonder no Popish Missionaries are sent from Maryland to labour in this Neglected Vineyard, who we know have Zeal enough to traverse Sea and Land on the Meritorious Errand of making converts.

Nor is it less Strange that some Wolf in Sheep's cloathing arrives not from New England to lead astray a Flock that has no shepherd. People uninstructed in any Religion are ready to embrace the first that offers. Tis natural for helpless man to adore his Maker in Some Form or other, and were there any exceptions to this Rule, I should expect it to be among the Hottentots of the Cape of Good Hope and of North Carolina.

There fell a great deal of Rain in the Night, accompany'd with a Strong Wind. The fellow-feeling we had for the poor Dismalites, on Account of this unkind Weather, render'd the Down we laid upon uneasy. We fancy'd them half-drown'd in their Wet Lodging, with the Trees blowing down about their Ears. These Were the Gloomy Images our Fears Suggested; tho' twas so much uneasiness clear gain. They happen'd to come off much better, by being luckily emcampt on the dry piece of Ground afore-mention'd.

17. They were, however, forct to keep the Sabbath in Spite of their Teeth, contrary to the Dispensation our good Chaplain had given them. Indeed, their Short allowance of Provision would have justify'd their making the best

of their way, without Distinction of days. Twas certainly a Work both of Necessity and Self-preservation, to save themselves from Starving. Nevertheless, the hard Rain had made every thing so thoroughly wet, that it was quite impossible to do any Business. They therefore made a vertue of what they could not help, and contentedly rested in their dry Situation.

Since the Surveyors had enter'd the Dismal, they had laid Eyes on no living Creature: neither Bird nor Beast, Insect nor Reptile came in View. Doubtless, the Eternal Shade that broods over this mighty Bog, and hinders the sun-beams from blessing the Ground, makes it an uncomfortable Habitation for any thing that has life. Not so much as a Zealand Frog cou'd endure so Aguish a Situation.

It had one Beauty, however, that delighted the Eye, tho' at the Expense of all the other Senses: the Moisture of the Soil preserves a continual Verdure, and makes every Plant an Evergreen, but at the same time the foul Damps ascend without ceasing, corrupt the Air, and render it unfit for Respiration. Not even a Turkey-Buzzard will venture to fly over it, no more than the Italian Vultures will over the filthy Lake Avernus, or the Birds in the Holy-Land over the Salt Sea, where Sodom and Gomorrah formerly stood.

In these sad Circumstances, the kindest thing we cou'd do for our Suffering Friends was to give them a place in the Litany. Our Chaplain, for his Part, did his Office, and rubb'd us up with a Seasonable Sermon. This was quite a new thing to our Brethren of North Carolina, who live in a climate where no clergyman can Breathe, any more than Spiders in Ireland.

For want of men in Holy Orders, both the Members of the Council and Justices of the Peace are empower'd by the Laws of that Country to marry all those who will not take One another's Word; but for the ceremony of Christening their children, they trust that to chance. If a Parson come in their way, they will crave a Cast of his office, as they call it, else they are content their Offspring should remain as Arrant Pagans as themselves. They account it among their greatest advantages that they are not Priest-ridden, not remembering that the Clergy is rarely guilty of Bestriding such as have the misfortune to be poor.

One thing may be said for the Inhabitants of that Province, that they are not troubled with any Religious Fumes, and have the least Super-

stition of any People living. They do not know Sunday from any other day, any more than Robinson Crusoe did, which would give them a great Advantage were they given to be industrious. But they keep so many Sabbaths every week, that their disregard of the Seventh Day has no manner of cruelty in it, either to Servants or Cattle.

It was with some difficulty we cou'd make our People quit the good cheer they met with at this House, so it was late before we took our Departure; but to make us amends, our Landlord was so good as to conduct us Ten Miles on our Way, as far as the Cypress Swamp, which drains itself into the Dismal. Eight Miles beyond that we forded the Waters of Coropeak, which tend the same way as do many others on that side. In Six Miles more we reacht the Plantation of Mr. Thomas Spight, a Grandee of N Carolina. We found the good Man upon his Crutches, being crippled with the Gout in both his Knees. Here we flatter'd ourselves we should by this time meet with good Tydings of the Surveyors, but had reckon'd, alas! without our Host: on the Contrary, we were told the Dismal was at least Thirty Miles wide at that Place. However, as nobody could say this on his own Knowledge, we Order'd Guns to be fired and a Drum to be beaten, but receiv'd no Answer, unless it was from that prating Nymph Echo, who, like a loquacious Wife, will always have the last Word, and Sometimes return three for one.

18. It was indeed no Wonder our Signal was not heard at that time, by the People in the Dismal, because, in Truth, they had not then penetrated one Third of their way. They had that Morning fallen to work with great Vigour; and, finding the Ground better than Ordinary, drove on the Line 2 Miles and 38 poles. This was reckon'd an Herculean day's Work, and yet they would not have Stopp'd there, had not an impenetrable cedar Thicket chekt their Industry. Our Landlord had seated Himself on the Borders of this Dismal, for the Advantage of the Green Food His Cattle find there all Winter, and for the Rooting that Supports His Hogs. This, I own, is some convenience to his Purse, for which his whole Family pay dear in their Persons, for they are devoured by musketas all the Summer, and have Agues every Spring and Fall, which Corrupt all the Juices of their Bodies, give them a cadaverous complexion, and besides a lazy, creeping Habit, which they never get rid of.

19. We Ordered Several Men to Patrole on the Edge of the Dismal, both towards the North and towards the South, and to fire Guns at proper Distances. This they perform'd very punctually, but cou'd hear nothing in return, nor gain any Sort of Intelligence. In the mean time whole Flocks of Women and Children flew hither to Stare at us, with as much curiosity as if we had lately Landed from Bantam or Morocco.

. . .

None of our Visitors could, however, tell us any News of the Surveyors, nor Indeed was it possible any of them shou'd at that time, They being still laboring in the Midst of the Dismal.

It seems they were able to carry the Line this Day no further than one mile and 61 Poles, and that whole distance was thro' a Miry cedar Bogg, where the ground trembled under their Feet most frightfully. In many places too their Passage was retarded by a great number of fallen Trees, that lay Horsing upon one Another.

Tho' many circumstances concurr'd to make this an unwholesome Situation, yet the Poor men had no time to be sick, nor can one conceive a more Calamitous Case than it would have been to be laid up in that uncomfortable Quagmire. Never were Patients more tractable, or willing to take Physick, than these honest Fellows; but it was from a Dread of laying their Bones in a Bogg that wou'd soon spew them up again. That Consideration also put them upon more caution about their Lodging.

They first cover'd the Ground with Square Pieces of Cypress bark, which now, in the Spring, they cou'd easily Slip off the Tree for that purpose. On this they Spread their Bedding; but unhappily the Weight and Warmth of their Bodies made the Water rise up betwixt the Joints of the Bark, to their great Inconvenience. Thus they lay not only moist, but also exceedingly cold, because their Fires were continually going out. For no sooner was the Trash upon the Surface burnt away, but immediately the Fire was extinguisht by the Moisture of the Soil, Insomuch that it was great part of the Centinel's Business to rekindle it again in a Fresh Place, every Quarter of an Hour. Nor cou'd they indeed do their duty better, because Cold was the only Enemy they had to Guard against in a miserable Morass, where nothing can inhabit.

20. We could get no Tidings yet of our Brave Adventurers, notwithstanding we despatcht men to the likeliest Stations to enquire after them. They were still Scuffling in the Mire, and could not Possibly forward the Line this whole day more than one Mile and 64 Chains. Every Step of this Day's Work was thro' a cedar Bog, where the Trees were somewhat Smaller and grew more into a Thicket. It was not a great Misfortune to the Men to find their Provisions grow less as their Labour grew greater; They were all forct to come to short Allowance, and consequently to work hard without filling their Bellies. Tho' this was very severe upon English Stomachs, yet the People were so far from being discomfited at it, that they still kept up their good Humour, and merrily told a young Fellow in the Company, who lookt very Plump and Wholesome, that he must expect to go first to Pot, if matters shou'd come to Extremity.

. . .

21. The Surveyors and their Attendants began now in good Earnest to be alarm'd with Apprehensions of Famine, nor could they forbear looking with Some Sort of Appetite upon a dog that had been the faithful Companion of their Travels.

Their Provisions were now near exhausted. They had this Morning made the last Distribution, that so each might Husband his small Pittance as he pleas'd. Now it was that the fresh Colour'd Young Man began to tremble every Joint of Him, having dreamed, the Night before, that the Indians were about to Barbacue him over live coals.

The Prospect of Famine determin'd the People, at last, with one consent, to abandon the Line for the Present, which advanced but slowly, and make the best of their way to firm Land. Accordingly they sat off very early, and, by the help of the Compass which they carried along with them, Steer'd a direct Westwardly Course. They marcht from Morning till Night, and Computed their Journey to amount to about 4 Miles, which was a great way, considering the difficulties of the Ground. It was all along a Cedar-Swamp, so dirty and perplext, that if they had not travell'd for their Lives, they cou'd not have reacht so far.

On their way they espied a Turkey-Buzzard, that flew prodigiously high to get above the Noisome Exhalations that ascend from that filthy place. This they were willing to understand as a good Omen, according to the Superstitions of the Ancients, who had great Faith in the Flight of Vultures. However, after all this tedious Journey, they could yet discover no End of their toil, which made them very pensive, especially after they had eat the last Morsel of their Provisions. But to their unspeakable comfort, when all was husht in the Evening, they heard the Cattle low, and the Dogs bark, very distinctly, which, to Men in that distress, was more delightful Music than Faustina or Farinelli cou'd have made. In the mean time the Commissioners could get no News of them from any of their Visiters, who assembled from every Point of the Compass.

. . .

22. Our Patrole happen'd not to go far enough to the Northward this Morning, if they had, the People in the Dismal might have heard the Report of their Guns. For this Reason they return'd without any Tydings, which threw us into a great tho' unnecessary Per-

plexity. This was now the Ninth day since they enter'd into that inhospitable Swamp, and consequently we had reason to believe their Provisions were quite Spent.

. . .

However long we might think the time, yet we were cautious of Shewing our uneasiness, for fear of Mortifying our Landlord. He had Done his best for us, and therefore we were unwilling he should think us dissatisfy'd with our Entertainment. In the midst of our concern, we were most agreeably surpriz'd, just after Dinner, with the News that the Dismalites were all Safe. These blessed Tidings were brought to us by Mr. Swan, the Carolina-Surveyor, who came to us in a very tatter'd condition.

After very short Salutations, we got about Him as if He had been a Hottentot, and began to Inquire into his Adventures.

1728   1841

JONATHAN EDWARDS

1703–1758

THE NAME of Jonathan Edwards has come to stand for all that is harsh and cruel in the religion of the later Puritans. He was the man, according to this myth, who rejoiced in the punishment of the damned, who condemned innocent babes to the tortures of Hell-fire. All that most Americans seem to remember about him is the title of his notorious Enfield sermon, "Sinners in the Hands of an Angry God." As most readers of Dante rarely follow him through Purgatory to Paradise, so few today have penetrated the fire of Edwards's imprecatory sermons to catch his vision of Heaven. He was a mystic and therefore found it difficult to express the ineffable experiences of his soul. Men halted before his vision of Hell, which he drew for them in order that God's grace, in restoring some men to Heaven, might seem the more remarkable. That Edwards is remembered only for his Inferno is not the least of the ironies which pursued him in life and beyond the grave.

As a boy Edwards showed a remarkable power of observation and logical analysis which might have led, in another environment, to a career as a scientist or a philosopher. At Yale College, which he entered at thirteen, he read the "new" philosophers, Locke and Newton. While studying theology he passed, in 1721, through a religious conversion so profound, and so beautifully recorded (in his "Personal Narrative") that it reminds one of the ecstasies of the mystics of the medieval church. After serving as the pastor of a Presbyterian congregation in New York and as a tutor at Yale, Edwards became, in 1726, the colleague of his grandfather, the Rev. Solomon Stoddard, in Northampton, Massachusetts. This was to be his home for twenty-four years, until that sad day in 1750 when, after two years of contention between them, he preached to his flock his "Farewell Sermon."

At Stockbridge, on the Massachusetts frontier, where Edwards settled in 1751 as pastor of the church and missionary to the Indians, he had leisure to write the two important treatises, "The Nature of True Virtue" and "Concerning the End for which God Created the World," and his greatest work, *A Careful and Strict Enquiry into the Modern Prevailing Notions of that Freedom of Will which is supposed to be Essential to Moral Agency, Vertue and Vice, Reward and Punishment, Praise and Blame* (1754). In 1757 he accepted the presidency of the College of New Jersey (now Princeton), though he modestly doubted whether he was qualified for the office. Less than three months after his arrival in Princeton he died of a smallpox inoculation.

In his efforts to purify Calvinistic thought and make it acceptable to an heretical age, Edwards erected a wonderfully consistent system of theology. The tragedy is that though his readers might have to bow to his logic, they had been swept too far along in the new currents of thought to be persuaded in their hearts. The basis of his thought and so of his conviction was not rational, for his mysticism determined the idealistic trend of his philosophy. It evoked as well the premise of his theology: God's sovereignty in choosing whom he would to eternal life and rejecting whom he pleased, leaving them eternally to perish and be everlastingly tormented in Hell. Before his conversion this seemed to Edwards a horrible doctrine. Thereafter it appeared "exceeding pleasant, bright and sweet." If one loves God sufficiently, has "sweet complacency in Him," is visited by His grace so that the rectitude of human nature, lost by original sin, is restored, the fate of the rest of mankind becomes of slight consequence. God, far from showing Himself arbitrary and vindictive in saving or rejecting whom He will, should be adored because He condescends to consider man. His mercy is remarkable because He has deigned, without obligation, to show any at all. Man, once glorious, became vile through Adam, but God, with infinite tenderness, still allows him to regain Eden. Lost in Him, as matter is dissolved in spirit, the elect no more dread the pain of Hell than we tremble for the thunder when we know that it cannot harm us.

With those who lived in the mid-eighteenth century such doctrine could not prevail. Some followed the Arminian heresy that man's will is free. Some, revolted by the idea of total depravity, adopted the notions of Hutcheson and Shaftesbury, which allow man a moral sense by which he may understand and choose virtue. Some preferred to believe, with Hobbes and Mandeville, that man is ruled by self-love, and found in this belief no imputation of sin. Though to Edwards the "higher argument" remained, like Milton, he wrote in an "age too late."

The Works of President Edwards, S. Austin, ed., 8 vols., Worcester, 1808–1809.

Complete Works, Perry Miller, general ed., New Haven, 1957, *et seq.*

Jonathan Edwards, Representative Selections, with Introduction, Bibliography, and Notes (American Writers Series), C. H. Faust and T. M. Johnson, eds., New York, 1935.

H. N. Gardiner, *Selected Sermons of Jonathan Edwards*, New York, 1904.

A. B. Crabtree, *Jonathan Edwards' View of Man: A Study in Eighteenth Century Calvinism*, Wellington, England, 1948.

Perry Miller, *Jonathan Edwards*, New York, 1949.

» » [SARAH PIERREPONT]¹ « «

They say there is a young lady in [New Haven] who is beloved of that Great Being, who made and rules the world, and that there are certain seasons in which this Great Being, in some way or other invisible, comes to her and fills her mind with exceeding sweet de-

¹ Edwards married Sarah Pierrepont July 28, 1721. This note was written in 1723 when Sarah was thirteen and Edwards twenty.

light, and that she hardly cares for anything, except to meditate on him—that she expects after a while to be received up where he is, to be raised up out of the world and caught up into heaven; being assured that he loves her too well to let her remain at a distance from him always. There she is to dwell with him, and to be ravished with his love and delight forever. Therefore, if you present all the world before
10 her, with the richest of its treasures, she disregards it and cares not for it, and is unmindful of any pain or affliction. She has a strange sweetness in her mind, and singular purity in her affections; is most just and conscientious in all her conduct; and you could not persuade her to do any thing wrong or sinful, if you would give her all the world, lest she should offend this Great Being. She is of a wonderful sweetness, calmness and universal benevolence of mind; especially after this Great God has manifested himself to her mind. She will sometimes go about from place to place, singing sweetly; and seems to be always full of joy and pleasure; and no one knows for what. She loves to be alone, walking in the fields and groves, and seems to have some one invisible always conversing with her.

1723   1829

» » [PERSONAL NARRATIVE] « «

20   I had a variety of concerns and exercises about my soul from my childhood; [2] but I had two more remarkable seasons of awakening, before I met with that change, by which I was brought to those new dispositions, and that new sense of things, that I have since had. The first time was when I was a boy, some years before I went to college, at a time of remarkable awakening in my father's congregation. I was then very much affected for many months,
30 and concerned about the things of religion, and my soul's salvation; and was abundant in [religious] duties. I used to pray five times a day in secret, and to spend much time in religious talk with other boys; and used to meet with them to pray together. I experienced I know not what kind of delight in religion. My mind was much engaged in it, and had much self-righteous pleasure; and it was my delight to abound in religious duties. I, with some of
40 my school-mates, joined together, and built a booth in a swamp, in a very retired spot, for a place of prayer. And besides, I had particular secret places of my own in the woods, where I used to retire by myself; and was from time to time much affected. My affections seemed to be lively and easily moved, and I seemed to be in my element, when engaged in religious duties. And I am ready to think, many are deceived with such affections, and such a kind of delight
50 as I then had in religion, and mistake it for grace.

But, in process of time, my convictions and affections wore off; and I entirely lost all those affections and delights and left off secret prayer, at least as to any constant performance of it; and returned like a dog to his vomit, and went on in the ways of sin. Indeed, I was at times very uneasy, especially towards the latter part of my time at college; when it pleased God, to seize me with a pleurisy; in which he brought me nigh to the grave, and shook me over the pit of hell. And yet, it was not long after my recovery, before I fell again into my old ways of sin. But God would not suffer me to go on with any quietness; I had great and violent inward struggles, till, after many conflicts with wicked inclinations, repeated resolutions, and bonds that I laid myself under by a kind of vows to God, I was brought wholly to break off all former wicked ways, and all ways of known outward sin; and to apply myself to seek salvation, and practise many religious duties; but without that kind of affection and delight which I had formerly experienced. My concern now wrought more by inward struggles and conflicts, and self-reflections. I made seeking my salvation the main business of my life. But yet, it seems to me, I sought it after a miserable manner; which has made me sometimes since to question, whether ever it issued in that which was saving; being ready to doubt, whether such miserable seeking ever succeeded. I was indeed brought to seek salvation in a manner that I never was before; I felt a spirit to part with all things in the world, for an interest in Christ. My concern continued and prevailed, with many exercising thoughts and inward struggles; but yet it never seemed

[2] Spent in East Windsor, Connecticut.

to be proper to express that concern by the name of terror.

From my childhood up, my mind had been full of objections against the doctrine of God's sovereignty, in choosing whom he would to eternal life, and rejecting whom he pleased; leaving them eternally to perish, and be everlastingly tormented in hell. It used to appear like a horrible doctrine to me. But I remember the time very well, when I seemed to be convinced, and fully satisfied, as to this sovereignty of God, and his justice in thus eternally disposing of men, according to his sovereign pleasure. But never could give an account, how, or by what means, I was thus convinced, not in the least imagining at the time, nor a long time after, that there was any extraordinary influence of God's Spirit in it; but only that now I saw further, and my reason apprehended the justice and reasonableness of it. However, my mind rested in it; and it put an end to all those cavils and objections. And there has been a wonderful alteration in my mind, in respect to the doctrine of God's sovereignty, from that day to this; so that I scarce ever have found so much as the rising of an objection against it, in the most absolute sense, in God's shewing mercy to whom he will shew mercy, and hardening whom he will. God's absolute sovereignty and justice, with respect to salvation and damnation, is what my mind seems to rest assured of, as much as of any thing that I see with my eyes; at least it is so at times. But I have often, since that first conviction, had quite another kind of sense of God's sovereignty than I had then. I have often since had not only a conviction, but a delightful conviction. The doctrine has very often appeared exceedingly pleasant, bright, and sweet. Absolute sovereignty is what I love to ascribe to God. But my first conviction was not so.

The first instance that I remember of that sort of inward, sweet delight in God and divine things, that I have lived much in since, was on reading those words, 1 Tim. i. 17. *Now unto the King eternal, immortal, invisible, the only wise God, be honour and glory for ever and ever, Amen.* As I read the words, there came into my soul, and was as it were diffused through it, a sense of the glory of the Divine Being; a new sense, quite different from any thing I ever experienced before. Never any words of scripture seemed to me as these words did. I thought with myself, how excellent a Being that was,

and how happy I should be, if I might enjoy that God, and be rapt up to him in heaven, and be as it were swallowed up in him for ever! I kept saying, and as it were singing over these words of scripture to myself; and went to pray to God that I might enjoy him, and prayed in a manner quite different from what I used to do; with a new sort of affection. But it never came into my thought, that there was any thing spiritual, or of a saving nature in this.   10

From about that time, I began to have a new kind of apprehensions and ideas of Christ, and the work of redemption, and the glorious way of salvation by him. An inward, sweet sense of these things, at times, came into my heart; and my soul was led away in pleasant views and contemplations of them. And my mind was greatly engaged to spend my time in reading and meditating on Christ, on the beauty and excellency of his person, and the lovely way of   20 salvation by free grace in him. I found no books so delightful to me, as those that treated of these subjects. Those words Cant. ii. 1., used to be abundantly with me, *I am the Rose of Sharon, and the Lily of the valleys.* The words seemed to me, sweetly to represent the loveliness and beauty of Jesus Christ. The whole book of Canticles used to be pleasant to me, and I used to be much in reading it, about that time; and found, from time to time, an inward   30 sweetness, that would carry me away, in my contemplations. This I know not how to express otherwise, than by a calm, sweet abstraction of soul from all the concerns of this world; and sometimes a kind of vision, or fixed ideas and imaginations, of being alone in the mountains, or some solitary wilderness, far from all mankind, sweetly conversing with Christ, and wrapt and swallowed up in God. The sense I had of divine things, would often of a sudden   40 kindle up, as it were, a sweet burning in my heart; an ardor of soul, that I know not how to express.

Not long after I first began to experience these things, I gave an account to my father of some things that had passed in my mind. I was pretty much affected by the discourse we had together; and when the discourse was ended, I walked abroad alone, in a solitary place in my father's pasture, for contemplation. And as I   50 was walking there, and looking upon the sky and clouds, there came into my mind so sweet a sense of the glorious *majesty* and *grace* of God, as I know not how to express. I seemed to see them both in a sweet conjunction; majesty and meekness joined together: it was a sweet, and gentle, and holy majesty; and also a majestic meekness; and awful sweetness; a high, and great, and holy gentleness.

After this my sense of divine things gradually increased, and became more and more lively, and had more of that inward sweetness. The appearance of every thing was altered;
10 there seemed to be, as it were, a calm, sweet cast, or appearance of divine glory, in almost every thing. God's excellency, his wisdom, his purity and love, seemed to appear in every thing; in the sun, moon and stars; in the clouds and blue sky; in the grass, flowers, trees; in the water and all nature; which used greatly to fix my mind. I often used to sit and view the moon for continuance; and in the day, spent much time in viewing the clouds and sky, to behold
20 the sweet glory of God in these things: in the mean time, singing forth, with a low voice, my contemplations of the Creator and Redeemer. And scarce any thing, among all the works of nature, was so sweet to me as thunder and lightning; formerly, nothing had been so terrible to me. Before, I used to be uncommonly terrified with thunder, and to be struck with terror when I saw a thunder storm rising; but now, on the contrary, it rejoiced me. I felt God,
30 so to speak, at the first appearance of a thunder storm; and used to take the opportunity, at such times, to fix myself in order to view the clouds, and see the lightnings play, and hear the majestic and awful voice of God's thunder, which oftentimes was exceedingly entertaining, leading me to sweet contemplations of my great and glorious God. While thus engaged, it always seemed natural to me to sing, or chant forth my meditations; or, to speak my thoughts
40 in soliloquies with a singing voice.

I felt then great satisfaction, as to my good state; but that did not content me. I had vehement longings of soul after God and Christ, and after more holiness, wherewith my heart seemed to be full, and ready to break; which often brought to my mind the words of the Psalmist, Psal. cxix. 28. *My soul breaketh for the longing it hath.* I often felt a mourning and lamenting in my heart, that I had not turned
50 to God sooner, that I might have had more time to grow in grace. My mind was greatly fixed on divine things; almost perpetually in the contemplation of them. I spent most of my time in thinking of divine things, year after

year; often walking alone in the woods, and solitary places, for meditation, soliloquy, and prayer, and converse with God; and it was always my manner, at such times, to sing forth my contemplations. I was almost constantly in ejaculatory prayer, wherever I was. Prayer seemed to be natural to me, as the breath by which the inward burnings of my heart had vent. The delights which I now felt in the things of religion, were of an exceedingly different kind from those before mentioned, that I had when a boy; and what I then had no more notion of, than one born blind has of pleasant and beautiful colors. They were of a more inward, pure, soul animating and refreshing nature. Those former delights never reached the heart; and did not arise from any sight of the divine excellency of the things of God; or any taste of the soul-satisfying and life-giving good there is in them.

My sense of divine things seemed gradually to increase, till I went to preach at Newyork,[3] which was about a year and a half after they began; and while I was there, I felt them, very sensibly, in a much higher degree, than I had done before. My longings after God, and holiness, were much increased. Pure and humble, holy and heavenly, Christianity, appeared exceedingly amiable to me. I felt a burning desire to be in every thing a complete Christian; and conformed to the blessed image of Christ; and that I might live, in all things, according to the pure, sweet and blessed rules of the gospel. I had an eager thirsting after progress in these things; which put me upon pursuing and pressing after them. It was my continual strife day and night, and constant inquiry, how I should *be* more holy, and *live* more holily, and more becoming a child of God, and a disciple of Christ. I now sought an increase of grace and holiness, and a holy life, with much more earnestness, than ever I sought grace before I had it. I used to be continually examining myself, and studying and contriving for likely ways and means, how I should live holily, with far greater diligence and earnestness, than ever I pursued anything in my life; but yet with too great a dependence on my own strength; which afterwards proved a great damage to me. My experience had not then taught me, as it has done since, my extreme feebleness and impotence, every manner of way; and the bottomless depths of secret corruption and deceit there

[3] August, 1722.

was in my heart. However, I went on with my eager pursuit after more holiness, and conformity to Christ.

The heaven I desired was a heaven of holiness; to be with God, and to spend my eternity in divine love, and holy communion with Christ. My mind was very much taken up with contemplations on heaven, and the enjoyments there; and living there in perfect holiness, humility and love: And it used at that time to appear a great part of the happiness of heaven, that there the saints could express their love to Christ. It appeared to me a great clog and burden, that what I felt within, I could not express as I desired. The inward ardor of my soul, seemed to be hindered and pent up, and could not freely flame out as it would. I used often to think, how in heaven this principle should freely and fully vent and express itself. Heaven appeared exceedingly delightful, as a world of love; and that all happiness consisted in living in pure, humble, heavenly, divine love.

I remember the thoughts I used then to have of holiness; and said sometimes to myself, "I do certainly know that I love holiness, such as the gospel prescribes." It appeared to me, that there was nothing in it but what was ravishingly lovely; the highest beauty and amiableness—a *divine* beauty; far purer than any thing here upon earth; and that every thing else was like mire and defilement, in comparison of it.

Holiness, as I then wrote down some of my contemplations on it, appeared to me to be of a sweet, pleasant, charming, serene, calm nature; which brought an inexpressible purity, brightness, peacefulness and ravishment to the soul. In other words, that it made the soul like a field or garden of God, with all manner of pleasant flowers; all pleasant, delightful, and undisturbed; enjoying a sweet calm, and the gently vivifying beams of the sun. The soul of a true Christian, as I then wrote my meditations, appeared like such a little white flower as we see in the spring of the year; low and humble on the ground, opening its bosom to receive the pleasant beams of the sun's glory; rejoicing, as it were, in a calm rapture; diffusing around a sweet fragrancy; standing peacefully and lovingly, in the midst of other flowers round about; all in like manner opening their bosoms, to drink in the light of the sun. There was no part of creature holiness, that I had so great a sense of its loveliness, as humility, brokenness of heart and poverty of spirit; and there was

nothing that I so earnestly longed for. My heart panted after this, to lie low before God, as in the dust; that I might be nothing, and that God might be ALL, that I might become as a little child.

While at Newyork, I was sometimes much affected with reflections on my past life, considering how late it was before I began to be truly religious; and how wickedly I had lived till then; and once so as to weep abundantly, 10 and for a considerable time together.

On January 12, 1723, I made a solemn dedication of myself to God, and wrote it down; giving up myself, and all that I had to God; to be for the future, in no respect, my own; to act as one that had no right to himself, in any respect. And solemnly vowed, to take God for my whole portion and felicity; looking on nothing else, as any part of my happiness, nor acting as if it were; and his law for the constant rule of 20 my obedience: engaging to fight, with all my might, against the world, the flesh, and the devil, to the end of my life. But I have reason to be infinitely humbled, when I consider, how much I have failed, of answering my obligation.

I had, then, abundance of sweet, religious conversation, in the family where I lived, with Mr. John Smith, and his pious mother. My heart was knit in affection, to those, in whom were appearances of true piety; and I could 30 bear the thoughts of no other companions, but such as were holy, and the disciples of the blessed Jesus. I had great longings, for the advancement of Christ's kingdom in the world; and my secret prayer used to be, in great part, taken up in praying for it. If I heard the least hint, of any thing that happened, in any part of the world, that appeared, in some respect or other, to have a favorable aspect, on the interests of Christ's kingdom, my soul eagerly 40 catched at it; and it would much animate and refresh me. I used to be eager to read public news-letters, mainly for that end; to see if I could not find some news, favorable to the interest of religion in the world.

I very frequently used to retire into a solitary place, on the banks of Hudson's River, at some distance from the city, for contemplation on divine things and secret converse with God: and had many sweet hours there. Sometimes Mr. 50 Smith and I walked there together, to converse on the things of God; and our conversation used to turn much on the advancement of Christ's kingdom in the world, and the glorious things that God would accomplish for his church in the latter days. I had then, and at other times, the greatest delight in the holy scriptures, of any book whatsoever. Oftentimes in reading it, every word seemed to touch my heart. I felt a harmony between something in my heart, and those sweet and powerful words. I seemed often to see so much light exhibited by every sentence, and such a refreshing food communicated, that I could not get along in reading; often dwelling long on one sentence, to see the wonders contained in it; and yet almost every sentence seemed to be full of wonders.

I came away from Newyork in the month of April, 1723, and had a most bitter parting with Madam Smith and her son. My heart seemed to sink within me, at leaving the family and city, where I had enjoyed so many sweet and pleasant days. I went from Newyork to Wethersfield, by water; and as I sailed away, I kept sight of the city as long as I could. However, that night after this sorrowful parting, I was greatly comforted in God at Westchester, where we went ashore to lodge: and had a pleasant time of it all the voyage to Saybrook. It was sweet to me to think of meeting dear Christians in heaven, where we should never part more. At Saybrook we went ashore to lodge on Saturday, and there kept the Sabbath; where I had a sweet and refreshing season, walking alone in the fields.

After I came home to Windsor, I remained much in a like frame of mind, as when at Newyork; only sometimes I felt my heart ready to sink, with the thoughts of my friends at Newyork. My support was in contemplations on the heavenly state; as I find in my Diary of May 1, 1723. It was a comfort to think of that state, where there is fulness of joy; where reigns heavenly, calm, and delightful love, without alloy; where there are continually the dearest expressions of this love; where is the enjoyment of the persons loved, without ever parting; where those persons who appear so lovely in this world, will really be inexpressibly more lovely and full of love to us. And how sweetly will the mutual lovers join together, to sing the praises of God and the Lamb! How will it fill us with joy to think, that this enjoyment, these sweet exercises will never cease, but will last to all eternity. . . . I continued much in the same frame, in the general, as when at Newyork, till I went to Newhaven, as Tutor of the College: particularly, once at Bol-

ton, on a journey from Boston, while walking out alone in the fields. After I went to Newhaven, I sunk in religion; my mind being diverted from my eager pursuits after holiness, by some affairs, that greatly perplexed and distracted my thoughts.

In September, 1725, I was taken ill at Newhaven, and while endeavouring to go home to Windsor, was so ill at the North Village, that I could go no farther; where I lay sick, for about a quarter of a year. In this sickness, God was pleased to visit me again, with the sweet influences of his Spirit. My mind was greatly engaged there, on divine and pleasant contemplations, and longings of soul. I observed, that those who watched with me, would often be looking out wishfully for the morning; which brought to my mind those words of the Psalmist, and which my soul with delight made its own language, *My soul waiteth for the Lord, more than they 'that watch for the morning; I say, more than they that watch for the morning;* and when the light of day came in at the window, it refreshed my soul, from one morning to another. It seemed to be some image of the light of God's glory.

I remember, about that time, I used greatly to long for the conversion of some, that I was concerned with; I could gladly honour them, and with delight be a servant to them, and lie at their feet, if they were but truly holy. But some time after this, I was again greatly diverted with some temporal concerns, that exceedingly took up my thoughts, greatly to the wounding of my soul; and went on, through various exercises, that it would be tedious to relate, which gave me much more experience of my own heart, than ever I had before.

Since I came to this town,[4] I have often had sweet complacency in God, in views of his glorious perfections and the excellency of Jesus Christ. God has appeared to me a glorious and lovely Being, chiefly on account of his holiness. The holiness of God has always appeared to me the most lovely of all his attributes. The doctrines of God's absolute sovereignty, and free grace, in shewing mercy to whom he would shew mercy; and man's absolute dependance on the operations of God's Holy Spirit, have very often appeared to me as sweet and glorious doctrines. These doctrines have been much my delight. God's sovereignty has ever appeared to me, great part of his glory. It has

[4] Northampton, Massachusetts.

often been my delight to approach God, and adore him as a sovereign God, and ask sovereign mercy of him.

I have loved the doctrines of the gospel; they have been to my soul like green pastures. The gospel has seemed to me the richest treasure; the treasure that I have most desired, and longed that it might dwell richly in me. The way of salvation by Christ has appeared, in a general way, glorious and excellent, most pleasant and most beautiful. It has often seemed to me, that it would in a great measure spoil heaven, to receive it in any other way. That text has often been affecting and delightful to me, Isa. xxxii. 2. *A man shall be an hiding place from the wind, and a covert from the tempest, &c.*

It has often appeared to me delightful, to be united to Christ; to have him for my head, and to be a member of his body; also to have Christ for my teacher and prophet. I very often think with sweetness, and longings, and pantings of soul, of being a little child, taking hold of Christ, to be led by him through the wilderness of this world. That text, Matth. xviii. 3, has often been sweet to me, *except ye be converted and become as little children, &c.* I love to think of coming to Christ, to receive salvation of him, poor in spirit, and quite empty of self, humbly exalting him alone; cut off entirely from my own root, in order to grow into, and out of Christ; to have God in Christ to be all in all; and to live by faith in the Son of God, a life of humble unfeigned confidence in him. That scripture has often been sweet to me, Psal. cxv. 1. *Not unto us, O Lord, not unto us, but to thy name give glory, for thy mercy, and for thy truth's sake.* And those words of Christ, Luke x. 21. *In that hour Jesus rejoiced in spirit, and said, I thank thee, O Father, Lord of heaven and earth, that thou hast hid these things from the wise and prudent, and hast revealed them unto babes: Even so, Father, for so it seemed good in thy sight.* That sovereignty of God which Christ rejoiced in, seemed to me worthy of such joy; and that rejoicing seemed to show the excellency of Christ, and of what spirit he was.

Sometimes, only mentioning a single word caused my heart to burn within me; or only seeing the name of Christ, or the name of some attribute of God. And God has appeared glorious to me, on account of the Trinity. It has made me have exalting thoughts of God, that he subsists in three persons; Father, Son and Holy Ghost. The sweetest joys and delights I have experienced, have not been those that have arisen from a hope of my own good estate; but in a direct view of the glorious things of the gospel. When I enjoy this sweetness, it seems to carry me above the thoughts of my own estate; it seems at such times a loss that I cannot bear, to take off my eye from the glorious, pleasant object I behold without me, to turn my eye in upon myself, and my own good estate. 10

My heart has been much on the advancement of Christ's kingdom in the world. The histories of the past advancement of Christ's kingdom have been sweet to me. When I have read histories of past ages, the pleasantest thing in all my reading has been, to read of the kingdom of Christ being promoted. And when I have expected, in my reading, to come to any such thing, I have rejoiced in the prospect, all the way as I read. And my mind has been much entertained and delighted with the scripture promises and prophecies, which relate to the future glorious advancement of Christ's kingdom upon earth. 20

I have sometimes had a sense of the excellent fulness of Christ, and his meetness and suitableness as a Saviour; whereby he has appeared to me, far above all, the chief of ten thousands. His blood and atonement have appeared sweet, and his righteousness sweet; which was always accompanied with ardency of spirit; and inward strugglings and breathings, and groanings that cannot be uttered, to be emptied of myself, and swallowed up in Christ. 30

Once, as I rode out into the woods for my health, in 1737, having alighted from my horse in a retired place, as my manner commonly has been, to walk for divine contemplation and prayer, I had a view that for me was extraordinary, of the glory of the Son of God, as Mediator between God and man, and his wonderful, great, full, pure and sweet grace and love, and meek and gentle condescension. This grace that appeared so calm and sweet, appeared also great above the heavens. The person of Christ appeared ineffably excellent with an excellency great enough to swallow up all thought and conception . . . which continued as near as I can judge, about an hour; which kept me the greater part of the time in a flood of tears, and weeping aloud. I felt an ardency of soul to 40 50 be, what I know not otherwise how to express, emptied and annihilated; to lie in the dust, and to be full of Christ alone; to love him with a holy and pure love; to trust in him; to live upon him; to serve and follow him; and to be perfectly sanctified and made pure, with a divine and heavenly purity. I have, several other times, had views very much of the same nature, and which have had the same effects.

I have many times had a sense of the glory of the third person in the Trinity, in his office of Sanctifier; in his holy operations, communicating divine light and life to the soul. God, in the communications of his Holy Spirit, has appeared as an infinite fountain of divine glory and sweetness; being full, and sufficient to fill and satisfy the soul; pouring forth itself in sweet communications; like the sun in its glory, sweetly and pleasantly diffusing light and life. And I have sometimes had an affecting sense of the excellency of the word of God, as a word of life; as the light of life; a sweet, excellent lifegiving word; accompanied with a thirsting after that word, that it might dwell richly in my heart.

Often, since I lived in this town, I have had very affecting views of my own sinfulness and vileness; very frequently to such a degree as to hold me in a kind of loud weeping, sometimes for a considerable time together; so that I have often been forced to shut myself up. I have had a vastly greater sense of my own wickedness, and the badness of my heart, than ever I had before my conversion. It has often appeared to me, that if God should mark iniquity against me, I should appear the very worst of all mankind; of all that have been, since the beginning of the world to this time; and that I should have by far the lowest place in hell. When others, that have come to talk with me about their soul concerns, have expressed the sense they have had of their own wickedness, by saying that it seemed to them, that they were as bad as the devil himself; I thought their expression seemed exceedingly faint and feeble, to represent my wickedness.

My wickedness, as I am in myself, has long appeared to me perfectly ineffable, and swallowing up all thought and imagination; like an infinite deluge, or mountains over my head. I know not how to express better what my sins appear to me to be, than by heaping infinite upon infinite, and multiplying infinite by infinite. Very often, for these many years, these expressions are in my mind, and in my mouth,

"Infinite upon infinite . . . Infinite upon infinite!" When I look into my heart, and take a view of my wickedness, it looks like an abyss infinitely deeper than hell. And it appears to me, that were it not for free grace, exalted and raised up to the infinite height of all the fulness and glory of the great Jehovah, and the arm of his power and grace stretched forth in all the majesty of his power, and in all the glory of his sovereignty, I should appear sunk down in my sins below hell itself; far beyond the sight of every thing, but the eye of sovereign grace, that can pierce even down to such a depth. And yet, it seems to me, that my conviction of sin is exceedingly small, and faint; it is enough to amaze me, that I have no more sense of my sin. I know certainly, that I have very little sense of my sinfulness. When I have had turns of weeping and crying for my sins, I thought I knew at the time, that my repentance was nothing to my sin.

I have greatly longed of late, for a broken heart, and to lie low before God; and, when I ask for humility, I cannot bear the thoughts of being no more humble than other Christians. It seems to me, that though their degrees of humility may be suitable for them, yet it would be a vile selfexaltation in me, not to be the lowest in humility of all mankind. Others speak of their longing to be "humbled to the dust"; that may be a proper expression for them, but I always think of myself, that I ought, and it is an expression that has long been natural for me to use in prayer, "to lie infinitely low before God." And it is affecting to think, how ignorant I was, when a young Christian, of the bottomless, infinite depths of wickedness, pride, hypocrisy and deceit, left in my heart.

I have a much greater sense of my universal, exceeding dependence on God's grace and strength, and mere good pleasure, of late, than I used formerly to have; and have experienced more of an abhorrence of my own righteousness. The very thought of any joy arising in me, on any consideration of my own amiableness, performances, or experiences, or any goodness of heart or life, is nauseous and detestable to me. And yet I am greatly afflicted with a proud and selfrighteous spirit, much more sensibly than I used to be formerly. I see that serpent rising and putting forth its head continually, every where, all around me.

Though it seems to me, that, in some respects, I was a far better Christian, for two or three years after my first conversion, than I am now; and lived in a more constant delight and pleasure; yet, of late years, I have had a more full and constant sense of the absolute sovereignty of God, and a delight in that sovereignty; and have had more of a sense of the glory of Christ, as a Mediator revealed in the gospel. On one Saturday night, in particular, I had such a discovery of the excellency of the gospel above all other doctrines, that I could not but say to myself, "This is my chosen light, my chosen doctrine"; and of Christ, "This is my chosen Prophet." It appeared sweet, beyond all expression, to follow Christ, and to be taught, and enlightened, and instructed by him; to learn of him, and to live to him. Another Saturday night, (January, 1739) I had such a sense,

how sweet and blessed a thing it was to walk in the way of duty; to do that which was right and meet to be done, and agreeable to the holy mind of God; that it caused me to break forth into a kind of loud weeping, which held me some time, so that I was forced to shut myself up, and fasten the doors. I could not but, as it were, cry out, "How happy are they which do that which is right in the sight of God! They are blessed indeed, they are the happy ones!" [10] I had, at the same time, a very affecting sense, how meet and suitable it was that God should govern the world, and order all things according to his own pleasure; and I rejoiced in it, that God reigned, and that his will was done.

c. 1740   1808

From: SINNERS IN THE HANDS OF AN ANGRY GOD [5]

» »   « «

APPLICATION [OF THE TEXT]

Deuteronomy xxxii. 35.—*Their foot shall slide in due time.*

The use of this awful subject may be for awakening unconverted persons in this congregation. This that you have heard is the case of every one of you that are out of Christ.— That world of misery, that lake of burning brimstone, is extended abroad under you. There is the dreadful pit of the glowing flames of the wrath of God; there is hell's wide gaping mouth open; and you have nothing to stand upon, nor any thing to take hold of; there is nothing between you and hell but the air; it is only the power and mere pleasure of God that holds you up.

You probably are not sensible of this; you find you are kept out of hell, but do not see the hand of God in it; but look at other things, as the good state of your bodily constitution, your care of your own life, and the means you use for your own preservation. But indeed these things are nothing; if God should withdraw his hand, they would avail no more to keep you from falling, than the thin air to hold up a person that is suspended in it.

Your wickedness makes you as it were heavy as lead, and to tend downwards with great weight and pressure towards hell; and if God should let you go, you would immediately sink

[5] This imprecatory sermon, preached at Enfield, Connecticut, in 1741, produced "such a breathing of distress, and weeping, that the preacher was obliged to speak to the people and desire silence, that he might be heard."

and swiftly descend and plunge into the bottomless gulf, and your healthy constitution, and [23] your own care and prudence, and best contrivance, and all your righteousness, would have no more influence to uphold you and keep you out of hell, than a spider's web would have to stop a fallen rock. Were it not for the sovereign pleasure of God, the earth would not bear [30] you one moment; for you are a burden to it; the creation groans with you; the creature is made subject to the bondage of your corruption, not willingly; the sun does not willingly shine upon you to give you light to serve sin and Satan; the earth does not willingly yield her increase to satisfy your lusts; nor is it willingly a stage for your wickedness to be acted upon; the air does not willingly serve you for breath to maintain the flame of life in your [40] vitals, while you spend your life in the service of God's enemies. God's creatures are good, and were made for men to serve God with, and do not willingly subserve to any other purpose, and groan when they are abused to purposes so directly contrary to their nature and end. And the world would spew you out, were it not for the sovereign hand of him who hath subjected it in hope. There are black clouds of God's wrath now hanging directly over your heads, [50] full of the dreadful storm, and big with thunder; and were it not for the restraining hand of God, it would immediately burst forth upon you. The sovereign pleasure of God, for the present, stays his rough wind; otherwise it would come with fury, and your destruction would come like a whirlwind, and you would be like the chaff of the summer threshing floor.

The wrath of God is like great waters that are dammed for the present; they increase more and more, and rise higher and higher, till an outlet is given; and the longer the stream is stopped, the more rapid and mighty is its course, when once it is let loose. It is true, that judgment against your evil works has not been executed hitherto; the floods of God's vengeance have been withheld; but your guilt in the mean time is constantly increasing, and you are every day treasuring up more wrath; the waters are continually rising, and waxing more and more mighty; and there is nothing but the mere pleasure of God, that holds the waters back, that are unwilling to be stopped, and press hard to go forward. If God should only withdraw his hand from the flood-gate, it would immediately fly open, and the fiery floods of the fierceness and wrath of God, would rush forth with inconceivable fury, and would come upon you with omnipotent power; and if your strength were ten thousand times greater than it is, yea, ten thousand times greater than the strength of the stoutest, sturdiest devil in hell, it would be nothing to withstand or endure it.

The bow of God's wrath is bent, and the arrow made ready on the string, and justice bends the arrow at your heart, and strains the bow, and it is nothing but the mere pleasure of God, and that of an angry God, without any promise or obligation at all, that keeps the arrow one moment from being made drunk with your blood. Thus all you that never passed under a great change of heart, by the mighty power of the Spirit of God upon your souls; all you that were never born again, and made new creatures, and raised from being dead in sin, to a state of new, and before altogether unexperienced light and life, are in the hands of an angry God. However you may have reformed your life in many things, and may have had religious affections, and may keep up a form of religion in your families and closets, and in the house of God, it is nothing but his mere pleasure that keeps you from being this moment swallowed up in everlasting destruction. However unconvinced you may now be of the truth of what you hear, by and by you will be fully convinced of it. Those that are gone from being in the like circumstances with you, see that it was so with them; for destruction came suddenly upon most of them; when they expected

nothing of it, and while they were saying, Peace and safety: now they see, that those things on which they depended for peace and safety, were nothing but thin air and empty shadows.

The God that holds you over the pit of hell, much as one holds a spider, or some lothsome insect over the fire, abhors you, and is dreadfully provoked: his wrath towards you burns like fire; he looks upon you as worthy of nothing else, but to be cast into the fire; he is of purer eyes than to bear to have you in his sight; you are ten thousand times more abominable in his eyes, than the most hateful venomous serpent is in ours. You have offended him infinitely more than ever a stubborn rebel did his prince; and yet it is nothing but his hand that holds you from falling into the fire every moment. It is to be ascribed to nothing else, that you did not go to hell the last night; that you was suffered to awake again in this world, after you closed your eyes to sleep. And there is no other reason to be given why you have not dropped into hell since you arose in the morning, but that God's hand has held you up. There is no other reason to be given why you have not gone to hell, since you have sat here in the house of God, provoking his pure eyes by your sinful wicked manner of attending his solemn worship. Yea, there is nothing else that is to be given as a reason why you do not this very moment drop down into hell.

O sinner! Consider the fearful danger you are in: it is a great furnace of wrath, a wide and bottomless pit, full of the fire of wrath, that you are held over in the hand of that God, whose wrath is provoked and incensed as much against you, as against many of the damned in hell. You hang by a slender thread, with the flames of divine wrath flashing about it, and ready every moment to singe it, and burn it asunder; and you have no interest in any Mediator, and nothing to lay hold of to save yourself, nothing to keep off the flames of wrath, nothing of your own, nothing that you ever have done, nothing that you can do, to induce God to spare you one moment. . . .

How dreadful is the state of those that are daily and hourly in the danger of this great wrath and infinite misery! But this is the dismal case of every soul in this congregation that has not been born again, however moral and strict, sober and religious, they may otherwise be. Oh that you would consider it, whether you be young or old! There is reason to think, that there are many in this congregation now hearing this discourse, that will actually be the subjects of this very misery to all eternity. We know not who they are, or in what seats they sit, or what thoughts they now have. It may be they are now at ease, and hear all these things without much disturbance, and are now flattering themselves that they are not the persons, promising themselves that they shall escape. If we knew that there was one person, and but one, in the whole congregation, that was to be the subject of this misery, what an awful thing would it be to think of! If we knew who it was, what an awful sight would it be to see such a person! How might all the rest of the congregation lift up a lamentable and bitter cry over him! But, alas! instead of one, how many is it likely will remember this discourse in hell? And it would be a wonder if some that are now present should not be in hell in a very short time, even before this year is out. And it would be no wonder if some persons, that now sit here in some seats of this meeting-house, in health, quiet and secure, should be there before to-morrow morning. Those of you that finally continue in a natural condition, that shall keep out of hell longest will be there in a little time! Your damnation does not slumber; it will come swiftly and, in all probability, very suddenly upon many of you. You have reason to wonder that you are not already in hell. It is doubtless the case of some whom you have seen and known, that never deserved hell more than you, and that heretofore appeared as likely to have been now alive as you. Their case is past all hope; they are crying in extreme misery and perfect despair; but here you are in the land of the living and in the house of God, and have an opportunity to obtain salvation. What would not those poor damned hopeless souls give for one day's such opportunity as you now enjoy!

And now you have an extraordinary opportunity, a day wherein Christ has thrown the door of mercy wide open, and stands in the door calling and crying with a loud voice to poor sinners; a day wherein many are flocking to him, and pressing into the kingdom of God. Many are daily coming from the east, west, north and south; many that were very likely in the same miserable condition that you are in, are now in a happy state, with their hearts filled with love to him who has loved them, and washed them from their sins in his own blood, and rejoicing in hope of the glory of God. How awful is it to be left behind at such a day! To see so many others feasting, while you are pining and perishing! To see so many rejoicing and singing for joy of heart, while you have cause to mourn for sorrow of heart, and howl for vexation of spirit! How can you rest one moment in such a condition? Are not your souls as precious as the souls of the people at Suffield, where they are flocking from day to day to Christ? 10

Are there not many here that have lived long in the world and are not to this day born again? and so are aliens from the commonwealth of Israel, and have done nothing ever since they have lived, but treasure up wrath against the day of wrath? Oh, sirs, your case, in an especial manner, is extremely dangerous. Your guilt and hardness of heart is extremely great. Do you not see how generally persons of your years are passed over and left, in the present remarkable 20 and wonderful dispensation of God's mercy? You had need to consider yourselves, and wake thoroughly out of sleep. You cannot bear the fierceness and wrath of the infinite God.— And you, young men, and young women, will you neglect this precious season which you now enjoy, when so many others of your age are renouncing all youthful vanities, and flocking to Christ? You especially have now an extraordinary opportunity; but if you neglect it, 30 it will soon be with you as it is with those persons who spent all the precious days of youth in sin, and are now come to such a dreadful pass in blindness and hardness.—And you, children, who are unconverted, do not you know that you are going down to hell, to bear the dreadful wrath of that God, who is now angry with you every day and every night? Will you be content to be the children of the devil, when so many other children in the 40 land are converted, and are become the holy and happy children of the King of kings?

And let every one that is yet out of Christ, and hanging over the pit of hell, whether they be old men and women, or middle aged or young people, or little children, now hearken to the loud calls of God's word and providence. This acceptable year of the Lord, a day of such great favours to some, will doubtless be a day of as remarkable vengeance to others. 50 Men's hearts harden, and their guilt increases apace at such a day as this, if they neglect their souls; and never was there so great danger of such persons being given up to hardness of heart and blindness of mind. God seems now to be hastily gathering in his elect in all parts of the land; and probably the greater part of adult persons that ever shall be saved, will be brought in now in a little time, and that it will be as it was on that great out-pouring of the Spirit upon the Jews in the apostles' days; the election will obtain, and the rest will be blinded. If this should be the case with you, you will eternally curse this day, and will curse the day that ever you was born, to see such a season of the pouring out of God's Spirit, and will wish that you had died and gone to hell before you had seen it. Now undoubtedly it is,

as it was in the days of John the Baptist, the axe is in an extraordinary manner laid at the root of the trees, that every tree that brings not forth good fruit, may be hewn down and cast into the fire.

Therefore, let every one that is out of Christ, now awake and fly from the wrath to come. The wrath of Almighty God is now undoubtedly hanging over great part of this congregation: Let every one fly out of Sodom: *"Haste and escape for your lives, look not behind you, escape to the mountain, lest you be consumed."*

1741

» »   [TO THE TRUSTEES OF THE COLLEGE OF NEW JERSEY AT PRINCETON]   « «

Stockbridge, Oct. 19, 1757

Rev. and Hon. Gentlemen,

I was not a little surprised, on receiving the unexpected notice, of your having made choice of me, to succeed the late President Burr, as the Head of Nassau Hall.—I am much in doubt, whether I am called to undertake the business, which you have done me the unmerited honour to choose me for.—If some regard may be had to my outward comfort, I might mention the many inconveniences, and great detriment, which may be sustained, by my removing, with my numerous family, so far from all the estate I have in the world, (without any prospect of disposing of it, under present circumstances, but with great loss,) now when we have scarcely got over the trouble and damage sustained by our removal from Northmapton, and have but just begun to have our affairs in a comfortable situation, for a subsistence in this place; and the expense I must immediately be at, to put myself into circumstances, tolerably comporting with the needful support of the honours of the office I am invited to; which will not well consist with my ability.

But this is not my main objection. The chief difficulties in my mind, in the way of accepting this important and arduous office, are these two: First, my own defects, unfitting me for such an undertaking, many of which are generally known; beside others, of which my own heart is conscious.—I have a constitution, in many respects peculiarly unhappy, attended with flaccid solids, vapid, sizy and scarce fluids, and a low tide of spirits; often occasioning a kind of childish weakness and contemptibleness of speech, presence, and demeanor, with a disagreeable dulness and stiffness, much unfitting me for conversation, but more especially for the government of a college.—This makes me shrink at the thoughts of taking upon me, in the decline of life, such a new and great business, attended with such a multiplicity of cares, and requiring such a degree of activity, alertness, and spirit of government; especially as succeeding one so remarkably well qualified in these respects, giving occasion to every one to remark the wide difference. I am also deficient in some parts of learning, particularly in Algebra, and the higher parts of Mathematics, and in the Greek Classics; my Greek learning having been chiefly in the New Testament.—The other thing is this; that my engaging in this business will not well consist with those views, and that course of employ in my study, which have long engaged and swallowed up my mind, and been the chief entertainment and delight of my life.

And here, honoured Sirs, (emboldened, by the testimony I have now received of your unmerited esteem, to rely on your candour,) I will with freedom open myself to you.

My method of study, from my first beginning the work of the ministry, has been very much by writing; applying myself, in this way, to improve every important hint; pursuing the clue to my utmost, when any thing in reading, meditation, or conversation, has been suggested to my mind, that seemed to promise light, in any weighty point; thus penning what appeared to me my best thoughts, on innumerable subjects, for my own benefit.—The longer I prosecuted my studies, in this method, the more habitual it became, and the more pleasant and profitable I found it.—The farther I travelled in this way, the more and wider the field opened, which has occasioned my laying out many things in my mind, to do in this manner, if God should spare my life, which my heart hath been much upon; particularly many things against most of the prevailing errors of the present day, which I cannot with any patience see maintained, (to the utter subverting of the gospel of Christ,) with so high a hand, and so long continued a triumph, with so little control, when it appears so evident to me, that there is truly no foundation for any of this glorying and insult. I have already published something on one of the main points in dispute between the Arminians and Calvinists: and have it in view, God willing, (as I have already signified to the public,) in like manner to consider all the other controverted points, and have done much towards a preparation for it.—But beside these, I have had on my mind and heart, (which I long ago began, not with any view to publication,) a great work, which I call a *History of the Work of Redemption,* a body of divinity in an entire new method, being thrown into the form of a history; considering the affair of Christian Theology, as the whole of it, in each part, stands in reference to the great work of redemption by Jesus Christ; which I suppose to be, of all others, the grand design of God, and the *summum* and *ultimum* of all the divine operations and decrees; particularly considering all parts of the grand scheme, in their historical order.—The order of their existence, or their being brought forth to view, in the course of divine dispensations, or the wonderful series of successive acts and events; beginning from eternity, and descending from thence to the great work and successive dispensations of the infinitely wise God, in time, considering the chief events coming to pass in the church of God, and revolutions in the world of mankind, affecting the state of the church and the affair of redemption, which we have an account of in history or prophecy; till at last, we come to the general resurrection, last judgment, and consummation of all things; when it shall be said, *It is done. I am Alpha and Omega, the Beginning and the End.*—Concluding my work, with the consideration of that perfect state of things, which shall be finally settled, to last for eternity.—This history will be carried on with regard to all three worlds, heaven, earth and hell; considering the connected, successive events and alterations in each, so far as the scriptures give any light; introducing all parts of divinity in that order which is most scriptural and most natural; a method which appears to me the most beautiful and entertaining, wherein every divine doctrine will appear to the greatest advantage, in the brightest light, in the most striking manner, shewing the admirable contexture and harmony of the whole.

I have also, for my own profit and entertainment, done much towards another great work, which I call the *Harmony of the Old and New Testament,* in three parts. The first, considering the Prophecies of the Messiah, his redemption and kingdom; the evidences of their references to the Messiah, etc. comparing them all one with another, demonstrating their agreement, true scope, and sense; also considering all the various particulars wherein those prophecies have their exact fulfilment; shewing the universal, precise, and admirable correspondence between predictions and events. The second part, considering the Types of the Old Testament, shewing the evidence of their being intended as representations of the great things of the gospel of Christ; and the agreement of the type with the antitype. The third and great part, considering the Harmony of the Old and New Testament, as to doctrine and precept. In the course of this work, I find there will be occasion for an explanation of a very great part of the holy Scriptures; which may, in such a view, be explained in a method, which to me seems the most entertaining and profitable, best tending to lead the mind to a view of the true spirit, design, life and soul of the scriptures, as well as their proper use and improvement.—I have also many other things in hand, in some of which I have made great progress, which I will not trouble you with an account of. Some of these things, if divine providence favour, I should be willing to attempt a publication of. So far as I myself am able to judge of what talents I have, for benefitting my fellow creatures by word, I think I can write better than I can speak.

My heart is so much in these studies, that I cannot find it in my heart to be willing to put myself into an incapacity to pursue them any more in the future part of my life, to such a degree as I must, if I undertake to go through the same course of employ, in the office of president, that Mr. Burr did, instructing in all the languages, and taking the whole care of the instruction of one of the classes, in all parts of learning, besides his other labours. If I should see light to determine me to accept the place offered me, I should be willing to take upon me the work of a president, so far as it consists in the general inspection of the whole society; and to be subservient to the school, as to their order and methods of study and instruction, assisting, myself, in the immediate instruction in the arts and sciences, (as discretion should direct, and occasion serve, and the state of things require,) especially of the senior class; and added to all, should be willing to do the whole work of a professor of divinity, in public and private lectures, proposing questions to be answered, and some to be discussed in writing and free conversation, in meetings of graduates, and others, appointed in proper seasons, for these ends. It would be now out of my way, to spend time, in a constant teaching of the languages; unless it be the Hebrew tongue; which I should be willing to improve myself in, by instructing others.

On the whole, I am much at a loss, with respect to the way of duty, in this important affair: I am in doubt, whether, if I should engage in it, I should not do what both you and I would be sorry for afterwards. Nevertheless, I think the greatness of the affair, and the regard due to so worthy and venerable a body, as that of the trustees of Nassau Hall, requires my taking the matter into serious consideration. And unless you should appear to be discouraged, by the things which I have now represented, as to any farther expectation from me, I shall proceed to ask advice, of such as I esteem most wise, friendly and faithful: if, after the mind of the Commissioners in Boston is known, it appears that they consent to leave me at liberty, with respect to the business they have employed me in here.

1757   1829

BENJAMIN FRANKLIN

1706–1790

WHEN FRANKLIN, the son of a Boston tallow-chandler, died at eighty-four, he was the first citizen of the world. The judgment of John Adams is not exaggerated:

His reputation was more universal than that of Leibnitz or Newton, Frederick or Voltaire, and his character more beloved and esteemed than any or all of them. . . . His name was familiar to government and people, to kings, courtiers, nobility, clergy, and philosophers, as well as plebeians, to such a degree that there was scarcely a peasant or a citizen, a *valet de chambre*, coachman or footman, a lady's chambermaid or a scullion in a kitchen, who was not familiar with it, and who did not consider him as a friend to human kind.

Franklin's greatness is not derived from what he wrote: there were eighteenth-century thinkers who were more profound. Nor does it depend on what he discovered, important and useful as his scientific work was. But none of his contemporaries so entirely represents the age as Franklin; none had pushed its fundamental assumptions into every field of thought and activity as he had done. He most completely exemplified the aims of the Enlightenment—to master the mysteries of the universe and place knowledge at the service of mankind.

His many-sided life falls into three periods. Until 1757 he is Franklin the printer, the creator of Poor Richard, the public-spirited Philadelphian and Pennsylvanian. Most of the next eighteen years he spent in London, as the shrewd diplomatic agent for several of the colonies. After a brief stay in America (May, 1775–October, 1776), during which he helped to frame the Declaration of Independence, he was sent to France. There his difficult task was to secure

French aid, and then, after the Revolutionary War ended, to assist in the negotiations for peace. Only five years of his life remained when he returned to Philadelphia in 1785.

Franklin was proud of his trade. He had learned it from his brother James in Boston and, at sixteen, had even published his paper for him when James was in trouble with the authorities. In Philadelphia, whither he migrated in 1723, his rise was rapid and he was soon one of the leading printers in the colonies. So well had he prospered that in 1748 he could withdraw from active participation in business. Meanwhile, in these busy years, he had striven to improve himself. In 1727 he formed the Junto, the members of which were required to debate each week profitable questions in ethics, science, literature, and the mechanic arts. Somewhere he found time to learn to read French, Spanish, Italian, and Latin.

In 1731 Franklin's public service began with his founding of the Philadelphia Library Company. He also helped to establish, in 1744, the American Philosophical Society and the Academy (1749) which later grew into the University of Pennsylvania. He became clerk of the Assembly of the colony in 1736, was made Philadelphia's postmaster in 1737, and in 1753 deputy postmaster of the colonies. In 1754 he proposed the farsighted Albany Plan of union.

Meanwhile his significant electrical experiments had been published in London (1751). When he arrived there to work for the colonial cause in 1757, he found himself famous. Honors showered upon him and men of influence sought his friendship. His first diplomatic efforts were successful: he won for Pennsylvania the right to tax the proprietors; his incontrovertible answers, before the bar of the House, to the questions about the Stamp Act had much to do with its repeal. During the next eight years, as events moved toward revolution, Franklin was regarded by the English government as an incendiary, whereas, actually, he was a moderating influence. A final effort to discredit him was made when the Solicitor-General abused Franklin before the Privy Council in a tirade lasting an hour. The next day he was deprived of the postmastership.

Though the burdens of office were severe for an aging man during his years in France (1776–1785), there were compensations in his friendships with Voltaire ("Qu'il est charmant de voir embrasser Solon et Sophocle"), Madame Helvétius, le Veillard, the Mayor of Passy (where Franklin lived), and the members of the Masonic lodge of the Nine Sisters, who made him their *Vénérable*. Even when the peace treaty with England was signed in 1783, his grateful but exacting country would not let Franklin come home. After he did return, his counsel was still needed in framing the new constitution. He was the only one of the Revolutionary patriots to sign all four of the documents on which the Republic rests: the Declaration of Independence, the treaty of alliance with France (1778), the Treaty of Paris, and the Constitution.

Like Dr. Johnson, Franklin was never at a loss for an opinion; his vast knowledge and his common sense were always sharp and ready for work. As a young man, revolting from the Calvinism of his home, he became a Deist, influenced by his reading in Collins and Shaftesbury. His contact with Newtonianism, during his first stay in London, gave a scientific bent to his Deism and turned his interests from ethics to the laws of nature. He realized the importance of mathematics in the new science and lamented that his deficiency in it made him "like a Man searching for some thing in a dark Room where I can only grope and guess."

Franklin's political ideas derive from Locke's version of the social contract and the prevailing notion of natural rights. Longer than many of the colonial statesmen he was an imperialist and strove to show Parliament how the colonies might be persuaded to be loyal members of the Empire. As an opponent of mercantilism, however, he was of necessity an advocate of free trade. He adopted and helped to spread the doctrine of laissez faire. Agriculture, he believed, is the only honest way for a government to acquire wealth: the other means are war, which is robbery, and commerce, which is generally cheating.

In 1784 Franklin wrote: "I have always set a greater value on the character of a *doer of good* than on any other kind of reputation." This desire did not originate in humanitarian enthusiasm. Though Franklin was a friend of Whitefield, the Methodist evangelist, he had no great faith in the universal goodness of the human heart. He believed in doing good—and what American has done more?—because it was a reasonable way to live and because he had a genius for it.

The Writings of Benjamin Franklin, A. H. Smyth, ed., 10 vols., New York, 1905–1907.
The Papers of Benjamin Franklin, L. W. Labaree, W. J. Bell, Jr., *et al.*, eds., New Haven, 1959, *et seq.*
Benjamin Franklin, Representative Selections, with Introduction, Bibliography, and Notes (American Writers Series), F. L. Mott and C. H. Jorgensen, eds., New York, 1936.
Bernard Fay, *Franklin, the Apostle of Modern Times*, Boston, 1929.
Carl Van Doren, *Benjamin Franklin*, New York, 1938.

From: AUTOBIOGRAPHY [1]

TWYFORD, *at the Bishop of St. Asaph's, 1771*

Dear Son; I have ever had a pleasure in obtaining any little anecdotes of my ancestors. You may remember the enquiries I made among the remains of my relations when you were with me in England and the journey I undertook for that purpose. Imagining it may be equally agreeable to you to know the circumstances of *my* life—many of which you are yet unacquainted with—and expecting a week's uninterrupted leisure in my present country retirement, I sit down to write them for you. Besides, there are some other inducements that excite me to this undertaking. From the poverty and obscurity in which I was born and in which I passed my earliest years, I have raised myself to a state of affluence and some degree of celebrity in the world. As constant good fortune has accompanied me even to an advanced period of life, my posterity will perhaps be desirous of learning the means, which I employed, and which, thanks to Providence, so well succeeded with me. They may also deem them fit to be imitated, should any of them find themselves in similar circumstances. That good fortune, when I reflected on it, which is frequently the case, has induced me sometimes to say that were it left to my choice, I should have no objection to go over the same life from its beginning to the end, only asking

the advantage authors have of correcting in a second edition some faults of the first. So would I also wish to change some incidents of it for others more favourable. Notwithstanding, if this condition were denied, I should still accept the offer. But as this repetition is not to be expected, that which resembles most living one's life over again, seems to be to recall all the circumstances of it; and, to render this remembrance more durable, to record them in writing. . . .

Josiah, my father, married young and carried his wife with three children to New England about 1682. The conventicles being at that time forbidden by law and frequently disturbed, some considerable men of his acquaintance determined to go to that country; and he was prevailed with to accompany them thither, where they expected to enjoy the exercise of their religion with freedom. By the same wife, my father had four children more born there, and by a second wife ten others—in all seventeen, of which I remember often to have seen thirteen sitting together at his table, who all grew up to years of maturity and married. I was the youngest son and the youngest of all the children except two daughters. I was born in Boston, in New England.

My mother, the second wife, was Abiah Folger, daughter of Peter Folger, one of the first settlers of New England, of whom honourable mention is made by Cotton Mather in his ecclesiastical history of that country, entitled *Magnalia Christi Americana,* as a "godly and

---

[1] The text here followed is that established by Max Farrand and represents the wording of the final version to pass under Franklin's eyes.

learned Englishman," if I remember the words rightly. I have heard that he wrote several small occasional pieces, but only one of them was printed, which I saw many years since. It was written in 1675, in familiar verse according to the taste of the time and people, and addressed to those then concerned in the government there. It asserts the liberty of conscience, and in behalf of the Anabaptists, Quakers, and other sectaries that had been persecuted. He attributes to this persecution the Indian Wars and other calamities that had befallen the country, regarding them as so many judgments of God to punish so heinous an offence, and exhorting a repeal of those laws, so contrary to charity. This piece appeared to me as written with manly freedom and a pleasing simplicity. The six last lines I remember, though I have forgotten the two first; the purport of them was that his censures proceeded from good will, and therefore he would be known to be the author.

> Because to be a libeller (says he),
>   I hate it with my heart.
> From Sherburne Town [1] where now I dwell,
>   My name I do put here,
> Without offence, your real friend,
>   It is Peter Folgier.

My elder brothers were all put apprentices to different trades. I was put to the grammar school at eight years of age, my father intending to devote me as the tithe of his sons to the service of the church. My early readiness in learning to read (which must have been very early, as I do not remember when I could not read) and the opinion of all his friends that I should certainly make a good scholar, encouraged him in this purpose of his. My uncle Benjamin, too, approved of it and proposed to give me all his shorthand volumes of sermons to set up with, if I would learn his shorthand. I continued, however, at the grammar school rather less than a year, though in that time I had risen gradually from the middle of the class of that year to be at the head of the same class, and was removed into the next class, whence I was to be placed in the third at the end of the year. But my father, burdened with a numerous family, was unable without inconvenience to support the expence of a college education, considering, moreover, as he said to one of his friends in my presence, the little encouragement that line of life afforded to those

[1] In the island of Nantucket.

educated for it. He gave up his first intentions, took me from the grammar school, and sent me to a school for writing and arithmetic kept by a then famous man, Mr. Geo. Brownell. He was a skillful master, and successful in his profession, employing the mildest and most encouraging methods. Under him I learned to write a good hand pretty soon, but I failed in the arithmetic and made no progress in it. At ten years old, I was taken home to help my father in his business, which was that of a tallow chandler and soap boiler—a business he was not bred to but had assumed on his arrival in New England, because he found his dyeing trade, being in little request, would not maintain his family. Accordingly, I was employed in cutting wick for the candles, filling the molds for cast candles, attending the shop, going of errands, etc.

I disliked the trade and had a strong inclination to go to sea, but my father declared against it; however, living near the water, I was much in it and on it. I learned early to swim well and to manage boats; and when embarked with other boys, I was commonly allowed to govern, especially in any case of difficulty; and upon other occasions I was generally the leader among the boys and sometimes led them into scrapes, of which I will mention one instance as it shows an early projecting public spirit, tho' not then justly conducted.

There was a salt marsh that bounded part of the mill pond, on the edge of which at high water, we used to stand to fish for minnows. By much trampling we had made it a mere quagmire. My proposal was to build a wharf there for us to stand upon, and I showed my comrades a large heap of stones which were intended for a new house near the marsh and which would very well suit our purpose. Accordingly, in the evening when the workmen were gone home, I assembled a number of my playfellows, and we worked diligently like so many emmets, sometimes two or three to a stone, 'till we brought them all to make our little wharf. The next morning the workmen were surprised at missing the stones, which had formed our wharf; enquiry was made after the authors of this transfer; we were discovered, complained of; several of us were corrected by our fathers, and tho' I demonstrated the utility of our work, mine convinced me that that which was not honest could not be truly useful . . .

From my infancy I was passionately fond of

reading, and all the little money that came into my hands was laid out in the purchasing of books. I was very fond of voyages. My first acquisition was Bunyan's works in separate little volumes. I afterwards sold them to enable me to buy R. Burton's historical collections; they were small chapmen's books and cheap, forty or fifty in all. My father's little library consisted chiefly of books in polemic divinity, most of which I read. I have since often regretted that at a time when I had such a thirst for knowledge, more proper books had not fallen in my way, since it was now resolved I should not be bred to divinity. There was among them Plutarch's *Lives,* in which I read abundantly, and I still think that time spent to great advantage. There was also a book of Defoe's called an *Essay on Projects* and another of Dr. Mather's called *Essays to do Good,* which perhaps gave me a turn of thinking that had an influence on some of the principal future events of my life.

This bookish inclination at length determined my father to make me a printer, though he had already one son (James) of that profession. In 1717 my brother, James, returned from England with a press and letters to set up his business in Boston. I liked it much better than that of my father, but still had a hankering for the sea. To prevent the apprehended effect of such an inclination, my father was impatient to have me bound to my brother. I stood out some time, but at last was persuaded and signed the indenture, when I was yet but twelve years old. I was to serve as apprentice till I was twenty-one years of age, only I was to be allowed journeyman's wages during the last year. In a little time I made a great progress in the business and became a useful hand to my brother. I now had access to better books. An acquaintance with the apprentices of booksellers enabled me sometimes to borrow a small one, which I was careful to return soon and clean. Often I sat up in my room reading the greatest part of the night, when the book was borrowed in the evening and to be returned early in the morning, lest it should be found missing or wanted.

After some time a merchant, an igenious, sensible man, Mr. Matthew Adams, who had a pretty collection of books and who frequented our printing house, took notice of me, invited me to see his library, and very kindly proposed to lend me such books as I chose to read. I now took a fancy to poetry and made some little pieces. My brother, supposing it might turn to account, encouraged me and induced me to compose two occasional ballads. One was called the "Lighthouse Tragedy," and contained an account of the shipwreck of Capt. Worthilake with his two daughters; the other was a "Sailor's Song on the Taking of the Famous *Teach,* or Blackbeard, the Pirate." They were wretched stuff, in street ballad style; and when they were printed, he sent me about the town to sell them. The first sold prodigiously, the event being recent and having made a great noise. This success flattered my vanity, but my father discouraged me by ridiculing my performances and telling me verse-makers were generally beggars. Thus I escaped being a poet and probably a very bad one. But as prose writing has been of great use to me in the course of my life and was a principal means of my advancement, I shall tell you how in such a situation I acquired what little ability I may be supposed to have in that way.

There was another bookish lad in the town, John Collins by name, with whom I was intimately acquainted. We sometimes disputed, and very fond we were of argument, and very desirous of confuting one another—which disputatious turn, by the way, is apt to become a very bad habit, making people often extremely disagreeable in company, by the contradiction that is necessary to bring it into practice; and thence besides souring and spoiling the conversation, it is productive of disgusts and perhaps enmities where you may have occasion for friendship. I had caught it by reading my father's books of dispute on religion. Persons of good sense, I have since observed, seldom fall into it, except lawyers, university men, and men of all sorts who have been bred at Edinburgh. A question was once somehow or other started between Collins and me on the propriety of educating the female sex in learning and their abilities for study. He was of opinion that it was improper and that they were naturally unequal to it. I took the contrary side, perhaps a little for dispute sake. He was naturally more eloquent, having a greater plenty of words, and sometimes, as I thought, I was vanquished more by his fluency than by the strength of his reasons. As we parted without settling the point and were not to see one another again for some time, I sat down to put my arguments in writing, which I copied fair and sent to him. He answered and I replied. Three or four letters on a side had passed, when my father happened to find my papers and read them. Without entering into the subject in dispute, he took occasion to talk with me about my manner of writing, observed that though I had the advantage of my antagonist in correct spelling and pointing (which I owed to the printing house) I fell far short in elegance of expression, in method, and in perspicuity—of which he convinced me by several instances. I saw the justice of his remarks and thence grew more attentive to my manner of writing, and determined to endeavour to improve my style.

About this time I met with an odd volume of the *Spectator*. It was the third. I had never before seen any of them. I bought it, read it over and over, and was much delighted with it. I thought the writing excellent and wished if possible to imitate it. With that view, I took some of the papers, and making short hints of the sentiment in each sentence, laid them by a few days, and then without looking at the book, tried to complete the papers again by expressing each hinted sentiment at length and as fully as it had been expressed before, in any suitable words that should occur to me. Then I compared my *Spectator* with the original, discovered some of my faults, and corrected them. But I found I wanted a stock of words or a readiness in recollecting and using them, which I thought I should have acquired before that time if I had gone on making verses; since the continual search for words of the same import but of different length to suit the measure, or of different sound for the rhyme would have laid me under a constant necessity of searching for variety, and also have tended to fix that variety in my mind, and make me master of it. Therefore I took some of the tales in the *Spectator* and turned them into verse, and after a time, when I had pretty well forgotten the prose, turned them back again. I also sometimes jumbled my collections of hints into confusion, and after some weeks endeavoured to reduce them into the best order before I began to form the full sentences and complete the paper. This was to teach me method in the arrangement of the thoughts. By comparing my work afterwards with the original, I discovered many faults and corrected them; but I sometimes had the pleasure of fancying that in certain particulars of small import I had been lucky enough to improve the method or the language, and this encouraged me to think that I might possibly in time come to be a tolerable English writer, of which I was extremely ambitious.

The time I allotted for these exercises and for reading, was at night after work, or before it began in the morning, or on Sundays, when I contrived to be in the printing house alone, avoiding as much as I could the common attendance on public worship which my father used to exact of me when I was under his care —and which, indeed, I still thought a duty, though I could not, as it seemed to me, afford the time to practise it. . . .

While I was intent on improving my language, I met with an English grammar (I think it was Greenwood's) at the end of which there were two little sketches on the arts of rhetoric and logic, the latter finishing with a dispute in the Socratic method. And soon after I procured Xenophon's *Memorable Things of Socrates*, wherein there are many examples of the same method. I was charmed with it, adopted it, dropped my abrupt contradiction and positive argumentation, and put on the humble enquirer. And being then, from reading Shaftsbury and Collins, made a doubter, as I already was in many points of our religious doctrines, I found this method the safest for myself and very embarrassing to those against whom I used it; therefore, I took a delight in it, practised it continually, and grew very artful and expert in drawing people, even of superior knowledge, into concessions the consequences of which they did not foresee, entangling them in difficulties out of which they could not extricate themselves, and so obtaining victories that neither myself nor my cause always deserved. I continued this method some few years but gradually left it, retaining only the habit of expressing myself in terms of modest diffidence, never using when I advance anything that may possibly be disputed the words, "certainly," "undoubtedly," or any others that give the air of positiveness to an opinion; but rather say, "I conceive or apprehend a thing to be so or so," "It appears to me," or "I should think it so or so, for such and such reasons," or "I imagine it to be so," or "It is so if I am not mistaken." This habit, I believe, has been of great advantage to me when I have had occasion to inculcate my opinions and persuade men into measures that I have been from time to time engaged in promoting. And as the chief ends of conversation are to *inform*, or to be *informed*, to *please* or to *persuade*, I wish well-meaning and sensible men would not lessen their power of doing good by a positive, assuming manner that seldom fails to disgust, tends to create opposition, and to defeat every one of those purposes for which speech was given to us. In fact, if you wish to instruct others, a positive, dogmatical manner in advancing your sentiments may provoke contradiction and prevent a candid attention. If you desire instruction and improvement from the knowledge of others, you should not at the same time express yourself as firmly fixed in your present opinions; modest and sensible men, who do not love disputation, will probably leave you undisturbed in the possession of your error. In adopting such a manner you can seldom expect to please your hearers, or to persuade those whose concurrence you desire. Pope judiciously observes,

Men must be taught as if you taught them not,
And things unknown propos'd as things forgot.

He also recommends it to us,

To speak, though sure, with seeming diffidence.

And he might have joined with this line that which he has coupled with another, I think less properly,

For want of modesty is want of sense.

If you ask why *less properly,* I must repeat the lines,

Immodest words admit of no defence,
For want of modesty is want of sense.

Now is not the "want of sense" (where a man is so unfortunate as to want it) some apology for his "want of modesty"? and would not the lines stand more justly thus?

Immodest words admit but this defense
That want of modesty is want of sense.

This, however, I should submit to better judgments.

My brother had in 1720 or '21 begun to print a newspaper. It was the second that appeared in America and was called *The New England Courant.* The only one before it was *The Boston Newsletter.* I remember his being dissuaded by some of his friends from the undertaking as not likely to succeed, one newspaper being in their judgment enough for America. At this time, 1771, there are not less than five-and-twenty. He went on, however, with the undertaking; I was employed to carry the papers to the customers, after having worked in composing the types and printing off the sheets. He had some ingenious men among his friends who amused themselves by writing little pieces for this paper, which gained it credit and made it more in demand; and these gentlemen often visited us. Hearing their conversations and their accounts of the approbation their papers were received with, I was excited to try my hand among them. But being still a boy and suspecting that my brother would object to printing anything of mine in his paper if he knew it to be mine, I contrived to disguise my hand; and writing an anonymous paper, I put it at night under the door of the printing house. It was found in the morning and communicated to his writing friends when they called in as usual. They read it, commented on it in my hearing, and I had the exquisite pleasure of finding it met with their approbation, and that in their different guesses at the author, none were named but men of some character among us for learning and ingenuity. I suppose now that I was rather lucky in my judges and that perhaps they were not really so very good as I then believed them to be. Encouraged, however, by this attempt, I wrote and sent in the same way to the press several other pieces, which were equally approved, and I kept my secret till my small fund of sense for such performances was pretty well exhausted, and then I discovered it, when I began to be considered a little more by my brother's acquaintance. However, that did not quite please him as he thought that it tended to make me too vain.

This might be one occasion of the differences we began to have about this time. Though a brother, he considered himself as my master and me as his apprentice, and accordingly expected the same services from me as he would from another; while I thought he degraded me too much in some he required of me, who from a brother expected more indulgence. Our disputes were often brought before our father, and I fancy I was either generally in the right or else a better pleader, because the judgment was generally in my favour. But my brother was passionate and had often beaten me, which I took extremely amiss. I fancy his harsh and tyrannical treatment of me might be a means of impressing me with that aversion to arbitrary power that has stuck to me through my whole life. Thinking my apprenticeship very tedious, I was continually wishing for some opportunity of shortening it, which at length offered in a manner unexpected.

One of the pieces in our newspaper on some political point which I have now forgotten, gave offence to the Assembly. He was taken up, censured, and imprisoned for a month by the Speaker's warrant, I suppose because he would not discover the author. I, too, was taken up and examined before the Council; but though I did not give them any satisfaction, they contented themselves with admonishing me and dismissed me, considering me, perhaps, as an apprentice who was bound to keep his master's secrets. During my brother's confinement, which I resented a good deal notwithstanding our private differences, I had the management of the paper, and I made bold to give our rulers some rubs in it, which my brother took very kindly, while others began to consider me in an unfavourable light as a young genius that had a turn for libelling and satire. My brother's discharge was accompanied with an order from the House (a very odd one) that "James Franklin should no longer print the paper called the *New England Courant*." There was a consultation held in our printing house amongst his friends in this conjuncture. Some proposed to elude the order by changing the name of the paper; but my brother seeing inconveniences in that, it was finally concluded on as a better way to let it be printed for the future under the name of "Benjamin Franklin"; and to avoid the censure of the Assembly that might fall on him as still printing it by his apprentice, the contrivance was that my old indenture should be returned to me with a full discharge on the back of it, to show in case of necessity; but to secure to him the benefit of my service, I should sign new indentures for the remainder of the term, which were to be kept private. A very flimsy scheme it was, but, however, it was immediately executed, and the paper went on accordingly under my name for several months. At length a fresh difference arising between my brother and me, I took upon me to assert my freedom, presuming that he would not venture to produce the new indentures. It was not fair in me to take this advantage, and this I therefore reckon one of the first errata of my life. But the unfairness of it weighed little with me, when under the impressions of resentment for the blows his passion too often urged him to bestow upon me, though he was otherwise not an ill-natured man. Perhaps I was too saucy and provoking. . . .

The inclination I had had for the sea was by this time done away, or I might now have gratified it. But having another profession and conceiving myself a pretty good workman, I offered my services to the printer [in New York], old Mr. Wm. Bradford (who had been the first printer in Pennsylvania, but had removed thence in consequence of a quarrel with the Governor, Geo. Keith). He could give me no employment, having little to do and hands enough already. "But," says he, "my son at Philadelphia has lately lost his principal hand, Aquila Rose, by death. If you go thither I believe he may employ you."

Philadelphia was a hundred miles farther. I set out, however, in a boat for Amboy, leaving my chest and things to follow me round by sea. In crossing the bay we met with a squall that tore our rotten sails to pieces, prevented our getting into the kill, and drove us upon Long Island. In our way a drunken Dutchman who was a passenger, too, fell overboard; when he was sinking, I reached through the water to his shock pate and drew him up so that we got him in again. His ducking sobered him a little, and he went to sleep, taking first out of his pocket a book which he desired I would dry for him. It proved to be my old favourite author Bunyan's *Pilgrim's Progress* in Dutch, finely printed on good paper with copper cuts, a dress better than I had ever seen it wear in its own language. I have since found that it has been translated into most of the languages of Europe, and suppose it has been more generally read than any other book except, perhaps, the Bible. Honest John was the first that I know of who mixes narration and dialogue, a method of writing very engaging to the reader, who in the most interesting parts finds himself, as it were, admitted into the company and present at the conversation. Defoe has imitated him successfully in his *Robinson Crusoe*, in his *Moll Flanders*, and other pieces; and Richardson has done the same in his *Pamela*, etc.

On approaching the island, we found it was in a place where there could be no landing, there being a great surf on the stony beach. So we dropped anchor and swung out our cable towards the shore. Some people came down to the water edge and hallooed to us, as we did to them, but the wind was so high and the surf so loud that we could not understand each other. There were some canoes on the shore, and we made signs and called to them to fetch us, but they either did not comprehend us or thought it impracticable, so they went off. Night approaching, we had no remedy but to have patience till the wind abated, and in the meantime the boatman and I concluded to sleep if we could, and so we crowded into the scuttle with the Dutchman who was still wet, and the spray breaking over the head of our boat leaked through to us, so that we were soon almost as wet as he. In this manner we lay all night with very little rest; but the wind abating the next day, we made a shift to reach Amboy before night, having been thirty hours on the water without victuals or any drink but a bottle of filthy rum, the water we sailed on being salt.

In the evening I found myself very feverish and went to bed; but having read somewhere that cold water drank plentifully was good for a fever, I followed the prescription, sweat plentifully most of the night, my fever left me, and in the morning crossing the ferry, I proceeded on my journey on foot, having fifty miles to Burlington, where I was told I should find boats that would carry me the rest of the way to Philadelphia.

It rained very hard all the day, I was thoroughly soaked and by noon a good deal tired, so I stopped at a poor inn, where I stayed all night, beginning now to wish I had never left home. I made so miserable a figure, too, that I found by the questions asked me I was suspected to be some runaway servant, and in danger of being taken up on that suspicion. However, I proceeded the next day, and got in the evening to an inn within eight or ten miles of Burlington, kept by one Dr. Brown.

He entered into conversation with me while I took some refreshment and, finding I had read a little, became very sociable and friendly. Our acquaintance continued all the rest of his life. He had been, I imagine, an itinerant doctor, for there was no town in England or any country in Europe of which he could not give a very particular account. He had some letters and was ingenious, but he was an infidel and wickedly undertook some years after to travesty the Bible in doggerel verse as Cotton had done with Virgil. By this means he set many of the facts in a very ridiculous light and might have done mischief with weak minds if his work had been published, but it never was. At his house I lay that night, and the next morning reached Burlington, but had the mortification to find that the regular boats were gone a little before and no

other expected to go before Tuesday, this being Saturday. Wherefore, I returned to an old woman in the town of whom I had bought some gingerbread to eat on the water and asked her advice; she invited me to lodge at her house till a passage by water should offer; and being tired with my foot travelling, I accepted the invitation. Understanding I was a printer, she would have had me remain in that town and follow my business, being ignorant of the stock necessary to begin with. She was very hospitable, gave me a dinner of ox cheek with great goodwill, accepting only a pot of ale in return. And I thought myself fixed till Tuesday should come. However, walking in the evening by the side of the river, a boat came by, which I found was going towards Philadelphia with several people in her. They took me in, and as there was no wind, we rowed all the way; and about midnight, not having yet seen the city, some of the company were confident we must have passed it and would row no farther; the others knew not where we were, so we put towards the shore, got into a creek, landed near an old fence, with the rails of which we made a fire, the night being cold in October, and there we remained till daylight. Then one of the company knew the place to be Cooper's Creek, a little above Philadelphia, which we saw as soon as we got out of the creek, and arrived there about eight or nine o'clock, on the Sunday morning and landed at the Market Street wharf.

I have been the more particular in this description of my journey, and shall be so of my first entry into that city, that you may in your mind compare such unlikely beginnings with the figure I have since made there. I was in my working dress, my best clothes being to come round by sea. I was dirty from my journey; my pockets were stuffed out with shirts and stockings; I knew no soul, nor where to look for lodging. Fatigued with walking, rowing, and want of sleep, I was very hungry, and my whole stock of cash consisted of a Dutch dollar and about a shilling in copper coin, which I gave to the boatmen for my passage. At first they refused it on account of my having rowed, but I insisted on their taking it. A man is sometimes more generous when he has little money than when he has plenty, perhaps through fear of being thought to have but little. I walked towards the top of the street, gazing about till near Market Street, where I met a boy with bread. I have often made a meal of dry bread, and inquiring where he had bought it, I went immediately to the baker's he directed me to. I asked for biscuit, meaning such as we had in Boston, but that sort, it seems, was not made in Philadelphia. I then asked for a threepenny loaf and was told they had none such. Not knowing the different prices nor the names of the different sorts of bread, I told him to give me three pennyworth of any sort. He gave me accordingly three great puffy rolls. I was surprized at the quantity but took it, and having no room in my pockets, walked off with a roll under each arm and eating the other. Thus I went up Market Street as far as Fourth Street, passing by the door of Mr. Read, my future wife's father, when she, standing at the door, saw me, and thought I made—as I certainly did—a most awkward, ridiculous appearance. Then I turned and went down Chestnut Street and part of Walnut Street, eating my roll all the way, and coming round, found myself again at Market Street wharf near the boat I came in, to which I went for a draught of the river water, and being filled with one of my rolls, gave the other two to a woman and her child that came down the river in the boat with us and were waiting to go farther. Thus refreshed, I walked again up the street, which by this time had many clean dressed people in it who were all walking the same way; I joined them, and thereby was led into the great meetinghouse of the Quakers near the market. I sat down among them, and after looking round awhile and hearing nothing said, being very drowsy through labour and want of rest the preceding night, I fell fast asleep and continued so till the meeting broke up, when someone was kind enough to rouse me. This was therefore the first house I was in or slept in, in Philadelphia.

I then walked down again towards the river, and looking in the faces of everyone, I met a young Quaker man whose countenance pleased me, and accosting him requested he would tell me where a stranger could get a lodging. We were then near the Sign of the Three Mariners. "Here," says he, "is a house where they receive strangers, but it is not a reputable one; if thee wilt walk with me, I'll show thee a better one." He conducted me to the Crooked Billet in Water Street. There I got a dinner. And while I was eating, several sly questions were asked me, as from my youth and appearance I was suspected of being a runaway. After dinner my sleepiness returned; and being shown to a bed, I lay down without undressing and slept till six in the evening, when I was called to supper. I went to bed again very early and slept soundly till next morning. Then I dressed myself as neat as I could, and went to Andrew Bradford, the printer's. I found in the shop the old man his father, whom I had seen at New York, and who travelling on horseback, had got to Philadelphia before me. He introduced me to his son, who received me civilly, gave me a breakfast, but told me he did not at present want a hand, being lately supplied with one. But there was another printer in town lately set up, one Keimer, who perhaps might employ me; if not, I should be welcome to lodge at his house, and he would give me a little work to do now and then till fuller business should offer.

The old gentleman said he would go with me to the new printer. And when we found him, "Neighbor," says Bradford, "I have brought to see you a young man of your business; perhaps you may want such a one." He asked me a few questions, put a composing stick in my hand to see how I worked, and then said he would employ me soon, though he had just then nothing for me to do. And taking old Bradford, whom he had never seen before, to be one of the townspeople that had a good will for him, entered into a conversation on his present undertaking and prospects; while Bradford, not discovering that he was the other printer's father, on Keimer's saying he expected soon to get the greatest part of the business into his own hands, drew him on by artful questions and starting little doubts to explain all his views, what influence he relied on, and in what manner he intended to proceed. I, who stood by and heard all, saw immediately that one of them was a crafty old sophister, and the other a true novice. Bradford left me with Keimer, who was greatly surprized when I told him who the old man was.

Keimer's printing house, I found, consisted of an old damaged press and a small worn-out fount of English types, which he was then using himself, composing an elegy on Aquila Rose, before-mentioned, an ingenious young man of excellent character, much respected in the town, secretary to the Assembly, and a pretty poet. Keimer made verses, too, but indifferently. He could not be said to write them, for his method was to compose them in the types directly out of his head; so there being no copy but one pair of cases, and the elegy probably requiring all the letter, no one could help him. I endeavoured to put his press (which he had not yet used, and of which he understood nothing) into order fit to be worked with; and promising to come and print off his elegy as soon as he should have got it ready, I returned to Bradford's, who gave me a little job to do for the present, and there I lodged and dieted. A few days after Keimer sent for me to print off the elegy. And now he had got another pair of cases, and a pamphlet to reprint, on which he set me to work.

These two printers I found poorly qualified for their business. Bradford had not been bred to it and was very illiterate; and Keimer, though something of a scholar, was a mere compositor, knowing nothing of presswork. He had been one of the French prophets and could act their enthusiastic agitations. At this time he did not profess any particular religion, but something of all on occasion, was very ignorant of the world, and had—as I afterwards found—a good deal of the knave in his composition. He did not like my lodging at Bradford's while I worked with him. He had a house, indeed, but without furniture, so he could not lodge me; but he got me a lodging at Mr. Read's, before-mentioned, who was the owner of his house. And my chest and clothes being come by this time, I made rather a more respectable appearance in the eyes of Miss Read than I had done when she first happened to see me eating my roll in the street. . . .

It was about this time I conceived the bold and arduous project of arriving at moral perfection. I wished to live without committing any fault at any time; I would conquer all that either natural inclination, custom, or company might lead me into. As I knew, or thought I knew, what was right and wrong, I did not see why I might not *always* do the one and avoid the other. But I soon found I had undertaken a task of more difficulty than I had imagined. While my attention was taken up and care employed in guarding against one fault, I was often surprised by another. Habit took the advantage of inattention. Inclination was sometimes too strong for reason. I concluded at length that the mere speculative conviction that it was our interest to be completely virtuous was not sufficient to prevent our slipping, and that the contrary habits must be broken and good ones acquired and established before we can have any dependence on a steady, uni-

form rectitude of conduct. For this purpose I therefore contrived the following method.

In the various enumerations of the moral virtues I had met with in my reading, I found the catalogue more or less numerous, as different writers included more or fewer ideas under the same name. Temperance, for example, was by some confined to eating and drinking, while by others it was extended to mean the moderating every other pleasure, appetite, inclination, or passion—bodily or mental, even to our avarice and ambition. I proposed to myself, for the sake of clearness, to use rather more names with fewer ideas annexed to each than a few names with more ideas; and I included under thirteen names of virtues all that at that time occurred to me as necessary or desirable, and annexed to each a short precept which fully expressed the extent I gave to its meaning.

These names of virtues with their precepts were

1. TEMPERANCE

Eat not to dulness. Drink not to elevation.

2. SILENCE

Speak not but what may benefit others or yourself. Avoid trifling conversation.

3. ORDER

Let all your things have their places. Let each part of your business have its time.

4. RESOLUTION

Resolve to perform what you ought. Perform without fail what you resolve.

5. FRUGALITY

Make no expence but to do good to others or yourself; i.e., waste nothing.

6. INDUSTRY

Lose no time. Be always employed in something useful. Cut off all unnecessary actions.

7. SINCERITY

Use no hurtful deceit. Think innocently and justly; and, if you speak, speak accordingly.

8. JUSTICE

Wrong none by doing injuries or omitting the benefits that are your duty.

9. MODERATION

Avoid extremes. Forbear resenting injuries so much as you think they deserve.

10. CLEANLINESS

Tolerate no uncleanness in body, clothes or habitation.

11. TRANQUILITY

Be not disturbed at trifles or at accidents common or unavoidable.

12. CHASTITY

Rarely use venery but for health or offspring —never to dulness, weakness, or the injury of your own or another's peace or reputation.

13. HUMILITY

Imitate Jesus and Socrates.

My intention being to acquire the *habitude* of all these virtues, I judged it would be well not to distract my attention by attempting the whole at once but to fix it on one of them at a time, and when I should be master of that, then to proceed to another, and so on till I should have gone thro' the thirteen. And as the previous acquisition of some might facilitate the acquisition of certain others, I arranged them with that view as they stand above. *Temperance* first, as it tends to procure that coolness and clearness of head which is so necessary where constant vigilance was to be kept up, and guard maintained, against the unremitting attraction of ancient habits, and the force of perpetual temptations. This being acquired and established, *Silence* would be more easy, and my desire being to gain knowledge at the same time that I improved in virtue, and considering that in conversation it was obtained rather by the use of the ear than of the tongue, and therefore wishing to break a habit I was getting into of prattling, punning, and joking, which only made me acceptable to trifling company, I gave *Silence* the second place. This and the next, *Order,* I expected would allow me more time for attending to my project and my studies. *Resolution,* once become habitual, would keep me firm in my endeavours to obtain all the subsequent virtues; *Frugality* and *Industry,* freeing me from my remaining debt and, producing affluence and independence, would make more easy the practice of *Sincerity* and *Justice,* etc., etc. Conceiving then that agreeable to the advice of Pythagoras in his golden verses, daily examination would be necessary, I contrived the following method for conducting that examination.

I made a little book in which I allotted a page for each of the virtues. I ruled each page with red ink so as to have seven columns, one for each day of the week, marking each column with a letter for the day. I crossed these columns with thirteen red lines, marking the beginning of each line with the first letter of one of the virtues, on which line and in its proper column I might mark by a little black spot every fault I found upon examination to have been committed respecting that virtue upon that day.

I determined to give a week's strict attention to each of the virtues successively. Thus in the first week my great guard was to avoid even the least offence against temperance, leaving the other virtues to their ordinary chance, only marking every evening the faults of the day. Thus if in the first week I could keep my first line marked "T." clear of spots, I supposed the habit of that virtue so much strengthened and its opposite weakened that I might venture extending my attention to include the next, and for the following week keep both lines clear of spots. Proceeding thus to the last, I could go thro' a course complete in thirteen weeks, and four courses in a year. And like him who, having a garden to weed, does not attempt to eradicate all the bad herbs at once, which would exceed his reach and his strength, but works on one of the beds at a time, and having accomplished the first, proceeds to a second; so I should have (I hoped) the encouraging pleasure of seeing on my pages the progress I made in virtue by clearing successively my lines of their spots, till in the end by a number of courses, I should be happy in viewing a clean book after a thirteen weeks' daily examination. . . .

My scheme of *Order* gave me the most trouble, and I found that tho' it might be practicable where a man's business was such as to leave him the disposition of his time, that of a journeyman printer for instance, it was not possible to be exactly observed by a master, who must mix with the world and often receive people of business at their own hours. Order, too, with regard to places for things, papers, etc., I found extremely difficult to acquire. I had not been early accustomed to *method,* and having an exceeding good memory, I was not so sensible of the inconvenience attending want of method. This article therefore cost me so much painful attention, and my faults in it vexed me so much, and I made so little progress in amendment and had such frequent relapses, that I was almost ready to give up the attempt and content myself with a faulty character in that respect. Like the man who in buying an ax of a smith my neighbour, desired to have the whole of its surface as bright as the edge; the smith consented to grind it bright for him if he would turn the wheel. He turned while the smith pressed the broad face of the ax hard and heavily on the stone, which made the turning of it very fatiguing. The man came every now and then from the wheel to see how the work went on; and at length would take his ax as it was, without further grinding. "No," says the smith, "turn on, turn on; we shall have it bright by and by; as yet 'tis only speckled." "Yes," says the man, *but I think I like a speckled ax best.* And I believe this may have been the case with many who having, for want of some such means as I employed, found the difficulty of obtaining good and breaking bad habits in other points of vice and virtue, have given up the struggle and concluded that "a speckled ax was best." For something that pretended to be reason was every now and then suggesting to me that such extreme nicety as I exacted of myself might be a kind of foppery in morals, which if it were known would make me ridiculous; that a perfect character might be attended with the inconvenience of being envied and hated; and that a benevolent man should allow a few faults in himself, to keep his friends in countenance. . . .

My list of virtues contained at first but twelve. But a Quaker friend having kindly informed me that I was generally thought proud, that my pride showed itself frequently in conversation, that I was not content with being in the right when discussing any point, but was overbearing and rather insolent—of which he convinced me by mentioning several instances—I determined endeavouring to cure myself if I could of this vice or folly among the rest, and I added *Humility* to my list, giving an extensive meaning to the word. I cannot boast of much success in acquiring the *reality* of this virtue, but I had a good deal with regard to the *appearance* of it. I made it a rule to forbear all direct contradiction to the sentiments of others and all positive assertion of my own. I even forbade myself agreeable to the old laws of our Junto, the use of every word or expression in the language that imported a fixed opinion, such as "certainly,"

"undoubtedly," etc.; and I adopted instead of them, "I conceive," "I apprehend," or "I imagine" a thing to be so or so, or "It so appears to me at present." When another asserted something that I thought an error, I denied myself the pleasure of contradicting him abruptly and of showing immediately some absurdity in his proposition; and in answering I began by observing that in certain cases or circumstances his opinion would be right, but that in the present case there "appeared" or "seemed to me" some difference, etc. I soon found the advantage of this change in my manners: The conversations I engaged in went on more pleasantly; the modest way in which I proposed my opinions procured them a readier reception and less contradiction; I had less mortification when I was found to be in the wrong, and I more easily prevailed with others to give up their mistakes and join with me when I happened to be in the right. And this mode, which I at first put on with some violence to natural inclination, became at length so easy and so habitual to me that perhaps for these fifty years no one has ever heard a dogmatical expression escape me. And to this habit (after my character of integrity) I think it principally owing that I had early so much weight with my fellow citizens when I proposed new institutions or alterations in the old, and so much influence in public councils when I became a member. For I was but a bad speaker, never eloquent, subject to much hesitation in my choice of words, hardly correct in language, and yet I generally carried my point.

In reality there is perhaps no one of our natural passions so hard to subdue as *pride;* disguise it, struggle with it, beat it down, stifle it, mortify it as much as one pleases, it is still alive and will every now and then peep out and show itself. You will see it perhaps often in this history. For even if I could conceive that I had completely overcome it, I should probably be proud of my humility.

[Thus far written at Passy, 1784] [1]

In 1732 I first published my *Almanac*, under the name of Richard Saunders; it was continued by me about twenty-five years, commonly called *Poor Richard's Almanac.* I endeavoured to make it both entertaining and useful, and it accordingly came to be in such demand that I reaped considerable profit from it, vending annually near ten thousand. And observ-

Square brackets are Franklin's.

ing that it was generally read, scarce any neighbourhood in the province being without it, I considered it as a proper vehicle for conveying instruction among the common people, who bought scarce any other books. I therefore filled all the little spaces that occurred between the remarkable days in the calendar with proverbial sentences, chiefly such as inculcated industry and frugality as the means of procuring wealth and thereby securing virtue —it being more difficult for a man in want to act always honestly, as (to use here one of those proverbs) "it is hard for an empty sack to stand upright." These proverbs, which contained the wisdom of many ages and nations, I assembled and formed into a connected discourse prefixed to the *Almanac* of 1757, as the harangue of a wise old man to the people attending an auction. The bringing all these scattered counsels thus into a focus enabled them to make greater impression. The piece, being universally approved, was copied in all the newspapers of the Continent, reprinted in Britain on a broadside to be stuck up in houses, two translations were made of it in French, and great numbers bought by the clergy and gentry to distribute gratis among their poor parishioners and tenants. In Pennsylvania, as it discouraged useless expence in foreign superfluities, some thought it had its share of influence in producing that growing plenty of money which was observable for several years after its publication. . . .

In 1746 being at Boston, I met there with a Dr. Spence, who was lately arrived from Scotland, and showed me some electric experiments. They were imperfectly performed, as he was not very expert; but being on a subject quite new to me, they equally surprized and pleased me. Soon after my return to Philadelphia, our library company received from Mr. Peter Colinson, F.R.S., of London, a present of a glass tube, with some account of the use of it in making such experiments. I eagerly seized the opportunity of repeating what I had seen at Boston, and by much practice acquired great readiness in performing those also which we had an account of from England, adding a number of new ones I say much practice, for my house was continually full for some time with people who came to see these new wonders. To divide a little this incumbrance among my friends, I caused a number of similar tubes to be blown at our glass house, with which they furnished themselves, so that we

had at length several performers. Among these the principal was Mr. Kinnersley, an ingenious neighbour, who, being out of business, I encouraged to undertake showing the experiments for money, and drew up for him two lectures in which the experiments were ranged in such order and accompanied with explanations, in such method as that the foregoing should assist in comprehending the following. He procured an elegant apparatus for the purpose, in which all the little machines that I had roughly made for myself were nicely formed by instrument makers. His lectures were well attended and gave great satisfaction and after some time he went thro' the Colonies exhibiting them in every capital town and picked up some money. In the West India Islands, indeed, it was with difficulty the experiments could be made, from the general moisture of the air.

Obliged as we were to Mr. Colinson for his present of the tube, etc., I thought it right he should be informed of our success in using it and wrote him several letters containing accounts of our experiments. He got them read in the Royal Society, where they were not at first thought worth so much notice as to be printed in their transactions. One paper which I wrote for Mr. Kinnersley, on the sameness of lightning with electricity, I sent to Dr. Mitchel, an acquaintance of mine and one of the members also of that Society, who wrote me word that it had been read but was laughed at by the connoisseurs. The papers, however, being shown to Dr. Fothergill, he thought them of too much value to be stifled and advised the printing of them. Mr. Colinson then gave them to Cave for publication in his *Gentleman's Magazine;* but he chose to print them separately in a pamphlet, and Dr. Fothergill wrote the preface. Cave, it seems, judged rightly for his profit; for by the additions that arrived afterwards, they swelled to a quarto volume, which has had five editions and cost him nothing for copy-money. . . .

What gave my book the more sudden and general celebrity was the success of one of its proposed experiments, made by Messrs. Dalibard and Delor at Marly for drawing lightning from the clouds. This engaged the public attention everywhere. M. Delor, who had an apparatus for experimental philosophy and lectured in that branch of science, undertook to repeat what he called the "Philadelphia Experiments," and after they were performed before the King and court, all the curious of Paris flocked to see them. I will not swell this narrative with an account of that capital experiment, nor of the infinite pleasure I received in the success of a similar one I made soon after with a kite at Philadelphia, as both are to be found in the histories of electricity. Dr. Wright, an English physician then at Paris, wrote to a friend who was of the Royal Society an account of the high esteem my experiments were in among the learned abroad, and of their wonder that my writings had been so little noticed in England. The Society on this resumed the consideration of the letters that had been read to them, and the celebrated Dr. Watson drew up a summary account of them and of all I had afterwards sent to England on the subject, which he accompanied with some praise of the writer. This summary was then printed in their transactions. And some members of the Society in London, particularly the very ingenious Mr. Canton, having verified the experiment of procuring lightning from the clouds by a pointed rod and acquainting them with the success, they soon made me more than amends for the slight with which they had before treated me. Without my having made any application for that honour, they chose me a member and voted that I should be excused the customary payments, which would have amounted to twenty-five guineas,

and ever since have given me their transactions gratis. They also presented me with the gold medal of Sir Godfrey Copley for the year 1753, the delivery of which was accompanied by a very handsome speech of the president, Lord Macclesfield, wherein I was highly honoured.

Our new Governor, Capt. Denny, brought over for me the before-mentioned medal from the Royal Society, which he presented to me at an entertainment given him by the city. He accompanied it with very polite expressions of his esteem for me, having, as he said, been long acquainted with my character. After dinner, when the company, as was customary at that time, were engaged in drinking, he took me aside into another room and acquainted me that he had been advised by his friends in England to cultivate a friendship with me, as one who was capable of giving him the best advice and of contributing most effectually to the making his administration easy, that he therefore desired of all things to have a good understanding with me; and he begged me to be assured of his readiness on all occasions to render me every service that might be in his power. He said much to me also of the Proprietor's good dispositions towards the province and of the advantage it might be to us all, and to me in particular, if the opposition that had been so long continued to his measures . . .

» » THE WAY TO WEALTH [8] « «

[Preface to *Poor Richard Improved*, 1758]

COURTEOUS READER,

I have heard that nothing gives an author so great pleasure as to find his works respectfully quoted by other learned authors. This pleasure I have seldom enjoyed; for tho' I have been, if I may say it without vanity, an eminent author of almanacks annually now a full quarter of a century, my brother authors in the same way, for what reason I know not, have ever been very sparing in their applauses; and no other author has taken the least notice of me; so that did not my writings produce me some solid pudding, the great deficiency of praise would have quite discouraged me.

I concluded at length that the people were the best judges of my merit, for they buy my works; and besides, in my rambles, where I am not personally known, I have frequently heard one or other of my adages repeated, with, *as Poor Richard says,* at the end on't. This gave me some satisfaction, as it showed not only that my instructions were regarded, but discovered likewise some respect for my authority; and I own, that to encourage the practice of remembering and repeating those wise sentences, I have sometimes quoted myself with great gravity.

Judge, then, how much I must have been gratified by an incident I am going to relate to you. I stopt my horse lately where a great number of people were collected at a vendue of merchant goods. The hour of sale not being come, they were conversing on the badness of

[8] Franklin began publishing his almanacs, in which Poor Richard's maxims were scattered, in 1732. Some of these proverbs Franklin assembled in this famous speech of Father Abraham. It has been reprinted hundreds of times.

the times, and one of the company call'd to a plain clean old man, with white locks, "Pray, Father Abraham, what think you of the times? Won't these heavy taxes quite ruin the country? How shall we be ever able to pay them? What would you advise us to?" Father Abraham stood up, and reply'd, "If you'd have my advice, I'll give it you in short, for *A word to the wise is enough,* and *Many words won't fill a bushel,* as *Poor Richard* says." They all join'd in desiring him to speak his mind, and gathering round him, he proceeded as follows:

"Friends," says he, "and neighbors, the taxes are indeed very heavy, and if those laid on by the government were the only ones we had to pay, we might more easily discharge them; but we have many others, and much more grievous to some of us. We are taxed twice as much by our idleness, three times as much by our pride, and four times as much by our folly; and from these taxes the commissioners cannot ease or deliver us by allowing an abatement. However, let us hearken to good advice, and something may be done for us; *God helps them that help themselves,* as *Poor Richard* says, in his Almanack of 1733.

It would be thought a hard government that should tax its people one-tenth part of their time, to be employed in its service. But idleness taxes many of us much more, if we reckon all that is spent in absolute sloth, or doing of nothing, with that which is spent in idle employments or amusements that amount to nothing. Sloth, by bringing on diseases, absolutely shortens life. *Sloth, like rust, consumes faster than labor wears; while the used key is always bright,* as *Poor Richard* says. *But dost thou love life, then do not squander time, for that's the stuff life is made of,* as *Poor Richard* says. How much more than is necessary do we spend in sleep, forgetting that *The sleeping fox catches no poultry,* and that *There will be sleeping enough in the grave,* as *Poor Richard* says.

If Time be of all things the most precious, wasting of time must be, as *Poor Richard* says, *the greatest prodigality;* since, as he elsewhere tells us, *Lost time is never found again; and what we call time enough, always proves little enough.* Let us then up and be doing, and doing to the purpose; so by diligence shall we do more with less perplexity. *Sloth makes all things difficult, but industry all easy,* as *Poor Richard* says; and *He that riseth late must trot all day, and shall scarce overtake his business at night;* while *laziness travels so slowly, that*

poverty soon overtakes him, as we read in *Poor Richard,* who adds, *Drive thy business, let not that drive thee;* and *Early to bed, and early to rise, makes a man healthy, wealthy, and wise.*

So what signifies wishing and hoping for better times. We may make these times better, if we bestir ourselves. *Industry need not wish,* as *Poor Richard* says, *and he that lives upon hope will die fasting. There are no gains without pains; then help, hands, for I have no lands,* [10] or if I have, they are smartly taxed. And, as *Poor Richard* likewise observes, *He that hath a trade hath an estate; and he that hath a calling, hath an office of profit and honor;* but then the trade must be worked, and the calling well followed, or neither the estate nor the office will enable us to pay our taxes. If we are industrious, we shall never starve; for, as *Poor Richard* says, *At the working man's house hunger looks in, but dares not enter.* Nor will [20] the bailiff or the constable enter, for *Industry pays debts, while despair encreaseth them,* says *Poor Richard.* What though you have found no treasure, nor has any rich relation left you a legacy; *Diligence is the mother of good-luck,* as *Poor Richard* says, *and God gives all things to industry. Then plough deep, while sluggards sleep, and you shall have corn to sell and to keep,* says *Poor Dick.* Work while it is called to-day, for you know not how much you may be [30] hindered to-morrow, which makes *Poor Richard* say, *One to-day is worth two to-morrows,* and farther, *Have you somewhat to do to-morrow? do it to-day.* If you were a servant, would you not be ashamed that a good master should catch you idle? Are you then your own master? *Be ashamed to catch yourself idle,* as *Poor Dick* says. When there is so much to be done for yourself, your family, your country, and your gracious King, be up by peep of day; [40] *Let not the sun look down and say, inglorious here he lies.* Handle your tools without mittens; remember that *The cat in gloves catches no mice,* as *Poor Richard* says. 'Tis true there is much to be done, and perhaps you are weak-handed; but stick to it steadily; and you will see great effects, for *Constant dropping wears away stones,* and *by diligence and patience the mouse ate in two the cable;* and *little strokes fell great oaks,* as *Poor Richard* says in his Al- [50] manack, the year I cannot just now remember.

Methinks I hear some of you say, *Must a man afford himself no leisure?* I will tell thee, my friend, what *Poor Richard* says: *Employ thy time well, if thou meanest to gain leisure; and,* since thou art not sure of a minute, 'throw not away an hour. Leisure is time for doing something useful: this leisure the diligent man will obtain, but the lazy man never; so that, as *Poor Richard* says, *A life of leisure and a life of laziness are 'two things.* Do you imagine that sloth will afford you more comfort than labour? No, for as *Poor Richard* says, *Trouble springs from idleness, and grievous toil from needless ease.*

10 *Many without labour would live by their wits only, but they break for want of stock.* Whereas industry gives comfort, and plenty, and respect; *Fly pleasures, and they'll follow you.* The diligent spinner has a large shift; and now I have a sheep and a cow, every body bids me good morrow; all which is well said by *Poor Richard.*

But with our industry, we must likewise be steady, settled, and careful, and oversee our own affairs with our own eyes, and not trust

20 too much to others; for as *Poor Richard* says,

> I never saw an oft-removed tree,
> Nor yet an oft-removed family,
> That throve so well as those that settled be.

And again, *three removes is as bad as a fire;* and again, *keep thy shop, and thy shop will keep thee;* and again, *if you would have your business done, go; if not, send.* And again,

> He that by the plough would thrive
> Himself must either hold or drive.

33 And again, *The eye of a master will do more work than both his hands;* and again, *want of care does us more damage than want of knowledge;* and again, *not to oversee workmen is to leave them your purse open.* Trusting too much to others' care is the ruin of many; for, as the Almanack says, *In the affairs of this world, men*

40 *are saved, not by faith, but by the want of it;* but a man's own care is profitable; for saith *Poor Dick, learning is to the studious, and riches to the careful,* as well as, *power to the bold, and Heaven to the virtuous.* And farther, *If you would have a faithful servant, and one that you like, serve yourself.* And again, he adviseth to circumspection and care, even in the smallest matters, because sometimes, *A little neglect may breed great mischief;* adding, *for*

50 *want of a nail the shoe was lost; for want of a shoe the horse was lost; and for want of a horse the rider was lost,* being overtaken and slain by the enemy; all for want of care about a horse-shoe nail.

So much for industry, my friends, and atten-

tion to one's own business; but to these we must add frugality, if we would make our industry more certainly successful. A man may, if he knows not how to save as he gets, keep his nose all his life to the grindstone, and die not worth a groat at last. *A fat kitchen makes a lean will,* as *Poor Richard* says; and

> *Many estates are spent in the getting,*
> *Since women for tea forsook spinning and knitting,*
> *And men for punch forsook hewing and splitting.*

If you would be wealthy, says he in another Almanack, *think of saving as well as of getting: The Indies have not made Spain rich, because her outgoes are greater than her incomes.*

Away then with your expensive follies, and you will not then have so much cause to complain of hard times, heavy taxes, and chargeable families; for, as *Poor Dick* says,

> *Women and wine, game and deceit,*
> *Make the wealth small and the wants great.*

And farther, *What maintains one vice, would bring up two children.* You may think perhaps, that a *little* tea, or a *little* punch now and then, diet a *little* more costly, clothes a *little* finer, and a *little* entertainment now and then, can be no *great* matter; but remember what *Poor Richard* says: *Many a little makes a mickle;* and farther, *beware of little expences; a small leak will sink a great ship;* and again, *who dainties love, shall beggars prove;* and moreover, *fools make feasts, and wise men eat them.*

Here you are all got together at this vendue of fineries and knicknacks. You call them goods; but if you do not take care, they will prove evils to some of you. You expect they will be sold cheap, and perhaps they may for less than they cost; but if you have no occasion for them, they must be dear to you. Remember what *Poor Richard* says: *Buy what thou hast no need of, and ere long thou shalt sell thy necessaries.* And again, *At a great pennyworth pause a while.* He means that perhaps the cheapness is apparent only, and not real; or the bargain, by straitening thee in thy business may do thee more harm than good. For in another place he says, *Many have been ruined by buying good pennyworths.* Again, *Poor Richard* says, *'Tis foolish to lay out money in a purchase of repentance;* and yet this folly is practised every day at vendues, for want of minding the Almanack. *Wise men,* as *Poor Dick* says, *learn by others' harms; fools scarcely by their own;* but *felix quem faciunt aliena pericula cautum.*

Many a one, for the sake of finery on the back, have gone with a hungry belly, and half-starved their families. *Silks and sattins, scarlet and velvet,* as *Poor Richard* says, *put out the kitchen fire.*

These are not the necessaries of life; they can scarcely be called the conveniences; and yet only because they look pretty, how many want to have them! The artificial wants of mankind thus become more numerous than the natural, and, as *Poor Dick* says, *For one poor person, there are an hundred indigent.* By these, and other extravagancies, the genteel are reduced to poverty, and forced to borrow of those whom they formerly despised, but who through industry and frugality have maintained their standing; in which case it appears plainly, that *A ploughman on his legs is higher than a gentleman on his knees,* as *Poor Richard* says. Perhaps they have had a small estate left them, which they knew not the getting of; they think, *'tis day, and will never be night;* that a little to be spent out of so much is not worth minding; *A child and a fool,* as *Poor Richard* says, *imagine twenty shillings and twenty years can never be spent;* but *always taking out of the meal-tub, and never putting in, soon comes to the bottom;* as *Poor Dick* says, *When the well's dry, they know the worth of water.* But this they might have known before, if they had taken his advice; *If you would know the value of money, go and try to borrow some; for, he that goes a borrowing goes a sorrowing;* and indeed so does he that lends to such people, when he goes to get it in again. *Poor Dick* farther advises, and says,

> *Fond pride of dress is sure a very curse;*
> *E'er fancy you consult, consult your purse.*

And again, *Pride is as loud a beggar as want, and a great deal more saucy.* When you have bought one fine thing, you must buy ten more, that your appearance may be all of a piece; but *Poor Dick* says, *'Tis easier to suppress the first desire, than to satisfy all that follow it.* And 'tis as truly folly for the poor to ape the rich, as for the frog to swell in order to equal the ox.

> *Great estates may venture more,*
> *But little boats should keep near shore.*

'Tis, however, a folly soon punished; for, *pride that dines on vanity, sups on contempt,* as *Poor Richard* says. And in another place, *pride breakfasted with plenty, dined with poverty, and supped with infamy.* And after all, of what

use is this pride of appearance, for which so much is risked, so much is suffered? It cannot promote health, or ease pain; it makes no increase of merit in the person, it creates envy, it hastens misfortune.

> *What is a butterfly? At best*
> *He's but a caterpillar drest;*
> *The gaudy fop's his picture just,*

as *Poor Richard* says.

But what madness must it be to run in debt for these superfluities! We are offered, by the terms of this vendue, six months' credit; and that perhaps has induced some of us to attend it, because we cannot spare the ready money, and hope now to be fine without it. But, ah, think what you do when you run in debt; you give to another power over your liberty! If you cannot pay at the time, you will be ashamed to see your creditor; you will be in fear when you speak to him; you will make poor pitiful sneaking excuses, and by degrees come to lose your veracity, and sink into base downright lying; for, as *Poor Richard* says, *The second vice is lying; the first is running in debt.* And again, to the same purpose, *Lying rides upon debt's back.* Whereas a free-born Englishman ought not to be ashamed or afraid to see or speak to any man living. But poverty often deprives a man of all spirit and virtue: *'Tis hard for an empty bag to stand upright,* as *Poor Richard* truly says.

What would you think of that prince, or that government, who should issue an edict forbidding you to dress like a gentleman or a gentlewoman, on pain of imprisonment or servitude? Would you not say that you were free, have a right to dress as you please, and that such an edict would be a breach of your privileges, and such a government tyrannical? And yet you are about to put yourself under that tyranny, when you run in debt for such dress! Your creditor has authority at his pleasure to deprive you of your liberty, by confining you in gaol for life, or to sell you for a servant, if you should not be able to pay him! When you have got your bargain, you may, perhaps, think little of payment; but *creditors,* Poor Richard tells us, *have better memories than debtors;* and in another place says, *creditors are a superstitious sect, great observers of set days and times.* The day comes round before you are aware, and the demand is made before you are prepared to satisfy it; or if you bear your debt in mind, the term which at first seemed so long, will, as it lessens, appear extremely short. Time will seem to have added wings to his heels, as well as shoulders. *Those have a short Lent, saith Poor Richard, who owe money to be paid at Easter.* Then since, as he says, *The borrower is a slave to the lender, and the debtor to the creditor;* disdain the chain, preserve your freedom; and maintain your independency; be industrious and free; be frugal and free. At present, perhaps, you may think yourself in thriving circumstances, and that you can bear a little extravagance without injury; but,

    For age and want, save while you may;
    No morning sun lasts a whole day,

as *Poor Richard* says. Gain may be temporary and uncertain, but ever while you live, expence is constant and certain; and *'Tis easier to build two chimnies, than to keep one in fuel,* as *Poor Richard* says. So, *rather go to bed supperless than rise in debt.*

    Get what you can, and what you get, hold;
    'Tis the stone that will turn all your lead into gold,

as *Poor Richard* says. And when you have got the philosopher's stone, sure you will no longer complain of bad times, or the difficulty of paying taxes.

This doctrine, my friends, is reason and wisdom; but after all, do not depend too much upon your own industry, and frugality, and prudence, though excellent things; for they may all be blasted without the blessing of Heaven; and therefore, ask that blessing humbly, and be not uncharitable to those that at present seem to want it, but comfort and help them. Remember, Job suffered, and was afterwards prosperous.

And now to conclude, *Experience keeps a dear school, but fools will learn in no other, and scarce in that;* for it is true, *we may give advice, but we cannot give conduct,* as *Poor Richard* says. However, remember this, *They that won't be counselled, can't be helped,* as *Poor Richard* says; and farther, that, *if you will not hear reason, she'll surely rap your knuckles.*

Thus the old Gentleman ended his harangue. The people heard it, and approved the doctrine, and immediately practised the contrary, just as if it had been a common sermon; for the vendue opened, and they began to buy extravagantly, notwithstanding his cautions and their own fear of taxes. I found the good man had thoroughly studied my Almanacks, and digested all I had dropt on these topicks during the course of five and twenty years. The frequent mention he made of me must have tired any one else, but my vanity was wonderfully delighted with it, though I was conscious that not a tenth part of the wisdom was my own, which he ascribed to me, but rather the gleanings I had made of the sense of all ages and nations. However, I resolved to be the better for the echo of it; and though I had at first determined to buy stuff for a new coat, I went away resolved to wear my old one a little longer. Reader, if thou wilt do the same, thy profit will be as great as mine. *I am, as ever, thine to serve thee,*   RICHARD SAUNDERS.
1757   1758

» » THE WHISTLE [9] « «

TO MADAM BRILLON

PASSY, *November 10, 1779.*

I received my dear friend's two letters, one for Wednesday and one for Saturday. This is again Wednesday. I do not deserve one for to-day, because I have not answered the former. But, indolent as I am, and averse to writing, the fear of having no more of your pleasing epistles, if I do not contribute to the correspondence, obliges me to take up my pen; and as Mr. B. has kindly sent me word, that he sets out to-morrow to see you, instead of spending this Wednesday evening as I have done its namesakes, in your delightful company, I sit down to spend it in thinking of you, in writing to you, and in reading over and over again your letters.

I am charmed with your description of Paradise, and with your plan of living there; and I approve much of your conclusion, that, in the mean time, we should draw all the good we can from this world. In my opinion, we might all draw more good from it than we do, and suffer less evil, if we would take care not to give too much for *whistles.* For to me it seems, that most of the unhappy people we meet with, are become so by neglect of that caution.

[9] Though Madame Brillon called Franklin "Papa" their relations were flirtatious.

You ask what I mean? You love stories, and will excuse my telling one of myself.

When I was a child of seven years old, my friends, on a holiday, filled my pocket with coppers. I went directly to a shop where they sold toys for children; and, being charmed with the sound of a *whistle,* that I met by the way in the hands of another boy, I voluntarily offered and gave all my money for one. I then came home, and went whistling all over the house, much pleased with my *whistle,* but disturbing all the family. My brothers, and sisters, and cousins, understanding the bargain I had made, told me I had given four times as much for it as it was worth; put me in mind what good things I might have bought with the rest of the money; and laughed at me so much for my folly, that I cried with vexation; and the reflection gave me more chagrin than the *whistle* gave me pleasure.

This however was afterwards of use to me, the impression continuing on my mind; so that often, when I was tempted to buy some unnecessary thing, I said to myself, *Don't give too much for the whistle;* and I saved my money.

As I grew up, came into the world, and observed the actions of men, I thought I met with many, very many, who *gave too much for the whistle.*

When I saw one too ambitious of court favour, sacrificing his time in attendance on levees, his repose, his liberty, his virtue, and perhaps his friends, to attain it, I have said to myself, *This man gives too much for his whistle.*

When I saw another fond of popularity, constantly employing himself in political bustles, neglecting his own affairs, and ruining them by that neglect, *He pays, indeed,* said I, *too much for his whistle.*

If I knew a miser, who gave up every kind of comfortable living, all the pleasure of doing good to others, all the esteem of his fellow-citizens, and the joys of benevolent friendship, for the sake of accumulating wealth, *Poor man,* said I, *you pay too much for your whistle.*

When I met with a man of pleasure, sacrificing every laudable improvement of the mind, or of his fortune, to mere corporeal sensations, and ruining his health in their pursuit, *Mistaken man,* said I, *you are providing pain for yourself, instead of pleasure; you give too much for your whistle.*

If I see one fond of appearance, or fine clothes, fine houses, fine furniture, fine equipages, all above his fortune, for which he contracts debts, and ends his career in a prison, *Alas!* say I, *he has paid dear, very dear, for his whistle.*

When I see a beautiful, sweet-tempered girl married to an ill-natured brute of a husband, *What a pity,* say I, *that she should pay so much for a whistle!*

In short, I conceive that great part of the miseries of mankind are brought upon them by the false estimates they have made of the value of things, and by their *giving too much for their whistles.*

Yet I ought to have charity for these unhappy people, when I consider, that, with all this wisdom of which I am boasting, there are certain things in the world so tempting, for example, the apples of King John, which happily are not to be bought; for if they were put to sale by auction, I might very easily be led to ruin myself in the purchase, and find that I had once more given too much for the *whistle.*

Adieu, my dear friend, and believe me ever yours very sincerely and with unalterable affection,   B. FRANKLIN.

» » DIALOGUE BETWEEN FRANKLIN AND THE GOUT [10] « «

MIDNIGHT, *October 22, 1780.*
Franklin. Eh! Oh! Eh! What have I done to merit these cruel sufferings?

Gout. Many things: you have ate and drank too freely, and too much indulged those legs of yours in their indolence.

Franklin. Who is it that accuses me?

Gout. It is I, even I, the Gout.

[10] Enclosed in a letter to Madame Brillon.

Franklin. What! my enemy in person?

Gout. No, not your enemy.

Franklin. I repeat it; my enemy; for you would not only torment my body to death, but ruin my good name; you reproach me as a glutton and a tippler; now all the world, that knows me, will allow that I am neither the one nor the other.

Gout. The world may think as it pleases;

it is always very complaisant to itself, and sometimes to its friends; but I very well know that the quantity of meat and drink proper for a man who takes a reasonable degree of exercise, would be too much for another, who never takes any.

Franklin. I take—Eh! Oh!—as much exercise—Eh!—as I can, Madam Gout. You know my sedentary state, and on that account, it would seem, Madam Gout, as if you might spare me a little, seeing it is not altogether my own fault.

Gout. Not a jot; your rhetoric and your politeness are thrown away; your apology avails nothing. If your situation in life is a sedentary one, your amusements, your recreations, at least, should be active. You ought to walk or ride; or, if the weather prevents that, play at billiards. But let us examine your course of life. While the mornings are long, and you have leisure to go abroad, what do you do? Why, instead of gaining an appetite for breakfast by salutary exercise, you amuse yourself with books, pamphlets, or newspapers, which commonly are not worth the reading. Yet you eat an inordinate breakfast,—four dishes of tea, with cream, and one or two buttered toasts, with slices of hung beef, which, I fancy, are not things the most easily digested. Immediately afterward you sit down to write at your desk, or converse with persons who apply to you on business. Thus the time passes till one, without any kind of bodily exercise. But all this I could pardon, in regard, as you say, to your sedentary condition. But what is your practice after dinner? Walking in the beautiful gardens of those friends with whom you have dined, would be the choice of a man of sense; yours is to be fixed down to chess, where you are found engaged for two or three hours! This is your perpetual recreation, which is the least eligible of any for a sedentary man, because, instead of accelerating the motion of the fluids, the rigid attention it requires helps to retard the circulation and obstruct internal secretions. Wrapt in the speculations of this wretched game, you destroy your constitution. What can be expected from such a course of living, but a body replete with stagnant humors, ready to fall a prey to all kinds of dangerous maladies, if I, the Gout, did not occasionally bring you relief by agitating those humors, and so purifying or dissipating them? If it was in some nook or alley in Paris, deprived of walks, that you played awhile at chess after dinner, this might

be excusable; but the same taste prevails with you in Passy, Auteuil, Montmartre, or Savoy, —places where there are the finest gardens and walks, a pure air, beautiful women, and most agreeable and instructive conversation; all of which you might enjoy by frequenting the walks. But these are rejected for this abominable game of chess. Fie, then, Mr. Franklin! But, amidst my instructions, I had almost forgot to administer my wholesome corrections; so take that twinge,—and that!

Franklin. Oh! Eh! Oh! Ohhh! As much instruction as you please, Madam Gout, and as many reproaches; but pray, madam, a truce with your corrections!

Gout. No, sir, no: I will not abate a particle of what is so much for your good, —therefore—

Franklin. Oh! Ehhh!—It is not fair to say I take no exercise, when I do very often, going out to dine, and returning in my carriage.

Gout. That, of all imaginable exercises, is the most slight and insignificant, if you allude to the motion of a carriage suspended on springs. By observing the degree of heat obtained by different kinds of motion, we may form an estimate of the quantity of exercise given by each. Thus, for example, if you turn out to walk in winter with cold feet, in an hour's time you will be in a glow all over; ride on horseback, the same effect will scarcely be perceived by four hours' round trotting; but if you loll in a carriage, such as you have mentioned, you may travel all day, and gladly enter the last inn to warm your feet by the fire. Flatter yourself then no longer, that half an hour's airing in your carriage deserves the name of exercise. Providence has appointed few to roll in carriages, while he has given to all a pair of legs, which are machines infinitely more commodious and serviceable. Be grateful, then, and make a proper use of yours. Would you know how they forward the circulation of your fluids, in the very action of transporting you from place to place: observe, when you walk, that all your weight is alternately thrown from one leg to the other; this occasions a great pressure on the vessels of the foot, and repels their contents; when relieved, by the weight of being thrown on the other foot, the vessels of the first are allowed to replenish, and, by a return of this weight, this repulsion again succeeds; thus accelerating the circulation of the blood. The heat produced in any given time depends on the degree of this acceleration; the fluids are shaken, the humors alternated, the secretions facilitated, and all goes well; the cheeks are ruddy, and health is established. Behold your fair friend at Auteuil; [11] a lady who received from bounteous nature more really useful science than half a dozen such pretenders to philosophy as you have been able to extract from all your books. When she honors you with a visit, it is on foot. She walks all hours of the day, and leaves indolence and its concomitant maladies to be endured by her horses. In this see at once the preservative of her health and personal charms. But when you go to Auteuil, you must have your carriage, though it is no further from Passy to Auteuil than from Auteuil to Passy.

Franklin. Your reasonings grow very tiresome.

Gout. I stand corrected. I will be silent and continue my office; take that, and that.

Franklin. Oh! Ohh! Talk on, I pray you!

Gout. No, no; I have a good number of twinges for you to-night, and you may be sure of some more to-morrow.

Franklin. What, with such a fever! I shall go distracted. Oh! Eh! Can no one bear it for me?

Gout. Ask that of your horses; they have served you faithfully.

Franklin. How can you so cruelly sport with my torments?

Gout. Sport! I am very serious. I have here a list of offenses against your own health distinctly written, and can justify every stroke inflicted on you.

Franklin. Read it, then.

Gout. It is too long a detail; but I will briefly mention some particulars.

Franklin. Proceed. I am all attention.

Gout. Do you remember how often you have promised yourself, the following morning, a walk in the grove of Boulogne, in the Garden de la Muette, or in your own garden, and have violated your promise, alleging at one time it was too cold, at another too warm, too windy, too moist, or what else you pleased; when in truth it was too nothing but your insuperable love of ease?

Franklin. That, I confess, may have happened occasionally; probably ten times in a year.

Gout. Your confession is very far short of the truth; the gross amount is one hundred and ninety-nine times.

[11] Madame Helvétius. See note 12.

Franklin. Is it possible?

Gout. So possible that it is fact; you may rely on the accuracy of my statement. You know M. Brillon's gardens, and what fine walks they contain; you know the handsome flight of an hundred steps, which lead from the terrace above to the lawn below. You have been in the practice of visiting this amiable family twice a week after dinner, and it is a maxim of your own, that "a man may take as much exercise in walking a mile, up and down stairs, as in ten on level ground." What an opportunity was here for you to have had exercise in both these ways! Did you embrace it, and how often?

Franklin. I cannot immediately answer that question.

Gout. I will do it for you. Not once.

Franklin. Not once?

Gout. Even so. During the summer you went there at six o'clock. You found the charming lady with her lovely children and friends, eager to walk with you and entertain you with their agreeable conversation; and what has been your choice? Why, to sit on the terrace, satisfy yourself with the fine prospect, and passing your eye over the beauties of the garden below, without taking one step to descend and walk about in them. On the contrary, you call for tea and the chessboard; and lo! you are occupied in your seat till nine o'clock, and that besides two hours' play after dinner; and then, instead of walking home, which would have bestirred you a little, you step into your carriage. How absurd to suppose that all this carelessness can be reconcilable with health, without my interposition!

Franklin. I am convinced now of the justness of Poor Richard's remark, that "Our debts and our sins are always greater than we think for."

Gout. So it is. You philosophers are sages in your maxims, and fools in your conduct.

Franklin. But do you charge among my crimes that I return in a carriage from M. Brillon's?

Gout. Certainly; for, having been seated all the while, you cannot object the fatigue of the day, and cannot want, therefore, the relief of a carriage.

Franklin. What then would you have me do with my carriage?

Gout. Burn it if you choose: you would at least get heat out of it once in this way; or, if you dislike that proposal, here's another for

you: observe the poor peasants, who work in the vineyards and grounds about the villages of Passy, Auteuil, Chaillot, etc., you may find every day among these deserving creatures, four or five old men and women, bent and perhaps crippled by weight of years and too long and too great labor. After a most fatiguing day, these people have to trudge a mile or two to their smoky huts. Order your coachman to
10 set them down. This is an act that will be good for your soul; and at the same time after your visit to the Brillons, if you return on foot, that will be good for your body.

Franklin. Ah! how tiresome you are!

Gout. Well, then, to my office; it should not be forgotten that I am your physician. There!

Franklin. Oh-h-h! What a devil of a physician!

20 *Gout.* How ungrateful you are to say so! Is it not I who, in the character of your physician, have saved you from the palsy, dropsy, and apoplexy? one or other of which would have done for you long ago, but for me.

Franklin. I submit, and thank you for the past, but entreat the discontinuance of your
28 visits for the future; for, in my mind, one had

better die than be cured so dolefully. Permit me just to hint, that I have also not been unfriendly to you. I never feed physician or quack of any kind, to enter the list against you; if then you do not leave me to my repose, it may be said you are ungrateful too.

Gout. I can scarcely acknowledge that as an objection. As to quacks, I despise them; they may kill you indeed, but cannot injure me. And, as to regular physicians, they are at last convinced that the gout, in such a subject as you are, is no disease, but a remedy; and wherefore cure a remedy?—But to our business; there!

Franklin. Oh! Oh!—for Heaven's sake leave me, and I promise faithfully never more to play at chess, but to take exercise daily and live temperately.

Gout. I know you too well. You promise fair; but after a few months of good health you will return to your old habits; your fine promises will be forgotten like the forms of the last year's clouds. Let us then finish the account, and I will go. But I leave you with an assurance of visiting you again at a proper time and place; for my object is your good, and you are sensible now that I am your *real friend.*

» » À MADAME HELVÉTIUS [12] « «

Chargriné de votre résolution barbare, prononcée si positivement hier au soir, de rester seule pendant la vie en honneur de votre cher mari, je me retirois chez moi, tombois sur mon lit, me croyois mort, et que je me trouvois dans les Champs-Elisées.
40 On me demande si j'avois envie de voir quelques personnages particuliers. "Menez-moi chez les philosophes." "Il y en a deux qui demeurent ici près dans ce jardin; ils sont de très-bons voisins, et très-amis l'un de l'autre." "Qui sont-ils?" "Socrate et Helvétius." "Je les estime prodigieusement tous les deux; mais faites-moi voir premièrement Helevétius, parce que j'entends un peu de François et pas un mot de Grec."—Il m'a reçu avec beaucoup de
50 courtoisie, m'ayant connu, disoit-il, de réputation il y avoit quelque temps. Il me demanda

mille choses sur la guerre, et sur l'état présent de la religion, de la liberté, et du gouvernement en France. "Vous ne demandez donc rien," lui dis-je, "de votre chère amie Madame Helvétius; et cependant elle vous aime encore excessivement, et il n'y a qu'une heure que j'étois chez elle." "Ah!" dit-il, "vous me faites ressouvenir de mon ancienne félicité. Mais il faut l'oublier pour être heureux ici. Pendant plusieurs des premières années, je n'ai pensé qu'à elle. Enfin je suis consolé. J'ai pris une autre femme; la plus semblable à elle que j'ai pu trouver. Elle n'est pas, il est vrai, tout-à-fait si belle, mais elle a autant de bon sens, beaucoup d'esprit, et elle m'aime infiniment. Son étude continuelle est de me plaire, et elle est sortie actuellement chercher le meilleur nectar et ambroisie pour me régaler ce soir; restez avec moi et vous la verrez." "J'apperçois," dis-je, "que votre ancienne amie est plus fidelle que vous; car plusieurs bons partis lui ont été

[12] Madame Helvétius, a rich and charming widow, was Franklin's neighbor. Perhaps in earnest, but probably in gallantry, Franklin proposed marriage to her. This letter records his supposed dream the night following her refusal to have him.

offerts qu'elle a refusés tous. Je vous confesse que je l'ai aimée, moi, à la folie; mais elle étoit dure à mon égard, et m'a rejeté absolument pour l'amour de vous." "Je vous plains," dit-il, "de votre malheur; car vraiment c'est une bonne et belle femme, et bien aimable. Mais l'Abbé de la R[oche], et l'Abbé M[orellet], ne sont-ils pas encore quelquefois chez elle?" "Oui assurément; car elle n'a pas perdu un seul de vos amis." "Si vous aviez gagné l'Abbé M[orellet] (avec du bon café à la crême) à parler pour vous, vous auriez peut-être réussi; car il est raisonneur subtil comme Duns Scotus ou St. Thomas; il met ses arguments en si bon ordre qu'ils deviennent presque irrésistibles. Et si l'Abbé de la R[oche] avoit été gagné (par quelque belle édition d'un vieux classique) à parler *contre* vous, cela auroit été mieux; car j'ai toujours observé, que quand il lui conseilla quelque chose, elle avoit un penchant très-fort à faire le revers." A ces mots entra la nouvelle Madame Helevétius avec la nectar; à l'instant je l'ai reconnue pour être Madame Franklin, mon ancienne amie Américaine. Je l'ai réclamée, mais elle me dit froidement; "J'ai été votre bonne femme qaurante-neuf années et quatre mois;—presqu'un demi-siècle; soyez content de cela. J'ai formé ici une nouvelle connexion, qui durera à l'éternité."

Indigné de ce refus de mon Eurydice, je pris de suite la résolution de quitter ces ombres ingrates, et revenir en ce bon monde, revoir le soleil et vous.—*Me voici!*—*Vengeons-nous!*

[To Madame Helvétius

Saddened by your barbarous resolution, pronounced so positively yesterday evening, to remain single all your life long in honor of your dear husband, I went home, threw myself on the bed, thought myself dead and in the Elysian Fields.

They asked if I wanted to see any particular people. "Lead me to the philosophers." "There are two who live near here, in this garden; they are very good neighbors and very good friends." "Who are they?" "Socrates and Helvétius." "I admire them both prodigiously, but let me see Helvétius first, for I understand a little French and not a word of Greek."—He received me with great courtesy, having known me, he said, by reputation for some time. He asked me a thousand things about the war and about the present state of religion, liberty, and government in France. "You ask nothing," I said to him, "about your beloved Madame Helvétius and yet she still loves you excessively and only an hour ago I was at her house." "Ah!" said he, "you make me recall my former felicity. But we must forget that to be happy here. During most of my first years I thought only of her. At last I consoled myself. I took another wife, the woman most nearly like her I could find. She is not, it is true, quite so beautiful, but she has as much good sense, great wit, and loves me infinitely. It is her continual study to please me, and she has gone out at the moment to find the best nectar and ambrosia to regale me this evening; stay with me and you shall see her." "I perceive," said I, "that your former beloved is more faithful than you, for several good matches have been offered her, all of which she has refused. I will confess to you that I loved her myself to distraction, but she was unmoved by my esteem and refused me absolutely, for love of you." "I pity you," said he, "for your misfortune, for truly she is a good and beautiful woman, and very lovable. But the Abbé de la R[oche], and the Abbé M[orellet], are they not still sometimes at her house?" "Yes, certainly, for she has not lost a single one of your friends." "If you had won the Abbé M[orellet] (with a good cup of coffee with cream) to speak for you, you would perhaps have succeeded, for he is as subtle a pleader as Duns Scotus or St. Thomas; he puts his arguments in such good order that they become practically irresistible. And if the Abbé de la R[oche] had been won (by some fine edition of an ancient classic) to speak *against* you, that would have been even better, for I have always noticed that when he advises something she has a very strong inclination to do the opposite." At these words in came the new Madame Helvétius with the nectar; instantly I recognized her as Madame Franklin, my former American wife. I tried to reclaim her but she said coldly, "I was your good wife for forty-nine years and four months—almost half a century; be content with that. I have formed, here, a new connection which will last through eternity."

Angered by my Eurydice's refusal, I instantly resolved to leave these ungrateful shades and return to the good world, see the sun again, and you.—Here I am!—*Let us avenge ourselves!*]

JOHN WOOLMAN

1720–1772

HENRY CRABBE ROBINSON, friend of the English Romantic poets, wrote in his diary, under the date of January 22, 1824: "An illiterate tailor [Woolman], writes in the style of the most exquisite purity and grace. His moral qualities are transferred to his writings. Had he not been so very humble, he would have written a still better book; for, fearing to indulge in vanity, he conceals the events in which he was a great actor. His religion is love. His whole existence and all his passions were love. . . . His Christianity is most inviting—it is fascinating." Charles Lamb's advice, in his "A Quakers' Meeting" is well known: "Get the writings of John Woolman by heart; and love the early Quakers."

Woolman was, to be sure, a tailor by trade, but hardly illiterate, as his *Journal* and his more formal works prove. Though Mt. Holly, in the province of West Jersey, was his home, he made frequent visits to Quaker meetings as far distant as Maryland and New England, to further the unity of his people and the cause of Negro emancipation. On a missionary trip to England, undertaken in 1772, he was stricken with the smallpox and died in York.

Like other Quakers in the vicinity of Philadelphia, Woolman worked to perpetuate William Penn's policy of friendship toward the Indians, even in face of the insistence of the frontiersmen that the Pennsylvania government adopt warlike measures against them. Early in 1763, in spite of warning that the Susquehanna Indians were raiding settlements, Woolman made his memorable journey over the Wyalusing trail to visit friendly Indians in northeastern Pennsylvania. Six months after his return Pontiac's conspiracy broke out.

The excerpt from the *Journal* here printed begins on the eighth day of the Indian journey.

The Journal and Essays of John Woolman, A. M. Gummere, ed., New York, 1922.
Janet Whitney, *John Woolman: American Quaker*, Boston, 1942.

» » *From:* THE JOURNAL OF JOHN WOOLMAN « «

[1763]

[13 June] the Sun appearing we set forward, and as I rode over the barren Hills my meditations were on the Alterations of the Circumstances of the Natives of this land since the coming in of the English. The Lands near the Sea are conveniently scituated for fishing. The lands near the Rivers where the tides flow, and some above, are in many places fertile, and not mountainous; while the Running of the Tides makes passing up and down easie with any kind of Traffick. Those natives have in some places for [small] considerations sold their Inheritance so favourably Scituated and in other places been driven back by superior force. So that in many places as their way of Clothing themselves is now altered from what it was, and they far remote from us have to pass over Mountains, Swamps, and Barran deserts, where Traveling is very troublesome, in bringing their furs & skins to trade with us.

By the Extending of English Settlements and partly by English Hunters, those wild Beasts they chiefly depend on for a subsistence are not so plenty as they were. And people too often for the Sake of gain open a Door for them to waste their Skins & furs, in purchasing a Liquor which tends to the ruin of them & their Families.

My own will and desire being now very much broken, and my heart with much earnestness turned to the Lord, to whom alone I looked for help in the dangers before me, I had a prospect of the English along the Coast for upwards of nine hundred miles where I have traveled. And the favourable Scituation of the English, and the difficulties attending the natives [and the Slaves amongst us,] were open before me, and a weighty and Heavenly care came over my mind, and love filled my heart toward all mankind, in which I felt a Strong Engagement that we might be [faithful] to the Lord while His mercies [are yet extended] to us, and so attend to pure Universal Righteousness as to give no just cause of offence to the gentiles who do not profess christianity, Whether the Blacks from Africa, or the Native Inhabitants of this Continent: And here I was led into a close, laborious Enquiry, whether I as an individual kept clear from all things which tended to Stir up, or were connected with wars, Either in this Land or Africa, and my heart was deeply concerned that in future I might in all things keep steadily to the pure Truth, & live and walk in the plainness and Simplicity of a Sincere follower of Christ. And in this lonely Journey, I did this day greatly bewail the spreading of a wrong Spirit, believing that the prosperous Conveniant Scituation of the English, requires a Constant Attention to Divine love & wisdom, to guide and Support us in a way answerable to the will of that Good, Gracious, & Almighty Being who hath an Equal regard to all mankind. And here Luxury and Covetousness, with the numerous Opressions and other evils attending them, appeared very Afflicting to me, and I felt in that which is Immutable that the Seeds of great Calamity and desolation are Sown & growing fast on this Continent. Nor have I words sufficient to set forth that longing I then felt, that we who are placed along the Coast, & have tasted the Love and Goodness of God, might arise in his Strength, and like faithful Messengers Labour to check the growth of those Seeds that they may not ripen to the Ruin of our posterity.

We reached the Indian Settlement at Wioming [1] & here we were told that an Indian Runner had been at that place a day or two before us and brought news of the Indians taking an English Fort Westward, and destroying the people, and that they were endeavouring to Take another. And also that another Indian

Runer came there about [midnight, the night next] before we got there, who came from a Town about ten miles above Wahalowsing,[2] and brought news that some Indian Warriors from distant parts, came to that Town with two English Scalps, and told the people that it was War with the English.

Our [pilots] took us to the House of a Very Antient man, and soon after we had put in our baggage there came a man from another Indian House some distance off, and I perceiving there was a man near the door, went out, and he having a Tomahock wraped under his matchcoat out of sight, as I approached him he took it in his hand. I, however, went forward, and Speaking to him in a friendly way, perceived he understood some English, my companion then coming out we had some talk with him concerning the nature of our Visit in these parts, and then he going into the House with us, and talking with our [pilots] soon appeared friendly & Sat down and smoaked his pipe. Though his taking [his] hatchet in his hand at the instant I drew near him, had a disagreeable appearance, I believed he had no other intent than to be in readiness in case any violence was offered to him.

Hearing the news brought by these Indian Runers, and being told by the Indians where we lodged that what Indians were about Wioming Expected in a few days to move to some larger Towns, I thought that, to all outward appearance it was dangerous traveling at this time; and after a hard days journey [was] brought into a painfull Exercise at night, in which I had to trace back, and [feel] over the steps I had taken from my first moving in the visit, and though I had to bewail some weakness which at times had attended me, yet I could not find that I had ever given way to a wilfull disobedience: and [then] as I believed I had under a Sence of duty come thus far, I was now earnest in Spirit beseeching the Lord to Shew me what I ought to do.

In this great distress I grew jealous of myself, lest the desire of Reputation, as a man firmly settled to persevere through dangers; Or the fear of disgrace ariseing on my returning without performing the visit might have some place in me. Thus I lay full of thoughts, great part of the night, while my Beloved Companion lay & Slept by me; Till the Lord my Gracious Father, who saw the conflicts of my Soul,

---

[1] Wyoming (in Pennsylvania), the scene of the famous massacre of July, 1778.

[2] Now Wyalusing, fifty miles northwest of Scranton. The Wyalusing trail is now traversed by the Lehigh Valley Railroad.

was pleased to give quietness, and therein I was renewedly confirmed that it was my duty to go forward. Then was I again Strengthened to commit my Life, and all things relating thereto, into His Heavenly hands, and geting a little sleep toward day, when morning came we arose [and then on the]

[14 June], we sought out and visited all the Indians hereabouts that we could meet with, they being chiefly in one place about a mile from where we lodged in all perhaps twenty. Here I Exprest the care I had on my mind for their good, and told them that true Love had made me willing thus to leave my home & family to come & see the Indians, and Speak with them in their houses. Some of them understood English and appeared kind & friendly, So we took our leave of those Indians, and went up the River Susquehannah about three miles to the House of an Indian called Jacob January, who had killed his hog, and the women were making Store of Bread, and preparing to move up the River. Here our Pilots left their canow when they came down in the spring, which lying dry was leaky So that we being detained Some hours, had a good deal of friendly conversation with the family, and Eating Diner with them, we made some small presents. Then puting our Baggage in the Canow, Some of them pushed Slowly up the Stream, and the rest of us rode our Horses, and Swiming them over a Creek called Lehawahamunk,[3] we pitched our Tent a little above, there being a Shower in the evening: and in a Sence of Gods goodness in helping me in my Distress, Sustaining me under Tryals, and Enclineing my heart to Trust in Him, I lay down in an humble bowed frame of mind & had a comfortable nights lodging.

[15 June] proceeded forward till afternoon, and then a storm appearing we met our Canoe at An Appointed place, and the Rain continuing we Stayed all night, which was so heavy that it [ran] through our Tent & wet us and our Baggage.

[16] we found on our way abundance of Trees blown down with the Storm yesterday, and had ocasion reverendly to consider the kind dealing of the Lord who provided a Safe place in the valley, for us while this Storm continued. By the falling of Abundance of Trees across our path we were much hindered and in Some Swamps our way was so Stoped that we got throu—with extre[am] difficulty. I had this day

[3] ? Lackawanna.

often to consider mySelf as a Sojourner in this world, and a belief in the Allsufficiency of God to Support his people in their pilgrimage felt comfortable to me, and I was Industerously Employ'd to get to a state of perfect Resignation.

We seldom saw our Canow but at appointed places by reason of the Path going off from the River, and this afternoon Job Chilaway an Indian from Wahalowsing who talks good English, & is acquainted with Several people in & about Philadelphia, [he meeting] our people on the River, and understanding where we Expected to lodge, pushed back about Six miles and came to us after night and in a while our own Canow came, it being hard work pushing up Stream. Job told us that an Indian came in haiste to their Town yesterday, and told them that three warriors coming from Some distance, lodged in a Town above Wahalowsing a few nights past, and that these three men were going against the English at Juniatta. Job was going down the River to the Province Store at Shamokin.

Though I was so far favoured with health as to continue traveling, yet through the various difficulties in our Journey, and the different way of living from what I had been used to, I grew weak, and the news of these warriors being on their march so near us, and not knowing whether we might not fall in with them it was a fresh Tryal of my Faith, and though through the Strength of Divine Love I had Several times been enabled to commit myself to the Divine Disposal, I still found the want of my Strength [to be] renewed, that I might persevere therein, and my cries for help were put up to the Lord who in great Mercy gave me a resigned heart, in which I found quietness.

[17 June] parting [with] Job Chillaway we went on, & reached Wahalowsing about the middle of the afternoon: The first Indian that we Saw was a woman of a modest countenance, with a Babe. She first spake to our [Pilot] and then with a harmonious voice expressed her gladness at seeing us, [they] having before heard of our coming. Then by the direction of our [pilot] we sat down on a log, and he went to the Town to tell the people we were come. My companion & I Seting thus together in a deep inward stillness the poor woman came and sat near us, and great awfulness coming over us, we rejoyced in a sence of Gods Love manifested to our poor Souls. After a while, we heard a Konkshell blow several times & then came John Curtis and another Indian man, who kindly invited us into a House near the Town, where we found I suppose about Sixty people, Seting in Silence and after [Seting] a Short time I stood up and in Some tenderness of Spirit acquainted them with the nature of my visit, and that a concern for their good had made me willing to come thus far to see them: all in a few short Sentences which some of them understanding Interpreted to the others, and there appeared gladness amongst them. Then I Shewed them my Certificate, which was Explained to them, and the Moravian [4] who overtook us on the way being now here [bid] me wellcome.

[18 June] We rested ourselves this forenoon, & the Indians knowing that the Moravian and I were of different Religious Societies, and as some of their people had encouraged him to come & Stay a while with them were I believe concern'd that no jarring or discord might be in their meetings, & they I suppose having conferred together acquainted me that the People at my request would at any time come together & hold meetings, & allso told me that they Expected the Moravian would speak in their setled meetings which are commonly held morning and near evening. So I found liberty in my heart to Speak to the Moravian, & told him of the care I felt on my mind for the good of these people, & that I believed no ill Effects would follow it, if I sometimes Spake in their meetings when love engaged me thereto, without calling them together at times when they did not meet of course: whereupon he expresst his good-will toward my Speaking at any time, all that I found in my heart to say. So near evening I was at their meeting where the pure Gospel love was felt, to the tendering Some of our Hearts, and the Interpreters endeavouring to Acquaint the people with what I said in Short Sentences found some difficulty as none of them were quite perfect in the English and Delaware Tongues; So they helped one another, and we Laboured along, Divine Love attending, and afterwards, feeling my mind covered with the Spirit of Prayer, I told [those who] Interpreted that I found it in my heart to pray to God, & believed if I prayed Aright he would hear me, & Expresst my willingness for them to Omit Interpreting. So our meeting ended with a degree of Divine Love, & before the people went

out, I observed [Papoonal] the man who had been Zealous in Labouring for a Reformation in that Town being then very tender Spoke to one of the Interpreters, and I was afterwards told that he said in substance as follows, "I Love to Feel where words come from."

[19 June, Sunday] This morning in the meeting the Indian who came up with the Moravian being allso a member of that Society prayed, and then the Moravian Spake a Short time to the people. And in the afternoon, they coming together, and my heart being filled with a Heavenly care for their good, I spake to them awhile by Interpreters, but none of them being perfect in the work, & I feeling the Current of Love run Strong, told the Interpreters that I believed Some of the people would understand me, & so proceeded: In which exercise I believe the Holy [Ghost] wrought on Some hearts to Edification where all the words were not understood. I looked upon it as a time of Divine Favour, & my Heart was tendered and truly thankfull before the Lord: and after I Sat down one of the Interpreters Seemed Spirited up to give the Indians the Substance of what I said.

Before our first meeting this morning, [my mind] was led to meditate on the manifold difficulties of these Indians, who by permission of the Six Nations dwell in these parts, and a Near Sympathy with them was raised in me, And my Heart being enlarged in the Love of [Christ] I thought that the Affectionate care of a good man for his only Brother in Affliction, does not exceed what I then felt for that people.

I came to this place through much trouble, & though through the Mercies of God, I believed that if I died in the Journey it would be well with me, yet the thoughts of falling into the hands of [those] Indian warriors, was in times of weakness afflicting to me. And being of a Tender Constitution of Body the thoughts of captivity amongst them was at times grievous, as Supposing that they being strong & hardy might demand service of me beyound what I could well bear; but the Lord alone was my helper, and I believed if I went into captivity it would be for Some good end, and thus from time to time my mind was centered in Resignation in which I always found quietness. And now this day, though I had the Same Dangerous Wilderness between me & home, was inwardly Joyfull that the Lord had Strengthened me to come on this Visit, and Manifested a Fatherly care over me in my poor lowly con-

10

20

30

40

50

4 David Zeisberger, who was a Moravian missionary to the Indians for sixty-two years.

dition, when in mine own eyes I appear'd inferior to many amongst the Indians.

When the last mentioned meeting was ended it being night, [Papoonal] went to Bed, and one of the Interpreters Seting by me, I observed [Papoonal] Spoke with an harmonious voice I suppose a minute or two and I asking the Interpreter, was told that he was Expressing "his Thankfullness to God for the favours he had received that day, and Prayed that he would continue to favour him with that same which he had experienced in that meeting." [That though Papoonal] had before agreed to receive the Moravian, and to join with them, he still appeared kind & Loving to us.

[20 June] was at two meetings, & Silent in [both]. [21 June] This morning in Meeting my heart was Enlarged in pure love amongst them, and in Short plain Sentences Expresst several things that rested upon me; which one of the Interpreters gave the people pretty readily after which the meeting ended in Supplication, and I had cause humbly to acknowledge the Loving kindness of the Lord toward us; And then I believed that a Door remained open for the Faithfull disciples of Jesus Christ to Labour amongst these people.

I feeling my mind at Liberty to return, took my leave of them in general at the Conclusion of what I said in meeting, and so we prepared to go homeward, but some of their most active men told us, that when we were ready to move the people would choose to come & shake hands with us; which those who usually came to meeting [generally] did, & from a secret [draft] in my mind I went amongst some who did not use to go to meetings & took my leave of them allso, and the Moravian and his Indian Interpreter appeared respectful to us at parting. This Town stands on the bank of Susquehannah & consists I believe of about forty Houses mostly compact together; Some about thirty feet long, & Eighteen wide, some biger, & some less, mostly built of Split plank, one end set in the ground & the other piñed to a plate, [and then] Rafters, and covered with Bark. I understand a great Flood last winter overflowed the Chief part of the ground where the Town Stands, and some were now about moveing their Houses to higher ground.

We Expected only two Indians to be our Company, but when we were ready to go we found many of them were going to Bethlehem with Skins and Furs, who chose to go in company with us: So they loaded two Canows,

which they desired us to go in, telling us that the Waters were so raised with the Rains that the Horses should be taken by Such who were better Acquainted with the fording places. So we with several Indians went in the Canows, and others went on Horses, there being Seven besides ours, and we met with the Horsemen once on the way by Appointment, and then near night, a little below A Branch called Tankhannah [5] we lodged there, and some of the young men going out a little before dusk with their Guns brought in a Deer.

[22 June] Through diligence we reached Wioming before Night, and understood the Indians were mostly gone from this place; here we went up a Small Creek into the woods with our Canows, and pitching our Tent, carried out our Baggage, and before dark our Horses came to us.

[23 June] In the morning their Horses were loaded, & we prepar'd our Baggage and so Set forward being in all fourteen, and with diligent Traveling were favoured to get near half way to Fort Allen. The Land on this Road from Wioming to Our Frontier being mostly poor, & good grass Scarce, they chose a piece of low ground to lodge on, as the best for graseing; and I having Swet much in Traveling, and being weary Slept sound. I perceiv'd in the Night that I had taken cold; of which I was favoured to get better soon.

[24 June] We passed fort Allen, & lodged near it in the woods; having forded the westerly branch of Delaware three times, and thereby had a shorter way, & mist going over the highest part of the Blue Mountains, called the Second Ridge. In the Second time fording where the River cuts through the Mountain, the waters being Rapid and pretty deep, And my companion's mare being a tall & Tractable Animal, He Sundry times drove her back through the River, & they loaded her with the Burthens of some Small Horses, which they thought not Sufficient to [venture] through with their Loads.

The Troubles Westward and the difficulty for Indians to pass through our Frontier, I apprehend was one Reason why so many came as Expecting that our being in Company would prevent the outside Inhabitants from being Surprised.

[25 June] We reached Bethlehem takeing care on the way to keep foremost, and to Acquaint people on & near the Road who these

5 Tunkhannock.

Indians were. This we found very needfull for the Frontier Inhabitants were often alarmed at the Report of English being killed by Indians Westward.

Amongst our Company were Some who I did not remember to have Seen at Meeting, and some of these at first were very reserved; But we being several days together, and behaving friendly toward them, & making them sutable returns for the Services they did us, they became more free and Sociable.

[26 June, Sunday] Having carefully endeavoured to Settle all Affairs with the Indians relative to our Journey, we took leave of them and I thought they generally parted with us Affectionately. So we geting to Richland had a very Comfortable Meeting amongst our Friends: here I parted with my kind [& Beloved] Companion Benjamin Parvin, and accompanied by my Friend Samuel Foulke we rode to John Cadwaladers, from whence I reached home the Next day, where I found my Family midling well, and they & my Friends all along appear'd glad to see me return from a Journey which they apprehended Dangerous, but my mind while I was out, had been Employed in Striving for a perfect Resignation; I had often been confirmed in a Belief that whatever the Lord might be pleased to allot for me would work for good. [And] I was now carefull lest I should admit any degree of Selfishness in being glad overmuch; And Laboured to Improve by those Tryals in Such a maner as my Gracious Father & Protector [may] intend for me.

Between the English Inhabitants and Wahalowsing, we had only a narrow path, which in many places is much grown up with Bushes, and Interrupted by abundance of Trees lying across it; which together with the Mountains, Swamps, and rough Stones, it is a difficult road to Travel, and the more so for that Rattle-Snakes abound there, of which we killed four. That people who have never been in such places, have but an Imperfect Idea of them. But I was not only taught patience, but also made thankful to God who thus led me about and instructed me, that I might have a quick and lively feeling of the Afflictions of my fellow-Creatures, whose Scituation in life is difficult.   1774

WILLIAM BARTRAM

1739–1823

FEW AMERICAN BOOKS have had as great an influence on European writers as William Bartram's *Travels through North & South Carolina, Georgia, East & West Florida, the Cherokee Country, the Extensive Territories of the Muscogulges, or Creek Confederacy, and the Country of the Chactaws* (Philadelphia, 1791). The son of the Philadelphia Quaker scientist John Bartram, whom Linnaeus called "the greatest natural botanist in the world," William had accompanied his father on two expeditions before he undertook the journey which furnished the materials for the *Travels*. Aided by funds supplied by an English Quaker, Dr. John Fothergill, Bartram embarked in April, 1773, on a five-year expedition which covered the country from Savannah to the Mississippi. Illuminating in its topographical descriptions and its accounts of the strange beasts and flowers he discovered, the *Travels* have delighted both scientists and poets. The fourth part of the book discusses the "character, customs and persons of the American aborigines." With Quaker humanity Bartram moved freely among the Indians and was one of the first Americans to write accurately of them. The Seminoles called him "Puc-Puggy" (the Flower-hunter).

When the *Travels* were published in London in 1792, the English romantic writers found in the book justification for their ideas of the noble savage and the beneficence of nature. Wordsworth, Coleridge, and Southey borrowed heavily from it. Chateaubriand, in France, pillaged whole passages to give exotic beauty to his *Le Voyage en Amérique* and *Atala*. Bartram's chief gift to all these writers was a new sensuous vocabulary with which to describe the glory of the natural world.

Meanwhile the shy and modest man who had caused such a stir abroad, continued to hoe in his father's famous botanical garden outside Philadelphia.

Bartram characterized himself with finality in a passage in the *Travels:* "Continually impelled by a restless spirit of curiosity, in pursuit of new productions of nature, my chief happiness consisted in tracing and admiring the infinite power, majesty, and perfection of the great Almighty Creator, and in the contemplation, that through divine aid and permission, I might be instrumental in discovering, and introducing into my native country, some original productions of nature, which might become useful to society."

The Travels of William Bartram, Francis Harper, ed., New Haven, 1958.

Ernest Earnest, *John and William Bartram: Botanists and Explorers,* Philadelphia, 1940.

N. B. Fagin, *William Bartram, Interpreter of the American Landscape,* Baltimore, 1933.

From: TRAVELS THROUGH NORTH & SOUTH CAROLINA, GEORGIA, EAST & WEST FLORIDA

PART II. CHAPTER V [1]

The little lake, which is an expansion of the river, now appeared in view; on the east side are extensive marshes, and on the other high forests and orange groves, and then a bay, lined with vast cypress swamps, both coasts gradually approaching each other, to the opening of the river again, which is in this place about
10 three hundred yards wide. Evening now drawing on, I was anxious to reach some high bank of the river, where I intended to lodge; and agreeably to my wishes, I soon discovered on the west shore, a little promontory, at the turning of the river, contracting it here to about one hundred and fifty yards in width. This promontory is a peninsula, containing about three acres of high ground, and is one entire orange grove, with a few live oaks, magnolias and
20 palms. Upon doubling the point, I arrived at the landing, which is a circular harbour, at the foot of the bluff, the top of which is about twelve feet high; and back of it is a large cypress swamp, that spreads each way, the right wing forming the west coast of the little lake, and the left stretching up the river many miles, and encompassing a vast space of low grassy marshes. From this promontory, looking eastward across the river, we beheld a landscape of
30 low country, unparalleled as I think; on the

left is the east coast of the little lake, which I had just passed; and from the orange bluff at the lower end, the high forests begin, and increase in breadth from the shore of the lake, making a circular sweep to the right, and contain many hundred thousand acres of meadow; and this grand sweep of high forest encircles, as I apprehend, at least twenty miles of these green fields, interspersed with hommocks or islets of evergreen trees, where the sovereign magnolia and lordly palm stand conspicuous. The islets are high shelly knolls, on the sides of creeks or branches of the river, which wind about and drain off the superabundant waters that cover these meadows during the winter season.

The evening was temperately cool and calm. The crocodiles began to roar and appear in uncommon numbers along the shores and in the river. I fixed my camp in an open plain, near the utmost projection of the promontory, under the shelter of a large live oak, which stood on the highest part of the ground and but a few yards from my boat. From this open, high situation, I had a free prospect of the river, which was a matter of no trivial consideration to me, having good reason to dread the subtle attacks of the alligators, who were crowding about my harbour. Having collected a good quantity of wood for the purpose of keeping up a light and smoke during the night, I began to think of preparing my supper, when, upon examining my stores, I found but a scanty provision. I thereupon determined, as the most

[1] This chapter of Bartram's *Travels* made a deep impression on S. T. Coleridge and he copied many passages from it into his *Note Book.* Professor J. L. Lowes, in *The Road to Xanadu,* 1930, pp. 46–47, gives an account of the way in which the chapter's marvels entered into the imagery of "The Ancient Mariner."
    The river referred to in the first sentence is the St. Juan, in Florida.

expeditious way of supplying my necessities, to take my bob and try for some trout. About one hundred yards above my harbour began a cove or bay of the river, out of which opened a large lagoon. The mouth or entrance from the river to it was narrow, but the waters soon after spread and formed a little lake, extending into the marshes. Its entrance and shores within I observed to be verged with floating lawns of the pistia and nymphea and other aquatic plants; these I knew were excellent haunts for trout.

The verges and islets of the lagoon were elegantly embellished with flowering plants and shrubs; the laughing coots with wings half spread were tripping over the little coves and hiding themselves in the tufts of grass; young broods of the painted summer teal, skimming the still surface of the waters, and following the watchful parent unconscious of danger, were frequently surprised by the voracious trout; and he, in turn, as often by the subtle, greedy alligator. Behold him rushing forth from the flags and reeds. His enormous body swells. His plaited tail brandished high, floats upon the lake. The waters like a cataract descend from his opening jaws. Clouds of smoke issue from his dilated nostrils. The earth trembles with his thunder. When immediately from the opposite coast of the lagoon, emerges from the deep his rival champion. They suddenly dart upon each other. The boiling surface of the lake marks their rapid course, and a terrific conflict commences. They now sink to the bottom folded together in horrid wreaths. The water becomes thick and discoloured. Again they rise, their jaws clap together, re-echoing through the deep surrounding forests. Again they sink, when the contest ends at the muddy bottom of the lake, and the vanquished makes a hazardous escape, hiding himself in the muddy turbulent waters and sedge on a distant shore. The proud victor exulting returns to the place of action. The shores and forest resound his dreadful roar, together with the triumphing shouts of the plaited tribes around, witnesses of the horrid combat.

· · ·

The noise of the crocodiles kept me awake the greater part of the night, but when I arose in the morning, contrary to my expectations, there was perfect peace; very few of them to be seen, and those were asleep on the shore. Yet I was not able to suppress my fears and apprehensions of being attacked by them in future; and indeed yesterday's combat with them, notwithstanding I came off in a manner victorious, or at least made a safe retreat, had left sufficient impression on my mind to damp my courage; and it seemed too much for one of my strength, being alone in a very small boat, to encounter such collected danger. To pursue my voyage up the river, and be obliged every evening to pass such dangerous defiles, appeared to me as perilous as running the 10 gauntlet betwixt two rows of Indians armed with knives and firebrands. I however resolved to continue my voyage one day longer, if I possibly could with safety, and then return down the river, should I find the like difficulties to oppose. Accordingly I got everything on board, charged my gun, and set sail cautiously along shore. As I passed by Battle Lagoon, I began to tremble and keep a good lookout; when suddenly a huge alligator rushed out of 20 the reeds, and with a tremendous roar came up, and darted as swift as an arrow under my boat, emerging upright on my lee quarter, with open jaws, and belching water and smoke that fell upon me like rain in a hurricane. I laid soundly about his head with my club, and beat him off; and after plunging and darting about my boat, he went off on a straight line through the water, seemingly with the rapidity of lightning, and entered the cape of the 30 lagoon. I now employed my time to the very best advantage in paddling close along shore, but could not forbear looking now and then behind me, and presently perceived one of them coming up again. The water of the river hereabouts was shoal and very clear; the monster came up with the usual roar and menaces, and passed close by the side of my boat, when I could distinctly see a young brood of alligators, to the number of one hun- 40 dred or more, following after her in a long train. They kept close together in a column, without straggling off to the one side or the other; the young appeared to be an equal size, about fifteen inches in length, almost black, with pale yellow transverse waved clouds or blotches, much like rattlesnakes in colour. I now lost sight of my enemy again.

Still keeping close along shore, on turning a point or projection of the river bank, at once 50 I beheld a great number of hillocks or small pyramids, resembling haycocks, ranged like an encampment along the banks. They stood fifteen or twenty yards distant from the water, on a high marsh, about four feet perpendicular above the water. I knew them to be the nests of the crocodile, having had a description of them before, and now expected a furious and general attack, as I saw several large crocodiles swimming abreast of these buildings. These nests being so great a curiosity to me, I was determined at all events immediately to land and examine them. Accordingly I ran my bark on shore at one of their landing places, which was a sort of nick or little dock, from which ascended a sloping path or road up to the edge of the meadow, where their nests were; most of them were deserted, and the great thick whitish egg-shells lay broken and scattered upon the ground round about them.

The nests or hillocks are of the form of an obtuse cone, four feet high and four or five feet in diameter at their bases; they are constructed with mud, grass and herbage. At first they lay a floor of this kind of tempered mortar on the ground, upon which they deposit a layer of eggs, and upon this a stratum of mortar, seven or eight inches in thickness, and then another layer of eggs, and in this manner one stratum upon another, nearly to the top. I believe they commonly lay from one to two hundred eggs in a nest. These are hatched, I suppose, by the heat of the sun; and perhaps the vegetable substances mixed with the earth, being acted upon by the sun, may cause a small degree of fermentation, and so increase the heat in those hillocks. The ground for several acres about these nests shewed evident marks of a continual resort of alligators; the grass was every where beaten down, hardly a blade or straw was left standing; whereas, all about, at a distance, it was five or six feet high, and as thick as it could grow together. The female, as I imagine, carefully watches her own nest of eggs until they are hatched; or perhaps while she is attending her own brood, she takes under her care and protection as many as she can get at one time, either from her own particular nest or others; but certain it is, that the young are not left to shift for themselves, having had frequent opportunities of seeing the female alligator leading about the shores her train of young ones, just like a hen does her brood of chickens; and she is equally assiduous and courageous in defending the young, which are under [her] care, and providing for their subsistence; and when she is basking upon the warm banks, with her brood around her, you may hear the young ones continually whining

and barking, like young puppies. I believe but few of a brood live to the years of full growth and magnitude, as the old feed on the young as long as they can make prey of them.

The alligator when full grown is a very large and terrible creature, and of prodigious strength, activity and swiftness in the water. I have seen them twenty feet in length, and some are supposed to be twenty-two or twenty-three feet. Their body is as large as that of a horse; their shape exactly resembles that of a lizard, except their tail, which is flat or cuneiform, being compressed on each side, and gradually diminishing from the abdomen to the extremity, which, with the whole body is covered with horny plates or squammæ, impenetrable when on the body of the live animal, even to a rifle ball, except about their head and just behind their fore-legs or arms, where it is said they are only vulnerable. The head of a full grown one is about three feet, and the mouth opens nearly the same length; the eyes are small in proportion, and seem sunk deep in the head, by means of the prominency of the brows; the nostrils are large; inflated and prominent on the top, so that the head in the water resembles, at a distance, a great chunk of wood floating about. Only the upper jaw moves, which they raise almost perpendicular, so as to form a right angle with the lower one. In the forepart of the upper jaw, on each side, just under the nostrils, are two very large, thick, strong teeth or tusks, not very sharp, but rather the shape of a cone; these are as white as the finest polished ivory, and are not covered by any skin or lips, and always in sight, which gives the creature a frightful appearance; in the lower jaw are holes opposite to these teeth, to receive them; when they clap their jaws together it causes a surprising noise, like that which is made by forcing a heavy plank with violence upon the ground, and may be heard at a great distance.

But what is yet more surprising to a stranger, is the incredible loud and terrifying roar, which they are capable of making, especially in the spring season, their breeding time. It most resembles very heavy distant thunder, not only shaking the air and waters, but causing the earth to tremble; and when hundreds and thousands are roaring at the same time, you can scarcely be persuaded, but that the whole globe is violently and dangerously agitated. . . .

Here is in this river, and in the waters all over Florida, a very curious and handsome bird. The people call them snake birds. I think I have seen paintings of them on the Chinese screens and other India pictures: they seem to be a species of cormorant or loon (*Colymbus cauda elongata*) but far more beautiful and delicately formed than any other species that I have ever seen. The head and neck of this bird are extremely small and slender, the latter very long indeed, almost out of all proportion, the bill long, straight, and slender, tapering from its ball to a sharp point; all the upper side, the abdomen and thighs, are as black and glossy as a raven's, covered with feathers so firm and elastic, that they in some degree resemble fish-scales; the breast and upper part of the belly are covered with feathers of a cream colour; the tail is very long, of a deep black, and tipped with a silvery white, and when spread, represents an unfurled fan. They delight to sit in little peaceful communities, on the dry limbs of trees, hanging over the still waters, with their wings and tails expanded, I suppose to cool and air themselves, when at the same time they behold their images in the watery mirror. At such times, when we approach them, they drop off the limbs into the water as if dead, and for a minute or two are not to be seen; when on a sudden, at a vast distance, their long slender head and neck only appear, and have very much the appearance of a snake, and no other part of them to be seen when swimming in the water, except sometimes the tip end of the tail. In the heat of the day they are seen in great numbers, sailing very high in the air, over lakes and rivers.

I doubt not but if this bird had been an inhabitant of the Tiber in Ovid's days, it would have furnished him with a subject for some beautiful and entertaining metamorphoses. I believe it feeds intirely on fish, for its flesh smells and tastes intolerably strong of it; it is scarcely to be eaten, unless constrained by insufferable hunger.

I had now swamps and marshes on both sides of me, and evening coming on apace, I began to look out for high land to encamp on; but the extensive marshes seemed to have no bounds, and it was almost dark when I found a tolerably suitable place, and at last was constrained to take up with a narrow strip of high shelly bank, on the west side. Great numbers of crocodiles were in sight on both shores. I ran my bark on shore at a perpendicular bank four or five feet above the water, just by the roots and under the spreading limbs of a great live oak: this appeared to have been an ancient camping place by Indians and strolling adventurers, from ash heaps and old rotten firebrands and chunks, scattered about on the surface of the ground; but was now evidently the harbour and landing-place of some sovereign alligator: there led up from it a deep beaten path or road, and was a convenient ascent.

I did not approve of my intended habitation from these circumstances; and no sooner had I landed and moored my canoe to the roots of the tree, than I saw a huge crocodile rising up from the bottom close by me, who, when he perceived that I saw him, plunged down again under my vessel. This determined me to be on my guard, and in time to provide against a troublesome night. I took out of my boat every movable, which I carried upon the bank, then chose my lodging close to my canoe, under the spreading oak; as hereabouts only, the ground was open and clear of high grass and bushes, and consequently I had some room to stir and look round about. I then proceeded to collect firewood, which I found difficult to procure. Here were standing a few orange trees. As for provisions, I had saved one or two barbecued trout, the remains of my last evening's collection, in tolerable good order, though the sultry heats of the day had injured them; yet by stewing them up afresh with the lively juice of oranges, they served well enough for my supper, having by this time little relish or appetite for my victuals; for constant watching at night against the attacks of alligators, stinging of musquitoes and sultry heats of the day, together with the fatigues of working my bark, had almost deprived me of every desire but that of ending my troubles as speedy as possible. I had the good fortune to collect together a sufficiency of dry sticks, to keep up a light and smoke, which I laid by me, and then spread my skins and blankets upon the ground, kindled up a little fire, and supped before it was quite dark. The evening was however, extremely pleasant, a brisk cool breeze sprang up, and the skies were perfectly serene, the stars twinkling with uncommon brilliancy. I stretched myself along before my fire; having the river, my little harbour, and the stern of my vessel in view; and now through

fatigue and weariness I fell asleep. But this happy temporary release from cares and troubles I enjoyed but a few moments, when I was awakened and greatly surprised, by the terrifying screams of owls in the deep swamps around me; and what increased my extreme misery was the difficulty of getting quite awake, and yet hearing at the same time such screaming and shouting, which increased and spread
10 every way for miles around, in dreadful peals vibrating through the dark extensive forests, meadows, and lakes. I could not after this surprise recover my former peaceable state and tranquility of mind and repose, during the long night; and I believe it was happy for me that I was awakened, for at that moment the crocodile was dashing my canoe against the roots of the tree, endeavouring to get into her for the fish, which I however prevented. An-
20 other time in the night I believe I narrowly escaped being dragged into the river by him, for when again through excessive fatigue I had fallen asleep, but was again awakened by the screaming owl, I found the monster on the top of the bank, his head towards me, not above two yards distant; when starting up and seizing my fusee well loaded, which I always kept under my head in the night time, he drew back and plunged into the water. After this I roused
30 up my fire, and kept a light during the remaining part of the night, being determined not to be caught napping so again; indeed the musquitoes alone would have been abundantly sufficient to keep any creature awake that possessed their perfect senses; but I was overcome, and stupified with incessant watching and labour. As soon as I discovered the first signs of day-light, I arose, got all my effects and implements on board and set sail, proceed-
40 ing upwards, hoping to give the musquitoes the slip, who were now, by the cool morning dews and breezes, driven to their shelter and hiding places. I was mistaken however in these conjectures, for great numbers of them, which had concealed themselves in my boat, as soon as the sun arose, began to revive, and sting me on my legs, which obliged me to land in order to get bushes to beat them out of their
49 quarters.

. . .

The air continued sultry, and scarcely enough wind to flutter the leaves on the trees. The eastern coast of the river now opens, and presents to view ample plains, consisting of grassy marshes and green meadows, and affords a prospect almost unlimited and extremely pleasing. The opposite shore presents to view a sublime contrast; a high bluff bearing magnificent forests of grand magnolia, glorious palms, fruitful orange groves, live oaks, bays and others. This grand elevation continues four or five hundred yards, describing a gentle curve on the river, ornamented by a sublime grove of palms, consisting of many hundreds of trees together; they entirely shade the ground under them. Above and below the bluff the grounds gradually descend to the common level swamps on the river; back of this eminence opens to view expansive green meadows or savannas, in which are to be seen glittering ponds of water, surrounded at a great distance by high open pine forests and hommocks, and islets of oaks and bays projecting into the savannas. After ranging about these solitary groves and peaceful shades, I re-embarked and continued some miles up the river, between elevated banks of the swamps or low lands; when on the east shore, in a capacious cove or winding of the river, were pleasing floating fields of pistia; and in the bottom of this cove opened to view a large creek or branch of the river, which I knew to be the entrance to a beautiful lake, on the banks of which was the farm I was going to visit, and which I designed should be the last extent of my voyage up the river.

About noon the weather became extremely sultry, not a breath of wind stirring, hazy or cloudy, with very heavy distant thunder, which is answered by the crocodiles, sure presage of a storm!

Soon after ascending this branch of the river, on the right hand presents to view a delightful little bluff, consisting chiefly of shells, and covered with a dark grove of red cedar, zanthoxylon and myrtle. I could not resist the temptation to stop here, although the tremendous thunder all around the hemisphere alarmed me greatly, having a large lake to cross. From this grove presents to view an expansive and pleasing prospect. The beauteous long lake in front, about north east from me, its most distant east shores adorned with dark, high forests of stately trees; north and south almost endless green plains and meadows, embellished with islets and projecting promontories of high, dark forests, where the pyramidal magnolia grandiflora, palma elata, and shady oak, conspiciously tower.

Being heretofore so closely invested by high forests and deep swamps of the great river, I was prevented from seeing the progress and increase of the approaching tempest, the terrific appearance of which now at once confounded me. How purple and firey appeared the tumultuous clouds, swiftly ascending or darting from the horizon upwards! they seemed to oppose and dash against each other; the skies appeared streaked with blood and purple flame overhead, the flaming lightning streaming and darting about in every direction around, seems to fill the world with fire; whilst the heavy thunder keeps the earth in a constant tremor. I had yet some hopes of crossing the lake to the plantation in sight. On the opposite shore of the creek before me, and on the cape as we enter the lake, stood a large islet or grove of oaks and palms. Here I intended to seek shelter and abide till the fury of the hurricane was overpast, if I found it too violent to permit me to cross the lake. In consequence of this precipitate determination, I stepped into my boat and pushed off. What a dreadful rushing and roaring there was every where around me! and to my utter confusion and astonishment, I could not find from what particular quarter its strongest current or direction came, whereby I might have a proper chance of taking measures of securing a harbour or running from it. The high forests behind me bend to the blast, and the sturdy limbs of the trees crack. I had by this time got up abreast of the grove or hommock; the hurricane close by, pursuing me, I found it dangerous and imprudent in the highest degree to put in here, as the groves were already torn up, and the spreading limbs of the ancient live oaks were flying over my head, and carried about in the air as leaves and stubble. I ran by and boldly entered the lake (being hurried in by a strong current, which seemed a prodigy, the violent wind driving the stream of the creek back again into the lake), and as soon as possible took shelter under the high reedy bank of the lake, made fast my bark to the boughs of a low shrubby hickory, that leaned over the water. Such was the violence of the wind, that it raised the waters on the opposite shores of the lake several feet perpendicular, and there was a rapid flow of water from the creek into it, which was contrary to its natural course. Such floods of rain fell during the space of half or three quarters of an hour that my boat was filled, and I expected every moment when I should see her

sink to the bottom of the lake; and the violence of the wind kept the cable so constantly extended, that it was beyond my ability to get to her. My box, which contained my books of specimens and other collections, was floating about in her; and for a great part of the time the rain came down with such rapidity and fell in such quantities, that every object was totally obscured, excepting the continual streams or rivers of lightning, pouring from the clouds. All seemed a frightful chaos. When the wind and rain abated, I was overjoyed to see the face of nature again appear.

It took me an hour or more to clear the water out of my bark. I then crossed the lake before a brisk and favourable breeze (it was about a mile over) and landed safely at the plantation.

. . .

Since I have turned my observations upon the birds of this country, I shall notice another very singular one, though already most curiously and exactly figured by Catesby, yet it seems to be nearly allied to those before mentioned, I mean the bird which he called the wood pelican. This is a large bird, perhaps near three feet high when standing erect. The bill is very long and strong, bending with a moderate curve, from the base to the tip; the upper mandible is the largest, and receives the edges of the nether one into it its whole length; the edges are very sharp and firm; the whole of a dark ash or horn colour; the forehead round the base of the beak and sides of the head is bare of feathers, and of a dark greenish colour, in which space is placed the eyes, which are very large; the remainder of the head and neck is of a nut brown colour; the back of a light bluish grey; upper part of the wings, breast, and belly, almost white, with some slight dashes of grey; the quill-feathers and tail, which are very short, are of a dark slate colour, almost black; the legs, which are very long and bare of feathers a great length above the knees, are of a dark dull greenish colour; they have a small bag or pouch under their throat; they feed on serpents, young alligators, frogs, and other reptiles.

This solitary bird does not associate in flocks, but is generally seen alone; commonly near the banks of great rivers, in vast marshes or meadows, especially such as are caused by inundations; and also in the vast deserted rice plantations; he stands alone on the topmost limb of tall dead cypress trees, his neck contracted or drawn in upon his shoulders, and beak resting like a long scythe upon his breast: in this pensive posture and solitary situation, they look extremely grave, sorrowful, and melancholy, as if in the deepest thought. They are never seen on the salt sea coast, and yet are never found at a great distance from it. I take this bird to be of a different genus from the tantalus, and perhaps approaches the nearest to the Egyptian ibis of any other bird yet known.

• • •

Having agreeably diverted away the intolerable heats of sultry noon in fruitful fragrant groves, with renewed vigour I again resume my sylvan pilgrimage. The afternoon and evening moderately warm, and exceeding pleasant views from the river and its varied shores. I passed by Battle Lagoon and the bluff, without much opposition; but the crocodiles were already assembling in the pass. Before night I came to, at a charming orange grove bluff, on the east side of the little lake; and after fixing my camp on a high open situation, and collecting a plenty of dry wood for fuel, I had time to get some fine trout for supper and joyfully return to my camp.

What a most beautiful creature is this fish before me! gliding to and fro, and figuring in the still clear waters, with his orient attendants and associates: the yellow bream or sun fish. It is about eight inches in length, nearly of the shape of the trout, but rather larger in proportion over the shoulders and breast; the mouth large, and the branchiostega opens wide; the whole fish is of a pale gold (or burnished brass) colour, darker on the back and upper sides; the scales are of a proportionable size, regularly placed, and every where variably powdered with red, russet, silver, blue, and green specks, so laid on the scales as to appear like real dust or opaque bodies, each apparent particle being so projected by light and shade, and the various attitudes of the fish, as to deceive the sight; for in reality nothing can be of a more plain or polished surface than the scales and whole body of the fish. The fins are of an orange colour; and, like all the species of the bream, the ultimate angle of the branchiostega terminates by a little spatula, the extreme end of which represents a crescent of the finest ultramarine blue, encircled with silver and velvet black, like the eye in the feathers of a pea-

cock's train. He is a fish of prodigious strength and activity in the water; a warrior in a gilded coat of mail, and gives no rest or quarter to small fish, which he preys upon. They are delicious food and in great abundance.

• • •

At evening I arrived at Cedar Point, my former safe and pleasant harbour, at the east cape of the Great Lake, where I had noticed some curious shrubs and plants; here I rested, and on the smooth and gentle current launch again into the little ocean of Lake George, meaning now, on my return, to coast his western shores in search of new beauties in the bounteous kingdom of Flora.

I was however induced to deviate a little from my intended course, and touch at the inchanting little Isle of Palms. This delightful spot, planted by nature, is almost an entire grove of palms, with a few pyramidal magnolias, live oaks, golden orange, and the animating Zanthoxylon. What a beautiful retreat is here! blessed unviolated spot of earth, rising from the limpid waters of the lake: its fragrant groves and blooming lawns invested and protected by encircling ranks of the Yucca gloriosa. A fascinating atmosphere surrounds this blissful garden; the balmy Lantana, ambrosial Citra, perfumed Crinum, perspiring their mingled odours, wafted through Zanthoxylon groves. I at last broke away from the enchanting spot, and stepped on board my boat, hoisted sail, and soon approached the coast of the main, at the cool eve of day: then traversing a capacious semicircular cove of the lake, verged by low, extensive grassy meadows, I at length by dusk made a safe harbour, in a little lagoon, on the sea shore or strand of a bold sandy point, which descended from the surf of the lake. This was a clean sandy beach, hard and firm by the beating surf, when the wind sets from the east coast. I drew up my vessel on the sloping shore, that she might be safe from the beating waves in case of sudden storm of wind in the night. A few yards back the land was a little elevated, and over-grown with thickets of shrubs and low trees, consisting chiefly of Zanthoxylon, Olea Americana, Rhamnus frangula, Sideroxylon, Morus, Ptela, Halesia, Querci, Myruca cerifera, and others. These groves were but low, yet sufficiently high to shelter me from the chilling dews; and being but a few yards distance from my vessel, here I fixed my encampment. A brisk wind arising from the lake, drove away the clouds of musquitoes into the thickets. I now, with difficulty and industry, collected a sufficiency of dry wood to keep up a light during the night, and to roast some trout which I had caught when descending the river; their heads I stewed in the juice of oranges, which, with boiled rice, afforded me a wholesome and delicious supper: I hung the remainder of my broiled fish on the snags of some shrubs over my head. I at last, after reconnoitring my habitation, returned, spread abroad my skins and blanket upon the clean sands by my fireside, and betook myself to repose.

How glorious the powerful sun, minister of the Most High in the rule and government of this earth, leaves our hemisphere, retiring from our sight beyond the western forests! I behold with gratitude his departing smiles, ringing the fleecy roseate clouds, now riding far away on the eastern horizon; behold they vanish from sight in the azure skies!

All now silent and peaceable, I suddenly fell asleep. At midnight I awake; when, raising my head erect, I find myself alone in the wilderness of Florida, on the shores of Lake George. Alone indeed, but under the care of the Almighty, and protected by the invisible hand of my guardian angel.

When quite awake, I started at the heavy tread of some animal; the dry limbs of trees upon the ground crack under his feet; the close shrubby thickets part and bend under him as he rushes off.

I rekindled up my sleepy fire, lay in contact the exfoliated smoking brands damp with the dew of heaven.

The bright flame ascends and illuminates the ground and groves around me.

When looking up, I found my fish carried off, though I had thought them safe on the shrubs, just over my head; but their scent, carried to a great distance by the damp nocturnal breezes, I suppose were too powerful attractions to resist.

Perhaps it may not be time lost, to rest a while here, and reflect on the unexpected and unaccountable incident, which however pointed out to me an extraordinary deliverance or protection of my life, from the rapacious wolf that stole my fish from over my head.

How much easier and more eligible might it have been for him to have leaped upon my breast in the dead of sleep, and torn my throat, which would have instantly deprived

me of life, and then glutted his stomach for the present with my warm blood, and dragged off my body, which would have been a feast afterwards for him and his howling associates! I say, would not this have been a wiser step, than to have made protracted and circular approaches, and then after, by chance, espying the fish over my head, with the greatest caution and silence rear up, and take them off the snags one by one, then make off with them, 10 and that so cunningly as not to waken me until he had fairly accomplished his purpose?

The morning being clear, I set sail with a favourable breeze, coasting along the shores; when on a sudden the waters became transparent, and discovered the sandy bottom, and the several nations of fish, passing and repassing each other. Following this course I led to the cape of the little river, descending from Six Mile Springs, and meanders six miles from 20 its source through green meadows. I entered this pellucid stream, sailing over the heads of innumerable squadrons of fish, which although many feet deep in the water, were distinctly to be seen. I passed by charming islets of flourishing trees, as palm, red bay, ash, maple, nyssa, and others. As I approached the distant high forest on the main, the river widens, floating fields of green Pistia surrounded me, the rapid stream winding through them. What an alluring 30 scene was now before me! A vast bason or little lake of crystal waters, half encircled by swelling hills clad with orange and odoriferous illicium groves, the towering magnolia, itself a grove, and the exalted palm, as if conscious of their transcendent glories, tossed about their lofty heads, painting, with mutable shades, the green floating fields beneath. The social prattling coot enrobed in blue, and the squeeling water-hen, with wings half expanded, tripped 40 after each other, over the watery mirrour.

I put in at an ancient landing place, which is a sloping ascent to a level grassy plain, an old Indian field. As I intended to make my most considerable collections at this place, I proceeded immediately to fix my encampment by a few yards from my safe harbour, where I securely fastened my boat to a live oak, which overshadowed my port. 49

. . .

The trees and shrubs which cover these extensive wilds are about five or six feet high, and seem to be kept down by the annual firing of the deserts, rather than the barrenness of the soil, as I saw a few large live oaks, mulberry trees, and hiccories, which evidently have withstood the devouring flames. These adjoining wild plains, forests, and savannas, are situated lower than the hilly groves on the banks of the lake and river; but what should be the natural cause of it I cannot even pretend to conjecture, unless one may suppose that those high hills, which we call bluffs, on the banks of this great river and its lakes, and which support those magnificent groves and high forests, and are generally composed of shells and sand, were thrown up to their present height by the winds and waves, when the bed of the river was nearer the level of the present surface of the earth; but then, to rest upon such a supposition, would be admitting that the waters were heretofore in greater quantities than at this time, or that their present channels and receptacles are worn deeper into the earth.

I now directed my steps towards my encampment, in a different direction. I seated myself upon a swelling green knoll, at the head of the crystal bason. Near me, on the left, was a point or projection of an entire grove of the aromatic Illicium Floridanum; on my right, and all around behind me, was a fruitful orange grove, with palms, and magnolias, interspersed; in front, just under my feet, was the inchanting and amazing crystal fountain, which incessantly threw up, from dark, rocky caverns below, tons of water every minute, forming a bason, capacious enough for large shallops to ride in, and a creek of four or five feet depth of water, and near twenty yards over, which meanders six miles through green meadows, pouring its limpid waters into the great Lake George, where they seem to remain pure and unmixed. About twenty yards from the upper edge of the bason, and directly opposite to the mouth or outlet of the creek, is a continual and amazing ebullition, where the waters are thrown up in such abundance and amazing force, as to jet and swell up two or three feet above the common surface; white sand and small particles of shells are thrown up with the waters, near to the top, when they diverge from the center, subside with the expanding flood, and gently sink again, forming a large rim or funnel round about the aperture or mouth of the fountain, which is a vast perforation through a bed of rocks, the ragged points of which are projected out on every side. Thus far I know to be matter of real fact, and I have related it as near as I could conceive or express

myself. But there are yet remaining scenes inexpressibly admirable and pleasing.

Behold, for instance, a vast circular expanse before you, the waters of which are so extremely clear as to be absolutely diaphanous or transparent as the ether; the margin of the bason ornamented with a great variety of fruitful and floriferous trees, shrubs, and plants, the pendant golden orange dancing with the melody of the merry birds, tenants of the encircling aromatic grove.

At the same instant innumerable bands of fish are seen, some clothed in the most brilliant colours; the voracious crocodile stretched along at full length, as the great trunk of a tree in size; the devouring garfish, inimical trout, and all the varieties of gilded painted bream; the barbed catfish, dreaded sting-ray, skate, and flounder, spotted bass, sheeps head and ominous drum; all in their separate bands and communities, with free unsuspicious intercourse performing their evolutions; there are no signs of enmity, no attempt to devour each other; the different bands seem peaceably and complaisantly to move a little aside, as it were to make room for others to pass by.

But behold yet something far more admirable, see whole armies descending into an abyss, into the mouth of the bubbling fountain; they disappear! are they gone for ever? is it real? I raise my eyes with terror and astonishment,—I look down again to the fountain with anxiety, when behold them as it were emerging from the blue ether of another world, apparently at a vast distance; at their first appearance, no bigger than flies or minnows; now gradually enlarging, their brilliant colours begin to paint the fluid.

Now they come forward rapidly, and instantly emerge, with the elastic expanding column of crystalline waters, into the circular bason or funnel; see now how gently they rise, some upright, other obliquely, or seem to [lie] as it were on their sides, suffering themselves to be gently lifted or borne up by the expanding fluid towards the surface, sailing or floating like butterflies in the cerulean ether; then again they as gently descend, diverge and move off; when they rally, form again, and rejoin their kindred tribes.

This amazing and delightful scene, though real, appears at first but as a piece of excellent painting; there seems no medium; you imagine the picture to be within a few inches of your eyes, and that you may without the least difficulty touch any one of the fish, or put your finger upon the crocodile's eye, when it really is twenty or thirty feet under water.

And although this paradise of fish may seem to exhibit a just representation of the peaceable and happy state of nature which existed before the fall, yet in reality it is a mere representation; for the nature of the fish is the same as if they were in Lake George or the river; but here the water or element in which they live and move, is so perfectly clear and transparent, it places them all on an equality with regard to their ability to injure or escape from one another; (as all river fish of prey, or such as feed upon each other, as well as the unwieldy crocodile, take their prey by surprise; secreting themselves under covert or in ambush, until an opportunity offers, when they rush suddenly upon them) but here is no covert, no ambush; here the trout freely passes by the very nose of the alligator, and laughs in his face, and the bream by the trout.

But what is really surprising is, that the consciousness of each other's safety, or some other latent cause, should so absolutely alter their conduct, for here is not the least attempt made to injure or disturb one another.

. . .   1791

FRANCIS HOPKINSON

1737–1791

FRANCIS HOPKINSON was a valuable citizen in the young republic. Eminent in many activities, though pre-eminent in none, he performed useful services for Pennsylvania and New Jersey, his country, and the arts of music, painting, and poetry. A son of Thomas Hopkinson, friend of Franklin and Judge of the Admiralty, young Francis attended the Academy which held its first commencement as the College of Philadelphia (now the University of Pennsylvania) the year he was graduated (1757). After a journey to England, where his kinsman the Bishop of Worcester assisted him in his efforts to secure a post, Hopkinson returned to America and married the daughter of the founder of Bordentown, New Jersey. At the outbreak of the Revolution he was collector of customs at Newcastle, Delaware. A delegate to the first Continental Congress, and a signer of the Declaration of Independence, he served during the War as Chairman of the Continental Navy Board. In 1779 he became Judge of the Admiralty, and in 1789 a Federal judge in the newly created district of Eastern Pennsylvania.

During the Revolution Hopkinson helped to support the morale of his countrymen by his writing. Earlier he had earned some fame as a lyric poet. The struggle evoked his talents as a satirist in prose and verse. *A Pretty Story* (1774), an allegorical presentation of English misrule, appeared at the right moment to put fight into the members of the First Continental Congress. His "Battle of the Kegs" was sung by the troops on the march. Though he is by no means to be compared with Swift, in whose company his admiring friend Dr. Benjamin Rush placed him, Hopkinson deserves to be remembered with John Trumbull and Philip Freneau, poets whose art was improved by their devotion to the principles of the new nation.

The Miscellaneous Essays and Occasional Writings of Francis Hopkinson, Esq., 3 vols., Philadelphia, 1792.
G. E. Hastings, *The Life and Works of Francis Hopkinson*, Chicago, 1926.
O. G. Sonneck, *Francis Hopkinson, the First American Poet-Composer*, Washington, 1905.

THE BATTLE OF THE KEGS [1]

Gallants attend and hear a friend,
　　Trill forth harmonious ditty,
Strange things I'll tell which late befel
　　In Philadelphia city.

'Twas early day, as poets say,
　　Just when the sun was rising,
A soldier stood on a log of wood,
　　And saw a thing surprising.

As in amaze he stood to gaze,
　　The truth can't be denied, sir,　　10
He spied a score of kegs or more
　　Come floating down the tide, sir.

A sailor too in jerkin blue,
　　This strange appearance viewing,
First damn'd his eyes, in great surprise,
　　Then said Some mischief's brewing.

These kegs, I'm told, the rebels bold,
　　Pack'd up like pickling herring;
And they're come down t'attack the town,
　　In this new way of ferrying.　　20

The soldier flew, the sailor too,
　　And scar'd almost to death, sir,
Wore out their shoes, to spread the news,
　　And ran till out of breath, sir.

Now up and down throughout the town,
　　Most frantic scenes were acted;
And some ran here, and others there,
　　Like men almost distracted.

Some fire cry'd, which some denied,
　　But said the earth had quaked;　　30
And girls and boys, with hideous noise,
　　Ran thro' the streets half naked.

Sir William [2] he, snug as a flea,
　　Lay all this time a snoring,
Nor dream'd of harm as he lay warm,
　　In bed with Mrs. L——g.

Now in a fright, he starts upright,
　　Awak'd by such a clatter;
He rubs both eyes, and boldly cries,
　　For God's sake, what's the matter?　　40

[1] N.B. This ballad was occasioned by a real incident. Certain machines, in the form of kegs, charg'd with gun powder, were sent down the river to annoy the British shipping then at Philadelphia. The danger of these machines being discovered, the British manned the wharfs and shipping, and discharged their small arms and cannons at every thing they saw floating in the river during the ebb tide. [Hopkinson's note.]
[2] Sir William Howe.

At his bed-side he then espy'd,
　　Sir Erskine at command, sir,
Upon one foot, he had one boot,
　　And th'other in his hand, sir.

"Arise, arise, sir Erskine cries,
　　The rebels—more's the pity,
Without a boat are all afloat,
　　And rang'd before the city.

"The motly crew, in vessels new,
　　With Satan for their guide, sir,　　50
Pack'd up in bags, or wooden kegs,
　　Come driving down the tide, sir.

"Therefore prepare for bloody war,
　　These kegs must all be routed,
Or surely we despised shall be,
　　And British courage doubted."

The royal band, now ready stand
　　All rang'd in dread array, sir,
With stomach stout to see it out,
　　And make a bloody day, sir.　　60

The cannons roar from shore to shore,
　　The small arms make a rattle;
Since wars began I'm sure no man
　　E'er saw so strange a battle.

The rebel dales, the rebel vales,
　　With rebel trees surrounded;
The distant wood, the hills and floods,
　　With rebel echos sounded.

The fish below swam to and fro,
　　Attack'd from ev'ry quarter;　　70
Why sure, thought they, the devil's to pay,
　　'Mongst folks above the water.

The kegs, 'tis said, tho' strongly made,
　　Of rebel staves and hoops, sir,
Could not oppose their powerful foes,
　　The conqu'ring British troops, sir.

From morn to night these men of might
　　Display'd amazing courage;
And when the sun was fairly down,
　　Retir'd to sup their porrage.　　80

An hundred men with each a pen,
　　Or more upon my word, sir,
It is most true would be too few,
　　Their valour to record, sir.

Such feats did they perform that day,
  Against these wick'd kegs, sir,
That years to come, if they get home,
  They'll make their boasts and brags, sir.
                                    1778

SONG

I

My gen'rous heart disdains
  The slave of love to be,
I scorn his servile chains,
  And boast my liberty.
        This wining
        And pining
And wasting with care,
Are not to my taste, be she ever so fair.

II

Shall a girl's capricious frown
Sink my noble spirits down?   10
Shall a face of white and red
Make me droop my silly head?
Shall I set me down and sigh
For an eye-brow or an eye?
For a braided lock of hair,
Curse my fortune and despair?
    My gen'rous heart disdains, &c.

III

Still uncertain is to-morrow,
Not quite certain is to-day—
Shall I waste my time in sorrow?   20
Shall I languish life away?
All because a cruel maid,
Hath not Love with Love repaid.
    My gen'rous heart disdains, &c.   1778

» » « «

» » THE NEW ROOF [3] « «

The roof [of] a certain Mansion-house was observed to be in a very bad condition,[4] and quite insufficient for the purpose of protection from the inclemencies of the weather. This was matter of surprise and speculation, as it was well known that the roof was not more than twelve years old, and therefore its defects could not be ascribed to a natural decay by time.

Although there were many different opinions respecting the causes of this deficiency, yet all agreed that the family could not sleep in comfort or safety under it.

At last it was determined to employ some skilful architects to survey and examine this defective roof, to make report of its condition, and to point out such alterations and repairs as might be found necessary.

These skilful architects accordingly met together; and after a thorough examination of the faulty roof, they found,

1st   That the whole fabric was too weak.

2nd   That there were indeed *thirteen* rafters; but that these rafters were not connected by any braces or ties, so as to form a union of strength.

3d   That some of these rafters were thick and heavy, and others too slight; and as the whole had been put together whilst the timber was yet green, some had warped outwards, and of course sustained an undue proportion of   10 weight, whilst others, warping inwards, had shrunk from bearing any weight at all.

4th   That the shingling and lathing had not been secured with iron nails, but only wooden pegs,[5] which swelling and shrinking by successions of wet and dry weather, had left the shingles so loose, that many of them had been blown away by the wind; and that before long, the whole would, probably, in like manner be blown away.

5th   That the cornice was so ill propor-   20 tioned, and so badly put up, as to be neither an ornament nor of use: and,

6th   That the roof was so flat as to admit the most idle servants in the family, their playmates and acquaintances, to trample upon and abuse it.[6]

Having made these observations, these ju-

[3] In December 1788 the convention of Philadelphia assembled to consider the constitution or frame of government for the United States, drawn up by the late general convention of the states, and by them recommended to the consideration of the people at large. After three weeks deliberation, the proposed constitution was adopted by the convention of Pennsylvania, by a majority of two thirds of that body. The following allegory contains in substance the principal arguments used in that important debate. [Hopkinson's note.]
[4] The old Confederation. [Hopkinson's note.]

[5] Paper Currency. [Hopkinson's note.]
[6] Want of dignity in government. [Hopkinson's note.]

dicious architects were of opinion, that it would be altogether vain and fruitless to attempt any alterations or repairs in a roof so defective in all points, and therefore proposed to have it entirely removed; and that a new roof, of a better construction, should be erected over the mansion-house: and they also prepared a drawing or plan of a new roof, such as they thought most excellent for security, duration, and ornament. In forming this plan, they consulted the most celebrated authors in ancient and modern architecture, and brought into their design the most approved parts, selected from the models before them; and finally endeavoured to proportion the whole to the size of the building and the strength of the walls.

This proposal of a new roof, it may well be imagined, became the principal subject of conversation in the family: and the opinions of it were various, according to the judgment, interests, or ignorance of the disputants.

On a certain day the servants of the family had assembled in the great hall to discuss the important question. Amongst these was JAMES,[7] the architect, who had been one of the surveyors of the old roof, and had a principal hand in forming the plan of the new one. A great number of tenants had also gathered out of doors, and crowded the windows and avenues to the hall, which were left open for them, that they might hear the arguments for and against the new roof.

Now, there was an old woman, known by the name of *Margery the midwife,* who had got a comfortable apartment in the mansion-house. This woman was of an intriguing spirit, of a restless and inveterate temper, fond of tattle, and a great mischief-maker. In this situation, and with these talents, she unavoidably acquired an influence in the family; by the exercise of which, according to her natural propensity, she had long kept the house in confusion, and sown discord and discontent amongst the servants.

Margery was, for many reasons, an irreconcilable enemy to the new roof, and the architects who had contrived it. Amongst these, two reasons were very obvious. First: the mantlepiece, on which her cups and platters were placed, was made of a portion of the great cornice; and she boiled her pot with the shingles that blew off from the defective roof: and, secondly, it so happened that, in the construc-

tion of the new roof, her apartment would be considerably lessened.

No sooner, therefore, did she hear of the plan proposed by the architects, but she put on her old red cloak, and was day and night trudging amongst the servants and tenants, crying out against the new roof, and the framers thereof. Amongst these she had selected *William, Jack,* and *Robert,* three of the servants, and instigated them to oppose the plan recommended. She caused them to be sent to the great hall on the day of debate, and furnished them with innumerable alarms and fears, cunning arguments, and specious objections.

Now, the principal argument and objections with which *Margery* had instructed William, Jack, and Robert, were these.

1st   That the architects had not exhibited a bill of scantling [8] for the new roof, as they ought to have done; and, therefore, the carpenters, under the pretence of providing timber for it, might lay waste whole forests, to the ruin of the farm.

2dly   That no provision was made in the plan for a trap door [9] for the servants to pass through with water, if the chimney should take fire, and that in case of such an accident it might hereafter be deemed penal to break a hole in the roof, for access, to save the whole building from destruction.

3dly   That this roof was to be guarded by battlements,[10] which in stormy seasons, would prove dangerous to the family, as the bricks might be blown down and fall on their heads.

4thly   It was observed, that the old roof was ornamented with twelve pedestals,[11] ranged along the ridge, which had been objects of universal admiration. Whereas, according to the new plan, these pedestals were only to be placed along the eaves of the roof over the walls. As to the cupola, some of the objectors said it was too heavy, and would prove a dangerous burden to the building; whilst others insisted that it was too light, and would certainly be blown away by the wind.

5thly   It was urged, that the thirteen rafters would be so strongly braced together, that the individual and separate strength of each rafter would be lost in the compounded and united

---

[7] James Wilson, one of the leading Pennsylvania delegates to the Constitutional Convention.

[8] Bill of rights. (This note and the notes which follow are by Hopkinson.)
[9] Liberty of the press.
[10] Standing army.
[11] Trial by jury.

strength of the whole;[12] and so this roof might be considered as one solid mass of timber, and not as composed of distinct rafters like the old roof.

6[thly] That, according to the proposed plan, the several parts of the roof were so framed as to mutually strengthen and support each other; and therefore, there was great reason to fear, that the whole might stand independent of the walls; and, that in time the walls might moulder away, and the roof remain suspended in the air, threatening destruction to all who should come under it.[13]

To these objections, JAMES, the architect, in substance replied.

1st As to the want of a bill of scantling, he observed, that if the timber for this roof was to be purchased from a stranger, it would have been quite proper to have such a bill, lest the stranger should charge in account more than he was entitled to; but as the timber was to be cut from our own lands, a bill of scantling was both useless and improper. It was of no use, because the wood always was, and always would be, the property of the family, whether growing in the forest, or fabricated into a roof for the mansion-house; and improper, because the carpenters would be bound by the bill of scantling; which, if it should not be perfectly accurate, a circumstance not to be expected, either the roof would be defective for want of sufficient materials, or the carpenters must cut from the forest, without authority, which is penal by the laws of the house.

2[dly] To the second objection, he said, that a trap-door was not properly a part of the frame of a roof; but there could be no doubt but that the carpenters would take care to make such a door in the shingling for the family to carry water through, *dirty* or *clean,* to extinguish fire, either in the chimney or on the roof; and that this was the only proper way of making such a door.

3[dly] As to the battlements, he insisted, that they were absolutely necessary for the protection of the whole house. 1st Because, in case of a sudden attack by robbers, the family could defend themselves behind these battlements, and annoy and disperse the enemy. 2[dly] If any of the adjoining buildings should take fire, the battlements would screen the roof from the destructive flames. And, 3[dly], they would re-

tain the rafters in their respective places, in case any of them should, from rottenness or warping, be in danger of falling from the general union, and injuring the other parts of the roof: observing also, that the battlements should always be ready for these purposes, as there would be neither time nor opportunity for raising battlements after an assault was actually made, or a conflagration begun. As to the bricks being blown down, and falling on the heads of the people, he said the whole would always be in the power of the family, who could at any time repair or remove any loose and dangerous parts; and there could be no doubt but that their vigilance would be fully sufficient to prevent accidents of this kind.

4[thly] With respect to the twelve pedestals, he acknowledged their use and beauty; but observed that these, like all other things, were only so in their proper places, and under circumstances suited to their nature and design: and he insisted that the ridge of a roof was not the place for pedestals, which should rest on the solid wall, being made of the same materials; and ought, in propriety, to be considered as so many projections, or continuations of the wall itself, and not as component parts of the wooden roof. As to the cupola, he said, that all agreed that there should be one of some kind or other; as well for a proper finish to the building, as for the purpose of indicating the winds, and containing a bell to sound the alarm in case of necessity. The objections to the proposed cupola, he said, were too contradictory to merit a reply.

5[thly] To the fifth objection, he answered: that the intention really was to make a firm and substantial roof, by uniting the strength of the thirteen rafters; but that this was so far from annihilating the several rafters, and rendering them of no use individually, that it was manifest, from a bare inspection of the plan, that the strength of each contributed to the strength of the whole, and that the existence of each and all was essential to the existence of the fabric as a roof.

6[thly] And lastly, he said, that the roof was, in truth, so framed as that the parts should mutually support and check each other. But it was absolutely absurd, and contrary to the known laws of nature, to infer from thence, that the whole frame could stand self-supported in the air. For, however its component parts might be combined with respect to each

---

[12] That the sovereignties of the several states would be absorbed in the general government.

[13] That it would be a consolidated government, and might exist independent of the people or of the states.

other, the whole must necessarily rest upon and be supported by the walls. That the walls might, indeed, stand for a few years in a ruinous and uninhabitable condition, without any roof; but the roof could not, for a moment, stand without the support of the walls: and finally, that of all dangers and apprehensions, this of the roof's remaining after the walls are gone, was the most absurd and impossible.

It was mentioned before, that whilst this debate was going on in the great hall, the windows and doors were crowded with attendants. Amongst these, was a half crazy fellow, who was suffered to go at large as a harmless lunatic.[14] *Margery,* however, thought he might be a serviceable engine in promoting opposition to the new roof. As people of deranged understandings are easily irritated, she exasperated this poor fellow against the architects, and filled him with terrible apprehensions from the new roof; making him believe that the architects had provided a dark hole in the garret, where he was to be chained for life. Having by these suggestions filled his mind with rage and terror, she turned him loose amongst the crowd, where he roared and bawled to the great annoyance of the bye-standers. . . .   1787

[14] A furious writer under the signature of *Philadelphiensis.*

The Connecticut Wits

THE SO-CALLED Connecticut or Hartford Wits constitute the first school of American writers. The chief members of the group are John Trumbull (1751–1831), Timothy Dwight (1752–1817), David Humphreys (1752–1818), and Joel Barlow (1754–1812). Less important are Lemuel Hopkins (1750–1801), Richard Alsop (1751–1815), and Theodore Dwight (1764–1846). Though each of these gentlemen was a man of parts and of marked individuality, the fate which has continuously herded them together in literary histories is not altogether undeserved. Even in their own time their solidarity was recognized, and the traits they have in common are, in the main, more numerous than their dissimilarities. Almost all of them were noted for their promise and brilliance as Yale undergraduates; several had some local reputation as poets before the Revolution and were consciously striving to provide the colonies with a literature commensurate with their increasing importance in the British Empire. The Revolutionary War enlisted their sympathies and poetical talents, but their propaganda poetry for the cause lacks the causticity of Freneau's. Save for the renegade Barlow, they were by no means political radicals. Once the Revolution was over, their fundamental conservatism, fortified by their religious orthodoxy, reasserted itself. As men of weight in Connecticut life they became alarmed at the atheistical and democratic spirit abroad in the land. Tom Paine and Thomas Jefferson were as odious to them as King George and Lord North had been in '76.

The Connecticut Wits (American Authors Series), V. L. Parrington, ed., New York, 1926.
H. A. Beers, *The Connecticut Wits and Other Essays,* New Haven, 1920.
Alexander Cowie, *John Trumbull, Connecticut Wit,* Chapel Hill, 1936.
Charles E. Cunningham, *Timothy Dwight, 1752–1817: A Biography,* New York, 1942.
Leon Howard, *The Connecticut Wits,* Chicago, 1943.
C. B. Todd, *Life and Letters of Joel Barlow, LL.D.,* New York, 1886.
M. C. Tyler, *Three Men of Letters,* New York, 1895 (Dwight and Barlow).
J. L. Woodress, *A Yankee's Odyssey: The Life of Joel Barlow,* Philadelphia, 1958.
T. A. Zunder, *The Early Days of Joel Barlow, a Connecticut Wit,* New Haven, 1934.

JOHN TRUMBULL

1751–1831

T HE PRECOCIOUS Trumbull was prepared to enter Yale at the age of seven, but was not the solemn boy such an achievement suggests. At college, which he entered at thirteen, he resented the pedantry of the curriculum so deeply that when he became a tutor at Yale (1771–1773) he encouraged his students in English studies, an unheard of innovation. During this period he wrote and published (1772–1773) an amusing satirical poem on the follies of education, *The Progress of Dulness.* The first part details the career of Tom Brainless at college; the second shows Dick Hairbrain, a farmer's son, transformed there from a boor into a fop; the third part turns to the education of females in coquetry and useless needlework.

In Boston, where Trumbull was admitted to the bar in 1773, he was, with some reluctance, swept into the current of revolutionary enthusiasm. Having moved back to New Haven in 1774, he published early in 1776 the first canto of *M'Fingal,* a Hudibrastic narrative of a Scotch Tory who refuses to be persuaded to hate Britain and is finally tarred and feathered by his fellow townsmen. The whole poem was not issued until 1782. Though it had little effect on the revolutionary cause, *M'Fingal* was immensely popular from 1782 until the 1820's.

Trumbull wrote little of account after *M'Fingal.* He collaborated with his Hartford friends in the Federalist *Anarchiad* and *Echo,* but most of the rest of his life was spent as a lawyer, judge, and acknowledged leader of the Connecticut Wits.

» » *From:* M'FINGAL [1] « «

CANTO SECOND

THE TOWN-MEETING. P.M.

The Sun, who never stops to dine,
Two hours had pass'd the mid-way line,
And driving at his usual rate,
Lash'd on his downward car of state.
And now expired the short vacation,
And dinner done in epic fashion,
While all the crew beneath the trees,
Eat pocket-pies, or bread and cheese,
(Nor shall we, like old Homer, care
To versify their bill of fare)   10
Each active party, feasted well,
Throng'd in, like sheep, at sound of bell;
With equal spirit took their places,
And meeting oped with three *Oh Yesses:*
When first, the daring Whigs t' oppose,
Again the great M'FINGAL rose,

Stretch'd magisterial arm amain,
And thus resumed the accusing strain.
    "Ye Whigs attend, and hear affrighted
The crimes whereof ye stand indicted;   20
The sins and follies past all compass,
That prove you guilty, or *non compos.*
I leave the verdict to your senses,
And jury of your consciences;
Which though they're neither good nor true,
Must yet convict you and your crew.
    "Ungrateful sons! a factious band,
That rise against your parent-land.
Ye viper race, that burst in strife
The genial womb that gave you life,   30
Tear with sharp fangs and forked tongue
The indulgent bowels whence ye sprung;
And scorn the debt and obligation,
You justly owe the British nation,
Which, since you cannot pay, your crew
Affect to swear was never due.
    "Did not the deeds of England's primate [2]
First drive your fathers to this climate.

[1] This narrative poem tells of the troubles of a Massachusetts Tory squire during the Revolution. Its four cantos are entitled: The Town-Meeting, A.M.; The Town-Meeting, P.M.; The Liberty Pole; The Vision.

[2] Archbishop Laud.

Whom jails and fines and every ill
Forced to their good against their will?   40
Ye owe to their obliging temper
The peopling your new-fangled empire,
While every British act and canon
Stood forth your *causa sine qua non.*
Who'd seen, except for these restraints,
Your witches, quakers, whigs and saints,
Or heard of Mather's famed *Magnalia,*
If Charles and Laud had chanced to fail you?
Did they not send your charters o'er
And give you lands you own'd before,   50
Permit you all to spill your blood,
And drive out heathens where you could;
On these mild terms, that, conquest won,
The realm you gain'd should be their own?
And when of late attack'd by those,
Whom her connection made your foes,
Did they not then, distress'd by war,
Send generals to your help from far,
Whose aid you own'd, in terms less haughty,
And thankfully o'erpaid your quota?   60
Say, at what period did they grudge
To send you Governor or Judge,
With all your Missionary crew,
To teach you law and gospel too?
They brought all felons in the nation
To help you on in population;
Proposed their Bishops to surrender,
And made their Priests a legal tender,
Who only ask'd, in surplice clad,
The simple tithe of all you had: 70
And now, to keep all knaves in awe,
Have sent their troops t' establish law,
And with gunpowder, fire and ball,
Reform your people, one and all.
Yet when their insolence and pride
Have anger'd all the world beside;
When fear and want at once invade,
Can you refuse to lend them aid,
And rather risk your heads in fight,
Than gratefully throw in your mite?   80
Can they for debts make satisfaction,
Should they dispose their realm at auction,
And sell off Britain's goods and land all
To France and Spain, by inch of candle?
Shall good King George, with want oppress'd,
Insert his name in bankrupt list,
And shut up shop, like failing merchant,
That fears the bailiffs should make search in't;
With poverty shall princes strive,
And nobles lack wheron to live?   90
Have they not rack'd their whole inventions
To feed their brats on posts and pensions;
Made their Scotch friends with taxes groan,

And pick'd poor Ireland to the bone:
Yet have on hand, as well deserving,
Ten thousand bastards, left for starving?
And can you now, with conscience clear,
Refuse them an asylum here,
And not maintain, in manner fitting,
These genuine sons of mother Britain?   100
"T' evade these crimes of blackest grain
You prate of liberty in vain,
And strive to hide your vile designs
In terms abstruse, like school-divines.
"Your boasted patriotism is scarce,
And country's love is but a farce:
For after all the proofs you bring,
We Tories know there's no such thing.
Hath not Dalrymple show'd in print,
And Johnson too, there's nothing in't;   110
Produced you demonstration ample,
From others' and their own example,
That self is still, in either faction,
The only principle of action;
The loadstone, whose attracting tether
Keeps the politic world together:
And spite of all your double dealing,
We all are sure 'tis so, from feeling.
"Who heeds your babbling of transmitting
Freedom to brats of your begetting,   120
Or will proceed, as tho' there were a tie,
And obligation to posterity?
We get them, bear them, breed and nurse,
What has posterity done for us,
That we, lest they their rights should lose,
Should trust our necks to gripe of noose?
"And who believes you will not run?
Ye're cowards, every mother's son;
And if you offer to deny,
We've witnesses to prove it by.   130
Attend th' opinion first, as referee,
Of your old general, stout Sir Jeffery; [3]
Who swore that with five thousand foot
He'd rout you all, and in pursuit
Run thro' the land, as easily
As camel thro' a needle's eye?
Did not the mighty Colonel Grant
Against your courage pour his rant,
Affirm your universal failure
In every principle of valour,   140
And swear no scamperers e'er could match you,
So swift, a bullet scarce could catch you?
And will you not confess, in this
A judge most competent he is;
Well skill'd on running to decide,
As what himself has often tried?
'Twould not methinks be labor lost,

[3] Sir Jeffrey Amherst.

If you'd sit down and count the cost,
And ere you call your Yankies out,
First think what work you've set about.　150
Have you not roused, his force to try on,
That grim old beast, the British Lion;
And know you not, that at a sup
He's large enough to eat you up?
Have you survey'd his jaws beneath,
Drawn inventories of his teeth,
Or have you weigh'd, in even balance,
His strength and magnitude of talons?
His roar would change your boasts to fear,
As easily, as sour small beer;　160
And make your feet from dreadful fray,
By native instinct run away.
Britain, depend on't, will take on her
T' assert her dignity and honor,
And ere she'd lose your share of pelf,
Destroy your country, and herself.
For has not North declared they fight
To gain substantial rev'nue by't,
Denied he'd ever deign to treat,
Till on your knees and at his feet?　170
And feel you not a trifling ague
From Van's *"Delanda est Carthago?"*
For this now Britain has projected,
Think you she has not means t' effect it?
Has she not set at work all engines
To spirit up the native Indians,
Send on your backs the tawney band,
With each an hatchet in his hand,
T' amuse themselves with scalping knives,
And butcher children and your wives;　180
And paid them for your scalps at sale
More than your heads would fetch by tale;
That she might boast again with vanity,
Her English national humanity?
For now in its primeval sense
This term, *humanity,* comprehends
All things of which, on this side hell,
The *human mind* is capable;
And thus 'tis well, by writers sage,
Applied to Britain and to Gage.　190
On this brave work to raise allies,
She sent her duplicate of Guys,
To drive at different parts at once on,
Her stout Guy Carlton and Guy Johnson;
To each of whom, to send again you,
Old Guy of Warwick were a ninny,
Though the dun cow he fell'd in war,
These killcows are his betters far.
　"And has she not essay'd her notes
To rouse your slaves to cut your throats;　200
Sent o'er ambassadors with guineas,
To bribe your blacks in Carolinas?

And has not Gage, her missionary,
Turn'd many an Afric to a Tory;
Made the New-England Bishop's see grow,
By many a new-converted negro?
As friends to government when he
Your slaves at Boston late set free,
Enlisted them in black parade,
Emboss'd with regimental red;　210
While flared the epaulette, like flambeau,
On Captain Cuff and Ensign Sambo:
And were they not acquainted then
Among his very bravest men?
And when such means she stoops to take,
Think you she is not wide awake?
As the good man of old in Job
Own'd wondrous allies through the globe,
Had brought the stones along the street
To ratify a cov'nant meet,　220
And every beast, from lice to lions,
To join in leagues of strict alliance:
Has she not cringed, in spite of pride,
For like assistance, far and wide,
Till all this formidable league rose
Of Indians, British troops and Negroes?
And can you break these triple bands
By all your workmanship of hands?"
　"Sir," quoth Honorius, "we presume
You guess from past feats what's to come,　230
And from the mighty deeds of Gage
Fortell how fierce the war he'll wage.
You doubtless recollected here
The annals of his first great year:
While, wearying out the Tories' patience,
He spent his breath in proclamations;
While all his mighty noise and vapour
Was used in wrangling upon paper,
And boasted military fits
Closed in the straining of his wits;　240
While troops, in Boston commons placed,
Laid nought, but quires of paper, waste;
While strokes alternate stunn'd the nation,
Protest, Address and Proclamation,
And speech met speech, fib clash'd with fib,
And Gage still answer'd, squib for squib.
　"Though this not all his time was lost on;
He fortified the town of Boston,
Built breastworks, that might lend assistance
To keep the patriots at a distance;　250
For howsoe'er the rogues might scoff,
He liked them best the farthest off;
Works of important use to aid
His courage, when he felt afraid,
And whence right off, in manful station,
He'd boldly pop his proclamation.
Our hearts must in our bosoms freeze,

At such heroic deeds as these."

"Vain," said the 'Squire, "you'll find to sneer
At Gage's first triumphant year;   260
For Providence, disposed to teaze us,
Can use what instruments it pleases.
To pay a tax, at Peter's wish,
His chief cashier was once a fish;
An ass, in Balaam's sad disaster,
Turn'd orator and saved his master;
A goose, placed sentry on his station,
Preserved old Rome from desolation;
An English bishop's cur of late
Disclosed rebellions 'gainst the state;   270
So frogs croak'd Pharaoh to repentance,
And lice delay'd the fatal sentence:
And heaven can ruin you at pleasure,
By Gage, as soon as by a Cæsar.
Yet did our hero in these days
Pick up some laurel wreaths of praise.
And as the statuary of Seville
Made his crackt saint an exc'llent devil;
So though our war small triumph brings,
We gain'd great fame in other things.   280
   "Did not our troops show great discerning,
And skill your various arts in learning?
Outwent they not each native noodle
By far, in playing Yankee-doodle,
Which as 'twas your New-England tune,
'Twas marvellous they took so soon?
And ere the year was fully through,
Did not they learn to foot it too,
And such a dance, as ne'er was known,
For twenty miles on end lead down?   290
Did they not lay their heads together,
And gain your art to tar and feather,
When Colonel Nesbit, thro' the town,
In triumph bore the country-clown?
Oh what a glorious work to sing
The veteran troops of Britain's king,
Adventuring for th' heroic laurel
With bag of feathers and tar-barrel!
To paint the cart where culprits ride,
And Nesbit marching at its side,   300
Great executioner and proud,
Like hangman high on Holborn road;
And o'er the slow-drawn rumbling car,
The waving ensign of the war!
And when a triumph Rome decreed
For great Caligula's valiant deed,
Who had subdued the British seas,
By gath'ring cockles from their base;
In pompous car the conq'ror bore
His captive scallops from the shore,   310
Ovations gain'd his crabs for fetching,
And mighty feats of oyster-catching:

'Gainst Yankies thus the war begun,
They tarr'd, and triumph'd over, one;
And fought and boasted through the season,
With force as great and equal reason.
   "Yet thus though skill'd in vict'ry's toils,
They boast, not unexpert, in wiles.
For gain'd they not an equal fame in
The arts of secrecy and scheming;   320
In stratagem show'd wondrous force,
And modernized the Trojan horse,
Play'd o'er again the tricks Ulyssean,
In their famed Salem expedition?
For as that horse, the poets tell ye,
Bore Grecian armies in its belly,
Till their full reckoning run, with joy
Shrewd Sinon midwived them in Troy:
So in one ship was Leslie bold
Cramm'd with three hundred men in hold,   330
Equipp'd for enterprize and sail,
Like Jonas stow'd in womb of whale.
To Marblehead in depth of night
The cautious vessel wing'd her flight.
And now the sabbath's silent day
Call'd all your Yankies off to pray;
Safe from each prying jealous neighbour,
The scheme and vessel fell in labor.
Forth from its hollow womb pour'd hast'ly
The Myrmidons of Colonel Leslie.   340
Not thicker o'er the blacken'd strand,
The frogs detachment, rush'd to land,
Furious by onset and surprize
To storm th' entrenchment of the mice.
Through Salem straight, without delay,
The bold battalion took its way,
March'd o'er a bridge, in open sight
Of several Yankies arm'd for fight;
Then without loss of time or men,
Veer'd round for Boston back again,   350
And found so well their projects thrive,
That every soul got home alive.
   "Thus Gage's arms did fortune bless
With triumph, safety and success.
But mercy is without dispute
His first and darling attribute;
So great, it far outwent and conquer'd
His military skill at Concord.
There, when the war he chose to wage,
Shone the benevolence of Gage;   360
Sent troops to that ill-omen'd place,
On errands mere of special grace;
And all the work, he chose them for,
Was to *prevent a civil war;*
For which kind purpose he projected
The only certain way t' effect it,
To seize your powder, shot and arms,

And all your means of doing harms;
As prudent folks take knives away,
Lest children cut themselves at play.   370
And yet, when this was all his scheme,
The war you still will charge on him;
And tho' he oft has swore and said it,
Stick close to facts, and give no credit.
Think you, he wish'd you'd brave and beard
     him?
Why, 'twas the very thing, that scared him.
He'd rather you should all have run,
Than staid to fire a single gun.
So, for the civil war you lament,
Faith, you yourselves must take the blame
     in't;   380
For had you then, as he intended,
Given up your arms, it must have ended:
Since that's no war, each mortal knows,
Where one side only gives the blows,
And t'other bears them; on reflection
The most we call it is correction.
Nor could the contest have gone higher,
If you had ne'er returned the fire:
But when you shot, and not before,
It then commenced a civil war.   390
Else Gage, to end this controversy,
Had but corrected you in mercy;
Whom mother Britain, old and wise,
Sent o'er, the colonies to chastise;
Command obedience on their peril
Of ministerial whip and ferule;
And since they ne'er must come of age,
Govern'd and tutor'd them by Gage.
Still more, that mercy was their errand,
The army's conduct makes apparent.   400
What though at Lexington you can say,
They kill'd a few, they did not fancy;
At Concord then with manful popping,
Discharged a round, the ball to open;
Yet when they saw your rebel rout
Determined still to brave it out,
Did they not show their love of peace,
Their wish that discord straight might cease;
Demonstrate, and by proofs uncommon,
Their orders were to injure no man?   410
For did not every regular run,
As soon as e'er you fired a gun;
Take the first shot you sent them, greeting,
As meant their signal for retreating;
And fearful, if they staid for sport,
You might by accident be hurt,
Convey themselves with speed away
Full twenty miles in half a day;
Race till their legs were grown so weary,
They scarce sufficed their weight to carry?   420

Whence Gage extols, from general hearsay,
The great activity of Lord Percy;
Whose brave example led them on,
And spirited the troops to run;
Who now may boast, at royal levees,
A Yankee-chace worth forty Chevys.
     "Yet you, as vile as they were kind,
Pursued, like tygers, still behind;
Fired on them at your will, and shut
The town, as though you'd starve them out;   430
And with parade preposterous hedged,
Affect to hold them there besieged:
Though Gage, whom proclamations call
Your Gov'rnor and Vice-Admiral,
Whose power gubernatorial still
Extends as far as Bunker's hill,
Whose admiralty reaches, clever,
Near half a mile up Mistic river,
Whose naval force yet keeps the seas,
Can run away whene'er he'd please.   440
Nay, stern with rage grim Putnam boiling
Plunder'd both Hogg and Noddle Island; [4]
Scared troops of Tories into town,
Burn'd all their hay and houses down,
And menaced Gage, unless he'd flee,
To drive him headlong to the sea;
As once, to faithless Jews a sign,
The De'el, turn'd hog-reeve, did the swine.
     "But now your triumphs all are o'er;
For see from Britain's angry shore,   450
With deadly hosts of valor join
Her Howe, her Clinton and Burgoyne!
As comets thro' th' affrighted skies
Pour baleful ruin as they rise;
As Ætna with infernal roar
In conflagration sweeps the shore;
Or as Abijah White, when sent
Our Marshfield friends to represent,
Himself while dread array involves,
Commissions, pistols, swords, resolves,   460
In awful pomp descending down
Bore terror on the factious town:
Not with less glory and affright,
Parade these generals forth to fight.
No more each Bristol colonel runs
From whizzing beetles, as air-guns;
Thinks horn-bugs bullets, or thro' fears
Muskitoes takes for musketeers;
Nor scapes, as if you'd gain'd supplies,
From Beelzebub's whole host of flies.   470
No bug these warlike hearts appalls;
They better know the sound of balls.
I hear the din of battle bray;
The trump of horror mark its way.

[4] Islands in Boston Harbor.

I see afar the sack of cities,
The gallows strung with Whig-committees;
Your moderators triced, like vermin,
And gate-posts graced with heads of chairmen;
Your Congress for wave-off'rings hanging,
And ladders throng'd with priests harangu-
    ing.   480
What pillories glad the Tories' eyes
With patriot ears for sacrifice!
What whipping-posts your chosen race
Admit successive in embrace,
While each bears off his sins, alack!
Like Bunyans' pilgrim, on his back!
Where then, when Tories scarce get clear,
Shall Whigs and Congresses appear?
What rocks and mountains will you call
To wrap you over with their fall,   490
And save your heads, in these sad weathers,
From fire and sword, and tar and feathers?
For lo! with British troops tar-bright,
Again our Nesbitt heaves in sight;
He comes, he comes, your lines to storm,
And rig your troups in uniform.
To meet such heroes will ye brag,
With fury arm'd, and feather-bag,
Who wield their missile pitch and tar
With engines new in British war?   500
    "Lo! where our mighty navy brings
Destruction on her canvass wings,
While through the deep the British thunder
Shall sound th' alarm, to rob and plunder!
As Phœbus first, so Homer speaks,
When he march'd out t' attack the Greeks,
'Gainst mules sent forth his arrows fatal,
And slew th' auxiliaries, their cattle:
So where our ships shall stretch the keel,
What vanquish'd oxen shall they steal!   510
What heroes, rising from the deep,
Invade your marshall'd hosts of sheep;
Disperse whole troops of horse, and pressing,
Make cows surrender at discretion;
Attack your hens, like Alexanders,
And regiments rout of geese and ganders;
Or where united arms combine,
Lead captive many a herd of swine!
Then rush in dreadful fury down
To fire on every seaport town;   520
Display their glory and their wits,
Fright helpless children into fits,
And stoutly, from the unequal fray,
Make many a woman run away.
    "And can ye doubt, whene'er we please,
Our chiefs shall boast such deeds as these?
Have we not chiefs transcending far
The old famed *thunderbolts of war;*

Beyond the brave knight-errant fighters,
Stiled swords of death, by novel-writers; 530
Nor in romancing ages e'er rose
So terrible a tier of heroes.
From Gage what sounds alarm the waves!
How loud a blunderbuss is Graves!
How Newport dreads the blustering sallies,
That thunder from our popgun, Wallace,
While noise in formidable strains,
Spouts from his thimble-full of brains!
I see you sink in awed surprise!
I see our Tory brethren rise!   540
And as the sec'tries Sandemanian,
Our friends, describe their hoped millennium;
Boast how the world in every region
At once shall own their true religion,
For heaven shall knock, with vengeance dread,
All unbelievers on the head;
And then their church, the meek in spirit,
The earth, as promised, shall inherit
From the dead wicked, as heirs male,
Or next remainder-men in tail: 550
Such ruin shall the Whigs oppress;
Such spoils our Tory friends shall bless;
While Confiscation at command
Shall stalk in terror through the land,
Shall give all whig-estates away,
And call our brethren into play.
    "And can you pause, or scruple more?
These things are near you, at the door.
Behold! for though to reasoning blind,
Signs of the times you still might mind,   560
And view impending fate, as plain
As you'd foretell a shower of rain.
    "Hath not heaven warn'd you what must
        ensue,
And providence declared against you?
Hung forth the dire portents of war
By fires and beacons in the air;
Alarm'd old women all around
With fearful noises under ground,
While earth, for many a hundred leagues,
Groan'd with her dismal load of Whigs?   570
Was there a meteor, far and wide,
But muster'd on the Tory side;
A star malign, that has not bent
Its aspects for the parliament,
Forboding your defeat and misery,
As once they fought against old Sisera?
Was there a cloud, that spread the skies,
But bore our armies of allies,
While dreadful hosts of flame stood forth
In baleful streamers from the north?   580
Which plainly show'd what part they join'd;
For North's the minister, ye mind;

Whence oft your quibblers in gazettes
On *Northern blasts* have strain'd their wits;
And think you not, the clouds know how
To make the pun, as well [as] you?
Did there arise an apparition,
But grinn'd forth ruin to sedition;
A death-watch, but has join'd our leagues,
And click'd destruction to the Whigs? 590
Heard ye not, when the wind was fair,
At night our prophets in the air,
Who, loud, like admiralty libel,
Read awful chapters from the Bible,
And war and plague and death denounced,
And told you how you'd soon be trounced?
I see, to join our conq'ring side,
Heaven, earth and hell at once allied;
See from your overthrow and end,
The Tory paradise ascend, 600
Like that new world, which claims its station,
Beyond the final conflagration.
I see the day, that lots your share
In utter darkness and despair;
The day of joy, when North, our lord,
His faithful fav'rites shall reward.
No Tory then shall set before him
Small wish of 'Squire and Justice Quorum;
But to his unmistaken eyes
See lordships, posts and pension rise. 610
    "Awake to gladness then, ye Tories!
Th' unbounded prospect lies before us.
The power display'd in Gage's banners,
Shall cut their fertile lands to manors;
And o'er our happy conquer'd ground,
Dispense estates and titles round.
Behold! the world shall stare at new setts,
Of home-made Earls in Massachusetts;
Admire, array'd in ducal tassels,
Your Ol'vers, Hutchinsons and Vassals; 620
See join'd in ministerial work
His Grace of Albany, and York.
What lordships from each carved estate,
On our New-York Assembly wait!
What titled Jauncys, Gales and Billops;
Lord Brush, Lord Wilkins and Lord Philips!
In wide-sleeved pomp of godly guise,
What solemn rows of Bishops rise!
Aloft a Cardinal's hat is spread
O'er punster Cooper's reverend head. 630
In Vardell, that poetic zealot,
I view a lawn-bedizen'd Prelate;
While mitres fall, as 'tis their duty,
On heads of Chandler and Auchmuty! [5]
Knights, Viscounts, Barons, shall ye meet,

[5] Tories in New York; Cooper was President of King's College
(Columbia).

As thick as pebbles in the street;
E'en I perhaps (heaven speed my claim!)
Shall fix a *Sir* before my name.
For titles all our foreheads ache,
For what blest changes can they make! 640
Place Reverence, Grace and Excellence,
Where neither claim'd the least pretence;
Transform by patent's magic words
Men, likest devils, into Lords;
Whence commoners, to Peers translated,
Are justly said to be *created*.
Now where commissioners you saw,
Shall boards of nobles deal you law;
Long-robed comptrollers judge your rights,
And tide-waiters start up in knights. 650
While Whigs subdued, in slavish awe,
Our wood shall hew, our water draw,
And bless the mildness, when past hope,
That saved their necks from noose of rope.
For since our leaders have decreed,
Their blacks, who join us, shall be freed,
To hang the conquer'd whigs, we all see,
Would prove but weak, and thriftless policy,
Except their Chiefs: the vulgar knaves
Will do more good, preserved for slaves." 660
    " 'Tis well," Honorius cried; "your scheme
Has painted out a pretty dream.
We can't confute your second-sight;
We shall be slaves and you a knight.
These things must come, but I divine,
They'll come not in your day, nor mine.
    "But, oh my friends, my brethren, hear;
And turn for once th' attentive ear.
Ye see how prompt to aid our woes
The tender mercies of our foes; 670
Ye see with what unvaried rancour
Still for our blood their minions hanker;
Nor aught can sate their mad ambition,
From us, but death, or worse, submission.
Shall these then riot in our spoil,
Reap the glad harvest of our toil,
Rise from their country's ruins proud,
And roll their chariot-wheels in blood?
See Gage, with inauspicious star,
Has oped the gates of civil war, 680
When streams of gore, from freemen slain,
Encrimson'd Concord's fatal plain;
Whose warning voice, with awful sound,
Still cries, like Abel's, from the ground;
And heaven, attentive to its call,
Shall doom the proud oppressor's fall.
    "Rise then, ere ruin swift surprize,
To victory, to vengeance, rise.
Hark, how the distant din alarms;
The echoing trumpet breathes, to arms. 690

From provinces remote afar,
The sons of glory rouse to war.
'Tis Freedom calls! the raptured sound
The Apalachian hills rebound.
The Georgian coasts her voice shall hear,
And start from lethargies of fear.
From the parch'd zone, with glowing ray
Where pours the sun intenser day,
To shores where icy waters roll,
And tremble to the glimm'ring pole,   700
Inspired by freedom's heavenly charms,
United nations wake to arms.
The star of conquest lights their way,
And guides their vengeance on their prey.
Yes, though tyrannic force oppose,
Still shall they triumph o'er their foes;
Till heaven the happy land shall bless
With safety, liberty and peace.
    "And ye, whose souls of dastard mould
Start at the bravery of the bold;   710
To love your country who pretend,
Yet want all spirit to defend;
Who feel your fancies so prolific,
Engend'ring visions, whims terrific,
O'errun with horrors of coercion,
Fire, blood and thunder in reversion,
King's standards, pill'ries, confiscations,
And Gage's scare-crow proclamations;
Who scarce could rouse, if caught in fray,
Presence of mind to run away;   720
See nought but halters rise to view,
In all your dreams, and deem them true;
And while these phantoms haunt your brains,
Bow down your willing necks to chains.
Heavens! are ye sons of sires so great,
Immortal in the fields of fate,
Who braved all deaths, by land or sea,
Who bled, who conquer'd, to be free?
Hence coward souls, the worst disgrace
Of our forefathers' valiant race;   730
Hie homeward from the glorious field,
There turn the wheel, the distaff wield;
Act what ye are, nor dare to stain
The warrior's arms with touch profane;
There beg your more heroic wives
To guard your own, your children's, lives;
Beneath their aprons seek a screen,
Nor dare to mingle more with men."
    As thus he spake, the Tories' anger
Could now restrain itself no longer;   740
Who tried before by many a freak, or
Insulting noise, to stop the speaker;
Swung th' un-oil'd hinge of each pew-door,
Their feet kept shuffling on the floor;
Made their disapprobation known

By many a murmur, hum and groan,
That to his speech supplied the place
Of counterpart in thorough bass.
Thus bagpipes, while the tune they breathe,
Still drone and grumble underneath;   750
And thus the famed Demosthenes
Harangued the rumbling of the seas,
Held forth with elocution grave,
To audience loud of wind and wave;
And had a stiller congregation,
Than Tories are, to hear th' oration.
The uproar now grew high and louder,
As nearer thund'rings of a cloud are,
And every soul with heart and voice
Supplied his quota of the noise.   760
Each listening ear was set on torture,
Each Tory bellowing, "Order, Order";
And some, with tongue not low or weak,
Were clam'ring fast, for leave to speak;
The Moderator, with great vi'lence,
The cushion thump'd with, "Silence, Silence!"
The Constable to every prater
Bawl'd out, "Pray hear the moderator";
Some call'd the vote, and some in turn
Were screaming high, "Adjourn, Adjourn."   770
Not Chaos heard such jars and clashes,
When all the el'ments fought for places.
The storm each moment fiercer grew;
His sword the great M'FINGAL drew,
Prepared in either chance to share,
To keep the peace, or aid the war.
Nor lack'd they each poetic being,
Whom bards alone are skill'd in seeing;
Plumed Victory stood perch'd on high,
Upon the pulpit-canopy,   780
To join, as is her custom tried,
Like Indians, on the strongest side;
The Destinies, with shears and distaff,
Drew near their threads of life to twist off;
The Furies 'gan to feast on blows,
And broken head, and bloody nose:
When on a sudden from without
Arose a loud terrific shout;
And straight the people all at once heard
Of tongues an universal concert;   790
Like Æsop's times, as fable runs,
When every creature talk'd at once,
Or like the variegated gabble,
That crazed the carpenters of Babel.
Each party soon forsook the quarrel,
And let the other go on parol,
Eager to know what fearful matter
Had conjured up such general clatter;
And left the church in thin array,
As though it had been lecture-day.   800

Our 'Squire M'FINGAL straitway beckon'd
The Constable to stand his second;
And sallied forth with aspect fierce
The crowd assembled to disperse.
  The Moderator, out of view,
Beneath the desk had lain perdue;

Peep'd up his head to view the fray,
Beheld the wranglers run away,
And left alone, with solemn face
Adjourn'd them without time or place.   810
              1775 (two cantos)
              1782 (complete poem)

JOEL BARLOW

1754–1812

JOEL BARLOW was the apostate among the Connecticut Wits. Until 1788 the pattern of his life coincides with that of his friends in the Hartford group—a successful career at Yale, a chaplaincy in the army, an attempt to support himself by the law, work on a long poem which would show the stuff that was in him. The first sketch of his "regular Epic Poem, on the discovery of America," Barlow had made while he was still at Yale; finally, in 1787 *The Vision of Columbus*, dedicated to Louis XVI and subscribed for by all the great in America, burst upon his grateful countrymen. Unfortunately he was not content to let its nine books and five thousand lines stand as first printed. In 1807 it appeared as *The Columbiad*, new-dressed and enlarged to fit the magnitude of America's position among the nations of the world.

Meanwhile Barlow had traveled far from the religious and political conservatism of Hartford and New Haven. After the failure of the Scioto Land Company which he represented in Europe, he settled in England, where he became the friend of Tom Paine, Horne Tooke, and other radicals. His new revolutionary sympathy was displayed in an inflammatory poem, *The Conspiracy of Kings* (1792), and an admirable prose tract, *Advice to the Privileged Orders* (1792), designed "to induce statesmen" to adopt principles of the American and French revolutions.

The tract ranks with Paine's *Rights of Man* (both were written in reply to Burke's *Reflections on the French Revolution*) as an eloquent statement of the novel concept of the state as the guardian of the rights of all the people rather than the conserver of property, the prevailing Whig doctrine. Barlow further advanced the extremely modern idea that the state is bound to furnish the man who is born of poor parents with the means of subsistence.

She ought not only to instruct him in the artificial laws by which property is secured, but in the artificial industry by which it is obtained. She is bound, in *justice* as well as policy, to give him some art or trade. For the reason of his incapacity is, that *she* has usurped his birth-right; and this is restoring it to him in another form, more convenient for both parties. The failure of society in this branch of her duty, is the occasion of much the greater part of the evils that call for criminal jurisprudence.

Barlow was honored with French citizenship and made a fortune in the French funds. After serving as American consul at Algiers, he returned in 1805 to the United States and established himself in a great house on the Potomac. Six years later he died of exposure near Cracow in Poland while on a mission to Napoleon, as American minister to France.

» » THE HASTY PUDDING [6] « «

CANTO I

Ye Alps audacious, through the heavens that
  rise,
To cramp the day and hide me from the skies;
Ye Gallic flags, that o'er their heights unfurled,
Bear death to kings and freedom to the world,
I sing not you. A softer theme I choose,
A virgin theme, unconscious of the muse,
But fruitful, rich, well suited to inspire
The purest frenzy of poetic fire.
  Despise it not, ye bards to terror steeled,   9
Who hurl your thunders round the epic field;
Nor ye who strain your midnight throats to sing
Joys that the vineyard and the stillhouse bring;
Or on some distant fair your notes employ,
And speak of raptures that you ne'er enjoy.
I sing the sweets I know, the charms I feel,
My morning incense, and my evening meal,—
The sweets of Hasty Pudding. Come, dear
  bowl,
Glide o'er my palate, and inspire my soul.
The milk beside thee, smoking from the kine,
Its substance mingled, married in with thine,
Shall cool and temper thy superior heat,   21
And save the pains of blowing while I eat.
  Oh! could the smooth, the emblematic song
Flow like the genial juices o'er my tongue,
Could those mild morsels in my numbers chime,
And, as they roll in substance, roll in rime,
No more thy awkward, unpoetic name
Should shun the muse or prejudice thy fame;
But, rising grateful to the accustomed ear,
All bards should catch it, and all realms revere!
  Assist me first with pious toil to trace   31
Through wrecks of time, thy lineage and thy
  race;
Declare what lovely squaw, in days of yore,
(Ere great Columbus sought thy native shore)
First gave thee to the world; her works of fame
Have lived indeed, but lived without a name.
Some tawny Ceres, goddess of her days,
First learned with stones to crack the well-dried
  maize,
Through the rough sieve to shake the golden
  shower,
In boiling water stir the yellow flour: 40
The yellow flour, bestrewed and stirred with
  haste,

Swells in the flood and thickens to a paste,
Then puffs and wallops, rises to the brim,
Drinks the dry knobs that on the surface swim;
The knobs at last the busy ladle breaks,
And the whole mass its true consistence takes.
  Could but her sacred name, unknown so
  long,
Rise, like her labors, to the son of song,
To her, to them I'd consecrate my lays,
And blow her pudding with the breath of
  praise.   50
If 'twas Oella whom I sang before,
I here ascribe her one great virtue more.
Not through the rich Peruvian realms alone
The fame of Sol's sweet daughter should be
  known,
But o'er the world's wide climes should live se-
  cure,
Far as his rays extend, as long as they endure.
  Dear Hasty Pudding, what unpromised joy
Expands my heart, to meet thee in Savoy!
Doomed o'er the world through devious paths
  to roam,
Each clime my country, and each house my
  home,   60
My soul is soothed, my cares have found an
  end;
I greet my long-lost, unforgotten friend.
  For thee through Paris, that corrupted town,
How long in vain I wandered up and down,
Where shameless Bacchus, with his drenching
  hoard,
Cold from his cave usurps the morning board.
London is lost in smoke and steeped in tea;
No Yankee there can lisp the name of thee;
The uncouth word, a libel on the town,
Would call a proclamation from the crown.   70
For climes oblique, that fear the sun's full rays,
Chilled in their fogs, exclude the generous
  maize;
A grain whose rich, luxuriant growth requires
Short, gentle showers, and bright, ethereal fires.
  But here, though distant from our native
  shore,
With mutual glee, we meet and laugh once
  more.
The same! I know thee by that yellow face,
That strong complexion of true Indian race,
Which time can never change, nor soil impair,
Nor Alpine snows, nor Turkey's morbid air;   80
For endless years, through every mild domain,

[6] Said to have been written during a fit of homesickness, when
Barlow was living in Savoy.

Where grows the maize, there thou art sure to
    reign.
    But man, more fickle, the bold licence claims,
In different realms to give thee different names.
Thee the soft nations round the warm Levant
Polanta call; the French, of course, *Polante.*
E'en in thy native regions, how I blush
To hear the Pennsylvanians call thee *Mush!*
On Hudson's banks, while men of Belgic spawn
Insult and eat thee by the name *Suppawn.*   90
All spurious appellations, void of truth;
I've better known thee from my earliest youth:
Thy name is *Hasty Pudding!* thus my sire
Was wont to greet thee fuming from his fire;
And while he argued in thy just defense
With logic clear he thus explained the sense:
"In haste the boiling caldron, o'er the blaze,
Receives and cooks the ready powdered maize;
In haste 'tis served, and then in equal haste,
With cooling milk, we make the sweet repast.
No carving to be done, no knife to grate   101
The tender ear and wound the stony plate;
But the smooth spoon, just fitted to the lip,
And taught with art the yielding mass to dip,
By frequent journeys to the bowl well stored,
Performs the hasty honors of the board."
Such is thy name, significant and clear,
A name, a sound to every Yankee dear,
But most to me, whose heart and palate chaste
Preserve my pure, hereditary taste.   110
    There are who strive to stamp with disrepute
The luscious food, because it feeds the brute;
In tropes of high-strained wit, while gaudy
    prigs
Compare thy nursling, man, to pampered pigs;
With sovereign scorn I treat the vulgar jest,
Nor fear to share thy bounties with the beast.
What though the generous cow gives me to
    quaff
The milk nutritious: am I then a calf?
Or can the genius of the noisy swine,
Though nursed on pudding, thence lay claim to
    mine?   120
Sure the sweet song I fashion to thy praise,
Runs more melodious than the notes they raise.
    My song, resounding in its grateful glee,
No merit claims: I praise myself in thee.
My father loved thee through his length of
    days!
For thee his fields were shaded o'er with maize;
From thee what health, what vigor he pos-
    sessed,
Ten sturdy freemen from his loins attest;
Thy constellation ruled my natal morn,
And all my bones were made of Indian corn.

Delicious grain, whatever form it take,   131
To roast or boil, to smother or to bake,
In every dish 'tis welcome still to me,
But most, my Hasty Pudding, most in thee.
    Let the green succotash with thee contend;
Let beans and corn their sweetest juices blend;
Let butter drench them in its yellow tide,
And a long slice of bacon grace their side;
Not all the plate, how famed soe'er it be,
Can please my palate like a bowl of thee.   140
Some talk of hoe-cake, fair Virginia's pride!
Rich johnny-cake this mouth has often tried;
Both please me well, their virtues much the
    same,
Alike their fabric, as allied their fame,
Except in dear New England, where the last
Receives a dash of pumpkin in the paste,
To give it sweetness and improve the taste.
But place them all before me, smoking hot,
The big, round dumpling, rolling from the pot;
The pudding of the bag, whose quivering
    breast,   150
With suet lined, leads on the Yankee feast;
The charlotte brown, within whose crusty sides
A belly soft the pulpy apple hides;
The yellow bread whose face like amber glows,
And all of Indian that the bakepan knows,—
You tempt me not; my favorite greets my eyes,
To that loved bowl my spoon by instinct flies

CANTO II

To mix the food by vicious rules of art,
To kill the stomach and to sink the heart,
To make mankind to social virtue sour,
Cram o'er each dish, and be what they devour;
For this the kitchen muse first framed her book,
Commanding sweats to stream from every
    cook;
Children no more their antic gambols tried,
And friends to physic wondered why they died.
    Not so the Yankee: his abundant feast,
With simples furnished and with plainness
    dressed,   10
A numerous offspring gathers round the board,
And cheers alike the servant and the lord;
Whose well-bought hunger prompts the joyous
    taste,
And health attends them from the short repast.
    While the full pail rewards the milkmaid's
    toil,
The mother sees the morning caldron boil;
To stir the pudding next demands their care;
To spread the table and the bowls prepare;
To feed the household as their portions cool
And send them all to labor or to school.   20

Yet may the simplest dish some rules impart,
For nature scorns not all the aids of art.
E'en Hasty Pudding, purest of all food,
May still be bad, indifferent, or good,
As sage experience the short process guides,
Or want of skill, or want of care presides.
Whoe'er would form it on the surest plan,
To rear the child and long sustain the man;
To shield the morals while it mends the size,
And all the powers of every food supplies,— 30
Attend the lesson that the muse shall bring,
Suspend your spoons, and listen while I sing.
　　But since, O man! thy life and health demand
Not food alone, but labor from thy hand,
First, in the field, beneath the sun's strong rays,
Ask of thy mother earth the needful maize;
She loves the race that courts her yielding soil,
And gives her bounties to the sons of toil.
　　When now the ox, obedient to thy call,
Repays the loan that filled the winter stall,　40
Pursue his traces o'er the furrowed plain,
And plant in measured hills the golden grain;
But when the tender germ begins to shoot,
And the green spire declares the sprouting root,
Then guard your nursling from each greedy foe,
The insidious worm, the all-devouring crow.
A little ashes sprinkled round the spire,
Soon steeped in rain, will bid the worm retire;
The feathered robber with his hungry maw
Swift flies the field before your man of straw,
A frightful image, such as schoolboys bring　51
When met to burn the Pope or hang the King.
　　Thrice in the season, through each verdant row,
Wield the strong plowshare and the faithful hoe;
The faithful hoe, a double task that takes,
To till the summer corn and roast the winter cakes.
　　Slow springs the blade, while checked by chilling rains,
Ere yet the sun the seat of Cancer gains;
But when his fiercest fires emblaze the land,
Then start the juices, then the roots expand;
Then, like a column of Corinthian mold,　61
The stalk struts upward and the leaves unfold;
The bushy branches all the ridges fill,
Entwine their arms, and kiss from hill to hill.
Here cease to vex them; all your cares are done:
Leave the last labors to the parent sun;
Beneath his genial smiles, the well-dressed field,
When autumn calls, a plenteous crop shall yield.

Now the strong foliage bears the standards high,
And shoots the tall top-gallants to the sky;　7（
The suckling ears their silky fringes bend,
And pregnant grown, their swelling coats distend;
The loaded stalk, while still the burden grows,
O'erhangs the space that runs between the rows;
High as a hop-field waves the silent grove,
A safe retreat for little thefts of love,
When the pledged roasting-ears invite the maid
To meet her swain beneath the new-formed shade;
His generous hand unloads the cumberous hill,
And the green spoils her ready basket fill;　8o
Small compensation for the twofold bliss,
The promised wedding, and the present kiss.
　　Slight depredations these; but now the moon
Calls from his hollow tree the sly raccoon;
And while by night he bears his prize away,
The bolder squirrel labors through the day.
Both thieves alike, but provident of time,
A virtue rare, that almost hides their crime.
Then let them steal the little stores they can,
And fill their granaries from the toils of man;
We've one advantage where they take no part—　91
With all their wiles, they ne'er have found the art
To boil the Hasty Pudding; here we shine
Superior far to tenants of the pine;
This envied boon to man shall still belong,
Unshared by them in substance or in song.
　　At last the closing season browns the plain,
And ripe October gathers in the grain;
Deep-loaded carts the spacious corn-house fill,
The sack distended marches to the mill;　1oo
The laboring mill beneath the burden groans,
And showers the future pudding from the stones;
Till the glad housewife greets the powdered gold,
And the new crop exterminates the old.
Ah who can sing what every wight must feel,
The joy that enters with the bag of meal,
A general jubilee pervades the house,
Wakes every child and gladdens every mouse.

CANTO III

The days grow short; but though the falling sun
To the glad swain proclaims his day's work done,

Night's pleasing shades his various tasks pro-
    long,
And yield new subjects to my various song.
For now, the corn-house filled, the harvest
    home,
The invited neighbors to the husking come;
A frolic scene, where work, and mirth, and play,
Unite their charms to chase the hours away.
    Where the huge heap lies centered in the
        hall,
The lamp suspended from the cheerful wall,
Brown, corn-fed nymphs, and strong, hard-
    handed beaux,   11
Alternate ranged, extend in circling rows,
Assume their seats, the solid mass attack;
The dry husks rustle, and the corncobs crack;
The song, the laugh, alternate notes resound,
And the sweet cider trips in silence round.
    The laws of husking every wight can tell;
And sure no laws he ever keeps so well:
For each red ear a general kiss he gains,
With each smut ear she smuts the luckless
    swains;   20
But when to some sweet maid a prize is cast,
Red as her lips and taper as her waist,
She walks the round and culls one favored
    beau,
Who leaps the luscious tribute to bestow.
Various the sport, as are the wits and brains
Of well-pleased lasses and contending swains;
Till the vast mound of corn is swept away,
And he that gets the last ear wins the day.
    Meanwhile, the housewife urges all her care,
The well-earned feast to hasten and prepare.
The sifted meal already waits her hand,   31
The milk is strained, the bowls in order stand,
The fire flames high; and as a pool—that takes
The headlong stream that o'er the milldam
    breaks—
Foams, roars, and rages with incessant toils,
So the vexed caldron rages, roars, and boils.
    First with clean salt she seasons well the
        food,
Then strews the flour, and thickens all the flood.
Long o'er the simmering fire she lets it stand;
To stir it well demands a stronger hand;   40
The husband takes his turn: and round and
    round
The ladle flies; at last the toil is crowned;
When to the board the thronging huskers pour,
And take their seats as at the corn before.
    I leave them to their feast. There still belong
More useful matters to my faithful song.
For rules there are, though ne'er unfolded
    yet,

Nice rules and wise, how pudding should be
    eat.   48
    Some with molasses line the luscious treat,
And mix, like bards, the useful with the sweet.
A wholesome dish, and well deserving praise,
A great resource in those bleak wintry days,
When the chilled earth lies buried deep in
    snow,
And raging Boreas dries the shivering cow.
    Blest cow! thy praise shall still my notes em-
        ploy,
Great source of health, the only source of joy;
Mother of Egypt's god,—but sure, for me,
Were I to leave my God, I'd worship thee.
How oft thy teats these pious hands have
    prest!
How oft thy bounties proved my only feast!   60
How oft I've fed thee with my favorite grain!
And roared, like thee, to see thy children slain!
    Ye swains who know her various worth to
        prize,
Ah! house her well from winter's angry skies.
Potatoes, pumpkins, should her sadness cheer,
Corn from your crib, and mashes from your
    beer;
When spring returns, she'll well acquit the loan,
And nurse at once your infants and her own.
Milk then with pudding I should always choose;
To this in future I confine my muse,   70
Till she in haste some further hints unfold,
Well for the young, nor useless to the old.
First in your bowl the milk abundant take,
Then drop with care along the silver lake
Your flakes of pudding; these at first will hide
Their little bulk beneath the swelling tide;
But when their growing mass no more can sink,
When the soft island looms above the brink,
Then check your hand; you've got the portion
    due;
So taught our sires, and what they taught is
    true.   80
    There is a choice in spoons. Though small
        appear
The nice distinction, yet to me 'tis clear.
The deep-bowled Gallic spoon, contrived to
    scoop
In ample draughts the thin, diluted soup,
Performs not well in those substantial things,
Whose mass adhesive to the metal clings;
Where the strong labial muscles must embrace
The gentle curve, and sweep the hollow space
With ease to enter and discharge the freight,
A bowl less concave, but still more dilate,   90
Becomes the pudding best. The shape, the size,
A secret rests, unknown to vulgar eyes.

Experienced feeders can alone impart
A rule so much above the lore of art.
These tuneful lips that thousand spoons have
    tried,
With just precision could the point decide,
Though not in song; the muse but poorly
    shines
In cones, and cubes, and geometric lines;
Yet the true form, as near as she can tell,
Is that small section of a goose-egg shell,   100
Which in two equal portions shall divide
The distance from the center to the side.

Fear not to slaver; 'tis no deadly sin.
Like the free Frenchman, from your joyous
    chin
Suspend the ready napkin; or, like me,
Poise with one hand your bowl upon your
    knee;
Just in the zenith your wise head project,
Your full spoon, rising in a line direct,
Bold as a bucket, heeds no drops that fall;
The wide-mouthed bowl will surely catch them
    all!   110
1792–1793   1796

PHILIP FRENEAU

1752–1832

PHILIP FRENEAU, now chiefly remembered as the poet whose ballads put heart into the American soldiers during the Revolution, was also the first writer of stature in the new republic. His father, of Huguenot descent, was a well-to-do New York shipping merchant. Freneau spent his vacations from school at the family estate, "Mount Pleasant," near the present village of Freneau, New Jersey. In later years, whenever he was disappointed in his alternate vocations of sea-captain and editor, he returned to "Mount Pleasant" to farm and write poetry.

At Princeton, from which he was graduated in 1771, he moved in the circle of young Whigs which included H. H. Brackenridge, "Light Horse Harry" Lee, William Bradford, who would later be United States Attorney General, and James Madison, the future President. After teaching school under Brackenridge for a brief period, Freneau spent most of the time from 1775 to 1778 at Santa Cruz in the Lesser Antilles. In 1779 he contributed to the *United States Magazine* conducted by Brackenridge. On the way to the West Indies in 1780 his ship was captured by the British, and Freneau was imprisoned on the *Scorpion* in New York harbor. His war poems henceforth ring with the emotion of a participant. During the next decade he assisted in publishing two papers, the *Freeman's Journal* of Philadelphia (1781–1783) and the *New York Daily Advertiser* (1790).

Encouraged by Madison and others to undertake a paper in Philadelphia in support of anti-Federalist principles, Freneau established the *National Gazette*. From 1791 to 1793 it blasted away twice a week at Fenno's *Gazette of the United States*, the organ of the Hamiltonians. As the leading democratic paper, Freneau's *National Gazette* spread the doctrines of French radicalism into the remote corners of the land. At the height of the furore over Citizen Genêt, Freneau went farther than any of the democrats in support of the illegal activities of that ambassadorial trouble-maker. In spite of this embarrassment Jefferson, who had given Freneau a post as translator in the State Department, refused to discharge him, even at the behest of Washington who, in a rage, referred to the editor as "that rascal Freneau." "I will not do it," Jefferson declared; "his paper has saved our constitution which was galloping fast into monarchy."

Twice in later years Freneau edited his own paper: the *Jersey Chronicle* in 1795–1796 and the New York *Time Piece and Literary Companion* in 1797–1798. His contributions to the Philadelphia *Aurora*, under the pseudonym of Robert Slender, attracted readers to that staunch Jeffersonian paper from 1799 to 1814. From 1809 till his death in 1832, Freneau lived at his farm in New Jersey. He died, at eighty-one, of exposure, having lost his way in a bog while walking home at night from the village.

Freneau's fame has too long been colored by the hatred of his Federalist opponents who would have liked to dismiss him, as did President Dwight of Yale, as "mere incendiary or rather as a despicable tool of bigger incendiaries." He should be remembered as the first popularizer of the political beliefs to which the followers of Jefferson, Jackson, and Wilson have adhered in successive generations. He often signed himself, in derision, O.S.M. (One of the Swinish Multitude), but his friends, the democratic leaders, were men of cultivation like himself—Jefferson, Lee, Madison, Judge Tucker of Williamsburg, George Clinton, Governor of New York, and DeWitt Clinton, his nephew, the builder of the Erie Canal.

In spite of the sharpness of his pen, Freneau was a genial, pacific man, a lover of the classic poets and of the sea and the rural scenes which abound in his poems. Some have lamented that so gifted a poet should have "wasted" his talents in propaganda. Such a sentimental view of his activities fails to take into account the depth of his humanitarian sympathies. His devotion to the democratic cause inspired, actually, much of his best work in prose and verse.

Five collections of Freneau's writings were published during his life. One of these contained prose as well as poetry.

The Poems of Philip Freneau, Poet of the Revolution, F. L. Pattee, ed., 3 vols., Princeton, 1902–1907.
The Last Poems of Philip Freneau, Lewis Leary, ed., New Brunswick, 1946.
The Prose of Philip Freneau, P. M. Marsh, ed., New Brunswick, 1955.
N. F. Adkins, *Philip Freneau and the Cosmic Enigma,* New York, 1949.
Lewis Leary, *That Rascal Freneau: A Study in Literary Failure,* New Brunswick, 1941.

» » *From:* THE HOUSE OF NIGHT[1] « «

A VISION

1

Trembling I write my dream, and recollect
A fearful vision at the midnight hour;
So late, Death o'er me spread his sable wings,
Painted with fancies of malignant power!

. . .

6

By some sad means, when Reason holds no
    sway,
Lonely I rov'd at midnight o'er a plain
Where murmuring streams and mingling rivers
    flow
Far to their springs, or seek the sea again.

7

Sweet vernal May! tho' then thy woods in
    bloom   9

[1] In its first form, as published in 1779, the poem consisted of seventy-three stanzas.

Flourish'd, yet nought of this could Fancy see,
No wild pinks bless'd the meads, no green the
    fields,
And naked seem'd to stand each lifeless tree:

8

Dark was the sky, and not one friendly star
Shone from the zenith or horizon, clear,
Mist sate upon the woods, and darkness rode
In her black chariot, with a wild career.

9

And from the woods the late resounding note
Issued of the loquacious Whip-poor-will,
Hoarse, howling dogs, and nightly roving
    wolves
Clamour'd from far off cliffs invisible.   20

10

Rude, from the wide extended Chesapeke
I heard the winds the dashing waves assail,
And saw from far, by picturing fancy form'd,
The black ship travelling through the noisy
    gale.

11

At last, by chance and guardian fancy led,
I reach'd a noble dome, rais'd fair and high,
And saw the light from upper windows flame,
Presage of mirth and hospitality.

12

And by that light around the dome appear'd
A mournful garden of autumnal hue,   30
Its lately pleasing flowers all drooping stood
Amidst high weeds that in rank plenty grew.

13

The Primrose there, the violet darkly blue,
Daisies and fair Narcissus ceas'd to rise,
Gay spotted pinks their charming bloom with-
drew.
And Polyanthus quench'd its thousand dyes.

14

No pleasant fruit or blossom gaily smil'd,
Nought but unhappy plants or trees were seen,
The yew, the myrtle, and the church-yard elm,
The cypress, with its melancholy green.   40

15

There cedars dark, the osier, and the pine,
Shorn tamarisks, and weeping willows grew,
The poplar tall, the lotos, and the lime,
And pyracantha did her leaves renew.

16

The poppy there, companion to repose,
Display'd her blossoms that began to fall,
And here the purple amaranthus rose
With mint strong-scented, for the funeral.

17

And here and there with laurel shrubs between
A tombstone lay, inscrib'd with strains of
woe,   50
And stanzas sad, throughout the dismal green,
Lamented for the dead that slept below.

18

Peace to this awful dome!—when strait I heard
The voice of men in a secluded room,
Much did they talk of death, and much of life,
Of coffins, shrouds, and horrors of a tomb.

. . .

23

Then up three winding stairs my feet were
brought

To a high chamber, hung with mourning sad,
The unsnuff'd candles glar'd with visage dim,
'Midst grief, in ecstasy of woe run mad.   60

24

A wide leaf'd table stood on either side,
Well fraught with phials, half their liquids
spent,
And from a couch, behind the curtain's veil,
I heard a hollow voice of loud lament.

25

Turning to view the object whence it came,
My frighted eyes a horrid form survey'd;
Fancy, I own thy power—Death on the couch,
With fleshless limbs, at rueful length, was laid.

26

And o'er his head flew jealousies and cares,
Ghosts, imps, and half the black Tartarian
crew,   70
Arch-angels damn'd, nor was their Prince re-
mote,
Borne on the vaporous wings of Stygian dew.

27

Around his bed, by the dull flambeaux' glare,
I saw pale phantoms—Rage to madness vext,
Wan, wasting grief, and ever musing care,
Distressful pain, and poverty perplext.

28

Sad was his countenance, if we can call
That countenance, where only bones were seen
And eyes sunk in their sockets, dark and low,
And teeth, that only show'd themselves to
grin.   80

29

Reft was his scull of hair, and no fresh bloom
Of chearful mirth sate on his visage hoar:
Sometimes he rais'd his head, while deep-
drawn groans
Were mixt with words that did his fate deplore.

30

Oft did he wish to see the daylight spring,
And often toward the window lean'd to hear,
Fore-runner of the scarlet-mantled morn,
The early note of wakeful Chanticleer.

31

Thus he—But at my hand a portly youth
Of comely countenance, began to tell,   90
"That this was Death upon his dying bed,
"Sullen, morose, and peevish to be well;

32

"Fixt is his doom—the miscreant reigns no
more
"The tyrant of the dying or the dead;
"This night concludes his all-consuming reign,
"Pour out, ye heav'ns, your vengeance on his
head.

33

"But since, my friend (said he), chance leads
you here,
"With me this night upon the sick attend.
"You on this bed of death must watch, and I
"Will not be distant from the fretful fiend." 100

. . .

46

So said, at Death's left side I sate me down,
The mourning youth toward his right reclin'd;
Death in the middle lay, with all his groans,
And much he toss'd and tumbled, sigh'd and
pin'd.

47

But now this man of hell toward me turn'd,
And strait, in hideous tone, began to speak;
Long held he sage discourse, but I forbore
To answer him, much less his news to seek.

48

He talk'd of tomb-stones and of monuments,
Of equinoctial climes and India shores, 110
He talk'd of stars that shed their influence,
Fevers and plagues, and all their noxious stores.

49

He mention'd, too, the guileful *calenture*,
Tempting the sailor on the deep sea main,
That paints gay groves upon the ocean floor,
Beckoning her victim to the faithless scene.

50

Much spoke he of the myrtle and the yew,
Of ghosts that nightly walk the church-yard
o'er, 118
Of storms that through the wint'ry ocean blow
And dash the well-mann'd galley to the shore.

51

O broad-mouth'd cannons, and the thunderbolt,
O sieges and convulsions, dearth and fire,
Of poisonous weeds—but seem'd to sneer at
these
Who by the laurel o'er him did aspire.

. . .

103

Scarce had he spoke, when on the lofty dome
Rush'd from the clouds a hoarse resounding
blast—
Round the four eaves so loud and sad it play'd
As though all music were to breathe its last.

104

Warm was the gale, and such as travelers say
Sport with the winds on Zaara's barren waste;
Black was the sky, a mourning carpet spread,
Its azure blotted, and its stars o'ercast! 132

105

Lights in the air like burning stars were hurl'd,
Dogs howl'd, heaven mutter'd, and the tempest
blew,
The red half-moon peeped from behind a cloud
As if in dread the amazing scene to view.

106

The mournful trees that in the garden stood
Bent to the tempest as it rush'd along,
The elm, the myrtle, and the cypress sad
More melancholy tun'd its bellowing song. 140

107

No more that elm its noble branches spread,
The yew, the cypress, or the myrtle tree,
Rent from the roots the tempest tore them
down,
And all the grove in wild confusion lay.

108

Yet, mindful of his dread command, I part
Glad from the magic dome—nor found relief;
Damps from the dead hung heavier round my
heart,
While sad remembrance rous'd her stores of
grief.

109

O'er a dark field I held my dubious way 149
Where Jack-a-lanthorn walk'd his lonely round,
Beneath my feet substantial darkness lay,
And screams were heard from the distemper'd
ground.

110

Nor look'd I back, till to a far off wood,
Trembling with fear, my weary feet had sped—
Dark was the night, but at the inchanted dome
I saw the infernal windows flaming red.

111

And from within the howls of Death I heard,
Cursing the dismal night that gave him birth,
Damning his ancient sire, and mother sin,
Who at the gates of hell, accursed, brought him
    forth.   160

112

(For fancy gave to my enraptur'd soul
An eagle's eye, with keenest glance to see,
And bade those distant sounds distinctly roll,
Which, waking, never had affected me.)

113

Oft his pale breast with cruel hand he smote,
And tearing from his limbs a winding sheet,
Roar'd to the black skies, while the woods
    around,
As wicked as himself, his words repeat.

114

Thrice tow'rd the skies his meagre arms he
    rear'd,
Invok'd all hell, and thunders on his head,   170
Bid light'nings fly, earth yawn, and tempests
    roar,
And the sea wrap him in its oozy bed.

115

"My life for one cool draught!—O, fetch your
    springs,
"Can one unfeeling to my woes be found!
"No friendly visage comes to my relief,
"But ghosts impend, and spectres hover round.

116

"Though humbled now, dishearten'd and dis-
    trest,
"Yet, when admitted to the peaceful ground,
"With heroes, kings, and conquerors I shall
    rest,   179
"Shall sleep as safely, and perhaps as sound."

117

Dim burnt the lamp, and now the phantom
    Death
Gave his last groans in horror and despair—
"All hell demands me hence,"—he said, and
    threw
The red lamp hissing through the midnight air.

118

Trembling, across the plain my course I held,
And found the grave-yard, loitering through
    the gloom,

And, in the midst, a hell-red, wandering light,
Walking in fiery circles round the tomb.

119

Among the graves a spiry building stood,
Whose tolling bell, resounding through the
    shade,   190
Sung doleful ditties to the adjacent wood,
And many a dismal drowsy thing it said.

120

This fabrick tall, with towers and chancels
    grac'd,
Was rais'd by sinners' hands, in ages fled;
The roof they painted, and the beams they
    brac'd,
And texts from scripture o'er the walls they
    spread:

121

But wicked were their hearts, for they re-
    fus'd
To aid the helpless orphan, when distrest,
The shivering, naked stranger they misus'd,
And banish'd from their doors the starving
    guest.   200

122

By laws protected, cruel and profane,
The poor man's ox these monsters drove
    away;—
And left Distress to attend her infant train,
No friend to comfort, and no bread to stay.

123

But heaven look'd on with keen, resentful eye,
And doom'd them to perdition and the grave,
That as they felt not for the wretch distrest,
So heaven no pity on their souls would have.

124

In pride they rais'd this building tall and
    fair,
Their hearts were on perpetual mischief bent,
With pride they preach'd, and pride was in
    their prayer,   211
With pride they were deceiv'd, and so to hell
    they went.

125

At distance far approaching to the tomb,
By lamps and lanthorns guided through the
    shade,

A coal-black chariot hurried through the gloom,
Spectres attending, in black weeds array'd.

126

Whose woeful forms yet chill my soul with
    dread,
Each wore a vest in Stygian chambers wove,
Death's kindred all—Death's horses they be-
    strode,
And gallop'd fiercely, as the chariot drove. 220

127

Each horrid face a grizly mask conceal'd,
Their busy eyes shot terror to my soul
As now and then, by the pale lanthorn's glare,
I saw them for their parted friend condole.

128

Before the hearse Death's chaplain seem'd to
    go,
Who strove to comfort, what he could, the
    dead;
Talk'd much of Satan, and the land of woe,
And many a chapter from the scriptures read.

129

At last he rais'd the swelling anthem high,
In dismal numbers seem'd he to complain; 230
The captive tribes that by Euphrates wept,
Their song was jovial to this dreary strain.

130

That done, they plac'd the carcase in the tomb,
To dust and dull oblivion now resign'd,
Then turn'd the chariot tow'rd the House of
    Night,
Which soon flew off, and left no trace behind.

131

But as I stoop'd to write the appointed verse,
Swifter than thought the airy scene decay'd;
Blushing the morn arose, and from the east
With her gay streams of light dispell'd the
    shade. 240

132

What is this Death, ye deep read sophists,
    say?—
Death is no more than one unceasing change;
New forms arise, while other forms decay,
Yet all is Life throughout creation's range.

133

The towering Alps, the haughty Apennine,
The Andes, wrapt in everlasting snow,
The Apalachian and the Ararat
Sooner or later must to ruin go.

134

Hills sink to plains, and man returns to dust,
That dust supports a reptile or a flower; 250
Each changeful atom by some other nurs'd
Takes some new form, to perish in an hour.

135

Too nearly join'd to sickness, toils, and pains,
(Perhaps for former crimes imprison'd here)
True to itself the immortal soul remains,
And seeks new mansions in the starry sphere.

136

When Nature bids thee from the world retire,
With joy thy lodging leave, a fated guest;
In Paradise, the land of thy desire,
Existing always, always to be blest. 260
               1779, 1786

» »   « «

TO THE MEMORY OF THE BRAVE AMERICANS

Under General Greene, in South
Carolina, Who Fell in the Action
of September 8, 1781

At Eutaw Springs the valiant died;
   Their limbs with dust are covered o'er—
Weep on, ye springs, your tearful tide;
   How many heroes are no more!

If in this wreck of ruin, they
   Can yet be thought to claim a tear,
O smite your gentle breast, and say
   The friends of freedom slumber here!

Thou, who shalt trace this bloody plain,
   If goodness rules thy generous breast, 10
Sigh for the wasted rural reign;
   Sigh for the shepherds, sunk to rest!

Stranger, their humble graves adorn;
   You too may fall, and ask a tear;

'Tis not the beauty of the morn
  That proves the evening shall be clear.—

They saw their injured country's woe;
  The flaming town, the wasted field;
Then rushed to meet the insulting foe;
  They took the spear—but left the shield.   20

Led by thy conquering genius, Greene,
  The Britons they compelled to fly;
None distant viewed the fatal plain,
  None grieved, in such a cause to die—

But, like the Parthian, famed of old,
  Who, flying, still their arrows threw,
These routed Britons, full as bold,
  Retreated, and retreating slew.

Now rest in peace, our patriot band;
  Though far from nature's limits thrown,   30
We trust they find a happier land,
  A brighter sunshine of their own.
                                    1781

THE WILD HONEY-SUCKLE

Fair flower, that dost so comely grow,
Hid in this silent, dull retreat,
Untouched thy honied blossoms blow,
Unseen thy little branches greet;
  No roving foot shall crush thee here,
  No busy hand provoke a tear.

By Nature's self in white arrayed,
She bade thee shun the vulgar eye,
And planted here the guardian shade,
And sent soft waters murmuring by;   10
  Thus quietly thy summer goes,
  Thy days declining to repose.

Smit with those charms, that must decay,
I grieve to see your future doom;
They died—nor were those flowers more gay,
The flowers that did in Eden bloom;
  Unpitying frosts, and Autumn's power
  Shall leave no vestige of this flower.

From morning suns and evening dews
At first thy little being came: 20
If nothing once, you nothing lose,
For when you die you are the same;
  The space between, is but an hour,
  The frail duration of a flower.
                                    1786

TO AN AUTHOR

Your leaves bound up compact and fair,
In neat array at length prepare,
To pass their hour on learning's stage,
To meet the surly critic's rage;
The statesman's slight, the smatterer's sneer—
Were these, indeed, your only fear,
You might be tranquil and resigned:
What most should touch your fluttering mind;
Is that, few critics will be found
To sift your works, and deal the wound.   10

Thus, when one fleeting year is past
On some bye-shelf your book is cast—
Another comes, with something new,
And drives you fairly out of view:

With some to praise, but more to blame,
The mind returns to—whence it came;
And some alive, who scarce could read
Will publish satires on the dead.

Thrice happy Dryden, who could meet
Some rival bard in every street!   20
When all were bent on writing well
It was some credit to excel:—

Thrice happy Dryden, who could find
A Milbourne for his sport designed—
And Pope, who saw the harmless rage
Of Dennis bursting o'er his page
Might justly spurn the critic's aim,
Who only helped to swell his fame.

On these bleak climes by Fortune thrown,
Where rigid reason reigns alone,   30
Where lovely Fancy has no sway,
Nor magic forms about us play—
Nor nature takes her summer hue
Tell me, what has the muse to do?—

An age employed in edging steel
Can no poetic raptures feel;
No solitude's attracting power,
No leisure of the noon day hour,
No shaded stream, no shaded grove
Can this fantastic century move;   40

The muse of love in no request—
Go—try your fortune with the rest,
One of the nine you should engage,
To meet the follies of the age:—

On one, we fear, your choice must fall—
The least engaging of them all—

Her visage stern—an angry style—
A clouded brow—malicious smile—
A mind on murdered victims placed—
She, only she, can please the taste!   50
                                        1788

THE INDIAN BURYING GROUND [2]

In spite of all the learned have said,
    I still my old opinion keep;
The posture, that we give the dead,
    Points out the soul's eternal sleep.

Not so the ancients of these lands—
    The Indian, when from life released,
Again is seated with his friends,
    And shares again the joyous feast.

His imaged birds, and painted bowl,
    And venison, for a journey dressed,   10
Bespeak the nature of the soul,
    Activity, that knows no rest.

His bow, for action ready bent,
    And arrows, with a head of stone,
Can only mean that life is spent,
    And not the old ideas gone.

Thou, stranger, that shalt come this way,
    No fraud upon the dead commit—
Observe the swelling turf, and say
    They do not lie, but here they sit.   20

Here still a lofty rock remains,
    On which the curious eye may trace
(Now wasted, half, by wearing rains)
    The fancies of a ruder race.

Here still an aged elm aspires,
    Beneath whose far-projecting shade
(And which the shepherd still admires)
    The children of the forest played!

There oft a restless Indian queen
    (Pale Shebah, with her braided hair)   30
And many a barbarous form is seen
    To chide the man that lingers there.

By midnight moons, o'er moistening dews;
    In habit for the chase arrayed,

[2] The North Americans bury their dead in a sitting posture; decorating the corpse with wampum, the images of birds, quadrupeds, &; And (if that of a warrior) with bows, arrows, tomhawks, and other military weapons. [Freneau's note.]

The hunter still the deer pursues,
    The hunter and the deer, a shade!

And long shall timorous fancy see
    The painted chief, and pointed spear,
And Reason's self shall bow the knee
    To shadows and delusions here.   40
                                        1788

EPISTLE

From Dr. Franklin (deceased) to his Poeti-
    cal Panegyrists, on some of their
            Absurd Compliments

"Good Poets, why so full of pain,
Are you sincere—or do you feign?
Love for your tribe I never had,
Nor penned three stanzas, good or bad.

At funerals, sometimes, grief appears,
Where legacies have purchased tears:
'Tis folly to be sad for nought,
From me you never gained a groat.

To better trades I turned my views,
And never meddled with the muse;   10
Great things I did for rising States,
And kept the lightning from some pates.

This grand discovery, you adore it
But ne'er will be the better for it:
You still are subject to those fires,
For poets' houses have no spires.

Philosophers are famed for pride;
But, pray, be modest—when I died,
No "sighs disturbed old ocean's bed,"
No "Nature wept" for Franklin dead!   20

That day, on which I left the coast,
A beggar-man was also lost
If "Nature wept," you must agree
She wept for *him*—as well as *me*.

There's reason even in telling lies—
In such profusion of her "sighs,"
She was too sparing of a tear—
In Carolina, all was clear:

And, if there fell some snow and sleet,
Why must it be my winding sheet?   30
Snows oft have clothed the April plain,
Have melted, and will melt again.

Poets, I pray you, say no more,
Or say what Nature said before;
That reason should your pens direct,
Or else you pay me no respect.

Let reason be your constant rule,
And Nature, trust me, is no fool—
When to the dust great men she brings,
MAKE HER DO—SOME UNCOMMON THINGS." 40
                                    1790

THE AMERICAN SOLDIER

[A Picture from the Life]

Deep in a vale, a stranger now to arms,
Too poor to shine in courts, too proud to beg,
He, who once warr'd on Saratoga's plains,
Sits musing o'er his scars, and wooden leg.

Remembering still the toil of former days,
To other hands he sees his earnings paid;—
They share the due reward—he feeds on praise,
Lost in the abyss of want, misfortune's shade.

Far, far from domes where splendid tapers glare,
'Tis his from dear bought peace no wealth to win,   10
Remov'd alike from courtly cringing 'squires,
The great-man s Levee, and the proud man's grin.

Sold are those arms which once on Britons blaz'd,
When, flush'd with conquest, to the charge they came;
That power repell'd, and Freedom's fabrick rais'd,
She leaves her soldier—famine and a name!
?1790   1795

ON THE ANNIVERSARY

Of the Storming of the Bastille, at Paris, July 14th, 1789

The chiefs that bow to Capet's reign,
In mourning, now, their weeds display;
But we, that scorn a monarch's chain,

Combine to celebrate the day
To Freedom's birth that put the seal,
And laid in dust the proud Bastille.

To Gallia's rich and splendid crown,
This mighty Day gave such a blow
As Time's recording hand shall own
No former age had power to do: 10
No single gem some Brutus stole,
But instant ruin seiz'd the whole.

Now tyrants rise, once more to bind
In royal chains a nation freed—
Vain hope! for they, to death consign'd,
Shall soon, like perjur'd Louis, bleed:
O'er every king, o'er every queen
Fate hangs the sword, and guillotine.

"Plung'd in a gulf of deep distress
France turns her back—(so traitors say)   20
Kings, priests, and nobles, round her press,
Resolv'd to seize their destin'd prey:
Thus Europe swears (in arms combin'd)
To Poland's doom is France consign'd."

Yet those, who now are thought so low
From conquests that were basely gain'd,
Shall rise tremendous from the blow
And free Two Worlds, that still are chain'd,
Restrict the Briton to his isle,
And Freedom plant in every soil.   30

Ye sons of this degenerate clime,
Haste, arm the barque, expand the sail;
Assist to speed that golden time
When Freedom rules, and monarchs fail;
All left to France—new powers may join,
And help to crush the cause divine.

Ah! while I write, dear France Allied,
My ardent wish I scarce restrain,
To throw these Sybil leaves aside,
And fly to join you on the main: 40
Unfurl the topsail for the chace
And help to crush the tyrant race!   1793

ODE[3]

God save the Rights of Man!
Give us a heart to scan
Blessings so dear:

[3] Sung at the Civic Feast given in honor of Citizen Genêt, Philadelphia, June 1, 1793. The tune is "God Save the King" ("America").

Let them be spread around
Wherever man is found,
And with the welcome sound
Ravish his ear.

Let us with France agree,
And bid the world be free,
While tyrants fall!   10
Let the rude savage host
Of their vast numbers boast—
Freedom's almighty trust
Laughs at them all!

Though hosts of slaves conspire
To quench fair Gallia's fire,
Still shall they fail:
Though traitors round her rise,
Leagu'd with her enemies,
To war each patriot flies,   20
And will prevail.

No more is valour's flame
Devoted to a name,
Taught to adore—
Soldiers of Liberty
Disdain to bow the knee,
But teach Equality
To every shore.

The world at last will join
To aid thy grand design,   30
Dear Liberty!
To Russia's frozen lands
The generous flame expands:
On Afric's burning sands
Shall man be free!

In this our western world
Be Freedom's flag unfurl'd
Through all its shores!
May no destructive blast
Our heaven of joy o'ercast,   40
May Freedom's fabric last
While time endures.

If e'er her cause require!—
Should tyrants e'er aspire
To aim their stroke,
May no proud despot daunt—
Should he his standard plant,
Freedom will never want
Her hearts of oak!
?1791   1795

ON A HONEY BEE

Drinking from a Glass of Wine and Drowned Therein

Thou, born to sip the lake or spring,
Or quaff the waters of the stream,
Why hither come on vagrant wing?—
Does Bacchus tempting seem—
Did he, for you, this glass prepare?—
Will I admit you to a share?

Did storms harass or foes perplex,
Did wasps or king-birds bring dismay—
Did wars distress, or labours vex,
Or did you miss your way?—   10
A better seat you could not take
Than on the margin of this lake.

Welcome!—I hail you to my glass:
All welcome, here, you find;
Here, let the cloud of trouble pass,
Here, be all care resigned.—
This fluid never fails to please,
And drown the griefs of men or bees.

What forced you here, we cannot know,
And you will scarcely tell—   20
But cheery we would have you go
And bid a glad farewell:
On lighter wings we bid you fly,
Your dart will now all foes defy.

Yet take not, oh! too deep a drink,
And in this ocean die;
Here bigger bees than you might sink,
Even bees full six feet high.
Like Pharaoh, then, you would be said
To perish in a sea of red.   30

Do as you please, your will is mine;
Enjoy it without fear—
And your grave will be this glass of wine,
Your epitaph—a tear—
Go, take your seat in Charon's boat,
We'll tell the hive, you died afloat.   1809

ON THE UNIVERSALITY AND OTHER ATTRIBUTES OF THE GOD OF NATURE

All that we see, about, abroad,
What is it all, but nature's God?

In meaner works discover'd here
No less than in the starry sphere.

In seas, on earth, this God is seen;
All that exist, upon him lean;
He lives in all, and never stray'd
A moment from the works he made:

His system fix'd on general laws
Bespeaks a wise creating cause;   10
Impartially he rules mankind
And all that on this globe we find.

Unchanged in all that seems to change,
Unbounded space is his great range;

To one vast purpose always true,
No time, with him, is old or new.

In all the attributes divine
Unlimited perfectings shine;
In these enwrapt, in these complete,
All virtues in that centre meet.   20

This power who doth all powers transcend,
To all intelligence a friend,
Exists, the *greatest and the best*
Through all the worlds, to make them blest.

All that he did he first approved
He all things into *being* loved;
O'er all he made he still presides,
For them in life, or death provides.   1815

» » « «

» » *From:* THE PHILOSOPHER OF THE FOREST « «

x

THE PAST AND FUTURE OF AMERICA[4]

When nature first brought forth her infant, the American world, to enjoy the blessings and vivifying influences of the new created sun, as if conscious of the injuries this part of her creation was to suffer in future ages, she seemed particularly industrious, she took especial care to plant it in such a situation that many hundreds of centuries, and immense number of years must elapse, before it could possibly be discovered by the greedy natives of the eastern continent.—"Till more than five thousand years have passed away (said she) it shall be inaccessible to all, except a few tribes of wandering Tartars, who from time to time may find their way thither by accident; literally *the children of nature,* wild as the wind and waves, and free as the animals that wander in the woody or the watry waste. The magnet alone, continued she, shall enable the polished people of the eastern regions to discover and ravage the delectable lands I have formed in the opposite hemisphere; but that fossil, the invaluable loadstone, I will bury deep in the

[4] One in the series of essays which Freneau contributed to *The Freeman's Journal.*

earth, unobserved its wonderful properties, till destiny and over-ruling fate, whose decrees no one can obviate, to my extremest grief, shall disclose it to the eye of avarice, ambition, and scrutinizing curiosity, and prompt a bold and daring *Columbus* to go in quest of those shores which it will not be in my power any longer to conceal."—

So spoke Nature, the mother of all men, and all things. In the mean time ages rolled away: the old world was peopled, unpeopled, and peopled again. Nations grew and flourished: they quarrelled, they fought, and made peace: the *four great monarchies* succeeded each other, and fell again into decay, with their emperors, kings and heroes, by far less durable than the lifeless marble columns which to this day mark the spot where their proudest capitals stood, or where their most famous battles were fought. These nations had their ages of politeness and barbarism, ignorance and science, misery and felicity: the follies of one age were acted over again by another, and each retired in its turn of the receptacles of silence, solitude and darkness, to make room for succeeding generations.

But still America lay unknown and undiscovered, with all her islands, lakes, mountains, woods, plains, capacious harbours and extended shores. Here the fish sported in the waters, undisturbed by hooks or nets, and the beasts of the forest enjoyed a secure repose. The poets of the eastern world were in the mean time amusing their iron hearted contemporaries with the fictions of a golden age; their fabulous Arcadias and Saturnian kingdoms; the ideas and notions of which must have owed their existence to the magic power of fancy alone, as they were wholly ignorant that the happy scenes, the innocent people and pastoral ages, of which they sung, were at that moment realizing in another quarter of the globe, as yet unexplored and unknown.—But, in process of time, as nature had foreseen, this immense continent was at length raised from its long night of obscurity to the view of astonished nations: the inhabitants, like the country, seemed to be a new race of mortals; of different natures, ideas and inclinations from those already known. They, also, gazed at the Europeans as a species of men differing in all respects from themselves, and, as far as regarded power and abilities, beings of a superior nature.

As the Europeans had the *means*, they of course conceived they had also the *right* to extirpate the innocent natives, or drive them from the sea coasts to the interior parts of the country. The most specious pretext for this procedure seems to have been, that the Aborigines, or old inhabitants of America, did not sufficiently exert themselves to cultivate and improve the lands nature had so liberally bestowed upon them: they were content with the productions of the simple genius of the earth, and *therefore* were scarcely to be considered, according to these casuists, as legal proprietors of the immense territories that were now discovered.

Full of this idea, the Europeans flocked over, and carefully examined the soil and productions of this new-found region: the best lands in North America were observed to lie in a temperate climate, and the new-comers soon found it their interest to cultivate and improve a soil that promised so much to the hand of industry. They roused the jealousy of the natives, who, unwilling to part with their pleasant abodes in the neighbourhood of the sea, made many attempts, (and sometimes not unsuccessfully) to annihilate these intruding strangers; but, as the several divisions of the old world were at that time overstocked with inhabitants, who constantly waged bloody wars with each other, notwithstanding the devastation and destruction of the human species occasioned

thereby, it became absolutely necessary that many should emigrate. Providence gave permission to the arm of tyranny to expel thousands from their native lands; and many, in hopes of bettering their fortunes, submitted to become voluntary exiles. Among the rest, Britain seemed very busy in virtually banishing and expelling her subjects to this remote region, who chose the northern coast, as knowing of no other asylum, excepting the grave, from the scourge of oppression. These, with a mixture of adventurers from various nations, at length humbled the savage tribes, and by the mere force of industry rendered a large proportion of this new country rich and flourishing. Britain soon cast a greedy eye upon the hard-earned possessions of this exiled race; she claimed them as subjects, and took them under her protection; but at the same time said in her heart, *They shall hereafter be my slaves.*

The children of the first emigrants immediately forgot the wrongs and injuries their forefathers had experienced, and strictly united themselves to her, not as yet aware of her insidious designs: but nature disregarded the connexion; and whispering in the ear of reason, was heard to say, "The union cannot be lasting."

Her words have proved true: the people of the present age have seen the unnatural bonds in a moment dissolved, the union broken, and the connexion at an end! Tell me, ye advocates for the dependence of these states upon the remote island of Britain; ye who assert that their happiness, their interest, and their glory is bound up in such a dependence, would you not esteem him a madman who should attempt amidst the rage of contending winds and waves to bind together two bulky ships with a single thread of silk for their mutual safety? Just as reasonable is it to suppose that America and the comparatively paltry and oppositely interested island of Britain can be happily united under one and the same sovereign.

What a spectacle of derision do the infatuated Britons now exhibit to the world, in seriously attempting to subjugate a country to which nature never gave them a shadow of right, and whose immense extent is, of itself, a standing and insurmountable obstacle to their success! An island, situated on the extremities of the ocean, on the verge of polar darkness, incumbered with rugged mountains, traversed by uncouth savages of horrid mien; barren heaths, and useless, broken lands; a spot, whose strength is merely artificial, sending out on impracticable conquests her fleets and armies, the flower of her youth and her ablest commanders, who, the moment they come within the vortex, the sphere of attraction of this huge unwieldy body, the American world, are instantly swallowed up, like straws in a whirlpool, and irrecoverably lost!

What a nation of numerous and ingenious mechanics and manufacturers were the English only ten years ago! With the fleeces of their sheep they warmed the inhabitants of either frigid zone: the fine linens of their island were in high estimation in every clime; but in order to prosecute their mad scheme of reducing to unconditional submission or desolating a country naturally invincible, they have taken the weaver from the loom and the cobler from his stall; the back of the pedlar is released from its burden, and he who of yore was honestly and profitably occupied in fitting garments to the shoulders of his brethren, fancying himself on a sudden an *Alexander* or an *Hernando Cortez;* in search of glory, in quest of never fading laurels, and for the support of his idol, Royalty, traverses the wide extended ocean, and leads to imaginary conquests and devastations in the trans-Atlantic world!

It is not easy to conceive what will be the greatness and importance of North America in a century or two to come, if the present fabric of Nature is upheld, and the people retain those bold and manly sentiments of freedom, which actuate them at this day. Agriculture, the basis of a nation's greatness, will here, most probably, be advanced to its summit of perfection; and its attendant, commerce, will so agreeably and usefully employ mankind, that wars will be forgotten; nations, by a free intercourse with this vast and fertile continent, and this continent with the whole world, will again become brothers after so many centuries of hatred and jealousy, and no longer treat each other as savages and monsters. The iron generation will verge to decay, and those days of felicity advance which have been so often wished for by all good men, and which are so beautifully described by the prophetic sages of ancient times.

My friend, the clergyman, informs me, that after passing a ridge of lofty mountains extending on the western frontiers of these republics, a new and most enchanting region opens, of inexpressible beauty and fertility. The lands are *there* of a quality far superior to those situated in the neighbourhood of the sea coast: the trees of the forest are stately and tall, the meadows and pastures spacious, supporting vast herds of the native animals of the country; which own no master, nor expect their sustenance from the hands of men. The climate, he says, is moderate and agreeable; there the rivers no longer bend their courses eastward to the Atlantic, but inclining to the west and south, and moving with a gentle current through the channels that Nature has opened, fall at length into that grand repository of a thousand dreams, *Mississippi,* who collecting his waters, derived from a source remote and unknown, rolls onward through the frozen regions of the north, and stretching his prodigiously extended arms to the east and west, embraces those savage groves and dreary solitudes, as yet uninvestigated by the traveller, unsung by the poet, and unmeasured by the chain of the geometrician; till uniting with the *Ohio* and turning due south, receiving afterwards the *Missouri* and a hundred others, this prince of rivers, in comparison of whom the *Nile* is but a small rivulet, and the *Danube* a ditch, hurries with his immense flood of waters into the Mexican sea, laving the shores of many fertile countries in his passage, inhabited by savage nations to this day almost unknown and without a name.

It is a standing rule in philosophy, that Nature does nothing in vain. A potent nation, now at war with these republics, has proclaimed her resolution *to lay waste what she cannot reclaim by conquest, and schemes are projected to oblige such to re-emigrate to Europe as shall escape the fury of the destroyers.* But if this new world was not to become at some time or another the receptacle of numerous civilized nations, from one extremity to the other, for what visible purpose could Nature have formed these vast lakes in the bosom of her infant empire, which surprise and astonish the traveller, who, leaving the salt ocean behind him to the east, finds, unexpectedly, new oceans of a prodigious extent in those tracts where Fancy would have furnished nothing but endless hills, inhospitable wilds and dreary forests existed? These lakes having, severally, a communication with each other, and lastly with the Atlantic ocean, towards the north-east; approaching also very near, by the west, to several of the navigable branches of the Mississippi, from an easy communication through a long tract of country, the intercourse between the various parts of which would, in future times, at least for the purposes of commerce, be extremely difficult and laborious, were it not for this continuation of waters, that for ages have been waiting to receive the barque of traffic, urged forward by the sail or the stroke of the springy oar; as the soil bordering thereon has no less impatiently expected the operations of the industrious plough.

During a very considerable part of the year, the south west wind blows unremittedly on the face of this serpentine river, the Ohio; and even at other times, the current of air is more prevalent in that direction than in any other, which being directly opposed to the course of the stream, moving at the rate of one mile hourly, is it not evident that Providence, Nature, or Fate, has so ordered this matter, that the commercial vessels hereafter sailing northward thereon may have favourable gales to make an answerable progress against a current that is still contrary and the same, and that those bound to the south may have the assistance of the ebbing stream to combat the adverse winds with more advantage.—It would

carry me far beyond the bounds of a short essay, to point out every particular, indicating the future importance of this newly discovered country; and it is really astonishing, as I intimated before, that a nation endued with the divine gift of reason, if they would exercise that gift, should at this day entertain a serious thought of reducing, by force of arms, this immense continent to their absolute sway; a continent beholding two hemispheres, abounding with a hardy and active race of inhabitants, producing every thing within itself proper for its own maintenance and defence; a continent extending thro' such a number of degrees of latitude and longitude, from the limits of the torrid zone, the circle of the northern tropic, to those frozen streams and icy mountains, where, chilled with the extreme rigours of perpetual winter, Nature seems to have lost her vegetative powers; and where a few of the human race, the natives of the polar regions, that are found to exist in those unjoyous climes, bears so little resemblance in the features of the mind to what the civilized world calls a *man,* that they scarcely deserve the name.   1782, 1788

RULES FOR CHANGING A LIMITED » » REPUBLICAN GOVERNMENT INTO AN « « UNLIMITED HEREDITARY ONE[5]

I. It being necessary, in order to effect the change, to get rid of constitutional shackles, and popular prejudices, all possible means and occasions are to be used for both these purposes.

II. Nothing being more likely to prepare the vulgar mind for aristocratical ranks and hereditary powers, than Titles, endeavour in the offset of the government to confer these on its most dignified officers. If the principal magistrate should happen to be particularly venerable in the eyes of the people, take advantage of that fortunate circumstance in setting the example.

III. Should the attempt fail, through his republican aversion to it, or from the danger of alarming the people, do not abandon the enterprise altogether, but lay up the proposition in record. Time may gain it respect, and it will be there always ready cut and dried for any favourable conjuncture that may offer.

IV. In drawing all bills, resolutions, and reports, keep constantly in view that the limitations in the constitution are ultimately to be explained away. Precedents and phrases may thus be shuffled in, without being adverted to by candid or weak people, of which good use may afterwards be made.

V. As the novelty and bustle of inaugurating the government will for some time keep the public mind in a heedless and unsettled state, let the *Press,* during this period be busy in propagating the doctrines of monarchy and aristocracy. For this purpose it will be particularly useful to confound a mobbish democracy with a representative republic, that by exhibiting all the turbulent examples and enormities of the former, an odium may be thrown on the character of the latter. Review all the civil contests, convulsions, factions, broils, squabbles, bickerings, black eyes and bloody noses of ancient, middle, and modern ages, caricature them into the most frightful forms and colours that can be imagined, and unfold

[5] One of Freneau's anti-Hamiltonian editorials in the Jeffersonian *National Gazette,* which Freneau edited.

one scene of the horrible tragedy after another, 'till the people be made, if possible, to tremble at their own shadows.—*Let the discourses on* —then contrast with these pictures of terror the quiet of hereditary succession, the reverence claimed by birth and nobility, and the fascinating influence of stars, and ribbands, and garters; cautiously suppressing all the bloody tragedies and unceasing oppression which form the history of this species of government. No pains should be spared in this part of the undertaking, for the greatest will be wanted, it being extremely difficult, especially when a people have been taught to reason and feel their rights, to convince them that a king who is always an enemy to the people, and a nobility who are perhaps still more so, will take better care of the people than the people will take of themselves.

VI. But the grand *nostrum* will be a Public Debt, provided enough of it can be got, and it be medicated with the proper ingredients. If by good fortune a debt be ready at hand, the most is to be made of it. Stretch it and swell it to the utmost the items will bear. Allow as many extra claims as decency will permit. Assume all the debts of your neighbours: In a word, get as much debt as can be raked and scraped together, and when you have got all you can, "advertise" for more, and have the debt made *as big as possible*. This object being accomplished, the next will be to make it *as perpetual as possible;* and the next to that, to get it into *as few hands as possible*. The more effectually to bring this about, modify the debt, complicate it, divide it, subdivide it, subtract it, postpone it, let there be one third of two thirds, and two thirds of one third, and two thirds of two thirds: let there be three per cents and four per cents, and six per cents, and present six per cents, and future six per cents. To be brief, let the whole be such a mystery that a *few only* can understand it; and let all possible opportunities and informations fall in the way of *these few*, to clinch their advantages over the many.

VII. It must not be forgotten that the members of the legislative body are to have a deep stake in the game. This is an essential point, and happily is attended with no difficulty. A sufficient number, properly disposed, can alternately legislate and speculate, and speculate and legislate, and buy and sell, and sell and buy, until a due portion of the property of their constituents has passed into their hands to give them an interest against their constituents, and to ensure the part they are to act. All this however must be carried on under cover of the closest secrecy; and it is particularly lucky that dealings in paper admit of more secrecy than any other. Should a discovery take place, the whole plan may be blown up.

VIII. The ways in which a great debt, so constituted and applied, will contribute to the ultimate end in view, are both numerous and obvious. 1. The *favourite few*, thus possessed of it, whether within or without the government, will feel the staunchest fealty to it, and will go through thick and thin to support it in all its oppressions and usurpations. 2. Their money will give them consequence and influence, even among those who have been tricked out of it. 3. They will be the readiest materials that can be found for an hereditary aristocratic order, whenever matters are ripe for one. 4. A great debt will require great taxes, great taxes many taxgatherers and other officers: and all officers are auxiliaries of power. 5. Heavy taxes may produce discontents; these may threaten resistance; and in proportion to this danger will be the pretence for a *standing army* to repel it. 6. A standing army in its turn will increase the moral force of the government by means of its appointments, and give it physical force by means of the sword; thus doubly forwarding the main object.

IX. The management of a great funded debt and an extensive system of taxes will afford a plea not to be neglected, for establishing a great incorporated bank. The use of such a machine is well understood. If the constitution, according to its fair meaning, should not authorize it, so much the better. Push it through by a forced meaning, and you will get in the bargain an admirable precedent for future misconstructions. In fashioning the bank remember that it is to be made particularly instrumental in enriching and aggrandizing the elect few, who are to be called in due season to the honors and felicities of the *kingdom* preparing for them; and who are the pillars that must support it. It will be easy to throw the benefit entirely into their hands, and to make it a solid edition of 50, or 60, or 70 per cent to their former capitals of 800 per cent, or 900 per cent, without costing them a shilling; whilst it will be so difficult to explain to the people that this gain of the few is at the cost of the many, that the *contrary* may be boldly and safely pretended. The bank will be pregnant with other important advantages. It will admit the same men to be, at the same time, members of the bank and members of the government. The two institutions will thus be soddered together, and each made the stronger. Money will be put under the direction of the government, and the government under the direction of money. To crown the whole, the bank will have a proper interest in *swelling and perpetuating the public debt and public taxes,* with all the blessings of both, because its agency and its profits will be extended in exact proportion.

X. "Divide and govern" is a maxim consecrated by the experience of ages, and should be as familiar in its use to every politician as the knife he carries in his pocket. In the work here to be executed the best effects may be produced by this maxim, and with peculiar facility. An extensive republic made up of lesser republics, necessarily contains various sorts of people, distinguished by local and other interests and prejudices. Let the whole group be well examined in all its parts and relations, geographical and political, metaphysical and metaphorical; let there be first a northern and a southern section by a line running east and west, and then an eastern and western section, by a line running north and south. By a suitable nomenclature, the landholders cultivating different articles can be discriminated from one another, all from the class of merchants, and both from that of manufacturers. One of the subordinate republics may be represented as a commercial state, another as a navigation state, another as a manufacturing state, others as agricultural states; and although the great body of the people in each be really agricultural, and the other characters be more or less common to all, still it will be politic to take advantage of such an arrangement. Should the members of the great republic be of different size, and subject to little jealousies on that account, another important division will be ready formed to your hand. Add again the divisions that may be carved out of *personal interests,* political opinions, and local parties—With so convenient an assortment of votes, especially with the help of the *marked ones,* a majority may be packed for any question with as much ease as the odd trick by an adroit gamester, and any

measure whatever be carried or defeated, as the great revolution to be brought about, may require. It is only necessary therefore, to recommend that full use be made of the resource: and to remark that, besides the direct benefit to be drawn from these artificial divisions, they will tend to smother the true and natural one, existing in all societies between the few who are always impatient of political equality, and the many who can never rise above it; between those who are to mount to the prerogatives, and those who are to be saddled with the burthens, of the hereditary government to be introduced; in one word, between the general mass of the people, attached to their republican government and republican interests, and the chosen band devoted to monarchy and mammon. It is of infinite importance that this distinction should be kept out of sight. The success of the project absolutely requires it.

XI. As soon as sufficient progress in the intended change shall have been made, and the public mind duly prepared, according to the rules already laid down, it will be proper to venture on another and a bolder step towards a removal of the constitutional landmarks. Here the aid of the former encroachments, and all the other precedents and way paving manoeuvres will be called in of course. But, in order to render success the more certain, it will be of special moment to give the most plausible and popular name that can be found, to the power that is to be usurped. It may be called, for example, a power for the common safety or the public good, or, "the general welfare." If the people should not be too much enlightened, the name will have a most imposing effect. It will escape attention that it means, in fact, the same thing with a power to do anything the government pleases "in all cases whatsoever." To oppose the power may consequently seem to the ignorant, and be called by the artful, opposing the "general welfare," and may be cried down under that deception. As the people, however, may not run so readily into the snare as might be wished, it will be prudent to bait it well with some specious popular interest, such as the encouragement of manufacturers, or even of agriculture; taking due care not even to mention any unpopular object to which the power is equally applicable, such as religion, &c. &c. &c. By this contrivance, particular classes of people may possibly be taken in, who will be a valuable reinforcement. With respect to the patronage of agriculture there is not indeed much to be expected from it. It will be too quickly seen through by the owners and tillers of the soil, that to tax them with one hand and pay back a part only with the other, is a losing game on their side. From the power over manufactures more is to be hoped. It will not be so easily perceived that the premium bestowed may not be equal to the circuitous tax on consumption which pays it. There are particular reasons, for pushing the experiment on this class of citizens. 1. As they live in towns and can act together, it is of vast consequence to gain them over to the interest of monarchy. 2. If the power over them be once established, the government can grant favours or monopolies, as it pleases; can raise or repress this or that place, as it pleases; can gratify this or that individual, as it pleases; in a word, by creating a dependence in so numerous and important a class of citizens, it will increase its own independence of every class and be more free to pursue the grand object in contemplation. 3. The expense of this operation will not in the end cost the government a shilling; for the moment any branch of manufacture has been brought to a state of tolerable maturity *the exciseman will be ready* with the constable and his search-warrant to demand a reimbursement, and as much more as can be squeezed out of the article. All this, it is to be remembered, supposes that the manufacturers will be weak enough to be cheated, in some respects, out of their own *interests,* and wicked enough, in others, to betray *those* of their fellow citizens; a supposition that, if known, would totally mar the experiment. Great care, therefore, must be taken to prevent it from leaking out.

XII.   The expediency of seizing every occasion of external danger for augmenting and perpetuating the standing military force, is too obvious to escape. So important is this matter, that for any loss or disaster whatever attending the national arms, there will be ample consolation and compensation in the opportunities for enlarging the establishment. A military defeat will become a political victory, and the loss of a little vulgar blood contributes to ennoble that which flows in the veins of our future dukes and marquisses.

XIII.   The same prudence will improve the opportunity afforded by an increase of the military expenditures, for perpetuating the taxes required for them. If the inconsistency and absurdity of establishing a *perpetual* tax for a temporary service should produce any difficulty in the business, *Rule* 10 must be resorted to. Throw in as many extraneous motives as will make up a majority, and the thing is effected in an instant. What was before evil will become good as easily as black could be made white by the same magical operation.

XIV.   Throughout this great undertaking it will be wise to have some particular model constantly in view. The work can then be carried on more systematically, and every measure be fortified, in the progress, by apt illustrations and authorities. Should there exist a particular monarchy against which there are fewer prejudices than against any other: Should it contain a mixture of the representative principle so as to present on one side the semblance of a republican aspect; should it moreover have a great, funded, complicated, irredeemable debt, with all the apparatus and appurtenances of excises, banks, &c. &c. &c., upon that a steady eye is to be kept. In all cases it will assist, and in most its statute book will furnish a precise pattern by which there may be cut out any moneyed or monarchical project that may be wanted.

XV.   As it is not to be expected that the change of a republic into a monarchy, with the rapidity desired, can be carried through without occasional suspicions and alarms, it will be necessary to be prepared for such events. The best general rule on the subject is to be taken from the example of crying "Stop thief" first —Neither lungs nor pens must be spared in charging every man who whispers, or even thinks that the revolution on foot is meditated, with being himself an enemy to the established government, and meaning to overturn it. Let the charge be reiterated and reverberated till at last such confusion and uncertainty be produced, that the people being not able to find out where the truth lies, withdraw their attention from the contest.

Many other rules of great wisdom and efficacy might be added: but it is conceived that the above will be abundantly enough for the purpose. This will certainly be the case, if the people can be either kept asleep so as not to discover, or be thrown into artificial divisions, so as not [to] resist what is silently going forward—Should it be found impossible, however, to prevent the people from awaking and uniting; should all artificial distinctions give way to the natural division between the lordly minded few and the well disposed many; should all who have common interest make a common cause and shew an inflexible attach- ment to republicanism in opposition to a government of monarchy and of money; why then—

July 4 and 7, 1792

HUGH HENRY BRACKENRIDGE

1748–1816

BRACKENRIDGE came to the College of New Jersey (now Princeton) from the frontier county of York, Pennsylvania. As an undergraduate he was conspicuous for his Whig ardor. With his classmates James Madison and Philip Freneau he organized the American Whig Society and contributed to the satiric war against its Tory rival, the Cliosophic Society. At the commencement of 1771 he recited a poem on *The Rising Glory of America* which he and Freneau had written. After graduation he taught school. During this time he wrote a play, *The Battle of Bunkers-Hill* (1776), for his pupils; served as a very unpacifistic army chaplain; and edited in Philadelphia the *United States Magazine* to prove "that we are able to cultivate the *belles lettres*, even disconnected with Great-Britain."

In 1781, on being admitted to the bar, Brackenridge made the great decision of his life: to go west (to Pittsburgh) and cast in his lot with the frontiersmen. He believed strongly that "in new countries the human genius will receive a spring, which it cannot have in the old. . . . The strongest minds, and the most enterprising, go there. They are thrown upon the vigor of their own intellect. . . . The plodding cub stays at home, while the more active tatterdemalion quits his paternal roof, and goes to build a cabin, and make a new roof for himself, in the wild woods of Tennessee, or elsewhere." Henceforth a leader in western Pennsylvania, Brackenridge became, in 1799, a judge in the supreme court of the state.

Brackenridge was a true democrat. He had no more fear of revolution than Jefferson. In the Whiskey Insurrection of 1794 his sympathies were with the frontiersmen. On the other hand, he respected such conserving forces of society as the Constitution, the common law, and the judiciary. He loved the classical authors he had read at Princeton, as the form and substance of his picaresque novel, *Modern Chivalry*, show.

The first part of *Modern Chivalry* (1792–1793, 1797) recounts the adventures of Captain Farrago in trying to restrain his ambitious bog-trotting servant Teague from becoming a legislator, a preacher, a lawyer, and a diplomat. In the second part (1804–1805), which discusses a variety of subjects of contemporary interest, the narrative is almost completely abandoned. The whole work was published in 1815.

Because *Modern Chivalry* is directed mainly at the fickleness of the people and their readiness to elect to public office persons who are unqualified, it has often been mistaken for an attack on democracy. A careful reading of a few pages will show how absurd this notion is. The effort of Brackenridge's whole life, as editor, legislator, judge, and satirist, was to educate his constituents to make them fit to rule themselves. A discerning reader will see that what he dislikes more than demagogues are the monarchists and the Society of the Cincinnati, and all self-acknowledged aristocrats who, while pretending to act for the common good, quietly distribute privilege to their own class.

Modern Chivalry, C. M. Newlin, ed., New York, 1937.
C. M. Newlin, *The Life and Writings of Hugh Henry Brackenridge*, Princeton, 1932.

» » *From:* MODERN CHIVALRY « «

PART I, VOLUME I, BOOK I, CHAPTER 3

[TEAGUE ESCAPES BEING MADE
A SENATOR]

The Captain rising early next morning, and setting out on his way, had now arrived at a place where a number of people were convened, for the purpose of electing persons to represent them in the legislature of the state. There was a weaver who was a candidate for this appointment, and seemed to have a good deal of interest among the people. But another, who was a man of education, was his competitor. Relying on some talent of speaking which he thought he possessed, he addressed the multitude.

Fellow citizens, said he, I pretend not to any great abilities; but am conscious to myself that I have the best good will to serve you. But it is very astonishing to me, that this weaver should conceive himself qualified for the trust. For though my acquirements are not great, yet his are still less. The mechanical business which he pursues, must necessarily take up so much of his time, that he cannot apply himself to political studies. I should therefore think it would be more answerable to your dignity, and conducive to your interest, to be represented by a man at least of some letters, than by an illiterate handicraftsman like this. It will be more honourable for himself, to remain at his loom and knot threads, than to come forward in a legislative capacity: because, in the one case, he is in the sphere where God and nature has placed him; in the other, he is like a fish out of water, and must struggle for breath in a new element.

Is it possible he can understand the affairs of government, whose mind has been concentered to the small object of weaving webs; to the price by the yard, the grist of the thread, and such like matters as concern a manufacturer of cloths? The feet of him who weaves, are more occupied than the head, or at least as much; and therefore the whole man must be, at least, but in half accustomed to exercise his mental powers. For these reasons, all other things set aside, the chance is in my favour, with respect to information. However, you will decide, and give your suffrages to him or to me, as you shall judge expedient.

The Captain hearing these observations, and looking at the weaver, could not help advancing, and undertaking to subjoin something in support of what had been just said. Said he, I have no prejudice against a weaver more than another man. Nor do I know any harm in the trade; save that from the sedentary life in a damp place, there is usually a paleness of the countenance: but this is a physical, not a moral evil. Such usually occupy subterranean apartments; not for the purpose, like Demosthenes, of shaving their heads, and writing over eight times the history of Thucydides, and perfecting a stile of oratory; but rather to keep the thread moist; or because this is considered but as an inglorious sort of trade, and is frequently thrust away into cellars, and damp outhouses, which are not occupied for a better use.

But to rise from the cellar to the senate house, would be an unnatural hoist. To come from counting threads, and adjusting them to the splits of a reed, to regulate the finances of a government, would be preposterous; there being no congruity in the case. There is no analogy between knotting threads and framing laws. It would be a reversion of the order of things. Not that a manufacturer of linen or woolen, or other stuff, is an inferior character, but a different one, from that which ought to be employed in affairs of state. It is unnecessary to enlarge on this subject; for you must all be convinced of the truth and propriety of what I say. But if you will give me leave to take the manufacturer aside a little, I think I can explain to him my ideas on the subject; and very probably prevail with him to withdraw his pretensions. The people seeming to acquiesce, and beckoning to the weaver, they drew aside, and the Captain addressed him in the following words:

Mr. Traddle, said he, for that was the name of the manufacturer, I have not the smallest idea of wounding your sensibility; but it would seem to me, it would be more your interest to pursue your occupation, than to launch out into that of which you have no knowledge. When you go to the senate house, the application to you will not be to warp a web; but to make laws for the commonwealth. Now, suppose that the making these laws, requires a knowledge of commerce, or of the interest of agriculture, or those principles upon which the different manufactures depend, what service could you render. It is possible you might think justly enough; but could you speak? You are not in the habit of public speaking. You are not furnished with those common place ideas, with which even very ignorant men can pass for knowing something. There is nothing makes a man so ridiculous as to attempt what is above his sphere. You are no tumbler for instance; yet should you give out that you could vault upon a man's back; or turn head over heels, like the wheels of a cart; the stiffness of your joints would encumber you; and you would fall upon your backside to the ground. Such a squash as that would do you damage. The getting up to ride on the state is an unsafe thing to those who are not accustomed to such horsemanship. It is a disagreeable thing for a man to be laughed at, and there is no way of keeping ones self from it but by avoiding all affectation.

While they were thus discoursing, a bustle had taken place among the croud. Teague hearing so much about elections, and serving the government, took it into his head, that he could be a legislator himself. The thing was not displeasing to the people, who seemed to favour his pretensions; owing, in some degree, to there being several of his countrymen among the croud; but more especially to the fluctuation of the popular mind, and a disposition to what is new and ignoble. For though the weaver was not the most elevated object of choice, yet he was still preferable to this tatterdemalion, who was but a menial servant, and had so much of what is called the brogue on his tongue, as to fall far short of an elegant speaker.

The Captain coming up, and finding what was on the carpet, was greatly chagrined at not having been able to give the multitude a better idea of the importance of a legislative trust; alarmed also, from an apprehension of the loss of his servant. Under these impressions he resumed his address to the multitude. Said he, This is making the matter still worse, gentlemen: this servant of mine is but a bog-trotter; who can scarcely speak the dialect in which your laws ought to be written; but certainly has never read a single treatise on any political subject; for the truth is, he cannot read at all. The young people of the lower class, in Ireland, have seldom the advantage of a good education; especially the descendants

of the ancient Irish, who have most of them a great assurance of countenance, but little information, or literature. This young man, whose family name is Oregan, has been my servant for several years; and, except a too great fondness for women, which now and then brings him into scrapes, he has demeaned himself in a manner tolerable enough. But he is totally ignorant of the great principles of legislation; and more especially, the particular interests of the government. A free government is a noble possession to a people: and this freedom consists in an equal right to make laws, and to have the benefit of the laws when made. Though doubtless, in such a government, the lowest citizen may become chief magistrate; yet it is sufficient to possess the right; not absolutely necessary to exercise it. Or even if you should think proper, now and then, to shew your privilege, and exert, in a signal manner, the democratic prerogative, yet is it not descending too low to filch away from me a hireling, which I cannot well spare, to serve your purpose. You are surely carrying the matter too far, in thinking to make a senator of this hostler; to take him away from an employment to which he has been bred, and put him to another, to which he has served no apprenticeship: to set those hands which have been lately employed in currying my horse, to the draughting bills, and preparing business for the house.

The people were tenacious of their choice, and insisted on giving Teague their suffrages; and by the frown upon their brows, seemed to indicate resentment at what has been said; as indirectly charging them with want of judgment; or calling in question their privilege to do what they thought proper. It is a very strange thing, said one of them, who was a speaker for the rest, that after having conquered Burgoyne and Cornwallis, and got a government of our own, we cannot put in it whom we please. This young man may be your servant, or another man's servant; but if we chuse to make him a delegate, what is that to you. He may not be yet skilled in the matter, but there is a good day a-coming. We will impower him; and it is better to trust a plain man like him, than one of your high flyers, that will make laws to suit their own purposes.

Said the Captain, I had much rather you would send the weaver, though I thought that improper, than to invade my household, and thus detract from me the very person that I have about me to brush my boots, and clean my spurs. The prolocutor of the people gave him to understand that his surmises were useless, for the people had determined on the choice, and Teague they would have, for a representative.

Finding it answered no end to expostulate with the multitide, he requested to speak a word with Teague by himself. Stepping aside, he said to him, composing his voice, and addressing him in a soft manner: Teague, you are quite wrong in this matter they have put into your head. Do you know what it is to be a member of a deliberative body? What qualifications are necessary? Do you understand any thing of geography? If a question should be, to make a law to dig a canal in some part of the state, can you describe the bearing of the mountains, and the course of the rivers? Or if commerce is to be pushed to some new quarter, by the force of regulations, are you competent to decide in such a case? There will be questions of law, and astronomy on the carpet. How you must gape and stare like a fool, when you come to be asked your opinion on these subjects. Are you acquainted with the abstract principles of finance; with the funding public securities; the ways and means of raising the revenue; providing for the discharge of the public debts, and all other things which respect the economy of the government? Even if you had knowledge, have you a facility of speaking? I would suppose you would have too much pride to go to the house just to say, Ay, or No. This is not the fault of your nature, but of your education; having been accustomed to dig turf in your early years, rather than instructing yourself in the classics, or common school books.

When a man becomes a member of a public body, he is like a racoon, or other beast that climbs up the fork of a tree; the boys pushing at him with pitch-forks, or throwing stones, or shooting at him with an arrow, the dogs barking in the mean time. One will find fault with your not speaking; another with your speaking, if you speak at all. They will have you in the newspapers, and ridicule you as a perfect beast. There is what they call the caricatura; that is, representing you with a dog's head, or a cat's claw. As you have a red head, they will very probably make a fox of you, or a sorrel horse, or a brindled cow. It is the devil in hell to be exposed to the squibs and crackers of the gazette wits and publications. You know no

more about these matters than a goose; and yet you would undertake rashly, without advice, to enter on the office; nay, contrary to advice. For I would not for a thousand guineas, though I have not the half of it to spare, that the breed of the Oregans should come to this; bringing on them a worse stain than stealing sheep; to which they are addicted. You have nothing but your character, Teague, in a new country to depend upon. Let it never be said, that you quitted an honest livelihood, the taking care of my horse, to follow the new fangled whims of the times, and to be a statesman.

Teague was moved chiefly with the last part of the address, and consented to give up the object.

The Captain, glad of this, took him back to the people, and announced his disposition to decline the honour which they had intended him.

Teague acknowledged that he had changed his mind, and was willing to remain in a private station.

The people did not seem well pleased with the Captain; but as nothing more could be said about the matter, they turned their attention to the weaver, and gave him their suffrages.

BOOK II, CHAPTER I

[TEAGUE AND THE SOCIETY OF PHILOSOPHERS]

There was, in a certain great city, a society who called themselves Philosophers. They had published books they called Transactions. These contained dissertations on the nature and causes of things; from the stars of the heaven to the fire-flies of the earth; and from the sea-crab to the woodland buffaloe. Such disquisitions are doubtless useful and entertaining to an inquisitive mind.

There is no question, but there were in this body some very great men; whose investigations of the arcana of nature deserve attention. But so it was, there had been introduced, by some means, many individuals, who were no philosophers at all. This is no unusual thing with institutions of this nature; though, by the bye, it is a very great fault. For it lessens the incentives of honour, to have the access made so easy, that every one may obtain admission. It has been a reproach to some colleges, that a diploma could be purchased for half a crown. This society were still more moderate; for the bare scratching the backside of a member has been known to procure a fellowship. At least, there have been those admitted who appeared capable of nothing else.

Nevertheless, it was necessary, even in these cases, for the candidates to procure some token of a philosophical turn of mind; such as the skin of a dead cat, or some odd kind of a mouse-trap, or the like; or have some phrases in their mouths, about minerals and petrifactions; so as just to support some idea of natural knowledge, and pass muster. There was one who had got in by finding, accidentally, the tail of a rabbit, which had been taken off in a boy's trap. Another by means of a squirrel's scalp, which he had taken care to stretch and dry on a bit of osier, bended in the form of a hoop. The beard of an old fox, taken off and dried in the sun, was the means of introducing one whom I knew very well: Or rather, as I have already hinted, it was beforehand intended he should be introduced; and these exuviæ, or spoils of the animal kingdom, were but the tokens and apologies for admission.

It happened as the Captain was riding this day, and Teague trotting after him, he saw a large owl, that had been shot by some body, and was placed in the crotch of a tree about the height of a man's head from the ground, for those that passed by to look at. The Captain being struck with it, as somewhat larger than such birds usually are, desired Teague to reach it to him; and tying it to the hinder part of his saddle, rode along.

Passing by the house of one who belonged to the society, the bird was noticed at the saddle-skirts, and the philosopher coming out, made enquiry with regard to the genus and nature of the fowl. Said the Captain, I know nothing more about it, than that it is nearly as large as a turkey buzzard. It is doubtless, said the other, the great Canada owl, that comes from the Lakes; and if your honour will give me leave, I will take it and submit it to the society, and have yourself made a member. As to the first, the Captain consented; but as to the last, the being a member, he chose rather he decline it; conceiving himself unqualified for a place in such a body. The other assured him that he was under a very great mistake; for there were persons there who scarcely knew a B from a bull's foot. That may be, said the Captain; but if others chuse to degrade them-

selves, by suffering their names to be used in so preposterous a way as that, it was no reason he should.

The other gave him to understand, that the society would certainly wish to express their sense of his merit, and shew themselves not inattentive to a virtuoso; that as he declined the honour himself, he probably might not be averse to let his servant take a seat among them. 10

He is but a simple Irishman, said the Captain, and of a low education; his language being that spoken by the aborigines of his country. And if he speaks a little English, it is with the brogue on his tongue; which would be unbecoming in a member of your body. It would seem to me, that a philosopher ought to know how to write, or at least to read. But Teague can neither write nor read. He can sing a song, or whistle an Irish tune; but is 20 totally illiterate in all things else. I question much if he could tell you how many new moons there are in the year; or any the most common thing you could ask him. He is a long-legged fellow, it is true; and might be of service in clambering over rocks, or going to the shores of rivers, to gather curiosities. But could you not get persons to do this, without making them members? I have more respect for science, than to suffer this bog-trotter to be so advanced 30 at its expence.

In these American states, there is a wide field for philosophic search; and these researches may be of great use in agriculture, mechanics, and astronomy. There is but little immediate profit attending these pursuits; but if there can be inducements of honour, these may supply the place. What more alluring to a young man, than the prospect of being, one day, received into the society of men truly 40 learned; the admission being a test and a proof of distinguished knowledge. But the fountain of honour, thus contaminated by a sediment foreign from its nature, who would wish to drink of it?

Said the philosopher, At the first institution of the society by Dr. Franklin and others, it was put upon a narrow basis, and only men of science were considered proper to compose it; and this might be a necessary policy at that 50 time, when the institution was in its infancy, and could not bear much draw-back of ignorance. But it has not been judged so necessary of late years. The matter stands now on a broad and catholic bottom; and, like the gospel

itself, it is our orders to go out into the highways and hedges, and compel them to come in.
There are hundreds, whose names you may see
on our list, who are not more instructed than
this lad of yours.

They must be a sad set indeed then, said
the Captain.

Sad or not sad, said the other, it is the case;
and if you will let Teague go, I will engage
10 him a membership.

I take it very ill of you, Mr. Philosopher, said
the Captain, to put this nonsense in his head.
If you knew what trouble I have lately had
with a parcel of people that were for sending
him to Congress, you would be unwilling to
draw him from me for the purpose of making
him a philosopher. It is not an easy matter to
get hirelings now-a-days; and when you do
get one, it is a mere chance, whether he is
20 faithful, and will suit your purpose. It would
be a very great loss to me, to have him taken
off at this time, when I have equipped myself
for a journey.

Teague was a good deal incensed at this
refusal of his master, and insisted that he would
be a philosopher. You are an ignoramus, said
the Captain. It is not the being among philosophers will make you one.

Teague insisted that he had a right to make
30 the best of his fortune: and as there was a door
open to his advancement he did not see why
he might not make use of it.

The Captain finding that it answered no end
to dispute the matter with him, by words of
sense and reason, took a contrary way to manage him.

Teague, said he, I have a regard for you, and
would wish to see you do well. But before you
take this step, I would wish to speak a word
40 or two in private. If you will go, I may perhaps
suggest some things that may be of service to
you, for your future conduct in that body.

Teague consenting, they stepped aside; and
the Captain addressed him in the following
manner:

Teague, said he, do you know what you are
about? It is a fine thing at first sight, to be a
philosopher, and get into this body. And indeed, if you are a real philosopher, it might be
50 some honour, and also safe, to take that leap.
But do you think it is to make a philosopher
of you that they want you? Far from it. It is
their great study to find curiosities; and because this man saw you coming after me, with
a red head, trotting like an Esquimaux Indian,

it has struck his mind to pick you up, and pass
you for one. Nay, it is possible, they may
intend worse; and when they have examined
you awhile, take the skin off you, and pass you
for an overgrown otter, or a musk-rat; or some
outlandish animal, for which they will themselves invent a name. If you were at the
museum of one of these societies, to observe
the quantity of skins and skeletons they have,
you might be well assured they did not come
by them honestly. I know so much of these
people, that I am well persuaded they would
think no more of throwing you into a kettle
of boiling water, than they would a tarapin;
and having scraped you out to a shell, present
you as the relics of an animal they had procured, at an immense price, from some Guinea
merchant. Or if they should not at once turn
you to this use, how, in the mean time, will
they dispose of you? They will have you away
through the bogs and marshes, catching flies
and mire-snipes; or send you to the woods for
a polecat; or oblige you to descend into draw-
wells for fog, and phlogistic air, and the Lord
knows what. You must go into wolves dens, and
catch bears by the tail; run over mountains
like an opossum, and dig the earth like a
ground hog. You will have to climb upon trees,
and get yourself bit by flying squirrels. There
will be no end to the musquetoes you will have
to dissect. What is all this to diving into mill-
dams and rivers, to catch craw-fish? Or if you
go to the ocean there are alligators to devour
you like a cat-fish. Who knows but it may come
your turn, in a windy night, to go aloft to the
heavens, to rub down the stars, and give the
goats and rams that are there, fodder. The
keeping the stars clean, is a laborious work; a
great deal worse than scouring andirons, or
brass kettles. There is a bull there would think
no more of tossing you on his horns than he
would a puppy dog. If the crab should get you
into his claws he would squeeze you like a
lobster. But what is all that to your having no
place to stand on? How would you like to be up
at the moon, and to fall down when you had
missed your hold, like a boy from the top-mast
of a ship, and have your brains beat out upon
the top of some great mountain; where the
devil might take your skeleton and give it to
the turkey-buzzards?

Or if they should, in the mean time, excuse
you from such out of door services, they will
rack and torture you with hard questions. You
must tell them how long the rays of light are

coming from the sun; how many drops of rain fall in a thunder gust; what makes the grass-hopper chirp when the sun is hot; how muscle shells get up to the top of the mountains; how the Indians got over to America. You will have to prove absolutely that the negroes were once white; and that their flat noses came by some cause in the compass of human means to pro-duce. These are puzzling questions; and yet you must solve them all. Take my advice, and stay where you are. Many men have ruined themselves by their ambition, and made bad worse. There is another kind of philosophy, which lies more within your sphere; that is moral philosophy. Every hostler or hireling can study this, and you have the most excellent opportunity of acquiring this knowledge in our traverses through the country; or communica-tions at the different taverns or villages, where we may happen to sojourn.

Teague had, in his own mind, long ago given up all thoughts of the society; and would not for the world have any more to do with it; therefore, without bidding the philosopher adieu, they pursued their route as usual.

VOLUME II, BOOK V, CHAPTER 5

[CONGRESSIONAL DEBATES]

The next day, revolving everything in his mind, it occurred to the Captain that the Irish-man might have gone out of town, hearing of an election at a district, and have been elected to Congress. As that body was then sitting, he thought it could be no great trouble to go to the house, and cast an eye from the gallery, and see if the ragamuffin had got there. There was one that had a little of the brogue of Teague upon his tongue, but nothing of his physiognomy; others had a good deal of his manner; but there was none that came abso-lutely up to the physic of his person.

However, being here, the Captain tho't it not amiss to listen a while to the debates upon the carpet. A certain bill was depending, and made, it seems, the order of the day. Mr. Cogan being on the floor, spoke:—Sir, said he, addressing himself to the chair, the bill in contemplation, is, in my opinion, of a dan-gerous tendency. I will venture to foretel, that, if it goes into a law, the cows will have fewer calves, and the sheep less wool; hens will lay fewer eggs, and cocks forget to crow daylight.

The horses will be worse shod, and stumble more; our watches go too slow; corns grow upon our toes; young women have the stomach ach; old men the gout; and middle aged per-sons fainting fits. The larks will fall dead in the field; the frogs croak till they burst their bags; and the leaves of the trees fall before the autumn. Snow will be found in the heat of harvest, and dog days in winter. The rivers will revert; and the shadows fall to the east in 10 the morning. The moon will be eclipsed; and the equinoxes happen at a wrong season of the year. Was it not such a bill as this, that changed the old stile; that made the eclipse in the time of Julius Cesar; that produced an earthquake at Jamaica, and sunk Port Royal? All history, both ancient and modern, is full of the mischiefs of such a bill. I shall, therefore, vote against it.

Mr. Bogan was now on the floor, and advo- 20 cated the good effects of the bill.

Sir, said he, addressing himself to the chair, I appear in support of the bill. I say, it will have a good effect on the physical world es-pecially. The ducks will be fatter, the geese heavier, the swans whiter, the redbirds sing better, and partridges come more easily into traps. It will kill rats, muzzle calves, and cut colts; and multiply the breed of oysters, and pickle cod-fish. It will moderate the sun's heat, 30 and the winter's cold; prevent fogs, and cure the ague. It will help the natural brain; brace the nerves, cure sore eyes, and the cholic, and remove rheumatisms. Consult experience, and it will be found, that provisions of the nature proposed by this bill, have an astonishing influence in this respect, where they have been tried. I must take the liberty to say, the gentle-man's allegations are totally *unfounded;* and he has *committed* himself in the matter of his 40 history; the earthquake in Jamaica not hap-pening in the time of Julius Cesar; and there-fore could have nothing to do with the eclipse of the sun. I shall, therefore, vote in favour of the bill.

Mr. Cogan rose to explain; and said, that he did not say, that the earthquake at Jamaica was at the same time with the eclipse of the sun, which happened at the birth of Julius Cesar.

Mr. Bogan rose to correct the gentleman: 50 it was not at the birth of Julius Cesar, but at his death, that the earthquake happened.

Mr. Hogan was on the floor: Said, he thought he could reconcile the gentlemen on that head. It was well known Julius Cesar lived about the time of the rebellion in Scotland, a little after Nebuchadnezzar, king of the Jews. As to the earthquake, he did not remember what year it happened; and therefore could say nothing about it.

At this period, the question being called, it was put, and carried by a majority of 25.

The Captain, satisfied with the sample of Congressional debates, retired, and came to his
10 lodging.

PART II, VOLUME I, BOOK II

[PROLOGUE]

It has been asked, why, in writing this memoir; have I taken my clown, *from the Irish nation?* The character of the English clown,
20 I did not well understand; nor could I imitate the manner of speaking. That of the Scotch I have tried, as may be seen, in the character of Duncan. But I found it, in my hands, rather insipid. The character of the Irish clown, to use the language of Rousseau, "has more stuff in it." He will attempt any thing.

The American has in fact, yet, no character; neither the clown, nor the gentleman. So that I could not take one from our own country;
30 which I would much rather have done, as the scene lay here. But the midland states of America, and the western parts in general, being half Ireland, the character of the Irish clown will not be wholly misunderstood. It is true the clown is taken from the aboriginal Irish; a character not so well known in the North of that country; nevertheless, it is still so much known, even there, and amongst the emigrants here, or their descendants, that it will not be
40 wholly thrown away.

On the Irish stage, it is a standing character; and on the theatre in Britain, it is also introduced. I have not been able to do it justice, being but half an Irishman, myself, and not so well acquainted with the reversions, and idiom, of the genuine Thady, as I could wish. However, the imitation at a distance from the original, will better pass than if it had been written, and read, nearer home. Foreigners
50 will not so readily distinguish the incongruities; or, as it is the best we can produce for the present, will more indulgently consider them.

I think it the duty of every man who possesses a faculty, and perhaps a facility of drawing such images, as will amuse his neighbour,

to lend a hand, and do something. Have those authors done nothing for the world, whose works would seem to have had no other object but to amuse? In low health; after the fatigue of great mental exertion on solid disquisitions; in pain of mind, from disappointed passions; or broken with the sensibilities of sympathy, and affection; it is a relief to try not to think; and this is attainable, in some degree, by light reading. Under sensations of this kind, I have had recourse more than once to Don Quixotte; which doubtless contains a great deal of excellent moral sentiment. But, at the same time, has much, that can serve only to amuse. Even in health, and with a flow of spirits, from prosperous affairs, it diversifies enjoyments, and adds to that happiness of which the mind is capable. I trust, therefore, that the gravest persons will not be of opinion that I ought to be put out of the church, for any appearance of levity, which this work may seem to carry with it.

I know there have been instances, amongst the *Puritans,* of clergymen degraded for singing a Scotch pastoral. But music is a carnal thing compared with putting thoughts upon paper. It requires an opening of the mouth, and a rolling of the tongue, whereas thought is wholly spiritual, and depends, not on any modification of the corporeal organs. Music, however, even by the strictest sects, is admissable in sacred harmony, which is an acknowledgment, that even sound has its uses to soothe the mind or to fit it for contemplation.

I would ask, which is the most entertaining work, Smollet's History of England; or his Humphrey Clinker? For, as to the utility, so far as that depends upon truth, they are both alike. History has been well said to be *the Romance of the human mind; and Romance the history of the heart.* When the son of Robert Walpole asked his father, whether he should read to him out of a book of history; he said; *"he was not fond of Romance."* This minister had been long engaged in affairs; and from what he had seen of accounts of things within his own knowledge he had little confidence in the relation of things which he had not seen. Except memoirs of person's own times, biographical sketches by cotemporary writers: Voyages, and Travels, that have geographical exactness, there is little of the historical kind, in point of truth, before Roderick Random; or Gil Blass.

The Eastern nations in their tales, pretend

to nothing but fiction. Nor is the story with them the less amusing because it is not *true*. Nor is the moral of it less impressive, because the actors never had existence. This, I have thought it sufficient to say, by way of introduction in this place.

PART II, VOLUME IV, BOOK I, CHAPTER 4

[SHOULD BEASTS VOTE?]

The principle of universal suffrage was much agitated at this time: whether every poll, as the word imports, should poll, or have a vote; or that *property* should also vote. If property alone, the question would arise, whether *soil* only; or also goods and chattles. If soil only, to what quantity or quality, shall the suffrage be attached? An hundred acres of soil of a bad quality, may not have the intrinsic worth of one of good. How should an inspector, or judge of an election, determine on the quality, unless the owner brings a sample with him, as the man who had his house to sell, brought a brick. This would be an inconvenience; and would render it impracticable to escape frauds. For a man might dig a sample from his neighbours, and pass it for his own. And as to quantity, the occupier of the greater quantity, is the most worthless citizen; at least the one who occupies more than he cultivates; because he neither eats the hay, nor lets another eat it. It is preposterous that *soil* should vote; a dumb field, a dead tree with a crows nest upon it; an hazle bush; a morass, or a barren mountain; or even a hill with a tuft of oaks upon it. These are all inanimate substances; how can they vote? For goods and chattles something might be said; a *live beast* particularly; as the animal could speak, not with a viva voce vote, like a man; *more humano,* like a human creature. But with some guttural sound from the throat, or fauces, which might be called its own; and not like the tree with a turkey buzzard on it; and which is not its own voice. I mean that of the tree, said the speaker, who was running on in this manner; and yet it is advocated, that stocks and stones that go with the soil shall have a vote. There might be some reason in improvements voting; a brick house or a dutch barn; but none at all in the mere *brutum tellus* of an estate.

This led the way to an hypothesis, that property in moveables should alone entitle; and

this, after some debate, began to be narrowed down to property in *living animals;* especially to useful quadrupeds, and those of full growth, and who had come to years, I will not say of discretion, but of maturity. From the light thrown upon the subject, the right of suffrage to grown cattle had become so popular, that there was no resisting it; not that viva voce it was proposed or thought of that inarticulating speaking creatures should speak out, or name   10 their representatives, nor even that they should give in a ballot, but that they should be brought upon the ground to shew their faces, that there might be no imposition, the voters alleging that they had cattle when they had not.

But it was not to every owner's beast that it was advisable to extend the right; but only to the more valuable animals; or such as were of a good breed; Virginia horses that are fit for the saddle or the turf.   20

It may seem very strange; but actually the thing took; and at a polling some time after, it began to be carried into effect that beasts should be constituents, and have their representatives. It was not the principle, but to the individual beast that some exceptions took place; as for instance, an English bull was brought upon the hustings to give his vote. We will have no English bull said the inspectors. Not that a brute beast is not entitled to a vote;   30 nor that a bull cannot vote, or be voted for; but this is an *English bull*. No English bull can vote. You might as well bring an Englishman himself, to the polls. It is in right of the bull keeper, or rather bull-owner, that the bull claims the suffrage. If an Englishman himself, not naturalized, is excluded, how can his bull or his horse, or any other quadruped be admitted? It would be sufficient to set aside the election if his ticket was introduced. A bull indeed!   40 The name of John Bull is appropriate to an Englishman. An Irish bull is quite another matter; John Bull shall have no vote here.

In the mean time, a man on an iron-grey horse rode up to the window, which was open for receiving tickets, and unequivocally insisted on a vote for his horse. Vouchers stood by, who averred that he was foaled in the country, that, horse and colt, they had known him many years; that as to his paying taxes, they could   50 not so well say, unless his labour on the farm could be considered as paying tax.

In the mean time, the horse putting his nose in at the window, taking it for a rack, an inspector gave him a fillup on the snout, which resenting; the owner wheeling round, the horse wheeling under him, he rode over one or more of the bystanders who were in the way.

Certain it is, the horse was a meritorious horse, having seen service in the campaign under General Wayne against the Indians in 1793. Nevertheless, they that had been rode over did not brook the affront, or put up with it unrevenged; for calling out horse, horse, to which some added the word stolen, as fame increases as it goes, it was echoed along the lines *stolen horse;* upon which the man was apprehended, and carried before a magistrate, who not having heard of the right of beasts to vote, thought this story improbable as he related what had passed at the window of the election house, and for want of proper bail he was committed.

It may be material to mention that the horse's mane and tail were black to distinguish him from a grey horse that belonged to another person. I have known several that knew the horse; but who were not present on the occasion to which we refer, and so, will not undertake to vouch for the truth of it, not having charged their memory with it, or taken a note of it at the moment it occurred. Or it may be, they do not chuse to recollect it, or give information on the subject, thinking it prudent not to involve themselves on elective disputes, as there is no knowing, when parties run high, how far the bare vouching for a fact may involve one. Such is the result of strong passions when not under controul of reason and reflection. Weak persons are always the most positive, because they cannot afford the acknowledgment of an error. It will not do to admit fallibility; for there is no knowing how far the inference may be drawn.

Another man came up who brought a sheep to the polls; a merino ram, who, he said, was entitled to a vote, having resided in the country, since he had been brought in by Humphreys,[1] representing him to be of the breed of the great Fezzen ram, though there were those who thought it might be what is called a yankey trick; not but, that all Americans may be capable of substituting a thing for what it is not; and all are called Yankees by the British; but New-England men are distinguished; and called Yankee Doodles.

The ram is not entitled to a vote said the inspector, nor ought he to be permitted to put in a ticket, were he of the breed of the golden fleece guarded by the fiery dragons whom Jason

overcame; and brought away the wool; no; not if he was the very ram that was caught in the thicket; or that Daniel saw in his vision coupled with the he goat. But he is a Spanish ram born under despotism, how can he be expected to give a republican vote; of papist origin, he may bring the inquisition with him; coming here to vote. Besides, this is a very real sheep, that is offered; and not one whom we call a sheep in a figurative sense of the word. Where we call men horses, or asses, we do not mean always that they are so, *puris naturalibus,* without overalls on, with the horn and the hoof about them, but shadowing forth the same thing under a veil of metaphor, as the case may be. But not on this ground altogether do I reject him; and because he has wool on his back; but, because he is of barbary origin. The Moors brought the breed into Spain. You may cast a *sheep's eye* at the window as long as you please, master ram; but not a vote shall you have as long as I am here. I do not know whether you are not a half breed, and no genuine merino. So away with him, as the song says,

"To the ewe-boughts,[2] Marian."

Another person coming up, brought a large ox, which he called Thomas Jefferson; not out of respect to the ox, but to the man, as having a good name and reputation. Make way, said the voters, for Thomas Jefferson. We will have no Thomas Jeffersons, said the inspector; he is out of his district. I assert the contrary, said the owner; he was calved in this settlement. He is called the mammoth ox, and I had thought of driving him to Washington; but that I knew, however he might be made a present to Jefferson, the congress would eat him, as they did the mammoth cheese; so that the president would scarcely get a slice of him. For there are parasites in all countries; and the worthless are chiefly those who dance attendance upon men in office; and how can it be avoided to invite them to partake of civilities? You will certainly allow a vote to Thomas Jefferson.—No; not if he was the real Jefferson from Monticello, said the inspector. How can I tell but he may introduce the same politics? That is true, said another; break judges, abolish taxes, dismantle navies, build gunboats, lay embargoes, depress armies, pay tributes to barbary powers, issue proclamations, wear red breeches, receive ambassadors in pantaloons and slippers, collect prairie dogs, and horned frogs, dream of salt

[1] David Humphreys, the Connecticut poet, was minister to Lisbon and Madrid from 1791 to 1802. On his return to America he was allowed to export from Spain a flock of Merino sheep.

[2] Sheep-folds.

mountains, walk with Pedimetres, and be *under French influence*. We will have no Thomas Jefferson. You may drive off your ox. He shall have no vote here.

No doubt the judges and inspectors, being men of sense, saw the absurdity of carrying the principle so far into practice, as to admit the representation of property, by this property being itself, and in its own individual existence, the constituent. But not thinking it safe, or practicable, to resist this temporary phrenzy, and misconception of things, by a direct resistance, it became necessary, by indirect means to avoid it. To lay it down in the face of the multitude that these new voters had not a right, would not have been endured; but parrying it by questioning the right in a particular case, gave no umbrage. It was saving the principle, though it denied the exercise.

The man that had rode down the bystanders, and was taken up for a horse thief, was pardoned by the governor. This was done to get quit of the investigation; the governor thinking it for the credit of the country that there should be nothing said about the occasion, and manner of the felony; or the mistake under which the imputation had arisen.

But, party spirit at this time had begun to run high; some insisting on the right of suffrage to their cattle; and others considering it a burlesque. You might have seen shilelahs in the air, and several bullocks were knocked down that were brought up to the polls. A lad was tumbled from his palfry as he was riding him to water, under an idea that he was bringing him to aid the adverse ticket. The lad was somewhat hurt by the fall, and the steed ran off, and could not be caught again until salt was shewn him, and oats in a hat, some one crying cope, cope. The ram that had been offered, seeing arrive the sheep, cried ba; and it was insisted that he had been given his vote, which the candidate against whom it was taken down, resented; and hit the tup a stroke, that, in the sailor's phrase, brought him on his beam ends. —The blow, however, which was aimed at a pig in a poke, which a man was carrying home, and which was heard to squeal; struck the man himself: What, said the assailant, are you bringing here the swinish multitude to vote?

Nevertheless, it was not so much the admitting quadrupeds, but unqualified cattle that became the subject of the controversy; intelligent persons arguing that it was a thing shameful in itself, and unjust. Because it was a fraud upon the whole community, that stragglers should be brought forward, which the individuals concerned in the fraud reconciled to himself on the score of serving the party: That it required some refinement to be aware of the indelicacy of urging an improper vote. Was it reasonable to suppose that a horse creature could give an independent vote, that was in the power of his owner to be stinted of his oats, and rode faster or slower as he thought proper, on a journey? Was it reasonable to expect that the ox would think differently on political subjects from his master? Should he venture to dissent, a crack of the whip or the spur, would bring him to his senses. Even a rational creature, that may be supposed to have more fortitude, is usually in subjection to the master, in matter of opinion, where he is a slave. It is for this reason that slaves are excluded.—Whatever might plausibly be said as to the expediency of extending the privilege of citizenship to those animals that are *feræ naturæ*, and are at their own hands in a forest, it is quite another matter as far as it respects domesticated animals, that have no will of their own, but are under dominion, whether subjugated to a plough or a team. The wild animals that roam, have some spirit of independence. They would starve before they would tamely submit themselves to arbitrary rule, and government. Hence it is, that traps are used. It requires shooting to bring some of them to terms. But an ox may be goaded into acquiescence. He does not drink whiskey, it is true; and for that reason, it cannot be said that whiskey will purchase him; but is there nothing to be done with good grass? The inticements are various that might be held out to allure from the independence of his own judgment.

As to horses voting on the occasion we are speaking of, so far as matter of fact is concerned, I admit it has been denied. For, that though a great number of horses were seen to be ridden up; yet it is usual to go on horseback to elections, especially when the voters have to come from some distance; so that the mere circumstance of being on the ground, is no conclusive evidence of having given a vote; and this I am the more careful to note, as in the case of a new government, that like an individual, has a character, in some measure, to establish, it is of moment, that what is groundlessly alleged, be explained. At the same time, I am aware of the impolicy of denying a thing in toto where there is any foundation;—were there no other reason that would induce an his-

torian to adhere to the truth. For even where a man is pressing a matter that is difficult to be believed, and he has nothing in truth to concede, he will yield a little, skilfully, in order to give the impression of candour, and secure belief to the more important points. How much more does it behoove a writer to be careful of insisting on the freedom from all blame on the part of those whom he advocates, lest that he
10 bring in question the veracity of his relation, where he has every thing on his side. I do not therefore say positively, that the inspectors and judges of the election, in some districts, were not deceived, and their vigilance baffled; or that they did not connive. For that would be saying too much, considering the nature of affairs. The most vigilant cannot always watch; and the most severe in their notions of the rights of persons, may indulge. But, granting
20 that some horse creatures did vote, with their riders on their backs, does it follow that the inspectors had notice of it; or that the persons who usually stand by and vouch for the right of suffrage to the individual, were not to blame.— They may have announced their names as rational persons; and under that idea may have got their votes taken. I have been the more careful in throwing out these hints, because if it were once admitted that such votes did pass,
30 unless surreptitiously, and *sub silentio*, it might grow into precedent. And we well know, that in matters of political and legal law, precedent has the force of authority. It may be suggested as not fairly presumable that inspectors and judges could be deceived. I have seen too much of elections not to think that practice to be unfair, where an individual, powerful for wealth or family, is a candidate, or where there is a contest of party somewhat violent; and unprin-
40 cipled and daring individuals, will take their stations, and act as common vouchers on an

election day, as to the name, age, freedom, or estate of the person who offers a vote. He will be supported by pugilists, or persons prepared with clubs, who though they do not actually strike, will menace with this appearance of force, and intimidate those who might dispute the vouching that is given. I consider all this as immoral and unbecoming a good citizen. But I have seen even inspectors and judges intimidated by this shew of hostility; and I would not wonder if I were to hear that under this awe, in some places, improper votes were taken. Not that I would excuse this timidity of officers, as lessening it from a misdemeanor, to a mere neglect of duty. I reprehend both the overawing and the being overawed in the discharge of a public trust.

But in justice to the character of the country, I incline to think after all that has been reported to the contrary, that instances of beasts voting were more rare than is imagined; and that a considerable foundation of what has gone abroad on this head, was the epithets bestowed by the contending parties calling one another beasts; such as horses, asses, sheep, buffaloes, oxen, and the names of other cattle. All this metaphorically, just as persons of a less polished education, where they dispute on literary or theological subjects, call each other geese, sucking pigs, or turkey-buzzards. I have heard even well bred persons speak of their antagonists after a warm debate, as wood-peckers and mire-snipes. In political controversies, it is no uncommon thing to bestow the epithets of jackass. I have heard even an accomplished lady, use the term monkey, speaking on an individual of the other sex. It would be endless to enumerate such instances of the application of terms, that do not in themselves import the natural form or metamorphose of any person.

1815

CHARLES BROCKDEN BROWN

1771–1810

IF WE disregard such imitations of English models as W. H. Brown's *The Power of Sympathy* (1789) and Susanna Rowson's *Charlotte Temple* (1790), we may say that the art of fiction in America begins with the radical, forward-looking novels of Charles Brockden Brown, from whom a line of descent may be traced to Poe, Melville, Hawthorne, and Henry James. A precocious, humorless youth, grasping eagerly at knowledge, he speedily turned from the law to literature with full realization of what a precarious living it would yield. Moving from Philadelphia to New York in 1793, he found congenial company in the Friendly Club, whose membership included amateurs of letters like his friend Dr. Elihu Hubbard Smith, one of the Connecticut Wits, and William Dunlap, dramatist and painter, and Brown's future biographer.

Before the appearance of *Wieland* in 1798 Brown had written verse, a dialogue on the rights of women (*Alcuin: A Dialogue*, 1798), magazine essays, and a complete novel, *Sky-Walk*, which was printed but not issued. Between 1798 and 1801 novels sprouted from him; at one time he was engaged in writing five. In order of publication his important novels are: *Wieland* (1798), *Ormond* (1799), *Edgar Huntly* (1799), *Arthur Mervyn* (1799–1800), *Clara Howard* (1801), and *Jane Talbot* (1801). From 1803 until 1807 Brown edited a journal of distinction, the *Literary Magazine and American Register*, which encouraged the development of a native American literature. In the last seven years of his life he was increasingly interested in public affairs and finally abandoned fiction for political writing.

The novels of Brown mirror the turbulent ideas of contemporary French and English radical thinkers. Like them he was intensely interested in the influence of environment on character and contemptuous of corrupt social institutions which pervert the individual. His characters trust reason and despise sensibility. From Godwin, whom Brown greatly admired, he undoubtedly took his typical high-minded villain-hero (Welbeck in *Arthur Mervyn*, Carwin in *Wieland*, and Ormond). In the Advertisement to his unpublished *Sky-Walk* he gave a reason for preferring such heroes: "The world is governed, not by the simpleton, but by the man of soaring passions and intellectual energy. By the display of such only can we hope to enchain the attention and ravish the souls of those who study and reflect."

But Brown deserves to be remembered for more than his service in introducing Godwinian radicalism to America. He was our first novelist to place his story realistically in the American scene, whether that was the Indian-haunted Pennsylvania frontier, as in *Edgar Huntly*, or fever-infested Philadelphia, as in *Arthur Mervyn*. He was fascinated by the problems of abnormal psychology and made use of the "science" of his day—ventriloquism, somnambulism, spontaneous combustion—instead of Gothic ghosts to raise the goose flesh of his readers.

In Europe Brown was a favorite with the poets and novelists. Scott borrowed from him. Peacock said of Shelley that "nothing so blended itself with the structure of his interior mind as the creations of Brown." Keats, in writing to a friend of his delight over *Wieland*, concluded, "A strange American scion of the German trunk. Powerful genius—accomplished horror."

Ormond, Ernest Marchand, ed., New York, 1937.
D. L. Clark, *Charles Brockden Brown: Pioneer Voice of America*, Durham, N. C., 1952.
H. R. Warfel, *Charles Brockden Brown, American Gothic Novelist*, Gainesville, Florida, 1942.

» » *From:* EDGAR HUNTLY « «

TO THE PUBLIC

The flattering reception that has been given, by the public, to Arthur Mervyn, has prompted the writer to solicit a continuance of the same favour, and to offer to the world a new performance.

America has opened new views to the naturalist and politician, but has seldom furnished themes to the moral painter. That new springs of action and new motives to curiosity should operate, that the field of investigation, opened to us by our own country, should differ essentially from those which exist in Europe, may be readily conceived. The sources of amusement to the fancy and instruction to the heart, that are peculiar to ourselves, are equally numerous and inexhaustible. It is the purpose of this work to profit by some of these sources; to exhibit a series of adventures, growing out of the condition of our country, and connected with one of the most common and most wonderful diseases or affections of the human frame.

One merit the writer may at least claim: that of calling forth the passions and engaging the sympathy of the reader by means hitherto unemployed by preceding authors. Puerile superstition and exploded manners, Gothic castles and chimeras, are the materials usually employed for this end. The incidents of Indian hostility, and the perils of the Western wilderness, are far more suitable; and for a native of America to overlook these would admit of no apology. These, therefore, are, in part, the ingredients of this tale, and these he has been ambitious of depicting in vivid and faithful colours. The success of his efforts must be estimated by the liberal and candid reader.

CHAPTER XVII

Thus was I delivered from my prison, and restored to the enjoyment of the air and the light. Perhaps the chance was almost miraculous that led me to this opening. In any other direction, I might have involved myself in an inextricable maze and rendered my destruction sure; but what now remained to place me in absolute security? Beyond the fire I could see nothing; but, since the smoke rolled rapidly away, it was plain that on the opposite side the cavern was open to the air.

I went forward, but my eyes were fixed upon the fire; presently, in consequence of changing my station, I perceived several feet, and the skirts of blankets. I was somewhat startled at these appearances. The legs were naked and scored into uncouth figures. The moccasins which lay beside them, and which were adorned in a grotesque manner, in addition to other incidents, immediately suggested the suspicion that they were Indians. No spectacle was more adapted that this to excite wonder and alarm. Had some mysterious power snatched me from the earth, and cast me, in a moment, into the heart of the wilderness? Was I still in the vicinity of my parental habitation, or was I thousands of miles distant?

Were these the permanent inhabitants of this region, or were they wanderers and robbers? While in the heart of the mountain, I had entertained a vague belief that I was still within the precincts of Norwalk. This opinion was shaken for a moment by the objects which I now beheld, but it insensibly returned; yet how was this opinion to be reconciled to appearances so strange and uncouth, and what measure did a due regard to my safety enjoin me to take?

I now gained a view of four brawny and terrific figures, stretched upon the ground. They lay parallel to each other, on their left sides; in consequence of which their faces were turned from me. Between each was an interval where lay a musket. Their right hands seemed placed upon the stocks of their guns, as if to seize them on the first moment of alarm.

The aperture through which these objects were seen was at the back of the cave, and some feet from the ground. It was merely large enough to suffer a human body to pass. It was involved in profound darkness, and there was no danger of being suspected or discovered as long as I maintained silence and kept out of view.

It was easily imagined that these guests would make but a short sojourn in this spot. There was reason to suppose that it was now night, and that, after a short repose, they would start up and resume their journey. It was my first design to remain shrouded in this covert till their departure, and I prepared to endure imprisonment and thirst somewhat longer.

Meanwhile my thoughts were busy in accounting for this spectacle. I need not tell thee that Norwalk is the termination of a sterile and narrow tract which begins in the Indian country. It forms a sort of rugged and rocky vein, continues upwards of fifty miles. It is crossed in a few places by narrow and intricate paths, by which a communication is maintained between the farms and settlements on the opposite sides of the ridge.

During former Indian wars, this rude surface was sometimes traversed by the red-men, and they made, by means of it, frequent and destructive inroads into the heart of the English settlements. During the last war, notwithstanding the progress of population, and the multiplied perils of such an expedition, a band of them had once penetrated into Norwalk, and lingered long enough to pillage and murder some of the neighbouring inhabitants.

I have reason to remember that event. My father's house was placed on the verge of this solitude. Eight of these assassins assailed it at the dead of night. My parents and an infant child were murdered in their beds; the house was pillaged, and then burnt to the ground. Happily, myself and my two sisters were abroad upon a visit. The preceding day had been fixed for our return to our father's house; but a storm occurred, which made it dangerous to cross the river, and, by obliging us to defer our journey, rescued us from captivity or death.

Most men are haunted by some species of terror or antipathy, which they are, for the most part, able to trace to some incident which befell them in their early years. You will not be surprised that the fate of my parents, and the sight of the body of one of this savage band, who, in the pursuit that was made after them, was overtaken and killed, should produce lasting and terrific images in my fancy. I never looked upon or called up the image of a savage without shuddering.

I knew that, at this time, some hostilities had been committed on the frontier; that a long course of injuries and encroachments had lately exasperated the Indian tribes; that an implacable and exterminating war was generally expected. We imagined ourselves at an inaccessible distance from the danger, but I could not but remember that this persuasion was formerly as strong as at present, and that an expedition which had once succeeded might possibly be attempted again. Here was every token of enmity and bloodshed. Each prostrate figure was furnished with a rifled musket, and a leathern bag tied round his waist, which was, probably, stored with powder and ball.

From these reflections, the sense of my own danger was revived and enforced, but I likewise ruminated on the evils which might impend over others. I should, no doubt, be safe by remaining in this nook; but might not some means be pursued to warn others of their danger? Should they leave this spot without notice of their approach being given to the fearless and pacific tenants of the neighbouring district, they might commit, in a few hours, the most horrid and irreparable devastation.

The alarm could only be diffused in one way. Could I not escape, unperceived, and without alarming the sleepers, from this cavern? The slumber of an Indian is broken by the slightest noise; but, if all noise be precluded, it is commonly profound. It was possible, I conceived, to leave my present post, to descend into the cave, and issue forth without the smallest signal. Their supine posture assured me that they were asleep. Sleep usually

comes at their bidding, and if, perchance, they should be wakeful at an unseasonable moment, they always sit on their haunches, and, leaning their elbows on their knees, consume the tedious hours in smoking. My peril would be great. Accidents which I could not forsee, and over which I had no command, might occur to awaken someone at the moment I was passing the fire. Should I pass in safety, I might issue forth into a wilderness, of which I had no knowledge, where I might wander till I perished with famine, or where my footsteps might be noted and pursued and overtaken by these implacable foes. These perils were enormous and imminent; but I likewise considered that I might be at no great distance from the habitations of men, and that my escape might rescue them from the most dreadful calamities. I determined to make this dangerous experiment without delay.

I came nearer to the aperture, and had, consequently, a larger view of this recess. To my unspeakable dismay, I now caught a glimpse of one seated at the fire. His back was turned towards me so that I could distinctly survey his gigantic form and fantastic ornaments.

My project was frustrated. This one was probably commissioned to watch and to awaken his companions when a due portion of sleep had been taken. That he would not be unfaithful or remiss in the performance of the part assigned to him was easily predicted. To pass him without exciting his notice (and the entrance could not otherwise be reached) was impossible. Once more I shrunk back, and revolved with hopelessness and anguish the necessity to which I was reduced.

This interval of dreary foreboding did not last long. Some motion in him that was seated by the fire attracted my notice. I looked, and beheld him rise from his place and go forth from the cavern. This unexpected incident led my thoughts into a new channel. Could not some advantage be taken of his absence? Could not this opportunity be seized for making my escape? He had left his gun and hatchet on the ground. It was likely, therefore, that he had not gone far, and would speedily return. Might not these weapons be seized and some provision thus be made against the danger of meeting him without, or of being pursued?

Before a resolution could be formed, a new sound saluted my ear. It was a deep groan, succeeded by sobs that seemed struggling for utterance but were vehemently counteracted by the sufferer. This low and bitter lamentation apparently proceeded from some one within the cave. It could not be from one of this swarthy band. It must, then, proceed from a captive, whom they had reserved for torment or servitude, and who had seized the opportunity afforded by the absence of him that watched to give vent to his despair.

I again thrust my head forward, and beheld, lying on the ground, apart from the rest, and bound hand and foot, a young girl. Her dress was the coarse russet garb of the country, and bespoke her to be some farmer's daughter. Her features denoted the last degree of fear and anguish, and she moved her limbs in such a manner as showed that the ligatures by which she was confined produced, by their tightness, the utmost degree of pain.

My wishes were now bent not only to preserve myself and to frustrate the future attempts of these savages, but likewise to relieve this miserable victim. This could only be done by escaping from the cavern and returning with seasonable aid. The sobs of the girl were likely to rouse the sleepers. My appearance before her would prompt her to testify her surprise by some exclamation or shriek. What could hence be predicted but that the band would start on their feet and level their unerring pieces at my head!

I know not why I was insensible to these dangers. My thirst was rendered by these delays intolerable. It took from me, in some degree, the power of deliberation. The murmurs which had drawn me hither continued still to be heard. Some torrent or cascade could not be far distant from the entrance of the cavern, and it seemed as if one draught of clear water was a luxury cheaply purchased by death itself. This, in addition to considerations more disinterested, and which I have already mentioned, impelled me forward.

The girl's cheek rested on the hard rock, and her eyes were dim with tears. As they were turned towards me, however, I hoped that my movements would be noticed by her gradually and without abruptness. This expectation was fulfilled. I had not advanced many steps before she discovered me. This moment was critical beyond all others in the course of my existence. My life was suspended, as it were, by a spider's thread. All rested on the effect which this discovery should make upon this feeble victim.

I was watchful of the first movement of her eye which should indicate a consciousness of my presence. I laboured, by gestures and looks, to deter her from betraying her emotion. My attention was, at the same time, fixed upon the sleepers, and an anxious glance was cast towards the quarter whence the watchful savage might appear.

I stooped and seized the musket and hatchet. The space beyond the fire was, as I expected, open to the air. I issued forth with trembling steps. The sensations inspired by the dangers which environed me, added to my recent horrors, and the influence of the moon, which had now gained the zenith, and whose lustre dazzled my long-benighted senses, cannot be adequately described.

For a minute, I was unable to distinguish objects. This confusion was speedily corrected, and I found myself on the verge of a steep. Craggy eminences arose on all sides. On the left hand was a space that offered some footing, and hither I turned. A torrent was below me, and this path appeared to lead to it. It quickly appeared in sight, and all foreign cares were, for a time, suspended.

This water fell from the upper regions of the hill, upon a flat projecture which was continued on either side, and on part of which I was now standing. The path was bounded on the left by an inaccessible wall, and on the right terminated, at the distance of two or three feet from the wall, in a precipice. The water was eight or ten paces distant, and no impediment seemed likely to rise between us. I rushed forward with speed.

My progress was quickly checked. Close to the falling water, seated on the edge, his back supported by the rock, and his legs hanging over the precipice, I now beheld the savage who left the cave before me. The noise of the cascade and the improbability of interruption, at least from this quarter, had made him inattentive to my motions.

I paused. Along this verge lay the only road by which I could reach the water, and by which I could escape. The passage was completely occupied by this antagonist. To advance towards him, or to remain where I was, would produce the same effect. I should, in either case, be detected. He was unarmed; but his outcries would instantly summon his companions to his aid. I could not hope to overpower him, and pass him in defiance of his opposition. But, if this were effected, pursuit would be instantly commenced. I was unacquainted with the way. The way was unquestionably difficult. My strength was nearly annihilated; I should be overtaken in a moment, or their deficiency in speed would be supplied by the accuracy of their aim. Their bullets, at least, would reach me.

There was one method of removing this impediment. The piece which I held in my hand was cocked. There could be no doubt that it was loaded. A precaution of this kind would never be omitted by a warrior of this hue. At a greater distance than this, I should not fear to reach the mark. Should I not discharge it, and, at the same moment, rush forward to secure the road which my adversary's death would open to me?

Perhaps you will conceive a purpose like this to have argued a sanguinary and murderous disposition. Let it be remembered, however, that I entertained no doubts about the hostile designs of these men. This was sufficiently indicated by their arms, their guise, and the captive who attended them. Let the fate of my parents be, likewise, remembered. I was not certain but that these very men were the assassins of my family, and were those who had reduced me and my sisters to the condition of orphans and dependants. No words can describe the torments of my thirst. Relief to these torments, and safety to my life, were within view. How could I hesitate?

Yet I did hesitate. My aversion to bloodshed was not to be subdued but by the direst necessity. I knew, indeed, that the discharge of a musket would only alarm the enemies who remained behind; but I had another and a better weapon in my grasp. I could rive the head of my adversary, and cast him headlong, without any noise which should be heard, into the cavern.

Still I was willing to withdraw, to re-enter the cave, and take shelter in the darksome recesses from which I had emerged. Here I might remain, unsuspected, till these detested guests should depart. The hazards attending my reentrance were to be boldly encountered, and the torments of unsatisfied thirst were to be patiently endured, rather than imbrue my hands in the blood of my fellow-men. But this expedient would be ineffectual if my retreat should be observed by this savage. Of that I was bound to be incontestably assured. I retreated, therefore, but kept my eye fixed at the same time upon the enemy.

Some ill fate decreed that I should not retreat unobserved. Scarcely had I withdrawn three paces when he started from his seat, and, turning towards me, walked with a quick pace. The shadow of the rock, and the improbability of meeting an enemy here, concealed me for a moment from his observation. I stood still. The slightest motion would have attracted his notice. At present, the narrow space engaged all his vigilance. Cautious footsteps, and attention to the path, were indespensable to his safety. The respite was momentary, and I employed it in my own defence.

How otherwise could I act? The danger that impended aimed at nothing less than my life. To take the life of another was the only method of averting it. The means were in my hand, and they were used. In an extremity like this, my muscles would have acted almost in defiance of my will.

The stroke was quick as lightning, and the wound mortal and deep. He had not time to descry the author of his fate, but, sinking on the path, expired without a groan. The hatchet buried itself in his breast, and rolled with him to the bottom of the precipice.

Never before had I taken the life of a human creature. On this head I had, indeed, entertained somewhat of religious scruples. These scruples did not forbid me to defend myself, but they made me cautious and reluctant to decide. Though they could not withhold my hand when urged by a necessity like this, they were sufficient to make me look back upon the deed with remorse and dismay.

I did not escape all compunction in the present instance, but the tumult of my feelings was quickly allayed. To quench my thirst was a consideration by which all others were supplanted. I approached the torrent, and not only drank copiously, but laved my head, neck, and arms, in this delicious element.

CHAPTER XVIII

Never was any delight worthy of comparison with the raptures which I then experienced. Life, that was rapidly ebbing, appeared to return upon me with redoubled violence. My languors, my excruciating heat, vanished in a moment, and I felt prepared to undergo the labours of Hercules. Having fully supplied the demands of nature in this respect, I returned to reflection on the circumstances of my situation. The path winding round the hill was now free from all impediments. What remained but to precipitate my flight? I might speedily place myself beyond all danger. I might gain some hospitable shelter, where my fatigues might be repaired by repose, and my wounds be cured. I might likewise impart to my protectors seasonable information of the enemies who meditated their destruction.

I thought upon the condition of the hapless girl whom I had left in the power of the savages. Was it impossible to rescue her? Might I not relieve her from her bonds, and make her the companion of my flight? The exploit was perilous, but not impracticable. There was something dastardly and ignominious in withdrawing from the danger, and leaving a helpless being exposed to it. A single minute might suffice to snatch her from death or captivity. The parents might deserve that I should hazard or even sacrifice my life in the cause of their child.

After some fluctuation, I determined to return to the cavern and attempt the rescue of the girl. The success of this project depended on the continuance of their sleep. It was proper to approach with wariness, and to heed the smallest token which might bespeak their condition. I crept along the path, bending my ear forward to catch any sound that might arise. I heard nothing but the half-stifled sobs of the girl.

I entered with the slowest and most anxious circumspection. Every thing was found in its pristine state. The girl noticed my entrance with a mixture of terror and joy. My gestures and looks enjoined upon her silence. I stooped down, and, taking another hatchet, cut asunder the deer-skin thongs by which her wrists and ankles were tied. I then made signs for her to rise and follow me. She willingly complied with my directions; but her benumbed joints and lacerated sinews refused to support her. There was no time to be lost; I therefore lifted her in my arms, and, feeble and tottering as I was, proceeded with this burthen along the perilous steep and over a most rugged path.

I hoped that some exertion would enable her to retrieve the use of her limbs. I set her, therefore, on her feet, exhorting her to walk as well as she was able, and promising her my occasional assistance. The poor girl was not deficient in zeal, and presently moved along with light and quick steps. We speedily reached the bottom of the hill. . . .   1799

WASHINGTON IRVING

1783–1859

NO ONE but Washington Irving could have convinced the English, determined to believe that Americans were all but illiterate, that the arts could flourish here. Genial, liked by nearly everyone, he moved in the best London society without being in the slightest degree a tuft-hunter. In the 1820's in England three men of letters were the rage: Scott, Byron, and, after them, Irving. His *Sketch Book* (1819–1820) and *Bracebridge Hall* (1822) made the perfect rejoinder to the Reverend Sydney Smith's sneer of 1820: "In the four quarters of the globe who reads an American book?" The answer in London, at the moment, was "Everybody." Irving's fellow countrymen were not slow in their gratitude. When he returned home in 1832, after an absence of seventeen years, he was publicly feasted and attempts were made to thrust office upon him. American authors flattered him by imitation. Only writers with a robust and original genius, like Melville, protested against Irving's domination of our literature during the first half of the century.

Irving grew up in a provincially aristocratic New York which was soon to become the commercial metropolis of the country. Though frail, as a boy he roamed the town and the surrounding regions along the Hudson with his companions and enjoyed stealthy visits to the John Street Theater, forbidden by his Presbyterian father. In 1801 he began to read law, but though admitted to the bar he never followed the profession seriously. Back from a two-year visit to

Europe, during which he had seen much of the fashionable world, he was in 1806 the center of a group of literary young men called the "Nine Worthies." Out of their hilarious sessions at the Kemble House on the Passaic River came a periodical, *Salmagundi* (1807–1808), one of the innumerable imitations of the *Spectator*. New York was delighted and sufficiently scandalized. In the following year appeared Irving's first independent work, Diedrich Knickerbocker's *History of New York*, begun as a burlesque history but containing a good deal of topical satire against Jefferson. In 1810 Irving became a partner in the family's hardware business. Between this date and the time of his setting out for England (1815) to take over the firm's Liverpool branch, his only literary venture was the editorship of the *Analectic Magazine*, a pale American reflex of *Blackwood's*.

In 1818 the Irving firm went into bankruptcy. The moment was decisive. Irving took the bolder way and cast loose from business, determined to make a living by his pen. He was already known in London literary circles. Scott had entertained him warmly in Abbotsford in 1817. Nevertheless the risk was great for one who had written nothing in eight years. The success of the *Sketch Book*, with its diverting story of Rip van Winkle, was reassuring. *Bracebridge Hall* and *Tales of a Traveller* (1824) worked the same vein. In 1826 Irving went to Madrid as a member of the American Legation. The glamorous past of Spain stirred him emotionally. Under this stimulus his *Life and Voyages of Columbus* (1828), the *Conquest of Granada* (1829), and *The Alhambra* (1832) were written with unusual speed.

On returning to America in 1832 Irving made considerable effort to understand the tremendous changes which had taken place during his absence. America, with Jackson in power, was now a democracy in fact. Irving's experiences while on an expedition through the southwest in 1832, which was the basis of his *Tour on the Prairies* (1835), did little, however, to show him the significance of the frontier in American life. Nor did he, when employed by John Jacob Astor to write the history of his fur-trading company, penetrate in *Astoria* (1836) beneath the surface of adventure to the real story of exploitation with which a more acute historian would have had to deal. Aside from one other book dealing with the frontier, *Captain Bonneville* (1837), Irving's last work was a fairly pedestrian biography, *Goldsmith* (1840), *Mahomet* (1849–1850), and *Washington* (1855–1859). His leisured life at his gothic villa "Sunnyside," near Tarrytown, New York, was broken between 1842 and 1845 by his service as minister to Spain.

It was Irving's virtue as a writer that he knew his limitations. Composition was difficult for him; invention next to impossible. (His tales can easily be traced to their sources.) He wisely stuck to the sketch and short tale because, as he said, "I choose to take a line of writing peculiar to myself." The long biographies called into play his antiquarian enthusiasms, his ability to write a smooth narrative and to delineate character. Critics are fond of saying that with Irving the style is everything. Irving himself declared that he wished, "to write in such a manner that my productions may have more than the mere interest of narrative to recommend them, . . . something, if I dare use the phrase, of classic merit, i.e., depending upon style, etc." But style is always expressive of something. What Irving achieved was a perfect vehicle for the expression of his peculiar view of the world.

What was that view, which still invites, though we are aware that life was for Irving always a retreat into the past? He stands closer to the English preromantics, like Gray and Walpole, than to poets like Wordsworth and Emerson who represent the romantic movement in its more powerful manifestations. Like the preromantics, he was still a man of common sense, but he liked a little mystery added to the landscape if he were quite sure the mystery would not engulf him. This appetite for the picturesque, which induced him to shade and sentimentalize what he observed, prevented him from seeing all he might have seen in *A Tour on the Prairies*, but in

Bracebridge Hall it gave just the desired relish to the commonplaces of English country life. Neither account is true, but each reveals what thousands of readers were glad to believe was the truth.

For one who was in so good a position to observe the political scene in Europe and America Irving was singularly imperceptive. Compared with the judgments of Cooper, Emerson, and Melville, his remarks on American life are naive and uncritical. By inheritance a Federalist, Irving became, after his return to America, an adherent of the Democratic party, from which he received in 1842 the post of Minister to Spain. But for all his good-humored tolerance toward Jackson, of whom he said, "The more I see of this old cock of the woods, the more I relish his game qualities," Irving feared the "subversive" doctrines of the Loco-focos, the democratic radicals of the day. Any attempt to limit the power or wealth of the great trading and financial classes would, in his eyes, endanger the country.

Except for the anti-Jefferson satire in the *Salmagundi* papers and *Knickerbocker's History* there is little politics in Irving's prose. He was striving to create something which would outlive the times, and the intrusion of the issues of the moment would nullify that attempt. Yet his bias toward conservatism and compromise is evident whether he is writing of Abbotsford or Astoria. As V. L. Parrington significantly noted, Irving, in his last work, unconsciously returned to the political principles of his youth, and wrote an account of Washington's administrations deeply colored by his Federalist sources.

S. T. Williams and M. E. Edge, *A Bibliography of the Writings of Washington Irving: A Check List*, New York, 1936.
W. R. Langfield, *Washington Irving: A Bibliography*, New York, 1933.
The Works of Washington Irving, Author's uniform revised edition, 21 vols., New York, 1860–1861.
Washington Irving, Representative Selections, with Introduction, Bibliography, and Notes (American Writers Series), H. A. Pochmann, ed., New York, 1934.
P. M. Irving, *The Life and Letters of Washington Irving, by His Nephew*, 4 vols., New York, 1862–1864.
Laura Benet, *Washington Irving, Explorer of American Legend*, New York, 1944.
H. A. Pochmann, "Irving's German Sources in *The Sketch Book*," *Studies in Philology*, XXVII (July, 1930), 477–507.
S. T. Williams, *The Life of Washington Irving*, 2 vols., New York, 1935.

» » *From:* A HISTORY OF NEW YORK[1] « «

BOOK IV. CONTAINING THE
CHRONICLES OF THE REIGN
OF WILLIAM THE TESTY [2]

CHAPTER I

Showing the Nature of History in General; Containing, Farthermore, the Universal Acquirements of William the Testy, and How a Man May Learn So Much as to Render Himself Good for Nothing

When the lofty Thucydides is about to enter

upon his description of the plague that desolated Athens, one of his modern commentators assures the reader, that the history is now going to be exceeding solemn, serious, and pathetic; and hints, with that air of chuckling gratulation with which a good dame draws forth a choice morsel from a cupboard to regale a favorite, that this plague will give his history a most agreeable variety.

In like manner did my heart leap within me, when I came to the dolorous dilemma of Fort Goed Hope, which I at once perceived to be the forerunner of a series of great events and entertaining disasters. Such are the true subjects for the historic pen. For what is history, in fact, but a kind of Newgate calendar, a register of the crimes and miseries that man has in-

---

[1] "Diedrich Knickerbocker's" *History of New York, from the Beginning of the World to the End of the Dutch Dynasty* was revised several times by Irving, particularly for the editions of 1812 and 1848. The present text includes Irving's late revisions.
[2] Irving satirizes Thomas Jefferson under the name of William the Testy. The reader familiar with the Federalists' method of ridiculing Jefferson will notice here their reiterated taunts: that he was a pedant, a dabbler in science, a vivisectionist, a pacifist. Many events of Jefferson's administration are burlesqued.

flicted on his fellow-man? It is a huge libel on human nature, to which we industriously add page after page, volume after volume, as if we were building up a monument to the honor, rather than the infamy of our species. If we turn over the pages of these chronicles that man has written of himself, what are the characters dignified by the appellation of great, and held up to the admiration of posterity? Tyrants, robbers, conquerors, renowned only for the magnitude of their misdeeds, and the stupendous wrongs and miseries they have inflicted on mankind—warriors, who had hired themselves to the trade of blood, not from motives of virtuous patriotism, or to protect the injured and defenceless, but merely to gain the vaunted glory of being adroit and successful in massacring their fellow-beings! What are the great events that constitute a glorious era?—The fall of empires—the desolation of happy countries —splendid cities smoking in their ruins—the proudest works of art tumbled in the dust— the shrieks and groans of whole nations ascending unto heaven!

It is thus the historian may be said to thrive on the miseries of mankind, like birds of prey which hover over the field of battle, to fatten on the mighty dead. It was observed by a great projector of inland lock navigation, that rivers, lakes, and oceans, were only formed to feed canals.—In like manner I am tempted to believe, that plots, conspiracies, wars, victories, and massacres, are ordained by Providence only as food for the historian.

It is a source of great delight to the philosopher, in studying the wonderful economy of nature, to trace the mutual dependencies of things, how they are created reciprocally for each other, and how the most noxious and apparently unnecessary animal has its uses. Thus those swarms of flies, which are so often execrated as useless vermin, are created for the sustenance of spiders—and spiders, on the other hand, are evidently made to devour flies. So those heroes who have been such scourges to the world, were bounteously provided as themes for the poet and historian, while the poet and the historian were destined to record the achievements of heroes!

These, and many similar reflections, naturally arose in my mind, as I took up my pen to commence the reign of William Kieft: for now the stream of our history, which hitherto has rolled in a tranquil current, is about to depart forever from its peaceful haunts, and

brawl through many a turbulent and rugged scene.

As some sleek ox, sunk in the rich repose of a clover-field, dozing and chewing the cud, will bear repeated blows before it raises itself; so the province of Nieuw Nederlandts, having waxed fat under the drowsy reign of the Doubter, needed cuffs and kicks to rouse it into action. The reader will now witness the manner in which a peaceful community advances towards a state of war; which is apt to be like the approach of a horse to a drum, with much prancing and little progress, and too often with the wrong end foremost.

Wilhelmus Kieft, who, in 1634, ascended the gubernatorial chair (to borrow a favorite though clumsy appellation of modern phraseologists), was of a lofty descent, his father being inspector of wind-mills in the ancient town of Saardam; and our hero, we are told, when a boy, made very curious investigations into the nature and operation of these machines, which was one reason why he afterwards came to be so ingenious a governor. His name, according to the most authentic etymologists, was a corruption of Kyver; that is to say, a *wrangler* or *scolder;* and expressed the characteristic of his family, which, for nearly two centuries, had kept the windy town of Saardam in hot water, and produced more tartars and brimstones than any ten families in the place; and so truly did he inherit this family peculiarity, that he had not been a year in the government of the province, before he was universally denominated William the Testy. His appearance answered to his name. He was a brisk, wiry, waspish little old gentleman; such a one as may now and then be seen stumping about our city in a broad-skirted coat with huge buttons, a cocked hat stuck on the back of his head, and a cane as high as his chin. His face was broad, but his features were sharp; his cheeks were scorched into a dusky red, by two fiery little gray eyes; his nose turned up, and the corners of his mouth turned down, pretty much like the muzzle of an irritable pug-dog.

I have heard it observed by a profound adept in human physiology, that if a woman waxes fat with the progress of years, her tenure of life is somewhat precarious, but if haply she withers as she grows old, she lives forever. Such promised to be the case with William the Testy, who grew tough in proportion as he dried. He had withered, in fact, not through the process of years, but through the tropical fervor of his soul, which burnt like a vehement rush-light in his bosom; inciting him to incessant broils and bickerings. Ancient traditions speak much of his learning, and of the gallant inroads he had made into the dead languages, in which he had made captive a host of Greek nouns and Latin verbs; and brought off rich booty in ancient saws and apothegms; which he was wont to parade in his public harangues, as a triumphant general of yore, his *spolia opima.* Of metaphysics he knew enough to confound all hearers and himself into the bargain. In logic, he knew the whole family of syllogisms and dilemmas, and was so proud of his skill that he never suffered even a self-evident fact to pass unargued. It was observed, however, that he seldom got into an argument without getting into a perplexity, and then into a passion with his adversary for not being convinced gratis.

He had, moreover, skirmished smartly on the frontiers of several of the sciences, was fond of experimental philosophy, and prided himself upon inventions of all kinds. His abode, which he had fixed at a Bowerie or country-seat at a short distance from the city, just at what is now called Dutch-street, soon abounded with proofs of his ingenuity: patent smokejacks that required a horse to work them; Dutch ovens that roasted meat without fire; carts that went before the horses; weathercocks that turned against the wind; and other wrong-headed contrivances that astonished and confounded all beholders. The house, too, was beset with paralytic cats and dogs, the subjects of his experimental philosophy; and the yelling and yelping of the latter unhappy victims of science, while aiding in the pursuit of knowledge, soon gained for the place the name of "Dog's Misery," by which it continues to be known even at the present day.

It is in knowledge as in swimming; he who flounders and splashes on the surface, makes more noise, and attracts more attention, than the pearl-diver who quietly dives in quest of treasures to the bottom. The vast acquirements of the new governor were the theme of marvel among the simple burghers of New Amsterdam; he figured about the place as learned a man as a Bonze at Pekin, who has mastered one half of the Chinese alphabet: and was unanimously pronounced a "universal genius!"

I have known in my time many a genius of this stamp; but, to speak my mind freely, I never knew one who, for the ordinary purposes of life, was worth his weight in straw. In this respect, a little sound judgment and plain common sense is worth all the sparkling genius that ever wrote poetry or invented theories. Let us see how the universal acquirements of William the Testy aided him in the affairs of government.

CHAPTER II

How William the Testy Undertook to Conquer by Proclamation—How He Was a Great Man Abroad, but a Little Man in His Own House

No sooner had this bustling little potentate been blown by a whiff of fortune into the seat of government than he called his council together to make them a speech on the state of affairs.

Caius Gracchus, it is said, when he harangued the Roman populace, modulated his tone by an oratorical flute or pitchpipe; Wilhelmus Kieft, not having such an instrument at hand, availed himself of that musical organ or trump which nature has implanted in the midst of a man's face; in other words, he preluded his address by a sonorous blast of the nose; a preliminary flourish much in vogue among public orators.

He then commenced by expressing his humble sense of his utter unworthiness of the high post to which he had been appointed; which made some of the simple burghers wonder why he undertook it, not knowing that it is a point of etiquette with a public orator never to enter upon office without declaring himself unworthy to cross the threshold. He then proceeded in a manner highly classic and erudite to speak of government generally, and of the governments of ancient Greece in particular; together with the wars of Rome and Carthage; and the rise and fall of sundry outlandish empires which the worthy burghers had never read nor heard of. Having thus, after the manner of your learned orator, treated of things in general, he came by a natural, roundabout transition, to the matter in hand, namely, the daring aggressions of the Yankees.

As my readers are well aware of the advantage a potentate has of handling his enemies as he pleases in his speeches and bulletins, where he has the talk all on his own side, they may rest assured that William the Testy did not let such an opportunity escape of giving the Yankees what is called "a taste of his quality." In speaking of their inroads into the territories of their High Mightinesses, he compared them to the Gauls who desolated Rome; the Goths and Vandals who overran the fairest plains of Europe; but when he came to speak of the unparalleled audacity with which they of Weathersfield had advanced their patches up to the very walls of Fort Goed Hoop, and threatened to smother the garrison in onions, tears of rage started into his eyes, as though he nosed the very offence in question.

Having thus wrought up his tale to a climax, he assumed a most belligerent look, and assured the council that he had devised an instrument, potent in its effects, and which he trusted would soon drive the Yankees from the land. So saying, he thrust his hand into one of the deep pockets of his broad-skirted coat and drew forth, not an infernal machine, but an instrument in writing, which he laid with great emphasis upon the table.

The burghers gazed at it for a time in silent awe, as a wary housewife does at a gun, fearful it may go off half-cocked. The document in question had a sinister look, it is true; it was crabbed in text, and from a broad red ribbon dangled the great seal of the province, about the size of a buckwheat pancake. Still, after all, it was but an instrument in writing. Herein, however, existed the wonder of the invention. The document in question was a PROCLAMA-TION, ordering the Yankees to depart instantly from the territories of their High Mightinesses under pain of suffering all the forfeitures and punishments in such case made and provided. It was on the moral effect of this formidable instrument that Wilhelmus Kieft calculated; pledging his valor as a governor that, once fulminated against the Yankees, it would, in less than two months, drive every mother's son of them across the borders.

The council broke up in perfect wonder, and nothing was talked of for some time among the old men and women of New Amsterdam but the vast genius of the governor, and his new and cheap mode of fighting by proclamation.

As to Wilhelmus Kieft, having dispatched his proclamation to the frontiers, he put on his cocked hat and corduroy small-clothes, and mounting a tall raw-boned charger, trotted out to his rural retreat of Dog's Misery. Here, like the good Numa, he reposed from the toils of state, taking lessons in government, not from the nymph Egeria, but from the honored wife of his bosom; who was one of that class of females sent upon the earth a little after the flood, as a punishment for the sins of mankind, and commonly known by the appellation of *knowing women*. In fact, my duty as an historian obliges me to make known a circumstance which was a great secret at the time, and consequently was not a subject of scandal at more than half the tea-tables in New Amsterdam, but which, like many other great secrets, has leaked out in the lapse of years—and this was, that Wilhelmus the Testy, though one of the most potent little men that ever breathed, yet submitted at home to a species of government, neither laid down in Aristotle nor Plato; in short, it partook of the nature of a pure, unmixed tyranny, and is familiarly denominated *petticoat government.*—An absolute sway, which, although exceedingly common in these modern days, was very rare among the ancients, if we may judge from the rout made about the domestic economy of honest Socrates; which is the only ancient case on record.

The great Kieft, however, warded off all the sneers and sarcasms of his particular friends, who are ever ready to joke with a man on sore points of the kind, by alleging that it was a government of his own election, to which he submitted through choice; adding at the same time a profound maxim which he had found in an ancient author, that "he who would aspire to *govern*, should first learn to *obey*."

CHAPTER VII

Growing Discontents of New Amsterdam under the Government of William the Testy

It has been remarked by the observant writer of the Stuyvesant manuscript, that under the administration of William Kieft the disposition of the inhabitants of New Amsterdam experienced an essential change, so that they became very meddlesome and factious. The unfortunate propensity of the little governor to experiment and innovation, and the frequent exacerbations of his temper, kept his council in a continual worry; and the council being to the people at large what yeast or leaven is to a batch, they threw the whole community in a ferment; and the people at large being to the city what the mind is to the body, the unhappy commotions they underwent operated most disastrously upon New Amsterdam—insomuch that, in certain of their paroxysms of consternation and perplexity, they begat several of the most crooked, distorted, and abominable streets, lanes, and alleys, with which this metropolis is disfigured.

The fact was, that about this time, the community, like Balaam's ass, began to grow more enlightened than its rider, and to show a disposition for what is called "self government." This restive propensity was first evinced in certain popular meetings, in which the burghers
10 of New Amsterdam met to talk and smoke over the complicated affairs of the province, gradually obfuscating themselves with politics and tobacco-smoke. Hither resorted those idlers and squires of low degree who hang loose on society and are blown about by every wind of doctrine. Cobblers abandoned their stalls to give lessons on political economy; blacksmiths suffered their fires to go out while they stirred up the fires of faction; and even tailors, though said to be
20 the ninth parts of humanity, neglected their own measures to criticize the measures of government.

Strange! that the science of government, which seems to be so generally understood, should invariably be denied to the only one called upon to exercise it. Not one of the politicians in question, but, take his word for it, could have administered affairs ten times better than William the Testy.
30 Under the instructions of these political oracles the good people of New Amsterdam soon became exceedingly enlightened; and, as a matter of course, exceedingly discontented. They gradually found out the fearful error in which they had indulged, of thinking themselves the happiest people in creation; and were convinced that, all circumstances to the contrary notwithstanding, they were a very unhappy, deluded, and consequently ruined
40 people!

We are naturally prone to discontent, and avaricious after imaginary causes of lamentation. Like lubberly monks we belabor our own shoulders, and take a vast satisfaction in the music of our own groans. Nor is this said by way of paradox; daily experience shows the truth of these observations. It is almost impossible to elevate the spirits of a man groaning under ideal calamities; but nothing is easier
50 than to render him wretched, though on the pinnacle of felicity; as it would be an Herculean task to hoist a man to the top of a steeple, though the merest child could topple him off thence.

I must not omit to mention that these popular meetings were generally held at some noted tavern; these public edifices possessing what in modern times are thought the true fountains of political inspiration. The ancient Greeks deliberated upon a matter when drunk, and reconsidered it when sober. Mob politicians in modern times dislike to have two minds upon a subject; so they both deliberate and act when drunk; by this means a world of delay is spared; and as it is universally allowed that a man when drunk sees double, it follows conclusively that he sees twice as well as his sober neighbors.

CHAPTER XII

Containing the Rise of the Great Amphictyonic Council of the Pilgrims, with the Decline and Final Extinction of William the Testy

It was asserted by the wise men of ancient times, who had a nearer opportunity of ascertaining the fact, that at the gate of Jupiter's palace lay two huge tuns, one filled with blessings, the other with misfortunes; and it would verily seem as if the latter had been completely overturned and left to deluge the unlucky province of Nieuw Nederlands: for about this time, while harassed and annoyed from the south and the north, incessant forays were made by the border chivalry of Connecticut upon the pig-stys and hen-roosts of the Nederlanders. Every day or two some broad-bottomed express-rider, covered with mud and mire, would come floundering into the gate of New Amsterdam, freighted with some new tale of aggression from the frontier; whereupon Antony Van Corlear, seizing his trumpet, the only substitute for a newspaper in those primitive days, would sound the tidings from the ramparts with such doleful notes and disastrous cadence as to throw half the old women in the city into hysterics; all which tended greatly to increase his popularity; there being nothing for which the public are more grateful than being frequently treated to a panic; a secret well known to modern editors.

But, oh ye powers! into what a paroxysm of passion did each new outrage of the Yankees throw the choleric little governor! Letter after letter, protest after protest, bad Latin, worse English, and hideous Low Dutch, were incessantly fulminated upon them, and the four-and-twenty letters of the alphabet, which formed his standing army, were worn out by constant campaigning. All, however, was in-effectual; even the recent victory at Oyster Bay, which had shed such a gleam of sunshine between the clouds of his foul-weather reign, was soon followed by a more fearful gathering up of those clouds, and indications of more portentous tempest; for the Yankee tribe on the banks of the Connecticut, finding on this memorable occasion their incompetency to cope, in fair fight, with the sturdy chivalry of the Manhattoes, had called to their aid all the ten tribes of their brethren who inhabit the east country, which from them has derived the name of Yankee land. This call was promptly responded to. The consequence was a great confederacy of the tribes of Massachusetts, Connecticut, New Plymouth and New Haven, under the title of the "United Colonies of New England"; the pretended object of which was mutual defence against the savages; but the real object the subjugation of the Nieuw Neder-lands.

For, to let the reader into one of the great secrets of history, the Nieuw Nederlands had long been regarded by the whole Yankee race as the modern land of promise, and themselves as the chosen and peculiar people destined, one day or other, by hook or by crook, to get pos-session of it. In truth they are a wonderful and all-prevalent people; of that class who only re-quire an inch to gain an ell, or a halter to gain a horse. From the time they first gained a foot-hold on Plymouth Rock, they began to migrate, progressing and progressing from place to place, and land to land, making a little here and a little there, and controverting the old proverb, that a rolling stone gathers no moss. Hence they have facetiously received the nickname of THE PILGRIMS: that is to say, a people who are al-ways seeking a better country than their own.

The tidings of this great Yankee league struck William Kieft with dismay, and for once in his life he forgot to bounce on receiving a disagreeable piece of intelligence. In fact, on turning over in his mind all that he had read at the Hague about leagues and combinations, he found that this was a counterpart of the Amphictyonic league, by which the states of Greece attained such power and supremacy; and the very idea made his heart quake for the safety of his empire at the Manhattoes.

The affairs of the confederacy were managed by an annual council of delegates held at Bos-ton, which Kieft denominated the Delphos of this truly classic league. The very first meet-ing gave evidence of hostility to the Nieuw Nederlanders, who were charged, in their deal-ings with the Indians, with carrying on a traffic in "guns, powther and shott—a trade damnable and injurious to the colonists." It is true the Connecticut traders were fain to dabble a little in this damnable traffic; but then they always dealt in what were termed Yankee guns; in-geniously calculated to burst in the pagan hands which used them.

The rise of this potent confederacy was a death-blow to the glory of William the Testy, for from that day forward he never held up his head, but appeared quite crest-fallen. It is true, as the grand council augmented in power, and the league, rolling onward, gathered about the red hills of New Haven, threatening to overwhelm the Nieuw Nederlands, he con-tinued occasionally to fulminate proclamations and protests, as a shrewd sea-captain fires his guns into a water-spout; but alas! they had no more effect than so many blank cartridges.

Thus end the authenticated chronicles of the reign of William the Testy; for henceforth, in the troubles, perplexities, and confusion of the times, he seems to have been totally overlooked, and to have slipped for ever through the fingers of scrupulous history. It is a matter of deep con-cern that such obscurity should hang over his latter days; for he was in truth a mighty and great little man, and worthy of being utterly renowned, seeing that he was the first poten-tate that introduced into this land the art of fighting by proclamation, and defending a country by trumpeters and wind-mills.

It is true, that certain of the early provincial poets, of whom there were great numbers in the Nieuw Nederlands, taking advantage of his mysterious exit, have fabled, that, like Romu-lus, he was translated to the skies, and forms a very fiery little star, somewhere on the left claw of the crab; while others, equally fanciful, declare that he had experienced a fate similar to that of the good king Arthur; who, we are assured by ancient bards, was carried away to the delicious abodes of fairy land, where he still exists, in pristine worth and vigor, and will one day or another return to restore the gallantry, the honor, and the immaculate prob-ity, which prevailed in the glorious days of the Round Table.

All these, however, are but pleasing fan-tasies, the cobweb visions of those dreaming varlets, the poets, to which I would not have my judicious readers attach any credibility.

Neither am I disposed to credit an ancient and rather apocryphal historian, who asserts that the ingenious Wilhelmus was annihilated by the blowing down of one of his wind-mills; nor a writer of later times, who affirms that he fell a victim to an experiment in natural history, having the misfortune to break his neck from a garret window of the stadthouse in attempt-
10 ing to catch swallows by sprinkling salt upon their tails. Still less do I put my faith in the tradition that he perished at sea in conveying home to Holland a treasure of golden ore, discovered somewhere among the haunted regions of the Catskill mountains.

The most probable account declares, that
16 what with the constant troubles on his frontiers,

the incessant schemings and projects going on in his own pericranium, the memorials, petitions, remonstrances, and sage pieces of advice of respectable meetings of the sovereign people, and the refractory disposition of his councillors, who were sure to differ from him on every point, and uniformly to be in the wrong—his mind was kept in a furnace heat, until he became as completely burnt out as a Dutch family pipe which has passed through three generations of hard smokers. In this manner did he undergo a kind of animal combustion, consuming away like a farthing rush-light: so that when grim death finally snuffed him out, there was scarce left enough of him to bury!

1809, 1812, 1848

» » *From:* THE SKETCH BOOK « «

RIP VAN WINKLE

A Posthumous Writing of Diedrich Knickerbocker

By Woden, God of Saxons,
From whence comes Wensday, that is Wodensday.
Truth is a thing that ever I will keep
Unto thylke day in which I creep into
My sepulchre——   CARTWRIGHT.

31   (The following tale was found among the papers of the late Diedrich Knickerbocker, an old gentleman of New York, who was very curious in the Dutch history of the province, and the manners of the descendants from its primitive settlers. His historical researches, however, did not lie so much among books as among men; for the former are lamentably scanty on his favorite topics; whereas he found the old burghers, and still more their wives, rich in that legendary lore so invaluable to
40   true history. Whenever, therefore, he happened upon a genuine Dutch family, snugly shut up in its low-roofed farmhouse under a spreading sycamore, he looked upon it as a little clasped volume of black-letter, and studied it with the zeal of a book worm.

The result of all these researches was a history of the province during the reign of the Dutch governors, which he published some years since. There have been various opinions as to the literary character of his work, and, to tell the truth, it is not a
50   whit better than it should be. Its chief merit is its scrupulous accuracy, which indeed was a little questioned on its first appearance, but has since been completely established; and it is now admitted into all historical collections, as a book of unquestionable authority.

The old gentleman died shortly after the pub-

lication of his work, and now that he is dead and gone, it cannot do much harm to his memory to say that his time might have been much better employed in weightier labors. He, however, was apt to ride his hobby his own way; and though it did now and then kick up the dust a little in the eyes of his neighbors, and grieve the spirit of some friends, for whom he felt the truest deference and affection; yet his errors and follies are remembered "more in sorrow than in anger," and it begins to be suspected that he never intended to injure or offend. But however his memory may be appreciated by critics, it is still held dear by many folks, whose good opinion is worth having; particularly by certain biscuit bakers, who have gone so far as to imprint his likeness on their new-year cakes; and have thus given him a chance for immortality, almost equal to the being stamped on a Waterloo Medal, or a Queen Anne's Farthing.)

Whoever has made a voyage up the Hudson must remember the Kaatskill Mountains. They are a dismembered branch of the great Appalachian family, and are seen away to the west of the river, swelling up to a noble height, and lording it over the surrounding country. Every change of season, every change of weather, indeed every hour of the day, produces some change in the magical hues and shapes of these mountains, and they are regarded by all the good wives, far and near, as perfect barometers. When the weather is fair and settled, they are clothed in blue and purple, and print their bold outlines on the clear evening sky; but, sometimes when the rest of the landscape is cloudless they will gather a hood of gray vapors about their summits, which, in the last rays of the setting sun, will glow and light up like a crown of glory.

At the foot of these fairy mountains, the voyager may have described the light smoke curling up from a village, whose shingle-roofs gleam among the trees, just where the blue tints of the upland melt away into the fresh green of the nearer landscape. It is a little village of great antiquity, having been founded by some of the Dutch colonists in the early times of the province, just about the beginning of the government of the good Peter Stuyvesant, (may he rest in peace!) and there were some of the houses of the original settlers standing within a few years, built of small yellow bricks brought from Holland, having latticed windows and gable fronts, surmounted with weathercocks.

In that same village, and in one of these very houses (which, to tell the precise truth, was sadly time-worn and weather-beaten), there lived many years since, while the country was yet a province of Great Britain, a simple, good-natured fellow, of the name of Rip Van Winkle. He was a descendant of the Van Winkles who figured so gallantly in the chivalrous days of Peter Stuyvesant, and accompanied him to the siege of Fort Christina. He inherited, however, but little of the martial character of his ancestors. I have observed that he was a simple, good-natured man; he was, moreover, a kind neighbor, and an obedient hen-pecked husband. Indeed, to the latter circumstance might be owing that meekness of spirit which gained him such universal popularity; for those men are most apt to be obsequious and conciliating abroad, who are under the discipline of shrews at home. Their tempers, doubtless, are rendered pliant and malleable in the fiery furnace of domestic tribulation; and a curtain lecture is worth all the sermons in the world for teaching the virtues of patience and long-suffering. A termagant wife may, therefore, in some respects be considered a tolerable blessing; and if so, Rip Van Winkle was thrice blessed.

Certain it is, that he was a great favorite among all the good wives of the village, who, as usual with the amiable sex, took his part in all family squabbles; and never failed, whenever they talked those matters over in their evening gossipings, to lay all the blame on Dame Van Winkle. The children of the village, too, would shout with joy whenever he approached. He assisted at their sports, made their play-things, taught them to fly kites and shoot marbles, and told them long stories of ghosts, witches, and Indians. Whenever he went dodging about the village, he was surrounded by a troop of them, hanging on his skirts, clambering on his back, and playing a thousand tricks on him with impunity; and not a dog would bark at him throughout the neighborhood.

The great error in Rip's composition was an insuperable aversion to all kinds of profitable labor. It could not be from the want of assiduity or perseverance; for he would sit on a wet rock, with a rod as long and heavy as a Tartar's lance, and fish all day without a murmur, even though he should not be encouraged by a single nibble. He would carry a fowling-piece on his shoulder for hours together, trudging through woods and swamps, and up hill and down dale, to shoot a few squirrels or wild pigeons. He would never refuse to assist a neighbor even in the roughest toil, and was a foremost man at all country frolics for husking Indian corn, or building stone-fences; the women of the village, too, used to employ him to run their errands, and to do such little odd jobs as their less obliging husbands would not do for them. In a word, Rip was ready to attend to anybody's business but his own; but as to doing family duty, and keeping his farm in order, he found it impossible.

In fact, he declared it was of no use to work on his farm; it was the most pestilent little piece of ground in the whole country; everything about it went wrong, and would go wrong, in spite of him. His fences were continually falling to pieces; his cow would either go astray, or get among the cabbages; weeds were sure to grow quicker in his fields than anywhere else; the rain always made a point of setting in just as he had some out-door work to do; so that though his patrimonial estate had dwindled away under his management, acre by acre, until there was little more left than a mere patch of Indian corn and potatoes, yet it was the worst-conditioned farm in the neighborhood.

His children, too, were as ragged and wild as if they belonged to nobody. His son Rip, an urchin begotten in his own likeness, promised to inherit the habits, with the old clothes of his father. He was generally seen trooping like a colt at his mother's heels, equipped in a pair of his father's cast-off galligaskins, which he had much ado to hold up with one hand, as a fine lady does her train in bad weather.

Rip Van Winkle, however, was one of those happy mortals, of foolish, well-oiled dispositions, who take the world easy, eat white bread or brown, whichever can be got with least thought or trouble, and would rather starve on a penny than work for a pound. If left to himself, he would have whistled life away in perfect contentment; but his wife kept continually dinning in his ears about his idleness, his carelessness, and the ruin he was bringing on his family. Morning, noon, and night her tongue was incessantly going, and everything he said or did was sure to produce a torrent of household eloquence. Rip had but one way of replying to all lectures of the kind, and that, by frequent use, had grown into a habit. He shrugged his shoulders, shook his head, cast up his eyes, but said nothing. This, however, always provoked a fresh volley from his wife; so that he was fain to draw off his forces, and take to the outside of the house—the only side which, in truth, belongs to a henpecked husband.

Rip's sole domestic adherent was his dog Wolf, who was as much henpecked as his master; for Dame Van Winkle regarded them as companions in idleness, and even looked upon Wolf with an evil eye, as the cause of his master's going so often astray. True it is, in all points of spirit befitting an honorable dog, he was as courageous an animal as ever scoured the woods—but what courage can withstand the ever-during and all-besetting terrors of a woman's tongue? The moment Wolf entered the house his crest fell, his tail drooped to the ground, or curled between his legs, he sneaked about with a gallows air, casting many a sidelong glance at Dame Van Winkle, and at the least flourish of a broomstick or ladle he would fly to the door with yelping precipitation.

Times grew worse and worse with Rip Van Winkle as years of matrimony rolled on; a tart temper never mellows with age, and a sharp tongue is the only edged tool that grows keener with constant use. For a long while he used to console himself, when driven from home, by frequenting a kind of perpetual club of the sages, philosophers, and other idle personages of the village; which held its sessions on a bench before a small inn, designated by a rubicund portrait of His Majesty George the Third. Here they used to sit in the shade through a long lazy summer's day, talking listlessly over village gossip, or telling endless sleepy stories about nothing. But it would have

been worth any statesman's money to have heard the profound discussions that sometimes took place, when by chance an old newspaper fell into their hands, from some passing traveller. How solemnly they would listen to the contents, as drawled out by Derrick Van Bummel, the school-master, a dapper learned little man, who was not to be daunted by the most gigantic word in the dictionary; and how sagely they would deliberate upon public events some months after they had taken place.

The opinions of this junto were completely controlled by Nicholas Vedder, a patriarch of the village, and landlord of the inn, at the door of which he took his seat from morning till night, just moving sufficiently to avoid the sun and keep in the shade of a large tree; so that the neighbors could tell the hour by his movements as accurately as by a sundial. It is true he was rarely heard to speak, but smoked his pipe incessantly. His adherents, however (for every great man has his adherents), perfectly understood him, and knew how to gather his opinions. When anything that was read or related displeased him, he was observed to smoke his pipe vehemently, and to send forth short, frequent and angry puffs; but when pleased, he would inhale the smoke slowly and tranquilly, and emit it in light and placid clouds; and sometimes, taking the pipe from his mouth, and letting the fragrant vapor curl about his nose, would gravely nod his head in token of perfect approbation.

From even this stronghold the unlucky Rip was at length routed by his termagant wife, who would suddenly break in upon the tranquillity of the assemblage and call the members all to naught; nor was that august personage, Nicholas Vedder himself, sacred from the daring tongue of this terrible virago, who charged him outright with encouraging her husband in habits of idleness.

Poor Rip was at last reduced almost to despair; and his only alternative, to escape from the labor of the farm and clamor of his wife, was to take gun in hand and stroll away into the woods. Here he would sometimes seat himself at the foot of a tree, and share the contents of his wallet with Wolf, with whom he sympathized as a fellow-sufferer in persecution. "Poor Wolf," he would say, "thy mistress leads thee a dog's life of it; but never mind, my lad, whilst I live thou shalt never want a friend to stand by thee!" Wolf would wag his tail, look wistfully in his master's face, and if dogs can feel pity I verily believe he reciprocated the sentiment with all his heart.

In a long ramble of the kind on a fine autumnal day, Rip had unconsciously scrambled to one of the highest parts of the Kaatskill Mountains. He was after his favorite sport of squirrel shooting, and the still solitudes had echoed and reëchoed with the reports of his gun. Panting and fatigued, he threw himself, late in the afternoon, on a green knoll, covered with mountain herbage, that crowned the brow of a precipice. From an opening between the trees he could overlook all the lower country for many a mile of rich woodland. He saw at a distance the lordly Hudson, far, far below him, moving on its silent but majestic course, with the reflection of a purple cloud, or the sail of a lagging bark, here and there sleeping on its glassy bosom, and at last losing itself in the blue highlands.

On the other side he looked down into a deep mountain glen, wild, lonely, and shagged, the bottom filled with fragments from the impending cliffs, and scarcely lighted by the reflected rays of the setting sun. For some time Rip lay musing on this scene; evening was gradually advancing; the mountains began to throw their long blue shadows over the valleys; he saw that it would be dark long before he could reach the village, and he heaved a heavy sigh when he thought of encountering the terrors of Dame Van Winkle.

As he was about to descend, he heard a voice from a distance, hallooing, "Rip Van Winkle! Rip Van Winkle!" He looked round, but could see nothing but a crow winging its solitary flight across the mountain. He thought his fancy must have deceived him, and turned again to descend, when he heard the same cry ring through the still evening air: "Rip Van Winkle! Rip Van Winkle!"—at the same time Wolf bristled up his back, and giving a low growl, skulked to his master's side, looking fearfully down into the glen. Rip now felt a vague apprehension stealing over him; he looked anxiously in the same direction, and perceived a strange figure slowly toiling up the rocks, and bending under the weight of something he carried on his back. He was surprised to see any human being in this lonely and unfrequented place; but supposing it to be some one of the neighborhood in need of his assistance, he hastened down to yield it.

On nearer approach he was still more surprised at the singularity of the stranger's appearance. He was a short, square-built old fellow, with thick bushy hair, and a grizzled beard. His dress was of the antique Dutch fashion: a cloth jerkin strapped round the waist, several pair of breeches, the outer one of ample volume, decorated with rows of buttons down the sides, and bunches at the knees. He bore on his shoulder a stout keg, that seemed full of liquor, and made signs for Rip to approach and assist him with the load. Though rather shy and distrustful of this new acquaintance, Rip complied with his usual alacrity; and mutually relieving one another, they clambered up a narrow gully, apparently the dry bed of a mountain torrent. As they ascended, Rip every now and then heard long rolling peals, like distant thunder, that seemed to issue out of a deep ravine, or rather cleft, between lofty rocks, toward which their rugged path conducted. He paused for an instant, but supposing it to be the muttering of one of those transient thunder-showers which often take place in mountain heights, he proceeded. Passing through the ravine, they came to a hollow, like a small amphitheatre, surrounded by perpendicular precipices, over the brinks of which impending trees shot their branches, so that you only caught glimpses of the azure sky and the bright evening cloud. During the whole time Rip and his companion had labored on in silence; for though the former marvelled greatly what could be the object of carrying a keg of liquor up this wild mountain, yet there was something strange and incomprehensible about the unknown, that inspired awe and checked familiarity.

On entering the ampitheatre, new objects of wonder presented themselves. On a level spot in the centre was a company of odd-looking personages playing at ninepins. They were dressed in a quaint outlandish fashion; some wore short doublets, others jerkins, with long knives in their belts, and most of them had enormous breeches of similar style with that of the guide's. Their visages, too, were peculiar; one had a large beard, broad face, and small piggish eyes, the face of another seemed to consist entirely of nose, and was surmounted by a white sugar-loaf hat, set off with a little red cock's tail. They all had beards, of various shapes and colors. There was one who seemed to be the commander. He was a stout old gentleman, with a weather-beaten countenance; he wore a laced doublet, broad belt and hanger, high-crowned hat and feather, red stockings, and high-heeled shoes, with roses in them. The whole group reminded Rip of the figures in an old Flemish painting in the parlor of Dominie Van Shaick, the village parson, which had been brought over from Holland at the time of the settlement.

What seemed particularly odd to Rip was, that though these folks were evidently amusing themselves, yet they maintained the gravest faces, the most mysterious silence, and were, withal, the most melancholy party of pleasure he had ever witnessed. Nothing interrupted the stillness of the scene but the noise of the balls, which, whenever they were rolled, echoed along the mountains like rumbling peals of thunder.

As Rip and his companion approached them, they suddenly desisted from their play, and stared at him with such fixed, statue-like gaze, and such strange, uncouth, lack-lustre countenances, that his heart turned within him, and his knees smote together. His companion now emptied the contents of the keg into large flagons, and made signs to him to wait upon the company. He obeyed with fear and trembling; they quaffed the liquor in profound silence, and then returned to their game.

By degrees Rip's awe and apprehension subsided. He even ventured, when no eye was fixed upon him, to taste the beverage, which he found had much of the flavor of excellent Hollands. He was naturally a thirsty soul, and was soon tempted to repeat the draught. One taste provoked another; and he reiterated his visits to the flagon so often that at length his senses were overpowered, his eyes swam in his head, his head gradually declined, and he fell into a deep sleep.

On waking, he found himself on the green knoll whence he had first seen the old man of the glen. He rubbed his eyes—it was a bright sunny morning. The birds were hopping and twittering among the bushes, and the eagle was wheeling aloft, and breasting the pure mountain breeze. "Surely," thought Rip, "I have not slept here all night." He recalled the occurrences before he fell asleep. The strange man with a keg of liquor—the mountain ravine —the wild retreat among the rocks—the woebegone party at nine-pins—the flagon—"Oh! that flagon! that wicked flagon!" thought Rip —"what excuse shall I make to Dame Van Winkle?"

He looked round for his gun, but in place of the clean, well-oiled fowling-piece, he found an old firelock lying by him, the barrel incrusted with rust, the lock falling off, and the stock worm-eaten. He now suspected that the grave roysters of the mountain had put a trick upon him, and, having dosed him with liquor, had robbed him of his gun. Wolf, too, had disappeared, but he might have strayed away after a squirrel or partridge. He whistled after him and shouted his name, but all in vain; the echoes repeated his whistle and shout, but no dog was to be seen.

He determined to revisit the scene of the last evening's gambol, and if he met with any of the party, to demand his dog and gun. As he rose to walk, he found himself stiff in the joints, and wanting in his usual activity. "These mountain beds do not agree with me," thought Rip, "and if this frolic should lay me up with a fit of the rheumatism, I shall have a blessed time with Dame Van Winkle." With some difficulty he got down into the glen: he found the gully up which he and his companion had ascended the preceding evening; but to his astonishment a mountain stream was now foaming down it, leaping from rock to rock, and filling the glen with babbling murmurs. He, however, made shift to scramble up its sides, working his toilsome way through thickets of birch, sassafras, and witch-hazel, and sometimes tripped up or entangled by the wild grapevines that twisted their coils or tendrils from tree to tree, and spread a kind of network in his path.

At length he reached to where the ravine had opened through the cliffs to the amphitheatre; but no traces of such opening remained. The rocks presented a high impenetrable wall, over which the torrent came tumbling in a sheet of feathery foam, and fell into a broad, deep basin, black from the shadows of the surrounding forest. Here, then, poor Rip was brought to a stand. He again called and whistled after his dog; he was only answered by the cawing of a flock of idle crows, sporting high in air about a dry tree that overhung a sunny precipice; and who, secure in their elevation, seemed to look down and scoff at the poor man's perplexities. What was to be done? the morning was passing away, and Rip felt famished for want of his breakfast. He grieved to give up his dog and gun; he dreaded to meet his wife; but it would not do to starve among the mountains. He shook his head, shouldered the rusty firelock, and, with a heart full of trouble and anxiety, turned his steps homeward.

As he approached the village he met a number of people, but none whom he knew, which somewhat surprised him, for he had thought himself acquainted with every one in the country round. Their dress, too, was of a different fashion from that to which he was accustomed. They all stared at him with equal marks of surprise, and whenever they cast their eyes upon him, invariably stroked their chins. The constant recurrence of this gesture induced Rip, involuntarily, to do the same, when, to his astonishment, he found his beard had grown a foot long!

He had now entered the skirts of the village. A troop of strange children ran at his heels, hooting after him, and pointing at his gray beard. The dogs, too, not one of which he recognized for an old acquaintance, barked at him as he passed. The very village was altered; it was larger and more populous. There were rows of houses which he had never seen before, and those which had been his familiar haunts had disappeared. Strange names were over the doors—strange faces at the windows—everything was strange. His mind now misgave him; he began to doubt whether both he and the world around him were not bewitched. Surely this was his native village, which he had left but the day before. There stood the Kaatskill Mountains—there ran the silver Hudson at a distance—there was every hill and dale precisely as it had always been—Rip was sorely perplexed—"That flagon last night," thought he, "has addled my poor head sadly!"

It was with some difficulty that he found the way to his own house, which he approached with silent awe, expecting every moment to hear the shrill voice of Dame Van Winkle. He found the house gone to decay—the roof fallen in, the windows shattered, and the doors off the hinges. A half-starved dog that looked like Wolf was skulking about it. Rip called him by name, but the cur snarled, showed his teeth, and passed on. This was an unkind cut indeed—"My very dog," sighed poor Rip, "has forgotten me!"

He entered the house, which, to tell the truth, Dame Van Winkle had always kept in neat order. It was empty, forlorn, and apparently abandoned. This desolateness overcame all his connubial fears—he called loudly for his wife and children—the lonely chambers rang for a moment with his voice, and then again all was silence.

He now hurried forth, and hastened to his old resort, the village inn—but it, too, was gone. A large, rickety wooden building stood in its place, with great gaping windows, some of them broken and mended with old hats and petticoats, and over the door was painted, "The Union Hotel, by Jonathan Doolittle." Instead of the great tree that used to shelter the quiet little Dutch inn of yore, there now was reared a tall naked pole, with something on the top that looked like a red night-cap, and from it was fluttering a flag, on which was a singular assemblage of stars and stripes—all this was strange and incomprehensible. He recognized on the sign, however, the ruby face of King George, under which he had smoked so many a peaceful pipe; but even this was singularly metamorphosed. The red coat was changed for one of blue and buff, a sword was held in the hand instead of a sceptre, the head was decorated with a cocked hat, and underneath was painted in large characters, GENERAL WASHINGTON.

There was, as usual, a crowd of folk about the door, but none that Rip recollected. The very character of the people seemed changed. There was a busy, bustling, disputatious tone about it, instead of the accustomed phlegm and drowsy tranquillity. He looked in vain for the sage Nicholas Vedder, with his broad face, double chin, and fair long pipe, uttering clouds of tobacco-smoke instead of idle speeches; or Van Bummel, the schoolmaster, doling forth the contents of an ancient newspaper. In place of these, a lean, bilious-looking fellow, with his pockets full of handbills, was haranguing vehemently about rights of citizens—elections—members of congress—liberty—Bunker's Hill—heroes of seventy-six—and other words, which were a perfect Babylonish jargon to the bewildered Van Winkle.

The appearance of Rip, with his long grizzled beard, his rusty fowling-piece, his uncouth dress, and an army of women and children at his heels, soon attracted the attention of the tavern-politicians. They crowded round him, eyeing him from head to foot with great curiosity. The orator bustled up to him, and, drawing him partly aside, inquired "on which side he voted?" Rip stared in vacant stupidity. Another short but busy little fellow pulled him by the arm, and, rising on tiptoe, inquired in his ear, "Whether he was Federal or Democrat?" Rip was equally at a loss to comprehend the question; when a knowing, self-important old gentleman, in a sharp cocked hat, made his

way through the crowd, putting them to the right and left with his elbows as he passed, and planting himself before Van Winkle, with one arm akimbo, the other resting on his cane, his keen eyes and sharp hat penetrating, as it were, into his very soul, demanded in an austere tone, "what brought him to the election with a gun on his shoulder, and a mob at his heels, and whether he meant to breed a riot in the vil-
10 lage?"—"Alas! gentlemen," cried Rip, somewhat dismayed, "I am a poor quiet man, a native of the place, and a loyal subject of the king, God bless him!"

Here a general shout burst from the bystanders—"A tory! a tory! a spy! a refugee! hustle him! away with him!" It was with great difficulty that the self-important man in the cocked hat restored order; and, having assumed a tenfold austerity of brow, demanded again of
20 the unknown culprit what he came there for, and whom he was seeking? The poor man humbly assured him that he meant no harm, but merely came there in search of some of his neighbors, who used to keep about the tavern.

"Well—who are they?—name them."

Rip bethought himself a moment, and inquired, "Where's Nicholas Vedder?"

There was a silence for a little while, when
30 an old man replied, in a thin, piping voice: "Nicholas Vedder! why, he is dead and gone these eighteen years! There was a wooden tombstone in the churchyard that used to tell all about him, but that's rotten and gone too."

"Where's Brom Dutcher?"

"Oh, he went off to the army in the beginning of the war; some say he was killed at the storming of Stony Point—others say he was drowned in a squall at the foot of Antony's
40 Nose. I don't know—he never came back again."

"Where's Van Bummel, the schoolmaster?"

"He went off to the wars too, was a great militia general, and is now in Congress."

Rip's heart died away at hearing of these sad changes in his home and friends, and finding himself thus alone in the world. Every answer puzzled him too, by treating of such enormous lapses of time, and of matters which
50 he could not understand: war—Congress—Stony Point; he had no courage to ask after any more friends, but cried out in despair, "Does nobody here know Rip Van Winkle?"

"Oh, Rip Van Winkle!" exclaimed two or three, "Oh, to be sure! that's Rip Van Winkle yonder, leaning against the tree."

Rip looked, and beheld a precise counterpart of himself, as he went up the mountain: apparently as lazy, and certainly as ragged. The poor fellow was now completely confounded. He doubted his own identity, and whether he was himself or another man. In the midst of his bewilderment, the man in the cocked hat demanded who he was, and what was his name?

"God knows," exclaimed he, at his wit's end; "I'm not myself—I'm somebody else—that's me yonder—no—that's somebody else got into my shoes—I was myself last night, but I fell asleep on the mountain, and they've changed my gun, and everything's changed, and I'm changed, and I can't tell what's my name, or who I am!"

The by-standers began now to look at each other, nod, wink significantly, and tap their fingers against their foreheads. There was a whisper, also, about securing the gun, and keeping the old fellow from doing mischief, at the very suggestion of which the self-important man in the cocked hat retired with some precipitation. At this critical moment a fresh, comely woman pressed through the throng to get a peep at the gray-bearded man. She had a chubby child in her arms, which, frightened at his looks, began to cry. "Hush, Rip," cried she, "hush, you little fool; the old man won't hurt you." The name of the child, the air of the mother, the tone of her voice, all awakened a train of recollections in his mind. "What is your name, my good woman?" asked he.

"Judith Gardenier."

"And your father's name?"

"Ah, poor man, Rip Van Winkle was his name, but it's twenty years since he went away from home with his gun, and never has been heard of since,—his dog came home without him, but whether he shot himself, or was carried away by the Indians, nobody can tell. I was then but a little girl."

Rip had but one question more to ask; but he put it with a faltering voice:

"Where's your mother?"

"Oh, she too had died but a short time since; she broke a blood-vessel in a fit of passion at a New-England peddler."

There was a drop of comfort, at least, in this intelligence. The honest man could contain himself no longer. He caught his daughter and her child in his arms. "I am your father!" cried he—"Young Rip Van Winkle once—old Rip Van Winkle now! Does nobody know poor Rip Van Winkle?"

All stood amazed, until an old woman, tottering out from among the crowd, put her hand to her brow, and peering under it in his face for a moment, exclaimed, "Sure enough! it is Rip Van Winkle—it is himself! Welcome home again, old neighbor—Why, where have you been these twenty long years?"

Rip's story was soon told, for the whole twenty years had been to him but as one night. The neighbors stared when they heard it; some were seen to wink at each other, and put their tongues in their cheeks; and the self-important man in the cocked hat, who, when the alarm was over, had returned to the field, screwed down the corners of his mouth, and shook his head—upon which there was a general shaking of the head throughout the assemblage.

It was determined, however, to take the opinion of old Peter Vanderdonk, who was seen slowly advancing up the road. He was a descendant of the historian of that name, who wrote one of the earliest accounts of the province. Peter was the most ancient inhabitant of the village, and well versed in all the wonderful events and traditions of the neighborhood. He recollected Rip at once and corroborated his story in the most satisfactory manner. He assured the company that it was a fact, handed down from his ancestor the historian, that the Kaatskill mountains had always been haunted by strange beings. That it was affirmed that the great Hendrick Hudson, the first discoverer of the river and country, kept a kind of vigil there every twenty years, with his crew of the Half-moon; being permitted in this way to revisit the scenes of his enterprise, and keep a guardian eye upon the river and the great city called by his name. That his father had once seen them in their old Dutch dresses playing at ninepins in a hollow of the mountain; and that he himself had heard, one summer afternoon, the sound of their balls like distant peals of thunder.

To make a long story short, the company broke up, and returned to the more important concerns of the election. Rip's daughter took him home to live with her; she had a snug, well-furnished house, and a stout cheery farmer for a husband, whom Rip recollected for one of the urchins that used to climb upon his back.

As to Rip's son and heir, who was the ditto of himself, seen leaning against the tree, he was employed to work on the farm, but evinced an hereditary disposition to attend to anything else but his business.

Rip now resumed his old walks and habits; he soon found many of his former cronies, though all rather the worse for the wear and tear of time, and preferred making friends among the rising generation, with whom he soon grew into great favor.

Having nothing to do at home, and being arrived at that happy age when a man can be idle with impunity, he took his place once more on the bench at the inn door, and was reverenced as one of the patriarchs of the village, and a chronicle of the old times "before the war." It was some time before he could get into the regular track of gossip, or could be made to comprehend the strange events that had taken place during his torpor. How that there had been a revolutionary war—that the country had thrown off the yoke of old England—and that, instead of being a subject of his Majesty George the Third, he was now a free citizen of the United States. Rip, in fact, was no politician; the changes of states and empires made but little impression on him; but there was one species of despotism under which he had long groaned, and that was—petticoat government. Happily that was at an end; he had got his neck out of the yoke of matrimony, and could go in and out whenever he pleased, without dreading the tyranny of Dame Van Winkle. Whenever her name was mentioned, however, he shook his head, shrugged his shoulders, and cast up his eyes; which might pass either for an expression of resignation to his fate, or joy at his deliverance.

He used to tell his story to every stranger that arrived at Mr. Doolittle's hotel. He was observed, at first, to vary on some points every time he told it, which was, doubtless, owing to his having so recently awaked. It at last settled down precisely to the tale I have related, and not a man, woman, or child in the neighborhood but knew it by heart. Some always pretended to doubt the reality of it, and insisted that Rip had been out of his head, and that this was one point on which he always remained flighty. The old Dutch inhabitants, however, almost universally gave it full credit. Even to this day they never hear a thunder-storm of a summer afternoon about the Kaatskill, but they say Hendrick Hudson and his crew are at their game of ninepins; and it is a common wish of all henpecked husbands in the neighborhood, when life hangs heavy on their hands, that they might have a quieting draught out of Rip Van

6   Winkle's flagon.[3]   1819–1820

[3] The foregoing Tale, one would suspect, had been suggested to Mr. Knickerbocker by a little German superstition about the Emperor Frederick *der Rothbart*, and the Kypphäuser mountain; the subjoined note, however, which he had appended to the tale, shows that it is an absolute fact, narrated with his usual fidelity.

"The story of Rip Van Winkle may seem incredible to many, but nevertheless I give it my full belief, for I know the vicinity of our old Dutch settlements to have been very subject to marvellous events and appearances. Indeed, I have heard many stranger stories than this, in the villages along the Hudson; all of which were too well authenticated to admit of a doubt. I have even talked with Rip Van Winkle myself, who, when last I saw him, was a very venerable old man, and so perfectly rational and consistent on every other point, that I think no conscientious person could refuse to take this into the bargain; nay, I have seen a certificate on the subject taken before a country justice and signed with a cross, in the justice's own handwriting. The story, therefore, is beyond the possibility of doubt.
                                    D. K." [Irving's note.]

» » *From:* BRACEBRIDGE HALL « «

THE AUTHOR

WORTHY READER:—On again taking pen in hand, I would fain make a few observations at the outset, by way of bespeaking a right under-
20 standing. The volumes which I have already published have met with a reception far beyond my most sanguine expectations. I would willingly attribute this to their intrinsic merits; but, in spite of the vanity of authorship, I cannot but be sensible that their success has, in a great measure, been owing to a less flattering cause. It has been a matter of marvel, to my European readers, that a man from the wilds of America should express himself in
30 tolerable English. I was looked upon as something new and strange in literature; a kind of demi-savage, with a feather in his hand, instead of on his head; and there was a curiosity to hear what such a being had to say about civilized society.

This novelty is now at an end, and of course the feeling of indulgence which it produced. I must now expect to bear the scrutiny of sterner criticisms, and to be measured by the
40 same standard as contemporary writers; and the very favor shown to my previous writings will cause these to be treated with the greatest rigor, as there is nothing for which the world is apt to punish a man more severely than for having been over-praised. On this head, therefore, I wish to forestall the censoriousness of the reader, and I entreat he will not think the worse of me for the many injudicious things that may have been said in my commendation.
50 I am aware that I often travel over beaten ground, and treat of subjects that have already been discussed by abler pens. Indeed, various authors have been mentioned as my models, to whom I should feel flattered if I thought

I bore the slightest resemblance; but in truth I write after no model that I am conscious of, and I write with no idea of imitation or competition. In venturing occasionally on topics that have already been almost exhausted by English authors, I do it, not with the presumption of challenging a comparison, but with the hope that some new interest may be given to such topics, when discussed by the pen of a stranger.

If, therefore, I should sometimes be found dwelling with fondness on subjects trite and commonplace with the reader, I beg the circumstances under which I write may be kept in recollection. Having been born and brought up in a new country, yet educated from infancy in the literature of an old one, my mind was early filled with historical and poetical associations, connected with places, and manners, and customs of Europe, but which could rarely be applied to those of my own country. To a mind thus peculiarly prepared, the most ordinary objects and scenes, on arriving in Europe, are full of strange matter and interesting novelty. England is as classic ground to an American, as Italy is to an Englishman; and old London teems with as much historical association as mighty Rome.

Indeed, it is difficult to describe the whimsical medley of ideas that throng upon his mind on landing among English scenes. He for the first time sees a world about which he has been reading and thinking in every stage of his existence. The recollected ideas of infancy, youth, and manhood, of the nursery, the school, and the study, come swarming at once upon him; and his attention is distracted between great and little objects, each of which, perhaps, awakens an equally delightful train of remembrances.

But what more especially attracts his notice, are those peculiarities which distinguish an old country and an old state of society from a new one. I have never yet grown familiar enough with the crumbling monuments of past ages, to blunt the intense interest with which I at first beheld them. Accustomed always to scenes where history was, in a manner, anticipation; where everything in art was new and progressive, and pointed to the future rather than to the past; where, in short, the works of man gave no ideas but those of young existence and prospective improvement; there was something inexpressibly touching in the sight of enormous piles of architecture, gray with antiquity, and sinking to decay. I cannot describe the mute but deep-felt enthusiasm with which I have contemplated a vast monastic ruin, like Tintern Abbey, buried in the bosom of a quiet valley, and shut up from the world, as though it had existed merely for itself; or a warrior pile, like Conway Castle, standing in stern loneliness on its rocky height, a mere hollow yet threatening phantom of departed power. They spread a grand, and melancholy, and, to me, an unusual charm over the landscape; I for the first time beheld signs of national old age, and empire's decay, and proofs of the transient and perishing glories of art, amidst the ever-springing and reviving fertility of nature.

But, in fact, to me every thing was full of matter; the footsteps of history were everywhere to be traced; and poetry had breathed over and sanctified the land. I experienced the delightful freshness of feeling of a child, to whom everything is new. I pictured to myself a set of inhabitants and a mode of life for every habitation that I saw, from the aristocratical mansion, amidst the lordly repose of stately groves and solitary parks, to the straw-thatched cottage, with its scanty garden and its cherished woodbine. I thought I never could be sated with the sweetness and freshness of a country so completely carpeted with verdure; where every air breathed of the balmy pasture, and the honeysuckle hedge. I was continually coming upon some little document of poetry in the blossomed hawthorn, the daisy, the cowslip, the primrose, or some other simple object that has received a supernatural value from the muse. The first time that I heard the song of the nightingale, I was intoxicated more by the delicious crowd of remembered associations than by the melody of its notes; and I

shall never forget the thrill of ecstasy with which I first saw the lark rise, almost from beneath my feet, and wing its musical flight up into the morning sky.

In this way I traversed England, a grown-up child, delighted by every object, great and small; and betraying a wondering ignorance, and simple enjoyment, that provoked many a stare and a smile from my wiser and more experienced fellow-travellers. Such too was the 10 odd confusion of associations that kept breaking upon me as I first approached London. One of my earliest wishes had been to see this great metropolis. I had read so much about it in the earliest books put into my infant hands; and I had heard so much about it from those around me who had come from the "old countries," that I was familiar with the names of its streets and squares, and public places, before I knew those of my native city. It was, 20 to me, the great centre of the world, round which everything seemed to revolve. I recollect contemplating so wistfully, when a boy, a paltry little print of the Thames, and London Bridge, and St. Paul's, that was in front of an old magazine; and a picture of Kensington Gardens, with gentlemen in three-cornered hats and broad skirts, and ladies in hoops and lappets, that hung up in my bedroom; even the venerable cut of St. John's Gate, that has stood, 30 time out of mind, in front of the Gentleman's Magazine, was not without its charms to me; and I envied the odd-looking little men that appeared to be loitering about its arches.

How then did my heart warm when the towers of Westminster Abbey were pointed out to me, rising above the rich groves of St. James's Park, with a thin blue haze above their gray pinnacles! I could not behold this great mausoleum of what is most illustrious in our 40 paternal history, without feeling my enthusiasm in a glow. With what eagerness did I explore every part of the metropolis! I was not content with those matters which occupy the dignified research of the learned traveller; I delighted to call up all the feelings of childhood, and to seek after those objects which had been the wonders of my infancy. London Bridge, so famous in nursery song; the far-famed monument; Gog and Magog, and the Lions in the 50 Tower,—all brought back many a recollection of infantine delight, and of good old beings, now no more, who had gossiped about them to my wondering ear. Nor was it without a re-

currence of childish interest that I first peeped
into Mr. Newberry's shop, in St. Paul's Churchyard, that fountain-head of literature. Mr. Newberry was the first that ever filled my infant
mind with the idea of a great and good man.
He published all the picture-books of the day;
and, out of his abundant love for children, he
charged "nothing for either paper or print, and
only a penny-halfpenny for the binding"!

10   I have mentioned these circumstances,
worthy reader, to show you the whimsical
crowd of associations that are apt to beset my
mind on mingling among English scenes. I
hope they may, in some measure, plead my
apology, should I be found harping upon stale
and trivial themes, or indulging an over-fond-
ness for anything antique and obsolete. I know
it is the humor, not to say cant of the day, to
run riot about old times, old books, old cus-
20   toms, and old buildings; with myself, however,
as far as I have caught the contagion, the feeling is genuine. To a man from a young country, all old things are in a manner new; and he
may surely be excused in being a little curious
about antiquities, whose native land, unfortunately, cannot boast of a single ruin.

Having been brought up, also, in the comparative simplicity of a republic, I am apt to be
struck with even the ordinary circumstances
30   incident to an aristocratical state of society. If,
however, I should at any time amuse myself by
pointing out some of the eccentricities, and

some of the poetical characteristics of the latter, I would not be understood as pretending to
decide upon its political merits. My only aim
is to paint characters and manners. I am no
politician. The more I have considered the
study of politics, the more I have found it full
of perplexity; and I have contented myself, as
I have in my religion, with the faith in which I
was brought up, regulating my own conduct
by its precepts; but leaving to abler heads the
task of making converts.

I shall continue on, therefore, in the course I
have hitherto pursued; looking at things poetically, rather than politically; describing them
as they are, rather than pretending to point out
how they should be; and endeavoring to see
the world in as pleasant a light as circumstances will permit.

I have always had an opinion that much
good might be done by keeping mankind in
good humor with one another. I may be wrong
in my philosophy, but I shall continue to
practise it until convinced of its fallacy. When
I discover the world to be all that it has been
represented by sneering cynics and whining
poets, I will turn to and abuse it also; in the
meanwhile, worthy reader, I hope you will not
think lightly of me, because I cannot believe
this to be so very bad a world as it is represented.

Thine truly,
GEOFFREY CRAYON

» » *From:* A TOUR ON THE PRAIRIES « «

CHAPTER 20

The Camp of the Wild Horse

Hunters' Stories—Habits of the Wild Horse—The
Half-Breed and His Prize—A Horse Chase—A
Wild Spirit Tamed

We had encamped in a good neighborhood
for game, as the reports of rifles in various
directions speedily gave notice. One of our
hunters soon returned with the meat of a doe,
50   tied up in the skin, and slung across his shoulders. Another brought a fat buck across his
horse. Two other deer were brought in, and a
number of turkeys. All the game was thrown
down in front of the Captain's fire, to be por-
tioned out among the various messes. The spits

and camp-kettles were soon in full employ, and
throughout the evening there was a scene of
hunters' feasting and profusion.

We had been disappointed this day in our
hopes of meeting with buffalo, but the sight of
the wild horse had been a great novelty, and
gave a turn to the conversation of the camp for
the evening. There were several anecdotes told
of a famous gray horse, which has ranged the
prairies of this neighborhood for six or seven
years, setting at naught every attempt of the
hunters to capture him. They say he can pace
and rack (or amble) faster than the fleetest
horses can run. Equally marvellous accounts
were given of a black horse on the Brassos, who
grazed the prairies on that river's banks in the
Texas. For years he outstripped all pursuit. His
fame spread far and wide; offers were made for

him to the amount of a thousand dollars; the boldest and most hard-riding hunters tried incessantly to make prize of him, but in vain. At length he fell a victim to his gallantry, being decoyed under a tree by a tame mare, and a noose dropped over his head by a boy perched among the branches.

The capture of the wild horse is one of the most favorite achievements of the prairie tribes; and, indeed, it is from this source that the Indian hunters chiefly supply themselves. The wild horses which range those vast grassy plains, extending from the Arkansas to the Spanish settlements, are of various forms and colors, betraying their various descents. Some resemble the common English stock, and are probably descended from horses which have escaped from our border settlements. Others are of a low but strong make, and are supposed to be of the Andalusian breed, brought out by the Spanish discoverers.

Some fanciful speculatists have seen in them descendants of the Arab stock, brought into Spain from Africa, and thence transferred to this country; and have pleased themselves with the idea that their sires may have been of the pure coursers of the desert, that once bore Mahomet and his warlike disciples across the sandy plains of Arabia.

The habits of the Arab seem to have come with the steed. The introduction of the horse on the boundless prairies of the Far West changed the whole mode of living of their inhabitants. It gave them that facility of rapid motion, and of sudden and distant change of place, so dear to the roving propensities of man. Instead of lurking in the depths of gloomy forests, and patiently threading the mazes of a tangled wilderness on foot, like his brethren of the north, the Indian of the West is a rover of the plain; he leads a brighter and more sunshiny life; almost always on horseback, on vast flowery prairies and under cloudless skies.

I was lying by the Captain's fire, late in the evening, listening to stories about those coursers of the prairies, and weaving speculations of my own, when there was a clamor of voices and a loud cheering at the other end of the camp; and word was passed that Beatte, the half-breed, had brought in a wild horse.

In an instant every fire was deserted; the whole camp crowded to see the Indian and his prize. It was a colt about two years old, well grown, finely limbed, with bright prominent eyes, and a spirited yet gentle demeanor. He gazed about him with an air of mingled stupefaction and surprise, at the men, the horses, and the camp-fires; while the Indian stood before him with folded arms, having hold of the other end of the cord which noosed his captive, and gazing on him with a most imperturbable aspect. Beatte, as I have before observed, has a greenish olive complexion, with a strongly marked countenance, not unlike the bronze casts of Napoleon; and as he stood before his captive horse, with folded arms and fixed aspect, he looked more like a statue than a man.

If the horse, however, manifested the least restiveness, Beatte would immediately worry him with the lariat, jerking him first on one side, then on the other, so as almost to throw him on the ground; when he had thus rendered him passive, he would resume his statue-like attitude and gaze at him in silence.

The whole scene was singularly wild; the tall grove, partially illumined by the flashing fires of the camp, the horses tethered here and there among the trees, the carcasses of deer hanging around, and, in the midst of all, the wild huntsman and his wild horse, with an admiring throng of rangers almost as wild.

In the eagerness of their excitement, several of the young rangers sought to get the horse by purchase or barter, and even offered extravagant terms; but Beatte declined all their offers. "You give great price now," said he; "tomorrow you be sorry, and take back, and say d—d Indian!"

The young men importuned him with questions about the mode in which he took the horse, but his answers were dry and laconic; he evidently retained some pique at having been undervalued and sneered at by them; and at the same time looked down upon them with contempt as greenhorns little versed in the noble science of woodcraft.

Afterwards, however, when he was seated by our fire, I readily drew from him an account of his exploit; for, though taciturn among strangers, and little prone to boast of his actions, yet his taciturnity, like that of all Indians, had its times of relaxation.

He informed me, that on leaving the camp, he had returned to the place where we had lost sight of the wild horse. Soon getting upon its track, he followed it to the banks of the river. Here, the prints being more distinct in the sand, he perceived that one of the hoofs was broken and defective, so he gave up the pursuit.

As he was returning to the camp, he came upon a gang of six horses, which immediately made for the river. He pursued them across the stream, left his rifle on the river-bank, and putting his horse to full speed, soon came up with the fugitives. He attempted to noose one of them, but the lariat hitched on one of his ears, and he shook it off. The horses dashed up a hill, he followed hard at their heels, when, of a sudden, he saw their tails whisking in the air, and they plunging down a precipice. It was too late to stop. He shut his eyes, held in his breath, and went over with them—neck or nothing. The descent was between twenty and thirty feet, but they all came down safe upon a sandy bottom.

He now succeeded in throwing his noose round a fine young horse. As he galloped alongside of him, the two horses passed each side of a sapling, and the end of the lariat was jerked out of his hand. He regained it, but an intervening tree obliged him again to let it go. Having once more caught it, and coming to a more open country, he was enabled to play the young horse with the line until he gradually checked and subdued him, so as to lead him to the place where he had left his rifle.

He had another formidable difficulty in getting him across the river, where both horses stuck for a time in the mire, and Beatte was nearly unseated from his saddle by the force of the current and the struggles of his captive. After much toil and trouble, however, he got across the stream, and brought his prize safe into camp.

For the remainder of the evening the camp remained in a high state of excitement; nothing was talked of but the capture of wild horses; every youngster of the troop was for this harum-scarum kind of chase; every one promised himself to return from the campaign in triumph, bestriding one of these wild coursers of the prairies. Beatte had suddenly risen to great importance; he was the prime hunter, the hero of the day. Offers were made him by the best-mounted rangers, to let him ride their horses in the chase, provided he would give them a share of the spoil. Beatte bore his honors in silence, and closed with none of the offers. Our stammering, chattering, gasconading little Frenchman, however, made up for his taciturnity by vaunting as much upon the subject as if it were he that had caught the horse. Indeed he held forth so learnedly in the matter, and boasted so much of the many horses he had taken, that he began to be considered an oracle; and some of the youngsters were inclined to doubt whether he were not superior even to the taciturn Beatte.

The excitement kept the camp awake later than usual. The hum of voices, interrupted by occasional peals of laughter, was heard from the groups around the various fires, and the night was considerably advanced before all had sunk to sleep.

With the morning dawn the excitement revived, and Beatte and his wild horse were again the gaze and talk of the camp. The captive had been tied all night to a tree among the other horses. He was again led forth by Beatte, by a long halter or lariat, and, on his manifesting the least restiveness, was, as before, jerked and worried into passive submission. He appeared to be gentle and docile by nature, and had a beautifully mild expression of the eye. In his strange and forlorn situation, the poor animal seemed to seek protection and companionship in the very horse which had aided to capture him.

Seeing him thus gentle and tractable, Beatte, just as we were about to march, strapped a light pack upon his back, by way of giving him the first lesson in servitude. The native pride and independence of the animal took fire at this indignity. He reared, and plunged, and kicked, and tried in every way to get rid of the degrading burden. The Indian was too potent for him. At every paroxysm he renewed the discipline of the halter, until the poor animal, driven to despair, threw himself prostrate on the ground, and lay motionless, as if acknowledging himself vanquished. A stage hero, representing the despair of a captive prince, could not have played his part more dramatically. There was absolutely a moral grandeur in it.

The imperturbable Beatte folded his arms, and stood for a time, looking down in silence upon his captive; until seeing him perfectly subdued, he nodded his head slowly, screwed his mouth into a sardonic smile of triumph, and, with a jerk of the halter, ordered him to rise. He obeyed, and from that time forward offered no resistance. During that day he bore his pack patiently, and was led by the halter; but in two days he followed voluntarily at large among the supernumerary horses of the troop.

I could not but look with compassion upon this fine young animal, whose whole course of existence had been so suddenly reversed. From being a denizen of these vast pastures, ranging at will from plain to plain and mead to mead, cropping of every herb and flower, and drinking of every stream, he was suddenly reduced to perpetual and painful servitude, to pass his life under the harness and the curb, amid, perhaps, the din and dust and drudgery of cities. The transition in his lot was such as sometimes takes place in human affairs, and in the fortunes of towering individuals:—one day, a prince of the prairies—the next day, a packhorse!

1835

» » *From:* WOLFERT'S ROOST « «

THE CREOLE VILLAGE[4]

A Sketch from a Steamboat

In travelling about our motley country, I am often reminded of Ariosto's account of the moon, in which the good paladin Astolpho found everything garnered up that had been lost on earth. So I am apt to imagine that many things lost in the Old World are treasured up in the New; having been handed down from generation to generation, since the early days of the colonies. A European antiquary, therefore, curious in his researches after the ancient and almost obliterated customs and usages of his country, would do well to put himself upon the track of some early band of emigrants, follow them across the Atlantic, and rummage among their descendants on our shores.

In the phraseology of New England might be found many an old English provincial phrase, long since obsolete in the parent country; with some quaint relics of the Roundheads; while Virginia cherishes peculiarities characteristic of the days of Elizabeth and Sir Walter Raleigh.

In the same way, the sturdy yoemanry of New Jersey and Pennsylvania keep up many usages fading away in ancient Germany; while many an honest, broad-bottomed custom, nearly extinct in venerable Holland, may be found flourishing in pristine vigor and luxuriance in Dutch villages, on the banks of the Mohawk and the Hudson.

In no part of our country, however, are the customs and peculiarities imported from the old world by the earlier settlers kept up with more fidelity than in the little, poverty-stricken villages of Spanish and French origin, which border the rivers of ancient Louisiana. Their population is generally made up of the descendants of those nations, married and interwoven together, and occasionally crossed with a slight dash of the Indian. The French character, however, floats on top, as, from its buoyant qualities, it is sure to do, whenever it forms a particle, however small, of an intermixture.

In these serene and dilapidated villages, art and nature stand still, and the world forgets to turn round. The revolutions that distract other parts of this mutable planet, reach not here, or pass over without leaving any trace. The fortunate inhabitants have none of that public spirit which extends its cares beyond its horizon, and imports trouble and perplexity from all quarters in newspapers. In fact, newspapers are almost unknown in these villages; and, as French is the current language, the inhabitants have little community of opinion with their republican neighbors. They retain, therefore, their old habits of passive obedience to the decrees of government, as though they still lived under the absolute sway of colonial commandants, instead of being part and parcel of the sovereign people, and having a voice in public legislation.

A few aged men, who have grown gray on their hereditary acres, and are of the good old colonial stock, exert a patriarchal sway in all matters of public and private import; their opinions are considered oracular, and their word is law.

The inhabitants, moreover, have none of that eagerness for gain, and rage for improvement, which keep our people continually on the move, and our country towns incessantly in a state of transition. There the magic phrases, "town lots," "water privileges," "railroads," and other comprehensive and soul-stirring words from the speculator's vocabulary, are never heard. The residents dwell in the houses built by their forefathers, without thinking of enlarging or modernizing them, or pulling them down and turning them into granite stores. The

---

[4] Published for the first time in *The Magnolia* (an annual) for 1837. Later included in *Wolfert's Roost and other Papers* (1855).

trees under which they have been born, and have played in infancy, flourish undisturbed; though, by cutting them down, they might open new streets, and put money in their pockets. In a word, the almighty dollar, that great object of universal devotion throughout our land, seems to have no genuine devotees in these peculiar villages; and unless some of its missionaries penetrate there, and erect bank-ing-houses and other pious shrines, there is no knowing how long the inhabitants may remain in their present state of contented poverty.

In descending one of our great western rivers in a steamboat, I met with two worthies from one of these villages, who had been on a distant excursion, the longest they had ever made, as they seldom ventured far from home. One was the great man, or Grand Seigneur of the village; not that he enjoyed any legal privi-leges or power there, everything of the kind having been done away when the province was ceded by France to the United States. His sway over his neighbors was merely one of custom and convention, out of deference to his family. Beside, he was worth full fifty thousand dollars, an amount almost equal, in the imagi-nations of the villagers, to the treasures of King Solomon.

This very substantial old gentleman, though of the fourth or fifth generation in this country, retained the true Gallic feature and deport-ment, and reminded me of one of those provin-cial potentates that are to be met with in the remote parts of France. He was of a large frame, a ginger-bread complexion, strong fea-tures, eyes that stood out like glass knobs, and a prominent nose, which he frequently regaled from a gold snuff-box, and occasionally blew with a colored handkerchief, until it sounded like a trumpet.

He was attended by an old negro, as black as ebony, with a huge mouth, in a continual grin; evidently a privileged and favorite serv-ant, who had grown up and grown old with him. He was dressed in creole style, with white jacket and trousers, a stiff shirt-collar, that threatened to cut off his ears, a bright Madras handkerchief tied round his head, and large gold ear-rings. He was the politest negro I met with in a western tour, and that is saying a great deal, for, excepting the Indians, the negroes are the most gentlemanlike personages to be met with in those parts. It is true they differ from the Indians in being a little extra

polite and complimentary. He was also one of the merriest; and here, too, the negroes, how-ever we may deplore their unhappy condition, have the advantage of their masters. The whites are, in general, too free and prosperous to be merry. The cares of maintaining their rights and liberties, adding to their wealth, and making presidents, engross all their thoughts and dry up all the moisture of their souls. If you hear a broad, hearty, devil-may-care laugh, be assured it is a negro's.

Beside this African domestic, the seigneur of the village had another no less cherished and privileged attendant. This was a huge dog, of the mastiff breed, with a deep, hanging mouth, and a look of surly gravity. He walked about the cabin with the air of a dog perfectly at home, and who had paid for his passage. At dinner-time he took his seat beside his master, giving him a glance now and then out of a corner of his eye, which bespoke perfect confi-dence that he would not be forgotten. Nor was he. Every now and then a huge morsel would be thrown to him, peradventure the half-picked leg of a fowl, which he would receive with a snap like the springing of a steel trap,—one gulp, and all was down; and a glance of the eye told his master that he was ready for an-other consignment.

The other village worthy, travelling in com-pany with the seigneur, was of a totally differ-ent stamp. Small, thin, and weazen-faced, as Frenchmen are apt to be represented in carica-ture, with a bright, squirrel-like eye, and a gold ring in his ear. His dress was flimsy, and sat loosely on his frame, and he had altogether the look of one with but little coin in his pocket. Yet, though one of the poorest, I was assured he was one of the merriest and most popular personages in his native village.

Compère Martin, as he was commonly called, was the factotum of the place,—sports-man, schoolmaster, and land-surveyor. He could sing, dance, and, above all, play on the fiddle, an invaluable accomplishment in an old French creole village, for the inhabitants have a hereditary love for balls and *fêtes*. If they work but little, they dance a great deal; and a fiddle is the joy of their heart.

What had sent Compère Martin travelling with the Grand Seigneur I could not learn. He evidently looked up to him with great defer-ence, and was assiduous in rendering him petty attentions; from which I concluded that he lived at home upon the crumbs which fell from his table. He was gayest when out of his sight, and had his song and his joke when forward among the deck passengers; but, altogether, Compère Martin was out of his element on board of a steamboat. He was quite another being, I am told, when at home in his own village.

Like his opulent fellow-traveller, he too had his canine follower and retainer,—and one suited to his different fortunes,—one of the civilest, most unoffending little dogs in the world. Unlike the lordly mastiff, he seemed to think he had no right on board of the steamboat; if you did but look hard at him, he would throw himself upon his back, and lift up his legs, as if imploring mercy.

At table he took his seat a little distance from his master; not with the bluff, confident air of the mastiff, but quietly and diffidently; his head on one side, with one ear dubiously slouched, the other hopefully cocked up; his under-teeth projecting beyond his black nose, and his eye wistfully following each morsel that went into his master's mouth.

If Compère Martin now and then should venture to abstract a morsel from his plate, to give to his humble companion, it was edifying to see with what diffidence the exemplary little animal would take hold of it, with the very tip of his teeth, as if he would almost rather not, or was fearful of taking too great a liberty. And then with what decorum would he eat it! How many efforts would he make in swallowing it, as if it stuck in his throat; with what daintiness would he lick his lips; and then with what an air of thankfulness would he resume his seat, with his teeth once more projecting beyond his nose, and an eye of humble expectation fixed upon his master.

It was late in the afternoon when the steamboat stopped at the village which was the residence of these worthies. It stood on the high bank of the river, and bore traces of having been a frontier trading-post. There were the remains of stockades that once protected it from the Indians, and the houses were in the ancient Spanish and French colonial taste, the place having been successively under the domination of both those nations prior to the cession of Louisiana to the United States.

The arrival of the seigneur of fifty thousand dollars, and his humble companion, Compère Martin, had evidently been looked forward to as an event in the village. Numbers of men, women, and children, white, yellow, and black, were collected on the river bank; most of them clad in old-fashioned French garments, and their heads decorated with colored handkerchiefs or white nightcaps. The moment the steamboat came within sight and hearing, there was a waving of handkerchiefs, and a screaming and bawling of salutations and felicitations, that baffle all description. 10

The old gentleman of fifty thousand dollars was received by a train of relatives, and friends, and children, and grandchildren, whom he kissed on each cheek, and who formed a procession in his rear, with a legion of domestics, of all ages, following him to a large, old-fashioned French house, that domineered over the village.

His black *valet de chambre,* in white jacket and trousers, and gold ear-rings, was met on 20 the shore by a boon, though rustic companion, a tall negro fellow, with a long good-humored face, and the profile of a horse, which stood out from beneath a narrow-rimmed straw hat, stuck on the back of his head. The explosions of laughter of these two varlets on meeting and exchanging compliments, were enough to electrify the country round.

The most hearty reception, however, was that given to Compère Martin. Everybody, 30 young and old, hailed him before he got to land. Everybody had a joke for Compère Martin, and Compère Martin had a joke for everybody. Even his little dog appeared to partake of his popularity, and to be caressed by every hand. Indeed, he was quite a different animal the moment he touched the land. Here he was at home; here he was of consequence. He barked, he leaped, he frisked about his old friends, and then would skim round the place 40 in a wide circle, as if mad.

I traced Compère Martin and his little dog to their home. It was an old ruinous Spanish house, of large dimensions, with verandas overshadowed by ancient elms. The house had probably been the residence, in old times, of the Spanish commandant. In one wing of this crazy, but aristocratical abode, was nestled the family of my fellow-traveller; for poor devils are apt to be magnificently clad and lodged, in 50 the cast-off clothes and abandoned palaces of the great and wealthy.

The arrival of Compère Martin was welcomed by a legion of women, children, and mongrel curs; and, as poverty and gayety generally go hand-in-hand among the French and their descendants, the crazy mansion soon resounded with loud gossip and light-hearted laughter.

As the steamboat paused a short time at the village, I took occasion to stroll about the place. Most of the houses were in the French taste, with casements and rickety verandas, but most of them in flimsy and ruinous condition. All the wagons, ploughs, and other utensils about the place were of ancient and inconvenient Gallic construction, such as had been brought from France in the primitive days of the colony. The very looks of the people reminded me of the villages of France.

From one of the houses came the hum of a spinningwheel, accompanied by a scrap of an old French *chanson,* which I have heard many a time among the peasantry of Languedoc, doubtless a traditional song, brought over by the first French emigrants, and handed down from generation to generation.

Half a dozen young lasses emerged from the adjacent dwellings, reminding me, by their light step and gay costume, of scenes in ancient France, where taste in dress comes natural to every class of females. The trim bodice and colored petticoat, and little apron, with its pockets to receive the hands when in an attitude for conversation; the colored kerchief wound tastefully round the head, with a coquettish knot perking above one ear; and the neat slipper and tight-drawn stocking, with its braid of narrow ribbon embracing the ankle where it peeps from its mysterious curtain. It is from this ambush that Cupid sends his most inciting arrows.

While I was musing upon the recollections thus accidentally summoned up, I heard the sound of a fiddle from the mansion of Compère Martin, the signal, no doubt, for a joyous gathering. I was disposed to turn my steps thither, and witness the festivities of one of the very few villages I had met with in my wide tour that was yet poor enough to be merry; but the bell of the steamboat summoned me to reëmbark.

As we swept away from the shore, I cast back a wistful eye upon the moss-grown roofs and ancient elms of the village, and prayed that the inhabitants might long retain their happy ignorance, their absence of all enterprise and improvement, their respect for the fiddle, and their contempt for the almighty dollar.[5] I fear, however, my prayer is doomed to be of no avail. In a little while the steamboat whirled me to an American town, just springing into bustling and prosperous existence.

The surrounding forest had been laid out in town lots; frames of wooden buildings were rising from among stumps and burnt trees. The place already boasted a court-house, a jail, and two banks, all built of pine boards, on the model of Grecian temples. There were rival hotels, rival churches, and rival newspapers; together with the usual number of judges and generals and governors; not to speak of doctors by the dozen, and lawyers by the score.

The place, I was told, was in an astonishing career of improvement, with a canal and two railroads in embryo. Lots doubled in price every week; everybody was speculating in land; everybody was rich; and everybody was growing richer. The community, however, was torn to pieces by new doctrines in religion and in political economy; there were camp-meetings, and agrarian meetings; and an election was at hand, which, it was expected, would throw the whole country into a paroxysm.

Alas! with such an enterprising neighbor, what is to become of the poor little creole village!   1837

[5] This phrase, used for the first time in this sketch, has since passed into current circulation, and by some has been questioned as savoring of irreverence. The author, therefore, owes it to his orthodoxy to declare that no irreverence was intended even to the dollar itself; which he is aware is daily becoming more and more an object of worship. [Irving's note.]

JAMES FENIMORE COOPER

1789–1851

COOPER'S early environment was aristocratic, and the impressions he received from it resulted in his settled belief that the democratic maxim "that 'one man is as good as another' is true in neither nature, revealed morals, or political theory." His father, William Cooper, acquired in 1785 a patent of thousands of acres on the headwaters of the Susquehanna in New York State. Here, after the family's removal from New Jersey in 1790, he ruled the 40,000 souls holding land under him like an English lord of the manor. In the frontier village of Cooperstown the future novelist mingled with the prototypes of the characters in his Leather-Stocking Tales.

Cooper was prepared for college by the rector of St. Peter's in Albany, an Englishman who had the "profoundest contempt for republics and republican institutions." After his dismissal from Yale (which came about because he defied the rules of the College once too often), he enlisted (1806) as a midshipman, intending to make a career in the Navy. His experiences during the next five years later made him infallible as a novelist of the sea. A further strengthening of the ties which held him to the older aristocratic order in America resulted from his marriage in 1811 to Susan DeLancey. The DeLanceys were Tories whose estate, Heathcote Hill, on Long Island Sound, rivaled Judge Cooper's on Otsego Lake. For the next eleven years young Cooper lived as a country squire, but by 1817 he was heavily in debt.

Cooper's first published fiction was *Precaution* (1820). By imitating the style and content of contemporary English women novelists who wrote about fashionable society, he hoped to produce a bestseller. His attempt succeeded well enough to encourage him to go on. The following year he turned to the American scene with *The Spy*, an excellent story of the adventures of Harvey Birch, trusted messenger of Washington during the New York campaign. The unprecedented sale of *The Spy* made it inevitable that Cooper should turn writer. Before June, 1826, when he sailed for Europe to educate his children and establish better connections with publishers, he had written the first of the Leather-Stocking series (*The Pioneers*, 1823; *The Last of the Mohicans*, 1826) and *The Pilot* (1824) which he had been provoked to undertake because of the lack of nautical authenticity in Scott's *The Pirate*. Cooper would never be so popular with his countrymen as he was at the moment of leaving for his seven-year stay abroad.

Moving from one European city to another, Cooper soon enjoyed the friendship of liberal leaders in France and England. Through his intimacy with Lafayette his interest in French affairs, and then in the contrast between American and European institutions, became intense. Two important literary ventures resulted from this new concern with political ideas: a trilogy of novels displaying the evils of feudal society (*The Bravo*, 1831; *The Heidenmauer*, 1832; *The Headsman*, 1833) and a series of travel letters, *Gleanings in Europe*, in which he pointed out the social consequences in England and the Continental countries of the faults in their governmental systems.

When Cooper returned home he at once set about instructing his fellow Americans. Though he continued to be a defender of America, his belief, henceforth frequently expressed, that a landed aristocratic class was needed to maintain standards in education, government, and the arts, was anathema to the Jacksonian democrats. Beginning with his *Letter to His Countrymen* (1834), Cooper was for the rest of his life in constant controversy with editors and critics. Though he won his libel suits against defamatory Whig editors and reduced the critics of his *History of the Navy of the United States of America* (1839) to a grumbling silence, he was never again popular. Yet much of his best work, produced at incredible speed, was done during these years: *The American Democrat* (1838), an admirable defense and critique of our social order; the remaining novels in the Leather-Stocking group; and three novels of purpose dealing with the Anti-rent War in New York State (1839–1846). In these, Cooper's sympathy with his class generates a swiftly moving story. The novels, of which *Satanstoe* (1845) is the best, cover the period of settlement in northern New York from the time of the granting of the patents to the struggle of the tenant farmers to change the conditions of feudal tenure by which the descendants of the patentees still ruled.

The critic of Cooper must admit at once the novelist's many defects. Not one of his female characters has any life in her. They are effective only in blushing and fainting. His attempts to reproduce wit and eloquence are ludicrous. He is guilty of many absurdities of plotting: in *The Spy* George Washington skulks around the countryside in the disguise of the benevolent Mr. Harper. Too often his narrative formula takes the reader round and round the circle of pursuit-capture-escape-pursuit-capture-escape until he wishes the hero would stay captured or be shot so that he cannot escape again.

But Cooper's faults weigh less than his qualities. He knew how to make judicious use of history in fiction, and through his familiarity with the terrain he describes, with frontier conditions, and with life on shipboard, he is able to write as one having authority. A few of his main characters—Natty Bumppo, Chingachgook, Harvey Birch—are, as one says, immortal, but equally memorable are a number of his minor characters, which present a wide range of American types from the first contented slave in American fiction (Caesar, in *The Spy*) to Newcome, the close-dealing Yankee in *The Chainbearer*. Even the most sophisticated American, if his blood is red, can be thrilled by the Pilot's handling of the frigate in the storm (Chapter V) or the desperate race against time on the ice floes, in *Satanstoe*, or the siege of the blockhouse in *Wyandotté*.

In Spanish-America, in the last century, the "Espy," Señor Birch, was believed to be one of the great heroes of our revolution. In France, today, when children play at "peaux rouges," each small boy clamors to be "Bas-de-cuir."

R. E. Spiller and P. C. Blackburn, *A Descriptive Bibliography of the Writings of James Fenimore Cooper*, New York, 1934.
Novels (with illustrations by F. D. C. Darley), 32 vols., New York, 1859–1861.
James Fenimore Cooper, Representative Selections, with Introduction, Bibliography, and Notes (American Writers Series), R. E. Spiller, ed., New York, 1936.
The Leatherstocking Saga, Allan Nevins, ed., New York, 1954.
The Letters and Journals of James Fenimore Cooper, J. F. Beard, ed., 2 vols., Cambridge, 1960, *et seq.*
H. W. Boynton, *James Fenimore Cooper*, New York, 1931.
W. B. S. Clymer, *James Fenimore Cooper*, Boston, 1900.
M. E. Cunningham, ed., *James Fenimore Cooper, a Re-appraisal*, Cooperstown, New York, 1954.
James Grossman, *James Fenimore Cooper*, New York, 1949.
T. R. Lounsbury, *James Fenimore Cooper*, Boston, 1882.
J. F. Ross, *The Social Criticism of Fenimore Cooper*, Berkeley, Calif., 1933.
R. E. Spiller, *Fenimore Cooper, Critic of His Times*, New York, 1931.

» » *From:* THE PIONEERS[1] « «

CHAPTER XXXII

. . . It has been already said that the "court of common pleas and general sessions of the peace," or, as it is commonly called, the "county court," over which Judge Temple presided, held one of its stated sessions on the following morning. The attendants of Richard were officers who had come to the village, as much to discharge their usual duties at this court, as to escort the prisoners; and the Sheriff knew their habits too well, not to feel confident he should find most, if not all of them, in the public room of the jail, discussing the qualities of the keeper's liquors. Accordingly he held his way through the silent streets of the village, di-

[1] The first of the novels in which Natty Bumppo (Leatherstocking) appeared. In the order of the events which they chronicle (though not in the order of their composition) the Leather-stocking tales are *The Deerslayer*, *The Last of the Mohicans*, *The Pathfinder*, *The Pioneers*, and *The Prairie*. Judge Temple in *The Pioneers* is a partial portrait of Cooper's father.

rectly to the small and insecure building that contained all the unfortunate debtors, and some of the criminals of the county, and where justice was administered to such unwary applicants as were so silly as to throw away two dollars, in order to obtain one from their neighbors. The arrival of four malefactors in the custody of a dozen officers, was an event, at that day, in Templeton; and when the Sheriff reached the jail, he found every indication that his subordinates intended to make a night of it.

The nod of the Sheriff brought two of his deputies to the door, who in their turn drew off six or seven of the constables. With this force Richard led the way through the village, towards the bank of the lake, undisturbed by any noise, except the barking of one or two curs, who were alarmed by the measured tread of the party, and by the low murmurs that ran through their own numbers, as a few cautious questions and answers were exchanged, relative to the object of their expedition. When they had crossed the little bridge of hewn logs that was thrown over the Susquehanna, they left the highway, and struck into that field which had been the scene of the victory over the pigeons. From this they followed their leader into the low bushes of pines and chestnuts which had sprung up along the shores of the lake, where the plough had not succeeded the fall of the trees, and soon entered the forest itself. Here Richard paused, and collected his troop around him.

"I have required your assistance, my friends," he said, in a low voice, "in order to arrest Nathaniel Bumppo, commonly called the Leatherstocking. He has assaulted a magistrate, and resisted the execution of a search-warrant, by threatening the life of a constable with his rifle. In short, my friends, he has set an example of rebellion to the laws, and has become a kind of outlaw. He is suspected of other misdemeanors and offences against private rights; and I have this night taken on myself, by the virtue of my office of Sheriff, to arrest the said Bumppo, and bring him to the county jail, that he may be present and forthcoming to answer to these heavy charges before the court to-morrow morning. In executing this duty, friends and fellow-citizens, you are to use courage and discretion. Courage, that you may not be daunted by any lawless attempts that this man may make with his rifle and his dogs, to oppose you; and discretion, which here means caution and prudence, that he may not escape from this

sudden attack—and for other good reasons that I need not mention. You will form yourselves in a complete circle around his hut, and at the word 'advance,' called aloud by me, you will rush forward, and, without giving the criminal time for deliberation, enter his dwelling by force, and make him your prisoner. Spread yourselves for this purpose, while I shall descend to the shore with a deputy, to take charge of that point; and all communications must be made directly to me, under the bank in front of the hut, where I shall station myself, and remain in order to receive them."

This speech, which Richard had been studying during his walk, had the effect that all similar performances produce, of bringing the dangers of the expedition immediately before the eyes of his forces. The men divided, some plunging deeper into the forest, in order to gain their stations without giving an alarm, and others continuing to advance, at a gait that would allow the whole party to go in order: but all devising the best plan to repulse the attack of a dog, or to escape a rifle bullet. It was a moment of dread expectation and interest.

When the Sheriff thought time enough had elapsed for the different divisions of his force to arrive at their stations, he raised his voice in the silence of the forest, and shouted the watchword. The sounds played among the arched branches of the trees in hollow cadences; but when the last sinking tone was lost on the ear, in place of the expected howls of the dogs, no other noises were returned but the crackling of torn branches and dried sticks, as they yielded before the advancing steps of the officers. Even this soon ceased, as if by a common consent, when the curiosity and impatience of the Sheriff getting the complete ascendency over discretion, he rushed up the bank, and in a moment stood on the little piece of cleared ground in front of the spot where Natty had so long lived. To his amazement, in place of the hut he saw only its smouldering ruins.

The party gradually drew together about the heap of ashes and the ends of smoking logs; while a dim flame in the centre of the ruin, which still found fuel to feed its lingering life, threw its pale light, flickering with the passing currents of the air, around the circle,—now showing a face with eyes fixed in astonishment, and then glancing to another countenance, leaving the former shaded in the obscurity of night. Not a voice was raised in inquiry, nor an exclamation made in astonishment. The transition from excitement to disappointment was too powerful for speech; and even Richard lost the use of an organ that was seldom known to fail him.

The whole group were yet in the fulness of their surprise, when a tall form stalked from the gloom into the circle, treading down the hot ashes and dying embers with callous feet; and standing over the light, lifted his cap, and exposed the bare head and weather-beaten features of the Leather-stocking. For a moment he gazed at the dusky figures who surrounded him, more in sorrow than in anger, before he spoke.

"What would ye with an old and helpless man?" he said. "You've driven God's creaters from the wilderness, where his providence had put them for his own pleasure: and you've brought in the troubles and divilties of the law, where no man was ever known to disturb another. You have driven me, that have lived forty long years of my appointed time in this very spot, from my home and the shelter of my head, lest you should put your wicked feet and wasty ways in my cabin. You've driven me to burn these logs, under which I've eaten and drunk—the first of Heaven's gifts, and the other of the pure springs—for the half of a hundred years; and to mourn the ashes under my feet, as a man would weep and mourn for the children of his body. You've rankled the heart of an old man, that has never harmed you or your'n, with bitter feelings towards his kind, at a time when his thoughts should be on a better world; and you've driven him to wish that the beasts of the forest, who never feast on the blood of their own families, was his kindred and race: and now, when he has come to see the last brand of his hut, before it is melted into ashes, you follow him up, at midnight, like hungry hounds on the track of a worn-out and dying deer. What more would ye have? for I am here—one to many. I come to mourn, not to fight; and, if it is God's pleasure, work your will on me."

When the old man ended, he stood, with the light gilmmering around his thinly-covered head, looking earnestly at the group, which receded from the pile with an involuntary movement, without the reach of the quivering rays, leaving a free passage for his retreat into the bushes, where pursuit, in the dark, would have been fruitless. Natty seemed not to regard this advantage; but stood facing each individual in the circle in succession, as if to see who would

be the first to arrest him. After a pause of a few moments, Richard began to rally his confused faculties; and, advancing, apologized for his duty, and made him his prisoner. The party now collected; and, preceded by the Sheriff, with Natty in their centre, they took their way towards the village.

During the walk, divers questions were put to the prisoner concerning his reasons for burning the hut, and whither Mohegan had retreated; but to all of them he observed a profound silence, until, fatigued with their previous duties, and the lateness of the hour, the Sheriff and his followers reached the village, and dispersed to their several places of rest, after turning the key of a jail on the aged and apparently friendless Leather-stocking.

CHAPTER XXXIII

Fetch here the stocks, ho!
You stubborn ancient knave, you reverend braggart,
We'll teach you.   *Lear.*

The long days and early sun of July allowed time for a gathering of the interested, before the little bell of the academy announced that the appointed hour had arrived for administering right to the wronged, and punishment to the guilty. Ever since the dawn of day, the highways and woodpaths that, issuing from the forests, and winding along the sides of the mountains, centred in Templeton, had been thronged with equestrians and footmen, bound to the haven of justice. There was to be seen a well-clad yeoman, mounted on a sleek, switch-tailed steed, ambling along the highway, with his red face elevated in a manner that said, "I have paid for my land, and fear no man"; while his bosom was swelling with the pride of being one of the grand inquest for the county. At his side rode a companion, his equal in independence of feeling, perhaps, but his inferior in thrift, as in property and consideration. This was a professed dealer in lawsuits,—a man whose name appeared in every calendar,—whose substance, gained in the multifarious expedients of a settler's changeable habits, was wasted in feeding the harpies of the courts. He was endeavoring to impress the mind of the grand juror with the merits of a cause now at issue. Along with these was a pedestrian, who, having thrown a rifle frock over his shirt, and placed his best wool hat above his sun-burnt visage, had issued from his retreat in the woods by a footpath, and was striving to keep company with the others, on his way to hear and to decide the disputes of his neighbors, as a petit juror. Fifty similar little knots of countrymen might have been seen, on that morning, journeying towards the shire-town on the same errand.

By ten o'clock the streets of the village were filled with busy faces; some talking of their private concerns, some listening to a popular expounder of political creeds; and others gaping in at the open stores, admiring the finery, or examining scythes, axes, and such other manufactures as attracted their curiosity or excited their admiration. A few women were in the crowd, most carrying infants, and followed, at a lounging, listless gait, by their rustic lords and masters. There was one young couple, in whom connubial love was yet fresh, walking at a respectful distance from each other; while the swain directed the timid steps of his bride, by a gallant offering of a thumb!

At the first stroke of the bell, Richard issued from the door of the "Bold Dragoon," flourishing a sheathed sword, that he was fond of saying his ancestors had carried in one of Cromwell's victories, and crying, in an authoritative tone, to "clear the way for the court." The order was obeyed promptly, though not servilely, the members of the crowd nodding familiarly to the members of the procession as it passed. A party of constables with their staves followed the Sheriff, preceding Marmaduke, and four plain, grave-looking yeomen, who were his associates on the bench. There was nothing to distinguish these subordinate judges from the better part of the spectators, except gravity, which they affected a little more than common, and that one of their number was attired in an old-fashioned military coat, with skirts that reached no lower than the middle of his thighs, and bearing two little silver epaulettes, not half so big as a modern pair of shoulder-knots. This gentleman was a colonel of the militia, in attendance on a court-martial, who found leisure to steal a moment from his military to attend to his civil jurisdiction; but this incongruity excited neither notice nor comment. Three or four clean-shaved lawyers followed, as meekly as if they were lambs going to the slaughter. One or two of their number had contrived to obtain an air of scholastic gravity by wearing spectacles. The rear was brought up by another posse of constables, and the mob followed the whole into the room where the court held its sittings.

The edifice was composed of a basement of squared logs, perforated here and there with small grated windows, through which a few wistful faces were gazing at the crowd without. Among the captives were the guilty, downcast countenances of the counterfeiters, and the simple but honest features of the Leather-stocking. The dungeons were to be distinguished, externally, from the debtors' apartments only by the size of the apertures, the thickness of the grates, and by the heads of the spikes that were driven into the logs as a protection against the illegal use of edge-tools. The upper story was of frame-work, regularly covered with boards, and contained one room decently fitted up for the purposes of justice. A bench, raised on a narrow platform to the height of a man above the floor, and protected in front by a light railing, ran along one of its sides. In the centre was a seat, furnished with rude arms, that was always filled by the presiding judge. In front, on a level with the floor of the room, was a large table covered with green baize, and surrounded by benches; and at either of its ends were rows of seats, rising one over the other, for jury boxes. Each of these divisions was surrounded by a railing. The remainder of the room was an open space, appropriated to the spectators.

When the judges were seated, the lawyers had taken possession of the table, and the noise of moving feet had ceased in the area, the proclamations were made in the usual form, the jurors were sworn, the charge was given, and the court proceeded to hear the business before them.

We shall not detain the reader with a description of the captious discussions that occupied the court for the first two hours. Judge Temple had impressed on the jury, in his charge, the necessity for despatch on their part, recommending to their notice, from motives of humanity, the prisoners in the jail, as the first objects of their attention. Accordingly, after the period we have mentioned had elapsed, the cry of the officer to "clear the way for the grand jury," announced the entrance of that body. The usual forms were observed, when the foreman handed up to the bench two bills, on both of which the Judge observed, at the first glance of his eye, the name of Nathaniel Bumppo. It was a leisure moment with the court; some low whispering passed between the bench and the Sheriff, who gave a signal to his officers, and in a very few minutes the silence that prevailed was interrupted by a general movement in the outer crowd; when presently the Leather-stocking made his appearance, ushered into the criminal's bar under the custody of two constables. The hum ceased, the people closed into the open space again, and the silence soon became so deep, that the hard breathing of the prisoner was audible.

Natty was dressed in his buck-skin garments, without his coat, in place of which he wore only a shirt of coarse linen-check, fastened at his throat by the sinew of a deer, leaving his red neck and weather-beaten face exposed and bare. It was the first time that he had ever crossed the threshold of a court of justice, and curiosity seemed to be strongly blended with his personal feelings. He raised his eyes to the bench, thence to the jury-boxes, the bar, and the crowd without, meeting every where looks fastened on himself. After surveying his own person, as searching the cause of this unusual attraction, he once more turned his face around the assemblage, and opened his mouth in one of his silent and remarkable laughs.

"Prisoner, remove your cap," said Judge Temple.

The order was either unheard or unheeded.

"Nathaniel Bumppo, be uncovered," repeated the Judge.

Natty started at the sound of his name, and raising his face earnestly towards the bench, he said—

"Anan!"

Mr. Lippet arose from his seat at the table, and whispered in the ear of the prisoner; when Natty gave him a nod of assent, and took the deer-skin covering from his head.

"Mr. District Attorney," said the Judge, "the prisoner is ready; we wait for the indictment."

The duties of public prosecutor were discharged by Dirck Van der School, who adjusted his spectacles, cast a cautious look around him at his brethren of the bar, which he ended by throwing his head aside so as to catch one glance over the glasses, when he proceeded to read the bill aloud. It was the usual charge for an assault and battery on the person of Hiram Doolittle, and was couched in the ancient language of such instruments, especial care having been taken by the scribe not to omit the name of a single offensive weapon known to the law. When he had done, Mr. Van der School removed his spectacles, which he closed and placed in his pocket, seemingly for the pleasure of again opening and replacing them on his nose. After this evolution was repeated once or twice, he handed the bill over to Mr. Lippet,

with a cavalier air, that said as much as "Pick a hole in that if you can."

Natty listened to the charge with great attention, leaning forward towards the reader with an earnestness that denoted his interest; and when it was ended, he raised his tall body to the utmost, and drew a long sigh. All eyes were turned to the prisoner, whose voice was vainly expected to break the stillness of the room.

"You have heard the presentment that the grand jury have made, Nathaniel Bumppo," said the Judge; "what do you plead to the charge?"

The old man dropped his head for a moment in a reflecting attitude, and then raising it, he laughed before he answered—

"That I handled the man a little rough or so, is not to be denied; but that there was occasion to make use of all the things that the gentleman has spoken of, is downright untrue. I am not much of a wrestler, seeing that I'm getting old; but I was out among the Scotch-Irishers—lets me see—it must have been as long ago as the first year of the old war——"

"Mr. Lippet, if you are retained for the prisoner," interrupted Judge Temple, "instruct your client how to plead; if not, the court will assign him counsel."

Aroused from studying the indictment by this appeal, the attorney got up, and after a short dialogue with the hunter in a low voice, he informed the court that they were ready to proceed.

"Do you plead guilty or not guilty?" said the Judge.

"I may say not guilty with a clean conscience," returned Natty; "for there's no guilt in doing what's right; and I'd rather died on the spot, than had him put foot in the hut at that moment."

Richard started at this declaration, and bent his eyes significantly on Hiram, who returned the look with a slight movement of his eyebrows.

"Proceed to open the cause, Mr. District Attorney," continued the Judge. "Mr. Clerk, enter the plea of not guilty."

After a short opening address from Mr. Van der School, Hiram was summoned to the bar to give his testimony. It was delivered to the letter, perhaps, but with all that moral coloring which can be conveyed under such expressions as, "thinking no harm," "feeling it my bounden duty as a magistrate," and "seeing that the constable was back'ard in the business." When he had done, and the district attorney declined putting any further interrogatories, Mr. Lippet arose, with an air of keen investigation, and asked the following questions:

"Are you a constable of this county, sir?"

"No, sir," said Hiram, "I'm only a justice-peace."

"I ask you, Mr. Doolittle, in the face of this court, putting it to your conscience and your knowledge of the law, whether you had any right to enter that man's dwelling?"

"Hem!" said Hiram, undergoing a violent struggle between his desire for vengeance and his love of legal fame; "I do suppose—that in —that is—strict law—that supposing—maybe I hadn't a real—lawful right;—but as the case was—and Billy was so back'ard—I thought I might come for'ard in the business."

"I ask you again, sir," continued the lawyer, following up his success, "whether this old, this friendless old man, did or did not repeatedly forbid your entrance?"

"Why, I must say," said Hiram, "that he was considerable cross-grained; not what I call clever, seeing that it was only one neighbor wanting to go into the house of another."

"Oh! then you own it was only meant for a neighborly visit on your part, and without the sanction of law. Remember, gentlemen, the words of the witness, 'one neighbor wanting to enter the house of another.' Now, sir, I ask you if Nathaniel Bumppo did not again and again order you not to enter?"

"There was some words passed between us," said Hiram, "but I read the warrant to him aloud."

"I repeat my question; did he tell you not to enter his habitation?"

"There was a good deal passed betwixt us— but I've the warrant in my pocket; maybe the court would wish to see it?"

"Witness," said Judge Temple, "answer the question directly; did or did not the prisoner forbid your entering his hut?"

"Why, I some think——"

"Answer without equivocation," continued the Judge, sternly.

"He did."

"And did you attempt to enter after this order?"

"I did; but the warrant was in my hand."

"Proceed, Mr. Lippet, with your examination."

But the attorney saw that the impression was in favor of his client, and, waving his hand with a supercilious manner, as if unwilling to insult the understanding of the jury with any further defence, he replied—

"No, sir; I leave it for your honor to charge; I rest my case here."

"Mr. District Attorney," said the Judge, "have you any thing to say?"

Mr. Van der School removed his spectacles, folded them, and replacing them once more on his nose, eyed the other bill which he held in his hand, and then said, looking at the bar over the top of his glasses—

"I shall rest the prosecution here, if the court please."

Judge Temple arose and began the charge.

"Gentlemen of the Jury," he said, "you have heard the testimony, and I shall detain you but a moment. If an officer meet with resistance in the execution of a process, he has an undoubted right to call any citizen to his assistance; and the acts of such assistant come within the protection of the law. I shall leave you to judge, gentlemen, from the testimony, how far the witness in this prosecution can be so considered, feeling less reluctance to submit the case thus informally to your decision, because there is yet another indictment to be tried, which involves heavier charges against the unfortunate prisoner."

The tone of Marmaduke was mild and insinuating, and as his sentiments were given with such apparent impartiality, they did not fail of carrying due weight with the jury. The grave-looking yeomen, who composed this tribunal, laid their heads together for a few minutes, without leaving the box, when the foreman arose, and after the forms of the court were duly observed, he pronounced the prisoner to be—

"Not guilty."

"You are acquitted of this charge, Nathaniel Bumppo," said the Judge.

"Anan!" said Natty.

"You are found not guilty of striking and assaulting Mr. Doolittle."

"No, no, I'll not deny but that I took him a little roughly by the shoulders," said Natty, looking about him with great simplicity, "and that I——"

"You are acquitted," interrupted the Judge, "and there is nothing further to be said or done in the matter."

A look of joy lighted up the features of the old man, who now comprehended the case, and placing his cap eagerly on his head again, he threw up the bar of his little prison, and said feelingly—

"I must say this for you, Judge Temple, that the law has not been so hard on me as I dreaded. I hope God will bless you for the kind things you've done to me this day."

But the staff of the constable was opposed to his egress, and Mr. Lippet whispered a few words in his ear, when the aged hunter sank back into his place, and, removing his cap, stroked down the remnants of his grey and sandy locks, with an air of mortification mingled with submission.

"Mr. District Attorney," said Judge Temple, affecting to busy himself with his minutes, "proceed with the second indictment."

Mr. Van der School took great care that no part of the presentment, which he now read, should be lost on his auditors. It accused the prisoner of resisting the execution of a search-warrant, by force of arms, and particularized, in the vague language of the law, among a variety of other weapons, the use of the rifle. This was indeed a more serious charge than an ordinary assault and battery, and a corresponding degree of interest was manifested by the spectators in its result. The prisoner was duly arraigned, and his plea again demanded. Mr. Lippet had anticipated the answers of Natty, and in a whisper advised him how to plead. But the feelings of the old hunter were awakened by some of the expressions of the indictment, and, forgetful of his caution, he exclaimed—

"'Tis a wicked untruth; I crave no man's blood. Them thieves, the Iroquois, won't say it to my face, that I ever thirsted after man's blood. I have fou't as a soldier that feared his Maker and his officer, but I never pulled trigger on any but a warrior that was up and awake. No man can say that I ever struck even a Mingo in his blanket. I believe there's some who thinks there's no God in a wilderness!"

"Attend to your plea, Bumppo," said the Judge; "you hear that you are accused of using your rifle against an officer of justice? are you guilty or not guilty?"

By this time the irritated feelings of Natty had found vent; and he rested on the bar for a moment, in a musing posture, when he lifted his face, with his silent laugh, and, pointing to where the wood-chopper stood, he said—

"Would Billy Kirby be standing there, d'ye think, if I had used the rifle?"

"Then you deny it," said Mr. Lippet; "you plead not guilty?"

"Sartain," said Natty; "Billy knows that I never fired at all. Billy, do you remember the turkey last winter? ah! me! that was better than common firing; but I can't shoot as I used to could."

"Enter the plea of not guilty," said Judge Temple, strongly affected by the simplicity of the prisoner.

Hiram was again sworn, and his testimony given on the second charge. He had discovered his former error, and proceeded more cautiously than before. He related very distinctly, and for the man, with amazing terseness, the suspicion against the hunter, the complaint, the issuing of the warrant, and the swearing in of Kirby; all of which, he affirmed, were done in due form of law. He then added the manner in which the constable had been received; and stated distinctly, that Natty had pointed the rifle at Kirby, and threatened his life, if he attempted to execute his duty. All this was confirmed by Jotham, who was observed to adhere closely to the story of the magistrate. Mr. Lippet conducted an artful cross-examination of these two witnesses, but after consuming much time, was compelled to relinquish the attempt to obtain any advantage, in despair.

At length the district attorney called the wood-chopper to the bar. Billy gave an extremely confused account of the whole affair, although he evidently aimed at the truth, until Mr. Van der School aided him, by asking some direct questions:—

"It appears from examining the papers, that you demanded admission into the hut legally; so you were put in bodily fear by his rifle and threats?"

"I didn't mind them that, man," said Billy, snapping his fingers; "I should be a poor stick to mind old Leather-stocking."

"But I understood you to say, (referring to your previous words (as delivered here in court) in the commencement of your testimony) that you thought he meant to shoot you?"

"To be sure I did; and so would you too, squire, if you had seen the chap dropping a muzzle that never misses, and cocking an eye that has a natural squint by long practice. I thought there would be a dust on't, and my back was up at once; but Leather-stocking gi'n up the skin, and so the matter ended."

"Ah! Billy," said Natty, shaking his head,

 'twas a lucky thought in me to throw out the
hide, or there might have been blood spilt; and
I'm sure, if it had been your'n, I should have
mourn'd it sorely the little while I have to
stay."

"Well, Leather-stocking," returned Billy, facing the prisoner with a freedom and familiarity
that utterly disregarded the presence of the
court, "as you are on the subject, it may be that
you've no——"

"Go on with your examination, Mr. District
Attorney."

That gentleman eyed the familiarity between
his witness and the prisoner with manifest disgust, and indicated to the court that he was
done.

"Then you didn't feel frightened, Mr. Kirby?"
said the counsel for the prisoner.

"Me! no," said Billy, casting his eyes over his
own huge frame with evident self-satisfaction;
"I'm not to be skeared so easy."

"You look like a hardy man; where were you
born, sir?"

"Varmount state; 'tis a mountaynious place,
but there's a stiff soil, and it's pretty much
wooded with beech and maple."

"I have always heard so," said Mr. Lippet,
soothingly. "You have been used to the rifle
yourself, in that country?"

"I pull the second best trigger in this county.
I knock under to Natty Bumppo there, sin' he
shot the pigeon."

Leather-stocking raised his head, and laughed
again, when he abruptly thrust out a wrinkled
hand, and said—

"You're young yet, Billy, and hav'n't seen the
matches that I have; but here's my hand; I
bear no malice to you, I don't."

Mr. Lippet allowed this conciliatory offering
to be accepted, and judiciously paused, while
the spirit of peace was exercising its influence
over the two; but the Judge interposed his
authority.

"This is an improper place for such dialogues," he said. "Proceed with your examination of this witness, Mr. Lippet, or I shall order
the next."

The attorney started, as if unconscious of
any impropriety, and continued—

"So you settled the matter with Natty ami-
cably on the spot, did you?"

"He gi'n me the skin, and I didn't want to
quarrel with an old man; for my part, I see no
such mighty matter in shooting a buck!"

"And you parted friends? and you would

never have thought of bringing the business
up before a court, hadn't you been subpœ-
naed?"

"I don't think I should; he gi'n the skin, and
I didn't feel a hard thought, though Squire
Doolittle got some affronted."

"I have done, sir," said Mr. Lippet, probably relying on the charge of the Judge, as he
again seated himself, with the air of a man
who felt that his success was certain.

When Mr. Van der School arose to address
the jury, he commenced by saying—

"Gentlemen of the jury, I should have interrupted the leading questions put by the prisoner's counsel (by leading questions I mean
telling him what to say), did I not feel confident that the law of the land was superior to
any advantages (I mean legal advantages)
which he might obtain by his art. The counsel
for the prisoner, gentlemen, has endeavored to
persuade you, in opposition to your own good
sense, to believe that pointing a rifle at a constable (elected or deputed) is a very innocent
affair; and that society (I mean the commonwealth, gentlemen) shall not be endangered
thereby. But let me claim your attention, while
we look over the particulars of this heinous
offence." Here Mr. Van der School favored the
jury with an abridgment of the testimony, recounted in such a manner as utterly to confuse
the faculties of his worthy listeners. After this
exhibition he closed as follows:—"And now,
gentlemen, having thus made plain to your
senses the crime of which this unfortunate man
has been guilty (unfortunate both on account
of his ignorance and his guilt), I shall leave you
to your own consciences; not in the least doubting that you will see the importance (notwithstanding the prisoner's counsel (doubtless
relying on your former verdict) wishes to appear so confident of success) of punishing
the offender, and asserting the dignity of the
laws."

It was now the duty of the Judge to deliver
his charge. It consisted of a short, comprehensive summary of the testimony, laying bare
the artifice of the prisoner's counsel, and placing the facts in so obvious a light, that they
could not well be misunderstood. "Living as
we do, gentlemen," he concluded, "on the
skirts of society, it becomes doubly necessary
to protect the ministers of the law. If you believe the witnesses, in their construction of the
acts of the prisoner, it is your duty to convict
him; but if you believe that the old man, who

this day appears before you, meant not to harm the constable, but was acting more under the influence of habit than by the instigations of malice, it will be your duty to judge him, but to do it with lenity."

As before, the jury did not leave their box; but, after a consultation of some little time, their foreman arose, and pronounced the prisoner—

10 "Guilty."

There was but little surprise manifested in the court room at this verdict, as the testimony, the greater part of which we have omitted, was too clear and direct to be passed over. The judges seemed to have anticipated this sentiment, for a consultation was passing among them also, during the deliberation of the jury, and the preparatory movements of the "bench" announced the coming sentence.

20 "Nathaniel Bumppo," commenced the Judge, making the customary pause.

The old hunter, who had been musing again, with his head on the bar, raised himself, and cried, with a prompt, military tone—

"Here."

The Judge waved his hand for silence, and proceeded—

"In forming their sentence, the court have been governed as much by the consideration of 30 your ignorance of the laws, as by a strict sense of the importance of punishing such outrages as this of which you have been found guilty. They have therefore passed over the obvious punishment of whipping on the bare back, in mercy to your years; but as the dignity of the law requires an open exhibition of the consequences of your crime, it is ordered, that you be conveyed from this room to the public stocks, where you are to be confined for one 40 hour: that you pay a fine to the state of one hundred dollars; and that you be imprisoned in the jail of this county for one calendar month, and furthermore, that your imprisonment do not cease until the said fine shall be paid. I feel it my duty, Nathaniel Bumppo——"

"And where should I get the money?" interrupted the Leather-stocking, eagerly; "where should I get the money? you'll take away the bounty on the painters, because I cut the throat 50 of a deer; and how is an old man to find so much gold or silver in the woods? No, no, Judge: think better of it, and don't talk of shutting me up in a jail for the little time I have to stay."

"If you have any thing to urge against the passing of the sentence, the court will yet hear you," said the Judge, mildly.

"I have enough to say ag'in it," cried Natty, grasping the bar on which his fingers were working with a convulsed motion. "Where am I to get the money? Let me out into the woods and hills, where I've been used to breathe the clear air, and though I'm threescore and ten, if you've left game enough in the country, I'll travel night and day but I'll make you up the sum afore the season is over. Yes, yes—you see the reason of the thing, and the wickedness of shutting up an old man, that has spent his days, as one may say, where he could always look into the windows of heaven."

"I must be governed by the law——"

"Talk not to me of law, Marmaduke Temple," interrupted the hunter. "Did the beast of the forest mind your laws, when it was thirsty and hungering for the blood of your own child! She was kneeling to her God for a greater favor than I ask, and he heard her; and if you now say no to my prayers, do you think he will be deaf?"

"My private feelings must not enter into——"

"Hear me, Marmaduke Temple," interrupted the old man, with melancholy earnestness, "and hear reason. I've travelled these mountains when you was no judge, but an infant in your mother's arms; and I feel as if I had a right and a privilege to travel them ag'in afore I die. Have you forgot the time that you come on to the lake-shore, when there wasn't even a jail to lodge in; and didn't I give you my own bear-skin to sleep on, and the fat of a noble buck to satisfy the cravings of your hunger? Yes, yes—you thought it no sin then to kill a deer! And this I did, though I had no reason to love you, for you had never done any thing but harm to them that loved and sheltered me. And now, will you shut me up in your dungeons to pay me for my kindness? A hundred dollars! where should I get the money? No, no—there's them that says hard things of you, Marmaduke Temple, but you an't so bad as to wish to see an old man die in a prison, because he stood up for the right. Come, friend, let me pass; it's long sin' I've been used to such crowds, and I crave to be in the woods ag'in. Don't fear me, Judge—I bid you not to fear me; for if there's beaver enough left on the streams, or the buckskins will sell for a shilling a-piece, you shall have the last penny of the fine. Where are ye, pups! come away, dogs! come away! we have a grievous toil to do for our years, but it shall be done—yes, yes, I've promised it, and it shall be done!"

It is unnecessary to say, that the movement of the Leather-stocking was again intercepted by the constable; but before he had time to speak, a bustling in the crowd, and a loud hem, drew all eyes to another part of the room.

Benjamin had succeeded in edging his way through the people, and was now seen balancing his short body, with one foot in a window and the other on the railing of the jury-box. To the amazement of the whole court, the steward was evidently preparing to speak. After a good deal of difficulty, he succeeded in drawing from his pocket a small bag, and then found utterance.

"If-so-be," he said, "that your honor is agreeable to trust the poor fellow out on another cruise among the beasts, here's a small matter that will help to bring down the risk, seeing that there's just thirty-five of your Spaniards in it; and I wish, from the bottom of my heart, that they was raal British guineas, for the sake of the old boy. But 'tis as it is; and if Squire Dickens will just be so good as to overhaul this small bit of an account, and take enough from the bag to settle the same, he's welcome to hold on upon the rest, till such time as the Leather-stocking can grapple with them said beaver, or, for that matter, for ever, and no thanks asked."

As Benjamin concluded, he thrust out the wooden register of his arrears to the "Bold Dragoon" with one hand, while he offered his bag of dollars with the other. Astonishment at this singular interruption produced a profound stillness in the room, which was only interrupted by the Sheriff, who struck his sword on the table, and cried—

"Silence!"

"There must be an end to this," said the Judge, struggling to overcome his feelings. "Constable, lead the prisoner to the stocks. Mr. Clerk, what stands next on the calendar?"

Natty seemed to yield to his destiny, for he sank his head on his chest, and followed the officer from the courtroom in silence. The crowd moved back for the passage of the prisoner, and when his tall form was seen descending from the outer door, a rush of the people to the scene of his disgrace followed.

CHAPTER XXXIV

Ha! ha! look! he wears cruel garters!   *Lear.*

The punishments of the common law were still known, at the time of our tale, to the people of New York; and the whipping-post, and its companion, the stocks, were not yet supplanted by the more merciful expedients of the public prison. Immediately in front of the jail those relics of the elder times were situated, as a lesson of precautionary justice to the evildoers of the settlement.

Natty followed the constables to this spot, bowing his head with submission to a power that he was unable to oppose, and surrounded by the crowd that formed a circle about his person, exhibiting in their countenances strong curiosity. A constable raised the upper part of the stocks, and pointed with his finger to the holes where the old man was to place his feet. Without making the least objection to the punishment, the Leather-stocking quietly seated himself on the ground, and suffered his limbs to be laid in the openings, without even a murmur; though he cast one glance about him, in quest of that sympathy that human nature always seems to require under suffering. If he met no direct manifestations of pity, neither did he see any unfeeling exultation, or hear a single reproachful epithet. The character of the mob, if it could be called by such a name, was that of attentive subordination.

The constable was in the act of lowering the upper plank, when Benjamin, who had pressed close to the side of the prisoner, said, in his hoarse tones, as if seeking for some cause to create a quarrel—

"Where away, master constable, is the use of clapping a man in them here bilboes? it neither stops his grog nor hurts his back; what for is it that you do the thing?"

"'Tis the sentence of the court, Mr. Penguillium, and there's law for it, I s'pose."

"Ay, ay, I know that there's law for the thing; but where away do you find the use, I say? it does no harm, and it only keeps a man by the heels for the small matter of two glasses."

"Is it no harm, Benny Pump," said Natty, raising his eyes with a piteous look in the face of the steward—"is it no harm to show off a man in his seventy-first year, like a tame bear, for the settlers to look on! Is it no harm to put an old soldier, that has sarved through the war of 'fifty-six, and seen the inimy in the 'seventy-six business, into a place like this, where the boys can point at him and say, I have known the time when he was a spectacle for the county! Is it no harm to bring down the pride of an honest man to be the equal of the beasts of the forest!"

Benjamin stared about him fiercely, and could he have found a single face that ex-
10 pressed contumely, he would have been prompt to quarrel with its owner; but meeting every-where with looks of sobriety, and occasionally of commiseration, he very deliberately seated himself by the side of the hunter, and placing his legs in the two vacant holes of the stocks, he said—

"Now lower away, master constable, lower away, I tell ye! If-so-be there's such a thing hereabouts as a man that wants to see a bear,
20 let him look and be d—d, and he shall find two of them, and mayhap one of the same that can bite as well as growl."

"But I have no orders to put you in the stocks, Mr. Pump," cried the constable; "you must get up, and let me do my duty."

"You've my orders, and what do you need better to meddle with my own feet? so lower away, will ye, and let me see the man that chooses to open his mouth with a grin on it."
30 "There can't be any harm in locking up a creater that will enter the pound," said the con-stable, laughing, and closing the stocks on them both.

It was fortunate that this act was executed with decision, for the whole of the spectators, when they saw Benjamin assume the position he took, felt an inclination for merriment, which few thought it worth while to suppress. The steward struggled violently for his liberty
40 again, with an evident intention of making battle on those who stood nearest to him; but the key was already turned, and all his efforts were vain.

"Hark ye, master constable," he cried, "just clear away your bilboes for the small matter of a log-glass, will ye, and let me show some of them there chaps who it is that they are so merry about."

"No, no, you would go in, and you can't
50 come out," returned the officer, "until the time has expired that the Judge directed for the keeping of the prisoner."

Benjamin, finding that his threats and his struggles were useless, had good sense enough to learn patience from the resigned manner of

his companion, and soon settled himself down by the side of Natty, with a contemptuousness expressed in his hard features, that showed he had substituted disgust for rage. When the violence of the steward's feelings had in some measure subsided, he turned to his fellow-sufferer, and, with a motive that might have vindicated a worse effusion, he attempted the charitable office of consolation.

"Taking it by and large, Master Bump-ho, 'tis but a small matter after all," he said. "Now, I've known very good sort of men, aboard of the Boadishey, laid by the heels, for nothing, mayhap, but forgetting that they'd drunk their allowance already, when a glass of grog has come in their way. This is nothing more than riding with two anchors ahead, waiting for a turn in the tide, or a shift of wind, d'ye see, with a soft bottom and plenty of room for the sweep of your hawse. Now I've seen many a man, for over-shooting his reckoning, as I told ye, moored head and starn, where he couldn't so much as heave his broadside round, and mayhap a stopper clapt on his tongue too, in the shape of a pump-bolt lashed athwart-ship his jaws, all the same as an out-rigger along-side of a taffrel-rail."

The hunter appeared to appreciate the kind intentions of the other, though he could not understand his eloquence; and raising his hum-bled countenance, he attempted a smile, as he said—

"Anan!"

" 'Tis nothing, I say, but a small matter of a squall that will soon blow over," continued Benjamin. "To you that has such a length of keel, it must be all the same as nothing; tho'f, seeing that I'm a little short in my lower tim-bers, they've triced my heels up in such a way as to give me a bit of a cant. But what cares I, Master Bump-ho, if the ship strains a little at her anchor; it's only for a dog-watch, and dam'me but she'll sail with you then on that cruise after them said beaver. I'm not much used to small arms, seeing that I was stationed at the ammunition-boxes, being sum'mat too low-rigged to see over the hammock-cloths; but I can carry the game, d'ye see, and mayhap make out to lend a hand with the traps; and if-so-be you're any way so handy with them as ye be with your boat-hook, 'twill be but a short cruise after all. I've squared the yards with Squire Dickens this morning, and I shall send him word that he needn't bear my name on the books again till such time as the cruise is over."

"You're used to dwell with men, Benny," said Leather-stocking, mournfully, "and the ways of the woods would be hard on you, if——"

"Not a bit—not a bit," cried the steward; "I'm none of your fair-weather chaps, Master Bump-ho, as sails only in smooth water. When I find a friend, I sticks by him, d'ye see. Now, there's no better man a'going than Squire Dickens, and I love him about the same as I loves Mistress Hollister's new keg of Jamaiky." The steward paused, and turning his uncouth visage on the hunter, he surveyed him with a roguish leer of his eye, and gradually suffered the muscles of his hard features to relax, until his face was illuminated by the display of his white teeth, when he dropped his voice, and added,—"I say, Master Leather-stocking, 'tis fresher and livelier than any Hollands you'll get in Garnsey. But we'll send a hand over and ask the woman for a taste, for I'm so jamb'd in these here bilboes, that I begin to want sum-'mat to lighten my upper works."

Natty sighed, and gazed about him on the crowd, that already began to disperse, and which had now diminished greatly, as its members scattered in their various pursuits. He looked wistfully at Benjamin, but did not reply; a deeply seated anxiety seeming to absorb every other sensation, and to throw a melancholy gloom over his wrinkled features, which were working with the movements of his mind.

The steward was about to act on the old principle, that silence gives consent, when Hiram Doolittle, attended by Jotham, stalked out of the crowd, across the open space, and approached the stocks. The magistrate passed by the end where Benjamin was seated, and posted himself, at a safe distance from the steward, in front of the Leather-stocking. Hiram stood, for a moment, cowering before the keen looks that Natty fastened on him, and suffering under an embarrassment that was quite new; when, having in some degree recovered himself, he looked at the heavens, and then at the smoky atmosphere, as if it were only an ordinary meeting with a friend, and said, in his formal hesitating way—

"Quite a scurcity of rain lately; I some think we shall have a long drought on't."

Benjamin was occupied in untying his bag of dollars, and did not observe the approach of the magistrate, while Natty turned his face, in which every muscle was working, away from him in disgust, without answering. Rather en-couraged than daunted by this exhibition of dislike, Hiram, after a short pause, continued.

"The clouds look as if they'd no water in them, and the earth is dreadfully parched. To my judgment, there'll be short crops this season, if the rain doesn't fall quite speedily."

The air with which Mr. Doolittle delivered this prophetical opinion was peculiar to his species. It was a jesuitical, cold, unfeeling, and selfish manner, that seemed to say, "I have kept within the law," to the man he had so cruelly injured. It quite overcame the restraint that the old hunter had been laboring to impose on himself, and he burst out in a warm glow of indignation.

"Why should the rain fall from the clouds," he cried, "when you force the tears from the eyes of the old, the sick, and the poor! Away with ye—away with ye! you may be formed in the image of the Maker, but Satan dwells in your heart. Away with ye, I say! I am mournful, and the sight of ye brings bitter thoughts."

Benjamin ceased thumbing his money, and raised his head at the instant that Hiram, who was thrown off his guard by the invectives of the hunter, unluckily trusted his person within reach of the steward, who grasped one of his legs, with a hand that had the grip of a vice, and whirled the magistrate from his feet, before he had either time to collect his senses or to exercise the strength he did really possess. Benjamin wanted neither proportions nor manhood in his head, shoulders, and arms, though all the rest of his frame appeared to be originally intended for a very different sort of a man. He exerted his physical powers on the present occasion, with much discretion; and as he had taken his antagonist at a great disadvantage, the struggle resulted, very soon, in Benjamin getting the magistrate fixed in a posture somewhat similar to his own, and manfully placed face to face.

"You're a ship's cousin, I tell ye, Master Doo-but-little," roared the steward; "some such matter as a ship's cousin, sir. I know you, I do, with your fair-weather speeches to Squire Dickens, to his face, and then you go and sarve out your grumbling to all the old women in the town, do ye. An't it enough for any Christian, let him harbor never so much malice, to get an honest old fellow laid by the heels in this fashion, without carrying sail so hard on the poor dog, as if you would run him down as he lay at his anchors? But I've logged many a hard thing against your name, master, and now the time's come to foot up the day's work, d'ye see; so square yourself, you lubber, square yourself, and we'll soon know who's the better man."

"Jotham!" cried the frightened magistrate—"Jotham! call in the constables. Mr. Penguillium, I command the peace—I order you to keep the peace."

"There's been more peace than love atwixt us, master," cried the steward, making some very unequivocal demonstrations towards hostility; "so mind yourself! square yourself, I say! do you smell this here bit of a sledge-hammer?"

"Lay hands on me if you dare!" exclaimed Hiram, as well as he could under the grasp which the steward held on his throttle—"lay hands on me if you dare!"

"If ye call this laying, master, you are welcome to the eggs," roared the steward.

It becomes our disagreeable duty to record here, that the acts of Benjamin now became violent; for he darted his sledge-hammer violently on the anvil of Mr. Doolittle's countenance, and the place became, in an instant, a scene of tumult and confusion. The crowd rushed in a dense circle around the spot, while some ran to the courtroom to give the alarm, and one or two of the more juvenile part of the multitude had a desperate trial of speed to see who should be the happy man to communicate the critical situation of the magistrate to his wife.

Benjamin worked away with great industry and a good deal of skill, at his occupation, using one hand to raise up his antagonist, while he knocked him over with the other; for he would have been disgraced in his own estimation, had he struck a blow on a fallen adversary. By this considerate arrangement he had found means to hammer the visage of Hiram out of all shape, by the time Richard succeeded in forcing his way through the throng to the point of combat. The Sheriff afterwards declared that, independently of his mortification, as preserver of the peace of the county, at this interruption to its harmony, he was never so grieved in his life, as when he saw this breach of unity between his favorites. Hiram had in some degree become necessary to his vanity, and Benjamin, strange as it may appear, he really loved. This attachment was exhibited in the first words that he uttered.

"Squire Doolittle! Squire Doolittle! I am ashamed to see a man of your character and office forget himself so much as to disturb the peace, insult the court, and beat poor Benjamin in this manner!"

At the sound of Mr. Jones's voice, the steward ceased his employment, and Hiram had an opportunity of raising his discomfited visage towards the mediator. Emboldened by the sight of the Sheriff, Mr. Doolittle again had recourse to his lungs.

"I'll have the law on you for this," he cried desperately; "I'll have the law on you for this. I call on you, Mr. Sheriff, to seize this man, and I demand that you take his body into custody."

By this time Richard was master of the true state of the case, and, turning to the steward, he said, reproachfully—

"Benjamin, how came you in the stocks? I always thought you were mild and docile as a lamb. It was for your docility that I most esteemed you. Benjamin! Benjamin! you have not only disgraced yourself, but your friends, by this shameless conduct. Bless me! bless me! Mr. Doolittle, he seems to have knocked your face all of one side."

Hiram by this time had got on his feet again, and without the reach of the steward, when he broke forth in violent appeals for vengeance. The offence was to apparent to be passed over, and the Sheriff, mindful of the impartiality exhibited by his cousin in the recent trial of the Leather-stocking, came to the painful conclusion that it was necessary to commit his majordomo to prison. As the time of Natty's punishment was expired, and Benjamin found that they were to be confined, for that night at least, in the same apartment, he made no very strong objections to the measure, nor spoke of bail, though, as the Sheriff preceded the party of constables that conducted them to the jail, he uttered the following remonstrance:—

"As to being berthed with Master Bump-ho for a night or so, it's but little I think of it, Squire Dickens, seeing that I calls him an honest man, and one as has a handy way with boat-hooks and rifles; but as for owning that a man desarves any thing worse than a double allowance, for knocking that carpenter's face a-one-side, as you call it, I'll maintain it's ag'in reason and Christianity. If there's a bloodsucker in this 'ere county, it's that very chap. Ay! I know him! and if he hasn't got all the same as dead wood in his head-works, he knows sum-'mat of me. Where's the mighty harm, Squire, that you take it so much to heart? It's all the same as any other battle, d'ye see, sir, being broadside to broadside, only that it was fout at anchor, which was what we did in Port Praya roads, when Suff'ring came in among us; and a suff'ring time he had of it, before he got out again."

Richard thought it unworthy of him to make any reply to this speech; but when his prisoners were safely lodged in an outer dungeon, ordering the bolts to be drawn and the key turned, he withdrew.

Benjamin held frequent and friendly dialogues with different people, through the iron gratings, during the afternoon; but his companion paced their narrow limits, in his mocassins, with quick, impatient treads, his face hanging on his breast in dejection, or when lifted, at moments, to the idlers at the window, lighted, perhaps, for an instant, with the childish aspect of aged forgetfulness, which would vanish directly in an expression of deep and obvious anxiety.

At the close of the day, Edwards was seen at the window, in earnest dialogue with his friend; and after he departed, it was thought that he had communicated words of comfort to the hunter, who threw himself on his pallet, and was soon in a deep sleep. The curious spectators had exhausted the conversation of the steward, who had drunk good fellowship with half of his acquaintance, and as Natty was no longer in motion, by eight o'clock, Billy Kirby, who was the last lounger at the window, retired into the "Templetown Coffee-house," when Natty rose and hung a blanket before the opening, and the prisoners apparently retired for the night.

CHAPTER XXXV

And to avoid the foe's pursuit,
With spurring put their cattle to't;
And till all four were out of wind,
And danger too, ne'er look'd behind.
                                   Hudibras.

As the shades of evening approached, the jurors, witnesses, and other attendants on the court, began to disperse, and before nine o'clock the village was quiet, and its streets nearly deserted. At that hour Judge Temple and his daughter, followed at a short distance by Louisa Grant, walked slowly down the avenue, under the slight shadows of the young poplars, holding the following discourse:—

"You can best soothe his wounded spirit, my child," said Marmaduke; "but it will be dangerous to touch on the nature of his offence; the sanctity of the laws must be respected."

"Surely, sir," cried the impatient Elizabeth, "those laws that condemn a man like the Leather-stocking to so severe a punishment, for an offence that even I must think very venial, cannot be perfect in themselves."

"Thou talkest of what thou dost not understand, Elizabeth," returned her father. "Society cannot exist without wholesome restraints. Those restraints cannot be inflicted, without security and respect to the persons of those who administer them; and it would sound ill indeed to report, that a judge had extended favor to a convicted criminal, because he had saved the life of his child."

"I see—I see the difficulty of your situation, dear sir," cried the daughter; "but in appreciating the offence of poor Natty, I cannot separate the minister of the law from the man."

"There thou talkest as a woman, child; it is not for an assault on Hiram Doolittle, but for threatening the life of a constable, who was in the performance of——"

"It is immaterial whether it be one or the other," interrupted Miss Temple, with a logic that contained more feeling than reason; "I know Natty to be innocent, and, thinking so, I must think all wrong who oppress him."

"His judge among the number! thy father, Elizabeth?"

"Nay, nay, nay; do not put such questions to me; give me my commission, father, and let me proceed to execute it."

The Judge paused a moment, smiling fondly on his child, and then dropped his hand affectionately on her shoulder, as he answered—

"Thou hast reason, Bess, and much of it too, but thy heart lies too near thy head. But listen: in this pocket-book are two hundred dollars. Go to the prison—there are none in this place to harm thee—give this note to the jailor, and when thou seest Bumppo, say what thou wilt to the poor old man; give scope to the feelings of thy warm heart; but try to remember, Elizabeth, that the laws alone remove us from the condition of the savages; that he has been criminal, and that his judge was thy father."

Miss Temple made no reply, but she pressed the hand that held the pocket-book to her bosom, and taking her friend by the arm, they issued together from the enclosure into the principal street of the village.

As they pursued their walk in silence, under the row of houses, where the deeper gloom of the evening effectually concealed their persons, no sound reached them, excepting the slow tread of a yoke of oxen, with the rattling of a cart, that were moving along the street in the same direction with themselves. The figure of the teamster was just discernible by the dim light, lounging by the side of his cattle with a listless air, as if fatigued by the toil of the day. At the corner, where the jail stood, the progress of the ladies was impeded, for a moment, by the oxen, who were turned up to the side of the building, and given a lock of hay, which they had carried on their necks, as a reward for their patient labor. The whole of this was so natural, and so common, that Elizabeth saw nothing to induce a second glance at the team, until she heard the teamster speaking to his cattle in a low voice:—

"Mind yourself, Brindle; will you, sir! will you!"

The language itself was unusual to oxen, with which all who dwell in a new country are familiar; but there was something in the voice also, that startled Miss Temple. On turning the corner, she necessarily approached the man, and her look was enabled to detect the person of Oliver Edwards, concealed under the coarse garb of a teamster. Their eyes met at the same instant, and, notwithstanding the gloom, and the enveloping cloak of Elizabeth, the recognition was mutual.

"Miss Temple!" "Mr. Edwards!" was exclaimed simultaneously, though a feeling that seemed common to both, rendered the words nearly inaudible.

"Is it possible!" exclaimed Edwards, after the moment of doubt had passed; "do I see you so nigh the jail! but you are going to the Rectory; I beg pardon, Miss Grant, I believe; I did not recognise you at first."

The sigh which Louisa uttered was so faint, that it was only heard by Elizabeth, who replied quickly—

"We are going not only to the jail, Mr. Edwards, but into it. We wish to show the Leather-stocking that we do not forget his services, and that at the same time we must be just, we are also grateful. I suppose you are on a similar errand; but let me beg that you will give us leave to precede you ten minutes. Good night, sir; I—I—am quite sorry, Mr. Edwards,

to see you reduced to such labor; I am sure my father would——"

"I shall wait your pleasure, madam," interrupted the youth, coldly. "May I beg that you will not mention my being here?"

"Certainly," said Elizabeth, returning his bow by a slight inclination of her head, and urging the tardy Louisa forward. As they entered the jailor's house, however, Miss Grant found leisure to whisper—

"Would it not be well to offer part of your money to Oliver? half of it will pay the fine of Bumppo; and he is so unused to hardships! I am sure my father would subscribe much of his little pittance, to place him in a station that is more worthy of him."

The involuntary smile that passed over the features of Elizabeth was blended with an expression of deep and heartfelt pity. She did not reply, however, and the appearance of the jailor soon recalled the thoughts of both to the object of their visit.

The rescue of the ladies, and their consequent interest in his prisoner, together with the informal manners that prevailed in the country, all united to prevent any surprise, on the part of the jailor, at their request for admission to Bumppo. The note of Judge Temple, however, would have silenced all objections, if he had felt them, and he led the way without hesitation to the apartment that held the prisoners. The instant the key was put into the lock, the hoarse voice of Benjamin was heard, demanding—

"Yo! hoy! who comes there?"

"Some visitors that you'll be glad to see," returned the jailor. "What have you done to the lock, that it won't turn?"

"Handsomely, handsomely, master," cried the steward; "I have just drove a nail into a berth along-side of this here bolt, as a stopper, d'ye see, so that master Doo-but-little can't be running in and breezing up another fight atwixt us; for, to my account, there'll be but a ban-yan with me soon, seeing that they'll mulct me of my Spaniards, all the same as if I'd overflogged the lubber. Throw your ship into the wind, and lay by for a small matter, will ye? and I'll soon clear a passage."

The sounds of hammering gave an assurance that the steward was in earnest, and in a short time the lock yielded, when the door was opened.

Benjamin had evidently been anticipating the seizure of his money, for he had made frequent demands on the favorite cask at the "Bold Dragoon," during the afternoon and evening, and was now in that state which by marine imagery is called "half-seas-over." It was no easy thing to destroy the balance of the old tar by the effects of liquor, for, as he expressed it himself, "he was too low-rigged not to carry sail in all weathers"; but he was precisely in that condition which is so expressively termed "muddy." When he perceived who the visitors were, he retreated to the side of the room where his pallet lay, and, regardless of the presence of his young mistress, seated himself on it with an air of great sobriety, placing his back firmly against the wall.

"If you undertake to spoil my locks in this manner, Mr. Pump," said the jailor, "I shall put a stopper, as you call it, on your legs, and tie you down to your bed."

"What for should ye, master?" grumbled Benjamin; "I've rode out one squall to-day anchored by the heels, and I wants no more of them. Where's the harm of doing all the same as yourself? Leave that there door free outboard, and you'll find no locking inboard, I'll promise ye."

"I must shut up for the night at nine," said the jailor, "and it's now forty-two minutes past eight." He placed the little candle on a rough pine-table, and withdrew.

"Leather-stocking!" said Elizabeth, when the key of the door was turned on them again, "my good friend Leather-stocking! I have come on a message of gratitude. Had you submitted to the search, worthy old man, the death of the deer would have been a trifle, and all would have been well——"

"Submit to the sarch!" interrupted Natty, raising his face from resting on his knees, without rising from the corner where he had seated himself; "d'ye think, gal, I would let such a varmint into my hut? No, no—I wouldn't have opened the door to your own sweet countenance then. But they are wilcome to sarch among the coals and ashes now; they'll find only some such heap as is to be seen at every pot-ashery in the mountains."

The old man dropped his face again on one hand, and seemed to be lost in melancholy.

"The hut can be rebuilt, and made better than before," returned Miss Temple; "and it shall be my office to see it done, when your imprisonment is ended."

"Can ye raise the dead, child?" said Natty, in a sorrowful voice: "can ye go into the place where you've laid your fathers, and mothers, and children, and gather together their ashes, and make the same men and women of them as afore? You do not know what 'tis to lay your head for more than forty years under the cover of the same logs, and to look on the same things for the better part of a man's life. You are young yet, child, but you are one of the most precious of God's creaters. I had a hope for ye that it might come to pass, but it's all over now; this put to that, will drive the thing quite out of his mind for ever."

Miss Temple must have understood the meaning of the old man better than the other listeners; for, while Louisa stood innocently by her side, commiserating the griefs of the hunter, she bent her head aside, so as to conceal her features. The action and the feeling that caused it lasted but a moment.

"Other logs, and better, though, can be had, and shall be found for you, my old defender," she continued. "Your confinement will soon be over, and, before that time arrives, I shall have a house prepared for you, where you may spend the close of your harmless life in ease and plenty."

"Ease and plenty! house!" repeated Natty, slowly. "You mean well, you mean well, and I quite mourn that it cannot be; but he has seen me a sight and a laughingstock for——"

"Damn your stocks," said Benjamin, flourishing his bottle with one hand, from which he had been taking hasty and repeated draughts, while he made gestures of disdain with the other; "who cares for his bilboes? there's a leg that's been stuck up an end like a jib-boom for an hour, d'ye see, and what's it the worse for't, ha! canst tell me, what's it the worser, ha!"

"I believe you forget, Mr. Pump, in whose presence you are," said Elizabeth.

"Forget you, Miss Lizzy," returned the steward; "if I do, dam'me; you are not to be forgot, like Goody Prettybones, up at the big house there. I say, old sharp-shooter, she may have pretty bones, but I can't say so much for her flesh, d'ye see, for she looks somewhat like an atomy with another man's jacket on. Now, for the skin of her face, it's all the same as a new top-sail with a taut bolt-rope, being snug at the leaches, but all in a bight about the inner cloths."

"Peace—I command you to be silent, sir!" said Elizabeth.

"Ay, ay, ma'am," returned the steward.

"You didn't say I shouldn't drink, though."

"We will not speak of what is to become of others," said Miss Temple, turning again to the hunter—"but of your own fortunes, Natty. It shall be my care to see that you pass the rest of your days in ease and plenty."

"Ease and plenty!" again repeated the Leather-stocking; "what ease can there be to an old man, who must walk a mile across the open fields, before he can find a shade to hide him from a scorching sun! or what plenty is there where you may hunt a day, and not start a buck, or see any thing bigger than a mink, or maybe a stray fox! Ah! I shall have a hard time after them very beavers, for this fine. I must go low toward the Pennsylvany line in sarch of the creaters, maybe a hundred mile; for they are not to be got here-away. No, no,— your betterments and clearings have druv the knowing things out of the country; and instead of beaver-dams, which is the nater of the animal, and according to Providence, you turn back the waters over the low grounds with your mill-dams, as if 'twas in man to stay the drops from going where He wills them to go. —Benny, unless you stop your hand from going so often to your mouth, you won't be ready to start when the time comes."

"Hark'ee, Master Bump-ho," said the steward; "don't you fear for Ben. When the watch is called, set me on my legs, and give me the bearings and distance of where you want to steer, and I'll carry sail with the best of you, I will."

"The time has come now," said the hunter, listening; "I hear the horns of the oxen rubbing ag'in the side of the jail."

"Well, say the word, and then heave ahead, shipmate," said Benjamin.

"You won't betray us, gal?" said Natty, looking simply into the face of Elizabeth—"you won't betray an old man, who craves to breathe the clear air of heaven? I mean no harm; and if the law says that I must pay the hundred dollars, I'll take the season through, but it shall be forthcoming; and this good man will help me."

"You catch them," said Benjamin, with a sweeping gesture of his arm, "and if they get away again, call me a slink, that's all."

"But what mean you?" cried the wondering Elizabeth. "Here you must stay for thirty days; but I have the money for your fine in this purse. Take it; pay it in the morning, and summon patience for your month. I will come often to

see you, with my friend; we will make up your clothes with our own hands; indeed, indeed, you shall be comfortable."

"Would ye, children?" said Natty, advancing across the floor with an air of kindness, and taking the hand of Elizabeth; "would ye be so kearful of an old man, and just for shooting the beast which cost him nothing? Such things doesn't run in the blood, I believe, for you seem not to forget a favor. Your little fingers couldn't do much on a buck-skin, nor be you used to such a thread as sinews. But if he hasn't got past hearing, he shall hear it and know it, that he may see, like me, there is some who know how to remember a kindness."

"Tell him nothing," cried Elizabeth, earnestly; "if you love me, if you regard my feelings, tell him nothing. It is of yourself only I would talk, and for yourself only I act. I grieve, Leather-stocking, that the law requires that you should be detained here so long; but, after all, it will be only a short month, and—"

"A month!" exclaimed Natty, opening his mouth with his usual laugh; "not a day, nor a night, nor an hour, gal. Judge Temple may sintence, but he can't keep, without a better dungeon than this. I was taken once by the French, and they put sixty-two of us in a block-house, nigh hand to old Frontinac; but 'twas easy to cut through a pine log to them that was used to timber." The hunter paused, and looked cautiously around the room, when, laughing again, he shoved the steward gently from his post, and removing the bed-clothes, discovered a hole recently cut in the logs with a mallet and chisel. "It's only a kick, and the outside piece is off, and then——"

"Off! ay, off!" cried Benjamin, rousing from his stupor; "well, here's off. Ay! ay! you catch 'em, and I'll hold on to them said beaver-hats."

"I fear this lad will trouble me much," said Natty; " 'twill be a hard pull for the mountain, should they take the scent soon, and he is not in a state of mind to run."

"Run!" echoed the steward; "no, sheer alongside, and let's have a fight of it."

"Peace!" ordered Elizabeth.

"Ay, ay, ma'am."

"You will not leave us, surely, Leather-stocking," continued Miss Temple; "I beseech you, reflect that you will be driven to the woods entirely, and that you are fast getting old. Be patient for a little time, when you can go abroad openly, and with honor."

"Is there beaver to be catched here, gal?"

"If not, here is money to discharge the fine, and in a month you are free. See, here it is in gold."

"Gold!" said Natty, with a kind of childish curiosity; "it's long sin' I've seen a gold piece. We used to get the broad joes, in the old war, as plenty as the bears be now. I remember there was a man in Dieskau's army, that was killed, who had a dozen of the shining things sewed up in his shirt. I didn't handle them myself, but I seen them cut out with my own eyes; they was bigger and brighter than them be."

"These are English guineas, and are yours," said Elizabeth; "an earnest of what shall be done for you."

"Me! why should you give me this treasure?" said Natty, looking earnestly at the maiden.

"Why! have you not saved my life? did you not rescue me from the jaws of the beast?" exclaimed Elizabeth, veiling her eyes, as if to hide some hideous object from her view.

The hunter took the money, and continued turning it in his hand for some time, piece by piece, talking aloud during the operation.

"There's a rifle, they say, out on the Cherry Valley, that will carry a hundred rods and kill. I've seen good guns in my day, but none quite equal to that. A hundred rods with any sartainty is great shooting! Well, well—I'm old, and the gun I have will answer my time. Here, child, take back your gold. But the hour has come; I hear him talking to the cattle, and I must be going. You won't tell of us, gal—you won't tell of us, will ye?"

"Tell of you!" echoed Elizabeth. "But take the money, old man; take the money, even if you go into the mountains."

"No, no," said Natty, shaking his head kindly; "I would not rob you so for twenty rifles. But there's one thing you can do for me, if ye will, that no other is at hand to do."

"Name it—name it."

"Why, it's only to buy a canister of powder; —'twill cost two silver dollars. Benny Pump has the money ready, but we daren't come into the town to get it. Nobody has it but the Frenchman. 'Tis of the best, and just suits a rifle. Will you get it for me, gal?—say, will you get it for me?"

"Will I! I will bring it to you, Leather-stocking, though I toil a day in quest of you through the woods. But where shall I find you, and how?"

"Where!" said Natty, musing a moment—

"tomorrow, on the Vision; on the very top of the Vision, I'll meet you, child, just as the sun gets over our heads. See that it's the fine grain; you'll know it by the gloss, and the price."

"I will do it," said Elizabeth, firmly.

Natty now seated himself, and, placing his feet in the hole, with a slight effort he opened a passage through into the street. The ladies heard the rustling of hay, and well understood the reason why Edwards was in the capacity of a teamster.

"Come, Benny," said the hunter; "'twill be no darker to-night, for the moon will rise in an hour."

"Stay!" exclaimed Elizabeth; "it should not be said that you escaped in the presence of the daughter of Judge Temple. Return, Leather-stocking, and let us retire, before you execute your plan."

Natty was about to reply, when the approach footsteps of the jailor announced the necessity of his immediate return. He had barely time to regain his feet, and to conceal the hole with the bed-clothes, across which Benjamin very opportunely fell, before the key was turned, and the door of the apartment opened.

"Isn't Miss Temple ready to go?" said the civil jailor:—"it's the usual hour for locking up."

"I follow you, sir," returned Elizabeth, "good night, Leather-stocking."

"It's a fine grain, gal, and I think 'twill carry lead further than common. I am getting old, and can't follow up the game with the step that I used to could."

Miss Temple waved her hand for silence, and preceded Louisa and the keeper from the apartment. The man turned the key once, and observed that he would return and secure his prisoners, when he had lighted the ladies to the street. Accordingly, they parted at the door of the building, when the jailor retired to his dungeons, and the ladies walked, with throbbing hearts, towards the corner.

"Now the Leather-stocking refuses the money," whispered Louisa, "it can all be given to Mr. Edwards, and that added to——"

"Listen!" said Elizabeth; "I hear the rustling of the hay; they are escaping at this moment. Oh! they will be detected instantly!"

By this time they were at the corner, where Edwards and Natty were in the act of drawing the almost helpless body of Benjamin through the aperture. The oxen had started back from their hay, and were standing with their heads down the street, leaving room for the party to act in.

"Throw the hay into the cart," said Edwards, "or they will suspect how it has been done. Quick, that they may not see it."

Natty had just returned from executing this order, when the light of the keeper's candle shone through the hole, and instantly his voice was heard in the jail, exclaiming for his prisoners.

"What is to be done now?" said Edwards— "this drunken fellow will cause our detection, and we have not a moment to spare."

"Who's drunk, ye lubber!" muttered the steward.

"A break-jail! a break-jail!" shouted five or six voices from within.

"We must leave him," said Edwards.

" 'Twouldn't be kind, lad," returned Natty; "he took half the disgrace of the stocks on himself to-day, and the creater has feeling."

At this moment two or three men were heard issuing from the door of the "Bold Dragoon," and among them the voice of Billy Kirby.

"There's no moon yet," cried the wood-chopper; "but it's a clear night. Come, who's for home? Hark! what a rumpus they're kicking up in the jail—here's go and see what it's about."

"We shall be lost," said Edwards, "if we don't drop this man."

At that instant Elizabeth moved close to him, and said rapidly, in a low voice—

"Lay him in the cart, and start the oxen; no one will look there."

"There's a woman's quickness in the thought," said the youth.

The proposition was no sooner made than executed. The steward was seated on the hay, and enjoined to hold his peace, and apply the goad that was placed in his hand, while the oxen were urged on. So soon as this arrangement was completed, Edwards and the hunter stole along the houses for a short distance, when they disappeared through an opening that led into the rear of the buildings. The oxen were in brisk motion, and presently the cries of pursuit were heard in the street. The ladies quickened their pace, with a wish to escape the crowd of constables and idlers that were approaching, some execrating, and some laughing at the exploit of the prisoners. In the confusion, the voice of Kirby was plainly distinguishable above all the others, shouting and swearing that he would have the fugitives, threatening to bring back Natty in one pocket, and Benjamin in the other.

"Spread yourselves, men," he cried, as he passed the ladies, his heavy feet sounding along the street like the tread of a dozen; "spread yourselves; to the mountains; they'll be in the mountain in a quarter of an hour, and then look out for a long rifle."

His cries were echoed from twenty mouths, for not only the jail, but the taverns had sent forth their numbers, some earnest in the pursuit, and others joining it as in sport.

As Elizabeth turned in at her father's gate, she saw the wood-chopper stop at the cart, when she gave Benjamin up for lost. While they were hurrying up the walk, two figures, stealing cautiously but quickly under the shades of the trees, met the eyes of the ladies, and in a moment Edwards and the hunter crossed their path.

"Miss Temple, I may never see you again," exclaimed the youth; "let me thank you for all your kindness; you do not, cannot know, my motives."

"Fly! fly!" cried Elizabeth:—"the village is alarmed. Do not be found conversing with me at such a moment, and in these grounds."

"Nay, I must speak, though detection were certain."

"Your retreat to the bridge is already cut off; before you can gain the wood your pursuers will be there.—If—"

"If what?" cried the youth. "Your advice has saved me once already; I will follow it to death."

"The street is now silent and vacant," said Elizabeth, after a pause; "cross it, and you will find my father's boat in the lake. It would be easy to land from it where you please in the hills."

"But Judge Temple might complain of the trespass."

"His daughter shall be accountable, sir."

The youth uttered something in a low voice, that was heard only by Elizabeth, and turned to execute what she had suggested. As they were separating, Natty approached the females, and said—

"You'll remember the canister of powder, children. Them beavers must be had, and I and the pups be getting old; we want the best of ammunition."

"Come, Natty," said Edwards, impatiently.

"Coming, lad, coming. God bless you, young

ones, both of ye, for ye mean well and kindly to the old man."

The ladies paused until they had lost sight of the retreating figures, when they immediately entered the Mansion-house.

While this scene was passing in the walk, Kirby had overtaken the cart, which was his own, and had been driven by Edwards without asking the owner, from the place where the patient oxen usually stood at evening, waiting the pleasure of their master.

"Woa—come hither, Golden," he cried; "why, how come you off the end of the bridge, where I left you, dummies?"

"Heave ahead," muttered Benjamin, giving a random blow with his lash, that alighted on the shoulder of the other.

"Who the devil be you?" cried Billy, turning round in surprise, but unable to distinguish, in the dark, the hard visage that was just peering over the cart-rails.

"Who be I? why I'm helmsman aboard of this here craft, d'ye see, and a straight wake I'm making of it. Ay, ay! I've got the bridge right ahead, and the bilboes dead-aft; I calls that good steerage, boy. Heave ahead."

"Lay your lash in the right spot, Mr. Benny Pump," said the wood-chopper, "or I'll put you in the palm of my hand, and box your ears. Where be you going with my team?"

"Team!"

"Ay, my cart and oxen."

"Why, you must know, Master Kirby, that the Leather-stocking and I—that's Benny Pump—you knows Ben?—well, Benny and I —no, me and Benny; dam'me if I know how 'tis; but some of us are bound after a cargo of beaver-skins, d'ye see, and so we've pressed the cart to ship them 'ome in. I say, Master Kirby, what a lubberly oar you pull—you handle an oar, boy, pretty much as a cow would a musket, or a lady would a marling-spike."

Billy had discovered the state of the steward's mind, and he walked for some time alongside of the cart, musing with himself, when he took the goad from Benjamin (who fell back on the hay, and was soon asleep), and drove his cattle down the street, over the bridge, and up the mountain, towards a clearing, in which he was to work the next day, without any other interruption than a few hasty questions from parties of the constables.

Elizabeth stood for an hour at the window of her room, and saw the torches of the pursuers gliding along the side of the mountain, and heard their shouts and alarms; but, at the end of that time, the last party returned, wearied and disappointed, and the village became as still as when she issued from the gate on her mission to the jail.   1823

WILLIAM CULLEN BRYANT

1794–1878

WHEN the young Bryant, urged on by Henry Sedgwick and Gulian Verplanck, two far-sighted New Yorkers, left his law practice in Great Barrington, Massachusetts, to edit the *New-York Review*, those who had watched his career as a poet were dismayed. They had further reason to fear that America had lost her most promising poet to the vulgar trade of journalism when Bryant assumed in 1829 the editorship of the *New York Evening Post*, a position which he would occupy for a half century. The elder Richard H. Dana, himself a poet and jealous for the dignity of American letters, remarked that "If Bryant must write in a paper to get his bread, I pray God he may get a bellyful." The forebodings of Bryant's admirers were not justified, for he continued to be a poet, but it is a fact that one-third of his poetry, including most of what we now remember, was written before 1829. After 1836 he gave up all thought of a career outside journalism and bent his efforts toward making the *Post* the great liberal paper it became under his leadership.

A farm boy from Cummington in the Berkshire hills of Massachusetts, Bryant was encouraged in his precocious devotion to poetry by his father, the village doctor. At nine he was turning off Popean couplets with ease. An anti-Jefferson satire, *The Embargo, or Sketches of the Times*, so pleased his Federalist father that he had it published at Boston in 1808 and again in 1809 with other verses added. After a year at Williams College (1810–1811) Bryant succumbed to the law, the inevitable profession of a literary man in the early days of the Republic. He had practiced nine years in Great Barrington before his flight to New York. Meanwhile American lovers of poetry had marked him for a great future when they read "Thanatopsis" in 1817 and his slender volume of *Poems* in 1821.

By inheritance a conservative in religion and politics, Bryant early broke away from his Calvinist and Federalist upbringing. As a young editor he defended the principles of the more radical democrats. The *Post* supported low tariffs, upheld the right of laborers to organize unions, and attacked the Bank of the United States, but when the Democratic party became openly the party of slavery Bryant abandoned it for the new Republican party of Lincoln, whose ability he early recognized. The *Post* urged a vigorous prosecution of the Civil War but advocated moderation in the days of Reconstruction. As the years passed Bryant was looked up to as the first citizen of New York. Shy and reserved in manner and uncomfortable at public gatherings in which he had a part, he wrote with devastating wit and force. By his courage, learning, and urbanity he raised the standards of American journalism immeasurably.

As a poet Bryant was the first in America to feel the surge of the romantic revolution in England. The first draft of "Thanatopsis" (1811), beginning in what is now the seventeenth line, betrays the sixteen-year-old boy's reading of Blair and Gray and a deistic attitude taken over from the Augustan poets. When the introductory lines were added in 1821 he had experienced his Wordsworthian conversion. His first reading of *Lyrical Ballads* had caused a "thousand springs . . . to gush up at once into [his] heart and the face of Nature, of a sudden, to change into a strange freshness and life." Yet Bryant is not merely an American Wordsworth. To both poets as young men, it is true, the colors and forms of nature were an appetite, a feeling and a love, but Bryant seldom loses himself pantheistically in nature. One feels still, in his more ambitious poems, the awfulness of the Puritan God though He is transformed into a "presence" or a "majesty."

If this awesome nature of Bryant's poetry is alien to us, we can still enjoy "A Winter Piece" and "Summer Wind," first of a long procession of poems inspired by the New England countryside. It must be remembered that he was the first poet to awaken other poets and readers of poetry to the beauty of our scenery, strange as it may seem that anyone ever had to be convinced that Monument Mountain and Green River are as fit for poetry as Skiddaw or the Severn. We should recall, too, his other services to his art. He lectured sensibly about poetry; he helped to end the tyranny of the heroic couplet by his use of varying meters; as reviewer and editor he encouraged younger poets like Emerson and Longfellow. He believed that it was only a matter of time before America would have her own poetical tradition. As he said in his lectures before the Athenaeum Society in New York in 1826: "If . . . our poetry should finally fail of rivaling that of Europe, it will be because Genius sits idle in the midst of its treasures."

The Life and Works of William Cullen Bryant, Parke Godwin, ed., 6 vols., New York, 1883–1884.

William Cullen Bryant, Representative Selections, with Introduction, Bibliography, and Notes (American Writers Series), Tremaine McDowell, ed., New York, 1935.

Allan Nevins, *The Evening Post: A Century of Journalism*, New York, 1922.

H. H. Peckham, *Gotham Yankee: A Biography of William Cullen Bryant*, New York, 1950.

THANATOPSIS [1]

To him who in the love of Nature holds
Communion with her visible forms, she speaks
A various language; for his gayer hours
She has a voice of gladness, and a smile
And eloquence of beauty, and she glides
Into his darker musings, with a mild
And healing sympathy, that steals away
Their sharpness, ere he is aware. When thoughts
Of the last bitter hour come like a blight
Over thy spirit, and sad images   10
Of the stern agony, and shroud, and pall,
And breathless darkness, and the narrow house,
Make thee to shudder, and grow sick at
    heart;—
Go forth, under the open sky, and list
To Nature's teachings, while from all around—
Earth and her waters, and the depths of air—
Comes a still voice—
                Yet a few days, and thee
The all-beholding sun shall see no more
In all his course; nor yet in the cold ground, 20
Where thy pale form was laid, with many tears,
Nor in the embrace of ocean, shall exist
Thy image. Earth, that nourished thee, shall
    claim
Thy growth, to be resolved to earth again,
And, lost each human trace, surrendering up
Thine individual being, shalt thou go
To mix for ever with the elements,
To be a brother to the insensible rock
And to the sluggish clod, which the rude swain
Turns with his share, and treads upon. The
    oak   30
Shall send his roots abroad, and pierce thy
    mould.

Yet not to thine eternal resting-place
Shalt thou retire alone, nor couldst thou wish
Couch more magnificent. Thou shalt lie down
With patriarchs of the infant world—with
    kings,
The powerful of the earth—the wise, the good,
Fair forms, and hoary seers of ages past,
All in one mighty sepulchre. The hills
Rock-ribbed and ancient as the sun,—the vales
Stretching in pensive quietness between;   40
The venerable woods—rivers that move
In majesty, and the complaining brooks
That make the meadows green; and, poured
    round all,
Old Ocean's gray and melancholy waste,—

[1] The first version of "Thanatopsis" was written when Bryant was sixteen. In 1821 he added an introduction (ll. 1–17) and a conclusion (ll. 66–81).

Are but the solemn decorations all
Of the great tomb of man. The golden sun,
The planets, all the infinite host of heaven,
Are shining on the sad abodes of death,
Through the still lapse of ages. All that tread
The globe are but a handful to the tribes   50
That slumber in its bosom.—Take the wings
Of morning, pierce the Barcan wilderness,
Or lose thyself in the continuous woods
Where rolls the Oregon, and hears no sound,
Save his own dashings—yet the dead are there:
And millions in those solitudes, since first
The flight of years began, have laid them down
In their last sleep—the dead reign there alone.
So shalt thou rest, and what if thou withdraw
In silence from the living, and no friend   60
Take note of thy departure? All that breathe
Will share thy destiny. The gay will laugh
When thou art gone, the solemn brood of care
Plod on, and each one as before will chase
His favorite phantom; yet all these shall leave
Their mirth and their employments, and shall
    come
And make their bed with thee. As the long
    train
Of ages glide away, the sons of men,
The youth in life's green spring, and he who
    goes
In the full strength of years, matron and
    maid,   70
The speechless babe, and the gray-headed
    man—
Shall one by one be gathered to thy side
By those, who in their turn shall follow them.

So live that when thy summons comes to
    join
The innumerable caravan, which moves
To that mysterious realm, where each shall take
His chamber in the silent halls of death,
Thou go not, like the quarry-slave at night,
Scourged to his dungeon, but, sustained and
    soothed
By an unfaltering trust, approach thy grave, 80
Like one who wraps the drapery of his couch
About him, and lies down to pleasant dreams.
1811   1817, 1821

THE YELLOW VIOLET

When beechen buds begin to swell,
    And woods the blue-bird's warble know,
The yellow violet's modest bell
    Peeps from the last year's leaves below.

Ere russet fields their green resume,
  Sweet flower, I love, in forest bare,
To meet thee, when thy faint perfume
  Alone is in the virgin air.

Of all her train, the hands of Spring
  First plant thee in the watery mould,   10
And I have seen thee blossoming
  Beside the snow-bank's edges cold.

Thy parent sun, who bade thee view
  Pale skies, and chilling moisture sip,
Has bathed thee in his own bright hue,
  And streaked with jet thy glowing lip.

Yet slight thy form, and low thy seat,
  And earthward bent thy gentle eye,
Unapt the passing view to meet,
  When loftier flowers are flaunting nigh.   20

Oft, in the sunless April day,
  Thy early smile has stayed my walk;
But midst the gorgeous blooms of May,
  I passed thee on thy humble stalk.

So they, who climb to wealth, forget
  The friends in darker fortunes tried.
I copied them—but I regret
  That I should ape the ways of pride.

And when again the genial hour
  Awakes the painted tribes of light,   30
I'll not o'erlook the modest flower
  That made the woods of April bright.
1814   1821

TO A WATERFOWL

Whither, midst falling dew,
While glow the heavens with the last steps of
    day,
Far, through their rosy depths, dost thou
    pursue
  Thy solitary way?

Vainly the fowler's eye
Might mark thy distant flight to do thee wrong,
As, darkly seen against the crimson sky,
  Thy figure floats along.

Seek'st thou the plashy brink
Of weedy lake, or marge of river wide,   10
Or where the rocking billows rise and sink
  On the chafed ocean-side?

There is a Power whose care
Teaches thy way along that pathless coast—
The desert and illimitable air—
  Lone wandering, but not lost.

All day thy wings have fanned,
At that far height, the cold, thin atmosphere,
Yet stoop not, weary, to the welcome land,
  Though the dark night is near.   20

And soon that toil shall end;
Soon shalt thou find a summer home, and rest,
And scream among thy fellows; reeds shall
    bend,
  Soon, o'er thy sheltered nest.

Thou'rt gone, the abyss of heaven
Hath swallowed up thy form; yet, on my heart
Deeply has sunk the lesson thou hast given,
  And shall not soon depart.

He who, from zone to zone,
Guides through the boundless sky thy certain
    flight,   30
In the long way that I must tread alone,
  Will lead my steps aright.
1815   1818

A WINTER PIECE

  The time has been that these wild solitudes,
Yet beautiful as wild, were trod by me
Oftener than now; and when the ills of life
Had chafed my spirit—when the unsteady
    pulse
Beat with strange flutterings—I would wander
    forth
And seek the woods. The sunshine on my path
Was to me as a friend. The swelling hills,
The quiet dells retiring far between,
With gentle invitation to explore
Their windings, were a calm society   10
That talked with me and soothed me. Then
    the chant
Of birds, and chime of brooks, and soft caress
Of the fresh sylvan air, made me forget
The thoughts that broke my peace, and I began
To gather simples by the fountain's brink,
And lose myself in day-dreams. While I stood
In Nature's loneliness, I was with one
With whom I early grew familiar, one
Who never had a frown for me, whose voice
Never rebuked me for the hours I stole   20
From cares I loved not, but of which the world

Deems highest, to converse with her. When
shrieked
The bleak November winds, and smote the
woods,
And the brown fields were herbless, and the
shades,
That met above the merry rivulet,
Were spoiled, I sought, I loved them still; they
seemed
Like old companions in adversity.
Still there was beauty in my walks; the brook,
Bordered with sparkling frost-work, was as gay
As with its fringe of summer flowers. Afar,   30
The village with its spires, the path of streams
And dim receding valleys, hid before
By interposing trees, lay visible
Through the bare grove, and my familiar
haunts
Seemed new to me. Nor was I slow to come
Among them, when the clouds, from their still
skirts,
Had shaken down on earth their feathery snow,
And all was white. The pure keen air abroad,
Albeit it breathed no scent of herb, nor heard
Love-call of bird nor merry hum of bee,   40
Was not the air of death. Bright mosses crept
Over the spotted trunks, and the close buds,
That lay along the boughs, instinct with life,
Patient, and waiting the soft breath of Spring,
Feared not the piercing spirit of the North.
The snow-bird twittered on the beechen bough,
And 'neath the hemlock, whose thick branches
bent
Beneath its bright cold burden, and kept dry
A circle, on the earth, of withered leaves,
The partridge found a shelter. Through the
snow   50
The rabbit sprang away. The lighter track
Of fox, and the raccoon's broad path, were
there,
Crossing each other. From his hollow tree
The squirrel was abroad, gathering the nuts
Just fallen, that asked the winter cold and
sway
Of winter blast, to shake them from their hold.

But Winter has yet brighter scenes—he
boasts
Splendors beyond what gorgeous Summer
knows;
Or Autumn with his many fruits, and woods
All flushed with many hues. Come when the
rains   60
Have glazed the snow and clothed the trees
with ice,

While the slant sun of February pours
Into the bowers a flood of light. Approach!
The incrusted surface shall upbear thy steps,
And the broad arching portals of the grove
Welcome thy entering. Look! the massy trunks
Are cased in the pure crystal; each light spray,
Nodding and tinkling in the breath of heaven,
Is studded with its trembling water-drops,
That glimmer with an amethystine light.   70
But round the parent-stem the long low boughs
Bend, in a glittering ring, and arbors hide
The glassy floor. Oh! you might deem the spot
The spacious cavern of some virgin mine,
Deep in the womb of earth—where the gems
grow,
And diamonds put forth radiant rods and bud
With amethyst and topaz—and the place
Lit up, most royally, with the pure beam
That dwells in them. Or haply the vast hall
Of fairy palace, that outlasts the night,   80
And fades not in the glory of the sun;—
Where crystal columns send forth slender
shafts
And crossing arches; and fantastic aisles
Wind from the sight in brightness, and are lost
Among the crowded pillars. Raise thine eye;
Thou seest no cavern roof, no palace vault;
There the blue sky and the white drifting cloud
Look in. Again the wildered fancy dreams
Of spouting fountains, frozen as they rose,
And fixed, with all their branching jets, in
air,   90
And all their sluices sealed. All, all is light;
Light without shade. But all shall pass away
With the next sun. From numberless vast trunks
Loosened, the crashing ice shall make a sound
Like the far roar of rivers, and the eve
Shall close o'er the brown woods as it was wont.

And it is pleasant, when the noisy streams
Are just set free, and milder suns melt off
The plashy snow, save only the firm drift
In the deep glen or the close shade of
pines—   100
'Tis pleasant to behold the wreaths of smoke
Roll up among the maples of the hill,
Where the shrill sound of youthful voices
wakes
The shriller echo, as the clear pure lymph,
That from the wounded trees, in twinkling
drops,
Falls, mid the golden brightness of the morn,
Is gathered in with brimming pails, and oft,
Wielded by sturdy hands, the stroke of axe
Makes the woods ring. Along the quiet air,

Come and float calmly off the soft light
    clouds,   110
Such as you see in summer, and the winds
Scarce stir the branches. Lodged in sunny
    cleft,
Where the cold breezes come not, blooms alone
The little wind-flower, whose just opened eye
Is blue as the spring heaven it gazes at—
Startling the loiterer in the naked groves
With unexpected beauty, for the time
Of blossoms and green leaves is yet afar.
And ere it comes, the encountering winds shall
    oft
Muster their wrath again, and rapid clouds 120
Shade heaven, and bounding on the frozen
    earth
Shall fall their volleyed stores, rounded like
    hail
And white like snow, and the loud North again
Shall buffet the vexed forest in his rage.
1820   1825

SPAIN

Aye, wear the chain—ye who for once have
    known
The sweets of freedom—yet could crouch
    again
In blind and trembling worship of a throne;
Aye wear—for ye are worthy—wear the chain
And bow, till ye are weary, to the yoke
    Your patriot fathers broke.

Degenerate Spaniards! let the priestly band
Possess your realm again; and let them wake
The fires of pious murder in your land,
And drag your best and bravest to the stake, 10
And tread down truth, and in the dungeon bind
    The dreaded strength of mind.

Give up the promise of bright days that cast
A glory of your nation from afar;
Call back the darkness of the ages past
To quench that holy dawn's new-risen star;
Let only tyrants and their slaves be found
    Alive on Spanish ground.

Yet mark! ye cast the gift of heaven away,
And your best blood for this shall yet be
    shed;   20
The fire shall waste your borders, and the way
Be covered with its heaps of festering dead,
And vultures of the cliff on every plain
    Feast high upon the slain.

The spirit that of yore had slept so long,
Then woke, and drove the Moors to Afric's
    shore,
Lives, and repressed, shall rise one day more
    strong—
Rise and redeem your shackled race once more,
And crush, mid showers of blood and shrieks
    and groans,
    Mitres and stars and throne.   30
1822   1823

THE DEATH OF THE FLOWERS [2]

The melancholy days are come, the saddest of
    the year,
Of wailing winds, and naked woods, and
    meadows brown and sere;
Heaped in the hollows of the grove, the autumn
    leaves lie dead;
They rustle to the eddying gust, and to the
    rabbit's tread;
The robin and the wren are flown, and from
    the shrubs the jay,
And from the wood-top calls the crow through
    all the gloomy day.

Where are the flowers, the fair young flowers,
    that lately sprang and stood
In brighter light and softer airs, a beauteous
    sisterhood?
Alas! they all are in their graves, the gentle
    race of flowers
Are lying in their lowly beds, with the fair and
    good of ours.   10
The rain is falling where they lie, but the cold
    November rain
Calls not from out the gloomy earth the lovely
    ones again.

The wind-flower and the violet, they perished
    long ago,
And the brier-rose and the orchis died amid
    the summer glow;
But on the hills the golden-rod, and the aster
    in the wood,
And the yellow sunflower by the brook in
    autumn beauty stood,
Till fell the frost from the clear cold heaven,
    as falls the plague on men,
And the brightness of their smile was gone,
    from upland, glade, and glen.

And now, when comes the calm mild day, as
    still such days will come,

[2] Written in memory of Bryant's sister, who died in 1824.

To call the squirrel and the bee from out their
    winter home;   20
When the sound of dropping nuts is heard,
    though all the trees are still,
And twinkle in the smoky light the waters of
    the rill,
The south wind searches for the flowers whose
    fragrance late he bore,
And sighs to find them in the wood and by the
    stream no more.

And then I think of one who in her youthful
    beauty died,
The fair meek blossom that grew up and faded
    by my side.
In the cold moist earth we laid her, when the
    forests cast the leaf,
And we wept that one so lovely should have a
    life so brief:
Yet not unmeet it was that one, like that young
    friend of ours,
So gentle and so beautiful, should perish with
    the flowers.   30
1825   1825

A SUMMER RAMBLE

The quiet August noon has come;
    A slumberous silence fills the sky,
The fields are still, the woods are dumb,
    In glassy sleep the waters lie.

And mark yon soft white clouds that rest
    Above our vale, a moveless throng;
The cattle on the mountain's breast
    Enjoy the grateful shadow long.

Oh, how unlike those merry hours,
    In early June, when Earth laughs out,   10
When the fresh winds make love to flowers,
    And woodlands sing and waters shout—

When in the grass sweet voices talk,
    And strains of tiny music swell
From every moss-cup of the rock,
    From every nameless blossom's bell!

But now a joy too deep for sound,
    A peace no other season knows,
Hushes the heavens and wraps the ground,
    The blessing of supreme repose.   20

Away! I will not be, to-day,
    The only slave of toil and care;

Away from desk and dust! away!
    I'll be as idle as the air.

Beneath the open sky abroad,
    Among the plants and breathing things,
The sinless, peaceful works of God,
    I'll share the calm the season brings.

Come, thou, in whose soft eyes I see
    The gentle meanings of thy heart,   30
One day amid the woods with me,
    From men and all their cares apart.

And where, upon the meadow's breast,
    The shadow of the thicket lies,
The blue wild-flowers thou gatherest
    Shall glow yet deeper near thine eyes.

Come, and when mid the calm profound,
    I turn, those gentle eyes to seek,
They, like the lovely landscape round,
    Of innocence and peace shall speak.   40

Rest here, beneath the unmoving shade,
    And on the silent valleys gaze,
Winding and widening, till they fade
    In yon soft ring of summer haze.

The village trees their summits rear
    Still as its spire, and yonder flock
At rest in those calm fields appear
    As chiselled from the lifeless rock.

One tranquil mount the scene o'erlooks—
    There the hushed winds their sabbath
    keep,   50
While a near hum from bees and brooks
    Comes faintly like the breath of sleep.

Well may the gazer deem that when,
    Worn with the struggle and the strife,
And heart-sick at the wrongs of men,
    The good forsakes the scene of life,

Like this deep quiet that, awhile,
    Lingers the lovely landscape o'er,
Shall be the peace whose holy smile
    Welcomes him to a happier shore.   60
1826   1826

HYMN OF THE CITY

Not in the solitude
Alone may man commune with Heaven, or see,

Only in savage wood
And sunny vale, the present Deity;
    Or only hear his voice
Where the winds whisper and the waves re-
    joice.

    Even here do I behold
Thy steps, Almighty!—here, amid the crowd
    Through the great city rolled,
With everlasting murmur deep and loud—   10
    Choking the ways that wind
'Mong the proud piles, the work of human kind.

    Thy golden sunshine comes
From the round heaven, and on their dwelling
    lies
    And lights their inner homes;
For them thou fill'st with air the unbounded
    skies,
    And givest them the stores
Of ocean, and the harvests of its shores.

    Thy Spirit is around,   19
Quickening the restless mass that sweeps along;
    And this eternal sound—
Voices and footfalls of the numberless throng—
    Like the resounding sea,
Or like the rainy tempest, speaks of Thee.

    And when the hour of rest
Comes, like a calm upon the mid-sea brine,
    Hushing its billowy breast—
The quiet of that moment too is thine;
    It breathes of Him who keeps
The vast and hapless city while it sleeps.   30
1830   1830

THE PRAIRIES [3]

These are the gardens of the Desert, these
The unshorn fields, boundless and beautiful,
For which the speech of England has no
    name—
The Prairies. I behold them for the first,
And my heart swells, while the dilated sight
Takes in the encircling vastness. Lo! they
    stretch
In airy undulations, far away,
As if the Ocean, in his gentlest swell,
Stood still, with all his rounded billows fixed
And motionless forever. Motionless?—   10
No—they are all unchained again. The clouds
Sweep over with their shadows, and, beneath,

[3] Bryant visited Illinois in 1832.

The surface rolls and fluctuates to the eye;
Dark hollows seem to glide along and chase
The sunny ridges. Breezes of the South!
Who toss the golden and the flame-like flowers,
And pass the prairie-hawk that, poised on high,
Flaps his broad wings, yet moves not—ye have
    played
Among the palms of Mexico and vines   19
Of Texas, and have crisped the limpid brooks
That from the fountains of Sonora glide
Into the calm Pacific—have ye fanned
A nobler or a lovelier scene than this?
Man hath no part in all this glorious work:
The hand that built the firmament hath heaved
And smoothed these verdant swells, and sown
    their slopes
With herbage, planted them with island-groves,
And hedged them round with forests. Fitting
    floor
For this magnificent temple of the sky—   29
With flowers whose glory and whose multitude
Rival the constellations! The great heavens
Seem to stoop down upon the scene in love,—
A nearer vault, and of a tenderer blue,
Than that which bends above our Eastern hills.

    As o'er the verdant waste I guide my steed,
Among the high rank grass that sweeps his
    sides,
The hollow beating of his footstep seems
A sacrilegious sound. I think of those
Upon whose rest he tramples. Are they here—
The dead of other days?—and did the dust   40
Of these fair solitudes once stir with life
And burn with passion? Let the mighty mounds
That overlook the rivers, or that rise
In the dim forest crowded with old oaks,
Answer. A race, that long has passed away,
Built them; a disciplined and populous race
Heaped, with long toil, the earth, while yet the
    Greek
Was hewing the Pentelicus to forms
Of symmetry, and rearing on its rock   49
The glittering Parthenon. These ample fields
Nourished their harvests, here their herds were
    fed,
When haply by their stalls the bison lowed,
And bowed his manèd shoulder to the yoke.
All day this desert murmured with their toils,
Till twilight blushed, and lovers walked, and
    wooed
In a forgotten language, and old tunes,
From instruments of unremembered form,
Gave the soft winds a voice. The red-man
    came—

The roaming hunter-tribes, warlike and fierce,
And the mound-builders vanished from the
earth.   60
The solitude of centuries untold
Has settled where they dwelt. The prairie-wolf
Hunts in their meadows, and his fresh-dug den
Yawns by my path. The gopher mines the
ground
Where stood their swarming cities. All is gone;
All—save the piles of earth that hold their
bones,
The platforms where they worshipped unknown
gods,
The barriers which they builded from the soil
To keep the foe at bay—till o'er the walls   69
The wild beleaguerers broke, and, one by one,
The strongholds of the plain were forced, and
heaped
With corpses. The brown vultures of the wood
Flocked to those vast uncovered sepulchres,
And sat, unscared and silent, at their feast.
Haply some solitary fugitive,
Lurking in marsh and forest, till the sense
Of desolation and of fear became
Bitterer than death, yielded himself to die.
Man's better nature triumphed then. Kind
words
Welcomed and soothed him; the rude conquer-
ors   80
Seated the captive with their chiefs; he chose
A bride among their maidens, and at length
Seemed to forget—yet ne'er forgot—the wife
Of his first love, and her sweet little ones
Butchered, amid their shrieks, with all his race.

  Thus change the forms of being. Thus arise
Races of living things, glorious in strength,
And perish, as the quickening breath of God
Fills them, or is withdrawn. The red-man, too,
Has left the blooming wilds he ranged so
long,   90
And, nearer to the Rocky Mountains, sought

A wilder hunting-ground. The beaver builds
No longer by these streams, but far away,
On waters whose blue surface ne'er gave back
The white man's face—among Missouri's
springs,
And pools whose issues swell the Oregon—
He rears his little Venice. In these plains
The bison feeds no more. Twice twenty leagues
Beyond remotest smoke of hunter's camp,
Roams the majestic brute, in herds that shake
The earth with thundering steps—yet here I
meet   101
His ancient footprints stamped beside the pool.

  Still this great solitude is quick with life.
Myriads of insects, gaudy as the flowers
They flutter over, gentle quadrupeds,
And birds, that scarce have learned the fear of
man,
Are here, and sliding reptiles of the ground,
Startlingly beautiful. The graceful deer
Bounds to the wood at my approach. The bee,
A more adventurous colonist than man,   110
With whom he came across the eastern deep,
Fills the savannas with his murmurings,
And hides his sweets, as in the golden age,
Within the hollow oak. I listen long
To his domestic hum, and think I hear
The sound of that advancing multitude
Which soon shall fill these deserts. From the
ground
Comes up the laugh of children, the soft voice
Of maidens, and the sweet and solemn hymn
Of Sabbath worshippers. The low of herds   120
Blends with the rustling of the heavy grain
Over the dark brown furrows. All at once
A fresher wind sweeps by, and breaks my
dream,
And I am in the wilderness alone.
1832   1833

» »   « «

» » *From:* LECTURES ON POETRY [4] « «

LECTURE III

ON POETRY IN ITS RELATION TO OUR AGE AND COUNTRY

An opinion prevails, which neither wants the

[4] Only recently arrived in New York, Bryant was asked in 1826 to speak on poetry before the Athenaeum Society. He delivered four lectures.

support of respectable names nor of plausible reasonings, that the art of poetry, in common with its sister arts, painting and sculpture, cannot in the present age be cultivated with the same degree of success as formerly. It has been supposed that the progress of reason, of science, and of the useful arts has a tendency to narrow the sphere of the imagination, and to repress the enthusiasm of the affections. Poetry, it is alleged, whose office it was to nurse the infancy of the human race, and to give it its first lessons of wisdom, having fulfilled the part to which she was appointed, now resigns her charge to severer instructors. Others, again, refining upon this idea, maintain that not only the age in which we live must fail to produce anything to rival the productions of the ancient masters of song, but that our own country, of all parts of the globe, is likely to remain the most distant from such a distinction.

Our citizens are held to possess, in a remarkable degree, the heedful, calculating, prosaic spirit of the age, while our country is decried as peculiarly barren of the materials of poetry. The scenery of our land these reasoners admit to be beautiful, but they urge that it is the beauty of a face without expression; that it wants the associations of tradition which are the soul and interest of scenery; that it wants the national superstitions which linger yet in every district in Europe, and the legends of distant and dark ages and of wild and unsettled times of which the old world reminds you at every step. Nor can our country, they say, ever be more fruitful of these materials than at present. For this is not an age to give birth to new superstitions, but to explode and root out old, however harmless and agreeable they may be, while half the world is already wondering how little the other half will finally believe. Is it likely, then, that a multitude of interesting traditions will spring up in our land to ally themselves with every mountain, every hill, every forest, every river, and every tributary brook? There may be some passages of our early history which associate themselves with particular places, but the argument is that the number of these will never be greatly augmented. The genius of our nation is quiet and commercial. Our people are too much in love with peace and gain, the state of society is too settled, and the laws too well enforced and respected, to allow of wild and strange adventures. There is no romance either in our character, our history, or our condition of society; and, therefore, it is neither likely to encourage poetry, nor capable of supplying it with those materials—materials drawn from domestic traditions and manners—which render it popular.

If these views of the tendency of the present age, and the state of things in our own country, are to be received as true, it must be acknowl-edged that they are not only exceedingly discouraging to those who make national literature a matter of pride, but, what is worse, that they go far toward causing that very inferiority on which they so strongly insist. Not that there is any danger that the demand for contemporary poetry will entirely cease. Verses have always been, and always will be written, and will always find readers; but it is of some consequence that they should be good verses, that they should exert the healthful and beneficial influences which I consider as belonging to the highest productions of the art; not feebly and imperfectly, but fully and effectually.

If, however, excellence in any art is believed to be unattainable, it will never be attained. There is, indeed, no harm in representing it as it really is, in literature as in every other pursuit, as rare and difficult, for by this means they who aspire to it are incited to more vigorous exertions. The mind of man glories in nothing more than in struggling successfully with difficulty, and nothing more excites our interest and admiration than the view of this struggle and triumph. The distinction of having done what few are able to do is the more enviable from its unfrequency, and attracts a multitude of competitors who catch each other's ardor and imitate each other's diligence. But if you go a step farther, and persuade those who are actuated by a generous ambition that this difficulty amounts to an impossibility, you extinguish their zeal at once. You destroy hope, and with it strength; you drive from the attempt those who were most likely and most worthy to succeed, and you put in their place a crowd of inferior contestants, satisfied with a low measure of excellence, and incapable of apprehending anything higher. Should, then, the views of this subject of which I have spoken be untrue, we may occasion much mischief by embracing them; and it becomes us, before we adopt them, to give them an attentive examination, and to be perfectly satisfied of their soundness.

But, if it be a fact that poetry in the present age is unable to attain the same degree of excellence as formerly, it cannot certainly be ascribed to any change in the original and natural faculties and dispositions of mind by which it is produced and by which it is enjoyed. The theory that men have degenerated in their mental powers and moral temperament is even more absurd than the notion of a decline in their physical strength, and is too fanciful to be combated by grave reasoning. It would be difficult, I fancy, to persuade the easiest credulity that the imagination of man has become, with the lapse of ages, less active and less capable of shaping the materials at its command into pictures of majesty and beauty. Is anybody whimsical enough to suppose that the years that have passed since the days of Homer have made men's hearts cold and insensible, or deadened the delicacy of their moral perceptions, or rendered them less susceptible of cultivation? All the sources of poetry in the mind, and all the qualities to which it owes its power over the mind, are assuredly left us. Degeneracy, if it has taken place, must be owing to one of two things—either to the absence of those circumstances which, in former times, developed and cherished the poetical faculty to an extraordinary degree, or to the existence of other intellectual interests which, in the present age, tend to repress its natural exercise.

What, then, were the circumstances which fostered the art of poetry in ancient times? They have been defined to be the mystery impressed on all the operations of nature as yet not investigated and traced to their laws—the beautiful systems of ancient mythology, and, after their extinction, the superstitions that linger like ghosts in the twilight of a later age. Let us examine separately each of these alleged advantages. That there is something in whatever is unknown and inscrutable which strongly excites the imagination and awes the heart, particularly when connected with things of unusual vastness and grandeur, is not to be denied. But I deny that much of this mystery is apparent to an ignorant age, and I maintain that no small degree of inquiry and illumination is necessary to enable the mind to perceive it. He who takes all things to be as they appear, who supposes the earth to be a great plain, the sun a moving ball of fire, the heavens a vault of sapphire, and the stars a multitude of little flames lighted up in its arches—what does he think of mysteries, or care for them? But enlighten him a little further. Teach him that the earth is an immense sphere; that the wide land whose bounds he knows so imperfectly is an isle in the great oceans that flow all over it; talk to him of the boundlessness of the skies, and the army of worlds that move through them—and, by means of the knowledge that you communicate, you have opened to him a vast field of the unknown and the wonderful. Thus it ever was and ever will be with the human mind; everything

which it knows introduces to its observation a greater multitude of things which it does not know; the clearing up of one mystery conducts it to another; all its discoveries are bounded by a circle of doubt and ignorance which is wide in proportion to the knowledge it enfolds. It is a pledge of the immortal destinies of the human intellect that it is forever drawn by a strong attraction to the darker edge of this circle, and forever attempting to penetrate the obscurities beyond. The old world, then, is welcome to its mysteries; we need not envy it on that account: for, in addition to our superior knowledge and as a consequence of it, we have even more of them than it, and they are loftier, deeper, and more spiritual.

But the mythologies of antiquity!—in particular, the beautiful mythologies of Greece and Rome, of which so much enters into the charming remains of ancient poetry! Beautiful those mythologies unquestionably were, and exceedingly varied and delightfully adapted to many of the purposes of poetry; yet it may be doubted whether, on the whole, the art gained more by them than it lost. For remark that, so far as mystery is a quality of poetry, it has been taken away almost entirely by the myth. The fault of the myth was that it accounted for everything. It had a god for every operation of nature—a Jupiter to distil the showers and roll the thunder, a Phœbus to guide the chariot of the sun, a divinity to breathe the winds, a divinity to pour out every fountain. It left nothing in obscurity; everything was seen. Its very beauty consisted in minute disclosures. Thus the imagination was delighted, but neither the imagination nor the feelings were stirred up from their utmost depths. That system gave us the story of a superior and celestial race of beings, to whom human passions were attributed, and who were, like ourselves, susceptible of suffering; but it elevated them so far above the creatures of earth in power, in knowledge, and in security from the calamities of our condition, that they could be the subjects of little sympathy. Therefore it is that the mythological poetry of the ancients is as cold as it is beautiful, as unaffecting as it is faultless. And the genius of this mythological poetry, carried into the literature of a later age, where it was cultivated with a less sincere and earnest spirit, has been the destruction of all nature and simplicity. Men forsook the sure guidance of their own feelings and impressions, and fell into gross offences against taste. They wished to describe

the passion of love, and they talked of Venus and her boy Cupid and his bow; they would speak of the freshness and glory of morning, and they fell to prattling of Phœbus and his steeds. No wonder that poetry has been thought a trifling art when thus practiced. For my part I cannot but think that human beings, placed among the things of this earth, with their affections and sympathies, their joys and sorrow,
10   and the accidents of fortune to which they are liable, are infinitely a better subject for poetry than any imaginary race of creatures whatever. Let the fountain tell me of the flocks that have drunk at it; of the village girl that has gathered spring flowers on its margin; the traveller that has slaked his thirst there in the hot noon, and blessed its waters; the schoolboy that has pulled the nuts from the hazels that hang over it as it leaps and sparkles in its cool basin; let it speak
20   of youth and health and purity and gladness, and I care not for the naiad that pours it out. If it must have a religious association, let it murmur of the invisible goodness that fills and feeds its reservoirs in the darkness of the earth. The admirers of poetry, then, may give up the ancient mythology without a sigh. Its departure has left us what is better than all it has taken away: it has left us men and women; it has left us the creatures and things of God's universe,
30   to the simple charm of which the cold splendor of that system blinded men's eyes, and to the magnificence of which the rapid progress of science is every day adding new wonders and glories. It has left us, also, a more sublime and affecting religion, whose truths are broader, higher, nobler than any outlook to which its random conjectures ever attained.

With respect to later superstitions, traces of which linger yet in many districts of the civi-
40   lized world—such as the belief in witchcraft, astrology, the agency of foul spirits in the affairs of men, in ghosts, fairies, water-sprites, and goblins of the wood and the mine—I would observe that the ages which gave birth to this fantastic brood are not those which have produced the noblest specimens of poetry. Their rise supposes a state of society too rude for the successful cultivation of the art. Nor does it seem to me that the bigoted and implicit recep-
50   tion of them is at all favorable to the exercise of poetic talent. Poetry, it is true, sometimes produces a powerful effect by appealing to that innate love of the supernatural which lies at the bottom of every man's heart and mind, and which all are willing to indulge, some freely

and some by stealth, but it does this for the most part by means of those superstitions which exist rather in tradition than in serious belief. It finds them more flexible and accommodating; it is able to mould them to its purposes, and at liberty to reject all that is offensive. Accordingly, we find that even the poets of superstitious ages have been fond of going back to the wonders and prodigies of elder days. Those who invented fictions for the age of chivalry, which one would be apt to think had marvels enough of its own, delighted to astonish their readers with tales of giants, dragons, hippogriffs, and enchanters, the home of which was laid in distant ages, or, at least, in remote countries. The best witch ballad, with the exception, perhaps, of "Tam o'Shanter," that I know of is Hogg's "Witch of Fife," yet both these were written long after the belief in witches had been laughed out of countenance.

It is especially the privilege of an age which has no engrossing superstitions of its own, to make use in its poetry of those of past ages; to levy contributions from the credulity of all time, and thus to diversify indefinitely the situations in which its human agents are placed. If these materials are managed with sufficient skill to win the temporary assent of the reader to the probability of the supernatural circumstances related, the purpose of the poet is answered. This is precisely the condition of the present age; it has the advantage over all ages that have preceded it in the abundance of those collected materials, and its poets have not been slow to avail themselves of their aid.

In regard to the circumstances which are thought in the present age to repress and limit the exercise of the poetical faculty, the principal if not the only one is supposed to be the prevalence of studies and pursuits unfavorable to the cultivation of the imagination and to enthusiasm of feeling. True it is that there are studies and pursuits which principally call into exercise other faculties of the mind, and that they are competitors with Poetry for the favor of the public. But it is not certain that the patronage bestowed on them would be extended to her, even if they should cease to exist. Nay, there is strong reason to suppose that they have done something to extend her influence, for they have certainly multiplied the number of readers, and everybody who reads at all sometimes reads poetry, and generally professes to admire what the best judges pronounce excellent, and, perhaps, in time come to enjoy it.

Various inclinations continue, as heretofore, to impel one individual to one pursuit, and another to another—one to chemistry and another to poetry—yet I cannot see that their different labors interfere with each other, or that, because the chemist prosecutes his science successfully, therefore the poet should lose his inspiration. Take the example of Great Britain. In no country are the sciences studied with greater success, yet in no country is poetry pursued with more ardor. Spring and autumn reign hand in hand in her literature; it is loaded at once with blossoms and fruits. Does the poetry of that island of the present day—the poetry of Wordsworth, Scott, Coleridge, Byron, Southey, Shelley, and others—smack of the chilling tendencies of the physical sciences? Or, rather, is it not bold, varied, impassioned, irregular, and impatient of precise laws, beyond that of any former age? Indeed, has it not the freshness, the vigor, and perhaps also the disorder, of a new literature?

The amount of knowledge necessary to be possessed by all who would keep pace with the age, as much greater as it is than formerly, is not, I apprehend, in danger of oppressing and smothering poetical talent. Knowledge is the material with which Genius builds her fabrics. The greater its abundance, the more power is required to dispose it into order and beauty, but the more vast and magnificent will be the structure. All great poets have been men of great knowledge. Some have gathered it from books, as Spenser and Milton; others from keen observation of men and things, as Homer and Shakespeare. On the other hand, the poetry of Ossian, whether genuine or not, is an instance of no inconsiderable poetical talent struggling with the disadvantages of a want of knowledge. It is this want which renders it so singularly monotonous. The poverty of the poet's ideas confined his mind to a narrow circle, and his poems are a series of changes rung upon a few thoughts and a few images. Single passages are beautiful and affecting, but each poem, as a whole, is tiresome and uninteresting.

I come, in the last place, to consider the question of our own expectations in literature, and the probability of our producing in the new world anything to rival the immortal poems of the old. Many of the remarks already made on the literary spirit of the present age will apply also to this part of the subject. Indeed, in this point of view, we should do ill to despair of our country, at least until the lapse of many years shall seem to have settled the question against us. Where the fountains of knowledge are by the roadside, and where the volumes from which poetic enthusiasms are caught and fed are in everybody's hands, it would be singularly strange if, amid the multitude of pursuits which occupy our citizens, nobody should think of taking verse as a path to fame. Yet, if it shall be chosen and pursued with the characteristic ardor of our countrymen, what can prevent its being brought to the same degree of perfection here as in other countries? Not the want of encouragement surely, for the literary man needs but little to stimulate his exertions, and with that little his exertions are undoubtedly greater. Who would think of fattening a racehorse? Complaints of the poverty of poets are as old as their art, but I never heard that they wrote the worse verse for it. It is enough, probably, to call forth their most vigorous efforts, that poetry is admired and honored by their countrymen. With respect to the paucity of national traditions, it will be time to complain of it when all those of which we are possessed are exhausted. Besides, as I have already shown, it is the privilege of poets, when they suppose themselves in need of materials, to seek them in other countries. The best English poets have done this. The events of Spenser's celebrated poem take place within the shadowy limits of fairy-land. Shakespeare has laid the scene of many of his finest tragedies in foreign countries. Milton went out of the world for the subject of his two epics. Byron has taken the incidents of all his poems from outside of England. Southey's best work is a poem of Spain— of chivalry, and of the Roman Church. For the story of one of his narrative poems, Moore went to Persia; for that of another, to the antediluvian world. Wordsworth and Crabbe, each in a different way, and each with great power, abjuring all heroic traditions and recollections, and all aid from the supernatural and the marvellous, have drawn their subjects from modern manners and the simple occurrences of common life. Are they read, for that reason, with any the less avidity by the multitudes who resort to their pages for pastime, for edification, for solace, for noble joy, and for the ecstasies of pure delight?

It has been urged by some, as an obstacle to the growth of elegant literature among us, that our language is a transplanted one, framed for a country and for institutions different from ours, and, therefore, not likely to be wielded by us with such force, effect, and grace, as it would have been if it had grown up with our nation, and received its forms and its accessions from the exigences of our experience. It seems to me that this is one of the most unsubstantial of all the brood of phantoms which have been conjured up to alarm us. Let those who press this opinion descend to particulars. Let them point out the peculiar defects of our 10 language in its application to our natural and political situation. Let them show in what respects it refuses to accommodate itself easily and gracefully to all the wants of expression that are felt among us. Till they do this, let us be satisfied that the copious and flexible dialect we speak is as equally proper to be used at the equator as at the poles, and at any intermediate latitude; and alike in monarchies or republics. It has grown up, as every forcible and beauti-20 ful language has done, among a simple and unlettered people; it has accommodated itself, in the first place, to the things of nature, and, as civilization advanced, to the things of art; and thus it has become a language full of picturesque forms of expression, yet fitted for the 26 purposes of science. If a new language were to

arise among us in our present condition of society, I fear that it would derive too many of its words from the roots used to signify canals, railroads, and steam-boats—things which, however well thought of at present, may perhaps a century hence be superseded by still more ingenious inventions. To try this notion about a transplanted dialect, imagine one of the great living poets of England emigrated to this country. Can anybody be simple enough to suppose that his poetry would be the worse for it?

I infer, then, that all the materials of poetry exist in our own country, with all the ordinary encouragements and opportunities for making a successful use of them. The elements of beauty and grandeur, intellectual greatness and moral truth, the stormy and the gentle passions, the casualties and the changes of life, and the light shed upon man's nature by the story of past times and the knowledge of foreign manners, have not made their sole abode in the old world beyond the waters. If under these circumstances our poetry should finally fail of rivalling that of Europe, it will be because Genius sits idle in the midst of its treasures.   1884

» » FRIAR TUCK LEGISLATION [5] « «

A famous thief was Robin Hood;
But Scotland had a thief as good,
It was—it was the great Rob Roy.
Old Ballad.

A speaker, Mr. Thomas Gisborne, at one of the recent meetings of the Anti-Corn Law League, made a happy allusion to what he called Friar Tuck Legislation. He had in his mind the story which is told in some of the old 40 chronicles of Robin Hood and his merry foresters, when they were once assembled in Congress to deliberate upon the proper distribution of a pretty large amount of spoils. These legislators, persuaded by the soft and honied words of Friar Tuck, left it to him to frame a law for the proper adjustment of their claims. When the law was reported, by the able committee which had it in charge, it became instantly evident that Friar Tuck himself would get much 50 the largest share. Public opinion, continues the history, thereupon went against the holy man, and a league was formed to resist the iniquity of his decision.

Now, what did the good Friar in the emergency? Why, he met the people boldly and openly, and said, "For whose benefit are laws made, I should like to know?" And then immediately answering his own question, lest some silly objector might give it another turn, he went on, "First, for the benefit of those who make them, and afterward as it may happen." Nor did the disinterested judge stop there, but he proceeded, "Am I not the lawmaker, and shall I not profit by my own law?" The story runs, we believe, that the good man next quietly pocketed his share of the booty, and left his unreasonable companions to make the best of what remained.

Friar Tuck represents a class; he is a type and pattern of a large circle of imitators; his peculiar method of legislation is not obsolete. There are many persons at this day whose morality seems to be framed according to the same standard. Members of the United States Congress, for instance, who pass tariff laws to put money into their own pockets, are the legitimate descendants of Friar Tuck.

[5] Bryant was a staunch free-trader. This editorial is from the *Evening Post* for April 26, 1844.

It is quite remarkable how many are the points of resemblance between this legislation of Sherwood Forest and that of the manufacturers at Washington. In the first place, the plunder to be distributed is raised from the people, in either case, without their being formally consulted; in the one by high duties, and in the other by the strong arm. Then the persons who take upon themselves to decide how this plunder is to be divided, like Friar Tuck, have a deep interest in the result, and generally manage to appropriate to themselves the largest share. They are the owners of manufacturing capital, and they contrive to make this capital return an enormous interest. "For whose benefit," they gravely ask, "are laws made?" and then answer, "First for the benefit of those who make them, and afterward as it may happen." Let us impose high duties; let us fill our pockets; let us who make the laws take all that we can get—and as to the people, the mass of laborers and consumers, why that's as it may happen! This is virtually the reasoning of one sort of our just and disinterested legislators.

But there is one point in which the resemblance does not hold. Friar Tuck was a bold, straight-forward, open-mouthed statesman, willing to proclaim his principles and justify the consequences to which they led. His followers in Congress act upon precisely the same principles, but assign another reason. He avowed that he wished to cram his pocket; they hold up some mock pretense of public good. "Shall I not benefit by my own law?" he said, and gathered up his gains; but they gather the gain and leave the reason unsaid, or rather hypocritically resort to some more palatable reason. The advantage of consistency is on the side of Robin Hood's priest. There is a frankness in his philosophy which throws the sneaking duplicity of the legislators of the cotton mills quite into the shade.

1844   1844

EDGAR ALLAN POE

1809–1849

THE LEGEND which has grown up around Poe long obscured both the facts of his career and the true nature of his genius. Among the many causes of the legend are the extravagant stories Poe told about himself, in order to impress his hearers; the inability of his friends or his foes, in their devotion or dislike, to tell the truth about their relations with him; the false statements made by the Reverend Rufus Griswold, Poe's erstwhile enemy and unfortunately his literary executor; and finally, the kind of writing Poe did. When an author writes stories like "Berenice" and poems like "The Conqueror Worm," fantastic in theme and gruesome in detail, there is bound to be speculation over the sort of person he must be in his private life. So prevalent was the belief in his moral delinquency that, when in 1865 there was a proposal to erect a memorial to him in Baltimore, William Cullen Bryant refused to contribute, on the grounds that "there should be some decided element of goodness in the character of those to whom a public monument directs the attention of the world."

Poe's mother, an actress, died in poverty in Richmond when her son was two. His father, David Poe, is said to have died ten months before. The child was taken into the home of a wealthy merchant, John Allan, though not legally adopted by him. Edgar, as he grew up, had reason to expect that Mr. Allan would treat him as a son. He went with the Allans to England and attended school there (from 1815–1820); Allan sent him to the University of Virginia in 1826. When the two quarreled over the young man's gambling debts, Poe ran off to Boston, where he published his first book, the excessively rare *Tamerlane and Other Poems* (1827). Since starvation was ahead of him he enlisted in the army. In 1829 Allan bought his release from the service, and the next year Poe was at West Point. Because of another quarrel with Allan, he got himself dismissed from the Academy. In 1833 a measure of success came to him through winning a short-story prize offered by the *Baltimore Saturday Visiter*. This event brought Poe the friendship of one of the judges of the story contest, the novelist John P. Kennedy, who helped Poe secure a place with the *Southern Literary Messenger* of Richmond, the first of many magazines to which he brought fame because of his skill as an editor and the worth of his contributions. The course of his connection with this magazine would be repeated often thereafter: a series of drunken sprees and frequent disagreements with the publisher, which ended in dismissal.

In 1836 Poe married his cousin, Virginia Clemm. Her mother became the patient and resourceful mainstay of their strange household. In Philadelphia, from 1838 to 1843, Poe was associated with several magazines, notably *Graham's*. The *Tales of the Grotesque and Arabesque* were published in 1839 (1840). During the New York years which followed (1844–1849) Poe attained notoriety, if not fame. His spectacular recitations of "The Raven" at private parties were town talk, and his series of essays on living American writers, "Literati," made him feared and hated. While he struggled to obtain a magazine of his own, Virginia was dying of consumption in the bare cottage at Fordham, then some miles out of the city. After her death in 1847 Poe slipped his life's anchor. On his way North from a trip to Richmond in September, 1849, he was found in a Baltimore tavern near death from drink and, it was thought, the mauling he had received from an election gang.

Poe's admirers and disciples, particularly among the French, have done their best to picture him as an original genius whose unearthly visions, often induced by drink, had little connection with his daily life. Without minimizing the originality of his tales and poems, the critic of Poe is bound to correct the faults in this picture. Poe, as an editor, was conscientious, hard-working, and successful, when drink and poverty allowed him to be. He was, moreover, keenly aware of the issues, political and artistic, of the day and had much to say on them in his reviews. Of science he had more than a layman's knowledge, and he was immoderately proud of his powers of reasoning. Even the tales in the vein of the grotesque reflected rather than created the taste of the time for stories about premature burial, escapes from the Inquisition, and other Gothic horrors. His greatness as an artist derives quite as much from the rigor with which he practiced his theories about the art of writing, both prose and verse, as from the power of his imagination.

In Poe's time two views of the poet's function were in the ascendant. American poets like Longfellow maintained what Poe called "the didactic heresy," that it is the poet's final aim to teach a lesson. The poets of the romantic generation in England and their American followers emphasized the communication of a definite and detailed emotional experience. These two doctrines Poe opposed. To him the poet's business is to concentrate on the "poem simply for the poem's sake"; to *create* the poem, not teach a moral by it or transcribe an experience. For by means of the beauty created by the poet the soul will be pleasurably elevated and may indeed even catch a glimpse of the supernal beauty. Since Poe excluded morality and truth from the category of beauty, his own poetry, designed to arouse the reader's soul to the contemplation of beauty, is limited. By intent it contains none of the "impurities" of didactic, reflective, imagistic, or metaphysical verse.

In Poe's aestheticism the Symbolist poets in France and the Pre-Raphaelites in England found confirmation of their ideas and inspiration for their own poetry. Indeed, while Americans were still arguing whether a man given to drink, cadging money from his friends, and accusing Longfellow of plagiarism could really be accepted among the great, Mallarmé had decided that the bright flower of Poe's thought, transplanted to France, had found there its true soil.

In England Rossetti reversed the situation in "The Raven" and wrote "The Blessed Damozel," and M. Dupin, the first detective in literature, was honored by the adoption of his analytical methods by Sherlock Holmes.

J. B. Hubbell, "Poe," in *Eight American Authors, A Review of Research and Criticism*, New York, 1956, pp. 1–46.
The Complete Works of Edgar Allan Poe, J. A. Harrison, ed., 17 vols., New York, 1902.
The Poems of Edgar Allan Poe, Killis Campbell, ed., Boston, 1917.
The Letters of Edgar Allan Poe, John Ostrom, ed., 2 vols., Cambridge, 1948.
Hervey Allen, *Israfel: The Life and Times of Edgar Allan Poe*, New York, 1926.
C. P. Cambiaire, *The Influence of Edgar Allan Poe in France*, New York, 1927.
Killis Campbell, *The Mind of Poe and Other Studies*, Cambridge, 1933.
T. H. Chivers, Life of Poe, R. B. Davis, ed., New York, 1952.
E. H. Davidson, *Poe—A Critical Study*, Cambridge, 1957.
N. B. Fagin, *The Histrionic Mr. Poe*, Baltimore, 1949.
Una Pope-Hennessey, *Edgar Allan Poe (1809–1849), A Critical Biography*, London, 1934.
A. H. Quinn, *Edgar Allan Poe: A Critical Biography*, New York, 1941.
G. E. Woodberry, *The Life of Edgar Allan Poe, Personal and Literary*, 2 vols., Boston, 1909.

» »   « «

ROMANCE

Romance, who loves to nod and sing,
With drowsy head and folded wing,
Among the green leaves as they shake
Far down within some shadowy lake,
To me a painted paroquet
Hath been—a most familiar bird—
Taught me my alphabet to say
To lisp my very earliest word,
While in the wild wood I did lie,
A child—with a most knowing eye.   10

Of late, eternal Condor years
So shake the very Heaven on high
With tumult as they thunder by,
I have no time for idle cares
Through gazing on the unquiet sky.
And when an hour with calmer wings
Its down upon my spirit flings—
That little time with lyre and rhyme
To while away—forbidden things!
My heart would feel to be a crime   20
Unless it trembled with the strings.
                                   1829

TO HELEN

Helen, thy beauty is to me
   Like those Nicéan barks of yore,
That gently, o'er a perfumed sea,
   The weary, way-worn wanderer bore
   To his own native shore.

On desperate seas long wont to roam,
   Thy hyacinth hair, thy classic face,
Thy Naiad airs have brought me home
   To the glory that was Greece,
   And the grandeur that was Rome.   10

Lo! in yon brilliant window-niche
   How statue-like I see thee stand,
The agate lamp within thy hand!
   Ah, Psyche, from the regions which
   Are Holy-Land!   1831

ISRAFEL

And the angel Israfel, whose heart-strings are a
lute, and who has the sweetest voice of all God's
creatures.—KORAN.

In Heaven a spirit doth dwell
   "Whose heart-strings are a lute";
None sing so wildly well
As the angel Israfel,
And the giddy stars (so legends tell)
Ceasing their hymns, attend the spell
   Of his voice, all mute.

Tottering above
   In her highest noon,
   The enamoured moon   10
Blushes with love,
   While, to listen, the red levin
   (With the rapid Pleiads, even.
   Which were seven,)
   Pauses in Heaven.

And they say (the starry choir
    And the other listening things)
That Israfeli's fire
Is owing to that lyre
    By which he sits and sings—   20
The trembling living wire
Of those unusual strings.

But the skies that angel trod,
    Where deep thoughts are a duty,
Where Love's a grown-up God,
    Where the Houri glances are
Imbued with all the beauty
    Which we worship in a star.

Therefore, thou art not wrong,
    Israfeli, who despisest   30
An unimpassioned song;
To thee the laurels belong,
    Best bard, because the wisest!
Merrily live, and long!

The ecstasies above
    With thy burning measures suit—
Thy grief, thy joy, thy hate, thy love,
    With the fervour of thy lute—
Well may the stars be mute!

Yes, Heaven is thine; but this   40
    Is a world of sweets and sours;
    Our flowers are merely—flowers,
And the shadow of thy perfect bliss
    Is the sunshine of ours.

If I could dwell
Where Israfel
    Hath dwelt, and he where I,
He might not sing so wildly well
    A mortal melody,
While a bolder note than this might swell
From my lyre within the sky.   51
                    1831

THE CITY IN THE SEA[1]

Lo! Death has reared himself a throne
In a strange city lying alone
Far down within the dim West,
Where the good and the bad and the worst
    and the best
Have gone to their eternal rest.

[1] This poem was much revised between 1831 and 1845.

There shrines and palaces and towers
(Time-eaten towers that tremble not!)
Resemble nothing that is ours.
Around, by lifting winds forgot,
Resignedly beneath the sky   10
The melancholy waters lie.

No rays from the holy heaven come down
On the long night-time of that town;
But light from out the lurid sea
Streams up the turrets silently—
Gleams up the pinnacles far and free—
Up domes—up spires—up kingly halls—

Up fanes—up Babylon-like walls—
Up shadowy long-forgotten bowers
Of sculptured ivy and stone flowers—   20
Up many and many a marvellous shrine
Whose wreathèd friezes intertwine
The viol, the violet, and the vine.

Resignedly beneath the sky
The melancholy waters lie.
So blend the turrets and shadows there
That all seem pendulous in air,
While from a proud tower in the town
Death looks gigantically down.

There open fanes and gaping graves   30
Yawn level with the luminous waves;
But not the riches there that lie
In each idol's diamond eye—
Not the gayly-jewelled dead
Tempt the waters from their bed;
For no ripples curl, alas!
Along that wilderness of glass—
No swellings tell that winds may be
Upon some far-off happier sea—
No heavings hint that winds have been   40
On seas less hideously serene.

But lo, a stir is in the air!
The wave—there is a movement there!
As if the towers had thrust aside,
In slightly sinking, the dull tide—
As if their tops had feebly given
A void within the filmy Heaven.
The waves have now a redder glow—
The hours are breathing faint and low—
And when, amid no earthly moans,   50
Down, down that town shall settle hence,
Hell, rising from a thousand thrones,
Shall do it reverence.   1831, 1845

LENORE

Ah, broken is the golden bowl!—the spirit
flown forever!
Let the bell toll!—a saintly soul floats on the
Stygian river:—
And, Guy De Vere, hast *thou* no tear?—weep
now or never more!
See! on yon drear and rigid bier low lies thy
love, Lenore!
Come, let the burial rite be read—the funeral
song be sung!—
An anthem for the queenliest dead that ever
died so young—
A dirge for her the doubly dead in that she died
so young.

"Wretches! ye loved her for her wealth, and ye
hated her for her pride;
And, when she fell in feeble health, ye blessed
her—that she died:—
How *shall* the ritual, then, be read—the requiem how be sung   10
By you—by yours, the evil eye,—by yours, the
slanderous tongue
That did to death the innocence that died, and
died so young?"

Peccavimus; yet rave not thus! but let a Sabbath song
Go up to God so solemnly the dead may feel
no wrong!
The sweet Lenore hath gone before, with Hope
that flew beside,
Leaving thee wild for the dear child that should
have been thy bride—
For her, the fair and debonair, that now so
lowly lies,
The life upon her yellow hair, but not within
her eyes—
The life still there upon her hair, the death
upon her eyes.

"Avaunt!—avaunt! to friends from fiends the
indignant ghost is riven—   20
From Hell unto a high estate within the utmost
Heaven—
From moan and groan to a golden throne be-
side the King of Heaven:—
Let *no* bell toll, then, lest her soul, amid its
hallowed mirth,
Should catch the note as it doth float up from
the damnèd Earth!

And I—to-night my heart is light:—no dirge
will I upraise,
But waft the angel on her flight with a Pæan of
old days!"   1831

THE COLISEUM [2]

Type of the antique Rome! Rich reliquary
Of lofty contemplation left to Time
By buried centuries of pomp and power!
At length—at length—after so many days
Of weary pilgrimage and burning thirst
(Thirst for the springs of lore that in thee lie),
I kneel, an altered and an humble man,
Amid thy shadows, and so drink within
My very soul thy grandeur, gloom, and glory!

Vastness! and Age! and Memories of Eld!   10
Silence! and Desolation! and dim Night!
I feel ye now—I feel ye in your strength—
O spells more sure than e'er Judæan king
Taught in the gardens of Gethsemane!
O charms more potent than the rapt Chaldee
Ever drew down from out the quiet stars!

Here, where a hero fell, a column falls!
Here, where the mimic eagle glared in gold,
A midnight vigil holds the swarthy bat!
Here, where the dames of Rome their gilded
hair   20
Waved to the wind, now wave the reed and
thistle!
Here, where on golden throne the monarch
lolled,
Glides, spectre-like, unto his marble home,
Lit by the wan light of the hornèd moon,
The swift and silent lizard of the stones!

But stay! these walls—these ivy-clad arcades—
These mouldering plinths—these sad and
blackened shafts—
These vague entablatures—this crumbling
frieze—
These shattered cornices—this wreck—this
ruin—
These stones—alas! these gray stones—are they
all—   30
All of the famed and the colossal left
By the corrosive Hours to Fate and me?

"Not all"—the Echoes answer me—"not all!
Prophetic sounds and loud, arise forever

[2] Poe submitted this poem in the *Baltimore Saturday Visiter's* prize
competition (1833) in which his "MS Found in a Bottle" won one
hundred dollars.

From us, and from all Ruin, unto the wise,
As melody from Memnon to the Sun.
We rule the hearts of mightiest men—we rule
With a despotic sway all giant minds.
We are not impotent—we pallid stones.
Not all our power is gone—not all our fame—
Not all the magic of our high renown—   41
Not all the wonder that encircles us—
Not all the mysteries that in us lie—
Not all the memories that hang upon
And cling around about us as a garment,
Clothing us in a robe of more than glory."
                                        1833

TO ONE IN PARADISE

Thou wast all that to me, love,
    For which my soul did pine—
A green isle in the sea, love,
    A fountain and a shrine,
All wreathed with fairy fruits and flowers,
    And all the flowers were mine.

Ah, dream too bright to last!
    Ah, starry Hope! that didst arise
But to be overcast!
    A voice from out the Future cries,   10
"On! on!"—but o'er the Past
    (Dim gulf!) my spirit hovering lies
Mute, motionless, aghast!

For, alas! alas! with me
    The light of Life is o'er!
No more—no more—no more—
(Such language holds the solemn sea
    To the sands upon the shore)
Shall bloom the thunder-blasted tree,
    Or the stricken eagle soar!   20

And all my days are trances,
    And all my nightly dreams
Are where thy grey eye glances,
    And where thy footstep gleams—
In what ethereal dances,
    By what eternal streams.   1834

SONNET—SILENCE

There are some qualities—some incorporate
    things,
That have a double life, which thus is made
A type of that twin entity which springs
From matter and light, evinced in solid and
    shade.

There is a two-fold *Silence*—sea and shore—
Body and soul. One dwells in lonely places,
Newly with grass o'ergrown; some solemn
    graces,
Some human memories and tearful lore,
Render him terrorless: his name's "No More."
He is the corporate Silence: dread him not!   10
No power hath he of evil in himself;
But should some urgent fate (untimely lot!)
Bring thee to meet his shadow (nameless elf,
That haunteth the lone regions where hath
    trod
No foot of man), commend thyself to God!
                                        1840

THE RAVEN [3]

Once upon a midnight dreary, while I pon-
    dered, weak and weary,
Over many a quaint and curious volume of
    forgotten lore—
While I nodded, nearly napping, suddenly
    there came a tapping,
As of some one gently rapping, rapping at my
    chamber door.
" 'Tis some visiter," I muttered, "tapping at
    my chamber door—
    Only this and nothing more."

Ah, distinctly I remember it was in the bleak
    December;
And each separate dying ember wrought its
    ghost upon the floor.
Eagerly I wished the morrow;—vainly I had
    sought to borrow
From my books surcease of sorrow—sorrow
    for the lost Lenore—   10
For the rare and radiant maiden whom the
    angels name Lenore—
    Nameless *here* for evermore.

And the silken, sad, uncertain rustling of each
    purple curtain
Thrilled me—filled me with fantastic terrors
    never felt before;
So that now, to still the beating of my heart, I
    stood repeating,
" 'Tis some visiter entreating entrance at my
    chamber door—
Some late visiter entreating entrance at my
    chamber door;—
    This it is and nothing more."

[3] Poe revised "The Raven" frequently. It exists in at least sixteen
different forms. See Poe's remarks on the poem in "The Philosophy
of Composition."

Presently my soul grew stronger; hesitating
  then no longer,
"Sir," said I, "or Madam, truly your forgiveness
  I implore;   20
But the fact is I was napping, and so gently
  you came rapping,
And so faintly you came tapping, tapping at
  my chamber door,
That I scarce was sure I heard you"—here I
  opened wide the door;—
    Darkness there and nothing more.

Deep into that darkness peering, long I stood
  there wondering, fearing,
Doubting, dreaming dreams no mortal ever
  dared to dream before;
But the silence was unbroken, and the stillness gave no token,
And the only word there spoken was the whispered word, "Lenore?"
This I whispered, and an echo murmured back
  the word, "Lenore!"
    Merely this and nothing more.   30

Back into the chamber turning, all my soul
  within me burning,
Soon again I heard a tapping somewhat louder
  than before.
"Surely," said I, "surely that is something at
  my window lattice;
Let me see, then, what thereat is, and this
  mystery explore—
Let my heart be still a moment and this mystery explore;—
    'Tis the wind and nothing more!"

Open here I flung the shutter, when, with
  many a flirt and flutter,
In there stepped a stately Raven of the saintly
  days of yore;
Not the least obeisance made he; not a minute
  stopped or stayed he;
But, with mien of lord or lady, perched above
  my chamber door—   40
Perched upon a bust of Pallas just above my
  chamber door—
    Perched, and sat, and nothing more.

Then this ebony bird beguiling my sad fancy
  into smiling,
By the grave and stern decorum of the coun-
  tenance it wore,
"Though thy crest be shorn and shaven, thou,"
  I said, "art sure no craven,

Ghastly grim and ancient Raven wandering
  from the Nightly shore—
Tell me what thy lordly name is on the Night's
  Plutonian shore!"
    Quoth the Raven, "Nevermore."

Much I marvelled this ungainly fowl to hear
  discourse so plainly,
Though its answer little meaning—little relevancy bore;   50
For we cannot help agreeing that no living
  human being
Ever yet was blessed with seeing bird above
  his chamber door—
Bird or beast upon the sculptured bust above
  his chamber door,
    With such name as "Nevermore."

But the Raven, sitting lonely on the placid
  bust, spoke only
That one word, as if his soul in that one word
  he did outpour.
Nothing farther then he uttered—not a feather
  then he fluttered—
Till I scarcely more than muttered "Other
  friends have flown before—
On the morrow *he* will leave me, as my Hopes
  have flown before."
    Then the bird said, "Nevermore."   60

Startled at the stillness broken by reply so
  aptly spoken,
"Doubtless," said I, "what it utters is its only
  stock and store
Caught from some unhappy master whom unmerciful Disaster
Followed fast and followed faster till his songs
  one burden bore—
Till the dirges of his Hope that melancholy
  burden bore
    Of 'Never—nevermore.'"

But the Raven still beguiling all my fancy
  into smiling,
Straight I wheeled a cushioned seat in front
  of bird and bust and door;
Then, upon the velvet sinking, I betook myself to linking
Fancy unto fancy, thinking what this ominous
  bird of yore—   70
What this grim, ungainly, ghastly, gaunt, and
  ominous bird of yore
    Meant in croaking "Nevermore."

This I sat engaged in guessing, but no syllable expressing
To the fowl whose fiery eyes now burned into my bosom's core;
This and more I sat divining, with my head at ease reclining
On the cushion's velvet lining that the lamp-light gloated o'er,
But whose velvet-violet lining with the lamp-light gloating o'er,
   She shall press, ah, nevermore!

Then, methought, the air grew denser, perfumed from an unseen censer
Swung by seraphim whose foot-falls tinkled on the tufted floor.   80
"Wretch," I cried, "thy God hath lent thee—by these angels he hath sent thee
Respite—respite and nepenthe from thy memories of Lenore;
Quaff, oh quaff this kind nepenthe and forget this lost Lenore!"
   Quoth the Raven, "Nevermore."

"Prophet!" said I, "thing of evil!—prophet still, if bird or devil!—
Whether Tempter sent, or whether tempest tossed thee here ashore,
Desolate yet all undaunted, on this desert land enchanted—
On this home by Horror haunted—tell me truly, I implore—
Is there—*is* there balm in Gilead?—tell me—tell me, I implore!"
   Quoth the Raven, "Nevermore."   90

"Prophet!" said I, "thing of evil!—prophet still, if bird or devil!
By that Heaven that bends above us—by that God we both adore—
Tell this soul with sorrow laden if, within the distant Aidenn,
It shall clasp a sainted maiden whom the angels name Lenore—
Clasp a rare and radiant maiden whom the angels name Lenore."
   Quoth the Raven, "Nevermore."

"Be that word our sign of parting, bird or fiend!" I shrieked, upstarting—
"Get thee back into the tempest and the Night's Plutonian shore!
Leave no black plume as a token of that lie thy soul hath spoken!

Leave my loneliness unbroken!—quit the bust above my door!   100
Take thy beak from out my heart, and take thy form from off my door!"
   Quoth the Raven, "Nevermore."

And the Raven, never flitting, still is sitting, *still* is sitting
On the pallid bust of Pallas just above my chamber door;
And his eyes have all the seeming of a demon's that is dreaming,
And the lamp-light o'er him streaming throws his shadow on the floor;
And my soul from out that shadow that lies floating on the floor
   Shall be lifted—nevermore!   1845

ULALUME—A BALLAD

The skies they were ashen and sober;
   The leaves they were crispèd and sere—
   The leaves they were withering and sere:
It was night in the lonesome October
   Of my most immemorial year:
It was hard by the dim lake of Auber,
   In the misty mid region of Weir—
It was down by the dank tarn of Auber,
   In the ghoul-haunted woodland of Weir.

Here once, through an alley Titanic,   10
   Of cypress, I roamed with my Soul—
   Of cypress, with Psyche, my Soul.
These were days when my heart was volcanic
   As the scoriac rivers that roll—
   As the lavas that restlessly roll
Their sulphurous currents down Yaanek
   In the ultimate climes of the Pole—
That groan as they roll down Mount Yaanek
   In the realms of the Boreal Pole.

Our talk had been serious and sober,   20
   But our thoughts they were palsied and sere—
   Our memories were treacherous and sere;
For we knew not the month was October,
   And we marked not the night of the year
   (Ah, night of all nights in the year!)—
We noted not the dim lake of Auber
   (Though once we had journeyed down here)—
We remembered not the dank tarn of Auber,
   Nor the ghoul-haunted woodland of Weir.

And now, as the night was senescent 30
  And star-dials pointed to morn—
  As the star-dials hinted of morn—
At the end of our path a liquescent
  And nebulous lustre was born,
Out of which a miraculous crescent
  Arose with a duplicate horn—
Astarte's bediamonded crescent
  Distinct with its duplicate horn.

And I said: "She is warmer than Dian;
  She rolls through an ether of sighs— 40
  She revels in a region of sighs.
She has seen that the tears are not dry on
  These cheeks, where the worm never dies,
And has come past the stars of the Lion,
  To point us the path to the skies—
  To the Lethean peace of the skies—
Come up, in despite of the Lion,
  To shine on us with her bright eyes—
Come up through the lair of the Lion,
  With love in her luminous eyes." 50

But Psyche, uplifting her finger,
  Said: "Sadly this star I mistrust—
  Her pallor I strangely mistrust:
Ah, hasten!—ah, let us not linger!
  Ah, fly!—let us fly!—for we must."
In terror she spoke, letting sink her
  Wings till they trailed in the dust—
In agony sobbed, letting sink her
  Plumes till they trailed in the dust—
  Till they sorrowfully trailed in the dust. 60

I replied: "This is nothing but dreaming:
  Let us on by this tremulous light!
  Let us bathe in this crystalline light!
Its Sibyllic splendor is beaming
  With Hope and in Beauty to-night:—
See!—it flickers up the sky through the night!
Ah, we safely may trust to its gleaming,
  And be sure it will lead us aright—
We surely may trust to a gleaming,
  That cannot but guide us aright, 70
  Since it flickers up to Heaven through the
    night."

Thus I pacified Psyche and kissed her,
  And tempted her out of her gloom—
  And conquered her scruples and gloom;
And we passed to the end of the vista,
  But were stopped by the door of a tomb—
  By the door of a legended tomb;
And I said: "What is written, sweet sister,
  On the door of this legended tomb?"

She replied: "Ulalume—Ulalume!— 80
  'Tis the vault of thy lost Ulalume!"

Then my heart it grew ashen and sober
  As the leaves that were crispèd and sere—
  As the leaves that were withering and sere;
And I cried: "It was surely October
  On *this* very night of last year
That I journeyed—I journeyed down here!—
  That I brought a dread burden down here—
  On this night of all nights in the year,
Ah, what demon hath tempted me here? 90
Well I know, now, this dim lake of Auber—
  This misty mid region of Weir—
Well I know, now, this dank tarn of Auber,
  This ghoul-haunted woodland of Weir."

Said we, then—the two, then: "Ah, can it
  Have been that the woodlandish ghouls—
  The pitiful, the merciful ghouls—
To bar up our way and to ban it
  From the secret that lies in these wolds—
  From the thing that lies hidden in these
    wolds— 100
Have drawn up the spectre of a planet
  From the limbo of lunary souls—
This sinfully scintillant planet
  From the Hell of the planetary souls?"
                                      1847, 1850

THE BELLS[4]

I

Hear the sledges with the bells—
      Silver bells!
What a world of merriment their melody fore-
    tells!
  How they tinkle, tinkle, tinkle,
    In the icy air of night!
  While the stars that oversprinkle
  All the heavens, seem to twinkle
    With a crystalline delight;
    Keeping time, time, time,
    In a sort of Runic rhyme, 10
To the tintinnabulation that so musically wells
  From the bells, bells, bells, bells,
      Bells, bells, bells—
From the jingling and the tinkling of the bells.

II

Hear the mellow wedding bells—
      Golden bells!

4 In its first form "The Bells" consisted of only eighteen lines.

What a world of happiness their harmony
    foretells!
  Through the balmy air of night
  How they ring out their delight!—
      From the molten-golden notes,   20
          And all in tune,
      What a liquid ditty floats
To the turtle-dove that listens, while she gloats
          On the moon!
  Oh, from out the sounding cells,
What a gush of euphony voluminously wells!
          How it swells!
          How it dwells
      On the Future!—how it tells
      Of the rapture that impels   30
    To the swinging and the ringing
      Of the bells, bells, bells—
      Of the bells, bells, bells, bells,
          Bells, bells, bells—
To the rhyming and the chiming of the bells!

III

  Hear the loud alarum bells—
      Brazen bells!
What a tale of terror, now, their turbulency
    tells!
    In the startled ear of night
    How they scream out their affright!   40
        Too much horrified to speak,
        They can only shriek, shriek,
          Out of tune,
In a clamorous appealing to the mercy of the
    fire,
In a mad expostulation with the deaf and
    frantic fire,
      Leaping higher, higher, higher,
      With a desperate desire,
      And a resolute endeavor
      Now—now to sit, or never,
  By the side of the pale-faced moon.   50
      Oh, the bells, bells, bells!
      What a tale their terror tells
          Of Despair!
    How they clang, and clash, and roar!
    What a horror they outpour
On the bosom of the palpitating air!
      Yet the ear, it fully knows,
        By the twanging
        And the clanging,
      How the danger ebbs and flows;   60
  Yet the ear distinctly tells,
        In the jangling
        And the wrangling,
      How the danger sinks and swells,

By the sinking or the swelling in the anger of
    the bells—
        Of the bells—
    Of the bells, bells, bells, bells,
        Bells, bells, bells—
In the clamor and the clangor of the bells!

IV

Hear the tolling of the bells—   70
      Iron bells!
What a world of solemn thought their monody
    compels!
    In the silence of the night,
    How we shiver with affright
At the melancholy menace of their tone!
      For every sound that floats
      From the rust within their throats
          Is a groan.
    And the people—ah, the people—
    They that dwell up in the steeple,   80
          All alone,
    And who, tolling, tolling, tolling,
      In that muffled monotone,
    Feel a glory in so rolling
      On the human heart a stone—
  They are neither man nor woman—
  They are neither brute nor human—
        They are Ghouls:—
  And their king it is who tolls:—
  And he rolls, rolls, rolls,   90
        Rolls
      A pæan from the bells!
  And his merry bosom swells
    With the pæan of the bells!
  And he dances, and he yells;
  Keeping time, time, time,
  In a sort of Runic rhyme,
    To the pæan of the bells:—
        Of the bells:—
  Keeping time, time, time,   100
  In a sort of Runic rhyme,
    To the throbbing of the bells—
  Of the bells, bells, bells—
    To the sobbing of the bells;
  Keeping time, time, time,
    As he knells, knells, knells,
  In a happy Runic rhyme,
    To the rolling of the bells—
  Of the bells, bells, bells:—
    To the tolling of the bells—   110
  Of the bells, bells, bells, bells,
        Bells, bells, bells—
To the moaning and the groaning of the bells.
1848–1849   1849

TO MY MOTHER[5]

Because I feel that, in the Heavens above,
The angels, whispering to one another,
Can find, among their burning terms of love,
None so devotional as that of "Mother,"
Therefore by that dear name I long have called
    you—
You who are more than mother unto me,
And fill my heart of hearts, where Death in-
    stalled you
In setting my Virginia's spirit free.
My mother—my own mother, who died early,
Was but the mother of myself; but you   10
Are mother to the one I loved so dearly,
And thus are dearer than the mother I knew
By that infinity with which my wife
Was dearer to my soul than its soul-life.
1849   1850

ANNABEL LEE

It was many and many a year ago,
    In a kingdom by the sea,
That a maiden there lived whom you may
    know
    By the name of ANNABEL LEE;
And this maiden she lived with no other
    thought
    Than to love and be loved by me.

She was a child and *I* was a child,
    In this kingdom by the sea,
But we loved with a love that was more than
    love—
    I and my ANNABEL LEE—   10
With a love that the wingèd seraphs of heaven
    Coveted her and me.

[5] Mrs. Clemm, the mother of Poe's child-wife Virginia.

And this was the reason that, long ago,
    In this kingdom by the sea,
A wind blew out of a cloud, chilling
    My beautiful ANNABEL LEE;
So that her high-born kinsmen came
    And bore her away from me,
To shut her up in a sepulchre
    In this kingdom by the sea.   20

The angels, not half so happy in Heaven,
    Went envying her and me—
Yes!—that was the reason (as all men know,
    In this kingdom by the sea)
That the wind came out of the cloud by night,
    Chilling and killing my ANNABEL LEE.

But our love it was stronger by far than the
    love
    Of those who were older than we—
    Of many far wiser than we—
And neither the angels in Heaven above,   30
    Nor the demons down under the sea,
Can ever dissever my soul from the soul
    Of the beautiful ANNABEL LEE:

For the moon never beams, without bringing
    me dreams
    Of the beautiful ANNABEL LEE;
And the stars never rise, but I see the bright
    eyes
    Of the beautiful ANNABEL LEE:
And so, all the night-tide, I lie down by the
    side
Of my darling, my darling, my life and my
    bride,
    In the sepulchre there by the sea—   40
    In her tomb by the side of the sea.   1849

« «   » »

» » THE FALL OF THE HOUSE OF USHER « «

Son cœur est un luth suspendu;
Sitôt qu'on le touche il résonne.
                    BÉRANGER.

During the whole of a dull, dark, and soundless day in the autumn of the year, when the
clouds hung oppressively low in the heavens,
I had been passing alone, on horseback,
through a singularly dreary tract of country,
and at length found myself, as the shades of
the evening drew on, within view of the melancholy House of Usher. I know not how it was
—but, with the first glimpse of the building, a
sense of insufferable gloom pervaded my spirit.
I say insufferable; for the feeling was unrelieved by any of that half-pleasurable, because
poetic, sentiment with which the mind usually

receives even the sternest natural images of the desolate or terrible. I looked upon the scene before me—upon the mere house, and the simple landscape features of the domain, upon the bleak walls, upon the vacant eye-like windows, upon a few rank sedges, and upon a few white trunks of decayed trees—with an utter depression of soul which I can compare to no earthly sensation more properly than to the after-
10 dream of the reveller upon opium: the bitter lapse into everyday life, the hideous dropping off of the veil. There was an iciness, a sinking, a sickening of the heart, an unredeemed dreariness of thought which no goading of the imagination could torture into aught of the sublime. What was it—I paused to think—what was it that so unnerved me in the contemplation of the House of Usher? It was a mystery all insoluble; nor could I grapple with the shadowy
20 fancies that crowded upon me as I pondered. I was forced to fall back upon the unsatisfactory conclusion, that while, beyond doubt, there *are* combinations of very simple natural objects which have the power of thus affecting us, still the analysis of this power lies among considerations beyond our depth. It was possible, I reflected, that a mere different arrangement of the particulars of the scene, of the details of the picture, would be sufficient to
30 modify, or perhaps to annihilate, its capacity for sorrowful impression; and acting upon this idea, I reined my horse to the precipitous brink of a black and lurid tarn that lay in unruffled lustre by the dwelling, and gazed down—but with a shudder even more thrilling than before —upon the remodelled and inverted images of the gray sedge, and the ghastly tree-stems, and the vacant and eye-like windows.

Nevertheless, in this mansion of gloom I
40 now proposed to myself a sojourn of some weeks. Its proprietor, Roderick Usher, had been one of my boon companions in boyhood; but many years had elapsed since our last meeting. A letter, however, had lately reached me in a distant part of the country—a letter from him—which in its wildly importunate nature had admitted of no other than a personal reply. The MS. gave evidence of nervous agitation. The writer spoke of acute bodily illness, of a
50 mental disorder which oppressed him, and of an earnest desire to see me, as his best and indeed his only personal friend, with a view of attempting, by the cheerfulness of my society, some alleviation of his malady. It was the manner in which all this, and much more, was

said—it was the apparent *heart* that went with his request—which allowed me no room for hesitation; and I accordingly obeyed forthwith what I still considered a very singular summons.

Although as boys we had been even intimate associates, yet I really knew little of my friend. His reserve had been always excessive and habitual. I was aware, however, that his very ancient family had been noted, time out of mind, for a peculiar sensibility of temperament, displaying itself, through long ages, in many works of exalted art, and manifested of late in repeated deeds of munificent yet unobtrusive charity, as well as in a passionate devotion to the intricacies, perhaps even more than to the orthodox and easily recognizable beauties, of musical science. I had learned, too, the very remarkable fact that the stem of the Usher race, all time-honored as it was, had put forth at no period any enduring branch; in other words, that the entire family lay in the direct line of descent, and had always, with very trifling and very temporary variation, so lain. It was this deficiency, I considered, while running over in thought the perfect keeping of the character of the premises with the accredited character of the people, and while speculating upon the possible influence which the one, in the long lapse of centuries, might have exercised upon the other—it was this deficiency, perhaps, of collateral issue, and the consequent undeviating transmission from sire to son of the patrimony with the name, which had, at length, so identified the two as to merge the original title of the estate in the quaint and equivocal appellation of the "House of Usher" —an appellation which seemed to include, in the minds of the peasantry who used it, both the family and the family mansion.

I have said that the sole effect of my somewhat childish experiment, that of looking down within the tarn, had been to deepen the first singular impression. There can be no doubt that the consciousness of the rapid increase of my superstition—for why should I not so term it?—served mainly to accelerate the increase itself. Such, I have long known, is the paradoxical law of all sentiments having terror as a basis. And it might have been for this reason only, that, when I again uplifted my eyes to the house itself, from its image in the pool, there grew in my mind a strange fancy— a fancy so ridiculous, indeed, that I but mention it to show the vivid force of the sensations which oppressed me. I had so worked upon my imagination as really to believe that about the whole mansion and domain there hung an atmosphere peculiar to themselves and their immediate vicinity: an atmosphere which had no affinity with the air of heaven, but which had reeked up from the decayed trees, and the gray wall, and the silent tarn: a pestilent and mystic vapor, dull, sluggish, faintly discernible, and leaden-hued.

Shaking off from my spirit what *must* have been a dream, I scanned more narrowly the real aspect of the building. Its principal feature seemed to be that of an excessive antiquity. The discoloration of ages had been great. Minute fungi overspread the whole exterior, hanging in a fine tangled webwork from the eaves. Yet all this was apart from any extraordinary dilapidation. No portion of the masonry had fallen; and there appeared to be a wild inconsistency between its still perfect adaptation of parts and the crumbling condition of the individual stones. In this there was much that reminded me of the specious totality of old wood-work which has rotted for long years in some neglected vault, with no disturbance from the breath of the external air. Beyond this indication of extensive decay, however, the fabric gave little token of instability. Perhaps the eye of a scrutinizing observer might have discovered a barely perceptible fissure, which, extending from the roof of the building in front, made its way down the wall in a zigzag direction, until it became lost in the sullen waters of the tarn.

Noticing these things, I rode over a short causeway to the house. A servant in waiting took my horse, and I entered the Gothic archway of the hall. A valet, of stealthy step, thence conducted me, in silence, through many dark and intricate passages in my progress to the studio of his master. Much that I encountered on the way contributed, I know not how, to heighten the vague sentiments of which I have already spoken. While the objects around me —while the carvings of the ceilings, the sombre tapestries of the walls, the ebon blackness of the floors, and the phantasmagoric armorial trophies which rattled as I strode, were but matters to which, or to such as which, I had been accustomed from my infancy—while I hesitated not to acknowledge how familiar was all this—I still wondered to find how unfamiliar were the fancies which ordinary images were stirring up. On one of the staircases, I met the physician of the family. His countenance, I thought, wore a mingled expression of low cunning and perplexity. He accosted me with trepidation and passed on. The valet now threw open a door and ushered me into the presence of his master.

The room in which I found myself was very large and lofty. The windows were long, narrow, and pointed, and at so vast a distance from the black oaken floor as to be altogether inaccessible from within. Feeble gleams of encrimsoned light made their way through the trellised panes, and served to render sufficiently distinct the more prominent objects around; the eye, however, struggled in vain to reach the remoter angles of the chamber, or the recesses of the vaulted and fretted ceiling. Dark draperies hung upon the walls. The general furniture was profuse, comfortless, antique, and tattered. Many books and musical instruments lay scattered about, but failed to give any vitality to the scene. I felt that I breathed an atmosphere of sorrow. An air of stern, deep, and irredeemable gloom hung over and pervaded all.

Upon my entrance, Usher arose from a sofa on which he had been lying at full length, and greeted me with a vivacious warmth which had much in it, I at first thought, of an overdone cordiality—of the constrained effort of the *ennuyé* man of the world. A glance, however, at his countenance convinced me of his perfect sincerity. We sat down; and for some moments, while he spoke not, I gazed upon him with a feeling half of pity, half of awe. Surely man had never before so terribly altered, in so brief a period, as had Roderick Usher! It was with difficulty that I could bring myself to admit the identity of the wan being before me with the companion of my early boyhood. Yet the character of his face had been at all times remarkable. A cadaverousness of complexion; an eye large, liquid, and luminous beyond comparison; lips somewhat thin and very pallid, but of a surpassingly beautiful curve; a nose of a delicate Hebrew model, but with a breadth of nostril unusual in similar formations; a finely moulded chin, speaking, in its want of prominence, of a want of moral energy; hair of a more than web-like softness and tenuity; these features, with an inordinate expansion above the regions of the temple, made up altogether a countenance not easily to be forgotten. And now in the mere exaggeration of the prevailing character of these features, and of the expression they were wont to convey, lay so much of change that I doubted to whom I spoke. The now ghastly pallor of the skin, and the now miraculous lustre of the eye, above all things startled and even awed me. The silken hair, too, had been suffered to grow all unheeded, and as, in its wild gossamer texture, it floated rather than fell about the face, I could not, even with effort, connect its arabesque expression with any idea of simple humanity.

In the manner of my friend I was at once struck with an incoherence, an inconsistency; and I soon found this to arise from a series of feeble and futile struggles to overcome an habitual trepidancy, an excessive nervous agitation. For something of this nature I had indeed been prepared, no less by his letter than by reminiscences of certain boyish traits, and by conclusions deduced from his peculiar physical conformation and temperament. His action was alternately vivacious and sullen. His voice varied rapidly from a tremulous indecision (when the animal spirits seemed utterly in abeyance) to that species of energetic concision—that abrupt, weighty, unhurried, and hollow-sounding enunciation—that leaden, self-balanced and perfectly modulated guttural utterance—which may be observed in the lost drunkard, or the irreclaimable eater of opium, during the periods of his most intense excitement.

It was thus that he spoke of the object of my visit, of his earnest desire to see me, and of the solace he expected me to afford him. He entered, at some length, into what he conceived to be the nature of his malady. It was, he said, a constitutional and a family evil, and one for which he despaired to find a remedy—a mere nervous affection, he immediately added, which would undoubtedly soon pass off. It displayed itself in a host of unnatural sensations. Some of these, as he detailed them, interested and bewildered me; although, perhaps, the terms and the general manner of the narration had their weight. He suffered much from a morbid acuteness of the senses; the most insipid food was alone endurable; he could wear only garments of certain texture; the odors of all flowers were oppressive; his eyes were tortured by even a faint light; and there were but peculiar sounds, and these from stringed instruments, which did not inspire him with horror.

To an anomalous species of terror I found him a bounden slave. "I shall perish," said he, "I *must* perish in this deplorable folly. Thus,

thus, and not otherwise, shall I be lost. I dread the events of the future, not in themselves, but in their results. I shudder at the thought of any, even the most trivial, incident, which may operate upon this intolerable agitation of soul. I have, indeed, no abhorrence of danger, except in its absolute effect—in terror. In this unnerved—in this pitiable condition, I feel that the period will sooner or later arrive when I must abandon life and reason together, in some struggle with the grim phantasm, FEAR."

I learned moreover at intervals, and through broken and equivocal hints, another singular feature of his mental condition. He was enchained by certain superstitious impressions in regard to the dwelling which he tenanted, and whence, for many years, he had never ventured forth—in regard to an influence whose supposititious force was conveyed in terms too shadowy here to be restated—an influence which some peculiarities in the mere form and substance of his family mansion, had, by dint of long sufferance, he said, obtained over his spirit—an effect which the physique of the gray walls and turrets, and of the dim tarn into which they all looked down, had, at length, brought about upon the morale of his existence.

He admitted, however, although with hesitation, that much of the peculiar gloom which thus afflicted him could be traced to a more natural and far more palpable origin—to the severe and long-continued illness, indeed to the evidently approaching dissolution, of a tenderly beloved sister—his sole companion for long years, his last and only relative on earth. "Her decease," he said, with a bitterness which I can never forget, "would leave him (him the hopeless and the frail) the last of the ancient race of the Ushers." While he spoke the lady Madeline (for so was she called) passed slowly through a remote portion of the apartment, and, without having noticed my presence, disappeared. I regarded her with an utter astonishment not unmingled with dread, and yet I found it impossible to account for such feelings. A sensation of stupor oppressed me, as my eyes followed her retreating steps. When a door, at length, closed upon her, my glance sought instinctively and eagerly the countenance of the brother; but he had buried his face in his hands, and I could only perceive that a far more than ordinary wanness had overspread the emaciated fingers through which trickled many passionate tears.

The disease of the lady Madeline had long

baffled the skill of her physicians. A settled apathy, a gradual wasting away of the person, and frequent although transient affections of a partially cataleptical character, were the unusual diagnosis. Hitherto she had steadily borne up against the pressure of her malady, and had not betaken herself finally to bed; but, on the closing in of the evening of my arrival at the house, she succumbed (as her brother told me at night with inexpressible agitation) to the prostrating power of the destroyer; and I learned that the glimpse I had obtained of her person would thus probably be the last I should obtain—that the lady, at least while living, would be seen by me no more.

For several days ensuing, her name was unmentioned by either Usher or myself; and during this period I was busied in earnest endeavors to alleviate the melancholy of my friend. We painted and read together; or I listened, as if in a dream, to the wild improvisations of his speaking guitar. And thus, as a closer and still closer intimacy admitted me more unreservedly into the recesses of his spirit, the more bitterly did I perceive the futility of all attempt at cheering a mind from which darkness, as if an inherent positive quality, poured forth upon all objects of the moral and physical universe, in one unceasing radiation of gloom.

I shall ever bear about me a memory of the many solemn hours I thus spent alone with the master of the House of Usher. Yet I should fail in any attempt to convey an idea of the exact character of the studies, or of the occupations, in which he involved me, or led me the way. An excited and highly distempered ideality threw a sulphureous lustre over all. His long improvised dirges will ring forever in my ears. Among other things, I hold painfully in mind a certain singular perversion and amplification of the wild air of the last waltz of Von Weber. From the paintings over which his elaborate fancy brooded, and which grew, touch by touch, into vaguenesses at which I shuddered the more thrillingly because I shuddered knowing not why;—from these paintings (vivid as their images now are before me) I would in vain endeavor to educe more than a small portion which should lie within the compass of merely written words. By the utter simplicity, by the nakedness of his designs, he arrested and overawed attention. If ever mortal painted an idea, that mortal was Roderick Usher. For me at least, in the circumstances then surrounding me, there arose, out of the pure abstractions which the hypochondriac contrived to throw upon his canvas, an intensity of intolerable awe, no shadow of which felt I ever yet in the contemplation of the certainly glowing yet too concrete reveries of Fuseli.

One of the phantasmagoric conceptions of my friend, partaking not so rigidly of the spirit of abstraction, may be shadowed forth, although feebly, in words. A small picture presented the interior of an immensely long and rectangular vault or tunnel, with low walls, smooth, white, and without interruption or device. Certain accessory points of the design served well to convey the idea that this excavation lay at an exceeding depth below the surface of the earth. No outlet was observed in any portion of its vast extent, and no torch or other artificial source of light was discernible; yet a flood of intense rays rolled throughout, and bathed the whole in a ghastly and inappropriate splendor.

I have just spoken of that morbid condition of the auditory nerve which rendered all music intolerable to the sufferer, with the exception of certain effects of stringed instruments. It was, perhaps, the narrow limits to which he thus confined himself upon the guitar, which gave birth, in great measure, to the fantastic character of his performances. But the fervid *facility* of his impromptus could not be so accounted for. They must have been, and were, in the notes, as well as in the words of his wild fantasias (for he not unfrequently accompanied himself with rhymed verbal improvisations), the result of that intense mental collectedness and concentration to which I have previously alluded as observable only in particular moments of the highest artificial excitement. The words of one of these rhapsodies I have easily remembered. I was, perhaps, the more forcibly impressed with it, as he gave it, because, in the under or mystic current of its meaning, I fancied that I perceived, and for the first time, a full consciousness, on the part of Usher, of the tottering of his lofty reason upon her throne. The verses, which were entitled "The Haunted Palace," ran very nearly, if not accurately, thus:

I

In the greenest of our valleys
By good angels tenanted,
Once a fair and stately palace—
Radiant palace—reared its head.

In the monarch Thought's dominion,
    It stood there!
Never seraph spread a pinion
    Over fabric half so fair!

II

Banners yellow, glorious, golden,
    On its roof did float and flow,
(This—all this—was in the olden
    Time long ago)
10 And every gentle air that dallied,
    In that sweet day,
Along the ramparts plumed and pallid,
    A wingèd odor went away.

III

Wanderers in that happy valley,
    Through two luminous windows, saw
Spirits moving musically
    To a lute's well-tunèd law,
Round about a throne where, sitting,
20   Porphyrogene!
In state his glory well befitting,
    The ruler of the realm was seen.

IV

And all with pearl and ruby glowing
    Was the fair palace door,
Through which came flowing, flowing, flowing
    And sparkling evermore,
A troop of Echoes, whose sweet duty
    Was but to sing,
30 In voices of surpassing beauty,
    The wit and wisdom of their king.

V

But evil things, in robes of sorrow,
    Assailed the monarch's high estate.
(Ah, let us mourn!—for never morrow
    Shall dawn upon him, desolate!)
And round about his home the glory
    That blushed and bloomed
Is but a dim-remembered story
    Of the old time entombed.

VI

42 And travellers, now, within that valley,
    Through the red-litten windows see
Vast forms that move fantastically
    To a discordant melody;
While, like a ghastly rapid river,
    Through the pale door
A hideous throng rush out forever,
    And laugh—but smile no more.

50 I well remember that suggestions arising
from this ballad led us into a train of thought,
wherein there became manifest an opinion of
Usher's which I mention not so much on account of its novelty, (for other men have
thought thus), as on account of the pertinacity

with which he maintained it. This opinion, in
its general form, was that of the sentience of all
vegetable things. But in his disordered fancy
the idea had assumed a more daring character,
and trespassed, under certain conditions, upon
the kingdom of inorganization. I lack words to
express the full extent, or the earnest *abandon*
of his persuasion. The belief, however, was
connected (as I have previously hinted) with
the gray stones of the home of his forefathers.
The conditions of the sentience had been here,
he imagined, fulfilled in the method of collocation of these stones—in the order of their arrangement, as well as in that of the many fungi
which overspread them, and of the decayed
trees which stood around—above all, in the
long undisturbed endurance of this arrangement, and in its reduplication in the still waters
of the tarn. Its evidence—the evidence of the
sentience—was to be seen, he said (and I here
started as he spoke), in the gradual yet certain
condensation of an atmosphere of their own
about the waters and the walls. The result was
discoverable, he added, in that silent, yet importunate and terrible influence which for centuries had moulded the destinies of his family,
and which made *him* what I now saw him—
what he was. Such opinions need no comment,
and I will make none.

Our books—the books which, for years, had
formed no small portion of the mental existence
of the invalid—were, as might be supposed, in
strict keeping with this character of phantasm.
We pored together over such works as the
Ververt and *Chartreuse* of Gresset; the *Belphe-
gor* of Machiavelli; the *Heaven and Hell* of
Swedenborg; the *Subterranean Voyage of
Nicholas Klimm* by Holberg; the *Chiromancy*
of Robert Flud, of Jean D'Indaginé, and of De
la Chambre; the *Journey into the Blue Distance* of Tieck; and the *City of the Sun* of
Campanella. One favorite volume was a small
octavo edition of the *Directorium Inquisitorum*
by the Dominican Eymeric de Gironne; and
there were passages in Pomponius Mela, about
the old African Satyrs and Ægipans, over
which Usher would sit dreaming for hours. His
chief delight, however, was found in the perusal
of an exceedingly rare and curious book in
quarto Gothic—the manual of a forgotten
church—the *Vigiliæ Mortuorum Secundum
Chorum Ecclesiæ Maguntinæ.*

I could not help thinking of the wild ritual of
this work, and of its probable influence upon
the hypochondriac, when one evening, having

informed me abruptly that the lady Madeline was no more, he stated his intention of preserving her corpse for a fortnight, (previously to its final interment,) in one of the numerous vaults within the main walls of the building. The worldly reason, however, assigned for this singular proceeding, was one which I did not feel at liberty to dispute. The brother had been led to his resolution (so he told me) by consideration of the unusual character of the malady of the deceased, of certain obtrusive and eager inquiries on the part of her medical men, and of the remote and exposed situation of the burial-ground of the family. I will not deny that when I called to mind the sinister countenance of the person whom I met upon the staircase, on the day of my arrival at the house, I had no desire to oppose what I regarded as at best but a harmless, and by no means an unnatural precaution.

At the request of Usher, I personally aided him in the arrangements for the temporary entombment. The body having been encoffined, we two alone bore it to its rest. The vault in which we placed it (and which had been so long unopened that our torches, half smothered in its oppressive atmosphere, gave us little opportunity for investigation) was small, damp, and entirely without means of admission for light; lying, at great depth, immediately beneath that portion of the building in which was my own sleeping apartment. It had been used, apparently, in remote feudal times, for the worst purposes of a donjon-keep, and in later days as a place of deposit for powder, or some other highly combustible substance, as a portion of its floor, and the whole interior of a long archway through which we reached it, were carefully sheathed with copper. The door, of massive iron, had been, also, similarly protected. Its immense weight caused an unusually sharp grating sound, as it moved upon its hinges.

Having deposited our mournful burden upon tressels within this region of horror, we partially turned aside the yet unscrewed lid of the coffin, and looked upon the face of the tenant. A striking similitude between the brother and sister now first arrested my attention; and Usher, divining, perhaps, my thoughts, murmured out some few words from which I learned that the deceased and himself had been twins, and that sympathies of a scarcely intelligible nature had always existed between them. Our glances, however, rested not long upon the dead—for we could not regard her unawed. The disease which had thus entombed the lady in the maturity of youth, had left, as usual in all maladies of a strictly cataleptical character, the mockery of a faint blush upon the bosom and the face, and that suspiciously lingering smile upon the lip which is so terrible in death. We replaced and screwed down the lid, and, having secured the door of iron, made our way, with toil, into the scarcely less gloomy apartments of the upper portion of the house. 10

And now, some days of bitter grief having elapsed, an observable change came over the features of the mental disorder of my friend. His ordinary manner had vanished. His ordinary occupations were neglected or forgotten. He roamed from chamber to chamber with hurried, unequal, and objectless step. The pallor of his countenance had assumed, if possible, a 20 more ghastly hue—but the luminousness of his eye had utterly gone out. The once occasional huskiness of his tone was heard no more; and a tremulous quaver, as if of extreme terror, habitually characterized his utterance. There were times, indeed, when I thought his unceasingly agitated mind was laboring with some oppressive secret, to divulge which he struggled for the necessary courage. At times, again, I was obliged to resolve all into the mere in- 30 explicable vagaries of madness, for I beheld him gazing upon vacancy for long hours, in an attitude of the profoundest attention, as if listening to some imaginary sound. It was no wonder that his condition terrified—that it infected me. I felt creeping upon me, by slow yet certain degrees, the wild influences of his own fantastic yet impressive superstitions.

It was, especially, upon retiring to bed late in the night of the seventh or eighth day after 40 the placing of the lady Madeline within the donjon, that I experienced the full power of such feelings. Sleep came not near my couch, while the hours waned and waned away. I struggled to reason off the nervousness which had dominion over me. I endeavored to believe that much, if not all, of what I felt was due to the bewildering influence of the gloomy furniture of the room—of the dark and tattered draperies which, tortured into motion by the 50 breath of a rising tempest, swayed fitfully to and fro upon the walls, and rustled uneasily about the decorations of the bed. But my efforts were fruitless. An irrepressible tremor gradually pervaded my frame; and at length there sat upon my very heart an incubus of utterly causeless alarm. Shaking this off with a gasp and a struggle, I uplifted myself upon the pillows, and, peering earnestly within the intense darkness of the chamber, hearkened—I know not why, except that an instinctive spirit prompted me—to certain low and indefinite sounds which came, through the pauses of the storm, at long intervals, I knew not whence. Overpowered by an intense sentiment of horror, unaccountable yet unendurable, I threw on my clothes with haste (for I felt that I should sleep no more during the night,) and endeavored to arouse myself from the pitiable condition into which I had fallen, by pacing rapidly to and fro through the apartment.

I had taken but few turns in this manner, when a light step on an adjoining staircase arrested my attention. I presently recognized it as that of Usher. In an instant afterward he rapped with a gentle touch at my door, and entered, bearing a lamp. His countenance was, as usual, cadaverously wan—but, moreover, there was a species of mad hilarity in his eyes —an evidently restrained hysteria in his whole demeanor. His air appalled me—but anything was preferable to the solitude which I had so long endured, and I even welcomed his presence as a relief.

"And you have not seen it?" he said abruptly, after having stared about him for some moments in silence—"you have not then seen it? —but, stay! you shall." Thus speaking, and having carefully shaded his lamp, he hurried to one of the casements, and threw it freely open to the storm.

The impetuous fury of the entering gust nearly lifted us from our feet. It was, indeed, a tempestuous yet sternly beautiful night, and one wildly singular in its terror and its beauty. A whirlwind had apparently collected its force in our vicinity; for there were frequent and violent alterations in the direction of the wind; and the exceeding density of the clouds (which hung so low as to press upon the turrets of the house) did not prevent our perceiving the lifelike velocity with which they flew careering from all points against each other, without passing away into the distance. I say that even their exceeding density did not prevent our perceiving this; yet we had no glimpse of the moon or stars, nor was there any flashing forth of the lightning. But the under surfaces of the huge masses of agitated vapor, as well as all terrestrial objects immediately around us, were glowing in the unnatural light of a faintly luminous and distinctly visible gaseous exhalation which hung about and enshrouded the mansion.

"You must not—you shall not behold this!" said I, shudderingly, to Usher, as I led him with a gentle violence from the window to a seat. "These appearances, which bewilder you, are merely electrical phenomena not uncommon—or it may be that they have their ghastly origin in the rank miasma of the tarn. Let us close this casement; the air is chilling and dangerous to your frame. Here is one of your favorite romances. I will read, and you shall listen;—and so we will pass away this terrible night together."

The antique volume which I had taken up was the *Mad Trist* of Sir Launcelot Canning; but I had called it a favorite of Usher's more in sad jest than in earnest; for, in truth, there is little in its uncouth and unimaginative prolixity which could have had interest for the lofty and spiritual ideality of my friend. It was, however, the only book immediately at hand; and I indulged a vague hope that the excitement which now agitated the hypochondriac might find relief (for the history of mental disorder is full of similar anomalies) even in the extremeness of the folly which I should read. Could I have judged, indeed, by the wild overstrained air of vivacity with which he hearkened, or apparently hearkened, to the words of the tale, I might well have congratulated myself upon the success of my design.

I had arrived at that well-known portion of the story where Ethelred, the hero of the *Trist*, having sought in vain for peaceable admission into the dwelling of the hermit, proceeds to make good an entrance by force. Here, it will be remembered, the words of the narrative run thus:

"And Ethelred, who was by nature of a doughty heart, and who was now mighty withal, on account of the powerfulness of the wine which he had drunken, waited no longer to hold parley with the hermit, who, in sooth, was of an obstinate and maliceful turn, but, feeling the rain upon his shoulders, and fearing the rising of the tempest, uplifted his mace outright, and with blows made quickly room in the plankings of the door for his gauntleted hand; and now pulling therewith sturdily, he so cracked, and ripped, and tore all asunder, that the noise of the dry and hollow-sounding wood alarumed and reverberated throughout the forest."

At the termination of this sentence I started, and for a moment paused; for it appeared to me (although I at once concluded that my excited fancy had deceived me)—it appeared to me that from some very remote portion of the mansion there came, indistinctly, to my ears, what might have been, in its exact similarity of character, the echo (but a stifled and dull one certainly) of the very cracking and ripping sound which Sir Launcelot had so particularly described. It was, beyond doubt, the coincidence alone which had arrested my attention; for, amid the rattling of the sashes of the casements, and the ordinary commingled noises of the still increasing storm, the sound, in itself, had nothing, surely, which should have interested or disturbed me. I continued the story:

"But the good champion Ethelred, now entering within the door, was sore enraged and amazed to perceive no signal of the maliceful hermit; but, in the stead thereof, a dragon of a scaly and prodigious demeanor, and of a fiery tongue, which sate in guard before a palace of gold, with a floor of silver; and upon the wall there hung a shield of shining brass with this legend enwritten—

Who entereth herein, a conqueror hath bin;
Who slayeth the dragon, the shield he shall win.

And Ethelred uplifted his mace, and struck upon the head of the dragon, which fell before him, and gave up his pesty breath, with a shriek so horrid and harsh, and withal so piercing, that Ethelred had fain to close his ears with his hands against the dreadful noise of it, the like whereof was never before heard."

Here again I paused abruptly, and now with a feeling of wild amazement; for there could be no doubt whatever that, in this instance, I did actually hear (although from what direction it proceeded I found it impossible to say) a low and apparently distant, but harsh, protracted, and most unusual screaming or grating sound—the exact counterpart of what my fancy had already conjured up for the dragon's unnatural shriek as described by the romancer. Oppressed, as I certainly was, upon the occurrence of this second and most extraordinary coincidence, by a thousand conflicting sensations, in which wonder and extreme terror were predominant, I still retained sufficient presence of mind to avoid exciting, by any observation, the sensitive nervousness of my companion. I was by no means certain that he had noticed the sounds in question; although, assuredly, a strange alteration had during the last few minutes taken place in his demeanor. From a position fronting my own, he had gradually brought round his chair, so as to sit with his face to the door of the chamber; and thus I could but partially perceive his features, although I saw that his lips trembled as if he were murmuring inaudibly. His head had dropped upon his breast—yet I knew that he was not asleep, from the wide and rigid opening of the eye as I caught a glance of it in profile. The motion of his body, too, was at variance with this idea—for he rocked from side to side with a gentle yet constant and uniform sway. Having rapidly taken notice of all this, I resumed the narrative of Sir Launcelot, which thus proceeded:

"And now, the champion, having escaped from the terrible fury of the dragon, bethinking himself of the brazen shield, and of the breaking up of the enchantment which was upon it, removed the carcass from out of the way before him, and approached valourously over the silver pavement of the castle to where the shield was upon the wall; which in sooth tarried not for his full coming, but fell down at his feet upon the silver floor, with a mighty great and terrible ringing sound."

No sooner had these syllables passed my lips, than—as if a shield of brass had indeed at the moment, fallen heavily upon a floor of silver—I became aware of a distinct, hollow, metallic and clangorous yet apparently muffled reverberation. Completely unnerved, I leaped to my feet; but the measured rocking movement of Usher was undisturbed. I rushed to the chair in which he sat. His eyes were bent fixedly before him, and throughout his whole countenance there reigned a stony rigidity. But as I placed my hand upon his shoulder, there came a strong shudder over his whole person; a sickly smile quivered about his lips; and I saw that he spoke in a low, hurried, and gibbering murmur, as if unconscious of my presence. Bending closely over him, I at length drank in the hideous import of his words.

"Not hear it?—yes, I hear it, and *have* heard it. Long—long—long—many minutes, many hours, many days, have I heard it—yet I dared not—oh, pity me, miserable wretch that I am!—I dared not—I *dared* not speak! *We have put her living in the tomb!* Said I not that my senses were acute? I *now* tell you that I heard her first feeble movements in the hollow coffin. I heard them—many, many days ago—yet I dared not—*I dared not speak!* And now—to-night—Ethelred—ha! ha!—the breaking of the

hermit's door, and the deathcry of the dragon, and the clangor of the shield!—say, rather, the rending of her coffin, and the grating of the iron hinges of her prison, and her struggles within the coppered archway of the vault! Oh, whither shall I fly? Will she not be here anon? Is she not hurrying to upbraid me for my haste? Have I not heard her footstep on the stair? Do I not distinguish that heavy and horrible beat-
10 ing of her heart? Madman!"—here he sprang furiously to his feet, and shrieked out his syllables, as if in the effort he were giving up his soul—"*Madman! I tell you that she now stands without the door!*"

As if in the superhuman energy of his utter-ance there had been found the potency of a spell, the huge antique panels to which the speaker pointed threw slowly back, upon the instant, their ponderous and ebony jaws. It
20 was the work of the rushing gust—but then without those doors there *did* stand the lofty and enshrouded figure of the lady Madeline of Usher. There was blood upon her white robes, and the evidence of some bitter struggle upon every portion of her emaciated frame. For a moment she remained trembling and reeling
27 to and fro upon the threshold—then, with a

low moaning cry, fell heavily inward upon the person of her brother, and, in her violent and now final death agonies, bore him to the floor a corpse, and a victim to the terrors he had anticipated.

From that chamber, and from that mansion, I fled aghast. The storm was still abroad in all its wrath as I found myself crossing the old causeway. Suddenly there shot along the path a wild light, and I turned to see whence a gleam so unusual could have issued; for the vast house and its shadows were alone behind me. The radiance was that of the full, setting, and blood-red moon, which now shone vividly through that once barely discernible fissure, of which I have before spoken as extending from the roof of the building, in a zigzag direction, to the base. While I gazed, this fissure rapidly widened—there came a fierce breath of the whirlwind—the entire orb of the satellite burst at once upon my sight—my brain reeled as I saw the mighty walls rushing asunder—there was a long tumultuous shouting sound like the voice of a thousand waters—and the deep and dank tarn at my feet closed sullenly and silently over the fragments of the "*House of Usher.*"
1839

» » THE MURDERS IN THE RUE MORGUE[6] « «

What song the Syrens sang, or what name Achilles assumed when he hid himself among women, although puzzling questions are not beyond *all* conjecture.   SIR THOMAS BROWNE: *Urn-Burial*

The mental features discoursed of as the analytical are, in themselves, but little sus-ceptible of analysis. We appreciate them only in their effects. We know of them, among other
40 things, that they are always to their possessor, when inordinately possessed, a source of the liveliest enjoyment. As the strong man exults in his physical ability, delighting in such exer-cises as call his muscles into action, so glories the analyst in that moral activity which *dis-entangles*. He derives pleasure from even the most trivial occupations bringing his talents into play. He is fond of enigmas, of conun-drums, of hieroglyphics; exhibiting in his solu-
50 tions of each a degree of *acumen* which ap-pears to the ordinary apprehension preter-natural. His results brought about by the very soul and essence of method, have, in truth, the whole air of intuition.

[6] This is the first tale ever written in the detective-story genre.

The faculty of resolution is possibly much invigorated by mathematical study, and es-pecially by that highest branch of it, which, unjustly, and merely on account of its retro-grade operations, has been called, as if *par excellence*, analysis. Yet to calculate is not in itself to analyze. A chess-player, for example, does the one, without effort at the other. It fol-lows that the game of chess, in its effects upon mental character, is greatly misunderstood. I am not now writing a treatise, but simply prefacing a somewhat peculiar narrative by observations very much at random; I will, therefore, take occasion to assert that the higher powers of the reflective intellect are more decidedly and more usefully tasked by the un-ostentatious game of draughts than by all the elaborate frivolity of chess. In this latter, where the pieces have different and *bizarre* motions, with various and variable values, what is only complex is mistaken (a not unusual error) for what is profound. The *attention* is here called powerfully into play. If it flag for an instant, an oversight is committed, resulting in injury or defeat. The possible moves being not only manifold, but involute, the chances of such oversights are multiplied; and in nine cases out of ten, it is the more concentrative rather than the more acute player who conquers. In draughts, on the contrary, where the moves are *unique* and have but little variation, the probabilities of inadvertence are diminished, and the mere attention being left comparatively unemployed, what advantages are obtained by either party are obtained by superior acumen. To be less abstract: Let us suppose a game of draughts where the pieces are reduced to four kings, and where, of course, no oversight is to be expected. It is obvious that here the victory can be decided (the players being at all equal) only by some *recherché* movement, the result of some strong exertion of the intellect. Deprived of ordinary resources, the analyst throws himself into the spirit of his opponent, identifies himself therewith, and not unfrequently sees thus, at a glance, the sole methods (sometimes indeed absurdly simple ones) by which he may seduce into error or hurry into miscalculation.

Whist has long been noted for its influence upon what is termed the calculating power; and men of the highest order of intellect have been known to take an apparently unaccountable delight in it, while eschewing chess as frivolous. Beyond doubt there is nothing of a similar nature so greatly tasking the faculty of analysis. The best chess-player in Christendom *may* be little more than the best player of chess; but proficiency in whist implies capacity for success in all these more important undertakings where mind struggles with mind. When I say proficiency, I mean that perfection in the game which includes a comprehension of *all* the sources whence legitimate advantage may be derived. These are not only manifold, but multiform, and lie frequently among recesses of thought altogether inaccessible to the ordinary understanding. To observe attentively is to remember distinctly; and, so far, the concentrative chess-player will do very well at whist; while the rules of Hoyle (themselves based upon the mere mechanism of the game) are sufficiently and generally comprehensible. Thus to have a retentive memory, and to proceed by "the book," are points commonly regarded as the sum total of good playing. But it is in matters beyond the limits of mere rule that the skill of the analyst is evinced. He makes, in

silence, a host of observations and inferences. So, perhaps, do his companions; and the difference in the extent of the information obtained lies, not so much in the validity of the inference, as in the quality of the observation. The necessary knowledge is that of *what* to observe. Our player confines himself not at all; nor, because the game is the object, does he reject deductions from things external to the game. He examines the countenance of his partner, comparing it carefully with that of each of his opponents. He considers the mode of assorting the cards in each hand; often counting trump by trump, and honor by honor, through the glances bestowed by their holders upon each. He notes every variation of face as the play progresses, gathering a fund of thought from the differences in the expression of certainty, of surprise, of triumph, or chagrin. From the manner of gathering up a trick he judges whether the person taking it can make another in the suit. He recognizes what is played through feint, by the air with which it is thrown upon the table. A casual or inadvertent word; the accidental dropping or turning of a card, with the accompanying anxiety or carelessness in regard to its concealment; the counting of the tricks, with the order of their arrangement; embarrassment, hesitation, eagerness or trepidation—all afford, to his apparently intuitive perception, indications of the true state of affairs. The first two or three rounds having been played, he is in full possession of the contents of each hand, and thenceforward puts down his cards with as absolute a precision of purpose as if the rest of the party had turned outward the faces of their own.

The analytical power should not be confounded with simple ingenuity; for while the analyst is necessarily ingenious, the ingenious man is often remarkably incapable of analysis. The constructive or combining power, by which ingenuity is usually manifested, and to which the phrenologists (I believe erroneously) have assigned a separate organ, supposing it a primitive faculty, has been so frequently seen in those whose intellect bordered otherwise upon idiocy, as to have attracted general observation among writers on morals. Between ingenuity and the analytic ability there exists a difference far greater, indeed, than that between the fancy and the imagination, but of a character very strictly analogous. It will be found, in fact, that the ingenious are always fanciful, and the *truly* imaginative never otherwise than analytic.

The narrative which follows will appear to the reader somewhat in the light of a commentary upon the propositions just advanced.

Residing in Paris during the spring and part of the summer of 18—, I there became acquainted with a Monsieur C. Auguste Dupin. This young gentleman was of an excellent— indeed of an illustrious—family, but, by a variety of untoward events, had been reduced to such poverty that the energy of his character succumbed beneath it, and he ceased to bestir himself in the world or to care for the retrieval of his fortunes. By courtesy of his creditors, there still remained in his possession a small remnant of his patrimony; and upon the income arising from this he managed, by means of a rigorous economy, to procure the necessaries of life, without troubling himself about its superfluities. Books, indeed, were his sole luxuries, and in Paris these are easily obtained.

Our first meeting was at an obscure library in the Rue Montmartre, where the accident of our both being in search of the same very rare and very remarkable volume brought us into closer communion. We saw each other again and again. I was deeply interested in the little family history which he detailed to me with all that candor which a Frenchman indulges whenever mere self is the theme. I was astonished, too, at the vast extent of his reading; and, above all, I felt my soul enkindled within me by the wild fervor and the vivid freshness of his imagination. Seeking in Paris the objects I then sought, I felt that the society of such a man would be to me a treasure beyond price; and this feeling I frankly confided to him. It was at length arranged that we should live together during my stay in the city; and, as my worldly circumstances were somewhat less embarrassed than his own, I was permitted to be at the expense of renting, and furnishing in a style which suited the rather fantastic gloom of our common temper, a time-eaten and grotesque mansion, long deserted, through superstitions into which we did not inquire, and tottering to its fall in a retired and desolate portion of the Faubourg St. Germain.

Had the routine of our life at this place been known to the world, we should have been regarded as madmen—although, perhaps, as madmen of a harmless nature. Our seclusion was perfect. We admitted no visitors. Indeed, the locality of our retirement had been carefully kept a secret from my own former associates; and it had been many years since Dupin had ceased to know or be known in Paris. We existed within ourselves alone.

It was a freak of fancy in my friend (for what else shall I call it?) to be enamored of the Night for her own sake; and into this *bizarrerie,* as into all his others, I quietly fell; giving myself up to his wild whims with a perfect *abandon.* The sable divinity would not herself dwell with us always; but we could counterfeit her presence. At the first dawn of the morning we closed all the massy shutters of our old building; lighted a couple of tapers which, strongly perfumed, threw out only the ghastliest and feeblest of rays. By the aid of these we then busied our souls in dreams— reading, writing, or conversing, until warned by the clock of the advent of the true Darkness. Then we sallied forth into the streets, arm and arm, continuing the topics of the day, or roaming far and wide until a late hour, seeking, amid the wild lights and shadows of the populous city, that infinity of mental excitement which quiet observation can afford.

At such times I could not help remarking and admiring (although from his rich ideality I had been prepared to expect it) a peculiar analytic ability in Dupin. He seemed, too, to take an eager delight in its exercise—if not exactly in its display—and did not hesitate to confess the pleasure thus derived. He boasted to me, with a low chuckling laugh, that most men, in respect to himself, wore windows in their bosoms, and was wont to follow up such assertions by direct and very startling proofs of his intimate knowledge of my own. His manner at these moments was frigid and abstract; his eyes were vacant in expression; while his voice, usually a rich tenor, rose into a treble which would have sounded petulantly but for the deliberateness and entire distinctness of the enunciation. Observing him in these moods I often dwelt meditatively upon the old philosophy of the Bi-Part Soul, and amused myself with the fancy of a double Dupin—the creative and the resolvent.

Let it not be supposed from what I have just said that I am detailing any mystery, or penning any romance. What I have described in the Frenchman was merely the result of an excited, or perhaps of a diseased, intelligence. But of the character of his remarks at the periods in question an example will best convey the idea.

We were strolling one night down a long dirty street, in the vicinity of the Palais Royal. Being both, apparently, occupied with thought, neither of us had spoken a syllable for fifteen minutes at least. All at once Dupin broke forth with these words:

"He is a very little fellow, that's true, and would do better for the *Théâtre des Variétés*."

"There can be no doubt of that," I replied unwittingly, and not at first observing (so much had I been absorbed in reflection) the extraordinary manner in which the speaker had chimed in with my meditations. In an instant afterward I recollected myself, and my astonishment was profound.

"Dupin," said I, gravely, "this is beyond my comprehension. I do not hesitate to say that I am amazed, and can scarcely credit my senses. How was it possible you should know I was thinking of—?" Here I paused, to ascertain beyond a doubt whether he really knew of whom I thought.

—"of Chantilly," said he, "why do you pause? You were remarking to yourself that his diminutive figure unfitted him for tragedy."

This was precisely what had formed the subject of my reflections. Chantilly was a *quondam* cobbler of the Rue St. Denis, who, becoming stage-mad, had attempted the *rôle* of Xerxes, in Crébillon's tragedy so called, and been notoriously Pasquinaded for his pains.

"Tell me, for Heaven's sake," I exclaimed, "the method—if method there is—by which you have been enabled to fathom my soul in this matter." In fact, I was even more startled than I would have been willing to express.

"It was the fruiterer," replied my friend, "who brought you to the conclusion that the mender of soles was not of sufficient height for Xerxes *et id genus omne*."

"The fruiterer!—you astonish me—I know no fruiterer whomsoever."

"The man who ran up against you as we entered the street—it may have been fifteen minutes ago."

I now remembered that, in fact, a fruiterer, carrying upon his head a large basket of apples, had nearly thrown me down, by accident, as we passed from the Rue C—— into the thoroughfare where we stood; but what this had to do with Chantilly I could not possibly understand.

There was not a particle of *charlatanerie*

about Dupin. "I will explain," he said, "and, that you may comprehend all clearly, we will first retrace the course of your meditations, from the moment in which I spoke to you until that of the *rencontre* with the fruiterer in question. The larger links of the chain run thus—Chantilly, Orion, Dr. Nichols, Epicurus, Stereotomy, the street stones, the fruiterer."

There are few persons who have not, at some period of their lives, amused themselves in retracing the steps by which particular conclusions of their own minds have been attained. The occupation is often full of interest; and he who attempts it for the first time is astonished by the apparently illimitable distance and incoherence between the starting-point and the goal. What, then, must have been my amazement when I heard the Frenchman speak what he had just spoken, and when I could not help acknowledging that he had spoken the truth? He continued:

"We had been talking of horses, if I remember aright, just before leaving the Rue C——. This was the last subject we discussed. As we crossed into this street, a fruiterer, with a large basket upon his head, brushing quickly past us, thrust you upon a pile of paving-stones collected at a spot where the causeway is undergoing repair. You stepped upon one of the loose fragments, slipped, slightly strained your ankle, appeared vexed or sulky, muttered a few words, turned to look at the pile, and then proceeded in silence. I was not particularly attentive to what you did; but observation has become with me, of late, a species of necessity.

"You kept your eyes upon the ground—glancing, with a petulant expression, at the holes and ruts in the pavement (so that I saw you were still thinking of the stones), until we reached the little alley called Lamartine, which had been paved, by way of experiment, with the overlapping and riveted blocks. Here your countenance brightened up, and, perceiving your lips move, I could not doubt that you murmured the word 'stereotomy,' a term very affectedly applied to this species of pavement. I knew that you could not say to yourself 'stereotomy' without being brought to think of atomies, and thus of the theories of Epicurus; and since, when we discussed this subject not very long ago, I mentioned to you how singularly, yet with how little notice, the vague guesses of that noble Greek had met with confirmation in the late nebular cosmogony, I felt that you could not avoid casting your eyes upward to the great *nebula* in Orion, and I certainly expected that you would do so. You did look up; and I was now assured that I had correctly followed your steps. But in that bitter *tirade* upon Chantilly, which appeared in yesterday's *Musée,* the satirist, making some disgraceful allusions to the cobbler's change of name upon assuming the buskin, quoted a Latin line about which we have often conversed. I mean the line

'Perdidit antiquum litera prima sonum.'

I had told you that this was in reference to Orion, formerly written Urion; and, from certain pungencies connected with this explanation, I was aware that you could not have forgotten it. It was clear, therefore, that you would not fail to combine the two ideas of Orion and Chantilly. That you did combine them I saw by the character of the smile which passed over your lips. You thought of the poor cobbler's immolation. So far, you had been stooping in your gait; but now I saw you draw yourself up to your full height. I was then sure that you reflected upon the diminutive figure of Chantilly. At this point I interrupted your meditations to remark that as, in fact, he *was* a very little fellow—that Chantilly—he would do better at the *Théâtre des Variétés."*

Not long after this, we were looking over an evening edition of the *Gazette des Tribunaux,* when the following paragraphs arrested our attention:

"Extraordinary Murders.—This morning, about three o'clock, the inhabitants of the Quarter St. Roch were aroused from sleep by a succession of terrific shrieks, issuing apparently from the fourth story of a house in the Rue Morgue, known to be in the sole occupancy of one Madame L'Espanaye, and her daughter, Mademoiselle Camille L'Espanaye. After some delay, occasioned by a fruitless attempt to procure admission in the usual manner, the gateway was broken in with a crowbar, and eight or ten of the neighbors entered, accompanied by two *gendarmes.* By this time the cries had ceased; but, as the party rushed up the first flight of stairs, two or more rough voices, in angry contention, were distinguished, and seemed to proceed from the upper part of the house. As the second landing was reached, these sounds also had ceased, and everything remained perfectly quiet. The party spread themselves, and hurried from room to room.

Upon arriving at a large back chamber in the fourth story (the door of which, being found locked, with the key inside, was forced open), a spectacle presented itself which struck every one present not less with horror than with astonishment.

"The apartment was in the wildest disorder —the furniture broken and thrown about in all directions. There was only one bedstead; and from this the bed had been removed, and thrown into the middle of the floor. On a chair lay a razor, besmeared with blood. On the hearth were two or three long and thick tresses of grey human hair, also dabbled in blood, and seeming to have been pulled out by the roots. Upon the floor were found four Napoleons, an ear-ring of topaz, three large silver spoons, three small of *métal d'Alger,* and two bags, containing nearly four thousand francs in gold. The drawers of a *bureau,* which stood in one corner, were open, and had been, apparently, rifled, although many articles still remained in them. A small iron safe was discovered under the *bed* (not under the bedstead). It was open, with the key still in the door. It had no contents beyond a few old letters, and other papers of little consequence.

"Of Madame L'Espanaye no traces were here seen; but an unusual quantity of soot being observed in the fireplace, a search was made in the chimney, and (horrible to relate!) the corpse of the daughter, head downward, was dragged therefrom; it having been thus forced up the narrow aperture for a considerable distance. The body was quite warm. Upon examining it, many excoriations were perceived, no doubt occasioned by the violence with which it had been thrust up and disengaged. Upon the face were many severe scratches, and upon the throat, dark bruises, and deep indentations of fingernails, as if the deceased had been throttled to death.

"After a thorough investigation of every portion of the house, without farther discovery, the party made its way into a small paved yard in the rear of the building, where lay the corpse of the old lady, with her throat so entirely cut that, upon an attempt to raise her, the head fell off. The body, as well as the head, was fearfully mutilated—the former so much so as scarcely to retain any semblance of humanity.

"To this horrible mystery there is not as yet, we believe, the slightest clew."

The next day's paper had these additional particulars.

"The Tragedy in the Rue Morgue. Many individuals have been examined in relation to the most extraordinary and frightful affair" [the word *"affaire"* has not yet, in France, that levity of import which it conveys with us], "but nothing whatever has transpired to throw light upon it. We give below all the material testimony elicited.

"Pauline Dubourg, laundress, deposes that she has known both the deceased for three years, having washed for them during that period. The old lady and her daughter seemed on good terms—very affectionate towards each other. They were excellent pay. Could not speak in regard to their mode or means of living. Believed that Madame L. told fortunes for a living. Was reputed to have money put by. Never met any persons in the house when she called for the clothes or took them home. Was sure that they had no servant in employ. There appeared to be no furniture in any part of the building except in the fourth story.

"Pierre Moreau, tobacconist, deposes that he has been in the habit of selling small quantities of tobacco and snuff to Madame L'Espanaye for nearly four years. Was born in the neighborhood, and has always resided there. The deceased and her daughter had occupied the house in which the corpses were found, for more than six years. It was formerly occupied by a jeweller, who underlet the upper rooms to various persons. The house was the property of Madame L. She became dissatisfied with the abuse of the premises by her tenant, and moved into them herself, refusing to let any portion. The old lady was childish. Witness had seen the daughter some five or six times during the six years. The two lived an exceedingly retired life—were reputed to have money. Had heard it said among the neighbors that Madame L. told fortunes—did not believe it. Had never seen any person enter the door except the old lady and her daughter, a porter once or twice, and a physician some eight or ten times.

"Many other persons, neighbors, gave evidence to the same effect. No one was spoken of as frequenting the house. It was not known whether there were any living connections of Madame L. and her daughter. The shutters of the front windows were seldom opened. Those in the rear were always closed, with the exception of the large back room, fourth story.

The house was a good house—not very old.

"Isidore Musèt, gendarme, deposes that he was called to the house about three o'clock in the morning, and found some twenty or thirty persons at the gateway, endeavoring to gain admittance. Forced it open, at length, with a bayonet—not with a crowbar. Had but little difficulty in getting it open, on account of its being a double or folding gate, and bolted neither at bottom nor top. The shrieks were continued until the gate was forced—and then suddenly ceased. They seemed to be screams of some person (or persons) in great agony—were loud and drawn out, not short and quick. Witness led the way upstairs. Upon reaching the first landing, heard two voices in loud and angry contention: the one a gruff voice, the other much shriller—a very strange voice. Could distinguish some words of the former, which was that of a Frenchman. Was positive that it was not a woman's voice. Could distinguish the words *'sacré'* and *'diable.'* The shrill voice was that of a foreigner. Could not be sure whether it was the voice of a man or of a woman. Could not make out what was said, but believed the language to be Spanish. The state of the room and of the bodies was described by this witness as we described them yesterday.

"Henri Duval, a neighbor, and by trade a silversmith, deposes that he was one of the party who first entered the house. Corroborates the testimony of Musèt in general. As soon as they forced an entrance, they reclosed the door, to keep out the crowd, which collected very fast, notwithstanding the lateness of the hour. The shrill voice, this witness thinks, was that of an Italian. Was certain it was not French. Could not be sure that it was a man's voice. It might have been a woman's. Was not acquainted with the Italian language. Could not distinguish the words, but was convinced, by the intonation, that the speaker was an Italian. Knew Madame L. and her daughter. Had conversed with both frequently. Was sure that the shrill voice was not that of either of the deceased.

"——— Odenheimer, restaurateur. This witness volunteered his testimony. Not speaking French, was examined through an interpreter. Is a native of Amsterdam. Was passing the house at the time of the shrieks. They lasted for several minutes—probably ten. They were long and loud—very awful and distressing. Was one of those who entered the building. Corrobo-

rated the previous evidence in every respect but one. Was sure that the shrill voice was that of a man—of a Frenchman. Could not distinguish the words uttered. They were loud and quick—unequal—spoken apparently in fear as well as in anger. The voice was harsh—not so much shrill as harsh. Could not call it a shrill voice. The gruff voice said repeatedly, '*sacré*,' '*diable*,' and once '*mon Dieu*.'

"*Jules Mignaud*, banker, of the firm of Mignaud et Fils, Rue Deloraine. Is the elder Mignaud. Madame L'Espanaye had some property. Had opened an account with his banking house in the spring of the year —— (eight years previously). Made frequent deposits in small sums. Had checked for nothing until the third day before her death, when she took out in person the sum of 4000 francs. This sum was paid in gold, and a clerk sent home with the money.

"*Adolphe Le Bon*, clerk to Mignaud et Fils, deposes that on the day in question, about noon, he accompanied Madame L'Espanaye to her residence with the 4000 francs, put up in two bags. Upon the door being opened, Mademoiselle L. appeared and took from his hands one of the bags, while the old lady relieved him of the other. He then bowed and departed. Did not see any person in the street at the time. It is a by-street—very lonely.

"*William Bird*, tailor, deposes that he was one of the party who entered the house. Is an Englishman. Has lived in Paris two years. Was one of the first to ascend the stairs. Heard the voices in contention. The gruff voice was that of a Frenchman. Could make out several words, but cannot now remember all. Heard distinctly '*sacré*' and '*mon Dieu*.' There was a sound at the moment as if of several persons struggling —a scraping and scuffling sound. The shrill voice was very loud—louder than the gruff one. Is sure that it was not the voice of an Englishman. Appeared to be that of a German. Might have been a woman's voice. Does not understand German.

"Four of the above-named witnesses, being recalled, deposed that the door of the chamber in which was found the body of Mademoiselle L. was locked on the inside when the party reached it. Everything was perfectly silent—no groans or noises of any kind. Upon forcing the door no person was seen. The windows, both of the back and front room, were down and firmly fastened from within. A door between the two rooms was closed, but not locked. The door leading from the front room into the passage was locked, with the key on the inside. A small room in the front of the house, on the fourth story, at the head of the passage, was open, the door being ajar. This room was crowded with old beds, boxes, and so forth. These were carefully removed and searched. There was not an inch of any portion of the house which was not carefully searched. Sweeps were sent up and down the chimneys. The house was a four-story one with garrets (*mansardes*). A trap-door on the roof was nailed down very securely—did not appear to have been opened for years. The time elapsing between the hearing of the voices in contention and the breaking open of the room door, was variously stated by the witnesses. Some made it as short as three minutes—some as long as five. The door was opened with difficulty.

"*Alfonzo Garcio*, undertaker, deposes that he resides in the Rue Morgue. Is a native of Spain. Was one of the party who entered the house. Did not proceed upstairs. Is nervous, and was apprehensive of the consequences of agitation. Heard the voices in contention. The gruff voice was that of a Frenchman. Could not distinguish what was said. The shrill voice was that of an Englishman—is sure of this. Does not understand the English language, but judges by the intonation.

"*Alberto Montani*, confectioner, deposes that he was among the first to ascend the stairs. Heard the voices in question. The gruff voice was that of a Frenchman. Distinguished several words. The speaker appeared to be expostulating. Could not make out the words of the shrill voice. Spoke quick and unevenly. Thinks it the voice of a Russian. Corroborates the general testimony. Is an Italian. Never conversed with a native of Russia.

"Several witnesses, recalled, here testified that the chimneys of all the rooms on the fourth story were too narrow to admit the passage of a human being. By 'sweeps' were meant cylindrical sweeping-brushes, such as are employed by those who clean chimneys. These brushes were passed up and down every flue in the house. There is no back passage by which any one could have descended while the party proceeded upstairs. The body of Mademoiselle L'Espanaye was so firmly wedged in the chimney that it could not be got down until four or five of the party united their strength.

"*Paul Dumas*, physician, deposes that he was called to view the bodies about daybreak. They were both then lying on the sacking of the bedstead in the chamber where Mademoiselle L. was found. The corpse of the young lady was much bruised and excoriated. The fact that it had been thrust up the chimney would sufficiently account for these appearances. The throat was greatly chafed. There were several deep scratches just below the chin, together with a series of livid spots which were evidently the impression of fingers. The face was fearfully discolored, and the eyeballs protruded. The tongue had been partially bitten through. A large bruise was discovered upon the pit of the stomach, produced, apparently, by the pressure of a knee. In the opinion of M. Dumas, Mademoiselle L'Espanaye had been throttled to death by some person or persons unknown. The corpse of the mother was horribly mutilated. All the bones of the right leg and arm were more or less shattered. The left *tibia* much splintered, as well as all the ribs of the left side. Whole body dreadfully bruised and discolored. It was not possible to say how the injuries had been inflicted. A heavy club of wood, or a broad bar of iron—a chair—any large, heavy, and obtuse weapon would have produced such results, if wielded by the hands of a very powerful man. No woman could have inflicted the blows with any weapon. The head of the deceased, when seen by witness, was entirely separated from the body, and was also greatly shattered. The throat had evidently been cut with some very sharp instrument— probably with a razor.

"*Alexandre Étienne,* surgeon, was called with M. Dumas to view the bodies. Corroborated the testimony, and the opinions of M. Dumas.

"Nothing farther of importance was elicited, although several other persons were examined. A murder so mysterious, and so perplexing in all its particulars, was never before committed in Paris—if indeed a murder has been committed at all. The police are entirely at fault —an unusual occurrence in affairs of this nature. There is not, however, the shadow of a clew apparent."

The evening edition of the paper stated that the greatest excitement still continued in the Quartier St. Roch—that the premises in question had been carefully re-searched, and fresh examinations of witnesses instituted, but all to no purpose. A postscript, however, mentioned that Adolphe Le Bon had been arrested and imprisoned, although nothing appeared to criminate him, beyond the facts already detailed.

Dupin seemed singularly interested in the progress of this affair—at least so I judged from his manner, for he made no comments. It was only after the announcement that Le Bon had been imprisoned, that he asked me my opinion respecting the murders.

I could merely agree with all Paris in considering them an insoluble mystery. I saw no means by which it would be possible to trace the murderer.

"We must not judge of the means," said Dupin, "by this shell of an examination. The Parisian police, so much extolled for *acumen,* are cunning, but no more. There is no method in their proceedings, beyond the method of the moment. They make a vast parade of measures; but, not unfrequently, these are so ill adapted to the objects proposed, as to put us in mind of Monsieur Jourdain's calling for his *robe-de-chambre—pour mieux entendre la musique.* The results attained by them are not unfrequently surprising, but, for the most part, are brought about by simple diligence and activity. When these qualities are unavailing, their schemes fail. Vidocq, for example, was a good guesser, and a persevering man. But, without educated thought, he erred continually by the very intensity of his investigations. He impaired his vision by holding the object too close. He might see, perhaps, one or two points with unusual clearness, but in so doing he, necessarily, lost sight of the matter as a whole. Thus there is such a thing as being too profound. Truth is not always in a well. In fact, as regards the more important knowledge, I do believe that she is invariably superficial. The depth lies in the valleys where we seek her, and not upon the mountain-tops where she is found. The modes and sources of this kind of error are well typified in the contemplation of the heavenly bodies. To look at a star by glances— to view it in a sidelong way, by turning toward it the exterior portions of the *retina* (more susceptible of feeble impressions of light than the interior), is to behold the star distinctly— is to have the best appreciation of its lustre: a lustre which grows dim just in proportion as we turn our vision *fully* upon it. A greater number of rays actually fall upon the eye in the latter case, but, in the former, there is the more refined capacity for comprehension. By undue profundity we perplex and enfeeble thought, and it is possible to make even Venus herself vanish from the firmament by a scrutiny too sustained, too concentrated, or too direct.

"As for these murders, let us enter into some examinations for ourselves, before we make up an opinion respecting them. An inquiry will afford us amusement" (I thought this an odd term, so applied, but said nothing), "and, besides, Le Bon once rendered me a service for which I am not ungrateful. We will go and see the premises with our own eyes. I know G——, the Prefect of Police, and shall have no difficulty in obtaining the necessary permission."

The permission was obtained, and we proceeded at once to the Rue Morgue. This is one of those miserable thoroughfares which intervene between the Rue Richelieu and the Rue St. Roch. It was late in the afternoon when we reached it, as this quarter is at a great distance from that in which we resided. The house was readily found; for there were still many persons gazing up at the closed shutters, with an objectless curiosity, from the opposite side of the way. It was an ordinary Parisian house, with a gateway, on one side of which was a glazed watch-box, with a sliding panel in the window, indicating a *loge de concierge*. Before going in we walked up the street, turned down an alley, and then, again turning, passed in the rear of the building—Dupin, meanwhile, examining the whole neighborhood, as well as the house, with a minuteness of attention for which I could see no possible object.

Retracing our steps, we came again to the front of the dwelling, rang, and, having shown our credentials, were admitted by the agents in charge. We went upstairs—into the chamber where the body of Mademoiselle L'Espanaye had been found, and where both the deceased still lay. The disorders of the room had, as usual, been suffered to exist. I saw nothing beyond what had been stated in the *Gazette des Tribunaux*. Dupin scrutinized everything, not excepting the bodies of the victims. We then went into the other rooms, and into the yard; a *gendarme* accompanying us throughout. The examination occupied us until dark, when we took our departure. On our way home my companion stepped in for a moment at the office of one of the daily papers.

I have said that the whims of my friend were manifold, and that *Je les ménagais;*—for this phrase there is no English equivalent. It was his humor, now, to decline all conversation on the subject of the murder, until about noon the next day. He then asked me, suddenly, if I had observed anything *peculiar* at the scene of the atrocity.

There was something in his manner of emphasizing the word "peculiar," which caused me to shudder, without knowing why.

"No, nothing *peculiar*," I said; "nothing more, at least, than we both saw stated in the paper."

"The *Gazette*," he replied, "has not entered, I fear, into the unusual horror of the thing. But dismiss the idle opinions of this print. It appears to me that this mystery is considered insoluble, for the very reason which should cause it to be regarded as easy of solution—I mean, for the *outré* character of its features. The police are confounded by the seeming absence of motive: not for the murder itself, but for the atrocity of the murder. They are puzzled, too, by the seeming impossibility of reconciling the voices heard in contention with the facts that no one was discovered upstairs but the assassinated Mademoiselle L'Espanaye, and that there were no means of egress without the notice of the party ascending. The wild disorder of the room; the corpse thrust, with the head downward, up the chimney; the frightful mutilation of the body of the old lady; these considerations, with those just mentioned, and others which I need not mention, have sufficed to paralyze the powers, by putting completely at fault the boasted *acumen*, of the government agents. They have fallen into the gross but common error of confounding the unusual with the abstruse. But it is by these deviations from the plane of the ordinary that reason feels its way, if at all, in its search for the true. In investigations such as we are now pursuing, it should not be so much asked 'what has occurred,' as 'what has occurred that has never occurred before.' In fact, the facility with which I shall arrive, or have arrived, at the solution of this mystery is in the direct ratio of its apparent insolubility in the eyes of the police."

I stared at the speaker in mute astonishment.

"I am now awaiting," continued he, looking toward the door of our apartment—"I am now awaiting a person who, although perhaps not the perpetrator of these butcheries, must have been in some measure implicated in their perpetration. Of the worst portion of the crimes committed it is probable that he is innocent. I hope that I am right in this supposition; for upon it I build my expectation of reading the entire riddle. I look for the man here—in this room—every moment. It is true that he may not arrive; but the probability is that he will. Should he come, it will be necessary to detain him. Here are pistols; and we both know how to use them when occasion demands their use."

I took the pistols, scarcely knowing what I did, or believing what I heard, while Dupin went on, very much as if in a soliloquy. I have already spoken of his abstract manner at such times. His discourse was addressed to myself; but his voice, although by no means loud, had that intonation which is commonly employed in speaking to some one at a great distance. His eyes, vacant in expression, regarded only the wall.

"That the voices heard in contention," he said, "by the party upon the stairs, were not the voices of the women themselves, was fully proved by the evidence. This relieves us of all doubt upon the question whether the old lady could have first destroyed the daughter, and afterward have committed suicide. I speak of this point chiefly for the sake of method; for the strength of Madame L'Espanaye would have been utterly unequal to the task of thrusting her daughter's corpse up the chimney as it was found; and the nature of the wounds upon her own person entirely precludes the idea of self-destruction. Murder, then, has been committed by some third party; and the voices of this third party were those heard in contention. Let me now advert—not to the whole testimony respecting these voices—but to what was *peculiar* in that testimony. Did you observe, anything peculiar about it?"

I remarked that, while all the witnesses agreed in supposing the gruff voice to be that of a Frenchman, there was much disagreement in regard to the shrill, or, as one individual termed it, the harsh voice.

"That was the evidence itself," said Dupin, "but it was not the peculiarity of the evidence. You have observed nothing distinctive. Yet there *was* something to be observed. The witnesses, as you remark, agreed about the gruff voice; they were here unanimous. But in regard to the shrill voice, the peculiarity is—not that they disagreed—but that, while an Italian, an Englishman, a Spaniard, a Hollander, and a Frenchman attempted to describe it, each one spoke of it as that *of a foreigner*. Each is sure that it was not the voice of one of his own countrymen. Each likens it—not to the voice of an individual of any nation with whose language he is conversant—but the converse. The Frenchman supposes it the voice of a Spaniard, and 'might have distinguished some words *had he been acquainted with the Spanish.*' The Dutchman maintains it to have been that of a Frenchman; but we find it stated that '*not understanding French, 'this witness was examined through an interpreter.*' The Englishman thinks it the voice of a German, and '*does not understand German.*' The Spaniard 'is sure' that it was that of an Englishman, but 'judges by the intonation' altogether, '*as he has no knowledge of the English.*' The Italian believes it the voice of a Russian, but '*has never conversed with a native of Russia.*' The second Frenchman differs, moreover, with the first, and is positive that the voice was that of an Italian; but, *not being cognizant of that tongue,* is, like the Spaniard, 'convinced by the intonation.' Now, how strangely unusual must that voice have really been, about which such testimony as this *could* have been elicited!—in whose *tones,* even, denizens of the five great divisions of Europe could recognize nothing familiar! You will say that it might have been the voice of an Asiatic—of an African. Neither Asiatics nor Africans abound in Paris; but, without denying the inference, I will now merely call your attention to three points. The voice is termed by one witness 'harsh rather than shrill.' It is represented by two others to have been 'quick and *unequal.*' No words—no sounds resembling words—were by any witness mentioned as distinguishable.

"I know not," continued Dupin, "what impression I may have made, so far, upon your own understanding; but I do not hesitate to say that legitimate deductions even from this portion of the testimony—the portion respecting the gruff and shrill voices—are in themselves sufficient to engender a suspicion which should give direction to all farther progress in the investigation of the mystery. I said 'legitimate deductions'; but my meaning is not thus fully expressed. I designed to imply that the deductions are the *sole* proper ones, and that the suspicion arises *inevitably* from them as the single result. What the suspicion is, however, I will not say just yet. I merely wish you to bear in mind that, with myself, it was sufficiently forcible to give a definite form, a certain tendency, to my inquiries in the chamber.

"Let us now transport ourselves, in fancy, to this chamber. What shall we first seek here? The means of egress employed by the murderers. It is not too much to say that neither of us believes in preternatural events. Madame and Mademoiselle L'Espanaye were not destroyed by spirits. The doers of the deed were material, and escaped materially. Then how? Fortunately, there is but one mode of reasoning upon the point, and that mode *must* lead us to a definite decision.—Let us examine, each by each, the possible means of egress. It is clear that the assassins were in the room where Mademoiselle L'Espanaye was found, or at least in the room adjoining, when the party ascended the stairs. It is then only from these two apartments that we have to seek issues. The police have laid bare the floors, the ceilings, and the masonry of the walls, in every direction. No *secret* issues could have escaped their vigilance. But, not trusting to *their* eyes, I examined with my own. There were, then, *no* secret issues. Both doors leading from the rooms into the passage were securely locked, with the keys inside. Let us turn to the chimneys. These, although of ordinary width for some eight or ten feet above the hearths, will not admit, throughout their extent, the body of a large cat. The impossibility of egress, by means already stated, being thus absolute, we are reduced to the windows. Through those of the front room no one could have escaped without notice from the crowd in the street. The murderers *must* have passed, then, through those of the back room. Now, brought to this conclusion in so unequivocal a manner as we are, it is not our part, as reasoners, to reject it on account of apparent impossibilities. It is only left for us to prove that these apparent 'impossibilities' are, in reality, not such.

"There are two windows in the chamber. One of them is unobstructed by furniture, and is wholly visible. The lower portion of the other is hidden from view by the head of the unwieldy bedstead which is thrust close up against it. The former was found securely fastened from within. It resisted the utmost force of those who endeavored to raise it. A large gimlet-hole had been pierced in its frame to the left, and a very stout nail was found fitted therein, nearly to the head. Upon examining the other window, a similar nail was seen similarly fitted in it; and a vigorous attempt to raise this sash failed also. The police were now entirely satisfied that egress had not been in these directions. And, *therefore*, it was thought a matter of supererogation to withdraw the nails and open the windows.

"My own examination was somewhat more particular, and was so for the reason I have just given; because here it was, I knew, that all apparent impossibilities *must* be proved to be not such in reality.

"I proceeded to think thus—*a posteriori*. The murderers *did* escape from one of these windows. This being so, they could not have refastened the sashes from the inside, as they were found fastened: the consideration which put a stop, through its obviousness, to the scrutiny of the police in this quarter. Yet the sashes *were* fastened. They *must*, then, have the power of fastening themselves. There was no escape from this conclusion. I stepped to the unobstructed casement, withdrew the nail with some difficulty, and attempted to raise the sash. It resisted all my efforts, as I had anticipated. A concealed spring must, I now knew, exist; and this corroboration of my idea convinced me that my premises, at least, were correct, however mysterious still appeared the circumstances attending the nails. A careful search soon brought to light the hidden spring. I pressed it, and, satisfied with the discovery, forbore to upraise the sash.

"I now replaced the nail and regarded it attentively. A person passing out through this window might have reclosed it, and the spring would have caught—but the nail could not have been replaced. The conclusion was plain, and again narrowed in the field of my investigations. The assassins *must* have escaped through the other window. Supposing, then, the springs upon each sash to be the same, as was probable, there *must* be found a difference between the nails, or at least between the modes of their fixture. Getting upon the sacking of the bedstead, I looked over the head-board minutely at the second casement. Passing my hand down behind the board, I readily discovered and pressed the spring, which was, as I had supposed, identical in character with its neighbor. I now looked at the nail. It was as stout as the other, and apparently fitted in the same manner—driven in nearly up to the head.

"You will say that I was puzzled; but, if you think so, you must have misunderstood the nature of the inductions. To use a sporting phrase, I had not been once 'at fault.' The scent had never for an instant been lost. There was no flaw in any link of the chain. I had traced the secret to its ultimate result,—and that result was *the nail*. It had, I say, in every respect, the appearance of its fellow in the other window;

but this fact was an absolute nullity (conclusive as it might seem to be) when compared with the consideration that here, at this point, terminated the clew. 'There *must* be something wrong,' I said, 'about the nail.' I touched it; and the head, with about a quarter of an inch of the shank, came off in my fingers. The rest of the shank was in the gimlet-hole, where it had been broken off. The fracture was an old one (for its edges were incrusted with rust), and had apparently been accomplished by the blow of a hammer, which had partially imbedded, in the top of the bottom sash, the head portion of the nail. I now carefully replaced this head portion in the indentation whence I had taken it, and the resemblance to a perfect nail was complete—the fissure was invisible. Pressing the spring, I gently raised the sash for a few inches; the head went up with it, remaining firm in its bed. I closed the window, and the semblance of the whole nail was again perfect.

"The riddle, so far, was now unriddled. The assassin had escaped through the window which looked upon the bed. Dropping of its own accord upon his exit (or perhaps purposely closed), it had become fastened by the spring; and it was the retention of this spring which had been mistaken by the police for that of the nail,—farther inquiry being thus considered unnecessary.

"The next question is that of the mode of descent. Upon this point I had been satisfied in my walk with you around the building. About five feet and a half from the casement in question there runs a lightning-rod. From this rod it would have been impossible for any one to reach the window itself, to say nothing of entering it. I observed, however, that the shutters of the fourth story were of the peculiar kind called by Parisian carpenters *ferrades*—a kind rarely employed at the present day, but frequently seen upon very old mansions at Lyons and Bordeaux. They are in the form of an ordinary door (a single, not a folding door), except that the upper half is latticed or worked in open trellis—thus affording an excellent hold for the hands. In the present instance these shutters are fully three feet and a half broad. When we saw them from the rear of the house, they were both about half open—that is to say, they stood off at right angles from the wall. It is probable that the police, as well as myself examined the back of the tenement; but, if so, in looking at these *ferrades* in the line of their breadth (as they must have done), they did not perceive this great breadth itself, or, at all events, failed to take it into due consideration. In fact, having once satisfied themselves that no egress could have been made in this quarter, they would naturally bestow here a very cursory examination. It was clear to me, however, that the shutter belonging to the window at the head of the bed would, if swung fully back to the wall, reach to within two feet of the lightning-rod. It was also evident that, by exertion of a very unusual degree of activity and courage, an entrance into the window, from the rod, might have been thus effected. By reaching to the distance of two feet and a half (we now suppose the shutter open to its whole extent), a robber might have taken a firm grasp upon the trelliswork. Letting go, then, his hold upon the rod, placing his feet securely against the wall, and springing boldly from it, he might have swung the shutter so as to close it, and, if we imagine the window open at the time, might even have swung himself into the room.

"I wish you to bear especially in mind I have spoken of a *very* unusual degree of activity as requisite to success in so hazardous and so difficult a feat. It is my design to show you, first, that the thing might possibly have been accomplished: but, secondly and *chiefly*, I wish to impress upon your understanding the *very extraordinary*, the almost preternatural, character of that agility which could have accomplished it.

"You will say, no doubt, using the language of the law, that 'to make out my case' I should rather undervalue than insist upon a full estimation of the activity required in this matter. This may be the practice in law, but it is not the usage of reason. My ultimate object is only the truth. My immediate purpose is to lead you to place in juxtaposition that *very unusual* activity, of which I have just spoken, with that *very peculiar* shrill (or harsh) and *unequal* voice, about whose nationality no two persons could be found to agree, and in whose utterance no syllabification could be detected."

At these words a vague and half-formed conception of the meaning of Dupin flitted over my mind. I seemed to be upon the verge of comprehension, without power to comprehend; as men, at times, find themselves upon the brink of remembrance, without being able, in the end, to remember. My friend went on with his discourse.

"You will see," he said, "that I have shifted

the question from the mode of egress to that of ingress. It was my design to suggest that both were effected in the same manner, at the same point. Let us now revert to the interior of the room. Let us survey the appearances here. The drawers of the bureau, it is said, had been rifled, although many articles of apparel still remained within them. The conclusion here is absurd. It is a mere guess—a very silly one—and no more. How are we to know that the articles found in the drawers were not all these drawers had originally contained? Madame L'Espanaye and her daughter lived an exceedingly retired life—saw no company, seldom went out, had little use for numerous changes of habiliment. Those found were at least of as good quality as any likely to be possessed by these ladies. If a thief had taken any, why did he not take the best—why did he not take all? In a word, why did he abandon four thousand francs in gold to encumber himself with a bundle of linen? The gold *was* abandoned. Nearly the whole sum mentioned by Monsieur Mignaud, the banker, was discovered, in bags, upon the floor. I wish you, therefore, to discard from your thoughts the blundering idea of *motive*, engendered in the brains of the police by that portion of the evidence which speaks of money delivered at the door of the house. Coincidences ten times as remarkable as this (the delivery of the money, and murder committed within three days upon the party receiving it) happen to all of us every hour of our lives, without attracting even momentary notice. Coincidences, in general, are great stumbling-blocks in the way of that class of thinkers who have been educated to know nothing of the theory of probabilities: that theory to which the most glorious objects of human research are indebted for the most glorious of illustration. In the present instance, had the gold been gone, the fact of its delivery three days before would have formed something more than a coincidence. It would have been corroborative of this idea of motive. But, under the real circumstances of the case, if we are to suppose gold the motive of this outrage, we must also imagine the perpetrator so vacillating an idiot as to have abandoned his gold and his motive together.

"Keeping now steadily in mind the points to which I have drawn your attention—that peculiar voice, that unusual agility, and that startling absence of motive in a murder so singularly atrocious as this—let us glance at the butchery itself. Here is a woman strangled to death by manual strength, and thrust up a chimney, head downward. Ordinary assassins employ no such modes of murder as this. Least of all, do they thus dispose of the murdered. In the manner of thrusting the corpse up the chimney, you will admit that there was something *excessively outré*—something altogether irreconcilable with our common notions of human action, even when we suppose the actors the most depraved of men. Think, too, how great must have been that strength which could have thrust the body *up* such an aperture so forcibly that the united vigor of several persons was found barely sufficient to drag it *down!*

"Turn, now, to other indications of the employment of a vigor most marvellous. On the hearth were thick tresses—very thick tresses—of grey human hair. These had been torn out by the roots. You are aware of the great force necessary in tearing thus from the head even twenty or thirty hairs together. You saw the locks in question as well as myself. Their roots (a hideous sight!) were clotted with fragments of the flesh of the scalp: sure token of the prodigious power which had been exerted in uprooting perhaps half a million of hairs at a time. The throat of the old lady was not merely cut, but the head absolutely severed from the body: the instrument was a mere razor. I wish you also to look at the *brutal* ferocity of these deeds. Of the bruises upon the body of Madame L'Espanaye I do not speak. Monsieur Dumas, and his worthy coadjutor Monsieur Étienne, have pronounced that they were inflicted by some obtuse instrument; and so far these gentlemen are very correct. The obtuse instrument was clearly the stone pavement in the yard, upon which the victim had fallen from the window which looked in upon the bed. This idea, however simple it may now seem, escaped the police for the same reason that the breadth of the shutters escaped them—because, by the affair of the nails, their perceptions had been hermetically sealed against the possibility of the windows having ever been opened at all.

"If now, in addition to all these things, you have properly reflected upon the odd disorder of the chamber, we have gone so far as to combine the ideas of an agility astounding, a strength superhuman, a ferocity brutal, a butchery without motive, a *grotesquerie* in horror absolutely alien from humanity, and a voice foreign in tone to the ears of men of many nations, and devoid of all distinct or intelligible syllabification. What result, then, has ensued?

What impression have I made upon your fancy?"

I felt a creeping of the flesh as Dupin asked me the question. "A madman," I said, "has done this deed—some raving maniac, escaped from a neighboring *Maison de Santé*."

"In some respects," he replied, "your idea is not irrelevant. But the voices of madmen, even in their wildest paroxysms, are never found to tally with that peculiar voice heard upon the stairs. Madmen are of some nation, and their language, however incoherent in its words, has always the coherence of syllabification. Besides, the hair of a madman is not such as I now hold in my hand. I disentangled this little tuft from the rigidly clutched fingers of Madame L'Espanaye. Tell me what you can make of it."

"Dupin!" I said, completely unnerved; "this hair is most unusual—this is no *human* hair."

"I have not asserted that it is," said he; "but, before we decide this point, I wish you to glance at the little sketch I have here traced upon this paper. It is a *fac-simile* drawing of what has been described in one portion of the testimony as 'dark bruises, and deep indentations of finger-nails,' upon the throat of Mademoiselle L'Espanaye, and in another (by Messrs. Dumas and Étienne) as a 'series of livid spots, evidently the impression of fingers.'

"You will perceive," continued my friend, spreading out the paper upon the table before us, "that this drawing gives the idea of a firm and fixed hold. There is no *slipping* apparent. Each finger has retained—possibly until the death of the victim—the fearful grasp by which it originally imbedded itself. Attempt, now, to place all your fingers, at the same time, in the respective impressions as you see them."

I made the attempt in vain.

"We are possibly not giving this matter a fair trial," he said. "The paper is spread out upon a plane surface; but the human throat is cylindrical. Here is a billet of wood, the circumference of which is about that of the throat. Wrap the drawing around it, and try the experiment again."

I did so; but the difficulty was even more obvious than before. "This," I said, "is the mark of no human hand."

"Read now," replied Dupin, "this passage from Cuvier."

It was a minute anatomical and generally descriptive account of the large fulvous Ourang-Outang of the East Indian Islands. The gigantic stature, the prodigious strength and activity, the wild ferocity, and the imitative propensities of these mammalia are sufficiently well known to all. I understood the full horrors of the murder at once.

"The description of the digits," said I, as I made an end of reading, "is in exact accordance with this drawing. I see that no animal but an Ourang-Outang, of the species here mentioned, could have impressed the indentations as you have traced them. This tuft of tawny hair, too, is identical in character with that of the beast of Cuvier. But I cannot possibly comprehend the particulars of this frightful mystery. Besides, there were *two* voices heard in contention, and one of them was unquestionably the voice of a Frenchman."

"True; and you will remember an expression attributed almost unanimously, by the evidence, to this voice,—the expression, 'mon Dieu.' This, under the circumstances, has been justly characterized by one of the witnesses (Montani, the confectioner) as an expression of remonstrance or expostulation. Upon these two words, therefore, I have mainly built my hopes of a full solution of the riddle. A Frenchman was cognizant of the murder. It is possible—indeed it is far more than probable—that he was innocent of all participation in the bloody transactions which took place. The Ourang-Outang may have escaped from him. He may have traced it to the chamber; but, under the agitating circumstances which ensued, he could never have recaptured it. It is still at large. I will not pursue these guesses—for I have no right to call them more—since the shades of reflection upon which they are based are scarcely of sufficient depth to be appreciable by my own intellect, and since I could not pretend to make them intelligible to the understanding of another. We will call them guesses, then, and speak of them as such. If the Frenchman in question is indeed, as I suppose, innocent of this atrocity, this advertisement, which I left last night, upon our return home, at the office of *Le Monde* (a paper devoted to the shipping interest, and much sought by sailors), will bring him to our residence."

He handed me a paper, and I read thus:

"Caught—*In the Bois de Boulogne, early in the morning of the —— inst.* (the morning of the murder), *a very large, tawny Ourang-Outang of the Bornese species. The owner (who is ascertained to be a sailor, belonging to a Maltese vessel) may have the animal again, upon identifying it satisfactorily, and paying a few charges arising from its capture and keeping. Call at No. ——, Rue ——, Faubourg St. Germain—au troisième."*

"How was it possible," I asked, "that you should know the man to be a sailor, and belonging to a Maltese vessel?"

"I do *not* know it," said Dupin. "I am not sure of it. Here, however, is a small piece of ribbon, which, from its form, and from its greasy appearance, has evidently been used in tying the hair in one of those long *queues* of which sailors are so fond. Moreover, this knot is one which few besides sailors can tie, and is peculiar to the Maltese. I picked the ribbon up at the foot of the lightning rod. It could not have belonged to either of the deceased. Now if, after all, I am wrong in my induction from this ribbon, that the Frenchman was a sailor belonging to a Maltese vessel, still I can have done no harm in saying what I did in the advertisement. If I am in error, he will merely suppose that I have been misled by some circumstance into which he will not take the trouble to inquire. But if I am right, a great point is gained. Cognizant although innocent of the murder, the Frenchman will naturally hesitate about replying to the advertisement—about demanding the Ourang-Outang. He will reason thus: 'I am innocent; I am poor; my Ourang-Outang is of great value—to one in my circumstances a fortune of itself—why should I lose it through idle apprehensions of danger? Here it is, within my grasp. It was found in the Bois de Boulogne—at a vast distance from the scene of that butchery. How can it ever be suspected that a brute beast should have done the deed? The police are at fault; they have failed to procure the slightest clew. Should they even trace the animal, it would be impossible to prove me cognizant of the murder, or to implicate me in guilt on account of that cognizance. Above all, *I am known.* The advertiser designates me as the possessor of the beast. I am not sure to what limit his knowledge may extend. Should I avoid claiming a property of so great value, which it is known that I possess, I will render the animal, at least, liable to suspicion. It is not my policy to attract attention either to myself or to the beast. I will answer the advertisement, get the Ourang-Outang, and keep it close until this matter has blown over.'"

At this moment we heard a step upon the stairs.

"Be ready," said Dupin, "with your pistols, but neither use them nor show them until at a signal from myself."

The front door of the house had been left open, and the visitor had entered, without ringing, and advanced several steps upon the staircase. Now, however, he seemed to hesitate. Presently we heard him descending. Dupin was moving quickly to the door, when we again heard him coming up. He did not turn back a second time, but stepped up with decision, and rapped at the door of our chamber.

"Come in," said Dupin, in a cheerful and hearty tone.

A man entered. He was a sailor, evidently, —a tall, stout, and muscular-looking person, with a certain dare-devil expression of countenance, not altogether unprepossessing. His face, greatly sunburnt, was more than half hidden by whisker and *mustachio.* He had with him a huge oaken cudgel, but appeared to be otherwise unarmed. He bowed awkwardly, and bade us "Good-evening," in French accents, which although somewhat Neufchâtelish, were still sufficiently indicative of a Parisian origin.

"Sit down, my friend," said Dupin. "I suppose you have called about the Ourang-Outang. Upon my word, I almost envy you the possession of him; a remarkably fine and no doubt a very valuable animal. How old do you suppose him to be?"

The sailor drew a long breath, with the air of a man relieved of some intolerable burden, and then replied, in an assured tone:

"I have no way of telling—but he can't be more than four or five years old. Have you got him here?"

"Oh, no; we had no conveniences for keeping him here. He is at a livery stable in the Rue Dubourg, just by. You can get him in the morning. Of course you are prepared to identify the property?"

"To be sure I am, sir."

"I shall be sorry to part with him," said Dupin.

"I don't mean that you should be at all this trouble for nothing, sir," said the man. "Couldn't expect it. Am very willing to pay a reward for the finding of the animal—that is to say, anything in reason."

"Well," replied my friend, "that is all very fair, to be sure. Let me think!—what should I have? Oh! I will tell you. My reward shall be this. You shall give me all the information in your power about these murders in the Rue Morgue."

Dupin said the last words in a very low tone, and very quietly. Just as quietly, too, he walked toward the door, locked it, and put the key in his pocket. He then drew a pistol from his bosom and placed it, without the least flurry, upon the table.

The sailor's face flushed up as if he were struggling with suffocation. He started to his feet and grasped his cudgel; but the next moment he fell back into his seat, trembling violently, and with the countenance of death itself. He spoke not a word. I pitied him from the bottom of my heart.

"My friend," said Dupin, in a kind tone, "you are alarming yourself unnecessarily—you are indeed. We mean you no harm whatever. I pledge you the honor of a gentleman, and of a Frenchman, that we intend you no injury. I perfectly well know that you are innocent of the atrocities in the Rue Morgue. It will not do, however, to deny that you are in some measure implicated in them. From what I have already said, you must know that I have had means of information about this matter—means of which you could never have dreamed. Now the thing stands thus. You have done nothing which you could have avoided—nothing, certainly, which renders you culpable. You were not even guilty of robbery, when you might have robbed with impunity. You have nothing to conceal. You have no reason for concealment. On the other hand, you are bound by every principle of honor to confess all you know. An innocent man is now imprisoned, charged with the crime of which you can point out the perpetrator."

The sailor had recovered his presence of mind, in a great measure, while Dupin uttered these words; but his original boldness of bearing was all gone.

"So help me God," said he, after a brief pause, "I *will* tell you all I know about this affair; but I do not expect you to believe one half I say—I would be a fool indeed if I did. Still, I *am* innocent, and I will make a clean breast if I die for it."

What he stated was, in substance, this. He had lately made a voyage to the Indian Archipelago. A party, of which he formed one, landed at Borneo, and passed into the interior on an excursion of pleasure. Himself and a companion had captured the Ourang-Outang. This companion dying, the animal fell into his own exclusive possession. After great trouble, occasioned by the intractable ferocity of his captive during the home voyage, he at length succeeded in lodging it safely at his own residence in Paris, where, not to attract toward himself the unpleasant curiosity of his neighbors, he kept it carefully secluded, until such time as it should recover from a wound in the foot, received from a splinter on board ship. His ultimate design was to sell it. [10]

Returning home from some sailors' frolic on the night, or rather in the morning, of the murder, he found the beast occupying his own bedroom, into which it had broken from a closet adjoining, where it had been, as was thought, securely confined. Razor in hand, and fully lathered, it was sitting before a looking-glass, attempting the operation of shaving, in which it had no doubt previously watched its master through the key-hole of the closet. Terrified at the sight of so dangerous a weapon in the possession of an animal so ferocious, and so well able to use it, the man for some moments was at a loss what to do. He had been accustomed, however, to quiet the creature, even in its fiercest moods, by the use of a whip, and to this he now resorted. Upon sight of it, the Ourang-Outang sprang at once through the door of the chamber, down the stairs, and thence, through a window, unfortunately open, into the street. [20] [30]

The Frenchman followed in despair; the ape, razor still in hand, occasionally stopping to look back and gesticulate at its pursuer, until the latter had nearly come up with it. It then again made off. In this manner the chase continued for a long time. The streets were profoundly quiet, as it was nearly three o'clock in the morning. In passing down an alley in the rear of the Rue Morgue, the fugitive's attention was arrested by a light gleaming from the open window of Madame L'Espanaye's chamber, in the fourth story of her house. Rushing to the building, it perceived the lightning-rod, clambered up with inconceivable agility, grasped the shutter, which was thrown fully back against the wall, and, by its means, swung itself directly upon the headboard of the bed. The whole feat did not occupy a minute. The shutter was kicked open again by the Ourang-Outang as it entered the room. [40] [50]

The sailor, in the meantime, was both rejoiced and perplexed. He had strong hopes of now recapturing the brute, as it could scarcely escape from the trap into which it had ventured, except by the rod, where it might be intercepted as it came down. On the other hand, there was much cause for anxiety as to what it might do in the house. This latter reflection urged the man still to follow the fugitive. A lightning-rod is ascended without difficulty, especially by a sailor; but, when he had arrived as high as the window, which lay far to his left, his career was stopped; the most that he could accomplish was to reach over so as to obtain a glimpse of the interior of the room. At this glimpse he nearly fell from his hold through excess of horror. Now it was that those hideous shrieks arose upon the night, which had startled from slumber the inmates of the Rue Morgue. Madame L'Espanaye and her daughter, habited in their night-clothes, had apparently been occupied in arranging some papers in the iron chest already mentioned, which had been wheeled into the middle of the room. It was open, and its contents lay beside it on the floor. The victims must have been sitting with their backs toward the windows; and, from the time elapsing between the ingress of the beast and the screams, it seems probable that it was not immediately perceived. The flapping-to of the shutter would naturally have been attributed to the wind.

As the sailor looked in, the gigantic animal had seized Madame L'Espanaye by the hair (which was loose, as she had been combing it), and was flourishing the razor about her face, in imitation of the motions of a barber. The daughter lay prostrate and motionless: she had swooned. The screams and struggles of the old lady (during which the hair was torn from her head) had the effect of changing the probably pacific purposes of the Ourang-Outang into those of wrath. With one determined sweep of its muscular arm it nearly severed her head from her body. The sight of blood inflamed its anger into frenzy. Gnashing its teeth, and flashing fire from its eyes, it flew upon the body of the girl, and imbedded its fearful talons in her throat, retaining its grasp until she expired. Its wandering and wild glances fell at this moment upon the head of the bed, over which the face of its master, rigid with horror, was just discernible. The fury of the beast, who no doubt bore still in mind the dreaded whip, was instantly converted into fear. Conscious of having deserved punishment, it seemed desirous of concealing its

bloody deeds, and skipped about the chamber in an agony of nervous agitation; throwing down and breaking the furniture as it moved, and dragging the bed from the bedstead. In conclusion, it seized first the corpse of the daughter, and thrust it up the chimney, as it was found; then that of the old lady, which it immediately hurled through the window headlong.

As the ape approached the casement with its mutilated burden, the sailor shrank aghast to the rod, and, rather gliding than clambering down it, hurried at once home—dreading the consequences of the butchery, and gladly abandoning, in his terror, all solicitude about the fate of the Ourang-Outang. The words heard by the party upon the staircase were the Frenchman's exclamations of horror and affright, commingled with the fiendish jabberings of the brute.

I have scarcely anything to add. The Ourang-Outang must have escaped from the chamber, by the rod, just before the breaking of the door. It must have closed the window as it passed through it. It was subsequently caught by the owner himself, who obtained for it a very large sum at the *Jardin des Plantes*. Le Bon was instantly released, upon our narration of the circumstances (with some comments from Dupin) at the bureau of the Prefect of Police. This functionary, however well disposed to my friend, could not altogether conceal his chagrin at the turn which affairs had taken, and was fain to indulge in a sarcasm or two, about the propriety of every person minding his own business.

"Let him talk," said Dupin, who had not thought it necessary to reply. "Let him discourse; it will ease his conscience. I am satisfied with having defeated him in his own castle. Nevertheless, that he failed in the solution of this mystery is by no means that matter for wonder which he supposes it; for, in truth, our friend the Prefect is somewhat too cunning to be profound. In his wisdom is no *stamen*. It is all head and no body, like the pictures of the Goddess Laverna,—or, at best, all head and shoulders, like a codfish. But he is a good creature after all. I like him especially for one master-stroke of cant, by which he has attained his reputation for ingenuity. I mean the way he has '*de nier ce qu'est et d'expliquer ce que n'est pas.*'"   1841

» » THE PHILOSOPHY OF COMPOSITION « «

Charles Dickens, in a note now lying before me, alluding to an examination I once made of the mechanism of "Barnaby Rudge," says— "By the way, are you aware that Godwin wrote his 'Caleb Williams' backwards? He first involved his hero in a web of difficulties, forming the second volume, and then, for the first, cast about him for some mode of accounting for what had been done."

I cannot think this the *precise* mode of procedure on the part of Godwin—and indeed what he himself acknowledges, is not altogether in accordance with Mr. Dickens' idea— but the author of "Caleb Williams" was too good an artist not to perceive the advantage derivable from at least a somewhat similar process. Nothing is more clear than that every plot, worth the name, must be elaborated to its *dénouement* before anything be attempted with the pen. It is only with the *dénouement* constantly in view that we can give a plot its indispensable air of consequence, or causation, by making the incidents, and especially the tone at all points, tend to the development of the intention.

There is a radical error, I think, in the usual mode of constructing a story. Either history affords a thesis—or one is suggested by an incident of the day—or, at best, the author sets himself to work in the combination of striking events to form merely the basis of his narrative—designing, generally, to fill in with description, dialogue, or autorial comment, whatever crevices of fact, or action, may, from page to page, render themselves apparent.

I prefer commencing with the consideration of an *effect*. Keeping originality *always* in view —for he is false to himself who ventures to dispense with so obvious and so easily attainable a source of interest—I say to myself, in the first place,—"Of the innumerable effects, or impressions, of which the heart, the intellect, or (more generally) the soul is susceptible, what one shall I, on the present occasion, select?" Having chosen a novel, first, and secondly a vivid effect, I consider whether it can be best wrought by incident or tone—whether by ordinary incidents and peculiar tone, or the converse, or by peculiarity both of incident and tone—afterward looking about me (or rather within) for such combinations of event, or

tone, as shall best aid me in the construction of the effect.

I have often thought how interesting a magazine paper might be written by any author who would—that is to say who could—detail, step by step, the processes by which any one of his compositions attained its ultimate point of completion. Why such a paper has never been given to the world, I am much at a loss to say—but, perhaps, the autorial vanity has had more to do with the omission than any one other cause. Most writers—poets in especial—prefer having it understood that they compose by a species of fine frenzy—an ecstatic intuition—and would positively shudder at letting the public take a peep behind the scenes, at the elaborate and vacillating crudities of thought—at the true purposes seized only at the last moment—at the innumerable glimpses of idea that arrived not at the maturity of full view—at the fully matured fancies discarded in despair as unmanageable—at the cautious selections and rejections—at the painful erasures and interpolations—in a word, at the wheels and pinions—the tackle for scene-shifting—the step-ladders and demon-traps— the cock's feathers, the red paint and the black patches, which, in the ninety-nine cases out of the hundred, constitute the properties of the literary *histrio*.

I am aware, on the other hand, that the case is by no means common, in which an author is at all in condition to retrace the steps by which his conclusions have been attained. In general, suggestions, having arisen pell-mell, are pursued and forgotten in a similar manner.

For my own part, I have neither sympathy with the repugnance alluded to, nor, at any time the least difficulty in recalling to mind the progressive steps of any of my compositions; and, since the interest of an analysis, or reconstruction, such as I have considered a *desideratum*, is quite independent of any real or fancied interest in the thing analyzed, it will not be regarded as a breach of decorum on my part to show the *modus operandi* by which some one of my own works was put together. I select "The Raven," as most generally known. It is my design to render it manifest that no one point in its composition is referrible either to accident or intuition—that the work proceeded, step by step, to its completion with the precision and rigid consequence of a mathematical problem.

Let us dismiss, as irrelevant to the poem, *per se,* the circumstance—or say the necessity—which, in the first place, gave rise to the intention of composing *a* poem that should suit at once the popular and the critical taste.

We commence, then, with this intention.

The initial consideration was that of extent. If any literary work is too long to be read at one sitting, we must be content to dispense with the immensely important effect derivable from unity of impression—for, if two sittings be required, the affairs of the world interfere, and everything like totality is at once destroyed. But since, *ceteris paribus,* no poet can afford to dispense with *anything* that may advance his design, it but remains to be seen whether there is, in extent, any advantage to counterbalance the loss of unity which attends it. Here I say no, at once. What we term a long poem is, in fact, merely a succession of brief ones—that is to say, of brief poetical effects. It is needless to demonstrate that a poem is such, only inasmuch as it intensely excites, by elevating, the soul; and all intense excitements are, through a psychal necessity, brief. For this reason, at least one half of the "Paradise Lost" is essentially prose—a succession of poetical excitements interspersed, *inevitably,* with corresponding depressions—the whole being deprived, through the extremeness of its length, of the vastly important artistic element, totality, or unity, of effect.

It appears evident, then, that there is a distinct limit, as regards length, to all works of literary art—the limit of a single sitting—and that, although in certain classes of prose composition, such as "Robinson Crusoe" (demanding no unity), this limit may be advantageously overpassed, it can never properly be overpassed in a poem. Within this limit, the extent of a poem may be made to bear mathematical relation to its merit—in other words, to the excitement or elevation—again in other words, to the degree of the true poetical effect which it is capable of inducing; for it is clear that the brevity must be in direct ratio of the intensity of the intended effect:—this, with one proviso—that a certain degree of duration is absolutely requisite for the production of any effect at all.

Holding in view these considerations, as well as that degree of excitement which I deemed not above the popular, while not below the critical, taste, I reached at once what I conceived the proper *length* for my intended poem—a length of about one hundred lines. It is, in fact, a hundred and eight.

My next thought concerned the choice of an impression, or effect, to be conveyed: and here I may as well observe that, throughout the construction, I kept steadily in view the design of rendering the work *universally* appreciable. I should be carried too far out of my immediate topic were I to demonstrate a point upon which I have repeatedly insisted, and which, with the poetical, stands not in the slightest need of demonstration—the point, I mean, that Beauty is the sole legitimate province of the poem. A few words, however, in elucidation of my real meaning, which some of my friends have evinced a disposition to misrepresent. That pleasure which is at once the most intense, the most elevating, and the most pure, is, I believe, found in the contemplation of the beautiful. When, indeed, men speak of Beauty, they mean, precisely, not a quality, as is supposed, but an effect—they refer, in short, just to that intense and pure elevation of *soul*—*not* of intellect, or of heart—upon which I have commented, and which is experienced in consequence of contemplating "the beautiful." Now I designate Beauty as the province of the poem, merely because it is an obvious rule of Art that effects should be made to spring from direct causes—that objects should be attained through means best adapted for their attainment—no one as yet having been weak enough to deny that the peculiar elevation alluded to is *most readily* attained in the poem. Now the object Truth, or the satisfaction of the intellect, and the object Passion, or the excitement of the heart, are, although attainable, to a certain extent, in poetry, far more readily attainable in prose. Truth, in fact, demands a precision, and Passion a *homeliness* (the truly passionate will comprehend me) which are absolutely antagonistic to that Beauty which, I maintain, is the excitement, or pleasurable elevation, of the soul. It by no means follows from anything here said, that passion, or even truth, may not be introduced, and even profitably introduced, into a poem—for they may serve in elucidation, or aid the general effect, as do discords in music, by contrast—but the true artist will always contrive, first, to tone them into proper subservience to the predominant aim, and, secondly, to enveil them, as far as possible, in that Beauty which is the atmosphere and the essence of the poem.

Regarding, then, Beauty as my province, my next question referred to the *tone* of its highest manifestation—and all experience has shown that this tone is one of *sadness*. Beauty of whatever kind, in its supreme development, invariably excites the sensitive soul to tears. Melancholy is thus the most legitimate of all the poetical tones.

The length, the province, and the tone, being thus determined, I betook myself to ordinary induction, with the view of obtaining some artistic piquancy which might serve me as a key-note in the construction of the poem—some pivot upon which the whole structure might turn. In carefully thinking over all the usual artistic effects—or more properly *points,* in the theatrical sense—I did not fail to perceive immediately that no one had been so universally employed as that of the *refrain.* The universality of its employment sufficed to assure me of its intrinsic value, and spared me the necessity of submitting it to analysis. I considered it, however, with regard to its susceptibility of improvement, and soon saw it to be in a primitive condition. As commonly used, the *refrain,* or burden, not only is limited to lyric verse, but depends for its impression upon the force of monotone—both in sound and thought. The pleasure is deduced solely from the sense of identity—of repetition. I resolved to diversify, and so heighten, the effect, by adhering, in general, to the monotone of sound, while I continually varied that of thought: that is to say, I determined to produce continuously novel effects, by the variation *of the application* of the *refrain*—the refrain itself remaining, for the most part, unvaried.

These points being settled, I next bethought me of the *nature* of my *refrain.* Since its application was to be repeatedly varied, it was clear that the *refrain* itself must be brief, for there would have been an insurmountable difficulty in frequent variations of application in any sentence of length. In proportion to the brevity of the sentence, would, of course, be the facility of the variation. This led me at once to a single word as the best *refrain.*

The question now arose as to the *character* of the word. Having made up my mind to a *refrain,* the division of the poem into stanzas was, of course, a corollary: the *refrain* forming the close to each stanza. That such a close, to

have force, must be sonorous and susceptible of protracted emphasis, admitted no doubt: and these considerations, inevitably led me to the long *o* as the most sonorous vowel, in connection with *r* as the most producible consonant.

The sound of the *refrain* being thus determined, it became necessary to select a word embodying this sound, and at the same time in the fullest possible keeping with that melancholy which I had predetermined as the tone of the poem. In such a search it would have been absolutely impossible to overlook the word "Nevermore." In fact, it was the very first which presented itself.

The next *desideratum* was a pretext for the continuous use of the one word "nevermore." In observing the difficulty which I at once found in inventing a sufficiently plausible reason for its continuous repetition, I did not fail to perceive that this difficulty arose solely from the pre-assumption that the word was to be so continuously or monotonously spoken by a *human* being—I did not fail to perceive, in short, that the difficulty lay in the reconciliation of this monotony with the exercise of reason on the part of the creature repeating the word. Here, then, immediately arose the idea of a *non*-reasoning creature capable of speech; and, very naturally, a parrot, in the first instance, suggested itself, but was superseded forthwith by a Raven, as equally capable of speech, and infinitely more in keeping with the intended *tone.*

I had now gone so far as the conception of a Raven—the bird of ill omen—monotonously repeating the one word, "Nevermore," at the conclusion of each stanza, in a poem of melancholy tone, and in length about one hundred lines. Now, never losing sight of the object *supremeness,* or perfection, at all points, I asked myself—"Of all melancholy topics, what, according to the *universal* understanding of mankind, is the *most* melancholy?" Death—was the obvious reply. "And when," I said, "is this most melancholy of topics most poetical?" From what I have already explained at some length, the answer, here also, is obvious—"When it most closely allies itself to *Beauty:* the death, then, of a beautiful woman is, unquestionably, the most poetical topic in the world—and equally is it beyond doubt that the lips best suited for such topic are those of a bereaved lover."

I had now to combine the two ideas, of a

lover lamenting his deceased mistress and a
Raven continuously repeating the word "Nevermore."—I had to combine these, bearing in
mind my design of varying at every turn the
application of the word repeated; but the only
intelligible mode of such combination is that
of imagining the Raven employing the word in
answer to the queries of the lover. And here it
was that I saw at once the opportunity afforded
for the effect on which I had been depending
—that is to say, the effect of the *variation of
application*. I saw that I could make the first
query propounded by the lover—the first query
to which the Raven should reply "Nevermore"
—that I could make this first query a commonplace one—the second less so—the third still
less, and so on—until at length the lover,
startled from his original *nonchalance* by the
melancholy character of the word itself—by its
frequent repetition—and by a consideration of
the ominous reputation of the fowl that uttered
it—is at length excited to superstition, and
wildly propounds queries of a far different
character—queries whose solution he has passionately at heart—propounds them half in
superstition and half in that species of despair
which delights in self-torture—propounds them
not altogether because he believes in the prophetic or demoniac character of the bird
(which, reason assures him, is merely repeating a lesson learned by rote) but because he experiences a frenzied pleasure in so modeling his
questions as to receive from the *expected*
"Nevermore" the most delicious because the
most intolerable of sorrow. Perceiving the opportunity thus afforded me—or, more strictly,
thus forced upon me in the progress of the construction—I first established in mind the climax, or concluding query—that query to
which "Nevermore" should be in the last place
an answer—that in reply to which this word
"Nevermore" should involve the uttermost conceivable amount of sorrow and despair.

Here then the poem may be said to have its
beginning—at the end, where all works of art
should begin—for it was here, at this point of
my preconsiderations, that I first put pen to
paper in the composition of the stanza:

"Prophet," said I, "thing of evil! prophet still if
  bird or devil!
By that heaven that bends above us—by that God
  we both adore,
Tell this soul with sorrow laden, if within the distant Aidenn,

It shall clasp a sainted maiden whom the angels
  name Lenore—
Clasp a rare and radiant maiden whom the angels
  name Lenore."
    Quoth the Raven "Nevermore."

I composed this stanza, at this point, first
that, by establishing the climax, I might the
better vary and graduate, as regards seriousness and importance, the preceding queries of
the lover—and, secondly, that I might definitely settle the rhythm, the metre, and the
length and general arrangement of the stanza—
as well as graduate the stanzas which were to
precede, so that none of them might surpass
this in rhythmical effect. Had I been able, in
the subsequent composition, to construct more
vigorous stanzas, I should, without scruple,
have purposely enfeebled them, so as not to interfere with the climacteric effect.

And here I may as well say a few words of
the versification. My first object (as usual)
was originality. The extent to which this has
been neglected, in versification, is one of the
most unaccountable things in the world. Admitting that there is little possibility of variety
in mere *rhythm*, it is still clear that the possible
varieties of metre and stanza are absolutely
infinite—and yet, *for centuries, no man, in
verse, has ever done, or ever seemed to think of
doing, an original thing*. The fact is, that originality (unless in minds of very unusual force)
is by no means a matter, as some suppose, of
impulse or intuition. In general, to be found, it
must be elaborately sought, and although a
positive merit of the highest class, demands in
its attainment less of invention than negation.

Of course, I pretend to no originality in
either the rhythm or metre of the "Raven."
The former is trochaic—the latter is octameter
acatalectic, alternating with heptameter catalectic repeated in the *refrain* of the fifth verse,
and terminating with tetrameter catalectic.
Less pedantically—the feet employed throughout (trochees) consist of a long syllable followed by a short: the first line of the stanza
consists of eight of these feet—the second of
seven and a half (in effect two-thirds)—the
third of eight—the fourth of seven and a half—
the fifth the same—the sixth three and a half.
Now, each of these lines, taken individually,
has been employed before, and what originality the "Raven" has, is in their *combination
into stanza*; nothing even remotely approaching this combination has ever been attempted.
The effect of this originality of combination is

aided by other unusual, and some altogether
novel effects, arising from an extension of the
application of the principles of rhyme and
alliteration.

The next point to be considered was the
mode of bringing together the lover and the
Raven—and the first branch of this consideration was the *locale*. For this the most natural
suggestion might seem to be a forest, or the
fields—but it has always appeared to me that a
close *circumscription of space* is absolutely
necessary to the effect of insulated incident:—
it has the force of a frame to a picture. It has
an indisputable moral power in keeping concentrated the attention, and, of course, must
not be confounded with mere unity of place.

I determined, then, to place the lover in his
chamber—in a chamber rendered sacred to
him by memories of her who had frequented it.
The room is represented as richly furnished—
this in mere pursuance of the ideas I have already explained on the subject of Beauty, as the
sole true poetical thesis.

The *locale* being thus determined, I had
now to introduce the bird—and the thought of
introducing him through the window, was inevitable. The idea of making the lover suppose,
in the first instance, that the flapping of the
wings of the bird against the shutter, is a
"tapping" at the door, originated in the wish
to increase, by prolonging, the reader's curiosity, and in a desire to admit the incidental effect arising from the lover's throwing open the
door, finding all dark, and thence adopting the
half-fancy that it was the spirit of his mistress
that knocked.

I made the night tempestuous, first, to account for the Raven's seeking admission, and
secondly, for the effect of contrast with the
(physical) serenity within the chamber.

I made the bird alight on the bust of Pallas,
also for the effect of contrast between the
marble and the plumage—it being understood
that the bust was absolutely *suggested* by the
bird—the bust of *Pallas* being chosen, first, as
most in keeping with the scholarship of the
lover, and, secondly, for the sonorousness of
the word, Pallas, itself.

About the middle of the poem, also, I have
availed myself of the force of contrast, with a
view of deepening the ultimate impression.
For example, an air of the fantastic—approaching as nearly to the ludicrous as was admissible
—is given to the Raven's entrance. He comes
in "with many a flirt and flutter."

Not the *least obeisance made he*—not a moment
  stopped or stayed he,
But with mien of lord or lady, perched above my
  chamber door.

In the two stanzas which follow, the design
is more obviously carried out:—

Then this ebony bird beguiling my sad fancy into
  smiling
By the *grave and stern decorum of the countenance* 10
  it wore,
"Though thy *crest be shorn and shaven* thou," I
  said, "art sure no craven,
Ghastly grim and ancient Raven wandering from
  the nightly shore—
Tell me what thy lordly name is on the Night's
  Plutonian shore?"
    Quoth the Raven "Nevermore."

Much I marvelled *this ungainly fowl* to hear discourse so plainly   20
Though its answer little meaning—little relevancy
  bore;
For we cannot help agreeing that no living human
  being
Ever yet was blessed with seeing bird above his
  chamber door—
Bird or beast upon the sculptured bust above his
  chamber door,
    With such name as "Nevermore."

The effect of the *dénouement* being thus pro- 30
vided for, I immediately drop the fantastic for
a tone of the most profound seriousness:—this
tone commencing in the stanza directly following the one last quoted, with the line,

But the Raven, sitting lonely on that placid bust,
  spoke only, etc.

From this epoch the lover no longer jests—
no longer sees anything even of the fantastic
in the Raven's demeanor. He speaks of him as 40
a "grim, ungainly, ghastly, gaunt, and ominous bird of yore," and feels the "fiery eyes"
burning into his "bosom's core." This revolution of thought, or fancy, on the lover's part, is
intended to induce a similar one on the part of
the reader—to bring the mind into a proper
frame for the *dénouement*—which is now
brought about as rapidly and as *directly* as possible.

With the *dénouement* proper—with the 50
Raven's reply, "Nevermore," to the lover's final
demand if he shall meet his mistress in another
world—the poem, in its obvious phase, that of
a simple narrative, may be said to have its
completion. So far, everything is within the

limits of the accountable—of the real. A raven, having learned by rote the single word "Nevermore," and having escaped from the custody of its owner, is driven at midnight, through the violence of a storm, to seek admission at a window from which a light still gleams—the chamber-window of a student, occupied half in poring over a volume, half in dreaming of a beloved mistress deceased. The casement being
10 thrown open at the fluttering of the bird's wings, the bird itself perches on the most convenient seat out of the immediate reach of the student, who, amused by the incident and the oddity of the visitor's demeanor, demands of it, in jest and without looking for a reply, its name. The raven addressed, answers with its customary word, "Nevermore"—a word which finds immediate echo in the melancholy heart of the student, who, giving utterance aloud to
20 certain thoughts suggested by the occasion, is again startled by the fowl's repetition of "Nevermore." The student now guesses the state of the case, but is impelled, as I have before explained, by the human thirst for self-torture, and in part by superstition, to propound such queries to the bird as will bring him, the lover, the most of the luxury of sorrow, through the anticipated answer "Nevermore." With the indulgence, to the extreme, of this self-torture,
30 the narration, in what I have termed its first or obvious phase, has a natural termination, and so far there has been no overstepping of the limits of the real.

But in subjects so handled, however skilfully, or with however vivid an array of incident, there is always a certain hardness or nakedness, which repels the artistical eye. Two things are invariably required—first, some amount of complexity, or more properly, adap-
40 tation; and, secondly, some amount of suggestiveness—some under-current, however indefi-

nite, of meaning. It is this latter, in especial, which imparts to a work of art so much of that *richness* (to borrow from colloquy a forcible term) which we are too fond of confounding with *the ideal.* It is the *excess* of the suggested meaning—it is the rendering this the upper instead of the under current of the theme—which turns into prose (and that of the very flattest kind) the so-called poetry of the so-called transcendentalists.

Holding these opinions, I added the two concluding stanzas of the poem—their suggestiveness being thus made to pervade all the narrative which has preceded them. The under-current of meaning is rendered first apparent in the lines—

"Take thy beak from out *my heart,* and take thy
    form from off my door!"
        Quoth the Raven, "Nevermore!"

It will be observed that the words, "from out my heart," involve the first metaphorical expression in the poem. They, with the answer, "Nevermore," dispose the mind to seek a moral in all that has been previously narrated. The reader begins now to regard the Raven as emblematical—but it is not until the very last line of the very last stanza, that the intention of making him emblematical of *Mournful and Never-ending Remembrance* is permitted distinctly to be seen:

And the Raven, never flitting, still is sitting, still
    is sitting,
On the pallid bust of Pallas, just above my chamber
    door;
And his eyes have all the seeming of a demon's that
    is dreaming,
And the lamplight o'er him streaming throws his
    shadow on the floor;
And my soul *from out that shadow* that lies floating
    on the floor
        Shall be lifted—nevermore.   1846

» » THE POETIC PRINCIPLE « «

In speaking of the Poetic Principle, I have no design to be either thorough or profound. While discussing very much at random the
50 essentiality of what we call Poetry, my principal purpose will be to cite for consideration some few of those minor English or American poems which best suit my own taste, or which, upon my own fancy, have left the most definite impression. By "minor poems" I mean, of

course, poems of little length. And here, in the beginning, permit me to say a few words in regard to a somewhat peculiar principle, which, whether rightfully or wrongfully, has always had its influence in my own critical estimate of the poem. I hold that a long poem does not exist. I maintain that the phrase, "a long poem," is simply a flat contradiction in terms.

I need scarcely observe that a poem deserves its title only inasmuch as it excites, by elevating the soul. The value of the poem is in the ratio of this elevating excitement. But all excitements are, through a psychal necessity, transient. That degree of excitement which would entitle a poem to be so called at all, cannot be sustained throughout a composition of any great length. After the lapse of half an hour, at the very utmost, it flags—fails—a revulsion ensues—and then the poem is, in effect, and in fact, no longer such.

There are, no doubt, many who have found difficulty in reconciling the critical dictum that the *Paradise Lost* is to be devoutly admired throughout, with the absolute impossibility of maintaining for it, during perusal, the amount of enthusiasm which that critical dictum would demand. This great work, in fact, is to be regarded as poetical only when, losing sight of that vital requisite in all works of Art, Unity, we view it merely as a series of minor poems. If, to preserve its Unity—its totality of effect or impression—we read it (as would be necessary) at a single sitting, the result is but a constant alternation of excitement and depression. After a passage of what we feel to be true poetry, there follows, inevitably, a passage of platitude which no critical pre-judgment can force us to admire; but if, upon completing the work, we read it again, omitting the first book—that is to say, commencing with the second—we shall be surprised at now finding that admirable which we before condemned—the damnable which we had previously so much admired. It follows from all this that the ultimate, aggregate, or absolute effect of even the best epic under the sun, is a nullity—and this is precisely the fact.

In regard to the *Iliad*, we have, if not positive proof, at least very good reason, for believing it intended as a series of lyrics; but, granting the epic intention, I can say only that the work is based in an imperfect sense of art. The modern epic is, of the supposititious ancient model, but an inconsiderate and blindfold imitation. But the day of these artistic anomalies is over. If, at any time, any very long poem *were* popular in reality—which I doubt—it is at least clear that no very long poem will ever be popular again.

That the extent of a poetical work is, *ceteris paribus*, the measure of its merit, seems undoubtedly, when we thus state it, a proposition sufficiently absurd—yet we are indebted for it to the Quarterly Reviews. Surely there can be nothing in mere *size*, abstractly considered—there can be nothing in mere *bulk*, so far as a volume is concerned, which has so continuously elicited admiration from these saturnine pamphlets! A mountain, to be sure, by the mere sentiment of physical magnitude which it conveys, *does* impress us with a sense of the sublime—but no man is impressed after *this* fashion by the material grandeur of even *The Columbiad*. Even the Quarterlies have not instructed us to be so impressed by it. *As yet*, they have not *insisted* on our estimating Lamartine by the cubic foot, or Pollok by the pound —but what else are we to *infer* from their continued prating about "sustained effort"? If, by "sustained effort," any little gentleman has accomplished an epic, let us frankly commend him for the effort—if this indeed be a thing commendable—but let us forbear praising the epic on the effort's account. It is to be hoped that common sense, in the time to come, will prefer deciding upon a work of art rather by the impression it makes, by the effect it produces, than by the time it took to impress the effect, or by the amount of "sustained effort" which had been found necessary in effecting the impression. The fact is, that perseverance is one thing, and genius quite another—nor can all the Quarterlies in Christendom confound them. By and by, this proposition, with many which I have just been urging, will be received as self-evident. In the mean time, by being generally condemned as falsities, they will not be essentially damaged as truths.

On the other hand, it is clear that a poem may be improperly brief. Undue brevity degenerates into mere epigrammatism. A *very* short poem, while now and then producing a brilliant or vivid, never produces a profound or enduring effect. There must be the steady pressing down of the stamp upon the wax. De Béranger has wrought innumerable things, pungent and spirit-stirring; but in general they have been too imponderous to stamp themselves deeply into the public attention, and thus, as so many feathers of fancy, have been blown aloft only to be whistled down the wind.

A remarkable instance of the effect of undue brevity in depressing a poem—in keeping it out of the popular view—is afforded by the following exquisite little Serenade:

> "I arise from dreams of thee
> In the first sweet sleep of night,
> When the winds are breathing low,
> And the stars are shining bright;

I arise from dreams of thee,
   And a spirit in my feet
Has led me—who knows how?—
   To thy chamber-window, sweet!

"The wandering airs, they faint
   On the dark, the silent stream—
The champak odors fail
   Like sweet thoughts in a dream;
The nightingale's complaint,
10   It dies upon her heart,
As I must die on thine,
   O, beloved as thou art!

"O, lift me from the grass!
   I die, I faint, I fail!
Let thy love in kisses rain
   On my lips and eyelids pale.
My cheek is cold and white, alas!
   My heart beats loud and fast:
20 Oh! press it close to thine again,
   Where it will break at last!"

Very few perhaps are familiar with these
lines—yet no less a poet than Shelley is their
author. Their warm, yet delicate and ethereal
imagination will be appreciated by all—but by
none so thoroughly as by him who has himself
arisen from sweet dreams of one beloved to
bathe in the aromatic air of a southern mid-
30 summer night.
   One of the finest poems by Willis, the very
best in my opinion which he has ever written,
has no doubt, through this same defect of undue brevity, been kept back from its proper
position, not less in the critical than in the
popular view.

"The shadows lay along Broadway,
   'Twas near the twilight tide—
And slowly there a lady fair
40   Was walking in her pride.
Alone walked she; but, viewlessly,
   Walked spirits at her side.

"Peace charm'd the street beneath her feet,
   And Honor charm'd the air;
And all astir looked kind on her,
   And called her good as fair—
For all God ever gave to her
   She kept with chary care.

50 "She kept with care her beauties rare
   From lovers warm and true—
For her heart was cold to all but gold,
   And the rich came not to woo—
But honor'd well are charms to sell,
   If priests the selling do.

"Now walking there was one more fair—
   A slight girl, lily-pale;
And she had unseen company
   To make the spirit quail—
'Twixt Want and Scorn she walk'd forlorn,
   And nothing could avail.

"No mercy now can clear her brow
   For this world's peace to pray;
For, as love's wild prayer dissolved in air,
   Her woman's heart gave way!—
But the sin forgiven by Christ in Heaven
   By man is cursed alway!"

In this composition we find it difficult to
recognize the Willis who has written so many
mere "verses of society." The lines are not only
richly ideal, but full of energy; while they
breathe an earnestness, an evident sincerity of
sentiment, for which we look in vain throughout all the other works of this author.
   While the epic mania—while the idea that,
to merit in poetry, prolixity is indispensable—
has for some years past been gradually dying
out of the public mind by mere dint of its own
absurdity, we find it succeeded by a heresy too
palpably false to be long tolerated, but one
which, in the brief period it has already endured, may be said to have accomplished more
in the corruption of our Poetical Literature than
all its other enemies combined. I allude to the
heresy of *The Didactic.* It has been assumed,
tacitly and avowedly, directly and indirectly,
that the ultimate object of all Poetry is Truth.
Every poem, it is said, should inculcate a moral;
and by this moral is the poetical merit of the
work to be adjudged. We Americans especially
have patronized this happy idea; and we Bostonians very especially have developed it in
full. We have taken it into our heads that to
write a poem simply for the poem's sake, and
to acknowledge such to have been our design,
would be to confess ourselves radically wanting
in the true Poetic dignity and force:—but the
simple fact is, that, would we but permit ourselves to look into our own souls, we should
immediately there discover that under the sun
there neither exists nor *can* exist any work more
thoroughly dignified, more supremely noble
than this very poem, this poem *per se,* this
poem which is a poem and nothing more, this
poem written solely for the poem's sake.
   With as deep a reverence for the True as
ever inspired the bosom of man, I would nevertheless limit, in some measure, its modes of inculcation. I would limit to enforce them. I
would not enfeeble them by dissipation. The

demands of Truth are severe. She has no sympathy with the myrtles. All *that* which is so indispensable in Song, is precisely all *that* with which *she* has nothing whatever to do. It is but making her a flaunting paradox, to wreathe her in gems and flowers. In enforcing a truth, we need severity rather than efflorescence of language. We must be simple, precise, terse. We must be cool, calm, unimpassioned. In a word, we must be in that mood which, as nearly as possible, is the exact converse of the poetical. *He* must be blind indeed who does not perceive the radical and chasmal differences between the truthful and the poetical modes of inculcation. He must be theory-mad beyond redemption who, in spite of these differences, shall still persist in attempting to reconcile the obstinate oils and waters of Poetry and Truth.

Dividing the world of mind into its three most immediately obvious distinctions, we have the Pure Intellect, Taste, and the Moral Sense. I place Taste in the middle because it is just this position which, in the mind, it occupies. It holds intimate relations with either extreme; but from the Moral Sense is separated by so faint a difference that Aristotle has not hesitated to place some of its operations among the virtues themselves. Nevertheless, we find the *offices* of the trio marked with a sufficient distinction. Just as the Intellect concerns itself with Truth, so Taste informs us of the Beautiful, while the Moral Sense is regardful of Duty. Of this latter, while Conscience teaches the obligation, and Reason the expediency, Taste contents herself with displaying the charms, waging war upon Vice solely on the ground of her deformity, her disproportion, her animosity to the fitting, to the appropriate, to the harmonious, in a word, to Beauty.

An immortal instinct, deep within the spirit of man, is thus, plainly, a sense of the Beautiful. This it is which administers to his delight in the manifold forms, and sounds, and odors, and sentiments, amid which he exists. And just as the lily is repeated in the lake, or the eyes of Amaryllis in the mirror, so is the mere oral or written repetition of these forms, and sounds, and colors, and odors, and sentiments, a duplicate source of delight. But this mere repetition is not poetry. He who shall simply sing, with however glowing enthusiasm, or with however vivid a truth of description, of the sights, and sounds, and odors, and colors, and sentiments, which greet *him* in common with all mankind

—he, I say, has yet failed to prove his divine title. There is still a something in the distance which he has been unable to attain. We have still a thirst unquenchable, to allay which he has not shown us the crystal springs. This thirst belongs to the immortality of Man. It is at once a consequence and an indication of his perennial existence. It is the desire of the moth for the star. It is no mere appreciation of the Beauty before us—but a wild effort to reach the Beauty above. Inspired by an ecstatic prescience of the glories beyond the grave, we struggle, by multiform combinations among the things and thoughts of Time, to attain a portion of that Loveliness whose very elements, perhaps, appertain to eternity alone. And thus when by Poetry—or when by Music, the most entrancing of the Poetic moods—we find ourselves melted into tears, we weep then—not as the Abbate Gravina supposes—through excess of pleasure, but through a certain, petulant, impatient sorrow at our inability to grasp *now*, wholly, here on earth, at once and forever, those divine and rapturous joys, of which *through* the poem, or *through* the music, we attain to but brief and indeterminate glimpses.

The struggle to apprehend the supernal Loveliness—this struggle, on the part of souls fittingly constituted—has given to the world all *that* which it (the world) has ever been enabled at once to understand and to *feel* as poetic.

The Poetic Sentiment, of course, may develop itself in various modes—in Painting, in Sculpture, in Architecture, in the Dance—very especially in Music—and very peculiarly, and with a wide field, in the composition of the Landscape Garden. Our present theme, however, has regard only to its manifestation in words. And here let me speak briefly on the topic of rhythm. Contenting myself with the certainty that Music, in its various modes of metre, rhythm, and rhyme, is of so vast a moment in Poetry as never to be wisely rejected —is so vitally important an adjunct, that he is simply silly who declines its assistance, I will not now pause to maintain its absolute essentiality. It is in Music, perhaps, that the soul most nearly attains the great end for which, when inspired by the Poetic Sentiment, it struggles—the creation of supernal Beauty. It *may* be, indeed, that here this sublime end is, now and then, attained in *fact*. We are often made to feel, with a shivering delight, that from an earthly harp are stricken notes which *cannot* have been unfamiliar to the angels. And thus there can be little doubt that in the union of Poetry with Music in its popular sense, we shall find the widest field for the Poetic development. The old Bards and Minnesingers had advantages which we do not possess—and Thomas Moore, singing his own songs, was, in the most legitimate manner, perfecting them as poems.

To recapitulate, then:—I would define, in brief, the Poetry of words as *The Rhythmical Creation of Beauty*. Its sole arbiter is Taste. With the Intellect or with the Conscience, it has only collateral relations. Unless incidentally, it has no concern whatever either with Duty or with Truth.

A few words, however, in explanation. *That* pleasure which is at once the most pure, the most elevating, and the most intense, is derived, I maintain, from the contemplation of the Beautiful. In the contemplation of Beauty we alone find it possible to attain that pleasurable elevation, or excitement, *of the soul,* which we recognize as the Poetic Sentiment, and which is so easily distinguished from Truth, which is the satisfaction of the Reason, or from Passion, which is the excitement of the heart. I make Beauty, therefore,—using the word as inclusive of the sublime,—I make Beauty the province of the poem, simply because it is an obvious rule of Art that effects should be made to spring as directly as possible from their causes:—no one as yet having been weak enough to deny that the peculiar elevation in question is at least *most readily* attainable in the poem. It by no means follows, however, that the incitements of Passion, or the precepts of Duty, or even the lessons of Truth, may not be introduced into a poem, and with advantage; for they may subserve, incidentally, in various ways, the general purposes of the work:—but the true artist will always contrive to tone them down in proper subjection to that *Beauty* which is the atmosphere and the real essence of the poem.

I cannot better introduce the few poems which I shall present for your consideration, than by the citation of the Proëm to Mr. Longfellow's "Waif":

"The day is done, and the darkness
    Falls from the wings of Night,
As a feather is wafted downward
    From an eagle in his flight.

"I see the lights of the village
    Gleam through the rain and the mist,
And a feeling of sadness comes o'er me,
    That my soul cannot resist;

"A feeling of sadness and longing,
    That is not akin to pain,
And resembles sorrow only
    As the mist resembles the rain.

"Come, read to me some poem,
    Some simple and heartfelt lay,
That shall soothe this restless feeling,
    And banish the thoughts of day.

"Not from the grand old masters,
    Not from the bards sublime,
Whose distant footsteps echo
    Through the corridors of Time.

"For, like strains of martial music,
    Their mighty thoughts suggest
Life's endless toil and endeavor;
    And to-night I long for rest.

"Read from some humbler poet,
    Whose songs gushed from his heart,
As showers, from the clouds of summer,
    Or tears from the eyelids start;

"Who through long days of labor,
    And nights devoid of ease,
Still heard in his soul the music
    Of wonderful melodies.

"Such songs have power to quiet
    The restless pulse of care,
And come like the benediction
    That follows after prayer.

"Then read from the treasured volume
    The poem of thy choice,
And lend to the rhyme of the poet
    The beauty of thy voice.

"And the night shall be filled with music,
    And the cares, that infest the day,
Shall fold their tents, like the Arabs,
    And as silently steal away."

With no great range of imagination, these lines have been justly admired for their delicacy of expression. Some of the images are very effective. Nothing can be better than

"The bards sublime
Whose distant footsteps echo
Down the corridors of Time "

The idea of the last quatrain is also very effective. The poem, on the whole, however, is chiefly to be admired for the graceful *insouciance* of its metre, so well in accordance with the character of the sentiments, and especially for the *ease* of the general manner. This "ease" or naturalness, in a literary style, it has long been the fashion to regard as ease in appearance alone—as a point of really difficult attainment. But not so: a natural manner is difficult only to him who should never meddle with it—to the unnatural. It is but the result of writing with the understanding, or with the instinct, that *the tone*, in composition, should always be that which the mass of mankind would adopt—and must perpetually vary, of course, with the occasion. The author who, after the fashion of the *North American Review*, should be upon *all* occasions merely "quiet," must necessarily upon *many* occasions be simply silly, or stupid; and has no more right to be considered "easy" or "natural" than a Cockney exquisite, or than the sleeping Beauty in the wax-works.

Among the minor poems of Bryant, none has so much impressed me as the one which he entitles "June." I quote only a portion of it:

"There, through the long, long summer hours,
    The golden light should lie,
And thick young herbs and groups of flowers
    Stand in their beauty by.
The oriole should build and tell
    His love-tale, close beside my cell;
        The idle butterfly
Should rest him there, and there be heard
The housewife-bee and humming bird.

"And what if cheerful shouts, at noon,
    Come, from the village sent,
Or songs of maids, beneath the moon,
    With fairy laughter blent?
And what, if in the evening light,
Betrothed lovers walk in sight
    Of my low monument?
I would the lovely scene around
Might know no sadder sight nor sound.

"I know, I know I should not see
    The season's glorious show,
Nor would its brightness shine for me,
    Nor its wild music flow;
But if, around my place of sleep,
The friends I love should come to weep,
    They might not haste to go.
Soft airs, and song, and light, and bloom
Should keep them lingering by my tomb.

"These to their softened hearts should bear
    The thought of what has been,
And speak of one who cannot share
    The gladness of the scene;
Whose part, in all the pomp that fills
The circuit of the summer hills,
    Is—that his grave is green;
And deeply would their hearts rejoice
To hear again his living voice."

The rhythmical flow here is even voluptuous—nothing could be more melodious. The poem has always affected me in a remarkable manner. The intense melancholy which seems to well up, perforce, to the surface of all the poet's cheerful sayings about his grave, we find thrilling us to the soul—while there is the truest poetic elevation in the thrill. The impression left is one of a pleasurable sadness. And if, in the remaining compositions which I shall introduce to you, there be more or less of a similar tone always apparent, let me remind you that (how or why we know not) this certain taint of sadness is inseparably connected with all the higher manifestations of true Beauty. It is, nevertheless,

"A feeling of sadness and longing
    That is not akin to pain,
And resembles sorrow only
    As the mist resembles the rain."

The taint of which I speak is clearly perceptible even in a poem so full of brilliancy and spirit as the "Health" of Edward Coate Pinckney.

"I fill this cup to one made up
    Of loveliness alone,
A woman, of her gentle sex
    The seeming paragon;
To whom the better elements
    And kindly stars have given
A form so fair, that, like the air,
    'Tis less of earth than heaven.

"Her every tone is music's own,
    Like those of morning birds,
And something more than melody
    Dwells ever in her words;
The coinage of her heart are they,
    And from her lips each flows
As one may see the burdened bee
    Forth issue from the rose.

"Affections are as thoughts to her,
    The measures of her hours;
Her feelings have the fragrancy,
    The freshness of young flowers

And lovely passions, changing oft,
  So fill her, she appears
The image of themselves by turns,—
  The idol of past years!

"Of her bright face one glance will trace
  A picture on the brain,
And of her voice in echoing hearts
  A sound must long remain;
But memory, such as mine of her,
  So very much endears,
When death is nigh, my latest sigh
  Will not be life's, but hers.

"I fill this cup to one made up
  Of loveliness alone,
A woman, of her gentle sex
  The seeming paragon—
Her health! and would on earth there stood
  Some more of such a frame,
That life might be all poetry,
  And weariness a name."

It was the misfortune of Mr. Pinckney to have been born too far south. Had he been a New Englander, it is probable that he would have been ranked as the first of American lyrists, by that magnanimous cabal which has so long controlled the destinies of American Letters, in conducting the thing called the *North American Review.* The poem just cited is especially beautiful; but the poetic elevation which it induces, we must refer chiefly to our sympathy in the poet's enthusiasm. We pardon his hyperboles for the evident earnestness with which they are uttered.

It was by no means my design, however, to expatiate upon the *merits* of what I should read you. These will necessarily speak for themselves. Boccalini, in his *Advertisements from Parnassus,* tells us that Zoilus once presented Apollo a very caustic criticism upon a very admirable book:—whereupon the god asked him for the beauties of the work. He replied that he only busied himself about the errors. On hearing this, Apollo, handing him a sack of unwinnowed wheat, bade him pick out *all the chaff* for his reward.

Now this fable answers very well as a hit at the critics—but I am by no means sure that the god was in the right. I am by no means certain that the true limits of the critical duty are not grossly misunderstood. Excellence, in a poem especially, may be considered in the light of an axiom, which need only be properly *put,* to become self-evident. It is *not* excellence if it require to be demonstrated as such:—and thus to point out too particularly the merits of a work of Art, is to admit that they are *not* merits altogether.

Among the "Melodies" of Thomas Moore is one whose distinguished character as a poem proper seems to have been singularly left out of view. I allude to his lines beginning— "Come, rest in this bosom." The intense energy of their expression is not surpassed by anything in Byron. There are two of the lines in which a sentiment is conveyed that embodies the *all in all* of the divine passion of love—a sentiment which, perhaps, has found its echo in more, and in more passionate, human hearts than any other single sentiment ever embodied in words:

"Come, rest in this bosom, my own stricken deer,
Though the herd have fled from thee, thy home is
  still here;
Here still is the smile, that no cloud can o'ercast,
And a heart and a hand all thy own to the last.

"Oh! what was love made for, if 'tis not the same
Through joy and through torment, through glory
  and shame?
I know not, I ask not, if guilt's in that heart,
I but know that I love thee, whatever thou art.

"Thou hast call'd me thy Angel in moments of
  bliss,
And thy Angel I'll be, 'mid the horrors of this,—
Through the furnace, unshrinking, thy steps to
  pursue,
And shield thee, and save thee,—or perish there
  too!"

It has been the fashion of late days to deny Moore imagination, while granting him fancy —a distinction originating with Coleridge— than whom no man more fully comprehended the great powers of Moore. The fact is, that the fancy of this poet so far predominates over all his other faculties, and over the fancy of all other men, as to have induced, very naturally, the idea that he is fanciful *only.* But never was there a greater mistake. Never was a grosser wrong done the fame of a true poet. In the compass of the English language I can call to mind no poem more profoundly—more weirdly *imaginative,* in the best sense, than the lines commencing—"I would I were by that dim lake"—which are the composition of Thomas Moore. I regret that I am unable to remember them.

One of the noblest—and, speaking of fancy, one of the most singularly fanciful of modern poets, was Thomas Hood. His "Fair Ines" had always for me an inexpressible charm:

> "O saw ye not fair Ines!
>   She's gone into the West,
> To dazzle when the sun is down,
>   And rob the world of rest:
> She took our daylight with her,
>   The smiles that we love best,
> With morning blushes on her cheek,
>   And pearls upon her breast.
>
> "O turn again, fair Ines,
>   Before the fall of night,
> For fear the Moon should shine alone,
>   And stars unrivall'd bright;
> And blessed will the lover be
>   That walks beneath their light,
> And breathes the love against thy cheek
>   I dare not even write!
>
> "Would I had been, fair Ines,
>   That gallant cavalier,
> Who rode so gaily by thy side,
>   And whisper'd thee so near!
> Were there no bonny dames at home,
>   Or no true lovers here,
> That he should cross the seas to win
>   The dearest of the dear?
>
> "I saw thee, lovely Ines,
>   Descend along the shore,
> With bands of noble gentlemen,
>   And banners wav'd before;
> And gentle youth and maidens gay,
>   And snowy plumes they wore;
> It would have been a beauteous dream,
>   If it had been no more!
>
> "Alas, alas, fair Ines,
>   She went away with song,
> With Music waiting on her steps,
>   And shoutings of the throng;
> But some were sad, and felt no mirth,
>   But only Music's wrong,
> In sounds that sang farewell, farewell,
>   To her you've loved so long.
>
> "Farewell, farewell, fair Ines,
>   That vessel never bore
> So fair a lady on its deck,
>   Nor danced so light before,—
> Alas for pleasure on the sea,
>   And sorrow on the shore!
> The smile that blest one lover's heart
>   Has broken many more!"

"The Haunted House," by the same author, is one of the truest poems ever written, one of the *truest*, one of the most unexceptionable, one of the most thoroughly artistic, both in its theme and in its execution. It is, moreover, powerfully ideal—imaginative. I regret that its length renders it unsuitable for the purposes of this Lecture. In place of it, permit me to offer the universally appreciated "Bridge of Sighs":

> "One more Unfortunate,
>   Weary of breath,
> Rashly importunate,
>   Gone to her death!
>
> Take her up tenderly,
>   Lift her with care;—
> Fashion'd so slenderly,
>   Young, and so fair!
>
> "Look at her garments
>   Clinging like cerements;
> Whilst the wave constantly
>   Drips from her clothing;
> Take her up instantly,
>   Loving, not loathing.—
>
> "Touch her not scornfully;
>   Think of her mournfully,
> Gently and humanly;
>   Not of the stains of her,
> All that remains of her
>   Now, is pure womanly.
>
> "Make no deep scrutiny
>   Into her mutiny
> Rash and undutiful;
>   Past all dishonor,
> Death has left on her
>   Only the beautiful.
>
> "Still, for all slips of hers,
>   One of Eve's family—
> Wipe those poor lips of hers
>   Oozing so clammily,
> Loop up her tresses
>   Escaped from the comb,
> Her fair auburn tresses;
>   Whilst wonderment guesses
> Where was her home?
>
> "Who was her father?
>   Who was her mother?
> Had she a sister?
>   Had she a brother?
> Or was there a dearer one
>   Still, and a nearer one
> Yet, than all other?
>
> "Alas! for the rarity
>   Of Christian charity
> Under the sun!
>   Oh! it was pitiful!
> Near a whole city full,
>   Home she had none.

"Sisterly, brotherly,
Fatherly, motherly
Feelings had changed:
Love, by harsh evidence,
Thrown from its eminence,
Even God's providence
Seeming estranged.

"Where the lamps quiver
So far in the river,
With many a light
From window and casement,
From garret to basement,
She stood, with amazement,
Houseless by night.

"The bleak wind of March
Made her tremble and shiver;
But not the dark arch,
Or the black flowing river:
Mad from life's history,
Glad to death's mystery,
Swift to be hurl'd—
Anywhere, anywhere
Out of the world!

"In she plunged boldly,
No matter how coldly
The rough river ran,—
Over the brink of it,
Picture it—think of it,
Dissolute Man!
Lave in it, drink of it
Then, if you can!

"Take her up tenderly,
Lift her with care;
Fashion'd so slenderly,
Young, and so fair!

Ere her limbs frigidly
Stiffen too rigidly,
Decently,—kindly,—
Smooth, and compose them;
And her eyes, close them,
Staring so blindly!

"Dreadfully staring
Through muddy impurity,
As when with the daring
Last look of despairing
Fixed on futurity.
Perishing gloomily,
Spurred by contumely,
Cold inhumanity,
Burning insanity,
Into her rest,—
Cross her hands humbly,
As if praying dumbly,
Over her breast!
Owning her weakness,

Her evil behavior,
And leaving, with meekness,
Her sins to her Savior!"

The vigor of this poem is no less remarkable than its pathos. The versification, although carrying the fanciful to the very verge of the fantastic, is nevertheless admirably adapted to the wild insanity which is the thesis of the poem.

Among the minor poems of Lord Byron is one which has never received from the critics the praise which it undoubtedly deserves:

"Though the day of my destiny's over,
    And the star of my fate hath declined,
Thy soft heart refused to discover
    The faults which so many could find;
Though thy soul with my grief was acquainted,
    It shrunk not to share it with me,
And the love which my spirit hath painted
    It never hath found but in *thee*.

"Then when nature around me is smiling,
    The last smile which answers to mine,
I do not believe it beguiling,
    Because it reminds me of thine;
And when winds are at war with the ocean,
    As the breasts I believed in with me,
If their billows excite an emotion,
    It is that they bear me from *thee*.

"Though the rock of my last hope is shivered,
    And its fragments are sunk in the wave,
Though I feel that my soul is delivered
    To pain—it shall not be its slave.
There is many a pang to pursue me:
    They may crush, but they shall not contemn—
They may torture, but shall not subdue me—
    'Tis of *thee* that I think—not of them.

"Though human, thou didst not deceive me,
    Though woman, thou didst not forsake,
Though loved, thou forborest to grieve me,
    Though slandered, thou never couldst shake,—
Though trusted, thou didst not disclaim me,
    Though parted, it was not to fly,
Though watchful, 'twas not to defame me,
    Nor mute, that the world might belie.

"Yet I blame not the world, nor despise it,
    Nor the war of the many with one—
If my soul was not fitted to prize it,
    'Twas folly not sooner to shun:
And if dearly that error hath cost me,
    And more than I once could foresee,
I have found that whatever it lost me,
    It could not deprive me of *thee*.

"From the wreck of the past, which hath perished,
    Thus much I at least may recall,

It hath taught me that which I most cherished
  Deserved to be dearest of all:
In the desert a fountain is springing,
  In the wide waste there still is a tree,
And a bird in the solitude singing,
  Which speaks to my spirit of *thee*."

Although the rhythm here is one of the most difficult, the versification could scarcely be improved. No nobler *theme* ever engaged the pen of poet. It is the soul-elevating idea that no man can consider himself entitled to complain of Fate while, in his adversity, he still retains the unwavering love of woman.

From Alfred Tennyson—although in perfect sincerity I regard him as the noblest poet that ever lived—I have left myself time to cite only a very brief specimen. I call him, and *think* him the noblest of poets—*not* because the impressions he produces are at *all* times the most profound—*not* because the poetical excitement which he induces is at *all* times the most intense —but because it *is* at all times the most ethereal—in other words, the most elevating and the most pure. No poet is so little of the earth, earthy. What I am about to read is from his last long poem, *The Princess:*

"Tears, idle tears, I know not what they mean,
Tears from the depth of some divine despair
Rise in the heart, and gather to the eyes,
In looking on the happy Autumn-fields,
And thinking of the days that are no more.

"Fresh as the first beam glittering on a sail
That brings our friends up from the underworld,
Sad as the last which reddens over one
That sinks with all we love below the verge;
So sad, so fresh, the days that are no more.

"Ah, sad and strange as in dark summer dawns
The earliest pipe of half-awaken'd birds
To dying ears, when unto dying eyes
The casement slowly grows a glimmering square;
So sad, so strange, the days that are no more.

"Dear as remember'd kisses after death,
And sweet as those by hopeless fancy feign'd
On lips that are for others; deep as love,
Deep as first love, and wild with all regret;
O Death in Life, the days that are no more."

Thus, although in a very cursory and imperfect manner, I have endeavored to convey to you my conception of the Poetic Principle. It has been my purpose to suggest that, while this Principle itself is strictly and simply the Human Aspiration for Supernal Beauty, the manifestation of the Principle is always found in *an elevating excitement of the Soul,* quite independent of that passion which is the intoxication of the Heart, or of that Truth which is the satisfaction of the Reason. For in regard to Passion, alas! its tendency is to degrade rather than to elevate the Soul. Love, on the contrary—Love—the true, the divine Eros— the Uranian as distinguished from the Dionæan Venus—is unquestionably the purest and truest of all poetical themes. And in regard to Truth —if, to be sure, through the attainment of a truth we are led to perceive a harmony where none was apparent before, we experience at once the true poetical effect—but this effect is referable to the harmony alone, and not in the least degree to the truth which merely served to render the harmony manifest.

We shall reach, however, more immediately a distinct conception of what the true Poetry is, by mere reference to a few of the simple elements which induce in the Poet himself the true poetical effect. He recognizes the ambrosia which nourishes his soul, in the bright orbs that shine in Heaven—in the volutes of the flower—in the clustering of low shrubberies— in the waving of the grain-fields—in the slanting of tall Eastern trees—in the blue distance of mountains—in the grouping of clouds—in the twinkling of half-hidden brooks—in the gleaming of silver rivers—in the repose of sequestered lakes—in the star-mirroring depths of lonely wells. He perceives it in the songs of birds—in the harp of Æolus—in the sighing of the night-wind—in the repining voice of the forest—in the surf that complains to the shore —in the fresh breath of the woods—in the scent of the violet—in the voluptuous perfume of the hyacinth—in the suggestive odor that comes to him at eventide from far-distant, undiscovered islands, over dim oceans, illimitable and unexplored. He owns it in all noble thoughts—in all unworldly motives—in all holy impulses—in all chivalrous, generous, and self-sacrificing deeds. He feels it in the beauty of woman—in the grace of her step—in the lustre of her eye—in the melody of her voice—in her soft laughter—in her sigh—in the harmony of the rustling of her robes. He deeply feels it in her winning endearments—in her burning enthusiasms—in her gentle charities—in her meek and devotional endurances—but above all—ah, far above all—he kneels to it, he worships it in the faith, in the purity, in the strength, in the altogether divine majesty— of her *love.*

Let me conclude by the recitation of yet an-other brief poem—one very different in character from any that I have before quoted. It is by Motherwell, and is called "The Song of the Cavalier." With our modern and altogether rational ideas of the absurdity and impiety of warfare, we are not precisely in that frame of mind best adapted to sympathise with the sentiments, and thus to appreciate the real excellence of the poem. To do this fully we must identify ourselves in fancy with the soul of the old cavalier.

"Then mounte! then mounte, brave gallants, all,
  And don your helmes amaine:
Deathe's couriers, Fame and Honor, call
  Us to the field againe.
No shrewish teares shall fill our eye
  When the sword-hilt's in our hand,—
Heart-whole we'll part, and no whit sighe
  For the fayrest of the land;
Let piping swaine, and craven wight,
  Thus weepe and puling crye,
Our business is like men to fight,
  And hero-like to die!"   1850

THOMAS HOLLEY CHIVERS

1809–1858

WHEN DANTE GABRIEL ROSSETTI read Chivers's *The Lost Pleiad* (1845) he was amused "at a certain combination of helter-skelter fervour and profusion, and of oddity" in it. James Russell Lowell called Chivers a "droll illustration of the shell of Shelley." Yet Rossetti owed a literary debt to Chivers, which he never acknowledged, and Chivers had more real poetry in him than Lowell. He was in fact a genius who, a few times, put his feet on the ground.

A native of Georgia, born, probably, in 1809, he graduated in medicine at Transylvania University in Kentucky, but practiced only a short time. *The Path of Sorrow*, the first of eleven volumes of verse, was issued in 1832, from a newspaper press in Franklin, Tennessee. In 1837 he married Harriet Hunt of Springfield, Massachusetts. A previous marriage had ended in a tragic separation. The rest of his life he lived much in the North, but he considered Georgia his home and in 1847 invited Poe to live with him there. The friendship between the two poets began in 1842, and though each accused the other of plagiarism and Poe called Chivers "at the same time one of the best and one of the worst poets in America," they were still friends when Poe died.

The eleven volumes of verse Chivers published, most of them at his own expense, bear such fantastic titles as *Eonchs of Ruby, A Gift of Love* (1851), and *Memoralia; or Phials of Amber Full of the Tears of Love; A Gift for the Beautiful* (1853). In criticizing the kind of poetry these volumes contain Poe spoke with the sure judgment he often displayed in writing of his contemporaries: "[Chivers's] productions affect one as a wild dream—strange, incongruous, full of images of more than arabesque monstrosity and snatches of sweet, unsustained song. Even his worst nonsense (and some of it is horrible) has an indefinite charm of sentiment and melody. We can never be sure that there is *any* meaning in his words,—neither is there any meaning in many of our finest musical airs—but the effect is very similar in both. His figures of speech are metaphors run mad, and his grammar is often none at all. Yet there are as fine individual passages to be found in the poems of Dr. Chivers as in those of any poet whatsoever."

Complete Works, E. L. Chase and L. F. Parke, eds., Providence, R. I., 1957 *et seq.*
S. F. Damon, *Thomas Holley Chivers, Friend of Poe*, New York, 1930.
C. H. Watts, *Thomas Holley Chivers, His Literary Career and His Poetry*, Athens, Georgia, 1956.

FAITH

Faith is the flower that blooms unseen
By mountains of immortal green—
A hoped-for harvest in the skies,
In which the reaper never dies—
A tree to which the power is given
To lift its branches into heaven;
And from whose boughs of gorgeous fruit
A loftier tree shall take its root.

Lord! we are grafted into thine,
When broken off from Adam's vine;   10
And so, from that degenerate tree,
We grow into the life of thee!
For, by the prunings of thy word,
Are we then purged into the Lord;
And like Mount Zion we shall stand
The Temples of our native land.

Lord! if the stars should take their flight,
And vanish from the halls of night;
And if the morning should appear,
And vanish from the evening near;   20
And if the rivers should run dry,
And every flower that decks them die;
And if the world should cease to be—
I would not lose my trust in thee.
1827   1837

THE DYING BEAUTY

She died in beauty, like the moon that rose
  In golden glory on the brow of night,
And passed off gently, like the evening's close,
  When day's last steps upon the heavens are
    bright.
She died in beauty, like the trampled flower
  That yields its fragrance to the passer's feet,
For all her life was as an April shower,
  That kept the tear-drops of her parting
    sweet.
And like the rainbows of the sunny skies,
  The dew-drop fillet of the brow of even—   10
That blends its colours as the evening dies—
  Her beauty melted in the light of heaven.

She died in softness, like the last sad tone
  That lingers gently on the midnight ear,
When beauty wanders from her bower alone,
  And no one answers, but the voice is near.
She died in beauty, like the lonesome dove
  That seeks her fledglings in the desert air,
And hastes away from out the flowery grove
  To seek the little ones that nestled there.   20
And like the humming-bird that seeks the
    bower,
  But wings her swiftly from the place away,
And bears the dew-drop from the fading
    flower—
  Her spirit wandered to the isle of day.

She died in meekness, like the noiseless lamb
  When slain upon the altar by the knife,
And lay reclining on her couch so calm,
  That all who saw her said she still had life.
She died in softness, like the Dorian flute,
  When heard melodious on the hills at
    night,   30
When every voice but that loved one is mute,
  And all the holy heavens above are bright.
And like the turtle that has lost her love,
  She hastened quickly from the world to rest,
And passed off gently to the realms above,
  To reign forever in her FATHER'S breast.

She died in glory, like the setting sun,
  Whose radiance mingles with the azure skies,
That blends so softly they appear but one,
  And, dying, lives the life that never dies. 40
She died in sweetness, like the ocean shell,
  Whose tones are lost upon the moaning deep,
And lay so calmly that we could not tell
  Her slumber differed from an infant's sleep.
And like the lake with swans upon its breast,
  The ripples waving to the reedy shore—
She settled softly to her final rest,
  And met her Father to be grieved no more.
                                        1837

SONNET,—TO ISA SLEEPING

Sleep on, and dream of Heaven awhile!—Rogers.

As graceful as the Babylonian willow
Bending, at noontide, over some clear stream
In Palestine, in beauty did she seem
Upon the cygnet-down of her soft pillow;
And now her breast heaved like some gentle
    billow
Swayed by the presence of the full round
    moon—
Voluptuous as the summer South at noon—
Her cheeks as rosy as the radiant dawn,
When heaven is cloudless! When she breathed,
    the air
Around was perfume! Timid as the fawn,   10
And meeker than the dove, her soft words were

Like gentle music heard at night, when all
Around is still—until the soul of care
Was soothed, as noontime by some waterfall.
1838　　　　　　　　　　　　　　　　1845

APOLLO

What are stars, but hieroglyphics of God's glory
　　writ in lightning
　　On the wide-unfolded pages of the azure
　　scroll above?
But the quenchless apotheoses of thoughts for-
　　ever brightening
　　In the mighty Mind immortal of the God
　　whose name is Love?
Diamond letters sculptured, rising, on the azure
　　ether pages,
　　That now sing to one another—unto one
　　another shine—
God's eternal scripture talking, through the
　　midnight, to the Ages,
　　Of the life that is immortal, of the life that
　　is divine—
Life that *cannot* be immortal, but the life
　　that is divine.

Like some deep impetuous river from the
　　fountains everlasting,　　　　　　　　10
　　Down the serpentine soft valley of the vistas
　　of all Time,
Over cataracts of adamant uplifted into moun-
　　tains,

Soared his soul to God in thunder on the
　　wings of thought sublime.
With the rising golden glory of the sun in
　　ministrations,
　　Making oceans metropolitan of splendor for
　　the dawn—
Piling pyramid on pyramid of music for the
　　nations—
　　Sings the Angel who sits shining everlasting
　　in the sun,
　　For the stars, which are the echoes of the
　　shining of the sun.

Like the lightnings piled on lightnings, ever
　　rising, never reaching,
　　In one monument of glory towards the
　　golden gates of God—　　　　　　　　20
Voicing out themselves in thunder upon thun-
　　der in their preaching,
　　Piled this Cyclop up his Epic where the
　　Angels never trod.
Like the fountains everlasting that forever more
　　are flowing
　　From the throne within the centre of the City
　　built on high,
With their genial irrigation life forever more
　　bestowing—
　　Flows his lucid, liquid river through the
　　gardens of the sky,
　　For the stars forever blooming in the gardens
　　of the sky.　　　　　　　　　　　　1853

RALPH WALDO EMERSON

1803–1882

IF EMERSON had died in his late twenties his career would have paralleled that of scores of sober-minded New England young men who endured privation that they might live in the spirit and minister to others. Seven generations of parsons stretched back of him, and a Unitarian pulpit was inevitable. In 1829 he became assistant pastor of the Second Church in Boston. Between his graduation from Harvard in 1821 and the time of his call he had taught school to help support his mother and sisters, attended the Harvard Divinity School, and lived a year in the South for his health. In 1832, a decisive date in his life, he resigned his pastorate because he was not willing to administer the Lord's Supper. The reason was deeper than a disinclination to observe the simple forms of his church. He had written in his journal months before: "In the Bible you are not directed to be a Unitarian, or a Calvinist, or an Episcopalian. . . . If a man is wise he will say to himself, I am not a member of that or of any party. I am God's child, a disciple of Christ, or, in the eye of God, a fellow disciple with Christ. . . . A sect or party is an elegant incognito devised to save a man from the vexation of thinking." Henceforth he would belong to no party; he would devote his life to thinking and to teaching what he had thought out to a conclusion, by occasional preaching, by lecturing near and far over America, and by his published essays.

Immediately following his resignation he traveled in Europe, where he met Landor, Words-worth, Coleridge, and Carlyle. With the last named there opened a friendship which was kept alive by forty years of correspondence. In 1834 he settled in Concord and brought there, in 1835, his second wife, Lydia Jackson. He entered fully into the life of this remarkable village, which could number among its citizens Hawthorne, Thoreau, the Alcotts, and Margaret Fuller. His first civic office, scrupulously filled, was that of hog-reeve. He tried out his new lectures on the audience of the local Lyceum, where even those who could not follow the argument listened approvingly because they loved the man.

All his life Emerson kept a journal, half-diary, half a collection of *pensées*. From time to time he gathered together the best things he had written down on Friendship or Nature or History or Manners and molded them into a lecture. When this had been delivered for a season—his annual lecture tours supplied a good share of the family income—it was later reworked into an essay. His first book was *Nature* (1836) which contains, in germ, most of his principal ideas. In 1837 came the vigorous Phi Beta Kappa address at Harvard, "The American Scholar," and in 1838 he angered the orthodox clergy of New England by his Divinity School Address before the graduating class. Not for many years was he again welcome in the lecture rooms of his Alma Mater. *Essays*, in two series, appeared in 1841 and 1844. His other books are *Poems* (1847), *Representative Men* (1850), *English Traits* (1856), *Conduct of Life* (1860), *May Day and Other Pieces* (1867), *Society and Solitude* (1870), and *Letters and Social Aims* (1875).

In his last years Emerson had a host of disciples among those in the West who had awaited his lectures year after year and in men of ability like Moncure D. Conway and James Cabot, his biographer, who had been fired in their youth by his iconoclastic teaching. This time of his fame was clouded by aphasia, so that at the end the poet and thinker whose words had such power could no longer even name his friends.

Emerson is not a philosopher in the sense that he constructed a self-contained system, written down in the language of the schools. But he is by no means the eclectic thinker some critics, Matthew Arnold among them, have made him out to be. The general outline of a consistent philosophy is to be found in his lectures and essays. What is more important, one can trace a development in his thought, as the facts of the new science were borne in upon him, from the first somewhat misty idealism, tending toward pantheism, to a kind of evolutionary monism. Even in his early period he can speak of "the Efficient Nature, *natura naturans*, the quick cause before which all forms flee as the driven snows; itself secret, its works driven before it in flocks and multitudes . . . arriving at consummate results without shock or leap." His earlier position is best represented by the rapturous *Nature*, but the transcendental views expressed in it were soon modified. These changes are clearly seen in his "Method of Nature," an address delivered at Waterville, Maine, in 1841.

The characteristics of Emerson's style, to some extent devices deliberately employed, tend to conceal the essential unity of his thought. His words pour out in a staccato enthusiasm which distracts one from the logical structure beneath. Instead of argument he uses parable, analogy, and image. To shock his materialistic countrymen out of their complacency he speaks hyper-bolically and in absolutes. The whole tone is prophetic. Thus it is that one finds the premises of his thought only after reading many of his essays and so meeting again and again, in new guises, his leading ideas.

Emerson's emphasis on the necessity of individual self-reliance, his doctrine of compensation, for which he has often been called a blind optimist, his idea of the over-soul—each of these peculiar Emersonian concepts is derived from his intuitions of Nature. Of many key-sentences one might choose, these two may suffice to show the foundations on which the essays rest: "Let man, then, learn the revelation of all nature and all thought to his heart; this namely, that the Highest dwells with him: that the sources of nature are in his own mind, if the sentiment of duty is there." "Our compound nature differences us from God, but our reason is not to be distinguished from the Divine Essence. . . . It is in all men, even the worst, and constitutes them men. In bad men it is dormant, in the good efficient, but it is perfect and identical in all, underneath the peculiarities, the vices, and the errors of the individual."

Floyd Stovall, "Emerson," in *Eight American Authors, A Review of Research and Criticism*, New York, 1956, pp. 47–99.

The Complete Works of Ralph Waldo Emerson, 12 vols., Boston, 1903–1904.

The Journals of Ralph Waldo Emerson, E. W. Emerson and W. E. Forbes, eds., 10 vols., Boston, 1900–1914.

The Letters of Ralph Waldo Emerson, R. L. Rusk, ed., 6 vols., New York, 1939.

The Journals and Miscellaneous Notebooks of Ralph Waldo Emerson. W. H. Gilman, Cambridge, 1960.

J. E. Cabot, *A Memoir of Ralph Waldo Emerson*, 2 vols., Boston, 1887.

F. I. Carpenter, *Emerson and Asia*, Cambridge, 1930.

———, *Emerson Handbook*, New York, 1953.

H. D. Gray, *Emerson: A Statement of New England Transcendentalism as Expressed in the Philosophy of its Chief Exponent*, Stanford, 1917.

V. C. Hopkins, *Spires of Form: A Study of Emerson's Aesthetic Theory*, Cambridge, 1951.

R. L. Rusk, *The Life of Ralph Waldo Emerson*, New York (1949), 1957.

Stephen Whicher, *Freedom and Fate: An Inner Life of Ralph Waldo Emerson*, Philadelphia, 1953.

THE RHODORA

On Being Asked, Whence Is the Flower?

In May, when sea-winds pierced our solitudes,
I found the fresh Rhodora in the woods,
Spreading its leafless blooms in a damp nook,
To please the desert and the sluggish brook.
The purple petals, fallen in the pool,
Made the black water with their beauty gay;
Here might the red-bird come his plumes to cool,
And court the flower that cheapens his array.
Rhodora! if the sages ask thee why
This charm is wasted on the earth and sky,   10
Tell them, dear, that if eyes were made for seeing,
Then Beauty is its own excuse for being:
Why thou wert there, O rival of the rose!
I never thought to ask, I never knew:
But, in my simple ignorance, suppose
The self-same Power that brought me there
    brought you.

1834   1839

EACH AND ALL

Little thinks, in the field, yon red-cloaked
    clown
Of thee from the hill-top looking down;
The heifer that lows in the upland farm,
Far-heard, lows not thine ear to charm;
The sexton, tolling his bell at noon,
Deems not that great Napoleon
Stops his horse, and lists with delight,
Whilst his files sweep round yon Alpine height;
Nor knowest thou what argument
Thy life to thy neighbor's creed has lent.   10
All are needed by each one;
Nothing is fair or good alone.
I thought the sparrow's note from heaven,
Singing at dawn on the alder bough;
I brought him home, in his nest, at even;
He sings the song, but it pleases not now,
For I did not bring home the river and sky;—
He sang to my ear,—they sang to my eye.
The delicate shells lay on the shore;
The bubbles of the latest wave   20
Fresh pearls to their enamel gave;

And the bellowing of the savage sea
Greeted their safe escape to me.
I wiped away the weeds and foam,
I fetched my sea-born treasures home;
But the poor, unsightly, noisome things
Had left their beauty on the shore
With the sun and the sand and the wild uproar.
The lover watched his graceful maid,
As 'mid the virgin train she strayed, 30
Nor knew her beauty's best attire
Was woven by the snow-white choir.
At last she came to his hermitage,
Like the bird from the woodlands to the
    cage;—
The gay enchantment was undone,
A gentle wife, but fairy none.
Then I said, "I covet truth;
Beauty is unripe childhood's cheat;
I leave it behind with the games of youth:"—
As I spoke, beneath my feet 40
The ground-pine curled its pretty wreath,
Running over the club-moss burrs;
I inhaled the violet's breath;
Around me stood the oaks and firs;
Pine-cones and acorns lay on the ground;
Over me soared the eternal sky,
Full of light and of deity;
Again I saw, again I heard,
The rolling river, the morning bird;—
Beauty through my senses stole; 50
I yielded myself to the perfect whole.
? 1834   1839

CONCORD HYMN

Sung at the Completion of the
Battle Monument, July 4, 1837

By the rude bridge that arched the flood,
    Their flag to April's breeze unfurled,
Here once the embattled farmers stood
    And fired the shot heard round the world.

The foe long since in silence slept;
    Alike the conqueror silent sleeps;
And Time the ruined bridge has swept
    Down the dark stream which seaward creeps.

On this green bank, by this soft stream,
    We set to-day a votive stone; 10
That memory may their deed redeem,
    When, like our sires, our sons are gone.

Spirit, that made those heroes dare
    To die, and leave their children free,

Bid Time and Nature gently spare
    The shaft we raise to them and thee.

THE PROBLEM

I like a church; I like a cowl;
I love a prophet of the soul;
And on my heart monastic aisles
Fall like sweet strains, or pensive smiles;
Yet not for all his faith can see
Would I that cowlèd churchman be.

Why should the vest on him allure,
Which I could not on me endure?

Not from a vain or shallow thought
His awful Jove young Phidias brought; 10
Never from lips of cunning fell
The thrilling Delphic oracle;
Out from the heart of nature rolled
The burdens of the Bible old;
The litanies of nations came,
Like the volcano's tongue of flame,
Up from the burning core below,—
The canticles of love and woe:
The hand that rounded Peter's dome
And groined the aisles of Christian Rome 20
Wrought in a sad sincerity:
Himself from God he could not free;
He builded better than he knew;—
The conscious stone to beauty grew.

Know'st thou what wove yon woodbird's nest
Of leaves, and feathers from her breast?
Or how the fish outbuilt her shell,
Painting with morn her annual cell?
Or how the sacred pine-tree adds
To her old leaves new myriads? 30
Such and so grew these holy piles,
Whilst love and terror laid the tiles.
Earth proudly wears the Parthenon,
As the best gem upon her zone,
And Morning opes with haste her lids
To gaze upon the Pyramids;
O'er England's abbeys bends the sky,
As on its friends, with kindred eye;
For out of Thought's interior sphere
These wonders rose to upper air; 40
And Nature gladly gave them place,
Adopted them into her race,
And granted them an equal date
With Andes and with Ararat.

These temples grew as grows the grass;
Art might obey, but not surpass.

The passive Master lent his hand
To the vast soul that o'er him planned;
And the same power that reared the shrine
Bestrode the tribes that knelt within.   50
Ever the fiery Pentecost
Girds with one flame the countless host,
Trances the heart through chanting choirs,
And through the priest the mind inspires.
The word unto the prophet spoken
Was writ on tables yet unbroken;
The word by seers or sibyls told,
In groves of oak, or fanes of gold,
Still floats upon the morning wind,
Still whispers to the willing mind.   60
One accent of the Holy Ghost
The heedless world hath never lost.
I know what say the fathers wise,—
The Book itself before me lies,
Old *Chrysostom*, best Augustine,
And he who blent both in his line,
The younger *Golden Lips* or mines,
Taylor, the Shakespeare of divines.
His words are music in my ear,
I see his cowlèd portrait dear;   70
And yet, for all his faith could see,
I would not the good bishop be.
1839   1840

URIEL

It fell in the ancient periods
    Which the brooding soul surveys,
Or ever the wild Time coined itself
    Into calendar months and days.

This was the lapse of Uriel,
Which in Paradise befell.
Once, among the Pleiads walking,
Seyd overheard the young gods talking;
And the treason, too long pent,
To his ears was evident.   10
The young deities discussed
Laws of form, and metre just,
Orb, quintessence, and sunbeams,
What subsisteth, and what seems.
One, with low tones that decide,
And doubt and reverend use defied,
With a look that solved the sphere,
And stirred the devils everywhere,
Gave his sentiment divine
Against the being of a line.   20
"Line in nature is not found;
Unit and universe are round;
In vain produced, all rays return;

Evil will bless, and ice will burn."
As Uriel spoke with piercing eye,
A shudder ran around the sky;
The stern old war-gods shook their heads,
The seraphs frowned from myrtle-beds;
Seemed to the holy festival
The rash word boded ill to all;   30
The balance-beam of Fate was bent;
The bounds of good and ill were rent;
Strong Hades could not keep his own,
But all slid to confusion.

A sad self-knowledge, withering, fell
On the beauty of Uriel;
In heaven once eminent, the god
Withdrew, that hour, into his cloud;
Whether doomed to long gyration
In the sea of generation,   40
Or by knowledge grown too bright
To hit the nerve of feebler sight.
Straightway, a forgetting wind
Stole over the celestial kind,
And their lips the secret kept,
If in ashes the fire-seed slept.
But now and then, truth-speaking things
Shamed the angels' veiling wings;
And, shrilling from the solar course,
Or from fruit of chemic force,   50
Procession of a soul in matter,
Or the speeding change of water,
Or out of the good of evil born,
Came Uriel's voice of cherub scorn,
And a blush tinged the upper sky,
And the gods shook, they knew not why.
1838   1846

THE SNOW-STORM

Announced by all the trumpets of the sky,
Arrives the snow, and, driving o'er the fields,
Seems nowhere to alight: the whited air
Hides hills and woods, the river, and the
    heaven,
And veils the farm-house at the garden's end.
The sled and traveller stopped, the courier's
    feet
Delayed, all friends shut out, the housemates
    sit
Around the radiant fireplace, enclosed
In a tumultuous privacy of storm.

Come see the north-wind's masonry.   10
Out of an unseen quarry evermore
Furnished with tile, the fierce artificer

Curves his white bastions with projected roof
Round every windward stake, or tree, or door.
Speeding, the myriad-handed, his wild work
So fanciful, so savage, nought cares he
For number or proportion. Mockingly,
On coop or kennel he hangs Parian wreaths;
A swan-like form invests the hidden thorn;
Fills up the farmer's lane from wall to wall,   20
Maugre the farmer's sighs; and at the gate
A tapering turret overtops the work.
And when his hours are numbered, and the
    world
Is all his own, retiring, as he were not,
Leaves, when the sun appears, astonished Art
To mimic in slow structures, stone by stone,
Built in an age, the mad wind's night-work,
The frolic architecture of the snow.   1841

THE SPHINX

The Sphinx is drowsy,
    Her wings are furled:
Her ear is heavy,
    She broods on the world.
"Who'll tell me my secret,
    The ages have kept?—
I awaited the seer
    While they slumbered and slept:—

"The fate of the man-child,
    The meaning of man;   10
Known fruit of the unknown;
    Dædalian plan;
Out of sleeping a waking,
    Out of waking a sleep;
Life death overtaking;
    Deep underneath deep?

"Erect as a sunbeam,
    Upspringeth the palm;
The elephant browses,
    Undaunted and calm;   20
In beautiful motion
    The thrush plies his wings;
Kind leaves of his covert,
    Your silence he sings.

"The waves, unashamèd,
    In difference sweet,
Play glad with the breezes,
    Old playfellows meet;
The journeying atoms,
    Primordial wholes,   30
Firmly draw, firmly drive,
    By their animate poles.

"Sea, earth, air, sound, silence,
    Plant, quadruped, bird,
By one music enchanted,
    One deity stirred,—
Each the other adorning,
    Accompany still;
Night veileth the morning,
    The vapor the hill.   40

"The babe by its mother
    Lies bathèd in joy;
Glide its hours uncounted,—
    The sun is its toy;
Shines the peace of all being,
    Without cloud, in its eyes;
And the sum of the world
    In soft miniature lies.

"But man crouches and blushes,
    Absconds and conceals;   50
He creepeth and peepeth,
    He palters and steals;
Infirm, melancholy,
    Jealous glancing around,
An oaf, an accomplice,
    He poisons the ground.

"Out spoke the great mother,
    Beholding his fear;—
At the sound of her accents
    Cold shuddered the sphere:—   60
'Who has drugged my boy's cup?
    Who has mixed my boy's bread?
Who, with sadness and madness,
    Has turned my child's head?'"

I heard a poet answer
    Aloud and cheerfully,
"Say on, sweet Sphinx! thy dirges
    Are pleasant songs to me.
Deep love lieth under
    These pictures of time;   70
They fade in the light of
    Their meaning sublime.

"The fiend that man harries
    Is love of the Best;
Yawns the pit of the Dragon,
    Lit by rays from the Blest.
The Lethe of Nature
    Can't trance him again,
Whose soul sees the perfect,
    Which his eyes seek in vain.   80

"To vision profounder,
    Man's spirit must dive;

His aye-rolling orb
  At no goal will arrive;
The heavens that now draw him
  With sweetness untold,
Once found,—for new heavens
  He spurneth the old.

"Pride ruined the angels,
  Their shame them restores;   90
Lurks the joy that is sweetest
  In stings of remorse.
Have I a lover
  Who is noble and free?—
I would he were nobler
  Than to love me.

"Eterne alternation
  Now follows, now flies;
And under pain, pleasure,—
  Under pleasure, pain lies.   100
Love works at the centre,
  Heart-heaving alway;
Forth speed the strong pulses
  To the borders of day.

"Dull Sphinx, Jove keep thy five wits;
  Thy sight is growing blear;
Rue, myrrh, and cummin for the Sphinx,
  Her muddy eyes to clear!"
The old Sphinx bit her thick lip,—
  Said, "Who taught thee me to name? 110
I am thy spirit, yoke-fellow;
  Of thine eye I am eyebeam.

"Thou art the unanswered question;
  Couldst see thy proper eye,
Alway it asketh, asketh;
  And each answer is a lie.
So take thy quest through nature,
  It through thousand natures ply;
Ask on, thou clothed eternity;
  Time is the false reply."   120

Uprose the merry Sphinx,
  And crouched no more in stone;
She melted into purple cloud,
  She silvered in the moon;
She spired into a yellow flame;
  She flowered in blossoms red;
She flowed into a foaming wave:
  She stood Monadnoc's head.

Through a thousand voices
  Spoke the universal dame;   130
"Who telleth one of my meanings
  Is master of all I am."   1841

BACCHUS

Bring me wine, but wine which never grew
In the belly of the grape,
Or grew on vine whose tap-roots, reaching
  through
Under the Andes to the Cape,
Suffered no savor of the earth to scape.

Let its grapes the morn salute
From a nocturnal root,
Which feels the acrid juice
Of Styx and Erebus;
And turns the woe of Night,   10
By its own craft, to a more rich delight.

We buy ashes for bread;
We buy diluted wine;
Give me of the true,—
Whose ample leaves and tendrils curled
Among the silver hills of heaven,
Draw everlasting dew;
Wine of wine,
Blood of the world,
Form of forms, and mould of statures,   20
That I intoxicated,
And by the draught assimilated,
May float at pleasure through all natures;
The bird-language rightly spell,
And that which roses say so well.

Wine that is shed
Like the torrents of the sun
Up the horizon walls,
Or like the Atlantic streams, which run
When the South Sea calls.   30

Water and bread,
Food which needs no transmuting,
Rainbow-flowering, wisdom-fruiting,
Wine which is already man,
Food which teach and reason can.

Wine which Music is,—
Music and wine are one,—
That I, drinking this,
Shall hear far Chaos talk with me;
Kings unborn shall walk with me;   40
And the poor grass shall plot and plan
What it will do when it is man.
Quickened so, will I unlock
Every crypt of every rock.

I thank the joyful juice
For all I know;—

Winds of remembering
Of the ancient being blow,
And seeming-solid walls of use
Open and flow.   50

Pour, Bacchus! the remembering wine;
Retrieve the loss of me and mine!
Vine for vine be antidote,
And the grape requite the lote!
Haste to cure the old despair,—
Reason in Nature's lotus drenched,
The memory of ages quenched;
Give them again to shine;
Let wine repair what this undid;
And where the infection slid,   60
A dazzling memory revive;
Refresh the faded tints,
Recut the aged prints,
And write my old adventures with the pen
Which on the first day drew,
Upon the tablets blue,
The dancing Pleiads and eternal men.
1846   1847

ODE

Inscribed to W. H. Channing [1]

Though loath to grieve
The evil time's sole patriot,
I cannot leave
My honied thought
For the priest's cant,
Or statesman's rant.

If I refuse
My study for their politique,
Which at the best is trick,
The angry Muse   10
Puts confusion in my brain.

But who is he that prates
Of the culture of mankind,
Of better arts and life?
Go, blindworm, go,
Behold the famous States
Harrying Mexico
With rifle and with knife!

Or who, with accent bolder,
Dare praise the freedom-loving mountaineer? 20

I found by thee, O rushing Contoocook!
And in thy valleys, Agiochook!
The jackals of the negro-holder.

The God who made New Hampshire
Taunted the lofty land
With little men;—
Small bat and wren
House in the oak:—
If earth-fire cleave
The upheaved land, and bury the folk,   30
The southern crocodile would grieve.
Virtue palters; Right is hence;
Freedom praised, but hid;
Funeral eloquence
Rattles the coffin-lid.

What boots thy zeal,
O glowing friend,
That would indignant rend
The northland from the south?
Wherefore? to what good end?   40
Boston Bay and Bunker Hill
Would serve things still;—
Things are of the snake.

The horseman serves the horse,
The neatherd serves the neat,
The merchant serves the purse,
The eater serves his meat;
'Tis the day of the chattel,
Web to weave, and corn to grind;
Things are in the saddle,   50
And ride mankind.

There are two laws discrete,
Not reconciled,—
Law for man, and law for thing;
The last builds town and fleet,
But it runs wild,
And doth the man unking.

'Tis fit the forest fall,
The steep be graded,
The mountain tunnelled,   60
The sand shaded,
The orchard planted,
The glebe tilled,
The prairie granted,
The steamer built.

Let man serve law for man;
Live for friendship, live for love,
For truth's and harmony's behoof;

[1] The nephew of William Ellery Channing, the famous Unitarian preacher, was a zealous humanitarian. Though Emerson, in this poem, refuses to join actively in the antislavery movement, at the time of John Brown's crusade he changed his position and began to speak out eloquently on abolition.

The state may follow how it can,
As Olympus follows Jove.   70

   Yet do not I implore
The wrinkled shopman to my sounding woods,
Nor bid the unwilling senator
Ask votes of thrushes in the solitudes.
Every one to his chosen work;—
Foolish hands may mix and mar;
Wise and sure the issues are.
Round they roll till dark is light,
Sex to sex, and even to odd;—
The over-god   80
Who marries Right to Might,
Who peoples, unpeoples,—
He who exterminates
Races by stronger races,
Black by white faces,—
Knows to bring honey
Out of the lion;
Grafts gentlest scion
On pirate and Turk.

The Cossack eats Poland,   90
Like stolen fruit;
Her last noble is ruined,
Her last poet mute:
Straight, into double band
The victors divide;
Half for freedom strike and stand;—
The astonished Muse finds thousands at her
   side.   1847

MUSKETAQUID [2]

Because I was content with these poor fields,
Low, open meads, slender and sluggish streams,
And found a home in haunts which others
   scorned,
The partial wood-gods overpaid my love,
And granted me the freedom of their state,
And in their secret senate have prevailed
With the dear, dangerous lords that rule our
   life,
Made moon and planets parties to their bond,
And through my rock-like, solitary wont
Shot million rays of thought and tenderness. 10
For me, in showers, in sweeping showers, the
   Spring
Visits the valley;—break away the clouds,—
I bathe in the morn's soft and silvered air,
And loiter willing by yon loitering stream.
Sparrows far off, and nearer, April's bird,
Blue-coated,—flying before from tree to tree,

[2] The Concord River.

Courageous sing a delicate overture
To lead the tardy concert of the year.
Onward and nearer rides the sun of May;
And wide around, the marriage of the plants 20
Is sweetly solemnized. Then flows amain
The surge of summer's beauty; dell and crag,
Hollow and lake, hillside, and pine arcade,
Are touched with genius. Yonder ragged cliff
Has thousand faces in a thousand hours.

Beneath low hills, in the broad interval
Through which at will our Indian rivulet
Winds mindful still of sannup and of squaw,
Whose pipe and arrow oft the plough unburies,
Here in pine houses built of new-fallen trees, 30
Supplanters of the tribe, the farmers dwell.
Traveller, to thee, perchance, a tedious road,
Or, it may be, a picture; to these men,
The landscape is an armory of powers,
Which, one by one, they know to draw and use.
They harness beast, bird, insect, to their work;
They prove the virtues of each bed of rock,
And, like the chemist 'mid his loaded jars,
Draw from each stratum its adapted use
To drug their crops or weapon their arts
   withal.   40
They turn the frost upon their chemic heap,
They set the wind to winnow pulse and grain,
They thank the spring-flood for its fertile slime,
And, on cheap summit-levels of the snow,
Slide with the sledge to inaccessible woods
O'er meadows bottomless. So, year by year,
They fight the elements with elements,
(That one would say, meadow and forest
   walked,
Transmuted in these men to rule their like,)
And by the order in the field disclose   50
The order regnant in the yeoman's brain.

What these strong masters wrote at large in
   miles,
I followed in small copy in my acre;
For there's no rood has not a star above it;
The cordial quality of pear or plum
Ascends as gladly in a single tree
As in broad orchards resonant with bees;
And every atom poises for itself,
And for the whole. The gentle deities
Showed me the lore of colors and of sounds, 60
The innumerable tenements of beauty,
The miracle of generative force,
Far-reaching concords of astronomy
Felt in the plants and in the punctual birds;
Better, the linkèd purpose of the whole,
And, chiefest prize, found I true liberty
In the glad home plain-dealing nature gave.

The polite found me impolite; the great
Would mortify me, but in vain; for still
I am a willow of the wilderness,   70
Loving the wind that bent me. All my hurts
My garden spade can heal. A woodland walk,
A quest of river-grapes, a mocking thrush,
A wild-rose, or rock-loving columbine,
Salve my worst wounds.
For thus the wood-gods murmured in my ear:
"Dost love our manners? Canst thou silent lie?
Canst thou, thy pride forgot, like nature pass
Into the winter night's extinguished mood?
Canst thou shine now, then darkle,   80
And being latent feel thyself no less?
As, when the all-worshipped moon attracts the
    eye,
The river, hill, stems, foliage are obscure,
Yet envies none, none are unenviable."
                                                         1847

THE APOLOGY

Think me not unkind and rude
    That I walk alone in grove and glen;
I go to the god of the wood
    To fetch his word to men.

Tax not my sloth that I
    Fold my arms beside the brook;
Each cloud that floated in the sky
    Writes a letter in my book.

Chide me not, laborious band,
    For the idle flowers I brought;   10
Every aster in my hand
    Goes home loaded with a thought.

There was never mystery
    But 't is figured in the flowers;
Was never secret history
    But birds tell it in the bowers.

One harvest from thy field
    Homeward brought the oxen strong;
A second crop thine acres yield
    Which I gather in a song.   20
                                                      1847

HAMATREYA [3]

Bulkeley, Hunt, Willard, Hosmer, Meriam,
    Flint,

[3] This poem reflects the idea in a passage in the *Vishnu Purana*
which Emerson copied into his journal in 1845: "These were the
verses, Maitreya, which earth recited and by listening to which ambition fades away like snow before the sun."

Possessed the land which rendered to their toil
Hay, corn, roots, hemp, flax, apples, wool and
    wood.
Each of these landlords walked amidst his
    farm,
Saying, " 'Tis mine, my children's and my
    name's.
How sweet the west wind sounds in my own
    trees!
How graceful climb those shadows on my hill!
I fancy these pure waters and the flags
Know me, as does my dog: we sympathize;
And, I affirm, my actions smack of the soil." 10

Where are these men? Asleep beneath their
    grounds:
And strangers, fond as they, their furrows
    plough.
Earth laughs in flowers, to see her boastful
    boys
Earth-proud, proud of the earth which is not
    theirs;
Who steer the plough, but cannot steer their
    feet
Clear of the grave.
They added ridge to valley, brook to pond,
And sighed for all that bounded their domain;
"This suits me for a pasture; that's my park;
We must have clay, lime, gravel, granite-
    ledge,   20
And misty lowland, where to go for peat.
The land is well,—lies fairly to the south.
'Tis good, when you have crossed the sea and
    back,
To find the sitfast acres where you left them."
Ah! the hot owner sees not Death, who adds
Him to his land, a lump of mould the more.
Hear what the Earth says:

EARTH-SONG

"Mine and yours;
Mine, not yours.
Earth endures;   30
Stars abide—
Shine down in the old sea;
Old are the shores;
But where are old men?
I who have seen much,
Such have I never seen.

"The lawyer's deed
Ran sure,
In tail,
To them, and to their heirs   40

Who shall succeed,
Without fail,
Forevermore.

"Here is the land,
Shaggy with wood,
With its old valley,
Mound and flood.
But the heritors?—
Fled like the flood's foam.
The lawyer, and the laws,   50
And the kingdom,
Clean swept herefrom.

"They called me theirs,
Who so controlled me;
Yet every one
Wished to stay, and is gone,
How am I theirs,
If they cannot hold me,
But I hold them?"

When I heard the Earth-song   60
I was no longer brave;
My avarice cooled
Like lust in the chill of the grave.   1847

DAYS

Daughters of Time, the hypocritic Days,
Muffled and dumb like barefoot dervishes,
And marching single in an endless file,
Bring diadems and fagots in their hands.
To each they offer gifts after his will,
Bread, kingdoms, stars, and sky that holds them
    all.
I, in my pleachèd garden, watched the pomp,
Forgot my morning wishes, hastily
Took a few herbs and apples, and the Day
Turned and departed silent. I, too late,   10
Under her solemn fillet saw the scorn.
1852   1857

WALDEINSAMKEIT

I do not count the hours I spend
In wandering by the sea;
The forest is my loyal friend,
Like God it useth me.

In plains that room for shadows make
Of skirting hills to lie,
Bound in by streams which give and take
Their colors from the sky;

Or on the mountain-crest sublime,
Or down the oaken glade,   10
O what have I to do with time?
For this the day was made.

Cities of mortals woe-begone
Fantastic care derides,
But in the serious landscape lone
Stern benefit abides.

Sheen will tarnish, honey cloy,
And merry is only a mask of sad,
But, sober on a fund of joy,
The woods at heart are glad.   20

There the great Planter plants
Of fruitful worlds the grain,
And with a million spells enchants
The souls that walk in pain.

Still on the seeds of all he made
The rose of beauty burns;
Through times that wear and forms that fade,
Immortal youth returns.

The black ducks mounting from the lake,
The pigeon in the pines,   30
The bittern's boom, a desert make
Which no false art refines.

Down in yon watery nook,
Where bearded mists divide,
The gray old gods whom Chaos knew,
The sires of Nature, hide.

Aloft, in secret veins of air,
Blows the sweet breath of song,
O, few to scale those uplands dare,
Though they to all belong!   40

See thou bring not to field or stone
The fancies found in books;
Leave authors' eyes, and fetch your own,
To brave the landscape's looks.

Oblivion here thy wisdom is,
Thy thrift, the sleep of cares;
For a proud idleness like this
Crowns all thy mean affairs.
1857   1858

BRAHMA

If the red slayer think he slays,
    Or if the slain think he is slain,

They know not well the subtle ways
  I keep, and pass, and turn again.

Far or forgot to me is near;
  Shadow and sunlight are the same;
The vanished gods to me appear;
  And one to me are shame and fame.

They reckon ill who leave me out;
  When me they fly, I am the wings;   10
I am the doubter and the doubt,
  And I the hymn the Brahmin sings.

The strong gods pine for my abode,
  And pine in vain the sacred Seven;
But thou, meek lover of the good!
  Find me, and turn thy back on heaven.
1856   1857

TWO RIVERS

Thy summer voice, Musketaquit,
Repeats the music of the rain;
But sweeter rivers pulsing flit
Through thee, as thou through Concord Plain.

Thou in thy narrow banks art pent:
The stream I love unbounded goes
Through flood and sea and firmament;
Through light, through life, it forward flows.

I see the inundation sweet,
I hear the spending of the stream   10
Through years, through men, through Nature
    fleet,
Through love and thought, through power and
    dream.

Musketaquit, a goblin strong,
Of shard and flint makes jewels gay;
They lose their grief who hear his song,
And where he winds is the day of day.

So forth and brighter fares my stream,—
Who drink it shall not thirst again;
No darkness stains its equal gleam,
And ages drop in it like rain.   20
1856   1858

SEASHORE

I heard or seemed to hear the chiding Sea
Say, Pilgrim, why so late and slow to come?
Am I not always here, thy summer home?

Is not my voice thy music, morn and eve?
My breath thy healthful climate in the heats,
My touch thy antidote, my bay thy bath?
Was ever building like my terraces?
Was ever couch magnificent as mine?
Lie on the warm rock-ledges, and there learn
A little hut suffices like a town.   10
I make your sculptured architecture vain,
Vain beside mine. I drive my wedges home,
And carve the coastwise mountain into caves.
Lo! here is Rome and Nineveh and Thebes,
Karnak and Pyramid and Giant's Stairs
Half piled or prostrate; and my newest slab
Older than all thy race.

              Behold the Sea,
The opaline, the plentiful and strong,
Yet beautiful as is the rose in June,
Fresh as the trickling rainbow of July;   20
Sea full of food, the nourisher of kinds,
Purger of earth, and medicine of men;
Creating a sweet climate by my breath,
Washing out harms and griefs from memory,
And, in my mathematic ebb and flow,
Giving a hint of that which changes not.
Rich are the sea-gods:—who gives gifts but
    they?
They grope the sea for pearls, but more than
    pearls:
They pluck Force thence, and give it to the
    wise.
For every wave is wealth to Dædalus,   30
Wealth to the cunning artist who can work
This matchless strength. Where shall he find,
    O waves!
A load your Atlas shoulders cannot lift?

I with my hammer pounding evermore
The rocky coast, smite Andes into dust,
Strewing my bed, and, in another age,
Rebuild a continent of better men.
Then I unbar the doors: my paths lead out
The exodus of nations: I disperse
Men to all shores that front the hoary main. 40

  I too have arts and sorceries;
Illusion dwells forever with the wave.
I know what spells are laid. Leave me to deal
With credulous and imaginative man;
For, though he scoop my water in his palm,
A few rods off he deems it gems and clouds.
Planting strange fruits and sunshine on the
    shore,
I make some coast alluring, some lone isle,
To distant men, who must go there, or die.
c. 1857   1867

» » NATURE « «

A subtle chain of countless rings
The next unto the farthest brings;
The eye reads omens where it goes,
And speaks all languages the rose;
And, striving to be man, the worm
Mounts through all the spires of form.

INTRODUCTION

Our age is retrospective. It builds the sepulchres of the fathers. It writes biographies, histories, and criticism. The foregoing generations beheld God and nature face to face; we, through their eyes. Why should not we also enjoy an original relation to the universe? Why should not we have a poetry and philosophy of insight and not of tradition, and a religion by revelation to us, and not the history of theirs? Embosomed for a season in nature, whose floods of life stream around and through us, and invite us by the powers they supply, to action proportioned to nature, why should we grope among the dry bones of the past, or put the living generation into masquerade out of its faded wardrobe? The sun shines to-day also. There is more wool and flax in the fields. There are new lands, new men, new thoughts. Let us demand our own works and laws and worship.

Undoubtedly we have no questions to ask which are unanswerable. We must trust the perfection of the creation so far, as to believe that whatever curiosity the order of things has awakened in our minds, the order of things can satisfy. Every man's condition is a solution in hieroglyphic to those inquiries he would put. He acts it as life, before he apprehends it as truth. In like manner, nature is already, in its forms and tendencies, describing its own design. Let us interrogate the great apparition that shines so peacefully around us. Let us inquire, to what end is nature?

All science has one aim, namely, to find a theory of nature. We have theories of races and of functions, but scarcely yet a remote approach to an idea of creation. We are now so far from the road to truth, that religious teachers dispute and hate each other, and speculative men are esteemed unsound and frivolous. But to a sound judgment, the most abstract truth is the most practical. Whenever a true theory appears, it will be its own evidence. Its test is, that it will explain all phenomena. Now many are thought not only unexplained but inexplicable; as language, sleep, madness, dreams, beasts, sex.

Philosophically considered, the universe is composed of Nature and the Soul. Strictly speaking, therefore, all that is separate from us, all which Philosophy distinguishes as the NOT ME, that is, both nature and art, all other men and my own body, must be ranked under this name, NATURE. In enumerating the values of nature and casting up their sum, I shall use the word in both senses,—in its common and in its philosophical import. In inquiries so general as our present one, the inaccuracy is not material; no confusion of thought will occur. *Nature*, in the common sense, refers to essences unchanged by man; space, the air, the river, the leaf. *Art* is applied to the mixture of his will with the same things, as in a house, a canal, a statue, a picture. But his operations taken together are so insignificant, a little chipping, baking, patching, and washing, that in an impression so grand as that of the world on the human mind, they do not vary the result.

I. NATURE

To go into solitude, a man needs to retire as much from his chamber as from society. I am not solitary whilst I read and write, though nobody is with me. But if a man would be alone, let him look at the stars. The rays that come from those heavenly worlds will separate between him and what he touches. One might think the atmosphere was made transparent with this design, to give man, in the heavenly bodies, the perpetual presence of the sublime. Seen in the streets of cities, how great they are! If the stars should appear one night in a thousand years, how would men believe and adore; and preserve for many generations the remembrance of the city of God which had been shown! But every night come out these envoys of beauty, and light the universe with their admonishing smile.

The stars awaken a certain reverence, because though always present, they are inaccessible; but all natural objects make a kindred impression, when the mind is open to their influence. Nature never wears a mean appearance. Neither does the wisest man extort her secret, and lose his curiosity by finding out all her perfection. Nature never became a toy to a wise spirit. The flowers, the animals, the mountains, reflected the wisdom of his best hour, as much as they had delighted the simplicity of his childhood.

When we speak of nature in this manner, we have a distinct but most poetical sense in the mind. We mean the integrity of impression made by manifold natural objects. It is this which distinguishes the stick of timber of the wood-cutter, from the tree of the poet. The charming landscape which I saw this morning is indubitably made up of some twenty or thirty farms. Miller owns this field, Locke that, and Manning the woodland beyond. But none of them owns the landscape. There is a property in the horizon which no man has but he whose eye can integrate all the parts, that is, the poet. This is the best part of these men's farms, yet to this their warranty-deeds give no title.

To speak truly, few adult persons can see nature. Most persons do not see the sun. At least they have a very superficial seeing. The sun illuminates only the eye of the man, but shines into the eye and the heart of the child. The lover of nature is he whose inward and outward senses are still truly adjusted to each other; who has retained the spirit of infancy even into the era of manhood. His intercourse with heaven and earth becomes part of his daily food. In the presence of nature a wild delight runs through the man, in spite of real sorrows. Nature says,—he is my creature, and maugre all his impertinent griefs, he shall be glad with me. Not the sun or the summer alone, but every hour and season yields its tribute of delight; for every hour and change corresponds to and authorizes a different state of the mind, from breathless noon to grimmest midnight. Nature is a setting that fits equally well a comic or a mourning piece. In good health, the air is a cordial of incredible virtue. Crossing a bare common, in snow puddles, at twilight, under a clouded sky, without having in my thoughts any occurrence of special good fortune, I have enjoyed a perfect exhilaration. I am glad to the brink of fear. In the woods, too, a man casts off his years, as the snake his slough, and at what period soever of life, is always a child. In the woods is perpetual youth. Within these plantations of God, a decorum and sanctity reign, a perennial festival is dressed, and the guest sees not how he should tire of them in a thousand years. In the woods, we return to reason and

faith. There I feel that nothing can befall me in life,—no disgrace, no calamity (leaving me my eyes), which nature cannot repair. Standing on the bare ground,—my head bathed by the blithe air, and uplifted into infinite space,—all mean egotism vanishes. I become a transparent eye-ball; I am nothing; I see all; the currents of the Universal Being circulate through me; I am part or parcel of God. The name of the nearest friend sounds then foreign and accidental: to be brothers, to be acquaintances, master or servant, is then a trifle and a disturbance. I am the lover of uncontained and immortal beauty. In the wilderness, I find something more dear and connate than in streets or villages. In the tranquil landscape, and especially in the distant line of the horizon, man beholds somewhat as beautiful as his own nature.

The greatest delight which the fields and woods minister is the suggestion of an occult relation between man and the vegetable. I am not alone and unacknowledged. They nod to me, and I to them. The waving of the boughs in the storm is new to me and old. It takes me by surprise, and yet is not unknown. Its effect is like that of a higher thought or a better emotion coming over me, when I deemed I was thinking justly or doing right.

Yet it is certain that the power to produce this delight does not reside in nature, but in man, or in a harmony of both. It is necessary to use these pleasures with great temperance. For nature is not always tricked in holiday attire, but the same scene which yesterday breathed perfume and glittered as for the frolic of the nymphs, is overspread with melancholy to-day. Nature always wears the colors of the spirit. To a man laboring under calamity, the heat of his own fire hath sadness in it. Then there is a kind of contempt of the landscape felt by him who has just lost by death a dear friend. The sky is less grand as it shuts down over less worth in the population.

II. COMMODITY

Whoever considers the final cause of the world will discern a multitude of uses that enter as parts into that result. They all admit of being thrown into one of the following classes: Commodity; Beauty; Language; and Discipline.

Under the general name of commodity, I rank all those advantages which our senses owe to nature. This, of course, is a benefit which is temporary and mediate, not ultimate, like its service to the soul. Yet although low, it is perfect in its kind, and is the only use of nature which all men apprehend. The misery of man appears like childish petulance, when we explore the steady and prodigal provision that has been made for his support and delight on this green ball which floats him through the heavens. What angels invented these splendid ornaments, these rich conveniences, this ocean of air above, this ocean of water beneath, this firmament of earth between? this zodiac of lights, this tent of dropping clouds, this striped coat of climates, this fourfold year? Beasts, fire, water, stones, and corn serve him. The field is at once his floor, his work-yard, his playground, his garden, and his bed.

> "More servants wait on man
> Than he'll take notice of."

Nature, in its ministry to man, is not only the material, but is also the process and the result. All the parts incessantly work into each other's hands for the profit of man. The wind sows the seed; the sun evaporates the sea; the wind blows the vapor to the field; the ice, on the other side of the planet, condenses rain on this; the rain feeds the plant; the plant feeds the animal; and thus the endless circulations of the divine charity nourish man.

The useful arts are reproductions or new combinations by the wit of man, of the same natural benefactors. He no longer waits for favoring gales, but by means of steam, he realizes the fable of Æolus's bag, and carries the two and thirty winds in the boiler of his boat. To diminish friction, he paves the road with iron bars, and, mounting a coach with a ship-load of men, animals, and merchandise behind him, he darts through the country, from town to town, like an eagle or a swallow through the air. By the aggregate of these aids, how is the face of the world changed, from the era of Noah to that of Napoleon! The private poor man hath cities, ships, canals, bridges, built for him. He goes to the post-office, and the human race run on his errands; to the book-shop, and the human race read and write of all that happens, for him; to the court-house, and nations repair his wrongs. He sets his house upon the road, and the human race go forth every morning, and shovel out the snow, and cut a path for him.

But there is no need of specifying particulars in this class of uses. The catalogue is endless, and the examples so obvious, that I shall leave them to the reader's reflection, with the general remark, that this mercenary benefit is one which has respect to a farther good. A man is fed, not that he may be fed, but that he may work.

III. BEAUTY

A nobler want of man is served by nature, namely, the love of Beauty.

The ancient Greeks called the world κόσμος, beauty. Such is the constitution of all things, or such the plastic power of the human eye, that the primary forms, as the sky, the mountain, the tree, the animal, give us a delight *in and for themselves;* a pleasure arising from outline, color, motion, and grouping. This seems partly owing to the eye itself. The eye is the best of artists. By the mutual action of its structure and of the laws of light, perspective is produced, which integrates every mass of objects, of what character soever, into a well colored and shaded globe, so that where the particular objects are mean and unaffecting, the landscape which they compose is round and symmetrical. And as the eye is the best composer, so light is the first of painters. There is no object so foul that intense light will not make beautiful. And the stimulus it affords to the sense, and a sort of infinitude which it hath, like space and time, make all matter gay. Even the corpse has its own beauty. But besides this general grace diffused over nature, almost all the individual forms are agreeable to the eye, as is proved by our endless imitations of some of them, as the acorn, the grape, the pine-cone, the wheat-ear, the egg, the wings and forms of most birds, the lion's claw, the serpent, the butterfly, sea-shells, flames, clouds, buds, leaves, and the forms of many trees, as the palm.

For better consideration, we may distribute the aspects of Beauty in a threefold manner.

1. First, the simple perception of natural forms is a delight. The influence of the forms and actions in nature is so needful to man, that, in its lowest functions, it seems to lie on the confines of commodity and beauty. To the body and mind which have been cramped by noxious work or company, nature is medicinal and restores their tone. The tradesman, the attorney comes out of the din and craft of the street and sees the sky and the woods, and is a man again. In their eternal calm, he finds himself. The health of the eye seems to demand a horizon. We are never tired, so long as we can see far enough.

But in other hours, Nature satisfies by its

loveliness, and without any mixture of corporeal benefit. I see the spectacle of morning from the hilltop over against my house, from daybreak to sunrise, with emotions which an angel might share. The long slender bars of cloud float like fishes in the sea of crimson light. From the earth, as a shore, I look out into that silent sea. I seem to partake its rapid transformations; the active enchantment reaches my dust, and I dilate and conspire with the morning wind. How does Nature deify us with a few and cheap elements! Give me health and a day, and I will make the pomp of emperors ridiculous. The dawn is my Assyria; the sunset and moonrise my Paphos, and unimaginable realms of faerie; broad noon shall be my England of the senses and the understanding; the night shall be my Germany of mystic philosophy and dreams.

Not less excellent, except for our less susceptibility in the afternoon, was the charm, last evening, of a January sunset. The western clouds divided and subdivided themselves into pink flakes modulated with tints of unspeakable softness; and the air had so much life and sweetness that it was a pain to come within doors. What was it that nature would say? Was there no meaning in the live repose of the valley behind the mill, and which Homer or Shakespeare could not re-form for me in words? The leafless trees become spires of flame in the sunset, with the blue east for their background, and the stars of the dead calices of flowers, and every withered stem and stubble rimed with frost, contribute something to the mute music.

The inhabitants of cities suppose that the country landscape is pleasant only half the year. I please myself with the graces of the winter scenery, and believe that we are as much touched by it as by the genial influences of summer. To the attentive eye, each moment of the year has its own beauty, and in the same field, it beholds, every hour, a picture which was never seen before, and which shall never be seen again. The heavens change every moment, and reflect their glory or gloom on the plains beneath. The state of the crop in the surrounding farms alters the expression of the earth from week to week. The succession of native plants in the pastures and roadsides, which makes the silent clock by which time tells the summer hours, will make even the divisions of the day sensible to a keen observer. The tribes of birds and insects, like the plants punctual to their time, follow each other, and

the year has room for all. By watercourses, the variety is greater. In July, the blue pontederia or pickerel-weed blooms in large beds in the shallow parts of our pleasant river, and swarms with yellow butterflies in continual motion. Art cannot rival this pomp of purple and gold. Indeed the river is a perpetual gala, and boasts each month a new ornament.

But this beauty of Nature which is seen and felt as beauty, is the least part. The shows of day, the dewy morning, the rainbow, mountains, orchards in blossom, stars, moonlight, shadows in still water, and the like, if too eagerly hunted, become shows merely, and mock us with their unreality. Go out of the house to see the moon, and 't is mere tinsel; it will not please as when its light shines upon your necessary journey. The beauty that shimmers in the yellow afternoons of October, who ever could clutch it? Go forth to find it, and it is gone; 't is only a mirage as you look from the windows of diligence.

2. The presence of a higher, namely, of the spiritual element is essential to its perfection. The high and divine beauty which can be loved without effeminacy, is that which is found in combination with the human will. Beauty is the mark God sets upon virtue. Every natural action is graceful. Every heroic act is also decent, and causes the place and the bystanders to shine. We are taught by great actions that the universe is the property of every individual in it. Every rational creature has all nature for his dowry and estate. It is his, if he will. He may divest himself of it; he may creep into a corner, and abdicate his kingdom, as most men do, but he is entitled to the world by his constitution. In proportion to the energy of his thought and will, he takes up the world into himself. "All those things for which men plough, build, or sail, obey virtue"; said Sallust. "The winds and waves," said Gibbon, "are always on the side of the ablest navigators." So are the sun and moon and all the stars of heaven. When a noble act is done,—perchance in a scene of great natural beauty; when Leonidas and his three hundred martyrs consume one day in dying, and the sun and moon come each and look at them once in the steep defile of Thermopylæ; when Arnold Winkelried, in the high Alps, under the shadow of the avalanche, gathers in his side a sheaf of Austrian spears to break the line for his comrades; are not these heroes entitled to add the beauty of the scene to the beauty of the deed? When the bark of Columbus nears

the shore of America;—before it, the beach lined with savages, fleeing out of all their huts of cane; the sea behind; and the purple mountains of the Indian Archipelago around, can we separate the man from the living picture? Does not the New World clothe his form with her palm-groves and savannahs as fit drapery? Ever does natural beauty steal in like air, and envelope great actions. When Sir Harry Vane was dragged up the Tower-hill, sitting on a sled, to suffer death as the champion of the English laws, one of the multitude cried out to him, "You never sat on so glorious a seat!" Charles II., to intimidate the citizens of London, caused the patriot Lord Russell to be drawn in an open coach through the principal streets of the city on his way to the scaffold. "But," his biographer says, "the multitude imagined they saw liberty and virtue sitting by his side." In private places, among sordid objects, an act of truth or heroism seems at once to draw to itself the sky as its temple, the sun as its candle. Nature stretches out her arms to embrace man, only let his thoughts be of equal greatness. Willingly does she follow his steps with the rose and the violet, and bend her lines of grandeur and grace to the decoration of her darling child. Only let his thoughts be of equal scope, and the frame will suit the picture. A virtuous man is in unison with her works, and makes the central figure of the visible sphere. Homer, Pindar, Socrates, Phocion, associate themselves fitly in our memory with the geography and climate of Greece. The visible heavens and earth sympathize with Jesus. And in common life, whosoever has seen a person of powerful character and happy genius will have remarked how easily he took all things along with him,—the persons, the opinions, and the day, and nature became ancillary to a man.

3. There is still another aspect under which the beauty of the world may be viewed, namely, as it becomes an object of the intellect. Beside the relation of things to virtue, they have a relation to thought. The intellect searches out the absolute order of things as they stand in the mind of God, and without the colors of affection. The intellectual and the active powers seem to succeed each other, and the exclusive activity of the one generates the exclusive activity of the other. There is something unfriendly in each to the other, but they are like the alternate periods of feeding and working in animals; each prepares and will be followed by the other. Therefore does beauty, which, in relation to actions, as we have seen, comes unsought, and comes because it is unsought, remain for the apprehension and pursuit of the intellect; and then again, in its turn, of the active power. Nothing divine dies. All good is eternally reproductive. The beauty of nature re-forms itself in the mind, and not for barren contemplation, but for new creation.

All men are in some degree impressed by the face of the world; some men even to delight. This love of beauty is Taste. Others have the same love in such excess, that, not content with admiring, they seek to embody it in new forms. The creation of beauty is Art.

The production of a work of art throws a light upon the mystery of humanity. A work of art is an abstract or epitome of the world. It is the result or expression of nature, in miniature. For, although the works of nature are innumerable and all different, the result or the expression of them all is similar and single. Nature is a sea of forms radically alike and even unique. A leaf, a sunbeam, a landscape, the ocean, make an analogous impression on the mind. What is common to them all,—that perfectness and harmony, is beauty. The standard of beauty is the entire circuit of natural forms,—the totality of nature; which the Italians expressed by defining beauty "il piu nell' uno." Nothing is quite beautiful alone; nothing but is beautiful in the whole. A single object is only so far beautiful as it suggests this universal grace. The poet, the painter, the sculptor, the musician, the architect, seek each to concentrate this radiance of the world on one point, and each in his several work to satisfy the love of beauty which stimulates him to produce. Thus is Art a nature passed through the alembic of man. Thus in art does Nature work through the will of a man filled with the beauty of her first works.

The world thus exists to the soul to satisfy the desire of beauty. This element I call an ultimate end. No reason can be asked or given why the soul seeks beauty. Beauty, in its largest and profoundest sense, is one expression for the universe. God is the all-fair. Truth and goodness and beauty are but different faces of the same All. But beauty in nature is not ultimate. It is the herald of inward and internal beauty, and is not alone a solid and satisfactory good. It must stand as a part, and not as yet the last or highest expression of the final cause of Nature.

IV. LANGUAGE

Language is a third use which Nature subserves to man. Nature is the vehicle of thought, and in a simple, double, and three-fold degree.

1. Words are signs of natural facts.

2. Particular natural facts are symbols of particular spiritual facts.

3. Nature is the symbol of spirit.

1. Words are signs of natural facts. The use of natural history is to give us aid in supernatural history; the use of the outer creation, to give us language for the beings and changes of the inward creation. Every word which is used to express a moral or intellectual fact, if traced to its root, is found to be borrowed from some material appearance. *Right* means *straight; wrong* means *twisted. Spirit* primarily means *wind; transgression,* the crossing of a *line; supercilious,* the *raising of the eyebrow.* We say the *heart* to express emotion, the *head* to denote thought; and *thought* and *emotion* are words borrowed from sensible things, and now appropriated to spiritual nature. Most of the process by which this transformation is made is hidden from us in the remote time when language was framed; but the same tendency may be daily observed in children. Children and savages use only nouns or names of things, which they convert into verbs, and apply to analogous mental acts.

2. But this origin of all words that convey a spiritual import,—so conspicuous a fact in the history of language,—is our least debt to nature. It is not words only that are emblematic; it is things which are emblematic. Every natural fact is a symbol of some spiritual fact. Every appearance in nature corresponds to some state of the mind, and that state of the mind can only be described by presenting that natural appearance as its picture. An enraged man is a lion, a cunning man is a fox, a firm man is a rock, a learned man is a torch. A lamb is innocence; a snake is subtle spite; flowers express to us the delicate affections. Light and darkness are our familiar expression for knowledge and ignorance; and heat for love. Visible distance behind and before us is respectively our image of memory and hope.

Who looks upon a river in a meditative hour, and is not reminded of the flux of all things? Throw a stone into the stream, and the circles that propagate themselves are the beautiful type of all influence. Man is conscious of a universal soul within or behind his individual life, wherein, as in a firmament, the natures of Justice, Truth, Love, Freedom, arise and shine. This universal soul he calls Reason: it is not mine or thine, or his, but we are its; we are its property and men. And the blue sky in which the private earth is buried, the sky with its eternal calm, and full of everlasting orbs, is the type of Reason. That which intellectually considered we call Reason, considered in relation to nature, we call Spirit. Spirit is the Creator. Spirit hath life in itself. And man in all ages and countries embodies it in his language, as the FATHER.

It is easily seen that there is nothing lucky or capricious in these analogies, but that they are constant, and pervade nature. These are not the dreams of a few poets, here and there, but man is an analogist, and studies relations in all objects. He is placed in the centre of beings, and a ray of relation passes from every other being to him. And neither can man be understood without these objects, nor these objects without man. All the facts in natural history taken by themselves, have no value, but are barren, like a single sex. But marry it to human history, and it is full of life. Whole floras, all Linnæus' and Buffon's volumes, are dry catalogues of facts; but the most trivial of these facts, the habit of a plant, the organs, or work, or noise of an insect, applied to the illustration of a fact in intellectual philosophy, or in any way associated to human nature, affects us in the most lively and agreeable manner. The seed of a plant,—to what affecting analogies in the nature of man is that little fruit made use of, in all discourse, up to the voice of Paul, who calls the human corpse a seed,—"It is sown a natural body; it is raised a spiritual body." The motion of the earth round its axis, and round the sun, makes the day, and the year. These are certain amounts of brute light and heat. But is there no intent of an analogy between man's life and the seasons? And do the seasons gain no grandeur or pathos from that analogy? The instincts of the ant are very unimportant, considered as the ant's; but the moment a ray of relation is seen to extend from it to man, and the little drudge is seen to be a monitor, a little body with a mighty heart, then all its habits, even that said to be recently observed, that it never sleeps, become sublime.

Because of this radical correspondence between visible things and human thoughts, savages, who have only what is necessary, converse in figures. As we go back in history, language becomes more picturesque, until its infancy, when it is all poetry; or all spiritual facts are represented by natural symbols. The same symbols are found to make the original elements of all languages. It has moreover been observed, that the idioms of all languages approach each other in passages of the greatest eloquence and power. And as this is the first language, so is it the last. This immediate dependence of language upon nature, this conversion of an outward phenomenon into a type of somewhat inhuman life, never loses its power to affect us. It is this which gives that piquancy to the conversation of a strong-natured farmer or backwoodsman, which all men relish.

A man's power to connect his thought with its proper symbol, and so to utter it, depends on the simplicity of his character, that is, upon his love of truth, and his desire to communicate it without loss. The corruption of man is followed by the corruption of language. When simplicity of character and the sovereignty of ideas is broken up by the prevalence of secondary desires, the desire of riches, of pleasure, of power, and of praise,—and duplicity and falsehood take place of simplicity and truth, the power over nature as an interpreter of the will is in a degree lost; new imagery ceases to be created, and old words are perverted to stand for things which are not; a paper currency is employed, when there is no bullion in the vaults. In due time the fraud is manifest, and words lose all power to stimulate the understanding or the affections. Hundreds of writers may be found in every long-civilized nation, who for a short time believe, and make others believe, that they see and utter truths, who do not of themselves clothe one thought in its natural garment, but who feed unconsciously on the language created by the primary writers of the country, those, namely, who hold primarily on nature.

But wise men pierce this rotten diction and fasten words again to visible things; so that picturesque language is at once a commanding certificate that he who employs it is a man in alliance with truth and God. The moment our discourse rises above the ground line of familiar facts and is inflamed with passion or exalted by thought, it clothes itself in images. A man conversing in earnest, if he watch his intellectual processes, will find that a material image, more or less luminous, arises in his mind, contemporaneous with every thought, which furnishes the vestment of the thought. Hence, good writing and brilliant discourse are perpetual allegories. This imagery is spontaneous. It is the blending of experience with the present action of the mind. It is proper creation. It is the working of the Original Cause through the instruments he has already made.

These facts may suggest the advantage which the country life possesses for a powerful mind, over the artificial and curtailed life of cities. We know more from nature than we can at will communicate. Its light flows into the mind evermore, and we forget its presence. The poet, the orator, bred in the woods, whose senses have been nourished by their fair and appeasing changes, year after year, without design and without heed,—shall not lose their lesson altogether, in the roar of cities or the broil of politics. Long hereafter, amidst agitation and terror in national councils,—in the hour of revolution,—these solemn images shall reappear in their morning lustre, as fit symbols and words of the thoughts which the passing events shall awaken. At the call of a noble sentiment, again the woods wave, the pines murmur, the river rolls and shines, and the cattle low upon the mountains, as he saw and heard them in his infancy. And with these forms, the spells of persuasion, the keys of power are put into his hands.

3. We are thus assisted by natural objects in the expression of particular meanings. But how great a language to convey such peppercorn informations! Did it need such noble races of creatures, this profusion of forms, this host of orbs in heaven, to furnish man with the dictionary and grammar of his municipal speech? Whilst we use this grand cipher to expedite the affairs of our pot and kettle, we feel that we have not yet put it to its use, neither are able. We are like travellers using the cinders of a volcano to roast their eggs. Whilst we see that it always stands ready to clothe what we would say, we cannot avoid the question, whether the characters are not significant of themselves. Have mountains, and waves, and skies, no significance but what we consciously give them when we employ them as emblems of our thoughts? The world is emblematic. Parts of speech are metaphors, because the whole of nature is a metaphor of the human mind. The laws of moral nature answer to those of matter as face to face in a

glass. "The visible world and the relation of its parts, is the dial plate of the invisible." The axioms of physics translate the laws of ethics. Thus, "the whole is greater than its part"; "reaction is equal to action"; "the smallest weight may be made to lift the greatest, the difference of weight being compensated by time"; and many the like propositions, which have an ethical as well as physical sense. These propositions have a much more extensive and universal sense when applied to human life, than when confined to technical use.

In like manner, the memorable words of history and the proverbs of nations consist usually of a natural fact, selected as a picture or parable of a moral truth. Thus; A rolling stone gathers no moss; A bird in the hand is worth two in the bush; A cripple in the right way will beat a racer in the wrong; Make hay while the sun shines; 'T is hard to carry a full cup even; Vinegar is the son of wine; The last ounce broke the camel's back; Long-lived trees make roots first;—and the like. In their primary sense these are trivial facts, but we repeat them for the value of their analogical import. What is true of proverbs, is true of all fables, parables, and allegories.

This relation between the mind and matter is not fancied by some poet, but stands in the will of God, and so is free to be known by all men. It appears to men, or it does not appear. When in fortunate hours we ponder this miracle, the wise man doubts if at all other times he is not blind and deaf;

> "Can such things be,
> And overcome us like a summer's cloud,
> Without our special wonder?"

for the universe becomes transparent, and the light of higher laws than its own shines through it. It is the standing problem which has exercised the wonder and the study of every fine genius since the world began; from the era of the Egyptians and the Brahmins to that of Pythagoras, of Plato, of Bacon, of Leibnitz, of Swedenborg. There sits the Sphinx at the roadside, and from age to age, as each prophet comes by, he tries his fortune at reading her riddle. There seems to be a necessity in spirit to manifest itself in material forms; and day and night, river and storm, beast and bird, acid and alkali, preëxist in necessary Ideas in the mind of God, and are what they are by virtue of preceding affections in the world of spirit. A Fact is the end or last issue of spirit.

The visible creation is the terminus or the circumference of the invisible world. "Material objects," said a French philosopher, "are necessarily kinds of *scoriæ* of the substantial thoughts of the Creator, which must always preserve an exact relation to their first origin; in other words, visible nature must have a spiritual and moral side."

This doctrine is abstruse, and though the images of "garment," "scoriæ," "mirror," etc., may stimulate the fancy, we must summon the aid of subtler and more vital expositors to make it plain. "Every scripture is to be interpreted by the same spirit which gave it forth," is the fundamental law of criticism. A life in harmony with nature, the love of truth and of virtue, will purge the eyes to understand her text. By degrees we may come to know the primitive sense of the permanent objects of nature, so that the world shall be to us an open book, and every form significant of its hidden life and final cause.

A new interest surprises us, whilst, under the view now suggested, we contemplate the fearful extent and multitude of objects; since "every object rightly seen unlocks a new faculty of the soul." That which was unconscious truth, becomes, when interpreted and defined in an object, a part of the domain of knowledge,—a new weapon in the magazine of power.

V. DISCIPLINE

In view of the significance of nature, we arrive at once at a new fact, that nature is a discipline. This use of the world includes the preceding uses, as parts of itself.

Space, time, society, labor, climate, food, locomotion, the animals, the mechanical forces, give us sincerest lessons, day by day, whose meaning is unlimited. They educate both the Understanding and the Reason. Every property of matter is a school for the understanding,— its solidity or resistance, its inertia, its extension, its figure, its divisibility. The understanding adds, divides, combines, measures, and finds nutriment and room for its activity in this worthy scene. Meantime, Reason transfers all these lessons into its own world of thought, by perceiving the analogy that marries Matter and Mind.

1. Nature is a discipline of the understanding in intellectual truths. Our dealing with sensible objects is a constant exercise in the necessary lessons of difference, of likeness, of

order, of being and seeming, of progressive arrangement; of ascent from particular to general; of combination to one end of manifold forces. Proportioned to the importance of the organ to be formed, is the extreme care with which its tuition is provided,—a care pretermitted in no single case. What tedious training, day after day, year after year, never ending, to form the common sense; what continual reproduction of annoyances, inconveniences, dilemmas; what rejoicing over us of little men; what disputing of prices, what reckonings of interest,—and all to form the Hand of the mind;—to instruct us that "good thoughts are no better than good dreams, unless they be executed!"

The same good office is performed by Property and its filial systems of debt and credit. Debt, grinding debt, whose iron face the widow, the orphan, and the sons of genius fear and hate;—debt, which consumes so much time, which so cripples and disheartens a great spirit with cares that seem so base, is a preceptor whose lessons cannot be foregone, and is needed most by those who suffer from it most. Moreover, property, which has been well compared to snow,—"if it fall level to-day, it will be blown into drifts to-morrow,"—is the surface action of internal machinery, like the index on the face of a clock. Whilst now it is the gymnastics of the understanding, it is hiving, in the foresight of the spirit, experience in profounder laws.

The whole character and fortune of the individual are affected by the least inequalities in the culture of the understanding; for example, in the perception of differences. Therefore is Space, and therefore Time, that man may know that things are not huddled and lumped, but sundered and individual. A bell and a plough have each their use, and neither can do the office of the other. Water is good to drink, coal to burn, wool to wear; but wool cannot be drunk, nor water spun, nor coal eaten. The wise man shows his wisdom in separation, in gradation, and his scale of creatures and of merits is as wide as nature. The foolish have no range in their scale, but suppose every man is as every other man. What is not good they call the worst, and what is not hateful, they call the best.

In like manner, what good heed Nature forms in us! She pardons no mistakes. Her yea is yea, and her nay, nay.

The first steps in Agriculture, Astronomy, Zoölogy (those first steps which the farmer, the hunter, and the sailor take), teach that Nature's dice are always loaded; that in her heaps and rubbish are concealed sure and useful results.

How calmly and genially the mind apprehends one after another the laws of physics! What noble emotions dilate the mortal as he enters into the councils of the creation, and feels by knowledge the privilege to BE! His insight refines him. The beauty of nature shines in his own breast. Man is greater that he can see this, and the universe less, because Time and Space relations vanish as laws are known.

Here again we are impressed and even daunted by the immense Universe to be explored. "What we know is a point to what we do not know." Open any recent journal of science, and weigh the problems suggested concerning Light, Heat, Electricity, Magnetism, Physiology, Geology, and judge whether the interest of natural science is likely to be soon exhausted.

Passing by many particulars of the discipline of nature, we must not omit to specify two.

The exercise of the Will, or the lesson of power, is taught in every event. From the child's successive possession of his several senses up to the hour when he saith, "Thy will be done!" he is learning the secret that he can reduce under his will not only particular events but great classes, nay the whole series of events, and so conform all facts to his character. Nature is thoroughly mediate. It is made to serve. It receives the dominion of man as meekly as the ass on which the Savior rode. It offers all its kingdoms to man as the raw material which he may mould into what is useful. He is never weary of working it up. He forges the subtile and delicate air into wise and melodious words, and gives them wing as angels of persuasion and command. One after another, his victorious thought comes up with and reduces all things, until the world becomes at last only a realized will,—the double of the man.

2. Sensible objects conform to the premonitions of Reason and reflect the conscience. All things are moral; and in their boundless changes have an unceasing reference to spiritual nature. Therefore is nature glorious with form, color, and motion; that every globe in the remotest heaven, every chemical change

from the rudest crystal up to the laws of life, every change of vegetation from the first principle of growth in the eye of a leaf, to the tropical forest and antediluvian coal-mine, every animal function from the sponge up to Hercules, shall hint or thunder to man the laws of right and wrong, and echo the Ten Commandments. Therefore is nature ever the ally of Religion: lends all her pomp and riches to the religious sentiment. Prophet and priest, David, Isaiah, Jesus, have drawn deeply from this source. This ethical character so penetrates the bone and marrow of nature, as to seem the end for which it was made. Whatever private purpose is answered by any member or part, this is its public and universal function, and is never omitted. Nothing in nature is exhausted in its first use. When a thing has served an end to the uttermost, it is wholly new for an ulterior service. In God, every end is converted into a new means. Thus the use of commodity, regarded by itself, is mean and squalid. But it is to the mind an education in the doctrine of Use, namely, that a thing is good only so far as it serves; that a conspiring of parts and efforts to the production of an end is essential to any being. The first and gross manifestation of this truth is our inevitable and hated training in values and wants, in corn and meat.

It has already been illustrated, that every natural process is a version of a moral sentence. The moral law lies at the centre of nature and radiates to the circumference. It is the pith and marrow of every substance, every relation, and every process. All things with which we deal preach to us. What is a farm but a mute gospel? The chaff and the wheat, weeds and plants, blight, rain, insects, sun,—it is a sacred emblem from the first furrow of spring to the last stack which the snow of winter overtakes in the fields. But the sailor, the shepherd, the miner, the merchant, in their several resorts, have each an experience precisely parallel, and leading to the same conclusion: because all organizations are radically alike. Nor can it be doubted that this moral sentiment which thus scents the air, grows in the grain, and impregnates the waters of the world, is caught by man and sinks into his soul. The moral influence of nature upon every individual is that amount of truth which it illustrates to him. Who can estimate this? Who can guess how much firmness the sea-beaten rock has taught the fisherman? how much tranquillity has been reflected to man from the azure sky, over whose unspotted deeps the winds forevermore drive flocks of stormy clouds, and leave no wrinkle or stain? how much industry and providence and affection we have caught from the pantomime of brutes? What a searching preacher of self-command is the varying phenomenon of Health!

Herein is especially apprehended the unity of Nature,—the unity in variety,—which meets us everywhere. All the endless variety of things make an identical impression. Xenophanes complained in his old age, that, look where he would, all things hastened back to unity: he was weary of seeing the same entity in the tedious variety of forms. The fable of Proteus has a cordial truth. A leaf, a drop, a crystal, a moment of time, is related to the whole, and partakes of the perfection of the whole. Each particle is a microcosm, and faithfully renders the likeness of the world.

Not only resemblances exist in things whose analogy is obvious, as when we detect the type of the human hand in the flipper of the fossil saurus, but also in objects wherein there is great superficial unlikeness. Thus architecture is called "frozen music," by De Staël and Goethe. Vitruvius thought an architect should be a musician. "A Gothic church," said Coleridge, "is a petrified religion." Michael Angelo maintained, that, to an architect, a knowledge of anatomy is essential. In Haydn's oratorios, the notes present to the imagination not only motions, as of the snake, the stag, and the elephant, but colors also; as the green grass. The law of harmonic sound reappears in the harmonic colors. The granite is differenced in its laws only by the more or less of heat, from the river that wears it away. The river, as it flows, resembles the air that flows over it; the air resembles the light which traverses it with more subtle currents; the light resembles the heat which rides with it through Space. Each creature is only a modification of the other; the likeness in them is more than the difference, and their radical law is one and the same. A rule of one art, or a law of one organization, holds true throughout nature. So intimate is this Unity, that, it is easily seen, it lies under the undermost garment of nature, and betrays its source in Universal Spirit. For it pervades Thought also. Every universal truth which we express in words implies or supposes every other truth. *Omne verum vero consonat.* It is like a great circle on a sphere, comprising all possible circles; which, however, may be drawn and comprise it in like manner. Every such truth is the absolute Ens seen from one side. But it has innumerable sides.

The central Unity is still more conspicuous in actions. Words are finite organs of the infinite mind. They cannot cover the dimensions of what is in truth. They break, chop, and impoverish it. An action is the perfection and publication of thought. A right action seems to fill the eye, and to be related to all nature. "The wise man, in doing one thing, does all; or, in the one thing he does rightly, he sees the likeness of all which is done rightly."

Words and actions are not the attributes of brute nature. They introduce us to the human form, of which all other organizations appear to be degradations. When this appears among so many that surround it, the spirit prefers it to all others. It says: "From such as this have I drawn joy and knowledge; in such as this have I found and beheld myself; I will speak to it; it can speak again; it can yield me thought already formed and alive." In fact, the eye—the mind—is always accompanied by these forms, male and female; and these are incomparably the richest informations of the power and order that lie at the heart of things. Unfortunately, every one of them bears the marks as of some injury; is marred and superficially defective. Nevertheless, far different from the deaf and dumb nature around them, these all rest like fountain-pipes on the unfathomed sea of thought and virtue whereto they alone, of all organizations, are the entrances.

It were a pleasant inquiry to follow into detail their ministry to our education, but where would it stop? We are associated in adolescent and adult life with some friends, who, like skies and waters, are coextensive with our idea; who, answering each to a certain affection of the soul, satisfy our desire on that side; whom we lack power to put at such focal distance from us, that we can mend or even analyze them. We cannot choose but love them. When much intercourse with a friend has supplied us with a standard of excellence, and has increased our respect for the resources of God who thus sends a real person to outgo our ideal; when he has, moreover, become an object of thought, and, whilst his character retains all its unconscious effect, is converted in the mind into solid and sweet wisdom,—it is a sign to us that his office is closing, and he is commonly withdrawn from our sight in a short time.

VI. IDEALISM

Thus is the unspeakable but intelligible and practicable meaning of the world conveyed to man, the immortal pupil, in every object of sense. To this one end of Discipline, all parts of nature conspire.

A noble doubt perpetually suggests itself,—whether this end be not the Final Cause of the Universe; and whether nature outwardly exists. It is a sufficient account of that Appearance we call the World, that God will teach a human mind, and so makes it the receiver of a certain number of congruent sensations, which we call sun and moon, man and woman, house and trade. In my utter impotence to test the authenticity of the report of my senses, to know whether the impressions they make on me correspond with outlying objects, what difference does it make, whether Orion is up there in heaven, or some god paints the image in the firmament of the soul? The relations of parts and the end of the whole remaining the same, what is the difference, whether land and sea interact, and worlds revolve and intermingle without number or end,—deep yawning under deep, and galaxy balancing galaxy, throughout absolute space,—or whether, without relations of time and space, the same appearances are inscribed in the constant faith of man? Whether nature enjoy a substantial existence without, or is only in the apocalypse of the mind, it is alike useful and alike venerable to me. Be it what it may, it is ideal to me, so long as I cannot try the accuracy of my senses.

The frivolous make themselves merry with the Ideal theory, as if its consequences were burlesque; as if it affected the stability of nature. It surely does not. God never jests with us, and will not compromise the end of nature by permitting any inconsequence in its procession. Any distrust of the permanence of laws would paralyze the faculties of man. Their permanence is sacredly respected, and his faith therein is perfect. The wheels and springs of man are all set to the hypothesis of the permanence of nature. We are not built like a ship to be tossed, but like a house to stand. It is a natural consequence of this structure, that, so long as the active powers predominate over the reflective, we resist with indignation any hint that nature is more short-lived or mutable than spirit. The broker, the wheelwright, the carpenter, the tollman, are much displeased at the intimation.

But whilst we acquiesce entirely in the permanence of natural laws, the question of the absolute existence of nature still remains open. It is the uniform effect of culture on the human mind, not to shake our faith in the stability of particular phenomena, as of heat, water, azote; but to lead us to regard nature as a phenomenon, not a substance; to attribute necessary existence to spirit; to esteem nature as an accident and an effect.

To the senses and the unrenewed understanding, belongs a sort of instinctive belief in the absolute existence of nature. In their view, man and nature are indissolubly joined. Things are ultimates, and they never look beyond their sphere. The presence of Reason mars this faith. The first effort of thought tends to relax this despotism of the senses, which binds us to nature as if we were a part of it, and shows us nature aloof, and, as it were, afloat. Until this higher agency intervened, the animal eye sees, with wonderful accuracy, sharp outlines and colored surfaces. When the eye of Reason opens, to outline and surface are at once added grace and expression. These proceed from imagination and affection, and abate somewhat of the angular distinctness of objects. If the Reason be stimulated to more earnest vision, outlines and surfaces become transparent, and are no longer seen; causes and spirits are seen through them. The best moments of life are these delicious awakenings of the higher powers, and the reverential withdrawing of nature before its God.

Let us proceed to indicate the effects of culture.

1. Our first institution in the Ideal philosophy is a hint from Nature herself.

Nature is made to conspire with spirit to emancipate us. Certain mechanical changes, a small alteration in our local position apprises us of a dualism. We are strangely affected by seeing the shore from a moving ship, from a balloon, or through the tints of an unusual sky. The least change in our point of view gives the whole world a pictorial air. A man who seldom rides, needs only to get into a coach and traverse his own town, to turn the street into a puppet-show. The men, the women,—talking, running, bartering, fighting,—the earnest mechanic, the lounger, the beggar, the boys, the dogs, are unrealized at once, or at least wholly detached from all relation to the observer, and seen as apparent, not substantial beings. What new thoughts are suggested by seeing a face of country quite familiar, in the rapid movement of the railroad car! Nay, the most wonted objects, (make a very slight change in the point of vision,) please us most. In a camera obscura, the butcher's cart, and the figure of one of our own family amuse us. So a portrait of a well-known face gratifies us. Turn the eyes upside down, by looking at the landscape through your legs, and how agreeable is the picture, though you have seen it any time these twenty years!

In these cases, by mechanical means, is suggested the difference between the observer and the spectacle—between man and nature. Hence arises a pleasure mixed with awe; I may say, a low degree of the sublime is felt, from the fact, probably, that man is hereby apprised that whilst the world is a spectacle, something in himself is stable.

2. In a higher manner, the poet communicates the same pleasure. By a few strokes he delineates, as on air, the sun, the mountain, the camp, the city, the hero, the maiden, not different from what we know them, but only lifted from the ground and afloat before the eye. He unfixes the land and the sea, makes them revolve around the axis of his primary thought, and disposes them anew. Possessed himself by a heroic passion, he uses matter as symbols of it. The sensual man conforms thoughts to things; the poet conforms things to his thoughts. The one esteems nature as rooted and fast; the other, as fluid, and impresses his being thereon. To him, the refractory world is ductile and flexible; he invests dust and stones with humanity, and makes them the words of the Reason. The Imagination may be defined to be the use which the Reason makes of the material world. Shakspeare possesses the power of subordinating nature for the purposes of expression, beyond all poets. His imperial muse tosses the creation like a bauble from hand to hand, and uses it to embody any caprice of thought that is uppermost in his mind. The remotest spaces of nature are visited, and the farthest sundered things are brought together, by a subtile spiritual connection. We are made aware that magnitude of material things is relative, and all objects shrink and expand to serve the passion of the poet. Thus in his sonnets, the lays of birds, the scents and dyes of flowers, he finds to be the *shadow* of his beloved; time, which

keeps her from him, is his *chest;* the suspicion she has awakened, is her *ornament;*

> The ornament of beauty is Suspect,
> A crow which flies in heaven's sweetest air.

His passion is not the fruit of chance; it swells, as he speaks, to a city, or a state.

> No, it was builded far from accident;
> It suffers not in smiling pomp, nor falls
> Under the brow of thralling discontent;
> It fears not policy, that heretic,
> That works on leases of short numbered hours,
> But all alone stands hugely politic.

In the strength of his constancy, the Pyramids seem to him recent and transitory. The freshness of youth and love dazzles him with its resemblance to morning;

> Take those lips away
> Which so sweetly were forsworn;
> And those eyes,—the break of day,
> Lights that do mislead the morn.

The wild beauty of this hyperbole, I may say in passing, it would not be easy to match in literature.

This transfiguration which all material objects undergo through the passion of the poet,—this power which he exerts to dwarf the great, to magnify the small,—might be illustrated by a thousand examples from his Plays. I have before me the Tempest, and will cite only these few lines.

> Ariel. The strong based promontory
> Have I made shake, and by the spurs plucked up
> The pine and cedar.

Prospero calls for music to soothe the frantic Alonzo, and his companions;

> A solemn air, and the best comforter
> To an unsettled fancy, cure thy brains
> Now useless, boiled within thy skull.

Again;

> The charm dissolves apace,
> **And, as the** morning steals upon the night,
> **Melting the** darkness, so their rising senses
> **Begin to** chase the ignorant fumes that mantle
> Their clearer reason.
>   Their understanding
> Begins to swell: and the approaching tide
> Will shortly fill the reasonable shores
> That now lie foul and muddy.

The perception of real affinities between events (that is to say, of *ideal* affinities, for those only are real) enables the poet thus to make free with the most imposing forms and phenomena of the world, and to assert the predominance of the soul.

3. Whilst thus the poet animates nature with his own thoughts, he differs from the philosopher only herein, that the one proposes Beauty as his main end; the other Truth. But the philosopher, not less than the poet, postpones the apparent order and relations of things to the empire of thought. "The problem of philosophy," according to Plato, "is, for all that exists conditionally, to find a ground unconditioned and absolute." It proceeds on the faith that a law determines all phenomena, which being known, the phenomena can be predicted. That law, when in the mind, is an idea. Its beauty is infinite. The true philosopher and the true poet are one, and a beauty, which is truth, and a truth, which is beauty, is the aim of both. Is not the charm of one of Plato's or Aristotle's definitions strictly like that of the Antigone of Sophocles? It is, in both cases, that a spiritual life has been imparted to nature; that the solid seeming block of matter has been pervaded and dissolved by a thought; that this feeble human being has penetrated the vast masses of nature with an informing soul, and recognized itself in their harmony, that is, seized their law. In physics, when this is attained, the memory disburthens itself of its cumbrous catalogues of particulars, and carries centuries of observation in a single formula.

Thus even in physics, the material is degraded before the spiritual. The astronomer, the geometer, rely on their irrefragable analysis, and disdain the results of observation. The sublime remark of Euler on his law of arches, "This will be found contrary to all experience, yet is true," had already transferred nature into the mind, and left matter like an outcast corpse.

4. Intellectual science has been observed to beget invariably a doubt of the existence of matter. Turgot said, "He that has never doubted the existence of matter may be assured he has no aptitude for metaphysical inquiries." It fastens the attention upon immortal necessary uncreated natures, that is, upon Ideas; and in their presence we feel that the outward circumstance is a dream and a shade. Whilst we wait in this Olympus of gods, we think of nature as an appendix to the soul. We ascend into their region, and know that these are the thoughts of the Su-

preme Being. "These are they who were set up from everlasting, from the beginning, or ever the earth was. When he prepared the heavens, they were there; when he established the clouds above, when he strengthened the fountains of the deep. Then they were by him, as one brought up with him. Of them took he counsel."

Their influence is proportionate. As objects of science they are accessible to few men. Yet all men are capable of being raised by piety or by passion into their region. And no man touches these divine natures, without becoming, in some degree, himself divine. Like a new soul, they renew the body. We become physically nimble and lightsome; we tread on air; life is no longer irksome, and we think it will never be so. No man fears age or misfortune or death in their serene company, for he is transported out of the district of change. Whilst we behold unveiled the nature of Justice and Truth, we learn the difference between the absolute and the conditional or relative. We apprehend the absolute. As it were, for the first time, *we exist*. We become immortal, for we learn that time and space are relations of matter; that, with a perception of truth, or a virtuous will, they have no affinity.

5. Finally, religion and ethics, which may be fitly called the practice of ideas, or the introduction of ideas into life, have an analogous effect with all lower culture, in degrading nature and suggesting its dependence on spirit. Ethics and religion differ herein; that the one is the system of human duties commencing from man; the other, from God. Religion includes the personality of God; Ethics does not. They are one to our present design. They both put nature under foot. The first and last lesson of religion is, "The things that are seen, are temporal; the things that are unseen, are eternal." It puts an affront upon nature. It does that for the unschooled, which philosophy does for Berkeley and Viasa. The uniform language that may be heard in the churches of the most ignorant sects is,—"Contemn the unsubstantial shows of the world; they are vanities, dreams, shadows, unrealities; seek the realities of religion." The devotee flouts nature. Some theosophists have arrived at a certain hostility and indignation towards matter, as the Manichean and Plotinus. They distrusted in themselves any looking back to these fleshpots of Egypt. Plotinus was ashamed of his body. In short, they might all say of matter,

what Michael Angelo said of external beauty, "It is the frail and weary weed, in which God dresses the soul which he has called into time."

It appears that motion, poetry, physical and intellectual science, and religion, all tend to affect our convictions of the reality of the external world. But I own there is something ungrateful in expanding too curiously the particulars of the general proposition, that all culture tends to imbue us with idealism. I have no hostility to nature, but a child's love to it. I expand and live in the warm day like corn and melons. Let us speak her fair. I do not wish to fling stones at my beautiful mother, nor soil my gentle nest. I only wish to indicate the true position of nature in regard to man, wherein to establish man, all right education tends; as the ground which to attain is the object of human life, that is, of man's connection with nature. Culture inverts the vulgar views of nature, and brings the mind to call that apparent which it uses to call real, and that real which it uses to call visionary. Children, it is true, believe in the external world. The belief that it appears only, is an afterthought, but with culture this faith will as surely arise on the mind as did the first.

The advantage of the ideal theory over the popular faith is this, that it presents the world in precisely that view which is most desirable to the mind. It is, in fact, the view which Reason, both speculative and practical, that is, philosophy and virtue, take. For, seen in the light of thought, the world always is phenomenal; and virtue subordinates it to the mind. Idealism sees the world in God. It beholds the whole circle of persons and things, of actions and events, of country and religion, not as painfully accumulated, atom after atom, act after act, in an aged creeping Past, but as one vast picture which God paints on the instant eternity for the contemplation of the soul. Therefore the soul holds itself off from a too trivial and microscopic study of the universal tablet. It respects the end too much to immerse itself in the means. It sees something more important in Christianity than the scandals of ecclesiastical history or the niceties of criticism; and, very incurious concerning persons or miracles, and not at all disturbed by chasms of historical evidence, it accepts from God the phenomenon, as it finds it, as the pure and awful form of religion in the world. It is not hot and passionate at the appearance of what it calls its own good or bad fortune, at the union or opposition of other persons. No man is its enemy. It accepts whatsoever befalls, as part of its lesson. It is a watcher more than a doer, and it is a doer, only that it may the better watch.

VII. SPIRIT

It is essential to a true theory of nature and of man, that it should contain somewhat progressive. Uses that are exhausted or that may be, and facts that end in the statement, cannot be all that is true of this brave lodging wherein man is harbored, and wherein all his faculties find appropriate and endless exercise. And all the uses of nature admit of being summed in one, which yields the activity of man an infinite scope. Through all its kingdoms, to the suburbs and outskirts of things, it is faithful to the cause whence it had its origin. It always speaks of Spirit. It suggests the absolute. It is a perpetual effect. It is a great shadow pointing always to the sun behind us.

The aspect of nature is devout. Like the figure of Jesus, she stands with bended head, and hands folded upon the breast. The happiest man is he who learns from nature the lesson of worship.

Of that ineffable essence which we call Spirit, he that thinks most, will say least. We can foresee God in the coarse, and, as it were, distant phenomena of matter; but when we try to define and describe himself, both language and thought desert us, and we are as helpless as fools and savages. That essence refuses to be recorded in propositions, but when man has worshipped him intellectually, the noblest ministry of nature is to stand as the apparition of God. It is the organ through which the universal spirit speaks to the individual, and strives to lead back the individual to it.

When we consider Spirit, we see that the views already presented do not include the whole circumference of man. We must add some related thoughts.

Three problembs are put by nature to the mind: What is matter? Whence is it? and Whereto? The first of these questions only, the ideal theory answers. Idealism saith: matter is a phenomenon, not a substance. Idealism acquaints us with the total disparity between the evidence of our own being and the evidence of the world's being. The one is perfect; the other, incapable of any assurance; the mind is a part of the nature of things; the world is a divine dream, from which we may presently awake to the glories and certainties of day. Idealism is a hypothesis to account for nature by other principles than those of carpentry and chemistry. Yet, if it only deny the existence of matter, it does not satisfy the demands of the spirit. It leaves God out of me. It leaves me in the splendid labyrinth of my perceptions, to wander without end. Then the heart resists it, because it balks the affections in denying substantive being to men and women. Nature is so pervaded with human life that there is something of humanity in all and in every particular. But this theory makes nature foreign to me, and does not account for that consanguinity which we acknowledge to it.

Let it stand then, in the present state of our knowledge, merely as a useful introductory hypothesis, serving to apprise us of the eternal distinction between the soul and the world.

But when, following the invisible steps of thought, we come to inquire, Whence is matter? and Whereto? many truths arise to us out of the recesses of consciousness. We learn that the highest is present to the soul of man; that the dread universal essence, which is not wisdom, or love, or beauty, or power, but all in one, and each entirely, is that for which all things exist, and that by which they are; that spirit creates; that behind nature, throughout nature, spirit is present; one and not compound, it does not act upon us from without, that is, in space and time, but spiritually, or through ourselves: therefore, that spirit, that is, the Supreme Being, does not build up nature around us, but puts it forth through us, as the life of the tree puts forth new branches and leaves through the pores of the old. As a plant upon the earth, so a man rests upon the bosom of God; he is nourished by unfailing fountains, and draws, at his need, inexhaustible power. Who can set bounds to the possibilities of man? Once inhale the upper air, being admitted to behold the absolute natures of justice and truth, and we learn that man has access to the entire mind of the Creator, is himself the creator in the finite. This view, which admonishes me where the sources of wisdom and power lie, and points to virtue as to

"The golden key
Which opes the palace of eternity,"

carries upon its face the highest certificate of truth, because it animates me to create my own world through the purification of my soul.

The world proceeds from the same spirit as the body of man. It is a remoter and inferior incarnation of God, a projection of God in the unconscious. But it differs from the body in one important respect. It is not, like that, now subjected to the human will. Its serene order is inviolable by us. It is, therefore, to us, the present expositor of the divine mind. It is a fixed point whereby we may measure our departure. As we degenerate, the contrast between us and our house is more evident. We are as much strangers in nature as we are aliens from God. We do not understand the notes of birds. The fox and the deer run away from us; the bear and tiger rend us. We do not know the uses of more than a few plants, as corn and the apple, the potato and the vine. Is not the landscape, every glimpse of which hath a grandeur, a face of him? Yet this may show us what discord is between man and nature, for you cannot freely admire a noble landscape if laborers are digging in the field hard by. The poet finds something ridiculous in his delight until he is out of the sight of men.

VIII. PROSPECTS

In inquiries respecting the laws of the world and the frame of things, the highest reason is always the truest. That which seems faintly possible, it is so refined, is often faint and dim because it is deepest seated in the mind among the eternal verities. Empirical science is apt to cloud the sight, and, by the very knowledge of functions and processes, to bereave the student of the manly contemplation of the whole. The savant becomes unpoetic. But the best read naturalist who lends an entire and devout attention to truth, will see that there remains much to learn of his relation to the world, and that it is not to be learned by any addition or subtraction or other comparison of known quantities, but is arrived at by untaught sallies of the spirit, by a continual self-recovery, and by entire humility. He will perceive that there are far more excellent qualities in the student than preciseness and infallibility; that a guess is often more fruitful than an indisputable affirmation, and that a dream may let us deeper into the secret of nature than a hundred concerted experiments.

For the problems to be solved are precisely those which the physiologist and the naturalist omit to state. It is not so pertinent to man to know all the individuals of the animal kingdom, as it is to know whence and whereto is this tyrannizing unity in his constitution, which evermore separates and classifies things, endeavoring to reduce the most diverse to one form. When I behold a rich landscape, it is less to my purpose to recite correctly the order and superposition of the strata, than to know why all thought of multitude is lost in a tranquil sense of unity. I cannot greatly honor minuteness in details, so long as there is no hint to explain the relation between things and thoughts; no ray upon the *metaphysics* of conchology, of botany, of the arts, to show the relation of the forms of flowers, shells, animals, architecture, to the mind, and build science upon ideas. In a cabinet of natural history, we become sensible of a certain occult recognition and sympathy in regard to the most unwieldy and eccentric forms of beast, fish, and insect. The American who has been confined, in his own country, to the sight of buildings designed after foreign models, is surprised on entering York Minster or St. Peter's at Rome, by the feeling that these structures are imitations also, —faint copies of an invisible archetype. Nor has science sufficient humanity, so long as the naturalist overlooks that wonderful congruity which subsists between man and the world; of which he is lord, not because he is the most subtile inhabitant, but because he is its head and heart, and finds something of himself in every great and small thing, in every mountain stratum, in every new law of color, fact of astronomy, or atmospheric influence which observation or analysis lays open. A perception of this mystery inspires the muse of George Herbert, the beautiful psalmist of the seventeenth century. The following lines are part of his little poem on Man.

Man is all symmetry,
Full of proportions, one limb to another,
   And all to all the world besides.
Each part may call the farthest, brother;
For head with foot hath private amity,
   And both with moons and tides.

Nothing hath got so far
But man hath caught and kept it as his prey;
   His eyes dismount the highest star:
   He is in little all the sphere.
Herbs gladly cure our flesh, because that they
   Find their acquaintance there.

For us, the winds do blow,
The earth doth rest, heaven move, and fountains
   flow;

Nothing we see, but means our good,
As our delight, or as our treasure;
The whole is either our cupboard of food,
Or cabinet of pleasure.

The stars have us to bed:
Night draws the curtain; which the sun withdraws.
Music and light attend our head.
All things unto our flesh are kind,
In their descent and being; to our mind,
10   In their ascent and cause.

More servants wait on man
Than he'll take notice of. In every path,
He treads down that which doth befriend him
When sickness makes him pale and wan.
Oh mighty love! Man is one world, and hath
Another to attend him.

The perception of this class of truths makes the attraction which draws men to science, but 20 the end is lost sight of in attention to the means. In view of this half-sight of science, we accept the sentence of Plato, that "poetry comes nearer to vital truth than history." Every surmise and vaticination of the mind is entitled to a certain respect, and we learn to prefer imperfect theories, and sentences which contain glimpses of truth, to digested systems which have no one valuable suggestion. A wise writer will feel that the ends of study and 30 composition are best answered by announcing undiscovered regions of thought, and so communicating, through hope, new activity to the torpid spirit.

I shall therefore conclude this essay with some traditions of man and nature, which a certain poet sang to me; and which, as they have always been in the world, and perhaps reappear to every bard, may be both history and prophecy.

40   "The foundations of man are not in matter, but in spirit. But the element of spirit is eternity. To it, therefore, the longest series of events, the oldest chronologies are young and recent. In the cycle of the universal man, from whom the known individuals proceed, centuries are points, and all history is but the epoch of one degradation.

"We distrust and deny inwardly our sympathy with nature. We own and disown our re- 50 lation to it, by turns. We are, like Nebuchadnezzar, dethroned, bereft of reason, and eating grass like an ox. But who can set limits to the remedial force of spirit?

"A man is a god in ruins. When men are innocent, life shall be longer, and shall pass into the immortal, as gently as we awake from dreams. Now, the world would be insane and rabid, if these disorganizations should last for hundreds of years. It is kept in check by death and infancy. Infancy is the perpetual Messiah, which comes into the arms of fallen men, and pleads with them to return to paradise.

"Man is the dwarf of himself. Once he was permeated and dissolved by spirit. He filled nature with his overflowing currents. Out from him sprang the sun and moon; from man the sun, from woman the moon. The laws of his mind, the periods of his actions externized themselves into day and night, into the year and the seasons. But, having made for himself this huge shell, his waters retired; he no longer fills the veins and veinlets; he is shrunk to a drop. He sees that the structure still fits him, but fits him colossally. Say, rather, once it fitted him, now it corresponds to him from far and on high. He adores timidly his own work. Now is man the follower of the sun, and woman the follower of the moon. Yet sometimes he starts in his slumber, and wonders at himself and his house, and muses strangely at the resemblance betwixt him and it. He perceives that if his law is still paramount, if still he have elemental power, if his word is sterling yet in nature, it is not conscious power, it is not inferior but superior to his will. It is instinct." Thus my Orphic poet sang.

At present, man applies to nature but half his force. He works on the world with his understanding alone. He lives in it, and masters it by a penny-wisdom; and he that works most in it is but a half-man, and whilst his arms are strong and his digestion good, his mind is imbruted, and he is a selfish savage. His relation to nature, his power over it, is through the understanding, as by manure; the economic use of fire, wind, water, and the mariner's needle; steam, coal, chemical agriculture; the repairs of the human body by the dentist and the surgeon. This is such a resumption of power as if a banished king should buy his territories inch by inch, instead of vaulting at once into his throne. Meantime, in the thick darkness, there are not wanting gleams of a better light, —occasional examples of the action of man upon nature with his entire force,—with reason as well as understanding. Such examples are, the traditions of miracles in the earliest antiquity of all nations; the history of Jesus Christ; the achievements of a principle, as in religious and political revolutions, and in the abolition of the slave-trade; the miracles of enthusiasm, as those reported of Swedenborg, Hohenlohe, and the Shakers; many obscure and yet contested facts, now arranged under the name of Animal Magnetism; prayer; eloquence; self-healing; and the wisdom of children. These are examples of Reason's momentary grasp of the sceptre; the exertions of a power which exists not in time or space, but an instantaneous in-streaming causing power. The difference between the actual and the ideal force of man is happily figured by the schoolmen, in saying, that the knowledge of man is an evening knowledge, *vespertina cognitio,* but that of God is a morning knowledge, *matutina cognitio.*

The problem of restoring to the world original and eternal beauty is solved by the redemption of the soul. The ruin or the blank that we see when we look at nature, is in our own eye. The axis of vision is not coincident with the axis of things, and so they appear not transparent but opaque. The reason why the world lacks unity, and lies broken and in heaps, **is,** because man is disunited with himself. He cannot be a naturalist until he satisfies all the demands of the spirit. Love is as much its demand as perception. Indeed, neither can be perfect without the other. In the uttermost meaning of the words, thought is devout, and devotion is thought. Deep calls unto deep. But in actual life, the marriage is not celebrated. There are innocent men who worship God after the tradition of their fathers, but their sense of duty has not yet extended to the use of all their faculties. And there are patient naturalists, but they freeze their subject under the wintry light of the understanding. Is not prayer also a study of truth,—a sally of the soul into the unfound infinite? No man ever prayed heartily without learning something. But when a faithful thinker, resolute to detach every object from personal relations and see it in the light of thought, shall, at the same time, kindle science with the fire of the holiest affections, then will God go forth anew into the creation.

It will not need, when the mind is prepared for study, to search for objects. The invariable mark of wisdom is to see the miraculous in the common. What is a day? What is a year? What is summer? What is woman? What is a child? What is sleep? To our blindness, these things seem unaffecting. We make fables to hide the baldness of the fact and conform it, as we say, to the higher law of the mind. But when the fact is seen under the light of an idea, the gaudy fable fades and shrivels. We behold the real higher law. To the wise, therefore, a fact is true poetry, and the most beautiful of fables. These wonders are brought to our own door. You also are a man. Man and woman and their social life, poverty, labor, sleep, fear, fortune, are known to you. Learn that none of these things is superficial, but that each phenomenon has its roots in the faculties and affections of the mind. Whilst the abstract question occupies your intellect, nature brings it in the concrete to be solved by your hands. It were a wise inquiry for the closet, to compare, point by point, especially at remarkable crises in life, our daily history with the rise and progress of ideas in the mind.

So shall we come to look at the world with new eyes. It shall answer the endless inquiry of the intellect,—What is truth? and of the affections,—What is good? by yielding itself passive to the educated Will. Then shall come to pass what my poet said: "Nature is not fixed but fluid. Spirit alters, moulds, makes it. The immobility or bruteness of nature is the absence of spirit; to pure spirit it is fluid, it is volatile, it is obedient. Every spirit builds itself a house, and beyond its house a world, and beyond its world a heaven. Know then that the world exists for you. For you is the phenomenon perfect. What we are, that only can we see. All that Adam had, all that Cæsar could, you have and can do. Adam called his house, heaven and earth; Cæsar called his house, Rome; you perhaps call yours, a cobbler's trade; a hundred acres of ploughed land; or a scholar's garret. Yet line for line and point for point your dominion is as great as theirs, though without fine names. Build therefore your own world. As fast as you conform your life to the pure idea in your mind, that will unfold its great proportions. A correspondent revolution in things will attend the influx of the spirit. So fast will disagreeable appearances, swine, spiders, snakes, pests, mad-houses, prisons, enemies, vanish; they are temporary and shall be no more seen. The sordor and filths of nature, the sun shall dry up, and the wind exhale. As when the summer comes from the south the snow-banks melt and the face of the earth becomes green before it, so shall the advancing spirit create its ornaments along its path, and carry with it the beauty it visits and the song which enchants it; it shall draw beautiful faces, warm hearts, wise discourse, and heroic acts, around its way, until evil is no more seen. The kingdom of man over nature, which cometh not with observation,—a domin- ion such as now is beyond his dream of God, —he shall enter without more wonder than the blind man feels who is gradually restored to perfect sight."   1836

» » THE AMERICAN SCHOLAR[4] « «

Mr. President and Gentlemen, I greet you on the recommencement of our literary year. Our anniversary is one of hope, and, per- haps, not enough of labor. We do not meet for games of strength or skill, for the recitation of histories, tragedies, and odes, like the ancient Greeks; for parliaments of love and poesy, like the Troubadours; nor for the advancement of science, like our contemporaries in the British and European capitals. Thus far, our holiday has been simply a friendly sign of the survival of the love of letters amongst a people too busy to give to letters any more. As such, it is precious as the sign of an indestructible in- stinct. Perhaps the time is already come when it ought to be, and will be, something else; when the sluggard intellect of this continent will look from under its iron lids, and fill the postponed expectation of the world with some- thing better than the exertions of mechanical skill. Our day of dependence, our long ap- prenticeship to the learning of other lands, draws to a close. The millions that around us are rushing into life, cannot always be fed on the sere remains of foreign harvests. Events, ac- tions arise, that must be sung, that will sing themselves. Who can doubt that poetry will revive and lead in a new age, as the star in the constellation Harp, which now flames in our zenith, astronomers announce, shall one day be the pole-star for a thousand years?

In this hope, I accept the topic which not only usage but the nature of our association seem to prescribe to this day,—the American Scholar. Year by year we come up hither to read one more chapter of his biography. Let us inquire what light new days and events have thrown on his character and his hopes.

It is one of those fables, which, out of an unknown antiquity, convey an unlooked-for wisdom, that the gods, in the beginning, di- vided Man into men, that he might be more helpful to himself; just as the hand was divided into fingers, the better to answer its end.

The old fable covers a doctrine ever new and sublime; that there is One Man,—pres- ent to all particular men only partially, or through one faculty; and that you must take the whole society to find the whole man. Man is not a farmer, or a professor, or an engineer, but he is all. Man is priest, and scholar, and statesman, and producer, and soldier. In the *divided* or social state these functions are par- celled out to individuals, each of whom aims to do his stint of the joint work, whilst each other performs his. The fable implies that the in- dividual, to possess himself, must sometimes return from his own labor to embrace all the other laborers. But, unfortunately, this original unit, this fountain of power, has been so dis- tributed to multitudes, has been so minutely subdivided and peddled out, that it is spilled into drops, and cannot be gathered. The state of society is one in which the members have suffered amputation from the trunk, and strut about so many walking monsters,—a good finger, a neck, a stomach, an elbow, but never a man.

Man is thus metamorphosed into a thing, into many things. The planter, who is Man sent out into the field to gather food, is seldom cheered by any idea of the true dignity of his ministry. He sees his bushel and his cart, and nothing beyond, and sinks into the farmer, in- stead of Man on the farm. The tradesman scarcely ever gives an ideal worth to his work, but is ridden by the routine of his craft, and the soul is subject to dollars. The priest be- comes a form; the attorney a statute-book; the mechanic a machine; the sailor a rope of the ship.

In this distribution of functions the scholar is the delegated intellect. In the right state, he is *Man Thinking*. In the degenerate state, when the victim of society, he tends to become a mere thinker, or, still worse, the parrot of other men's thinking.

In this view of him, as Man Thinking, the theory of his office is contained. Him Nature solicits with all her placid, all her monitory

---

[4] The oration delivered before the Phi Beta Kappa Society, at Cambridge, August 31, 1837.

pictures; him the past instructs; him the future invites. Is not indeed every man a student, and do not all things exist for the student's behoof? And, finally, is not the true scholar the only true master? But the old oracle said, "All things have two handles: beware of the wrong one." In life, too often, the scholar errs with mankind and forfeits his privilege. Let us see him in his school, and consider him in reference to the main influences he receives.

I. The first in time and the first in importance of the influences upon the mind is that of nature. Every day, the sun; and, after the sunset, night and her stars. Ever the winds blow; ever the grass grows. Every day, men and women, conversing, beholding and beholden. The scholar is he of all men whom this spectacle most engages. He must settle its value in his mind. What is nature to him? There is never a beginning, there is never an end, to the inexplicable continuity of this web of God, but always circular power returning into itself. Therein it resembles his own spirit, whose beginning, whose ending, he never can find,— so entire, so boundless. Far too as her splendors shine, system on system shooting like rays, upward, downward, without centre, without circumference,—in the mass and in the particle, nature hastens to render account of herself to the mind. Classification begins. To the young mind, every thing is individual, stands by itself. By and by, it finds how to join two things, and see in them one nature; then three, then three thousand; and so, tyrannized over by its own unifying instinct, it goes on tying things together, diminishing anomalies, discovering roots running under ground whereby contrary and remote things cohere and flower out from one stem. It presently learns that since the dawn of history there has been a constant accumulation and classifying of facts. But what is classification but the perceiving that these objects are not chaotic, and are not foreign, but have a law which is also a law of the human mind? The astronomer discovers that geometry, a pure abstraction of the human mind, is the measure of planetary motion. The chemist finds proportions and intelligible method throughout matter; and science is nothing but the finding of analogy, identity, in the most remote parts. The ambitious soul sits down before each refractory fact: one after another, reduces all strange constitutions, all new powers, to their class and their law, and goes on forever to animate the last fibre of organization, the outskirts of nature, by insight.

Thus to him, to this school-boy under the bending dome of day, is suggested that he and it proceed from one root; one is leaf and one is flower; relation, sympathy, stirring in every vein. And what is that root? Is not that the soul of his soul? A thought too bold; a dream too wild. Yet when this spiritual light shall have revealed the law of more earthly natures,—when he has learned to worship the soul, and to see that the natural philosophy that now is, is only the first gropings of its gigantic hand, he shall look forward to an ever expanding knowledge as to a becoming creator. He shall see that nature is the opposite of the soul, answering to it part for part. One is seal, and one is print. Its beauty is the beauty of his own mind. Its laws are the laws of his own mind. Nature then becomes to him the measure of his attainments. So much of nature as he is ignorant of, so much of his own mind does he not yet possess. And, in fine, the ancient precept, "Know thyself," and the modern precept, "Study nature," become at last one maxim.

II. The next great influence into the spirit of the scholar is the mind of the Past,—in whatever form, whether of literature, of art, of institutions, that mind is inscribed. Books are the best type of the influence of the past, and perhaps we shall get at the truth,—learn the amount of this influence more conveniently, —by considering their value alone.

The theory of books is noble. The scholar of the first age received into him the world around; brooded thereon; gave it the new arrangement of his own mind, and uttered it again. It came into him life; it went out from him truth. It came to him short-lived actions; it went out from him immortal thoughts. It came to him business; it went from him poetry. It was dead fact; now, it is quick thought. It can stand, and it can go. It now endures, it now flies, it now inspires. Precisely in proportion to the depth of mind from which it issued, so high does it soar, so long does it sing.

Or, I might say, it depends on how far the process had gone, of transmuting life into truth. In proportion to the completeness of the distillation, so will the purity and imperishableness of the product be. But none is quite perfect. As no air-pump can by any means make a perfect vacuum, so neither can any artist entirely exclude the conventional, the local, the perishable from his book, or write a book of pure thought, that shall be as efficient, in all respects, to a remote posterity, as to contemporaries, or rather to the second age. Each age, it is found, must write its own books; or rather, each generation for the next succeeding. The books of an older period will not fit this.

10   Yet hence arises a grave mischief. The sacredness which attaches to the act of creation, the act of thought, is transferred to the record. The poet chanting was felt to be a divine man: henceforth the chant is divine also. The writer was a just and wise spirit: henceforward it is settled, the book is perfect; as love of the hero corrupts into worship of his statue. Instantly, the book becomes noxious: the guide is a tyrant. The sluggish and per-
20 verted mind of the multitude, slow to open to the incursions of Reason, having once so opened, having once received this book, stands upon it, and makes an outcry if it is disparaged. Colleges are built on it. Books are written on it by thinkers, not by Man Thinking; by men of talent, that is, who start wrong, who set out from accepted dogmas, not from their own sight of principles. Meek young men grow up in libraries, believing it their duty to ac-
30 cept the views which Cicero, which Locke, which Bacon, have given; forgetful that Cicero, Locke, and Bacon were only young men in libraries when they wrote these books.

    Hence, instead of Man Thinking, we have the bookworm. Hence the book-learned class, who value books, as such; not as related to nature and the human constitution, but as making a sort of Third Estate with the world and the soul. Hence, the restorers of readings,
40 the emendators, the bibliomaniacs of all degrees.

    Books are the best of things, well used; abused, among the worst. What is the right use? What is the one end which all means go to effect? They are for nothing but to inspire. I had better never see a book than to be warped by its attraction clean out of my own orbit, and made a satellite instead of a system. The one thing in the world, of value,
50 is the active soul. This every man is entitled to; this every man contains within him, although in almost all men obstructed, and as yet unborn. The soul active sees absolute truth; and utters truth, or creates. In this action it is genius; not the privilege of here and

there a favorite, but the sound estate of every man. In its essence it is progressive. The book, the college, the school of art, the institution of any kind, stop with some past utterance of genius. This is good, say they,—let us hold by this. They pin me down. They look backward and not forward. But genius looks forward; the eyes of man are set in his forehead, not in his hindhead; man hopes; genius creates. Whatever talents may be, if the man create not, the pure efflux of the Deity is not his; cinders and smoke there may be, but not yet flame. There are creative manners, there are creative actions, and creative words; manners, actions, words, that is, indicative of no custom or authority, but springing spontaneous from the mind's own sense of good and fair.

    On the other part, instead of being its own seer, let it receive from another mind its truth, though it were in torrents of light, without periods of solitude, inquest, and self-recovery, and a fatal disservice is done. Genius is always sufficiently the enemy of genius by overinfluence. The literature of every nation bears me witness. The English dramatic poets have Shakspearized now for two hundred years.

    Undoubtedly there is a right way of reading, so it be sternly subordinated. Man Thinking must not be subdued by his instruments. Books are for the scholar's idle times. When he can read God directly, the hour is too precious to be wasted in other men's transcripts of their readings. But when the intervals of darkness come, as come they must,— when the sun is hid and the stars withdraw their shining,—we repair to the lamps which were kindled by their ray, to guide our steps to the East again, where the dawn is. We hear, that we may speak. The Arabian proverb says, "A fig tree, looking on a fig tree, becometh fruitful."

    It is remarkable, the character of the pleasure we derive from the best books. They impress us with the conviction that one nature wrote and the same reads. We read the verses of one of the great English poets, of Chaucer, of Marvell, of Dryden, with the most modern joy,—with a pleasure, I mean, which is in great part caused by the abstraction of all *time* from their verses. There is some awe mixed with the joy of our surprise, when this poet, who lived in some past world, two or three hundred years ago, says that which lies close to my own soul, that which I also had well-nigh thought and said. But for the evidence thence afforded to the philosophical doctrine of the identity of all minds, we should suppose some preëstablished harmony, some foresight of souls that were to be, and some preparation of stores for their future wants, like the fact observed in insects, who lay up food before death for the young grub they shall never see.

I would not be hurried by any love of system, by any exaggeration of instincts, to underrate the Book. We all know, that as the human body can be nourished on any food, though it were boiled grass and the broth of shoes, so the human mind can be fed by any knowledge. And great and heroic men have existed who had almost no other information than by the printed page. I only would say that it needs a strong head to bear that diet. One must be an inventor to read well. As the proverb says, "He that would bring home the wealth of the Indies, must carry out the wealth of the Indies." There is then creative reading as well as creative writing. When the mind is braced by labor and invention, the page of whatever book we read becomes luminous with manifold allusion. Every sentence is doubly significant, and the sense of our author is as broad as the world. We then see, what is always true, that as the seer's hour of vision is short and rare among heavy days and months, so is its record, perchance, the least part of his volume. The discerning will read, in his Plato or Shakspeare, only that least part, —only the authentic utterances of the oracle; —all the rest he rejects, were it never so many times Plato's and Shakspeare's.

Of course there is a portion of reading quite indispensable to a wise man. History and exact science he must learn by laborious reading. Colleges, in like manner, have their indispensable office,—to teach elements. But they can only highly serve us when they aim not to drill, but to create; when they gather from far every ray of various genius to their hospitable halls, and, by the concentrated fires, set the hearts of their youth on flame. Thought and knowledge are natures in which apparatus and pretension avail nothing. Gowns, and pecuniary foundations, though of towns of gold, can never countervail the least sentence or syllable of wit. Forget this, and our American colleges will recede in their public importance, whilst they grow richer every year.

III. There goes in the world a notion that the scholar should be a recluse, a valetudinarian,—as unfit for any handiwork or public labor as a pen-knife for an axe. The so-called "practical men" sneer at speculative men, as if, because they speculate or *see*, they could do nothing. I have heard it said that the clergy, —who are always, more universally than any other class, the scholars of their day,—are addressed as women; that the rough, spontaneous conversation of men they do not hear, but only a mincing and diluted speech. They are often virtually disfranchised; and, indeed, there are advocates for their celibacy. As far as this is true of the studious classes, it is not just and wise. Action is with the scholar subordinate, but it is essential. Without it, he is not yet man. Without it, thought can never ripen into truth. Whilst the world hangs before the eye as a cloud of beauty, we cannot even see its beauty. Inaction is cowardice, but there can be no scholar without the heroic mind. The preamble of thought, the transition through which it passes from the unconscious to the conscious, is action. Only so much do I know, as I have lived. Instantly we know whose words are loaded with life, and whose not.

The world,—this shadow of the soul, or *other me*,—lies wide around. Its attractions are the keys which unlock my thoughts and make me acquainted with myself. I run eagerly into this resounding tumult. I grasp the hands of those next me, and take my place in the ring to suffer and to work, taught by an instinct that so shall the dumb abyss be vocal with speech. I pierce its order; I dissipate its fear; I dispose of it within the circuit of my expanding life. So much only of life as I know by experience, so much of the wilderness have I vanquished and planted, or so far have I extended my being, my dominion. I do not see how any man can afford, for the sake of his nerves and his nap, to spare any action in which he can partake. It is pearls and rubies to his discourse. Drudgery, calamity, exasperation, want, are instructors in eloquence and wisdom. The true scholar grudges every opportunity of action past by, as a loss of power. It is the raw material out of which the intellect moulds her splendid products. A strange process too, this, by which experience is converted into thought, as a mulberry leaf is converted into satin. The manufacture goes forward at all hours.

The actions and events of our childhood and youth are now matters of calmest observation. They lie like fair pictures in the air. Not so with our recent actions,—with the business which we now have in hand. On this we are quite unable to speculate. Our affections as yet circulate through it. We no more feel or know it than we feel the feet, or the hand, or the brain of our body. The new deed is yet a part of life,—remains for a time immersed in our unconscious life. In some contemplative hour it detaches itself from the life like a ripe fruit, to become a thought of the mind. Instantly it is raised, transfigured; the corruptible has put on incorruption. Henceforth it is an object of beauty, however base its origin and neighborhood. Observe too the impossibility of antedating this act. In its grub state, it cannot fly, it cannot shine, it is a dull grub. But suddenly, without observation, the selfsame thing unfurls beautiful wings, and is an angel of wisdom. So is there no fact, no event, in our private history, which shall not, sooner or later, lose its adhesive, inert form, and astonish us by soaring from our body into the empyrean. Cradle and infancy, school and playground, the fear of boys, and dogs, and ferules, the love of little maids and berries, and many another fact that once filled the whole sky, are gone already; friend and relative, profession and party, town and country, nation and world, must also soar and sing.

Of course, he who has put forth his total strength in fit actions has the richest return of wisdom. I will not shut myself out of this globe of action, and transplant an oak into a flowerpot, there to hunger and pine; nor trust the revenue of some single faculty, and exhaust one vein of thought, much like those Savoyards, who, getting their livelihood by carving shepherds, shepherdesses, and smoking Dutchmen, for all Europe, went out one day to the mountain to find stock, and discovered that they had whittled up the last of their pine-trees. Authors we have, in numbers, who have written out their vein, and who, moved by a commendable prudence, sail for Greece or Palestine, follow the trapper into the prairie, or ramble round Algiers, to replenish their merchantable stock.

If it were only for a vocabulary, the scholar would be covetous of action. Life is our dictionary. Years are well spent in country labors; in town; in the insight into trades and manufactures; in frank intercourse with many men and women; in science; in art; to the one end of mastering in all their facts a language by which to illustrate and embody our percep-

tions. I learn immediately from any speaker how much he has already lived, through the poverty or the splendor of his speech. Life lies behind us as the quarry from whence we get tiles and copestones for the masonry of to-day. This is the way to learn grammar. Colleges and books only copy the language which the field and the work-yard made.

But the final value of action, like that of books, and better than books, is that it is a resource. That great principle of Undulation in nature, that shows itself in the inspiring and expiring of the breath; in desire and satiety; in the ebb and flow of the sea; in day and night; in heat and cold; and, as yet more deeply ingrained in every atom and every fluid, is known to us under the name of Polarity,—these "fits of easy transmission and reflection," as Newton called them, are the law of nature because they are the law of spirit.

The mind now thinks; now acts; and each fit reproduces the other. When the artist has exhausted his materials, when the fancy no longer paints, when thoughts are no longer apprehended, and books are a weariness,—he has always the resource *to live*. Character is higher than intellect. Thinking is the function. Living is the functionary. The stream retreats to its source. A great soul will be strong to live, as well as strong to think. Does he lack organ or medium to impart his truths? He can still fall back on this elemental force of living them. This is a total act. Thinking is a partial act. Let the grandeur of justice shine in his affairs. Let the beauty of affection cheer his lowly roof. Those "far from fame," who dwell and act with him, will feel the force of his constitution in the doings and passages of the day better than it can be measured by any public and designed display. Time shall teach him that the scholar loses no hour which the man lives. Herein he unfolds the sacred germ of his instinct, screened from influence. What is lost in seemliness is gained in strength. Not out of those on whom systems of education have exhausted their culture, comes the helpful giant to destroy the old or to build the new, but out of unhandselled savage nature; out of terrible Druids and Berserkers come at last Alfred and Shakspeare.

I hear therefore with joy whatever is beginning to be said of the dignity and necessity of labor to every citizen. There is virtue yet in the hoe and the spade, for learned as well as for unlearned hands. And labor is everywhere welcome; always we are invited to work; only be this limitation observed, that a man shall not for the sake of wider activity sacrifice any opinion to the popular judgments and modes of action.

I have now spoken of the education of the scholar by nature, by books, and by action. It remains to say somewhat of his duties.

They are such as become Man Thinking. They may all be comprised in self-trust. The office of the scholar is to cheer, to raise, and to guide men by showing them facts amidst appearances. He plies the slow, unhonored, and unpaid task of observation. Flamsteed and Herschel, in their glazed observatories, may catalogue the stars with the praise of all men, and, the results being splendid and useful, honor is sure. But he, in his private observatory, cataloguing obscure and nebulous stars of the human mind, which as yet no man has thought of as such,—watching days and months sometimes for a few facts; correcting still his old records,—must relinquish display and immediate fame. In the long period of his preparation he must betray often an ignorance and shiftlessness in popular arts, incurring the disdain of the able who shoulder him aside. Long he must stammer in his speech; often forego the living for the dead. Worse yet, he must accept—how often!—poverty and solitude. For the ease and pleasure of treading the old road, accepting the fashions, the education, the religion of society, he takes the cross of making his own, and, of course, the self-accusation, the faint heart, the frequent uncertainty and loss of time, which are the nettles and tangling vines in the way of the self-relying and self-directed; and the state of virtual hostility in which he seems to stand to society, and especially to educated society. For all this loss and scorn, what offset? He is to find consolation in exercising the highest functions of human nature. He is one who raises himself from private considerations, and breathes and lives on public and illustrious thoughts. He is the world's eye. He is the world's heart. He is to resist the vulgar prosperity that retrogrades ever to barbarism, by preserving and communicating heroic sentiments, noble biographies, melodious verse, and the conclusions of history. Whatsoever oracles the human heart, in all emergencies, in all solemn hours, has uttered as its commentary on the world of actions,—these he shall receive and impart. And whatsoever new verdict Reason from her inviolable seat pronounces on the passing men and events of to-day,—this he shall hear and promulgate.

These being his functions, it becomes him to feel all confidence in himself, and to defer never to the popular cry. He and he only knows the world. The world of any moment is the merest appearance. Some great decorum, some fetish of a government, some ephemeral trade, or war, or man, is cried up by half mankind and cried down by the other half, as if all depended on this particular up or down. The odds are that the whole question is not worth the poorest thought which the scholar has lost in listening to the controversy. Let him not quit his belief that a popgun is a popgun, though the ancient and honorable of the earth affirm it to be the crack of doom. In silence, in steadiness, in severe abstraction, let him hold by himself; add observation to observation, patient of neglect, patient of reproach, and bide his own time,—happy enough if he can satisfy himself alone that this day he has seen something truly. Success treads on every right step. For the instinct is sure, that prompts him to tell his brother what he thinks. He then learns that in going down into the secrets of his own mind he has descended into the secrets of all minds. He learns that he who has mastered any law in his private thoughts, is master to that extent of all men whose language he speaks, and of all into whose language his own can be translated. The poet, in utter solitude remembering his spontaneous thoughts and recording them, is found to have recorded that which men in crowded cities find true for them also. The orator distrusts at first the fitness of his frank confessions, his want of knowledge of the person he addresses, until he finds that he is the complement of his hearers; that they drink his words because he fulfils for them their own nature; the deeper he dives into his privatest, secretest presentiment, to his wonder he finds this is the most acceptable, most public, and universally true. The people delight in it; the better part of every man feels, This is my music; this is myself.

In self-trust all the virtues are comprehended. Free should the scholar be,—free and brave. Free even to the definition of freedom, "without any hindrance that does not arise out of his own constitution." Brave; for fear is a thing which a scholar by his very function puts behind him. Fear always springs from ignorance. It is a shame to him if his tranquillity, amid dangerous times, arise from the presumption that, like children and women, his is a protected class; or if he seek a temporary peace by the diversion of his thoughts from politics or vexed questions, hiding his head like an ostrich in the flowering bushes, peeping into microscopes, and turning rhymes, as a boy whistles to keep his courage up. So is the danger a danger still; so is the fear worse. Manlike let him turn and face it. Let him look into its eye and search its nature, inspect its origin,—see the whelping of this lion,—which lies no great way back; he will then find in himself a perfect comprehension of its nature and extent; he will have made his hands meet on the other side, and can henceforth defy it, and pass on superior. The world is his who can see through its pretension. What deafness, what stone-blind custom, what overgrown error you behold is there only by sufferance,—by your sufferance. See it to be a lie, and you have already dealt it its mortal blow.

Yes, we are the cowed,—we the trustless. It is a mischievous notion that we are come late into nature; that the world was finished a long time ago. As the world was plastic and fluid in the hands of God, so it is ever to so much of his attributes as we bring to it. To ignorance and sin, it is flint. They adapt themselves to it as they may; but in proportion as a man has any thing in him divine, the firmament flows before him and takes his signet and form. Not he is great who can alter matter, but he who can alter my state of mind. They are the kings of the world who give the color of their present thought to all nature and all art, and persuade men by the cheerful serenity of their carrying the matter, that this thing which they do is the apple which the ages have desired to pluck, now at last ripe, and inviting nations to the harvest. The great man makes the great thing. Wherever Macdonald sits, there is the head of the table. Linnæus makes botany the most alluring of studies, and wins it from the farmer and the herb-woman; Davy, chemistry; and Cuvier, fossils. The day is always his who works in it with serenity and great aims. The unstable estimates of men crowd to him whose mind is filled with a truth, as the heaped waves of the Atlantic follow the moon.

For this self-trust, the reason is deeper than can be fathomed,—darker than can be enlightened. I might not carry with me the feeling of my audience in stating my own belief. But I have already shown the ground of my hope, in adverting to the doctrine that man is one. I believe man has been wronged; he has wronged himself. He has almost lost the light that can lead him back to his prerogatives. Men are become of no account. Men in history, men in the world of to-day are bugs, are spawn, and are called "the mass" and "the herd." In a century, in a millennium, one or two men; that is to say, one or two approximations to the right state of every man. All the rest behold in the hero or the poet their own green and crude being,—ripened; yes, and are content to be less, so *that* may attain to its full stature. What a testimony, full of grandeur, full of pity, is borne to the demands of his own nature, by the poor clansman, the poor partisan, who rejoices in the glory of his chief. The poor and the low find some amends to their immense moral capacity, for their acquiescence in a politcial and social inferiority. They are content to be brushed like flies from the path of a great person, so that justice shall be done by him to that common nature which it is the dearest desire of all to see enlarged and glorified. They sun themselves in the great man's light, and feel it to be their own element. They cast the dignity of man from their downtrod selves upon the shoulders of a hero, and will perish to add one drop of blood to make that great heart beat, those giant sinews combat and conquer. He lives for us, and we live in him.

Men such as they are, very naturally seek money or power; and power because it is as good as money,—the "spoils," so called, "of office." And why not? for they aspire to the highest, and this, in their sleep-walking, they dream is highest. Wake them, and they shall quit the false good, and leap to the true, and leave governments to clerks and desks. This revolution is to be wrought by the gradual domestication of the idea of Culture. The main enterprise of the world for splendor, for extent, is the upbuilding of a man. Here are the materials strewn along the ground. The private life of one man shall be a more illustrious monarchy, more formidable to its enemy, more sweet and serene in its influence to its friend, than any kingdom in history. For a man, rightly viewed, comprehendeth the particular natures of all men. Each philosopher, each bard, each actor has only done for me, as by a delegate, what one day I can do for myself. The books which once we valued more than the apple of the eye, we have quite exhausted. What is that but saying that we have come up with the point of view which the universal mind took through the eyes of one scribe; we have been that man, and have passed on. First, one; then another; we drain all cisterns, and, waxing greater by all these supplies, we crave a better and more abundant food. The man has never lived that can feed us ever. The human mind cannot be enshrined in a person who shall set a barrier on any one side to this unbounded, unboundable empire. It is one central fire, which, flaming now out of the lips of Etna, lightens the capes of Sicily, and now out of the throat of Vesuvius, illuminates the towers and vineyards of Naples. It is one light which beams out of a thousand stars. It is one soul which animates all men.

But I have dwelt perhaps tediously upon this abstraction of the Scholar. I ought not to delay longer to add what I have to say of nearer reference to the time and to this country.

Historically, there is thought to be a difference in the ideas which predominate over successive epochs, and there are data for marking the genius of the Classic, of the Romantic, and now of the Reflective or Philosophical age. With the views I have intimated of the oneness or the identity of the mind through all individuals, I do not much dwell on these differences. In fact, I believe each individual passes through all three. The boy is a Greek; the youth, romantic; the adult reflective. I deny not, however, that a revolution in the leading idea may be distinctly enough traced.

Our age is bewailed as the age of Introversion. Must that needs be evil? We, it seems, are critical; we are embarrassed with second thoughts; we cannot enjoy any thing for hankering to know whereof the pleasure consists; we are lined with eyes; we see with our feet; the time is infected with Hamlet's unhappiness,—

"Sicklied o'er with the pale cast of thought."

It is so bad then? Sight is the last thing to be pitied. Would we be blind? Do we fear lest we should outsee nature and God, and drink truth dry? I look upon the discontent of the literary class as a mere announcement of the fact that they find themselves not in the state of mind of their fathers, and regret the coming state as untried; as a boy dreads the water before he has learned that he can swim. If there is any period one would desire to be born in, is it not the age of Revolution; when the old and the new stand side by side and admit of being compared; when the energies of all men are searched by fear and by hope; when the historic glories of the old can be compensated by the rich possibilities of the new era? This time, like all times, is a very good one, if we but know what to do with it.

I read with some joy of the auspicious signs of the coming days, as they glimmer already through poetry and art, through philosophy and science, through church and state.

One of these signs is the fact that the same movement which effected the elevation of what was called the lowest class in the state, assumed in literature a very marked and as benign an aspect. Instead of the sublime and beautiful, the near, the low, the common, was explored and poetized. That which had been negligently trodden under foot by those who were harnessing and provisioning themselves for long journeys into far countries, is suddenly found to be richer than all foreign parts. The literature of the poor, the feelings of the child, the philosophy of the street, the meaning of household life, are the topics of the time. It is a great stride. It is a sign—is it not?—of new vigor when the extremities are made active, when currents of warm life run into the hands and the feet. I ask not for the great, the remote, the romantic; what is doing in Italy or Arabia; what is Greek art, or Provençal minstrelsy; I embrace the common, I explore and sit at the feet of the familiar, the low. Give me insight into to-day, and you may have the antique and future worlds. What would we really know the meaning of? The meal in the firkin; the milk in the pan; the ballad in the street; the news of the boat; the glance of the eye; the form and the gait of the body;—show me the ultimate reason of these matters; show me the sublime presence of the highest spiritual cause lurking, as always it does lurk, in these suburbs and extremities of nature; let me see every trifle bristling with the polarity that ranges it instantly on an eternal law; and the shop, the plough, and the ledger referred to the like cause by which light undulates and poets sing;—and the world lies no longer a dull miscellany and lumber-room, but has form and order; there is no trifle, there is no puzzle, but one design unites and animates the farthest pinnacle and the lowest trench.

This idea has inspired the genius of Goldsmith, Burns, Cowper, and, in a newer time, of Goethe, Wordsworth, and Carlyle. This idea they have differently followed and with various success. In contrast with their writing, the style of Pope, of Johnson, of Gibbon, looks cold and pedantic. This writing is blood-warm. Man is surprised to find that things near are not less beautiful and wondrous than things remote. The near explains the far. The drop is a small ocean. A man is related to all nature. This perception of the worth of the vulgar is fruitful in discoveries. Goethe, in this very thing the most modern of the moderns, has shown us, as none ever did, the genius of the ancients.

There is one man of genius who has done much for this philosophy of life, whose literary value has never yet been rightly estimated;—I mean Emanuel Swedenborg. The most imaginative of men, yet writing with the precision of a mathematician, he endeavored to engraft a purely philosophical Ethics on the popular Christianity of his time. Such an attempt of course must have difficulty which no genius could surmount. But he saw and showed the connection between nature and the affections of the soul. He pierced the emblematic or spiritual character of the visible, audible, tangible world. Especially did his shade-loving muse hover over and interpret the lower parts of nature; he showed the mysterious bond that allies moral evil to the foul material forms, and has given in epical parables a theory of insanity, of beasts, of unclean and fearful things.

Another sign of our times, also marked by an analogous political movement, is the new importance given to the single person. Every thing that tends to insulate the individual,—to surround him with barriers of natural respect, so that each man shall feel the world is his, and man shall treat with man as a sovereign state with a sovereign state,—tends to true union as well as greatness. "I learned," said the melancholy Pestalozzi, "that no man in God's wide earth is either willing or able to help any other man." Help must come from the bosom alone. The scholar is that man who must take up into himself all the ability of the time, all the contributions of the past, all the hopes of the future. He must be an university of knowledges. If there be one lesson more than another which should pierce his ear, it is: The world is nothing, the man is all; in yourself is the law of all nature, and you know not yet how a globule of sap ascends; in yourself slumbers the whole of Reason; it is for you to know all; it is for you to dare all. Mr. President and Gentlemen, this confidence in the unsearched might of man belongs, by all motives, by all prophecy, by all preparation, to the American Scholar. We have listened too long to the courtly muses of Europe. The spirit of the American freeman is already suspected to be timid, imitative, tame. Public and private avarice make the air we breathe thick and fat. The scholar is decent, indolent, complaisant. See already the tragic consequence. The mind of this country, taught to aim at low objects, eats upon itself. There is no work for any but the decorous and the complaisant. Young men of the fairest promise, who begin life upon our shores, inflated by the mountain winds, shined upon by all the stars of God, find the earth below not in unison with these, but are hindered from action by the disgust which the principles on which business is managed inspire, and turn drudges, or die of disgust, some of them suicides. What is the remedy? They did not yet see, and thousands of young men as hopeful now crowding to the barriers for the career do not yet see, that if the single man plant himself indomitably on his instincts, and there abide, the huge world will come round to him. Patience,—patience; with the shades of all the good and great for company; and for solace the perspective of your own infinite life; and for work the study and the communication of principles, the making those instincts prevalent, the conversion of the world. Is it not the chief disgrace in the world, not to be an unit;—not to be reckoned one character;—not to yield that peculiar fruit which each man was created to bear, but to be reckoned in the gross, in the hundred, or the thousand, of the party, the section, to which we belong; and our opinion predicted geographically, as the north, or the south? Not so, brothers and friends,—please God, ours shall not be so. We will walk on our own feet; we will work with our own hands; we will speak our own minds. The study of letters shall be no longer a name for pity, for doubt, and for sensual indulgence. The dread of man and the love of man shall be a wall of defence and a wreath of joy around all. A nation of men will for the first time exist, because each believes himself inspired by the Divine Soul which also inspires all men.   1837

»   »   THE POET   «   «

A moody child and wildly wise
Pursued the game with joyful eyes,
Which chose, like meteors, their way,
And rived the dark with private ray:
They overleapt the horizon's edge,
Searched with Apollo's privilege;
Through man, and woman, and sea, and star,
Saw the dance of nature forward far;
Through worlds, and races, and terms, and times,
Saw musical order, and pairing rhymes.

Olympian bards who sung
Divine ideas below,
Which always find us young,
And always keep us so.

Those who are esteemed umpires of taste are often persons who have acquired some knowledge of admired pictures or sculptures, and have an inclination for whatever is elegant; but if you inquire whether they are beautiful souls, and whether their own acts are like fair pictures, you learn that they are selfish and sensual. Their cultivation is local, as if you should rub a log of dry wood in one spot to produce fire, all the rest remaining cold. Their knowledge of the fine arts is some study of rules and particulars, or some limited judgment of color or form, which is exercised for amusement or for show. It is a proof of the shallowness of the doctrine of beauty, as it lies in the minds of our amateurs, that men seem to have lost the perception of the instant dependence of form upon soul. There is no doctrine of forms in our philosophy. We were put into our bodies, as fire is put into a pan to be carried about; but there is no accurate adjustment between the spirit and the organ, much less is the latter the germination of the former. So in regard to other forms, the intellectual men do not believe in any essential dependence of the material world on thought and volition. Theologians think it a pretty air-castle to talk of the spiritual meaning of a ship or a cloud, of a city or a contract, but they prefer to come again to the solid ground of historical evidence; and even the poets are contented with a civil and conformed manner of living, and to write poems from the fancy, at a safe distance from their own experience. But the highest minds of the world have never ceased to explore the double meaning, or, shall

I say, the quadruple, or the centuple, or much more manifold meaning, of every sensuous fact: Orpheus, Empedocles, Heraclitus, Plato, Plutarch, Dante, Swedenborg, and the masters of sculpture, picture, and poetry. For we are not pans and barrows, nor even porters of the fire and torch-bearers, but children of the fire, made of it, and only the same divinity transmuted, and at two or three removes, when we know least about it. And this hidden truth, that the fountains whence all this river of Time, and its creatures, floweth, are intrinsically ideal and beautiful, draws us to the consideration of the nature and functions of the Poet, or the man of Beauty, to the means and materials he uses, and to the general aspect of the art in the present time.

The breadth of the problem is great, for the poet is representative. He stands among partial men for the complete man, and apprises us not of his wealth, but of the common-wealth. The young man reveres men of genius, because, to speak truly, they are more himself than he is. They receive of the soul as he also receives, but they more. Nature enhances her beauty, to the eye of loving men, from their belief that the poet is beholding her shows at the same time. He is isolated among his contemporaries, by truth and by his art, but with this consolation in his pursuits, that they will draw all men sooner or later. For all men live by truth, and stand in need of expression. In love, in art, in avarice, in politics, in labor, in games, we study to utter our painful secret. The man is only half himself, the other half is his expression.

Notwithstanding this necessity to be published, adequate expression is rare. I know not how it is that we need an interpreter; but the great majority of men seem to be minors, who have not yet come into possession of their own, or mutes, who cannot report the conversation they have had with nature. There is no man who does not anticipate a supersensual utility in the sun, and stars, earth and water. These stand and wait to render him a peculiar service. But there is some obstruction, or some excess of phlegm in our constitution, which does not suffer them to yield the due effect. Too feeble fall the impressions of nature on us to make us artists. Every touch should thrill. Every man should be so much an artist that he could report in conversation what had befallen him. Yet, in our experience, the rays or appulses have sufficient force to arrive at the senses, but not enough to reach the quick and compel the reproduction of themselves in speech. The poet is the person in whom these powers are in balance, the man without impediment, who sees and handles that which others dream of, traverses the whole scale of experience, and is representative of man, in virtue of being the largest power to receive and to impart.

For the Universe has three children, born at one time, which reappear, under different names, in every system of thought, whether they be called cause, operation, and effect; or, more poetically, Jove, Pluto, Neptune; or, theologically, the Father, the Spirit, and the Son; but which we will call here the Knower, the Doer, and the Sayer. These stand respectively for the love of truth, for the love of good, and for the love of beauty. These three are equal. Each is that which he is essentially, so that he cannot be surmounted or analyzed, and each of these three has the power of the others latent in him, and his own patent.

The poet is the sayer, the namer, and represents beauty. He is a sovereign, and stands on the centre. For the world is not painted, or adorned, but is from the beginning beautiful; and God has not made some beautiful things, but Beauty is the creator of the universe. Therefore the poet is not any permissive potentate, but is emperor in his own right. Criticism is infested with a cant of materialism, which assumes that manual skill and activity is the first merit of all men, and disparages such as say and do not, overlooking the fact that some men, namely, poets, are natural sayers, sent into the world to the end of expression, and confounds them with those whose province is action, but who quit it to imitate the sayers. But Homer's words are as costly and admirable to Homer, as Agamemnon's victories are to Agamemnon. The poet does not wait for the hero or the sage, but, as they act and think primarily, so he writes primarily what will and must be spoken, reckoning the others, though primaries also, yet, in respect to him, secondaries and servants; as sitters or models

in the studio of a painter or as assistants who bring building materials to an architect.

For poetry was all written before time was, and whenever we are so finely organized that we can penetrate into that region where the air is music, we hear those primal warblings, and attempt to write them down, but we lose ever and anon a word, or a verse, and substitute something of our own, and thus miswrite the poem. The men of more delicate ear write down these cadences more faithfully, and these transcripts, though imperfect, become the songs of the nations. For nature is as truly beautiful as it is good, or as it is reasonable, and must as much appear, as it must be done, or be known. Words and deeds are quite indifferent modes of the divine energy. Words are also actions, and actions are a kind of words.

The sign and credentials of the poet are, that he announces that which no man foretold. He is the true and only doctor; he knows and tells; he is the only teller of news, for he was present and privy to the appearance which he describes. He is a beholder of ideas, and an utterer of the necessary and causal. For we do not speak now of men of poetical talents, or of industry and skill in metre, but of the true poet. I took part in a conversation, the other day, concerning a recent writer of lyrics, a man of subtle mind, whose head appeared to be a music-box of delicate tunes and rhythms, and whose skill and command of language we could not sufficiently praise. But when the question arose, whether he were not only a lyrist, but a poet, we were obliged to confess that he is plainly a contemporary, not an eternal man. He does not stand out of our low limitations, like a Chimborazo under the line, running up from the torrid base through all the climates of the globe, with belts of the herbage of every latitude on its high and mottled sides; but this genius is the landscape-garden of a modern house, adorned with fountains and statues, with well-bred men and women standing and sitting in the walks and terraces. We hear, through all the varied music, the ground-tone of conventional life. Our poets are men of talents who sing, and not the children of music. The argument is secondary, the finish of the verses is primary.

For it is not metres, but a metre-making argument, that makes a poem,—a thought so passionate and alive, that, like the spirit of a plant or an animal, it has an architecture of its own, and adorns nature with a new thing. The thought and the form are equal in the order of time, but in the order of genesis the thought is prior to the form. The poet has a new thought: he has a whole new experience to unfold; he will tell us how it was with him, and all men will be the richer in his fortune. For the experience of each new age requires a new confession, and the world seems always waiting for its poet. I remember, when I was young, how much I was moved one morning by tidings that genius had appeared in a youth who sat near me at table. He had left his work, and gone rambling none knew whither, and had written hundreds of lines, but could not tell whether that which was in him was therein told: he could tell nothing but that all was changed—man, beast, heaven, earth, and sea. How gladly we listened! how credulous! Society seemed to be compromised. We sat in the aurora of a sunrise which was to put out all the stars. Boston seemed to be at twice the distance it had the night before, or was much farther than that. Rome,—what was Rome? Plutarch and Shakspeare were in the yellow leaf, and Homer no more should be heard of. It is much to know that poetry has been written this very day, under this very roof, by your side. What! that wonderful spirit has not expired! These stony moments are still sparkling and animated! I had fancied that the oracles were all silent, and nature had spent her fires; and behold! all night, from every pore, these fine auroras have been streaming. Every one has some interest in the advent of the poet, and no one knows how much it may concern him. We know that the secret of the world is profound, but who or what shall be our interpreter, we know not. A mountain ramble, a new style of face, a new person, may put the key into our hands. Of course, the value of genius to us is in the veracity of its report. Talent may frolic and juggle; genius realizes and adds. Mankind, in good earnest, have gone so far in understanding themselves and their work, and the foremost watchman on the peak announces his news. It is the truest word ever spoken, and the phrase will be the fittest, most musical, and the unerring voice of the world for that time.

All that we call sacred history attests that the birth of a poet is the principal event in chronology. Man, never so often deceived, still watches for the arrival of a brother who can hold him steady to a truth, until he has made

it his own. With what joy I begin to read a poem, which I confide in as an inspiration! And now my chains are to be broken; I shall mount above these clouds and opaque airs in which I live,—opaque, though they seem transparent,—and from the heaven of truth I shall see and comprehend my relations. That will reconcile me to life, and renovate nature, to see trifles animated by a tendency, and to know what I am doing. Life will no more be 10 a noise; now I shall see men and women, and know the signs by which they may be discerned from fools and satans. This day shall be better than my birthday: then I became an animal: now I am invited into the science of the real. Such is the hope, but the fruition is postponed. Oftener it falls that this winged man, who will carry me into the heaven, whirls me into mists, then leaps and frisks about with me as it were from cloud to cloud, still affirming 20 that he is bound heavenward; and I, being myself a novice, am slow in perceiving that he does not know the way into the heavens, and is merely bent that I should admire his skill to rise, like a fowl or a flying-fish, a little way from the ground or the water; but the all-piercing, all-feeding, and ocular air of heaven, that man shall never inhabit. I tumble down again soon into my old nooks, and lead the life of exaggerations as before, and have 30 lost my faith in the possibility of any guide who can lead me thither where I would be.

But, leaving these victims of vanity, let us, with new hope, observe how nature, by worthier impulses, has insured the poet's fidelity to his office of announcement and affirming, namely, by the beauty of things, which becomes a new and higher beauty when expressed. Nature offers all her creatures to him as a picture-language. Being used as a type, 40 a second wonderful value appears in the object, far better than its old value, as the carpenter's stretched cord, if you hold your ear close enough, is musical in the breeze. "Things more excellent than every image," says Jamblichus, "are expressed through images." Things admit of being used as symbols, because nature is a symbol, in the whole, and in every part. Every line we can draw in the sand has expression; and there is no body with- 50 out its spirit or genius. All form is an effect of character; all condition, of the quality of the life; all harmony, of health; (and, for this reason, a perception of beauty should be sympathetic, or proper, only to the good). The beautiful rests on the foundations of the necessary. The soul makes the body, as the wise Spenser teaches:

> "So every spirit, as it is most pure,
> And hath in it the more of heavenly light,
> So it the fairer body doth procure
> To habit in, and it more fairly dight,
> With cheerful grace and amiable sight.
> For, of the soul, the body form doth take,
> For soul is form, and doth the body make."

12   Here we find ourselves, suddenly, not in a critical speculation, but in a holy place, and should go very warily and reverently. We stand before the secret of the world, there where Being passes into Appearance, and Unity into Variety.

The Universe is the externization of the soul. Wherever the life is, that bursts into appear-
20 ance around it. Our science is sensual, and therefore superficial. The earth and the heavenly bodies, physics and chemistry, we sensually treat, as if they were self-existent; but these are the retinue of that Being we have. "The mighty heaven," said Proclus, "exhibits, in its transfigurations, clear images of the splendor of intellectual perceptions; being moved in conjunction with the unapparent periods of intellectual natures." Therefore,
30 science always goes abreast with the just elevation of the man, keeping step with religion and metaphysics; or, the state of science is an index of our self-knowledge. Since every thing in nature answers to a moral power, if any phenomenon remains brute and dark, it is because the corresponding faculty in the observer is not yet active.

No wonder, then, if these waters be so deep, that we hover over them with a re-
40 ligious regard. The beauty of the fable proves the importance of the sense; to the poet, and to all others; or, if you please, every man is so far a poet as to be susceptible of these enchantments of nature: for all men have the thoughts whereof the universe is the celebration. I find that the fascination resides in the symbol. Who loves nature? Who does not? Is it only poets, and men of leisure and cultivation, who live with her? No; but also hunters, farmers,
50 grooms, and butchers, though they express their affection in their choice of life, and not in their choice of words. The writer wonders what the coachman or the hunter values in riding, in horses, and dogs. It is not superficial qualities. When you talk with him, he holds these at as slight a rate as you. His worship is sympathetic; he has no definitions, but he is commanded in nature, by the living power which he feels to be there present. No imitation, or playing of these things, would content him; he loves the earnest of the north wind, of rain, of stone, and wood, and iron. A beauty not explicable is dearer than a beauty which we can see to the end of. It is nature the symbol, nature certifying the supernatural, body overflowed by life, which he worships with coarse, but sincere rites.

The inwardness and mystery of this attachment drive men of every class to the use of emblems. The schools of poets and philosophers are not more intoxicated with their symbols, than the populace with theirs. In our political parties, compute the power of badges and emblems. See the huge ball which they roll from Baltimore to Bunker Hill! In the political processions, Lowell goes in a loom, and Lynn in a shoe, and Salem in a ship. Witness the cider-barrel, the log-cabin, the hickory-stick, the palmetto, and all the cognizances of party. See the power of national emblems. Some stars, lilies, leopards, a crescent, a lion, an eagle, or other figure, which came into credit God knows how, on an old rag of bunting, blowing in the wind on a fort, at the ends of the earth, shall make the blood tingle under the rudest or the most conventional exterior. The people fancy they hate poetry, and they are all poets and mystics!

Beyond this universality of the symbolic language, we are apprised of the divineness of this superior use of things, whereby the world is a temple whose walls are covered with emblems, pictures, and commandments of the Deity, in this, that there is no fact in nature which does not carry the whole sense of nature; and the distinctions which we make in events, and in affairs, of low and high, honest and base, disappear when nature is used as a symbol. Thought makes everything fit for use. The vocabulary of an omniscient man would embrace words and images excluded from polite conversation. What would be base, or even obscene, to the obscene, becomes illustrious, spoken in a new connection of thought. The piety of the Hebrew prophets purges their grossness. The circumcision is an example of the power of poetry to raise the low and offensive. Small and mean things serve as well as great symbols. The meaner the type by which a law is expressed, the more pungent it is, and the more lasting in the memories of men: just as we choose the smallest box or case in which any needful utensil can be carried. Bare lists of words are found suggestive to an imaginative and excited mind; as it is related of Lord Chatham, that he was accustomed to read in Bailey's Dictionary when he was preparing to speak in Parliament. The poorest experience is rich enough for all the purposes of expressing thought. Why covet a knowledge of new facts? Day and night, house and garden, a few books, a few actions, serve us as well as would all trades and all spectacles. We are far from having exhausted the significance of the few symbols we use. We can come to use them yet with a terrible simplicity. It does not need that a poem should be long. Every word was once a poem. Every new relation is a new word. Also, we use defects and deformities to a sacred purpose, so expressing our sense that the evils of the world are such only to the evil eye. In the old mythology, mythologists observe, defects are ascribed to divine natures, as lameness to Vulcan, blindness to Cupid, and the like, to signify exuberances.

For, as it is dislocation and detachment from the life of God that makes things ugly, the poet, who re-attaches things to nature and the Whole,—re-attaching even artificial things, and violations of nature, to nature, by a deeper insight,—disposes very easily of the most disagreeable facts. Readers of poetry see the factory-village and the railway, and fancy that the poetry of the landscape is broken up by these; for these works of art are not yet consecrated in their reading; but the poet sees them fall within the great Order not less than the beehive or the spider's geometrical web. Nature adopts them very fast into her vital circles, and the gliding train of cars she loves like her own. Besides, in a centred mind, it signifies nothing how many mechanical inventions you exhibit. Though you add millions, and never so surprising, the fact of mechanics has not gained a grain's weight. The spiritual fact remains unalterable, by many or by few particulars; as no mountain is of any appreciable height to break the curve of the sphere. A shrewd country-boy goes to the city for the first time, and the complacent citizen is not satisfied with his little wonder. It is not that he does not see all the fine houses, and know that he never saw such before, but he disposes of them as easily as the poet finds place for the railway. The chief value of the new fact, is to enhance the great and constant fact of Life, which can dwarf any and every circumstance, and to which the belt of wampum, and the commerce of America, are alike.

The world being thus put under the mind for verb and noun, the poet is he who can articulate it. For, though life is great, and fascinates, and absorbs,—and though all men are intelligent of the symbols through which it is named,—yet they cannot originally use them. We are symbols, and inhabit symbols; workmen, work, and tools, words and things, birth and death, all are emblems; but we sympathize with the symbols, and, being infatuated with the economical uses of things, we do not know that they are thoughts. The poet, by an ulterior intellectual perception, gives them a power which makes their old use forgotten, and puts eyes and a tongue into every dumb and inanimate object. He perceives the independence of the thought on the symbol, the stability of the thought, the accidency and fugacity of the symbol. As the eyes of Lyncæus were said to see through the earth, so the poet turns the world to glass, and shows us all things in their right series and procession. For, through that better perception, he stands one step nearer to things, and sees the flowing or metamorphosis; perceives that thought is multiform; that within the form of every creature is a force impelling it to ascend into a higher form; and, following with his eyes the life, uses the forms which express that life, and so his speech flows with the flowing of nature. All the facts of the animal economy, sex, nutriment, gestation, birth, growth, are symbols of the passage of the world into the soul of man, to suffer there a change, and reappear a new and higher fact. He uses forms according to the life and not according to the form. This is true science. The poet alone knows astronomy, chemistry, vegetation, and animation, for he does not stop at these facts, but employs them as signs. He knows why the plain or meadow of space was strown with these flowers we call suns and moons and stars; why the great deep is adorned with animals, with men, and gods; for in every word he speaks he rides on them as the horses of thought.

By virtue of this science the poet is the Namer or Language-maker, naming things sometimes after their appearance, sometimes after their essence, and giving to every one its own name and not another's, thereby rejoicing the intellect, which delights in detachment or boundary. The poets made all the words, and therefore language is the archives of history, and, if we must say it, a sort of tomb of the muses. For, though the origin of most of our words is forgotten, each word was at first a stroke of genius, and obtained currency, because for the moment it symbolized the world to the first speaker and to the hearer. The etymologist finds the deadest word to have been once a brilliant picture. Language is fossil poetry. As the limestone of the continent consists of infinite masses of the shells of animalcules, so language is made up of images, or tropes, which now, in their secondary use, have long ceased to remind us of their poetic origin. But the poet names the thing because he sees it, or comes one step nearer to it than any other. This expression, or naming, is not art, but a second nature, grown out of the first, as a leaf out of a tree. What we call nature is a certain self-regulated motion or change; and nature does all things by her own hands, and does not leave another to baptize her, but baptizes herself; and this through the metamorphosis again. I remember that a certain poet described it to me thus:—

Genius is the activity which repairs the decays of things, whether wholly or partly of a material and finite kind. Nature, through all her kingdoms, insures herself. Nobody cares for planting the poor fungus: so she shakes down from the gills of one agaric countless spores, any one of which, being preserved, transmits new billions of spores to-morrow or next day. The new agaric of this hour has a chance which the old one had not. This atom of seed is thrown into a new place, not subject to the accidents which destroyed its parent two rods off. She makes a man; and having brought him to ripe age, she will no longer run the risk of losing this wonder at a blow, but she detaches from him a new self, that the kind may be safe from accidents to which the individual is exposed. So when the soul of the poet has come to ripeness of thought, she detaches and sends away from it its poems or songs,— a fearless, sleepless, deathless progeny, which is not exposed to the accidents of the weary kingdom of time; a fearless, vivacious offspring, clad with wings (such was the virtue of the soul out of which they came), which carry them fast and far, and infix them irrevocably into the hearts of men. These wings are the beauty of the poet's soul. The songs, thus flying

immortal from their mortal parent, are pursued by clamorous flights of censures, which swarm in far greater numbers, and threaten to devour them; but these last are not winged. At the end of a very short leap they fall plump down, and rot, having received from the souls out of which they came no beautiful wings. But the melodies of the poet ascend, and leap, and pierce into the deeps of infinite time.

So far the bard taught me, using his freer speech. But nature has a higher end, in the production of new individuals, than security, namely, *ascension,* or, the passage of the soul into higher forms. I knew, in my younger days, the sculptor who made the statue of the youth which stands in the public garden. He was, as I remember, unable to tell, directly, what made him happy, or unhappy, but by wonderful indirections he could tell. He rose one day, according to his habit, before the dawn, and saw the morning break, grand as the eternity out of which it came, and, for many days after, he strove to express this tranquillity, and, lo! his chisel had fashioned out of marble the form of a beautiful youth, Phosphorus, whose aspect is such that, it is said, all persons who look on it become silent. The poet also resigns himself to his mood, and that thought which agitated him is expressed, but *alter idem,* in a manner totally new. The expression is organic, or, the new type which things themselves take when liberated. As, in the sun, objects paint their images on the retina of the eye, so they, sharing the aspiration of the whole universe, tend to paint a far more delicate copy of their essence in his mind. Like the metamorphosis of things into higher organic forms, is their change into melodies. Over everything stands its dæmon, or soul, and, as the form of the thing is reflected by the eye, so the soul of the thing is reflected by a melody. The sea, the mountain-ridge, Niagara, and every flower-bed, pre-exist, or superexist, in pre-cantations, which sail like odors in the air, and when any man goes by with an ear sufficiently fine, he overhears them, and endeavors to write down the notes, without diluting or depraving them. And herein is the legitimation of criticism, in the mind's faith that the poems are a corrupt version of some text in nature, with which they ought to be made to tally. A rhyme in one of our sonnets should not be less pleasing than the iterated nodes of a sea-shell, or the resembling difference of a group of flowers. The pairing of the birds is an idyl, not tedious as our idyls are; a tempest is a rough ode, without falsehood or rant; a summer, with its harvest sown, reaped, and stored, is an epic song, subordinating how many admirably executed parts. Why should not the symmetry and truth that modulate these, glide into our spirits, and we participate the invention of nature?

This insight, which expresses itself by what is called Imagination, is a very high sort of seeing, which does not come by study, but by the intellect being where and what it sees; by sharing the path or circuit of things through forms, and so making them translucid to others. The path of things is silent. Will they suffer a speaker to go with them? A spy they will not suffer; a lover, a poet, is the transcendency of their own nature,—him they will suffer. The condition of true naming, on the poet's part, is his resigning himself to the divine *aura* which breathes through forms, and accompanying that.

It is a secret which every intellectual man quickly learns, that, beyond the energy of his possessed and conscious intellect, he is capable of a new energy (as of an intellect doubled on itself), by abandonment to the nature of things; that, beside his privacy of power as an individual man, there is a great public power, on which he can draw, by unlocking, at all risks, his human doors, and suffering the ethereal tides to roll and circulate through him: then he is caught up into the life of the Universe, his speech is thunder, his thought is law, and his words are universally intelligible as the plants and animals. The poet knows that he speaks adequately, then only when he speaks somewhat wildly, or, "with the flower of the mind"; not with the intellect, used as an organ, but with the intellect released from all service, and suffered to take its direction from its celestial life; or, as the ancients were wont to express themselves, not with intellect alone, but with the intellect inebriated by nectar. As the traveller who has lost his way throws his reins on his horse's neck, and trusts to the instinct of the animal to find his road, so must we do with the divine animal who carries us through the world. For if in any manner we can stimulate this instinct, new passages are opened for us into nature, the mind flows into and through things hardest and highest, and the metamorphosis is possible.

This is the reason why bards love wine, mead, narcotics, coffee, tea, opium, the fumes of sandal-wood and tobacco, or whatever other procurers of animal exhilaration. All men avail themselves of such means as they can, to add this extraordinary power to their normal powers; and to this end they prize conversation, music, pictures, sculpture, dancing, theatres, travelling, war, mobs, fires, gaming, politics, or love, or science, or animal intoxication, which are several coarser or finer *quasi*-mechanical substitutes for the true nectar, which is the ravishment of the intellect by coming nearer to the fact. These are auxiliaries to the centrifugal tendency of a man, to his passage out into free space, and they help him to escape the custody of that body in which he is pent up, and of that jail-yard of individual relations in which he is enclosed. Hence a great number of such as were professionally expressers of Beauty, as painters, poets, musicians, and actors, have been more than others wont to lead a life of pleasure and indulgence: all but the few who received the true nectar; and, as it was a spurious mode of attaining freedom, as it was an emancipation not into the heavens, but into the freedom of baser places, they were punished for that advantage they won, by a dissipation and deterioration. But never can any advantage be taken of nature by a trick. The spirit of the world, the great calm presence of the Creator, comes not forth to the sorceries of opium or of wine. The sublime vision comes to the pure and simple soul in a clean and chaste body. That is not an inspiration which we owe to narcotics, but some counterfeit excitement and fury. Milton says that the lyric poet may drink wine and live generously, but the epic poet, he who shall sing of the gods, and their descent unto men, must drink water out of a wooden bowl. For poetry is not "Devil's wine," but God's wine. It is with this as it is with toys. We fill the hands and nurseries of our children with all manner of dolls, drums, and horses, withdrawing their eyes from the plain face and sufficing objects of nature, the sun, and moon, the animals, the water, and stones, which should be their toys. So the poet's habit of living should be set on a key so low that the common influences should delight him. His cheerfulness should be the gift of the sunlight; the air should suffice for his inspiration, and he should be tipsy with water. That spirit which suffices quiet hearts, which seems to come forth to such from every dry knoll of sere grass, from every pine stump and half-embedded stone, on which the dull March sun shines, comes forth to the poor and hungry, and such as are of simple taste. If thou fill thy brain with Boston and New York, with fashion and covetousness, and wilt stimulate thy jaded senses with wine and French coffee, thou shalt find no radiance of wisdom in the lonely waste of the pine-woods.

If the imagination intoxicates the poet, it is not inactive in other men. The metamorphosis excites in the beholder an emotion of joy. The use of symbols has a certain power of emancipation and exhilaration for all men. We seem to be touched by a wand, which makes us dance and run about happily, like children. We are like persons who come out of a cave or cellar into the open air. This is the effect on us of tropes, fables, oracles, and all poetic forms. Poets are thus liberating gods. Men have really got a new sense, and found within their world another world, or nest of worlds; for, the metamorphosis once seen, we divine that it does not stop. I will not now consider how much this makes the charm of algebra and the mathematics, which also have their tropes, but it is felt in every definition; as, when Aristotle defines *space* to be an immovable vessel, in which things are contained; or, when Plato defines a *line* to be a flowing point; or, *figure* to be a bound of solid; and many the like. What a joyful sense of freedom we have, when Vitruvius announces the old opinion of artists that no architect can build any house well who does not know something of anatomy. When Socrates, in Charmides, tells us that the soul is cured of its maladies by certain incantations, and that these incantations are beautiful reasons, from which temperance is generated in souls; when Plato calls the world an animal, and Timæus affirms that plants also are animals: or affirms a man to be a heavenly tree, growing with his root, which is his head, upward; and, as George Chapman, following him, writes,—

"So in our tree of man, whose nervie root
Springs in his top;"

when Orpheus speaks of hoariness as "that white flower which marks extreme old age"; when Proclus calls the universe the statue of the intellect; when Chaucer, in his praise of "Gentilesse," compares good blood in mean condition to fire, which, though carried to the darkest house betwixt this and the mount of Caucasus, will yet hold its natural office, and burn as bright as if twenty thousand men did it behold; when John saw, in the Apocalypse, the ruin of the world through evil, and the stars fall from Heaven, as the fig-tree casteth her untimely fruit; when Æsop reports the whole catalogue of common daily relations through the masquerade of birds and beasts; —we take the cheerful hint of the immortality of our essence, and its versatile habits and escapes, as when the gypsies say of themselves "It is in vain to hang them, they cannot die."

The poets are thus liberating gods. The ancient British bards had for the title of their order, "Those who are free throughout the world." They are free, and they make free. An imaginative book renders us much more service at first, by stimulating us through its tropes, than afterward, when we arrive at the precise sense of the author. I think nothing is of any value in books, excepting the transcendental and extraordinary. If a man is inflamed and carried away by his thought, to that degree that he forgets the authors and the public, and heeds only this one dream, which holds him like an insanity, let me read his paper, and you may have all the arguments and histories and criticism. All the value which attaches to Pythagoras, Paracelsus, Cornelius Agrippa, Cardan, Kepler, Swedenborg, Schelling, Oken, or any other who introduces questionable facts into his cosmogony, as angels, devils, magic, astrology, palmistry, mesmerism, and so on, is the certificate we have of departure from routine, and that here is a new witness. That also is the best success in conversation, the magic of liberty, which puts the world, like a ball, in our hands. How cheap even the liberty then seems; how mean to study, when an emotion communicates to the intellect the power to sap and upheave nature: how great the perspective! nations, times, systems, enter and disappear, like threads in tapestry of large figure and many colors; dream delivers us to dream, and, while the drunkenness lasts, we will sell our bed, our philosophy, our religion, in our opulence.

There is good reason why we should prize this liberation. The fate of the poor shepherd, who, blinded and lost in the snowstorm, perishes in a drift within a few feet of his cottage door, is an emblem of the state of man. On the brink of the waters of life and truth, we are miserably dying. The inaccessibleness of every thought but that we are in, is wonderful. What if you come near to it,—you are as remote when you are nearest, as when you are farthest. Every thought is also a prison; every Heaven is also a prison. Therefore we love the poet, the inventor, who in any form, whether in an ode, or in an action, or in looks and behavior, has yielded us a new thought. He unlocks our chains, and admits us to a new scene.

This emancipation is dear to all men; and the power to impart it, as it must come from greater depth and scope of thought, is a measure of intellect. Therefore all books of the imagination endure, all which ascend to that truth, that the writer sees nature beneath him, and uses it as his exponent. Every verse or sentence, possessing this virtue, will take care of its own immortality. The religions of the world are the ejaculations of a few imaginative men.

But the quality of the imagination is to flow, and not to freeze. The poet did not stop at the color, or the form, but read their meaning; neither may he rest in this meaning, but he makes the same objects exponents of his new thought. Here is the difference betwixt the poet and the mystic, that the last nails a symbol to one sense, which was a true sense for a moment, but soon becomes old and false. For all symbols are fluxional; all language is vehicular and transitive, and is good, as ferries and horses are, for conveyance, not as farms and houses are, for homestead. Mysticism consists in the mistake of an accidental and individual symbol for an universal one. The morning-redness happens to be the favorite meteor to the eyes of Jacob Behmen, and comes to stand to him for truth and faith; and he believes should stand for the same realities to every reader. But the first reader prefers as naturally the symbol of a mother and child, or a gardener and his bulb, or a jeweller polishing a gem. Either of these, or of a myriad more, are equally good to the person to whom they are significant. Only they must be held lightly, and be very willingly translated into the equivalent terms which others use. And the mystic must be steadily told,— All that you say is just as true without the tedious use of that symbol as with it. Let us have a little algebra, instead of this trite rhetoric,—universal signs, instead of these village symbols,—and we shall both be gainers. The history of hierarchies seems to show that all religious error consisted in making the symbol too stark and solid, and, at last, nothing but an excess of the organ of language.

Swedenborg, of all men in the recent ages, stands eminently for the translator of nature into thought. I do not know the man in history to whom things stood so uniformly for words. Before him the metamorphosis continually plays. Everything on which his eye rests, obeys the impulses of moral nature. The figs become grapes whilst he eats them. When some of his angels affirmed a truth, the laurel twig which they held blossomed in their hands. The noise which at a distance appeared like gnashing and thumping, on coming nearer was found to be the voice of disputants. The men, in one of his visions, seen in heavenly light, appeared like dragons, and seemed in darkness; but to each other they appeared as men, and, when the light from heaven shone into their cabin, they complained of the darkness, and were compelled to shut the window that they might see.

There was this perception in him, which makes the poet or seer an object of awe and terror, namely, that the same man, or society of men, may wear one aspect to themselves and their companions, and a different aspect to higher intelligences. Certain priests, whom he describes as conversing very learnedly together, appeared to the children, who were at some distance, like dead horses; and many the like misappearances. And instantly the mind inquires whether these fishes under the bridge, yonder oxen in the pasture, those dogs in the yard, are immutably fishes, oxen, and dogs, or only so appear to me, and perchance to themselves appear upright men; and whether I appear as a man to all eyes. The Brahmins and Pythagoras propounded the same question, and if any poet has witnessed the transformation, he doubtless found in it harmony with various experiences. We have all seen changes as considerable in wheat and caterpillars. He is the poet, and shall draw us with love and terror, who sees, through the flowing vest, the firm nature, and can declare it.

I look in vain for the poet whom I describe. We do not, with sufficient plainness, or sufficient profoundness, address ourselves to life, nor dare we chaunt our own times and social circumstance. If we filled the day with bravery, we should not shrink from celebrating it. Time and nature yield us many gifts, but not yet the timely man, the new religion, the reconciler, whom all things await. Dante's praise is, that he dared to write his autobiography in colossal cipher, or into universality. We have yet had no genius in America, with tyrannous eye, which knew the value of our incomparable materials, and saw, in the barbarism and materialism of the times, another carnival of the same gods whose picture he so much admires in Homer; then in the middle age; then in Calvinism. Banks and tariffs, the newspaper and caucus, Methodism and Unitarianism, are flat and dull to dull people, but rest on the same foundations of wonder as the town of Troy and the temple of Delphi, and are as swiftly passing away. Our log-rolling, our stumps and their politics, our fisheries, our Negroes, and Indians, our boats, and our repudiations, the wrath of rogues, and the pusillanimity of honest men, the northern trade, the southern planting, the western clearing, Oregon and Texas, are yet unsung. Yet America is a poem in our eyes; its ample geography dazzles the imagination, and it will not wait long for metres. If I have not found that excellent combination of gifts in my countrymen which I seek, neither could I aid myself to fix the idea of the poet by reading now and then in Chalmers's collection of five centuries of English poets. These are wits, more than poets, though there have been poets among them. But when we adhere to the ideal of the poet, we have our difficulties even with Milton and Homer. Milton is too literary, and Homer too literal and historical.

But I am not wise enough for a national criticism, and must use the old largeness a little longer, to discharge my errand from the muse to the poet concerning his art.

Art is the path of the creator to his work. The paths, or methods, are ideal and eternal, though few men ever see them, not the artist himself for years, or for a lifetime, unless he come into the conditions. The painter, the sculptor, the composer, the epic rhapsodist, the orator, all partake one desire, namely, to express themselves symmetrically and abundantly, not dwarfishly and fragmentarily. They found or put themselves in certain conditions, as, the painter and sculptor before some impressive human figures; the orator, into the assembly of the people; and the others, in such scenes as each has found exciting to his intellect; and each presently feels the new desire. He hears a voice, he sees a beckoning. Then he is apprised, with wonder, what herds of dæmons hem him in. He can no more rest; he says, with the old painter, "By God, it is in me, and must go forth of me." He pursues a beauty, half seen, which flies before him. The poet pours out verses in every solitude. Most of the things he says are conventional, no doubt; but by and by he says something which is original

and beautiful. That charms him. He would say nothing else but such things. In our way of talking, we say, "That is yours, this is mine"; but the poet knows well that it is not his; that it is as strange and beautiful to him as to you; he would fain hear the like eloquence at length. Once having tasted this immortal ichor, he cannot have enough of it, and, as an admirable creative power exists in these intellections, it is of the last importance that these things get spoken. What a little of all we know is said! What drops of all the sea of our science are baled up! and by what accident it is that these are exposed, when so many secrets sleep in nature! Hence the necessity of speech and song; hence these throbs and heart-beatings in the orator, at the door of the assembly, to the end, namely, that thought may be ejaculated as Logos, or Word.

Doubt not, O poet, but persist. Say, "It is in me, and shall out." Stand there, balked and dumb, stuttering and stammering, hissed and hooted, stand and strive, until, at last, rage draw out of thee that *dream*-power which every night shows thee is thine own; a power transcending all limit and privacy, and by virtue of which a man is the conductor of the whole river of electricity. Nothing walks, or creeps, or grows, or exists, which must not in turn arise and walk before him as exponent of his meaning. Comes he to that power, his genius is no longer exhaustible. All the creatures, by pairs and by tribes, pour into his mind as into a Noah's ark, to come forth again to people a new world. This is like the stock of air for our respiration, or for the combustion of our fireplace, not a measure of gallons, but the entire atmosphere if wanted. And therefore the rich poets, as Homer, Chaucer, Shakspeare, and Raphael, have obviously no limits to their works, except the limits of their lifetime, and resemble a mirror carried through the street, ready to render an image of every created thing.

O poet! a new nobility is conferred in groves and pastures, and not in castles, or by the sword-blade, any longer. The conditions are hard, but equal. Thou shalt leave the world, and know the muse only. Thou shalt not know any longer the time, customs, graces, politics, or opinions of men, but shalt take all from the muse. For the time of towns is tolled from the world by funeral chimes, but in nature the universal hours are counted by succeeding tribes of animals and plants, and by growth of joy on joy. God wills also that thou abdicate a manifold and duplex life, and that thou be content that others speak for thee. Others shall be thy gentlemen, and shall represent all courtesy and worldly life for thee; others shall do the great and resounding actions also. Thou shalt lie close hid with nature, and canst not be afforded to the Capitol or the Exchange. The world is full of renunciations and apprenticeships, and this is thine; thou must pass for a fool and a churl for a long season. This is the screen and sheath in which Pan has protected his well-beloved flower, and thou shalt be known only to thine own, and they shall console thee with tenderest love. And thou shalt not be able to rehearse the names of thy friends in thy verse, for an old shame before the holy ideal. And this is the reward: that the ideal shall be real to thee, and the impressions of the actual world shall fall like summer rain, copious, but not troublesome, to thy invulnerable essence. Thou shalt have the whole land for thy park and manor, the sea for thy bath and navigation, without tax and without envy; the woods and the rivers thou shalt own; and thou shalt possess that wherein others are only tenants and boarders. Thou true land-lord! sea-lord! air-lord! Wherever snow falls, or water flows, or birds fly, wherever day and night meet in twilight, wherever the blue heaven is hung by clouds, or sown with stars, wherever are forms with transparent boundaries, wherever are outlets into celestial space, wherever is danger, and awe, and love, there is Beauty, plenteous as rain, shed for thee, and though thou shouldst walk the world over, thou shalt not be able to find a condition inopportune or ignoble.

1844

» » NAPOLEON; OR, THE MAN OF THE WORLD[5] « «

Among the eminent persons of the nineteenth century, Bonaparte is far the best known, and the most powerful; and owes his predominance to the fidelity with which he expresses the tone of thought and belief, the aims of the masses of active and cultivated men. It is Swedenborg's theory, that every organ is made up of homogeneous particles; or, as it is sometimes expressed, every whole is made of similars; that is, the lungs are composed of infinitely small lungs; the liver, of infinitely small livers; the kidney, of little kidneys, &c. Following this analogy, if any man is found to carry with him the power and affections of vast numbers, if Napoleon is France, if Napoleon is Europe, it is because the people whom he sways are little Napoleons.

In our society, there is a standing antagonism between the conservative and the democratic classes; between those who have made their fortunes, and the young and the poor who have fortunes to make; between the interests of dead labor,—that is, the labor of hands long ago still in the grave, which labor is now entombed in money stocks, or in land and buildings owned by idle capitalists,—and the interests of living labor, which seeks to possess itself of land, and buildings, and money stocks. The first class is timid, selfish, illiberal, hating innovation, and continually losing numbers by death. The second class is selfish also, encroaching, bold, self-relying, always outnumbering the other, and recruiting its numbers every hour by births. It desires to keep open every avenue to the competition of all, and to multiply avenues;—the class of business men in America, in England, in France, and throughout Europe; the class of industry and skill. Napoleon is its representative. The instinct of active, brave, able men, throughout the middle class every where, has pointed out Napoleon as the incarnate Democrat. He had their virtues and their vices; above all, he had their spirit or aim. That tendency is material, pointing at a sensual success, and employing the richest and most various means to that end; conversant with mechanical powers, highly intellectual, widely and accurately learned and skilful, but subordinating all intellectual and spiritual forces into means to a material success. To be the rich man, is the end. "God has granted," says the Koran, "to every people a prophet in its own tongue." Paris, and London, and New York, the spirit of commerce, of money, and material power, were also to have their prophet; and Bonaparte was qualified and sent.

Every one of the million readers of anecdotes, or memoirs, or lives of Napoleon, delights in the page, because he studies in it his

---

[5] The sixth of the essays published as *Representative Men* in 1850. Emerson had previously used them as lectures.

own history. Napoleon is thoroughly modern, and, at the highest point of his fortunes, has the very spirit of the newspapers. He is no saint,—to use his own word, "no capuchin," and he is no hero, in the high sense. The man in the street finds in him the qualities and powers of other men in the street. He finds him, like himself, by birth a citizen, who, by very intelligible merits, arrived at such a commanding position, that he could indulge all those tastes which the common man possesses, but is obliged to conceal and deny: good society, good books, fast travelling, dress, dinners, servants without number, personal weight, the execution of his ideas, the standing in the attitude of a benefactor to all persons about him, the refined enjoyments of pictures, statues, music, palaces, and conventional honors,—precisely what is agreeable to the heart of every man in the nineteenth century,—this powerful man possessed.

It is true that a man of Napoleon's truth of adaptation to the mind of the masses around him, becomes not merely representative, but actually a monopolizer and usurper of other minds. Thus Mirabeau plagiarized every good thought, every good word, that was spoken in France. Dumont relates, that he sat in the gallery of the Convention, and heard Mirabeau make a speech. It struck Dumont that he could fit it with a peroration, which he wrote in pencil immediately, and showed it to Lord Elgin, who sat by him. Lord Elgin approved it, and Dumont, in the evening, showed it to Mirabeau. Mirabeau read it, pronounced it admirable, and declared he would incorporate it into his harangue, tomorrow, to the Assembly. "It is impossible," said Dumont, "as, unfortunately, I have shown it to Lord Elgin." "If you have shown it to Lord Elgin, and to fifty persons beside, I shall still speak it to-morrow": and he did speak it, with much effect, at the next day's session. For Mirabeau, with his overpowering personality, felt that these things, which his presence inspired, were as much his own, as if he had said them, and that his adoption of them gave them their weight. Much more absolute and centralizing was the successor to Mirabeau's popularity, and to much more than his predominance in France. Indeed, a man of Napoleon's stamp almost ceases to have a private speech and opinion. He is so largely receptive, and is so placed, that he comes to be a bureau for all the intelligence, wit, and power, of the age and country. He gains the battle; he makes the code; he makes the system of weights and measures; he levels the Alps; he builds the road. All distinguished engineers, savans, statists, report to him: so, likewise, do all good heads in every kind: he adopts the best measures, sets his stamp on them, and not these alone, but on every happy and memorable expression. Every sentence spoken by Napoleon, and every line of his writing, deserves reading, as it is the sense of France.

Bonaparte was the idol of common men, because he had in transcendent degree the qualities and powers of common men. There is a certain satisfaction in coming down to the lowest ground of politics, for we get rid of cant and hypocrisy. Bonaparte wrought, in common with that great class he represented, for power and wealth,—but Bonaparte, specially, without any scruple as to the means. All the sentiments which embarrass men's pursuit of these objects, he set aside. The sentiments were for women and children. Fontanes, in 1804, expressed Napoleon's own sense, when, in behalf of the Senate, he addressed him,—"Sire, the desire of perfection is the worst disease that ever afflicted the human mind." The advocates of liberty, and of progress, are "ideologists";— a word of contempt often in his mouth;— "Necker is an ideologist": "Lafayette is an ideologist."

An Italian proverb, too well known, declares that, "if you would succeed, you must not be too good." It is an advantage, within certain limits, to have renounced the dominion of the sentiments of piety, gratitude, and generosity; since, what was an impassable bar to us, and still is to others, becomes a convenient weapon for our purposes; just as the river which was a formidable barrier, winter transforms into the smoothest of roads.

Napoleon renounced, once for all, sentiments and affections, and would help himself with his hands and his head. With him is no miracle, and no magic. He is a worker in brass, in iron, in wood, in earth, in roads, in buildings, in money, and in troops, and a very consistent and wise master-workman. He is never weak and literary, but acts with the solidity and the precision of natural agents. He has not lost his native sense and sympathy with things. Men give way before such a man, as before natural events. To be sure, there are men enough who are immersed in things, as farmers, smiths, sailors, and mechanics generally; and we know how real and solid such men appear in the presence of scholars and grammarians: but these men ordinarily lack the power of arrangement, and are like hands without a head. But Bonaparte superadded to this mineral and animal force, insight and generalization, so that men saw in him combined the natural and the intellectual power, as if the sea and land had taken flesh and begun to cipher. Therefore the land and sea seem to presuppose him. He came unto his own, and they received him. This ciphering operative knows what he is working with, and what is the product. He knew the properties of gold and iron, of wheels and ships, of troops and diplomatists, and required that each should do after its kind.

The art of war was the game in which he exerted his arithmetic. It consisted, according to him, in having always more forces than the enemy, on the point where the enemy is attacked, or where he attacks: and his whole talent is strained by endless manoeuvre and evolution, to march always on the enemy at an angle, and destroy his forces in detail. It is obvious that a very small force, skilfully and rapidly manoeuvring, so as always to bring two men against one at the point of engagement, will be an overmatch for a much larger body of men.

The times, his constitution, and his early circumstances, combined to develop this pattern democrat. He had the virtues of his class, and the conditions for their activity. That common sense, which no sooner respects any end, than it finds the means to effect it; the delight in the use of means; in the choice, simplification, and combining of means; the directness and thoroughness of his work; the prudence with which all was seen, and the energy with which all was done, make him the natural organ and head of what I may almost call, from its extent, the *modern* party.

Nature must have far the greatest share in every success, and so in his. Such a man was wanted, and such a man was born; a man of stone and iron, capable of sitting on horseback sixteen or seventeen hours, of going many days together without rest or food, except by snatches, and with the speed and spring of a tiger in action; a man not embarrassed by any scruples; compact, instant, selfish, prudent, and of a perception which did not suffer itself to be baulked or misled by any pretences of others, or any superstition, or any heat or haste of his own. "My hand of iron," he said, "was not at the extremity of my arm; it was immediately connected with my head." He respected the power of nature and fortune, and ascribed to it his superiority, instead of valuing himself, like inferior men, on his opinionativeness, and waging war with nature. His favorite rhetoric lay in allusion to his star; and he pleased himself, as well as the people, when he styled himself the "Child of Destiny." "They charge me," he said, "with the commission of great crimes: men of my stamp do not commit crimes. Nothing has been more simple than my elevation: 'tis in vain to ascribe it to intrigue or crime: it was owing to the peculiarity of the times, and to my reputation of having fought well against the enemies of my country. I have always marched with the opinion of great masses, and with events. Of what use, then, would crimes be to me?" Again he said, speaking of his son, "My son can not replace me; I could not replace myself. I am the creature of circumstances."

He had a directness of action never before combined with so much comprehension. He is a realist, terrific to all talkers, and confused truth-obscuring persons. He sees where the matter hinges, throws himself on the precise point of resistance, and slights all other considerations. He is strong in the right manner, namely, by insight. He never blundered into victory, but won his battles in his head, before he won them on the field. His principal means are in himself. He asks counsel of no other. In 1796, he writes to the Directory; "I have conducted the campaign without consulting any one. I should have done no good, if I had been under the necessity of conforming to the notions of another person. I have gained some advantages over superior forces, and when totally destitute of every thing, because, in the persuasion that your confidence was reposed in me, my actions were as prompt as my thoughts."

History is full, down to this day, of the imbecility of kings and governors. They are a class of persons much to be pitied, for they know not what they should do. The weavers strike for bread; and the king and his ministers, not knowing what to do, meet them with bayonets. But Napoleon understood his business. Here was a man who, in each moment and emergency, knew what to do next. It is an immense comfort and refreshment to the spirits, not only of kings, but of citizens. Few men have any next; they live from hand to mouth, without plan, and are ever at the end of their line, and, after each action, wait for an impulse from abroad. Napoleon had been the first man of the world, if his ends had been purely public. As he is, he inspires confidence and vigor by the extraordinary unity of his action. He is firm, sure, self-denying, self-postponing, sacrificing every thing to his aim,— money, troops, generals, and his own safety also, to his aim; not misled, like common adventurers, by the splendor of his own means. "Incidents ought not to govern policy," he said, "but policy, incidents." "To be hurried away by every event, is to have no political system at all." His victories were only so many doors, and he never for a moment lost sight of his way onward, in the dazzle and uproar of the present circumstance. He knew what to do, and he flew to his mark. He would shorten a straight line to come at his object. Horrible anecdotes may, no doubt, be collected from his history, of the price at which he bought his successes; but he must not therefore be set down as cruel; but only as one who knew no impediment to his will; not bloodthirsty, not cruel,—but woe to what thing or person stood in his way! Not bloodthirsty, but not sparing of blood,—and pitiless. He saw only the object: the obstacle must give way. "Sire, General Clarke can not combine with General Junot, for the dreadful fire of the Austrian battery."—"Let him carry the battery."—"Sire, every regiment that approaches the heavy artillery is sacrificed: Sire, what orders?"—"Forward, forward!" Seruzier, a colonel of artillery, gives, in his *Military Memoirs*, the following sketch of a scene after the battle of Austerlitz.—"At the moment in which the Russian army was making its retreat, painfully, but in good order, on the ice of the lake, the Emperor Napoleon came riding at full speed toward the artillery. 'You are losing time,' he cried; 'fire upon those masses; they must be engulfed: fire upon the ice.' The order remained unexecuted for ten minutes. In vain several officers and myself were placed on the slope of a hill to produce the effect: their balls and mine rolled upon the ice, without breaking it up. Seeing that, I tried a simple method of elevating light howitzers. The almost perpendicular fall of the heavy projectiles

produced the desired effect. My method was immediately followed by the adjoining batteries, and in less than no time we buried" some [6] "thousands of Russians and Austrians under the waters of the lake."

In the plenitude of his resources, every obstacle seemed to vanish. "There shall be no Alps," he said; and he built his perfect roads, climbing by graded galleries their steepest precipices, until Italy was as open to Paris as any town in France. He laid his bones to, and wrought for his crown. Having decided what was to be done, he did that with might and main. He put out all his strength. He risked every thing, and spared nothing, neither ammunition, nor money, nor troops, nor generals, nor himself.

We like to see every thing do its office after its kind, whether it be a milch-cow or a rattlesnake; and, if fighting be the best mode of adjusting national differences, (as large majorities of men seem to agree,) certainly Bonaparte was right in making it thorough. "The grand principle of war," he said, "was, that an army ought always to be ready, by day and by night, and at all hours, to make all the resistance it is capable of making." He never economized his ammunition, but, on a hostile position, rained a torrent of iron,—shells, balls, grape-shot,—to annihilate all defence. On any point of resistance, he concentrated squadron on squadron in overwhelming numbers, until it was swept out of existence. To a regiment of horse-chasseurs at Lobenstein, two days before the battle of Jena, Napoleon said, "My lads, you must not fear death; when soldiers brave death, they drive him into the enemy's ranks." In the fury of assault, he no more spared himself. He went to the edge of his possibility. It is plain that in Italy he did what he could, and all that he could. He came, several times, within an inch of ruin; and his own person was all but lost. He was flung into the marsh at Arcola. The Austrians were between him and his troops, in the melée, and he was brought off with desperate efforts. At Lonato, and at other places, he was on the point of being taken prisoner. He fought sixty battles. He had never enough. Each victory was a new weapon. "My power would fall, were I not to support it by new achievements. Conquest has made me what I am, and conquest must maintain me." He felt, with every

---

[6] As I quote at second hand, and cannot produce Seruzier, I dare not adopt the high figure I find. [Author's note.]

wise man, that as much life is needed for conservation, as for creation. We are always in peril, always in a bad plight, just on the edge of destruction, and only to be saved by invention and courage.

This vigor was guarded and tempered by the coldest prudence and punctuality. A thunderbolt in the attack, he was found invulnerable in his intrenchments. His very attack was never the inspiration of courage, but the result of calculation. His idea of the best defence consists in being still the attacking party. "My ambition," he says, "was great, but was of a cold nature." In one of his conversations with Las Casas, he remarked, "As to moral courage, I have rarely met with the two-o'clock-in-the-morning kind: I mean unprepared courage, that which is necessary on an unexpected occasion; and which, in spite of the most unforeseen events, leaves full freedom of judgment and decision": and he did not hesitate to declare that he was himself eminently endowed with this "two-o'clock-in-the-morning courage, and that he had met with few persons equal to himself in this respect."

Every thing depended on the nicety of his combinations, and the stars were not more punctual than his arithmetic. His personal attention descended to the smallest particulars. "At Montebello, I ordered Kellermann to attack with eight hundred horse, and with these he separated the six thousand Hungarian grenadiers, before the very eyes of the Austrian cavalry. This cavalry was half a league off, and required a quarter of an hour to arrive on the field of action; and I have observed, that it is always these quarters of an hour that decide the fate of a battle." "Before he fought a battle, Bonaparte thought little about what he should do in case of success, but a great deal about what he should do in case of a reverse of fortune." The same prudence and good sense mark all his behavior. His instructions to his secretary at the Tuilleries are worth remembering. "During the night, enter my chamber as seldom as possible. Do not awake me when you have any good news to communicate; with that there is no hurry. But when you bring bad news, rouse me instantly, for then there is not a moment to be lost." It was a whimsical economy of the same kind which dictated his practice, when general in Italy, in regard to his burdensome correspondence. He directed Bourrienne to leave all letters unopened for three weeks, and then observed with satisfaction how large a part of the correspondence had thus disposed of itself, and no longer required an answer. His achievement of business was immense, and enlarges the known powers of man. There have been many working kings, from Ulysses to William of Orange, but none who accomplished a tithe of this man's performance.

To these gifts of nature, Napoleon added the advantage of having been born to a private and humble fortune. In his later days, he had the weakness of wishing to add to his crowns and badges the prescription of aristocracy: but he knew his debt to his austere education, and made no secret of his contempt for the born kings, and for "the hereditary asses," as he coarsely styled the Bourbons. He said that, "in their exile, they had learned nothing, and forgot nothing." Bonaparte had passed through all the degrees of military service, but also was citizen before he was emperor, and so has the key to citizenship. His remarks and estimates discover the information and justness of measurement of the middle class. Those who had to deal with him, found that he was not to be imposed upon, but could cipher as well as another man. This appears in all parts of his Memoirs, dictated at St. Helena. When the expenses of the empress, of his household, of his palaces, had accumulated great debts, Napoleon examined the bills of the creditors himself, detected overcharges and errors, and reduced the claims by considerable sums.

His grand weapon, namely, the millions whom he directed, he owed to the representative character which clothed him. He interests us as he stands for France and for Europe; and he exists as captain and king, only as far as the Revolution, or the interest of the industrious masses, found an organ and a leader in him. In the social interests, he knew the meaning and value of labor, and threw himself naturally on that side. I like an incident mentioned by one of his biographers at St. Helena. "When walking with Mrs. Balcombe, some servants, carrying heavy boxes, passed by on the road, and Mrs. Balcombe desired them, in rather an angry tone, to keep back. Napoleon interfered, saying, 'Respect the burden, Madam.'" In the time of the empire, he directed attention to the improvement and embellishment of the markets of the capital. "The market-place," he said, "is the Louvre of the common people." The principal works that have survived him are his magnificent roads. He filled the troops with his spirit, and a sort of freedom and companionship grew up between him and them, which the forms of his court never permitted between the officers and himself. They performed, under his eye, that which no others could do. The best document of his relation to his troops is the order of the day on the morning of the battle of Austerlitz, in which Napoleon promises the troops that he will keep his person out of reach of fire. This declaration, which is the reverse of that ordinarily made by generals and sovereigns on the eve of a battle, sufficiently explains the devotion of the army to their leader.

But though there is in particulars this identity between Napoleon and the mass of the people, his real strength lay in their conviction that he was their representative in his genius and aims, not only when he courted, but when he controlled and even when he decimated them by his conscriptions. He knew, as well as any Jacobin in France, how to philosophize on liberty and equality; and, when allusion was made to the precious blood of centuries, which was spilled by the killing of the Duc d'Enghien, he suggested, "Neither is my blood ditch-water." The people felt that no longer the throne was occupied, and the land sucked of its nourishment, by a small class of legitimates, secluded from all community with the children of the soil, and holding the ideas and superstitions of a long-forgotten state of society. Instead of that vampyre, a man of themselves held, in the Tuilleries, knowledge and ideas like their own, opening, of course, to them and their children, all places of power and trust. The day of sleepy, selfish policy, ever narrowing the means and opportunities of young men, was ended, and a day of expansion and demand was come. A market for all the powers and productions of man was opened; brilliant prizes glittered in the eyes of youth and talent. The old, iron-bound, feudal France was changed into a young Ohio or New York; and those who smarted under the immediate rigors of the new monarch, pardoned them, as the necessary severities of the military system which had driven out the oppressor. And even when the majority of the people had begun to ask, whether they had really gained any thing under the exhausting levies of men and money of the new master,—the whole talent of the country, in every rank and kindred, took his part, and defended him as its natural patron. In 1814, when advised to rely on the higher classes, Napoleon said to those around him, "Gentlemen, in the situation in which I stand, my only nobility is the rabble of the Faubourgs."

Napoleon met this natural expectation. The necessity of his position required a hospitality to every sort of talent, and its appointment to trusts; and his feeling went along with this policy. Like every superior person, he undoubtedly felt a desire for men and compeers, and a wish to measure his power with other masters, and an impatience of fools and underlings. In Italy, he sought for men, and found none. "Good God!" he said, "how rare men are! There are eighteen millions in Italy, and I have with difficulty found two,—Dandolo and Melzi." In later years, with larger experience, his respect for mankind was not increased. In a moment of bitterness, he said, to one of his oldest friends, "Men deserve the contempt with which they inspire me. I have only to put some gold lace on the coat of my virtuous republicans, and they immediately become just what I wish them." This impatience at levity was, however, an oblique tribute of respect to those able persons who commanded his regard, not only when he found them friends and coadjutors, but also when they resisted his will. He could not confound Fox and Pitt, Carnot, Lafayette, and Bernadotte, with the danglers of his court; and, in spite of the detraction which his systematic egotism dictated toward the great captains who conquered with and for him, ample acknowledgments are made by him to Lannes, Duroc, Kleber, Dessaix, Massena, Murat, Ney, and Augereau. If he felt himself their patron, and the founder of their fortunes, as when he said, "I made my generals out of mud," he could not hide his satisfaction in receiving from them a seconding and support commensurate with the grandeur of his enterprise. In the Russian campaign, he was so much impressed by the courage and resources of Marshal Ney, that he said, "I have two hundred millions in my coffers, and I would give them all for Ney." The characters which he has drawn of several of his marshals, are discriminating, and, though they did not content the insatiable vanity of French officers, are, no doubt, substantially just. And, in fact, every species of merit was sought and advanced under his government. "I know," he said, "the depth and draught of water of every one of my generals." Natural power was sure to be well received at his court. Seventeen men, in his time, were raised from common soldiers to the rank of king, marshal, duke, or general; and the crosses of his Legion of Honor were given to personal valor, and not to family connexion. "When soldiers have been baptized in the fire of a battle-field, they have all one rank in my eyes."

When a natural king becomes a titular king, every body is pleased and satisfied. The Revolution entitled the strong populace of the Faubourg St. Antoine, and every horse-boy and powder-monkey in the army, to look on Napoleon, as flesh of his flesh, and the creature of *his* party: but there is something in the success of grand talent which enlists an universal sympathy. For, in the prevalence of sense and spirit over stupidity and malversation, all reasonable men have an interest; and, as intellectual beings, we feel the air purified by the electric shock, when material force is overthrown by intellectual energies. As soon as we are removed out of the reach of local and accidental partialities, man feels that Napoleon fights for him; these are honest victories; this strong steam-engine does our work. Whatever appeals to the imagination, by transcending the ordinary limits of human ability, wonderfully encourages and liberates us. This capacious head, revolving and disposing sovereignly trains of affairs, and animating such multitudes of agents; this eye, which looked through Europe; this prompt invention; this inexhaustible resource;—what events! what romantic pictures! what strange situations!— when spying the Alps, by a sunset in the Sicilian sea; drawing up his army for battle, in sight of the Pyramids, and saying to his troops, "From the tops of those pyramids, forty centuries look down on you"; fording the Red Sea; wading in the gulf of the Isthmus of Suez. On the shore of Plotemais, gigantic projects agitated him. "Had Acre fallen, I should have changed the face of the world." His army, on the night of the battle of Austerlitz, which was the anniversary of his inauguration as Emperor, presented him with a bouquet of forty standards taken in the fight. Perhaps it is a little puerile, the pleasure he took in making these contrasts glaring; as when he pleased himself with making kings wait in his antechambers, at Tilsit, at Paris, and at Erfurt.

We cannot, in the universal imbecility, indecision, and indolence of men, sufficiently congratulate ourselves on this strong and ready

actor, who took occasion by the beard, and showed us how much may be accomplished by the mere force of such virtues as all men possess in less degrees; namely, by punctuality, by personal attention, by courage, and thoroughness. "The Austrians," he said, "do not know the value of time." I should cite him, in his earlier years, as a model of prudence. His power does not consist in any wild or extravagant force; in any enthusiasm, like Mahomet's; or singular power of persuasion; but in the exercise of common sense on each emergency, instead of abiding by rules and customs. The lesson he teaches is that which vigor always teaches,—that there is always room for it. To what heaps of cowardly doubts is not that man's life an answer. When he appeared, it was the belief of all military men that there could be nothing new in war; as it is the belief of men to-day, that nothing new can be undertaken in politics, or in church or in letters, or in trade, or in farming, or in our social manners and customs; and as it is, at all times, the belief of society that the world is used up. But Bonaparte knew better than society; and, moreover, knew that he knew better. I think all men know better than they do; know that the institutions we so volubly commend are go-carts and baubles; but they dare not trust their presentiments. Bonaparte relied on his own sense, and did not care a bean for other people's. The world treated his novelties just as it treats every body's novelties,—made infinite objection; mustered all the impediments: but he snapped his finger at their objections. "What creates great difficulty," he remarks, "in the profession of the land-commander, is the necessity of feeding so many men and animals. If he allows himself to be guided by the commissaries, he will never stir, and all his expeditions will fail." An example of his common sense is what he says of the passage of the Alps in winter, which, all writers, one repeating after the other, had described as impracticable. "The winter," says Napoleon, "is not the most unfavorable season for the passage of lofty mountains. The snow is then firm, the weather settled, and there is nothing to fear from avalanches, the real and only danger to be apprehended in the Alps. On those high mountains, there are often very fine days in December, of a dry cold, with extreme calmness in the air." Read his account, too, of the way in which battles are gained. "In all battles, a moment occurs, when the bravest troops, after having made the greatest efforts, feel inclined to run. That terror proceeds from a want of confidence in their own courage; and it only requires a slight opportunity, a pretence, to restore confidence to them. The art is to give rise to the opportunity, and to invent the pretence. At Arcola, I won the battle with twenty-five horsemen. I seized that moment of lassitude, gave every man a trumpet, and gained the day with this handful. You see that two armies are two bodies which meet, and endeavor to frighten each other: a moment of panic occurs, and that moment must be turned to advantage. When a man has been present in many actions, he distinguishes that moment without difficulty: it is as easy as casting up an addition."

This deputy of the nineteenth century added to his gifts a capacity for speculation on general topics. He delighted in running through the range of practical, of literary, and of abstract questions. His opinion is always original, and to the purpose. On the voyage to Egypt, he liked, after dinner, to fix on three or four persons to support a proposition, and as many to oppose it. He gave a subject, and the discussions turned on questions of religion, the different kinds of government, and the art of war. One day, he asked, whether the planets were inhabited? On another, what was the age of the world? Then he proposed to consider the probability of the destruction of the globe, either by water or by fire: at another time, the truth or fallacy of presentiments, and the interpretation of dreams. He was very fond of talking of religion. In 1806, he conversed with Fournier, bishop of Montpellier, on matters of theology. There were two points on which they could not agree, viz., that of hell, and that of salvation out of the pale of the church. The Emperor told Josephine, that he disputed like a devil on these two points, on which the bishop was inexorable. To the philosophers he readily yielded all that was proved against religion as the work of men and time; but he would not hear of materialism. One fine night, on deck, amid a clatter of materialism, Bonaparte pointed to the stars, and said, "You may talk as long as you please, gentlemen, but who made all that?" He delighted in the conversation of men of science, particularly of Monge and Berthollet; but the men of letters he slighted; "they were manufacturers of phrases." Of medicine, too, he was fond of talking, and

with those of its practitioners whom he most esteemed,—with Corvisart at Paris, and with Antonomarchi at St. Helena. "Believe me," he said to the last, "we had better leave off all these remedies: life is a fortress which neither you nor I know any thing about. Why throw obstacles in the way of its defence? Its own means are superior to all the apparatus of your laboratories. Corvisart candidly agreed with me, that all your filthy mixtures are good for nothing. Medicine is a collection of uncertain prescriptions, the result of which, taken collectively, are more fatal than useful to mankind. Water, air, and cleanliness, are the chief articles in my pharmacopeia."

His memoirs, dictated to Count Montholon and General Gourgaud, at St. Helena, have great value, after all the deduction that, it seems, is to be made from them, on account of his known disingenuousness. He has the good-nature of strength and conscious superiority. I admire his simple, clear narrative of his battles;—good as Caesar's; his good-natured and sufficiently respectful account of Marshal Wurmser and his other antagonists, and his own equality as a writer to his varying subject. The most agreeable portion is the Campaign in Egypt.

He had hours of thought and wisdom. In intervals of leisure, either in the camp or the palace, Napoleon appears as a man of genius, directing on abstract questions the native appetite for truth, and the impatience of words, he was wont to show in war. He could enjoy every play of invention, a romance, a *bon mot*, as well as a stratagem in a campaign. He delighted to fascinate Josephine and her ladies, in a dim-lighted apartment, by the terrors of a fiction, to which his voice and dramatic power lent every addition.

I call Napoleon the agent or attorney of the middle class of modern society; of the throng who fill the markets, shops, counting-houses, manufactories, ships, of the modern world, aiming to be rich. He was the agitator, the destroyer of prescription, the internal improver, the liberal, the radical, the inventor of means, the opener of doors and markets, the subverter of monopoly and abuse. Of course, the rich and aristocratic did not like him. England, the centre of capital, and Rome and Austria, centres of tradition and genealogy, opposed him. The consternation of the dull and conservative classes, the terror of the foolish old men and old women of the Roman conclave,

—who in their despair took hold of any thing, and would cling to red-hot iron,—the vain attempts of statists to amuse and deceive him, of the emperor of Austria to bribe him; and the instinct of the young, ardent, and active men, every where, which pointed him out as the giant of the middle class, make his history bright and commanding. He had the virtues of the masses of his constituents: he had also their vices. I am sorry that the brilliant picture has its reverse. But that is the fatal quality which we discover in our pursuit of wealth, that it is treacherous, and is bought by the breaking or weakening of the sentiments: and it is inevitable that we should find the same fact in the history of this champion, who proposed to himself simply a brilliant career, without any stipulation or scruple concerning the means.

Bonaparte was singularly destitute of generous sentiments. The highest-placed individual in the most cultivated age and population of the world,—he has not the merit of common truth and honesty. He is unjust to his generals; egotistic, and monopolizing; meanly stealing the credit of their great actions from Kellermann, from Bernadotte; intriguing to involve his faithful Junot in hopeless bankruptcy, in order to drive him to a distance from Paris, because the familiarity of his manners offends the new pride of his throne. He is a boundless liar. The official paper, his "Moniteurs," and all his bulletins, are proverbs for saying what he wished to be believed; and worse,—he sat, in his premature old age, in his lonely island, coldly falsifying facts, and dates, and characters, and giving to history a theatrical eclat. Like all Frenchmen, he has a passion for stage effect. Every action that breathes of generosity is poisoned by this calculation. His star, his love of glory, his doctrine of the immortality of the soul, are all French. "I must dazzle and astonish. If I were to give the liberty of the press, my power could not last three days." To make a great noise is his favorite design. "A great reputation is a great noise: the more there is made, the farther off it is heard. Laws, institutions, monuments, nations, all fall; but the noise continues, and resounds in after ages." His doctrine of immortality is simply fame. His theory of influence is not flattering. "There are two levers for moving men,—interest and fear. Love is a silly infatuation, depend upon it. Friendship is but a name. I love nobody. I do not even love my brothers: perhaps Joseph, a little, from habit, and because he is my elder; and Duroc, I love him too; but why?—because his character pleases me: he is stern and resolute, and, I believe, the fellow never shed a tear. For my part, I know very well that I have no true friends. As long as I continue to be what I am, I may have as many pretended friends as I please. Leave sensibility to women: but men should be firm in heart and purpose, or they should have nothing to do with war and government." He was thoroughly unscrupulous. He would steal, slander, assassinate, drown, and poison, as his interest dictated. He had no generosity; but mere vulgar hatred: he was intensely selfish: he was perfidious: he cheated at cards: he was a prodigious gossip; and opened letters; and delighted in his infamous police; and rubbed his hands with joy when he had intercepted some morsel of intelligence concerning the men and women about him, boasting that "he knew every thing"; and interfered with the cutting the dresses of the women; and listened after the hurrahs and the compliments of the street, incognito. His manners were coarse. He treated women with low familiarity. He had the habit of pulling their ears, and pinching their cheeks, when he was in good humor, and of pulling the ears and whiskers of men, and of striking and horse-play with them, to his last days. It does not appear that he listened at keyholes, or, at least, that he was caught at it. In short, when you have penetrated through all the circles of power and splendor, you were not dealing with a gentleman, at last; but with an impostor and a rogue: and he fully deserves the epithet of *Jupiter Scapin,* or a sort of Scamp Jupiter.

In describing the two parties into which modern society divides itself,—the democrat and the conservative,—I said, Bonaparte represents the Democrat, or the party of men of business, against the stationary or conservative party. I omitted then to say, what is material to the statement, namely, that these two parties differ only as young and old. The democrat is a young conservative; the conservative is an old democrat. The aristocrat is the democrat ripe, and gone to seed,—because both parties stand on the one ground of the supreme value of property, which one endeavors to get, and the other to keep. Bonaparte may be said to represent the whole history of this party, its youth and its age; yes, and with poetic justice, its fate, in his own. The counter-revolution, the counter-party, still waits for its organ and representative, in a lover and a man of truly public and universal aims.

Here was an experiment, under the most favorable conditions, of the powers of intellect without conscience. Never was such a leader so endowed, and so weaponed; never leader found such aids and followers. And what was the result of this vast talent and power, of these immense armies, burned cities, squandered treasures, immolated millions of men, of this demoralized Europe? It came to no result. All passed away, like the smoke of his artillery, and left no trace. He left France smaller, poorer, feebler, than he found it; and the whole contest for freedom was to be begun again. The attempt was, in principle, suicidal. France served him with life, and limb, and estate, as long as it could identify its interest with him; but when men saw that after victory was another war; after the destruction of armies, new conscriptions; and they who had toiled so desperately were never nearer to the reward,—they could not spend what they had earned, nor repose on their down-beds, nor strut in their chateaux,—they deserted him. Men found that his absorbing egotism was deadly to all other men. It resembled the torpedo, which inflicts a succession of shocks on any one who takes hold of it, producing spasms which contract the muscles of the hand, so that the man can not open his fingers; and the animal inflicts new and more violent shocks, until he paralyzes and kills his victim. So, this exorbitant egotist narrowed, impoverished, and absorbed the power and existence of those who served him; and the universal cry of France, and of Europe, in 1814, was, "enough of him"; "*assez de Bonaparte.*"

It was not Bonaparte's fault. He did all that in him lay, to live and thrive without moral principle. It was the nature of things, the eternal law of man and of the world, which baulked and ruined him; and the result, in a million experiments, will be the same. Every experiment, by multitudes or by individuals, that has a sensual and selfish aim, will fail. The pacific Fourier will be as inefficient as the pernicious Napoleon. As long as our civilization is essentially one of property, of fences, of exclusiveness, it will be mocked by delusions. Our riches will leave us sick; there will be bitterness in our laughter; and our wine will burn our mouth. Only that good profits, which we can taste with all doors open, and which serves all men. 1850

HENRY DAVID THOREAU

1817–1862

THOREAU IS the Transcendentalist who has the most to say to our generation. He has indeed only in recent years received his proper recognition. In his lifetime it was easy for his contemporaries to misconstrue his personality and his ideas. To many he was only a pale reflection of Emerson. To his neighbors in Concord he appeared as a man who had not fulfilled the promise of his youth, the captain of a huckleberry party instead of being, as Emerson said he might have been, "the head of American engineers." The plutocratic era after the Civil War saw him as a charming writer of nature essays, kin to Burroughs and Muir. His pungent social criticism, so destructive of the "values" of the Gilded Age, was disregarded. Finally, the judgements of two writers whose pronouncements carried weight at that time, Lowell and Stevenson, fixed the popular impression of Thoreau as Emerson's man and a "skulker" who avoided life instead of facing it robustly. Now we can see clearly that Thoreau's attack on fundamental problems was deep and that his conclusions are continuously useful. Europeans like Tolstoi and Gandhi and the leaders of the Socialist movement in England, all of whom have acknowledged their debt to him, were able to perceive his unique qualities sooner than his countrymen did.

With considerable sacrifice on his family's part Thoreau was sent to Harvard, where he acquired the lifelong habit of making productive use of the College library. He returned to Concord; in spirit he had scarcely left it and was never to leave it thereafter except on lecture tours or surveying trips or brief excursions for pleasure. For a time he and his brother John conducted a private school, on startlingly modern principles, but already he had resolved to work at earning a living only as often as he had to in order that his body might be clothed, fed, and housed. Time was too precious to be wasted in money-grubbing, and he had ambitions to be a writer. He helped with the family business of making lead pencils and graphite, tutored, lectured (when audiences would have him), and acted as handy man in Emerson's household for two different periods. The only profession he followed was surveying, but he complained that his clients generally did not want him to do a really good job.

There was plenty of time to walk the woods and fields near Concord, to explore the Musket-aquid in his homemade boat, and to go farther afield in search of new trees and animals and village lore and the pleasures of along-the-road conversation. These trips would bear fruit in articles later on. In 1839 he made, with his beloved brother John, the famous two weeks' journey which furnished the materials for *A Week on the Concord and Merrimack Rivers*, published in 1849. In 1846 he visited the Maine woods around Katahdin where he could still see the remnants of the primeval forest. Three years later he explored Cape Cod, the first of four excursions which eventually got inside the covers of his posthumous *Cape Cod*, the gayest of his travel writing. On a surveying trip to Perth Amboy in 1856 he met Walt Whitman, took his measure, and concluded that he was "a great fellow." On the last of his excursions, to Minnesota in 1861, he was in search of health. The quest was unsuccessful.

Thoreau asked nothing of the State but that it should leave him alone, but from the middle forties he was drawn into the political controversies of the day. When the liberty of all men was threatened by the new American imperialism and the iniquities of the Fugitive Slave Law his own liberty was in danger and he was prepared to act. He moved from the doctrine of passive resistance, expressed in "Civil Disobedience" in 1849 to the high indignation of "Slavery in Massachusetts" in 1854. When John Brown was on trial, Thoreau, who had known and assisted him, raised his voice to plead "for his immortal life" and his cause, which was no longer Brown's, but the cause of all just men.

The most famous episode of Thoreau's life, his sojourn at Walden Pond from July 4, 1845, till September 6, 1847, has been often misinterpreted, although his purpose in building his hut and "retiring" a mile and a half from Concord is emphatically stated in *Walden* (1854). He wanted to live deliberately there, to front only the essential facts of life. "I did not wish to live what was not life, living is so dear; nor did I wish to practise resignation, unless it was quite necessary." By finding out how much of one's time is required to supply the body's needs, he would know how much was left for the "soul's life." For him the soul's necessities were leisure for the observation and enjoyment of nature, time for reading and meditation and writing and friendship. He did not leave Walden Pond to preach a gospel but to prepare his report. He did not urge his mode of life on others; his only desire was that each young man "be very careful to find out and pursue *his own* way, and not his father's or his mother's or his neighbor's instead."

Walden is one of the deep books of the world's literature, capable of disturbing the consciences of those who really read it. Its economic teaching has nothing to do with price levels and business cycles but goes to first principles, which professional economists safely ignore. *Walden* is the distillation of a personality. In it is the Thoreau who loved nature with a pagan warmth which sometimes alarmed Emerson, who approached it as a hierophant. Behind it one feels

Thoreau's extraordinary wisdom, the fusion of his learning, his hard-won, self-reliant thought, and his humanity. The book is a work of art because he had worked as hard to be a writer as he did at driving life into a corner to get the meanness and the sublimity of it. In his life he had time to complete only two books, the *Week* and *Walden*, but he had time to make these live.

Lewis Leary, "Thoreau," in *Eight American Authors, A Review of Research and Criticism*, New York, 1956, pp. 153–206.
The Writings of Henry David Thoreau, 20 vols., Boston, 1906.
The Correspondence of Henry David Thoreau, Carle Bode, ed., New York, 1958.
The Heart of Thoreau's Journals, Odell Shepard, ed., Boston, 1927.
H. S. Canby, *Thoreau*, Boston, 1939.
R. L. Cook, *Passage to Walden*, Boston, 1949.
W. R. Harding, ed., *Thoreau: A Century of Criticism*, Dallas, 1954.
———, *A Thoreau Handbook*, New York, 1959.
J. W. Krutch, *Henry David Thoreau*, New York, 1948.
F. B. Sanborn, *The Life of Henry David Thoreau*, Boston, 1917.
J. Lyndon Shanley, *The Making of Walden*, Chicago, 1957.

INSPIRATION [1]

If with light head erect I sing,
    Though all the Muses lend their force,
From my poor love of any thing,
    The verse is weak and shallow as its source.

But if with bended neck I grope,
    Listening behind me for my wit,
With faith superior to hope,
    More anxious to keep back than forward it,—

Making my soul accomplice there
    Unto the flame my heart hath lit,—   10
Then will the verse forever wear:
    Time cannot bend the line which God hath writ.

Always the general show of things
    Floats in review before my mind,
And such true love and reverence brings,
    That sometimes I forget that I am blind.

But now there comes, unsought, unseen,
    Some clear divine electuary,
And I, who had but sensual been,
    Grow sensible, and as God is, am wary.   20

I hearing get, who had but ears,
    And sight, who had but eyes before;
I moments live, who lived but years,
    And truth discern, who knew but learning's lore.

I hear beyond the range of sound,
    I see beyond the range of sight,
New earths and skies and seas around,
    And in my day the sun doth pale his light.

A clear and ancient harmony
    Pierces my soul through all its din,   30
As through its utmost melody,—
    Farther behind than they, farther within.

More swift its bolt than lightning is,
    Its voice than thunder is more loud,
It doth expand my privacies
    To all, and leave me single in the crowd.

It speaks with such authority,
    With so serene and lofty tone,
That idle Time runs gadding by,
    And leaves me with Eternity alone.   40

Now chiefly is my natal hour,
    And only now my prime of life;
Of manhood's strength it is the flower,
    'Tis peace's end, and war's beginning strife.
                                    1849

INDEPENDENCE

My life more civil is and free
    Than any civil polity.

Ye princes, keep your realms
    And circumscribèd power,
Not wide as are my dreams,
    Nor rich as is this hour.

[1] Lines from this poem are interspersed through *A Week on the Concord and Merrimack Rivers*. The version here given omits the first stanza and the last nine stanzas of the poem.

What can ye give which I have not?
What can you take which I have got?
   Can ye defend the dangerless?
   Can ye inherit nakedness?   *10*

To all true wants Time's ear is deaf,
Penurious States lend no relief
   Out of their pelf:
   But a free soul—thank God—
   Can help itself.

Be sure your fate
Doth keep apart its state,   1841

Not linked with any band,
Even the noblest of the land;

In tented fields with cloth of gold   *20*
   No place doth hold,
But is more chivalrous than they are,
And sigheth for a nobler war;
A finer strain its trumpet sings,
A brighter gleam its armor flings.

The life that I aspire to live
   No man proposeth me;
No trade upon the street
   Wears its emblazonry.   1863

»   »   *From:* WALDEN [2]   «   «

ECONOMY

(CHAPTER I)

When I wrote the following pages, or rather the bulk of them, I lived alone, in the woods, a mile from any neighbor, in a house which I had built myself, on the shore of Walden Pond, in Concord, Massachusetts, and earned my living by the labor of my hands only. I lived there two years and two months. At present I am a sojourner in civilized life again.

I should not obtrude my affairs so much on the notice of my readers if very particular inquiries had not been made by my townsmen concerning my mode of life, which some would call impertinent, though they do not appear to me at all impertinent, but, considering the circumstances, very natural and pertinent. Some have asked what I got to eat; if I did not feel lonesome; if I was not afraid; and the like. Others have been curious to learn what portion of my income I devoted to charitable purposes; and some, who have large families, how many poor children I maintained. I will therefore ask those of my readers who feel no particular interest in me to pardon me if I undertake to answer some of these questions in this book. In most books, the *I*, or first person, is omitted; in this it will be retained; that, in respect to egotism, is the main difference. We commonly do not remember that it is, after all, always the first person that is speaking. I should not talk

[2] Thoreau lived at Walden Pond from July, 1845, until September, 1847. Parts of *Walden* were read as lectures at the Concord Lyceum.

so much about myself if there were anybody else whom I knew as well. Unfortunately, I am confined to this theme by the narrowness of my experience. Moreover, I, on my side, require of every writer, first or last, a simple and sincere account of his own life, and not merely what he has heard of other men's lives; some such account as he would send to his kindred from a distant land; for if he has lived sincerely, it must have been in a distant land to *10* me. Perhaps these pages are more particularly addressed to poor students. As for the rest of my readers, they will accept such portions as apply to them. I trust that none will stretch the seams in putting on the coat, for it may do good service to him whom it fits.

I would fain say something, not so much concerning the Chinese and Sandwich Islanders as you who read these pages, who are said to live in New England; something about your *20* condition, especially your outward condition or circumstances in this world, in this town, what it is, whether it is necessary that it be as bad as it is, whether it cannot be improved as well as not. I have travelled a good deal in Concord; and everywhere, in shops, and offices, and fields, the inhabitants have appeared to me to be doing penance in a thousand remarkable ways. What I have heard of Bramins sitting exposed to four fires and looking in the face *30* of the sun; or hanging suspended, with their heads downward, over flames; or looking at the heavens over their shoulders "until it becomes impossible for them to resume their natural position, while from the twist of the neck nothing but liquids can pass into the stomach"; or dwelling, chained for life, at the foot of a tree; or measuring with their bodies, like caterpillars, the breadth of vast empires; or standing on one leg on the tops of pillars,—even these forms of conscious penance are hardly more incredible and astonishing than the scenes which I daily witness. The twelve labors of Hercules were trifling in comparison with those which my neighbors have undertaken; for they were only twelve, and had an end; but I could never see that these men slew or captured any monster or finished any labor. They have no friend Iolaus to burn with a hot iron the root of the hydra's head, but as soon as one head is crushed, two spring up.

I see young men, my townsmen, whose misfortune it is to have inherited farms, houses, barns, cattle, and farming tools; for these are more easily acquired than got rid of. Better if they had been born in the open pasture and suckled by a wolf, that they might have seen with clearer eyes what field they were called to labor in. Who made them serfs of the soil? Why should they eat their sixty acres, when man is condemned to eat only his peck of dirt? Why should they begin digging their graves as soon as they are born? They have got to live a man's life, pushing all these things before them, and get on as well as they can. How many a poor immortal soul have I met well-nigh crushed and smothered under its load, creeping down the road of life, pushing before it a barn seventy-five feet by forty, its Augean stables never cleansed, and one hundred acres of land, tillage, mowing, pasture, and wood-lot! The portionless, who struggle with no such unnecessary inherited encumbrances, find it labor enough to subdue and cultivate a few cubic feet of flesh.

But men labor under a mistake. The better part of the man is soon plowed into the soil for compost. By a seeming fate, commonly called necessity, they are employed, as it says in an old book, laying up treasures which moth and rust will corrupt and thieves break through and steal. It is a fool's life, as they will find when they get to the end of it, if not before. It is said that Deucalion and Pyrrha created men by throwing stones over their heads behind them:—

"Inde genus durum sumus, experiensque laborum,
  Et documenta damus quâ simus origine nati."

Or, as Raleigh rhymes it in his sonorous way.—

"From thence our kind hard-hearted is, enduring
  pain and care,
Approving that our bodies of a stony nature are."

So much for a blind obedience to a blundering oracle, throwing the stones over their heads behind them, and not seeing where they fell.

Most men, even in this comparatively free country, through mere ignorance and mistake, are so occupied with the factitious cares and superfluously coarse labors of life that its finer fruits cannot be plucked by them. Their fingers, from excessive toil, are too clumsy and tremble too much for that. Actually, the laboring man has not leisure for a true integrity day by day; he cannot afford to sustain the manliest relations to men; his labor would be depreciated in the market. He has no time to be anything but a machine. How can he remember well his ignorance—which his growth requires—who has so often to use his knowledge? We should feed and clothe him gratuitously sometimes, and recruit him with our cordials, before we judge of him. The finest qualities of our nature, like the bloom on fruits, can be preserved only by the most delicate handling. Yet we do not treat ourselves nor one another thus tenderly.

Some of you, we all know, are poor, find it hard to live, are sometimes, as it were, gasping for breath. I have no doubt that some of you who read this book are unable to pay for all the dinners which you have actually eaten, or for the coats and shoes which are fast wearing or are already worn out, and have come to this page to spend borrowed or stolen time, robbing your creditors of an hour. It is very evident what mean and sneaking lives many of you live, for my sight has been whetted by experience; always on the limits, trying to get into business and trying to get out of debt, a very ancient slough, called by the Latins *æs alienum*, another's brass, for some of their coins were made of brass; still living, and dying, and buried by this other's brass; always promising to pay, promising to pay, to-morrow, and dying to-day, insolvent; seeking to curry favor, to get custom, by how many modes, only not state-prison offences; lying, flattering, voting, contracting yourselves into a nutshell of civility, or dilating into an atmosphere of thin and vaporous generosity, that you may persuade your neighbor to let you make his shoes, or his hat, or his coat, or his carriage, or import his groceries for him; making yourself sick, that you may lay up something against a sick day, something to be tucked away in an old chest, or in a stocking behind the plastering, or, more safely, in the brick bank; no matter where, no matter how much or how little.

I sometimes wonder that we can be so frivolous, I may almost say, as to attend to the gross but somewhat foreign form of servitude called Negro Slavery, there are so many keen and subtle masters that enslave both North and South. It is hard to have a Southern overseer; it is worse to have a Northern one; but worst of all when you are the slave-driver of yourself. Talk of a divinity in man! Look at the teamster on the highway, wending to market by day or night; does any divinity stir within him? His highest duty to fodder and water his horses! What is his destiny to him compared with the shipping interests? Does not he drive for Squire Make-a-stir? How godlike, how immortal, is he? See how he cowers and sneaks, how vaguely all the day he fears, not being immortal nor divine, but the slave and prisoner of his own opinion of himself, a fame won by his own deeds. Public opinion is a weak tyrant compared with our own private opinion. What a man thinks of himself, that it is which determines, or rather indicates, his fate. Self-emancipation even in the West Indian provinces of the fancy and imagination,—what Wilberforce is there to bring that about? Think, also, of the ladies of the land weaving toilet cushions against the last day, not to betray too green an interest in their fates! As if you could kill time without injuring eternity.

The mass of men lead lives of quiet desperation. What is called resignation is confirmed desperation. From the desperate city you go into the desperate country, and have to console yourself with the bravery of minks and muskrats. A stereotyped but unconscious despair is concealed even under what are called the games and amusements of mankind. There is no play in them, for this comes after work. But it is a characteristic of wisdom not to do desperate things.

When we consider what, to use the words of the catechism, is the chief end of man, and what are the true necessaries and means of life, it appears as if men had deliberately chosen the common mode of living because they preferred it to any other. Yet they honestly think there is no choice left. But alert and healthy natures remember that the sun rose clear. It is never too late to give up our prejudices. No way of thinking or doing, however

ancient, can be trusted without proof. What everybody echoes or in silence passes by as true to-day may turn out to be falsehood tomorrow, mere smoke of opinion, which some had trusted for a cloud that would sprinkle fertilizing rain on their fields. What old people say you cannot do, you try and find that you can. Old deeds for old people, and new deeds for new. Old people did not know enough once, perchance, to fetch fresh fuel to keep the fire 10 a-going; new people put a little dry wood under a pot, and are whirled round the globe with the speed of birds, in a way to kill old people, as the phrase is. Age is no better, hardly so well, qualified for an instructor as youth, for it has not profited so much as it has lost. One may almost doubt if the wisest man has learned anything of absolute value by living. Practically, the old have no very important advice to give the young, their own ex- 20 perience has been so partial, and their lives have been such miserable failures, for private reasons, as they must believe; and it may be that they have some faith left which belies that experience, and they are only less young than they were. I have lived some thirty years on this planet, and I have yet to hear the first syllable of valuable or even earnest advice from my seniors. They have told me nothing, and probably cannot tell me anything, to the pur- 30 pose. Here is life, an experiment to a great extent untried by me; but it does not avail me that they have tried it. If I have any experience which I think valuable, I am sure to reflect that this my Mentors said nothing about.

One farmer says to me, "You cannot live on vegetable food solely, for it furnishes nothing to make bones with"; and so he religiously devotes a part of his day to supplying his system with the raw material of bones; walking all the 40 while he talks behind his oxen, which, with vegetable-made bones, jerk him and his lumbering plow along in spite of every obstacle. Some things are really necessaries of life in some circles, the most helpless and diseased, which in others are luxuries merely, and in others still are entirely unknown.

The whole ground of human life seems to some to have been gone over by their predecessors, both the heights and the valleys, and 50 all things to have been cared for. According to Evelyn, "the wise Solomon prescribed ordinances for the very distances of trees; and the Roman prætors have decided how often you may go into your neighbor's land to gather the acorns which fall on it without trespass, and what share belongs to that neighbor." Hippocrates has even left directions how we should cut our nails; that is, even with the ends of the fingers, neither shorter nor longer. Undoubtedly the very tedium and ennui which presume to have exhausted the variety and the joys of life are as old as Adam. But man's capacities have never been measured; nor are we to judge of what he can do by any precedents, so little has been tried. Whatever have been thy failures hitherto, "be not afflicted, my child, for who shall assign to thee what thou hast left undone?"

We might try our lives by a thousand simple tests; as, for instance, that the same sun which ripens my beans illumines at once a system of earths like ours. If I had remembered this it would have prevented some mistakes. This was not the light in which I hoed them. The stars are the apexes of what wonderful triangles! What distant and different beings in the various mansions of the universe are contemplating the same one at the same moment! Nature and human life are as various as our several constitutions. Who shall say what prospect life offers to another? Could a greater miracle take place than for us to look through each other's eyes for an instant? We should live in all the ages of the world in an hour; ay, in all the worlds of the ages. History, Poetry, Mythology!—I know of no reading of another's experience so startling and informing as this would be.

The greater part of what my neighbors call good I believe in my soul to be bad, and if I repent of anything, it is very likely to be my good behavior. What demon possessed me that I behaved so well? You may say the wisest thing you can, old man,—you who have lived seventy years, not without honor of a kind,— I hear an irresistible voice which invites me away from all that. One generation abandons the enterprises of another like stranded vessels.

I think that we may safely trust a good deal more than we do. We may waive just so much care of ourselves as we honestly bestow elsewhere. Nature is as well adapted to our weakness as to our strength. The incessant anxiety and strain of some is a well-nigh incurable form of disease. We are made to exaggerate the importance of what work we do; and yet how much is not done by us! or, what if we had been taken sick? How vigilant we are! determined not to live by faith if we can avoid it; all the day long on the alert, at night we unwillingly say our prayers and commit ourselves to uncertainties. So thoroughly and sincerely are we compelled to live, reverencing our life, and denying the possibility of change. This is the only way, we say; but there are as many ways as there can be drawn radii from one centre. All change is a miracle to contemplate; but it is a miracle which is taking place every instant. Confucius said, "To know that we know what we know, and that we do not know what we do not know, that is true knowledge." When one man has reduced a fact of the imagination to be a fact to his understanding, I foresee that all men will at length establish their lives on that basis.

Let us consider for a moment what most of the trouble and anxiety which I have referred to is about, and how much it is necessary that we be troubled, or, at least, careful. It would be some advantage to live a primitive and frontier life, though in the midst of an outward civilization, if only to learn what are the gross necessaries of life and what methods have been taken to obtain them; or even to look over the old day-books of the merchants, to see what it was that men most commonly bought at the stores, what they stored, that is, what are the grossest groceries. For the improvements of ages have had but little influence on the essential laws of man's existence: as our skeletons, probably, are not to be distinguished from those of our ancestors.

By the words, *necessary of life,* I mean whatever, of all that man obtains by his own exertions, has been from the first, or from long use has become, so important to human life that few, if any, whether from savageness, or poverty, or philosophy, ever attempt to do without it. To many creatures there is in this sense but one necessary of life—Food. To the bison of the prairie it is a few inches of palatable grass, with water to drink; unless he seeks the Shelter of the forest or the mountain's shadow. None of the brute creation requires more than Food and Shelter. The necessaries of life for man in this climate may, accurately enough, be distributed under the several heads of Food, Shelter, Clothing, and Fuel; for not till we have secured these are we prepared to entertain the true problems of life with freedom and a prospect of success. Man has invented, not only houses, but clothes and cooked food; and possibly from the accidental discovery of the warmth of fire, and the consequent use of it, at first a luxury, arose the present necessity to sit by it. We observe cats and dogs acquiring the same second nature. By proper Shelter and Clothing we legitimately retain our own internal heat; but with an excess of these, or of Fuel, that is, with an external heat greater than our own internal, may not cookery properly be said to begin? Darwin, the naturalist, says of the inhabitants of Tierra del Fuego, that while his own party, who were well clothed and sitting close to a fire, were far from too warm, these naked savages, who were farther off, were observed, to his great surprise, "to be streaming with perspiration at undergoing such a roasting." So, we are told, the New Hollander goes naked with impunity, while the European shivers in his clothes. Is it impossible to combine the hardiness of these savages with the intellectualness of the civilized man? According to Liebig, man's body is a stove, and food the fuel which keeps up the internal combustion in the lungs. In cold weather we eat more, in warm less. The animal heat is the result of a slow combustion, and disease and death take place when this is too rapid; or for want of fuel, or from some defect in the draught, the fire goes out. Of course the vital heat is not to be confounded with fire; but so much for analogy. It appears, therefore, from the above list, that the expression, *animal life,* is nearly synonymous with the expression, *animal heat;* for while Food may be regarded as the Fuel which keeps up the fire within us —and Fuel serves only to prepare that Food or to increase the warmth of our bodies by addition from without,—Shelter and Clothing also serve only to retain the *heat* thus generated and absorbed.

The grand necessity, then, for our bodies, is to keep warm, to keep the vital heat in us. What pains we accordingly take, not only with our Food, and Clothing, and Shelter, but with our beds, which are our night-clothes, robbing the nests and breasts of birds to prepare this shelter within a shelter, as the mole has its bed of grass and leaves at the end of its burrow! The poor man is wont to complain that this is a cold world; and to cold, no less physical than social, we refer directly a great part of our ails. The summer, in some climates, makes possible to man a sort of Elysian life. Fuel, except to cook his Food, is then unnecessary; the sun is his fire, and many of the fruits are sufficiently cooked by its rays; while Food generally is more various, and more easily obtained, and Clothing and Shelter are wholly or half unnecessary. At the present day, and in this country, as I find by my own experience, a few implements, a knife, an axe, a spade, a wheelbarrow, &c., and for the studious, lamplight, stationery, and access to a few books, rank next to necessaries, and can all be obtained at a trifling cost. Yet some, not wise, go to the other side of the globe, to barbarous and unhealthy regions, and devote themselves to trade for ten or twenty years, in order that they may live,—that is, keep comfortably warm,—and die in New England at last. The luxuriously rich are not simply kept comfortably warm, but unnaturally hot; as I implied before, they are cooked, of course *à la mode.*

Most of the luxuries, and many of the so-called comforts of life, are not only not indispensable, but positive hindrances to the elevation of mankind. With respect to luxuries and comforts, the wisest have ever lived a more simple and meagre life than the poor. The ancient philosophers, Chinese, Hindoo, Persian, and Greek, were a class than which none has been poorer in outward riches, none so rich in inward. We know not much about them. It is remarkable that *we* know so much of them as we do. The same is true of the more modern reformers and benefactors of their race. None can be an impartial or wise observer of human life but from the vantage ground of what *we* should call voluntary poverty. Of a life of luxury the fruit is luxury, whether in agriculture, or commerce, or literature, or art. There are nowadays professors of philosophy, but not philosophers. Yet it is admirable to profess because it was once admirable to live. To be a philosopher is not merely to have subtle thoughts, nor even to found a school, but so to love wisdom as to live according to its dictates, a life of simplicity, independence, magnanimity, and trust. It is to solve some of the problems of life, not only theoretically, but practically. The success of great scholars and thinkers is commonly a courtier-like success, not kingly, not manly. They make shift to live merely by conformity, practically as their fathers did, and are in no sense the progenitors of a nobler race of men. But why do men degenerate ever? What makes families run out? What is the nature of the luxury which enervates and destroys nations? Are we sure that there is none of it in our own lives?

The philosopher is in advance of his age even in the outward form of his life. He is not fed, sheltered, clothed, warmed, like his contemporaries. How can a man be a philosopher and not maintain his vital heat by better methods than other men?

When a man is warmed by the several modes which I have described, what does he want next? Surely not more warmth of the same kind, as more and richer food, larger and more splendid houses, finer and more abundant clothing, more numerous, incessant, and hotter fires, and the like. When he has obtained those things which are necessary to life, there is another alternative than to obtain the superfluities; and that is, to adventure on life now, his vacation from humbler toil having commenced. The soil, it appears, is suited to the seed, for it has sent its radicle downward, and it may now send its shoot upward also with confidence. Why has man rooted himself thus firmly in the earth, but that he may rise in the same proportion into the heavens above?—for the nobler plants are valued for the fruit they bear at last in the air and light, far from the ground, and are not treated like the humbler esculents, which, though they may be biennials, are cultivated only till they have perfected their root, and often cut down at top for this purpose, so that most would not know them in their flowering season.

I do not mean to prescribe rules to strong and valiant natures, who will mind their own affairs whether in heaven or hell, and perchance build more magnificently and spend more lavishly than the richest, without ever impoverishing themselves, not knowing how they live,—if, indeed, there are any such, as has been dreamed; nor to those who find their encouragement and inspiration in precisely the present condition of things, and cherish it with the fondness and enthusiasm of lovers,—and, to some extent, I reckon myself in this number; I do not speak to those who are well employed, in whatever circumstances, and they know whether they are well employed or not;—but mainly to the mass of men who are discontented, and idly complaining of the hardness of their lot or of the times, when they might improve them. There are some who complain most energetically and inconsolably of any, because they are, as they say, doing their duty. I also have in my mind that seemingly wealthy, but most terribly impoverished class of all, who have accumulated dross, but know not how to use it, or get rid of it, and thus have forged their own golden or silver fetters.

If I should attempt to tell how I have desired to spend my life in years past, it would probably surprise those of my readers who are somewhat acquainted with its actual history; it would certainly astonish those who know nothing about it. I will only hint at some of the enterprises which I have cherished.

In any weather, at any hour of the day or night, I have been anxious to improve the nick of time, and notch it on my stick too; to stand on the meeting of two eternities, the past and future, which is precisely the present moment; to toe that line. You will pardon some obscurities, for there are more secrets in my trade than in most men's, and yet not voluntarily kept, but inseparable from its very nature. I would gladly tell all that I know about it, and never paint "No Admittance" on my gate.

I long ago lost a hound, a bay horse, and a turtledove, and am still on their trail. Many are the travellers I have spoken concerning them, describing their tracks and what calls they answered to. I have met one or two who had heard the hound, and the tramp of the horse, and even seen the dove disappear behind a cloud, and they seemed as anxious to recover them as if they had lost them themselves.

To anticipate, not the sunrise and the dawn merely, but, if possible, Nature herself! How many mornings, summer and winter, before yet any neighbor was stirring about his business, have I been about mine! No doubt, many of my townsmen have met me returning from this enterprise, farmers starting for Boston in the twilight, or woodchoppers going to their work. It is true, I never assisted the sun materially in his rising, but, doubt not, it was of the last importance only to be present at it.

So many autumn, ay, and winter days, spent outside the town, trying to hear what was in the wind, to hear and carry it express! I wellnigh sunk all my capital in it, and lost my own breath into the bargain, running in the face of it. If it had concerned either of the political parties, depend upon it, it would have appeared in the Gazette with the earliest intelligence. At other times watching from the observatory of some cliff or tree, to telegraph any new arrival; or waiting at evening on the hill-tops, for the sky to fall, that I might catch something, though I never caught much, and that, manna-wise, would dissolve again in the sun.

For a long time I was reporter to a journal, of no very wide circulation, whose editor has never yet seen fit to print the bulk of my contributions, and, as is too common with writers, I got only my labor for my pains. However, in this case my pains were their own reward.

For many years I was self-appointed inspector of snow storms and rain storms, and did my duty faithfully; surveyor, if not of highways, then of forest paths and all across-lot routes, keeping them open, and ravines bridged and passable at all seasons, where the public heel had testified to their utility.

I have looked after the wild stock of the town, which give a faithful herdsman a good deal of trouble by leaping fences; and I have had an eye to the unfrequented nooks and corners of the farm; though I did not always know whether Jonas or Solomon worked in a particular field to-day; that was none of my business. I have watered the red huckleberry, the sand cherry and the nettle tree, the red pine and the black ash, the white grape and the yellow violet, which might have withered else in dry seasons.

In short, I went on thus for a long time (I may say it without boasting) faithfully minding my business, till it became more and more evident that my townsmen would not after all admit me into the list of town officers, nor make my place a sinecure with a moderate allowance. My accounts, which I can swear to have kept faithfully, I have, indeed, never got audited, still less accepted, still less paid and settled. However, I have not set my heart on that.

Not long since, a strolling Indian went to sell baskets at the house of a well-known lawyer in my neighborhood. "Do you wish to buy any baskets?" he asked. "No, we do not want any," was the reply. "What!" exclaimed the Indian, as he went out the gate, "do you mean to starve us?" Having seen his industrious white neighbors so well off,—that the lawyer had only to weave arguments, and by some magic, wealth and standing followed,—he had said to himself: I will go into business; I will weave baskets; it is a thing which I can do. Thinking that when he had made the baskets he would have done his part, and then it would be the white man's to buy them. He had not discovered that it was necessary for him to make it worth the other's while to buy them, or at least make him think that it was so, or to make something else which it would be worth his while to buy. I too had woven a kind of basket of a delicate texture, but I had not made it worth any one's while to buy them. Yet not the less, in my case, did I think it worth my while to weave them, and instead of studying how to make it worth men's while to buy my baskets, I studied rather how to avoid the necessity of selling them. The life which men praise and regard as successful is but one kind. Why should we exaggerate any one kind at the expense of the others?

Finding that my fellow-citizens were not likely to offer me any room in the court-house, or any curacy or living anywhere else, but I must shift for myself, I turned my face more exclusively than ever to the woods, where I was better known. I determined to go into business at once, and not wait to acquire the usual capital, using such slender means as I had already got. My purpose in going to Walden Pond was not to live cheaply nor to live dearly there, but to transact some private business with the fewest obstacles; to be hindered from accomplishing which for want of a little common-sense, a little enterprise and business talent, appeared not so sad as foolish.

I have always endeavored to acquire strict business habits; they are indispensable to every man. If your trade is with the Celestial Empire, then some small counting house on the coast, in some Salem harbor, will be fixture enough. You will export such articles as the country affords, purely native products, much ice and pine timber and a little granite, always in native bottoms. These will be good ventures. To oversee all the details yourself in person; to be at once pilot and captain, and owner and underwriter; to buy and sell and keep the accounts; to read every letter received, and write or read every letter sent; to superintend the discharge of imports night and day; to be upon many parts of the coast almost at the same time,—often the richest freight will be discharged upon a Jersey shore;—to be your own telegraph, unweariedly sweeping the horizon, speaking all passing vessels bound coastwise; to keep up a steady despatch of commodities, for the supply of such a distant and exorbitant market; to keep yourself informed of the state of the markets, prospects of

war and peace everywhere, and anticipate the tendencies of trade and civilization,—taking advantage of the results of all exploring expeditions, using new passages and all improvements in navigation;—charts to be studied, the position of reefs and new lights and buoys to be ascertained, and ever, and ever, the logarithmic tables to be corrected, for by the error of some calculator the vessel often splits upon a rock
10 that should have reached a friendly pier,— there is the untold fate of La Pérouse[3];—universal science to be kept pace with, studying the lives of all great discoverers and navigators, great adventurers and merchants, from Hanno and the Phœnicians down to our day; in fine, account of stock to be taken from time to time, to know how you stand. It is a labor to task the faculties of a man,—such problems of profit and loss, of interest, of tare and tret, and
20 gauging of all kinds in it, as demand a universal knowledge.

I have thought that Walden Pond would be a good place for business, not solely on account of the railroad and the ice trade; it offers advantages which it may not be good policy to divulge; it is a good port and a good foundation. No Neva marshes to be filled; though you must everywhere build on piles of your own driving. It is said that a flood-tide, with a
30 westerly wind, and ice in the Neva, would sweep St. Petersburg from the face of the earth.

As this business was to be entered into without the usual capital, it may not be easy to conjecture where those means, that will still be indispensable to every such undertaking, were to be obtained. As for Clothing, to come at once to the practical part of the question,
40 perhaps we are led oftener by the love of novelty and a regard for the opinions of men, in procuring it, than by a true utility. Let him who has work to do recollect that the object of clothing is, first, to retain the vital heat, and secondly, in this state of society, to cover nakedness, and he may judge how much of any necessary or important work may be accomplished without adding to his wardrobe. Kings and queens who wear a suit but once, though
50 made by some tailor or dressmaker to their majesties, cannot know the comfort of wearing a suit that fits. They are no better than wooden horses to hang the clean clothes on. Every day

[3] An explorer, seeking the Northwest Passage, who disappeared in 1788.

our garments become more assimilated to ourselves, receiving the impress of the wearer's character, until we hesitate to lay them aside without such delay and medical appliances and some such solemnity even as our bodies. No man ever stood the lower in my estimation for having a patch in his clothes; yet I am sure that there is greater anxiety, commonly, to have fashionable, or at least clean and unpatched clothes, than to have a sound conscience. But even if the rent is not mended, perhaps the worst vice betrayed is improvidence. I sometimes try my acquaintances by such tests as this,—who could wear a patch, or two extra seams only, over the knee? Most behave as if they believed that their prospects for life would be ruined if they should do it. It would be easier for them to hobble to town with a broken leg than with a broken pantaloon. Often if an accident happens to a gentleman's legs, they can be mended; but if a similar accident happens to the legs of his pantaloons, there is no help for it; for he considers, not what is truly respectable, but what is respected. We know but few men, a great many coats and breeches. Dress a scarecrow in your last shift, you standing shiftless by, who would not soonest salute the scarecrow? Passing a cornfield the other day, close by a hat and coat on a stake, I recognized the owner of the farm. He was only a little more weather-beaten than when I saw him last. I have heard of a dog that barked at every stranger who approached his master's premises with clothes on, but was easily quieted by a naked thief. It is an interesting question how far men would retain their relative rank if they were divested of their clothes. Could you, in such a case, tell surely of any company of civilized men, which belonged to the most respected class? When Madam Pfeiffer, in her adventurous travels round the world, from east to west, had got so near home as Asiatic Russia, she says that she felt the necessity of wearing other than a travelling dress, when she went to meet the authorities, for she "was now in a civilized country, where . . . people are judged of by their clothes." Even in our democratic New England towns the accidental possession of wealth, and its manifestation in dress and equipage alone, obtain for the possessor almost universal respect. But they who yield such respect, numerous as they are, are so far heathen, and need to have a missionary sent to them. Beside, clothes introduced sewing, a kind of work which you may call endless; a woman's dress, at least, is never done.

A man who has at length found something to do will not need to get a new suit to do it in; for him the old will do, that has lain dusty in the garret for an indeterminate period. Old shoes will serve a hero longer than they have served his valet,—if a hero ever has a valet,—bare feet are older than shoes, and he can make them do. Only they who go to soirées and legislative halls must have new coats, coats to change as often as the man changes in them. But if my jacket and trousers, my hat and shoes, are fit to worship God in, they will do; will they not? Who ever saw his old clothes,—his old coat, actually worn out, resolved into its primitive elements, so that it was not a deed of charity to bestow it on some poor boy, by him perchance to be bestowed on some poorer still, or shall we say richer, who could do with less? I say, beware of all enterprises that require new clothes, and not rather a new wearer of clothes. If there is not a new man, how can the new clothes be made to fit? If you have any enterprise before you, try it in your old clothes. All men want, not something to *do with,* but something to *do,* or rather something to *be.* Perhaps we should never procure a new suit, however ragged or dirty the old, until we have so conducted, so enterprised or sailed in some way, that we feel like new men in the old, and that to retain it would be like keeping new wine in old bottles. Our moulting season, like that of the fowls, must be a crisis in our lives. The loon retires to solitary ponds to spend it. Thus also the snake casts its slough, and the caterpillar its wormy coat, by an internal industry and expansion; for clothes are but our outmost cuticle and mortal coil. Otherwise we shall be found sailing under false colors, and be inevitably cashiered at last by our own opinion, as well as that of mankind.

We don garment after garment, as if we grew like exogenous plants by addition without. Our outside and often thin and fanciful clothes are our epidermis or false skin, which partakes not of our life, and may be stripped off here and there without fatal injury; our thicker garments, constantly worn, are our cellular integument, or cortex; but our shirts are our liber or true bark, which cannot be removed without girdling and so destroying the man. I believe that all races at some seasons wear something equivalent to the shirt. It is desirable that a man be clad so simply that he can lay his hands

on himself in the dark, and that he live in all respects so compactly and preparedly that, if an enemy take the town, he can, like the old philosopher, walk out the gate empty-handed without anxiety. While one thick garment is, for most purposes, as good as three thin ones, and cheap clothing can be obtained at prices really to suit customers; while a thick coat can be bought for five dollars, which will last as many years, thick pantaloons for two dollars, cowhide boots for a dollar and a half a pair, a summer hat for a quarter of a dollar, and a winter cap for sixty-two and a half cents, or a better be made at home at a nominal cost, where is he so poor that, clad in such a suit, *of his own earning,* there will not be found wise men to do him reverence?

When I ask for a garment of a particular form, my tailoress tells me gravely, "They do not make them so now," not emphasizing the "They" at all, as if she quoted an authority as impersonal as the Fates, and I find it difficult to get made what I want, simply because she cannot believe that I mean what I say, that I am so rash. When I hear this oracular sentence, I am for a moment absorbed in thought, emphasizing to myself each word separately that I may come at the meaning of it, that I may find out by what degree of consanguinity *They* are related to *me,* and what authority they may have in an affair which affects me so nearly; and, finally, I am inclined to answer her with equal mystery, and without any more emphasis of the "they,"—"It is true, they did not make them so recently, but they do now." Of what use this measuring of me if she does not measure my character, but only the breadth of my shoulders, as it were a peg to hang the coat on? We worship not the Graces, nor the Parcæ, but Fashion. She spins and weaves and cuts with full authority. The head monkey at Paris puts on a traveller's cap, and all the monkeys in America do the same. I sometimes despair of getting anything quite simple and honest done in this world by the help of men. They would have to be passed through a powerful press first, to squeeze their old notions out of them, so that they would not soon get upon their legs again; and then there would be some one in the company with a maggot in his head, hatched from an egg deposited there nobody knows when, for not even fire kills these things, and you would have lost your labor. Nevertheless, we will not forget that some Egyptian wheat was handed down to us by a mummy.

On the whole, I think that it cannot be maintained that dressing has in this or any country risen to the dignity of an art. At present men make shift to wear what they can get. Like shipwrecked sailors, they put on what they can find on the beach, and at a little distance, whether of space or time, laugh at each other's masquerade. Every generation laughs at the old fashions, but follows religiously the new. We are amused at beholding the costume of Henry VIII., or Queen Elizabeth, as much as if it was that of the King and Queen of the Cannibal Islands. All costume off a man is pitiful or grotesque. It is only the serious eye peering from and the sincere life passed within it, which restrain laughter and consecrate the costume of any people. Let Harlequin be taken with a fit of the colic and his trappings will have to serve that mood too. When the soldier is hit by a cannon-ball, rags are as becoming as purple.

The childish and savage taste of men and women for new patterns keeps how many shaking and squinting through kaleidoscopes that they may discover the particular figure which this generation requires to-day. The manufacturers have learned that this taste is merely whimsical. Of two patterns which differ only by a few threads more or less of a particular color, the one will be sold readily, the other lie on the shelf, though it frequently happens that after the lapse of a season the latter becomes the most fashionable. Comparatively, tattooing is not the hideous custom which it is called. It is not barbarous merely because the printing is skin-deep and unalterable.

I cannot believe that our factory system is the best mode by which men may get clothing. The condition of the operatives is becoming every day more like that of the English; and it cannot be wondered at, since, as far as I have heard or observed, the principal object is, not that mankind may be well and honestly clad, but, unquestionably, that the corporations may be enriched. In the long run men hit only what they aim at. Therefore, though they should fail immediately, they had better aim at something high.

As for a Shelter, I will not deny that this is now a necessary of life, though there are instances of men having done without it for long periods in colder countries than this. Samuel Laing says that "The Laplander in his skin dress, and in a skin bag which he puts over his head and shoulders, will sleep night after night on the snow . . . in a degree of cold which would extinguish the life of one exposed to it in any woollen clothing." He had seen them asleep thus. Yet he adds, "They are not hardier than other people." But, probably, man did not live long on earth without discovering the convenience which there is in a house, the domestic comforts, which phrase may have originally signified the satisfactions of the house more than of the family; though these must be extremely partial and occasional in those climates where the house is associated in our thoughts with winter or the rainy season chiefly, and two thirds of the year, except for a parasol, is unnecessary. In our climate, in the summer, it was formerly almost solely a covering at night. In the Indian gazettes a wigwam was the symbol of a day's march, and a row of them cut or painted on the bark of a tree signified that so many times they had camped. Man was not made so large limbed and robust but that he must seek to narrow his world, and wall in a space such as fitted him. He was at first bare and out of doors; but though this was pleasant enough in serene and warm weather, by daylight, the rainy season and the winter, to say nothing of the torrid sun, would perhaps have nipped his race in the bud if he had not made haste to clothe himself with the shelter of a house. Adam and Eve, according to the fable, wore the bower before other clothes. Man wanted a home, a place of warmth, or comfort, first of physical warmth, then the warmth of the affections.

We may imagine a time when, in the infancy of the human race, some enterprising mortal crept into a hollow in a rock for shelter. Every child begins the world again, to some extent, and loves to stay outdoors, even in wet and cold. It plays house, as well as horse, having an instinct for it. Who does not remember the interest with which, when young, he looked at shelving rocks, or any approach to a cave? It was the natural yearning of that portion of our most primitive ancestor which still survived in us. From the cave we have advanced to roofs of palm leaves, of bark and boughs, of linen woven and stretched, of grass and straw, of boards and shingles, of stones and tiles. At last, we know not what it is to live in the open air, and our lives are domestic in more senses than we think. From the hearth to the field is a great distance. It would be well perhaps if we were to spend more of our days and nights without any obstruction between us and the celestial bodies, if the poet did not speak so much from under a roof, or the saint dwell there so long. Birds do not sing in caves, nor do doves cherish their innocence in dovecots.

However, if one designs to construct a dwelling-house, it behooves him to exercise a little Yankee shrewdness, lest after all he find himself in a workhouse, a labyrinth without a clew, a museum, an almshouse, a prison, or a splendid mausoleum instead. Consider first how slight a shelter is absolutely necessary. I have seen Penobscot Indians, in this town, living in tents of thin cotton cloth, while the snow was nearly a foot deep around them, and I thought that they would be glad to have it deeper to keep out the wind. Formerly, when how to get my living honestly, with freedom left for my proper pursuits, was a question which vexed me even more than it does now, for unfortunately I am become somewhat callous, I used to see a large box by the railroad, six feet long by three wide, in which the laborers locked up their tools at night; and it suggested to me that every man who was hard pushed might get such a one for a dollar, and, having bored a few auger holes in it, to admit the air at least, get into it when it rained and at night, and hook down the lid, and so have freedom in his love, and in his soul be free. This did not appear the worst, nor by any means a despicable alternative. You could sit up as late as you pleased, and, whenever you got up, go abroad without any landlord or house-lord dogging you for rent. Many a man is harassed to death to pay the rent of a larger and more luxurious box who would not have frozen to death in such a box as this. I am far from jesting. Economy is a subject which admits of being treated with levity, but it cannot so be disposed of. A comfortable house for a rude and hardy race, that lived mostly out of doors, was once made here almost entirely of such materials as Nature furnished ready to their hands. Gookin, who was superintendent of the Indians subject to the Massachusetts Colony, writing in 1674, says, "The best of their houses are covered very neatly, tight and warm, with barks of trees, slipped from their bodies at those seasons when the sap is up, and made into great flakes, with pressure of weighty timber, when they are green. . . . The meaner sort are covered with mats which they make of a kind of bulrush, and are also indifferently tight and warm, but not so good as the former. . . . Some I have seen, sixty or a hundred feet long and thirty feet broad. . . . I have often lodged in their wigwams, and found them as warm as the best English houses." He adds, that they were commonly carpeted and lined within with well-wrought embroidered mats, and were furnished with various utensils. The Indians had advanced so far as to regulate the effect of the wind by a mat suspended over the hole in the roof and moved by a string. Such a lodge was in the first instance constructed in a day or two at most, and taken down and put up in a few hours; and every family owned one, or its apartment in one.

In the savage state every family owns a shelter as good as the best, and sufficient for its coarser and simpler wants; but I think that I speak within bounds when I say that, though the birds of the air have their nests, and the foxes their holes, and the savages their wigwams, in modern civilized society not more than one half of the families own a shelter. In the large towns and cities, where civilization especially prevails, the number of those who own a shelter is a very small fraction of the whole. The rest pay an annual tax for this outside garment of all, become indispensable summer and winter, which would buy a village of Indian wigwams, but now helps to keep them poor as long as they live. I do not mean to insist here on the disadvantage of hiring compared with owning, but it is evident that the savage owns his shelter because it costs so little, while the civilized man hires his commonly because he cannot afford to own it; nor can he, in the long run, any better afford to hire. But, answers one, by merely paying this tax the poor civilized man secures an abode which is a palace compared with the savage's. An annual rent of from twenty-five to a hundred dollars (these are the country rates) entitles him to the benefit of the improvements of centuries, spacious apartments, clean paint and paper, Rumford fire-place, back plastering, Venetian blinds, copper pump, spring lock, a commodious cellar, and many other things. But how happens it that he who is said to enjoy these things is so commonly a *poor* civilized man, while the savage, who has them not, is rich as a savage? If it is asserted that civilization is a real advance in the condition of man,—and I think that it is, though only the wise improve their advantages,—it must be shown that it has produced better dwellings without making them more costly; and the cost of a thing is the amount of what I will call life which is required to be exchanged for it, immediately or in the long run. An average house in this neighborhood costs perhaps eight hundred dollars, and to lay up this sum will take from ten to fifteen years of the laborer's life, even if he is not encumbered with a family,—estimating the pecuniary value of every man's labor at one dollar a day, for if some receive more, others receive less;—so that he must have spent more than half his life commonly before *his* wigwam will be earned. If we suppose him to pay a rent instead, this is but a doubtful choice of evils. Would the savage have been wise to exchange his wigwam for a palace on these terms?

It may be guessed that I reduce almost the whole advantage of holding this superfluous property as a fund in store against the future, so far as the individual is concerned, mainly to the defraying of funeral expenses. But perhaps a man is not required to bury himself. Nevertheless this points to an important distinction between the civilized man and the savage; and, no doubt, they have designs on us for our benefit, in making the life of a civilized people an *institution,* in which the life of the individual is to a great extent absorbed, in order to preserve and perfect that of the race. But I wish to show at what a sacrifice this advantage is at present obtained, and to suggest that we may possibly so live as to secure all the advantage without suffering any of the disadvantage. What mean ye by saying that the poor ye have always with you, or that the fathers have eaten sour grapes, and the children's teeth are set on edge?

"As I live, saith the Lord God, ye shall not have occasion any more to use this proverb in Israel.

"Behold, all souls are mine; as the soul of the father, so also the soul of the son is mine: the soul that sinneth it shall die."

When I consider my neighbors, the farmers of Concord, who are at least as well off as the other classes, I find that for the most part they have been toiling twenty, thirty, or forty years, that they may become the real owners of their farms, which commonly they have inherited with encumbrances, or else bought with hired money,—and we may regard one third of that toil as the cost of their houses,—but commonly they have not paid for them yet. It is true, the encumbrances sometimes outweigh the value of the farm, so that the farm itself becomes one great encumbrance, and still a man is found to inherit it, being well acquainted with it, as he

says. On applying to the assessors, I am surprised to learn that they cannot at once name a dozen in the town who own their farms free and clear. If you would know the history of these homesteads, inquire at the bank where they are mortgaged. The man who has actually paid for his farm with labor on it is so rare that every neighbor can point to him. I doubt if there are three such men in Concord. What has been said of the merchants, that a very large majority, even ninety-seven in a hundred, are sure to fail, is equally true of the farmers. With regard to the merchants, however, one of them says pertinently that a great part of their failures are not genuine pecuniary failures, but merely failures to fulfil their engagements, because it is inconvenient; that is, it is the moral character that breaks down. But this puts an infinitely worse face on the matter, and suggests, beside, that probably not even the other three succeed in saving their souls, but are perchance bankrupt in a worse sense than they who fail honestly. Bankruptcy and repudiation are the springboards from which much of our civilization vaults and turns its somersets, but the savage stands on the unelastic plank of famine. Yet the Middlesex Cattle Show goes off here with *éclat* annually, as if all the joints of the agricultural machine were suent.

The farmer is endeavoring to solve the problem of a livelihood by a formula more complicated than the problem itself. To get his shoestrings he speculates in herds of cattle. With consummate skill he has set his trap with a hair springe to catch comfort and independence, and then, as he turned away, got his own leg into it. This is the reason he is poor; and for a similar reason we are all poor in respect to a thousand savage comforts, though surrounded by luxuries. As Chapman sings,—

"The false society of men—
        —for earthly greatness
All heavenly comforts rarefies to air."

And when the farmer has got his house, he may not be the richer but the poorer for it, and it be the house that has got him. As I understand it, that was a valid objection urged by Momus against the house which Minerva made, that she "had not made it movable, by which means a bad neighborhood might be avoided"; and it may still be urged, for our houses are such unwieldy property that we are often imprisoned rather than housed in them; and the bad neighborhood to be avoided is our own scurvy selves. I know one or two families, at least, in this town, who, for nearly a generation, have been wishing to sell their houses in the outskirts and move into the village, but have not been able to accomplish it, and only death will set them free.

Granted that the *majority* are able at last either to own or hire the modern house with all its improvements. While civilization has been improving our houses, it has not equally improved the men who are to inhabit them. It has created palaces, but it was not so easy to create noblemen and kings. And *if the civilized man's pursuits are no worthier than the savage's, if he is employed the greater part of his life in obtaining gross necessaries and comforts merely, why should he have a better dwelling than the former?*

But how do the poor *minority* fare? Perhaps it will be found that just in proportion as some have been placed in outward circumstances above the savage, others have been degraded below him. The luxury of one class is counterbalanced by the indigence of another. On the one side is the palace, on the other are the almshouse and "silent poor." The myriads who built the pyramids to be the tombs of the Pharaohs were fed on garlic, and it may be were not decently buried themselves. The mason who finishes the cornice of the palace returns at night perchance to a hut not so good as a wigwam. It is a mistake to suppose that, in a country where the usual evidences of civilization exist, the condition of a very large body of the inhabitants may not be as degraded as that of savages. I refer to the degraded poor, not now to the degraded rich. To know this I should not need to look farther than to the shanties which everywhere border our railroads, that last improvement in civilization; where I see in my daily walks human beings living in sties, and all winter with an open door, for the sake of light, without any visible, often imaginable, wood-pile, and the forms of both old and young are permanently contracted by the long habit of shrinking from cold and misery, and the development of all their limbs and faculties is checked. It certainly is fair to look at that class by whose labor the works which distinguish this generation are accomplished. Such too, to a greater or less extent, is the condition of the operatives of every denomination in England, which is the great workhouse of the world. Or I could refer you to Ireland, which is marked as one of the white

or enlightened spots on the map. Contrast the physical condition of the Irish with that of the North American Indian, or the South Sea Islander, or any other savage race before it was degraded by contact with the civilized man. Yet I have no doubt that that people's rulers are as wise as the average of civilized rulers. Their condition only proves what squalidness may consist with civilization. I hardly need refer now to the laborers in our Southern States who produce the staple exports of this country, and are themselves a staple production of the South. But to confine myself to those who are said to be in *moderate* circumstances.

Most men appear never to have considered what a house is, and are actually though needlessly poor all their lives because they think that they must have such a one as their neighbors have. As if one were to wear any sort of coat which the tailor might cut out for him, or, gradually leaving off palm-leaf hat or cap of woodchuck skin, complain of hard times because he could not afford to buy him a crown! It is possible to invent a house still more convenient and luxurious than we have, which yet all would admit that man could not afford to pay for. Shall we always study to obtain more of these things, and not sometimes to be content with less? Shall the respectable citizen thus gravely teach, by precept and example, the necessity of the young man's providing a certain number of superfluous glow-shoes, and umbrellas, and empty guest chambers for empty guests, before he dies? Why should not our furniture be as simple as the Arab's or the Indian's? When I think of the benefactors of the race, whom we have apotheosized as messengers from heaven, bearers of divine gifts to man, I do not see in my mind any retinue at their heels, any carload of fashionable furniture. Or what if I were to allow—would it not be a singular allowance?—that our furniture should be more complex than the Arab's, in proportion as we are morally and intellectually his superiors! At present our houses are cluttered and defiled with it, and a good housewife would sweep out the greater part into the dusthole, and not leave her morning's work undone. Morning work! By the blushes of Aurora and the music of Memnon, what should be man's *morning work* in this world? I had three pieces of limestone on my desk, but I was terrified to find that they required to be dusted daily, when the furniture of my mind was all undusted still, and I threw them out the window in disgust. How, then, could I have a furnished house? I would rather sit in the open air, for no dust gathers on the grass, unless where man has broken ground.

It is the luxurious and dissipated who set the fashions which the herd so diligently follow. The traveller who stops at the best houses, so called, soon discovers this, for the publicans presume him to be a Sardanapalus, and if he resigned himself to their tender mercies he would soon be completely emasculated. I think that in the railroad car we are inclined to spend more on luxury than on safety and convenience, and it threatens without attaining these to become no better than a modern drawing-room, with its divans, and ottomans, and sunshades, and a hundred other oriental things, which we are taking west with us, invented for the ladies of the harem and the effeminate natives of the Celestial Empire, which Jonathan should be ashamed to know the names of. I would rather sit on a pumpkin and have it all to myself, than to be crowded on a velvet cushion. I would rather ride on earth in an ox cart with a free circulation, than go to heaven in the fancy car of an excursion train and breathe a *malaria* all the way.

The very simplicity and nakedness of man's life in the primitive ages imply this advantage at least, that they left him still but a sojourner in nature. When he was refreshed with food and sleep he contemplated his journey again. He dwelt, as it were, in a tent in this world, and was either threading the valleys, or crossing the plains, or climbing the mountain-tops. But lo! men have become the tools of their tools. The man who independently plucked the fruits when he was hungry is become a farmer; and he who stood under a tree for shelter, a housekeeper. We now no longer camp as for a night, but have settled down on earth and forgotten heaven. We have adopted Christianity merely as an improved method of *agri*-culture. We have built for this world a family mansion, and for the next a family tomb. The best works of art are the expression of man's struggle to free himself from this condition, but the effect of our art is merely to make this low state comfortable and that higher state to be forgotten. There is actually no place in this village for a work of *fine* art, if any had come down to us, to stand, for our lives, our houses and streets, furnish no proper pedestal for it. There is not a nail to hang a picture on, nor a shelf to receive the bust of a hero or a saint. When I consider how our houses are built and paid for, or not paid for, and their internal economy managed and sustained, I wonder that the floor does not give way under the visitor while he is admiring the gewgaws upon the mantel-piece, and let him through into the cellar, to some solid and honest, though earthy foundation. I cannot but perceive that this so-called rich and refined life is a thing jumped at, and I do not get on in the enjoyment of the *fine* arts which adorn it, my attention being wholly occupied with the jump; for I remember that the greatest genuine leap, due to human muscles alone, on record, is that of certain wandering Arabs, who are said to have cleared twenty-five feet on level ground. Without factitious support, man is sure to come to earth again beyond that distance. The first question which I am tempted to put to the proprietor of such great impropriety is, Who bolsters you? Are you one of the ninety-seven who fail, or the three who succeed? Answer me these questions, and then perhaps I may look at your bawbles and find them ornamental. The cart before the horse is neither beautiful nor useful. Before we can adorn our houses with beautiful objects the walls must be stripped, and our lives must be stripped, and beautiful housekeeping and beautiful living be laid for a foundation: now, a taste for the beautiful is most cultivated out of doors, where there is no house and no housekeeper.

Old Johnson,[4] in his "Wonder-Working Providence," speaking of the first settlers of this town, with whom he was contemporary, tells us that "they burrow themselves in the earth for their first shelter under some hillside, and, casting the soil aloft upon timber, they make a smoky fire against the earth, at the highest side." They did not "provide them houses," says he, "till the earth, by the Lord's blessing, brought forth bread to feed them," and the first year's crop was so light that "they were forced to cut their bread very thin for a long season." The secretary of the Province of New Netherland, writing in Dutch, in 1650, for the information of those who wished to take up land there, states more particularly that "those in New Netherland, and especially in New England, who have no means to build farm-houses at first according to their wishes, dig a square pit in the ground, cellar fashion, six or seven feet deep, as long and as broad as they think proper, case the earth inside with

---

[4] Edward Johnson's *Wonder-Working Providence of Sion's Saviour in New England* (1654).

wood all round the wall, and line the wood with the bark of trees or something else to prevent the caving in of the earth; floor this cellar with plank, and wainscot it overhead for a ceiling, raise a roof of spars clear up, and cover the spars with bark or green sods, so that they can live dry and warm in these houses with their entire families for two, three, and four years, it being understood that partitions are run through those cellars which are adapted to the size of the family. The wealthy and principal men in New England, in the beginning of the colonies, commenced their first dwelling-houses in this fashion for two reasons: firstly, in order not to waste time in building, and not to want food the next season; secondly, in order not to discourage poor laboring people whom they brought over in numbers from Fatherland. In the course of three or four years, when the country became adapted to agriculture, they built themselves handsome houses, spending on them several thousands."

In this course which our ancestors took there was a show of prudence at least, as if their principle were to satisfy the more pressing wants first. But are the more pressing wants satisfied now? When I think of acquiring for myself one of our luxurious dwellings, I am deterred, for, so to speak, the country is not yet adapted to *human* culture, and we are still forced to cut our *spiritual* bread far thinner than our forefathers did their wheaten. Not that all architectural ornament is to be neglected even in the rudest periods; but let our houses first be lined with beauty, where they come in contact with our lives, like the tenement of the shell-fish, and not overlaid with it. But, alas! I have been inside one or two of them, and know what they are lined with.

Though we are not so degenerate but that we might possibly live in a cave or a wigwam, or wear skins to-day, it certainly is better to accept the advantages, though so dearly bought, which the invention and industry of mankind offer. In such a neighborhood as this, boards and shingles, lime and bricks, are cheaper and more easily obtained than suitable caves, or whole logs, or bark in sufficient quantities, or even well-tempered clay or flat stones. I speak understandingly on this subject, for I have made myself acquainted with it both theoretically and practically. With a little more wit, we might use these materials so as to become richer than the richest now are, and make our civilization a blessing. The civilized man is a more experienced and wiser savage. But to make haste to my own experiment.

Near the end of March 1845 I borrowed an axe and went down to the woods by Walden Pond, nearest to where I intended to build my house, and began to cut down some tall, arrowy white pines, still in their youth, for timber. It is difficult to begin without borrowing, but perhaps it is the most generous course thus to permit your fellow-men to have an interest in your enterprise. The owner of the axe, as he released his hold on it, said that it was the apple of his eye; but I returned it sharper than I received it. It was a pleasant hillside where I worked, covered with pine woods, through which I looked out on the pond, and a small open field in the woods where pines and hickories were springing up. The ice in the pond was not yet dissolved, though there were some open spaces, and it was all dark-colored and saturated with water. There were some slight flurries of snow during the days that I worked there; but for the most part when I came out on to the railroad, on my way home, its yellow sand-heap stretched away gleaming in the hazy atmosphere, and the rails shone in the spring sun, and I heard the lark and peewee and other birds already come to commence another year with us. They were pleasant spring days, in which the winter of man's discontent was thawing as well as the earth, and the life that had lain torpid began to stretch itself. One day, when my axe had come off and I had cut a green hickory for a wedge, driving it with a stone, and had placed the whole to soak in a pond hole in order to swell the wood, I saw a striped snake run into the water, and he lay on the bottom, apparently without inconvenience, as long as I stayed there, or more than a quarter of an hour; perhaps because he had not yet fairly come out of the torpid state. It appeared to me that for a like reason men remain in their present low and primitive condition; but if they should feel the influence of the spring of springs arousing them, they would of necessity rise to a higher and more ethereal life. I had previously seen the snakes in frosty mornings in my path with portions of their bodies still numb and inflexible, waiting for the sun to thaw them. On the 1st of April it rained and melted the ice, and in the early part of the day, which was very foggy, I heard a stray goose groping about over the pond and cackling as if lost, or like the spirit of the fog.

So I went on for some days cutting and hewing timber, and also studs and rafters, all with my narrow axe, not having many communicable or scholar-like thoughts, singing to myself,—

> Men say they know many things;
> But lo! they have taken wings,—
> The arts and sciences,
> And a thousand appliances;
> The wind that blows
> Is all that anybody knows.

I hewed the main timbers six inches square, most of the studs on two sides only, and the rafters and floor timbers on one side, leaving the rest of the bark on, so that they were just as straight and much stronger than sawed ones. Each stick was carefully mortised or tenoned by its stump, for I had borrowed other tools by this time. My days in the woods were not very long ones; yet I usually carried my dinner of bread and butter, and read the newspaper in which it was wrapped, at noon, sitting amid the green pine boughs which I had cut off, and to my bread was imparted some of their fragrance, for my hands were covered with a thick coat of pitch. Before I had done I was more the friend than the foe of the pine tree, though I had cut down some of them, having become better acquainted with it. Sometimes a rambler in the wood was attracted by the sound of my axe, and we chatted pleasantly over the chips which I had made.

By the middle of April, for I made no haste in my work, but rather made the most of it, my house was framed and ready for the raising. I had already bought the shanty of James Collins, an Irishman who worked on the Fitchburg Railroad, for boards. James Collins' shanty was considered an uncommonly fine one. When I called to see it he was not at home. I walked about the outside, at first unobserved from within, the window was so deep and high. It was of small dimensions, with a peaked cottage roof, and not much else to be seen, the dirt being raised five feet all around as if it were a compost heap. The roof was the soundest part, though a good deal warped and made brittle by the sun. Doorsill there was none, but a perennial passage for the hens under the door-board. Mrs. C. came to the door and asked me to view it from the inside. The hens were driven in by my approach. It was dark, and had a dirt floor for the most part, dank, clammy, and aguish, only here a board and there a board which would not bear removal. She lighted a lamp to show me the inside of the roof and the walls, and also that the board floor extended under the bed, warning me not to step into the cellar, a sort of dust-hole two feet deep. In her own words, they were "good boards overhead, good boards all around, and a good window,"—of two whole squares originally, only the cat had passed out that way lately. There was a stove, a bed, and a place to sit, an infant in the house where it was born, a silk parasol, gilt-framed looking-glass, and a patent new coffee-mill nailed to an oak sapling, all told. The bargain was soon concluded, for James had in the meanwhile returned. I to pay four dollars and twenty-five cents to-night, he to vacate at five to-morrow morning, selling to nobody else meanwhile: I to take possession at six. It were well, he said, to be there early, and anticipate certain indistinct but wholly unjust claims on the score of ground rent and fuel. This he assured me was the only encumbrance. At six I passed him and his family on the road. One large bundle held their all,—bed, coffee-mill, looking-glass, hens,—all but the cat; she took to the woods and became a wild cat, and, as I learned afterward, trod in a trap set for woodchucks, and so became a dead cat at last.

I took down this dwelling the same morning, drawing the nails, and removed it to the pond-side by small cartloads, spreading the boards on the grass there to bleach and warp back again in the sun. One early thrush gave me a note or two as I drove along the woodland path. I was informed treacherously by a young Patrick that neighbor Seeley, an Irishman, in the intervals of the carting, transferred the still tolerable, straight, and drivable nails, staples, and spikes to his pocket, and then stood when I came back to pass the time of day, and look freshly up, unconcerned, with spring thoughts, at the devastation; there being a dearth of work, as he said. He was there to represent spectatordom, and help make this seemingly insignificant event one with the removal of the gods of Troy.

I dug my cellar in the side of a hill sloping to the south, where a woodchuck had formerly dug his burrow, down through sumach and blackberry roots, and the lowest stain of vegetation, six feet square by seven deep, to a fine sand where potatoes would not freeze in any winter. The sides were left shelving, and not stoned; but the sun having never shone on them, the sand still keeps its place. It was but two hours' work. I took particular pleasure in this breaking of ground, for in almost all latitudes men dig into the earth for an equable temperature. Under the most splendid house in the city is still to be found the cellar where they store their roots as of old, and long after the superstructure has disappeared posterity remark its dent in the earth. The house is still but a sort of porch at the entrance of a burrow.

At length, in the beginning of May, with the help of some of my acquaintances, rather to improve so good an occasion for neighborliness than from any necessity, I set up the frame of my house. No man was ever more honored in the character of his raisers than I. They are destined, I trust, to assist at the raising of loftier structures one day. I began to occupy my house on the 4th of July, as soon as it was boarded and roofed, for the boards were carefully feather-edged and lapped, so that it was perfectly impervious to rain, but before boarding I laid the foundation of a chimney at one end, bringing two cartloads of stones up the hill from the pond in my arms. I built the chimney after my hoeing in the fall, before a fire became necessary for warmth, doing my cooking in the meanwhile out of doors on the ground, early in the morning: which mode I still think *is* in some respects more convenient and agreeable than the usual one. When it stormed before my bread was baked, I fixed a few boards over the fire, and sat under them to watch my loaf, and passed some pleasant hours in that way. In those days, when my hands were much employed, I read but little, but the least scraps of paper which lay on the ground, my holder, or tablecloth, afforded me as much entertainment, in fact, answered the same purpose as the Iliad.

It would be worth the while to build still more deliberately than I did, considering, for instance, what foundation a door, a window, a cellar, a garret, have in the nature of man, and perchance never raising any superstructure until we found a better reason for it than our temporal necessities even. There is some of the same fitness in a man's building his own house that there is in a bird's building its own nest. Who knows but if men constructed their dwellings with their own hands, and provided food for themselves and families simply and honestly enough, the poetic faculty would be universally developed, as birds universally sing when they are so engaged? But alas! we do like

cowbirds and cuckoos, which lay their eggs in nests which other birds have built, and cheer no traveller with their chattering and unmusical notes. Shall we forever resign the pleasure of construction to the carpenter? What does architecture amount to in the experience of the mass of men? I never in all my walks came across a man engaged in so simple and natural an occupation as building his house. We belong to the community. It is not the tailor alone who is the ninth part of a man; it is as much the preacher, and the merchant, and the farmer. Where is this division of labor to end? and what object does it finally serve? No doubt another *may* also think for me; but it is not therefore desirable that he should do so to the exclusion of my thinking for myself.

True, there are architects so-called in this country, and I have heard of one at least possessed with the idea of making architectural ornaments have a core of truth, a necessity, and hence a beauty, as if it were a revelation to him. All very well perhaps from his point of view, but only a little better than the common dilettantism. A sentimental reformer in architecture, he began at the cornice, not at the foundation. It was only how to put a core of truth within the ornaments, that every sugar plum in fact might have an almond or caraway seed in it,—though I hold that almonds are most wholesome without the sugar,—and not how the inhabitant, the indweller, might build truly within and without, and let the ornaments take care of themselves. What reasonable man ever supposed that ornaments were something outward and in the skin merely,—that the tortoise got his spotted shell, or the shell-fish its mother-o'-pearl tints, by such a contract as the inhabitants of Broadway their Trinity Church? But a man has no more to do with the style of architecture of his house than a tortoise with that of its shell: nor need the soldier be so idle as to try to paint the precise *color* of his virtue on his standard. The enemy will find it out. He may turn pale when the trial comes. This man seemed to me to lean over the cornice, and timidly whisper his half truth to the rude occupants who really knew it better than he. What of architectural beauty I now see, I know has gradually grown from within outward, out of the necessities and character of the indweller, who is the only builder,—out of some unconscious truthfulness, and nobleness, without ever a thought for the appearance; and whatever additional beauty of this kind is destined

to be produced will be preceded by a like unconscious beauty of life. The most interesting
dwellings in this country, as the painter knows,
are the most unpretending, humble log huts
and cottages of the poor commonly; it is the life
of the inhabitants whose shells they are, and
not any peculiarity in their surfaces merely,
which makes them *picturesque;* and equally
interesting will be the citizen's suburban box,
when his life shall be as simple and as agreeable to the imagination, and there is as little
straining after effect in the style of his dwelling.
A great proportion of architectural ornaments
are literally hollow, and a September gale
would strip them off, like borrowed plumes,
without injury to the substantials. They can do
without *architecture* who have no olives nor
wines in the cellar. What if an equal ado were
made about the ornaments of style in literature,
and the architects of our bibles spent as much
time about their cornices as the architects of
our churches do? So are made the *belles-lettres*
and the *beaux-arts* and their professors. Much
it concerns a man, forsooth, how a few sticks
are slanted over him or under him, and what
colors are daubed upon his box. It would signify somewhat, if, in any earnest sense, *he*
slanted them and daubed it; but the spirit having departed out of the tenant, it is of a piece
with constructing his own coffin,—the architecture of the grave,—and "carpenter" is but another name for "coffin-maker." One man says,
in his despair or indifference to life, take up a
handful of the earth at your feet, and paint
your house that color. Is he thinking of his last
and narrow house? Toss up a copper for it as
well. What an abundance of leisure he must
have! Why do you take up a handful of dirt?
Better paint your house your own complexion;
let it turn pale or blush for you. An enterprise
to improve the style of cottage architecture!
When you have got my ornaments ready, I
will wear them.

Before winter I built a chimney, and shingled
the sides of my house, which were already impervious to rain, with imperfect and sappy
shingles made of the first slice of the log, whose
edges I was obliged to straighten with a plane.

I have thus a tight shingled and plastered
house, ten feet wide by fifteen long, and eight-
feet posts, with a garret and a closet, a large
window on each side, two trap-doors, one door
at the end, and a brick fireplace opposite. The
exact cost of my house, paying the usual price
for such materials as I used, but not counting

the work, all of which was done by myself, was
as follows; and I give the details because very
few are able to tell exactly what their houses
cost, and fewer still, if any, the separate cost of
the various materials which compose them:—

Boards	$8 03½,	mostly shanty boards.
Refuse shingles for roof and sides	4 00	
Laths	1 25	
Two second-hand windows with glass . .	2 43	
One thousand old brick	4 00	
Two casks of lime . .	2 40	That was high.
Hair	0 31	More than I needed.
Mantle-tree iron . .	0 15	
Nails	3 90	
Hinges and screws . .	0 14	
Latch	0 10	
Chalk	0 01	I carried a good part on my back.
Transportation . . .	1 40	
In all . . .	$28 12½	

These are the materials excepting the timber, stones, and sand, which I claimed by
squatter's right. I have also a small wood-shed
adjoining, made chiefly of the stuff which was
left after building the house.

I intend to build me a house which will surpass any on the main street in Concord in grandeur and luxury, as soon as it pleases me as
much and will cost me no more than my present one.

I thus found that the student who wishes for
a shelter can obtain one for a lifetime at an expense not greater than the rent which he now
pays annually. If I seem to boast more than is
becoming, my excuse is that I brag for humanity
rather than for myself; and my shortcomings
and inconsistencies do not affect the truth of
my statement. Notwithstanding much cant and
hypocrisy,—chaff which I find it difficult to
separate from my wheat, but for which I am as
sorry as any man,—I will breathe freely and
stretch myself in this respect, it is such a relief
to both the moral and physical system; and I
am resolved that I will not through humility
become the devil's attorney. I will endeavor to
speak a good word for the truth. At Cambridge
College the mere rent of a student's room,
which is only a little larger than my own, is
thirty dollars each year, though the corporation
had the advantage of building thirty-two side
by side and under one roof, and the occupant
suffers the inconvenience of many and noisy

neighbors, and perhaps a residence in the fourth story. I cannot but think that if we had more true wisdom in these respects, not only less education would be needed, because, forsooth, more would already have been acquired, but the pecuniary expense of getting an education would in a great measure vanish. Those conveniences which the student requires at Cambridge or elsewhere cost him or somebody else ten times as great a sacrifice of life as they would with proper management on both sides. Those things for which the most money is demanded are never the things which the student most wants. Tuition, for instance, is an important item in the term bill, while for the far more valuable education which he gets by associating with the most cultivated of his contemporaries no charge is made. The mode of founding a college is, commonly, to get up a subscription of dollars and cents, and then, following blindly the principles of a division of labor to its extreme,—a principle which should never be followed but with circumspection,—to call in a contractor who makes this a subject of speculation, and he employs Irishmen or other operatives actually to lay the foundations, while the students that are to be are said to be fitting themselves for it; and for these oversights successive generations have to pay. I think that it would be *better than this*, for the students, or those who desire to be benefited by it, even to lay the foundation themselves. The student who secures his coveted leisure and retirement by systematically shirking any labor necessary to man obtains but an ignoble and unprofitable leisure, defrauding himself of the experience which alone can make leisure fruitful. "But," says one, "you do not mean that the students should go to work with their hands instead of their heads?" I do not mean that exactly, but I mean something which he might think a good deal like that; I mean that they should not *play* life, or *study* it merely, while the community supports them at this expensive game, but earnestly *live* it from beginning to end. How could youths better learn to live than by at once trying the experiment of living? Methinks this would exercise their minds as much as mathematics. If I wished a boy to know something about the arts and sciences, for instance, I would not pursue the common course, which is merely to send him into the neighborhood of some professor, where anything is professed and practised but the art of life;—to survey the world through a telescope or a microscope, and never with his natural eye; to study chemistry, and not learn how his bread is made, or mechanics, and not learn how it is earned; to discover new satellites to Neptune, and not detect the motes in his eyes, or to what vagabond he is a satellite himself; or to be devoured by the monsters that swarm all around him, while contemplating the monsters in a drop of vinegar. Which would have advanced the most at the end of a month,—the boy who had made his own jackknife from the ore which he had dug and smelted, reading as much as would be necessary for this,—or the boy who had attended the lectures on metallurgy at the Institute in the meanwhile, and had received a Rogers' penknife from his father? Which would be most likely to cut his fingers? . . . To my astonishment I was informed on leaving college that I had studied navigation!—why, if I had taken one turn down the harbor I should have known more about it. Even the *poor* student studies and is taught only *political* economy, while that economy of living which is synonymous with philosophy is not even sincerely professed in our colleges. The consequence is, that while he is reading Adam Smith, Ricardo, and Say, he runs his father in debt irretrievably.

As with our colleges, so with a hundred "modern improvements": there is an illusion about them; there is not always a positive advance. The devil goes on exacting compound interest to the last for his early share and numerous succeeding investments in them. Our inventions are wont to be pretty toys, which distract our attention from serious things. They are but improved means to an unimproved end, an end which it was already but too easy to arrive at; as railroads lead to Boston or New York. We are in great haste to construct a magnetic telegraph from Maine to Texas; but Maine and Texas, it may be, have nothing important to communicate. Either is in such a predicament as the man who was earnest to be introduced to a distinguished deaf woman, but when he was presented, and one end of her ear trumpet was put into his hand, had nothing to say. As if the main object were to talk fast and not to talk sensibly. We are eager to tunnel under the Atlantic and bring the old world some weeks nearer to the new; but perchance the first news that will leak through into the broad, flapping American ear will be that the Princess Adelaide has the whooping cough. After all, the man whose horse trots a mile in a minute does not carry the most important messages; he is not an evangelist, nor does he come round eating locusts and wild honey. I doubt if Flying Childers ever carried a peck of corn to the mill.

One says to me, "I wonder that you do not lay up money; you love to travel; you might take the cars and go to Fitchburg to-day and see the country." But I am wiser than that. I have learned that the swiftest traveller is he that goes afoot. I say to my friend, Suppose we try who will get there first. The distance is thirty miles; the fare ninety cents. That is almost a day's wages. I remember when wages were sixty cents a day for laborers on this very road. Well, I start now on foot, and get there before night; I have travelled at that rate by the week together. You will in the meanwhile have earned your fare, and arrive there some time to-morrow, or possibly this evening, if you are lucky enough to get a job in season. Instead of going to Fitchburg, you will be working here the greater part of the day. And so, if the railroad reached round the world, I think that I should keep ahead of you; and as for seeing the country and getting experience of that kind, I should have to cut your acquaintance altogether.

Such is the universal law, which no man can ever outwit, and with regard to the railroad even we may say it is as broad as it is long. To make a railroad round the world available to all mankind is equivalent to grading the whole surface of the planet. Men have an indistinct notion that if they keep up this activity of joint stocks and spades long enough all will at length ride somewhere, in next to no time, and for nothing; but though a crowd rushes to the depot, and the conductor shouts "All aboard!" when the smoke is blown away and the vapor condensed, it will be perceived that a few are riding, but the rest are run over,—and it will be called, and will be, "A melancholy accident." No doubt they can ride at last who shall have earned their fare, that is, if they survive so long, but they will probably have lost their elasticity and desire to travel by that time. This spending of the best part of one's life earning money in order to enjoy a questionable liberty during the least valuable part of it, reminds me of the Englishman who went to India to make a fortune first, in order that he might return to England and live the life of a poet. He should have gone up garret at once. "What!" exclaim a million Irishmen, starting up from all the shanties in the land, "is not this railroad which we have built a good thing?" Yes, I answer, *comparatively* good, that is, you might have done worse; but I wish, as you are brothers of mine, that you could have spent your time better than digging in this dirt.

Before I finished my house, wishing to earn ten or twelve dollars by some honest and agreeable method, in order to meet my unusual expenses, I planted about two acres and a half of light and sandy soil near it chiefly with beans, but also a small part with potatoes, corn, peas, and turnips. The whole lot contains eleven acres, mostly growing up to pines and hickories, and was sold the preceding season for eight dollars and eight cents an acre. One farmer said that it was "good for nothing but to raise cheeping squirrels on." I put no manure whatever on this land, not being the owner, but merely a squatter, and not expecting to cultivate so much again, and I did not quite hoe it all once. I got out several cords of stumps in plowing, which supplied me with fuel for a long time, and left small circles of virgin mould, easily distinguishable through the summer by the greater luxuriance of the beans there. The dead and for the most part unmerchantable wood behind my house, and the driftwood from the pond, have supplied the remainder of my fuel. I was obliged to hire a team and a man for the plowing, though I held the plow myself. My farm outgoes for the first season were, for implements, seed, work, &c., $14.72½. The seed corn was given me. This never costs anything to speak of, unless you plant more than enough. I got twelve bushels of beans, and eighteen bushels of potatoes, beside some peas and sweet corn. The yellow corn and turnips were too late to come to anything. My whole income from the farm was

	$23 44.
Deducting the outgoes . . .	14 72½
There are left	8 71½,

beside produce consumed and on hand at the time this estimate was made of the value of $4.50,—the amount on hand much more than balancing a little grass which I did not raise. All things considered, that is, considering the importance of a man's soul and of to-day, notwithstanding the short time occupied by my experiment, nay, partly even because of its transient character, I believe that that was doing better than any farmer in Concord did that year.

The next year I did better still, for I spaded up all the land which I required, about a third of an acre, and I learned from the experience of both years, not being in the least awed by many celebrated works on husbandry, Arthur Young among the rest, that if one would live simply and eat only the crop which he raised, and raise no more than he ate, and not exchange it for an insufficient quantity of more luxurious and expensive things, he would need to cultivate only a few rods of ground, and that it would be cheaper to spade up that than to use oxen to plow it, and to select a fresh spot from time to time than to manure the old, and he could do all his necessary farm work as it were with his left hand at odd hours in the summer; and thus he would not be tied to an ox, or horse, or cow, or pig, as at present. I desire to speak impartially on this point, and as one not interested in the success or failure of the present economical and social arrangements. I was more independent than any farmer in Concord, for I was not anchored to a house or farm, but could follow the bent of my genius, which is a very crooked one, every moment. Beside being better off than they already, if my house had been burned or my crops had failed, I should have been nearly as well off as before.

I am wont to think that men are not so much the keepers of herds as herds are the keepers of men, the former are so much the freer. Men and oxen exchange work; but if we consider necessary work only, the oxen will be seen to have greatly the advantage, their farm is so much the larger. Man does some of his part of the exchange work in his six weeks of haying, and it is no boy's play. Certainly no nation that lived simply in all respects, that is, no nation of philosophers, would commit so great a blunder as to use the labor of animals. True, there never was and is not likely soon to be a nation of philosophers, nor am I certain it is desirable that there should be. However, *I* should never have broken a horse or bull and taken him to board for any work he might do for me, for fear I should become a horse-man or a herds-man merely; and if society seems to be the gainer by so doing, are we certain that what is one man's gain is not another's loss, and that the stable-boy has equal cause with his master to be satisfied? Granted that some public works would not have been constructed without this aid, and let man share the glory of such with the ox and horse; does it follow that he could not have accomplished works yet more worthy of himself in that case? When men begin to do, not merely unnecessary or artistic, but luxurious and idle work, with their assistance, it is inevitable that a few do all the exchange work with the oxen, or, in other words, become the slaves of the strongest. Man thus not only works for the animal within him, but, for a symbol of this, he works for the animal without him. Though we have many substantial houses of brick or stone, the prosperity of the farmer is still measured by the degree to which the barn overshadows the house. This town is said to have the largest houses for oxen, cows, and horses hereabouts, and it is not behindhand in its public buildings; but there are very few halls for free worship or free speech in this county. It should not be by their architecture, but why not even by their power of abstract thought, that nations should seek to commemorate themselves? How much more admirable the Bhagvat-Geeta than all the ruins of the East! Towers and temples are the luxury of princes. A simple and independent mind does not toil at the bidding of any prince. Genius is not a retainer to any emperor, nor is its material silver, or gold, or marble, except to a trifling extent. To what end, pray, is so much stone hammered? In Arcadia, when I was there, I did not see any hammering stone. Nations are possessed with an insane ambition to perpetuate the memory of themselves by the amount of hammered stone they leave. What if equal pains were taken to smooth and polish their manners? One piece of good sense would be more memorable than a monument as high as the moon. I love better to see stones in place. The grandeur of Thebes was a vulgar grandeur. More sensible is a rod of stone wall that bounds an honest man's field than a hundred-gated Thebes that has wandered farther from the true end of life. The religion and civilization which are barbaric and heathenish build splendid temples; but what you might call Christianity does not. Most of the stone a nation hammers goes toward its tomb only. It buries itself alive. As for the Pyramids, there is nothing to wonder at in them so much as the fact that so many men could be found degraded enough to spend their lives constructing a tomb for some ambitious booby, whom it would have been wiser and manlier to have drowned in the Nile, and then given his body to the dogs. I might possibly invent some excuse for them and him, but I have no time for it. As for the religion and love of art of the builders, it is much the same all the world over, whether the building be an Egyptian temple or the United States Bank. It costs more than it comes to. The mainspring is vanity, assisted by the love of garlic and bread and butter. Mr. Balcom, a promising young architect, designs it on the back of his Vitruvius, with hard pencil and ruler, and the job is let out to Dobson & Sons, stonecutters. When the thirty centuries begin to look down on it, mankind begin to look up at it. As for your high towers and monuments, there was a crazy fellow once in this town who undertook to dig through to China, and he got so far that, as he said, he heard the Chinese pots and kettles rattle; but I think that I shall not go out of my way to admire the hole which he made. Many are concerned about the monuments of the West and the East,—to know who built them. For my part, I should like to know who in those days did not build them,—who were above such trifling. But to proceed with my statistics.

By surveying, carpentry, and day-labor of various other kinds in the village in the meanwhile, for I have as many trades as fingers, I had earned $13.34. The expense of food for eight months, namely, from July 4th to March 1st, the time when these estimates were made, though I lived there more than two years,—not counting potatoes, a little green corn, and some peas, which I had raised, nor considering the value of what was on hand at the last date, was—

Rice	$1 73½	
Molasses . . .	1 73	Cheapest form of the saccharine.
Rye meal . .	1 04¾	
Indian meal .	0 99¾	Cheaper than rye.
Pork	0 22	
Flour . .	0 88	Costs more than Indian meal, both money and trouble.
Sugar . . .	0 80	
Lard . . .	0 65	
Apples . . .	0 25	
Dried apple . .	0 22	
Sweet potatoes .	0 10	
One pumpkin .	0 6	
One water-melon	0 2	
Salt	0 3	

All experiments which failed.

Yes, I did eat $8.74, all told; but I should not thus unblushingly publish my guilt, if I did not know that most of my readers were equally guilty with myself, and that their deeds would look no better in print. The next year I sometimes caught a mess of fish for my dinner, and once I went so far as to slaughter a woodchuck which ravaged my bean-field,—effect his transmigration, as a Tartar would say,—and devour him, partly for experiment's sake; but though it afforded me a momentary enjoyment, notwithstanding a musky flavor, I saw that the longest use would not make that a good practice, however it might seem to have your woodchucks ready dressed by the village butcher.

Clothing and some incidental expenses within the same dates, though little can be inferred from this item, amounted to

	$8 40¾
Oil and some household utensils .	2 00

So that all the pecuniary outgoes, excepting for washing and mending, which for the most part were done out of the house, and their bills have not yet been received,—and these are all and more than all the ways by which money necessarily goes out in this part of the world,—were

House, ...	$28 12½
Farm one year, ...	14 72½
Food eight months, . . .	8 74
Clothing, etc., eight months, .	8 40¾
Oil, etc., eight months, . . .	2 00
In all, ...	$61 99¾

I address myself now to those of my readers who have a living to get. And to meet this I have for farm produce sold

	$23 44
Earned by day-labor, . . .	13 34
In all, ...	$36 78,

which subtracted from the sum of the outgoes leaves a balance of $25.21¾ on the one side,—this being very nearly the means with which I started, and the measure of expenses to be incurred,—and on the other, beside the leisure and independence and health thus secured, a comfortable house for me as long as I choose to occupy it.

These statistics, however accidental and therefore uninstructive they may appear, as they have a certain completeness, have a certain value also. Nothing was given me of which I have not rendered some account. It appears from the above estimate, that my food alone cost me in money about twenty-seven cents a week. It was, for nearly two years after this, rye and Indian meal without yeast, potatoes, rice, a very little salt pork, molasses, and salt; and my drink, water. It was fit that I should live on rice, mainly, who loved so well the philosophy of India. To meet the objections of some inveterate cavillers, I may as well state, that if I dined out occasionally, as I always had done, and I trust shall have opportunities to do again, it was frequently to the detriment of my domestic arrangements. But the dining out, being, as I have stated, a constant element, does not in the least affect a comparative statement like this.

I learned from my two years' experience that it would cost incredibly little trouble to obtain one's necessary food even in this latitude; that a man may use as simple a diet as the animals, and yet retain health and strength. I have made a satisfactory dinner, satisfactory on several accounts, simply off a dish of purslane (*Portulaca oleracea*) which I gathered in my cornfield, boiled and salted. I give the Latin on account of the savoriness of the trivial name. And pray what more can a reasonable man desire, in peaceful times, in ordinary noons, than a sufficient number of ears of green sweet corn boiled, with the addition of salt? Even the little variety which I used was a yielding to the demands of appetite, and not of health. Yet men have come to such a pass that they frequently starve, not for want of necessaries, but for want of luxuries; and I know a good woman who thinks that her son lost his life because he took to drinking water only.

The reader will perceive that I am treating the subject rather from an economic than a dietetic point of view, and he will not venture to put my abstemiousness to the test unless he has a well-stocked larder.

Bread I at first made of pure Indian meal and salt, genuine hoe-cakes, which I baked before my fire out of doors on a shingle or the end of a stick of timber sawed off in building my house; but it was wont to get smoked and to have a piny flavor. I tried flour also; but have at last found a mixture of rye and Indian meal most convenient and agreeable. In cold weather it was no little amusement to bake several small loaves of this in succession, tending and turning them as carefully as an Egyptian his hatching eggs. They were a real cereal fruit which I ripened, and they had to my senses a fragrance like that of other noble fruits, which I

kept in as long as possible by wrapping them in cloths. I made a study of the ancient and indispensable art of bread-making, consulting such authorities as offered, going back to the primitive days and first invention of the unleavened kind, when from the wildness of nuts and meats men first reached the mildness and refinement of this diet, and travelling gradually down in my studies through that accidental souring of the dough which, it is supposed, taught the leavening process, and through the various fermentations thereafter, till I came to "good, sweet, wholesome bread," the staff of life. Leaven, which some deem the soul of bread, the *spiritus* which fills its cellular tissue, which is religiously preserved like the vestal fire,—some precious bottleful, I suppose, first brought over in the Mayflower, did the business for America, and its influence is still rising, swelling, spreading, in cerealian billows over the land,—this seed I regularly and faithfully procured from the village, till at length one morning I forgot the rules and scalded my yeast; by which accident I discovered that even this was not indispensable,—for my discoveries were not by the synthetic but analytic process, —and I have gladly omitted it since, though most housewives earnestly assured me that safe and wholesome bread without yeast might not be, and elderly people prophesied a speedy decay of the vital forces. Yet I find it not to be an essential ingredient, and after going without it for a year am still in the land of the living; and I am glad to escape the trivialness of carrying a bottleful in my pocket, which would sometimes pop and discharge its contents to my discomfiture. It is simpler and more respectable to omit it. Man is an animal who more than any other can adapt himself to all climates and circumstances. Neither did I put any sal soda, or other acid or alkali, into my bread. It would seem that I made it according to the recipe which Marcus Porcius Cato gave about two centuries before Christ. "Panem depsticium sic facito. Manus mortariumque bene lavato. Farinam in mortarium indito, aquae paulatim addito, subigitoque pulchre. Ubi bene subegeris, defingito, coquitoque sub testu." Which I take to mean, "Make kneaded bread thus. Wash your hands and trough well. Put the meal into the trough, add water gradually, and knead it thoroughly. When you have kneaded it well, mould it, and bake it under a cover," that is, in a baking-kettle. Not a word about leaven. But I did not always use this staff of life. At one time, owing to the emptiness of my purse, I saw none of it for more than a month.

Every New Englander might easily raise all his own breadstuffs in this land of rye and Indian corn, and not depend on distant and fluctuating markets for them. Yet so far are we from simplicity and independence that, in Concord, fresh and sweet meal is rarely sold in the shops, and hominy and corn in a still coarser form are hardly used by any. For the most part the farmer gives to his cattle and hogs the grain of his own producing, and buys flour, which is at least no more wholesome, at a greater cost, at the store. I saw that I could easily raise my bushel or two of rye and Indian corn, for the former will grow on the poorest land, and the latter does not require the best, and grind them in a hand-mill, and so do without rice and pork; and if I must have some concentrated sweet, I found by experiment that I could make a very good molasses either of pumpkins or beets, and I knew that I needed only to set out a few maples to obtain it more easily still, and while these were growing I could use various substitutes beside those which I have named. "For," as the Forefathers sang,—

"we can make liquor to sweeten our lips
Of pumpkins and parsnips and walnut-tree chips."

Finally, as for salt, that grossest of groceries, to obtain this might be a fit occasion for a visit to the seashore, or, if I did without it altogether, I should probably drink the less water. I do not learn that the Indians ever troubled themselves to go after it.

Thus I could avoid all trade and barter, so far as my food was concerned, and having a shelter already, it would only remain to get clothing and fuel. The pantaloons which I now wear were woven in a farmer's family,—thank Heaven there is so much virtue still in man; for I think the fall from the farmer to the operative as great and memorable as that from the man to the farmer;—and in a new country fuel is an encumbrance. As for a habitat, if I were not permitted still to squat, I might purchase one acre at the same price for which the land I cultivated was sold—namely, eight dollars and eight cents. But as it was, I considered that I enhanced the value of the land by squatting on it.

There is a certain class of unbelievers who sometimes ask me such questions as, if I think that I can live on vegetable food alone; and to strike at the root of the matter at once,—for the root is faith,—I am accustomed to answer such, that I can live on board nails. If they cannot understand that, they cannot understand much that I have to say. For my part, I am glad to hear of experiments of this kind being tried; as that a young man tried for a fortnight to live on hard, raw corn on the ear, using his teeth for all mortar. The squirrel tribe tried the same and succeeded. The human race is interested in these experiments, though a few old women who are incapacitated for them, or who own their thirds in mills, may be alarmed.

My furniture, part of which I made myself,—and the rest cost me nothing of which I have not rendered an account,—consisted of a bed, a table, a desk, three chairs, a looking-glass three inches in diameter, a pair of tongs and andirons, a kettle, a skillet, and a frying-pan, a dipper, a wash-bowl, two knives and forks, three plates, one cup, one spoon, a jug for oil, a jug for molasses, and a japanned lamp. None is so poor that he need sit on a pumpkin. That is shiftlessness. There is a plenty of such chairs as I like best in the village garrets to be had for taking them away. Furniture! Thank God, I can sit and I can stand without the aid of a furniture warehouse. What man but a philosopher would not be ashamed to see his furniture packed in a cart and going up country exposed to the light of heaven and the eyes of men, a beggarly account of empty boxes? That is Spaulding's furniture. I could never tell from inspecting such a load whether it belonged to a so-called rich man or a poor one; the owner always seemed poverty-stricken. Indeed, the more you have of such things the poorer you are. Each load looks as if it contained the contents of a dozen shanties; and if one shanty is poor, this is a dozen times as poor. Pray, for what do we *move* ever but to get rid of our furniture, our *exuviæ;* at last to go from this world to another newly furnished, and leave this to be burned? It is the same as if all these traps were buckled to a man's belt, and he could not move over the rough country where our lines are cast without dragging them,—dragging his trap. He was a lucky fox that left his tail in the trap. The muskrat will gnaw his third leg off to be free. No wonder man has lost his elasticity. How often he is at a dead set! "Sir, if I may be so bold, what do you mean by a dead set?" If you are a seer, whenever you meet a man you will see all that he owns, ay, and much that he pretends to disown, behind him, even to his kitchen furniture and all the trumpery which he saves and will not burn, and he will appear to be harnessed to it and making what headway he can. I think that the man is at a dead set who has got through a knot-hole or gateway where his sledge load of furniture cannot follow him. I cannot but feel compassion when I hear some trig, compact-looking man, seemingly free, all girded and ready, speak of his "furniture," as whether it is insured or not. "But what shall I do with my furniture?" My gay butterfly is entangled in a spider's web then. Even those who seem for a long while not to have any, if you inquire more narrowly you will find have some stored in somebody's barn. I look upon England to-day as an old gentleman who is travelling with a great deal of baggage, trumpery which has accumulated from long housekeeping, which he has not the courage to burn; great trunk, little trunk, bandbox, and bundle. Throw away the first three at least. It would surpass the powers of a well man nowadays to take up his bed and walk, and I should certainly advise a sick one to lay down his bed and run. When I have met an immigrant tottering under a bundle which contained his all,—looking like an enormous wen which had grown out of the nape of his neck,—I have pitied him, not because that was his all, but because he had all *that* to carry. If I have got to drag my trap, I will take care that it be a light one and do not nip me in a vital part. But perchance it would be wisest never to put one's paw into it.

I would observe, by the way, that it costs me nothing for curtains, for I have no gazers to shut out but the sun and moon, and I am willing that they should look in. The moon will not sour milk nor taint meat of mine, nor will the sun injure my furniture or fade my carpet; and if he is sometimes too warm a friend, I find it still better economy to retreat behind some curtain which nature has provided, than to add a single item to the details of housekeeping. A lady once offered me a mat, but as I had no room to spare within the house, nor time to spare within or without to shake it, I declined it, preferring to wipe my feet on the sod before my door. It is best to avoid the beginnings of evil.

Not long since I was present at the auction of a deacon's effects, for his life had not been ineffectual:—

"The evil that men do lives after them."

As usual, a great proportion was trumpery which had begun to accumulate in his father's day. Among the rest was a dried tapeworm. And now, after lying half a century in his garret and other dust holes, these things were not burned; instead of a *bonfire,* or purifying destruction of them, there was an *auction,* or increasing of them. The neighbors eagerly collected to view them, bought them all, and carefully transported them to their garrets and dust holes, to lie there till their estates are settled, when they will start again. When a man dies he kicks the dust.

The customs of some savage nations might, perchance, be profitably imitated by us, for they at least go through the semblance of casting their slough annually; they have the idea of the thing, whether they have the reality or not. Would it not be well if we were to celebrate such a "busk," or "feast of first fruits," as Bartram describes to have been the custom of the Mucclasse Indians? "When a town celebrates the busk," says he, "having previously provided themselves with new clothes, new pots, pans, and other household utensils and furniture, they collect all their worn out clothes and other despicable things, sweep and cleanse their houses, squares, and the whole town, of their filth, which, with all the remaining grain and other old provisions they cast together into one common heap, and consume it with fire. After having taken medicine, and fasted for three days, all the fire in the town is extinguished. During this fast they abstain from the gratification of every appetite and passion whatever. A general amnesty is proclaimed; all malefactors may return to their town."

"On the fourth morning, the high priest, by rubbing dry wood together, produces new fire in the public square, from whence every habitation in the town is supplied with the new and pure flame."

They then feast on the new corn and fruits, and dance and sing for three days, "and the four following days they receive visits and rejoice with their friends from neighboring towns who have in like manner purified and prepared themselves."

The Mexicans also practised a similar purification at the end of every fifty-two years, in the belief that it was time for the world to come to an end.

I have scarcely heard of a truer sacrament, that is, as the dictionary defines it, "outward and visible sign of an inward and spiritual grace," than this, and I have no doubt that they were originally inspired directly from Heaven to do thus, though they have no bibli
9 cal record of the revelation.

For more than five years I maintained myself thus solely by the labor of my hands, and I found, that, by working about six weeks in a year, I could meet all the expenses of living. The whole of my winters, as well as most of my summers, I had free and clear for study. I have thoroughly tried school-keeping, and found that my expenses were in proportion, or rather out of proportion, to my income, for I was
20 obliged to dress and train, not to say think and believe, accordingly, and I lost my time into the bargain. As I did not teach for the good of my fellow-men, but simply for a livelihood, this was a failure. I have tried trade; but I found that it would take ten years to get under way in that, and that then I should probably be on my way to the devil. I was actually afraid that I might by that time be doing what is called a good business. When formerly I was looking
30 about to see what I could do for a living, some sad experience in conforming to the wishes of friends being fresh in my mind to tax my ingenuity, I thought often and seriously of picking huckleberries; that surely I could do, and its small profits might suffice,—for my greatest skill has been to want but little,—so little capital it required, so little distraction from my wonted moods, I foolishly thought. While my acquaintances went unhesitantly into trade or
40 the professions, I contemplated this occupation as most like theirs; ranging the hills all summer to pick the berries which came in my way, and thereafter carelessly dispose of them; so, to keep the flocks of Admetus. I also dreamed that I might gather the wild herbs, or carry evergreens to such villagers as loved to be reminded of the woods, even to the city, by hay-cart loads. But I have since learned that trade curses everything it handles; and though
50 you trade in messages from heaven, the whole curse of trade attaches to the business.

As I preferred some things to others, and especially valued my freedom, as I could fare hard and yet succeed well, I did not wish to spend my time in earning rich carpets or other fine furniture, or delicate cookery, or a house in the Grecian or the Gothic style just yet. If there are any to whom it is no interruption to acquire these things, and who know how to use them when acquired, I relinquish to them the pursuit. Some are "industrious," and appear to love labor for its own sake, or perhaps because it keeps them out of worse mischief; to such I have at present nothing to say. Those who would not know what to do with more leisure than they now enjoy, I might advise to work twice as hard as they do,—work till they pay for themselves, and get their free papers. For myself I found that the occupation of a day-laborer was the most independent of any, especially as it required only thirty or forty days in a year to support one. The laborer's day ends with the going down of the sun, and he is then free to devote himself to his chosen pursuit, independent of his labor; but his employer, who speculates from month to month, has no respite from one end of the year to the other.

In short, I am convinced, both by faith and experience, that to maintain one's self on this earth is not a hardship but a pastime, if we will live simply and wisely; as the pursuits of the simpler nations are still the sports of the more artificial. It is not necessary that a man should earn his living by the sweat of his brow, unless he sweats easier than I do.

One young man of my acquaintance, who has inherited some acres, told me that he thought he should live as I did, *if he had the means.* I would not have any one adopt *my* mode of living on any account; for, beside that before he has fairly learned it I may have found out another for myself, I desire that there may be as many different persons in the world as possible; but I would have each one be very careful to find out and pursue *his own* way, and not his father's or his mother's or his neighbor's instead. The youth may build or plant or sail, only let him not be hindered from doing that which he tells me he would like to do. It is by a mathematical point only that we are wise, as the sailor or the fugitive slave keeps the pole-star in his eye; but that is sufficient guidance for all our life. We may not arrive at our port within a calculable period, but we would preserve the true course.

Undoubtedly, in this case, what is true for one is truer still for a thousand, as a large house is not proportionally more expensive than a small one, since one roof may cover, one cellar underlie, and one wall separate several apartments. But for my part, I preferred the solitary dwelling. Moreover, it will commonly be cheaper to build the whole yourself than to convince another of the advantage of the common wall; and when you have done this, the common partition, to be much cheaper, must be a thin one, and that other may prove a bad neighbor, and also not keep his side in repair. The only coöperation which is commonly possible is exceedingly partial and superficial; and what little true coöperation there is, is as if it were not, being a harmony inaudible to men. If a man has faith he will coöperate with equal faith everywhere; if he has not faith, he will continue to live like the rest of the world, whatever company he is joined to. To coöperate, in the highest as well as the lowest sense, means *to get our living together*. I heard it proposed lately that two young men should travel together over the world, the one without money, earning his means as he went, before the mast and behind the plow, the other carrying a bill of exchange in his pocket. It was easy to see that they could not long be companions or coöperate, since one would not *operate* at all. They would part at the first interesting crisis in their adventures. Above all, as I have implied, the man who goes alone can start today; but he who travels with another must wait till that other is ready, and it may be a long time before they get off.

But all this is very selfish, I have heard some of my townsmen say. I confess that I have hitherto indulged very little in philanthropic enterprises. I have made some sacrifices to a sense of duty, and among others have sacrificed this pleasure also. There are those who have used all their arts to persuade me to undertake the support of some poor family in the town; and if I had nothing to do—for the devil finds employment for the idle—I might try my hand at some such pastime as that. However, when I have thought to indulge myself in this respect, and lay their Heaven under an obligation by maintaining certain poor persons in all respects as comfortably as I maintain myself, and have even ventured so far as to make them the offer, they have one and all unhesitatingly preferred to remain poor. While my townsmen and women are devoted in so many ways to the good of their fellows, I trust that one at least may be spared to other and less humane pursuits. You must have a genius for charity as well as for anything else. As for Doing-good, that is one of the professions which are full. Moreover, I have tried it fairly, and, strange as it may seem, am satisfied that it does not agree with my constitution. Probably I should not consciously and deliberately forsake my particular calling to do the good which society demands of me, to save the universe from annihilation; and I believe that a like but infinitely greater steadfastness elsewhere is all that now preserves it. But I would not stand between any man and his genius; and to him who does this work, which I decline, with his whole heart and soul and life, I would say, Persevere, even if the world call it doing evil, as it is most likely they will.

I am far from supposing that my case is a peculiar one; no doubt many of my readers would make a similar defence. At doing something,—I will not engage that my neighbors shall pronounce it good,—I do not hesitate to say that I should be a capital fellow to hire; but what that is, it is for my employer to find out. What *good* I do, in the common sense of that word, must be aside from my main path, and for the most part wholly unintended. Men say, practically, Begin where you are and such as you are, without aiming mainly to become of more worth, and with kindness aforethought go about doing good. If I were to preach at all in this strain, I should say rather, Set about being good. As if the sun should stop when he had kindled his fires up to the splendor of a moon or a star of the sixth magnitude, and go about like a Robin Goodfellow, peeping in at every cottage window, inspiring lunatics, and tainting meats, and making darkness visible, instead of steadily increasing his genial heat and beneficence till he is of such brightness that no mortal can look him in the face, and then, in the meanwhile too, going about the world in his own orbit, doing it good, or rather, as a truer philosophy has discovered, the world going about him getting good. When Phaeton, wishing to prove his heavenly birth by his beneficence, had the sun's chariot but one day, and drove out of the beaten track, he burned several blocks of houses in the lower streets of heaven, and scorched the surface of the earth, and dried up every spring, and made the great desert of Sahara, till at length Jupiter hurled him headlong to the earth with a thunderbolt, and the sun, through grief at his death, did not shine for a year.

There is no odor so bad as that which arises from goodness tainted. It is human, it is divine, carrion. If I knew for a certainty that a man was coming to my house with the conscious design of doing me good, I should run for my life, as from that dry and parching wind of the African deserts called the simoom, which fills the mouth and nose and ears and eyes with dust till you are suffocated, for fear that I should get some of his good done to me,—some of its virus mingled with my blood. No,—in this case I would rather suffer evil the natural way. A man is not a good *man* to me because he will feed me if I should be starving, or warm me if I should be freezing, or pull me out of a ditch if I should ever fall into one. I can find you a Newfoundland dog that will do as much. Philanthropy is not love for one's fellow-man in the broadest sense. Howard was no doubt an exceedingly kind and worthy man in his way, and has his reward; but, comparatively speaking, what are a hundred Howards to *us*, if their philanthropy do not help *us* in our best estate, when we are most worthy to be helped? I never heard of a philanthropic meeting in which it was sincerely proposed to do any good to me, or the like of me.

The Jesuits were quite balked by those Indians who, being burned at the stake, suggested new modes of torture to their tormentors. Being superior to physical suffering, it sometimes chanced that they were superior to any consolation which the missionaries could offer; and the law to do as you would be done by fell with less persuasiveness on the ears of those who, for their part, did not care how they were done by, who loved their enemies after a new fashion, and came very near freely forgiving them all they did.

Be sure that you give the poor the aid they most need, though it be your example which leaves them far behind. If you give money, spend yourself with it, and do not merely abandon it to them. We make curious mistakes sometimes. Often the poor man is not so cold and hungry as he is dirty and ragged and gross. It is partly his taste, and not merely his misfortune. If you give him money, he will perhaps buy more rags with it. I was wont to pity the clumsy Irish laborers who cut ice on the pond, in such mean and ragged clothes, while I shivered in my more tidy and somewhat more fashionable garments, till, one bitter cold day, one who had slipped into the water came to my house to warm him, and I saw him strip off three pairs of pants and two pairs of stockings ere he got down to the skin, though they were

dirty and ragged enough, it is true, and that he could afford to refuse the *extra* garments which I offered him, he had so many *intra* ones. This ducking was the very thing he needed. Then I began to pity myself, and I saw that it would be a greater charity to bestow on me a flannel shirt than a whole slop-shop on him. There are a thousand hacking at the branches of evil to one who is striking at the root, and it may be that he who bestows the largest amount of time and money on the needy is doing the most by his mode of life to produce that misery which he strives in vain to relieve. It is the pious slave-breeder devoting the proceeds of every tenth slave to buy a Sunday's liberty for the rest. Some show their kindness to the poor by employing them in their kitchens. Would they not be kinder if they employed themselves there? You boast of spending a tenth part of your income in charity: maybe you should spend the nine tenths so, and done with it. Society recovers only a tenth part of the property then. Is this owing to the generosity of him in whose possession it is found, or to the remissness of the officers of justice?

Philanthropy is almost the only virtue which is sufficiently appreciated by mankind. Nay, it is greatly overrated; and it is our selfishness which overrates it. A robust poor man, one sunny day here in Concord, praised a fellow-townsman to me, because, as he said, he was kind to the poor, meaning himself. The kind uncles and aunts of the race are more esteemed than its true spiritual fathers and mothers. I once heard a reverend lecturer on England, a man of learning and intelligence, after enumerating her scientific, literary, and political worthies, Shakespeare, Bacon, Cromwell, Milton, Newton, and others, speak next of her Christian heroes, whom, as if his profession required it of him, he elevated to a place far above all the rest, as the greatest of the great. They were Penn, Howard, and Mrs. Fry. Every one must feel the falsehood and cant of this. The last were not England's best men and women; only, perhaps, her best philanthropists.

I would not subtract anything from the praise that is due to philanthropy, but merely demand justice for all who by their lives and works are a blessing to mankind. I do not value chiefly a man's uprightness and benevolence, which are, as it were, his stem and leaves. Those plants of whose greenness withered we make herb tea for the sick serve but a humble use, and are most employed by quacks. I want the flower and fruit of a man; that some fragrance be wafted over from him to me, and some ripeness flavor our intercourse. His goodness must not be a partial and transitory act, but a constant superfluity, which costs him nothing and of which he is unconscious. This is a charity that hides a multitude of sins. The philanthropist too often surrounds mankind with the remembrance of his own cast-off griefs as an atmosphere, and calls it sympathy. We should impart our courage, and not our despair, our health and ease, and not our disease, and take care that this does not spread by contagion. From what southern plains comes up the voice of wailing? Under what latitudes reside the heathen to whom we would send light? Who is that intemperate and brutal man whom we would redeem? If anything ail a man, so that he does not perform his functions, if he have a pain in his bowels even,—for that is the seat of sympathy,—he forthwith sets about reforming—the world. Being a microcosm himself, he discovers—and it is a true discovery, and he is the man to make it—that the world has been eating green apples; to his eyes, in fact, the globe itself is a great green apple, which there is danger awful to think of that the children of men will nibble before it is ripe; and straightway his drastic philanthropy seeks out the Esquimaux and the Patagonian, and embraces the populous Indian and Chinese villages; and thus, by a few years of philanthropic activity, the powers in the meanwhile using him for their own ends, no doubt, he cures himself of his dyspepsia, the globe acquires a faint blush on one or both of its cheeks, as if it were beginning to be ripe, and life loses its crudity and is once more sweet and wholesome to live. I never dreamed of any enormity greater than I have committed. I never knew, and never shall know, a worse man than myself.

I believe that what so saddens the reformer is not his sympathy with his fellows in distress, but, though he be the holiest son of God, is his private ail. Let this be righted, let the spring come to him, the morning rise over his couch, and he will forsake his generous companions without apology. My excuse for not lecturing against the use of tobacco is, that I never chewed it, that is a penalty which reformed tobacco-chewers have to pay; though there are things enough I have chewed which I could lecture against. If you should ever be betrayed into any of these philanthropies, do not let your left hand know what your right hand does, for it is not worth knowing. Rescue the drowning and tie your shoe-strings. Take your time, and set about some free labor.

Our manners have been corrupted by communication with the saints. Our hymn-books resound with a melodious cursing of God and enduring Him forever. One would say that even the prophets and redeemers had rather consoled the fears than confirmed the hopes of man. There is nowhere recorded a simple and irrepressible satisfaction with the gift of life, any memorable praise of God. All health and success does me good, however far off and withdrawn it may appear; all disease and failure helps to make me sad and does me evil, however much sympathy it may have with me or I with it. If, then, we would indeed restore mankind by truly Indian, botanic, magnetic, or natural means, let us first be as simple and well as Nature ourselves, dispel the clouds which hang over our own brows, and take up a little life into our pores. Do not stay to be an overseer of the poor, but endeavor to become one of the worthies of the world.

I read in the Gulistan, or Flower Garden, of Sheik Sadi of Shiraz, that "They asked a wise man, saying; Of the many celebrated trees which the Most High God has created lofty and umbrageous, they call none azad, or free, excepting the cypress, which bears no fruit; what mystery is there in this? He replied: Each has its appropriate produce, and appointed season, during the continuance of which it is fresh and blooming, and during their absence dry and withered; to neither of which states is the cypress exposed, being always flourishing; and of this nature are the azads, or religious independents.—Fix not thy heart on that which is transitory; for the Dijlah, or Tigris, will continue to flow through Bagdad after the race of caliphs is extinct: if thy hand has plenty, be liberal as the date tree; but if it affords nothing to give away, be an azad, or free man, like the cypress."

WHERE I LIVED, AND WHAT I LIVED FOR

(CHAPTER 2)

At a certain season of our life we are accustomed to consider every spot as the possible site of a house. I have thus surveyed the country on every side within a dozen miles of where I live. In imagination I have bought all the farms in succession, for all were to be bought, and I knew their price. I walked over each farmer's premises, tasted his wild apples, discoursed on husbandry with him, took his farm at his price, at any price, mortgaging it to him in my mind; even put a higher price on it,—took everything but a deed of it,—took his word for his deed, for I dearly love to talk,—cultivated it, and him too to some extent, I trust, and withdrew when I had enjoyed it long enough, leaving him to carry it on. This experience entitled me to be regarded as a sort of real-estate broker by my friends. Wherever I sat, there I might live, and the landscape radiated from me accordingly. What is a house but a *sedes*, a seat?—better if a country seat. I discovered many a site for a house not likely to be soon improved, which some might have thought too far from the village, but to my eyes the village was too far from it. Well, there I might live, I said; and there I did live, for an hour, a summer and a winter life; saw how I could let the years run off, buffet the winter through, and see the spring come in. The future inhabitants of this region, wherever they may place their houses, may be sure that they have been anticipated. An afternoon sufficed to lay out the land into orchard, wood-lot, and pasture, and to decide what fine oaks or pines should be left to stand before the door, and whence each blasted tree could be seen to the best advantage; and then I let it lie, fallow perchance, for a man is rich in proportion to the number of things which he can afford to let alone.

My imagination carried me so far that I even had the refusal of several farms,—the refusal was all I wanted,—but I never got my fingers burned by actual possession. The nearest that I came to actual possession was when I bought the Hollowell place, and had begun to sort my seeds, and collected materials with which to make a wheelbarrow to carry it on or off with; but before the owner gave me a deed of it, his wife—every man has such a wife—changed her mind and wished to keep it, and he offered me ten dollars to release him. Now, to speak the truth, I had but ten cents in the world, and it surpassed my arithmetic to tell, if I was that man who had ten cents, or who had a farm, or ten dollars, or all together. However, I let him keep the ten dollars and the farm too, for I had carried it far enough; or rather, to be generous, I sold him the farm for just what I gave for it, and, as he was not a rich man, made him a present of ten dollars, and still had my ten cents, and seeds, and materials for a wheelbarrow left. I found thus that I had been a rich man without any damage to my poverty. But I retained the landscape, and I have since annually carried off what it yielded without a wheelbarrow. With respect to landscapes,—

> "I am monarch of all I *survey*,
> My right there is none to dispute."

I have frequently seen a poet withdraw, having enjoyed the most valuable part of a farm, while the crusty farmer supposed that he had got a few wild apples only. Why, the owner does not know it for many years when a poet has put his farm in rhyme, the most admirable kind of invisible fence, has fairly impounded it, milked it, skimmed it, and got all the cream, and left the farmer only the skimmed milk.

The real attractions of the Hollowell farm, to me, were: its complete retirement, being about two miles from the village, half a mile from the nearest neighbor, and separated from the highway by a broad field; its bounding on the river, which the owner said protected it by its fogs from frosts in the spring, though that was nothing to me; the gray color and ruinous state of the house and barn, and the dilapidated fences, which put such an interval between me and the last occupant; the hollow and lichen-covered apple trees, gnawed by rabbits, showing what kind of neighbors I should have; but above all, the recollection I had of it from my earliest voyages up the river, when the house was concealed behind a dense grove of red maples, through which I heard the house-dog bark. I was in haste to buy it, before the proprietor finished getting out some rocks, cutting down the hollow apple trees, and grubbing up some young birches which had sprung up in the pasture, or, in short, had made any more of his improvements. To enjoy these advantages I was ready to carry it on; like Atlas, to take the world on my shoulders,—I never heard what compensation he received for that,—and do all those things which had no other motive or excuse but that I might pay for it and be unmolested in my possession of it; for I knew all the while that it would yield the most abundant crop of the kind I wanted, if I could only afford to let it alone. But it turned out as I have said.

All that I could say, then, with respect to farming on a large scale—I have always cultivated a garden—was, that I had had my seeds ready. Many think that seeds improve with age. I have no doubt that time discriminates between the good and the bad; and when at last I shall plant, I shall be less likely to be disappointed. But I would say to my fellows, once for all, As long as possible live free and uncommitted. It makes but little difference whether you are committed to a farm or the county jail.

Old Cato, whose "De Re Rusticâ" is my "Cultivator," says,—and the only translation I have seen makes sheer nonsense of the passage, —"When you think of getting a farm turn it thus in your mind, not to buy greedily; nor spare your pains to look at it, and do not think it enough to go round it once. The oftener you go there the more it will please you, if it is good." I think I shall not buy greedily, but go round and round it as long as I live, and be buried in it first, that it may please me the more at last.

The present was my next experiment of this kind, which I purpose to describe more at length, for convenience putting the experience of two years into one. As I have said, I do not propose to write an ode to dejection, but to brag as lustily as chanticleer in the morning, standing on his roost, if only to wake my neighbors up.

When first I took up my abode in the woods, that is, began to spend my nights as well as days there, which, by accident, was on Independence Day, on the Fourth of July, 1845, my house was not finished for winter, but was merely a defence against the rain, without plastering or chimney, the walls being of rough weather-stained boards, with wide chinks, which made it cool at night. The upright white hewn studs and freshly planed door and window casings gave it a clean and airy look, especially in the morning, when its timbers were saturated with dew, so that I fancied that by noon some sweet gum would exude from them. To my imagination it retained throughout the day more or less of this auroral character, reminding me of a certain house on a mountain which I had visited the year before. This was an airy and unplastered cabin, fit to entertain a travelling god, and where a goddess might trail her garments. The winds which passed over my dwelling were such as sweep over the ridges of mountains, bearing the broken strains, or celestial parts only, of terrestrial music. The morning wind forever blows, the poem of creation is uninterrupted; but few are the ears that hear it. Olympus is but the outside of the earth everywhere.

The only house I had been the owner of before, if I except a boat, was a tent, which I used occasionally when making excursions in the summer, and this is still rolled up in my garret; but the boat, after passing from hand to hand, has gone down the stream of time. With this more substantial shelter about me, I had made some progress toward settling in the world. This frame, so slightly clad, was a sort of crystallisation around me, and reacted on the builder. It was suggestive somewhat as a picture in outlines. I did not need to go out doors to take the air, for the atmosphere within had lost none of its freshness. It was not so much within-doors as behind a door where I sat, even in the rainiest weather. The Harivansa says, "An abode without birds is like a meat without seasoning." Such was not my abode, for I found myself suddenly neighbor to the birds; not by having imprisoned one, but having caged myself near them. I was not only nearer to some of those which commonly frequent the garden and the orchard, but to those wilder and more thrilling songsters of the forest which never, or rarely, serenade a villager,—the wood thrush, the veery, the scarlet tanager, the field-sparrow, the whip-poor-will, and many others.

I was seated by the shore of a small pond, about a mile and a half south of the village of Concord and somewhat higher than it, in the midst of an extensive wood between that town and Lincoln, and about two miles south of that our only field known to fame, Concord Battle Ground; but I was so low in the woods that the opposite shore, half a mile off, like the rest, covered with wood, was my most distant horizon. For the first week, whenever I looked out on the pond it impressed me like a tarn high up on the side of a mountain, its bottom far above the surface of other lakes, and, as the sun arose, I saw it throwing off its nightly clothing of mist, and here and there, by degrees, its soft ripples or its smooth reflecting surface was revealed, while the mists, like ghosts, were stealthily withdrawing in every direction into the woods, as at the breaking up of some nocturnal conventicle. The very dew seemed to hang upon the trees later into the day than usual, as on the sides of mountains.

This small lake was of most value as a neighbor in the intervals of a gentle rain-storm in August, when, both air and water being perfectly still, but the sky overcast, mid-afternoon had all the serenity of evening, and the wood thrush sang around, and was heard from shore to shore. A lake like this is never smoother than at such a time; and the clear portion of the air above it being shallow and darkened by clouds, the water, full of light and reflections, becomes a lower heaven itself so much the more important. From a hill-top near by, where the wood had been recently cut off, there was a pleasing vista southward across the pond, through a wide indentation in the hills which form the shore there, where their opposite sides sloping toward each other suggested a stream flowing out in that direction through a wooded valley, but stream there was none. That way I looked between and over the near green hills to some distant and higher ones in the horizon, tinged with blue. Indeed, by standing on tiptoe I could catch a glimpse of some of the peaks of the still bluer and more distant mountain ranges in the northwest, those true-blue coins from heaven's own mint, and also of some portion of the village. But in other directions, even from this point, I could not see over or beyond the woods which surrounded me. It is well to have some water in your neighborhood, to give buoyancy to and float the earth. One value even of the smallest well is, that when you look into it you see that earth is not continent but insular. This is as important as that it keeps butter cool. When I looked across the pond from this peak toward the Sudbury meadows, which in time of flood I distinguished elevated perhaps by a mirage in their seething valley, like a coin in a basin, all the earth beyond the pond appeared like a thin crust insulated and floated even by this small sheet of intervening water, and I was reminded that this on which I dwelt was but *dry land.*

Though the view from my door was still more contracted, I did not feel crowded or confined in the least. There was pasture enough for my imagination. The low shrub oak plateau

to which the opposite shore arose stretched away toward the prairies of the West and the steppes of Tartary, affording ample room for all the roving families of men. "There are none happy in the world but beings who enjoy freely a vast horizon,"—said Damodara, when his herds required new and larger pastures.

Both place and time were changed, and I dwelt nearer to those parts of the universe and to those eras in history which had most attracted me. Where I lived was as far off as many a region viewed nightly by astronomers. We are wont to imagine rare and delectable places in some remote and more celestial corner of the system, behind the constellation of Cassiopeia's Chair, far from noise and disturbance. I discovered that my house actually had its site in such a withdrawn, but for ever new and unprofaned, part of the universe. If it were worth the while to settle in those parts near to the Pleiades or the Hyades, to Aldebaran or Altair, then I was really there, or at an equal remoteness from the life which I had left behind, dwindled and twinkling with as fine a ray to my nearest neighbor, and to be seen only in moonless nights by him. Such was that part of creation where I had squatted;—

"There was a shepherd that did live,
    And held his thoughts as high
As were the mounts whereon his flocks
    Did hourly feed him by."

What should we think of the shepherd's life if his flocks always wandered to higher pastures than his thoughts?

Every morning was a cheerful invitation to make my life of equal simplicity, and I may say innocence, with Nature herself. I have been as sincere a worshipper of Aurora as the Greeks. I got up early and bathed in the pond; that was a religious exercise, and one of the best things which I did. They say that characters were engraven on the bathing tub of king Tching-thang to this effect: "Renew thyself completely each day; do it again, and again, and forever again." I can understand that. Morning brings back the heroic ages. I was as much affected by the faint hum of a mosquito making its invisible and unimaginable tour through my apartment at earliest dawn, when I was sitting with door and windows open, as I could be by any trumpet that ever sang of fame. It was Homer's requiem; itself an Iliad and Odyssey in the air, singing its own wrath and wanderings. There was something cosmical about it; a standing advertisement, till forbidden, of the everlasting vigor and fertility of the world. The morning, which is the most memorable season of the day, is the awakening hour. Then there is least somnolence in us; and for an hour, at least, some part of us awakes which slumbers all the rest of the day and night. Little is to be expected of that day, if it can be called a day, to which we are not awakened by our Genius, but by the mechanical nudgings of some servitor, are not awakened by our own newly acquired force and aspirations from within, accompanied by the undulations of celestial music, instead of factory bells, and a fragrance filling the air—to a higher life than we fell asleep from; and thus the darkness bear its fruit, and prove itself to be good, no less than the light. That man who does not believe that each day contains an earlier, more sacred, and auroral hour than he has yet profaned, has despaired of life, and is pursuing a descending and darkening way. After a partial cessation of his sensuous life, the soul of man, or its organs rather, are reinvigorated each day, and his Genius tries again what noble life it can make. All memorable events, I should say, transpire in morning time and in a morning atmosphere. The Vedas say, "All intelligences awake with the morning." Poetry and art, and the fairest and most memorable of the actions of men, date from such an hour. All poets and heroes, like Memnon, are the children of Aurora, and emit their music at sunrise. To him whose elastic and vigorous thought keeps pace with the sun, the day is a perpetual morning. It matters not what the clocks say or the attitudes and labors of men. Morning is when I am awake and there is a dawn in me. Moral reform is the effort to throw off sleep. Why is it that men give so poor an account of their day if they have not been slumbering? They are not such poor calculators. If they had not been overcome with drowsiness, they would have performed something. The millions are awake enough for physical labor; but only one in a million is awake enough for effective intellectual exertion, only one in a hundred millions to a poetic or divine life. To be awake is to be alive. I have never yet met a man who was quite awake. How could I have looked him in the face?

We must learn to reawaken and keep ourselves awake, not by mechanical aids, but by an infinite expectation of the dawn, which does not forsake us in our soundest sleep. I know of no more encouraging fact than the unquestionable ability of man to elevate his life by a conscious endeavor. It is something to be able to paint a particular picture, or to carve a statue, and so to make a few objects beautiful; but it is far more glorious to carve and paint the very atmosphere and medium through which we look, which morally we can do. To affect the quality of the day, that is the highest of arts. Every man is tasked to make his life, even in its details, worthy of the contemplation of his most elevated and critical hour. If we refused, or rather used up, such paltry information as we get, the oracles would distinctly inform us how this might be done.

I went to the woods because I wished to live deliberately, to front only the essential facts of life, and see if I could not learn what it had to teach, and not, when I came to die, discover that I had not lived. I did not wish to live what was not life, living is so dear; nor did I wish to practise resignation, unless it was quite necessary. I wanted to live deep and suck out all the marrow of life, to live so sturdily and Spartan-like as to put to rout all that was not life, to cut a broad swath and shave close, to drive life into a corner, and reduce it to its lowest terms, and, if it proved to be mean, why then to get the whole and genuine meanness of it, and publish its meanness to the world; or if it were sublime, to know it by experience, and be able to give a true account of it in my next excursion. For most men, it appears to me, are in a strange uncertainty about it, whether it is of the devil or of God, and have *somewhat hastily* concluded that it is the chief end of man here to "glorify God and enjoy Him forever."

Still we live meanly, like ants; though the fable tells us that we were long ago changed into men; like pygmies we fight with cranes; it is error upon error, and clout upon clout, and our best virtue has for its occasion a superfluous and evitable wretchedness. Our life is frittered away by detail. An honest man has hardly need to count more than his ten fingers, or in extreme cases he may add his ten toes, and lump the rest. Simplicity, simplicity, simplicity! I say, let your affairs be as two or three, and not a hundred or a thousand; instead of a million count half a dozen, and keep your accounts on your thumb-nail. In the midst of this chopping sea of civilized life, such are the clouds and storms and quicksands and thousand-and-one items to be allowed for, that a man has to live, if he would not founder and go to the bottom and not make his port at all, by dead reckoning, and he must be a great calculator indeed who succeeds. Simplify, simplify. Instead of three meals a day, if it be necessary eat but one; instead of a hundred dishes, five; and reduce other things in proportion. Our life is like a German Confederacy, made up of petty states, with its boundary forever fluctuating, so that even a German cannot tell you how it is bounded at any moment. The nation itself, with all its so-called internal improvements, which, by the way are all external and superficial, is just such an unwieldy and overgrown establishment, cluttered with furniture and tripped up by its own traps, ruined by luxury and heedless expense, by want of calculation and a worthy aim, as the million households in the land; and the only cure for it as for them is in a rigid economy, a stern and more than Spartan simplicity of life and elevation of purpose. It lives too fast. Men think that it is essential that the *Nation* have commerce, and export ice, and talk through a telegraph, and ride thirty miles an hour, without a doubt, whether *they* do or not; but whether we should live like baboons or like men, is a little uncertain. If we do not get out sleepers, and forge rails, and devote days and nights to the work, but go to tinkering upon our *lives* to improve *them,* who will build railroads? And if railroads are not built, how shall we get to heaven in season? But if we stay at home and mind our business, who will want railroads? We do not ride on the railroad; it rides upon us. Did you ever think what those sleepers are that underlie the railroad? Each one is a man, an Irishman, or a Yankee man. The rails are laid on them, and they are covered with sand, and the cars run smoothly over them. They are sound sleepers, I assure you. And every few years a new lot is laid down and run over; so that, if some have the pleasure of riding on a rail, others have the misfortune to be ridden upon. And when they run over a man that is walking in his sleep, a supernumerary sleeper in the wrong position, and wake him up, they suddenly stop the cars, and make a hue and cry about it, as if this were an exception. I am glad to know that it takes a gang of men for every five miles to keep the sleepers down and level in their beds as it is, for this is a sign that they may sometime get up again.

Why should we live with such hurry and waste of life? We are determined to be starved before we are hungry. Men say that a stitch in time saves nine, and so they take a thousand stitches to-day to save nine to-morrow. As for *work*, we haven't any of any consequence. We have the Saint Vitus' dance, and cannot possibly keep our heads still. If I should only give a few pulls at the parish bell-rope, as for a fire, that is, without setting the bell, there is hardly a man on his farm in the outskirts of Concord, notwithstanding that press of engagements which was his excuse so many times this morning, nor a boy, nor a woman, I might almost say, but would forsake all and follow that sound, not mainly to save property from the flames, but, if we will confess the truth, much more to see it burn, since burn it must, and we, be it known, did not set it on fire,—or to see it put out, and have a hand in it, if that is done as handsomely; yes, even if it were the parish church itself. Hardly a man takes a half-hour's nap after dinner, but when he wakes he holds up his head and asks, "What's the news?" as if the rest of mankind had stood his sentinels. Some give directions to be waked every half-hour, doubtless for no other purpose; and then to pay for it, they tell what they have dreamed. After a night's sleep the news is as indispensable as the breakfast. "Pray, tell me anything new that has happened to a man anywhere on this globe,"—and he reads it over his coffee and rolls, that a man has had his eyes gouged out this morning on the Wachito River; never dreaming the while that he lives in the dark unfathomed mammoth cave of this world, and has but the rudiment of an eye himself.

For my part, I could easily do without the post-office. I think that there are very few important communications made through it. To speak critically, I never received more than one or two letters in my life—I wrote this some years ago—that were worth the postage. The penny-post is, commonly, an institution through which you seriously offer a man that penny for his thoughts which is so often safely offered in jest. And I am sure that I never read any memorable news in a newspaper. If we read of one man robbed, or murdered, or killed by accident, or one house burned, or one vessel wrecked, or one steamboat blown up, or one cow run over on the Western Railroad, or one mad dog killed, or one lot of grasshoppers in the winter,—we never need read of another. One is enough. If you are acquainted with the

principle, what do you care for a myriad instances and applications? To a philosopher all
news, as it is called, is gossip, and they who
edit and read it are old women over their tea.
Yet not a few are greedy after this gossip.
There was such a rush, as I hear, the other day
at one of the offices to learn the foreign news by
the last arrival, that several large squares of
plate glass belonging to the establishment were
broken by the pressure,—news which I seriously think a ready wit might write a twelvemonth or twelve years beforehand with sufficient accuracy. As for Spain, for instance, if
you know how to throw in Don Carlos and
the Infanta, and Don Pedro and Seville and
Granada, from time to time in the right proportions,—they may have changed the names
a little since I saw the papers,—and serve up
a bull-fight when other entertainments fail, it
will be true to the letter, and give us as good
an idea of the exact state or ruin of things in
Spain as the most succinct and lucid reports
under this head in the newspapers: and as for
England, almost the last significant scrap of
news from that quarter was the Revolution of
1649; and if you have learned the history of
her crops for an average year, you never need
attend to that thing again, unless your speculations are of a merely pecuniary character. If
one may judge who rarely looks into the newspapers, nothing new does ever happen in foreign parts, a French Revolution not excepted.

What news! how much more important to
know what that is which was never old!
"Kieou-he-yu (great dignitary of the state of
Wei) sent a man to Khoung-tseu to know his
news. Khoung-tseu caused the messenger to
be seated near him, and questioned him in
these terms: What is your master doing? The
messenger answered with respect: My master
desires to diminish the number of his faults,
but he cannot come to the end of them. The
messenger being gone, the philosopher remarked: What a worthy messenger! What a
worthy messenger!" The preacher, instead of
vexing the ears of drowsy farmers on their day
of rest at the end of the week,—for Sunday is
the fit conclusion of an ill-spent week, and not
the fresh and brave beginning of a new one,
—with this one other draggle-tail of a sermon,
should shout with thundering voice, "Pause!
Avast! Why so seeming fast, but deadly slow?"

Shams and delusions are esteemed for soundest truths, while reality is fabulous. If men
would steadily observe realities only, and not
allow themselves to be deluded, life, to compare it with such things as we know, would be
like a fairy tale and the Arabian Nights' Entertainments. If we respected only what is inevitable and has a right to be, music and
poetry would resound along the streets. When
we are unhurried and wise, we perceive that
only great and worthy things have any permanent and absolute existence,—that petty
fears and petty pleasures are but the shadow
of the reality. This is always exhilarating and
sublime. By closing the eyes and slumbering,
and consenting to be deceived by shows, men
establish and confirm their daily life of routine
and habit everywhere, which still is built on
purely illusory foundations. Children, who play
life, discern its true law and relations more
clearly than men, who fail to live it worthily,
but who think that they are wiser by experience, that is, by failure. I have read in a
Hindoo book, that "there was a king's son, who,
being expelled in infancy from his native city,
was brought up by a forester, and, growing up
to maturity in that state, imagined himself to
belong to the barbarous race with which he
lived. One of his father's ministers having discovered him, revealed to him what he was, and
the misconception of his character was removed, and he knew himself to be a prince.
So soul," continues the Hindoo philosopher,
"from the circumstances in which it is placed,
mistakes its own character, until the truth is
revealed to it by some holy teacher, and then
it knows itself to be *Brahme.*" I perceive that
we inhabitants of New England live this mean
life that we do because our vision does not
penetrate the surface of things. We think that
that *is* which *appears* to be. If a man should
walk through this town and see only the reality,
where, think you, would the "Mill-dam" go
to? If he should give us an account of the
realities he beheld there, we should not recognize the place in his description. Look at a
meeting-house, or a court-house, or a jail, or
a shop, or a dwelling-house, and say what that
thing really is before a true gaze, and they
would all go to pieces in your account of them.
Men esteem truth remote, in the outskirts of
the system, behind the farthest star, before
Adam and after the last man. In eternity there
is indeed something true and sublime. But all
these times and places and occasions are now
and here. God Himself culminates in the
present moment, and will never be more divine
in the lapse of all the ages. And we are

enabled to apprehend at all what is sublime and noble only by the perpetual instilling and drenching of the reality that surrounds us. The universe constantly and obediently answers to our conceptions; whether we travel fast or slow, the track is laid for us. Let us spend our lives in conceiving then. The poet or the artist never yet had so fair and noble a design but some of his posterity at least could accomplish it.

Let us spend one day as deliberately as Nature, and not be thrown off the track by every nutshell and mosquito's wing that falls on the rails. Let us rise early and fast, or break fast, gently and without perturbation; let company come and let company go, let the bells ring and the children cry,—determined to make a day of it. Why should we knock under and go with the stream? Let us not be upset and overwhelmed in that terrible rapid and whirlpool called a dinner, situated in the meridian shadows. Weather this danger and you are safe, for the rest of the way is down hill. With unrelaxed nerves, with morning vigor, sail by it, looking another way, tied to the mast like Ulysses. If the engine whistles, let it whistle till it is hoarse for its pains. If the bell rings, why should we run? We will consider what kind of music they are like. Let us settle ourselves, and work and wedge our feet downward through the mud and slush of opinion, and prejudice, and tradition, and delusion, and appearance, that alluvion which covers the globe, through Paris and London, through New York and Boston and Concord, through church and state, through poetry and philosophy and religion, till we come to a hard bottom and rocks in place, which we can call *reality*, and say, This is, and no mistake; and then begin, having a *point d'appui*, below freshet and frost and fire, a place where you might found a wall or a state, or set a lamp-post safely, or perhaps a gauge, not a Nilometer, but a Realometer, that future ages might know how deep a freshet of shams and appearances had gathered from time to time. If you stand right fronting and face to face to a fact, you will see the sun glimmer on both its surfaces, as if it were a cimeter, and feel its sweet edge dividing you through the heart and marrow, and so you will happily conclude your mortal career. Be it life or death, we crave only reality. If we are really dying, let us hear the rattle in our throats and feel cold in the extremities; if we are alive, let us go about our business.

Time is but the stream I go a-fishing in. I drink at it; but while I drink I see the sandy bottom and detect how shallow it is. Its thin current slides away, but eternity remains. I would drink deeper; fish in the sky, whose bottom is pebbly with stars. I cannot count one. I know not the first letter of the alphabet. I have always been regretting that I was not as wise as the day I was born. The intellect is a cleaver; it discerns and rifts its way into the secret of things. I do not wish to be any more busy with my hands than is necessary. My head is hands and feet. I feel all my best faculties concentrated in it. My instinct tells me that my head is an organ for burrowing, as some creatures use their snout and forepaws, and with it I would mine and burrow my way through these hills. I think that the richest vein is somewhere hereabouts; so by the divining rod and thin rising vapors I judge; and here I will begin to mine.

BAKER FARM

(CHAPTER 10)

Sometimes I rambled to pine groves, standing like temples, or like fleets at sea, full-rigged, with wavy boughs, and rippling with light, so soft and green and shady that the Druids would have forsaken their oaks to worship in them; or to the cedar wood beyond Flint's Pond, where the trees, covered with hoary blue berries, spiring higher and higher, are fit to stand before Valhalla, and the creeping juniper covers the ground with wreaths full of fruit; or to swamps where the usnea lichen hangs in festoons from the white spruce trees, and toadstools, round tables of the swamp gods, cover the ground, and more beautiful fungi adorn the stumps, like butterflies or shells, vegetable winkles; where the swamp-pink and dogwood grow, the red alder berry glows like eyes of imps, the waxwork grooves and crushes the hardest woods in its folds, and the wild holly berries make the beholder forget his home with their beauty, and he is dazzled and tempted by nameless other wild forbidden fruits, too fair for mortal taste. Instead of calling on some scholar, I paid many a visit to particular trees, of kinds which are rare in this neighborhood, standing far away in the middle of some pasture, or in the depths of a wood or swamp, or on a hilltop; such as the black birch, of which we have some handsome specimens two feet in diameter; its cousin, the yellow birch, with its loose golden vest, perfumed like the first; the beech, which has so neat a bole and beautifully lichen-painted, perfect in all its details, of which, excepting scattered specimens, I know but one small grove of sizable trees left in the township, supposed by some to have been planted by the pigeons that were once baited with beech nuts near by; it is worth the while to see the silver grain sparkle when you split this wood; the bass; the hornbeam; the *Celtis occidentalis,* or false elm, of which we have but one well-grown; some taller mast of a pine, a shingle tree, or a more perfect hemlock than usual, standing like a pagoda in the midst of the woods; and many others I could mention. These were the shrines I visited both summer and winter.

Once it chanced that I stood in the very abutment of a rainbow's arch, which filled the lower stratum of the atmosphere, tinging the grass and leaves around, and dazzling me as if I looked through colored crystal. It was a lake of rainbow light, in which, for a short while, I lived like a dolphin. If it had lasted longer it might have tinged my employments and life. As I walked on the railroad causeway, I used to wonder at the halo of light around my shadow, and would fain fancy myself one of the elect. One who visited me declared that the shadows of some Irishmen before him had no halo about them, that it was only natives that were so distinguished. Benvenuto Cellini tells us in his memoirs, that, after a certain terrible dream or vision which he had during his confinement in the castle of St. Angelo a respendent light appeared over the shadow of his head at morning and evening, whether he was in Italy or France, and it was particularly conspicuous when the grass was moist with dew. This was probably the same phenomenon to which I have referred, which is especially observed in the morning, but also at other times, and even by moonlight. Though a constant one, it is not commonly noticed, and, in the case of an excitable imagination like Cellini's, it would be basis enough for superstition. Beside, he tells us that he showed it to very few. But are they not indeed distinguished who are conscious that they are regarded at all?

I set out one afternoon to go a-fishing to Fair Haven, through the woods, to eke out my scanty fare of vegetables. My way led through Pleasant Meadow, an adjunct of the Baker Farm, that retreat of which a poet has since sung, beginning,—

> "Thy entry is a pleasant field,
> Which some mossy fruit trees yield
> Partly to a ruddy brook,
> By gliding musquash undertook,
> And mercurial trout,
> Darting about."

I thought of living there before I went to Walden. I "hooked" the apples, leaped the brook, and scared the musquash and the trout. It was one of those afternoons which seem indefinitely long before one, in which many events may happen, a large portion of our natural life, though it was already half spent when I started. By the way there came up a shower, which compelled me to stand half an hour under a pine, piling boughs over my head, and wearing my handkerchief for a shed; and when at length I had made one cast over the pickerelweed, standing up to my middle in water, I found myself suddenly in the shadow of a cloud, and the thunder began to rumble with such emphasis that I could do no more than listen to it. The gods must be proud, thought I, with such forked flashes to rout a poor unarmed fisherman. So I made haste for shelter to the nearest hut, which stood half a mile from any road, but so much the nearer to the pond, and had long been uninhabited:—

> "And here a poet builded,
> In the completed years,
> For behold a trivial cabin
> That to destruction steers."

So the Muse fables. But therein, as I found, dwelt now John Field, an Irishman, and his wife, and several children, from the broad-faced boy who assisted his father at his work, and now came running by his side from the bog to escape the rain, to the wrinkled, sibyl-like, cone-headed infant that sat upon its father's knee as in the palaces of nobles, and looked out from its home in the midst of wet and hunger inquisitively upon the stranger, with the privilege of infancy, not knowing but it was the last of a noble line, and the hope and cynosure of the world, instead of John Field's poor starveling brat. There we sat together under that part of the roof which leaked the least, while it showered and thundered without. I had sat there many times of old before the ship was built that floated this family to America. An honest, hard-working, but shiftless man plainly was John Field; and his wife—she too was brave to cook so many successive dinners in the recesses of that lofty stove; with round greasy face and bare breast, still thinking to improve her condition one day; with the never absent mop in one hand, and yet no effects of it visible anywhere. The chickens, which had also taken shelter here from the rain, stalked about the room like members of the family, too humanised methought to roast well. They stood and looked in my eye or pecked at my shoe significantly. Meanwhile my host told me his story, how hard he worked "bogging" for a neighboring farmer, turning up a meadow with a spade or bog hoe at the rate of ten dollars an acre and the use of the land with manure for one year, and his little broad-faced son worked cheerfully at his father's side the while, not knowing how poor a bargain the latter had made. I tried to help him with my experience, telling him that he was one of my nearest neighbors, and that I too, who came a-fishing here, and looked like a loafer, was getting my living like himself; that I lived in a tight, light, and clean house, which hardly cost more than the annual rent of such a ruin as his commonly amounts to; and how, if he chose, he might in a month or two build himself a palace of his own; that I did not use tea, nor coffee, nor butter, nor milk, nor fresh meat, and so did not have to work to get them; again, as I did not work hard, I did not have to eat hard, and it cost me but a trifle for my food; but as he began with tea, and coffee, and butter, and milk, and beef, he had to work hard to pay for them, and when he had worked hard he had to eat hard again to repair the waste of his system,—and so it was as broad as it was long, indeed it was broader than it was long, for he was discontented and wasted his life into the bargain; and yet he had rated it as a gain in coming to America, that here you could get tea, and coffee, and meat every day. But the only true America is that country where you are at liberty to pursue such a mode of life as may enable you to do without these, and where the state does not endeavor to compel you to sustain the slavery and war and other superfluous expenses which directly or indirectly result from the use of such things. For I purposely talked to him as if he were a philosopher, or desired to be one. I should be glad if all the meadows on the earth were left in a wild state, if that were the consequence of men's beginning to redeem themselves. A man will not need to study history to find out what is best for his own culture. But alas! the culture of an Irishman is an enterprise to be undertaken with a sort of moral bog hoe. I told him, that as he worked so hard at bogging, he required thick boots and stout clothing, which yet were soon soiled and worn out, but I wore light shoes and thin clothing, which cost not half so much, though he might think that I was dressed like a gentleman (which, however, was not the case), and in an hour or two, without labor, but as a recreation, I could, if I wished, catch as many fish as I should want for two days, or earn enough money to support me a week. If he and his family would live simply, they might all go a-huckleberrying in the summer for their amusement. John heaved a sigh at this, and his wife stared with arms a-kimbo, and both appeared to be wondering if they had capital enough to begin such a course with, or arithmetic enough to carry it through. It was sailing by dead reckoning to them, and they saw not clearly how to make their port so; therefore I suppose they still take life bravely, after their fashion, face to face, giving it tooth and nail, not having skill to split its massive columns with any fine entering wedge, and rout it in detail—thinking to deal with it roughly, as one should handle a thistle. But they fight at an overwhelming disadvantage—living, John Field, alas! without arithmetic, and failing so.

"Do you ever fish?" I asked. "Oh yes, I catch a mess now and then when I am lying by; good perch I catch." "What's your bait?" "I catch shiners with fishworms, and bait the perch with them." "You'd better go now, John," said his wife, with glistening and hopeful face; but John demurred.

The shower was now over, and a rainbow above the eastern woods promised a fair evening; so I took my departure. When I had got without I asked for a drink, hoping to get a sight of the well bottom, to complete my survey of the premises; but there, alas! are shallows and quicksands, and rope broken withal, and bucket irrecoverable. Meanwhile the right culinary vessel was selected, water was seemingly distilled, and after consultation and long delay passed out to the thirsty one,—not yet suffered to cool, not yet to settle. Such gruel sustains life here, I thought; so, shutting my eyes, and excluding the motes by a skilfully directed undercurrent, I drank to genuine hospitality the heartiest draught I could. I am not squeamish in such cases when manners are concerned.

As I was leaving the Irishman's roof after the rain, bending my steps again to the pond, my haste to catch pickerel, wading in retired meadows, in sloughs and bog-holes, in forlorn and savage places, appeared for an instant trivial to me who had been sent to school and college; but as I ran down the hill toward the reddening west, with the rainbow over my shoulder, and some faint tinkling sounds borne to my ear through the cleansed air, from I know not what quarter, my Good Genius seemed to say,—Go fish and hunt far and wide day by day,—farther and wider,—and rest thee by many brooks and hearth-sides without misgiving. Remember thy Creator in the days of thy youth. Rise free from care before the dawn, and seek adventures. Let the noon find thee by other lakes, and the night overtake thee everywhere at home. There are no larger fields than these, no worthier games than may here be played. Grow wild according to thy nature, like these sedges and brakes, which will never become English hay. Let the thunder rumble; what if it threaten ruin to farmers' crops? that is not its errand to thee. Take shelter under the cloud, while they flee to carts and sheds. Let not to get a living be thy trade, but thy sport. Enjoy the land, but own it not. Through want of enterprise and faith men are where they are, buying and selling, and spending their lives like serfs.

O Baker Farm!

"Landscape where the richest element
Is a little sunshine innocent." . . .

"No one runs to revel
On thy rail-fenced lea." . . .

"Debate with no man hast thou,
    With questions art never perplexed,
As tame at the first sight as now,
    In thy plain russet gabardine dressed." . . .

"Come ye who love,
    And ye who hate,
Children of the Holy Dove,
    And Guy Faux of the state,
And hang conspiracies
From the tough rafters of the trees!"

Men come tamely home at night only from the next field or street, where their household echoes haunt, and their life pines because it breathes its own breath over again; their shadows morning and evening reach farther than their daily steps. We should come home from far, from adventures, and perils, and discoveries every day, with new experience and character.

Before I had reached the pond some fresh impulse had brought out John Field, with altered mind, letting go "bogging" ere this sunset. But he, poor man, disturbed only a couple of fins while I was catching a fair string, and he said it was his luck; but when we changed seats in the boat luck changed seats too. Poor John Field!—I trust he does not read this, unless he will improve by it,—thinking to live by some derivative old-country mode in this primitive new country,—to catch perch with shiners. It is good bait sometimes, I allow. With his horizon all his own, yet he a poor man, born to be poor, with his inherited Irish poverty or poor life, his Adam's grandmother and boggy ways, not to rise in this world, he nor his posterity, till their wading, webbed, bog-trotting feet get *talaria* to their heels.

HIGHER LAWS

(CHAPTER 11)

As I came home through the woods with my string of fish, trailing my pole, it being now quite dark, I caught a glimpse of a woodchuck stealing across my path, and felt a strange thrill of savage delight, and was strongly tempted to seize and devour him raw; not that I was hungry then, except for that wildness which he represented. Once or twice, however, while I lived at the pond, I found myself ranging the woods, like a half-starved hound, with a strange abandonment, seeking some kind of venison which I might devour, and no morsel could have been too savage for me. The wildest scenes had become unaccountably familiar. I found in myself, and still find, an instinct toward a higher, or, as it is named, spiritual life, as do most men, and another toward a primitive rank and savage one, and I reverence them both. I love the wild not less than the good. The wildness and adventure that are in fishing still recommend it to me. I like sometimes to take rank hold on life and spend my day more as the animals do. Perhaps I have owed to this employment and to hunting, when quite young, my closest acquaintance with Nature. They early introduce us to and detain us in scenery with which otherwise, at that age, we should have little acquaintance. Fishermen, hunters, woodchoppers, and others, spending their lives in the fields and woods, in a peculiar sense a part of Nature themselves, are often in a more favorable mood for observing her, in the intervals of their pursuits, than philosophers or poets even, who approach her with expectation. She is not afraid to exhibit herself to them. The traveller on the prairie is naturally a hunter, on the head waters of the Missouri and Columbia a trapper, and at the Falls of St. Mary a fisherman. He who is only a traveller learns things at second-hand and by the halves, and is poor authority. We are most interested when science reports what those men already know practically or instinctively, for that alone is a true *humanity*, or account of human experience.

They mistake who assert that the Yankee has few amusements, because he has not so many public holidays, and men and boys do not play so many games as they do in England, for here the more primitive but solitary amusements of hunting, fishing, and the like have not yet given place to the former. Almost every New England boy among my contemporaries shouldered a fowling-peice between the ages of ten and fourteen; and his hunting and fishing grounds were not limited like the preserves of an English nobleman, but were more boundless even than those of a savage. No wonder, then, that he did not oftener stay to play on the common. But already a change is taking place, owing, not to an increased humanity, but to an increased scarcity of game, for perhaps the hunter is the greatest friend of the animals hunted, not excepting the Humane Society.

Moreover, when at the pond, I wished sometimes to add fish to my fare for variety. I have actually fished from the same kind of necessity that the first fishers did. Whatever humanity I might conjure up against it was all factitious, and concerned my philosophy more than my feelings. I speak of fishing only now, for I had long felt differently about fowling, and sold my gun before I went to the woods. Not that I am less humane than others, but I did not perceive that my feelings were much affected. I did not pity the fishes nor the worms. This was habit. As for fowling, during the last years that I carried a gun my excuse was that I was studying ornithology, and sought only new or rare birds. But I confess that I am now inclined to think that there is a finer way of studying ornithology than this. It requires so much closer attention to the habits of the birds, that, if for that reason only, I have been willing to omit the gun. Yet

notwithstanding the objection on the score of humanity, I am compelled to doubt if equally valuable sports are ever substituted for these; and when some of my friends have asked me anxiously about their boys, whether they should let them hunt, I have answered, yes,—remembering that it was one of the best parts of my education,—*make* them hunters, though sportsmen only at first, if possible, mighty hunters at last, so that they shall not find game large enough for them in this or any vegetable wilderness,—hunters as well as fishers of men. Thus far I am of the opinion of Chaucer's nun,[5] who

"yave not of the text a pulled hen
That saith that hunters ben not holy men."

There is a period in the history of the individual, as of the race, when the hunters are the "best men," as the Algonquins called them. We cannot but pity the boy who has never fired a gun; he is no more humane, while his education has been sadly neglected. This was my answer with respect to those youths who were bent on this pursuit, trusting that they would soon outgrow it. No humane being, past the thoughtless age of boyhood, will wantonly murder any creature which holds its life by the same tenure that he does. The hare in its extremity cries like a child. I warn you, mothers, that my sympathies do not always make the usual phil*anthropic* distinctions.

Such is oftenest the young man's introduction to the forest, and the most original part of himself. He goes thither at first as a hunter and fisher, until at last, if he has the seeds of a better life in him, he distinguishes his proper objects, as a poet or naturalist it may be, and leaves the gun and fish-pole behind. The mass of men are still and always young in this respect. In some countries a hunting parson is no uncommon sight. Such a one might make a good shepherd's dog, but is far from being the Good Shepherd. I have been surprised to consider that the only obvious employment, except wood-chopping, ice-cutting, or the like business, which ever to my knowledge detained at Walden Pond for a whole half day any of my fellow-citizens, whether fathers or children of the town, with just one exception, was fishing. Commonly they did not think that they were lucky, or well paid for their time, unless they got a long string of fish, though they had

[5] Thoreau should have said, and it really makes some difference, Chaucer's Monk.

*t*he opportunity of seeing the pond all the while. They might go there a thousand times before the sediment of fishing would sink to the bottom and leave their purpose pure; but no doubt such a clarifying process would be going on all the while. The governor and his council faintly remember the pond, for they went a-fishing there when they were boys; but now they are too old and dignified to go a-fishing, and so they know it no more forever. Yet even they expect to go to heaven at last. If the legislature regards it, it is chiefly to regulate the number of hooks to be used there; but they know nothing about the hook of hooks with which to angle for the pond itself, impaling the legislature for a bait. Thus, even in civilized communities, the embryo man passes through the hunter stage of development.

I have found repeatedly, of late years, that I cannot fish without falling a little in self-respect. I have tried it again and again. I have skill at it, and, like many of my fellows, a certain instinct for it, which revives from time to time, but always when I have done I feel that it would have been better if I had not fished. I think that I do not mistake. It is a faint intimation, yet so are the first streaks of morning. There is unquestionably this instinct in me which belongs to the lower orders of creation; yet with every year I am less a fisherman, though without more humanity or even wisdom; at present I am no fisherman at all. But I see that if I were to live in a wilderness I should again be tempted to become a fisher and hunter in earnest. Beside, there is something essentially unclean about this diet and all flesh, and I began to see where house-work commences, and whence the endeavor, which costs so much, to wear a tidy and respectable appearance each day, to keep the house sweet and free from all ill odors and sights. Having been my own butcher and scullion and cook, as well as the gentleman for whom the dishes were served up, I can speak from an unusually complete experience. The practical objection to animal food in my case was its uncleanness; and besides, when I had caught and cleaned and cooked and eaten my fish, they seemed not to have fed me essentially. It was insignificant and unnecessary, and cost more than it came to. A little bread or a few potatoes would have done as well, with less trouble and filth. Like many of my contemporaries, I had rarely for many years used animal food, or tea, or coffee, &c.; not so much because of any ill effects which I had traced to them, as because they were not agreeable to my imagination. The repugnance to animal food is not the effect of experience, but is an instinct. It appeared more beautiful to live low and fare hard in many respects; and though I never did so, I went far enough to please my imagination. I believe that every man who has ever been earnest to preserve his higher or poetic faculties in the best condition has been particularly inclined to abstain from animal food, and from much food of any kind. It is a significant fact, stated by entomologists,—I find it in Kirby and Spence,—that "some insects in their perfect state, though furnished with organs of feeding, make no use of them"; and they lay it down as "a general rule, that almost all insects in this state eat much less than in that of larvæ. The voracious caterpillar when transformed into a butterfly . . . and the gluttonous maggot when become a fly" content themselves with a drop or two of honey or some other sweet liquid. The abdomen under the wings of the butterfly still represents the larva. This is the tid-bit which tempts his insectivorous fate. The gross feeder is a man in the larva state; and there are whole nations in that condition, nations without fancy or imagination, whose vast abdomens betray them.

It is hard to provide and cook so simple and clean a diet as will not offend the imagination; but this, I think, is to be fed when we feed the body; they should both sit down at the same table. Yet perhaps this may be done. The fruits eaten temperately need not make us ashamed of our appetites, nor interrupt the worthiest pursuits. But put an extra condiment into your dish, and it will poison you. It is not worth the while to live by rich cookery. Most men would feel shame if caught preparing with their own hands precisely such a dinner, whether of animal or vegetable food, as is every day prepared for them by others. Yet till this is otherwise we are not civilized, and, if gentlemen and ladies, are not true men and women. This certainly suggests what change is to be made. It may be vain to ask why the imagination will not be reconciled to flesh and fat. I am satisfied that it is not. Is it not a reproach that man is a carnivorous animal? True, he can and does live, in a great measure, by preying on other animals; but this is a miserable way,—as any one who will go to snaring rabbits, or slaughtering lambs, may learn,—and he will be regarded as a benefactor of his race who shall teach man to confine himself to a more innocent and wholesome diet. Whatever my own practice may be, I have no doubt that it is a part of the destiny of the human race, in its gradual improvement, to leave off eating animals, as surely as the savage tribes have left off eating each other when they came in contact with the more civilized.

If one listens to the faintest but constant suggestions of his genius, which are certainly true, he sees not to what extremes, or even insanity, it may lead him; and yet that way, as he grows more resolute and faithful, his road lies. The faintest assured objection which one healthy man feels will at length prevail over the arguments and customs of mankind. No man ever followed his genius till it misled him. Though the result were bodily weakness, yet perhaps no one can say that the consequences were to be regretted, for these were a life in conformity to higher principles. If the day and the night are such that you greet them with joy, and life emits a fragrance like flowers and sweet-scented herbs, is more elastic, more starry, more immortal,—that is your success. All nature is your congratulation, and you have cause momentarily to bless yourself. The greatest gains and values are farthest from being appreciated. We easily come to doubt if they exist. We soon forget them. They are the highest reality. Perhaps the facts most astounding and most real are never communicated by man to man. The true harvest of my daily life is somewhat as intangible and indescribable as the tints of morning or evening. It is a little star-dust caught, a segment of the rainbow which I have clutched.

Yet, for my part, I was never unusually squeamish; I could sometimes eat a fried rat with a good relish, if it were necessary. I am glad to have drunk water so long, for the same reason that I prefer the natural sky to an opium-eater's heaven. I would fain keep sober always; and there are infinite degrees of drunkenness. I believe that water is the only drink for a wise man; wine is not so noble a liquor; and think of dashing the hopes of a morning with a cup of warm coffee, or of an evening with a dish of tea! Ah, how low I fall when I am tempted by them! Even music may be intoxicating. Such apparently slight causes destroyed Greece and Rome, and will destroy England and America. Of all ebriosity, who does not prefer to be intoxicated by the air he breathes? I have found it to be the most serious objection to coarse labors long continued, that

they compelled me to eat and drink coarsely also. But to tell the truth, I find myself at present somewhat less particular in these respects. I carry less religion to the table, ask no blessing; not because I am wiser than I was, but, I am obliged to confess, because, however much it is to be regretted, with years I have grown more coarse and indifferent. Perhaps these questions are entertained only in youth, as most believe of poetry. My practice is "nowhere," my opinion is here. Nevertheless I am far from regarding myself as one of those privileged ones to whom the Ved refers when it says, that "he who has true faith in the Omnipresent Supreme Being may eat all that exists," that is, is not bound to inquire what is his food, or who prepares it; and even in their case it is to be observed, as a Hindoo commentator has remarked, that the Vedant limits this privilege to "the time of distress."

Who has not sometimes derived an inexpressible satisfaction from his food in which appetite had no share? I have been thrilled to think that I owed a mental perception to the commonly gross sense of taste, that I have been inspired through the palate, that some berries which I had eaten on a hillside had fed my genius. "The soul not being mistress of herself," says Thseng-tseu, "one looks, and one does not see; one listens, and one does not hear; one eats, and one does not know the savor of food." He who distinguishes the true savor of his food can never be a glutton; he who does not cannot be otherwise. A puritan may go to his brown-bread crust with as gross an appetite as ever an alderman to his turtle. Not that food which entereth into the mouth defileth a man, but the appetite with which it is eaten. It is neither the quality nor the quantity, but the devotion to sensual savors; when that which is eaten is not a viand to sustain our animal, or inspire our spiritual life, but food for the worms that possess us. If the hunter has a taste for mud-turtles, muskrats, and other such savage tidbits, the fine lady indulges a taste for jelly made of a calf's foot, or for sardines from over the sea, and they are even. He goes to the mill-pond, she to her preserve-pot. The wonder is how they, how you and I, can live this slimy beastly life, eating and drinking.

Our whole life is startlingly moral. There is never an instant's truce between virtue and vice. Goodness is the only investment that never fails. In the music of the harp which trembles round the world it is the insisting on this which thrills us. The harp is the travelling patterer for the Universe's Insurance Company, recommending its laws, and our little goodness is all the assessment that we pay. Though the youth at last grows indifferent, the laws of the universe are not indifferent, but are for ever on the side of the most sensitive. Listen to every zephyr for some reproof, for it is surely there, and he is unfortunate who does not hear it. We cannot touch a string or move a stop but the charming moral transfixes us. Many an irksome noise, go a long way off, is heard as music, a proud sweet satire on the meanness of our lives.

We are conscious of an animal in us, which awakens in proportion as our higher nature slumbers. It is reptile and sensual, and perhaps cannot be wholly expelled; like the worms which, even in life and health, occupy our bodies. Possibly we may withdraw from it, but never change its nature. I fear that it may enjoy a certain health of its own; that we may be well, yet not pure. The other day I picked up the lower jaw of a hog, with white and sound teeth and tusks, which suggested that there was an animal health and vigor distinct from the spiritual. This creature succeeded by other means than temperance and purity. "That in which men differ from brute beasts," says Mencius, "is a thing very inconsiderable; the common herd lose it very soon; superior men preserve it carefully." Who knows what sort of life would result if we had attained to purity? If I knew so wise a man as could teach me purity I would go to seek him forthwith. "A command over our passions, and over the external senses of the body, and good acts, are declared by the Ved to be indispensable in the mind's approximation to God." Yet the spirit can for the time pervade and control every member and function of the body, and transmute what in form is the grossest sensuality into purity and devotion. The generative energy, which, when we are loose, dissipates and makes us unclean, when we are continent invigorates and inspires us. Chastity is the flowering of man; and what are called Genius, Heroism, Holiness, and the like, are but various fruits which succeed it. Man flows at once to God when the channel of purity is open. By turns our purity inspires and our impurity casts us down. He is blessed who is assured that the animal is dying out in him day by day, and the divine being established. Perhaps there is none but has cause for shame on account of the inferior and brutish nature to which he is allied. I fear that we are such gods or demigods only as fauns and satyrs, the divine allied to beasts, the creatures of appetite, and that, to some extent, our very life is our disgrace—

"How happy's he who hath due place assigned
To his beasts and disaforested his mind!
. . .
Can use his horse, goat, wolf, and ev'ry beast,
And is not ass himself to all the rest!
Else man not only is the herd of swine,
But he's those devils too which did incline
Them to a headlong rage, and made them worse."

All sensuality is one, though it takes many forms; all purity is one. It is the same whether a man eat, or drink, or cohabit, or sleep sensually. They are but one appetite, and we only need to see a person do any one of these things to know how great a sensualist he is. The impure can neither stand nor sit with purity. When the reptile is attacked at one mouth of his burrow, he shows himself at another. If you would be chaste, you must be temperate. What is chastity? How shall a man know if he is chaste? He shall not know it. We have heard of this virtue, but we know not what it is. We speak conformably to the rumor which we have heard. From exertion come wisdom and purity; from sloth ignorance and sensuality. In the student sensuality is a sluggish habit of mind. An unclean person is universally a slothful one, one who sits by a stove, whom the sun shines on prostrate, who reposes without being fatigued. If you would avoid uncleanness, and all the sins, work earnestly, though it be at cleaning a stable. Nature is hard to be overcome, but she must be overcome. What avails it that you are Christian, if you are not purer than the heathen, if you deny yourself no more, if you are not more religious? I know of many systems of religion esteemed heathenish whose precepts fill the reader with shame, and provoke him to new endeavors, though it be to the performance of rites merely.

I hesitate to say these things, but it is not because of the subject,—I care not how obscene my *words* are,—but because I cannot speak of them without betraying my impurity. We discourse freely without shame of one form of sensuality, and are silent about another. We are so degraded that we cannot speak simply of the necessary functions of human nature. In earlier ages, in some countries, every function was reverently spoken of and regulated by law.

Nothing was too trivial for the Hindoo law-giver, however offensive it may be to modern taste. He teaches how to eat, drink, cohabit, void excrement and urine, and the like, elevating what is mean, and does not falsely excuse himself by calling these things trifles.

Every man is the builder of a temple, called his body, to the god he worships, after a style purely his own, nor can he get off by hammering marble instead. We are all sculptors and painters, and our material is our own flesh and blood and bones. Any nobleness begins at once to refine a man's features, any meanness or sensuality to imbrute them.

John Farmer sat at his door one September evening, after a hard day's work, his mind still running on his labor more or less. Having bathed, he sat down to re-create his intellectual man. It was a rather cool evening, and some of his neighbors were apprehending a frost. He had not attended to the train of his thoughts long when he heard some one playing on a flute, and that sound harmonized with his mood. Still he thought of his work; but the burden of his thought was, that though this kept running in his head, and he found himself planning and contriving it against his will, yet it concerned him very little. It was no more than the scurf of his skin, which was constantly shuffled off. But the notes of the flute came home to his ears out of a different sphere from that he worked in, and suggested work for certain faculties which slumbered in him. They gently did away with the street, and the village, and the state in which he lived. A voice said to him,—Why do you stay here and live this mean moiling life, when a glorious existence is possible for you? Those same stars twinkle over other fields than these.—But how to come out of this condition and actually migrate thither? All that he could think of was to practise some new austerity, to let his mind descend into his body and redeem it, and treat himself with ever increasing respect.

CONCLUSION

(CHAPTER 18)

To the sick the doctors wisely recommend a change of air and scenery. Thank Heaven, here is not all the world. The buck-eye does not grow in New England, and the mocking-bird is rarely heard here. The wild goose is more of a cosmopolite than we; he breaks his fast in Canada, takes a luncheon in the Ohio, and plumes himself for the night in a southern bayou. Even the bison, to some extent, keeps pace with the seasons, cropping the pastures of the Colorado only till a greener and sweeter grass awaits him by the Yellowstone. Yet we think that if rail-fences are pulled down, and stone-walls piled up on our farms, bounds are henceforth set to our lives and our fates decided. If you are chosen town-clerk, forsooth, you cannot go to Tierra del Fuego this summer: but you may go to the land of infernal fire nevertheless. The universe is wider than our views of it.

Yet we should oftener look over the tafferel of our craft, like curious passengers, and not make the voyage like stupid sailors picking oakum. The other side of the globe is but the home of our correspondent. Our voyaging is only great-circle sailing, and the doctors prescribe for diseases of the skin merely. One hastens to southern Africa to chase the giraffe; but surely that is not the game he would be after. How long, pray, would a man hunt giraffes if he could? Snipes and woodcocks also may afford rare sport; but I trust it would be nobler game to shoot one's self.—

"Direct your eye right inward, and you'll find
A thousand regions in your mind
Yet undiscovered. Travel them, and be
Expert in home-cosmography."

What does Africa—what does the West stand for? Is not our own interior white on the chart? black though it may prove, like the coast, when discovered? Is it the source of the Nile, or the Niger, or the Mississippi, or a North-West Passage around this continent, that we would find? Are these the problems which most concern mankind? Is Franklin the only man who is lost, that his wife should be so earnest to find him? Does Mr. Grinnell know where he himself is? Be rather the Mungo Park, the Lewis and Clarke and Frobisher, of your own streams and oceans; explore your own higher latitudes,— with shiploads of preserved meats to support you, if they be necessary, and pile the empty cans sky-high for a sign. Were preserved meats invented to preserve meat merely? Nay, be a Columbus to whole new continents and worlds within you, opening new channels, not of trade, but of thought. Every man is the lord of a realm beside which the earthly empire of the Czar is but a petty state, a hummock left by the ice. Yet some can be patriotic who have no *self-*

respect, and sacrifice the greater to the less. They love the soil which makes their graves, but have no sympathy with the spirit which may still animate their clay. Patriotism is a maggot in their heads. What was the meaning of that South-Sea Exploring Expedition, with all its parade and expense, but an indirect recognition of the fact that there are continents and seas in the moral world, to which every man is an isthmus or an inlet, yet unexplored by him, but that it is easier to sail many thousand miles through cold and storm and cannibals, in a government ship, with five hundred men and boys to assist one, than it is to explore the private sea, the Atlantic and Pacific Ocean of one's being alone.—

> "Erret, et extremos alter scrutetur Iberos.
> Plus habet hic vitae, plus habet ille viae."

Let them wander and scrutinize the outlandish
  Australians:
I have more of God, they more of the road.

It is not worth the while to go round the world to count the cats in Zanzibar. Yet do this even till you can do better, and you may perhaps find some "Symmes' Hole," by which to get at the inside at last. England and France, Spain and Portugal, Gold Coast and Slave Coast, all front on this private sea; but no bark from them has ventured out of sight of land, though it is without doubt the direct way to India. If you would learn to speak all tongues and conform to the customs of all nations, if you would travel farther than all travellers, be naturalized in all climes, and cause the Sphinx to dash her head against a stone, even obey the precept of the old philosopher, and Explore thyself. Herein are demanded the eye and the nerve. Only the defeated and deserters go to the wars, cowards that run away and enlist. Start now on that farthest western way, which does not pause at the Mississippi or the Pacific, nor conduct toward a worn-out China or Japan, but leads on direct, a tangent to this sphere, summer and winter, day and night, sun down, moon down, and at last earth down too.

It is said that Mirabeau took to highway robbery "to ascertain what degree of resolution was necessary in order to place one's self in formal opposition to the most sacred laws of society." He declared that "a soldier who fights in the ranks does not require half so much courage as a foot-pad,"—"that honor and religion have never stood in the way of a well-considered and a firm resolve." This was manly, as the world goes; and yet it was idle, if not desperate. A saner man would have found himself often enough "in formal opposition" to what are deemed "the most sacred laws of society," through obedience to yet more sacred laws, and so have tested his resolution without going out of his way. It is not for a man to put himself in such an attitude to society, but to maintain himself in whatever attitude he finds himself through obedience to the laws of his being, which will never be one of opposition to a just government, if he should chance to meet with such.

I left the woods for as good a reason as I went there. Perhaps it seemed to me that I had several more lives to live, and could not spare any more time for that one. It is remarkable how easily and insensibly we fall into a particular route, and make a beaten track for ourselves. I had not lived there a week before my feet wore a path from my door to the pond-side; and though it is five or six years since I trod it, it is still quite distinct. It is true, I fear that others may have fallen into it, and so helped to keep it open. The surface of the earth is soft and impressible by the feet of men; and so with the paths which the mind travels. How worn and dusty, then, must be the highways of the world, how deep the ruts of tradition and conformity! I did not wish to take a cabin passage, but rather to go before the mast and on the deck of the world, for there I could best see the moonlight amid the mountains. I do not wish to go below now.

I learned this, at least, by my experiment: that if one advances confidently in the direction of his dreams, and endeavors to live the life which he has imagined, he will meet with a success unexpected in common hours. He will put some things behind, will pass an invisible boundary; new, universal, and more liberal laws will begin to establish themselves around and within him; or the old laws be expanded, and interpreted in his favor in a more liberal sense, and he will live with the license of a higher order of beings. In proportion as he simplifies his life, the laws of the universe will appear less complex, and solitude will not be solitude, nor poverty poverty, nor weakness weakness. If you have built castles in the air, your work need not be lost; that is where they should be. Now put the foundations under them.

It is a ridiculous demand which England and

America make, that you shall speak so that they can understand you. Neither men nor toadstools grow so. As if that were important, and there were not enough to understand you without them. As if Nature could support but one order of understandings, could not sustain birds as well as quadrupeds, flying as well as creeping things, and *hush* and *whoa,* which Bright can understand, were the best English. As if there were safety in stupidity alone. I fear chiefly lest my expression may not be *extra-vagant* enough, may not wander far enough beyond the narrow limits of my daily experience, so as to be adequate to the truth of which I have been convinced. *Extra vagance!* it depends on how you are yarded. The migrating buffalo, which seeks new pastures in another latitude, is not extravagant like the cow which kicks over the pail, leaps the cowyard fence, and runs after her calf, in milking time. I desire to speak somewhere *without* bounds; like a man in a waking moment, to men in their waking moments; for I am convinced that I cannot exaggerate enough even to lay the foundation of a true expression. Who that has heard a strain of music feared then lest he should speak extravagantly any more for ever? In view of the future or possible, we should live quite laxly and undefined in front, our outlines dim and misty on that side; as our shadows reveal an insensible perspiration toward the sun. The volatile truth of our words should continually betray the inadequacy of the residual statement. Their truth is instantly *translated;* its literal monument alone remains. The words which express our faith and piety are not definite; yet they are significant and fragrant like frankincense to superior natures.

Why level downward to our dullest perception always, and praise that as common sense? The commonest sense is the sense of men asleep, which they express by snoring. Sometimes we are inclined to class those who are once-and-a-half-witted with the half-witted, because we appreciate only a third part of their wit. Some would find fault with the morning red, if they ever got up early enough. "They pretend," as I hear, "that the verses of Kabir have four different senses; illusion, spirit, intellect, and the exoteric doctrine of the Vedas"; but in this part of the world it is considered a ground for complaint if a man's writings admit of more than one interpretation. While England endeavors to cure the potato-rot, will not any endeavor to cure the brain-rot, which prevails so much more widely and fatally?

I do not suppose that I have attained to obscurity, but I should be proud if no more fatal fault were found with my pages on this score than was found with the Walden ice. Southern customers objected to its blue color, which is the evidence of its purity, as if it were muddy, and preferred the Cambridge ice, which is white, but tastes of weeds. The purity men love is like the mists which envelope the earth, and not like the azure ether beyond.

Some are dinning in our ears that we Americans, and moderns generally, are intellectual dwarfs compared with the ancients, or even the Elizabethan men. But what is that to the purpose? A living dog is better than a dead lion. Shall a man go and hang himself because he belongs to the race of pygmies, and not be the biggest pygmy that he can? Let every one mind his own business, and endeavor to be what he was made.

Why should we be in such desperate haste to succeed and in such desperate enterprises? If a man does not keep pace with his companions, perhaps it is because he hears a different drummer. Let him step to the music which he hears, however measured or far away. It is not important that he should mature as soon as an apple tree or an oak. Shall he turn his spring into summer? If the condition of things which we were made for is not yet, what were any reality which we can substitute? We will not be shipwrecked on a vain reality. Shall we with pains erect a heaven of blue glass over ourselves, though when it is done we shall be sure to gaze still at the true ethereal heaven far above, as if the former were not?

There was an artist in the city of Kouroo who was disposed to strive after perfection. One day it came into his mind to make a staff. Having considered that in an imperfect work time is an ingredient, but into a perfect work time does not enter, he said to himself, It shall be perfect in all respects, though I should do nothing else in my life. He proceeded instantly to the forest for wood, being resolved that it should not be made of unsuitable material; and as he searched for and rejected stick after stick, his friends gradually deserted him, for they grew old in their works and died, but he grew not older by a moment. His singleness of purpose and resolution, and his elevated piety, endowed him, without his knowledge, with perennial youth. As he made no compromise with Time, Time kept out of his way, and only sighed at a distance because he could not overcome him. Before he had found a stock in all respects suitable the city of Kouroo was a hoary ruin, and he sat on one of its mounds to peel the stick. Before he had given it the proper shape the dynasty of the Candahars was at an end, and with the point of the stick he wrote the name of the last of that race in the sand, and then resumed his work. By the time he had smoothed and polished the staff Kalpa was no longer the pole-star; and ere he had put on the ferule and the head adorned with precious stones, Brahma had awoke and slumbered many times. But why do I stay to mention these things? When the finishing stroke was put to his work, it suddenly expanded before the eyes of the astonished artist into the fairest of all the creations of Brahma. He had made a new system in making a staff, a world with full and fair proportions; in which, though the old cities and dynasties had passed away, fairer and more glorious ones had taken their places. And now he saw by the heap of shavings still fresh at his feet, that, for him and his work, the former lapse of time had been an illusion, and that no more time had elapsed than is required for a single scintillation from the brain of Brahma to fall on and inflame the tinder of a mortal brain. The material was pure, and his art was pure; how could the result be other than wonderful?

No face which we can give to a matter will stead us so well at last as the truth. This alone wears well. For the most part, we are not where we are, but in a false position. Through an infirmity of our natures, we suppose a case and put ourselves into it, and hence are in two cases at the same time, and it is doubly difficult to get out. In sane moments we regard only the facts, the case that is. Say what you have to say, not what you ought. Any truth is better than make-believe. Tom Hyde, the tinker, standing on the gallows, was asked if he had anything to say. "Tell the tailors," said he, "to remember to make a knot in their thread before they take the first stitch." His companion's prayer is forgotten.

However mean your life is, meet it and live it; do not shun it and call it hard names. It is not so bad as you are. It looks poorest when you are richest. The fault-finder will find faults even in paradise. Love your life, poor as it is.

You may perhaps have some pleasant, thrilling, glorious hours, even in a poorhouse. The setting sun is reflected from the windows of the almshouse as brightly as from the rich man's abode; the snow melts before its door as early in the spring. I do not see but a quiet mind may live as contentedly there, and have as cheering thoughts, as in a palace. The town's poor seem to me often to live the most independent lives of any. Maybe they are simply great enough to receive without misgiving. Most think that they are above being supported by the town; but it oftener happens that they are not above supporting themselves by dishonest means, which should be more disreputable. Cultivate poverty like a garden herb, like sage. Do not trouble yourself much to get new things, whether clothes or friends. Turn the old; return to them. Things do not change: we change. Sell your clothes and keep your thoughts. God will see that you do not want society. If I were confined to a corner of a garret all my days, like a spider, the world would be just as large to me while I had my thoughts about me. The philosopher said: "From an army of three divisions one can take away its general, and put it in disorder; from the man the most abject and vulgar one cannot take away his thought." Do not seek so anxiously to be developed, to subject yourself to many influences to be played on; it is all dissipation. Humility like darkness reveals the heavenly lights. The shadows of poverty and meanness gather around us, "and lo! creation widens to our view." We are often reminded that if there were bestowed on us the wealth of Crœsus, our aims must still be the same, and our means essentially the same. Moreover, if you are restricted in your range by poverty, if you cannot buy books and newspapers, for instance, you are but confined to the most significant and vital experiences; you are compelled to deal with the material which yields the most sugar and the most starch. It is life near the bone where it is sweetest. You are defended from being a trifler. No man loses ever on a lower level by magnanimity on a higher. Superfluous wealth can buy superfluities only. Money is not required to buy one necessary of the soul.

I live in the angle of a leaden wall, into whose composition was poured a little alloy of bell metal. Often, in the repose of my midday, there reaches my ears a confused *tintinnabulum* from without. It is the noise of my contemporaries. My neighbors tell me of their adventures with famous gentlemen and ladies, what notabilities they met at the dinner-table; but I am no more interested in such things than in the contents of the Daily Times. The interest and the conversation are about costume and manners chiefly; but a goose is a goose still, dress it as you will. They tell me of California and Texas, of England and the Indies, of the Hon. Mr. —— of Georgia or of Massachusetts, all transient and fleeting phenomena, till I am ready to leap from their court-yard like the Mameluke bey. I delight to come to my bearings,—not walk in procession with pomp and parade, in a conspicuous place, but to walk even with the Builder of the universe, if I may, —not to live in this restless, nervous, bustling, trivial Nineteenth Century, but stand or sit thoughtfully while it goes by. What are men celebrating? They are all on a committee of arrangements, and hourly expect a speech from somebody. God is only the president of the day, and Webster is his orator. I love to weigh, to settle, to gravitate toward that which most strongly and rightfully attracts me;—not hang by the beam of the scale and try to weigh less, —not suppose a case, but take the case that is; to travel the only path I can, and that on which no power can resist me. It affords me no satisfaction to commence to spring an arch before I have got a solid foundation. Let us not play at kittlybenders.[6] There is a solid bottom everywhere. We read that the traveller asked the boy if the swamp before him had a hard bottom. The boy replied that it had. But presently the traveller's horse sank in up to the girths, and he observed to the boy, "I thought you said that this bog had a hard bottom." "So it has," answered the latter, "but you have not got half way to it yet." So it is with the bogs and quicksands of society; but he is an old boy that knows it. Only what is thought, said, or done at a certain rare coincidence is good. I would not be one of those who will foolishly drive a nail into mere lath and plastering; such a deed would keep me awake nights. Give me a hammer, and let me feel for the furring. Do not depend on the putty. Drive a nail home and clinch it so faithfully that you can wake up in the night and think of your work with satisfaction,—a work at which you would not be ashamed to invoke the Muse. So will help you God, and so only. Every nail driven should

6 Skating on thin ice.

be as another rivet in the machine of the universe, you carrying on the work.

Rather than love, than money, than fame, give me truth. I sat at a table where were rich food and wine in abundance, and obsequious attendance, but sincerity and truth were not; and I went away hungry from the inhospitable board. The hospitality was as cold as the ices. I thought that there was no need of ice to freeze them. They talked to me of the age of the wine and the fame of the vintage; but I thought of an older, a newer, and purer wine, of a more glorious vintage, which they had not got, and could not buy. The style, the house and grounds and "entertainment" pass for nothing with me. I called on the king, but he made me wait in his hall, and conducted like a man incapacitated for hospitality. There was a man in my neighborhood who lived in a hollow tree. His manners were truly regal. I should have done better had I called on him.

How long shall we sit in our porticoes practising idle and musty virtues, which any work would make impertinent? As if one were to begin the day with long-suffering, and hire a man to hoe his potatoes; and in the afternoon go forth to practise Christian meekness and charity with goodness aforethought! Consider the China pride and stagnant self-complacency of mankind. This generation inclines a little to congratulate itself on being the last of an illustrious line; and in Boston and London and Paris and Rome, thinking of its long descent, it speaks of its progress in art and science and literature with satisfaction. There are the Records of the Philosophical Societies, and the public Eulogies of *Great Men!* It is the good Adam contemplating his own virtue. "Yes, we have done great deeds, and sung divine songs, which shall never die,"—that is, as long as *we* can remember them. The learned societies and great men of Assyria,—where are they? What youthful philosophers and experimentalists we are! There is not one of my readers who has yet lived a whole human life. These may be but the spring months in the life of the race. If we have had the seven-years' itch, we have not seen the seventeen-year locust yet in Concord. We are acquainted with a mere pellicle of the globe on which we live. Most have not delved six feet beneath the surface, nor leaped as many above it. We know not where we are. Beside, we are sound asleep nearly half our time. Yet we esteem ourselves wise, and have an established order on the surface. Truly, we are deep thinkers, we are ambitious spirits! As I stand over the insect crawling amid the pine needles on the forest floor, and endeavoring to conceal itself from my sight, and ask myself why it will cherish those humble thoughts, and hide its head from me who might, perhaps, be its benefactor, and impart to its race some cheering information, I am reminded of the greater Benefactor and Intelligence that stands over me, the human insect.

There is an incessant influx of novelty into the world, and yet we tolerate incredible dulness. I need only suggest what kind of sermons are still listened to in the most enlightened countries. There are such words as joy and sorrow, but they are only the burden of a psalm, sung with a nasal twang, while we believe in the ordinary and mean. We think that we can change our clothes only. It is said that the British Empire is very large and respectable, and that the United States are a first-rate power. We do not believe that a tide rises and falls behind every man which can float the British Empire like a chip, if he should ever harbor it in his mind. Who knows what sort of seventeen-year locust will next come out of the ground? The government of the world I live in was not framed, like that of Britain, in after-dinner conversations over the wine.

The life in us is like the water in the river. It may rise this year higher than man has ever known it, and flood the parched uplands; even this may be the eventful year, which will drown out all our muskrats. It was not always dry land where we dwell. I see far inland the banks which the stream anciently washed, before science began to record its freshets. Every one has heard the story which has gone the rounds of New England, of a strong and beautiful bug which came out of the dry leaf of an old table of apple-tree wood, which had stood in a farmer's kitchen for sixty years, first in Connecticut, and afterward in Massachusetts, —from an egg deposited in the living tree many years earlier still, as appeared by counting the annual layers beyond it; which was heard gnawing out for several weeks, hatched perchance by the heat of an urn. Who does not feel his faith in a resurrection and immortality strengthened by hearing of this? Who knows what beautiful and winged life, whose egg has been buried for ages under many concentric layers of woodenness in the dead dry life of society, deposited at first in the alburnum of the green and living tree, which has been gradually converted into the semblance of its well-seasoned tomb,—heard perchance gnawing out now for years by the astonished family of man, as they sat round the festive board,—may unexpectedly come forth from amidst society's most trivial and hand-selled furniture, to enjoy its perfect summer life at last!

I do not say that John or Jonathan will realize all this; but such is the character of that morrow which mere lapse of time can never make to dawn. The light which puts out our eyes is darkness to us. Only that day dawns to which we are awake. There is more day to dawn. The sun is but a morning star.   1854

NATHANIEL HAWTHORNE

1804–1864

NO AMERICAN WRITER waited longer for his public than Hawthorne. Indeed it was almost accidental that he emerged into the light at all. At Bowdoin College he did not distinguish himself as a student though, strangely enough, since shyness was already inveterate with him, he made friends who were to assist him later on. He had evidently resolved to become a writer, foolhardy decision for the scion of a Puritan family which had produced only sea captains and members of the learned professions.

He went about the business in a curious fashion. He did not try to break into literature as Longfellow did, by way of scholarship, or as Poe did, over the rough road of journalism, or as his friend Melville did, by exploiting his personal adventures in fiction. He returned to the silent Salem house of his widowed mother, climbed to his room under the eaves there and tried, for eleven years, to write. With his own hands he destroyed the manuscript of a collection of stories and the unsold copies of a novel, *Fanshawe* (1828). Some of his short stories had appeared in gift books and magazines, but Hawthorne was almost a defeated man when in 1836 he became editor of *The American Magazine of Useful and Entertaining Knowledge*. In 1837 his *Twice-Told Tales*, the printing of which was guaranteed by his college friend Bridge, established his reputation.

All his life Hawthorne was aware of the barriers between him and other men which his shyness and sense of isolation had erected. In these years he made some effort to surmount them and to find out what life in mid-century materialistic America was like. It was necessary for him to earn a living, for one thing, and he realized as well that his writing was attenuated because of his inability to do more than observe mankind from the fringes of the crowd. Twice in the next decade Hawthorne earned a grubby livelihood as a customs official, once in Boston and later in Salem. For a time (1841) he was a member of the Brook Farm community at West Roxbury. Though his marriage to Sophia Peabody, which took place in 1842, was entirely happy, it was a union of two isolated individuals, for she was as much devoted to the misty ideals of the Transcendentalists as he was habituated to seeing events symbolically and allegorically. This way of viewing the world, as he said of himself, led him to "invest his plots and characters with the aspect of scenery and people in the clouds, and to steal away the human warmth out of his compositions."

In 1850 he suddenly became a popular writer. He had completed *The Scarlet Letter*, his first novel, but hesitated to show it to Fields, the publisher, fearing that since it was "positively a hell-fired story" into which he had found it almost impossible to throw any "cheering light," the public would refuse to enter its dark and dismal passages. Fields's faith was justified; two thousand copies were sold in ten days. Hawthorne was famous at forty-six.

The rest of his productive life was crowded into eight years. In 1851 came *The House of the Seven Gables;* the next year *The Blithedale Romance*. In the latter he aired his views on the Brook Farm experiment and egoistic reformers in general. His college friend, President Pierce, whose campaign biography Hawthorne had written, appointed him Consul at Liverpool in 1853. This irksome post he left in 1856, going from England to Italy where the pagan and Catholic civilization of Rome profoundly disturbed his New England nature. His last important work, *The Marble Faun*, was the result. When he returned to Concord in 1860 he was a broken man. Though he tried to continue writing, he produced nothing of importance save a travel-book (*Our Old Home*, 1863) based on his years in England.

Few American writers (perhaps none except Henry James) have so well understood their own limitations and powers as Hawthorne. He admired realists like Trollope and would have been glad to emulate them, but knew he should not try. Like Cooper, Melville, and Thoreau, he looked on the American scene with a critical eye but he did not attempt robust satire. "Earth's Holocaust" and "The Celestial Railroad" are sharp attacks on contemporary follies but, like his tales, they are cast in his habitual allegorical mold. His longer works he called "Romances," defining them as presenting the truth of the human heart though set deliberately in such "an atmospherical medium as to bring out or mellow the lights and deepen and enrich the shadows of the picture." The human situations of his romances are real and terrible enough: in *The Scarlet Letter* the effect of guilt on Hester who confesses her sin and on Dimmesdale who keeps his secret: in *The House of the Seven Gables* the operation of the ancestral curse on the three warped and unhuman descendants who inherit it: in *The Blithedale Romance* the egoism of an obsessed reformer assaulted by the passion of the vengeful woman who loves him: in *The Marble Faun* the sense of guilt which invades Hilda's innocence because she has been an inadvertent witness of the crime of Miriam and Donatello.

Each of the romances is set against a background which throws a sinister light over the story. In none, characteristically, does Hawthorne make his scene the normal life of America of his day. For this reason, and because he so often saw his men and women less as human beings than as moral abstractions, Hawthorne lacks the stature of the greatest novelists. But it should be remembered that no writer before him in America had attempted themes so serious in their import or had looked so deeply into human motives; only Poe was so completely an artist. In Hawthorne Puritan New England at last had its novelist. As his biographer, who was, in a sense his disciple, said of him, "No one has had just his vision of life, and no one has had a literary form that more successfully expressed his vision."

Walter Blair, "Hawthorne," in *Eight American Authors, A Review of Research and Criticism*, New York, 1956, pp. 100–152.
The Complete Works of Nathaniel Hawthorne, G. P. Lathrop, ed., 12 vols., Boston, 1883.
The Complete Novels and Selected Tales of Nathaniel Hawthorne (Modern Library), N. H. Pearson, ed., New York, 1937.
The American Notebooks, Randall Stewart, ed., New Haven, 1932.
R. H. Fogle, *Hawthorne's Fiction: The Light and the Dark*, Norman, Oklahoma, 1952.
Julian Hawthorne, *Nathaniel Hawthorne and His Wife*, 2 vols., Boston, 1885.
Henry James, *Hawthorne* (English Men of Letters), New York and London, 1879.
R. R. Male, *Hawthorne's Tragic Vision*, Austin, Texas, 1957.
Randall Stewart, *Nathaniel Hawthorne, A Biography*, New Haven, 1948.
H. H. Waggoner, *Hawthorne; A Critical Study*, Cambridge, 1955.

» » YOUNG GOODMAN BROWN « «

Young Goodman Brown came forth at sunset into the street at Salem village; but put his head back, after crossing the threshold, to exchange a parting kiss with his young wife. And Faith, as the wife was aptly named, thrust her own pretty head into the street, letting the wind play with the pink ribbons of her cap while she called to Goodman Brown.

"Dearest heart," whispered she, softly and rather sadly, when her lips were close to his ear, "prithee put off your journey until sunrise and sleep in your own bed to-night. A lone woman is troubled with such dreams and such thoughts that she's afeard of herself sometimes. Pray tarry with me this night, dear husband, of all nights in the year."

"My love and my Faith," replied young Goodman Brown, "of all nights in the year, this one night must I tarry away from thee. My journey, as thou callest it, forth and back again, must needs be done 'twixt now and sunrise. What, my sweet, pretty wife, dost thou doubt me already, and we but three months married?"

"Then God bless you!" said Faith, with the pink ribbons; "and may you find all well when you come back."

"Amen!" cried Goodman Brown. "Say thy prayers, dear Faith, and go to bed at dusk, and no harm will come to thee."

So they parted; and the young man pursued his way until, being about to turn the corner by the meeting-house, he looked back and saw the head of Faith still peeping after him with a melancholy air, in spite of her pink ribbons.

"Poor little Faith!" thought he, for his heart smote him. "What a wretch am I to leave her on such an errand! She talks of dreams, too. Methought as she spoke there was trouble in her face, as if a dream had warned her what work is to be done to-night. But no, no; 'twould kill her to think it. Well, she's a blessed angel on earth; and after this one night I'll cling to her skirts and follow her to heaven."

With this excellent resolve for the future, Goodman Brown felt himself justified in making more haste on his present evil purpose. He had taken a dreary road, darkened by all the gloomiest trees of the forest, which barely stood aside to let the narrow path creep through, and closed immediately behind. It was all as lonely as could be; and there is this peculiarity in such a solitude, that the traveller knows not who may be concealed by the innumerable trunks and the thick boughs overhead; so that with lonely footsteps he may yet be passing through an unseen multitude.

"There may be a devilish Indian behind every tree," said Goodman Brown to himself; and he glanced fearfully behind him as he added, "What if the devil himself should be at my very elbow!"

His head being turned back, he passed a crook of the road, and, looking forward again, beheld the figure of a man, in grave and decent attire, seated at the foot of an old tree. He arose at Goodman Brown's approach and walked onward side by side with him.

"You are late, Goodman Brown," said he. "The clock of the Old South was striking as I came through Boston, and that is full fifteen minutes agone."

"Faith kept me back a while," replied the young man, with a tremor in his voice, caused by the sudden appearance of his companion, though not wholly unexpected.

It was now deep dusk in the forest, and deepest in that part of it where these two were journeying. As nearly as could be discerned, the second traveller was about fifty years old, apparently in the same rank of life as Goodman Brown, and bearing a considerable resemblance to him, though perhaps more in expression than features. Still they might have been taken for father and son. And yet, though the elder person was as simply clad as the younger, and as simple in manner too, he had an indescribable air of one who knew the world, and who would not have felt abashed at the governor's dinner table or in King William's court, were it possible that his affairs should call him thither. But the only thing about him that could be fixed upon as remarkable was his staff, which bore the likeness of a great black snake, so curiously wrought that it might almost be seen to twist and wriggle itself like a living serpent. This, of course, must have been an ocular deception, assisted by the uncertain light.

"Come, Goodman Brown," cried his fellow-traveller, "this is a dull pace for the beginning of a journey. Take my staff, if you are so soon weary."

"Friend," said the other, exchanging his slow pace for a full stop, "having kept covenant by meeting thee here, it is my purpose now to return whence I came. I have scruples touching the matter thou wot'st of."

"Sayest thou so?" replied he of the serpent, smiling apart. "Let us walk on, nevertheless, reasoning as we go; and if I convince thee not thou shalt turn back. We are but a little way in the forest yet."

"Too far! too far!" exclaimed the goodman, unconsciously resuming his walk. "My father never went into the woods on such an errand, nor his father before him. We have been a race of honest men and good Christians since the days of the martyrs; and shall I be the first of the name of Brown that ever took this path and kept—"

"Such company, thou wouldst say," observed the elder person, interpreting his pause. "Well said, Goodman Brown! I have been as well acquainted with your family as with every one among the Puritans; and that's no trifle to say. I helped your grandfather, the constable, when he lashed the Quaker woman so smartly through the streets of Salem; and it was I that brought your father a pitch-pine knot, kindled at my own hearth, to set fire to an Indian village, in King Philip's war. They were my good friends, both; and many a pleasant walk have we had along this path, and returned merrily after midnight. I would fain be friends with you for their sake."

"If it be as thou sayest," replied Goodman Brown, "I marvel they never spoke of these matters; or, verily, I marvel not, seeing that the least rumor of the sort would have driven them from New England. We are a people of prayer, and good works to boot, and abide no such wickedness."

"Wickedness or not," said the traveller with the twisted staff, "I have a very general acquaintance here in New England. The deacons of many a church have drunk the communion wine with me; the selectmen of divers towns make me their chairman; and a majority of the Great and General Court are firm supporters of my interest. The governor and I, too—But these are state secrets."

"Can this be so?" cried Goodman Brown, with a stare of amazement at his undisturbed companion. "Howbeit, I have nothing to do with the governor and council; they have their own ways, and are no rule for a simple husbandman like me. But, were I to go on with thee, how should I meet the eye of that good old man, our minister, at Salem village? Oh, his voice would make me tremble both Sabbath day and lecture day."

Thus far the elder traveller had listened with due gravity; but now burst into a fit of irrepressible mirth, shaking himself so violently that his snake-like staff actually seemed to wriggle in sympathy.

"Ha! ha! ha!" shouted he again and again; then composing himself, "Well, go on, Goodman Brown, go on; but, prithee, don't kill me with laughing."

"Well, then, to end the matter at once," said Goodman Brown, considerably nettled, "there is my wife, Faith. It would break her dear little heart; and I'd rather break my own."

"Nay, if that be the case," answered the other, "e'en go thy ways, Goodman Brown. I would not for twenty old women like the one hobbling before us that Faith should come to any harm."

As he spoke he pointed his staff at a female figure on the path, in whom Goodman Brown recognized a very pious and exemplary dame, who had taught him his catechism in youth, and was still his moral and spiritual adviser, jointly with the minister and Deacon Gookin.

"A marvel, truly, that Goody Cloyse should be so far in the wilderness at nightfall," said he. "But with your leave, friend, I shall take a cut through the woods until we have left this Christian woman behind. Being a stranger to you, she might ask whom I was consorting with and whither I was going."

"Be it so," said his fellow-traveller. "Betake you to the woods, and let me keep the path."

Accordingly the young man turned aside, but took care to watch his companion, who advanced softly along the road until he had come within a staff's length of the old dame. She, meanwhile, was making the best of her way, with singular speed for so aged a woman, and mumbling some indistinct words—a prayer, doubtless—as she went. The traveller put forth his staff and touched her withered neck with what seemed the serpent's tail.

"The devil!" screamed the pious old lady.

"Then Goody Cloyse knows her old friend?" observed the traveller, confronting her and leaning on his writhing stick.

"Ah, forsooth, and is it your worship indeed?" cried the good dame. "Yea, truly is it, and in the very image of my old gossip, Goodman Brown, the grandfather of the silly fellow that now is. But—would your worship believe it?—my broomstick hath strangely disappeared, stolen, as I suspect, by that unhanged witch, Goody Cory, and that, too, when I was all anointed with the juice of smallage, and cinquefoil, and wolf's bane—"

"Mingled with fine wheat and the fat of a new-born babe," said the shape of old Goodman Brown.

"Ah, your worship knows the recipe," cried the old lady, cackling aloud. "So, as I was saying, being all ready for the meeting, and no horse to ride on, I made up my mind to foot it; for they tell me there is a nice young man to be taken into communion to-night. But now your good worship will lend me your arm, and we shall be there in a twinkling."

"That can hardly be," answered her friend. "I may not spare you my arm, Goody Cloyse; but here is my staff, if you will."

So saying, he threw it down at her feet, where, perhaps, it assumed life, being one of the rods which its owner had formerly lent to the Egyptian magi. Of this fact, however, Goodman Brown could not take cognizance. He had cast up his eyes in astonishment, and, looking down again, beheld neither Goody Cloyse nor the serpentine staff, but his fellow-traveller alone, who waited for him as calmly as if nothing had happened.

"That old woman taught me my catechism," said the young man; and there was a world of meaning in this simple comment.

They continued to walk onward, while the elder traveller exhorted his companion to make good speed and persevere in the path, discoursing so aptly that his arguments seemed rather to spring up in the bosom of his auditor than to be suggested by himself. As they went, he plucked a branch of maple to serve for a walking stick, and began to strip it of the twigs and little boughs, which were wet with evening dew. The moment his fingers touched them they became strangely withered and dried up as with a week's sunshine. Thus the pair proceeded, at a good free pace, until suddenly, in a gloomy hollow of the road, Goodman Brown sat himself down on the stump of a tree and refused to go any farther.

"Friend," said he, stubbornly, "my mind is made up. Not another step will I budge on this errand. What if a wretched old woman do choose to go to the devil when I thought she was going to heaven: is that any reason why I should quit my dear Faith and go after her?"

"You will think better of this by and by," said his acquaintance, composedly. "Sit here and rest yourself a while; and when you feel like moving again, there is my staff to help you along."

Without more words, he threw his companion the maple stick, and was as speedily out of sight as if he had vanished into the deepening gloom. The young man sat a few moments by the roadside, applauding himself greatly, and thinking with how clear a conscience he should meet the minister in his morning walk, nor shrink from the eye of good old Deacon Gookin. And what calm sleep would be his that very night, which was to have been spent so wickedly, but so purely and sweetly now, in the arms of Faith! Amidst these pleasant and praiseworthy meditations, Goodman Brown heard the tramp of horses along the road, and deemed it advisable to conceal himself within the verge of the forest, conscious of the guilty purpose that had brought him thither, though now so happily turned from it.

On came the hoof tramps and the voices of the riders, two grave old voices, conversing soberly as they drew near. These mingled sounds appeared to pass along the road, within a few yards of the young man's hiding-place; but, owing doubtless to the depth of the gloom at that particular spot, neither the travellers nor their steeds were visible. Though their figures brushed the small boughs by the wayside, it could not be seen that they intercepted, even for a moment, the faint gleam from the strip of bright sky athwart which they must have passed. Goodman Brown alternately crouched and stood on tiptoe, pulling aside the branches and thrusting forth his head as far as he durst without discerning so much as a shadow. It vexed him the more, because he could have sworn, were such a thing possible, that he recognized the voices of the minister and Deacon Gookin, jogging along quietly, as they were wont to do, when bound to some ordination or ecclesiastical council. While yet within hearing, one of the riders stopped to pluck a switch.

"Of the two, reverend sir," said the voice like the deacon's, "I had rather miss an ordination dinner than to-night's meeting. They tell me that some of our community are to be here from Falmouth and beyond, and others from Connecticut and Rhode Island, besides several of the Indian powwows, who, after their fashion, know almost as much deviltry as the best of us. Moreover, there is a goodly young woman to be taken into communion."

"Mighty well, Deacon Gookin!" replied the solemn old tones of the minister. "Spur up, or we shall be late. Nothing can be done, you know, until I get on the ground."

The hoofs clattered again; and the voices, talking so strangely in the empty air, passed on through the forest, where no church had ever been gathered or solitary Christian prayed. Whither, then, could these holy men be journeying so deep into the heathen wilderness? Young Goodman Brown caught hold of a tree for support, being ready to sink down on the ground, faint and overburdened with the heavy sickness of his heart. He looked up to the sky, doubting whether there really was a heaven above him. Yet there was the blue arch, and the stars brightening in it.

"With heaven above and Faith below, I will yet stand firm against the devil!" cried Goodman Brown.

While he still gazed upward into the deep arch of the firmament and had lifted his hands to pray, a cloud, though no wind was stirring, hurried across the zenith and hid the brightening stars. The blue sky was still visible, except directly overhead, where this black mass of cloud was sweeping swiftly northward. Aloft in the air, as if from the depths of the cloud, came a confused and doubtful sound of voices. Once the listener fancied that he could distinguish the accents of townspeople of his own, men and women, both pious and ungodly, many of whom he had met at the communion table, and had seen others rioting at the tavern. The next moment, so indistinct were the sounds, he doubted whether he had heard aught but the murmur of the old forest, whispering without a wind. Then came a stronger swell of those familiar tones, heard daily in the sunshine at Salem village, but never until now from a cloud of night. There was one voice, of a young woman, uttering lamentations, yet with an uncertain sorrow, and entreating for some favor, which, perhaps, it would grieve her to obtain; and all the unseen multitude, both saints and sinners, seemed to encourage her onward.

"Faith!" shouted Goodman Brown, in a voice of agony and desperation; and the echoes of the forest mocked him, crying, "Faith! Faith!" as if bewildered wretches were seeking her all through the wilderness.

The cry of grief, rage, and terror was yet piercing the night, when the unhappy husband held his breath for a response. There was a scream, drowned immediately in a louder murmur of voices, fading into far-off laughter, as the dark cloud swept away, leaving the clear and silent sky above Goodman Brown. But something fluttered lightly down through the air and caught on the branch of a tree. The young man seized it, and beheld a pink ribbon.

"My Faith is gone!" cried he, after one stupefied moment. "There is no good on earth; and sin is but a name. Come, devil; for to thee is this world given."

And, maddened with despair, so that he laughed loud and long, did Goodman Brown grasp his staff and set forth again, at such a rate that he seemed to fly along the forest path rather than to walk or run. The road grew wilder and drearier and more faintly traced, and vanished at length, leaving him in the heart of the dark wilderness, still rushing onward with the instinct that guides mortal man to evil. The whole forest was peopled with frightful sounds—the creaking of the trees, the howling of wild beasts, and the yell of Indians; while sometimes the wind tolled like a distant church bell, and sometimes gave a broad roar around the traveller, as if all Nature were laughing him to scorn. But he was himself the chief horror of the scene, and shrank not from its other horrors.

"Ha! ha! ha!" roared Goodman Brown when the wind laughed at him. "Let us hear which will laugh loudest. Think not to frighten me with your deviltry. Come witch, come wizard, come Indian powwow, come devil himself, and here comes Goodman Brown. You may as well fear him as he fear you."

In truth, all through the haunted forest there could be nothing more frightful than the figure of Goodman Brown. On he flew among the black pines, brandishing his staff with frenzied gestures, now giving vent to an inspiration of horrid blasphemy, and now shouting forth such laughter as set all the echoes of the forest laughing like demons around him. The fiend in his own shape is less hideous than when he rages in the breast of man. Thus sped the demoniac on his course, until, quivering among the trees, he saw a red light before him, as when the felled trunks and branches of a clearing have been set on fire, and throw up their lurid blaze against the sky, at the hour of midnight. He paused, in a lull of the tempest that had driven him onward, and heard the swell of what seemed a hymn, rolling solemnly from a distance with the weight of many voices. He knew the tune; it was a familiar one in the choir of the village meeting-house. The verse died heavily away, and was lengthened by a chorus, not of human voices, but of all the sounds of the benighted wilderness pealing in awful harmony together. Goodman Brown cried out, and his cry was lost to his own ear by its unison with the cry of the desert.

In the interval of silence he stole forward until the light glared full upon his eyes. At one extremity of an open space, hemmed in by the dark wall of the forest, arose a rock, bearing some rude, natural resemblance either to an altar or a pulpit, and surrounded by four blazing pines, their tops aflame, their stems untouched, like candles at an evening meeting. The mass of foliage that had overgrown the summit of the rock was all on fire, blazing high into the night and fitfully illuminating the whole field. Each pendent twig and leafy festoon was in a blaze. As the red light arose and fell, a numerous congregation alternately shone forth, then disappeared in shadow, and again grew, as it were, out of the darkness, peopling the heart of the solitary woods at once.

"A grave and dark-clad company," quoth Goodman Brown.

In truth they were such. Among them, quivering to and fro between gloom and splendor, appeared faces that would be seen next day at the council board of the province, and others which, Sabbath after Sabbath, looked devoutly heavenward, and benignantly over the crowded pews, from the holiest pulpits in the land. Some affirm that the lady of the governor was there. At least there were high dames well known to her, and wives of honored husbands, and widows, a great multitude, and ancient maidens, all of excellent repute, and fair young girls, who trembled lest their mothers should espy them. Either the sudden gleams of light flashing over the obscure field bedazzled Goodman Brown, or he recognized a score of the church members of Salem village famous for their especial sanctity. Good old Deacon Gookin had arrived, and waited at the skirts of that venerable saint, his revered pastor. But, irreverently consorting with these grave, reputable, and pious people, these elders of the church, these chaste dames and dewy virgins, there were men of dissolute lives and women of spotted fame, wretches given over to all mean and filthy vice, and suspected even of horrid crimes. It was strange to see that the good shrank not from the wicked, nor were the sinners abashed by the saints. Scattered also among their pale-faced enemies were the Indian priests, or powwows, who had often scared their native forest with more hideous incantations than any known to English witchcraft.

"But where is Faith?" thought Goodman Brown; and, as hope came into his heart, he trembled.

Another verse of the hymn arose, a slow and mournful strain, such as the pious love, but joined to words which expressed all that our nature can conceive of sin, and darkly hinted at far more. Unfathomable to mere mortals is the lore of fiends. Verse after verse was sung; and still the chorus of the desert swelled between like the deepest tone of a mighty organ; and with the final peal of that dreadful anthem there came a sound, as if the roaring wind, the rushing streams, the howling beasts, and every other voice of the unconcerted wilderness were mingling and according with the voice of guilty man in homage to the prince of all. The four blazing pines threw up a loftier flame, and obscurely discovered shapes and visages of horror on the smoke wreaths above the impious assembly. At the same moment the fire on the rock shot redly forth and formed a glowing arch above its base, where now appeared a figure. With reverence be it spoken, the figure bore no slight similitude, both in garb and manner, to some grave divine of the New England churches.

"Bring forth the converts!" cried a voice that echoed through the field and rolled into the forest.

At the word, Goodman Brown stepped forth from the shadow of the trees and approached the congregation, with whom he felt a loathful brotherhood by the sympathy of all that was wicked in his heart. He could have well-nigh sworn that the shape of his own dead father beckoned him to advance, looking downward from a smoke wreath, while a woman, with dim features of despair, threw out her hand to warn him back. Was it his mother? But he had no power to retreat one step, nor to resist, even in thought, when the minister and good old Deacon Gookin seized his arm and led him to the blazing rock. Thither came also the slender form of a veiled female, led between

Goody Cloyse, that pious teacher of the catechism, and Martha Carrier, who had received the devil's promise to be queen of hell. A rampant hag was she. And there stood the proselytes beneath the canopy of fire.

"Welcome, my children," said the dark figure, "to the communion of your race. Ye have found thus young your nature and your destiny. My children, look behind you!"

They turned; and flashing forth, as it were, in a sheet of flame, the fiend worshippers were seen; the smile of welcome gleamed darkly on every visage.

"There," resumed the sable form, "are all whom ye have reverenced from youth. Ye deemed them holier than yourselves, and shrank from your own sin, contrasting it with their lives of righteousness and prayerful aspirations heavenward. Yet here are they all in my worshipping assembly. This night it shall be granted you to know their secret deeds: how hoary-bearded elders of the church have whispered wanton words to the young maids of their households; how many a woman, eager for widows' weeds, has given her husband a drink at bedtime and let him sleep his last sleep in her bosom; how beardless youths have made haste to inherit their fathers' wealth; and how fair damsels—blush not, sweet ones— have dug little graves in the garden, and bidden me, the sole guest, to an infant's funeral. By the sympathy of your human hearts for sin ye shall scent out all the places—whether in church, bedchamber, street, field, or forest—where crime has been committed, and shall exult to behold the whole earth one stain of guilt, one mighty blood spot. Far more than this. It shall be yours to penetrate, in every bosom, the deep mystery of sin, the fountain of all wicked arts, and which inexhaustibly supplies more evil impulses than human power—than my power at its utmost—can make manifest in deeds. And now, my children, look upon each other."

They did so; and, by the blaze of the hell-kindled torches, the wretched man beheld his Faith, and the wife her husband, trembling before that unhallowed altar.

"Lo, there ye stand, my children," said the figure, in a deep and solemn tone, almost sad with its despairing awfulness, as if his once angelic nature could yet mourn for our miserable race. "Depending upon one another's hearts, ye had still hoped that virtue were not all a dream. Now are ye undeceived. Evil is the nature of mankind. Evil must be your only happiness. Welcome again, my children, to the communion of your race."

"Welcome," repeated the fiend worshippers, in one cry of despair and triumph.

And there they stood, the only pair, as it seemed, who were yet hesitating on the verge of wickedness in this dark world. A basin was hollowed, naturally, in the rock. Did it contain water, reddened by the lurid light? or was it blood? or, perchance, a liquid flame? Herein did the shape of evil dip his hand and prepare to lay the mark of baptism upon their foreheads, that they might be partakers of the mystery of sin, more conscious of the secret guilt of others, both in deed and thought, than they could now be of their own. The husband cast one look at his pale wife, and Faith at him. What polluted wretches would the next glance show them to each other, shuddering alike at what they disclosed and what they saw!

"Faith! Faith!" cried the husband, "look up to heaven, and resist the wicked one."

Whether Faith obeyed he knew not. Hardly had he spoken when he found himself amid calm night and solitude, listening to a roar of the wind which died heavily away through the forest. He staggered against the rock, and felt it chill and damp; while a hanging twig, that had been all on fire, besprinkled his cheek with the coldest dew.

The next morning young Goodman Brown came slowly into the street of Salem village, staring around him like a bewildered man. The good old minister was taking a walk along the graveyard to get an appetite for breakfast and meditate his sermon, and bestowed a blessing, as he passed, on Goodman Brown. He shrank from the venerable saint as if to avoid an anathema. Old Deacon Gookin was at domestic worship, and the holy words of his prayer were heard through the open window. "What God doth the wizard pray to?" quoth Goodman Brown. Goody Cloyse, that excellent old Chris-

tian, stood in the early sunshine at her own lattice, catechizing a little girl who had brought her a pint of morning's milk. Goodman Brown snatched away the child as from the grasp of the fiend himself. Turning the corner by the meeting-house, he spied the head of Faith, with the pink ribbons, gazing anxiously forth, and bursting into such joy at sight of him that she skipped along the street and almost kissed her husband before the whole village. But 10 Goodman Brown looked sternly and sadly into her face, and passed on without a greeting.

Had Goodman Brown fallen asleep in the forest and only dreamed a wild dream of a witch-meeting?

Be it so if you will; but, alas! it was a dream of evil omen for young Goodman Brown. A stern, a sad, a darkly meditative, a distrustful, if not a desperate man did he become from the night of that fearful dream. On the Sabbath 20 day, when the congregation were singing a holy psalm, he could not listen because an anthem of sin rushed loudly upon his ear and drowned all the blessed strain. When the minister spoke from the pulpit with power and fervid eloquence, and, with his hand on the open Bible, of the sacred truths of our religion, and of saint-like lives and triumphant deaths, and of future bliss or misery unutterable, then did Goodman Brown turn pale, dreading lest the 30 roof should thunder down upon the gray blasphemer and his hearers. Often, awaking suddenly at midnight, he shrank from the bosom of Faith; and at morning or eventide, when the family knelt down at prayer, he scowled and muttered to himself, and gazed sternly at his wife, and turned away. And when he had lived long, and was borne to his grave a hoary corpse, followed by Faith, an aged woman, and children and grandchildren, a 40 goodly procession, besides neighbors not a few, they carved no hopeful verse upon his tombstone, for his dying hour was gloom.   1835

» » THE GRAY CHAMPION « «

There was once a time when New England groaned under the actual pressure of heavier wrongs than those threatened ones which brought on the Revolution. James II, the bigoted successor of Charles the Voluptuous, had annulled the charters of all the colonies, and sent a harsh and unprincipled soldier to take

away our liberties and endanger our religion. The administration of Sir Edmund Andros 50 lacked scarcely a single characteristic of tyranny: a Governor and Council, holding office from the King, and wholly independent of the country; laws made and taxes levied without concurrence of the people, immediate or by their representatives; the rights of private citizens violated, and the titles of all landed property declared void; the voice of complaint stifled by restrictions on the press; and, finally, disaffection overawed by the first band of mercenary troops that ever marched on our free soil. For two years our ancestors were kept in sullen submission, by that filial love which had invariably secured their allegiance to the mother country, whether its head chanced to be a Parliament, Protector, or Popish Monarch. Till these evil times, however, such allegiance had been merely nominal, and the colonists had ruled themselves, enjoying far more freedom, than is even yet the privilege of the native subjects of Great Britain.

At length, a rumor reached our shores that the Prince of Orange had ventured on an enterprise, the success of which would be the triumph of civil and religious rights and the salvation of New England. It was but a doubtful whisper; it might be false, or the attempt might fail; and, in either case, the man, that stirred against King James, would lose his head. Still, the intelligence produced a marked effect. The people smiled mysteriously in the streets, and threw bold glances at their oppressors; while, far and wide, there was a subdued and silent agitation, as if the slightest signal would rouse the whole land from its sluggish despondency. Aware of their danger, the rulers resolved to avert it by an imposing display of strength, and perhaps to confirm their despotism by yet harsher measures. One afternoon in April, 1689, Sir Edmund Andros and his favorite councillors, being warm with wine, assembled the red-coats of the Governor's Guard, and made their appearance in the streets of Boston. The sun was near setting when the march commenced.

The roll of the drum, at that unquiet crisis, seemed to go through the streets, less as the martial music of the soldiers, than as a muster call to the inhabitants themselves. A multitude, by various avenues, assembled in King Street, which was destined to be the scene, nearly a century afterwards, of another encounter between the troops of Britain, and a people struggling against her tyranny. Though more than sixty years had elapsed, since the Pilgrims came, this crowd of their descendants still showed the strong and sombre features of their character, perhaps more strikingly in such a stern emergency than on happier occasions. There were the sober garb, the general severity of mien, the gloomy but undismayed expression, the scriptural forms of speech, and the confidence in Heaven's blessing on a righteous cause, which would have marked a band of the original Puritans, when threatened by some peril of the wilderness. Indeed, it was not yet time for the old spirit to be extinct; since there were men in the street, that day, who had worshipped there beneath the trees, before a house was reared to the God for whom they had become exiles. Old soldiers of the Parliament were here, too, smiling grimly at the thought, that their aged arms might strike another blow against the house of Stuart. Here, also, were the veterans of King Philip's war, who had burned villages and slaughtered young and old, with pious fierceness, while the godly souls throughout the land were helping them with prayer. Several ministers were scattered among the crowd, which, unlike all other mobs, regarded them with such reverence, as if there were sanctity in their very garments. These holy men exerted their influence to quiet the people, but not to disperse them. Meantime, the purpose of the Governor, in disturbing the peace of the town, at a period when the slightest commotion might throw the country into a ferment, was almost the universal subject of inquiry, and variously explained.

"Satan will strike his master-stroke presently," cried some, "because he knoweth that his time is short. All our godly pastors are to be dragged to prison! We shall see them at a Smithfield fire in King Street!"

Hereupon the people of each parish gathered closer round their minister, who looked calmly upwards and assumed a more apostolic dignity, as well befitted a candidate for the highest honor of his profession, the crown of martyrdom. It was actually fancied, at that period, that New England might have a John Rogers of her own, to take the place of that worthy in the Primer.

"The Pope of Rome has given orders for a new St. Bartholomew!" cried others. "We are to be massacred, man and male child!"

Neither was this rumor wholly discredited, although the wiser class believed the Governor's object somewhat less atrocious. His predecessor under the old charter, Bradstreet, a venerable companion of the first settlers, was known to be in town. There were grounds for conjecturing, that Sir Edmund Andros intended, at once, to strike terror, by a parade of military force, and to confound the opposite faction by possessing himself of their chief.

"Stand firm for the old charter Governor!" shouted the crowd, seizing upon the idea. "The good old Governor Bradstreet!"

While this cry was at the loudest, the people were surprised by the well-known figure of Governor Bradstreet himself, a patriarch of nearly ninety, who appeared on the elevated steps of a door, and, with characteristic mildness, besought them to submit to the constituted authorities.

"My children," concluded this venerable person, "do nothing rashly. Cry not aloud, but pray for the welfare of New England, and expect patiently what the Lord will do in this matter!"

The event was soon to be decided. All this time, the roll of the drum had been approaching through Cornhill, louder and deeper, till with reverberations from house to house, and the regular tramp of martial footsteps, it burst into the street. A double rank of soldiers made their appearance, occupying the whole breadth of the passage, with shouldered matchlocks, and matches burning, so as to present a row of fires in the dusk. Their steady march was like the progress of a machine, that would roll irresistibly over everything in its way. Next, moving slowly, with a confused clatter of hoofs on the pavement, rode a party of mounted gentlemen, the central figure being Sir Edmund Andros, elderly, but erect and soldier-like. Those around him were his favorite councillors, and the bitterest foes of New England. At his right hand rode Edward Randolph, our arch-enemy, that "blasted wretch," as Cotton Mather calls him, who achieved the downfall of our ancient government, and was followed with a sensible curse, through life and to his grave. On the other side was Bullivant, scattering jests and mockery as he rode along. Dudley came behind, with a downcast look, dreading, as well he might, to meet the indignant gaze of the people, who beheld him, their only countryman by birth, among the oppressors of his native land. The captain of a frigate in the harbor, and two or three civil officers under the Crown, were also there. But the figure which most attracted the public eye, and stirred up the deepest feeling, was the Episcopal clergyman of King's Chapel, riding haughtily among the magistrates in his priestly vestments, the fitting representative of prelacy and persecution, the union of church and state, and all those abominations which had driven the Puritans to the wilderness. Another guard of soldiers, in double rank, brought up the rear.

The whole scene was a picture of the condition of New England, and its moral, the deformity of any government that does not grow out of the nature of things and the character of the people. On one side the religious multitude, with their sad visages and dark attire, and on the other, the group of despotic [10] rulers, with the high churchman in the midst, and here and there a crucifix at their bosoms, all magnificently clad, flushed with wine, proud of unjust authority, and scoffing at the universal groan. And the mercenary soldiers, waiting but the word to deluge the street with blood, showed the only means by which obedience could be secured.

"O Lord of Hosts," cried a voice among the crowd, "provide a Champion for thy people!" [20]

This ejaculation was loudly uttered, and served as a herald's cry, to introduce a remarkable personage. The crowd had rolled back, and were now huddled together nearly at the extremity of the street, while the soldiers had advanced no more than a third of its length. The intervening space was empty—a paved solitude, between lofty edifices, which threw almost a twilight shadow over it. Suddenly, there was seen the figure of an ancient man, [30] who seemed to have emerged from among the people, and was walking by himself along the centre of the street, to confront the armed band. He wore the old Puritan dress, a dark cloak and a steeple-crowned hat, in the fashion of at least fifty years before, with a heavy sword upon his thigh, but a staff in his hand to assist the tremulous gait of age.

When at some distance from the multitude, the old man turned slowly round, displaying a [40] face of antique majesty, rendered doubly venerable by the hoary beard that descended on his breast. He made a gesture at once of encouragement and warning, then turned again, and resumed his way.

"Who is this gray patriarch?" asked the young men of their sires.

"Who is this venerable brother?" asked the old men among themselves.

But none could make reply. The fathers of [50] the people, those of fourscore years and upwards, were disturbed, deeming it strange that they should forget one of such evident authority, whom they must have known in their early days, the associate of Winthrop, and all the old councillors, giving laws, and making prayers, and leading them against the savage. The elderly men ought to have remembered him, too, with locks as gray in their youth, as their own were now. And the young! How could he have passed so utterly from their memories—that hoary sire, the relic of long-departed times, whose awful benediction had surely been bestowed on their uncovered heads, in childhood?

"Whence did he come? What is his purpose? Who can this old man be?" whispered the wondering crowd.

Meanwhile, the venerable stranger, staff in hand, was pursuing his solitary walk along the centre of the street. As he drew near the advancing soldiers, and as the roll of their drum came full upon his ear, the old man raised himself to a loftier mien, while the decrepitude of age seemed to fall from his shoulders, leaving him in gray but unbroken dignity. Now, he marched onward with a warrior's step, keeping time to the military music. Thus the aged form advanced on one side, and the whole parade of soldiers and magistrates on the other, till, when scarcely twenty yards remained between, the old man grasped his staff by the middle, and held it before him like a leader's truncheon.

"Stand!" cried he.

The eye, the face, and attitude of command; the solemn, yet warlike peal of that voice, fit either to rule a host in the battle field or be raised to God in prayer, were irresistible. At the old man's word and outstretched arm, the roll of the drum was hushed at once, and the advancing line stood still. A tremulous enthusiasm seized upon the multitude. That stately form, combining the leader and the saint, so gray, so dimly seen, in such an ancient garb, could only belong to some old champion of the righteous cause, whom the oppressor's drum had summoned from his grave. They raised a shout of awe and exultation, and looked for the deliverance of New England.

The Governor, and the gentlemen of his party, perceiving themselves brought to an unexpected stand, rode hastily forward, as if they would have pressed their snorting and affrighted horses right against the hoary apparition. He, however, blenched not a step, but glancing his severe eye round the group, which half encompassed him, at last bent it sternly on Sir Edmund Andros. One would have thought that the dark old man was chief ruler

there, and that the Governor and Council, with soldiers at their back, representing the whole power and authority of the Crown, had no alternative but obedience.

"What does this old fellow here?" cried Edward Randolph, fiercely. "On, Sir Edmund! Bid the soldiers forward, and give the dotard the same choice that you give all his countrymen—to stand aside or be trampled on!"

"Nay, nay, let us show respect to the good grandsire," said Bullivant, laughing. "See you not, he is some old round-headed dignitary, who hath lain asleep these thirty years, and knows nothing of the change of times? Doubtless, he thinks to put us down with a proclamation in Old Noll's name!"

"Are you mad, old man?" demanded Sir Edmund Andros, in loud and harsh tones. "How dare you stay the march of King James's Governor?"

"I have stayed the march of a king himself, ere now," replied the gray figure, with stern composure. "I am here, Sir Governor, because the cry of an oppressed people hath disturbed me in my secret place; and beseeching this favor earnestly of the Lord, it was vouchsafed me to appear once again on earth, in the good old cause of his saints. And what speak ye of James? There is no longer a Popish tyrant on the throne of England, and by to-morrow noon, his name shall be a byword in this very street, where ye would make it a word of terror. Back, thou that wast a Governor, back! With this night thy power is ended—to-morrow, the prison!—back, lest I foretell the scaffold!"

The people had been drawing nearer and nearer, and drinking in the words of their champion, who spoke in accents long disused, like one unaccustomed to converse, except with the dead of many years ago. But his voice stirred their souls. They confronted the soldiers, not wholly without arms, and ready to convert the very stones of the street into deadly weapons. Sir Edmund Andros looked at the old man; then he cast his hard and cruel eye over the multitude, and beheld them burning with that lurid wrath, so difficult to kindle or to quench; and again he fixed his gaze on the aged form, which stood obscurely in an open space, where neither friend nor foe had thrust himself. What were his thoughts, he uttered no word which might discover. But whether the oppressor were overawed by the Gray Champion's look, or perceived his peril in the threatening attitude of the people, it is certain that he gave back, and ordered his soldiers to commence a slow and guarded retreat. Before another sunset, the Governor, and all that rode so proudly with him, were prisoners, and long ere it was known that James had abdicated, King William was proclaimed throughout New England.

But where was the Gray Champion? Some reported, that when the troops had gone from King Street, and the people were thronging tumultuously in their rear, Bradstreet, the aged Governor, was seen to embrace a form more aged than his own. Others soberly affirmed, that while they marvelled at the venerable grandeur of his aspect, the old man had faded from their eyes, melting slowly into the hues of twilight, till, where he stood, there was an empty space. But all agreed that the hoary shape was gone. The men of that generation watched for his reappearance, in sunshine and in twilight, but never saw him more, nor knew when his funeral passed, nor where his gravestone was.

And who was the Gray Champion? Perhaps his name might be found in the records of that stern Court of Justice, which passed a sentence, too mighty for the age, but glorious in all after times, for its humbling lesson to the monarch and its high example to the subject. I have heard, that whenever the descendants of the Puritans are to show the spirit of their sires, the old man appears again. When eighty years had passed, he walked once more in King Street. Five years later, in the twilight of an April morning, he stood on the green, beside the meeting-house, at Lexington, where now the obelisk of granite, with a slab of slate inlaid, commemorates the first fallen of the Revolution. And when our fathers were toiling at the breastwork on Bunker's Hill, all through that night the old warrior walked his rounds. Long, long may it be, ere he comes again! His hour is one of darkness, and adversity, and peril. But should domestic tyranny oppress us, or the invader's step pollute our soil, still may the Gray Champion come; for he is the type of New England's hereditary spirit; and his shadowy march, on the eve of danger, must ever be the pledge, that New England's sons will vindicate their ancestry. 1835

» » THE MINISTER'S BLACK VEIL « «

A PARABLE [1]

The sexton stood in the porch of Milford meeting-house, pulling busily at the bell rope. The old people of the village came stooping along the street. Children with bright faces, tripped merrily beside their parents, or mimicked a graver gait, in the conscious dignity of their Sunday clothes. Spruce bachelors looked sidelong at the pretty maidens, and fancied that the Sabbath sunshine made them prettier than on week days. When the throng had mostly streamed into the porch, the sexton began to toll the bell, keeping his eye on the Reverend Mr. Hooper's door. The first glimpse of the clergyman's figure, was the signal for the bell to cease its summons.

"But what has good Parson Hooper got upon his face?" cried the sexton in astonishment.

All within hearing immediately turned about, and beheld the semblance of Mr. Hooper, pacing slowly his meditative way towards the meeting-house. With one accord they started, expressing more wonder than if some strange minister were coming to dust the cushions of Mr. Hooper's pulpit.

"Are you sure it is our parson?" inquired Goodman Gray of the sexton.

"Of a certainty it is good Mr. Hooper," replied the sexton. "He was to have exchanged pulpits with Parson Shute, of Westbury; but Parson Shute sent to excuse himself yesterday, being to preach a funeral sermon."

The cause of so much amazement may appear sufficiently slight. Mr. Hooper, a gentlemanly person, of about thirty, though still a bachelor, was dressed with due clerical neatness, as if a careful wife had starched his band, and brushed the weekly dust from his Sunday's garb. There was but one thing remarkable in his appearance. Swathed about his forehead, and hanging down over his face, so low as to

[1] Another clergyman in New England, Mr. Joseph Moody, of York, Maine, who died about eighty years since, made himself remarkable by the same eccentricity that is here related of the Reverend Mr. Hooper. In his case, however, the symbol had a different import. In early life he had accidentally killed a beloved friend; and from that day till the hour of his own death, he hid his face from men. [Hawthorne's note.]

be shaken by his breath, Mr. Hooper had on a black veil. On a nearer view, it seemed to consist of two folds of crape, which entirely concealed his features, except the mouth and chin, but probably did not intercept his sight, further than to give a darkened aspect to all living and inanimate things. With this gloomy shade before him, good Mr. Hooper walked onward, at a slow and quiet pace, stooping somewhat, and looking on the ground, as is customary with abstracted men, yet nodding kindly to those of his parishioners who still waited on the meeting-house steps. But so wonder-struck were they, that his greeting hardly met with a return.

"I can't really feel as if good Mr. Hooper's face was behind that piece of crape," said the sexton.

"I don't like it," muttered an old woman, as she hobbled into the meeting-house. "He has changed himself into something awful, only by hiding his face."

"Our parson has gone mad!" cried Goodman Gray, following him across the threshold.

A rumor of some unaccountable phenomenon had preceded Mr. Hooper into the meeting-house, and set all the congregation astir. Few could refrain from twisting their heads towards the door, many stood upright, and turned directly about; while several little boys clambered upon the seats, and came down again with a terrible racket. There was a general bustle, a rustling of the women's gowns and shuffling of the men's feet, greatly at variance with that hushed repose which should attend the entrance of the minister. But Mr. Hooper appeared not to notice the perturbation of his people. He entered with an almost noiseless step, bent his head mildly to the pews on each side, and bowed as he passed his oldest parishioner, a white-haired great-grandsire, who occupied an arm chair in the centre of the aisle. It was strange to observe how slowly this venerable man became conscious of something singular in the appearance of his pastor. He seemed not fully to partake of the prevailing wonder, till Mr. Hooper had ascended the stairs, and showed himself in the pulpit, face to face with his congregation, except for the black veil. That mysterious emblem was never once withdrawn. It shook with his measured breath, as he gave out the psalm; it threw its obscurity between him and the holy page, as he read the Scriptures; and while he prayed, the veil lay heavily on his uplifted countenance. Did he seek to hide it from the dread Being whom he was addressing?

Such was the effect of this simple piece of crape, that more than one woman of delicate nerves was forced to leave the meeting-house. Yet perhaps the pale-faced congregation was almost as fearful a sight to the minister, as his black veil to them.

Mr. Hooper had the reputation of a good preacher, but not an energetic one: he strove to win his people heavenward by mild, persuasive influences, rather than to drive them thither by the thunders of the Word. The sermon which he now delivered, was marked by the same characteristics of style and manner, as the general series of his pulpit oratory. But there was something, either in the sentiment of the discourse itself, or in the imagination of the auditors, which made it greatly the most powerful effort that they had ever heard from their pastor's lips. It was tinged, rather more darkly than usual, with the gentle gloom of Mr. Hooper's temperament. The subject had reference to secret sin, and those sad mysteries which we hide from our nearest and dearest, and would fain conceal from our own consciousness, even forgetting that the Omniscient can detect them. A subtle power was breathed into his words. Each member of the congregation, the most innocent girl, and the man of hardened breast, felt as if the preacher had crept upon them, behind his awful veil, and discovered their hoarded iniquity of deed or thought. Many spread their clasped hands on their bosoms. There was nothing terrible in what Mr. Hooper said, at least, no violence; and yet, with every tremor of his melancholy voice, the hearers quaked. An unsought pathos came hand in hand with awe. So sensible were the audience of some unwonted attribute in their minister, that they longed for a breath of wind to blow aside the veil, almost believing that a stranger's visage would be discovered, though the form, gesture, and voice were those of Mr. Hooper.

At the close of the services, the people hurried out with indecorous confusion, eager to communicate their pent-up amazement, and conscious of lighter spirits, the moment they lost sight of the black veil. Some gathered in little circles, huddled closely together, with their mouths all whispering in the centre; some went homeward alone, wrapt in silent meditation; some talked loudly, and profaned the Sabbath day with ostentatious laughter. A few shook their sagacious heads, intimating that they could penetrate the mystery; while one or two affirmed that there was no mystery at all, but only that Mr. Hooper's eyes were so weakened by the midnight lamp, as to require a shade. After a brief interval, forth came good Mr. Hooper also, in the rear of his flock. Turning his veiled face from one group to another, he paid due reverence to the hoary heads, saluted the middle aged with kind dignity, as their friend and spiritual guide, greeted the young with mingled authority and love, and laid his hands on the little children's heads to bless them. Such was always his custom on the Sabbath day. Strange and bewildered looks repaid him for his courtesy. None, as on former occasions, aspired to the honor of walking by their pastor's side. Old Squire Saunders, doubtless by an accidental lapse of memory, neglected to invite Mr. Hooper to his table, where the good clergyman had been wont to bless the food, almost every Sunday since his settlement. He returned, therefore, to the parsonage, and, at the moment of closing the door, was observed to look back upon the people, all of whom had their eyes fixed upon the minister. A sad smile gleamed faintly from beneath the black veil, and flickered about his mouth, glimmering as he disappeared.

"How strange," said a lady, "that a simple black veil, such as any woman might wear on her bonnet, should become such a terrible thing on Mr. Hooper's face!"

"Something must surely be amiss with Mr. Hooper's intellects," observed her husband, the physician of the village. "But the strangest part of the affair is the effect of this vagary, even on a sober-minded man like myself. The black veil, though it covers only our pastor's face, throws its influence over his whole person, and makes him ghostlike from head to foot. Do you not feel it so?"

"Truly do I," replied the lady; "and I would not be alone with him for the world. I wonder he is not afraid to be alone with himself!"

"Men sometimes are so," said her husband.

The afternoon service was attended with similar circumstances. At its conclusion, the bell tolled for the funeral of a young lady. The relatives and friends were assembled in the house, and the more distant acquaintances stood about the door, speaking of the good qualities of the deceased, when their talk was interrupted by the appearance of Mr. Hooper, still covered with his black veil. It was now an appropriate emblem. The clergyman stepped into the room where the corpse was laid, and bent over the coffin, to take a last farewell of his deceased parishioner. As he stooped, the veil hung straight down from his forehead, so that, if her eyelids had not been closed forever, the dead maiden might have seen his face. Could Mr. Hooper be fearful of her glance, that he so hastily caught back the black veil? A person who watched the interview between the dead and living, scrupled not to affirm, that, at the instant when the clergyman's features were disclosed, the corpse had slightly shuddered, rustling the shroud and muslin cap, though the countenance retained the composure of death. A superstitious old woman was the only witness of this prodigy. From the coffin Mr. Hooper passed into the chamber of the mourners, and thence to the head of the staircase, to make the funeral prayer. It was a tender and heart-dissolving prayer, full of sorrow, yet so imbued with celestial hopes, that the music of a heavenly harp, swept by the fingers of the dead, seemed faintly to be heard among the saddest accents of the minister. The people trembled, though they but darkly understood him when he prayed that they, and himself, and all of mortal race, might be ready, as he trusted this young maiden had been, for the dreadful hour that should snatch the veil from their faces. The bearers went heavily forth, and the mourners followed, saddening all the street, with the dead before them, and Mr. Hooper in his black veil behind.

"Why do you look back?" said one in the procession to his partner.

"I had a fancy," replied she, "that the minister and the maiden's spirit were walking hand in hand."

"And so had I, at the same moment," said the other.

That night, the handsomest couple in Milford village were to be joined in wedlock. Though reckoned a melancholy man, Mr. Hooper had a placid cheerfulness for such occasions, which often excited a sympathetic smile, where livelier merriment would have been thrown away. There was no quality of his disposition which made him more beloved than this. The company at the wedding awaited his arrival with impatience, trusting that the strange awe, which had gathered over him throughout the day, would now be dispelled. But such was not the result. When Mr. Hooper came, the first thing that their eyes rested on was the same horrible black veil, which had added deeper gloom to the funeral, and could portend nothing but evil to the wedding. Such was its immediate effect on the guests, that a cloud seemed to have rolled duskily from beneath the black crape, and dimmed the light of the candles. The bridal pair stood up before the minister. But the bride's cold fingers quivered in the tremulous hand of the bridegroom, and her deathlike paleness caused a whisper, that the maiden who had been buried a few hours before, was come from her grave to be married. If ever another wedding were so dismal, it was that famous one, where they tolled the wedding knell. After performing the• ceremony, Mr. Hooper raised a glass of wine to his lips, wishing happiness to the new-married couple, in a strain of mild pleasantry that ought to have brightened the features of the guests, like a cheerful gleam from the hearth. At that instant, catching a glimpse of his figure in the looking glass, the black veil involved his own spirit in the horror with which it overwhelmed all others. His frame shuddered—his lips grew white—he spilt the untasted wine upon the carpet—and rushed forth into the darkness. For the Earth, too, had on her Black Veil.

The next day, the whole village of Milford talked of little else than Parson Hooper's black veil. That, and the mystery concealed behind it, supplied a topic for discussion between acquaintances meeting in the street, and good women gossiping at their open windows. It was the first item of news that the tavern keeper told to his guests. The children babbled of it on their way to school. One imitative little imp covered his face with an old black handkerchief, thereby so affrighting his playmates that the panic seized himself, and he well nigh lost his wits by his own waggery.

It was remarkable that, of all the busybodies and impertinent people in the parish, not one ventured to put the plain question to Mr. Hooper, wherefore he did this thing. Hitherto, whenever there appeared the slightest call for such interference, he had never lacked advisers, nor shown himself averse to be guided by their judgment. If he erred at all, it was by so painful a degree of self-distrust, that even the mildest censure would lead him to consider an indifferent action as a crime. Yet, though so well acquainted with this amiable weakness, no individual among his parishioners chose to make the black veil a subject of friendly remonstrance. There was a feeling of dread, neither

plainly confessed nor carefully concealed, which caused each to shift the responsibility upon another, till at length it was found expedient to send a deputation of the church, in order to deal with Mr. Hooper about the mystery, before it should grow into a scandal. Never did an embassy so ill discharge its duties. The minister received them with friendly courtesy, but became silent, after they were seated, leaving to his visitors the whole burden of introducing their important business. The topic, it might be supposed, was obvious enough. There was the black veil, swathed round Mr. Hooper's forehead, and concealing every feature above his placid mouth, on which, at times, they could perceive the glimmering of a melancholy smile. But that piece of crape, to their imagination, seemed to hang down before his heart, the symbol of a fearful secret between him and them. Were the veil but cast aside, they might speak freely of it, but not till then. Thus they sat a considerable time, speechless, confused, and shrinking uneasily from Mr. Hooper's eye, which they felt to be fixed upon them with an invisible glance. Finally, the deputies returned abashed to their constituents, pronouncing the matter too weighty to be handled, except by a council of the churches, if, indeed, it might not require a general synod.

But there was one person in the village, unappalled by the awe with which the black veil had impressed all beside herself. When the deputies returned without an explanation, or even venturing to demand one, she, with the calm energy of her character, determined to chase away the strange cloud that appeared to be settling round Mr. Hooper, every moment more darkly than before. As his plighted wife, it should be her privilege to know what the black veil concealed. At the minister's first visit, therefore, she entered upon the subject, with a direct simplicity, which made the task easier both for him and her. After he had seated himself, she fixed her eyes steadfastly upon the veil, but could discern nothing of the dreadful gloom that had so overawed the multitude: it was but a double fold of crape, hanging down from his forehead to his mouth, and slightly stirring with his breath.

"No," said she aloud, and smiling, "there is nothing terrible in this piece of crape, except that it hides a face which I am always glad to look upon. Come, good sir, let the sun shine from behind the cloud. First lay aside your black veil: then tell me why you put it on."

Mr. Hooper's smile glimmered faintly.

"There is an hour to come," said he, "when all of us shall cast aside our veils. Take it not amiss, beloved friend, if I wear this piece of crape till then."

"Your words are a mystery, too," returned the young lady. "Take away the veil from them, at least."

"Elizabeth, I will," said he, "so far as my vow may suffer me. Know, then, this veil is a type and a symbol, and I am bound to wear it ever, both in light and darkness, in solitude and before the gaze of multitudes, and as with strangers, so with my familiar friends. No mortal eye will see it withdrawn. This dismal shade must separate me from the world: even you, Elizabeth, can never come behind it!"

"What grievous affliction hath befallen you," she earnestly inquired, "that you should thus darken your eyes forever?"

"If it be a sign of mourning," replied Mr. Hooper, "I, perhaps, like most other mortals, have sorrows dark enough to be typified by a black veil."

"But what if the world will not believe that it is the type of an innocent sorrow?" urged Elizabeth. "Beloved and respected as you are, there may be whispers, that you hide your face under the consciousness of secret sin. For the sake of your holy office, do away this scandal!"

The color rose into her cheeks as she intimated the nature of the rumors that were already abroad in the village. But Mr. Hooper's mildness did not forsake him. He even smiled again—that same sad smile, which always appeared like a faint glimmering of light, proceeding from the obscurity beneath the veil.

"If I hide my face for sorrow, there is cause enough," he merely replied; "and if I cover it for secret sin, what mortal might not do the same?"

And with this gentle, but unconquerable obstinacy did he resist all her entreaties. At length Elizabeth sat silent. For a few moments she appeared lost in thought, considering, probably, what new methods might be tried, to withdraw her lover from so dark a fantasy, which, if it had no other meaning, was perhaps a symptom of mental disease. Though of a firmer character than his own, the tears rolled down her cheeks. But, in an instant, as it were, a new feeling took the place of sorrow: her eyes were fixed insensibly on the black veil, when, like a sudden twilight in the air, its ter-

rors fell around her. She arose, and stood trembling before him.

"And do you feel it then at last?" said he mournfully.

She made no reply, but covered her eyes with her hand and turned to leave the room. He rushed forward and caught her arm.

"Have patience with me, Elizabeth!" cried he passionately. "Do not desert me, though this veil must be between us here on earth. Be 10 mine, and hereafter there shall be no veil over my face, no darkness between our souls! It is but a mortal veil—it is not for eternity! O! you know not how lonely I am, and how frightened, to be alone behind my black veil. Do not leave me in this miserable obscurity forever!"

"Lift the veil but once, and look me in the face," said she.

"Never! It cannot be!" replied Mr. Hooper.

"Then farewell!" said Elizabeth. 20

She withdrew her arm from his grasp, and slowly departed, pausing at the door, to give one long shuddering gaze, that seemed almost to penetrate the mystery of the black veil. But, even amid his grief, Mr. Hooper smiled to think that only a material emblem had separated him from happiness, though the horrors, which it shadowed forth, must be drawn darkly between the fondest of lovers.

From that time no attempts were made to 30 remove Mr. Hooper's black veil, or, by a direct appeal, to discover the secret which it was supposed to hide. By persons who claimed a superiority to popular prejudice, it was reckoned merely an eccentric whim, such as often mingles with the sober actions of men otherwise rational, and tinges them all with its own semblance of insanity. But with the multitude, good Mr. Hooper was irreparably a bugbear. He could not walk the street with any peace of 40 mind, so conscious was he that the gentle and timid would turn aside to avoid him, and that others would make it a point of hardihood to throw themselves in his way. The impertinence of the latter class compelled him to give up his customary walk, at sunset, to the burial ground; for when he leaned pensively over the gate, there would always be faces behind the gravestones, peeping at his black veil. A fable went the rounds, that the stare of the dead people 50 drove him thence. It grieved him, to the very depth of his kind heart, to observe how the children fled from his approach, breaking up their merriest sports, while his melancholy figure was yet afar off. Their instinctive dread caused him to feel, more strongly than aught else, that a preternatural horror was interwoven with the threads of the black crape. In truth, his own antipathy to the veil was known to be so great, that he never willingly passed before a mirror, nor stooped to drink at a still fountain, lest, in its peaceful bosom, he should be affrighted by himself. This was what gave plausibility to the whispers, that Mr. Hooper's conscience tortured him for some great crime too horrible to be entirely concealed, or otherwise than so obscurely intimated. Thus, from beneath the black veil, there rolled a cloud into the sunshine, an ambiguity of sin or sorrow, which enveloped the poor minister, so that love or sympathy could never reach him. It was said, that ghost and fiend consorted with him there. With self-shudderings and outward terrors, he walked continually in its shadow, groping darkly within his own soul, or gazing through a medium that saddened the whole world. Even the lawless wind, it was believed, respected his dreadful secret, and never blew aside the veil. But still good Mr. Hooper sadly smiled at the pale visages of the worldly throng as he passed by.

Among all its bad influences, the black veil had the one desirable effect, of making its wearer a very efficient clergyman. By the aid of his mysterious emblem—for there was no other apparent cause—he became a man of awful power, over souls that were in agony for sin. His converts always regarded him with a dread peculiar to themselves, affirming, though but figuratively, that, before he brought them to celestial light, they had been with him behind the black veil. Its gloom, indeed, enabled him to sympathize with all dark affections. Dying sinners cried aloud for Mr. Hooper, and would not yield their breath till he appeared; though ever, as he stooped to whisper consolation, they shuddered at the veiled face so near their own. Such were the terrors of the black veil, even when Death had bared his visage! Strangers came long distances to attend service at his church, with the mere idle purpose of gazing at his figure, because it was forbidden them to behold his face. But many were made to quake ere they departed! Once, during Governor Belcher's administration, Mr. Hooper was appointed to preach the election sermon. Covered with his black veil, he stood before the chief magistrate, the council, and the representatives, and wrought so deep an impression, that the legislative measures of that year were characterized by all the gloom and piety of our earliest ancestral sway.

In this manner Mr. Hooper spent a long life, irreproachable in outward act, yet shrouded in dismal suspicions; kind and loving, though unloved, and dimly feared; a man apart from men, shunned in their health and joy, but ever summoned to their aid in mortal anguish. As years wore on, shedding their snows above his sable veil, he acquired a name throughout the New England churches, and they called him Father Hooper. Nearly all his parishioners, who were of mature age when he was settled, had been borne away by many a funeral: he had one congregation in the church, and a more crowded one in the churchyard; and having wrought so late into the evening, and done his work so well, it was now good Father Hooper's turn to rest.

Several persons were visible by the shaded candle-light, in the death chamber of the old clergyman. Natural connections he had none. But there was the decorously grave, though unmoved physician, seeking only to mitigate the last pangs of the patient whom he could not save. There were the deacons, and other eminently pious members of his church. There, also, was the Reverend Mr. Clark, of Westbury, a young and zealous divine, who had ridden in haste to pray by the bedside of the expiring minister. There was the nurse, no hired handmaiden of death, but one whose calm affection had endured thus long in secrecy, in solitude, amid the chill of age, and would not perish, even at the dying hour. Who, but Elizabeth! And there lay the hoary head of good Father Hooper upon the death pillow, with the black veil still swathed about his brow, and reaching down over his face, so that each more difficult gasp of his faint breath caused it to stir. All through life that piece of crape had hung between him and the world: it had separated him from cheerful brotherhood and woman's love, and kept him in that saddest of all prisons, his own heart; and still it lay upon his face, as if to deepen the gloom of his darksome chamber, and shade him from the sunshine of eternity.

For some time previous, his mind had been confused, wavering doubtfully between the past and the present, and hovering forward, as it were, at intervals, into the indistinctness of the world to come. There had been feverish turns, which tossed him from side to side, and wore away what little strength he had. But in his most convulsive struggles, and in the wildest vagaries of his intellect, when no other thought retained its sober influence, he still showed an awful solicitude lest the black veil should slip aside. Even if his bewildered soul could have forgotten, there was a faithful woman at his pillow, who, with averted eyes, would have covered that aged face, which she had last beheld in the comeliness of manhood. At length the death-stricken old man lay quietly in the torpor of mental and bodily exhaustion, with an imperceptible pulse, and breath that grew fainter and fainter, except when a long, deep, and irregular inspiration seemed to prelude the flight of his spirit.

The minister of Westbury approached the bedside.

"Venerable Father Hooper," said he, "the moment of your release is at hand. Are you ready for the lifting of the veil, that shuts in time from eternity?"

Father Hooper at first replied merely by a feeble motion of his head; then, apprehensive, perhaps, that his meaning might be doubtful, he exerted himself to speak.

"Yea," said he, in faint accents, "my soul hath a patient weariness until that veil be lifted."

"And is it fitting," resumed the Reverend Mr. Clark, "that a man so given to prayer, of such a blameless example, holy in deed and thought, so far as mortal judgment may pronounce; is it fitting that a father in the church should leave a shadow on his memory, that may seem to blacken a life so pure? I pray you, my venerable brother, let not this thing be! Suffer us to be gladdened by your triumphant aspect, as you go to your reward. Before the veil of eternity be lifted, let me cast aside this black veil from your face!"

And thus speaking, the Reverend Mr. Clark bent forward to reveal the mystery of so many years. But, exerting a sudden energy, that made all the beholders stand aghast, Father Hooper snatched both his hands from beneath the bed clothes, and pressed them strongly on the black veil, resolute to struggle, if the minister of Westbury would contend with a dying man.

"Never!" cried the veiled clergyman. "On earth, never!"

"Dark old man!" exclaimed the affrighted minister, "with what horrible crime upon your soul are you now passing to the judgment?"

Father Hooper's breath heaved; it rattled in his throat; but, with a mighty effort, grasping forward with his hands, he caught hold of life, and held it back till he should speak. He even raised himself in bed; and there he sat, shivering with the arms of death around him, while the black veil hung down, awful, at that last moment, in the gathered terrors of a lifetime. And yet the faint, sad smile, so often there, now seemed to glimmer from its obscurity, and linger on Father Hooper's lips.

"Why do you tremble at me alone?" cried he, turning his veiled face round the circle of pale spectators. "Tremble also at each other! Have men avoided me, and women shown no pity, and children screamed and fled, only for my black veil? What, but the mystery which it obscurely typifies, has made this piece of crape so awful? When the friend shows his inmost heart to his friend; the lover to his best beloved; when man does not vainly shrink from the eye of his Creator, loathsomely treasuring up the secret of his sin; then deem me a monster, for the symbol beneath which I have lived, and die! I look around me, and, lo! on every visage a Black Veil!"

While his auditors shrank from one another, in mutual affright, Father Hooper fell back upon his pillow, a veiled corpse, with a faint smile lingering on the lips. Still veiled, they laid him in his coffin, and a veiled corpse they bore him to the grave. The grass of many years has sprung up and withered on that grave, the burial stone is moss-grown, and good Mr. Hooper's face is dust; but awful is still the thought, that it mouldered beneath the Black Veil!   1836

» » RAPPACCINI'S DAUGHTER « «

(*From the* WRITINGS OF AUBÉPINE)

We do not remember to have seen any translated specimens of the productions of M. de l'Aubépine—a fact the less to be wondered at, as his very name is unknown to many of his own countrymen as well as to the student of foreign literature. As a writer, he seems to occupy an unfortunate position between the Transcendentalists (who, under one name or another, have their share in all the current literature of the world) and the great body of pen-and-ink men who address the intellect and sympathies of the multitude. If not too refined, at all events too remote, too shadowy, and unsubstantial in his modes of development to suit the taste of the latter class, and yet too popular to satisfy the spiritual or metaphysical requisitions of the former, he must necessarily find himself without an audience, except here and there an individual or possibly an isolated clique. His writings, to do them justice, are not altogether destitute of fancy and originality; they might have won him greater reputation but for an inveterate love of allegory, which is apt to invest his plots and characters with the aspect of scenery and people in the clouds and to steal away the human warmth out of his conceptions. His fictions are sometimes historical, sometimes of the present day, and sometimes, so far as can be discovered, have little or no reference either to time or space. In any case, he generally contents himself with a very slight embroidery of outward manners,—the faintest possible counterfeit of real life,—and endeavors to create an interest by some less obvious peculiarity of the subject. Occasionally a breath of Nature, a raindrop of pathos and tenderness, or a gleam of humor will find its way into the midst of his fantastic imagery, and make us feel as if, after all, we were yet within the limits of our native earth. We will only add to this very cursory notice that M. de l'Aubépine's productions, if the reader chance to take them in precisely the proper point of view, may amuse a leisure hour as well as those of a brighter man; if otherwise, they can hardly fail to look excessively like nonsense.

Our author is voluminous; he continues to write and publish with as much praiseworthy and indefatigable prolixity as if his efforts were crowned with the brilliant success that so justly attends those of Eugene Sue. His first appearance was by a collection of stories in a long series of volumes entitled *Contes deux fois racontées*. The titles of some of his more recent works (we quote from memory) are as follows: *Le Voyage Céleste à Chemin de Fer*, 3 tom., 1838. *Le nouveau Père Adam et la nouvelle Mère Eve*, 2 tom., 1839. *Roderic; ou le Serpent à l'estomac*, 2 tom., 1840. *Le Culte du Feu*, a folio volume of ponderous research into the religion and ritual of the old Persian Ghebers, published in 1841. *La Soirée du Chateau en Espagne*, 1 tom. 8vo., 1842; and *L'Artiste du Beau; ou le Papillon Mécanique*, 5 tom. 4to., 1843. Our somewhat wearisome perusal of this startling catalogue of volumes has left behind it a certain personal affection and sympathy, though by no means admiration, for M. de l'Aubépine; and we would fain do the little in our power towards introducing him favorably to the American public. The ensuing tale is a translation of his *Beatrice; ou la Belle Empoisonneuse*, recently published in *La Revue Anti-Aristocratique*. This jour-

nal, edited by the Comte de Bearhaven, has for some years past led the defence of liberal principles and popular rights with a faithfulness and ability worthy of all praise.

A young man, named Giovanni Guasconti, came, very long ago, from the more southern region of Italy, to pursue his studies at the University of Padua. Giovanni, who had but a scanty supply of gold ducats in his pocket, took lodgings in a high and gloomy chamber of an old edifice which looked not unworthy to have been the palace of a Paduan noble, and which, in fact, exhibited over its entrance the armorial bearings of a family long since extinct. The young stranger, who was not unstudied in the great poem of his country, recollected that one of the ancestors of this family, and perhaps an occupant of this very mansion, had been pictured by Dante as a partaker of the immortal agonies of his Inferno. These reminiscences and associations, together with the tendency to heartbreak natural to a young man for the first time out of his native sphere, caused Giovanni to sigh heavily as he looked around the desolate and ill-furnished apartment.

"Holy Virgin, signor!" cried old Dame Lisabetta, who, won by the youth's remarkable beauty of person, was kindly endeavoring to give the chamber a habitable air, "what a sigh was that to come out of a young man's heart! Do you find this old mansion gloomy? For the love of Heaven, then, put your head out of the window, and you will see as bright sunshine as you have left in Naples."

Guasconti mechanically did as the old woman advised, but could not quite agree with her that the Paduan sunshine was as cheerful as that of southern Italy. Such as it was, however, it fell upon a garden beneath the window and expended its fostering influences on a variety of plants, which seemed to have been cultivated with exceeding care.

"Does this garden belong to the house?" asked Giovanni.

"Heaven forbid, signor, unless it were fruitful of better pot herbs than any that grow there now," answered old Lisabetta. "No; that garden is cultivated by the own hands of Signor Giacomo Rappaccini, the famous doctor, who, I warrant him, has been heard of as far as Naples. It is said that he distils these plants into medicines that are as potent as a charm. Oftentimes you may see the signor doctor at work, and perchance the signora, his daughter, too, gathering the strange flowers that grow in the garden."

The old woman had now done what she could for the aspect of the chamber; and, commending the young man to the protection of the saints, took her departure.

Giovanni still found no better occupation than to look down into the garden beneath his window. From its appearance, he judged it to be one of those botanic gardens which were of earlier date in Padua than elsewhere in Itay or in the world. Or, not improbably, it might once have been the pleasure-place of an opulent family; for there was the ruin of a marble fountain in the centre, sculptured with rare art, but so wofully shattered that it was impossible to trace the original design from the chaos of remaining fragments. The water, however, continued to gush and sparkle into the sunbeams as cheerfully as ever. A little gurgling sound ascended to the young man's window and made him feel as if the fountain were an immortal spirit, that sung its song unceasingly and without heeding the vicissitudes around it, while one century imbodied it in marble and another scattered the perishable garniture on the soil. All about the pool into which the water subsided grew various plants, that seemed to require a plentiful supply of moisture for the nourishment of gigantic leaves, and, in some instances, flowers gorgeously magnificent. There was one shrub in particular, set in a marble vase in the midst of the pool, that bore a profusion of purple blossoms, each of which had the lustre and richness of a gem; and the whole together made a show so resplendent that it seemed enough to illuminate the garden, even had there been no sunshine. Every portion of the soil was peopled with plants and herbs, which, if less beautiful, still bore tokens of assiduous care, as if all had their individual virtues, known to the scientific mind that fostered them. Some were placed in urns, rich with old carving, and others in common garden pots; some crept serpent-like along the ground or climbed on high, using whatever means of ascent was offered them. One plant had wreathed itself round a statue of Vertumnus, which was thus quite veiled and shrouded in a drapery of hanging foliage, so happily arranged that it might have served a sculptor for a study.

While Giovanni stood at the window he heard a rustling behind a screen of leaves, and became aware that a person was at work in the garden. His figure soon emerged into view, and showed itself to be that of no common laborer, but a tall, emaciated, sallow, and sickly-looking man, dressed in a scholar's garb of black. He was beyond the middle term of life, with gray hair, a thin, gray beard, and a face singularly marked with intellect and cultivation, but which could never, even in his more youthful days, have expressed much warmth of heart.

Nothing could exceed the intentness with which this scientific gardener examined every shrub which grew in his path: it seemed as if he was looking into their inmost nature, making observations in regard to their creative essence, and discovering why one leaf grew in this shape and another in that, and wherefore such and such flowers differed among themselves in hue and perfume. Nevertheless, in spite of this deep intelligence on his part, there was no approach to intimacy between himself and these vegetable existences. On the contrary, he avoided their actual touch or the direct inhaling of their odors with a caution that impressed Giovanni most disagreeably; for the man's demeanor was that of one walking among malignant influences, such as savage beasts, or deadly snakes, or evil spirits, which, should he allow them one moment of license, would wreak upon him some terrible fatality. It was strangely frightful to the young man's imagination to see this air of insecurity in a person cultivating a garden, that most simple and innocent of human toils, and which had been alike the joy and labor of the unfallen parents of the race. Was this garden, then, the Eden of the present world? And this man, with such perception of harm in what his own hands caused to grow,—was he the Adam?

The distrustful gardener, while plucking away the dead leaves or pruning the too luxuriant growth of the shrubs, defended his hands with a pair of thick gloves. Nor were these his only armor. When, in his walk through the garden, he came to the magnificent plant that hung its purple gems beside the marble fountain, he placed a kind of mask over his mouth and nostrils, as if all this beauty did but conceal a deadlier malice; but, finding his task still too dangerous, he drew back, removed the mask, and called loudly, but in the infirm voice of a person affected with inward disease,—

"Beatrice! Beatrice!"

"Here am I, my father. What would you?" cried a rich and youthful voice from the window of the opposite house—a voice as rich as a tropical sunset, and which made Giovanni, though he knew not why, think of deep hues of purple or crimson and of perfumes heavily delectable. "Are you in the garden?"

"Yes, Beatrice," answered the gardener; "and I need your help."

Soon there emerged from under a sculptured portal the figure of a young girl, arrayed with as much richness of taste as the most splendid of the flowers, beautiful as the day, and with a bloom so deep and vivid that one shade more would have been too much. She looked redundant with life, health, and energy; all of which attributes were bound down and compressed, as it were, and girdled tensely, in their luxuriance, by her virgin zone. Yet Giovanni's fancy must have grown morbid while he looked down into the garden; for the impression which the fair stranger made upon him was as if here were another flower, the human sister of those vegetable ones, as beautiful as they, more beautiful than the richest of them, but still to be touched only with a glove, nor to be approached without a mask. As Beatrice came down the garden path, it was observable that she handled and inhaled the odor of several of the plants which her father had most sedulously avoided.

"Here, Beatrice," said the latter, "see how many needful offices require to be done to our chief treasure. Yet, shattered as I am, my life might pay the penalty of approaching it so closely as circumstances demand. Henceforth, I fear, this plant must be consigned to your sole charge."

"And gladly will I undertake it," cried again the rich tones of the young lady, as she bent towards the magnificent plant and opened her arms as if to embrace it. "Yes, my sister, my splendor, it shall be Beatrice's task to nurse and serve thee; and thou shalt reward her with thy kisses and perfumed breath, which to her is as the breath of life."

Then, with all the tenderness in her manner that was so strikingly expressed in her words, she busied herself with such attentions as the plant seemed to require; and Giovanni, at his lofty window, rubbed his eyes and almost doubted whether it were a girl tending her favorite flower, or one sister performing the duties of affection to another. The scene soon terminated. Whether Dr. Rappaccini had finished his labors in the garden, or that his watchful eye had caught the stranger's face, he now took his daughter's arm and retired. Night was already closing in; oppressive exhalations seemed to proceed from the plants and steal upward past the open window; and Giovanni, closing the lattice, went to his couch and dreamed of a rich flower and beautiful girl. Flower and maiden were different, and yet the same, and fraught with some strange peril in either shape.

But there is an influence in the light of morning that tends to rectify whatever errors of fancy, or even of judgment, we may have incurred during the sun's decline, or among the shadows of the night, or in the less wholesome glow of moonshine. Giovanni's first movement, on starting from sleep, was to throw open the window and gaze down into the garden which his dreams had made so fertile of mysteries. He was surprised, and a little ashamed, to find how real and matter-of-fact an affair it proved to be, in the first rays of the sun which gilded the dewdrops that hung upon leaf and blossom, and, while giving a brighter beauty to each rare flower, brought every thing within the limits of ordinary experience. The young man rejoiced that, in the heart of the barren city, he had the privilege of overlooking this spot of lovely and luxuriant vegetation. It would serve, he said to himself, as a symbolic language to keep him in communion with Nature. Neither the sickly and thoughtworn Dr. Giacomo Rappaccini, it is true, nor his brilliant daughter, were now visible; so that Giovanni could not determine how much of the singularity which he attributed to both was due to their own qualities and how much to his wonder-working fancy; but he was inclined to take a most rational view of the whole matter.

In the course of the day he paid his respects to Signor Pietro Baglioni, professor of medicine in the university, a physician of eminent repute, to whom Giovanni had brought a letter of introduction. The professor was an elderly personage, apparently of genial nature and habits that might almost be called jovial. He kept the young man to dinner, and made himself very agreeable by the freedom and liveliness of his conversation, especially when warmed by a flask or two of Tuscan wine. Giovanni, conceiving that men of science, inhabitants of the same city, must needs be on familiar terms with one another, took an opportunity to mention the name of Dr. Rappaccini. But the professor did not respond with so much cordiality as he had anticipated.

"Ill would it become a teacher of the divine art of medicine," said Professor Pietro Baglioni, in answer to a question of Giovanni, "to with-hold due and well-considered praise of a physician so eminently skilled as Rappaccini; but, on the other hand, I should answer it but scantily to my conscience were I to permit a worthy youth like yourself, Signor Giovanni, the son of an ancient friend, to imbibe erroneous ideas respecting a man who might hereafter chance to hold your life and death in his hands. The truth is, our worshipful Dr. Rappaccini has as much science as any member of the faculty—with perhaps one single exception—in Padua, or all Italy; but there are certain grave objections to his professional character."

"And what are they?" asked the young man.

"Has my friend Giovanni any disease of body or heart, that he is so inquisitive about physicians?" said the professor, with a smile. "But as for Rappaccini, it is said of him—and I, who know the man well, can answer for its truth—that he cares infinitely more for science than for mankind. His patients are interesting to him only as subjects for some new experiment. He would sacrifice human life, his own among the rest, or whatever else was dearest to him, for the sake of adding so much as a grain of mustard seed to the great heap of his accumulated knowledge."

"Methinks he is an awful man indeed," remarked Guasconti, mentally recalling the cold and purely intellectual aspect of Rappaccini. "And yet, worshipful professor, is it not a noble spirit? Are there many men capable of so spiritual a love of science?"

"God forbid," answered the professor, somewhat testily; "at least, unless they take sounder views of the healing art than those adopted by Rappaccini. It is his theory that all medicinal virtues are comprised within those substances which we term vegetable poisons. These he cultivates with his own hands, and is said even to have produced new varieties of poison, more horribly deleterious than Nature, without the assistance of this learned person, would ever have plagued the world withal. That the signor doctor does less mischief than might be expected with such dangerous substances, is undeniable. Now and then, it must be owned, he has effected, or seemed to effect, a marvellous cure; but, to tell you my private mind, Signor Giovanni, he should receive little credit for such instances of success,—they being probably the work of chance,—but should be held strictly accountable for his failures, which may justly be considered his own work."

The youth might have taken Baglioni's opinions with many grains of allowance had he known that there was a professional warfare of long continuance between him and Dr. Rappaccini, in which the latter was generally thought to have gained the advantage. If the reader be inclined to judge for himself, we refer him to certain black-letter tracts on both sides, preserved in the medical department of the University of Padua. 10

"I know not, most learned professor," returned Giovanni, after musing on what had been said of Rappaccini's exclusive zeal for science,—"I know not how dearly this physician may love his art; but surely there is one object more dear to him. He has a daughter."

"Aha!" cried the professor, with a laugh. "So now our friend Giovanni's secret is out. You have heard of this daughter, whom all the young men in Padua are wild about, though 20 not half a dozen have ever had the good hap to see her face. I know little of the Signora Beatrice save that Rappaccini is said to have instructed her deeply in his science, and that, young and beautiful as fame reports her, she is already qualified to fill a professor's chair. Perchance her father destines her for mine! Other absurd rumors there be, not worth talking about or listening to. So now, Signor Giovanni, drink off your glass of lachryma." 30

Guasconti returned to his lodgings somewhat heated with the wine he had quaffed, and which caused his brain to swim with strange fantasies in reference to Dr. Rappaccini and the beautiful Beatrice. On his way, happening to pass by a florist's, he bought a fresh bouquet of flowers.

Ascending to his chamber, he seated himself near the window, but within the shadow thrown by the depth of the wall, so that he 40 could look down into the garden with little risk of being discovered. All beneath his eye was a solitude. The strange plants were basking in the sunshine, and now and then nodding gently to one another, as if in acknowledgment of sympathy and kindred. In the midst, by the shattered fountain, grew the magnificent shrub, with its purple gems clustering all over it; they glowed in the air, and gleamed back again out of the depths of the pool, which thus seemed 50 to overflow with colored radiance from the rich reflection that was steeped in it. At first, as we have said, the garden was a solitude. Soon, however,—as Giovanni had half hoped, half feared, would be the case,—a figure appeared beneath the antique sculptured portal, and came down between the rows of plants, inhaling their various perfumes as if she were one of those beings of old classic fable that lived upon sweet odors. On again beholding Beatrice, the young man was even startled to perceive how much her beauty exceeded his recollection of it; so brilliant, so vivid, was its character, that she glowed amid the sunlight, and, as Giovanni whispered to himself, positively illuminated the more shadowy intervals of the garden path. Her face being now more revealed than on the former occasion, he was struck by its expression of simplicity and sweetness— qualities that had not entered into his idea of her character, and which made him ask anew what manner of mortal she might be. Nor did he fail again to observe, or imagine, an analogy between the beautiful girl and the gorgeous shrub that hung its gemlike flowers over the fountain—a resemblance which Beatrice seemed to have indulged a fantastic humor in heightening, both by the arrangement of her dress and the selection of its hues.

Approaching the shrub, she threw open her arms, as with a passionate ardor, and drew its branches into an intimate embrace—so intimate that her features were hidden in its leafy bosom and her glistening ringlets all intermingled with the flowers.

"Give me thy breath, my sister," exclaimed Beatrice; "for I am faint with common air. And give me this flower of thine, which I separate with gentlest fingers from the stem and place it close beside my heart."

With these words the beautiful daughter of Rappaccini plucked one of the richest blossoms of the shrub, and was about to fasten it in her bosom. But now, unless Giovanni's draughts of wine had bewildered his senses, a singular incident occurred. A small orange-colored reptile, of the lizard or chameleon species, chanced to be creeping along the path, just at the feet of Beatrice. It appeared to Giovanni,—but, at the distance from which he gazed, he could scarcely have seen anything so minute,—it appeared to him, however, that a drop or two of moisture from the broken stem of the flower descended upon the lizard's head. For an instant the reptile contorted itself violently, and then lay motionless in the sunshine. Beatrice observed this remarkable phenomenon, and crossed herself, sadly, but without surprise; nor did she therefore hesitate to arrange the fatal flower in her bosom. There it

blushed, and almost glimmered with the dazzling effect of a precious stone, adding to her dress and aspect the one appropriate charm which nothing else in the world could have supplied. But Giovanni, out of the shadow of his window, bent forward and shrank back, and murmured and trembled.

"Am I awake? Have I my senses?" said he to himself. "What is this being? Beautiful shall I call her, or inexpressibly terrible?"

Beatrice now strayed carelessly through the garden, approaching closer beneath Giovanni's window, so that he was compelled to thrust his head quite out of its concealment in order to gratify the intense and painful curiosity which she excited. At this moment there came a beautiful insect over the garden wall: it had, perhaps, wandered through the city, and found no flowers or verdure among those antique haunts of men until the heavy perfumes of Dr. Rappaccini's shrubs had lured it from afar. Without alighting on the flowers, this winged brightness seemed to be attracted by Beatrice, and lingered in the air and fluttered about her head. Now, here it could not be but that Giovanni Guasconti's eyes deceived him. Be that as it might, he fancied that, while Beatrice was gazing at the insect with childish delight, it grew faint and fell at her feet; its bright wings shivered; it was dead—from no cause that he could discern, unless it were the atmosphere of her breath. Again Beatrice crossed herself and sighed heavily as she bent over the dead insect.

An impulsive movement of Giovanni drew her eyes to the window. There she beheld the beautiful head of the young man—rather a Grecian than an Italian head, with fair, regular features, and a glistening of gold among his ringlets—gazing down upon her like a being that hovered in mid air. Scarcely knowing what he did, Giovanni threw down the bouquet which he had hitherto held in his hand.

"Signora," said he, "there are pure and healthful flowers. Wear them for the sake of Giovanni Guasconti."

"Thanks, signor," replied Beatrice, with her rich voice, that came forth as it were like a gush of music, and with a mirthful expression half childish and half womanlike. "I accept your gift, and would fain recompense it with this precious purple flower; but, if I toss it into the air, it will not reach you. So Signor Guasconti must even content himself with my thanks."

She lifted the bouquet from the ground, and

then, as if inwardly ashamed at having stepped aside from her maidenly reserve to respond to a stranger's greeting, passed swiftly homeward through the garden. But, few as the moments were, it seemed to Giovanni, when she was on the point of vanishing beneath the sculptured portal, that his beautiful bouquet was already beginning to wither in her grasp. It was an idle thought; there could be no possibility of distinguishing a faded flower from a fresh one at so great a distance.

For many days after this incident the young man avoided the window that looked into Dr. Rappaccini's garden, as if something ugly and monstrous would have blasted his eyesight had he been betrayed into a glance. He felt conscious of having put himself, to a certain extent, within the influence of an unintelligible power by the communication which he had opened with Beatrice. The wisest course would have been, if his heart were in any real danger, to quit his lodgings and Padua itself at once; the next wiser, to have accustomed himself, as far as possible, to the familiar and daylight view of Beatrice—thus bringing her rigidly and systematically within the limits of ordinary experience. Least of all, while avoiding her sight, ought Giovanni to have remained so near this extraordinary being that the proximity and possibility even of intercourse should give a kind of substance and reality to the wild vagaries which his imagination ran riot continually in producing. Guasconti had not a deep heart—or, at all events, its depths were not sounded now; but he had a quick fancy, and an ardent southern temperament, which rose every instant to a higher fever pitch. Whether or no Beatrice possessed those terrible attributes, that fatal breath, the affinity with those so beautiful and deadly flowers which were indicated by what Giovanni had witnessed, she had at least instilled a fierce and subtle poison into his system. It was not love, although her rich beauty was a madness to him; nor horror, even while he fancied her spirit to be imbued with the same baneful essence that seemed to pervade her physical frame; but a wild offspring of both love and horror that had each parent in it, and burned like one and shivered like the other. Giovanni knew not what to dread; still less did he know what to hope; yet hope and dread kept a continual warfare in his breast, alternately vanquishing one another and starting up afresh to renew the contest. Blessed are all simple emotions, be they dark or bright! It is the lurid intermixture of the two that produces the illuminating blaze of the infernal regions.

Sometimes he endeavored to assuage the fever of his spirit by a rapid walk through the streets of Padua or beyond its gates: his footsteps kept time with the throbbings of his brain, so that the walk was apt to accelerate itself to a race. One day he found himself arrested; his arm was seized by a portly personage, who had turned back on recognizing the young man and expended much breath in overtaking him.

"Signor Giovanni! Stay, my young friend!" cried he. "Have you forgotten me? That might well be the case if I were as much altered as yourself."

It was Baglioni, whom Giovanni had avoided ever since their first meeting, from a doubt that the professor's sagacity would look too deeply into his secrets. Endeavoring to recover himself, he stared forth wildly from his inner world into the outer one and spoke like a man in a dream.

"Yes; I am Giovanni Guasconti. You are Professor Pietro Baglioni. Now let me pass!"

"Not yet, not yet, Signor Giovanni Guasconti," said the professor, smiling, but at the same time scrutinizing the youth with an earnest glance. "What! did I grow up side by side with your father? and shall his son pass me like a stranger in these old streets of Padua? Stand still, Signor Giovanni; for we must have a word or two before we part."

"Speedily, then, most worshipful professor, speedily," said Giovanni, with feverish impatience. "Does not your worship see that I am in haste?"

Now, while he was speaking there came a man in black along the street, stooping and moving feebly like a person in inferior health. His face was all overspread with a most sickly and sallow hue, but yet so pervaded with an expression of piercing and active intellect that an observer might easily have overlooked the merely physical attributes and have seen only this wonderful energy. As he passed, this person exchanged a cold and distant salutation with Baglioni, but fixed his eyes upon Giovanni with an intentness that seemed to bring out whatever was within him worthy of notice. Nevertheless, there was a peculiar quietness in the look, as if taking merely a speculative, not a human, interest in the young man.

"It is Dr. Rappaccini!" whispered the professor when the stranger had passed. "Has he ever seen your face before?"

"Not that I know," answered Giovanni, starting at the name.

"He *has* seen you! he must have seen you!" said Baglioni hastily. "For some purpose or other, this man of science is making a study of you. I know that look of his! It is the same that coldly illuminates his face as he bends over a bird, a mouse, or a butterfly; which, in pursuance of some experiment, he has killed by the perfume of a flower; a look as deep as Nature itself, but without Nature's warmth of love. Signor Giovanni, I will stake my life upon it, you are the subject of one of Rappaccini's experiments!"

"Will you make a fool of me?" cried Giovanni passionately. *"That,* signor professor, were an untoward experiment."

"Patience! patience!" replied the imperturbable professor. "I tell thee, my poor Giovanni, that Rappaccini has a scientific interest in thee. Thou hast fallen into fearful hands! And the Signora Beatrice,—what part does she act in this mystery?"

But Guasconti, finding Baglioni's pertinacity intolerable, here broke away, and was gone before the professor could again seize his arm. He looked after the young man intently and shook his head.

"This must not be," said Baglioni to himself. "The youth is the son of my old friend, and shall not come to any harm from which the arcana of medical science can preserve him. Besides, it is too insufferable an impertinence in Rappaccini thus to snatch the lad out of my own hands, as I may say, and make use of him for his infernal experiments. This daughter of his! It shall be looked to. Perchance, most learned Rappaccini, I may foil you where you little dream of it!"

Meanwhile Giovanni had pursued a circuitous route, and at length found himself at the door of his lodgings. As he crossed the threshold he was met by old Lisabetta, who smirked and smiled, and was evidently desirous to attract his attention; vainly, however, as the ebullition of his feelings had momentarily subsided into a cold and dull vacuity. He turned his eyes full upon the withered face that was puckering itself into a smile, but seemed to behold it not. The old dame, therefore, laid her grasp upon his cloak.

"Signor! signor!" whispered she, still with a smile over the whole breadth of her visage, so that it looked not unlike a grotesque carving in wood, darkened by centuries. "Listen, signor! There is a private entrance into the garden!"

"What do you say?" exclaimed Giovanni, turning quickly about, as if an inanimate thing should start into feverish life. "A private entrance into Dr. Rappaccini's garden?"

"Hush! hush! not so loud!" whispered Lisabetta, putting her hand over his mouth. "Yes; into the worshipful doctor's garden, where you may see all his fine shrubbery. Many a young man in Padua would give gold to be admitted among those flowers."

Giovanni put a piece of gold into her hand.

"Show me the way," said he.

A surmise, probably excited by his conversation with Baglioni, crossed his mind, that this interposition of old Lisabetta might perchance be connected with the intrigue, whatever were its nature, in which the professor seemed to suppose that Dr. Rappaccini was involving him. But such a suspicion, though it disturbed Giovanni, was inadequate to restrain him. The instant that he was aware of the possibility of approaching Beatrice, it seemed an absolute necessity of his existence to do so. It mattered not whether she were angel or demon; he was irrevocably within her sphere, and must obey the law that whirled him onward, in everlessening circles, towards a result which he did not attempt to foreshadow; and yet, strange to say, there came across him a sudden doubt whether this intense interest on his part were not delusory; whether it were really of so deep and positive a nature as to justify him in now thrusting himself into an incalculable position; whether it were not merely the fantasy of a young man's brain, only slightly or not at all connected with his heart.

He paused, hesitated, turned half about, but again went on. His withered guide led him along several obscure passages, and finally undid a door, through which, as it was opened, there came the sight and sound of rustling leaves, with the broken sunshine glimmering among them. Giovanni stepped forth, and, forcing himself through the entanglement of a shrub that wreathed its tendrils over the hidden entrance, stood beneath his own window in the open area of Dr. Rappaccini's garden.

How often is it the case that, when impossibilities have come to pass and dreams have condensed their misty substance into tangible realities, we find ourselves calm, and even coldly self-possessed, amid circumstances which it would have been a delirium of joy or agony to anticipate! Fate delights to thwart us thus. Passion will choose his own time to rush upon the scene, and lingers sluggishly behind when an appropriate adjustment of events would seem to summon his appearance. So was it now with Giovanni. Day after day his pulses had throbbed with feverish blood at the improbable idea of an interview with Beatrice, and of standing with her, face to face, in this very garden, basking in the Oriental sunshine of her beauty, and snatching from her full gaze the mystery which he deemed the riddle of his own existence. But now there was a singular and untimely equanimity within his breast. He threw a glance around the garden to discover if Beatrice or her father were present, and, perceiving that he was alone, began a critical observation of the plants.

The aspect of one and all of them dissatisfied him; their gorgeousness seemed fierce, passionate, and even unnatural. There was hardly an individual shrub which a wanderer, straying by himself through a forest, would not have been startled to find growing wild, as if an unearthly face had glared at him out of the thicket. Several also would have shocked a delicate instinct by an appearance of artificialness indicating that there had been such commixture, and, as it were, adultery, of various vegetable species, that the production was no longer of God's making, but the monstrous offspring of man's depraved fancy, glowing with only an evil mockery of beauty. They were probably the result of experiment, which in one or two cases had succeeded in mingling plants individually lovely into a compound possessing the questionable and ominous character that distinguished the whole growth of the garden. In fine, Giovanni recognized but two or three plants in the collection, and those of a kind that he well knew to be poisonous. While busy with these contemplations he heard the rustling of a silken garment, and, turning, beheld Beatrice emerging from beneath the sculptured portal.

Giovanni had not considered with himself what should be his deportment; whether he should apologize for his intrusion into the garden, or assume that he was there with the privity at least, if not by the desire, of Dr. Rappaccini or his daughter; but Beatrice's manner placed him at his ease, although leaving him still in doubt by what agency he had gained admittance. She came lightly along the path and met him near the broken fountain.

There was surprise in her face, but brightened by a simple and kind expression of pleasure.

"You are a connoisseur in flowers, signor," said Beatrice, with a smile, alluding to the bouquet which he had flung her from the window. "It is no marvel, therefore, if the sight of my father's rare collection has tempted you to take a nearer view. If he were here, he could tell you many strange and interesting facts as to the nature and habits of these shrubs; for he has spent a lifetime in such studies, and this garden is his world."

"And yourself, lady," observed Giovanni, "if fame says true,—you likewise are deeply skilled in the virtues indicated by these rich blossoms and these spicy perfumes. Would you deign to be my instructress, I should prove an apter scholar than if taught by Signor Rappaccini himself."

"Are there such idle rumors?" asked Beatrice, with the music of a pleasant laugh. "Do people say that I am skilled in my father's science of plants? What a jest is there! No; though I have grown up among these flowers, I know no more of them than their hues and perfume; and sometimes methinks I would fain rid myself of even that small knowledge. There are many flowers here, and those not the least brilliant, that shock and offend me when they meet my eye. But pray, signor, do not believe these stories about my science. Believe nothing of me save what you see with your own eyes."

"And must I believe all that I have seen with my own eyes?" asked Giovanni, pointedly, while the recollection of former scenes made him shrink. "No, signora; you demand too little of me. Bid me believe nothing save what comes from your own lips."

It would appear that Beatrice understood him. There came a deep flush to her cheek; but she looked full into Giovanni's eyes, and responded to his gaze of uneasy suspicion with a queenlike haughtiness.

"I do so bid you, signor," she replied. "Forget whatever you may have fancied in regard to me. If true to the outward senses, still it may be false in its essence; but the words of Beatrice Rappaccini's lips are true from the depths of the heart outward. Those you may believe."

A fervor glowed in her whole aspect and beamed upon Giovanni's consciousness like the light of truth itself; but while she spoke there was a fragrance in the atmosphere around her, rich and delightful, though evanescent, yet which the young man, from an indefinable reluctance, scarcely dared to draw into his lungs. It might be the odor of the flowers. Could it be Beatrice's breath which thus enbalmed her words with a strange richness, as if by steeping them in her heart? A faintness passed like a shadow over Giovanni and flitted away; he seemed to gaze through the beautiful girl's eyes into her transparent soul, and felt no more doubt or fear.

The tinge of passion that had colored Beatrice's manner vanished; she became gay, and appeared to derive a pure delight from her communion with the youth not unlike what the maiden of a lonely island might have felt conversing with a voyager from the civilized world. Evidently her experience of life had been confined within the limits of that garden. She talked now about matters as simple as the daylight or summer clouds, and now asked questions in reference to the city, or Giovanni's distant home, his friends, his mother, and his sisters—questions indicating such seclusion, and such lack of familiarity with modes and forms, that Giovanni responded as if to an infant. Her spirit gushed out before him like a fresh rill that was just catching its first glimpse of the sunlight and wondering at the reflections of earth and sky which were flung into its bosom. There came thoughts, too, from a deep source, and fantasies of a gemlike brilliancy, as if diamonds and rubies sparkled upward among the bubbles of the fountain. Ever and anon there gleamed across the young man's mind a sense of wonder that he should be walking side by side with the being who had so wrought upon his imagination, whom he had idealized in such hues of terror, in whom he had positively witnessed such manifestations of dreadful attributes,—that he should be conversing with Beatrice like a brother, and should find her so human and so maidenlike. But such reflections were only momentary; the effect of her character was too real not to make itself familiar at once.

In this free intercourse they had strayed through the garden, and now, after many turns among its avenues, were come to the shattered fountain, beside which grew the magnificent shrub, with its treasury of glowing blossoms. A fragrance was diffused from it which Giovanni recognized as identical with that which he had attributed to Beatrice's breath, but incomparably more powerful. As her eyes fell upon it, Giovanni beheld her

press her hand to her bosom as if her heart were throbbing suddenly and painfully.

"For the first time in my life," murmured she, addressing the shrub, "I had forgotten thee."

"I remember, signora," said Giovanni, "that you once promised to reward me with one of these living gems for the bouquet which I had the happy boldness to fling to your feet. Permit me now to pluck it as a memorial of this interview."

He made a step towards the shrub with extended hand; but Beatrice darted forward, uttering a shriek that went through his heart like a dagger. She caught his hand and drew it back with the whole force of her slender figure. Giovanni felt her touch thrilling through his fibres.

"Touch it not!" exclaimed she, in a voice of agony. "Not for thy life! It is fatal!"

Then, hiding her face, she fled from him and vanished beneath the sculptured portal. As Giovanni followed her with his eyes, he beheld the emaciated figure and pale intelligence of Dr. Rappaccini, who had been watching the scene, he knew not how long, within the shadow of the entrance.

No sooner was Guasconti alone in his chamber than the image of Beatrice came back to his passionate musings, invested with all the witchery that had been gathering around it ever since his first glimpse of her, and now likewise imbued with a tender warmth of girlish womanhood. She was human; her nature was endowed with all gentle and feminine qualities; she was worthiest to be worshipped; she was capable, surely, on her part, of the height and heroism of love. Those tokens which he had hitherto considered as proofs of a frightful peculiarity in her physical and moral system were now either forgotten or by the subtle sophistry of passion transmitted into a golden crown of enchantment, rendering Beatrice the more admirable by so much as she was the more unique. Whatever had looked ugly was now beautiful; or, if incapable of such a change, it stole away and hid itself among those shapeless half ideas which throng the dim region beyond the daylight of our perfect consciousness. Thus did he spend the night, nor fell asleep until the dawn had begun to awake the slumbering flowers in Dr. Rappaccini's garden, whither Giovanni's dreams doubtless led him. Up rose the sun in his due season, and, flinging his beams upon the young man's eyelids, awoke him to a sense of pain. When thoroughly aroused, he became sensible of a burning and tingling agony in his hand—in his right hand—the very hand which Beatrice had grasped in her own when he was on the point of plucking one of the gemlike flowers. On the back of that hand there was now a purple print like that of four small fingers, and the likeness of a slender thumb upon his wrist.

Oh, how stubbornly does love,—or even that cunning semblance of love which flourishes in the imagination, but strikes no depth of root into the heart,—how stubbornly does it hold its faith until the moment comes when it is doomed to vanish into thin mist! Giovanni wrapped a handkerchief about his hand and wondered what evil thing had stung him, and soon forgot his pain in a reverie of Beatrice.

After the first interview, a second was in the inevitable course of what we call fate. A third; a fourth; and a meeting with Beatrice in the garden was no longer an incident in Giovanni's daily life, but the whole space in which he might be said to live; for the anticipation and memory of that ecstatic hour made up the remainder. Nor was it otherwise with the daughter of Rappaccini. She watched for the youth's appearance and flew to his side with confidence as unreserved as if they had been playmates from early infancy—as if they were such playmates still. If, by any unwonted chance, he failed to come at the appointed moment, she stood beneath the window and sent up the rich sweetness of her tones to float around him in his chamber and echo and reverberate throughout his heart: "Giovanni! Giovanni! Why tarriest thou? Come down!" And down he hastened into that Eden of poisonous flowers.

But, with all this intimate familiarity, there was still a reserve in Beatrice's demeanor, so rigidly and invariably sustained that the idea of infringing it scarcely occurred to his imagination. By all appreciable signs, they loved; they had looked love with eyes that conveyed the holy secret from the depths of one soul into the depths of the other, as if it were too sacred to be whispered by the way; they had even spoken love in those gushes of passion when their spirits darted forth in articulated breath like tongues of long hidden flame; and yet there had been no seal of lips, no clasp of hands, nor any slightest caress such as love claims and hallows. He had never touched one of the gleaming ringlets of her hair; her garment—so marked was the physical barrier between them—had never been waved against him by a breeze. On the few occasions when Giovanni had seemed tempted to overstep the limit, Beatrice grew so sad, so stern, and withal wore such a look of desolate separation, shuddering at itself, that not a spoken word was requisite to repel him. At such times he was startled at the horrible suspicions that rose, monster-like, out of the caverns of his heart and stared him in the face; his love grew thin and faint as the morning mist; his doubts alone had substance. But, when Beatrice's face brightened again after the momentary shadow, she was transformed at once from the mysterious, questionable being whom he had watched with so much awe and horror; she was now the beautiful and unsophisticated girl whom he felt that his spirit knew with a certainty beyond all other knowledge.

A considerable time had now passed since Giovanni's last meeting with Baglioni. One morning, however, he was disagreeably surprised by a visit from the professor, whom he had scarcely thought of for whole weeks, and would willingly have forgotten still longer. Given up as he had long been to a pervading excitement, he could tolerate no companions except upon condition of their perfect sympathy with his present state of feeling. Such sympathy was not to be expected from Professor Baglioni.

The visitor chatted carelessly for a few moments about the gossip of the city and the university, and then took up another topic. "I have been reading an old classic author lately," said he, "and met with a story that strangely interested me. Possibly you may remember it. It is of an Indian prince, who sent a beautiful woman as a present to Alexander the Great. She was as lovely as the dawn and gorgeous as the sunset; but what especially distinguished her was a certain rich perfume in her breath—richer than a garden of Persian roses. Alexander, as was natural to a youthful conqueror, fell in love at first sight with this magnificent stranger; but a certain sage physician, happening to be present, discovered a terrible secret in regard to her."

"And what was that?" asked Giovanni, turning his eyes downward to avoid those of the professor.

"That this lovely woman," continued Baglioni, with emphasis, "had been nourished with poisons from her birth upward, until her whole nature was so imbued with them that she herself had become the deadliest poison in existence. Poison was her element of life. With that rich perfume of her breath she blasted the very air. Her love would have been poison—her embrace death. Is not this a marvellous tale?"

"A childish fable," answered Giovanni, nervously starting from his chair. "I marvel how your worship finds time to read such nonsense among your graver studies."

"By the by," said the professor, looking uneasily about him, "what singular fragrance is this in your apartment? Is it the perfume of your gloves? It is faint, but delicious; and yet, after all, by no means agreeable. Were I to breathe it long, methinks it would make me ill. It is like the breath of a flower; but I see no flowers in the chamber."

"Nor are there any," replied Giovanni, who had turned pale as the professor spoke; "nor, I think, is there any fragrance except in your worship's imagination. Odors, being a sort of element combined of the sensual and the spiritual, are apt to deceive us in this manner. The recollection of a perfume, the bare idea of it, may easily be mistaken for a present reality."

"Ay; but my sober imagination does not often play such tricks," said Baglioni; "and, were I to fancy any kind of odor, it would be that of some vile apothecary drug, wherewith my fingers are likely enough to be imbued. Our worshipful friend Rappaccini, as I have heard, tinctures his medicaments with odors richer than those of Araby. Doubtless, likewise, the fair and learned Signora Beatrice would minister to her patients with draughts as sweet as a maiden's breath; but woe to him that sips them!"

Giovanni's face evinced many contending emotions. The tone in which the professor alluded to the pure and lovely daughter of Rappaccini was a torture to his soul; and yet the intimation of a view of her character, opposite to his own, gave instantaneous distinctness to a thousand dim suspicions, which now grinned at him like so many demons. But he strove hard to quell them and to respond to Baglioni with a true lover's perfect faith.

"Signor professor," said he, "you were my father's friend; perchance, too, it is your purpose to act a friendly part towards his son. I would fain feel nothing towards you save respect and deference; but I pray you to observe, signor, that there is one subject on which we must not speak. You know not the Signora Beatrice. You cannot, therefore, estimate the wrong—the blasphemy, I may even say—that is offered to her character by a light or injurious word."

"Giovanni! my poor Giovanni!" answered the professor, with a calm expression of pity, "I know this wretched girl far better than yourself. You shall hear the truth in respect to the poisoner Rappaccini and his poisonous daughter; yes, poisonous as she is beautiful. Listen; for, even should you do violence to my gray hairs, it shall not silence me. That old fable of the Indian woman has become a truth by the deep and deadly science of Rappaccini and in the person of the lovely Beatrice."

Giovanni groaned and hid his face.

"Her father," continued Baglioni, "was not restrained by natural affection from offering up his child in this horrible manner as the victim of his insane zeal for science; for, let us do him justice, he is as true a man of science as ever distilled his own heart in an alembic. What, then, will be your fate? Beyond a doubt you are selected as the material of some new experiment. Perhaps the result is to be death; perhaps a fate more awful still. Rappaccini, with what he calls the interest of science before his eyes, will hesitate at nothing."

"It is a dream," muttered Giovanni to himself; "surely it is a dream."

"But," resumed the professor, "be of good cheer, son of my friend. It is not yet too late for the rescue. Possibly we may even succeed in bringing back this miserable child within the limits of ordinary nature, from which her father's madness has estranged her. Behold this little silver vase! It was wrought by the hands of the renowned Benvenuto Cellini, and is well worthy to be a love gift to the fairest dame in Italy. But its contents are invaluable. One little sip of this antidote would have rendered the most virulent poisons of the Borgias innocuous. Doubt not that it will be as efficacious against those of Rappaccini. Bestow the vase, and the precious liquid within it, on your Beatrice, and hopefully await the result."

Baglioni laid a small, exquisitely wrought silver vial on the table and withdrew, leaving what he had said to produce its effect upon the young man's mind.

"We will thwart Rappaccini yet," thought he, chuckling to himself, as he descended the stairs; "but, let us confess the truth of him, he is a wonderful man—a wonderful man indeed; a vile empiric, however, in his practice, and therefore not to be tolerated by those who respect the good old rules of the medical profession."

Throughout Giovanni's whole acquaintance with Beatrice, he had occasionally, as we have said, been haunted by dark surmises as to her character; yet so thoroughly had she made herself felt by him as a simple, natural, most affectionate, and guileless creature, that the image now held up by Professor Baglioni looked as strange and incredible as if it were not in accordance with his own original conception. True, there were ugly recollections connected with his first glimpses of the beautiful girl; he could not quite forget the bouquet that withered in her grasp, and the insect that perished amid the sunny air, by no ostensible agency save the fragrance of her breath. These incidents, however, dissolving in the pure light of her character, had no longer the efficacy of facts, but were acknowledged as mistaken fantasies, by whatever testimony of the senses they might appear to be substantiated. There is something truer and more real than what we can see with the eyes and touch with the finger. On such better evidence had Giovanni founded his confidence in Beatrice, though rather by the necessary force of her high attributes than by any deep and generous faith on his part. But now his spirit was incapable of sustaining itself at the height to which the early enthusiasm of passion had exalted it; he fell down, grovelling among earthly doubts, and defiled therewith the pure whiteness of Beatrice's image. Not that he gave her up; he did but distrust. He resolved to institute some decisive test that should satisfy him, once for all, whether there were those dreadful peculiarities in her physical nature which could not be supposed to exist without some corresponding monstrosity of soul. His eyes, gazing down afar, might have deceived him as to the lizard, the insect, and the flowers; but if he could witness, at the distance of a few paces, the sudden blight of one fresh and healthful flower in Beatrice's hand, there would be room for no further question. With this idea he hastened to the florist's and purchased a bouquet that was still gemmed with the morning dew-drops.

It was now the customary hour of his daily interview with Beatrice. Before descending into the garden, Giovanni failed not to look at his figure in the mirror—a vanity to be expected in a beautiful young man, yet, as displaying itself at that troubled and feverish moment, the token of a certain shallowness of feeling and insincerity of character. He did gaze, however, and said to himself that his features had never before possessed so rich a grace, nor his eyes such vivacity, nor his cheeks so warm a hue of superabundant life.

"At least," thought he, "her poison has not yet insinuated itself into my system. I am no flower to perish in her grasp."

With that thought he turned his eyes on the bouquet, which he had never once laid aside from his hand. A thrill of indefinable horror shot through his frame on perceiving that those dewy flowers were already beginning to droop; they wore the aspect of things that had been fresh and lovely yesterday. Giovanni grew white as marble, and stood motionless before the mirror, staring at his own reflection there as at the likeness of something frightful. He remembered Baglioni's remark about the fragrance that seemed to pervade the chamber. It must have been the poison in his breath! Then he shuddered—shuddered at himself. Recovering from his stupor, he began to watch with curious eye a spider that was busily at work hanging its web from the antique cornice of the apartment, crossing and recrossing the artful system of interwoven lines—as vigorous and active a spider as ever dangled from an old ceiling. Giovanni bent towards the insect, and emitted a deep, long breath. The spider suddenly ceased its toil; the web vibrated with a tremor originating in the body of the small artisan. Again Giovanni sent forth a breath, deeper, longer, and imbued with a venomous feeling out of his heart: he knew not whether he were wicked, or only desperate. The spider made a convulsive gripe with his limbs and hung dead across the window.

"Accursed! accursed!" muttered Giovanni, addressing himself. "Hast thou grown so poisonous that this deadly insect perishes by thy breath?"

At that moment a rich, sweet voice came floating up from the garden.

"Giovanni! Giovanni! It is past the hour! Why tarriest thou? Come down!"

"Yes," muttered Giovanni again. "She is the only being whom my breath may not slay! Would that it might!"

He rushed down, and in an instant was standing before the bright and loving eyes of

Beatrice. A moment ago his wrath and despair had been so fierce that he could have desired nothing so much as to wither her by a glance; but with her actual presence there came influences which had too real an existence to be at once shaken off; recollections of the delicate and benign power of her feminine nature, which had so often enveloped him in a religious calm; recollections of many a holy and passionate outgush of her heart, when the pure fountain had been unsealed from its depths and made visible in its transparency to his mental eye; recollections which, had Giovanni known how to estimate them, would have assured him that all this ugly mystery was but an earthly illusion, and that, whatever mist of evil might seem to have gathered over her, the real Beatrice was a heavenly angel. Incapable as he was of such high faith, still her presence had not utterly lost its magic. Giovanni's rage was quelled into an aspect of sullen insensibility. Beatrice, with a quick spiritual sense, immediately felt that there was a gulf of blackness between them which neither he nor she could pass. They walked on together, sad and silent, and came thus to the marble fountain and to its pool of water on the ground, in the midst of which grew the shrub that bore gem-like blossoms. Giovanni was affrighted at the eager enjoyment—the appetite, as it were—with which he found himself inhaling the fragrance of the flowers.

"Beatrice," asked he, abruptly, "whence came this shrub?"

"My father created it," answered she, with simplicity.

"Created it! created it!" repeated Giovanni. "What mean you, Beatrice?"

"He is a man fearfully acquainted with the secrets of Nature," replied Beatrice; "and, at the hour when I first drew breath, this plant sprang from the soil, the offspring of his science, of his intellect, while I was but his earthly child. Approach it not!" continued she, observing with terror that Giovanni was drawing nearer to the shrub. "It has qualities that you little dream of. But I, dearest Giovanni,—I grew up and blossomed with the plant and was nourished with its breath. It was my sister, and I loved it with a human affection; for, alas! —hast thou not suspected it?—there was an awful doom."

Here Giovanni frowned so darkly upon her that Beatrice paused and trembled. But her faith in his tenderness reassured her, and made her blush that she had doubted for an instant.

"There was an awful doom," she continued, "the effect of my father's fatal love of science, which estranged me from all society of my kind. Until Heaven sent thee, dearest Giovanni, O, how lonely was thy poor Beatrice!"

"Was it a hard doom?" asked Giovanni, fixing his eyes upon her.

"Only of late have I known how hard it was," answered she, tenderly. "O, yes; but my heart was torpid, and therefore quiet."

Giovanni's rage broke forth from his sullen gloom like a lightning flash out of a dark cloud.

"Accursed one!" cried he, with venomous scorn and anger. "And, finding thy solitude wearisome, thou hast severed me likewise from all the warmth of life and enticed me into thy region of unspeakable horror!"

"Giovanni!" exclaimed Beatrice, turning her large bright eyes upon his face. The force of his words had not found its way into her mind; she was merely thunderstruck.

"Yes, poisonous thing!" repeated Giovanni, beside himself with passion. "Thou hast done it! Thou hast blasted me! Thou hast filled my veins with poison! Thou hast made me as hateful, as ugly, as loathsome and deadly a creature as thyself—a world's wonder of hideous monstrosity! Now, if our breath be happily as fatal to ourselves as to all others, let us join our lips in one kiss of unutterable hatred, and so die!"

"What has befallen me?" murmured Beatrice, with a low moan out of her heart. "Holy Virgin, pity me, a poor heart-broken child!"

"Thou,—dost thou pray?" cried Giovanni, still with the same fiendish scorn. "Thy very prayers, as they come from thy lips, taint the atmosphere with death. Yes, yes; let us pray! Let us to church and dip our fingers in the holy water at the portal! They that come after us will perish as by a pestilence! Let us sign crosses in the air! It will be scattering curses abroad in the likeness of holy symbols!"

"Giovanni," said Beatrice, calmly, for her grief was beyond passion, "why dost thou join thyself with me thus in those terrible words? I, it is true, am the horrible thing thou namest me. But thou,—what hast thou to do, save with one other shudder at my hideous misery to go forth out of the garden and mingle with thy race, and forget that there ever crawled on earth such a monster as poor Beatrice?"

"Dost thou pretend ignorance?" asked Giovanni, scowling upon her. "Behold! this power have I gained from the pure daughter of Rappaccini."

There was a swarm of summer insects flitting through the air in search of the food promised by the flower odors of the fatal garden. They circled round Giovanni's head, and were evidently attracted towards him by the same influence which had drawn them for an instant within the sphere of several of the shrubs. He sent forth a breath among them, and smiled bitterly at Beatrice as at least a score of the insects fell dead upon the ground.

"I see it! I see it!" shrieked Beatrice. "It is my father's fatal science! No, no, Giovanni; it was not I! Never! never! I dreamed only to love thee and be with thee a little time, and so to let thee pass away, leaving but thine image in mine heart; for, Giovanni, believe it, though my body be nourished with poison, my spirit is God's creature, and craves love as its daily food. But my father,—he has united us in this fearful sympathy. Yes; spurn me, tread upon me, kill me! Oh, what is death after such words as thine? But it was not I. Not for a world of bliss would I have done it."

Giovanni's passion had exhausted itself in its outburst from his lips. There now came across him a sense, mournful, and not without tenderness, of the intimate and peculiar relationship between Beatrice and himself. They stood, as it were, in an utter solitude, which would be made none the less solitary by the densest throng of human life. Ought not, then, the desert of humanity around them to press this insulated pair closer together? If they should be cruel to one another, who was there to be kind to them? Besides, thought Giovanni, might there not still be a hope of his returning within the limits of ordinary nature, and leading Beatrice, the redeemed Beatrice, by the hand? O, weak, and selfish, and unworthy spirit, that could dream of an earthly union and earthly happiness as possible, after such deep love had been so bitterly wronged as was Beatrice's love by Giovanni's blighting words! No, no; there could be no such hope. She must pass heavily, with that broken heart, across the borders of Time—she must bathe her hurts in some fount of paradise, and forget her grief in the light of immortality, and *there* be well.

But Giovanni did not know it.

"Dear Beatrice," said he, approaching her, while she shrank away as always at his approach, but now with a different impulse, "dearest Beatrice, our fate is not yet so desperate. Behold! there is a medicine, potent, as a wise physician has assured me, and almost divine in its efficacy. It is composed of ingredients the most opposite to those by which thy awful father has brought this calamity upon thee and me. It is distilled of blessed herbs. Shall we not quaff it together, and thus be purified from evil?"

"Give it me!" said Beatrice, extending her hand to receive the little silver vial which Giovanni took from his bosom. She added, with a peculiar emphasis, "I will drink; but do thou await the result."

She put Baglioni's antidote to her lips; and, at the same moment, the figure of Rappaccini emerged from the portal and came slowly towards the marble fountain. As he drew near, the pale man of science seemed to gaze with a triumphant expression at the beautiful youth and maiden, as might an artist who should spend his life in achieving a picture or a group of statuary and finally be satisfied with his success. He paused; his bent form grew erect with conscious power; he spread out his hands over them in the attitude of a father imploring a blessing upon his children; but those were the same hands that had thrown poison into the stream of their lives. Giovanni trembled. Beatrice shuddered nervously, and pressed her hand upon her heart.

"My daughter," said Rappaccini, "thou art no longer lonely in the world. Pluck one of those precious gems from thy sister shrub and bid thy bridegroom wear it in his bosom. It will not harm him now. My science and the sympathy between thee and him have so wrought within his system that he now stands apart from common men, as thou dost, daughter of my pride and triumph, from ordinary women. Pass on, then, through the world, most dear to one another and dreadful to all besides!"

"My father," said Beatrice, feebly,—and still as she spoke she kept her hand upon her heart, —"wherefore didst thou inflict this miserable doom upon thy child?"

"Miserable!" exclaimed Rappaccini. "What mean you, foolish girl? Dost thou deem it misery to be endowed with marvellous gifts against which no power nor strength could avail an enemy—misery, to be able to quell the mightiest with a breath—misery, to be as terrible as thou art beautiful? Wouldst thou, then, have preferred the condition of a weak woman, exposed to all evil and capable of none?"

"I would fain have been loved, not feared," murmured Beatrice, sinking down upon the ground. "But now it matters not. I am going, father, where the evil which thou hast striven to mingle with my being will pass away like a dream—like the fragrance of these poisonous flowers, which will no longer taint my breath
10 among the flowers of Eden. Farewell, Giovanni! Thy words of hatred are like lead within my heart; but they, too, will fall away as I ascend. Oh, was there not, from the first, more poison in thy nature than in mine?"

To Beatrice,—so radically had her earthly part been wrought upon by Rappaccini's skill, —as poison had been life, so the powerful antidote was death; and thus the poor victim of man's ingenuity and of thwarted nature, and of the fatality that attends all such efforts of perverted wisdom, perished there, at the feet of her father and Giovanni. Just at that moment Professor Pietro Baglioni looked forth from the window, and called loudly, in a tone of triumph mixed with horror, to the thunder-stricken man of science,—

"Rappaccini! Rappaccini! and is *this* the upshot of your experiment!"   1844

» » ETHAN BRAND « «

A CHAPTER FROM AN ABORTIVE ROMANCE

23   Bartram the lime-burner, a rough, heavy-looking man, begrimed with charcoal, sat watching his kiln, at nightfall, while his little son played at building houses with the scattered fragments of marble, when, on the hillside below them, they heard a roar of laughter, not mirthful, but slow, and even solemn, like
30 a wind shaking the boughs of the forest.

"Father, what is that?" asked the little boy, leaving his play, and pressing betwixt his father's knees.

"Oh, some drunken man, I suppose," answered the lime-burner; "some merry fellow from the barroom in the village, who dared not laugh loud enough within doors, lest he should blow the roof of the house off. So here he is, shaking his jolly sides at the foot of Graylock."
40   "But, father," said the child, more sensitive than the obtuse, middle-aged clown, "he does not laugh like a man that is glad. So the noise frightens me!"

"Don't be a fool, child!" cried his father, gruffly. "You will never make a man, I do believe; there is too much of your mother in you. I have known the rustling of a leaf startle you. Hark! Here comes the merry fellow now. You shall see that there is no harm in him."
50   Bartram and his little son, while they were talking thus, sat watching the same lime-kiln that had been the scene of Ethan Brand's solitary and meditative life, before he began his search for the Unpardonable Sin. Many years, as we have seen, had now elapsed, since that

portentous night when the IDEA was first developed. The kiln, however, on the mountain-side, stood unimpaired, and was in nothing changed since he had thrown his dark thoughts into the intense glow of its furnace, and melted them, as it were, into the one thought that took possession of his life. It was a rude, round, tower-like structure about twenty feet high, heavily built of rough stones, and with a hillock of earth heaped about the larger part of its circumference; so that the blocks and fragments of marble might be drawn by cartloads, and thrown in at the top. There was an opening at the bottom of the tower, like an oven-mouth, but large enough to admit a man in a stooping posture, and provided with a massive iron door. With the smoke and jets of flame issuing from the chinks and crevices of this door, which seemed to give admittance into the hill-side, it resembled nothing so much as the private entrance to the infernal regions, which the shepherds of the Delectable Mountains were accustomed to show to pilgrims.

There are many such lime-kilns in that tract of country, for the purpose of burning the white marble which composes a large part of the substance of the hills. Some of them, built years ago, and long deserted, with weeds growing in the vacant round of the interior, which is open to the sky, and grass and wild-flowers rooting themselves into the chinks of the stones, look already like relics of antiquity, and may yet be overspread with the lichens of centuries to come. Others, where the lime-burner still feeds his daily and night-long fire, afford points of interest to the wanderer among the hills, who seats himself on a log of wood or a fragment of marble, to hold a chat with the solitary man. It is a lonesome, and, when the character is inclined to thought, may be an intensely thoughtful occupation; as it proved in the case of Ethan Brand, who had mused to such strange purpose, in days gone by, while the fire in this very kiln was burning.

The man who now watched the fire was of a different order, and troubled himself with no thoughts save the very few that were requisite to his business. At frequent intervals, he flung back the clashing weight of the iron door, and, turning his face from the insufferable glare, thrust in huge logs of oak, or stirred the immense brands with a long pole. Within the furnace were seen the curling and riotous flames, and the burning marble, almost molten with the intensity of heat; while without, the reflection of the fire quivered on the dark intricacy of the surrounding forest, and showed in the foreground a bright and ruddy little picture of the hut, the spring beside its door, the athletic and coal-begrimed figure of the lime-burner, and the half-frightened child, shrinking into the protection of his father's shadow. And when again the iron door was closed, then reappeared the tender light of the half-full moon, which vainly strove to trace out the indistinct shapes of the neighboring mountains; and, in the upper sky, there was a flitting congregation of clouds, still faintly tinged with the rosy sunset, though thus far down into the valley the sunshine had vanished long and long ago.

The little boy now crept still closer to his father, as footsteps were heard ascending the hill-side, and a human form thrust aside the bushes that clustered beneath the trees.

"Halloo! who is it?" cried the lime-burner, vexed at his son's timidity, yet half infected by it. "Come forward, and show yourself, like a man, or I'll fling this chunk of marble at your head!"

"You offer me a rough welcome," said a gloomy voice, as the unknown man drew nigh. "Yet I neither claim nor desire a kinder one, even at my own fireside."

To obtain a distincter view, Bartram threw open the iron door of the kiln, whence immediately issued a gush of fierce light, that smote full upon the stranger's face and figure. To a careless eye there appeared nothing very remarkable in his aspect, which was that of a man in a coarse, brown, country-made suit of clothes, tall and thin, with the staff and heavy shoes of a wayfarer. As he advanced, he fixed his eyes—which were very bright—intently upon the brightness of the furnace, as if he beheld, or expected to behold, some object worthy of note within it.

"Good evening, stranger," said the lime-burner; "whence come you, so late in the day?"

"I come from my search," answered the wayfarer; "for, at last, it is finished."

"Drunk!—or crazy!" muttered Bartram to himself. "I shall have trouble with the fellow. The sooner I drive him away, the better."

The little boy, all in a tremble, whispered to his father, and begged him to shut the door of the kiln, so that there might not be so much light; for that there was something in the man's face which he was afraid to look at, yet could not look away from. And, indeed, even the lime-burner's dull and torpid sense began to be impressed by an indescribable something in that thin, rugged, thoughtful visage, with the grizzled hair hanging wildly about it, and those deeply-sunken eyes, which gleamed like fires within the entrance of a mysterious cavern. But, as he closed the door, the stranger turned towards him, and spoke in a quiet, familiar way, that made Bartram feel as if he were a sane and sensible man, after all.

"Your task draws to an end, I see," said he. "This marble has already been burning three days. A few hours more will convert the stone to lime."

"Why, who are you?" exclaimed the lime-burner. "You seem as well acquainted with my business as I am myself."

"And well I may be," said the stranger; "for I followed the same craft many a long year, and here, too, on this very spot. But you are a new comer in these parts. Did you never hear of Ethan Brand?"

"The man that went in search of the Unpardonable Sin?" asked Bartram, with a laugh.

"The same," answered the stranger. "He has found what he sought, and therefore he comes back again."

"What! then you are Ethan Brand himself?" cried the lime-burner, in amazement. "I am a new comer here, as you say, and they call it eighteen years since you left the foot of Graylock. But, I can tell you, the good folks still talk about Ethan Brand, in the village yonder, and what a strange errand took him away from his lime-kiln. Well, and so you have found the Unpardonable Sin?"

"Even so!" said the stranger, calmly.

"If the question is a fair one," proceeded Bartram, "where might it be?"

Ethan Brand laid his finger on his own heart. "Here!" replied he.

And then, without mirth in his countenance, but as if moved by an involuntary recognition of the infinite absurdity of seeking throughout the world for what was the closest of all things to himself, and looking into every heart, save his own, for what was hidden in no other breast, he broke into a laugh of scorn. It was the same slow, heavy laugh, that had almost appalled the lime-burner when it heralded the wayfarer's approach.

The solitary mountain-side was made dismal by it. Laughter, when out of place, mistimed, or bursting forth from a disordered state of feeling, may be the most terrible modulation of the human voice. The laughter of one asleep, even if it be a little child,—the madman's laugh,—the wild, screaming laugh of a born idiot,—are sounds that we sometimes tremble to hear, and would always willingly forget. Poets have imagined no utterance of fiends or hobgoblins so fearfully appropriate as a laugh. And even the obtuse lime-burner felt his nerves shaken, as this strange man looked inward at his own heart, and burst into laughter that rolled away into the night, and was indistinctly reverberated among the hills.

"Joe," said he to his little son, "scamper down to the tavern in the village, and tell the jolly fellows there that Ethan Brand has come back, and that he has found the Unpardonable Sin!"

The boy darted away on his errand, to which Ethan Brand made no objection, nor seemed hardly to notice it. He sat on a log of wood, looking steadfastly at the iron door of the kiln. When the child was out of sight, and his swift and light footsteps ceased to be heard treading first on the fallen leaves and then on the rocky mountain-path, the lime-burner began to regret his departure. He felt that the little fellow's presence had been a barrier between his guest and himself, and that he must now deal, heart to heart, with a man who, on his own confession, had committed the one only crime for which Heaven could afford no mercy. That crime, in its indistinct blackness, seemed to overshadow him. The lime-burner's

own sins rose up within him, and made his memory riotous with a throng of evil shapes that asserted their kindred with the Master Sin, whatever it might be, which it was within the scope of man's corrupted nature to conceive and cherish. They were all of one family; they went to and fro between his breast and Ethan Brand's, and carried dark greetings from one to the other.

Then Bartram remembered the stories which had grown traditionary in reference to this strange man, who had come upon him like a shadow of the night, and was making himself at home in his old place, after so long absence that the dead people, dead and buried for years, would have had more right to be at home, in any familiar spot, than he. Ethan Brand, it was said, had conversed with Satan himself in the lurid blaze of this very kiln. The legend had been matter of mirth heretofore, but looked grisly now. According to this tale, before Ethan Brand departed on his search, he had been accustomed to evoke a fiend from the hot furnace of the lime-kiln, night after night, in order to confer with him about the Unpardonable Sin; the man and the fiend each laboring to frame the image of some mode of guilt which could neither be atoned for nor forgiven. And, with the first gleam of light upon the mountain-top, the fiend crept in at the iron door, there to abide the intensest element of fire, until again summoned forth to share in the dreadful task of extending man's possible guilt beyond the scope of Heaven's else infinite mercy.

While the lime-burner was struggling with the horror of these thoughts, Ethan Brand rose from the log, and flung open the door of the kiln. The action was in such accordance with the idea in Bartram's mind, that he almost expected to see the Evil One issue forth, red-hot, from the raging furnace.

"Hold! hold!" cried he, with a tremulous attempt to laugh; for he was ashamed of his fears, although they overmastered him. "Don't, for mercy's sake, bring out your devil now!"

"Man!" sternly replied Ethan Brand, "what need have I of the devil? I have left him behind me, on my track. It is with such half-way sinners as you that he busies himself. Fear not, because I open the door. I do but act by old custom, and am going to trim your fire, like a lime-burner, as I was once."

He stirred the vast coals, thrust in more wood, and bent forward to gaze into the hollow prison-house of the fire, regardless of the fierce glow that reddened upon his face. The lime-burner sat watching him, and half suspected his strange guest of a purpose, if not to evoke a fiend, at least to plunge bodily into the flames, and thus vanish from the sight of man. Ethan Brand, however, drew quietly back, and closed the door of the kiln.

"I have looked," said he, "into many a human heart that was seven times hotter with sinful passions than yonder furnace is with fire. But I found not there what I sought. No, not the Unpardonable Sin!"

"What is the Unpardonable Sin?" asked the lime-burner; and then he shrank farther from his companion, trembling lest his question should be answered.

"It is a sin that grew within my own breast," replied Ethan Brand, standing erect, with a pride that distinguishes all enthusiasts of his stamp. "A sin that grew nowhere else! The sin of an intellect that triumphed over the sense of brotherhood with man and reverence for God, and sacrificed everything to its own mighty claims! The only sin that deserves a recompense of immortal agony! Freely, were it to do again, would I incur the guilt. Unshrinkingly I accept the retribution!"

"The man's head is turned," muttered the lime-burner to himself. "He may be a sinner like the rest of us,—nothing more likely,—but, I'll be sworn, he is a madman too."

Nevertheless, he felt uncomfortable at his situation, alone with Ethan Brand on the wild mountain-side, and was right glad to hear the rough murmur of tongues, and the footsteps of what seemed a pretty numerous party, stumbling over the stones and rustling through the underbrush. Soon appeared the whole lazy regiment that was wont to infest the village tavern, comprehending three or four individuals who had drunk flip beside the bar-room fire through all the winters, and smoked their pipes beneath the stoop through all the summers, since Ethan Brand's departure. Laughing boisterously, and mingling all their voices together in unceremonious talk, they now burst into the moonshine and narrow streaks of fire-light that illuminated the open space before the lime-kiln. Bartram set the door ajar again, flooding the spot with light, that the whole company might get a fair view of Ethan Brand, and he of them.

There, among other old acquaintances, was a once ubiquitous man, now almost extinct, but whom we were formerly sure to encounter at the hotel of every thriving village throughout the country. It was the stage-agent. The present speciman of the genus was a wilted and smoke-dried man, wrinkled and red-nosed, in a smartly-cut, brown, bob-tailed coat, with brass buttons, who, for a length of time unknown, had kept his desk and corner in the bar-room, and was still puffing what seemed to be the same cigar that he had lighted twenty years before. He had great fame as a dry joker, though, perhaps, less on account of any intrinsic humor than from a certain flavor of brandy-toddy and tobacco-smoke, which impregnated all his ideas and expressions, as well as his person. Another well-remembered though strangely altered face was that of Lawyer Giles, as people still call him in courtesy; an elderly ragamuffin, in his soiled shirt-sleeves and tow-cloth trousers. This poor fellow had been an attorney, in what he called his better days, a sharp practitioner, and in great vogue among the village litigants; but flip, and sling, and toddy, and cocktails, imbibed at all hours, morning, noon and night, had caused him to slide from intellectual to various kinds and degrees of bodily labor, till, at last, to adopt his own phrase, he slid into a soap-vat. In other words, Giles was now a soap-boiler, in a small way. He had come to be but the fragment of a human being, a part of one foot having been chopped off by an axe, and an entire hand torn away by the devilish grip of a steam-engine. Yet, though the corporeal hand was gone, a spiritual member remained; for, stretching forth the stump, Giles steadfastly averred that he felt an invisible thumb and fingers with as vivid a sensation as before the real ones were amputated. A maimed and miserable wretch he was; but one, nevertheless, whom the world could not trample on, and had no right to scorn, either in this or any previous stage of his misfortunes, since he had still kept up the courage and spirit of a man, asked nothing in charity, and with his one hand—and that the left one—fought a stern battle against want and hostile circumstances.

Among the throng, too, came another personage, who, with certain points of similarity to Lawyer Giles, had many more of difference. It was the village doctor; a man of some fifty years, whom, at an earlier period of his life, we introduced as paying a professional visit to Ethan Brand during the latter's supposed insanity. He was now a purple-visaged, rude, and

brutal, yet half-gentlemanly figure, with something wild, ruined, and desperate in his talk,
and in all the details of his gesture and manners. Brandy possessed this man like an evil
spirit, and made him as surly and savage as a
wild beast, and as miserable as a lost soul; but
there was supposed to be in him such wonderful skill, such native gifts of healing, beyond
any which medical science could impart, that
society caught hold of him, and would not let
him sink out of its reach. So, swaying to and
fro upon his horse, and grumbling thick accents
at the bedside, he visited all the sick chambers
for miles about among the mountain towns, and
sometimes raised a dying man, as it were, by
miracle, or quite as often, no doubt, sent his
patient to a grave that was dug many a year
too soon. The doctor had an everlasting pipe
in his mouth, and, as somebody said, in allusion
to his habit of swearing, it was always alight
with hell-fire.

These three worthies pressed forward, and
greeted Ethan Brand each after his own fashion, earnestly inviting him to partake of the
contents of a certain black bottle, in which,
as they averred, he would find something far
better worth seeking for than the Unpardonable Sin. No mind, which has wrought itself
by intense and solitary meditation into a high
state of enthusiasm, can endure the kind of
contact with low and vulgar modes of thought
and feeling to which Ethan Brand was now
subjected. It made him doubt—and, strange
to say, it was a painful doubt—whether he had
indeed found the Unpardonable Sin, and found
it within himself. The whole question on which
he had exhausted life, and more than life,
looked like a delusion.

"Leave me," he said bitterly, "ye brute
beasts, that have made yourselves so, shrivel-
ling up your souls with fiery liquors! I have
done with you. Years and years ago, I groped
into your hearts, and found nothing there for
my purpose. Get ye gone!"

"Why, you uncivil scoundrel," cried the
fierce doctor, "is that the way you respond to
the kindness of your best friends? Then let me
tell you the truth. You have no more found
the Unpardonable Sin than yonder boy Joe
has. You are but a crazy fellow,—I told you so
twenty years ago,—neither better nor worse
than a crazy fellow, and the fit companion of
old Humphrey, here!"

He pointed to an old man, shabbily dressed,
with long white hair, thin visage, and unsteady
eyes. For some years past this aged person had
been wandering about among the hills, inquiring of all travelers whom he met for his
daughter. The girl, it seemed, had gone off
with a company of circus-performers; and occasionally tidings of her came to the village,
and fine stories were told of her glittering
appearance as she rode on horseback in the
ring, or performed marvelous feats on the tight-
rope.

The white-haired father now approached
Ethan Brand, and gazed unsteadily into his
face.

"They tell me you have been all over the
earth," said he, wringing his hands with earnestness. "You must have seen my daughter,
for she makes a grand figure in the world, and
everybody goes to see her. Did she send any
word to her old father, or say when she was
coming back?"

Ethan Brand's eye quailed beneath the old
man's. That daughter, from whom he so earnestly desired a word of greeting, was the
Esther of our tale, the very girl whom, with
such cold and remorseless purpose, Ethan
Brand had made the subject of a psychological
experiment, and wasted, absorbed, and perhaps
annihilated her soul, in the process.

"Yes," murmured he, turning away from the
hoary wanderer; "it is no delusion. There is an
Unpardonable Sin!"

While these things were passing, a merry
scene was going forward in the area of cheerful
light, beside the spring and before the door of
the hut. A number of the youth of the village,
young men and girls, had hurried up the hillside, impelled by curiosity to see Ethan Brand,
the hero of so many a legend familiar to their
childhood. Finding nothing, however, very
remarkable in his aspect,—nothing but a sun-
burnt wayfarer, in plain garb and dusty shoes,
who sat looking into the fire, as if he fancied
pictures among the coals,—these young people
speedily grew tired of observing him. As it
happened, there was other amusement at hand.
An old German Jew, traveling with a diorama
on his back, was passing down the mountain-
road towards the village just as the party
turned aside from it, and, in hopes of eking
out the profits of the day, the showman had
kept them company to the lime-kiln.

"Come, old Dutchman," cried one of the
young men, "let us see your pictures, if you
can swear they are worth looking at!"

"Oh, yes, Captain," answered the Jew,—

whether as a matter of courtesy or craft, he styled everybody Captain,—"I shall show you, indeed, some very superb pictures!"

So, placing his box in a proper position, he invited the young men and girls to look through the glass orifices of the machine, and proceeded to exhibit a series of the most outrageous scratchings and daubings, as specimens of the fine arts, that ever an itinerant showman had the face to impose upon his circle of spectators. The pictures were worn out, moreover, tattered, full of cracks and wrinkles, dingy with tobacco-smoke, and otherwise in a most pitiable condition. Some purported to be cities, public edifices, and ruined castles in Europe; others represented Napoleon's battles and Nelson's sea-fights; and in the midst of these would be seen a gigantic, brown, hairy hand,—which might have been mistaken for the Hand of Destiny, though, in truth, it was only the showman's,—pointing its forefinger to various scenes of the conflict, while its owner gave historical illustrations. When, with much merriment at its abominable deficiency of merit, the exhibition was concluded, the German bade little Joe put his head into the box. Viewed through the magnifying glasses, the boy's round, rosy visage assumed the strangest imaginable aspect of an immense Titanic child, the mouth grinning broadly, and the eyes and every other feature overflowing with fun at the joke. Suddenly, however, that merry face turned pale, and its expression changed to horror, for this easily impressed and excitable child had become sensible that the eye of Ethan Brand was fixed upon him through the glass.

"You make the little man to be afraid, Captain," said the German Jew, turning up the dark and strong outline of his visage, from his stooping posture. "But look again, and, by chance, I shall cause you to see somewhat that is very fine, upon my word!"

Ethan Brand gazed into the box for an instant, and then starting back, looked fixedly at the German. What had he seen? Nothing, apparently; for a curious youth, who had peeped in almost at the same moment, beheld only a vacant space of canvas.

"I remember you now," muttered Ethan Brand to the showman.

"Ah, Captain," whispered the Jew of Nuremberg, with a dark smile, "I find it to be a heavy matter in my show-box,—this Unpardonable Sin! By my faith, Captain, it has wearied my shoulders, this long day, to carry it over the mountain."

"Peace," answered Ethan Brand, sternly, "or get thee into the furnace yonder!"

The Jew's exhibition had scarcely concluded, when a great, elderly dog,—who seemed to be his own master, as no person in the company laid claim to him,—saw fit to render himself the object of public notice. Hitherto, he had shown himself a very quiet, well-disposed old dog, going round from one to another, and, by way of being sociable, offering his rough head to be patted by any kindly hand that would take so much trouble. But now, all of a sudden, this grave and venerable quadruped, of his own mere motion, and without the slightest suggestion from anybody else, began to run round after his tail, which, to heighten the absurdity of the proceeding, was a great deal shorter than it should have been. Never was seen such headlong eagerness in pursuit of an object that could not possibly be attained; never was heard such a tremendous outbreak of growling, snarling, barking, and snapping,—as if one end of the ridiculous brute's body were at deadly and most unforgivable enmity with the other. Faster and faster, round about went the cur; and faster and still faster fled the unapproachable brevity of his tail; and louder and fiercer grew his yells of rage and animosity; until, utterly exhausted, and as far from the goal as ever, the foolish old dog ceased his performance as suddenly as he had begun it. The next moment he was as mild, quiet, sensible, and respectable in his deportment, as when he first scraped acquaintance with the company.

As may be supposed, the exhibition was greeted with universal laughter, clapping of hands, and shouts of encore, to which the canine performer responded by wagging all that there was to wag of his tail, but appeared totally unable to repeat his very successful effort to amuse the spectators.

Meanwhile, Ethan Brand had resumed his seat upon the log, and moved, it might be, by a perception of some remote analogy between his own case and that of this self-pursuing cur, he broke into the awful laugh, which, more than any other token, expressed the condition of his inward being. From that moment, the merriment of the party was at an end; they stood aghast, dreading lest the inauspicious sound should be reverberated around the horizon, and that mountain would thunder it to mountain, and so the horror be prolonged upon their ears. Then, whispering one to another that it was late,—that the moon was almost down,—that the August night was growing chill,—they hurried homewards, leaving the lime-burner and little Joe to deal as they might with their unwelcome guest. Save for these three human beings, the open space on the hill-side was a solitude, set in a vast gloom of forest. Beyond that darksome verge, the fire-light glimmered on the stately trunks and almost black foliage of pines, intermixed with the lighter verdure of sapling oaks, maples, and poplars, while here and there lay the gigantic corpses of dead trees, decaying on the leaf-strewn soil. And it seemed to little Joe—a timorous and imaginative child—that the silent forest was holding its breath, until some fearful thing should happen.

Ethan Brand thrust more wood into the fire, and closed the door of the kiln; then looking over his shoulder at the lime-burner and his son, he bade, rather than advised, them to retire to rest.

"For myself, I cannot sleep," said he. "I have matters that it concerns me to meditate upon. I will watch the fire, as I used to do in the old time."

"And call the devil out of the furnace to keep you company, I suppose," muttered Bartram, who had been making intimate acquaintance with the black bottle above-mentioned. "But watch, if you like, and call as many devils as you like! For my part, I shall be all the better for a snooze. Come, Joe!"

As the boy followed his father into the hut, he looked back at the wayfarer, and the tears came into his eyes, for his tender spirit had an intuition of the bleak and terrible loneliness in which this man had enveloped himself.

When they had gone, Ethan Brand sat listening to the crackling of the kindled wood, and looking at the little spirts of fire that issued through the chinks of the door. These trifles, however, once so familiar, had but the slightest hold of his attention, while deep within his mind he was reviewing the gradual but marvelous change that had been wrought upon him by the search to which he had devoted himself. He remembered how the night dew had fallen upon him,—how the dark forest had whispered to him,—how the stars had gleamed upon him,—a simple and loving man, watching his fire in the years gone by, and ever musing as it burned. He remembered with

what tenderness, with what love and sympathy for mankind, and what pity for human guilt and woe, he had first begun to contemplate those ideas which afterwards became the inspiration of his life; with what reverence he had then looked into the heart of man, viewing it as a temple originally divine, and, however desecrated, still to be held sacred by a brother; with what awful fear he had deprecated the success of his pursuit, and prayed that the Unpardonable Sin might never be revealed to him. Then ensued that vast intellectual development, which, in its progress, disturbed the counterpoise between his mind and heart. The Idea that possessed his life had operated as a means of education; it had gone on cultivating his powers to the highest point of which they were susceptible; it had raised him from the level of an unlettered laborer to stand on a star-lit eminence, whither the philosophers of the earth, laden with the lore of universities, might vainly strive to clamber after him. So much for the intellect! But where was the heart? That, indeed, had withered—had contracted—had hardened—had perished! It had ceased to partake of the universal throb. He had lost his hold of the magnetic chain of humanity. He was no longer a brother-man, opening the chambers or the dungeons of our common nature by the key of holy sympathy, which gave him a right to share in all its secrets; he was now a cold observer, looking on mankind as the subject of his experiment, and, at length, converting man and woman to be his puppets, and pulling the wires that moved them to such degrees of crime as were demanded for his study.

Thus Ethan Brand became a fiend. He began to be so from the moment that his moral nature had ceased to keep the pace of improvement with his intellect. And now, as his highest effort and inevitable development,—as the bright and gorgeous flower, and rich, delicious fruit of his life's labor,—he had produced the Unpardonable Sin!

"What more have I to seek? What more to achieve?" said Ethan Brand to himself. "My task is done, and well done!"

Starting from the log with a certain alacrity in his gait, and ascending the hillock of earth that was raised against the stone circumference of the lime-kiln, he thus reached the top of the structure. It was a space of perhaps ten feet across, from edge to edge, presenting a view of the upper surface of the immense mass of broken marble with which the kiln was heaped. All these innumerable blocks and fragments of marble were red-hot and vividly on fire, sending up great spouts of blue flame, which quivered aloft and danced madly, as within a magic circle, and sank and rose again, with continual and multitudinous activity. As the lonely man bent forward over this terrible body of fire, the blasting heat smote up against his person with a breath that, it might be supposed, would have scorched and shrivelled him up in a moment.

Ethan Brand stood erect, and raised his arms on high. The blue flames played upon his face, and imparted the wild and ghastly light which alone could have suited its expression; it was that of a fiend on the verge of plunging into his gulf of intensest torment.

"O Mother Earth," cried he, "who art no more my Mother, and into whose bosom this frame shall never be resolved! O mankind, whose brotherhood I have cast off, and trampled thy great heart beneath my feet! O stars of heaven, that shone on me of old, as if to light me onward and upward!—farewell all, and forever. Come, deadly element of Fire, —henceforth my familiar frame! Embrace me, as I do thee!"

That night the sound of a fearful peal of laughter rolled heavily through the sleep of the lime-burner and his little son; dim shapes of horror and anguish haunted their dreams, and seemed still present in the rude hovel, when they opened their eyes to the daylight.

"Up, boy, up!" cried the lime-burner, staring about him. "Thank Heaven, the night is gone, at last; and rather than pass such another, I would watch my lime-kiln, wide awake, for a twelvemonth. This Ethan Brand, with his humbug of an Unpardonable Sin, has done me no such mighty favor, in taking my place!"

He issued from the hut, followed by little Joe, who kept fast hold of his father's hand. The early sunshine was already pouring its gold upon the mountain-tops; and though the valleys were still in shadow, they smiled cheerfully in the promise of the bright day that was hastening onward. The village, completely shut in by hills, which swelled away gently about it, looked as if it had rested peacefully in the hollow of the great hand of Providence. Every dwelling was distinctly visible; the little spires of the two churches pointed upwards, and caught a fore-glimmering of brightness from the sun-gilt skies upon their gilded weather-cocks. The tavern was astir, and the figure of the old, smoke-dried stage-agent, cigar in mouth, was seen beneath the stoop. Old Graylock was glorified with a golden cloud upon his head. Scattered likewise over the breasts of the surrounding mountains, there were heaps of hoary mist, in fantastic shapes, some of them far down into the valley, others high up towards the summits, and still others of the same family of mist or cloud, hovering in the gold radiance of the upper atmosphere. Stepping from one to another of the clouds that rested on the hills, and thence to the loftier brotherhood that sailed in air, it seemed almost as if a mortal man might thus ascend into the heavenly regions. Earth was so mingled with sky that it was a day-dream to look at it.

To supply that charm of the familiar and homely, which Nature so readily adopts into a scene like this, the stage-coach was rattling down the mountain-road, and the driver sounded his horn, while echo caught up the notes, and intertwined them into a rich and varied and elaborate harmony, of which the original performer could lay claim to little share. The great hills played a concert among themselves, each contributing a strain of airy sweetness.

Little Joe's face brightened at once.

"Dear father," cried he, skipping cheerily to and fro, "that strange man is gone, and the sky and the mountains all seem glad of it!"

"Yes," growled the lime-burner, with an oath, "but he has let the fire go down, and no thanks to him if five hundred bushels of lime are not spoiled. If I catch the fellow hereabouts again, I shall feel like tossing him into the furnace!"

With his long pole in his hand, he ascended to the top of the kiln. After a moment's pause, he called to his son.

"Come up here, Joe!" said he.

So little Joe ran up the hillock, and stood by his father's side. The marble was all burnt into perfect, snow-white lime. But on its surface, in the midst of the circle,—snow-white too, and thoroughly converted into lime,—lay a human skeleton, in the attitude of a person who, after long toil, lies down to long repose. Within the ribs—strange to say—was the shape of a human heart.

"Was the fellow's heart made of marble?" cried Bartram, in some perplexity at this phenomenon. "At any rate, it is burnt into what looks like special good lime; and, taking all the bones together, my kiln is half a bushel the richer for him."

So saying, the rude lime-burner lifted his pole, and, letting it fall upon the skeleton, the relics of Ethan Brand were crumbled into fragments.   1850

» » *From:* OUR OLD HOME « «

OUTSIDE GLIMPSES OF ENGLISH POVERTY.

Becoming an inhabitant of a great English
13 town, I often turned aside from the prosperous thoroughfares, (where the edifices, the shops, and the bustling crowd differed not so much from scenes with which I was familiar in my own country,) and went designedly astray among precincts that reminded me of some of Dickens's grimiest pages. There I caught
20 glimpses of a people and a mode of life that were comparatively new to my observation, a sort of sombre phantasmagoric spectacle, exceedingly undelightful to behold, yet involving a singular interest and even fascination in its ugliness.

Dirt, one would fancy, is plenty enough all over the world, being the symbolic accompaniment of the foul incrustation which began to settle over and bedim all earthly things as soon
30 as Eve had bitten the apple; ever since which hapless epoch, her daughters have chiefly been engaged in a desperate and unavailing struggle to get rid of it. But the dirt of a poverty-stricken English street is a monstrosity unknown on our side of the Atlantic. It reigns supreme within its own limits, and is inconceivable everywhere beyond them. We enjoy the great advantage, that the brightness and dryness of our atmosphere keep everything
40 clean that the sun shines upon, converting the larger portion of our impurities into transitory dust which the next wind can sweep away, in contrast with the damp, adhesive grime that incorporates itself with all surfaces (unless continually and painfully cleansed) in the chill moisture of the English air. Then the all-pervading smoke of the city, abundantly inter-
47 mingled with the sable snow-flakes of bituminous coal, hovering overhead, descending, and alighting on pavements and rich architectural fronts, on the snowy muslin of the ladies, and the gentlemen's starched collars and shirt-bosoms, invests even the better streets in a half-mourning garb. It is beyond the resources of Wealth to keep the smut away from its

premises or its own fingers' ends; and as for Poverty, it surrenders itself to the dark influence without a struggle. Along with disastrous circumstances, pinching need, adversity so lengthened out as to constitute the rule of life, there comes a certain chill depression of the spirits which seems especially to shudder at cold water. In view of so wretched a state of things, we accept the ancient Deluge not merely as an insulated phenomenon, but as a periodical necessity, and acknowledge that nothing less than such a general washing-day could suffice to cleanse the slovenly old world of its moral and material dirt.

Gin-shops, or what the English call spirit-vaults, are numerous in the vicinity of these poor streets, and are set off with the magnificence of gilded door-posts, tarnished by contact with the unclean customers who haunt there. Ragged children come thither with old shaving-mugs, or broken-nosed teapots, or any such make-shift receptacle, to get a little poison or madness for their parents, who deserve no better requital at their hands for having engendered them. Inconceivably sluttish women enter at noonday and stand at the counter among boon-companions of both sexes, stirring up misery and jollity in a bumper together, and quaffing off the mixture with a relish. As for the men, they lounge there continually, drinking till they are drunken,—drinking as long as they have a halfpenny left, and then, as it seemed to me, waiting for a sixpenny miracle to be wrought in their pockets, so as to enable them to be drunken again. Most of these establishments have a significant advertisement of "Beds," doubtless for the accommodation of their customers in the interval between one intoxication and the next. I never could find it in my heart, however, utterly to condemn these sad revellers, and should certainly wait till I had some better consolation to offer before depriving them of their dram of gin, though death itself were in the glass; for methought their poor souls needed such fiery stimulant to lift them a little way out of the smothering squalor of both their outward and

interior life, giving them glimpses and suggestions, even if bewildering ones, of a spiritual
existence that limited their present misery. The
temperance-reformers unquestionably derive
their commission from the Divine Beneficence,
but have never been taken fully into its counsels. All may not be lost, though those good
men fail.

Pawn-brokers' establishments, distinguished
by the mystic symbol of the three golden balls,
were conveniently accessible; though what
personal property these wretched people could
possess, capable of being estimated in silver or
copper, so as to afford a basis for a loan, was
a problem that still perplexes me. Old clothes-
men, likewise, dwelt hard by, and hung out
ancient garments to dangle in the wind. There
were butchers' shops, too, of a class adapted to
the neighborhood, presenting no such generously fattened carcasses as Englishmen love
to gaze at in the market, no stupendous halves
of mighty beeves, no dead hogs or muttons
ornamented with carved bas-reliefs of fat on
their ribs and shoulders, in a peculiarly British
style of art,—not these, but bits and gobbets of
lean meat, selvages snipt off from steaks, tough
and stringy morsels, bare bones smitten away
from joints by the cleaver, tripe, liver, bullocks' feet, or whatever else was cheapest and
divisible into the smallest lots. I am afraid that
even such delicacies came to many of their
tables hardly oftener than Christmas. In the
windows of other little shops you saw half a
dozen wizened herrings, some eggs in a basket,
looking so dingily antique that your imagination smelt them, fly-speckled biscuits, segments
of a hungry cheese, pipes and papers of tobacco. Now and then a sturdy milk-woman
passed by with a wooden yoke over her shoulders, supporting a pail on either side, filled with
a whitish fluid, the composition of which was
water and chalk and the milk of a sickly cow,
who gave the best she had, poor thing! but
could scarcely make it rich or wholesome,
spending her life in some close city-nook and
pasturing on strange food. I have seen, once
or twice, a donkey coming into one of these
streets with panniers full of vegetables, and
departing with a return cargo of what looked
like rubbish and street-sweepings. No other
commerce seemed to exist, except, possibly, a
girl might offer you a pair of stockings or a
worked collar, or a man whisper something
mysterious about wonderfully cheap cigars.
And yet I remember seeing female hucksters

in those regions, with their wares on the edge
of the sidewalk and their own seats right in
the carriage-way, pretending to sell half-de-
cayed oranges and apples, toffy, Ormskirk
cakes, combs and cheap jewelry, the coarsest
kind of crockery, and little plates of oysters,—
knitting patiently all day long, and removing
their undiminished stock in trade at nightfall.
All indispensable importations from other
quarters of the town were on a remarkably
diminutive scale: for example, the wealthier
inhabitants purchased their coal by the wheel-
barrow-load, and the poorer ones by the peck-
measure. It was a curious and melancholy
spectacle, when an overladen coal-cart happened to pass through the street and drop a
handful or two of its burden in the mud, to see
half a dozen women and children scrambling
for the treasure-trove, like a flock of hens and
chickens gobbling up some spilt corn. In this
connection I may as well mention a commodity of boiled snails (for such they appeared to
me, though probably a marine production)
which used to be peddled from door to door,
piping hot, as an article of cheap nutriment.

The population of these dismal abodes appeared to consider the sidewalks and middle of
the street as their common hall. In a drama of
low life, the unity of place might be arranged
rigidly according to the classic rule, and the
street be the one locality in which every scene
and incident should occur. Courtship, quarrels,
plot and counterplot, conspiracies for robbery
and murder, family difficulties or agreements,
—all such matters, I doubt not are constantly
discussed or transacted in this sky-roofed saloon, so regally hung with its sombre canopy
of coal-smoke. Whatever the disadvantages of
the English climate, the only comfortable or
wholesome part of life, for the city poor, must
be spent in the open air. The stifled and
squalid rooms where they lie down at night,
whole families and neighborhoods together, or
sulkily elbow one another in the daytime, when
a settled rain drives them within doors, are
worse horrors than it is worth while (without
a practical object in view) to admit into one's
imagination. No wonder that they creep forth
from the foul mystery of their interiors, stumble down from their garrets, or scramble up
out of their cellars, on the upper step of which
you may see the grimy housewife, before the
shower is ended, letting the raindrops gutter
down her visage; while her children (an imp-
ish progeny of cavernous recesses below the

common sphere of humanity) swarm into the daylight and attain all that they know of personal purification in the nearest mud-puddle. It might almost make a man doubt the existence of his own soul, to observe how Nature has flung these little wretches into the street and left them there, so evidently regarding them as nothing worth, and how all mankind acquiesce in the great mother's estimate of her offspring. For, if they are to have no immortality, what superior claim can I assert for mine? And how difficult to believe that anything so precious as a germ of immortal growth can have been buried under this dirt-heap, plunged into this cesspool of misery and vice! As often as I beheld the scene, it affected me with surprise and loathsome interest, much resembling, though in a far intenser degree, the feeling with which, when a boy, I used to turn over a plank or an old log that had long lain on the damp ground, and found a vivacious multitude of unclean and devilish-looking insects scampering to and fro beneath it. Without an infinite faith, there seemed as much prospect of a blessed futurity for those hideous bugs and many-footed worms as for these brethren of our humanity and co-heirs of all our heavenly inheritance. Ah, what a mystery! Slowly, slowly, as after groping at the bottom of a deep, noisome, stagnant pool, my hope struggles upward to the surface, bearing the half-drowned body of a child along with it, and heaving it aloft for its life, and my own life, and all our lives. Unless these slime-clogged nostrils can be made capable of inhaling celestial air, I know not how the purest and most intellectual of us can reasonably expect ever to taste a breath of it. The whole question of eternity is staked there. If a single one of those helpless little ones be lost, the world is lost!

The women and children greatly preponderate in such places; the men probably wandering abroad in quest of that daily miracle, a dinner and a drink, or perhaps slumbering in the daylight that they may the better follow out their cat-like rambles through the dark. Here are women with young figures, but old, wrinkled, yellow faces, tanned and blear-eyed with the smoke which they cannot spare from their scanty fires,—it being too precious for its warmth to be swallowed by the chimney. Some of them sit on the door-steps, nursing their unwashed babies at bosoms which we will glance aside from, for the sake of our mothers and all womanhood, because the fairest spectacle is here the foulest. Yet motherhood, in these dark abodes, is strangely identical with what we have all known it to be in the happiest homes. Nothing, as I remember, smote me with more grief and pity (all the more poignant because perplexingly entangled with an inclination to smile) than to hear a gaunt and ragged mother priding herself on the pretty ways of her ragged and skinny infant, just as a young matron might, when she invites her lady friends to admire her plump, white-robed darling in the nursery. Indeed, no womanly characteristic seemed to have altogether perished out of these poor souls. It was the very same creature whose tender torments make the rapture of our young days, whom we love, cherish, and protect, and rely upon in life and death, and whom we delight to see beautify her beauty with rich robes and set it off with jewels, though now fantastically masquerading in a garb of tatters, wholly unfit for her to handle. I recognized her, over and over again, in the groups round a door-step or in the descent of a cellar, chatting with prodigious earnestness about intangible trifles, laughing for a little jest, sympathizing at almost the same instant with one neighbor's sunshine and another's shadow, wise, simple, sly, and patient, yet easily perturbed, and breaking into small feminine ebullitions of spite, wrath, and jealousy, tornadoes of a moment, such as vary the social atmosphere of her silken-skirted sisters, though smothered into propriety by dint of a well-bred habit. Not that there was an absolute deficiency of good breeding, even here. It often surprised me to witness a courtesy and deference among these ragged folks, which, having seen it, I did not thoroughly believe in, wondering whence it should have come. I am persuaded, however, that there were laws of intercourse which they never violated,—a code of the cellar, the garret, the common staircase, the door-step, and the pavement, which perhaps had as deep a foundation in natural fitness as the code of the drawing-room.

Yet again I doubt whether I may not have been uttering folly in the last two sentences, when I reflect how rude and rough these specimens of feminine character generally were. They had a readiness with their hands that reminded me of Molly Seagrim and other heroines in Fielding's novels. For example, I have seen a woman meet a man in the street, and, for no reason perceptible to me, suddenly clutch him by the hair and cuff his ears,—an infliction which he bore with exemplary patience, only snatching the very earliest opportunity to take to his heels. Where a sharp tongue will not serve the purpose they trust to the sharpness of their finger-nails, or incarnate a whole vocabulary of vituperative words in a resounding slap, or the downright blow of a doubled fist. All English people, I imagine, are influenced in a far greater degree than ourselves by this simple and honest tendency, in cases of disagreement, to batter one another's persons; and whoever has seen a crowd of English ladies (for instance, at the door of the Sistine Chapel, in Holy Week) will be satisfied that their belligerent propensities are kept in abeyance only by a merciless rigor on the part of society. It requires a vast deal of refinement to spiritualize their large physical endowments. Such being the case with the delicate ornaments of the drawing-room, it is the less to be wondered at that women who live mostly in the open air, amid the coarsest kind of companionship and occupation, should carry on the intercourse of life with a freedom unknown to any class of American females, though still, I am resolved to think, compatible with a generous breadth of natural propriety. It shocked me, at first, to see them (of all ages, even elderly, as well as infants that could just toddle across the street alone) going about in the mud and mire, or through the dusky snow and slosh of a severe week in winter, with petticoats high uplifted above bare, red feet and legs; but I was comforted by observing that both shoes and stockings generally reappeared with better weather, having been thriftily kept out of the damp for the convenience of dry feet within doors. Their hardihood was wonderful, and their strength greater than could have been expected from such spare diet as they probably lived upon. I have seen them carrying on their heads great burdens under which they walked as freely as if they were fashionable bonnets; or sometimes the burden was huge enough almost to cover the whole person, looked at from behind,—as in Tuscan villages you may see the girls coming in from the country with great bundles of green twigs upon their backs, so that they resemble locomotive masses of verdure and fragrance. But these poor English women seemed to be laden with rubbish, incongruous and indescribable, such as bones and rags, the sweepings of the house and of the street, a merchandise gathered up from what poverty itself had thrown away, a heap of filthy stuff analogous to Christian's bundle of sin.

Sometimes, though very seldom, I detected a certain gracefulness among the younger women that was altogether new to my observation. It was a charm proper to the lowest class. One girl I particularly remember, in a garb none of the cleanest and nowise smart, and her self exceedingly coarse in all respects, but yet endowed with a sort of witchery, a native charm, a robe of simple beauty and suitable behavior that she was born in and had never been tempted to throw off, because she had really nothing else to put on. Eve herself could not have been more natural. Nothing was affected, nothing imitative; no proper grace was vulgarized by an effort to assume the manners or adornments of another sphere. This kind of beauty, arrayed in a fitness of its own, is probably vanishing out of the world, and will certainly never be found in America, where all the girls, whether daughters of the upper-tendom, the mediocrity, the cottage, or the kennel, aim at one standard of dress and deportment, seldom accomplishing a perfectly triumphant hit or an utterly absurd failure. Those words, "genteel" and "ladylike," are terrible ones and do us infinite mischief, but it is because (at least, I hope so) we are in a transition state, and shall emerge into a higher mode of simplicity than has ever been known to past ages.

In such disastrous circumstances as I have been attempting to describe, it was beautiful to observe what a mysterious efficacy still asserted itself in character. A woman, evidently poor as the poorest of her neighbors, would be knitting or sewing on the door-step, just as fifty other women were; but round about her skirts (though wofully patched) you would be sensible of a certain sphere of decency, which, it seemed to me, could not have been kept more impregnable in the cosiest little sitting-room, where the tea-kettle on the hob was humming its good old song of domestic peace. Maidenhood had a similar power. The evil habit that grows upon us in this harsh world makes me faithless to my own better perceptions and yet I have seen girls in these wretched streets, on whose virgin purity, judging merely from their impression on my instincts as they passed by, I should have deemed it safe, at the moment, to stake my life. The next moment, however, as the surrounding flood of moral uncleanness surged over their footsteps, I would not have staked a spike of thistle-down on the same wager. Yet the miracle was within the scope of Providence, which is equally wise and equally beneficent, (even to those poor girls, though I acknowledge the fact without the remotest comprehension of the mode of it,) whether they were pure or what we fellow-sinners call vile. Unless your faith be deep-rooted and of most vigorous growth, it is the safer way not to turn aside into this region so suggestive of miserable doubt. It was a place "with dreadful faces thronged," wrinkled and grim with vice and wretchedness; and, thinking over the line of Milton here quoted, I come to the conclusion that those ugly lineaments which startled Adam and Eve, as they looked backward to the closed gate of Paradise, were no fiends from the pit, but the more terrible foreshadowings of what so many of their descendants were to be. God help them, and us likewise, their brethren and sisters! Let me add, that, forlorn, ragged, care-worn, hopeless, dirty, haggard, hungry, as they were, the most pitiful thing of all was to see the sort of patience with which they accepted their lot, as if they had been born into the world for that and nothing else. Even the little children had this characteristic in as perfect development as their grandmothers.

The children, in truth, were the ill-omened blossoms from which another harvest of precisely such dark fruitage as I saw ripened around me was to be produced. Of course you would imagine these to be lumps of crude iniquity, tiny vessels as full as they could hold of naughtiness; nor can I say a great deal to the contrary. Small proof of parental discipline could I discern, save when a mother (drunken, I sincerely hope) snatched her own imp out of a group of pale, half-naked, humor-eaten abortions that were playing and squabbling together in the mud, turned up its tatters, brought down her heavy hand on its poor little tenderest part, and let it go again with a shake. If the child knew what the punishment was for, it was wiser than I pretend to be. It yelled, and went back to its playmates in the mud. Yet let me bear testimony to what was beautiful, and more touching than anything that I ever witnessed in the intercourse of happier children. I allude to the superintendence which some of these small people (too small, one would think, to be sent into the street alone, had there been any other nursery for them)

exercised over still smaller ones. Whence they derived such a sense of duty, unless immediately from God, I cannot tell; but it was wonderful to observe the expression of responsibility in their deportment, the anxious fidelity with which they discharged their unfit office, the tender patience with which they linked their less pliable impulses to the wayward foot-steps of an infant, and let it guide them whithersoever it liked. In the hollow-cheeked, large-eyed girl of ten, whom I saw giving a cheerless oversight to her baby-brother, I did not so much marvel at it. She had merely come a little earlier than usual to the perception of what was to be her business in life. But I admired the sickly-looking little boy, who did violence to his boyish nature by making himself the servant of his little sister,—she too small to walk, and he too small to take her in his arms,—and therefore working a kind of miracle to transport her from one dirt-heap to another. Beholding such works of love and duty, I took heart again, and deemed it not so impossible, after all, for these neglected children to find a path through the squalor and evil of their circumstances up to the gate of heaven. Perhaps there was this latent good in all of them, though generally they looked brutish, and dull even in their sports; there was little mirth among them, nor even a fully awakened spirit of blackguardism. Yet sometimes, again, I saw, with surprise and a sense as if I had been asleep and dreaming, the bright, intelligent, merry face of a child whose dark eyes gleamed with vivacious expression through the dirt that incrusted its skin, like sunshine struggling through a very dusty window-pane. . . .

After making myself as familiar as I decently could with the poor streets, I became curious to see what kind of a home was provided for the inhabitants at the public expense, fearing that it must needs be a most comfortless one, or else their choice (if choice it were) of so miserable a life outside was truly difficult to account for. Accordingly, I visited a great alms-house, and was glad to observe how unexceptionably all the parts of the establishment were carried on, and what an orderly life, full-fed, sufficiently reposeful, and undisturbed by the arbitrary exercise of authority, seemed to be led there. Possibly, indeed, it was that very orderliness, and the cruel necessity of being neat and clean, and even the comfort resulting from these and other Christian-like restraints and regulations, that constituted the principal grievance on the part of the poor, shiftless inmates, accustomed to a life-long luxury of dirt and harum-scarumness. The wild life of the streets has perhaps as unforgettable a charm, to those who have once thoroughly imbibed it, as the life of the forest or the prairie. But I conceive rather that there must be insuperable difficulties, for the majority of the poor, in the way of getting admittance to the almshouse, than that a merely æsthetic preference for the street would incline the pauper-class to fare scantily and precariously, and expose their raggedness to the rain and snow, when such a hospitable door stood wide open for their entrance. It might be that the roughest and darkest side of the matter was not shown me, there being persons of eminent station and of both sexes in the party which I accompanied; and, of course, a properly trained public functionary would have deemed it a monstrous rudeness, as well as a great shame, to exhibit anything to people of rank that might too painfully shock their sensibilities.

The women's ward was the portion of the establishment which we especially examined. It could not be questioned that they were treated with kindness as well as care. No doubt, as has been already suggested, some of them felt the irksomeness of submission to general rules of orderly behavior, after being accustomed to that perfect freedom from the minor proprieties, at least, which is one of the compensations of absolutely hopeless poverty, or of any circumstances that set us fairly below the decencies of life. I asked the governor of the house whether he met with any difficulty in keeping peace and order among his inmates; and he informed me that his troubles among the women were incomparably greater than with the men. They were freakish, and apt to be quarrelsome, inclined to plague and pester one another in ways that it was impossible to lay hold of, and to thwart his own authority by the like intangible methods. He said this with the utmost good-nature, and quite won my regard by so placidly resigning himself to the inevitable necessity of letting the women throw dust into his eyes. They certainly looked peaceable and sisterly enough, as I saw them, though still it might be faintly perceptible that some of them were consciously playing their parts before the governor and his distinguished visitors.

This governor seemed to me a man thoroughly fit for his position. An American, in an office of similar responsibility, would doubtless be a much superior person, better educated, possessing a far wider range of thought, more naturally acute, with a quicker tact of external observation and a readier faculty of dealing with difficult cases. The women would not succeed in throwing half so much dust into his eyes. Moreover, his black coat, and thin, sallow visage, would make him look like a scholar, and his manners would indefinitely approximate to those of a gentleman. But I cannot help questioning, whether, on the whole, these higher endowments would produce decidedly better results. The Englishman was thoroughly plebeian both in aspect and behavior, a bluff, ruddy-faced, hearty, kindly, yeoman-like personage, with no refinement whatever, nor any superfluous sensibility, but gifted with a native wholesomeness of character which must have been a very beneficial element in the atmosphere of the almshouse. He spoke to his pauper family in loud, good-humored, cheerful tones, and treated them with a healthy freedom that probably caused the forlorn wretches to feel as if they were free and healthy likewise. If he had understood them a little better, he would not have treated them half so wisely. We are apt to make sickly people more morbid, and unfortunate people more miserable, by endeavoring to adapt our deportment to their especial and individual needs. They eagerly accept our well-meant efforts; but it is like returning their own sick breath back upon themselves, to be breathed over and over again, intensifying the inward mischief at every repetition. The sympathy that would really do them good is of a kind that recognizes their sound and healthy parts, and ignores the part affected by disease, which will thrive under the eye of a too close observer like a poisonous weed in the sunshine. My good friend the governor had no tendencies in the latter direction, and abundance of them in the former, and was consequently as wholesome and invigorating as the west wind with a little spice of the north in it, brightening the dreary visages that encountered us as if he had carried a sunbeam in his hand. He expressed himself by his whole being and personality, and by works more than words, and had the not unusual English merit of knowing what to do much better than how to talk about it.

The women, I imagine, must have felt one

imperfection in their state, however comfortable otherwise. They were forbidden, or, at all events, lacked the means, to follow out their natural instinct of adorning themselves; all were dressed in one homely uniform of blue-checked gowns, with such caps upon their heads as English servants wear. Generally, too, they had one dowdy English aspect, and a vulgar type of features so nearly alike that they seemed literally to constitute a sisterhood. We have few of these absolutely unilluminated faces among our native American population, individuals of whom must be singularly unfortunate, if, mixing as we do, no drop of gentle blood has contributed to refine the turbid element, no gleam of hereditary intelligence has lighted up the stolid eyes, which their forefathers brought from the Old Country. Even in this English almshouse, however, there was at least one person who claimed to be intimately connected with rank and wealth. The governor, after suggesting that this person would probably be gratified by our visit, ushered us into a small parlor, which was furnished a little more like a room in a private dwelling than others that we entered, and had a row of religious books and fashionable novels on the mantelpiece. An old lady sat at a bright coal fire, reading a romance, and rose to receive us with a certain pomp of manner and elaborate display of ceremonious courtesy, which, in spite of myself, made me inwardly question the genuineness of her aristocratic pretensions. But, at any rate, she looked like a respectable old soul, and was evidently gladdened to the very core of her frost-bitten heart by the awful punctiliousness with which we responded to her gracious and hospitable, though unfamiliar welcome. After a little polite conversation, we retired; and the governor, with a lowered voice and an air of deference, told us that she had been a lady of quality, and had ridden in her own equipage, not many years before, and now lived in continual expectation that some of her rich relatives would drive up in their carriages to take her away. Meanwhile, he added, she was treated with great respect by her fellow-paupers. I could not help thinking, from a few criticisable peculiarities in her talk and manner, that there might have been a mistake on the governor's part, and perhaps a venial exaggeration on the old lady's, concerning her former position in society; but what struck me was the forcible instance of that most prevalent of English

vanities, the pretension to aristocratic connection, on one side, and the submission and reverence with which it was accepted by the governor and his household, on the other. Among ourselves, I think, when wealth and eminent position have taken their departure, they seldom leave a pallid ghost behind them, —or, if it sometimes stalks abroad, few recognize it.

We went into several other rooms, at the doors of which, pausing on the outside, we could hear the volubility, and sometimes the wrangling, of the female inhabitants within, but invariably found silence and peace when we stepped over the threshold. The women were grouped together in their sitting-rooms, sometimes three or four, sometimes a larger number, classified by their spontaneous affinities, I suppose, and all busied, so far as I can remember, with the one occupation of knitting coarse yarn stockings. Hardly any of them, I am sorry to say, had a brisk or cheerful air, though it often stirred them up to a momentary vivacity to be accosted by the governor, and they seemed to like being noticed, however slightly, by the visitors. The happiest person whom I saw there (and, running hastily through my experiences, I hardly recollect to have seen a happier one in my life, if you take a careless flow of spirits as happiness) was an old woman that lay in bed among ten or twelve heavy-looking females, who plied their knitting-work round about her. She laughed, when we entered, and immediately began to talk to us, in a thin, little, spirited quaver, claiming to be more than a century old; and the governor (in whatever way he happened to be cognizant of the fact) confirmed her age to be a hundred and four. Her jauntiness and cackling merriment were really wonderful. It was as if she had got through with all her actual business in life two or three generations ago, and now, freed from every responsibility for herself or others, had only to keep up a mirthful state of mind till the short time, or long time, (and, happy as she was, she appeared not to care whether it were long or short,) before Death, who had misplaced her name in his list, might remember to take her away. She had gone quite round the circle of human existence, and come back to the playground again. And so she had grown to be a kind of miraculous old pet, the plaything of people seventy or eighty years younger than herself, who talked and laughed with her as if she were a child, finding great delight in her wayward and strangely playful responses, into some of which she cunningly conveyed a gibe that caused their ears to tingle a little. She had done getting out of bed in this world, and lay there to be waited upon like a queen or a baby.

In the same room sat a pauper who had once been an actress of considerable repute, but was compelled to give up her profession by a softening of the brain. The disease seemed to have stolen the continuity out of her life, and disturbed all healthy relationship between the thoughts within her and the world without. On our first entrance, she looked cheerfully at us, and showed herself ready to engage in conversation; but suddenly, while we were talking with the century-old crone, the poor actress began to weep, contorting her face with extravagant stage-grimaces, and wringing her hands for some inscrutable sorrow. It might have been a reminiscence of actual calamity in her past life, or, quite as probably, it was but a dramatic woe, beneath which she had staggered and shrieked and wrung her hands with hundreds of repetitions in the sight of crowded theatres, and been as often comforted by thunders of applause. But my idea of the mystery was, that she had a sense of wrong in seeing the aged woman (whose empty vivacity was like the rattling of dry peas in a bladder) chosen as the central object of interest to the visitors, while she herself, who had agitated thousands of hearts with a breath, sat starving for the admiration that was her natural food. I appeal to the whole society of artists of the Beautiful and the Imaginative,— poets, romancers, painters, sculptors, actors,— whether or no this is a grief that may be felt even amid the torpor of a dissolving brain!

We looked into a good many sleeping-chambers, where were rows of beds, mostly calculated for two occupants, and provided with sheets and pillow-cases that resembled sackcloth. It appeared to me that the sense of beauty was insufficiently regarded in all the arrangements of the almshouse; a little cheap luxury for the eye, at least, might do the poor folks a substantial good. But, at all events, there was the beauty of perfect neatness and orderliness, which, being heretofore known to few of them, was perhaps as much as they could well digest in the remnant of their lives. We were invited into the laundry, where a great washing and drying were in process, the whole atmosphere being hot and vaporous with the steam of wet garments and bedclothes. This atmosphere was the pauper-life of the past week or fortnight resolved into a gaseous state, and breathing it, however fastidiously, we were forced to inhale the strange element into our inmost being. Had the Queen been there, I know not how she could have escaped the necessity. What an intimate brotherhood is this in which we dwell, do what we may to put an artificial remoteness between the high creature and the low one! A poor man's breath, borne on the vehicle of tobacco-smoke, floats into a palace-window and reaches the nostrils of a monarch. It is but an example, obvious to the sense, of the innumerable and secret channels by which, at every moment of our lives, the flow and reflux of a common humanity pervade us all. How superficial are the niceties of such as pretend to keep aloof! Let the whole world be cleansed, or not a man or woman of us all can be clean.

By and by we came to the ward where the children were kept, on entering which, we saw, in the first place, several unlovely and unwholesome little people lazily playing together in a courtyard. And here a singular incommodity befell one member of our party. Among the children was a wretched, pale, half-torpid little thing, (about six years old, perhaps, but I know not whether a girl or a boy,) with a humor in its eyes and face, which the governor said was the scurvy, and which appeared to bedim its powers of vision, so that it toddled about gropingly, as if in quest of it did not precisely know what. This child—this sickly, wretched, humor-eaten infant, the offspring of unspeakable sin and sorrow, whom it must have required several generations of guilty progenitors to render so pitiable an object as we beheld it—immediately took an unaccountable fancy to the gentleman just hinted at. It prowled about him like a pet kitten, rubbing against his legs, following everywhere at his heels, pulling at his coat-tails, and, at last, exerting all the speed that its poor limbs were capable of, got directly before him and held forth its arms, mutely insisting on being taken up. It said not a word, being perhaps underwitted and incapable of prattle. But it smiled up in his face,—a sort of woful gleam was that smile, through the sickly blotches that covered its features,—and found means to express such a perfect confidence that it was going to be fondled and made much of, that there was no possibility in a human heart of balking its expectation. It was as if God had promised the poor child this favor on behalf of that individual, and he was bound to fulfil the contract, or else no longer call himself a man among men. Nevertheless, it could be no easy thing for him to do, he being a person burdened with more than an Englishman's customary reserve, shy of actual contact with human beings, afflicted with a peculiar distaste for whatever was ugly, and, furthermore, accustomed to that habit of observation from an insulated stand-point which is said (but, I hope, erroneously) to have the tendency of putting ice into the blood.

So I watched the struggle in his mind with a good deal of interest, and am seriously of opinion that he did an heroic act, and effected more than he dreamed of towards his final salvation, when he took up the loathsome child and caressed it as tenderly as if he had been its father. To be sure, we all smiled at him, at the time, but doubtless would have acted pretty much the same in a similar stress of circumstances. The child, at any rate, appeared to be satisfied with his behavior; for when he had held it a considerable time, and set it down, it still favored him with its company, keeping fast hold of his forefinger till we reached the confines of the place. And on our return through the courtyard, after visiting another part of the establishment, here again was this same little Wretchedness waiting for its victim, with a smile of joyful, and yet dull recognition about its scabby mouth and in its rheumy eyes. No doubt, the child's mission in reference to our friend was to remind him that he was responsible, in his degree, for all the sufferings and misdemeanors of the world in which he lived, and was not entitled to look upon a particle of its dark calamity as if it were none of his concern: the offspring of a brother's iniquity being his own blood-relation, and the guilt, likewise, a burden on him, unless he expiated it by better deeds.

All the children in this ward seemed to be invalids, and, going up-stairs, we found more of them in the same or a worse condition than the little creature just described, with their mothers (or more probably other women, for the infants were mostly foundlings) in attendance as nurses. The matron of the ward, a middle-aged woman, remarkably kind and motherly in aspect, was walking to and fro across the chamber—on that weary journey in which careful mothers and nurses travel so continually and so far, and gain never a step

of progress—with an unquiet baby in her arms. She assured us that she enjoyed her occupation, being exceedingly fond of children; and, in fact, the absence of timidity in all the little people was a sufficient proof that they could have had no experience of harsh treatment, though, on the other hand, none of them appeared to be attracted to one individual more than another. In this point they differed widely from the poor child below-stairs. They seemed to recognize a universal motherhood in womankind, and cared not which individual might be the mother of the moment. I found their tameness as shocking as did Alexander Selkirk that of the brute subjects of his else solitary kingdom. It was a sort of tame familiarity, a perfect indifference to the approach of strangers, such as I never noticed in other children. I accounted for it partly by their nerveless, unstrung state of body, incapable of the quick thrills of delight and fear which play upon the lively harp-strings of a healthy child's nature, and partly by their woful lack of acquaintance with a private home, and their being therefore destitute of the sweet homebred shyness, which is like the sanctity of heaven about a mother-petted child. Their condition was like that of chickens hatched in an oven, and growing up without the especial guardianship of a matron-hen: both the chicken and the child, methinks, must needs want something that is essential to their respective characters.

In this chamber (which was spacious, containing a large number of beds) there was a clear fire burning on the hearth, as in all the other occupied rooms; and directly in front of the blaze sat a woman holding a baby, which, beyond all reach of comparison, was the most horrible object that ever afflicted my sight. Days afterwards—nay, even now, when I bring it up vividly before my mind's eye—it seemed to lie upon the floor of my heart, polluting my moral being with the sense of something grievously amiss in the entire conditions of humanity. The holiest man could not be otherwise than full of wickedness, the chastest virgin seemed impure, in a world where such a babe was possible. The governor whispered me, apart, that, like nearly all the rest of them, it was the child of unhealthy parents. Ah, yes! There was the mischief. This spectral infant, a hideous mockery of the visible link which Love creates between man and woman, was born of disease and sin. Diseased Sin was its father, and Sinful Disease its mother, and their offspring lay in the woman's arms like a nursing Pestilence, which, could it live and grow up, would make the world a more accursed abode than ever heretofore. Thank Heaven, it could not live! This baby, if we must give it that sweet name, seemed to be three or four months old, but, being such an unthrifty changeling, might have been considerably older. It was all covered with blotches, and preternaturally dark and discolored; it was withered away, quite shrunken and fleshless; it breathed only amid pantings and gaspings, and moaned painfully at every gasp. The only comfort in reference to it was the evident impossibility of its surviving to draw many more of those miserable, moaning breaths; and it would have been infinitely less heart-depressing to see it die, right before my eyes, than to depart and carry it alive in my remembrance, still suffering the incalculable torture of its little life. I can by no means express how horrible this infant was, neither ought I to attempt it. And yet I must add one final touch. Young as the poor little creature was, its pain and misery had endowed it with a premature intelligence, insomuch that its eyes seemed to stare at the by-standers out of their sunken sockets knowingly and appealingly, as if summoning us one and all to witness the deadly wrong of its existence. At least, I so interpreted its look, when it positively met and responded to my own awe-stricken gaze, and therefore I lay the case, as far as I am able, before mankind, on whom God has imposed the necessity to suffer in soul and body till this dark and dreadful wrong be righted.

Thence we went to the school-rooms, which were underneath the chapel. The pupils, like the children whom we had just seen, were, in large proportion, foundlings. Almost without exception, they looked sickly, with marks of eruptive trouble in their doltish faces, and a general tendency to diseases of the eye. Moreover, the poor little wretches appeared to be uneasy within their skins, and screwed themselves about on the benches in a disagreeably suggestive way, as if they had inherited the evil habits of their parents as an innermost garment of the same texture and material as the shirt of Nessus, and must wear it with unspeakable discomfort as long as they lived. I saw only a single child that looked healthy; and on my pointing him out, the governor informed me that this little boy, the sole exception to the miserable aspect of his school-fellows, was not a foundling, nor properly a work-house child, being born of respectable parentage, and his father one of the officers of the institution. As for the remainder,—the hundred pale abortions to be counted against one rosy-cheeked boy,—what shall we say or do? Depressed by the sight of so much misery, and uninventive of remedies for the evils that force themselves on my perception, I can do little more than recur to the idea already hinted at in the early part of this article, regarding the speedy necessity of a new deluge. So far as these children are concerned, at any rate, it would be a blessing to the human race, which they will contribute to enervate and corrupt, —a greater blessing to themselves, who inherit no patrimony but disease and vice, and in whose souls if there be a spark of God's life, this seems the only possible mode of keeping it aglow,—if every one of them could be drowned tonight, by their best friends, instead of being put tenderly to bed. This heroic method of treating human maladies, moral and material, is certainly beyond the scope of man's discretionary rights, and probably will not be adopted by Divine Providence until the opportunity of milder reformation shall have been offered us, again and again, through a series of future ages.

It may be fair to acknowledge that the humane and excellent governor, as well as other persons better acquainted with the subject than myself, took a less gloomy view of it, though still so dark a one as to involve scanty consolation. They remarked that individuals of the male sex, picked up in the streets and nurtured in the work-house, sometimes succeed tolerably well in life, because they are taught trades before being turned into the world, and, by dint of immaculate behavior and good luck, are not unlikely to get employment and earn a livelihood. The case is different with the girls. They can only go to service, and are invariably rejected by families of respectability on account of their origin, and for the better reason of their unfitness to fill satisfactorily even the meanest situations in a well-ordered English household. Their resource is to take service with people only a step or two above the poorest class, with whom they fare scantily, endure harsh treatment, lead shifting and precarious lives, and finally drop into the slough of evil, through which, in their best estate, they do but pick their slimy way on stepping-stones.

From the schools we went to the bake-house,

and the brew-house, (for such cruelty is not harbored in the heart of a true Englishman as to deny a pauper his daily allowance of beer), and through the kitchens, where we beheld an immense pot over the fire, surging and walloping with some kind of a savory stew that filled it up to its brim. We also visited a tailor's shop, and a shoemaker's shop, in both of which a number of men, and pale, diminutive apprentices, were at work, diligently enough, though seemingly with small heart in the business. Finally, the governor ushered us into a shed, inside of which was piled up an immense quantity of new coffins. They were of the plainest description, made of pine boards, probably of American growth, not very nicely smoothed by the plane, neither painted nor stained with black, but provided with a loop of rope at either end for the convenience of lifting the rude box and its inmate into the cart that shall carry them to the burial-ground. There, in holes ten feet deep, the paupers are buried one above another, mingling their relics indistinguishably. In another world may they resume their individuality, and find it a happier one than here!

As we departed, a character came under our notice which I have met with in all almshouses, whether of the city or village, or in England or America. It was the familiar simpleton, who shuffled across the courtyard, clattering his wooden-soled shoes, to greet us with a howl or a laugh, I hardly know which, holding out his hand for a penny, and chuckling grossly when it was given him. All underwitted persons, so far as my experience goes, have this craving for copper coin, and appear to estimate its value by a miraculous instinct, which is one of the earliest gleams of human intelligence while the nobler faculties are yet in abeyance. There may come a time, even in this world, when we shall all understand that our tendency to the individual appropriation of gold and broad acres, fine houses, and such good and beautiful things as are equally enjoyable by a multitude, is but a trait of imperfectly developed intelligence, like the simpleton's cupidity of a penny. When that day dawns,—and probably not till then,—I imagine that there will be no more poor streets nor need of almshouses.

I was once present at the wedding of some poor English people, and was deeply impressed by the spectacle, though by no means with such proud and delightful emotions as seem to have affected all England on the recent occasion of the marriage of its Prince. It was in the Cathedral at Manchester, a particularly black and grim old structure, into which I had stepped to examine some ancient and curious wood-carvings within the choir. The woman in attendance greeted me with a smile, (which always glimmers forth on the feminine visage, I know not why, when a wedding is in question), and asked me to take a seat in the nave till some poor parties were married, it being the Easter holidays, and a good time for them to marry, because no fees would be demanded by the clergyman. I sat down accordingly, and soon the parson and his clerk appeared at the altar, and a considerable crowd of people made their entrance at a side-door, and ranged themselves in a long, huddled line across the chancel. They were my acquaintances of the poor streets, or persons in a precisely similar condition of life and were now come to their marriage-ceremony in just such garbs as I had always seen them wear: the men in their loafers' coats, out at elbows, or their laborers' jackets, defaced with grimy toil; the women drawing their shabby shawls tighter about their shoulders, to hide the raggedness beneath; all of them unbrushed, unshaven, unwashed, uncombed, and wrinkled with penury and care; nothing virgin-like in the brides, nor hopeful or energetic in the bridegrooms;—they were, in short, the mere rags and tatters of the human race, whom some east-wind of evil omen, howling along the streets, had chanced to sweep together into an unfragrant heap. Each and all of them, conscious of his or her individual misery, had blundered into the strange miscalculation of supposing that they could lessen the sum of it by multiplying it into the misery of another person. All the couples (and it was difficult, in such a confused crowd, to compute exactly their number) stood up at once, and had execution done upon them in the lump, the clergyman addressing only small parts of the service to each individual pair, but so managing the larger portion as to include the whole company without the trouble of repetition. By this compendious contrivance, one would apprehend, he came dangerously near making every man and woman the husband or wife of every other, nor, perhaps, would he have perpetrated much additional mischief by the mistake; but, after receiving a benediction in common, they assorted themselves in their own fashion, as they only knew how, and departed to the garrets, or the cellars, or the unsheltered street-corners, where their honeymoon and subsequent lives were to be spent. The parson smiled decorously, the clerk and the sexton grinned broadly, the female attendant tittered almost aloud, and even the married parties seemed to see something exceedingly funny in the affair; but for my part, though generally apt enough to be tickled by a joke, I laid it away in my memory as one of the saddest sights I ever looked upon.

Not very long afterwards, I happened to be passing the same venerable Cathedral, and heard a clang of joyful bells, and beheld a bridal party coming down the steps towards a carriage and four horses, with a portly coachman and two postilions, that waited at the gate. One parson and one service had amalgamated the wretchedness of a score of paupers; a Bishop and three or four clergymen had combined their spiritual might to forge the golden links of this other marriage-bond. The bridegroom's mien had a sort of careless and kindly English pride; the bride floated along in her white drapery, a creature so nice and delicate that it was a luxury to see her, and a pity that her silk slippers should touch anything so grimy as the old stones of the churchyard avenue. The crowd of ragged people, who always cluster to witness what they may of an aristocratic wedding, broke into audible admiration of the bride's beauty and the bridegroom's manliness, and uttered prayers and ejaculations (possibly paid for in alms) for the happiness of both. If the most favorable of earthly conditions could make them happy, they had every prospect of it. They were going to live on their abundance in one of those stately and delightful English homes, such as no other people ever created or inherited, a hall set far and safe within its own private grounds, and surrounded with venerable trees, shaven lawns, rich shrubbery, and trimmest pathways, the whole so artfully contrived and tended that summer rendered it a paradise, and even winter would hardly disrobe it of its beauty; and all this fair property seemed more exclusively and inalienably their own, because of its descent through many forefathers, each of whom had added an improvement or a charm, and thus transmitted it with a stronger stamp of rightful possession to his heir. And is it possible, after all, that there may be a flaw in the title-deeds? Is, or is not, the system wrong that gives one married pair so immense a superfluity of luxurious home, and shuts out a million others from any home whatever? One day or another safe as they deem themselves, and safe as the hereditary temper of the people really tends to make them, the gentlemen of England will be compelled to face this question. 1863

» » *From:* THE HOUSE OF THE SEVEN GABLES « «

PREFACE

When a writer calls his work a Romance, it need hardly be observed that he wishes to claim a certain latitude, both as to its fashion and material, which he would not have felt himself entitled to assume, had he professed to be writing a Novel. The latter form of composition is presumed to aim at a very minute fidelity, not merely to the possible, but to the probable and ordinary course of man's experience. The former—while, as a work of art, it must rigidly subject itself to laws, and while it sins unpardonably so far as it may swerve aside from the truth of the human heart—has fairly a right to present that truth under circumstances, to a great extent, of the writer's own choosing or creation. If he think fit, also, he may so manage his atmospherical medium as to bring out or mellow the lights and deepen and enrich the shadows of the picture. He will be wise, no doubt, to make a very moderate use of the privileges here stated, and, especially, to mingle the Marvellous rather as a slight, delicate, and evanescent flavor, than as any portion of the actual substance of the dish offered to the public. He can hardly be said, however, to commit a literary crime even if he disregard this caution.

In the present work, the author has proposed to himself—but with what success, fortunately, it is not for him to judge—to keep undeviatingly within his immunities. The point of view in which this tale comes under the Romantic definition lies in the attempt to connect a by-gone time with the very present that is flitting away from us. It is a legend, prolonging itself, from an epoch now gray in the distance, down into our own broad daylight, and bringing along with it some of its legendary mist, which the reader, according to his pleasure, may either disregard, or allow it to float almost imperceptibly about the characters and events for the sake of a picturesque effect. The narrative, it may be, is woven of so humble a texture as to require this advantage, and, at the same time, to render it the more difficult of attainment.

Many writers lay very great stress upon some definite moral purpose, at which they profess to aim their works. Not to be deficient in this particular, the author has provided himself with a moral;—the truth, namely, that the wrong-doing of one generation lives into the successive ones, and, divesting itself of every temporary advantage, becomes a pure and uncontrollable mischief; and he would feel it a singular gratification, if this romance might effectually convince mankind—or, indeed, any one man—of the folly of tumbling down an avalanche of ill-gotten gold, or real estate, on the heads of an unfortunate posterity, thereby to maim and crush them, until the accumulated mass shall be scattered abroad in its original atoms. In good faith, however, he is not sufficiently imaginative to flatter himself with the slightest hope of this kind. When romances do really teach anything, or produce any effective operation, it is usually through a far more subtile process than the ostensible one. The author has considered it hardly worth his while, therefore, relentlessly to impale the story with its moral, as with an iron rod,—or, rather, as by sticking a pin through a butterfly,—thus at once depriving it of life, and causing it to stiffen in an ungainly and unnatural attitude. A high truth, indeed, fairly, finely, and skilfully wrought out, brightening at every step,

and crowning the final development of a work of fiction, may add an artistic glory, but is never any truer, and seldom any more evident, at the last page than at the first.

The reader may perhaps choose to assign an actual locality to the imaginary events of this narrative. If permitted by the historical connection,—which, though slight, was essential to his plan,—the author would very willingly have avoided anything of this nature. Not to speak of other objections, it exposes the romance to an inflexible and exceedingly dangerous species of criticism, by bringing his fancy-pictures almost into positive contact with the realities of the moment. It has been no part of his object, however, to describe local manners, nor in any way to meddle with the characteristics of a community for whom he cherishes a proper respect and natural regard. He trusts not to be considered as unpardonably offending, by laying out a street that infringes upon nobody's private rights, and appropriating a lot of land which had no visible owner, and building a house, of materials long in use for constructing castles in the air. The personages of the tale—though they give themselves out to be of ancient stability and considerable prominence—are really of the author's own making, or, at all events, of his own mixing; their virtues can shed no lustre, nor their defects redound, in the remotest degree, to the discredit of the venerable town of which they profess to be inhabitants. He would be glad, therefore, if—especially in the quarter to which he alludes—the book may be read strictly as a Romance, having a great deal more to do with the clouds overhead than with any portion of the actual soil of the County of Essex.   1851

» » *From:* THE MARBLE FAUN « «

PREFACE

This Romance was sketched out during a residence of considerable length in Italy, and has been rewritten and prepared for the press in England. The author proposed to himself merely to write a fanciful story, evolving a thoughtful moral, and did not purpose attempting a portraiture of Italian manners and character. He has lived too long abroad not to be aware that a foreigner seldom acquires that knowledge of a country at once flexible and

profound, which may justify him in endeavoring to idealize its traits.

Italy, as the site of his Romance, was chiefly valuable to him as affording a sort of poetic or fairy precinct, where actualities would not be so terribly insisted upon as they are, and must needs be, in America. No author, without a trial, can conceive of the difficulty of writing a romance about a country where there is no shadow, no antiquity, no mystery, no picturesque and gloomy wrong, nor anything but a commonplace prosperity in broad and simple daylight, as is happily the case with my dear native land. It will be very long, I trust, before romance-writers may find congenial and easily handled themes, either in the annals of our stalwart republic, or in any characteristic and probable events of our individual lives. Romance and poetry, ivy, lichens, and wall-flowers need ruin to make them grow. . . .

1860

HERMAN MELVILLE

1819–1891

EVEN INTO the early 1920's Herman Melville was only a name in histories of literature. The reasons for his disappearance below the horizon are manifold: his own refusal to go on writing books of South Sea adventure which delighted his first public; his persistence in writing novels like *Mardi*, *Moby-Dick*, and *Pierre* which troubled his readers with metaphysical problems presented in dark symbols and allegories; the boldness with which he attacked the beliefs of a genteel age; the almost complete cessation of his career as a writer before he and his public and the critics had come to terms. But there have always been Melville enthusiasts, in England as well as America, and it was no surprise to them that the generation of the 1920's should proclaim him the most powerful writer America has produced.

Melville's father was a New Englander of Scotch ancestry; his mother never forgot her pride in her Dutch forebears. The humiliation of his father's bankruptcy and the years of the family's genteel poverty (following his father's death) had lasting effects on the boy, who early realized that he must make his own way in the world, in spite of the "expectations" to which he was heir. Like so many youths of his time he sought his fortune at sea, shipping first, at nineteen, on a voyage to Liverpool, and then, at twenty-two, on a four years' venture in the South Seas. Leaving his whaling ship at the Marquesas, he spent a month among the cannibals on Nuku-hiva. Escaping on another whaler he reached Tahiti, and eventually sailed from Honolulu on the American frigate *United States* in August, 1843, arriving in Boston in October, 1844.

The amazing adventures of these four years furnished Melville with material for a series of books, for he settled to the business of writing as soon as he reached his mother's house near Albany. *Typee*, the first (1846), brought him profitable but irksome renown as the "man who had lived among the cannibals." *Omoo* (1847) recounted his picaresque adventures in Tahiti, where he was for a time imprisoned as a mutineer. *Mardi* (1849), though foreshadowing his later more serious books, made use of the sea and island scenes for setting and atmosphere. In *Redburn* (1849) Melville turned his memories of his first voyage into an affecting tale of a sensitive boy's venture into a world where tyranny, fraud, and inhumanity are rampant. *White-Jacket* (1850) is a story of brutality and heroism aboard a United States man-of-war. It was written with some intention of helping to reform conditions in the navy. The *Neversink* of the story is patently the *United States* of Melville's homeward voyage. An eager public had reached for all these books because Melville could spin a yarn in language that smelled of the sea. A whole new world was discovered in them: the common sailor at last had a spokesman; the cannibals' home life was spied upon; missionary ineptitude was ridiculed. The prudish were shocked; everyone else was delighted.

Meanwhile Melville had tasted the pleasures of New York literary society, from 1847–1850, and had wearied of its mediocrity. He removed to Pittsfield, Massachusetts, which was to be his home for the next thirteen years, and settled to the writing of what he intended should be an important book. *Moby-Dick* was, he wrote Hawthorne, "broiled in hell-fire." Into it he poured his life's blood. He followed it the next year, in 1852, with another novel planned on a big scale, *Pierre*. His creative powers apparently exhausted by these two books, the first of which puzzled his readers while the second revolted them, Melville wrote only a short novel and tales, some of them admirable ("Benito Cereno," "The Encantadas"), before the *Confidence Man* of 1857. The rest of his life he produced nothing save four volumes of verse and some scattered pieces, unpublished at his death. He supported his family by lecturing (1857–1860) and for twenty years as a Customs Inspector in New York. Occasionally some admirer, an English writer or an undergraduate who had chanced on his books, would seek him in his obscurity and be surprised to find a cultivated, widely read gentleman, eager to discuss philosophy but politely unwilling to talk about the South Sea paradise from which he had long ago escaped.

Melville took upon his shoulders the weight of the nineteenth century. The habit of speculation grew upon him, until, in his own image, the head overcame the heart. Born while the doctrines of Calvinism were still issues in men's lives, he debated ceaselessly with himself after 1850 "fixed fate, free will, foreknowledge absolute." Hawthorne noted in his journal, when Melville visited him in Liverpool in 1856: "It is strange how he persists—and has persisted ever since I knew him [1850], and probably long before—in wandering to and fro over these deserts, as dismal and monotonous as the sandhills amid which we were sitting." Melville's great quest was for some answer to the nature of ultimate reality. At first, in *Mardi* where Truth is sought in the guise of the lovely evanescent Yillah, he hoped the Truth behind the universe might prove to be beneficent. In *Moby-Dick*, where it is incarnated in the White Whale, a question mark has replaced the hope. Captain Ahab does not know whether the white whale he pursues over the seven seas is principal or agent, whether indeed there is any sentient force behind its apparent malignancy. The symbolic and highly significant "The Whiteness of the Whale" chapter raises the whole question whether ultimate reality, seemingly incarnate in the monster, may not be a void and an illusion. At least, Melville plainly hints, Ahab has himself conjured up these torments and is driven to pursue the whale, not by fate, but by his own mad hates. In *Pierre* the hero of the novel seeks the nature of moral truth. He has followed what he believes is his moral duty, in giving his illegitimate half-sister his name in marriage, only to feel the whole weight of society against him. Is Truth ambiguous, born of heaven and earth, so that the righteous man can never live while on earth by heaven's time?

To this main preoccupation of Melville's thought must be added his speculations on the destiny of American democracy, on the significance of the industrialism which was changing fundamentally the whole life of the nation, on the imminence of the class struggle, on the inadequacy of science, the new god, to answer any of the problems the new age must solve, including those raised by its own advent. Melville's epical poem *Clarel* (1876) deals with these concerns. The Civil War aroused him both intellectually and emotionally and produced his best volume of verse, *Battle Pieces* (1866).

Finally Melville ceased to put his doubts and conclusions on paper and kept them for his own study and his solitary walks about New York. Among his papers, however, was found all but completed at his death, a remarkably fine story, *Billy Budd*, the purport of which is resignation. He had come finally to that full realization of the tragic sense of life felt by men like Sophocles and Shakespeare. The young sailor, Billy Budd, unjustly accused of treason, is condemned to die by the captain who is terribly troubled by the execution he must order. But here is the tragic fact, made endurable only because of man's heroism which fate cannot conquer.

S. T. Williams, "Melville," in *Eight American Authors, A Review of Research and Criticism*, New York, 1956, pp. 207–270.

The Works of Herman Melville, Standard Edition, 16 vols., London, 1922–1924.

Herman Melville, Representative Selections, with Introduction, Bibliography, and Notes (American Writers Series), Willard Thorp, ed., New York, 1938.

The Letters of Herman Melville, M. R. Davis and W. H. Gilman, eds., New Haven, 1960.

C. R. Anderson, *Melville in the South Seas*, New York, 1939.

Leon Howard, *Herman Melville, A Biography*, Berkeley, California, 1951.

Jay Leyda, *The Melville Log: A Documentary Life of Herman Melville, 1819–1891*, New York, 1951.

Lawrance Thompson, *Melville's Quarrel with God*, Princeton, 1952.

» » *From:* MARDI [1] « «

AND A VOYAGE THITHER

CHAPTER CLXI

THEY HEARKEN UNTO A VOICE FROM THE GODS

Next day we retraced our voyage northward, to visit that section of Vivenza.[2]

In due time we landed.

To look round was refreshing. Of all the lands we had seen, none looked more promising. The groves stood tall and green; the fields spread lush and broad; the dew of the first morning seemed hardly vanished from the grass. On all sides was heard the fall of waters, the swarming of bees, and the rejoicing hum of a thriving population.

"Ha, ha!" laughed Yoomy, "Labor laughs in this land; and claps his hands in the jubilee groves! methinks that Yillah will yet be found."

Generously entertained, we tarried in this land; till at length from over the Lagoon, came full tidings of the eruption we had witnessed in Franko,[3] with many details. The conflagration [4] had spread through Porpheero; and the kings were to and fro hunted, like malefactors by blood-hounds; all that part of Mardi was heaving with throes.

With the utmost delight, these tidings were welcomed by many; yet others heard them with boding concern.

Those, too, there were, who rejoiced that the kings were cast down; but mourned that the people themselves stood not firmer. A victory, turned to no wise and enduring account, said they, is no victory at all. Some victories revert to the vanquished.

But day by day great crowds ran down to the beach, in wait for canoes periodically bringing further intelligence. Every hour new cries startled the air. "Hurrah! another kingdom is burnt down to the earth's edge; another demi-god is unhelmed; another republic is dawning. Shake hands, freemen, shake hands! Soon will we hear of Dominora down in the dust; of hapless Verdanna [5] free as ourselves; all Porpheero's volcanoes are bursting! Who may withstand the people? The times tell terrible tales to tyrants! Ere we die, freemen, all Mardi will be free."

Overhearing these shouts, Babbalanja thus addressed Media:—"My lord, I can not but believe, that these men, are far more excited than those with whom they so ardently sympathize. But no wonder. The single discharges which are heard in Porpheero; here come condensed in one tremendous report. Every arrival is a firing off of events by platoons."

Now, during this tumultuous interval, King Media very prudently kept himself exceedingly quiet. He doffed his regalia; and in all things carried himself with a dignified discretion. And many hours he absented himself; none

---

[1] Under the guise of a narration of adventure in the South Seas Melville satirizes in *Mardi* the political and religious institutions of his time. The voyagers include Yoomy, a poet; Babbalanja, a philosopher; Media, a king.

[2] Vivenza = America.

[3] Franko = France.

[4] The revolutions of 1848.

[5] Dominora = England. Verdanna = Ireland.

knowing whither he went, or what his employment.

So also with Babbalanja. But still pursuing our search, at last we all journeyed into a great valley, whose inhabitants were more than commonly inflated with the ardor of the times.

Rambling on, we espied a clamorous crowd gathered about a conspicuous palm, against which, a scroll was fixed.

The people were violently agitated; storming out maledictions against the insolent knave, who, over night, must have fixed there, that scandalous document. But whoever he may have been, certain it was, he had contrived to hood himself effectually.

After much vehement discussion, during which sundry inflammatory harangues were made from the stumps of trees near by, it was proposed, that the scroll should be read aloud, so that all might give ear.

Seizing it, a fiery youth mounted upon the bowed shoulders of an old man, his sire; and with a shrill voice, ever and anon interrupted by outcries, read as follows:—

"Sovereign-kings of Vivenza! it is fit you should hearken to wisdom. But well aware, that you give ear to little wisdom except your own; and that as freemen, you are free to hunt down him who dissents from your majesties; I deem it proper to address you anonymously.

"And if it please you, you may ascribe this voice to the gods: for never will you trace it to man.

"It is not unknown, sovereign-kings! that in these boisterous days, the lessons of history are almost discarded, as superseded by present experiences. And that while all Mardi's Present has grown out of its Past, it is becoming obsolete to refer to what has been. Yet, peradventure, the Past is an apostle.

"The grand error of this age, sovereign-kings! is the general supposition, that the very special Diabolus is abroad; whereas, the very special Diabolus has been abroad ever since Mardi began.

"And the grand error of your nation, sovereign-kings! seems this:—The conceit that Mardi is now in the last scene of the last act of her drama; and that all preceding events were ordained to bring about the catastrophe you believe to be at hand,—a universal and permanent Republic.

"May it please you, those who hold to these things are fools, and not wise.

"Time is made up of various ages; and each thinks its own a novelty. But imbedded in the walls of the pyramids, which outrun all chronologies, sculptured stones are found, belonging to yet older fabrics. And as in the mound-building period of yore, so every age thinks its erections will forever endure. But as your forests grow apace, sovereign-kings! overrunning the tumuli in your western vales; so, while deriving their substance from the past, succeeding generations overgrow it; but in time, themselves decay.

"Oro [6] decrees these vicissitudes.

"In chronicles of old, you read, sovereign-kings! that an eagle from the clouds presaged royalty to the fugitive Taquinoo; [7] and a king, Taquinoo reigned; No end to my dynasty, thought he.

"But another omen descended, foreshadowing the fall of Zooperbi, his son; and Zooperbi returning from his camp, found his country a fortress against him. No more kings would she have. And for five hundred twelve-moons the Regifugium or King's-flight, was annually celebrated like your own jubilee day. And rampant young orators stormed out detestation of kings; and augurs swore that their birds presaged immortality to freedom.

"Then, Romara's free eagles flew over all Mardi, and perched on the topmost diadems of the east.

"Ever thus must it be.

"For, mostly, monarchs are as gemmed bridles upon the world, checking the plungings of a steed from the Pampas. And republics are as vast reservoirs, draining down all streams to one level; and so, breeding a fulness which can not remain full, without overflowing. And thus, Romara flooded all Mardi, till scarce an Ararat was left of the lofty kingdoms which had been.

"Thus, also, did Franko, fifty twelve-moons ago. Thus may she do again. And though not yet, have you, sovereign-kings! in any large degree done likewise, it is because you overflow your redundancies within your own mighty borders; having a wild western waste, which many shepherds with their flocks could not overrun in a day. Yet overrun at last it will be; and then, the recoil must come.

"And, may it please you, that thus far your chronicles had narrated a very different story, had your population been pressed and packed, like that of your old sire-land Dominora. Then, your great experiment might have proved an

---

[6] Oro = God.
[7] This parable deals with the Tarquin dynasty in Rome.

explosion; like the chemist's who, stirring his mixture, was blown by it into the air.

"For though crossed, and recrossed by many brave quarterings, and boasting the great Bull in your pedigree; yet, sovereign-kings! you are not meditative philosophers like the people of a small republic of old; nor enduring stoics, like their neighbors. Pent up, like them, may it please you, your thirteen original tribes had proved more turbulent, than so many mutinous legions. Free horses need wide prairies; and fortunate for you, sovereign-kings! that you have room enough, wherein to be free.

"And, may it please you, you are free, partly, because you are young. Your nation is like a fine, florid youth, full of fiery impulses, and hard to restrain; his strong hand nobly championing his heart. On all sides, freely he gives, and still seeks to acquire. The breath of his nostrils is like smoke in spring air; every tendon is electric with generous resolves. The oppressor he defies to his beard; the high walls of old opinions he scales with a bound. In the future he sees all the domes of the East.

"But years elapse, and this bold boy is transformed. His eyes open not as of yore; his heart is shut up as a vice. He yields not a groat; and seeking no more acquisitions, is only bent on preserving his hoard. The maxims once trampled under foot, are now printed on his front; and he who hated oppressors, is become an oppressor himself.

"Thus, often, with men; thus, often, with nations. Then marvel not, sovereign-kings! that old states are different from yours; and think not, your own must forever remain liberal as now.

"Each age thinks its own is eternal. But though for five hundred twelve-moons, all Romara, by courtesy of history, was republican; yet, at last, her terrible king-tigers came, and spotted themselves with gore.

"And time was, when Dominora was republican, down to her sturdy back-bone. The son of an absolute monarch became the man Karolus; [8] and his crown and head both rolled in the dust. And Dominora had her patriots by thousands; and lusty Defenses and glorious Areopagiticas were written, not since surpassed; and no turban was doffed save in homage of Oro.

"Yet, may it please you, to the sound of pipe and tabor, the second King Karolus returned in good time; and was hailed gracious majesty by high and low.

[8] Charles I of England.

"Throughout all eternity, the parts of the past are but parts of the future reversed. In the old foot-prints, up and down, you mortals go, eternally travelling your Sierras. And not more infallible the ponderings of the Calculating Machine than the deductions from the decimals of history.

"In nations, sovereign-kings! there is a transmigration of souls; in you, is a marvellous destiny. The eagle of Romara revives in your own mountain bird, and once more is plumed for her flight. Her screams are answered by the vauntful cries of a hawk; his red comb yet reeking with slaughter. And one East, one West, those bold birds may fly, till they lock pinions in the midmost beyond.

"But, soaring in the sky over the nations that shall gather their broods under their wings, that bloody hawk may hereafter be taken for the eagle.

"And though crimson republics may rise in constellations, like fiery Aldebarans, speeding to their culminations; yet, down must they sink at last, and leave the old sultan-sun in the sky; in time, again to be deposed.

"For little longer, may it please you, can republics subsist now, than in days gone by. For assuming that Mardi is wiser than of old; nevertheless, though all men approached sages in intelligence, some would yet be more wise than others; and so, the old degrees be preserved. And no exemption would an equality of knowledge furnish, from the inbred servility of mortal to mortal; from all the organic causes, which inevitably divide mankind into brigades and battalions, with captains at their head.

"Civilization has not ever been the brother of equality. Freedom was born among the wild eyries in the mountains; and barbarous tribes have sheltered under her wings, when the enlightened people of the plain have nestled under different pinions.

"Though, thus far, for you, sovereign-kings! your republic has been fruitful of blessings; yet, in themselves, monarchies are not utterly evil. For many nations, they are better than republics; for many, they will ever so remain. And better, on all hands, that peace should rule with a scepter, than that the tribunes of the people should brandish their broadswords. Better be the subject of a king, upright and just; than a freeman in Franko, with the executioner's axe at every corner.

"It is not the prime end, and chief blessing, to be politically free. And freedom is only good as a means; is no end in itself. Nor, did man fight it out against his masters to the haft, not then, would he uncollar his neck from the yoke. A born thrall to the last, yelping out his liberty, he still remains a slave unto Oro; and well is it for the universe, that Oro's scepter is absolute.

"World-old the saying, that it is easier to govern others than oneself. And that all men should govern themselves as nations, needs that all men be better, and wiser, than the wisest of one-man rulers. But in no stable democracy do all men govern themselves. Though an army be all volunteers, martial law must prevail. Delegate your power, you leagued mortals must. The hazard you must stand. And though unlike King Bello of Dominora, your great chieftain, sovereign-kings! may not declare war of himself; nevertheless, has he done a still more imperial thing:—gone to war without declaring intentions. You yourselves were precipitated upon a neighboring nation,[9] ere you knew your spears were in your hands.

"But, as in stars you have written it on the welkin, sovereign-kings! you are a great and glorious people. And verily, yours is the best and happiest land under the sun. But not wholly, because you, in your wisdom, decreed it: your origin and geography necessitated it. Nor, in their germ, are all your blessings to be ascribed to the noble sires, who of yore fought in your behalf, sovereign-kings! Your nation enjoyed no little independence before your Declaration declared it. Your ancient pilgrims fathered your liberty; and your wild woods harbored the nursling. For the state that to-day is made up of slaves, can not to-morrow transmute her bond into free; though lawlessness may transform them into brutes. Freedom is the name for a thing that is *not* freedom; this, a lesson never learned in an hour or an age. By some tribes it will never be learned.

"Yet, if it please you, there may be such a thing as being free under Caesar. Ages ago, there were as many vital freemen as breathe vital air to-day.

"Names make not distinctions; some despots rule without swaying scepters. Though King Bello's palace was not put together by yoked men; your federal temple of freedom, sovereign-kings! was the handiwork of slaves.

"It is not gildings, and gold maces, and crown-jewels alone that makes a people servile.

[9] The Mexican War.

There is much bowing and cringing among you yourselves, sovereign-kings! Poverty is abased before riches, all Mardi over; any where, it is hard to be a debtor; any where, the wise will lord it over fools; every where, suffering is found.

"Thus, freedom is more social than political. And its real felicity is not to be shared. *That* is of a man's own individual getting and holding. It is not, who rules the state, but who rules me. Better be secure under one king, than exposed to violence from twenty millions of monarchs, though oneself be of the number.

"But superstitious notions you harbor, sovereign-kings! Did you visit Dominora, you would not be marched straight into a dungeon. And though you would behold sundry sights displeasing, you would start to inhale such liberal breezes; and hear crowds boasting of their privileges; as you, of yours. Nor has the wine of Dominora, a monarchical flavor.

"Now, though far and wide, to keep equal pace with the times, great reforms, of a verity, be needed; nowhere are bloody revolutions required. Though it be the most certain of remedies, no prudent invalid opens his veins, to let out his disease with his life. And though all evils may be assuaged; all evils cannot be done away. For evil is the chronic malady of the universe; and checked in one place, breaks forth in another.

"Of late, on this head, some wild dreams have departed.

"There are many who erewhile believed that the age of pikes and javelins was passed; that after a heady and blustering youth, old Mardi was at last settling down into a serene old age; and that the Indian summer, first discovered in your land, sovereign-kings! was the hazy vapor emitted from its tranquil pipe. But it has not so proved. Mardi's peaces are but truces. Long absent, at last the red comets have returned. And return they must, though their periods be ages. And should Mardi endure till mountain melt into mountain, and all the isles form one table-land; yet, would it but expand the old battle-plain.

"Students of history are horror-struck at the massacres of old; but in the shambles, men are being murdered to-day. Could time be reversed, and the future change places with the past, the past would cry out against us, and our future, full as loudly, as we against the ages foregone. All the Ages are his children, calling each other names.

"Hark ye, sovereign-kings! cheer not on the yelping pack too furiously. Hunters have been torn by their hounds. Be advised; wash your hands. Hold aloof. Oro has poured out an ocean for an everlasting barrier between you and the worst folly which other republics have perpetrated. That barrier hold sacred. And swear never to cross over to Porpheero, by manifesto or army, unless you traverse dry land.

"And be not too grasping, nearer home. It is not freedom to filch. Expand not your area too widely, now. Seek you proselytes? Neighboring nations may be free, without coming under your banner. And if you cannot lay your ambition, know this: that it is best served by waiting events.

"Time, but Time only, may enable you to cross the equator; and give you the Arctic Circles for your boundaries." . . .

1849

» » *From:* WHITE-JACKET « «

CHAPTER LX

A MAN-OF-WAR'S-MAN SHOT AT

There was a seaman belonging to the foretop—a mess-mate, though not a top-mate of mine, and no favorite of the Captain's—who, for certain venial transgressions, had been prohibited from going ashore on liberty when the ship's company went. Enraged at the deprivation—for he had not touched earth in upward of a year—he, some nights after, lowered himself overboard, with the view of gaining a canoe, attached by a rope to a Dutch galiot some cables'-length distant. In this canoe he proposed paddling himself ashore. Not being a very expert swimmer, the commotion he made in the water attracted the ear of the sentry on that side of the ship, who, turning about in his walk, perceived the faint white spot where the fugitive was swimming in the frigate's shadow. He hailed it; but no reply.

"Give the word, or I fire!"

Not a word was heard.

The next instant there was a red flash, and, before it had completely ceased illuminating the night, the white spot was changed into crimson. Some of the officers, returning from a party at the Beach of the Flamingoes, happened to be drawing near the ship in one of her cutters. They saw the flash, and the bounding body it revealed. In a moment the top-man was dragged into the boat, a handkerchief was used for a tourniquet, and the wounded fugitive was soon on board the frigate, when, the Surgeon being called, the necessary attentions were rendered.

Now, it appeared, that at the moment the sentry fired, the top-man—in order to elude discovery, by manifesting the completest quietude—was floating on the water, straight and horizontal, as if reposing on a bed. As he was not far from the ship at the time, and the sentry was considerably elevated above him—pacing his platform, on a level with the upper part of the hammock-nettings—the ball struck with great force, with a downward obliquity, entering the right thigh just above the knee, and, penetrating some inches, glanced upward along the bone, burying itself somewhere, so that it could not be felt by outward manipulation. There was no dusky discoloration to mark its internal track, as in the case when a partly spent ball—obliquely hitting—after entering the skin, courses on, just beneath the surface, without penetrating further. Nor was there any mark on the opposite part of the thigh to denote its place, as when a ball forces itself straight through a limb, and lodges, perhaps, close to the skin on the other side. Nothing was visible but a small, ragged puncture, bluish about the edges, as if the rough point of a tenpenny nail had been forced into the flesh, and withdrawn. It seemed almost impossible, that through so small an aperture, a musket-bullet could have penetrated.

The extreme misery and general prostration of the man, caused by the great effusion of blood—though, strange to say, at first he said he felt no pain from the wound itself—induced the Surgeon, very reluctantly, to forgo an immediate search for the ball, to extract it, as that would have involved the dilating of the wound by the knife; an operation which, at that juncture, would have been almost certainly attended with fatal results. A day or two, therefore, was permitted to pass, while simple dressings were applied.

The surgeons of the other American ships of war in harbor occasionally visited the Neversink, to examine the patient, and incidentally to listen to the expositions of our own Surgeon, their senior in rank. But Cadwallader Cuticle, who, as yet, has been but incidentally alluded to, now deserves a chapter by himself.

CHAPTER LXI

THE SURGEON OF THE FLEET

10　Cadwallader Cuticle, M.D., and Honorary Member of the most distinguished Colleges of Surgeons both in Europe and America, was our Surgeon of the Fleet. Nor was he at all blind to the dignity of his position; to which, indeed, he was rendered peculiarly competent, if the reputation he enjoyed was deserved. He had the name of being the foremost Surgeon in the Navy, a gentleman of remarkable science, and a veteran practitioner.

20　He was a small, withered man, nearly, perhaps quite, sixty years of age. His chest was shallow, his shoulders bent, his pantaloons hung round skeleton legs, and his face was singularly attenuated. In truth, the corporeal vitality of this man seemed, in a good degree, to have died out of him. He walked abroad, a curious patchwork of life and death, with a wig, one glass eye, and a set of false teeth, while his voice was husky and thick; but his

30　mind seemed undebilitated as in youth; it shone out of his remaining eye with basilisk brilliancy.

Like most old physicians and surgeons who have seen much service, and have been promoted to high professional place for their scientific attainments, this Cuticle was an enthusiast in his calling. In private, he had once been heard to say, confidentially, that he would rather cut off a man's arm than dismember the

40　wing of the most delicate pheasant. In particular, the department of Morbid Anatomy was his peculiar love; and in his state-room below he had a most unsightly collection of Parisian casts, in plaster and wax, representing all imaginable malformations of the human members, both organic and induced by disease. Chief among these was a cast, often to be met with in the Anatomical Museums of Europe, and no doubt an unexaggerated copy of a gen-

50　uine original; it was the head of an elderly woman, with an aspect singularly gentle and meek, but at the same time wonderfully expressive of a gnawing sorrow, never to be relieved. You would almost have thought it the

face of some abbess, for some unspeakable crime voluntarily sequestered from human society, and leading a life of agonized penitence without hope; so marvellously sad and tearfully pitiable was this head. But when you first beheld it, no such emotions ever crossed your mind. All your eyes and all your horrified soul were fast fascinated and frozen by the sight of a hideous, crumpled horn, like that of a ram, downward, growing out from the forehead, and partly shadowing the face; but as you gazed, the freezing fascination of its horribleness gradually waned, and then your whole heart burst with sorrow, as you contemplated those aged features, ashy pale and wan. The horn seemed the mark of a curse for some mysterious sin, conceived and committed before the spirit had entered the flesh. Yet that sin seemed something imposed, and not voluntarily sought; some sin growing out of the heartless necessities of the predestination of things; some sin under which the sinner sank in sinless woe.

But no pang of pain, not the slightest touch of concern, ever crossed the bosom of Cuticle when he looked on this cast. It was immovably fixed to a bracket, against the partition of his state-room, so that it was the first object that greeted his eyes when he opened them from his nightly sleep. Nor was it to hide the face, that upon retiring, he always hung his Navy cap upon the upward curling extremity of the horn, for that obscured it but little.

The Surgeon's cot-boy, the lad who made up his swinging bed and took care of his room, often told us of the horror he sometimes felt when he would find himself alone in his master's retreat. At times he was seized with the idea that Cuticle was a preternatural being; and once entering his room in the middle watch of the night, he started at finding it enveloped in a thick, bluish vapor, and stifling with the odors of brimstone. Upon hearing a low groan from the smoke, with a wild cry he darted from the place, and, rousing the occupants of the neighboring state-rooms, it was found that the vapor proceeded from smoldering bunches of Lucifer matches, which had become ignited through the carelessness of the Surgeon. Cuticle, almost dead, was dragged from the suffocating atmosphere, and it was several days ere he completely recovered from its effects. This accident took place immediately over the powder magazine; but as Cuticle, during his sickness, paid dearly enough for transgressing the laws prohibiting combustibles in the gun-room, the Captain contented himself with privately remonstrating with him.

Well knowing the enthusiasm of the Surgeon for all specimens of morbid anatomy, some of the ward-room officers used to play upon his credulity, though, in every case, Cuticle was not long in discovering their deceptions. Once, when they had some sago pudding for dinner, and Cuticle chanced to be ashore, they made up a neat parcel of this bluish-white, firm, jelly-like preparation, and placing it in a tin box, carefully sealed with wax, they deposited it on the gun-room table, with a note, purporting to come from an eminent physician in Rio, connected with the Grand National Museum on the Praca d'Acclamacao, begging leave to present the scientific Senhor Cuticle—with the donor's compliments—an uncommonly fine specimen of a cancer.

Descending to the ward-room, Cuticle spied the note, and no sooner read it, than, clutching the case, he opened it, and exclaimed, "Beautiful! splendid! I have never seen a finer specimen of this most interesting disease."

"What have you there, Surgeon Cuticle?" said a Lieutenant, advancing.

"Why, sir, look at it; did you ever see anything more exquisite?"

"Very exquisite indeed; let me have a bit of it, will you, Cuticle?"

"Let you have a bit of it!" shrieked the Surgeon, starting back. "Let you have one of my limbs! I wouldn't mar so large a specimen for a hundred dollars; but what can you want of it? You are not making collections!"

"I'm fond of the article," said the Lieutenant; "it's a fine cold relish to bacon or ham. You know, I was in New Zealand last cruise, Cuticle, and got into sad dissipation there among the cannibals; come, let's have a bit, if it's only a mouthful."

"Why, you infernal Feejee!" shouted Cuticle, eyeing the other with a confounded expression; "you don't really mean to eat a piece of this cancer?"

"Hand it to me, and see whether I will not," was the reply.

"In God's name, take it!" cried the Surgeon, putting the case into his hands, and then standing with his own uplifted.

"Steward!" cried the Lieutenant, "the castor —quick! I always use plenty of pepper with this dish, Surgeon; it's oystery. Ah! this is really delicious," he added, smacking his lips over a mouthful. "Try it now, Surgeon, and you'll never keep such a fine dish as this, lying uneaten on your hands, as a mere scientific curiosity."

Cuticle's whole countenance changed; and, slowly walking up to the table, he put his nose close to the tin case, then touched its contents with his finger and tasted it. Enough. Buttoning up his coat, in all the tremblings of an old man's rage he burst from the ward-room, and, calling for a boat, was not seen again for twenty-four hours.

But though, like all other mortals, Cuticle was subject at times to these fits of passion—at least under outrageous provocation—nothing could exceed his coolness when actually employed in his imminent vocation. Surrounded by moans and shrieks, by features distorted with anguish inflicted by himself, he yet maintained a countenance almost supernaturally calm; and unless the intense interest of the operation flushed his wan face with a momentary tinge of professional enthusiasm, he toiled away, untouched by the keenest misery coming under a fleet-surgeon's eye. Indeed, long habituation to the dissecting-room and the amputation-table had made him seemingly impervious to the ordinary emotions of humanity. Yet you could not say that Cuticle was essentially a cruel-hearted man. His apparent heartlessness must have been of a purely scientific origin. It is not to be imagined even that Cuticle would have harmed a fly, unless he could procure a microscope powerful enough to assist him in experimenting on the minute vitals of the creature.

But notwithstanding his marvellous indifference to the sufferings of his patients, and spite even of his enthusiasm in his vocation—not cooled by frosting old age itself—Cuticle, on some occasions, would affect a certain disrelish of his profession, and declaim against the necessity that forced a man of his humanity to perform a surgical operation. Especially was it apt to be thus with him, when the case was one of more than ordinary interest. In discussing it, previous to setting about it, he would veil his eagerness under an aspect of great circumspection, curiously marred, however, by continual sallies of unsuppressible impatience. But the knife once in his hand, the compassionless surgeon himself, undisguised, stood before you. Such was Cadwallader Cuticle, our Surgeon of the Fleet.

CHAPTER LXII

A CONSULTATION OF MAN-OF-WAR SURGEONS

It seems customary for the Surgeon of the Fleet, when any important operation in his department is on the anvil, and there is nothing to absorb professional attention from it, to invite his brother surgeons, if at hand at the time, to a ceremonious consultation upon it. And this, in courtesy, his brother surgeons expect.

In pursuance of this custom, then, the surgeons of the neighboring American ships of war were requested to visit the Neversink in a body, to advise concerning the case of the top-man, whose situation had now become critical. They assembled on the half-deck, and were soon joined by their respected senior, Cuticle. In a body they bowed as he approached, and accosted him with deferential regard.

"Gentlemen," said Cuticle, unostentatiously seating himself on a camp-stool, handed him by his cot-boy, "we have here an extremely interesting case. You have all seen the patient, I believe. At first I had hopes that I should have been able to cut down to the ball, and remove it; but the state of the patient forbade. Since then, the inflammation and sloughing of the part has been attended with a copious suppuration, great loss of substance, extreme debility and emaciation. From this, I am convinced that the ball has shattered and deadened the bone, and now lies impacted in the medullary canal. In fact, there can be no doubt that the wound is incurable, and that amputation is the only resource. But, gentlemen, I find myself placed in a very delicate predicament. I assure you I feel no professional anxiety to perform the operation. I desire your advice, and if you will now again visit the patient with me, we can then return here, and decide what is best to be done. Once more, let me say, that I feel no personal anxiety whatever to use the knife."

The assembled surgeons listened to this address with the most serious attention, and, in accordance with their superior's desire, now descended to the sick-bay, where the patient was languishing. The examination concluded, they returned to the half-deck, and the consultation was renewed.

"Gentlemen," began Cuticle, again seating himself, "you have now just inspected the limb; you have seen that there is no resource but amputation; and now, gentlemen, what do you say? Surgeon Bandage, of the Mohawk, will you express your opinion?"

"The wound is a very serious one," said Bandage—a corpulent man, with a high German forehead—shaking his head solemnly.

"Can anything save him but amputation?" demanded Cuticle.

"His constitutional debility is extreme," observed Bandage, "but I have seen more dangerous cases."

"Surgeon Wedge, of the Malay," said Cuticle, in a pet, "be pleased to give *your* opinion; and let it be definitive, I entreat:" this was said with a severe glance toward Bandage.

"If I thought," began Wedge, a very spare, tall man, elevating himself still higher on his toes, "that the ball had shattered and divided the whole *femur*, including the *Greater* and *Lesser Trochanter*, the *Linear aspera*, the *Digital fossa*, and the *Intertrochanteric*, I should certainly be in favor of amputation; but that, sir, permit me to observe, is not my opinion."

"Surgeon Sawyer, of the Buccaneer," said Cuticle, drawing in his thin lower lip with vexation, and turning to a round-faced, florid, frank, sensible-looking man, whose uniform coat very handsomely fitted him, and was adorned with an unusual quantity of gold lace; "Surgeon Sawyer, of the Buccaneer, let us now hear *your* opinion, if you please. Is not amputation the only resource, sir?"

"Excuse me," said Sawyer, "I am decidedly opposed to it; for if hitherto the patient has not been strong enough to undergo the extraction of the ball, I do not see how he can be expected to endure a far more severe operation. As there is no immediate danger of mortification, and you say the ball cannot be reached without making large incisions, I should support him, I think, for the present, with tonics, and gentle antiphlogistics, locally applied. On no account would I proceed to amputation until further symptoms are exhibited."

"Surgeon Patella, of the Algerine," said Cuticle, in an ill-suppressed passion, abruptly turning round on the person addressed, "will *you* have the kindness to say whether *you* do not think that amputation is the only resource?"

Now Patella was the youngest of the company, a modest man, filled with a profound reverence for the science of Cuticle, and desirous of gaining his good opinion, yet not wishing to commit himself altogether by a decided reply, though, like Surgeon Sawyer, in his own mind he might have been clearly against the operation.

"What you have remarked, Mr. Surgeon of the Fleet," said Patella, respectfully hemming, "concerning the dangerous condition of the limb, seems obvious enough; amputation would certainly be a cure to the wound; but then, as, notwithstanding his present debility, the patient seems to have a strong constitution, he might rally as it is, and by your scientific treatment, Mr. Surgeon of the Fleet"—bowing—"be entirely made whole, without risking an amputation. Still, it is a very critical case, and amputation may be indispensable; and if it *is* to be performed, there ought to be no delay whatever. That is my view of the case, Mr. Surgeon of the Fleet."

"Surgeon Patella, then, gentlemen," said Cuticle, turning round triumphantly, "is clearly of opinion that amputation should be immediately performed. For my own part—individually, I mean, and without respect to the patient—I am sorry to have it so decided. But this settles the question, gentlemen—in my own mind, however, it was settled before. At ten o'clock to-morrow morning the operation will be performed. I shall be happy to see you all on the occasion, and also your juniors" (alluding to the absent *Assistant Surgeons*). "Good-morning, gentlemen; at ten o'clock, remember."

And Cuticle retreated to the Ward-room.

CHAPTER LXIII

THE OPERATION

Next morning, at the appointed hour, the surgeons arrived in a body. They were accompanied by their juniors, young men ranging in age from nineteen years to thirty. Like the senior surgeons, these young gentlemen were arrayed in their blue navy uniforms, displaying a profusion of bright buttons, and several broad bars of gold lace about the wristbands. As in honor of the occasion, they had put on their best coats; they looked exceedingly brilliant.

The whole party immediately descended to the half-deck, where preparations had been made for the operation. A large garrison-ensign was stretched across the ship by the main-mast, so as completely to screen the space behind. This space included the whole extent aft to the bulk-head of the Commodore's cabin, at the door of which the marine-orderly paced, in plain sight, cutlass in hand.

Upon two gun-carriages, dragged amidships, the Death-board (used for burials at sea) was horizontally placed, covered with an old royal-stun'-sail. Upon this occasion, to do duty as an amputation-table, it was widened by an additional plank. Two match-tubs, near by, placed one upon another, at either end supported another plank, distinct from the table, whereon was exhibited an array of saws and knives of various and peculiar shapes and sizes; also, a sort of steel, something like the dinner-table implement, together with long needles, crooked at the end for taking up the arteries, and large darning-needles, thread and bee's-wax, for sewing up a wound.

At the end nearest the larger table was a tin basin of water, surrounded by small sponges, placed at mathematical intervals. From the long horizontal pole of a great-gun rammer—fixed in its usual place overhead—hung a number of towels, with "U.S." marked in the corners.

All these arrangements had been made by the "surgeon's steward," a person whose important functions in a man-of-war will, in a future chapter, be entered upon at large. Upon the present occasion, he was bustling about, adjusting and readjusting the knives, needles, and carver, like an over-conscientious butler fidgeting over a dinner-table just before the convivialists enter.

But by far the most striking object to be seen behind the ensign was a human skeleton, whose every joint articulated with wires. By a rivet at the apex of the skull, it hung dangling from a hammock-hook fixed in a beam above. Why this object was here, will presently be seen; but why it was placed immediately at the foot of the amputation-table, only Surgeon Cuticle can tell.

While the final preparations were being made, Cuticle stood conversing with the assembled Surgeons and Assistant Surgeons, his invited guests.

"Gentlemen," said he, taking up one of the glittering knives and artistically drawing the steel across it; "Gentlemen, though these scenes are very unpleasant, and in some moods, I may say, repulsive to me—yet how much better for our patient to have the contusions and lacerations of his present wound—with all its dangerous symptoms—converted into a clean incision, free from these objections, and occasioning so much less subsequent anxiety to himself and the Surgeon. Yes," he added, tenderly feeling the edge of his knife, "amputation is our only resource. Is it not so, Surgeon Patella?" turning toward that gentleman, as if relying upon some sort of an assent, however clogged with conditions.

"Certainly," said Patella, "amputation is your only resource, Mr. Surgeon of the Fleet; that is, I mean, if you are fully persuaded of its necessity."

The other surgeons said nothing, maintaining a somewhat reserved air, as if conscious that they had no positive authority in the case, whatever might be their own private opinions; but they seemed willing to behold, and, if called upon, to assist at the operation, since it could not now be averted.

The young men, their Assistants, looked very eager, and cast frequent glances of awe upon so distinguished a practitioner as the venerable Cuticle.

"They say he can drop a leg in one minute and ten seconds from the moment the knife touches it," whispered one of them to another.

"We shall see," was the reply, and the speaker clapped his hand to his fob, to see if his watch would be forthcoming when wanted.

"Are you all ready here?" demanded Cuticle, now advancing to his steward; "have not those fellows got through yet?" pointing to three men of the carpenter's gang, who were placing bits of wood under the gun-carriages supporting the central table.

"They are just through, sir," respectfully answered the Steward, touching his hand to his forehead, as if there were a cap-front there.

"Bring up the patient, then," said Cuticle.

"Young gentleman," he added, turning to the row of Assistant Surgeons, "seeing you here reminds me of the classes of students once under my instruction at the Philadelphia College of Physicians and Surgeons. Ah, those were happy days!" he sighed, applying the extreme corner of his handkerchief to his glass eye. "Excuse an old man's emotions, young gentlemen; but when I think of the numerous rare cases that then came under my treatment, I cannot but give way to my feelings. The town,

the city, the metropolis, young gentlemen, is the place for you students; at least in these dull times of peace, when the army and navy furnish no inducements for a youth ambitious of rising in our honorable profession. Take an old man's advice, and if the war now threatening between the States and Mexico should break out, exchange your Navy commissions for commissions in the army. From having no military marine herself, Mexico has always been backward in furnishing subjects for the amputation-tables of foreign navies. The cause of science has languished in her hands. The army, young gentlemen, is your best school; depend upon it. You will hardly believe it, Surgeon Bandage," turning to that gentleman, "but this is my first important case of surgery in a nearly three years' cruise. I have been almost wholly confined in this ship to doctor's practice—prescribing for fevers and fluxes. True, the other day a man fell from the mizen-top-sail yard; but that was merely an aggravated case of dislocations and bones splintered and broken. No one, sir, could have made an amputation of it, without severely contusing his conscience. And mine—I may say it, gentlemen, without ostentation—is peculiarly susceptible."

And so saying, the knife and carver touchingly dropped to his sides, and he stood for a moment fixed in a tender reverie. But a commotion being heard beyond the curtain, he started, and, briskly crossing and recrossing the knife and carver, exclaimed, "Ah, here comes our patient; surgeons, this side of the table, if you please; young gentlemen, a little farther off, I beg. Steward, take off my coat—so; my neckerchief now; I must be perfectly unencumbered, Surgeon Patella, or I can do nothing whatever."

These articles being removed, he snatched off his wig, placing it on the gun-deck capstan; then took out his set of false teeth, and placed it by the side of the wig; and, lastly, putting his forefinger to the inner angle of his blind eye, spirted out the glass optic with professional dexterity, and deposited that, also, next to the wig and false teeth.

Thus divested of nearly all inorganic appurtenances, what was left of the surgeon slightly shook itself, to see whether anything more could be spared to advantage.

"Carpenter's mates," he now cried, "will you never get through with that job?"

"Almost through, sir—just through," they replied, staring round in search of the strange, unearthly voice that addressed them; for the absence of his teeth had not at all improved the conversational tones of the Surgeon of the Fleet.

With natural curiosity, these men had purposely been lingering, to see all they could; but now, having no further excuse, they snatched up their hammers and chisels, and —like the stage-builders decamping from a public meeting at the eleventh hour, after just completing the rostrum in time for the first speaker—the Carpenter's gang withdrew.

The broad ensign now lifted, revealing a glimpse of the crowd of man-of-war's-men outside, and the patient, borne in the arms of two of his mess-mates, entered the place. He was much emaciated, weak as an infant, and every limb visibly trembled, or rather jarred, like the head of a man with the palsy. As if an organic and involuntary apprehension of death had seized the wounded leg, its nervous motions were so violent that one of the mess-mates was obliged to keep his hand upon it.

The top-man was immediately stretched upon the table, the attendants steadying his limbs, when, slowly opening his eyes, he glanced about at the glittering knives and saws, the towels and sponges, the armed sentry at the Commodore's cabin-door, the row of eager-eyed students, the meagre death's-head of a Cuticle, now with his shirt sleeves rolled up upon his withered arms and knife in hand, and, finally, his eye settled in horror upon the skeleton, slowly vibrating and jingling before him, with the slow, slight roll of the frigate in the water.

"I would advise perfect repose of your every limb, my man," said Cuticle, addressing him; "the precision of an operation is often impaired by the inconsiderate restlessness of the patient. But if you consider, my good fellow," he added, in a patronizing and almost sympathetic tone, and slightly pressing his hand on the limb, "if you consider how much better it is to live with three limbs than to die with four, and especially if you but knew to what torments both sailors and soldiers were subjected before the time of Celsus, owing to the lamentable ignorance of surgery then prevailing, you would certainly thank God from the bottom of your heart that *your* operation has been postponed to the period of this enlightened age, blessed with a Bell, a Brodie, and a Lally. My man, before Celsus's time, such was the general ignorance of our noble science, that, in order to prevent the excessive effusion of blood, it was deemed indispensable to operate with a red-hot knife" —making a professional movement toward the thigh—"and pour scalding oil upon the parts" —elevating his elbow, as if with a tea-pot in his hand—"still further to sear them, after amputation had been performed."

"He is fainting!" said one of his mess-mates; "quick! some water!" The steward immediately hurried to the top-man with the basin.

Cuticle took the top-man by the wrist, and feeling it a while, observed, "Don't be alarmed, men," addressing the two mess-mates; "he'll recover presently; this fainting very generally takes place." And he stood for a moment, tranquilly eyeing the patient.

Now the Surgeon of the Fleet and the top-man presented a spectacle which, to a reflecting mind, was better than a churchyard sermon on the mortality of man.

Here was a sailor, who, four days previous, had stood erect—a pillar of life—with an arm like a royal-mast and a thigh like a windlass. But the slightest conceivable finger-touch of a bit of crooked trigger had eventuated in stretching him out, more helpless than an hour-old babe, with a blasted thigh, utterly drained of its brawn. And who was it that now stood over him like a superior being, and, as if clothed himself with the attributes of immortality indifferently discoursed of carving up his broken flesh, and thus piecing out his abbreviated days? Who was it that in capacity of Surgeon, seemed enacting the part of a Regenerator of life? The withered, shrunken, one-eyed, toothless, hairless Cuticle; with a trunk half dead— a *memento mori* to behold!

And while, in those soul-sinking and panic-striking premonitions of speedy death which almost invariably accompany a severe gun-shot wound, even with the most intrepid spirits; while thus drooping and dying, this once robust top-man's eye was now waning in his head like a Lapland moon being eclipsed in clouds—Cuticle, who for years had still lived in his withered tabernacle of a body—Cuticle, no doubt sharing in the common self-delusion of old age—Cuticle must have felt his hold of life as secure as the grim hug of a grizzly bear. Verily, Life is more awful than Death; and let no man, though his live heart beat in him like a canon—let him not hug his life to himself; for, in the predestined necessities of things, that bounding life of his is not a whit more secure than the life of a man on his death-bed.

To-day we inhale the air with expanding lungs, and life runs through us like a thousand Niles; but to-morrow we may collapse in death, and all our veins be dry as the Brook Kedron in a drought.

"And now, young gentlemen," said Cuticle, turning to the Assistant Surgeons, "while the patient is coming to, permit me to describe to you the highly-interesting operation I am about to perform."

"Mr. Surgeon of the Fleet," said Surgeon Bandage, "if you are about to lecture, permit me to present you with your teeth; they will make your discourse more readily understood." And so saying, Bandage, with a bow, placed the two semicircles of ivory into Cuticle's hands.

"Thank you, Surgeon Bandage," said Cuticle, and slipped the ivory into its place.

"In the first place, now, young gentlemen, let me direct your attention to the excellent preparation before you. I have had it unpacked from its case, and set up here from my state-room, where it occupies the spare berth; and all this for your express benefit, young gentlemen. This skeleton I procured in person from the Hunterian department of the Royal College of Surgeons in London. It is a master-piece of art. But we have no time to examine it now. Delicacy forbids that I should amplify at a juncture like this"—casting an almost benignant glance toward the patient, now beginning to open his eyes; "but let me point out to you upon this thigh-bone"—disengaging it from the skeleton, with a gentle twist—"the precise place where I propose to perform the operation. *Here,* young gentlemen, *here* is the place. You perceive it is very near the point of articulation with the trunk."

"Yes," interposed Surgeon Wedge, rising on his toes, "yes, young gentlemen, the point of articulation with the *acetabulum* of the *os innominatum.*"

"Where's your 'Bell on Bones,' Dick?" whispered one of the assistants to the student next him. "Wedge has been spending the whole morning over it, getting out the hard names."

"Surgeon Wedge," said Cuticle, looking round severely, "we will dispense with your commentaries, if you please, at present. Now, young gentlemen, you cannot but perceive, that the point of operation being so near the trunk and the vitals, it becomes an unusually beautiful one, demanding a steady hand and a true eye; and, after all, the patient may die under my hands."

"Quick, Steward! water, water; he's fainting again!" cried the two mess-mates.

"Don't be alarmed for your comrade, men," said Cuticle, turning round. "I tell you it is not an uncommon thing for the patient to betray some emotion upon these occasions—most usually manifested by swooning; it is quite natural it should be so. But we must not delay the operation. Steward, that knife—no, the next one—there, that's it. He is coming to, I think" —feeling the top-man's wrist. "Are you all ready, sir?"

This last observation was addressed to one of the Neversink's assistant surgeons, a tall, lank, cadaverous young man, arrayed in a sort of shroud of white canvas, pinned about his throat, and completely enveloping his person. He was seated on a match-tub—the skeleton swinging near his head—at the foot of the table, in readiness to grasp the limb, as when a plank is being severed by a carpenter and his apprentice.

"The sponges, Steward," said Cuticle, for the last time taking out his teeth, and drawing up his shirt sleeve still farther. Then, taking the patient by the wrist, "Stand by, now, you mess-mates; keep hold of his arms; pin him down. Steward, put your hand on the artery; I shall commence as soon as his pulse begins to —*now, now!*" Letting fall the wrist, feeling the thigh carefully, and bowing over it an instant, he drew the fatal knife unerringly across the flesh. As it first touched the part, the row of surgeons simultaneously dropped their eyes to the watches in their hands, while the patient lay, with eyes horribly distended, in a kind of waking trance. Not a breath was heard; but as the quivering flesh parted in a long, lingering gash, a spring of blood welled up between the living walls of the wound, and two thick streams, in opposite directions, coursed down the thigh. The sponges were instantly dipped in the purple pool; every face present was pinched to a point with suspense; the limb writhed; the man shrieked; his mess-mates pinioned him; while round and round the leg went the unpitying cut.

"The saw!" said Cuticle.

Instantly it was in his hand.

Full of the operation, he was about to apply it, when, looking up, and turning to the assistant surgeons, he said, "Would any of you young gentlemen like to apply the saw? A splendid subject!"

Several volunteered; when, selecting one, Cuticle surrendered the instrument to him, saying, "Don't be hurried, now; be steady."

While the rest of the assistants looked upon their comrade with glances of envy, he went rather timidly to work; and Cuticle, who was earnestly regarding him, suddenly snatched the saw from his hand "Away, butcher! you disgrace the profession. Look at *me!*"

For a few moments the thrilling, rasping sound was heard; and then the top-man seemed parted in twain at the hip, as the leg slowly slid into the arms of the pale, gaunt man in the shroud, who at once made away with it, and tucked it out of sight under one of the guns.

"Surgeon Sawyer," now said Cuticle, courteously turning to the surgeon of the Mohawk, "would you like to take up the arteries? They are quite at your service, sir."

"Do, Sawyer; be prevailed upon," said Surgeon Bandage.

Sawyer complied; and while, with some modesty, he was conducting the operation, Cuticle, turning to the row of assistants, said, "Young gentlemen, we will now proceed with our illustration. Hand me that bone, Steward." And taking the thigh-bone in his still bloody hands, and holding it conspicuously before his auditors, the Surgeon of the Fleet began:

"Young gentlemen, you will perceive that precisely at this spot—*here*—to which I previously directed your attention—at the corresponding spot precisely—the operation has been performed. About here, young gentlemen, *here*"—lifting his hand some inches from the bone—"about *here* the great artery was. But you noticed that I did not use the tourniquet; I never do. The forefinger of my steward is far better than a tourniquet, being so much more manageable, and leaving the smaller veins uncompressed. But I have been told, young gentlemen, that a certain Seignior Seignioroni, a surgeon of Seville, has recently invented an admirable substitute for the clumsy, old-fashioned tourniquet. As I understand it, it is something like a pair of *calipers*, working with a small Archimedes screw—a very clever invention, according to all accounts. For the padded points at the end of the arches"—arching his forefinger and thumb—"can be so worked as to approximate in such a way, as to

—but you don't attend to me, young gentlemen," he added, all at once starting.

Being more interested in the active proceedings of Surgeon Sawyer, who was now threading a needle to sew up the over-lapping of the stump, the young gentlemen had not scrupled to turn away their attention altogether from the lecturer.

A few moments more, and the top-man, in a swoon, was removed below into the sick-bay. As the curtain settled again after the patient had disappeared, Cuticle, still holding the thigh-bone of the skeleton in his ensanguined hands, proceeded with his remarks upon it; and having concluded them, added, "Now, young gentlemen, not the least interesting consequence of this operation will be the finding of the ball, which, in case of non-amputation, might have long eluded the most careful search. That ball, young gentlemen, must have taken a most circuitous route. Nor, in cases where the direction is oblique, is this at all unusual. Indeed, the learned Henner gives us a most remarkable—I had almost said an incredible—case of a soldier's neck, where the bullet, entering at the part called Adam's Apple—"

"Yes," said Surgeon Wedge, elevating himself, "the *pomum Adami.*"

"Entering the point called *Adam's Apple*," continued Cuticle, severely emphasizing the last two words, "ran completely round the neck, and, emerging at the same hole it had entered, shot the next man in the ranks. It was afterward extracted, says Henner, from the second man, and pieces of the other's skin were found adhering to it. But examples of foreign substances being received into the body with a ball, young gentlemen, are frequently observed. Being attached to a United States ship at the time, I happened to be near the spot of the battle of Ayacucho, in Peru. The day after the action, I saw in the barracks of the wounded a trooper, who, having been severely injured in the brain, went crazy, and, with his own holster-pistol, committed suicide in the hospital. The ball drove inward a portion of his woollen nightcap—"

"In the form of a *cul-de-sac*, doubtless," said the undaunted Wedge.

"For once, Surgeon Wedge, you use the only term that can be employed; and let me avail myself of this opportunity to say to you, young gentlemen, that a man of true science"

—expanding his shallow chest a little—"uses but few hard words, and those only when none other will answer his purpose; whereas the smatterer in science"—slightly glancing toward Wedge—"thinks, that by mouthing hard words, he proves that he understands hard things. Let this sink deep in your minds, young gentlemen; and, Surgeon Wedge"—with a stiff bow—"permit me to submit the reflection to yourself.

10 Well, young gentlemen, the bullet was afterward extracted by pulling upon the external parts of the *cul-de-sac*—a simple, but exceedingly beautiful operation. There is a fine example, somewhat similar, related in Guthrie; but, of course, you must have met with it, in so well-known a work as his Treatise upon Gunshot Wounds. When, upward of twenty years ago, I was with Lord Cochrane, then admiral of the fleets of this very country"—pointing

20 shoreward, out of a port-hole—"a sailor of the vessel to which I was attached, during the blockade of Bahia, had his leg—" But by this time the fidgets had completely taken possession of his auditors, especially of the senior surgeons; and turning upon them abruptly, he added, "But I will not detain you longer, gentlemen"—turning round upon all the surgeons—"your dinners must be waiting you on board your respective ships. But, Surgeon Sawyer,

30 perhaps you may desire to wash your hands before you go. There is the basin, sir; you will find a clean towel on the rammer. For myself, I seldom use them"—taking out his handkerchief. "I must leave you now, gentlemen"—bowing. "To-morrow, at ten, the limb will be upon the table, and I shall be happy to see you all upon the occasion. Who's there?" turning to the curtain, which then rustled.

"Please, sir," said the steward, entering, "the patient is dead."

"The body also, gentlemen, at ten precisely," said Cuticle, once more turning round upon his guests. "I predicted that the operation might prove fatal; he was very much run down. Good-morning;" and Cuticle departed.

"He does not, surely, mean to touch the body?" exclaimed Surgeon Sawyer, with much excitement.

"Oh, no!" said Patella, "that's only his way; he means, doubtless, that it may be inspected previous to being taken ashore for burial."

The assemblage of gold-laced surgeons now ascended to the quarter-deck; the second cutter was called away by the bugler, and, one by one, they were dropped aboard of their respective ships.

The following evening the mess-mates of the top-man rowed his remains ashore, and buried them in the ever-vernal Protestant cemetery, hard by the Beach of the Flamingoes, in plain sight from the bay.

1849   1850

» » *From:* MOBY-DICK [10] « «

OR, THE WHALE

CHAPTER CXXXIII

THE CHASE—FIRST DAY

43 That night, in the mid-watch, when the old man—as his wont at intervals—stepped forth from the scuttle in which he leaned, and went to his pivot-hole, he suddenly thrust out his face fiercely, snuffing up the sea air as a sagacious ship's dog will, in drawing nigh to some barbarous isle. He declared that a whale must

50 be near. Soon that peculiar odor, sometimes to a great distance given forth by the living sperm whale, was palpable to all the watch; nor was any mariner surprised when, after inspecting the compass, and then the dog-vane, and then

[10] These chapters are the last three of the novel.

ascertaining the precise bearing of the odor as nearly as possible, Ahab rapidly ordered the ship's course to be slightly altered, and the sail to be shortened.

The acute policy dictating these movements was sufficiently vindicated at daybreak, by the sight of a long sleek on the sea directly and lengthwise ahead, smooth as oil, and resembling in the pleated watery wrinkles bordering it, the polished metallic-like marks of some swift tide-rip, at the mouth of a deep, rapid stream.

"Man the mast-heads! Call all hands!"

Thundering with the butts of three clubbed handspikes on the forecastle deck, Daggoo roused the sleepers with such judgment claps that they seemed to exhale from the scuttle, so instantaneously did they appear with their clothes in their hands.

"What d'ye see?" cried Ahab, flattening his face to the sky.

"Nothing, nothing, sir!" was the sound hailing down in reply.

"T'-gallant-sails!—stunsails! alow and aloft, and on both sides!"

All sail being set, he now cast loose the life-line, reserved for swaying him to the main royal-mast head; and in a few moments they were hoisting him thither, when, while but two thirds of the way aloft, and while peering ahead through the horizontal vacancy between the main-top-sail and top-gallant-sail, he raised a gull-like cry in the air, "There she blows!—there she blows! A hump like a snow-hill! It is Moby Dick!"

Fired by the cry which seemed simultaneously taken up by the three look-outs, the men on deck rushed to the rigging to behold the famous whale they had so long been pursuing. Ahab had now gained his final perch, some feet above the other look-outs, Tashtego standing just beneath him on the cap of the top-gallant-mast, so that the Indian's head was almost on a level with Ahab's heel. From this height the whale was now seen some mile or so ahead, at every roll of the sea revealing his high sparkling hump, and regularly jetting his silent spout into the air. To the credulous mariners it seemed the same silent spout they had so long ago beheld in the moonlit Atlantic and Indian Oceans.

"And did none of ye see it before?" cried Ahab, hailing the perched men all around him.

"I saw him almost that same instant, sir, that Captain Ahab did, and I cried out," said Tashtego.

"Not the same instant; not the same—no, the doubloon is mine, Fate reserved the doubloon for me. *I* only; none of ye could have raised the White Whale first. There she blows! there she blows!—there she blows! There again!—there again!" he cried, in long-drawn, lingering, methodic tones, attuned to the gradual prolongings of the whale's visible jets. "He's going to sound! In stunsails! Down top-gallant-sails! Stand by three boats. Mr. Starbuck, remember, stay on board, and keep the ship. Helm there! Luff, luff a point! So; steady, man, steady! There go flukes! No, no; only black water! All ready the boats there? Stand by, stand by! Lower me, Mr. Starbuck; lower, lower,—quick,

quicker!" and he slid through the air to the deck.

"He is heading straight to leeward, sir," cried Stubb, "right away from us; cannot have seen the ship yet."

"Be dumb, man! Stand by the braces! Hard down the helm!—brace up! Shiver her!—shiver her!—So; well that! Boats, boats!"

Soon all the boats but Starbuck's were dropped; all the boat-sails set—all the paddles plying; with rippling swiftness, shooting to leeward; and Ahab heading the onset. A pale, death-glimmer lit up Fedallah's sunken eyes; a hideous motion gnawed his mouth.

Like noiseless nautilus shells, their light prows sped through the sea; but only slowly they neared the foe. As they neared him, the ocean grew still more smooth; seemed drawing a carpet over its waves; seemed a noon-meadow, so serenely it spread. At length the breathless hunter came so nigh his seemingly unsuspecting prey, that his entire dazzling hump was distinctly visible, sliding along the sea as if an isolated thing, and continually set in a revolving ring of finest, fleecy, greenish foam. He saw the vast, involved wrinkles of the slightly projecting head beyond. Before it, far out on the soft Turkish-rugged waters, went the glistening white shadow from his broad, milky forehead, a musical rippling playfully accompanying the shade; and behind, the blue waters interchangeably flowed over into the moving valley of his steady wake; and on either hand bright bubbles arose and danced by his side. But these were broken again by the light toes of hundreds of gay fowl softly feathering the sea, alternate with their fitful flight; and like to some flagstaff rising from the painted hull of an argosy, the tall but shattered pole of a recent lance projected from the white whale's back; and at intervals one of the cloud of soft-toed fowls hovering, and to and fro skimming like a canopy over the fish, silently perched and rocked on this pole, the long tail feathers streaming like pennons.

A gentle joyousness—a mighty mildness of repose in swiftness, invested the gliding whale. Not the white bull Jupiter swimming away with ravished Europa clinging to his graceful horns; his lovely, leering eyes sideways intent upon the maid; with smooth bewitching fleetness, rippling straight for the nuptial bower in Crete; not Jove, not that great majesty Supreme! did surpass the glorified White Whale as he so divinely swam.

On each soft side—coincident with the parted swell, that but once leaving him, flowed so wide away—on each bright side, the whale shed off enticings. No wonder there had been some among the hunters who namelessly transported and allured by all this serenity, had ventured to assail it; but had fatally found that quietude but the vesture of tornadoes. Yet calm, enticing calm, oh, whale! thou glidest on, to all who for the first time eye thee, no matter how many in that same way thou may'st have bejuggled and destroyed before.

And thus, through the serene tranquillities of the tropical sea, among waves whose hand-clappings were suspended by exceeding rapture, Moby Dick moved on, still withholding from sight the full terrors of his submerged trunk, entirely hiding the wrenched hideousness of his jaw. But soon the fore part of him slowly rose from the water; for an instant his whole marbleized body formed a high arch, like Virginia's Natural Bridge, and warningly waving his bannered flukes in the air, the grand god revealed himself, sounded, and went out of sight. Hoveringly halting, and dipping on the wing, the white sea-fowls longingly lingered over the agitated pool that he left.

With oars apeak, and paddles down, the sheets of their sails adrift, the three boats now stilly floated, awaiting Moby Dick's reappearance.

"An hour," said Ahab, standing rooted in his boat's stern; and he gazed beyond the whale's place, towards the dim blue spaces and wide wooing vacancies to leeward. It was only an instant; for again his eyes seemed whirling round in his head as he swept the watery circle. The breeze now freshened; the sea began to swell.

"The birds!—the birds!" cried Tashtego.

In long Indian file, as when herons take wing, the white birds were now all flying towards Ahab's boat; and when within a few yards began fluttering over the water there, wheeling round and round, with joyous, expectant cries. Their vision was keener than man's; Ahab could discover no sign in the sea. But suddenly as he peered down and down into its depths, he profoundly saw a white living spot no bigger than a white weasel, with wonderful celerity uprising, and magnifying as it rose, till it turned, and then there were plainly revealed two long crooked rows of white, glistening teeth, floating up from the

undiscoverable bottom. It was Moby Dick's open mouth and scrolled jaw; his vast, shadowed bulk still half blending with the blue of the sea. The glittering mouth yawned beneath the boat like an open-doored marble tomb; and giving one sidelong sweep with his steering oar, Ahab whirled the craft aside from this tremendous apparition. Then, calling upon Fedallah to change places with him, went forward to the bows, and seizing Perth's harpoon, commanded his crew to grasp their oars and stand by to stern.

Now, by reason of this timely spinning round the boat upon its axis, its bow, by anticipation, was made to face the whale's head while yet under water. But as if perceiving this stratagem, Moby Dick, with that malicious intelligence ascribed to him, sidelingly transplanted himself, as it were, in an instant, shooting his pleated head lengthwise beneath the boat.

Through and through; through every plank and each rib, it thrilled for an instant, the whale obliquely lying on his back, in the manner of a biting shark, slowly and feelingly taking its bows full within his mouth, so that the long, narrow, scrolled lower jaw curled high up into the open air, and one of the teeth caught in a row-lock. The bluish pearl-white of the inside of the jaw was within six inches of Ahab's head, and reached higher than that. In this attitude the White Whale now shook the slight cedar as a mildly cruel cat her mouse. With unastonished eyes Fedallah gazed, and crossed his arms; but the tiger-yellow crew were tumbling over each other's heads to gain the uttermost stern.

And now, while both elastic gunwales were springing in and out, as the whale dallied with the doomed craft in this devilish way; and from his body being submerged beneath the boat, he could not be darted at from the bows, for the bows were almost inside of him, as it were; and while the other boats involuntarily paused, as before a quick crisis impossible to withstand, then it was that monomaniac Ahab, furious with this tantalizing vicinity of his foe, which placed him all alive and helpless in the very jaws he hated; frenzied with all this, he seized the long bone with his naked hands, and wildly strove to wrench it from its gripe. As now he thus vainly strove, the jaw slipped from him; the frail gunwales bent in, collapsed, and snapped, as both jaws, like an enormous shears, sliding further aft, bit the craft completely in twain, and locked themselves fast again in the sea, midway between the two floating wrecks. These floated aside, the broken ends drooping, the crew at the stern-wreck clinging to the gunwales, and striving to hold fast to the oars to lash them across.

At the preluding moment, ere the boat was yet snapped, Ahab, the first to perceive the whale's intent, by the crafty upraising of his head, a movement that loosed his hold for the time; at that moment his hand had made one final effort to push the boat out of the bite. But only slipping further into the whale's mouth, and tilting over sideways as it slipped, the boat had shaken off his hold on the jaw; spilled him out of it, as he leaned to the push; and so he fell flat-faced upon the sea.

Ripplingly withdrawing from his prey, Moby Dick now lay at a little distance, vertically thrusting his oblong white head up and down in the billows; and at the same time slowly revolving his whole spindled body; so that when his vast wrinkled forehead rose—some twenty or more feet out of the water—the now rising swells, with all their confluent waves, dazzlingly broke against it; vindictively tossing their shivered spray still higher into the air.[11] So, in a gale, the but half baffled Channel billows only recoil from the base of the Eddystone, triumphantly to overleap its summit with their scud.

But soon resuming his horizontal attitude, Moby Dick swam swiftly round and round the wrecked crew; sideways churning the water in his vengeful wake, as if lashing himself up to still another and more deadly assault. The sight of the splintered boat seemed to madden him, as the blood of grapes and mulberries cast before Antiochus's elephants in the book of Maccabees. Meanwhile Ahab half smothered in the foam of the whale's insolent tail, and too much of a cripple to swim,—though he could still keep afloat, even in the heart of such a whirlpool as that; helpless Ahab's head was seen, like a tossed bubble which the least chance shock might burst. From the boat's fragmentary stern, Fedallah incuriously and mildly eyed him; the clinging crew, at the other drifting end, could not succor him; more than enough

was it for them to look to themselves. For so revolvingly appalling was the White Whale's aspect, and so planetarily swift the ever-contracting circles he made, that he seemed horizontally swooping upon them. And though the other boats, unharmed, still hovered hard by; still they dared not pull into the eddy to strike, lest that should be the signal for the instant destruction of the jeopardized castaways, Ahab and all; nor in that case could they themselves hope to escape. With straining eyes, then, they remained on the outer edge of the direful zone, whose centre had now become the old man's head.

Meantime, from the beginning all this had been descried from the ship's mast heads; and squaring her yards, she had borne down upon the scene; and was now so nigh, that Ahab in the water hailed her;—"Sail on the"—but that moment a breaking sea dashed on him from Moby Dick, and whelmed him for the time. But struggling out of it again, and chancing to rise on a towering crest, he shouted,—"Sail on the whale!—Drive him off!"

The *Pequod's* prows were pointed; and breaking up the charmed circle, she effectually parted the white whale from his victim. As he sullenly swam off, the boats flew to the rescue.

Dragged into Stubb's boat with blood-shot, blinded eyes, the white brine caking in his wrinkles; the long tension of Ahab's bodily strength did crack, and helplessly he yielded to his body's doom: for a time, lying all crushed in the bottom of Stubb's boat, like one trodden under foot of herds of elephants. Far inland, nameless wails came from him, as desolate sounds from out ravines.

But this intensity of his physical prostration did but so much the more abbreviate it. In an instant's compass, great hearts sometimes condense to one deep pang, the sumtotal of those shallow pains kindly diffused through feebler men's whole lives. And so, such hearts, though summary in each one suffering; still, if the gods decree it, in their lifetime aggregate a whole age of woe, wholly made up of instantaneous intensities; for even in their pointless centres, those noble natures contain the entire circumferences of inferior souls.

"The harpoon," said Ahab, half way rising, and draggingly leaning on one bended arm—"is it safe?"

[11] This motion is peculiar to the sperm whale. It receives its designation (pitchpoling) from its being likened to that preliminary up-and-down poise of the whale-lance, in the exercise called pitchpoling, previously described. By this motion the whale must best and most comprehensively view whatever objects may be encircling him. [Melville's note.]

"Aye, sir, for it was not darted; this is it," said Stubb, showing it.

"Lay it before me;—any missing men?"

"One, two, three, four, five;—there were five oars, sir, and here are five men."

"That's good.—Help me, man; I wish to stand. So, so, I see him! there! there! going to leeward still; what a leaping spout!—Hands off from me! The eternal sap runs up in Ahab's bones again! Set the sail; out oars; the helm!"

It is often the case that when a boat is stove, its crew, being picked up by another boat, help to work that second boat; and the chase is thus continued with what is called double-banked oars. It was thus now. But the added power of the boat did not equal the added power of the whale, for he seemed to have treble-banked his every fin; swimming with a velocity which plainly showed, that if now, under these circumstances, pushed on, the chase would prove an indefinitely prolonged, if not a hopeless one; nor could any crew endure for so long a period, such an unintermitted, intense straining at the oar; a thing barely tolerable only in some one brief vicissitude. The ship itself, then, as it sometimes happens, offered the most promising intermediate means of overtaking the chase. Accordingly, the boats now made for her, and were soon swayed up to their cranes—the two parts of the wrecked boat having been previously secured by her—and then hoisting everything to her side, and stacking her canvas high up, and sideways outstretching it with stunsails, like the double-jointed wings of an albatross; the *Pequod* bore down in the leeward wake of Moby Dick. At the well known, methodic intervals, the whale's glittering spout was regularly announced from the manned mast-heads; and when he would be reported as just gone down, Ahab would take the time, and then pacing the deck, binnacle-watch in hand, so soon as the last second of the allotted hour expired, his voice was heard.—"Whose is the doubloon now? D'ye see him?" and if the reply was, No, sir! straightway he commanded them to lift him to his perch. In this way the day wore on; Ahab, now aloft and motionless; anon, unrestingly pacing the planks.

As he was thus walking, uttering no sound, except to hail the men aloft, or to bid them hoist a sail still higher, or to spread one to a still greater breadth—thus to and fro pacing, beneath his slouched hat, at every turn he passed his own wrecked boat, which had been dropped upon the quarter-deck, and lay there reversed; broken bow to shattered stern. At last he paused before it; and as in an already over-clouded sky fresh troops of clouds will sometimes sail across, so over the old man's face there now stole some such added gloom as this.

Stubb saw him pause; and perhaps intending, not vainly, though, to evince his own unabated fortitude, and thus keep up a valiant place in his Captain's mind, he advanced, and eyeing the wreck exclaimed—"The thistle the ass refused; it pricked his mouth too keenly, sir, ha! ha!"

"What soulless thing is this that laughs before a wreck? Man, man! did I not know thee brave as fearless fire (and as mechanical) I could swear thou wert a poltroon. Groan nor laugh should be heard before a wreck."

"Aye, sir," said Starbuck, drawing near, "'tis a solemn sight; an omen, and an ill one."

"Omen? omen?—the dictionary! If the gods think to speak outright to man, they will honorably speak outright; not shake their heads, and give an old wives' darkling hint.—Begone! Ye two are the opposite poles of one thing; Starbuck is Stubb reversed, and Stubb is Starbuck; and ye two are all mankind; and Ahab stands alone among the millions of the peopled earth, nor gods nor men his neighbors! Cold, cold—I shiver!—How now? Aloft there! D'ye see him? Sing out for every spout, though he spout ten times a second!"

The day was nearly done; only the hem of his golden robe was rustling. Soon it was almost dark, but the look-out men still remained unset.

"Can't see the spout now, sir;—too dark"—cried a voice from the air.

"How heading when last seen?"

"As before, sir,—straight to leeward."

"Good! he will travel slower now 'tis night. Down royals and top-gallant stun-sails, Mr. Starbuck. We must not run over him before morning; he's making a passage now, and may heave-to a while. Helm there! keep her full before the wind!—Aloft! come down!—Mr. Stubb, send a fresh hand to the fore-mast head, and see it manned till morning."—Then advancing towards the doubloon in the main-mast—"Men, this gold is mine, for I earned it; but I shall let it abide here till the White Whale is dead; and then, whosoever of ye first raises him, upon the day he shall be killed, this gold is that man's; and if on that day I shall again raise him, then, ten times its sum shall be divided among all of ye! Away now!—the deck is thine, sir."

And so saying, he placed himself half way within the scuttle, and slouching his hat, stood there till dawn, except when at intervals rousing himself to see how the night wore on.

CHAPTER CXXXIV

THE CHASE—SECOND DAY

At day-break, the three mast-heads were punctually manned afresh.

"D'ye see him?" cried Ahab, after allowing a little space for the light to spread.

"See nothing, sir."

"Turn up all hands and make sail! he travels faster than I thought for;—the top-gallant sails! —aye, they should have been kept on her all night. But no matter—'tis but resting for the rush."

Here be it said, that this pertinacious pursuit of one particular whale, continued through day into night, and through night into day, is a thing by no means unprecedented in the South sea fishery. For such is the wonderful skill, prescience of experience, and invincible confidence acquired by some great natural geniuses among the Nantucket commanders; that from the simple observation of a whale when last descried, they will, under certain given circumstances, pretty accurately foretell both the direction in which he will continue to swim for a time, while out of sight, as well as his probable rate of progression during that period. And, in these cases, somewhat as a pilot, when about losing sight of a coast, whose general trending he well knows, and which he desires shortly to return to again, but at some further point; like as this pilot stands by his compass, and takes the precise bearing of the cape at present visible, in order the more certainly to hit aright the remote, unseen headland, eventually to be visited: so does the fisherman, at his compass, with the whale; for after being chased, and diligently marked, through several hours of daylight, then, when night obscures the fish, the creature's future wake through the darkness is almost as established to the sagacious mind of the hunter, as the pilot's coast is to him. So that to this hunter's wondrous skill, the proverbial evanescence of a thing writ in water, a wake, is to all desired

purposes well nigh as reliable as the steadfast land. And as the mighty iron Leviathan of the modern railway is so familiarly known in its every pace, that, with watches in their hands, men time his rate as doctors that of a baby's pulse; and lightly say of it, the up train or the down train will reach such or such a spot, at such or such an hour; even so, almost, there are occasions when these Nantucketers time that other Leviathan of the deep, according to the observed humor of his speed; and say to themselves, so many hours hence this whale will have gone two hundred miles, will have about reached this or that degree of latitude or longitude. But to render this acuteness at all successful in the end, the wind and the sea must be the whaleman's allies; for of what present avail to the becalmed or windbound mariner is the skill that assures him he is exactly ninety-three leagues and a quarter from his port? Inferable from these statements, are many collateral subtile matters touching the chase of whales.

The ship tore on; leaving such a furrow in the sea as when a cannon-ball, missent, becomes a plough-share and turns up the level field.

"By salt and hemp!" cried Stubb, "but this swift motion of the deck creeps up one's legs and tingles at the heart. This ship and I are two brave fellows!—Ha! ha! Some one take me up, and launch me, spine-wise, on the sea,— for by live-oaks! my spine's a keel. Ha, ha! we go the gait that leaves no dust behind!"

"There she blows—she blows!—she blows! —right ahead!" was now the mast-head cry.

"Aye, aye!" cried Stubb, "I knew it—ye can't escape—blow on and split your spout, O whale! the mad fiend himself is after ye! blow your trump—blister your lungs!—Ahab will dam off your blood, as a miller shuts his water-gate upon the stream!"

And Stubb did but speak out for well nigh all that crew. The frenzies of the chase had by this time worked them bubblingly up, like old wine worked anew. Whatever pale fears and forebodings some of them might have felt before; these were not only now kept out of sight through the growing awe of Ahab, but they were broken up, and on all sides routed, as timid prairie hares that scatter before the bounding bison. The hand of Fate had snatched all their souls; and by the stirring perils of the previous day; the rack of the past night's suspense; the fixed, unfearing, blind, reckless way in which their wild craft went plunging towards its flying mark; by all these things, their hearts were bowled along. The wind that made great bellies of their sails, and rushed the vessel on by arms invisible as irresistible; this seemed the symbol of that unseen agency which so enslaved them to the race.

They were one man, not thirty. For as the one ship that held them all; though it was put together of all contrasting things—oak, and maple, and pine wood; iron, and pitch, and hemp—yet all these ran into each other in the one concrete hull, which shot on its way, both balanced and directed by the long central keel; even so, all the individualities of the crew, this man's valor, that man's fear; guilt and guiltiness, all varieties were welded into oneness, and were all directed to that fatal goal which Ahab their one lord and keel did point to.

The rigging lived. The mast-heads, like the tops of tall palms, were outspreadingly tufted with arms and legs. Clinging to a spar with one hand, some reached forth the other with impatient wavings; others, shading their eyes from the vivid sunlight, sat far out on the rocking yards; all the spars in full bearing of mortals, ready and ripe for their fate. Ah! how they still strove through that infinite blueness to seek out the thing that might destroy them!

"Why sing ye not out for him, if ye see him?" cried Ahab, when, after the lapse of some minutes since the first cry, no more had been heard. "Sway me up, men; ye have been deceived; not Moby Dick casts one odd jet that way, and then disappears."

It was even so; in their headlong eagerness, the men had mistaken some other thing for the whale-spout, as the event itself soon proved; for hardly had Ahab reached his perch; hardly was the rope belayed to its pin on deck, when he struck the key-note to an orchestra, that made the air vibrate as with the combined discharges of rifles. The triumphant halloo of thirty buckskin lungs was heard, as—much nearer to the ship than the place of the imaginary jet, less than a mile ahead—Moby Dick bodily burst into view! For not by any calm and indolent spoutings; not by the peaceable gush of that mystic fountain in his head, did the White Whale now reveal his vicinity; but by the far more wondrous phenomenon of breaching. Rising with his utmost velocity from the furthest depths, the Sperm Whale thus

booms his entire bulk into the pure element of air, and piling up a mountain of dazzling foam, shows his place to the distance of seven miles and more In those moments, the torn, enraged waves he shakes off, seem his mane; in some cases, this breaching is his act of defiance.

"There she breaches! there she breaches!" was the cry, as in his immeasurable bravadoes the White Whale tossed himself salmon-like to Heaven. So suddenly seen in the blue plain of the sea, and relieved against the still bluer margin of the sky, the spray that he raised, for the moment, intolerably glittered and glared like a glacier; and stood there gradually fading and fading away from its first sparkling intensity, to the dim mistiness of an advancing shower in a vale.

"Aye, breach your last to the sun, Moby Dick!" cried Ahab, "thy hour and thy harpoon are at hand!—Down! down all of ye, but one man at the fore. The boats!—stand by!"

Unmindful of the tedious rope-ladders of the shrouds, the men, like shooting stars, slid to the deck, by the isolated backstays and halyards; while Ahab, less dartingly, but still rapidly, was dropped from his perch.

"Lower away," he cried, so soon as he had reached his boat—a spare one, rigged the afternoon previous. "Mr. Starbuck, the ship is thine—keep away from the boats, but keep near them. Lower, all!"

As if to strike a quick terror into them, by this time being the first assailant himself, Moby Dick had turned, and was now coming for the three crews. Ahab's boat was central; and cheering his men, he told them he would take the whale head-and-head,—that is, pull straight up to his forehead,—a not uncommon thing; for when within a certain limit, such a course excludes the coming onset from the whale's sidelong vision. But ere that close limit was gained, and while yet all three boats were plain as the ship's three masts to his eye; the White Whale churning himself into furious speed, almost in an instant as it were, rushing among the boats with open jaws, and a lashing tail, offered appalling battle on every side; and heedless of the irons darted at him from every boat, seemed only intent on annihilating each separate plank of which those boats were made. But skilfully manœuvred, incessantly wheeling like trained chargers in the field; the boats for a while eluded him; though, at times, but by a plank's breadth; while all the time,

Ahab's unearthly slogan tore every other cry but his to shreds.

But at last in his untraceable evolutions, the White Whale so crossed and recrossed, and in a thousand ways entangled the slack of the three lines now fast to him, that they foreshortened, and, of themselves, warped the devoted boats towards the planted irons in him; though now for a moment the whale drew aside a little, as if to rally for a more tremendous charge. Seizing that opportunity, Ahab first paid out more line: and then was rapidly hauling and jerking in upon it again—hoping that way to disencumber it of some snarls—when lo!—a sight more savage than the embattled teeth of sharks!

Caught and twisted—corkscrewed in the mazes of the line—loose harpoons and lances, with all their bristling barbs and points, came flashing and dripping up to the chocks in the bows of Ahab's boat. Only one thing could be done. Seizing the boat-knife, he critically reached within—through—and then, without —the rays of steel; dragged in the line beyond, passed it, inboard, to the bowsman, and then, twice sundering the rope near the chocks—dropped the intercepted fagot of steel into the sea; and was all fast again. That instant, the White Whale made a sudden rush among the remaining tangles of the other lines; by so doing, irresistibly dragged the more involved boats of Stubb and Flask towards his flukes; dashed them together like two rolling husks on a surf-beaten beach, and then, diving down into the sea, disappeared in a boiling maelstrom, in which, for a space, the odorous cedar chips of the wrecks danced round and round, like the grated nutmeg in a swiftly stirred bowl of punch.

While the two crews were yet circling in the waters, reaching out after the revolving line-tubs, oars, and other floating furniture, while aslope little Flask bobbed up and down like an empty vial, twitching his legs upwards to escape the dreaded jaws of sharks; and Stubb was lustily singing out for some one to ladle him up; and while the old man's line—now parting—admitted of his pulling into the creamy pool to rescue whom he could:—in that wild simultaneousness of a thousand concreted perils,—Ahab's yet unstricken boat seemed drawn up towards Heaven by invisible wires,—as, arrow-like, shooting perpendicularly from the sea, the White Whale dashed his broad forehead against its bottom, and sent it,

turning over and over, into the air; till it fell again—gunwale downwards—and Ahab and his men struggled out from under it, like seals from a seaside cave.

The first uprising momentum of the whale —modifying its direction as he struck the surface—involuntarily launched him along it, to a little distance from the centre of the destruction he had made; and with his back to it, he now lay for a moment slowly feeling with his flukes from side to side; and whenever a stray oar, bit of plank, the least chip or crumb of the boats touched his skin, his tail swiftly drew back, and came sideways, smiting the sea. But soon, as if satisfied that his work for that time was done, he pushed his pleated forehead through the ocean, and trailing after him the intertangled lines, continued his leeward way at a traveller's methodic pace.

As before, the attentive ship having descried the whole fight, again came bearing down to the rescue, and dropping a boat, picked up the floating mariners, tubs, oars, and whatever else could be caught at, and safely landed them on her decks. Some sprained shoulders, wrists, and ankles; livid contusions; wrenched harpoons and lances; inextricable intricacies of rope; shattered oars and planks; all these were there; but no fatal or even serious ill seemed to have befallen any one. As with Fedallah the day before, so Ahab was now found grimly clinging to his boat's broken half, which afforded a comparatively easy float; nor did it so exhaust him as the previous day's mishap.

But when he was helped to the deck, all eyes were fastened upon him; as instead of standing by himself he still half-hung upon the shoulder of Starbuck, who had thus far been the foremost to assist him. His ivory leg had been snapped off, leaving but one short sharp splinter.

"Aye, aye, Starbuck, 'tis sweet to lean sometimes, be the leaner who he will; and would old Ahab had leaned oftener than he has."

"The ferrule has not stood, sir," said the carpenter, now coming up; "I put good work into that leg."

"But no bones broken, sir, I hope," said Stubb with true concern.

"Aye! and all splintered to pieces, Stubb! —d'ye see it.—But even with a broken bone, old Ahab is untouched; and I account no living bone of mine one jot more me, than this dead one that's lost. Nor white whale, nor man, nor fiend, can so much as graze old Ahab in his own proper and inaccessible being. Can any lead touch yonder floor, any mast scrape yonder roof?—Aloft there! which way?"

"Dead to leeward, sir."

"Up helm, then; pile on the sail again, ship keepers! down the rest of the spare boats and rig them—Mr. Starbuck, away, and muster the boat's crews."

"Let me first help thee towards the bulwarks, sir."

"Oh, oh, oh! how this splinter gores me now! Accursed fate! that the unconquerable captain in the soul should have such a craven mate!"

"Sir?"

"My body, man, not thee. Give me something for a cane—there, that shivered lance will do. Muster the men. Surely I have not seen him yet. By heaven, it cannot be!—missing?—quick! call them all."

The old man's hinted thought was true. Upon mustering the company, the Parsee was not there.

"The Parsee!" cried Stubb—"he must have been caught in——"

"The black vomit wrench thee!—run all of ye above, alow, cabin, forecastle—find him —not gone—not gone!"

But quickly they returned to him with the tidings that the Parsee was nowhere to be found.

"Aye, sir," said Stubb—"caught among the tangles of your line—I thought I saw him dragging under."

"*My* line? *my* line? Gone?—gone? What means that little word?—What death-knell rings in it, that old Ahab shakes as if he were the belfry. The harpoon, too!—toss over the litter there,—d'ye see it?—the forged iron, men, the white whale's—no, no, no,—blistered fool! this hand did dart it!—'tis in the fish! —Aloft there! Keep him nailed—Quick!—all hands to the rigging of the boats—collect the oars—harpooneers! the irons, the irons!—hoist the royals higher—a pull on all the sheets!— helm there! steady, steady for your life! I'll ten times girdle the unmeasured globe; yea and dive straight through it, but I'll slay him yet!"

"Great God! but for one single instant show thyself," cried Starbuck; "never, never wilt thou capture him, old man—In Jesus' name no more of this, that's worse than devil's madness. Two days chased; twice stove to splinters; thy very leg once more snatched from under thee; thy

evil shadow gone—all good angels mobbing thee with warnings:—what more wouldst thou have?—Shall we keep chasing this murderous fish till he swamps the last man? Shall we be dragged by him to the bottom of the sea? Shall we be towed by him to the infernal world? Oh, oh,—Impiety and blasphemy to hunt him more!"

"Starbuck, of late I've felt strangely moved to thee; ever since that hour we both saw —thou know'st what, in one another's eyes. But in this matter of the whale, be the front of thy face to me as the palm of this hand —a lipless, unfeatured blank. Ahab is for ever Ahab, man. This whole act's immutably decreed. 'Twas rehearsed by thee and me a billion years before this ocean rolled. Fool! I am the Fates' lieutenant; I act under orders. Look thou, underling! that thou obeyest mine.— Stand round me, men. Ye see an old man cut down to the stump; leaning on a shivered lance; propped up on a lonely foot. 'Tis Ahab —his body's part; but Ahab's soul's a centipede, that moves upon a hundred legs. I feel strained, half-stranded, as ropes that tow dismasted frigates in a gale; and I may look so. But ere I break, ye'll hear me crack; and till ye hear *that,* know that Ahab's hawser tows his purpose yet. Believe ye, men, in the things called omens? Then laugh aloud, and cry encore! For ere they drown, drowning things will twice rise to the surface; then rise again, to sink for evermore. So with Moby Dick—two days he's floated—to-morrow will be the third. Aye, men, he'll rise once more—but only to spout his last! D'ye feel brave men, brave?"

"As fearless fire," cried Stubb.

"And as mechanical," muttered Ahab. Then as the men went forward, he muttered on: "The things called omens! And yesterday I talked the same to Starbuck there, concerning my broken boat. Oh! how valiantly I seek to drive out of others' hearts what's clinched so fast in mine!—The Parsee—the Parsee!—gone, gone? and he was to go before:—but still was to be seen again ere I could perish—How's that?—There's a riddle now might baffle all the lawyers backed by the ghosts of the whole line of judges:—like a hawk's beak it pecks my brain. *I'll, I'll* solve it, though!"

When dusk descended, the whale was still in sight to leeward.

So once more the sail was shortened, and everything passed nearly as on the previous night; only, the sound of hammers, and the hum of the grindstone was heard till nearly daylight, as the men toiled by lanterns in the complete and careful rigging of the spare boats and sharpening their fresh weapons for the morrow. Meantime, of the broken keel of Ahab's wrecked craft the carpenter made him another leg; while still as on the night before, slouched Ahab stood fixed within his scuttle; his hid, heliotrope glance anticipatingly gone backward on its dial; sat due eastward for the earliest sun.

CHAPTER CXXXV

THE CHASE—THIRD DAY

The morning of the third day dawned fair and fresh, and once more the solitary night-man at the fore-mast-head was relieved by crowds of the daylight look-outs, who dotted every mast and almost every spar.

"D'ye see him?" cried Ahab; but the whale was not yet in sight.

"In his infallible wake, though; but follow that wake, that's all. Helm there; steady, as thou goest, and hast been going. What a lovely day again! were it a new-made world, and made for a summer-house to the angels, and this morning the first of its throwing open to them, a fairer day could not dawn upon that world. Here's food for thought, had Ahab time to think; but Ahab never thinks; he only feels, feels, feels; *that's* tingling enough for mortal man! to think's audacity. God only has that right and privilege. Thinking is, or ought to be, a coolness and a calmness; and our poor hearts throb, and our poor brains beat too much for that. And yet, I've sometimes thought my brain was very calm—frozen calm, this old skull cracks so, like a glass in which the contents turn to ice, and shiver it. And still this hair is growing now; this moment growing, and heat must breed it; but no, it's like that sort of common grass that will grow anywhere, between the earthy clefts of Greenland ice or in Vesuvius lava. How the wild winds blow it; they whip it about me as the torn shreds of split sails lash the tossed ship they cling to. A vile wind that has no doubt blown ere this through prison corridors and cells, and wards of hospitals, and ventilated them, and now comes blowing hither as innocent as fleeces. Out upon it!—it's tainted. Were I the wind, I'd blow no more on such a wicked, miserable world. I'd crawl somewhere to a cave, and slink there. And yet, 'tis a noble and heroic thing, the wind! who ever conquered it? In every fight it has the last and bitterest blow. Run tilting at it, and you but run through it. Ha! a coward wind that strikes stark naked men, but will not stand to receive a single blow. Even Ahab is a braver thing—a nobler thing than *that*. Would now the wind but had a body; but all the things that most exasperate and outrage mortal man, all these things are bodiless, but only bodiless as objects, not as agents. There's a most special, a most cunning, oh, a most malicious difference! And yet, I say again, and swear it now, that there's something all glorious and gracious in the wind. These warm Trade Winds, at least, that in the clear heavens blow straight on, in strong and steadfast, vigorous mildness; and veer not from their mark, however the baser currents of the sea may turn and tack, and mightiest Mississippies of the land shift and swerve about, uncertain where to go at last. And by the eternal Poles! these same Trades that so directly blow my good ship on; these Trades, or something like them—something so unchangeable, and full as strong, blow my keeled soul along! To it! Aloft there! What d'ye see?"

"Nothing, sir."

"Nothing! and noon at hand! The doubloon goes a-begging! See the sun! Aye, aye, it must be so. I've over-sailed him. How, got the start? Aye, he's chasing *me* now; not I, *him*—that's bad; I might have known it, too. Fool! the lines —the harpoons he's towing. Aye, aye, I have run him by last night. About! about! Come down, all of ye, but the regular look-outs! Man the braces!"

Steering as she had done, the wind had been somewhat on the *Pequod's* quarter, so that now being pointed in the reverse direction, the braced ship sailed hard upon the breeze as she rechurned the cream in her own white wake.

"Against the wind he now steers for the open jaw," murmured Starbuck to himself, as he coiled the new-hauled main-brace upon the rail. "God keep us, but already my bones feel damp within me, and from the inside wet my flesh. I misdoubt me that I disobey my God in obeying him!"

"Stand by to sway me up!" cried Ahab, advancing to the hempen basket. "We should meet him soon."

"Aye, aye, sir," and straightway Starbuck

did Ahab's bidding, and once more Ahab swung on high.

A whole hour now passed; gold-beaten out to ages. Time itself now held long breaths with keen suspense. But at last, some three points off the weather bow, Ahab descried the spout again, and instantly from the three mast-heads three shrieks went up as if the tongues of fire had voiced it.

10 "Forehead to forehead I meet thee, this third time, Moby Dick! On deck there!—brace sharper up; crowd her into the wind's eye. He's too far off to lower yet, Mr. Starbuck. The sails shake! Stand over that helmsman with a top-maul! So, so; he travels fast, and I must down. But let me have one more good round look aloft here at the sea; there's time for that. An old, old sight, and yet somehow so young; aye, and not changed a wink since I first saw
20 it, a boy, from the sand-hills of Nantucket! The same!—the same!—the same to Noah as to me. There's a soft shower to leeward. Such lovely leewardings! They must lead somewhere—to something else than common land, more palmy than the palms. Leeward! the white whale goes that way; look to windward, then; the better if the bitterer quarter. But good bye, good bye, old mast-head! What's this?—green? aye, tiny mosses in these warped cracks. No such green
30 weather stains on Ahab's head! There's the difference now between man's old age and matter's. But aye, old mast, we both grow old together; sound in our hulls, though, are we not, my ship? Aye, minus a leg, that's all. By heaven, this dead wood has the better of my live flesh every way. I can't compare with it; and I've known some ships made of dead trees outlast the lives of men made of the most vital stuff of vital fathers. What's that he said?
40 he should still go before me, my pilot; and yet to be seen again? But where? Will I have eyes at the bottom of the sea, supposing I descend those endless stairs? and all night I've been sailing from him, wherever he did sink to. Aye, aye, like many more thou told'st direful truth as touching thyself, O Parsee; but, Ahab, there thy shot fell short. Good bye, mast-head—keep a good eye upon the whale, the while I'm gone. We'll talk to-morrow, nay, to-night, when the
50 white whale lies down there, tied by head and tail."

He gave the word; and still gazing round him, was steadily lowered through the cloven blue air to the deck.

In due time the boats were lowered; but as standing in his shallop's stern, Ahab just hovered upon the point of the descent, he waved to the mate,—who held one of the tackle-ropes on deck—and bade him pause.

"Starbuck!"

"Sir?"

"For the third time my soul's ship starts upon this voyage, Starbuck."

"Aye, sir, thou wilt have it so."

"Some ships sail from their ports, and ever afterwards are missing, Starbuck!"

"Truth, sir: saddest truth."

"Some men die at ebb tide; some at low water; some at the full of the flood;—and I feel now like a billow that's all one crested comb, Starbuck. I am old;—shake hands with me, man."

Their hands met; their eyes fastened; Starbuck's tears the glue.

"Oh, my captain, my captain!—noble heart —go not—go not!—see, it's a brave man that weeps; how great the agony of the persuasion then!"

"Lower away!"—cried Ahab, tossing the mate's arm from him. "Stand by the crew!"

In an instant the boat was pulling round close under the stern.

"The sharks! the sharks!" cried a voice from the low cabin-window there; "O master, my master, come back!"

But Ahab heard nothing; for his own voice was high-lifted then; and the boat leaped on.

Yet the voice spake true; for scarce had he pushed from the ship, when numbers of sharks, seemingly rising from out the dark waters beneath the hull, maliciously snapped at the blades of the oars, every time they dipped in the water; and in this way accompanied the boat with their bites. It is a thing not uncommonly happening to the whale-boats in those swarming seas; the sharks at times apparently following them in the same prescient way that vultures hover over the banners of marching regiments in the east. But these were the first sharks that had been observed by the *Pequod* since the White Whale had been first descried; and whether it was that Ahab's crew were all such tiger-yellow barbarians, and therefore their flesh more musky to the senses of the sharks—a matter sometimes well known to affect them,—however it was, they seemed to follow that one boat without molesting the others.

"Heart of wrought steel!" murmured Starbuck, gazing over the side, and following with his eyes the receding boat—"canst thou yet ring boldly to that sight?—lowering thy keel among ravening sharks, and followed by them, open-mouthed, to the chase; and this the critical third day?—For when three days flow together in one continuous intense pursuit; be sure the first is the morning, the second the noon, and the third the evening and the end of that thing—be that end what it may. Oh! my God! what is this that shoots through me, and leaves me so deadly calm, yet expectant, —fixed at the top of a shudder! Future things swim before me, as in empty outlines and skeletons; all the past is somehow grown dim. Mary, girl! thou fadest in pale glories behind me; boy! I seem to see but thy eyes grown wondrous blue. Strangest problems of life seem clearing; but clouds sweep between—Is my journey's end coming? My legs feel faint; like his who has footed it all day. Feel thy heart,—beats it yet?—Stir thyself, Starbuck!—stave it off— move, move! speak aloud!—Mast-head there! See ye my boy's hand on the hill?—Crazed;— aloft there!—keep thy keenest eye upon the boats:—mark well the whale!—Ho! again!— drive off that hawk! see! he pecks—he tears the vane"—pointing to the red flag flying at the main-truck—"Ha! he soars away with it!— Where's the old man now? see'st thou that sight, oh Ahab!—shudder, shudder!"

The boats had not gone very far, when by a signal from the mast-heads—a downward-pointed arm, Ahab knew that the whale had sounded; but intending to be near him at the next rising, he held on his way a little sideways from the vessel; the becharmed crew maintaining the profoundest silence, as the head-beat waves hammered and hammered against the opposing bow.

"Drive, drive in your nails, oh ye waves! to their uttermost heads drive them in! ye but strike a thing without a lid; and no coffin and no hearse can be mine:—and hemp only can kill me! Ha! Ha!"

Suddenly the waters around them slowly swelled in broad circles; then quickly upheaved, as if sideways sliding from a submerged berg of ice, swiftly rising to the surface. A low rumbling sound was heard; a subterraneous hum; and then all held their breaths; as bedraggled with trailing ropes, and harpoons, and lances, a vast form shot lengthwise, but obliquely from the sea. Shrouded in a thin drooping veil of mist, it hovered for a moment in the rainbowed air; and then fell swamping

back into the deep. Crushed thirty feet upwards, the waters flashed for an instant like heaps of fountains, then brokenly sank in a shower of flakes, leaving the circling surface creamed like new milk round the marble trunk of the whale.

"Give way!" cried Ahab to the oarsmen, and the boats darted forward to the attack; but maddened by yesterday's fresh irons that corroded in him, Moby Dick seemed combinely possessed by all the angels that fell from heaven. The wide tiers of welded tendons overspreading his broad white forehead, beneath the transparent skin, looked knitted together; as head on, he came churning his tail among the boats; and once more flailed them apart; spilling out the irons and lances from the two mates' boats, and dashing in one side of the upper part of their bows, but leaving Ahab's almost without a scar.

While Daggoo and Queequeg were stopping the strained planks; and as the whale swimming out from them, turned, and showed one entire flank as he shot by them again; at that moment a quick cry went up. Lashed round and round to the fish's back; piniooned in the turns upon turns in which, during the past night, the whale had reeled the involutions of the lines around him, the half torn body of the Parsee was seen; his sable raiment frayed to shreds; his distended eyes turned full upon old Ahab.

The harpoon dropped from his hand.

"Befooled, befooled!"—drawing in a long lean breath—"Aye, Parsee! I see thee again.— Aye, and thou goest before; and this, *this* then is the hearse that thou didst promise. But I hold thee to the last letter of thy word. Where is the second hearse? Away, mates, to the ship! those boats are useless now; repair them if ye can in time, and return to me; if not, Ahab is enough to die—Down, men! the first thing that but offers to jump from this boat I stand in, that thing I harpoon. Ye are not other men, but my arms and my legs; and so obey me.—Where's the whale? gone down again?"

But he looked too nigh the boat; for as if bent upon escaping with the corpse he bore, and as if the particular place of the last encounter had been but a stage in his leeward voyage, Moby Dick was now again steadily swimming forward; and had almost passed the ship,—which thus far had been sailing in the contrary direction to him, though for the present her headway had been stopped. He seemed swimming with his utmost velocity, and now only intent upon pursuing his own straight path in the sea.

"Oh! Ahab," cried Starbuck, "not too late is it, even now, the third day, to desist. See! Moby Dick seeks thee not. It is thou, thou, that madly seekest him!"

Setting sail to the rising wind, the lonely boat was swiftly impelled to leeward, by both oars and canvas. And at last when Ahab was sliding by the vessel, so near as plainly to distinguish Starbuck's face as he leaned over the rail, he hailed him to turn the vessel about, and follow him, not too swiftly, at a judicious interval. Glancing upward, he saw Tashtego, Queequeg, and Daggoo, eagerly mounting to the three mast-heads; while the oarsmen were rocking in the two staved boats which had just been hoisted to the side, and were busily at work in repairing them. One after the other, through the port-holes, as he sped, he also caught flying glimpses of Stubb and Flask, busying themselves on deck among bundles of new irons and lances. As he saw all this; as he heard the hammers in the broken boats; far other hammers seemed driving a nail into his heat. But he rallied. And now marking that the vane or flag was gone from the main-mast-head, he shouted to Tashtego, who had just gained the perch, to descend again for another flag, and a hammer and nails, and so nail it to the mast.

Whether fagged by the three days' running chase, and the resistance to his swimming in the knotted hamper he bore; or whether it was some latent deceitfulness and malice in him: whichever was true, the White Whale's way now began to abate, as it seemed, from the boat so rapidly nearing him once more; though indeed the whale's last start had not been so long a one as before. And still as Ahab glided over the waves the unpitying sharks accompanied him; and so pertinaciously stuck to the boat; and so continually bit at the plying oars, that the blades became jagged and crunched, and left small splinters in the sea, at almost every dip.

"Heed them not! those teeth but give new rowlocks to your oars. Pull on! 'tis the better rest, the shark's jaw than the yielding water."

"But at every bite, sir, the thin blades grow smaller and smaller!"

"They will last long enough! pull on!—But who can tell"—he muttered—"whether these sharks swim to feast on the whale or on Ahab?

—But pull! on! Aye, all alive, now—we near him. The helm! take the helm; let me pass," —and so saying, two of the oarsmen helped him forward to the bows of the still flying boat.

At length as the craft was cast to one side, and ran ranging along with the White Whale's flank, he seemed strangely oblivious of its advance—as the whale sometimes will—and Ahab was fairly within the smoky mountain mist, which, thrown off from the whale's spout, curled round his great, Monadnock [12] hump; he was even thus close to him; when, with body arched back, and both arms lengthwise high-lifted to the poise, he darted his fierce iron, and his far fiercer curse into the hated whale. As both steel and curse sank to the socket, as if sucked into a morass, Moby Dick sideways writhed; spasmodically rolled his nigh flank against the bow, and, without staving a hole in it, so suddenly canted the boat over, that had it not been for the elevated part of the gunwale to which he then clung, Ahab would once more have been tossed into the sea. As it was, three of the oarsmen—who foreknew not the precise instant of the dart, and were therefore unprepared for its effects—these were flung out; but so fell, that, in an instant two of them clutched the gunwale again, and rising to its level on a combing wave, hurled themselves bodily inboard again; the third man helplessly dropping astern, but still afloat and swimming.

Almost simultaneously, with a mighty volition of ungraduated, instantaneous swiftness, the White Whale darted through the weltering sea. But when Ahab cried out to the steersman to take new turns with the line, and hold it so; and commanded the crew to turn round on their seats, and tow the boat up to the mark; the moment the treacherous line felt that double strain and tug, it snapped in the empty air!

"What breaks in me? Some sinew cracks!— 'tis whole again; oars! oars! Burst in upon him!"

Hearing the tremendous rush of the sea-crashing boat, the whale wheeled round to present his blank forehead at bay; but in that evolution, catching sight of the nearing black hull of the ship; seemingly seeing in it the source of all his persecutions; bethinking it— it may be—a larger and nobler foe; of a sudden, he bore down upon its advancing prow, smiting his jaws amid fiery showers of foam.

Ahab staggered; his hand smote his forehead. "I grow blind; hands! stretch out before

[12] A mountain in southern New Hampshire.

me that I may yet grope my way. Is't night?"

"The whale! The ship!" cried the cringing oarsmen.

"Oars! oars! Slope downwards to thy depths, O sea, that ere it be for ever too late, Ahab may slide this last, last time upon his mark! I see: the ship! the ship! Dash on, my men! Will ye not save my ship?"

But as the oarsmen violently forced their boat through the sledge-hammering seas, the before whale-smitten bow-ends of two planks burst through, and in an instant almost, the temporarily disabled boat lay nearly level with the waves; its half-wading, splashing crew, trying hard to stop the gap and bale out the pouring water.

Meantime, for that one beholding instant, Tashtego's mast-head hammer remained suspended in his hand; and the red flag, half-wrapping him as with a plaid, then streamed itself straight out from him, as his own forward-flowing heart; while Starbuck and Stubb, standing upon the bowsprit beneath, caught sight of the down-coming monster just as soon as he.

"The whale, the whale! Up helm, up helm! Oh, all ye sweet powers of air, now hug me close! Let not Starbuck die, if die he must, in a woman's fainting fit. Up helm, I say—ye fools, the jaw! the jaw! Is this the end of all my bursting prayers? all my lifelong fidelities? Oh, Ahab, Ahab, lo, thy work. Steady! helmsman, steady. Nay, nay! Up helm again! He turns to meet us! Oh, his unappeasable brow drives on towards one, whose duty tells him he cannot depart. My God, stand by me now!

"Stand not by me, but stand under me, whoever you are that will now help Stubb; for Stubb, too, sticks here. I grin at thee, thou grinning whale! Who ever helped Stubb, or kept Stubb awake, but Stubb's own unwinking eye? And now poor Stubb goes to bed upon a mattress that is all too soft; would it were stuffed with brushwood! I grin at thee, thou grinning whale! Look ye, sun, moon, and stars! I call ye assassins of as good a fellow as ever spouted up his ghost. For all that, I would yet ring glasses with ye, would ye but hand the cup! Oh, oh! oh, oh! thou grinning whale, but there'll be plenty of gulping soon! Why fly ye not, O Ahab! For me, off shoes and jacket to it; let Stubb die in his drawers! A most mouldy and over-salted death, though;—cherries! cherries! cherries! Oh, Flask, for one red cherry ere we die!"

"Cherries? I only wish that we were where they grow. Oh, Stubb, I hope my poor mother's drawn my part-pay ere this: if not, few coppers will now come to her, for the voyage is up."

From the ship's bows, nearly all the seamen now hung inactive; hammers, bits of plank, lances, and harpoons, mechanically retained in their hands, just as they had darted from their various employments; all their enchanted eyes intent upon the whale, which from side to side strangely vibrating his predestinating head, sent a broad band of overspreading semicircular foam before him as he rushed. Retribution, swift vengeance, eternal malice were in his whole aspect, and spite of all that mortal man could do, the solid white buttress of his forehead smote the ship's starboard bow, till men and timbers reeled. Some fell flat upon their faces. Like dislodged trucks, the heads of the harpooneers aloft shook on their bull-like necks. Through the breach, they heard the waters pour, as mountain torrents down a flume.

"The ship! The hearse!—the second hearse!" cried Ahab from the boat; "its wood could only be American!"

Diving beneath the settling ship, the whale ran quivering along its keel; but turning under water, swiftly shot to the surface again, far off the other bow, but within a few yards of Ahab's boat, where, for a time, he lay quiescent.

"I turn my body from the sun. What ho, Tashtego! let me hear thy hammer. Oh! ye three unsurrendered spires of mine; thou uncracked keel; and only god-bullied hull; thou firm deck, and haughty helm, and Pole-pointed prow,—death-glorious ship! must ye then perish, and without me? Am I cut off from the last fond pride of meanest shipwrecked captains? Oh, lonely death on lonely life! Oh, now I feel my topmost greatness lies in my topmost grief. Ho, ho! from all your furthest bounds, pour ye now in, ye bold billows of my whole foregone life, and top this one piled comber of my death! Towards thee I roll, thou all-destroying but unconquering whale; to the last I grapple with thee; from hell's heart I stab at thee; for hate's sake I spit my last breath at thee. Sink all coffins and all hearses to one common pool! and since neither can be mine, let me then tow to pieces, while still chasing thee, though tied to thee, thou damned whale! *Thus*, I give up the spear!"

The harpoon was darted; the stricken whale flew forward; with igniting velocity the line ran through the groove;—ran foul. Ahab

stooped to clear it; he did clear it; but the flying turn caught him round the neck, and voice-
lessly as Turkish mutes bowstring their victim,
he was shot out of the boat, ere the crew knew
he was gone. Next instant, the heavy eye-splice
in the rope's final end flew out of the stark-
empty tub, knocked down an oarsman, and
smiting the sea, disappeared in its depths.

For an instant, the tranced boat's crew stood
still; then turned. "The ship? Great God, where
is the ship?" Soon they through dim, bewildering mediums saw her sidelong fading phantom,
as in the gaseous Fata Morgana; only the uppermost masts out of water; while fixed by infatuation, or fidelity, or fate, to their once lofty
perches, the pagan harpooneers still maintained
their sinking lookouts on the sea. And now,
concentric circles seized the lone boat itself,
and all its crew, and each floating oar, and
every lance-pole, and spinning, animate and
inanimate, all round and round in one vortex,
carried the smallest chip of the Pequod out of
sight.

But as the last whelmings intermixingly
poured themselves over the sunken head of the
Indian at the mainmast, leaving a few inches
of the erect spar yet visible, together with long
streaming yards of the flag, which calmly un-
dulated, with ironical coincidings, over the
destroying billows they almost touched;—at
that instant, a red arm and a hammer hovered
backwardly uplifted in the open air, in the act
of nailing the flag faster and yet faster to the
subsiding spar. A sky-hawk that tauntingly had
followed the main-truck downwards from its
natural home among the stars, pecking at the
flag, and incommoding Tashtego there; this
bird now chanced to intercept its broad fluttering wing between the hammer and the wood;
and simultaneously feeling that ethereal thrill,
the submerged savage beneath, in his death-
gasp, kept his hammer frozen there; and so the
bird of heaven, with archangelic shrieks, and
his imperial beak thrust upwards, and his
whole captive form folded in the flag of Ahab,
went down with his ship, which, like Satan,
would not sink to hell till she had dragged a
living part of heaven along with her, and hel-
meted herself with it.

Now small fowls flew screaming over the yet
yawning gulf; a sullen white surf beat against
its steep sides; then all collapsed, and the great
shroud of the sea rolled on as it rolled five
thousand years ago.   1851

» » *From:* THE ENCANTADAS [13] « «

OR, ENCHANTED ISLES

SKETCH FIRST

THE ISLES AT LARGE

'—That may not be, said then the ferryman,
Least we unweeting hap to be fordonne;
For those same islands seeming now and than,
Are not firme land, nor any certein wonne,
But stragling plots which to and froe do ronne
In the wide waters; therefore are they hight
The Wandering Islands; therefore do them shonne;
For they have oft drawne many a wandring wight
Into most deadly daunger and distressed plight;
For whosoever once hath fastened
His foot thereon may never it secure
But wandreth evermore uncertein and unsure.'

'Darke, dolefull, dreary, like a greedy grave,
That still for carrion carcasses doth crave;
On top whereof ay dwelt the ghastly owl,
Shrieking his balefull note, which ever drave
Far from that haunt all other cheerful fowl,
And all about it wandring ghosts did wayle and howl.'

Take five-and-twenty heaps of cinders
dumped here and there in an outside city lot;
imagine some of them magnified into mountains, and the vacant lot the sea; and you will

[13] First published in *Putnam's Monthly Magazine;* republished in
The Piazza Tales, 1856.

have a fit idea of the general aspect of the
Encantadas, or Enchanted Isles. A group rather
of extinct volcanoes than of isles; looking much
as the world at large might, after a penal conflagration.

It is to be doubted whether any spot of
earth can, in desolateness, furnish a parallel
to this group. Abandoned cemeteries of long
ago, old cities by piecemeal tumbling to their
ruin, these are melancholy enough; but, like
all else which has but once been associated
with humanity, they still awaken in us some
thoughts of sympathy, however sad. Hence,
even the Dead Sea, along with whatever other
emotions it may at times inspire, does not fail
to touch in the pilgrim some of his less un-
pleasurable feelings.

And as for solitariness; the great forests of
the north, the expanses of unnavigated waters,
the Greenland ice-fields, are the profoundest
of solitudes to a human observer; still the

magic of their changeable tides and seasons mitigates their terror; because, though unvisited by men, those forests are visited by the May; the remotest seas reflect familiar stars even as Lake Erie does; and in the clear air of a fine Polar day, the irradiated, azure ice shows beautifully as malachite.

But the special curse, as one may call it, of the Encantadas, that which exalts them in desolation above Idumea and the Pole, is, that to them change never comes; neither the change of seasons nor of sorrows. Cut by the Equator, they know not autumn, and they know not spring; while already reduced to the lees of fire, ruin itself can work little more upon them. The showers refresh the deserts; but in these isles rain never falls. Like split Syrian gourds left withering in the sun, they are cracked by an everlasting drought beneath a torrid sky. "Have mercy upon me," the wailing spirit of the Encantadas seems to cry, "and send Lazarus that he may dip the tip of his finger in water and cool my tongue, for I am tormented in this flame."

Another feature in these isles is their emphatic uninhabitableness. It is deemed a fit type of all-forsaken overthrow, that the jackal should den in the wastes of weedy Babylon; but the Encantadas refuse to harbor even the outcasts of the beasts. Man and wolf alike disown them. Little but reptile life is here found: tortoises, lizards, immense spiders, snakes, and that strangest anomaly of outlandish nature, the *aguano*. No voice, no low, no howl is heard; the chief sound of life here is a hiss.

On most of the isles where vegetation is found at all, it is more ungrateful than the blankness of Aracama. Tangled thickets of wiry bushes, without fruit and without a name, springing up among deep fissures of calcined rock, and treacherously masking them; or a parched growth of distorted cactus trees.

In many places the coast is rock-bound, or, more properly, clinker-bound; tumbled masses of blackish or greenish stuff like the dross of an iron-furnace, forming dark clefts and caves here and there, into which a ceaseless sea pours a fury of foam; overhanging them with a swirl of gray, haggard mist, amidst which sail screaming flights of unearthly birds heightening the dismal din. However calm the sea without, there is no rest for those swells and those rocks; they lash and are lashed, even when the outer ocean is most at peace with itself. On the oppressive, clouded days, such as are peculiar to this part of the watery Equator, the dark, vitrified masses, many of which raise themselves among white whirlpools and breakers in detached and perilous places off the shore, present a most Plutonian sight. In no world but a fallen one could such lands exist.

Those parts of the strand free from the marks of fire stretch away in wide level beaches of multitudinous dead shells, with here and there decayed bits of sugar-cane, bamboos, and cocoa-nuts, washed upon this other and darker world from the charming palm isles to the westward and southward; all the way from Paradise to Tartarus; while mixed with the relics of distant beauty you will sometimes see fragments of charred wood and mouldering ribs of wrecks. Neither will anyone be surprised at meeting these last, after observing the conflicting currents which eddy throughout nearly all the wide channels of the entire group. The capriciousness of the tides of air sympathizes with those of the sea. Nowhere is the wind so light, baffling, and every way unreliable, and so given to perplexing calms, as at the Encantadas. Nigh a month has been spent by a ship going from one isle to another, though but ninety miles between; for owing to the force of the current, the boats employed to tow barely suffice to keep the craft from sweeping upon the cliffs, but do nothing toward accelerating her voyage. Sometimes it is impossible for a vessel from afar to fetch up with the group itself, unless large allowances for prospective leeway have been made ere its coming in sight. And yet, at other times, there is a mysterious indraft, which irresistibly draws a passing vessel among the isles, though not bound to them.

True, at one period, as to some extent at the present day, large fleets of whalemen cruised for spermaceti upon what some seamen call the Enchanted Ground. But this, as in due place will be described, was off the great outer isle of Albemarle, away from the intricacies of the smaller isles, where there is plenty of searoom; and hence, to that vicinity, the above remarks do not altogether apply; though even there the current runs at times with singular force, shifting, too, with as singular a caprice.

Indeed, there are seasons when currents quite unaccountable prevail for a great distance round about the total group, and are so strong and irregular as to change a vessel's course against the helm, though sailing at the rate of four or five miles the hour. The difference in the reckonings of navigators, produced by these causes, along with the light and variable winds, long nourished a persuasion, that there existed two distinct clusters of isles in the parallel of the Encantadas, about a hundred leagues apart. Such was the idea of their earlier visitors, the Bucaniers; and as late as 1750, the charts of that part of the Pacific accorded with the strange delusion. And this apparent fleetingness and unreality of the locality of the isles was most probably one reason for the Spaniards calling them the Encantada, or Enchanted Group.

But not uninfluenced by their character, as they now confessedly exist, the modern voyager will be inclined to fancy that the bestowal of this name might have in part originated in that air of spell-bound desertness which so significantly invests the isles. Nothing can better suggest the aspect of once living things malignly crumbled from ruddiness into ashes. Apples of Sodom, after touching, seem these isles.

However wavering their place may seem by reason of the currents, they themselves, at least to one upon the shore, appear invariably the same; fixed, cast, glued into the very body of cadaverous death.

Nor would the appellation, enchanted, seem misapplied in still another sense. For concerning the peculiar reptile inhabitant of these wilds—whose presence gives the group its second Spanish name, Gallipagos—concerning the tortoises found here, most mariners have long cherished a superstition, not more frightful than grotesque. They earnestly believe that all wicked sea-officers, more especially commodores and captains, are at death (and, in some cases, before death) transformed into tortoises; thenceforth dwelling upon these hot aridities, sole solitary lords of Asphaltum.

Doubtless, so quaintly dolorous a thought was originally inspired by the woebegone landscape itself; but more particularly, perhaps, by the tortoises. For, apart from their strictly physical features, there is something strangely self-condemned in the appearance of these creatures. Lasting sorrow and penal hopelessness are in no animal form so suppliantly expressed as in theirs; while the thought of their wonderful longevity does not fail to enhance the impression.

Nor even at the risk of meriting the charge of absurdly believing in enchantments, can I restrain the admission that sometimes, even now, when leaving the crowded city to wander out July and August among the Adirondack Mountains, far from the influences of towns and proportionally nigh to the mysterious ones of nature; when at such times I sit me down in the mossy head of some deep-wooded gorge, surrounded by prostrate trunks of blasted pines, and recall, as in a dream, my other and far-distant rovings in the baked heart of the charmed isles; and remember the sudden glimpses of dusky shells, and long languid necks protruded from the leafless thickets; and again have beheld the vitreous inland rocks worn down and grooved into deep ruts by ages and ages of the slow draggings of tortoises in quest of pools of scanty water; I can hardly resist the feeling that in my time I have indeed slept upon evilly enchanted ground.

Nay, such is the vividness of my memory, or the magic of my fancy, that I know not whether I am not the occasional victim of optical delusion concerning the Gallipagos. For, often in scenes of social merriment, and especially at revels held by candle-light in old-fashioned mansions, so that shadows are thrown into the further recesses of an angular and spacious room, making them put on a look of haunted undergrowth of lonely woods, I have drawn the attention of my comrades by my fixed gaze and sudden change of air, as I have seemed to see, slowly emerging from those imagined solitudes, and heavily crawling along the floor, the ghost of a gigantic tortoise, with "Memento * * * *" burning in live letters upon his back.

SKETCH EIGHTH

NORFOLK ISLE AND THE CHOLA WIDOW

'At last they in an island did espy
A seemly woman sitting by the shore,
That with great sorrow and sad agony
Seemed some great misfortune to deplore,
And loud to them for succor called evermore.'

'Black his eye as the midnight sky,
White his neck as the driven snow,
Red his cheek as the morning light;—
Cold he lies in the ground below.
    My love is dead,
        Gone to his death-bed, ys
All under the cactus tree.'

'Each lonely scene shall thee restore,
For thee the tear be duly shed;
Belov'd till life can charm no more,
And mourned till Pity's self be dead.'

Far to the north-east of Charles's Isle, sequestered from the rest, lies Norfolk Isle; and, however insignificant to most voyagers, to me, through sympathy, that lone island has become a spot made sacred by the strangest trials of humanity.

It was my first visit to the Encantadas. Two days had been spent ashore in hunting tortoises. There was not time to capture many; so on the third afternoon we loosed our sails. We were just in the act of getting under way, the uprooted anchor yet suspended and invisibly swaying beneath the wave, as the good ship gradually turned her heel to leave the isle behind, when the seaman who heaved with me at the windlass paused suddenly, and directed my attention to something moving on the land, not along the beach, but somewhat back, fluttering from a height.

In view of the sequel of this little story, be it here narrated how it came to pass, that an object which partly from its being so small was quite lost to every other man on board, still caught the eye of my handspike companion. The rest of the crew, myself included, merely stood up to our spikes in heaving, whereas, unwontedly exhilarated, at every turn of the ponderous windlass, my belted comrade leaped atop of it, with might and main giving a downward, thewey, perpendicular heave, his raised eye bent in cheery animation upon the slowly receding shore. Being high lifted above all others was the reason he perceived the object, otherwise unperceivable; and this elevation of his eye was owing to the elevation of his spirits; and this again—for truth must out—to a dram of Peruvian Pisco, in guerdon for some kindness done, secretly administered to him that morning by our mulatto steward. Now, certainly, Pisco does a deal of mischief in the world; yet seeing that, in the present case, it was the means, though indirect, of rescuing a human being from the most dreadful fate, must we not also needs admit that sometimes Pisco does a deal of good?

Glancing across the water in the direction pointed out, I saw some white thing hanging from an inland rock, perhaps half a mile from the sea.

"It is a bird; a white-winged bird; perhaps a—no; it is—it is a handkerchief!"

"Ay, a handkerchief!" echoed my comrade, and with a louder shout apprised the captain.

Quickly now—like the running out and training of a great gun—the long cabin spyglass was thrust through the mizen-rigging from the high platform of the poop; whereupon

a human figure was plainly seen upon the inland rock, eagerly waving toward us what seemed to be the handkerchief.

Our captain was a prompt, good fellow. Dropping the glass, he lustily ran forward, ordering the anchor to be dropped again; hands to stand by a boat, and lower away.

In a half-hour's time the swift boat returned. It went with six and came with seven; and the seventh was a woman.

It is not artistic heartlessness, but I wish I could but draw in crayons; for this woman was a most touching sight; and crayons, tracing softly melancholy lines, would best depict the mournful image of the dark-damasked Chola widow.

Her story was soon told, and though given in her own strange language was as quickly understood; for our captain, from long trading on the Chilian coast, was well versed in the Spanish. A Cholo, or half-breed Indian woman of Payta in Peru, three years gone by, with her young new-wedded husband Felipe, of pure Castilian blood, and her one only Indian brother, Truxill, Hunilla had taken passage on the main in a French whaler, commanded by a joyous man; which vessel, bound to the cruising-grounds beyond the Enchanted Isles, proposed passing close by their vicinity. The object of the little party was to procure tortoise oil, a fluid which for its great purity and delicacy is held in high estimation wherever known; and it is well known all along this part of the Pacific coast. With a chest of clothes, tools, cooking utensils, a rude apparatus for trying out the oil, some casks of biscuit, and other things, not omitting two favorite dogs, of which faithful animal all the Cholos are very fond, Hunilla and her companions were safely landed at their chosen place; the Frenchman, according to the contract made ere sailing, engaged to take them off upon returning from a four months' cruise in the westward seas; which interval the three adventurers deemed quite sufficient for their purposes.

On the isle's lone beach they paid him in silver for their passage out, the stranger having declined to carry them at all except upon that condition; though willing to take every means to ensure the due fulfilment of his promise. Felipe had striven hard to have this payment put off to the period of the ship's return. But in vain. Still they thought they had, in another way, ample pledge of the good faith of the Frenchman. It was arranged that the expenses of the passage home should not be payable in silver, but in tortoises; one hundred tortoises ready captured to the returning captain's hand. These the Cholos meant to secure after their own work was done, against the probable time of the Frenchman's coming back; and no doubt in prospect already felt, that in those hundred tortoises—now somewhere ranging the isle's interior—they possessed one hundred hostages. Enough: the vessel sailed; the gazing three on shore answered the loud glee of the singing crew; and ere evening, the French craft was hull down in the distant sea, its masts three faintest lines which quickly faded from Hunilla's eye.

The stranger had given a blithesome promise, and anchored it with oaths; but oaths and anchors equally will drag; naught else abides on fickle earth but unkept promises of joy. Contrary winds from out unstable skies, or contrary moods of his more varying mind, or shipwreck and sudden death in solitary waves; whatever was the cause, the blithe stranger never was seen again.

Yet, however dire a calamity was here in store, misgivings of it ere due time never disturbed the Cholos' busy mind, now all intent upon the toilsome matter which had brought them hither. Nay, by swift doom coming like a thief at night, ere seven weeks went by, two of the little party were removed from all anxieties of land or sea. No more they sought to gaze with feverish fear, or still more feverish hope, beyond the present's horizon line; but into the furthest future their own silent spirits sailed. By persevering labor beneath that burning sun, Felipe and Truxill had brought down to their hut many scores of tortoises, and tried out the oil, when, elated with their good success, and to reward themselves for such hard work, they, too hastily, made a catamaran, or Indian raft, much used on the Spanish main, and merrily started on a fishing trip, just without a long reef with many jagged gaps, running parallel with the shore, about half a mile from it. By some bad tide or hap, or natural negligence of joyfulness (for though they could not be heard, yet by their gestures they seemed singing at the time) forced in deep water against that iron bar, the ill-made catamaran was overset, and came all to pieces; when dashed by broad-chested swells between their broken logs and the sharp teeth of the reef, both adventurers perished before Hunilla's eyes.

Before Hunilla's eyes they sank. The real woe of this event passed before her sight as some sham tragedy on the stage. She was seated on a rude bower among the withered thickets, crowning a lofty cliff, a little back from the beach. The thickets were so disposed, that in looking upon the sea at large she peered out from among the branches as from the lattice of a high balcony. But upon the day we speak of here, the better to watch the adventure of those two hearts she loved, Hunilla had withdrawn the branches to one side, and held them so. They formed an oval frame, through which the bluely boundless sea rolled like a painted one. And there, the invisible painter painted to her view the wave-tossed and disjointed raft, its once level logs slantingly upheaved, as raking masts, and the four struggling arms undistinguishable among them; and then all subsided into smooth-flowing creamy waters, slowly drifting the splintered wreck; while first and last, no sound of any sort was heard. Death in a silent picture; a dream of the eye; such vanishing shapes as the mirage shows.

So instant was the scene, so trance-like its mild pictorial effect, so distant from her blasted bower and her common sense of things, that Hunilla gazed and gazed, nor raised a finger or a wail. But as good to sit thus dumb, in stupor staring on that dumb show, for all that otherwise might be done. With half a mile of sea between, how could her two enchanted arms aid those four fated ones? The distance long, the time one sand. After the lightning is beheld, what fool shall stay the thunder-bolt? Felipe's body was washed ashore, but Truxill's never came; only his gay, braided hat of golden straw—that same sunflower thing he waved to her, pushing from the strand—and now, to the last gallant, it still saluted her. But Felipe's body floated to the marge, with one arm encirclingly outstretched. Lock-jawed in grim death, the lover-husband softly clasped his bride, true to her even in death's dream. Ah, heaven, when man thus keeps his faith, wilt thou be faithless who created the faithful one? But they cannot break faith who never plighted it.

It needs not to be said what nameless misery now wrapped the lonely widow. In telling her own story she passed this almost entirely over, simply recounting the event. Construe the comment of her features as you might, from her mere words little would you have weened that

Hunilla was herself the heroine of her tale. But not thus did she defraud us of our tears. All hearts bled that grief could be so brave.

She but showed us her soul's lid, and the strange ciphers thereon engraved; all within, with pride's timidity, was withheld. Yet was there one exception. Holding out her small olive hand before our captain, she said in mild and slowest Spanish, "Señor, I buried him"; then paused, struggled as against the writhed coilings of a snake, and cringing suddenly, leaped up, repeating in impassioned pain, "I buried him, my life, my soul!"

Doubtless, it was by half-unconscious, automatic motions of her hands, that this heavy-hearted one performed the final office for Felipe, and planted a rude cross of withered sticks —no green ones might be had—at the head of that lonely grave, where rested now in lasting uncomplaint and quiet haven he whom untranquil seas had overthrown.

But some dull sense of another body that should be interred, of another cross that should hallow another grave—unmade as yet—some dull anxiety and pain touching her undiscovered brother, now haunted the oppressed Hunilla. Her hands fresh from the burial earth, she slowly went back to the beach, with unshaped purposes wandering there, her spell-bound eye bent upon the incessant waves. But they bore nothing to her but a dirge, which maddened her to think that murderers should mourn. As time went by, and these things came less dreamingly to her mind, the strong persuasions of her Romish faith, which sets peculiar store by consecrated urns, prompted her to resume in waking earnest that pious search which had but been begun as in somnambulism. Day after day, week after week, she trod the cindery beach, till at length a double motive edged every eager glance. With equal longing she now looked for the living and the dead; the brother and the captain; alike vanished, never to return. Little accurate note of time had Hunilla taken under such emotions as were hers, and little, outside herself, served for calendar or dial. As to poor Crusoe in the self-same sea, no saint's bell pealed forth the lapse of week or month; each day went by unchallenged; no chanticleer announced those sultry dawns, no lowing herds those poisonous nights. All wonted and steadily recurring sounds, human, or humanised by sweet fellowship with man, but one stirred that torrid trance—the cry of dogs; save which naught but the rolling

sea invaded it, an all-pervading monotone; and to the widow that was the least loved voice she could have heard.

No wonder, that as her thoughts now wandered to the unreturning ship, and were beaten back again, the hope against hope so struggled in her soul, that at length she desperately said, "Not yet, not yet; my foolish heart runs on too fast." So she forced patience for some further weeks. But to those whom earth's sure indraft draws, patience or impatience is still the same.

Hunilla now sought to settle precisely in her mind, to an hour, how long it was since the ship had sailed; and then, with the same precision, how long a space remained to pass. But this proved impossible. What present day or month it was she could not say. Time was her labyrinth, in which Hunilla was entirely lost. And now follows——

Against my own purposes a pause descends upon me here. One knows not whether nature doth not impose some secrecy upon him who has been privy to certain things. At least, it is to be doubted whether it be good to blazon such. If some books are deemed most baneful and their sale forbid, how, then, with deadlier facts, not dreams of doting men? Those whom books will hurt will not be proof against events. Events, not books, should be forbid. But in all things man sows upon the wind, which bloweth just there whither it listeth; for ill or good, man cannot know. Often ill comes from the good, as good from ill.

When Hunilla——

Dire sight it is to see some silken beast long dally with a golden lizard ere she devour. More terrible, to see how feline Fate will sometimes dally with a human soul, and by a nameless magic make it repulse a sane despair with a hope which is but mad. Unwittingly I imp this cat-like thing, sporting with the heart of him who reads; for if he feel not he reads in vain. —"The ship sails this day, to-day," at last said Hunilla to herself; "this gives me certain time to stand on; without certainty I go mad. In loose ignorance I have hoped and hoped; now in firm knowledge I will but wait. Now I live and no longer perish in bewilderings. Holy Virgin, aid me! Thou wilt waft back the ship. Oh, past length of weary weeks— all to be dragged over—to buy the certainty of to-day, I freely give ye, though I tear ye from me!"

As mariners, tossed in tempest on some desolate ledge, patch them a boat out of the remnants of their vessel's wreck, and launch it in the self-same waves, see here Hunilla, this lone ship-wrecked soul, out of treachery invoking trust. Humanity, thou strong thing, I worship thee, not in the laurelled victor, but in this vanquished one.

Truly Hunilla leaned upon a reed, a real one; no metaphor; a real Eastern reed. A piece of hollow cane, drifted from unknown isles, and found upon the beach, its once jagged ends rubbed smoothly even as by sandpaper; its golden glazing gone. Long ground between the sea and land, upper and nether stone, the unvarnished substance was filed bare, and wore another polish now, one with itself, the polish of its agony. Circular lines at intervals cut all round this surface, divided it into six panels of unequal length. In the first were scored the days, each tenth one marked by a longer and deeper notch; the second was scored for the number of sea-fowl eggs for sustenance, picked out from the rocky nests; the third, how many fish had been caught from the shore; the fourth, how many small tortoises found inland; the fifth, how many days of sun; the sixth, of clouds; which last, of the two, was the greater one. Long night of busy numbering, misery's mathematics, to weary her too-wakeful soul to sleep; yet sleep for that was none.

The panel of the days was deeply worn— the long tenth notches half effaced, as alphabets of the blind. Ten thousand times the longing widow had traced her finger over the bamboo—dull flute, which played on, gave no sound—as if counting birds flown by in air would hasten tortoises creeping through the woods.

After the one hundred and eightieth day no further mark was seen; that last one was the faintest, as the first the deepest.

"There were more days," said our captain; "many, many more; why did you not go on and notch them, too, Hunilla?"

"Señor, ask me not."

"And meantime, did no other vessel pass the isle?"

"Nay, señor;—but——"

"You do not speak; but *what*, Hunilla?"

"Ask me not, señor."

"You saw ships pass, far away; you waved to them; they passed on;—was that it, Hunilla?"

"Señor, be it as you say."

Braced against her woe, Hunilla would not, durst not trust the weakness of her tongue.

Then when our captain asked whether any whale-boats had——

But no, I will not file this thing complete for scoffing souls to quote, and call it firm proof upon their side. The half shall here remain untold. Those two unnamed events which befell Hunilla on this isle, let them abide between her and her God. In nature, as in law, it may be libellous to speak some truths.

Still, how it was that, although our vessel had lain three days anchored nigh the isle, its one human tenant should not have discovered us till just upon the point of sailing, never to revisit so lone and far a spot, this needs explaining ere the sequel come.

The place where the French captain had landed the little party was on the further and opposite end of the isle. There, too, it was that they had afterward built their hut. Nor did the widow in her solitude desert the spot where her loved ones had dwelt with her, and where the dearest of the twain now slept his last long sleep, and all her plaints awaked him not, and he of husbands the most faithful during life.

Now, high broken land rises between the opposite extremities of the isle. A ship anchored at one side is invisible from the other. Neither is the isle so small, but a considerable company might wander for days through the wilderness of one side, and never be seen, or their halloos heard, by any stranger holding aloof on the other. Hence Hunilla, who naturally associated the possible coming of ships with her own part of the isle, might to the end have remained quite ignorant of the presence of our vessel, were it not for a mysterious presentiment, borne to her, so our mariners averred, by this isle's enchanted air. Nor did the widow's answer undo the thought.

"How did you come to cross the isle this morning, then, Hunilla?" said our captain.

"Señor, something came flitting by me. It touched my cheek, my heart, señor."

"What do you say, Hunilla?"

"I have said, señor, something came through the air."

It was a narrow chance. For when in crossing the isle Hunilla gained the high land in the centre, she must then for the first have perceived our masts, and also marked that their sails were being loosed, perhaps even heard the echoing chorus of the windlass song. The strange ship was about to sail, and she behind. With all haste she now descends the height on the hither side, but soon loses sight of the ship among the sunken jungles at the mountain's base. She struggles on through the withered branches, which seek at every step to bar her path, till she comes to the isolated rock, still some way from the water. This she climbs, to reassure herself. The ship is still in plainest sight. But now, worn out with over-tension, Hunilla all but faints; she fears to step down from her giddy perch; she is fain to pause, there where she is, and as a last resort catches the turban from her head, unfurls and waves it over the jungles toward us.

During the telling of her story the mariners formed a voiceless circle round Hunilla and the captain; and when at length the word was given to man the fastest boat, and pull round to the isle's thither side, to bring away Hunilla's chest and the tortoise-oil, such alacrity of both cheery and sad obedience seldom before was seen. Little ado was made. Already the anchor had been recommitted to the bottom, and the ship swung calmly to it.

But Hunilla insisted upon accompanying the boat as indispensable pilot to her hidden hut. So being refreshed with the best the steward could supply, she started with us. Nor did ever any wife of the most famous admiral, in her husband's barge, receive more silent reverence of respect than poor Hunilla from this boat's crew.

Rounding many a vitreous cape and bluff, in two hours' time we shot inside the fatal reef; wound into a secret cove, looked up along a green many-gabled lava wall, and saw the island's solitary dwelling.

It hung upon an impending cliff, sheltered on two sides by tangled thickets, and half screened from view in front by juttings of the rude stairway, which climbed the precipice from the sea. Built of canes, it was thatched with long, mildewed grass. It seemed an abandoned hay-rick, whose haymakers were now no more. The roof inclined but one way; the eaves coming to within two feet of the ground. And here was a simple apparatus to collect the dews, or rather doubly distilled and finest winnowed rains, which, in mercy or in mockery, the night-skies sometimes drop upon these blighted Encantadas. All along beneath the eaves, a spotted sheet, quite weather-stained, was spread, pinned to short, upright stakes, set in the shallow sand. A small clinker, thrown into the cloth, weighed its middle down, thereby straining all moisture into a calabash placed below. This vessel supplied each drop of water

ever drunk upon the isle by the Cholos. Hunilla told us the calabash would sometimes, but not often, be half filled overnight. It held six quarts, perhaps. "But," said she, "we were used to thirst. At sandy Payta, where I live, no shower from heaven ever fell; all the water there is brought on mules from the inland vales."

Tied among the thickets were some twenty moaning tortoises, supplying Hunilla's lonely larder; while hundreds of vast tableted black bucklers, like displaced, shattered tombstones of dark slate, were also scattered round. These were the skeleton backs of those great tortoises from which Felipe and Truxill had made their precious oil. Several large calabashes and two goodly kegs were filled with it. In a pot near by were the caked crusts of a quantity which had been permitted to evaporate. 'They meant to have strained it off next day,' said Hunilla, as she turned aside.

I forgot to mention the most singular sight of all, though the first that greeted us after landing.

Some ten small, soft-haired, ringleted dogs, of a beautiful breed, peculiar to Peru, set up a concert of glad welcomings when we gained the beach, which was responded to by Hunilla. Some of these dogs had, since her widowhood, been born upon the isle, the progeny of the two brought from Payta. Owing to the jagged steeps and pitfalls, torturous thickets, sunken clefts, and perilous intricacies of all sorts in the interior, Hunilla, admonished by the loss of one favorite among them, never allowed these delicate creatures to follow her in her occasional birds'-nests climbs and other wanderings; so that, through long habituation, they offered not to follow, when that morning she crossed the land, and her own soul was then too full of other things to heed their lingering behind. Yet, all along she had so clung to them, that, besides what moisture they lapped up at early daybreak from the small scoopholes among the adjacent rocks, she had shared the dew of her calabash among them; never laying by any considerable store against those prolonged and utter droughts which, in some disastrous seasons, warp these isles.

Having pointed out, at our desire, what few things she would like transported to the ship— her chest, the oil, not omitting the live tortoises which she intended for a grateful present to our captain—we immediately set to work, carrying them to the boat down the long, sloping stair of deeply shadowed rock. While my comrades were thus employed, I looked and Hunilla had disappeared.

It was not curiosity alone, but, it seems to me, something different mingled with it, which prompted me to drop my tortoise, and once more gaze slowly around. I remembered the husband buried by Hunilla's hands. A narrow pathway led into a dense part of the thickets. Following it through many mazes, I came out upon a small, round, open space, deeply chambered there.

The mound rose in the middle; a bare heap of finest sand, like that unverdured heap found at the bottom of an hour-glass run out. At its head stood the cross of withered sticks; the dry, peeled bark still fraying from it; its transverse limb tied up with rope, and forlornly adroop in the silent air.

Hunilla was partly prostrate upon the grave; her dark head bowed, and lost in her long, loosened Indian hair; her hands extended to the cross-foot, with a little brass crucifix clasped between; a crucifix worn featureless, like an ancient graven knocker long plied in vain. She did not see me, and I made no noise, but slid aside, and left the spot.

A few moments ere all was ready for our going, she reappeared among us. I looked into her eyes, but saw no tear. There was something which seemed strangely haughty in her air, and yet it was the air of woe. A Spanish and an Indian grief, which would not visibly lament. Pride's height in vain abased to proneness on the rack; nature's pride subduing nature's torture.

Like pages the small and silken dogs surrounded her, as she slowly descended toward the beach. She caught the two most eager creatures in her arms:—"Mia Teeta! Mia Tomoteeta!" and fondling them, inquired how many could we take on board.

The mate commanded the boat's crew; not a hard-hearted man, but his way of life had been such that in most things, even in the smallest, simple utility was his leading motive.

"We cannot take them all, Hunilla; our supplies are short; the winds are unreliable; we may be a good many days going to Tombez. So take those you have, Hunilla; but no more."

She was in the boat; the oarsmen, too, were seated; all save one, who stood ready to push off and then spring himself. With the sagacity of their race, the dogs now seemed aware that they were in the very instant of being deserted upon a barren strand. The gunwales of the boat were high; its prow—presented inland—was lifted; so owing to the water, which they seemed instinctively to shun, the dogs could not well leap into the little craft. But their busy paws hard scraped the prow, as it had been some farmer's door shutting them out from shelter in a winter storm. A clamorous agony of alarm. They did not howl, or whine; they all but spoke.

"Push off! Give way!" cried the mate. The boat gave one heavy drag and lurch, and next moment shot swiftly from the beach, turned on her heel, and sped. The dogs ran howling along the water's marge; now pausing to gaze at the flying boat, then motioning as if to leap in chase, but mysteriously withheld themselves; and again ran howling along the beach. Had they been human beings, hardly would they have more vividly inspired the sense of desolation. The oars were plied as confederate feathers of two wings. No one spoke. I looked back upon the beach, and then upon Hunilla, but her face was set in a stern dusky calm. The dogs crouching in her lap vainly licked her rigid hands. She never looked behind her; but sat motionless, till we turned a promontory of the coast and lost all sights and sounds astern. She seemed as one who, having experienced the sharpest of mortal pangs, was henceforth content to have all lesser heartstrings riven, one by one. To Hunilla, pain seemed so necessary, that pain in other beings, though by love and sympathy made her own, was unrepiningly to be borne. A heart of yearning in a frame of steel. A heart of earthly yearning, frozen by the frost which falleth from the sky.

The sequel is soon told. After a long passage, vexed by calms and baffling winds, we made the little port of Tombez in Peru, there to recruit the ship. Payta was not very distant. Our captain sold the tortoise oil to a Tombez merchant; and adding to the silver a contribution from all hands, gave it to our silent passenger, who knew not what the mariners had done.

The last seen of lone Hunilla she was passing into Payta town, riding upon a small gray ass; and before her on the ass's shoulders, she eyed the jointed workings of the beast's armorial cross.   1854

» »   « «

THE PORTENT

(1859)

Hanging from the beam,
   Slowly swaying (such the law),
Gaunt the shadow on your green,
   Shenandoah!
The cut is on the crown
   (Lo, John Brown),
And the stabs shall heal no more.

Hidden in the cap
   Is the anguish none can draw;
So your future veils its face,   10
   Shenandoah!
But the streaming beard is shown
   (Weird John Brown),
The meteor of the war.   1866

MALVERN HILL

(July, 1862)

Ye elms that wave on Malvern Hill
   In prime of morn and May,
Recall ye how McClellan's men
   Here stood at bay?
While deep within yon forest dim
   Our rigid comrades lay—
Some with the cartridge in their mouth,
Others with fixed arms lifted South—
   Invoking so
The cypress glades? Ah wilds of woe!   10

The spires of Richmond, late beheld
   Through rifts in musket-haze,
Were closed from view in clouds of dust
   On leaf-walled ways,
Where streamed our wagons in caravan;
   And the Seven Nights and Days
Of march and fast, retreat and fight,
Pinched our grimed faces to ghastly plight—
   Does the elm wood
Recall the haggard beards of blood?   20

The battle-smoked flag, with stars eclipsed,
   We followed (it never fell!)—
In silence husbanded our strength—
   Received their yell;
Till on this slope we patient turned
   With cannon ordered well;
Reverse we proved was not defeat;

But ah, the sod what thousands meet!—
   Does Malvern Wood
Bethink itself, and muse and brood?   30

    We elms of Malvern Hill
      Remember everything;
    But sap the twig will fill;
    Wag the world how it will,
      Leaves must be green in Spring.

                     1866

SHERIDAN AT CEDAR CREEK

(October, 1864)

Shoe the steed with silver
   That bore him to the fray,
When he heard the guns at dawning—
   Miles away;
When he heard them calling, calling—
   Mount! nor stay:
     Quick, or all is lost;
     They've surprised and stormed the post,
     They push your routed host—
Gallop! retrieve the day.   10

House the horse in ermine—
   For the foam-flake blew
White through the red October;
   He thundered into view;
They cheered him in the looming,
   Horseman and horse they knew.
     The turn of the tide began,
     The rally of bugles ran,
     He swung his hat in the van;
The electric hoof-spark flew.   20

Wreathe the steed and lead him—
   For the charge he led
Touched and turned the cypress
   Into amaranths for the head
Of Philip, king of riders,
   Who raised them from the dead.
     The camp (at dawning lost),
     By eve, recovered—forced,
     Rang with laughter of the lost
And belated Early fled.   30

Shroud the horse in sable—
   For the mounds they heap!
There is firing in the Valley,
   And yet no strife they keep;
It is the parting volley,
   It is the pathos deep.

There is glory for the brave
Who lead, and nobly save,
But no knowledge in the grave
Where the nameless followers sleep.   *40*
                                              1866

FAR OFF-SHORE

Look, the raft, a signal flying,
    Thin—a shred;
None upon the lashed spars lying,
    Quick or dead.

Cries the sea-fowl, hovering over,
    "Crew, the crew?"
And the billow, reckless rover,
    Sweeps anew!   1888

THE ENVIABLE ISLES

(From "Rammon") [14]

Through storms you reach them and from
        storms are free.
Afar descried, the foremost drear in hue,
But, nearer, green; and, on the marge, the sea
Makes thunder low and mist of rainbowed
        dew.

But, inland, where the sleep that folds the hills
A dreamier sleep, the trance of God, instills—
On uplands hazed, in wandering airs aswoon,
Slow-swaying palms salute love's cypress tree
Adown in vale where pebbly runlets croon
A song to lull all sorrow and all glee.   *10*

Sweet-fern and moss in many a glade are here,
    Where, strown in flocks, what cheek-flushed
        myriads lie
Dimpling in dream—unconscious slumberers
        mere,
    While billows endless round the beaches die.
                                              1888

LONE FOUNTS

Though fast youth's glorious fable flies,
View not the world with worldling's eyes;
Nor turn with weather of the time.
Foreclose the coming of surprise:

Stand where Posterity shall stand;
And, dipping in lone founts thy hand,
Drink of the never-varying lore:
Wise once, and wise thence evermore.   1891

ART

In placid hours well-pleased we dream
Of many a brave unbodied scheme.
But form to lend, pulsed life create,
What unlike things must meet and mate:
A flame to melt—a wind to freeze;
Sad patience—joyous energies;
Humility—yet pride and scorn;
Instinct and study; love and hate;
Audacity—reverence. These must mate
And fuse with Jacob's mystic heart,   *10*
To wrestle with the angel—Art.   1891

EPILOGUE FROM CLAREL [15]

If Luther's day expand to Darwin's year,
Shall that exclude the hope—foreclose the fear?

Unmoved by all the claims our times avow,
The ancient Sphinx still keeps the porch of
        shade
And comes Despair, whom not her calm may
        cow,
And coldly on that adamantine brow
Scrawls undeterred his bitter pasquinade.
But Faith (who from the scrawl indignant
        turns),
With blood warm oozing from her wounded
        trust,   *9*
Inscribes even on her shards of broken urns
The sign o' the cross—*the spirit above the dust!*

Yea, ape and angel, strife and old debate—
The harps of heaven and dreary gongs of hell;
Science the feud can only aggravate—
No umpire she betwixt the chimes and knell:
The running battle of the star and clod
Shall run for ever—if there be no God.

Degrees we know, unknown in days before;
The light is greater, hence the shadow more;
And tantalized and apprehensive Man   *20*
Appealing—Wherefore ripen us to pain?
Seems there the spokesman of dumb Nature's
        train.

---

[14] Melville's poem "Rammon, the Enviable Isles" was never completed.

[15] A long narrative poem in which the characters discuss Christianity, Democracy, and Science.

But through such strange illusions have they
   passed
Who in life's pilgrimage have baffled striven—
Even death may prove unreal at the last,
And stoics be astounded into heaven.

Then keep thy heart, though yet but ill-
   resigned—
Clarel, thy heart, the issues there but mind;

That like the crocus budding through the
   snow—
That like a swimmer rising from the deep—
That like a burning secret that doth go   31
Even from the bosom that would hoard and
   keep;
Emerge thou mayst from the last whelming sea,
And prove that death but routs life into victory.
                            1876

JOHN GREENLEAF WHITTIER

1807–1892

UNLIKE Holmes and Longfellow, Whittier was not the heir of the prosperous orthodoxy of New England. The son of a Quaker farmer, and for a time a shoemaker, he worked so hard as a boy that he was in later life a semi-invalid. Had it not been for a schoolmaster who showed him the poetry of Burns and the chance that his first poem was published in William Lloyd Garrison's Newburyport *Free Press*, he might have continued to cobble shoes all his life. Through the influence of the abolitionist leader Whittier was started on his career as an editor and a poet and was roused to become an active participant in the antislavery movement. The immediate result of Garrison's interest was Whittier's appointment as editor of a pro-Clay paper in Boston. From 1828, the date of his going to Boston, until the late 1840's, he was a constant contributor to and frequent editor of abolitionist papers in various parts of the country.

Though his stirring pamphlet *Justice and Expediency* (1833) was one of the greatest of antislavery pronouncements, as a sincere Quaker Whittier did not favor the tactics of violence condoned by many of his associates. While other workers in the cause claimed John Brown as their protomartyr, Whittier wrote soberly to Sumner: "The distinction should be made clear between the natural sympathy with the man and approval of his mad, and, as I think, most dangerous and unjustifiable act." Whittier favored political action and worked effectively as a lobbyist to persuade slippery congressmen to the antislavery side. To Garrison and others who thought all compromise ignoble and were ready to risk civil war to bring about emancipation, he seemed lukewarm if not traitorous. But he continued to fight in his own way, as editor, politician, and poetical propagandist until war came.

As a writer Whittier underwent several transformations before he discovered what he could best do. His first extended efforts were prose legends about New England's past. Much of his early verse shows him trying to be deliberately "literary," now in the style of Burns (he actually wrote some poems in Scottish dialect), now imitating Tom Moore or Mrs. Hemans. Not until abolitionism gave him a subject to his heart did he cease to be imitative. It is astonishing, in fact, to see how few of the poems every schoolchild knows there are in the ornate collected *Poems* issued in 1849, when he was forty-two. James Russell Lowell in *The Fable for Critics* speaks of him a year earlier solely as a poet who leads metaphorical fights for reform and whatever "they call human rights." It was not until the slave was free and Whittier had retired from the battle to outlive all of his compeers except Holmes, that the image of the benevolent white-bearded creator of "The Barefoot Boy" and "Maud Muller" captivated his nostalgic countrymen.

Most of Whittier's poetry, we should admit, is third-rate. He judged himself well in the "Proem," written to introduce the *Poems* of 1849, in which he says he cannot breathe "the marvellous notes" of the true lyric poet. By nature and inheritance too ascetic to enjoy the sensuous beauty of the world, he can seldom create images which are better than flat and second-hand. His verse flows too easily, which is one reason why he succeeds best in the ballad, where the story sets a limit to the number of stanzas. Yet some of his verse deserves to survive for its intrinsic value. "Snow Bound" brings us close to a New England which was vanishing in his day under the smoke of industrialism. The "Kansas Emigrants" still echoes with the voices which sang it on the westward trail. His *Songs of Labor* are genuine proletarian poetry, though Whittier believed the interests of the rich and poor "are one and same, inseparable evermore" ("The Problem").

T. F. Currier, *A Bibliography of John Greenleaf Whittier*, Cambridge, 1937.
The Writings of John Greenleaf Whittier, 7 vols., Boston, 1888–1889.
S. T. Pickard, *Life and Letters of John Greenleaf Whittier*, 2 vols., Boston (1894), 1907.
Whitman Bennett, *Whittier, Bard of Freedom*, Chapel Hill, North Carolina, 1941.
W. S. Kennedy, *John G. Whittier, The Poet of Freedom* (American Reformers), New York, 1892.
J. A. Pollard, *John Greenleaf Whittier, Friend of Man*, Boston, 1949.
F. M. Pray, *A Study of Whittier's Apprenticeship as a Poet*, Pennsylvania State College, 1930.

PROEM [1]

I love the old melodious lays
Which softly melt the ages through,
      The songs of Spenser's golden days,
      Arcadian Sidney's silvery phrase,
Sprinkling our noon of time with freshest morning dew.

      Yet, vainly in my quiet hours
To breathe their marvellous notes I try;
      I feel them, as the leaves and flowers
      In silence feel the dewy showers,
And drink with glad, still lips the blessing of
      the sky.   10

The rigor of a frozen clime,
The harshness of an untaught ear,
      The jarring words of one whose rhyme
      Beat often Labor's hurried time,
Or Duty's rugged march through storm and
      strife, are here.

      Of mystic beauty, dreamy grace,
No rounded art the lack supplies;
      Unskilled the subtle lines to trace,
      Or softer shades of Nature's face,
I view her common forms with unanointed
      eyes.   20

      Nor mine the seer-like power to show
The secrets of the heart and mind;

[1] This poem was placed by Whittier as a proem to the first collected edition of his poems (1848, dated 1849).

To drop the plummet-line below
Our common world of joy and woe,
A more intense despair or brighter hope to find.

      Yet here at least an earnest sense
Of human right and weal is shown;
      A hate of tyranny intense,
      And hearty in its vehemence,
As if my brother's pain and sorrow were my
      own.   30

      O Freedom! if to me belong
Nor mighty Milton's gift divine,
      Nor Marvel's wit and graceful song,
      Still with a love as deep and strong
As theirs, I lay, like them, my best gifts on thy
      shrine!
1847   1849

MEMORIES

A beautiful and happy girl,
      With step as light as summer air,
Eyes glad with smiles, and brow of pearl,
Shadowed by many a careless curl
      Of unconfined and flowing hair;
A seeming child in everything,
      Save thoughtful brow and ripening charms,
As Nature wears the smile of Spring
When sinking into Summer's arms.

A mind rejoicing in the light   10
      Which melted through its graceful bower,

Leaf after leaf, dew-moist and bright,
And stainless in its holy white,
  Unfolding like a morning flower:
A heart, which, like a fine-toned lute,
With every breath of feeling woke,
And, even when the tongue was mute,
  From eye and lip in music spoke.

How thrills once more the lengthening chain
  Of memory, at the thought of thee!   20
Old hopes which long in dust have lain,
Old dreams, come thronging back again,
  And boyhood lives again in me;
I feel its glow upon my cheek,
  Its fulness of the heart is mine,
As when I leaned to hear thee speak,
  Or raised my doubtful eye to thine.

I hear again thy low replies,
  I feel thy arm within my own,
And timidly again uprise   30
The fringèd lids of hazel eyes,
  With soft brown tresses overblown.
Ah! memories of sweet summer eves,
  Of moonlit wave and willowy way,
Of stars and flowers, and dewy leaves,
  And smiles and tones more dear than they!

Ere this, thy quiet eye hath smiled
  My picture of thy youth to see,
When, half a woman, half a child,
Thy very artlessness beguiled,   40
  And folly's self seemed wise in thee;
I too can smile, when o'er that hour
  The lights of memory backward stream,
Yet feel the while that manhood's power
  Is vainer than my boyhood's dream.

Years have passed on, and left their trace,
  Of graver care and deeper thought;
And unto me the calm, cold face
Of manhood, and to thee the grace
  Of woman's pensive beauty brought.   50
More wide, perchance, for blame than praise,
  The school-boy's humble name has flown;
Thine, in the green and quiet ways
  Of unobtrusive goodness known.

And wider yet in thought and deed
  Diverge our pathways, one in youth;
Thine the Genevan's sternest creed,
While answers to my spirit's need
  The Derby dalesman's simple truth.
For thee, the priestly rite and prayer,   60
  And holy day, and solemn psalm;

For me, the silent reverence where
  My brethren gather, slow and calm.

Yet hath thy spirit left on me
  An impress Time has worn not out,
And something of myself in thee,
A shadow from the past, I see,
  Lingering, even yet, thy way about;
Not wholly can the heart unlearn
  That lesson of its better hours,   70
Not yet has Time's dull footstep worn
  To common dust that path of flowers.

Thus, while at times before our eyes
  The shadows melt, and fall apart,
And, smiling through them, round us lies
The warm light of our morning skies,—
  The Indian Summer of the heart!
In secret sympathies of mind,
  In founts of feeling which retain
Their pure, fresh flow, we yet may find   80
  Our early dreams not wholly vain!
1841   1843

MASSACHUSETTS TO VIRGINIA [2]

The blast from Freedom's Northern hills, upon
    its Southern way,
Bears greeting to Virginia from Massachusetts
    Bay:
No word of haughty challenging, nor battle
    bugle's peal,
Nor steady tread of marching files, nor clang
    of horsemen's steel,

No trains of deep-mouthed cannon along our
    highways go;
Around our silent arsenals untrodden lies the
    snow;
And to the land-breeze of our ports, upon their
    errands far,
A thousand sails of commerce swell, but none
    are spread for war.

We hear thy threats, Virginia! thy stormy
    words and high
Swell harshly on the Southern winds which
    melt along our sky;   10

---

[2] Written on reading an account of the proceedings of the citizens of Norfolk, Va., in reference to George Latimer, the alleged fugitive slave, who was seized in Boston without warrant at the request of James B. Grey, of Norfolk, claiming to be his master. The case caused great excitement North and South, and led to the presentation of a petition to Congress, signed by more than fifty thousand citizens of Massachusetts, calling for such laws and proposed amendments to the Constitution as should relieve the Commonwealth from all further participation in the crime of oppression. George Latimer himself was finally given free papers for the sum of four hundred dollars. [Whittier's note.]

Yet, not one brown, hard hand foregoes its
    honest labor here,
No hewer of our mountain oaks suspends his
    axe in fear.

Wild are the waves which lash the reefs along
    St. George's bank;
Cold on the shores of Labrador the fog lies
    white and dank;
Through storm, and wave, and blinding mist,
    stout are the hearts which man
The fishing-smacks of Marblehead, the sea-
    boats of Cape Ann.

The cold north light and wintry sun glare on
    their icy forms,
Bent grimly o'er their straining lines or wres-
    tling with the storms;
Free as the winds they drive before, rough as
    the waves they roam,
They laugh to scorn the slaver's threat against
    their rocky home.   20

What means the Old Dominion? Hath she
    forgot the day
When o'er her conquered valleys swept the
    Briton's steel array?
How, side by side with sons of hers, the
    Massachusetts men
Encountered Tarleton's charge of fire, and
    stout Cornwallis, then?

Forgets she how the Bay State, in answer to
    the call
Of her old House of Burgesses, spoke out from
    Faneuil Hall?
When, echoing back her Henry's cry, came
    pulsing on each breath
Of Northern winds, the thrilling sounds of
    "Liberty or Death!"

What asks the Old Dominion? If now her sons
    have proved
False to their fathers' memory, false to the
    faith they loved;   30
If she can scoff at Freedom, and its great
    charter spurn,
Must we of Massachusetts from truth and
    duty turn?

We hunt your bondmen, flying from Slavery's
    hateful hell;
Our voices, at your bidding, take up the blood-
    hound's yell;

We gather, at your summons, above our
    fathers' graves,
From Freedom's holy altar-horns to tear your
    wretched slaves!

Thank God! not yet so vilely can Massachu-
    setts bow;
The spirit of her early time is with her even
    now;
Dream not because her Pilgrim blood moves
    slow and calm and cool,
She thus can stoop her chainless neck, a
    sister's slave and tool!   40

All that a *sister* State should do, all that a *free*
    State may,
Heart, hand, and purse we proffer, as in our
    early day;
But that one dark loathsome burden ye must
    stagger with alone,
And reap the bitter harvest which ye yourselves
    have sown!

Hold, while ye may, your struggling slaves,
    and burden God's free air
With woman's shriek beneath the lash, and
    manhood's wild despair;
Cling closer to the "cleaving curse" that writes
    upon your plains
The blasting of Almighty wrath against a
    land of chains.

Still shame your gallant ancestry, the cavaliers
    of old,
By watching round the shambles where human
    flesh is sold;   50
Gloat o'er the new-born child, and count his
    market value, when
The maddened mother's cry of woe shall
    pierce the slaver's den!

Lower than plummet soundeth, sink the Vir-
    ginia name;
Plant, if ye will, your fathers' graves with
    rankest weeds of shame;
Be, if ye will, the scandal of God's fair uni-
    verse;
We wash our hands forever, of your sin and
    shame and curse.

A voice from lips whereon the coal from
    Freedom's shrine hath been,
Thrilled, as but yesterday, the hearts of Berk-
    shire's mountain men:

The echoes of that solemn voice are sadly
   lingering still
In all our sunny valleys, on every windswept
   hill. 60

And when the prowling man-thief came hunt-
   ing for his prey
Beneath the very shadow of Bunker's shaft
   of gray,
How, through the free lips of the son, the
   father's warning spoke;
How, from its bonds of trade and sect, the
   Pilgrim city broke!

A hundred thousand right arms were lifted up
   on high,
A hundred thousand voices sent back their
   loud reply;
Through the thronged towns of Essex the
   startling summons rang,
And up from bench and loom and wheel her
   young mechanics sprang!

The voice of free, broad Middlesex, of thousands as of one,
The shaft of Bunker calling to that of Lexington; 70
From Norfolk's ancient villages, from Plymouth's rocky bound
To where Nantucket feels the arms of ocean
   close her round;

From rich and rural Worcester, where through
   the calm repose
Of cultured vales and fringing woods the gentle
   Nashua flows,
To where Wachuset's wintry blasts the moun-
   tain larches stir,
Swelled up to Heaven the thrilling cry of
   "God save Latimer!"

And sandy Barnstable rose up, wet with the
   salt sea spray;
And Bristol sent her answering shout down
   Narragansett Bay!
Along the broad Connecticut old Hampden
   felt the thrill,
And the cheer of Hampshire's woodmen swept
   down from Holyoke Hill. 80

The voice of Massachusetts! Of her free sons
   and daughters,
Deep calling unto deep aloud, the sound of
   many waters!

Against the burden of that voice what tyrant
   power shall stand?
No fetters in the Bay State! No slave upon her
   land!

Look to it well, Virginians! In calmness we
   have borne,
In answer to our faith and trust, your insult
   and your scorn;
You've spurned our kindest counsels; you've
   hunted for our lives;
And shaken round our hearths and homes
   your manacles and gyves!

We wage no war, we lift no arm, we fling no
   torch within
The fire-damps of the quaking mine beneath
   your soil of sin; 90
We leave ye with your bondmen, to wrestle,
   while ye can,
With the strong upward tendencies and god-
   like soul of man!

But for us and for our children, the vow
   which we have given
For freedom and humanity, is registered in
   heaven;
No slave-hunt in our borders,—no pirate on
   our strand!
No fetters in the Bay State,—no slave upon
   our land!
1842   1843

ICHABOD [3]

So fallen! so lost! the light withdrawn
   Which once he wore!
The glory from his gray hairs gone
   Forevermore!

Revile him not, the Tempter hath
   A snare for all;
And pitying tears, not scorn and wrath,
   Befit his fall!

Oh, dumb be passion's stormy rage,
   When he who might 10
Have lighted up and led his age,
   Falls back in night.

[3] This poem was the outcome of the surprise and grief and forecast of evil consequences which I felt on reading the Seventh of
March speech of Daniel Webster in support of the "Compromise,"
and the Fugitive Slave Law. No partisan or personal enmity dictated it. On the contrary my admiration of the splendid personality
and intellectual power of the great senator was never stronger than
when I laid down his speech, and, in one of the saddest moments of
my life, penned my protest. . . . [Whittier's note.]

Scorn! would the angels laugh, to mark
   A bright soul driven,
Fiend-goaded, down the endless dark,
   From hope and heaven!

Let not the land once proud of him
   Insult him now,
Nor brand with deeper shame his dim,
   Dishonored brow.   20

But let its humbled sons, instead,
   From sea to lake,
A long lament, as for the dead,
   In sadness make.

Of all we loved and honored, naught
   Save power remains;
A fallen angel's pride of thought,
   Still strong in chains.

All else is gone; from those great eyes
   The soul has fled: 30
When faith is lost, when honor dies,
   The man is dead!

Then pay the reverence of old days
   To his dead fame;
Walk backward, with averted gaze,
   And hide the shame!
1850   1850

DEDICATION

[To *Songs of Labor*]

I would the gift I offer here
   Might graces from thy favor take,
And, seen through Friendship's atmosphere,
On softened lines and coloring, wear
The unaccustomed light of beauty, for thy
   sake.

Few leaves of Fancy's spring remain:
   But what I have I give to thee,
The o'er-sunned bloom of summer's plain,
And paler flowers, the latter rain
Calls from the westering slope of life's autumnal
   lea.   10

Above the fallen groves of green,
   Where youth's enchanted forest stood,
Dry root and mossèd trunk between,
A sober after-growth is seen,
As springs the pine where falls the gay-leafed
   maple wood!

Yet birds will sing, and breezes play
   Their leaf-harps in the sombre tree;
And through the bleak and wintry day
It keeps its steady green alway,—
So, even my after-thoughts may have a charm
   for thee.   20

Art's perfect forms no moral need,
   And beauty is its own excuse;
But for the dull and flowerless weed
Some healing virtue still must plead,
And the rough ore must find its honors in its
   use.

So haply these, my simple lays
   Of homely toil, may serve to show
The orchard bloom and tasselled maize
That skirt and gladden duty's ways,
The unsung beauty hid life's common things
   below.   30

Haply from them the toiler, bent
   Above his forge or plough, may gain
A manlier spirit of content,
And feel that life is wisest spent
Where the strong working hand makes strong
   the working brain.

The doom which to the guilty pair
   Without the walls of Eden came,
Transforming sinless ease to care
And rugged toil, no more shall bear
The burden of old crime, or mark of primal
   shame.   40

A blessing now, a curse no more;
   Since He, whose name we breathe with
   awe,
The coarse mechanic vesture wore,
A poor man toiling with the poor,
In labor, as in prayer, fulfilling the same law.
   1850

THE LUMBERMEN [4]

Wildly round our woodland quarters
   Sad-voiced Autumn grieves;
Thickly down these swelling waters
   Float his fallen leaves.
Through the tall and naked timber,
   Column-like and old,
Gleam the sunsets of November,
   From their skies of gold.

[4] One of the *Songs of Labor*.

O'er us, to the southland heading,
 Screams the gray wild-goose; 10
On the night-frost sounds the treading
 Of the brindled moose.
Noiseless creeping, while we're sleeping,
 Frost his task-work plies;
Soon, his icy bridges heaping,
 Shall our log-piles rise.

When, with sounds of smothered thunder,
 On some night of rain,
Lake and river break asunder
 Winter's weakened chain, 20
Down the wild March flood shall bear them
 To the saw-mill's wheel,
Or where Steam, the slave, shall tear them
 With his teeth of steel.

Be it starlight, be it moonlight,
 In these vales below,
When the earliest beams of sunlight
 Streak the mountain's snow,
Crisps the hoar-frost, keen and early,
 To our hurrying feet, 30
And the forest echoes clearly,
 All our blows repeat.

Where the crystal Ambijejis
 Stretches broad and clear,
And Millnoket's pine-black ridges
 Hide the browsing deer;
Where, through lakes and wide morasses,
 Or through rocky walls,
Swift and strong, Penobscot passes
 White with foamy falls; 40

Where, through clouds, are glimpses given
 Of Katahdin's sides,—
Rock and forest piled to heaven,
 Torn and ploughed by slides!
Far below, the Indian trapping,
 In the sunshine warm;
Far above, the snow-cloud wrapping
 Half the peak in storm!

Where are mossy carpets better
 Than the Persian weaves, 50
And than Eastern perfumes sweeter
 Seem the fading leaves;
And a music wild and solemn,
 From the pine-tree's height,
Rolls its vast and sea-like volume
 On the wind of night;

Make we here our camp of winter;
 And, through sleet and snow,

Pitchy knot and beechen splinter
 On our hearth shall glow. 60
Here, with mirth to lighten duty,
 We shall lack alone
Woman's smile and girlhood's beauty,
 Childhood's lisping tone.

But their hearth is brighter burning
 For our toil to-day;
And the welcome of returning
 Shall our loss repay,
When, like seamen from the waters,
 From the woods we come, 70
Greeting sisters, wives, and daughters,
 Angels of our home!

Not for us the measured ringing
 From the village spire,
Not for us the Sabbath singing
 Of the sweet-voiced choir:
Ours the old, majestic temple,
 Where God's brightness shines
Down the dome so grand and ample,
 Propped by lofty pines! 80

Through each branch-enwoven skylight,
 Speaks He in the breeze,
As of old beneath the twilight
 Of lost Eden's trees!
For His ear, the inward feeling
 Needs no outward tongue;
He can see the spirit kneeling
 While the axe is swung.

Heeding truth alone, and turning
 From the false and dim, 90
Lamp of toil or altar burning
 Are alike to Him.
Strike, then, comrades! Trade is waiting
 On our rugged toil;
Far ships waiting for the freighting
 Of our woodland spoil!

Ships, whose traffic links these highlands
 Bleak and cold, of ours,
With the citron-planted islands
 Of a clime of flowers; 100
To our frosts the tribute bringing
 Of eternal heats;
In our lap of winter flinging
 Tropic fruits and sweets.

Cheerly, on the axe of labor,
 Let the sunbeams dance,
Better than the flash of sabre
 Or the gleam of lance!

Strike! With every blow is given
  Freer sun and sky,   110
And the long-hid earth to heaven
  Looks, with wondering eye!

Loud behind us grow the murmurs
  Of the age to come;
Clang of smiths, and tread of farmers,
  Bearing harvest home!
Here her virgin lap with treasures
  Shall the green earth fill;
Waving wheat and golden maize-ears
  Crown each beechen hill.   120

Keep who will the city's alleys,
  Take the smooth-shorn plain;
Give to us the cedarn valleys,
  Rocks and hills of Maine!
In our North-land, wild and woody,
  Let us still have part:
Rugged nurse and mother sturdy,
  Hold us to thy heart!

Oh, our free hearts beat the warmer
  For thy breath of snow;   130
And our tread is all the firmer
  For thy rocks below.
Freedom, hand in hand with labor,
  Walketh strong and brave;
On the forehead of his neighbor
  No man writeth Slave!

Lo, the day breaks! old Katahdin's
  Pine-trees show its fires,
While from these dim forest gardens
  Rise their blackened spires.   140
Up, my comrades! up and doing!
  Manhood's rugged play
Still renewing, bravely hewing
  Through the world our way!
1845   1845

FIRST-DAY THOUGHTS

In calm and cool and silence, once again
  I find my old accustomed place among
  My brethren, where, perchance, no human
    tongue
  Shall utter words; where never hymn is
    sung,
  Nor deep-toned organ blown, nor censer
    swung,
  Nor dim light falling through the pictured
    pane!

There, syllabled by silence, let me hear
The still small voice which reached the
    prophet's ear;
Read in my heart a still diviner law
Than Israel's leader on his tables saw!   10
There let me strive with each besetting sin
  Recall my wandering fancies, and restrain
  The sore disquiet of a restless brain;
  And, as the path of duty is made plain,
May grace be given that I may walk therein,
  Not like the hireling, for his selfish gain,
With backward glances and reluctant tread,
Making a merit of his coward dread,
  But, cheerful, in the light around me thrown,
  Walking as one to pleasant service led;   20
  Doing God's will as if it were my own,
Yet trusting not in mine, but in His strength
    alone!   1852

THE BAREFOOT BOY

Blessings on thee, little man,
Barefoot boy, with cheek of tan!
With thy turned-up pantaloons,
And thy merry whistled tunes;
With thy red lip, redder still
Kissed by strawberries on the hill;
With the sunshine on thy face,
Through thy torn brim's jaunty grace;
From my heart I give thee joy,—
I was once a barefoot boy!   10
Prince thou art,—the grown-up man
Only is republican.
Let the million-dollared ride!
Barefoot, trudging at his side,
Thou hast more than he can buy
In the reach of ear and eye,—
Outward sunshine, inward joy:
Blessings on thee, barefoot boy!

Oh for boyhood's painless play,
Sleep that wakes in laughing day,   20
Health that mocks the doctor's rules,
Knowledge never learned of schools,
Of the wild bee's morning chase,
Of the wild-flower's time and place,
Flight of fowl and habitude
Of the tenants of the wood;
How the tortoise bears his shell,
How the woodchuck digs his cell,
And the ground-mole sinks his well;
How the robin feeds her young,   30
How the oriole's nest is hung;
Where the whitest lilies blow,

Where the freshest berries grow,
Where the ground-nut trails its vine,
Where the wood-grape's clusters shine;
Of the black wasp's cunning way,
Mason of his walls of clay,
And the architectural plans
Of gray hornet artisans!
For, eschewing books and tasks,   40
Nature answers all he asks;
Hand in hand with her he walks,
Face to face with her he talks,
Part and parcel of her joy,—
Blessings on the barefoot boy!

Oh for boyhood's time of June,
Crowding years in one brief moon,
When all things I heard or saw,
Me, their master, waited for.
I was rich in flowers and trees,   50
Humming-birds and honey-bees;
For my sport the squirrel played,
Plied the snouted mole his spade;
For my taste the blackberry cone
Purpled over hedge and stone;
Laughed the brook for my delight
Through the day and through the night,
Whispering at the garden wall,
Talked with me from fall to fall;
Mine the sand-rimmed pickerel pond,   60
Mine the walnut slopes beyond,
Mine, on bending orchard trees,
Apples of Hesperides!
Still as my horizon grew,
Larger grew my riches too;
All the world I saw or knew
Seemed a complex Chinese toy,
Fashioned for a barefoot boy!

Oh for festal dainties spread,
Like my bowl of milk and bread;   70
Pewter spoon and bowl of wood,
On the door-stone, gray and rude!
O'er me, like a regal tent,
Cloudy-ribbed, the sunset bent,
Purple-curtained, fringed with gold,
Looped in many a wind-swung fold;
While for music came the play
Of the pied frogs' orchestra;
And, to light the noisy choir,
Lit the fly his lamp of fire.   80
I was monarch: pomp and joy
Waited on the barefoot boy!

Cheerily, then, my little man,
Live and laugh, as boyhood can!

Though the flinty slopes be hard,
Stubble-speared the new-mown sward,
Every morn shall lead thee through
Fresh baptisms of the dew;
Every evening from thy feet
Shall the cool wind kiss the heat: 90
All too soon these feet must hide
In the prison cells of pride,
Lose the freedom of the sod,
Like a colt's for work be shod,
Made to tread the mills of toil,
Up and down in ceaseless moil:
Happy if their track be found
Never on forbidden ground;
Happy if they sink not in
Quick and treacherous sands of sin.   100
Ah! that thou couldst know thy joy,
Ere it passes, barefoot boy!
1855   1856

THE KANSAS EMIGRANTS

We cross the prairie as of old
    The pilgrims crossed the sea,
To make the West, as they the East,
    The homestead of the free!

We go to rear a wall of men
    On Freedom's southern line,
And plant beside the cotton-tree
    The rugged Northern pine!

We're flowing from our native hills
    As our free rivers flow: 10
The blessing of our Mother-land
    Is on us as we go.

We go to plant her common schools
    On distant prairie swells,
And give the Sabbaths of the wild
    The music of her bells.

Upbearing, like the Ark of old,
    The Bible in our van,
We go to test the truth of God
    Against the fraud of man.   20

No pause, no rest, save where the streams
    That feed the Kansas run,
Save where our Pilgrim gonfalon
    Shall flout the setting sun!

We'll tread the prairie as of old
    Our fathers sailed the sea,

And make the West, as they the East,
   The homestead of the free!
1854   1856

FOR RIGHTEOUSNESS' SAKE

Inscribed to Friends under Arrest for
Treason against the Slave Power

The age is dull and mean. Men creep,
   Not walk; with blood too pale and tame
To pay the debt they owe to shame;
Buy cheap, sell dear; eat, drink, and sleep
   Down-pillowed, deaf to moaning want;
Pay tithes for soul-insurance; keep
   Six days to Mammon, one to Cant.

In such a time, give thanks to God,
   That somewhat of the holy rage
With which the prophets in their age 10
On all its decent seemings trod,
   Has set your feet upon the lie,
That man and ox and soul and clod
   Are market stock to sell and buy!

The hot words from your lips, my own,
   To caution trained, might not repeat;
But if some tares among the wheat
Of generous thought and deed were sown,
   No common wrong provoked your zeal;
The silken gauntlet that is thrown   20
   In such a quarrel rings like steel.

The brave old strife the fathers saw
   For Freedom calls for men again
Like those who battled not in vain
For England's Charter, Alfred's law;
   And right of speech and trial just
Wage in your name their ancient war
   With venal courts and perjured trust.

God's ways seem dark, but, soon or late,
   They touch the shining hills of day;   30
The evil cannot brook delay,
   The good can well afford to wait.
Give ermined knaves their hour of crime;
   Ye have the future grand and great,
The safe appeal of Truth to Time!
1855   1856

SKIPPER IRESON'S RIDE [5]

Of all the rides since the birth of time,
Told in story or sung in rhyme,—

[5] Whittier heard the story of the Skipper when he was a student at the Haverhill Academy in 1828. Though he began the ballad then, he did not finish it until 1857. The events described in it took place at Marblehead in 1808.

On Apuleius's Golden Ass,
Or one-eyed Calendar's horse of brass,
Witch astride of a human back,
Islam's prophet on Al-Borák,—
The strangest ride that ever was sped
Was Ireson's, out from Marblehead!
   Old Floyd Ireson, for his hard heart,
   Tarred and feathered and carried in a cart
   By the women of Marblehead!   11

Body of turkey, head of owl,
Wings a-droop like a rained-on fowl,
Feathered and ruffled in every part,
Skipper Ireson stood in the cart.
Scores of women, old and young,
Strong of muscle, and glib of tongue,
Pushed and pulled up the rocky lane,
Shouting and singing the shrill refrain:
   "Here's Flud Oirson, fur his horrd horrt,   20
   Torr'd an' futherr'd an' corr'd in a corrt
   By the women o' Morble'ead!"

Wrinkled scolds with hands on hips,
Girls in bloom of cheek and lips,
Wild-eyed, free-limbed, such as chase
Bacchus round some antique vase,
Brief of skirt, with ankles bare,
Loose of kerchief and loose of hair,
With conch-shells blowing and fish-horns'
   twang,
Over and over the Mænads sang: 30
   "Here's Flud Oirson, fur his horrd horrt,
   Torr'd an' futherr'd an' corr'd in a corrt
   By the women o' Morble'ead!"

Small pity for him!—He sailed away
From a leaking ship in Chaleur Bay,—
Sailed away from a sinking wreck,
With his own town's-people on her deck!
"Lay by! lay by!" they called to him.
Back he answered, 'Sink or swim!
Brag of your catch of fish again!"   40
And off he sailed through the fog and rain!
   Old Floyd Ireson, for his hard heart,
   Tarred and feathered and carried in a cart
   By the women of Marblehead!

Fathoms deep in dark Chaleur
That wreck shall lie forevermore.
Mother and sister, wife and maid,
Looked from the rocks of Marblehead
Over the moaning and rainy sea,—
Looked for the coming that might not be!   50
What did the winds and the sea-birds say

Of the cruel captain who sailed away?—
  Old Floyd Ireson, for his hard heart,
  Tarred and feathered and carried in a cart
    By the women of Marblehead!

Through the street, on either side,
Up flew windows, doors swung wide;
Sharp-tongued spinsters, old wives gray,
Treble lent the fish-horn's bray.
Sea-worn grandsires, cripple-bound,   60
Hulks of old sailors run aground,
Shook head, and fist, and hat, and cane,
And cracked with curses the hoarse refrain:
  "Here's Flud Oirson, fur his horrd horrt,
  Torr'd an' futherr'd an' corr'd in a corrt
    By the women o' Morble'ead!"

Sweetly along the Salem road
Bloom of orchard and lilac showed.
Little the wicked skipper knew
Of the fields so green and the sky so blue. 70
Riding there in his sorry trim,
Like an Indian idol glum and grim,
Scarcely he seemed the sound to hear
Of voices shouting, far and near:
  "Here's Flud Oirson, fur his horrd horrt,
  Torr'd an' futherr'd an' corr'd in a corrt
    By the women o' Morble'ead!"

"Hear me, neighbors!" at last he cried,—
"What to me is this noisy ride?
What is the shame that clothes the skin   80
To the nameless horror that lives within?
Waking or sleeping, I see a wreck,
And hear a cry from a reeling deck!
Hate me and curse me,—I only dread
The hand of God and the face of the dead!"
  Said old Floyd Ireson, for his hard heart,
  Tarred and feathered and carried in a cart
    By the women of Marblehead!

Then the wife of the skipper lost at sea
Said, "God has touched him! why should
    we!"   90
Said an old wife mourning her only son,
"Cut the rogue's tether and let him run!"
So with soft relentings and rude excuse,
Half scorn, half pity, they cut him loose,
And gave him a cloak to hide him in,
And left him alone with his shame and sin.
  Poor Floyd Ireson, for his hard heart,
  Tarred and feathered and carried in a cart
    By the women of Marblehead!
1828, 1857   1857

TELLING THE BEES [6]

Here is the place; right over the hill
  Runs the path I took;
You can see the gap in the old wall still,
  And the stepping-stones in the shallow
    brook.

There is the house, with the gate red-barred,
  And the poplars tall;
And the barn's brown length, and the cattle-
    yard,
  And the white horns tossing above the wall.

There are the bee hives ranged in the sun;
  And down by the brink   10
Of the brook are her poor flowers, weed-
    o'errun,
  Pansy and daffodil, rose and pink.

A year has gone, as the tortoise goes,
  Heavy and slow;
And the same rose blows, and the same sun
    glows,
  And the same brook sings of a year ago.

There's the same sweet clover-smell in the
    breeze;
  And the June sun warm
Tangles his wings of fire in the trees,
  Setting, as then, over Fernside farm.   20

I mind me how with a lover's care
  From my Sunday coat
I brushed off the burrs, and smoothed my hair,
  And cooled at the brookside my brow and
    throat.

Since we parted, a month had passed,—
  To love, a year;
Down through the beeches I looked at last
  On the little red gate and the well-sweep
    near.

I can see it all now,—the slantwise rain
  Of light through the leaves,   30
The sundown's blaze on her window-pane,
  The bloom of her roses under the eaves.

Just the same as a month before,—
  The house and the trees,

[6] A remarkable custom, brought from the Old Country, formerly prevailed in the rural districts of New England. On the death of a member of the family, the bees were at once informed of the event, and their hives dressed in mourning. This ceremonial was supposed to be necessary to prevent the swarms from leaving their hives and seeking a new home. [Whittier's note.]

The barn's brown gable, the vine by the
    door,—
Nothing changed but the hives of bees.

Before them, under the garden wall,
    Forward and back,
Went drearily singing the chore-girl small,
    Draping each hive with a shred of black.   40

Trembling, I listened: the summer sun
    Had the chill of snow;
For I knew she was telling the bees of one
    Gone on the journey we all must go!

Then I said to myself, "My Mary weeps
    For the dead to-day:
Haply her blind old grandsire sleeps
    The fret and the pain of his age away."

But her dog whined low; on the doorway sill,
    With his cane to his chin,   50
The old man sat; and the chore-girl still
    Sung to the bees stealing out and in.

And the song she was singing ever since
    In my ear sounds on:—
"Stay at home, pretty bees, fly not hence!
    Mistress Mary is dead and gone!"   1858

LAUS DEO![7]

It is done!
    Clang of bell and roar of gun
Send the tidings up and down.
    How the belfries rock and reel!
    How the great guns, peal on peal,
Fling the joy from town to town!

Ring, O bells!
    Every stroke exulting tells
Of the burial hour of crime.
    Loud and long, that all may hear,   10
    Ring for every listening ear
Of Eternity and Time!

Let us kneel:
    God's own voice is in that peal,
And this spot is holy ground.
    Lord, forgive us! What are we,

[7] The poem was suggested to Whittier when, as he sat in the Friends' meeting, he heard the bells and cannon announcing the passage of the constitutional amendment abolishing slavery.

That our eyes this glory see,
That our ears have heard the sound!

For the Lord
    On the whirlwind is abroad;   20
In the earthquake He has spoken:
    He has smitten with his thunder
    The iron walls asunder,
And the gates of brass are broken!

Loud and long
    Lift the old exulting song;
Sing with Miriam by the sea,
    He has cast the mighty down;
    Horse and rider sink and drown;
"He hath triumphed gloriously!"   30

Did we dare,
    In our agony of prayer,
Ask for more than He has done?
    When was ever his right hand
    Over any time or land
Stretched as now beneath the sun?

How they pale,
    Ancient myth and song and tale,
In this wonder of our days,
    When the cruel rod of war   40
    Blossoms white with righteous law,
And the wrath of man is praise!

Blotted out!
    All within and all about
Shall a fresher life begin;
    Freer breathe the universe
    As it rolls its heavy curse
On the dead and buried sin!

It is done!
    In the circuit of the sun   50
Shall the sound thereof go forth.
    It shall bid the sad rejoice,
    It shall give the dumb a voice,
It shall belt with joy the earth!

Ring and swing,
    Bells of joy! On morning's wing
Send the song of praise abroad!
    With a sound of broken chains
    Tell the nations that He reigns,
Who alone is Lord and God!   60

1865   1865

SNOW-BOUND [8]

A Winter Idyl

The sun that brief December day
Rose cheerless over hills of gray,
And, darkly circled, gave at noon
A sadder light than waning moon.
Slow tracing down the thickening sky
Its mute and ominous prophecy,
A portent seeming less than threat,
It sank from sight before it set.
A chill no coat, however stout,
Of homespun stuff could quite shut out,　　10
A hard, dull bitterness of cold,
That checked, mid-vein, the circling race
Of life-blood in the sharpened face,
The coming of the snow-storm told.
The wind blew east; we heard the roar
Of Ocean on his wintry shore,
And felt the strong pulse throbbing there
Beat with low rhythm our inland air.

Meanwhile we did our nightly chores,—
Brought in the wood from out of doors,　　20
Littered the stalls, and from the mows
Raked down the herd's-grass for the cows:
Heard the horse whinnying for his corn;
And, sharply clashing horn on horn,
Impatient down the stanchion rows
The cattle shake their walnut bows;
While, peering from his early perch
Upon the scaffold's pole of birch,
The cock his crested helmet bent
And down his querulous challenge sent.　　30

Unwarmed by any sunset light
The gray day darkened into night,
A night made hoary with the swarm
And whirl-dance of the blinding storm,

As zigzag, wavering to and fro,
Crossed and recrossed the wingèd snow:
And ere the early bedtime came
The white drift piled the window-frame,
And through the glass the clothes-line posts
Looked in like tall and sheeted ghosts.　　40

So all night long the storm roared on:
The morning broke without a sun;
In tiny spherule traced with lines
Of Nature's geometric signs,
In starry flake, and pellicle,
All day the hoary meteor fell;
And, when the second morning shone,
We looked upon a world unknown,
On nothing we could call our own.
Around the glistening wonder bent　　50
The blue walls of the firmament,
No cloud above, no earth below,—
A universe of sky and snow!
The old familiar sights of ours
Took marvellous shapes; strange domes and
　　　towers
Rose up where sty or corn-crib stood,
Or garden-wall, or belt of wood;
A smooth white mound the brush-pile showed,
A fenceless drift what once was road;
The bridle-post an old man sat　　60
With loose-flung coat and high cocked hat;
The well-curb had a Chinese roof;
And even the long sweep, high aloof,
In its slant splendor, seemed to tell
Of Pisa's leaning miracle.

A prompt, decisive man, no breath
Our father wasted: "Boys, a path!"
Well pleased (for when did farmer boy
Count such a summons less than joy?)
Our buskins on our feet we drew;　　70
With mittened hands, and caps drawn low,
To guard our necks and ears from snow,
We cut the solid whiteness through.
And, where the drift was deepest, made
A tunnel walled and overlaid
With dazzling crystal: we had read
Of rare Aladdin's wondrous cave,
And to our own his name we gave,
With many a wish the luck were ours
To test his lamp's supernal powers.　　80
We reached the barn with merry din,
And roused the prisoned brutes within.
The old horse thrust his long head out,
And grave with wonder gazed about;
The cock his lusty greeting said,
And forth his speckled harem led;

---

[8] The inmates of the family at the Whittier homestead who are referred to in the poem were my father, mother, my brother and two sisters, and my uncle and aunt, both unmarried. In addition, there was the district schoolmaster, who boarded with us. The "not unfeared, half-welcome guest" was Harriet Livermore, daughter of Judge Livermore, of New Hampshire, a young woman of fine natural ability, enthusiastic, eccentric, with slight control over her violent temper, which sometimes made her religious profession doubtful. She was equally ready to exhort in school-house prayer-meetings and dance in a Washington ball-room, while her father was a member of Congress. She early embraced the doctrine of the Second Advent, and felt it her duty to proclaim the Lord's speedy coming. With this message she crossed the Atlantic and spent the greater part of a long life in travelling over Europe and Asia. She lived some time with Lady Hester Stanhope, a woman as fantastic and mentally strained as herself, on the slope of Mt. Lebanon, but finally quarrelled with her in regard to two white horses with red marks on their backs which suggested the idea of saddles, on which her titled hostess expected to ride into Jerusalem with the Lord. A friend of mine found her, when quite an old woman, wandering in Syria with a tribe of Arabs, who with the Oriental notion that madness is inspiration, accepted her as their prophetess and leader. At the time referred to in "Snow-Bound" she was boarding at the Rocks Village, about two miles from us. . . . [Whittier's note.]

The oxen lashed their tails, and hooked,
And mild reproach of hunger looked;
The hornèd patriarch of the sheep,
Like Egypt's Amun roused from sleep,   90
Shook his sage head with gesture mute,
And emphasized with stamp of foot.

All day the gusty north-wind bore
The loosening drift its breath before;
Low circling round its southern zone,
The sun through dazzling snow-mist shone.
No church-bell lent its Christian tone
To the savage air, no social smoke
Curled over woods of snow-hung oak.
A solitude made more intense   100
By dreary-voicèd elements,
The shrieking of the mindless wind,
The moaning tree-boughs swaying blind,
And on the glass the unmeaning beat
Of ghostly finger-tips of sleet.
Beyond the circle of our hearth
No welcome sound of toil or mirth
Unbound the spell, and testified
Of human life and thought outside.
We minded that the sharpest ear   110
The buried brooklet could not hear,
The music of whose liquid lip
Had been to us companionship,
And, in our lonely life, had grown
To have an almost human tone.

As night drew on, and, from the crest
Of wooded knolls that ridged the west,
The sun, a snow-blown traveller, sank
From sight beneath the smothering bank,
We piled, with care, our nightly stack   120
Of wood against the chimney-back,—
The oaken log, green, huge, and thick,
And on its top the stout back-stick;
The knotty forestick laid apart,
And filled between with curious art
The ragged brush; then, hovering near,
We watched the first red blaze appear,
Heard the sharp crackle, caught the gleam
On whitewashed wall and sagging beam,
Until the old, rude-furnished room   130
Burst, flower-like, into rosy bloom;
While radiant with a mimic flame
Outside the sparkling drift became,
And through the bare-boughed lilac-tree
Our own warm hearth seemed blazing free.
The crane and pendent trammels showed,
The Turks' heads on the andirons glowed;
While childish fancy, prompt to tell
The meaning of the miracle,

Whispered the old rhyme: "*Under the tree,*   140
When fire outdoors burns merrily,
There the witches are making tea."

The moon above the eastern wood
Shone at its full; the hill-range stood
Transfigured in the silver flood,
Its blown snows flashing cold and keen,
Dead white, save where some sharp ravine
Took shadow, or the sombre green
Of hemlocks turned to pitchy black
Against the whiteness at their back.   150
For such a world and such a night
Most fitting that unwarming light,
Which only seemed where'er it fell
To make the coldness visible.

Shut in from all the world without,
We sat the clean-winged hearth about,
Content to let the north-wind roar
In baffled rage at pane and door,
While the red logs before us beat
The frost-line back with tropic heat;   160
And ever, when a louder blast
Shook beam and rafter as it passed,
The merrier up its roaring draught
The great throat of the chimney laughed;
The house-dog on his paws outspread
Laid to the fire his drowsy head,
The cat's dark silhouette on the wall
A couchant tiger's seemed to fall;
And, for the winter fireside meet,
Between the andirons' straddling feet,   170
The mug of cider simmered slow,
The apples sputtered in a row,
And, close at hand, the basket stood
With nuts from brown October's wood.

What matter how the night behaved?
What matter how the north-wind raved?
Blow high, blow low, not all its snow
Could quench our hearth-fire's ruddy glow.
O Time and Change!—with hair as gray
As was my sire's that winter day,   180
How strange it seems, with so much gone
Of life and love, to still live on!
Ah, brother! only I and thou
Are left of all that circle now,—
The dear homes faces whereupon
That fitful firelight paled and shone.
Henceforward, listen as we will,
The voices of that hearth are still;
Look where we may, the wide earth o'er,
Those lighted faces smile no more.   190

We tread the paths their feet have worn,
 We sit beneath their orchard trees,
 We hear, like them, the hum of bees
And rustle of the bladed corn;
We turn the pages that they read,
 Their written words we linger o'er,
But in the sun they cast no shade,
No voice is heard, no sign is made,
 No step is on the conscious floor!
Yet Love will dream, and Faith will trust, 200
(Since He who knows our need is just,)
That somehow, somewhere, meet we must.
Alas for him who never sees
The stars shine through his cypress-trees!
Who, hopeless, lays his dead away,
Nor looks to see the breaking day
Across the mournful marbles play!
Who hath not learned, in hours of faith,
 The truth to flesh and sense unknown,
That Life is ever lord of Death, 210
 And Love can never lose its own!

We sped the time with stories old,
Wrought puzzles out, and riddles told,
Or stammered from our school-book lore
"The Chief of Gambia's golden shore."
How often since, when all the land
Was clay in Slavery's shaping hand,
As if a far-blown trumpet stirred
The languorous sin-sick air, I heard:
"Does not the voice of reason cry, 220
 Claim the first right which Nature gave,
From the red scourge of bondage fly,
 Nor deign to live a burdened slave!"
Our father rode again his ride
On Memphremagog's wooded side;
Sat down again to moose and samp
In trapper's hut and Indian camp;
Lived o'er the old idyllic ease
Beneath St. Francois' hemlock-trees;
Again for him the moonlight shone 230
On Norman cap and boffced zone;
Again he heard the violin play
Which led the village dance away,
And mingled in its merry whirl
The grandam and the laughing girl.
Or, nearer home, our steps he led
Where Salisbury's level marshes spread
 Mile-wide as flies the laden bee;
Where merry mowers, hale and strong,
Swept, scythe on scythe, their swaths along 240
 The low green prairies of the sea.
We shared the fishing off Boar's Head,
 And round the rocky Isles of Shoals
 The hake-broil on the drift-wood coals;

The chowder on the sand-beach made,
Dipped by the hungry, steaming hot,
With spoons of clam-shell from the pot.
We heard the tales of witchcraft old,
And dream and sign and marvel told
To sleepy listeners as they lay 250
Stretched idly on the salted hay,
Adrift along the winding shores,
When favoring breezes deigned to blow
The square sail of the gundelow
And idle lay the useless oars.

Our mother, while she turned her wheel
Or run the new-knit stocking-heel,
Told how the Indian hordes came down
At midnight on Cocheco town,
And how her own great-uncle bore 260
His cruel scalp-mark to fourscore.
Recalling, in her fitting phrase,
 So rich and picturesque and free,
 (The common unrhymed poetry
Of simple life and country ways,)
The story of her early days,—
She made us welcome to her home;
Old hearths grew wide to give us room;
We stole with her a frightened look
At the gray wizard's conjuring-book, 270
The fame whereof went far and wide
Through all the simple country-side;
We heard the hawks at twilight play,
The boat-horn on Piscataqua,
The loon's weird laughter far away;
We fished her little trout-brook, knew
What flowers in wood and meadow grew,
What sunny hillsides autumn-brown
She climbed to shake the ripe nuts down,
Saw where in sheltered cove and bay 280
The ducks' black squadron anchored lay,
And heard the wild-geese calling loud
Beneath the gray November cloud.

Then, haply, with a look more grave,
And soberer tone, some tale she gave
From painful Sewel's ancient tome,
Beloved in every Quaker home,
Of faith fire-winged by martyrdom,
Or Chalkley's Journal, old and quaint,—
Gentlest of skippers, rare sea-saint! 290
Who, when the dreary calms prevailed,
And water-butt and bread-cask failed,
And cruel, hungry eyes pursued
His portly presence mad for food,
With dark hints muttered under breath
Of casting lots for life or death,
Offered, if Heaven withheld supplies,

To be himself the sacrifice.
Then, suddenly, as if to save
The good man from his living grave,   300
A ripple on the water grew,
A school of porpoise flashed in view.
"Take, eat," he said, "and be content;
These fishes in my stead are sent
By Him who gave the tangled ram
To spare the child of Abraham."

Our uncle, innocent of books,
Was rich in lore of fields and brooks,
The ancient teachers never dumb
Of Nature's unhoused lyceum.   310
In moons and tides and weather wise,
He read the clouds as prophecies,
And foul or fair could well divine,
By many an occult hint and sign,
Holding the cunning-warded keys
To all the woodcraft mysteries;
Himself to Nature's heart so near
That all her voices in his ear
Of beast or bird had meanings clear,
Like Apollonius of old,   320
Who knew the tales the sparrows told,
Or Hermes, who interpreted
What the sage cranes of Nilus said;
A simple, guileless, childlike man,
Content to live where life began;
Strong only on his native grounds,
The little world of sights and sounds
Whose girdle was the parish bounds,
Whereof his fondly partial pride
The common features magnified,   330
As Surrey hills to mountains grew
In White of Selborne's loving view,—
He told how teal and loon he shot,
And how the eagle's eggs he got,
The feats on pond and river done,
The prodigies of rod and gun;
Till, warming with the tales he told,
Forgotten was the outside cold,
The bitter wind unheeded blew,
From ripening corn the pigeons flew,   340
The partridge drummed i' the wood, the mink
Went fishing down the river-brink.
In fields with bean or clover gay,
The woodchuck, like a hermit gray,
   Peered from the doorway of his cell;
The muskrat plied the mason's trade,
And tier by tier his mud-walls laid;
And from the shagbark overhead
   The grizzled squirrel dropped his shell.

Next, the dear aunt, whose smile of cheer   350
And voice in dreams I see and hear—

The sweetest woman ever Fate
Perverse denied a household mate,
Who, lonely, homeless, not the less
Found peace in love's unselfishness,
And welcome whereso'er she went,
A calm and gracious element,
Whose presence seemed the sweet income
And womanly atmosphere of home—
Called up her girlhood memories,   360
The huskings and the apple-bees,
The sleigh-rides and the summer sails,
Weaving through all the poor details
And homespun warp of circumstance
A golden woof-thread of romance.
For well she kept her genial mood
And simple faith of maidenhood;
Before her still a cloud-land lay,
The mirage loomed across her way;
The morning dew, that dries so soon   370
With others, glistened at her noon;
Through years of toil and soil and care,
From glossy tress to thin gray hair,
All unprofaned she held apart
The virgin fancies of the heart.
Be shame to him of woman born
Who hath for such but thought of scorn.

There, too, our elder sister plied
Her evening task the stand beside;
A full, rich nature, free to trust,   380
Truthful and almost sternly just,
Impulsive, earnest, prompt to act,
And make her generous thought a fact,
Keeping with many a light disguise
The secret of self-sacrifice.
O heart sore-tried! thou hast the best,
That Heaven itself could give thee,—rest,
Rest from all bitter thoughts and things!
   How many a poor one's blessing went
      With thee beneath the low green tent   390
Whose curtain never outward swings!

As one who held herself a part
Of all she saw, and let her heart
   Against the household bosom lean,
Upon the motley-braided mat
Our youngest and our dearest sat,
Lifting her large, sweet, asking eyes,
   Now bathed in the unfading green
And holy peace of Paradise.
Oh, looking from some heavenly hill,   400
   Or from the shade of saintly palms,
      Or silver reach of river calms,
Do those large eyes behold me still?
With me one little year ago:—

The chill weight of the winter snow
   For months upon her grave has lain;
And now, when summer south-winds blow
   And brier and harebell bloom again,
I tread the pleasant paths we trod,
I see the violet-sprinkled sod   410
Whereon she leaned, too frail and weak
The hillside flowers she loved to seek,
Yet following me wher'er I went
With dark eyes full of love's content.
The birds are glad; the brier-rose fills
The air with sweetness; all the hills
Stretch green to June's unclouded sky;
But still I wait with ear and eye
For something gone which should be nigh,
A loss in all familiar things,   420
In flower that blooms, and bird that sings.
And yet, dear heart! remembering thee,
   Am I not richer than of old?
Safe in thy immortality,
   What change can reach the wealth I hold?
   What chance can mar the pearl and gold
Thy love hath left in trust with me?
And while in life's late afternoon,
   Where cool and long the shadows grow,
I walk to meet the night that soon   430
   Shall shape and shadow overflow,
I cannot feel that thou art far,
Since near at need the angels are;
And when the sunset gates unbar,
   Shall I not see thee waiting stand,
And, white against the evening star,
   The welcome of thy beckoning hand?

Brisk wielder of the birch and rule,
The master of the district school
Held at the fire his favored place,   440
Its warm glow lit a laughing face
Fresh-hued and fair, where scarce appeared
The uncertain prophecy of beard.
He teased the mitten-blinded cat,
Played cross-pins on my uncle's hat,
Sang songs, and told us what befalls
In classic Dartmouth's college halls.
Born the wild Northern hills among,
From whence his yeoman father wrung
By patient toil subsistence scant,   450
Not competence and yet not want,
He early gained the power to pay
His cheerful, self-reliant way;
Could doff at ease his scholar's gown
To peddle wares from town to town;
Or through the long vacation's reach
In lonely lowland districts teach,
Where all the droll experience found

At stranger hearths in boarding round,
The moonlit skater's keen delight,   460
The sleigh-drive through the frosty night,
The rustic-party, with its rough
Accompaniment of blind-man's-buff,
And whirling-plate, and forfeits paid,
His winter task a pastime made.
Happy the snow-locked homes wherein
He tuned his merry violin,
Or played the athlete in the barn,
Or held the good dame's winding-yarn,
Or mirth-provoking versions told   470
Of classic legends rare and old,
Wherein the scenes of Greece and Rome
Had all the commonplace of home,
And little seemed at best the odds
'Twixt Yankee pedlers and old gods;
Where Pindus-born Arachthus took
The guise of any grist-mill brook,
And dread Olympus at his will
Became a huckleberry hill.

A careless boy that night he seemed;   480
   But at his desk he had the look
And air of one who wisely schemed,
   And hostage from the future took
   In trainèd thought and lore of book.
Large-brained, clear-eyed, of such as he
Shall Freedom's young apostles be,
Who, following in War's bloody trail,
Shall every lingering wrong assail;
All chains from limb and spirit strike,
Uplift the black and white alike;   490
Scatter before their swift advance
The darkness and the ignorance,
The pride, the lust, the squalid sloth,
Which nurtured Treason's monstrous growth,
Made murder pastime, and the hell
Of prison-torture possible;
The cruel lie of caste refute,
Old forms remould, and substitute
For Slavery's lash the freeman's will,
For blind routine, wise-handed skill;   500
A school-house plant on every hill,
Stretching in radiate nerve-lines thence
The quick wires of intelligence;
Till North and South together brought
Shall own the same electric thought,
In peace a common flag salute,
And, side by side in labor's free
And unresentful rivalry,
Harvest the fields wherein they fought.

Another guest that winter night   510
Flashed back from lustrous eyes the light.

Unmarked by time, and yet not young,
The honeyed music of her tongue
And words of meekness scarcely told
A nature passionate and bold,
Strong, self-concentred, spurning guide,
Its milder features dwarfed beside
Her unbent will's majestic pride.
She sat among us, at the best,
A not unfeared, half-welcome guest,   520
Rebuking with her cultured phrase
Our homeliness of words and ways.
A certain pard-like, treacherous grace
Swayed the lithe limbs and dropped the lash,
Lent the white teeth their dazzling flash;
And under low brows, black with night,
Rayed out at times a dangerous light;
The sharp heat-lightnings of her face
Presaging ill to him whom Fate
Condemned to share her love or hate.   530
A woman tropical, intense
In thought and act, in soul and sense,
She blended in a like degree
The vixen and the devotee,
Revealing with each freak or feint
    The temper of Petruchio's Kate,
The raptures of Siena's saint.
Her tapering hand and rounded wrist
Had facile power to form a fist;
The warm, dark languish of her eyes   540
Was never safe from wrath's surprise.
Brows saintly calm and lips devout
Knew every change of scowl and pout;
And the sweet voice had notes more high
And shrill for social battle-cry.

Since then what old cathedral town
Has missed her pilgrim staff and gown,
What convent-gate has held its lock
Against the challenge of her knock!
Through Smyrna's plague-hushed thorough-
    fares,   550
Up sea-set Malta's rocky stairs,
Gray olive slopes of hills that hem
Thy tombs and shrines, Jerusalem,
Or startling on her desert throne
The crazy Queen of Lebanon
With claims fantastic as her own,
Her tireless feet have held their way;
And still, unrestful, bowed, and gray,
She watches under Eastern skies,
    With hope each day renewed and fresh,   560
    The Lord's quick coming in the flesh,
Whereof she dreams and prophesies!

Where'er her troubled path may be,
    The Lord's sweet pity with her go!

The outward wayward life we see,
    The hidden springs we may not know.
Nor is it given us to discern
    What threads the fatal sisters spun,
    Through what ancestral years has run
The sorrow with the woman born,   570
What forged her cruel chain of moods,
What set her feet in solitudes,
    And held the love within her mute,
What mingled madness in the blood,
    A life-long discord and annoy,
    Water of tears with oil of joy,
And hid within the folded bud
    Perversities of flower and fruit.
It is not ours to separate
The tangled skein of will and fate,   580
To show what metes and bounds should stand
Upon the soul's debatable land,
And between choice and Providence
Divide the circle of events;
But He who knows our frame is just,
Merciful and compassionate,
And full of sweet assurances
And hope for all the language is,
That He remembereth we are dust!

At last the great logs, crumbling low,   590
Sent out a dull and duller glow,
The bull's-eye watch that hung in view,
Ticking its weary circuit through,
Pointed with mutely warning sign
Its black hand to the hour of nine.
That sign the pleasant circle broke:
My uncle ceased his pipe to smoke,
Knocked from its bowl the refuse gray,
And laid it tenderly away;
Then roused himself to safely cover   600
The dull red brands with ashes over.
And while, with care, our mother laid
The work aside, her steps she stayed
One moment, seeking to express
Her grateful sense of happiness
For food and shelter, warmth and health,
And love's contentment more than wealth,
With simple wishes (not the weak,
Vain prayers which no fulfilment seek,
But such as warm the generous heart,   610
O'er-prompt to do with Heaven its part)
That none might lack, that bitter night,
For bread and clothing, warmth and light.

Within our beds awhile we heard
The wind that round the gables roared,
With now and then a ruder shock,
Which made our very bedsteads rock.

We heard the loosened clapboards tost,
The board-nails snapping in the frost;
And on us, through the unplastered wall,   620
Felt the light sifted snow-flakes fall.
But sleep stole on, as sleep will do
When hearts are light and life is new;
Faint and more faint the murmurs grew,
Till in the summer-land of dreams
They softened to the sound of streams,
Low stir of leaves, and dip of oars,
And lapsing waves on quiet shores.

Next morn we wakened with the shout
Of merry voices high and clear;   630
And saw the teamsters drawing near
To break the drifted highways out.
Down the long hillside treading slow
We saw the half-buried oxen go,
Shaking the snow from heads uptost,
Their straining nostrils white with frost.
Before our door the straggling train
Drew up, an added team to gain.
The elders threshed their hands a-cold,
   Passed, with the cider-mug, their jokes   640
   From lip to lip; the younger folks
Down the loose snow-banks, wrestling, rolled,
Then toiled again the cavalcade
   O'er windy hill, through clogged ravine,
   And woodland paths that wound between
Low drooping pine-boughs winter-weighed.
From every barn a team afoot,
At every house a new recruit,
Where, drawn by Nature's subtlest law,
Haply the watchful young men saw   650
Sweet doorway pictures of the curls
And curious eyes of merry girls,
Lifting their hands in mock defence
Against the snow-ball's compliments,
And reading in each missive tost
The charm with Eden never lost.

We heard once more the sleigh-bells' sound;
   And, following where the teamsters led,
The wise old Doctor went his round,
Just pausing at our door to say,   660
In the brief autocratic way
Of one who, prompt at Duty's call,
Was free to urge her claim on all,
   That some poor neighbor sick abed
At night our mother's aid would need.
For, one in generous thought and deed,
   What mattered in the sufferer's sight
   The Quaker matron's inward light,
The Doctor's mail of Calvin's creed?

All hearts confess the saints elect   670
   Who, twain in faith, in love agree,
And melt not in an acid sect
   The Christian pearl of charity!

So days went on: a week had passed
Since the great world was heard from last.
The Almanac we studied o'er,
Read and reread our little store
Of books and pamphlets, scarce a score;
One harmless novel, mostly hid
From younger eyes, a book forbid,   680
And poetry, (or good or bad,
A single book was all we had,)
Where Ellwood's meek, drab-skirted Muse,
   A stranger to the heathen Nine,
   Sang, with a somewhat nasal whine,
The wars of David and the Jews.
At last the floundering carrier bore
The village paper to our door.
Lo! broadening outward as we read,
To warmer zones the horizon spread;   690
In panoramic length unrolled
We saw the marvels that it told.
Before us passed the painted Creeks,
   And daft McGregor on his raids
   In Costa Rica's everglades.
And up Taygetos winding slow
Rode Ypsilanti's Mainote Greeks,
A Turk's head at each saddle-bow!
Welcome to us its week-old news,
Its corner for the rustic Muse,   700
   Its monthly gauge of snow and rain,
Its record, mingling in a breath
The wedding bell and dirge of death:
Jest, anecdote, and love-lorn tale,
The latest culprit sent to jail;
Its hue and cry of stolen and lost,
Its vendue sales and goods at cost,
   And traffic calling loud for gain.
We felt the stir of hall and street,
The pulse of life that round us beat;   710
The chill embargo of the snow
Was melted in the genial glow;
Wide swung again our ice-locked door,
And all the world was ours once more!

Clasp, Angel of the backward look
   And folded wings of ashen gray
   And voice of echoes far away,
The brazen covers of thy book;
The weird palimpsest old and vast,
Wherein thou hid'st the spectral past;   720
Where, closely mingling, pale and glow
The characters of joy and woe;

The monographs of outlived years,
Or smile-illumed or dim with tears,
    Green hills of life that slope to death,
And haunts of home, whose vistaed trees
Shade off to mournful cypresses
    With the white amaranths underneath.
Even while I look, I can but heed
    The restless sands' incessant fall,   730
Importunate hours that hours succeed,
Each clamorous with its own sharp need,
    And duty keeping pace with all.
Shut down and clasp the heavy lids;
I hear again the voice that bids
The dreamer leave his dream midway
For larger hopes and graver fears:
Life greatens in these later years,
The century's aloe flowers to-day!

Yet, haply, in some lull of life,   740
Some Truce of God which breaks its strife,
The worldling's eyes shall gather dew,
    Dreaming in throngful city ways
Of winter joys his boyhood knew;
And dear and early friends—the few
Who yet remain—shall pause to view
    These Flemish pictures of old days;
Sit with me by the homestead hearth,
And stretch the hands of memory forth
    To warm them at the wood-fire's blaze! 750
And thanks untraced to lips unknown
Shall greet me like the odors blown
From unseen meadows newly mown,
Or lilies floating in some pond,
Wood-fringed, the wayside gaze beyond;
The traveller owns the grateful sense
Of sweetness near, he knows not whence,
And, pausing, takes with forehead bare
The benediction of the air.
1865   1866

A MYSTERY

The river hemmed with leaning trees
    Wound through its meadows green;
A low, blue line of mountains showed
    The open pines between.

One sharp, tall peak above them all
    Clear into sunlight sprang:

I saw the river of my dreams,
    The mountain that I sang!

No clue of memory led me on,
    But well the ways I knew;   10
A feeling of familiar things
    With every footstep grew.

Not otherwise above its crag
    Could lean the blasted pine;
Not otherwise the maple hold
    Aloft its red ensign.

So up the long and shorn foot-hills
    The mountain road should creep;
So, green and low, the meadow fold
    Its red-haired kine asleep.   20

The river wound as it should wind;
    Their place the mountains took;
The white torn fringes of their clouds
    Wore no unwonted look.

Yet ne'er before that river's rim
    Was pressed by feet of mine,
Never before mine eyes had crossed
    That broken mountain line.

A presence, strange at once and known,
    Walked with me as my guide;   30
The skirts of some forgotten life
    Trailed noiseless at my side.

Was it a dim-remembered dream?
    Or glimpse through æons old?
The secret which the mountains kept
    The river never told.

But from the vision ere it passed
    A tender hope I drew,
And, pleasant as a dawn of spring,
    The thought within me grew,   40

That love would temper every change,
    And soften all surprise,
And, misty with the dreams of earth,
    The hills of Heaven arise.
1873   1873

» » « «

HENRY WADSWORTH LONGFELLOW

1807–1882

DURING HIS LIFETIME a comfortable income and an international popularity, which made him even more famous than Tennyson, insulated Longfellow from what little adverse criticism of his poetry entered his study. Since his death the acid of time has eaten away at the 650 pages of his collected verse until there is little which we can honestly place beside the best of Emerson and Thoreau and of his most impertinent critic, Poe. But the modern critic's task is by no means done when he has selected that best which remains and has analyzed the defects of the rest. Longfellow's popularity is a phenomenon of our culture, and of mid-nineteenth century culture in general, and must be accounted for.

Longfellow's energetic father, a successful lawyer of Portland, Maine, intended that his son should follow his profession. Young Longfellow, by the time he was a senior at Bowdoin, had decided otherwise. In a letter home he wrote boldly: "The fact is . . . I most eagerly aspire after future eminence in literature, my whole soul burns most ardently after it, and every earthly thought centers in it. There may be something visionary in *this*, but I flatter myself, that I have prudence enough to keep my enthusiasm from defeating its own object by too great haste." Both father and son knew how impractical a "decision" (at the age of seventeen) this was. No poet or novelist in America had ever supported himself entirely by creative writing. But the young man knew that America would have no literature until men with talent made it their exclusive occupation. "Poetry with us has never yet been anything but a pastime," he told the audience at his commencement the next year, in his oration on "Our Native Writers." Fortunately father and son did not have to break over the momentous question. Bowdoin needed a Professor of Modern Languages, and the post was offered young Longfellow on the condition that he prepare for his task by studying abroad.

The next three years in France, Spain, Italy, and Germany were hardly spent in the ways intended by Stephen Longfellow and the eminent scholar George Ticknor, recently returned from his European studies and now a professor at Harvard, whose advice had been asked. In hours he should have passed studying the literatures and institutions of the countries he visited, in hearing lectures and meeting men of affairs, Longfellow was idling through the countryside, playing the dandy in Paris, and reading such poets as he fancied. The fact is, that though he later performed his duties faithfully as a professor of modern languages at Bowdoin (1829–1833) and at Harvard (1836–1854) and did his bewildered best to prepare for these tasks by two sojourns in Europe, he had no real calling to be a scholar. The struggle to be free would culminate in his resignation from his Harvard chair in 1854.

Before that date Longfellow had published constantly in the magazines, chiefly belletristic articles, reviews, and verse translations. A novel, *Hyperion*, concealing the anguished story of his temporarily unsuccessful courtship of Frances Appleton, appeared in 1839. This was also the year of his first collection of verse, *Voices of the Night*. *Evangeline* was issued in 1847; *Hiawatha* the year after his resignation.

When we consider Longfellow's defects as a poet, we note first the significant fact that in his twenties, when many lyricists do their finest work, Longfellow wrote only a half-dozen pieces. To be a poet after thirty requires qualities of mind which he lacked: intellectual passion, a sense of the past, and a knowledge of mankind. For one who had read so much, Longfellow was a singularly ignorant man. Nature was little more than a collection of metaphors to him. The new science troubled him not at all. In history he glanced at the picturesque and the romantic. Though he lived in dangerous times when revolutions exploded in Europe and civil war rent America, there is scarcely a repercussion of these events in his poetry. The result of Longfellow's failure to establish contact with what is reality to most men was more serious than the mere limitation of his subjects to legend and the permissible emotions. A poet's vitality is revealed by his imagery, and since Longfellow, isolated in his dreamworld, could summon up only time-worn metaphors, his poetry is anemic. It seldom surprises us with revelations from the poet's larger world.

Why, then, did the Emperor of Brazil translate "Robert of Sicily" and why is it that "Hiawatha" can be read in Latin as well as nearly all the modern languages? As far as translation is concerned, one must remember that Longfellow translates easily. There are no obscurities of thought, no diffused images, no subtle poetic ambiguities or personal symbols to vex the translator. The popularity of Longfellow is readily understood when one recalls that he flourished in the heyday of Tom Moore and the gift books, *The Moss-Rose* and *The Opal*. He was a more masculine Lydia Sigourney. The taste which praised Mrs. Browning's "Lady Geraldine's Courtship" and Tennyson's *Princess* elevated *Evangeline* above Goethe's *Hermann und Dorothea*.

Longfellow will not disappear below the horizon. As a significant figure he cannot. As one who fought for the poet's place in American life he should not. Moreover there is in his work a residue of real poetry, as the following selections prove. Strange irony that the most revered poet of his time should confess revealingly, in a letter to his sister: "But with me, all deep impressions are silent ones." In the occasional instances when he violated this reticence, which was his inheritance and which the convention of the day imposed, he showed a genuine poetic intensity.

L. S. Livingston, *A Bibliography of the First Editions in Book Form of the Writings of Henry Wadsworth Longfellow*, New York, 1908.
The Works of Henry Wadsworth Longfellow, Samuel Longfellow, ed., 14 vols., Boston, 1886–1891. (Contains S. Longfellow's 3 vol. *Life* of H. W. Longfellow.)
The Complete Poetical Works of Henry Wadsworth Longfellow (Cambridge Edition), Boston, 1893.
Henry Wadsworth Longfellow, Representative Selections (American Writers Series), New York, 1934.
S. Longfellow, *Life of Henry W. Longfellow*, 3 vols., Boston, 1891.
Lawrance Thompson, *Young Longfellow*, New York, 1938.
E. C. Wagenknecht, *Longfellow; A Full Length Portrait*, New York, 1955.

A PSALM OF LIFE

What the Heart of the Young Man Said to the Psalmist

Tell me not, in mournful numbers,
　Life is but an empty dream!—
For the soul is dead that slumbers,
　And things are not what they seem.

Life is real! Life is earnest!
　And the grave is not its goal;
Dust thou art, to dust returnest,
　Was not spoken of the soul.

Not enjoyment, and not sorrow,
　Is our destined end or way;　　10
But to act, that each to-morrow
　Find us farther than to-day.

Art is long, and Time is fleeting,
　And our hearts, though stout and brave,
Still, like muffled drums, are beating
　Funeral marches to the grave.

In the world's broad field of battle,
　In the bivouac of Life,
Be not like dumb, driven cattle!
　Be a hero in the strife!　　20

Trust no Future, howe'er pleasant!
　　Let the dead Past bury its dead!
Act,—act in the living Present!
　　Heart within, and God o'erhead!

Lives of great men all remind us
　　We can make our lives sublime,
And, departing, leave behind us
　　Footprints on the sands of time;

Footprints, that perhaps another,
　　Sailing o'er life's solemn main, 　　　30
A forlorn and shipwrecked brother,
　　Seeing, shall take heart again.

Let us, then, be up and doing,
　　With a heart for any fate;
Still achieving, still pursuing,
　　Learn to labor and to wait.
1838 　　　　　　　　　　　　　　　1839

THE BELEAGUERED CITY [1]

I have read, in some old, marvellous tale,
　　Some legend strange and vague,
That a midnight host of spectres pale
　　Beleaguered the walls of Prague.

Beside the Moldau's rushing stream,
　　With the wan moon overhead,
There stood, as in an awful dream,
　　The army of the dead.

White as a sea-fog, landward bound,
　　The spectral camp was seen, 　　　10
And, with a sorrowful, deep sound,
　　The river flowed between.

No other voice nor sound was there,
　　No drum, nor sentry's pace;
The mist-like banners clasped the air
　　As clouds with clouds embrace.

But when the old cathedral bell
　　Proclaimed the morning prayer,
The white pavilions rose and fell
　　On the alarmèd air. 　　　　　　20

Down the broad valley fast and far
　　The troubled army fled;
Up rose the glorious morning star,
　　The ghastly host was dead.

I have read, in the marvellous heart of man,
　　That strange and mystic scroll,
That an army of phantoms vast and wan
　　Beleaguer the human soul.

Encamped beside Life's rushing stream,
　　In Fancy's misty light, 　　　　　30
Gigantic shapes and shadows gleam
　　Portentous through the night.

Upon its midnight battle-ground
　　The spectral camp is seen,
And, with a sorrowful, deep sound,
　　Flows the River of Life between.

No other voice nor sound is there,
　　In the army of the grave;
No other challenge breaks the air,
　　But the rushing of Life's wave. 　　40

And when the solemn and deep church-bell
　　Entreats the soul to pray,
The midnight phantoms feel the spell,
　　The shadows sweep away.

Down the broad Vale of Tears afar
　　The spectral camp is fled;
Faith shineth as a morning star,
　　Our ghastly fears are dead.
1839 　　　　　　　　　　　　　　1839

THE SKELETON IN ARMOR [2]

"Speak! speak! thou fearful guest!
Who, with thy hollow breast
Still in rude armor drest,
　　Comest to daunt me!
Wrapt not in Eastern balms,
But with thy fleshless palms
Stretched, as if asking alms,
　　Why dost thou haunt me?"

Then, from those cavernous eyes
Pale flashes seemed to rise, 　　　10
As when the Northern skies
　　Gleam in December;
And, like the water's flow
Under December's snow,
Came a dull voice of woe
　　From the hearts chamber.

[1] Longfellow's idea for this poem came from a note in Scott's *Border Minstrelsy:* "Similar to this was the *Nacht Lager*, a midnight camp, which seemed nightly to beleaguer the walls of Prague, but which disappeared at the recitation of the magical words, *Vezelé, Vezelé, ho! ho! ho!*"

[2] This ballad was suggested to me while riding on the seashore at Newport. A year or two previous a skeleton had been dug up at Fall River clad in broken and corroded armor; and the idea occurred to me of connecting it with the Round Tower at Newport. . . . [Longfellow's note.]

"I was a Viking old!
My deeds, though manifold,
No Skald in song has told,
   No Saga taught thee!   20
Take heed that in thy verse
Thou dost the tale rehearse,
Else dread a dead man's curse;
   For this I sought thee.

"Far in the Northern Land,
By the wild Baltic's strand,
I, with my childish hand,
   Tamed the gerfalcon;
And, with my skates fast-bound,
Skimmed the half-frozen Sound,   30
That the poor whimpering hound
   Trembled to walk on.

"Oft to his frozen lair
Tracked I the grisly bear,
While from my path the hare
   Fled like a shadow;
Oft through the forest dark
Followed the were-wolf's bark,
Until the soaring lark
   Sang from the meadow.   40

"But when I older grew,
Joining a corsair's crew,
O'er the dark sea I flew
   With the marauders.
Wild was the life we led;
Many the souls that sped,
Many the hearts that bled,
   By our stern orders.

"Many a wassail-bout
Wore the long winter out;   50
Often our midnight shout
   Set the cocks crowing,
As we the Berserk's tale
Measured in cups of ale,
Draining the oaken pail,
   Filled to o'erflowing.

"Once as I told in glee
Tales of the stormy sea,
Soft eyes did gaze on me,
   Burning yet tender;   60
And as the white stars shine
On the dark Norway pine,
On that dark heart of mine
   Fell their soft splendor.

"I wooed the blue-eyed maid,
Yielding, yet half afraid,

And in the forest's shade
   Our vows were plighted.
Under its loosened vest
Fluttered her little breast,   70
Like birds within their nest
   By the hawk frighted.

"Bright in her father's hall
Shields gleamed upon the wall,
Loud sang the minstrels all,
   Chanting his glory;
When of old Hildebrand
I asked his daughter's hand,
Mute did the minstrels stand
   To hear my story.   80

"While the brown ale he quaffed,
Loud then the champion laughed,
And as the wind-gusts waft
   The sea-foam brightly,
So the loud laugh of scorn
Out of those lips unshorn,
From the deep drinking-horn
   Blew the foam lightly.

"She was a Prince's child,
I but a Viking wild,   90
And though she blushed and smiled,
   I was discarded!
Should not the dove so white
Follow the sea-mew's flight,
Why did they leave that night
   Her nest unguarded?

"Scarce had I put to sea,
Bearing the maid with me,
Fairest of all was she
   Among the Norsemen!   100
When on the white sea-strand,
Waving his armèd hand,
Saw we old Hildebrand,
   With twenty horsemen.

"Then launched they to the blast,
Bent like a reed each mast,
Yet we were gaining fast,
   When the wind failed us;
And with a sudden flaw
Came round the gusty Skaw,   110
So that our foe we saw
   Laugh as he hailed us.

"And as to catch the gale
Round veered the flapping sail,
'Death!' was the helmsman's hail,
   'Death without quarter!'

Midships with iron keel
Struck we her ribs of steel;
Down her black hulk did reel
   Through the black water!   120

"As with his wings aslant,
Sails the fierce cormorant,
Seeking some rocky haunt,
   With his prey laden,—
So toward the open main,
Beating to sea again,
Through the wild hurricane,
   Bore I the maiden.

"Three weeks we westward bore,
And when the storm was o'er,   130
Cloud-like we saw the shore
   Stretching to leeward;
There for my lady's bower
Built I the lofty tower,
Which, to this very hour,
   Stands looking seaward.

"There lived we many years;
Time dried the maiden's tears;
She had forgot her fears,
   She was a mother;   140
Death closed her mild blue eyes,
Under that tower she lies;
Ne'er shall the sun arise
   On such another!

"Still grew my bosom then,
Still as a stagnant fen!
Hateful to me were men,
   The sunlight hateful!
In the vast forest here,
Clad in my warlike gear,   150
Fell I upon my spear,
   Oh, death was grateful!

"Thus, seamed with many scars,
Bursting these prison bars
Up to its native stars
   My soul ascended!
There from the flowing bowl
Deep drinks the warrior's soul,
Skoal! to the Northland! *skoal!*"
   Thus the tale ended.   160

1840   1841

NUREMBERG

In the valley of the Pegnitz, where across broad
   meadow-lands

Rise the blue Franconian mountains, Nuremberg, the ancient, stands.

Quaint old town of toil and traffic, quaint old
   town of art and song,
Memories haunt thy pointed gables, like the
   rooks that round them throng:

Memories of the Middle Ages, when the emperors, rough and bold,
Had their dwelling in thy castle, time-defying,
   centuries old;

And thy brave and thrifty burghers boasted,
   in their uncouth rhyme,
That their great imperial city stretched its
   hand through every clime.

In the court-yard of the castle, bound with
   many an iron band,
Stands the mighty linden planted by Queen
   Cunigunde's hand;   10

On the square the oriel window, where in old
   heroic days
Sat the poet Melchior singing Kaiser Maxi-
   milian's praise,

Everywhere I see around me rise the wondrous
   world of Art:
Fountains wrought with richest sculpture
   standing in the common mart;

And above cathedral doorways saints and
   bishops carved in stone,
By a former age commissioned as apostles to
   our own.

In the church of sainted Sebald sleeps enshrined his holy dust,
And in bronze the Twelve Apostles guard
   from age to age their trust;

In the church of sainted Lawrence stands a
   pix of sculpture rare,
Like the foamy sheaf of fountains, rising
   through the painted air.   20

Here, when Art was still religion, with a simple, reverent heart,
Lived and labored Albrecht Dürer, the Evangelist of Art;

Hence in silence and in sorrow, toiling still with
   busy hand,

Like an emigrant he wandered, seeking for the
    Better Land.

Emigravit is the inscription on the tombstone
    where he lies;
Dead he is not, but departed,—for the artist
    never dies.

Fairer seems the ancient city, and the sunshine
    seems more fair,
That he once has trod its pavement, that he
    once has breathed its air!

Through these streets so broad and stately,
    these obscure and dismal lanes,
Walked of yore the Mastersingers, chanting
    rude poetic strains.   30

From remote and sunless suburbs came they to
    the friendly guild,
Building nests in Fame's great temple, as in
    spouts the swallows build.

As the weaver plied the shuttle, wove he too
    the mystic rhyme,
And the smith his iron measures hammered to
    the anvil's chime;

Thanking God, whose boundless wisdom makes
    the flowers of poesy bloom
In the forge's dust and cinders, in the tissues
    of the loom.

Here Hans Sachs, the cobbler-poet, laureate of
    the gentle craft,
Wisest of the Twelve Wise Masters, in huge
    folios sang and laughed.

But his house is now an ale-house, with a nicely
    sanded floor,
And a garland in the window, and his face
    above the door;   40

Painted by some humble artist, as in Adam
    Puschman's song,
As the old man gray and dove-like, with his
    great beard white and long.

And at night the swart mechanic comes to
    drown his cark and care,
Quaffing ale from pewter tankards, in the mas-
    ter's antique chair.

Vanished is the ancient splendor, and before
    my dreamy eye

Wave these mingled shapes and figures, like a
    faded tapestry.

Not thy Councils, not thy Kaisers, win for thee
    the world's regard;
But thy painter, Albrecht Dürer, and Hans
    Sachs thy cobbler bard.

Thus, O Nuremberg, a wanderer from a region
    far away,
As he paced thy streets and court-yards, sang
    in thought his careless lay: 50

Gathering from the pavement's crevice, as a
    floweret of the soil,
The nobility of labor,—the long pedigree of
    toil.
1844   1844

THE DAY IS DONE

The day is done, and the darkness
    Falls from the wings of Night,
As a feather is wafted downward
    From an eagle in his flight.

I see the lights of the village
    Gleam through the rain and the mist,
And a feeling of sadness comes o'er me,
    That my soul cannot resist:

A feeling of sadness and longing,
    That is not akin to pain,   10
And resembles sorrow only
    As the mist resembles the rain.

Come, read to me some poem,
    Some simple and heartfelt lay,
That shall soothe this restless feeling,
    And banish the thoughts of day.

Not from the grand old masters,
    Not from the bards sublime,
Whose distant footsteps echo
    Through the corridors of Time.   20

For, like strains of martial music,
    Their mighty thoughts suggest
Life's endless toil and endeavor;
    And to-night I long for rest.

Read from some humbler poet,
    Whose songs gushed from his heart,
As showers from the clouds of summer,
    Or tears from the eyelids start;

Who, through long days of labor,
    And nights devoid of ease,   *30*
Still heard in his soul the music
    Of wonderful melodies.

Such songs have power to quiet
    The restless pulse of care,
And come like the benediction
    That follows after prayer.

Then read from the treasured volume
    The poem of thy choice,
And lend to the rhyme of the poet
    The beauty of thy voice.   *40*

And the night shall be filled with music,
    And the cares that infest the day,
Shall fold their tents, like the Arabs,
    And as silently steal away.
1844   1844

THE FIRE OF DRIFT-WOOD

Devereux Farm, near Marblehead

We sat within the farm-house old,
    Whose windows, looking o'er the bay,
Gave to the sea-breeze damp and cold,
    An easy entrance, night and day.

Not far away we saw the port,
    The strange, old-fashioned, silent town,
The lighthouse, the dismantled fort,
    The wooden houses, quaint and brown.

We sat and talked until the night,
    Descending, filled the little room: *10*
Our faces faded from the sight,
    Our voices only broke the gloom.

We spake of many a vanished scene,
    Of what we once had thought and said,
Of what had been, and might have been,
    And who was changed, and who was dead;

And all that fills the hearts of friends,
    When first they feel, with secret pain,
Their lives thenceforth have separate ends,
    And never can be one again;   *20*

The first slight swerving of the heart,
    That words are powerless to express,
And leave it still unsaid in part,
    Or say it in too great excess.

The very tones in which we spake
    Had something strange, I could but mark;
The leaves of memory seemed to make
    A mournful rustling in the dark.

Oft died the words upon our lips,
    As suddenly, from out the fire   *30*
Built of the wreck of stranded ships,
    The flames would leap and then expire.

And, as their splendor flashed and failed,
    We thought of wrecks upon the main,
Of ships dismasted, that were hailed
    And sent no answer back again.

The windows, rattling in their frames,
    The ocean, roaring up the beach,
The gusty blast, the bickering flames,
    All mingled vaguely in our speech;   *40*

Until they made themselves a part
    Of fancies floating through the brain,
The long-lost ventures of the heart,
    That send no answers back again.

O flames that glowed! O hearts that yearned!
    They were indeed too much akin,
The drift-wood fire without that burned,
    The thoughts that burned and glowed within.
1846   1848

IN THE CHURCHYARD
AT CAMBRIDGE

In the village churchyard she lies,
Dust is in her beautiful eyes,
    No more she breathes, nor feels, nor stirs;
At her feet and at her head
Lies a slave to attend the dead,
    But their dust is white as hers.

Was she, a lady of high degree,
So much in love with the vanity
    And foolish pomp of this world of ours?
Or was it Christian charity,   *10*
And lowliness, and humility,
    The richest and rarest of all dowers?

Who shall tell us? No one speaks;
No color shoots into those cheeks,
    Either of anger or of pride,
At the rude question we have asked;
Nor will the mystery be unmasked
    By those who are sleeping at her side.

Hereafter?—And do you think to look
On the terrible pages of that Book   20
    To find her failings, faults, and errors?
Ah, you will then have other cares,
In your own shortcomings and despairs,
    In your own secret sins and terrors!
1851

THE WARDEN OF THE
CINQUE PORTS [3]

A mist was driving down the British Channel,
    The day was just begun,
And through the window-panes, on floor and
        panel,
    Streamed the red autumn sun.

It glanced on flowing flag and rippling pennon,
    And the white sails of ships;
And, from the frowning rampart, the black can-
        non
    Hailed it with feverish lips.

Sandwich and Romney, Hastings, Hithe, and
        Dover
    Were all alert that day,   10
To see the French war-steamers speeding over,
    When the fog cleared away.

Sullen and silent, and like couchant lions,
    Their cannon, through the night,
Holding their breath, had watched, in grim de-
        fiance,
    The sea-coast opposite.

And now they roared at drum-beat from their
        stations
    On every citadel;
Each answering each, with morning salutations,
    That all was well.   20

And down the coast, all taking up the burden,
    Replied the distant forts,
As if to summon from his sleep the Warden
    And Lord of the Cinque Ports.

Him shall no sunshine from the fields of azure,
    No drum-beat from the wall,
No morning gun from the black fort's embra-
        sure,
    Awaken with its call!

[3] Warden of the Cinque Ports was one of the many titles held by the Duke of Wellington, whose death (in 1852) Longfellow commemorated in this poem.

No more, surveying with an eye impartial
    The long line of the coast,   30
Shall the gaunt figure of the old Field Marshal
    Be seen upon his post!

For in the night, unseen, a single warrior,
    In sombre harness mailed,
Dreaded of man, and surnamed the Destroyer,
    The rampart wall had scaled.

He passed into the chamber of the sleeper,
    The dark and silent room,
And as he entered, darker grew, and deeper,
    The silence and the gloom.   40

He did not pause to parley or dissemble,
    But smote the Warden hoar;
Ah! what a blow! that made all England trem-
        ble
    And groan from shore to shore.

Meanwhile, without, the surly cannon waited,
    The sun rose bright o'erhead;
Nothing in Nature's aspect intimated
    That a great man was dead.
1852   1852

THE JEWISH CEMETERY
AT NEWPORT

How strange it seems! These Hebrews in their
        graves,
    Close by the street of this fair seaport town,
Silent beside the never-silent waves,
    At rest in all this moving up and down!

The trees are white with dust, that o'er their
        sleep
    Wave their broad curtains in the south-wind's
        breath,
While underneath these leafy tents they keep
    The long, mysterious Exodus of Death.   8

And these sepulchral stones, so old and brown,
    That pave with level flags their burial-place,
Seem like the tablets of the Law, thrown down
    And broken by Moses at the mountain's base.

The very names recorded here are strange,
    Of foreign accent, and of different climes;
Alvares and Rivera interchange
    With Abraham and Jacob of old times.

"Blessed be God, for he created Death!"
    The mourners said, "and Death is rest and
        peace";
Then added, in the certainty of faith,
    "And giveth Life that nevermore shall cease."

Close are the portals of their Synagogue,   21
    No Psalms of David now the silence break,
No Rabbi reads the ancient Decalogue
    In the grand dialect the Prophets spake.

Gone are the living, but the dead remain,
    And not neglected; for a hand unseen,
Scattering its bounty, like a summer rain,
    Still keeps their graves and their remem-
        brance green.

How came they here? What burst of Christian
        hate,
    What persecution, merciless and blind,   30
Drove o'er the sea—that desert desolate—
    These Ishmaels and Hagars of mankind?

They lived in narrow streets and lanes obscure,
    Ghetto and Judenstrass, in mirk and mire;
Taught in the school of patience to endure
    The life of anguish and the death of fire.

All their lives long, with the unleavened bread
    And bitter herbs of exile and its fears,
The wasting famine of the heart they fed,
    And slaked its thirst with marah of their
        tears.   40

Anathema maranatha! was the cry
    That rang from town to town, from street to
        street;
At every gate the accursed Mordecai
    Was mocked and jeered, and spurned by
        Christian feet.

Pride and humiliation hand in hand
    Walked with them through the world
        where'er they went;
Trampled and beaten were they as the sand,
    And yet unshaken as the continent.

For in the background figures vague and vast
    Of patriarchs and of prophets rose sublime,
And all the great traditions of the Past   51
    They saw reflected in the coming time.

And thus forever with reverted look
    The mystic volume of the world they read,
Spelling it backward, like a Hebrew book,
    Till life became a Legend of the Dead.

But ah! what once has been shall be no more!
    The groaning earth in travail and in pain
Brings forth its races, but does not restore,
    And the dead nations never rise again.   60
1852   1852

THE TWO ANGELS

Two angels, one of Life and one of Death,
    Passed o'er our village as the morning broke;
The dawn was on their faces, and beneath,
    The sombre houses hearsed with plumes of
        smoke.

Their attitude and aspect were the same,
    Alike their features and their robes of white;
But one was crowned with amaranth, as with
        flame,
    And one with asphodels, like flakes of light.

I saw them pause on their celestial way;
    Then said I, with deep fear and doubt op-
        pressed,   10
"Beat not so loud, my heart, lest thou betray
    The place where thy beloved are at rest!"

And he who wore the crown of asphodels,
    Descending, at my door began to knock,
And my soul sank within me, as in wells
    The waters sink before an earthquake's
        shock.

I recognized the nameless agony,
    The terror and the tremor and the pain,
That oft before had filled or haunted me,
    And now returned with threefold strength
        again.   20

The door I opened to my heavenly guest,
    And listened, for I thought I heard God's
        voice;
And, knowing whatsoe'er He sent was best,
    Dared neither to lament nor to rejoice.

Then with a smile, that filled the house with
        light,
    "My errand is not Death, but Life," he said;
And ere I answered, passing out of sight,
    On his celestial embassy he sped.

'Twas at thy door, O friend! and not at mine,
    The angel with the amaranthine wreath,   30
Pausing, descended, and with voice divine
    Whispered a word that had a sound like
        Death.

Then fell upon the house a sudden gloom,
    A shadow on those features fair and thin;
And softly, from that hushed and darkened
        room,
    Two angels issued, where but one went in.

All is of God! If he but wave his hand,
    The mists collect, the rain falls thick and
        loud,
Till, with a smile of light on sea and land,
    Lo! he looks back from the departing cloud.

Angels of Life and Death alike are his;   41
    Without his leave they pass no threshold o'er;
Who, then, would wish or dare, believing this,
    Against his messengers to shut the door?
1854   1854

MY LOST YOUTH

Often I think of the beautiful town [4]
    That is seated by the sea;
Often in thought go up and down
The pleasant streets of that dear old town,
    And my youth comes back to me.
        And a verse of a Lapland song
        Is haunting my memory still:
        "A boy's will is the wind's will,
And the thoughts of youth are long, long
        thoughts."

I can see the shadowy lines of its trees,   10
    And catch, in sudden gleams,
The sheen of the far-surrounding seas,
And islands that were the Hesperides
    Of all my boyish dreams.
        And the burden of that old song,
        It murmurs and whispers still:
        "A boy's will is the wind's will,
And the thoughts of youth are long, long
        thoughts."

I remember the black wharves and the slips,
    And the sea-tides tossing free;   20
And Spanish sailors with bearded lips,
And the beauty and mystery of the ships,
    And the magic of the sea.
        And the voice of that wayward song
        Is singing and saying still:
        "A boy's will is the wind's will,
And the thoughts of youth are long, long
        thoughts."

[4] Portland, Maine.

I remember the bulwarks by the shore,
    And the fort upon the hill;
The sunrise gun, with its hollow roar,   30
The drum-beat repeated o'er and o'er,
    And the bugle wild and shrill.
        And the music of that old song
        Throbs in my memory still:
        "A boy's will is the wind's will,
And the thoughts of youth are long, long
        thoughts."

I remember the sea-fight far away, [5]
    How it thundered o'er the tide!
And the dead captains, as they lay   39
In their graves, o'erlooking the tranquil bay
    Where they in battle died.
        And the sound of that mournful song
        Goes through me with a thrill:
        "A boy's will is the wind's will,
And the thoughts of youth are long, long
        thoughts."

I can see the breezy dome of groves,
    The shadows of Deering's Woods;
And the friendships old and the early loves
Come back with a Sabbath sound, as of doves
    In quiet neighborhoods.   50
        And the verse of that sweet old song,
        It flutters and murmurs still:
        "A boy's will is the wind's will,
And the thoughts of youth are long, long
        thoughts."

I remember the gleams and glooms that dart
    Across the school-boy's brain;
The song and the silence in the heart,
That in part are prophecies, and in part
    Are longings wild and vain.
        And the voice of that fitful song   60
        Sings on, and is never still:
        "A boy's will is the wind's will,
And the thoughts of youth are long, long
        thoughts."

There are things of which I may not speak;
    There are dreams that cannot die;
There are thoughts that make the strong heart
        weak,
And bring a pallor into the cheek,
    And a mist before the eye.
        And the words of that fatal song
        Come over me like a chill: 70
        "A boy's will is the wind's will,

[5] Between the *Enterprise* and *Boxer*, in 1813.

And the thoughts of youth are long, long
  thoughts."

Strange to me now are the forms I meet
  When I visit the dear old town;
But the native air is pure and sweet,
And the trees that o'ershadow each well-known
    street,
  As they balance up and down,
  Are singing the beautiful song,
  Are sighing and whispering still:
  "A boy's will is the wind's will,   80
And the thoughts of youth are long, long
  thoughts."

And Deering's Woods are fresh and fair,
  And with joy that is almost pain
My heart goes back to wander there,
And among the dreams of the days that were,
  I find my lost youth again.
  And the strange and beautiful song,
  The groves are repeating it still:
  "A boy's will is the wind's will,
And the thoughts of youth are long, long
  thoughts."   90
1855   1855

THE CHILDREN'S HOUR

Between the dark and the daylight,
  When the night is beginning to lower,
Comes a pause in the day's occupations,
  That is known as the Children's Hour.

I hear in the chamber above me
  The patter of little feet,
The sound of a door that is opened,
  And voices soft and sweet.

From my study I see in the lamplight,
  Descending the broad hall stair,   10
Grave Alice, and laughing Allegra,
  And Edith with golden hair.

A whisper, and then a silence:
  Yet I know by their merry eyes
They are plotting and planning together
  To take me by surprise.

A sudden rush from the stairway,
  A sudden raid from the hall!
By three doors left unguarded
  They enter my castle wall!   20

They climb up into my turret
  O'er the arms and back of my chair;
If I try to escape, they surround me;
  They seem to be everywhere.

They almost devour me with kisses,
  Their arms about me entwine,
Till I think of the Bishop of Bingen
  In his Mouse-Tower on the Rhine!

Do you think, O blue-eyed banditti,
  Because you have scaled the wall,   30
Such an old mustache as I am
  Is not a match for you all!

I have you fast in my fortress,
  And will not let you depart,
But put you down into the dungeon
  In the round-tower of my heart.

And there will I keep you forever,
  Yes, forever and a day,
Till the walls shall crumble to ruin,
  And moulder in dust away!   40
1859   1859

PAUL REVERE'S RIDE [6]

Listen, my children, and you shall hear
Of the midnight ride of Paul Revere,
On the eighteenth of April, in Seventy-five;
Hardly a man is now alive
Who remembers that famous day and year.

He said to his friend, "If the British march
By land or sea from the town to-night,
Hang a lantern aloft in the belfry arch
Of the North Church tower as a signal light,—
One, if by land, and two, if by sea;   10
And I on the opposite shore will be,
Ready to ride and spread the alarm
Through every Middlesex village and farm,
For the country folk to be up and to arm."

Then he said, "Good-night!" and with muffled
    oar
Silently rowed to the Charlestown shore,
Just as the moon rose over the bay,
Where swinging wide at her moorings lay
The Somerset, British man-of-war;
A phantom ship, with each mast and spar   20
Across the moon like a prison bar,
And a huge black hulk, that was magnified
By its own reflection in the tide.

[6] The first of the *Tales of a Wayside Inn*.

Meanwhile, his friend, through alley and street,
Wanders and watches with eager ears,
Till in the silence around him he hears
The muster of men at the barrack door,
The sound of arms, and the tramp of feet,
And the measured tread of the grenadiers,
Marching down to their boats on the shore.   30

Then he climbed the tower of the Old North
    Church
By the wooden stairs, with stealthy tread,
To the belfry-chamber overhead,
And startled the pigeons from their perch
On the sombre rafters, that round him made
Masses and moving shapes of shade,—
By the trembling ladder, steep and tall,
To the highest window in the wall,
Where he paused to listen and look down
A moment on the roofs of the town,   40
And the moonlight flowing over all.

Beneath, in the churchyard, lay the dead,
In their night-encampment on the hill,
Wrapped in silence so deep and still
That he could hear, like a sentinel's tread,
The watchful night-wind, as it went
Creeping along from tent to tent,
And seeming to whisper, "All is well!"
A moment only he feels the spell
Of the place and the hour, and the secret dread
Of the lonely belfry and the dead;   51
For suddenly all his thoughts are bent
On a shadowy something far away,
Where the river widens to meet the bay,—
A line of black that bends and floats
On the rising tide, like a bridge of boats.

Meanwhile, impatient to mount and ride,
Booted and spurred, with a heavy stride
On the opposite shore walked Paul Revere.
Now he patted his horse's side,   60
Now gazed at the landscape far and near,
Then, impetuous, stamped the earth,
And turned and tightened his saddle-girth;
But mostly he watched with eager search
The belfry-tower of the Old North Church,
As it rose above the graves on the hill,
Lonely and spectral and sombre and still.
And lo! as he looks, on the belfry's height
A glimmer, and then a gleam of light!
He springs to the saddle, the bridle he turns,
But lingers and gazes, till full on his sight   71
A second lamp in the belfry burns!

A hurry of hoofs in a village street,
A shape in the moonlight, a bulk in the dark,
And beneath, from the pebbles, in passing, a
    spark
Struck out by a steed flying fearless and fleet:
That was all! And yet, through the gloom and
    the light,
The fate of a nation was riding that night;
And the spark struck out by that steed, in his
    flight,
Kindled the land into flame with its heat.   80

He has left the village and mounted the steep,
And beneath him, tranquil and broad and deep,
Is the Mystic, meeting the ocean tides;
And under the alders that skirt its edge,
Now soft on the sand, now loud on the ledge,
Is heard the tramp of his steed as he rides.

It was twelve by the village clock,
When he crossed the bridge into Medford
    town.
He heard the crowing of the cock,
And the barking of the farmer's dog,   90
And felt the damp of the river fog,
That rises after the sun goes down.

It was one by the village clock,
When he galloped into Lexington.
He saw the gilded weathercock
Swim in the moonlight as he passed,
And the meeting-house windows, blank and
    bare,
Gaze at him with a spectral glare,
As if they already stood aghast
At the bloody work they would look upon.   100

It was two by the village clock,
When he came to the bridge in Concord town.
He heard the bleating of the flock,
And the twitter of birds among the trees,
And felt the breath of the morning breeze
Blowing over the meadows brown.
And one was safe and asleep in his bed
Who at the bridge would be first to fall,
Who that day would be lying dead,
Pierced by a British musket-ball.   110

You know the rest. In the books you have read,
How the British Regulars fired and fled,—
How the farmers gave them ball for ball,
From behind each fence and farm-yard wall,
Chasing the red-coats down the lane,
Then crossing the fields to emerge again
Under the trees at the turn of the road,
And only pausing to fire and load.

So through the night rode Paul Revere;
And so through the night went his cry of alarm
To every Middlesex village and farm,— 121
A cry of defiance and not of fear,
A voice in the darkness, a knock at the door,
And a word that shall echo forevermore!
For, borne on the night-wind of the Past,
Through all our history, to the last,
In the hour of darkness and peril and need,
The people will waken and listen to hear
The hurrying hoof-beats of that steed,
And the midnight message of Paul Revere. 130
1860   1861

HAWTHORNE

May 23, 1864

How beautiful it was, that one bright day
    In the long week of rain!
Though all its splendor could not chase away
    The omnipresent pain.

The lovely town was white with apple-blooms,
    And the great elms o'erhead
Dark shadows wove on their aerial looms
    Shot through with golden thread.

Across the meadows, by the gray old manse,
    The historic river flowed: 10
I was as one who wanders in a trance,
    Unconscious of his road.

The faces of familiar friends seemed strange;
    Their voices I could hear,
And yet the words they uttered seemed to
        change
    Their meaning to my ear.

For the one face I looked for was not there,
    The one low voice was mute;
Only an unseen presence filled the air,
    And baffled my pursuit.   20

Now I look back, and meadow, manse, and
        stream
    Dimly my thought defines;
I only see—a dream within a dream—
    The hill-top hearsed with pines.

I only hear above his place of rest
    Their tender undertone,
The infinite longings of a troubled breast,
    The voice so like his own.

There in seclusion and remote from men
    The wizard hand lies cold,   30
Which at its topmost speed let fall the pen,
    And left the tale half told.

Ah! who shall lift that wand of magic power,
    And the lost clew regain?
The unfinished window in Aladdin's tower
    Unfinished must remain!
1864   1864

DIVINA COMMEDIA[7]

I

Oft have I seen at some cathedral door
A laborer, pausing in the dust and heat,
Lay down his burden, and with reverent feet
Enter, and cross himself, and on the floor
Kneel to repeat his paternoster o'er;
Far off the noises of the world retreat;
The loud vociferations of the street
Become an undistinguishable roar.
So, as I enter here from day to day,
And leave my burden at this minster gate,   10
Kneeling in prayer, and not ashamed to pray,
The tumult of the time disconsolate
To inarticulate murmurs dies away,
While the eternal ages watch and wait.
1864   1864

II

How strange the sculptures that adorn these
        towers!
This crowd of statues, in whose folded sleeves
Birds build their nests; while canopied with
        leaves
Parvis and portal bloom like trellised bowers,
And the vast minster seems a cross of flowers!
But fiends and dragons on the gargoyled eaves
Watch the dead Christ between the living
        thieves,   21
And, underneath, the traitor Judas lowers!
Ah! from what agonies of heart and brain,
What exultations trampling on despair,
What tenderness, what tears, what hate of
        wrong,
What passionate outcry of a soul in pain,
Uprose this poem of the earth and air,
This mediæval miracle of song!
1864   1866

III

I enter, and I see thee in the gloom
Of the long aisles, O poet saturnine!   30

[7] These sonnets were written to be published with Longfellow's translation of Dante's *Divine Comedy*.

And strive to make my steps keep pace with
    thine.
The air is filled with some unknown perfume;
The congregation of the dead make room
For thee to pass; the votive tapers shine;
Like rooks that haunt Ravenna's groves of
    pine
The hovering echoes fly from tomb to tomb.
From the confessionals I hear arise
Rehearsals of forgotten tragedies,
And lamentations from the crypts below;
And then a voice celestial that begins   40
With the pathetic words, "Although your sins
As scarlet be," and ends with "as the snow."
1865   1866

IV

With snow-white veil and garments as of
    flame,
She stands before thee, who so long ago
Filled thy young heart with passion and the
    woe
From which thy song and all its splendors
    came;
And while with stern rebuke she speaks thy
    name,
The ice about thy heart melts as the snow
On mountain heights, and in swift overflow
Comes gushing from thy lips in sobs of shame.
Thou makest full confession; and a gleam,   51
As of the dawn on some dark forest cast,
Seems on thy lifted forehead to increase;
Lethe and Eunoë—the remembered dream
And the forgotten sorrow—bring at last
That perfect pardon which is perfect peace.
1867   1867

V

I lift mine eyes, and all the windows blaze
With forms of Saints and holy men who died,
Here martyred and hereafter glorified;
And the great Rose upon its leaves displays 60
Christ's Triumph, and the angelic roundelays,
With splendor upon splendor multiplied;
And Beatrice again at Dante's side
No more rebukes, but smiles her words of
    praise.
And then the organ sounds, and unseen choirs
Sing the old Latin hymns of peace and love

And benedictions of the Holy Ghost;
And the melodious bells among the spires
O'er all the house-tops and through heaven
    above
Proclaim the elevation of the Host!   70
1865   1866

VI

O star of morning and of liberty!
O bringer of the light, whose splendor shines
Above the darkness of the Apennines,
Forerunner of the day that is to be!
The voices of the city and the sea,
The voices of the mountains and the pines,
Repeat thy song, till the familiar lines
Are footpaths for the thought of Italy!
Thy flame is blown abroad from all the heights,
Through all the nations, and a sound is heard,
As of a mighty wind, and men devout,   81
Strangers of Rome, and the new proselytes,
In their own language hear the wondrous
    word,
And many are amazed and many doubt.
1866   1866

THE THREE SILENCES OF MOLINOS [8]

Three Silences there are: the first of speech,
The second of desire, the third of thought;
This is the lore a Spanish monk, distraught
With dreams and visions, was the first to teach.
These Silences, commingling each with each,
Made up the perfect Silence that he sought
And prayed for, and wherein at times he caught
Mysterious sounds from realms beyond our
    reach.
O thou, whose daily life anticipates
The life to come, and in whose thought and
    word   10
The spiritual world preponderates,
Hermit of Amesbury! thou too hast heard
Voices and melodies from beyond the gates,
And speakest only when thy soul is stirred!
1877   1878

[8] Written for the dinner given by *The Atlantic Monthly* in honor of
Whittier's seventieth birthday.

»   »   «   «

OLIVER WENDELL HOLMES

1809–1894

FOR A HALF-CENTURY Dr. Holmes was to Bostonians the perfect representative of the New England Brahmin caste which he was the first to describe. His latest witticisms passed from mouth to mouth along Beacon Street. We still, in fact, sadly misquote them without acknowledgment. No anniversary celebration in Cambridge or Boston could properly come to an end without a poem from him commemorating the occasion. If these poems now seem merely good topical verse, yet Holmes's prose will always be read, as Lamb's is, for the personality which shines through it. As we idle through his remarks on trotting horses, sculling, Calvinism, sparring, the length of women's skirts, love, ghosts, *et al.*, watching for the earthy phrases of this Autocrat who has "his straw at the bunghole of the universe," we soon perceive how close to the little truths of life his words are.

"I am a Cambridge boy!" Holmes said proudly at seventy-one. His youth was spent in the old gambrel-roofed house on the Common, the historic parsonage of the First Congregational Church, of which his father had been pastor since 1795. Harvard College graduated him in 1829 along with S. F. Smith, the author of "America." After a few months spent in studying law, which he found "very cold and cheerless about the threshold," he decided on medicine as a profession. Before sailing for Europe in 1833, to find in Paris the best training then available, Holmes had already shown that literature would occupy a large part in his life. "Old Ironsides," published in a Boston paper when he was twenty-one, rang through the country. Two rambling essays, entitled "The Autocrat of the Breakfast-Table," appeared in the *New England Magazine* (1831–1833). This early venture in prose accounts for the quizzical opening remark of the famous Autocrat series in the *Atlantic* (1857–1858): "I was just going to say, when I was interrupted. . . . " The interruption had lasted a quarter of a century!

Holmes's two years abroad were important in his career. His contact in Paris with the best minds in the medical profession fired him with the desire for eminence, with the result that his studies led in 1847 to his appointment as Parkman Professor of Anatomy at the Harvard Medical School. This post he held until his retirement in 1882. His European experiences gave him a largeness of view which tempered his provincialism. Though the Boston State House was for him the hub of the solar system, he was more conscious of the planets revolving at a respectful distance from it than were most of the literary Brahmins.

In 1857 Holmes found his true medium as a writer. Lowell, the first editor of the new *Atlantic Monthly*, made it a "condition precedent" when he accepted the editorship, that Holmes should be a contributor. Thus began the monthly papers called *The Autocrat of the Breakfast-Table*, purporting to be the table-talk, at a Boston boarding-house, of a genial dogmatist who conversed, as Holmes did, endlessly, brilliantly, and usually without staying for an answer. When the Autocrat, in the twelfth paper, married the schoolmistress and the series ended, a new one was begun with the Professor in the chair. In each book the relations of the boarders evolved into a slight plot. Evidently encouraged by his success with these excursions into fiction, Holmes published in the *Atlantic* for 1860 a "medicated" novel, *The Professor's Story*, called *Elsie Venner* in book form (1861). The bizarre plot, which tells of the blighted life of a girl who inherits from her mother snakelike characteristics, conceals an attack on the doctrine of predestination. With

Holmes Puritan cruelty was almost an obsession, and this novel was his most vigorous effort to kill what remained of Calvinism in New England. Holmes's best writing was done in the years between 1857 and the Civil War. His later novels and *The Poet at the Breakfast-Table* (1872) show a falling off.

E. M. Tilton, ed., *A Bibliography of Oliver Wendell Holmes*, New York, 1953.
The Writings of Oliver Wendell Holmes, 13 vols., Boston, 1891.
Oliver Wendell Holmes, Representative Selections, with Introduction, Bibliography, and Notes (American Writers Series), S. I. Hayakawa and H. M. Jones, eds., New York, 1939.
M. A. DeW. Howe, *Holmes of the Breakfast Table*, New York, 1939.
J. T. Morse, Jr., *Life and Letters of Oliver Wendell Holmes*, 2 vols., Boston, 1896.
E. M. Tilton, *Amiable Autocrat: A Biography of Dr. Oliver Wendell Holmes*, New York, 1953.

OLD IRONSIDES[1]

Ay, tear her tattered ensign down!
  Long has it waved on high,
And many an eye has danced to see
  That banner in the sky;
Beneath it rung the battle shout,
  And burst the cannon's roar;—
The meteor of the ocean air
  Shall sweep the clouds no more.

Her deck, once red with heroes' blood,
  Where knelt the vanquished foe,   10
When winds were hurrying o'er the flood,
  And waves were white below,
No more shall feel the victor's tread,
  Or know the conquered knee;—
The harpies of the shore shall pluck
  The eagle of the sea!

Oh, better that her shattered hulk
  Should sink beneath the wave;
Her thunders shook the mighty deep,
  And there should be her grave;   20
Nail to the mast her holy flag,
  Set every threadbare sail,
And give her to the god of storms,
  The lightning and the gale!
1830   1830

THE LAST LEAF[2]

I saw him once before,
As he passed by the door,
  And again
The pavement stones resound,
As he totters o'er the ground
  With his cane.

They say that in his prime,
Ere the pruning-knife of Time
  Cut him down,
Not a better man was found   10
By the Crier on his round
  Through the town.

But now he walks the streets,
And he looks at all he meets
  Sad and wan,
And he shakes his feeble head,
That it seems as if he said,
  "They are gone."

The mossy marbles rest
On the lips that he has prest   20
  In their bloom,
And the names he loved to hear
Have been carved for many a year
  On the tomb.

My grandmamma has said—
Poor old lady, she is dead
  Long ago—
That he had a Roman nose,
And his cheek was like a rose
  In the snow.   30

But now his nose is thin,
And it rests upon his chin
  Like a staff,
And a crook is in his back,
And a melancholy crack
  In his laugh.

I know it is a sin
For me to sit and grin
  At him here;
But the old three-cornered hat,   40
And the breeches, and all that,
  Are so queer!

[1] This poem prevented the destruction of the *Constitution* and made Holmes famous.
[2] The subject of the poem is Major Thomas Melville, Herman Melville's grandfather.

And if I should live to be
The last leaf upon the tree
   In the spring,
Let them smile, as I do now,
At the old forsaken bough
   Where I cling.

?1831   1833

A SONG

For the Centennial Celebration of Harvard College, 1836

When the Puritans came over,
   Our hills and swamps to clear,
The woods were full of catamounts,
   And Indians red as deer,
With tomahawks and scalping-knives,
   That make folks' heads look queer;—
Oh the ship from England used to bring
   A hundred wigs a year!

The crows came cawing through the air
   To pluck the Pilgrims' corn,   10
The bears came snuffing round the door
   Whene'er a babe was born,
The rattlesnakes were bigger round
   Than the butt of the old ram's horn
The deacon blew at meeting time
   On every "Sabbath" morn.

But soon they knocked the wigwams down,
   And pine-tree trunk and limb
Began to sprout among the leaves
   In shape of steeples slim;   20
And out the little wharves were stretched
   Along the ocean's rim,
And up the little school-house shot
   To keep the boys in trim.

And when at length the College rose,
   The sachem cocked his eye
At every tutor's meagre ribs
   Whose coat-tails whistled by:
But when the Greek and Hebrew words
   Came tumbling from his jaws,   30
The copper-colored children all
   Ran screaming to the squaws.

And who was on the Catalogue
   When college was begun?
Two nephews of the President,
   And *the* Professor's son;
(They turned a little Indian by,

As brown as any bun;)
Lord! how the seniors knocked about
   The freshman class of one!   40

They had not then the dainty things
   That commons now afford,
But *succotash* and *hominy*
   Were smoking on the board;
They did not rattle round in gigs,
   Or dash in long-tailed blues,
But always on Commencement days
   The tutors blacked their shoes.

God bless the ancient Puritans!
   Their lot was hard enough;   50
But honest hearts make iron arms,
   And tender maids are tough;
So love and faith have formed and fed
   Our true-born Yankee stuff,
And keep the kernel in the shell
   The British found so rough!

THE MORNING VISIT

A sick man's chamber, though it often boast
The grateful presence of a literal toast,
Can hardly claim, amidst its various wealth,
The right unchallenged to propose a health;
Yet though its tenant is denied the feast,
Friendship must launch his sentiment at least,
As prisoned damsels, locked from lovers' lips,
Toss them a kiss from off their fingers' tips.

The morning visit,—not till sickness falls
In the charmed circles of your own safe walls;
Till fever's throb and pain's relentless rack   11
Stretch you all helpless on your aching back;
Not till you play the patient in your turn,
The morning visit's mystery shall you learn.

'Tis a small matter in your neighbor's case,
To charge your fee for showing him your face;
You skip up-stairs, inquire, inspect, and touch,
Prescribe, take leave, and off to twenty such.

But when at length, by fate's transferred
   decree,
The visitor becomes the visitee,   20
Oh, then, indeed, it pulls another string;
Your ox is gored, and that's a different thing!
Your friend is sick: phlegmatic as a Turk,
You write your recipe and let it work;
Not yours to stand the shiver and the frown,

And sometimes worse, with which your draught
   goes down.
Calm as a clock your knowing hand directs,
Rhei, jalapæ ana grana sex,
Or traces on some tender missive's back,
Scrupulos duos pulveris ipecac;   30
And leaves your patient to his qualms and
   gripes,
Cool as a sportsman banging at his snipes.

But change the time, the person, and the place,
And be yourself "the interesting case,"
You'll gain some knowledge which it's well to
   learn;
In future practice it may serve your turn.
Leeches, for instance,—pleasing creatures
   quite;
Try them,—and bless you,—don't you find
   they bite?
You raise a blister for the smallest cause,
But be yourself the sitter whom it draws,   40
And trust my statement, you will not deny
The worst of draughtsmen is your Spanish fly!
It's mighty easy ordering when you please,
Infusi sennæ capiat uncias tres;
It's mighty different when you quackle down
Your own three ounces of the liquid brown.

Pilula, pulvis,—pleasant words enough,
When other throats receive the shocking stuff;
But oh, what flattery can disguise the groan
That meets the gulp which sends it through
   your own!   50
Be gentle, then, though Art's unsparing rules
Give you the handling of her sharpest tools;
Use them not rashly,—sickness is enough;
Be always "ready," but be never "rough."

Of all the ills that suffering man endures,
The largest fraction liberal Nature cures;
Of those remaining, 't is the swellest part
Yields to the efforts of judicious Art;
But simple *Kindness,* kneeling by the bed
To shift the pillow for the sick man's head,   60
Give the fresh draught to cool the lips that
   burn,
Fan the hot brow, the weary frame to turn,—
Kindness, untutored by our grave M.D.'s
But Nature's graduate, when she schools to
   please,
Wins back more sufferers with her voice and
   smile
Than all the trumpery in the druggist's pile.

Once more, be *quiet:* coming up the stair,
Don't be a plantigrade, a human bear,

But, stealing softly on the silent toe,
Reach the sick chamber ere you're heard be-
   low.   70
Whatever changes there may greet your eyes,
Let not your looks proclaim the least surprise;
It's not your business by your face to show
All that your patient does not want to know;
Nay, use your optics with considerate care,
And don't abuse your privilege to stare.
But if your eyes may probe him overmuch,
Beware still further how you rudely touch;
Don't clutch his carpus in your icy fist,
But warm your fingers ere you take the wrist.
If the poor victim needs must be percussed,   81
Don't make an anvil of his aching bust;
(Doctors exist within a hundred miles
Who thump a thorax as they'd hammer piles;)
If you must listen to his doubtful chest,
Catch the essentials, and ignore the rest.
Spare him; the sufferer wants of you and art
A track to steer by, not a finished chart.
So of your questions: don't in mercy try
To pump your patient absolutely dry;   90
He's not a mollusk squirming in a dish,
You're not Agassiz, and he's not a fish.

And last, not least, in each perplexing case,
Learn the sweet magic of a *cheerful face;*
Not always smiling, but at least serene,
When grief and anguish cloud the anxious
   scene.
Each look, each movement, every word and
   tone,
Should tell your patient you are all his own;
Not the mere artist, purchased to attend,
But the warm, ready, self-forgetting friend,   100
Whose genial visit in itself combines
The best of cordials, tonics, anodynes.

Such is the *visit* that from day to day
Sheds o'er my chamber its benignant ray.
I give his health, who never cared to claim
Her babbling homage from the tongue of
   Fame;
Unmoved by praise, he stands by all confest,
The truest, noblest, wisest, kindest, best.
1849   1888

THE DEACON'S MASTERPIECE [3]

Or, the Wonderful "One-Hoss Shay": a Logical Story

[3] An attack, by means of allegory, on Calvinism. It is one of the
poems in *The Autocrat of the Breakfast-Table.*

Have you heard of the wonderful one-hoss
    shay,
That was built in such a logical way
It ran a hundred years to a day,
And then, of a sudden, it—ah, but stay,
I'll tell you what happened without delay,
Scaring the parson into fits,
Frightening people out of their wits,—
Have you ever heard of that, I say?

Seventeen hundred and fifty-five.
Georgius Secundus was then alive,—   10
Snuffy old drone from the German hive.
That was the year when Lisbon-town
Saw the earth open and gulp her down,
And Braddock's army was done so brown,
Left without a scalp to its crown.
It was on the terrible Earthquake-day
That the Deacon finished the one-hoss shay.

Now in building of chaises, I tell you what
There is always *somewhere* a weakest spot,—
In hub, tire, felloe, in spring or thill,   20
In panel, or crossbar, or floor, or sill,
In screw, bolt, thoroughbrace,—lurking still,
Find it somewhere you must and will,—
Above or below, or within or without,—
And that's the reason, beyond a doubt,
That a chaise *breaks down,* but doesn't *wear
    out.*

But the Deacon swore (as Deacons do,
With an "I dew vum," or an "I tell *yeou,*")
He would build one shay to beat the taown
'N' the keounty 'n' all the kentry raoun';   30
It should be so built that it *couldn'* break
    daown:
"Fur," said the Deacon, " 't's mighty plain
Thut the weakes' place mus' stan' the strain;
'N' the way t' fix it, uz I maintain,
   Is only jest
T' make that place uz strong uz the rest."

So the Deacon inquired of the village folk
Where he could find the strongest oak,
That couldn't be split nor bent nor broke,—
That was for spokes and floor and sills;   40
He sent for lancewood to make the thills;
The crossbars were ash, from the straightest
    trees;
The panels of white-wood, that cuts like cheese,
But lasts like iron for things like these;
The hubs of logs from the "Settler's ellum,"—
Last of its timber,—they couldn't sell 'em,
Never an axe had seen their chips,

And the wedges flew from between their lips,
Their blunt ends frizzled like celery-tips;
Step and prop-iron, bolt and screw,   50
Spring, tire, axle, and linchpin too,
Steel of the finest, bright and blue;
Thoroughbrace bison-skin, thick and wide;
Boot, top, dasher, from tough old hide
Found in the pit when the tanner died.
That was the way he "put her through."
"There!" said the Deacon, "naow she'll dew!"

Do! I tell you, I rather guess
She was a wonder, and nothing less!
Colts grew horses, beards turned gray,   60
Deacon and deaconess dropped away,
Children and grandchildren—where were
    they?
But there stood the stout old one-hoss shay
As fresh as on Lisbon-earthquake-day!

Eighteen hundred;—it came and found
The Deacon's masterpiece strong and sound.
Eighteen hundred increased by ten;—
"Hahnsum kerridge" they called it then.
Eighteen hundred and twenty came;—
Running as usual; much the same.   70
Thirty and forty at last arrive,
And then come fifty, and fifty-five.

Little of all we value here
Wakes on the morn of its hundredth year
Without both feeling and looking queer.
In fact, there's nothing that keeps its youth,
So far as I know, but a tree and truth.
(This is a moral that runs at large;
Take it.—You're welcome.—No extra charge.)

First of November,—the Earthquake-day.—
There are traces of age in the one-hoss shay,
A general flavor of mild decay,   82
But nothing local, as one may say.
There couldn't be,—for the Deacon's art
Had made it so like in every part
That there wasn't a chance for one to start.
For the wheels were just as strong as the
    thills,
And the floor was just as strong as the sills,
And the panels just as strong as the floor,
And the whipple-tree neither less nor more,   90
And the back crossbar as strong as the fore,
And spring and axle and hub *encore.*
And yet, *as a whole,* it is past a doubt
In another hour it will be *worn out!*

First of November, 'Fifty-five!
This morning the parson takes a drive.

Now, small boys, get out of the way!
Here comes the wonderful one-horse shay,
Drawn by a rat-tailed, ewe-necked bay.   99
"Huddup!" said the parson.—Off went they.
The parson was working his Sunday's text,—
Had got to *fifthly*, and stopped perplexed
At what the—Moses—was coming next.
All at once the horse stood still,
Close by the meet'n'-house on the hill.
First a shiver, and then a thrill,
Then something decidedly like a spill,—
And the parson was sitting upon a rock,
At half-past nine by the meet'n'-house clock,—
Just the hour of the Earthquake shock!   110
What do you think the parson found,
When he got up and stared around?
The poor old chaise in a heap or mound,
As if it had been to the mill and ground!
You see, of course, if you're not a dunce,
How it went to pieces all at once,—
All at once and nothing first,—
Just as bubbles do when they burst.

End of the wonderful one-hoss shay.
Logic is logic. That's all I say.   120
                                        1858

THE MORAL BULLY

Yon whey-faced brother, who delights to
    wear
A weedy flux of ill-conditioned hair,
Seems of the sort that in a crowded place
One elbows freely into smallest space;
A timid creature, lax of knee and hip,
Whom small disturbance whitens round the lip;
One of those harmless spectacled machines,
The Holy-Week of Protestants convenes;
Whom school-boys question if their walk tran-
    scends
The last advices of maternal friends;   10
Whom John, obedient to his master's sign,
Conducts, laborious, up to *ninety-nine*,
While Peter, glistening with luxurious scorn,
Husks his white ivories like an ear of corn;
Dark in the brow and bilious in the cheek,
Whose yellowish linen flowers but once a
    week,
Conspicuous, annual, in their threadbare suits,
And the laced high-lows which they call their
    boots,
Well mayst thou *shun* that dingy front severe,
But him, O stranger, him thou canst not
    fear!   20

Be slow to judge, and slower to despise,
Man of broad shoulders and heroic size!
The tiger, writhing from the boa's rings,
Drops at the fountain where the cobra stings.
In that lean phantom, whose extended glove
Points to the text of universal love,
Behold the master that can tame thee down
To crouch, the vassal of his Sunday frown;
His velvet throat against thy corded wrist, 29
His loosened tongue against thy doubled fist!

The MORAL BULLY, though he never swears,
Nor kicks intruders down his entry stairs,
Though meekness plants his backward-sloping
    hat,
And non-resistance ties his white cravat,
Though his black broadcloth glories to be seen
In the same plight with Shylock's gaberdine,
Hugs the same passion to his narrow breast
That heaves the cuirass on the trooper's chest,
Hears the same hell-hounds yelling in his rear
That chase from port the maddened buccaneer,
Feels the same comfort while his acrid words
Turn the sweet milk of kindness into curds, 42
Or with grim logic prove, beyond debate,
That all we love is worthiest of our hate,
As the scarred ruffian of the pirate's deck,
When his long swivel rakes the staggering
    wreck!

Heaven keep us all! Is every rascal clown
Whose arm is stronger free to knock us down?
Has every scarecrow, who cachectic soul   49
Seems fresh from Bedlam, airing on parole,
Who, though he carries but a doubtful trace
Of angel visits on his hungry face,
From lack of marrow or the coins to pay,
Has dodged some vices in a shabby way,
The right to stick us with his cutthroat terms,
And bait his homilies with his brother worms?
                                        1862

From: *WIND-CLOUDS AND STAR-DRIFTS*⁴

From the Young Astronomer's Poem

VI

Questioning

I am not humble; I was shown my place,
Clad in such robes as Nature had at hand;

⁴ One of the poems in *The Poet at the Breakfast-Table*.

Took what she gave, nor chose; I know no
    shame,
No fear for being simply what I am.
I am not proud, I hold my every breath
At Nature's mercy. I am as a babe
Borne in a giant's arms, he knows not where;
Each several heart-beat, counted like the coin
A miser reckons, is a special gift
As from an unseen hand; if that withhold 10
Its bounty for a moment, I am left
A clod upon the earth to which I fall.

Something I find in me that well might claim
The love of beings in a sphere above
This doubtful twilight world of right and
    wrong;
Something that shows me of the self-same clay
That creeps or swims or flies in humblest form.
Had I been asked, before I left my bed
Of shapeless dust, what clothing I would wear,
I would have said, More angel and less
    worm; 20
But for their sake who are even such as I,
Of the same mingled blood, I would not choose
To hate that meaner portion of myself
Which makes me brother to the least of men.

I dare not be a coward with my lips
Who dare to question all things in my soul;
Some men may find their wisdom on their
    knees,
Some prone and grovelling in the dust like
    slaves;
Let the meek glowworm glisten in the dew;
I ask to lift my taper to the sky 30

As they who hold their lamps above their
    heads,
Trusting the larger currents up aloft,
Rather than crossing eddies round their breast,
Threatening with every puff the flickering
    blaze.

My life shall be a challenge, not a truce!
This is my homage to the mightier powers,
To ask my boldest question, undismayed
By muttering threats that some hysteric sense
Of wrong or insult will convulse the throne
Where wisdom reigns supreme; and if I err, 40
They all must err who have to feel their way
As bats that fly at noon; for what are we
But creatures of the night, dragged forth by
    day,
Who needs must stumble, and with stammering
    steps
Spell out their paths in syllables of pain?

Thou wilt not hold in scorn the child who
    dares
Look up to Thee, the Father,—dares to ask
More than thy wisdom answers. From Thy
    hand
The worlds were cast; yet every leaflet claims
From that same hand its little shining sphere
Of star-lit dew; thine image, the great sun, 51
Girt with his mantle of tempestuous flame,
Glares in mid-heaven; but to his noon-tide
    blaze
The slender violet lifts its lidless eye,
And from his splendor steals its fairest hue,
In sweetest perfume from his scorching fire.
                 1872

» »   « «

» » *From:* THE AUTOCRAT OF THE BREAKFAST-TABLE « «

IV

[I am so well pleased with my boarding-house that I intend to remain there, perhaps for years. Of course I shall have a great many conversations to report, and they will necessarily be of different tone and on different subjects. The talks are like the breakfasts,—sometimes dipped toast, and sometimes dry. You must take them as they come. How can I do what all these letters ask me to? No. 1. wants serious and earnest thought. No. 2. (letter

smells of bad cigars) must have more jokes; wants me to tell a "good storey" which he has copied out for me. (I suppose two letters before the word "good" refer to some Doctor of Divinity who told the story.) No. 3. (in female hand)—more poetry. No. 4. wants something that would be of use to a practical man. (*Prahctical mahn* he probably pronounces it.) No. 5. (gilt-edged, sweet-scented)—"more sentiment,"—"heart's outpourings."—

My dear friends, one and all, I can do nothing but report such remarks as I happen to have made at our breakfast-table. Their character will depend on many accidents,—a good deal on the particular persons in the company to whom they were addressed. It so happens that those which follow were mainly intended for the divinity-student and the schoolmistress; though others, whom I need not mention, saw fit to interfere, with more or less propriety, in the conversation. This is one of my privileges as a talker; and of course, when I was not talking for our whole company, I don't expect all the readers of this periodical to be interested in my notes of what was said. Still, I think there may be a few that will rather like this vein,—possibly prefer it to a livelier one,— serious young men, and young women generally, in life's roseate parenthesis from —— years of age to —— inclusive.

Another privilege of talking is to misquote. —Of course it wasn't Proserpina that actually cut the yellow hair,—but Iris. (As I have since told you) it was the former lady's regular business, but Dido had used herself ungenteelly and Madame d'Enfer stood firm on the point of etiquette. So the bathycolpian Here,—Juno, in Latin,—sent down Iris instead. But I was mightily pleased to see that one of the gentlemen that do the heavy articles for the celebrated "Oceanic Miscellany" misquoted Campbell's line without any excuse. "Waft us *home* the *message*" of course it ought to be. [Will he be duly grateful for the correction?]

—The more we study the body and the mind, the more we find both to be governed, not *by,* but *according to* laws, such as we observe in the larger universe.—You think you know all about *walking,*—don't you, now? Well, how do you suppose your lower limbs are held to your body? They are sucked up by two cupping vessels ("cotyloid"—cuplike—cavities), and held there as long as you live, and longer. At any rate, you think you move them backward and forward at such a rate as your will determines, don't you? On the contrary, they swing just as any other pendulums swing, at a fixed rate, determined by their length. You can alter this by muscular power, as you can take hold of the pendulum of a clock and make it move faster or slower; but your ordinary gait is timed by the same mechanism as the movements of the solar system.

[My friend, the Professor, told me all this, referring me to certain German physiologists by the name of Weber for proof of the facts, which, however, he said he had often verified.

I appropriated it to my own use; what can one do better than this, when one has a friend that tells him anything worth remembering?

The Professor seems to think that man and the general powers of the universe are in partnership. Some one was saying that it had cost nearly half a million to move the Leviathan only so far as they had got it already.—Why, —said the Professor,—they might have hired an EARTHQUAKE for less money!]

Just as we find a mathematical rule at the bottom of many of the bodily movements, just so thought may be supposed to have its regular cycles. Such or such a thought comes round periodically, in its turn. Accidental suggestions, however, so far interfere with the regular cycles, that we may find them practically beyond our power of recognition. Take all this for what it is worth, but at any rate you will agree that there are certain particular thoughts that do not come up once a day, nor once a week, but that a year would hardly go round without your having them pass through your mind. Here is one which comes up at intervals in this way. Some one speaks of it, and there is an instant and eager smile of assent in the listener or listeners. Yes, indeed; they have often been struck by it.

All at once a conviction flashes through us that we have been in the same precise circumstances as at the present instant, once or many times before.

O, dear, yes!—said one of the company,— everybody has had that feeling.

The landlady didn't know anything about such notions; it was an idee in folks' heads, she expected.

The schoolmistress said, in a hesitating sort of way, that she knew the feeling well, and didn't like to experience it; it made her think she was a ghost, sometimes.

The young fellow whom they call John said he knew all about it; he had just lighted a cheroot the other day, when a tremendous conviction all at once came over him that he had done just the same thing ever so many times before. I looked severely at him, and his countenance immediately fell—*on the side toward me;* I cannot answer for the other, for he can wink and laugh with either half of his face without the other half's knowing it.

—I have noticed—I went on to say—the following circumstances connected with these sudden impressions. First, that the condition which seems to be the duplicate of a former one is often very trivial,—one that might have presented itself a hundred times. Secondly, that the impression is very evanescent, and that it is rarely, if ever, recalled by any voluntary effort, at least after any time has elapsed. Thirdly, that there is a disinclination to record the circumstances, and a sense of incapacity to reproduce the state of mind in words. Fourthly, I have often felt that the duplicate condition had not only occurred once before, but that it was familiar and, as it seemed, habitual. Lastly, I have had the same convictions in my dreams.

How do I account for it?—Why, there are several ways that I can mention, and you may take your choice. The first is that which the young lady hinted at;—that these flashes are sudden recollections of a previous existence. I don't believe that; for I remember a poor student I used to know told me he had such a conviction one day when he was blacking his boots, and I can't think he had ever lived in another world where they use Day and Martin.

Some think that Dr. Wigan's doctrine of the brain's being a double organ, its hemispheres working together like the two eyes, accounts for it. One of the hemispheres hangs fire, they suppose, and the small interval between the perceptions of the nimble and the sluggish half seems an indefinitely long period and therefore the second perception appears to be the copy of another, ever so old. But even allowing the centre of perception to be double, I can see no good reason for supposing this indefinite lengthening of the time, nor any analogy that bears it out. It seems to me most likely that the coincidence of circumstances is very partial, but that we take this partial resemblance for identity, as we occasionally do resemblances of persons. A momentary posture of circumstances is so far like some preceding one that we accept it as exactly the same, just as we accost a stranger occasionally, mistaking him for a friend. The apparent similarity may be owing perhaps, quite as much to the mental state at the time, as to the outward circumstances.

—Here is another of these curiously recurring remarks. I have said it and heard it many times, and occasionally met with something like it in books,—somewhere in Bulwer's novels, I think, and in one of the works of Mr. Olmsted, I know.

Memory, imagination, old sentiments and associations, are more readily reached through the sense of SMELL *than by almost any other channel.*

Of course the particular odors which act upon each person's susceptibilities differ.—O, yes! I will tell you some of mine. The smell of *phosphorus* is one of them. During a year or two of adolescence I used to be dabbling in chemistry a good deal, and as about that time I had my little aspirations and passions like another, some of these things got mixed up with each other: orange-colored fumes of nitrous acid, and visions as bright and transient; reddening litmus paper, and blushing cheeks; —*eheu!*

"Soles occidere et redire possunt,"

but there is no reagent that will redden the faded roses of eighteen hundred and —— spare them! But, as I was saying, phosphorus fires this train of associations in an instant; its luminous vapors with their penetrating odor throw me into a trance; it comes to me in a double sense "trailing clouds of glory." Only the confounded Vienna matches, *ohne phosphor-geruch,* have worn my sensibilities a little.

Then there is the *marigold.* When I was of smallest dimensions, and wont to ride impacted between the knees of fond parental pair, we would sometimes cross the bridge to the next village-town and stop opposite a low, brown "gambrel-roofed" cottage. Out of it would come one Sally, sister of its swarthy tenant, swarthy herself, shady-lipped, sad-voiced, and, bending over her flower-bed, would gather a "posy," as she called it, for the little boy. Sally lies in the churchyard with a slab of blue slate at her head, lichen-crusted, and leaning a little within the last few years. Cottage, garden-beds, posies, grenadier-like rows of seedling onions, —stateliest of vegetables,—all are gone, but the breath of a marigold brings them all back to me.

Perhaps the herb *everlasting,* the fragrant *immortelle* of our autumn fields, has the most suggestive odor to me of all those that set me dreaming. I can hardly describe the strange thoughts and emotions which come to me as I inhale the aroma of its pale, dry, rustling flowers. A something it has of sepulchral spicery, as if it had been brought from the core of some great pyramid, where it had lain on the breast of a mummied Pharaoh. Something, too, of immortality in the sad, faint sweetness lingering so long in its lifeless petals. Yet this does not tell why it fills my eyes with tears and carries me in blissful thoughts to the banks of asphodel that border the River of Life.

—I should not have talked so much about these personal susceptibilities, if I had not a remark to make about them which I believe is a new one. It is this. There may be a physical reason for the strange connection between the sense of smell and the mind. The olfactory nerve,—so my friend, the Professor, tells me,—is the only one directly connected with the hemispheres of the brain, the parts in which, as we have every reason to believe, the intellectual processes are performed. To speak more truly, the olfactory "nerve" is not a nerve at all, he says, but a part of the brain, in intimate connection with its anterior lobes. Whether this anatomical arrangement is at the bottom of the facts I have mentioned, I will not decide, but it is curious enough to be worth remembering. Contrast the sense of taste, as a source of suggestive impressions, with that of smell. Now the Professor assures me that you will find the nerve of taste has no immediate connection with the brain proper, but only with the prolongation of the spinal cord.

[The old gentleman opposite did not pay much attention, I think, to this hypothesis of mine. But while I was speaking about the sense of smell he nestled about in his seat, and presently succeeded in getting out a large red bandanna handkerchief. Then he lurched a little to the other side, and after much tribulation at last extricated an ample round snuffbox. I looked as he opened it and felt for the wonted pugil. Moist rappee, and a Tonkabean lying therein. I made the manual sign understood of all mankind that use the precious dust, and presently my brain, too, responded to the long unused stimulus.—O boys,—that were,—actual papas and possible grandpapas, —some of you with crowns like billiard-balls, —some in locks of sable silvered, and some of silver sabled,—do you remember, as you doze over this, those after-dinners at the Trois Frères, when the Scotch-plaided snuffbox went round and the dry Lundy-Foot tickled its way along into our happy sensoria? Then it was that the Chambertin or the Clos Vougeot came in, slumbering in its straw cradle. And one among you,—do you remember how he would sit dreaming over his Burgundy, and tinkle his fork against the sides

of the bubble-like glass, saying that he was hearing the cow-bells as he used to hear them, when the deep-breathing kine came home at twilight from the huckleberry pasture, in the old home a thousand leagues towards the sunset?]

Ah me! what strains and strophes of unwritten verse pulsate through my soul when I open a certain closet in the ancient house where I was born! On its shelves used to lie bundles of sweet-marjoram and pennyroyal and lavender and mint and catnip; there apples were stored until their seeds should grow black, which happy period there were sharp little milk-teeth always ready to anticipate; there peaches lay in the dark, thinking of the sunshine they had lost, until, like the hearts of saints who dream of heaven in their sorrow, they grew fragrant as the breath of angels. The odorous echo of a score of dead summers lingers yet in those dim recesses.

—Do I remember Byron's line about "striking the electric chain"?—To be sure I do. I sometimes think the less the hint that stirs the automatic machinery of association, the more easily this moves us. What can be more trivial than that old story of opening the folio Shakespeare that used to lie in some ancient English hall and finding the flakes of Christmas pastry between its leaves, shut up in them perhaps a hundred years ago? And, lo! as one looks on these poor relics of a bygone generation, the universe changes in the twinkling of an eye; old George the Second is back again, and the elder Pitt is coming into power, and General Wolfe is a fine, promising young man, and over the Channel they are pulling the Sieur Damiens to pieces with wild horses, and across the Atlantic the Indians are tomahawking Hirams and Jonathans and Jonases at Fort William Henry; all the dead people who have been in the dust so long—even to the stout-armed cook that made the pastry—are alive again; the planet unwinds a hundred of its luminous coils, and the procession of the equinoxes is retraced on the dial of heaven! All this for a bit of pie-crust!

—I will thank you for that pie,—said the provoking young fellow whom I have named repeatedly. He looked at it for a moment, and put his hands to his eyes as if moved,—I was thinking,—he said indistinctly—

—How? What is't?—said our landlady.

—I was thinking—said he—who was the

king of England when this old pie was baked, —and it made me feel bad to think how long he must have been dead.

[Our landlady is a decent body, poor, and a widow of course; *celà va sans dire*. She told me her story once; it was as if a grain of corn that had been ground and bolted had tried to individualize itself by a special narrative. There was the wooing and the wedding,—the start in life,—the disappointment,—the children she had buried,—the struggle against fate,—the dismantling of life, first of its small luxuries, and then of its comforts,—the broken spirits,—the altered character of the one on whom she leaned,—and at last the death that came and drew the black curtain between her and all her earthly hopes.

I never laughed at my landlady after she had told me her story, but I often cried,—not those pattering tears that run off the eaves upon our neighbors' grounds, the *stillicidium* of self-conscious sentiment, but those which steal noiselessly through their conduits until they reach the cisterns lying round about the heart; those tears that we weep inwardly with unchanging features;—such did I shed for her often when the imps of the boarding-house Inferno tugged at her soul with their red-hot pincers.]

Young man,—I said—the pasty you speak lightly of is not old, but courtesy to those who labor to serve us, especially if they are of the weaker sex, is very old, and yet well worth retaining. May I recommend to you the following caution, as a guide, whenever you are dealing with a woman, or an artist, or a poet, —if you are handling an editor or politician, it is superfluous advice. I take it from the back of one of those little French toys which contain pasteboard figures moved by a small running stream of fine sand; Benjamin Franklin [5] will translate it for you: *"Quoiqu'elle soit très solidement montée, il faut ne pas* BRUTALISER *la machine."*—I will thank you for the pie, if you please.

[I took more of it than was good for me, —as much as 85°, I should think,—and had an indigestion in consequence. While I was suffering from it, I wrote some sadly desponding poems, and a theological essay which took a very melancholy view of creation. When I got better I labelled them all "Pie-crust," and laid them by as scarecrows and solemn

[5] The landlady's youngest son.

warnings. I have a number of books on my shelves which I should like to label with some such title; but, as they have great names on their title-pages,—Doctors of Divinity, some of them,—it wouldn't do.]

—My friend, the Professor, whom I have mentioned to you once or twice, told me yesterday that somebody had been abusing him in some of the journals of his calling. I told him that I didn't doubt he deserved it; that I hoped he did deserve a little abuse occasionally, and would for a number of years to come; that nobody could do anything to make his neighbors wiser or better without being liable to abuse for it; especially that people hated to have their little mistakes made fun of, and perhaps he had been doing something of the kind.—The Professor smiled.—Now, said I, hear what I am going to say. It will not take many years to bring you to the period of life when men, at least the majority of writing and talking men, do nothing but praise. Men, like peaches and pears, grow sweet a little while before they begin to decay. I don't know what it is,—whether a spontaneous change, mental or bodily, or whether it is a thorough experience of the thanklessness of critical honesty,—but it is a fact, that most writers, except sour and unsuccessful ones, get tired of finding fault at about the time when they are beginning to grow old. As a general thing, I would not give a great deal for the fair words of a critic, if he is himself an author, over fifty years of age. At thirty we are all trying to cut our names in big letters upon the walls of this tenement of life; twenty years later we have carved it, or shut up our jack-knives. Then we are ready to help others, and more anxious not to hinder any, because nobody's elbows are in our way. So I am glad you have a little life left; you will be saccharine enough in a few years.

—Some of the softening effects of advancing age have struck me very much in what I have heard or seen here and elsewhere. I just now spoke of the sweetening process that authors undergo. Do you know that in the gradual passage from maturity to helplessness the harshest characters sometimes have a period in which they are gentle and placid as young children? I have heard it said, but I cannot be sponsor for its truth, that the famous chieftain, Lochiel, was rocked in a cradle like a baby, in his old age. An old man, whose studies had been of the severest scholastic kind, used to love to hear little nursery-stories read over and over to him. One who saw the Duke of Wellington in his last years describes him as very gentle in his aspect and demeanor. I remember a person of singularly stern and lofty bearing who became remarkably gracious and easy in all his ways in the later period of his life.

10   And that leads me to say that men often remind me of pears in their way of coming to maturity. Some are ripe at twenty, like human Jargonelles, and must be made the most of, for their day is soon over. Some come into their perfect condition late, like the autumn kinds, and they last better than the summer fruit. And some, that, like the Winter-Nelis, have been hard and uninviting until all the rest have had their season, get their glow
20 and perfume long after the frost and snow have done their worst with the orchards. Beware of rash criticisms; the rough and astringent fruit you condemn may be an autumn or a winter pear, and that which you have picked up beneath the same bough in August may have been only its worm-eaten windfalls. Milton was a Saint-Germain with a graft of the roseate Early-Catherine. Rich, juicy, lively, fragrant, russet skinned old Chaucer was an
30 Easter-Beurré; the buds of a new summer were swelling when he ripened.

    —There is no power I envy so much,—said the divinity-student,—as that of seeing analogies and making comparisons. I don't understand how it is that some minds are continually coupling thoughts or objects that seem not in the least related to each other, until all at once they are put in a certain light and you wonder that you did not always see that they were as
40 like as a pair of twins. It appears to me a sort of miraculous gift.

    [He is a rather nice young man, and I think has an appreciation of the higher mental qualities remarkable for one of his years and training. I try his head occasionally as housewives try eggs,—give it an intellectual shake and hold it up to the light, so to speak, to see if it has life in it, actual or potential, or only contains lifeless albumen.]

50   You call it *miraculous,*—I replied,—tossing the expression with my facial eminence, a little smartly, I fear.—Two men are walking by the polyphlœsbœan ocean, one of them having a small tin cup with which he can scoop up a gill of sea-water when he will, and the other

nothing but his hands, which will hardly hold water at all,—and you call the tin cup a miraculous possession! It is the ocean that is the miracle, my infant apostle! Nothing is clearer than that all things are in all things, and that just according to the intensity and extension of our mental being we shall see the many in the one and the one in the many. Did Sir Isaac think what he was saying when he made *his* speech about the ocean,—the child and the pebbles, you know? Did he mean to speak slightingly of a pebble? Of a spherical solid which stood sentinel over its compartment of space before the stone that became the pyramids had grown solid, and has watched it until now! A body which knows all the currents of force that traverse the globe; which holds by invisible threads to the ring of Saturn and the belt of Orion! A body from the contemplation of which an archangel could infer the entire inorganic universe as the simplest of corollaries! A throne of the all-pervading Deity, who has guided its every atom since the rosary of heaven was strung with beaded stars!

So,—to return to *our* walk by the ocean, —if all that poetry has dreamed, all that insanity has raved, all that maddening narcotics have driven through the brains of men, or smothered passion nursed in the fancies of women,—if the dreams of colleges and convents and boarding schools,—if every human feeling that sighs, or smiles, or curses, or shrieks, or groans should bring all their innumerable images, such as come with every hurried heart-beat,—the epic which held them all, though its letters filled the zodiac, would be but a cupful from the infinite ocean of similitudes and analogies that rolls through the universe.

[The divinity-student honored himself by the way in which he received this. He did not swallow it at once, neither did he reject it; but he took it as a pickerel takes the bait, and carried it off with him to his hole (in the fourth story) to deal with it at his leisure.]

    —Here is another remark made for his especial benefit.—There is a natural tendency in many persons to run their adjectives together in *triads,* as I have heard them called, —thus: He was honorable, courteous, and brave; she was graceful, pleasing, and virtuous. Dr. Johnson is famous for this; I think it was Bulwer who said you could separate a paper in the "Rambler" into three distinct essays.

Many of our writers show the same tendency, —my friend, the Professor, especially. Some think it is in humble imitation of Johnson, —some that it is for the sake of the stately sound only. I don't think they get to the bottom of it. It is, I suspect, an instinctive and involuntary effort of the mind to present a thought or image with the *three dimensions* which belong to every solid,—an unconscious handling of an idea as if it had length, breadth, and thickness. It is a great deal easier to say this than to prove it, and a great deal easier to dispute it than to disprove it. But mind this: the more we observe and study, the wider we find the range of the automatic and instinctive principles in body, mind, and morals, and the narrower the limits of the self-determining conscious movement.

—I have often seen piano-forte players and singers make such strange motions over their instruments or song-books that I wanted to laugh at them. "Where did our friends pick up all these fine ecstatic airs?" I would say to myself. Then I would remember My Lady in "Marriage à la Mode," and amuse myself with thinking how affectation was the same thing in Hogarth's time and in our own. But one day I bought me a Canary-bird and hung him up in a cage at my window. By-and-by he found himself at home, and began to pipe his little tunes; and there he was, sure enough, swimming and waving about, with all the droopings and liftings and languishing side-turnings of the head that I had laughed at. And now I should like to ask, WHO taught him all this? —and me, through him, that the foolish head was not the one swinging itself from side to side and bowing and nodding over the music, but that other which was passing its shallow and self-satisfied judgment on a creature made of finer clay than the frame which carried that same head upon its shoulders?

—Do you want an image of the human will or the self-determining principle, as compared with its pre-arranged and impassable restrictions? A drop of water, imprisoned in a crystal; you may see such a one in any mineralogical collection. One little fluid particle in the crystalline prism of the solid universe!

—Weaken moral obligations?—No, not weaken but define them. When I preach that sermon I spoke of the other day, I shall have to lay down some principles not fully recognized in some of your text-books.

I should have to begin with one most for- midable preliminary. You saw an article the other day in one of the journals, perhaps, in which some old Doctor or other said quietly that patients were very apt to be fools and cowards. But a great many of the clergyman's patients are not only fools and cowards, but also liars.

[Immense sensation at the table.—Sudden retirement of the angular female in oxydated bombazine. Movement of adhesion—as they say in the Chamber of Deputies—on the part of the young fellow they call John. Falling of the old-gentleman-opposite's lower jaw— (gravitation is beginning to get the better of him.) Our landlady to Benjamin Franklin, briskly,—Go to school right off, there's a good boy! Schoolmistress curious,—takes a quick glance at divinity-student. Divinity-student slightly flushed; draws his shoulders back a little, as if a big falsehood,—or truth,—had hit him in the forehead. Myself calm.]

—I should not make such a speech as that, you know, without having pretty substantial indorsers to fall back upon, in case my credit should be disputed. Will you run upstairs, Benjamin Franklin (for B. F. had *not* gone right off, of course), and bring down a small volume from the left upper corner of the right-hand shelves?

[Look at the precious little black, ribbed backed, clean-typed, vellum-papered 32mo. "DESIDERII ERASMI COLLOQUIA. Amstelodami. Typis Ludovici Elzevirii. 1650." Various names written on title-page. Most conspicuous this: Gul. Cookeson, E. Coll. Omn. Anim. 1725. Oxon.

—O William Cookeson, of All-Souls College, Oxford,—then writing as I now write,—now in the dust, where I shall lie,—is this line all that remains to thee of earthly remembrance? Thy name is at least once more spoken by living men;—is it a pleasure to thee? Thou shalt share with me my little draught of immortality,—its week, its month, its year,— whatever it may be,—and then we will go together into the solemn archives of Oblivion's Uncatalogued Library!]

—If you think I have used rather strong language, I shall have to read something to you out of the book of this keen and witty scholar, —the great Erasmus,—who "laid the egg of the Reformation which Luther hatched." Oh, you never read his *Naufragium*, or "Shipwreck," did you? Of course not; for, if you had, I don't think you would have given me credit,

—or discredit,—for entire originality in that speech of mine. That men are cowards in the contemplation of futurity he illustrates by the extraordinary antics of many on board the sinking vessel; that they are fools, by their praying to the sea, and making promises to bits of wood from the true cross, and all manner of similar nonsense; that they are fools, cowards, and liars all at once, by this story:

I will put it into rough English for you.—"I couldn't help laughing to hear one fellow bawling out, so that he might be sure to be heard, a promise to Saint Christopher of Paris —the monstrous statue in the great church there,—that he would give him a wax taper as big as himself. 'Mind what you promise!' said an acquaintance who stood near him, poking him with his elbow; 'you couldn't pay for it, if you sold all your things at auction.' 'Hold your tongue, you donkey!' said the fellow,—but softly, so that Saint Christopher should not hear him,—'do you think I'm in earnest? If I once get my foot on dry ground, catch me giving him so much as a tallow candle!' "

Now, therefore, remembering that those who have been loudest in their talk about the great subject of which we were speaking have not necessarily been wise, brave, and true men, but, on the contrary, have very often been wanting in one or two or all of the qualities these words imply, I should expect to find a good many doctrines current in the schools which I should be obliged to call foolish, cowardly, and false.

—So you would abuse other people's beliefs, Sir, and yet not tell us your own creed!—said the divinity-student, coloring up with a spirit for which I liked him all the better.

—I have a creed,—I replied;—none better, and none shorter. It is told in two words,—the two first of the Paternoster. And when I say these words I mean them. And when I compared the human will to a drop in a crystal, and said I meant to *define* moral obligations, and not weaken them, this was what I intended to express: that the fluent, self-determining power of human beings is a very strictly limited agency in the universe. The chief planes of its enclosing solid are, of course, organization, education, condition. Organization may reduce the power of the will to nothing, as in some idiots; and from this zero the scale mounts upwards by slight gradations. Education is only second to nature. Imagine all the infants born

this year in Boston and Timbuctoo to change places! Condition does less, but "Give me neither poverty nor riches" was the prayer of Agur, and with good reason. If there is any improvement in modern theology, it is in getting out of the region of pure abstractions and taking these every-day working forces into account. The great theological question now heaving and throbbing in the minds of Christian men is this:—

No, I won't talk about these things now. My remarks might be repeated, and it would give my friends pain to see with what personal incivilities I should be visited. Besides, what business has a mere boarder to be talking about such things at a breakfast-table? Let him make puns. To be sure, he was brought up among the Christian fathers, and learned his alphabet out of a quarto "Concilium Tridentinum." He has also heard many thousand theological lectures by men of various denominations; and it is not at all to the credit of these teachers, if he is not fit by this time to express an opinion on theological matters.

I know well enough that there are some of you who had a great deal rather see me stand on my head than use it for any purpose of thought. Does not my friend, the Professor, receive at least two letters a week, requesting him to ...., —on the strength of some youthful antic of his, which, no doubt, authorizes the intelligent constituency of autograph-hunters to address him as a harlequin?

—Well, I can't be savage with you for wanting to laugh, and I like to make you laugh well enough, when I can. But then observe this: if the sense of the ridiculous is one side of an impressible nature, it is very well; but if that is all there is in a man, he had better have been an ape at once, and so have stood at the head of his profession. Laughter and tears are meant to turn the wheels of the same machinery of sensibility; one is wind-power, and the other water-power; that is all. I have often heard the Professor talk about hysterics as being Nature's cleverest illustration of the reciprocal convertibility of the two states of which these acts are the manifestations. But you may see it every day in children; and if you want to choke with stifled tears at the sight of the transition, as it shows itself in older years, go and see Mr. Blake play *Jesse Rural.*

It is a very dangerous thing for a literary man to indulge his love for the ridiculous.

People laugh *with* him just so long as he amuses them; but if he attempts to be serious, they must still have their laugh, and so they laugh *at* him. There is in addition, however, a deeper reason for this than would at first appear. Do you know that you feel a little superior to every man who makes you laugh, whether by making faces or verses? Are you aware that you have a pleasant sense of patronizing him, when you condescend so far as to let him turn somersets, literal or literary, for your royal delight? Now if a man can only be allowed to stand on a daïs, or raised platform, and look down on his neighbor who is exerting his talent for him, oh, it is all right!—first-rate performance!—and all the rest of the fine phrases. But if all at once the performer asks the gentleman to come upon the floor, and, stepping upon the platform, begins to talk down at him,—ah, that wasn't in the programme!

I have never forgotten what happened when Sydney Smith—who, as everybody knows, was an exceedingly sensible man, and a gentleman, every inch of him—ventured to preach a sermon on the Duties of Royalty. The "Quarterly," "so savage and tartarly," came down upon him in the most contemptuous style, as "a joker of jokes," a "diner-out of the first water," in one of his own phrases; sneering at him, insulting him, as nothing but a toady of a court, sneaking behind the anonymous, would ever have been mean enough to do a man of his position and genius, or to any decent person even.—If I were giving advice to a young fellow of talent, with two or three facets to his mind, I would tell him by all means to keep his wit in the background until after he had made a reputation by his more solid qualities. And so to an actor: *Hamlet* first, and *Bob Logic* afterwards, if you like; but don't think, as they say poor Liston used to, that people will be ready to allow that you can do anything great with *Macbeth's* dagger after flourishing about with *Paul Pry's* umbrella. Do you know, too, that the majority of men look upon all who challenge their attention,—for a while, at least,—as beggars, and nuisances? They always try to get off as cheaply as they can; and the cheapest of all things they can give a literary man—pardon the forlorn pleasantry!—is the *funny*-bone. That is all very well so far as it goes, but satisfies no man, and makes a good many angry, as I told you on a former occasion.

—Oh, indeed, no!—I am not ashamed to make you laugh, occasionally. I think I could read you something I have in my desk which would probably make you smile. Perhaps I will read it one of these days, if you are patient with me when I am sentimental and reflective; not just now. The ludicrous has its place in the universe; it is not a human invention, but one of the Divine ideas, illustrated in the practical jokes of kittens and monkeys long before Aristophanes or Shakspeare. How curious it is that we always consider solemnity and the absence of all gay surprises and encounter of wits as essential to the idea of the future life of those whom we thus deprive of half their faculties and then call *blessed!* There are not a few who, even in this life, seem to be preparing themselves for that smileless eternity to which they look forward, by banishing all gayety from their hearts and all joyousness from their countenances. I meet one such in the street not unfrequently, a person of intelligence and education, but who gives me (and all that he passes) such a rayless and chilling look of recognition,—something as if he were one of Heaven's assessors, come down to "doom" every acquaintance he met,—that I have sometimes begun to sneeze on the spot, and gone home with a violent cold, dating from that instant. I don't doubt he would cut his kitten's tail off, if he caught her playing with it. Please tell me, who taught her to play with it?

No, no!—give me a chance to talk to you, my fellow-boarders, and you need not be afraid that I shall have any scruples about entertaining you, if I can do it, as well as giving you some of my serious thoughts, and perhaps my sadder fancies. I know nothing in English or any other literature more admirable than that sentiment of Sir Thomas Browne, "EVERY MAN TRULY LIVES, SO LONG AS HE ACTS HIS NATURE, OR SOME WAY MAKES GOOD THE FACULTIES OF HIMSELF."

I find the great thing in this world is not so much where we stand, as in what direction we are moving: To reach the port of heaven, we must sometimes sail with the wind and sometimes against it,—but we must sail, and not drift, nor lie at anchor. There is one very sad thing in old friendships, to every mind which is really moving onward. It is this: that one cannot help using his early friends as the seaman uses the log, to mark his progress. Every now and then, we throw an old schoolmate over the stern with a string of thought tied to him, and look,—I am afraid with a kind of luxurious and sanctimonious compassion,—to see the rate at which the string reels off, while he lies there bobbing up and down, poor fellow! and we are dashing along with the white foam and bright sparkle at our bows;—the ruffled bosom of prosperity and progress, with a sprig of diamonds stuck in it! But this is only the sentimental side of the matter; for grow we must, if we outgrow all that we love.

Don't misunderstand that metaphor of heaving the log, I beg you. It is merely a smart way of saying that we cannot avoid measuring our rate of movement by those with whom we have long been in the habit of comparing ourselves; and when they once become stationary, we can get our reckoning from them with painful accuracy. We see just what we were when they were our peers, and can strike the balance between that and whatever we may feel ourselves to be now. No doubt we may sometimes be mistaken. If we change our last simile to that very old and familiar one of a fleet leaving a harbor and sailing in company for some distant region, we can get what we want out of it. There is one of our companions;—her streamers were torn into rags before she had got into the open sea, then by and by her sails blew out of the ropes one after another, the waves swept her deck, and as night came on we left her a seeming wreck, as we flew under our pyramid of canvas. But lo! at dawn she is still in sight,—it may be in advance of us. Some deep ocean-current has been moving her on, strong, but silent,—yes, stronger than these noisy winds that puff our sails until they are swollen as the cheeks of jubilant cherubim. And when at last the black steam-tug with the skeleton arms, which comes out of the mist sooner or later and takes us all in tow, grapples her and goes off panting and groaning with her, it is to that harbor where all wrecks are refitted and where, alas! we, towering in our pride, may never come.

So you will not think I mean to speak lightly of old friendships, because we cannot help instituting comparisons between our present and former selves by the aid of those who were what we were, but are not what we are. Nothing strikes one more, in the race of life, than to see how many give out in the first half of the course. "Commencement day" always reminds me of the start for the "Derby," when the beautiful high-bred three-year-olds of the season are brought up for trial. That day is the

start, and life is the race. Here we are at Cambridge, and a class is just "graduating." Poor Harry! he was to have been there too, but he has paid forfeit; step out here into the grass behind the church; ah! there it is:—

"HUNC LAPIDEM POSUERUNT
SOCII MŒRENTES"

But this is the start, and here they are,—coats bright as silk, and manes as smooth as *eau lustrale* can make them. Some of the best of the colts are pranced round, a few minutes each, to show their paces. What is that old gentleman crying about? and the old lady by him, and the three girls, what are they all covering their eyes for? Oh, that is *their* colt which has just been trotted up on the stage. Do they really think those little thin legs can do anything in such a slashing sweepstakes as is coming off in these next forty years? Oh, this terrible gift of second-sight that comes to some of us when we begin to look through the silvered rings of the *arcus senilis!*

Ten years gone. First turn in the race. A few broken down; two or three bolted. Several show in advance of the ruck. *Cassock*, a black colt, seems to be ahead of the rest; those black colts commonly get the start, I have noticed, of the others, in the first quarter. *Meteor* has pulled up.

Twenty years. Second corner turned. *Cassock* has dropped from the front, and *Judex*, an iron-gray, has the lead. But look! how they have thinned out! Down flat,—five,—six,—how many? They lie still enough! they will not get up again in this race, be very sure! And the rest of them, what a "tailing off"! Anybody can see who is going to win,—perhaps.

Thirty years. Third corner turned. *Dives*, bright sorrel, ridden by the fellow in a yellow jacket, begins to make play fast; is getting to be the favorite with many. But who is that other one that has been lengthening his stride from the first, and now shows close up to the front? Don't you remember the quiet brown colt *Asteroid*, with the star in his forehead? That is he; he is one of the sort that lasts; look out for him! The black "colt," as we used to call him, is in the background, taking it easily in a gentle trot. There is one they used to call *the Filly*, on account of a certain feminine air he had; well up, you see; the Filly is not to be despised, my boy!

Forty years. More dropping off,—but places much as before.

Fifty years. Race over. All that are on the course are coming in at a walk; no more running. Who is ahead? Ahead? What! and the winning-post a slab of white or gray stone standing out from that turf where there is no more jockeying or straining for victory! Well, the world marks their places in its betting-book; but be sure that these matter very little, if they have run as well as they knew how!

—Did I not say to you a little while ago that the universe swam in an ocean of similitudes and analogies? I will not quote Cowley, or Burns, or Wordsworth, just now, to show you what thoughts were suggested to them by the simplest natural objects, such as a flower or a leaf; but I will read you a few lines, if you do not object, suggested by looking at a section of one of those chambered shells to which is given the name of Pearly Nautilus. We need not trouble ourselves about the distinction between this and the Paper Nautilus, the *Argonauta* of the ancients. The name applied to both shows that each had long been compared to a ship, as you may see more fully in Webster's Dictionary, or the "Encyclopedia," to which he refers. If you will look into Roget's Bridgewater Treatise, you will find a figure of one of these shells and a section of it. The last will show you the series of enlarging compartments successively dwelt in by the animal that inhabits the shell, which is built in a widening spiral. Can you find no lesson in this?

The Chambered Nautilus

This is the ship of pearl, which, poets feign,
  Sails the unshadowed main,—
  The venturous bark that flings

On the sweet summer wind its purpled wings
In gulfs enchanted, where the siren sings,
  And coral reefs lie bare,
Where the cold sea-maids rise to sun their streaming hair.

Its webs of living gauze no more unfurl;
  Wrecked is the ship of pearl!
  And every chambered cell,
Where its dim dreaming life was wont to dwell,
As the frail tenant shaped his growing shell,
  Before thee lies revealed,—
Its irised ceiling rent, its sunless crypt unsealed!

Year after year beheld the silent toil
  That spread his lustrous coil;
  Still, as the spiral grew,
He left the past year's dwelling for the new,
Stole with soft step its shining archway through,
  Built up its idle door,
Stretched in his last-found home, and knew the old no more.

Thanks for the heavenly message brought by thee,
  Child of the wandering sea,
  Cast from her lap forlorn!
From thy dead lips a clearer note is born
Than ever Triton blew from wreathèd horn!
  While on mine ear it rings,
Through the deep caves of thought I hear a voice that sings:—

Build thee more stately mansions, O my soul,
  As the swift seasons roll!
  Leave thy low-vaulted past!
Let each new temple, nobler than the last,
Shut thee from heaven with a dome more vast,
  Till thou at length art free,
Leaving thine outgrown shell by life's unresting sea!

                                    1857–1858

JAMES RUSSELL LOWELL

1819–1891

"IN LOWELL," wrote his good friend, William Dean Howells, "I was always conscious of an older and closer and stricter civilization than my own, an unbroken tradition, a more authoritative status. His democracy was more of the head and mine more of the heart, and his denied the equality which mine affirmed." Lowell was indeed the last great literary brahmin in a changing Boston. The son of a Unitarian minister, he was born at Elmwood House in Cambridge, an old colonial mansion screened in leafage and surrounded by smooth lawns, easy of access from Harvard College, and disturbed only by the bells of horse-cars passing in Brattle

Street. His education was in Cambridge: Wells's classical school, Harvard (1838), Harvard Law (1840). Students coming over from the Yard during his long professorship at Harvard (1856–1876) would find him in his crowded study at Elmwood, reserved, handsome behind his reddish beard, with a book on his knees and a pipe in his mouth.

His marriage to Maria White in 1844 gave new direction to Lowell's life. She was an ardent abolitionist, a gifted poet, and an extremely beautiful girl. And it was she, primarily, who drew Lowell out of his basic conservatism and into the torrent of antislavery discussion which in the mid-forties had already begun to split the country into factions. Lowell's great year was the fourth of his marriage, 1848, when he became corresponding editor of the *National Anti-Slavery Standard* of New York, published his *Poems*, second series, composed *A Fable for Critics* and *The Vision of Sir Launfal*, and collected the first series of *The Biglow Papers*. But domestic misfortunes crowded in. Of the four children only one survived infancy, and when his wife died two months before their ninth wedding anniversary, a light went out in Lowell.

Lowell's indolence was a legend among his contemporaries, but all three periods of his life after college disprove the accusation. While his wife lived he produced with incredible speed much of his best work. Although he wrote little between 1849 and 1864, and began to think that his poetical moon had set, he studied in Europe (1851–1852, and again in 1855–1856), labored assiduously in his Harvard professorship, edited the *Atlantic Monthly* from its inception in 1857 until his resignation in 1861, and began in 1864 an editorial association with Charles Eliot Norton on the *North American Review*. To this period also belong *Fireside Travels* (1864), *The Biglow Papers*, second series (1867), and the critical essays growing out of his professorial lectures (*Among My Books*, 1870, second series, 1876; *My Study Windows*, 1871). These are wise and savory essays whose consistently high literary quality makes them still good reading, though their frequent failure to grasp central issues places them nearer to appreciation than to criticism. In 1877, as if to set another milestone to his career, he saw through the press his complete poetical works.

After the mid-century Lowell's conservatism gradually deepened, while his personal austerity was heightened by his diplomatic service in Spain and England. Through Howells's intercession, President Hayes appointed Lowell Minister to Spain (1877–1880) and afterward to the Court of St. James (1880–1885). In view of his former enmity toward England it was ironic that he should now take her so rapidly to his heart. But he liked the "comfortably padded environment" of London, said Howells, and on his return to private life affected the ambassadorial frock-coat and topper in place of the unostentatious clothes he had hitherto worn. Of his last six summers he spent four in England, near Whitby, before he returned to the quiet of Elmwood to die.

The impressionistic mode of criticism which mars many of Lowell's critical essays serves him well in *A Fable for Critics*, which is comparable to Leigh Hunt's *Feast of The Poets*, and displays a Byronic brilliance in concocting startling rhymes.

The Biglow Papers are topical and controversial. The war with Mexico (1846–1848), through which Texas was brought into the Union, was very unpopular among abolitionists and free-soilers in New England. Most Texans were proslavery, and the new territory greatly enlarged slave-holding areas. Thoreau saw the war as one of conquest in the interest of slave-mongers. No less antagonistic was Hosea Biglow, a young Jaalam farmer whom Lowell created as a mouthpiece for his own opinions. "My ingenious young parishioner," says Rev. Homer Wilbur, Hosea's fictitious and pedantic editor, "brought to my study a copy of verses touching the acquisition of territory resulting from the Mexican War, and the folly of leaving the question of

slavery or freedom to the adjudication of chance." Although Hosea is "kind o' prest with
Hayin' " on the farm, he finds time to compose nine commonsense poems in his Yankee dialect.
These are Lowell's contribution to the growth of the Republican (Liberty or Free-soil) Party,
which wished to exclude slavery from all newly acquired territory. The papers appeared serially during the war. Less successful is the second series, begun in the *Atlantic* in 1861, and later
collected. Having passed the storm-and-stress period of the forties, Lowell now speaks as a conservative Republican, less interested in slavery than in the preservation of the Union. His criticism of England for espousing the Confederate cause has something of the old fire. But in
general his fierce humanitarianism has cooled to sober citizenship, though one should not forget
his best occasional poem, the *Ode Recited at the Harvard Commemoration*, with its impassioned tribute to the martyred Lincoln.

G. W. Cooke, *A Bibliography of James Russell Lowell*, Boston, 1906.
The Complete Writings of James Russell Lowell, 16 vols., Cambridge, 1904.
The Letters of James Russell Lowell, C. E. Norton, ed., 2 vols., New York, 1894.
New Letters of James Russell Lowell, M. A. DeW. Howe, ed., New York, 1932.
Leon Howard, *Victorian Knight-errant: A Study of the Early Literary Career of James Russell Lowell*, Berkeley, Cali-
fornia, 1952.
J. J. Reilly, *James Russell Lowell as a Critic*, New York, 1915.

» » *From:* A FABLE FOR CRITICS « «

. . .

I called this a "Fable for Critics"; you think
    it's
More like a display of my rhythmical trinkets;
My plot, like an icicle, 's slender and slippery,
Every moment more slender, and likely to slip
    awry,
And the reader unwilling *in loco desipere*,
Is free to jump over as much of my frippery
As he fancies, and, if he's a provident skipper,
    he
May have like Odysseus control of the gales,
And get safe to port, ere his patience quite fails;
Moreover, although 'tis a slender return   10
For your toil and expense, yet my paper will
    burn,
And, if you have manfully struggled thus far
    with me,
You may e'en twist me up, and just light your
    cigar with me:
If too angry for that, you can tear me in pieces,
And my *membra disjecta* consign to the
    breezes,
A fate like great Ratzau's, whom one of those
    bores,
Who beflead with bad verses poor Louis
    Quatorze,
Describes (the first verse somehow ends with
    victoire),

As *dispersant partout et ses membres et sa
    gloire;*
Or, if I were over-desirous of earning   20
A repute among noodles for classical learning,
I could pick you a score of allusions, I wis,
As new as the jests of *Didaskalos tis;*
Better still, I could make out a good solid list
From authors recondite who do not exist,—
But that would be naughty: at least, I could
    twist
Something out of Absyrtus, or turn your in-
    quiries
After Milton's prose metaphor, drawn from
    Osiris;—
But, as Cicero says he won't say this or that
(A fetch, I must say, most transparent and
    flat),   30
After saying whate'er he could possibly think
    of,—
I simply will state that I pause on the brink of
A mire, ankle-deep, of deliberate confusion,
Made up of old jumbles of classic allusion:
So, when you were thinking yourselves to be
    pitied,
Just conceive how much harder your teeth
    you'd have gritted,
An 'twere not for the dulness I've kindly
    omitted.

. . .

"There comes Emerson first, whose rich words, every one,
Are like gold nails in temples to hang trophies on,
Whose prose is grand verse, while his verse, the Lord knows,   40
Is some of it pr— No, 'tis not even prose;
I'm speaking of metres; some poems have welled
From those rare depths of soul that have ne'er been excelled;
They're not epics, but that doesn't matter a pin,
In creating, the only hard thing's to begin;
A grass-blade's no easier to make than an oak;
If you've once found the way, you've achieved the grand stroke;
In the worst of his poems are mines of rich matter,
But thrown in a heap with a crush and a clatter;
Now it is not one thing nor another alone   50
Makes a poem, but rather the general tone,
The something pervading, uniting the whole,
The before unconceived, unconceivable soul,
So that just in removing this trifle or that, you
Take away, as it were, a chief limb of the statue;
Roots, wood, bark, and leaves singly perfect may be,
But, clapt hodge-podge together, they don't make a tree.

"But, to come back to Emerson (whom, by the way,
I believe we left waiting),—his is, we may say,
A Greek head on right Yankee shoulders, whose range   60
Has Olympus for one pole, for t'other the Exchange;
He seems, to my thinking (although I'm afraid
The comparison must, long ere this, have been made),
A Plotinus-Montaigne, where the Egyptian's gold mist
And the Gascon's shrewd wit cheek-by-jowl coexist;
All admire, and yet scarcely six converts he's got
To I don't (nor they either) exactly know what;
For though he builds glorious temples, 'tis odd
He leaves never a doorway to get in a god.
'Tis refreshing to old-fashioned people like me   70
To meet such a primitive Pagan as he,
In whose mind all creation is duly respected

As parts of himself—just a little projected;
And who's willing to worship the stars and the sun,
A convert to—nothing but Emerson.
So perfect a balance there is in his head,
That he talks of things sometimes as if they were dead;
Life, nature, love, God, and affairs of that sort,
He looks at as merely ideas; in short,
As if they were fossils stuck round in a cabinet,   80
Of such vast extent that our earth's a mere dab in it;
Composed just as he is inclined to conjecture her,
Namely, one part pure earth, ninety-nine parts pure lecturer;
You are filled with delight at his clear demonstration,
Each figure, word, gesture, just fits the occasion,
With the quiet precision of science he'll sort 'em,
But you can't help suspecting the whole a *post mortem.*

"There are persons, mole-blind to the soul's make and style,
Who insist on a likeness 'twixt him and Carlyle;
To compare him with Plato would be vastly fairer,   90
Carlyle's the more burly, but E. is the rarer;
He sees fewer objects, but clearlier, truelier,
If C.'s as original, E.'s more peculiar;
That he's more of a man you might say of the one,
Of the other he's more of an Emerson;
C.'s the Titan, as shaggy of mind as of limb,—
E. the clear-eyed Olympian, rapid and slim;
The one's two thirds Norseman, the other half Greek,
Where the one's most abounding, the other's to seek;
C.'s generals require to be seen in the mass,—   100
E.'s specialties gain if enlarged by the glass;
C. gives nature and God his own fits of the blues,
And rims common-sense things with mystical hues,—
E. sits in a mystery calm and intense,
And looks coolly around him with sharp common sense;
C. shows you how every-day matters unite
With the dim transdiurnal recesses of night,—

While E., in a plain, preternatural way,
Makes mysteries matters of mere every day;
C. draws all his characters quite *à la*
Fuseli,—   110
Not sketching their bundles of muscles and
thews illy,
He paints with a brush so untamed and profuse,
They seem nothing but bundles of muscles and
thews;
E. is rather like Flaxman, lines strait and severe,
And a colorless outline, but full, round, and
clear;—
To the men he thinks worthy he frankly accords
The design of a white marble statue in words.
C. labors to get at the centre, and then
Take a reckoning from there of his actions and
men;
E. calmly assumes the said centre as granted,
And, given himself, has whatever is wanted. 121

. . .

"There is Whittier, whose swelling and ve-
hement heart
Strains the strait-breasted drab of the Quaker
apart,
And reveals the live Man, still supreme and
erect,
Underneath the bemummying wrappers of
sect;
There was ne'er a man born who had more of
the swing
Of the true lyric bard and all that kind of thing;
And his failures arise (though he seem not to
know it)
From the very same cause that has made him
a poet,—
A fervor of mind which knows no separa-
tion   130
'Twixt simple excitement and pure inspiration,
As my Pythoness erst sometimes erred from not
knowing
If 'twere I or mere wind through her tripod
was blowing;
Let his mind once get head in its favorite
direction
And the torrent of verse bursts the dams of
reflection,
While, borne with the rush of the metre along,
The poet may chance to go right or go wrong,
Content with the whirl and delirium of song;
Then his grammar's not always correct, nor his
rhymes,
And he's prone to repeat his own lyrics some-
times,   140

Not his best, though, for those are struck off at
white-heats
When the heart in his breast like a trip-hammer
beats,
And can ne'er be repeated again any more
Than they could have been carefully plotted
before:
Like old what's-his-name there at the battle of
Hastings
(Who, however, gave more than mere rhyth-
mical bastings),
Our Quaker leads off metaphorical fights
For reform and whatever they call human
rights,
Both singing and striking in front of the war
And hitting his foes with the mallet of Thor; 150
Anne haec, one exclaims, on beholding his
knocks,
Vestis filii tui, O leather-clad Fox?
Can that be thy son, in the battle's mid din,
Preaching brotherly love and then driving it in
To the brain of the tough old Goliath of sin,
With the smoothest of pebbles from Castaly's
spring
Impressed on his hard moral sense with a sling?

. . .

"There is Hawthorne, with genius so shrink-
ing and rare
That you hardly at first see the strength that is
there;
A frame so robust, with a nature so sweet, 160
So earnest, so graceful, so lithe and so fleet,
Is worth a descent from Olympus to meet;
'Tis as if a rough oak that for ages had stood,
With his gnarled bony branches like ribs of the
wood,
Should bloom, after cycles of struggle and
scathe,
With a single anemone trembly and rathe;
His strength is so tender, his wildness so meek,
That a suitable parallel sets one to seek,—
He's a John Bunyan Fouqué, a Puritan Tieck;
When nature was shaping him, clay was not
granted   170
For making so full-sized a man as she wanted,
So, to fill out her model, a little she spared
From some finer-grained stuff for a woman
prepared,
And she could not have hit a more excellent
plan
For making him fully and perfectly man.
The success of her scheme gave her so much
delight,

That she tried it again, shortly after, in Dwight;
Only, while she was kneading and shaping the
clay,
She sang to her work in her sweet childish way,
And found, when she'd put the last touch to
his soul,   180
That the music had somehow got mixed with
the whole.

"Here's Cooper, who's written six volumes
to show
He's as good as a lord: well, let's grant that
he's so;
If a person prefer that description of praise,
Why, a coronet's certainly cheaper than bays;
But he need take no pains to convince us he's
not
(As his enemies say) the American Scott.
Choose any twelve men, and let C. read aloud
That one of his novels of which he's most
proud,
And I'd lay any bet that, without ever quit-
ting   190
Their box, they'd be all, to a man, for ac-
quitting.
He has drawn you one character, though, that
is new,
One wildflower he's plucked that is wet with
the dew
Of this fresh Western world, and, the thing
not to mince,
He has done naught but copy it ill ever since;
His Indians, with proper respect be it said,
Are just Natty Bumppo, daubed over with red,
And his very Long Toms are the same useful
Nat,
Rigged up in duck pants and a sou'wester hat
(Though once in a Coffin, a good chance was
found   200
To have slipped the old fellow a way under-
ground).
All his other men-figures are clothes upon
sticks,
The dernière chemise of a man in a fix
(As a captain besieged, when his garrison's
small,
Sets up caps upon poles to be seen o'er the
wall);
And the women he draws from one model don't
vary,
All sappy as maples and flat as a prairie.
When a character's wanted, he goes to the task
As a cooper would do in composing a cask;
He picks out the staves, of their qualities
heedful,   210

Just hoops them together as tight as is needful,
And, if the best fortune should crown the attempt, he
Has made at the most something wooden and
empty.

"Don't suppose I would underrate Cooper's
abilities;
If I thought you'd do that, I should feel very
ill at ease;
The men who have given to one character life
And objective existence are not very rife;
You may number them all, both prose-writers
and singers,
Without overrunning the bounds of your
fingers,
And Natty won't go to oblivion quicker   220
Than Adams the parson or Primrose the vicar.

"There is one thing in Cooper I like, too,
and that is
That on manners he lectures his countrymen
gratis;
Not precisely so either, because, for a rarity,
He is paid for his tickets in unpopularity.
Now he may overcharge his American pictures,
But you'll grant there's a good deal of truth in
his strictures;
And I honor the man who is willing to sink
Half his present repute for the freedom to
think,
And, when he has thought, be his cause strong
or weak,   230
Will risk t'other half for the freedom to speak,
Caring naught for what vengeance the mob has
in store,
Let that mob be the upper ten thousand or
lower.

            .   .   .

"There comes Poe, with his raven, like
Barnaby Rudge,
Three fifths of him genius and two fifths sheer
fudge,
Who talks like a book of iambs and pentame-
ters,
In a way to make people of common sense
damn metres,
Who has written some things quite the best of
their kind,
But the heart somehow seems all squeezed out
by the mind,
Who—but hey-day! What's this? Messieurs
Mathews and Poe,   240
You mustn't fling mud-balls at Longfellow so,

Does it make a man worse that his character's
such
As to make his friends love him (as you think)
too much?
Why, there is not a bard at this moment alive
More willing than he that his fellows should
thrive:
While you are abusing him thus, even now
He would help either one of you out of a
slough;
You may say that he's smooth and all that till
you're hoarse,
But remember that elegance also is force;
After polishing granite as much as you will, 250
The heart keeps its tough old persistency still;
Deduct all you can, *that* still keeps you at bay;
Why, he'll live till men weary of Collins and
Gray.
I'm not over-fond of Greek metres in English,
To me rhyme's a gain, so it be not too jinglish,
And your modern hexameter verses are no more
Like Greek ones than sleek Mr. Pope is like
Homer;
As the roar of the sea to the coo of a pigeon
is,
So, compared to your moderns, sounds old
Melesigenes;
I may be too partial, the reason, perhaps,
o't is   260
That I've heard the old blind man recite his
own rhapsodies,
And my ear with that music impregnate may
be,
Like the poor exiled shell with the soul of the
sea,
Or as one can't bear Strauss when his nature is
cloven

To its deeps within deeps by the stroke of
Beethoven;
But, set that aside, and 'tis truth that I speak,
Had Theocritus written in English, not Greek,
I believe that his exquisite sense would scarce
change a line
In that rare, tender, virgin-like pastoral Evan-
geline.
That's not ancient nor modern, its place is
apart   270
Where time has no sway, in the realm of pure
Art,
'Tis a shrine of retreat from Earth's hubbub
and strife
As quiet and chaste as the author's own life.

          .   .   .

"There is Lowell, who's striving Parnassus
to climb
With a whole bale of *isms* tied together with
rhyme,
He might get on alone, spite of brambles and
boulders,
But he can't with that bundle he has on his
shoulders,
The top of the hill he will ne'er come nigh
reaching
Till he learns the distinction 'twixt singing and
preaching;
His lyre has some chords that would ring pretty
well,   280
But he'd rather by half make a drum of the
shell,
And rattle away till he's old as Methusalem,
At the head of a march to the last new
Jerusalem. . . .

1848   1848

» » *From:* THE BIGLOW PAPERS « «

FIRST SERIES

NO. I

A LETTER

From Mr. Ezekiel Biglow of Jaalam to the Hon.
Joseph T. Buckingham, Editor of the Boston
Courier, Inclosing a Poem of His Son, Mr. Ho-
sea Biglow

JAYLEM, june 1846

MISTER EDDYTER:—Our Hosea wuz down to
Boston last week, and he see a cruetin Sarjunt

a struttin round as popler as a hen with 1 chick-
ing, with 2 fellers a drummin and fifin arter him
like all nater. the sarjunt he thout Hosea hed
n't gut his i teeth cut cos he looked a kindo's
though he'd jest com down, so he cal'lated to
hook him in, but Hosy woodn't take none o' his
sarse for all he hed much as 20 Rooster's tales
stuck onto his hat and eenamost enuf brass a
bobbin up and down on his shoulders and fig-
ureed onto his coat and trousis, let alone wut
nater hed sot in his featers, to make a 6 pounder
out on.

wal, Hosea he com home considerabal riled, and arter I'd gone to bed I heern Him a thrashin round like a short-tailed Bull in fli-time. The old Woman ses she to me ses she, Zekle, ses she, our Hosee's gut the chollery or suthin anuther ses she, don't you Bee skeered, ses I, he's oney amakin pottery[1] ses i, he's ollers on hand at that ere busynes like Da & martin, and shure enuf, cum mornin, Hosy he cum down stares full chizzle, hare on eend and cote tales flyin, and sot rite of to go reed his varses to Parson Wilbur bein he haint aney grate shows o' book larnin himself, bimeby he cum back and sed the parson wuz dreffle tickled with 'em as i hoop you will Be, and said they wuz True grit.

Hosea ses taint hardly fair to call 'em hisn now, cos the parson kind o' slicked off sum o' the last varses, but he told Hosee he didn't want to put his ore in to tetch to the Rest on 'em, bein they wuz verry well As thay wuz, and then Hosy ses he sed suthin a nuther about Simplex Mundishes or sum sech feller, but I guess Hosea kind o' didn't hear him, for I never hearn o' nobody o' that name in this vil-ladge, and I've lived here man and boy 76 year cum next tater diggin, and thair aint no wheres a kitting spryer 'n I be.

If you print 'em I wish you'd jest let folks know who hosy's father is, cos my ant Keziah used to say it's nater to be curus ses she, she aint livin though and he's a likely kind o' lad.

 EZEKIEL BIGLOW

Thrash away, you'll *hev* to rattle
  On them kittle-drums o' yourn,—
'Taint a knowin' kind o' cattle
  Thet is ketched with mouldy corn;
Put in stiff, you fifer feller,
  Let folks see how spry you be,—
Guess you'll toot till you are yeller
  'Fore you git ahold o' me!

Thet air flag's a leetle rotten,
  Hope it aint your Sunday's best;—   10
Fact! it takes a sight o' cotton
  To stuff out a soger's chest:
Sence we farmers hev to pay fer 't,
  Ef you must wear humps like these,
Sposin' you should try salt hay fer 't,
  It would du ez slick ez grease.

'Twould n't suit them Southun fellers,
  They 're a dreffle graspin' set,

Aut insanit, aut versos facit.—H. W. [Lowell's note.]

We must ollers blow the bellers
  Wen they want their irons het;   20
May be it's all right ez preachin',
  But *my* narves it kind o' grates,
Wen I see the overreachin'
  O' them nigger-drivin' States.

Them thet rule us, them slave-traders,
  Haint they cut a thunderin' swarth
(Helped by Yankee renegaders),
  Thru the vartu o' the North!
We begin to think it's nater
  To take sarse an' not be riled;—   30
Who'd expect to see a tater
  All on eend at bein' biled?

Ez fer war, I call it murder,—
  There you hev it plain an' flat;
I don't want to go no furder
  Than my Testyment fer that;
God hez sed so plump an' fairly,
  It's ez long ez it is broad,
An' you've gut to git up airly
  Ef you want to take in God.   40

'Taint your eppyletts an' feathers
  Make the thing a grain more right;
'Taint afollerin' your bell-wethers
  Will excuse ye in His sight;
Ef you take a sword an' dror it,
  An' go stick a feller thru,
Guv'ment aint to answer for it,
  God'll send the bill to you.

Wut's the use o' meetin'-goin'
  Every Sabbath, wet or dry,   50
Ef it's right to go amowin'
  Feller-men like oats an' rye?
I dunno but wut it's pooty
  Trainin' round in bobtail coats,—
But it's curus Christian dooty
  This 'ere cuttin' folks's throats.

They may talk o' Freedom's airy
  Tell they're pupple in the face,—
It's a grand gret cemetary
  Fer the barthrights of our race;   60
They jest want this Californy
  So's to lug new slave-states in
To abuse ye, an' to scorn ye,
  An' to plunder ye like sin.

Aint it cute to see a Yankee
  Take sech everlastin' pains,
All to git the Devil's thankee

Helpin' on 'em weld their chains?
Wy, it's jest ez clear ez figgers,
   Clear ez one an' one makes two,   70
Chaps thet make black slaves o' niggers
   Want to make wite slaves o' you.

Tell ye jest the eend I've come to
   Arter cipherin' plaguy smart,
An' it makes a handy sum, tu,
   Any gump could larn by heart;
Laborin' man an' laborin' woman
   Hev one glory an' one shame.
Ev'y thin' thet's done inhuman
   Injers all on 'em the same.   80

'Taint by turnin' out to hack folks
   You're agoin' to git your right,
Nor by lookin' down on black folks
   Coz you're put upon by wite;
Slavery aint o' nary color,
   'Taint the hide thet makes it wus,
All it keers fer in a feller
   'S jest to make him fill its pus.

Want to tackle *me* in, du ye?
   I expect you'll hev to wait;   90
Wen cold lead puts daylight thru ye
   You'll begin to kal'late;
S'pose the crows wun't fall to pickin'
   All the carkiss from your bones,
Coz you helped to give a lickin'
   To them poor half-Spanish drones?

Jest go home an' ask our Nancy
   Wether I'd be sech a goose
Ez to jine ye,—guess you'd fancy
   The etarnal bung wuz loose!   100
She wants me fer home consumption,
   Let alone the hay's to mow,—
Ef you're arter folks o' gumption,
   You've a darned long row to hoe.

Take them editors thet's crowin'
   Like a cockerel three months old,—
Don't ketch any on 'em goin',
   Though they *be* so blasted bold;
Aint they a prime lot o' fellers?
   'Fore they think on't guess they'll sprout
(Like a peach thet's got the yellers),   111
   With the meanness bustin' out.

Wal, go 'long to help 'em stealin'
   Bigger pens to cram with slaves,   1846

Help the men thet's ollers dealin'
   Insults on your fathers' graves;
Help the strong to grind the feeble,
   Help the many agin the few,
Help the men thet call your people   119
   Witewashed slaves an' peddlin' crew!

Massachusetts, God forgive her,
   She's akneelin' with the rest,
She, thet ough' to ha' clung ferever
   In her grand old eagle-nest;
She thet ough' to stand so fearless
   W'ile the wracks are round her hurled,
Holdin' up a beacon peerless
   To the oppressed of all the world!

Ha'n't they sold your colored seamen?
   Ha'n't they made your env'ys w'iz?   130
Wut'll make ye act like freemen?
   Wut'll git your dander riz?
Come, I'll tell ye wut I'm thinkin'
   Is our dooty in this fix,
They'd ha' done 't ez quick ez winkin'
   In the days o' seventy-six.

Clang the bells in every steeple,
   Call all true men to disown
The tradoocers of our people,
   The enslavers o' their own;   140
Let our dear old Bay State proudly
   Put the trumpet to her mouth,
Let her ring this messidge loudly
   In the ears of all the South:—

"I'll return ye good fer evil
   Much ez we frail mortils can,
But I wun't go help the Devil
   Makin' man the cus o' man;
Call me coward, call me traiter,
   Jest ez suits your mean idees,—   150
Here I stand a tyrant-hater,
   An' the friend o' God an' Peace!"

Ef I'd *my* way I hed ruther
   We should go to work an' part,—
They take one way, we take t' other,
   Guess it wouldn't break my heart;
Man hed ough' to put asunder
   Them thet God has noways jined;
An' I shouldn't gretly wonder
   Ef there's thousands o' my mind.   160
                                      1846

» » « «

» » THOREAU « «

What contemporary, if he was in the fighting period of his life, (since Nature sets limits about her conscription for spiritual fields, as the state does in physical warfare), will ever forget what was somewhat vaguely called the "Transcendental Movement" of thirty years ago? Apparently set astir by Carlyle's essays on the "Signs of the Times," and on "History," the final and more immediate impulse seemed to be given by "Sartor Resartus." At least the republication in Boston of that wonderful Abraham à Sancta Clara sermon on Lear's text of the miserable forked radish gave the signal for a sudden mental and moral mutiny. *Ecce nunc tempus acceptabile!* was shouted on all hands with every variety of emphasis, and by voices of every conceivable pitch, representing the three sexes of men, women, and Lady Mary Wortley Montagues. The nameless eagle of the tree Ygdrasil was about to sit at last, and wild-eyed enthusiasts rushed from all sides, each eager to thrust under the mystic bird that chalk egg from which the new and fairer Creation was to be hatched in due time. *Redeunt Saturnia regna,*—so far was certain, though in what shape, or by what methods, was still a matter of debate. Every possible form of intellectual and physical dyspepsia brought forth its gospel. Bran had its prophets, and the pre-sartorial simplicity of Adam its martyrs, tailored impromptu from the tar-pot by incensed neighbors, and sent forth to illustrate the "feathered Mercury," as defined by Webster and Worcester. Plainness of speech was carried to a pitch that would have taken away the breath of George Fox; and even swearing had its evangelists, who answered a simple inquiry after their health with an elaborate ingenuity of imprecation that might have been honorably mentioned by Marlborough in general orders. Everybody had a mission (with a capital M) to attend to everybody else's business. No brain but has its private maggot, which must have found pitiably short commons sometimes. Not a few inpecunious zealots abjured the use of money (unless earned by other people), professing to live on the internal revenues of the spirit. Some had an assurance of instant millennium so soon as hooks and eyes should be substituted for buttons. Communities were established where everything was to be common but common-sense. Men renounced their old gods, and hesitated only whether to bestow their furloughed allegiance on Thor or Budh. Conventions were held for every hitherto inconceivable purpose. The belated gift of tongues, as among the Fifth Monarchy men, spread like a contagion, rendering its victims incomprehensible to all Christian men; whether equally so to the most distant possible heathen or not was unexperimented, though many would have subscribed liberally that a fair trial might be made. It was the pentecost of Shinar. The day of utterances reproduced the day of rebuses and anagrams, and there was nothing so simple that uncial letters and the style of Diphilus the Labyrinth could not turn it into a riddle. Many foreign revolutionists out of work added to the general misunderstanding their contribution of broken English in every most ingenious form of fracture. All stood ready at a moment's notice to reform everything but themselves. The general motto was:—

> "And we'll *talk* with them, too,
> And take upon's the mystery of things
> As if we were God's spies."

Nature is always kind enough to give even her clouds a humorous lining. I have barely hinted at the comic side of the affair, for the material was endless. This was the whistle and trailing fuse of the shell, but there was a very solid and serious kernel, full of the most deadly explosiveness. Thoughtful men divined it, but the generality suspected nothing. The word "transcendental" then was the maid of all work for those who could not think, as "Pre-Raphaelite" has been more recently for people of the same limited housekeeping. The truth is, that there was a much nearer metaphysical relation and a much more distant æsthetic and literary relation between Carlyle and the Apostles of the Newness, as they were called in New England, than has commonly been supposed. Both represented the reaction and revolt against *Philisterei,* a renewal of the old battle begun in modern times by Erasmus and Reuchlin, and continued by Lessing, Goethe, and, in a far narrower sense, by Heine in Germany, and of which Fielding, Sterne, and Wordsworth in different ways have been the leaders in England. It was simply a struggle for fresh air, in which, if the windows could not be opened, there was danger that panes would be broken, though painted with images of saints and martyrs. Light, colored by these reverend effigies, was none the more respirable for being picturesque. There is only one thing better than tradition, and that is the original and eternal life out of which all tradition takes its rise. It was this life which the reformers demanded, with more or less clearness of consciousness and expression, life in politics, life in literature, life in religion. Of what use to import a gospel from Judæa, if we leave behind the soul that made it possible, the God who keeps it forever real and present? Surely Abana and Pharpar *are* better than Jordan, if a living faith be mixed with those waters and none with these.

Scotch Presbyterianism as a motive of spiritual progress was dead; New England Puritanism was in like manner dead; in other words, Protestantism had made its fortune and no longer protested; but till Carlyle spoke out in the Old World and Emerson in the New, no one had dared to proclaim, *Le roi est mort: vive le roi!* The meaning of which proclamation was essentially this: the vital spirit has long since departed out of this form once so kingly, and the great seal has been in commission long enough; but meanwhile the soul of man, from which all power emanates and to which it reverts, still survives in undiminished royalty; God still survives, little as you gentlemen of the Commission seem to be aware of it,—nay, will possibly outlive the whole of you, incredible as it may appear. The truth is, that both Scotch Presbyterianism and New England Puritanism made their new avatar in Carlyle and Emerson, the heralds of their formal decease, and the tendency of the one toward Authority and of the other toward Independency might have been prophesied by whoever had studied history. The necessity was not so much in the men as in the principles they represented and the traditions which overruled them. The Puritanism of the past found its unwilling poet in Hawthorne, the rarest creative imagination of the century, the rarest in some ideal respects since Shakespeare; but the Puritanism that cannot die, the Puritanism that made New England what it is, and is destined to make America what it should be, found its voice in Emerson. Though holding himself aloof from all active partnership in movements of reform, he has been the sleeping partner who has supplied a great part of their capital.

The artistic range of Emerson is narrow, as every well-read critic must feel at once; and so is that of Æschylus, so is that of Dante, so is that of Montaigne, so is that of Schiller, so is that of nearly every one except Shakespeare; but there is a gauge of height no less than of breadth, of individuality as well as of comprehensiveness, and, above all, there is the standard of genetic power, the test of the masculine as distinguished from the receptive minds. There are staminate plants in literature, that make no fine show of fruit, but without whose pollen, quintessence of fructifying gold, the garden had been barren. Emerson's mind is emphatically one of these, and there is no man to whom our æsthetic culture owes so much. The Puritan revolt had made us ecclesiastically and the Revolution politically independent, but we were still socially and intellectually moored to English thought, till Emerson cut the cable and gave us a chance at the dangers and the glories of blue water. No man young enough to have felt it can forget or cease to be grateful for the mental and moral *nudge* which he received from the writings of his high-minded and brave-spirited countryman. That we agree with him, or that he always agrees with himself, is aside from the question; but that he arouses in us something that we are the better for having awakened, whether that something be of opposition or assent, that he speaks always to what is highest and least selfish in us, few Americans of the generation younger than his own would be disposed to deny. His oration before the Phi Beta Kappa Society at Cambridge, some thirty years ago, was an event without any former parallel in our literary annals, a scene to be always treasured in the memory for its picturesqueness and its inspiration. What crowded and breathless aisles, what windows clustering with eager heads, what enthusiasm of approval, what grim silence of foregone dissent! It was our Yankee version of a lecture by Abelard, our Harvard parallel to the last public appearances of Schelling.

I said that the Transcendental Movement was the protestant spirit of Puritanism seeking a new outlet and an escape from forms and creeds which compressed rather than expressed it. In its motives, its preaching, and its results, it differed radically from the doctrine of Carlyle. The Scotchman, with all his genius, and his humor gigantesque as that of Rabelais, has grown shriller and shriller with years, degenerating sometimes into a common scold, and emptying very unsavory vials of wrath on the head of the sturdy British Socrates of worldly common sense. The teaching of Emerson tended much more exclusively to self-culture and the independent development of the individual man. It seemed to many almost Pythagorean in its voluntary seclusion from commonwealth affairs. Both Carlyle and Emerson were disciples of Goethe, but Emerson in a far truer sense; and while the one, from his bias toward the eccentric, has degenerated more and more into mannerism, the other has clarified steadily toward perfection of style,—exquisite fineness of material, unobtrusive lowness of tone and simplicity of fashion, the most high-bred garb of expression. Whatever may be said of his thought, nothing can be finer than the delicious limpidness of his phrase. If it was ever questionable whether democracy could develop a gentleman, the problem has been affirmatively solved at last. Carlyle, in his cynicism and his admiration of force in and for itself, has become at last positively inhuman; Emerson, reverencing strength, seeking the highest outcome of the individual, has found that society and politics are also main elements in the attainment of the desired end, and has drawn steadily manward and worldward. The two men represent respectively those grand personifications in the drama of Æschylus, Βία and Κράτος.

Among the pistillate plants kindled to fruitage by the Emersonian pollen, Thoreau is thus far the most remarkable; and it is something eminently fitting that his posthumous works should be offered us by Emerson, for they are strawberries from his own garden. A singular mixture of varieties, indeed, there is;—alpine, some of them, with the flavor of rare mountain air; others wood, tasting of sunny roadside banks or shy openings in the forest; and not a few seedlings swollen hugely by culture, but lacking the fine natural aroma of the more modest kinds. Strange books these are of his, and interesting in many ways,—instructive chiefly as showing how considerable a crop may be raised on a comparatively narrow close of mind, and how much a man may make of his life if he will assiduously follow it, though perhaps never truly finding it at last.

I have just been renewing my recollection of Mr. Thoreau's writings, and have read through his six volumes in the order of their production. I shall try to give an adequate report of their impression upon me both as critic and as mere reader. He seems to me to have been a man with so high a conceit of himself that he accepted without questioning, and insisted on our accepting, his defects and weaknesses of character as virtues and powers peculiar to himself. Was he indolent, he finds none of the activities which attract or employ the rest of mankind worthy of him. Was he wanting in the qualities that make success, it is success that is contemptible, and not himself that lacks persistency and purpose. Was he poor, money was an unmixed evil. Did his life seem a selfish one, he condemns doing good as one of the weakest of superstitions. To be of use was with him the most killing bait of the wily tempter Uselessness. He had no faculty of generalization from outside of himself, or at least no experience which would supply the material of such, and he makes his own whim the law, his own range the horizon of the universe. He condemns a world, the hollowness of whose satisfactions he had never had the means of testing, and we recognize Apemantus behind the mask of Timon. He had little active imagination; of the receptive he had much. His appreciation is of the highest quality; his critical power, from want of continuity of mind, very limited and inadequate. He somewhere cites a simile from Ossian, as an example of the superiority of the old poetry to the new, though, even were the historic evidence less convincing, the sentimental melancholy of those poems should be conclusive of their modernness. He had none of the artistic mastery which controls a great work to the serene balance of completeness, but exquisite mechanical skill in the shaping of sentences and paragraphs, or (more rarely) short bits of verse for the expression of a detached thought, sentiment, or image. His works give one the feeling of a sky full of stars,—something impressive and exhilarating certainly, something high overhead and freckled thickly with spots of isolated brightness; but whether these have any mutual relation with each other, or have any concern with our mundane matters, is for the most part matter of conjecture,—astrology as yet, and not astronomy.

It is curious, considering what Thoreau afterwards became, that he was not by nature an observer. He only saw the things he looked for, and was less poet than naturalist. Till he built his Walden shanty, he did not know that the hickory grew in Concord. Till he went to Maine, he had never seen phosphorescent wood, a phenomenon early familiar to most

country boys. At forty he speaks of the seed-
ing of the pine as a new discovery, though one
should have thought that its gold-dust of blowing pollen might have earlier drawn his eye.
Neither his attention nor his genius was of the
spontaneous kind. He discovered nothing. He
thought everything a discovery of his own,
from moonlight to the planting of acorns and
nuts by squirrels. This is a defect in his character, but one of his chief charms as a writer.
Everything grows fresh under his hand. He
delved in his mind and nature; he planted
them with all manner of native and foreign
seeds, and reaped assiduously. He was not
merely solitary, he would be isolated, and succeeded at last in almost persuading himself
that he was autochthonous. He valued everything in proportion as he fancied it to be exclusively his own. He complains in "Walden"
that there is no one in Concord with whom he
could talk of Oriental literature, though the
man was living within two miles of his hut who
had introduced him to it. This intellectual
selfishness becomes sometimes almost painful
in reading him. He lacked that generosity of
"communication" which Johnson admired in
Burke. De Quincey tells us that Wordsworth
was impatient when any one else spoke of
mountains, as if he had a peculiar property in
them. And we can readily understand why it
should be so: no one is satisfied with another's
appreciation of his mistress. But Thoreau seems
to have prized a lofty way of thinking (often
we should be inclined to call it a remote one)
not so much because it was good in itself as
because he wished few to share it with him.
It seems now and then as if he did not seek to
lure others up "above our lower region of turmoil," but to leave his own name cut on the
mountain peak as the first climber. This itch
of originality infects his thought and style. To
be misty is not to be mystic. He turns commonplaces end for end, and fancies it makes
something new of them. As we walk down Park
Street, our eye is caught by Dr. Winship's
dumb-bells, one of which bears an inscription
testifying that it is the heaviest ever put up at
arm's length by any athlete; and in reading Mr.
Thoreau's books we cannot help feeling as if he
sometimes invited our attention to a particular
sophism or paradox as the biggest yet maintained by any single writer. He seeks, at all
risks, for perversity of thought, and revives the
age of *concetti* while he fancies himself going
back to a pre-classical nature. "A day," he says,

"passed in the society of those Greek sages,
such as described in the Banquet of Xenophon,
would not be comparable with the dry wit of
decayed cranberry-vines and the fresh Attic salt
of the moss-beds." It is not so much the True
that he loves as the Out-of-the-Way. As the
Brazen Age shows itself in other men by exaggeration of phrase, so in him by extravagance of
statement. He wishes always to trump your suit
and to *ruff* when you least expect it. Do you
love Nature because she is beautiful? He will
find a better argument in her ugliness. Are you
tired of the artificial man? He instantly dresses
you up an ideal in a Penobscot Indian, and attributes to this creature of his otherwise-mind-
edness as peculiarities things that are common
to all woodsmen, white or red, and this simply
because he has not studied the pale-faced variety.

This notion of an absolute originality, as if
one could have a patent-right in it, is an absurdity. A man cannot escape in thought, any
more than he can in language, from the past
and the present. As no one ever invents a word,
and yet language somehow grows by general
contribution and necessity, so it is with thought.
Mr. Thoreau seems to me to insist in public on
going back to flint and steel, when there is a
match-box in his pocket which he knows very
well how to use at a pinch. Originality consists
in power of digesting and assimilating thoughts,
so that they become part of our life and substance. Montaigne, for example, is one of the
most original of authors, though he helped
himself to ideas in every direction. But they
turn to blood and coloring in his style, and give
a freshness of complexion that is forever charming. In Thoreau much seems yet to be foreign
and unassimilated, showing itself in symptoms
of indigestion. A preacher-up of Nature, we
now and then detect under the surly and stoic
garb something of the sophist and the senti-
mentalizer. I am far from implying that this was
conscious on his part. But it is much easier for
a man to impose on himself when he measures
only with himself. A greater familiarity with
ordinary men would have done Thoreau good,
by showing him how many fine qualities are
common to the race. The radical vice of his
theory of life was that he confounded physical
with spiritual remoteness from men. A man is
far enough withdrawn from his fellows if he
keep himself clear of their weaknesses. He is
not so truly withdrawn as exiled, if he refuse
to share in their strength. "Solitude," says Cow-

ley, "can be well fitted and set right but upon a very few persons. They must have enough knowledge of the world to see the vanity of it, and enough virtue to despise all vanity." It is a morbid self-consciousness that pronounces the world of men empty and worthless before trying it, the instinctive evasion of one who is sensible of some innate weakness, and retorts the accusation of it before any has made it but himself. To a healthy mind, the world is a constant challenge of opportunity. Mr. Thoreau had not a healthy mind, or he would not have been so fond of prescribing. His whole life was a search for the doctor. The old mystics had a wiser sense of what the world was worth. They ordained a severe apprenticeship to law, and even ceremonial, in order to the gaining of freedom and mastery over these. Seven years of service for Rachel were to be rewarded at last with Leah. Seven other years of faithfulness with her were to win them at last the true bride of their souls. Active Life was with them the only path to the contemplative.

Thoreau had no humor, and this implies that he was a sorry logician. Himself an artist in rhetoric, he confounds thought with style when he undertakes to speak of the latter. He was forever talking of getting away from the world, but he must be always near enough to it, nay, to the Concord corner of it, to feel the impression he makes there. He verifies the shrewd remark of Sainte-Beuve, "On touche encore à son temps et très-fort, même quand on le repousse." [1] This egotism of his is a Stylites pillar after all, a seclusion which keeps him in the public eye. The dignity of man is an excellent thing, but therefore to hold one's self too sacred and precious is the reverse of excellent. There is something delightfully absurd in six volumes addressed to a world of such "vulgar fellows" as Thoreau affirmed his fellow men to be. I once had a glimpse of a genuine solitary who spent his winters one hundred and fifty miles beyond all human communication, and there dwelt with his rifle as his only confidant. Compared with this, the shanty on Walden Pond has something the air, it must be confessed, of the Hermitage of La Chevrette. I do not believe that the way to a true cosmopolitanism carries one into the woods or the society of musquashes. Perhaps the narrowest provincialism is that of Self; that of Kleinwinkel is nothing to it. The natural man, like the

singing birds, comes out of the forest as inevitably as the natural bear and the wildcat stick there. To seek to be natural implies a consciousness that forbids all naturalness forever. It is as easy—and no easier—to be natural in a *salon* as in a swamp, if one do not aim at it, for what we call unnaturalness always has its spring in a man's thinking too much about himself. "It is impossible," said Turgot, "for a vulgar man to be simple."

I look upon a great deal of the modern sentimentalism about Nature as a mark of disease. It is one more symptom of the general liver-complaint. To a man of wholesome constitution the wilderness is well enough for a mood or a vacation, but not for a habit of life. Those who have most loudly advertised their passion for seclusion and their intimacy with nature, from Petrarch down, have been mostly sentimentalists, unreal men, misanthropes on the spindle side, solacing an uneasy suspicion of themselves by professing contempt for their kind. They make demands on the world in advance proportioned to their inward measure of their own merit, and are angry that the world pays only by the visible measure of performance. It is true of Rousseau, the modern founder of the sect, true of Saint Pierre, his intellectual child, and of Châteaubriand, his grandchild, the inventor, we might almost say, of the primitive forest, and who first was touched by the solemn falling of a tree from natural decay in the windless silence of the woods. It is a very shallow view that affirms trees and rocks to be healthy, and cannot see that men in communities are just as true to the laws of their organization and destiny; that can tolerate the puffin and the fox, but not the fool and the knave; that would shun politics because of its demagogues, and snuff up the stench of the obscene fungus. The divine life of Nature is more wonderful, more various, more sublime in man than in any other of her works, and the wisdom that is gained by commerce with men, as Montaigne and Shakespeare gained it, or with one's own soul among men, as Dante, is the most delightful, as it is the most precious, of all. In outward nature it is still man that interests us, and we care far less for the things seen than the way in which they are seen by poetic eyes like Wordsworth's or Thoreau's, and the reflections they cast there. To hear the to-do that is often made over the simple fact that a man sees the image of himself in the outward world, one is re-

---

[1] *One is affected constantly and powerfully by his own epoch, even when he turns his back upon it.*

minded of a savage when he for the first time catches a glimpse of himself in a looking-glass. "Venerable child of Nature," we are tempted to say, "to whose science in the invention of the tobacco-pipe, to whose art in the tattooing of thine undegenerate hide not yet enslaved by tailors, we are slowly striving to climb back, the miracle thou beholdest is sold in my unhappy country for a shilling!" If matters go on as they have done, and everybody must needs blab of all the favors that have been done him by roadside and river-brink and woodland walk, as if to kiss and tell were no longer treachery, it will be a positive refreshment to meet a man who is as superbly indifferent to Nature as she is to him. By and by we shall have John Smith, of No. –12–12th Street, advertising that he is not the J. S. who saw a cow-lily on Thursday last, as he never saw one in his life, would not see one if he could, and is prepared to prove an alibi on the day in question.

Solitary communion with Nature does not seem to have been sanitary or sweetening in its influence on Thoreau's character. On the contrary, his letters show him more cynical as he grew older. While he studied with respectful attention the minks and woodchucks, his neighbors, he looked with utter contempt on the august drama of destiny of which his country was the scene, and on which the curtain had already risen. He was converting us back to a state of nature "so eloquently," as Voltaire said of Rousseau, "that he almost persuaded us to go on all fours," while the wiser fates were making it possible for us to walk erect for the first time. Had he conversed more with his fellows, his sympathies would have widened with the assurance that his peculiar genius had more appreciation, and his writings a larger circle of readers, or at least a warmer one, than he dreamed of. We have the highest testimony[2] to the natural sweetness, sincerity, and nobleness of his temper, and in his books an equally irrefragable one to the rare quality of his mind. He was not a strong thinker, but a sensitive feeler. Yet his mind strikes us as cold and wintry in its purity. A light snow has fallen everywhere in which he seems to come on the track of the shier sensations that would elsewhere leave no trace. We think greater compression would have done more for his fame. A feeling of sameness comes

[2] Mr. Emerson, in the Biographical Sketch prefixed to the *Excursions*. [Lowell's note.]

over us as we read so much. Trifles are recorded with an over-minute punctuality and conscientiousness of detail. He registers the state of his personal thermometer thirteen times a day. We cannot help thinking sometimes of the man who

> "Watches, starves, freezes, and sweats
> To learn but catechisms and alphabets
> Of unconcerning things, matters of fact,"

and sometimes of the saying of the Persian poet, that "when the owl would boast, he boasts of catching mice at the edge of a hole." We could readily part with some of his affectations. It was well enough for Pythagoras to say, once for all, "When I was Euphorbus at the siege of Troy"; not so well for Thoreau to travesty it into "When I was a shepherd on the plains of Assyria." A naïve thing said over again is anything but naïve. But with every exception, there is no writing comparable with Thoreau's in kind, that is comparable with it in degree where it is best; where it disengages itself, that is, from the tangled roots and dead leaves of a second-hand Orientalism, and runs limpid and smooth and broadening as it runs, a mirror for whatever is grand and lovely in both worlds.

George Sand says neatly, that "Art is not a study of positive reality" (*actuality* were the fitter word,) "but a seeking after ideal truth." It would be doing very inadequate justice to Thoreau if we left it to be inferred that this ideal element did not exist in him, and that too in larger proportion, if less obtrusive, than his nature-worship. He took nature as the mountain-path to an ideal world. If the path wind a good deal, if he record too faithfully every trip over a root, if he botanize somewhat wearisomely, he gives us now and then superb outlooks from some jutting crag, and brings us out at last into an illimitable ether, where the breathing is not difficult for those who have any true touch of the climbing spirit. His shanty-life was a mere impossibility, so far as his own conception of it goes, as an entire independency of mankind. The tub of Diogenes had a sounder bottom. Thoreau's experiment actually presupposed all that complicated civilization which it theoretically abjured. He squatted on another man's land; he borrows an axe; his boards, his nails, his bricks, his mortar, his books, his lamp, his fish-hooks, his plough, his hoe, all turn state's evidence against him as an accomplice in the sin of that artificial civilization which rendered it possible that such a person as Henry D. Thoreau should exist at all. *Magnis tamen excidit ausis.* His aim was a noble and a useful one, in the direction of "plain living and high thinking." It was a practical sermon on Emerson's text that "things are in the saddle and ride mankind," an attempt to solve Carlyle's problem (con-densed from Johnson) of "lessening your de-nominator." His whole life was a rebuke of the waste and aimlessness of our American luxury, which is an abject enslavement to tawdry up-holstery. He had "fine translunary things" in him. His better style as a writer is in keeping with the simplicity and purity of his life. We have said that his range was narrow, but to be a master is to be a master. He had caught his English at its living source, among the poets and prose-writers of its best days; his litera-ture was extensive and recondite; his quota-tions are always nuggets of the purest ore: there are sentences of his as perfect as any-thing in the language, and thoughts as clearly crystallized; his metaphors and images are al-ways fresh from the soil; he had watched Na-ture like a detective who is to go upon the stand; as we read him, it seems as if all-out-of-doors had kept a diary and become its own Montaigne; we look at the landscape as in a Claude Lorraine glass; compared with his, all other books of similar aim, even White's "Sel-borne," seem dry as a country clergyman's meteorological journal in an old almanac. He belongs with Donne and Browne and Novalis; if not with the originally creative men, with the scarcely smaller class who are peculiar, and whose leaves shed their invisible thought-seed like ferns.

1865   1865

» » ON A CERTAIN CONDESCENSION IN FOREIGNERS « «

Walking one day toward the Village, as we used to call it in the good old days, when al-most every dweller in the town had been born in it, I was enjoying that delicious sense of dis-enthralment from the actual which the deep-ening twilight brings with it, giving as it does a sort of obscure novelty to things familiar. The coolness, the hush, broken only by the distant bleat of some belated goat, querulous to be disburthened of her milky load, the few faint stars, more guessed as yet than seen, the sense that the coming dark would so soon fold me in the secure privacy of its disguise,—all things combined in a result as near absolute peace as can be hoped for by a man who knows that there is a writ out against him in the hands of the printer's devil. For the moment, I was en-joying the blessed privilege of thinking with-out being called on to stand and deliver what I thought to the small public who are good enough to take any interest therein. I love old ways, and the path I was walking felt kindly to the feet it had known for almost fifty years. How many fleeting impressions it had shared with me! How many times I had lingered to study the shadows of the leaves mezzotinted upon the turf that edged it by the moon, of the bare boughs etched with a touch beyond Rem-brandt by the same unconscious artist on the smooth page of snow! If I turned round, through dusky tree-gaps came the first twinkle of evening lamps in the dear old homestead. On Corey's hill I could see these tiny pharoses of love and home and sweet domestic thoughts flash out one by one across the blackening salt-meadow between. How much has not kero-sene added to the cheerfulness of our evening landscape! A pair of night-herons flapped heavily over me toward the hidden river. The war was ended. I might walk townward with-out that aching dread of bulletins that had darkened the July sunshine and twice made the scarlet leaves of October seem stained with blood. I remembered with a pang, half-proud, half-painful, how, so many years ago, I had walked over the same path and felt round my finger the soft pressure of a little hand that was one day to harden with faithful grip of sabre. On how many paths, leading to how many homes where proud Memory does all she can to fill up the fireside gaps with shining shapes, must not men be walking in just such pensive mood as I? Ah, young heroes, safe in immortal youth as those of Homer, you at least carried your ideal hence untarnished! It is locked for you beyond moth or rust in the treasure-chamber of Death.

Is not a country, I thought, that has had

such as they in it, that could give such as they
a brave joy in dying for it, worth something,
then? And as I felt more and more the soothing magic of evening's cool palm upon my temples, as my fancy came home from its revery,
and my senses, with reawakened curiosity, ran
to the front windows again from the viewless
closet of abstraction, and felt a strange charm
in finding the old tree and shabby fence still
there under the travesty of falling night, nay,
were conscious of an unsuspected newness in
familiar stars and the fading outlines of hills
my earliest horizon, I was conscious of an immortal soul, and could not but rejoice in the
unwaning goodliness of the world into which I
had been born without any merit of my own.
I thought of dear Henry Vaughan's rainbow,
"Still young and fine!" I remembered people
who had to go over to the Alps to learn what
the divine silence of snow was, who must run
to Italy before they were conscious of the miracle wrought every day under their very noses
by the sunset, who must call upon the Berkshire hills to teach them what a painter autumn was, while close at hand the Fresh Pond
meadows made all oriels cheap with hues that
showed as if a sunset-cloud had been wrecked
among their maples. One might be worse off
than even in America, I thought. There are
some things so elastic that even the heavy roller
of democracy cannot flatten them altogether
down. The mind can weave itself warmly in
the cocoon of its own thoughts and dwell a hermit anywhere. A country without traditions,
without ennobling associations, a scramble of
parvenus, with a horrible consciousness of
shoddy running through politics, manners, art,
literature, nay, religion itself? I confess, it did
not seem so to me there in that illimitable
quiet, that serene self-possession of nature,
where Collins might have brooded his "Ode to
Evening," or where those verses on Solitude in
Dodsley's Collection, that Hawthorne liked so
much, might have been composed. Traditions?
Granting that we had none, all that is worth
having in them is the common property of
the soul,—an estate in gavelkind for all the
sons of Adam,—and, moreover, if a man cannot stand on his two feet (the prime quality of
whoever has left any tradition behind him),
were it not better for him to be honest about it
at once, and go down on all fours? And for associations, if one have not the wit to make
them for himself out of native earth, no ready-
made ones of other men will avail much. Lex-

ington is none the worse to me for not being in
Greece, not Gettysburg that its name is not
Marathon. "Blessed old fields," I was just exclaiming to myself, like one of Mrs. Radcliffe's
heroes, "dear acres, innocently secure from
history, which these eyes first beheld, may you
be also those to which they shall at last slowly
darken!" when I was interrupted by a voice
which asked me in German whether I was the
Herr Professor, Doctor, So-and-so? The "Doctor" was by brevet or vaticination, to make the
grade easier to my pocket.

One feels so intimately assured that one is
made up, in part, of shreds and leavings of the
past, in part of the interpolations of other people, that an honest man would be slow in saying *yes* to such a question. But "my name is
So-and-so" is a safe answer, and I gave it.
While I had been romancing with myself, the
street-lamps had been lighted, and it was under one of these detectives that had robbed
the Old Road of its privilege of sanctuary after
nightfall that I was ambushed by my foe. The
inexorable villain had taken my description, it
appears, that I might have the less chance to
escape him. Dr. Holmes tells us that we change
our substance, not every seven years, as was
once believed, but with every breath we draw.
Why had I not the wit to avail myself of the
subterfuge, and, like Peter, to renounce my
identity, especially, as in certain moods of
mind, I have often more than doubted of it
myself? When a man is, as it were, his own
front-door, and is thus knocked at, why may
he not assume the right of that sacred wood to
make every house a castle, by denying himself
to all visitations? I was truly not at home
when the question was put to me, but had to
recall myself from all out-of-doors, and to piece
my self-consciousness hastily together as well
as I could before I answered it.

I knew perfectly well what was coming. It
is seldom that debtors or good Samaritans
waylay people under gas-lamps in order to
force money upon them, so far as I have seen
or heard. I was also aware, from considerable
experience, that every foreigner is persuaded
that, by doing this country the favor of coming
to it, he has laid every native thereof under an
obligation, pecuniary or other, as the case may
be, whose discharge he is entitled to on demand duly made in person or by letter. Too
much learning (of this kind) had made me mad
in the provincial sense of the word. I had begun life with the theory of giving something to

every beggar that came along, though sure of never finding a native-born countryman among them. In a small way, I was resolved to emulate Hatem Tai's tent, with its three hundred and sixty-five entrances, one for every day in the year,—I know not whether he was astronomer enough to add another for leap-years. The beggars were a kind of German-silver aristocracy; not real plate, to be sure, but better than nothing. Where everybody was overworked, they supplied the comfortable equipoise of absolute leisure, so æsthetically needful. Besides, I was but too conscious of a vagrant fibre in myself, which too often thrilled me in my solitary walks with the temptation to wander on into infinite space, and by a single spasm of resolution to emancipate myself from the drudgery of prosaic serfdom to respectability and the regular course of things. This prompting has been at times my familiar demon, and I could not but feel a kind of respectful sympathy for men who had dared what I had only sketched out to myself as a splendid possibility. For seven years I helped maintain one heroic man on an imaginary journey to Portland,—as fine an example as I have ever known of hopeless loyalty to an ideal. I assisted another so long in a fruitless attempt to reach Mechlenburg-Schwerin, that at last we grinned in each other's faces when we met, like a couple of augurs. He was possessed by this harmless mania as some are by the North Pole, and I shall never forget his look of regretful compassion (as for one who was sacrificing his higher life to the fleshpots of Egypt) when I at last advised him somewhat strenuously to go to the D——, whither the road was so much travelled that he could not miss it. General Banks, in his noble zeal for the honor of his country, would confer on the Secretary of State the power of imprisoning, in case of war, all these seekers of the unattainable, thus by a stroke of the pen annihilating the single poetic element in our humdrum life. Alas! not everybody has the genius to be a Bobbin-Boy, or doubtless all these also would have chosen that more prosperous line of life! But moralists, sociologists, political economists, and taxes have slowly convinced me that my beggarly sympathies were a sin against society. Especially was the Buckle doctrine of averages (so flattering to our free-will) persuasive with me; for as there must be in every year a certain number who would bestow an alms on these abridged editions of the Wandering Jew, the withdrawal of my quota

could make no possible difference, since some destined proxy must always step forward to fill my gap. Just so many misdirected letters every year and no more! Would it were as easy to reckon up the number of men on whose backs fate has written the wrong address, so that they arrive by mistake in Congress and other places where they do not belong! May not these wanderers of whom I speak have been sent into the world without any proper address at all? Where is our Dead-Letter Office for such? And if wiser social arrangements should furnish us with something of the sort, fancy (horrible thought!) how many a workingman's friend (a kind of industry in which the labor is light and the wages heavy) would be sent thither because not called for in the office where he at present lies!

But I am leaving my new acquaintance too long under the lamp-post. The same Gano which had betrayed me to him revealed to me a well-set young man of about half my own age, as well dressed, so far as I could see, as I was, and with every natural qualification for getting his own livelihood as good, if not better, than my own. He had been reduced to the painful necessity of calling upon me by a series of crosses beginning with the Baden Revolution (for which, I own, he seemed rather young,—but perhaps he referred to a kind of revolution practised every season at Baden-Baden), continued by repeated failures in business, for amounts which must convince me of his entire respectability, and ending with our Civil War. During the latter, he had served with distinction as a soldier, taking a main part in every important battle, with a rapid list of which he favored me, and no doubt would have admitted that, impartial as Jonathan Wild's great ancestor, he had been on both sides, had I baited him with a few hints of conservative opinions on a subject so distressing to a gentleman wishing to profit by one's sympathy and unhappily doubtful as to which way it might lean. For all these reasons, and, as he seemed to imply, for his merit in consenting to be born in Germany, he considered himself my natural creditor to the extent of five dollars, which he would handsomely consent to accept in greenbacks, though he preferred specie. The offer was certainly a generous one, and the claim presented with an assurance that carried conviction. But, unhappily, I had been led to remark a curious natural phenomenon. If I was ever weak enough to

give anything to a petitioner of whatever nationality, it always rained decayed compatriots
of his for a month after. *Post hoc ergo prop-
ter hoc* may not always be safe logic, but here
I seemed to perceive a natural connection of
cause and effect. Now, a few days before I had
been so tickled with a paper (professedly written by a benevolent American clergyman) certifying that the bearer, a hard-working German, had long "sofered with rheumatic paints
in his limps," that, after copying the passage
into my note-book, I thought it but fair to pay
a trifling *honorarium* to the author. I had
pulled the string of the shower-bath! It had
been running shipwrecked sailors for some
time, but forthwith it began to pour Teutons,
redolent of *lager-bier.* I could not help associating the apparition of my new friend with this
series of otherwise unaccountable phenomena.
I accordingly made up my mind to deny the
debt, and modestly did so, pleading a native
bias towards impecuniosity to the full as strong
as his own. He took a high tone with me at
once, such as an honest man would naturally
take with a confessed repudiator. He even
brought down his proud stomach so far as to
join himself to me for the rest of my townward
walk, that he might give me his views of the
American people, and thus inclusively of myself.

I know not whether it is because I am pig-
eon-livered and lack gall, or whether it is from
an over-mastering sense of drollery, but I am
apt to submit to such bastings with a patience
which afterwards surprises me, being not without my share of warmth in the blood. Perhaps
it is because I so often meet with young persons who know vastly more than I do, and especially with so many foreigners whose knowledge of this country is superior to my own.
However it may be, I listened for some time
with tolerable composure as my self-appointed
lecturer gave me in detail his opinions of my
country and its people. America, he informed
me, was without arts, science, literature, culture, or any native hope of supplying them.
We were a people wholly given to money-get-
ting, and who, having got it, knew no other use
for it than to hold it fast. I am fain to confess
that I felt a sensible itching of the biceps, and
that my fingers closed with such a grip as he
had just informed me was one of the effects of
our unhappy climate. But happening just then
to be where I could avoid temptation by dodging down a by-street, I hastily left him to finish
his diatribe to the lamp-post, which could stand
it better than I. That young man will never
know how near he came to being assaulted
by a respectable gentleman of middle age, at
the corner of Church Street. I have never felt
quite satisfied that I did all my duty by him in
not knocking him down. But perhaps he might
have knocked *me* down, and then?

The capacity of indignation makes an essential part of the outfit of every honest man, but
I am inclined to doubt whether he is a wise one
who allows himself to act upon its first hints.
It should be rather, I suspect, a *latent* heat in
the blood, which makes itself felt in character,
a steady reserve for the brain, warming the
ovum of thought to life, rather than cooking it
by a too hasty enthusiasm in reaching the boil-
ing-point. As my pulse gradually fell back to
its normal beat, I reflected that I had been un-
comfortably near making a fool of myself,—a
handy salve of euphuism for our vanity, though
it does not always make a just allowance to
Nature for her share in the business. What
possible claim had my Teutonic friend to rob
me of my composure? I am not, I think, specially thin-skinned as to other people's opinions
of myself, having, as I conceive, later and fuller
intelligence on that point than anybody else
can give me. Life is continually weighing us in
very sensitive scales, and telling every one of
us precisely what his real weight is to the last
grain of dust. Whoever at fifty does not rate
himself quite as low as most of his acquaintance would be likely to put him, must be either
a fool or a great man, and I humbly disclaim
being either. But if I was not smarting in person from any scattering shot of my late companion's commination, why should I grow hot
at any implication of my country therein?
Surely *her* shoulders are broad enough, if yours
or mine are not, to bear up under a considerable avalanche of this kind. It is the bit of
truth in every slander, the hint of likeness in
every caricature, that makes us smart. "Art
thou *there,* old Truepenny?" How did your
blade know its way so well to that one loose
rivet in our armor? I wondered whether Americans were over-sensitive in this respect, whether
they were more touchy than other folks. On
the whole, I thought we were not. Plutarch,
who at least had studied philosophy, if he
had not mastered it, could not stomach something Herodotus had said of Bœotia, and devoted an essay to showing up the delightful
old traveller's malice and ill-breeding. French

editors leave out of Montaigne's "Travels" some remarks of his about France, for reasons best known to themselves. Pachydermatous Deutschland, covered with trophies from every field of letters, still winces under that question which Père Bouhours put two centuries ago, *Si un Allemand peut être belesprit?* John Bull grew apoplectic with angry amazement at the audacious persiflage of Pückler-Muskau. To be sure, he was a prince,—but that was not all of it, for a chance phrase of gentle Hawthorne sent a spasm through all the journals of England. Then this tenderness is not peculiar to *us?* Console yourself, dear man and brother, whatever else you may be sure of, be sure at least of this, that you are dreadfully like other people. Human nature has a much greater genius for sameness than for originality, or the world would be at a sad pass shortly. The surprising thing is that men have such a taste for this somewhat musty flavor, that an Englishman, for example, should feel himself defrauded, nay, even outraged, when he comes over here and finds a people speaking what he admits to be something like English, and yet so very different from (or, as he would say, to) those he left at home. Nothing, I am sure, equals *my* thankfulness when I meet an Englishman who is *not* like every other, or, I may add, an American of the same odd turn.

Certainly it is no shame to a man that he should be as nice about his country as about his sweetheart, and who ever heard even the friendliest appreciation of that unexpressive she that did not seem to fall infinitely short? Yet it would hardly be wise to hold every one an enemy who could not see her with our own enchanted eyes. It seems to be the common opinion of foreigners that Americans are *too* tender upon this point. Perhaps we are; and if so, there must be a reason for it. Have we had fair play. Could the eyes of what is called Good Society (though it is so seldom true either to the adjective or noun) look upon a nation of democrats with any chance of receiving an undistorted image? Were not those, moreover, who found in the old order of things an earthly paradise, paying them quarterly dividends for the wisdom of their ancestors, with the punctuality of the seasons, unconsciously bribed to misunderstand if not to misrepresent us? Whether at war or at peace, there we were, a standing menace to all earthly paradises of that kind, fatal underminers of the very credit on which the dividends were based,

all the more hateful and terrible that our destructive agency was so insidious, working invisible in the elements, as it seemed, active while they slept, and coming upon them in the darkness like an armed man. *Could* Laius have the proper feelings of a father towards Œdipus, announced as his destined destroyer by infallible oracles, and felt to be such by every conscious fibre of his soul? For more than a century the Dutch were the laughing-stock of polite Europe. They were butter-firkins, swillers of beer and schnaps, and their *vrouws* from whom Holbein painted the all-but loveliest of Madonnas, Rembrandt the graceful girl who sits immortal on his knee in Dresden, and Rubens his abounding goddesses, were the synonymes of clumsy vulgarity. Even so late as Irving the ships of the greatest navigators in the world were represented as sailing equally well stern-foremost. That the aristocratic Venetians should have

"Riveted with gigantic piles
Thorough the centre their new-catchèd miles,"

was heroic. But the far more marvellous achievement of the Dutch in the same kind was ludicrous even to republican Marvell. Meanwhile, during that very century of scorn, they were the best artists, sailors, merchants, bankers, printers, scholars, jurisconsults, and statesmen in Europe, and the genius of Motley has revealed them to us, earning a right to themselves by the most heroic struggle in human annals. But, alas! they were not merely simple burghers who had fairly made themselves High Mightinesses, and could treat on equal terms with anointed kings, but their commonwealth carried in its bosom the germs of democracy. They even unmuzzled, at least after dark, that dreadful mastiff, the Press, whose scent is, or ought to be, so keen for wolves in sheep's clothing and for certain other animals in lions' skins. They made fun of Sacred Majesty, and, what was worse, managed uncommonly well without it. In an age when periwigs made so large a part of the natural dignity of man, people with such a turn of mind were dangerous. How could they seem other than vulgar and hateful?

In the natural course of things we succeeded to this unenviable position of general butt. The Dutch had thriven under it pretty well, and there was hope that we could at least contrive to worry along. And we certainly did in a very redoubtable fashion. Perhaps we deserved some of the sarcasm more than our Dutch predecessors in office. We had nothing to boast of in arts or letters, and were given to bragging overmuch of our merely material prosperity, due quite as much to the virtue of our continent as to our own. There was some truth in Carlyle's sneer, after all. Till we had succeeded in some higher way than this, we had only the success of physical growth. Our greatness, like that of enormous Russia, was greatness on the map,—barbarian mass only; but had we gone down, like that other Atlantis, in some vast cataclysm, we should have covered but a pin's point on the chart of memory, compared with those ideal spaces occupied by tiny Attica and cramped England. At the same time, our critics somewhat too easily forgot that material must make ready the foundation for ideal triumphs, that the arts have no chance in poor countries. But it must be allowed that democracy stood for a great deal in our shortcoming. The Edinburgh Review never would have thought of asking, "Who reads a Russian book?" and England was satisfied with iron from Sweden without being impertinently inquisitive after her painters and statuaries. Was it that they expected too much from the mere miracle of Freedom? Is it not the highest art of a Republic to make men of flesh and blood, and not the marble ideals of such? It may be fairly doubted whether we have produced this higher type of man yet. Perhaps it is the collective, not the individual, humanity that is to have a chance of nobler development among us. We shall see. We have a vast amount of imported ignorance, and, still worse, of native ready-made knowledge, to digest before even the preliminaries of such a consummation can be arranged. We have got to learn that statesmanship is the most complicated of all arts, and to come back to the apprenticeship-system too hastily abandoned. At present, we trust a man with making constitutions on less proof of competence than we should demand before we gave him our shoe to patch. We have nearly reached the limit of the reaction from the old notion, which paid too much regard to birth and station as qualifications for office, and have touched the extreme point in the opposite direction, putting the highest of human functions up at auction to be bid for by any creature capable of going upright on two legs. In some places, we have arrived at a point at which civil society is no longer possible, and already another reaction has begun, not backwards to the old system, but towards fitness either from natural aptitude or special training. But will it always be safe to let evils work their own cure by becoming unendurable? Every one of them leaves its taint in the constitution of the body-politic, each in itself, perhaps, trifling, yet all together powerful for evil.

But whatever we might do or leave undone, we were not genteel, and it was uncomfortable to be continually reminded that, though we should boast that we were the Great West till we were black in the face, it did not bring us an inch nearer to the world's West-End. That sacred enclosure of respectability was tabooed to us. The Holy Alliance did not inscribe us on its visiting-list. The Old World of wigs and orders and liveries would shop with us, but we must ring at the area-bell, and not venture to awaken the more august clamors of the knocker. Our manners, it must be granted, had none of those graces that stamp the caste of Vere de Vere, in whatever museum of British antiquities they may be hidden. In short, we were vulgar.

This was one of those horribly vague accusations, the victim of which has no defence. An umbrella is of no avail against a Scotch mist. It envelops you, it penetrates at every pore, it wets you through without seeming to wet you at all. Vulgarity is an eighth deadly sin, added to the list in these latter days, and worse than all the others put together, since it perils your salvation in *this* world,—far the more important of the two in the minds of most men. It profits nothing to draw nice distinctions between essential and conventional, for the convention in this case *is* the essence, and you may break every command of the decalogue with perfect good-breeding, nay, if you are adroit, without losing caste. We, indeed, had it not to lose, for we had never gained it. "*How* am I vulgar?" asks the culprit, shudderingly. "Because thou art not like unto Us," answers Lucifer, Son of the Morning, and there is no more to be said. The god of this world may be a fallen angel, but he has us *there!* We were as clean,—so far as my observation goes, I think we were cleaner, morally and physically, than the English, and therefore, of course, than everybody else. But we did not pronounce the diphthong *ou* as they did, and we said *eether* and not *eyther*, following therein the fashion of our ancestors, who unhappily could bring over no English better than Shakespeare's; and we did not stammer as they had learned to do from the courtiers, who in this way flattered the Hanoverian king, a foreigner among the people he had come to reign over. Worse than all, we might have the noblest ideas and the finest sentiments in the world, but we vented them through that organ by which men are led rather than leaders, though some physiologists would persuade us that Nature furnishes her captains with a fine handle to their faces that Opportunity may get a good purchase on them for dragging them to the front.

This state of things was so painful that excellent people were not wanting who gave their whole genius to reproducing here the original Bull, whether by gaiters, the cut of their whiskers, by a factitious brutality in their tone, or by an accent that was forever tripping and falling flat over the tangled roots of our common tongue. Martyrs to a false ideal, it never occurred to them that nothing is more hateful to gods and men than a second-rate Englishman, and for the very reason that this planet never produced a more splendid creature than the first-rate one, witness Shakespeare and the Indian mutiny. Witness that truly sublime self-abnegation of those prisoners lately among the bandits of Greece, where average men gave an example of quiet fortitude for which all the stoicism of antiquity can show no match. Witness the wreck of the Birkenhead, an example of disciplined heroism, perhaps the most precious, as the rarest, of all. If we could contrive to be not too unobtrusively our simple selves, we should be the most delightful of human beings, and the most original; whereas, when the plating of Anglicism rubs off, as it always will in points that come to much wear, we are liable to very unpleasing conjectures about the quality of the metal underneath. Perhaps one reason why the average Briton spreads himself here with such an easy air of superiority may be owing to the fact that he meets with so many bad imitations as to conclude himself the only real thing in a wilderness of shams. He fancies himself moving through an endless Bloomsbury, where his mere apparition confers honor as an avatar of the court-end of the universe. Not a Bull of them all but is persuaded he bears Europa upon his back. This is the sort of fellow whose patronage is so divertingly insufferable. Thank Heaven he is not the only specimen of cater-cousinship from the dear old Mother Island that is shown to us! Among genuine things, I know nothing more

genuine than the better men whose limbs were made in England. So manly-tender, so brave, so true, so warranted to wear, they make us proud to feel that blood is thicker than water.

But it is not merely the Englishman; every European candidly admits in himself some right of primogeniture in respect of us, and pats this shaggy continent on the back with a lively sense of generous unbending. The German who plays the bass-viol has a well-founded contempt, which he is not always nice in concealing, for a country so few of whose children ever take that noble instrument between their knees. His cousin, the Ph. D. from Göttingen, cannot help despising a people who do not grow loud and red over Aryans and Turanians, and are indifferent about their descent from either. The Frenchman feels an easy mastery in speaking his mother tongue, and attributes it to some native superiority of parts that lifts him high above us barbarians of the West. The Italian *prima donna* sweeps a curtsy of careless pity to the over-facile pit which unsexes her with the *bravo!* innocently meant to show a familiarity with foreign usage. But all without exception make no secret of regarding us as the goose bound to deliver them a golden egg in return for *their* cackle. Such men as Agassiz, Guyot, and Goldwin Smith come with gifts in their hands; but since it is commonly European failures who bring hither their remarkable gifts and acquirements, this view of the case is sometimes just the least bit in the world provoking. To think what a delicious seclusion of contempt we enjoyed till California and our own ostentatious *parvenus,* flinging gold away in Europe that might have endowed libraries at home, gave us the ill repute of riches! What a shabby downfall from the Arcadia which the French officers of our Revolutionary War fancied they saw here through Rousseau-tinted spectacles! Something of Arcadia there really was, something of the Old Age; and that divine provincialism were cheaply repurchased could we have it back again in exchange for the tawdry upholstery that has taken its place.

For some reason or other, the European has rarely been able to see America except in caricature. Would the first Review of the world have printed the *niaiseries* of M. Maurice Sand as a picture of society in any civilized country? M. Sand, to be sure, has inherited nothing of his famous mother's literary outfit, except the pseudonym. But since the con-

ductors of the *Revue* could not have published his story because it was clever, they
must have thought it valuable for its truth.
As true as the last-century Englishman's picture of Jean Crapaud! We do not ask to be
sprinkled with rosewater, but may perhaps
fairly protest against being drenched with the
rinsings of an unclean imagination. The next
time the *Revue* allows such ill-bred persons
to throw their slops out of its first-floor windows, let it honestly preface the discharge with
à gare l'eau! that we may run from under in
season. And M. Duvergier de Hauranne, who
knows how to be entertaining! I know that *le
Français est plutôt indiscret que confiant,* and
the pen slides too easily when indiscretions
will fetch so much a page; but should we not
have been *tant-soit-peu* more cautious had we
been writing about people on the other side of
the Channel? But then it is a fact in the natural history of the American long familiar to
Europeans, that he abhors privacy, knows not
the meaning of reserve, lives in hotels because
of their greater publicity, and is never so
pleased as when his domestic affairs (if he may
be said to have any) are paraded in the newspapers. Barnum, it is well known, represents
perfectly the average national sentiment in
this respect. However it be, we are not treated
like other people, or perhaps I should say like
people who are ever likely to be met with in
society.

Is it in the climate? Either I have a false
notion of European manners, or else the atmosphere affects them strangely when ex-
ported hither. Perhaps they suffer from the
sea-voyage like some of the more delicate
wines. During our Civil War an English gentleman of the highest description was kind enough
to call upon me, mainly, as it seemed, to inform
me how entirely he sympathized with the
Confederates, and how sure he felt that we
could never subdue them,—"they were the
gentlemen of the country, you know." Another,
the first greetings hardly over, asked me how
I accounted for the universal meagreness of
my countrymen. To a thinner man than I, or
from a stouter man than he, the question *might*
have been offensive. The Marquis of Harting-
ton [3] wore a secession badge at a public hall

[3] One of Mr. Lincoln's neatest strokes of humor was his treatment
of this gentleman when a laudable curiosity induced him to be presented to the President of the Broken Bubble. Mr. Lincoln persisted in
calling him Mr. Partington. Surely the refinement of good-breeding
could go no further. Giving the young man his real name (already
notorious in the newspapers) would have made his visit an insult.
Had Henri IV. done this, it would have been famous. [Lowell's
note.]

in New York. In a civilized country he might
have been roughly handled; but here, where
the *biensèances* are not so well understood, of
course nobody minded it. A French traveller
told me he had been a good deal in the British
colonies, and had been astonished to see how
soon the people became Americanized. He
added, with delightful *bonhomie,* and as if he
were sure it would charm me, that "they even
began to talk through their noses, just like   10
you!" I was naturally ravished with this testimony to the assimilating power of democracy,
and could only reply that I hoped they would
never adopt our democratic patent-method of
seeming to settle one's honest debts, for they
would find it paying through the nose in the
long-run. I am a man of the New World, and
do not know precisely the present fashion of
May-Fair, but I have a kind of feeling that if
an American (*mutato nomine, de te* is always   20
frightfully possible) were to do this kind of
thing under a European roof, it would induce
some disagreeable reflections as to the ethical
results of democracy. I read the other day in
print the remark of a British tourist who had
eaten large quantities of our salt, such as it is
(I grant it has not the European savor), that
the Americans were hospitable, no doubt, but
that it was partly because they longed for
foreign visitors to relieve the tedium of their   30
dead-level existence, and partly from ostentation. What shall we do? Shall we close our
doors? Not I, for one, if I should so have for-
feited the friendship of L. S., most lovable of
men. He somehow seems to find us human, at
least, and so did Clough, whose poetry will one
of these days, perhaps, be found to have been
the best utterance in verse of this generation.
And T. H., the mere grasp of whose manly
hand carries with it the pledge of frankness   40
and friendship, of an abiding simplicity of nature as affecting as it is rare!

The fine old Tory aversion of former times
was not hard to bear. There was something
even refreshing in it, as in a northeaster to a
hardy temperament. When a British parson,
travelling in Newfoundland while the slash
of our separation was still raw, after prophesy-
ing a glorious future for an island that continued to dry its fish under the ægis of Saint   50
George, glances disdainfully over his spectacles in parting at the U. S. A., and forebodes
for them a "speedy relapse into barbarism,"
now that they have madly cut themselves off
from the humanizing influences of Britain, I

smile with barbarian self-conceit. But this kind of thing became by degrees an unpleasant anachronism. For meanwhile the young giant was growing, was beginning indeed to feel tight in his clothes, was obliged to let in a gore here and there in Texas, in California, in New Mexico, in Alaska, and had the scissors and needle and thread ready for Canada when the time came. His shadow loomed like a Brocken-spectre over against Europe,—the shadow of what they were coming to, that was the unpleasant part of it. Even in such misty image as they had of him, it was painfully evident that his clothes were not of any cut hitherto fashionable, nor conceivable by a Bond Street tailor,—and this in an age, too, when everything depends upon clothes, when, if we do not keep up appearances, the seeming-solid frame of this universe, nay, your very God, would slump into himself, like a mockery king of snow, being nothing, after all, but a prevailing mode, a make-believe of believing. From this moment the young giant assumed the respectable aspect of a phenomenon, to be got rid of if possible, but at any rate as legitimate a subject of human study as the glacial period or the silurian what-d'ye-call-ems. If the man of the primeval drift-heaps be so absorbingly interesting, why not the man of the drift that is just beginning, of the drift into whose irresistible current we are just being sucked whether we will or no? If I were in their place, I confess I should not be frightened. Man has survived so much, and contrived to be comfortable on this planet after surviving so much! I am something of a protestant in matters of government also, and am willing to get rid of vestments and ceremonies and to come down to bare benches, if only faith in God take the place of a general agreement to profess confidence in ritual and sham. Every mortal man of us holds stock in the only public debt that is absolutely sure of payment, and that is the debt of the Maker of this Universe to the Universe he has made. I have no notion of selling out my shares in a panic.

It was something to have advanced even to the dignity of a phenomenon, and yet I do not know that the relation of the individual American to the individual European was bettered by it; and that, after all, must adjust itself comfortably before there can be a right understanding between the two. We had been a desert, we became a museum. People came hither for scientific and not social ends. The very cockney could not complete his education without taking a vacant stare at us in passing. But the sociologists (I think they call themselves so) were the hardest to bear. There was no escape. I have even known a professor of this fearful science to come disguised in petticoats. We were cross-examined as a chemist cross-examines a new substance. Human? yes, all the elements are present, though abnormally combined. Civilized? Hm! that needs a stricter assay. No entomologist could take a more friendly interest in a strange bug. After a few such experiences, I, for one, have felt as if I were merely one of those horrid things preserved in spirits (and very bad spirits, too) in a cabinet. I was not the fellow-being of these explorers: I was a curiosity; I was a *specimen.* Hath not an American organs, dimensions, senses, affections, passions even as a European hath? If you prick us, do we not bleed? If you tickle us, do we not laugh? I will not keep on with Shylock to his next question but one.

Till after our Civil War it never seemed to enter the head of any foreigner, especially of any Englishman, that an American had what could be called a country, except as a place to eat, sleep, and trade in. Then it seemed to strike them suddenly. "By Jove, you know, fellahs don't fight like that for a shop-till!" No, I rather think not. To Americans America is something more than a promise and an expectation. It has a past and traditions of its own. A descent from men who sacrificed everything and came hither, not to better their fortunes, but to plant their idea in virgin soil, should be a good pedigree. There was never colony save this that went forth, not to seek gold, but God. Is it not as well to have sprung from such as these as from some burly beggar who came over with Wilhelmus Conquestor, unless, indeed, a line grow better as it runs farther away from stalwart ancestors? And for our history, it is dry enough, no doubt, in the books, but, for all that, is of a kind that tells in the blood. I have admitted that Carlyle's sneer had a show of truth in it. But what does he himself, like a true Scot, admire in the Hohenzollerns? First of all, that they were *canny,* a thrifty, forehanded race. Next, that they made a good fight from generation to generation with the chaos around them. That is precisely the battle which the English race on this continent has been pushing doughtily forward for two centuries and a half. Doughtily and silently, for you cannot hear in Europe "that crash, the death-song of the perfect tree," that has been going on here from sturdy father to sturdy son, and making this continent habitable for the weaker Old World breed that has swarmed to it during the last half-century. If ever men did a good stroke of work on this planet, it was the forefathers of those whom you are wondering whether it would not be prudent to acknowledge as far-off cousins. Alas, man of genius, to whom we owe so much, could you see nothing more than the burning of a foul chimney in that clash of Michael and Satan which flamed up under your very eyes?

Before our war we were to Europe but a huge mob of adventurers and shopkeepers. Leigh Hunt expressed it well enough when he said that he could never think of America without seeing a gigantic counter stretched all along the seaboard. And Leigh Hunt, without knowing it, had been more than half Americanized, too! Feudalism had by degrees made commerce, the great civilizer, contemptible. But a tradesman with sword on thigh and very prompt of stroke was not only redoubtable, he had become respectable also. Few people, I suspect, alluded twice to a needle in Sir John Hawkwood's presence, after that doughty fighter had exchanged it for a more dangerous tool of the same metal. Democracy had been hitherto only a ludicrous effort to reverse the laws of nature by thrusting Cleon into the place of Pericles. But a democracy that could fight for an abstraction, whose members held life and goods cheap compared with that larger life which we call country, was not merely unheard-of, but portentous. It was the nightmare of the Old World taking upon itself flesh and blood, turning out to be substance and not dream. Since the Norman crusader clanged down upon the throne of the *porphyro-geniti*, carefully-draped appearances had never received such a shock, had never been so rudely called on to produce their titles to the empire of the world. Authority has had its periods not unlike those of geology, and at last comes Man claiming kingship in right of his mere manhood. The world of the Saurians might be in some respects more picturesque, but the march of events is inexorable, and that world is bygone.

The young giant had certainly got out of long-clothes. He had become the *enfant terrible* of the human household. It was not and will not be easy for the world (especially for our British cousins) to look upon us as grown up. The youngest of nations, its people must also be young and to be treated accordingly, was the syllogism,—as if libraries did not make all nations equally old in all those respects, at least, where age is an advantage and not a defect. Youth, no doubt, has its good qualities, as people feel who are losing it, but boyishness is another thing. We had been somewhat boyish as a nation, a little loud, a little pushing, a little braggart. But might it not partly have been because we felt that we had certain claims to respect that were not admitted? The war which established our position as a vigorous nationality has also sobered us. A nation, like a man, cannot look death in the eye for four years without some strange reflections, without arriving at some clearer consciousness of the stuff it is made of, without some great moral change. Such a change, or the beginning of it, no observant person can fail to see here. Our thought and our politics, our bearing as a people, are assuming a manlier tone. We have been compelled to see what was weak in democracy as well as what was strong. We have begun obscurely to recognize that things do not go of themselves, and that popular government is not in itself a panacea, is no better than any other form except as the virtue and wisdom of the people make it so, and that when men undertake to do their own kingship, they enter upon the dangers and responsibilities as well as the privileges of the function. Above all, it looks as if we were on the way to be persuaded that no government can be carried on by declamation. It is noticeable also that facility of communication has made the best English and French thought far more directly operative here than ever before. Without being Europeanized, our discussion of important questions in statesmanship, in political economy, in æsthetics, is taking a broader scope and a higher tone. It had certainly been provincial, one might almost say local, to a very unpleasant extent. Perhaps our experience in soldiership has taught us to value training more than we have been popularly wont. We may possibly come to the conclusion, one of these days, that self-made men may not be always equally skilful in the manufacture of wisdom, may not be divinely commissioned to fabricate the higher qualities of opinion on all possible topics of human interest.

So long as we continue to be the most common-schooled and the least cultivated people in the world, I suppose we must consent to endure this condescending manner of foreigners toward us. The more friendly they mean to be, the more ludicrously prominent it becomes. They can never appreciate the immense amount of silent work that has been done here, making this continent slowly fit for the abode of man, and which will demonstrate itself, let us hope, in the character of the people. Outsiders can only be expected to judge a nation by the amount it has contributed to the civilization of the world; the amount, that is, that can be seen and handled. A great place in history can only be achieved by competitive examinations, nay, by a long course of them. How much new thought have we contributed to the common stock? Till that question can be triumphantly answered, or needs no answer, we must continue to be simply interesting as an experiment, to be studied as a problem, and not respected as an attained result or an accomplished solution. Perhaps, as I have hinted, their patronizing manner toward us is the fair result of their failing to see here anything more than a poor imitation, a plaster-cast of Europe. And are they not partly right? If the tone of the uncultivated American has too often the arrogance of the barbarian, is not that of the cultivated as often vulgarly apologetic? In the America they meet with is there the simplicity, the manliness, the absence of sham, the sincere human nature, the sensitiveness to duty and implied obligation, that in any way distinguishes us from what our orators call "the effete civilization of the Old World"? Is there a politician among us daring enough (except a Dana here and there) to risk his future on the chance of our keeping our word with the exactness of superstitious communities like England? Is it certain that we shall be ashamed of a bankruptcy of honor, if we can only keep the letter of our bond? I hope we shall be able to answer all these questions with a frank *yes*. At any rate, we would advise our visitors that we are not merely curious creatures, but belong to the family of man, and that, as individuals, we are not to be always subjected to the competitive examination above mentioned, even if we acknowledged their competence as an examining board. Above all, we beg them to remember that America is not to us, as to them, a mere object of external interest to be discussed and analyzed, but *in* us, part of our very marrow. Let them not suppose that we conceive of ourselves as exiles from the graces and amenities of an older date than we, though very much at home in a state of things not yet all it might be or should be, but which we mean to make so, and which we find both wholesome and pleasant for men (though perhaps not for *dilettanti*) to live in. "The full tide of human existence" may be felt here as keenly as Johnson felt it at Charing Cross, and in a larger sense. I know one person who is singular enough to think Cambridge the very best spot on the habitable globe. "Doubtless God *could* have made a better, but doubtless he never did."

It will take England a great while to get over her airs of patronage toward us, or even passably to conceal them. She cannot help confounding the people with the country, and regarding us as lusty juveniles. She has a conviction that whatever good there is in us is wholly English, when the truth is that we are worth nothing except so far as we have disinfected ourselves of Anglicism. She is especially condescending just now, and lavishes sugar-plums on us as if we had not outgrown them. I am no believer in sudden conversions, especially in sudden conversions to a favorable opinion of people who have just proved you to be mistaken in judgment and therefore unwise in policy. I never blamed her for not wishing well to democracy,—how should she?—but Alabamas are not wishes. Let her not be too hasty in believing Mr. Reverdy Johnson's pleasant words. Though there is no thoughtful man in America who would not consider a war with England the greatest calamities, yet the feeling towards her here is very far from cordial, whatever our Minister may say in the effusion that comes after ample dining. Mr. Adams, with his famous "My Lord, this means war," perfectly represented his country. Justly or not, we have a feeling that we have been wronged, not merely insulted. The only sure way of bringing about a healthy relation between the two countries is for Englishmen to clear their minds of the notion that we are always to be treated as a kind of inferior and deported Englishman whose nature they perfectly understand, and whose back they accordingly stroke the wrong way of the fur with amazing perseverance. Let them learn to treat us naturally on our merits as human beings, as they would a German or a Frenchman, and not as if we were a kind of counterfeit Briton whose crime appeared in every shade of difference, and before long there would come that right feeling which we naturally call a good understanding. The common blood, and still more the common language, are fatal instruments of misapprehension. Let them give up *trying* to understand us, still more thinking that they do, and acting in various absurd ways as the necessary consequence, for they will never arrive at that devoutly-to-be-wished consummation, till they learn to look at us as we are and not as they suppose us to be. Dear old long-estranged mother-in-law, it is a great many years since we parted. Since 1660, when you married again, you have been a step-mother to

us. Put on your spectacles, dear madam. Yes, we *have* grown, and changed likewise. You would not let us darken your doors, if you could help it. We know that perfectly well. But pray, when we look to be treated as men, don't shake that rattle in our faces, nor talk baby to us any longer.

"Do, child, go to it grandam, child;
Give grandam kingdom, and it grandam will
Give it a plum, a cherry, and a fig!"

1868   1869

HARRIET BEECHER STOWE

1811–1896

THE HEAVY WEIGHT of the fame of *Uncle Tom's Cabin* has almost obliterated Harriet Beecher Stowe's real importance as a novelist of New England. Even her literary contemporaries spoke of the book as the high-water mark to which her genius—George Sand said that she had genius but not talent—never rose again. To the modern reader the best character in *Uncle Tom's Cabin* is a minor one, the New England spinster, Miss Ophelia, aunt to St. Clare.

Her sympathetic knowledge and understanding of Calvinist New England Harriet Beecher Stowe owed in large part to her father, Lyman Beecher, and her five reverend brothers. With Henry Ward, two years younger than she, she walked, from childhood "always hand-in-hand."

Lyman Beecher, when his sixth child, Harriet, was born in 1811, was pastor of the Congregational Church in Lichfield, Connecticut. In 1832 he was appointed to the presidency of Lane Theological Seminary in Cincinnati. There Harriet became interested in the abolitionist cause. There she met and married, in 1836, Calvin Ellis Stowe, Professor of Biblical Literature at the Seminary. In 1850 he was called to Bowdoin College in Brunswick, Maine; in 1853, to the Theological Seminary at Andover.

It was as a member of the Semi-Colon Club in Cincinnati that Harriet became aware of her gift for story writing. "Prize Tale: a New England Sketch" was published in the *Western Monthly Magazine* in 1834, and she soon found that she could command two dollars a page at any time, a page that she could write in fifteen minutes. Her husband admired and encouraged her as a "literary woman," but, dreamy and distrait, with none of the New England "faculty" she hymns so admiringly in her stories, she made a sad muddle of the attempt to combine the labors of Victorian housekeeping, the bringing up of six children, and the duty of preaching and earning with her pen. Nevertheless, a little woman, "tired far into the future," as Mrs. Hawthorne described her, she kept at it bravely. She published more than thirty books beside a perpetual flow of articles, "sketches," "papers," domestic advice, and stories for children. "Sermons, essays, lives of distinguished people," she wrote to her publisher James T. Fields, "I can write to order at times and seasons. A story comes, grows like a flower, sometimes will and sometimes won't, like a pretty woman." "She could bring her soul under discipline," as V. L. Parrington has shrewdly observed, "but not her art. . . . The creative instinct was strong in her but the critical was wholly lacking."

When she was fired to write something for the cause of the slave Harriet Beecher Stowe made two commonplace attempts before the inspiration came for *Uncle Tom's Cabin* (1852). The book, she said, was less composed by her than imposed upon her. It "insisted upon getting itself into being, and would take no denial." For the storm of praise and contumely that greeted it she was completely unprepared. *Dred: a Tale of the Great Dismal Swamp* (1856), which continued the discussion of the negro question, was well reasoned but had small emotional appeal.

Uncle Tom's Cabin sold three hundred thousand copies in a year in America and a million and a half in the British Empire, but it did not make a fortune for its author. There was money enough, though, for travel in Europe, where Mrs. Stowe was greeted by throngs at every railway station, loaded with gifts for the antislavery cause, and formed close friendships with the Duchess of Sutherland, the Brownings, and Lady Byron.

The sketches of New England life with which Harriet Beecher Stowe began her literary career grew to substantial proportions in the twenty years when her fame was at its height. *The Minister's Wooing* (1859) had as its chief character her hero Samuel Hopkins, the apostle of her supreme hero Jonathan Edwards. *The Pearl of Orr's Island* (1862) took its genesis from the days in Brunswick, Maine. *Oldtown Folks* (1869), the best of her books, was a novelizing of her husband's recollections of his boyhood in Natick, Massachusetts; *Poganuc People* (1878), a romanticized biography of her own Connecticut childhood. Of them all she seems to have enjoyed most and worked hardest over the Oldtown tales. "It is more to me than a story," she wrote; "it is my résumé of the whole spirit and body of New England, a country that is now exerting such an influence on the civilized world that to know it truly becomes an object."

The Writings of Harriet Beecher Stowe, 16 vols., Boston, 1896.
Annie Fields, "Days with Mrs. Stowe," in *Authors and Friends*, Boston, 1893; *Life and Letters of Harriet Beecher Stowe*, Boston, 1897.
C. H. Foster, *The Rungless Ladder; Harriet Beecher Stowe and New England Puritanism*, Durham, N. C., 1954.
Catherine Gilbertson, *Harriet Beecher Stowe*, New York, 1937.
C. E. and L. B. Stowe, *Harriet Beecher Stowe*, Boston, 1911.
Forrest Wilson, *Crusader in Crinoline*, Philadelphia, 1941.

» » *From:* OLDTOWN FOLKS « «

CHAPTER V

THE OLD MEETING-HOUSE

. . . It was the custom, on the first Sabbath after a bereavement, for the whole family circle to be present together in church, to request, in a formal note, the prayers of the congregation that the recent death might be sanctified to them. It was a point of honor for all family connections to be present at this service, even though they should not attend the funeral; and my Uncle Bill, a young Sophomore in Cambridge College, had come down duly to be with us on the occasion. He was a joyous, spirited, jolly, rollicking young fellow, not in the slightest degree given to funereal reflec-

tions, and his presence in the house always brought a certain busy cheerfulness which I felt lighten my darkness.

One thing certainly had a tendency in that direction, which was that Aunt Lois was always perceptibly ameliorated by Uncle Bill's presence. Her sharp, spare features wore a relaxed and smiling aspect, her eyes had a softer light, and she belied her own frequent disclaimer, that she never had any beauty, by looking almost handsome.

Poor Aunt Lois! I am afraid my reader will not do justice to her worth by the specimens of her ways and words which I have given. Any one that has ever pricked his fingers in trying to force open a chestnut-burr may perhaps have moralized at the satin lining, so smooth and soft, that lies inside of that sharpness. It is an emblem of a kind of nature very frequent in New England, where the best and kindest and most desirable of traits are enveloped in an outside wrapping of sharp austerity.

. . .

Aunt Lois was a good Christian, but she made that particular mistake in repeating the Lord's Prayer which so many of us quite unconsciously do,—she always said, *My* will be done, instead of Thy will. Not in so many words, of course,—it was the secret inner voice of her essential nature that spoke and said one thing, while her tongue said another. But then who can be sure enough of himself in this matter, to cast the first stone at Aunt Lois?

It was the fashion of the Calvinistic preaching of that time to put the doctrine of absolute and unconditional submission to God in the most appalling forms, and to exercise the conscience with most severe supposititious tests. After many struggles and real agonies, Aunt Lois had brought herself to believe that she would be willing to resign her eternal salvation to the Divine glory; that she could consent to the eternal perdition of those on whom her heart was most particularly set, were it God's will; and thus her self-will, as she supposed, had been entirely annihilated, whereas it was only doubled back on itself, and ready to come out with tenfold intensity in the unsuspected little things of this life, where she looked less at Divine agency than human instrumentality. No law, as she supposed, required her to submit to people's acting foolishly in their worldly matters, particularly when she was able and willing to show them precisely how they ought to act.

. . .

It was according to all the laws of moral gravitation that, as soon as my father died, my mother became an obedient satellite in Aunt Lois's orbit. She was one of those dear, helpless little women, who, like flowers by the wayside, seem to be at the disposal of the first strong hand that wants to gather them. She was made to be ruled over; and so we all felt this first Sunday morning that we had come home to be under the dominion of Aunt Lois. She put on my mother's mourning-bonnet and tied it under her meek, unresisting chin, turning her round and round to get views of her from different points, and arranging her ribbons and veil and pins as if she had been a lay figure going to exhibition; and then she tied our collars, and gave a final twitch to our jackets, and warned us not to pull out the pins from the crape bands on our new hats, nor to talk and look round in meeting, strengthening the caution with, "Just so sure as you do, there's Mr. Israel Scran, the tithing-man, will come and take you and set you on the pulpit stairs." 10

Now Mr. Israel Scran on week-days was a rather jolly, secular-looking individual, who sat on the top of a barrel in his store, and told good stories; but Israel Scran on Sundays was a tithing-man, whose eyes were supposed to be as a flame of fire to search out little boys that played in meeting, and bring them to awful retribution. And I must say that I shook in my shoes at the very idea of his entering into judgment with me for any misdemeanor. 20

Going to church on the present occasion was rather a severe and awful ceremony to my childish mind, second only to the dreary horror of the time when we stood so dreadfully still around the grave, and heard those heavy clods thud upon the coffin. I ventured a timid inquiry of my mother as to what was going to be done there.

Aunt Lois took the word out of her mouth. "Now, Horace, hush your talk, and don't worry 30 your mother. She's going to put up a note to be prayed for to-day, and we are all going to join; so you be a good boy, and don't talk."

Being good was so frequently in those days represented to me as synonymous with keeping silence, that I screwed my little mouth up firmly as I walked along to the meeting-house, behind my mother, holding my brother Bill's hand, and spoke not a word, though he made several overtures towards conversation by in- 40 forming me that he saw a chipmunk, and that if it was only Monday he'd hit him smack; and also telling me that Sam Lawson had promised to go pout-fishing with us on Tuesday, with other boy temporalities of a nature equally worldly.

The meeting-house to which our steps were tending was one of those huge, shapeless, barn-like structures, which our fathers erected apparently as a part of that well-arranged system 50 by which they avoided all resemblance to those fair, poetic ecclesiastical forms of the Old World, which seemed in their view as "garments spotted by the flesh."

The interior of it was revealed by the light

of two staring rows of windows, which let in the glare of the summer sun, and which were so loosely framed, that, in wintry and windy weather, they rattled and shook, and poured in a perfect whirlwind of cold air, which disported itself over the shivering audience.

It was a part of the theory of the times never to warm these buildings by a fire; and the legend runs that once in our meeting-house the communion was administered under a temperature which actually froze the sacred elements while they were being distributed. Many a remembrance of winter sessions in that old meeting-house rose to my mind, in which I sat with my poor dangling feet perfectly numb and paralyzed with cold, and blew on my finger-ends to keep a little warmth in them, and yet I never thought of complaining; for everybody was there,—mother, aunts, grandmother, and all the town. We all sat and took our hardships in common, as a plain, necessary fact of existence.

Going to meeting, in that state of society into which I was born, was as necessary and inevitable a consequence of waking up on Sunday morning as eating one's breakfast. Nobody thought of staying away,—and, for that matter, nobody wanted to stay away. Our weekly life was simple, monotonous, and laborious; and the chance of seeing the whole neighborhood together in their best clothes on Sunday was a thing which, in the dearth of all other sources of amusement, appealed to the idlest and most unspiritual of loafers. They who did not care for the sermon or the prayers wanted to see Major Broad's scarlet coat and laced ruffles, and his wife's brocade dress, and the new bonnet which Lady Lothrop had just had sent up from Boston. Whoever had not seen these would be out of society for a week to come, and not be able to converse understandingly on the topics of the day.

The meeting on Sunday united in those days, as nearly as possible, the whole population of a town,—men, women, and children. There was then in a village but one fold and one shepherd, and long habit had made the tendency to this one central point so much a necessity to every one, that to stay away from "meetin'" for any reason whatever was always a secret source of uneasiness. I remember in my early days, sometimes when I had been left at home by reason of some of the transient ailments of childhood, how ghostly and supernatural the stillness of the whole house and village outside the meeting-house used to appear to me, how loudly the clock ticked and the flies buzzed down the window-pane, and how I listened in the breathless stillness to the distant psalm-singing, the solemn tones of the long prayer, and then to the monotone of the sermon, and then again to the closing echoes of the last hymn, and thought sadly, what if some day I should be left out, when all my relations and friends had gone to meeting in the New Jerusalem, and hear afar the music from the crystal walls.

As our Sunday gathering at meeting was a complete picture of the population of our village, I shall, as near as possible, daguerreotype our Sunday audience, as the best means of placing my readers in sympathy with the scene and actors of this history.

The arrangement of our house of worship in Oldtown was somewhat peculiar, owing to the fact of its having originally been built as a mission church for the Indians. The central portion of the house, usually appropriated to the best pews, was in ours devoted to them; and here were arranged benches of the simplest and most primitive form, on which were collected every Sunday the thin and wasted remnants of what once was a numerous and powerful tribe. There were four or five respectable Indian families, who owned comfortable farms in the neighborhood, and came to meeting in their farm-wagons, like any of their white neighbors.

Conspicuous among these, on the front bench, facing the pulpit, sat the Indian head-magistrate, Justice Waban,—tall and erect as an old pine-tree, and of a grave and reverend aspect. Next to him was seated the ecclesiastical superior of that portion of the congregation, Deacon Ephraim. Mild, intelligent, and devout, he was the perfect model of the praying Indian formed in the apostolic traditions of the good Eliot. By his side sat his wife, Keturah, who, though she had received Christian baptism, still retained in most respects the wild instincts and untamed passions of the savage. Though she attended church and allowed her children to be baptized, yet, in spite of minister, elder, and tithing-man, she obstinately held on to the practice of many of her old heathen superstitions.

Old Keturah was one of the wonders of my childhood. She was spoken of among the gossips with a degree of awe, as one who possessed more knowledge than was good for her;

and in thunder-storms and other convulsions of nature she would sit in her chimney-corner and chant her old Indian incantations, to my mingled terror and delight. I remember distinctly three syllables that occurred very often, —"ah-mah-ga, ah-mah-ga,"—sometimes pronounced in wild, plaintive tones, and sometimes in tones of menace and denunciation. In fact, a century before, Keturah must have had a hard time of it with her Christian neighbors; but our minister was a gentleman and a scholar, and only smiled benignly when certain elderly ladies brought him terrible stories of Keturah's proceedings.

Next to Keturah was seated Deborah Kummacher, an Indian woman, who had wisely forsaken the unprofitable gods of the wild forest, and taken to the Christian occupation of fruit-growing, and kept in nice order a fruit farm near my grandfather's, where we children delighted to resort in the season, receiving from her presents of cherries, pears, peaches, or sweet apples, which she informed us she was always ready to give to good children who said their prayers and made their manners when they came into her house. Next behind her came Betty Poganut, Patty Pegan, and old Sarah Wonsamug,—hard-visaged, high-cheekboned females, with snaky-black eyes, principally remarkable, in my mind, for the quantity of cider they could drink. I had special reason to remember this, as my grandmother's house was their favorite resort, and drawing cider was always the work of the youngest boy.

Then there was Lem Sudock, a great, coarse, heavy-moulded Indian, with gigantic limbs and a savage face, but much in request for laying stone walls, digging wells, and other tasks for which mere physical strength was the chief requisite. Beside him was Dick Obscue, a dull, leering, lazy, drinking old fellow, always as dry as an empty sponge, but with an endless capacity for imbibing. Dick was of a class which our modern civilization would never see inside of a church, though he was in his seat in our meeting-house as regularly as any of the deacons; but on weekdays his principal employment seemed to be to perambulate the country, making stations of all the kitchen firesides, where he would tell stories, drink cider, and moralize, till the patience or cider-pitchers of his hosts ran dry, when he would rise up slowly, adj st his old straw hat, hitch up his dangling nether garments a little tighter, and, with a patronizing nod, say, "Wal, naow, 'f you can spare me I'll go."

Besides our Indian population, we had also a few negroes, and a side gallery was appropriated to them. Prominent there was the stately form of old Boston Foodah, an African prince, who had been stolen from the coast of Guinea in early youth, and sold in Boston at some period of antiquity whereto the memory of man runneth not. All the Oldtown people, and their fathers and grandfathers, remembered Old Boston just as he then existed, neither older nor younger. He was of a majestic stature, slender and proudly erect, and perfectly graceful in every movement, his woolly hair as white as the driven snow. He was servant to General Hull in the Revolutionary war, and at its close was presented by his master with a full suit of his military equipments, including three-cornered hat, with plume, epaulets, and sword. Three times a year,—at the spring training, the fall muster, and on Thanksgiving day,—Boston arrayed himself in full panoply, and walked forth a really striking and magnificent object. In the eyes of us boys, on these days, he was a hero, and he patronized us with a condescension which went to our hearts. His wife, Jinny, was a fat, roly-poly little body, delighting in red and yellow bonnets, who duly mustered into meeting a troop of black-eyed, fat, woolly-headed little negroes, whom she cuffed and disciplined during sermon-time with a matronly ferocity designed to show white folks that she was in earnest in their religious training.

Near by was old Primus King, a gigantic, retired whaleman, black as a coal, with enormous hands and feet, universally in demand in all the region about as assistant in butchering operations.

. . .

The houses of the colored people formed a little settlement by themselves in the north part of the village, where they lived on most amicable terms with all the inhabitants.

In the front gallery of the meeting-house, opposite the pulpit, was seated the choir of the church. The leader of our music was old Mump Morse, a giant of a man, in form not unlike a cider-hogshead, with a great round yellow head, and a voice like the rush of mighty winds, who was wont to boast that he could chord with thunder and lightning better than any man in the parish. Next to him came

our friend Sam Lawson, whose distinguished
peculiarity it was, that he could strike into any
part where his voice seemed most needed; and
he often showed the miscellaneous nature of
his accomplishments by appearing as tenor,
treble, or counter, successively, during the
rendering of one psalm. If we consider that he
also pitched the tunes with his pitch-pipe, and
played on his bass-viol, we shall see increasing
10 evidence of that versatility of genius for which
he was distinguished.

Another principal bass-singer was old Joe
Stedman, who asserted his democratic right to
do just as he had a mind to by always appearing every Sunday in a clean leather apron
of precisely the form he wore about his weekly
work. Of course all the well-conducted upper
classes were scandalized, and Joe was privately
admonished of the impropriety, which greatly
20 increased his satisfaction, and caused him to
regard himself as a person of vast importance.
It was reported that the minister had told him
that there was more pride in his leather apron
than in Captain Browne's scarlet cloak; but
Joe settled the matter by declaring that the
apron was a matter of conscience with him, and
of course after that there was no more to be
said.

These leading characters, with a train of
30 young men and maidens who practised in the
weekly singing-school, used to conduct the
musical devout exercises much to their own
satisfaction, if not always to that of our higher
circle.

And now, having taken my readers through
the lower classes in our meeting-house, I must,
in order of climax, represent to them our
higher orders.

Social position was a thing in those days
40 marked by lines whose precision and distinctness had not been blurred by the rough
handling of democracy. Massachusetts was, in
regard to the aroma and atmosphere of her
early days, an aristocratic community. The
seeds of democratic social equality lay as yet
ungerminated in her soil. The State was a
garden laid out with the old formal parallelo-
grams and clipped hedges of princely courts
and titled ranks, but sown with seeds of a new
50 and rampant quality, which were destined to
overgrow them all.

Even our little town had its court circle,
its House of Lords and House of Commons,
with all the etiquette and solemn observances
thereto appertaining. At the head stood the

minister and his wife, whose rank was expressed by the pew next the pulpit. Then came
Captain Browne, a retired English merchant
and ship-owner, who was reported to have
ballasted himself with a substantial weight of
worldly substance. Captain Browne was a tall,
upright, florid man, a little on the shady side
of life, but carrying his age with a cheerful
greenness. His long, powdered locks hung in
a well-tended queue down his back, and
he wore a scarlet coat, with a white vest
and stock, and small-clothes, while long silk
stockings with knee and shoe buckles of the
best paste, sparkling like real diamonds, completed his attire. His wife rustled by his side
in brocade which might almost stand alone for
stiffness, propped upon heels that gave a majestic altitude to her tall, thin figure.

Next came the pew of Miss Mehitable Rossiter, who, in right of being the only surviving
member of the family of the former minister,
was looked upon with reverence in Oldtown,
and took rank decidedly in the Upper House,
although a very restricted and limited income
was expressed in the quality of her attire. Her
Sunday suit in every article spoke of ages past,
rather than of the present hour. Her laces were
darned, though still they were laces; her satin
gown had been turned and made over, till
every possible capability of it was exhausted;
and her one Sunday bonnet exhibited a power
of coming out in fresh forms, with each revolving season, that was quite remarkable, particularly as each change was somewhat odder
than the last. But still, as everybody knew that
it was Miss Mehitable Rossiter, and no meaner
person, her queer bonnets and dyed gowns
were accepted as a part of those inexplicable
dispensations of the Providence that watches
over the higher classes, which are to be received by faith alone.

In the same pew with Miss Mehitable sat
Squire Jones, once, in days of colonial rule,
rejoicing in the dignity of Sheriff of the County.
During the years of the Revolutionary war, he
had mysteriously vanished from view, as many
good Tories did; but now that the new social
status was well established, he suddenly reappeared in the neighborhood, and took his
place as an orderly citizen, unchallenged and
unquestioned. It was enough that the Upper
House received him. The minister gave him his
hand, and Lady Lothrop courtesied to him,
and called on his wife, and that, of course,
settled the manner in which the parish were

to behave; and, like an obedient flock, they all jumped the fence after their shepherd. Squire Jones, besides, was a well-formed, well-dressed man, who lived in a handsome style, and came to meeting in his own carriage; and these are social virtues not to be disregarded in any well-regulated community.

There were certain well-established ranks and orders in social position in Oldtown, which it is important that I should distinctly define. People who wore ruffles round their hands, and rode in their own coaches, and never performed any manual labor, might be said to constitute in Oldtown our House of Lords,—and they might all have been counted on two or three of my fingers. It was, in fact, confined to the personages already enumerated. There were the minister, Captain Browne, and Sheriff Jones.

But below these, yet associating with them on terms of strict equality, were a more numerous body of Commons,—men of substance and influence, but who tilled the earth with their own hands, or pursued some other active industrial calling.

Distinguished among these, sitting in the next pew to the Sheriff, was Major Broad, a practical farmer, who owned a large and thriving farm of the best New England type, and presented that true blending of the laboring man and the gentleman which is nowhere else found. He had received his military rank for meritorious services in the late Revolutionary war, and he came back to his native village with that indefinable improvement in air and manner which is given by the habits of military life. With us he owed great prestige to a certain personal resemblance to General Washington which he was asserted to have by one of our townsfolk, who had often seen him and the General on the same field, and who sent the word abroad in the town that whoever wanted to know how General Washington looked had only to look upon Major Broad. The Major was too much of a real man to betray the slightest consciousness of this advantage, but it invested him with an air of indefinable dignity in the eyes of all his neighbors, especially those of the lower ranks.

Next came my grandfather's family pew; and in our Oldtown House of Commons I should say that none stood higher than he. In his Sunday suit my grandfather was quite a well-made, handsome man. His face was marked by grave, shrewd reflection, and a certain gentle cast of humor, which rarely revealed itself even in a positive smile, and yet often made me feel as if he were quietly and interiorly smiling at his own thoughts. His well-brushed Sunday coat and small-clothes, his bright knee and shoe buckles, his long silk stockings, were all arranged with a trim neatness refreshing to behold. His hair, instead of being concealed by a wig, or powdered and tied in a queue, after the manner of the aristocracy, fell in long curls on his shoulders, and was a not unbecoming silvery frame to the placid picture of his face. He was a man by nature silent and retiring, indisposed to anything like hurry or tumult, rather easy and generously free in his business habits, and quietly sanguine in his expectations. In point of material possessions he was reputed well to do, as he owned a large farm and two mills, and conducted the business thereof with a quiet easiness which was often exceedingly provoking to my grandmother and Aunt Lois. No man was more popular in the neighborhood, and the confidence of his fellow-townsmen was yearly expressed in town-meeting by his reappointment to every office of trust which he could be induced to accept. He was justice of the peace, deacon of the church, selectman, —in short, enjoyed every spiritual and temporal office by the bestowal of which his fellow-men could express confidence in him. This present year, indeed, he bore the office of tithing-man, in association with Mr. Israel Scran. It had been thought that it would be a good thing, in order to check the increasing thoughtlessness of the rising generation in regard to Sunday-keeping, to enlist in this office an authority so much respected as Deacon Badger; but the manner in which he performed its duties was not edifying to the minds of strictly disposed people. The Deacon in his official capacity was expected to stalk forth at once as a terror to evil-doers, whereas he seemed to have no capacity for terrifying anybody. When a busy individual informed him that this or that young person was to be seen walking out in the fields, or picking flowers in their gardens of a Sabbath afternoon, the Deacon always placidly answered that he had n't seen them; from which the ill-disposed would infer that he looked another way, of set purpose, and the quiet internal smile that always illuminated the Deacon's face gave but too much color to this idea.

In those days the great war of theology

which has always divided New England was rife, and every man was marked and ruled as to his opinions, and the theologic lines passed even through the conjugal relation, which often, like everything else, had its Calvinistic and Arminian side.

My grandfather was an Arminian,[1] while my grandmother was, as I have said, an earnest, ardent Calvinist. Many were the controversies I have overheard between them, in which the texts of Scripture flew thick and fast, until my grandfather at last would shut himself up in that final fortress of calm and smiling silence which is so provoking to feminine ardor. There intrenched, he would look out upon his assailants with a quiet, imperturbable good-humor which quite drove them to despair.

It was a mystery to my grandmother how a good man, as she knew my grandfather to be, *could* remain years unmoved in the very hearing of such unanswerable arguments as she had a thousand times brought up, and still, in the very evening of his days, go on laying his serene old head on an Arminian pillow! My grandfather was a specimen of that class of men who can walk amid the opinions of their day, encircled by a halo of serene and smiling individuality which quarrels with nobody, and, without shocking any one's prejudices, preserves intact the liberty of individual dissent. He silently went on thinking and doing exactly as he pleased, and yet was always spoken of as the *good* Deacon. His calm, serene, benignant figure was a sort of benediction as he sat in his pew of a Sunday; and if he did not see the little boys that played, or, seeing them, only smilingly brought them to a sense of duty by passing them a head of fennel through the slats of the pews, still Deacon Badger was reckoned about the best man in the world.

By the side of my grandfather sat his eldest born, Uncle Jacob, a hale, thrifty young farmer, who, with his equally hale and thrifty wife, was settled on a well-kept farm at some distance from ours. Uncle Jacob was a genuine son of the soil, whose cheeks were ruddy as clover, and teeth as white as new milk. He had grown up on a farm, as quietly as a tree grows, and had never been ten miles from his birthplace. He was silent, contented, and industrious. He was in his place to be prayed for as one of a bereaved family, of course, this morning; but

[1] The Dutch theologian Arminius doubted the Calvinistic doctrine of unconditional predestination. His teachings helped to undermine the theology of the New England Puritans.

there was scarcely more capability of mourning in his plump, healthy body than there is in that of a well-fed, tranquil steer. But he took his weekly portion of religion kindly. It was the thing to do on Sunday, as much as making hay or digging potatoes on Monday. His wife by his side displayed no less the aspect of calm, respectable, well-to-do content. Her Sunday bonnet was without spot, her Sunday gown without wrinkle; and she had a great bunch of fennel in her pocket-handkerchief, which, from time to time, she imparted to us youngsters with a benevolent smile.

·   ·   ·   ·

But time would fail me to go on and describe all the quiddities and oddities of our Sunday congregation. Suffice it to say, that we all grew in those days like the apple-trees in our back lot. Every man had his own quirks and twists, and threw himself out freely in the line of his own individuality; and so a rather jerky, curious, original set of us there was. But such as we were, high and low, good and bad, refined and illiterate, barbarian and civilized, negro and white, the old meeting-house united us all on one day of the week, and its solemn services formed an insensible but strong bond of neighborhood charity.

We may rail at Blue Laws and Puritan strictness as much as we please, but certainly those communities where our fathers carried out their ideas fully had their strong points; and, rude and primitive as our meeting-houses were, this weekly union of all classes in them was a most powerful and efficient means of civilization. The man or woman cannot utterly sink who on every seventh day is obliged to appear in decent apparel, and to join with all the standing and respectability of the community in a united act of worship.

Nor were our Sunday services, though simple, devoid of their solemn forms. The mixed and motley congregation came in with due decorum during the ringing of the first bell, and waited in their seats the advent of the minister. The tolling of the bell was the signal for him that his audience were ready to receive him, and he started from his house. The clerical dress of the day, the black silk gown, the spotless bands, the wig and three-cornered hat and black gloves, were items of professional fitness which, in our minister's case, never failed of a due attention. When, with his wife leaning on his arm, he entered at the door of the meeting-house, the whole congregation rose and remained reverently standing until he had taken his seat in the pulpit. The same reverential decorum was maintained after service was over, when all remained standing and uncovered while the minister and his family passed down the broad aisle and left the house. Our fathers were no man-worshippers, but they regarded the minister as an ambassador from the great Sovereign of the universe, and paid reverence to Him whose word he bore in their treatment of him.

On the Sunday following the funeral of any one in the parish, it was customary to preach a sermon having immediate reference to the event which had occurred, in the course of which the nearest friends and relatives were directly addressed, and stood up in their seats to receive the pastoral admonition and consolation. I remember how wan and faded, like a shimmering flower, my poor mother rose in her place, while I was forcibly held down by Aunt Lois's grasp on my jacket till the "orphan children" were mentioned, when I was sent up on my feet with an impetus like a Jack in a box; and afterward the whole family circle arose and stood, as the stream of admonition and condolence became more general. We were reminded that the God of the widow and orphan never dies,—that this life is the shadow, and the life to come the substance,—that there is but one thing needful,—that as our departed friend is today, so we may all be tomorrow; and then the choir sung, to the tune of Old Darwen,

"Shall man, O God of life and light,
    Forever moulder in the grave?
Hast thou forgot thy glorious work,
    Thy promise and thy power to save?"

I cannot say much for our country psalmody. Its execution was certainly open to severe criticism; and Uncle Eliakim, on every occasion of especial solemnity, aggravated its peculiarities by tuning up in a high, cracked voice a weird part, in those days called "counter," but which would in our days insure his being taken out of the house as a possessed person. But, in spite of all this, those old minor-keyed funeral hymns in which our fathers delighted always had a quality in them that affected me powerfully. The music of all barbarous nations is said to be in the minor key, and there is in its dark combinations something that gives piercing utterance to that undertone of doubt, mystery, and sorrow by which a sensitive spirit always is encompassed in this life.

I was of a peculiarly sensitive organization; my nerves shivered to every touch, like harpstrings. What might have come over me had I heard the solemn chants of cathedrals, and the deep pulsations of the old organ-hearts that beat there, I cannot say, but certain it is that the rude and primitive singing in our old meeting-house always excited me powerfully. It brought over me, like a presence, the sense of the infinite and eternal, the yearning and the fear and the desire of the poor finite being, so ignorant and so helpless. I left the church lifted up as if walking on air, with the final words of the psalm floating like an illuminated cloud around me,—

"Faith sees the bright eternal doors
    Unfold to make His children way;
They shall be crowned with endless life,
    And shine in everlasting day."

1869

WALT WHITMAN

1819–1892

WHITMAN'S LONG LIFE was one of many occupations: office boy and printer's devil in Brooklyn, country school-teacher (1836–1838), editor at various times of nine newspapers, including the *Daily Eagle* (1846–1847), *The Freeman*, a Free-soil paper (1848), and the *Daily Times* (1857–1859), all of Brooklyn. A son of Long Island—"fish-shape Paumanok"—he came later to know at first hand many of the states which his poems celebrate, as war nurse in Washington and in the army hospitals in Virginia (1863–1864), as traveler in the West (1879) and in Canada (1880); and he assumed willingly the role of prophet and public voice for American democracy. At the end of the war his appointment to a job in the Indian Bureau, Department of the Interior, was taken from him by Secretary James Harlan because of the alleged obscenity of his poetry. But with successive editions of *Leaves of Grass* (1855, 1856, 1860, 1867, 1871) his fame was spreading as far abroad as England and France, and recognition of Whitman in America was furthered by the publication of *Drum-Taps* (1865) and *Democratic Vistas* (1871). The figure of Good, Gray Poet was one which pleased him and which he admired; unlike his contemporary, Tennyson, he did not try to compel awe by acting the part of one who stands aloof from the importunate crowd.

The death of his mother, and a severe illness and partial paralysis of his own, darkened the year 1873. But his removal to Camden, New Jersey, with summers at near-by Stafford Farm, helped him regain strength. The 1881 edition of *Leaves of Grass* was much revised and augmented, and was followed by *Specimen Days* in 1882. In 1884 Whitman bought the famous house on Mickle Street, Camden, where he died after having completed a final revised edition of *Leaves of Grass* in the last year of his life.

The Whitman legend is somewhat faded now. Events have made their comment on the democratic prophecies, and much of the vast welter of words in which he sang his country and himself has lost its power to please. There remains, of course, much that is fine and stirring still in the rolling catalogues and the loud assertions: a sense of the common man and common things of Whitman's America. And certainly Whitman as a political man must not be ignored, even though it is critical folly to attempt to rationalize his politics with their contradictions and confusions at the expense of much of his finest poetry. For Whitman is as a rule less the poet in his public incantations than in those poems in which, stepping from the rostrum, abandoning the gazetteer and the inventory, he looks into himself for private purposes—though the occasion may be public, as in *When Lilacs Last in the Dooryard Bloomed*, *The Wound Dresser*, and *Vigil Strange I Kept in the Field One Night*. It is in such poems as these, and in others—*On the Beach at Night*, *Out of the Cradle Endlessly Rocking*—that his virtues emerge most clearly: his tenderness, his responsiveness to the mystery and sadness of life, his love of man, too often forced into self-conscious attitudinizing.

It is at these moments that his lines lose the slackness of the catalogues, the brassiness of the theatrical yawp, and (retaining their characteristic cadences) acquire something of the concentration which poetry achieves when words and emotion are sufficient to each other. One might turn his poem *When I Heard the Learn'd Astronomer* into a kind of parable, and seeing Whitman himself as the astronomer (with his charts and diagrams, adding, dividing, measuring, lecturing with much applause in the lecture room) follow him most willingly when he "wanders off by himself" and

> In the mystical moist night-air, and from time to time
> Looks up in perfect silence at the stars.

Willard Thorp, "Whitman," in *Eight American Authors, A Review of Research and Criticism*, New York, 1956, pp. 271–318.

The Complete Writings of Walt Whitman, 10 vols., New York, 1902.

Walt Whitman's Poems, G. W. Allen and C. T. Davis, eds., New York, 1955.

G. W. Allen, *The Solitary Singer: A Critical Biography of Walt Whitman*, New York, 1955.

———, *Walt Whitman Handbook*, Chicago, 1946.

H. S. Canby, *Walt Whitman, an American: A Study in Biography*, Boston, 1943.

Milton Hindus, ed., *Leaves of Grass One Hundred Years After*, Stanford, 1955.

Emory Holloway, *Whitman, An Interpretation in Narrative*, New York, 1926.

Horace Traubel, *With Walt Whitman in Camden*, 3 vols., N. Y., 1906–14; IV, Phil., 1953; V, Carbondale, Ill., 1959.

» » From: SONG OF MYSELF [1] « «

1

I celebrate myself, and sing myself,
And what I assume you shall assume,
For every atom belonging to me as good belongs to you.

I loafe and invite my soul,
I lean and loafe at my ease observing a spear of summer grass.

My tongue, every atom of my blood, form'd from this soil, this air,
Born here of parents born here from parents the same, and their parents the same,
I, now thirty-seven years old in perfect health begin,
Hoping to cease not till death.

Creeds and schools in abeyance,   10
Retiring back a while sufficed at what they are, but never forgotten,
I harbor for good or bad, I permit to speak at every hazard,
Nature without check with original energy.

2

Houses and rooms are full of perfumes, the shelves are crowded with perfumes,
I breathe the fragrance myself and know it and like it,
The distillation would intoxicate me also, but I shall not let it.

The atmosphere is not a perfume, it has no taste of the distillation, it is odorless,
It is for my mouth forever, I am in love with it,
I will go to the bank by the wood and become undisguised and naked,
I am mad for it to be in contact with me.   20

The smoke of my own breath,
Echoes, ripples, buzz'd whispers, love-root, silk-thread, crotch and vine,
My respiration and inspiration, the beating of my heart, the passing of blood and air through my lungs,
The sniff of green leaves and dry leaves, and of the shore and dark-color'd sea-rocks, and of hay in the barn,

The sound of the belch'd words of my voice loos'd to the eddies of the wind,
A few light kisses, a few embraces, a reaching around of arms,
The play of shine and shade on the trees as the supple boughs wag,
The delight alone or in the rush of the streets, or along the fields and hill-sides,
The feeling of health, the full-noon trill, the song of me rising from bed and meeting the sun.

Have you reckon'd a thousand acres much? have you reckon'd the earth much?   30
Have you practis'd so long to learn to read?
Have you felt so proud to get at the meaning of poems?

Stop this day and night with me and you shall possess the origin of all poems,
You shall possess the good of the earth and sun, (there are millions of suns left,)
You shall no longer take things at second or third hand, nor look through the eyes of the dead, nor feed on the spectres in books,
You shall not look through my eyes either, nor take things from me,
You shall listen to all sides and filter them from your self.

3

I have heard what the talkers were talking, the talk of the beginning and the end,
But I do not talk of the beginning or the end.

There was never any more inception than there is now,   40
Nor any more youth or age than there is now,
And will never be any more perfection than there is now,
Nor any more heaven or hell than there is now.

Urge and urge and urge,
Always the procreant urge of the world.
Out of the dimness opposite equals advance, always substance and increase, always sex,
Always a knit of identity, always distinction, always a breed of life.

To elaborate is no avail, learn'd and unlearn'd feel that it is so.

[1] Called "Walt Whitman" or "A Poem of Walt Whitman an American" in the first five editions; first given its present title in the edition of 1881, whence the present version is drawn.

Sure as the most certain sure, plumb in the
  uprights, well entretied, braced in the beams,
Stout as a horse, affectionate, haughty, electrical,   50
I and this mystery here we stand.

Clear and sweet is my soul, and clear and
  sweet is all that is not my soul.

Lack one lacks both, and the unseen is proved
  by the seen,
Till that becomes unseen and receives proof
  in its turn.

Showing the best and dividing it from the
  worst age vexes age,
Knowing the perfect fitness and equanimity
  of things, while they discuss I am silent, and
  go bathe and admire myself.

Welcome is every organ and attribute of me,
  and of any man hearty and clean,
Not an inch nor a particle of an inch is vile,
  and none shall be less familiar than the rest.

I am satisfied—I see, dance, laugh, sing;
As the hugging and loving bed-fellow sleeps
  at my side through the night, and withdraws at the peep of the day with stealthy
  tread,   60
Leaving me baskets cover'd with white towels
  swelling the house with their plenty,
Shall I postpone my acceptation and realization and scream at my eyes,
That they turn from gazing after and down
  the road,
And forthwith cipher and show me to a cent,
Exactly the value of one and exactly the value
  of two, and which is ahead?

4

Trippers and askers surround me,
People I meet, the effect upon me of my early
  life or the ward and city I live in, or the
  nation,
The latest dates, discoveries, inventions, societies, authors old and new,
My dinner, dress, associates, looks, compliments, dues,
The real or fancied indifference of some man or
  woman I love,   70
The sickness of one of my folks or of myself,
  or ill-doing or loss or lack of money, or
  depressions or exaltations,

Battles, the horrors of fratricidal war, the fever
  of doubtful news, the fitful events;
These come to me days and nights and go
  from me again,
But they are not the Me myself.

Apart from the pulling and hauling stands what
  I am,
Stands amused, complacent, compassionating,
  idle, unitary,
Looks down, is erect, or bends an arm on an
  impalpable certain rest,
Looking with side-curved head curious what
  will come next,
Both in and out of the game and watching and
  wondering at it.

Backward I see in my own days where I
  sweated through fog with linguists and con-
  tenders,   80
I have no mockings or arguments, I witness and
  wait.

5

I believe in you my soul, the other I am
  must not abase itself to you,
And you must not be abased to the other.

Loafe with me on the grass, loose the stop
  from your throat,
Not words, not music or rhyme I want, not
  custom or lecture, not even the best,
Only the lull I like, the hum of your valvèd
  voice.

I mind how once we lay such a transparent
  summer morning,
How you settled your head athwart my hips
  and gently turn'd over upon me,
And parted the shirt from my bosom-bone, and
  plunged your tongue to my bare-stript heart,
And reach'd till you felt my beard, and reach'd
  till you held my feet.   90

Swiftly arose and spread around me the peace
  and knowledge that pass all the argument
  of the earth,
And I know that the hand of God is the promise
  of my own,
And I know that the spirit of God is the brother
  of my own,
And that all the men ever born are also my
  brothers, and the women my sisters and
  lovers,

And that a kelson of the creation is love,
And limitless are leaves stiff or drooping in the
fields,
And brown ants in the little wells beneath
them,
And mossy scabs of the worm fence, heap'd
stones, elder, mullein and poke-weed.

6

A child said *What is the grass?* fetching it to
me with full hands,
How could I answer the child? I do not know
what it is any more than he.   100
I guess it must be the flag of my disposition, out
of hopeful green stuff woven.

Or I guess it is the handkerchief of the Lord,
A scented gift and remembrancer designedly
dropt,
Bearing the owner's name someway in the
corners, that we may see and remark, and
say *Whose?*

Or I guess the grass is itself a child, the
produced babe of the vegetation.

Or I guess it is a uniform hieroglyphic,
And it means, Sprouting alike in broad zones
and narrow zones,
Growing among black folks as among white,
Kanuck, Tuckahoe, Congressman, Cuff, I give
them the same, I receive them the same.

And now it seems to me the beautiful uncut
hair of graves.   110

Tenderly will I use you curling grass,
It may be you transpire from the breasts of
young men,
It may be if I had known them I would have
loved them,
It may be you are from old people, or from
offspring taken soon out of their mothers'
laps,
And here you are the mothers' laps.

This grass is very dark to be from the white
heads of old mothers,
Darker than the colorless beards of old men,
Dark to come from under the faint red roofs of
mouths.

O I perceive after all so many uttering tongues,
And I perceive they do not come from the roofs
of mouths for nothing.   120

I wish I could translate the hints about the
dead young men and women,
And the hints about old men and mothers, and
the offspring taken soon out of their laps.

What do you think has become of the young
and old men?
And what do you think has become of the
women and children?

They are alive and well somewhere,
The smallest sprout shows there is really no
death,
And if ever there was it led forward life, and
does not wait at the end to arrest it,
And ceas'd the moment life appear'd.

All goes onward and outward, nothing collapses,
And to die is different from what any one
supposed, and luckier.   130

7

Has any one supposed it lucky to be born?
I hasten to inform him or her it is just as lucky
to die, and I know it.

I pass death with the dying and birth with the
new-wash'd babe, and am not contain'd between my hat and boots,
And peruse manifold objects, no two alike and
every one good,
The earth good and the stars good, and their
adjuncts all good.

I am not an earth nor an adjunct of an earth,
I am the mate and companion of people, all
just as immortal and fathomless as myself,
(They do not know how immortal, but I
know.)

Every kind for itself and its own, for me mine
male and female,
For me those that have been boys and that
love women,   140
For me the man that is proud and feels how
it stings to be slighted,
For me the sweet-heart and the old maid, for
me mothers and mothers of mothers,
For me lips that have smiled, eyes that have
shed tears,
For me children and the begetters of children.

Undrape! you are not guilty to me, nor stale
    nor discarded,
I see through the broadcloth and gingham
    whether or no,
And am around, tenacious, acquisitive, tireless,
    and cannot be shaken away.

8

The little one sleeps in its cradle,
I lift the gauze and look a long time, and si-
    lently brush away flies with my hand.

The youngster and the red-faced girl turn aside
    up the bushy hill,   150
I peeringly view them from the top.

The suicide sprawls on the bloody floor of the
    bedroom,
I witness the corpse with its dabbled hair, I
    note where the pistol has fallen.

The blab of the pave, tires of carts, sluff of
    boot-soles, talk of the promenaders,
The heavy omnibus, the driver with his inter-
    rogating thumb, the clank of the shod horses
    on the granite floor,
The snow-sleighs, clinking, shouted jokes, pelts
    of snow-balls,
The hurrahs for popular favorites, the fury of
    rous'd mobs,
The flap of the curtain'd litter, a sick man
    inside borne to the hospital,
The meeting of enemies, the sudden oath, the
    blows and fall,
The excited crowd, the policeman with his star
    quickly working his passage to the centre of
    the crowd,   160
The impassive stones that receive and return
    so many echoes,
What groans of over-fed or half-starv'd who
    fall sunstruck or in fits,
What exclamations of women taken suddenly
    who hurry home and give birth to babes,
What living and buried speech is always vi-
    brating here, what howls restrain'd by de-
    corum,
Arrests of criminals, slights, adulterous offers
    made, acceptances, rejections with convex
    lips,
I mind them or the show or resonance of them
    —I come and I depart.

9

The big doors of the country barn stand open
    and ready,
The dried grass of the harvest-time loads the
    slow-drawn wagon,
The clear light plays on the brown gray and
    green intertinged,
The armfuls are pack'd to the sagging mow. 170

I am there, I help, I came stretch'd atop of the
    load,
I felt its soft jolts, one leg reclined on the other,
I jump from the cross-beams and seize the
    clover and timothy,
And roll head over heels and tangle my hair
    full of wisps.

10

Alone far in the wilds and mountains I hunt,
Wandering amazed at my own lightness and
    glee,
In the late afternoon choosing a safe spot to
    pass the night,
Kindling a fire and broiling the fresh-kill'd
    game,
Falling asleep on the gather'd leaves with my
    dog and gun by my side.

The Yankee clipper is under her sky-sails, she
    cuts the sparkle and scud,   180
My eyes settle the land, I bend at her prow or
    shout joyously from the deck.

The boatmen and clam-diggers arose early and
    stopt for me,
I tuck'd my trowser-ends in my boots and went
    and had a good time;
You should have been with us that day round
    the chowder-kettle.

I saw the marriage of the trapper in the open
    air in the far west, the bride was a red girl,
Her father and his friends sat near cross-legged
    and dumbly smoking, they had moccasins to
    their feet and large thick blankets hanging
    from their shoulders,
On a bank lounged the trapper, he was drest
    mostly in skins, his luxuriant beard and curls
    protected his neck, he held his bride by the
    hand,
She had long eyelashes, her head was bare, her
    coarse straight locks descended upon her
    voluptuous limbs and reach'd to her feet.

The runaway slave came to my house and stopt outside,
I heard his motions crackling the twigs of the woodpile, 190
Through the swung half-door of the kitchen I saw him limpsy and weak,
And went where he sat on a log and led him in and assured him,
And brought water and fill'd a tub for his sweated body and bruis'd feet,
And gave him a room that enter'd from my own, and gave him some coarse clean clothes,
And remember perfectly well his revolving eyes and his awkwardness,
And remember putting plasters on the galls of his neck and ankles;
He staid with me a week before he was recuperated and pass'd north,
I had him sit next me at table, my fire-lock lean'd in the corner.

11

Twenty-eight young men bathe by the shore,
Twenty-eight young men and all so friendly;
Twenty-eight years of womanly life and all so lonesome. 201

She owns the fine house by the rise of the bank,
She hides handsome and richly drest aft the blinds of the window.

Which of the young men does she like the best?
Ah the homeliest of them is beautiful to her.

Where are you off to, lady? for I see you,
You splash in the water there, yet stay stock still in your room.

Dancing and laughing along the beach came the twenty-ninth bather,
The rest did not see her, but she saw them and loved them.

The beards of the young men glisten'd with wet, it ran from their long hair, 210
Little streams pass'd all over their bodies.

An unseen hand also pass'd over their bodies,
It descended tremblingly from their temples and ribs.

The young men float on their backs, their white bellies bulge to the sun, they do not ask who seizes fast to them,
They do not know who puffs and declines with pendant and bending arch,
They do not think whom they souse with spray.

12

The butcher-boy puts off his killing-clothes, or sharpens his knife at the stall in the market,
I loiter enjoying his repartee and his shuffle and break-down.

Blacksmiths with grimed and hairy chests environ the anvil,
Each has his main-sledge, they are all out, there is a great heat in the fire. 220

From the cinder-strew'd threshold I follow their movements,
The lithe sheer of their waists plays even with their massive arms,
Overhand the hammers swing, overhand so slow, overhand so sure,
They do not hasten, each man hits in his place.

13

The negro holds firmly the reins of his four horses, the block swags underneath on its tied-over chain,
The negro that drives the long dray of the stone-yard, steady and tall he stands pois'd on one leg on the string-piece,
His blue shirt exposes his ample neck and breast and loosens over his hip-band,
His glance is calm and commanding, he tosses the slouch of his hat away from his forehead,
The sun falls on his crispy hair and mustache, falls on the black of his polish'd and perfect limbs.

I behold the picturesque giant and love him, and I do not stop there, 230
I go with the team also.

In me the caresser of life wherever moving, backward as well as forward sluing,
To niches aside and junior bending, not a person or object missing,
Absorbing all to myself and for this song.

Oxen that rattle the yoke and chain or halt in the leafy shade, what is that you express in your eyes?
It seems to me more than all the print I have read in my life.

My tread scares the wood-drake and wood-duck
  on my distant and day-long ramble,
They rise together, they slowly circle around.

I believe in those wing'd purposes,
And acknowledge red, yellow, white, playing
  within me,   240
And consider green and violet and the tufted
  crown intentional,
And do not call the tortoise unworthy because
  she is not something else,
And the jay in the woods never studied the
  gamut, yet trills pretty well to me,
And the look of the bay mare shames silliness
  out of me.

14

The wild gander leads his flock through the
  cool night,
Ya-honk he says, and sounds it down to me
  like an invitation,
The pert may suppose it meaningless, but I
  listening close,
Find its purpose and place up there toward the
  wintry sky.

The sharp-hoof'd moose of the north, the cat on
  the house-sill, the chickadee, the prairie-dog,
The litter of the grunting sow as they tug at
  her teats,   250
The brood of the turkey-hen and she with her
  half-spread wings,
I see in them and myself the same old law.

The press of my foot to the earth springs a hundred affections,
They scorn the best I can do to relate them.

I am enamour'd of growing out-doors,
Of men that live among cattle or taste of the
  ocean or woods,
Of the builders and steerers of ships and the
  wielders of axes and mauls, and the drivers
  of horses,
I can eat and sleep with them week in and
  week out.

What is commonest, cheapest, nearest, easiest,
  is Me,
Me going in for my chances, spending for vast
  returns,   260
Adorning myself to bestow myself on the first
  that will take me,

Not asking the sky to come down to my good
  will,
Scattering it freely forever.

15

The pure contralto sings in the organ loft,
The carpenter dresses his plank, the tongue of
  his foreplane whistles its wild ascending lisp,
The married and unmarried children ride home
  to their Thanksgiving dinner,
The pilot seizes the king-pin, he heaves down
  with a strong arm,
The mate stands braced in the whale-boat,
  lance and harpoon are ready,
The duck-shooter walks by silent and cautious
  stretches,
The deacons are ordain'd with cross'd hands at
  the altar,   270
The spinning-girl retreats and advances to the
  hum of the big wheel,
The farmer stops by the bars as he walks on a
  First-day loaf and looks at the oats and rye,
The lunatic is carried at last to the asylum a
  confirm'd case,
(He will never sleep any more as he did in the
  cot in his mother's bed-room;)
The jour printer with gray head and gaunt jaws
  works at his case,
He turns his quid of tobacco while his eyes
  blurr with the manuscript;
The malform'd limbs are tied to the surgeon's
  table,
What is removed drops horribly in a pail;
The quadroon girl is sold at the auction-stand,
  the drunkard nods by the bar-room stove,
The machinist rolls up his sleeves, the policeman travels his beat, the gate-keeper marks
  who pass,   280
The young fellow drives the express-wagon, (I
  love him, though I do not know him;)
The half-breed straps on his light boots to com-
  pete in the race,
The western turkey-shooting draws old and
  young, some lean on their rifles, some sit on
  logs,
Out from the crowd steps the marksman, takes
  his position, levels his piece;
The groups of newly-come immigrants cover
  the wharf or levee,
As the woolly-pates hoe in the sugar-field, the
  overseer views them from his saddle,
The bugle calls in the ball-room, the gentlemen
  run for their partners, the dancers bow to
  each other,

The youth lies awake in the cedar-roof'd garret and harks to the musical rain,
The Wolverine sets traps on the creek that helps fill the Huron,   289
The squaw wrapt in her yellow-hemm'd cloth is offering moccasins and bead-bags for sale,
The connoisseur peers along the exhibition-gallery with half-shut eyes bent sideways,
As the deck-hands make fast the steamboat the plank is thrown for the shore-going passengers,
The young sister holds out the skein while the elder sister winds it off in a ball, and stops now and then for the knots,
The one-year wife is recovering and happy having a week ago borne her first child,
The clean-hair'd Yankee girl works with her sewing-machine or in the factory or mill,
The paving-man leans on his two-handed rammer, the reporter's lead flies swiftly over the note-book, the sign-painter is lettering with blue and gold,
The canal boy trots on the tow-path, the book-keeper counts at his desk, the shoemaker waxes his thread,
The conductor beats time for the band and all the performers follow him,
The child is baptized, the convert is making his first professions,
The regatta is spread on the bay, the race is begun, (how the white sails sparkle!)   300
The drover watching his drove sings out to them that would stray,
The pedler sweats with his pack on his back, (the purchaser higgling about the odd cent;)
The bride unrumples her white dress, the minute-hand of the clock moves slowly,
The opium-eater reclines with rigid head and just-open'd lips,
The prostitute draggles her shawl, her bonnet bobs on her tipsy and pimpled neck,
The crowd laugh at her blackguard oaths, the men jeer and wink to each other,
(Miserable! I do not laugh at your oaths nor jeer you;)
The President holding a cabinet council is surrounded by the great Secretaries,
On the piazza walk three matrons stately and friendly with twined arms,
The crew of the fish-smack pack repeated layers of halibut in the hold,   310
The Missourian crosses the plains toting his wares and his cattle,
As the fare-collector goes through the train he gives notice by the jingling of loose change,

The floor-men are laying the floor, the tinners are tinning the roof, the masons are calling for mortar,
In single file each shouldering his hod pass onward the laborers;
Seasons pursuing each other the indescribable crowd is gather'd, it is the fourth of Seventh-month, (what salutes of cannon and small arms!)
Seasons pursuing each other the plougher ploughs, the mower mows, and the winter-grain falls in the ground;
Off on the lakes the pike-fisher watches and waits by the hole in the frozen surface,
The stumps stand thick round the clearing, the squatter strikes deep with his axe,
Flatboatmen make fast towards dusk near the cotton-wood or pecan-trees,
Coon-seekers go through the regions of the Red river or through those drain'd by the Tennessee, or through those of the Arkansas,   320
Torches shine in the dark that hangs on the Chattahooche or Altamahaw,
Patriarchs sit at supper with sons and grandsons and great-grandsons around them,
In walls of adobie, in canvas tents, rest hunters and trappers after their day's sport,
The city sleeps and the country sleeps,
The living sleep for their time, the dead sleep for their time,
The old husband sleeps by his wife and the young husband sleeps by his wife;
And these tend inward to me, and I tend outward to them,
And such as it is to be of these more or less I am,
And of these one and all I weave the song of myself.

16

I am of old and young, of the foolish as much as the wise,   330
Regardless of others, ever regardful of others,
Maternal as well as paternal, a child as well as a man,
Stuff'd with the stuff that is coarse and stuff'd with the stuff that is fine,
One of the Nation of many nations, the smallest the same and the largest the same,
A Southerner soon as a Northerner, a planter nonchalant and hospitable down by the Oconee I live,
A Yankee bound my own way ready for trade, my joints the limberest joints on earth and the sternest joints on earth,

A Kentuckian walking the vale of the Elkhorn
in my deer-skin leggings, a Louisianian or
Georgian,
A boatman over lakes or bays or along coasts,
a Hoosier, Badger, Buckeye;
At home on Kanadian snow-shoes or up in the
bush, or with fishermen off Newfoundland,
At home in the fleet of ice-boats, sailing with
the rest and tacking,   340
At home on the hills of Vermont or in the woods
of Maine, or the Texan ranch,
Comrade of Californians, comrade of free
North-Westerners, (loving their big proportions,)
Comrade of raftsmen and coalmen, comrade of
all who shake hands and welcome to drink
and meat,
A learner with the simplest, a teacher of the
thoughtfullest,
A novice beginning yet experient of myriads of
seasons,
Of every hue and caste am I, of every rank and
religion,
A farmer, mechanic, artist, gentleman, sailor,
quaker,
Prisoner, fancy-man, rowdy, lawyer, physician,
priest.

I resist any thing better than my own diversity,
Breathe the air but leave plenty after me,   350
And am not stuck up, and am in my place.

(The moth and the fish-eggs are in their place,
The bright suns I see and the dark suns I cannot see are in their place,
The palpable is in its place and the impalpable
is in its place.)

17

These are really the thoughts of all men in all
ages and lands, they are not original with
me,
If they are not yours as much as mine they are
nothing, or next to nothing,
If they are not the riddle and the untying of the
riddle they are nothing,
If they are not just as close as they are distant
they are nothing.

This is the grass that grows wherever the land
is and the water is,
This the common air that bathes the globe. 360

· · ·

24

Walt Whitman, a kosmos, of Manhattan the
son,
Turbulent, fleshy, sensual, eating, drinking and
breeding,
No sentimentalist, no stander above men and
women or apart from them,
No more modest than immodest.

Unscrew the locks from the doors!
Unscrew the doors themselves from their
jambs!

Whoever degrades another degrades me,
And whatever is done or said returns at last
to me.

Through me the afflatus surging and surging,
through me the current and index.

I speak the pass-word primeval, I give the sign
of democracy,   370
By God! I will accept nothing which all cannot
have their counterpart of on the same terms.

Through me many long dumb voices,
Voices of the interminable generations of pris-
oners and slaves,
Voices of the diseas'd and despairing and of
thieves and dwarfs,
Voices of cycles of preparation and accretion,
And of the threads that connect the stars, and
of wombs and of the father-stuff,

And of the rights of them the others are down
upon,
Of the deform'd, trivial, flat, foolish, despised,
Fog in the air, beetles rolling balls of dung.

Through me forbidden voices,   380
Voices of sexes and lusts, voices veil'd and I
remove the veil,
Voices indecent by me clarified and transfig-
ur'd.

I do not press my fingers across my mouth,
I keep as delicate around the bowels as around
the head and heart,
Copulation is no more rank to me than death is.

I believe in the flesh and the appetites,
Seeing, hearing, feeling, are miracles, and each
part and tag of me is a miracle.
Divine am I inside and out, and I make holy
whatever I touch or am touch'd from,

The scent of these arm-pits aroma finer than
   prayer,
This head more than churches, bibles, and all
   the creeds.   390

If I worship one thing more than another it
   shall be the spread of my own body, or any
   part of it,
Translucent mould of me it shall be you!
Shaded ledges and rests it shall be you!
Firm masculine colter it shall be you!
Whatever goes to the tilth of me it shall be
   you!
You my rich blood! your milky stream pale
   strippings of my life!
Breast that presses against other breasts it shall
   be you!
My brain it shall be your occult convolutions!
Root of wash'd sweet-flag! timorous pond-snipe!
   nest of guarded duplicate eggs! it shall be
   you!
Mix'd tussled hay of head, beard, brawn, it
   shall be you!   400
Trickling sap of maple, fibre of manly wheat, it
   shall be you!
Sun so generous it shall be you!
Vapors lighting and shading my face it shall be
   you!
You sweaty brooks and dews it shall be you!
Winds whose soft-tickling genitals rub against
   me it shall be you!
Broad muscular fields, branches of live oak,
   loving lounger in my winding paths, it shall
   be you!
Hands I have taken, face I have kiss'd, mortal
   I have ever touch'd, it shall be you.

I dote on myself, there is that lot of me and
   all so luscious,
Each moment and whatever happens thrills me
   with joy,
I cannot tell how my ankles bend, nor whence
   the cause of my faintest wish,   410
Nor the cause of the friendship I emit, nor the
   cause of the friendship I take again.

That I walk up my stoop, I pause to consider
   if it really be,
A morning-glory at my window satisfies me
   more than the metaphysics of books.

To behold the day-break!
The little light fades the immense and diapha-
   nous shadows,
The air tastes good to my palate.

Hefts of the moving world at innocent gambols
   silently rising, freshly exuding,
Scooting obliquely high and low.

Something I cannot see puts upward libidinous
   prongs,
Seas of bright juice suffuse heaven.   420

The earth by the sky staid with, the daily close
   of their junction,
The heav'd challenge from the east that moment over my head,
The mocking taunt, See then whether you shall
   be master!

. . .

31

I believe a leaf of grass is no less than the
   journey-work of the stars,
And the pismire is equally perfect, and a grain
   of sand, and the egg of the wren,
And the tree-toad is a chef-d'œuvre for the
   highest,
And the running blackberry would adorn the
   parlors of heaven,
And the narrowest hinge in my hand puts to
   scorn all machinery,
And the cow crunching with depress'd head
   surpasses any statue,
And a mouse is miracle enough to stagger sex-
   tillions of infidels.   430

I find I incorporate gneiss, coal, long-threaded
   moss, fruits, grains, esculent roots,
And am stucco'd with quadrupeds and birds all
   over,
And have distanced what is behind me for good
   reasons,
But call any thing back again when I desire it.

In vain the speeding or shyness,
In vain the plutonic rocks send their old heat
   against my approach,
In vain the mastodon retreats beneath its own
   powder'd bones,
In vain objects stand leagues off and assume
   manifold shapes,
In vain the ocean settling in hollows and the
   great monsters lying low,
In vain the buzzard houses herself with the
   sky,   440
In vain the snake slides through the creepers
   and logs,

In vain the elk takes to the inner passes of the woods,
In vain the razor-bill'd auk sails far north to Labrador,
I follow quickly, I ascend to the nest in the fissure of the cliff.

32

I think I could turn and live with animals, they're so placid and self-contain'd,
I stand and look at them long and long.

They do not sweat and whine about their condition,
They do not lie awake in the dark and weep for their sins,
They do not make me sick discussing their duty to God,
Not one is dissatisfied, not one is demented with the mania of owning things,   450
Not one kneels to another, nor to his kind that lived thousands of years ago,
Not one is respectable or unhappy over the whole earth.

So they show their relations to me and I accept them,
They bring me tokens of myself, they evince them plainly in their possession.

I wonder where they get those tokens,
Did I pass that way huge times ago and negligently drop them?

Myself moving forward then and now and forever,
Gathering and showing more always and with velocity,
Infinite and omnigenous, and the like of these among them,
Not too exclusive toward the reachers of my remembrancers,   460
Picking out here one that I love, and now go with him on brotherly terms.

A gigantic beauty of a stallion, fresh and responsive to my caresses,
Head high in the forehead, wide between the ears,
Limbs glossy and supple, tail dusting the ground,
Eyes full of sparkling wickedness, ears finely cut, flexibly moving.

His nostrils dilate as my heels embrace him,
His well-built limbs tremble with pleasure as we race around and return.
I but use you a minute, then I resign you, stallion,
Why do I need your paces when I myself outgallop them?   469
Even as I stand or sit passing faster than you.

33

Space and Time! now I see it is true, what I guess'd at,
What I guess'd when I loaf'd on the grass,
What I guess'd while I lay alone in my bed,
And again as I walk'd the beach under the paling stars of the morning.

My ties and ballasts leave me, my elbows rest in sea-gaps,
I skirt sierras, my palms cover continents,
I am afoot with my vision.

. . .

I ascend to the foretruck,
I take my place late at night in the crow's-nest,
We sail the arctic sea, it is plenty light enough,
Through the clear atmosphere I stretch around on the wonderful beauty,   481
The enormous masses of ice pass me and I pass them, the scenery is plain in all directions,
The white-topt mountains show in the distance, I fling out my fancies toward them,
We are approaching some great battle-field in which we are soon to be engaged,
We pass the colossal outposts of the encampment, we pass with still feet and caution,
Or we are entering by the suburbs some vast and ruin'd city,
The blocks and fallen architecture more than all the living cities of the globe.

I am a free companion, I bivouac by invading watchfires,
I turn the bridegroom out of bed and stay with the bride myself,
I tighten her all night to my thighs and lips.

My voice is the wife's voice, the screech by the rail of the stairs,   491
They fetch my man's body up dripping and drown'd.

I understand the large hearts of heroes,
The courage of present times and all times,

How the skipper saw the crowded and rudder-
less wreck of the steam-ship, and Death chasing it up and down the storm,
How he knuckled tight and gave not back an
inch, and was faithful of days and faithful
of nights,
And chalk'd in large letters on a board, *Be of
good cheer, we will not desert you;*
How he follow'd with them and tack'd with
them three days and would not give it up,
How he saved the drifting company at last,
How the lank loose-gown'd women look'd when
boated from the side of their prepared
graves,   500
How the silent old-faced infants and the lifted
sick, and the sharp-lipp'd unshaven men;
All this I swallow, it tastes good, I like it well,
it becomes mine,
I am the man, I suffer'd, I was there.

The disdain and calmness of martyrs,
The mother of old, condemn'd for a witch,
burnt with dry wood, her children gazing on,
The hounded slave that flags in the race, leans
by the fence, blowing, cover'd with sweat.
The twinges that sting like needles his legs and
neck, the murderous buckshot and the bullets
All these I feel or am.

I am the hounded slave, I wince at the bite of
the dogs,
Hell and despair are upon me, crack and again
crack the marksmen,   510
I clutch the rails of the fence, my gore drips,
thinn'd with the ooze of my skin,
I fall on the weeds and stones,
The riders spur their unwilling horses, haul
close,
Taunt my dizzy ears and beat me violently over
the head with whip-stocks.

Agonies are one of my changes of garments,
I do not ask the wounded person how he feels,
I myself become the wounded person,
My hurts turn livid upon me as I lean on a cane
and observe.

I am the mash'd fireman with breast-bone
broken,
Tumbling walls buried me in their debris,
Heat and smoke I inspired, I heard the yelling
shouts of my comrades,   520
I heard the distant click of their picks and
shovels,

They have clear'd the beams away, they tenderly lift me forth.

I lie in the night air in my red shirt, the pervading hush is for my sake,
Painless after all I lie exhausted but not so unhappy,
White and beautiful are the faces around me,
the heads are bared of their fire-caps,
The kneeling crowd fades with the light of the
torches.

Distant and dead resuscitate,
They show as the dial or move as the hands of
me, I am the clock myself.

I am an old artillerist, I tell of my fort's bom-
bardment,
I am there again.   530

Again the long roll of the drummers,
Again the attacking cannon, mortars,
Again to my listening ears the cannon respon-
sive.

I take part, I see and hear the whole,
The cries, curses, roar, the plaudits for well-
aim'd shots,
The ambulanza slowly passing trailing its red
drip,
Workmen searching after damages, making indispensable repairs,
The fall of grenades through the rent roof, the
fan-shaped explosion,
The whizz of limbs, heads, stone, wood, iron,
high in the air.

Again gurgles the mouth of my dying general,
he furiously waves with his hand,   540
He gasps through the clot *Mind not me—mind
—the entrenchments.*

. . .

40

Flaunt of the sunshine I need not your bask—
lie over!
You light surfaces only, I force surfaces and
depths also.

Earth! you seem to look for something at my
hands,
Say, old top-knot, what do you want?

Man or woman, I might tell how I like you,
but cannot,
And might tell what it is in me and what it is
in you, but cannot,
And might tell that pining I have, that pulse of
my nights and days.

Behold, I do not give lectures or a little charity,
When I give I give myself.   550

You there, impotent, loose in the knees,
Open your scarf'd chops till I blow grit within
you,
Spread your palms and lift the flaps of your
pockets,
I am not to be denied, I compel, I have stores
plenty and to spare,
And any thing I have I bestow.

I do not ask who you are, that is not important
to me,
You can do nothing and be nothing but what I
will infold you.

To cotton-field drudge or cleaner of privies I
lean,
On his right cheek I put the family kiss,   559
And in my soul I swear I never will deny him.

On women fit for conception I start bigger and
nimbler babes,
(This day I am jetting the stuff of far more arrogant republics.)

To any one dying, thither I speed and twist the
knob of the door,
Turn the bed-clothes toward the foot of the
bed,
Let the physician and the priest go home.

I seize the descending man and raise him with
resistless will,
O despairer, here is my neck,
By God, you shall not go down! hang your
whole weight upon me.

I dilate you with tremendous breath, I buoy
you up,
Every room of the house do I fill with an arm'd
force,   570
Lovers of me, bafflers of graves.

Sleep—I and they keep guard all night,
Not doubt, not decease shall dare to lay finger
upon you,

I have embraced you, and henceforth possess
you to myself,
And when you rise in the morning you will find
what I tell you is so.

. . .

46

I know I have the best of time and space, and
was never measured and never will be measured.

I tramp a perpetual journey, (come listen all!)
My signs are a rain-proof coat, good shoes, and
a staff cut from the woods,
No friend of mine takes his ease in my chair,
I have no chair, no church, no philosophy, 580
I lead no man to a dinner-table, library, ex-
change,
But each man and each woman of you I lead
upon a knoll,

My left hand hooking you round the waist,
My right hand pointing to landscapes of continents and the public road.

Not I, not any one else can travel that road for
you,
You must travel it for yourself.

It is not far, it is within reach,
Perhaps you have been on it since you were
born and did not know,
Perhaps it is everywhere on water and on land.

Shoulder your duds dear son, and I will mine,
and let us hasten forth,   590
Wonderful cities and free nations we shall fetch
as we go.

If you tire, give me both burdens, and rest the
chuff of your hand on my hip,
And in due time you shall repay the same service to me,
For after we start we never lie by again.

This day before dawn I ascended a hill and
look'd at the crowded heaven,
And I said to my spirit *When we become the*
enfolders of those orbs, and the pleasure and
knowledge of every thing in them, shall we
be fill'd and satisfied then?
And my spirit said *No, we but level that lift to*
pass and continue beyond.

You are also asking me questions and I hear
you,
I answer that I cannot answer, you must find
out for yourself.

Sit a while dear son,   600
Here are biscuits to eat and here is milk to
drink,
But as soon as you sleep and renew yourself in
sweet clothes, I kiss you with a good-by kiss
and open the gate for your egress hence.

Long enough have you dream'd contemptible
dreams,
Now I wash the gum from your eyes,
You must habit yourself to the dazzle of the
light and of every moment of your life.

Long have you timidly waded holding a plank
by the shore,
Now I will you to be a bold swimmer,
To jump off in the midst of the sea, rise again,
nod to me, shout, and laughingly dash with
your hair.

47

I am the teacher of athletes,
He that by me spreads a wider breast than my
own proves the width of my own,   610
He most honors my style who learns under it to
destroy the teacher.

The boy I love, the same becomes a man not
through derived power, but in his own right,
Wicked rather than virtuous out of conformity
or fear,
Fond of his sweetheart, relishing well his steak,
Unrequited love or a slight cutting him worse
than sharp steel cuts,
First-rate to ride, to fight, to hit the bull's eye,
to sail a skiff, to sing a song or play on the
banjo,
Preferring scars and the beard and faces pitted
with small-pox over all latherers,
And those well-tann'd to those that keep out of
the sun.

I teach straying from me, yet who can stray
from me?
I follow you whoever you are from the present
hour,   620
My words itch at your ears till you understand
them.
I do not say these things for a dollar or to fill
up the time while I wait for a boat,

(It is you talking just as much as myself, I act
as the tongue of you,
Tied in your mouth, in mind it begins to be
loosen'd.)

I swear I will never again mention love or death
inside a house,
And I swear I will never translate myself at all,
only to him or her who privately stays with
me in the open air.
If you would understand me go to the heights
or water-shore,
The nearest gnat is an explanation, and a drop
or motion of waves a key,
The maul, the oar, the hand-saw, second my
words.

No shutter'd room or school can commune with
me,   630
But roughs and little children better than they.

The young mechanic is closest to me, he knows
me well,
The woodman that takes his axe and jug with
him shall take me with him all day,
The farm-boy ploughing in the field feels good
at the sound of my voice,
In vessels that sail my words sail, I go with
fishermen and seamen and love them.

The soldier camp'd or upon the march is mine,
On the night ere the pending battle many seek
me, and I do not fail them,
On that solemn night (it may be their last)
those that know me seek me.

My face rubs to the hunter's face when he lies
down alone in his blanket,
The driver thinking of me does not mind the
jolt of his wagon,   640
The young mother and old mother comprehend
me,
The girl and the wife rest the needle a moment
and forget where they are,
They and all would resume what I have told
them.

48

I have said that the soul is not more than the
body,
And I have said that the body is not more than
the soul,
And nothing, not God, is greater to one than
one's self is,

And whoever walks a furlong without sympathy
  walks to his own funeral drest in his shroud,
And I or you pocketless of a dime may purchase
  the pick of the earth,
And to glance with an eye or show a bean in its
  pod confounds the learning of all times,
And there is no trade or employment but the
  young man following it may become a hero,
And there is no object so soft but it makes a
  hub for the wheel'd universe,   651
And I say to any man or woman, Let your soul
  stand cool and composed before a million
  universes.

And I say to mankind, Be not curious about
  God,
For I who am curious about each am not curi-
  ous about God,
(No array of terms can say how much I am at
  peace about God and about death.)

I hear and behold God in every object, yet
  understand God not in the least,
Nor do I understand who there can be more
  wonderful than myself.

Why should I wish to see God better than this
  day?
I see something of God each hour of the
  twenty-four, and each moment then,
In the faces of men and women I see God, and
  in my own face in the glass,   660
I find letters from God dropt in the street, and
  every one is sign'd by God's name,
And I leave them where they are, for I know
  that wheresoe'er I go,
Others will punctually come for ever and ever.

49

And as to you Death, and you bitter hug of
  mortality, it is idle to try to alarm me.

To his work without flinching the accoucheur
  comes,
I see the elder-hand pressing receiving supporting,
I recline by the sills of the exquisite flexible
  doors,
And mark the outlet, and mark the relief and
  escape.

And as to you Corpse I think you are good
  manure, but that does not offend me,

I smell the white roses sweet-scented and growing,   670
I reach to the leafy lips, I reach to the polish'd
  breasts of melons.

And as to you Life I reckon you are the leavings
  of many deaths,
(No doubt I have died myself ten thousand
  times before.)

I hear you whispering there O stars of heaven,
O suns—O grass of graves—O perpetual transfers and promotions,
If you do not say any thing how can I say any
  thing?

Of the turbid pool that lies in the autumn
  forest,
Of the moon that descends the steeps of the
  soughing twilight,
Toss, sparkles of day and dusk—toss on the
  black stems that decay in the muck,   679
Toss to the moaning gibberish of the dry limbs.

I ascend from the moon, I ascend from the
  night,
I perceive that the ghastly glimmer is noonday
  sunbeams reflected,
And debouch to the steady and central from
  the offspring great or small.

50

There is that in me—I do not know what it is
  —but I know it is in me.

Wrench'd and sweaty—calm and cool then my
  body becomes,
I sleep—I sleep long.

I do not know it—it is without name—it is a
  word unsaid,
It is not in any dictionary, utterance, symbol.

Something it swings on more than the earth I
  swing on,
To it the creation is the friend whose embracing
  awakes me.   690

Perhaps I might tell more. Outlines! I plead for
  my brothers and sisters.

Do you see O my brothers and sisters?
It is not chaos or death—it is form, union, plan
  —it is eternal life—it is Happiness.

51

The past and present wilt—I have fill'd them,
  emptied them,
And proceed to fill my next fold of the future.

Listener up there! what have you to confide to
  me?
Look in my face while I snuff the sidle of evening,
(Talk honestly, no one else hears you, and I
  stay only a minute longer.)

Do I contradict myself?
Very well then I contradict myself,   700
(I am large, I contain multitudes.)

I concentrate toward them that are nigh, I wait
  on the door-slab.

Who has done his day's work? who will soonest
  be through with his supper?
Who wishes to walk with me?

Will you speak before I am gone? will you
  prove already too late?

52

The spotted hawk swoops by and accuses me,
  he complains of my gab and my loitering.

I too am not a bit tamed, I too am untranslatable,
I sound my barbaric yawp over the roofs of the
  world.

The last scud of day holds back for me,
It flings my likeness after the rest and true as
  any on the shadow'd wilds,   710
It coaxes me to the vapor and the dusk.

I depart as air, I shake my white locks at the
  runaway sun,
I effuse my flesh in eddies, and drift it in lacy
  jags.

I bequeath myself to the dirt to grow from the
  grass I love,
If you want me again look for me under your
  boot-soles.

You will hardly know who I am or what I
  mean,
But I shall be good health to you nevertheless,
And filter and fibre your blood.

Failing to fetch me at first keep encouraged,
Missing me one place search another,   720
I stop somewhere waiting for you.
1855   1881

» »   « «

CROSSING BROOKLYN FERRY

1

Flood-tide below me! I see you face to face!
Clouds of the west—sun there half an hour
  high—I see you also face to face.

Crowds of men and women attired in the usual
  costumes, how curious you are to me!
On the ferry-boats the hundreds and hundreds
  that cross, returning home, are more curious
  to me than you suppose,
And you that shall cross from shore to shore
  years hence are more to me, and more in my
  meditations, than you might suppose.

2

The impalpable sustenance of me from all
  things at all hours of the day,

The simple, compact, well-join'd scheme, myself disintegrated, every one disintegrated
  yet part of the scheme,
The similitudes of the past and those of the
  future,
The glories strung like beads on my smallest
  sights and hearings, on the walk in the street
  and the passage over the river,
The current rushing so swiftly and swimming
  with me far away,   10
The others that are to follow me, the ties between me and them,
The certainty of others, the life, love, sight,
  hearing of others.

Others will enter the gates of the ferry and
  cross from shore to shore,
Others will watch the run of the flood-tide,
Others will see the shipping of Manhattan
  north and west, and the heights of Brooklyn
  to the south and east,

Others will see the islands large and small;

Fifty years hence, others will see them as they cross, the sun half an hour high,

A hundred years hence, or ever so many hundred years hence, others will see them,

Will enjoy the sunset, the pouring-in of the flood-tide, the falling-back to the sea of the ebb-tide.

3

It avails not, time nor place—distance avails not,   20

I am with you, you men and women of a generation, or ever so many generations hence,

Just as you feel when you look on the river and sky, so I felt,

Just as any of you is one of a living crowd, I was one of a crowd,

Just as you are refresh'd by the gladness of the river and the bright flow, I was refresh'd,

Just as you stand and lean on the rail, yet hurry with the swift current, I stood yet was hurried,

Just as you look on the numberless masts of ships and the thick-stemm'd pipes of steamboats, I look'd.

I too many and many a time cross'd the river of old,

Watched the Twelfth-month sea-gulls, saw them high in the air floating with motionless wings, oscillating their bodies,

Saw how the glistening yellow lit up parts of their bodies and left the rest in strong shadow,

Saw the slow-wheeling circles and the gradual edging toward the south,   30

Saw the reflection of the summer sky in the water,

Had my eyes dazzled by the shimmering track of beams,

Look'd at the fine centrifugal spokes of light round the shape of my head in the sunlit water,

Look'd on the haze on the hills southward and south-westward,

Look'd on the vapor as it flew in fleeces tinged with violet,

Look'd toward the lower bay to notice the vessels arriving,

Saw their approach, saw aboard those that were near me,

Saw the white sails of schooners and sloops, saw the ships at anchor,

The sailors at work in the rigging or out astride the spars,

The round masts, the swinging motion of the hulls, the slender serpentine pennants,   40

The large and small steamers in motion, the pilots in their pilot-houses,

The white wake left by the passage, the quick tremulous whirl of the wheels,

The flags of all nations, the falling of them at sunset,

The scallop-edged waves in the twilight, the ladled cups, the frolicsome crests and glistening,

The stretch afar growing dimmer and dimmer, the gray walls of the granite storehouses by the docks,

On the river the shadowy group, the big steamtug closely flank'd on each side by the barges, the hay-boat, the belated lighter,

On the neighboring shore the fires from the foundry chimneys burning high and glaringly into the night,

Casting their flicker of black contrasted with wild red and yellow light over the tops of houses, and down into the clefts of streets.

4

These and all else were to me the same as they are to you,

I loved well those cities, loved well the stately and rapid river,   50

The men and women I saw were all near to me,

Others the same—others who looked back on me because I look'd forward to them,

(The time will come, though I stop here to-day and to-night.)

5

What is it then between us?

What is the count of the scores or hundreds of years between us?

Whatever it is, it avails not—distance avails not, and place avails not,

I too lived, Brooklyn of ample hills was mine,

I too walk'd the streets of Manhattan island, and bathed in the waters around it,

I too felt the curious abrupt questionings stir within me,

In the day among crowds of people sometimes they came upon me,   60

In my walks home late at night or as I lay in my bed they came upon me,

I too had been struck from the float forever
held in solution,
I too had receiv'd identity by my body,
That I was I knew was of my body, and what I
should be I knew I should be of my body.

6

It is not upon you alone the dark patches fall,
The dark threw its patches down upon me also,
The best I had done seem'd to me blank and
suspicious,
My great thoughts as I supposed them, were
they not in reality meagre?
Nor is it you alone who know what it is to be
evil,
I am he who knew what it was to be evil,   70
I too knitted the old knot of contrariety,
Blabb'd, blush'd, resented, lied, stole, grudg'd,
Had guile, anger, lust, hot wishes I dared not
speak,
Was wayward, vain, greedy, shallow, sly, cow-
ardly, malignant,
The wolf, the snake, the hog, not wanting in
me,
The cheating look, the frivolous word, the
adulterous wish, not wanting,
Refusals, hates, postponements, meanness, lazi-
ness, none of these wanting,
Was one with the rest, the days and haps of
the rest,
Was call'd my nighest name by clear loud
voices of young men as they saw me ap-
proaching or passing,
Felt their arms on my neck as I stood, or the
negligent leaning of their flesh against me as
I sat,   80
Saw many I loved in the street or ferry-boat or
public assembly, yet never told them a word,
Lived the same life with the rest, the same old
laughing, gnawing, sleeping,
Play'd the part that still looks back on the
actor or actress,
The same old role, the role that is what we
make it, as great as we like,
Or as small as we like, or both great and small.

7

Closer yet I approach you,
What thought you have of me now, I had as
much of you—I laid in my stores in advance,
I consider'd long and seriously of you before
you were born.
Who was to know what should come home to
me?

Who knows but I am enjoying this?   90
Who knows, for all the distance, but I am as
good as looking at you now, for all you cannot see me?

8

Ah, what can ever be more stately and admirable to me than mast-hemm'd Manhattan?
River and sunset and scallop-edg'd waves of
flood-tide?
The sea-gulls oscillating their bodies, the hay-
boat in the twilight, and the belated lighter?

What gods can exceed these that clasp me by
the hand, and with voices I love call me
promptly and loudly by my nighest name
as I approach?

What is more subtle than this which ties me to
the woman or man that looks in my face?
Which fuses me into you now, and pours my
meaning into you?

We understand then do we not?
What I promis'd without mentioning it, have
you not accepted?
What the study could not teach—what the
preaching could not accomplish is accomplish'd, is it not?   100

9

Flow on, river! flow with the flood-tide, and
ebb with the ebb-tide!
Frolic on, crested and scallop-edg'd waves!
Gorgeous clouds of the sunset! drench with
your splendor me, or the men and women
generations after me!
Cross from shore to shore, countless crowds of
passengers!
Stand up, tall masts of Mannahatta! stand up,
beautiful hills of Brooklyn!
Throb, baffled and curious brain! throw out
questions and answers!
Suspend here and everywhere, eternal float of
solution!
Gaze, loving and thirsting eyes, in the house or
street or public assembly!
Sound out, voices of young men! loudly and
musically call me by my nighest name!
Live, old life! play the part that looks back on
the actor or actress!   110
Play the old role, the role that is great or small
according as one makes it!
Consider, you who peruse me, whether I may
not in unknown ways be looking upon you;

Be firm, rail over the river, to support those who
     lean idly, yet haste with the hasting current;
Fly on, sea-birds! fly sideways, or wheel in large
     circles high in the air;
Receive the summer sky, you water, and faith-
     fully hold it till all downcast eyes have time
     to take it from you!
Diverge, fine spokes of light, from the shape
     of my head, or any one's head, in the sunlit
     water!
Come on, ships from the lower bay! pass up
     or down, white-sail'd schooners, sloops,
     lighters!
Flaunt away, flags of all nations! be duly
     lower'd at sunset!
Burn high your fires, foundry chimneys! cast
     black shadows at nightfall! cast red and yel-
     low light over the tops of the houses!
Appearances, now or henceforth, indicate what
     you are,   120
You necessary film, continue to envelop the
     soul,
About my body for me, and your body for you,
     be hung our divinest aromas,
Thrive, cities—bring your freight, bring your
     shows, ample and sufficient rivers,
Expand, being than which none else is perhaps
     more spiritual,
Keep your places, objects than which none
     else is more lasting.

You have waited, you always wait, you dumb,
     beautiful ministers,
We receive you with free sense at last, and are
     insatiate henceforward,
Not you any more shall be able to foil us, or
     withhold yourselves from us,
We use you,—and do not cast you aside—we
     plant you permanently within us,
We fathom you not—we love you—there is
     perfection in you also,   130
You furnish your parts toward eternity,
Great or small, you furnish your parts toward
     the soul.   1856

OUT OF THE CRADLE ENDLESSLY ROCKING [2]

Out of the cradle endlessly rocking,
Out of the mocking-bird's throat, the musical
     shuttle,
Out of the Ninth-month midnight,

[2] First printed under another title in the New York *Saturday Press*,
December 24, 1859. The present version is that of 1881.

Over the sterile sands and the fields beyond,
     where the child leaving his bed wander'd
     alone, bareheaded, barefoot,
Down from the shower'd halo,
Up from the mystic play of shadows twining
     and twisting as if they were alive,
Out from the patches of briers and black-
     berries,
From the memories of the bird that chanted to
     me,
From your memories sad brother, from the fit-
     ful risings and fallings I heard,
From under that yellow half-moon late-risen
     and swollen as if with tears,   10
From those beginning notes of yearning and
     love there in the mist,
From the thousand responses of my heart never
     to cease,
From the myriad thence-arous'd words,
From the word stronger and more delicious
     than any,
From such as now they start the scene re-
     visiting,
As a flock, twittering, rising, or overhead pass-
     ing,
Borne hither, ere all eludes me, hurriedly,
A man, yet by these tears a little boy again,
Throwing myself on the sand, confronting the
     waves,
I, chanter of pains and joys, uniter of here and
     hereafter,   20
Taking all hints to use them, but swiftly leap-
     ing beyond them,
A reminiscence sing.

Once Paumanok,
When the lilac-scent was in the air and Fifth-
     month grass was growing,
Up this seashore in some briers,
Two feather'd guests from Alabama, two to-
     gether,
And their nest, and four light-green eggs
     spotted with brown,
And everyday the he-bird to and fro near at
     hand,
And every day the she-bird crouch'd on her
     nest, silent, with bright eyes,
And every day I, a curious boy, never too close,
     never disturbing them,   30
Cautiously peering, absorbing, translating.

Shine! shine! shine!
Pour down your warmth, great sun!
While we bask, we two together.

Two together!
Winds blow south, or winds blow north,
Day come white, or night come black,
Home, or rivers and mountains from home,
Singing all time, minding no time,
While we two keep together.　　　40

Till of a sudden,
May-be kill'd, unknown to her mate,
One forenoon that she-bird crouch'd not on
　　the nest,
Nor return'd that afternoon, nor the next,
Nor ever appear'd again.

And thenceforward all summer in the sound
　　of the sea,
And at night under the full of the moon in
　　calmer weather,
Over the hoarse surging of the sea,
Or flitting from brier to brier by day,
I saw, I heard at intervals the remaining one,
　　the he-bird,　　　50
The solitary guest from Alabama.

Blow! blow! blow!
Blow up sea-winds along Paumanok's shore;
I wait and I wait till you blow my mate to me.

Yes, when the stars glisten'd,
All night long on the prong of a moss-scallop'd
　　stake,
Down almost amid the slapping waves,
Sat the lone singer wonderful causing tears.

He call'd on his mate,
He pour'd forth the meanings which I of all
　　men know.　　　60

Yes my brother I know,
The rest might not, but I have treasur'd every
　　note,
For more than once dimly down to the beach
　　gliding,
Silent, avoiding the moonbeams, blending my-
　　self with the shadows,
Recalling now the obscure shapes, the echoes,
　　the sounds and sights after their sorts,
The white arms out in the breakers tirelessly
　　tossing,
I, with bare feet, a child, the wind wafting my
　　hair,
Listen'd long and long.

Listen'd to keep, to sing, now translating the
　　notes,
Following you my brother.　　　70

Soothe! soothe! soothe!
Close on its wave soothes the wave behind,
And again another behind embracing and lap-
　　ping, every one close,
But my love soothes not me, not me.

Low hangs the moon, it rose late,
It is lagging—O I think it is heavy with love,
　　with love.

O madly the sea pushes upon the land,
With love, with love.

O night! do I not see my love fluttering out
　　among the breakers?
What is that little black thing I see there in the
　　white?　　　80

Loud! loud! loud!
Loud I call to you, my love!
High and clear I shoot my voice over the
　　waves,
Surely you must know who is here, is here,
You must know who I am, my love.

Low-hanging moon!
What is that dusky spot in your brown yellow?
O it is the shape, the shape of my mate!
O moon do not keep her from me any longer.

Land! land! O land!　　　90
Whichever way I turn, O I think you could give
　　me my mate back again if you only would,
For I am almost sure I see her dimly which-
　　ever way I look.

O rising stars!
Perhaps the one I want so much will rise, will
　　rise with one of you.

O throat! O trembling throat!
Sound clearer through the atmosphere!
Pierce the woods, the earth,
Somewhere listening to catch you must be the
　　one I want.

Shake out carols!
Solitary here, the night's carols!　　　100
Carols of lonesome love! death's carols!
Carols under that lagging, yellow, waning
　　moon!

*O under that moon where she droops almost
    down into the sea!*
O reckless despairing carols.

But soft! sink low!
Soft! let me just murmur,
*And do you wait a moment you husky-nois'd
    sea,*
*For somewhere I believe I heard my mate re-
    sponding to me,*
So faint, I must be still, be still to listen,
*But not altogether still, for then she might not
    come immediately to me.*   110

Hither my love!
Here I am! here!
*With this just-sustain'd note I announce my-
    self to you,*
This gentle call is for you my love, for you.

Do not be decoy'd elsewhere,
*That is the whistle of the wind, it is not my
    voice,*
That is the fluttering, the fluttering of the spray,
Those are the shadows of leaves.

O darkness! O in vain!
O I am very sick and sorrowful.   120

*O brown halo in the sky near the moon, droop-
    ing upon the sea!*
O troubled reflection in the sea!
O throat! O throbbing heart!
And I singing uselessly, uselessly all the night.

O past! O happy life! O songs of joy!
In the air, in the woods, over fields,
Loved! loved! loved! loved! loved!
But my mate no more, no more with me!
We two together no more.

The aria sinking,   130
All else continuing, the stars shining,
The winds blowing, the notes of the bird con-
    tinuous echoing,
With angry moans the fierce old mother in-
    cessantly moaning,
On the sands of Paumanok's shore gray and
    rustling,
The yellow half-moon enlarged, sagging down,
    drooping, the face of the sea almost touch-
    ing,
The boy ecstatic, with his bare feet the waves,
    with his hair the atmosphere dallying,

The love in the heart long pent, now loose, now
    at last tumultuously bursting,
The aria's meaning, the ears, the soul, swiftly
    depositing,
The strange tears down the cheeks coursing,
The colloquy there, the trio, each uttering, 140
The undertone, the savage old mother inces-
    santly crying,
To the boy's soul's questions sullenly timing,
    some drown'd secret hissing,
To the outsetting bard.
Demon or bird! (said the boy's soul,)
Is it indeed toward your mate you sing? or is it
    really to me?
For I, that was a child, my tongue's use sleep-
    ing, now I have heard you,
Now in a moment I know what I am for, I
    awake,
And already a thousand singers, a thousand
    songs, clearer, louder and more sorrowful
    than yours,
A thousand warbling echoes have started to
    life within me, never to die.

O you singer solitary, singing by yourself,
    projecting me,   150
O solitary me listening, never more shall I
    cease perpetuating you,
Never more shall I escape, never more the
    reverberations,
Never more the cries of unsatisfied love be
    absent from me,
Never again leave me to be the peaceful child
    I was before what there in the night,
By the sea under the yellow and sagging moon,
The messenger there arous'd, the fire, the sweet
    hell within,
The unknown want, the destiny of me.

O give me the clew! (it lurks in the night here
    somewhere,)
O if I am to have so much, let me have more!

A word then, (for I will conquer it,)   160
The word final, superior to all,
Subtle, sent up—what is it?—I listen;
Are you whispering it, and have been all the
    time, you sea-waves?
Is that it from your liquid rims and wet sands?

Whereto answering, the sea,
Delaying not, hurrying not,
Whisper'd me through the night, and very
    plainly before daybreak,
Lisp'd to me the low and delicious word death,

And again death, death, death, death,
Hissing melodious, neither like the bird nor
    like my arous'd child's heart,   170
But edging near as privately for me rustling at
    my feet,
Creeping thence steadily up to my ears and
    laving me softly all over,
Death, death, death, death, death.

Which I do not forget,
But fuse the song of my dusky demon and
    brother,
That he sang to me in the moonlight on
    Paumanok's gray beach,
With the thousand responsive songs at random,
My own songs awaked from that hour,
And with them the key, the word up from the
    waves,
The word of the sweetest song and all songs,
That strong and delicious word which, creeping
    to my feet,   181
(Or like some old crone rocking the cradle,
    swathed in sweet garments, bending aside,)
The sea whisper'd me.   1859

BY THE BIVOUAC'S FITFUL FLAME

By the bivouac's fitful flame,
A procession winding around me, solemn and
    sweet and slow—but first I note,
The tents of the sleeping army, the fields' and
    the woods' dim outline,
The darkness lit by spots of kindled fire, the
    silence,
Like a phantom far or near an occasional figure
    moving,
The shrubs and trees, (as I lift my eyes they
    seem to be stealthily watching me,)
While wind in procession thoughts, O tender
    and wondrous thoughts,
Of life and death, of home and the past and
    loved, and of those that are far away;
A solemn and slow procession there as I sit on
    the ground,
By the bivouac's fitful flame.   10
    1865

VIGIL STRANGE I KEPT ON THE
FIELD ONE NIGHT

Vigil strange I kept on the field one night;
When you my son and my comrade dropt at
    my side that day,
One look I but gave which your dear eyes re-
    turn'd with a look I shall never forget,

One touch of your hand to mine O boy, reach'd
    up as you lay on the ground,
Then onward I sped in the battle, the even-
    contested battle,
Till late in the night reliev'd to the place at
    last again I made my way,
Found you in death so cold dear comrade,
    found your body son of responding kisses,
    (never again on earth responding,)
Bared your face in the starlight, curious the
    scene, cool blew the moderate night-wind,
Long there and then in vigil I stood, dimly
    around me the battle-field spreading,
Vigil wondrous and vigil sweet there in the
    fragrant silent night,   10
But not a tear fell, not even a long-drawn sigh,
    long, long I gazed,
Then on the earth partially reclining sat by
    your side leaning my chin in my hands,
Passing sweet hours, immortal and mystic hours
    with you dearest comrade—not a tear, not
    a word,
Vigil of silence, love and death, vigil for you
    my son and my soldier,
As onward silently stars aloft, eastward new
    ones upward stole,
Vigil final for you brave boy, (I could not
    save you, swift was your death,
I faithfully loved you and cared for you living,
    I think we shall surely meet again,)
Till at latest lingering of the night, indeed
    just as the dawn appear'd,
My comrade I wrapt in his blanket, envelop'd
    well his form,
Folded the blanket well, tucking it carefully
    over head and carefully under feet,   20
And there and then and bathed by the rising
    sun, my son in his grave, in his rude-dug
    grave I deposited,
Ending my vigil strange with that, vigil of
    night and battle-field dim,
Vigil for boy of responding kisses, (never again
    on earth responding,)
Vigil for comrade swiftly slain, vigil I never
    forget, how as day brighten'd,
I rose from the chill ground and folded my
    soldier well in his blanket,
And buried him where he fell.   1865

AS TOILSOME I WANDER'D
VIRGINIA'S WOODS

As toilsome I wander'd Virginia's woods,
To the music of rustling leaves kick'd by my
    feet, (for 'twas autumn,)

I mark'd at the foot of a tree the grave of a
  soldier;
Mortally wounded he and buried on the retreat,
  (easily all could I understand,)
The halt of a mid-day hour, when up! no time
  to lose—yet this sign left,
On a tablet scrawl'd and nail'd on the tree by
  the grave,
"Bold, cautious, true, and my loving comrade."
Long, long I muse, then on my way go wandering,
Many a changeful season to follow, and many
  a scene of life,
Yet at times through changeful season and
  scene, abrupt, alone, or in the crowded
  street,   10
Comes before me the unknown soldier's grave,
  comes the inscription rude in Virginia's
  woods,
"Bold, cautious, true, and my loving comrade."   1865

THE WOUND-DRESSER

1

An old man bending I come among new faces,
Years looking backward resuming in answer to
  children,
Come tell us old man, as from young men and
  maidens that love me,
(Arous'd and angry, I'd thought to beat the
  alarum, and urge relentless war,
But soon my fingers fail'd me, my face droop'd
  and I resign'd myself,
To sit by the wounded and soothe them, or
  silently watch the dead;)
Years hence of these scenes, of these furious
  passions, these chances,
Of unsurpass'd heroes, (was one side so brave?
  the other was equally brave;)
Now be witness again, paint the mightiest
  armies of earth,
Of those armies so rapid so wondrous what
  saw you to tell us?   10
What stays with you latest and deepest? of
  curious panics,
Of hard-fought engagements or sieges tremendous what deepest remains?

2

O maidens and young men I love and that love
  me,
What you ask of my days those the strangest
  and sudden your talking recalls,

Soldier alert I arrive after a long march cover'd
  with sweat and dust,
In the nick of time I come, plunge in the fight,
  loudly shout in the rush of successful charge,
Enter the captur'd works—yet lo, like a swift-
  running river they fade,
Pass and are gone they fade—I dwell not on
  soldiers' perils or soldiers' joys,
(Both I remember well—many the hardships,
  few the joys, yet I was content.)

But in silence, in dreams' projections,   20
While the world of gain and appearance and
  mirth goes on,
So soon what is over forgotten, and waves wash
  the imprints off the sand,
With hinged knees returning I enter the doors,
  (while for you up there,
Whoever you are, follow without noise and be
  of strong heart.)

Bearing the bandages, water and sponge,
Straight and swift to my wounded I go,
Where they lie on the ground after the battle
  brought in,
Where their priceless blood reddens the grass
  the ground,
Or to the rows of the hospital tent, or under
  the roof'd hospital,
To the long rows of cots up and down each
  side I return,   30
To each and all one after another I draw near,
  not one do I miss,
An attendant follows holding a tray, he carries
  a refuse pail,
Soon to be fill'd with clotted rags and blood,
  emptied, and fill'd again.

I onward go, I stop,
With hinged knees and steady hand to dress
  wounds,
I am firm with each, the pangs are sharp yet
  unavoidable,
One turns to me his appealing eyes—poor
  boy! I never knew you,
Yet I think I could not refuse this moment to
  die for you, if that would save you.

3

On, on I go, (open doors of time! open hospital
  doors!)
The crush'd head I dress, (poor crazed hand
  tear not the bandage away,)   40
The neck of the cavalry-man with the bullet
  through and through I examine,

Hard the breathing rattles, quite glazed already the eye, yet life struggles hard,
(Come sweet death! be persuaded O beautiful death!
In mercy come quickly.)
From the stump of the arm, the amputated hand,
I undo the clotted lint, remove the slough, wash off the matter and blood,
Back on his pillow the soldier bends with curv'd neck and side-falling head,
His eyes are closed, his face is pale, he dares not look on the bloody stump,
And has not yet look'd on it.

I dress a wound in the side, deep, deep,   50
But a day or two more, for see the frame all wasted and sinking,
And the yellow-blue countenance see.

I dress the perforated shoulder, the foot with the bullet-wound,
Cleanse the one with a gnawing and putrid gangrene, so sickening, so offensive,
While the attendant stands behind aside me holding the tray and pail.

I am faithful, I do not give out,
The fractur'd thigh, the knee, the wound in the abdomen,
These and more I dress with impassive hand, (yet deep in my breast a fire, a burning flame.)

4

Thus in silence in dreams' projections,
Returning, resuming, I thread my way through the hospitals,   60
The hurt and wounded I pacify with soothing hand,
I sit by the restless all the dark night, some are so young,
Some suffer so much, I recall the experience sweet and sad,
(Many a soldier's loving arms about this neck have cross'd and rested,
Many a soldier's kiss dwells on these bearded lips.)   1865

WHEN I HEARD THE LEARN'D ASTRONOMER

When I heard the learn'd astronomer,
When the proofs, the figures, were ranged in columns before me,
When I was shown the charts and diagrams, to add, divide, and measure them,
When I sitting heard the astronomer where he lectured with much applause in the lecture-room,
How soon unaccountable I became tired and sick,
Till rising and gliding out I wander'd off by myself,
In the mystical moist night-air, and from time to time,
Look'd up in perfect silence at the stars.   1865

GIVE ME THE SPLENDID SILENT SUN

1

Give me the splendid silent sun with all his beams full-dazzling,
Give me juicy autumnal fruit ripe and red from the orchard,
Give me a field where the unmow'd grass grows,
Give me an arbor, give me the trellis'd grape,
Give me fresh corn and wheat, give me serene-moving animals teaching content,
Give me nights perfectly quiet as on high plateaus west of the Mississippi, and I looking up at the stars,
Give me odorous at sunrise a garden of beautiful flowers where I can walk undisturb'd,
Give me for marriage a sweet-breath'd woman of whom I should never tire,
Give me a perfect child, give me away aside from the noise of the world a rural domestic life,
Give me to warble spontaneous songs recluse by myself, for my own ears only,   10
Give me solitude, give me Nature, give me again O Nature your primal sanities!

These demanding to have them, (tired with ceaseless excitement, and rack'd by the war-strife,)
These to procure incessantly asking, rising in cries from my heart,
While yet incessantly asking still I adhere to my city,
Day upon day and year upon year O city, walking your streets,
Where you hold me enchain'd a certain time refusing to give me up,

Yet giving to make me glutted, enrich'd of
soul, you give me forever faces;
(O I see what I sought to escape, confronting,
reversing my cries,
I see my own soul trampling down what it
ask'd for.)

2

Keep your splendid silent sun,   20
Keep your woods O Nature, and the quiet
places by the woods,
Keep your fields of clover and timothy, and
your corn-fields and orchards,
Keep the blossoming buckwheat fields where
the Ninth-month bees hum;
Give me faces and streets—give me these
phantoms incessant and endless along the
trottoirs!
Give me interminable eyes—give me women
—give me comrades and lovers by the
thousand!
Let me see new ones every day—let me hold
new ones by the hand every day!
Give me such shows—give me the streets of
Manhattan!
Give me Broadway, with the soldiers marching
—give me the sound of the trumpets and
drums!
(The soldiers in companies or regiments—some
starting away, flush'd and reckless,
Some, their time up, returning with thinn'd
ranks, young, yet very old, worn, marching,
noticing nothing;)   30
Give me the shores and wharves heavy-fringed
with black ships!
O such for me! O an intense life, full to reple-
tion and varied!
The life of the theatre, bar-room, huge hotel,
for me!
The saloon of the steamer! the crowded excursion for me! the torchlight procession!
The dense brigade bound for the war, with
high piled military wagons following;
People, endless, streaming, with strong voices,
passions, pageants,
Manhattan streets with their powerful throbs,
with beating drums as now,
The endless and noisy chorus, the rustle and
clank of muskets, (even the sight of the
wounded,)
Manhattan crowds, with their turbulent musical chorus!
Manhattan faces and eyes forever for me.   40
                                    1865

WHEN LILACS LAST IN THE DOORYARD BLOOM'D

1

When lilacs last in the dooryard bloom'd,
And the great star early droop'd in the western
sky in the night,
I mourn'd, and yet shall mourn with ever
returning spring.

Ever-returning spring, trinity sure to me you
bring,
Lilac blooming perennial and drooping star in
the west,
And thought of him I love.

2

O powerful western fallen star!
O shades of night—O moody, tearful night!
O great star disappear'd—O the black murk
that hides the star!
O cruel hands that hold me powerless—O help-
less soul of me!   10
O harsh surrounding cloud that will not free
my soul.

3

In the dooryard fronting an old farm-house
near the white-wash'd palings,
Stands the lilac-bush tall-growing with heart-
shaped leaves of rich green,
With many a pointed blossom rising delicate,
with the perfume strong I love,
With every leaf a miracle—and from this bush
in the dooryard,
With delicate-color'd blossoms and heart-
shaped leaves of rich green,
A sprig with its flower I break.

4

In the swamp in secluded recesses,
A shy and hidden bird is warbling a song.

Solitary the thrush,   20
The hermit withdrawn to himself, avoiding
the settlements,
Sings by himself a song.

Song of the bleeding throat,
Death's outlet song of life, (for well dear
brother I know,
If thou wast not granted to sing thou would'st
surely die.)

5

Over the breast of the spring, the land, amid cities,
Amid lanes and through old woods, where lately the violets peep'd from the ground, spotting the gray debris,
Amid the grass in the fields each side of the lanes, passing the endless grass,
Passing the yellow-spear'd wheat, every grain from its shroud in the dark-brown fields up- risen,
Passing the apple-tree blows of white and pink in the orchards,   30
Carrying a corpse to where it shall rest in the grave,
Night and day journeys a coffin.

6

Coffin that passes through lanes and streets,
Through day and night with the great cloud darkening the land,
With the pomp of the inloop'd flags with the cities draped in black,
With the show of the states themselves as of crape-veil'd women standing,
With processions long and winding and the flambeaus of the night,
With the countless torches lit, with the silent sea of faces and the unbared heads,
With the waiting depot, the arriving coffin, and the sombre faces,
With dirges through the night, with the thou- sand voices rising strong and solemn,   40
With all the mournful voices of the dirges pour'd around the coffin,
The dim-lit churches and the shuddering or- gans—where amid these you journey,
With the tolling tolling bells' perpetual clang,
Here, coffin that slowly passes,
I give you my sprig of lilac.

7

(Nor for you, for one alone,
Blossoms and branches green to coffins all I bring,
For fresh as the morning, thus would I chant a song for you O sane and sacred death.

All over bouquets of roses,
O death, I cover you over with roses and early lilies,   50
But mostly and now the lilac that blooms the first,

Copious I break, I break the sprigs from the bushes,
With loaded arms I come, pouring for you,
For you and the coffins all of you O death.)

8

O western orb sailing the heaven,
Now I know what you must have meant as a month since I walk'd,
As I walk'd in silence the transparent shadowy night,
As I saw you had something to tell as you bent to me night after night,
As you droop'd from the sky low down as if to my side, (while the other stars all look'd on,)
As we wander'd together the solemn night, (for something I know not what kept me from sleep,)   60
As the night advanced, and I saw on the rim of the west how full you were of woe,
As I stood on the rising ground in the breeze in the cool transparent night,
As I watch'd where you pass'd and was lost in the netherward black of the night,
As my soul in its trouble dissatisfied sank, as where you sad orb,
Concluded, dropt in the night, and was gone.

9

Sing on there in the swamp,
O singer bashful and tender, I hear your notes, I hear your call,
I hear, I come presently, I understand you,
But a moment I linger, for the lustrous star has detain'd me,
The star my departing comrade holds and de- tains me.   70

10

O how shall I warble myself for the dead one there I loved?
And how shall I deck my song for the large sweet soul that has gone?
And what shall my perfume be for the grave of him I love?

Sea-winds blown from east and west,
Blown from the Eastern sea and blown from the Western sea, till there on the prairies meeting,
These and with these and the breath of my chant,
I'll perfume the grave of him I love.

11

O what shall I hang on the chamber walls?
And what shall the pictures be that I hang on
the walls,
To adorn the burial-house of him I love?   80

Pictures of growing spring and farms and
homes,
With the Fourth-month eve at sundown, and
the gray smoke lucid and bright,
With floods of the yellow gold of the gorgeous,
indolent, sinking sun, burning, expanding the
air,
With the fresh sweet herbage under foot, and
the pale green leaves of the trees prolific,
In the distance the flowing glaze, the breast
of the river, with a wind-dapple here and
there,
With ranging hills on the banks, with many a
line against the sky, and shadows,
And the city at hand with dwellings so dense,
and stacks of chimneys,
And all the scenes of life and the workshops,
and the workmen homeward returning.

12

Lo, body and soul—this land,
My own Manhattan with spires, and the sparkling and hurrying tides, and the ships,   90
The varied and ample land, the South and
the North in the light, Ohio's shores and
flashing Missouri,
And ever the far-spreading prairies cover'd
with grass and corn.

Lo, the most excellent sun so calm and haughty,
The violet and purple morn with just-felt
breezes,
The gentle soft-born measureless light,
The miracle spreading bathing all, the fulfill'd
noon,
The coming eve delicious, the welcome night
and the stars,
Over my cities shining all, enveloping man and
land.

13

Sing on, sing on you gray-brown bird,
Sing from the swamps, the recesses, pour your
chant from the bushes,   100
Limitless out of the dusk, out of the cedars and
pines.

Sing on dearest brother, warble your reedy
song,
Loud human song, with voice of uttermost woe.

O liquid and free and tender!
O wild and loose to my soul—O wondrous
singer!
You only I hear—yet the star holds me, (but
will soon depart,)
Yet the lilac with mastering odor holds me.

14

Now while I sat in the day and look'd forth,
In the close of the day with its light and the
fields of spring, and the farmers preparing
their crops,
In the large unconscious scenery of my land
with its lakes and forests,   110
In the heavenly aerial beauty, (after the per-
turb'd winds and the storms,)
Under the arching heavens of the afternoon
swift passing, and the voices of children and
women,
The many-moving sea-tides, and I saw the
ships how they sail'd,
And the summer approaching with richness,
and the fields all busy with labor,
And the infinite separate houses, how they all
went on, each with its meals and minutia of
daily usages,
And the streets how their throbbings throbb'd,
and the cities pent—lo, then and there,
Falling upon them all and among them all,
enveloping me with the rest,
Appear'd the cloud, appear'd the long black
trail,
And I knew death, its thought, and the sacred
knowledge of death.

Then with the knowledge of death as walking
one side of me,   120
And the thought of death close-walking the
other side of me,
And I in the middle as with companions, and
as holding the hands of companions,
I fled forth to the hiding receiving night that
talks not,
Down to the shores of the water, the path by
the swamp in the dimness,
To the solemn shadowy cedars and ghostly
pines so still.

And the singer so shy to the rest receiv'd me,
The gray-brown bird I know receiv'd us comrades three,

And he sang the carol of death, and a verse
for him I love.

From deep secluded recesses,
From the fragrant cedars and the ghostly pines
so still,   130
Came the carol of the bird.

And the charm of the carol rapt me,
As I held as if by their hands my comrades in
the night,
And the voice of my spirit tallied the song of
the bird.

Come lovely and soothing death,
Undulate round the world, serenely arriving,
arriving,
In the day, in the night, to all, to each,
Sooner or later delicate death.

Prais'd be the fathomless universe,
For life and joy, and for objects and knowledge
curious,   140
And for love, sweet love—but praise! praise!
praise!
For the sure-enwinding arms of cool-enfolding
death.

Dark mother always gliding near with soft
feet,
Have none chanted for thee a chant of fullest
welcome?
Then I chant it for thee, I glorify thee above
all,
I bring thee a song that when thou must indeed
come, come unfalteringly.

Approach strong deliveress,
When it is so, when thou hast taken them,
I joyously sing the dead,
Lost in the loving floating ocean of thee,
Laved in the flood of thy bliss O death.   150

From me to thee glad serenades,
Dances for thee I propose saluting thee, adorn-
ments and feastings for thee,
And the sights of the open landscape and the
high-spread sky are fitting,
And life and the fields, and the huge and
thoughtful night.

The night in silence under many a star,
The ocean shore and the husky whispering
wave whose voice I know,
And the soul turning to thee O vast and well-
veil'd death,
And the body gratefully nestling close to thee.

Over the tree-tops I float thee a song,
Over the rising and sinking waves, over the
myriad fields and the prairies wide,   160
Over the dense-pack'd cities all and the teem-
ing wharves and ways,
I float this carol with joy, with joy to thee
O death.

15

To the tally of my soul,
Loud and strong kept up the gray-brown bird,
With pure deliberate notes spreading filling the
night.
Loud in the pines and cedars dim,
Clear in the freshness moist and swamp-per-
fume,
And I with my comrades there in the night.

While my sight that was bound in my eyes
unclosed,
As to long panoramas of visions.   170

And I saw askant the armies,
I saw as in noiseless dreams hundreds of battle-
flags,
Borne through the smoke of the battles and
pierc'd with missiles I saw them,
And carried hither and yon through the smoke,
and torn and bloody,
And at last but a a few shreds left on the staffs,
(and all in silence,)
And the staffs all splinter'd and broken.

I saw battle-corpses, myriads of them,
And the white skeletons of young men, I saw
them,
I saw the debris and debris of all the slain
soldiers of the war,
But I saw they were not as was thought,   180
They themselves were fully at rest, they
suffer'd not,
The living remain'd and suffer'd, the mother
suffer'd,
And the wife and the child and the musing
comrade suffer'd,
And the armies that remain'd suffer'd.

16

Passing the visions, passing the night,
Passing, unloosing the hold of my comrades' hands,
Passing the song of the hermit bird and the tallying song of my soul,
Victorious song, death's outlet song, yet varying ever-altering song,
As low and wailing, yet clear the notes, rising and falling, flooding the night,
Sadly sinking and fainting, as warning and warning, and yet again bursting with joy, 190
Covering the earth and filling the spread of the heaven,
As that powerful psalm in the night I heard from recesses,
Passing, I leave thee lilac with heart-shaped leaves,
I leave thee there in the door-yard, blooming, returning with spring.

I cease from my song for thee,
From my gaze on thee in the west, fronting the west, communing with thee,
O comrade lustrous with silver face in the night.
Yet each to keep and all, retrievements out of the night,
The song, the wondrous chant of the gray-brown bird,
And the tallying chant, the echo arous'd in my soul, 200
With the lustrous and drooping star with the countenance full of woe,
With the holders holding my hand nearing the call of the bird,
Comrades mine and I in the midst, and their memory ever to keep, for the dead I loved so well,
For the sweetest, wisest soul of all my days and lands—and this for his dear sake,
Lilac and star and bird twined with the chant of my soul,
There in the fragrant pines and the cedars dusk and dim. 1865–66

YEARS OF THE MODERN

Years of the modern! years of the unperform'd!
Your horizon rises, I see it parting away for more august dramas,
I see not America only, not only Liberty's nation but other nations preparing,
I see tremendous entrances and exits, new combinations, the solidarity of races,
I see that force advancing with irresistible power on the world's stage,
(Have the old forces, the old wars, played their parts? are the acts suitable to them closed?)
I see Freedom, completely arm'd and victorious and very haughty, with Law on one side and Peace on the other,
A stupendous trio all issuing forth against the idea of caste;
What historic denouements are these we so rapidly approach?
I see men marching and countermarching by swift millions, 10
I see the frontiers and boundaries of the old aristocracies broken,
I see the landmarks of European kings removed,
I see this day the People beginning their landmarks, (all others give way;)
Never were such sharp questions ask'd as this day,
Never was average man, his soul, more energetic, more like a God,
Lo, how he urges and urges, leaving the masses no rest!
His daring foot is on land and sea everywhere, he colonizes the Pacific, the archipelagoes,
With the steamship, the electric telegraph, the newspaper, the wholesale engines of war,
With these and the world-spreading factories he interlinks all geography, all lands;
What whispers are these O lands, running ahead of you, passing under the seas? 20
Are all nations communing? is there going to be but one heart to the globe?
Is humanity forming en-masse? for lo, tyrants tremble, crowns grow dim,
The earth, restive, confronts a new era, perhaps a general divine war,
No one knows what will happen next, such portents fill the days and nights;
Years prophetical! the space ahead as I walk, as I vainly try to pierce it, is full of phantoms,
Unborn deeds, things soon to be, project their shapes around me,
This incredible rush and heat, this strange ecstatic fever of dreams O years!
Your dreams O years, how they penetrate through me! (I know not whether I sleep or wake;)
The perform'd America and Europe grow dim, retiring in shadow behind me,

The unperform'd, more gigantic than ever,
advance, advance upon me. 30
1865

A NOISELESS PATIENT SPIDER

A noiseless patient spider,
I mark'd where on a little promontory it stood
isolated,
Mark'd how to explore the vacant vast surrounding,
It launch'd forth filament, filament, filament,
out of itself,
Ever unreeling them, ever tirelessly speeding
them.

And you O my soul where you stand,
Surrounded, detached, in measureless oceans
of space,
Ceaselessly musing, venturing, throwing, seeking the spheres to connect them,
Till the bridge you will need be form'd, till the
ductile anchor hold,
Till the gossamer thread you fling catch somewhere, O my soul. 10
1868

ON THE BEACH AT NIGHT

On the beach at night,
Stands a child with her father,
Watching the east, the autumn sky.

Up through the darkness,
While ravening clouds, the burial clouds, in
black masses spreading,
Lower sullen and fast athwart and down the
sky,
Amid a transparent clear belt of ether yet left
in the east,
Ascends large and calm the lord-star Jupiter,
And nigh at hand, only a very little above,
Swim the delicate sisters the Pleiades. 10

From the beach the child holding the hand of
her father,
Those burial-clouds that lower victorious soon
to devour all,
Watching, silently weeps.

Weep not, child,
Weep not, my darling,
With these kisses let me remove your tears,

The ravening clouds shall not long be victorious,
They shall not long possess the sky, they devour the stars only in apparition,
Jupiter shall emerge, be patient, watch again
another night, the Pleiades shall emerge,
They are immortal, all those stars both silvery
and golden shall shine out again, 20
The great stars and the little ones shall shine
out again, they endure,
The vast immortal suns and the long-enduring
pensive moons shall again shine.

Then dearest child mournest thou only for
Jupiter?
Considerest thou alone the burial of the stars?

Something there is,
(With my lips soothing thee, adding I whisper,
I give thee the first suggestion, the problem
and indirection,)
Something there is more immortal even than
the stars,
(Many the burials, many the days and nights,
passing away,)
Something that shall endure longer even than
lustrous Jupiter, 30
Longer than sun or any revolving satellite,
Or the radiant sisters the Pleiades. 1871

PASSAGE TO INDIA

1

Singing my days,
Singing the great achievements of the present,
Singing the strong light works of engineers,
Our modern wonders, (the antique ponderous
Seven outvied,)
In the Old World the east the Suez canal,
The New by its mighty railroad spann'd,
The seas inlaid with eloquent gentle wires;
Yet first to sound, and ever sound, the cry with
thee O soul,
The Past! the Past! the Past!

The Past—the dark unfathom'd retrospect! 10
The teeming gulf—the sleepers and the
shadows!
The past—the infinite greatness of the past!
For what is the present after all but a growth
out of the past?
(As a projectile form'd, impell'd, passing a
certain line, still keeps on,

So the present, utterly form'd, impell'd by the past.)

2

Passage O soul to India!
Eclaircise the myths Asiatic, the primitive fables.
Not you alone proud truths of the world,
Nor you alone ye facts of modern science,
But myths and fables of eld, Asia's, Africa's fables,   20
The far-darting beams of the spirit, the un-loos'd dreams,
The deep diving bibles and legends,
The daring plots of the poets, the elder religions;
O you temples fairer than lilies pour'd over by the rising sun!
O you fables spurning the known, eluding the hold of the known, mounting to heaven!
You lofty and dazzling towers, pinnacled, red as roses, burnish'd with gold!
Towers of fables immortal fashion'd from mortal dreams!
You too I welcome and fully the same as the rest!
You too with joy I sing.

Passage to India!   30
Lo, soul, seest thou not God's purpose from the first?
The earth to be spann'd, connected by network,
The races, neighbors, to marry and be given in marriage,
The oceans to be cross'd, the distant brought near,
The lands to be welded together.

A worship new I sing,
You captains, voyagers, explorers, yours,
You engineers, you architects, machinists, yours,
You, not for trade or transportation only,
But in God's name, and for thy sake O soul.   40

3

Passage to India!
Lo soul for thee of tableaus twain,
I see in one the Suez canal initiated, open'd,
I see the procession of steamships, the Empress Eugenie's leading the band,
I mark from on deck the strange landscape, the pure sky, the level sand in the distance,
I pass swiftly the picturesque groups, the workmen gather'd,
The gigantic dredging machines.

In one again, different, (yet thine, all thine, O soul, the same,)
I see over my own continent the Pacific railroad surmounting every barrier,
I see continual trains of cars winding along the Platte carrying freight and passengers,   50
I hear the locomotives rushing and roaring, and the shrill steam-whistle,
I hear the echoes reverberate through the grandest scenery in the world,
I cross the Laramie plains, I note the rocks in grotesque shapes, the buttes,
I see the plentiful larkspur and wild onions, the barren, colorless, sage-deserts,
I see in glimpses afar or towering immediately above me the great mountains, I see the Wind river and the Wahsatch mountains,
I see the Monument mountain and the Eagle's Nest, I pass the Promontory, I ascend the Nevadas,
I scan the noble Elk mountain and wind around its base,
I see the Humboldt range, I thread the valley and cross the river,
I see the clear waters of lake Tahoe, I see forests of majestic pines,
Or crossing the great desert, the alkaline plains, I behold enchanting mirages of waters and meadows,   60
Marking through these and after all, in duplicate slender lines,
Bridging the three or four thousand miles of land travel,
Tying the Eastern to the Western sea,
The road between Europe and Asia.

(Ah Genoese thy dream! thy dream!
Centuries after thou art laid in thy grave,
The shore thou foundest verifies thy dream.)

4

Passage to India!
Struggles of many a captain, tales of many a sailor dead,
Over my mood stealing and spreading they come,   70
Like clouds and cloudlets in the unreach'd sky.

Along all history, down the slopes,
As a rivulet running, sinking now, and now again to the surface rising,

A ceaseless thought, a varied train—lo, soul,
to thee, thy sight, they rise,
The plans, the voyages again, the expeditions;
Again Vasco da Gama sails forth,
Again the knowledge gain'd, the mariner's
compass,
Lands found and nations born, thou born
America,
For purpose vast, man's long probation fill'd,
Thou rondure of the world at last accomplish'd.   80

5

O vast Rondure, swimming in space,
Cover'd all over with visible power and beauty,
Alternate light and day and the teeming spiritual darkness,
Unspeakable high processions of sun and moon
and countless stars above,
Below, the manifold grass and waters, animals,
mountains, trees,
With inscrutable purpose, some hidden prophetic intention,
Now first it seems my thought begins to span
thee.

Down from the gardens of Asia descending
radiating,
Adam and Eve appear, then their myriad
progeny after them,
Wandering, yearning, curious, with restless explorations,   90
With questionings, baffled, formless, feverish,
with never-happy hearts,
With that sad incessant refrain, Wherefore unsatisfied soul? and Whither O mocking life?

Ah who shall soothe these feverish children?
Who justify these restless explorations?
Who speak the secret of impassive earth?
Who bind it to us? what is this separate Nature
so unnatural?
What is this earth to our affections? (unloving
earth, without a throb to answer ours,
Cold earth, the place of graves.)

Yet soul be sure the first intent remains, and
shall be carried out,
Perhaps even now the time has arrived.   100

After the seas are all cross'd, (as they seem already cross'd,)
After the great captains and engineers have accomplish'd their work,

After the noble inventors, after the scientists,
the chemist, the geologist, ethnologist,
Finally shall come the poet worthy that name,
The true son of God shall come singing his
songs.

Then not your deeds only O voyagers, O scientists and inventors, shall be justified,
All these hearts as of fretted children shall be
sooth'd,
All affection shall be fully responded to, the
secret shall be told,
All these separations and gaps shall be taken
up and hook'd and link'd together,
The whole earth, this cold, impassive, voiceless
earth, shall be completely justified,   110
Trinitas divine shall be gloriously accomplish'd
and compacted by the true son of God, the
poet,
(He shall indeed pass the straits and conquer
the mountains,
He shall double the cape of Good Hope to some
purpose,)
Nature and Man shall be disjoin'd and diffused
no more,
The true son of God shall absolutely fuse them.

6

Year at whose wide-flung door I sing!
Year of the purpose accomplish'd!
Year of the marriage of continents, climates
and oceans!
(No mere doge of Venice now wedding the
Adriatic,)
I see O year in you the vast terraqueous globe
given and giving all,   120
Europe to Asia, Africa join'd, and they to the
New World,
The lands, geographies, dancing before you,
holding a festival garland,
As brides and bridegrooms hand in hand.

Passage to India!
Cooling airs from Caucasus far, soothing cradle
of man,
The river Euphrates flowing, the past lit up
again.

Lo soul, the retrospect brought forward,
The old, most populous, wealthiest of earth's
lands,
The streams of the Indus and the Ganges and
their many affluents,

(I my shores of America walking to-day be-
hold, resuming all,)   130
The tale of Alexander on his warlike marches
suddenly dying,
On one side China and on the other side Persia
and Arabia,
To the south the great seas and the bay of
Bengal,
The flowing literatures, tremendous epics, re-
ligions, castes,
Old occult Brahma interminably far back, the
tender and junior Buddha,
Central and southern empires and all their be-
longings, possessors,
The wars of Tamerlane, the reign of Aurung-
zebe,
The traders, rulers, explorers, Moslems, Vene-
tians, Byzantium, the Arabs, Portuguese,
The first travelers famous yet, Marco Polo,
Batouta the Moor,
Doubts to be solv'd, the map incognita, blanks
to be fill'd,   140
The foot of man unstay'd, the hands never at
rest,
Thyself O soul that will not brook a challenge.

The mediæval navigators rise before me,
The world of 1492, with its awaken'd enter-
prise,
Something swelling in humanity now like the
sap of the earth in spring,
The sunset splendor of chivalry declining.

And who art thou sad shade?
Gigantic, visionary, thyself a visionary,
With majestic limbs and pious beaming eyes,
Spreading around with every look of thine a
golden world,   150
Enhuing it with gorgeous hues.

As the chief histrion,
Down to the footlights walks in some great
scena,
Dominating the rest I see the Admiral himself,
(History's type of courage, action, faith,)
Behold him sail from Palos leading his little
fleet,
His voyage behold, his return, his great fame,
His misfortunes, calumniators, behold him a
prisoner, chain'd,
Behold his dejection, poverty, death.

(Curious in time I stand, noting the efforts of
heroes,   160

Is the deferment long? bitter the slander,
poverty, death?
Lies the seed unreck'd for centuries in the
ground? lo, to God's due occasion,
Uprising in the night, it sprouts, blooms,
And fills the earth with use and beauty.)

                        7

Passage indeed O soul to primal thought,
Not lands and seas alone, thy own clear fresh-
ness,
The young maturity of brood and bloom,
To realms of budding bibles.

O soul, repressless, I with thee and thou with
me,
Thy circumnavigation of the world begin, 170
Of man, the voyage of his mind's return,
To reason's early paradise,
Back, back to wisdom's birth, to innocent in-
tuitions,
Again with fair creation.

                        8

O we can wait no longer,
We too take ship O soul,
Joyous we too launch out on trackless seas,
Fearless for unknown shores on waves of ec-
stasy to sail,
Amid the wafting winds, (thou pressing me to
thee, I thee to me, O soul,)
Caroling free, singing our song of God, 180
Chanting our chant of pleasant exploration.

With laugh and many a kiss,
(Let others deprecate, let others weep for sin,
remorse, humiliation,)
O soul thou pleasest me, I thee.

Ah more than any priest O soul we too believe
in God,
But with the mystery of God we dare not dally.

O soul thou pleasest me, I thee,
Sailing these seas or on the hills, or waking in
the night,
Thoughts, silent thoughts, of Time and Space
and Death, like waters flowing,
Bear me indeed as through the regions infinite,   190
Whose air I breathe, whose ripples hear, lave
me all over,

Bathe me O God in thee, mounting to thee,
I and my soul to range in range of thee.

O Thou transcendent,
Nameless, the fibre and the breath,
Light of the light, shedding forth universes,
    thou centre of them,
Thou mightier centre of the true, the good, the
    loving,
Thou moral, spiritual fountain—affection's
    source—thou reservoir,
(O pensive soul of me—O thirst unsatisfied—
    waitest not there?
Waitest not haply for us somewhere there the
    Comrade perfect?)   200
Thou pulse—thou motive of the stars, suns,
    systems,
That, circling, move in order, safe, harmonious,
Athwart the shapeless vastnesses of space,
How should I think, how breathe a single
    breath, how speak, if, out of myself,
I could not launch, to those, superior universes?

Swiftly I shrivel at the thought of God,
At Nature and its wonders, Time and Space
    and Death,
But that I, turning, call to thee O soul, thou
    actual Me,
And lo, thou gently masterest the orbs,
Thou matest Time, smilest content at Death,
And fillest, swellest full the vastnesses of
    Space.   211

Greater than stars or suns,
Bounding O soul thou journeyest forth;
What love than thine and ours could wider
    amplify?
What aspirations, wishes, outvie thine and ours
    O soul?
What dreams of the ideal? what plans of purity,
    perfection, strength?
What cheerful willingness for others' sake to
    give up all?
For others' sake to suffer all?

Reckoning ahead O soul, when thou, the time
    achiev'd,
The seas all cross'd, weather'd the capes, the
    voyage done,   220
Surrounded, copest, frontest God, yieldest, the
    aim attain'd,
As fill'd with friendship, love complete, the
    Elder Brother found,
The Younger melts in fondness in his arms.

9

Passage to more than India!
Are thy wings plumed indeed for such far
    flights?
O soul, voyagest thou indeed on voyages like
    those?
Disportest thou on waters such as those?
Soundest below the Sanscrit and the Vedas?
Then have thy bent unleash'd.

Passage to you, your shores, ye aged fierce
    enigmas!   230
Passage to you, to mastership of you, ye stran-
    gling problems!
You, strew'd with the wrecks of skeletons, that,
    living, never reach'd you.

Passage to more than India!
O secret of the earth and sky!
Of you O waters of the sea! O winding creeks
    and rivers!
Of you O woods and fields! of you strong
    mountains of my land!
Of you O prairies! of you gray rocks!
O morning red! O clouds! O rain and snows!
O day and night, passage to you!

O sun and moon and all you stars! Sirius and
    Jupiter!   240
Passage to you!

Passage, immediate passage! the blood burns
    in my veins!
Away O soul! hoist instantly the anchor!
Cut the hawsers—haul out—shake out every
    sail!
Have we not stood here like trees in the ground
    long enough?
Have we not grovel'd here long enough, eating
    and drinking like mere brutes?
Have we not darken'd and dazed ourselves
    with books long enough?

Sail forth—steer for the deep waters only,
Reckless O soul, exploring, I with thee, and
    thou with me,
For we are bound where mariner has not yet
    dared to go,   250
And we will risk the ship, ourselves and all.

O my brave soul!
O farther farther sail!

O daring joy, but safe! are they not all the seas of God?
O farther, farther, farther sail!   1871

PRAYER OF COLUMBUS

A batter'd, wreck'd old man,
Thrown on this savage shore, far, far from home,
Pent by the sea and dark rebellious brows, twelve dreary months,
Sore, stiff with many toils, sicken'd and nigh to death,
I take my way along the island's edge,
Venting a heavy heart.

I am too full of woe!
Haply I may not live another day;
I cannot rest O God, I cannot eat or drink or sleep,
Till I put forth myself, my prayer, once more to Thee,   10
Breathe, bathe myself once more in Thee, commune with Thee,
Report myself once more to Thee.

Thou knowest my years entire, my life,
My long and crowded life of active work, not adoration merely;
Thou knowest the prayers and vigils of my youth,
Thou knowest my manhood's solemn and visionary meditations,
Thou knowest how before I commenced I devoted all to come to Thee,
Thou knowest I have in age ratified all those vows and strictly kept them,
Thou knowest I have not once lost nor faith nor ecstasy in Thee,
In shackles, prison'd, in disgrace, repining not,   20
Accepting all from Thee, as duly come from Thee.

All my emprises have been fill'd with Thee,
My speculations, plans, begun and carried on in thoughts of Thee,
Sailing the deep or journeying the land for Thee;
Intentions, purports, aspirations mine, leaving results to Thee.
O I am sure they really came from Thee,
The urge, the ardor, the unconquerable will,
The potent, felt, interior command, stronger than words,

A message from the Heavens whispering to me even in sleep,
These sped me on.   30

By me and these the work so far accomplish'd,
By me earth's elder cloy'd and stifled lands uncloy'd, unloos'd,
By me the hemispheres rounded and tied, the unknown to the known.

The end I know not, it is all in Thee,
Or small or great I know not—haply what broad fields, what lands,
Haply the brutish measureless human undergrowth I know,
Transplanted there may rise to stature, knowledge worthy Thee,
Haply the swords I know may there indeed be turn'd to reaping-tools,
Haply the lifeless cross I know, Europe's dead cross, may bud and blossom there.

One effort more, my altar this bleak sand;   40
That Thou O God my life hast lighted,
With ray of light, steady, ineffable, vouchsafed of Thee,
Light rare untellable, lighting the very light,
Beyond all signs, descriptions, languages;
For that O God, be it my latest word, here on my knees,
Old, poor, and paralyzed, I thank Thee.

My terminus near,
The clouds already closing in upon me,
The voyage balk'd, the course disputed, lost,
I yield my ships to Thee.   50

My hands, my limbs grow nerveless,
My brain feels rack'd, bewilder'd,
Let the old timbers part, I will not part,
I will cling fast to Thee, O God, though the waves buffet me,
Thee, Thee at least I know.

Is it the prophet's thought I speak, or am I raving?
What do I know of life? what of myself?
I know not even my own work past or present,
Dim ever-shifting guesses of it spread before me,
Of newer better worlds, their mighty parturition,
Mocking, perplexing me.   61

And these things I see suddenly, what mean
  they?
As if some miracle, some hand divine unseal'd
  my eyes,
Shadowy vast shapes smile through the air and
  sky,
And on the distant waves sail countless ships,
And anthems in new tongues I hear saluting
  me.   1874

PATROLING BARNEGAT

Wild, wild the storm, and the sea high running,
Steady the roar of the gale, with incessant
  undertone muttering,
Shouts of demoniac laughter fitfully piercing
  and pealing,
Waves, air, midnight, their savagest trinity lashing,
Out in the shadows there milk-white combs
  careering,
On beachy slush and sand spirts of snow fierce
  slanting,
Where through the murk the easterly death-
  wind breasting,
Through cutting swirl and spray watchful and
  firm advancing,
(That in the distance! is that a wreck? is the
  red signal flaring?)
Slush and sand of the beach tireless till daylight
  wending,   10
Steadily, slowly, through hoarse roar never re-
  mitting,
Along the midnight edge by those milk-white
  combs careering,
A group of dim, weird forms, struggling, the
  night confronting,
That savage trinity warily watching.   1880

SPIRIT THAT FORM'D THIS SCENE

Written in Platte Cañon, Colorado

Spirit that form'd this scene,
These tumbled rock-piles grim and red,
These reckless heaven-ambitious peaks,
These gorges, turbulent-clear streams, this na-
  ked freshness,
These formless wild arrays, for reasons of their
  own,
I know thee, savage spirit—we have communed
  together,
Mine too such wild arrays, for reasons of their
  own;
Was't charged against my chants they had for-
  gotten art?
To fuse within themselves its rules precise and
  delicatesse?
The lyrist's measur'd beat, the wrought-out
  temple's grace—column and polish'd arch
  forgot?   10
But thou that revelest here—spirit that form'd
  this scene,
They have remember'd thee.   1881

YOUTH, DAY, OLD AGE AND NIGHT

Youth, large, lusty, loving—youth full of grace,
  force, fascination,
Do you know that Old Age may come after you
  with equal grace, force, fascination?

Day full-blown and splendid—day of the immense sun, action, ambition, laughter,
The Night follows close with millions of suns,
  and sleep and restoring darkness.   1881

» »   « «

» » *From:* DEMOCRATIC VISTAS « «

. . . America, filling the present with greatest deeds and problems, cheerfully accepting
the past, including feudalism, (as, indeed, the
present is but the legitimate birth of the past,
including feudalism,) counts, as I reckon, for
her justification and success, (for who, as yet,
dare claim success?) almost entirely on the
future. Nor is that hope unwarranted. Today,
ahead, though dimly yet, we see, in vistas, a
copious, sane, gigantic offspring. For our New
World I consider far less important for what it
has done, or what it is, than for results to come.
Sole among nationalities, these States have assumed the task to put in forms of lasting power
and practicality, on areas of amplitude rivaling
the operations of the physical kosmos, the moral

political speculations of ages, long, long deferr'd, the democratic republican principle, and the theory of development and perfection by voluntary standards, and self-reliance. Who else, indeed, except the United States, in history, so far, have accepted in unwitting faith, and, as we now see, stand, act upon, and go security for, these things? . . .

10 To him or her within whose thought rages the battle, advancing, retreating, between democracy's convictions, aspirations, and the people's crudeness, vice, caprices, I mainly write this essay. I shall use the words America and democracy as convertible terms. Not an ordinary one is the issue. The United States are destined either to surmount the gorgeous history of feudalism, or else prove the most tremendous failure of time. Not the least doubtful am I on any prospects of their material suc-
20 cess. The triumphant future of their business, geographic and productive departments, on larger scales and in more varieties than ever, is certain. In those respects the republic must soon (if she does not already) outstrip all examples hitherto afforded, and dominate the world.

Admitting all this, with the priceless value of our political institutions, general suffrage, (and fully acknowledging the latest, widest
30 opening of the doors,) I say that, far deeper than these, what finally and only is to make of our western world a nationality superior to any hither known, and outtopping the past, must be vigorous, yet unsuspected Literatures, perfect personalities and sociologies, original, transcendental, and expressing (what, in highest sense, are not yet express'd at all) democracy and the modern. . . .

                    . . .

41 For my part, I would alarm and caution even the political and business reader, and to the utmost extent, against the prevailing delusion that the establishment of free political institutions, and plentiful intellectual smartness, with general good order, physical plenty, industry, &c., (desirable and precious advantages as they all are,) do, of themselves, determine and yield to our experiment of de-
50 mocracy the fruitage of success. With such advantages at present fully, or almost fully, possess'd—the Union just issued, victorious, from the struggle with the only foes it need ever fear, (namely, those within itself, the interior ones,) and with unprecedented materialistic

advancement—society, in these States, is canker'd, crude, superstitious, and rotten. Political, or law-made society is, and private, or voluntary society, is also. In any vigor, the element of moral conscience, the most important, the verteber to State or man, seems to me either entirely lacking, or seriously enfeebled or ungrown.

I say we had best look our times and lands searchingly in the face, like a physician diagnosing some deep disease. Never was there, perhaps, more hollowness at heart than at present, and here in the United States. Genuine belief seems to have left us. The underlying principles of the States are not honestly believ'd in, (for all this hectic glow, and these melo-dramatic screamings,) nor is humanity itself believ'd in. What penetrating eye does not everywhere see through the mask? The spectacle is appaling. We live in an atmosphere of hypocrisy throughout. The men believe not in the women, nor the women in the men. A scornful superciliousness rules in literature. The aim of all the *littérateurs* is to find something to make fun of. A lot of churches, sects, &c., the most dismal phantasms I know, usurp the name of religion. Conversation is a mass of badinage. From deceit in the spirit, the mother of all false deeds, the offspring is already incalculable. . . .

                    . . .

I say the mission of government, henceforth, in civilized lands, is not repression alone, and not authority alone, not even of law, nor by that favorite standard of the eminent writer, the rule of the best men, the born heroes and captains of the race, (as if such ever, or one time out of a hundred, get into the big places, elective or dynastic)—but higher than the highest arbitrary rule, to train communities through all their grades, beginning with individuals and ending there again, to rule themselves. . . .

For it is not that democracy is of exhaustive account, in itself. Perhaps, indeed, it is, (like Nature,) of no account in itself. It is that, as we see, it is the best, perhaps only, fit and full means, formulater, general caller-forth, trainer, for the million, not for grand material personalities only, but for immortal souls. To be a voter with the rest is not so much; and this, like every institute, will have its imperfections. But to become an enfranchised man, and now, impediments removed, to stand and start without humiliation, and equal with the rest; to commence, or have the road clear'd to commence, the grand experiment of development, whose end, (perhaps requiring several generations,) may be the forming of a full-grown man or woman—that *is* something. To ballast the State is also secured, and in our times is to be secured, in no other way.

We do not, (at any rate I do not,) put it either on the ground that the People, the masses, even the best of them, are, in their latent or exhibited qualities, essentially sensible and good—nor on the ground of their rights; but that good or bad, rights or no rights, the democratic formula is the only safe and preservative one for coming times. We endow the masses with the suffrage for their own sake, no doubt; then, perhaps still more, from another point of view, for community's sake. Leaving the rest to the sentimentalists, we present freedom as sufficient in its scientific aspect, cold as ice, reasoning, deductive, clear and passionless as crystal.

Democracy too is law, and of the strictest, amplest kind. Many suppose, (and often in its own ranks the error,) that it means a throwing aside of law, and running riot. But, briefly, it is the superior law, not alone that of physical force, the body, which, adding to, it supersedes with that of the spirit. Law is the unshakable order of the universe forever; and the law over all, and law of laws, is the law of successions; that of the superior law, in time, gradually supplanting and overwhelming the inferior one. (While, for myself, I would cheerfully agree—first covenanting that the formative tendencies shall be administer'd in favor, or at least not against it, and that this reservation be closely construed—that until the individual or community show due signs, or be so minor and fractional as not to endanger the State, the condition of authoritative tutelage may continue, and self-government must abide its time.) Nor is the esthetic point, always an important one, without fascination for highest aiming souls. The common ambition strains for elevations, to become some privileged exclusive. The master sees greatness and health in being part of the mass; nothing will do as well as common ground. Would you have in yourself the divine, vast, general law? Then merge yourself in it.

And topping democracy, this most alluring record, that it alone can bind, and ever seeks to bind, all nations, all men, of however various

and distant lands, into a brotherhood, a family. It is the old, yet ever-modern dream of earth, out of her eldest and her youngest, her fond philosophers and poets. Not that half only, individualism, which isolates. There is another half, which is adhesiveness or love, that fuses, ties, and aggregates, making the races comrades, and fraternizing all. Both are to be vitalized by religion, (sole worthiest elevator of man or State,) breathing into the proud, material tissues, the breath of life. For I say at the core of democracy, finally, is the religious element. All the religions, old and new, are there. Nor may the scheme step forth, clothed in resplendent beauty and command, till these, bearing the best, the latest fruit, the spiritual, shall fully appear.

. . .

What is the reason our time, our lands, that we see no fresh local courage, sanity, of our own—the Mississippi, stalwart Western men, real mental and physical facts, Southerners, &c., in the body of our literature? especially the poetic part of it. But always, instead, a parcel of dandies and ennuyees, dapper little gentlemen from abroad, who flood us with their thin sentiment of parlors, parasols, piano-songs, tinkling rhymes, the five-hundredth importation—or whimpering and crying about something, chasing one aborted conceit after another, and forever occupied in dyspeptic amours with dyspeptic women. While, current and novel, the grandest events and revolutions, and stormiest passions of history, are crossing today with unparallel'd rapidity and magnificence over the stages of our own and all the continents, offering new materials, opening new vistas, with largest needs, inviting the daring launching forth of conceptions in literature, inspired by them, soaring in highest regions, serving art in its highest, (which is only the other name for serving God, and serving humanity,) where is the man of letters, where is the book, with any nobler aim than to follow in the old track, repeat what has been said before—, and, as its utmost triumph, sell well, and be erudite or elegant?

Mark the roads, the processes, through which these States have arrived, standing easy, henceforth ever-equal, ever-compact, in their range today. European adventures? the most antique? Asiatic or African? old history—miracles—romances? Rather, our own unquestion'd facts. They hasten, incredible, blazing bright as fire.

From the deeds and days of Columbus down to the present, and including the present—and especially the late Secession war—when I con them, I feel, every leaf, like stopping to see if I have not made a mistake, and fall'n on the splendid figments of some dream. But it is no dream. We stand, live, move, in the huge flow of our age's materialism—in its spirituality. We have had founded for us the most positive of lands. The founders have pass'd to other spheres—but what are these terrible duties they have left us?

. . .

And still, providing for contingencies, I fain confront the fact, the need of powerful native philosophs and orators and bards, these States, as rallying points to come, in times of danger, and to fend off ruin and defection. For history is long, long, long. Shift and turn the combinations of the statement as we may, the problem of the future of America, is in certain respects as dark as it is vast. Pride, competition, segregation, vicious wilfulness, and license beyond example, brood already upon us. Unwieldy and immense, who shall hold in behemoth? who bridle leviathan? Flaunt it as we choose, athwart and over the roads of our progress loom huge uncertainty, and dreadful, threatening gloom. It is useless to deny it: Democracy grows rankly up the thickest, noxious, deadliest plants and fruits of all—brings worse and worse invaders —needs newer, larger, stronger, keener compensations and compellers.

Our lands, embracing so much, (embracing indeed the whole, rejecting none,) hold in their breast that flame also, capable of consuming themselves, consuming us all. Short as the span of our national life has been, already have death and downfall crowded close upon us—and will again crowd close, no doubt, even if warded off. Ages to come may never know, but I know, how narrowly during the late secession war— and more than once, and more than twice or thrice—our Nationality, (wherein bound up, as in a ship in a storm, depended, and yet depend, all our best life, all hope, all value,) just grazed, just by a hair escaped destruction. Alas! to think of them! the agony and bloody sweat of certain of those hours! those cruel, sharp, suspended crises!

Even today, amid these whirls, incredible flippancy, and blind fury of parties, infidelity, entire lack of first-class captains and leaders, added to the plentiful meanness and vulgarity of the ostensible masses—that problem, the labor question, beginning to open like a yawning gulf, rapidly widening every year—what prospect have we? We sail a dangerous sea of seething currents, cross and under-currents, vortices—all so dark, untried—and whither shall we turn? It seems as if the Almighty had spread before this nation charts of imperial destinies, dazzling as the sun, yet with many a deep, intestine difficulty, and human aggregate of cankerous imperfection,—saying, lo! the roads, the only plans of development, long and varied with all terrible balks and ebullitions. You said in your soul, I will be empire of empires, overshadowing all else, past and present, putting the history of old-world dynasties, conquests behind me, as of no account—making a new history, a history of democracy, making old history a dwarf—I alone inaugurating largeness, culminating time. If these, O lands of America, are indeed the prizes, the determinations of your soul, be it so. But behold the cost, and already specimens of the cost. Thought you greatness was to ripen for you like a pear? If you would have greatness, know that you must conquer it through ages, centuries—must pay for it with a proportionate price. For you too, as for all lands, the struggle, the traitor, the wily person in office, scrofulous wealth, the surfeit of prosperity, the demonism of greed, the hell of passion, the decay of faith, the long postponement, the fossil-like lethargy, the ceaseless need of revolutions, prophets, thunderstorms, deaths, births, new projections and invigorations of ideas and men.   1871

» » « «

EMILY DICKINSON

1830–1886

THE OUTWARD FACTS of Emily Dickinson's life are so few that it is no wonder certain biographers have resorted to fiction in attempting to describe a poet whose inner life, as revealed in her verse, must have been intense. Born into the cultivated, though austere and provincial society of Amherst, when the infant college was ten years old, she lived the normal life of a girl of her time in New England. The excellent Amherst Academy prepared her to enter the middle class at the newly founded Mount Holyoke Seminary (now Mount Holyoke College), where she remained only one year. Her education did not cease when she returned to Amherst. All the rest of her life she was in touch with the currents of thought of the age, though she was not a learned woman like her admired Elizabeth Barrett Browning and George Eliot.

In 1854 Emily made a visit to Washington and Philadelphia while her father was a member of Congress. It is probable that in the latter city she met the man who inspired the most remarkable love poems written by an American. That he was a clergyman and already married could not quench her love, though this obstacle, of course, made their marriage impossible. He saw her several times in later years, but there was never any hope that they might become lovers in fact. For Emily "all had no codicil." Gradually she withdrew from the social life of the town and was seen only by her family and by a few friends who knew how to pass the barrier. But she was by no means the anchoress legend has pictured her. To the children in her brother's house next door she was a fourth playmate, an abettor of their little treasons. Tender and gay with them, she poured her fine scorn on stupid and trivial grown-ups. It was lucky for some visitors to the Dickinson home that they never knew what Miss Emily said about them when they had taken their leave.

In her younger days Emily Dickinson knew and was admired by several men—her father, as the town's leading citizen and the treasurer of the College, kept his doors hospitably open. From some of these she learned much and gave much in return; there may have been more than friendship between her and one of them, for one of her finest poems begins "My life closed twice before its close." Of a different, though equally influential nature, were her friendships with two literary men of the time, Samuel Bowles, the vigorous, liberal editor of the *Springfield Republican*, and Thomas Wentworth Higginson, to whom she sent a handful of her poems in 1862, to ask him whether her verse was alive. Though the public was to know nothing of her poetry until after her death, a fairly large number of persons, aside from such literary mentors as Bowles and Higginson, knew that the recluse of the Dickinson house, whose white dress disappeared into the dusk of a passageway when callers came, was an extraordinary poet. Friends in Amherst were honored with her delicately penned verses sent with gifts of flowers or newly baked bread, and wisely cherished them. "Sister Sue," the wife of her brother Austin Dickinson, received hundreds of these poetical missives.

Possibly it is not to be regretted that her fame was confined to a discriminating few. What would America have made of her poems in 1870? For a time after the three series of them were issued in 1890, 1891, and 1896, there was a considerable, though temporary interest in her name, but her real resurrection did not come until the 1920's, as a result of the publication by her niece, the surviving member of the family, of new poems and letters and of significant biographical material. The generation after the first World War which rediscovered Donne and Marvell and whose idols were Pound and Eliot, first realized that Emily Dickinson was one of America's major poets.

One can, in fact, find few poets who have accomplished so much with so few tools. Confining herself almost entirely to the meters of the hymn tunes of her childhood, she made out of her acquaintance with nature, from a love affair lived only in the imagination, and from her intimations of immortality, nearly eighteen hundred poems, whose freshness can still evoke in us a fine surprise. The paradoxes of her life—an ecstatic delight in the natural world untouched by any pantheistic mists, a pagan joy of living mixed with an anguish which would have undone another, a sense of the concrete immediacy of the world balanced by constant meditating on the place where life meets death—these perceptions, as they are transmuted in her poems, make a world in which the finite moment acquires the perspective of eternity.

A. L. Hampson, *Emily Dickinson: A Bibliography*, Northampton, Mass., 1930.
The Poems of Emily Dickinson, T. H. Johnson, ed., 3 vols., Cambridge, 1958.
Selected Poems of Emily Dickinson, Conrad Aiken, ed., New York, The Modern Library, 1948.
The Complete Poems of Emily Dickinson, ed. T. H. Johnson 1 vol., Boston, 1960.
The Letters of Emily Dickinson, T. H. Johnson, ed., 3 vols., Cambridge, 1958.
C. R. Anderson, *Emily Dickinson's Poetry: Stairway of Surprise*, New York, 1960.
M. T. Bingham, *Emily Dickinson's Home*, New York, 1955.
———, *Ancestors' Brocades: The Literary Debut of Emily Dickinson*, New York, 1945.
Glauco Cambon, "Violence and Abstraction in Emily Dickinson," *Sewanee Review*, LXVIII (Summer, 1960), 450–464.
MacGregor Jenkins, *Emily Dickinson, Friend and Neighbor*, Boston (1930), 1939.
T. H. Johnson, *Emily Dickinson, An Interpretive Biography*, Cambridge, 1955.
Genevieve Taggard, *The Life and Mind of Emily Dickinson*, New York, 1930.
G. F. Whicher, *This Was a Poet: A Critical Biography of Emily Dickinson*, New York, 1938.

1

I hav'nt told my garden yet—
Lest that should conquer me
I hav'nt quite the strength now
To break it to the Bee—

I will not name it in the street
For shops w'd stare at me—
That one so shy—so ignorant
Should have the face to die.

The hillsides must not know it—
Where I have rambled so—   10
Nor tell the loving forests
The day that I shall go—

Nor lisp it at the table—
Nor heedless by the way
Hint that within the Riddle
One will walk today—
Ca. 1858

2 [1]

Safe in their Alabaster Chambers—
Untouched by Morning

[1] Version of 1859 consists of stanzas 1 and 2 above. Version of 1861 reads *Lie* for *Sleep* in stanza 1, omits stanza 2, and adds stanza 3.

And untouched by Noon—
Sleep the meek members of the Resurrection—
Rafter of satin,
And Roof of stone.

[Light laughs the breeze
In her Castle above them—
Babbles the Bee in a stolid Ear,
Pipe the Sweet Birds in ignorant cadence—10
Ah, what Sagacity perished here!]

Grand go the Years—in the Crescent—above
    them—
Worlds scoop their Arcs—
And Firmaments—row—
Diadems—drop—and Doges—surrender—
Soundless as dots—on a Disc of Snow.
1859–1861

3

There's a certain Slant of light,
Winter Afternoons—
That oppresses, like the Heft
Of Cathedral Tunes—

Heavenly Hurt, it gives us—
We can find no scar,
But internal difference,
Where the Meanings, are—

None may teach it—Any—
'Tis the Seal Despair—   10
An imperial affliction
Sent us of the Air—

When it comes, the Landscape listens—
Shadows—hold their breath—
When it goes, 'tis like the Distance
On the look of Death—
Ca. 1861

4

Wild Nights—Wild Nights!
Were I with thee,
Wild Nights should be
Our luxury!

Futile—the Winds—
To a Heart in port—
Done with the Compass—
Done with the Chart!

Rowing in Eden—
Ah, the Sea!   10
Might I but moor—Tonight—
In Thee!
Ca. 1861

5

Of all the Souls that stand create—
I have elected—One—
When Sense from Spirit—flies away—
And Subterfuge—is done—

When that which is—and that which was—
Apart—intrinsic—stand—
And this brief Tragedy of Flesh—
Is shifted—like a Sand—

When Figures show their royal Front—
And Mists—are carved away,   10
Behold the Atom—I preferred—
To all the lists of Clay!
Ca. 1862

6

I cannot live with You—
It would be Life—
And Life is over there—
Behind the Shelf
The Sexton keeps the Key to—

Putting up
Our Life—His Porcelain—
Like a Cup—

Discarded of the Housewife—
Quaint—or Broke—   10
A newer Sevres pleases—
Old Ones crack—

I could not die—with You,
For One must wait
To shut the Other's Gaze down—
You—could not—

And I—could I stand by
And see You—freeze—
Without my Right of Frost—
Death's privilege?   20

Nor could I rise—with You—
Because Your Face
Would put out Jesus'—
That New Grace

Glow plain—and foreign
On my homesick Eye—
Except that You than He
Shone closer by—

They'd judge Us—How—
For You—served Heaven—You know,   30
Or sought to—
I could not—

Because You saturated Sight
And I had no more Eyes
For sordid excellence
As Paradise

And were You lost, I would be—
Though My Name
Rang loudest
On the Heavenly fame—   40

And were You—saved—
And I—condemned to be
Where You were not—
That self—were Hell to Me—

So We must keep apart—
You there—I—here—
With just the Door ajar
That Oceans are—and Prayer,
And that White Sustenance—
Despair—   50
Ca. 1862

7

The Soul selects her own Society—
Then—shuts the Door—
To her divine Majority—
Present no more—

Unmoved—she notes the Chariots—pausing—
At her low Gate—
Unmoved—an Emperor be kneeling
Upon her Mat—

I've known her—from an ample nation—
Choose One—   10
Then—close the Valves of her attention—
Like Stone—
Ca. 1862

8

It was not Death, for I stood up,
And all the Dead, lie down—
It was not Night, for all the Bells
Put out their Tongues, for Noon.

It was not Frost, for on my Flesh
I felt Siroccos—crawl—
Nor Fire—for just my Marble feet
Could keep a Chancel, cool—

And yet, it tasted, like them all,
The Figures I have seen   10
Set orderly, for Burial,
Reminded me, of mine—

As if my life were shaven,
And fitted to a frame,
And could not breathe without a key,
And 'twas like Midnight, some—

When everything that ticked—has stopped—
And Space stares all around—
Or Grisly frosts—first Autumn morns—
Repeal the Beating Ground—   20

But most, like Chaos—Stopless—cool—
Without a Chance, or Spar—
Or even a Report of Land
To justify—Despair.
1862

9

A Bird came down the Walk—
He did not know I saw—

He bit an Angle-worm in halves
And ate the fellow, raw,

And then he drank a Dew
From a convenient Grass—
And then hopped sidewise to the Wall
To let a Beetle pass—

He glanced with rapid eyes
That hurried all around—   10
They looked like frightened Beads, I thought—
He stirred his Velvet Head

Like one in danger, Cautious,
I offered him a Crumb,
And he unrolled his feathers
And rowed him softer home—

Than Oars divide the Ocean,
Too silver for a seam—
Or Butterflies, off Banks of Noon,
Leap, plashless as they swim.   20
1862

10

Because I could not stop for Death—
He kindly stopped for me—
The Carriage held but just Ourselves—
And Immortality.

We slowly drove—He knew no haste
And I had out away
My labor and my leisure too,
For His Civility—

We passed the School, where Children strove
At Recess—in the Ring—   10
We passed the Fields of Gazing Grain—
We passed the Setting Sun—

Or rather—He passed Us—
The Dews drew quivering and chill—
For only Gossamer, my gown—
My Tippet—only Tulle—

We paused before a House that seemed
A Swelling of the Ground—
The Roof was scarcely visible—
The Cornice—in the Ground—   20

Since then—'tis centuries—and yet
Feels shorter than the Day
I first surmised the Horses Heads
Were toward Eternity—
Ca. 1863

11

He preached upon "Breadth" till it argued him
    narrow—
The Broad are too broad to define
And of "Truth" until it proclaimed him a
    Liar—
The Truth never flaunted a sign—

Simplicity fled from his counterfeit presence
As Gold the Pyrites would shun—
What confusion would cover the innocent Jesus
To meet so enabled a Man!   10
1872

12

The Spider as an Artist
Has never been employed—
Though his surpassing Merit
Is freely certified

By every Broom and Bridget
Throughout a Christian Land,
Neglected Son of Genius,
I take thee by the Hand.
Ca. 1873

13

Not with a Club, the Heart is broken
Nor with a Stone—
A Whip so small you could not see it
I've known

To lash the Magic Creature
Till it fell,
Yet that Whip's Name
Too noble then to tell.

Magnanimous as Bird
By Boy descried—   10
Singing unto the Stone
Of which it died—

Shame need not crouch
In such an Earth as Our's—
Shame—stand erect—
The Universe is your's.
Ca. 1874

14

Let me not mar that perfect Dream
By an Auroral stain
But so adjust my daily Night
That it will come again.

Not when we know, the Power accosts—
The Garment of Surprise
Was all our timid Mother wore,
At Home—in Paradise.
Ca. 1875

15

A Route of Evanescence
With a revolving wheel—
A Resonance of Emerald—
A Rush of Cochineal—

And every Blossom on the Bush
Adjusts it's tumbled Head—
The Mail from Tunis, probably,
An easy Morning's Ride—
Ca. 1879

16

Elysium is as far as to
The very nearest Room
If in that Room a Friend await
Felicity or Doom—

What fortitude the Soul contains,
That it can so endure
The accent of a coming Foot,
The opening of a Door—
Ca. 1882

17

Lightly stepped a yellow star
To it's lofty place
Loosed the Moon her silver hat
From her lustral Face
All of Evening softly lit
As an Astral Hall—
Father I observed to Heaven
You are punctual—
?

18

My life closed twice before its close;
It yet remains to see
If Immortality unveil
A third event to me,

So huge, so hopeless to conceive
As these that twice befell.
Parting is all we know of heaven,
And all we need of hell.
?

BRET HARTE

1836–1902

THE ADVANCE PUBLICITY which heralded Bret Harte's return to the East in the winter of 1871 was such as might have been accorded a visiting potentate. The preceding year had seen the publication in Boston of *The Luck of Roaring Camp and Other Sketches*, and the volume had seized the imagination of Easterners eager for a firsthand report of life in California mining communities. If Bret Harte's admirers had expected to see a miner in rough boots and flannel shirt, they were disappointed when he alighted from the train in Boston: a slender, dignified figure of middle height, with neat mustaches and side-whiskers, the white hands of a sedentary worker, and clothes stylish to the point of foppery. Bostonians may not have remembered that in fact as well as in appearance, Harte was an Easterner, son of an Albany, New York, school-teacher whose vain search for pedagogical advancement had taken him and his family to half a dozen cities on the Atlantic seaboard before his death in 1845. For nine years thereafter the widow and her four children lived in Brooklyn and Manhattan, so that Bret was seventeen before he left the East.

The all-important move to California was occasioned by Mrs. Harte's marriage to Col. Andrew Williams, who subsequently became the first mayor of Oakland, California. In 1856, Bret tried tutoring for a year, and then moved north into the wild region near the Trinity River diggings, where he served for a while as stage-driver for Wells, Fargo, and Company. That he ever became a prospector is improbable. Instead he taught school, helped a doctor put up prescriptions, and was general factotum to *The Northern Californian*, a boom-town newspaper.

Back in San Francisco in 1861 he worked successively in the office of the surveyor-general and at the Mint, contributed scores of sketches and poems to the *Golden Era*, and finally struck literary gold when he became first editor of the *Overland Monthly*. The second number of this magazine (August, 1868) contained "The Luck of Roaring Camp," and the issue of January, 1869, carried "The Outcasts of Poker Flat." His reputation was further enhanced by the famous dialect poem, "Plain Language from Truthful James" (1870), more generally known as "The Heathen Chinee." The immediate result of his trip east was a $10,000 contract with the *Atlantic Monthly* for the rights to his literary output during 1872. But he signally failed to live up to expectations. Disdaining the West he lived chiefly in New York, and in six years produced two volumes of short stories, *Mrs. Skaggs's Husbands* (1873) and *Tales of the Argonauts* (1875), a disappointing novel, and two unsuccessful plays, on one of which, *Ah Sin* (1877), he collaborated with Mark Twain. The rest of his story is one of financial extravagance, appointments to consulates in Crefeld, Prussia (1878–1880), and Glasgow (1880–1885), and residence in London (1885–1902), where his reputation still held despite the uninspired potboilers which he continued to write, empty redactions of the California material which had made him famous.

Except for historical reasons Harte's local color work is worth little. Even the best of his stories are second-rate, but they have been perpetuated largely because of their adventitious connection with California during the colorful era in the fifties and sixties which saw the exploitation of the mineral resources of the state.

G. R. Stewart, *A Bibliography of the Writings of Bret Harte in the Magazines and Newspapers of California, 1857–1871,* Berkeley, California, 1933.
The Writings of Bret Harte (Standard Library Edition), 19 vols., Boston, 1896–1903.
H. W. Boynton, *Bret Harte,* New York, 1903.
A. F. Harlow, *Bret Harte of the Old West,* New York, 1943.
G. R. Stewart, *Bret Harte, Argonaut and Exile,* Boston, 1931.

» » THE LUCK OF ROARING CAMP « «

There was commotion in Roaring Camp. It could not have been a fight, for in 1850 that was not novel enough to have called together the entire settlement. The ditches and claims were not only deserted, but "Tuttle's grocery" had contributed its gamblers, who, it will be remembered, calmly continued their game the day that French Pete and Kanaka Joe shot each other to death over the bar in the front room. The whole camp was collected before a rude cabin on the outer edge of the clearing. Conversation was carried on in a low tone, but the name of a woman was frequently repeated. It was a name familiar enough in the camp,— "Cherokee Sal."

Perhaps the less said of her the better. She was a coarse and, it is to be feared, a very sinful woman. But at that time she was the only woman in Roaring Camp, and was just then lying in sore extremity, when she most needed the ministration of her own sex. Dissolute, abandoned, and irreclaimable, she was yet suffering a martyrdom hard enough to bear even when veiled by sympathizing womanhood, but now terrible in her loneliness. The primal curse had come to her in that original isolation which must have made the punishment of the first transgression so dreadful. It was, perhaps, part of the expiation of her sin that, at a moment when she most lacked her sex's intuitive tenderness and care, she met only the half-contemptuous faces of her masculine associates. Yet a few of the spectators were, I think, touched by her sufferings. Sandy Tipton thought it was "rough on Sal," and, in the contemplation of her condition, for a moment rose superior to the fact that he had an ace and two bowers in his sleeve.

It will be seen also that the situation was novel. Deaths were by no means uncommon in Roaring Camp, but a birth was a new thing.

People had been dismissed the camp effectively, finally, and with no possibility of return; but this was the first time that anybody had been introduced *ab initio.* Hence the excitement.

"You go in there, Stumpy," said a prominent citizen known as "Kentuck," addressing one of the loungers. "Go in there, and see what you kin do. You've had experience in them things."

Perhaps there was a fitness in the selection. Stumpy, in other climes, had been the putative head of two families; in fact, it was owing to some legal informality in these proceedings that Roaring Camp—a city of refuge—was indebted to his company. The crowd approved the choice, and Stumpy was wise enough to bow to the majority. The door closed on the extempore surgeon and midwife, and Roaring Camp sat down outside, smoked its pipe, and awaited the issue.

The assemblage numbered about a hundred men. One or two of these were actual fugitives from justice, some were criminal, and all were reckless. Physically they exhibited no indication of their past lives and character. The greatest scamp had a Raphael face, with a profusion of blonde hair; Oakhurst, a gambler, had the melancholy air and intellectual abstraction of a Hamlet; the coolest and most courageous man was scarcely over five feet in height, with a soft voice and an embarrassed, timid manner. The term "roughs" applied to them was a distinction rather than a definition. Perhaps in the minor details of fingers, toes, ears, etc., the camp may have been deficient, but these slight omissions did not detract from their aggregate force. The strongest man had but three fingers on his right hand; the best shot had but one eye.

Such was the physical aspect of the men that

were dispersed around the cabin. The camp lay in a triangular valley between two hills and a river. The only outlet was a steep trail over the summit of a hill that faced the cabin, now illuminated by the rising moon. The suffering woman might have seen it from the rude bunk whereon she lay,—seen it winding like a silver thread until it was lost in the stars above.

A fire of withered pine boughs added so-
10 ciability to the gathering. By degrees the natural levity of Roaring Camp returned. Bets were freely offered and taken regarding the result. Three to five that "Sal would get through with it"; even that the child would survive; side bets as to the sex and complexion of the coming stranger. In the midst of an excited discussion an exclamation came from those nearest the door, and the camp stopped to listen. Above the swaying and moaning of the pines, the
20 swift rush of the river, and the crackling of the fire rose a sharp, querulous cry,—a cry unlike anything heard before in the camp. The pines stopped moaning, the river ceased to rush, and the fire to crackle. It seemed as if Nature had stopped to listen, too.

The camp rose to its feet as one man! It was proposed to explode a barrel of gunpowder; but in consideration of the situation of the mother, better counsels prevailed, and only a
30 few revolvers were discharged; for whether owing to the rude surgery of the camp, or some other reason, Cherokee Sal was sinking fast. Within an hour she had climbed, as it were, that rugged road that led to the stars, and so passed out of Roaring Camp, its sin and shame, forever. I do not think that the announcement disturbed them much, except in speculation as to the fate of the child. "Can he live now?" was asked of Stumpy. The answer was doubtful.
40 The only other being of Cherokee Sal's sex and maternal condition in the settlement was an ass. There was some conjecture as to fitness, but the experiment was tried. It was less problematical than the ancient treatment of Romulus and Remus, and apparently as successful.

When these details were completed, which exhausted another hour, the door was opened, and the anxious crowd of men, who had already formed themselves into a queue, en-
50 tered in single file. Beside the low bunk or shelf, on which the figure of the mother was starkly outlined below the blankets, stood a pine table. On this a candle-box was placed, and within it, swathed in staring red flannel, lay the last arrival at Roaring Camp. Beside the

candle-box was placed a hat. Its use was soon indicated. "Gentlemen," said Stumpy, with a singular mixture of authority and *ex officio* complacency,—"gentlemen will please pass in at the front door, round the table, and out at the back door. Them as wishes to contribute anything toward the orphan will find a hat handy." The first man entered with his hat on; he uncovered, however, as he looked about him, and so unconsciously set an example to the next. In such communities good and bad actions are catching. As the procession filed in comments were audible,—criticisms addressed perhaps rather to Stumpy in the character of showman: "Is that him?" "Mighty small specimen"; "Hasn't more'n got the color"; "Ain't bigger nor a derringer." The contributions were as characteristic: A silver tobacco box; a doubloon; a navy revolver, silver mounted; a gold specimen; a very beautifully embroidered lady's handkerchief (from Oakhurst the gambler); a diamond breastpin; a diamond ring (suggested by the pin, with the remark from the giver that he "saw that pin and went two diamonds better"); a slung-shot; a Bible (contributor not detected); a golden spur; a silver teaspoon (the initials, I regret to say, were not the giver's); a pair of surgeon's shears; a lancet; a Bank of England note for £5; and about $200 in loose gold and silver coin. During these proceedings Stumpy maintained a silence as impassive as the dead on his left, a gravity as inscrutable as that of the newly born on his right. Only one incident occurred to break the monotony of the curious procession. As Kentuck bent over the candle-box half curiously, the child turned, and, in a spasm of pain, caught at his groping finger, and held it fast for a moment. Kentuck looked foolish and embarrassed. Something like a blush tried to assert itself in his weather-beaten cheek. "The d—d little cuss!" he said, as he extricated his finger, with perhaps more tenderness and care than he might have been deemed capable of showing. He held that finger a little apart from its fellows as he went out, and examined it curiously. The examination provoked the same original remark in regard to the child. In fact, he seemed to enjoy repeating it. "He rastled with my finger," he remarked to Tipton, holding up the member, "the d—d little cuss!"

It was four o'clock before the camp sought repose. A light burnt in the cabin where the watchers sat, for Stumpy did not go to bed that night. Nor did Kentuck. He drank quite freely, and related with great gusto his experience, invariably ending with his characteristic condemnation of the newcomer. It seemed to relieve him of any unjust implication of sentiment, and Kentuck had the weaknesses of the nobler sex. When everybody else had gone to bed, he walked down to the river and whistled reflectingly. Then he walked up the gulch past the cabin, still whistling with demonstrative unconcern. At a large redwood-tree he paused and retraced his steps, and again passed the cabin. Halfway down to the river's bank he again paused, and then returned and knocked at the door. It was opened by Stumpy. "How goes it?" said Kentuck, looking past Stumpy toward the candle-box. "All serene!" replied Stumpy. "Anything up?" "Nothing." There was a pause —an embarrassing one—Stumpy still holding the door. Then Kentuck had recourse to his finger, which he held up to Stumpy. "Rastled with it,—the d—d little cuss," he said, and retired.

The next day Cherokee Sal had such rude sepulture as Roaring Camp afforded. After her body had been committed to the hillside, there was a formal meeting of the camp to discuss what should be done with her infant. A resolution to adopt it was unanimous and enthusiastic. But an animated discussion in regard to the manner and feasibility of providing for its wants at once sprang up. It was remarkable that the argument partook of none of those fierce personalities with which discussions were usually conducted at Roaring Camp. Tipton proposed that they should send the child to Red Dog,—a distance of forty miles,—where female attention could be procured. But the unlucky suggestion met with fierce and unanimous opposition. It was evident that no plan which entailed parting from their new acquisition would for a moment be entertained. "Besides," said Tom Ryder, "them fellows at Red Dog would swap it, and ring in somebody else on us." A disbelief in the honesty of other camps prevailed at Roaring Camp, as in other places.

The introduction of a female nurse in the camp also met with objection. It was argued that no decent woman could be prevailed to accept Roaring Camp as her home, and the speaker urged that "they didn't want any more of the other kind." This unkind allusion to the defunct mother, harsh as it may seem, was the first spasm of propriety,—the first symptom of the camp's regeneration. Stumpy advanced

nothing. Perhaps he felt a certain delicacy in interfering with the selection of a possible successor in office. But when questioned, he averred stoutly that he and "Jinny"—the mammel before alluded to—could manage to rear the child. There was something original, independent, and heroic about the plan that pleased the camp. Stumpy was retained. Certain articles were sent for to Sacramento. "Mind," said the treasurer, as he pressed a bag of gold-dust into the expressman's hand, "the best that can be got,—lace, you know, and filigree-work and frills,—d—n the cost!"

Strange to say, the child thrived. Perhaps the invigorating climate of the mountain camp was compensation for material deficiencies. Nature took the foundling to her broader breast. In that rare atmosphere of the Sierra foothills, —that air pungent with balsamic odor, that ethereal cordial at once bracing and exhilarating,—he may have found food and nourishment, or a subtle chemistry that transmuted ass's milk to lime and phosphorus. Stumpy inclined to the belief that it was the latter and good nursing. "Me and that ass," he would say, "has been father and mother to him! Don't you," he would add, apostrophizing the helpless bundle before him, "never go back on us."

By the time he was a month old the necessity of giving him a name became apparent. He had generally been known as "The Kid," "Stumpy's Boy," "The Coyote" (an allusion to his vocal powers), and even by Kentuck's endearing diminutive of "The d—d little cuss." But these were felt to be vague and unsatisfactory, and were at last dismissed under another influence. Gamblers and adventurers are generally superstitious, and Oakhurst one day declared that the baby had brought "the luck" to Roaring Camp. It was certain that of late they had been successful. "Luck" was the name agreed upon, with the prefix of Tommy for greater convenience. No allusion was made to the mother, and the father was unknown. "It's better," said the philosophical Oakhurst, "to take a fresh deal all round. Call him Luck, and start him fair." A day was accordingly set apart for the christening. What was meant by this ceremony the reader may imagine who has already gathered some idea of the reckless irreverence of Roaring Camp. The master of ceremonies was one "Boston," a noted wag, and the occasion seemed to promise the greatest facetiousness. This ingenious satirist had spent two days in preparing a burlesque of the Church service, with pointed local allusions. The choir was properly trained, and Sandy Tipton was to stand godfather. But after the procession had marched to the grove with music and banners, and the child had been deposited before a mock altar, Stumpy stepped before the expectant crowd. "It ain't my style to spoil fun, boys," said the little man, stoutly eying the faces around him, "but it strikes me that this thing ain't exactly on the squar. It's playing it pretty low down on this yer baby to ring in fun on him that he ain't goin' to understand. And ef there's goin' to be any godfathers round, I'd like to see who's got any better rights than me." A silence followed Stumpy's speech. To the credit of all humorists be it said that the first man to acknowledge its justice was the satirist thus stopped of his fun. "But," said Stumpy, quickly following up his advantage, "we're here for a christening, and we'll have it. I proclaim you Thomas Luck, according to the laws of the United States and the State of California, so help me God." It was the first time that the name of the Deity had been otherwise uttered than profanely in the camp. The form of christening was perhaps even more ludicrous than the satirist had conceived; but strangely enough, nobody saw it and nobody laughed. "Tommy" was christened as seriously as he would have been under a Christian roof, and cried and was comforted in as orthodox fashion.

And so the work of regeneration began in Roaring Camp. Almost imperceptibly a change came over the settlement. The cabin assigned to "Tommy Luck"—or "The Luck," as he was more frequently called—first showed signs of improvement. It was kept scrupulously clean and whitewashed. Then it was boarded, clothed, and papered. The rosewood cradle, packed eighty miles by mule, had, in Stumpy's way of putting it, "sorter killed the rest of the furniture." So the rehabilitation of the cabin became a necessity. The men who were in the habit of lounging in at Stumpy's to see "how 'The Luck' got on" seemed to appreciate the change, and in self-defense the rival establishment of "Tuttle's grocery" bestirred itself and imported a carpet and mirrors. The reflections of the latter on the appearance of Roaring Camp tended to produce stricter habits of personal cleanliness. Again Stumpy imposed a kind of quarantine upon those who aspired to the honor and privilege of holding The Luck.

It was a cruel mortification to Kentuck—who, in the carelessness of a large nature and the habits of frontier life, had begun to regard all garments as a second cuticle, which, like a snake's, only sloughed off through decay—to be debarred this privilege from certain prudential reasons. Yet such was the subtle influence of innovation that he thereafter appeared regularly every afternoon in a clean shirt and face still shining from his ablutions. Nor were moral and social sanitary laws neglected. "Tommy," who was supposed to spend his whole existence in a persistent attempt to repose, must not be disturbed by noise. The shouting and yelling, which had gained the camp its infelicitous title, were not permitted within hearing distance of Stumpy's. The men conversed in whispers or smoked with Indian gravity. Profanity was tacitly given up in these sacred precincts, and throughout the camp a popular form of expletive, known as "D—n the luck!" and "Curse the luck!" was abandoned, as having a new personal bearing. Vocal music was not interdicted, being supposed to have a soothing, tranquilizing quality; and one song, sung by "Man-o'-War Jack," an English sailor from her Majesty's Australian colonies, was quite popular as a lullaby. It was a lugubrious recital of the exploits of "the Arethusa, Seventy-four," in a muffled minor, ending with a prolonged dying fall at the burden of each verse, "On b-oo-o-ard of the Arethusa." It was a fine sight to see Jack holding The Luck, rocking from side to side as if with the motion of a ship, and crooning forth this naval ditty. Either through the peculiar rocking of Jack or the length of his song,—it contained ninety stanzas, and was continued with conscientious deliberation to the bitter end,—the lullaby generally had the desired effect. At such times the men would lie at full length under the trees in the soft summer twilight, smoking their pipes and drinking in the melodious utterances. An indistinct idea that this was pastoral happiness pervaded the camp. "This 'ere kind o' think," said the Cockney Simmons, meditatively reclining on his elbow, "is 'evingly." It reminded him of Greenwich.

On the long summer days The Luck was usually carried to the gulch from whence the golden store of Roaring Camp was taken. There, on a blanket spread over pine boughs, he would lie while the men were working in the ditches below. Latterly there was a rude attempt to decorate this bower with flowers and sweet-smelling shrubs, and generally some one would bring him a cluster of wild honey-suckles, azaleas, or the painted blossoms of Las Mariposas. The men had suddenly awakened to the fact that there were beauty and significance in these trifles, which they had so long trodden carelessly beneath their feet. A flake of glittering mica, a fragment of variegated quartz, a bright pebble from the bed of the creek, became beautiful to eyes thus cleared and strengthened, and were invariably put aside for The Luck. It was wonderful how many treasures the woods and hillsides yielded that "would do for Tommy." Surrounded by playthings such as never child out of fairyland had before, it is to be hoped that Tommy was content. He appeared to be serenely happy, albeit there was an infantine gravity about him, a contemplative light in his round gray eyes, that sometimes worried Stumpy. He was always tractable and quiet, and it is recorded that once, having crept beyond his "corral," —a hedge of tessellated pine boughs, which surrounded his bed,—he dropped over the bank on his head in the soft earth, and remained with his mottled legs in the air in that position for at least five minutes with unflinching gravity. He was extricated without a murmur. I hesitate to record the many other instances of his sagacity, which rest, unfortunately, upon the statements of prejudiced friends. Some of them were not without a tinge of superstition. "I crep' up the bank just now," said Kentuck one day, in a breathless state of excitement, "and dern my skin if he wasn't a-talking to a jaybird as was a-sittin' on his lap. There they was, just as free and sociable as anything you please, a-jawin' at each other just like two cherrybums." Howbeit, whether creeping over the pine boughs or lying lazily on his back blinking at the leaves above him, to him the birds sang, the squirrels chattered, and the flowers bloomed. Nature was his nurse and playfellow. For him she would let slip between the leaves golden shafts of sunlight that fell just within his grasp; she would send wandering breezes to visit him with the balm of bay and resinous gum; to him the tall redwoods nodded familiarly and sleepily, the bumble-bees buzzed, and the rooks cawed a slumbrous accompaniment.

Such was the golden summer of Roaring Camp. They were "flush times," and the luck was with them. The claims had yielded enormously. The camp was jealous of its privileges and looked suspiciously on strangers. No encouragement was given to immigration, and, to make their seclusion more perfect, the land on either side of the mountain wall that surrounded the camp they duly preëmpted. This, and a reputation for singular proficiency with the revolver, kept the reserve of Roaring Camp inviolate. The expressman—their only connecting link with the surrounding world—sometimes told wonderful stories of the camp. He would say, "They've a street up there in 'Roaring' that would lay over any street in Red Dog. They've got vines and flowers round their houses, and they wash themselves twice a day. But they're mighty rough on strangers, and they worship an Ingin baby."

With the prosperity of the camp came a desire for further improvement. It was proposed to build a hotel in the following spring, and to invite one or two decent families to reside there for the sake of The Luck, who might perhaps profit by female companionship. The sacrifice that this concession to the sex cost these men, who were fiercely skeptical in regard to its general virtue and usefulness, can only be accounted for by their affection for Tommy. A few still held out. But the resolve could not be carried into effect for three months, and the minority meekly yielded in the hope that something might turn up to prevent it. And it did.

The winter of 1851 will long be remembered in the foothills. The snow lay deep on the Sierras, and every mountain creek became a river, and every river a lake. Each gorge and gulch was transformed into a tumultuous water-course that descended the hillsides, tearing down giant trees and scattering its drift and débris along the plain. Red Dog had been twice under water, and Roaring Camp had been forewarned. "Water put the gold into them gulches," said Stumpy. "It's been here once and will be here again!" And that night the North Fork suddenly leaped over its banks and swept up the triangular valley of Roaring Camp.

In the confusion of rushing water, crashing trees, and crackling timber, and the darkness which seemed to flow with the water and blot out the fair valley, but little could be done to collect the scattered camp. When the morning broke, the cabin of Stumpy, nearest the river-bank, was gone. Higher up the gulch they found the body of its unlucky owner; but the pride, the hope, the joy, The Luck, of Roaring

Camp had disappeared. They were returning with sad hearts when a shout from the bank recalled them.

It was a relief-boat from down the river. They had picked up, they said, a man and an infant, nearly exhausted, about two miles below. Did anybody know them, and did they belong here?

It needed but a glance to show them Kentuck lying there, cruelly crushed and bruised, but still holding The Luck of Roaring Camp in his arms. As they bent over the strangely assorted pair, they saw that the child was cold and pulseless. "He is dead," said one. Kentuck opened his eyes. "Dead?" he repeated feebly. "Yes, my man, and you are dying too." A smile lit the eyes of the expiring Kentuck. "Dying!" he repeated; "he's a-taking me with him. Tell the boys I've got The Luck with me now"; and the strong man, clinging to the frail babe as a drowning man is said to cling to a straw, drifted away into the shadowy river that flows forever to the unknown sea.

1868   1868

"MARK TWAIN," SAMUEL LANGHORNE CLEMENS

1835–1910

MARK TWAIN lived the American fairy tale: He was a poor boy who made spectacularly good. A child of the middle-western frontier, a jack-of-all-trades before turning to writing as a profession, he ultimately saw the world on its most imposing levels. He was also, to complete the picture, a victim of the get-rich-quick impulse which is a part of the fairy tale, though he could satirize this impulse magnificently in *The Gilded Age*. And it is possible that he was always a bit uneasy in the face of an older and more impressive culture than that of the frontier—the culture of Europe or New England—the uneasiness making itself felt at its extremes in the brash iconoclasm of his travel books and in his abject apologies for the Whittier dinner speech. But he did not become a snob, or cramp himself in the genteel mold of a Boston Brahmin. His apologies for the Whittier speech are less characteristic of him than the speech itself, with its frontier exaggerations, its easy colloquialism, its refusal to be frightened by important names.

Yet Mark Twain knew moments of bitterness, and his view of life was that of one who had seen enough of it not to be particularly hopeful of human beings or their accomplishments. "My idea of our civilization," he wrote during the Boer War (his sympathies were with the Boers), "is that it is a shoddy, poor thing & full of cruelties, vanities, arrogancies, meannesses, & hypocrisies." The pessimism in such a comment has caused much wrangling among critics attempting either to explain it or to explain it away, as though it were surprising that one who saw human nature as essentially mean should express himself in comic terms. For however we explain his inner life, Mark Twain's function in his best work was that of the great comic writer in any age—to expose the ironic contradictions between pretense or delusion, and actuality. The king and the duke in *Huckleberry Finn* are American scalawags of the nineteenth-century frontier, but they are human in more general terms, and if one ventures (recalling the episode of the orphan girls) to regard them as distant relatives of Molière's Tartuffe, it is not to force a literary reference, but to point out their place in the great comic tradition. Here would belong also, for their varying qualities, others of Mark Twain's finest characters—Colonel Sellers in *The Gilded Age*, and the whole society of *The Man That Corrupted Hadleyburg*. And, providing a standard of decency and dignity against which scoundrels, frauds, and deadbeats might be measured, there is Nigger Jim, the noblest of Mark Twain's people.

For Twain knew the world. At twelve, when his father died, he had begun to serve apprenticeship on the Hannibal, Missouri, *Courier*, and for ten years thereafter he roved the land—in New York, Pennsylvania, Ohio, and Iowa. For four years he was a Mississippi river-pilot, happily navigating 1,200 miles of yellow water in proud fulfillment of a boyhood ambition. Then he moved west, to Carson City, and jumping to Virginia City, which he saw in its tough heyday, as a reporter for the local *Enterprise*. After two more years (1864–1866) in San Francisco, his wanderlust drew him to the Sandwich Islands, back to California, and then to New York *via* the Isthmus of Panama. Having got Eastern fame with his *Jumping Frog* collection of tall Western tales, he was soon off on an expedition to the Holy Land (*The Innocents Abroad*, 1869).

Following his marriage to Olivia Langdon in 1870 he settled to literary work in Hartford, Connecticut. Succeeding years saw great books like *Roughing It* (1872); *The Gilded Age* (with Charles Dudley Warner, 1873); *Old Times on the Mississippi* (1875); *Tom Sawyer* (1876); *A Tramp Abroad* (1880); *Huckleberry Finn* (1884); *A Connecticut Yankee in King Arthur's Court* (1889); and *Pudd'nhead Wilson* (1894). To recoup a languishing fortune he began in 1895 a lecture-tour around the world. His triumphant return in 1900 was a national event, and Yale and Oxford decorated him with honorary degrees. There is no more characteristic photograph of Mark than that in which he appears after the Oxford ceremony, delightedly swaggering in his red robes.

Mark Twain's work grew out of the traditions of frontier humor, with its relish for the strange behavior so abundant in a new country, its love of exaggeration and the anecdote. At times he is tempted too far by this love, and his work suffers—he was unable to sustain a long narrative with complete success. But, summing up the humorous methods of the frontier, he converted them to lasting comedy—a comedy without affectation (there is in his work none of Meredith's pirouetting with the Comic Muse), and enduringly alive in the dry shrewd speech and the easy rhythms of the American language.

H. H. Clark, "Mark Twain," in *Eight American Authors, A Review of Research and Criticism*, New York, 1956, pp. 319–363.

The Writings of Mark Twain, A. B. Paine, ed., 37 vols., New York, 1922–1925. (Paine also edited Twain's *Letters, Speeches, Autobiography* and *Notebooks*.)

Ivan Benson, *Mark Twain's Western Years*, Stanford, 1938.

Walter Blair, *Mark Twain & Huck Finn*, Berkeley, Cal., 1960.

M. M. Brashear, *Mark Twain, Son of Missouri*, Chapel Hill, N. C., 1934.

Bernard DeVoto, *Mark Twain's America*, Boston, 1932; *Mark Twain in Eruption*, New York, 1940; *Mark Twain at Work*, Cambridge, 1942.

W. D. Howells, *My Mark Twain: Reminiscences and Criticism*, New York, 1910.

E. H. Long, *Mark Twain Handbook*, New York, 1957.

A. B. Paine, *Mark Twain, A Biography*, 3 vols., New York, 1912.

E. C. Wagenknecht, *Mark Twain: The Man and His Work*, New Haven, 1935.

» » JIM SMILEY AND HIS JUMPING FROG « «

[THE CELEBRATED JUMPING FROG OF CALAVERAS COUNTY] [1]

In compliance with the request of a friend of mine, who wrote me from the East, I called on good-natured, garrulous old Simon Wheeler, and inquired after my friend's friend *Leonidas W. Smiley*, as requested to do, and I hereunto append the result. I have a lurking suspicion that *Leonidas W.* Smiley is a myth; that my

[1] In the New York *Saturday Press*, where it first appeared November 18, 1865, the piece bore the title, "Jim Smiley and his Jumping Frog." Worth perusal is Mark Twain's own redaction, *The Jumping Frog: in English, then in French, then clawed back into a civilized language once more by patient, unremunerated toil* (New York, 1903).

friend never knew such a personage; that he only conjectured that, if I asked old Wheeler about him, it would remind him of his infamous *Jim* Smiley, and he would go to work and bore me nearly to death with some infernal reminiscence of him as long and tedious as it should be useless to me. If that was the design, it certainly succeeded.

I found Simon Wheeler dozing comfortably by the barroom stove of the old, dilapidated tavern in the ancient mining camp of Angel's, and I noticed that he was fat and bald-headed, and had an expression of winning gentleness and simplicity upon his tranquil countenance. He roused up and gave me good-day. I told him a friend of mine had commissioned me to make some inquiries about a cherished companion of his boyhood named *Leonidas W.* Smiley—*Rev. Leonidas W.* Smiley—a young minister of the Gospel, who he had heard was at one time a resident of Angel's Camp. I added that, if Mr. Wheeler could tell me anything about this Rev. Leonidas W. Smiley, I would feel under many obligations to him.

Simon Wheeler backed me into a corner and blockaded me there with his chair, and sat me down and reeled off the monotonous narrative which follows this paragraph. He never smiled, he never betrayed the slightest suspicion of enthusiasm; but all through the interminable narrative there ran a vein of impressive earnestness and sincerity, which showed me plainly that, so far from his imagining that there was anything ridiculous or funny about his story, he regarded it as a really important matter, and admired its two heroes as men of transcendent genius in *finesse*. To me, the spectacle of a man drifting serenely along through such a queer yarn without ever smiling, was exquisitely absurd. As I said before, I asked him to tell me what he knew of Rev. Leonidas W. Smiley, and he replied as follows. I let him go on in his own way, and never interrupted him once:

There was a feller here once by the name of *Jim* Smiley, in the winter of '49—or may be it was the spring of '50—I don't recollect exactly, somehow, though what makes me think it was one or the other is because I remember the big flume wasn't finished when he first came to the camp; but any way, he was the curiosest man about always betting on any thing that turned up you ever see, if he couldn't, he'd change sides. Any way that suited the other man would suit him—any way just so's he got a bet, *he* was satisfied. But still he was lucky, uncommon lucky; he most always come out winner. He was always ready and laying for a chance; there couldn't be no solitary thing mentioned but that feller'd offer to bet on it, and take any side you please, as I was telling you. If there was a horse-race, you'd find him flush, or you'd find him busted at the end of it; if there was a dog-fight, he'd bet on it; if there was a cat-fight, he'd bet on it; if there was a chicken-fight, he'd bet on it; why, if there was two birds setting on a fence, he would bet you which one would fly first; or if there was a camp-meeting, he would be there reg'lar, to bet on Parson Walker, which he judged to be the best exhorter about there, and so he was, too, and a good man. If he even seen a straddle-bug start to go anywheres, he would bet you how long it would take him to get wherever he was going to, and if you took him up, he would follow that straddle-bug to Mexico but what he would find out where he was bound for and how long he was on the road. Lots of the boys here has seen that Smiley, and can tell you about him. Why, it never made no difference to *him*—he would bet on *any* thing—the dangdest feller. Parson Walker's wife laid very sick once, for a good while, and it seemed as if they warn't going to save her; but one morning he come in, and Smiley asked how she was, and he said she was considerable better—thank the Lord for his inf'nit mercy—and coming on so smart that, with the blessing of Prov'dence, she'd get well yet; and Smiley, before he thought, says "Well, I'll risk two-and-a-half that she won't, any way."

Thish-yer Smiley had a mare—the boys called her fifteen-minute nag, but that was only in fun, you know, because, of course, she was faster than that—and he used to win money on that horse, for all she was so slow and always had the asthma, or the distemper, or the consumption, or something of that kind. They used to give her two or three hundred yards start, and then pass her under way; but always at the fag-end of the race she'd get excited and desperate-like, and come cavorting and straddling up, and scattering her legs around limber, sometimes in the air, and sometimes out to one side amongst the fences, and kicking up m-o-r-e dust, and raising m-o-r-e racket with her coughing and sneezing and blowing her nose—and always fetch up at the stand just about a neck ahead, as near as you could cypher it down.

And he had a little small bull pup, that to look at him you'd think he wa'n't worth a cent, but to set around and look ornery, and lay for a chance to steal something. But as soon as money was up on him, he was a different dog; his underjaw'd begin to stick out like the fo'castle of a steamboat, and his teeth would uncover, and shine savage like the furnaces. And a dog might tackle him, and bullyrag him, and bite him, and throw him over his shoulder two or three times, and Andrew Jackson—which was the name of the pup—Andrew Jackson would never let on but what *he* was satisfied, and hadn't expected nothing else—and the bets being doubled and doubled on the other side all the time, till the money was all up; and then all of a sudden he would grab that other dog just by the j'int of his hind leg and freeze it—not chaw, you understand, but only jest grip and hang on till they throwed up the sponge, if it was a year. Smiley always come out winner on that pup, till he harnessed a dog once that didn't have no hind legs, because they'd been sawed off by a circular saw, and when the thing had gone along far enough, and the money was all up, and he come to make a snatch for his pet holt, he saw in a minute how he'd been imposed on, and how the other dog had him in the door, so to speak, and he 'peared surprised, and then he looked sorter discouraged-like, and didn't try no more to win the fight, and so he got shucked out bad. He gave Smiley a look, as much as to say his heart was broke, and it was *his* fault, for putting up a dog that hadn't no hind legs for him to take holt of, which was his main dependence in a fight, and then he limped off a piece and laid down and died. It was a good pup, was that Andrew Jackson, and would have made a name for hisself if he'd lived, for the stuff was in him, and he a genius—I know it, because he hadn't had no opportunity to speak of, and it don't stand to reason that a dog could make such a fight as he could under them circumstances, if he hadn't no talent. It always makes me feel sorry when I think of that last fight of his'n, and the way it turned out.

Well, thish-yer Smiley had rat-terriers, and chicken cocks, and tom-cats, and them kind of things, till you couldn't rest, and you could't fetch nothing for him to bet on but

he'd match you. He ketched a frog one day, and took him home, and said he cal'klated to edercate him; and so he never done nothing for three months but set in his back yard and learn that frog to jump. And you bet he *did* learn him, too. He'd give him a little punch behind, and the next minute you'd see that frog whirling in the air like a doughnut—see him turn one summerset, or may be a couple, if he got a good start, and come down flat-footed and all right, like a cat. He got him up so in the matter of catching flies, and kept him in practice so constant, that he'd nail a fly every time as far as he could see him. Why, I've seen him set Dan'l Webster down here on this floor—Dan'l Webster was the name of the frog—and sing out, "Flies, Dan'l, flies!" and quicker'n you could wink, he'd spring straight up, and snake a fly off'n the counter there, and flop down on the floor again as solid as a gob of mud, and fall to scratching the side of his head with his hind foot as indifferent as if he hadn't no idea he'd been doin' any more'n any frog might do. You never see a frog so modest and straightfor'ard as he was, for all he was so gifted. And when it come to fair and square jumping on a dead level, he could get over more ground at one straddle than any animal of his breed you ever see. Jumping on a dead level was his strong suit, you understand; and when it come to that, Smiley would ante up money on him as long as he had a red. Smiley was monstrous proud of his frog, and well he might be, for fellers that had traveled and been everywheres, all said he laid over any frog that ever *they* see.

Well, Smiley kept the beast in a little lattice box, and he used to fetch him down town sometimes and lay for a bet. One day a feller —a stranger in the camp, he was—come across him with his box, and says:

'What might it be that you've got in the box?'

And Smiley says, sorter indifferent like, 'It might be a parrot, or it might be a canary, may be, but it ain't—it's only just a frog.'

And the feller took it, and looked at it careful, and turned it round this way and that, and says, 'H'm—so 't is. Well, what's *he* good for?'

'Well,' Smiley says, easy and careless, 'He's good enough for *one* thing, I should judge—he can outjump ary frog in Calaveras county.'

The feller took the box again, and took

THE AMERICAN LITERARY RECORD

another long, particular look, and give it back
to Smiley, and says, very deliberate, 'Well, I
don't see no p'ints about that frog that's any
better'n any other frog.'

'May be you don't,' Smiley says. 'May be you
understand frogs, and may be you don't understand 'em; may be you've had experience, and
may be you an't only a amature, as it were.
Anyways, I've got *my* opinion, and I'll risk
forty dollars he can outjump any frog in
Calaveras county.'

And the feller studied a minute, and then
says, kinder sad like, 'Well, I'm only a stranger
here, and I an't got no frog, but if I had a frog,
I'd bet you.'

And then Smiley says, 'That's all right—
that's all right—if you'll hold my box a minute,
I'll go and get you a frog.' And so the feller
took the box, and put up his forty dollars along
with Smiley's, and set down to wait.

So he set there a good while thinking and
thinking to hisself, and then he got the frog
out and prized his mouth open and took a
teaspoon and filled him full of quail shot
—filled him pretty near up to his chin—and
set him on the floor. Smiley he went to the
swamp and slopped around in the mud for
a long time, and finally he ketched a frog, and
fetched him in, and give him to this feller,
and says:

'Now, if you're ready, set him alongside of
Dan'l, with his fore-paws just even with Dan'l,
and I'll give the word.' Then he says, 'One
—two—three—jump!' and him and the feller
touched up the frogs from behind, and the
new frog hopped off, but Dan'l give a heave,
and hysted up his shoulders—so—like a
Frenchman, but it wa'n't no use—couldn't
budge; he was planted as solid as an anvil,
and he couldn't no more stir than if he was
anchored out. Smiley was a good deal surprised, and he was disgusted too, but he didn't

have no idea what the matter was, of course.

The feller took the money and started away;
and when he was going out of the door, he
sorter jerked his thumb over his shoulders—
this way—at Dan'l, and says again, very deliberate, 'Well, *I* don' see no p'ints about that
frog that's any better'n any other frog.'

Smiley he stood scratching his head and
looking down at Dan'l a long time, and at last
he says, 'I do wonder what in the nation that
frog throw'd off for—I wonder if there ain't
something the matter with him—he 'pears to
look mighty baggy, somehow.' And he ketched
Dan'l by the nap of the neck, and lifted him
up and says, 'Why, blame my cats, if he don't
weigh five pound!' and turned him upside
down, and he belched out a double handful
of shot. And then he see how it was, and he
was the maddest man—he set the frog down
and took out after that feller, but he never
ketched him. And—

[Here Simon Wheeler heard his name called
from the front yard, and got up to see what
was wanted.] And turning to me as he moved
away, he said: 'Just set where you are, stranger, and rest easy—I an't going to be gone a
second.'

But, by your leave, I did not think that a
continuation of the history of the enterprising
vagabond *Jim* Smiley would be likely to afford
me much information concerning the Rev.
Leonidas W. Smiley, and so I started away.

At the door I met the sociable Wheeler
returning, and he button-holed me and recommenced:

'Well, thish-yer Smiley had a yaller one-
eyed cow that didn't have no tail, only jest
a short stump like a bannanner, and—'

'Oh! hang Smiley and his afflicted cow!'
I muttered, good-naturedly, and bidding the
old gentleman good-day, I departed.
1865   1865

» » *From:* OLD TIMES ON THE MISSISSIPPI[2] « «

I

[AMBITION]

When I was a boy, there was but one perma-

[2] *Old Times on the Mississippi*, later called *Life on the Mississippi*,
was first printed in the *Atlantic Monthly* in six parts January-June,
1875). The present extracts are from the first two installments.

nent ambition among my comrades in our
village on the west bank of the Mississipi
River. That was, to be a steamboatman. We
had transient ambitions of other sorts, but they
were only transient. When a circus came and
went, it left us all burning to become clowns;

the first negro minstrel show that ever came to our section left us all suffering to try that kind of life; now and then we had a hope that, if we lived and were good, God would permit us to be pirates. These ambitions faded out, each in its turn; but the ambition to be a steamboat-man always remained.

Once a day a cheap, gaudy packet arrived upward from St. Louis, and another downward from Keokuk. Before these events, the day was glorious with expectancy; after they had transpired, the day was a dead and empty thing. Not only the boys, but the whole village, felt this. After all these years I can picture that old time to myself now, just as it was then: the white town drowsing in the sunshine of a summer's morning; the streets empty, or pretty nearly so; one or two clerks sitting in front of the Water Street stores, with their splint-bottomed chairs tilted back against the walls, chins on breasts, hats slouched over their faces, asleep—with shingle-shavings enough around to show what broke them down; a sow and a litter of pigs loafing along the sidewalk, doing a good business in watermelon rinds and seeds; two or three lonely little freight piles scattered about the "levee"; a pile of "skids" on the slope of the stone-paved wharf, and the fragrant town drunkard asleep in the shadow of them; two or three wood flats at the head of the wharf, but nobody to listen to the peaceful lapping of the wavelets against them; the great Mississippi, the majestic, the magnificent Mississippi, rolling its mile-wide tide along, shining in the sun; the dense forest away on the other side; the "point" above the town, and the "point" below, bounding the river-glimpse and turning it into a sort of sea, and withal a very still and brilliant and lonely one. Presently a film of dark smoke appears above one of those remote "points"; instantly a negro dray-man, famous for his quick eye and prodigious voice, lifts up the cry, "S-t-e-a-m-boat a-comin'!" and the scene changes! The town drunkard stirs, the clerks wake up, a furious clatter of drays follows, every house and store pours out a human contribution, and all in a twinkling the dead town is alive and moving. Drays, carts, men, boys, all go hurrying from many quarters to a common center, the wharf. Assembled there, the people fasten their eyes upon the coming boat as upon a wonder they are seeing for the first time. And the boat *is* rather a handsome sight, too. She is long and sharp and trim and pretty; she has two tall, fancy-topped chimneys, with a gilded device of some kind swung between them; a fanciful pilot-house, all glass and "gingerbread," perched on top of the "texas" deck behind them; the paddle-boxes are gorgeous with a picture or with gilded rays above the boat's name; the boiler-deck, the hurricane-deck, and the texas deck are fenced and ornamented with clean white railings; there is a flag gallantly flying from the jack-staff; the furnace doors are open and the fires glaring bravely; the upper decks are black with passengers; the captain stands by the big bell, calm, imposing, the envy of all; great volumes of the blackest smoke are rolling and tumbling out of the chimneys—a husbanded grandeur created with a bit of pitch-pine just before arriving at a town; the crew are grouped on the forecastle; the broad stage is run far out over the port bow, and an envied deck-hand stands picturesquely on the end of it with a coil of rope in his hand; the pent steam is screaming through the gauge-cocks; the captain lifts his hand, a bell rings, the wheels stop; then they turn back, churning the water to foam, and the steamer is at rest. Then such a scramble as there is to get aboard, and to get ashore, and to take in freight and to discharge freight, all at one and the same time; and such a yelling and cursing as the mates facilitate it all with! Ten minutes later the steamer is under way again, with no flag on the jack-staff and no black smoke issuing from the chimneys. After ten more minutes the town is dead again, and the town drunkard asleep by the skids once more.

My father was a justice of the peace, and I supposed he possessed the power of life and death over all men, and could hang anybody that offended him. This was distinction enough for me as a general thing; but the desire to be a steamboatman kept intruding, nevertheless. I first wanted to be a cabin-boy, so that I could come out with a white apron on and shake a table-cloth over the side, where all my old comrades could see me; later I thought I would rather be the deck-hand who stood on the end of the stage-plank with the coil of rope in his hand, because he was particularly conspicuous. But these were only day-dreams —they were too heavenly to be contemplated as real possibilities. By and by one of our boys went away. He was not heard of for a long time. At last he turned up as apprentice engineer or "striker" on a steamboat. This thing shook the bottom out of all my Sunday-school teachings. That boy had been notoriously worldly, and I just the reverse; yet he was exalted to this eminence, and I left in obscurity and misery. There was nothing generous about this fellow in his greatness. He would always manage to have a rusty bolt to scrub while his boat tarried at our town, and he would sit on the inside guard and scrub it, where we all could see him and envy him and loathe him. And whenever his boat was laid up he would come home and swell around the town in his blackest and greasiest clothes, so that nobody could help remembering that he was a steamboatman; and he used all sorts of steamboat technicalities in his talk, as if he were so used to them that he forgot common people could not understand them. He would speak of the "labboard" side of a horse in an easy, natural way that would make one wish he was dead. And he was always talking about "St. Looy" like an old citizen; he would refer casually to occasions when he was "coming down Fourth Street," or when he was "passing by the Planter's House," or when there was a fire and he took a turn on the brakes of "the old Big Missouri"; and then he would go on and lie about how many towns the size of ours were burned down there that day. Two or three of the boys had long been persons of consideration among us because they had been to St. Louis once and had a vague general knowledge of its wonders, but the day of their glory was over now. They lapsed into humble silence, and learned to disappear when the ruthless "cub"-engineer approached. This fellow had money, too, and hair oil. Also an ignorant silver watch and a shiny brass watch chain. He wore a leather belt and used no suspenders. If ever a youth was cordially admired and hated by his comrades, this one was. No girl could withstand his charms. He "cut out" every boy in the village. When his boat blew up at last, it diffused a tranquil contentment among us such as we had not known for months. But when he came home the next week, alive, renowned, and appeared in church all battered up and bandaged, a shining hero, stared at and wondered over by everybody, it seemed to us that the partiality of Providence for an undeserving reptile had reached a point where it was open to criticism.

. . .

[CUB PILOT]

What with lying on the rocks four days at Louisville, and some other delays, the poor old *Paul Jones* fooled away about two weeks in making the voyage from Cincinnati to New Orleans. This gave me a chance to get acquainted with one of the pilots, and he taught me how to steer the boat, and thus made the fascination of river life more potent than ever for me.

It also gave me a chance to get acquainted with a youth who had taken deck passage—more's the pity; for he easily borrowed six dollars of me on a promise to return to the boat and pay it back to me the day after we should arrive. But he probably died or forgot, for he never came. It was doubtless the former, since he had said his parents were wealthy, and he only traveled deck passage because it was cooler.[3]

I soon discovered two things. One was that a vessel would not be likely to sail for the mouth of the Amazon under ten or twelve years; and the other was that the nine or ten dollars still left in my pocket would not suffice for so impossible an exploration as I had planned, even if I could afford to wait for a ship. Therefore it followed that I must contrive a new career. The *Paul Jones* was now bound for St. Louis. I planned a siege against my pilot, and at the end or three hard days he surrendered. He agreed to teach me the Mississippi River from New Orleans to St. Louis for five hundred dollars, payable out of the first wages I should receive after graduating. I entered upon the small enterprise of "learning" twelve or thirteen hundred miles of the great Mississippi River with the easy confidence of my time of life. If I had really known what I was about to require of my faculties, I should not have had the courage to begin. I supposed that all a pilot had to do was to keep his boat in the river, and I did not consider that that could be much of a trick, since it was so wide.

The boat backed out from New Orleans at four in the afternoon, and it was "our watch" until eight. Mr. B[ixby], my chief, "straightened her up," plowed her along past the sterns of the other boats that lay at the Levee, and then said, "Here, take her; shave those steamships as close as you'd peel an apple." I took

[3] "Deck" passage—*i.e.* steerage passage. [Author's note.]

the wheel, and my heartbeat fluttered up into the hundreds; for it seemed to me that we were about to scrape the side off every ship in the line, we were so close. I held my breath and began to claw the boat away from the danger; and I had my own opinion of the pilot who had known no better than to get us into such peril, but I was too wise to express it. In half a minute I had a wide margin of safety intervening between the *Paul Jones* and the ships; and within ten seconds more I was set aside in disgrace, and Mr. B[ixby] was going into danger again and flaying me alive with abuse of my cowardice. I was stung, but I was obliged to admire the easy confidence with which my chief loafed from side to side of his wheel, and trimmed the ships so closely that disaster seemed ceaselessly imminent. When he had cooled a little he told me that the easy water was close ashore and the current outside, and therefore we must hug the bank, up-stream, to get the benefit of the former, and stay well out, down-stream, to take advantage of the latter. In my own mind I resolved to be a down-stream pilot and leave the up-streaming to people dead to prudence.

Now and then Mr. B[ixby] called my attention to certain things. Said he, "This is Six-Mile Point." I assented. It was pleasant enough information, but I could not see the bearing of it. I was not conscious that it was a matter of any interest to me. Another time he said, "This is Nine-Mile Point." Later he said, "This is Twelve-Mile Point." They were all about level with the water's edge; they all looked about alike to me; they were monotonously unpicturesque. I hoped Mr. B[ixby] would change the subject. But no; he would crowd up around a point, hugging the shore with affection, and then say: "The slack water ends here, abreast this bunch of China trees; now we cross over." So he crossed over. He gave me the wheel once or twice, but I had no luck. I either came near chipping off the edge of a sugar-plantation, or I yawed too far from shore, and so dropped back into disgrace again and got abused.

The watch was ended at last, and we took supper and went to bed. At midnight the glare of a lantern shone in my eyes, and the night watchman said:

"Come, turn out!"

And then he left. I could not understand this extraordinary procedure; so I presently gave up trying to, and dozed off to sleep. Pretty soon the watchman was back again, and

this time he was gruff. I was annoyed. I said:

"What do you want to come bothering around here in the middle of the night for? Now, as like as not, I'll not get to sleep again to-night."

The watchman said:

"Well, if this ain't good, I'm blessed."

The "off-watch" was just turning in, and I heard some brutal laughter from them, and such remarks as "Hello, watchman! ain't the new cub turned out yet? He's delicate, likely. Give him some sugar in a rag, and send for the chambermaid to sing 'Rock-a-by Baby,' to him."

About this time Mr. B[ixby] appeared on the scene. Something like a minute later I was climbing the pilot-house steps with some of my clothes on and the rest in my arms. Mr. B[ixby] was close behind, commenting. Here was something fresh—this thing of getting up in the middle of the night to go to work. It was a detail in piloting that had never occurred to me at all. I knew that boats ran all night, but somehow I had never happened to reflect that somebody had to get up out of a warm bed to run them. I began to fear that piloting was not quite so romantic as I had imagined it was; there was something very real and worklike about this new phase of it.

It was a rather dingy night, although a fair number of stars were out. The big mate was at the wheel, and he had the old tub pointed at a star and was holding her straight up the middle of the river. The shores on either hand were not much more than half a mile apart, but they seemed wonderfully far away and ever so vague and indistinct. The mate said:

"We've got to land at Jones's plantation, sir."

The vengeful spirit in me exulted. I said to myself, "I wish you joy of your job, Mr. B[ixby]; you'll have a good time finding Mr. Jones's plantation such a night as this; and I hope you never *will* find it as long as you live."

Mr. B[ixby] said to the mate:

"Upper end of the plantation, or the lower?"

"Upper."

"I can't do it. The stumps there are out of water at this stage. It's no great distance to the lower, and you'll have to get along with that."

"All right, sir. If Jones don't like it, he'll have to lump it, I reckon."

And then the mate left. My exultation began

to cool and my wonder to come up. Here was a man who not only proposed to find this plantation on such a night, but to find either end of it you preferred. I dreadfully wanted to ask a question, but I was carrying about as many short answers as my cargo-room would admit of, so I held my peace. All I desired to ask Mr. B[ixby] was the simple question whether he was ass enough to really imagine he was going to find that plantation on a night when all plantations were exactly alike and all of the same color. But I held in. I used to have fine inspirations of prudence in those days.

Mr. B[ixby] made for the shore and soon was scraping it, just the same as if it had been daylight. And not only that, but singing:

"Father in heaven, the day is declining," etc.

It seemed to me that I had put my life in the keeping of a peculiarly reckless outcast. Presently he turned on me and said:

"What's the name of the first point above New Orleans?"

I was gratified to be able to answer promptly, and I did. I said I didn't know.

"Don't *know?*"

This manner jolted me. I was down at the foot again, in a moment. But I had to say just what I had said before.

"Well, you're a smart one!" said Mr. B[ixby]. "What's the name of the *next* point?"

Once more I didn't know.

"Well, this beats anything. Tell me the name of *any* point or place I told you."

I studied awhile and decided that I couldn't.

"Look here! What do you start out from, above Twelve-Mile Point, to cross over?"

"I—I—don't know."

"You—you—don't know?" mimicking my drawling manner of speech. "What *do* you know?"

"I—I—nothing, for certain."

"By the great Cæsar's ghost, I believe you! You're the stupidest dunderhead I ever saw or ever heard of, so help me Moses! The idea of *you* being a pilot—*you!* Why, you don't know enough to pilot a cow down a lane."

Oh, but his wrath was up! He was a nervous man, and he shuffled from one side of his wheel to the other as if the floor was hot. He would boil awhile to himself, and then overflow and scald me again.

"Look here! What do you suppose I told you the names of those points for?"

I tremblingly considered a moment, and then the devil of temptation provoked me to say:

"Well to—to—be entertaining, I thought."

This was a red rag to the bull. He raged and stormed so (he was crossing the river at the time) that I judged it made him blind, because he ran over the steering-oar of a trading-scow. Of course the traders sent up a volley of red-hot profanity. Never was a man so grateful as Mr. B[ixby] was; because he was brimful, and here were subjects who could *talk back.* He threw open a window, thrust his head out, and such an irruption followed as I never had heard before. The fainter and farther away the scowmen's curses drifted, the higher Mr. B[ixby] lifted his voice and the weightier his adjectives grew. When he closed the window he was empty. You could have drawn a seine through his system and not caught curses enough to disturb your mother with. Presently he said to me in the gentlest way:

"My boy, you must get a little memorandum-book; and every time I tell you a thing, put it down right away. There's only one way to be a pilot, and that is to get this entire river by heart. You have to know it just like A B C."

That was a dismal revelation to me; for my memory was never loaded with anything but blank cartridges. However, I did not feel discouraged long. I judged that it was best to make some allowance, for doubtless Mr. Bixby was "stretching." Presently he pulled a rope and struck a few strokes on the big bell. The stars were all gone now, and the night was as black as ink. I could hear the wheels churn along the bank, but I was not entirely certain that I could see the shore. The voice of the invisible watchman called up from the hurricane-deck:

"What's this, sir?"

"Jones's plantation."

I said to myself, "I wish I might venture to offer a small bet that it isn't." But I did not chirp. I only waited to see. Mr. B[ixby] handled the engine-bells, and in due time the boat's nose came to the land, a torch glowed from the forecastle, a man skipped ashore, a darkey's voice on the bank said: "Gimme de k'yarpet-bag, Mass' Jones," and the next moment we were standing up the river again, all serene. I reflected deeply awhile, and then said—but not aloud—"Well, the finding of that plantation was the luckiest accident that ever happened; but it couldn't happen again in a hundred years." And I fully believed it *was* an accident, too.

By the time we had gone seven or eight hundred miles up the river, I had learned to be a tolerably plucky up-stream steersman, in daylight; and before we reached St. Louis I had made a trifle of progress in night work, but only a trifle. I had a note-book that fairly bristled with the names of towns, "points," bars, islands, bends, reaches, etc.; but the information was to be found only in the note-book—none of it was in my head. It made my heart ache to think I had only got half of the river set down; for as our watch was four hours off and four hours on, day and night, there was a long four-hour gap in my book for every time I had slept since the voyage began.

My chief was presently hired to go on a big New Orleans boat, and I packed my satchel and went with him. She was a grand affair. When I stood in her pilot-house I was so far above the water that I seemed perched on a mountain; and her decks stretched so far away, fore and aft, below me, that I wondered how I could ever have considered the little *Paul Jones* a large craft. There were other differences, too. The *Paul Jones's* pilot-house was a cheap, dingy, battered rattle trap, cramped for room; but here was a sumptuous glass temple; room enough to have a dance in; showy red and gold window-curtains; an imposing sofa; leather cushions and a back to the high bench where visiting pilots sit, to spin yarns and "look at the river"; bright, fanciful "cuspi-

dores," instead of a broad wooden box filled with sawdust; nice new oilcloth on the floor; a hospitable big stove for winter; a wheel as high as my head, costly with inlaid work; a wire tiller-rope; bright brass knobs for the bells; and a tidy, white-aproned, black "texas-tender," to bring up tarts and ices and coffee during mid-watch, day and night. Now this was "something like"; and so I began to take heart once more to believe that piloting was a romantic sort of occupation after all. The moment we were under way I began to prowl about the great steamer and fill myself with joy. She was as clean and as dainty as a drawing-room; when I looked down her long, gilded saloon, it was like gazing through a splendid tunnel; she had an oil-picture, by some gifted sign-painter, on every stateroom door; she glittered with no end of prism-fringed chandeliers; the clerk's office was elegant, the bar was marvelous, and the barkeeper had been barbered and upholstered at incredible cost. The boiler-deck (*i.e.*, the second story of the boat, so to speak) was as spacious as a church, it seemed to me; so with the forecastle; and there was no pitiful handful of deck-hands, firemen, and roustabouts down there, but a whole battalion of men. The fires were fiercely glaring from a long row of furnaces, and over them were eight huge boilers! This was unutterable pomp. The mighty engines—but enough of this. I had never felt so fine before. And when I found that the regiment of natty servants respectfully "sir'd" me, my satisfaction was complete.
1874   1875

» » THE WHITTIER DINNER SPEECH⁴ « «
ADDRESS OF SAMUEL L. CLEMENS (MARK TWAIN)

MR. CHAIRMAN,—This is an occasion peculiarly meet for the digging up of pleasant reminiscences concerning literary folk, therefore I will drop lightly into history myself. Standing here on the shore of the Atlantic, and contemplating certain of its largest literary billows, I am reminded of a thing which happened to me thirteen years ago, when I had just succeeded in stirring up a little Nevadian

⁴ From a report of the dinner given by the publishers of the *Atlantic Monthly* in honor of the Seventieth Anniversary of the Birth of John Greenleaf Whittier, at the Hotel Brunswick, Boston, December 17, 1877, as published in the Boston *Evening Transcript*, December 18, 1877.

literary puddle myself, whose spume-flakes were beginning to blow thinly Californiaward. I started an inspection tramp through the southern mines of California. I was callow and conceited, and I resolved to try the virtue of my NOM DE GUERRE. I very soon had an opportunity. I knocked at a miner's lonely log cabin in the foothills of the Sierras just at nightfall. It was snowing at the time. A jaded, melancholy man of fifty, barefooted, opened the door to me. When he heard my NOM DE GUERRE he looked more dejected than before.

He let me in—pretty reluctantly, I thought—and after the customary bacon and beans, black coffee and hot whisky, I took a pipe. This sorrowful man had not said three words up to this time. Now he spoke up, and said, in the voice of one who is secretly suffering, "You're the fourth—I'm going to move." "The fourth what?" said I. "The fourth littery man that has been here in twenty-four hours—I'm going to move." "You don't tell me!" said I; "who were the others?" "Mr. Longfellow, Mr. Emerson, and Mr. Oliver Wendell Holmes—confound the lot!"

You can easily believe I was interested. I supplicated—three hot whiskies did the rest—and finally the melancholy miner began. Said he:

"They came here just at dark yesterday evening, and I let them in, of course. Said they were going to the Yosemite. They were a rough lot, but that's nothing; everybody looks rough that travels afoot. Mr. Emerson was a seedy little bit of a chap, red-headed. Mr. Holmes was as fat as a balloon; he weighed as much as three hundred, and had double chins all the way down to his stomach. Mr. Longfellow was built like a prize-fighter. His head was cropped and bristly, like as if he had a wig made of hairbrushes. His nose lay straight down in his face, like a finger with the end joint tilted up. They had been drinking, I could see that. And what queer talk they used! Mr. Holmes inspected this cabin, then he took me by the button-hole and says he:

" 'Through the deep caves of thought
I hear a voice that sings,
'Build thee more stately mansions,
O my soul!' "

"Says I, 'I can't afford it, Mr. Holmes, and moreover I don't want to.' Blamed if I liked it pretty well, either, coming from a stranger that way. However, I started to get out my bacon and beans when Mr. Emerson came and looked on awhile, and then HE takes me aside by the buttonhole and says:

"Give me agates for my meat;
Give me cantharids to eat;
From air and ocean bring me foods,
From all zones and altitudes."

"Says I, 'Mr. Emerson, if you'll excuse me, this ain't no hotel.' You see, it sort of riled me—I warn't used to the ways of littery swells. But I went on a-sweating over my work, and

next comes Mr. Longfellow and buttonholes me and interrupts me. Says he:

" 'Honor be to Mudjekeewis!
You shall hear how Pau-Puk-Keewis—'

"But I broke in, and says I, 'Beg your pardon, Mr. Longfellow, if you'll be so kind as to hold your yawp for about five minutes and let me get this grub ready, you'll do me proud.' Well, sir, after they'd filled up I set out the jug. Mr. Holmes looks at it and then he fires up all of a sudden and yells:

" 'Flash out a stream of blood-red wine!
For I would drink to other days.'

"By George, I was getting kind of worked up. I don't deny it, I was getting kind of worked up. I turns to Mr. Holmes and says I, 'Looky here, my fat friend, I'm a-running this shanty, and if the court knows herself you'll take whisky straight or you'll go dry.' Them's the very words I said to him. Now I don't want to sass such famous littery people, but you see they kind of forced me. There ain't nothing onreasonable 'bout me. I don't mind a passel of guests a-treadin' on my tail three or four times, but when it comes to STANDING on it it's different, 'and if the court knows herself,' I says, 'you'll take whisky straight or you'll go dry.' Well, between drinks they'd swell around the cabin and strike attitudes and spout; and pretty soon they got out a greasy old deck and went to playing euchre at ten cents a corner—on trust. I began to notice some pretty suspicious things. Mr. Emerson dealt, looked at his hand, shook his head, says—

" 'I am the doubter and the doubt—'

and calmly bunched the hands and went to shuffling for a new lay-out. Says he:

" 'They reckon ill who leave me out;
They know not well the subtle ways I keep.
I pass and deal AGAIN!'

Hang'd if he didn't go ahead and do it, too! Oh, he was a cool one! Well, in about a minute things were running pretty tight, but all of a sudden I see by Mr. Emerson's eye he judged he had 'em. He had already corralled two tricks and each of the others one. So now he kind of lifts a little in his chair and says,

" 'I tire of globes and aces!—
Too long the game is played!'

and down he fetched a right bower. Mr. Long-fellow smiles as sweet as pie and says,

" 'Thanks, thanks to thee, my worthy friend,
    For the lesson thou hast taught,'

and blamed if he didn't down with ANOTHER right bower! Emerson claps his hand on his bowie, Longfellow claps his on his revolver, and I went under a bunk. There was going to be trouble; but that monstrous Holmes rose up, wobbling his double chins, and says he, 'Order, gentlemen; the first man that draws I'll lay down on him and smother him!' All quiet on the Potomac, you bet!

"They were pretty how-come-you-so by now, and they begun to blow. Emerson says, 'The noblest thing I ever wrote was "Barbara Frietchie." ' Says Longfellow, 'It don't begin with my "Bigelow Papers." ' Says Holmes, 'My "Thanatopsis" lays over 'em both.' They mighty near ended in a fight. Then they wished they had some more company, and Mr. Emerson pointed to me and says:

" 'Is yonder squalid peasant all
    That this proud nursery could breed?'

He was a-whetting his bowie on his boot—so I let it pass. Well, sir, next they took it into their heads that they would like some music; so they made me stand up and sing, 'When Johnny Comes Marching Home' till I dropped —at thirteen minutes past four this morning.

That's what I've been through, my friend. When I woke at seven they were leaving, thank goodness, and Mr. Longfellow had my only boots on and his'n under his arm. Says I, 'Hold on there, Evangeline, what are you going to do with THEM?' He says, 'Going to make tracks with 'em, because—

"Lives of great men all remind us
    We can make our lives sublime;
And, departing, leave behind us   10
    Footprints on the sands of time.'

As I said, Mr. Twain, you are the fourth in twenty-four hours—and I'm going to move; I ain't suited to a littery atmosphere."

I said to the miner, "Why, my dear sir, THESE were not the gracious singers to whom we and the world pay loving reverence and homage; these were impostors."

The miner investigated me with a calm eye   20 for a while; then said he, "Ah! impostors, were they? Are you?"

I did not pursue the subject, and since then I have not traveled on my NOM DE GUERRE enough to hurt. Such was the reminiscence I was moved to contribute, Mr. Chairman. In my enthusiasm I may have exaggerated the details a little, but you will easily forgive me that fault, since I believe it is the first time I have ever deflected from perpendicular fact on   30 an occasion like this.

1877   1877

» » THE MAN THAT CORRUPTED HADLEYBURG « «

I

It was many years ago. Hadleyburg was the most honest and upright town in all the region around about. It had kept that reputation unsmirched during three generations, and was prouder of it than of any other of its possessions. It was so proud of it, and so anxious to insure its perpetuation, that it began to teach the principles of honest dealing to its babies in the cradle, and made the like teachings the staple of their culture thenceforward through all the years devoted to their education. Also, throughout the formative years temptations were kept out of the way of the young people, so that their honesty could have every chance to harden and solidify, and become a part of their very bone. The neighboring towns were

jealous of this honorable supremacy, and affected to sneer at Hadleyburg's pride in it and call it vanity; but all the same they were   40 obliged to acknowledge that Hadleyburg was in reality an incorruptible town; and if pressed they would also acknowledge that the mere fact that a young man hailed from Hadleyburg was all the recommendation he needed when he went forth from his natal town to seek for responsible employment.

But at last, in the drift of time, Hadleyburg had the ill luck to offend a passing stranger—possibly without knowing it, certainly without   50 caring, for Hadleyburg was sufficient unto itself, and cared not a rap for strangers or their opinions. Still, it would have been well to make an exception in this one's case, for he was a bitter man and revengeful. All through his wanderings during a whole year he kept his injury in mind, and gave all his leisure moments to trying to invent a compensating satisfaction for it. He contrived many plans, and all of them were good, but none of them was quite sweeping enough; the poorest of them would hurt a great many individuals, but what he wanted was a plan which would comprehend the entire town, and not let so much as one person escape unhurt. At last he had a fortunate idea, and when it fell into his brain it lit up his whole head with an evil joy. He began to form a plan at once, saying to himself, "That is the thing to do—I will corrupt the town."

Six months later he went to Hadleyburg, and arrived in a buggy at the house of the old cashier of the bank about ten at night. He got a sack out of the buggy, shouldered it, and staggered with it through the cottage yard, and knocked at the door. A woman's voice said "Come in," and he entered, and set his sack behind the stove in the parlor, saying politely to the old lady who sat reading the Missionary Herald by the lamp:

"Pray keep your seat, madam, I will not disturb you. There—now it is pretty well concealed; one would hardly know it was there. Can I see your husband a moment, madam?"

No, he was gone to Brixton, and might not return before morning.

"Very well, madam, it is no matter. I merely wanted to leave that sack in his care, to be delivered to the rightful owner when he shall be found. I am a stranger; he does not know me; I am merely passing through the town to-night to discharge a matter which has been long in my mind. My errand is now completed, and I go pleased and a little proud, and you will never see me again. There is a paper attached to the sack which will explain everything. Good night, madam."

The old lady was afraid of the mysterious big stranger, and was glad to see him go. But her curiosity was roused, and she went straight to the sack and brought away the paper. It began as follows:

TO BE PUBLISHED; or, the right man sought out by private inquiry—either will answer. This sack contains gold coin weighing a hundred and sixty pounds four ounces—

"Mercy on us, and the door not locked!"

Mrs. Richards flew to it all in a tremble and locked it, then pulled down the window-shades and stood frightened, worried, and wondering if there was anything else she could do toward making herself and the money more safe. She listened awhile for burglars, then surrendered to curiosity and went back to the lamp and finished reading the paper:

I am a foreigner, and am presently going back to my own country, to remain there permanently. I am grateful to America for what I have received at her hands during my long stay under her flag; and to one of her citizens—a citizen of Hadleyburg—I am especially grateful for a great kindness done me a year or two ago. Two great kindnesses, in fact. I will explain. I was a gambler. I say I was. I was a ruined gambler. I arrived in this village at night, hungry and without a penny. I asked for help—in the dark; I was ashamed to beg in the light. I begged of the right man. He gave twenty dollars—that is to say, he gave me life, as I considered it. He also gave me fortune; for out of that money I have made myself rich at the gaming-table. And finally, a remark which he made to me has remained with me to this day, and has at last conquered me; and in conquering has saved the remnant of my morals; I shall gamble no more. Now I have no idea who that man was, but I want him found, and I want him to have this money, to give away, throw away, or keep, as he pleases. It is merely my way of testifying my gratitude to him. If I could stay, I would find him myself; but no matter, he will be found. This is an honest town, an incorruptible town, and I know I can trust it without fear. This man can be identified by the remark which he made to me; I feel persuaded that he will remember it.

And now my plan is this: If you prefer to conduct the inquiry privately, do so. Tell the contents of this present writing to any one who is likely to be the right man. If he shall answer, 'I am the man; the remark I made was so-and-so' apply the test—to wit; open the sack, and in it you will find a sealed envelope containing that remark. If the remark mentioned by the candidate tallies with it, give him the money, and ask no further questions, for he is certainly the right man.

But if you shall prefer a public inquiry, then publish this present writing in the local paper—with these instructions added, to wit: Thirty days from now, let the candidate appear at the town-hall at eight in the evening (Friday), and hand his remark, in a sealed envelope, to the Rev. Mr. Burgess (if he will be kind enough to act); and let Mr. Burgess there and then destroy the seals of the sack, open it, and see if the remark is correct; if correct, let the money be delivered, with my sincere gratitude, to my benefactor thus identified.

Mrs. Richards sat down, gently quivering with excitement, and was soon lost in thinkings

—after this pattern; "What a strange thing it is! . . . And what a fortune for that kind man who set his bread afloat upon the waters! . . . If it had only been my husband that did it!—for we are so poor, so old and poor! . . ." Then, with a sigh—"But it was not my Edward; no, it was not he that gave a stranger twenty dollars. It is a pity, too; I see it now. . . ." Then, with a shudder—"But it is gambler's money! The wages of sin; we couldn't take it; we couldn't touch it. I don't like to be near it; it seems a defilement." She moved to a farther chair. . . . "I wish Edward would come and take it to the bank; a burglar might come at any moment; it is dreadful to be here all alone with it."

At eleven Mr. Richards arrived, and while his wife was saying, "I am so glad you've come!" he was saying, "I'm so tired—tired clear out; it is dreadful to be poor, and have to make these dismal journeys at my time of life. Always at the grind, grind, grind, on a salary—another man's slave, and he sitting at home in his slippers, rich and comfortable."

"I am so sorry for you, Edward, you know that; but be comforted; we have our livelihood; we have our good name—"

"Yes, Mary, and that is everything. Don't mind my talk—it's just a moment's irritation and doesn't mean anything. Kiss me—there, it's all gone now, and I am not complaining any more. What have you been getting? What's in the sack?"

Then his wife told him the great secret. It dazed him for a moment; then he said:

"It weighs a hundred and sixty pounds? Why, Mary, it's for-ty thou-sand dollars—think of it—a whole fortune! Not ten men in this village are worth that much. Give me the paper."

He skimmed through it and said:

"Isn't it an adventure! Why, it's a romance; it's like the impossible things one reads about in books, and never sees in life." He was well stirred up now; cheerful, even gleeful. He tapped his old wife on the cheek, and said, humorously, "Why, we're rich, Mary, rich; all we've got to do is bury the money and burn the papers. If the gambler ever comes to inquire, we'll merely look coldly upon him and say: 'What is this nonsense you are talking? We have never heard of you and your sack of gold before'; and then he would look foolish, and—"

"And in the mean time, while you are running on with your jokes, the money is still here, and it is fast getting along toward burglar-time."

"True. Very well, what shall we do—make the inquiry private? No, not that: it would spoil the romance. The public method is better. Think what a noise it will make! And it will make all the other towns jealous; for no stranger would trust such a thing to any town but Hadleyburg, and they know it. It's a great card for us. I must get to the printing-office now, or I shall be too late."

"But stop—stop—don't leave me here alone with it, Edward!"

But he was gone. For only a little while, however. Not far from his own house he met the editor-proprietor of the paper, and gave him the document, and said, "Here is a good thing for you, Cox—put it in."

"It may be too late, Mr. Richards, but I'll see."

At home again he and his wife sat down to talk the charming mystery over; they were in no condition for sleep. The first question was, who could the citizen have been who gave the stranger the twenty dollars? It seemed a simple one; both answered it in the same breath:

"Barclay Goodson."

"Yes," said Richards, "he could have done it, and it would have been like him, but there's not another in the town."

"Everybody will grant that, Edward—grant it privately, anyway. For six months, now, the village has been its own proper self once more—honest, narrow, self-righteous, and stingy."

"It is what he always called it, to the day of his death—said it right out publicly, too."

"Yes, and he was hated for it."

"Oh, of course; but he didn't care. I reckon he was the best-hated man among us, except the Reverend Burgess."

"Well, Burgess deserves it—he will never get another congregation here. Mean as the town is, it knows how to estimate him. Edward, doesn't it seem odd that the stranger should appoint Burgess to deliver the money?"

"Well, yes—it does. That is—that is—"

"Why so much that-is-ing? Would you select him?"

"Mary, maybe the stranger knows him better than this village does."

"Much that would help Burgess!"

The husband seemed perplexed for an answer; the wife kept a steady eye upon him, and waited. Finally Richards said, with the hesitancy of one who is making a statement which is likely to encounter doubt:

"Mary, Burgess is not a bad man."

His wife was certainly surprised.

"Nonsense!" she exclaimed.

"He is not a bad man. I know. The whole of his unpopularity had its foundation in that one thing—the thing that made so much noise."

"That 'one thing,' indeed! As if that 'one thing' wasn't enough, all by itself."

"Plenty. Plenty. Only he wasn't guilty of it."

"How you talk! Not guilty of it! Everybody knows he was guilty."

"Mary, I give you my word—he was innocent."

"I can't believe it, and I don't. How do you know?"

"It is a confession. I am ashamed, but I will make it. I was the only man who knew he was innocent. I could have saved him, and—and—well, you know how the town was wrought up—I hadn't the pluck to do it. It would have turned everybody against me. I felt mean, ever so mean; but I didn't dare; I hadn't the manliness to face that."

Mary looked troubled, and for a while was silent. Then she said, stammeringly:

"I—I don't think it would have done for you to—to—One mustn't—er—public opinion—one has to be so careful—so—" It was a difficult road, and she got mired, but after a little she got started again. "It was a great pity, but—Why, we couldn't afford it, Edward—we couldn't indeed. Oh, I wouldn't have had you do it for anything!"

"It would have lost us the good will of so many people, Mary; and then—and then—"

"What troubles me now is, what he thinks of us, Edward."

"He? He doesn't suspect that I could have saved him."

"Oh," exclaimed the wife, in a tone of relief, "I am glad of that! As long as he doesn't know that you could have saved him, he—he—well, that makes it a great deal better. Why, I might have known he didn't know, because he is always trying to be friendly with us, as little encouragement as we give him. More than once people had twitted me with it. There's the Wilsons, and the Wilcoxes, and the Harknesses, they take a mean pleasure in saying, 'your friend Burgess,' because they know it pesters me. I wish he wouldn't persist in liking us so; I can't think why he keeps it up."

"I can explain it. It's another confession.

When the thing was new and hot, and the town made a plan to ride him on a rail, my conscience hurt me so that I couldn't stand it, and I went privately and gave him notice, and he got out of the town and staid out till it was safe to come back."

"Edward! If the town had found it out—"

"Don't! It scares me yet, to think of it. I repented of it the minute it was done; and I was even afraid to tell you, lest your face might betray it to somebody. I didn't sleep any that night, for worrying. But after a few days I saw that no one was going to suspect me, and after that I got to feeling glad I did it. And I feel glad yet, Mary—glad through and through."

"So do I, now, for it would have been a dreadful way to treat him. Yes, I'm glad; for really you did owe him that, you know. But, Edward, suppose it should come out yet, some day!"

"It won't."

"Why?"

"Because everybody thinks it was Goodson."

"Of course they would!"

"Certainly. And of course he didn't care. They persuaded poor old Sawlsberry to go and charge it on him, and he went blustering over there and did it. Goodson looked him over, like as if he was hunting for a place on him that he could despise the most, then he says, 'So you are the Committee of Inquiry, are you?' Sawlsberry said that was about what he was. 'Hm. So they require particulars, or do you reckon a kind of a general answer will do?' 'If they require particulars, I will come back, Mr. Goodson; I will take the general answer first.'

"Very well, then, tell them to go to hell—I reckon that's general enough. And I'll give you some advice, Sawlsberry; when you come back for the particulars, fetch a basket to carry the relics of yourself home in.'"

"Just like Goodson; it's got all the marks. He had only one vanity: he thought he could give advice better than any other person."

"It settled the business, and saved us, Mary. The subject was dropped."

"Bless you, I'm not doubting that."

Then they took up the gold-sack mystery again, with strong interest. Soon the conversation began to suffer breaks—interruptions caused by absorbed thinkings. The breaks grew more and more frequent. At last Richards lost himself wholly in thought. He sat long, gazing vacantly at the floor, and by and by he began to punctuate his thoughts with little nervous movements of his hands that seemed to indicate vexation. Meantime his wife too had relapsed into a thoughtful silence, and her movements were beginning to show a troubled discomfort. Finally Richards got up and strode aimlessly about the room, plowing his hands through his hair, much as a somnambulist might do who was having a bad dream. Then he seemed to arrive at a definite purpose; and without a word he put on his hat and passed quickly out of the house. His wife sat brooding, with a drawn face, and did not seem to be aware that she was alone. Now and then she murmured, "Lead us not into t— . . . but— but—we are so poor, so poor! . . . Lead us not into . . . Ah, who would be hurt by it?— and no one would ever know. . . . Lead us . . ." The voice died out in mumblings. After a little she glanced up and muttered in a half-frightened, half-glad way:

"He is gone! But, oh dear, he may be too late—too late . . . Maybe not—maybe there is still time." She rose and stood thinking, nervously clasping and unclasping her hands. A slight shudder shook her frame, and she said, out of a dry throat, "God forgive me— It's awful to think such things—but . . . Lord, how we are made—how strangely we are made!"

She turned the light low, and slipped stealthily over and kneeled down by the sack and felt of its ridgy sides with her hands, and fondled them lovingly; and there was a gloating light in her poor old eyes. She fell into fits of absence; and came half out of them at times to mutter, "If we had only waited!—oh, if we had only waited a little, and not been in such a hurry!"

Meantime Cox had gone home from his office and told his wife all about the strange thing that had happened, and they had talked it over eagerly, and guessed that the late Goodson was the only man in the town who could have helped a suffering stranger with so noble a sum as twenty dollars. Then there was a pause, and the two became thoughtful and silent. And by and by nervous and fidgety. At last the wife said, as if to herself:

"Nobody knows this secret but the Richardses . . . and us . . . nobody."

The husband came out of his thinkings with a slight start, and gazed wistfully at his wife, whose face was become very pale; then he hesitatingly rose, and glanced furtively at his hat, then at his wife—a sort of mute inquiry.

Mrs Cox swallowed once or twice, with her hand at her throat, then in place of speech she nodded her head. In a moment she was alone, and mumbling to herself.

And now Richards and Cox were hurrying through the deserted streets, from opposite directions. They met, panting, at the foot of the printing-office stairs; by the night light there they read each other's face. Cox whispered:

"Nobody knows about this but us?"

The whispered answer was,

"Not a soul—on honor, not a soul!"

"If it isn't too late to—"

The men were starting up-stairs; at this moment they were overtaken by a boy, and Cox asked:

"Is that you, Johnny?"

"Yes, sir."

"You needn't ship the early mail—nor any mail; wait till I tell you."

"It's already gone, sir."

"Gone?" It had the sound of an unspeakable disappointment in it.

"Yes sir. Time-table for Brixton and all the towns beyond changed to-day, sir—had to get the papers in twenty minutes earlier than common. I had to rush; if I had been two minutes later—"

The men turned and walked slowly away, not waiting to hear the rest. Neither of them spoke during ten minutes; then Cox said, in a vexed tone:

"What possessed you to be in such a hurry, I can't make out."

The answer was humble enough:

"I see it now, but somehow I never thought, you know, until it was too late. But the next time—"

"Next time be hanged! It won't come in a thousand years."

Then the friends separated without a good night, and dragged themselves home with the gait of mortally stricken men. At their homes their wives sprang up with an eager "Well?" —then saw the answer with their eyes and sank down sorrowing, without waiting for it to come in words. In both houses a discussion followed of a heated sort—a new thing; there had been discussions before, but not heated ones, not ungentle ones. The discussions to-night were a sort of seeming plagiarisms of each other. Mrs. Richards said,

"If you had only waited, Edward—if you had only stopped to think; but no, you must run straight to the printing-office and spread it all over the world.'"

"It said publish it."

"That is nothing; it also said do it privately, if you liked. There, now—is that true, or not?"

"Why, yes—yes, it is true; but when I thought what a stir it would make, and what a compliment it was to Hadleyburg that a stranger should trust it so—"

10 "Oh, certainly, I know all that; but if you had only stopped to think, you would have seen that you couldn't find the right man, because he is in his grave, and hasn't left chick nor child nor relation behind him; and as long as the money went to somebody that awfully needed it, and nobody would be hurt by it, and—and—"

She broke down, crying. Her husband tried to think of some comforting thing to say, and 20 presently came out with this:

"But after all, Mary, it must be for the best —it must be; we know that. And we must remember that it was so ordered—"

"Ordered! Oh, everythin's ordered, when a person has to find some way out when he has been stupid. Just the same, it was ordered that the money should come to us in this special way, and it was you that must take it on yourself to go meddling with the designs of Provi-30 dence—and who gave you the right? It was wicked, that is what it was—just blasphemous presumption, and no more becoming to a meek and humble professor of—"

"But, Mary, you know how we have been trained all our lives long, like the whole village, till it is absolutely second nature to us to stop not a single moment to think when there's an honest thing to be done—"

"Oh, I know it, I know it—it's been one 40 everlasting training and training and training in honesty—honesty shielded, from the very cradle, against every possible temptation, and so it's artificial honesty, and weak as water when temptation comes, as we have seen this night. God knows I never had shade nor shadow of a doubt of my petrified and indestructible honesty until now—and now, under the very first big and real temptation, I— Edward, it is my belief that this town's honesty 50 is as rotten as mine is; as rotten as yours is. It is a mean town, a hard, stingy town, and hasn't a virtue in the world but this honesty it is so celebrated for and so conceited about; and so help me, I do believe that if ever the day comes that its honesty falls under great temp-

tation, its grand reputation will go to ruin like a house of cards. There, now I've made confession, and I feel better; I am a humbug, and I've been one all my life, without knowing it. Let no man call me honest again—I will not have it."

"I—well, Mary, I feel a good deal as you do; I certainly do. It seems strange, too, so strange. I never could have believed it—never."

A long silence followed; both were sunk in thought. At last the wife looked up and said:

"I know what you are thinking, Edward."

Richards had the embarrassed look of a person who is caught.

"I am ashamed to confess it, Mary, but—"

"It's no matter, Edward, I was thinking the same question myself."

"I hope so. State it."

"You were thinking, if a body could only guess out what the remark was that Goodson made to the stranger."

"It's perfectly true. I feel guilty and ashamed. And you?"

"I'm past it. Let us make a pallet here; we've got to stand watch till the bank vault opens in the morning and admits the sack. . . . Oh dear—if we hadn't made the mistake!"

The pallet was made, and Mary said:

"The open sesame—what could it have been? I do wonder what that remark could have been? But come; we will get to bed now."

"And sleep?"

"No: think."

"Yes, think."

By this time the Coxes too had completed their spat and their reconciliation, and were turning in—to think, to think, and toss, and fret, and worry over what the remark could possibly have been which Goodson made to the stranded derelict; that golden remark; that remark worth forty thousand dollars, cash.

The reason that the village telegraph-office was open later than usual that night was this: The foreman of Cox's paper was the local representative of the Associated Press. One might say its honorary representative, for it wasn't four times a year that he could furnish thirty words that would be accepted. But this time it was different. His despatch stating what he had caught got an instant answer:

Send the whole thing—all the details— twelve hundred words.

A colossal order! The foreman filled the bill; and he was the proudest man in the State. By breakfast-time the next morning the name of

Hadleyburg the Incorruptible was on every lip in America, from Montreal to the Gulf, from the glaciers of Alaska to the orange-groves of Florida; and millions and millions of people were discussing the stranger and his money-sack, and wondering if the right man would be found, and hoping some more news about the matter would come soon—right away.

II

Hadleyburg village woke up world-celebrated—astonished—happy—vain. Vain beyond imagination. Its nineteen principal citizens and their wives went about shaking hands with each other, and beaming, and smiling, and congratulating, and saying this thing adds a new word to the dictionary—Hadleyburg, synonym for incorruptible—destined to live in dictionaries forever! And the minor and unimportant citizens and their wives went around acting in much the same way. Everybody ran to the bank to see the gold-sack; and before noon grieved and envious crowds began to flock in from Brixton and all neighboring towns; and that afternoon and next day reporters began to arrive from everywhere to verify the sack and history and write the whole thing up anew, and make dashing free-hand pictures of the sack, and of Richards's house, and the bank, and the Presbyterian church, and the Baptist church, and the public square, and the town-hall where the test would be applied and the money delivered; and damnable portraits of the Richardses, and Pinkerton the banker, and Cox, and the foreman, and Reverend Burgess, and the post-master—and even of Jack Halliday, who was the loafing, good-natured, no-account, irreverent fisherman, hunter, boys' friend, stray-dogs' friend, typical "Sam Lawson" of the town. The little mean, smirking, oily Pinkerton showed the sack to all comers, and rubbed his sleek palms together pleasantly, and enlarged upon the town's fine old reputation for honesty and upon this wonderful indorsement of it, and hoped and believed that the example would now spread far and wide over the American world, and be epoch-making in the matter of moral regeneration. And so on, and so on.

By the end of a week things had quieted down again; the wild intoxication of pride and joy had sobered to a soft, sweet, silent delight—a sort of deep, nameless, unutterable content. All faces bore a look of peaceful, holy happiness.

Then a change came. It was a gradual change: so gradual that its beginnings were hardly noticed; maybe were not noticed at all, except by Jack Halliday, who always noticed everything; and always made fun of it, too, no matter what it was. He began to throw out chaffing remarks about people not looking quite so happy as they did a day or two ago; and next he claimed that the new aspect was deepening to positive sadness; next, that it was taking on a sick look; and finally he said that everybody was become so moody, thoughtful, and absent-minded that he could rob the meanest man in town of a cent out of the bottom of his breeches pocket and not disturb his revery.

At this stage—or at about this stage—a saying like this was dropped at bedtime—with a sigh, usually—by the head of each of the nineteen principal households: "Ah, what could have been the remark that Goodson made?"

And straightway—with a shudder—came this, from the man's wife:

"Oh, don't! What horrible thing are you mulling in your mind? Put it away from you, for God's sake!"

But that question was wrung from those men again the next night—and got the same retort. But weaker.

And the third night the men uttered the question yet again—with anguish, and absently. This time—and the following night—the wives fidgeted feebly, and tried to say something. But didn't.

And the night after that they found their tongues and responded—longingly:

"Oh, if we could only guess!"

Halliday's comments grew daily more and more sparklingly disagreeable and disparaging. He went diligently about, laughing at the town, individually and in mass. But his laugh was the only one left in the village: it fell upon a hollow and mournful vacancy and emptiness. Not even a smile was findable anywhere. Halliday carried a cigar-box around on a tripod, playing that it was a camera, and halted all passers and aimed the thing and said, "Ready!—now look pleasant, please," but not even this capital joke could surprise the dreary faces into any softening.

So three weeks passed—one week was left. It was Saturday evening—after supper. Instead of the aforetime Saturday-evening flutter and bustle and shopping and larking, the streets were empty and desolate. Richards and his old wife sat apart in their little parlor—miserable and thinking. This was become their evening habit now: the lifelong habit which had preceded it, of reading, knitting, and contented chat, or receiving or paying neighborly calls, was dead and gone and forgotten, ages ago— two or three weeks ago; nobody talked now, nobody read, nobody visited—the whole village sat at home, sighing, worrying, silent. Trying to guess out that remark.

10   The postman left a letter. Richards glanced listlessly at the superscription and the postmark —unfamiliar, both—and tossed the letter on the table and resumed his might-have-beens and his hopeless dull miseries where he had left them off. Two or three hours later his wife got wearily up and was going away to bed without a good night—custom now—but she stopped near the letter and eyed it awhile with a dead interest, then broke it open, and began to skim
20 it over. Richards, sitting there with his chair tilted back against the wall and his chin between his knees, heard something fall. It was his wife. He sprang to her side, but she cried out:

"Leave me alone. I am too happy. Read the letter—read it!"

He did. He devoured it, his brain reeling. The letter was from a distant state, and it said:

30   I am a stranger to you, but no matter: I have something to tell. I have just arrived home from Mexico, and learned about that episode. Of course you do not know who made that remark, but I know, and I am the only person living who does know. It was GOODSON. I knew him well, many years ago. I passed through your village that very night, and was his guest till the midnight train came along. I overheard him make that remark to the stranger in the dark—it was in Hale Alley. He and I talked of it the rest of the way home,
40 and while smoking in his house. He mentioned many of your villagers in the course of his talk— most of them in a very uncomplimentary way, but two or three favorably; among these latter yourself. I say "favorably"—nothing stronger. I remember his saying he did not actually LIKE any person in the town—not one; but that you—I THINK he said you—am almost sure—had done him a very great service once, possibly without knowing the full value of it, and he wished he had a fortune, he would leave it to you when he
50 died, and a curse apiece for the rest of the citizens. Now, then, if it was you that did him that service, you are his legitimate heir, and entitled to the sack of gold. I know that I can trust to your honor and honesty, for in a citizen of Hadleyburg these virtues are an unfailing inheritance, and so I am going to reveal to you the remark, well satisfied

that if you are not the right man you will seek and find the right one and see that poor Goodson's debt of gratitude for the service referred to is paid. This is the remark: "You are Far from Being a BAD Man: GO, and reform."

Howard L. Stephenson.

"Oh, Edward, the money is ours, and I am so grateful, oh, so grateful—kiss me, dear, it's forever since we kissed—and we needed it so —the money—and now you are free of Pinkerton and his bank, and nobody's slave any more; it seems to me I could fly for joy."

It was a happy half-hour that the couple spent there on the settee caressing each other; it was the old days come again—days that had begun with their courtship and lasted without a break till the stranger brought the deadly money. By and by the wife said:

"Oh, Edward, how lucky it was you did him that grand service, poor Goodson! I never like him, but I love him now. And it was fine and beautiful of you never to mention it or brag about it." Then, with a touch of reproach, "But you ought to have told me, Edward, you ought to have told your wife, you know."

"Well, I—er—well, Mary, you see—"

"Now stop hemming and hawing, and tell me about it, Edward. I always loved you, and now I'm proud of you. Everybody believes there was only one good generous soul in this village, and now it turns out that you—Edward, why don't you tell me?"

"Well—er—er— Why, Mary, I can't!"

"You can't? Why can't you?"

"You see, he—well, he—he made me promise I wouldn't."

The wife looked him over, and said, very slowly:

"Made—you—promise? Edward, what do you tell me that for?"

"Mary, do you think I would lie?"

She was troubled and silent for a moment, then she laid her hand within his and said:

"No . . . no. We have wandered far enough from our bearings—God spare us that! In all your life you have never uttered a lie. But now —now that the foundations of things seem to be crumbling from under us, we—we—" She lost her voice for a moment, then said, brokenly, "Lead us not into temptation. . . . I think you made the promise, Edward. Let it rest so. Let us keep away from the ground. Now—that is all gone by; let us be happy again; it is no time for clouds."

Edward found it something of an effort to

comply, for his mind kept wandering—trying to remember what the service was that he had done Goodson.

The couple lay awake the most of the night, Mary happy and busy, Edward busy but not so happy. Mary was planning what she would do with the money. Edward was trying to recall that service. At first his conscience was sore on account of the lie he had told Mary—if it was a lie. After much reflection—suppose it was a lie? What then? Was it such a great matter? Aren't we always acting lies? Then why not tell them? Look at Mary—look what she had done. While he was hurrying off on his honest errand, what was she doing? Lamenting because the papers hadn't been destroyed and the money kept! Is theft better than lying?

That point lost its sting—the lie dropped into the background and left comfort behind it. The next point came to the front: Had he rendered that service? Well, here was GOODSON's own evidence as reported in Stephenson's letter; there could be no better evidence than that—it was even proof that he had rendered it. Of course. So that point was settled. . . . No, not quite. He recalled with a wince that his unknown Mr. Stephenson was just a trifle unsure as to whether the performer of it was Richards or some other—and, oh dear, he had put whither that money must go—and Mr. Stephenson was not doubting that if he was the wrong man he would go honorably and find the right one. Oh, it was odious to put a man in such a situation—ah, why couldn't Stephenson have left out that doubt! What did he want to intrude that for?

Further reflection. How did it happen that Richards's name remained in Stephenson's mind as indicating the right man, and not some other man's name? That looked good. Yes, that looked very good. In fact, it went on looking better and better, straight along—until by and by it grew into positive proof. And then Richards put the matter at once out of his mind, for he had a private instinct that a proof once established is better left so.

He was feeling reasonably comfortable now, but there was still one other detail that kept pushing itself on his notice; of course he had done that service—that was settled; but what was that service? He must recall it—he would not go to sleep till he had recalled it; it would make his peace of mind perfect. And so he thought and thought. He thought of a dozen things—possible services, even probable services—but none of them seemed adequate, none of them seemed large enough—none of them seemed worth the money—worth the fortune Goodson had wished he could leave in his will. And besides, he couldn't remember having done them, anyway. Now, then—now, then—what kind of a service would it be that would make a man so inordinately grateful? Ah—the saving of his soul! That must be it. Yes, he could remember, now, how he once set himself to the task of converting Goodson, and labored at it as much as—he was going to say three months, then to a week, then to a day, then to nothing. Yes, he remembered now, and with unwelcome vividness, that Goodson had told him to go to thunder and mind his own business—he wasn't hankering to follow Hadleyburg to heaven!

So that solution was a failure—he hadn't saved Goodson's soul. Richards was discouraged. Then after a little came another idea; had he saved Goodson's property? No, that wouldn't do—he hadn't any. His life? That is it! Of course. Why, he might have thought of it before. This time he was on the right track, sure. His imagination-mill was hard at work in a minute, now.

Thereafter during a stretch of two exhausting hours he was busy saving Goodson's life. He saved it in all kinds of difficult and perilous way. In every case he got it saved satisfactorily up to a certain point; then, just as he was beginning to get well persuaded that it had really happened, a troublesome detail would turn up which made the whole thing impossible. As in the matter of drowning, for instance. In that case he had swum out and tugged Goodson ashore in an unconscious state with a great crowd looking on and applauding, but when he had got it all thought out and was just beginning to remember all about it, a whole swarm of disqualifying details arrived on the ground: the town would have known of the circumstance, Mary would have known of it, it would glare like a limelight in his own memory instead of being an inconspicuous service which he had possibly rendered "without knowing its full value." And at this point he remembered that he couldn't swim, anyway.

Ah—there was a point which he had been overlooking from the start: it had to be a service which he had rendered "possibly without knowing the full value of it." Why, really, that ought to be an easy hunt—much easier than those others. And sure enough, by and by he found it. Goodson, years and years ago, came near marrying a very sweet and pretty girl, named Nancy Hewitt, but in some way or other the match had been broken off; the girl died, Goodson remained a bachelor, and by and by became a soured one and a frank despiser of the human species. Soon after the girl's death the village found out, or thought it had found out, that she carried a spoonful of negro blood in her veins. Richards worked at these details a good while, and in the end he thought he remembered things concerning them which must have gotten mislaid in his memory through long neglect. He seemed to dimly remember that it was he that found out about the negro blood; that it was he that told the village; that the village told Goodson where they got it; that he thus saved Goodson from marrying the tainted girl; that he had done him this great service "without knowing the full value of it," in fact without knowing that he was doing it; but that Goodson knew the value of it, and what a narrow escape he had had, and so went to his grave grateful to his benefactor and wishing he had a fortune to leave him. It was all clear and simple now, and the more he went over it the more luminous and certain it grew; and at last, when he nestled to sleep satisfied and happy, he remembered the whole thing just as if it had been yesterday. In fact, he dimly remembered Goodson's telling him his gratitude once. Meantime Mary had spent six thousand dollars on a new house for herself and a pair of slippers for her pastor, and then had fallen peacefully to rest.

That same Saturday evening the postman had delivered a letter to each of the principal citizens—nineteen letters in all. No two of the envelopes were alike, and no two of the superscriptions were in the same hand, but the letters inside were just exact copies of the letter received by Richards—handwriting and all—and were all signed by Stephenson, but in place of RICHARDS's name each receiver's own name appeared.

All night long eighteen principal citizens did what their caste-brother Richards was doing at the same time—they put in their energies trying to remember what notable service it was that they had unconsciously done Barclay Goodson. In no case was it a holiday job; still they succeeded.

And while they were at this work, which was difficult, their wives put in the night spending the money, which was easy. During that night the nineteen wives spent an average of seven thousand dollars each out of the forty thousand in the sack—a hundred and thirty-three thousand altogether.

Next day there was a surprise for Jack Halliday. He noticed that the faces of the nineteen chief citizens and their wives bore that expression of peaceful and holy happiness again. He could not understand it, neither was he able to invent any remarks about it that could damage it or disturb it. And so it was his turn to be dissatisfied with life. His private guesses at the reasons for the happiness failed in all instances, upon examination. When he met Mrs. Wilcox and noticed the placid ecstasy in her face, he said to himself, "Her cat has had kittens"—and went and asked the cook: it was not so; the cook had detected the happiness, but did not know the cause. When Halliday found the duplicate ecstasy in the face of "Shadbelly" Billson (village nickname) he was sure some neighbor of Billson's had broken his leg, but inquiry showed that this had not happened. The subdued ecstasy in Gregory Yates's face could mean but one thing—he was a mother-in-law short; It was another mistake. "And Pinkerton—Pinkerton—he has collected ten cents that he thought he was going to lose." And so on, and so on. In some cases the guesses had to remain in doubt, in the others they proved distinctly errors. In the end Halliday said to himself, "Anyway it foots up that there's nineteen Hadleyburg families temporarily in heaven: I don't know how it happened; I only know Providence is off duty to-day."

An architect and builder from the next state had lately ventured to set up a small business in this unpromising village, and his sign had now been hanging out a week. Not a customer yet; he was a discouraged man, and sorry he had come. But his weather changed suddenly now. First one and then another chief citizens's wife said to him privately:

"Come to my house Monday week—but say nothing about it for the present. We think of building."

He got eleven invitations that day. That night he wrote his daughter and broke off her match with her student. He said she could marry a mile higher than that.

Pinkerton the banker and two or three other well-to-do men planned country seats—but waited. That kind don't count their chickens until they are hatched.

The Wilsons devised a grand new thing—a

fancydress ball. They made no actual promises, but told all their acquaintanceship in confidence that they were thinking the matter over and thought they should give it—"and if we do, you will be invited, of course." People were surprised, and said, one to another, "Why they are crazy, those poor Wilsons, they can't afford it." Several among the nineteen said privately to their husbands, "It is a good idea: we will keep still till their cheap thing is over, then we will give one that will make it sick."

The days drifted along, and the bill of future squanderings rose higher and higher, wilder and wilder, more and more foolish and reckless. It began to look as if every member of the nineteen would not only spend his whole forty thousand dollars before receiving-day, but be actually in debt by the time he got the money. In some cases light-headed people did not stop with planning to spend, they really spent—on credit. They bought land, mortgages, farms, speculative stocks, fine clothes, horses, and various other things, paid down the bonus, and made themselves liable for the rest—at ten days. Presently the sober second thought came, and Halliday noticed that a ghastly anxiety was beginning to show up in a good many faces. Again he was puzzled, and didn't know what to make of it. "The Wilcox kittens aren't dead, for they weren't born; nobody's broken a leg; there's no shrinkage in mother-in-laws; nothing has happened—it is an unsolvable mystery."

There was another puzzled man, too—the Rev. Mr. Burgess. For days, wherever he went, people seemed to follow him or to be watching him or too, if he ever found himself in a retired spot, a member of the nineteen would be sure to appear, thrust an envelope privately into his hand, whisper "To be opened at the Town-hall Friday evening," then vanish away like a guilty thing. He was expecting that there might be one claimant for the sack—doubtful, however, Goodson being dead—but it never occurred to him that all this crowd might be claimants. When the great Friday came at last he found that he had nineteen envelopes.

III

The town-hall had never looked finer. The platform at the end of it was backed by a showy draping of flags; at intervals along the walls were festoons of flags; the gallery fronts were clothed in flags; the supporting columns were swathed in flags; all this was to impress the stranger, for he would be there in considerable force, and in a large degree he would be connected with the press. The house was full. The 412 fixed seats were occupied; also the 68 extra chairs which had been packed into the aisles; the steps of the platform were occupied; some distinguished strangers were given seats on the platform; at the horseshoe of tables which fenced the front and sides of the platform sat a strong force of special correspondents who had come from everywhere. It was the best-dressed house the town had ever produced. There were some tolerable expensive toilets there, and in several cases the ladies who wore them had the look of being unfamiliar with that kind of clothes. At least the town thought they had that look, but the notion could have arisen from the town's knowledge of the fact that these ladies had never inhabited such clothes before.

The gold-sack stood on a little table at the front of the platform where all the house could see it. The bulk of the house gazed at it with a burning interest, a mouth-watering interest, a wistful and pathetic interest; a minority of nineteen couples gazed at it tenderly, lovingly, proprietarily, and the male half of this minority kept saying over to themselves the moving little impromptu speeches of thankfulness for the audience's applause and congratulations which they were presently going to get up and deliver. Every now and then one of these got a piece of paper out of his vest pocket and privately glanced at it to refresh his memory.

Of course there was a buzz of conversation going on—there always is: but at last when the Rev. Mr. Burgess rose and laid his hand on the sack he could hear his microbes gnaw, the place was so still. He related the curious history of the sack, then went on to speak in warm terms of Hadleyburg's old and well-earned reputation for spotless honesty, and of the town's just pride in this reputation. He said that this reputation was a treasure of priceless value; that under Providence its value had now become inestimably enhanced, for the recent episode had spread this fame far and wide, and thus had focussed the eyes of the American world upon this village, and made its name for all time, as he hoped and believed, a synonym for commercial incorruptibility. (APPLAUSE) "And who is to be the guardian of this noble treasure—the community as a whole? No! The responsibility is individual, not communal.

From this day forth each and every one of you is in his own person its special guardian, and individually responsible that no harm shall come to it. Do you—does each of you—accept this great trust? (TUMULTUOUS ASSENT) Then all is well. Transmit it to your children and to your children's children. To-day your purity is beyond reproach—see to it that it shall remain so. To-day there is not a person in your community who could be beguiled to touch a penny not his own—see to it that you abide in this grace. ("WE WILL! WE WILL!") This is not the place to make comparisons between ourselves and other communities—some of them ungracious toward us; they have their ways, we have ours; let us be content. (APPLAUSE) I am done. Under my hand, my friends, rests a stranger's eloquent recognition of what we are; through him the world will always henceforth know what we are. We do not know who he is, but in your name I utter your gratitude, and ask you to raise your voices in indorsement."

The house rose in a body and made the walls quake with the thunders of its thankfulness for the space of a long minute. Then it sat down, and Mr. Burgess took the envelope out of his pocket. The house held its breath while he slit the envelope open and took from it a slip of paper. He read its contents—slowly and impressively—the audience listening with tranced attention to this magic document, each of whose words stood for an ingot of gold:

" 'THE REMARK WHICH I MADE TO THE DISTRESSED STRANGER WAS THIS: "YOU ARE VERY FAR FROM BEING A BAD MAN: GO, AND REFORM." ' " Then he continued: "We shall know in a moment now whether the remark here quoted corresponds with the one concealed in the sack; and if that shall prove to be so—and it undoubtedly will—this sack of gold belongs to a fellow-citizen who will henceforth stand before the nation as the symbol of the special virtue which has made our town famous throughout the land—Mr. Billson!"

The house had gotten itself all ready to burst into the proper tornado of applause; but instead of doing it, it seemed stricken with a paralysis; there was a deep hush for a moment or two, then a wave of whispered murmurs swept the place—of about this tenor: "BILLSON! oh, come, this is TOO thin! Twenty dollars to a stranger—or anybody—BILLSON! Tell it to the marines!" And now at this point the house caught its breath all of a sudden in a new access of astonishment, for it discovered that whereas in one part of the hall Deacon Billson was standing up with his head meekly bowed, in another part of it Lawyer Wilson was doing the same. There was a wondering silence now for a while. Everybody was puzzled, and nineteen couples were surprised and indignant.

Billson and Wilson turned and stared at each other. Billson asked, bitingly,

"Why do YOU rise, Mr. Wilson?"

"Because I have a right to. Perhaps you will be good enough to explain to the house why YOU rise?"

"With great pleasure. Because I wrote that paper."

"It is an impudent falsity! I wrote it myself."

It was Burgess's turn to be paralyzed. He stood looking vacantly at first one of the men and then the other, and did not seem to know what to do. The house was stupefied. Lawyer Wilson spoke up, now, and said,

"I ask the Chair to read the name signed to that paper."

That brought the Chair to itself, and it read out the name,

" 'John Wharton BILLSON.' "

"There!" shouted Billson, "what have you got to say for yourself, now? And what kind of apology are you going to make to me and to this insulted house for the imposture which you have attempted to play here?"

"No apologies are due, sir; and as for the rest of it, I publicly charge you with pilfering my note from Mr. Burgess and substituting a copy of it signed with your own name. There is no other way by which you could have gotten hold of the test-remark; I alone, of living men, possessed the secret of its wording."

There was likely to be a scandalous state of things if this went on; everybody noticed with distress that the short-hand scribes were scribbling like mad; many people were crying "Chair, Chair! Order! order!" Burgess rapped with his gavel, and said:

"Let us not forget the proprieties due. There has evidently been a mistake somewhere, but surely that is all. If Mr. Wilson gave me an envelope—and I remember now that he did— I still have it."

He took one out of his pocket, opened it, glanced at it, looked surprised and worried, and stood silent a few moments. Then he waved his hand in a wandering and mechanical way, and made an effort or two to say something, then gave it up, despondently. Several voices cried out:

"Read it! read it! What is it?"

So he began in a dazed and sleep-walker fashion:

" 'THE REMARK WHICH I MADE TO THE UNHAPPY STRANGER WAS THIS: "YOU ARE FAR FROM BEING A BAD MAN. (The house gazed at him, marvelling.) GO, AND REFORM." ' (MURMURS: "Amazing! what can this mean?") This one," said the Chair, "is signed Thurlow G. Wilson."

"There!" cried Wilson, "I reckon that settles it! I knew perfectly well my note was purloined."

"Purloined!" retorted Billson. "I'll let you know that neither you nor any man of your kidney must venture to—"

THE CHAIR. "Order, gentlemen, order! Take your seats, both of you, please."

They obeyed, shaking their heads and grumbling angrily. The house was profoundly puzzled; it did not know what to do with this curious emergency. Presently Thompson got up. Thompson was the hatter. He would have liked to be a Nineteener; but such was not for him; his stock of hats was not considerable enough for the position. He said:

"Mr. Chairman, if I may be permitted to make a suggestion, can both of these gentlemen be right? I put it to you, sir, can both have happened to say the very same words to the stranger? It seems to me—"

The tanner got up and interrupted him. The tanner was a disgruntled man; he believed himself entitled to be a Nineteener, but he couldn't get recognition. It made him a little unpleasant in his ways and speech. Said he:

"Sho, THAT's not the point! THAT could happen—twice in a hundred years—but not the other thing. NEITHER of them gave the twenty dollars!" (A RIPPLE OF APPLAUSE)

BILLSON. "I did!"

WILSON. "I did!"

Then each accused the other of pilfering.

THE CHAIR. "Order! Sit down, if you please—both of you. Neither of the notes has been out of my possession at any moment."

A VOICE. "Good—that settles THAT!"

THE TANNER. "Mr. Chairman, one thing is now plain; one of these men has been eavesdropping under the other one's bed, and filching family secrets. If it is not unparliamentary to suggest it, I will remark that both are equal to it. (THE CHAIR. "Order! order!") I withdraw the remark, sir, and will confine myself to suggesting that IF one of them has over-

heard the other reveal the test-remark to his wife, we shall catch him now."

A VOICE. "How?"

THE TANNER. "Easily. The two have not quoted the remark in exactly the same words. You would have noticed that, if there hadn't been a considerable stretch of time and an exciting quarrel inserted between the two readings."

A VOICE. "Name the difference."

THE TANNER. "The word VERY is in Billson's note, and not in the other."

MANY VOICES. "That's so—he's right!"

THE TANNER. "And so, if the Chair will examine the test-remark in the sack, we shall know which of these two frauds—(THE CHAIR —"Order!")—which of these two adventurers —(THE CHAIR. "Order! order!")—which of these gentlemen—(LAUGHTER AND APPLAUSE) —is entitled to wear the belt as being the first dishonest blatherskite ever bred in this town —which he has dishonored, and which will be a sultry place for him from now out!" (VIGOROUS APPLAUSE)

MANY VOICES. "Open it—open the sack!"

Mr. Burgess made a slit in the sack, slid his hand in and brought out an envelope. In it were a couple of folded notes. He said:

"One of these is marked, 'Not to be examined until all written communications which have been addressed to the Chair—if any— shall have been read.' The other is marked 'THE TEST.' Allow me. . . . It is worded—to wit:

" 'I do not require that the first half of the remark which was made to me by my benefactor shall be quoted with exactness, for it was not striking, and could be forgotten; but its closing fifteen words are quite striking, and I think easily rememberable; unless THESE shall be accurately reproduced, let the applicant be regarded as an impostor. My benefactor began by saying he seldom gave advice to any one, but that it always bore the hall-mark of high value when he did give it. Then he said this—and it has never faded from my memory: "YOU ARE FAR FROM BEING A BAD MAN—" ' "

FIFTY VOICES. "That settles it—the money's Wilson's! Wilson! Wilson! Speech! Speech!"

People jumped up and crowded around Wilson, wringing his hand and congratulating fervently—meantime the Chair was hammering with the gavel and shouting:

"Order, gentlemen! Order! Order! Let me

finish reading, please." When quiet was restored, the reading was resumed—as follows:

"'"Go, and reform—or, mark my words—some day, for your sins, you will die and go to hell or Hadleyburg—try and make it the former."'"

A ghastly silence followed. First an angry cloud began to settle darkly upon the faces of the citizen-ship; after a pause the cloud began to rise, and a tickled expression tried to take its place; tried so hard that it was only kept under with great and painful difficulty; the reporters, the Brixtonites, and other strangers bent their heads down and shielded their faces with their hands, and managed to hold in by main strength and heroic courtesy. At this most inopportune time burst upon the stillness the roar of a solitary voice—Jack Halliday's:
"That's got the hall-mark on it!"

Then the house let go, strangers and all. Even Mr. Burgess's gravity broke down presently, then the audience considered itself officially absolved from all restraint, and it made the most of its privilege. It was a good long laugh, and a tempestuously whole-hearted one, but it ceased at last—long enough for Mr. Burgess to try to resume, and for the people to get their eyes partially wiped; then it broke out again; and afterward yet again; then at last Burgess was able to get out these serious words:

"It is useless to try to disguise the fact—we find ourselves in the presence of a matter of grave import. It involves the honor of your town, it strikes at the town's good name. The difference of a single word between the test-remarks offered by Mr. Wilson and Mr. Billson was itself a serious thing, since it indicated that one or the other of these gentlemen had committed a theft—"

The two men were sitting limp, nerveless, crushed; but at these words both were electrified into movement, and started to get up—

"Sit down!" said the Chair, sharply, and they obeyed. "That, as I have said, was a serious thing. And it was—but for only one of them. But the matter has become graver; for the honor of both is now in formidable peril. Shall I go even further, and say in inextricable peril? Both left out the crucial fifteen words." He paused. During several moments he allowed the pervading stillness to gather and deepen its impressive effects, then added: "There would seem to be but one way whereby this could happen. I ask these gentlemen—Was there collision?—agreement?"

A low murmur sifted through the house; its import was, "He's got them both."

Billson was not used to emergencies; he sat in a helpless collapse. But Wilson was a lawyer. He struggled to his feet, pale and worried, and said:

"I ask the indulgence of the house while I explain this most painful matter. I am sorry to say what I am about to say, since it must inflict irreparable injury upon Mr. Billson, whom I have always esteemed and respected until now, and in whose invulnerability to temptation I entirely believed—as did you all. But for the preservation of my own honor I must speak—and with frankness. I confess with shame—and I now beseech your pardon for it—that I said to the ruined stranger all of the words contained in the test-remark, including the disparaging fifteen. (sensation) When the late publication was made I recalled them, and I resolved to claim the sack of coin, for by every right I was entitled to it. Now I will ask you to consider this point, and weigh it well: that stranger's gratitude to me that night knew no bounds; he said himself that he could find no words for it that were adequate, and that if he should ever be able he would repay me a thousandfold. Now, then, I ask you this: could I expect—could I believe—could I even remotely imagine—that, feeling as he did, he would do so ungrateful a thing as to add those quite unnecessary fifteen words to his test?—set a trap for me?—expose me as a slanderer of my own town before my own people assembled in a public hall? It was preposterous; it was impossible. His test would contain only the kindly opening clause of my remark. Of that I had no shadow of doubt. You would have thought as I did. You would not have expected a base betrayal from one whom you had befriended and against whom you had committed no offence. And so, with perfect confidence, perfect trust, I wrote on a piece of paper the opening words—ending with 'Go, and reform,'—and signed it. When I was about to put it in an envelope I was called into my back office, and without thinking I left the paper lying open on my desk." He stopped, turned his head slowly toward Billson, waited a moment, then added: "I ask you to note this: when I returned, a little later, Mr. Billson was retiring by my street door." (sensation)

In a moment Billson was on his feet and shouting:

"It's a lie! It's an infamous lie!"

THE CHAIR. "Be seated, sir! Mr. Wilson has the floor."

Billson's friends pulled him into his seat and quieted him, and Wilson went on:

"Those are the simple facts. My note was now lying in a different place on the table from where I had left it. I noticed that, but attached no importance to it, thinking a draught had blown it there. That Mr. Billson would read a private paper was a thing which could not occur to me; he was an honorable man, and he would be above that. If you will allow me to say it, I think his extra word 'VERY' stands explained; it is attributable to a defect of memory. I was the only man in the world who could furnish here any detail of the test-mark —by HONORABLE means. I have finished."

There is nothing in the world like a persuasive speech to fuddle the mental apparatus and upset the convictions and debauch the emotions of an audience not practised in the tricks and delusions of oratory. Wilson sat down victorious. The house submerged him in tides of approving applause; friends swarmed to him and shook him by the hand and congratulated him, and Billson was shouted down and not allowed to say a word. The Chair hammered and hammered with its gavel, and kept shouting,

"But let us proceed, gentlemen, let us proceed!"

At last there was a measurable degree of quiet, and the hatter said,

"But what is there to proceed with, sir, but to deliver the money?"

VOICES. "That's it! That's it! Come forward, Wilson!"

THE HATTER. "I move three cheers for Mr. Wilson, Symbol of the special virtue which—"

The cheers burst forth before he could finish; and in the midst of them—and in the midst of the clamor of the gavel also—some enthusiasts mounted Wilson on a big friend's shoulder and were going to fetch him in triumph to the platform. The Chair's voice now rose above the noise—

"Order! To your places! You forget that there is still a document to be read." When quiet had been restored he took up the document, and was going to read it, but laid it down again, saying, "I forgot; this is not to be read until all written communications received by me have first been read." He took an envelope out of his pocket, removed its enclosure, glanced at it—seemed astonished— held it out and gazed at it—stared at it.

Twenty or thirty voices cried out:

"What is it? Read it! read it!"

And he did—slowly, and wondering:

"'The remark which I made to the stranger —(VOICES. "Hello! how's this?")—was this: "You are far from being a bad man. (VOICES. "Great Scott!") Go, and reform."' (VOICE. "Oh, saw my leg off!") Signed by Mr. Pinkerton the banker."

The pandemonium of delight which turned itself loose now was of a sort to make the judicious weep. Those whose withers were unwrung laughed till the tears ran down; the reporters, in throes of laughter, set down disordered pot-hooks which would never in the world be decipherable; and a sleeping dog jumped up, scared out of its wits, and barked itself crazy at the turmoil. All manner of cries were scattered through the din: "We're getting rich—TWO Symbols of Incorruptibility!—without counting Billson!" "THREE!—count Shadbelly in—we can't have too many!" "All right —Billson's elected!" "Alas, poor Wilson—victim of TWO thieves!"

A POWERFUL VOICE. "Silence! The Chair's fished up something more out of its pocket."

VOICES. "Hurrah! Is it something fresh? Read it! read! read!"

THE CHAIR (reading). "'The remark which I made,' etc. 'You are far from being a bad man. Go,' etc. Signed, 'Gregory Yates.'"

TORNADO OF VOICES. "Four Symbols!" "'Rah for Yates!" "Fish again!"

The house was in a roaring humor now, and ready to get all the fun out of the occasion that might be in it. Several Nineteeners, looking pale and distressed, got up and began to work their way toward the aisles, but a score of shouts went up:

"The doors, the doors—close the doors; no Incorruptible shall leave this place! Sit down, everybody!"

The mandate was obeyed.

"Fish again! Read! read!

The Chair fished again, and once more the familiar words began to fall from its lips— "'You are far from being a bad man—'"

"Name! name! What's his name?"

"'L. Ingoldsby Sargent.'"

"Five elected! Pile up the Symbols! Go on, go on!"

"'You are far from being a bad—'"

"Name! name!"

"'Nicholas Whitworth.'"

"Hooray! hooray! it's a symbolical day!"

Somebody wailed in, and began to sing this rhyme (leaving out "it's") to the lovely "Mikado" tune of "When a man's afraid of a beautiful maid"; the audience joined in, with joy; then, just in time, somebody contributed another line—

"And don't you this forget—"

The house roared it out. A third line was at once furnished—

"Corruptibles far from Hadleyburg are—"

The house roared that one too. As the last note died, Jack Halliday's voice rose high and clear, freighted with a final line—

"But the Symbols are here, you bet!"

That was sung, with booming enthusiasm. Then the happy house started in at the beginning and sang the four lines through twice, with immense swing and dash, and finished up with a crashing three-times-three and a tiger for "Hadleyburg the Incorruptible and all Symbols of it which we shall find worthy to receive the hall-mark to-night."

Then the shoutings at the Chair began again, all over the place:

"Go on! go on! Read! read some more! Read all you've got!"

"That's it—go on! We are winning eternal celebrity!"

A dozen men got up now and began to protest. They said that this farce was the work of some abandoned joker, and was an insult to the whole community. Without a doubt these signatures were all forgeries—

"Sit down! sit down! Shut up! You are confessing. We'll find YOUR names in the lot."

"Mr. Chairman, how many of those envelopes have you got?"

The Chair counted.

"Together with those that have been already examined, there are nineteen."

A storm of derisive applause broke out.

"Perhaps they all contain the secret. I move that you open them all and read every signature that is attached to a note of that sort—and

read also the first eight words of the note."

"Second the motion!"

It was put and carried—uproariously. Then poor old Richards got up, and his wife rose and stood at his side. Her head was bent down, so that none might see that she was crying. Her husband gave her his arm, and so supporting her, he began to speak in a quavering voice:

"My friends, you have known us two—Mary and me—all our lives, and I think you have liked us and respected us—"

The Chair interrupted him:

"Allow me. It is quite true—that which you are saying, Mr. Richards; this town DOES know you two; it DOES like you; it DOES respect you; more—it honors you and LOVES you—"

Halliday's voice rang out:

"That's the hall-marked truth, too! If the Chair is right, let the house speak up and say it. Rise! Now, then—hip! hip! hip!—all together!"

The house rose in mass, faced toward the old couple eagerly, filled the air with a snow-storm of waving handkerchiefs, and delivered the cheers with all its affectionate heart.

The Chair then continued:

"What I was going to say is this: We know your good heart, Mr. Richards, but this is not a time for the exercise of charity toward offenders. (Shouts of "Right! right!") I see your generous purpose in your face, but I cannot allow you to plead for these men—"

"But I was going to—"

"Please take your seat, Mr. Richards. We must examine the rest of these notes—simple fairness to the men who have already been exposed requires this. As soon as that has been done—I give you my word for this—you shall be heard."

MANY VOICES. "Right!—the Chair is right —no interruption can be permitted at this stage! Go on!—the names! the names!—according to the terms of the motion!"

The old couple sat reluctantly down, and the husband whispered to the wife, "It is pitifully hard to have to wait; the shame will be greater than ever when they find we were only going to plead for OURSELVES."

Straightway the jollity broke loose again with the reading of the names.

"'You are far from being a bad man—' Signature, 'Robert J. Titmarsh.'"

"'You are far from being a bad man—' Signature, 'Eliphalet Weeks.'"

" 'You are far from being a bad man—' Signature, 'Oscar B. Wilder.' "

At this point the house lit upon the idea of taking the eight words out of the Chairman's hands. He was not unthankful for that. Thenceforward he held up each note in its turn, and waited. The house droned out the eight words in a massed and measured and musical deep volume of sound (with a daringly close resemblance to a well-known church chant)—" 'You are f-a-r from being a b-a-a-a-d man.' " Then the Chair said, "Signature, 'Archibald Wilcox.' " And so on, and so on, name after name, and everybody had an increasingly and gloriously good time except the wretched Nineteen. Now and then, when a particularly shining name was called, the house made the Chair wait while it chanted the whole of the test-remark from the beginning to the closing words, "And go to hell or Hadleyburg—try and make it the for-or-m-e-r!" and in these special cases they added a grand and agonized and imposing "A-a-a-a-MEN!"

The list dwindled, dwindled, dwindled, poor old Richards keeping tally of the count, wincing when a name resembling his own was pronounced, and waiting in miserable suspense for the time to come when it would be his humiliating privilege to rise with Mary and finish his plea, which he was intending to word thus: ". . . for until now we have never done any wrong thing, but have gone our humble way unreproached. We are very poor, we are old, and have no chick nor child to help us; we were sorely tempted, and we fell. It was my purpose when I got up before to make confession and beg that my name might not be read out in this public place, for it seemed to us that we could not bear it; but I was prevented. It was just; it was our place to suffer with the rest. It has been hard for us. It is the first time we have ever heard our name fall from any one's lips—sullied. Be merciful—for the sake of the better days; make our shame as light to bear as in your charity you can." At this point in his revery Mary nudged him, perceiving that his mind was absent. The house was chanting, "You are f-a-r," etc.

"Be ready," Mary whispered. "Your name comes now; he has read eighteen."

The chant ended.

"Next! next! next!" came volleying from all over the house.

Burgess put his hand into his pocket. The old couple, trembling, began to rise. Burgess fumbled a moment, then said,

"I find I have read them all."

Faint with joy and surprise, the couple sank into their seats, and Mary whispered,

"Oh, bless God, we are saved!—he has lost ours—I wouldn't give this for a hundred of those sacks!"

The house burst out with its "Mikado" travesty, and sang it three times with ever-increasing enthusiasm, rising to its feet when it reached for the third time the closing line—

"But the Symbols are here, you bet!"

and finishing up with cheers and a tiger for "Hadleyburg purity and our eighteen immortal representatives of it."

Then Wingate, the saddler, got up and proposed cheers "for the cleanest man in town, the one solitary important citizen in it who didn't try to steal that money—Edward Richards."

They were given with great and moving heartiness; then somebody proposed that Richards be elected sole Guardian and Symbol of the now Sacred Hadleyburg Tradition, with power and right to stand up and look the whole sarcastic world in the face."

Passed, by acclamation; then they sang the "Mikado" again, and ended it with

"And there's ONE Symbol left, you bet!"

There was a pause; then—

A VOICE. "Now, then, who's to get the sack?"

THE TANNER (with bitter sarcasm). "That's easy. The money has to be divided among the eighteen Incorruptibles. They gave the suffering stranger twenty dollars apiece—and that remark—each in his turn—it took twenty-two minutes for the procession to move past. Staked the stranger—total contribution, $360. All they want is just the loan back—and interest—forty thousand dollars altogether."

MANY VOICES (derisively). "That's it! Divvy! divvy! Be kind to the poor—don't keep them waiting!"

THE CHAIR. "Order! I now offer the stranger's remaining document. It says: 'If no claimant shall appear (grand chorus of groans) I desire that you open the sack and count out the money to the principal citizens of your town, they to take it in trust (Cries of Oh! Oh! Oh!), and use it in such ways as to them shall seem best for the propagation and preservation of your community's noble reputation for in-

corruptible honesty (more cries)—a reputation to which their names and their efforts will
add a new and far-reaching lustre.' (Enthusiastic outburst of sarcastic applause) That seems
to be all. No—here is a postscript:

"'P.S.—CITIZENS OF HADLEYBURG: There
IS no test-remark—nobody made one. (GREAT
SENSATION) There wasn't any pauper stranger,
nor any twenty dollar contribution, nor any
10   accompanying benediction and compliment—
these are all inventions. (General buzz and
hum of astonishment and delight) Allow me to
tell my story—it will take but a word or two.
I passed through your town at a certain time,
and received a deep offence which I had not
earned. Any other man would have been content to kill one or two of you and call it square,
but to me that would have been a trivial revenge, and inadequate; for the dead do not
20   SUFFER. Besides, I could not kill you all—and,
anyway, made as I am, even that would not
have satisfied me. I wanted to damage every
man in the place, and every woman—and not
in their bodies or in their estate, but in their
vanity—the place where feeble and foolish
people are most vulnerable. So I disguised myself and came back and studied you. You were
easy game. You had an old and lofty reputation
for honesty, and naturally you were proud of
30   it—it was your treasure of treasures, the very
apple of your eye. As soon as I found out that
you carefully and vigilantly kept yourselves
and your children OUT OF TEMPTATION, I knew
how to proceed. Why, you simple creatures,
the weakest of all weak things is a virtue which
has not been tested in the fire. I laid a plan,
and gathered a list of names. My project was
to corrupt Hadleyburg the Incorruptible. My
idea was to make liars and thieves of nearly
40   half a hundred smirchless men and women
who had never in their lives uttered a lie or
stolen a penny. I was afraid of Goodson. He
was neither born nor reared in Hadleyburg.
I was afraid that if I started to operate my
scheme by getting my letter laid before you,
you would say to yourselves, "Goodson is the
only man among us who would give away
twenty dollars to a poor devil'—and then you
might not bite at my bait. But Heaven took
50   Goodson; then I knew I was safe, and I set my
trap and baited it. It may be that I shall not
catch all the men to whom I mailed the pretended test secret, but I shall catch the most of
them, if I know Hadleyburg nature. (VOICES.

"Right—he got every last one of them.") I
believe they will even steal ostensible GAMBLE-
money, rather than miss, poor, tempted, and
mistrained fellows. I am hoping to eternally
and everlastingly squelch your vanity and give
Hadleyburg a new renown—one that will
STICK—and spread far. If I have succeeded,
open the sack and summon the Committee on
Propagation and Preservation of the Hadleyburg Reputation.'"

A CYCLONE OF VOICES. "Open it! Open it!
The Eighteen to the front! Committee on
Propagation of the Tradition! Forward—the
Incorruptibles!"

The Chair ripped the sack wide, and gathered up a handful of bright, broad, yellow
coins, shook them together, then examined
them—

"Friends, they are only gilded disks of lead!"

There was a crashing outbreak of delight
over this news, and when the noise had subsided, the tanner called out:

"By right of apparent seniority in this business, Mr. Wilson is Chairman of the Committee on Propagation of the Tradition. I suggest that he step forward on behalf of his
pals, and receive in trust the money."

A HUNDRED VOICES. "Wilson! Wilson! Wilson! Speech! Speech!"

WILSON (in a voice trembling with anger)
"You will allow me to say, and without apologies for my language, DAMN the money!"

A VOICE. "Oh, and him a Baptist!"

A VOICE. "Seventeen Symbols left! Step
up, gentlemen, and assume your trust!"

There was a pause—no response.

THE SADDLER. "Mr. Chairman, we've got
ONE clean man left, anyway, out of the late
aristocracy; and he needs money and deserves
it. I move that you appoint Jack Halliday to get
up there and auction off that sack of gilt
twenty-dollar pieces, and give the result to
the right man—the man whom Hadleyburg
delights to honor—Edward Richards."

This was received with great enthusiasm,
the dog taking a hand again; the saddler
started the bids at a dollar, the Brixton folk
and Barnum's representative fought hard for
it, the people cheered every jump that the bids
made, the excitement climbed moment by moment higher and higher, the bidders got on
their mettle and grew steadily more and more
daring, more and more determined, the jumps
went from a dollar up to five, then to ten, then

to twenty, then fifty, then to a hundred, then—

At the beginning of the auction Richards whispered in distress to his wife: "Oh, Mary, can we allow it? It—it—you see, it is an honor-reward, a testimonial to purity of character, and—and—can we allow it? Hadn't I better get up and—Oh, Mary, what ought we to do?—what do you think we—" (HAL-LIDAY'S VOICE. "FIFTEEN I'M BID!—FIFTEEN FOR THE SACK!—TWENTY!—AH? THANKS!——THIRTY—THANKS AGAIN! THIRTY, THIRTY, THIRTY!—DO I HEAR FORTY?—FORTY IT IS! KEEP THE BALL ROLLING, GENTLEMEN, KEEP IT ROLLING!—FIFTY!—THANKS, NOBLE ROMAN!—GOING AT FIFTY, FIFTY, FIFTY!—SEVENTY!—NINETY!—SPLENDID!—A HUNDRED!—PILE IT UP, PILE IT UP!—HUNDRED AND TWENTY—FORTY!—JUST IN TIME!—HUNDRED AND FIFTY!—TWO HUNDRED!—SUPERB! DO I HEAR TWO H—THANKS!—TWO HUNDRED AND FIFTY!—")

"It is another temptation, Edward—I'm all in a tremble,—but oh, we've escaped ONE temptation, and that ought to warn us, to— ("SIX DID I HEAR?—THANKS!—SIX FIFTY, SIX F—SEVEN HUNDRED!") And yet, Edward, when you think—nobody susp— ("EIGHT HUNDRED DOLLARS!—HURRAH!—MAKE IT NINE!—MR. PARSONS? DID I HEAR YOU SAY—THANKS!—NINE!—THIS NOBLE SACK OF VIRGIN LEAD GOING AT ONLY NINE HUNDRED DOLLARS, GILDING AND ALL—COME! DO I HEAR—A THOUSAND!—GRATEFULLY YOURS!—DID SOME ONE SAY ELEVEN?—A SACK WHICH IS GOING TO BE THE MOST CELEBRATED IN THE WHOLE UNI—") Oh, Edward" (beginning to sob) "we are so poor!—but—but—do as you think best—do as you think best."

Edward fell—that is, he sat still; sat with a conscience which was not satisfied, but which was overpowered by circumstances.

Meantime a stranger, who looked like an amateur detective gotten up as an impossible English earl, had been watching the evening's proceedings with manifest interest, and with a contented expression in his face; and he had been privately commenting to himself. He was now soliloquizing somewhat like this: "None of the Eighteen are bidding; that is not satisfactory; I must change that—the dramatic unities require it; they must buy the sack they tried to steal; they must pay a heavy price, too —some of them are rich. And another thing, when I make a mistake in Hadleyburg nature the man that puts that error upon me is en-

titled to a high honorarium, and some one must pay it. This poor old Richards has brought my judgment to shame; he is an honest man:—I don't understand it, but I acknowledge it. Yes, he saw my deuces—AND with a straight flush, and by rights the pot is his. And it shall be a jack-pot, too, if I can manage it. He disappointed me, but let that pass."

He was watching the bidding. At a thousand, the market broke: the prices tumbled swiftly. He waited—and still watched. One competitor dropped out; then another, and another. He put in a bid or two, now. When the bids had sunk to ten dollars, he added a five; some one raised him a three; he waited a moment, then flung in a fifty dollar jump, and the sack was his—at $1282. The house broke out in cheers—then stopped; for he was on his feet, and had lifted his hand. He began to speak.

"I desire to say a word, and ask a favor. I am a speculator in rarities, and I have dealings with persons interested in numismatics all over the world. I can make a profit on this purchase, just as it stands; but there is a way, if I can get your approval, whereby I can make every one of these leaden twenty-dollar pieces worth its face in gold, and perhaps more. Grant me that approval, and I will give part of my gains to your Mr. Richards, whose invulnerable probity you have so justly and so cordially recognized to-night; his share shall be ten thousand dollars, and I will hand him the money to-morrow. (GREAT APPLAUSE FROM THE HOUSE) But the "invulnerable probity" made the Richardses blush prettily; however, it went for modesty, and did no harm. If you will pass my proposition by a good majority—I would like a two-thirds vote—I will regard that as the town's consent, and that is all I ask. Rarities are always helped by any device which will rouse curiosity and compel remark. Now if I may have your permission to stamp upon the faces of each of these ostensible coins the names of the eighteen gentlemen who—"

Nine-tenths of the audience were on their feet in a moment—dog and all—and the proposition was carried with a whirlwind of approving applause and laughter.

They sat down, and all the Symbols except "Dr." Clay Harkness got up, violently protesting against the proposed outrage, and threatening to—

"I beg you not to threaten me," said the stranger, calmly. "I know my legal rights, and am not accustomed to being frightened at bluster." (APPLAUSE) He sat down. "Dr." Harkness saw an opportunity here. He was one of the two very rich men of the place, and Pinkerton was the other. Harkness was proprietor of a mint; that is to say, a popular patent medicine. He was running for the Legislature on one ticket, and Pinkerton on the other. It was a close race and a hot one and getting hotter every day. Both had strong appetites for money; each had bought a great tract of land, with a purpose; there was going to be a new railway, and each wanted to be in the Legislature and help locate the route to his own advantage; a single vote might make the decision, and with it two or three fortunes. The stake was large, and Harkness was a daring speculator. He was sitting close to the stranger. He leaned over while one or another of the other Symbols was entertaining the house with protests and appeals, and asked, in a whisper,

"What is your price for the sack?"

"Forty thousand dollars."

"I'll give you twenty."

"No."

"Twenty-five."

"No."

"Say thirty."

"The price is forty thousand dollars; not a penny less."

"All right, I'll give it. I will come to the hotel at ten in the morning. I don't want it known; will see you privately."

"Very good." Then the stranger got up and said to the house:

"I find it late. The speeches of these gentlemen are not without merit, not without interest, not without grace; yet if I may be excused I will take my leave. I thank you for the great favor which you have shown me in granting my petition. I ask the Chair to keep the sack for me until to-morrow, and to hand these three five-hundred dollar notes to Mr. Richards." They were passed up to the Chair. "At nine I will call for the sack, and at eleven will deliver the rest of the ten thousand to Mr. Richards in person, at his home. Good-night."

Then he slipped out, and left the audience making a vast noise, which was composed of a mixture of cheers, the "Mikado" song, dog-disapproval, and the chant, "You are f-a-r from being a b-a-a-d man—a-a-a-a-men!"

IV

At home the Richardses had to endure congratulations and compliments until midnight. Then they were left to themselves. They looked a little sad, and they sat silent and thinking. Finally Mary sighed and said,

"Do you think we are to blame, Edward—MUCH to blame?" and her eyes wandered to the accusing triplet of big bank-notes lying on the table, where the congratulators had been gloating over them and reverently fingering them. Edward did not answer at once; then he brought out a sigh and said, hesitatingly:

"We—we couldn't help it, Mary. It—well, it was ordered. ALL things are."

Mary glanced up and looked at him steadily, but he didn't return the look. Presently she said:

"I thought congratulations and praises always tasted good. But—it seems to me, now —Edward?"

"Well?"

"Are you going to stay in the bank?"

"N-no."

"Resign?"

"In the morning—by note."

"It does seem best."

Richards bowed his head in his hands and muttered:

"Before, I was not afraid to let oceans of people's money pour through my hands, but —Mary, I am so tired, so tired—"

"We will go to bed."

At nine in the morning the stranger called for the sack and took it to the hotel in a cab. At ten Harkness had a talk with him privately. The stranger asked for and got five checks on a metropolitan bank—drawn to "Bearer,"— four for $1500 each, and one for $34,000. He put one of the former in his pocket-book, and the remainder, representing $38,500, he put in an envelope, and with these he added a note, which he wrote after Harkness was gone. At eleven he called at the Richards house and knocked. Mrs. Richards peeped through the shutters, then went and received the envelope, and the stranger disappeared without a word. She came back flushed and a little unsteady on her legs, and gasped out:

"I am sure I recognized him! Last night it

seemed to me that maybe I had seen him somewhere before."

"He is the man that brought the sack here?"

"I am almost sure of it."

"Then he is the ostensible Stephenson too, and sold every important citizen in this town with his bogus secret. Now if he has sent checks instead of money, we are sold too, after we thought we had escaped. I was beginning to feel fairly comfortable once more, after my night's rest, but the look of that envelope makes me sick. It isn't fat enough; $8500 in even the largest bank-notes makes more bulk than that."

"Edward, why do you object to checks?"

"Checks signed by Stephenson! I am resigned to take the $8500 if it could come in bank-notes—for it does seem that it was so ordered, Mary—but I have never had much courage, and I have not the pluck to try to market a check signed with that disastrous name. It would be a trap. That man tried to catch me; we escaped somehow or other; and now he is trying a new way. If it is checks—"

"Oh, Edward, it is TOO bad!" and she held up the checks and began to cry.

"Put them in the fire! quick! we mustn't be tempted. It is a trick to make the world laugh at US, along with the rest, and—Give them to ME, since you can't do it!" He snatched them and tried to hold his grip till he could get to the stove; but he was human, he was a cashier, and he stopped a moment to make sure of the signature. Then he came near to fainting.

"Fan me, Mary, fan me! They are the same as gold!"

"Oh, how lovely, Edward! Why?"

"Signed by Harkness. What can the mystery of that be, Mary?"

"Edward, do you think—"

"Look here—look at this! Fifteen—fifteen —fifteen—thirty-four. Thirty-eight thousand five hundred! Mary, the sack isn't worth twelve dollars, and Harkness—apparently—has paid about par for it."

"And does it all come to us, do you think— instead of the ten thousand?"

"Why, it looks like it. And the checks are made to 'Bearer,' too."

"Is that good, Edward? What is it for?"

"A hint to collect them at some distant bank, I reckon. Perhaps Harkness doesn't want the matter known. What is that—a note?"

"Yes. It was with the checks."

It was in the "Stephenson" handwriting, but there was no signature. It said:

"I am a disappointed man. Your honesty is beyond the reach of temptation. I had a different idea about it, but I wronged you in that, and I beg pardon, and do it sincerely. I honor you—and that is sincere too. This town is not worthy to kiss the hem of your garment. Dear sir, I made a square bet with myself that there were nineteen debauchable men in your self-righteous community. I have lost. Take the whole pot, you are entitled to it."

Richards drew a deep sigh, and said:

"It seems written with fire—it burns so. Mary—I am miserable again."

"I, too. Ah, dear, I wish—"

"To think, Mary—he BELIEVES in me."

"Oh, don't, Edward—I can't bear it."

"If those beautiful words were deserved, Mary—and God knows I believed I deserved them once—I think I could give the forty thousand dollars for them. And I would put that paper away, as representing more than gold and jewels, and keep it always. But now —We could not live in the shadow of its accusing presence, Mary."

He put it in the fire.

A messenger arrived and delivered an envelope. Richards took from it a note and read it; it was from Burgess.

"You saved me, in a difficult time. I saved you last night. It was at cost of a lie, but I made the sacrifice freely, and out of a grateful heart. None in this village knows so well as I know how brave and good and noble you are. At bottom you cannot respect me, knowing as you do of that matter of which I am accused, and by the general voice condemned; but I beg that you will at least believe that I am a grateful man; it will help me to bear my burden.

(Signed)

"Burgess."

"Saved, once more. And on such terms!" He put the note in the fire. "I—I wish I were dead, Mary, I wish I were out of it all."

"Oh, these are bitter, bitter days, Edward. The stabs, through their very generosity, are so deep—and they come so fast!"

Three days before the election each of two thousand voters suddenly found himself in possession of a prized memento—one of the renowned bogus double-eagles. Around one of its faces was stamped these words: "THE REMARK I MADE TO THE POOR STRANGER WAS—."

Around the other face was stamped these: "GO, AND REFORM. (SIGNED) PINKERTON." Thus the entire remaining refuse of the renowned joke was emptied upon a single head, and with calamitous effect. It revived the recent vast laugh and concentrated it upon Pinkerton; and Harkness's election was a walk-over.

Within twenty-four hours after the Richardses had received their checks their consciences were quieting down, discouraged; the old couple were learning to reconcile themselves to the sin which they had committed. But they were to learn, now, that a sin takes on new and real terrors when there seems a chance that it is going to be found out. This gives it a fresh and most substantial and important aspect. At church the morning sermon was of the usual pattern; it was the same old things said in the same old way; they had heard them a thousand times and found them innocuous, next to meaningless, and easy to sleep under; but now it was different; the sermon seemed to bristle with accusations; it seemed aimed straight and specially at people who were concealing deadly sins. After church they got away from the mob of congratulators as soon as they could, and hurried homeward, chilled to the bone at they did not know what —vague, shadowy, indefinite fears. And by chance they caught a glimpse of Mr. Burgess as he turned a corner. He paid no attention to their nod of recognition! He hadn't seen it; but they did not know that. What could his conduct mean? It might mean—it might mean —oh, a dozen dreadful things. Was it possible that he knew that Richards could have cleared him of guilt in that bygone time, and had been silently waiting for a chance to even up accounts? At home, in their distress they got to imagining that their servant might have been in the next room listening when Richards revealed the secret to his wife that he knew of Burgess's innocence; next, Richards began to imagine that he had heard the swish of a gown in there at that time; next, he was sure he HAD heard it. They would call Sarah in, on a pretext, and watch her face: if she had been betraying them to Mr. Burgess, it would show in her manner. They asked her some questions —questions which were so random and incoherent and seemingly purposeless that the girl felt sure that the old people's minds had been affected by their sudden good fortune; the sharp and watchful gaze which they bent upon her frightened her, and that completed the business. She blushed, she became nervous and confused, and to the old people these were plain signs of guilt—guilt of some fearful sort or other—without doubt she was a spy and a traitor. When they were alone again they began to piece many unrelated things together and get horrible results out of the combination. When things had got about to the worst, Richards was delivered of a sudden gasp, and his wife asked,

"Oh, what is it?—what is it?"

"The note—Burgess's note! Its language was sarcastic, I see it now." He quoted: "'At bottom you cannot respect me, KNOWING, as you do, of THAT MATTER of which I am accused' —oh, it is perfectly plain, now, God help me! He knows that I know! You see the ingenuity of the phrasing. It was a trap—and like a fool, I walked into it. And Mary—?"

"Oh, it is dreadful—I know what you are going to say—he didn't return your transcript of the pretended test-remark."

"No—kept it to destroy us with. Mary, he has exposed us to some already. I know it— I know it, well. I saw it in a dozen faces after church. Ah, he wouldn't answer our nod of recognition—HE knew what he had been doing!"

In the night the doctor was called. The news went around in the morning that the old couple were rather seriously ill—prostrated by the exhausting excitement growing out of their great windfall, the congratulations, and the late hours, the doctor said. The town was sincerely distressed; for these old people were about all it had left to be proud of, now.

Two days later the news was worse. The old couple were delirious, and were doing strange things. By witness of the nurses, Richards had exhibited checks—for $8500? No— for an amazing sum—$38,500! What could be the explanation of this gigantic piece of luck?

The following day the nurses had more news —and wonderful. They had concluded to hide the checks, lest harm come to them; but when they searched they were gone from under the patient's pillow—vanished away. The patient said:

"Let the pillow alone; what do you want?"

"We thought it best that the checks—"

"You will never see them again—they are destroyed. They came from Satan. I saw the hell-brand on them, and I knew they were sent to betray me to sin." Then he fell to gabbling strange and dreadful things which were not clearly understandable, and which the doctor admonished them to keep to themselves.

Richards was right; the checks were never seen again.

A nurse must have talked in her sleep, for within two days the forbidden gabblings were the property of the town; and they were of a surprising sort. They seemed to indicate that Richards had been a claimant for the sack himself, and that Burgess had concealed that fact and then maliciously betrayed it.

Burgess was taxed with this and stoutly denied it. And he said it was not fair to attach weight to the chatter of a sick old man who was out of his mind. Still, suspicion was in the air, and there was much talk.

After a day or two it was reported that Mrs. Richards's delirious deliveries were getting to be duplicates of her husband's. Suspicion flamed up into conviction, now, and the town's pride in the purity of its one undiscredited important citizen began to dim down, and flicker toward extinction.

Six days passed, then came more news. The old couple were dying. Richards's mind cleared in his latest hour, and he sent for Burgess. Burgess said:

"Let the room be cleared. I think he wishes to say something in privacy."

"No!" said Richards; "I want witnesses. I want you all to hear my confession, so that I may die a man, and not a dog. I was clean —artificially—like the rest; and like the rest I fell when temptation came. I signed a lie, and claimed the miserable sack. Mr. Burgess remembered that I had done him a service, and in gratitude (and ignorance) he suppressed my claim and saved me. You know the thing that was charged against Burgess years ago. My testimony, and mine alone, could have cleared him, and I was a coward, and left him to suffer disgrace—"

"No—no—Mr. Richards, you—"

"My servant betrayed my secret to him—"

"No one has betrayed anything to me—"

—"and then he did a natural and justifiable thing—he repented of the saving kindness which he had done me, and he EXPOSED me— as I deserved—"

"Never!—I make oath—"

"Out of my heart I forgive him."

Burgess's impassioned protestations fell upon deaf ears; the dying man passed away without knowing that once more he had done poor Burgess a wrong. The old wife died that night.

The last of the sacred Nineteen had fallen a prey to the fiendish sack; the town was stripped of the last rag of its ancient glory. Its mourning was not showy, but it was deep.

By act of the Legislature—upon prayer and petition—Hadleyburg was allowed to change its name to (never mind what—I will not give it away), and leave one word out of the motto that for many generations had graced the town's official seal.[5]

It is an honest town once more, and the man will have to rise early that catches it napping again.   1899

[5] Printed at the end (p. 54) of the story when it appeared in *Harper's Magazine*, C, 29–54 (December, 1899) were the two seals. The original motto was "Lead us not into temptation." The revised motto omits the negative.

WILLIAM DEAN HOWELLS

1837–1920

IN 1884, when young Hamlin Garland made his pilgrimage to Boston, the mecca of light and learning, he found another self-taught Westerner already firmly established in the hierarchy of the mighty. One moment's interview with William Dean Howells, thought Garland, would have been a sufficiently rich reward "for a youth who had only just escaped from spreading manure on an Iowa farm." When Howells talked kindly to him for an hour, he went away exalted.

Howells had risen more rapidly than Garland was to do. Born to a Swedenborgian newspaperman in Martin's Ferry, Ohio, he got what schooling he could as the family zigzagged from one Ohio town to another. His substitutes for high school and college were the newspapers for which he worked, particularly the *Ohio State Journal* of Columbus. A successful campaign biography of Lincoln in 1860 gained Howells an appointment to the American consulate at Venice which lasted until Lincoln's assassination. Back in Boston in 1866 he was soon made subeditor of the nine-year-old *Atlantic Monthly*, whose publisher, James T. Fields, he had met during a pilgrimage to Boston in 1860. After five years he became editor-in-chief, in which capacity he continued until 1881. Before 1871 he had published little but the Lincoln biography, some poetry, and two books on Italy. During his decade as editor-in-chief he produced seven urbane, good-humored, but relatively inconsequential novels, of which the best is *The Lady of the Aroostook* (1879). In 1881 Howells left the *Atlantic* and in 1891 moved from Boston to New York, a mild apostate from Bostonian tradition who drew new life from his changed environment. Although he not infrequently recurred to the novel of manners, his strongest writing belongs to the period 1882-1899. Of the twenty novels which he completed in as many years the best are his study of marital incompatibility, *A Modern Instance* (1882); *The Minister's Charge* (1887), which looks Boston squarely and not too politely in the eye; *A Hazard of New Fortunes* (1890), whose action includes a New York streetcar strike; and *The Rise of Silas Lapham* (1885), his account of a self-made man in brahmin Boston.

For twenty-five years before his death, Howells was known as the "Dean of American Letters," and not without good reason. As novelist, critic, and editor, he sought to liberate American fiction from sterile didacticism, romanticism, and devotion to the exotic. His *Criticism and Fiction* (1891) asks revaluation of art in terms of the real world, the American scene, and the democratic principle. American novelists must be "as American as they unconsciously can"; the arts must look rather to the "work-worn, care-worn, brave, kindly face" of the everyday world than to "the romantic, the bizarre, the heroic." Howells owes to Tolstoy, whom he worshiped, his high concept of fiction as "one in aim with all the other great civilizing forces" which lead toward reform of individuals and social institutions. And yet in practice Howells is rather the "historian of feeling and character" than the propagandist. His satire and irony are always incidental, his sympathies wide, his attitude detached. Modern readers squirm at his talk of "exquisiteness" and "respectability." He did not always choose "nice subjects," but he generally treated them with corseted decorum. Yet he desired only to keep a proper perspective on sex in the novel, and he found the pitiless morality of Zola a sufficient antidote for the Frenchman's occasional indecencies.

Several times Howells was moved to write novels of social purpose. The spectacle of human cruelty and the miseries attendant on capitalistic expansion troubled him increasingly from the eighties onward. Always before his eyes was the example of Tolstoy, the exponent of simple Christian socialism, who he said taught him "to see life . . . as a field of endeavor toward the happiness of the whole human family." Howells' sense of fair play led him to defend the accused during the trial of the Chicago anarchists in 1886. In fiction, besides dozens of other Utopian romances, there was the persuasive teaching of Bellamy's *Looking Backward* (1888), that "forecast . . . of the next stage in the industrial and social development of humanity." Bellamy's hero falls asleep in 1887, awaking in the year 2000 to a new America in which a form of socialism has eliminated class distinctions, religious sectarianism, war, and the profit system.

Some of Bellamy's theorizing reappears in Howells' *A Traveller from Altruria* (1894). To a New England resort hotel comes Aristides Homos, emissary from the recently discovered continent of Altruria (cf. *altruism*), a moneyless, agrarian commonwealth to which (in a sequel, *Through the Eye of the Needle*, 1907) Homos returns with a New York bride. Too long for inclusion here are the final chapters of *A Traveller*, where Homos describes his country's evolution from capitalism to state socialism. But Howells' position is Fabian rather than Marxian: "You can have a righteous public only by the slow process of having righteous men and women."

W. M. Gibson, *A Bibliography of William Dean Howells*, New York, 1948.

Life in Letters of William Dean Howells, Mildred Howells, ed., 2 vols., New York, 1928.

Mark Twain—Howells Letters, H. N. Smith and W. M. Gibson, eds., Cambridge, 1960.

G. N. Bennett, *William Dean Howells; The Development of a Novelist*, Norman, Oklahoma, 1959.

E. H. Cady, *The Road to Realism; The Early Years, 1837–1885, of William Dean Howells*, Syracuse, N. Y., 1956.

_____, *The Realist at War; The Mature Years, 1885–1920, of William Dean Howells*, Syracuse, N. Y., 1958.

Everett Carter, *Howells and the Age of Realism*, Philadelphia, 1954.

D. G. Cooke, *William Dean Howells: A Critical Study*, New York, 1922.

O. W. Firkins, *William Dean Howells: A Study*, Cambridge, 1924.

» » *From:* A TRAVELLER FROM ALTRURIA* « «

CHAPTER II

We left the hotel, and I began to walk my friend across the meadow toward the lake. I wished him to see the reflection of the afterglow in its still waters, with the noble lines of the mountain range that glassed itself there; the effect is one of the greatest charms of that lovely region, the sojourn of the sweetest summer in the world, and I am always impatient to show it to strangers.

We climbed the meadow wall and passed through a stretch of woods, to a path leading down to the shore, and as we loitered along in the tender gloom of the forest, the music of the hermit-thrushes rang all round us, like crystal bells, like silver flutes, like the drip of fountains, like the choiring of still-eyed cherubim. We stopped from time to time and listened, while the shy birds sang unseen in their covert of shadows; but we did not speak till we emerged from the trees and suddenly stood upon the naked knoll overlooking the lake.

Then I explained, "The woods used to come down to the shore here, and we had their mystery and music to the water's edge; but last winter the owner cut the timber off. It looks rather ragged now." I had to recognize the fact, for I saw the Altrurian staring about him over the clearing, in a kind of horror. It was a squalid ruin, a graceless desolation, which not even the pitying twilight could soften. The stumps showed their hideous mutilation everywhere; the brush had been burned,

and the fires had scorched and blackened the lean soil of the hill slope, and blasted it with sterility. A few weak saplings, withered by the flames, drooped and straggled about; it would be a century before the forces of nature could repair the waste.

"You say the owner did this," said the Altrurian. "Who is the owner?"

"Well, it does seem too bad," I answered evasively. "There has been a good deal of feeling about it. The neighbors tried to buy him off before he began the destruction, for they knew the value of the woods as an attraction to summer-boarders; the city cottagers, of course, wanted to save them, and together they offered for the land pretty nearly as much as the timber was worth. But he had got it into his head that the land here by the lake would sell for building lots if it was cleared, and he could make money on that as well as on the trees; and so they had to go. Of course, one might say that he was deficient in public spirit, but I don't blame him, altogether."

"No," the Altrurian assented, somewhat to my surprise, I confess.

I resumed, "There was no one else to look after his interests, and it was not only his right but his duty to get the most he could for himself and his own, according to his best light. That is what I tell people when they fall foul of him for his want of public spirit."

"The trouble seems to be, then, in the system that obliges each man to be the guardian of his own interests. Is that what you blame?"

"No, I consider it a very perfect system. It is based upon individuality, and we believe that individuality is the principle that differences civilized men from savages, from the lower animals, and makes us a nation instead of a tribe or a herd. There isn't one of us, no matter how much he censured this man's want of public spirit, but would resent the slightest interference with his property rights. The woods were his; he had the right to do what he pleased with his own."

10   "Do I understand you that, in America, a man may do what is wrong with his own?"

"He may do anything with his own."

"To the injury of others?"

"Well, not in person or property. But he may hurt them in taste and sentiment as much as he likes. Can't a man do what he pleases with his own in Altruria?"

"No, he can only do right with his own."

"And if he tries to do wrong, or what the
20   community thinks is wrong?"

"Then the community takes his own from him." Before I could think of anything to say to this he went on: "But I wish you would explain to me why it was left to this man's neighbors to try and get him to sell his portion of the landscape?"

"Why, bless my soul!" I exclaimed, "who else was there? You wouldn't have expected to take up a collection among the summer-
30   boarders?"

"That wouldn't have been so unreasonable; but I didn't mean that. Was there no provision for such an exigency in your laws? Wasn't the state empowered to buy him off at the full value of his timber and his land?"

"Certainly not," I replied. "That would be rank paternalism."

It began to get dark, and I suggested that we had better be going back to the hotel. The
40   talk seemed already to have taken us away from all pleasure in the prospect; I said, as we found our way through the rich, balsam-scented twilight of the woods, where one joy-haunted thrush was still singing, "You know that in America the law is careful not to meddle with a man's private affairs, and we don't attempt to legislate personal virtue."

"But marriage," he said, "surely you have the institution of marriage?"

50   I was really annoyed at this. I returned sarcastically, "Yes, I am glad to say that there we can meet your expectation; we have marriage, not only consecrated by the church, but established and defended by the state. What has that to do with the question?"

"And you consider marriage," he pursued, "the citadel of morality, the fountain of all that is pure and good in your private life, the source of home and the image of heaven?"

"There are some marriages," I said with a touch of our national humor, "that do not quite fill the bill, but that is certainly our ideal of marriage."

"Then why do you say that you have not legislated personal virtue in America?" he asked. "You have laws, I believe, against theft and murder, and slander and incest, and perjury and drunkenness?"

"Why, certainly."

"Then it appears to me that you have legislated honesty, regard for human life, regard for character, abhorrence of unnatural vice, good faith and sobriety. I was told on the train coming up, by a gentleman who was shocked at the sight of a man beating his horse, that you even had laws against cruelty to animals."

"Yes, and I am happy to say that they are enforced to such a degree that a man cannot kill a cat cruelly without being punished for it." The Altrurian did not follow up his advantage, and I resolved not to be outdone in magnanimity. "Come, I will own that you have the best of me on those points. I must say you've trapped me very neatly, too; I can enjoy a thing of that kind when it's well done, and I frankly knock under. But I had in mind something altogether different when I spoke. I was thinking of those idealists who want to bind us hand and foot, and render us the slaves of a state where the most intimate relations of life shall be penetrated by legislation, and the very hearthstone shall be a tablet of laws."

"Isn't marriage a rather intimate relation of life?" asked the Altrurian. "And I understood that gentleman on the train to say that you had laws against cruelty to children, and societies established to see them enforced. You don't consider such laws an invasion of the home, do you, or a violation of its immunities? I imagine," he went on, "that the difference between your civilization and ours is only one of degree, after all, and that America and Altruria are really one at heart."

I thought his compliment a bit hyperbolical, but I saw that it was honestly meant, and as we Americans are first of all patriots, and vain for our country before we are vain for ourselves, I was not proof against the flattery it conveyed to me civically if not personally.

CHAPTER III

The Altrurian did not try to detain me this time. He said he should be very glad indeed to meet my friends, and I led the way toward a little group at the corner of the piazza. They were men whom I particularly liked, for one reason or another; they were intelligent and open-minded, and they were thoroughly American. One was a banker; another was a minister; there was a lawyer, and there was a doctor; there was a professor of political economy in one of our colleges; and there was a retired manufacturer—I do not know what he used to manufacture: cotton or iron, or something like that. They all rose politely as I came up with my Altrurian, and I fancied in them a sensation of expectancy created by the rumor of his eccentric behavior which must have spread through the hotel. But they controlled this if they had it, and I could see, as the light fell upon his face from a spray of electrics on the nearest pillar, that sort of liking kindle in theirs which I had felt myself at first sight of him.

I said, "Gentlemen, I wish to introduce my friend, Mr. Homos," and then I presented them severally to him by name. We all sat down, and I explained: "Mr. Homos is from Altruria. He is visiting our country for the first time, and is greatly interested in the working of our institutions. He has been asking me some rather hard questions about certain phases of our civilization; and the fact is that I have launched him upon you because I don't feel quite able to cope with him."

They all laughed civilly at this sally of mine, but the professor asked, with a sarcasm that I thought I hardly merited, "What point in our polity can be obscured to the author of 'Glove and Gauntlet' and 'Airs and Graces'?"

They all laughed again, not so civilly, I felt, and then the banker asked my friend, "Is it long since you left Altruria?"

"It seems a great while ago," the Altrurian answered, "but it is really only a few weeks."

"You came by way of England, I suppose?"

"Yes; there is no direct line to America," said the Altrurian.

"That seems rather odd," I ventured, with some patriotic grudge.

"Oh, the English have direct lines everywhere," the banker instructed me.

"The tariff has killed our shipbuilding," said the professor. No one took up this firebrand, and the professor added, "Your name is Greek, isn't it, Mr. Homos?"

"Yes; we are of one of the early Hellenic families," said the Altrurian.

"And do you think," asked the lawyer, who, like most lawyers, was a lover of romance, and was well read in legendary lore especially, "that there is any reason for supposing that Altruria is identical with the fabled Atlantis?"

"No, I can't say that I do. We have no traditions of a submergence of the continent, and there are only the usual evidences of a glacial epoch which you find everywhere to support such a theory. Besides, our civilization is strictly Christian, and dates back to no earlier period than that of the first Christian commune after Christ. It is a matter of history with us that one of these communists, when they were dispersed, brought the gospel to our continent; he was cast away on our eastern coast on his way to Britian."

"Yes, we know that," the minister intervened, "but it is perfectly astonishing that an island so large as Altruria should have been lost to the knowledge of the rest of the world ever since the beginning of our era. You would hardly think that there was a space of the ocean's surface a mile square which had not been traversed by a thousand keels since Columbus sailed westward."

"No, you wouldn't. And I wish," the doctor suggested in his turn, "that Mr. Homos would tell us something about his country, instead of asking us about ours."

"Yes," I coincided, "I'm sure we should all find it a good deal easier. At least I should; but I brought our friend up in the hope that the professor would like nothing better than to train a battery of hard facts upon a defenceless stranger." Since the professor had given me that little stab, I was rather anxious to see how he would handle the desire for information in the Altrurian which I had found so prickly.

This turned the laugh on the professor, and he pretended to be as curious about Altruria as the rest, and said he would rather hear of it. But the Altrurian said: "I hope you will excuse me. Sometime I shall be glad to talk of Altruria as long as you like; or if you will come to us, I shall be still happier to show you many things that I couldn't make you understand at a distance. But I am in America to learn, not to teach, and I hope you will have patience with my ignorance. I begin to be afraid that it is so great as to seem a little incredible. I have fancied in my friend here," he went on, with a smile toward me, "a suspicion that I was not entirely single in some of the inquiries I have made, but that I had some ulterior motive, some wish to censure or satirize."

"Oh, not at all!" I protested, for it was not polite to admit a conjecture so accurate. "We are so well satisfied with our condition that we have nothing but pity for the darkened mind of the foreigner, though we believe in it fully: we are used to the English tourist."

My friends laughed and the Altrurian continued: "I am very glad to hear it, for I feel myself at a peculiar disadvantage among you. I am not only a foreigner, but I am so alien to you in all the traditions and habitudes that I find it very difficult to get upon common ground with you. Of course I know theoretically what you are, but to realize it practically is another thing. I had read so much about America and understood so little that I could not rest without coming to see for myself. Some of the apparent contradictions were so colossal"—

"We have everything on a large scale here," said the banker, breaking off the ash of his cigar with the end of his little finger, "and we rather pride ourselves on the size of our inconsistencies, even. I know something of the state of things in Altruria, and, to be frank with you, I will say that it seems to me preposterous. I should say it was impossible, if it were not an accomplished fact; but I always feel bound to recognize the thing done. You have hitched your wagon to a star, and you have made the star go; there is never any trouble with wagons, but stars are not easily broken to harness, and you have managed to get yours well in hand. As I said, I don't believe in you, but I respect you." I thought this charming, myself; perhaps because it stated my own mind about Altruria so exactly and in terms so just and generous.

"Pretty good," said the doctor, in a murmur of satisfaction, at my ear, "for a bloated bond-holder."

"Yes," I whispered back, "I wish I had said it. What an American way of putting it! Emerson would have liked it himself. After all, *he* was our prophet."

"He must have thought so from the way we kept stoning him," said the doctor, with a soft laugh.

"Which of our contradictions," asked the banker, in the same tone of gentle bonhomie, "has given you and our friend pause, just now?"

The Altrurian answered after a moment: "I am not sure that it is a contradiction, for as yet I have not ascertained the facts I was seeking. Our friend was telling me of the great change that had taken place in regard to work, and the increased leisure that your professional people are now allowing themselves; and I was asking him where your workingmen spent their leisure."

He went over the list of those he had specified, and I hung my head in shame and pity; it really had such an effect of mawkish sentimentality. But my friends received it in the best possible way. They did not laugh; they heard him out, and then they quietly deferred to the banker, who made answer for us all:

"Well, I can be almost as brief as the historian of Iceland in his chapter on snakes: those people have no leisure to spend."

"Except when they go out on a strike," said the manufacturer, with a certain grim humor of his own; I never heard anything more dramatic than the account he once gave of the way he broke up a labor-union. "I have seen a good many of them at leisure then."

"Yes," the doctor chimed in, "and in my younger days, when I necessarily had a good deal of charity-practice, I used to find them at leisure when they were 'laid off.' It always struck me as such a pretty euphemism. It seemed to minify the harm of the thing so. It seemed to take all the hunger and cold and sickness out of the fact. To be simply 'laid off' was so different from losing your work and having to face beggary or starvation!"

"Those people," said the professor, "never put anything by. They are wasteful and improvident, almost to a man; and they learn nothing by experience, though they know as well as we do that it is simply a question of demand and supply, and that the day of overproduction is sure to come, when their work must stop unless the men that give them work are willing to lose money."

"And I've seen them lose it, sometimes, rather than shut down," the manufacturer remarked; "lose it hand over hand, to keep the men at work; and then as soon as the tide turned the men would strike for higher wages. You have no idea of the ingratitude of those people." He said this towards the minister, as if he did not wish to be thought hard; and in fact he was a very kindly man.

"Yes," replied the minister, "that is one of

the most sinister features of the situation. They seem really to regard their employers as their enemies. I don't know how it will end."

1894

1894

PAUL HAMILTON HAYNE

1830–1886

AS A YOUNG MAN Hayne was a member of the cultivated ante-bellum society of Charleston, South Carolina. Hayne's father, a naval officer, died when the boy was an infant, so he grew up in the home of his uncle Senator Robert Y. Hayne, Webster's opponent in the famous two-weeks-long debate of 1830. After graduating from the College of Charleston, young Hayne tried the law, but soon abandoned it for writing. When a group of the city's literary men founded, in 1857, *Russell's Magazine*, named for its backer, the leading bookseller of Charleston, Hayne was made editor. Before the Civil War interrupted his career, he had published three volumes of verse: *Poems* (1855), *Sonnets and Other Poems* (1857), and *Avolio* (1860).

During the war Hayne's Charleston house and most of his library were destroyed. After the war ended he built a shack, furnished with packing boxes and papered with magazine illustrations, at "Copse Hill," in the pine-barrens near Augusta, Georgia. Here, in extreme poverty but contented with his life, he wrote his later poems, gathered into the *Collected Poems* of 1882. During these years he corresponded with Longfellow, Bryant, Sidney Lanier, Holmes, Lowell, Tennyson, and Swinburne. As his war poems had done much to put fight into the Confederate soldiers, so his later verses, as well as his charitable attitude toward the victors, helped to heal the breach between North and South.

Hayne's poetry, save for a few good lyrics, is sentimental and often pointlessly descriptive. His deliberate exclusion from his verse of all save "poetic" subjects endeared him to the English Pre-Raphaelites.

Poems of Paul Hamilton Hayne, Boston, 1882. (Contains a brief biographical sketch by Margaret J. Preston.)
Kate H. Beecher, *Paul Hamilton Hayne: Life and Letters*, Belmont, N. C., 1951.
The Correspondence of Bayard Taylor and Paul Hamilton Hayne, Charles Duffy, ed., Baton Rouge, La., 1945.
C. R. Anderson, "Charles Gayarre and Paul Hayne: The Last Literary Cavaliers," in *American Studies in Honor of William Kenneth Boyd*, Durham, N. C., 1940, pp. 221–281.

ASPECTS OF THE PINES

Tall, sombre, grim, against the morning sky
  They rise, scarce touched by melancholy airs,
Which stir the fadeless foliage dreamfully,
  As if from realms of mystical despairs.

Tall, sombre, grim, they stand with dusky gleams
  Brightening to gold within the woodland's core,

Beneath the gracious noontide's tranquil beams—
  But the weird winds of morning sigh no more.

A stillness, strange, divine, ineffable,
  Broods round and o'er them in the wind's surcease,   10
And on each tinted copse and shimmering dell
  Rests the mute rapture of deep-hearted peace.

Last, sunset comes—the solemn joy and might
  Borne from the West when cloudless day
    declines—
Low, flutelike breezes sweep the waves of
    light,
  And lifting dark green tresses of the pines,

Till every lock is luminous—gently float,
  Fraught with hale odors up the heavens
    afar
To faint when twilight on her virginal throat
  Wears for a gem the tremulous vesper
    star.   20
                      1858

THE COTTAGE ON THE HILL

On a steep hillside, to all airs that blow,
Open, and open to the varying sky,
Our cottage homestead, smiling tranquilly,
Catches morn's earliest and eve's latest glow;
Here, far from worldly strife, and pompous
    show,
The peaceful seasons glide serenely by,
Fulfil their missions, and as calmly die,
As waves on quiet shores when winds are low.
Fields, lonely paths, the one small glimmering
    rill
That twinkles like a wood-fay's mirthful eye, 10
Under moist bay-leaves, clouds fantastical
That float and change at the light breeze's
    will,—
To me, thus lapped in sylvan luxury,
Are more than death of kings, or empires' fall.
                      1872

TWO EPOCHS

Lovers by a dim sea strand
Looking wave-ward, hand in hand;
Silent, trembling with the bliss
Of their first betrothal kiss:

Lovers still, tho' wedded long!
(Time true love can never wrong!)
Gazing—faithful hand in hand,
O'er a darker sea and strand;

Ah! one lover's face is wan
As a wave the moon shines on;   10
But those strange tides stretched afar
Know not sun, nor moon, nor star!
                      1882

THE MOCKING-BIRD

A golden pallor of voluptuous light
Filled the warm southern night:
The moon, clear orbed, above the sylvan scene
Moved like a stately queen,
So rife with conscious beauty all the while,
What could she do but smile
At her own perfect loveliness below,
Glassed in the tranquil flow
Of crystal fountains and unruffled streams?
Half lost in waking dreams,   10
As down the loneliest forest dell I strayed,
Lo! from a neighboring glade,
Flashed through the drifts of moonshine,
    swiftly came
A fairy shape of flame.
It rose in dazzling spirals overhead,
Whence to wild sweetness wed,
Poured marvelous melodies, silvery trill on trill;
The very leaves grew still
On the charmed trees to hearken; while for me,
Heart-trilled to ecstasy,   20
I followed—followed the bright shape that
    flew,
Still circling up the blue,
Till as a fountain that has reached its height,
Falls back in sprays of light
Slowly dissolved, so that enrapturing lay
Divinely melts away
Through tremulous spaces to a music-mist,
Soon by the fitful breeze
  How gently kissed
Into remote and tender silences.   30
                      1882

» »   « «

SIDNEY LANIER

1842–1881

DESPITE THE STERILITIES of army and business life, despite constant poverty, pain, weariness, and sickness, wrote Lanier to his father in 1873, "think how . . . these two figures of music and poetry have steadily kept in my heart so that I could not banish them." He had spent four-fifths of his life in uncongenial occupations. Now, half-apologetically, he said that he must follow the bent of his genius. But little time remained: he had fought tuberculosis for eight years; in another eight the disease would kill him.

Not far from Lanier's birthplace in Macon, Georgia, stood the Presbyterian university, Ogle-thorpe, whence he was graduated (1860) at the top of his class, and to whose faculty he was immediately appointed. Dreams of study in Germany were destroyed by the Civil War. As a volunteer private, Lanier saw action under Lee during Grant's attack on Petersburg (described in his novel, *Tiger Lilies*, 1867), and in 1864 was assigned to naval scout duty, helping Confederate shipping run the blockade off Wilmington, N. C. Captured at sea, Lanier spent four hellish months in prison camp at Point Lookout, Maryland, with men dying around him at the rate of twenty a day. Upon his release, half-dead of lung inflammation and starvation, he managed somehow to limp home to Macon and several months' illness from the effects of which he never recovered.

In the dark days of so-called Reconstruction, Lanier felt strongly the "drought and famine" of his intellectual life. "With us of the younger generation in the South since the war, pretty much the whole of life has been not dying." But having come north to Baltimore in 1873, he began the long-deferred pursuit of those "two sublime arts," music and poetry, filled with an enthusiasm that belied his ebbing strength. Despite continued poverty and ill-health, he managed one by one to fulfill his ambitions: playing in Baltimore's symphony orchestra, publishing a collection of poetry (Philadelphia, 1876, dated 1877), and lecturing on poetry and the novel at Johns Hopkins (1879–1881).

Music, which he regarded as the highest of the arts, is the touchstone of Lanier's poetics. His cryptic definition of music as "love in search of a word" is elaborated by one of the characters in *Tiger Lilies:* "Music means harmony, harmony means love, love means—God!" But he is less transcendental in his pioneering study of poetic technique, *The Science of English Verse* (1880), which seeks to establish a musical basis for the analysis of poetic metre. Thus blank verse can be read in "three-four" time, while the tone-color of a symphony can be duplicated in poetry through the considered arrangement of assonance, rhyme, consonantal alliteration, and euphonic vowels. In his own poetry Lanier achieved effects which resemble, without consciously imitating, those of Swinburne and the young Tennyson. His critical precepts triumphantly survive the test of practice in poems like "The Marshes of Glynn."

The Centennial Edition of Sidney Lanier, C. R. Anderson, ed., 10 vols., Baltimore, 1945.
The Letters of Sidney Lanier: Selections from His Correspondence, 1866–1881, H. W. Lanier, ed., New York, 1899.
M. C. Jones, *Sidney Lanier: A Chronological Record of Authenticated Facts,* Macon, Georgia, 1940.
A. H. Starke, *Sidney Lanier,* Chapel Hill, 1933.
Richard Webb and E. R. Coulson, *Sidney Lanier, Poet and Prosodist,* Athens, Georgia, 1941.

» » THE SYMPHONY « «

"O Trade! O Trade! would thou wert dead!
The time needs heart—'tis tired of head:
We're all for love," the violins said.
"Of what avail the rigorous tale
Of bill for coin and box for bale?
Grant thee, O Trade! thine uttermost hope:
Level red gold with blue sky-slope,
And base it deep as devils grope:
When all's done, what hast thou won
Of the only sweet that's under the sun?   10
Ay, canst thou buy a single sigh
Of true love's least, least ecstasy?"
Then, with a bridegroom's heart-beats trem-
    bling,
All the mightier strings assembling
Ranged them on the violins' side
As when the bridegroom leads the bride,
And, heart in voice, together cried:
"Yea, what avail the endless tale
Of gain by cunning and plus by sale?
Look up the land, look down the land   20
The poor, the poor, the poor, they stand
Wedged by the pressing of Trade's hand
Against an inward-opening door
That pressure tightens evermore:
They sigh a monstrous foul-air sigh
For the outside leagues of liberty,
Where Art, sweet lark, translates the sky
Into a heavenly melody.
'Each day, all day' (these poor folks say),
'In the same old year-long, drear-long way,   30
We weave in the mills and heave in the kilns,
We sieve mine-meshes under the hills,
And thieve much gold from the Devil's bank
    tills,
To relieve, O God, what manner of ills?—
The beasts, they hunger, and eat, and die;
And so do we, and the world's a sty;
Hush, fellow-swine: why nuzzle and cry?
Swinehood hath no remedy
Say many men, and hasten by,
Clamping the nose and blinking the eye.   40
But who said once, in the lordly tone,
Man shall not live by bread alone
But all that cometh from the Throne?
    Hath God said so?
    But Trade saith *No:*
And the kilns and the curt-tongued mills say
    Go!
There's plenty that can, if you can't: we know.
Move out, if you think you're underpaid.

The poor are prolific; we're not afraid;
    Trade is trade.' "   50
Thereat this passionate protesting
Meekly changed, and softened till
It sank to sad requesting
And suggesting sadder still:
"And oh, if men might some time see
How piteous-false the poor decree
That trade no more than trade must be!
Does business mean, *Die, you—live, I?*
Then 'Trade is trade' but sings a lie:
'Tis only war grown miserly.   60
If business is battle, name it so:
War-crimes less will shame it so,
And widows less will blame it so.
Alas, for the poor to have some part
In yon sweet living lands of Art,
Makes problem not for head, but heart.
Vainly might Plato's brain revolve it:
Plainly the heart of a child could solve it."

And then, as when from words that seem but
    rude
We pass to silent pain that sits abrood   70
Back in our heart's great dark and solitude,
So sank the strings to gentle throbbing
Of long chords change-marked with sobbing—
Motherly sobbing, not distinctlier heard
Than half wing-openings of the sleeping bird,
Some dream of danger to her young hath
    stirred.
Then stirring and demurring ceased, and lo!
Every least ripple of the strings' song-flow
Died to a level with each level bow   79
And made a great chord tranquil-surfaced so,
As a brook beneath his curving bank doth go
To linger in the sacred dark and green
Where many boughs the still pool overlean
And many leaves make shadow with their
    sheen.
    But presently
A velvet flute-note fell down pleasantly
Upon the bosom of that harmony,
And sailed and sailed incessantly,
As if a petal from a wild-rose blown
Had fluttered down upon that pool of tone   90
And boatwise dropped o' the convex side
And floated down the glassy tide
And clarified and glorified
The solemn places where the shadows bide.
From the warm concave of that fluted note

Somewhat, half song, half odor, forth did float,
As if a rose might somehow be a throat:
"When Nature from her far-off glen
Flutes her soft messages to men,
  The flute can say them o'er again;   100
  Yea, Nature, singing sweet and lone,
Breathes through life's strident polyphone
The flute-voice in the world of tone.
  Sweet friends,
  Man's love ascends
To finer and diviner ends
Than man's mere thought e'er comprehends.
For I, e'en I,
As here I lie,
A petal on a harmony,   110
Demand of Science whence and why
Man's tender pain, man's inward cry,
When he doth gaze on earth and sky?
I am not overbold:
  I hold
Full powers from Nature manifold.
I speak for each no-tonguéd tree
That, spring by spring, doth nobler be,
And dumbly and most wistfully
His mighty prayerful arms outspreads   120
Above men's oft-unheeding heads,
And his big blessing downward sheds.
I speak for all-shaped blooms and leaves,
Lichens on stones and moss on eaves,
Grasses and grains in ranks and sheaves;
Broad-fronded ferns and keen-leaved canes,
And briery mazes bounding lanes,
And marsh-plants, thirsty-cupped for rains,
And milky stems and sugary veins;
For every long-armed woman-vine   130
That round a piteous tree doth twine;
For passionate odors, and divine
Pistils, and petals crystalline;
All purities of shady springs,
All shynesses of film-winged things
That fly from tree-trunks and bark-rings;
All modesties of mountain-fawns
That leap to covert from wild lawns,
And tremble if the day but dawns;
All sparklings of small beady eyes   140
Of birds, and sidelong glances wise
Wherewith the jay hints tragedies;
All piquancies of prickly burs,
And smoothnesses of downs and furs
Of eiders and of minevers;
All limpid honeys that do lie
At stamen-bases, nor deny
The humming-birds' fine roguery,
Bee-thighs, nor any butterfly;
All gracious curves of slender wings,   150

Bark-mottlings, fibre-spiralings,
Fern-wavings and leaf-flickerings;
Each dial-marked leaf and flower-bell
Wherewith in every lonesome dell
Time to himself his hours doth tell;
All tree-sounds, rustlings of pine cones,
Wind-sighings, doves' melodious moans,
And night's unearthly under-tones;
All placid lakes and waveless deeps,
All cool reposing mountain-steeps,   160
Vale-calms and tranquil lotos-sleeps;—
Yea, all fair forms, and sounds and lights,
And warmths, and mysteries, and mights,
Of Nature's utmost depths and heights,
—These doth my timid tongue present,
Their mouthpiece and leal instrument
And servant, all love-eloquent.
I heard, when '*All for love*' the violins cried:
So, Nature calls through all her system wide,
Give me thy love, O man, so long denied.   170
Much time is run, and man hath changed his
    ways,
Since Nature, in the antique fable-days,
Was hid from man's true love by proxy fays,
False fauns and rascal gods that stole her
    praise.
The nymphs, cold creatures of man's colder
    brain,
Chilled Nature's streams till man's warm heart
    was fain
Never to lave its love in them again.
Later, a sweet Voice *Love thy neighbor* said;
Then first the bounds of neighborhood out-
    spread
Beyond all confines of old ethnic dread.   180
Vainly the Jew might wag his covenant head:
'*All men are neighbors,*' so the sweet Voice
    said.
So, when man's arms had circled all man's race,
The liberal compass of his warm embrace
Stretched bigger yet in the dark bounds of
    space;
With hands a-grope he felt smooth Nature's
    grace,
Drew her to breast and kissed her sweetheart
    face:
Yea man found neighbors in great hills and
    trees
And streams and clouds and suns and birds
    and bees,
And throbbed with neighbor-loves in loving
    these.   190
But oh, the poor! the poor! the poor!
That stand by the inward-opening door
Trade's hand doth tighten ever more,

And sigh their monstrous foul-air sigh
For the outside hills of liberty,
Where Nature spreads her wild blue sky
For Art to make into melody!
Thou Trade! thou king of the modern days!
   Change thy ways,
   Change thy ways;   200
Let the sweaty laborers file
   A little while,
   A little while,
Where Art and Nature sing and smile.
Trade! is thy heart all dead, all dead?
And hast thou nothing but a head?
I'm all for heart," the flute-voice said,
And into sudden silence fled,
Like as a blush that while 'tis red
Dies to a still, still white instead.   210

   Thereto a thrilling calm succeeds,
Till presently the silence breeds
A little breeze among the reeds
That seems to blow by sea-marsh weeds:
Then from the gentle stir and fret
Sings out the melting clarionet,
Like as a lady sings while yet
Her eyes with salty tears are wet.
"O Trade! O Trade!" the Lady said,
"I too will wish thee utterly dead   220
If all thy heart is in thy head.
For O my God! and O my God!
What shameful ways have women trod
At beckoning of Trade's golden rod!
Alas when sighs are traders' lies,
And heart's-ease eyes and violet eyes
   Are merchandise!
O purchased lips that kiss with pain!
O cheeks coin-spotted with smirch and stain!
O trafficked hearts that break in twain!   230
—And yet what wonder at my sisters' crime?
So hath Trade withered up Love's sinewy
     prime,
Men love not women as in olden time.
Ah, not in these cold merchantable days
Deem men their life an opal gray, where plays
The one red Sweet of gracious ladies'-praise.
Now, comes a suitor with sharp prying eye—
Says, *Here, you Lady, if you'll sell, I'll buy:*
Come, heart for heart—a trade? What! weep-
    ing? why?
Shame on such wooers' dapper mercery!   240
I would my lover kneeling at my feet
In humble manliness should cry, *O sweet!*
I know not if thy heart my heart will greet:
I ask not if thy love my love can meet:
Whate'er thy worshipful soft tongue shall say,

I'll kiss thine answer, be it yea or nay:
I do but know I love thee, and I pray
To be thy knight until my dying day.
Woe him that cunning trades in hearts con-
    trives!   249
Base love good women to base loving drives.
If men loved larger, larger were our lives;
And wooed they nobler, won they nobler
    wives."

There thrust the bold straightforward horn
To battle for that lady lorn,
With heartsome voice of mellow scorn,
Like any knight in knighthood's morn.
   "Now comfort thee," said he,
    "Fair Lady.
For God shall right thy grievous wrong,
And man shall sing thee a true-love song,   260
Voiced in act his whole life long,
   Yea, all thy sweet life long,
    Fair Lady.
Where's he that craftily hath said,
The day of chivalry is dead?
I'll prove that lie upon his head,
   Or I will die instead,
    Fair Lady.
Is Honor gone into his grave?
Hath Faith become a caitiff knave,   270
And Selfhood turned into a slave,
   To work in Mammon's cave,
    Fair Lady?
Will Truth's long blade ne'er gleam again?
Hath Giant Trade in dungeons slain
All great contempts of mean-got gain
   And hates of inward stain,
    Fair Lady?
For aye shall name and fame be sold,
And place be hugged for the sake of gold,   280
And smirch-robed Justice feebly scold
   At Crime all money-bold,
    Fair Lady?
Shall self-wrapt husbands aye forget
Kiss-pardons for the daily fret
Wherewith sweet wifely eyes are wet—
   Blind to lips kiss-wise set—
    Fair Lady?
Shall lovers higgle, heart for heart,
Till wooing grows a trading mart   290
Where much for little, and all for part,
   Make love a cheapening art,
    Fair Lady?
Shall woman scorch for a single sin
That her betrayer may revel in,
And she be burnt, and he but grin

When that the flames begin,
  Fair Lady?
Shall ne'er prevail the woman's plea,
We maids would far, far whiter be 300
If that our eyes might sometimes see
  Men maids in purity,
    Fair Lady?
Shall Trade aye salve his conscience-aches
With jibes at Chivalry's old mistakes—
The wars that o'erhot knighthood makes
  For Christ's and ladies' sakes,
    Fair Lady?
Now by each knight that e'er hath prayed
To fight like a man and love like a maid, 310
Since Pembroke's life, as Pembroke's blade,
  I' the scabbard, death, was laid,
    Fair Lady,
I dare avouch my faith is bright
That God doth right and God hath might.
Nor time hath changed His hair to white,
  Nor His dear love to spite,
    Fair Lady.
I doubt no doubts: I strive, and shrive my clay,
And fight my fight in the patient modern way
For true love and for thee—ah me! and pray
  To be thy knight until my dying day, 322
    Fair Lady."
Made end the knightly horn, and spurred away
Into the thick of the melodious fray.

And then the hautboy played and smiled,
And sang like any large-eyed child,
Cool-hearted and all undefiled.
  "Huge Trade!" he said,
"Would thou wouldst lift me on thy head 330
And run where'er my finger led!
Once said a Man—and wise was He—
Never shalt thou the heavens see,
Save as a little child thou be."

Then o'er sea-lashings of commingling tunes
The ancient wise bassoons,
  Like weird
  Gray-beard
Old harpers sitting on the high sea-dunes,
  Chanted runes: 340
"Bright-waved gain, gray-waved loss,
The sea of all doth lash and toss,
One wave forward and one across:
But now 'twas trough, now 'tis crest,
And worst doth foam and flash to best,
  And curst to blest.

Life! Life! thou sea-fugue, writ from east to
    west
  Love, Love alone can pore
  On thy dissolving score
  Of harsh half-phrasings, 350
    Blotted ere writ,
  And double erasings
  Of chords most fit.
Yea, Love, sole music-master blest,
May read thy weltering palimpsest.
To follow Time's dying melodies through,
And never to lose the old in the new,
And ever to solve the discords true—
  Love alone can do.
And ever Love hears the poor-folks' crying,
And ever Love hears the women's sighing, 361
And ever sweet knighthood's death-defying,
And ever wise childhood's deep implying,
But never a trader's glozing and lying.

And yet shall Love himself be heard,
Though long deferred, though long deferred:
O'er the modern waste a dove hath whirred:
Music is Love in search of a word."
Baltimore, 1875   1875

» » UNCLE JIM'S BAPTIST REVIVAL HYMN « «

By Sidney and Clifford Lanier

(Not long ago a certain Georgia cotton-planter, driven to desperation by awaking each morning to find that the grass had quite outgrown the cotton overnight, and was likely to choke it, in defiance of his lazy freedmen's hoes and ploughs, set the whole State in a laugh by exclaiming to a group of fellow-sufferers: "It's all stuff about Cincinnatus leaving the plough to go into politics *for patriotism;* he was just a-runnin' from grass!"

This state of things—when the delicate young rootlets of the cotton are struggling against the hardier multitudes of the grass-suckers—is universally described in plantation parlance by the phrase "in the grass"; and Uncle Jim appears to have found in it so much similarity to the condition of his own ("Baptis'") church, overrun, as it was, by the cares of this world, that he has embodied it in the refrain of a revival hymn such as the colored improvisator of the South not infrequently constructs from his daily surroundings. He has drawn all the ideas of his stanzas from the early morning phenomena of those critical weeks when the loud plantation-horn is blown before daylight, in order to rouse all hands for a long day's fight against the common enemy of cotton-planting mankind.

In addition to these exegetical commentaries, the Northern reader probably needs to be informed that the phrase "peerten up" means substantially *to spur up*, and is an active form of the adjective "peert" (probably a corruption of *pert*), which is so common in the South, and which has much the signification of "smart" in New England, as e.g., a "peert" horse, in antithesis to a "sorry"—i.e. poor, mean, lazy one.)

Solo.—   Sin's rooster's crowed, Ole Mahster's
              riz,
          De sleepin'-time is pas';
          Wake up dem lazy Baptissis,
Chorus.—   *Dey's mightily in de grass, grass,*
            Dey's mightily in de grass.

          Ole Mahster's blowed de mornin'-
              horn,
          He's blowed a powerful blas';
          O Baptis' come, come hoe de corn,
              You's mightily in de grass, grass,
              You's mightily in de grass.   10

          De Meth'dis team's done hitched; O
              fool,
          De day's a-breakin' fas';
          Gear up dat lean ole Baptis' mule,
              Dey's mightily in de grass, grass,
              Dey's mightily in de grass.

          De workmen's few an' mons'rous
              slow,
          De cotton's sheddin' fas';
          Whoop, look, jes' look at de Baptis'
              row,
              Hit's mightily in de grass, grass,
              Hit's mightily in de grass.   20

          De jay-bird squeal to de mockin'-
              bird: "Stop!
          Don' gimme none o' yo' sass;
          Better sing one song for de Baptis'
              crop,
              Dey's mightily in de grass, grass,
              Dey's mightily in de grass."

          And de ole crow croak: "Don' work,
              no, no;
          But de fiel'-lark say, "Yaas, yaas,
          An' I spec' you mighty glad, you deb-
              blish crow,
              Dat de Baptissis's in de grass,
                  grass,   29
              Dat de Baptissis's in de grass!"

          Lord, thunder us up to de plowin'-
              match,
          Lord, peerten de hoein' fas',
          Yea, Lord, hab mussy on de Baptis'
              patch,
              Dey's mightily in de grass, grass,
              Dey's mightily in de grass.
1876   1876

» » THE MARSHES OF GLYNN [1] « «

Glooms of the live-oaks, beautiful-braided and
     woven
With intricate shades of the vines that myriad-
     cloven
     Clamber the forks of the multiform
         boughs,—
         Emerald twilights,—
         Virginal shy lights,
     Wrought of the leaves to allure to the whis-
         per of vows,
When lovers pace timidly down through the
     green colonnades
Of the dim sweet woods, of the dear dark
     woods,
Of the heavenly woods and glades,
That run to the radiant marginal sand-beach
     within   10
     The wide sea-marshes of Glynn;—

Beautiful glooms, soft dusks in the noon-day
     fire,—
Wildwood privacies, closets of lone desire,
Chamber from chamber parted with wavering
     arras of leaves,—
Cells for the passionate pleasure of prayer to
     the soul that grieves,
Pure with a sense of the passing of saints
     through the wood,
Cool for the dutiful weighing of ill with
     good;—

[1] A monument to Lanier has been erected on the edge of the marshes, which are in the vicinity of Brunswick, Georgia.

O braided dusks of the oak and woven shades
of the vine,
While the riotous noon-day sun of the June-
day long did shine
Ye held me fast in your heart and I held you
fast in mine;   20
But now when the noon is no more, and riot is
rest,
And the sun is a-wait at the ponderous gate of
the West,
And the slant yellow beam down the wood-
aisle doth seem
Like a lane into heaven that leads from a
dream,—
Ay, now, when my soul all day hath drunken
the soul of the oak,
And my heart is at ease from men, and the
wearisome sound of the stroke
Of the scythe of time and the trowel of
trade is low,
And belief overmasters doubt, and I know
that I know,
And my spirit is grown to a lordly great
compass within,
That the length and the breadth and the sweep
of the marshes of Glynn   30
Will work me no fear like the fear they have
wrought me of yore
When length was fatigue, and when breadth
was but bitterness sore,
And when terror and shrinking and dreary un-
namable pain
Drew over me out of the merciless miles of the
plain,—

Oh, now, unafraid, I am fain to face
The vast sweet visage of space.
To the edge of the wood I am drawn, I am
drawn,
Where the gray beach glimmering runs, as a
belt of the dawn,
For a mete and a mark
To the forest-dark:—   40
So:
Affable live-oak, leaning low,—
Thus—with your favor—soft, with a reverent
hand,
(Not lightly touching your person, Lord of the
land!)
Bending your beauty aside, with a step I stand
On the firm-packed sand,
Free
By a world of marsh that borders a world of
sea.

Sinuous southward and sinuous northward
the shimmering band
Of the sand-beach fastens the fringe of the
marsh to the folds of the land.   50
Inward and outward to northward and southward the beach-lines linger and curl
As a silver-wrought garment that clings to and
follows the firm sweet limbs of a girl.
Vanishing, swerving, evermore curving again
into sight,
Softly the sand-beach wavers away to a dim
gray looping of light.
And what if behind me to westward the wall
of the woods stands high?
The world lies east: how ample, the marsh and
the sea and the sky!
A league and a league of marsh-grass, waist-
high, broad in the blade,
Green, and all of a height, and unflecked with
a light or a shade,
Stretch leisurely off, in a pleasant plain,
To the terminal blue of the main.   60

Oh, what is abroad in the marsh and the terminal sea?
Somehow my soul seems suddenly free
From the weighing of fate and the sad discussion of sin,
By the length and the breadth and the sweep
of the marshes of Glynn.

Ye marshes, how candid and simple and noth-
ing-withholding and free
Ye publish yourselves to the sky and offer yourselves to the sea!
Tolerant plains, that suffer the sea and the
rains and the sun,
Ye spread and span like the catholic man who
hath mightily won
God out of knowledge and good out of infinite pain
And sight out of blindness and purity out of a
stain.   70

As the marsh-hen secretly builds on the watery
sod,
Behold I will build me a nest on the greatness
of God:
I will fly in the greatness of God as the marsh-
hen flies
In the freedom that fills all the space 'twixt
the marsh and the skies:
By so many roots as the marsh-grass sends in
the sod

I will heartily lay me a-hold on the greatness
  of God:
Oh, like to the greatness of God is the greatness within
The range of the marshes, the liberal marshes
  of Glynn.

And the sea lends large, as the marsh: lo, out
  of his plenty the sea
Pours fast: full soon the time of the flood-tide
  must be: 80
Look how the grace of the sea doth go
About and about through the intricate channels
  that flow
  Here and there,
    Everywhere,
Till his waters have flooded the uttermost
  creeks and the low-lying lanes,
And the marsh is meshed with a million veins,
That like as with rosy and silvery essences flow
  In the rose-and-silver evening glow.
    Farewell, my lord Sun!
The creeks overflow: a thousand rivulets run

'Twixt the roots of the sod; the blades of the
  marsh-grass stir;   91
Passeth a hurrying sound of wings that westward whirr;
Passeth, and all is still; and the currents cease
  to run;
And the sea and the marsh are one.

How still the plains of the waters be!
The tide is in his ecstasy.
The tide is at his highest height:
    And it is night.

And now from the Vast of the Lord will the
  waters of sleep
Roll in on the souls of men,   100
But who will reveal to our waking ken
The forms that swim and the shapes that creep
    Under the waters of sleep?
And I would I could know what swimmeth
  below when the tide comes in
On the length and the breadth of the marvel-
  lous marshes of Glynn.

Baltimore 1878   1879

GEORGE WASHINGTON CABLE

1844–1925

THE READING PUBLIC in New Orleans, and indeed in the whole South, was so incensed by Cable's treatment of the Negro question in *The Grandissimes* (1880) and *The
Silent South* (1885) that when Cable moved away from New Orleans to Northampton, Massachusetts, his extreme unpopularity was commonly, though erroneously, credited with having
been the cause. Yet the incident is meaningful. Cable was by nature both a man of letters and a
reformer; he not only felt the instinct to recreate human nature in fiction, he was also impelled
by a strong urge to reform it in real life. When the two motives operated together, he produced
his best work, *Old Creole Days* (1879) and *The Grandissimes;* when they did not, his work is usually too sentimental, and suffers from a limpness of artistic form, as in *Dr. Sevier* (1885) and the
other later novels.

The time-span of Cable's life runs through one of those periods of great events which Matthew Arnold believed necessary for greatness in art. The struggle between the North and the
South was the dominating influence of Cable's career. It is involved even in his heredity, for his
father came of an old Virginia slave-holding family and his mother was of New England ancestry. Cable did not have an easy childhood. Born in New Orleans where his family had moved
for business reasons, he was forced by the death of his father to assume the support of his mother
and sisters when he was but fifteen years old. A few years later, the Civil War brought the
Union forces into New Orleans, and the Cables had to leave the city for refusing to take the

Yankee oath of allegiance. During the remainder of the War he fought for the South in a Mississippi cavalry regiment.

New Orleans properly provided the scenery for Cable's best literary work. From the archives of the city he drew material for his Creole writings. The first of his short stories, " 'Sieur George," appeared in *Scribner's Magazine* in 1873, and was reprinted six years later in the collection of stories called *Old Creole Days*. Strongly local in color, and weak in structure as well as too sentimental, these stories are nevertheless subtle accounts of Creole life and temperament, of the gay early days in New Orleans when the octoroon balls were more brilliant than the best efforts of higher society. One finds in them both the excitement of a temperamental Latin society at its height and the sadness of its decline, the contrasting figures of proud French aristocracy and of refined but outcast mulatto society. The issues at stake are those raised by racial mixture and by social decay, and Cable's extreme sensitivity to them pervades *Old Creole Days*.

The Grandissimes is Cable's best novel. Like his short stories it is based upon the French civilization of New Orleans, this time in the days of the Louisiana Purchase. The main theme of the book is a feud between two French families, the Grandissimes and the De Grapions, but the incidental nature of the plot and the semihumorous treatment of the characters are driven along by an intense and bitter sense of the injustice with which the Negro slaves were ruled, and of the prevailing social discrimination against half-castes. Yet there is great understanding also, and in the novel as a whole Cable expressed a point of view many decades in advance of both his Northern and his Southern contemporaries.

Lucy L. Cable Bikle, *George W. Cable, His Life and Letters*, New York, 1928.
Arlin Turner, *George Washington Cable, a Biography*, Durham, N. C., 1956.

» » 'TITE POULETTE[1] « «

Kristian Koppig was a rosy-faced, beardless young Dutchman. He was one of that army of gentlemen who, after the purchase of Louisiana, swarmed from all parts of the commercial world, over the mountains of Franco-Spanish exclusiveness, like the Goths over the Pyrenees, and settled down in New Orleans to pick up their fortunes, with the diligence of hungry pigeons. He may have been a German; the distinction was too fine for Creole haste and disrelish.

He made his home in a room with one dormer window looking out, and somewhat down, upon a building opposite, which still stands, flush with the street, a century old. Its big, round-arched windows in a long, second-story row, are walled up, and two or three from time to time have had smaller windows let into them again, with odd little latticed peep-holes in their batten shutters. This had already been done when Kristian Koppig first began to

[1] Published first in *Scribner's Monthly*, October, 1874, " 'Tite Poulette" is one of the stories in *Old Creole Days* (1879). It is a preliminary study for the novelette *Madame Delphine*.

look at them from his solitary dormer window.

All the features of the building lead me to guess that it is a remnant of the old Spanish Barracks, whose extensive structure fell by government sale into private hands a long time ago. At the end toward the swamp a great, oriental-looking passage is left, with an arched entrance, and a pair of ponderous wooden doors. You look at it, and almost see Count O'Reilly's artillery come bumping and trundling out, and dash around into the ancient Plaza to bang away at King St. Charles's birthday.

I do not know who lives there now. You might stand about on the opposite *banquette* for weeks and never find out. I suppose it is a residence, for it does not look like one. That is the rule in that region.

In the good old times of duels, and bagatelleclubs, and theatre-balls, and Cayetano's circus, Kristian Koppig rooming as described, there lived in the portion of this house, partly overhanging the archway, a palish handsome woman, by the name—or going by the name—of Madame John. You would hardly have thought of her being "colored." Though fading, she was still of very attractive countenance, fine, rather severe features, nearly straight hair carefully kept, and that vivid black eye so peculiar to her kind. Her smile, which came and went with her talk, was sweet and exceedingly intelligent; and something told you, as you looked at her, that she was one who had had to learn a great deal in this troublesome life.

"But!" —the Creole lads in the street would say— "—her daughter!" and there would be lifting of arms, wringing of fingers, rolling of eyes, rounding of mouths, gaspings and clasping of hands. "So beautiful, beautiful, beautiful! White?—white like a water lily! White—like a magnolia!"

Applause would follow, and invocation of all the saints to witness.

And she could sing.

"Sing?" (disdainfully)—"if a mocking-bird can *sing!* Ha!"

They could not tell just how old she was; they "would give her about seventeen."

Mother and daughter were very fond. The neighbors could hear them call each other pet names, and see them sitting together, sewing, talking happily to each other in the unceasing French way, and see them go out and come in together on their little tasks and errands. " 'Tite Poulette," the daughter was called; she never went out alone.

And who was this Madame John?

"Why, you know!—she was" —said the wigmaker at the corner to Kristian Koppig— "I'll tell you. You know?—she was" —and the rest atomized off in a rasping whisper. She was the best yellow-fever nurse in a thousand yards round; but that is not what the wig-maker said.

A block nearer the river stands a house altogether different from the remnant of old barracks. It is of frame, with a deep front gallery over which the roof extends. It has become a den of Italians, who sell fuel by daylight, and by night are up to no telling what extent of deviltry. This was once the home of a gay gentleman, whose first name happened to be John. He was a member of the Good Children Social Club. As his parents lived with him, his wife would, according to custom, have been called Madame John; but he had no wife. His father died, then his mother; last of all,

himself. As he is about to be off, in comes Madame John, with 'Tite Poulette, then an infant, on her arm.

"Zalli," said he, "I am going."

She bowed her head, and wept.

"You have been very faithful to me, Zalli."

She wept on.

"Nobody to take care of you now, Zalli."

Zalli only went on weeping.

"I want to give you this house, Zalli; it is for you and the little one."

An hour after, amid the sobs of Madame John, she and the "little one" inherited the house, such as it was. With the fatal caution which characterizes ignorance, she sold the property and placed the proceeds in a bank, which made haste to fail. She put on widow's weeds, and wore them still when 'Tite Poulette "had seventeen," as the frantic lads would say.

How they did chatter over her. Quiet Kristian Koppig had never seen the like. He wrote to his mother, and told her so. A pretty fellow at the corner would suddenly double himself up with beckoning to a knot of chums; these would hasten up; recruits would come in from two or three other directions; as they reached the corner their countenances would quickly assume a genteel severity, and presently, with her mother, 'Tite Poulette would pass—tall, straight, lithe, her great black eyes made tender by their sweeping lashes, the faintest tint of color in her Southern cheek, her form all grace, her carriage a wonder of simple dignity.

The instant she was gone every tongue was let slip on the marvel of her beauty; but, though theirs were only the loose New Orleans morals of over fifty years ago, their unleashed tongues never had attempted any greater liberty than to take up the pet name, 'Tite Poulette. And yet the mother was soon to be, as we shall discover, a paid dancer at the *Salle de Condé.*

To Zalli, of course, as to all "quadroon ladies," the festivities of the Conde-street ballroom were familiar of old. There, in the happy days when dear Monsieur John was young, and the eighteenth century old, she had often repaired under guard of her mother—dead now, alas!—and Monsieur John would slip away from the dull play and dry society of Théâtre d'Orléans, and come around with his crowd of elegant friends; and through the long sweet hours of the ball she had danced, and laughed, and coquetted under her satin mask, even to the baffling and tormenting of that prince of

gentlemen, dear Monsieur John himself. No
man of questionable blood dare set his foot
within the door. Many noble gentlemen were
pleased to dance with her. Colonel De ——
and General La ——: city councilmen and officers from the Government House. There were
no paid dancers then. Every thing was decorously conducted indeed! Every girl's mother
was there, and the more discreet always left
before there was too much drinking. Yes, it
was gay, gay!—but sometimes dangerous. Ha!
more times than a few had Monsieur John
knocked down some long-haired and long-
knifed rowdy, and kicked the breath out of
him for looking saucily at her; but that was
like him, he was so brave and kind;—and he is
gone!

There was no room for widow's weeds there.
So when she put these on, her glittering eyes
never again looked through her pink and white
mask, and she was glad of it; for never, never
in her life had they so looked for anybody but
her dear Monsieur John, and now he was in
heaven—so the priest said—and she was a
sick-nurse.

Living was hard work; and, as Madame John
had been brought up tenderly, and had done
what she could to rear her daughter in the
same mistaken way, with, of course, no more
education than the ladies in society got, they
knew nothing beyond a little music and embroidery. They struggled as they could, faintly;
now giving a few private dancing lessons, now
dressing hair, but ever beat back by the steady
detestation of their imperious patronesses; and,
by and by, for want of that priceless worldly
grace known among the flippant as "money-
sense," these two poor children, born of misfortune and the complacent badness of the
times, began to be in want.

Kristian Koppig noticed from his dormer
window one day a man standing at the big
archway opposite, and clanking the brass
knocker on the wicket that was in one of the
doors. He was a smooth man, with his hair
parted in the middle, and his cigarette poised
on a tiny gold holder. He waited a moment,
politely cursed the dust, knocked again, threw
his slender sword-cane under his arm, and
wiped the inside of his hat with his handkerchief.

Madame John held a parley with him at
the wicket. 'Tite Poulette was nowhere seen.
He stood at the gate while Madame John went
up-stairs. Kristian Koppig knew him. He knew

him as one knows a snake. He was the manager
of the Salle de Condé. Presently Madame
John returned with a little bundle, and they
hurried off together.

And now what did this mean? Why, by any
one of ordinary acuteness the matter was easily
understood, but, to tell the truth, Kristian
Koppig was a trifle dull, and got the idea at
once that some damage was being planned
against 'Tite Poulette. It made the gentle
Dutchman miserable not to be minding his
own business, and yet—

"But the woman certainly will not attempt"
—said he to himself— "no, no! she cannot."
Not being able to guess what he meant, I cannot say whether she could or not. I know that
next day Kristian Koppig, glancing eagerly
over the "Ami des Lois," read an advertisement which he had always before skipped with
a frown. It was headed, "Salle de Condé,"
and, being interpreted, signified that a new
dance was to be introduced, the Danse de
Chinois, and that a young lady would follow it
with the famous "Danse du Shawl."

It was the Sabbath. The young man watched
the opposite window steadily and painfully
from early in the afternoon until the moon
shown bright; and from the time the moon
shone bright until Madame John!—joy!—Madame John! and not 'Tite Poulette, stepped
through the wicket, much dressed and well
muffled, and hurried off toward the Rue Condé.
Madame John was the "young lady"; and
the young man's mind, glad to return to its
own unimpassioned affairs, relapsed into quietude.

Madame John danced beautifully. It had
to be done. It brought some pay, and pay was
bread; and every Sunday evening, with a
touch here and there of paint and powder, the
mother danced the dance of the shawl, the
daughter remaining at home alone.

Kristian Koppig, simple, slow-thinking young
Dutchman, never noticing that he staid at
home with his window darkened for the very
purpose, would see her come to her window
and look out with a little wild, alarmed look
in her magnificent eyes, and go and come
again, and again, until the mother, like a
storm-driven bird, came panting home.

Two or three months went by.

One night, on the mother's return, Kristian
Koppig coming to his room nearly at the same
moment, there was much earnest conversation,
which he could see, but not hear.

"'Tite Poulette," said Madame John, "you are seventeen."

"True, Maman."

"Ah! my child, I see not how you are to meet the future." The voice trembled plaintively.

"But how, Maman?"

"Ah! you are not like others; no fortune, no pleasure, no friend."

"Maman!"

"No, no;—I thank God for it; I am glad you are not; but you will be lonely, lonely, all your poor life long. There is no place in this world for us poor women. I wish that we were either white or black!" —and the tears, two "shining ones," stood in the poor quadroon's eyes.

The daughter stood up, her eyes flashing.

"God made us, Maman," she said with a gentle, but stately smile.

"Ha!" said the mother, her keen glance darting through her tears, "Sin made *me*, yes."

"No," said 'Tite Poulette, "God made us. He made us just as we are; not more white, not more black."

"He made you, truly!" said Zalli. "You are so beautiful; I believe it well." She reached and drew the fair form to a kneeling posture. "My sweet, white daughter!"

Now the tears were in the girl's eyes. "And could I be whiter than I am?" she asked.

"Oh, no, no! 'Tite Poulette," cried the other; "but if we were only *real white!*—both of us; so that some gentleman might come to see me and say 'Madame John, I want your pretty little chick. She is so beautiful. I want to take her home. She is so good—I want her to be my wife.' Oh, my child, my child, to see that I would give my life—I would give my soul! Only you should take me along to be your servant. I walked behind two young men tonight; they were coming home from their office; presently they began to talk about you."

'Tite Poulette's eyes flashed fire.

"No, my child, they spoke only the best things. One laughed a little at times and kept saying 'Beware!' but the other—I prayed the Virgin to bless him, he spoke such kind and noble words. Such gentle pity; such a holy heart! 'May God defend her,' he said, *cherie;* he said, 'May God defend her, for I see no help for her.' The other one laughed and left him. He stopped in the door right across the street. Ah, my child, do you blush? Is that something to bring the rose to your cheek?

Many fine gentlemen at the ball ask me often, 'How is your daughter, Madame John?'"

The daughter's face was thrown into the mother's lap, not so well satisfied, now, with God's handiwork. Ah, how she wept! Sob, sob, sob; gasps and sighs and stifled ejaculations, her small right hand clinched and beating on her mother's knee; and the mother weeping over her.

Kristian Koppig shut his window. Nothing but a generous heart and a Dutchman's phlegm could have done so at that moment. And even thou, Kristian Koppig!—for the window closed very slowly.

He wrote to his mother, thus:

"In this wicked city, I see none so fair as the poor girl who lives opposite me, and who, alas! though so fair, is one of those whom the taint of caste has cursed. She lives a lonely, innocent life in the midst of corruption, like the lilies I find here in the marshes, and I have great pity for her. 'God defend her,' I said tonight to a fellow clerk, 'I see no help for her.' I know there is a natural, and I think proper, horror of mixed blood (excuse the mention, sweet mother), and I feel it, too; and yet if she were in Holland today, not one of a hundred suitors would detect the hidden blemish."

In such strain this young man wrote on trying to demonstrate the utter impossibility of his ever loving the lovable unfortunate, until the midnight tolling of the cathedral clock sent him to bed.

About the same hour Zalli and 'Tite Poulette were kissing good-night.

"'Tite Poulette, I want you to promise me one thing."

"Well, Maman?"

"If any gentleman should ever love you and ask you to marry,—not knowing, you know,—promise me you will not tell him you are not white."

"It can never be," said 'Tite Poulette.

"But if it should," said Madame John pleadingly.

"And break the law?" asked 'Tite Poulette, impatiently.

"But the law is unjust," said the mother.

"But it is the law!"

"But you will not, dearie, will you?"

"I would surely tell him!" said the daughter.

When Zalli, for some cause, went next morning to the window, she started.

"'Tite Poulette!"—she called softly without moving. The daughter came. The young man, whose idea of propriety had actuated him to this display, was sitting in the dormer window, reading. Mother and daughter bent a steady gaze at each other. It meant in French, "If he saw us last night!"—

"Ah! dear," said the mother, her face beaming with fun—

"What can it be, Maman?"

"He speaks—oh! ha, ha!—he speaks—such miserable French!"

It came to pass one morning at early dawn that Zalli and 'Tite Poulette, going to mass, passed a café, just as—who should be coming out but Monsieur, the manager of the *Salle de Condé*. He had not yet gone to bed. Monsieur was astonished. He had a Frenchman's eye for the beautiful, and certainly there the beautiful was. He had heard of Madame John's daughter, and had hoped once to see her, but did not; but could this be she?

They disappeared within the cathedral. A sudden pang of piety moved him; he followed. 'Tite Poulette was already kneeling in the aisle. Zalli, still in the vestibule, was just taking her hand from the font of holy-water.

"Madame John," whispered the manager.

She courtesied.

"Madame John, that young lady—is she your daughter?"

"She—she—is my daughter," said Zalli, with somewhat of alarm in her face, which the manager misinterpreted.

"I think not, Madame John." He shook his head, smiling as one too wise to be fooled.

"Yes, Monsieur, she is my daughter."

"O no, Madame John, it is only make-believe, I think."

"I swear she is, Monsieur de la Rue."

"Is that possible?" pretending to waver, but convinced in his heart of hearts, by Zalli's alarm, that she was lying. "But how? Why does she not come to our ball-room with you?"

Zalli, trying to get away from him, shrugged and smiled. "Each to his taste, Monsieur; it pleases her not."

She was escaping, but he followed one step more. "I shall come to see you, Madame John."

She whirled and attacked him with her eyes. "Monsieur must not give himself the trouble!" she said, the eyes at the same time adding, "Dare to come!" She turned again, and knelt to her devotions. The manager dipped in the font, crossed himself, and departed.

Several weeks went by, and M. de la Rue

had not accepted the fierce challenge of Madame John's eyes. One or two Sunday nights she had succeeded in avoiding him, though fulfilling her engagement in the *Salle;* but by and by pay-day,—a Saturday,—came round, and though the pay was ready, she was loath to go up to Monsieur's little office.

It was an afternoon in May. Madame John came to her own room, and, with a sigh, sank into a chair. Her eyes were wet.

"Did you go to his office, dear mother?" asked 'Tite Poulette.

"I could not," she answered, dropping her face in her hands.

"Maman, he has seen me at the window!"

"While I was gone?" cried the mother.

"He passed on the other side of the street. He looked up purposely, and saw me." The speaker's cheeks were burning red.

Zalli wrung her hands.

"It is nothing, mother; do not go near him."

"But the pay, my child."

"The pay matters not."

"But he will bring it here; he wants the chance."

That was the trouble, sure enough.

About this time Kristian Koppig lost his position in the German importing house where, he had fondly told his mother, he was indispensable.

"Summer was coming on," the senior said, "and you see our young men are almost idle. Yes, our engagement *was* for a year, but ah— we could not foresee"—etc., etc., "besides" (attempting a parting flattery), "your father is a rich gentleman, and you can afford to take the summer easy. If we can ever be of any service to you," etc., etc.

So the young Dutchman spent the afternoons at his dormer window reading and glancing down at the little casement opposite, where a small, rude shelf had lately been put out, holding a row of cigar-boxes with wretched little botanical specimens in them trying to die. 'Tite Poulette was their gardener; and it was odd to see,—dry weather or wet,—how many waterings per day those plants could take. She never looked up from her task; but I know she performed it with that unacknowledged pleasure which all girls love and deny, that of being looked upon by noble eyes.

On this peculiar Saturday afternoon in May, Kristian Koppig had been witness of the distressful scene over the way. It occurred to 'Tite Poulette that such might be the case, and she stepped to the casement to shut it. As she did so, the marvellous delicacy of Kristian Koppig moved him to draw in one of his shutters. Both young heads came out at one moment, while at the same instant—

"Rap, rap, rap, rap, rap!" clanked the knocker on the wicket. The black eyes of the maiden and the blue over the way, from looking into each other for the first time in life, glanced down to the arched doorway upon Monsieur the manager. Then the black eyes disappeared within, and Kristian Koppig thought again, and re-opening his shutter, stood up at the window prepared to become a bold spectator of what might follow.

But for a moment nothing followed.

"Trouble over there," thought the rosy Dutchman, and waited. The manager waited too, rubbing his hat and brushing his clothes with the tips of his kidded fingers.

"They do not wish to see him," slowly concluded the spectator.

"Rap, rap, rap, rap, rap!" quoth the knocker, and M. de la Rue looked up around at the windows opposite and noticed the handsome young Dutchman looking at him.

"Dutch!" said the manager softly, between his teeth.

"He is staring at me," said Kristian Koppig to himself;— "but then I am staring at him, which accounts for it."

A long pause, and then another long rapping.

"They want him to go away," thought Koppig.

"Knock hard!" suggested a street youngster, standing by.

"Rap, rap"— The manager had no sooner recommenced than several neighbors looked out of doors and windows.

"Very bad," thought our Dutchman; "somebody should make him go off. I wonder what they will do."

The manager stepped into the street, looked up at the closed window, returned to the knocker, and stood with it in his hand.

"They are all gone out, Monsieur," said the street-youngster.

"You lie!" said the cynosure of neighboring eyes.

"Ah!" thought Kristian Koppig; "I will go down and ask him"— Here his thoughts lost outline; he was only convinced that he had somewhat to say to him, and turned to go down stairs. In going he became a little vexed with himself because he could not help hurrying. He noticed, too, that his arm holding the stair-rail trembled in a silly way, whereas he was perfectly calm. Precisely as he reached the street-door the manager raised the knocker; but the latch clicked and the wicket was drawn slightly ajar.

Inside could just be descried Madame John. The manager bowed, smiled, talked, talked on, held money in his hand, bowed, smiled, talked on, flourished the money, smiled, bowed, talked on and plainly persisted in some intention to which Madame John was steadfastly opposed.

The window above, too,—it was Kristian Koppig who noticed that,—opened a wee bit, like the shell of a terrapin. Presently the manager lifted his foot and put forward an arm, as though he would enter the gate by pushing, but as quick as gunpowder it clapped—in his face!

You could hear the fleeing feet of Zalli pounding up the staircase.

As the panting mother re-entered her room, "See, Maman," said 'Tite Poulette, peeping at the window, "the young gentleman from over the way has crossed!"

"Holy Mary bless him!" said the mother.

"I will go over," thought Kristian Koppig, "and ask him kindly if he is not making a mistake."

"What are they doing, dear?" asked the mother, with clasped hands.

"They are talking; the young man is tranquil, but 'Sieur de la Rue is very angry," whispered the daughter; and just then—pang! came a sharp, keen sound rattling up the walls on either side of the narrow way, and "Aha!" and laughter and clapping of female hands from two or three windows.

"Oh! what a slap!" cried the girl, half in fright, half in glee, jerking herself back from the casement simultaneously with the report. But the "ahas" and laughter, and clapping of feminine hands, which still continued, came from another cause. 'Tite Poulette's rapid action had struck the slender cord that held up an end of her hanging garden, and the whole rank of cigar-boxes slid from their place, turned gracefully over as they shot through the air, and emptied themselves plump upon the head of the slapped manager. Breathless, dirty, pale as whitewash, he gasped a threat to be heard from again, and, getting round the corner as quick as he could walk, left Kristian

Koppig, standing motionless, the most astonished man in that street.

"Kristian Koppig, Kristian Koppig," said Greatheart to himself, slowly dragging upstairs, "what a mischief you have done. One poor woman certainly to be robbed of her bitter wages, and another—so lovely!—put to the burning shame of being the subject of a street brawl! What will this silly neighborhood say? 'Has the gentleman a heart as well as a hand?' 'Is it jealousy?'" There he paused, afraid himself to answer the supposed query; and then—"Oh! Kristian Koppig, you have been such a dunce!" "And I cannot apologize to them. Who in this street would carry my note, and not wink and grin over it with low surmises? I cannot even make restitution. Money? They would not dare receive it. Oh! Kristian Koppig, why *did* you not mind your own business? Is she any thing to you? Do you love her? *Of course not!* Oh!—such a dunce!"

The reader will eagerly admit that however faulty this young man's course of reasoning, his conclusion was correct. For mark what he did.

He went to his room, which was already growing dark, shut his window, lighted his big Dutch lamp, and sat down to write. "Something *must* be done," said he aloud, taking up his pen; "I will be calm and cool; I will be distant and brief; but—I shall have to be kind or I may offend. Ah! I shall have to write in French; I forgot that; I write it so poorly, dunce that I am, when all my brothers and sisters speak it so well." He got out his French dictionary. Two hours slipped by. He made a new pen, washed and refilled his inkstand, mended his "abominable!" chair, and after two hours more made another attempt, and another failure. "My head aches," said he, and lay down on his couch, the better to frame his phrases.

He was awakened by the Sabbath sunlight. The bells of the Cathedral and the Ursulines' chapel were ringing for high mass, and a mocking-bird, perching on a chimney-top above Madame John's rooms, was carolling, whistling, mewing, chirping, screaming, and trilling with the ecstasy of a whole May in his throat. "Oh! sleepy Kristian Koppig," was the young man's first thought, "—such a dunce!"

Madame John and daughter did not go to mass. The morning wore away, and their casement remained closed. "They are offended," said Kristian Koppig, leaving the house, and

wandering up to the little Protestant affair known as Christ Church.

"No, possibly they are not," he said, returning and finding the shutters thrown back.

By a sad accident, which mortified him extremely, he happened to see, late in the afternoon,—hardly conscious that he was looking across the street,—that Madame John was—dressing. Could it be that she was going to the *Salle de Condé*? He rushed to his table, and began to write.

He had guessed aright. The wages were too precious to be lost. The manager had written her a note. He begged to assure her that he was a gentleman of the clearest cut. If he had made a mistake the previous afternoon, he was glad no unfortunate result had followed except his having been assaulted by a ruffian; that the *Danse du Shawl* was promised in his advertisement, and he hoped Madame John (whose wages were in hand waiting for her) would not fail to assist as usual. Lastly, and delicately put, he expressed his conviction that Mademoiselle was wise and discreet in declining to entertain gentlemen at her home.

So, against much beseeching on the part of 'Tite Poulette, Madame John was going to the ball-room. "Maybe I can discover what 'Sieur de la Rue is planning against Monsieur over the way," she said, knowing certainly the slap would not be forgiven; and the daughter, though tremblingly, at once withdrew her objections.

The heavy young Dutchman, now thoroughly electrified, was writing like mad. He wrote and tore up, wrote and tore up, lighted his lamp, started again, and at last signed his name. A letter by a Dutchman in French!—what can be made of it in English? We will see:

"Madame and Mademoiselle:

"A stranger, seeking not to be acquainted, but seeing and admiring all days the goodness and high honor, begs to be pardoned of them for the mistakes, alas! of yesterday, and to make reparation and satisfaction in destroying the ornaments of the window, as well as the loss of compensation from Monsieur the manager, with the enclosed bill of the *Banque de la Louisiane* for fifty dollars ($50). And, hoping they will seeing what he is meaning, remains, respectfully,

"Kristian Koppig.

"P.S.—Madame must not go to the ball."

He must bear the missive himself. He must speak in French. What should the words be? A moment of study—he has it, and is off down the long three-story stairway. At the same moment Madame John stepped from the wicket, and glided off to the *Salle de Condé*, a trifle late.

"I shall see Madame John, of course," thought the young man, crushing a hope, and rattled the knocker. 'Tite Poulette sprang up from praying for her mother's safety. "What has she forgotten?" she asked herself, and
10 hastened down. The wicket opened. The two innocents were stunned.

"Aw—aw"—said the pretty Dutchman, "aw,"—blurted out something in virgin Dutch, . . . handed her the letter, and hurried down street.

"Alas! what have I done?" said the poor girl, bending over her candle, and bursting into tears that fell on the unopened letter. "And what shall I do? It may be wrong to open it—
20 and worse not to." Like her sex, she took the benefit of the doubt, and intensified her perplexity and misery by reading and misconstruing the all but unintelligible contents. What then? Not only sobs and sighs, but moaning and beating of little fists together, and outcries of soul-felt agony stifled against the bedside, and temples pressed into knitted palms, because of one who "sought *not to be* acquainted," but offered money—money!—in
30 pity to a poor—shame on her for saying that! —a poor *nigresse*.

And now our self-confessed dolt turned back from a half-hour's walk, concluding there might be an answer to his note. "Surely Madame John will appear this time." He knocked. The shutter stirred above, and something white came fluttering wildly down like a shot dove. It was his own letter containing the fifty dollar bill. He bounded to the wicket, and softly but
40 eagerly knocked again.

"Go away," said a trembling voice from above.

"Madame John?" said he; but the window closed, and he heard a step, the same step on the stair. Step, step, every step one step deeper into his heart. 'Tite Poulette came to the closed door.

"What will you?" said the voice within.

"I—I—don't wish to see you. I wish to see
50 Madame John."

"I must pray Monsieur to go away. My mother is at the *Salle de Condé*."

"At the ball!" Kristian Koppig strayed off, repeating the words for want of definite thought. All at once it occurred to him that at the ball he could make Madame John's acquaintance with impunity. "Was it courting sin to go?" By no means; he should, most likely, save a woman from trouble, and help the poor in their distress.

Behold Kristian Koppig standing on the floor of the *Salle de Condé*. A large hall, a blaze of lamps, a bewildering flutter of fans and floating robes, strains of music, columns of gay promenaders, a long row of turbaned mothers lining either wall, gentlemen of the portlier sort filling the recesses of the windows, whirling waltzers gliding here and there—smiles and grace, smiles and grace; all fair, orderly, elegant, bewitching. A young Creole's laugh mayhap a little loud, and—truly there were many sword-canes. But neither grace nor foulness satisfied the eye of the zealous young Dutchman.

Suddenly a muffled woman passed him, leaning on a gentleman's arm. It looked like—it must be, Madame John. Speak quick, Kristian Koppig; do not stop to notice the man!

"Madame John"—bowing—"I am your neighbor, Kristian Koppig."

Madame John bows low, and smiles—a ballroom smile, but is frightened, and her escort, —the manager,—drops her hand and slips away.

"Ah! Monsieur," she whispers excitedly, "you will be killed if you stay here a moment. Are you armed? No. Take this." She tried to slip a dirk into his hands, but he would not have it.

"Oh, my dear young man, go! Go quickly!" she plead, glancing furtively down the hall.

"I wish you not to dance," said the young man.

"I have danced already; I am going home. Come; be quick! we will go together." She thrust her arm through his, and they hastened into the street. When a square had been passed there came a sound of men running behind them.

"Run, Monsieur, run!" she cried, trying to drag him; but Monsieur Dutchman would not.

"*Run*, Monsieur! Oh, my God! it is 'Sieur"—

"*That* for yesterday!" cried the manager, striking fiercely with his cane. Kristian Koppig's fist rolled him in the dirt.

"*That* for 'Tite Poulette!" cried another man dealing the Dutchman a terrible blow from behind.

"And *that* for me!" hissed a third, thrusting at him with something bright.

"*That* for yesterday!" screamed the manager, bounding like a tiger; "That!" "THAT!" "Ha!"

Then Kristian Koppig knew that he was stabbed.

"That!" and "That!" and "That!" and the poor Dutchman struck wildly here and there, grasped the air, shut his eyes, staggered, reeled, fell, rose half up, fell again for good, and they were kicking him and jumping on him. All at once they scampered. Zalli had found the night-watch.

"Buz-z-z-z!" went a rattle. "Buz-z-z-z!" went another.

"Pick him up."

"Is he alive?"

"Can't tell; hold him steady; lead the way, misses."

"He's bleeding all over my breeches."

"This way—here—around this corner."

"This way now—only two squares more."

"Here we are."

"Rap-rap-rap!" on the old brass knocker. Curses on the narrow wicket, more on the dark archway, more still on the twisting stairs.

Up at last and into the room.

"Easy, easy, push this under his head! never mind his boots!"

So he lies—on 'Tite Poulette's own bed.

The watch are gone. They pause under the corner lamp to count profits;—a single bill—*Banque de la Louisiane*, fifty dollars. Providence is kind—tolerably so. Break it at the "Guillaume Tell." "But did you ever hear any one scream like that girl did?"

And there lies the young Dutch neighbor. His money will not flutter back to him this time; nor will any voice behind a gate "beg Monsieur to go away." O, Woman!—that knows no enemy so terrible as man! Come nigh, poor Woman, you have nothing to fear. Lay your strange, electric touch upon the chilly flesh; it strikes no eager mischief along the fainting veins. Look your sweet looks upon the grimy face, and tenderly lay back the locks from the congested brows; no wicked misinterpretation lurks to bite your kindness. Be motherly, be sisterly, fear nought. Go, watch him by night; you may sleep at his feet and he will not stir. Yet he lives, and shall live—may live to forget you, who knows? But for all that, be gentle and watchful; be womanlike, we ask no more; and God reward you!

Even while it was taking all the two women's strength to hold the door against Death, the sick man himself laid a grief upon them.

"Mother," he said to Madame John, quite a master of French in his delirium, "dear mother, fear not; trust your boy; fear nothing. I will not marry 'Tite Poulette; I cannot. She is fair, dear mother, but ah! she is not—don't you know, mother? don't you know? The race! the race! Don't you know that she is jet black? Isn't it?"

The poor nurse nodded "Yes," and gave a sleeping draught; but before the patient quite slept he started once and stared.

"Take her away,"—waving his hand—"take your beauty away. She is jet white. Who could take a jet white wife? O, no, no, no, no!"

Next morning his brain was right.

"Madame," he weakly whispered, "I was delirious last night?"

Zalli shrugged. "Only a very, very, wee, wee trifle of a bit."

"And did I say something wrong or—foolish?"

"O, no, no," she replied; "you only clasped your hands, so, and prayed, prayed all the time to the dear Virgin."

"To the virgin?" asked the Dutchman, smiling incredulously.

"And St. Joseph—yes, indeed," she insisted; "you may strike me dead."

And so, for politeness' sake, he tried to credit the invention, but grew suspicious instead.

Hard was the battle against death. Nurses are sometimes amazons, and such were these. Through the long, enervating summer, the contest lasted; but when at last the cool airs of October came stealing in at the bedside like long-banished little children, Kristian Koppig rose upon his elbow and smiled them a welcome.

The physician, blessed man, was kind beyond measure; but said some inexplicable things, which Zalli tried in vain to make him speak in an undertone. "If I knew Monsieur John?" he said, "certainly! Why, we were chums at school. And he left you so much as that, Madame John? Ah! my old friend John, always noble! And you had it all in that naughty bank? Ah, well, Madame John, it matters little. No, I shall not tell 'Tite Poulette. Adieu."

And another time:—"If I will let you tell me something? With pleasure, Madame John. No, and not tell anybody, Madame John. No, Madame, not even 'Tite Poulette. What?"—a long whistle—"is that pos-si-ble?—and Monsieur John knew it?—encouraged it?—eh, well, eh, well!—But—can I believe you, Madame John? Oh! you have Monsieur John's sworn statement. Ah! very good, truly, but—you *say* you have it; but where is it? Ah! to-morrow!" a sceptical shrug. "Pardon me, Madame John, I think perhaps, *perhaps* you are telling the truth.

"If I think you did right? Certainly! What nature keeps back, accident sometimes gives, Madame John; either is God's will. Don't cry. 'Stealing from the dead?' No! It was giving, yes! They are thanking you in heaven, Madame John."

Kristian Koppig, lying awake, but motionless and with closed eyes, hears in part, and, fancying he understands, rejoices with silent intensity. When the doctor is gone he calls Zalli.

"I give you a great deal of trouble, eh, Madame John?"

"No, no; you are no trouble at all. Had you the yellow fever—ah! then!"

She rolled her eyes to signify the superlative character of the tribulations attending yellow fever.

"I had a lady and gentleman once—a Spanish lady and gentleman, just off the ship; both sick at once with the fever—delirious—could not tell their names. Nobody to help me but sometimes Monsieur John! I never had such a time,—never before, never since,—as that time. Four days and nights this head touched not a pillow."

"And they died!" said Kristian Koppig.

"The third night the gentleman went. Poor Señor! 'Sieur John,—he did not know the harm,—gave him some coffee and toast! The fourth night it rained and turned cool, and just before day the poor lady"—

"Died!" said Koppig.

Zalli dropped her arms listlessly into her lap and her eyes ran brimful.

"And left an infant!" said the Dutchman, ready to shout with exultation.

"Ah! no, Monsieur," said Zalli.

The invalid's heart sank like a stone.

"Madame John,"—his voice was all in a tremor,—"tell me the truth. Is 'Tite Poulette your own child?"

"Ah-h-h, ha! ha! what foolishness! Of course she is my child!" And Madame gave vent to a true Frenchwoman's laugh.

It was too much for the sick man. In the pitiful weakness of his shattered nerves he turned his face into his pillow and wept like a child.

Zalli passed into the next room to hide her emotion.

"Maman, dear Maman," said 'Tite Poulette, who had overheard nothing, but only saw the tears.

"Ah! my child, my child, my task—my task is too great—too great for me. Let me go now —another time. Go and watch at his bedside."

"But, Maman,"—for 'Tite Poulette was frightened,—"he needs no care now."

"Nay, but go, my child; I wish to be alone."

The maiden stole in with averted eyes and tiptoed to the window—*that window.* The patient, already a man again, gazed at her till she could feel the gaze. He turned his eyes from her a moment to gather resolution. And now, stout heart, farewell; a word or two of friendly parting—nothing more.

" 'Tite Poulette."

The slender figure at the window turned and came to the bedside.

"I believe I owe my life to you," he said.

She looked down meekly, the color rising in her cheek.

"I must arrange to be moved across the street, tomorrow, on a litter."

She did not stir or speak.

"And I must now thank you, sweet nurse, for your care. Sweet nurse! Sweet nurse!"

She shook her head in protestation.

"Heaven bless you, 'Tite Poulette!"

Her face sank lower.

"God has made you very beautiful, 'Tite Poulette!"

She stirred not. He reached, and gently took her little hand, and as he drew her one step nearer, a tear fell from her long lashes. From the next room, Zalli, with a face of agonized suspense, gazed upon the pair, undiscovered. The young man lifted the hand to lay it upon his lips, when, with a mild, firm force, it was drawn away, yet still rested in his own upon the bedside, like some weak thing snared, that could only not get free.

"Thou wilt not have my love, 'Tite Poulette?"

No answer.

"Thou wilt not, beautiful?"

"Cannot!" was all that she could utter, and upon their clasped hands the tears ran down.

"Thou wrong'st me, 'Tite Poulette. Thou dost not trust me; thou fearest the kiss may loosen the hands. But I tell thee nay. I have struggled hard, even to this hour, against Love, but I yield me now; I yield; I am his unconditioned prisoner forever. God forbid that I ask aught but that you will be my wife."

Still the maiden moved not, looked not up, only rained down tears.

"Shall it not be, 'Tite Poulette?" He tried in vain to draw her.

"'Tite Poulette?" So tenderly he called! And then she spoke.

"It is against the law."

"It is not!" cried Zalli, seizing her round the waist and dragging her forward. "Take her! she is thine. I have robbed God long enough. Here are the sworn papers—here! Take her; she is as white as snow—so! Take her, kiss her; Mary be praised! I never had a child—she is the Spaniard's daughter!"   1874

JOEL CHANDLER HARRIS

1848–1908

TURNWOLD was one of several flourishing plantations in Putnam County, Georgia, over which Sherman's raiders swept like a blight during their march to the sea in November, 1864. Its proprietor, Joseph Addison Turner, had for some years been publishing the weekly *Countryman*, with printing-offices on the plantation. Astride the rail fence which bordered the Milledgeville Road, watching Sherman's men as they made off with most of the livestock and some of Turner's hundred-odd slaves, sat the *Countryman's* typesetter and Turner's protégé, a red-headed lad of sixteen named Joel Chandler Harris. In 1862 he had come to Turnwold from his birthplace in near-by Eatonton, where his mother was the village dressmaker. War presently compelled Turner to abandon the *Countryman*. But Harris, as boy and man, as printer's devil and editor, continued to work for Georgia newspapers during forty years. Much of his subsequent fame as a reporter of Negro dialect he admittedly owed to evenings with such masterful story-tellers as Old Uncle George Terrell in the slave-cabins at Turnwold.

After further apprenticeship on papers in Macon, New Orleans, and Savannah, Harris moved in 1876 to Atlanta, where he remained for a quarter of a century as editorial and feature-writer on the proud old *Atlanta Constitution*. The enthusiastic reception of some Georgia sketches which he published in the newspaper opened his eyes to Negro folklore as a subject for fictional exploitation. Of his ten books on Uncle Remus, the fullest and freshest are the first two, *Uncle Remus: His Songs and His Sayings* (1880) and *Nights with Uncle Remus* (1883). But the high quality of the series is adequately sustained in such later volumes as *Uncle Remus and His Friends* (1892), from which the present selections are drawn. Unlike much plantation literature, these tales are seldom marred by sentimental nostalgia. The genuineness of Uncle Remus is striking. At great pains to present real folklore in an authentic setting, Harris carefully verified his sources and aimed at exact phonetic transcription of Middle Georgia Negro dialect. To his discomfiture, ethnologists accepted him as a fellow-scientist, and sent him literary analogues for the Remus animal stories which they had found among Indian legends in North and South America.

The Uncle Remus books are clearly Harris's best. Some of the sketches in volumes like *Mingo* (1884) and *Free Joe* (1887) perhaps deserve wider fame, but he is ill at ease in the novel form, and his fugitive essays, collected in 1931, are interesting chiefly for his opinions on the Negro question. As a modest journalist, however, Harris made no claim to literary distinction. In the editorial rooms of the *Constitution*, his portly figure, red mustache, wide black hat, and string tie, were long a familiar sight. For the rest, he defied lionization, living quietly in his unpretentious Atlanta home, "Wren's Nest," and occasionally entertaining such close friends as the Hoosier dialect poet, James Whitcomb Riley, known to the Harris children as "Uncle Jeems" and to the nation as the creator of "Little Orphant Annie."

Julia C. Harris, *The Life and Letters of Joel Chandler Harris*, Boston, 1918. (Contains bibliography.)
Joel Chandler Harris, Editor and Essayist, Julia C. Harris, ed., Chapel Hill, N. C., 1931.
Stella Brookes, *Joel Chandler Harris, Folklorist*, Athens, Georgia, 1950.
A. F. Harlow, *Joel Chandler Harris (Uncle Remus): Plantation Storyteller*, New York, 1941.
J. H. Nelson, *The Negro Character in American Literature*, Lawrence, Kansas, 1926, pp. 107–119.
R. L. Wiggins, *The Life of Joel Chandler Harris from Obscurity in Boyhood to Fame in Early Manhood*, Nashville, Tennessee, 1918.

» » *From:* UNCLE REMUS AND HIS FRIENDS « «

DEATH AND THE NEGRO MAN

One day Uncle Remus was grinding the axe with which he chopped kindling for the kitchen and the big house. The axe was very dull. It was full of "gaps," and the work of putting an edge on it was neither light nor agreeable. A negro boy turned the grindstone, and the little boy poured on water when water was needed.

10   "Ef dis yer axe wuz a yard longer, it ud be a cross cut saw, en den ef we had de lumber we could saw it up en build us a house," said the old man.

The negro boy rolled his eyes and giggled, seeing which Uncle Remus bore so heavily on the axe that the grindstone could hardly be turned. The negro boy ceased giggling, but he continued to roll his eyes.

"Turn it!" exclaimed the old man. "Turn it!

20   Ef you don't turn it, I'll make you stan' dar plum twel night gwine thoo de motions. I'll make you do like de nigger man done when he got tired er work."

The old man stopped talking, but the grinding went on. After awhile, the little boy asked,—

"What did the man do when he got tired of work?"

"Dat's a tale, honey, en tellin' tales is playin'."

30   replied Uncle Remus. He wiped the blade of the axe on the palm of his hand, and tried the edge with his thum. "She won't shave," he said, by way of comment, "but I speck she'll do ter knock out kindlin'. Yit ef I had de time, I'd like ter stan' here en see how long dish yer triflin' vilyun would roll dem eyes at me."

In a little while the axe was supposed to be sharp enough, and then, dismissing the negro boy, Uncle Remus seated himself on one end of the frame that supported the grindstone, wiped his forehead on his coat sleeve, and proceeded to enjoy what he called a breathing spell.

"Dat ar nigger man you hear me talk about," he remarked, "wuz a-gittin' sorter ol', en he got so he ain't want ter work nohow you kin fix it. When folks hangs back fum work what dey bin set ter do, hit natchully makes bad matters wuss, en dat de way 't wuz with dish yer nigger man. He helt back, en he hung back, en den de white folks got fretted wid 'im en sot 'im a task. Gentermens! dat nigger man wuz mad. He wuz one er deze yer Affiky niggers, en you know how dey is—bowlegged en bad tempered. He quoiled en he quoiled when he 'uz by his own lone se'f, en he quoiled when he 'uz wid tudder folks.

"He got so mad dat he say he hope ole Gran'sir Death'll come take him off, en take his marster en de overseer 'long wid 'im. He talk so long en so loud, dat de white folks hear what he say. Den de marster en de overseer make it up 'mongst deyse'f dat dey gwine ter play a prank on dat nigger man.

"So den, one night, a leetle atter midnight, de marster got 'm a white counterpane, he did, en wrop hisse'f in it, en den he cut two eye-holes in a piller-case, en drawed it down over his head, en went down ter de house whar de nigger man stay. Nigger man ain't gon ter bed. He been fryin' meat en bakin' ashcake, en he sot dar in de cheer noddin', wid grease in his mouf en big hunk er ashcake in his han'. De door wuz half-way open, en de fire burnin' low.

"De marster walk in, he did, en sorter cle'r up his th'oat. Nigger man ain't wake up. Ef he make any movement, it uz ter clinch de ashcake a leetle tighter. Den de marster knock on de door—*blim-blim-blim!* Nigger man sorter fling his head back, but 't wan't long 'fo' hit drapt forrerd ag'in, en he went on wid his noddin' like nothin' ain't happen. De marster knock some mo'—*blam-blam-blam!* Dis time de nigger wake up en roll his eye-balls roun'. He see de big white thing, en he skeered ter move. His han' shake so he tu'n de ashcake loose.

"Nigger man 'low, 'Who dat?'

"De marster say: 'You call me, en I come.'

"Nigger man say: 'I ain't call you. What yo' name?'

"Marster 'low, 'Grandsir Death.'

"Nigger man shake so he can't skacely set still. De col' sweat come out on 'im. He 'low, 'Marse Death, I ain't call you. Somebody been fool you.'

"De marster 'low, 'I been hear you call me p'intedly. I listen at you ter-day, en yistiddy, en day 'fo' yistiddy. You say you want me ter take you en yo' marster en de overseer. Now I done come at yo' call.'

"Nigger man shake wuss. He say: 'Marse Death, go git de overseer fust. He lots bigger en fatter dan what I is. You'll like him de bes'. Please, suh, don't take me dis time, en I won't bodder you no mo' long ez I live.'

"De marster 'low, 'I come fer de man dat call me! I'm in a hurry! Daylight mus'n't ketch me here. Come on!'

"Well, suh, dat nigger man make a break for de winder, he did, en he went thoo it like a frog divin' in de mill pon'. He tuck ter de woods, en he 'uz gone mighty nigh a week. When he come back home he went ter work, en he work harder dan any er de res'. Somebody come 'long en try ter buy 'im, but his marster 'low he won't take lev'm hunder'd dollars for 'im,—cash money, paid down in his han'!"

1891   1892

BROTHER RABBIT'S MONEY MINT

One day the little boy was telling Uncle Remus about how much money one of his mother's brothers was going to make. Oh, it was ever so much—fifty, a hundred, maybe a thousand bales of cotton in one season. Uncle Remus groaned a little during this recital.

"Wharbouts he gwine ter make it?" the old man inquired with some asperity.

"Oh, in Mississippi," said the little boy. "Uncle James told papa that the cotton out there grows so high that a man sitting on his horse could hide in it."

"Did Marse Jeems see dat cotton hisse'f?" asked Uncle Remus.

"Yes, he did. He's been out there, and he saw it with his own eyes. He says he can make ever so many hundred dollars in Mississippi where he makes one here."

"Marse John ain't gwine, is he?"

"No; I heard papa tell mamma that Uncle James was drawing his long bow, and then mamma said she reckoned that her kinfolks were as truthful as anybody else's."

Immediately Uncle Remus's features lost their severity, and he lay back in his chair to laugh.

"Dat Miss Sally, up en down. Hit her kinnery en you got ter hit her. But yo' pa know Marse Jeems, en I been knowin' 'im sence he wuz in his teens; en when he git ter talkin' he'll stretch his blanket spite er de worl'. He allers would do dat, en he allers will. Now, dat des de long en de short un it. I don't keer ef he is kin ter Miss Sally, he'll talk wil'.

"Bless yo' soul, honey. I done hear talk er Massasip long 'fo' you wuz bornded. I done seed um go dar, en I done seed um come back, en eve'y time I hear folks talk 'bout makin' mo' money off dar dan dey kin anywhars nigher home, it put me in min' er de time when Brer Fox went huntin' de place whar dey make money."

"Is it a story, Uncle Remus?" asked the little boy.

"Well, 't ain't ez you may say one er deze yer reg'lar up en down tales, what runs crossways. Dish yer tale goes right straight. Brer Fox meet up wid Brer Rabbit in de big road, en dey pass de time er day, en ax one er nudder how der fambly connection is. Brer Fox say he sorter middlin' peart, en Brer Rabbit say he sorter betwix *'My gracious!'* en *'Thank gracious!'* Whiles dey er runnin' on en confabbin', Brer Fox hear sump'n rattlin' in Brer Rabbit's pocket.

"He 'low, 'Ef I ain't mighty much mistaken, Brer Rabbit, I hear money rattlin'.'

"Brer Rabbit sorter grin slow en hol' his head keerless.

"He say, ''T ain't nothin' much—des some small change what I bleedz ter take wid me in de case er needcessity.'

"Wid dat he drawed out a big han'ful er speeshy-dollars, en quarters, en sev'mpunces, en thrips, en all right spang-bang new. Hit shined in de sun twel it fair blin' yo' eyes.

"Brer Fox 'low, 'Laws a massy, Brer Rabbit! I ain't seed so much money sence I sol' my watermilions las' year. Ain't you skeerd some un'll fling you down en take it 'way fum you?'

"Brer Rabbit say, 'Dem what man 'nuff ter take it kin have it'; en he des strut 'long de road dar mo' samer dan one er deze yer milliumterry mens what got yaller stripes on der britches.

"Brer Fox 'low, 'Whar de name er goodness you git so much new speeshy, Brer Rabbit?"

"Brer Rabbit say, 'I git it whar dey make it at; dat whar I git it.'

"Brer Fox stop by de side er de road, en look 'stonish. He 'low, 'Wharbouts does dey make dish yer speeshy at?'

"Brer Rabbit say, 'Fust in one place en den in anudder. You got ter do like me, Brer Fox; you got ter keep yo' eye wide open.'

"Brer Fox 'low, 'Fer massy sake, Brer Rabbit, tell me how I gwine ter fine de place.'

"He beg en he beg, Brer Fox did, en Brer Rabbit look at 'im hard, like he got some doubts on his min'. Den Brer Rabbit sot down by de side er de road en mark in de san' wid his walkin' cane.

"Bimeby he say, 'Well, spozen I tell you, you'll go blabbin' it 'roun' de whole neighborhoods, en den dey'll git it all, en we won't git none 't all.'

"But Brer Fox des vow en declar' ter gracious dat he won't tell a livin' soul, en den ole Brer Rabbit sorter bent hisse'f back en cle'r up his th'oat.

"He say, ''T ain't much atter you fine it out, Brer Fox; all you got ter do is ter watch de road twel you see a waggin come 'long. Ef you'll look right close, you'll see dat de waggin, ef hit's de right kind er waggin, is got two front wheels en two behime wheels; en you'll see fuddermo' dat de front wheels is lots littler dan de behime wheels. Now, when you see dat, what is you bleedz ter b'lieve?'

"Brer Fox study little while, en den shuck his head. He 'low, 'You too much fer me, Brer Rabbit.'

"Brer Rabbit look like he feel sorry kaze Brer Fox sech a numbskull. He say, 'When you see dat, you bleedz ter b'lieve dat atter so long a time de big wheel gwine ter ketch de little one. Yo' common sense ought ter tell you dat.'

"Brer Fox 'low, 'Hit sholy look so.'

"Brer Rabbit say, 'Ef you know dat de big wheel gwine ter ketch de little wheel, en dat bran new money gwine ter drap fum betwixt um when dey grind up 'ginst one anudder, what you gwine do den?'

"Still Brer Fox study, en shake his head. Brer Rabbit look like he gittin' sick.

"He say, 'You kin set down en let de waggin go on by, ef you don't want no bran new money. Den agin, ef you want de money, you kin foller 'long en keep watch, en see when de behime wheels overtake de front uns en be on han' when de money starts ter drappin'.'

"Brer Fox look like he got de idee. He sorter laugh.

"Brer Rabbit say, 'Nex' time you see a waggin gwine by, Brer Fox, des holler for me ef you don't want ter take no chances. Des bawl out! I ain't got 'nuff speeshy, en I ain't gwine ter have 'nuff.'

"Brer Fox, he broke off a broom straw en 'gun ter chaw on it, en des 'bout dat time, dey hear a waggin comin' 'cross de hill.

"Brer Rabbit 'low, 'Des say de word, Brer Fox, en ef you ain't gwine 'long atter de waggin, I'll go myse'f!'

"Brer Fox say, 'Maybe de wheels done grinded tergedder back yonder a piece.'

"Brer Rabbit 'low, 'I ain't got time ter 'spute, Brer Fox. Ef you ain't gwine, des say de word!'

"Brer Fox sorter laugh like he shame. He say, 'I b'lieve I'll go a little piece er de way en see how de wheels run.'

"Wid dat," said Uncle Remus, looking up at the ceiling with a peculiar smile, "Brer Rabbit wish Brer Fox good luck, en went on 'bout his business. Yit he ain't go so fur dat he can't watch Brer Fox's motions. At de rise er de nex' hill he look back, en dar he see Brer Fox trottin' 'long atter de waggin. When he see dat, Brer Rabbit des lay down in de grass en kick up his heels en holler."

Uncle Remus laughed, and the little boy laughed. The old negro's merriment was as keen as that of the youngster, for his humor swept over a wide field of human experience. The little boy laughed at the transparent trick;

Uncle Remus no doubt beheld in his imagination a long procession of human Brer Foxes "polin' 'long," up hill and down hill, waiting for the hind wheels to overtake the front ones. After a while the little boy asked what became of Brother Fox.

"Well, honey," said Uncle Remus, "he des foller 'long, trottin' en gallopin', waitin' fer

de wheels ter ketch up wid one anudder. Ef he ain't in Massasip by dis time, I'm mighty much mistaken. I boun' yo' Unc' Jeems'll see 'im when he go out dar! Brer Fox had ter take his foot in his han', en git dar de bes' way he kin; yo' Unc' Jeems gwine by conveyance."

1891   1892

HENRY JAMES

1843–1916

IN A STRIDENT young nation where other young men customarily went west, there was a kind of inevitability in Henry James's decision to move eastward. From William James, the millionaire merchant of Albany, Henry James the elder, father of the novelist, inherited funds sufficient to lead the contemplative life and to raise four sturdy sons as gentlemen of the cosmopolis. Born in New York City, Henry James at seventeen was already thoroughly familiar with most of the great European capitals, in which even then he had spent nearly a third of his life. In 1866 the family established permanent residence in Cambridge, Massachusetts. Having previously sojourned at Harvard Law School, and having been refused participation in the Civil War because of a physical infirmity, Henry began at twenty-two to publish stories in the *Atlantic Monthly* and in *The Galaxy*, and criticism in *The Nation*. But in 1869 and 1873 there were trips to Europe, and in 1876 he settled in London, as it turned out, for the duration of his life. After 1876 he returned to America only four times, twice on visits occasioned by family deaths, and again in 1904–5 "after so many years' absence," said Hamlin Garland, "that many people had forgotten he was alive."

Unstintingly for the fifty years between the Civil War and the First World War, Henry James devoted his energies to the development of the novel form, with a singleness of purpose that has made his name the most distinguished and his influence the most powerful in the history of modern prose fiction. The first five years of his residence in London saw the publication of many novelettes and short stories, among them *Roderick Hudson* (1876); *The American* (1877); *The Europeans* (1878); *Daisy Miller* and *An International Episode* (1879); and *The Portrait of a Lady* and *Washington Square* (1881). As some of the titles indicate, James's primary interest during this period lay in conflicts resulting from contrasts between American and European character. Now also he wrote the brilliant essays on *French Poets and Novelists* (1878), and the life of *Hawthorne* (1879), where, in a famous paragraph, he enumerates America's disadvantages while idealizing life in England.

In the decade 1886–1896, having temporarily abandoned the theme of Americans on the Continent, James turned to such thoroughly English pieces as *The Princess Casamassima* (1886). The conflict between the artistic person and his environment is a strong motivating force in his long novel, *The Tragic Muse* (1890), and in a succession of novelettes like *The Aspern Papers* (1888) and *The Lesson of the Master* (1892). James's mastery of the art of dictation and his removal from the distractions of London society to Lamb House, Rye, made the next few years especially productive. Besides short stories, and novelettes like *The Spoils of Poynton* (1896) and

What Maisie Knew (1897), he wrote three long novels, *The Wings of the Dove* (1902), *The Ambassadors* (1903), and *The Golden Bowl* (1904), which amply compensate for the expenditure of patience required to read them, and show a new appreciation of the basic virtues of the American national character.

But the visit James made to America in 1910 soon drove him back to England, though the solid structure of continental life as he had known it was beginning rapidly to crumble. Besides a serious illness of his own, and the death of his philosopher brother William (1910), he was obliged to endure the spectacle of barbarism rising like a black tide across the world. In 1914 he began *The Ivory Tower*, a novel about America which he could not finish, and in the year before his death, partly to protest America's continued neutrality, he became a British subject.

James was the first able practitioner satisfactorily to codify the aesthetic of prose fiction, and thereby to raise the genre to the dignity of fine art. The main body of critical dicta was contained in his prefaces to separate volumes of the New York edition of his works (1907–1917). In 1934 these essays were collected under the title, *The Art of the Novel*, with a valuable introduction by R. P. Blackmur. It is central to James's aesthetics that life around us is clumsy, gross, without meaning in itself. The task of art is to render form upon this chaos, and the novel is clearly a transmutational agent in which the artist assists "true meanings to be born." Art thus creates a new and inner world by extracting the quintessence of meaningful experience. In this world James's characters move.

"What a man thinks and feels," said James, "are the history and character of what he does." But James saw that the detachment necessary to close psychological analysis could not be achieved in the conventional novel form. So through dozens of experiments he evolved a technique which he found satisfactory and which has been immeasurably influential in the development of prose fiction during the present century. Writers as far apart in subject matter as Joyce, Virginia Woolf, Hemingway, and Faulkner, owe him a technical debt, and he is properly the father of the stream-of-consciousness novel. His attempt "to pump the case [of every situation] gaspingly dry" gives to his novelettes a kind of brimming fullness which none of his successors has matched.

In abjuring grosser elements, James naturally, and perhaps unfortunately, limited the range of his subject matter. His interest is in the adjustment of finely tempered minds to their environments. The novels are either leisure-class comedies of manners, or tragedies resulting from the sensitive individual's failure to orient himself in society. And his Utopia, as his secretary assures us, "was an anarchy where nobody would be responsible for any other human being, but only for his own civilized character."

Leon Edel and D. H. Laurence, *A Bibliography of Henry James*, London, 1957.

The Novels and Tales of Henry James (New York Edition), 26 vols., New York, 1907–1917.

The Letters of Henry James, Percy Lubbock, ed., 2 vols., New York, 1920.

The Notebooks of Henry James, F. O. Matthiessen and K. B. Murdock, eds., New York, 1947.

Quentin Anderson, *The American Henry James*, New Brunswick, N. J., 1957.

Van Wyck Brooks, *The Pilgrimage of Henry James*, New York, 1925.

F. C. Crews, *The Tragedy of Manners; Moral Drama in the Later Novels of Henry James*, New Haven, 1957.

F. W. Dupee, ed., *The Question of Henry James: A Collection of Critical Essays*, New York, 1945.

Leon Edel, *Henry James*, Philadelphia, 1953.

Hound and Horn, VII (April–June, 1934). Henry James issue.

Kenyon Review, V (August, 1943), 481–617. Henry James issue.

» » THE PUPIL « «

I

The poor young man hesitated and procrastinated: it cost him such an effort to broach the subject of terms, to speak of money to a person who spoke only of feelings and, as it were, of the aristocracy. Yet he was unwilling to take leave, treating his engagement as settled, without some more conventional glance in that direction than he could find an opening for in the manner of the large affable lady who sat there drawing a pair of soiled gants de Suède through a fat jewelled hand, and, at once pressing and gliding, repeated over and over everything but the thing he would have liked to hear. He would have liked to hear the figure of his salary; but just as he was nervously about to sound that note the little boy came back—the little boy Mrs. Moreen had sent out of the room to fetch her fan. He came back without the fan, only with the casual observation that he couldn't find it. As he dropped this cynical confession he looked straight and hard at the candidate for the honour of taking his education in hand. This personage reflected somewhat grimly that the first thing he should have to teach his little charge would be to appear to address himself to his mother when he spoke to her and especially not to make her such an improper answer as that.

When Mrs. Moreen bethought herself of this pretext for getting rid of their companion Pemberton supposed it was precisely to approach the delicate subject of his remuneration. But it had been only to say some things about her son that it was better a boy of eleven shouldn't catch. They were extravagantly to his advantage save when she lowered her voice to sigh, tapping her left side familiarly, "And all over-clouded by *this,* you know; all at the mercy of a weakness—!" Pemberton gathered that the weakness was in the region of that heart. He had known the poor child was not robust: this was the basis on which he had been invited to treat, through an English lady, an Oxford acquaintance, then at Nice, who happened to know both his needs and those of the amiable American family looking out for something really superior in the way of a resident tutor.

The young man's impression of his prospective pupil, who had come into the room as if to see for himself the moment Pemberton was admitted, was not quite the soft solicitation the visitor had taken for granted. Morgan Moreen was somehow sickly without being "delicate," and that he looked intelligent—it is true Pemberton wouldn't have enjoyed his being stupid—only added to the suggestion that, as with his big mouth and big ears he really couldn't be called pretty, he might too utterly fail to please. Pemberton was modest, was even timid; and the chance that his small scholar would prove cleverer than himself had quite figured, to his anxiety, among the dangers of an untried experiment. He reflected, however, that these were risks one had to run when one accepted a position, as it was called, in a private family; when as yet one's university honours had, pecuniarily speaking, remained barren. At any rate when Mrs. Moreen got up as to intimate, that, since it was understood he would enter upon his duties within the week she would let him off now, he succeeded, in spite of the presence of the child, in squeezing out a phrase about the rate of payment. It was not the fault of the conscious smile which seemed a reference to the lady's expensive identity, it was not the fault of this demonstration, which had, in a sort, both vagueness and point, if the allusion didn't sound rather vulgar. This was exactly because she became still more gracious to reply: "Oh I can assure you that all that will be quite regular."

Pemberton only wondered, while he took up his hat, what "all that" was to amount to—people had such different ideas. Mrs. Moreen's words, however, seemed to commit the family to a pledge definite enough to elicit from the child a strange little comment in the shape of the mocking foreign ejaculation "Oh la-la!"

Pemberton, in some confusion, glanced at him as he walked slowly to the window with his back turned, his hands in his pockets and the air in his elderly shoulders of a boy who didn't play. The young man wondered if he should be able to teach him to play, though his mother had said it would never do and that this was why school was impossible. Mrs. Moreen exhibited no discomfiture; she only continued blandly: "Mr. Moreen will be delighted to meet your wishes. As I told you, he has been called to London for a week. As soon as he comes back you shall have it out with him."

This was so frank and friendly that the young man could only reply, laughing as his hostess laughed: "Oh I don't imagine we shall have much of a battle."

"They'll give you anything you like," the boy remarked unexpectedly, returning from the window. "We don't mind what anything costs—we live awfully well."

"My darling, you're too quaint!" his mother exclaimed, putting out to caress him a practised but ineffectual hand. He slipped out of it, but looked with intelligent innocent eyes at Pemberton, who had already had time to notice that from one moment to the other his small satiric face seemed to change its time of life. At this moment it was infantine, yet it appeared also to be under the influence of curious intuitions and knowledges. Pemberton rather disliked precocity and was disappointed to find gleams of it in a disciple not yet in his teens. Nevertheless he divined on the spot that Morgan wouldn't prove a bore. He would prove on the contrary a source of agitation. This idea held the young man, in spite of a certain repulsion.

"You pompous little person! We're not extravagant!" Mrs. Moreen gaily protested, making another unsuccessful attempt to draw the boy to her side. "You must know what to expect," she went on to Pemberton.

"The less you expect the better!" her companion interposed. "But we *are* people of fashion."

"Only so far as *you* make us so!" Mrs. Moreen tenderly mocked. "Well, then, on Friday—don't tell me you're superstitious—and mind you don't fail us. Then you'll see us all. I'm so sorry the girls are out. I guess you'll like the girls. And, you know, I've another son, quite different from this one."

"He tries to imitate me," Morgan said to their friend.

"He tries? Why he's twenty years old!" cried Mrs. Moreen.

"You're very witty," Pemberton remarked to the child—a proposition his mother echoed with enthusiasm, declaring Morgan's sallies to be the delight of the house.

The boy paid no heed to this; he only enquired abruptly of the visitor, who was surprised afterwards that he hadn't struck him as offensively forward: "Do you *want* very much to come?"

"Can you doubt it after such a description of what I shall hear?" Pemberton replied. Yet he didn't want to come at all; he was coming because he had to go somewhere, thanks to the collapse of his fortune at the end of a year abroad spent on the system of putting his scant patrimony into a single full wave of experience. He had had his full wave but couldn't pay the score at his inn. Moreover he had caught in the boy's eyes the glimpse of a far-off appeal.

"Well, I'll do the best I can for you," said Morgan; with which he turned away again. He passed out of one of the long windows; Pemberton saw him go and lean on the parapet of the terrace. He remained there while the young man took leave of his mother, who, on Pemberton's looking as if he expected a farewell from him, interposed with: "Leave him, leave him; he's so strange!" Pemberton supposed her to fear something he might say. "He's a genius—you'll love him," she added. "He's much the most interesting person in the family." And before he could invent some civility to oppose to this she wound up with: "But we're all good, you know!"

"He's a genius—you'll love him!" were words that recurred to our aspirant before the Friday, suggesting among many things that geniuses were not invariably loveable. However, it was all the better if there was an element that would make tutorship absorbing: he had perhaps taken too much for granted it would only disgust him. As he left the villa after his interview he looked up at the balcony and saw the child leaning over it. "We shall have great larks!" he called up.

Morgan hung fire a moment and then gaily returned: "By the time you come back I shall have thought of something witty!"

This made Pemberton say to himself "After all he's rather nice."

II

On the Friday he saw them all, as Mrs. Moreen had promised, for her husband had come back and the girls and the other son were at home. Mr. Moreen had a white moustache, a confiding manner and, in his buttonhole, the ribbon of a foreign order—bestowed, as Pemberton eventually learned, for services. For what services he never clearly ascertained: this was a point—one of a large number—that

Mr. Moreen's manner never confided. What it emphatically did confide was that he was even more a man of the world than you might first make out. Ulick, the firstborn, was in visible training for the same profession—under the disadvantage as yet, however, of no pretensions to type. The girls had hair and figures and manners and small fat feet, but had never been out alone. As for Mrs. Moreen Pemberton saw on a nearer view that her elegance was intermittent and her parts didn't always match. Her husband, as she had promised, met with enthusiasm Pemberton's ideas in regard to a salary. The young man had endeavoured to keep these stammerings modest, and Mr. Moreen made it no secret that *he* found them wanting in "style." He further mentioned that he aspired to be intimate with his children, to be their best friend, and that he was always looking out for them. That was what he went off for, to London and other places—to look out; and this vigilance was the theory of life, as well as the real occupation, of the whole family. They all looked out, for they were very frank on the subject of its being necessary. They desired it to be understood that they were earnest people, and also that their fortune, though quite adequate for earnest people, required the most careful administration. Mr. Moreen, as the parent bird, sought sustenance for the nest. Ulick invoked support mainly at the club, where Pemberton guessed that it was usually served on green cloth. The girls used to do up their hair and their frocks themselves, and our young man felt appealed to to be glad, in regard to Morgan's education, that, though it must naturally be of the best, it didn't cost too much. After a little he *was* glad, forgetting at times his own needs in the interest inspired by the child's character and culture and the pleasure of making easy terms for him.

During the first weeks of their acquaintance Morgan had been as puzzling as a page in an unknown language—altogether different from the obvious little Anglo-Saxons who had misrepresented childhood to Pemberton. Indeed the whole mystic volume in which the boy had been amateurishly bound demanded some practice in translation. To-day, after a considerable interval, there is something phantasmagoric, like a prismatic reflection or a serial novel, in Pemberton's memory of the queerness of the Moreens. If it were not for a few tangible tokens—a lock of Morgan's hair cut by his own hand, and the half-dozen letters received from him when they were disjoined —the whole episode and the figures peopling it would seem too inconsequent for anything but dreamland. Their supreme quaintness was their success—as it appeared to him for a while at the time; since he had never seen a family so brilliantly equipped for failure. Wasn't it success to have kept him so hatefully long? Wasn't it success to have drawn him in that first morning at déjeuner, the Friday he came—it was enough to *make* one superstitious—so that he utterly committed himself, and this not by calculation or on a signal, but from a happy instinct which made them, like a band of gipsies, work so neatly together? They amused him as much as if they had really been a band of gipsies. He was still young and had not seen much of the world—his English years had been properly arid; therefore the reversed conventions of the Moreens—for they had *their* desperate proprieties—struck him as topsy-turvy. He had encountered nothing like them at Oxford; still less had any such note been struck to his younger American ear during the four years at Yale in which he had richly supposed himself to be reacting against a Puritan strain. The reaction of the Moreens, at any rate, went ever so much further. He had thought himself very sharp that first day in hitting them all off in his mind with the "cosmopolite" label. Later it seemed feeble and colourless—confessedly helplessly provisional.

He yet when he first applied it felt a glow of joy—for an instructor he was still empirical —rise from the apprehension that living with them would really be to see life. Their sociable strangeness was an intimation of that—their chatter of tongues, their gaiety and good humour, their infinite dawdling (they were always getting themselves up, but it took forever, and Pemberton had once found Mr. Moreen shaving in the drawing-room), their French, their Italian and cropping up in the foreign fluencies, their cold tough slices of American. They lived on maccaroni and coffee —they had these articles prepared in perfection—but they knew recipes for a hundred other dishes. They overflowed with music and song, were always humming and catching each other up, and had a sort of professional acquaintance with Continental cities. They talked of "good places" as if they had been pickpockets or strolling players. They had at Nice a villa, a carriage, a piano, and a banjo, and they went to official parties. They were a perfect calendar of the "days" of their friends, which Pemberton knew them, when they were indisposed, to get out of bed to go to, and which made the week larger than life when Mrs. Moreen talked of them with Paula and Amy. Their initiations gave their new inmate at first an almost dazzling sense of culture. Mrs. Moreen had translated something at some former period—an author whom it made Pemberton feel *borné* never to have heard of. They could imitate Venetian and sing Neapolitan, and when they wanted to say something very particular communicated with each other in an ingenious dialect of their own, an elastic spoken cipher which Pemberton at first took for some *patois* of one of their countries, but which he "caught on to" as he would not have grasped provincial development of Spanish or German.

"It's the family language—Ultramoreen," Morgan explained to him drolly enough; but the boy rarely condescended to use it himself, though he dealt in colloquial Latin as if he had been a little prelate.

Among all the "days" with which Mrs. Moreen's memory was taxed she managed to squeeze in one of her own, which her friends sometimes forgot. But the house drew a frequented air from the number of fine people who were freely named there and from several mysterious men with foreign titles and English clothes whom Morgan called the Princes and who, on sofas with the girls, talked French very loud—though sometimes with some oddity of accent—as if to show they were saying nothing improper. Pemberton wondered how the Princes could ever propose in that tone and so publicly: he took for granted cynically that this was what was desired of them. Then he recognised that even for the chance of such an advantage Mrs. Moreen would never allow Paula and Amy to receive alone. These young ladies were not at all timid, but it was just the safeguards that made them so candidly free. It was a houseful of Bohemians who wanted tremendously to be Philistines.

In one respect, however, certainly, they achieved no rigour—they were wonderfully amiable and ecstatic about Morgan. It was a genuine tenderness, an artless admiration, equally strong in each. They even praised his beauty, which was small, and were as afraid of him as if they felt him of finer clay. They spoke of him as a little angel and a prodigy

—they touched on his want of health with long, vague faces. Pemberton feared at first an extravagance that might make him hate the boy, but before this happened he had become extravagant himself. Later, when he had grown rather to hate the others, it was a bribe to patience for him that they were at any rate nice about Morgan, going on tiptoe if they fancied he was showing symptoms, and even giving up somebody's "day" to procure him a pleasure. Mixed with this too was the oddest wish to make him independent, as if they had felt themselves not good enough for him. They passed him over to the new members of their circle very much as if wishing to force some charity of adoption on so free an agent and get rid of their own charge. They were delighted when they saw Morgan take so to his kind playfellow, and could think of no higher praise for the young man. It was strange how they contrived to reconcile the appearance, and indeed the essential fact, of adoring the child with their eagerness to wash their hands of him. Did they want to get rid of him before he should find them out? Pemberton was finding them out month by month. The boy's fond family, however this might be, turned their backs with exaggerated delicacy, as if to avoid the reproach of interfering. Seeing in time how little he had in common with them—it was by *them* he first observed it; they proclaimed it with complete humility—his companion was moved to speculate on the mysteries of transmission, the far jumps of heredity. Where his detachment from most of the things they represented had come from was more than an observer could say—it certainly had burrowed under two or three generations.

As for Pemberton's own estimate of his pupil, it was a good while before he got the point of view, so little had he been prepared for it by the smug young barbarians to whom the tradition of tutorship, as hitherto revealed to him, had been adjusted. Morgan was scrappy and surprising, deficient in many properties supposed common to the *genus* and abounding in others that were the portion only of the supernaturally clever. One day his friend made a great stride: it cleared up the question to perceive that Morgan *was* supernaturally clever and that, though the formula was temporarily meagre, this would be the only assumption on which one could successfully deal with him. He had the general quality of a child for whom life had not been simplified by school, a kind of home-bred sensibility which might have been bad for himself but was charming for others, and a whole range of refinement and perception—little musical vibrations as taking as picked-up airs—begotten by wandering about Europe at the tail of his migratory tribe. This might not have been an education to recommend in advance, but its results with so special a subject were as appreciable as the marks on a piece of fine porcelain. There was at the same time in him a small strain of stoicism, doubtless the fruit of having had to begin early to bear pain, which counted for pluck and made it of less consequence that he might have been thought at school rather a polyglot little beast. Pemberton indeed quickly found himself rejoicing that school was out of the question: in any million of boys it was probably good for all but one, and Morgan was that millionth. It would have made him comparative and superior—it might have made him really require kicking. Pemberton would try to be school himself—a bigger seminary than five hundred grazing donkeys, so that, winning no prizes, the boy would remain unconscious and irresponsible and amusing—amusing, because, though life was already intense in his childish nature, freshness still made there a strong draught for jokes. It turned out that even in the still air of Morgan's various disabilities jokes flourished greatly. He was a pale lean acute undeveloped little cosmopolite, who liked intellectual gymnastics and who also, as regards the behaviours of mankind, had noticed more things than you might suppose, but who nevertheless had his proper playroom of superstitions, where he smashed a dozen toys a day.

III

At Nice once, toward evening, as the pair rested in the open air after a walk, and looked over the sea at the pink western lights, he said suddenly to his comrade: "Do you like it, you know—being with us all in this intimate way?"

"My dear fellow, why should I stay if I didn't?"

"How do I know you'll stay? I'm almost sure you won't, very long."

"I hope you don't mean to dismiss me," said Pemberton.

Morgan debated, looking at the sunset. "I think if I did right, I ought to."

"Well, I know I'm supposed to instruct you in virtue; but in that case don't do right."

"You're very young—fortunately," Morgan went on, turning to him again.

"Oh yes, compared with you!"

"Therefore it won't matter so much if you do lose a lot of time."

"That's the way to look at it," said Pemberton accommodatingly.

They were silent a minute; after which the boy asked: "Do you like my father and mother very much?"

"Dear me, yes. Charming people."

Morgan received this with another silence; then unexpectedly, familiarly, but at the same time affectionately, he remarked: "You're a jolly old humbug!"

For a particular reason the words made our young man change colour. The boy noticed in an instant that he had turned red, whereupon he turned red himself and pupil and master exchanged a longish glance in which there was a consciousness of many more things than are usually touched upon, even tacitly, in such a relation. It produced for Pemberton an embarrassment; it raised in a shadowy form a question—this was the first glimpse of it—destined to play a singular and, as he imagined, owing to the altogether peculiar conditions, an unprecedented part in his intercourse with his little companion. Later, when he found himself talking with the youngster in a way in which few youngsters could ever have been talked with, he thought of that clumsy moment on the bench at Nice as the dawn of an understanding that had broadened. What had added to the clumsiness then was that he thought it his duty to declare to Morgan that he might abuse him, Pemberton, as much as he liked, but must never abuse his parents. To this Morgan had the easy retort that he hadn't dreamed of abusing them; which appeared to be true; it put Pemberton in the wrong.

"Then why am I a humbug for saying I think them charming?" the young man asked, conscious of a certain rashness.

"Well—they're not your parents."

"They love you better than anything in the world—never forget that," said Pemberton.

"Is that why you like them so much?"

"They're very kind to me," Pemberton replied evasively.

"You *are* a humbug!" laughed Morgan, passing an arm into his tutor's. He leaned against him looking off at the sea again and swinging his long thin legs.

"Don't kick my shins," said Pemberton while

he reflected "Hang it, I can't complain of them to the child!"

"There's another reason too," Morgan went on, keeping his legs still.

"Another reason for what?"

"Besides their not being your parents."

"I don't understand you," said Pemberton.

"Well, you will before long. All right!"

He did understand fully before long, but he made a fight even with himself before he confessed it. He thought it the oddest thing to have a struggle with the child about. He wondered he didn't hate the hope of the Moreens for bringing the struggle on. But by the time it began any such sentiment for that scion was closed to him. Morgan was a special case, and to know him was to accept him on his own odd terms. Pemberton had spent his aversion to special cases before arriving at knowledge. When at last he did arrive his quandary was great. Against every interest he had attached himself. They would have to meet things together. Before they went home that evening at Nice the boy had said, clinging to his arm:

"Well, at any rate you'll hang on to the last."

"To the last?"

"Till you're fairly beaten."

"*You* ought to be fairly beaten!" cried the young man, drawing him closer.

IV

A year after he had come to live with them Mr. and Mrs. Moreen suddenly gave up the villa at Nice. Pemberton had got used to suddenness, having seen it practised on a considerable scale during two jerky little tours —one in Switzerland the first summer, and the other late in the winter, when they all ran down to Florence and then, at the end of ten days, liking it much less than they had intended, straggled back in mysterious depression. They had returned to Nice "for ever," as they said; but this didn't prevent their squeezing, one rainy muggy May night, into a second-class railway-carriage—you could never tell by which class they would travel—where Pemberton helped them to stow away a wonderful collection of bundles and bags. The explanation of this manoeuvre was that they had determined to spend the summer "in some bracing place"; but in Paris they dropped into a small furnished apartment—a fourth floor in a third-rate avenue, where there was a smell on the staircase and the portier was hateful —and passed the next four months in blank indigence.

The better part of this baffled sojourn was for the preceptor and his pupil, who, visiting the Invalides and Notre Dame, the Conciergerie and all the museums, took a hundred remunerative rambles. They learned to know their Paris, which was useful, for they came back another year for a longer stay, the general character of which in Pemberton's memory to-day mixes pitiably and confusedly with that of the first. He sees Morgan's shabby knickerbockers—the everlasting pair that didn't match his blouse and that as he grew longer could only grow faded. He remembers the particular holes in his three or four pair of coloured stockings.

Morgan was dear to his mother, but he never was better dressed than was absolutely necessary—partly, no doubt, by his own fault, for he was as indifferent to his appearance as a German philosopher. "My dear fellow, you *are* coming to pieces," Pemberton would say to him in sceptical remonstrance; to which the child would reply, looking at him serenely up and down: "My dear fellow, so are you! I don't want to cast you in the shade." Pemberton could have no rejoinder for this—the assertion so closely represented the fact. If however the deficiencies of his own wardrobe were a chapter by themselves he didn't like his little charge to look too poor. Later he used to say "Well, if we're poor, why, after all, shouldn't we look it?" and he consoled himself with thinking there was something rather elderly and gentlemanly in Morgan's disrepair—it differed from the untidiness of the urchin who plays and spoils his things. He could trace perfectly the degrees by which, in proportion as her little son confined himself to his tutor for society, Mrs. Moreen shrewdly forbore to renew his garments. She did nothing that didn't show, neglected him because he escaped notice, and then, as he illustrated this clever policy, discouraged at home his public appearances. Her position was logical enough—those members of her family who did show had to be showy.

During this period and several others Pemberton was quite aware of how he and his comrade might strike people; wandering languidly through the Jardin des Plantes as if they had nowhere to go, sitting on the winter days in the galleries of the Louvre, so splendidly ironical to the homeless, as if for the advantage of the *calorifère*. They joked about it sometimes: it was the sort of joke that was perfectly within the boy's compass. They figured themselves as part of the vast vague hand-to-mouth multitude of the enormous city and pretended they were proud of their position in it—it showed them "such a lot of life" and made them conscious of a democratic brotherhood. If Pemberton couldn't feel a sympathy in destitution with his small companion—for after all Morgan's fond parents would never have let him really suffer—the boy would at least feel it with him, so it came to the same thing. He used sometimes to wonder what people would think they were—to fancy they were looked askance at, as if it might be a suspected case of kidnapping. Morgan wouldn't be taken for a young patrician with a preceptor—he wasn't smart enough; though he might pass for his companion's sickly little brother. Now and then he had a five-franc piece, and except once, when they bought a couple of lovely neckties, one of which he made Pemberton accept, they laid it out scientifically in old books. This was sure to be a great day, always spent on the quays, in a rummage of the dusty boxes that garnish the parapets. Such occasions helped them to live, for their books ran low very soon after the beginning of their acquaintance. Pemberton had a good many in England, but he was obliged to write to a friend and ask him kindly to get some fellow to give him something for them.

If they had to relinquish that summer the advantage of the bracing climate the young man couldn't but suspect this failure of the cup when at their very lips to have been the effect of a rude jostle of his own. This had represented his first blow-out, as he called it, with his patrons; his first successful attempt —though there was little other success about it—to bring them to a consideration of his impossible position. As the ostensible eve of a costly journey the moment had struck him as favourable to an earnest protest, the presentation of an ultimatum. Ridiculous as it sounded, he had never yet been able to compass an uninterrupted private interview with the elder pair or with either of them singly. They were always flanked by their elder children, and poor Pemberton usually had his own little charge at his side. He was conscious of its

being a house in which the surface of one's delicacy got rather smudged; nevertheless he had preserved the bloom of his scruple against announcing to Mr. and Mrs. Moreen with publicity that he shouldn't be able to go on longer without a little money. He was still simple enough to suppose Ulick and Paula and Amy might not know that since his arrival he had only had a hundred and forty francs; and he was magnanimous enough to wish not to compromise their parents in their eyes. Mr. Moreen now listened to him, as he listened to every one and to everything, like a man of the world, and seemed to appeal to him—though not of course too grossly—to try to be a little more of one himself. Pemberton recognised in fact the importance of the character—from the advantage it gave Mr. Moreen. He was not even confused or embarrassed, whereas the young man in his service was more so than there was any reason for. Neither was he surprised—at least any more than a gentleman had to be who freely confessed himself a little shocked—though not perhaps strictly at Pemberton.

"We must go into this, mustn't we, dear?" he said to his wife. He assured his young friend that the matter should have his very best attention; and he melted into space as elusively as if, at the door, he were taking an inevitable but deprecatory precedence. When, the next moment, Pemberton found himself alone with Mrs. Moreen it was to hear her say "I see, I see"—stroking the roundness of her chin and looking as if she were only hesitating between a dozen easy remedies. If they didn't make their push Mr. Moreen could at least disappear for several days. During his absence his wife took up the subject again spontaneously, but her contribution to it was merely that she had thought all the while they were getting on so beautifully. Pemberton's reply to this revelation was that unless they immediately put down something on account he would leave them on the spot and for ever. He knew she would wonder how he would get away, and for a moment expected her to enquire. She didn't, for which he was almost grateful to her, so little was he in a position to tell.

"You won't, you *know* you won't—you're too interested," she said. "You *are* interested, you know you are, you dear kind man!" She laughed with almost condemnatory archness, as if it were a reproach—though she wouldn't

insist; and flirted a soiled pocket handkerchief
at him.

Pemberton's mind was fully made up to take
his step the following week. This would give
him time to get an answer to a letter he had
dispatched to England. If he did in the event
nothing of the sort—that is if he stayed another
year and then went away only for three months
—it was not merely because before the answer
to his letter came (most unsatisfactory when
it did arrive) Mr. Moreen generously counted
out to him, and again with the sacrifice to
"form" of a marked man of the world, three
hundred francs in elegant ringing gold. He
was irritated to find that Mrs. Moreen was
right, that he couldn't at the pinch bear to
leave the child. This stood out clearer for the
very reason that, the night of his desperate
appeal to his patrons, he had seen fully for the
first time where he was. Wasn't it another
proof of the success with which those patrons
practised their arts that they had managed to
avert for so long the illuminating flash? It
descended on our friend with a breadth of
effect which perhaps would have struck a
spectator as comical, after he had returned to
his little servile room, which looked into a
close court where a bare dirty opposite wall
took, with the sound of shrill clatter, the
reflexion of lighted back windows. He had
simply given himself away to a band of adventurers. The idea, the word itself, wore a
romantic horror for him—he had always lived
on such safe lines. Later it assumed a more
interesting, almost a soothing, sense: it pointed
a moral, and Pemberton could enjoy a moral.
The Moreens were adventurers not merely because they didn't pay their debts, because they
lived on society, but because their whole view
of life, dim and confused and instinctive, like
that of clever colour-blind animals, was speculative and rapacious and mean. Oh they were
"respectable," and that only made them more
immondes! The young man's analysis, while he
brooded, put it at last very simply—they were
adventurers because they were toadies and
snobs. That was the completest account of
them—it was the law of their being. Even
when this truth became vivid to their ingenious
inmate he remained unconscious of how much
his mind had been prepared for it by the extraordinary little boy who had now become
such a complication in his life. Much less could
he then calculate on the information he was still
to owe the extraordinary little boy.

V

But it was during the ensuing time that the
real problem came up—the problem of how
far it was excusable to discuss the turpitude
of parents with a child of twelve, of thirteen,
of fourteen. Absolutely inexcusable and quite
impossible it of course at first appeared; and
indeed the question didn't press for some time
after Pemberton had received his three hundred francs. They produced a temporary lull,
a relief from the sharpest pressure. The young
man frugally amended his wardrobe and even
had a few francs in his pocket. He thought the
Moreens looked at him as if he were almost
too smart, as if they ought to take care not to
spoil him. If Mr. Moreen hadn't been such a
man of the world he would perhaps have
spoken of the freedom of such neckties on the
part of a subordinate. But Mr. Moreen was always enough a man of the world to let things
pass—he had certainly shown that. It was
singular how Pemberton guessed that Morgan,
though saying nothing about it, knew something had happened. But three hundred francs,
especially when one owed money, couldn't last
for ever; and when the treasure was gone—the
boy knew when it had failed—Morgan did
break ground. The party had returned to Nice
at the beginning of the winter, but not to the
charming villa. They went to an hotel, where
they stayed three months, and then moved
to another establishment, explaining that they
had left the first because, after waiting and waiting, they couldn't get the rooms they wanted.
These apartments, the rooms they wanted, were
generally very splendid; but fortunately they
never *could* get them—fortunately, I mean,
for Pemberton, who reflected always that if
they had got them, there would have been a
still scanter educational fund. What Morgan
said at last was said suddenly, irrelevantly,
when the moment came, in the middle of a
lesson, and consisted of the apparently unfeeling words: "You ought to *filer,* you know—
you really ought."

Pemberton stared. He had learnt enough
French slang from Morgan to know that to
filer meant to cut sticks. "Ah my dear fellow,
don't turn me off!"

Morgan pulled a Greek lexicon toward him
—he used a Greek-German—to look out a
word, instead of asking it of Pemberton. "You
can't go on like this, you know."

"Like what, my boy?"

"You know they don't pay you up," said Morgan, blushing and turning his leaves.

"Don't pay me?" Pemberton stared again and feigned amazement. "What on earth put that into your head?"

"It has been there a long time," the boy replied rummaging his book.

Pemberton was silent, then he went on: "I say, what are you hunting for? They pay me beautifully."

"I'm hunting for the Greek for awful whopper," Morgan dropped.

"Find that rather for gross impertinence and disabuse your mind. What do I want of money?"

"Oh that's another question!"

Pemberton wavered—he was drawn in different ways. The severely correct thing would have been to tell the boy that such a matter was none of his business and bid him go on with his lines. But they were really too intimate for that; it was not the way he was in the habit of treating him; there had been no reason it should be. On the other hand Morgan had quite lighted on the truth—he really shouldn't be able to keep it up much longer; therefore why not let him know one's real motive for forsaking him? At the same time it wasn't decent to abuse to one's pupil the family of one's pupil; it was better to misrepresent than to do that. So in reply to his comrade's last exclamation he just declared, to dismiss the subject, that he had received several payments.

"I say—I say!" the boy ejaculated, laughing.

"That's all right," Pemberton insisted. "Give me your written rendering."

Morgan pushed a copybook across the table, and he began to read the page, but with something running in his head that made it no sense. Looking up after a minute or two he found the child's eyes fixed on him and felt in them something strange. Then Morgan said: "I'm not afraid of the stern reality."

"I haven't yet seen the thing you *are* afraid of—I'll do you that justice!"

This came out with a jump—it was perfectly true—and evidently gave Morgan pleasure. "I've thought of it for a long time," he presently resumed.

"Well, don't think of it any more."

The boy appeared to comply, and they had a comfortable and even an amusing hour. They had a theory that they were very thorough, and yet they seemed always to be in the amusing part of lessons, the intervals between the dull dark tunnels, where there were waysides and jolly views. Yet the morning was brought to a violent end by Morgan's suddenly leaning his arms on the table, burying his head in them and bursting into tears: at which Pemberton was the more startled that, as it then came over him, it was the first time he had ever seen the boy cry and that the impression was consequently quite awful.

The next day, after much thought, he took a decision and, believing it to be just, immediately acted on it. He cornered Mr. and Mrs. Moreen again and let them know that if on the spot they didn't pay him all they owed him he wouldn't only leave their house but would tell Morgan exactly what had brought him to it.

"Oh you *haven't* told him?" cried Mrs. Moreen with a pacifying hand on her well-dressed bosom.

"Without warning you? For what do you take me?" the young man returned.

Mr. and Mrs. Moreen looked at each other; he could see that they appreciated, as tending to their security, his superstition of delicacy, and yet that there was a certain alarm in their relief. "My dear fellow," Mr. Moreen demanded, "what use *can* you have, leading the quiet life we all do, for such a lot of money?" —a question to which Pemberton made no answer, occupied as he was in noting that what passed in the mind of his patrons was something like: "Oh then, if we've felt that the child, dear little angel, has judged us and how he regards us, and we haven't been betrayed, he must have guessed—and in short it's *general!*" an inference that rather stirred up Mr. and Mrs. Moreen, as Pemberton had desired it should. At the same time, if he had supposed his threat would do something towards bringing them round, he was disappointed to find them taking for granted—how vulgar their perception *had* been!—that he had already given them away. There was a mystic uneasiness in their parental breasts, and that had been the inferior sense of it. None the less, however, his threat did touch them; for if they had escaped it was only to meet a new danger. Mr. Moreen appealed to him, on every precedent, as a man of the world; but his wife had recourse, for the first time since his domestication with them, to a fine *hauteur*, reminding him that a devoted mother, with her child, had arts that protected her against gross misrepresentation.

"I should misrepresent you grossly if I accused you of common honesty!" our friend replied; but as he closed the door behind him sharply, thinking he had not done himself much good, while Mr. Moreen lighted another cigarette, he heard his hostess shout after him more touchingly:

"Oh you do, you *do,* put the knife to one's throat!"

10 The next morning, very early, she came to his room. He recognised her knock, but had no hope she brought him money; as to which he was wrong, for she had fifty francs in her hand. She squeezed forward in her dressing-gown, and he received her in his own, between his bath-tub and his bed. He had been tolerably schooled by this time to the "foreign ways" of his hosts. Mrs. Moreen was ardent, and when she was ardent she didn't care what she did; so she now sat down on his bed, his clothes 20 being on the chairs, and, in her preoccupation, forgot, as she glanced round, to be ashamed of giving him such a horrid room. What Mrs. Moreen's ardour now bore upon was the design of persuading him that in the first place she was very good-natured to bring him fifty francs, and that in the second, if he would only see it, he was really too absurd to expect to be *paid.* Wasn't he paid enough without perpetual money—wasn't he paid by the comfortable 30 luxurious home he enjoyed with them all, without a care, an anxiety, a solitary want? Wasn't he sure of his position, and wasn't that everything to a young man like him, quite unknown, with singularly little to show, the ground of whose exorbitant pretensions it had never been easy to discover? Wasn't he paid above all by the sweet relation he had established with Morgan—quite ideal as from master to pupil— and by the simple, privilege of knowing and 40 living with so amazingly gifted a child; than whom really (and she meant literally what she said) there was no better company in Europe? Mrs. Moreen herself took to appealing to him as a man of the world; she said "Voyons, mon cher," and "My dear man, look here now"; and urged him to be reasonable, putting it before him that it was truly a chance for him. She spoke as if, according as he *should* be reasonable, he would prove himself worthy to be her 50 son's tutor and of the extraordinary confidence they had placed in him.

After all, Pemberton reflected, it was only a difference of theory and the theory didn't matter much. They had hitherto gone on that of remunerated, as now they would go on that of

gratuitous service; but why should they have so many words about it? Mrs. Moreen at all events continued to be convincing; sitting there with her fifty francs she talked and reiterated, as women reiterate, and bored and irritated him, while he leaned against the wall with his hands in the pockets of his wrapper, drawing it together round his legs and looking over the head of his visitor at the grey negations of his window. She wound up with saying: "You see I bring you a definite proposal."

"A definite proposal?"

"To make our relations regular, as it were— to put them on a comfortable footing."

"I see—it's a system," said Pemberton. "A kind of organised blackmail."

Mrs. Moreen bounded up, which was exactly what he wanted. "What do you mean by that?"

"You practise on one's fears—one's fears about the child if one should go away."

"And pray what would happen to him in that event?" she demanded with majesty.

"Why he'd be alone with *you.*"

"And pray with whom *should* a child be but with those whom he loves most?"

"If you think that, why don't you dismiss me?"

"Do you pretend he loves you more than he loves *us?*" cried Mrs. Moreen.

"I think he ought to. I make sacrifices for him. Though I've heard of those you make I don't see them."

Mrs. Moreen stared a moment; then with emotion she grasped her inmate's hand. "*Will* you make it—the sacrifice?"

He burst out laughing. "I'll see. I'll do what I can. I'll stay a little longer. Your calculation's just—I *do* hate intensely to give him up; I'm fond of him and he thoroughly interests me, in spite of the inconvenience I suffer. You know my situation perfectly. I haven't a penny in the world and, occupied as you see me with Morgan, am unable to earn money."

Mrs. Moreen tapped her undressed arm with her folded bank-note. "Can't you write articles? Can't you translate as I do?"

"I don't know about translating; it's wretchedly paid."

"I'm glad to earn what I can," said Mrs. Moreen with prodigious virtue.

"You ought to tell me who you do it for." Pemberton paused a moment, and she said nothing; so he added: "I've tried to turn off some little sketches, but the magazines won't have them—they're declined with thanks."

"You see then you're not such a phoenix," his visitor pointedly smiled—"to pretend to abilities you're sacrificing for our sake."

"I haven't time to do things properly," he ruefully went on. Then as it came over him that he was almost abjectly good-natured to give these explanations he added: "If I stay on longer it must be on one condition—that Morgan shall know distinctly on what footing I am."

Mrs. Moreen demurred. "Surely you don't want to show off to a child?"

"To show *you* off, do you mean?"

Again she cast about, but this time it was to produce a still finer flower. "And *you* talk of blackmail!"

"You can easily prevent it," said Pemberton.

"And *you* talk of practising on fears!" she bravely pushed on.

"Yes, there's no doubt I'm a great scoundrel."

His patroness met his eyes—it was clear she was in straits. Then she thrust out her money at him. "Mr. Moreen desired me to give you this on account."

"I'm much obliged to Mr. Moreen, but we *have* no account."

"You won't take it?"

"That leaves me more free," said Pemberton.

"To poison my darling's mind?" groaned Mrs. Moreen.

"Oh your darling's mind—!" the young man laughed.

She fixed him a moment, and he thought she was going to break out tormentedly, pleadingly: "For God's sake, tell me what *is* in it!" But she checked this impulse—another was stronger. She pocketed the money—the crudity of the alternative was comical—and swept out of the room with the desperate concession: "You may tell him any horror you like!"

VI

A couple of days after this, during which he had failed to profit by so free a permission, he had been for a quarter of an hour walking with his charge in silence when the boy became sociable again with the remark: "I'll tell you how I know it; I know it through Zénobie."

"Zénobie? Who in the world is *she?*"

"A nurse I used to have—ever so many years ago. A charming woman. I liked her awfully, and she liked me."

"There's no accounting for tastes. What is it you know through her?"

"Why, what their idea is. She went away because they didn't fork out. She did like me awfully, and she stayed two years. She told me all about it—that at last she could never get her wages. As soon as they saw how much she liked me they stopped giving her anything. They thought she'd stay for nothing—just *because,* don't you know?" And Morgan had a queer little conscious lucid look. "She did stay ever so long—as long as she could. She was only a poor girl. She used to send money to her mother. At last she couldn't afford it any longer, and went away in a fearful rage one night—I mean of course in a rage against *them.* She cried over me tremendously, she hugged me nearly to death. She told me all about it," the boy repeated. "She told me it was their idea. So I guessed, ever so long ago, that they have had the same idea with you."

"Zénobie was very sharp," said Pemberton. "And she made you so."

"Oh that wasn't Zénobie; that was nature. And experience!"

Morgan laughed.

"Well, Zénobie was a part of your experience."

"Certainly I was a part of hers, poor dear!" the boy wisely sighed. "And I'm part of yours."

"A very important part. But I don't see how you know I've been treated like Zénobie."

"Do you take me for the biggest dunce you've known?" Morgan asked. "Haven't I been conscious of what we've been through together?"

"What we've been through?"

"Our privations—our dark days."

"Oh our days have been bright enough."

Morgan went on in silence for a moment. Then he said: "My dear chap, you're a hero!"

"Well, you're another!" Pemberton retorted.

"No I'm not, but I ain't a baby. I won't stand it any longer. You must get some occupation that pays. I'm ashamed, I'm ashamed!" quavered the boy with a ring of passion, like some high silver note from a small cathedral chorister, that deeply touched his friend.

"We ought to go off and live somewhere together," the young man said.

"I'll go like a shot if you'll take me."

"I'd get some work that would keep us both afloat," Pemberton continued.

"So would I. Why shouldn't I work? I ain't such a beastly little muff as *that* comes to."

"The difficulty is that your parents wouldn't hear of it. They'd never part with you; they worship the ground you tread on. Don't you see the proof of it?" Pemberton developed. "They don't dislike me; they wish me no harm; they're very amiable people; but they're perfectly ready to expose me to any awkwardness in life for your sake."

The silence in which Morgan received his fond sophistry struck Pemberton somehow as expressive. After a moment the child repeated: "You *are* a hero!" Then he added: "They leave me with you altogether. You've all the responsibility. They put me off on you from morning till night. Why then should they object to my taking up with you completely? I'd help you."

"They're not particularly keen about my being helped, and they delight in thinking of you as *theirs*. They're tremendously proud of you."

"I'm not proud of *them*. But you know that," Morgan returned.

"Except for the little matter we speak of they're charming people," said Pemberton, not taking up the point made for his intelligence, but wondering greatly at the boy's own, and especially at this fresh reminder of something he had been conscious of from the first—the strangest thing in his friend's large little composition, a temper, a sensibility, even a private ideal, which made him as privately disown the stuff his people were made of. Morgan had in secret a small loftiness which made him acute about betrayed meanness; as well as a critical sense for the manners immediately surrounding him that was quite without precedent in a juvenile nature, especially when one noted that it had not made this nature "old-fashioned," as the word is of children—quaint or wizened or offensive. It was as if he had been a little gentleman and had paid the penalty by discovering that he was the only such person in his family. This comparison didn't make him vain, but it could make him melancholy and a trifle austere. While Pemberton guessed at these dim young things, shadows of shadows, he was partly drawn on and partly checked, as for a scruple, by the charm of attempting to sound the little cool shallows that were so quickly growing deeper. When he tried to figure to himself the morning twilight of childhood, so as to deal with it safely, he saw it was never fixed, never arrested that ignorance, at the instant he touched it, was already flushing faintly into knowledge, that there was nothing that at a given moment you could say an intelligent child didn't know. It seemed to him that he

himself knew too much to imagine Morgan's simplicity and too little to disembroil his angle.

The boy paid no heed to his last remark; he only went on: "I'd have spoken to them about their idea, as I call it, long ago, if I hadn't been sure what they'd say."

"And what would they say?"

"Just what they said about what poor Zénobie told me—that it was a horrid dreadful story, that they had paid her every penny they owed her."

"Well, perhaps they had," said Pemberton.

"Perhaps they've paid you!"

"Let us pretend they have, and *n'en parlons plus*."

"They accused her of lying and cheating"— Morgan stuck to historic truth. "That's why I don't want to speak to them."

"Lest they should accuse me too?" To this Morgan made no answer, and his companion, looking down at him—the boy turned away his eyes, which had filled—saw that he couldn't have trusted himself to utter. "You're right. Don't worry them," Pemberton pursued. "Except for that, they *are* charming people."

"Except for *their* lying and *their* cheating?"

"I say—I say!" cried Pemberton, imitating a little tone of the lad's which was itself an imitation.

"We must be frank, at the last; we *must* come to an understanding," said Morgan with the importance of the small boy who lets himself think he is arranging great affairs—almost playing at shipwreck or at Indians. "I know all about everything."

"I dare say your father has his reasons," Pemberton replied, but too vaguely, as he was aware.

"For lying and cheating?"

"For saving and managing and turning his means to the best account. He has plenty to do with his money. You're an expensive family."

"Yes, I'm very expensive," Morgan concurred in a manner that made his preceptor burst out laughing.

"He's saving for *you*," said Pemberton. "They think of you in everything they do."

"He might, while he's about it, save a little—" The boy paused, and his friend waited to hear what. Then Morgan brought out coldly: "A little reputation."

"Oh there's plenty of that. That's all right!"

"Enough of it for the people they know, no doubt. The people they know are awful."

"Do you mean the princes? We mustn't abuse the princes."

"Why not? They haven't married Paula—they haven't married Amy. They only clean out Ulick."

"You *do* know everything!" Pemberton declared.

"No I don't after all. I don't know what they live on, or how they live, or *why* they live! What have they got and how did they get it? Are they rich, are they poor, or have they a *modeste aisance?* Why are they always chiveying me about—living one year like ambassadors and the next like paupers? Who are they, anyway, and what are they? I've thought of all that—I've thought of a lot of things. They're so beastly worldly. That's what I hate most—oh I've *seen* it! All they care about is to make an appearance and to pass for something or other. What the dickens do they want to pass for? What *do* they, Mr. Pemberton?"

"You pause for a reply," said Pemberton, treating the question as a joke, yet wondering too and greatly struck with his mate's intense if imperfect vision. "I haven't the least idea."

"And what good does it do? Haven't I seen the way people treat them—the 'nice' people, the ones they want to know? They'll take anything from them—they'll lie down and be trampled on. The nice ones hate that—they just sicken them. You're the only really nice person we know."

"Are you sure? They don't lie down for me!"

"Well, you shan't lie down for them. You've got to go—that's what you've got to do," said Morgan.

"And what will become of you?"

"Oh I'm growing up. I shall get off before long. I'll see you later."

"You had better let me finish you," Pemberton urged, lending himself to the child's strange superiority.

Morgan stopped in their walk, looking up at him. He had to look up much less than a couple of years before—he had grown, in his loose leanness, so long and high. "Finish me?" he echoed.

"There are such a lot of jolly things we can do together yet. I want to turn you out—I want you to do me credit."

Morgan continued to look at him. "To give you credit—do you mean?"

"My dear fellow, you're too clever to live."

"That's just what I'm afraid you think. No, no; it isn't fair—I can't endure it. We'll separate next week. The sooner it's over the sooner to sleep."

"If I hear of anything—any other chance—I promise to go," Pemberton said.

Morgan consented to consider this. "But you'll be honest," he demanded; "you won't pretend you haven't heard?"

"I'm much more likely to pretend I have."

"But what can you hear of, this way, stuck in a hole with us? You ought to be on the spot, to go to England—you ought to go to America."

"One would think you were *my* tutor!" said Pemberton.

Morgan walked on and after a little had begun again: "Well, now that you know I know and that we look at the facts and keep nothing back—it's much more comfortable, isn't it?"

"My dear boy, it's so amusing, so interesting, that it will surely be quite impossible for me to forego such hours as these."

This made Morgan stop once more. "You *do* keep something back. Oh you're not straight—I am!"

"How am I not straight?"

"Oh you've got your idea!"

"My idea?"

"Why that I probably shan't make old—make older—bones, and that you can stick it out till I'm removed."

"You *are* too clever to live!" Pemberton repeated.

"I call it a mean idea," Morgan pursued. "But I shall punish you by the way I hang on."

"Look out or I'll poison you!" Pemberton laughed.

"I'm stronger and better every year. Haven't you noticed that there hasn't been a doctor near me since you came?"

"*I'm* your doctor," said the young man, taking his arm and drawing him tenderly on again.

Morgan proceeded and after a few steps gave a sigh of mingled weariness and relief. "Ah now that we look at the facts it's all right!"

VII

They looked at the facts a good deal after this; and one of the first consequences of their doing so was that Pemberton stuck it out, in his friend's parlance, for the purpose. Morgan made the facts so vivid and so droll, and at the same time so bald and so ugly, that there was fascination in talking them over with him, just as there would have been heartlessness in leaving him alone with them. Now that the pair had such perceptions in common it was useless for them to pretend they didn't judge such people; but the very judgment and the exchange of perceptions created another tie. Morgan had never been so interesting as now that he himself was made plainer by the sidelight of these confidences. What came out in it most was the small fine passion of his pride. He had plenty of that, Pemberton felt—so much that one might perhaps wisely wish for it some early bruises. He would have liked his people to have a spirit and had waked up to the sense of their perpetually eating humble-pie. His mother would consume any amount, and his father would consume even more than his mother. He had a theory that Ulick had wriggled out of an "affair" at Nice: there had once been a flurry at home, a regular panic, after which they all went to bed and took medicine, not to be accounted for on any other supposition. Morgan had a romantic imagination, fed by poetry and history, and he would have liked those who "bore his name"—as he used to say to Pemberton with the humour that made his queer delicacies manly—to carry themselves with an air. But their one idea was to get in with people who didn't want them and to take snubs as if they were honourable scars. Why people didn't want them more he didn't know —that was people's own affair; after all they weren't superficially repulsive, they were a hundred times cleverer than most of the dreary grandees, the "poor swells" they rushed about Europe to catch up with. "After all they *are* amusing—they are!" he used to pronounce with the wisdom of the ages. To which Pemberton always replied: "Amusing—the great Moreen troupe? Why they're altogether delightful; and if it weren't for the hitch that you and I (feeble performers!) make in the *ensemble* they'd carry everything before them."

What the boy couldn't get over was the fact that this particular blight seemed, in a tradition of self-respect, so undeserved and so arbitrary. No doubt people had a right to take the line they liked; but why should *his* people have liked the line of pushing and toadying and lying and cheating? What had their forefathers—all decent folk, so far as he knew—done to them, or what had *he* done to them? Who had poisoned their blood with the fifth-rate social ideal, the fixed idea of making smart acquaintances and getting into the *monde chic,* especially when it was foredoomed to failure and exposure? They showed so what they were after; that was what made the people they wanted not want *them.* And never a wince for dignity, never a throb of shame at looking each other in the face, never any independence or resentment or disgust. If his father or his brother would only knock some one down once or twice a year! Clever as they were they never guessed the impression they made. They were good-natured, yes—as good-natured as Jews at the doors of clothing-shops! But was that the model one wanted one's family to follow? Morgan had dim memories of an old grandfather, the maternal, in New York, whom he had been taken across the ocean at the age of five to see: a gentleman with a high neck-cloth and a good deal of pronunciation, who wore a dress-coat in the morning, which made one wonder what he wore in the evening, and had, or was supposed to have, "property" and something to do with the Bible Society. It couldn't have been but that *he* was a good type. Pemberton himself remembered Mrs. Clancy, a widowed sister of Mr. Moreen's, who was as irritating as a moral tale and had paid a fortnight's visit to the family at Nice shortly after he came to live with them. She was "pure and refined," as Amy said over the banjo, and had the air of not knowing what they meant when they talked, and of keeping something rather important back. Pemberton judged that what she kept back was an approval of many of their ways; therefore it was to be supposed that she too was of a good type, and that Mr. and Mrs. Moreen and Ulick and Paula and Amy might easily have been of a better one if they would.

But that they wouldn't was more and more perceptible from day to day. They continued to "chivey," as Morgan called it, and in due time became aware of a variety of reasons for proceeding to Venice. They mentioned a great many of them—they were always strikingly frank and had the brightest friendly chatter, at the late foreign breakfast in especial, before the ladies had made up their faces, when they leaned their arms on the table, had something to follow the *demi-tasse,* and, in the heat of familiar discussion as to what they "really ought" to do, fell inevitably into the languages in which they could *tutoyer.* Even Pemberton liked them then; he could endure even Ulick when he heard him give his little flat voice for the "sweet sea city." That was what made him have a sneaking kindness for them— that they were so out of the workaday world and kept him so out of it. The summer had waned when, with cries of ecstasy, they all passed out on the balcony that overhung the Grand Canal. The sunsets then were splendid and the Dorringtons had arrived. The Dorringtons were the only reason they hadn't talked of at breakfast; but the reasons they didn't talk of at breakfast always came out in the end. The Dorringtons on the other hand came out very little; or else when they did they stayed—as was natural—for hours, during which periods Mrs. Moreen and the girls sometimes called at their hotel (to see if they had returned) as many as three times running. The gondola was for the ladies, as in Venice too there were "days," which Mrs. Moreen knew in their order an hour after she arrived. She immediately took one herself, to which the Dorringtons never came, though on a certain occasion when Pemberton and his pupil were together at Saint Mark's—where, taking the best walks they had ever had and haunting a hundred churches, they spent a great deal of time—they saw the old lord turn up with Mr. Moreen and Ulick, who showed him the dim basilica as if it belonged to them. Pemberton noted how much less, among its curiosities, Lord Dorrington carried himself as a man of the world; wondering too whether, for such services, his companions took a fee from him. The autumn at any rate waned, the Dorringtons departed and Lord Verschoyle, the eldest son, had proposed neither for Amy nor for Paula.

One sad November day, while the wind roared round the old palace and the rain lashed the lagoon, Pemberton, for exercise and even somewhat for warmth—the Moreens were horribly frugal about fires; it was a cause of suffering to their inmate—walked up and down the big bare sala with his pupil. The scagliola floor was cold, the high battered casements shook in the storm, and the stately decay of the place was unrelieved by a particle of furniture. Pemberton's spirits were low, and it came over him that the fortune of the Moreens was now even lower. A blast of desolation, a portent of disgrace and disaster, seemed to draw through the comfortless hall. Mr. Moreen and Ulick were in the Piazza, looking out for something, strolling drearily, in mackintoshes, under the arcades; but still, in spite of mackintoshes, unmistakable men of the world. Paula and Amy were in bed—it might have been thought they were staying there to keep warm. Pemberton looked askance at the boy at his side, to see to what extent he was conscious of these dark omens. But Morgan, luckily for him, was now mainly conscious of growing taller and stronger and indeed of being in his fifteenth year. This fact was intensely interesting to him and the basis of a private theory—which, however, he had imparted to his tutor—that in a little while he should stand on his own feet. He considered that the situation would change—that in short he should be "finished," grown up, producible in the world of affairs and ready to prove himself of sterling ability. Sharply as he was capable at times of analysing, as he called it, his life, there were happy hours when he remained, as he also called it—and as the name, really, of their right ideal—"jolly" superficial; the proof of which was his fundamental assumption that he should presently go to Oxford, to Pemberton's college, and aided and abetted by Pemberton, do the most wonderful things. It depressed the young man to see how little in such a project he took account of ways and means: in other connexions he mostly kept to the measure. Pemberton tried to imagine the Moreens at Oxford and fortunately failed; yet unless they were to adopt it as a residence there would be no *modus vivendi* for Morgan. How could he live without an allowance, and where was the allowance to come from? He, Pemberton, might live on Morgan; but how could Morgan live on *him*? What was to become of him anyhow? Somehow the fact that he was a big boy now, with better prospects of health, made the question of his future more difficult. So long as he was markedly frail the great consideration he inspired seemed enough of an answer to it. But at the bottom of Pemberton's heart was the recognition of his probably being strong enough to live and not yet strong enough to struggle or to thrive. Morgan himself at any rate was in the first flush of the rosiest consciousness of adolescence, so that the beating of the tempest seemed to him after all but the voice of life and the challenge of fate. He had on his shabby little overcoat, with the collar up, but was enjoying his walk.

It was interrupted at last by the appearance of his mother at the end of the *sala*. She beckoned him to come to her, and while Pemberton saw him, complaisant, pass down the long vista and over the damp false marble, he wondered what was in the air. Mrs. Moreen said a word to the boy and made him go into the room she had quitted. Then, having closed the door after him, she directed her steps swiftly to Pemberton. There *was* something in the air, but his widest flight of fancy wouldn't have suggested

what it proved to be. She signified that she
had made a pretext to get Morgan out of the
way, and then she enquired—without hesitation—if the young man could favour her with
the loan of three louis. While, before bursting
into a laugh, he stared at her with surprise, she
declared that she was awfully pressed for the
money; she was desperate for it—it would save
her life.

10   "Dear lady, *c'est trop fort!*" Pemberton
laughed in the manner and with the borrowed
grace of idiom that marked the best colloquial,
the best anecdotic, moments of his friends
themselves. "Where in the world do you suppose I should get three louis, *du train dont
vous allez?*"
     "I thought you worked—wrote things. Don't
they pay you?"
     "Not a penny."
20   "Are you such a fool as to work for nothing?"
     "You ought surely to know that."
     Mrs. Moreen stared, then she coloured a
little. Pemberton saw she had quite forgotten
the terms—if "terms" they could be called—
that he had ended by accepting from herself;
they had burdened her memory as little as her
conscience. "Oh yes, I see what you mean—
you've been very nice about that; but why drag
it in so often?" She had been perfectly urbane
30 with him ever since the rough scene of explanation in his room the morning he made her accept *his* "terms"—the necessity of his making
his case known to Morgan. She had felt no resentment after seeing there was no danger Morgan would take the matter up with her. Indeed,
attributing this immunity to the good taste of
his influence with thê boy, she had once said to
Pemberton, "My dear fellow, it's an immense
comfort you're a gentleman." She repeated this
40 in substance now. "Of course you're a gentleman—that's a bother the less!" Pemberton reminded her that he had not "dragged in" anything that wasn't already in as much as his foot
was in his shoe; and she also repeated her
prayer that, somewhere and somehow, he
would find her sixty francs. He took the liberty
of hinting that if he could find them it wouldn't
be to lend them to *her*—as to which he consciously did himself injustice, knowing that if
50 he had them he would certainly put them at her
disposal. He accused himself, at bottom and not
unveraciously, of a fantastic, a demoralised
sympathy with her. If misery made strange bed-
fellows it also made strange sympathies. It was

moreover a part of the abasement of living with
such people that one had to make vulgar retorts, quite out of one's own tradition of good
manners. "Morgan, Morgan, to what pass have
I come for you?" he groaned while Mrs. Moreen
floated voluminously down the *sala* again to
liberate the boy, wailing as she went that everything was too odious.
     Before their young friend was liberated
there came a thump at the door communicating
with the staircase, followed by the apparition
of a dripping youth who poked in his head.
Pemberton recognised him as the bearer of a
telegram and recognised the telegram as addressed to himself. Morgan came back as, after
glancing at the signature—that of a relative in
London—he was reading the words: "Found
jolly job for you, engagement to coach opulent
youth on own terms. Come at once." The answer, happily, was paid, and the messenger
waited. Morgan, who had drawn near, waited
too, and looked hard at Pemberton; and Pemberton, after a moment, having met his look,
handed him the telegram. It was really by wise
looks—they knew each other so well now—
that, while the telegraph-boy, in his waterproof
cape, made a great puddle on the floor, the
thing was settled between them. Pemberton
wrote the answer with a pencil against the fres-
coed wall, and the messenger departed. When
he had gone the young man explained himself.
     "I'll make a tremendous charge; I'll earn a
lot of money in a short time, and we'll live on
it."
     "Well, I hope the opulent youth will be a
dismal dunce—he probably will," Morgan pa-
renthesised—"and keep you a long time a-ham-
mering of it in."
     "Of course the longer he keeps me the more
we shall have for our old age."
     "But suppose *they* don't pay you!" Morgan
awfully suggested.
     "Oh there are not two such—!" But Pember-
ton pulled up; he had been on the point of using too invidious a term. Instead of this he
said "Two such fatalities."
     Morgan flushed—the tears came to his eyes.
"*Dites toujours* two such rascally crews!" Then
in a different tone he added: "Happy opulent
youth!"
     "Not if he's a dismal dunce."
     "Oh they're happier then. But you can't have
everything, can you?" the boy smiled.
     Pemberton held him fast, hands on his shoul-

ders—he had never loved him so. "What will become of *you,* what will you do?" He thought of Mrs. Moreen, desperate for sixty francs.

"I shall become an *homme fait.*" And then as if he recognised all the bearings of Pemberton's allusion: "I shall get on with them better when you're not here."

"Ah don't say that—it sounds as if I set you against them!"

"You do—the sight of you. It's all right; you know what I mean. I shall be beautiful. I'll take their affairs in hand; I'll marry my sisters."

"You'll marry yourself!" joked Pemberton; as high, rather tense pleasantry would evidently be the right, or the safest, tone for their separation.

It was, however, not purely in this strain that Morgan suddenly asked: "But I say—how will you get to your jolly job? You'll have to telegraph to the opulent youth for money to come on."

Pemberton bethought himself. "They won't like that, will they?"

"Oh look out for them!"

Then Pemberton brought out his remedy. "I'll go to the American Consul; I'll borrow some money of him—just for the few days, on the strength of the telegram."

Morgan was hilarious. "Show him the telegram—then collar the money and stay!"

Pemberton entered into the joke sufficiently to reply that for Morgan he was really capable of that; but the boy, growing more serious, and to prove he hadn't meant what he said, not only hurried him off to the Consulate—since he was to start that evening, as he had wired to his friend—but made sure of their affair by going with him. They splashed through the tortuous perforations and over the humpbacked bridges, and they passed through the Piazza, where they saw Mr. Moreen and Ulick go into a jeweller's shop. The Consul proved accommodating—Pemberton said it wasn't the letter, but Morgan's grand air—and on their way back they went into Saint Mark's for a hushed ten minutes. Later they took up and kept up the fun of it to the very end; and it seemed to Pemberton a part of that fun that Mrs. Moreen, who was very angry when he had announced her his intention, she charged him, grotesquely and vulgarly and in reference to the loan she had vainly endeavoured to effect, with bolting lest they should "get something out" of him. On the other hand he had to do Mr. Moreen and Ulick the justice to recognise that when on coming in *they* heard the cruel news they took it like perfect men of the world.

VIII

When he got at work with the opulent youth, who was to be taken in hand for Balliol, he found himself unable to say if this aspirant had really such poor parts or if the appearance were only begotten of his own long association with an intensely living little mind. From Morgan he heard half a dozen times: the boy wrote charming young letters, a patchwork of tongues, with indulgent postscripts in the family Volapuk and, in little squares and rounds and crannies of the text, the drollest illustrations—letters that he was divided between the impulse to show his present charge as a vain, a wasted incentive, and the sense of something in them that publicity would profane. The opulent youth went up in due course and failed to pass; but it seemed to add to the presumption that brilliancy was not expected of him all at once that his parents, condoning the lapse, which they good-naturedly treated as little as possible as if it were Pemberton's, should have sounded the rally again, begged the young coach to renew the siege.

The young coach was now in a position to lend Mrs. Moreen three louis, and he sent her a post-office order even for a larger amount. In return for this favour he received a frantic scribbled line from her: "Implore you to come back instantly—Morgan dreadfully ill." They were on the rebound, once more in Paris—often as Pemberton had seen them depressed he had never seen them crushed—and communication was therefore rapid. He wrote to the boy to ascertain the state of his health, but awaited the answer in vain. He accordingly, after three days, took an abrupt leave of the opulent youth and, crossing the Channel, alighted at the small hotel, in the quarter of the Champs Elysées, of which Mrs. Moreen had given him the address. A deep if dumb dissatisfaction with this lady and her companions bore him company: they couldn't be vulgarly honest, but they could live at hotels, in velvety *entresols,* amid a smell of burnt pastilles, surrounded by the most expensive city in Europe. When he had left them in Venice it was with an irrepressible suspicion that something was going to happen; but the only thing that could have taken place was again their masterly retreat. "How is he? where is he?" he asked of Mrs. Moreen; but before she could speak these questions were answered by the pressure round his neck of a pair of arms, in shrunken sleeves, which still were perfectly capable of an effusive young foreign squeeze.

"Dreadfully ill—I don't see it!" the young man cried. And then to Morgan: "Why on earth didn't you relieve me? Why didn't you answer my letter?"

Mrs. Moreen declared that when she wrote he was very bad, and Pemberton learned at the same time from the boy that he had answered every letter he had received. This led to the clear inference that Pemberton's note had been kept from him so that the game to be practised should not be interfered with. Mrs. Moreen was prepared to see the fact exposed, as Pemberton saw the moment he faced her that she was prepared for a good many other things. She was prepared above all to maintain that she had acted from a sense of duty, that she was enchanted she had got him over, whatever they might say, and that it was useless of him to pretend he didn't know in all his bones that his place at such a time was with Morgan. He had taken the boy away from them and now had no right to abandon him. He had created for himself the gravest responsibilities and must at least abide by what he had done.

"Taken him away from you?" Pemberton exclaimed indignantly.

"Do it—do it for pity's sake; that's just what I want. I can't stand *this*—and such scenes. They're awful frauds—poor dears!" These words broke from Morgan, who had intermitted his embrace, in a key which made Pemberton turn quickly to him and see that he had suddenly seated himself, was breathing in great pain and was very pale.

"*Now* do you say he's not in a state, my precious pet?" shouted his mother, dropping on her knees before him with clasped hands, but touching him no more than if he had been a gilded idol. "It will pass—it's only for an instant; but don't say such dreadful things!"

"I'm all right—all right," Morgan panted to Pemberton, whom he sat looking up at with a strange smile, his hands resting on either side on the sofa.

"Now do you pretend I've been dishonest, that I've deceived?" Mrs. Moreen flashed at Pemberton as she got up.

"It isn't *he* says it, it's I!" the boy returned,

apparently easier but sinking back against the wall; while his restored friend, who had sat down beside him, took his hand and bent over him.

"Darling child, one does what one can; there are so many things to consider," urged Mrs. Moreen. "It's his *place*—his only place. You see *you* think it is now."

"Take me away—take me away," Morgan went on, smiling to Pemberton with his white face.

"Where shall I take you, and how—oh *how*, my boy?" the young man stammered, thinking of the rude way in which his friends in London held that, for his convenience, with no assurance of prompt return, he had thrown them over; of the just resentment with which they would already have called in a successor, and of the scant help to finding fresh employment that resided for him in the grossness of his having failed to pass his pupil.

"Oh we'll settle that. You used to talk about it," said Morgan. "If we can only go all the rest's a detail."

"Talk about it as much as you like, but don't think you can attempt it. Mr. Moreen would never consent—it would be so *very* hand-to-mouth," Pemberton's hostess beautifully explained to him. Then to Morgan she made it clearer: "It would destroy our peace, it would break our hearts. Now that he's back it will be all the same again. You'll have your life, your work and your freedom, and we'll all be happy as we used to be. You'll bloom and grow perfectly well, and we won't have any more silly experiments, will we? They're too absurd. It's Mr. Pemberton's place—every one in his place. You in yours, your papa in his, me in mine—*n'est-ce pas, chéri?* We'll all forget how foolish we've been and have lovely times."

She continued to talk and to surge vaguely about the little draped stuffy salon while Pemberton sat with the boy, whose colour gradually came back; and she mixed up her reasons, hinting that there were going to be changes, that the other children might scatter (who knew?—Paula had her ideas) and that then it might be fancied how much the poor old parent-birds would want the little nestling. Morgan looked at Pemberton, who wouldn't let him move; and Pemberton knew exactly how he felt at hearing himself called a little nestling. He admitted that he had had one or two bad days, but he protested afresh against the wrong of his mother's having made them the ground of a appeal to poor Pemberton. Poor Pemberton could laugh now, apart from the comicality of Mrs. Moreen's mustering so much philosophy for her defence—she seemed to shake it out of her agitated petticoats, which knocked over the light gilt chairs—so little did their young companion, *marked,* unmistakably marked at the best, strike him as qualified to repudiate any advantage.

He himself was in for it at any rate. He should have Morgan on his hands again indefinitely; though indeed he saw the lad had a private theory to produce which would be intended to smooth this down. He was obliged to him for it in advance; but the suggested amendment didn't keep his heart rather from sinking, any more than it prevented him from accepting the prospect on the spot, with some confidence moreover that he should do so even better if he could have a little supper. Mrs Moreen threw out more hints about the changes that were to be looked for, but she was such a mixture of smiles and shudders—she confessed she was very nervous—that he couldn't tell if she were in high feather or only in hysterics. If the family was really at last going to pieces why shouldn't she recognise the necessity of pitching Morgan into some sort of lifeboat? This presumption was fostered by the fact that they were established in luxurious quarters in the capital of pleasure; that was exactly where they naturally *would* be established in view of going to pieces. Moreover didn't she mention that Mr. Moreen and the others were enjoying themselves at the opera with Mr. Granger, and wasn't *that* also precisely where one would look for them on the eve of a smash? Pemberton gathered that Mr. Granger was a rich vacant American—a big bill with a flourishy heading and no items; so that one of Paula's "ideas" was probably that this time she hadn't missed fire—by which straight shot indeed she would have shattered the general cohesion. And if the cohesion was to crumble what would become of poor Pemberton? He felt quite enough bound up with them to figure to his alarm as a dislodged block in the edifice.

It was Morgan who eventually asked if no supper had been ordered for him; sitting with him below, later, at the dim delayed meal, in the presence of a great deal of corded green plush, a plate of ornamental biscuit and an aloofness marked on the part of the waiter. Mrs. Moreen had explained that they had been

obliged to secure a room for the visitor out of the house; and Morgan's consolation—he offered it while Pemberton reflected on the nastiness of luke-warm sauces—proved to be, largely, that this circumstance would facilitate their escape. He talked of their escape—recurring to it often afterwards—as if they were making up a "boy's book" together. But he likewise expressed his sense that there was something in the air, that the Moreens couldn't keep it up much longer. In point of fact, as Pemberton was to see, they kept it up for five or six months. All the while, however, Morgan's contention was designed to cheer him. Mr. Moreen and Ulick, whom he had met the day after his return, accepted that return like perfect men of the world. If Paula and Amy treated it even with less formality an allowance was to be made for them, inasmuch as Mr. Granger hadn't come to the opera after all. He had only placed his box at their service, with a bouquet for each of the party; there was even one apiece, embittering the thought of his profusion, for Mr. Moreen and Ulick. "They're all like that," was Morgan's comment; "at the very last, just when we think we've landed them they're back in the deep sea!"

Morgan's comments in these days were more and more free; they even included a large recognition of the extraordinary tenderness with which he had been treated while Pemberton was away. Oh yes, they couldn't do enough to be nice to him, to show him they had him on their mind and make up for his loss. That was just what made the whole thing so sad and caused him to rejoice after all in Pemberton's return—he had to keep thinking of their affection less, had less sense of obligation. Pemberton laughed out at this last reason, and Morgan blushed and said, "Well, dash it, you know what I mean." Pemberton knew perfectly what he meant; but there were a good many things that—dash it too!—it didn't make any clearer. This episode of his second sojourn in Paris stretched itself out wearily, with their resumed readings and wanderings and maunderings, their potterings on the quays, their hauntings of the museums, their occasional lingerings in the Palais Royal when the first sharp weather came on and there was a comfort in warm emanations, before Chevet's wonderful succulent window. Morgan wanted to hear all about the opulent youth—he took an immense interest in him. Some of the details of his opulence—Pemberton could spare him none of them—evidently fed the boy's appreciation of all his friend had given up to come back to him; but in addition to the greater reciprocity established by that heroism he had always his little brooding theory, in which there was a frivolous gaiety too, that their long probation was drawing to a close. Morgan's conviction that the Moreens couldn't go on much longer kept pace with the unexpended impetus with which, from month to month, they did go on. Three weeks after Pemberton had rejoined them they went on to another hotel, a dingier one than the first; but Morgan rejoiced that his tutor had at least still not sacrificed the advantage of a room outside. He clung to the romantic utility of this when the day, or rather the night, should arrive for their escape.

For the first time, in this complicated connexion, our friend felt his collar gall him. It was, as he had said to Mrs. Moreen in Venice, *trop fort*—everything was *trop fort*. He could neither really throw off his blighting burden nor find in it the benefit of a pacified conscience or of a rewarded affection. He had spent all the money accruing to him in England, and he saw his youth going and that he was getting nothing back for it. It was all very well of Morgan to count it for reparation that he should now settle on him permanently—there was an irritating flaw in such a view. He saw what the boy had in his mind; the conception that as his friend had had the generosity to come back he must show his gratitude by giving him his life. But the poor friend didn't desire the gift—what could he do with Morgan's dreadful little life? Of course at the same time that Pemberton was irritated he remembered the reason, which was very honourable to Morgan and which dwelt simply in his making one so forget that he was no more than a patched urchin. If one dealt with him on a different basis one's misadventures were one's own fault. So Pemberton waited in a queer confusion of yearning and alarm for the catastrophe which was held to hang over the house of Moreen, of which he certainly at moments felt the symptoms brush his cheek and as to which he wondered much in what form it would find its liveliest effect.

Perhaps it would take the form of sudden dispersal—a frightened *sauve qui peut*, a scuttling into selfish corners. Certainly they were less elastic than of yore; they were evidently looking for something they didn't find. The Dorringtons hadn't re-appeared, the princes had scattered; wasn't that the beginning of the end? Mrs. Moreen had lost her reckoning of the famous "days"; her social calendar was blurred—it had turned its face to the wall. Pemberton suspected that the great, the cruel discomfiture had been the unspeakable behaviour of Mr. Granger, who seemed not to know what he wanted, or, what was much worse, what *they* wanted. He kept sending flowers, as if to bestrew the path of his retreat, which was never the path of a return. Flowers were all very well, but—Pemberton could complete the proposition. It was now positively conspicuous that in the long run the Moreens were a social failure; so that the young man was almost grateful the run had not been short. Mr. Moreen indeed was still occasionally able to get away on business and, what was more surprising, was likewise able to get back. Ulick had no club, but you couldn't have discovered it from his appearance, which was as much as ever that of a person looking at life from the window of such an institution; therefore Pemberton was doubly surprised at an answer he once heard him make his mother in the desperate tone of a man familiar with the worst privations. Her question Pemberton had not quite caught; it appeared to be an appeal for a suggestion as to whom they might get to take Amy. "Let the Devil take her!" Ulick snapped; so that Pemberton could see that they had not only lost their amiability but had ceased to believe in themselves. He could also see that if Mrs. Moreen was trying to get people to take her children she might be regarded as closing the hatches for the storm. But Morgan would be the last she would part with.

One winter afternoon—it was a Sunday—he and the boy walked far together in the Bois de Boulogne. The evening was so splendid, the cold lemon-coloured sunset so clear, the stream of carriages and pedestrians so amusing and the fascination of Paris so great, that they stayed out later than usual and became aware that they should have to hurry home to arrive in time for dinner. They hurried accordingly, arm-in-arm, good-humoured and hungry, agreeing that there was nothing like Paris after all and that after everything too that had come and gone they were not yet sated with innocent pleasures. When they reached the hotel they found that, though scandalously late, they were in time for all the dinner they were likely to sit down to. Confusion reigned in the apartments of the Moreens—very shabby ones this time, but the best in the house—and before the interrupted service of the table, with objects displaced almost as if there had been a scuffle, and a great wine-stain from an overturned bottle, Pemberton couldn't blink the fact that there had been a scene of the last proprietary firmness. The storm had come—they were all seeking refuge. The hatches were down, Paula and Amy were invisible,—they had never tried the most casual art upon Pemberton, but he felt they had enough of an eye to him not to wish to meet him as young ladies whose frocks had been confiscated—and Ulick appeared to have jumped overboard. The host and his staff, in a word, had ceased to "go on" at the pace of their guests, and the air of embarrassed detention, thanks to a pile of gaping trunks in the passage, was strangely commingled with the air of indignant withdrawal.

When Morgan took all this in—and he took it in very quickly—he coloured to the roots of his hair. He had walked from his infancy among difficulties and dangers, but he had never seen a public exposure. Pemberton noticed in a second glance at him that the tears had rushed into his eyes and that they were tears of a new and untasted bitterness. He wondered an instant, for the boy's sake, whether he might successfully pretend not to understand. Not successfully, he felt, as Mr. and Mrs. Moreen, dinnerless by their extinguished hearth, rose before him in their little dishonoured salon, casting about with glassy eyes for the nearest port in such a storm. They were not prostrate but were horribly white, and Mrs. Moreen had evidently been crying. Pemberton quickly learned however that her grief was not for the loss of her dinner, much as she usually enjoyed it, but the fruit of a blow that struck even deeper, as she made all haste to explain. He would see for himself, so far as that went, how the great change had come, the dreadful bolt had fallen, and how they would now all have to turn themselves about. Therefore cruel as it was to them to part with their darling she must look to him to carry a little further the influence he had so fortunately acquired with the boy—to induce his young charge to follow him into some modest retreat. They depended on him—that was the fact—to take their delightful child temporarily under his protection: it would leave Mr. Moreen and herself so much more free to give the proper attention (too lit-

tle, alas! had been given) to the readjustment of their affairs.

"We trust you—we feel we *can*," said Mrs. Moreen, slowly rubbing her plump white hands and looking with compunction hard at Morgan, whose chin, not to take liberties, her husband stroked with a tentative paternal forefinger.

"Oh yes—we feel that we *can*. We trust Mr. Pemberton fully, Morgan," Mr. Moreen pursued.

Pemberton wondered again if he might pretend not to understand; but everything good gave way to the intensity of Morgan's understanding. "Do you mean he may take me to live with him for ever and ever?" cried the boy. "May take me away, away, anywhere he likes?"

"For ever and ever? *Comme vous-y-allez!*" Mr. Moreen laughed indulgently. "For as long as Mr. Pemberton may be so good."

"We've struggled, we've suffered," his wife went on; "But you've made him so your own that we've already been through the worst of the sacrifice."

Morgan had turned away from his father—he stood looking at Pemberton with a light in his face. His sense of shame for their common humiliated state had dropped; the case had another side—the thing was to clutch at *that*. He had a moment of boyish joy, scarcely mitigated by the reflexion that with this unexpected consecration of his hope—too sudden and too violent; the turn taken was away from a *good* boy's book—the "escape" was left on their hands. The boyish joy was there an instant, and Pemberton was almost scared at the rush of gratitude and affection that broke through his first abasement. When he stammered "My dear fellow, what do you say to *that*?" how could one not say something enthusiastic? But there was more need for courage at something else that immediately followed and that made the lad sit down quickly on the nearest chair. He had turned quite livid and had raised his hand to his left side. They were all three looking at him, but Mrs. Moreen suddenly bounded forward. "Ah his darling little heart!" she broke out; and this time, on her knees before him, and without respect for the idol, she caught him ardently in her arms. "You walked him too far, you hurried him too fast!" she hurled over her shoulder at Pemberton. Her son made no protest, and the next instant, still holding him, she sprang up with her face convulsed and with the terrified cry "Help, help! he's going, he's gone!" Pemberton saw with equal horror, by Morgan's own stricken face, that he was beyond their wildest recall. He pulled him half out of his mother's hands, and for a moment, while they held him together, they looked all their dismay into each other's eyes. "He couldn't stand it with his weak organ," said Pemberton—"the shock, the whole scene, the violent emotion."

"But I thought he *wanted* to go to you!" wailed Mrs. Moreen.

"I *told* you he didn't, my dear," her husband made answer. Mr. Moreen was trembling all over and was in his way as deeply affected as his wife. But after the very first he took his bereavement as a man of the world.

1890   1891

SARAH ORNE JEWETT

1849–1909

WHEN MISS JEWETT began to publish her stories in the *Atlantic Monthly*—the first was in 1869—the village of her birth, South Berwick, Maine, was already living on the memories of its great days when her grandfather was the owner of ships launched from the local yards. The stately white homes of the region had sent husbands and sons in these ships to the corners of the world. Tales of their exploits Miss Jewett heard as a girl from the women who survived them. To Miss Willa Cather she once remarked that "when an old house and an old woman came together in her brain with a click, she knew that a story was under way."

Through her father, the village doctor, Miss Jewett had come to know another side of the life of the countryside. Since she was a delicate child, he had often kept her from school to take her with him on his visits to lonely farmhouses on back roads. She saw sickness and sorrow with the eyes of a doctor who was sympathetic and at the same time, because his science demanded, observant and detached. These visits gave her material for her stories in later years and taught her ear the cadences of country speech. How deep the influence of her father was we can see from the portrait of him as Dr. Leslie in her novel *A Country Doctor* (1884).

Miss Jewett's first book, *Deephaven* (1877), is not a novel but a series of connected sketches, in this respect resembling her masterpiece, *The Country of the Pointed Firs* (1896). She ventured a full-length novel only three times: *A Country Doctor*, already mentioned, *A Marsh Island* (1885), and *The Tory Lover* (1901), in which she attempted to bring to life the proud past of Berwick in the time of the Revolution. Her short stories were collected between 1870 and 1900 in ten volumes.

Miss Jewett was recognized by belated Brahmins like T. B. Aldrich and Professor Norton as an important writer and worthy of their friendship. Of those in this circle only Howells seems really to have discerned how incomparable an artist she is. When one of her finest stories, "The Guests of Mrs. Timms," appeared, he wrote to her: "How you do make other people's joinery seem crude and clumsy! No, you are too friendly and kind for that, but it serves so, out of mere shame and a sense of its unworthiness."

She surpasses all the other so-called "local colorists" of the day, who had found a new delight in exploiting the legends, folklore, scenery, and quaint speech of their native regions, because with her the human situation is paramount and the "local color" the medium through which it is projected. But it is not enough to say that she knew her characters infallibly because they grew slowly in her imagination, as we know they did; or that she wisely attempted only that with which she was familiar or could justly imagine. The rightness of her feeling toward her characters is what counts above all else. Our emotions are never betrayed because she knew so exactly whether the scene should be touched with humor or pathos or tragedy. "The distinction between sentiment and sentimentality," she once wrote, "is a question of character, and is as deep as one can go in life, and kindness must have a sound tap-root." A writer must know the worth of his creatures, must take "them each in their relations to letters, to the world." The humblest life, so viewed, has nothing trivial about it, for a "master writer gives everything weight, and makes you feel the distinction and importance of it, and count it upon the right or the wrong side of a life's account."

She had no need to pin to her desk, for a constant reminder, as she did, two sentences she had copied from her admired Flaubert: "Écrire la vie ordinaire comme on écrit l'histoire," and "C'est ne pas de faire rire, ni de faire pleurer, ni de vous mettre à fureur, mais d'agir à la façon de la nature, c'est à dire de faire rêver." She knew this lesson as well as the master.

C. C. and C. J. Weber, *A Bibliography of the Published Writings of Sarah Orne Jewett*, Waterville, Me., 1949.
The Best Stories of Sarah Orne Jewett, Willa Cather, ed., 2 vols., Boston, 1925.
Letters of Sarah Orne Jewett, Richard Cary, ed., Waterville, Me., 1956.
F. O. Matthiessen, *Sarah Orne Jewett*, Boston, 1929.

» » THE ONLY ROSE [1] « «

I

Just where the village abruptly ended, and the green mowing fields began, stood Mrs. Bickford's house, looking down the road with all its windows, and topped by two prim chimneys that stood up like ears. It was placed with an end to the road, and fronted southward; you could follow a straight path from the gate past the front door and find Mrs. Bickford sitting by the last window of all in the kitchen, unless she were solemnly stepping about, prolonging the stern duties of her solitary housekeeping.

One day in early summer, when almost every one else in Fairfield had put her house plants out of doors, there were still three flower pots on a kitchen window sill. Mrs. Bickford spent but little time over her rose and geranium and Jerusalem cherry-tree, although they had gained a kind of personality born of long association. They rarely undertook to bloom, but had most courageously maintained life in spite of their owner's unsympathetic but conscientious care. Later in the season she would carry them out of doors, and leave them, until the time of frosts, under the shade of a great apple-tree, where they might make the best of what the summer had to give.

The afternoon sun was pouring in, the Jeru-

salem cherry-tree drooped its leaves in the heat and looked pale, when a neighbor, Miss Pendexter, came in from the next house but one to make a friendly call. As she passed the parlor with its shut blinds, and the sitting-room, also shaded carefully from the light, she wished, as she had done many times before, that somebody beside the owner might have the pleasure of living in and using so good and pleasant a house. Mrs. Bickford always complained of having so much care, even while she valued herself intelligently upon having the right to do as she pleased with one of the best houses in Fairfield. Miss Pendexter was a cheerful, even gay little person, who always brought a pleasant flurry of excitement, and usually had a genuine though small piece of news to tell, or some new aspect of already received information.

Mrs. Bickford smiled as she looked up to see this sprightly neighbor coming. She had no gift at entertaining herself, and was always glad, as one might say, to be taken off her own hands.

Miss Pendexter smiled back, as if she felt herself to be equal to the occasion.

"How be you to-day?" the guest asked kindly, as she entered the kitchen. "Why, what a sight o' flowers, Mis' Bickford! What be you goin' to do with 'em all?"

Mrs. Bickford wore a grave expression as she glanced over her spectacles. "My sister's boy fetched 'em over," she answered. "You know my sister Parsons's a great hand to raise flowers, an' this boy takes after her. He said his mother thought the gardin never looked handsomer, and she picked me these to send over. They was sendin' a team to Westbury for some fertilizer to put on the land, an' he come with the men, an' stopped to eat his dinner 'long o' me. He's been growin' fast, and looks peakéd. I expect sister 'Liza thought the ride, this pleasant day, would do him good. 'Liza sent word for me to come over and pass some days next week, but it ain't so that I can."

"Why, it's a pretty time of year to go off and make a little visit," suggested the neighbor encouragingly.

"I ain't got my sitting-room chamber carpet taken up yet," sighed Mrs. Bickford. "I do feel condemned. I might have done it to-day, but 't was all at end when I saw Tommy coming. There, he's a likely boy, an' so relished his dinner; I happened to be well prepared. I don't know but he's my favorite o' that family. Only I've been sittin' here thinkin', since he went, an' I can't remember that I ever was so belated with my spring cleaning."

"'T was owin' to the weather," explained Miss Pendexter. "None of us could be so smart as common this year, not even the lazy ones that always get one room done the first o' March, and brag of it to others' shame, and then never let on when they do the rest."

The two women laughed together cheerfully. Mrs. Bickford had put up the wide leaf of her large table between the windows and spread out the flowers. She was sorting them slowly into three heaps.

"Why, I do declare if you haven't got a rose in bloom yourself!" exclaimed Miss Pendexter abruptly, as if the bud had not been announced weeks before, and its progress regularly commented upon. "Ain't it a lovely rose? Why, Mis' Bickford!"

"Yes 'm, it's out to-day," said Mrs. Bickford, with a somewhat plaintive air. "I'm glad you come in so as to see it."

The bright flower was like a face. Somehow, the beauty and life of it were surprising in the plain room, like a gay little child who might suddenly appear in a doorway. Miss Pendexter forgot herself and her hostess and the tangled mass of garden flowers in looking at the red rose. She even forgot that it was incumbent upon her to carry forward the conversation. Mrs. Bickford was subject to fits of untimely silence which made her friends anxiously sweep the corners of their minds in search of something to say, but any one who looked at her now could easily see that it was not poverty of thought that made her speechless, but an overburdening sense of the inexpressible.

"Goin' to make up all your flowers into bo'quets? I think the short-stemmed kinds is often pretty in a dish," suggested Miss Pendexter compassionately.

"I thought I should make them into three bo'quets. I wish there wa'n't quite so many. Sister Eliza's very lavish with her flowers; she's always been a kind sister, too," said Mrs. Bickford vaguely. She was not apt to speak with so much sentiment, and as her neighbor looked at her narrowly she detected unusual signs of emotion. It suddenly became evident that the three nosegays were connected in her mind with her bereavement of three husbands, and Miss Pendexter's easily roused curiosity was quieted by the discovery that her friend was bent upon a visit to the burying-ground. It was the time of year when she was pretty sure to spend an afternoon there, and sometimes they had taken the walk in company. Miss Pendexter expected to receive the usual invitation, but there was nothing further said at the moment, and she looked again at the pretty rose.

Mrs. Bickford aimlessly handled the syringas and flowering almond sprays, choosing them out of the fragrant heap only to lay them down again. She glanced out of the window; then gave Miss Pendexter a long expressive look.

"I expect you're going to carry 'em over to the burying-ground?" inquired the guest, in a sympathetic tone.

"Yes 'm," said the hostess, now well started in conversation and in quite her every-day manner. "You see I was goin' over to my brother's folks to-morrow in South Fairfield, to pass the day; they said they were goin' to send over to-morrow to leave a wagon at the blacksmith's, and they'd hitch that to their best chaise, so I could ride back very comfortable. You know I have to avoid bein' out in the mornin' sun?"

Miss Pendexter smiled to herself at this moment; she was obliged to move from her chair at the window, the May sun was so hot on her back, for Mrs. Bickford always kept the curtains rolled high up, out of the way, for fear of fading and dust. The kitchen was a blaze of light. As for the Sunday chaise being sent, it was well known that Mrs. Bickford's married brothers and sisters comprehended the truth that she was a woman of property, and had neither chick nor child.

"So I thought 't was a good opportunity to just stop an' see if the lot was in good order, —last spring Mr. Wallis's stone hove with the frost; an' so I could take these flowers." She gave a sigh. "I ain't one that can bear flowers in a close room,—they bring on a headache; but I enjoy 'em as much as anybody to look at, only you never know what to put 'em in. If I could be out in the mornin' sun, as some do, and keep flowers in the house, I should have me a gardin, certain," and she sighed again.

"A garden's a sight o' care, but I don't begrudge none o' the care I give to mine. I have to scant on flowers so 's to make room for pole beans," said Miss Pendexter gayly. She had only a tiny strip of land behind her house, but she always had something to give away, and made riches out of her narrow poverty. "A few flowers gives me just as much pleasure as more would," she added. "You get acquainted with things when you've only got one or two roots. My sweet-williams is just like folks."

"Mr. Bickford was partial to sweet-williams," said Mrs. Bickford. "I never knew him to take notice of no other sort of flowers. When we'd be over to Eliza's, he' walk down her gardin, an' he'd never make no comments until he come to them, and then he'd say, 'Those is sweet-williams.' How many times I've heard him!"

"You ought to have a sprig of 'em for his bo'quet," suggested Miss Pendexter.

"Yes, I've put a sprig in," said her companion.

At this moment Miss Pendexter took a good look at the bouquets, and found that they were as nearly alike as careful hands could make them. Mrs. Bickford was evidently trying to reach absolute impartiality.

"I don't know but you think it's foolish to tie 'em up this afternoon," she said presently, as she wound the first with a stout string. "I thought I could put 'em in a bucket o' water out in the shed, where there's a draught o' air, and then I should have all my time in the morning. I shall have a good deal to do before I go. I always sweep the sitting-room and front entry Wednesdays. I want to leave everything nice, goin' away for all day so. So I meant to get the flowers out o' the way this afternoon. Why, it's most half past four, ain't it? But I sha'n't pick the rose till mornin'; 't will be blowed out better then."

"The rose?" questioned Miss Pendexter. "Why, are you goin' to pick that, too?"

"Yes, I be. I never like to let 'em fade on the bush. There, that's just what's a-troublin' me," and she turned to give a long, imploring look at the friend who sat beside her. Miss Pendexter had moved her chair before the table in order to be out of the way of the sun. "I don't seem to know which of 'em ought to have it," said Mrs. Bickford despondently. "I do so hate to make a choice between 'em; they all had their good points, especially Mr. Bickford, and I respected 'em all. I don't know but what I think of one on 'em 'most as much as I do of the other."

"Why, 't is difficult for you, ain't it?" responded Miss Pendexter. "I don't know 's I can offer advice."

"No, I s'pose not," answered her friend slowly, with a shadow of disappointment coming over her calm face. "I feel sure you would if you could, Abby."

Both of the women felt as if they were powerless before a great emergency.

"There's one thing,—they're all in a better world now," said Miss Pendexter, in a self-conscious and constrained voice; "they can't feel such little things or take note o' slights same's we can."

"No; I suppose 't is myself that wants to be just," answered Mrs. Bickford. "I feel under obligations to my last husband when I look about and see how comfortable he left me. Poor Mr. Wallis had his great projects, an' perhaps if he'd lived longer he'd have made a record; but when he died he'd failed all up, owing to that patent cornsheller he'd put everything into, and, as you know, I had to get along 'most any way I could for the next few years. Life was very disappointing with Mr. Wallis, but he meant well, an' used to be an amiable person to dwell with, until his temper got spoilt makin' so many hopes an' havin' 'em turn out failures. He had consider'ble of an air, an' dressed very handsome when I was first acquainted with him, Mr. Wallis did. I don't know 's you ever knew Mr. Wallis in his prime?"

"He died the year I moved over here from North Denfield," said Miss Pendexter, in a tone of sympathy. "I just knew him by sight. I was to his funeral. You know you lived in what we call the Wells house then, and I felt it wouldn't be an intrusion, we was such near neighbors. The first time I ever was in your house was just before that, when he was sick, an' Mary 'Becca

Wade an' I called to see if there was anything we could do."

"They used to say about town that Mr. Wallis went to an' fro like a mail-coach an' brought nothin' to pass," announced Mrs. Bickford without bitterness. "He ought to have had a better chance than he did in this little neighborhood. You see, he had excellent ideas, but he never'd learned the machinist's trade, and there was somethin' the matter with every model he contrived. I used to be real narrow-minded when he talked about moving 'way up to Lowell, or some o' them places; I hated to think of leaving my folks; and now I see that I never done right by him. His ideas was good. I know once he was on a jury, and there was a man stopping to the tavern where he was, near the court house, a man that traveled for a firm to Lowell; and they engaged in talk, an' Mr. Wallis let out some o' his notions an' contrivances, an' he said that man wouldn't hardly stop to eat, he was so interested, an' said he'd look for a chance for him up to Lowell. It all sounded so well that I kind of begun to think about goin' myself. Mr. Wallis said we'd close the house here, and go an' board through the winter. But he never heard a word from him, and the disappointment was one he never got over. I think of it now different from what I did then. I often used to be kind of disapproving to Mr. Wallis; but there, he used to be always tellin' over his great projects. Somebody told me once that a man by the same name of the one he met while he was to court had got some patents for the very things Mr. Wallis used to be workin' over; but 't was after he died, an' I don't know's 't was in him to ever really set things up so other folks could ha' seen their value. His machines always used to work kind of rickety, but folks used to come from all round to see 'em; they was curiosities if they wa'n't nothin' else, an' gave him a name."

Mrs. Bickford paused a moment, with some geranium leaves in her hand, and seemed to suppress with difficulty a desire to speak even more freely.

"He was a dreadful notional man," she said at last, regretfully, and as if this fact were a poor substitute for what had just been in her mind. "I recollect one time he worked all through the early winter over my churn, an' got it so it would go three quarters of an hour all of itself if you wound it up; an' if you'll believe it, he went an' spent all that time for

nothin' when the cow was dry, an' we was with difficulty borrowin' a pint o' milk a day somewheres in the neighborhood just to get along with." Mrs. Bickford flushed with displeasure, and turned to look at her visitor. "Now what do you think of such a man as that, Miss Pendexter?" she asked.

"Why, I don't know but 't was just as good for an invention," answered Miss Pendexter timidly; but her friend looked doubtful, and did not appear to understand.

"Then I asked him where it was, one day that spring when I'd got tired to death churnin', an' the butter wouldn't come in a churn I'd had to borrow, and he'd gone an' took ours all to pieces to get the works to make some other useless contrivance with. He had no sort of a business turn, but he was well meanin', Mr. Wallis was, an' full o' divertin' talk; they used to call him very good company. I see now that he never had no proper chance. I've always regretted Mr. Wallis," said she who was now the widow Bickford.

"I'm sure you always speak well of him," said Miss Pendexter. "'T was a pity he hadn't got among good business men, who could push his inventions an' do all the business part."

"I was left very poor an' needy for them next few years," said Mrs. Bickford mournfully; "but he never'd give up but what he should die worth his fifty thousand dollars. I don't see now how I ever did get along them next few years without him; but there, I always managed to keep a pig, an' sister Eliza gave me my potatoes, and I made out somehow. I could dig me a few greens, you know, in spring, and then't would come strawberry-time, and other berries a-follow-in' on. I was always decent to go to meetin' till within the last six months, an' then I went in bad weather, when folks wouldn't notice; but 't was a rainy summer, an' I managed to get considerable preachin' after all. My clothes looked proper enough when 't was a wet Sabbath. I often think o' them pinched days now, when I'm left so comfortable by Mr. Bickford."

"Yes'm, you've everything to be thankful for," said Miss Pendexter, who was as poor herself at that moment as her friend had ever been, and who could never dream of venturing upon the support and companionship of a pig. "Mr. Bickford was a very personable man," she hastened to say, the confidences were so intimate and interesting.

"Oh, very," replied Mrs. Bickford; "there was something about him that was very marked. Strangers would always ask who he was as he come into meetin'. His words counted; he never spoke except he had to. 'T was a relief at first after Mr. Wallis's being so fluent; but Mr. Wallis was splendid company for winter evenings,—'t would be eight o'clock before you knew it. I didn't use to listen to it all, but he had a great deal of information. Mr. Bickford was dreadful dignified; I used to be sort of meechin' with him along at the first, for fear he'd disapprove of me; but I found out 't wa'n't no need; he was always just that way, an' done everything by rule an' measure. He hadn't the mind of my other husbands, but he was a very dignified appearing man; he used 'most always to sleep in the evenin's, Mr. Bickford did."

"Them is lovely bo'quets, certain!" exclaimed Miss Pendexter. "Why, I couldn't tell 'em apart; the flowers are comin' out just right, aren't they?"

Mrs. Bickford nodded assent, and then, startled by sudden recollection, she cast a quick glance at the rose in the window.

"I always seem to forget about your first husband, Mr. Fraley," Miss Pendexter suggested bravely. "I've often heard you speak of him, too, but he'd passed away long before I ever knew you."

"He was but a boy," said Mrs. Bickford. "I thought the world was done for me when he died, but I've often thought since 't was a mercy for him. He come of a very melancholy family, and all his brothers an' sisters enjoyed poor health; it might have been his lot. Folks said we was as pretty a couple as ever come into church; we was both dark, with black eyes an' a good deal o' color,—you wouldn't expect it to see me now. Albert was one that held up his head, and looked as if he meant to own the town, an' he had a good word for everybody. I don't know what the years might have brought."

There was a long pause. Mrs. Bickford leaned over to pick up a heavy-headed Guelder-rose that had dropped on the floor.

"I expect 't was what they call fallin' in love," she added, in a different tone; "he wa'n't nothin' but a boy, an' I wa'n't nothin' but a girl, but we was dreadful happy. He didn't favor his folks,—they all had hay-colored hair and was faded-looking, except his mother; they

was alike, and looked alike, an' set everything by each other. He was just the kind of strong, hearty young man that goes right off if they get a fever. We was just settled on a little farm, an' he'd have done well if he'd had time; as it was, he left debts. He had a hasty temper, that was his great fault, but Albert had a lovely voice to sing; they said there wa'n't no such tenor voice in this part o' the State. I could hear him singin' to himself right out in the field a-ploughin' or hoein', an' he didn't know it half o' the time, no more'n a common bird would. I don't know's I valued his gift as I ought to, but there was nothin' ever sounded so sweet to me. I ain't one that ever had much fancy, but I knowed Albert had a pretty voice."

Mrs. Bickford's own voice trembled a little, but she held up the last bouquet and examined it critically. "I must hurry now an' put these in water," she said, in a matter of fact tone. Little Miss Pendexter was so quiet and sympathetic that her hostess felt no more embarrassed than if she had been talking only to herself.

"Yes, they do seem to droop some; 't is a little warm for them here in the sun," said Miss Pendexter; "but you'll find they'll all come up if you give them their fill o' water. They'll look very handsome to-morrow; folks'll notice them from the road. You've arranged them very tasty, Mis' Bickford."

"They do look pretty, don't they?" Mrs. Bickford regarded the three in turn. "I want to have them all pretty. You may deem it strange, Abby."

"Why, no, Mis' Bickford," said the guest sincerely, although a little perplexed by the solemnity of the occasion. "I know how 't is with friends,—that having one don't keep you from wantin' another; 't is just like havin' somethin' to eat, and then wantin' somethin' to drink just the same. I expect all friends find their places."

But Mrs. Bickford was not interested in this figure, and still looked vague and anxious as she began to brush the broken stems and wilted leaves into her wide calico apron. "I done the best I could while they was alive," she said, "and mourned 'em when I lost 'em, an' I feel grateful to be left so comfortable now when all is over. It seems foolish, but I'm still at a loss about that rose."

"Perhaps you'll feel sure when you first wake up in the morning," answered Miss Pendexter solicitously. "It's a case where I don't deem myself qualified to offer you any advice. But

I'll say one thing, seeing's you've been so friendly spoken and confiding with me. I never was married myself, Mis' Bickford, because it wa'n't so that I could have the one I liked."

"I suppose he ain't livin', then? Why, I wa'n't never aware you had met with a disappointment, Abby," said Mrs. Bickford instantly. None of her neighbors had ever suspected little Miss Pendexter of a romance.

"Yes'm, he's livin'," replied Miss Pendexter humbly. "No'm, I never have heard that he died."

"I want to know!" exclaimed the woman of experience. "Well, I'll tell you this, Abby: you may have regretted your lot, and felt lonesome and hardshipped, but they all have their faults, and a single woman's got her liberty, if she ain't got other blessin's."

"'T wouldn't have been my choice to live alone," said Abby, meeker than before. "I feel very thankful for my blessin's, all the same. You've always been a kind neighbor, Mis' Bickford."

"Why can't you stop to tea?" asked the elder woman, with unusual cordiality; but Miss Pendexter remembered that her hostess often expressed a dislike for unexpected company, and promptly took her departure after she had risen to go, glancing up at the bright flower as she passed outside the window. It seemed to belong most to Albert, but she had not liked to say so. The sun was low; the green fields stretched away southward into the misty distance.

II

Mrs. Bickford's house appeared to watch her out of sight down the road, the next morning. She had lost all spirit for her holiday. Perhaps it was the unusual excitement of the afternoon's reminiscences, or it might have been simply the bright moonlight night which had kept her broad awake until dawn, thinking of the past, and more and more concerned about the rose. By this time it had ceased to be merely a flower, and had become a definite symbol and assertion of personal choice. She found it very difficult to decide. So much of her present comfort and well-being was due to Mr. Bickford; still, it was Mr. Wallis who had been most unfortunate, and to whom she had done least justice. If she owed recognition to Mr. Bickford, she certainly owed amends to Mr. Wallis. If she gave him the rose, it would

be for the sake of affectionate apology. And then there was Albert, to whom she had no thought of being either indebted or forgiving. But she could not escape from the terrible feeling of decision.

It was a beautiful morning for a drive, but Mrs. Bickford was kept waiting some time for the chaise. Her nephew, who was to be her escort, had found much social advantage at the blacksmith's shop, so that it was after ten when she finally started with the three large flat-backed bouquets, covered with a newspaper to protect them from the sun. The petals of the almond flowers were beginning to scatter, and now and then little streams of water leaked out of the newspaper and trickled down the steep slope of her best dress to the bottom of the chaise. Even yet she had not made up her mind; she had stopped trying to deal with such an evasive thing as decision, and leaned back and rested as best she could.

"What an old fool I be!" she rebuked herself from time to time, in so loud a whisper that her companion ventured a respectful "What, ma'am?" and was astonished that she made no reply. John was a handsome young man, but Mrs. Bickford could never cease thinking of him as a boy. He had always been her favorite among the younger members of the family, and now returned this affectionate feeling, being possessed of an instinctive confidence in the sincerities of his prosaic aunt.

As they drove along, there had seemed at first to be something unsympathetic and garish about the beauty of the summer day. After the shade and shelter of the house, Mrs. Bickford suffered even more from a contracted and assailed feeling out of doors. The very trees by the roadside had a curiously fateful, trying way of standing back to watch her, as she passed in the acute agony of indecision, and she was annoyed and startled by a bird that flew too near the chaise in a moment of surprise. She was conscious of a strange reluctance to the movement of the Sunday chaise, as if she were being conveyed against her will; but the companionship of her nephew John grew every moment to be more and more a reliance. It was very comfortable to sit by his side, even though he had nothing to say; he was manly and cheerful, and she began to feel protected.

"Aunt Bickford," he suddenly announced, "I may's well out with it! I've got a piece o' news to tell you, if you won't let on to nobody. I expect you'll laugh, but you know I've set everything by Mary Lizzie Gifford ever since I was a boy. Well, sir!"

"Well, sir!" exclaimed aunt Bickford in her turn, quickly roused into most comfortable self-forgetfulness. "I am really pleased. She'll make you a good, smart wife, John. Ain't all the folks pleased, both sides?"

"Yes, they be," answered John soberly, with a happy, important look that became him well.

"I guess I can make out to do something for you to help along, when the right time comes," said aunt Bickford impulsively, after a moment's reflection. "I've known what it is to be starting out in life with plenty o' hope. You ain't calculatin' on gettin' married before fall, —or be ye?"

"'Long in the fall," said John regretfully. "I wish t' we could set up for ourselves right away this summer. I ain't got much ahead, but I can work well as anybody, an' now I'm out o' my time."

"She's a nice, modest, pretty girl. I thought she liked you, John," said the old aunt. "I saw her over to your mother's, last day I was there. Well, I expect you'll be happy."

"Certain," said John, turning to look at her affectionately, surprised by this outspokenness and lack of embarrassment between them. "Thank you, aunt," he said simply; "you're a real good friend to me"; and he looked away again hastily, and blushed a fine scarlet over his sun-browned face. "She's coming over to spend the day with the girls," he added. "Mother thought of it. You don't get over to see us very often."

Mrs. Bickford smiled approvingly. John's mother looked for her good opinion, no doubt, but it was very proper for John to have told his prospects himself, and in such a pretty way. There was no shilly-shallying about the boy.

"My gracious!" said John suddenly. "I'd like to have drove right by the burying-ground. I forgot we wanted to stop."

Strange as it may appear, Mrs. Bickford herself had not noticed the burying-ground, either, in her excitement and pleasure; now she felt distressed and responsible again, and showed it in her face at once. The young man leaped lightly to the ground, and reached for the flowers.

"Here, you just let me run up with 'em," he said kindly. "'T is hot in the sun to-day, an' you'll mind it risin' the hill. We'll stop as I fetch you back to-night, and you can go up comfortable an' walk the yard after sundown when it's cool, an' stay as long as you're a mind to. You seem sort of tired, aunt."

"I don't know but what I will let you carry 'em," said Mrs. Bickford slowly.

To leave the matter of the rose in the hands of fate seemed weakness and cowardice, but there was not a moment for consideration. John was a smiling fate, and his proposition was a great relief. She watched him go away with a terrible inward shaking, and sinking of pride. She had held the flowers with so firm a grasp that her hands felt weak and numb, and as she leaned back and shut her eyes she was afraid to open them again at first for fear of knowing the bouquets apart even at that distance, and giving instructions which she might regret. With a sudden impulse she called John once or twice eagerly; but her voice had a thin and piping sound, and the meditative early crickets that chirped in the fresh summer grass probably sounded louder in John's ears. The bright light on the white stones dazzled Mrs. Bickford's eyes; and then all at once she felt light-hearted, and the sky seemed to lift itself higher and wider from the earth, and she gave a sigh of relief as her messenger came back along the path. "I know who I do hope's got the right one," she said to herself. "There, what a touse I be in! I don't see what I had to go and pick the old rose for, anyway."

"I declare, they did look real handsome, aunt," said John's hearty voice as he approached the chaise. "I set 'em up just as you told me. This one fell out, an' I kept it. I don't know's you'll care. I can give it to Lizzie."

He faced her now with a bright, boyish look. There was something gay in his button-hole,—it was the red rose.

Aunt Bickford blushed like a girl. "Your choice is easy made," she faltered mysteriously, and then burst out laughing, there in front of the burying-ground. "Come, get right in, dear," she said. "Well, well! I guess the rose was made for you; it looks very pretty in your coat, John."

She thought of Albert, and the next moment the tears came into her old eyes. John was a lover, too.

"My first husband was just such a tall, straight young man as you be," she said as they drove along. "The flower he first give me was a rose." **1895**

HAMLIN GARLAND
1860–1940

HAMLIN GARLAND'S earliest memory was his father's return from the wars. With the "peculiar, measured, swinging stride . . . of Sherman's veterans," bearded, battle-scarred, emaciated, he reappeared one day in the Wisconsin coulee where in 1863 he had left his wife and children. The family afterward migrated in a covered wagon to Iowa and into Dakota Territory, pushed westward by Dick Garland's hunger for new lands, and sustained by the patient industry of his wife. In full consciousness of their silent heroism and not without bitterness, Hamlin Garland dedicated his first book to this pioneer couple, "whose half-century pilgrimage on the main-travelled road of life has brought them only toil and deprivation." It is their story which informs and strengthens *A Son of the Middle Border* (1917), and its continuation, *A Daughter of the Middle Border*, which won the Pulitzer Prize for 1922. Together these two volumes present the chronicle of a Midwestern family between the Civil War and the First World War.

Border life in the seventies and eighties was hard work. Rare joys like communal singing and turkey shoots could hardly compensate for the dispiriting dawn-to-dusk toil that was required of the boys as soon as they could handle the ploughshare and wield the dung-fork. Brief schooling in the seminary at Osage, Iowa, and a junket to New England, New York, and Washington when he was twenty-one opened new vistas for Garland. He mortgaged his claim in the Dakotas and went in 1884 to Boston. Hunched there over a boarding-house register, thinly dressed, underfed, he read day and night. While his purse grew flatter, he tells us, he skittered desperately from "pole to pole of the intellectual universe like an impatient bat." Through years of incredible effort and penury he gradually attained recognition, teaching at Moses Brown's school, preaching Henry George's land reform when he could, and placing an occasional book review. In Chicago, Joseph Kirkland, whose novel *Zury* he had praised, encouraged him to write frontier fiction, and he returned from a western visit determined to tell the truth about life on the Middle Border. Others might weep nostalgically over the little red schoolhouses, but Garland knew them as they were, boxlike, filthy, ill-heated, "sunsmit, bare as a nose" in the prairie mud. The farms were animal dens, and he hated the thought of his mother aging rapidly under the compulsion of endless toil, his father bent and graying in the stable-muck. "Why," he asked, "have these stern facts never been put into our literature as they have been used in Russia and in England?"

Garland's busiest years were the nineties. Championed by Howells and the aged Whitman, he joined the so-called revolt to realism in literature, lectured on agrarian reform for the Populist Party, bought his parents a comfortable Wisconsin homestead. In Chicago and after 1916 in New York, he rose gradually to eminence. His works include literary reminiscences, nineteen novels, and a biography of his father's old commander, U. S. Grant. But aside from the magnificent autobiographical volumes, Garland's reputation is likely to rest upon the short stories in *Main-Travelled Roads* (1891) and *Prairie Folks* (1893), which describe truthfully and well the loneliness, the futility, and the pathos of proletarian lives like Mrs. Ripley's.

Irving Bacheller, *et al.*, Biographical Reminiscences of Garland in *Mark Twain Quarterly*, IV (Summer, 1940).
J. T. Flanagan, "Hamlin Garland, Occasional Minnesotan," *Minnesota History*, XXII (June, 1941), 157–168.
W. D. Howells, "Mr. Garland's Books," *North American Review*, CXCVI (October, 1912), 523–528.
Allan Nevins, "Garland and the Prairies," *Literary Review*, II (August 19, 1922), 881–882.

» » From: MAIN-TRAVELLED ROADS « «

MRS. RIPLEY'S TRIP

The night was in windy November, and the blast, threatening rain, roared around the poor little shanty of Uncle Ripley, set like a chicken-trap on the vast Iowa prairie. Uncle Ethan was mending his old violin, with many York State "dums!" and "I gol darns!" totally oblivious of his tireless old wife, who, having "finished the supper-dishes," sat knitting a stocking, evidently for the little grandson who lay before the stove like a cat.

Neither of the old people wore glasses, and their light was a tallow candle; they couldn't afford "none o' them new-fangled lamps." The room was small, the chairs were wooden, and the walls bare—a home where poverty was a never-absent guest. The old lady looked pathetically little, weazened, and hopeless in her ill-fitting garments (whose original color had long since vanished), intent as she was on the stocking in her knotted, stiffened fingers, and there was a peculiar sparkle in her little black eyes, and an unusual resolution in the straight line of her withered and shapeless lips.

Suddenly she paused, stuck a needle in the spare knob of her hair at the back of her head, and looking at Ripley, said decisively: "Ethan Ripley, you'll haff to do your own cooking from now on to New Year's. I'm goin' back to Yaark State."

The old man's leather-brown face stiffened into a look of quizzical surprise for a moment; then he cackled, incredulously: "Ho! Ho! har! Sho! be y', now? I want to know if y' be."

"Well, you'll find out."

"Goin' to start to-morrow, mother?"

"No, sir, I ain't; but I am on Thursday. I want to get to Sally's by Sunday, sure, an' to Silas's on Thanksgivin'."

There was a note in the old woman's voice that brought genuine stupefaction into the face of Uncle Ripley. Of course in this case, as in all others, the money consideration was uppermost.

"Howgy 'xpect to get the money, mother? Anybody died an' left yeh a pile?"

"Never you mind where I get the money, so 's 't you don't haff to bear it. The land knows if I'd 'a' waited for you to pay my way—"

"You needn't twit me of bein' poor, old woman," said Ripley, flaming up after the

manner of many old people. "I've done my part t' get along. I've worked day in and day out—"

"Oh! I ain't done no work, have I?" snapped she, laying down the stocking and levelling a needle at him, and putting a frightful emphasis on "I."

"I didn't say you hadn't done no work."

"Yes, you did!"

"I didn't neither. I said—"

"I know what you said."

"I said I'd done my part!" roared the husband, dominating her as usual by superior lung power. "I didn't say you hadn't done your part," he added with an unfortunate touch of emphasis.

"I know y' didn't say it, but y' meant it. I don't know what y' call doin' my part, Ethan Ripley; but if cookin' for a drove of harvest hands and thrashin' hands, takin' care o' the eggs and butter, 'n' diggin' 'taters an' milkin' ain't my part, I don't never expect to do my part, 'n' you might as well know it fust 's last."

"I'm sixty years old," she went on, with a little break in her harsh voice, dominating him now by woman's logic, "an' I've never had a day to myself, not even Fourth o' July. If I've went a-visitin' 'r to a picnic, I've had to come home an' milk 'n' get supper for thirteen years in this house, 'n' it was just so in Davis County for ten more. For twenty-three years, Ethan Ripley, I've stuck right to the stove an' churn without a day or night off."

Her voice choked again, but she rallied, and continued impressively, "And now I'm a-goin' back to Yaark State."

Ethan was vanquished. He stared at her in speechless surprise, his jaw hanging. It was incredible.

"For twenty-three years," she went on musingly, "I've just about promised myself every year I'd go back an' see my folks." She was distinctly talking to herself now, and her voice had a touching, wistful cadence. "I've wanted to go back an' see the old folks, an' the hills where we played, an' eat apples off the old tree down by the well. I've had them trees an' hills in my mind days and days—nights, too— an' the girls I used to know, an' my own folks—"

She fell into a silent muse, which lasted so long that the ticking of the clock grew loud as a gong in the man's ears, and the wind outside seemed to sound drearier than usual. He returned to the money problem; kindly, though.

"But how y' goin' t' raise the money? I ain't got no extra cash this time. Agin Roach is paid, an' the intrest paid, we ain't got no hundred dollars to spare, Jane, not by a jugful."

"Wal, don't you lay awake nights studyin' on where I'm a-goin' to get the money," said the old woman, taking delight in mystifying him. She had him now, and he couldn't escape. He strove to show his indifference, however, by playing a tune or two on the violin.

"Come, Tukey, you better climb the wooden hill," Mrs. Ripley said, a half-hour later, to the little chap on the floor, who was beginning to get drowsy under the influence of his grandpa's fiddling. "Pa, you had orta 'a' put that string in the clock to-day—on the 'larm side the string is broke," she said, upon returning from the boy's bedroom. "I orta git up early to-morrow, to git some sewin' done. Land knows, I can't fix up much, but they is a little I c'n do. I want to look decent."

They were alone now, and they both sat expectantly.

"You 'pear to think, mother, that I'm agin yer goin'."

"Wal, it would kinder seem as if y' hadn't hustled yerself any t' help me git off."

He was smarting under the sense of being wronged. "Wal, I'm just as willin' you should go as I am for myself, but if I ain't got no money I don't see how I'm goin' to send—"

"I don't want ye to send; nobody ast ye to, Ethan Ripley. I guess if I had what I've earnt since we came on this farm I'd have enough to go to Jericho with."

"You've got as much out of it as I have," he replied gently. "You talk about your goin' back. Ain't I been wantin' to go back myself? And ain't I kep' still 'cause I see it wa'n't no use? I guess I've worked jest as long and as hard as you, an' in storms an' in mud an' heat, ef it comes t' that."

The woman was staggered, but she wouldn't give up; she must get in one more thrust.

"Wal, if you'd 'a' managed as well as I have, you'd have some money to go with." And she rose and went to mix her bread and set it "raisin'."

He sat by the fire twanging his fiddle softly. He was plainly thrown into gloomy retrospec-

tion, something quite unusual for him. But his fingers picking out the bars of a familiar tune set him to smiling, and whipping his bow across the strings, he forgot all about his wife's resolutions and his own hardships. "Trouble always slid off his back like punkins off a haystack, anyway," his wife said.

The old man still sat fiddling softly after his wife disappeared in the hot and stuffy little bedroom off the kitchen. His shaggy head bent lower over his violin. He heard her shoes drop —*one, two.* Pretty soon she called:

"Come, put up that squeakin' old fiddle, and go to bed. Seems as if you orta have sense enough not to set there keepin' everybody in the house awake."

"You hush up," retorted he. "I'll come when I git ready, and not till. I'll be glad when you're gone—"

"Yes, I warrant *that.*"

With which amiable good-night they went off to sleep, or at least she did, while he lay awake pondering on "where under the sun she was goin' t' raise that money."

The next day she was up bright and early, working away on her own affairs, ignoring Ripley entirely, the fixed look of resolution still on her little old wrinkled face. She killed a hen and dressed and baked it. She fried up a pan of doughnuts and made a cake. She was engaged in the doughnuts when a neighbor came in, one of these women who take it as a personal affront when any one in the neighborhood does anything without asking their advice. She was fat, and could talk a man blind in three minutes by the watch. Her neighbor said:

"What's this I hear, Mis' Ripley?"

"I dun know. I expect you hear about all they is goin' on in this neighborhood," replied Mrs. Ripley, with crushing bluntness; but the gossip did not flinch.

"Well, Sett Turner told *me* that her husband told *her* that Ripley told *him* this mornin' that you was goin' back East on a visit."

"Wal, what of it?"

"Well, air yeh?"

"The Lord willin' an' the weather permittin', I expect I be."

"Good land, I want to know! Well, well! I never was so astonished in my whole life. I said, says I, 'It can't be.' 'Well,' ses 'e, 'tha's what *she* told me,' ses 'e. 'But,' says I, 'she is the last woman in the world to gallavantin off East,' ses I. 'An',' ses he, 'but it comes from good authority, ses he. 'Well, then, it must be so,' ses I. But, land sakes! do tell me all about it. How come you to make up y'r mind? All these years you've been kind a' talkin' it over, an' now y'r actshelly goin'—well I *never!* 'I s'pose Ripley furnishes the money,' ses I to him. 'Well, no,' ses 'e. 'Ripley says he'll be blowed if he sees where the money's coming from,' ses 'e; and ses I, 'But maybe she's jest jokin',' ses I. 'Not much,' he says. S' 'e: 'Ripley believes she's goin' fast enough. He's jest as anxious to find out as we be—' "

Here Mrs. Doudney paused for breath; she had walked so fast and rested so little that her interminable flow of "ses I's" and "ses he's" ceased necessarily. She had reached, moreover, the point of most vital interest—the money.

"An' you'll find out jest 'bout as soon as he does," was the dry response from the figure hovering over the stove; and with all her manoeuvring that was all she got.

All day Ripley went about his work exceedingly thoughtful for him. It was cold blustering weather. The wind rustled among the corn-stalks with a wild and mournful sound, the geese and ducks went sprawling down the wind, and the horses' coats were ruffled and backs raised.

The old man was husking all alone in the field, his spare form rigged out in two or three ragged coats, his hands inserted in a pair of gloves minus nearly all the fingers, his thumbs done up in "stalls," and his feet thrust into huge coarse boots. The "down ears" wet and chapped his hands, already worn to the quick. Toward night it grew colder and threatened snow. In spite of all these attacks he kept his cheerfulness, and though he was very tired, he was softened in temper.

Having plenty of time to think matters over, he had come to the conclusion that the old woman needed a play-spell. "I ain't likely to be no richer next year than I am this one; if I wait till I'm able to send her she won't never go. I calc'late I c'n git enough out o' them shoats to send her. I'd kind a' lotted on eat'n them pigs done up in sassengers, but if the ol' woman goes East, Tukey an' me'll kind a' haff to pull through without 'em. We'll have a turkey f'r Thanksgivin', an' a chicken once 'n a while. Lord! but we'll miss the gravy on the flapjacks." (He smacked his lips over the thought of the lost dainty.) "But let 'er rip! We can stand it. Then there is my buffalo overcoat. I'd kind a' calc'lated on havin' a

buffalo—but that's gone up the spout along with them sassengers."

These heroic sacrifices having been determined upon, he put them into effect at once.

This he was able to do, for his corn-rows ran alongside the road leading to Cedarville, and his neighbors were passing almost all hours of the day.

It would have softened Jane Ripley's heart could she have seen his bent and stiffened form among the corn-rows, the cold wind piercing to the bone through his threadbare and insufficient clothing. The rising wind sent the snow rattling among the moaning stalks at intervals. The cold made his poor dim eyes water, and he had to stop now and then to swing his arms about his chest to warm them. His voice was hoarse with shouting at the shivering team.

That night as Mrs. Ripley was clearing the dishes away she got to thinking about the departure of the next day, and she began to soften. She gave way to a few tears when little Tewksbury Gilchrist, her grandson, came up and stood beside her.

"Gran'ma, you ain't goin' to stay away always, are yeh?"

"Why, course not, Tukey. What made y' think that?"

"Well, y' ain't told us nawthin' 't all about it. An' yeh kind 'o' look 's if yeh was mad."

"Well, I ain't mad; I'm jest a-thinkin', Tukey. Y' see, I come away from them hills when I was a little girl a'most; before I married y'r grandad. And I ain't never been back. 'Most all my folks is there, sonny, an' we've been s' poor all these years I couldn't seem t' never git started. Now, when I'm 'most ready t' go, I feel kind a queer—'s if I'd cry."

And cry she did, while little Tewksbury stood patting her trembling hands. Hearing Ripley's step on the porch, she rose hastily and, drying her eyes, plunged at the work again.

Ripley came in with a big armful of wood, which he rolled into the wood-box with a thundering crash. Then he pulled off his mittens, slapped them together to knock off the ice and snow, and laid them side by side under the stove. He then removed cap, coat, blouse, and finally his boots, which he laid upon the wood-box, the soles turned toward the stove-pipe.

As he sat down without speaking, he opened the front doors of the stove, and held the palms of his stiffened hands to the blaze. The light brought out a thoughtful look on his large, uncouth, yet kindly, visage. Life had laid hard lines on his brown skin, but it had not entirely soured a naturally kind and simple nature. It had made him penurious and dull and iron-muscled; had stifled all the slender flowers of his nature; yet there was warm soil somewhere hid in his heart.

"It's snowin' like all p'ssessed," he remarked finally. "I guess we'll have a sleigh-ride to-morrow. I calc'late t' drive y' daown in scrumptious style. If you must leave, why, we'll give yeh a whoopin' old send-off—won't we, Tukey?"

Nobody replying, he waited a moment. "I've ben a-thinkin' things over kind o' t'-day, mother, an' I've come t' the conclusion that we *have* been kind o' hard on yeh, without knowin' it, y' see. Y' see I'm kind o' easy-goin', an' little Tuke he's only a child, an' we ain't c'nsidered how you felt."

She didn't appear to be listening, but she was, and he didn't appear, on his part, to be talking to her, and he kept his voice as hard and dry as he could.

"An' I was tellin' Tukey t'-day that it was a dum shame our crops hadn't turned out better. An' when I saw ol' Hatfield go by I hailed him, an' asked him what he'd gimme for two o' m' shoats. Wal, the upshot is, I sent t' town for some things I calc'late you'd need. An' here's a ticket to Georgetown, and ten dollars. Why, ma, what's up?"

Mrs. Ripley broke down, and with her hands all wet with dish-water, as they were, covered her face, and sobbed. She felt like kissing him, but she didn't. Tewksbury began to whimper too; but the old man was astonished. His wife had not wept for years (before him). He rose and walking clumsily up to her timidly touched her hair—

"Why, mother! What's the matter? What've I done now? I was calc'latin' to sell them pigs anyway. Hatfield jest advanced the money on 'em."

She hopped up and dashed into the bed-room, and in a few minutes returned with a yarn mitten, tied around the wrist, which she laid on the table with a thump, saying: "I don't want yer money. There's money enough to take me where I want to go."

"Whee—ew! Thunder and gimpsum root! Where 'd ye get that? Didn't dig it out of a hole?"

"No, I jest saved it—a dime at a time—see!"

Here she turned it out on the table—some bills, but mostly silver dimes and quarters. "Thunder and scissors! Must be two er three hundred dollars there," he exclaimed.

"They's jest seventy-five dollars and thirty cents; jest about enough to go back on. Tickets is fifty-five dollars, goin' and comin'. That leaves twenty dollars for other expenses, not countin' what I've already spent, which is six-fifty," said she, recovering her self-possession. "It's plenty."

"But y' ain't calc'lated on no sleepers nor hotel bills."

"I ain't goin' on no sleeper. Mis' Doudney says it's jest scandalous the way things is managed on them cars. I'm goin' on the old-fashioned cars, where they ain't no half-dressed men runnin' around."

"But *you* needn't be afraid of them, mother; at your age—"

"There! you needn't throw my age an' home-liness into my face, Ethan Ripley. If I hadn't waited an' tended on you so long, I'd look a little more's I did when I married yeh."

Ripley gave it up in despair. He didn't realize fully enough how the proposed trip had unsettled his wife's nerves. She didn't realize it herself.

"As for the hotel bills, they won't be none. I ain't agoin' to pay them pirates as much for a day's board as we'd charge for a week's, and have nawthin' to eat but dishes. I'm goin' to take a chicken an' some hard-boiled eggs, an' I'm goin' right through to Georgetown."

"Wal, all right, mother; but here's the ticket I got."

"I don't want yer ticket."

"But you've got to take it."

"Well, I haint."

"Why, yes, ye have. It's bought, an' they won't take it back."

"Won't they?" She was perplexed again.

"Not much they won't. I ast 'em. A ticket sold is sold."

"Wal, if they won't—"

"You bet they won't."

"I s'pose I'll haff to use it." And that ended it.

They were a familiar sight as they rode down the road toward town next day. As usual, Mrs. Ripley sat up straight and stiff as "a half-drove wedge in a white-oak log." The day was cold and raw. There was some snow on the ground, but not enough to warrant the use of sleighs. It was "neither sleddin' nor wheelin'."

The old people sat on a board laid across the box, and had an old quilt or two drawn up over their knees. Tewksbury lay in the back part of the box (which was filled with hay), where he jounced up and down, in company with a queer old trunk and a brand-new imitation-leather hand-bag.

There is no ride quite so desolate and uncomfortable as a ride in a lumber-wagon on a cold day in autumn, when the ground is frozen, and the wind is strong and raw with threatening snow. The wagon wheels grind along in the snow, the cold gets in under the seat at the calves of one's legs, and the ceaseless bumping of the bottom of the box on the feet is almost intolerable.

There was not much talk on the way down, and what little there was related mainly to certain domestic regulations, to be strictly followed, regarding churning, pickles, pancakes, etc. Mrs. Ripley wore a shawl over her head, and carried her queer little black bonnet in her hand. Tewksbury was also wrapped in a shawl. The boy's teeth were pounding together like castanets by the time they reached Cedarville, and every muscle ached with the fatigue of shaking.

After a few purchases they drove down to the station, a frightful little den (common in the West), which was always too hot or too cold. It happened to be hot just now—a fact which rejoiced little Tewksbury.

"Now git my trunk *stamped*, 'r *fixed*, 'r whatever they call it," she said to Ripley, in a commanding tone, which gave great delight to the inevitable crowd of loafers beginning to assemble. "Now remember, Tukey, have grandad kill that biggest turkey night before Thanksgiving, an' then you run right over to Mis' Doudney's—she's got a nawful tongue, but she can bake a turkey first-rate—an' she'll fix up some squash-pies for yeh. You can warm up one o' them mince-pies. I wish ye could be with me, but ye can't; so do the best ye can."

Ripley returning now, she said: "Wal, now, I've fixed things up the best I could. I've baked bread enough to last a week, an' Mis' Doudney has promised to bake for yeh—"

"I don't like her bakin'!"

"Wal, you'll haff to stand it till I get back, 'n' you'll find a jar o' sweet pickles an' some crab-apple sauce down suller, 'n' you'd better melt up brown sugar for 'lasses, 'n' for goodness' sake don't eat all them mince-pies

up the fust week, 'n' see that Tukey ain't froze goin' to school. An' now you'd better get out for home. Good-by! an' remember them pies."

As they were riding home, Ripley roused up after a long silence.

"Did she—a—kiss you good-by, Tukey?"

"No, sir," piped Tewksbury.

"Thunder! didn't she?" After a silence: "She didn't me, neither. I guess she kind a' sort a' forgot it, bein' so flustrated, y' know."

One cold, windy, intensely bright day, Mrs. Stacey, who lives about two miles from Cedarville, looking out of the window, saw a queer little figure struggling along the road, which was blocked here and there with drifts. It was an old woman laden with a good half-dozen parcels, which the wind seemed determined to wrench from her.

She was dressed in black, with a full skirt, and her cloak being short, the wind had excellent opportunity to inflate her garments and sail her off occasionally into the deep snow outside the track, but she held out bravely till she reached the gate. As she turned in, Mrs. Stacey cried:

"Why! it's Gran'ma Ripley, just getting back from her trip. Why! how do you do? Come in. Why! you must be nearly frozen. Let me take off your hat and veil?"

"No, thank ye kindly, but I can't stop," was the given reply. "I must be gittin' back to Ripley. I expec' that man has jest let ev'rything go six ways f'r Sunday."

"Oh, you *must* sit down just a minute and warm."

"Wal, I will; but I've got to git home by sundown sure. I don't s'pose they's a thing in the house to eat," she said solemnly.

"Oh, dear! I wish Stacey was here, so he could take you home. An' the boys at school—"

"Don't need any help, if 't wa'nt for these bundles an' things. I guess I'll jest leave some of 'em here, an'—Here! take one of these apples. I brought 'em from Lizy Jane's suller, back to Yaark State."

"Oh! they're delicious! You must have had a lovely time."

"Pretty good. But I kep' thinkin' of Ripley an' Tukey all the time. I s'pose they have had a gay time of it" (she meant the opposite of gay). "Wal, as I told Lizy Jane, I've had my spree, an' now I've got to git back to work. They ain't no rest for such as we are. As I told

Lizy Jane, them folks in the big houses have Thanksgivin' dinners every day of their lives, and men an' women in splendid clo's to wait on 'em, so 't Thanksgivin' don't mean anything to 'em; but we poor critters, we make a great to-do if we have a good dinner onct a year. I've saw a pile o' this world, Mrs. Stacey—a pile of it! I didn't think they was so many big houses in the world as I saw b'tween here an' Chicago. Wal, I can't set here gabbin'." She rose resolutely. "I must get home to Ripley. Jest kind o' stow them bags away. I'll take two an' leave them three others. Good-by! I must be gittin' home to Ripley. He'll want his supper on time."

And off up the road the indomitable little figure trudged, head held down to the cutting blast—little snow-fly, a speck on a measureless expanse, crawling along with painful breathing, and slipping, sliding steps—"Gittin' home to Ripley an' the boy."

Ripley was out to the barn when she entered, but Tewksbury was building a fire in the old cook-stove. He sprang up with a cry of joy, and ran to her. She seized him and kissed him, and it did her so much good she hugged him close, and kissed him again and again crying hysterically.

"Oh, gran'ma, I'm so glad to see you! We've had an awful time since you've been gone."

She released him, and looked around. A lot of dirty dishes were on the table, the table-cloth was a "sight to behold" (as she afterward said), and so was the stove—kettle-marks all over the table-cloth, splotches of pancake batter all over the stove.

"Wal, I sh'd say as much," she dryly assented, untying her bonnet-strings.

When Ripley came in she had her regimentals on, the stove was brushed, the room swept, and she was elbow-deep in the dishpan. "Hullo, mother! Got back, hev yeh?"

"I sh'd say it was about *time*," she replied curtly, without looking up or ceasing work. "Has ol' 'Crumpy' dried up yit?" This was her greeting.

Her trip was a fact now; no chance could rob her of it. She had looked forward twenty-three years toward it, and now she could look back at it accomplished. She took up her burden again, never more thinking to lay it down.
1888   1888

AMBROSE BIERCE

1842–1914?

CIVILIZATION BE DINGED!—it is the mountains and the desert for me. . . . If you hear of my being stood up against a Mexican stone wall and shot to rags please know that I think that a pretty good way to depart this life. It beats old age, disease, or falling down the cellar stairs." Those were among the last words of Ambrose Bierce. His final letter was postmarked Chihuahua, Mexico, 26 December, 1913. Despite subsequent and wildly exotic rumors, one of which made him staff officer to Pancho Villa, no further word of this extremely handsome and straight-backed septuagenarian ever reached his friends. The best guess is that the white head and sharp blue eyes of the asthmatic old Gringo were last visible in the rifle-sight of some Mexican guerrilla in need of the gold in Bierce's belt.

Bierce's disappearance, heralded by such epistolary histrionics, was consistent with the somewhat stagey nature of his art; and it effectively capped an adventurous life begun in the religious settlement of Horse Cave in Meiggs County, Ohio. His early scorn for Marcus Aurelius Bierce, his poverty-and-piety-ridden father, was equalled by his admiration for a dashing soldier uncle, General Lucius Verus Bierce, who arranged, when the boy was seventeen, for his admittance to Kentucky Military Institute. Young Bierce was delighted at this release from the unwashed squalor of his early life, and when the Civil War broke he quickly volunteered in the Union Army, eager to follow his uncle, an ardent abolitionist.

Bierce was a born soldier and his best writing came out of the war. As sergeant in an infantry regiment (Ninth Indiana) he saw first service in what is now West Virginia, the background for *A Horseman in the Sky*. He was in the midst of the nightmare at Pittsburg Landing (*What I Saw of Shiloh*, in *Works*, I, 234ff.). Before Nashville, at Murfreesboro, and at Chickamauga (20 September, 1863), the young officer's gallantry under fire was conspicuous. Marching south as staff officer to General Hazen in the Army of the Cumberland, Bierce saw Brayle die (*Killed at Resaca*) and he himself nearly perished of a bad head-wound at Kenesaw Mountain (*One of the Missing*). He ended his military career as topographical engineer to Hazen on a postwar map-making expedition which took him to San Francisco. Here in 1866 he became a journalist.

In 1887 Bierce's reputation for acidulous wit earned him a well-paid job writing a column (*Prattle*) on Hearst's San Francisco *Examiner*, through which he rose to such local power and national vogue that he began erroneously to fancy himself a great artist. But his tales of the supernatural, *Can Such Things Be?* (1893), are merely good yarns, while his famous *Devil's Dictionary* (assembled in 1906) is a collection of rather shopworn epigrams. In 1909–1912 Bierce laboriously collected his works in twelve handsome volumes, ten of which could have been dispensed with. Soon afterward he vanished.

His romantic life has done more to enhance Bierce's reputation than his works are likely to do. But several of his war stories (*Tales of Soldiers and Civilians*, 1891, later re-titled *In the Midst of Life*) triumph over journalism, theatricality, and self-consciousness of style. Worth noticing among these are the psychological experiment of *An Occurrence at Owl Creek Bridge*, the magnificent organization of *A Horseman in the Sky*, the stabbing irony of the final sentence in *Killed at Resaca*, and the ghastly parody of Isaiah 11:6 in *Chickamauga*.

Vincent Starrett, *Ambrose Bierce, A Bibliography*, Philadelphia, 1929.
Collected Works of Ambrose Bierce, 12 vols., New York, 1909–1912.
The Letters of Ambrose Bierce, B. C. Pope, ed., San Francisco, 1922.
Paul Fatout, *Ambrose Bierce, the Devil's Lexicographer*, Norman, Oklahoma, 1921.
C. H. Grattan, *Bitter Bierce: A Mystery of American Letters*, New York, 1929.
Joseph Noel, *Footloose in Arcadia: A Personal Record of Jack London, George Stirling, Ambrose Bierce*, New York, 1940.
Franklin Walker, *Ambrose Bierce, the Wickedest Man in San Francisco*, New York, 1941.

» » CHICKAMAUGA « «

One sunny autumn afternoon a child strayed away from its rude home in a small field and entered a forest unobserved. It was happy in a new sense of freedom from control, happy in the opportunity of exploration and adventure; for this child's spirit, in bodies of its ancestors, had for thousands of years been trained to memorable feats of discovery and conquest—victories in battles whose critical moments were centuries, whose victors' camps were cities of hewn stone. From the cradle of its race it had conquered its way through two continents and passing a great sea had penetrated a third, there to be born to war and dominion as a heritage.

The child was a boy aged about six years, the son of a poor planter. In his younger manhood the father had been a soldier, had fought against naked savages and followed the flag of his country into the capital of a civilized race to the far South. In the peaceful life of a planter the warrior-fire survived; once kindled, it is never extinguished. The man loved military books and pictures and the boy had understood enough to make himself a wooden sword, though even the eye of his father would hardly have known it for what it was. This weapon he now bore bravely, as became the son of an heroic race, and pausing now and again in the sunny space of the forest assumed, with some exaggeration, the postures of aggression and defense that he had been taught by the engraver's art. Made reckless by the ease with which he overcame invisible foes attempting to stay his advance, he committed the common enough military error of pushing the pursuit to a dangerous extreme, until he found himself upon the margin of a wide but shallow brook, whose rapid waters barred his direct advance against the flying foe that had crossed with illogical ease. But the intrepid victor was not to be baffled; the spirit of the race which had passed the great sea burned unconquerable in that small breast and would not be denied. Finding a place where some bowlders in the bed of the stream lay but a step or a leap apart, he made his way across and fell again upon the rear-guard of his imaginary foe, putting all to the sword.

Now that the battle had been won, prudence required that he withdraw to his base of operations. Alas; like many a mightier conqueror, and like one, the mightiest, he could not

> *curb the lust for war,*
> *Nor learn that tempted Fate will leave the loftiest*
> *star.*

Advancing from the bank of the creek he suddenly found himself confronted with a new and more formidable enemy: in the path that he was following, sat, bolt upright, with ears erect and paws suspended before it, a rabbit! With a startled cry the child turned and fled, he knew not in what direction, calling with inarticulate cries for his mother, weeping, stumbling, his tender skin cruelly torn by brambles, his little heart beating hard with terror—breathless, blind with tears—lost in the forest! Then, for more than an hour, he wandered with erring feet through the tangled undergrowth, till at last, overcome by fatigue, he lay down in a narrow space between two rocks, within a few yards of the stream and still grasping his toy sword, no longer a weapon but a companion, sobbed himself to sleep. The wood birds sang merrily above his head; the squirrels, whisking their bravery of tail, ran barking from tree to tree, unconscious of the pity of it, and somewhere far away was a strange, muffled thunder, as if the partridges were drumming in celebration of nature's victory over the son of her immemorial enslavers. And back at the little plantation, where white men and black were hastily searching the fields and hedges in alarm, a mother's heart was breaking for her missing child.

Hours passed, and then the little sleeper rose to his feet. The chill of the evening was in his limbs, the fear of the gloom in his heart. But he had rested, and he no longer wept. With some blind instinct which impelled to action he struggled through the undergrowth about him and came to a more open ground—on his right the brook, to the left a gentle acclivity studded with infrequent trees; over all, the gathering gloom of twilight. A thin, ghostly mist rose along the water. It frightened and repelled him; instead of recrossing, in the direction whence he had come, he turned his back upon it, and went forward toward the dark enclosing wood. Suddenly he saw before him a strange moving object which he took to be some large animal—a dog, a pig—he could not name it; perhaps it was a bear. He had seen pictures of bears, but knew of nothing to their discredit and had vaguely wished to meet one. But something in form or movement of this object—something in the awkwardness of its approach—told him that it was not a bear, and curiosity was stayed by fear. He stood still and as it came slowly on gained courage every moment, for he saw that at least it had not the long, menacing ears of the rabbit. Possibly his impressionable mind was half conscious of something familiar in its shambling, awkward gait. Before it had approached near enough to resolve his doubts he saw that it was followed by another and another. To right and to left were many more; the whole open space about him was alive with them—all moving toward the brook.

They were men. They crept upon their hands and knees. They used their hands only, dragging their legs. They used their knees only, their arms hanging idle at their sides. They strove to rise to their feet, but fell prone in the attempt. They did nothing naturally, and nothing alike, save only to advance foot by foot in the same direction. Singly, in pairs and in little groups, they came on through the gloom, some halting now and again while others crept slowly past them, then resuming their movement. They came by dozens and by hundreds; as far on either hand as one could see in the deepening gloom they extended and the black wood behind them appeared to be inexhaustible. The very ground seemed in motion toward the creek. Occasionally one who had paused did not again go on, but lay motionless. He was dead. Some, pausing, made strange gestures with their hands, erected their arms and lowered them again, clasped their heads; spread their palms upward, as men are sometimes seen to do in public prayer.

Not all of this did the child note; it is what would have been noted by an elder observer; he saw little but that these were men, yet crept like babes. Being men, they were not terrible, though unfamiliarly clad. He moved among them freely, going from one to another and peering into their faces with childish curiosity. All their faces were singularly white and many were streaked and gouted with red. Something in this—something too, perhaps, in their grotesque attitudes and movements—reminded of the painted clown whom he had seen last summer in the circus, and he laughed as he watched them. But on and ever on they crept, these maimed and bleeding men, as heedless as he of the dramatic contrast between his laughter and their own ghastly gravity. To him it was a merry spectacle. He had seen his father's negroes creep upon their hands and knees for his amusement—had ridden them so, "making believe" they were his horses. He now approached one of these crawling figures from behind and with an agile movement mounted it astride. The man sank upon his breast, recovered, flung the small boy fiercely to the ground as an unbroken colt might have done, then turned upon him a face that lacked a lower jaw—from the upper teeth to the throat was a great red gap fringed with hanging shreds of flesh and splinters of bone. The unnatural prominence of nose, the absence of chin, the fierce eyes, gave this man the appearance of a great bird of prey crimsoned in throat and breast by the blood of its quarry. The man rose to his knees, the child to his feet. The man shook his fist at the child; the child, terrified at last, ran to a tree near by, got upon the farther side of it and took a more serious view of the situation. And so the clumsy multitude dragged itself slowly and painfully along in hideous pantomime—moved forward down the slope like a swarm of great black beetles, with never a sound of going—in silence profound, absolute.

Instead of darkening, the haunted landscape began to brighten. Through the belt of trees beyond the brook shone a strange red light, the trunks and branches of the trees making a black lacework against it. It struck the creeping figures and gave them monstrous shadows, which caricatured their movements on the lit grass. It fell upon their faces, touching their whiteness with a ruddy tinge, accentuating the stains with which so many of them were freaked and maculated. It sparkled on buttons and bits of metal in their clothing. Instinctively the child turned toward the growing splendor and moved down the slope with his horrible companions; in a few moments had passed the foremost of the throng—not much of a feat, considering his advantages. He placed himself in the lead, his wooden sword still in hand, and solemnly directed the march, conforming his pace to theirs and occasionally turning as if to see that his forces did not straggle. Surely such a leader never before had such a following.

Scattered about upon the ground now slowly narrowing by the encroachment of this awful march to water, were certain articles to which, in the leader's mind, were coupled no significant associations: an occasional blanket, tightly rolled lengthwise, doubled and the ends bound together with a string; a heavy knapsack here, and there a broken rifle—such things, in short, as are found in the rear of retreating troops, the "spoor" of men flying from their hunters. Everywhere near the creek, which here had a margin of lowland, the earth was trodden into mud by the feet of men and horses. An observer of better experience in the use of his eyes would have noticed that these footprints pointed in both directions; the ground had been twice passed over—in advance and in retreat. A few hours before, these desperate, stricken men, with their more fortunate and now distant comrades, had penetrated the forest in thousands. Their successive battalions, breaking into swarms and re-forming in lines, had passed the child on every side—had almost trodden on him as he slept. The rustle and murmur of their march had not awakened him. Almost within a stone's throw of where he lay they had fought a battle; but all unheard by him were the roar of the musketry, the shock of the cannon, "the thunder of the captains and the shouting." He had slept through it all, grasping his little wooden sword with perhaps a tighter clutch in unconscious sympathy with his martial environment, but as heedless of the grandeur of the struggle as the dead who had died to make the glory.

The fire beyond the belt of woods on the farther side of the creek, reflected to the earth from the canopy of its own smoke, was now suffusing the whole landscape. It transformed the sinuous line of mist to the vapor of gold. The water gleamed with dashes of red, and red, too, were many of the stones protruding above the surface. But that was blood; the less desperately wounded had stained them in crossing. On them, too, the child now crossed with eager steps; he was going to the fire. As he stood upon the farther bank he turned about to look at the companions of his march. The advance was arriving at the creek. The stronger had already drawn themselves to the brink and plunged their faces into the flood. Three or four who lay without motion appeared to have no heads. At this the child's eyes expanded with wonder; even his hospitable understanding could not accept a phenomenon implying such vitality as that. After slaking their thirst these men had not had the strength to back away from the water, nor to keep their heads above it. They were drowned. In rear of these, the open spaces of the forest showed the leader as many formless figures of his grim command as at first; but not nearly so many were in motion. He waved his cap for their encouragement and smilingly pointed with his weapon in the direction of the guiding light—a pillar of fire to this strange exodus.

Confident of the fidelity of his forces, he now entered the belt of woods, passed through it easily in the red illumination, climbed a fence, ran across a field, turning now and again to coquet with his responsive shadow, and so approached the blazing ruin of a dwelling. Desolation everywhere! In all the wide glare not a living thing was visible. He cared nothing for that; the spectacle pleased, and he danced with glee in imitation of the wavering flames. He ran about, collecting fuel, but every object that he found was too heavy for him to cast in from the distance to which the heat limited his approach. In despair he flung in his sword—a surrender to the superior forces of nature. His military career was at an end.

Shifting his position, his eyes fell upon some outbuildings which had an oddly familiar appearance, as if he had dreamed of them. He stood considering them with wonder, when suddenly the entire plantation, with its inclosing forest, seemed to turn as if upon a pivot. His little world swung half around; the points of the compass were reversed. He recognized the blazing building as his own home!

For a moment he stood stupefied by the power of the revelation, then ran with stumbling feet, making a half-circuit of the ruin. There, conspicuous in the light of the conflagration, lay the dead body of a woman—the white face turned upward, the hands thrown out and clutched full of grass, the clothing deranged, the long dark hair in tangles and full of clotted blood. The greater part of the forehead was torn away, and from the jagged hole the brain protruded, overflowing the temple, a frothy mass of gray, crowned with clusters of crimson bubbles—the work of a shell.

The child moved his little hands, making wild, uncertain gestures. He uttered a series of inarticulate and indescribable cries—something between the chattering of an ape and the gobbling of a turkey—a startling, soulless, unholy sound, the language of a devil. The child was a deaf mute.

Then he stood motionless, with quivering lips, looking down upon the wreck.

1890   1891

STEPHEN CRANE

1871–1900

To THAT ARCH-PRIEST of naturalism, Ernest Hemingway, Stephen Crane is one of the three good writers that America has produced. He died of tuberculosis in the Schwarzwald just short of twenty-nine, an inheritor, like Keats, of unfulfilled renown, and though there may be danger of overestimating the worth of his achievement, Crane's somber eye and honest voice arrest the discerning reader. But Crane, said Joseph Conrad, "had not the face of a lucky man."

Son of a New Jersey minister who named him "for his ancestor who signed the Declaration," Stevie attended Lafayette and Syracuse, but did not deign to graduate. He then worked as a reporter in New York, where he vainly peddled his ironic slum-novel, *Maggie, a Girl of the Streets*. Behind Crane's sudden rise to fame with *The Red Badge of Courage* (1895) lay the unremitting faith of his early champions, Garland and Howells, who helped him also with a volume of his tortured but strangely haunting verse, *The Black Riders* (1895). The impetus of first prosperity thrust him south to Mexico and west to Nebraska, where he gained impulse and setting for his best-known tale, Hemingway's favorite, *The Blue Hotel*.

By the irony that celebrated Crane for realistic reporting of a Civil War battle he had never seen, he seemed committed to the life of a war correspondent. Following the publication of *The Little Regiment and other episodes of the Civil War* (1896), he explored the Græco-Turkish fracas for Hearst. For twenty febrile days during the Spanish-American War, Crane followed the action at Guantanamo and San Juan Hill, so absorbed in the mad accents of suffering that he not only forgot to eat but also grew so callous of danger that Richard Harding Davis had once to knock him from the path of a Spanish bullet. His disgust with cheap jingoism and his remarkable gift for impressionistic epithet gave his war-reporting the strength of acidulous veracity. (See *Wounds in the Rain*, 1900.) Loaded with quinine and humorous cynicism, he returned to New York with a quite unearned reputation for riotous living. Partly to escape this "goulash of legendary lies," but chiefly because of his increasingly perilous physical condition, he fled overseas to the peace of Brede Place in Sussex and sudden death, which a dash to the Continent rather hastened than deterred.

The Open Boat, like much of Crane's best work, is a true episode, surcharged with poetic imagination and recorded with magnificent vigor. The scarcity of ordnance among 30,000 Cuban insurrectionists had stimulated gun-running along the Florida coast. In December, 1896, Crane shipped aboard the decrepit steamer *Commodore*, Captain Murphy, bound from Jacksonville on a devious errand. When the ship foundered, possibly through sabotage, Crane (the correspondent) clambered into the open boat with the captain and two others, of whom all but Higgins, the oiler, were finally saved. The story stands up well beside Conrad's great novel, *The Nigger of the Narcissus* (1897), Crane's enthusiasm for which led him to seek out Conrad in England. Both novel and tale depict a group of average men in the microcosm of a sea-swept craft, laboring heroically but in mutual perplexity under the inscrutable eye of the macrocosm. For his part, Conrad deeply admired *The Open Boat*, "which by the deep and simple humanity of its presentation seems somehow to illustrate the essentials of life itself, like a symbolic tale."

A. W. Williams and V. Starrett, *Stephen Crane, A Bibliography*, Glendale, California, 1948.

The Work of Stephen Crane, Wilson Follett, ed., 12 vols., New York, 1925–1926.

The Collected Poems of Stephen Crane, Wilson Follett, ed., New York, 1930.

The Letters of Stephen Crane, R. W. Stallman and Lilian Gilkes, eds., New York, 1960.

Thomas Beer, *Stephen Crane: A Study in American Letters*, New York, 1924.

John Berryman, *Stephen Crane*, New York, 1950.

Mrs. Joseph Conrad, "Recollections of Stephen Crane," *Bookman*, LXIII (April, 1926), 134–137.

H. R. Crane, "My Uncle, Stephen Crane," *American Mercury*, XXXI (January, 1934), 24–29.

Hamlin Garland, "Stephen Crane as I Knew Him," *Yale Review*, III (n. s.), (April, 1914), 494–506.

Daniel G. Hoffman, *The Poetry of Stephen Crane*, New York, 1957.

» » THE OPEN BOAT « «

A Tale Intended to Be After the Fact: Being the Experience of Four Men from the Sunk Steamer Commodore

I

None of them knew the color of the sky. Their eyes glanced level, and were fastened upon the waves that swept toward them. These waves were of the hue of slate, save for the tops, which were of foaming white, and all of the men knew the colors of the sea. The horizon narrowed and widened, and dipped and rose, and at all times its edge was jagged with waves that seemed thrust up in points like rocks. Many a man ought to have a bath-tub larger than the boat which here rode upon the sea. These waves were most wrongfully and barbarously abrupt and tall, and each froth-top was a problem in small-boat navigation.

The cook squatted in the bottom and looked with both eyes at the six inches of gunwale which separated him from the ocean. His sleeves were rolled over his fat forearms, and the two flaps of his unbuttoned vest dangled as he bent to bail out the boat. Often he said: "Gawd! That was a narrow clip." As he remarked it he invariably gazed eastward over the broken sea.

The oiler, steering with one of the two oars in the boat, sometimes raised himself suddenly to keep clear of water that swirled in over the stern. It was a thin little oar and it seemed often ready to snap.

The correspondent, pulling at the other oar, watched the waves and wondered why he was there.

The injured captain, lying in the bow, was at this time buried in that profound dejection and indifference which comes, temporarily at least, to even the bravest and most enduring when, willy nilly, the firm fails, the army loses, the ship goes down. The mind of the master of a vessel is rooted deep in the timbers of her, though he commanded for a day or a decade, and this captain had on him the stern impression of a scene in the greys of dawn of seven turned faces, and later a stump of a top-mast with a white ball on it that slashed to and fro at the waves, went low and lower, and down. Thereafter there was something strange in his voice. Although steady, it was deep with mourning, and of a quality beyond oration or tears.

"Keep 'er a little more south, Billie," said he.

"'A little more south,' sir," said the oiler in the stern.

A seat in this boat was not unlike a seat upon a bucking broncho, and by the same token, a broncho is not much smaller. The craft pranced and reared, and plunged like an animal. As each wave came, and she rose for it, she seemed like a horse making at a fence outrageously high. The manner of her scramble over these walls of water is a mystic thing, and, moreover, at the top of them were ordinarily these problems in white water, the foam racing down from the summit of each wave, requiring a new leap, and a leap from the air. Then, after scornfully bumping a crest, she would slide, and race, and splash down a long incline, and arrive bobbing and nodding in front of the next menace.

A singular disadvantage of the sea lies in the fact that after successfully surmounting one wave you discover that there is another behind it just as important and just as nervously anxious to do something effective in the way of swamping boats. In a ten-foot dingey one can get an idea of the resources of the sea in the line of waves that is not probable to the average experience which is never at sea in a dingey. As each slatey wall of water approached, it shut all else from the view of the men in the boat, and it was not difficult to imagine that this particular wave was the final outburst of the ocean, the last effort of the grim water. There was a terrible grace in the move of the waves, and they came in silence, save for the snarling of the crests.

In the wan light, the faces of the men must have been grey. Their eyes must have glinted in strange ways as they gazed steadily astern. Viewed from a balcony, the whole thing would doubtless have been weirdly picturesque. But the men in the boat had no time to see it, and if they had had leisure there were other things to occupy their minds. The sun swung steadily up the sky, and they knew it was broad day because the color of the sea changed from slate to emerald-green, streaked with amber lights, and the foam was like tumbling snow. The process of the breaking day was unknown to them. They were aware only of this effect upon the color of the waves that rolled toward them.

In disjointed sentences the cook and the correspondent argued as to the difference between a life-saving station and a house of refuge. The cook had said: "There's a house of refuge just north of the Mosquito Inlet Light, and as soon as they see us, they'll come off in their boat and pick us up."

"As soon as who see us?" said the correspondent.

"The crew," said the cook.

"Houses of refuge don't have crews," said the correspondent. "As I understand them, they are only places where clothes and grub are stored for the benefit of shipwrecked people. They don't carry crews."

"Oh, yes, they do," said the cook.

"No, they don't," said the correspondent.

"Well, we're not there yet, anyhow," said the oiler, in the stern.

"Well," said the cook, "perhaps it's not a house of refuge that I'm thinking of as being near Mosquito Inlet Light. Perhaps it's a life-saving station."

"We're not there yet," said the oiler, in the stern.

II

As the boat bounced from the top of each wave, the wind tore through the hair of the hatless men, and as the craft plopped her stern down again the spray splashed past them. The crest of each of these waves was a hill, from the top of which the men surveyed, for a moment, a broad tumultuous expanse, shining and wind-riven. It was probably splendid. It was probably glorious, this play of the free sea, wild with lights of emerald and white and amber.

"Bully good thing it's an on-shore wind," said the cook. "If not, where would we be? Wouldn't have a show."

"That's right," said the correspondent.

The busy oiler nodded his assent.

Then the captain, in the bow, chuckled in a way that expressed humor, contempt, tragedy, all in one. "Do you think we've got much of a show now, boys?" said he.

Whereupon the three were silent, save for a trifle of hemming and hawing. To express any particular optimism at this time they felt to be childish and stupid, but they all doubtless possessed this sense of the situation in their mind. A young man thinks doggedly at such times. On the other hand, the ethics of their condition was decidedly against any open suggestion of hopelessness. So they were silent.

"Oh, well," said the captain, soothing his children, "we'll get ashore all right."

But there was that in his tone which made them think, so the oiler quoth: "Yes! If this wind holds!"

The cook was bailing: "Yes! If we don't catch hell in the surf."

Canton flannel gulls flew near and far. Sometimes they sat down on the sea, near patches of brown seaweed that rolled on the waves with a movement like carpets on a line in a gale. The birds sat comfortably in groups, and they were envied by some in the dingey, for the wrath of the sea was no more to them than it was to a covey of prairie chickens a thousand miles inland. Often they came very close and stared at the men with black bead-like eyes. At these times they were uncanny and sinister in their unblinking scrutiny, and the men hooted angrily at them, telling them to be gone. One came, and evidently decided to alight on the top of the captain's head. The bird flew parallel to the boat and did not circle, but made short sidelong jumps in the air in chicken-fashion. His black eyes were wistfully fixed upon the captain's head. "Ugly brute," said the oiler to the bird. "You look as if you were made with a jack-knife." The cook and the correspondent swore darkly at the creature. The captain naturally wished to knock it away with the end of the heavy painter; but he did not dare do it, because anything resembling an emphatic gesture would have capsized this freighted boat, and so with his open hand, the captain gently and carefully waved the gull away. After it had been discouraged from the pursuit the captain breathed easier on account of his hair, and others breathed easier because the bird struck their minds at this time as being somehow grewsome and ominous.

In the meantime the oiler and the correspondent rowed. And also they rowed.

They sat together in the same seat, and each rowed an oar. Then the oiler took both oars; then the correspondent took both oars; then the oiler; then the correspondent. They rowed and they rowed. The very ticklish part of the business was when the time came for the reclining one in the stern to take his turn at the oars. By the very last star of truth, it is easier to steal eggs from under a hen than it was to change seats in the dingey. First the man in the stern slid his hand along the thwart and moved with care, as if he were of Sèvres. Then the man in the rowing seat slid his hand along the other thwart. It was all done with the most extraordinary care. As the two sidled past each other, the whole party kept watchful eyes on the coming wave, and the captain cried: "Look out now! Steady there!"

The brown mats of seaweed that appeared from time to time were like islands, bits of earth. They were traveling, apparently, neither one way nor the other. They were, to all intents, stationary. They informed the men in the boat that it was making progress slowly toward the land.

The captain, rearing cautiously in the bow, after the dingey soared on a great swell, said that he had seen the lighthouse at Mosquito Inlet. Presently the cook remarked that he had seen it. The correspondent was at the oars then, and for some reason he too wished to look at the lighthouse, but his back was toward the far shore and the waves were important, and for some time he could not seize an opportunity to turn his head. But at last there came a wave more gentle than the others, and when at the crest of it he swiftly scoured the western horizon.

"See it?" said the captain.

"No," said the correspondent slowly, "I didn't see anything."

"Look again," said the captain. He pointed. "It's exactly in that direction."

At the top of another wave, the correspondent did as he was bid, and this time his eyes chanced on a small still thing on the edge of the swaying horizon. It was precisely like the point of a pin. It took an anxious eye to find a lighthouse so tiny.

"Think we'll make it, captain?"

"If this wind holds and the boat don't swamp, we can't do much else," said the captain.

The little boat, lifted by each towering sea, and splashed viciously by the crests, made progress that in the absence of seaweed was not apparent to those in her. She seemed just a wee thing wallowing, miraculously top-up, at the mercy of five oceans. Occasionally, a great spread of water, like white flames, swarmed into her.

"Bail her, cook," said the captain serenely.

"All right, captain," said the cheerful cook.

III

It would be difficult to describe the subtle brotherhood of men that was here established on the seas. No one said that it was so. No one mentioned it. But it dwelt in the boat, and each man felt it warm him. They were a captain, an oiler, a cook, and a correspondent, and they were friends, friends in a more curiously ironbound degree than may be common. The hurt captain, lying against the water-jar in the bow, spoke always in a low voice and calmly, but he could never command a more ready and swiftly obedient crew than the motley three of the dingey. It was more than a mere recognition of what was best for the common safety. There was surely in it a quality that was personal and heartfelt. And after this devotion to the commander of the boat there was this comradeship that the correspondent, for instance, who had been taught to be cynical of men, knew even at the time was the best experience of his life. But no one said that it was so. No one mentioned it.

"I wish we had a sail," remarked the captain. "We might try my overcoat on the end of an oar and give you two boys a chance to rest." So the cook and the correspondent held the mast and spread wide the overcoat. The oiler steered, and the little boat made good way with her new rig. Sometimes the oiler had to scull sharply to keep a sea from breaking into the boat, but otherwise sailing was a success.

Meanwhile the lighthouse had been growing slowly larger. It had now almost assumed color, and appeared like a little grey shadow on the sky. The man at the oars could not be prevented from turning his head rather often to try for a glimpse of this little grey shadow.

At last, from the top of each wave the men in the tossing boat could see land. Even as the lighthouse was an upright shadow on the sky, this land seemed but a long black shadow on the sea. It certainly was thinner than paper. "We must be about opposite New Smyrna," said the cook, who had coasted this shore often in schooners. "Captain, by the way, I believe they abandoned that life-saving station there about a year ago."

"Did they?" said the captain.

The wind slowly died away. The cook and the correspondent were not now obliged to slave in order to hold high the oar. But the waves continued their old impetuous swooping at the dingey, and the little craft, no longer under way, struggled woundily over them. The oiler or the correspondent took the oars again.

Shipwrecks are *à propos* of nothing. If men could only train for them and have them occur when the men had reached pink condition, there would be less drowning at sea. Of the four in the dingey none had slept any time worth mentioning for two days and two nights previous to embarking in the dingey, and in the excitement of clambering about the deck of a foundering ship they had also forgotten to eat heartily.

For these reasons, and for others, neither the oiler nor the correspondent was fond of rowing at this time. The correspondent wondered ingenuously how in the name of all that was sane could there be people who thought it amusing to row a boat. It was not an amusement; it was a diabolical punishment, and even a genius of mental aberrations could never conclude that it was anything but a horror to the muscles and a crime against the back. He mentioned to the boat in general how the amusement of rowing struck him, and the weary-faced oiler smiled in full sympathy. Previously to the foundering, by the way, the oiler had worked double-watch in the engine-room of the ship.

"Take her easy, now, boys," said the captain. "Don't spend yourselves. If we have to run a surf you'll need all your strength, because we'll sure have to swim for it. Take your time."

Slowly the land arose from the sea. From a black line it became a line of black and a line of white, trees and sand. Finally, the captain said that he could make out a house on the shore. "That's the house of refuge, sure," said the cook. "They'll see us before long, and come out after us."

The distant lighthouse reared high. "The keeper ought to be able to make us out now, if he's looking through a glass," said the captain. "He'll notify the life-saving people."

"None of those other boats could have got ashore to give word of the wreck," said the oiler, in a low voice. "Else the life-boat would be out hunting us."

Slowly and beautifully the land loomed out of the sea. The wind came again. It had veered from the north-east to the south-east. Finally, a new sound struck the ears of the men in the boat. It was the low thunder of the surf on the shore. "We'll never be able to make the light-house now," said the captain. "Swing her head a little more north, Billie," said he.

" 'A little more north,' sir," said the oiler.

Whereupon the little boat turned her nose once more down the wind, and all but the oarsman watched the shore grow. Under the influence of this expansion doubt and direful apprehension was leaving the minds of the men. The management of the boat was still most absorbing, but it could not prevent a quiet cheerfulness. In an hour, perhaps, they would be ashore.

Their backbones had become thoroughly used to balancing in the boat, and they now rode this wild colt of a dingey like circus men. The correspondent thought that he had been drenched to the skin, but happening to feel in the top pocket of his coat, he found therein eight cigars. Four of them were soaked with sea-water; four were perfectly scathless. After a search, somebody produced three dry matches, and thereupon the four waifs rode impudently in their little boat, and with an assurance of an impending rescue shining in their eyes, puffed at the big cigars and judged well and ill of all men. Everybody took a drink of water.

IV

"Cook," remarked the captain, "there don't seem to be any signs of life about your house of refuge."

"No," replied the cook. "Funny they don't see us!"

A broad stretch of lowly coast lay before the eyes of the men. It was of dunes topped with dark vegetation. The roar of the surf was plain, and sometimes they could see the white lip of a wave as it spun up the beach. A tiny house was blocked out black upon the sky. Southward, the slim lighthouse lifted its little grey length.

Tide, wind, and waves were swinging the dingey northward. "Funny they don't see us," said the men.

The surf's roar was here dulled, but its tone was, nevertheless, thunderous and mighty. As the boat swam over the great rollers, the men sat listening to this roar. "We'll swamp sure," said everybody.

It is fair to say here that there was not a life-saving station within twenty miles in either direction, but the men did not know this fact,

and in consequence they made dark and op-
probrious remarks concerning the eyesight of
the nation's life-savers. Four scowling men sat
in the dingey and surpassed records in the invention of epithets.

"Funny they don't see us."

The lightheartedness of a former time had
completely faded. To their sharpened minds
it was easy to conjure pictures of all kinds
of incompetency and blindness and, indeed,
cowardice. There was the shore of the populous land, and it was bitter and bitter to them
that from it came no sign.

"Well," said the captain, ultimately, "I suppose we'll have to make a try for ourselves.
If we stay out here too long, we'll none of
us have strength left to swim after the boat
swamps."

And so the oiler, who was at the oars, turned
the boat straight for the shore. There was a
sudden tightening of muscle. There was some
thinking.

"If we don't all get ashore——" said the
captain. "If we don't all get ashore, I suppose
you fellows know where to send news of my
finish?"

They then briefly exchanged some addresses
and admonitions. As for the reflections of the
men, there was a great deal of rage in them.
Perchance they might be formulated thus: "If
I am going to be drowned—if I am going to
be drowned—if I am going to be drowned,
why, in the name of the seven mad gods who
rule the sea, was I allowed to come thus far
and contemplate sand and trees? Was I brought
here merely to have my nose dragged away
as I was about to nibble the sacred cheese
of life? It is preposterous. If this old ninny-
woman, Fate, cannot do better than this, she
should be deprived of the management of
men's fortunes. She is an old hen who knows
not her intention. If she has decided to drown
me, why did she not do it in the beginning
and save me all this trouble? The whole affair
is absurd. . . . But no, she cannot mean to
drown me. She dare not drown me. She cannot drown me. Not after all this work." Afterward the man might have had an impulse to
shake his fist at the clouds: "Just you drown
me, now, and then hear what I call you!"

The billows that came at this time were
more formidable. They seemed always just
about to break and roll over the little boat in a
turmoil of foam. There was a preparatory and
long growl in the speech of them. No mind

unused to the sea would have concluded that
the dingey could ascend these sheer heights in
time. The shore was still afar. The oiler was a
wily surfman. "Boys," he said swiftly, "she
won't live three minutes more, and we're too
far out to swim. Shall I take her to sea again,
captain?"

"Yes! Go ahead!" said the captain.

This oiler, by a series of quick miracles, and
fast and steady oarsmanship, turned the boat
in the middle of the surf and took her safely to
sea again.

There was a considerable silence as the boat
bumped over the furrowed sea to deeper water. Then somebody in gloom spoke. "Well,
anyhow, they must have seen us from the shore
by now."

The gulls went in slanting flight up the wind
toward the grey desolate east. A squall,
marked by dingy clouds, and clouds brick-red,
like smoke from a burning building, appeared
from the south-east.

"What do you think of those life-saving people? Ain't they peaches?"

"Funny they haven't seen us."

"Maybe they think we're out here for sport!
Maybe they think we're fishin'. Maybe they
think we're damned fools."

It was a long afternoon. A changed tide tried
to force them southward, but the wind and
wave said northward. Far ahead, where coast-
line, sea, and sky formed their mighty angle,
there were little dots which seemed to indicate
a city on the shore.

"St. Augustine?"

The captain shook his head. "Too near
Mosquito Inlet."

And the oiler rowed, and then the correspondent rowed. Then the oiler rowed. It was
a weary business. The human back can become the seat of more aches and pains than are
registered in books for the composite anatomy
of a regiment. It is a limited area, but it can
become the theatre of innumerable muscular
conflicts, tangles, wrenches, knots, and other
comforts.

"Did you ever like to row, Billie?" asked the
correspondent.

"No," said the oiler. "Hang it!"

When one exchanged the rowing-seat for a
place in the bottom of the boat, he suffered a
bodily depression that caused him to be careless of everything save an obligation to wiggle
one finger. There was cold sea-water swashing
to and fro in the boat, and he lay in it. His

head, pillowed on a thwart, was within an inch
of the swirl of a wave crest, and sometimes a
particularly obstreperous sea came in-board
and drenched him once more. But these matters did not annoy him. It is almost certain that
if the boat had capsized he would have tumbled comfortably out upon the ocean as if he
felt sure that it was a great soft mattress.

"Look! There's a man on the shore!"

"Where?"

"There! See 'im? See 'im?"

"Yes, sure! He's walking along."

"Now he's stopped. Look! He's facing us!"

"He's waving at us!"

"So he is! By thunder!"

"Ah, now we're all right! Now we're all
right! There'll be a boat out here for us in half-
an-hour."

"He's going on. He's running. He's going up
to that house there."

The remote beach seemed lower than the
sea, and it required a searching glance to discern the little black figure. The captain saw a
floating stick and they rowed to it. A bath-
towel was by some weird chance in the boat,
and, tying this on the stick, the captain waved
it. The oarsman did not dare turn his head, so
he was obliged to ask questions.

"What's he doing now?"

"He's standing still again. He's looking, I
think. . . . There he goes again. Toward the
house. . . . Now he's stopped again."

"Is he waving at us?"

"No, not now! he was, though."

"Look! There comes another man!"

"He's running."

"Look at him go, would you."

"Why, he's on a bicycle. Now he's met the
other man. They're both waving at us. Look!"

"There comes something up the beach."

"What the devil is that thing?"

"Why it looks like a boat."

"Why, certainly it's a boat."

"No, it's on wheels."

"Yes, so it is. Well, that must be the life-
boat. They drag them along shore on a wagon."

"That's the life-boat, sure."

"No, by——, it's—it's an omnibus."

"I tell you it's a life-boat."

"It is not! It's an omnibus. I can see it plain.
See? One of these big hotel omnibuses."

"By thunder, you're right. It's an omnibus,
sure as fate. What do you suppose they are
doing with an omnibus? Maybe they are going
around collecting the life-crew, hey?"

"That's it, likely. Look! There's a fellow
waving a little black flag. He's standing on the
steps of the omnibus. There comes those other
two fellows. Now they're all talking together.
Look at the fellow with the flag. Maybe he
ain't waving it."

"That ain't a flag, is it? That's his coat. Why,
certainly, that's his coat."

"So it is. It's his coat. He's taken it off and
is waving it around his head. But would you
look at him swing it."

"Oh, say, there isn't any life-saving station
there. That's just a winter resort hotel omnibus
that has brought over some of the boarders to
see us drown."

"What's that idiot with the coat mean?
What's he signaling, anyhow?"

"It looks as if he were trying to tell us to go
north. There must be a life-saving station up
there."

"No! He thinks we're fishing. Just giving us
a merry hand. See? Ah, there, Willie!"

"Well, I wish I could make something out of
those signals. What do you suppose he
means?"

"He don't mean anything. He's just playing."

"Well, if he'd just signal us to try the surf
again, or to go to sea and wait, or go north, or
go south, or go to hell—there would be some
reason in it. But look at him. He just stands
there and keeps his coat revolving like a wheel.
The ass!"

"There come more people."

"Now there's quite a mob. Look! Isn't that a
boat?"

"Where? Oh, I see where you mean. No,
that's no boat."

"That fellow is still waving his coat."

"He must think we like to see him do that.
Why don't he quit it? It don't mean anything."

"I don't know. I think he is trying to make
us go north. It must be that there's a life-saving
station there somewhere."

"Say, he ain't tired yet. Look at 'im wave."

"Wonder how long he can keep that up.
He's been revolving his coat ever since he
caught sight of us. He's an idiot. Why aren't
they getting men to bring a boat out? A fishing
boat—one of those big yawls—could come out
here all right. Why don't he do something?"

"Oh, it's all right, now."

"They'll have a boat out here for us in less
than no time, now that they've seen us."

A faint yellow tone came into the sky over
the low land. The shadows on the sea slowly

deepened. The wind bore coldness with it, and the men began to shiver.

"Holy smoke!" said one, allowing his voice to express his impious mood, "if we keep on monkeying out here! If we've got to flounder out here all night!"

"Oh, we'll never have to stay here all night! Don't you worry. They've seen us now, and it won't be long before they'll come chasing out after us."

The shore grew dusky. The man waving a coat blended gradually into this gloom, and it swallowed in the same manner the omnibus and the group of people. The spray, when it dashed uproariously over the side, made the voyagers shrink and swear like men who were being branded.

"I'd like to catch the chump who waved the coat. I feel like soaking him one, just for luck."

"Why? What did he do?"

"Oh, nothing, but then he seemed so damned cheerful."

In the meantime the oiler rowed, and then the correspondent rowed, and then the oiler rowed. Grey-faced and bowed forward, they mechanically, turn by turn, plied the leaden oars. The form of the lighthouse had vanished from the southern horizon, but finally a pale star appeared, just lifting from the sea. The streaked saffron in the west passed before the all-merging darkness, and the sea to the east was black. The land had vanished, and was expressed only by the low and drear thunder of the surf.

"If I am going to be drowned—if I am going to be drowned—if I am going to be drowned, why, in the name of the seven mad gods who rule the sea, was I allowed to come this far and contemplate sand and trees? Was I brought here merely to have my nose dragged away as I was about to nibble the sacred cheese of life?"

The patient captain, drooped over the water-jar, was sometimes obliged to speak to the oarsman.

"Keep her head up! Keep her head up!"

"'Keep her head up,' sir." The voices were weary and low.

This was surely a quiet evening. All save the oarsman lay heavily and listlessly in the boat's bottom. As for him, his eyes were just capable of noting the tall black waves that swept forward in a most sinister silence, save for an occasional subdued growl of a crest.

The cook's head was on a thwart, and he looked without interest at the water under his nose. He was deep in other scenes. Finally he spoke. "Billie," he murmured, dreamfully, "what kind of pie do you like best?"

V

"Pie," said the oiler and the correspondent, agitatedly. "Don't talk about those things, blast you!"

"Well," said the cook, "I was just thinking about ham sandwiches, and——"

A night on the sea in an open boat is a long night. As darkness settled finally, the shine of the light, lifting from the sea in the south, changed to full gold. On the northern horizon a new light appeared, a small bluish gleam on the edge of the waters. These two lights were the furniture of the world. Otherwise there was nothing but waves.

Two men huddled in the stern, and distances were so magnificent in the dingey that the rower was enabled to keep his feet partly warmed by thrusting them under his companions. Their legs indeed extended far under the rowing-seat until they touched the feet of the captain forward. Sometimes, despite the efforts of the tired oarsmen, a wave came piling into the boat, an icy wave of the night, and the chilling water soaked them anew. They would twist their bodies for a moment and groan, and sleep the dead sleep once more, while the water in the boat gurgled about them as the craft rocked.

The plan of the oiler and the correspondent was for one to row until he lost the ability, and then arouse the other from his sea-water couch in the bottom of the boat.

The oiler plied the oars until his head dropped forward, and the overpowering sleep blinded him. And he rowed yet afterward. Then he touched a man in the bottom of the boat, and called his name. "Will you spell me for a little while?" he said, meekly.

"Sure, Billie," said the correspondent, awakening and dragging himself to a sitting position. They exchanged places carefully, and the oiler, cuddling down in the sea-water at the cook's side, seemed to go to sleep instantly.

The particular violence of the sea had ceased. The waves came without snarling. The obligation of the man at the oars was to keep the boat headed so that the tilt of the rollers would not capsize her, and to preserve her from filling when the crests rushed past. The black waves were silent and hard to be seen in the darkness. Often one was almost upon the boat before the oarsman was aware.

In a low voice the correspondent addressed the captain. He was not sure that the captain was awake, although this iron man seemed to be always awake. "Captain, shall I keep her making for that light north, sir?"

The same steady voice answered him. "Yes. Keep it about two points off the port bow."

The cook had tied a life-belt around himself in order to get even the warmth which this clumsy cork contrivance could donate, and he seemed almost stove-like when a rower, whose teeth invariably chattered wildly as soon as he ceased his labor, dropped down to sleep.

The correspondent, as he rowed, looked down at the two men sleeping under-foot. The cook's arm was around the oiler's shoulders, and, with their fragmentary clothing and haggard faces, they were the babes of the sea, a grotesque rendering of the old babes in the wood.

Later he must have grown stupid at his work, for suddenly there was a growling of water, and a crest came with a roar and a swash into the boat, and it was a wonder that it did not set the cook afloat in his life-belt. The cook continued to sleep, but the oiler sat up, blinking his eyes and shaking with the new cold.

"Oh, I'm awful sorry, Billie," said the correspondent contritely.

"That's all right, old boy," said the oiler, and lay down again and was asleep.

Presently it seemed that even the captain dozed, and the correspondent thought that he was the one man afloat on all the oceans. The wind had a voice as it came over the waves, and it was sadder than the end.

There was a long, loud swishing astern of the boat, and a gleaming trail of phosphorescence, like blue flame, was furrowed on the black waters. It might have been made by a monstrous knife.

Then there came a stillness, while the correspondent breathed with the open mouth and looked at the sea.

Suddenly there was another swish and another long flash of bluish light, and this time it was alongside the boat, and might almost have been reached with an oar. The correspondent saw an enormous fin speed like a shadow through the water, hurling the crystalline spray and leaving the long glowing trail.

The correspondent looked over his shoulder at the captain. His face was hidden, and he seemed to be asleep. He looked at the babes of the sea. They certainly were asleep. So, being bereft of sympathy, he leaned a little way to one side and swore softly into the sea.

But the thing did not then leave the vicinity of the boat. Ahead or astern, on one side or the other, at intervals long or short, fled the long sparkling streak, and there was to be heard the whirroo of the dark fin. The speed and power of the thing was greatly to be admired. It cut the water like a gigantic and keen projectile.

The presence of this biding thing did not affect the man with the same horror that it would if he had been a picnicker. He simply looked at the sea dully and swore in an undertone.

Nevertheless, it is true that he did not wish to be alone. He wished one of his companions to awaken by chance and keep him company with it. But the captain hung motionless over the water-jar, and the oiler and the cook in the bottom of the boat were plunged in slumber.

VI

"If I am going to be drowned—if I am going to be drowned—if I am going to be drowned, why, in the name of the seven mad gods who rule the sea, was I allowed to come thus far and contemplate sand and trees?"

During this dismal night, it may be remarked that a man would conclude that it was really the intention of the seven mad gods to drown him, despite the abominable injustice of it. For it was certainly an abominable injustice to drown a man who had worked so hard, so hard. The man felt it would be a crime most unnatural. Other people had drowned at sea since galleys swarmed with painted sails, but still——

When it occurs to a man that nature does not regard him as important, and that she feels she would not maim the universe by disposing of him, he at first wishes to throw bricks at the temple, and he hates deeply the fact that there are no brick and no temples. Any visible expression of nature would surely be pelleted with his jeers.

Then, if there be no tangible thing to hoot he feels, perhaps, the desire to confront a personification and indulge in pleas, bowed to one knee, and with hands supplicant, saying: "Yes, but I love myself."

A high cold star on a winter's night is the word he feels that she says to him. Thereafter he knows the pathos of his situation.

The men in the dingey had not discussed these matters, but each had, no doubt, reflected upon them in silence and according to his mind. There was seldom any expression upon their faces save the general one of complete weariness. Speech was devoted to the business of the boat.

To chime the notes of his emotion, a verse mysteriously entered the correspondent's head. He had even forgotten that he had forgotten this verse, but it suddenly was in his mind.

"A soldier of the Legion lay dying in Algiers,
There was a lack of woman's nursing, there was dearth of woman's tears;
But a comrade stood beside him, and he took that comrade's hand,
And he said: 'I shall never see my own, my native land.'"

In his childhood, the correspondent had been made acquainted with the fact that a soldier of the Legion lay dying in Algiers, but he had never regarded the fact as important. Myriads of his school-fellows had informed him of the soldier's plight, but the dinning had naturally ended by making him perfectly indifferent. He had never considered it his affair that a soldier of the Legion lay dying in Algiers, nor had it appeared to him as a matter for sorrow. It was less to him than the breaking of a pencil's point.

Now, however, it quaintly came to him as a human, living thing. It was no longer merely a picture of a few throes in the breast of a poet, meanwhile drinking tea and warming his feet at the grate; it was an actuality—stern, mournful, and fine.

The correspondent plainly saw the soldier. He lay on the sand with his feet out straight and still. While his pale left hand was upon his chest in an attempt to thwart the going of his life, the blood came between his fingers. In the far Algerian distance, a city of low square forms was set against a sky that was faint with the last sunset hues. The correspondent, plying the oars and dreaming of the slow and slower movements of the lips of the soldier, was moved by a profound and perfectly impersonal comprehension. He was sorry for the soldier of the Legion who lay dying in Algiers.

The thing which had followed the boat and waited, had evidently grown bored at the delay. There was no longer to be heard the slash of the cut-water, and there was no longer the flame of the long trail. The light in the north still glimmered, but it was apparently no nearer to the boat. Sometimes the boom of the surf rang in the correspondent's ears, and he turned the craft seaward then and rowed harder. Southward, some one had evidently built a watch-fire on the beach. It was too low and too far to be seen, but it made a shimmering, roseate reflection upon the bluff back of it, and this could be discerned from the boat. The wind came stronger, and sometimes a wave suddenly raged out like a mountain-cat, and there was to be seen the sheen and sparkle of a broken crest.

The captain, in the bow, moved on his water-jar and sat erect. "Pretty long night," he observed to the correspondent. He looked at the shore. "Those life-saving people take their time."

"Did you see that shark playing around?"

"Yes, I saw him. He was a big fellow, all right."

"Wish I had known you were awake."

Later the correspondent spoke into the bottom of the boat.

"Billie!" There was a slow and gradual disentanglement. "Billie, will you spell me?"

"Sure," said the oiler.

As soon as the correspondent touched the cold comfortable sea-water in the bottom of the boat, and had huddled close to the cook's life-belt he was deep in sleep, despite the fact that his teeth played all the popular airs. This sleep was so good to him that it was but a moment before he heard a voice call his name in a tone that demonstrated the last stages of exhaustion. "Will you spell me?"

"Sure, Billie."

The light in the north had mysteriously vanished, but the correspondent took his course from the wide-awake captain.

Later in the night they took the boat farther out to sea, and the captain directed the cook to take one oar at the stern and keep the boat facing the seas. He was to call out if he should hear the thunder of the surf. This plan enabled the oiler and the correspondent to get respite together. "We'll give those boys a chance to get into shape again," said the captain. They curled down and, after a few preliminary chatterings and trembles, slept once more the dead

·leep. Neither knew they had bequeathed to the cook the company of another shark, or perhaps the same shark.

As the boat caroused on the waves, spray occasionally bumped over the side and gave them a fresh soaking, but this had no power to break their repose. The ominous slash of the wind and the water affected them as it would have affected mummies.

"Boys," said the cook, with the notes of every reluctance in his voice, "she's drifted in pretty close. I guess one of you had better take her to sea again." The correspondent, aroused, heard the crash of the toppled crests.

As he was rowing, the captain gave him some whisky-and-water, and this steadied the chills out of him. "If I ever get ashore and anybody shows me even a photograph of an oar——"

At last there was a short conversation.

"Billie. . . . Billie, will you spell me?"

"Sure," said the oiler.

VII

When the correspondent again opened his eyes, the sea and the sky were each of the grey hue of the dawning. Later, carmine and gold was painted upon the waters. The morning appeared finally, in its splendor, with a sky of pure blue, and the sunlight flamed on the tips of the waves.

On the distant dunes were set many little black cottages, and a tall white windmill reared above them. No man, nor dog, nor bicycle appeared on the beach. The cottages might have formed a deserted village.

The voyagers scanned the shore. A conference was held in the boat. "Well," said the captain, "if no help is coming we might better try a run through the surf right away. If we stay out here much longer we will be too weak to do anything for ourselves at all." The others silently acquiesced in this reasoning. The boat was headed for the beach. The correspondent wondered if none ever ascended the tall windtower, and if then they never looked seaward. This tower was a giant, standing with its back to the plight of the ants. It represented in a degree, to the correspondent, the serenity of nature amid the struggles of the individual— nature in the wind, and nature in the vision of men. She did not seem cruel to him then, nor beneficent, nor treacherous, nor wise. But she was indifferent, flatly indifferent. It is, perhaps, plausible that a man in this situation, impressed with the unconcern of the universe, should see the innumerable flaws of his life, and have them taste wickedly in his mind and wish for another chance. A distinction between right and wrong seems absurdly clear to him, then, in this new ignorance of the grave-edge, and he understands that if he were given another opportunity he would mend his conduct and his words, and be better and brighter during an introduction or at a tea.

"Now, boys," said the captain, "she is going to swamp, sure. All we can do is to work her in as far as possible, and then when she swamps, pile out and scramble for the beach. Keep cool now, and don't jump until she swamps sure."

The oiler took the oars. Over his shoulders he scanned the surf. "Captain," he said, "I think I'd better bring her about, and keep her head-on to the seas and back her in."

"All right, Billie," said the captain. "Back her in." The oiler swung the boat then and, seated in the stern, the cook and the correspondent were obliged to look over their shoulders to contemplate the lonely and indifferent shore.

The monstrous in-shore rollers heaved the boat high until the men were again enabled to see the white sheets of water scudding up the slanted beach. "We won't get in very close," said the captain. Each time a man could wrest his attention from the rollers, he turned his glance toward the shore, and in the expression of the eyes during this contemplation there was a singular quality. The correspondent, observing the others, knew that they were not afraid, but the full meaning of their glances was shrouded.

As for himself, he was too tired to grapple fundamentally with the fact. He tried to coerce his mind into thinking of it, but the mind was dominated at this time by the muscles, and the muscles said they did not care. It merely occurred to him that if he should drown it would be a shame.

There were no hurried words, no pallor, no plain agitation. The men simply looked at the shore. "Now, remember to get well clear of the boat when you jump," said the captain.

Seaward the crest of a roller suddenly fell with a thunderous crash, and the long white comber came roaring down upon the boat.

"Steady now," said the captain. The men were silent. They turned their eyes from the shore to the comber and waited. The boat slid up the incline, leaped at the furious top, bounced over it, and swung down the long back of the wave. Some water had been shipped and the cook bailed it out.

But the next crest crashed also. The tumbling, boiling flood of white water caught the boat and whirled it almost perpendicular. Water swarmed in from all sides. The correspondent had his hands on the gunwale at this time, and when the water entered at that place he swiftly withdrew his fingers, as if he objected to wetting them.

The little boat, drunken with this weight of water, reeled and snuggled deeper into the sea.

"Bail her out, cook! Bail her out," said the captain.

"All right, captain," said the cook.

"Now, boys, the next one will do for us, sure," said the oiler. "Mind to jump clear of the boat."

The third wave moved forward, huge, furious, implacable. It fairly swallowed the dingey, and almost simultaneously the men tumbled into the sea. A piece of life-belt had lain in the bottom of the boat, and as the correspondent went overboard he held this to his chest with his left hand.

The January water was icy, and he reflected immediately that it was colder than he had expected to find it on the coast of Florida. This appeared to his dazed mind as a fact important enough to be noted at the time. The coldness of the water was sad; it was tragic. This fact was somehow so mixed and confused with his opinion of his own situation that it seemed almost a proper reason for tears. The water was cold.

When he came to the surface he was conscious of little but the noisy water. Afterward he saw his companions in the sea. The oiler was ahead in the race. He was swimming strongly and rapidly. Off to the correspondent's left, the cook's great white and corked back bulged out of the water, and in the rear the captain was hanging with his one good hand to the keel of the overturned dingey.

There is a certain immovable quality to a shore, and the correspondent wondered at it amid the confusion of the sea.

It seemed also very attractive, but the correspondent knew that it was a long journey, and he paddled leisurely. The piece of life-preserver lay under him, and sometimes he whirled down the incline of a wave as if he were on a hand-sled.

But finally he arrived at a place in the sea where travel was beset with difficulty. He did not pause swimming to inquire what manner of current had caught him, but there his progress ceased. The shore was set before him like a bit of scenery on a stage, and he looked at it and understood with his eyes each detail of it.

As the cook passed, much farther to the left, the captain was calling to him, "Turn over on your back, cook! Turn over on your back and use the oar."

"All right, sir." The cook turned on his back, and, paddling with an oar, went ahead as if he were a canoe.

Presently the boat also passed to the left of the correspondent with the captain clinging with one hand to the keel. He would have appeared like a man raising himself to look over a board fence, if it were not for the extraordinary gymnastics of the boat. The correspondent marvelled that the captain could still hold to it.

They passed on, nearer to shore—the oiler, the cook, the captain—and following them went the water-jar, bouncing gaily over the seas.

The correspondent remained in the grip of this strange new enemy—a current. The shore, with its white slope of sand and its green bluff, topped with little silent cottages, was spread like a picture before him. It was very near to him then, but he was impressed as one who in a gallery looks at a scene from Brittany or Holland.

He thought: "I am going to drown? Can it be possible? Can it be possible? Can it be possible?" Perhaps an individual must consider his own death to be the final phenomenon of nature.

But later a wave perhaps whirled him out of this small, deadly current, for he found suddenly that he could again make progress toward the shore. Later still, he was aware that the captain, clinging with one hand to the keel of the dingey, had his face turned away from the shore and toward him, and was calling his name. "Come to the boat! Come to the boat!"

In his struggle to reach the captain and the boat, he reflected that when one gets properly wearied, drowning must really be a comfortable arrangement, a cessation of hostilities accompanied by a large degree of relief, and he was glad of it, for the main thing in his mind for some months had been horror of the temporary agony. He did not wish to be hurt.

Presently he saw a man running along the

shore. He was undressing with most remarkable speed. Coat, trousers, shirt, everything flew magically off him.

"Come to the boat," called the captain.

"All right, captain." As the correspondent paddled, he saw the captain let himself down to bottom and leave the boat. Then the correspondent performed his one little marvel of the voyage. A large wave caught him and flung him with ease and supreme speed completely over the boat and far beyond it. It struck him even then as an event in gymnastics, and a true miracle of the sea. An over-turned boat in the surf is not a plaything to a swimming man.

The correspondent arrived in water that reached only to his waist, but his condition did not enable him to stand for more than a moment. Each wave knocked him into a heap, and the under-tow pulled at him.

Then he saw the man who had been running and undressing, and undressing and running, come bounding into the water. He dragged ashore the cook, and then waded towards the captain, but the captain waved him away, and sent him to the correspondent. He was naked, naked as a tree in winter, but a halo was about his head, and he shone like a saint. He gave a strong pull, and a long drag, and a bully heave at the correspondent's hand. The cor-respondent, schooled in the minor formulæ, said: "Thanks, old man." But suddenly the man cried: "What's that?" He pointed a swift finger. The correspondent said: "Go."

In the shallows, face downward, lay the oiler. His forehead touched sand that was periodically, between each wave, clear of the sea.

The correspondent did not know all that transpired afterward. When he achieved safe ground he fell, striking the sand with each particular part of his body. It was as if he had dropped from a roof, but the thud was grateful to him.

It seems that instantly the beach was populated with men with blankets, clothes, and flasks, and women with coffee-pots and all the remedies sacred to their minds. The welcome of the land to the men from the sea was warm and generous, but a still and dripping shape was carried slowly up the beach, and the land's welcome for it could only be the different and sinister hospitality of the grave.

When it came night, the white waves paced to and fro in the moonlight, and the wind brought the sound of the great sea's voice to the men on shore, and they felt that they could then be interpreters.

1897   1898

FRANK NORRIS

1870–1902

TO HIS ELDEST SON Benjamin Franklin Norris gave his name and every educational advantage. As senior partner in a prosperous wholesale jewelry house in Chicago, he owned (like Jadwin, the speculator in *The Pit*) a Michigan Avenue mansion, some fine paintings, a stable of horses, and a country house on Lake Geneva, Wisconsin. In 1885 the family moved to the then opulent residential district just off San Francisco's Polk Street (the locale of *McTeague*). Frank attended boarding school near by until his father decided that the boy's artistic inclinations warranted study in a Paris atelier. After two years abroad, Frank returned to San Francisco with such bohemian mannerisms as spats, sideburns, a reverence for Zola, and a determination to write. Although an unfulfilled mathematics requirement prevented his graduation from the University of California with the class of 1894, he spent the academic year 1894–5 very profitably at Harvard as a special student in English 22, a course in writing.

As correspondent for the San Francisco *Chronicle* in the fall of 1895, Norris reached Johannesburg in time to be captured by the Boers, who deported him as soon as he recovered from a long siege of African fever. Back in California he joined the staff of *Wave*, a literary weekly, to which, between May 2, 1896, and September 24, 1898, he contributed upwards of fifty essays, sketches, and short stories. The Christmas number for 1897 contained his parodies of six prominent writers, with two of whom, Stephen Crane and Richard Harding Davis, he presently found himself serving as war correspondent in Cuba. But a severe recurrence of fever drove him to New York, where he worked as reader for a publishing house, and finished *McTeague* (1899), his closest approach to pure naturalism. The most memorable of Norris's single characters, the bull-shouldered, lion-maned dentist, gradually awakes from innocent if bestial torpor to a murderous fury of avarice, plagued by forces which he does not understand. Not dissimilar in theme is *Vandover and the Brute*. The unrevised manuscript of this novel, believed lost in the San Francisco earthquake, was tardily recovered and published in 1914. Like McTeague, Vandover fights a losing battle with the brute forces within his own nature. *Moran of the Lady Letty* (1898) and *A Man's Woman* (1900) are adventure yarns of love, the sea, and arctic exploration. The love-story of Condy Rivers, author-hero of *Blix* (1899), is partly autobiographical. Norris married at thirty, bought a California ranch, and died suddenly at thirty-two of peritonitis following an appendectomy, leaving his younger brother Charles to carry on as novelist in his stead.

His untimely death interrupted Norris's greatest work, a prose epic on wheat, or as someone called it a serial about cereal. Of the projected trilogy he was able to complete *The Octopus* (1901) and *The Pit* (posthumous, 1903). A third novel would presumably have examined an Old World famine induced by wheat-shortage. The short story here reprinted is a typical example of his attack on the gigantic evils of monopoly and speculation in vital foodstuffs. His treatment of the subject brought Norris to full stature, and in his hands the novel becomes an instrument of great documentary power. Through both novels the wheat flows eastward like an irresistible subterranean river. In *The Octopus*, wheatgrowers of California's San Joaquin valley are strangled by the steel tentacles of the mortgage-holding railroad. The wheat flows on. Curtis Jadwin, financier of *The Pit*, corners wheat in a bull market; but the mighty stream only sweeps his fortune and his health away. Growers and traders die and are forgotten; but the wheat becomes a symbol of immortality, of life constantly renewed and therefore everlasting.

For Norris's theory of the novel, see his *The Responsibilities of the Novelist* (New York, 1903).

K. A. Lohf and E. P. Sheahy, *Frank Norris, a Bibliography*, Los Gatos, California, 1959.
Collected Writings of Frank Norris, 10 vols., New York, 1928.
The Complete Works of Frank Norris, 10 vols., Garden City, N. Y., 1928.
Frank Norris of "The Wave": Stories and Sketches from the San Francisco Weekly, 1893–1897, Oscar Lewis, ed., San Francisco, 1931.
Ernest Marchand, *Frank Norris: A Study*, Stanford University Press, 1942.
C. G. Norris, *Frank Norris, 1870–1902*, New York, 1914 (pamphlet).
Franklin Walker, *Frank Norris, a Biography*, New York, 1932.

» » A DEAL IN WHEAT « «

I

THE BEAR—WHEAT AT SIXTY-TWO

As Sam Lewiston backed the horse into the shafts of his buckboard and began hitching the tugs to the whiffletree, his wife came out from the kitchen door of the house and drew near, and stood for some time at the horse's head, her arms folded and her apron rolled around them. For a long moment neither spoke. They had talked over the situation so long and so comprehensively the night before that there seemed to be nothing more to say.

The time was late in the summer, the place a ranch in southwestern Kansas, and Lewiston and his wife were two of a vast population of farmers, wheat growers, who at that moment were passing through a crisis—a crisis that at any moment might culminate in tragedy. Wheat was down to sixty-six.

At length Emma Lewiston spoke.

"Well," she hazarded, looking vaguely out across the ranch toward the horizon, leagues distant; "well, Sam, there's always that offer of brother Joe's. We can quit—and go to Chicago —if the worst comes."

"And give up!" exclaimed Lewiston, running the lines through the torets. "Leave the ranch! Give up! After all these years!"

His wife made no reply for the moment. Lewiston climbed into the buckboard and gathered up the lines. "Well, here goes for the last try, Emmie," he said. "Good-by, girl. Maybe things will look better in town to-day."

"Maybe," she said gravely. She kissed her husband good-by and stood for some time looking after the buckboard traveling toward the town in a moving pillar of dust.

"I don't know," she murmured at length; "I don't know just how we're going to make out."

When he reached town, Lewiston tied the horse to the iron railing in front of the Odd Fellows' Hall, the ground floor of which was occupied by the post-office, and went across the street and up the stairway of a building of brick and granite—quite the most pretentious structure of the town—and knocked at a door upon the first landing. The door was furnished with a pane of frosted glass, on which, in gold letters, was inscribed "Bridges & Co., Grain Dealers."

Bridges himself, a middle-aged man who wore a velvet skullcap and who was smoking a Pittsburg stogie, met the farmer at the counter and the two exchanged perfunctory greetings.

"Well," said Lewiston, tentatively, after a while.

"Well, Lewiston," said the other, "I can't take that wheat of yours at any better than sixty-two."

"Sixty-*two*."

"It's the Chicago price that does it, Lewiston. Truslow is bearing the stuff for all he's worth. It's Truslow and the bear clique that stick the knife into us. The price broke again this morning. We've just got a wire."

"Good heavens," murmured Lewiston, looking vaguely from side to side. "That—that ruins me. I *can't* carry my grain any longer—what with storage charges and—and—Bridges, I don't see just how I'm going to make out. Sixty-two cents a bushel! Why, man, what with this and with that it's cost me nearly a dollar a bushel to raise that wheat, and now Truslow—"

He turned away abruptly with a quick gesture of infinite discouragement.

He went down the stairs, and making his way to where his buckboard was hitched, got in, and, with eyes vacant, the reins slipping and sliding in his limp, half-open hands, drove slowly back to the ranch. His wife had seen him coming, and met him as he drew up before the barn.

"Well?" she demanded.

"Emmie," he said as he got out of the buckboard, laying his arm across her shoulder, "Emmie, I guess we'll take up with Joe's offer. We'll go to Chicago. We're cleaned out!"

II

THE BULL—WHEAT AT A DOLLAR-TEN

. . . —*and said Party of the Second Part further covenants and agrees to merchandise such wheat in foreign ports, it being understood and agreed between the Party of the First Part and the Party of the Second Part that the wheat hereinbefore mentioned is released and sold to the Party of the Second Part for export purposes only, and not for consumption or distribution within the boundaries of the United States of America or of Canada.*

"Now, Mr. Gates, if you will sign for Mr. Truslow, I guess that'll be all," remarked Hornung when he had finished reading.

Hornung affixed his signature to the two documents and passed them over to Gates, who signed for his principal client, Truslow—or, as he had been called ever since he had gone into the fight against Hornung's corner—the Great Bear. Hornung's secretary was called in and witnessed the signatures, and Gates thrust the contract into his Gladstone bag and stood up, smoothing his hat.

"You will deliver the warehouse receipts for the grain," began Gates.

"I'll send a messenger to Truslow's office before noon," interrupted Hornung. "You can pay by certified check through the Illinois Trust people."

When the other had taken himself off, Hornung sat for some moments gazing abstractedly toward his office windows, thinking over the whole matter. He had just agreed to release to Truslow, at the rate of one dollar and ten cents per bushel, one hundred thousand out of the two million and odd bushels of wheat that he, Hornung, controlled, or actually owned. And for the moment he was wondering if, after all, he had done wisely in not goring the Great Bear to actual financial death. He had made him pay one hundred thousand dollars. Truslow was good for this amount. Would it not have been better to have put a prohibitive figure on the grain and forced the Bear into bankruptcy? True, Hornung would then be without his enemy's money, but Truslow would have been eliminated from the situation, and that—so Hornung told himself—was always a consummation most devoutly, strenuously and diligently to be striven for. Truslow once dead was dead, but the Bear was never more dangerous than when desperate.

"But so long as he can't get *wheat*," muttered Hornung at the end of his reflections, "he can't hurt me. And he can't get it. That I *know*."

For Hornung controlled the situation. So far back as the February of that year an "unknown bull" had been making his presence felt on the floor of the Board of Trade. By the middle of March the commercial reports of the daily press had begun to speak of "the powerful bull clique"; a few weeks later that legendary condition of affairs implied and epitomized in the magic words "Dollar Wheat" had been attained, and by the first of April, when the price had been boosted to one dollar and ten cents a bushel, Hornung had disclosed his hand, and in place of mere rumors, the definite and authoritative news that May wheat had been cornered in the Chicago Pit went flashing around the world from Liverpool to Odessa and from Duluth to Buenos Ayres.

It was—as the veteran operators were persuaded—Truslow himself who had made Hornung's corner possible. The Great Bear had for once overreached himself, and, believing himself all-powerful, had hammered the price just the fatal fraction too far down. Wheat had gone to sixty-two—for the time, and under the circumstances, an abnormal price. When the reaction came it was tremendous. Hornung saw his chance, seized it, and in a few months had turned the tables, had cornered the product, and virtually driven the bear clique out of the pit.

On the same day that the delivery of the hundred thousand bushels was made to Truslow, Hornung met his broker at his lunch club.

"Well," said the latter, "I see you let go that line of stuff to Truslow."

Hornung nodded; but the broker added:

"Remember, I was against it from the very beginning. I know we've cleared up over a hundred thou'. I would have fifty times preferred to have lost twice that and *smashed Truslow dead.* Bet you what you like he makes us pay for it somehow."

"Huh!" grunted his principal. "How about insurance and warehouse charges, and carrying expenses on that lot? Guess we'd have had to pay those, too, if we'd held on."

But the other put up his chin, unwilling to be persuaded. "I won't sleep easy," he declared, "till Truslow is busted."

III

THE PIT

Just as Going mounted the steps on the edge of the pit the great gong struck, a roar of a hundred voices developed with the swiftness of successive explosions, the rush of a hundred men surging downward to the centre of the pit filled the air with the stamp and grind of feet, a hundred hands in eager strenuous gestures tossed upward from out the brown of the crowd, the official reporter in his cage on the margin of the pit leaned far forward with straining ear to catch the opening bid, and another day of battle was begun.

Since the sale of the hundred thousand bushels of wheat to Truslow the "Hornung crowd" had steadily shouldered the price higher until on this particular morning it stood at one dollar and a half. That was Hornung's price. No one else had any grain to sell.

But not ten minutes after the opening, Going was surprised out of all countenance to hear shouted from the other side of the pit these words:

"Sell May at one-fifty."

Going was for the moment touching elbows with Kimbark on one side and with Merriam on the other, all three belonging to the "Hornung crowd." Their answering challenge of "*Sold*" was as the voice of one man. They did not pause to reflect upon the strangeness of the circumstance. (That was for afterward.) Their response to the offer was as unconscious as reflex action and almost as rapid, and before the pit was well aware of what had happened the transaction of one thousand bushels was down upon Going's trading-card and fifteen hundred dollars had changed hands. But here was a marvel—the whole available supply of wheat cornered, Hornung master of the situation, invincible, unassailable; yet behold a man willing to sell, a Bear bold enough to raise his head.

"That was Kennedy, wasn't it, who made that offer?" asked Kimbark, as Going noted down the trade—"Kennedy, that new man?"

"Yes; who do you suppose he's selling for; who's willing to go short at this stage of the game?"

"Maybe he ain't short."

"Short! Great heavens, man; where'd he get the stuff?"

"Blamed if I know. We can account for every handful of May. Steady! Oh, there he goes again."

"Sell a thousand May at one-fifty," vociferated the bear-broker, throwing out his hand, one finger raised to indicate the number of "contracts" offered. This time it was evident that he was attacking the Hornung crowd deliberately, for, ignoring the jam of traders that swept toward him, he looked across the pit to where Going and Kimbark were shouting "*Sold! Sold!*" and nodded his head.

A second time Going made memoranda of the trade, and either the Hornung holdings were increased by two thousand bushels of May wheat or the Hornung bank account swelled by at least three thousand dollars of some unknown short's money.

Of late—so sure was the bull crowd of its position—no one had even thought of glancing at the inspection sheet on the bulletin board. But now one of Going's messengers hurried up to him with the announcement that this sheet showed receipts at Chicago for that morning of twenty-five thousand bushels, and not credited to Hornung. Some one had got hold of a line of wheat overlooked by the "clique" and was dumping it upon them.

"Wire the Chief," said Going over his shoulder to Merriam. This one struggled out of the

crowd, and on a telegraph blank scribbled:

"Strong bear movement—New man—Kennedy—Selling in lots of five contracts—Chicago receipts twenty-five thousand."

The message was despatched, and in a few moments the answer came back, laconic, of military terseness.

"Support the market."

And Going obeyed, Merriam and Kimbark [11] following, the new broker fairly throwing the wheat at them in thousand-bushel lots.

"Sell May at 'fifty; sell May; sell May." A moment's indecision, an instant's hesitation, the first faint suggestion of weakness, and the market would have broken under them. But for the better part of four hours they stood their ground, taking all that was offered, in constant communication with the Chief, and from time [20] to time stimulated and steadied by his brief, unvarying command:

"Support the market."

At the close of the session they had bought in the twenty-five thousand bushels of May. Hornung's position was as stable as a rock, and the price closed even with the opening figure —one dollar and a half.

But the morning's work was the talk of all La Salle Street. Who was back of that raid? [30] What was the meaning of this unexpected selling? For weeks the Pit trading had been merely nominal. Truslow, the Great Bear, from whom the most serious attack might have been expected, had gone to his country seat at Geneva Lake, in Wisconsin, declaring himself to be out of the market entirely. He went bass fishing every day. [38]

IV

THE BELT LINE

On a certain day toward the middle of the month, at a time when the mysterious Bear had unloaded some eighty thousand bushels upon Hornung, a conference was held in the library of Hornung's home. His broker attended it, and also a clean-faced, bright-eyed individual [50] whose name of Cyrus Ryder might have been found upon the pay-roll of a rather well-known detective agency. For upward of half an hour after the conference began the detective spoke, the other two listening attentively, gravely.

"Then, last of all," concluded Ryder, "I made out I was a hobo, and began stealing rides on the Belt Line Railroad. Know the road? It just circles Chicago. Truslow owns it. Yes? Well, then I began to catch on. I noticed that cars of certain numbers—thirty-one naught thirty-four, thirty-two one ninety—well, the numbers don't matter, but anyhow, these cars were always switched on to the sidings by Mr. Truslow's main elevator D soon as they came in. The wheat was shunted in, and they were pulled out again. Well, I spotted one car and stole a ride on her. Say, look here, *that car went right around the city on the Belt, and came back to D again, and the same wheat in her all the time.* The grain was reinspected— it was raw, I tell you—and the warehouse receipts made out just as though the stuff had come in from Kansas or Iowa."

"The same wheat all the time!" interrupted Hornung.

"The same wheat—your wheat, that you sold to Truslow."

"Great snakes!" ejaculated Hornung's broker. "Truslow never took it abroad at all."

"Took it abroad! Say, he's just been running it around Chicago, like the supers in 'Shenandoah,' round an' round, so you'd think it was a new lot, an' selling it back to you again."

"No wonder we couldn't account for so much wheat."

"Bought it from us at one-ten, and made us buy it back—our own wheat—at one-fifty."

Hornung and his broker looked at each other in silence for a moment. Then all at once Hornung struck the arm of his chair with his fist and exploded in a roar of laughter. The broker stared for one bewildered moment, then followed his example.

"Sold! Sold!" shouted Hornung almost gleefully. "Upon my soul it's as good as a Gilbert and Sullivan show. And we—Oh, Lord! Billy, shake on it, and hats off to my distinguished friend, Truslow. He'll be President some day. Hey! What? Prosecute him? Not I."

"He's done us out of a neat hatful of dollars for all that," observed the broker, suddenly grave.

"Billy, it's worth the price."

"We've got to make it up somehow."

"Well, tell you what. We were going to boost the price to one seventy-five next week, and make that our settlement figure."

"Can't do it now. Can't afford it."

"No. Here; we'll let out a big link; we'll put wheat at two dollars, and let it go at that."

"Two it is, then," said the broker.

V

THE BREAD LINE

The street was very dark and absolutely deserted. It was a district on the "South Side," not far from the Chicago River, given up largely to wholesale stores, and after nightfall was empty of all life. The echoes slept but lightly hereabouts, and the slightest footfall, the faintest noise, woke them upon the instant and sent them clamoring up and down the length of the pavement between the iron-shuttered fronts. The only light visible came from the side door of a certain "Vienna" bakery, where at one o'clock in the morning loaves of bread were given away to any who should ask. Every evening about nine o'clock the outcasts began to gather about the side door. The stragglers came in rapidly, and the line—the "bread line," as it was called—began to form. By midnight it was usually some hundred yards in length, stretching almost the entire length of the block.

Toward ten in the evening, his coat collar turned up against the fine drizzle that pervaded the air, his hands in his pockets, his elbows gripping his sides, Sam Lewiston came up and silently took his place at the end of the line.

Unable to conduct his farm upon a paying basis at the time when Truslow, the "Great Bear," had sent the price of grain down to sixty-two cents a bushel, Lewiston had turned over his entire property to his creditors, and, leaving Kansas for good, had abandoned farming, and had left his wife at her sister's boarding-house in Topeka with the understanding that she was to join him in Chicago so soon as he had found a steady job. Then he had come to Chicago and had turned workman. His brother Joe conducted a small hat factory on Archer Avenue, and for a time he found there a meagre employment. But difficulties had occurred, times were bad, the hat factory was involved in debts, the repealing of a certain import duty on manufactured felt overcrowded the home market with cheap Belgian and French products, and in the end his brother had resigned and gone to Milwaukee.

Thrown out of work, Lewiston drifted aimlessly about Chicago, from pillar to post, working a little, earning here a dollar, there a dime, but always sinking, sinking, till at last the ooze of the lowest bottom dragged at his feet and the rush of the great ebb went over him and engulfed him and shut him from the light, and a park bench became his home and the "bread line" his chief makeshift of subsistence.

He stood now in the infolding drizzle, sodden, stupefied with fatigue. Before and behind stretched the line. There was no talking. There was no sound. The street was empty. It was so still that the passing of a cable-car in the adjoining thoroughfare grated like prolonged rolling explosions, beginning and ending at immeasurable distances. The drizzle descended incessantly. After a long time midnight struck.

There was something ominous and gravely impressive in this interminable line of dark figures, close-pressed, soundless; a crowd, yet absolutely still; a close-packed, silent file, waiting, waiting in the vast deserted night-ridden street; waiting without a word, without a movement, there under the night and under the slow-moving mists of rain.

Few in the crowd were professional beggars. Most of them were workmen, long since out of work, forced into idleness by long-continued "hard times," by ill luck, by sickness. To them the "bread line" was a godsend. At least they could not starve. Between jobs here in the end was something to hold them up—a small platform, as it were, above the sweep of black water, where for a moment they might pause and take breath before the plunge.

The period of waiting on this night of rain seemed endless to those silent, hungry men; but at length there was a stir. The line moved. The side door opened. Ah, at last! They were going to hand out the bread.

But instead of the usual white-aproned under-cook with his crowded hampers there now appeared in the doorway a new man—a young fellow who looked like a bookkeeper's assistant. He bore in his hand a placard, which he tacked to the outside of the door. Then he disappeared within the bakery, locking the door after him.

A shudder of poignant despair, an unformed, inarticulate sense of calamity, seemed to run from end to end of the line. What had happened? Those in the rear, unable to read the placard, surged forward, a sense of bitter disappointment clutching at their hearts.

The line broke up, disintegrated into a shapeless throng—a throng that crowded forward and collected in front of the shut door whereon the placard was affixed. Lewiston, with the others, pushed forward. On the placard he read these words:

"Owing to the fact that the price of grain has been increased to two dollars a bushel, there will be no distribution of bread from this bakery until further notice."

Lewiston turned away, dumb, bewildered. Till morning he walked the streets, going on without purpose, without direction. But now at last his luck had turned. Overnight the wheel of his fortunes had creaked and swung upon its axis, and before noon he had found a job in the street-cleaning brigade. In the course of time he rose to be first shift-boss, then deputy inspector, then inspector, promoted to the dignity of driving a red wagon with rubber tires and drawing a salary instead of mere wages. The wife was sent for and a new start made.

But Lewiston never forgot. Dimly he began to see the significance of things. Caught once in the cogs and wheels of a great and terrible engine, he had seen—none better—its workings. Of all the men who had vainly stood in the "bread line" on that rainy night in early summer, he, perhaps, had been the only one who had struggled up to the surface again. How many others had gone down in the great ebb? Grim question; he dared not think how many.

He had seen the two ends of a great wheat operation—a battle between Bear and Bull. The stories (subsequently published in the city's press) of Truslow's counter move in selling Hornung his own wheat, supplied the unseen section. The farmer—he who raised the wheat—was ruined upon one hand; the working-man—he who consumed it—was ruined upon the other. But between the two, the great operators, who never saw the wheat they traded in, bought and sold the world's food, gambled in the nourishment of entire nations, practiced their tricks, their chicanery and oblique shifty "deals," were reconciled in their differences, and went on through their appointed way, jovial, contented, enthroned, and unassailable.

1901   1902

PAUL ELMER MORE

1864–1937

THREE MEMBERS of what was called in the 1920's "the older generation of critics" will not be forgotten: W. C. Brownell (1851–1928), Irving Babbitt (1865–1933), and Paul Elmer More. Of these More is acknowledged to have been the ablest. In seeking to ameliorate the crudeness and provincialism of our life and literature Brownell could only suggest that Americans cultivate taste and decorum, guided by French standards. Professor Babbitt's almost fanatical belief that all the ills of modern society can be ascribed to the influence of the heresies of the Romantics, especially Rousseau, narrowed his judgments and weakened his defenses. More was not subject to the disabilities which cramped Brownell and Babbitt. A scholar of the best kind, notwithstanding his dislike of the ways of modern literary scholarship, widely read in the ancient and modern literatures, More was also supported, as the other two men were not, by the Anglo-Catholic faith which gave substance and relevance to his critical beliefs.

Born in St. Louis in 1864, More was graduated from Washington University in 1887 and pursued graduate studies in Sanscrit and Pali at Harvard. His friendship with Irving Babbitt was formed during these years. After a brief experience as a teacher at Bryn Mawr, More decided that teaching was not his lifework. He retired in 1897 to a farmhouse near Shelburne, New Hampshire, and there "for three summers and two winters," as he later said, "with no human habitation in view, and with only a dog, named *Râj* after the canine hero of the last book of the *Mahâbhârata*, and a cat for constant companions, I took upon myself to live as a hermit after a mild Epicurean fashion of my own." In acknowledgment of the reading and thinking he accomplished in those years, More later called his critical writings, collected in eleven volumes between 1904 and 1921, *Shelburne Essays.*

From 1901 to 1903 More was literary editor of *The Independent*, and from 1903 to 1909 of *The New York Evening Post.* Many of his best critical essays appeared in the literary supplement of *The Post* and in *The Nation*, which he edited from 1909 until 1914. In 1914 he retired to Princeton, his home for the rest of his life. Princeton University welcomed him as a lecturer in Greek philosophy and here, in his later years, his ideas greatly influenced the work of a group of younger scholars in the humanities.

Between 1921 and 1931 More published *The Greek Tradition*, a work in five volumes which surveys the process through which Greek thought was merged in the Christian tradition. In 1928 he resumed the *Shelburne Essays* in a new series. The first of these three volumes contains, in "The Demon of the Absolute," the best statement of More's critical position. In the last year of his life appeared *Pages from an Oxford Diary*, which reveals, in moving prose, the nature of the faith which had sustained him. An earlier, more explicit and less personal, presentation of his religion is found in *The Sceptical Approach to Religion* (1934).

As a critic More was primarily moved by ethical considerations. Like the other Humanists of the 1920's he deplored the naturalism of contemporary writers and felt that such men as Anderson, Lewis, O'Neill, and Dos Passos had helped to rouse the beast that is in us, "by feeding it with suggestion until it dominates the soul." Since More was seldom concerned with the technical aspects of writing, the formal achievements of some of the new school did not, in his eyes, redeem their faults as "futilitarians."

Following an admirable exposition of the ethical foundations of art in "The Demon of the Absolute," More makes a statement which discloses his chief limitation as a critic: "So far I seem to see my way clear. If you should ask me by what rhetorical devices or by what instrument of representation one poem or one work of art appeals more successfully than another to the higher faculty within us . . . I would reply frankly that the solution of this problem of the imagination may be beyond my powers of critical analysis." Critics of the school of Mr. I. A. Richards would say that this problem is precisely the one on which literary critics should concentrate. In the years after the First World War when writers were especially interested in technical problems, More's indifference to them helped to separate him still farther from the creative writers of that generation.

In his later years, after the Humanist controversy was over, the integrity of More's ideas and the solidity of his judgments, particularly of the older American authors, became apparent to the chastened middle generation of critics. Many of them realized that in attempting to confute More they had been forced to discover their own critical philosophy. On the other side, More regretted the birchings he had given some of his detractors.

M. O. Young, *Paul Elmer More, A Bibliography*, Princeton, 1941.

S. G. Brown, "Toward an American Tradition: Paul Elmer More as Critic," *Sewanee Review*, XLVII (December, 1939), 476–497.

A. H. Dakin, *Paul Elmer More*, Princeton, 1960.

R. M. Davies, *The Humanism of Paul Elmer More*, New York, 1958.

L. J. A. Mercier, *The Challenge of Humanism*, New York, 1933, pp. 201–255.

W. J. Oates, "Paul Elmer More, A Quest of the Spirit," in *The Lives of Eighteen from Princeton*, Princeton, 1946, pp. 302–317.

H. W. Peck, "Some Aspects of the Criticism of Paul Elmer More," *Sewanee Rev.*, XXVI (Jan., 1918), 63–84.

Robert Shafer, *Paul Elmer More and American Criticism*, New Haven, 1935.

M. D. C. Tait, "The Humanism of Paul Elmer More," *University of Toronto Quarterly*, XVI (January, 1947), 109–122.

» » A NOTE ON POE'S METHOD « «

In the Authors Club of New York there hangs a life-size portrait of Poe which engages my attention as often as I visit those chambers. It is a face that might well haunt the dreams of a man for its pathos. On it is stamped the mark of defeat; the very lines of the mouth, the pronounced asymmetry of the two sides, tell only too clearly the secret of broken self-control and the long unsuccessful struggle with insidious habits. In this it is typical, unfortunately, of a whole class of supersensitive, physically unbalanced artists, who have given some basis to the plausible, but I think now rather discredited, theory that would explain all the phenomena of genius by a morbid psychology. But in one thing the face is unlike the type to which it otherwise belongs: there is not the least sign here of that mental relaxation, that loosening of the mind's grasp and determination, which often goes with what must be

called—though the phrase should not be wrongly interpreted in Poe's case—the breakdown of character. On the contrary, the eyes retain the look of intense concentration and logical grip.

And in these features the portrait is true to the original. For one of the distinguishing marks of Poe's work is just the combination of nervous irritability, running even into the morbid, with rigorous intellectual analysis. It is a combination not unknown in other writers of the ultra-romantic group; but it is the exception, and it is carried in Poe to an extreme for which it would be hard to find a parallel. Of his reasoning powers and his delight in the exercise of logical argument, no proof is required; it is sufficient merely to mention his story of *The Gold Bug*, his ingenious detective tales, his uncanny skill in predicting the development of one of Dickens' novels while running as a serial, his uncovering of the automatic chess-player, his *Eureka*. But you will observe that his mind is not directed to ethical abstractions and does not work upon ideas, after the fashion of his great contemporaries in the North; it is rather analytical, and interested in the detection of facts and the dissection of sensations. The difference may be illustrated by two stories in which Hawthorne and Poe have treated a similar theme. One of these is *Ethan Brand*, the most extraordinary and characteristic, in my judgement, of all Hawthorne's shorter works. It is the tale, you will remember, of a lime-burner who, in the long solitary watches of his furnace in the hills, meditates on the secret nature of the Unpardonable Sin, until his mind becomes possessed with this one idea, and he is driven to go down into the world and search among men for the key to the mystery. And he discovers it—discovers it in his own breast—and returns with his hideous knowledge to the lime-kiln. Yet he has committed no crime in the ordinary sense of the word; his wickedness lies in the mere search for the idea, and of his victims we hear only vaguely of a girl, "whom," as the account runs, "with such cold and remorseless purpose, [he] made the subject of a psychological experiment, and wasted, absorbed, and perhaps annihilated her soul, in the process." The effect of the story is ghostly, where Poe would have been ghastly. From *Ethan Brand* turn now to the tale of *The Man of the Crowd*, whom Poe pretends to see passing in the mob of a London street, and, fascinated by the singular countenance of the wretch, follows through the night and the day in his restless hurry from one thronged region of the city to another. "This old man," he exclaims at last, "is the type and genius of deep crime. He refuses to be alone. *He is the man of the crowd*. It will be in vain to follow; for I shall learn no more of him, nor of his deeds. The worst heart of the world is a grosser book than the *Hortulus Animæ*, and perhaps it is but one of the great mercies of God that *er lasst sich nicht lesen*." Poe's is a grim and unforgettable story, as original as Hawthorne's but different. Its power over our imagination depends on the analysis of the sensations connected with crime, whereas in *Ethan Brand* the interest is centred upon the search for the idea of evil in itself.

But if Poe differs from the ethical writers by avoiding what may be called the ideal use of the intellect, he differs also from the great mass of the romantic writers, with whom he is otherwise akin, by insistent use of the intellect in his own way. And this distinction comes out even more sharply in his criticism than in his practice. In three of his essays he has developed his critical theory elaborately and consistently, in *The Poetic Principle*, *The Rationale of Verse*, and *The Philosophy of Composition*, which together form one of the few æsthetic treatises in English of real value. In the first of these, a lecture which was read, it will be remembered in Boston, he lays down his definition of poetry "as *The Rhythmical Creation of Beauty*. Its sole arbiter is taste. With the intellect or with Conscience, it has only collateral relations. Unless incidentally, it has no concern whatever with Duty or with Truth." Some allowance must be made in this definition for the fact that Poe was flaunting his flag resolutely in the face of the ethical folk of Boston, and we shall see in a moment that his "collateral relations" of the intellect, as he expresses it, need a pretty wide interpretation. The next step in his theory brings us to these significant words: "It is in Music, perhaps, that the soul most nearly attains the great end for which, when inspired by the Poetic Sentiment, it struggles—the creation of Supernal Beauty."

This position he maintains in *The Rationale of Verse*, where he declares that verse "cannot be better designated than as an inferior or less capable Music." So far, of course, he is merely adopting one of the familiar commonplaces of the age. The conception of poetry as reaching its normal goal in music was constantly held forth by the early German theorists of the *Romantische Schule*. It is implied in Schleiermacher's declaration that the religious feeling should "accompany all the doings of a man as if it were a holy music; he should do all *with* religion, nothing *through* religion"; it is carried to its dogmatic extreme by Novalis, who sees the consummation of art in "poems which sound melodiously and are full of beautiful words, but without any sense or connexion." The theory may appear absurd, in fact is absurd, when stated in this bald manner; but it is held nevertheless in scarcely less extravagant terms by some of the radical critics of the present day. Now in their practice the poets of this school ordinarily have sought to attain the effect of musical evocation by throwing the thinking part of us under a kind of hypnotic spell which leaves the emotional part of us free to float off in a state of vague revery.

Thus, *Kubla Khan,* the typical poem of the *genre,* was actually composed by Coleridge in his sleep, and its charm upon us is that of a dreamlike magic, beginning anywhere and ending anywhere, lifting us up on luxurious waves of indolent music. No doubt there is verse of this pure evocative quality in our Poe, notably in *The Valley of Unrest* and *The City in the Sea,* and in these lulling cadences of *The Sleeper:*

> At midnight in the month of June,
> I stand beneath the mystic moon.
> An opiate vapour, dewy, dim,
> Exhales from out her golden rim,
> And, softly dripping, drop by drop,
> Upon the quiet mountain top,
> Steals drowsily and musically
> Into the universal valley.

There is, I maintain, an opiate magic in such lines as these equal in potency to anything ever produced by the rhapsodist of Highgate; but it is not, in my opinion, the most characteristic note of Poe. He is even more himself, not when he surrenders his genius to these flowing waves of revery, but when his mind is concentrated and works with a logical precision, with a logical hardness one might almost say, which is the opposite of the ordinary romantic manner. Consider, for instance, the logical structure and completeness of *The Bells:* there, if anywhere in the English tongue, poetry does become pure music and pure beauty, almost to the exclusion of ideas, yet the thing is worked out and its effects calculated with the mathematical finish of a Bach or any other master of counterpoint who composed before spontaneity became identified with genius.

And Poe not only practised this logical concentration, but raised it to a principle of art. We come thus to the third of his æsthetical treatises, that on *The Philosophy of Composition,* in which he sets forth with ruthless frankness the whole method employed by him in composing *The Raven.* According to this extraordinary exhibition of genius at work, having determined to produce a great poem, he first considered what effect he should aim to produce. As beauty in his view was "the sole legitimate province of the poem," his choice was so far decided for him. The "next question referred to the *tone* of its highest manifestation"; and here again his choice was fixed for him by his belief that "all experience has

shown this" tone to be one "of sadness. Beauty of whatever kind, in its supreme development, invariably excites the sensitive soul to tears." To evoke this effect, or any poetical effect, he saw that the refrain is the most universally employed and the most cogent instrument; he would therefore make a refrain the keynote of his poem, selecting for this purpose a word capable of protracted emphasis, melodious in itself, and in the fullest possible keeping with the tone of melancholy. These conditions led him immediately to the word "Nevermore" (suggested, probably, by Byron's famous use of it in *Don Juan*). The next step is the most curious of all. He felt the difficulty that "lay in the reconciliation of this monotony with the exercise of reason on the part of the creature repeating the word." It occurred to him that this difficulty might be obviated by putting the refrain into the mouth of a parrot, but he changed to a raven, "as equally capable of speech, and infinitely more in keeping with the intended *tone.*" He had now to consider what topic, "according to the *universal* understanding of mankind, is the *most* melancholy." Obviously this would be beauty associated with death, "the death, then, of a beautiful woman." This being determined, his task was to bring together his theme and the instrument of his refrain; but we need not pursue him through all the windings of his ingenious plot.

Now what shall be said of this cold-blooded piece of analysis? To many critics it has seemed to be a grand hoax or a bit of unparalleled effrontery. Or at least the whole thing must be taken as an *ex post facto* account, so to speak; for it is impossible that any poem deeply emotional and effective, or any true product of inspiration, should be thus put together like a piece of calculated machinery. And from the ordinary theory and practice of art such an opinion is right. But I am inclined to believe that *The Raven* was actually composed very much as the author explains, and that his essay is not only essentially true to facts but throws a remarkable light on one phase of his genius. I do not mean to say that in all details the reflection on the method to be adopted would precede by an appreciable moment of time the actual invention; the two processes may have gone on together in his mind. The point is that this *conscious* logical analysis was present with him throughout the whole work of composition to an abnormal degree, now preceding, now accompanying, now following the more inscrutable suggestions of the creative faculty. This, I take it, is Poe's original note, a quality which distinguishes his art from that of the other masters of unearthly revery. Here, too, lies the principal sphere of his influence on Baudelaire and the whole line of foreign poets who have imitated him without reaching his supremacy—they could borrow his method, they could not steal his brains.

Judged thus by the achievement in accordance with his own canon of art, Poe must rank high, if not first, among our American poets, and measured by the extent of his influence he would take a prominent place among the poets of Europe. But when we consider the character of his canon in itself, I fear that certain deductions must be made to his fame. We are forced then to question the very validity of his doctrine of truth and beauty. There is no uncertainty as to the nature of his principles, nor, as is often the case with others, is there any discrepancy in him between theory and practice. To go back to the beginning, let me recall a few words from his criticism of Hawthorne, in which he gives precision to his theory by contrasting the provinces of the tale and the poem. "The tale," he there says, "has a point of superiority over the poem. In fact, while the *rhythm* of this latter is an essential aid in the development of the poem's highest idea—the idea of the Beautiful—the artificialities of this rhythm are an insuperable bar to the development of all points of thought and expression which have their basis in *Truth*." We have here merely the insistent application of the doctrine promulgated in the essay on *The Poetic Principle*, that poetry is "the rhythmical creation of beauty," and that "the demands of truth are severe; she has no sympathy with the myrtle; all *that* which is indispensable in Song, is precisely all *that* with which *she* has nothing to do."

Now just what did Poe mean by this distinction, amounting to an opposition, between truth and beauty, and how did he carry it out in execution? In one sense it is manifest that no poet ever was truer than Poe; all that intense concentration of his mind, that logical grip of his theme, was directed in a way to the attainment of truth—to the perfectly and relentlessly true attainment of the effect which he had chosen to produce. Wherein lies the contrast between truth and beauty to which he was always returning in theory? It lies not in

any failure to deal truthfully with his material, but in the restriction of his material to a certain range of emotions and in the exclusion of what he brands as "the heresy of *The Didactic*." This he declares explicitly is the ground of his hostility to the contrary assumption that "the object of all Poetry is Truth." Had he confined his attack to didacticism as a mode of expression, it would have been well; but his unfortunate identification of didacticism with truth cut him off from a whole range of material, the highest and finest emotions of the human breast, which need not be didactical at all in form, but are connected with the intuition of moral truth. I mean that kind of emotion, to take an extreme case, which is stirred in Emerson's ethical epigrams. It is a question of values. Beautiful as is much of Poe's work, true as it is, I think an honest criticism must add that it leaves almost untouched the richest source of human feeling. Only perhaps one should except from this limitation the stanzas *To Helen*, in which Poe's distinctive sense of unearthly beauty lies close to the Platonic vision of the Ideal. If these stanzas were written, as tradition has it, when Poe was a mere boy (and they were certainly composed before he had reached his majority), they are one of the most astounding pieces of precocity in literary history—and that even though the two noblest lines stood originally in this comparatively flat form:

> To the beauty of fair Greece
> And the grandeur of old Rome.

And there is this also to be said. Taking truth and beauty as Poe did and as Keats did, Poe, I hold, was the more honest and the less mischievous theorizer than Keats. For taking truth and beauty as they did, Poe was manly and clear-headed in opposing them one to the other; whereas Keats delivered a doctrine as dangerous as it was misleading when he threw out those memorable words,

> Beauty is truth, truth beauty,—that is all
> Ye know on earth, and all ye need to know.

So much by way of extenuation. But we cannot forget, Poe himself never lets us forget, that he was a man to whom life in its outer circumstances was a long experience of unmerciful disaster, and that he had also to contend with an enemy in his own breast, the terrible physical taint whose ravages we see in his countenance. It is natural, but it is none the less unfortunate, that such a man should have developed an æsthetic theory which rejected from the province of poetry any claim of truth beyond that of fidelity to a chosen sensation, and which emphasized so strongly the element of melancholy inherent in the perception of physical beauty. His theory thus, instead of correcting the inevitable trend of a nature like his, rather confirmed him in his temperamental weakness. And so we see him often looking for beauty, and indeed finding it, in the ravages of disease and the ghastly secrets of the tomb. In this field of the abnormal Poe has wrought miracles, reaching his climax in that appalling song of madness which strikes the keynote of *The Fall of the House of Usher*. But we are merely darkening counsel if we set him in competition with those normal poets who deal with the larger and more universal aspects of nature and create loveliness out of the more wholesome emotions of our common humanity. Health is above disease in art as it is in life. Poe remains chiefly the poet of unripe boys and unsound men.

So much must be granted. Yet it is to the honour of Poe that in all his works you will come upon no single spot where the abnormal sinks to the unclean, or where there is an effort to intensify the effect of what is morbid emotionally by an appeal to what is morbid morally. The soul of this man was never tainted. 10 How much that means, how great and near was the danger, can be known by turning to certain of his Continental disciples. The line between them is narrow, but it separates two worlds. Poe does not hesitate to descend for his effects into the very grave where beauty and decay come together; but if you wish to understand the perils he escaped, read after *The Sleeper* one of the poems in which Baudelaire, Poe's avowed imitator and sponsor to Europe, gropes 20 with filthy hands among the mysteries of death.

1923

EDWIN ARLINGTON ROBINSON

1869–1935

THE READING PUBLIC of the nineties and the early years of our century was not ready for poetry such as Robinson's. *The Torrent and the Night Before* (1896), his first book, disregarded the canons of literary taste upheld by such prominent writers as E. C. Stedman, Thomas Bailey Aldrich, and R. W. Gilder. Critics of this school did not realize that Robinson was restoring life to American poetry. The spare, tough language and the conversational accent were the new elements in his style which were chiefly deplored by his earlier contemporaries. Not until 1916, with the publication of *The Man Against the Sky*, did the critics come to recognize his strength.

Robinson was brought up in Gardiner, Maine, the "Tilbury Town" of his poems. This background maintained a lasting influence on his life and thought. His family was prosperous in his boyhood and he grew up in a milieu that really did not understand his "bubble work that only fools pursue." Yet he continued to write—painfully and carefully—always troubled by the realization that his fellow-townsmen thought him an idle dreamer.

After two years at Harvard, Robinson went to New York. Odd jobs, sometimes of the most menial kind, never gave him the security he needed; even the intercession of President Roosevelt in 1905 resulted only in a temporary post in the New York Customs House. From 1911 he spent his summers in the MacDowell colony in Peterborough, New Hampshire, where he found, at last, the leisure and the society which he needed. In 1921 came the Pulitzer prize for his *Collected Poems;* in 1927, his *Tristram* brought him acclaim and financial success. He had justified his life in the eyes of Tilbury Town.

The years of struggle shadowed Robinson's work; failure and defeat as the world knows them became constant themes. *Captain Craig* (1902) tells of the man who has "failed" yet who has succeeded spiritually as those who condemn him have not. The same idea occurs in "Flammonde," *Matthias at the Door*, and many others. Seeing the First World War as the ruin of our materialistic society, Robinson held out a promise of a new order to come. *Merlin* (1917) and *Lancelot* (1920) portray allegorically the crash of the old order and the hope for the new.

These two Arthurian poems ushered in a succession of long narratives, culminating in *Tristram* (1927), the third member of the Arthurian trilogy. These, with *Captain Craig* and *Amaranth* (1934), are the most rewarding of the narratives; the others hold little interest for the ordinary reader.

Robinson's philosophy was stern but not fatalistic. He believed most men to be only partially alive. Matthias had to be re-born; Jasper saw too late that he was not living at all; Lancelot gave up Guinevere to find the redeeming light. The disparity between appearance and reality is Robinson's theme; his characters are New Englanders and his poetic method the ratiocination of these characters. His style suffers from two faults: the attempt to say too much in too little space, and the opposite tendency to enlarge on the trivial. At his worst he appears as a belated romantic, with no mythology on which to build. At his best he stands with Hawthorne and his contemporaries Frost and O'Neill in his powerful presentation of the interior drama of the soul.

Lillian Lippincott, *A Bibliography of the Writings and Criticisms of Edwin Arlington Robinson*, Boston, 1937.
Collected Poems of Edwin Arlington Robinson, New York, 1937.
Selected Letters of Edwin Arlington Robinson, New York, 1940.
Ellsworth Barnard, *Edwin Arlington Robinson, a Critical Study*, New York, 1952.
E. S. Fussell, *Edwin Arlington Robinson*, Berkeley, California, 1954.
Hermann Hagedorn, *Edwin Arlington Robinson, a Biography*, New York, 1938.
Emery Neff, *Edwin Arlington Robinson*, New York, 1948.
Yvor Winters, *Edwin Arlington Robinson*, New York, 1947.

RICHARD CORY

Whenever Richard Cory went down town,
We people on the pavement looked at him:
He was a gentleman from sole to crown,
Clean favored, and imperially slim.

And he was always quietly arrayed,
And he was always human when he talked;
But still he fluttered pulses when he said,
"Good-morning," and he glittered when he
    walked.

And he was rich—yes, richer than a king—
And admirably schooled in every grace: 10
In fine, we thought that he was every thing
To make us wish that we were in his place.

So on we worked, and waited for the light,
And went without the meat, and cursed the
    bread;

And Richard Cory, one calm summer night,
Went home and put a bullet through his head.
    1897

TWO MEN

There be two men of all mankind
    That I should like to know about;
But search and question where I will,
    I cannot ever find them out.

Melchizedek, he praised the Lord,
    And gave some wine to Abraham;
But who can tell what else he did
    Must be more learned than I am.

Ucalegon, he lost his house
    When Agamemnon came to Troy;   10
But who can tell me who he was—
    I'll pray the gods to give him joy.

There be two men of all mankind
  That I'm forever thinking on:
They chase me everywhere I go,—
  Melchizedek, Ucalegon.   1897

FOR A DEAD LADY

No more with overflowing light
Shall fill the eyes that now are faded,
Nor shall another's fringe with night
Their woman-hidden world as they did.
No more shall quiver down the days
The flowing wonder of her ways,
Whereof no language may requite
The shifting and the many-shaded.

The grace, divine, definitive,
Clings only as a faint forestalling;   10
The laugh that love could not forgive
Is hushed, and answers to no calling;
The forehead and the little ears
Have gone where Saturn keeps the years;
The breast where roses could not live
Has done with rising and with falling.

The beauty, shattered by the laws
That have creation in their keeping,
No longer trembles at applause,
Or ever children that are sleeping;   20
And we who delve in beauty's lore
Know all that we have known before
Of what inexorable cause
Makes Time so vicious in his reaping.
                         1909

THE MASTER[1]

(Lincoln)

A flying word from here and there
Had sown the name at which we sneered,
But soon the name was everywhere,
To be reviled and then revered:
A presence to be loved and feared,
We cannot hide it, or deny
That we, the gentlemen who jeered,
May be forgotten by and by.

He came when days were perilous
And hearts of men were sore beguiled;   10
And having made his note of us,

[1] Supposed to have been written not long after the Civil War.
[Robinson's note.]

He pondered and was reconciled.
Was ever master yet so mild
As he, and so untamable?
We doubted, even when he smiled,
Not knowing what he knew so well.

He knew that undeceiving fate
Would shame us whom he served unsought;
He knew that he must wince and wait—
The jest of those for whom he fought;   20
He knew devoutly what he thought
Of us and of our ridicule;
He knew that we must all be taught
Like little children in a school.

We gave a glamour to the task
That he encountered and saw through,
But little of us did he ask,
And little did we ever do.
And what appears if we review
The season when we railed and chaffed?   30
It is the face of one who knew
That we were learning while we laughed.

The face that in our vision feels
Again the venom that we flung,
Transfigured to the world reveals
The vigilance to which we clung.
Shrewd, hallowed, harassed, and among
The mysteries that are untold,
The face we see was never young
Nor could it wholly have been old.   40

For he, to whom we had applied
Our shopman's test of age and worth,
Was elemental when he died,
As he was ancient at his birth:
The saddest among kings of earth,
Bowed with a galling crown, this man
Met rancor with a cryptic mirth,
Laconic—and Olympian.

The love, the grandeur, and the fame
Are bounded by the world alone;   50
The calm, the smouldering, and the flame
Of awful patience were his own:
With him they are forever flown
Past all our fond self-shadowings,
Wherewith we cumber the Unknown
As with inept, Icarian wings.

For we were not as other men:
'Twas ours to soar and his to see;
But we are coming down again,
And we shall come down pleasantly;   60

Nor shall we longer disagree
On what it is to be sublime,
But flourish in our perigee
And have one Titan at a time.   1910

PASA THALASSA THALASSA

"The sea is everywhere the sea."

I

Gone—faded out of the story, the sea-faring
    friend I remember?
Gone for a decade, they say: never a word or a
    sign.
Gone with his hard red face that only his
    laughter could wrinkle,
Down where men go to be still, by the old way
    of the sea.

Never again will he come, with rings in his ears
    like a pirate,
Back to be living and seen, here with his roses
    and vines;
Here where the tenants are shadows and echoes
    of years uneventful,
Memory meets the event, told from afar by the
    sea.

Smoke that floated and rolled in the twilight
    away from the chimney
Floats and rolls no more. Wheeling and falling,
    instead,   10
Down with a twittering flash go the smooth
    and inscrutable swallows,
Down to the place made theirs by the cold
    work of the sea.

Roses have had their day, and the dusk is on
    yarrow and wormwood—
Dusk that is over the grass, drenched with
    memorial dew;
Trellises lie like bones in a ruin that once was
    a garden,
Swallows have lingered and ceased, shadows
    and echoes are all.

II

Where is he lying to-night, as I turn away
    down to the valley,
Down where the lamps of men tell me the
    streets are alive?
Where shall I ask, and of whom, in the town
    or on land or on water,
News of a time and a place buried alike and
    with him?   20

Few now remain who may care, nor may they
    be wiser for caring,
Where or what manner the doom, whether by
    day or by night;
Whether in Indian deeps or on flood-laden
    fields of Atlantis,
Or by the roaring Horn, shrouded in silence he
    lies.

Few now remain who return by the weed-
    weary path to his cottage,
Drawn by the scene as it was—met by the
    chill and the change;
Few are alive who report, and few are alive
    who remember,
More of him now than a name carved some-
    where on the sea.

"Where is he lying?" I ask, and the lights in
    the valley are nearer;
Down to the streets I go, down to the murmur
    of men.   30
Down to the roar of the sea in a ship may be
    well for another—
Down where he lies to-night, silent, and under
    the storms.   1910

MINIVER CHEEVY

Miniver Cheevy, child of scorn,
    Grew lean while he assailed the seasons;
He wept that he was ever born,
    And he had reasons.

Miniver loved the days of old
    When swords were bright and steeds were
        prancing;
The vision of a warrior bold
    Would set him dancing.

Miniver sighed for what was not,
    And dreamed, and rested from his labors;
He dreamed of Thebes and Camelot,   11
    And Priam's neighbors.

Miniver mourned the ripe renown
    That made so many a name so fragrant;
He mourned Romance, now on the town,
    And Art, a vagrant.

Miniver loved the Medici,
    Albeit he had never seen one;
He would have sinned incessantly
    Could he have been one.   20

Miniver cursed the commonplace
  And eyed a khaki suit with loathing:
He missed the mediæval grace
  Of iron clothing.

Miniver scorned the gold he sought,
  But sore annoyed was he without it;
Miniver thought, and thought, and thought,
  And thought about it.

Miniver Cheevy, born too late,
  Scratched his head and kept on thinking; 30
Miniver coughed, and called it fate,
  And kept on drinking.
1908?   1910

FLAMMONDE

The man Flammonde, from God knows where,
With firm address and foreign air,
With news of nations in his talk,
And something royal in his walk,
With glint of iron in his eyes,
But never doubt, nor yet surprise,
Appeared, and stayed, and held his head
As one by kings accredited.

Erect, with his alert repose
About him, and about his clothes,   10
He pictured all tradition hears
Of what we owe to fifty years.
His cleansing heritage of taste
Paraded neither want nor waste;
And what he needed for his fee
To live, he borrowed graciously.

He never told us what he was,
Or what mischance, or other cause,
Had banished him from better days
To play the Prince of Castaways.   20
Meanwhile he played surpassing well
A part, for most, unplayable;
In fine, one pauses, half afraid
To say for certain that he played.

For that, one may as well forego
Conviction as to yes or no;
Nor can I say just how intense
Would then have been the difference
To several, who, having striven
In vain to get what he was given,   30
Would see the stranger taken on
By friends not easy to be won.

Moreover, many a malcontent
He soothed and found munificent;
His courtesy beguiled and foiled
Suspicion that his years were soiled;
His mien distinguished any crowd,
His credit strengthened when he bowed;
And women, young and old, were fond
Of looking at the man Flammonde.   40

There was a woman in our town
On whom the fashion was to frown;
But while our talk renewed the tinge
Of a long-faded scarlet fringe,
The man Flammonde saw none of that,
And what he saw we wondered at—
That none of us, in her distress,
Could hide or find our littleness.

There was a boy that all agreed
Had shut within him the rare seed   50
Of learning. We could understand,
But none of us could lift a hand.
The man Flammonde appraised the youth,
And told a few of us the truth;
And thereby, for a little gold,
A flowered future was unrolled.

There were two citizens who fought
For years and years, and over nought;
They made life awkward for their friends,
And shortened their own dividends.   60
The man Flammonde said what was wrong
Should be made right; nor was it long
Before they were again in line,
And had each other in to dine.

And these I mention are but four
Of many out of many more.
So much for them. But what of him—
So firm in every look and limb?
What small satanic sort of kink
Was in his brain? What broken link   70
Withheld him from the destinies
That came so near to being his?

What was he, when we came to sift
His meaning, and to note the drift
Of incommunicable ways
That make us ponder while we praise?
Why was it that his charm revealed
Somehow the surface of a shield?
What was it that we never caught?
What was he, and what was he not?   80

How much it was of him we met
We cannot ever know; nor yet
Shall all he gave us quite atone
For what was his, and his alone;
Nor need we now, since he knew best,
Nourish an ethical unrest:
Rarely at once will nature give
The power to be Flammonde and live.

We cannot know how much we learn
From those who never will return,   90
Until a flash of unforeseen
Remembrance falls on what has been.
We've each a darkening hill to climb;
And this is why, from time to time
In Tilbury Town, we look beyond
Horizons for the man Flammonde.
1915–1916   1916

THE DARK HOUSE

Where a faint light shines alone,
Dwells a Demon I have known.
Most of you had better say
"The Dark House," and go your way.
Do not wonder if I stay.

For I know the Demon's eyes,
And their lure that never dies.
Banish all your fond alarms,
For I know the foiling charms
Of her eyes and of her arms,   10

And I know that in one room
Burns a lamp as in a tomb;
And I see the shadow glide,
Back and forth, of one denied
Power to find himself outside.

There he is who is my friend,
Damned, he fancies, to the end—
Vanquished, ever since a door
Closed, he thought, for evermore
On the life that was before.   20

And the friend who knows him best
Sees him as he sees the rest
Who are striving to be wise
While a Demon's arms and eyes
Hold them as a web would flies.

All the words of all the world,
Aimed together and then hurled,
Would be stiller in his ears

Than a closing of still shears
On a thread made out of years.   30

But there lives another sound,
More compelling, more profound;
There's a music, so it seems,
That assuages and redeems,
More than reason, more than dreams.

There's a music yet unheard
By the creature of the word,
Though it matters little more
Than a wave-wash on a shore—
Till a Demon shuts a door.   40

So, if he be very still
With his Demon, and one will,
Murmurs of it may be blown
To my friend who is alone
In a room that I have known.

After that from everywhere
Singing life will find him there;
Then the door will open wide,
And my friend, again outside,
Will be living, having died.   50
                                            1916

THE DARK HILLS

Dark hills at evening in the west,
    Where sunset hovers like a sound
Of golden horns that sang to rest
    Old bones of warriors under ground,
Far now from all the bannered ways
    Where flash the legions of the sun,
You fade—as if the last of days
    Were fading and all wars were done.
                                            1920

DEMOS

I

All you that are enamored of my name
    And least intent on what most I require,
    Beware; for my design and your desire,
Deplorably, are not as yet the same.
Beware, I say, the failure and the shame
    Of losing that for which you now aspire
    So blindly, and of hazarding entire
The gift that I was bringing when I came.

Give as I will, I cannot give you sight
    Whereby to see that with you there are
    some   10

To lead you, and be led. But they are dumb
Before the wrangling and the shrill delight
  Of your deliverance that has not come,
And shall not, if I fail you—as I might.

II

So little have you seen of what awaits
  Your fevered glimpse of a democracy
  Confused and foiled with an equality
Not equal to the envy it creates,
That you see not how near you are the gates
  Of an old king who listens fearfully   20
  To you that are outside and are to be
The noisy lords of imminent estates.

Rather be then your prayer that you shall have
  Your kingdom undishonored. Having all,
  See not the great among you for the small,
But hear their silence; for the few shall save
  The many, or the many are to fall—
Still to be wrangling in a noisy grave.   1920

MR. FLOOD'S PARTY

Old Eben Flood, climbing alone one night
Over the hill between the town below
And the forsaken upland hermitage
That held as much as he should ever know
On earth again of home, paused warily.
The road was his with not a native near;
And Eben, having leisure, said aloud,
For no man else in Tilbury Town to hear:

"Well, Mr. Flood, we have the harvest moon
Again, and we may not have many more;   10
The bird is on the wing, the poet says,
And you and I have said it here before.
Drink to the bird." He raised up to the light
The jug that he had gone so far to fill,
And answered huskily: "Well, Mr. Flood,
Since you propose it, I believe I will."

Alone, as if enduring to the end
A valiant armor of scarred hopes outworn,
He stood there in the middle of the road
Like Roland's ghost winding a silent horn.   20
Below him, in the town among the trees,
Where friends of other days had honored him,
A phantom salutation of the dead
Rang thinly till old Eben's eyes were dim.

Then, as a mother lays her sleeping child
Down tenderly, fearing it may awake,
He set the jug down slowly at his feet
With trembling care, knowing that most things
   break
And only when assured that on firm earth
It stood, as the uncertain lives of men   30
Assuredly did not, he paced away,
And with his hand extended paused again:

"Well, Mr. Flood, we have not met like this
In a long time; and many a change has come
To both of us, I fear, since last it was
We had a drop together. Welcome home!"
Convivially returning with himself,
Again he raised the jug up to the light;
And with an acquiescent quaver said:
"Well, Mr. Flood, if you insist, I might.   40

"Only a very little, Mr. Flood—
For auld lang syne. No more, sir; that will do."
So, for the time, apparently it did,
And Eben evidently thought so too;
For soon amid the silver loneliness
Of night he lifted up his voice and sang,
Secure, with only two moons listening,
Until the whole harmonious landscape rang—

"For auld lang syne." The weary throat gave
   out,
The last word wavered; and the song was
   done.   50
He raised again the jug regretfully
And shook his head, and was again alone.
There was not much that was ahead of him,
And there was nothing in the town below—
Where strangers would have shut the many
   doors
That many friends had opened long ago.
1919?   1921

» » « «

ROBERT FROST

1874–

FROST WAS NEARLY forty before his first book of poems appeared. The critical applause and popular acclaim which came in the next forty-five years did nothing to alter his humility, his humanity, or his honesty. Despite periods in which his work seemed out of fashion, or his tone too sly or top-lofty, he long ago won an unassailable position as dean of American poets. Three times a Pulitzer Prize winner, recipient of many honorary degrees both in England and at home, Academy member, Poetry Consultant to the Library of Congress, poet-in-residence at Amherst, Dartmouth, Michigan, and Harvard, the former mill-hand, farmer, poultryman, and school-teacher has been a familiar figure on lecture platforms for the best part of a full lifetime.

His career as writer began not long after his arrival (1885) in New England, with sister and widowed mother, from his birthplace in San Francisco. Between the earliest of his poems in the Nineties and his first published volume lay a twenty-year apprenticeship, marked by poverty and seeming failure, pride, perseverance, and courage. His education included the high school at Lawrence, Massachusetts, where he was valedictorian and class poet, a few months at Dartmouth, four semesters as special student at Harvard, and fifteen years as obscure farmer and teacher in New Hampshire. At twenty-one he married Elinor White (*ob.*, 1938) and in 1912 sold his farm and set out with wife and children for an extended stay in England. "I went to England to be in England," he has said. "I carried my MS. into London in my pocket, left it with David Nutt, and never had to show it to anyone else." When he returned after three years (1912–1915) abroad, his reputation as the maker of *A Boy's Will* (London, 1913) and *North of Boston* (London, 1914) had preceded his arrival, and American editions were soon in print.

Between these volumes and the *Complete Poems*, Frost published eight other collections of verse: *Mountain Interval* (1916), *New Hampshire* (1923), *West-running Brook* (1928), *A Further Range* (1936), *A Witness Tree* (1942), *A Masque of Reason* (1945), *Steeple Bush* (1947), and *A Masque of Mercy* (1947). His major forms are lyrical, including the sonnet in which he excels, but there are also a substantial number of blank-verse narratives and philosophic commentaries. The two masques are one-act playlets, the first a sardonic account of Job's relationship to God and Satan, and the second a latter-day encounter among people whose Biblical analogues include Jonah and St. Paul. Besides these volumes, Frost has published *Selected Poems* (1923, twice revised and enlarged), *Collected Poems* (1930, 1939), and *Complete Poems* (1949). Two valuable prose prefaces set forth his views on poetry: "The Figure A Poem Makes" in *Complete Poems*, and "The Constant Symbol" in the Modern Library edition of his poems.

Frost has rejected the regionalist tag, preferring to describe himself as synecdochist and universalist. To those who argue that his insistent embracement of the country life makes him an escapist, his reply, like that of Thoreau, is that he is a "pursuitist, not an escapist." Although he has suffered occasionally from contumely or critical indifference, he has lived to see the world make a path to his door without sacrifice of his integrity as poet. Nor has his best work shown signs of decay: his concept of organic form and his management of metaphor place him in close contiguity with other "moderns."

Under the almost Jacobean freedom of his blank verse, the iambic footfall is audible, if only as an echo. Yet there is more to his metrics than making fluid the old five-beat line. The secret lies in recapturing what Frost calls *the sound of sense* between which and mere *sound* he discerns an important difference. Folk-speech is musical without apparent artifice because it has a sound of sense which is rooted in the ear's daily experience. It conveys meaning not only through the words themselves but also through the tone and modulation, the speech-rhythm of the sentence. With Wordsworth and Emerson, Frost believes that "the beginning of literary form is in some turn given to the sentence in folk-speech." Poetic words are "the ordinary words that we hear about us, to which the imagination must give an iridescence." Frost is too well schooled in Greek and Latin, too skilled an etymologist, to accept overblown romantic diction. The epigrams in his prose have the spring-water savor of folk-proverbs although, like those in his poetry, they have undergone a considerable sophistication.

Louis and Esther Mertins, *The Intervals of Robert Frost: A Critical Bibliography*, Berkeley, California, 1947.
Complete Poems of Robert Frost, New York, 1949.
R. L. Cook, *The Dimensions of Robert Frost*, New York, 1959.
Sidney Cox, *A Swinger of Birches; A Portrait of Robert Frost*, New York, 1957.
J. F. Lynen, *The Pastoral Art of Robert Frost*, New Haven, 1960.
G. W. Nitchie, *Human Values in the Poetry of Robert Frost*, Durham, N. C., 1960.
E. S. Sergeant, *Robert Frost; The Trial By Existence*, New York, 1960.
Lawrance Thompson, *Fire and Ice: The Art and Thought of Robert Frost*, New York, 1942.
————, *Robert Frost*, Minneapolis, 1959.

» » *From:* A BOY'S WILL « «

MY NOVEMBER GUEST

My Sorrow, when she's here with me,
  Thinks these dark days of autumn rain
Are beautiful as days can be;
She loves the bare, the withered tree;
  She walks the sodden pasture lane.

Her pleasure will not let me stay.
  She talks and I am fain to list:
She's glad the birds are gone away,
She's glad her simple worsted grey
  Is silver now with clinging mist.   10

The desolate, deserted trees,
  The faded earth, the heavy sky,
The beauties she so truly sees,
She thinks I have no eye for these,
  And vexes me for reason why.

Not yesterday I learned to know
  The love of bare November days
Before the coming of the snow,
But it were vain to tell her so,
  And they are better for her praise.   20
                                        1912

A LATE WALK

When I go up through the mowing field,
  The headless aftermath,
Smooth-laid like thatch with the heavy dew,
  Half closes the garden path.

And when I come to the garden ground,
  The whir of sober birds
Up from the tangle of withered weeds
  Is sadder than any words.

A tree beside the wall stands bare,
  But a leaf that lingered brown,   10
Disturbed, I doubt not, by my thought,
  Comes softly rattling down.

I end not far from my going forth
  By picking the faded blue
Of the last remaining aster flower
  To carry again to you.   1913

STORM FEAR

When the wind works against us in the dark,
And pelts with snow

The lower chamber window on the east,
And whispers with a sort of stifled bark,
The beast,
'Come out! Come out!'—
It costs no inward struggle not to go,
Ah, no!
I count our strength,
Two and a child,   10

Those of us not asleep subdued to mark
How the cold creeps as the fire dies at length,—
How drifts are piled,
Dooryard and road ungraded,
Till even the comforting barn grows far away,
And my heart owns a doubt
Whether 'tis in us to arise with day
And save ourselves unaided.   1913

» » From: NORTH OF BOSTON « «

THE CODE

There were three in the meadow by the brook
Gathering up windrows, piling cocks of hay,
With an eye always lifted toward the west
Where an irregular sun-bordered cloud
Darkly advanced with a perpetual dagger
Flickering across its bosom. Suddenly
One helper, thrusting pitchfork in the ground,
Marched himself off the field and home. One
    stayed.
The town-bred farmer failed to understand.

'What is there wrong?'

            'Something you just now said.'

'What did I say?'   11

            'About our taking pains.'

'To cock the hay?—because it's going to
    shower?
I said that more than half an hour ago.
I said it to myself as much as you.'

'You didn't know. But James is one big fool.
He thought you meant to find fault with his
    work.
That's what the average farmer would have
    meant.
James would take time, of course, to chew it
    over
Before he acted: he's just got round to act.'

'He is a fool if that's the way he takes me.' 20

'Don't let it bother you. You've found out
    something.
The hand that knows his business won't be
    told
To do work better or faster—those two things.
I'm as particular as anyone:

Most likely I'd have served you just the same.
But I know you don't understand our ways.
You were just talking what was in your mind,
What was in all our minds, and you weren't
    hinting.
Tell you a story of what happened once:
I was up here in Salem at a man's   30
Named Sanders with a gang of four or five
Doing the haying. No one liked the boss.
He was one of the kind sports called a spider,
All wiry arms and legs that spread out wavy
From a humped body nigh as big's a biscuit.
But work! that man could work, especially
If by so doing he could get more work
Out of his hired help. I'm not denying
He was hard on himself. I couldn't find
That he kept any hours—not for himself.   40
Daylight and lantern-light were one to him:
I've heard him pounding in the barn all night.
But what he liked was someone to encourage.
Them that he couldn't lead he'd get behind
And drive, the way you can, you know, in
    mowing—
Keep at their heels and threaten to mow their
    legs off.
I'd seen about enough of his bulling tricks   47
(We call that bulling). I'd been watching him.
So when he paired off with me in the hayfield
To load the load, thinks I, Look out for trouble.
I built the load and topped it off; old Sanders
Combed it down with a rake and says, "O.K."
Everything went well till we reached the barn
With a big jag to empty in a bay.
You understand that meant the easy job
For the man up on top of throwing *down*
The hay and rolling it off wholesale,
Where on a mow it would have been slow lift-
    ing.
You wouldn't think a fellow'd need much
    urging   59
Under those circumstances, would you now?
But the old fool seizes his fork in both hands,

And looking up bewhiskered out of the pit,
Shouts like an army captain, "Let her come!"
Thinks I, D'ye mean it? "What was that you
    said?"
I asked out loud, so's there'd be no mistake,
"Did you say, Let her come?" "Yes, let her
    come."
He said it over, but he said it softer.
Never you say a thing like that to a man,
Not if he values what he is. God, I'd as soon
Murdered him as left out his middle name. 70
I'd built the load and knew right where to
    find it.
Two or three forkfuls I picked lightly round
    for
Like meditating, and then I just dug in
And dumped the rackful on him in ten lots.
I looked over the side once in the dust
And caught sight of him treading-water-like,
Keeping his head above. "Damn ye," I says,
"That gets ye!" He squeaked like a squeezed
    rat.
That was the last I saw or heard of him.
I cleaned the rack and drove out to cool off. 80
As I sat mopping hayseed from my neck,
And sort of waiting to be asked about it,
One of the boys sings out, "Where's the old
    man?"
"I left him in the barn under the hay.
If ye want him, ye can go and dig him out."
They realized from the way I swobbed my
    neck
More than was needed something must be up.
They headed for the barn; I stayed where I
    was.
They told me afterward. First they forked hay,
A lot of it, out into the barn floor.   90
Nothing! They listened for him. Not a rustle.
I guess they thought I'd spiked him in the
    temple
Before I buried him, or I couldn't have man-
    aged.
They excavated more. "Go keep his wife
Out of the barn." Someone looked in a window,
And curse me if he wasn't in the kitchen
Slumped way down in a chair, with both his
    feet
Against the stove, the hottest day that summer.
He looked so clean disgusted from behind
There was no one that dared to stir him
    up,   100
Or let him know that he was being looked at.
Apparently I hadn't buried him
(I may have knocked him down); but my just
    trying

To bury him had hurt his dignity.
He had gone to the house so's not to meet me.
He kept away from us all afternoon.
We tended to his hay. We saw him out
After a while pickin peas in his garden:
He couldn't keep away from doing something.'

'Weren't you relieved to find he wasn't
    dead?'   110

'No! and yet I don't know—it's hard to say.
I went about to kill him fair enough.'

'You took an awkward way. Did he discharge
    you?'

'Discharge me? No! He knew I did just right.'
                                               1914

THE WOODPILE

Out walking in the frozen swamp one grey
    day,
I paused and said, 'I will turn back from here.
No, I will go on farther—and we shall see.'
The hard snow held me, save where now and
    then
One foot went through. The view was all in
    lines
Straight up and down of tall slim trees
Too much alike to mark or name a place by
So as to say for certain I was here
Or somewhere else: I was just far from home.
A small bird flew before me. He was careful 10
To put a tree between us when he lighted,
And say no word to tell me who he was
Who was so foolish as to think what *he*
    thought.
He thought that I was after him for a feather—
The white one in his tail; like one who takes
Everything said as personal to himself.
One flight out sideways would have unde-
    ceived him.
And then there was a pile of wood for which
I forgot him and let his little fear
Carry him off the way I might have gone,   20
Without so much as wishing him good-night.
He went behind it to make his last stand.
It was a cord of maple, cut and split
And piled—and measured, four by four by
    eight.
And not another like it could I see.
No runner tracks in this year's snow looped
    near it.

And it was older sure than this year's cutting,
Or even last year's or the year's before.
The wood was grey and the bark warping off it
And the pile somewhat sunken. Clematis   30
Had wound strings round and round it like a
    bundle.
What held it though on one side was a tree
Still growing, and on one a stake and prop,

These latter about to fall. I thought that only
Someone who lived in turning to fresh tasks
Could so forget his handiwork on which
He spent himself, the labour of his axe,
And leave it there far from a useful fireplace
To warm the frozen swamp as best it could
With the slow smokeless burning of decay.   40
                                          1914

» » *From:* MOUNTAIN INTERVAL « «

BIRCHES

When I see birches bend to left and right
Across the line of straighter darker trees,
I like to think some boy's been swinging them.
But swinging doesn't bend them down to stay.
Ice-storms do that. Often you must have seen
    them
Loaded with ice a sunny winter morning
After a rain. They click upon themselves
As the breeze rises, and turn many-colored
As the stir cracks and crazes their enamel.
Soon the sun's warmth makes them shed crys-
    tal shells   10
Shattering and avalanching on the snow-
    crust—
Such heaps of broken glass to sweep away
You'd think the inner dome of heaven had
    fallen.
They are dragged to the withered bracken by
    the load,
And they seem not to break; though once they
    are bowed
So low for long, they never right themselves:
You may see their trunks arching in the woods
Years afterwards, trailing their leaves on the
    ground
Like girls on hands and knees that throw their
    hair
Before them over their heads to dry in the
    sun.   20
But I was going to say when Truth broke in
With all her matter-of-fact about the ice-storm
I should prefer to have some boy bend them
As he went out and in to fetch the cows—
Some boy too far from town to learn baseball
Whose only play was what he found himself,
Summer or winter, and could play alone.
One by one he subdued his father's trees
By riding them down over and over again
Until he took the stiffness out of them,   30
And not one but hung limp, not one was left

For him to conquer. He learned all there was
To learn about not launching out too soon
And so not carrying the tree away
Clear to the ground. He always kept his poise
To the top branches, climbing carefully
With the same pains you use to fill a cup
Up to the brim, and even above the brim.
Then he flung outward, feet first, with a
    swish,
Kicking his way down through the air to the
    ground.   40
So was I once myself a swinger of birches.
And so I dream of going back to be.
It's when I'm weary of considerations,
And life is too much like a pathless wood
Where your face burns and tickles with the
    cobwebs
Broken across it, and one eye is weeping
From a twig's having lashed across it open.
I'd like to get away from earth awhile
And then come back to it and begin over.
May no fate wilfully misunderstand me   50
And half grant what I wish and snatch me
    away
Not to return. Earth's the right place for love:
I don't know where it's likely to go better.
I'd like to go by climbing a birch tree,
And climb black branches up a snow-white
    trunk
Toward heaven, till the tree could bear no
    more,
But dipped its top and set me down again.
That would be good both going and coming
    back.
One could do worse than be a swinger of
    birches.   1915

AN OLD MAN'S WINTER NIGHT

All out of doors looked darkly in at him
Through the thin frost, almost in separate stars,

That gathers on the pane in empty rooms.
What kept his eyes from giving back the gaze
Was the lamp tilted near them in his hand.
What kept him from remembering the need
That brought him to that creaking room was
　age.
He stood with barrels round him—at a loss.
And having scared the cellar under him
In clomping there, he scared it once again 10
In clomping off:—and scared the outer night,
Which has its sounds, familiar, like the roar
Of trees and crack of branches, common
　things,
But nothing so like beating on a box.
A light he was to no one but himself
Where now he sat, concerned with he knew
　what,
A quiet light, and then not even that.
He consigned to the moon, such as she was,
So late-arising, to the broken moon   20
As better than the sun in any case
For such a charge, his snow upon the roof,
His icicles along the wall to keep;
And slept. The log that shifted with a jolt
Once in the stove, disturbed him and he
　shifted,
And eased his heavy breathing, but still slept.
One aged man—one man—can't keep a house,
A farm, a countryside, or if he can,
It's thus he does it of a winter night.   1916

THE COW IN APPLE TIME

Something inspires the only cow of late
To make no more of a wall than an open gate,
And think no more of wall-builders than fools.
Her face is flecked with pomace and she drools
A cider syrup. Having tasted fruit,
She scorns a pasture withering to the root.
She runs from tree to tree where lie and
　sweeten
The windfalls spiked with stubble and worm-
　eaten.
She leaves them bitten when she has to fly.
She bellows on a knoll against the sky.   10
Her udder shrivels and the milk goes dry.
                                          1914

'OUT, OUT—'

The buzz-saw snarled and rattled in the yard
And made dust and dropped stove-length
　sticks of wood,
Sweet-scented stuff when the breeze drew
　across it.
And from there those that lifted eyes could
　count
Five mountain ranges one behind the other
Under the sunset far into Vermont.
And the saw snarled and rattled, snarled and
　rattled,
As it ran light, or had to bear a load.
And nothing happened: day was all but done.
Call it a day, I wish they might have said   10
To please the boy by giving him the half hour
That a boy counts so much when saved from
　work.
His sister stood beside them in her apron
To tell them 'Supper.' At the word, the saw,
As if to prove saws knew what supper meant,
Leaped out at the boy's hand, or seemed to
　leap—
He must have given the hand. However it was,
Neither refused the meeting. But the hand!
The boy's first outcry was a rueful laugh,
As he swung toward them holding up the
　hand   20
Half in appeal, but half as if to keep
The life from spilling. Then the boy saw all—
Since he was old enough to know, big boy
Doing a man's work, though a child at heart—
He saw all spoiled. 'Don't let him cut my hand
　off—
The doctor, when he comes. Don't let him,
　sister!'
So. But the hand was gone already.
The doctor put him in the dark of ether.
He lay and puffed his lips out with his breath.
And then—the watcher at his pulse took
　fright.   30
No one believed. They listened at his heart.
Little—less—nothing!—and that ended it.
No more to build on there. And they, since
　they
Were not the one dead, turned to their affairs.
                                          1916

» » *From:* NEW HAMPSHIRE « «

THE RUNAWAY

Once when the snow of the year was beginning
  to fall,
We stopped by a mountain pasture to say,
  'Whose colt?'
A little Morgan had one forefoot on the wall,
The other curled at his breast. He dipped his
  head
And snorted at us. And then he had to bolt.
We heard the miniature thunder where he fled,
And we saw him or thought we saw him, dim
  and grey,
Like a shadow against the curtain of falling
  flakes.
'I think the little fellow's afraid of the snow.
He isn't winter-broken. It isn't play   10
With the little fellow at all. He's running away.
I doubt if even his mother could tell him,
  "Sakes,
It's only weather." He'd think she didn't know!
Where is his mother? He can't be out alone.'
And now he comes again with clatter of stone,
And mounts the wall again with whited eyes
And all his tail that isn't hair up straight.
He shudders his coat as if to throw off flies.
'Whoever it is that leaves him out so late,
When other creatures have gone to stall and
  bin,   20
Ought to be told to come and take him in.'
                                          1918

STOPPING BY WOODS ON A SNOWY
EVENING

Whose woods these are I think I know.
His house is in the village though;
He will not see me stopping here
To watch his woods fill up with snow.

My little horse must think it queer
To stop without a farmhouse near
Between the woods and frozen lake
The darkest evening of the year.

He gives his harness bells a shake
To ask if there is some mistake.   10
The only other sound's the sweep
Of easy wind and downy flake.

The woods are lovely, dark and deep.
But I have promises to keep,
And miles to go before I sleep,
And miles to go before I sleep.   1923

THE NEED OF BEING VERSED IN
COUNTRY THINGS

The house had gone to bring again
To the midnight sky a sunset glow.
Now the chimney was all of the house that
  stood,
Like a pistil after the petals go.

The barn opposed across the way,
That would have joined the house in flame
Had it been the will of the wind, was left
To bear forsaken the place's name.

No more it opened with all one end
For teams that came by the stony road   10
To drum on the floor with scurrying hoofs
And brush the mow with the summer load.

The birds that came to it through the air
At broken windows flew out and in,
Their murmur more like the sigh we sigh
From too much dwelling on what has been.

Yet for them the lilac renewed its leaf,
And the aged elm, though touched with fire;
And the dry pump flung up an awkward arm;
And the fence post carried a strand of wire. 20

For them there was really nothing sad.
But though they rejoiced in the nest they kept,
One had to be versed in country things
Not to believe the phoebes wept.   1920

» » « «

» » *From:* WEST RUNNING BROOK « «

A SOLDIER

He is that fallen lance that lies as hurled,
That lies unlifted now, come dew, come rust,
But still lies pointed as it plowed the dust.
If we who sight along it round the world,
See nothing worthy to have been its mark,
It is because like men we look too near,
Forgetting that as fitted to the sphere,

Our missiles always make too short an arc.
They fall, they rip the grass, they intersect
The curve of earth, and striking, break their
   own;   10
They make us cringe for metal-point on stone.
But this we know, the obstacle that checked
And tripped the body, shot the spirit on
Further than target ever showed or shone.
                    1928

» » *From:* A FURTHER RANGE « «

A LONE STRIKER

The swinging mill bell changed its rate
To tolling like the count of fate,
And though at that the tardy ran,
One failed to make the closing gate.
There was a law of God or man
That on the one who came too late
The gate for half an hour be locked,
His time be lost, his pittance docked.
He stood rebuked and unemployed.
The straining mill began to shake.   10
The mill, though many, many eyed,
Had eyes inscrutably opaque;
So that he couldn't look inside
To see if some forlorn machine
Was standing idle for his sake.
(He couldn't hope its heart would break.)

And yet he thought he saw the scene:
The air was full of dust of wool.
A thousand yarns were under pull,
But pull so slow, with such a twist,   20
All day from spool to lesser spool,
It seldom overtaxed their strength;
They safely grew in slender length.
And if one broke by any chance,
The spinner saw it at a glance.
The spinner still was there to spin.

That's where the human still came in.
Her deft hand showed with finger rings
Among the harp-like spread of strings.
She caught the pieces end to end   30
And, with a touch that never missed,
Not so much tied as made them blend.
Man's ingenuity was good.

He saw it plainly where he stood,
Yet found it easy to resist.

He knew another place, a wood,
And in it, tall as trees, were cliffs;
And if he stood on one of these,
'Twould be among the tops of trees,
Their upper branches round him wreathing, 40
Their breathing mingled with his breathing.
If—if he stood! Enough of ifs!
He knew a path that wanted walking;
He knew a spring that wanted drinking;
A thought that wanted further thinking;
A love that wanted re-renewing.
Nor was this just a way of talking
To save him the expense of doing.
With him it boded action, deed.

The factory was very fine;   50
He wished it all the modern speed.
Yet, after all, 'twas not divine,
That is to say, 'twas not a church.
He never would assume that he'd
Be any institution's need.
But he said then and still would say
If there should ever come a day
When industry seemed like to die
Because he left it in the lurch,
Or even merely seemed to pine   60
For want of his approval, why
Come get him—they knew where to search.
                    1933

A BLUE RIBBON AT AMESBURY

Such a fine pullet ought to go
All coiffured to a winter show,

And be exhibited, and win.
The answer is this one has been—

And come with all her honors home.
Her golden leg, her coral comb,
Her fluff of plumage, white as chalk,
Her style, were all the fancy's talk.

It seems as if you must have heard.
She scored an almost perfect bird.   10
In her we make ourselves acquainted
With one a Sewell might have painted.

Here common with the flock again,
At home in her abiding pen,
She lingers feeding at the trough,
The last to let night drive her off.

The one who gave her ankle-band,
Her keeper, empty pail in hand,
He lingers too, averse to slight
His chores for all the wintry night.   20

He leans against the dusty wall,
Immured almost beyond recall,
A depth past many swinging doors
And many litter-muffled floors.

He meditates the breeder's art.
He has a half a mind to start,
With her for Mother Eve, a race
That shall all living things displace.

'Tis ritual with her to lay
The full six days, then rest a day;   30

At which rate barring broodiness
She well may score an egg-success.

The gatherer can always tell
Her well-turned egg's brown sturdy shell,
As safe a vehicle of seed
As is vouchsafed to feathered breed.

No human spectre at the feast
Can scant or hurry her the least.
She takes her time to take her fill.
She whets a sleepy sated bill.   40

She groped across the pen alone
To peck herself a precious stone.
She waters at the patent fount.
And so to roost, the last to mount.

The roost is her extent of flight.
Yet once she rises to the height,
She shoulders with a wing so strong
She makes the whole flock move along.

The night is setting in to blow.
It scours the windowpane with snow,   50
But barely gets from them or her
For comment a complacent chirr.

The lowly pen is yet a hold
Against the dark and wind and cold
To give a prospect to a plan
And warrant prudence in a man.   1936

EDGAR LEE MASTERS

1869–1950

THE POSITION and personal philosophy of Masters is comparable to that of a prospector who once struck pay dirt, worked the lode to the end, and then spent the rest of a lonely life in embittered contemplation of the ore which he continued to turn up.

After a boyhood near the real Spoon River in Lewistown, Illinois, and a year (1889) at Knox College in Galesburg, he began to practice law in Chicago, where he married, got children, and talked to poets like Sandburg and Lindsay. Reading some of the satiric epigrams in the *Greek Anthology* and recalling his small-town life, he hit upon the idea of the *Spoon River Anthology*, first published serially in 1914, and afterwards immensely popular. The *vers libre* epitaphs, some kindly, some full of a savage indignation and misanthropic frankness which suggest Howe's

Story of a Country Town and Hardy's pessimistic poetry, achieve effective irony by pointing to the dichotomy between outward appearances and inner lives in a small town. In several other volumes of verse Masters continued in the same vein, but he also produced novels, verse-plays, essays, a history of Chicago, and four biographies. In his autobiography, *Across Spoon River* (1936), he detailed with utmost candor the marital, literary, and spiritual vicissitudes which clouded a good part of his life.

Across Spoon River; An Autobiography, New York, 1936.

E. L. Masters, "The Genesis of Spoon River," *American Mercury*, XXVIII (January, 1933), 38–55.

J. C. Chandler, "The Spoon River Country," *Journal of the Illinois State Historical Society*, XIV (1921–1922), 252–329.

H. E. Childs, "Agrarianism and Sex, Edgar Lee Masters and the Modern Spirit," *Sewanee Review*, XLI (July–September, 1933), 331–343.

Kimball Flaccus, *Edgar Lee Masters; A Biographical and Critical Study*, Montpelier, Vermont, 1955.

» » From: SPOON RIVER ANTHOLOGY « «

OLLIE McGEE

Have you seen walking through the village
A man with downcast eyes and haggard face?
That is my husband, by secret cruelty
Never to be told, robbed me of my youth and
my beauty;
Till at last, wrinkled and with yellow teeth,
And with broken pride and shameful humility,
I sank into the grave.
But what think you gnaws at my husband's
heart?
The face of what I was, the face of what he
made me!
These are driving him to the place where I
lie.   10
In death, therefore, I am avenged.   1915

FLETCHER McGEE

She took my strength by minutes,
She took my life by hours,
She drained me like a fevered moon
That saps the spinning world.
The days went by like shadows,
The minutes wheeled like stars.
She took the pity from my heart,
And made it into smiles.
She was a hunk of sculptor's clay,
My secret thoughts were fingers: 10
They flew behind her pensive brow
And lined it deep with pain.
They set the lips, and sagged the cheeks,
And drooped the eyes with sorrow.

My soul had entered in the clay,
Fighting like seven devils.
It was not mine, it was not hers;
She held it, but its struggles
Modeled a face she hated,
And a face I feared to see.   20
I beat the windows, shook the bolts.
I hid me in a corner—
And then she died and haunted me,
And hunted me for life.   1915

HARE DRUMMER

Do the boys and girls still go to Siever's
For cider, after school, in late September?
Or gather hazel nuts among the thickets
On Aaron Hatfield's farm when the frosts
begin?
For many times with the laughing girls and
boys
Played I along the road and over the hills
When the sun was low and the air was cool,
Stopping to club the walnut tree
Standing leafless against a flaming west.
Now, the smell of the autumn smoke,   10
And the dropping acorns,
And the echoes about the vales
Bring dreams of life. They hover over me.
They question me:
Where are those laughing comrades?
How many are with me, how many
In the old orchards along the way to Siever's,
And in the woods that overlook
The quiet water?   1915

CONRAD SIEVER

Not in that wasted garden
Where bodies are drawn into grass
That feeds no flocks, and into evergreens
That bear no fruit—
There where along the shaded walks
Vain sighs are heard,
And vainer dreams are dreamed
Of close communion with departed souls—
But here under the apple tree
I loved and watched and pruned   10
With gnarled hands
In the long, long years;
Here under the roots of this northern-spy
To move in the chemic change and circle of life,
Into the soil and into the flesh of the tree,
And into the living epitaphs
Of redder apples!   1915

A. D. BLOOD

If you in the village think that my work was a good one,
Who closed the saloons and stopped all playing at cards,
And haled old Daisy Fraser before Justice Arnett,
In many a crusade to purge the people of sin;
Why do you let the milliner's daughter Dora,
And the worthless son of Benjamin Pantier,
Nightly make my grave their unholy pillow?
                                        1915

THE CIRCUIT JUDGE

Take note, passers-by, of the sharp erosions
Eaten in my head-stone by the wind and rain—
Almost as if an intangible Nemesis or hatred
Were marking scores against me,
But to destroy, and not preserve, my memory.
I in life was the Circuit Judge, a maker of notches,
Deciding cases on the points the lawyers scored,
Not on the right of the matter.
O wind and rain, leave my head-stone alone!
For worse than the anger of the wronged,   10
The curses of the poor,
Was to lie speechless, yet with vision clear,
Seeing that even Hod Putt, the murderer,

Hanged by my sentence,
Was innocent in soul compared with me.
                                        1915

EDITOR WHEDON

To be able to see every side of every question;
To be on every side, to be everything, to be nothing long;
To pervert truth, to ride it for a purpose,
To use great feelings and passions of the human family
For base designs, for cunning ends,
To wear a mask like the Greek actors—
Your eight-page paper—behind which you huddle,
Bawling through the megaphone of big type:
"This is I, the giant."
Thereby also living the life of a sneak-thief,   10
Poisoned with the anonymous words
Of your clandestine soul.
To scratch dirt over scandal for money,
And exhume it to the winds for revenge,
Or to sell papers,
Crushing reputations, or bodies, if need be,
To win at any cost, save your own life.
To glory in demoniac power, ditching civilization,
As a paranoiac boy puts a log on the track
And derails the express train.   20
To be an editor, as I was.
Then to lie here close by the river over the place
Where the sewage flows from the village,
And the empty cans and garbage are dumped,
And abortions are hidden.   1915

ANNE RUTLEDGE

Out of me unworthy and unknown
The vibrations of deathless music;
"With malice toward none, with charity for all."
Out of me the forgiveness of millions toward millions,
And the beneficent face of a nation
Shining with justice and truth.
I am Anne Rutledge who sleep beneath these weeds,
Beloved in life of Abraham Lincoln,
Wedded to him, not through union,
But through separation.   10
Bloom forever, O Republic,
From the dust of my bosom!   1915

MAGRADY GRAHAM

Tell me, was Altgeld elected Governor?
For when the returns began to come in
And Cleveland was sweeping the East,
It was too much for you, poor old heart,
Who had striven for democracy
In the long, long years of defeat.
And like a watch that is worn
I felt you growing slower until you stopped.
Tell me, was Altgeld elected,
And what did he do?   10
Did they bring his head on a platter to a
    dancer,
Or did he triumph for the people?
For when I saw him
And took his hand,
The child-like blueness of his eyes
Moved me to tears,
And there was an air of eternity about him,
Like the cold, clear light that rests at dawn
On the hills!   1915

ARCHIBALD HIGBIE

I loathed you, Spoon River. I tried to rise
    above you,
I was ashamed of you. I despised you
As the place of my nativity.
And there in Rome, among the artists,
Speaking Italian, speaking French,
I seemed to myself at times to be free
Of every trace of my origin.
I seemed to be reaching the heights of art

And to breathe the air that the masters
    breathed,
And to see the world with their eyes.   10
But still they'd pass my work and say:
"What are you driving at, my friend?
Sometimes the face looks like Apollo's,
At others it has a trace of Lincoln's."
There was no culture, you know, in Spoon
    River,
And I burned with shame and held my peace.
And what could I do, all covered over
And weighted down with western soil,
Except aspire, and pray for another
Birth in the world, with all of Spoon River 20
Rooted out of my soul?   1915

JENNIE M'GREW

Not, where the stairway turns in the dark,
A hooded figure, shriveled under a flowing
    cloak!
Not yellow eyes in the room at night,
Staring out from a surface of cobweb gray!
And not the flap of a condor wing,
When the roar of life in your ears begins
As a sound heard never before!
But on a sunny afternoon,
By a country road,
Where purple rag-weeds bloom along a strag-
    gling fence,   10
And the field is gleaned, and the air is still,
To see against the sun-light something black,
Like a blot with an iris rim—
That is the sign to eyes of second sight. . . .
And that I saw!   1915

VACHEL LINDSAY

1879–1931

VACHEL LINDSAY of Springfield, Illinois, was a strange combination of child, reformer, artist, actor, and religious mystic, whose failure to integrate these somewhat immiscible propensities resulted in a tragic scattering of his force. A success neither by his own nor by bourgeois standards, he liked to see himself as a modern troubadour or nomadic tribal gleeman, rhythmically chanting his "gospel of beauty" in Y.M.C.A. dining halls, squatters' huts, general stores, and candy shops, and later in scores of college auditoriums throughout the nation. His audiences remember his somewhat pontifical platform presence, the bland smile and sweeping gesticulations which would have resembled those of a patent-medicine vendor had they not been strangely heightened by the mystical ecstasy which he seemed to derive from his sonorous incantations.

Lindsay's poetry is dominated by a strong religious and ethical bias, partly an inheritance from his strong-minded mother and his doctor father, staunch Campbellites who financed the boy through three years (1897–1900) at the denominational college in Hiram, Ohio. Although he spent the next six years studying art in Chicago and New York, inadequately supporting himself by clerking in a department store and serving as museum guide, Lindsay failed to obtain gainful employment either as artist or businessman. His idealism found happiest expression in occasional lectures before the Y.M.C.A., which he now saw as "an army in need of a singer." Always subject to dreams and visions, he had once written that "the flower of the Holy Spirit is the most wonderful and dangerous flower in the whole Universe. I have for good or ill eaten of it. And I have the desire as all those who eat. I would compass heaven and earth to make one proselyte." Vachel Lindsay began to gird himself for what he called his "roadside priesthood" as "teacher of the mysteries of beauty and the church of Beauty," and in 1906, 1908, and 1912 took long walking-tours through the South, East, and Southwest, penniless as a mendicant friar, preaching his "little one-page formula for making America lovelier." The people he approached were rarely inhospitable, taking leaflet copies of Lindsay's verse in exchange for bed and breakfast. These itinerant summers, which he describes in *Adventures While Preaching the Gospel of Beauty* (1914) and *A Handy Guide for Beggars* (1916), were probably the happiest of Lindsay's life.

Much of Lindsay's time between 1913 and his suicide was devoted to an effort to re-animate poetry by the use of music, elocution, pantomime, and communal responses, and to popularize native American subjects by frequent public readings of his own verse. The bulk of his work appeared in four volumes: *General William Booth Enters into Heaven* (1913), *The Congo, etc.* (1914), *The Chinese Nightingale, etc.* (1917), and the less popular *Golden Whales of California, etc.* (1920). Lindsay collected his verse in 1923 (revised 1925). Although he is best known for chants like *The Congo* and *General William Booth*, these bravura pieces give the reader less insight into the real Lindsay than his shorter lyrics, which include games and fantasies for children, poems on social reform, and much symbolist religious verse. "Let us seize," cried Lindsay, "these three ideals: Beauty, Freedom, Holiness; let us stamp them upon the innermost spirit of the land." His vision of the new America was a dream-world of his own imagining, peopled by a strange assortment of heroes: Lincoln, Whitman, Bryan, Tolstoi, Buddha, St. Francis of Assisi, and Johnny Appleseed.

Collected Poems, New York (1923), 1949.
Letters of Nicholas Vachel Lindsay to A. Joseph Armstrong, A. J. Armstrong, ed., Waco, Texas, 1940.
Stephen Graham, *Tramping with a Poet in the Rockies*, New York, 1922.
Mark Harris, *City of Discontent; an Interpretive Biography of Vachel Lindsay*, Indianapolis, 1952.
E. L. Masters, *Vachel Lindsay: A Poet in America*, New York, 1935.
J. B. Rittenhouse, "Vachel Lindsay," *South Atlantic Quarterly*, XXXII (July, 1933), 266–282.
Eleanor Ruggles, *The West-Going Heart; A Life of Vachel Lindsay*, New York, 1959.
A. E. Trombly, *Vachel Lindsay: Adventurer*, Columbia, Mo., 1929.

GENERAL WILLIAM BOOTH ENTERS INTO HEAVEN

[To be sung to the tune of *The Blood of the Lamb* with indicated instrument]

I

[*Bass drum beaten loudly.*]
Booth led boldly with his big bass drum—
(Are you washed in the blood of the Lamb?)

The Saints smiled gravely and they said:
    "He's come."
(Are you washed in the blood of the Lamb?)

Walking lepers followed, rank on rank,
Lurching bravoes from the ditches dank,
Drabs from the alleyways and drug fiends
    pale—
Minds still passion-ridden, soul-powers frail:—

Vermin-eaten saints with mouldy breath,
Unwashed legions with the ways of Death— 10
(Are you washed in the blood of the Lamb?)

[*Banjos.*]
Every slum had sent its half-a-score
The round world over. (Booth had groaned
    for more.)
Every banner that the wide world flies
Bloomed with glory and transcendent dyes.
Big-voiced lasses made their banjos bang,
Tranced, fanatical they shrieked and sang:—
"Are you washed in the blood of the Lamb?"
Hallelujah! It was queer to see
Bull-necked convicts with that land make
    free.   20
Loons with trumpets blowed a blare, blare,
    blare
On, on upward thro' the golden air!
(Are you washed in the blood of the Lamb?)

II

[*Bass drum slower and softer.*]
Booth died blind and still by Faith he trod,
Eyes still dazzled by the ways of God.
Booth led boldly, and he looked the chief,
Eagle countenance in sharp relief,
Beard-a-flying, air of high command
Unabated in that holy land.

[*Sweet flute music.*]
Jesus came from out the court-house door,   30
Stretched his hands above the passing poor.
Booth saw not, but led his queer ones there
Round and round the mighty court-house
    square.
Then, in an instant all that blear review
Marched on spotless, clad in raiment new.
The lame were straightened, withered limbs
    uncurled
And blind eyes opened on a new, sweet world.

[*Bass drum louder.*]
Drabs and vixens in a flash made whole!
Gone was the weasel-head, the snout, the jowl!
Sages and sibyls now, and athletes clean,   40
Rulers of empires, and of forests green!

[*Grand chorus of all instruments. Tam-
bourines to the foreground.*]
The hosts were sandalled, and their wings
    were fire!
(Are you washed in the blood of the Lamb?)
But their noise played havoc with the angel-
    choir.
(Are you washed in the blood of the Lamb?)
O, shout Salvation! It was good to see
Kings and Princes by the Lamb set free.
The banjos rattled and the tambourines
Jing-jing-jingled in the hands of Queens.

[*Reverently sung, no instruments.*]
And when Booth halted by the curb for
    prayer   50
He saw his Master thro' the flag-filled air.
Christ came gently with a robe and crown
For Booth the soldier, while the throng knelt
    down.
He saw King Jesus. They were face to face,
And he knelt a-weeping in that holy place.
Are you washed in the blood of the Lamb?
1912   1913

From: *THE CONGO* [1]

A Study of the Negro Race

I. THEIR BASIC SAVAGERY

Fat black bucks in a wine-barrel
    room,
Barrel-house kings, with feet un-
    stable,
Sagged and reeled and pounded on
    the table,
Pounded on the table,   *A deep rolling*
Beat an empty barrel with the   *bass.*
    handle of a broom,
Hard as they were able,
Boom, boom, BOOM,
With a silk umbrella and the handle
    of a broom,
Boomlay, boomlay, boomlay, BOOM.
THEN I had religion, THEN I had a
    vision.   10

[1] This poem, particularly the third section, was suggested by an
allusion in a sermon by my pastor, F. W. Burnham, to the heroic life
and death of Ray Eldred. Eldred was a missionary of the Disciples of
Christ who perished while swimming a treacherous branch of the
Congo. See "A Master Builder on the Congo," by Andrew F. Hen-
sey. [Lindsay's note.]

I could not turn from their revel in
  derision.

THEN I SAW THE CONGO, CREEPING
  THROUGH THE BLACK, *More deliberate. Solemnly chanted.*

CUTTING THROUGH THE FOREST
  WITH A GOLDEN TRACK.

Then along that riverbank
A thousand miles
Tattoed cannibals danced in files;
Then I heard the boom of the
  blood-lust song
And a thigh-bone beating on a tin-
  pan gong.

And "BLOOD" screamed the whistles
  and the fifes of the warriors, *A rapidly piling climax of speed and racket.*

"BLOOD" screamed the skull-faced,
  lean witch-doctors,   20
"Whirl ye the deadly voo-doo rattle,
Harry the uplands,
Steal all the cattle,
Rattle-rattle, rattle-rattle,
Bing!
Boomlay, boomlay, boomlay, BOOM,"
A roaring, epic, rag-time tune *With a philosophic pause.*
From the mouth of the Congo
To the Mountains of the Moon.

Death is an Elephant,   30
Torch-eyed and horrible, *Shrilly and with a heavily accented meter.*
Foam-flanked and terrible.
BOOM, steal the pygmies,
BOOM, kill the Arabs,
BOOM, kill the white men, *Like the wind in the chimney.*
Hoo, Hoo, Hoo.
Listen to the yell of Leopold's ghost
Burning in Hell for his hand-
  maimed host.
Hear how the demons chuckle and
  yell
Cutting his hands off, down in
  Hell.   40
Listen to the creepy proclamation,
Blown through the lairs of the
  forest-nation,
Blown past the white-ants' hill of
  clay,
Blown past the marsh where the
  butterflies play:—
"Be careful what you do,
Or Mumbo-Jumbo, God of the *All the "o" sounds very golden. Heavy accents very heavy.*
  Congo,
And all of the other

Gods of the Congo,
Mumbo-Jumbo will hoo-doo you, *Light accents very light. Last line whispered.*
Mumbo-Jumbo will hoo-doo
  you,   50
Mumbo-Jumbo will hoo-doo you."

II. THEIR IRREPRESSIBLE HIGH SPIRITS

Wild crap-shooters with a whoop *Rather shrill and high.*
  and a call
Danced the juba in their gambling
  hall
And laughed fit to kill, and shook
  the town,
And guyed the policemen and
  laughed them down
With a boomlay, boomlay, boomlay, BOOM.

THEN I SAW THE CONGO, CREEPING *Read exactly as in first section.*
  THROUGH THE BLACK,
CUTTING THROUGH THE FOREST
  WITH A GOLDEN TRACK.

A negro fairyland swung into view, *Lay emphasis on the delicate ideas. Keep as light-footed as possible.*
A minstrel river
Where dreams come true.   60
The ebony palace soared on high
Through the blossoming trees to
  the evening sky.
The inlaid porches and casements
  shone
With gold and ivory and elephant-
  bone.
And the black crowd laughed till
  their sides were sore
At the baboon butler in the agate
  door,
And the well-known tunes of the
  parrot band
That trilled on the bushes of that
  magic land.

A troupe of skull-faced witch-men *With pomposity.*
  came
Through the agate doorway in suits
  of flame,   70
Yea, long-tailed coats with a gold-
  leaf crust
And hats that were covered with
  diamond-dust.
And the crowd in the court gave a
  whoop and a call
And danced the juba from wall to
  wall.
But the witch-men suddenly stilled
  the throng

With a stern cold glare, and a stern
old song:—

"Mumbo-Jumbo   will   hoo-doo
you.". . .

With a great deliberation and ghostliness.

Just then from the doorway, as fat
as shotes,

Came the cake-walk princes in
their long red coats,

Canes with a brilliant lacquer
shine,   80

And tall silk hats that were red as
wine.

With overwhelming assurance, good cheer, and pomp.

And they pranced with their butterfly partners there,

Coal-black maidens with pearls in
their hair,

Knee-skirts trimmed with the jas-
samine sweet,

And bells on their ankles and little
black-feet.

And the couples railed at the chant
and the frown

Of the witch-men lean, and
laughed them down.

(Oh, rare was the revel, and well
worth while

That made those glowering witch-
men smile.)

With growing speed and sharply marked dance-rhythm.

The cake-walk royalty then began

To walk for a cake that was tall as
a man   91

To the tune of "Boomlay, boomlay,
Boom,"

While the witch-men laughed, with
a sinister air,

And sang with the scalawags
prancing there:—

"Walk with care, walk with care,

Or Mumbo-Jumbo, God of the
Congo,

And all of the other Gods of the
Congo,

Mumbo-Jumbo will hoo-doo you.

Beware, beware, walk with care,

Boomlay, boomlay, boomlay, boom.

Boomlay, boomlay, boomlay, boom.

Boomlay, boomlay, boomlay, boom.

Boomlay, boomlay, boomlay,   103

Boom."

With a touch of negro dialect, and as rapidly as possible to the end.

(Oh, rare was the revel, and well
worth while

That made those glowering witch-
men smile.)

Slow philosophic calm.

III. THE HOPE OF THEIR RELIGION

A good old negro in the slums of
the town

Preached at a sister for her velvet
gown.

Heavy bass. With a literal imitation of camp-meeting racket, and trance.

Howled at a brother for his low-
down ways,

His prowling, guzzling, sneak-thief
days.   110

Beat on the Bible till he wore it
out,

Starting the jubilee revival shout.

And some had visions, as they
stood on chairs,

And sang of Jacob, and the golden
stairs.

And they all repented, a thousand
strong,

From their stupor and savagery
and sin and wrong

And slammed with their hymn
books till they shook the room

With "Glory, glory, glory,"

And "Boom, boom, Boom."

THEN I SAW THE CONGO, CREEPING
THROUGH THE BLACK,   120

CUTTING THROUGH THE JUNGLE
WITH A GOLDEN TRACK.

Exactly as in the first section.

And the gray sky opened like a
new-rent veil

And showed the Apostles with their
coats of mail.

In bright white steel they were
seated round

And their fire-eyes watched where
the Congo wound.

And the twelve Apostles, from their
thrones on high,

Thrilled all the forest with their
heavenly cry:—

"Mumbo-Jumbo will die in the
jungle;

Never again will he hoo-doo you,

Never again will he hoo-doo you."

Sung to the tune of "Hark, ten thousand harps and voices."

Then along that river, a thousand
miles,   131

The vine-snared trees fell down in
files.

With growing deliberation and joy.

Pioneer angels cleared the way

For a Congo paradise, for babes at
play,

For sacred capitals, for temples
clean.

Gone were the skull-faced witch-

men lean.
There, where the wild ghost-gods had wailed *In a rather high key—as delicately as possible.*
A million boats of the angels sailed
With oars of silver, and prows of blue
And silken pennants that the sun shone through.   140
'Twas a land transfigured, 'twas a new creation.
Oh, a singing wind swept the negro nation;
And on through the backwoods clearing flew:—
"Mumbo-Jumbo is dead in the jungle.   *To the tune of "Hark, ten thousand*

Never again will he hoo-doo you.   *harps and voices."*
Never again will he hoo-doo you."

Redeemed were the forests, the beasts and the men,
And only the vulture dared again
By the far, lone mountains of the moon
To cry, in the silence, the Congo tune:—   150
"Mumbo-Jumbo will hoo-doo you,   *Dying down into a penetrating, terrified whisper.*
Mumbo-Jumbo will hoo-doo you.
Mumbo . . . Jumbo . . . will . . . hoo-doo . . . you."
1913   1914

» »   « «

THEODORE DREISER

1871–1945

FOR TWENTY YEARS Dreiser's novels formed the domain over which a fierce critical war was fought. On one side were ranged the defenders of reticence and moral values in literature; on the other the radical critics and novelists who were trying to break the grip of the genteel writers on American literature. As the storm-center of the controversy Dreiser stood, as his most vigorous champion, H. L. Mencken, said: "solid, granitic, without nerves." His first novel, *Sister Carrie* (1900), was, in effect, suppressed by its publishers. Not until 1907 was it formally issued in this country. The New York Society for the Suppression of Vice forced the publisher of *The "Genius"* (1915) to withdraw the book, though nearly five hundred writers, from which list some great names were conspicuously absent, were ready to testify that it is not an obscene novel. As late as 1927 Paul Elmer More, who had been active in the opposition, called *An American Tragedy* (1925), which Boston banned, a *monstrum informe cui lumen ademptum*.

Born in Terre Haute, Indiana, in 1871, Dreiser hated the poverty of his home and the narrow Catholic piety of his father. He longed to escape into the exciting world beyond. After two fumbling years in Chicago, he studied for a year at Indiana University. Back in Chicago in 1892, he became a reporter. He was ideally suited for this profession, which he subsequently followed in St. Louis, Pittsburgh, and New York.

In these years his observation of the brutality of life in large cities, his contacts with ruthless businessmen and politicians, and his reading in Herbert Spencer made him a believer in the philosophy of naturalism. There were to him only two kinds of people in the world, the strong and the weak. Whether a man goes up or down in the scale depends both upon his biological inheritance and the economic pressures to which he is subject. Sister Carrie moves up because there is in her a blind striving toward an ever shifting goal; Hurstwood, meanwhile, goes down because his physical need for Carrie asserts itself, with fatal consequences, at a crisis in his economic life. In *The Financier* (1912) and *The Titan* (1914), novels based on the career of Charles Yerkes, the Chicago robber baron, Cowperwood is dominated by two urges, sex and the lust for economic power. Far from condemning him for his ruthlessness, Dreiser is not a little impressed by it.

But Dreiser never became completely a naturalist. He had too much admiration for power as well as sympathy for the woes of others to maintain consistently the detached attitude toward his characters required of a naturalistic writer. The war between his heart and his mind had frequently induced him to make a melioristic compromise.

[Man] is becoming too wise to hearken always to instincts and desires; he is still too weak to always prevail against them. As a beast, the forces of life aligned him with them; as a man, he has not yet wholly learned to align himself with the forces. In this intermediate stage he wavers—neither drawn in harmony with nature by his instincts nor yet wisely putting himself into harmony by his own free-will. He is even as a wisp in the wind, moved by every breath of passion, acting now by his will and now by his instincts, erring with one, only to retrieve by the other, falling by one, only to rise by the other—a creature of incalculable variability.

Dreiser is at his best when he traces this "incalculable variability" in the actions of his characters. In none of his novels is the nexus of desire and will, influenced by inherited but ineffective moral standards, more painstakingly shown than in *An American Tragedy*. Based on an actual trial of 1906, it is the story of a young man who murders his pregnant sweetheart because she blocks his way into the glittering life which is opening before him. To Dreiser this is not just a sordid crime of passion but an act for which our American civilization is in large part responsible. No person or institution helped Clyde Griffiths to a better ideal of life than material success and self-gratification. In this novel Dreiser went far beyond the determinism of his earlier work and suggested that a better social order is possible. It was fitting that at the time of his death, Dreiser was professedly both a Christian and a Communist!

Letters of Theodore Dreiser: A Selection, R. H. Elias, ed., 3 vols., Philadelphia, 1959.
Dorothy Dudley, *Forgotten Frontiers. Dreiser and the Land of the Free*, New York, 1932.
R. H. Elias, *Theodore Dreiser, Apostle of Nature*, New York, 1949.
Alfred Kazin and Charles Shapiro, eds., *The Stature of Theodore Dreiser: A Critical Survey of the Man and his Work*, Bloomington, Indiana, 1955.
F. O. Matthiessen, *Theodore Dreiser*, New York, 1951.

» » FREE « «

The large and rather comfortable apartment of Rufus Haymaker, architect, in Central Park West, was very silent. It was scarcely dawn yet, and at the edge of the park, over the way, looking out from the front windows which graced this abode and gave it its charm, a stately line of poplars was still shrouded in a gray morning mist. From his bedroom at one end of the hall, where, also, a glimpse of the park was to be had, came Mr. Haymaker at this early hour to sit by one of these broader windows and contemplate these trees and a small lake beyond. He was very fond of Nature in its manifold art forms—quite poetic, in fact.

He was a tall and spare man of about sixty, not ungraceful, though slightly stoop-shouldered, with heavy overhanging eyebrows and hair, and a short, professionally cut gray mustache and beard, which gave him a severe and yet agreeable presence. For the present he was clad in a light-blue dressing gown with silver cords, which enveloped him completely. He had thin, pale, long-fingered hands, wrinkled at the back and slightly knotted at the joints, which bespoke the artist, in mood at least, and his eyes had a weary and yet restless look in them.

For only yesterday Doctor Storm, the family physician, who was in attendance on his wife, ill now for these three weeks past with a combination of heart lesion, kidney poisoning and neuritis, had taken him aside and said very softly and affectionately, as though he were trying to spare his feelings: "To-morrow, Mr. Haymaker, if your wife is no better I will call in my friend, Doctor Grainger, whom you know, for a consultation. He is more of an expert in these matters of the heart"—the heart, Mr. Haymaker had time to note ironically—"than I am. Together we will make a thorough examination, and then I hope we will be better able to say what the possibilities of her recovery really are. It's been a very trying case, a very stubborn one, I might say. Still, she has a great deal of vitality and is doing as well as could be expected, all things considered. At the same time, though I don't wish to alarm you unnecessarily—and there is no occasion for great alarm yet—still I feel it my duty to warn you that her condition is very serious indeed. Not that I wish you to feel that she is certain to die. I don't think she is. Not at all. Just the contrary. She may get well, and probably will, and live all of twenty years more." (Mentally Mr. Haymaker sighed a purely spiritual sigh.) "She has fine recuperative powers, so far as I can judge, but she has a bad heart, and this kidney trouble has not helped it any. Just now, when her heart should have the least strain, it has the most.

"She is just at that point where, as I may say, things are in the balance. A day or two, or three or four at the most, ought to show which way things will go. But, as I have said before, I do not wish to alarm you unnecessarily. We are not nearly at the end of our tether. We haven't tried blood transfusion yet, and there are several arrows to that bow. Besides, at any moment she may respond more vigorously to medication than she has heretofore—especially in connection with her kidneys. In that case the situation would be greatly relieved at once.

"However, as I say, I feel it my duty to speak to you in this way in order that you may be mentally prepared for any event, because in such an odd combination as this the worst may happen at any time. We never can tell. As an old friend of yours and Mrs. Haymaker's, and knowing how much you two mean to each other"—Mr. Haymaker merely stared at him vacantly—"I feel it my duty to prepare you in this way. We all of us have to face these things. Only last year I lost my dear Matilda, my youngest child, as you know. Just the same, as I say, I have the feeling that Mrs. Haymaker is not really likely to die soon, and that we—Doctor Grainger and myself—will still be able to pull her through. I really do."

Doctor Storm looked at Mr. Haymaker as though he were very sorry for him—an old man long accustomed to his wife's ways and likely to be made very unhappy by her untimely end; whereas Mr. Haymaker, though staring in an almost sculptural way, was really thinking what a farce it all was, what a dull mixture of error and illusion on the part of all. Here he was, sixty years of age, weary of all this, of life really—a man who had never been really happy in all the time that he had been married; and yet here was his wife, who from conventional reasons believed that he was or should be, and who on account of this was serenely happy herself, or nearly so. And this doctor, who imagined that he was old and weak and therefore in need of this loving woman's care and sympathy and understanding! Unconsciously he raised a deprecating hand.

Also his children, who thought him dependent on her and happy with her; his servants and her and his friends thinking the same thing, and yet he really was not. It was all a lie. He was unhappy. Always he had been unhappy, it seemed, ever since he had been married—for over thirty-one years now. Never in all that time, for even so much as a single day, had he ever done anything but long, long, long, in a pale, constrained way—for what, he scarcely dared think—not to be married any more—to be free—to be as he was before ever he saw Mrs. Haymaker.

And yet being conventional in mood and training and utterly domesticated by time and conditions over which he seemed not to have much control—nature, custom, public opinion, and the like, coming into play as forces—he had drifted, had not taken any drastic action. No, he had merely drifted, wondering if time, accident or something might not interfere and straighten out his life for him, but it never had. Now weary, old, or rapidly becoming so, he condemned himself for his inaction. Why hadn't he done something about it years before? Why hadn't he broken it up before it was too late, and saved his own soul, his longing for life, color? But no, he had not. Why complain so bitterly now?

All the time the doctor had talked this [way] before he had wanted to smile a wry, dry, cynical smile, for in reality he did not want Mrs. Haymaker to live—or at least at the moment he thought so. He was too miserably tired of it all. And so now, after nearly twenty-four hours of the same unhappy thought, sitting by this window looking at a not distant building which shone faintly in the haze, he ran his fingers through his hair as he gazed, and sighed.

How often in these weary months, and even years, past—ever since he and his wife had been living here, and before—had he come to these or similar windows while she was still asleep, to sit and dream! For some years now they had not even roomed together, so indifferent had the whole state become; though

she did not seem to consider that significant, either. Life had become more or less of a practical problem to her, one of position, place, prestige. And yet how often, viewing his life in retrospect, had he wished that his life had been as sweet as his dreams—that his dreams had come true.

. . .

Going to his office later this same day—it was in one of those tall buildings that face Madison Square—he had looked first, in passing, at the trees that line Central Park West, and then at the bright wall of apartment houses facing it, and meditated sadly, heavily. Here the sidewalks were crowded with nursemaids and children at play, and in between them, of course, the occasional citizen loitering or going about his errands. The day was so fine, so youthful, as spring days will seem at times. As he looked, especially at the children, and the young men bustling office-ward, mostly in new spring suits, he sighed and wished that he were young once more. Think how brisk and hopeful they were! Everything was before them. They could still pick and choose—no age or established conditions to stay them. Were any of them, he asked himself for the thousandth time, it seemed to him, as wearily connected as he had been at their age? Did they each have a charming young wife to love—one of whom they were passionately fond—such a one as he had never had; or did they not?

Wondering, he reached his office on one of the topmost floors of one of those highest buildings commanding a wide view of the city, and surveyed it wearily. Here were visible the two great rivers of the city, its towers and spires and far-flung walls. From these sometimes, even yet, he seemed to gain a patience to live, to hope. How in his youth all this had inspired him—or that other city that was then. Even now he was always at peace here, so much more so than in his own home, pleasant as it was. Here he could look out over this great scene and dream or he could lose the memory in his work that his love-life had been a failure. The great city, the buildings he could plan or supervise, the efficient help that always surrounded him—his help, not hers—aided to take his mind off himself and that deep-seated inner ache or loss.

The care of Mr. Haymaker's apartment during his wife's illness and his present absence throughout the day, devolved upon a middle-aged woman of great seriousness, Mrs. Elfridge by name, whom Mrs. Haymaker had employed years before; and under her a maid of all work, Hester, who waited on table, opened the door, and the like; and also at present two trained nurses, one for night and one for day service, who were in charge of Mrs. Haymaker. The nurses were both bright, healthy, blue-eyed girls, who attracted Mr. Haymaker and suggested all the youth he had never had—without really disturbing his poise. It would seem as though that could never be any more.

In addition, of course, there was the loving interest of his son Wesley and his daughter Ethelberta—whom his wife had named so in spite of him—both of whom had long since married and had children of their own and were living in different parts of the great city. In this crisis both of them came daily to learn how things were, and occasionally to stay for the entire afternoon or evening, or both. Ethelberta had wanted to come and take charge of the apartment entirely during her mother's illness, only Mrs. Haymaker, who was still able to direct, and fond of doing so, would not hear of it. She was not so ill but that she could still speak, and in this way could inquire and direct. Besides, Mrs. Elfridge was as good as Mrs. Haymaker in all things that related to Mr. Haymaker's physical comfort, or so she thought.

If the truth will come out—as it will in so many pathetic cases—it was never his physical so much as his spiritual or affectional comfort that Mr. Haymaker craved. As said before, he had never loved Mrs. Haymaker, or certainly not since that now long-distant period back in Muskegon, Michigan, where both had been born and where they had lived and met at the ages, she of fifteen, he of seventeen. It had been, strange as it might seem now, a love match at first sight with them. She had seemed so sweet, a girl of his own age or a little younger, the daughter of a local chemist. Later, when he had been forced by poverty to go out into the world to make his own way, he had written her much, and imagined her to be all that she had seemed at fifteen, and more—a dream among fair women. But Fortune, slow in coming to his aid and fickle in fulfilling his dreams, had brought it about that for several years more he had been compelled to stay away nearly all of the time, unable to marry her; during which period, unknown to

himself really, his own point of view had altered. How it had happened he could never tell really, but so it was. The great city, larger experiences—while she was still enduring the smaller ones—other faces, dreams of larger things, had all combined to destroy it or her, only he had not quite realized it then. He was always so slow in realizing the full import of the immediate thing, he thought.

That was the time, as he had afterward told himself—how often!—that he should have discovered his mistake and stopped. Later it always seemed to become more and more impossible. Then, in spite of some heartache to her and some distress to himself, no doubt, all would be well for him now. But no; he had been too inexperienced, too ignorant, too bound by all the conventions and punctilio of his simple Western world. He thought an engagement, however unsatisfactory it might come to seem afterward, was an engagement, and binding. An honorable man would not break one—or so his country moralists argued.

Yes, at that time he might have written her, he might have told her, then. But he had been too sensitive and kindly to speak of it. Afterward it was too late. He feared to wound her, to undo her, to undo her life. But now—now —look at his! He had gone back on several occasions before marriage, and might have seen and done and been free if he had had but courage and wisdom—but no; duty, order, the beliefs of the region in which he had been reared, and of America—what it expected and what she expected and was entitled to—had done for him completely. He had not spoken. Instead, he had gone on and married her without speaking of the change in himself, without letting her know how worse than ashes it had all become. God, what a fool he had been! how often since he had told himself over and over.

.   .   .

But even that was not the worst. No; that was not the worst, either. It had been the gradual realization coming along through the years that he had married an essentially small, narrow woman who could never really grasp his point of view—or, rather, the significance of his dreams or emotions—and yet with whom, nevertheless, because of this original promise or mistake, he was compelled to live. Grant her every quality of goodness, energy, industry, intent—as he did freely—still there was this; and it could never be adjusted, never. Essentially, as he had long since discovered, she was narrow, ultraconventional, whereas he was an artist by nature, brooding and dreaming strange dreams and thinking of far-off things which she did not or could not understand or did not sympathize with, save in a general and very remote way. The nuances of his craft, the wonders and subtleties of forms and angles—had she ever realized how significant these were to him, let alone to herself? No, never. She had not the least true appreciation of them—never had had. Architecture? Art? What could they really mean to her, desire as she might to appreciate them? And he could not now go elsewhere to discover that sympathy. No. He had never really wanted to, since the public and she would object, and he thinking it half evil himself.

Still, how was it, he often asked himself, that Nature could thus allow one conditioned or equipped with emotions and seekings such as his, not of an utterly conventional order, to seek out and pursue one like Ernestine, who was not fitted to understand him or to care what his personal moods might be? Was love truly blind, as the old saw insisted, or did Nature really plan, and cleverly, to torture the artist mind—as it did the pearl-bearing oyster with a grain of sand—with something seemingly inimical, in order that it might produce beauty? Sometimes he thought so. Perhaps the many interesting and beautiful buildings he had planned—the world called them so, at least—had been due to the loving care he lavished on them, being shut out from love and beauty elsewhere. Cruel Nature, that cared so little for the dreams of man—the individual man or woman!

At the time he had married Ernestine he was really too young to know exactly what it was he wanted to do or how it was he was going to feel in the years to come; and yet there was no one to guide him, to stop him. The custom of the time was all in favor of this dread disaster. Nature herself seemed to desire it—mere children being the be-all and the end-all of everything everywhere. Think of that as a theory! Later, when it became so clear to him what he had done, and in spite of all the conventional thoughts and conditions that seemed to bind him to this fixed condition, he had grown restless and weary, but never really irritable. No, he had never become that.

Instead he had concealed it all from her, persistently, in all kindness; only this hankering after beauty of mind and body in ways not represented by her had hurt so—grown finally almost too painful to bear. He had dreamed and dreamed of something different until it had become almost an obsession. Was it never to be, that something different, never, anywhere, in all time? What a tragedy! Soon he would be dead and then it would never be anywhere—anymore! Ernestine was charming, he would admit, or had been at first, though time had proved that she was not charming to him either mentally or physically in any compelling way; but how did that help him now? How could it? He had actually found himself bored by her for more than twenty-seven years now, and this other dream growing, growing, growing—until—

But now he was old, and she was dying, or might be, and it could not make so much difference what happened to him or to her; only it could, too, because he wanted to be free for a little while, just for a little while, before he died.

To be free! free!

One of the things that had always irritated him about Mrs. Haymaker was this, that in spite of his determination never to offend the social code in any way—he had felt for so many reasons, emotional as well as practical, that he could not afford so to do—and also in spite of the fact that he had been tortured by this show of beauty in the eyes and bodies of others, his wife, fearing perhaps in some strange psychic way that he might change, had always tried to make him feel or believe —premeditatedly and of a purpose, he thought—that he was not the kind of man who would be attractive to women; that he lacked some physical fitness, some charm that other men had, which would cause all young and really charming women to turn away from him. Think of it! He to whom so many women had turned with questioning eyes!

Also that she had married him largely because she had felt sorry for him! He chose to let her believe that, because he was sorry for her. Because other women had seemed to draw near to him at times in some appealing or seductive way she had insisted that he was not even a cavalier, let alone a Lothario; that he was ungainly, slow, uninteresting—to all women but her!

Persistently, he thought, and without any

real need, she had harped on this, fighting chimeras, a chance danger in the future; though he had never given her any real reason, and had never even planned to sin against her in any way—never. She had thus tried to poison his own mind in regard to himself and his art—and yet—and yet— Ah, those eyes of other women, their haunting beauty, the flitting something they said to him of infinite, inexpressible delight. Why had his life been so very hard?

One of the disturbing things about all this was the iron truth which it had driven home, namely, that Nature, unless it were expressed or represented by some fierce determination within, which drove one to do, be, cared no whit for him or any other man or woman. Unless one acted for oneself, upon some stern conclusion nurtured within, one might rot and die spiritually. Nature did not care. "Blessed be the meek"—yes. Blessed be the strong, rather, for they made their own happiness. All these years in which he had dwelt and worked in this knowledge, hoping for something but not acting, nothing had happened, except to him, and that in an unsatisfactory way. All along he had seen what was happening to him; and yet held by convention he had refused to act always, because somehow he was not hard enough to act. He was not strong enough, that was the real truth—had not been. Almost like a bird in a cage, an animal peeping out from behind bars, he had viewed the world of free thought and freer action. In many a drawing-room, on the street, or in his own home even, had he not looked into an eye, the face of someone who seemed to offer understanding, to know, to sympathize, though she might not have, of course; and yet religiously and moralistically, like an anchorite, because of duty and current belief and what people would say and think, Ernestine's position and faith in him, her comfort, his career and that of the children—he had put them all aside, out of his mind, forgotten them almost, as best he might. It had been hard at times, and sad, but so it had been.

And look at him now, old, not exactly feeble yet—no, not that yet, not quite!—but life weary and almost indifferent. All these years he had wanted, wanted—wanted—an understanding mind, a tender heart, the some one woman—she must exist somewhere—who would have sympathized with all the delicate shades and meanings of his own character, his

art, his spiritual as well as his material dreams — And yet look at him! Mrs. Haymaker had always been with him, present in the flesh or the spirit, and—so—

Though he could not even say that she was disagreeable to him in a material way—he could not say that she had ever been that exactly—still she did not correspond to his idea of what he needed, and so— Form had meant so much to him, color; the glorious perfectness of a glorious woman's body, for instance, the color of her thoughts, moods—exquisite they must be, like his own at times; but no, he had never had the opportunity to know one intimately. No, not one, though he had dreamed of her so long. He had never even dared whisper this to any one, scarcely to himself. It was not wise, not socially fit. Thoughts like this would tend to social ostracism in his circle, or rather hers—for had she not made the circle?

And here was the rub with Mr. Haymaker, at least, that he could not make up his mind whether in his restlessness and private mental complaints he were not even now guilty of a great moral crime in so thinking. Was it not true that men and women should be faithful in marriage whether they were happy or not? Was there not some psychic law governing this matter of union—one life, one love—which made the thoughts and the pains and the subsequent sufferings and hardships of the individual, whatever they might be, seem unimportant? The churches said so. Public opinion and the law seemed to accept this. There were so many problems, so much order to be disrupted, so much pain caused, many insoluable problems where children were concerned—if people did not stick. Was it not best, more blessed—socially, morally, and in every other way important—for him to stand by a bad bargain rather than to cause so much disorder and pain, even though he lost his own soul emotionally? He had thought so—or at least he had acted as though he thought so—and yet—How often had he wondered over this!

Take, now, some other phases. Granting first that Mrs. Haymaker had, according to the current code, measured up to the requirements of a wife, good and true, and that at first after marriage there had been just enough of physical and social charm about her to keep his state from becoming intolerable, still there was this old ache; and then newer things which came with the birth of the several children: First Elwell—named after a cousin of hers, not his—who had died only two years after he was born; and then Wesley; and then Ethelberta. How he had always disliked that name!—largely because he had hoped to call her Ottilie, a favorite name of his; or Janet, after his mother.

Curiously the arrival of these children and the death of poor little Elwell at two had somehow, in spite of his unrest, bound him to this matrimonial state and filled him with a sense of duty, and pleasure even—almost entirely apart from her, he was sorry to say—in these young lives; though if there had not been children, as he sometimes told himself, he surely would have broken away from her; he could not have stood it. They were so odd in their infancy, those little ones, so troublesome and yet so amusing—little Elwell, for instance, whose nose used to crinkle with delight when he would pretend to bite his neck, and whose gurgle of pleasure was so sweet and heart-filling that it positively thrilled and lured him. In spite of his thoughts concerning Ernestine —and always in those days they were rigidly put down as unmoral and even evil, a certain unsocial streak in him perhaps which was against law and order and social well-being—he came to have a deep and abiding feeling for Elwell. The latter, in some chemic, almost unconscious way, seemed to have arrived as a balm to his misery, a bandage for his growing wound —sent by whom, by what, how? Elwell had seized upon his imagination, and so his heartstrings—had come, indeed, to make him feel understanding and sympathy there in that little child; to supply, or seem to at least, what he lacked in the way of love and affection from one whom he could truly love. Elwell was never so happy apparently as when snuggling in his arms, not Ernestine's, or lying against his neck. And when he went for a walk or elsewhere there was Elwell always ready, arms up, to cling to his neck. He seemed, strangely enough, inordinately fond of his father, rather than his mother, and never happy without him. On his part, Haymaker came to be wildly fond of him—that queer little lump of a face, suggesting a little of himself and of his own mother, not so much of Ernestine, or so he thought, though he would not have objected to that. Not at all. He was not so small as that. Toward the end of the second year, when Elwell was just beginning to be able to utter a word or two, he had taught him that silly old rhyme which ran "There were three kittens,"

and when it came to "and they shall have no—" he would stop and say to Elwell, "What now?" and the latter would gurgle "puh!"—meaning, of course, pie.

Ah, those happy days with little Elwell, those walks with him over his shoulder or on his arm, those hours in which of an evening he would rock him to sleep in his arms! Always Ernestine was there, and happy in the thought of his love for little Elwell and her, her more than anything else perhaps; but it was an illusion—that latter part. He did not care for her even then as she thought he did. All his fondness was for Elwell, only she took it as evidence of his growing or enduring affection for her—another evidence of the peculiar working of her mind. Women were like that, he supposed—some women.

And then came that dreadful fever, due to some invading microbe which the doctors could not diagnose or isolate, infantile paralysis perhaps; and little Elwell had finally ceased to be as flesh and was eventually carried forth to the lorn, disagreeable graveyard near Woodlawn. How he had groaned internally, indulged in sad, despondent thoughts concerning the futility of all things human, when this had happened! It seemed for the time being as if all color and beauty had really gone out of his life for good.

"Man born of woman is of few days and full of troubles," the preacher whom Mrs. Haymaker had insisted upon having into the house at the time of the funeral had read. "He fleeth also as a shadow and continueth not."

Yes; so little Elwell had fled, as a shadow, and in his own deep sorrow at the time he had come to feel the first and only sad, deep sympathy for Ernestine that he had ever felt since marriage; and that because she had suffered so much—had lain in his arms after the funeral and cried so bitterly. It was terrible, her sorrow. Terrible—a mother grieving for her first-born! Why was it, he had thought at the time, that he had never been able to think or make her all she ought to be to him? Ernestine at this time had seemed better, softer, kinder, wiser, sweeter than she had ever seemed; more worthy, more interesting than ever he had thought her before. She had slaved so during the child's illness, stayed awake night after night, watched over him with such loving care —done everything, in short, that a loving human heart could do to rescue her young from the depths; and yet even then he had not really been able to love her. No, sad and un-kind as it might seem, he had not. He had just pitied her and thought her better, worthier! What cursed stars disordered the minds and moods of people so? Why was it that these virtues of people, their good qualities, did not make you love them, did not really bind them to you, as against the things you could not like? Why? He had resolved to do better in his thoughts, but somehow, in spite of himself, he had never been able so to do.

Nevertheless, at that time he seemed to real-ize more keenly than ever her order, industry, frugality, a sense of beauty within limits, a certain laudable ambition to do something and be somebody—only, only he could not sym-pathize with her ambitions, could not see that she had anything but a hopelessly common-place and always unimportant point of view. There was never any flare to her, never any true distinction of mind or soul. She seemed always, in spite of anything he might say or do, hopelessly to identify doing and being with money and current opinion—neighborhood public opinion, almost—and local social posi-tion, whereas he knew that distinguished doing might as well be connected with poverty and shame and disgrace as with these other things —wealth and station, for instance; a thing which she could never quite understand ap-parently, though he often tried to tell her, much against her mood always.

. . .

And in the matter of rearing and educating and marrying their two children, Wesley and Ethelberta, who had come after Elwell—what peculiar pains and feelings had not been in-volved in all this for him. In infancy both of these had seemed sweet enough, and so close to him, though never quite so wonderful as Elwell. But, as they grew, it seemed somehow as though Ernestine had come between him and them. First, it was the way she had raised them, the very stiff and formal manner in which they were supposed to move and be, copied from the few new-rich whom she had chanced to meet through him—and admired in spite of his warnings. That was the irony of architecture as a profession—it was always bringing such queer people close to one, and for the sake of one's profession, sometimes, particularly in the case of the young architect, one had to be nice to them. Later, it was the kind of school they should attend. He had half

imagined at first that it would be the public school, because they both had begun as simple people; but no, since they were prospering it had to be a private school for each, and not one of his selection, either—or hers, really— but one to which the Barlows and the Wester-velts, two families of means with whom Ernestine had become intimate, sent their children and therefore thought excellent!

The Barlows! Wealthy, but, to him, gross and mediocre people who had made a great deal of money in the manufacture of patent medicines out West, and who had then come to New York to splurge, and had been at-tracted to Ernestine—not him particularly, he imagined—because Haymaker had built a town house for them, and also because he was gaining a fine reputation. They were dreadful really, so *gauche*, so truly dull; and yet some-how they seemed to suit Ernestine's sense of fitness and worth at the time, because, as she said, they were good and kind—like her West-ern home folks; only they were not really. She just imagined so. They were worthy enough people in their way, though with no taste. Young Fred Barlow had been sent to the ex-pensive Gaillard School for Boys, near Morris-town, where they were taught manners and airs, and little else, as Haymaker always thought, though Ernestine insisted that they were given a religious training as well. And so Wesley had to go there—for a time, anyhow. It was the best school.

And similarly, because Mercedes Wester-velt, senseless, vain little thing, was sent to Briarcliff School, near White Plains, Ethelberta had to go there. Think of it! It was all so silly, so pushing. How well he remembered the long, delicate campaign which proceeded this, the logic and tactics employed, the importance of it socially to Ethelberta, the tears and cajolery. Mrs. Haymaker could always cry so easily, or seem to be on the verge of it, when she wanted anything; and somehow, in spite of the fact that he knew her tears were unimportant, or timed and for a purpose, he could never stand out against them, and she knew it. Always he felt moved or weakened in spite of himself. He had no weapon wherewith to fight them, though he resented them as a part of the argu-ment. Positively Mrs. Haymaker could be as sly and as ruthless as Machiavelli himself at times, and yet believe all the while that she was tender, loving, self-sacrificing, generous, moral and a dozen other things, all of which led to the final achievement of her own aims. Perhaps this was admirable from one point of view, but it irritated him always. But if one were unable to see himself or herself, their actual disturbing inconsistencies, what were you to do?

And again, he had by then been married so long that it was almost impossible to think of throwing her over, or so it seemed at the time. They had reached the place then where they had supposedly achieved position together, though in reality it was all his—and not such position as he was entitled to, at that. Ernestine —and he was thinking this in all kindness— could never attract the ideal sort. And anyhow, the mere breath of a scandal between them, separation or unfaithfulness, which he never really contemplated, would have led to endless bickering and social and commercial injury, or so he thought. All her strong friends—and his, in a way—those who had originally been his clients, would have deserted him. Their wives, their own social fears, would have compelled them to ostracize him! He would have been a scandal-marked architect, a brute for objecting to so kind and faithful and loving a wife. And perhaps he would have been, at that. He could never quite tell, it was all so mixed and tangled.

Take, again, the marriage of his son Wesley into the De Gaud family—George de Gaud *père* being nothing more than a retired real-estate speculator and promoter who had money, but nothing more; and Irma de Gaud, the daughter, being a gross, coarse, sensuous girl, physically attractive no doubt, and financially reasonably secure, or so she had seemed; but what else? Nothing, literally nothing; and his son had seemed to have at least some spiritual ideals at first. Ernestine had taken up with Mrs. George de Gaud—a miserable, narrow creature, so Haymaker thought—largely for Wesley's sake, he presumed. Anyhow, everything had been done to encourage Wesley in his suit and Irma in her toleration, and now look at them! De Gaud *père* had since failed and left his daughter practically nothing. Irma had been interested in anything but Wesley's career, had followed what she considered the smart among the new-rich—a smarter, wilder, newer new-rich than ever Ernestine had fancied, or could. To-day she was without a thought for anything besides teas and country clubs and theaters—and what else?

And long since Wesley had begun to realize it himself. He was an engineer now, in the employ of one of the great construction companies, a moderately successful man. But even Ernestine, who had engineered the match and thought it wonderful, was now down on her. She had begun to see through her some years ago, when Irma had begun to ignore her; only before it was always the De Gauds here, and the De Gauds there. Good gracious, what more could any one want than the De Gauds —Irma de Gaud, for instance? Then came the concealed dissension between Irma and Wesley, and now Mrs. Haymaker insisted that Irma had held, and was holding Wesley back. She was not the right woman for him. Almost —against all her prejudices—she was willing that he should leave her. Only, if Haymaker had broached anything like that in connection with himself!

And yet Mrs. Haymaker had been determined, because of what she considered the position of the De Gauds at that time, that Wesley should marry Irma. Wesley now had to slave at mediocre tasks in order to have enough to allow Irma to run in so-called fast society of a second or third rate. And even at that she was not faithful to him—or so Haymaker believed. There were so many strange evidences. And yet Haymaker felt that he did not care to interfere now. How could he? Irma was tired of Wesley, and that was all there was to it. She was looking elsewhere, he was sure.

Take but one more case, that of Ethelberta. What a name! In spite of all Ernestine's determination to make her so successful and thereby reflect some credit on her had she really succeeded in so doing? To be sure, Ethelberta's marriage was somewhat more successful financially than Wesley's had proved to be, but was she any better placed in other ways? John Kelso—"Jack," as she always called him—with his light ways and lighter mind, was he really any one!—anything more than a waster? His parents stood by him no doubt, but that was all; and so much the worse for him. According to Mrs. Haymaker at the time, he, too, was an ideal boy, admirable, just the man for Ethelberta, because the Kelsos, *père* and *mère*, had money. Horner Kelso had made a kind of fortune in Chicago in the banknote business, and had settled in New York, about the time that Ethelberta was fifteen, to spend it. Ethelberta had met Grace Kelso at school.

And now see! She was not unattractive, and had some pleasant, albeit highly affected, so-

cial ways; she had money, and a comfortable apartment in Park Avenue, but what had it all come to? John Kelso had never done anything really, nothing. His parents' money and indulgence and his early training for a better social state had ruined him if he had ever had a mind that amounted to anything. He was idle, pleasure-loving, mentally indolent, like Irma de Gaud. Those two should have met and mar-
10 ried, only they could never have endured each other. But how Mrs. Haymaker had courted the Kelsos in her eager and yet diplomatic way, giving teas and receptions and theater parties; and yet he had never been able to exchange ten significant words with either of them, or the younger Kelsos either. Think of it!

And somehow in the process Ethelberta, for all his early affection and tenderness and his
20 still kindly feeling for her, had been weaned away from him and had proved a limited and conventional girl, somewhat like her mother, and more inclined to listen to her than to him —though he had not minded that really. It had been the same with Wesley before her. Perhaps, however, a child was entitled to its likes and dislikes, regardless.

· · ·

30 The next morning, the second after his talk with Doctor Storm, found him sitting once more beside his front window in the early dawn, and so much of all this, and much more, was coming back to him as before. For the thousandth or the ten-thousandth time, as it seemed to him, in all the years that had gone, he was concluding again that his life was a failure. If only he were free for a little while just to be alone and think, perhaps to discover
40 what life might bring him yet; only on this occasion his thoughts were colored by a new turn in the situation. Yesterday afternoon, because Mrs. Haymaker's condition had grown worse, the consultation between Grainger and Storm was held, and to-day sometime transfusion was to be tried, that last grim stand taken by physicians in distress over a case; blood taken from a strong ex-cavalryman out of a position, in this case, and the best to be
50 hoped for, but not assured. In this instance his thoughts were as before wavering. Now supposing she really died, in spite of this? What would he think of himself then? He went back after a time and looked in on her where she was still sleeping. Now she was not so strong

as before, or so she seemed; her pulse was not so good, the nurse said. And now as before his mood changed in her favor, but only for a little while. For later, waking, she seemed to look and feel better.

· · ·

Haymaker merely stared at her from under his heavy gray eyebrows. He was so tired and gloomy, not only because he had not slept much of late himself but because of this sawing to and fro between his varying moods. Was he never to be able to decide for himself what he really wished? Was he never to be done with this interminable moral or spiritual problem? Why could he not make up his mind on the side of moral order, sympathy, and be at peace? Miss Filson pattered on about other heart cases, how so many people lived years and years after they were supposed to die of heart lesion; and he meditated as to the grayness and strangeness of it all, the worthlessness of his own life, the variability of his own moods. Why was he so? How queer—how almost evil, sinister—he had become at times; how weak at others. Last night as he had looked at Ernestine lying in bed, and this morning before he had seen her, he had thought if she only would die—if he were only really free once more, even at this late date. But then when he had seen her again this morning and now when Miss Filson spoke of transfusion, he felt sorry again. What good would it do him now? Why should he want to kill her? Could such evil ideas go unpunished either in this world or the next? Supposing his children could guess! Supposing she did die now—and he wished it so fervently only this morning—how would he feel? After all, Ernestine had not been so bad. She had tried, hadn't she?—only she had not been able to make a success of things, as he saw it, and he had not been able to love her, that was all. He reproached himself once more now with the hardness and the cruelty of his thoughts.

The opinion of the two physicians was that Mrs. Haymaker was not much better and that this first form of blood transfusion must be resorted to—injected straight via a pump— which should restore her greatly provided her heart did not bleed it out too freely. Before doing so, however, both men once more spoke to Haymaker, who in an excess of self-condemnation insisted that no expense must be spared. If her life was in danger, save it by any means

—all. It was precious to her, to him and to her children. So he spoke. Thus he felt that he was lending every force which could be expected of him, aside from fervently wishing for her recovery, which even now, in spite of himself, he could not do. He was too weary of it all, the conventional round of duties and obligations. But if she recovered, as her physicians seemed to think she might if transfusion were tried, if she gained even, it would mean that he would have to take her away for the summer to some quiet mountain resort—to be with her hourly during the long period in which she would be recovering. Well, he would not complain now. That was all right. He would do it. He would be bored of course, as usual, but it would be too bad to have her die when she could be saved. Yes, that was true. And yet—

He went down to his office again and in the meantime this first form of transfusion was tried, and proved a great success, apparently. She was much better, so the day nurse phoned at three; very much better. At five-thirty Mr. Haymaker returned, no unsatisfactory word having come in the interim, and there she was, resting on a raised pillow, if you please, and looking so cheerful, more like her old self than he had seen her in some time.

At once then his mood changed again. They were amazing, these variations in his own thoughts, almost chemic, not volitional, decidedly peculiar for a man who was supposed to know his own mind—only did one, ever? Now she would not die. Now the whole thing would go on as before. He was sure of it. Well, he might as well resign himself to the old sense of failure. He would never be free now. Everything would go on as before, the next and the next day the same. Terrible! Though he seemed glad—really grateful, in a way, seeing her cheerful and hopeful once more—still the obsession of failure and being once more bound forever returned now. In his own bed at midnight he said to himself: "Now she will really get well. All will be as before. I will never be free. I will never have a day—a day! Never!"

But the next morning, to his surprise and fear or comfort, as his moods varied, she was worse again; and then once more he reproached himself for his black thoughts. Was he not really killing her by what he thought? he asked himself—these constant changes in his mood? Did not his dark wishes have power? Was he not as good as a murderer in his way?

Think, if he had always to feel from now on that he had killed her by wishing so! Would not that be dreadful—an awful thing really? Why was he this way? Could he not be human, kind?

When Doctor Storm came at nine-thirty, after a telephone call from the nurse, and looked grave and spoke of horses' blood as being better, thicker than human blood—not so easily bled out of the heart when injected as a serum—Haymaker was beside himself with self-reproaches and sad, disturbing fear. His dark, evil thoughts of last night and all these days had done this, he was sure. Was he really a murderer at heart, a dark criminal, plotting her death?—and for what? Why had he wished last night that she would die? Her case must be very desperate.

"You must do your best," he now said to Doctor Storm. "Whatever is needful—she must not die if you can help it."

"No, Mr. Haymaker," returned the latter sympathetically. "All that can be done will be done. You need not fear. I have an idea that we didn't inject enough yesterday, and anyhow human blood is not thick enough in this case. She responded, but not enough. We will see what we can do to-day."

Haymaker, pressed with duties, went away, subdued and sad. Now once more he decided that he must not tolerate these dark ideas any more, must rid himself of these black wishes, whatever he might feel. It was evil. They would eventually come back to him in some dark way, he might be sure. They might be influencing her. She must be allowed to recover if she could without any opposition on his part. He must now make a further sacrifice of his own life, whatever it cost. It was only decent, only human. Why should he complain now, anyhow, after all these years! What difference would a few more years make? He returned at evening, consoled by his own good thoughts and a telephone message at three to the effect that his wife was much better. This second injection had proved much more effective. Horses' blood was plainly better for her. She was stronger, and sitting up again. He entered at five, and found her lying there pale and weak, but still with a better light in her eye, a touch of color in her cheeks—or so he thought—more force, and a very faint smile for him, so marked had been the change. How great and kind Doctor Storm really was! How resourceful! If she would only get well now! If this dread siege would only abate! Doctor Storm was coming again at eight.

"Well, how are you, dear?" she asked, looking at him sweetly and lovingly, and taking his hand in hers.

He bent and kissed her forehead—a Judas kiss, he had thought up to now, but not so to-night. To-night he was kind, generous—anxious, even, for her to live.

"All right, dearest; very good indeed. And how are you? It's such a fine evening out. You ought to get well soon so as to enjoy these spring days."

"I'm going to," she replied softly. "I feel so much better. And how have you been? Has your work gone all right?"

He nodded and smiled and told her bits of news. Ethelberta had phoned that she was coming, bringing violets. Wesley had said he would be here at six, with Irma! Such-and-such people had asked after her. How could he have been so evil, he now asked himself, as to wish her to die? She was not so bad—really quite charming in her way, an ideal wife for some one, if not him. She was as much entitled to live and enjoy her life as he was to enjoy his; and after all she was the mother of his children, had been with him all these years. Besides, the day had been so fine—it was now—a wondrous May evening. The air and sky were simply delicious. A lavender haze was in the air. The telephone bell now ringing brought still another of a long series of inquiries as to her condition. There had been so many of these during the last few days, the maid said, and especially to-day—and she gave Mr. Haymaker a list of names. See, he thought, she had even more friends than he, being so good, faithful, worthy. Why should he wish her ill?

He sat down to dinner with Ethelberta and Wesley when they arrived, and chatted quite gayly—more hopefully than he had in weeks. His own varying thoughts no longer depressing him, for the moment he was happy. How were they? What were the children all doing? At eight-thirty Doctor Storm came again, and announced that he thought Mrs. Haymaker was doing very well indeed, all things considered.

"Her condition is fairly promising, I must say," he said. "If she gets through another night or two comfortably without falling back I think she'll do very well from now on. Her strength seems to be increasing a fraction. However, we must not be too optimistic. Cases of this kind are very treacherous. To-morrow

we'll see how she feels, whether she needs any more blood."

He went away, and at ten Ethelberta and Wesley left for the night, asking to be called if she grew worse, thus leaving him alone once more. He sat and meditated. At eleven, after a few moments at his wife's bedside—absolute quiet had been the doctor's instructions these many days—he himself went to bed. He was very tired. His varying thoughts had afflicted him so much that he was always tired, it seemed—his evil conscience, he called it—but to-night he was sure he would sleep. He felt better about himself, about life. He had done better to-day. He should never have tolerated such dark thoughts. And yet—and yet—and yet—

He lay on his bed near a window which commanded a view of a small angle of the park, and looked out. There were the spring trees, as usual, silvered now by the light, a bit of lake showing at one end. Here in the city a bit of sylvan scenery such as this was so rare and so expensive. In his youth he had been so fond of water, any small lake or stream or pond. In his youth, also, he had loved the moon, and to walk in the dark. It had all, always, been so suggestive of love and happiness, and he had so craved love and happiness and never had it. Once he had designed a yacht club, the base of which suggested waves. Once, years ago, he had thought of designing a lovely cottage or country house for himself and some new love —that wonderful one—if ever she came and he were free. How wonderful it would all have been. Now—now—the thought at such an hour and especially when it was too late, seemed sacrilegious, hard, cold, unmoral, evil. He turned his face away from the moonlight and sighed, deciding to sleep and shut out these older and darker and sweeter thoughts if he could, and did.

Presently he dreamed, and it was as if some lovely spirit of beauty—that wondrous thing he had always been seeking—came and took him by the hand and led him out, out by dimpling streams and clear rippling lakes and a great, noble highway where were temples and towers and figures in white marble. And it seemed as he walked as if something had been, or were, promised him—a lovely fruition to something which he craved—only the world toward which he walked was still dark or shadowy, with something sad and repressing about it, a haunting sense of a still darker distance. He was going toward beauty apparently, but he was still seeking, seeking, and it was dark there when—

"Mr. Haymaker! Mr. Haymaker!" came a voice—soft, almost mystical at first, and then clearer and more disturbing, as a hand was laid on him. "Will you come at once? It's Mrs. Hay-maker!"

On the instant he was on his feet seizing the blue silk dressing gown hanging at his bed's head, and adjusting it as he hurried. Mrs. Elf-ridge and the nurse were behind him, very pale and distrait, wringing their hands. He could tell by that that the worst was at hand. When he reached the bedroom—her bedroom—there she lay as in life—still, peaceful, already limp, as though she were sleeping. Her thin, and as he sometimes thought, cold, lips were now parted in a faint, gracious smile, or trace of one. He had seen her look that way, too, at times; a really gracious smile, and wise, wiser than she was. The long, thin, graceful hands were open, the fingers spread slightly apart as though she were tired, very tired. The eyelids, too, rested wearily on tired eyes. Her form, spare as always, was outlined clearly under the thin coverlets. Miss Filson, the night nurse, was saying something about having fallen asleep for a moment, and waking only to find her so. She was terribly depressed and disturbed, possibly because of Doctor Storm.

Haymaker paused, greatly shocked and moved by the sight—more so than by anything since the death of little Elwell. After all, she had tried, according to her light. But now she was dead—and they had been together so long! He came forward, tears of sympathy springing to his eyes, then sank down beside the bed on his knees so as not to disturb her right hand where it lay.

"Ernie, dear," he said gently, "Ernie—are you really gone?" His voice was full of sorrow; but to himself it sounded false, traitorous.

He lifted the hand and put it to his lips sadly, then leaned his head against her, thinking of his long, mixed thoughts these many days, while both Mrs. Elfridge and the nurse began wiping their eyes. They were so sorry for him, he was so old now!

After a while he got up—they came forward to persuade him at last—looking tremendously sad and distrait, and asked Mrs. Elfridge and the nurse not to disturb his children. They could not aid her now. Let them rest until morning. Then he went back to his own room and sat down on the bed for a moment, gazing out on the same silvery scene that had attracted him before. It was dreadful. So then his dark wishing had come true at last? Possibly his black thoughts had killed her after all. Was that possible? Had his voiceless prayers been answered in this grim way? And did she know now what he had really thought? Dark thought. Where was she now? What was she thinking now if she knew? Would she hate him—haunt him? It was not dawn yet, only two or three in the morning, and the moon was still bright. And in the next room she was lying, pale and cool, gone forever now out of his life.

He got up after a time and went forward into that pleasant front room where he had so often loved to sit, then back into her room to view the body again. Now that she was gone, here more than elsewhere, in her dead presence, he seemed better able to collect his scattered thoughts. She might see or she might not—might know or not. It was all over now. Only he could not help but feel a little evil. She had been so faithful, if nothing more, so earnest in behalf of him and of his children. He might have spared her these last dark thoughts of these last few days. His feelings were so jumbled that he could not place them half the time. But at the same time the ethics of the past, of his own irritated feelings and moods in regard to her, had to be adjusted somehow before he could have peace. They must be adjusted, only how—how? He and Mrs. Elfridge had agreed not to disturb Doctor Storm any more to-night. They were all agreed to get what rest they could against the morning.

After a time he came forward once more to the front room to sit and gaze at the park. Here, perhaps, he could solve these mysteries for himself, think them out, find out what he did feel. He was evil for having wished all he had, that he knew and felt. And yet there was his own story, too—his life. The dawn was breaking by now; a faint grayness shaded the east and dimly lighted this room. A tall pier mirror between two windows now revealed him to himself—spare, angular, disheveled, his beard and hair astray and his eyes weary. The figure he made here as against his dreams of a happier life, once he were free, now struck him forcibly. What a farce! What a failure! Why should he, of all people, think of further happiness in love, even if he were free? Look at his reflection here in this mirror. What a picture—old, grizzled, done for! Had he not known that for so long? Was it not too ridiculous? Why should he have tolerated such vain thoughts? What could he of all people hope for now? No thing of beauty would have him now. Of course not. That glorious dream of his youth was gone forever. It was a mirage, an ignis fatuus. His wife might just as well have lived as died, for all the difference it would or could make to him. Only, he was really free just the same, almost as it were in spite of his varying moods. But he was old, weary, done for, a recluse and ungainly.

Now the innate cruelty of life, its blazing ironic indifference to him and so many grew rapidly upon him. What had he had? What all had he not missed? Dismally he stared first at his dark wrinkled skin; the crow's-feet at the sides of his eyes; the wrinkles across his forehead and between the eyes; his long, dark, wrinkled hands—handsome hands they once were, he thought; his angular, stiff body. Once he had been very much of a personage, he thought, striking, forceful, dynamic—but now! He turned and looked out over the park where the young trees were and the lake, to the pinking dawn—just a trace now—a significant thing in itself at this hour surely—the new dawn, so wondrously new for younger people —then back at himself. What could he wish for now—what hope for?

As he did so his dream came back to him— that strange dream of seeking and being led and promised and yet always being led forward into a dimmer, darker land. What did that mean? Had it any real significance? Was it all to be dimmer, darker still? Was it typical of his life? He pondered.

"Free!" he said after a time. "Free! I know now how that is. I am free now, at last! Free! . . . Free! . . . Yes—free . . . to die!"

So he stood there ruminating and smoothing his hair and his beard.   1918

SHERWOOD ANDERSON

1876–1941

THOUGH Sherwood Anderson often nibbled at the periphery of excellence, only occasionally did he reach the center, and one often finds him lingering in remote and shadowy eccentricities. "I dare say," he wrote once, "that the tragedy of Ring Lardner . . . that gorgeous talent of his so often smeared . . . is our common tragedy, the tragedy of every creative man, big or little, in our day." The tragedy of Anderson is that he might have been great had he disciplined his powers. He took refuge in the thought that human beings are lonely entities who cannot be completely known, even by themselves, and that their stories cannot be completely told, even by themselves. Lardner's perception of human depravity deepened his despondency, and sharpened his pen. Anderson's strong humanitarian sympathies too often led him into fumbling social theory or sentimental romancing. But his influence is still large and will be lasting. An eminent pioneer in the liberation of the short story, he contrived to thaw the frozen schemata by which the development of the form had been until his time severely inhibited.

"My notion," says a poem of Anderson's, "is one of escape." He came to literature tardily, gropingly, and by way of escape from business. His father was an itinerant harness-maker, gifted as a raconteur, shiftless as a paterfamilias. (See *A Story Teller's Story*, 1924, and the autobiographical novel, *Tar*, 1927.) From odd jobs around race-tracks (*Horses and Men*, 1923) and small Ohio towns, the boy escaped in his late teens to factory work in Chicago, to soldiering in the Spanish-American War, to advertising, to management of a flourishing paint-business in Elyria, Ohio. One day, struck by the direction his life had taken, he laughed mysteriously in the face of his stenographer and walked out of factory and town. At forty, he escaped into literary life with the publication of his first novel, and there he remained, contributing to periodicals and averaging, during his active years, a book a year. Part of 1922 he spent with Faulkner in New Orleans. In 1925 he bought a farm and later two weekly papers in Marion, Virginia, where he spent the final years of his life as a country editor. (See *Hello, Towns!* 1929.)

His seven novels develop the themes closest his heart: man's perplexity in the sterile world of machines and business, his equal befuddlement amidst the dark play of more intimate social forces. McPherson, McGregor, and McVey, respective heroes of *Windy McPherson's Son* (1916), *Marching Men* (1917), and *Poor White* (1920), all rise from poverty to eminence in business, but achieve little satisfaction in the process. The heroes of *Many Marriages* (1923) and *Dark Laughter* (1925) follow Anderson in abandoning business and marital ties in sudden resolutions based on cumulative dissatisfactions. In Southern textile towns the same old perplexities bother Red Oliver (*Beyond Desire*, 1933) and the titular heroine of *Kit Brandon* (1936).

But Anderson is never so good as in the volumes of short stories (*Winesburg, Ohio*, 1919; *The Triumph of the Egg*, 1921; *Horses and Men*, 1923; and *Death in The Woods*, 1933). The first of these he never excelled. As a young factory-hand in a Chicago boarding-house he tried to imagine the inner lives of the people he saw around him, and tied the stories together by giving them a common locale in the mythical Winesburg. They are a frustrated lot, "misfits, mutterers, crazy rebels, bedroom brooders, life-starved Americans drowned in stark solitude of soul." Anderson looks for the vital moments in their drab lives, their sudden impulses toward love or other forms of escape from the environmental husks that enclose them.

C. B. Chase, *Sherwood Anderson*, New York, 1927.
Nathan Fagin, "Sherwood Anderson," *South Atlantic Quarterly*, XLIII (July, 1944), 256–262.
Irving Howe, *Sherwood Anderson*, New York, 1951.
Alfred Kazin, *On Native Grounds*, New York, 1942, pp. 205–226.
Paul Rosenfeld, "Sherwood Anderson," *Dial*, LXXII (January, 1922), 29–42.
J. E. Schevill, *Sherwood Anderson, His Life and Work*, Denver, 1951.
Lionel Trilling, "Sherwood Anderson," *Kenyon Review*, III (Summer, 1941), 293–302.
Carl Van Doren, "Sinclair Lewis and Sherwood Anderson," *Century Magazine*, CX (July, 1925), 362–369.

» » *From:* WINESBURG, OHIO « «

MOTHER

Elizabeth Willard, the mother of George Willard, was tall and gaunt and her face was marked with smallpox scars. Although she was but forty-five, some obscure disease had taken the fire out of her figure. Listlessly she went about the disorderly old hotel looking at the faded wall-paper and the ragged carpets and, when she was able to be about, doing the work of a chambermaid among beds soiled by the slumbers of fat traveling men. Her husband, Tom Willard, slender, graceful man with square shoulders, a quick military step, and a black mustache, trained to turn sharply up at the ends, tried to put the wife out of his mind. The presence of the tall ghostly figure, moving slowly through the halls, he took as a reproach to himself. When he thought of her he grew angry and swore. The hotel was unprofitable and forever on the edge of failure and he wished himself out of it. He thought of the old house and the woman who lived there with him as things defeated and done for. The hotel in which he had begun life so hopefully was now a mere ghost of what a hotel should be. As he went spruce and businesslike through the streets of Winesburg, he sometimes stopped and turned quickly about as though fearing that the spirit of the hotel and of the woman would follow him even into the streets. "Damn such a life, damn it!" he sputtered aimlessly.

Tom Willard had a passion for village politics and for years had been the leading

Democrat in a strongly Republican community. Some day, he told himself, the tide of things political will turn in my favor and the years of ineffectual service count big in the bestowal of rewards. He dreamed of going to Congress and even of becoming governor. Once when a younger member of the party arose at a political conference and began to boast of his faithful service, Tom Willard grew white with fury. "Shut up, you," he roared, glaring about. "What do you know of service? What are you but a boy? Look at what I've done here! I was a Democrat here in Winesburg when it was a crime to be a Democrat. In the old days they fairly hunted us with guns."

Between Elizabeth and her one son George there was a deep unexpressed bond of sympathy, based on a girlhood dream that had long ago died. In the son's presence she was timid and reserved, but sometimes while he hurried about town intent upon his duties as a reporter, she went into his room and closing the door knelt by a little desk, made of a kitchen table, that sat near a window. In the room by the desk she went through a ceremony that was half a prayer, half a demand, addressed to the skies. In the boyish figure she yearned to see something half forgotten that had once been a part of herself recreated. The prayer concerned that. "Even though I die, I will in some way keep defeat away from you," she cried, and so deep was her determination that her whole body shook. Her eyes glowed and she clenched her fists. "If I am dead and see him becoming a meaningless drab figure like myself, I will come back," she declared. "I ask God now to give me that privilege. I demand it. I will pay for it. God may beat me with his fists. I will take any blow that may befall if but this my boy be allowed to express something for us both." Pausing uncertainly, the woman stared about the boy's room. "And do not let him become smart and successful either," she added vaguely.

The communion between George Willard and his mother was outwardly a formal thing without meaning. When she was ill and sat by the window in her room he sometimes went in the evening to make her a visit. They sat by a window that looked over the roof of a small frame building into Main Street. By turning their heads they could see, through another window, along an alleyway that ran behind the Main Street stores and into the back door of Abner Groff's bakery. Sometimes as they sat thus a picture of village life presented itself to them. At the back door of his shop appeared Abner Groff with a stick or an empty milk bottle in his hand. For a long time there was a feud between the baker and a grey cat that belonged to Sylvester West, the druggist. The boy and his mother saw the cat creep into the door of the bakery and presently emerge followed by the baker who swore and waved his arms about. The baker's eyes were small and red and his black hair and beard were filled with flour dust. Sometimes he was so angry that, although the cat had disappeared, he hurled sticks, bits of broken glass, and even some of the tools of his trade about. Once he broke a window at the back of Sinning's Hardware Store. In the alley the grey cat crouched behind barrels filled with torn paper and broken bottles above which flew a black swarm of flies. Once when she was alone, and after watching a prolonged and ineffectual outburst on the part of the baker, Elizabeth Willard put her head down on her long white hands and wept. After that she did not look along the alleyway any more, but tried to forget the contest between the bearded man and the cat. It seemed like a rehearsal of her own life, terrible in its vividness.

In the evening when the son sat in the room with his mother, the silence made them both feel awkward. Darkness came on and the evening train came in at the station. In the street below feet tramped up and down upon a board sidewalk. In the station yard, after the evening train had gone, there was a heavy silence. Perhaps Skinner Leason, the express agent, moved a truck the length of the station platform. Over on Main Street sounded a man's voice, laughing. The door of the express office banged. George Willard arose and crossing the room fumbled for the doorknob. Sometimes he knocked against a chair, making it scrape along the floor. By the window sat the sick woman, perfectly still, listless. Her long hands, white and bloodless, could be seen drooping over the ends of the arms of the chair. "I think you had better be out among the boys. You are too much indoors," she said, striving to relieve the embarrassment of the departure. "I thought I would take a walk," replied George Willard, who felt awkward and confused.

One evening in July, when the transient guests who made the New Willard House their temporary homes had become scarce, and the hallways, lighted only by kerosene lamps turned low, were plunged in gloom, Elizabeth Willard had an adventure. She had been ill in bed for several days and her son had not come to visit her. She was alarmed. The feeble blaze of life that remained in her body was blown into a flame by her anxiety and she crept out of bed, dressed and hurried along the hallway toward her son's room, shaking with exaggerated fears. As she went along she steadied herself with her hand, slipped along the papered walls of the hall and breathed with difficulty. The air whistled through her teeth. As she hurried forward she thought how foolish she was. "He is concerned with boyish affairs," she told herself. "Perhaps he has now begun to walk about in the evening with girls."

Elizabeth Willard had a dread of being seen by guests in the hotel that had once belonged to her father and the ownership of which still stood recorded in her name in the county courthouse. The hotel was continually losing patronage because of its shabbiness and she thought of herself as also shabby. Her own room was in an obscure corner and when she felt able to work she voluntarily worked among the beds, preferring the labor that could be done when the guests were abroad seeking trade among the merchants of Winesburg.

By the door of her son's room the mother knelt upon the floor and listened for some sound from within. When she heard the boy moving about and talking in low tones a smile came to her lips. George Willard had a habit of talking aloud to himself and to hear him doing so had always given his mother a peculiar pleasure. The habit in him, she felt, strengthened the secret bond that existed between them. A thousand times she had whispered to herself of the matter. "He is groping about, trying to find himself," she thought. "He is not a dull clod, all words and smartness. Within him there is a secret something that is striving to grow. It is the thing I let be killed in myself."

In the darkness in the hallway by the door the sick woman arose and started again toward her own room. She was afraid that the door would open and the boy come upon her. When she had reached a safe distance and was about to turn a corner into a second hallway she stopped and bracing herself with her hands waited, thinking to shake off a trembling fit of weakness that had come upon her. The presence of the boy in the room had made her happy. In her bed, during the long hours alone, the little fears that had visited her had become giants. Now they were all gone. "When I get back to my room I shall sleep," she murmured gratefully.

But Elizabeth Willard was not to return to her bed and to sleep. As she stood trembling in the darkness the door of her son's room opened and the boy's father, Tom Willard, stepped out. In the light that streamed out at the door he stood with the knob in his hand and talked. What he said infuriated the woman.

Tom Willard was ambitious for his son. He had always thought of himself as a successful man, although nothing he had ever done had turned out successfully. However, when he was out of sight of the New Willard House and had no fear of coming upon his wife, he swaggered and began to dramatize himself as one of the chief men of the town. He wanted his son to succeed. He it was who had secured for the boy the position on the *Winesburg Eagle.* Now, with a ring of earnestness in his voice, he was advising concerning some course of conduct. "I tell you what, George, you've got to wake up," he said sharply. "Will Henderson has spoken to me three times concerning the matter. He says you go along for hours not hearing when you are spoken to and acting like a gawky girl. What ails you?" Tom Willard laughed good-naturedly. "Well, I guess you'll get over it," he said. "I told Will that. You're not a fool and you're not a woman. You're Tom Willard's son and you'll wake up. I'm not afraid. What you say clears things up. If being a newspaper man has put the notion of becoming a writer into your mind that's all right. Only I guess you'll have to wake up to do that too, eh?"

Tom Willard went briskly along the hallway and down a flight of stairs to the office. The woman in the darkness could hear him laughing and talking with a guest who was striving to wear away a dull evening by dozing in a chair by the office door. She returned to the door of her son's room. The weakness had passed from her body as by a miracle and she stepped boldly along. A thousand ideas raced through her head. When she heard the scraping of a chair and the sound of a pen scratching upon paper, she again turned and went back along the hallway to her own room.

A definite determination had come into the mind of the defeated wife of the Winesburg

Hotel keeper. The determination was the result of long years of quiet and rather ineffectual thinking. "Now," she told herself, "I will act. There is something threatening my boy and I will ward it off." The fact that the conversation between Tom Willard and his son had been rather quiet and natural, as though an understanding existed between them, maddened her. Although for years she had hated her husband, her hatred had always before been a quite impersonal thing. He had been merely a part of something else that she hated. Now, and by the few words at the door, he had become the thing personified. In the darkness of her own room she clenched her fists and glared about. Going to a cloth bag that hung on a nail by the wall she took out a long pair of sewing scissors and held them in her hand like a dagger. "I will stab him," she said aloud. "He has chosen to be the voice of evil and I will kill him. When I have killed him something will snap within myself and I will die also. It will be a release for all of us."

In her girlhood and before her marriage with Tom Willard, Elizabeth had borne a somewhat shaky reputation in Winesburg. For years she had been what is called "stage-struck" and had paraded through the streets with traveling men guests at her father's hotel, wearing loud clothes and urging them to tell her of life in the cities out of which they had come. Once she startled the town by putting on men's clothes and riding a bicycle down Main Street.

In her own mind the tall dark girl had been in those days much confused. A great restlessness was in her and it expressed itself in two ways. First there was an uneasy desire for change, for some big definite movement to her life. It was this feeling that had turned her mind to the stage. She dreamed of joining some company and wandering over the world, seeing always new faces and giving something out of herself to all people. Sometimes at night she was quite beside herself with the thought, but when she tried to talk of the matter to the members of the theatrical companies that came to Winesburg and stopped at her father's hotel, she got nowhere. They did not seem to know what she meant, or if she did get something of her passion expressed, they only laughed. "It's not like that," they said. "It's as dull and uninteresting as this here. Nothing comes of it."

With the traveling men when she walked about with them, and later with Tom Willard, it was quite different. Always they seemed to understand and sympathize with her. On the side streets of the village, in the darkness under the trees, they took hold of her hand and she thought that something unexpressed in herself came forth and became a part of an unexpressed something in them.

And then there was the second expression of her restlessness. When that came she felt for a time released and happy. She did not blame the men who walked with her and later she did not blame Tom Willard. It was always the same, beginning with kisses and ending, after strange wild emotions, with peace and then sobbing repentance. When she sobbed she put her hand upon the face of the man and had always the same thought. Even though he were large and bearded she thought he had become suddenly a little boy. She wondered why he did not sob also.

In her room, tucked away in a corner of the old Willard House, Elizabeth Willard lighted a lamp and put it on a dressing table that stood by the door. A thought had come into her mind and she went to a closet and brought out a small square box and set it on the table. The box contained material for make-up and had been left with other things by a theatrical company that had once been stranded in Winesburg. Elizabeth Willard had decided that she would be beautiful. Her hair was still black and there was a great mass of it braided and coiled about her head. The scene that was to take place in the office below began to grow in her mind. No ghostly worn-out figure should confront Tom Willard, but something quite unexpected and startling. Tall and with dusky cheeks and hair that fell in a mass from her shoulders, a figure should come striding down the stairway before the startled loungers in the hotel office. The figure would be silent—it would be swift and terrible. As a tigress whose cub had been threatened would she appear, coming out of the shadows, stealing noiselessly along and holding the long wicked scissors in her hand.

With a little broken sob in her throat, Elizabeth Willard blew out the light that stood upon the table and stood weak and trembling in the darkness. The strength that had been as a miracle in her body left and she half reeled across the floor, clutching at the back of the chair in which she had spent so many long days staring out over the tin roofs into the main street of Winesburg. In the hallway there was the sound of footsteps and George Willard came in at the door. Sitting in a chair beside his mother he began to talk. "I'm going to get out of here," he said. "I don't know where I shall go or what I shall do but I am going away."

The woman in the chair waited and trembled. An impulse came to her. "I suppose you had better wake up," she said. "You think that? You will go to the city and make money, eh? It will be better for you, you think, to be a business man, to be brisk and smart and alive?" She waited and trembled.

The son shook his head. "I suppose I can't make you understand, but oh, I wish I could," he said earnestly. "I can't even talk to father about it. I don't try. There isn't any use. I don't know what I shall do. I just want to go away and look at people and think."

Silence fell upon the room where the boy and the woman sat together. Again, as on the other evenings, they were embarrassed. After a time the boy tried again to talk. "I suppose it won't be for a year or two but I've been thinking about it," he said, rising and going toward the door. "Something father said makes it sure that I shall have to go away." He fumbled with the door knob. In the room the silence became unbearable to the woman. She wanted to cry out with joy because of the words that had come from the lips of her son, but the expression of joy had become impossible to her. "I think you had better go out among the boys. You are too much indoors," she said. "I thought I would go for a little walk," replied the son, stepping awkwardly out of the room and closing the door.   1919

CARL SANDBURG

1878–

"I NEVER HAD supper with Abe Lincoln, nor a dish of soup with Jim Hill. But I've been around," said Sandburg. A proletarian Odysseus before he was twenty, he had roamed far and wide, working as stage-hand, harvest hand, house-painter, milkman, bus-boy, barber, and brick-maker. After six months in Puerto Rico with the Sixth Illinois Infantry during the Spanish-American War, he returned to his home in Galesburg, Illinois. There his Swedish-born parents lived; there he worked his way through Lombard College as tutor and janitor, and found time also to captain the basketball team and edit the undergraduate paper. After college his career gradually shaded from business through politics to newspaper work. During 1914 much of his work appeared in Harriet Monroe's *Poetry* and *Reedy's Mirror*. From 1917 to 1933, while his reputation steadily mounted with each of his books, Sandburg was associated with the Chicago *Daily News*, lecturing and guitar-strumming on the side. But by 1933 the uncompleted portion of his Lincoln biography (*The Prairie Years*, 2 vols., 1926; *The War Years*, 4 vols., 1939) claimed so much time that he retired from the *News* to a large house and workshop on the lakeshore sand-dunes near Harbert, Michigan. Harriet Monroe's prize poet became in 1940 Mr. Pulitzer's prize biographer-historian.

Sandburg's earlier volumes are part Whitman, part Imagist. More critical of what he saw than the omnivorous Whitman, Sandburg moved along the frontiers of commerce, "where smokestacks bite the sky with stub teeth." *Chicago Poems* (1916) are tough, defiant, working-class documents, framed in slangy vernacular. The poet frequents Jungheimer's, "the saloon with a soul," with stockyard pig-stickers and ice-handlers. He admires sturdy immigrants like Mrs. Giovannitti, pities the sweatshop girls that heaven forgot to protect. Social criticism is implicit also in *Smoke and Steel* (1920). Some of the free-verse biographies in *Cornhuskers* (1918), and the vignette on the Unknown Soldier in *Slabs of the Sunburnt West* (1922) could have served

Dos Passos as models for his sardonic profiles in *U. S. A.* Within the poet of the cacophonous city there was always another who hankered for the quiet prairie, the talk of wind with corn, the silent wheeling of constellations over Omaha. But Sandburg liked his landscapes with figures. "I am the people—the mob—the crowd—the mass," he said once in a Whitmanesque identification. The people, yes. He collected their folk-songs and ballads, scores of which had not hitherto seen print, in *American Songbag* (1927). He gave them free-verse history and a prophecy in *Good Morning, America* (1928). In *The People, Yes* (1936) he showed them that their slang, bulls, puns, tall tales, legends, and adages are the raw material of poetry. He crowned a useful life with a six-volume biography of the greatest man among them.

The people grope, asking, "Where now? What next?" Sandburg had a good answer in 1918, "We'll get along."

T. S. Shaw, *Carl Sandburg, a Bibliography*, Washington, 1948.
Complete Poems, New York, 1950.
Carl Sandburg, *Always the Young Strangers* (Autobiography), New York, 1952.
Rica Brenner, *Ten Modern Poets*, New York, 1930, pp. 119–148.
K. W. Detzer, *Carl Sandburg: A Study in Personality and Background*, New York, 1941.
Harry Hansen, *Midwest Portraits*, New York, 1923, pp. 17–91.
Journal of the Illinois State Historical Society, LXV (Winter, 1952). Carl Sandburg number.
Bruce Weirick, *From Whitman to Sandburg in American Poetry*, New York, 1928, pp. 210–221.
M. D. Zabel, "Sandburg's Testament," *Poetry*, XLIX (October, 1936), 33–45.

» » *From:* CHICAGO POEMS « «

GRAVES

I dreamed one man stood against a thousand,
One man damned as a wrongheaded fool.
One year and another he walked the streets,
And a thousand shrugs and hoots
Met him in the shoulders and mouths he
    passed.

    He died alone
And only the undertaker came to his funeral.

Flowers grow over his grave anod in the wind,
And over the graves of the thousand, too,
The flowers grow anod in the wind.   10

    Flowers and the wind,
Flowers anod over the graves of the dead,
Petals of red, leaves of yellow, streaks of white,
Masses of purple sagging . . .
I love you and your great way of forgetting.
    1916

» » *From:* CORNHUSKERS « «

THREE PIECES ON THE SMOKE OF AUTUMN

Smoke of autumn is on it all.
The streamers loosen and travel.
The red west is stopped with a gray haze.
They fill the ash trees, they wrap the oaks,
They make a long-tailed rider
In the pocket of the first, the earliest evening
    star.
    . . .

Three muskrats swim west on the Desplaines
    River.

There is a sheet of red ember glow on the
    river; it is dusk; and the muskrats one by one
    go on patrol routes west.   10

Around each slippery padding rat, a fan of
    ripples; in the silence of dusk a faint wash
    of ripples, the padding of the rats going
    west, in a dark and shivering river gold.

(A newspaper in my pocket says the Germans
pierce the Italian line; I have letters from
poets and sculptors in Greenwich Village;
I have letters from an ambulance man in
France and an I.W.W. man in Vladivo-
stok.)   19

I lean on an ash and watch the lights fall, the
red ember glow, and three muskrats swim
west in a fan of ripples on a sheet of river
gold.

. . .

Better the blue silence and the gray west,
The autumn mist on the river,
And not any hate and not any love,
And not anything at all of the keen and the
deep:
Only the peace of a dog head on the barn floor,
And the new corn shoveled in bushels
And the pumpkins brought from the corn rows,
Umber lights of the dark,   30
Umber lanterns of the loam dark.

Here a dog head dreams.
Not any hate, not any love.
Not anything but dreams.
Brother of dusk and umber.   1918

COOL TOMBS

When Abraham Lincoln was shoveled into the
tombs, he forgot the copperheads and the
assassin . . . in the dust, in the cool
tombs.

And Ulysses Grant lost all thought of con men
and Wall Street, cash and collateral turned
ashes . . . in the dust, in the cool tombs.

Pocahontas' body, lovely as a poplar, sweet as
a red haw in November or a pawpaw in
May, did she wonder? does she remember?
. . . in the dust, in the cool tombs?

Take any streetful of people buying clothes and
groceries, cheering a hero or throwing
confetti and blowing tin horns . . . tell
me if the lovers are losers . . . tell me if
any get more than the lovers . . . in the
dust . . . in the cool tombs.
1916   1916

MEMOIR OF A PROUD BOY [1]

He lived on the wings of storm.
The ashes are in Chihuahua.

Out of Ludlow and coal towns in Colorado
Sprang a vengeance of Slav miners, Italians,
Scots, Cornishmen, Yanks.
Killings ran under the spoken commands of this
boy
With eighty men and rifles on a hogback moun-
tain.

They killed swearing to remember
The shot and charred wives and children
In the burnt camp of Ludlow,
And Louis Tikas, the laughing Greek,   10
Plugged with a bullet, clubbed with a gun
butt.

As a home war
It held the nation a week
And one or two million men stood together
And swore by the retribution of steel.

It was all accidental.
He lived flecking lint off coat lapels
Of men he talked with.
He kissed the miner's babies
And wrote a Denver paper   20
Of picket silhouettes on a mountain line.
He had no mother but Mother Jones
Crying from a jail window of Trinidad:
"All I want is room enough to stand
And shake my fist at the enemies of the human
race."

Named by a grand jury as a murderer
He went to Chihuahua, forgot his old Scotch
name,
Smoked cheroots with Pancho Villa
And wrote letters of Villa as a rock of the
people.

How can I tell how Don Magregor went?   30

Three riders emptied lead into him.
He lay on the main street of an inland town.
A boy sat near all day throwing stones
To keep pigs away.

[1] Magregor was a young coal-miner who took to a Robin Hood
life after the famous Ludlow strike, when the State troops were
brought out against the strikers, and are alleged to have set on fire
the tents in which the women and children were sheltering because
they had been turned out of their homes, which belonged to the
coal-owners. Mother Jones is one of the leaders of the Industrial
Workers of the World. [Sandburg's note.]

The Villa men buried him in a pit
With twenty Carranzistas.

There is drama in that point . . .
. . . the boy and the pigs.
Griffith would make a movie of it to fetch sobs.
Victor Herbert would have the drums whirr
In a weave with a high fiddle-string's single
    clamor.   *41*

"And the muchacho sat there all day throwing
    stones
To keep the pigs away," wrote Gibbons to the
    Tribune.

Somewhere in Chihuahua or Colorado
Is a leather bag of poems and short stories.
                                                        1918

» » *From:* THE PEOPLE, YES « «

27

In the folded and quiet yesterdays
Put down in the book of the past
Is a scrawl of scrawny thumbs
And a smudge of clutching fingers
And the breath of hanged men,
Of thieves and vagabonds,
Of killers saying welcome as an ax fell,
Of traitors cut in four pieces
And their bowels thrust over their faces
According to the ancient Anglo-Saxon   10
Formula for the crime of treason,
Of persons covered with human filth
In due exaction of a penalty,
Of ears clipped, noses slit, fingers chopped
For the identification of vagrants,
Of loiterers and wanderers seared
"With a hot iron in the breast the mark V,"
Of violence as a motive lying deep
As the weather changes of the sea,
Of gang wars, tong wars, civil tumults,   20
Industrial strife, international mass murders,
Of agitators outlawed to live on thistles,
Of thongs for holding plainspoken men,
Of thought and speech being held a crime,
And a woman burned for saying,
"I listen to my voices and obey them,"
    And a thinker locked into stone and iron
        For saying, "The earth moves,"
        And the pity of men learning by shocks,
        By pain and practice,   30
        By plunges and struggles in a bitter pool.

In the folded and quiet yesterdays
How many times has it happened?
The leaders of the people estimated as to price
And bought with bribes signed and delivered
Or waylaid and shot or meshed by perjurers
Or hunted and sent into hiding
Or taken and paraded in garments of dung,
Fire applied to their footsoles:
    "Now will you talk?"   40
Their mouths basted with rubber hose:
    "Now will you talk?"
Thrown into solitary, fed on slops, hung by
    thumbs,
Till the mention of that uprising is casual, so-
    so,
As though the next revolt breeds somewhere
In the bowels of that mystic behemoth, the
    people.
"And when it comes again," say the watchers,
    "we are ready."
    How many times
    in the folded and quiet yesterdays
    has it happened?   50

    "You may burn my flesh and bones
    and throw the ashes to the four winds."
    smiled one of them,
    "Yet my voice shall linger on
    and in the years yet to come
    the young shall ask what was the idea
    for which you gave me death
    and what was I saying
    that I must die for what I said?"   1936

» »   « «

RING LARDNER

1885–1933

WHEN RING LARDNER was graduated from the high school in his home town of Niles, Michigan, his mother wanted him to be a clergyman. To his father's equally strong conviction that he would do well in engineering, the boy deferred to the extent of taking a degree at Chicago's Armour Institute of Technology. Then he turned to sports-writing, a career which he followed without interruption until his early death.

Like Crane, Harte, Bierce, Hemingway, and many another, Lardner found newspaper work a convenient stepping-stone to the writing of fiction. As columnist for various papers in St. Louis, Chicago, and Boston, he gained an early reputation as manhandler of the King's English. *You Know Me, Al* (1916) is a series of letters purportedly written by a bush-league pitcher named Jack Keefe, whose self-regard is as large as his brain is small. The title of the book, adaptable to a variety of situations, became a by-word with the A.E.F. abroad, and in many a parlor at home; from 1919 onwards, Lardner's work was widely circulated by Bell Syndicate, as his popularity grew. With the publication of *How to Write Short Stories (with samples)* in 1924, it became clear that Lardner was no mere slangster but rather a master in the difficult technique of character-portrayal through illiterate monologue. Five years later, when his best stories were collected in *Round-Up*, he began to look more like the melancholy Jacques than a former sportswriter turned humorist.

Gullible's Travels, the title of an early book, suggests a spiritual relationship between Lardner and Swift which the facts bear out. The late William Bolitho rightly said that Lardner's protagonists fall into two groups: fools and swine. His baseball players, prize fighters, golf fiends, and bridge addicts, his predatory females and his cheap, extroverted males, are Yahoos in the thinnest of disguises. Swiftian, too, is the black despondency which closed gradually around Lardner for a decade before his death.

N. F. Adkins, "Ring Lardner," *Dictionary of American Biography, Supplement One*, 1944.
Donald Elder, *Ring Lardner, A Biography*, Garden City, N. Y., 1956.
Maxwell Geismar, "Ring Lardner: Like Something Was Going to Happen," in *Writers in Crisis*, Boston, 1942.
Carl Van Doren, "Beyond Grammar: Ring W. Lardner, Philologist Among the Lowbrows," *Century Magazine*, XVI (July, 1923), 471–475.

» » *From:* ROUND UP « «

HAIRCUT

I got another barber that comes over from Carterville and helps me out Saturdays, but the rest of the time I can get along all right alone. You can see for yourself that this ain't no New York City and besides that, the most of the boys works all day and don't have no leisure to drop in here and get themselves prettied up.

You're a newcomer, ain't you? I thought I hadn't seen you round before. I hope you like it good enough to stay. As I say, we ain't no New York City or Chicago, but we have pretty good times. Not as good, though, since Jim Kendall got killed. When he was alive, him and Hod Meyers used to keep this town in an uproar. I bet they was more laughin' done here than any town its size in America.

Jim was comical, and Hod was pretty near

a match for him. Since Jim's gone, Hod tries to hold his end up just the same as ever, but it's tough goin' when you ain't got nobody to kind of work with.

They used to be plenty fun in here Saturdays. This place is jam-packed Saturdays, from four o'clock on. Jim and Hod would show up right after their supper, round six o'clock. Jim would set himself down in that big chair,
10 nearest the blue spittoon. Whoever had been settin' in that chair, why they'd get up when Jim come in and give it to him.

You'd of thought it was a reserved seat like they have sometimes in a theayter. Hod would generally always stand or walk up and down, or some Saturdays, of course, he'd be settin' in this chair part of the time, gettin' a haircut.

Well, Jim would set there a w'ile without openin' his mouth only to spit, and then finally
20 he'd say to me, "Whitey,"—my right name, that is, my right first name, is Dick, but everybody round here calls we Whitey—Jim would say, "Whitey, your nose looks like a rosebud tonight. You must of been drinkin' some of your aw de cologne."

So I'd say, "No, Jim, but you look like you'd been drinkin' somethin' of that kind or somethin' worse."

Jim would have to laugh at that, but then
30 he'd speak up and say, "No, I ain't had nothin' to drink, but that ain't sayin' I wouldn't like somethin'. I wouldn't even mind if it was wood alcohol."

Then Hod Meyers would say, "Neither would your wife." That would set everybody to laughin' because Jim and his wife wasn't on very good terms. She'd of divorced him only they wasn't no chance to get alimony and she didn't have no way to take care of herself and
40 the kids. She couldn't understand Jim. He *was* kind of rough, but a good fella at heart.

Him and Hod had all kinds of sport with Milt Sheppard. I don't suppose you've seen Milt. Well, he's got an Adam's apple that looks more like a mushmelon. So I'd be shavin' Milt and when I'd start to shave down here on his neck, Hod would holler, "Hey, Whitey, wait a minute! Before you cut into it, let's make up a pool and see who can guess closest to the num-
50 ber of seeds."

And Jim would say, "If Milt hadn't of been so hoggish, he'd of ordered a half a cantaloupe instead of a whole one and it might not of stuck in his throat."

All the boys would roar at this and Milt himself would force a smile, though the joke was on him. Jim certainly was a card!

There's his shavin' mug, settin' on the shelf, right next to Charley Vail's. "Charles M. Vail." That's the druggist. He comes in regular for his shave, three times a week. And Jim's is the cup next to Charley's. "James H. Kendall." Jim won't need no shavin' mug no more, but I'll leave it there just the same for old time's sake. Jim certainly was a character!

Years ago, Jim used to travel for a canned goods concern over in Carterville. They sold canned goods. Jim had the whole northern half of the State and was on the road five days out of every week. He'd drop in here Saturdays and tell his experiences for that week. It was rich.

I guess he paid more attention to playin' jokes than makin' sales. Finally the concern let him out and he come right home here and told everybody he'd been fired instead of sayin' he'd resigned like most fellas would of.

It was a Saturday and the shop was full and Jim got up out of that chair and says, "Gentlemen, I got an important announcement to make. I been fired from my job."

Well, they asked him if he was in earnest and he said he was and nobody could think of nothin' to say till Jim finally broke the ice himself. He says, "I been sellin' canned goods and now I'm canned goods myself."

You see, the concern he'd been workin' for was a factory that made canned goods. Over in Carterville. And now Jim said he was canned himself. He was certainly a card!

Jim had a great trick that he used to play w'ile he was travelin'. For instance, he'd be ridin' on a train and they'd come to some little town like, well, like, we'll say, like Benton. Jim would look out the train window and read the signs on the stores.

For instance, they'd be a sign, "Henry Smith, Dry Goods." Well, Jim would write down the name and the name of the town and when he got to wherever he was goin' he'd mail back a postal card to Henry Smith at Benton and not sign no name to it, but he'd write on the card, well, somethin' like "Ask your wife about that book agent that spent the afternoon last week," or "Ask your Missus who kept her from gettin' lonesome the last time you was in Carterville." And he'd sign the card, "A Friend."

Of course, he never knew what really come of none of these jokes, but he could picture what *probably* happened and that was enough.

Jim didn't work very steady after he lost his position with the Carterville people. What he did earn, doin' odd jobs round town, why he spent pretty near all of it on gin and his family might of starved if the stores hadn't of carried them along. Jim's wife tried her hand at dress-makin', but they ain't nobody goin' to get rich makin' dresses in this town.

As I say, she'd of divorced Jim, only she seen that she couldn't support herself and the kids and she was always hopin' that some day Jim would cut out his habits and give her more than two or three dollars a week.

They was a time when she would go to whoever he was workin' for and ask them to give her his wages, but after she done this once or twice, he beat her to it by borrowin' most of his pay in advance. He told it all round town, how he had outfoxed his Missus. He certainly was a caution!

But he wasn't satisfied with just outwittin' her. He was sore the way she had acted, tryin' to grab off his pay. And he made up his mind he'd get even. Well, he waited till Evans's Circus was advertised to come to town. Then he told his wife and two kiddies that he was goin' to take them to the circus. The day of the circus, he told them he would get the tickets and meet them outside the entrance to the tent.

Well, he didn't have no intentions of bein' there or buyin' tickets or nothin'. He got full of gin and laid round Wright's poolroom all day. His wife and the kids waited and waited and of course he didn't show up. His wife didn't have a dime with her, or nowhere else, I guess. So she finally had to tell the kids it was all off and they cried like they wasn't never goin' to stop.

Well, it seems, w'ile they was cryin' Doc Stair came along and he asked what was the matter, but Mrs. Kendall was stubborn and wouldn't tell him, but the kids told him and he insisted on takin' them and their mother in the show. Jim found this out afterwards and it was one reason why he had it in for Doc Stair.

Doc Stair come here about a year and a half ago. He's a mighty handsome young fella and his clothes always look like he has them made to order. He goes to Detroit two or three times a year and w'ile he's there he must have a tailor take his measure and then make him a suit to order. They cost pretty near twice as much, but they fit a whole lot better than if you just bought them in a store.

For a w'ile everybody was wonderin' why a young doctor like Doc Stair should come to a town like this where we already got old Doc Gamble and Doc Foote that's both been here for years and all the practice in town was always divided between the two of them.

Then they was a story got round that Doc Stair's gal had throwed him over, a gal up in the Northern Peninsula somewheres, and the reason he come here was to hide himself away and forget it. He said himself that he thought they wasn't nothin' like general practice in a place like ours to fit a man to be a good all round doctor. And that's why he'd came.

Anyways, it wasn't long before he was makin' enough to live on, though they tell me that he never dunned nobody for what they owed him, and the folks here certainly has got the owin' habit, even in my business. If I had all that was comin' to me for just shaves alone, I could go to Carterville and put up at the Mercer for a week and see a different picture every night. For instance, they's old George Purdy—but I guess I shouldn't ought to be gossipin'.

Well, last year, our coroner died, died of the flu. Ken Beatty, that was his name. He was the coroner. So they had to choose another man to be coroner in his place and they picked Doc Stair. He laughed at first and said he didn't want it, but they made him take it. It ain't no job that anybody would fight for and what a man makes out of it in a year would just about buy seeds for their garden. Doc's the kind, though, that can't say no to nothin' if you keep at him long enough.

But I was goin' to tell you about a poor boy we got here in town—Paul Dickson. He fell out of a tree when he was about ten years old. Lit on his head and it done somethin' to him and he ain't never been right. No harm in him, but just silly. Jim Kendall used to call him cuckoo; that's a name Jim had for anybody that was off their head, only he called people's head their bean. That was another of his gags, callin' head bean and callin' crazy people cuckoo. Only poor Paul ain't crazy, but just silly.

You can imagine that Jim used to have all kinds of fun with Paul. He'd send him to the White Front Garage for a left-handed monkey wrench. Of course they ain't no such a thing as a left-handed monkey wrench.

And once we had a kind of a fair here and they was a baseball game between the fats and the leans and before the game started Jim called Paul over and sent him way down to Schrader's hardware store to get a key for the pitcher's box.

They wasn't nothin' in the way of gags thet Jim couldn't think up, when he put his mind to it.

Poor Paul was always kind of suspicious of people, maybe on account of how Jim had kept foolin' him. Paul wouldn't have much to do with anybody only his own mother and Doc Stair and a girl here in town named Julie Gregg. That is, she ain't a girl no more, but pretty near thirty or over.

When Doc first come to town, Paul seemed to feel like here was a real friend and he hung round Doc's office most of the w'ile; the only time he wasn't there was when he'd go home to eat or sleep or when he seen Julie Gregg doin' her shoppin'.

When he looked out Doc's window and seen her, he'd run downstairs and join her and tag along with her to the different stores. The poor boy was crazy about Julie and she always treated him mighty nice and made him feel like he was welcome, though of course it wasn't nothin' but pity on her side.

Doc done all he could to improve Paul's mind and he told me once that he really thought the boy was gettin' better, that they was times when he was as bright and sensible as anybody else.

But I was goin' to tell you about Julie Gregg. Old Man Gregg was in the lumber business, but got to drinkin' and lost the most of his money and when he died, he didn't leave nothin' but the house and just enough insurance for the girl to skimp along on.

Her mother was a kind of a half invalid and didn't hardly ever leave the house. Julie wanted to sell the place and move somewheres else after the old man died, but the mother said she was born here and would die here. It was tough on Julie, as the young people round this town—well, she's too good for them.

She's been away to school and Chicago and New York and different places and they ain't no subject she can't talk on, where you take the rest of the young folks here and you mention anything to them outside of Gloria Swanson or Tommy Meighan and they think you're delirious. Did you see Gloria in Wages of Virtue? You missed somethin'!

Well, Doc Stair hadn't been here more than a week when he come in one day to get shaved and I recognized who he was as he had

been pointed out to me, so I told him about my old lady. She's been ailin' for a couple years and either Doc Gamble or Doc Foote, neither one, seemed to be helpin' her. So he said he would come out and see her, but if she was able to get out herself, it would be better to bring her to his office where he could make a completer examination.

So I took her to his office and w'ile I was waitin' for her in the reception room, in come Julie Gregg. When somebody comes in Doc Stair's office, they's a bell that rings in his inside office so as he can tell they's somebody to see him.

So he left my old lady inside and come out to the front office and that's the first time him and Julie met and I guess it was what they call love at first sight. But it wasn't fifty-fifty. This young fella was the slickest lookin' fella she'd ever seen in this town and she went wild over him. To him she was a young lady that wanted to see the doctor.

She'd came on about the same business I had. Her mother had been doctorin' for years with Doc Gamble and Doc Foote and without no results. So she'd heard they was a new doc in town and decided to give him a try. He promised to call and see her mother that same day.

I said a minute ago that it was love at first sight on her part. I'm not only judgin' by how she acted afterwards but how she looked at him that first day in his office. I ain't no mind reader, but it was wrote all over her face that she was gone.

Now Jim Kendall, besides bein' a jokesmith and a pretty good drinker, well, Jim was quite a lady-killer. I guess he run pretty wild durin' the time he was on the road for them Carterville people, and besides that, he'd had a couple little affairs of the heart right here in town. As I say, his wife could of divorced him, only she couldn't.

But Jim was like the majority of men, and women, too, I guess. He wanted what he couldn't get. He wanted Julie Gregg and worked his head off tryin' to land her. Only he'd of said bean instead of head.

Well, Jim's habits and his jokes didn't appeal to Julie and of course he was a married man, so he didn't have no more chance than, well, than a rabbit. That's an expression of Jim's himself. When somebody didn't have no chance to get elected or somethin', Jim would always say they didn't have no more chance than a rabbit.

He didn't make no bones about how he felt.

Right in here, more than once, in front of the whole crowd, he said he was stuck on Julie and anybody that could get her for him was welcome to his house and his wife and kids included. But she wouldn't have nothin' to do with him; wouldn't even speak to him on the street. He finally seen he wasn't gettin' nowheres with his usual line so he decided to try the rough stuff. He went right up to her house one evenin' and when she opened the door he forced his way in and grabbed her. But she broke loose and before he could stop her, she run in the next room and locked the door and phoned to Joe Barnes. Joe's the marshal. Jim could hear who she was phonin' to and he beat it before Joe got there.

Joe was an old friend of Julie's pa. Joe went to Jim the next day and told him what would happen if he ever done it again.

I don't know how the news of this little affair leaked out. Chances is that Joe Barnes told his wife and she told somebody else's wife and they told their husband. Anyways, it did leak out and Hod Meyers had the nerve to kid Jim about it, right here in this shop. Jim didn't deny nothin' and kind of laughed it off and said for us all to wait; that lots of people had tried to make a monkey out of him, but he always got even.

Meanw'ile everybody in town was wise to Julie's bein' wild mad over the Doc. I don't suppose she had any idear how her face changed when him and her was together; of course she couldn't of, or she'd of kept away from him. And she didn't know that we was all noticin' how many times she made excuses to go up to his office or pass it on the other side of the street and look up in his window to see if he was there. I felt sorry for her and so did most other people.

Hod Meyers kept rubbin' it into Jim about how the Doc had cut him out. Jim didn't pay no attention to the kiddin' and you could see he was plannin' one of his jokes.

One trick Jim had was the knack of changin' his voice. He could make you think he was a girl talkin' and he could mimic any man's voice. To show you how good he was along this line, I'll tell you the joke he played on me once.

You know, in most towns of any size, when a man is dead and needs a shave, why the barber that shaves him soaks him five dollars for the job; that is, he don't soak *him*, but whoever ordered the shave. I just charge three dollars because personally I don't mind shavin' a dead person. They lay a whole lot stiller than live customers. The only thing is that you don't feel like talkin' to them and you get kind of lonesome.

Well, about the coldest day we ever had here, two years ago last winter, the phone rung at the house w'ile I was home to dinner and I answered the phone and it was a woman's voice and she said she was Mrs. John Scott and her husband was dead and would I come out and shave him.

Old John had always been a good customer of mine. But they live seven miles out in the country, on the Streeter road. Still I didn't see how I could say no.

So I said I would be there, but would have to come in a jitney and it might cost three or four dollars besides the price of the shave. So she, or the voice, it said that was all right, so I got Frank Abbott to drive me out to the place and when I got there, who should open the door but old John himself! He wasn't no more dead than, well, than a rabbit.

It didn't take no private detective to figure out who had played me this little joke. Nobody could of thought it up but Jim Kendall. He certainly was a card!

I tell you this incident just to show you how he could disguise his voice and make you believe it was somebody else talkin'. I'd of swore it was Mrs. Scott had called me. Anyways, some woman.

Well, Jim waited till he had Doc Stair's voice down pat; then he went after revenge.

He called Julie up on a night when he knew Doc was over in Carterville. She never questioned but what it was Doc's voice. Jim said he must see her that night; he couldn't wait no longer to tell her somethin'. She was all excited and told him to come to the house. But he said he was expectin' an important long distance call and wouldn't she please forget her manners for once and come to his office. He said they couldn't nothin' hurt her and nobody would see her and he just *must* talk to her a little w'ile. Well, poor Julie fell for it.

Doc always keeps a night light in his office, so it looked to Julie like they was somebody there.

Meanw'ile Jim Kendall had went to Wright's poolroom, where they was a whole gang amusin' themselves. The most of them had drank plenty of gin, and they was a rough bunch even when sober. They was always strong for Jim's jokes and when he told them to come with him and see some fun they give up their card games and pool games and followed along.

Doc's office is on the second floor. Right outside his door they's a flight of stairs leadin' to the floor above. Jim and his gang hid in the dark behind these stairs.

Well, Julie come up to Doc's door and rung the bell and they was nothin' doin'. She rung it again and she rung it seven or eight times. Then she tried the door and found it locked. Then Jim made some kind of a noise and she heard it and waited a minute, and then she says, "Is that you, Ralph?" Ralph is Doc's first name.

They was no answer and it must of came to her all of a sudden that she'd been bunked. She pretty near fell downstairs and the whole gang after her. They chased her all the way home, hollerin', "Is that you, Ralph?" and "Oh, Ralphie, dear, is that you?" Jim says he couldn't holler it himself, as he was laughin' too hard.

Poor Julie! She didn't show up here on Main Street for a long, long time afterward.

And of course Jim and his gang told everybody in town, everybody but Doc Stair. They was scared to tell him, and he might of never knowed only for Paul Dickson. The poor cuckoo, as Jim called him, he was here in the shop one night when Jim was still gloatin' yet over what he'd done to Julie. And Paul took in as much of it as he could understand and he run to Doc with the story.

It's a cinch Doc went up in the air and swore he'd make Jim suffer. But it was a kind of a delicate thing, because if it got out that he had beat Jim up, Julie was bound to hear of it and then she'd know that Doc knew and of course knowin' that he knew would make it worse for her than ever. He was goin' to do somethin', but it took a lot of figurin'.

Well, it was a couple days later when Jim was here in the shop again, and so was the cuckoo. Jim was goin' duck-shootin' the next day and had came in lookin' for Hod Meyers to go with him. I happened to know that Hod had went over to Carterville and wouldn't be home till the end of the week. So Jim said he hated to go alone and he guessed he would call it off. Then poor Paul spoke up and said if Jim would take him he would go along. Jim thought a w'ile and then he said, well, he guessed a half-wit was better than nothin'.

I suppose he was plottin' to get Paul out in the boat and play some joke on him, like pushin' him in the water. Anyways, he said

Paul could go. He asked him had he ever shot a duck and Paul said no, he'd never even had a gun in his hands. So Jim said he could set in the boat and watch him and if he behaved himself, he might lend him his gun for a couple of shots. They made a date to meet in the mornin' and that's the last I seen of Jim alive.

Next mornin', I hadn't been open more than ten minutes when Doc Stair come in. He looked kind of nervous. He asked me had I seen Paul Dickson. I said no, but I knew where he was, out duck-shootin' with Jim Kendall. So Doc says that's what he had heard, and he couldn't understand it because Paul had told him he wouldn't never have no more to do with Jim as long as he lived.

He said Paul had told him about the joke Jim had played on Julie. He said Paul had asked him what he thought of the joke and the Doc had told him that anybody that would do a thing like that ought not to be let live.

I said it had been a kind of a raw thing, but Jim just couldn't resist no kind of a joke, no matter how raw. I said I thought he was all right at heart, but just bubblin' over with mischief. Doc turned and walked out.

At noon he got a phone call from old John Scott. The lake where Jim and Paul had went shootin' is on John's place. Paul had came runnin' up to the house a few minutes before and said they'd been an accident. Jim had shot a few ducks and then give the gun to Paul and told him to try his luck. Paul hadn't never handled a gun and he was nervous. He was shakin' so hard that he couldn't control the gun. He let fire and Jim sunk back in the boat dead.

Doc Stair, bein' the coroner, jumped in Frank Abbott's flivver and rushed out to Scott's farm. Paul and old John was down on the shore of the lake. Paul had rowed the boat to shore, but they'd left the body in it, waitin' for Doc to come.

Doc examined the body and said they might as well fetch it back to town. They was no use leavin' it there or callin' a jury as it was a plain case of accidental shootin'.

Personally I wouldn't never leave a person shoot a gun in the same boat I was in unless I was sure they knew somethin' about guns. Jim was a sucker to leave a new beginner have his gun, let alone a half-wit. It probably served Jim right, what he got. But still we miss him round here. He certainly was a card!

Comb it wet or dry?   1926

WILLA CATHER

1873–1947

WILLA CATHER is now so completely identified with her native region and village, Red Cloud, Nebraska, that it is hard to believe that she had been a writer for seventeen years before she turned back to the places and the people she had known when she was growing up. For many years after graduating from the University of Nebraska in 1895 she faced eastward, looking to New York and to Europe. In Pittsburgh she worked as a journalist and taught high school Latin and English. For six years (1906–1912) she was an editor, in New York, for S. S. McClure, one of the ablest magazine publishers of the day. During these years she produced a volume of verse and a book of short stories. In these first stories there is almost no mention of the high plains region of southern Nebraska, "The Divide," which she would later bring to life in her fiction.

In 1908 Sarah Orne Jewett, the subtlest of American regionalist writers, admonished Miss Cather to "find your own quiet center of life and write from that." Willa Cather was not yet ready to go back. Her first novel, *Alexander's Bridge* (1912), a study in the destructive process at work within its hero, is set in a sophisticated, Eastern milieu. But in the year of the novel's publication a decisive event in her life changed her career as a writer. She had resigned from *McClure's*, determined to support herself by fiction-writing. She and her brother Douglas made a journey into Arizona and New Mexico where the survivals of an old and primitive America excited her imagination and turned her thoughts back to her own beginnings.

In her next novel, *O Pioneers!* (1913), the Nebraska of the post-pioneer period was at last her setting. Technically the story belongs to Emil, whose adulterous love is punished by the wronged husband. Actually it centers on Emil's sister, Alexandra, the first of Miss Cather's strong-willed women who love this stern land and can make it blossom. The next novel, *The Song of the Lark* (1915), combined Miss Cather's new-found love for her region with her passion for music, particularly the opera (the heroine becomes a world-famous singer) but the attempt to unite the two worlds is not very successful. In *My Ántonia* (1918), undoubtedly her masterpiece, she uses the device of a narrator who has gone out into the great world but returns to Black Hawk to learn and tell the later story of Ántonia Shimerda's life. Though Ántonia had suffered much, she had endured and had become the kind of woman who lends herself "to immemorial human attitudes which we recognize by instinct as universal and true."

The first World War and its aftermath affected Miss Cather deeply. The values she cared for had vanished in the materialism of the new age. Her disillusionment shows in the novels written in the next years. The idyllic tone is gone and many of them are chronicles of moral failure, such as *A Lost Lady* (1923) and *My Mortal Enemy* (1926).

With *The Professor's House* (1925) Miss Cather began to look back beyond the pioneer times of her region to other places and times in which true heroism flourished. In this novel the backward glance—to the Cliff Dwellers in a New Mexico canyon—is only a framed interlude but it prefigures the two novels she would soon write about builders of civilization in North America, *Death Comes for the Archbishop* (1927) and *Shadows on the Rock* (1931), the one set in the southwest of the 1850's and the other in the Quebec of the time of Frontenac and Bishop Laval. At the time of their publication many critics noted that these were novels of escape but they failed to add that the escape was *to* something, to fortitude and creativity and loyalty.

There were two more novels to come, *Lucy Gayheart* (1935), another story of a musician who grows up in a village on the Platte, and *Sapphira and the Slave Girl* (1940), in which Miss Cather used her memories of her childhood years in the Shenandoah Valley of Virginia.

As a writer of fiction Miss Cather worked equally well in the three possible media, the novel, the short novel or nouvelle (*My Mortal Enemy*), and the short story. Three collections of stories were published during her lifetime, *The Troll Garden* (1905), *Youth and the Bright Medusa* (1920), and *Obscure Destinies* (1932). There is also one posthumous collection, *The Old Beauty and Others* (1948). Many of the stories—"Paul's Case," "Old Mrs. Harris," and the one printed here, "Neighbour Rosicky," for example,—have become as famous as the stories written by Miss Cather's mentor Sarah Orne Jewett.

The immediate impulse for the writing of "Neighbor Rosicky" was the death of her father, Charles Cather, in 1928. To Rosicky, who in real life was the husband of the original Ántonia, Miss Cather transferred her father's suffering and death from angina, and the story is filled with her affectionate remembrance of his gentleness and strength. In the story there is also her admiration for the Bohemian pioneers in the Red Cloud region. Of the many immigrant groups she had known in her childhood she had been closest to the Bohemians of neighbor Rosicky's kind.

P. M. Hutchinson, "The Writings of Willa Cather: A List of Works By and About Her," *Bulletin of the New York Public Library*, LX (June–August, 1956), 267–288, 338–356, 378–400.

The Novels and Stories of Willa Cather, 13 vols., Boston, 1937–1941.

Willa Cather in Europe: Her Own Story of the First Journey, George N. Kates, ed., New York, 1956.

E. K. Brown and Leon Edel, *Willa Cather: A Critical Biography*, New York, 1953.

David Daiches, *Willa Cather: A Critical Introduction*, Ithaca, New York 1951.

Maxwell Geismar, "Willa Cather: Lady in the Wilderness," *The Last of the Provincials: The American Novel, 1915–1925*, Boston, 1947, pp. 153–220.

Edith Lewis, *Willa Cather Living: A Personal Record*, New York, 1953.

J. H. Randall, *The Landscape and the Looking Glass. Willa Cather's Search for Value*, Boston, 1960.

E. S. Sergeant, *Willa Cather: A Memoir*, Philadelphia, 1953.

NEIGHBOUR ROSICKY

I

When Doctor Burleigh told neighbour Rosicky he had a bad heart, Rosicky protested.

"So? No, I guess my heart was always pretty good. I got a little asthma, maybe. Just a awful short breath when I was pitchin' hay last summer, dat's all."

"Well now, Rosicky, if you know more about it than I do, what did you come to me for? It's your heart that makes you short of breath, I tell you. You're sixty-five years old, and you've always worked hard, and your heart's tired. You've got to be careful from now on, and you can't do heavy work any more. You've got five boys at home to do it for you."

The old farmer looked up at the Doctor with a gleam of amusement in his queer triangular-shaped eyes. His eyes were large and lively, but the lids were caught up in the middle in a curious way, so that they formed a triangle. He did not look like a sick man. His brown face was creased but not wrinkled, he had a ruddy colour in his smooth-shaven cheeks and in his lips, under his long brown moustache. His hair was thin and ragged around his ears, but very little grey. His forehead, naturally high and crossed by deep parallel lines, now ran all the way up to his pointed crown. Rosicky's face had the habit of looking interested,—suggested a contented disposition and a reflective quality that was gay rather than grave. This gave him a certain detachment, the easy manner of an onlooker and observer.

"Well, I guess you ain't got no pills fur a bad heart, Doctor Ed. I guess the only thing is fur me to git me a new one."

Doctor Burleigh swung round in his desk-chair and frowned at the old farmer. "I think if I were you I'd take a little care of the old one, Rosicky."

Rosicky shrugged. "Maybe I don't know how. I expect you mean fur me not to drink my coffee no more."

"I wouldn't, in your place. But you'll do as you choose about that. I've never yet been able to separate a Bohemian from his coffee or his pipe. I've quit trying. But the sure thing is you've got to cut out farm work. You can feed the stock and do chores about the barn, but you can't do anything in the fields that makes you short of breath."

"How about shelling corn?"

"Of course not!"

Rosicky considered with puckered brows.

"I can't make my heart go no longer'n it wants to, can I, Doctor Ed?"

"I think it's good for five or six years yet, maybe more, if you'll take the strain off it. Sit around the house and help Mary. If I had a good wife like yours, I'd want to stay around the house."

His patient chuckled. "It ain't no place fur a man. I don't like no old man hanging round the kitchen too much. An' my wife, she's a awful hard worker her own self."

"That's it; you can help her a little. My Lord, Rosicky, you are one of the few men I know who has a family he can get some comfort out of; happy dispositions, never quarrel among themselves, and they treat you right. I want to see you live a few years and enjoy them."

"Oh, they're good kids, all right," Rosicky assented.

The Doctor wrote him a prescription and asked him how his oldest son, Rudolph, who had married in the spring, was getting on. Rudolph had struck out for himself, on rented land. "And how's Polly? I was afraid Mary mightn't like an American daughter-in-law, but it seems to be working out all right."

"Yes, she's a fine girl. Dat widder woman bring her daughters up very nice. Polly got lots of spunk, an' she got some style, too. Da's nice, for young folks to have some style." Rosicky inclined his head gallantly. His voice and his twinkly smile were an affectionate compliment to his daughter-in-law.

"It looks like a storm, and you'd better be getting home before it comes. In town in the car?" Doctor Burleigh rose.

"No, I'm in de wagon. When you got five boys, you ain't got much chance to ride round in de Ford. I ain't much for cars, noway."

"Well, it's a good road out to your place; but I don't want you bumping around in a wagon much. And never again on a hay-rake, remember!"

Rosicky placed the Doctor's fee delicately behind the desk-telephone, looking the other way, as if this were an absent-minded gesture. He put on his plush cap and his corduroy jacket with a sheepskin collar, and went out.

The Doctor picked up his stethoscope and frowned at it as if he were seriously annoyed with the instrument. He wished it had been telling tales about some other man's heart, some old man who didn't look the Doctor in the eye so knowingly, or hold out such a warm brown hand when he said good-bye. Doctor Burleigh had been a poor boy in the country before he went away to medical school; he had known Rosicky almost ever since he could remember, and he had a deep affection for Mrs. Rosicky.

Only last winter he had had such a good breakfast at Rosicky's, and that when he needed it. He had been out all night on a long, hard confinement case at Tom Marshall's,—a big rich farm where there was plenty of stock and plenty of feed and a great deal of expensive farm machinery of the newest model, and no comfort whatever. The woman had too many children and too much work, and she was no manager. When the baby was born at last, and handed over to the assisting neighbour woman, and the mother was properly attended to, Burleigh refused any breakfast in that slovenly house, and drove his buggy—the snow was too deep for a car—eight miles to Anton Rosicky's place. He didn't know another farm-house where a man could get such a warm welcome, and such good strong coffee with rich cream. No wonder the old chap didn't want to give up his coffee!

He had driven in just when the boys had come back from the barn and were washing up for breakfast. The long table, covered with a bright oilcloth, was set out with dishes waiting for them, and the warm kitchen was full of the smell of coffee and hot biscuit and sausage. Five big handsome boys, running from twenty to twelve, all with what Burleigh called natural good manners,—they hadn't a bit of the painful self-consciousness he himself had to struggle with when he was a lad. One ran to put his horse away, another helped him off with his fur coat and hung it up, and Josephine, the youngest child and the only daughter, quickly set another place under her mother's direction.

With Mary, to feed creatures was the natural expression of affection,—her chickens, the calves, her big hungry boys. It was a rare pleasure to feed a young man whom she seldom saw and of whom she was as proud as if he belonged to her. Some country housekeepers would have stopped to spread a white cloth over the oilcloth, to change the thick cups and plates for their best china, and the wooden-handled knives for plated ones. But not Mary.

"You must take us as you find us, Doctor Ed. I'd be glad to put out my good things for you if you was expected, but I'm glad to get you any way at all."

He knew she was glad,—she threw back her head and spoke out as if she were announcing him to the whole prairie. Rosicky hadn't said anything at all; he merely smiled his twinkling smile, put some more coal on the fire, and went into his own room to pour the Doctor a little drink in a medicine glass. When they were all seated, he watched his wife's face from his end of the table and spoke to her in Czech. Then, with the instinct of politeness which seldom failed him, he turned to the Doctor and said slyly: "I was just tellin' her not to ask you no questions about Mrs. Marshall till you eat some breakfast. My wife, she's terrible fur to ask questions."

The boys laughed, and so did Mary. She watched the Doctor devour her biscuit and sausage, too much excited to eat anything herself. She drank her coffee and sat taking in everything about her visitor. She had known him when he was a poor country boy, and was boastfully proud of his success, always saying: "What do people go to Omaha for, to see a doctor, when we got the best one in the State right here?" If Mary liked people at all, she felt physical pleasure in the sight of them, personal exultation in any good fortune that came to them. Burleigh didn't know many women like that, but he knew she was like that.

When his hunger was satisfied, he did, of course, have to tell them about Mrs. Marshall, and he noticed what the friendly interest the boys took in the matter.

Rudolph, the oldest one (he was living at home then), said: "The last time I was over there, she was lifting them big heavy milk-cans, and I knew she oughtn't to be doing it."

"Yes, Rudolph told me about that when he came home, and I said it wasn't right," Mary put in warmly. "It was all right for me to do them things up to the last, for I was terrible strong, but that woman's weakly. And do you think she'll be able to nurse it, Ed?" She sometimes forgot to give him the title she was so proud of. "And to think of your being up all night and then not able to get a decent breakfast! I don't know what's the matter with such people."

"Why, Mother," said one of the boys, "if Doctor Ed had got breakfast there, we wouldn't have him here. So you ought to be glad."

"He knows I'm glad to have him, John, any time. But I'm sorry for that poor woman, how bad she'll feel the Doctor had to go away in the cold without his breakfast."

"I wish I'd been in practice when these were getting born." The doctor looked down the row of close-clipped heads. "I missed some good breakfasts by not being."

The boys began to laugh at their mother because she flushed so red, but she stood her ground and threw up her head. "I don't care, you wouldn't have got away from this house without breakfast. No doctor ever did. I'd have had something ready fixed that Anton could warm up for you."

The boys laughed harder than ever, and exclaimed at her: "I'll bet you would!" "She would, that!"

"Father, did you get breakfast for the doctor when we were born?"

"Yes, and he used to bring me my breakfast, too, mighty nice. I was always awful hungry!" Mary admitted with a guilty laugh.

While the boys were getting the Doctor's horse, he went to the window to examine the house plants. "What do you do to your geraniums to keep them blooming all winter, Mary? I never pass this house that from the road I don't see your windows full of flowers."

She snapped off a dark red one, and a ruffled new green leaf, and put them in his buttonhole. "There, that looks better. You look too solemn for a young man, Ed. Why don't you git married? I'm worried about you. Settin' at breakfast, I looked at you real hard, and I seen you've got some grey hairs already."

"Oh, yes! They're coming. Maybe they'd come faster if I married."

"Don't talk so. You'll ruin your health eating at the hotel. I could send your wife a nice loaf of nut bread, if you only had one. I don't like to see a young man getting grey. I'll tell you something, Ed; you make some strong black tea and keep it handy in a bowl, and every morning just brush it into your hair, an' it'll keep the grey from showin' much. That's the way I do!"

Sometimes the Doctor heard the gossipers in the drug-store wondering why Rosicky didn't get on faster. He was industrious, and so were his boys, but they were rather free and easy, weren't pushers, and they didn't always show good judgment. They were comfortable, they were out of debt, but they didn't get much ahead. Maybe, Doctor Burleigh reflected, people as generous and warm-hearted and affectionate as the Rosickys never got ahead much; maybe you couldn't enjoy your life and put it into the bank, too.

II

When Rosicky left Doctor Burleigh's office he went into the farm-implement store to light his pipe and put on his glasses and read over the list Mary had given him. Then he went into the general merchandise place next door and stood about until the pretty girl with the plucked eyebrows, who always waited on him, was free. Those eyebrows, two thin India-ink strokes, amused him, because he remembered how they used to be. Rosicky always prolonged his shopping by a little joking; the girl knew the old fellow admired her, and she liked to chaff with him.

"Seems to me about every other week you buy ticking, Mr. Rosicky, and always the best quality," she remarked as she measured off the heavy bolt with red stripes.

"You see, my wife is always makin' goose-fedder pillows, an' de thin stuff don't hold in dem little down-fedders."

"You must have lots of pillows at your house."

"Sure. She makes quilts of dem, too. We sleeps easy. Now she's makin' a fedder quilt for my son's wife. You know Polly, that married my Rudolph. How much my bill, Miss Pearl?"

"Eight eighty-five."

"Chust make it nine, and put in some candy fur de women."

"As usual. I never did see a man buy so much candy for his wife. First thing you know, she'll be getting too fat."

"I'd like dat. I ain't much fur all dem slim women like what de style is now."

"That's one for me, I suppose, Mr. Bohunk!" Pearl sniffed and elevated her India-ink strokes.

When Rosicky went out to his wagon, it was beginning to snow,—the first snow of the season, and he was glad to see it. He rattled out of town and along the highway through a wonderfully rich stretch of country, the finest farms in the country. He admired this High Prairie, as it was called, and always liked to drive through it. His own place lay in a rougher territory, where there was some clay in the soil and it was not so productive. When he bought his land, he hadn't the money to buy on High Prairie; so he told his boys, when they grumbled, that if their land hadn't some clay in it, they wouldn't own it at all. All the same, he enjoyed looking at these fine farms, as he enjoyed looking at a prize bull.

After he had gone eight miles, he came to the graveyard, which lay just at the edge of his own hay-land. There he stopped his horses and sat still on his wagon seat, looking about at the snowfall. Over yonder on the hill he could see his own house, crouching low, with the clump of orchard behind and the windmill before, and all down the gentle hillslope the rows of pale gold cornstalks stood out against the white field. The snow was falling over the cornfield and the pasture and the hay-land, steadily, with very little wind,—a nice dry snow. The graveyard had only a light wire fence about it and was all overgrown with long red grass. The fine snow, settling into this red grass and upon the few little evergreens and the headstones, looked very pretty.

It was a nice graveyard, Rosicky reflected, sort of snug and homelike, not cramped or mournful,—a big sweep all round it. A man could lie down in the long grass and see the complete arch of the sky over him, hear the wagons go by; in summer the mowing-machine rattled right up to the wire fence. And it was so near home. Over there across the cornstalks his own roof and windmill looked so good to him that he promised himself to mind the Doctor and take care of himself. He was awful fond of his place, he admitted. He wasn't anxious to leave it. And it was a comfort to think that he would never have to go farther than the edge of his own hayfield. The snow, falling over his barnyard and the graveyard, seemed to draw things together like. And they were all old neighbours in the graveyard, most of them friends; there was nothing to feel awkward or embarrassed about. Embarrassment was the most disagreeable feeling Rosicky knew. He didn't often have it,—only with certain people whom he didn't understand at all.

Well, it was a nice snowstorm; a fine sight to see the snow falling so quietly and graciously over so much open country. On his cap and shoulders, on the horses' backs and manes, light, delicate, mysterious it fell; and with it a dry cool fragrance was released into the air. It meant rest for vegetation and men and beasts, for the ground itself; a season of long nights for sleep, leisurely breakfasts, peace by the fire. This and much more went through Rosicky's mind, but he merely told himself that winter was coming, clucked to his horses and drove on.

When he reached home, John, the youngest boy, ran out to put away his team for him, and he met Mary coming up from the outside cellar with her apron full of carrots. They went into the house together. On the table, covered with oilcloth figured with clusters of blue grapes, a place was set, and he smelled hot coffee-cake of some kind. Anton never lunched in town; he thought that extravagant, and anyhow he didn't like the food. So Mary always had something ready for him when he got home.

After he was settled in his chair, stirring his coffee in a big cup, Mary took out of the oven a pan of *kolache* stuffed with apricots, examined them anxiously to see whether they had got too dry, put them beside his plate, and then sat down opposite him.

Rosicky asked her in Czech if she wasn't going to have any coffee.

She replied in English, as being somehow the right language for transacting business: "Now what did Doctor Ed say, Anton? You tell me just what."

"He said I was to tell you some compliments, but I forgot 'em." Rosicky's eyes twinkled.

"About you, I mean. What did he say about your asthma?"

"He says I ain't got no asthma." Rosicky took one of the little rolls in his broad brown fingers. The thickened nail of his right thumb told the story of his past.

"Well, what is the matter? And don't try to put me off."

"He don't say nothing much, only I'm a little older, and my heart ain't so good like it used to be."

Mary started and brushed her hair back from her temples with both hands as if she were a little out of her mind. From the way she glared, she might have been in a rage with him.

"He says there's something the matter with your heart? Doctor Ed says so?"

"Now don't yell at me like I was a hog in de garden, Mary. You know I always did like to hear a woman talk soft. He didn't say anything de matter wid my heart, only it ain't so young like it used to be, an' he tell me not to pitch hay or run de corn-sheller."

Mary wanted to jump up, but she sat still. She admired the way he never under any circumstances raised his voice or spoke roughly. He was city-bred, and she was country-bred; she often said she wanted her boys to have their papa's nice ways.

"You never have no pain there, do you? It's your breathing and your stomach that's been wrong. I wouldn't believe nobody but Doctor Ed about it. I guess I'll go see him myself. Didn't he give you no advice?"

"Chust to take it easy like, an' stay round de house dis winter. I guess you got some carpenter work for me to do. I kin make some new shelves for you, and I want dis long time to build a closet in de boys' room and make dem two little fellers keep dere clo'es hung up."

Rosicky drank his coffee from time to time, while he considered. His moustache was of the soft long variety and came down over his mouth like the teeth of a buggy-rake over a bundle of hay. Each time he put down his cup, he ran his blue handkerchief over his lips. When he took a drink of water, he managed very neatly with the back of his hand.

Mary sat watching him intently, trying to find any change in his face. It is hard to see anyone who has become like your own body to you. Yes, his hair had got thin, and his high forehead had deep lines running from left to right. But his neck, always clean shaved except in the busiest seasons, was not loose or baggy. It was burned a dark reddish brown, and there were deep creases in it, but it looked firm and full of blood. His cheeks had a good colour. On either side of his mouth there was a half-moon down the length of his cheek, not wrinkles, but two lines that had come there from his habitual expression. He was shorter and broader than when she married him; his back had grown broad and curved, a good deal like the shell of an old turtle, and his arms and legs were short.

He was fifteen years older than Mary, but she had hardly ever thought about it before. He was her man, and the kind of man she liked. She was rough, and he was gentle,—city-bred, as she always said. They had been shipmates on a rough voyage and had stood by each other in trying times. Life had gone well with them because, at bottom, they had the same ideas about life. They agreed, without discussion, as to what was most important and what was secondary. They didn't often exchange opinions, even in Czech,—it was as if they had thought the same thought together. A good deal had to be sacrificed and thrown overboard in a hard life like theirs, and they had never disagreed as to the things that could go. It had been a hard life, and a soft life, too. There wasn't anything brutal in the short, broad-backed man with the three-cornered eyes and the forehead that went on to the top of his skull. He was a city man, a gentle man, and though he had married a rough farm girl, he had never touched her without gentleness.

They had been at one accord not to hurry through life, not to be always skimping and saving. They saw their neighbours buy more land and feed more stock than they did, without discontent. Once when the creamery agent came to the Rosickys to persuade them to sell him their cream, he told them how much money the Fasslers, their nearest neighbors, had made on their cream last year.

"Yes," said Mary, "and look at them Fassler children! Pale, pinched little things, they look like skimmed milk. I'd rather put some colour into my children's faces than put money into the bank."

The agent shrugged and turned to Anton.

"I guess we'll do like she says," said Rosicky.

III

Mary very soon got into town to see Doctor Ed, and then she had a talk with her boys and set a guard over Rosicky. Even John, the youngest, had his father on his mind. If Rosicky went to throw hay down from the loft, one of the boys ran up the ladder and took the fork from him. He sometimes complained that though he was getting to be an old man, he wasn't an old woman yet.

That winter he stayed in the house in the afternoons and carpentered, or sat in the chair between the window full of plants and the wooden bench where the two pails of drinking water stood. This spot was called "Father's corner," though it was not a corner at all. He had a shelf there, where he kept his Bohemian papers and his pipes and tobacco, and his shears and needles and thread and tailor's thimble. Having been a tailor in his youth, he couldn't bear to see a woman patching at his clothes, or at the boys'. He liked tailoring, and always patched all the overalls and jackets and work shirts. Occasionally he made over a pair of pants one of the older boys had outgrown, for the little fellow.

While he sewed, he let his mind run back over his life. He had a good deal to remember, really; life in three countries. The only part of his youth he didn't like to remember was the two years he had spent in London, in Cheapside, working for a German tailor who was wretchedly poor. Those days, when he was nearly always hungry, when his clothes were dropping off him for dirt, and the sound of a strange language kept him in continual bewilderment, had left a sore spot in his mind that wouldn't bear touching.

He was twenty when he landed at Castle Garden in New York, and he had a protector who got him work in a tailor shop in Vesey Street, down near the Washington Market. He looked upon that part of his life as very happy. He became a good workman, he was industrious, and his wages were increased from time to time. He minded his own business and envied nobody's good fortune. He went to night school and learned to read English. He often did overtime work and was well paid for it, but somehow he never saved anything. He couldn't refuse a loan to a friend, and he was self-indulgent. He liked a good dinner, and a little went for beer, a little for tobacco, a good deal went to the girls. He often stood through an opera on Saturday nights; he could get standing-room for a dollar. Those were the great days of opera in New York, and it gave a fellow something to think about for the rest of the week. Rosicky had a quick ear, and a childish love of all the stage splendour; the scenery, the costumes, the ballet. He usually went with a chum, and after the performance they had beer and maybe some oysters somewhere. It was a fine life, for the first five years or so it satisfied him completely. He was never hungry or cold or dirty, and everything amused him: a fire, a dog fight, a parade, a storm, a ferry ride. He thought New York the finest, richest, friendliest city in the world.

Moreover, he had what he called a happy home life. Very near the tailor shop was a small furniture-factory, where an old Austrian, Loeffler, employed a few skilled men and made unusual furniture, most of it to order, for the rich German housewives up-town. The top floor of Loeffler's five-storey factory was a loft, where he kept his choice lumber and stored the odd pieces of furniture left on his hands. One of the young workmen he employed was a Czech, and he and Rosicky became fast friends. They persuaded Loeffler to let them have a sleeping-room in one corner of the loft. They bought good beds and bedding and had their pick of the furniture kept up there. The loft was low-pitched, but light and airy, full of windows, and good-smelling by reason of the fine lumber put up there to season. Old Loeffler used to go down to the docks and buy wood from South America and the East from the sea captains. The young men were as foolish about their house as a bridal pair. Zichec, the young cabinet-maker, devised every sort of convenience, and Rosicky kept their clothes in order. At night and on Sundays, when the quiver of machinery underneath was still, it was the quietest place in the world, and on summer nights all the sea winds blew in. Zichec often practised on his flute in the evening. They were both fond of music and went to the opera together. Rosicky thought he wanted to live like that for ever.

But as the years passed, all alike, he began to get a little restless. When spring came round, he would begin to feel fretted, and he got to drinking. He was likely to drink too much of a Saturday night. On Sunday he was languid and heavy, getting over his spree. On Monday he plunged into work again. So he never had time to figure out what ailed him, though he knew something did. When the grass turned green in Park Place, and the lilac hedge at the back of Trinity churchyard put out its blossoms, he was tormented by a longing to run away. That was why he drank too much; to get a temporary illusion of freedom and wide horizons.

Rosicky, the old Rosicky, could remember as if it were yesterday the day when the young Rosicky found out what was the matter with him. It was on a Fourth of July afternoon, and he was sitting in Park Place in the sun. The lower part of New York was empty. Wall Street, Liberty Street, Broadway, all empty. So much stone and asphalt with nothing going on, so many empty windows. The emptiness was intense, like the stillness in a great factory when the machinery stops and the belts and bands cease running. It was too great a change, it took all the strength out of one. Those blank buildings, without the stream of life pouring through them, were like empty jails. It struck young Rosicky that this was the trouble with big cities; they built you in from the earth itself, cemented you away from any contact with the ground. You lived in an unnatural world, like the fish in an aquarium, who were probably much more comfortable than they ever were in the sea.

On that very day he began to think seriously about the articles he had read in the Bohemian papers, describing prosperous Czech farming communities in the West. He believed he would like to go out there as a farm hand; it was hardly possible that he could ever have land of his own. His people had always been workmen; his father and grandfather had worked in shops. His mother's parents had lived in the country, but they rented their farm and had a hard time to get along. Nobody in his family had ever owned any land,—that belonged to a different station of life altogether. Anton's mother died when he was little, and he was sent into the country to her parents. He stayed with them until he was twelve, and formed those ties with the earth and the farm animals and growing things which are never made at all unless they are made early. After his grandfather died, he went back to live with his father and stepmother, but she was very hard on him, and his father helped him to get passage to London.

After that Fourth of July day in Park Place, the desire to return to the country never left him. To work on another man's farm would be all he asked; to see the sun rise and set and to plant things and watch them grow. He was a very simple man. He was like a tree that has not many roots, but one tap-root that goes down deep. He subscribed for a Bohemian paper printed in Chicago, then for one printed in Omaha. His mind got farther and farther west. He began to save a little money to buy his liberty. When he was thirty-five, there was a great meeting in New York of Bohemian athletic societies, and Rosicky left the tailor shop and went home with the Omaha delegates to try his fortune in another part of the world.

IV

Perhaps the fact that his own youth was well over before he began to have a family was one reason why Rosicky was so fond of his boys. He had almost a grandfather's indulgence for them. He had never had to worry about any of them—except, just now, a little about Rudolph.

On Saturday night the boys always piled into the Ford, took little Josephine, and went to town to the moving-picture show. One Saturday morning they were talking at the breakfast table about starting early that evening, so that they would have an hour or so to see the Christmas things in the stores before the show began. Rosicky looked down the table.

"I hope you boys ain't disappointed, but I want you to let me have de car tonight. Maybe some of you can go in with de neighbours."

Their faces fell. They worked hard all week, and they were still like children. A new jack-knife or a box of candy pleased the older ones as much as the little fellow.

"If you and Mother are going to town," Frank said, "maybe you could take a couple of us along with you, anyway."

"No, I want to take de car down to Rudolph's, and let him an' Polly go in to de show. She don't git into town enough, an' I'm afraid she's gettin' lonesome, an' he can't afford no car yet."

That settled it. The boys were a good deal dashed. Their father took another piece of apple-cake and went on: "Maybe next Saturday night de two little fellers can go along wid dem."

"Oh, is Rudolph going to have the car every Saturday night?"

Rosicky did not reply at once; then he began to speak seriously: "Listen, boys; Polly ain't lookin' so good. I don't like to see nobody lookin' sad. It comes hard fur a town girl to be a farmer's wife. I don't want no trouble to start in Rudolph's family. When it starts, it ain't so easy to stop. An American girl don't git used to our ways all at once. I like to tell Polly she and Rudolph can have the car every Saturday night till after New Year's, if it's all right with you boys."

"Sure it's all right, Papa," Mary cut in. "And

it's good you thought about that. Town girls is used to more than country girls. I lay awake nights, scared she'll make Rudolph discontented with the farm."

The boys put as good a face on it as they could. They surely looked forward to their Saturday nights in town. That evening Rosicky drove the car the half-mile down to Rudolph's new, bare little house.

Polly was in a short-sleeved gingham dress, clearing away the supper dishes. She was a trim, slim little thing, with blue eyes and shingled yellow hair, and her eyebrows were reduced to a mere brush-stroke, like Miss Pearl's.

"Good evening, Mr. Rosicky. Rudolph's at the barn, I guess." She never called him father, or Mary mother. She was sensitive about having married a foreigner. She never in the world would have done it if Rudolph hadn't been such a handsome, persuasive fellow and such a gallant lover. He had graduated in her class in the high school in town, and their friendship began in the ninth grade.

Rosicky went in, though he wasn't exactly asked. "My boys ain't goin' to town tonight, an' I brought de car over fur you two to go in to de picture show."

Polly, carrying dishes to the sink, looked over her shoulder at him. "Thank you. But I'm late with my work tonight, and pretty tired. Maybe Rudolph would like to go in with you."

"Oh, I don't go to de shows! I'm too old-fashioned. You won't feel so tired after you ride in de air a ways. It's a nice clear night, an' it ain't cold. You go an' fix yourself up, Polly, an' I'll wash de dishes an' leave everything nice fur you."

Polly blushed and tossed her bob. "I couldn't let you do that, Mr. Rosicky. I wouldn't think of it."

Rosicky said nothing. He found a bib apron on a nail behind the kitchen door. He slipped it over his head and then took Polly by her two elbows and pushed her gently toward the door of her own room. "I washed up de kitchen many times for my wife, when de babies was sick or somethin'. You go an' make yourself look nice. I like you to look prettier'n any of dem town girls when you go in. De young folks must have some fun, an' I'm goin' to look out fur you, Polly."

That kind, reassuring grip on her elbows, the old man's funny bright eyes, made Polly want to drop her head on his shoulder for a second.

She restrained herself, but she lingered in his grasp at the door of her room, murmuring tearfully: "You always lived in the city when you were young, didn't you? Don't you ever get lonesome out here?"

As she turned round to him, her hand fell naturally into his, and he stood holding it and smiling into her face with his peculiar, knowing, indulgent smile without a shadow of reproach in it. "Dem big cities is all right fur de rich, but dey is terrible hard fur de poor."

"I don't know. Sometimes I think I'd like to take a chance. You lived in New York, didn't you?"

"An' London. Da's bigger still. I learned my trade dere. Here's Rudolph comin', you better hurry."

"Will you tell me about London some time?"

"Maybe. Only I ain't no talker, Polly. Run an' dress yourself up."

The bedroom door closed behind her, and Rudolph came in from the outside, looking anxious. He had seen the car and was sorry any of his family should come just then. Supper hadn't been a very pleasant occasion. Halting in the doorway, he saw his father in a kitchen apron, carrying dishes to the sink. He flushed crimson and something flashed in his eye. Rosicky held up a warning finger.

"I brought de car over fur you an' Polly to go to de picture show, an' I made her let me finish here so you won't be late. You go put on a clean shirt, quick!"

"But don't the boys want the car, Father?"

"Not tonight dey don't." Rosicky fumbled under his apron and found his pants pocket. He took out a silver dollar and said in a hurried whisper: "You go an' buy dat girl some ice cream an' candy tonight, like you was courtin'. She's awful good friends wid me."

Rudolph was very short of cash, but he took the money as if it hurt him. There had been a crop failure all over the county. He had more than once been sorry he'd married this year.

In a few minutes the young people came out, looking clean and a little stiff. Rosicky hurried them off, and then he took his own time with the dishes. He scoured the pots and pans and put away the milk and swept the kitchen. He put some coal in the stove and shut off the draughts, so the place would be warm for them when they got home late at night. Then he sat down and had a pipe and listened to the clock tick.

Generally speaking, marrying an American girl was certainly a risk. A Czech should marry a Czech. It was lucky that Polly was the daughter of a poor widow woman; Rudolph was proud, and if she had a prosperous family to throw up at him, they could never make it go. Polly was one of four sisters, and they all worked; one was book-keeper in the bank, one taught music, and Polly and her younger sister had been clerks, like Miss Pearl. All four of them were musical, had pretty voices, and sang in the Methodist choir, which the eldest sister directed.

Polly missed the sociability of a store position. She missed the choir, and the company of her sisters. She didn't dislike housework, but she disliked so much of it. Rosicky was a little anxious about this pair. He was afraid Polly would grow so discontented that Rudy would quit the farm and take a factory job in Omaha. He had worked for a winter up there, two years ago, to get money to marry on. He had done very well, and they would always take him back at the stockyards. But to Rosicky that meant the end of everything for his son. To be a landless man was to be a wage-earner, a slave, all your life; to have nothing, to be nothing.

Rosicky thought he would come over and do a little carpentering for Polly after the New Year. He guessed she needed jollying. Rudolph was a serious sort of chap, serious in love and serious about his work.

Rosicky shook out his pipe and walked home across the fields. Ahead of him the lamplight shone from his kitchen windows. Suppose he were still in a tailor shop on Vesey Street, with a bunch of pale, narrow-chested sons working on machines, all coming home tired and sullen to eat supper in a kitchen that was a parlour also; with another crowded, angry family quarrelling just across the dumb-waiter shaft, and squeaking pulleys at the windows where dirty washings hung on dirty lines above a court full of old brooms and mops and ash-cans. . . .

He stopped by the windmill to look up at the frosty winter stars and draw a long breath before he went inside. That kitchen with the shining windows was dear to him; but the sleeping fields and bright stars and the noble darkness were dearer still.

v

On the day before Christmas the weather set in very cold; no snow, but a bitter, biting wind that whistled and sang over the flat land and lashed one's face like fine wires. There was baking going on in the Rosicky kitchen all day, and Rosicky sat inside, making over a coat that Albert had outgrown into an overcoat for John. Mary had a big red geranium in bloom for Christmas, and a row of Jerusalem cherry trees, full of berries. It was the first year she had ever grown these; Doctor Ed brought her the seeds from Omaha when he went to some medical convention. They reminded Rosicky of plants he had seen in England; and all afternoon, as he stitched, he sat thinking about those two years in London, which his mind usually shrank from even after all this while.

He was a lad of eighteen when he dropped down into London, with no money and no connexions except the address of a cousin who was supposed to be working at a confectioner's. When he went to the pastry shop, however, he found that the cousin had gone to America. Anton tramped the streets for several days, sleeping in doorways and on the Embankment, until he was in utter despair. He knew no English, and the sound of the strange language all about him confused him. By chance he met a poor German tailor who had learned his trade in Vienna, and could speak a little Czech. This tailor, Lifschnitz, kept a repair shop in a Cheapside basement, underneath a cobbler. He didn't much need an apprentice, but he was sorry for the boy and took him in for no wages but his keep and what he could pick up. The pickings were supposed to be coppers given you when you took work home to a customer. But most of the customers called for their clothes themselves, and the coppers that came Anton's way were very few. He had, however, a place to sleep. The tailor's family lived upstairs in three rooms; a kitchen, a bedroom, where Lifschnitz and his wife and five children slept, and a living-room. Two corners of this living-room were curtained off for lodgers; in one Rosicky slept on an old horsehair sofa, with a feather quilt to wrap himself in. The other corner was rented to a wretched, dirty boy, who was studying the violin. He actually practised there. Rosicky was dirty, too. There was no way to be anything else. Mrs. Lifschnitz got the water she cooked and washed with from a pump in a brick court, four flights down. There were bugs in the place, and multitudes of fleas, though the poor woman did the best she could. Rosicky knew she often went empty to give another potato or a spoonful of

dripping to the two hungry, sad-eyed boys who lodged with her. He used to think he would never get out of there, never get a clean shirt to his back again. What would he do, he wondered, when his clothes actually dropped to pieces and the worn cloth wouldn't hold patches any longer?

It was still early when the old farmer put aside his sewing and his recollections. The sky had been a dark grey all day, with not a gleam of sun, and the light failed at four o'clock. He went to shave and change his shirt while the turkey was roasting. Rudolph and Polly were coming over for supper.

After supper they sat round in the kitchen, and the younger boys were saying how sorry they were it hadn't snowed. Everybody was sorry. They wanted a deep snow that would lie long and keep the wheat warm, and leave the ground soaked when it melted.

"Yes, sir!" Rudolph broke out fiercely; "if we have another dry year like last year, there's going to be hard times in this country."

Rosicky filled his pipe. "You boys don't know what hard times is. You don't owe nobody, you got plenty to eat an' keep warm, an' plenty water to keep clean. When you got them, you can't have it very hard."

Rudolph frowned, opened and shut his big right hand, and dropped it clenched upon his knee. "I've got to have a good deal more than that, Father, or I'll quit this farming gamble. I can always make good wages railroading, or at the packing house, and be sure of my money."

"Maybe so," his father answer dryly.

Mary, who had just come in from the pantry and was wiping her hands on the roller towel, thought Rudy and his father were getting too serious. She brought her darning-basket and sat down in the middle of the group.

"I ain't much afraid of hard times, Rudy," she said heartily. "We've had a plenty, but we've always come through. Your father wouldn't never take nothing very hard, not even hard times. I got a mind to tell you a story on him. Maybe you boys can't hardly remember the year we had that terrible hot wind, that burned everything up on the Fourth of July? All the corn an' the gardens. An' that was in the days when we didn't have alfalfa yet,— I guess it wasn't invented.

"Well, that very day your father was out cultivatin' corn, and I was here in the kitchen makin' plum preserves. We had bushels of plums that year. I noticed it was terrible hot, but it's always hot in the kitchen when you're preservin', an' I was too busy with my plums to mind. Anton come in from the field about three o'clock, an' I asked him what was the matter.

"'Nothin',' he says, 'but it's pretty hot, an' I think I won't work no more today.' He stood round for a few minutes, an' then he says: 'Ain't you near through? I want you should git up a nice supper for us tonight. It's Fourth of July.'

"I told him to git along, that I was right in the middle of preservin', but the plums would taste good on hot biscuit. 'I'm goin' to have fried chicken, too,' he says, and he went off an' killed a couple. You three oldest boys was little fellers, playin' round outside, real hot an' sweaty, an' your father took you to the horse tank down by the windmill an' took off your clothes an' put you in. Them two box-elder trees was little then, but they made shade over the tank. Then he took off all his own clothes, an' got in with you. While he was playin' in the water with you, the Methodist preacher drove into our place to say how all the neighbours was goin' to meet at the schoolhouse that night, to pray for rain. He drove right to the windmill, of course, and there was your father and you three with no clothes on. I was in the kitchen door, an' I had to laugh, for the preacher acted like he ain't never seen a naked man before. He surely was embarrassed, an' your father couldn't git to his clothes; they was all hangin' up on the windmill to let the sweat dry out of 'em. So he laid in the tank where he was, an' put one of you boys on top of him to cover him up a little, an' talked to the preacher.

"When you got through playin' in the water, he put clean clothes on you and a clean shirt on himself, an' by that time I'd begun to get supper. He says: 'It's too hot in here to eat comfortable. Let's have a picnic in the orchard. We'll eat our supper behind the mulberry hedge, under them linden trees.'

"So he carried our supper down, an' a bottle of my wild-grape wine, an' everything tasted good, I can tell you. The wind got cooler as the sun was goin' down, and it turned out pleasant, only I noticed how the leaves was curled up on the linden trees. That made me think, an' I asked your father if that hot wind all day hadn't been terrible hard on the gardens an' the corn.

"'Corn,' he says, 'there ain't no corn.'

"'What you talkin' about?' I said. 'Ain't we got forty acres?'

"'We ain't got an ear,' he says, 'nor nobody else ain't got none. All the corn in this country was cooked by three o'clock today, like you'd roasted it in an oven.'

"'You mean you won't get no crop at all?' I asked him. I couldn't believe it, after he'd worked so hard.

"'No crop this year,' he says. 'That's why we're havin' a picnic. We might as well enjoy what we got.'

"An' that's how your father behaved, when all the neighbours was so discouraged they couldn't look you in the face. An' we enjoyed ourselves that year, poor as we was, an' our neighbours wasn't a bit better off for bein' miserable. Some of 'em grieved till they got poor digestions and couldn't relish what they did have."

The younger boys said they thought their father had the best of it. But Rudolph was thinking that, all the same, the neighbours had managed to get ahead more, in the fifteen years since that time. There must be something wrong about his father's way of doing things. He wished he knew what was going on in the back of Polly's mind. He knew she liked his father, but he knew, too, that she was afraid of something. When his mother sent over coffee-cake or prune tarts or a loaf of fresh bread, Polly seemed to regard them with a certain suspicion. When she observed to him that his brothers had nice manners, her tone implied that it was remarkable they should have. With his mother she was stiff and on her guard. Mary's hearty frankness and gusts of good humour irritated her. Polly was afraid of being unusual or conspicuous in any way, of being "ordinary," as she said!

When Mary had finished her story, Rosicky laid aside his pipe.

"You boys like me to tell you about some of dem hard times I been through in London?" Warmly encouraged, he sat rubbing his forehead along the deep creases. It was bothersome to tell a long story in English (he nearly always talked to the boys in Czech), but he wanted Polly to hear this one.

"Well, you know about dat tailor shop I worked in in London? I had one Christmas dere I ain't never forgot. Times was awful bad before Christmas; de boss ain't got much work, an' have it awful hard to pay his rent. It ain't so much fun, bein' poor in a big city like London, I'll say! All de windows is full of good t'ings to eat, an' all de pushcarts in de streets is full, an' you smell 'em all de time, an' you ain't got no money,—not a damn bit. I didn't mind de cold so much, though I didn't have no overcoat, chust a short jacket I'd outgrowed so it wouldn't meet on me, an' my hands was chapped raw. But I always had a good appetite, like you all know, an' de sight of dem pork pies in de windows was awful fur me!

"Day before Christmas was terrible foggy dat year, an' dat fog gits into your bones and makes you all damp like. Mrs. Lifschnitz didn't give us nothin' but a little bread an' drippin' for supper, because she was savin' to try for to give us a good dinner on Christmas Day. After supper de boss say I can go an' enjoy myself, so I went into de streets to listen to de Christmas singers. Dey sing old songs an' make very nice music, an' I run round after dem a good ways, till I got awful hungry. I t'ink maybe if I go home, I can sleep till morning an' forget my belly.

"I went into my corner real quiet, and roll up in my fedder quilt. But I ain't got my head down, till I smell somet'ing good. Seem like it git stronger an' stronger, an' I can't git to sleep noway. I can't understand dat smell. Dere was a gas light in a hall across de court, dat always shine in at my window a little. I got up an' look round. I got a little wooden box in my corner fur a stool, 'cause I ain't got no chair. I picks up dat box, and under it dere is a roast goose on a platter! I can't believe my eyes. I carry it to de window where de light comes in, an' touch it and smell it to find out, an' den I taste it to be sure. I say, I will eat chust one little bite of dat goose, so I can go to sleep, and tomorrow I won't eat none at all. But I tell you, boys, when I stop, one half of dat goose was gone!"

The narrator bowed his head, and the boys shouted. But little Josephine slipped behind his chair and kissed him on the neck beneath his ear.

"Poor little Papa, I don't want him to be hungry!"

"Da's long ago, child. I ain't never been hungry since I had your mudder to cook fur me."

"Go on and tell us the rest, please," said Polly.

"Well, when I come to realize what I done, of course, I felt terrible. I felt better in de stomach, but very bad in de heart. I set on my bed wid dat platter on my knees, an' it all come to me; how hard dat poor woman save to buy dat goose, and how she get some neighbour to cook it dat got more fire, an' how she put it in my corner to keep it away from dem hungry children. Dey was a old carpet hung up to shut my corner off, an' de children wasn't allowed to go in dere. An' I know she put it in my corner because she trust me more'n she did de violin boy. I can't stand it to face her after I spoil de Christmas. So I put on my shoes and go out into de city. I tell myself I better throw myself in de river; but I guess I ain't dat kind of a boy.

"It was after twelve o'clock, an' terrible cold, an' I start out to walk about London all night. I walk along de river awhile, but dey was lots of drunks all along; men, and women too. I chust move along to keep away from de police. I git onto de Strand, an' den over to New Oxford Street, where dere was a big German restaurant on de ground floor, wid big windows all fixed up fine, an' I could see de people havin' parties inside. While I was lookin' in, two men and two ladies come out, laughin' and talkin' and feelin' happy about all dey been eatin' an' drinkin', and dey was speakin' Czech, —not like de Austrians, but like de home folks talk it.

"I guess I went crazy, an' I done what I ain't never done before nor since. I went right up to dem gay people an' begun to beg dem: 'Fellow-countrymen, for God's sake give me money enough to buy a goose!'

"Dey laugh, of course, but de ladies speak awful kind to me, an' dey take me back into de restaurant and give me hot coffee and cakes, an' make me tell all about how I happened to come to London, an' what I was doin' dere. Dey take my name and where I work down on paper, an' both of dem ladies give me ten shillings.

"De big market at Covent Garden ain't very far away, an' by dat time it was open. I go dere an' buy a big goose an' some pork pies, an' potatoes and onions, an' cakes an' oranges fur de children,—all I could carry! When I git home, everybody is still asleep. I pile all I bought on de kitchen table, an' go in an' lay down on my bed, an' I ain't waken up till I hear dat woman scream when she come out into her kitchen. My goodness, but she was surprise! She laugh an' cry at de same time, an' hug me and waken all de children. She ain't stop fur no breakfast; she git de Christmas dinner ready dat morning, and we all sit down an' eat all we can hold. I ain't never seen dat violin boy have all he can hold before.

"Two three days after dat, de two men come to hunt me up, an' dey ask my boss, and he give me a good report an' tell dem I was a steady boy all right. One of dem Bohemians was very smart an' run a Bohemian newspaper in New York, an' de odder was a rich man, in de importing business, an' dey been travelling togedder. Dey told me how t'ings was easier in New York, an' offered to pay my passage when dey was goin' home soon on a boat. My boss say to me: 'You go. You ain't got no chance here, an' I like to see you git ahead, fur you always been a good boy to my woman, and fur dat fine Christmas dinner you give us all.' An' da's how I got to New York."

That night when Rudolph and Polly, arm in arm, were running home across the fields with the bitter wind at their backs, his heart leaped for joy when she said she thought they might have his family come over for supper on New Year's Eve. "Let's get up a nice supper, and not let your mother help at all; make her be company for once."

"That would be lovely of you, Polly," he said humbly. He was a very simple, modest boy, and he, too, felt vaguely that Polly and her sisters were more experienced and worldly than his people.

VI

The winter turned out badly for farmers. It was bitterly cold, and after the first light snows before Christmas there was no snow at all,— and no rain. March was as bitter as February. On those days when the wind fairly punished the country, Rosicky sat by his window. In the fall he and the boys had put in a big wheat planting, and now the seed had frozen in the ground. All that land would have to be ploughed up and planted over again, planted in corn. It had happened before, but he was younger then, and he never worried about what had to be. He was sure of himself and of Mary; he knew they could bear what they had to bear, that they would always pull through somehow. But he was not so sure about the young ones, and he felt troubled because Rudolph and Polly were having such a hard start.

Sitting beside his flowering window while the panes rattled and the wind blew in under the door, Rosicky gave himself to reflection as he had not done since those Sundays in the loft of the furniture-factory in New York, long ago. Then he was trying to find what he wanted in life for himself; now he was trying to find what he wanted for his boys, and why it was he so hungered to feel sure they would be here, working this very land, after he was gone.

They would have to work hard on the farm, and probably they would never do much more than make a living. But if he could think of them as staying here on the land, he wouldn't have to fear any great unkindness for them. Hardships, certainly; it was a hardship to have the wheat freeze in the ground when seed was so high; and to have to sell your stock because you had no feed. But there would be other years when everything came along right, and you caught up. And what you had was your own. You didn't have to choose between bosses and strikers, and go wrong either way. You didn't have to do with dishonest and cruel people. They were the only things in his experience he had found terrifying and horrible; the look in the eyes of a dishonest and crafty man, of a scheming and rapacious woman.

In the country, if you had a mean neighbour, you could keep off his land and make him keep off yours. But in the city, all the foulness and misery and brutality of your neighbours was part of your life. The worst things he had come upon in his journey through the world were human,—depraved and poisonous specimens of man. To this day he could recall certain terrible faces in the London streets. There were mean people everywhere, to be sure, even in their own country town here. But they weren't tempered, hardened, sharpened, like the treacherous people in cities who live by grinding or cheating or poisoning their fellow-men. He had helped to bury two of his fellow-workmen in the tailoring trade, and he was distrustful of the organized industries that see one out of the world in big cities. Here, if you were sick, you had Doctor Ed to look after you; and if you died, fat Mr. Haycock, the kindest man in the world, buried you.

It seemed to Rosicky that for good, honest boys like his, the worst they could do on the farm was better than the best they would be likely to do in the city. If he'd had a mean boy, now, one who was crooked and sharp and tried to put anything over on his brothers, then town would be the place for him. But he had no such boy. As for Rudolph, the discontented one, he would give the shirt off his back to anyone who touched his heart. What Rosicky really hoped for his boys was that they could get through the world without ever knowing much about the cruelty of human beings. "Their mother and me ain't prepared them for that," he sometimes said to himself.

These thoughts brought him back to a grateful consideration of his own case. What an escape he had had, to be sure! He, too, in his time, had had to take money for repair work from the hand of a hungry child who let it go so wistfully; because it was money due his boss. And now, in all these years, he had never had to take a cent from any one in bitter need, —never had to look at the face of a woman become like a wolf's from struggle and famine. When he thought of these things, Rosicky would put on his cap and jacket and slip down to the barn and give his workhorses a little extra oats, letting them eat it out of his hand in their slobbery fashion. It was his way of expressing what he felt, and made him chuckle with pleasure.

The spring came warm, with blue skies,— but dry, dry as a bone. The boys began ploughing up the wheat-fields to plant them over in corn. Rosicky would stand at the fence corner and watch them, and the earth was so dry it blew up in clouds of brown dust that hid the horses and the sulky plough and the driver. It was a bad outlook.

The big alfalfa-field that lay between the home place and Rudolph's came up green, but Rosicky was worried because during that open windy winter a great many Russian thistle plants had blown in there and lodged. He kept asking the boys to rake them out; he was afraid their seed would root and "take the alfalfa." Rudolph said that was nonsense. The boys were working so hard planting corn, their father felt he couldn't insist about the thistles, but he set great store by that big alfalfa field. It was a feed you could depend on,—and there was some deeper reason, vague, but strong. The peculiar green of that clover woke early memories in old Rosicky, went back to something in his childhood in the old world. When he was a little boy, he had played in fields of that strong blue-green colour.

One morning, when Rudolph had gone to town in the car, leaving a work-team idle in his barn, Rosicky went over to his son's place,

put the horses to the buggy-rake, and set about quietly raking up those thistles. He behaved with guilty caution, and rather enjoyed stealing a march on Doctor Ed, who was just then taking his first vacation in seven years of practice and was attending a clinic in Chicago. Rosicky got the thistles raked up, but did not stop to burn them. That would take some time, and his breath was pretty short, so he thought he had better get the horses back to the barn.

He got them into the barn and to their stalls, but the pain had come on so sharp in his chest that he didn't try to take the harness off. He started for the house, bending lower with every step. The cramp in his chest was shutting him up like a jack-knife. When he reached the windmill, he swayed and caught at the ladder. He saw Polly coming down the hill, running with the swiftness of a slim greyhound. In a flash she had her shoulder under his armpit.

"Lean on me, Father, hard! Don't be afraid. We can get to the house all right."

Somehow they did, though Rosicky became blind with pain; he could keep on his legs, but he couldn't steer his course. The next thing he was conscious of was lying on Polly's bed, and Polly bending over him wringing out bath towels in hot water and putting them on his chest. She stopped only to throw coal into the stove, and she kept the tea-kettle and the black pot going. She put these hot applications on him for nearly an hour, she told him afterwards, and all that time he was drawn up stiff and blue, with the sweat pouring off him.

As the pain gradually loosed its grip, the stiffness went out of his jaws, the black circles round his eyes disappeared, and a little of his natural colour came back. When his daughter-in-law buttoned his shirt over his chest at last, he sighed.

"Da's fine, de way I feel now, Polly. It was a awful bad spell, an' I was so sorry it all come on you like it did."

Polly was flushed and excited. "Is the pain really gone? Can I leave you long enough to telephone over to your place?"

Rosicky's eyelids fluttered. "Don't telephone, Polly. It ain't no use to scare my wife. It's nice and quiet here, an' if I ain't too much trouble to you, just let me lay still till I feel like myself. I ain't got no pain now. It's nice here."

Polly bent over him and wiped the moisture from his face. "Oh, I'm so glad it's over!" she broke out impulsively. "It just broke my heart to see you suffer so, Father."

Rosicky motioned her to sit down on the chair where the tea-kettle had been, and looked up at her with that lively affectionate gleam in his eyes. "You was awful good to me, I won't never forgit dat. I hate it to be sick on you like dis. Down at de barn I say to myself, dat young girl ain't had much experience in sickness, I don't want to scare her, an' maybe she's got a baby comin' or somet'ing."

Polly took his hand. He was looking at her so intently and affectionately and confidingly; his eyes seemed to caress her face, to regard it with pleasure. She frowned with her funny streaks of eyebrows, and then smiled back at him.

"I guess maybe there is something of that kind going to happen. But I haven't told anyone yet, not my mother or Rudolph. You'll be the first to know."

His hand pressed hers. She noticed that it was warm again. The twinkle in his yellow-brown eyes seemed to come nearer.

"I like mighty well to see dat little child, Polly," was all he said. Then he closed his eyes and lay half-smiling. But Polly sat still, thinking hard. She had a sudden feeling that nobody in the world, not her mother, not Rudolph, or anyone, really loved her as much as old Rosicky did. It perplexed her. She sat frowning and trying to puzzle it out. It was as if Rosicky had a special gift for loving people, something that was like an ear for music or an eye for colour. It was quiet, unobtrusive; it was merely there. You saw it in his eyes,—perhaps that was why they were merry. You felt it in his hands, too. After he dropped off to sleep, she sat holding his warm, broad, flexible brown hand. She had never seen another in the least like it. She wondered if it wasn't a kind of gypsy hand, it was so alive and quick and light in its communications,—very strange in a farmer. Nearly all the farmers she knew had huge lumps of fists, like mauls, or they were knotty and bony and uncomfortable-looking, with stiff fingers. But Rosicky's was like quicksilver, flexible, muscular, about the colour of a pale cigar, with deep, deep creases across the palm. It wasn't nervous, it wasn't a stupid lump; it was a warm brown human hand, with some cleverness in it, a great deal of generosity, and something else which Polly could only call "gypsy-like,"—something nimble and lively and sure, in the way that animals are.

Polly remembered that hour long afterwards; it had been like an awakening to her. It seemed to her that she had never learned so much about life from anything as from old Rosicky's hand. It brought her to herself; it communicated some direct and untranslatable message.

When she heard Rudolph coming in the car, she ran out to meet him.

"Oh, Rudy, your father's been awful sick! He raked up those thistles he's been worrying about, and afterwards he could hardly get to the house. He suffered so I was afraid he was going to die."

Rudolph jumped to the ground. "Where is he now?"

"On the bed. He's asleep. I was terribly scared, because, you know, I'm so fond of your father." She slipped her arm through his and they went into the house. That afternoon they took Rosicky home and put him to bed, though he protested that he was quite well again.

The next morning he got up and dressed and sat down to breakfast with his family. He told Mary that his coffee tasted better than usual to him, and he warned the boys not to bear any tales to Doctor Ed when he got home. After breakfast he sat down by his window to do some patching and asked Mary to thread several needles for him before she went to feed her chickens,—her eyes were better than his, and her hands steadier. He lit his pipe and took up John's overalls. Mary had been watching him anxiously all morning, and as she went out of the door with her bucket of scraps, she saw that he was smiling. He was thinking, indeed, about Polly, and how he might never have known what a tender heart she had if he hadn't got sick over there. Girls nowadays didn't wear their heart on their sleeve. But now he knew Polly would make a fine woman after the foolishness wore off. Either a woman had that sweetness at her heart or she hadn't. You couldn't always tell by the look of them; but if they had that, everything came out right in the end.

After he had taken a few stitches, the cramp began in his chest, like yesterday. He put his pipe cautiously down on the window-sill and bent over to ease the pull. No use,—he had better try to get to his bed if he could. He rose and groped his way across the familiar floor, which was rising and falling like the deck of a ship. At the door he fell. When Mary came in, she found him lying there, and the moment she touched him she knew that he was gone.

Doctor Ed was away when Rosicky died,

and for the first few weeks after he got home he was hard driven. Every day he said to himself that he must get out to see that family that had lost their father. One soft, warm moonlight night in early summer he started for the farm. His mind was on other things, and not until his road ran by the graveyard did he realize that Rosicky wasn't over there on the hill where the red lamplight shone, but here, in the moonlight. He stopped his car, shut off the engine, and sat there for a while.

A sudden hush had fallen on his soul. Everything here seemed strangely moving and significant, though signifying what, he did not know. Close by the wire fence stood Rosicky's mowing-machine, where one of the boys had been cutting hay that afternoon; his own workhorses had been going up and down there. The new-cut hay perfumed all the night air. The moonlight silvered the long, billowy grass that grew over the graves and hid the fence; the few little evergreens stood out black in it, like shadows in a pool. The sky was very blue and soft, the stars rather faint because the moon was full.

For the first time it struck Doctor Ed that this was really a beautiful graveyard. He thought of city cemeteries; acres of shrubbery and heavy stone, so arranged and lonely and unlike anything in the living world. Cities of the dead, indeed; cities of the forgotten, of the "put away." But this was open and free, this little square of long grass which the wind forever stirred. Nothing but the sky overhead, and the many-coloured fields running on until they met that sky. The horses worked here in summer; the neighbours passed on their way to town; and over yonder, in the cornfield, Rosicky's own cattle would be eating fodder as winter came on. Nothing could be more undeathlike than this place; nothing could be more right for a man who had helped to do the work of great cities and had always longed for the open country and had got to it at last. Rosicky's life seemed to him complete and beautiful.

EZRA POUND

1885–

HARRIET MONROE once spoke of Pound's "love of stirring up and leading forth other minds." Amy Lowell, who felt his spell while usurping him as chief agent of the Imagist movement, said that "he could *make* you write." Carl Sandburg asserted that "he has done most of living men to incite new impulses in poetry." The assimilative mind and kinetic powers of Ezra Pound loom large indeed behind the poetic renascence whose flowering coincided approximately with the first World War. Polylingual, versatile, enthusiastic, generous with his time and interest, he aroused many an American poet to incandescence, at the same time turning out a respectable body of his own verse, including the loosely organized, allusive, autobiographical series of *Cantos*. His political intransigence, which resulted in his permanent exile to Rapallo, Italy, in the period after the second World War, is an unhappy aberration in the career of one who has served American poetry as a major catalyst through much of his life.

The cultural waste land of prewar America failed to hold Pound for long after his graduation from Hamilton College (Ph. B., 1905); his further experience of graduate study at the University of Pennsylvania and teaching at Wabash College (1906–7) was split by a voyage overseas in search of material for a doctor's thesis which he never wrote. The year 1908 found him established in London as a busy editor whose technical virtuosity, dogmatic assurance, and determination to burst free from the bonds of the immediate literary past soon made him many friends and a growing reputation. Among his associates he was soon to number Yeats,

Frost, T. E. Hulme, and F. S. Flint; with Aldington, H. D., and Amy Lowell, he launched the Imagist movement; he helped guide the fortunes of periodicals like *The Egoist*, *Blast*, and *The Little Review*, served Harriet Monroe as foreign correspondent and talent scout for *Poetry*, and after the war in Paris and Rapallo continued to throw his great energies and editorial skills into the rehabilitation of poetry.

Although Pound's persistent didacticism has not converted all his listeners, scores of poets have learned and are still learning from his poetic example. According to T. S. Eliot, who has freely acknowledged his debt to *il miglior fabbro*, Pound's free translations from the Anglo-Saxon, Provençal, Italian, Latin, Chinese, and Japanese have considerably enriched the techniques and vocabulary of present-day poetry. The same may be said, despite many lapses, of the whole range of Pound's poetry from the distinguished lucidity of *Hugh Selwyn Mauberley* (1920) through the *Cantos*, which began in 1925 with *A Draft of XVI Cantos* and have continued in the years between up to Canto CIX in 1959.

J. H. Edwards, *A Preliminary Checklist of the Writings of Ezra Pound*, New Haven, 1953.
The Cantos of Ezra Pound, New York, 1948.
The Pisan Cantos, New York, 1948.
Section: Rock-Drill: 85–95 de los cantares, New York, 1956.
Thornes: 96–109 de los cantares, New York, 1959.
Personae: The Collected Poems of Ezra Pound, New York (1926), 1949.
The Letters of Ezra Pound: 1907–1941, D. D. Paige, ed., New York, 1950.
Literary Essays, T. S. Eliot, ed., Norfolk, Connecticut, 1954.
A. S. Amdur, *The Poetry of Ezra Pound*, Cambridge, 1936.
T. S. Eliot, *Ezra Pound: His Metric and Poetry*, New York, 1917.
John Espey, *Ezra Pound's Mauberley*, Berkeley, California, 1955.
Hugh Kenner, *The Poetry of Ezra Pound*, London, 1951.
Lewis Leary, ed., *Motive and Method in the Cantos of Ezra Pound*, New York, 1954.
Charles Norman, *The Case of Ezra Pound*, New York, 1948.
_____, *Ezra Pound*, New York, 1960.
W. V. O'Connor and Edward Stone, *A Casebook on Ezra Pound*, New York, 1959.
Quarterly Review of Literature, V, no. 2 (1949). Ezra Pound issue.
M. L. Rosenthal, *A Primer of Ezra Pound*, New York, 1960.
Peter Russell, ed., *An Examination of Ezra Pound; A Collection of Essays*, Norfolk, Conn., 1950. (English title: *Ezra Pound; A Collection of Essays to be Presented to Ezra Pound on his Sixty-fifth Birthday*.)
H. H. Watts, *Ezra Pound and the Cantos*, Chicago, 1952.

A VIRGINAL

No, no! Go from me. I have left her lately.
I will not spoil my sheath with lesser brightness,
For my surrounding air hath a new lightness;
Slight are her arms, yet they have bound me straitly
And left me cloaked as with a gauze of æther;
As with sweet leaves; as with subtle clearness.
Oh, I have picke'd up magic in her nearness
To sheathe me half in half the things that sheathe her.
No, no! Go from me. I have still the flavour,
Soft as spring wind that's come from birchen bowers.   10

Green come the shoots, aye April in the branches,
As winter's wound with her sleight hand she staunches,
Hath of the trees a likeness of the savour:
As white their bark, so white this lady's hours.
                                                    1912

THE STUDY IN AESTHETICS

The very small children in patched clothing,
Being smitten with an unusual wisdom,
Stopped in their play as she passed them
And cried up from their cobbles:
    Guarda! Ahi, guarda! ch' è be'a! [1]

[1] Look, ah, look, how beautiful she is!

But three years after this
I heard the young Dante, whose last name I
   do not know—
For there are, in Sirmione, twenty-eight young
   Dantes and thirty-four Catulli;
And there had been a great catch of sardines,
And his elders   10
Were packing them in the great wooden boxes
For the market in Brescia, and he
Leapt about, snatching at the bright fish
And getting in both of their ways;
And in vain they commanded him to *sta
   fermo!* [2]
And when they would not let him arrange
The fish in the boxes
He stroked those which were already arranged,
Murmuring for his own satisfaction
This identical phrase: 20
   Ch' è be'a.
And at this I was mildly abashed.   1914

"SCATTERED MOLUCCAS"

Scattered Moluccas
Not knowing, day to day,
[2] Stand still.

The first day's end, in the next noon;
The placid water
Unbroken by the Simoon;

Thick foliage
Placid beneath warm suns,
Tawn fore-shores
Washed in the cobalt of oblivions;

Or through dawn-mist   10
The grey and rose
Of the juridical
Flamingoes;

A consciousness disjunct,
Being but this overblotted
Series
Of intermittences;

Coracle of Pacific voyages,
The unforecasted beach;
Then on an oar   20
Read this:

'I was
And I no more exist;
Here drifted
An hedonist.'   1920

» » *From:* HUGH SELWYN MAUBERLEY « «

I

E. P. ODE POUR L'ELECTION DE SON SEPULCHRE

For three years, out of key with his time,
He strove to resuscitate the dead art
Of poetry; to maintain "the sublime"
In the old sense. Wrong from the start—

No, hardly, but seeing he had been born
In a half savage country, out of date;
Bent resolutely on wringing lilies from the
   acorn;
Capaneus; trout for factitious bait;

Ἴδμεν γάρ τοι πάνθ', ὅο' ἐνὶ Τροίῃ   10
Caught in the unstopped ear;
Giving the rocks small lee-way
The chopped seas held him, therefore, that
   year.

His true Penelope was Flaubert,
He fished by obstinate isles;

Observed the elegance of Circe's hair
Rather than the mottoes on sun-dials.

Unaffected by "the march of events,"
He passed from men's memory in *l'an tren-
   tiesme*   20
De son eage; the case presents
No adjunct to the Muses' diadem.

II

The age demanded an image
Of its accelerated grimace,
Something for the modern stage,
Not, at any rate, an Attic grace;

Not, not certainly, the obscure reveries
Of the inward gaze;
Better mendacities   30
Than the classics in paraphrase!

The "age demanded" chiefly a mould in plaster,
Made with no loss of time,

A prose kinema, not, not assuredly, alabaster
Or the "sculpture" of rhyme.

III

The tea-rose tea-gown, etc.
Supplants the mousseline of Cos,
The pianola "replaces"
Sappho's barbitos.   40

Christ follows Dionysus,
Phallic and ambrosial
Made way for macerations;
Caliban casts out Ariel.

All things are a flowing,
Sage Heracleitus says;
But a tawdry cheapness
Shall outlast our days.

Even the Christian beauty
Defects—after Samothrace;   50
We see τὸ καλὸν
Decreed in the market place.

Faun's flesh is not to us,
Nor the saint's vision.
We have the press for wafer;
Franchise for circumcision.

All men, in law, are equals.
Free of Pisistratus,
We choose a knave or an eunuch
To rule over us.   60

O bright Apollo,
τίν' ἀνδρα, τίν' ἥρωα, τίνα θεὸν,
What god, man, or hero
Shall I place a tin wreath upon!

IV

These fought in any case,
and some believing,
                    pro domo, in any case . . .

Some quick to arm,
some for adventure,   70
some from fear of weakness,
some from fear of censure,
some for love of slaughter, in imagination,
learning later . . .
some in fear, learning love of slaughter;

Died some, pro patria,
                    non "dulce" non "et decor". . .
walked eye-deep in hell
believing in old men's lies, then unbelieving
came home, home to a lie,   80
home to many deceits,
home to old lies and new infamy;
usury age-old and age-thick
and liars in public places.

Daring as never before, wastage as never be-
    fore.
Young blood and high blood,
fair cheeks, and fine bodies;

fortitude as never before

frankness as never before,   90
disillusions as never told in the old days,
hysterias, trench confessions,
laughter out of dead bellies.

V

There died a myriad,
And of the best, among them,
For an old bitch gone in the teeth,
For a botched civilization,

Charm, smiling at the good mouth,
Quick eyes gone under earth's lid,

For two gross of broken statues,   100
For a few thousand battered books.

» » *From:* CANTOS « «

XLV

With usura hath no man a house of good stone
each block cut smooth and well fitting
that design might cover their face,
with usura
hath no man a painted paradise on his church
    wall

harpes et luthes
or where virgin receiveth message
and halo projects from incision,
with usura
seeth no man Gonzaga his heirs and his concu-
    bines
no picture is made to endure nor to live with
but it is made to sell and sell quickly

with usura, sin against nature,
is thy bread ever more of stale rags
is thy bread dry as paper,
with no mountain wheat, no strong flour
with usura the line grows thick
with usura is no clear demarcation
and no man can find site for his dwelling.
Stone cutter is kept from his stone
weaver is kept from his loom
WITH USURA
wool comes not to market
sheep bringeth no gain with usura
Usura is a murrain, usura
blunteth the needle in the maid's hand
and stoppeth the spinner's cunning. Pietro
    Lombardo
came not by usura
Duccio came not by usura
nor Pier della Francesca; Zuan Bellin' not by
    usura
nor was 'La Calunnia' painted.

Came not by usura Angelico; came not Am-
    brogio Praedis,
Came no church of cut stone signed: *Adamo
    me fecit.*
Not by usura St Trophime
Not by usura Saint Hilaire,
Usura rusteth the chisel
It rusteth the craft and the craftsman
It gnaweth the thread in the loom
None learneth to weave gold in her pattern;
Azure hath a canker by usura; cramoisi is un-
    broidered
Emerald findeth no Memling
Usura slayeth the child in the womb
It stayeth the young man's courting
It hath brought palsey to bed, lyeth
between the young bride and her bridegroom
                    CONTRA NATURAM
They have brought whores for Eleusis
Corpses are set to banquet
at behest of usura.   1937

"H. D.," HILDA DOOLITTLE

1886–

THE ANGLO-AMERICAN Imagist Movement was founded on the premise that "accurate description is a legitimate object of verse." Its reformational aims were nurtured in the rebellious aesthetic of T. E. Hulme, who called for a clear, concentrated, sinewy poetry, exact in epithet and employing ordinary language in fresh combinations. Ezra Pound advertised the movement by printing some of Hulme's own verse as an appendix to *Ripostes* (1912) and by issuing two years later an experimental anthology called *Des Imagistes.* Amy Lowell shortly assumed titular command of the group, issuing three Imagist year-books in the period 1915–1917. Although the movement soon passed into literary history, its effects continued to be both audible and visible for many postwar years, leaving its mark here and there in the work of such diverse poets as Pound, Sandburg, Eliot, William Carlos Williams, Hart Crane, and Wallace Stevens.

Besides Pound, Hulme, and Miss Lowell, the progenitors of Imagism included the English poets F. S. Flint and Richard Aldington and an American girl named Hilda Doolittle who had spent a shy girlhood in the environs of Philadelphia, briefly attended Bryn Mawr, and set off on a grand tour of Europe which ended in London and the masterful presence of Pound. Her marriage to Aldington, though it ended in divorce, brought together two very gifted young poets. Soon "H. D., *Imagiste,*" in Pound's cryptic designation, began to be heard of as a contributor to Harriet Monroe's *Poetry* (January, 1913) and her fame grew as more of her work appeared in the Imagist anthologies of Pound and Miss Lowell during the next four years.

Much of her best work was done by 1925. She will continue to be remembered for the technical perfection of such poems as *Garden, Orchard, Pear Tree,* for the hokku-like quality of

Oread, for the astringent freshness of poems like *Fragment 113* or *Orion Dead*. The spirit and texture of her strongest writing resembles the best of the Greek Anthology, and she has been called, not unreasonably, the glacial Sappho. But what most distinguished her early writing was her enthusiastic espousal and exemplification of Imagist principles. These are apparent in her revulsion from the saccharine, her quest and capture of salt and bitter cadences, her fierce dryad's exultation in the axe-bite of sharp edges, her almost Swinburnian ecstasy in the presence of the sea, and her conviction that "beauty without strength chokes out life."

Collected Poems of H. D., New York (1925), 1940.
R. P. Blackmur, "The Lesser Satisfactions," *Poetry*, XLI (November, 1932), 94–100.
Glenn Hughes, *Imagism and the Imagists*, Stanford University Press, 1931, pp. 109–124.

SEA POPPIES

Amber husk
fluted with gold,
fruit on the sand
marked with a rich grain,

treasure
spilled near the shrub-pines
to bleach on the boulders:

your stalk has caught root
among wet pebbles   10
and drift flung by the sea
and grated shells
and split conch-shells.

Beautiful, wide-spread,
fire upon leaf,
what meadow yields
so fragrant a leaf
as your bright leaf?   1916

FRAGMENT 113

"Neither honey nor bee for me."
—SAPPHO.

Not honey,
not the plunder of the bee
from meadow or sand-flower
or mountain-bush;
from winter-flower or shoot
born of the later heat:
not honey, not the sweet
stain on the lips and teeth:
not honey, not the deep
plunge of the soft belly   10
and the clinging of the gold-edged
pollen-dusted feet;

Not so—
though rapture blind my eyes,
and hunger crisp
dark and inert my mouth,
not honey, not the south,
not the tall stalk
of red twin-lilies,
nor light branch of fruit-tree   20
caught in flexible light branch;

not honey, not the south;
ah flower of purple iris,
flower of white,
or of the iris, withering the grass—
for fleck of the sun's fire,
gathers such heat and power,
that shadow-print is light,
cast through the petals
of the yellow iris flower;   30

not iris—old desire—old passion—
old forgetfulness—old pain—
not this, nor any flower,
but if you turn again,
seek strength of arm and throat,
touch as the god;
neglect the lyre-note;
knowing that you shall feel,
about the frame,

no trembling of the string   40
but heat, more passionate
of bone and the white shell
and fiery tempered steel.   1921

HELEN

All Greece hates
the still eyes in the white face,
the lustre as of olives

where she stands,
and the white hands.

All Greece reviles
the wan face when she smiles,
hating it deeper still
when it grows wan and white,
remembering past enchantments   10
and past ills.

Greece sees unmoved,
God's daughter, born of love,
the beauty of cool feet
and slenderest knees,
could love indeed the maid,
only if she were laid,
white ash amid funereal cypresses.   1924

OREAD

Whirl up, sea—
whirl your pointed pines,
splash your great pines
on our rocks,
hurl your green over us,
cover us with your pools of fir.   1924

ORION DEAD

(Artemis speaks.)

The cornel-trees
uplift from the furrows;

the roots at their bases
strike lower through the barley-sprays.

So arise and face me.
I am poisoned with rage of song.

I once pierced the flesh
of the wild deer,
now I am afraid to touch
the blue and the gold-veined hyacinths.   10

I will tear the full flowers
and the little heads
of the grape-hyacinths;
I will strip the life from the bulb
until the ivory layers
lie like narcissus petals
on the black earth.

Arise,
lest I bend an ash-tree
into a taut bow,   20
and slay—and tear
all the roots from the earth.

The cornel-wood blazes
and strikes through the barley-sprays
but I have lost heart for this.

I break a staff.
I break the tough branch.
I know no light in the woods.
I have lost pace with the wind.   1924

T. S. ELIOT

1888–

T. S. ELIOT is the most influential poet and critic of his generation. To a degree his influence has been pervasive because his ideas have constantly expanded from a center where they are closely interrelated. As he said in 1928, in the preface to a new edition of his epoch-making collection of essays, *The Sacred Wood:* "I have found the task [of revision] impossible, and perhaps even undesirable. For I discovered that what had happened in my own mind, in eight years, was not so much a change or reversal of opinions, as an expansion or development of interests." It is characteristic of Eliot that a hint or an allusion thrown out in one essay may find, years later, full development and expression. An opponent who attacked his ideas, as they were set forth in one context, found that he must cope with them in their transmutations in other fields. In our society, in which thinking is compartmentalized and is seldom rooted in faith, Eliot serves as a touchstone even for those who disagree with him.

T. S. Eliot was born in St. Louis in 1888. He attended Harvard, where he was graduated in

1909. Subsequently he studied at Harvard, the Sorbonne, and at Merton College, Oxford. Since 1914 he has lived in England. In 1927 he became a British subject.

While still an undergraduate Eliot wrote poetry with a marked individuality. His early verse gave evidence of his enthusiasm for the French symbolists, especially Laforgue, the Elizabethan dramatists, and Dante. From his friend Ezra Pound, "il miglior fabbro," to whom *The Waste Land* is dedicated, he learned much. Since his verse of this period helped to initiate a significant change in poetic style, a brief summary of its characteristics must be attempted.

Eliot's poetry written between 1917 and 1934 is allusive and recondite, though not really— as it has often been called—"obscure." Instead of being, as poetry had been for the past century, discursive and random in its aim, his verse is compact and precise. Each word bears many stresses. He uses as symbols persons in history and myth; lines, borrowed from other poets, which convey a maximum of emotion. The geographical movement of his themes and the constant shift from one moment to another in history universalize the ideas and the emotion. Finally, like the metaphysical poets, for whom Eliot created a new taste, he establishes a tension between moods in order to strike at the truth through paradox. Poetry of this sort is the very antithesis of the style which descended to the Victorians from the Romantics. Eliot was chiefly responsible, both in his verse and his criticism, for the repudiation of the romantic attitude.

Eliot's career as a poet can be divided into three stages. Through the composition of *The Waste Land* (1922) and *The Hollow Men* (1925) the mood is one of disgust with the sordidness and sterility of modern life. Yet behind the irony with which this life is treated is an intense desire for its purification. This serious mood, which is essentially religious, most of Eliot's contemporaries, who shared his disgust but not his aspiration, failed to perceive. They took their way to the political Left or pursued death in their books, as Hemingway did, or like H. L. Mencken, used the cutting tools of satire. Eliot made his way to the Anglo-Catholic Church. In *Ash Wednesday* (1930), seemingly the most personal of his poems, he makes his submission.

> Blessèd sister, holy mother, spirit of the fountain,
>   spirit of the garden,
> Suffer us not to mock ourselves with falsehood
> Teach us to care and not to care
> Teach us to sit still
> Even among these rocks,
> Our peace in His will

Aside from "Ash Wednesday" and the four "Ariel Poems," one of which is printed here ("Journey of the Magi"), Eliot published little verse between 1927 and 1936, the date of the first of the *Four Quartets*—"Burnt Norton." The other Quartets followed in fairly rapid succession: "East Coker" (1940); "The Dry Salvages" (1941); "Little Gidding" (1942). When the *Four Quartets* were issued in a single volume (1943), this work was at once recognized as one of the most impressive poems of our century.

While he was at work on "East Coker," Eliot conceived the idea of writing four poems, using the same structural pattern of five sections in each and carrying the developing theme from one Quartet to the next. In the *Quartets* Eliot abandoned his earlier impersonal and dramatic modes to speak directly. There are many styles in the poem, varying from the sharp satire of the soothsayers passage in "The Dry Salvages" (printed here) to the lyricism of "The dove descending breaks the air," which is the fourth section of "Little Gidding." The *Quartets* are "about" many things, but the principal theme is the struggle of finite man to transcend place and time and live momentarily out of time.

> For most of us, there is only the unattended
> Moment, the moment in and out of time,
> The distraction fit, lost in a shaft of sunlight,
> The wild thyme unseen, or the winter lightning
> Or the waterfall, or music heard so deeply
> That it is not heard at all, but you are the music
> While the music lasts.

Meanwhile Eliot's early interest in drama, which had shown itself in his use of the dramatic monologue ("The Love Song of J. Alfred Prufrock" and "Gerontion") and in his essays on the Elizabethan dramatists, led him to the writing of verse drama. In 1934 he prepared *The Rock*, a "pageant play," for the Forty-Five Churches Fund. At the Canterbury Festival in June 1935, his *Murder in the Cathedral* was performed with success. His next play, *The Family Reunion* (1939), proved to be too illusive and static for a popular audience. Eliot was not deterred. When he tried again, with *The Cocktail Party* (produced in 1949), he achieved the impossible: he had written a religious play in verse, which the audience did not *hear* as verse. The cocktail party chatter of the opening scene fooled audiences into believing they were witnessing a smart drawing-room comedy. Only gradually did they perceive the serious themes beneath the bantering words. Later plays are *The Confidential Clerk* (1954) and *The Elder Statesman* (1959).

Though Eliot's collected criticism fills only two volumes, *Selected Essays* (1932; revised, 1950) and *On Poetry and Poets* (1957), these essays represent a mere tithe of his critical writing. His criticism has molded the taste of a generation. Because of what he wrote about the Romantics and Victorians, their stock went down, while the reputation of the Jacobean dramatists, the metaphysical poets, Dryden, Dr. Johnson, Yeats, and Joyce correspondingly rose.

The early essays, in *The Sacred Wood* (1920), were largely concerned with two matters: critical theory and the triumphs or failures of particular authors (Marlowe, Jonson, Blake, Dante, and Swinburne). In this volume we find the first statements of many ideas to which Eliot returned in later essays. After he became an Anglo-Catholic, he was for a time pre-occupied with the relations between religion and literature (*For Lancelot Andrewes*, 1928, and *After Strange Gods*, 1934). In the 1940's, by which time he was internationally famous, Eliot summed up in several impressive addresses his views on such figures as Yeats and Virgil. His criticism has been continuously related to his self-education as a poet and dramatist but only lately, in such essays as "Milton II" (1947) and "Poetry and Drama" (1951) has he spoken explicitly of these relationships.

The essay published here, "Tradition and the Individual Talent," was chiefly useful, as the event proved, in providing a bridge by which contemporary writers might pass across and enter "the tradition." By means of it such innovators as Yeats and Joyce, who had obeyed "the necessity to conform," could already be seen as set among the great dead.

D. C. Gallup, *T. S. Eliot, A Bibliography*, New York, 1953.
Complete Poems and Plays, New York, 1952.
Selected Essays, New York, 1950.
On Poetry and Poets, New York, 1957.
Victor Brombert, *The Criticism of T. S. Eliot*, New Haven, 1949.

Elizabeth Drew, *T. S. Eliot, The Design of His Poetry*, New York, 1953.

Helen Gardner, *The Art of T. S. Eliot*, London, 1949.

D. E. S. Maxwell, *The Poetry of T. S. Eliot*, London, 1952.

F. O. Matthiessen, *The Achievement of T. S. Eliot*, Boston (1935), 1958.

B. Rajan, ed., *T. S. Eliot; A Study of His Writing by Several Hands*, London, 1948.

Kristian Smidt, *Poetry and Belief in the Work of T. S. Eliot*, Oslo, 1949.

Grover Smith, Jr., *T. S. Eliot's Poetry and Plays: A Study in Sources and Meaning*, Chicago, 1956.

Leonard Unger, ed., *T. S. Eliot: A Selected Critique*, New York, 1948.

George Williamson, *A Reader's Guide to T. S. Eliot: A Poem-By-Poem Analysis*, New York, 1953.

THE LOVE SONG OF J. ALFRED PRUFROCK

S'io credesse che mia risposta fosse
A persona che mai tornasse al mondo,
Questa fiamma staria senza piu scosse.
Ma perciocche giammai di questo fondo
Non torno vivo alcun, s'i'odo il vero,
Senza tema d'infamia ti rispondo. [1]

Let us go then, you and I,
When the evening is spread out against the
   sky
Like a patient etherised upon a table;
Let us go, through certain half-deserted streets,
The muttering retreats
Of restless nights in one-night cheap hotels
And sawdust restaurants with oyster-shells:
Streets that follow like a tedious argument
Of insidious intent
To lead you to an overwhelming question. . . .
Oh, do not ask, "What is it?"   11
Let us go and make our visit.

In the room the women come and go
Talking of Michelangelo.

The yellow fog that rubs its back upon the
   window-panes,
The yellow smoke that rubs its muzzle on the
   window-panes
Licked its tongue into the corners of the eve-
   ning,
Lingered upon the pools that stand in drains,
Let fall upon its back the soot that falls from
   chimneys,
Slipped by the terrace, made a sudden leap,
And seeing that it was a soft October night, 21
Curled once about the house, and fell asleep.

And indeed there will be time
For the yellow smoke that slides along the
   street,
Rubbing its back upon the window-panes;

[1] C. E. Norton translates: "If I believed that my reply were to a person who should ever return to the world, this flame would stand without more quiverings; but inasmuch as, if I hear truth, never did any one return alive from this depth, I answer thee without fear of infamy." (Dante's *Inferno*, XXVII, 61–66.)

There will be time, there will be time
To prepare a face to meet the faces that you
   meet;
There will be time to murder and create,
And time for all the works and days of hands
That lift and drop a question on your plate; 30
Time for you and time for me,
And time yet for a hundred indecisions,
And for a hundred visions and revisions,
Before the taking of a toast and tea.

In the room the women come and go
Talking of Michelangelo.

And indeed there will be time
To wonder, "Do I dare?" and, "Do I dare?"
Time to turn back and descend the stair,
With a bald spot in the middle of my hair— 40
(They will say: "How his hair is growing
   thin!")
My morning coat, my collar mounting firmly
   to the chin,
My necktie rich and modest, but asserted by
   a simple pin—
(They will say: "But how his arms and legs
   are thin!")
Do I dare
Disturb the universe?
In a minute there is time
For decisions and revisions which a minute
   will reverse.

For I have known them all already, known
   them all:
Have known the evenings, mornings, after-
   noons,   50
I have measured out my life with coffee
   spoons;
I know the voices dying with a dying fall
Beneath the music from a farther room.
   So how should I presume?

And I have known the eyes already, known
   them all—
The eyes that fix you in a formulated phrase,

And when I am formulated, sprawling on a pin,
When I am pinned and wriggling on the wall,
Then how should I begin
To spit out all the butt-ends of my days and ways?   60
   And how should I presume?
And I have known the arms already, known them all—
Arms that are braceleted and white and bare
(But in the lamplight, downed with light brown hair!)
Is it perfume from a dress
That makes me so digress?
Arms that lie along a table, or wrap about a shawl.
   And should I then presume?
   And how should I begin?

      . . .

Shall I say, I have gone at dusk through narrow streets   70
And watched the smoke that rises from the pipes
Of lonely men in shirt-sleeves, leaning out of windows? . . .
I should have been a pair of ragged claws
Scuttling across the floors of silent seas.

      . . .

And the afternoon, the evening, sleeps so peacefully!
Smoothed by long fingers,
Asleep . . . tired . . . or it malingers,
Stretched on the floor, here beside you and me.
Should I, after tea and cakes and ices,
Have the strength to force the moment to its crisis?   80
But though I have wept and fasted, wept and prayed,
Though I have seen my head (grown slightly bald) brought in upon a platter,
I am no prophet—and here's no great matter;
I have seen the moment of my greatness flicker,
And I have seen the eternal Footman hold my coat, and snicker,
And in short, I was afraid.

And would it have been worth it, after all,
After the cups, the marmalade, the tea,
Among the porcelain, among some talk of you and me,
Would it have been worth while,   90
To have bitten off the matter with a smile
To have squeezed the universe into a ball

To roll it toward some overwhelming question,
To say: 'I am Lazarus, come from the dead,
Come back to tell you all, I shall tell you all"—
If one, settling a pillow by her head,
   Should say: "That is not what I meant at all;
   That is not it, at all."

And would it have been worth it, after all,
Would it have been worth while,   100
After the sunsets and the dooryards and the sprinkled streets,
After the novels, after the teacups, after the skirts that trail along the floor—
And this, and so much more?—
It is impossible to say just what I mean!
But as if a magic lantern threw the nerves in patterns on a screen:
Would it have been worth while
If one, settling a pillow or throwing off a shawl,
And turning toward the window, should say:
   "That is not it at all,
   That is not what I meant, at all."   110

      . . .

No! I am not Prince Hamlet, nor was meant to be;
Am an attendant, lord, one that will do
To swell a progress, start a scene or two,
Advise the prince; no doubt, an easy tool,
Deferential, glad to be of use,
Politic, cautious, and meticulous;
Full of high sentence, but a bit obtuse;
At times, indeed, almost ridiculous—
Almost, at times, the Fool.

I grow old . . . I grow old . . .   120
I shall wear the bottoms of my trousers rolled.

Shall I part my hair behind? Do I dare to eat a peach?
I shall wear white flannel trousers, and walk upon the beach.
I have heard the mermaids singing, each to each.

I do not think that they will sing to me.

I have seen them riding seaward on the waves
Combing the white hair of the waves blown back
When the wind blows the water white and black.
We have lingered in the chambers of the sea

By sea-girls wreathed with seaweed red and
   brown   130
Till human voices wake us, and we drown.
                                   1915

GERONTION

Thou hast nor youth nor age
But as it were an after dinner sleep
Dreaming of both.

Here I am, an old man in a dry month,
Being read to by a boy, waiting for rain.
I was neither at the hot gates
Nor fought in the warm rain
Nor knee deep in the salt marsh, heaving a
   cutlass,
Bitten by flies, fought.
My house is a decayed house,
And the jew squats on the window sill, the
   owner,
Spawned in some estaminet of Antwerp,
Blistered in Brussels, patched and peeled in
   London.   10
The goat coughs at night in the field over
   head;
Rocks, moss, stonecrop, iron, merds.
The woman keeps the kitchen, makes tea,
Sneezes at evening, poking the peevish gutter.

                              I an old man,
A dull head among windy spaces.

Signs are taken for wonders. "We would see a
   sign"!
The word within a word, unable to speak a
   word,
Swaddled with darkness. In the juvescence
   of the year
Came Christ the tiger   20
In depraved May, dogwood and chestnut,
   flowering judas,
To be eaten, to be divided, to be drunk
Among whispers; by Mr. Silvero
With caressing hands, at Limoges
Who walked all night in the next room;

By Hakagawa, bowing among the Titians;
By Madame de Tornquist, in the dark room
Shifting the candles; Fräulein von Kulp
Who turned in the hall, one hand on the door.
   Vacant shuttles
Weave the wind. I have no ghosts,   30
An old man in a draughty house
Under a windy knob.

After such knowledge, what forgiveness? Think
   now
History has many cunning passages, contrived
   corridors
And issues, deceives with whispering ambi-
   tions,
Guides us by vanities. Think now
She gives when our attention is distracted
And what she gives, gives with such supple
   confusions
That the giving famishes the craving. Gives
   too late
What's not believed in, or if still believed,   40
In memory only, reconsidered passion. Gives
   too soon
Into weak hands, what's thought can be dis-
   pensed with
Till the refusal propagates a fear. Think
Neither fear nor courage saves us. Unnatural
   vices
Are fathered by our heroism. Virtues
Are forced upon us by our impudent crimes.
These tears are shaken from the wrath-bearing
   tree.

The tiger springs in the new year. Us he de-
   vours.
   Think at last
We have not reached conclusion, when I
Stiffen in a rented house. Think at last   50
I have not made this show purposely
And it is not by any concitation
Of the backward devils.
I would meet you upon this honestly.
I that was near your heart was removed there-
   from
To lose beauty in terror, terror in inquisition.
I have lost my passion: why should I need
   to keep it
Since what is kept must be adulterated?
I have lost my sight, smell, hearing, taste and
   touch: 59
How should I use it for your closer contact?

These with a thousand small deliberations
Protract the profit, of their chilled delirium,
Excite the membrane, when the sense has
   cooled,
With pungent sauces, multiply variety
In a wilderness of mirrors. What will the spider
   do,
Suspend its operations, will the weevil
Delay? De Bailhache, Fresca, Mrs. Cammel,
   whirled
Beyond the circuit of the shuddering Bear

In fractured atoms. Gull against the wind, in
    the windy straits
Of Belle Isle, or running on the Horn,   70
White feathers in the snow, the Gulf claims,
And an old man driven by the Trades
To a sleepy corner.
                  Tenants of the house,
Thoughts of a dry brain in a dry season.
                            1920

THE HOLLOW MEN

Mistah Kurtz—he dead.
          A penny for the Old Guy

I

We are the hollow men
We are the stuffed men
Leaning together
Headpiece filled with straw. Alas!
Our dried voices, when
We whisper together
Are quiet and meaningless
As wind in dry grass
Or rats' feet over broken glass
In our dry cellar   10

Shape without form, shade without colour,
Paralysed force, gesture without motion;
Those who have crossed
With direct eyes, to death's other Kingdom
Remember us—if at all—not as lost
Violent souls, but only
As the hollow men
The stuffed men.

II

Eyes I dare not meet in dreams
In death's dream kingdom   20
These do not appear:
There, the eyes are
Sunlight on a broken column
There, is a tree swinging
And voices are
In the wind's singing
More distant and more solemn
Than a fading star.

Let me be no nearer
In death's dream kingdom   30
Let me also wear
Such deliberate disguises

Rat's coat, crowskin, crossed staves
In a field
Behaving as the wind behaves
No nearer—

Not that final meeting
In the twilight kingdom

III

This is the dead land
This is cactus land   40
Here the stone images
Are raised, here they receive
The supplication of a dead man's hand
Under the twinkle of a fading star.

Is it like this
In death's other kingdom
Waking alone
At the hour when we are
Trembling with tenderness
Lips that would kiss   50
Form prayers to broken stone.

IV

The eyes are not here
There are no eyes here
In this valley of dying stars
In this hollow valley
This broken jaw of our lost kingdoms

In this last of meeting places
We grope together
And avoid speech
Gathered on this beach of the tumid river   60

Sightless, unless
The eyes reappear
As the perpetual star
Multifoliate rose
Of death's twilight kingdom
The hope only
Of empty men.

V

Here we go round the prickly pear
Prickly pear prickly pear
Here we go round the prickly pear
At five o'clock in the morning.   71

Between the idea
And the reality
Between the motion

And the act
Falls the Shadow
                    For Thine is the Kingdom

Between the conception
And the creation
Between the emotion   80
And the response
Falls the Shadow
                    Life is very long

Between the desire
And the spasm
Between the potency
And the existence
Between the essence
And the descent
Falls the Shadow   90
                    For Thine is the Kingdom

For Thine is
Life is
For Thine is the

This is the way the world ends
This is the way the world ends
This is the way the world ends
Not with a bang but a whimper.   1925

JOURNEY OF THE MAGI

'A cold coming we had of it,
Just the worst time of the year
For a journey, and such a long journey:
The ways deep and the weather sharp,
The very dead of winter.'
And the camels galled, sore-footed, refractory,
Lying down in the melting snow.
There were times we regretted
The summer palaces on slopes, the terraces,
And the silken girls bringing sherbet.
Then the camel men cursing and grumbling
And running away, and wanting their liquor
     and women,
And the night-fires going out, and the lack of
     shelters,

And the cities hostile and the towns unfriendly
And the villages dirty and charging high
     prices:
A hard time we had of it.
At the end we preferred to travel all night,
Sleeping in snatches,
With the voices singing in our ears, saying
That this was all folly.

     Then at dawn we came down to a temperate
          valley,
Wet, below the snow line, smelling of vegeta-
     tion;
With a running stream and a water-mill beat-
     ing the darkness,
And three trees on the low sky,
And an old white horse galloped away in the
     meadow.
Then we came to a tavern with vine-leaves
     over the lintel,
Six hands at an open door dicing for pieces of
     silver,
And feet kicking the empty wine-skins.
But there was no information, and so we con-
     tinued
And arrived at evening, not a moment too
     soon
Finding the place; it was (you may say) satis-
     factory.

     All this was a long time ago, I remember,
And I would do it again, but set down
This set down
This: were we led all that way for
Birth or Death? There was a Birth, certainly,
We had evidence and no doubt. I had seen
     birth and death,
But had thought they were different; this Birth
     was
Hard and bitter agony for us, like Death, our
     death.
We returned to our places, these Kingdoms,
But no longer at ease here, in the old dispensa-
     tion,
With an alien people clutching their gods.
I should be glad of another death.
                                              1927

» » *From:* THE DRY SALVAGES « «

                    v

To communicate with Mars, converse with
     spirits,

To report the behaviour of the sea monster,
Describe the horoscope, haruspicate or scry,
Observe disease in signatures, evoke
Biography from the wrinkles of the palm

And tragedy from fingers; release omens
By sortilege, or tea leaves, riddle the inevitable
With playing cards, fiddle with pentagrams
Or barbituric acids, or dissect
The recurrent image into pre-conscious ter-
   rors—   11
To explore the womb, or tomb, or dreams; all
   these are usual
Pastimes and drugs, and features of the press:
And always will be, some of them especially
When there is distress of nations and per-
   plexity
Whether on the shores of Asia, or in the Edg-
   ware Road.
Men's curiosity searches past and future
And clings to that dimension. But to appre-
   hend
The point of intersection of the timeless
With time, is an occupation for the saint— 20
No occupation either, but something given
And taken, in a lifetime's death in love,
Ardour and selflessness and self-surrender.
For most of us, there is only the unattended
Moment, the moment in and out of time,
The distraction fit, lost in a shaft of sunlight,
The wild thyme unseen, or the winter light-
   ning
Or the waterfall, or music heard so deeply

That it is not heard at all, but you are the
   music
While the music lasts. These are only hints
   and guesses,   31
Hints followed by guesses; and the rest
Is prayer, observance, discipline, thought and
   action.
The hint half guessed, the gift half under-
   stood, is Incarnation.
Here the impossible union.
Of spheres of existence is actual,
Here the past and future
Are conquered, and reconciled,
Where action were otherwise movement
Of that which is only moved   40
And has in it no source of movement—
Driven by daemonic, chthonic
Powers. And right action is freedom
From past and future also.
For most of us, this is the aim
Never here to be realised;
Who are only undefeated
Because we have gone on trying;
We, content at the last
If our temporal reversion nourish   50
(Not too far from the yew-tree)
The life of significant soil.

                                    1941

» » TRADITION AND THE INDIVIDUAL TALENT « «

I

In English writing we seldom speak of tradition, though we occasionally apply its name
in deploring its absence. We cannot refer to
"the tradition" or to "a tradition"; at most, we
employ the adjective in saying that the poetry
of So-and-so is "traditional" or even "too traditional." Seldom, perhaps, does the word appear except in a phrase of censure. If otherwise, it is vaguely approbative, with the implication, as to the work approved, of some
pleasing archæological reconstruction. You can
hardly make the word agreeable to English
ears without this comfortable reference to the
reassuring science of archæology.

Certainly the word is not likely to appear
in our appreciations of living or dead writers.
Every nation, every race, has not only its own
creative, but its own critical turn of mind; and
is even more oblivious of the shortcomings and
limitations of its critical habits than of those of
its creative genius. We know, or think we
know, from the enormous mass of critical
writing that has appeared in the French language the critical method or habit of the
French; we only conclude (we are such unconscious people) that the French are "more
critical' than we, and sometimes even plume
ourselves a little with the fact, as if the French
were the less spontaneous. Perhaps they are;
but we might remind ourselves that criticism 10
is as inevitable as breathing, and that we
should be none the worse for articulating what
passes in our minds when we read a book and
feel an emotion about it, for criticizing our
own minds in their work of criticism. One of
the facts that might come to light in this process is our tendency to insist, when we praise a
poet, upon those aspects of his work in which
he least resembles any one else. In these aspects or parts of his work we pretend to find 20
what is individual, what is the peculiar essence
of the man. We dwell with satisfaction upon

the poet's difference from his predecessors, especially his immediate predecessors; we endeavour to find something that can be isolated in order to be enjoyed. Whereas if we approach a poet without this prejudice we shall often find that not only the best, but the most individual parts of his work may be those in which the dead poets, his ancestors, assert their immortality most vigorously. And I do not
10 mean the impressionable period of adolescence, but the period of full maturity.

Yet if the only form of tradition, of handing down, consisted in following the ways of the immediate generation before us in a blind or timid adherence to its successes, "tradition" should positively be discouraged. We have seen many such simple currents soon lost in the sand; and novelty is better than repetition. Tradition is a matter of much wider signifi-
20 cance. It cannot be inherited, and if you want it you must obtain it by great labour. It involves, in the first place, the historical sense, which we may call nearly indispensable to any one who would continue to be a poet beyond his twenty-fifth year; and the historical sense involves a perception, not only of the pastness of the past, but of its presence; the historical sense compels a man to write not merely with his own generation in his bones, but with a
30 feeling that the whole of the literature of Europe from Homer and within it the whole of the literature of his own country has a simultaneous existence and composes a simultaneous order. This historical sense, which is a sense of the timeless as well of the temporal and of the timeless and of the temporal together, is what makes a writer traditional. And it is at the same time what makes a writer most acutely conscious of his place in time, of his
40 own contemporaneity.

No poet, no artist of any art, has his complete meaning alone. His significance, his appreciation is the appreciation of his relation to the dead poets and artists. You cannot value him alone; you must set him, for contrast and comparison, among the dead. I mean this as a principle of æsthetic, not merely historical, criticism. The necessity that he shall conform, that he shall cohere, is not onesided; what hap-
50 pens when a new work of art is created is something that happens simultaneously to all the works of art which preceded it. The existing monuments form an ideal order among themselves, which is modified by the introduction of the new (the really new) work of art

among them. The existing order is complete before the new work arrives; for order to persist after the supervention of novelty, the *whole* existing order must be, if ever so slightly, altered; and so the relations, proportions, values of each work of art toward the whole are readjusted; and this is conformity between the old and the new. Whoever has approved this idea of order, of the form of European, of English literature will not find it preposterous that the past should be altered by the present as much as the present is directed by the past. And the poet who is aware of this will be aware of great difficulties and responsibilities.

In a peculiar sense he will be aware also that he must inevitably be judged by the standards of the past. I say judged, not amputated, by them; not judged to be as good as, or worse or better than, the dead; and certainly not judged by the canons of dead critics. It is a judgment, a comparison, in which two things are measured by each other. To conform merely would be for the new work not really to conform at all; it would not be new, and would therefore not be a work of art. And we do not quite say that the new is more valuable because it fits in; but its fitting in is a test of its value—a test, it is true, which can only be slowly and cautiously applied, for we are none of us infallible judges of conformity. We say: it appears to conform, and is perhaps individual, or it appears individual, and may conform; but we are hardly likely to find that it is one and not the other.

To proceed to a more intelligible exposition of the relation of the poet to the past: he can neither take the past as a lump, an indiscriminate bolus, nor can he form himself wholly on one or two private admirations, nor can he form himself wholly upon one preferred period. The first course is inadmissible, the second is an important experience of youth, and the third is a pleasant and highly desirable supplement. The poet must be very conscious of the main current, which does not at all flow invariably through the most distinguished reputations. He must be quite aware of the obvious fact that art never improves, but that the material of art is never quite the same. He must be aware that the mind of Europe—the mind of his own country—a mind which he learns in time to be much more important than his own private mind—is a mind which changes, and that this change is a development which abandons nothing *en route*, which does not superannuate either Shakespeare, or Homer, or the rock drawing of the Magdalenian draughtsmen. That this development, refinement perhaps, complication certainly, is not, from the point of view of the artist, any improvement. Perhaps not even an improvement from the point of view of the psychologist or not to the extent which we imagine; perhaps only in the end based upon a complication in economics and machinery. But the difference between the present and the past is that the conscious present is an awareness of the past in a way and to an extent which the past's awareness of itself cannot show.

Someone said: "The dead writers are remote from us because we *know* so much more than they did." Precisely, and they are that which we know.

I am alive to a usual objection to what is clearly part of my programme for the *métier* of poetry. The objection is that the doctrine requires a ridiculous amount of erudition (pedantry), a claim which can be rejected by appeal to the lives of poets in any pantheon. It will even be affirmed that much learning deadens or perverts poetic sensibility. While, however, we persist in believing that a poet ought to know as much as will not encroach upon his necessary receptivity and necessary laziness, it is not desirable to confine knowledge to whatever can be put into a useful shape for examinations, drawing-rooms, or the still more pretentious modes of publicity. Some can absorb knowledge, the more tardy must sweat for it. Shakespeare acquired more essential history from Plutarch than most men could from the whole British Museum. What is to be insisted upon is that the poet must develop or procure the consciousness of the past and that he should continue to develop this consciousness throughout his career.

What happens is a continual surrender of himself as he is at the moment to something which is more valuable. The progress of an artist is a continual self-sacrifice, a continual extinction of personality.

There remains to define this process of depersonalization and its relation to the sense of tradition. It is in this depersonalization that art may be said to approach the condition of science. I, therefore, invite you to consider, as a suggestive analogy, the action which takes place when a bit of finely filiated platinum is introduced into a chamber containing oxygen and sulphur dioxide.

II

Honest criticism and sensitive appreciation are directed not upon the poet but upon the poetry. If we attend to the confused cries of the newspaper critics and the *susurrus* of popular repetition that follows, we shall hear the names of poets in great numbers; if we seek not Blue-book knowledge but the enjoyment of poetry, and ask for a poem, we shall seldom find it. I have tried to point out the importance of the relation of the poem to other poems by other authors, and suggested the conception of poetry as a living whole of all the poetry that has ever been written. The other aspect of this Impersonal theory of poetry is the relation of the poem to its author. And I hinted, by an analogy, that the mind of the mature poet differs from that of the immature one not precisely in any valuation of "personality," not being necessarily more interesting, or having "more to say," but rather by being a more finely perfected medium in which special, or very varied, feelings are at liberty to enter into new combinations.

The analogy was that of the catalyst. When the two gases previously mentioned are mixed in the presence of a filament of platinum, they form sulphurous acid. This combination takes place only if the platinum is present; nevertheless the newly formed acid contains no trace of platinum, and the platinum itself is apparently unaffected; has remained inert, neutral, and unchanged. The mind of the poet is the shred of platinum. It may partly or exclusively operate upon the experience of the man himself; but, the more perfect the artist, the more completely separate in him will be the man who suffers and the mind which creates; the more perfectly will the mind digest and transmute the passions which are its material.

The experience, you will notice, the elements which enter the presence of the transforming catalyst, are of two kinds: emotions and feelings. The effect of a work of art upon the person who enjoys it is an experience different in kind from any experience not of art. It may be formed out of one emotion, or may be a combination of several; and various feelings, inhering for the writer in particular words or phrases or images, may be added to compose the final result. Or great poetry may be made without the direct use of any emotion whatever: composed out of feelings solely. Canto XV of the *Inferno* (Brunetto Latini) is a working up of the emotion evident in the situation; but the effect, though single as that of any work of art, is obtained by considerable complexity of detail. The last quatrain gives an image, a feeling attaching to an image, which "came," which did not develop simply out of what precedes, but which was probably in suspension in the poet's mind until the proper combination arrived for it to add itself to. The poet's mind is in fact a receptacle for seizing and storing up numberless feelings, phrases, images, which remain there until all the particles which can unite to form a new compound are present together.

If you compare several representative passages of the greatest poetry you see how great is the variety of types of combination, and also how completely any semi-ethical criterion of "sublimity" misses the mark. For it is not the "greatness," the intensity, of the emotions, the components, but the intensity of the artistic process, the pressure, so to speak, under which the fusion takes place, that counts. The episode of Paolo and Francesca employs a definite emotion, but the intensity of the poetry is something quite different from whatever intensity in the supposed experience it may give the impression of. It is no more intense, furthermore, than Canto XXVI, the voyage of Ulysses, which has not the direct dependence upon an emotion. Great variety is possible in the process of transmutation of emotion: the murder of Agamemnon, or the agony of Othello, gives an artistic effect apparently closer to a possible original than the scenes from Dante. In the *Agamemnon,* the artistic emotion approximates to the emotion of an actual spectator; in *Othello* to the emotion of the protagonist himself. But the difference between art and the event is always absolute; the combination which is the murder of Agamemnon is probably as complex as that which is the voyage of Ulysses. In either case there has been a fusion of elements. The ode of Keats contains a number of feelings which have nothing particular to do with the nightingale, but which the nightingale, partly, perhaps, because of its attractive name, and partly because of its reputation, served to bring together.

The point of view which I am struggling to attack is perhaps related to the metaphysical theory of the substantial unity of the soul: for my meaning is, that the poet has, not a "personality" to express, but a particular medium, which is only a medium and not a personality, in which impressions and experiences combine in peculiar and unexpected ways. Impressions and experiences which are important for the man may take no place in the poetry, and those which become important in the poetry may play quite a negligible part in the man, the personality.

I will quote a passage which is unfamiliar enough to be regarded with fresh attention in the light—or darkness—of these observations:

And now methinks I could e'en chide myself
For doating on her beauty, though her death
Shall be revenged after no common action.
Does the silkworm expend her yellow labours
For thee? For thee does she undo herself?
Are lordships sold to maintain ladyships
For the poor benefit of a bewildering minute?
Why does yon fellow falsify highways,
And put his life between the judge's lips,
To refine such a thing—keep horse and men
To beat their valours for her? . . .[2]

In this passage (as is evident if it is taken in its context) there is a combination of positive and negative emotions: an intensely strong attraction toward beauty and an equally intense fascination by the ugliness which is contrasted with it and which destroys it. This balance of contrasted emotion is in the dramatic situation to which the speech is pertinent, but that situation alone is inadequate to it. This is, so to speak, the structural emotion, provided by the drama. But the whole effect, the dominant tone, is due to the fact that a number of floating feelings, having an affinity to this emotion by no means superficially evident, have combined to give us a new art emotion.

It is not in his personal emotions, the emotions provoked by particular events in his life, that the poet is in any way remarkable or interesting. His particular emotions may be simple, or crude, or flat. The emotion in his poetry will be a very complex thing, but not with the complexity of the emotions of people who have very complex or unusual emotions in life. One error, in fact, of eccentricity in poetry is to seek for new human emotions to express; and in this search for novelty in the wrong place it discovers the perverse. The business of

2 From Cyril Tourneur's *The Revenger's Tragedy*, III, 5.

the poet is not to find new emotions, but to use the ordinary ones and, in working them up into poetry, to express feelings which are not in actual emotions at all. And emotions which he has never experienced will serve his turn as well as those familiar to him. Consequently, we must believe that "emotion recollected in tranquillity" is an inexact formula. For it is neither emotion, nor recollection, nor, without distortion of meaning, tranquillity. It is a concentration, and a new thing resulting from the concentration, of a very great number of experiences which to the practical and active person would not seem to be experiences at all; it is a concentration which does not happen consciously or of deliberation. These experiences are not "recollected," and they finally unite in an atmosphere which is "tranquil" only in that it is a passive attending upon the event. Of course this is not quite the whole story. There is a great deal, in the writing of poetry, which must be conscious and deliberate. In fact, the bad poet is usually unconscious where he ought to be conscious, and conscious where he ought to be unconscious. Both errors tend to make him "personal." Poetry is not a turning loose of emotion, but an escape from emotion; it is not the expression of personality, but an escape from personality. But, of course, only those who have personality and emotions know what it means to want to escape from these things.

III

ὁ δὲ νοῦς ἴσως θειότερόν τι καὶ ἀπαθές ἐστιν.[3]

This essay proposes to halt at the frontier of metaphysics or mysticism, and confine itself to such practical conclusions as can be applied by the reasonable person interested in poetry. To divert interest from the poet to the poetry is a laudable aim: for it would conduce to a juster estimation of actual poetry, good and bad. There are many people who appreciate the expression of sincere emotion in verse, and there is a smaller number of people who can appreciate technical excellence. But very few know when there is an expression of *significant* emotion, emotion which has its life in the poem and not in the history of the poet. The emotion of art is impersonal. And the poet cannot reach this impersonality without surrendering himself wholly to the work to be done. And he is not likely to know what is to be done unless he lives in what is not merely the present, but the present moment of the past, unless he is conscious, not of what is dead, but of what is already living.   1919

[3] *Possibly the mind is too divine, and is therefore not affected.*

» » SECOND THOUGHTS ABOUT HUMANISM « «

In July, 1928, I published in *The Forum* the note on the Humanism of Irving Babbitt, which appears on the foregoing pages. I understand that Professor Babbitt considers that I misstated his views: but as I have not yet received detailed correction from any Humanist, I am still in the dark. It is quite likely that I am at fault, because I have meanwhile heard comments, from sympathetic friends, which indicate that they have misunderstood me. The present essay is therefore inspired rather by desire to make my own position clearer than by desire towards aggression. Here, I shall find it more useful to refer to Mr. Norman Foerster's brilliant book *American Criticism,* than to Mr. Babbitt's works. Mr. Foerster's book, as the work of a disciple, seems to give clearer hints of what Humanism is likely to become and do, than the work of Mr. Babbitt, which is more personal to himself.

My previous note has been interpreted, I am afraid, as an "attack" on humanism from a narrow sectarian point of view. It was not intended to be an attack. Having myself begun as a disciple of Mr. Babbitt, and feeling, as I do, that I have rejected nothing that seems to me positive in his teaching, I was hardly qualified to "attack" humanism. I was concerned rather to point out the weak points in its defences, before some genuine enemy took advantage of them. It can be—and is already—of immense value: but it must be subjected to criticism while there is still time.

One of the criticisms which I have heard of my criticism is this: that my criticism is all very well from the point of view of those who "believe"; but if I succeeded in proving that humanism is insufficient without religion, what is left for those who cannot believe? Now I have no desire to undermine the humanist position. But I fear that it may take on more and more of the character of a positive philosophy—and any philosophy, in our time, is likely to take on the character of a substitute for religious dogma. It is Humanism's positivistic tendencies that are alarming. In the work of the master, and still more in that of the disciples, there is a tendency towards a positive and exclusive dogma. Conceive a Comtism from which all the absurdities had been removed—and they form, I admit, a very important part of the Comtist scheme—and you have something like what I imagine Humanism might become.

In the actual Humanist position there is, as I have tried to show, on the one hand an admission that in the past Humanism has been allied with religion, and on the other hand a faith that it can in the future afford to ignore positive religion. This curious trick of identifying humanism and religion in one context, and contrasting them in another, plays a very large part in the Humanist formulation. Mr. Foerster says (p. 244):

"This centre to which humanism refers everything, this centripetal energy which counteracts the multifarious centrifugal impulses, this magnetic will which draws the flux of our sensations toward it while itself remaining at rest, is the reality which gives rise to religion. Pure humanism is content to describe it thus in physical terms, as an observed fact of experience; it hesitates to pass beyond its experimental knowledge to the dogmatic affirmations of any of the great religions. It cannot bring itself to accept a formal theology (any more than it can accept a romantic idealism) that has been set up in defiance of reason, for it holds that the value of supernatural intuition must be tested by the intellect. Again, it fears the asceticism to which religion tends in consequence of a too harsh dualism of the flesh and the spirit, for as we have said, humanism calls for completeness, wishing to use and not annihilate dangerous forces. Unlike religion, it assigns an important place to the instruments of both science and art. Nevertheless it agrees with religion in its perception of the ethical will as a power above the ordinary self, an impersonal reality in which all men may share despite the diversity of personal temperament and towards which their attitude must be one of subjection. This perception, immensely strengthened for us by Christianity, was already present in the humanism of the Greeks, who saw that the unpardonable sin is insolence or presumption, an overweening pride of passion or reason, a failure to be mindful of the Nemesis that lies in wait for disproportionate self-assertion. Humanism, no less than religion, enjoins the virtue of *humility*."

With all respect to Mr. Foerster's sound literary criticism, and his usual brilliance of statement which one cannot fail to admire, the passage I have just quoted seems to me a composition of ignorance, prejudice, confused thinking and bad writing. His first sentence, for the meaning of which I am at a loss, is a cloudy pseudo-scientific metaphor; and his remark that "pure humanism is content to describe it thus in physical terms" seems to give his hand away completely to what he calls "naturism." Either his first sentence is, as I think, merely a metaphor drawn from nineteenth-century physics—in which case it is not a "description," and no one can be content with it—or else the author is surrendering to the mechanistic ethics based upon old fashioned physics. "The reality which gives rise to religion" is a phrase which suggests the older school of anthropology; it is a guarded hint that religion is merely a state of feeling produced by certain physical or quasi-physical "realities" and "facts." Mr. Foerster's "hesitates" and "cannot bring itself" conceal dogmatism behind apparent prudence. Here he confuses, I think, the Humanist with Humanism. If an individual humanist hesitates or cannot bring himself, that is a perfectly natural human attitude, with which one has sympathy; but if the humanist affirms that *Humanism* hesitates and cannot bring itself, then he is making the hesitation, and the inability to bring itself, into a *dogma:* the humanist *Credo* is then a *Dubito*. He is asserting that there is a "pure Humanism" which is *incompatible* with religious faith. When he proceeds to distinguish Humanism from religion by saying that Humanism "holds that the value of supernatural intuition must be tested by the intellect," one wonders with what sort of religion he is contrasting it: for this kind of test was held by the Church long before the word Humanism was coined. Next, the "fear of asceticism" is characteristic, not only of Humanism, but of liberal Protestantism, from which Humanism sometimes seems to descend. The typical humanist, I agree, is not conceived as a cenobite; but *Humanism* if it goes so far as to include in its Creed, "I fear asceticism," is merely committing itself to another anti-religious dogma. Humanism, Mr. Foerster says, "wishes to use and not annihilate dangerous forces"; but does he really believe that the Christian religion, except in several heretical varieties, has ever tried to *annihilate* those dangerous forces? And if he thinks that religion depreciates science and art, I can only suppose that his religious training took place in the mountains of Tennessee.[4] Humanism, he says, agrees with religion in only one point: in believing in the ethical will. There was once an organization called the Ethical Culture Society, which held Sunday morning services: that seems to be the kind of liberal religion to which Mr. Foerster's Humanism comes down.

Mr. Foerster's Humanism, in fact, is too ethical to be true. Where do all these morals come from? One advantage of an orthodox religion, to my mind, is that it puts morals in their proper place. In spite of all the hard (and just) things Mr. Babbitt and Mr. More have said about Kant, the second generation of humanism seems to found its ethics on a similar basis to Kant's. Mr. Foerster finds that "the essential reality of experience is ethical." For the person with a definite religious faith, such a statement has one meaning; for the positivistic humanist, who repudiates religion, it must have another. And that meaning seems to rest upon obscurities and confusions. I can understand, though I do not approve, the naturalistic systems of morals founded upon biology and analytical psychology (what is valid in these consists largely of things that were always known); but I cannot understand a system of morals which seems to be founded on nothing but itself—which exists, I suspect, only by illicit relations with either psychology or religion or both, according to the bias of mind of the individual humanist.

Humanism depends very heavily, I believe, upon the tergiversations of the word "human"; and in general, upon implying clear and distinct philosophic ideas which are never there. My objection is that the humanist makes use, in his separation of the "human" from the "natural," of that "supernatural" which he denies. For I am convinced that if this "supernatural" is suppressed (I avoid the word "spiritual" because it can mean almost anything,) the *dualism* of man and nature collapses at once. Man is man because he can recognize supernatural realities, not because he can invent them. Either everything in man can be traced as a development from below, or something must come from above. There is no avoiding that dilemma: you must be either a naturalist or a supernaturalist. If you remove

from the word "human" all that the belief in the supernatural has given to man, you can view him finally as no more than an extremely clever, adaptable, and mischievous little animal. Mr. Foerster's ethics would be much more "reasonable" if they were those of Mr. Bertrand Russell; as they are, they are a form which is quite untenable and meaningless without a religious foundation.[5]

The real trouble, of course, is one of simple human fallibility. Mr. Foerster, like most humanists, was, I believe, trained as a man of letters; and Humanism bears the imprint of the academic man of letters. His approach to every other field of study is through literature. This is a perfectly proper approach; for we must all approach what we do not know with a limited equipment of the things that we do know. The trouble is that, for a modern humanist, literature thus becomes itself merely a means of approach to something else. If we try to make something do for something else, it is likely to become merely an amateur substitute for that other thing. Mr. Foerster and I would probably agree about the prevalent desiccation of the study of philosophy in universities.[6] Nevertheless, there is a philosophic training, and it is not the literary training; there are rules of the philosophic game about the use and definition of terms, and they are not the literary rules. One may consider the study of philosophy vain, but then one should not philosophise. What one is likely to do is to philosophise badly, because unconsciously. My objection is not to Humanism, but to Mr. Foerster for not being humanistic enough; and for playing the games of philosophy and theology without knowing the rules.

There is another aspect to Mr. Foerster's position which might earn him the title of "The Newest Laocoön": the interesting consideration that this trick of making literature do the work of philosophy, ethics and theology tends

---

[4] The reference is to the famous Scopes trial at Dayton, Tennessee, in 1925.

[5] Mr. Foerster's "reason" seems to me to differ from any Greek equivalent ($\lambda \acute{o} \gamma o s$) by being exclusively human; whereas to the Greek there was something inexplicable about $\lambda \acute{o} \gamma o s$ so that it was a participation of man in the divine. See the late Max Scheler's *Mensch und Geschichte* (Neue Schweizer Rundschau), p. 21. [Eliot's note.]

[6] Not, however, primarily the fault of the teachers, but of the whole educational system of which this teaching is a part. The teaching of philosophy to young men who have no background of *humanistic* education, the teaching of Plato and Aristotle to youths who know no Greek and are completely ignorant of ancient history, is one of the tragic farces of American education. We reap the whirlwind of pragmatists, behaviourists, etc. Incidentally, it is a public misfortune that Mr. Bertrand Russell did not have a classical education.

Humanism has done no greater service than in its criticism of modern education. See Mr. Babbitt's admirable essay on President Eliot in *The Forum*, several years ago. [Eliot's note.]

to vitiate one's judgment and sensibility in literature; but this aspect has been so well exposed in an essay by Mr. Allen Tate that I shall not linger over it here. But I should like to mention that Mr. Foerster, in seeking, as he says, "an ethos which has never existed," looks for guidance to:

10 "Greek sculpture (*of what period?*), Homer, Sophocles, Plato, Aristotle, Virgil, Horace, Jesus, Paul, Augustine, Francis of Assisi, Buddha, Confucius, Shakespeare, Milton and Goethe" (p. 242).

Mr. Foerster is not quite so silly as this list makes him seem, perilously as he does approach towards Five Foot Shelf Culture; he is merely confusing two points of view. For *culture* (and Mr. Foerster's culture is a propagation of Arnold's), these are the sorts of author-
20 ity to which we may properly look; and the man who has frequented them all will so far as that goes be a better, in the sense of being a *more cultured man,* than the man who has not. This is the best possible background. But the search for an "ethos" is a very much more serious and risky business than Mr. Foerster imagines; and Mr. Foerster is more likely to end in respectability than in perfection. Those who hunger and thirst after righteousness, and
30 are not satisfied with a snack-at-the-bar, will want a great deal more; and if they follow any one of these leaders, will not be able to follow all the rest. Boil down Horace, the Elgin Marbles, St. Francis and Goethe, and the result will be pretty thin soup. Culture, after all, is not enough, even though nothing is enough without culture.

With these odd mixed motives, Mr. Foerster does not make very much of Shakespeare,
40 though he gives him a patronizing word or two. Shakespeare is not a humanist. Mr. Foerster's judgment of Shakespeare is neither a literary nor a moral judgment. He seems to me to depreciate Shakespeare for the wrong reasons, just as, with all respect, Mr. Middleton Murry seems to me to extol him for the wrong reasons. If, as he says, Shakespeare was concerned "rather with mirroring life than with interpreting it," and with submitting "to actual-
50 ity rather than transcending it," I should say that such a good mirror, if you call that a mirror, is worth a great many interpretations, and that such submission is worth more than most transcendence. If you stick to a literary judgment, you cannot say that Shakespeare is in-

ferior to any poet who has ever written, unless you are prepared to substantiate your opinion by detailed analysis; and if you depreciate Shakespeare for his lower view of life, then you have issued out of literary criticism into social criticism; you are criticizing not so much the man but the age. I prefer the culture which produced Dante to the culture which produced Shakespeare; but I would not say that Dante was the greater poet, or even that he had the profounder mind; and if humanism chooses Goethe and leaves Shakespeare, then humanism is incapable of distinguishing between the chaff and the wheat.

Mr. Foerster is what I call a Heretic; that is, a person who seizes upon a truth and pushes it to the point at which it becomes a falsehood. In his hands, Humanism becomes something else, something more dangerous, because much more seductive to the best minds, than, let us say, Behaviourism. I wish to try to distinguish the functions of true Humanism from those imposed upon it by zealots.

I. The function of humanism is not to provide dogmas, or philosophical theories. Humanism, because it is general culture, is not concerned with philosophical foundations; it is concerned less with "reason" than with common sense. When it proceeds to exact definitions it becomes something other than itself.

II. Humanism makes for breadth, tolerance, equilibrium and sanity. It operates against fanaticism.

III. The world cannot get on without breadth, tolerance and sanity; any more than it can get on without narrowness, bigotry and fanaticism.

IV. It is not the business of humanism to refute anything. Its business is to *persuade,* according to its unformulable axioms of culture and good sense. It does not, for instance, overthrow the *arguments* or fallacies like Behaviourism; it operates by taste, by sensibility trained by culture. It is critical rather than constructive. It is necessary for the criticism of social life and social theories, political life and political theories.

Without humanism we could not cope with Mr. Shaw, Mr. Wells, Earl Russell, Mr. Mencken, Mr. Sandburg, M. Claudel, Herr Ludwig, Mrs. Macpherson, or the governments of America and Europe.

V. Humanism can have no positive theories about philosophy or theology. All that it can ask, in the most tolerant spirit, is: Is this particular philosophy or religion civilized or is it not?

VI. There is a type of person whom we call the Humanist, for whom humanism is enough. This type is valuable.

VII. Humanism is valuable (a) by itself, in the "pure humanist," who will not set up humanism as a substitute for philosophy and religion, and (b) as a mediating and corrective ingredient in a positive civilization founded on definite belief.[7]

VIII. Humanism, finally, is valid for a very small minority of *individuals.* But it is culture, not any subscription to a common programme or platform, which binds these individuals together. Such an "intellectual aristocracy" has not the economic bonds which unite the individuals of an "aristocracy of birth."

Such a modest limitation of Humanism as I have tried to indicate above (the list is not exhaustive or defining, but consists merely of the qualifications which occur immediately to my mind) will seem more than unsatisfactory to the more hopeful and ambitious devotees of the world. I wish to distinguish sharply, however, between what seems to me the correct and *necessarily* vague Humanism, and what T. E. Hulme means by Humanism in his notes in *Speculations.* I agree with what Hulme says; and I am afraid that many modern Humanists are explicitly or implicitly committed to the view which Hulme denounces; and that they are, in consequence, men of the Renaissance rather than men of our own time. For instance, Hulme gives as one characteristic of the Humanist (in his sense) the "refusal to believe any longer in the radical imperfection of either Man or Nature." I cannot help feeling that Mr. Foerster and even Mr. Babbitt are nearer to the view of Rousseau than they are to the religious view. For it is not enough to chastise the romantic visions of perfectibility, as they do; the modern humanistic view implies that man is either perfectible, or capable of indefinite improvement, because from that point of view the only difference is a difference of degree—so that there is always hope of a higher degree. It is to the immense credit of Hulme

[7] An interesting infusion of humanism in a remarkable religious personality is shown in the late Baron von Hügel's *Letters to a Niece.* [Eliot's note.]

that he found out for himself that there is an *absolute* to which Man can *never* attain. For the modern humanist, as for the romantic, "the problem of evil disappears, the conception of sin disappears." This is illustrated in Mr. Foerster's illusion of the *normally or typically human* (p. 241). (If Mr. Foerster met Jesus, Buddha, St. Francis or any one in the least like them, I question whether they would strike him as conforming to his ideal of 100 per cent normalcy.) Hulme put the matter into one paragraph:

"I hold the religious conception of ultimate values to be right, the humanist wrong. From the nature of things, these categories are not inevitable, like the categories of time and space, but are *equally objective.* In speaking of religion, it is to this level of abstraction that I wish to refer. I have none of the feelings of *nostalgia,* the reverence for tradition, the desire to recapture the sentiment of Fra Angelico, which seems to animate most modern defenders of religion. All that seems to me to be bosh. What is important, is what nobody seems to realize—the dogmas like that of Original Sin, which are the closest expression of the categories of the religious attitude. That man is in no sense perfect, but a wretched creature, who can yet apprehend perfection. It is not, then, that I put up with the dogma for the sake of the sentiment, but that I may possibly swallow the sentiment for the sake of the dogma."

This is a statement which Mr. Foerster, and all liberal theologians, would do well to ponder. Most people suppose that some people, because they enjoy the luxury of Christian sentiments and the excitement of Christian ritual, swallow or pretend to swallow incredible dogma. For some the process is exactly opposite. Rational assent may arrive late, intellectual conviction may come slowly, but they come inevitably without violence to honesty and nature. To put the sentiments in order is a later and an immensely difficult task: intellectual freedom is earlier and easier than complete spiritual freedom.

There is no opposition between the religious and the *pure* humanistic attitude: they are necessary to each other. It is because Mr. Foerster's brand of humanism seems to me *impure,* that I fear the ultimate discredit of all humanism.   1929

HART CRANE

1899–1932

THE TWO POETS whose work gives us the clearest perception of the confusions of the 1920's are T. S. Eliot and Hart Crane. But while Eliot was at that time dismayed by his "awareness of the decay of the individual consciousness and its fixed relation to the world," Crane, as Allen Tate says, believed that the poet by the exercise of his will and his imagination might still achieve an integration. His long poem, *The Bridge* (1930), which is epic in its scope, was an ardent attempt to give his countrymen a spiritual conviction about America which he felt he possessed. As he said in his essay "General Aims and Theories":

I feel persuaded that here are destined to be discovered certain as yet undefined spiritual quantities, perhaps a new hierarchy of faith not to be developed so completely elsewhere. And in this process I like to feel myself as a potential factor; certainly I must speak in its terms and what discoveries I may make are situated in its experience.

Yet for all the brilliance of its articulation and the beauty of its individual lyrics, *The Bridge* fails, because Crane had not really discovered these spiritual quantities in American civilization which the poem supposedly reveals. It is possible that the realization that his quest for a center to his existence was doomed, impelled him to commit suicide when he was not yet thirty-three. His had been an unhappy life, with a "curse of sundered parentage" over it and nights of dissipation in New York and Paris which make one think of Rimbaud, with whom he had more than this affinity. The wonder is that out of the chaos of his personal affairs could come verses so disciplined and images of such purity and force.

Crane may remain a "poet's poet." His method, described by Allen Tate as the "oblique presentation of theme" which is "formulated through a complex series of metaphors," baffles the casual reader. But the effort to fathom his implicit logis is rewarding. Crane was willing to discuss his practice. When Harriet Monroe, editor of Poetry, objected to the succession of "champion mixed metaphors" in "At Melville's Tomb," he wrote her a long letter of explication. This helpful letter is printed in the biographies by Horton and Weber, listed below.

In one matter of great concern to the modern artist Crane pointed the way to a proper solution. In the essay printed below he argues justly that since the machine plays such a part in our lives today, poetry must learn to absorb it, as it contrived, in the Middle Ages, to absorb the toughest theology. Crane's own poetry proves how this may be done. No modern poet, moreover, has made so much beauty out of the machine rhythms and the cacophonies of modern life.

White Buildings, New York, 1926. (With a foreword by Allen Tate.)
The Collected Poems of Hart Crane, Waldo Frank, ed., New York, 1946.
The Letters of Hart Crane, 1916–1932, New York, 1952.
Philip Horton, *Hart Crane*, New York, 1937. (Contains in the appendix four statements by Crane about his intentions as a poet. The essay "General Aims and Theories" is the first.)
G. B. Munson, *Destinations*, New York, 1928, pp. 160–177.
Brom Weber, *Hart Crane, A Biographical and Critical Study*, New York, 1948.

» » From: THE BRIDGE « «

Proem: TO BROOKLYN BRIDGE[1]

How many dawns, chill from his rippling rest
The seagull's wings shall dip and pivot him,
Shedding white rings of tumult, building high
Over the chained bay waters Liberty—

Then, with inviolate curve, forsake our eyes
As apparitional as sails that cross
Some page of figures to be filed away;
—Till elevators drop us from our day . . .

I think of cinemas, panoramic sleights
With multitudes bent toward some flashing
       scene   10
Never disclosed, but hastened to again,
Foretold to other eyes on the same screen;

And Thee, across the harbor, silver-paced
As though the sun took step of thee, yet left
Some motion ever unspent in thy stride,—
Implicitly thy freedom staying thee!

Out of some subway scuttle, cell or loft
A bedlamite speeds to thy parapets,
Tilting there momently, shrill shirt ballooning,
A jest falls from the speechless caravan.   20

Down Wall, from girder into street noon leaks,
A rip-tooth of the sky's acetylene;
All   afternoon   the   cloud-flown   derricks
       turn . . .
Thy cables breathe the North Atlantic still.

And obscure as that heaven of the Jews,
Thy guerdon . . . Accolade thou dost bestow
Of anonymity time cannot raise:
Vibrant reprieve and pardon thou dost show.

O harp and altar, of the fury fused,
(How could mere toil align thy choiring
       strings!)   30
Terrific threshold of the prophet's pledge,
Prayer of pariah, and the lover's cry,—

Again the traffic lights that skim thy swift
Unfractioned idiom, immaculate sigh of stars,
Beading thy path—condense eternity:
And we have seen night lifted in thine arms.

Under thy shadow by the piers I waited;
Only in darkness is thy shadow clear.
The City's fiery parcels all undone,
Already snow submerges an iron year . . .   40

O Sleepless as the river under thee,
Vaulting the sea, the prairies' dreaming sod,
Unto us lowliest sometime sweep, descend
And of the curveship lend a myth to God.
1926   1930

I

AVE MARIA[2]

Venient annis, sæcula seris,
Quibus Oceanus vincula rerum
Laxet et ingens pateat tellus
Tiphysque novos detegat orbes
Nec sit terris ultima Thule.
                    —SENECA

Be with me, Luis de San Angel,
       now—   Columbus
Witness before the tides can wrest   alone, gaz-
       away   ing toward
                                         Spain, in-
The word I bring, O you who   vokes the
       reined my suit   presence of
                                         two faithful
Into the Queen's great heart that   partisans of
       doubtful day;   his quest . . .
For I have seen now what no perjured breath
Of clown nor sage can riddle or gainsay;—
To you, too, Juan Perez, whose counsel fear
And greed adjourned,—I bring you back
       Cathay!

Here waves climb into dusk on gleaming mail;
Invisible valves of the sea,—locks, tendons 10
Crested and creeping, troughing corridors
That fall back yawning to another plunge.
Slowly the sun's red caravel drops light
Once more behind us. . . . It is morning
       there—
O where our Indian emperies lie revealed,
Yet lost, all, let this keel one instant yield!

I thought of Genoa; and this truth, now
       proved,
That made me exile in her streets, stood me
More absolute than ever—biding the moon
Till dawn should clear that dim frontier, first
       seen   20

---

[1] The poem begins and ends with an apostrophe to Brooklyn
Bridge, "symbol of our constructive future, one unique identity, in
which is also included our scientific hopes and achievements of
the future."

[2] Columbus is one of several figures in *The Bridge*—Pocahontas,
Rip Van Winkle, Walt Whitman, are others—who bring into the
poem the legends which cling to their names and who serve as
symbols and motifs.

—The Chan's great continent. . . . Then
faith, not fear
Nigh surged me witless. . . . Hearing the surf
near—
I, wonder-breathing, kept the watch,—saw
The first palm chevron the first lighted hill.

And lowered. And they came out to us crying,
"The Great White Birds!" (O Madre Maria,
still
One ship of these thou grantest safe returning;
Assure us through thy mantle's ageless blue!)
And record of more, floating in a casque,
Was tumbled from us under bare poles scud-
ding;   30
And later hurricanes may claim more
pawn. . . .
For here between two worlds, another, harsh,

This third, of water, tests the word; lo, here
Bewilderment and mutiny heap whelming
Laughter, and shadow cuts sleep from the
heart
Almost as though the Moor's flung scimitar
Found more than flesh to fathom in its fall.
Yet under tempest-lash and surfeitings
Some inmost sob, half-heard, dissuades the
abyss,
Merges the wind in measure to the waves,   40

Series on series, infinite,—till eyes
Starved wide on blackened tides, accrete—
enclose
This turning rondure whole, this crescent ring
Sun-cusped and zoned with modulated fire
Like pearls that whisper through the Doge's
hands
—Yet no delirium of jewels! Oh Fernando,
Take of that eastern shore, this western sea,
Yet yield thy God's, thy Virgin's charity!

—Rush down the plenitude, and you shall see
Isaiah counting famine on this lee!   50

*

An herb, a stray branch among salty teeth,
The jellied weeds that drag the shore,—per-
haps
Tomorrow's moon will grant us Saltes Bar—
Palos again,—a land cleared of long war.
Some Angelus environs the cordage tree;
Dark waters onward shake the dark prow free.

*

O Thou who sleepest on Thyself, apart
Like ocean athwart lanes of death and birth,

And all the eddying breath between dost
search
Cruelly with love thy parable of man,—   60
Inquisitor! incognizable word
Of Eden and the enchained Sepulchre,
Into thy steep savannahs, burning blue,
Utter to loneliness the sail is true.

Who grindest oar, and arguing the mast
Subscribest holocaust of ships, O Thou
Within whose primal scan consummately
The glistening seignories of Ganges swim;—
Who sendest greeting by the corposant,   69
And Teneriffe's garnet—flamed it in a cloud,
Urging through night our passage to the
Chan;—
Te Deum laudamus, for thy teeming span!

Of all that amplitude that time explores,
A needle in the sight, suspended north,—
Yielding by inference and discard, faith
And true appointment from the hidden shoal:
This disposition that thy night relates
From Moon to Saturn in one sapphire wheel:
The orbic wake of thy once whirling feet,
Elohim, still I hear thy sounding heel!   80

White toil of heaven's cordons, mustering
In holy rings all sails charged to the far
Hushed gleaming fields and pendant seething
wheat
Of knowledge,—round thy brows unhooded
now
—The kindled Crown! acceded of the poles
And biassed by full sails, meridians reel
Thy purpose—still one shore beyond desire!
The sea's green crying towers a-sway, Beyond

And kingdoms
            naked in the
                        trembling heart—
        Te Deum laudamus
                        O Thou Hand of Fire 90
1926   1930

II ³

4. THE DANCE

The swift red flesh, a winter king—
Who squired the glacier woman
    down the sky?
She ran the neighing canyons all
    the spring;

Then you
shall see her
truly—your
blood re-
membering
its first in-
vasion of her
secrecy, its

She spouted arms; she rose with
maize—to die.

first en-
counters
with her kin,
her chieftain
lover . . .
his shade
that haunts
the lakes and
hills

And in the autumn drouth, whose
burnished hands
With mineral wariness found out
the stone
Where prayers, forgotten, streamed the mesa
sands?
He holds the twilight's dim, perpetual throne.

Mythical brows we saw retiring—loth,
Disturbed and destined, into denser green. 10
Greeting they sped us, on the arrow's oath:
Now lie incorrigibly what years between . . .

There was a bed of leaves, and broken play;
There was a vail upon you, Pocahontas,
bride—
O Princess whose brown lap was virgin May;
And bridal flanks and eyes hid tawny pride.

I left the village for dogwood. By the canoe
Tugging below the mill-race, I could see
Your hair's keen crescent running, and the blue
First moth of evening take wing stealthily. 20

What laughing chains the water wove and
threw!
I learned to catch the trout's moon whisper; I
Drifted how many hours I never knew,
But, watching, saw that fleet young crescent
die,—

And one star, swinging, take its place, alone,
Cupped in the larches of the mountain pass—
Until, immortally, it bled into the dawn.
I left my sleek boat nibbling margin grass . . .

I took the portage climb, then chose
A further valley-shed; I could not stop. 30
Feet nozzled wat'ry webs of upper flows;
One white veil gusted from the very top.

O Appalachian Spring! I gained the ledge;
Steep, inaccessible smile that eastward bends
And northward reaches in that violet wedge
Of Adirondacks!—wisped of azure wands,

³ Part II of *The Bridge* is called "Powhatan's Daughter." Pocahontas is for Crane the "nature-symbol chosen to represent the
physical body of the continent." "The Dance" (the fourth of the
five sections of this part) describes the conflict of the Indians and
white men on American soil. Crane felt he had succeeded in this
section in becoming "identified with the Indian and his world before it is over, which is the only method possible of ever really possessing the Indian and his world as a cultural factor."

Over how many bluffs, tarns, streams I sped!
—And knew myself within some boding
shade:—
Grey tepees tufting the blue knolls ahead,
Smoke swirling through the yellow chestnut
glade . . . 40

A distant cloud, a thunder-bud—it grew,
That blanket of the skies: the padded foot
Within,—I heard it; 'til its rhythm drew,
—Siphoned the black pool from the heart's hot
root!

A cyclone threshes in the turbine crest,
Swooping in eagle feathers down your back;
Know, Maquokeeta, greeting; know death's
best;
—Fall, Sachem, strictly as the tamarack!

A birch kneels. All her whistling fingers fly.
The oak grove circles in a crash of leaves; 50
The long moan of a dance is in the sky.
Dance, Maquokeeta: Pocahontas grieves . . .

And every tendon scurries toward the twangs
Of lightning deltaed down your saber hair.
Now snaps the flint in every tooth; red fangs
And splay tongues thinly busy the blue
air . . .
Dance, Maquokeeta! snake that lives before,
That casts his pelt, and lives beyond! Sprout,
horn!
Spark, tooth! Medicine-man, relent, restore—
Lie to us,—dance us back the tribal morn! 60

Spears and assemblies: black drums thrusting
on—
O yelling battlements,—I, too, was liege
To rainbows currying each pulsant bone:
Surpassed the circumstance, danced out the
siege!

And buzzard-circleted, screamed from the
stake;
I could not pick the arrows from my side.
Wrapped in that fire, I saw more escorts
wake—
Flickering, sprint up the hill groins like a tide.

I heard the hush of lava wrestling your
arms, 69
And stag teeth foam about the raven throat;
Flame cataracts of heaven in seething swarms
Fed down your anklets to the sunset's moat.

O, like the lizard in the furious noon,
That drops his legs and colors in the sun,
—And laughs, pure serpent, Time itself, and
    moon
Of his own fate, I saw thy change begun!

And saw thee dive to kiss that destiny
Like one white meteor, sacrosanct and blent
At last with all that's consummate and free
There, where the first and last gods keep thy
    tent.   80

         ❋

Thewed of the levin, thunder-shod and lean,
Lo, through what infinite seasons dost thou
    gaze—
Across what bivouacs of thin angered slain,
And see'st thy bride immortal in the maize!

Totem and fire-gall, slumbering pyramid—
Though other calendars now stack the sky,
Thy freedom is her largesse, Prince, and hid
On paths thou knewest best to claim her by.

High unto Labrador the sun strikes free
Her speechless dream of snow, and stirred
    again,   90
She is the torrent and the singing tree;
And she is virgin to the last of men . . .

West, west and south! winds over Cumberland
And winds across the llano grass resume
Her hair's warm sibilance. Her breasts are
    fanned
O stream by slope and vineyard—into bloom!

And when the caribou slant down for salt
Do arrows thirst and leap? Do antlers shine
Alert, star-triggered in the listening vault
Of dusk?—And are her perfect brows to
    thine?   100

We danced, O Brave, we danced beyond their
    farms,
In cobalt desert closures made our vows . . .
Now is the strong prayer folded in thine arms,
The serpent with the eagle in the boughs.
1926   1930

      » »   « «

THE BROKEN TOWER

The bell-rope that gathers God at dawn
Dispatches me as though I dropped down the
    knell
Of a spent day—to wander the cathedral lawn
From pit to crucifix, feet chill on steps from
    hell.

Have you not heard, have you not seen that
    corps
Of shadows in the tower, whose shoulders
    sway
Antiphonal carillons launched before
The stars are caught and hived in the sun's
    ray?

The bells, I say, the bells break down their
    tower;
And swing I know not where. Their tongues
    engrave   10
Membrane through marrow, my long-scattered
    score
Of broken intervals. . . . And I, their sexton
    slave!

Oval encyclicals in canyons heaping
The impasse high with choir. Banked voices
    slain!
Pagodas, campaniles with reveilles outleap-
    ing—
O terraced echoes prostrate on the plain! . . .

And so it was I entered the broken world
To trace the visionary company of love, its
    voice
An instant in the wind (I know not whither
    hurled)   19
But not for long to hold each desperate choice.

My word I poured. But was it cognate, scored
Of that tribunal monarch of the air
Whose thigh embronzes earth, strikes crystal
    Word
In wounds pledged once to hope—cleft to de-
    spair?

The steep encroachments of my blood left me
No answer (could blood hold such a lofty
    tower
As flings the question true?)—or is it she
Whose sweet mortality stirs latent power?—

And through whose pulse I hear, counting the
    strokes
My veins recall and add, revived and sure 30
The angelus of wars my chest evokes:
What I hold healed, original now, and
    pure . . .

And builds, within, a tower that is not stone
(Not stone can jacket heaven)—but slip

Of pebbles—visible wings of silence sown
In azure circles, widening as they dip

The matrix of the heart, lift down the eye
That shrines the quiet lake and swells a
    tower . . .
The commodious, tall decorum of that sky 39
Unseals her earth, and lifts love in its shower.
1932   1932

» » MODERN POETRY « «

Modern poetry has long since passed the crest of its rebellion against many of the so-called classical strictures. Indeed the primary departures of the early intransigeants were often more in a classic direction, with respect to certain neglected early European traditions, than were many of the Victorian regulations that formed the immediate butt of attack.

Revolution flourishes still, but rather as a contemporary tradition in which the original obstacles to freedom have been, if not always eradicated, at least obscured by floods of later experimentation. Indeed, to the serious artist, revolution as an all-engrossing program no longer exists. It persists at a rapid momentum in certain groups or movements, but often in forms which are more constricting than liberation, in view of a generous choice of subject matter.

The poet's concern must be, as always, self-discipline toward a formal integration of experience. For poetry is an architectural art, based not on Evolution or the idea of progress, but on the articulation of the contemporary human consciousness *sub specie æternitatis,* and inclusive of all readjustments incident to science and other shifting factors related to that consciousness. The key to the process of free creative activity which Coleridge gave us in his "Lectures on Shakespeare" exposes the responsibilities of every poet, modern or ancient, and cannot be improved upon. "No work of true genius," he says, "dares want its appropriate form, neither indeed is there any danger of this. As it must not, so genius cannot, be lawless: for it is even this that constitutes its genius—*the power of acting creatively under laws of its own origination.*"

Poetry has at once a greater intimacy and a wider, more exact scope of implication than painting or any of the other arts. It is therefore more apt to be indicative of impending changes in other media such as painting or music. This is a logical deduction that facts do not always favor, as in the case of some modern composers such as Stravinsky, the full purport of whose inspiration seems to lie beyond the reach of current literary expression. Literature has a more tangible relationship to painting; and it is highly probable that the Symbolist 10 movement in French poetry was a considerable factor in the instigation first, of Impressionism, and later, of Cubism. Both arts have had parallel and somewhat analogous tendencies toward abstract statement and metaphysical representation. In this recent preoccupation it is certain that both media were responding to the shifting emphasis of the Western World away from religion toward science. Analysis and discovery, the two basic concerns of sci- 20 ence, became conscious objectives of both painter and poet. A great deal of modern painting is as independent of any representational motive as a mathematical equation; while some of the most intense and eloquent current verse derives sheerly from acute psychological analysis, quite independent of any dramatic motivation.

The function of poetry in a Machine Age is identical to its function in any other age; and 30 its capacities for presenting the most complete synthesis of human values remain essentially immune from any of the so-called inroads of science. The emotional stimulus of machinery is on an entirely different psychic plane from that of poetry. Its only menace lies in its capacities for facile entertainment, so easily accessible as to arrest the development of any but the most negligible esthetic responses. The ultimate influence of machinery in this respect 40 remains to be seen, but its firm entrenchment in our lives has already produced a series of challenging new responsibilities for the poet.

For unless poetry can absorb the machine, i.e., *acclimatize* it as naturally and casually as trees, cattle, galleons, castles and all other human associations of the past, then poetry has failed of its full contemporary function. This process does not infer any program of lyrical pandering to the taste of those obsessed by the importance of machinery; nor does it essentially involve even the specific mention of a single mechanical contrivance. It demands, however, along with the traditional qualifications of the poet, an extraordinary capacity for surrender, at least temporarily, to the sensations of urban life. This presupposes, of course, that the poet possesses sufficient spontaneity and gusto to convert this experience into positive terms. Machinery will tend to lose its sensational glamour and appear in its true subsidiary order in human life as use and continual poetic allusion subdue its novelty. For, contrary to general prejudice, the wonderment experienced in watching nose dives is of less immediate creative promise to poetry than the familiar gesture of a motorist in the modest act of shifting gears. I mean to say that mere romantic speculation on the power and beauty of machinery keeps it at a continual remove; it cannot act creatively in our lives until, like the unconscious nervous responses of our bodies, its connotations emanate from within—forming as spontaneous a terminology of poetic reference as the bucolic world of pasture, plow and barn.

The familiar contention that science is inimical to poetry is no more tenable than the kindred notion that theology has been proverbially hostile—with the "Commedia" of Dante to prove the contrary. The "truth" which science pursues is radically different from the metaphorical, extra-logical "truth" of the poet. When Blake wrote that "a tear is an intellectual thing, And a sigh is the sword of an Angel King"— he was not in any logical conflict with the principles of the Newtonian Universe. Similarly, poetic prophecy in the case of the seer has nothing to do with factual prediction or with futurity. It is a peculiar type of perception, capable of apprehending some absolute and timeless concept of the imagination with astounding clarity and conviction.

That the modern poet can profitably assume the roles of philosopher or theologian is questionable at best. Science, the uncanonized Deity of the times, seems to have automatically displaced the hierarchies of both Academy and Church. It is pertinent to cite the authors of the "Commedia" and "Paradise Lost" as poets whose verse survives the religious dogmas and philosophies of their respective periods, but it is fallacious to assume that either of these poets could have written important religious verse without the fully developed and articulated religious dogmas that each was heir to.

The future of American poetry is too complicated a speculation to be more than approached in this limited space. Involved in it are the host of considerations relative to the comparative influences of science, machinery and other factors which I have merely touched upon;—besides those influential traditions of early English prosody which form points of departure, at least, for any indigenous rhythms and forms which may emerge. The most typical and valid expression of the American *psychosis* seems to me still to be found in Whitman. His faults as a technician and his clumsy and indiscriminate enthusiasm are somewhat beside the point. He, better than any other, was able to coördinate those forces in America which seem most intractable, fusing them into a universal vision which takes on additional significance as time goes on. He was a revolutionist beyond the strict meaning of Coleridge's definition of genius, but his bequest is still to be realized in all its implications.

1929

ARCHIBALD MACLEISH

1892–

A NATIVE OF Glencoe, Illinois, and a graduate of Yale (1915) who was trained for the law at Harvard, MacLeish has ably combined the professions of poet, verse dramatist, journalist, librarian, teacher, and statesman. After service in France (1917–1919) in the first

World War, and a few years of law-practice, he took his family to Europe in 1923 for a lengthy sojourn as a member of that distinguished company of American expatriates which included Pound, Hemingway, Cowley, Tate, Hart Crane, Gertrude Stein, and William Carlos Williams. Paris was crowded with people intent upon fresh experimentation in all the arts, and MacLeish, who was already a competent lyrist, began to assemble a body of verse from which he proposed to omit "the sentimentality which passes among us for the ironic" and the "tags of wit" that are soon out of fashion. Besides Pound and Eliot, his masters were Rimbaud, Valéry, and Laforgue. Sensitive to the harsh dislocations which the war had left in its wake, he made frequent use of the elegiac mode, falling in love with the European past and fearful of the disintegrations of the future. His earliest long poem, *The Pot of Earth* (1925) uses an epigraph from Frazer's *Golden Bough* and is much indebted both in image and structure to Eliot's *Waste Land* (1922). The apogee of his apprenticeship came with *The Hamlet of A. MacLeish* (1928), a spiritual autobiography which ironically compares the plight of MacLeish's generation with that of Shakespeare's tragic hero.

A new and sometimes angry social consciousness marks the second phase of MacLeish's career. His Pulitzer Prize poem, *Conquistador* (1932) is a long narrative about the Spanish conquest of the Aztec empire in 1519–20. A masculine poem, full of the sea and sailing, long marches over stony ground, and bloody combat, it suggests sympathy with the soldiery and bitter irony over the waste of war. Published on the eve of those latter-day imperialisms which plunged first Spain and then the world into new disasters, *Conquistador* quietly anticipates the shape of much that lay ahead. Forthright and moving lyrics like "Lines for An Interment" and "Speech To Those Who Say Comrade" belong to the same harassed decade and the same cast of mind, while MacLeish's liberal political philosophy is well exemplified also in four early verse dramas: *Nobodaddy* (1926), *Panic* (1935), *The Fall of The City* (1937), and *Air Raid* (1938).

MacLeish's labors in literary and social causes earned him wide recognition and heavy responsibility during and after World War II. Following a term as Librarian of Congress (1939–1944) and another (1944–1945) as Assistant Secretary of State, he was appointed Boylston Professor at Harvard in 1949, and became chancellor of the American Academy of Arts and Letters in 1951. Throughout this period he continued his writing both in prose and verse. His *Collected Poems* won the National Book Award and a second Pulitzer Prize in 1953. Among his recent work in poetic drama may be mentioned *The Trojan Horse* (1952) which re-examines the ancient legend of the Trojans' capacity for self-deception; and the ambitious and controversial *J. B.*, founded on the Book of Job, which enjoyed a successful run on Broadway in 1958–59.

Arthur Mizener, *A Catalogue of the First Editions of Archibald MacLeish*, Yale University Library, 1938.
Collected Poems, 1917–1952, Boston, 1952.
A Time to Speak. The Selected Prose of Archibald MacLeish, Boston, 1941.
Cleanth Brooks, *Modern Poetry and the Tradition*, Chapel Hill, N. C., 1939, pp. 116–125.
Dudley Fitts, "To Karthage then I Came," *Hound & Horn*, IV (Summer, 1931), 637–641.
Llewellyn Jones, "Archibald MacLeish: A Modern Metaphysical," *English Journal*, XXIV (June, 1935), 441–451.
Arthur Mizener, "The Poetry of Archibald MacLeish," *Sewanee Review*, XLIV (October-December, 1938), 501–519.
H. H. Waggoner, "Archibald MacLeish and the Aspect of Eternity," *College English*, IV (April, 1943), 402–412.
M. D. Zabel, "The Cinema of Hamlet," *Literary Opinion in America*, New York, 1937, pp. 415–426.

YOU, ANDREW MARVELL

And here face down beneath the sun
And here upon earth's noonward height
To feel the always coming on
The always rising of the night

To feel creep up the curving east
The earthy chill of dusk and slow
Upon those under lands the vast
And ever climbing shadow grow

And strange at Ecbatan the trees
Take leaf by leaf the evening strange   10
The flooding dark about their knees
The mountains over Persia change

And now at Kermanshah the gate
Dark empty and the withered grass
And through the twilight now the late
Few travelers in the westward pass

And Baghdad darken and the bridge
Across the silent river gone
And through Arabia the edge
Of evening widen and steal on   20

And deepen on Palmyra's street
The wheel rut in the ruined stone
And Lebanon fade out and Crete
High through the clouds and overblown

And over Sicily the air
Still flashing with the landward gulls
And loom and slowly disappear
The sails above the shadowy hulls

And Spain go under and the shore
Of Africa the gilded sand   30
And evening vanish and no more
The low pale light across that land

Nor now the long light on the sea

And here face downward in the sun
To feel how swift how secretly
The shadow of the night comes on . . .
1926   1930

INVOCATION TO THE SOCIAL
MUSE

Señora it is true the Greeks are dead:

It is true also that we here are Americans:
That we use the machines: that a sight of the
     god is ususual:

That more people have more thoughts: that
     there are

Progress and science and tractors and revolu-
     tions and
Marx and the wars more antiseptic and mur-
     derous
And music in every home: there is also Hoo-
     ver:

Does the lady suggest we should write it out
     in The Word?
Does Madame recall our responsibilities? We
     are
Whores Fräulein: poets Fräulein are persons
     of   10

Known vocation following troops: they must
     sleep with
Stragglers from either prince and of both
     views:
The rules permit them to further the business
     of neither:

It is also strictly forbidden to mix in maneu-
     vers:
Those that infringe are inflated with praise on
     the plazas—
Their bones are resultantly afterwards found
     under newspapers:

Preferring life with the sons to death with the
     fathers
We also doubt on the record whether the sons
Will still be shouting around with the same
     huzzas—

For we hope Lady to live to lie with the
     youngest: 20
There are only a handful of things a man likes
Generation to generation hungry or

Well fed: the earth's one: life's
One: Mister Morgan is not one:

There is nothing worse for our trade than to be
     in style:

He that goes naked goes farther at last than
     another:
Wrap the bard in a flag or a school and they'll
     jimmy his
Door down and be thick in his bed—for a
     month:

(Who recalls the address now of the Imagists?)
But the naked man has always his own naked-
   ness: 30
People remember forever his live limbs:

They may drive him out of the camps but one
   will take him:
They may stop his tongue on his teeth with a
   rope's argument—
He will lie in a house and be warm when they
   are shaking:

Besides Tovarishch how to embrace an army?
How to take to one's chamber a million souls?
How to conceive in the name of a column of
   marchers?

The things of the poet are done to a man alone
As the things of love are done—or of death
   when he hears the
Step withdraw on the stair and the clock tick
   only: 40

Neither his class nor his kind nor his trade
   may come near him
There where he lies on his left arm and will
   die:
Nor his class nor his kind nor his trade when
   the blood is jeering

And his knee's in the soft of the bed where
   his love lies:

I remind you Barinya the life of the poet is
   hard—
A hardy life with a boot as quick as a fiver:

Is it just to demand of us also to bear arms?
      1932

LINES FOR AN INTERMENT

Now it is fifteen years you have lain in the
   meadow:
The boards at your face have gone through:
   the earth is
Packed down and the sound of the rain is
   fainter:
The roots of the first grass are dead:

It's a long time to lie in the earth with your
   honor:

The world Soldier the world has been moving
   on:

The girls wouldn't look at you twice in the
   cloth cap:
Six years old they were when it happened:

It bores them even in books: "Soissons be-
   sieged!"
As for the gents they have joined the American
   Legion: 10

Belts and a brass band and the ladies' auxiliaries:
The Californians march in the OD silk:

We are all acting again like civilized beings:
People mention it at tea . . .

The Facts of Life we have learned are Economic:
You were deceived by the detonations of
   bombs:

You thought of courage and death when you
   thought of warfare:
Hadn't they taught you the fine words were
   unfortunate?

Now that we understand we judge without
   bias: 19
We feel of course for those who had to die:

Women have written us novels of great passion
Proving the useless death of the dead was a
   tragedy:

Nevertheless it is foolish to chew gall:
The foremost writers on both sides have apologized:

The Germans are back in the Midi with
   cropped hair:
The English are drinking the better beer in
   Bavaria:

You can rest now in the rain in the Belgian
   meadow—
Now that it's all explained away and forgotten:
Now that the earth is hard and the wood rots:

Now you are dead . . .   30
      1933

SPEECH TO THOSE WHO SAY COMRADE

The brotherhood is not by the blood certainly:
But neither are men brothers by speech—by
    saying so:
Men are brothers by life lived and are hurt for
    it:

Hunger and hurt are the great begetters of
    brotherhood:
Humiliation has gotten much love:
Danger I say is the nobler father and mother:

Those are as brothers whose bodies have shared
    fear
Or shared harm or shared hurt or indignity.
Why are the old soldiers brothers and nearest?

For this: with their minds they go over the sea
    a little   10
And find themselves in their youth again as
    they were in
Soissons and Meaux and at Ypres and those
    cities:

A French loaf and the girls with their eyelids
    painted
Bring back to aging and lonely men
Their twentieth year and the metal odor of
    danger:

It is this in life which of all things is tender-
    est—
To remember together with unknown men the
    days
Common also to them and perils ended:

It is this which makes of many a generation—
A wave of men who having the same years 20
Have in common the same dead and the
    changes.

The solitary and unshared experience
Dies of itself like the violations of love
Or lives on as the dead live eerily:

The unshared and single man must cover his
Loneliness as a girl her shame for the way of
Life is neither by one man nor by suffering.

Who are the born brothers in truth? The pud-
    dlers
Scorched by the same flame in the same found-
    ries:

Those who have spit on the same boards with
    the blood in it: 30
Ridden the same rivers with green logs:
Fought the police in the parks of the same
    cities:
Grinned for the same blows: the same flogging:

Veterans out of the same ships—factories—
Expeditions for fame: the founders of conti-
    nents:
Those that hid in Geneva a time back:

Those that have hidden and hunted and all
    such—
Fought together: labored together: they carry
    the
Common look like a card and they pass touch-
    ing.

Brotherhood! No word said can make you
    brothers!   40
Brotherhood only the brave earn and by danger
    or
Harm or by bearing hurt and by no other.

Brotherhood here in the strange world is the
    rich and
Rarest giving of life and the most valued:
Not to be had for a word or a week's wishing.
1935   1936

THE LOST SPEAKERS

Never do sea birds sing

Never on earth's shingle
Any man—keeper of
Ocean-salted sheep—
Heard from the surge music

Neither were seamen used—
Light aloft in the east
And the soft night wind increasing—
Wakening to have heard
Wild music of birds   10

The sea makes all things silent—
Even these that in isles
And inland covert of thickets
Sing till the air is quick and the
Leaf stirs—creatures
Most formed for the sweet
Heartlessness of singing

Wings—not even the wing
Strongest of all things mortal
Gives to the mind before   20
Unending rings of horizon
Desire to sing

       *   *   *   *

            Their eyes
Changed: their work broken:
Many of ours who spoke in the
Inland years are dumb now
Seeing our march has come to the
Land's end and beyond is
Surf and the sea to wander

Restless at dusk they turn from the
Beach and the sea's churning   30
They do not look to the sea
They are silent: their mouths move se-
     cretly.   1936

"DOVER BEACH"—
A NOTE TO THAT POEM

      The wave withdrawing
Withers with seaward rustle of flimsy water
Sucking the sand down: dragging at empty
     shells:
The roil after it settling: too smooth:
     smothered. . . .

After forty a man's a fool to wait in the
Sea's face for the full force and the roaring of
Surf to come over him: droves of careening
     water.
After forty the tug's out and the salt and the
Sea follow it: less sound and violence: 9
Nevertheless the ebb has its own beauty—
Shells sand and all and the whispering rustle.
There's earth in it then and the bubbles of
     foam gone.

Moreover—and this too has its lovely uses—
It's the outward wave that spills the inward
     forward
Tripping the proud piled mute virginal
Mountain of water in wallowing welter of light
     and
Sound enough—thunder for miles back; it's a
     fine and a
Wild smother to vanish in: pulling down—
Tripping withoutward ebb the urgent inward.

Speaking alone for myself it's the steep hill
     and the   20
Toppling lift of the young men I am toward
     now—
Waiting for that as the wave for the next wave.
Let them go over us all I say with the thunder
     of
What's to be next in the world. It's we will be
     under it!   1936

THE ABSENCE [1]

Hunger nor thirst nor any bodily famine
Failing bread to be eaten: meat consumed:
Is comparable or any way to be likened to

This—this lack: this absence: this not to be
     found
Of you whom neither may tongue take nor
     fingers
Break to be broken nor the mouth devour—

Only by hands arms starved be with
Momentarily taking nothing away
But the need to return to you taking nothing
     away:

No hunger was ever sharp as this hunger—   10
The absence of you on a plain bed in this city
Counting the night out by the iron tongues.
                       1936

THE RECONCILIATION

Time like the repetitions of a child's piano
Brings me the room again the shallow lamp
     the love
The night the silence the slow bell the echoed
     answer.

By no thing here or lacking can the eyes dis-
     cover
The hundred winter evenings that have gone
     between
Nor know for sure the night is this and not
     that other.

The room is here the lamp is here: the mirror's
     leaning

[1] This and the following poem are the second and fifth poems in a group entitled *The Woman on the Stair*, published in *Public Speech* (1936).

Searches the same deep shadow where her
knees are caught:
All these are here within the room as I have
seen them.

Time has restored them all as in that rainy
autumn: 10
Even the echoes of that night return to this—
All as they were when first the earthy evening
brought them.

Between this night and that there is no human
distance:

There is no space an arm could not out-reach
by much—
And yet the stars most far apart are not more
distant.

Between my hand that touched and her soft
breast that touches
The irremediable past as steep as stone:
Wider than water: like all land and ocean
stretches:

We touch and by that touching farness are
alone.   1936

» »   « «

FOLK SONGS AND FOLK LORE

ONLY IN THE 1930's did we come fully to realize what a great wealth of folk lore America possesses. There are three principal reasons why ballads and folk tales have flourished so luxuriantly in our soil. The millions of immigrants from all the European countries who have sought our shores since the days of the New England and Virginia settlements brought with them their legends and songs, and the number they could bring was not limited by the size of their baggage. All this lore has been gradually transformed in the New World so that its Old World origins are often difficult to trace. The conditions of American life have continuously been just those, moreover, under which the making of ballads and legends flourishes. The Indian fights, the canal-boat brawls, the gold rush, the western trek, the seven wars we have fought inspired an incalculable number of them. Men all over America, doing the work of building a mighty nation, living an exciting life which every day gave them subjects for tragic or humorous or pathetic ballads, passed on to others what they heard or invented— cowboy ballads, songs of the shanty boys (lumberjacks), ballads of railroaders, hobo ballads, jailhouse songs, songs of the whalers and fishing fleets. Finally we must reckon in the songs of the Negro. The Negro invents a song as easily as he eats fried chicken. His spirituals, "shouts," workaday songs, chaingang songs, ballads of badmen like Joe Turner, and his blues constitute one of America's important contributions to Western culture.

Strictly speaking, a genuine folk song must be passed on orally, and in consequence it will exist in many versions; it must have been sung for a fair period of time, and the singers must have little or no sense of its origin. "Frankie and Johnny," of which some collectors possess more than a hundred versions, is a folk song; "America," although everyone in this country sings it, is not.

We know that even in Puritan New England common folk had their ballads, for Cotton Mather was so perturbed by their influence that he noted in his diary in 1713: "I am informed that the Minds and Manners of many people about the Countrey are much corrupted by foolish Songs and Ballads, which the Hawkers and Peddlars carry into all parts of the Countrey." In the Southern mountains, particularly, these ballads which came with the first settlers have lingered to this day. Of the "sacred list" of 305 ballads which Professor Francis James Child presented in his monumental *The English and Scottish Popular Ballads.* [5 vols., Boston, 1882–1898] over 100 have so far been discovered in this country.

In transmission these ballads lost their English place names and setting and came to sound throughly American. But the settlers soon began to make ballads of their own out of local calamities and sensational events. Two of the earliest of these, "Springfield Mountain" and "Lovewell's Fight," are printed here. As fast as new songs appeared—invented by some local singer, introduced by minstrel endmen or "vocalists" like the Hutchinson family, or imported from Europe—the people appropriated them, changed the words to fit their requirements, parodied them, passed them on. Many songs of the pioneers and the cowboys which seem on first hearing to have been invented on the trail can be traced back to some Eastern road show or amusement garden.

Collectors have been hunting ballads in America for more than half a century; the gathering of folk legends, weather lore, and proverbs has only begun. The results are likely to be just as rich. Folk lore of European origin is disseminated all over America. The native tall tales of the Southwestern frontier traveled westward and emerged in new surroundings. Mark Twain's "Celebrated Jumping Frog of Calaveras County," for example, was probably a Negro story of the Missouri frontier, but it was embellished in dozens of mining camps before Twain gave it definitive form. Legends about great folk heroes whom everyone had heard of, like Davy Crockett and Mike Fink and Paul Bunyan, crossed the continent and were finally appropriated by newspaper columnists, novelists, and playwrights. But each state has its local legendary Injun fighters and sons of Robin Hood whose deeds are legion and are still known only by old men who heard the tales about them from their grandfathers. Though the Indian lore, now at last put down in books, has had little influence on the white man's story-telling, the Negro, long before Joel Chandler Harris discovered Uncle Remus, shared his lore with his white friends.

A comprehensive bibliography of American folklore may be found in R. Spiller, W. Thorp, T. Johnson, H. Canby, eds., *Literary History of the United States*, New York, 1948, III, 192–217. See also Donald K. Wilgus, *Anglo-American Folksong Scholarship since 1898*, New Brunswick, New Jersey, 1959.

Journal of American Folk-Lore, 1888–.

Walter Blair and F. J. Meine, *Mike Fink, King of Mississippi Keelboatmen*, New York, 1933.

B. H. Bronson, *The Traditional Tunes of the Child Ballads; with their Texts, according to the Extant Records of Great Britain and America*, Princeton, 1959, *et seq.*

Olive Campbell and C. J. Sharp, *English Folk Songs from the Southern Appalachians*, New York, 1917. (Revised edition, 2 vols., 1932.)

J. C. Colcord, *Songs of American Sailormen*, New York, 1938.

J. H. Cox, *Folk-Songs of the South*, Cambridge, 1925.

A. K. Davis, Jr., *Traditional Ballads of Virginia*, Cambridge, 1929.

————, *Folk-Songs of Virginia*, Durham, N. C., 1949.

R. M. Dorson, *American Folklore*, Chicago, 1959.

W. A. Fisher, *Seventy Negro Spirituals*, Boston, 1926.

E. E. Gardner, *Folklore from the Schoharie Hills*, New York, 1937.

R. W. Gordon, *Folk-Songs of America*, New York, 1938. (Reprinted from articles in the *New York Times*.)

John Greenway, *American Folksongs of Protest*, Philadelphia, 1953.

W. C. Handy, *Blues*, New York, 1926.

G. P. Jackson, *Spiritual Folk-Songs of Early America*, New York, 1937.

George Korson, *Minstrels of the Mine Patch, Songs and Stories of the Anthracite Industry*, Philadelphia, 1938.

G. M. Laws, *Native American Balladry*, Philadelphia, 1950.

J. A. Lomax, *Songs of the Cattle Trail and Cow Camp*, New York, 1919.

J. A. Lomax and Alan Lomax, *American Ballads and Folk Songs*, New York, 1934.

Charles Neely, *Tales and Songs of Southern Illinois*, Menasha, Wisconsin, 1938.

W. W. Newell, *Games and Songs of American Children*, New York, 1883.

H. W. Odum and G. B. Johnson, *The Negro and His Songs*, Chapel Hill, N. C., 1925.

Louise Pound, *American Ballads and Songs*, New York, 1922.

Franz Rickaby, *Ballads and Songs of the Shanty-Boy*, Cambridge, 1926.

Carl Sandburg, *The American Songbag*, New York, 1927.

Esther Shephard, *Paul Bunyan*, New York, 1924.

Reed Smith, *South Carolina Ballads*, Cambridge, 1928.

H. W. Thompson, *Body, Boots & Britches*, Philadelphia, 1940. (New York State folk lore.)

Stith Thompson, *Motif-Index of Folk Literature*, 6 vols., Bloomington, Indiana, 1932–1936.

————, *Tales of the North American Indians*, Cambridge, 1929.

N. I. White, *American Negro Folk-Songs*, Cambridge, 1928.

————, ed., *The Frank C. Brown Collection of North Carolina Folklore*, 5 vols., 1952 *et seq.*

I. T. Whitfield, *Louisiana French Folk Songs*, Louisiana State University Press, 1939.

BARBARY ELLEN [1]

It was all in the month of May
  When the red-buds they were swelling,
He sent his servant John to town
  For the wants of Barbry Ellen.

Sweet William sent for you to come down
  That your name be Barbry Ellen;
She dressed herself in haste for to go
  And hated to deny him.

The very first words when she got there,
  Young man, I believe you're dying.   10
Oh, yes, I'm sick and mighty sick
  And death it is a-dwelling.

No better, no better will I ever be
  If I don't get Barbry Ellen.
Oh, yes, you're sick and mighty sick
  And death it is a dwelling.
No better, no better will you ever be
  Because you can't get Barbry Ellen.

He turned his pale face to the wall
  His back upon the army.   20
Adieu, adieu to the ladies all around,
  Be kind to Barbry Ellen.

She fell up against his bed-side
  A-screaming and a-crying.
I might have saved this young man's life
  If I only had been a-trying.

She had not got more than one mile to town
  Till she heard them death bells ringing.

They ring so clear they seemed for to say
  Hard-hearted Barbry Ellen.   30

She had not got more than two mile to town
  Till she saw the pale corpse coming.
Lie down, lie down, you pale corpse you,
  Let me take my last look upon you.

They tuck them both to the Van Catholic church
  And buried them side by side.
A rose growed on Sweet William's breast
  And a brier on Barbry Ellen's.

They growed as high as the Van Catholic church
  And could not grow any higher.   40
They tangled all around in a true lover's knot
  And no one could untie them.

LOVEWELL'S FIGHT [2]

Of worthy Captain Lovewell, I purpose now to sing,
How valiantly he served his country and his King;
He and his valiant soldiers, did range the woods full wide,
And hardships they endured to quell the Indians' pride.

'Twas nigh unto Pigwacket, on the eighth day of May,
They spied a rebel Indian soon after break of day;

[1] "Barbara Allen" is one of the most popular of the ballads brought over from England. Though the name of the unhappy lover changes from version to version, the cruel girl is always Barbara Allen. This version comes from Buchanan County, Virginia, and was published by Dorothy Scarborough in *A Song Catcher in Southern Mountains.*

[2] One of the earliest of our native ballads. It celebrates an actual fight at Fryeburg, Maine, on May 9, 1725. The text given here follows the version printed in Farmer and Moore's *Collections, Historical and Miscellaneous* (1824). It derives from a lost original issued by Franklin's printer brother, James.

He on a bank was walking, upon a neck of
land,
Which leads into a pond as we're made to understand.

Our men resolved to have him, and travelled
two miles round,
Until they met the Indian, who boldly stood
his ground;   10
Then speaks up Captain Lovewell, "Take you
good heed," says he,
"This rogue is to decoy us, I very plainly see.

"The Indians lie in ambush, in some place
nigh at hand,
In order to surround us upon this neck of land;
Therefore we'll march in order, and each man
leave his pack,
That we may briskly fight them when they
make their attack."

They came unto this Indian, who did them
thus defy,
As soon as they came nigh him, two guns he
did let fly,
Which wounded Captain Lovewell, and likewise one man more,
But when this rogue was running, they laid
him in his gore.   20

Then having scalped the Indian, they went
back to the spot,
Where they had laid their packs down, but
there they found them not;
For the Indians having spied them, when they
them down did lay,
Did seize them for their plunder, and carry
them away.

These rebels lay in ambush, this very place
hard by,
So that an English soldier did one of them
espy,
And cried out, "Here's an Indian," with that
they started out,
As fiercely as old lions, and hideously did
shout.

With that our valiant English all gave a loud
huzza,
To shew the rebel Indians they feared them not
a straw: 30
So now the fight began, as fiercely as could be;
The Indians ran up to them, but soon were
forced to flee.

Then spake up Captain Lovewell, when first
the fight began,
"Fight on, my valiant heroes! You see they fall
like rain."
For as we are informed, the Indians were so
thick,
A man could scarcely fire a gun, and not some
of them hit.

Then did the rebels try their best our soldiers
to surround,
But they could not accomplish it, because there
was a pond,
To which our men retreated and covered all
the rear,
The rogues were forced to flee them, altho'
they skulked for fear.   40

Two logs there were behind them, that close
together lay,
Without being discovered, they could not get
away;
Therefore our valiant English, they travelled
in a row,
And at a handsome distance as they were wont
to go.

'Twas ten o'clock in the morning, when first
the fight begun,
And fiercely did continue until the setting sun;
Excepting that the Indians some hours before
'twas night,
Drew off into the bushes, and ceased a while to
fight.

But soon again returned, in fierce and furious
mood,
Shouting as in the morning, but yet not half so
loud;   50
For as we are informed, so thick and fast they
fell,
Scarce twenty of their number, at night did
get home well.

And that our valiant English, till midnight
there did stay,
To see whether the rebels would have another
fray;
But they no more returning, they made off towards their home,
And brought away their wounded as far as
they could come.

Of all our valiant English, there were but
thirty-four,

And of the rebel Indians, there were about four
    score.
And sixteen of our English did safely home re-
    turn,
The rest were killed and wounded, for which
    we all must mourn.   60

Our worthy Captain Lovewell among them
    there did die,
They killed Lieutenant Robbins, and wounded
    good young Frye,
Who was our English chaplain; he many In-
    dians slew,
And some of them he scalped when bullets
    round him flew.

Young Fullam, too, I'll mention, because he
    fought so well,
Endeavoring to save a man, a sacrifice he fell;
But yet our valiant Englishmen in fight were
    ne'er dismayed.
But still they kept their motion, and Wyman's
    captain made,

Who shot the old chief Paugus, which did the
    foe defeat,
Then set his men in order, and brought off
    the retreat;   70
And braving many dangers and hardships in
    the way,
They safe arrived at Dunstable, the thirteenth
    day of May.
?1725

SPRINGFIELD MOUNTAIN [3]

On Springfield mountains there did dwell
A likeley youth was known full well
Lieutenant Merrick onley son
A likeley youth near twenty one.

One friday morning he did go
in to the medow and did mow
A round or two then he did feal
A pisen serpent at his heal.

When he received his deadly wond
he dropt his sythe a pon the ground   10
And strate for home wase his intent
Calling aloude still as he went,

tho all around his voys wase hered
but none of his friends to him apiere
they thought it wase some workmen calld
And there poor Timothy alone must fall.

So soon his Carfull father went
to seak his son with discontent
And there hes fond onley son he found
ded as a stone a pon the ground.   20

And there he lay down sopose to rest
withe both his hands Acrost his brest
his mouth and eyes Closed fast
And there poor man he slept his last.

his father vieude his track with greate concern
Where he had ran across the corn
unevin tracks where he did go
did apear to stagger two and frow.

The seventh of August sixty one
this fatull axadint was done   30
Let this a warning be to all
to be prepared when god does call.

CASEY JONES [4]

Come all you rounders, for I want you to hear,
The story of a brave engineer.
Casey Jones was the rounder's name.
On a big eight wheeler of a mighty fame.

Caller called Casey 'bout half-past four,
He kissed his wife at the station door,
Climbed to the cab with the orders in his hand,
He says, "This is my trip to the holy land."

Out of South Memphis yard on the fly,   9
Heard the fireman say, "You got a white eye."
Well, the switchmen knew by the engine moan
That the man at the throttle was Casey Jones.

The rain was comin' down five or six weeks.
The railroad track was like the bed of a creek.
They slowed her down to a thirty mile gait
And the south-bound mail was eight hours late.

Fireman says, "Casey, you're runnin' too fast,
You run that block board the last station you
    passed."

---

3 This ballad mourns a sad event which took place in 1761 in western Massachusetts. This version was first published in 1855 and would appear to be the original, which is said to have been composed by Timothy's sweetheart. In the later history of the ballad a girl—Sally or Molly—was introduced. Humorists like George H. Derby ("Phoenix") burlesqued it and a humorous version, "The Pesky Sarpent," was being sung in the music halls in the 1840's.

4 John Luther Jones, a crack engineer on the Illinois Central, ran the New Orleans Limited from Memphis to Canton. The wreck in which he was killed took place March 18, 1900. A Negro, Wallace Saunders, made up the first song about Casey. In 1909 a professional song-writer composed the ballad which caught on with the public.

Casey says, "I believe we'll make it though,
For she steams a lot better than I ever know."

Casey says, "Fireman, don't you fret,   21
Keep knockin' at the fire door, don't give up
    yet,
I'm going to run her till she leaves the rail,
Or make it on time with the south-bound mail."

Around he curve and down the dump,
Two locomotives was a bound to jump,
Fireman hollered, "Casey, it's just ahead,
We might jump and make it but we'll all be
    dead."

Around the curve comes a passenger train,
Casey blows the whistle, tells the fireman,
    "Ring the bell,"   30
Fireman jumps and says "Good-by,
Casey Jones, you're bound to die."

Well Casey Jones was all right.
He stuck to his duty day and night.
They loved his whistle and his ring number
    three,
And he came into Memphis on the old I. C.

Fireman goes down the depot track,
Begging his honey to take him back,
She says, "Oranges on the table, peaches on the
    shelf,   39
You're a goin' to get tired sleepin' by yourself."

Mrs. Casey Jones was a sittin' on the bed.
Telegram comes that Casey is dead.
She says, "Children, go to bed, and hush your
    cryin',
'Cause you got another papa on the Frisco
    line."

Headaches and heartaches and all kinds of
    pain.
They ain't apart from a railroad train.
Stories of brave men, noble and grand,
Belong to the life of a railroad man.

GO DOWN, MOSES

When Israel was in Egypt's land,
    Let my people go;
Oppressed so hard dey could not stand,
    Let my people go.

Go down, Moses,
    Way down in Egypt land,
Tell ole Pha-roh,
    Let my people go.

Thus saith the Lord, bold Moses said,
    Let my people go;   10
If not I'll smite your first-born dead,
    Let my people go.
        Go down, Moses, etc.

No more shall dey in bondage toil,
    Let my people go;
Let dem come out wid Egypt's spoil,
    Let my people go.
        Go down, Moses, etc.

ALL GOD'S CHILLUN GOT WINGS

I got a robe, you got a robe,
All o' God's chillun got a robe,
When I git to Heab'n I'm goin' to put on my
    robe,
I'm goin' to shout all ovah God's Heab'n,
Heab'n, Heab'n, I'm goin' to shout all over
    God's Heab'n.
        Ev'rybody talkin' 'bout Heab'n ain't goin'
        dere;
        Heab'n, Heab'n, I'm goin' to shout all ovah
        God's Heab'n.

I got wings, you got wings,
All o' God's chillun got wings,
When I git to Heab'n I'm goin' to put on my
    wings,   10
I'm goin' to fly all ovah God's Heab'n,
Heab'n, Heab'n, I'm goin' to fly all ovah God's
    Heab'n.
        Ev'rybody talkin' 'bout Heab'n ain't goin'
        dere;
        Heab'n, Heab'n, I'm goin' to fly all ovah
        God's Heab'n.

I got a harp, you got a harp,
All o' God's chillun got a harp,
When I git to Heab'n I'm goin' to take up my
    harp,
I'm goin' to play all ovah God's Heab'n,
Heab'n, Heab'n, I'm goin' to play all ovah
    God's Heab'n.
        Ev'rybody talkin' 'bout Heab'n ain't goin'
        dere;   20
        Heab'n, Heab'n, I'm goin' to play all ovah
        God's Heab'n.

I got shoes, you got shoes,
All o' God's chillun got shoes,
When I git to Heab'n I'm goin' to put on my
    shoes,
I'm goin' to walk all ovah God's Heab'n,
Heab'n, Heab'n, I'm goin' to walk all ovah
    God's Heab'n.
    Ev'rybody talkin' 'bout Heab'n ain't goin'
    dere;
    Heab'n, Heab'n, I'm goin' to walk all ovah
    God's Heab'n.

WATER-BOY [5]

Water-Boy, where are yo' hidin'?
If yo' don't-a come, I'm gwineter tell-a yo'
    Mammy.

Dere ain't no hammer dat's on-a dis mountain,
Dat ring-a like mine, boys, dat ring-a like mine.
Done bus' dis rock, boys, f'om hyah to Macon,
All de way to de jail, boys, yas, back to de jail.

Yo' Jack-o'-Di'monds, yo' Jack-o'-Di'monds,
I know yo' of old, boys, yas, I know yo' of old.
Yo' robbed ma pocket, yas, robba ma pocket,
Done-a robba ma pocket of silvah an' gold.   10

Water-Boy, where are yo' hidin'?
If yo' don't-a come, I'm gwineter tell-a yo'
    Mammy.
Oh—o, Water-Boy!

BEAR CAT DOWN IN GEORGIA

    I'll be back here,
    I'll be back here,

[5] "Water-Boy" and "Bear Cat Down in Georgia" are Negro
work songs.

Lawd, Lawd,
I'll be back here.

Bear cat, Lawd,
Bear cat, Lawd,
Turn to lion
Down in Georgia.

Look-a yonder,
Look-a yonder,   10
Lawd, Lawd,
Down in Georgia.

Ever see bear cat
Turn to lion,
Lawd, Lawd,
Down in Georgia?

My ol' bear cat,
My ol' bear cat,
Turn to lion,
Lawd, Lawd, Lawd.   20

Ever see a bear cat
Hug a lion,
Lawd, Lawd,
Down in Georgia?

If I make it,
If I make it,
Lawd, Lawd,
Down in Georgia.

Lord, I been fallin'
Lord, I been fallin'   30
Lawd, Lawd,
From my place.

'Fo long, Lawd,
Yes, 'fo long, Lawd,
I'll be back here,
I'll be back here.

» »   « «

» » FOUR FOLK HEROES « «

MIKE FINK BEATS DAVY CROCKETT AT A SHOOTING MATCH [6]

I expect, stranger, you think old Davy Crockett war never beat at the long rifle; but he war tho. I expect there's no man so strong, but what he will find some one stronger. If you havent heerd tell of one Mike Fink, I'll tell you something about him, for he war a helliferocious fellow, and made an almighty fine shot. Mike was a boatman on the Mississip, but he had a little cabbin on the head of the Cumberland, and a horrid handsome wife, that loved him the wickedest that ever you see. Mike only worked enough to find his wife in rags, and himself in powder, and lead, and whiskey, and the rest of the time he spent in nocking over bar and turkeys, and bouncing deer, and sometimes drawing a lead on an injun. So one night I fell in with him in the woods, where him and his wife shook down a blanket for me in his wigwam. In the morning sez Mike to me, 'I've got the handsomest wife, and the fastest horse, and the sharpest shooting iron in all Kentuck, and if any man dar doubt it, I'll be in his hair quicker than hell could scorch a feather.' This put my dander up, and sez I, 'I've nothing to say again your wife, Mike, for it cant be denied she's a shocking handsome woman, and Mrs. Crockett's in Tennessee, and I've got no horses. Mike, I dont exactly like to tell you you lie about what you say about your rifle, but I'm d—d if you speak the truth, and I'll prove it. Do you see that are cat sitting on the top rail of your potato patch, about a hundred and fifty yards off? If she ever hears agin, I'll be shot if it shant be without ears.' So I plazed away, and I'll bet you a horse, the ball cut off both the old tom cat's ears close to his head, and shaved the hair off clean across the skull, as slick as if I'd done it with a razor, and the critter never stirred, nor knew he'd lost his ears till he tried to scratch 'em. 'Talk about your rifle after that, Mike!' sez I. 'Do you see that are sow off furder than the eend of the world,' sez Mike, 'with a litter of pigs round

her,' and he lets fly. The old sow give a grunt, but never stirred in her tracks, and Mike falls to loading and firing for dear life, till he hadn't let one of them are pigs enough tail to make a tooth-pick on. 'Now,' sez he, 'Col. Crockett, I'll be preticularly ableedged to you if you'll put them are pig's tails on again,' sez he. 'That's onpossible, Mike,' sez I, 'but you've left one of 'em about an inch to steer by, and if it had a-been my work, I wouldn't have done it so wasteful. I'll mend your host,' and so I lets fly, and cuts off the apology he's left the poor cretur for decency. I wish I may drink the whole of Old Mississip, without a drop of the rale stuff in it, if you wouldn't have thort the tail had been drove in with a hammer. That made Mike a kinder sorter wrothy, and he sends a ball after his wife as she was going to the spring after a gourd full of water, and nocked half her koom out of her head, without stirring a hair, and calls out to her to stop for me to take a plizzard at what was left on it. The angeliferous critter stood still as a scarecrow in a cornfield for she'd got used to Mike's tricks by long practiss. 'No, no Mike,' sez I, 'Davy Crockett's hand would be sure to shake, if his iron was pointed within a hundred mile of a shemale, and I give up beat, Mike, and as we've had our eye-openers a-ready, we'll now take a flem-cutter, by way of an anti-formatic, and then we'll disperse.'

JOHN HENRY [7]

John Henry was a very small boy,
He sat on his daddy's knee;
He picked up a hammer, a little piece of steel,
Says, "This hammer'll be the death of me."

Captain told John Henry,
Says, "A man ain't nothin' but a man;
If you beat that steam drill down,
I'll lay a hundred dollars in your hand."

John Henry told the captain,
Says, "When you go to town

---

[6] From *The Crockett Almanac* for 1840; reprinted in Blair's *Native American Humor*, pp. 283–284. Mike Fink was a Mississippi keelboatman of mighty fame. Davy Crockett, after he left off shooting bears and Indians, sat in Congress for a time. He died in the defense of the Alamo.

[7] According to Professor L. W. Chappell (*John Henry, a Folk-Lore Study*) the ballad originated in a contest between the then new steam-drill and a Negro steel-driver during the building of the Big Bend Tunnel on the Chesapeake and Ohio Railroad, 1870–1873.

Bring John back a twelve-pound hammer,
And he'll sure whip your steam drill down."

John Henry told the captain,
"A man ain't nothin' but a man,
And if I don't beat your steam drill down
I'll die with a hammer in my hand, Lawd,
    Lawd."

John Henry went up on the mountain,
He came down on the side;
The rock was so tall, John Henry was so small,
That he laid down his hammer and he cried,
    "Lawd, Lawd."   20

Put John Henry on the right hand side,
That old steam drill on the left;
"Before I'll let that steam drill beat me down
I'll hammer my fool self to death."

John Henry said to his shaker boy,
Says, "Boy, you'd better pray,
For if I miss this six-foot steel
Tomorrow'll be your burying day."

The man that owned that old steam drill
Thought it was mighty fine,   30
But John Henry drove fourteen long feet
While the steam drill only made nine.

John Henry said to his loving little woman,
Says, "I'm sick and I want to go to bed;
Fix me a place to lay down, chile,
I got a rolling in my head."

John Henry had a pretty little woman,
The dress she wore was red;
She went down the track and she looked back,
Says, "I'm going where John Henry fell dead."

John Henry had a loving little woman,   41
The dress she wore was blue;
She went down the track, she never looked
    back,
Says, "John Henry, I've been true to you."

John Henry had a loving little woman,
The dress she wore was blue;
She went down the track, she never looked
    back,
Says, "John Henry, I'm leaving you."

John Henry had a loving little woman,
Her name was Polly Ann;   50

John Henry got sick and had to go to bed,
Polly bucked steel like a man.

JESSE JAMES

Jesse James was a lad that killed a-many a
    man;
He robbed the Danville train.
But that dirty little coward that shot Mister
    Howard [8]
Has laid poor Jesse in his grave.

Poor Jesse had a wife to mourn for his life,
Three children, they were brave.
But that dirty little coward that shot Mister
    Howard
Has laid poor Jesse in his grave.

It was Robert Ford, that dirty little coward,
I wonder how does he feel,   10
For he ate of Jesse's bread and he slept in
    Jesse's bed,
Then laid Jesse James in his grave.

Jesse was a man, a friend to the poor,
He never would see a man suffer pain;
And with his brother Frank he robbed the
    Chicago bank,
And stopped the Glendale train.

It was his brother Frank that robbed the
    Glendale bank,
And carried the money from the town;
It was in this very place that they had a little
    race,
For they shot Captain Sheets to the ground. 20

They went to the crossing not very far from
    there,
And there they did the same;
With the agent on his knees, he delivered up
    the keys
To the outlaws, Frank and Jesse James.

It was on a Wednesday night, the moon was
    shining bright,
They robbed the Glendale train;
The people, they did say, for many miles away,
It was robbed by Frank and Jesse James.

[8] Jesse's *alias*, under which he was living at St. Joseph, Missouri,
when Robert Ford, "that dirty little coward," shot him.

It was on a Saturday night, Jesse was at home,
Talking with his family brave;   30
Robert Ford came along like a thief in the
  night
And laid poor Jesse in his grave.

The people held their breath when they heard
  of Jesse's death,
And wondered how he ever came to die.

It was one of the gang called little Robert
  Ford,
He shot poor Jesse on the sly.

Jesse went to his rest with his hand on his
  breast;
The devil will be upon his knee.
He was born one day in the county of Clay
And came from a solitary race. . . .   40

EUGENE O'NEILL

1888–1953

NO OTHER AMERICAN dramatist has yet matched O'Neill either in the scope of his chosen themes or in persistent experiment with a variety of dramatic forms. In his earliest collection, *The Moon of the Caribbees, and Six Other Plays of the Sea* (1919) he drew equally upon his naturalistic imagination and his youthful adventures as a sailor. He soon showed that he was able, however, to leap from the naturalism of such plays as *Anna Christie* (1922) to the use of expressionistic devices in *The Hairy Ape* (1922), of formal masks in *The Great God Brown* (1926), of broad social satire in *Marco Millions* (1927), of subliminal speech in *Strange Interlude* (1928), and of sentimental family comedy in *Ah, Wilderness!* (1933). In his great trilogy of full-length plays, *Mourning Becomes Electra* (1931) he sought to develop a modern Freudian tragedy on the ground-plan of ancient Greek drama. In these and other plays he constantly cracked the frame of realistic representation. Yet his experimental impulse had little to do with theatrical fashions: he restlessly sought the dramatic form best suited to what he had to say, and since his vision of humankind was poetic rather than scientific or socially critical, he was rarely content to stay within the limits of conventional realism. In this respect, he is by no means unique. Similar efforts can be observed in such of his admired European predecessors as Ibsen and Strindberg, and to such of his youthful followers as Arthur Miller and Tennessee Williams. Yet O'Neill remains among the greatest of the modern experimentalists in the field of the drama.

Though born in New York, the son of a devout Catholic actor, he grew away from his theatrical heritage for a great part of his youth. At eighteen he entered Princeton but departed during his freshman year to work for a mail-order house in New York. In 1909 he accompanied a mining engineer on a gold-hunt in Spanish Honduras only to return in six months with malaria and no nuggets. As assistant manager of a stock company he toured the East and Midwest doing one-night stands in local "opera houses," but presently abandoned this harrowing experiment to work his way to South America before the mast on a Norwegian barque. In Buenos Aires he secured temporary jobs with several American companies, made an abortive voyage to South Africa, and returned to some months of beachcombing on the Argentine waterfront. Back in New York, he had tried both acting and journalism before he contracted tuberculosis. That year, 1913, marked a turning-point. The enforced leisure of the sanatorium made him long for literary action, and in 1914–15 he enrolled in Professor George Pierce Baker's 47 Workshop at Harvard.

The plays he did there and afterwards were frequently based on his own experience and observation. Besides those previously enumerated, his early productions include *Beyond the Horizon* (Pulitzer Prize Play for 1920), *The Straw* (1921), *Desire Under the Elms* and *All God's Chillun Got Wings* (both in 1924), *Lazarus Laughed* (1927), and *Dynamo* (1929). With *Mourning Becomes Electra* he reached full confidence and stature and from that time until his death he was widely acclaimed as the leading serious dramatist in his native country. In 1936 he was awarded the Nobel Prize for Literature. Ill health thereafter limited his hitherto immense productivity, but among the notable works of his later years must be mentioned *The Iceman Cometh* (1946) and *Long Day's Journey Into Night*, posthumously released and produced in 1956, and *A Touch of the Poet* (1957).

He was not uniformly successful in his attempt to communicate his conviction that dark and inscrutable forces underlie the blander appearances in human affairs; nor is his language always equal to the burden of meaning he seeks to load upon it. Yet his best dialogue is lively and strong, capable of holding and moving audiences, and of projecting a vision of life which many have found profoundly disturbing. Despite its rather stagey British and Negro dialect, *The Emperor Jones* (1920–21) is an arresting play which well exemplifies O'Neill's daring as an experimenter. He overcomes the difficulties inherent in so great a dependence upon monologue; he fuses the realistic plane with the symbolic in such a way that the actual is always seen against the background of the imagined without sacrifice of concrete psychological motivation. Thus he contrives to tell the story not only of an individual, or even of a rising race, but also to suggest something about the dimensions of man's courage, his fears and delusions, and his "high and mighty airs" ironically brought low.

The Plays of Eugene O'Neill, 12 vols., New York, 1934–1935.
Croswell Bowen, *The Curse of the Misbegotten; A Tale of the House of O'Neill*, New York, 1959.
B. H. Clark, *Eugene O'Neill: The Man and His Plays*, New York (1933), 1947.
E. A. Engel, *The Haunted Heroes of Eugene O'Neill*, Cambridge, 1953.
D. V. Falk, *Eugene O'Neill and the Tragic Tension; An Interpretive Study of the Plays*, New Brunswick, N. J., 1958.
J. T. Shipley, *The Art of Eugene O'Neill*, Seattle, 1928.
R. D. Skinner, *Eugene O'Neill: A Poet's Quest*, New York, 1935.
S. K. Winther, *Eugene O'Neill: A Critical Study*, New York, 1934.

» » THE EMPEROR JONES « «

CHARACTERS

BRUTUS JONES . . . . . . *Emperor*
HENRY SMITHERS . . *A Cockney Trader*
AN OLD NATIVE WOMAN
LEM . . . . A *Native Chief*
SOLDIERS . . . . . .*Adherents of Lem*
The Little Formless Fears; Jeff; The Negro Convicts; The Prison Guard; The Planters; The Auctioneer; The Slaves; The Congo Witch-Doctor; The Crocodile God.

The action of the play takes place on an island in the West Indies as yet not self-determined by White Marines. The form of native government is, for the time being, an Empire.

SCENE ONE

SCENE—*The audience chamber in the palace of the Emperor—a spacious, high-ceilinged room with bare, white-washed walls. The floor is of white tiles. In the rear, to the left of center, a wide archway giving out on a portico with white pillars. The palace is evidently situated on high ground for beyond the portico nothing can be seen but a vista of distant hills, their* summits crowned with thick groves of palm trees. In the right wall, center, a smaller arched doorway leading to the living quarters of the palace. The room is bare of furniture with the exception of one huge chair made of uncut wood which stands at center, its back to rear. This is very apparently the Emperor's throne. It is painted a dazzling, eye-smiting scarlet. There is a brilliant orange cushion on the seat and another smaller one is placed on the floor to serve as a footstool. Strips of matting, dyed scarlet, lead from the foot of the throne to the two entrances.

It is late afternoon but the sunlight still blazes yellowly beyond the portico and there is an oppressive burden of exhausting heat in the air.

As the curtain rises, a native negro woman sneaks in cautiously from the entrance on the right. She is very old, dressed in cheap calico, bare-footed, a red bandana handkerchief covering all but a few stray wisps of white hair. A bundle bound in colored cloth is carried over her shoulder on the end of a stick. She hesitates beside the doorway, peering back as if in extreme dread of being discovered. Then she begins to glide noiselessly, a step at a time, toward the doorway in the rear. At this moment, SMITHERS appears beneath the portico.

SMITHERS is a tall, stoop-shouldered man about forty. His bald head, perched on a long neck with an enormous Adam's apple, looks like an egg. The tropics have tanned his naturally pasty face with its small, sharp features to a sickly yellow, and native rum has painted his pointed nose to a startling red. His little, washy-blue eyes are red-rimmed and dart about him like a ferret's. His expression is one of unscrupulous meanness, cowardly and dangerous. He is dressed in a worn riding suit of dirty white drill, puttees, spurs, and wears a white cork helmet. A cartridge belt with an automatic revolver is around his waist. He carries a riding whip in his hand. He sees the woman and stops to watch her suspiciously. Then, making up his mind, he steps quickly on tiptoe into the room. The woman, looking back over her shoulder continually, does not see him until it is too late. When she does

SMITHERS springs forward and grabs her firmly by the shoulder. She struggles to get away, fiercely but silently.

SMITHERS [Tightening his grasp—roughly]: Easy! None o' that, me birdie. You can't wriggle out now. I got me 'ooks on yer.

WOMAN [Seeing the uselessness of struggling, gives way to frantic terror, and sinks to the ground, embracing his knees supplicatingly]: No tell him! No tell him, Mister!

SMITHERS [With great curiosity]: Tell 'im? [Then scornfully.] Oh, you mean 'is bloomin' Majesty. What's the gaime, any'ow? What are you sneakin' away for? Been stealin' a bit, I s'pose. [He taps her bundle with his riding whip significantly.]

WOMAN [Shaking her head vehemently]: No, me no steal.

SMITHERS: Bloody liar! But tell me what's up. There's somethin' funny goin' on. I smelled it in the air first thing I got up this mornin'. You blacks are up to some devilment. This palace of 'is is like a bleedin' tomb. Where's all the 'ands? [The woman keeps sullenly silent. SMITHERS raises his whip threateningly.] Ow, yer won't, won't yer? I'll show yer what's what.

WOMAN [Coweringly]: I tell, Mister. You no hit. They go—all go. [She makes a sweeping gesture toward the hills in the distance.]

SMITHERS: Run away—to the 'ills?

WOMAN: Yes, Mister. Him Emperor— Great Father. [She touches her forehead to the floor with a quick mechanical jerk.] Him sleep after eat. Then they go—all go. Me old woman. Me left only. Now me go too.

SMITHERS [His astonishment giving way to an immense, mean satisfaction]: Ow! so that's the ticket! Well, I know bloody well wot's in the air—when they runs orf to the 'ills. The tom-tom'll be thumping out there bloomin' soon. [With extreme vindictiveness.] And I'm bloody glad of it, for one! Serve 'im right! Puttin' on airs, the stinkin' nigger! 'Is Majesty! Gawd blimey! I only 'opes I'm there when they takes 'im out to shoot 'im. [Suddenly.] 'E's still 'ere all right, ain't 'e?

WOMAN: Yes. Him sleep.

SMITHERS: 'E's bound to find out soon as 'e wakes up. 'E's cunnin' enough to know when 'is time's come. [He goes to the doorway on right and whistles shrilly with his fingers in his mouth. The old woman springs to her feet and runs out of the doorway, rear. SMITHERS goes after her, reaching for his revolver.] Stop or I'll shoot! [*Then stopping—indifferently.*] Pop orf then, if yer like, yer black cow. [*He stands in the doorway, looking after her.*]

[*JONES enters from the right. He is a tall, powerfully-built, full-blooded negro of middle age. His features are typically negroid, yet there is something decidedly distinctive about his face—an underlying strength of will, a hardy, self-reliant confidence in himself that inspires respect. His eyes are alive with a keen, cunning intelligence. In manner he is shrewd, suspicious, evasive. He wears a light blue uniform coat, sprayed with brass buttons, heavy gold chevrons on his shoulders, gold braid on the collar, cuffs, etc. His pants are bright red with a light blue stripe down the side. Patent leather laced boots with brass spurs, and a belt with a long-barreled, pearl-handled revolver in a holster complete his make up. Yet there is something not altogether ridiculous about his grandeur. He has a way of carrying it off.*]

JONES [*Not seeing anyone—greatly irritated and blinking sleepily—shouts*]: Who dare whistle dat way in my palace? Who dare wake up de Emperor? I'll git de hide frayed off some o' you niggers sho'!

SMITHERS [*Showing himself—in a manner half-afraid and half-defiant*]: It was me whistled to yer. [*As JONES frowns angrily.*] I got news for yer.

JONES [*Putting on his suavest manner, which fails to cover up his contempt for the white man*]: Oh, it's you, Mister Smithers. [*He sits down on his throne with easy dignity.*] What news you got to tell me?

SMITHERS [*Coming close to enjoy his discomfiture*]: Don't yer notice nothin' funny to-day?

JONES [*Coldly*]: Funny? No. I ain't perceived nothin' of de kind!

SMITHERS: Then yer ain't so foxy as I thought yer was. Where's all your court? [*Sarcastically*] the Generals and the Cabinet Ministers and all?

JONES [*Imperturbably*]: Where dey mostly runs to minute I closes my eyes—drinkin' rum and talkin' big down in de town. [*Sarcastically.*] How come you don't know dat? Ain't you sousin' with 'em most every day?

SMITHERS [*Stung but pretending indifference—with a wink*]: That's part of the day's work. I got ter—ain't I—in my business?

JONES [*Contemptuously*]: Yo' business!

SMITHERS [*Imprudently enraged*]: Gawd blimey, you was glad enough for me ter take yer in on it when you landed here first. You didn't 'ave no 'igh and mighty airs in them days!

JONES [*His hand going to his revolver like a flash—menacingly*]: Talk polite, white man! Talk polite, you heah me! I'm boss heah now, is you fergettin'? [*The Cockney seems about to challenge this last statement with the facts but something in the other's eyes holds and cows him.*]

SMITHERS [*In a cowardly whine*]: No 'arm meant, old top.

JONES [*Condescendingly*]: I accepts yo' apology. [*Lets his hand fall from his revolver.*] No use'n you rakin' up ole times. What I was den is one thing. What I is now's another. You didn't let me in on yo' crooked work out o' no kind feelin's dat time. I done de dirty work fo' you—and most o' de brain work, too, fo' dat matter—and I was wu'th money to you, dat's de reason.

SMITHERS: Well, blimey, I give yer a start, didn't I—when no one else would. I wasn't afraid to 'ire yer like the rest was—'count of the story about your breakin' jail back in the States.

JONES: No, you didn't have no s'cuse to look down on me fo' dat. You been in jail you'-self more'n once.

SMITHERS [*Furiously*]: It's a lie! [*Then trying to pass it off by an attempt at scorn.*] Garn! Who told yer that fairy tale?

JONES: Dey's some tings I ain't got to be tole. I kin see 'em in folk's eyes. [*Then after a pause—meditatively.*] Yes, you sho' give me a start. And it didn't take long from dat time to git dese fool, woods' niggers right where I wanted dem. [*With pride.*] From stowaway to Emperor in two years! Dat's goin' some!

SMITHERS [*With curiosity*]: And I bet you got yer pile o' money 'id safe some place.

JONES [*With satisfaction*]: I sho' has! And it's in a foreign bank where no pusson don't ever git it out but me no matter what come. You didn't s'pose I was holdin' down dis Emperor job for de glory in it, did you? Sho'! De fuss and glory part of it, dat's only to turn de heads o' de low-flung, bush niggers dat's here. Dey wants de big circus show for deir money. I gives it to 'em an' I gits de money. [*With a grin.*] De long green, dat's me every time! [*Then rebukingly.*] But you ain't got no kick agin me, Smithers. I'se paid you back all you done for me many times. Ain't I pertected you and winked at all de crooked tradin' you been doin' right out in de broad day. Sho' I has— and me makin' laws to stop it at de same time! [*He chuckles.*]

SMITHERS [*Grinning*]: But, meanin' no 'arm, you been grabbin' right and left yourself, ain't yer? Look at the taxes you've put on 'em! Blimey! You've squeezed 'em dry!

JONES [*Chuckling*]: No, dey ain't *all* dry yet. I'se still heah, ain't I?

SMITHERS [*Smiling at his secret thought*]: They're dry right now, you'll find out. [*Changing the subject abruptly.*] And as for me breakin' laws, you've broke 'em all yerself just as fast as yer made 'em.

JONES: Ain't I de Emperor? De laws don't go for him. [*Judicially.*] You heah what I tells you, Smithers. Dere's little stealin' like you does, and dere's big stealin' like I does. For de little stealin' dey gits you in jail soon or late. For de big stealin' dey makes you Emperor and puts you in de Hall o' Fame when you croaks. [*Reminiscently.*] If dey's one thing I learns in ten years on de Pullman ca's listenin' to de white quality talk, it's dat same fact. And when I gits a chance to use it I winds up Emperor in two years.

SMITHERS [*Unable to repress the genuine admiration of the small fry for the large*]: Yes, yer turned the bleedin' trick, all right. Blimey, I never seen a bloke 'as 'ad the bloomin' luck you 'as.

JONES [*Severely*]: Luck? What you mean —luck?

SMITHERS: I suppose you'll say as that swank about the silver bullet ain't luck—and that was what first got the fool blacks on yer side the time of the revolution, wasn't it?

JONES [*With a laugh*]: Oh, dat silver bullet! Sho' was luck! But I makes dat luck, you heah? I loads de dice! Yessuh! When dat murderin' nigger ole Lem hired to kill me takes aim ten feet away and his gun misses fire and I shoots him dead, what you heah me say?

SMITHERS: You said yer'd got a charm so's no lead bullet'd kill yer. You was so strong only a silver bullet could kill yer, you told 'em. Blimey, wasn't that swank for yer—and plain, fat-'eaded luck?

JONES [*Proudly*]: I got brains and I uses 'em quick. Dat ain't luck.

SMITHERS: Yer know they wasn't 'ardly liable to get no silver bullets. And it was luck 'e didn't 'it you that time.

JONES [*Laughing*]: And dere all dem fool, bush niggers was kneelin' down and bumpin' deir heads on de ground like I was a miracle out o' de Bible. Oh Lawd, from dat time on I has dem all eatin' out of my hand. I cracks de whip and dey jumps through.

SMITHERS [*With a sniff*]: Yankee bluff done it.

JONES: Ain't a man's talkin' big what makes him big—long as he makes folks believe it? Sho', I talks large when I ain't got nothin' to back it up, but I ain't talkin' wild just de same. I knows I kin fool 'em—I *knows* it—and dat's backin' enough fo' my game. And ain't I got to learn deir lingo and teach some of dem English befo' I kin talk to' em? Ain't dat wuk? You ain't never learned ary word er it, Smithers, in de ten years you been heah, dough you knows it's money in you pocket tradin' wid 'em if you does. But you'se too shiftless to take de trouble.

SMITHERS [*Flushing*]: Never mind about me. What's this I've 'eard about yer really 'avin' a silver bullet moulded for yourself?

JONES: It's playin' out my bluff. I has de silver bullet molded and I tells 'em when de time comes I kills myself wid it. I tells 'em dat's 'cause I'm de on'y man in de world big enuff to git me. No use'n deir tryin'. And dey falls down and bumps deir heads. [*He laughs.*] I does dat so's I kin take a walk in peace widout no jealous nigger gunnin' at me from behind de trees.

SMITHERS [*Astonished*]: Then you 'ad it made—'onest?

JONES: Sho' did. Heah she be. [*He takes out his revolver, breaks it, and takes the silver bullet out of one chamber.*] Five lead an' dis silver baby at de last. Don't she shine pretty? [*He holds it in his hand, looking at it admiringly, as if strangely fascinated.*]

SMITHERS: Let me see. [*Reaches out his hand for it.*]

JONES [*Harshly*]: Keep yo' hands whar dey b'long, white man. [*He replaces it in the chamber and puts the revolver back on his hip.*]

SMITHERS [*Snarling*]: Gawd blimey! Think I'm a bleedin' thief, you would.

JONES: No, 'tain't dat. I knows you'se scared to steal from me. On'y I ain't 'lowin' nary body to touch dis baby. She's my rabbit's foot.

SMITHERS [*Sneering*]: A bloomin' charm, wot? [*Venomously.*] Well, you'll need all the bloody charms you 'as before long, s' 'elp me!

JONES [*Judicially*]:   Oh, I'se good for six months yit 'fore dey gits sick o' my game. Den, when I sees trouble comin', I makes my getaway.

SMITHERS: Ho! You got it all planned, ain't yer?

JONES: I ain't no fool. I knows dis Emperor's time is sho't. Dat why I make hay when de sun shine. Was you thinkin' I'se aimin' to hold down dis job for life? No, suh! What good is gittin' money if you stays back in dis raggedy country? I wants action when I spends. And when I sees dese niggers gittin' deir nerve to tu'n me out, and I'se got all de money in sight, I resigns on de spot and beats it quick.

SMITHERS: Where to?

JONES: None o' yo' business.

SMITHERS: Not back to the bloody States, I'll lay my oath.

JONES [*Suspiciously*]:   Why don't I? [*Then with an easy laugh.*] You mean 'count of dat story 'bout me breakin' from jail back dere? Dat's all talk.

SMITHERS [*Skeptically*]:   Ho, yes!

JONES [*Sharply*]:   You ain't 'sinuatin' I'se a liar, is you?

SMITHERS [*Hastily*]:   No, Gawd strike me! I was only thinkin' o' the bloody lies you told the blacks 'ere about killin' white men in the States.

JONES [*Angered*]:   How come dey're lies?

SMITHERS: You'd 'ave been in jail if you 'ad, wouldn't yer then? [*With venom.*] And from what I've 'eard, it ain't 'ealthy for a black to kill a white man in the States. They burns 'em in oil, don't they?

JONES [*With cool deadliness*]:   You mean lynchin' 'd scare me? Well, I tells you, Smithers, maybe I does kill one white man back dere. Maybe I does. And maybe I kills another right heah 'fore long if he don't look out.

SMITHERS [*Trying to force a laugh*]:   I was on'y spoofin' yer. Can't yer take a joke? And you was just sayin' you'd never been in jail.

JONES [*In the same tone—slightly boastful*]:   Maybe I goes to jail dere for gittin' in an argument wid razors ovah a crap game. Maybe I gits twenty years when dat colored man die. Maybe I gits in 'nother argument wid de prison guard was overseer ovah us when we're wukin' de roads. Maybe he hits me wid a whip and I splits his head wid a shovel and runs

away and files de chain off my leg and gits away safe. Maybe I does all dat an' maybe I don't. It's a story I tells you so's you knows I'se de kind of man dat if you evah repeats one word of it, I ends yo' stealin' on dis yearth mighty damn quick!

SMITHERS [*Terrified*]:   Think I'd peach on yer? Not me! Ain't I always been yer friend?

JONES [*Suddenly relaxing*]:   Sho' you has —and you better be.

SMITHERS [*Recovering his composure—and with it his malice*]:   And just to show yer I'm yer friend, I'll tell yer that bit o' news I was goin' to.

JONES: Go ahead! Shoot de piece. Must be bad news from de happy way you look.

SMITHERS [*Warningly*]:   Maybe it's gettin' time for you to resign—with that bloomin' silver bullet, wot? [*He finishes with a mocking grin.*]

JONES [*Puzzled*]:   What's dat you say? Talk plain.

SMITHERS: Ain't noticed any of the guards or servants about the place today, I 'aven't.

JONES [*Carelessly*]:   Dey're all out in de garden sleepin' under de trees. When I sleeps, dey sneaks a sleep, too, and I pretends I never suspicions it. All I got to do is to ring de bell and dey come flyin', makin' a bluff dey was wukin' all de time.

SMITHERS [*In the same mocking tone*]:   Ring the bell now an' you'll bloody well see what I means.

JONES [*Startled to alertness, but preserving the same careless tone*]:   Sho' I rings. [*He reaches below the throne and pulls out a big, common dinner bell which is painted the same vivid scarlet as the throne. He rings this vigorously—then stops to listen. Then he goes to both doors, rings again, and looks out.*]

SMITHERS [*Watching him with malicious satisfaction, after a pause—mockingly*]:   The bloody ship is sinkin' an' the bleedin' rats 'as slung their 'ooks.

JONES [*In a sudden fit of anger flings the bell clattering into a corner*]:   Low-flung, woods' niggers! [*Then catching Smithers' eye on him, he controls himself and suddenly bursts into a low chuckling laugh.*] Reckon I overplays my hand dis once! A man can't take de pot on a bob-tailed flush all de time. Was I sayin' I'd sit in six months mo'? Well, I'se changed my mind den. I cashes in and resigns de job of Emperor right dis minute.

SMITHERS [*With real admiration*]: Blimey, but you're a cool bird, and no mistake.

JONES: No use'n fussin'. When I knows de game's up I kisses it good-bye widout no long waits. Dey've all run off to de hills, ain't dey?

SMITHERS: Yes—every bleedin' man jack of 'em.

JONES: Den de revolution is at de post. And de Emperor better git his feet smokin' up de trail. [*He starts for the door in rear.*]

SMITHERS: Goin' out to look for your 'orse? Yer won't find any. They steals the 'orses first thing. Mine was gone when I went for 'im this mornin'. That's wot first give me a suspicion of wot was up.

JONES [*Alarmed for a second, scratches his head, then philosophically*]: Well, den I hoofs it. Feet, do yo' duty! [*He pulls out a gold watch and looks at it.*] Three-thuty. Sundown's at six-thuty or dere-abouts. [*Puts his watch back—with cool confidence.*] I got plenty o' time to make it easy.

SMITHERS: Don't be so bloomin' sure of it. They'll be after you 'ot and 'eavy. Ole Lem is at the bottom o' this business an' 'e 'ates you like 'ell. 'E'd rather do for you than eat 'is dinner, 'e would!

JONES [*Scornfully*]: Dat fool no-count nigger! Does you think I'se scared o' him? I stands him on his thick head more'n once befo' dis, and I does it again if he come in my way . . . [*Fiercely.*] And dis time I leave him a dead nigger fo' sho'!

SMITHERS: You'll 'ave to cut through the big forest—an' these blacks 'ere can sniff and follow a trail in the dark like 'ounds. You'd 'ave to 'ustle to get through that forest in twelve hours even if you knew all the bloomin' trails like a native.

JONES [*With indignant scorn*]: Look-a-heah, white man! Does you think I'se a natural bo'n fool? Give me credit fo' havin' some sense, fo' Lawd's sake! Don't you s'pose I'se looked ahead and made sho' of all de chances? I'se gone out in dat big forest, pretendin' to hunt, so many times dat I knows it high an' low like a book. I could go through on dem trails wid my eyes shut. [*With great contempt.*] Think dese ign'rent bush niggers dat ain't got brains enuff to know deir own names even can catch Brutus Jones? Huh, I s'pects not! Not on yo' life! Why, man, de white men went after me wid bloodhounds where I come from an' I jes' laughs at 'em. It's a shame to fool dese black trash around heah, dey're so easy. You watch

me, man. I'll make dem look sick, I will. I'll be 'cross de plain to de edge of de forest by time dark comes. Once in de woods in de night, dey got a swell chance o' findin' dis baby! Dawn tomorrow I'll be out at de oder side and on de coast whar dat French gunboat is stayin'. She picks me up, take me to Martinique when she go dar, and dere I is safe wid a mighty big bankroll in my jeans. It's easy as rollin' off a log.

SMITHERS [*Maliciously*]: But s'posin' somethin' 'appens wrong an' they do nab yer?

JONES [*Decisively*]: Dey don't—dat's de answer.

SMITHERS: But, just for argyment's sake—what'd you do?

JONES [*Frowning*]: I'se got five lead bullets in dis gun good enuff fo' common bush niggers —and after dat I got de silver bullet left to cheat 'em out o' gittin' me.

SMITHERS [*Jeeringly*]: Ho, I was fergettin' that silver bullet. You'll bump yourself orf in style, won't yer? Blimey!

JONES [*Gloomily*]: You kin bet yo' whole roll on one thing, white man. Dis baby plays out his string to de end and when he quits, he quits wid a bang de way he ought. Silver bullet ain't none too good for him when he go, dat's a fac'! [*Then shaking off his nervousness —with a confident laugh.*] Sho'! What is I talkin' about? Ain't come to dat yit and I never will—not wid trash niggers like dese yere. [*Boastfully.*] Silver bullet bring me luck anyway. I kin outguess, outrun, outfight, an' outplay de whole lot o' dem all ovah de board any time o' de day er night! You watch me! [*From the distant hills comes the faint, steady thump of a tom-tom, low and vibrating. It starts at a rate exactly corresponding to normal pulse beat —72 to the minute—and continues at a gradually accelerating rate from this point uninterruptedly to the very end of the play.*]

[JONES *starts at the sound. A strange look of apprehension creeps into his face for a moment as he listens. Then he asks, with an attempt to regain his most casual manner.*] What's dat drum beatin' fo'?

SMITHERS [*With a mean grin*]: For you. That means the bleedin' ceremony 'as started. I've 'eard it before and I knows.

JONES: Cer'mony? What cer'mony?

SMITHERS: The blacks is 'oldin' a bloody meetin', 'avin' a war dance, gettin' their courage worked up b'fore they starts after you.

JONES: Let dem! Dey'll sho' need it!

SMITHERS: And they're there 'oldin' their 'eathen religious service—makin' no end of devil spells and charms to 'elp 'em against your silver bullet. [*He guffaws loudly.*] Blimey, but they're balmy as 'ell!

JONES [*A tiny bit awed and shaken in spite of himself*]: Huh! Takes more'n dat to scare dis chicken!

SMITHERS [*Scenting the other's feeling—maliciously*]: Ternight when it's pitch black in the forest, they'll 'ave their pet devils and ghosts 'oundin' after you. You'll find yer bloody 'air 'll be standin' on end before termorrow mornin'. [*Seriously.*] It's a bleedin' queer place, that stinkin' forest, even in daylight. Yer don't know what might 'appen in there, it's that rotten still. Always sends the cold shivers down my back minute I gets in it.

JONES [*With a contemptuous sniff*]: I ain't no chicken-liver like you is. Trees an' me, we'se friends, and dar's a full moon comin' bring me light. And let dem po' niggers make all de fool spells dey'se a min' to. Does yo' s'pect I'se silly enuff to b'lieve in ghosts an' ha'nts an' all dat ole woman's talk? G'long, white man! You ain't talkin' to me. [*With a chuckle.*] Doesn't you know dey's got to do wid a man was member in good standin' o' de Baptist Church? Sho' I was dat when I was porter on de Pullmans, befo' I gits into my little trouble. Let dem try deir heathen tricks. De Baptist Church done pertect me and land dem all in hell. [*Then with more confident satisfaction.*] And I'se got little silver bullet o' my own, don't forgit.

SMITHERS: Ho! You 'aven't give much 'eed to your Baptist Church since you been down 'ere. I've 'eard myself you 'ad turned yer coat an' was takin' up with their blarsted witch-doctors, or whatever the 'ell yer calls the swine.

JONES [*Vehemently*]: I pretends to! Sho' I pretends! Dat's part o' my game from de fust. If I finds out dem niggers believes dat black is white, den I yells it out louder 'n deir loudest. It don't git me nothin' to do missionary work for de Baptist Church. I'se after de coin, an' I lays my Jesus on de shelf for de time bein'. [*Stops abruptly to look at his watch—alertly.*] But I ain't got de time to waste no more fool talk wid you. I'se gwine away from heah dis secon'. [*He reaches in under the throne and pulls out an expensive Panama hat with a bright multicolored band and sets it jauntily on his head.*] So long, white man! [*With a grin.*] See you in jail sometime, maybe!

SMITHERS: Not me, you won't. Well, I wouldn't be in yer bloody boots for no bloomin' money, but 'ere's wishin' yer luck just the same.

JONES [*Contemptuously*]: You're de frightenedest man evah I see! I tells you I'se safe's 'f I was in New York City. It takes dem niggers from now to dark to git up de nerve to start somethin'. By dat time, I'se got a head start dey never kotch up wid.

SMITHERS [*Maliciously*]: Give my regards to any ghosts yer meets up with.

JONES [*Grinning*]: If dat ghost got money, I'll tell him never ha'nt you less'n he wants to lose it.

SMITHERS [*Flattered*]: Garn! [*Then curiously.*] Ain't yer takin' no luggage with yer?

JONES: I travels light when I wants to move fast. And I got tinned grub buried on de edge o' de forest. [*Boastfully.*] Now say dat I don't look ahead an' use my brains! [*With a wide, liberal gesture.*] I will all dat's left in de palace to you—and you better grab all you kin sneak away wid befo' dey gits here.

SMITHERS [*Gratefully*]: Righto—and thanks ter yer. [*As* JONES *walks toward the door in rear—cautioningly.*] Say! Look 'ere, you ain't goin' out that way, are yer?

JONES: Does you think I'd slink out de back door like a common nigger? I'se Emperor yit, ain't I? And de Emperor Jones leaves de way he comes, and dat black trash don't dare stop him—not yit, leastways. [*He stops for a moment in the doorway, listening to the far-off but insistent beat of the tom-tom.*] Listen to dat roll-call, will you? Must be mighty big drum carry dat far. [*Then with a laugh.*] Well, if dey ain't no whole brass band to see me off, I sho' got de drum part of it. So long, white man. [*He puts his hands in his pockets and with studied carelessness, whistling a tune, he saunters out of the doorway and off to the left.*]

SMITHERS [*Looks after him with a puzzled admiration*]: 'E's got 'is bloomin' nerve with 'im, s'elp me! [*Then angrily.*] Ho—the bleedin' nigger—puttin' on 'is bloody airs! I 'opes they nabs 'im an' gives 'im what's what! [*Then putting business before the pleasure of this thought, looking around him with cupidity.*] A bloke ought to find a 'ole lot in this palace that'd go for a bit of cash. Let's take a look, 'Arry, me lad. [*He starts for the doorway on right as*

[*The curtain falls.*]

SCENE TWO

SCENE—*Nightfall. The end of the plain where the Great Forest begins. The foreground is sandy, level ground dotted by a few stones and clumps of stunted bushes cowering close against the earth to escape the buffeting of the trade wind. In the rear the forest is a wall of darkness dividing the world. Only when the eye becomes accustomed to the gloom can the outlines of separate trunks of the nearest trees be made out, enormous pillars of deeper blackness. A somber monotone of wind lost in the leaves moans in the air. Yet this sound serves but to intensify the impression of the forest's relentless immobility, to form a background throwing into relief its brooding, implacable silence.*

[*JONES enters from the left, walking rapidly. He stops as he nears the edge of the forest, looks around him quickly, peering into the dark as if searching for some familiar landmark. Then, apparently satisfied that he is where he ought to be, he throws himself on the ground, dog-tired.*]

Well, heah I is. In de nick o' time, too! Little mo' an' it'd be blacker'n de ace of spades heah-abouts. [*He pulls a bandana handkerchief from his hip pocket and mops off his perspiring face.*] Sho'! Gimme air! I'se tuckered out sho' 'nuff. Dat soft Emperor job ain't no trainin' fo' a long hike ovah dat plain in de brilin' sun. [*Then with a chuckle.*] Cheah up, nigger, de worst is yet to come. [*He lifts his head and stares at the forest. His chuckle peters out abruptly. In a tone of awe.*] My goodness, look at dem woods, will you? Dat no-count Smithers said dey'd be black an' he sho' called the turn. [*Turning away from them quickly and looking down at his feet, he snatches at a chance to change the subject— solicitously.*] Feet, you is holdin' up yo' end fine an' I sutinly hopes you ain't blisterin' none. It's time you git a rest. [*He takes off his shoes, his eyes studiously avoiding the forest. He feels of the soles of his feet gingerly.*] You is still in de pink—on'y a little mite feverish. Cool yo'selfs. Remember you done got a long journey yit befo' you. [*He sits in a weary attitude, listening to the rhythmic beating of the tom-tom. He grumbles in a loud tone to cover up a growing uneasiness.*] Bush niggers! Wonder dey wouldn' git sick o' beatin' dat drum. Sound louder, seem like. I wonder if dey's

startin' after me? [*He scrambles to his feet, looking back across the plain.*] Couldn't see dem now, nohow, if dey was hundred feet away. [*Then shaking himself like a wet dog to get rid of these depressing thoughts.*] Sho', dey's miles an' miles behind. What you gittin' fidgety about? [*But he sits down and begins to lace up his shoes in great haste, all the time muttering reassuringly.*] You know what? Yo' belly is empty, dat's what's de matter wid you. Come time to eat! Wid nothin' but wind on yo' stumach, o' course you feels jiggedy. Well, we eats right heah an' now soon's I gits dese pesky shoes laced up! [*He finishes lacing up his shoes.*] Dere! Now le's see. [*Gets on his hands and knees and searches the ground around him with his eyes.*] White stone, white stone, where is you? [*He sees the first white stone and crawls to it—with satisfaction.*] Heah you is! I knowed dis was de right place. Box of grub, come to me. [*He turns over the stone and feels in under it—in a tone of dismay.*] Ain't heah! Gorry, is I in de right place or isn't I? Dere's 'nother stone. Guess dat's it. [*He scrambles to the next stone and turns it over.*] Ain't heah, neither! Grub, whar is you? Ain't heah. Gorry, has I got to go hungry into dem woods—all de night? [*While he is talking he scrambles from one stone to another, turning them over in frantic haste. Finally, he jumps to his feet excitedly.*] Is I lost de place? Must have! But how dat happen when I was followin' de trail across de plain in broad daylight? [*Almost plaintively.*] I'se hungry, I is! I gotta git my feed. Whar's my strength gonna come from if I doesn't? Gorry, I gotta find dat grub high an' low somehow! Why it come dark so quick like dat? Can't see nothin'. [*He scratches a match on his trousers and peers about him. The rate of the beat of the far-off tom-tom increases perceptibly as he does so. He mutters in a bewildered voice.*] How come all dese white stones come heah when I only remembers one? [*Suddenly, with a frightened gasp, he flings the match on the ground and stamps on it.*] Nigger, is you gone crazy mad? Is you lightin' matches to show dem whar you is? Fo' Lawd's sake, use yo' haid. Gorry, I'se got to be careful! [*He stares at the plain behind him apprehensively, his hand on his revolver.*] But how come all dese white stones? And whar's dat tin box o' grub I hid all wrapped up in oil cloth?

[*While his back is turned, the LITTLE FORMLESS FEARS creep out from the deeper black-*

ness of the forest. They are black, shapeless, only their glittering little eyes can be seen. If they have any describable form at all it is that of a grubworm about the size of a creeping child. They move noiselessly, but with deliberate, painful effort, striving to raise themselves on end, failing and sinking prone again. JONES *turns about to face the forest. He stares up at the tops of the trees, seeking vainly to dis-*
10 *cover his whereabouts by their conformation.*]

Can't tell nothin' from dem trees! Gorry, nothin' 'round heah look like I evah seed it befo'. I'se done lost de place sho' 'nuff! [*With mornful foreboding.*] It's mighty queer! It's mighty queer! [*With sudden forced defiance —in an angry tone.*] Woods, is you tryin' to put somethin' ovah on me?

[*From the formless creatures on the ground in front of him comes a tiny gale of low mock-*
20 *ing laughter like a rustling of leaves. They squirm upward toward him in twisted attitudes.* JONES *looks down, leaps backward with a yell of terror, yanking out his revolver as he does so—in a quavering voice.*] What's dat? Who's dar? What is you? Git away from me befo' I shoots you up! You don't? . . .

[*He fires. There is a flash, a loud report, then silence broken only by the far-off, quickened throb of the tom-tom. The formless crea-*
30 *tures have scurried back into the forest.* JONES *remains fixed in his position, listening intently. The sound of the shot, the reassuring feel of the revolver in his hand, have somewhat restored his shaken nerve. He addresses himself with renewed confidence.*]

Dey're gone. Dat shot fix 'em. Dey was only little animals—little wild pigs, I reckon. Dey've maybe rooted out yo' grub an' eat it. Sho', you fool nigger, what you think dey is—ha'nts?
40 [*Excitedly.*] Gorry, you give de game away when you fire dat shot. Dem niggers heah dat fo' su'tin! Time you beat it in de woods widout no long waits. [*He starts for the forest—hesitates before the plunge—then urging himself in with manful resolution.*] Git in, nigger! What you skeered at? Ain't nothin' dere but de trees! Git in! [*He plunges boldly into the*
48 *forest.*]

SCENE THREE

SCENE—*Nine o'clock. In the forest. The moon has just risen. Its beams, drifting through the canopy of leaves, make a barely per-*

ceptible, suffused, eerie glow. A dense low wall of underbrush and creepers is in the nearer foreground, fencing in a small triangular clearing. Beyond this is the massed blackness of the forest like an encompassing barrier. A path is dimly discerned leading down to the clearing from left, rear, and winding away from it again toward the right. As the scene opens nothing can be distinctly made out. Except for the beating of the tom-tom, which is a trifle louder and quicker than in the previous scene, there is silence, broken every few seconds by a queer, clicking sound. Then gradually the figure of the negro, JEFF, *can be discerned crouching on his haunches at the rear of the triangle. He is middle-aged, thin, brown in color, is dressed in a Pullman porter's uniform, cap, etc. He is throwing a pair of dice on the ground before him, picking them up, shaking them, casting them out with the regular, rigid, mechanical movements of an automaton. The heavy, plodding footsteps of someone approaching along the trail from the left are heard and* JONES' *voice, pitched in a slightly higher key and strained in a cheering effort to overcome its own tremors.*

De moon's rizen. Does you heah dat, nigger? You gits more light from dis out. No mo' buttin' yo' fool head agin' de trunks an' scratchin' de hide off yo' legs in de bushes. Now you sees whar yo'se gwine. So cheer up! From now on you has a snap. [*He steps just to the rear of the triangular clearing and mops off his face on his sleeve. He has lost his Panama hat. His face is scratched, his brilliant uniform shows several large rents.*] What time's it gittin' to be, I wonder? I dassent light no match to find out. Phoo'. It's wa'm an' dat's a fac'! [*Wearily.*] How long I been makin' tracks in dese woods? Must be hours an' hours. Seems like fo'evah! Yit can't be, when de moon's jes' riz. Dis am a long night fo' yo', yo' Majesty! [*With a mournful chuckle.*] Majesty! Der ain't much majesty 'bout dis baby now. [*With attempted cheerfulness.*] Never min'. It's all part o' de game. Dis night come to an end like everything else. And when you gits dar safe and has dat bankroll in yo' hands you laughs at all dis. [*He starts to whistle but checks himself abruptly.*] What yo' whistlin' for, you po' dope! Want all de worl' to heah you? [*He stops talking to listen.*] Heah dat ole drum! Sho' gits nearer from de sound.

Dey're packin' it along wid 'em. Time fo' me to move. [*He takes a step forward, then stops—worriedly.*] What's dat odder queer clickety sound I heah? Dere it is! Sound close! Sound like—sound like—Fo' God sake, sound like some nigger was shootin' crap! [*Frightenedly.*] I better beat it quick when I gits dem notions. [*He walks quickly into the clear space—then stands transfixed as he sees* JEFF—*in a terrified gasp.*] Who dar? Who dat? Is dat you, Jeff? [*Starting toward the other, forgetful for a moment of his surroundings and readly believing it is a living man that he sees—in a tone of happy relief.*] Jeff! I'se sho' mighty glad to see you! Dey tol' me you done died from dat razor cut I gives you. [*Stopping suddenly, bewilderedly.*] But how you come to be heah, nigger? [*He stares fascinatedly at the other who continues his mechanical play with the dice.* JONES' *eyes begin to roll wildly. He stutters.*] Ain't you gwine—look up—can't you speak to me? Is you—is you—a ha'nt? [*He jerks out his revolver in a frenzy of terrified rage.*] Nigger, I kills you dead once. Has I got to kill you agin? You take it den. [*He fires. When the smoke clears away* JEFF *has disappeared.* JONES *stands trembling—then with a certain reassurance.*] He's gone, anyway. Ha'nt or no ha'nt, dat shot fix him. [*The beat of the far-off tom-tom is perceptibly louder and more rapid.* JONES *becomes conscious of it—with a start, looking back over his shoulder.*] Dey's gittin' near! Dey'se comin' fast! And heah I is shootin' shots to let 'em know jes' whar I is. Oh, Gorry, I'se got to run. [*Forgetting the path he plunges wildly into the underbrush in the rear and disappears in the shadow.*]

SCENE FOUR

SCENE—*Eleven o'clock. In the forest. A wide dirt road runs diagonally from right, front, to left, rear. Rising sheer on both sides the forest walls it in. The moon is now up. Under its light the road glimmers ghastly and unreal. It is as if the forest had stood aside momentarily to let the road pass through and accomplish its veiled purpose. This done, the forest will fold in upon itself again and the road will be no more.* JONES *stumbles in from the forest on the right. His uniform is ragged and torn. He looks about him with numbed surprise when he sees the road, his eyes*

blinking in the bright moonlight. He flops down exhaustedly and pants heavily for a while. Then with sudden anger.

I'm meltin' wid heat! Runnin' an' runnin' an' runnin'! Damn dis heah coat! Like a strait jacket! [*He tears off his coat and flings it away from him, revealing himself stripped to the waist.*] Dere! Dat's better! Now I kin breathe! [*Looking down at his feet, the spurs catch his eye.*] And to hell wid dese high-fangled spurs. Dey're what's been a-trippin' me up an' breakin my neck. [*He unstraps them and flings them away disgustedly.*] Dere! I gits rid o' dem frippety Emperor trappin's an' I travels lighter. Lawd! I'se tired! [*After a pause, listening to the insistent beat of the tom-tom in the distance.*] I must 'a put some distance between myself an' dem—runnin' like dat—and yit—dat damn drum sound jes' de same—nearer, even. Well, I guess I a'most holds my lead anyhow. Dey won't never catch up. [*With a sigh.*] If on'y my fool legs stands up. Oh, I'se sorry I evah went in for dis. Dat Emperor job is sho' hard to shake. [*He looks around him suspiciously.*] How'd dis road evah git heah? Good level road, too. I never remembers seein' it befo'. [*Shaking his head apprehensively.*] Dese woods is sho' full o' de queerest things at night. [*With a sudden terror.*] Lawd God, don't let me see no more o' dem ha'nts! Dey gits my goat! [*Then trying to talk himself into confidence.*] Ha'nts! You fool nigger, dey ain't no such things! Don't de Baptist parson tell you dat many time? Is you civilized. or is you like dese ign'rent black niggers heah? Sho'! Dat was all in yo' own head. Wasn't nothin' dere. Wasn't no Jeff! Know what? You jus' get seein' dem things 'cause yo' belly's empty and you's sick wid hunger inside. Hunger 'fects yo' head and yo' eyes. Any fool know dat. [*Then pleading fervently.*] But bless God, I don't come across no more o' dem, whatever dey is! [*Then cautiously.*] Rest! Don't talk! Rest! You needs it. Den you gits on yo' way again. [*Looking at the moon.*] Night's half gone a'most. You hits de coast in de mawning! Den you'se all safe.

[*From the right forward a small gang of negroes enter. They are dressed in striped convict suits, their heads are shaven, one leg drags limpingly, shackled to a heavy ball and chain. Some carry picks, the others shovels. They are followed by a white man dressed in the uniform of a prison guard. A Winchester rifle is slung across his shoulders and he carries a heavy whip. At a signal from the* GUARD *they stop on the road opposite where* JONES *is sitting.* JONES, *who has been staring up at the sky, unmindful of their noiseless approach, suddenly looks down and sees them. His eyes pop out, he tries to get to his feet and fly, but sinks back, too numbed by fright to move. His voices catches in a choking prayer.*]

Lawd Jesus!

10 [*The* PRISON GUARD *cracks his whip—noiselessly—and at that signal all the convicts start to work on the road. They swing their picks, they shovel, but not a sound comes from their labor. Their movements, like those of* JEFF *in the preceding scene, are those of automatons, —rigid, slow, and mechanical. The* PRISON GUARD *points sternly at* JONES *with his whip, motions him to take his place among the other shovelers.* JONES *gets to his feet in a hypnotized stupor. He mumbles subserviently.*]

20 Yes, suh! Yes, suh! I'se comin'.

[*As he shuffles, dragging one foot, over to his place, he curses under his breath with rage and hatred.*]

God damn yo' soul, I gits even wid you yit, sometime.

[*As if there were a shovel in his hands he goes through weary, mechanical gestures of digging up dirt, and throwing it to the roadside. Suddenly the* GUARD *approaches him*

30 *angrily, threateningly. He raises his whip and lashes* JONES *viciously across the shoulders with it.* JONES *winces with pain and cowers abjectly. The* GUARD *turns his back on him and walks away contemptuously. Instantly* JONES *straightens up. With arms upraised as if his shovel were a club in his hands he springs murderously at the unsuspecting* GUARD. *In the act of crashing down his shovel on the white man's skull,* JONES *suddenly becomes aware that his*

40 *hands are empty. He cries despairingly.*]

Whar's my shovel? Gimme my shovel 'till I splits his damn head! [*Appealing to his fellow convicts.*] Gimme a shovel, one o' you, fo' God's sake!

[*They stand fixed in motionless attitudes, their eyes on the ground. The* GUARD *seems to wait expectantly, his back turned to the attacker.* JONES *bellows with baffled, terrified rage, tugging frantically at his revolver.*]

50 I kills you, you white debil, if it's de last thing I evah does! Ghost or debil, I kill you again!

[*He frees the revolver and fires point blank at the* GUARD'S *back. Instantly the walls of the forest close in from both sides, the road and*

the figures of the convict gang are blotted out in an enshrouding darkness. The only sounds are a crashing in the underbrush as* JONES *leaps away in mad flight and the throbbing of the tom-tom, still far distant, but increased in volume of sound and rapidity of beat.*]

SCENE FIVE

SCENE—*One o'clock. A large circular clearing, enclosed by the serried ranks of gigantic trunks of tall trees whose tops are lost to view. In the center is a big dead stump worn by time into a curious resemblance to an auction block. The moon floods the clearing with a clear light.* JONES *forces his way in through the forest on the left. He looks wildly about the clearing with hunted, fearful glances. His pants are in tatters, his shoes cut and misshapen, flapping about his feet. He slinks cautiously to the stump in the center and sits down in a tense position, ready for instant flight. Then he holds his head in his hands and rocks back and forth, moaning to himself miserably.*

Oh Lawd, Lawd! Oh Lawd, Lawd! [*Suddenly he throws himself on his knees and raises his clasped hands to the sky—in a voice of agonized pleading.*] Lawd Jesus, heah my prayer! I'se a po' sinner, a po' sinner! I knows I done wrong, I knows it! When I cotches Jeff cheatin' wid loaded dice my anger overcomes me and I kills him dead! Lawd, I done wrong! When dat guard hits me wid de whip, my anger overcomes me, and I kills him dead. Lawd, I done wrong! And down heah whar dese fool bush niggers raises me up to the seat o' de mighty, I steals all I could grab. Lawd, I done wrong! I knows it! I'se sorry! Forgive me, Lawd! Forgive dis po' sinner! [*Then beseeching terrifiedly.*] And keep dem away, Lawd! Keep dem away from me! And stop dat drum soundin' in my ears! Dat begin to sound ha'nted, too. [*He gets to his feet, evidently slightly reassured by his prayer—with attempted confidence.*] De Lawd'll preserve me from dem ha'nts after dis. [*Sits down on the stump again.*] I ain't skeered o' real men. Let dem come. But dem odders . . . [*He shudders—then looks down at his feet, working his toes inside the shoes—with a groan.*] Oh, my po' feet! Dem shoes ain't no use no more 'ceptin' to hurt. I'se better off widout dem. [*He* unlaces them and pulls them off—holds the wrecks of the shoes in his hands and regards them mournfully.] You was real, A-one patin' leather, too. Look at you now. Emperor, you'se gittin' mighty low!

[*He sits dejectedly and remains with bowed shoulders, staring down at the shoes in his hands as if reluctant to throw them away. While his attention is thus occupied, a crowd of figures silently enter the clearing from all sides. All are dressed in Southern costumes of the period of the fifties of the last century. There are middle-aged men who are evidently well-to-do planters. There is one spruce, authoritative individual—the* AUCTIONEER. *There is a crowd of curious spectators, chiefly young belles and dandies who have come to the slave-market for diversion. All exchange courtly greetings in dumb show and chat silently together. There is something stiff, rigid, unreal, marionettish about their movements. They group themselves about the stump. Finally a batch of slaves are led in from the left by an attendant—three men of different ages, two women, one with a baby in her arms, nursing. They are placed to the left of the stump, beside* JONES.

The white planters look them over appraisingly as if they were cattle, and exchange judgments on each. The dandies point with their fingers and make witty remarks. The belles titter bewitchingly. All this in silence save for the ominous throb of the tom-tom. The AUCTIONEER *holds up his hand, taking his place at the stump. The groups strain forward attentively. He touches* JONES *on the shoulder peremptorily, motioning for him to stand on the stump—the auction block.*

JONES *looks up, sees the figures on all sides, looks wildly for some opening to escape, sees none, screams and leaps madly to the top of the stump to get as far away from them as possible. He stands there, cowering, paralyzed with horror. The* AUCTIONEER *begins his silent spiel. He points to* JONES, *appeals to the planters to see for themselves. Here is a good field hand, sound in wind and limb as they can see. Very strong still in spite of his being middle-aged. Look at that back. Look at those shoulders. Look at the muscles in his arms and his sturdy legs. Capable of any amount of hard labor. Moreover, of a good disposition, intelligent and tractable. Will any gentleman start the bidding? The* PLANTERS *raise their fingers, make their bids. They are apparently all eager*

to possess JONES. *The bidding is lively, the crowd interested. While this has been going on,* JONES *has been seized by the courage of desperation. He dares to look down and around him. Over his face abject terror gives way to mystification, to gradual realization—stutteringly.*]

What you all doin', white folks? What's all dis? What you all lookin' at me fo'? What you doin' wid me, anyhow? [*Suddenly convulsed* 10 *with raging hatred and fear.*] Is dis a auction? Is you sellin' me like dey uster befo' de war? [*Jerking out his revolver just as the* AUCTIONEER *knocks him down to one of the planters— glaring from him to the purchaser.*] And *you* sells me? And *you* buys me? I shows ycu I'se a free nigger, damn yo' souls! [*He fires at the* AUCTIONEER *and at the* PLANTER *with such rapidity that the two shots are almost simultaneous. As if this were a signal the walls of* 20 *the forest fold in. Only blackness remains and silence broken by* JONES *as he rushes off, crying with fear—and by the quickened, ever louder beat of the tom-tom.*]

SCENE SIX

SCENE—*Three o'clock. A cleared space in the forest. The limbs of the trees meet over it* 30 *forming a low ceiling about five feet from the ground. The interlocked ropes of creepers reaching upward to entwine the tree trunks give an arched appearance to the sides. The space thus inclosed is like the dark, noisome hold of some ancient vessel. The moonlight is almost completely shut out and only a vague, wan light filters through. There is the noise of someone approaching from the left,* 40 *stumbling and crawling through the undergrowth.* JONES' *voice is heard between chattering moans.*

Oh, Lawd, what I gwine do now? Ain't got no bullet left on'y de silver one. If mo' o' dem ha'nts come after me, how I gwine skeer dem away? Oh, Lawd, on'y de silver one left—an' I gotta save dat fo' luck. If I shoots dat one I'm a goner sho'! Lawd, it's black heah! Whar's de moon? Oh, Lawd, don't dis night evah come to 50 an end? [*By the sounds, he is feeling his way cautiously forward.*] Dere! Dis feels like a clear space. I gotta lie down an' rest. I don't care if dem niggers does cotch me. I gotta rest.

[*He is well forward now where his figure*

can be dimly made out. His pants have been so torn away that what is left of them is no better than a breech cloth. He flings himself full length, face downward on the ground, panting with exhaustion. Gradually it seems to grow lighter in the enclosed space and two rows of seated figures can be seen behind JONES. They are sitting in crumpled, despairing attitudes, hunched, facing one another with their backs touching the forest walls as if they were shackled to them. All negroes, naked save for loin cloths. At first they are silent and motionless. Then they begin to sway slowly forward toward each and back again in unison, as if they were laxly letting themselves follow the long roll of a ship at sea. At the same time, a low, melancholy murmur rises among them, increasing gradually by rhythmic degrees which seem to be directed and controlled by the throb of the tom-tom in the distance, to a long, tremulous wail of despair that reaches a certain pitch, unbearably acute, then falls by slow gradations of tone into silence and is taken up again. JONES starts, looks up, sees the figures, and throws himself down again to shut out the sight. A shudder of terror shakes his whole body as the wail rises up about him again. But the next time, his voice, as if under some uncanny compulsion, starts with the others. As their chorus lifts he rises to a sitting posture similar to the others, swaying back and forth. His voice reaches the highest pitch of sorrow, of desolation. The light fades out, the other voices cease, and only darkness is left. JONES can be heard scrambling to his feet and running off, his voice sinking down the scale and receding as he moves farther and farther away in the forest. The tom-tom beats louder, quicker, with a more insistent, triumphant pulsation.]

SCENE SEVEN

SCENE—Five o'clock. The foot of a gigantic tree by the edge of a great river. A rough structure of boulders, like an altar, is by the tree. The raised river bank is in the nearer background. Beyond this the surface of the river spreads out, brilliant and unruffled in the moonlight, blotted out and merged into a veil of bluish mist in the distance. JONES' voice is heard from the left rising and falling in the long, despairing wail of the chained slaves, to the rhythmic beat of the tom-tom. As his voice sinks into silence, he enters the open space. The expression of his face is fixed and stony, his eyes have an obsessed glare, he moves with a strange deliberation like a sleepwalker or one in a trance. He looks around at the tree, the rough stone altar, the moonlit surface of the river beyond, and passes his hand over his head with a vague gesture of puzzled bewilderment. Then, as if in obedience to some obscure impulse, he sinks into a kneeling, devotional posture before the altar. Then he seems to come to himself partly, to have an uncertain realization of what he is doing, for he straightens up and stares about him horrifiedly—in an incoherent mumble.

What—what is I doin'? What is—dis place? Seems like—seems like I know dat tree—an' dem stones—an' de river. I remember—seems like I been heah befo'. [Tremblingly.] Oh, Gorry, I'se skeered in dis place! I'se skeered! Oh, Lawd, pertect dis sinner!

[Crawling away from the altar, he cowers close to the ground, his face hidden, his shoulders heaving with sobs of hysterical fright. From behind the trunk of the tree, as if he had sprung out of it, the figure of the CONGO WITCH-DOCTOR appears. He is wizened and old, naked except for the fur of some small animal tied about his waist, its bushy tail hanging down in front. His body is stained all over a bright red. Antelope horns are on each side of his head, branching upward. In one hand he carries a bone rattle, in the other a charm stick with a bunch of white cockatoo feathers tied to the end. A great number of glass beads and bone ornaments are about his neck, ears, wrists, and ankles. He struts noiselessly with a queer prancing step to a position in the clear ground between JONES and the altar. Then with a preliminary, summoning stamp of his foot on the earth, he begins to dance and to chant. As if in response to his summons the beating of the tom-tom grows to a fierce, exultant boom whose throbs seem to fill the air with vibrating rhythm. JONES looks up, starts to spring to his feet, reaches a half-kneeling, half-squatting position and remains rigidly fixed there, paralyzed with awed fascination by this new apparition. The WITCH-DOCTOR sways, stamping with his foot, his bone rattle clicking the time. His voice rises and falls in a weird, monotonous croon, without articulate word di-

visions. Gradually his dance becomes clearly one of a narrative in pantomime, his croon is an incantation, a charm to allay the fierceness of some implacable deity demanding sacrifice. He flees, he is pursued by devils, he hides, he flees again. Ever wilder and wilder becomes his flight, nearer and nearer draws the pursuing evil, more and more the spirit of terror gains possession of him. His croon, rising to intensity, is punctuated by shrill cries. JONES *has become completely hypnotized. His voice joins in the incantation, in the cries, he beats time with his hands and sways his body to and fro from the waist. The whole spirit and meaning of the dance has entered into him, has become his spirit. Finally the theme to the pantomime halts on a howl of despair, and is taken up again in a note of savage hope. There is a salvation. The forces of evil demand sacrifice. They must be appeased. The* WITCH-DOCTOR *points with his wand to the sacred tree, to the river beyond, to the altar, and finally to* JONES *with a ferocious command.* JONES *seems to sense the meaning of this. It is he who must offer himself for sacrifice. He beats his forehead abjectly to the ground, moaning hystrically.]*

Mercy, Oh Lawd! Mercy! Mercy on dis po' sinner.

[The WITCH-DOCTOR *springs to the river bank. He stretches out his arms and calls to some God within its depths. Then he starts backward slowly, his arms remaining out. A huge head of a crocodile appears over the bank and its eyes, glittering greenly, fasten upon* JONES. *He stares into them fascinatedly. The* WITCH-DOCTOR *prances up to him, touches him with his wand, motions him with hideous command toward the waiting monster.* JONES *squirms on his belly nearer and nearer, moaning continually.]*

Mercy, Lawd! Mercy!

[The crocodile heaves more of his enormous hulk onto the land. JONES *squirms toward him. The* WITCH-DOCTOR'S *voice shrills out in furious exultation, the tom-tom beats madly.* JONES *cries out in a fierce, exhausted spasm of anguished pleading.]*

Lawd, save me! Lawd Jesus, heah my prayer!

[Immediately, in answer to his prayer, comes the thought of the one bullet left him. He snatches at his hip, shouting defiantly.]

De silver bullet! You don't git me yit!

[He fires at the green eyes in front of him.

The head of the crocodile sinks back behind the river bank, the WITCH-DOCTOR *springs behind the sacred tree and disappears.* JONES *lies with his face to the ground, his arms outstretched, whimpering with fear as the throb of the tom-tom fills the silence about him with a somber pulsation, a baffled but revengeful power.]*

SCENE EIGHT

SCENE—*Dawn. Same as Scene Two, the dividing line of forest and plain. The nearest tree trunks are dimly revealed but the forest behind them is still a mass of glooming shadow. The tom-tom seems on the very spot, so loud and continuously vibrating are its beats.* LEM *enters from the left, followed by a small squad of his soldiers, and by the Cockney trader,* SMITHERS. LEM *is a heavy-set, ape-faced old savage of the extreme African type, dressed only in a loin cloth. A revolver and cartridge belt are about his waist. His soldiers are in different degrees of rag-concealed nakedness. All wear broad palm-leaf hats. Each one carries a rifle.* SMITHERS *is the same as in Scene One. One of the soldiers, evidently a tracker, is peering about keenly on the ground. He grunts and points to the spot where* JONES *entered the forest.* LEM *and* SMITHERS *come to look.*

SMITHERS [*After a glance, turns away in disgust*]: That's where 'e went in right enough. Much good it'll do yer. 'E's miles orf by this an' safe to the Coast, damn 'is 'ide! I tole yer yer'd lose 'im, didn't I?—wastin' the 'ole bloomin' night beatin' yer bloody drum and castin' yer silly spells! Gawd blimey, wot a pack!

LEM [*Gutturally*]: We cotch him. You see. [*He makes a motion to his soldiers who squat down on their haunches in a semicircle.*]

SMITHERS [*Exasperatedly*]: Well, ain't yer goin' in an' 'unt 'im in the woods? What the 'ell's the good of waitin'?

LEM [*Imperturbably—squatting down himself*]: We cotch him.

SMITHERS [*Turning away from him contemptuously*]: Aw! Garn! 'E's a better man than the lot o' you put together. I 'ates the sight o' 'im but I'll say that for 'im. [*A sound of snapping twigs comes from the forest. The soldiers jump to their feet, cocking their rifles alertly.* LEM *remains sitting with an imperturbable expression, but listening intently. The sound from the woods is repeated.* LEM *makes a quick signal with his hand. His followers creep quickly but noiselessly into the forest, scattering so that each enters at a different spot.*]

SMITHERS [*In the silence that follows—in a contemptuous whisper*]:   You ain't thinkin' that would be 'im, I 'ope?

LEM [*Calmly*]:   We cotch him.

SMITHERS: Blarsted fat 'eads! [*Then after a second's thought—wonderingly.*] Still an' all, it might 'appen. If 'e lost 'is bloody way in these stinkin' woods 'e'd likely turn in a circle without 'is knowin' it. They all does.

LEM [*Peremptorily*]:   Sssh! [*The reports of several rifles sound from the forest, followed a second later by savage, exultant yells. The beating of the tom-tom abruptly ceases.* LEM *looks up at the white man with a grin of satisfaction.*] We cotch him. Him dead.

SMITHERS [*With a snarl*]:   'Ow d'yer know it's 'im an' 'ow d'yer know 'e's dead?

LEM: My mens dey got 'um silver bullets. Dey kill him shore.

SMITHERS [*Astonished*]:   They got silver bullets?

LEM: Lead bullet no kill him. He got um strong charm. I cook um money, make um silver bullet, make um strong charm, too.

SMITHERS [*Light breaking upon him*]:   So that's wot you was up to all night, wot? You was scared to put after 'im till you'd molded silver bullets, eh?

LEM [*Simply stating a fact*]:   Yes. Him got strong charm. Lead no good.

SMITHERS [*Slapping his thigh and guffawing*]:   Haw-haw! If yer don't beat all 'ell! [*Then recovering himself—scornfully.*] I'll bet yer it ain't 'im they shot at all, yer bleedin' looney!

LEM [*Calmly*]:   Dey come bring him now. [*The soldiers come out of the forest, carrying* JONES' *limp body. There is a little reddish-purple hole under his left breast. He is dead. They carry him to* LEM, *who examines his body with great satisfaction.*

SMITHERS [*Leans over his shoulder—in a tone of frightened awe*]:   Well, they did for yer right enough, Jonesey, me lad! Dead as a 'erring! [*Mockingly.*] Where's yer 'igh an' mighty airs now, yer bloomin' Majesty? [*Then with a grin.*] Silver bullets! Gawd blimey, but yer died in the 'eighth o' style, any'ow! [LEM *makes a motion to the soldiers to carry the body out left.* SMITHERS *speaks to him sneeringly.*]

SMITHERS: And I s'pose you think it's yer bleedin' charms and yer silly beatin' the drum that made 'im run in a circle when 'e'd lost 'imself, don't yer? [*But* LEM *makes no reply, does not seem to hear the question, walks out left after his men.* SMITHERS *looks after him with contemptuous scorn.*] Stupid as 'ogs, the lot of 'em! Blarsted niggers!

[*Curtain falls.*]

1920   1921

JOHN DOS PASSOS

1896–

BORN IN CHICAGO (his grandfather was an immigrant from Portugal), Dos Passos traveled as a child in Mexico and Belgium, spent a year at school in England, and prepared for college at Choate. At Harvard, where he was graduated *cum laude* in 1916, he was known as an intellectual, and the theme of his first two novels, *One Man's Initiation, 1917* (1920) and *Three Soldiers* (1921), is the brutal impact of war on young men with aesthetic sensibilities. Dos Passos got into the war when he went to Spain in 1916 to study architecture. He saw service with the French Ambulance Corps, the Italian Red Cross, and the A.E.F. medical corps. After the Armistice he spent some time in Paris. Back in America, he became active in left-wing causes, and went to jail in 1926 with Michael Gold after a protest meeting in the

Sacco-Vanzetti case. His *Manhattan Transfer* (1925) got him both fame and notoriety. Paul Elmer More called it "an explosion in a cesspool." Another critic warned, "Dos Passos has cast his lot with the enemies of civilized society." Actually *Manhattan Transfer* is a highly interesting technical experiment, informed by a desire to catch the speech-rhythms and the swift flow of images in modern urban life.

U. S. A. (1938) is a trilogy, containing *The 42nd. Parallel* (1930), *1919* (1932), and *The Big Money* (1936). No other work of fiction describes so abundantly the life of America in the decades that preceded the collapse of 1929. The protagonist is not an individual, but society itself, and to manage his complex subject, Dos Passos uses devices which carry him beyond the limits of conventional narrative technique. Characters are introduced from various social levels, and their stories alternate and occasionally coalesce. There are here and there brief biographies of important Americans; into these passages Dos Passos has put much of his best writing. Another recurrent device, the Newsreel, is compounded of newspaper headlines, scraps of news-stories and of popular songs, often juxtaposed with effective irony. The Camera Eye conveys in a stream-of-consciousness manner the author's own subjective impressions, thoughts, and memories.

These technical variations are not always successful (one wonders what the passing of time will do to the effectiveness of the Newsreels, while the Camera Eye is at best rather arty), but they do lend depth to the narrative and extend its frame of reference. They reveal the social causes that sweep the characters into war, the race for big money, and into frustration and disaster. It is an unhealthy civilization, but Dos Passos proposes no real solution to its ills.

Three later novels by Dos Passos, *Adventures of a Young Man* (1939), *Number One* (1943), and *The Grand Design* (1949), trace the misguided idealism and consequent misfortune of the two Spotswood brothers and their father. In the first novel of this trilogy, young Glenn Spotswood, a disillusioned American communist, dies in the Spanish Civil War, betrayed by members of the Party. In the second novel, Glenn's older brother, Tyler, is the reluctant brain behind a Huey Long type of native American fascist. The third novel, in which the boys' father, a radio commentator, serves as a "reflector" character, covers the Franklin Roosevelt years in Washington. By the time of its writing Dos Passos had lost faith, not only in left-wing liberalism, but also in the ameliorative measures of the New Deal. *The Grand Design* is total in its detestation of any kind of political action. There is no place for Americans to go but back, back to the Founders who, as he said in his *The Ground We Stand On* (1941), knew in their brighter day how to think and act. For some reason—Dos Passos has never said why—we have lost our way.

Jack Potter, *A Bibliography of John Dos Passos*, Chicago, 1950.

John Chamberlain, *John Dos Passos, A Biographical and Critical Essay* (pamphlet), New York, 1939.

Maxwell Geismar, "John Dos Passos: Conversion of a Hero," in *Writers in Crisis*, Boston, 1942, pp. 87–140.

Sinclair Lewis, *John Dos Passos's Manhattan Transfer*, New York, 1926.

Delmore Schwartz, "John Dos Passos and the Whole Truth," *Southern Review*, IV (Autumn, 1938), 351–367.

Mason Wade, "Novelist of America: John Dos Passos," *North American Review*, CCXLIV (Autumn, 1937), 349–367.

Harry R. Warfel, *American Novelists of Today*, New York, 1951, pp. 122–124.

T. K. Whipple, "Dos Passos and the U. S. A.," in *Study Out the Land*, Berkeley, California, 1943, pp. 85–92.

» » From: THE 42ND. PARALLEL « «

LOVER OF MANKIND

Debs was a railroad man, born in a weatherboarded shack at Terre Haute.

He was one of ten childern.

His father had come to America in a sailingship in '49,

an Alsatian from Colmar; not much of a money-maker, fond of music and reading,

10 he gave his children a chance to finish public school and that was about all he could do.

At fifteen Gene Debs was already working as a machinist on the Indianapolis and Terre Haute Railway.

He worked as locomotive fireman,

clerked in a store

joined the local of the Brotherhood of Locomotive Firemen, was elected secretary, trav-

20 eled all over the country as organizer.

He was a tall shamblefooted man, had a sort of gusty rhetoric that set on fire the railroad workers in their pineboarded halls

made them want the world he wanted,

a world brothers might own

where everybody would split even:

I am not a labor leader. I don't want you to follow me or anyone else. If you are looking for a Moses to lead you out of the capitalist

30 *wilderness you will stay right were you are. I would not lead you into this promised land if I could, because if I could lead you in, someone else would lead you out.*

That was how he talked to freighthandlers and gandywalkers, to firemen and switchmen and engineers, telling them it wasn't enough to organize the railroadmen, that all workers must be organized, that all workers must be organized in the worker's cooperative common-

40 wealth.

Locomotive fireman on many a long night's run,

under the smoke a fire burned him up, burned in gusty words that beat in pineboarded halls; he wanted his brothers to be free men.

That was what he saw in the crowd that met him at the Old Wells Street Depot when he came out of jail after the Pullman strike,

50 those were the men that chalked up nine hundred thousand votes for him in nineteen

twelve and scared the frockcoats and the tophats and diamonded hostesses at Saratoga Springs, Bar Harbor, Lake Geneva with the bogy of a socialist president.

But where were Gene Debs' brothers in nineteen eighteen when Woodrow Wilson had him locked up in Atlanta for speaking against war,

where were the big men fond of whisky and fond of each other, gentle rambling tellers of stories over bars in small towns in the Middle West,

quiet men who wanted a house with a porch to putter around and a fat wife to cook for them, a few drinks and cigars, a garden to dig in, cronies to chew the rag with

and wanted to work for it

and others to work for it;

where were the locomotive firemen and engineers when they hustled him off to Atlanta Penitentiary?

And they brought him back to die in Terre Haute

to sit on his porch in a rocker with a cigar in his mouth,

beside him American Beauty roses his wife fixed in a bowl;

and the people of Terre Haute and the people in Indiana and the people of the Middle West were fond of him and afraid of him and thought of him as an old kindly uncle who loved them, and wanted to be with him and to have him give them candy,

but they were afraid of him as if he had contracted a social disease, syphilis or leprosy, and thought it was too bad,

but on account of the flag

and prosperity

and making the world safe for democracy, they were afraid to be with him,

or to think much about him for fear they might believe him;

for he said:

While there is a lower class I am of it, while there is a criminal class I am of it, while there is a soul in prison I am not free.   1930

PROTEUS

Steinmetz was a hunch back,
son of a hunchback lithographer.

He was born in Breslau in eighteen sixtyfive, graduated with highest honors at seventeen from the Breslau Gymnasium, went to the University of Breslau to study mathematics;

mathematics to Steinmetz was muscular strength and long walks over the hills and the kiss of a girl in love and big evenings spent swilling beer with your friends;

on his broken back he felt the topheavy weight of society the way workingmen felt it on their straight backs, the way poor students felt it, was a member of a socialist club, editor of a paper called *The People's Voice.*

Bismarck was sitting in Berlin like a big paperweight to keep the new Germany feudal, to hold down the empire for his bosses the Hohenzollerns.

Steinmetz had to run off to Zurich for fear of going to jail; at Zurich his mathematics woke up all the professors at the Polytechnic;

but Europe in the eighties was no place for a penniless German student with a broken back and a big head filled with symbolic calculus and wonder about electricity that is mathematics made power

and a socialist at that.

With a Danish friend he sailed for America steerage on an old French line boat *La Champagne,*

lived in Brooklyn at first and commuted to Yonkers where he had a twelvedollar a week job with Rudolph Eichemeyer who was a German exile from fortyeight an inventor and electrician and owner of a factory where he made hatmaking machinery and electrical generators.

In Yonkers he worked out the theory of the Third Harmonics

and the law of hysteresis which states in a formula the hundredfold relations between the metallic heat, density, frequency when the poles change places in the core of a magnet under an alternating current.

It is Steinmetz's law of hysteresis that makes possible all the transformers that crouch in little boxes and gableroofed houses in all the hightension lines all over everywhere. The mathematical symbols of Steinmetz's law are the patterns of all transformers everywhere.

In eighteen ninetytwo when Eichemeyer sold out to the corporation that was to form General Electric, Steinmetz was entered in the contract along with other valuable appa-

ratus. All his life Steinmetz was a piece of apparatus belonging to General Electric.

First his laboratory was at Lynn, then it was moved and the little hunchback with it to Schenectady, the electric city.

General Electric humored him, let him be a socialist, let him keep a greenhouseful of cactuses lit up by mercury lights, let him have alligators, talking crows and a gila monster for 10 pets and the publicity department talked up the wizard, the medicine man who knew the symbols that opened up the doors of Ali Baba's cave.

Steinmetz jotted a formula on his cuff and next morning a thousand new powerplants had sprung up and the dynamos sang dollars and the silence of the transformers was all dollars,

and the publicity department poured oily stories into the ears of the American public 20 every Sunday and Steinmetz became the little parlor magician,

who made a toy thunderstorm in his laboratory and made all the toy trains run on time and the meat stay cold in the icebox and the lamp in the parlor and the great lighthouses and the searchlights and the revolving beams of light that guide airplanes at night towards Chicago, New York, St. Louis, Los Angeles,

and they let him be a socialist and believe 30 that human society could be improved the way you can improve a dynamo and they let him be pro-German and write a letter offering his services to Lenin because mathematicians are so impractical who make up formulas by which you can build powerplants, factories, subway systems, light, heat, air, sunshine but not human relations that affect the stockholders' money and the directors' salaries. 39

Steinmetz was a famous magician and he talked to Edison tapping with the Morse code on Edison's knee

because Edison was so very deaf

and he went out West

to make speeches that nobody understood

and he talked to Bryan about God on a railroad train

and all the reporters stood round while he and Einstein 50

met face to face,

but they couldn't catch what they said

and Steinmetz was the most valuable of apparatus General Electric had

until he wore out and died. 1930

» » *From:* U. S. A. « «

The young man walks fast by himself through the crowd that thins into the night streets; feet are tired from hours of walking; eyes greedy for warm curve of faces, answering flicker of eyes, the set of a head, the lift of a shoulder, the way hands spread and clench; blood tingles with wants; mind is a beehive of hopes buzzing and stinging; muscles ache for the knowledge of jobs, for the roadmender's pick and shovel work, the fisherman's knack
10 with a hook when he hauls on the slithery net from the rail of the lurching trawler, the swing of the bridgeman's arm as he slings down the whitehot rivet, the engineer's slow grip wise on the throttle, the dirtfarmer's use of his whole body when, whoaing the mules, he yanks the plow from the furrow. The young man walks by himself searching through the crowd with greedy eyes, greedy ears taut to hear, by himself, alone.
20 The streets are empty. People have packed into subways, climbed into streetcars and busses; in the stations they've scampered for suburban trains; they've filtered into lodgings and tenements, gone up in elevators into apartmenthouses. In a shopwindow two sallow windowdressers in their shirtsleeves are bringing out a dummy girl in a red evening dress, at a corner welders in masks lean into sheets of blue flame repairing a cartrack, a few drunk
30 bums shamble along, a sad streetwalker fidgets under an arclight. From the river comes the deep rumbling whistle of a steamboat leaving dock. A tug hoots far away.

The young man walks by himself, fast but not fast enough, far but not far enough (faces slide out of sight, talk trails into tattered scraps, footsteps tap fainter in alleys); he must catch the last subway, the streetcar, the bus, run up the gangplanks of all the steamboats,
40 register at all the hotels, work in the cities, answer the wantads, learn the trades, take up the jobs, live in all the boardinghouses, sleep in all the beds. One bed is not enough, one job is not enough, one life is not enough. At night, head swimming with wants, he walks by himself alone.

No job, no woman, no house, no city.

Only the ears busy to catch the speech are not alone; the ears are caught tight, linked tight by the tendrils of phrased words, the turn of a joke, the singsong fade of a story, the gruff fall of a sentence; linking tendrils of speech twine through the city blocks, spread over pavements, grow out along broad parked avenues, speed with the trucks leaving on their long night runs over roaring highways, whisper down sandy byroads past wornout farms, joining up cities and fillingstations, roundhouses, steamboats, planes groping along airways; words call out on mountain pastures, drift slow down rivers widening to the sea and the hushed beaches.

It was not in the long walks through jostling crowds at night that he was less alone, or in the training camp at Allentown, or in the day on the docks at Seattle, or in the empty reek of Washington City hot boyhood summer nights, or in the meal on Market Street, or in the swim off the red rocks at San Diego, or in the bed full of fleas in New Orleans, or in the cold razorwind off the lake, or in the gray faces trembling in the grind of gears in the street under Michigan Avenue, or in the smokers of limited expresstrains, or walking across country, or riding up the dry mountain canyons, or the night without a sleepingbag among frozen beartracks in the Yellowstone, or canoeing Sundays on the Quinnipiac;

but in his mother's words telling about longago, in his father's telling about when I was a boy, in the kidding stories of uncles, in lies the kids told at school, the hired man's yarns, the tall tales the doughboys told after taps;

it was the speech that clung to the ears, the link that tingled in the blood; U. S. A.

U. S. A. is the slice of a continent. U. S. A. is a group of holding companies, some aggregations of trade unions, a set of laws bound in calf, a radio network, a chain of moving picture theaters, a column of stock quotations rubbed out and written in by a Western Union boy on a blackboard, a publiclibrary full of old newspapers and dogeared historybooks with protests scrawled on the margins in pencil. U. S. A. is the world's greatest rivervalley fringed with mountains and hills, U. S. A. is a set of bigmouthed officials with too many bankaccounts. U. S. A. is a lot of men buried in their uniforms in Arlington Cemetery. U. S. A. is the letters at the end of an address when you are away from home. But mostly U. S. A. is the speech of the people. 1938

» » *From:* THE BIG MONEY « «

VAG

The young man waits at the edge of the concrete, with one hand he grips a rubbed suitcase of phony leather, the other hand almost making a fist, thumb up

that moves in ever so slight an arc when a car slithers past, a truck roars clatters; the wind of cars passing ruffles his hair, slaps grit in his face.

Head swims, hunger has twisted the belly tight,

he has skinned a heel through the torn sock, feet ache in the broken shoes, under the threadbare suit carefully brushed off with the hand, the torn drawers have a crummy feel, the feel of having slept in your clothes; in the nostrils lingers the staleness of discouraged carcasses crowded into a transient camp, the carbolic stench of the jail, on the taut cheeks the shamed flush from the boring eyes of cops and deputies, railroadbulls (they eat three squares a day, they are buttoned into well-made clothes, they have wives to sleep with, kids to play with after supper, they work for the big men who buy their way, they stick their chests out with the sureness of power behind their backs). Git the hell out, scram. Know what's good for you, you'll make yourself scarce. Gittin' tough, eh? Think you kin take it, eh?

The punch in the jaw, the slam on the head with the nightstick, the wrist grabbed and twisted behind the back, the big knee brought up sharp into the crotch,

the walk out of town with sore feet to stand and wait at the edge of the hissing speeding string of cars where the reek of ether and lead and gas melts into the silent grassy smell of the earth.

Eyes black with want seeking out the eyes of the drivers, a hitch, a hundred miles down the road.

Overhead in the blue a plane drones. Eyes follow the silver Douglas that flashes once in the sun and bores its smooth way out of sight into the blue.

(The transcontinental passengers sit pretty, big men with bankaccounts, highlypaid jobs, who are saluted by doormen; telephonegirls say goodmorning to them. Last night after a fine dinner, drinks with friends, they left Newark. Roar of climbing motors slanting up into the inky haze. Lights drop away. An hour staring along a silvery wing at a big lonesome moon hurrying west through curdling scum. Beacons flash in a line across Ohio.

At Cleveland the plane drops banking in a smooth spiral, the string of lights along the lake swings in a circle. Climbing roar of the motors again; slumped in the soft seat drowsing through the flat moonlight night.

Chi. A glimpse of the dipper. Another spiral swoop from cool into hot air thick with dust and the reek of burnt prairies.

Beyond the Mississippi dawn creeps up behind through the murk over the great plains. Puddles of mist go white in the Iowa hills, farms, fences, silos, steel glint from a river. The blinking eyes of the beacons reddening into day. Watercourses vein the eroded hills.

Omaha. Great cumulus clouds, from coppery churning to creamy to silvery white, trail brown skirts of rain oven the hot plains.

Cheyenne. The cool high air smells of sweetgrass.

The tightbaled clouds to westward burst and scatter in tatters over the strawcolored hills. Indigo mountains jut rimrock. The plane breasts a huge crumbling cloudbank and tobogans over bumpy air across green and crimson slopes into the sunny dazzle of Salt Lake.

The transcontinental passenger thinks contracts, profits, vacationtrips, mighty continent between Atlantic and Pacific, power, wires humming dollars, cities jammed, hills empty, the indiantrail leading into the wagonroad, the macadamed pike, the concrete skyway; trains, planes: history the billiondollar speedup,

and in the bumpy air over the desert ranges toward Las Vegas

sickens and vomits into the carton container the steak and mushrooms he ate in New York. No matter, silver in the pocket, greenbacks in the wallet, drafts, certified checks, plenty restaurants in L. A.)

The young man waits on the side of the road; the plane has gone; thumb moves in a small arc when a car tears hissing past. Eyes seek the drivers eyes. A hundred miles down the road. Head swims, belly tightens, wants crawl over his skin like ants:

10 went to school, books said opportunity, ads promised speed, own your home, shine bigger than your neighbor, the radiocrooner whispered girls, ghosts of platinum girls coaxed from the screen, millions in winnings were chalked up on the boards in the offices, paychecks were for hands willing to work, the cleared desk of an executive with three telephones on it;

waits with swimming head, needs knot the belly, idle hands numb, beside the speeding traffic.

A hundred miles down the road.

1936

» »   « «

WILLIAM FAULKNER

1897–

COLONEL WILLIAM Falkner, great-grandfather of the novelist, was a veteran of two wars, author of several successful books, and builder of a railroad between Oxford, Mississippi, and Memphis, Tennessee. Elected to the state legislature, he was promptly assassinated by a political enemy. The Colonel's famous descendant has kept clear of business and politics while developing his literary powers far beyond the level dreamed of, let alone achieved, by his eminent ancestor.

Born in rural Mississippi and a longtime resident of Oxford, William Faulkner began with *Sartoris* in 1929 to map and populate the fictional county of Yoknapatawpha. Although he has sometimes written of other localities, as in *Mosquitoes* (1927), *Pylon* (1935), or *A Fable* (1954), Yoknapatawpha has been for more than thirty years his visionary homeland. Fictional families like the Sartorises, Compsons, Sutpens, McCaslins, Varners, Bundrens, and Snopeses have become as real to their originator as the aristocrats, tradesmen, and poor whites of northern Mississippi from whom Faulkner has derived their modes of speech and thought, their violence and somnolence, their heroism and decadence, their humor and their tragedy. Thirty years after its inception the Yoknapatawpha cycle included a dozen novels and scores of short stories, the best part of a lifetime's work.

In his first ten years of fiction Faulkner earned a solid reputation with four memorable experiments in narrative method: *The Sound and the Fury* (1929); *As I Lay Dying* (1930); *Light in August* (1932), and *Absalom, Absalom!* (1936). Still regarded by many as his finest achievement, these books tell of the decay of the once-proud Compson clan; of the funeral journey of the poor-white Bundrens, bearing their dead matriarch to Jefferson for burial; of the fierce rebel Joe Christmas and the placid believer Lena Grove; and of the pride of Colonel Sutpen, whose dynastic plans fall to ashes with the destruction of his mansion and the disintegration of his family. For such works as these Faulkner was awarded the Nobel Prize for Literature for 1949.

Faulkner's world as it has gradually revealed itself is a remarkable composite of the near and known with a dark and grotesque gothicism which his followers in and out of the Deep South have been quick to imitate. One is reminded now of Twain's *Huckleberry Finn*, as with

Intruder in The Dust (1948), and now of Poe's "Black Cat" or "Tell-tale Heart," as in the murder-story here reprinted. Themes of guilt and expiation, distantly suggestive of Hawthorne, appear and reappear, as in the early shocker *Sanctuary* (1931) and its arresting sequel, *Requiem for a Nun* (1951). The miasmic atmosphere clears and brightens in *The Unvanquished* (1938), a spirited chronicle of the Sartoris family during and after the Civil War; it darkens again in *A Fable* (1954), a Christ-parable with a setting in war-torn France in 1918, which earned Faulkner a Pulitzer Prize and a National Book Award. The deeper grain of Faulkner's vision is tragic like Shakespeare's: we are likely to find a Lear in overalls or a de-intellectualized Hamlet; poetry grows in the minds of madmen like Darl Bundren or idiots like Benjy Compson and Ike Snopes. Like Shakespeare, too, Faulkner delights in the collocation of comic and tragic, as in his Snopes family trilogy—*The Hamlet* (1940), *The Town* (1957), and *The Mansion* (1959)—or in the contrasted tales of a womanizer and a woman-hater in *The Wild Palms* (1939).

"The Hound," first published in *Harper's* in 1931, was later rewritten as part of *The Hamlet*, where the murderer Ernest Cotton becomes Mink Snopes, whose misadventures hold together and bring to a climax the successive books of the trilogy.

J. B. Meriwether, "The Literary Career of William Faulkner: Catalogue of an Exhibition," *Princeton University Library Chronicle*, XXI (Spring, 1960), 111–164.
————, *William Faulkner: A Check List*, Princeton University Library, 1957.
Faulkner in the University (conferences at the University of Virginia), F. L. Gwynn and J. L. Blotner, eds., Charlottesville, Virginia, 1959.
Faulkner at Nagano (remarks on his writing made while on tour in Japan), R. A. Jelliffe, ed., Tokyo, 1956.
F. J. Hoffman and O. W. Vickery, eds., *William Faulkner: Two Decades of Criticism*, East Lansing, Michigan, 1951.
Irving Howe, *William Faulkner, A Critical Study*, New York, 1952.
W. L. Miner, *The World of William Faulkner*, Durham, N. C., 1952.
W. J. Slatoff, *Quest for Failure: A Study of William Faulkner*, Ithaca, New York, 1960.
O. W. Vickery, *The Novels of William Faulkner: A Critical Interpretation*, Baton Rouge, Louisiana, 1959.
H. H. Waggoner, *William Faulkner: From Jefferson to the World*, Lexington, Kentucky, 1959.

» » *From:* DOCTOR MARTINO AND OTHER STORIES « «

THE HOUND

To Cotton the shot was the loudest thing he had ever heard in his life. It was too loud to be heard all at once. It continued to build up about the thicket, the dim, faint road, long after the hammerlike blow of the ten-gage shotgun had shocked into his shoulder and long after the smoke of the black powder with which it was charged had dissolved, and after the maddened horse had whirled twice and then turned galloping, diminishing, the empty stirrups clashing against the empty saddle.

It made too much noise. It was outrageous, unbelievable—a gun which he had owned for twenty years. It stunned him with amazed outrage, seeming to press him down into the thicket, so that when he could make the second shot, it was too late and the hound too was gone.

Then he wanted to run. He had expected that. He had coached himself the night before. "Right after it you'll want to run," he told himself. "But you can't run. You got to finish it. You got to clean it up. It will be hard, but you got to do it. You got to set there in the bushes and shut your eyes and count slow until you can make to finish it." 10

He did that. He laid the gun down and sat where he had lain behind the log. His eyes were closed. He counted slowly, until he had stopped shaking and until the sound of the gun and the echo of the galloping horse had died out of his ears. He had chosen his place well. It was a quiet road, little used, marked not once in three months save by that departed horse; a short cut between the house where the owner of the horse lived and Varner's store; a quiet, fading, grass-grown trace along the edge of the river bottom, empty save for the two of them, the one squatting in the bushes, the other lying on his face in the road.

Cotton was a bachelor. He lived in a chinked log cabin floored with clay on the edge of the bottom, four miles away. It was dusk when he reached home. In the well-house at the back he drew water and washed his shoes. They were not muddier than usual, and he did not wear them save in severe weather, but he washed them carefully. Then he cleaned the shotgun and washed it too, barrel and stock; why, he could not have said, since he had never heard of finger prints, and immediately afterward he picked up the gun again and carried it into the house and put it away. He kept firewood, a handful of charred pine knots, in the chimney corner. He built a fire on the clay hearth and cooked his supper and ate and went to bed. He slept on a quilt pallet on the floor; he went to bed by barring the door and removing his overalls and lying down. It was dark after the fire burned out; he lay in the darkness. He thought about nothing at all save that he did not expect to sleep. He felt no triumph, vindication, nothing. He just lay there, thinking about nothing at all, even when he began to hear the dog. Usually at night he would hear dogs, single dogs ranging alone in the bottom, or coon- or cat-hunting packs. Having nothing else to do, his life, his heredity, and his heritage centered within a five-mile radius of Varner's store. He knew almost any dog he would hear by its voice, as he knew almost any man he would hear by his voice. He knew this dog's voice. It and the galloping horse with the flapping stirrups and the owner of the horse had been inseparable: where he saw one of them, the other two would not be far away—a lean, rangy brute that charged savagely at anyone who approached its master's house, with something of the master's certitude and overbearance; and to-day was not the first time he had tried to kill it, though only now did he know why he had not gone through with it. "I never knowed my own luck," he said to himself, lying on the pallet. "I never knowed.

If I had went ahead and killed it, killed the dog. . . ."

He was still not triumphant. It was too soon yet to be proud, vindicated. It was too soon. It had to do with death. He did not believe that a man could pick up and move that irrevocable distance at a moment's notice. He had completely forgotten about the body. So he lay with his gaunt, underfed body empty with waiting, thinking of nothing at all, listening to the dog. The cries came at measured intervals, timbrous, sourceless, with the sad, peaceful, abject quality of a single hound in the darkness, when suddenly he found himself sitting bolt upright on the pallet.

"Nigger talk," he said. He had heard (he had never known a negro himself, because of the antipathy, the economic jealousy, between his kind and negroes) how negroes claimed that a dog would howl at the recent grave of its master. "Hit's nigger talk," he said all the time he was putting on his overalls and his recently cleaned shoes. He opened the door. From the dark river bottom below the hill on which the cabin sat the howling of the dog came, bell-like and mournful. From a nail just inside the door he took down a coiled plowline and descended the slope.

Against the dark wall of the jungle fireflies winked and drifted; from beyond the black wall came the booming and grunting of frogs. When he entered the timber he could not see his own hand. The footing was treacherous with slime and creepers and bramble. They possessed the perversity of inanimate things, seeming to spring out of the darkness and clutch him with spiky tentacles. From the musing impenetrability ahead the voice of the hound came steadily. He followed the sound, muddy again; the air was chill, yet he was sweating. He was quite near the sound. The hound ceased. He plunged forward, his teeth drying under his dry lip, his hands clawed and blind, toward the ceased sound, the faint phosphorescent glare of the dog's eyes. The eyes vanished. He stopped, panting, stooped, the plowline in his hand, looking for the eyes. He cursed the dog, his voice a dry whisper. He could hear silence but nothing else.

He crawled on hands and knees, telling where he was by the shape of the trees on the sky. After a time, the brambles raking and slashing at his face, he found a shallow ditch. It was rank with rotted leaves; he waded ankle-deep in the pitch darkness, in something not earth and not water, his elbow crooked before his face. He stumbled upon something; an object with a slack feel. When he touched it, something gave a choked, infantlike cry, and he started back, hearing the creature scuttle away. "Just a possum," he said. "Hit was just a possum."

He wiped his hands on his flanks in order to pick up the shoulders. His flanks were foul with slime. He wiped his hands on his shirt, across his breast, then he picked up the shoulders. He walked backward, dragging it. From time to time he would stop and wipe his hands on his shirt. He stopped beside a tree, a rotting cypress shell, topless, about ten feet tall. He had put the coiled plowline into his bosom. He knotted it about the body and climbed the stump. The top was open, rotted out. He was not a large man, not as large as the body, yet he hauled it up to him hand over hand, bumping and scraping it along the stump, until it lay across the lip like a half-filled meal sack. The knot in the rope had slipped tight. At last he took out his knife and cut the rope and tumbled the body into the hollow stump.

It didn't fall far. He shoved at it, feeling around it with his hands for the obstruction; he tied the rope about the stub of a limb and held the end of it in his hands and stood on the body and began to jump up and down upon it, whereupon it fled suddenly beneath him and left him dangling on the rope.

He tried to climb the rope, rasping off with his knuckles the rotten fiber, a faint, damp powder of decay like snuff in his nostrils. He heard the stub about which the rope was tied crack and felt it begin to give. He leaped upward from nothing, scrabbling at the rotten wood, and got one hand over the edge. The wood crumbled beneath his fingers; he climbed perpetually without an inch of gain, his mouth cracked upon his teeth, his eyes glaring at the sky.

The wood stopped crumbling. He dangled by his hands, breathing. He drew himself up and straddled the edge. He sat there for a while. Then he climbed down and leaned against the hollow trunk.

When he reached his cabin he was tired, spent. He had never been so tired. He stopped at the door. Fireflies still blew along the dark band of timber, and owls hooted and the frogs still boomed and grunted. "I ain't never been so tired," he said leaning against the house, the wall which he had built log by log. "Like

ever thing had got outen hand. Climbing that stump, and the noise that shot made. Like I had got to be somebody else without knowing it, in a place where noise was louder, climbing harder to climb, without knowing it." He went to bed. He took off the muddy shoes, the overalls, and lay down; it was late then. He could tell by a summer star that came into the square window at two o'clock and after.

Then, as if it had waited for him to get settled and comfortable, the hound began to howl again. Lying in the dark, he heard the first cry come up from the river bottom, mournful, timbrous, profound.

Five men in overalls squatted against the wall of Varner's store. Cotton made the sixth. He sat on the top step, his back against a gnawed post which supported the wooden awning of the veranda. The seventh man sat in the single splint chair; a fat, slow man in denim trousers and a collarless white shirt, smoking a cob pipe. He was past middle-age. He was sheriff of the county. The man about whom they were talking was named Houston.

"He hadn't no reason to run off," one said. "To disappear. To send his horse back home with a empty saddle. He hadn't no reason. Owning his own land, his house. Making a good crop ever year. He was as well-fixed as ere a man in the county. A bachelor too. He hadn't no reason to disappear. You can mark it. He never run. I don't know what; but Houston never run."

"I don't know," a second said. "You can't tell what a man has got in his mind. Houston might a had reason that we don't know, for making it look like something had happened to him. For clearing outen the country and leaving it to look like something had happened to him. It's been done before. Folks before him has had reason to light out for Texas with a changed name."

Cotton sat a little below their eyes, his face lowered beneath his worn, stained, shabby hat. He was whittling at a stick, a piece of pine board.

"But a fellow can't disappear without leaving no trace," a third said. "Can he, Sheriff?"

"Well, I don't know," the Sheriff said. He removed the cob pipe and spat neatly across the porch into the dust. "You can't tell what a man will do when he's pinched. Except it will be something you never thought of. Never counted on. But if you can find just what pinched him you can pretty well tell what he done."

"Houston was smart enough to do ere a thing he taken a notion to," the second said. "If he'd wanted to disappear, I reckon we'd a known about what we know now."

"And what's that?" the third said.

"Nothing," the second said.

"That's a fact," the first said. "Houston was a secret man."

"He wasn't the only secret man around here," a fourth said. To Cotton it sounded sudden, since the fourth man had said no word before. He sat against the post, his hat slanted forward so that his face was invisible, believing that he could feel their eyes. He watched the sliver peel slow and smooth from the stick, ahead of his worn knife-blade. "I got to say something," he told himself.

"He warn't no smarter than nobody else," he said. Then he wished he had not spoken. He could see their feet beneath his hat-brim. He trimmed the stick, watching the knife, the steady sliver. "It's got to trim off smooth," he told himself. "It don't dast to break." He was talking; he could hear his voice: "Swelling around like he was the biggest man in the county. Setting that ere dog on folk's stock." He believed that he could feel their eyes, watching their feet, watching the sliver trim smooth and thin and unhurried beneath the knife blade. Suddenly he thought about the gun, the loud crash, the jarring shock. "Maybe I'll have to kill them all," he said to himself— a mild man in worn overalls, with a gaunt face and lackluster eyes like a sick man, whittling a stick with a thin hand, thinking about killing them. "Not them; just the words, the talk." But the talk was familiar, the intonation, the gestures; but so was Houston. He had known Houston all his life: that prosperous and over-bearing man. "With a dog," Cotton said, watching the knife return and bite into another sliver. "A dog that et better than me. I work, and eat worse than his dog. If I had been his dog, I would not have. . . . We're better off without him," he said, blurted. He could feel their eyes, sober, intent.

"He always did rile Ernest," the first said.

"He taken advantage of me," Cotton said, watching the infallible knife. "He taken advantage of ever man he could."

"He was a overbearing man," the Sheriff said.

Cotton believed that they were still watch-ing him, hidden behind their detached voices.

"Smart, though," the third said.

"He wasn't smart enough to win that suit against Ernest over that hog."

"That's so. How much did Ernest get outen that lawing? He ain't never told, has he?"

Cotton believed that they knew how much he had got from the suit. The hog had come into his lot one October. He penned it up; he tried by inquiry to find the owner. But none claimed it until he had wintered it on his corn. In the spring Houston claimed the hog. They went to court. Houston was awarded the hog, though he was assessed a sum for the winter-ing of it, and one dollar as pound-fee for a stray. "I reckon that's Ernest's business," the Sheriff said after a time.

Again Cotton heard himself talking, blurt-ing. "It was a dollar," he said, watching his knuckles whiten about the knife handle. "One dollar." He was trying to make his mouth stop talking. "After all I taken offen him. . . ."

"Juries does queer things," the Sheriff said, "in little matters. But in big matters they're mostly right."

Cotton whittled, steady and deliberate. "At first you'll want to run," he told himself. "But you got to finish it. You got to count a hun-dred, if it needs, and finish it."

"I heard that dog again last night," the third said.

"You did?" the Sheriff said.

"It ain't been home since the day the horse come in with the saddle empty," the first said.

"It's out hunting, I reckon," the Sheriff said. "It'll come in when it gets hungry."

Cotton trimmed at the stick. He did not move.

"Niggers claim a hound'll howl till a dead body's found," the second said.

"I've heard that," the Sheriff said. After a time a car came up and the Sheriff got into it. The car was driven by a deputy. "We'll be late for supper," the Sheriff said. The car mounted the hill; the sound died away. It was getting toward sundown.

"He ain't much bothered," the third said.

"Why should he be?" the first said. "After all, a man can leave his house and go on a trip without telling everybody."

"Looks like he'd a unsaddled that mare, though," the second said. "And there's some-thing the matter with that dog. It ain't been home since, and it ain't treed. I been hearing it ever night. It ain't treed. It's howling. It ain't been home since Tuesday. And that was the day Houston rid away from the store here on that mare."

Cotton was the last one to leave the store. It was after dark when he reached home. He ate some cold bread and loaded the shotgun and sat beside the open door until the hound began to howl. Then he descended the hill and entered the bottom.

The dog's voice guided him; after a while it ceased, and he saw its eyes. They were now motionless; in the red glare of the explosion he saw the beast entire in sharp relief. He saw it in the act of leaping into the ensuing welter of darkness; he heard the thud of its body. But he couldn't find it. He looked carefully, quartering back and forth, stopping to listen. But he had seen the shot strike it and hurl it backward, and he turned aside for about a hundred yards in the pitch darkness and came to a slough. He flung the shotgun into it, hearing the sluggish splash, watching the vague water break and recover, until the last ripple died. He went home and to bed.

He didn't go to sleep though, although he knew he would not hear the dog. "It's dead," he told himself, lying on his quilt pallet in the dark. "I saw the bullets knock it down. I could count the shot. The dog is dead." But still he did not sleep. He did not need sleep; he did not feel tired or stale in the mornings, though he knew it was not the dog. He knew he would not hear the dog again, and that sleep had nothing to do with the dog. So he took to spending the nights sitting up in a chair in the door, watching the fireflies and listening to the frogs and the owls.

He entered Varner's store. It was in mid-afternoon; the porch was empty, save for the clerk, whose name was Snopes. "Been looking for you for two-three days," Snopes said. "Come inside."

Cotton entered. The store smelled of cheese and leather and new earth. Snopes went behind the counter and reached from under the counter a shotgun. It was caked with mud. "This is yourn, ain't it?" Snopes said. "Vernon Tull said it was. A nigger squirl hunter found it in a slough."

Cotton came to the counter and looked at the gun. He did not touch it; he just looked at it. "It ain't mine," he said.

"Ain't nobody around here got one of them old Hadley ten-gages except you," Snopes said. "Tull says it's yourn."

"It ain't none of mine," Cotton said. "I got one like it. But mine's to home."

Snopes lifted the gun. He breeched it. "It had one empty and one load in it," he said. "Who you reckon it belongs to?"

"I don't know," Cotton said. "Mine's to home." He had come to purchase food. He bought it: crackers, cheese, a tin of sardines. It was not dark when he reached home, yet he opened the sardines and ate his supper. When he lay down he did not even remove his overalls. It was as though he waited for something, stayed dressed to move and go at once. He was still waiting for whatever it was when the window turned gray and then yellow and then blue; when, framed by the square window, he saw against the fresh morning a single soaring speck. By sunrise there were three of them, and then seven.

All that day he watched them gather, wheeling and wheeling, drawing their concentric black circles, watching the lower ones wheel down and down and disappear below the trees. He thought it was the dog. "They'll be through by noon," he said. "It wasn't a big dog."

When noon came they had not gone away; there were still more of them, while still the lower ones dropped down and disappeared below the trees. He watched them until dark came, until they went away, flapping singly and sluggishly up from beyond the trees. "I got to eat," he said. "With the work I got to do tonight." He went to the hearth and knelt and took up a pine knot, and he was kneeling, nursing a match into flame, when he heard the hound again; the cry deep, timbrous, unmistakable, and sad. He cooked his supper and ate.

With his axe in his hand he descended through his meager corn patch. The cries of the hound could have guided him, but he did not need it. He had not reached the bottom before he believed that his nose was guiding him. The dog still howled. He paid it no attention, until the beast sensed him and ceased, as it had done before; again he saw its eyes. He paid no attention to them. He went to the hollow cypress trunk and swung his axe into it, the axe sinking helve-deep into the rotten wood. While he was tugging at it something flowed silent and savage out of the darkness behind him and struck him a slashing blow.

The axe had just come free; he fell with the axe in his hand, feeling the hot reek of the dog's breath on his face and hearing the click of its teeth as he struck it down with his free hand. It leaped again; he saw its eyes now. He was on his knees, the axe raised in both hands now. He swung it, hitting nothing, feeling nothing; he saw the dog's eyes, crouched. He rushed at the eyes; they vanished. He waited
10 a moment, but heard nothing. He returned to the tree.

At the first stroke of the axe the dog sprang at him again. He was expecting it, so he whirled and struck with the axe at the two eyes and felt the axe strike something and whirl from his hands. He heard the dog whimper, he could hear it crawling away. On his hands and knees he hunted for the axe until he found it.

20 He began to chop at the base of the stump, stopping between blows to listen. But he heard nothing, saw nothing. Overhead the stars were swinging slowly past; he saw the one that looked into his window at two o'clock. He began to chop steadily at the base of the stump.

The wood was rotten; the axe sank helve-deep at each stroke, as into sand or mud; suddenly Cotton knew that it was not imagination he smelled. He dropped the axe and began to
30 tear at the rotten wood with his hands. The hound was beside him, whimpering; he did not know it was there, not even when it thrust its head into the opening, crowding against him, howling.

"Git away," he said, still without being conscious that it was the dog. He dragged at the body, feeling it slough upon its own bones, as though it were too large for itself; he turned his face away, his teeth glared, his breath
40 furious and outraged and restrained. He could feel the dog surge against his legs, its head in the orifice, howling.

When the body came free, Cotton went over backward. He lay on his back on the wet ground, looking up at a faint patch of starry sky. "I ain't never been so tired," he said. The dog was howling with an abject steadiness. "Shut up," Cotton said. "Hush. Hush." The dog didn't hush. "It'll be daylight soon." Cot-
50 ton said to himself. "I got to get up."

He got up and kicked at the dog. It moved away, but when he stooped and took hold of the legs and began to back away, the dog was there again, moaning to itself. When he would stop to rest, the dog would howl again; again

he kicked at it. Then it began to be dawn, the trees coming spectral and vast out of the miasmic darkness. He could see the dog plainly. It was gaunt, thin, with a long bloody gash across its face. "I'll have to get shut of you," he said. Watching the dog, he stooped and found a stick. It was rotten, foul with slime. He clutched it. When the hound lifted its muzzle to howl, he struck. The dog whirled; there was a long fresh scar running from shoulder to flank. It leaped at him, without a sound; he struck again. The stick took it fair between the eyes. He picked up the ankles and tried to run.

It was almost light. When he broke through the undergrowth upon the river bank the channel was invisible; a long bank of what looked like cotton batting, though he could hear the water beneath it somewhere. There was a freshness here; the edges of the mist licked into curling tongues. He stooped and lifted the body and hurled it into the bank of mist. At the instant of vanishing he saw it—a sluggish sprawl of three limbs instead of four, and he knew why it had been so hard to free from the stump. "I'll have to make another trip," he said; then he heard a pattering rush behind him. He didn't have time to turn when the hound struck him and knocked him down. It didn't pause. Lying on his back, he saw it in midair like a bird, vanish into the mist with a single short, choking cry.

He got to his feet and ran. He stumbled and caught himself and ran again. It was full light. He could see the stump and the black hole which he had chopped in it; behind him he could hear the swift, soft feet of the dog. As it sprang at him he stumbled and fell and saw it soar over him, its eyes like two cigar-coals; it whirled and leaped at him again before he could rise. He struck at its face with his bare hands and began to run. Together they reached the tree. It leaped at him again, slashing his arms as he ducked into the tree, seeking that member of the body which he did not know was missing until after he had released it into the mist, feeling the dog surging about his legs. Then the dog was gone. Then a voice said:

"We got him. You can come out, Ernest."

The countyseat was fourteen miles away. They drove to it in a battered Ford. On the back seat Cotton and the Sheriff sat, their inside wrists locked together by handcuffs. They had to drive for two miles before they reached the highroad. It was hot, ten o'clock in the morning. "You want to swap sides out of the sun?" the Sheriff said.

"I'm all right," Cotton said.

At two o'clock they had a puncture. Cotton and the Sheriff sat under a tree while the driver and the second deputy went across a field and returned with a glass jar of buttermilk and some cold food. They ate, repaired the tire, and went on.

When they were within three or four miles of town, they began to pass wagons and cars going home from market day in town, the wagon teams plodding homeward in their own inescapable dust. The Sheriff greeted them with a single gesture of his fat arm. "Home for supper, anyway," he said. "What's the matter, Ernest? Feeling sick? Here, Joe; pull up a minute."

"I'll hold my head out," Cotton said. "Never mind." The car went on. Cotton thrust his head out the V strut of the top stanchion. The Sheriff shifted his arm, giving him play, "Go on," Cotton said, "I'll be all right." The car went on. Cotton slipped a little farther down in the seat. By moving his head a little he could wedge his throat into the apex of the iron V, the uprights gripping his jaws beneath the ears. He shifted again until his head was tight in the vise, then he swung his legs over the door, drying to bring the weight of his body sharply down against his imprisoned neck. He could hear his vertebræ; he felt a kind of rage at his own toughness; he was struggling then against the jerk on the manacle, the hands on him.

Then he was lying on his back beside the road, with water on his face and in his mouth, though he could not swallow. He couldn't speak, trying to curse, cursing in no voice. Then he was in the car again, on the smooth street where children played in the big, shady yards in small bright garments, and men and women went home toward supper, to plates of food and cups of coffee in the long twilight of summer.

They had a doctor for him in his cell. When the doctor had gone he could smell supper cooking somewhere—ham and hot bread and coffee. He was lying on a cot; the last ray of copper sunlight slid through a narrow window, stippling the bars upon the wall above his head. His cell was near the common room, where the minor prisoners lived, the ones who were in jail for minor offenses or for three meals a day; the stairway from below came up into that room. It was occupied for the time by a group of negroes from the chain-gang that worked the streets, in jail for vagrancy or for selling a little whiskey or shooting craps for ten or fifteen cents. One of the negroes was at the window above the street, yelling down to someone. The others talked among themselves, their voices rich and murmurous, mellow and singsong. Cotton rose and went to the door of his cell and held to the bars, looking at the negroes.

"Hit," he said. His voice made no sound. He put his hand to his throat; he produced a dry croaking sound, at which the negroes ceased talking and looked at him, their eyeballs rolling. "It was all right," Cotton said, "until it started coming to pieces on me. I could a handled that dog." He held his throat his voice harsh, dry and croaking. "But it started coming to pieces on me. . . ."

"Who him?" one of the negroes said. They whispered among themselves, watching him, their eyeballs white in the dusk.

"It would a been all right," Cotton said, "but it started coming to pieces. . . ."

"Hush up, white man," one of the negroes said. "Don't you be telling us no truck like that."

"Hit would a been all right," Cotton said, his voice harsh, whispering. Then it failed him again altogether. He held to the bars with one hand, holding his throat with the other, while the negroes watched him, huddled, their eyeballs white and sober. Then with one accord they turned and rushed across the room, toward the staircase; he heard slow steps and then he smelled food, and he clung to the bars, trying to see the stairs. "Are they going to feed them niggers before they feed a white man?" he said, smelling the coffee and the ham.

1931

» »   « «

ERNEST HEMINGWAY

1899–

ACCEPTING THE Nobel Prize in 1954, Hemingway declared that a writer "should always try for something that has never been done or that others have tried and failed. Then sometimes, with great luck, he will succeed." Backed by this often reiterated belief, he has remained impervious to those critics who, while admiring his early technical brilliance, think that his continued preoccupation with athleticism, violence, death, courage, endurance, and romantic love indicates arrested development. His art has, however, been so closely founded on his personal observations and his enthusiasm for the active life has sustained him through such a variety of experiences that he is unlikely to change his writing subjects or his personal interests this side of the grave. His work derives its special quality from his ability to support a direct observation of natural and human events with a half-hidden symbolic structure whose moral overtones permeate the texture of all his best writing.

Born in Oak Park, Illinois, the son of a prosperous doctor, Hemingway quit formal education after high school, worked for the Kansas City *Star*, and in the first World War joined an ambulance corps on the Italian front. Badly wounded just before his nineteenth birthday, he returned home to begin serious writing until he resumed newspaper work as European correspondent for the Toronto *Star*. In Paris he joined the coterie of expatriates who were then gathering on the Left Bank, discovered Spanish bullfighting and Austrian skiing, turned to short fiction, was published in the little magazines, and began to be heard of at home. His first short stories, *In Our Time* (1925), effectively contrasted the squirrel-hunting days of his midwestern boyhood with man-hunting days on the Italian front in 1918. *The Sun Also Rises* (1926), his first novel, is a brilliant factual account of one segment of the postwar generation as they move from the gay life of Paris to the Fiesta of San Fermin in Pamplona, Spain.

Hemingway's essential romanticism is well exemplified in *A Farewell To Arms* (1929), which owes something to his experience of the war and his convalescence in Milan. From that time on he has roamed the Western world, examining the Spanish bullfight in *Death in the Afternoon* (1932); shooting on safari in *The Green Hills of Africa* (1935); saltwater fishing between Key West and Cuba in *To Have and Have Not* (1937); and serving as correspondent in Madrid during the Spanish Civil War, which provided him with materials for his political melodrama, *The Fifth Column* (1938) and most notably his great novel, *For Whom The Bell Tolls* (1940). In the second World War, he was again actively engaged—in the Caribbean aboard an armed yacht, as air observer over Europe, and on land with the invading Allies. His reminiscences of this time appear in the much-derogated *Across The River and Into The Trees* (1950), an account of the last days of an embittered professional soldier on a winter visit to Venice and the Veneto. *The Old Man and The Sea* (1952) tells of a Cuban fisherman's heroic struggle to capture a huge marlin only to lose his prize to sharks on the homeward voyage. A technical masterpiece, this novelette seemed to many the high point of Hemingway's achievement. *The Dangerous Summer*, excerpted in *Life* magazine in 1960, returns to the scenes and excitements of *Death in The Afternoon* with the story of the rivalry between two great young Spanish matadors in the summer of 1959.

The first forty-nine stories, collected in 1938, include "The Killers," probably the best extant short narrative of the gangster era. Written in Madrid in May, 1926, it remains remarkably undated.

Lee Samuels, *A Hemingway Check List*, New York, 1951.
Carlos Baker, ed., *Hemingway and His Critics: An International Anthology*, New York, 1961.
———, *Hemingway, The Writer As Artist*, Princeton (1952), 1956.
C. A. Fenton, *The Apprenticeship of Ernest Hemingway*, New York, 1954.
Edgar Johnson, "Farewell the Separate Peace," *Sewanee Review*, XLVIII (July–September, 1940), 289–300.
Delmore Schwartz, "Ernest Hemingway's Literary Situation," *Southern Review*, III (Spring, 1938), 769–789.
Gertrude Stein, "Ernest Hemingway and the Postwar Decade," *Atlantic*, CLII (August, 1933), 197–208. (A revised version printed in *The Autobiography of Alice B. Toklas*, New York, 1933, pp. 237–310.)
R. P. Warren, "Hemingway," *Kenyon Review*, IX (Winter, 1947), 1–28.
Philip Young, *Ernest Hemingway*, New York, 1952.

» » *From:* MEN WITHOUT WOMEN « «

THE KILLERS

The door of Henry's lunch-room opened and two men came in. They sat down at the counter.

"What's yours?" George asked them.

"I don't know," one of the men said. "What do you want to eat, Al?"

"I don't know," said Al. "I don't know what I want to eat."

Outside it was getting dark. The street-light came on outside the window. The two men at the counter read the menu. From the other end of the counter Nick Adams watched them. He had been talking to George when they came in.

"I'll have a roast pork tenderloin with apple sauce and mashed potatoes," the first man said.

"It isn't ready yet."

"What the hell do you put it on the card for?"

"That's the dinner," George explained. "You can get that at six o'clock."

George looked at the clock on the wall behind the counter.

"It's five o'clock."

"The clock says twenty minutes past five," the second man said.

"It's twenty minutes fast."

"Oh, to hell with the clock," the first man said. "What have you got to eat?"

"I can give you any kind of sandwiches," George said. "You can have ham and eggs, bacon and eggs, liver and bacon, or a steak."

"Give me chicken croquettes with green peas and cream sauce and mashed potatoes."

"That's the dinner."

"Everything we want's the dinner, eh? That's the way you work it."

"I can give you ham and eggs, bacon and eggs, liver—"

"I'll take ham and eggs," the man called Al said. He wore a derby hat and a black overcoat buttoned across the chest. His face was small and white and he had tight lips. He wore a silk muffler and gloves.

"Give me bacon and eggs," said the other man. He was about the same size as Al. Their faces were different, but they were dressed like twins. Both wore overcoats too tight for them. They sat leaning forward, their elbows on the counter.

"Got anything to drink?" Al asked.

"Silver beer, bevo, ginger-ale," George said.

"I mean you got anything to *drink?*"

"Just those I said."

"This is a hot town," said the other. "What do they call it?"

"Summit."

"Ever hear of it?" Al asked his friend.

"No," said the friend.

"What do you do here nights?" Al asked.

"They eat the dinner," his friend said. "They all come here and eat the big dinner."

"That's right," George said.

"So you think that's right?" Al asked George.

"Sure."

"You're a pretty bright boy, aren't you?"

"Sure," said George.

"Well, you're not," said the other little man. "Is he, Al?"

"He's dumb," said Al. He turned to Nick. "What's your name?"

"Adams."

"Another bright boy," Al said. "Ain't he a bright boy, Max?"

"The town's full of bright boys," Max said.

George put the two platters, one of ham and eggs, the other of bacon and eggs, on the counter. He set down two side-dishes of fried
10 potatoes and closed the wicket into the kitchen.

"Which is yours?" he asked Al.

"Don't you remember?"

"Ham and eggs."

"Just a bright boy," Max said. He leaned forward and took the ham and eggs. Both men ate with their gloves on. George watched them eat.

"What are *you* looking at?" Max looked at
20 George.

"Nothing."

"The hell you were. You were looking at me."

"Maybe the boy meant it for a joke, Max," Al said.

George laughed.

"*You* don't have to laugh," Max said to him. "*You* don't have to laugh at all, see?"

"All right," said George.
30 "So he thinks it's all right." Max turned to Al. "He thinks it's all right. That's a good one."

"Oh, he's a thinker," Al said. They went on eating.

"What's the bright boy's name down the counter?" Al asked Max.

"Hey, bright boy," Max said to Nick. "You go around on the other side of the counter with your boy friend."

"What's the idea?" Nick asked.
40 "There isn't any idea."

"You better go around, bright boy," Al said. Nick went around behind the counter.

"What's the idea?" George asked.

"None of your damn business," Al said. "Who's out in the kitchen?"

"The nigger."

"What do you mean the nigger?"

"The nigger that cooks."

"Tell him to come in."
50 "What's the idea?"

"Tell him to come in."

"Where do you think you are?"

"We know damn well where we are," the man called Max said. "Do we look silly?"

"You talk silly," Al said to him. "What the hell do you argue with this kid for? Listen," he said to George, "tell the nigger to come out here."

"What are you going to do to him?"

"Nothing. Use your head, bright boy. What would we do to a nigger?"

George opened the slit that opened back into the kitchen. "Sam," he called. "Come in here a minute."

The door to the kitchen opened and the nigger came in. "What was it?" he asked. The two men at the counter took a look at him.

"All right, nigger. You stand right there," Al said.

Sam, the nigger, standing in his apron, looked at the two men sitting at the counter. "Yes sir," he said. Al got down from his stool.

"I'm going back to the kitchen with the nigger and bright boy," he said. "Go on back to the kitchen, nigger. You go with him, bright boy." The little man walked after Nick and Sam, the cook, back into the kitchen. The door shut after them. The man called Max sat at the counter opposite George. He didn't look at George but looked in the mirror that ran along back of the counter. Henry's had been made over from a saloon into a lunch-counter.

"Well, bright boy," Max said, looking into the mirror, "why don't you say something?"

"What's it all about?"

"Hey Al," Max called, "bright boy wants to know what it's all about."

"Why don't you tell him?" Al's voice came from the kitchen.

"What do you think it's all about?"

"I don't know."

"What do you think?"

Max looked into the mirror all the time he was talking.

"I wouldn't say."

"Hey, Al, bright boy says he wouldn't say what he thinks it's all about."

"I can hear you, all right," Al said from the kitchen. He had propped open the slit that dishes passed through into the kitchen with a catsup bottle. "Listen, bright boy," he said from the kitchen to George. "Stand a little further along the bar. You move a little to the left, Max." He was like a photographer arranging for a group picture.

"Talk to me, bright boy," Max said. "What do you think's going to happen?"

George did not say anything.

"I'll tell you," Max said. "We're going to kill

a Swede. Do you know a big Swede named Ole Andreson?"

"Yes."

"He comes here to eat every night, don't he?"

"Sometimes he comes here."

"He comes here at six o'clock, don't he?"

"If he comes."

"We know all that, bright boy," Max said. "Talk about something else. Ever go to the movies?"

"Once in a while."

"You ought to go to the movies more. The movies are fine for a bright boy like you."

"What are you going to kill Ole Andreson for? What did he ever do to you?"

"He never had a chance to do anything to us. He never even seen us."

"And he's only going to see us once," Al said from the kitchen.

"What are you going to kill him for, then?" George asked.

"We're killing him for a friend. Just to oblige a friend, bright boy."

"Shut up," said Al from the kitchen. "You talk too goddam much."

"Well, I got to keep bright boy amused. Don't I, bright boy?"

"You talk too damn much," Al said. "The nigger and my bright boy are amused by themselves. I got them tied up like a couple of girl friends in the convent."

"I suppose you were in a convent."

"You never know."

"You were in a kosher convent. That's where you were."

George looked up at the clock.

"If anybody comes in you tell them the cook is off, and if they keep after it, you tell them you'll go back and cook yourself. Do you get that, bright boy?"

"All right," George said. "What you going to do with us afterward?"

"That'll depend," Max said. "That's one of those things you never know at the time."

George looked up at the clock. It was a quarter past six. The door from the street opened. A street-car motorman came in.

"Hello, George," he said. "Can I get supper?"

"Sam's gone out," George said. "He'll be back in about half an hour."

"I'd better go up the street," the motorman said. George looked at the clock. It was twenty minutes past six.

"That was nice, bright boy," Max said. "You're a regular little gentleman."

"He knew I'd blow his head off," Al said from the kitchen.

"No," said Max. "It ain't that. Bright boy is nice. He's a nice boy. I like him."

At six-fifty-five George said: "He's not coming."

Two other people had been in the lunchroom. Once George had gone out to the kitchen and made a ham-and-egg sandwich "to go" that a man wanted to take with him. Inside the kitchen he saw Al, his derby hat tipped back, sitting on a stool beside the wicket with the muzzle of a sawed-off shotgun resting on the ledge. Nick and the cook were back to back in the corner, a towel tied in each of their mouths. George had cooked the sandwich, wrapped it up in oiled paper, put it in a bag, brought it in, and the man had paid for it and gone out.

"Bright boy can do everything," Max said. "He can cook and everything. You'd make some girl a nice wife, bright boy."

"Yes?" George said. "Your friend, Ole Andreson, isn't going to come."

"We'll give him ten minutes," Max said.

Max watched the mirror and the clock. The hands of the clock marked seven o'clock, and then five minutes past seven.

"Come on, Al," said Max. "We better go. He's not coming."

"Better give him five minutes," Al said from the kitchen.

In the five minutes a man came in, and George explained that the cook was sick.

"Why the hell don't you get another cook?" the man asked. "Aren't you running a lunch-counter?" He went out.

"Come on, Al," Max said.

"What about the two bright boys and the nigger?"

"They're all right."

"You think so?"

"Sure. We're through with it."

"I don't like it," said Al. "It's sloppy. You talk too much."

"Oh, what the hell," said Max. "We got to keep amused, haven't we?"

"You talk too much, all the same," Al said. He came out from the kitchen. The cut-off barrels of the shotgun made a slight bulge under the waist of his too tight-fitting overcoat. He straightened his coat with his gloved hands.

"So long, bright boy," he said to George. "You got a lot of luck."

"That's the truth," Max said. "You ought to play the races, bright boy."

The two of them went out the door. George watched them, through the window, pass under the arc-light and cross the street. In their tight overcoats and derby hats they looked like a vaudeville team. George went back through the swinging-door into the kitchen and untied Nick and the cook.

"I don't want any more of that," said Sam, the cook. "I don't want any more of that."

Nick stood up. He had never had a towel in his mouth before.

"Say," he said. "What the hell?" He was trying to swagger it off.

"They were going to kill Ole Andreson," George said. "They were going to shoot him when he came in to eat."

"Ole Andreson?"

"Sure."

The cook felt the corners of his mouth with his thumbs.

"They all gone?" he asked.

"Yeah," said George. "They're gone now."

"I don't like it," said the cook. "I don't like any of it at all."

"Listen," George said to Nick. "You better go see Ole Andreson."

"All right."

"You better not have anything to do with it at all," Sam, the cook, said. "You better stay way out of it."

"Don't go if you don't want to," George said.

"Mixing up in this ain't going to get you anywhere," the cook said. "You stay out of it."

"I'll go see him," Nick said to George. "Where does he live?"

The cook turned away.

"Little boys always know what they want to do," he said.

"He lives up at Hirsch's rooming-house," George said to Nick.

"I'll go up there."

Outside the arc-light shone through the bare branches of a tree. Nick walked up the street beside the car-tracks and turned at the next arc-light down a side-street. Three houses up the street was Hirsch's rooming-house. Nick walked up the two steps and pushed the bell. A woman came to the door.

"Is Ole Andreson here?"

"Do you want to see him?"

"Yes, if he's in."

Nick followed the woman up a flight of stairs and back to the end of a corridor. She knocked on the door.

"Who is it?"

"It's somebody to see you, Mr. Andreson," the woman said.

"It's Nick Adams."

"Come in."

Nick opened the door and went into the room. Ole Andreson was lying on the bed with all his clothes on. He had been a heavyweight prizefighter and he was too long for the bed. He lay with his head on two pillows. He did not look at Nick.

"What was it?" he asked.

"I was up at Henry's," Nick said, "and two fellows came in and tied up me and the cook, and they said they were going to kill you."

It sounded silly when he said it. Ole Andreson said nothing.

"They put us out in the kitchen," Nick went on. "They were going to shoot you when you came in to supper.

Ole Andreson looked at the wall and did not say anything.

"George thought I better come and tell you about it."

"There isn't anything I can do about it," Ole Andreson said.

"I'll tell you what they were like."

"I don't want to know what they were like," Ole Andreson said. He looked at the wall. "Thanks for coming to tell me about it."

"That's all right."

Nick looked at the big man lying on the bed.

"Don't you want me to go and see the police?"

"No," Ole Andreson said. "That wouldn't do any good."

"Isn't there something I could do?"

"No. There ain't anything to do."

"Maybe it was just a bluff."

"No. It ain't just a bluff."

Ole Andreson rolled over toward the wall.

"The only thing is," he said, talking toward the wall, "I just can't make up my mind to go out. I been in here all day."

"Couldn't you get out of town?"

"No," Ole Andreson said. "I'm through with all that running around."

He looked at the wall.

"There ain't anything to do now."

"Couldn't you fix it up some way?"

"No. I got in wrong." He talked in the same

flat voice. "There ain't anything to do. After a while I'll make up my mind to go out."

"I better go back and see George," Nick said.

"So long," said Ole Andreson. He did not look toward Nick. "Thanks for coming around."

Nick went out. As he shut the door he saw Ole Andreson with all his clothes on, lying on the bed looking at the wall.

"He's been in his room all day," the landlady said down-stairs. "I guess he don't feel well. I said to him: 'Mr. Andreson, you ought to go out and take a walk on a nice fall day like this,' but he didn't feel like it."

"He doesn't want to go out."

"I'm sorry he don't feel well," the woman said. "He's an awfully nice man. He was in the ring, you know."

"I know it."

"You'd never know it except from the way his face is," the woman said. They stood talking just inside the street door. "He's just as gentle."

"Well, good-night, Mrs. Hirsch," Nick said.

"I'm not Mrs. Hirsch," the woman said. "She owns the place. I just look after it for her. I'm Mrs. Bell."

"Well, good-night, Mrs. Bell," Nick said.

"Good-night," the woman said.

Nick walked up the dark street to the corner under the arc-light, and then along the car-tracks to Henry's eating-house. George was inside, back of the counter.

"Did you see Ole?"

"Yes," said Nick. "He's in his room and he won't go out."

The cook opened the door from the kitchen when he heard Nick's voice.

"I don't even listen to it," he said and shut the door.

"Did you tell him about it?" George asked.

"Sure. I told him but he knows what it's all about." 10

"What's he going to do?"

"Nothing."

"They'll kill him."

"I guess they will."

"He must have got mixed up in something in Chicago."

"I guess so," said Nick.

"It's a hell of a thing."

"It's an awful thing," Nick said.

They did not say anything. George reached 20 down for a towel and wiped the counter.

"I wonder what he did?" Nick said.

"Double-crossed somebody. That's what they kill them for."

"I'm going to get out of this town," Nick said.

"Yes," said George. "That's a good thing to do."

"I can't stand to think about him waiting in the room and knowing he's going to get it. 30 It's too damned awful."

"Well," said George, "you better not think about it."

1926   1927

F. SCOTT FITZGERALD

1896–1940

AS A SCHOOLBOY in St. Paul, Minnesota, Fitzgerald wrote stories, kept a "Thought-book" in which he put down sharp impressions of people and his feelings about them, and produced plays of his own devising for his friends to act in. His adventures as an adolescent would later be transmuted into the nine Basil Duke Lee stories, which rank high among fictional accounts of the American boy on his way to manhood.

The young Fitzgerald had another ambition besides writing—to be an athlete. This he pursued with his habitual ardor at the Newman School and at Princeton, where it was finally extinguished. He was not fast enough or big enough (at five-feet-seven) to star on the football field. At Princeton he neglected his studies to the point of flunking out, was busy in Club politics, wrote the book for the Triangle Show, and took off for the theater and debutante parties in New York. Yet beneath the glitter of his life at college there was a steady seriousness about his writing. This was fostered by one of Princeton's most remarkable teachers, Christian Gauss, and by two campus writers, Edmund Wilson and John Peale Bishop.

With his war service completed (he did not go overseas) Fitzgerald worked for a time in an advertising agency. He was determined to marry Zelda Sayre of Montgomery, Alabama, whom he had met during the war. She would not consent unless there could be some financial stability in their lives. In July, 1919, he courageously quit his job and returned to the family attic in St. Paul to rewrite a novel in manuscript, "The Romantic Egoist," in which Dean Gauss and Scribner's had found too many flaws. From his Spartan months he emerged with *This Side of Paradise*, which was accepted by Scribner's and became an immediate success on publication in 1920.

This first novel is uneven in style (some of the scenes had appeared first in Princeton undergraduate magazines) but Fitzgerald had explored for the first time the ambitions and frustrations and the striving for purpose of his college generation. The glamor of the novel's wild nights concealed the fact that he had written the *Bildungsroman* of his time. He soon had many imitators. The "college novel" had arrived.

Success came suddenly. He was soon commanding top prices from the slick magazines for his short stories, and he turned them out in prodigious quantities. The total, in the end, was one hundred and sixty. The best of these Fitzgerald sorted out for reprinting in the four collections which appeared during his lifetime: *Flappers and Philosophers* (1920); *Tales of the Jazz Age* (1922); *All the Sad Young Men* (1926); and *Taps at Reveille* (1935).

The public image of Fitzgerald was quickly fixed and has been slow to fade: the successful but not very conscientious writer; the international playboy whose parties were the envy of the uninvited; and worse still, the man who wasted his talents and burned himself out. The image is a blurred one. Fitzgerald was, it is true, always in need of money, and he sometimes prostituted his art to get it. But he knew how to discriminate between the hack work which helped him buy gin and pay the doctors who tried to cure Zelda's mental illness and the other work by which he was determined to be famous. In college he had once remarked to Edmund Wilson, "I want to be one of the greatest writers that ever lived, don't you?" As his biographer, Arthur Mizener, says, "Though he lost the naïveté of this, he never lost its substance."

His second novel, *The Beautiful and Damned* (1922), is of its time, a story of a post-college couple who are determined to live richly but never worry about money. An inheritance eventually provides the money, but by then the beauty is gone and they are among the damned. Three years later Fitzgerald published what many critics believe is his best novel, *The Great Gatsby*. The theme is an important one: an American romantic from the wrong side of the tracks believes because he has made money (in the shady ways of the Prohibition era) that he can enter the charmed circle of Long Island society and carry off one of its lovely girls. He is defeated and is killed trying to protect the woman he wanted. The writing of this novel called into play Fitzgerald's best talents. It is as perfectly constructed as a novel by Henry James. The details are vivid and accurate. The theme of the outsider who can never enter what Dreiser once called "the walled city" is profoundly American.

When Fitzgerald's next novel, *Tender is the Night* (1934), appeared, America was in the midst of the Depression, and readers did not much relish this story of a young American psychiatrist living abroad and his wealthy patient whom he marries in order that he may cure her. When she is well, she is well enough to leave him for another man. This is Fitzgerald's most penetrating story about the behavior of the rich, but it sold only 13,000 copies in its first two years.

Burdened with debts—he estimated the sum at $40,000—Fitzgerald went to Hollywood in 1937 in order to recoup. He worked on scripts as faithfully as drinking bouts and his failing health permitted. The tortured end came in 1940 with a final heart attack. He left unfinished what might have been his greatest book, *The Last Tycoon*, a novel about Hollywood and American business. In 1941 his old friend Edmund Wilson published what he could assemble from notes and completed chapters. When Stephen Vincent Benét reviewed the volume, he said: "You can take off your hats, now, gentlemen, and I think perhaps you had better. This is not a legend, this is a reputation—and seen in perspective, it may well be one of the most secure reputations of our time."

F. Scott Fitzgerald, *The Stories of F. Scott Fitzgerald*, Malcolm Cowley, ed., New York, 1951.
————, *Three Novels: The Great Gatsby, Tender Is the Night, The Last Tycoon*, New York, 1953.
————, *Afternoon of an Author* (fourteen uncollected stories and six essays), Princeton, 1957.
Alfred Kazin, ed., *F. Scott Fitzgerald: The Man and His Work*, Cleveland, 1951.
J. E. Miller, *The Fictional Technique of Scott Fitzgerald*, The Hague, 1957.
Arthur Mizener, *The Far Side of Paradise, A Biography of F. Scott Fitzgerald*, Boston, 1951.
The Princeton University Library Chronicle, XII (Summer, 1951). Fitzgerald issue.

» *From:* ALL THE SAD YOUNG MEN «

THE RICH BOY

Begin with an individual, and before you know it you find that you have created a type; begin with a type, and you find that you have created—nothing. That is because we are all queer fish, queerer behind our faces and voices than we want any one to know or than we know ourselves. When I hear a man proclaiming himself an "average, honest, open fellow," I feel pretty sure that he has some definite and perhaps terrible abnormality which he has agreed to conceal—and his protestation of being average and honest and open is his way of reminding himself of his misprision.

There are no types, no plurals. There is a rich boy, and this is his and not his brothers' story. All my life I have lived among his brothers but this one has been my friend. Besides, if I wrote about his brothers I should have to begin by attacking all the lies that the poor have told about the rich and the rich have told about themselves—such a wild structure they have erected that when we pick up a book about the rich, some instinct prepares us for unreality. Even the intelligent and impassioned reporters of life have made the country of the rich as unreal as fairy-land.

Let me tell you about the very rich. They are different from you and me. They possess and enjoy early, and it does something to them, makes them soft where we are hard, and cynical where we are trustful, in a way that, unless you were born rich, it is very difficult to understand. They think, deep in their hearts, that they are better than we are because we had to discover the compensations and refuges of life for ourselves. Even when they enter deep into our world or sink below us, they still think that they are better than we are. They are different. The only way I can describe young Anson Hunter is to approach him as if he were a foreigner and cling stubbornly to my point of view. If I accept his for a moment I am lost—I have nothing to show but a preposterous movie.

II

Anson was the eldest of six children who would some day divide a fortune of fifteen million dollars, and he reached the age of reason—is it seven?—at the beginning of the century when daring young women were already gliding along Fifth Avenue in electric "mobiles." In those days he and his brother had an English governess who spoke the language very clearly and crisply and well, so that the two boys grew to speak as she did—their words and sentences were all crisp and clear and not run together as ours are. They didn't talk exactly like English children but acquired an accent that is peculiar to fashionable people in the city of New York.

In the summer the six children were moved from the house on 71st Street to a big estate in northern Connecticut. It was not a fashionable locality—Anson's father wanted to delay as long as possible his children's knowledge of that side of life. He was a man somewhat superior to his class, which composed New York society, and to his period, which was the snobbish and formalized vulgarity of the Gilded Age, and he wanted his sons to learn habits of concentration and have sound constitutions and grow up into right-living and successful men. He and his wife kept an eye on them as well as they were able until the two older boys went away to school, but in huge establishments this is difficult—it was much simpler in the series of small and medium-sized houses in which my own youth was spent—I was never far out of the reach of my mother's voice, of the sense of her presence, her approval or disapproval.

Anson's first sense of his superiority came to him when he realized the half-grudging American deference that was paid to him in the Connecticut village. The parents of the boys he played with always inquired after his father and mother, and were vaguely excited when their own children were asked to the Hunters' house. He accepted this as the natural state of things, and a sort of impatience with all groups of which he was not the center—in money, in position, in authority—remained with him for the rest of his life. He disdained to struggle with other boys for precedence—he expected it to be given him freely, and when it wasn't he withdrew into his family. His family was sufficient, for in the East money is still a somewhat feudal thing, a clan-forming thing. In the snobbish West, money separates families to form "sets."

At eighteen, when he went to New Haven, Anson was tall and thick-set, with a clear complexion and a healthy color from the ordered life he had led in school. His hair was yellow and grew in a funny way on his head, his nose was beaked—these two things kept him from being handsome—but he had a confident charm and a certain brusque style, and the upper-class men who passed him on the street knew without being told that he was a rich boy and had gone to one of the best schools. Nev-

ertheless, his very superiority kept him from being a success in college—the independence was mistaken for egotism, and the refusal to accept Yale standards with the proper awe seemed to belittle all those who had. So, long before he graduated, he began to shift the center of his life to New York.

He was at home in New York—there was his own house with "the kind of servants you can't get any more"—and his own family, of which, because of his good humor and a certain ability to make things go, he was rapidly becoming the centre, and the debutante parties, and the correct manly world of the men's clubs, and the occasional wild spree with the gallant girls whom New Haven only knew from the fifth row. His aspirations were conventional enough—they included even the irreproachable shadow he would some day marry, but they differed from the aspirations of the majority of young men in that there was no mist over them, none of that quality which is variously known as "idealism" or "illusion." Anson accepted without reservation the world of high finance and high extravagance, of divorce and dissipation, of snobbery and of privilege. Most of our lives end as a compromise—it was as a compromise that his life began.

He and I first met in the late summer of 1917 when he was just out of Yale, and, like the rest of us, was swept up into the systematized hysteria of the war. In the blue-green uniform of the naval aviation he came down to Pensacola, where the hotel orchestras played "I'm sorry, dear," and we young officers danced with the girls. Every one liked him, and though he ran with the drinkers and wasn't an especially good pilot, even the instructors treated him with a certain respect. He was always having long talks with them in his confident, logical voice—talks which ended by his getting himself, or, more frequently, another officer, out of some impending trouble. He was convivial, bawdy, robustly avid for pleasure, and we were all surprised when he fell in love with a conservative and rather proper girl.

Her name was Paula Legendre, a dark, serious beauty from somewhere in California. Her family kept a winter residence just outside of town, and in spite of her primness she was enormously popular; there is a large class of men whose egotism can't endure humor in a woman. But Anson wasn't that sort, and I couldn't understand the attraction of her "sincerity"—that was the thing to say about her—

for his keen and somewhat sardonic mind.

Nevertheless, they fell in love—and on her terms. He no longer joined the twilight gathering at the De Sota bar, and whenever they were seen together they were engaged in a long, serious dialogue, which must have gone on several weeks. Long afterward he told me that it was not about anything in particular but was composed on both sides of immature and even meaningless statements—the emotional content that gradually came to fill it grew up not out of the words but out of its enormous seriousness. It was a sort of hypnosis. Often it was interrupted, giving way to that emasculated humor we call fun; when they were alone it was resumed again, solemn, low-keyed, and pitched so as to give each other a sense of unity in feeling and thought. They came to resent any interruptions of it, to be unresponsive to facetiousness about life, even to the mild cynicism of their contemporaries. They were only happy when the dialogue was going on, and its seriousness bathed them like the amber glow of an open fire. Toward the end there came an interruption they did not resent—it began to be interrupted by passion.

Oddly enough, Anson was as engrossed in the dialogue as she was and as profoundly affected by it, yet at the same time aware that on his side much was insincere, and on hers much was merely simple. At first, too, he despised her emotional simplicity as well, but with his love her nature deepened and blossomed, and he could despise it no longer. He felt that if he could enter into Paula's warm safe life he would be happy. The long preparation of the dialogue removed any constraint—he taught her some of what he had learned from more adventurous women, and she responded with a rapt holy intensity. One evening after a dance they agreed to marry, and he wrote a long letter about her to his mother. The next day Paula told him that she was rich, that she had a personal fortune of nearly a million dollars.

III

It was exactly as if they could say "Neither of us has anything: we shall be poor together" —just as delightful that they should be rich instead. It gave them the same communion of adventure. Yet when Anson got leave in April, and Paula and her mother accompanied him North, she was impressed with the standing of his family in New York and with the scale on which they lived. Alone with Anson for the first time in the rooms where he had played as a boy, she was filled with a comfortable emotion, as though she were preeminently safe and taken care of. The pictures of Anson in a skull cap at his first school, of Anson on horseback with the sweetheart of a mysterious forgotten summer, of Anson in a gay group of ushers and bridesmaids at a wedding, made her jealous of his life apart from her in the past, and so completely did his authoritative person seem to sum up and typify these possessions of his that she was inspired with the idea of being married immediately and returning to Pensacola as his wife.

But an immediate marriage wasn't discussed —even the engagement was to be secret until after the war. When she realized that only two days of his leave remained, her dissatisfaction crystallized in the intention of making him as unwilling to wait as she was. They were driving to the country for dinner, and she determined to force the issue that night.

Now a cousin of Paula's was staying with them at the Ritz, a severe, bitter girl who loved Paula but was somewhat jealous of her impressive engagement, and as Paula was late in dressing, the cousin, who wasn't going to the party, received Anson in the parlor of the suite.

Anson had met friends at five o'clock and drunk freely and indiscreetly with them for an hour. He left the Yale Club at a proper time, and his mother's chauffeur drove him to the Ritz, but his usual capacity was not in evidence, and the impact of the steam-heated sitting-room made him suddenly dizzy. He knew it, and he was both amused and sorry.

Paula's cousin was twenty-five, but she was exceptionally naïve, and at first failed to realize what was up. She had never met Anson before, and she was surprised when he mumbled strange information and nearly fell off his chair, but until Paula appeared it didn't occur to her that what she had taken for the odor of a dry-cleaned uniform was really whiskey. But Paula understood as soon as she appeared; her only thought was to get Anson away before her mother saw him, and at the look in her eyes the cousin understood too.

When Paula and Anson descended to the limousine they found two men inside, both asleep; they were the men with whom he had been drinking at the Yale Club, and they were also going to the party. He had entirely forgotten their presence in the car. On the way to Hempstead they awoke and sang. Some of the songs were rough, and though Paula tried to reconcile herself to the fact that Anson had few verbal inhibitions, her lips tightened with shame and distaste.

Back at the hotel the cousin, confused and agitated, considered the incident, and then walked into Mrs. Legendre's bedroom, saying: "Isn't he funny?"

"Who is funny?"

10　"Why—Mr. Hunter. He seemed so funny." Mrs. Legendre looked at her sharply.

"How is he funny?"

"Why, he said he was French. I didn't know he was French."

"That's absurd. You must have misunderstood." She smiled: "It was a joke."

The cousin shook her head stubbornly.

"No. He said he was brought up in France. He said he couldn't speak any English, and

20　that's why he couldn't talk to me. And he couldn't!"

Mrs. Legendre looked away with impatience just as the cousin added thoughtfully, "Perhaps it was because he was so drunk," and walked out of the room.

This curious report was true. Anson, finding his voice thick and uncontrollable, had taken the unusual refuge of announcing that he spoke no English. Years afterward he used to tell that

30　part of the story, and he invariably communicated the uproarious laughter which the memory aroused in him.

Five times in the next hour Mrs. Legendre tried to get Hempstead on the phone. When she succeeded, there was a ten-minute delay before she heard Paula's voice on the wire.

"Cousin Jo told me Anson was intoxicated."

"Oh, no. . . ."

"Oh, yes. Cousin Jo says he was intoxicated.

40　He told her he was French and fell off his chair and behaved as if he was very intoxicated. I don't want you to come home with him."

"Mother, he's all right! Please don't worry about—"

"But I do worry. I think it's dreadful. I want you to promise me not to come home with him."

"I'll take care of it, mother. . . ."

"I don't want you to come home with him."

"All right, mother. Good-by."

50　"Be sure now, Paula. Ask some one to bring you."

Deliberately Paula took the receiver from her ear and hung it up. Her face was flushed with helpless annoyance. Anson was stretched asleep out in a bedroom upstairs, while the dinner-

party below was proceeding lamely toward conclusion.

The hour's drive had sobered him somewhat —his arrival was merely hilarious—and Paula hoped that the evening was not spoiled, after all, but two imprudent cocktails before dinner completed the disaster. He talked boisterously and somewhat offensively to the party at large for fifteen minutes, and then slid silently under the table; like a man in an old print—but, unlike an old print, it was rather horrible without being at all quaint. None of the young girls present remarked upon the incident—it seemed to merit only silence. His uncle and two other men carried him upstairs, and it was just after this that Paula was called to the phone.

An hour later Anson awoke in a fog of nervous agony, through which he perceived after a moment the figure of his Uncle Robert standing by the door.

". . . I said are you better?"

"What?"

"Do you feel better, old man?"

"Terrible," said Anson.

"I'm going to try you on another bromo-seltzer. If you can hold it down, it'll do you good to sleep."

With an effort Anson slid his legs from the bed and stood up.

"I'm all right," he said dully.

"Take it easy."

"I thin' if you gave me a glass brandy I could go downstairs."

"Oh, no—"

"Yes, that's the only thin'. I'm all right now. . . . I suppose I'm in dutch dow' there."

"They know you're a little under the weather," said his uncle deprecatingly. "But don't worry about it. Schuyler didn't even get here. He passed away in the locker-room over at the Links."

Indifferent to any opinion, except Paula's, Anson was nevertheless determined to save the débris of the evening, but when after a cold bath he made his appearance most of the party had already left. Paula got up immediately to go home.

In the limousine the old serious dialogue began. She had known that he drank, she admitted, but she had never expected anything like this—it seemed to her that perhaps they were not suited to each other, after all. Their ideas about life were too different, and so forth. When she finished speaking, Anson spoke in turn, very soberly. Then Paula said she'd have to think it over; she wouldn't decide tonight; she was not angry but she was terribly sorry. Nor would she let him come into the hotel with her, but just before she got out of the car she leaned and kissed him unhappily on the cheek.

The next afternoon Anson had a long talk with Mrs. Legendre while Paula sat listening in silence. It was agreed that Paula was to brood over the incident for a proper period and then, if mother and daughter thought it best, they would follow Anson to Pensacola. On his part he apologized with sincerity and dignity— that was all; with every card in her hand Mrs. Legendre was unable to establish any advantage over him. He made no promises, showed no humility, only delivered a few serious comments on life which brought him off with rather a moral superiority at the end. When they came South three weeks later, neither Anson in his satisfaction nor Paula in her relief at the reunion realized that the psychological moment had passed forever.

IV

He dominated and attracted her, and at the same time filled her with anxiety. Confused by his mixture of solidity and self-indulgence, of sentiment and cynicism—incongruities which her gentle mind was unable to resolve—Paula grew to think of him as two alternating personalities. When she saw him alone, or at a formal party, or with his casual inferiors, she felt a tremendous pride in his strong, attractive presence, the paternal, understanding stature of his mind. In other company she became uneasy when what had been a fine imperviousness to mere gentility showed its other face. The other face was gross, humorous, reckless of everything but pleasure. It startled her mind temporarily away from him, even led her into a short covert experiment with an old beau, but it was no use—after four months of Anson's enveloping vitality there was an anæmic pallor in all other men.

In July he was ordered abroad, and their tenderness and desire reached a crescendo. Paula considered a last-minute marriage—decided against it only because there were always cocktails on his breath now, but the parting itself made her physically ill with grief. After his departure she wrote him long letters of regret for the days of love they had missed by waiting. In August Anson's plane slipped down into the North Sea. He was pulled onto a destroyer after a night in the water and sent to hospital with pneumonia; the armistice was signed before he was finally sent home.

Then, with every opportunity given back to them, with no material obstacle to overcome, the secret weavings of their temperaments came between them, drying up their kisses and their tears, making their voices less loud to one another, muffling the intimate chatter of their hearts until the old communication was only possible by letters, from far away. One afternoon a society reporter waited for two hours in the Hunters' house for a confirmation of their engagement. Anson denied it; nevertheless an early issue carried the report as a leading paragraph—they were "constantly seen together at Southampton, Hot Springs, and Tuxedo Park." But the serious dialogue had turned a corner into a long-sustained quarrel, and the affair was almost played out. Anson got drunk flagrantly and missed an engagement with her, whereupon Paula made certain behavioristic demands. His despair was helpless before his pride and his knowledge of himself: the engagement was definitely broken.

"Dearest," said their letters now, "Dearest, Dearest, when I wake up in the middle of the night and realize that after all it was not to be, I feel that I want to die. I can't go on living any more. Perhaps when we meet this summer we may talk things over and decide differently —we were so excited and sad that day, and I don't feel that I can live all my life without you. You speak of other people. Don't you know there are no other people for me, but only you. . . ."

But as Paula drifted here and there around the East she would sometimes mention her gaieties to make him wonder. Anson was too acute to wonder. When he saw a man's name in her letters he felt more sure of her and a little disdainful—he was always superior to such things. But he still hoped that they would some day marry.

Meanwhile he plunged vigorously into all the movement and glitter of post-bellum New York, entering a brokerage house, joining half a dozen clubs, dancing late, and moving in three worlds—his own world, the world of young Yale graduates, and that section of the half-world which rests one end on Broadway. But there was always a thorough and infractible eight hours devoted to his work in Wall Street, where the combination of his influential family connection, his sharp intelligence, and his abundance of sheer physical energy brought him almost immediately forward. He had one of those invaluable minds with partitions in it; sometimes he appeared at his office refreshed by less than an hour's sleep, but such occurrences were rare. So early as 1920 his income in salary and commissions exceeded twelve thousand dollars.

10 As the Yale tradition slipped into the past he became more and more of a popular figure among his classmates in New York, more popular than he had ever been in college. He lived in a great house, and had the means of introducing young men into other great houses. Moreover, his life already seemed secure, while theirs, for the most part, had arrived again at precarious beginnings. They commenced to turn to him for amusement and escape, and 20 Anson responded readily, taking pleasure in helping people and arranging their affairs.

There were no men in Paula's letters now, but a note of tenderness ran through them that had not been there before. From several sources he heard that she had "a heavy beau," Lowell Thayer, a Bostonian of wealth and position, and though he was sure she still loved him, it made him uneasy to think that he might lose her, after all. Save for one unsatisfactory day she had not been in New York for almost 30 five months, and as the rumors multiplied he became increasingly anxious to see her. In February he took his vacation and went down to Florida.

Palm Beach sprawled plump and opulent between the sparkling sapphire of Lake Worth, flawed here and there by house-boats at anchor, and the great turquoise bar of the Atlantic Ocean. The huge bulks of the Breakers and the Royal Poinciana rose as twin paunches from 40 the bright level of the sand, and around them clustered the Dancing Glade, Bradley's House of Chance, and a dozen modistes and milliners with goods at triple prices from New York. Upon the trellissed veranda of the Breakers two hundred women stepped right, stepped left, wheeled, and slid in that then celebrated calisthenic known as the double-shuffle, while in half-time to the music two thousand bracelets clicked up and down on two hundred arms. 50 At the Everglades Club after dark Paula and Lowell Thayer and Anson and a casual fourth played bridge with hot cards. It seemed to Anson that her kind, serious face was wan and tired—she had been around now for four, five, years. He had known her for three.

"Two spades."

"Cigarette? . . . Oh, I beg your pardon. By me."

"By."

"I'll double three spades."

There were a dozen tables of bridge in the room, which was filling up with smoke. Anson's eyes met Paula's, held them persistently even when Thayer's glance fell between them. . . .

"What was bid?" he asked abstractedly.

"Rose of Washington Square"

sang the young people in the corners:

> *"I'm withering there*
> *In basement air—"*

The smoke banked like fog, and the opening of a door filled the room with blown swirls of ectoplasm. Little Bright Eyes streaked past the tables seeking Mr. Conan Doyle among the Englishmen who were posing as Englishmen about the lobby.

"You could cut it with a knife."

". . . cut it with a knife."

". . . a knife."

At the end of the rubber Paula suddenly got up and spoke to Anson in a tense, low voice. With scarcely a glance at Lowell Thayer, they walked out the door and descended a long flight of stone steps—in a moment they were walking hand in hand along the moonlit beach.

"Darling, darling. . . ." They embraced recklessly, passionately, in a shadow. . . . Then Paula drew back her face to let his lips say what she wanted to hear—she could feel the words forming as they kissed again. . . . Again she broke away, listening, but as he pulled her close once more she realized that he had said nothing—only *"Darling! Darling!"* in that deep, sad whisper that always made her cry. Humbly, obediently, her emotions yielded to him and the tears streamed down her face, but her heart kept on crying: "Ask me—oh, Anson, dearest, ask me!"

"Paula. . . . *Paula!*"

The words wrung her heart like hands, and Anson, feeling her tremble, knew that emotion was enough. He need say no more, commit their destinies to no practical enigma. Why should he, when he might hold her so, biding his own time, for another year—forever? He was considering them both, her more than himself. For a moment, when she said suddenly that she must go back to her hotel, he hesitated, thinking, first, "This is the moment, after all," and then: "No, let it wait—she is mine. . . ."

He had forgotten that Paula too was worn away inside with the strain of three years. Her mood passed forever in the night.

He went back to New York next morning filled with a certain restless dissatisfaction. Late in April, without warning, he received a telegram from Bar Harbor in which Paula told him that she was engaged to Lowell Thayer, and that they would be married immediately in Boston. What he never really believed could happen had happened at last.

Anson filled himself with whiskey that morning, and going to the office, carried on his work without a break—rather with a fear of what would happen if he stopped. In the evening he went out as usual, saying nothing of what had occurred; he was cordial, humorous, unabstracted. But one thing he could not help—for three days, in any place, in any company, he would suddenly bend his head into his hands and cry like a child.

V

In 1922 when Anson went abroad with the junior partner to investigate some London loans, the journey intimated that he was to be taken into the firm. He was twenty-seven now, a little heavy without being definitely stout, and with a manner older than his years. Old people and young people liked him and trusted him, and mothers felt safe when their daughters were in his charge, for he had a way, when he came into a room, of putting himself on a footing with the oldest and most conservative people there. "You and I," he seemed to say, "we're solid. We understand."

He had an instinctive and rather charitable knowledge of the weaknesses of men and women, and, like a priest, it made him the more concerned for the maintenance of outward forms. It was typical of him that every Sunday morning he taught in a fashionable Episcopal Sunday school—even though a cold shower and a quick change into a cutaway coat were all that separated him from the wild night before.

After his father's death he was the practical head of his family, and, in effect, guided the destinies of the younger children. Through a complication his authority did not extend to his father's estate, which was administrated by his Uncle Robert, who was the horsey member of the family, a good-natured, hard-drinking member of that set which centres about Wheatley Hills.

Uncle Robert and his wife, Edna, had been great friends of Anson's youth, and the former was disappointed when his nephew's superiority failed to take a horsey form. He backed him for a city club which was the most difficult in America to enter—one could only join if one's family had "helped to build up New York" (or, in other words, were rich before 1880)—and when Anson, after his election, neglected it for the Yale Club, Uncle Robert gave him a little talk on the subject. But when on top of that Anson declined to enter Robert Hunter's own conservative and somewhat neglected brokerage house, his manner grew cooler. Like a primary teacher who has taught all he knew, he slipped out of Anson's life.

There were so many friends in Anson's life— scarcely one for whom he had not done some unusual kindness and scarcely one whom he did not occasionally embarrass by his bursts of rough conversation or his habit of getting drunk whenever and however he liked. It annoyed him when any one else blundered in that regard—about his own lapses he was always humorous. Odd things happened to him and he told them with infectious laughter.

I was working in New York that spring, and I used to lunch with him at the Yale Club, which my university was sharing until the completion of our own. I had read of Paula's marriage, and one afternoon, when I asked him about her, something moved him to tell me the story. After that he frequently invited me to family dinners at his house and behaved as though there was a special relation between us, as though with his confidence a little of that consuming memory had passed into me.

I found that despite the trusting mothers, his attitude toward girls was not indiscriminately protective. It was up to the girl—if she showed an inclination toward looseness, she must take care of herself, even with him.

"Life," he would explain sometimes, "has made a cynic of me."

By life he meant Paula. Sometimes, especially when he was drinking, it became a little twisted in his mind, and he thought that she had callously thrown him over.

This "cynicism," or rather his realization that naturally fast girls were not worth sparing, led to his affair with Dolly Karger. It wasn't his only affair in those years, but it came nearest to touching him deeply, and it had a profound effect upon his attitude toward life.

Dolly was the daughter of a notorious "publicist" who had married into society. She herself grew up into the Junior League, came out at the Plaza, and went to the Assembly; and only a few old families like the Hunters could question whether or not she "belonged," for her picture was often in the papers, and she had more enviable attention than many girls who undoubtedly did. She was dark-haired, with carmine lips and a high, lovely color, which she concealed under pinkish-gray powder all through the first year out, because high color was unfashionable—Victorian-pale was the thing to be. She wore black, severe suits and stood with her hands in her pockets leaning a little forward, with a humorous restraint on her face. She danced exquisitely—better than anything she liked to dance—better than anything except making love. Since she was ten she had always been in love, and, usually, with some boy who didn't respond to her. Those who did —and there were many—bored her after a brief encounter, but for her failures she reserved the warmest spot in her heart. When she met them she would always try once more— sometimes she succeeded, more often she failed.

It never occurred to this gypsy of the unattainable that there was a certain resemblance in those who refused to love her—they shared a hard intuition that saw through to her weakness, not a weakness of emotion but a weakness of rudder. Anson perceived this when he first met her, less than a month after Paula's marriage. He was drinking rather heavily, and he pretended for a week that he was falling in love with her. Then he dropped her abruptly and forgot—immediately he took up the commanding position in her heart.

Like so many girls of that day Dolly was slackly and indiscreetly wild. The unconventionality of a slightly older generation had been simply one facet of a post-war movement to discredit obsolete manners—Dolly's was both older and shabbier, and she saw in Anson the two extremes which the emotionally shiftless woman seeks, an abandon to indulgence alternating with a protective strength. In his character she felt both the sybarite and the solid rock, and these two satisfied every need of her nature.

She felt that it was going to be difficult, but she mistook the reason—she thought that An-

son and his family expected a more spectacular marriage, but she guessed immediately that her advantage lay in his tendency to drink.

They met at the large débutante dances, but as her infatuation increased they managed to be more and more together. Like most mothers, Mrs. Karger believed that Anson was exceptionally reliable, so she allowed Dolly to go with him to distant country clubs and suburban houses without inquiring closely into their activities or questioning her explanations when they came in late. At first these explanations might have been accurate, but Dolly's worldly ideas of capturing Anson were soon engulfed in the rising sweep of her emotion. Kisses in the back of taxis and motor-cars were no longer enough; they did a curious thing:

They dropped out of their world for a while and made another world just beneath it where Anson's tippling and Dolly's irregular hours would be less noticed and commented on. It was composed, this world, of varying elements —several of Anson's Yale friends and their wives, two or three young brokers and bond salesmen and a handful of unattached men, fresh from college, with money and a propensity to dissipation. What this world lacked in spaciousness and scale it made up for by allowing them a liberty that it scarcely permitted itself. Moreover, it centred around them and permitted Dolly the pleasure of a faint condescension—a pleasure which Anson, whose whole life was a condescension from the certitudes of his childhood, was unable to share.

He was not in love with her, and in the long feverish winter of their affair he frequently told her so. In the spring he was weary—he wanted to renew his life at some other source—moreover, he saw that either he must break with her now or accept the responsibility of a definite seduction. Her family's encouraging attitude precipitated his decision—one evening when Mr. Karger knocked discreetly at the library door to announce that he had left a bottle of old brandy in the dining-room, Anson felt that life was hemming him in. That night he wrote her a short letter in which he told her that he was going on his vacation, and that in view of all the circumstances they had better meet no more.

It was June. His family had closed up the house and gone to the country, so he was living temporarily at the Yale Club. I had heard about his affair with Dolly as it developed— accounts salted with humor, for he despised unstable women, and granted them no place in the social edifice in which he believed—and when he told me that night that he was definitely breaking with her I was glad. I had seen Dolly here and there, and each time with a feeling of pity at the hopelessness of her struggle, and of shame at knowing so much about her that I had no right to know. She was what is known as "a pretty little thing," but there was a certain recklessness which rather fascinated me. Her dedication to the goddess of waste would have been less obvious had she been less spirited—she would most certainly throw herself away, but I was glad when I heard that the sacrifice would not be consummated in my sight.

Anson was going to leave the letter of farewell at her house next morning. It was one of the few houses left open in the Fifth Avenue district, and he knew that the Kargers, acting upon erroneous information from Dolly, had foregone a trip abroad to give their daughter her chance. As he stepped out the door of the Yale Club into Madison Avenue the postman passed him, and he followed back inside. The first letter that caught his eye was in Dolly's hand.

He knew what it would be—a lonely and tragic monologue, full of the reproaches he knew, the invoked memories, the "I wonder if's"—all the immemorial intimacies that he had communicated to Paula Legendre in what seemed another age. Thumbing over some bills, he brought it on top again and opened it. To his surprise it was a short, somewhat formal note, which said that Dolly would be unable to go to country with him for the week-end, because Perry Hull from Chicago had unexpectedly come to town. It added that Anson had brought this on himself: "—if I felt that you loved me as I love you I would go with you at any time, any place, but Perry is *so* nice, and he so much wants me to marry him—"

Anson smiled contemptuously—he had had experience with such decoy epistles. Moreover, he knew how Dolly had labored over this plan, probably sent for the faithful Perry and calculated the time of his arrival—even labored over the note so that it would make him jealous without driving him away. Like most compromises, it had neither force nor vitality but only a timorous despair.

Suddenly he was angry. He sat down in the lobby and read it again. Then he went to the phone, called Dolly and told her in his clear, compelling voice that he had received her note and would call for her at five o'clock as they had previously planned. Scarcely waiting for the pretended uncertainty of her "Perhaps I can see you for an hour," he hung up the receiver and went down to his office. On the way he tore his own letter into bits and dropped it in the street.

He was not jealous—she meant nothing to him—but at her pathetic ruse everything stubborn and self-indulgent in him came to the surface. It was a presumption from a mental inferior and it could not be overlooked. If she wanted to know to whom she belonged she would see.

He was on the door-step at quarter past five. Dolly was dressed for the street, and he listened in silence to the paragraph of "I can only see you for an hour," which she had begun on the phone.

"Put on your hat, Dolly," he said, "we'll take a walk."

They strolled up Madison Avenue and over to Fifth while Anson's shirt dampened upon his portly body in the deep heat. He talked little, scolding her, making no love to her, but before they had walked six blocks she was his again, apologizing for the note, offering not to see Perry at all as an atonement, offering anything. She thought that he had come because he was beginning to love her.

"I'm hot," he said when they reached 71st Street. "This is a winter suit. If I stop by the house and change, would you mind waiting for me downstairs? I'll only be a minute."

She was happy; the intimacy of his being hot, of any physical fact about him, thrilled her. When they came to the iron-grated door and Anson took out his key she experienced a sort of delight.

Downstairs it was dark, and after he ascended in the lift Dolly raised a curtain and looked out through opaque lace at the houses over the way. She heard the lift machinery stop, and with the notion of teasing him pressed the button that brought it down. Then on what was more than an impulse she got into it and sent it up to what she guessed was his floor.

"Anson," she called, laughing a little.

"Just a minute," he answered from his bedroom . . . then after a brief delay: "Now you can come in."

He had changed and was buttoning his vest. "This is my room," he said lightly. "How do you like it?"

She caught sight of Paula's picture on the wall and stared at it in fascination, just as Paula had stared at the pictures of Anson's childish sweethearts five years before. She knew something about Paula—sometimes she tortured herself with fragments of the story.

Suddenly she came close to Anson, raising her arms. They embraced. Outside the area window a soft artificial twilight already hovered, though the sun was still bright on a back roof across the way. In half an hour the room would be quite dark. The uncalculated opportunity overwhelmed them, made them both breathless, and they clung more closely. It was eminent, inevitable. Still holding one another, they raised their heads—their eyes fell together upon Paula's picture, staring down at them from the wall.

Suddenly Anson dropped his arms, and sitting down at his desk tried the drawer with a bunch of keys.

"Like a drink?" he asked in a gruff voice.

"No, Anson."

He poured himself half a tumbler of whiskey, swallowed it, and then opened the door into the hall.

"Come on," he said.

Dolly hesitated.

"Anson—I'm going to the country with you tonight, after all. You understand that, don't you?"

"Of course," he answered brusquely.

In Dolly's car they rode on to Long Island, closer in their emotions than they had ever been before. They knew what would happen—not with Paula's face to remind them that something was lacking, but when they were alone in the still, hot Long Island night they did not care.

The estate in Port Washington where they were to spend the week-end belonged to a cousin of Anson's who had married a Montana copper operator. An interminable drive began at the lodge and twisted under imported poplar saplings toward a huge, pink, Spanish house. Anson had often visited there before.

After dinner they danced at the Linx Club. About midnight Anson assured himself that his cousins would not leave before two—then he explained that Dolly was tired; he would take her home and return to the dance later. Trembling a little with excitement, they got into a borrowed car together and drove to Port Washington. As they reached the lodge he stopped and spoke to the night-watchman.

"When are you making a round, Carl?"

"Right away."

"Then you'll be here till everybody's in?"

"Yes, sir."

"All right. Listen: if any automobile, no matter whose it is, turns in at this gate, I want you to phone the house immediately." He put a five-dollar bill into Carl's hand. "Is that clear?"

"Yes, Mr. Anson." Being of the Old World, he neither winked nor smiled. Yet Dolly sat with her face turned slightly away.

Anson had a key. Once inside he poured a drink for both of them—Dolly left hers untouched—then he ascertained definitely the location of the phone, and found that it was within easy hearing distance of their rooms, both of which were on the first floor.

Five minutes later he knocked at the door of Dolly's room.

"Anson?" He went in, closing the door behind him. She was in bed, leaning up anxiously with elbows on the pillow; sitting beside her he took her in his arms.

"Anson, darling."

He didn't answer.

"Anson. . . . Anson! I love you. . . . Say you love me. Say it now—can't you say it now? Even if you don't mean it?"

He did not listen. Over her head he perceived that the picture of Paula was hanging here upon this wall.

He got up and went close to it. The frame gleamed faintly with thrice-reflected moonlight —within was a blurred shadow of a face that he saw he did not know. Almost sobbing, he turned around and stared with abomination at the little figure on the bed.

"This is all foolishness," he said thickly. "I don't know what I was thinking about. I don't love you and you'd better wait for somebody that loves you. I don't love you a bit, can't you understand?"

His voice broke, and he went hurriedly out. Back in the salon he was pouring himself a drink with uneasy fingers, when the front door opened suddenly, and his cousin came in.

"Why, Anson, I hear Dolly's sick," she began solicitously. "I hear she's sick. . . ."

"It was nothing," he interrupted, raising his voice so that it would carry into Dolly's room. "She was a little tired. She went to bed."

For a long time afterward Anson believed that a protective God sometimes interfered in human affairs. But Dolly Karger, lying awake and staring at the ceiling never again believed in anything at all.

VI

When Dolly married during the following autumn, Anson was in London on business. Like Paula's marriage, it was sudden, but it affected him in a different way. At first he felt that it was funny, and had an inclination to laugh when he thought of it. Later it depressed him—it made him feel old.

There was something repetitive about it— why, Paula and Dolly had belonged to different generations. He had a foretaste of the sensation of a man of forty who hears that the daughter of an old flame has married. He wired congratulations and, as was not the case with Paula, they were sincere—he had never really hoped that Paula would be happy.

When he returned to New York, he was made a partner in the firm, and, as his responsibilities increased, he had less time on his hands. The refusal of a life-insurance company to issue him a policy made such an impression on him that he stopped drinking for a year, and claimed that he felt better physically, though I think he missed the convivial recounting of those Celliniesque adventures which, in his early twenties, had played such a part of his life. But he never abandoned the Yale Club. He was a figure there, a personality, and the tendency of his class, who were now seven years out of college, to drift away to more sober haunts was checked by his presence.

His day was never too full nor his mind too weary to give any sort of aid to any one who asked it. What had been done at first through pride and superiority had become a habit and a passion. And there was always something—a younger brother in trouble at New Haven, a quarrel to be patched up between a friend and his wife, a position to be found for this man, an investment for that. But his specialty was the solving of problems for young married people. Young married people fascinated him and their apartments were almost sacred to him—he knew the story of their love-affair, advised them where to live and how, and remembered their babies' names. Toward young wives his attitude was circumspect: he never abused the trust which their husbands—strangely enough in view of his unconcealed irregularities—invariably reposed in him.

He came to take a vicarious pleasure in happy marriages, and to be inspired to an almost equally pleasant melancholy by those that went astray. Not a season passed that he did not witness the collapse of an affair that perhaps he himself had fathered. When Paula was divorced and almost immediately remarried to another Bostonian, he talked about her to me all one afternoon. He would never love any one as he had loved Paula, but he insisted that he no longer cared. 10

"I'll never marry," he came to say; "I've seen too much of it, and I know a happy marriage is a very rare thing. Besides, I'm too old."

But he did believe in marriage. Like all men who spring from a happy and successful marriage, he believed in it passionately—nothing he had seen would change his belief, his cynicism dissolved upon it like air. But he did really believe he was too old. At twenty-eight he began to accept with equanimity the prospect of 20 marrying without romantic love; he resolutely chose a New York girl of his own class, pretty, intelligent, congenial, above reproach—and set about falling in love with her. The things he had said to Paula with sincerity, to other girls with grace, he could no longer say at all without smiling, or with the force necessary to convince.

"When I'm forty," he told his friends, "I'll be ripe. I'll fall for some chorus girl like the rest." 30

Nevertheless, he persisted in his attempt. His mother wanted to see him married, and he could now well afford it—he had a seat on the Stock Exchange, and his earned income came to twenty-five thousand a year. The idea was agreeable: when his friends—he spent most of his time with the set he and Dolly had evolved —closed themselves in behind domestic doors at night, he no longer rejoiced in his freedom. He even wondered if he should have married 40 Dolly. Not even Paula had loved him more, and he was learning the rarity, in a single life, of encountering true emotion.

Just as this mood began to creep over him a disquieting story reached his ear. His aunt Edna, a woman just this side of forty, was carrying on an open intrigue with a dissolute, hard-drinking young man named Cary Sloane. Every one knew of it except Anson's Uncle Robert, who for fifteen years had talked long 50 in clubs and taken his wife for granted.

Anson heard the story again and again with increasing annoyance. Something of his old feeling for his uncle came back to him, a feeling that was more than personal, a reversion toward that family solidarity on which he had based his pride. His intuition singled out the essential point of the affair, which was that his uncle shouldn't be hurt. It was his first experiment in unsolicited meddling, but with his knowledge of Edna's character he felt that he could handle the matter better than a district judge or his uncle.

His uncle was in Hot Springs. Anson traced down the sources of the scandal so that there should be no possibility of mistake and then he called Edna and asked her to lunch with him at the Plaza next day. Something in his tone must have frightened her, for she was reluctant, but he insisted, putting off the date until she had no excuse for refusing.

She met him at the appointed time in the Plaza lobby, a lovely, faded, gray-eyed blonde in a coat of Russian sable. Five great rings, cold with diamonds and emeralds, sparkled on her slender hands. It occurred to Anson that it was his father's intelligence and not his uncle's that had earned the fur and the stones, the rich brilliance that buoyed up her passing beauty.

Though Edna scented his hostility, she was unprepared for the directness of his approach.

"Edna, I'm astonished at the way you've been acting," he said in a strong, frank voice. "At first I couldn't believe it."

"Believe what?" she demanded sharply.

"You needn't pretend with me, Edna. I'm talking about Cary Sloane. Aside from any other consideration, I didn't think you could treat Uncle Robert—"

"Now look here, Anson—" she began angrily, but his peremptory voice broke through hers:

"—and your children in such a way. You've been married eighteen years, and you're old enough to know better."

"You can't talk to me like that! You—"

"Yes, I can. Uncle Robert has always been my best friend." He was tremendously moved. He felt a real distress about his uncle, about his three young cousins.

Edna stood up, leaving her crab-flake cocktail untasted.

"This is the silliest thing—"

"Very well, if you won't listen to me I'll go to Uncle Robert and tell him the whole story— he's bound to hear it sooner or later. And afterward I'll go to old Moses Sloane."

Edna faltered back into her chair.

"Don't talk so loud," she begged him. Her eyes blurred with tears. "You have no idea how your voice carries. You might have chosen a less public place to make all these crazy accusations."

He didn't answer.

"Oh, you never liked me, I know," she went on. "You're just taking advantage of some silly gossip to try and break up the only interesting friendship I've ever had. What did I ever do to make you hate me so?"

Still Anson waited. There would be the appeal to his chivalry, then to his pity, finally to his superior sophistication—when he had shouldered his way through all these there would be admissions, and he could come to grips with her. By being silent, by being impervious, by returning constantly to his main weapon, which was his own true emotion, he bullied her into frantic despair as the luncheon hour slipped away. At two o'clock she took out a mirror and a handkerchief, shined away the marks of her tears and powdered the slight hollows where they had lain. She had agreed to meet him at her own house at five.

When he arrived she was stretched on a *chaise-longue* which was covered with cretonne for the summer, and the tears he had called up at luncheon seemed still to be standing in her eyes. Then he was aware of Cary Sloane's dark anxious presence upon the cold hearth.

"What's this idea of yours?" broke out Sloane immediately. "I understand you invited Edna to lunch and then threatened her on the basis of some cheap scandal."

Anson sat down.

"I have no reason to think it's only scandal."

"I hear you're going to take it to Robert Hunter, and to my father."

Anson nodded.

"Either you break it off—or I will," he said.

"What God damned business is it of yours, Hunter?"

"Don't lose your temper, Cary," said Edna nervously. "It's only a question of showing him how absurd—"

"For one thing, it's my name that's being handed around," interrupted Anson. "That's all that concerns you, Cary."

"Edna isn't a member of your family."

"She most certainly is!" His anger mounted. "Why—she owes this house and the rings on her fingers to my father's brains. When Uncle Robert married her she didn't have a penny."

They all looked at the rings as if they had a

significant bearing on the situation. Edna made a gesture to take them from her hand.

"I guess they're not the only rings in the world," said Sloane.

"Oh, this is absurd," cried Edna. "Anson, will you listen to me? I've found out how the silly story started. It was a maid I discharged who went right to the Chilicheffs—all these Russians pump things out of their servants and then put a false meaning on them." She brought down her fist angrily on the table: "And after Tom lent them the limousine for a whole month when we were South last winter—"

"Do you see?" demanded Sloane eagerly. "This maid got hold of the wrong end of the thing. She knew that Edna and I were friends, and she carried it to the Chilicheffs. In Russia they assume that if a man and a woman—"

He enlarged the theme to a disquisition upon social relations in the Caucasus.

"If that's the case it better be explained to Uncle Robert," said Anson dryly, "so that when the rumors do reach him he'll know they're not true."

Adopting the method he had followed with Edna at luncheon he let them explain it all away. He knew that they were guilty and that presently they would cross the line from explanation into justification and convict themselves more definitely than he could ever do. By seven they had taken the desperate step of telling him the truth—Robert Hunter's neglect, Edna's empty life, the casual dalliance that had flamed up into passion—but like so many true stories it had the misfortune of being old, and its enfeebled body beat helplessly against the armor of Anson's will. The threat to go to Sloane's father sealed their helplessness, for the latter, a retired cotton broker out of Alabama, was a notorious fundamentalist who controlled his son by a rigid allowance and the promise that at his next vagary the allowance would stop forever.

They dined at a small French restaurant, and the discussion continued—at one time Sloane resorted to physical threats, a little later they were both imploring him to give them time. But Anson was obdurate. He saw that Edna was breaking up, and that her spirit must not be refreshed by any renewal of their passion.

At two o'clock in a small night-club on 53d Street, Edna's nerves suddenly collapsed, and she cried to go home. Sloane had been drinking heavily all evening, and he was faintly maudlin, leaning on the table and weeping a little with his face in his hands. Quickly Anson gave them his terms. Sloane was to leave town for six months, and he must be gone within forty-eight hours. When he returned there was to be no resumption of the affair, but at the end of a year Edna might, if she wished, tell Robert Hunter that she wanted a divorce and go about it in the usual way.

He paused, gaining confidence from their faces for his final word.

"Or there's another thing you can do," he said slowly, "if Edna wants to leave her children, there's nothing I can do to prevent your running off together."

"I want to go home!" cried Edna again. "Oh, haven't you done enough to us for one day?"

Outside it was dark, save for a blurred glow from Sixth Avenue down the street. In that light those two who had been lovers looked for the last time into each other's tragic faces, realizing that between them there was not enough youth and strength to avert their eternal parting. Sloane walked suddenly off down the street and Anson tapped a dozing taxi-driver on the arm.

It was almost four; there was a patient flow of cleaning water along the ghostly pavement of Fifth Avenue, and the shadows of two night women flitted over the dark façade of St. Thomas's church. Then the desolate shrubbery of Central Park where Anson had often played as a child, and the mounting numbers, significant as names, of the marching streets. This was his city, he thought, where his name had flourished through five generations. No change could alter the permanence of its place here, for change itself was the essential substratum by which he and those of his name identified themselves with the spirit of New York. Resourcefulness and a powerful will—for his threats in weaker hands would have been less than nothing—had beaten the gathering dust from his uncle's name, from the name of his family, from even this shivering figure that sat beside him in the car.

Cary Sloane's body was found next morning on the lower shelf of a pillar of Queensboro Bridge. In the darkness and in his excitement he had thought that it was the water flowing black beneath him, but in less than a second it made no possible difference—unless he had planned to think one last thought of Edna, and call out her name as he struggled feebly in the water.

VII

Anson never blamed himself for his part in this affair—the situation which brought it about had not been of his making. But the just suffer with the unjust, and he found that his oldest and somehow his most precious friendship was over. He never knew what distorted story Edna told, but he was welcome in his uncle's house no longer.

Just before Christmas Mrs. Hunter retired to a select Episcopal heaven, and Anson became the responsible head of his family. An unmarried aunt who had lived with them for years ran the house, and attempted with helpless inefficiency to chaperone the younger girls. All the children were less self-reliant than Anson, more conventional both in their virtues and in their shortcomings. Mrs. Hunter's death had postponed the début of one daughter and the wedding of another. Also it had taken something deeply material from all of them, for with her passing the quiet, expensive superiority of the Hunters came to an end.

For one thing, the estate, considerably diminished by two inheritance taxes and soon to be divided among six children, was not a notable fortune any more. Anson saw a tendency in his youngest sisters to speak rather respectfully of families that hadn't "existed" twenty years ago. His own feeling of precedence was not echoed in them—sometimes they were conventionally snobbish, that was all. For another thing, this was the last summer they would spend on the Connecticut estate; the clamor against it was too loud: "Who wants to waste the best months of the year shut up in that dead old town?" Reluctantly he yielded —the house would go into the market in the fall, and next summer they would rent a smaller place in Westchester County. It was a step down from the expensive simplicity of his father's idea, and, while he sympathized with the revolt, it also annoyed him; during his mother's lifetime he had gone up there at least every other week-end—even in the gayest summers.

Yet he himself was part of this change, and his strong instinct for life had turned him in his twenties from the hollow obsequies of that abortive leisure class. He did not see this clearly—he still felt that there was a norm, a standard of society. But there was no norm, it was doubtful if there had ever been a true norm in New York. The few who still paid and fought to enter a particular set succeeded only to find that as a society it scarcely functioned —or, what was more alarming, that the Bohemia from which they fled sat above them at table.

At twenty-nine Anson's chief concern was his own growing loneliness. He was sure now that he would never marry. The number of weddings at which he had officiated as best man or usher was past all counting—there was a drawer at home that bulged with the official neckties of this or that wedding-party, neckties standing for romances that had not endured a year, for couples who had passed completely from his life. Scarfpins, gold pencils, cuff-buttons, presents from a generation of grooms had passed through his jewel-box and been lost— and with every ceremony he was less and less able to imagine himself in the groom's place. Under his hearty good-will toward all those marriages there was despair about his own.

And as he neared thirty he became not a little depressed at the inroads that marriage, especially lately, had made upon his friendships. Groups of people had a disconcerting tendency to dissolve and disappear. The men from his own college—and it was upon them he had expended the most time and affection —were the most elusive of all. Most of them were drawn deep into domesticity, two were dead, one lived abroad, one was in Hollywood writing continuities for pictures that Anson went faithfully to see.

Most of them, however, were permanent commuters with an intricate family life centring around some suburban country club, and it was from these that he felt his estrangement most keenly.

In the early days of their married life they had all needed him; he gave them advice about their slim finances, he exorcised their doubts about the advisability of bringing a baby into two rooms and a bath, especially he stood for the great world outside. But now their financial troubles were in the past and the fearfully expected child had evolved into an absorbing family. They were always glad to see old Anson, but they dressed up for him and tried to impress him with their present importance, and kept their troubles to themselves. They needed him no longer.

A few weeks before his thirtieth birthday the

last of his early and intimate friends was married. Anson acted in his usual rôle of best man, gave his usual silver tea-service, and went down to the usual *Homeric* to say good-by. It was a hot Friday afternoon in May, and as he walked from the pier he realized that Saturday closing had begun and he was free until Monday morning.

"Go where?" he asked himself.

The Yale Club, of course; bridge until dinner, then four or five raw cocktails in somebody's room and a pleasant confused evening. He regretted that this afternoon's groom wouldn't be along—they had always been able to cram so much into such nights: they knew how to attach women and how to get rid of them, how much consideration any girl deserved from their intelligent hedonism. A party was an adjusted thing—you took certain girls to certain places and spent just so much on their amusement; you drank a little, not much, more than you ought to drink, and at a certain time in the morning you stood up and said you were going home. You avoided college boys, sponges, future engagements, fights, sentiment, and indiscretions. That was the way it was done. All the rest was dissipation.

In the morning you were never violently sorry—you made no resolutions, but if you had overdone it and your heart was slightly out of order, you went on the wagon for a few days without saying anything about it, and waited until an accumulation of nervous boredom projected you into another party.

The lobby of the Yale Club was unpopulated. In the bar three very young alumni looked up at him, momentarily and without curiosity.

"Hello there, Oscar," he said to the bartender. "Mr. Cahill been around this afternoon?"

"Mr. Cahill's gone to New Haven."

"Oh . . . that so?"

"Gone to the ball game. Lot of men gone up."

Anson looked once again into the lobby, considered for a moment, and then walked out and over to Fifth Avenue. From the broad window of one of his clubs—one that he had scarcely visited in five years—a gray man with watery eyes stared down at him. Anson looked quickly away—that figure sitting in vacant resignation, in supercilious solitude, depressed him. He stopped and, retracing his steps, started over 47th Street toward Teak Warden's apartment. Teak and his wife had once been his most fa-

miliar friends—it was a household where he and Dolly Karger had been used to go in the days of their affair. But Teak had taken to drink, and his wife had remarked publicly that Anson was a bad influence on him. The remark reached Anson in an exaggerated form—when it was finally cleared up, the delicate spell of intimacy was broken, never to be renewed.

"Is Mr. Warden at home?" he inquired.

"They've gone to the country." 10

The fact unexpectedly cut at him. They were gone to the country and he hadn't known. Two years before he would have known the date, the hour, come up at the last moment for a final drink, and planned his first visit to them. Now they had gone without a word.

Anson looked at his watch and considered a week-end with his family, but the only train was a local that would jolt through the aggressive heat for three hours. And tomorrow in the 20 country, and Sunday—he was in no mood for porch-bridge with polite undergraduates, and dancing after dinner at a rural road-house, a diminutive of gaiety which his father had estimated too well.

"Oh, no," he said to himself. . . . "No."

He was a dignified, impressive young man, rather stout now, but otherwise unmarked by dissipation. He could have been cast for a pillar of something—at times you were sure it was 30 not society, at others nothing else—for the law, for the church. He stood for a few minutes motionless on the sidewalk in front of a 47th Street apartment-house; for almost the first time in his life he had nothing whatever to do.

Then he began to walk briskly up Fifth Avenue, as if he had just been reminded of an important engagement there. The necessity of dissimulation is one of the few characteristics that we share with dogs, and I think of Anson 40 on that day as some well-bred specimen who had been disappointed at a familiar back door. He was going to see Nick, once a fashionable bartender in demand at all private dances, and now employed in cooling non-alcoholic champagne among the labyrinthine cellars of the Plaza Hotel.

"Nick," he said, "what's happened to everything?"

"Dead," Nick said. 50

"Make me a whiskey sour." Anson handed a pint bottle over the counter. "Nick, the girls are different; I had a little girl in Brooklyn and she got married last week without letting me know."

"That a fact? Ha-ha-ha," responded Nick diplomatically. "Slipped it over on you."

"Absolutely," said Anson. "And I was out with her the night before."

"Ha-ha-ha," said Nick, "ha-ha-ha!"

"Do you remember the wedding, Nick, in Hot Springs where I had the waiters and the musicians singing 'God save the King'?"

"Now where was that, Mr. Hunter?" Nick concentrated doubtfully. "Seems to me that was—"

"Next time they were back for more, and I began to wonder how much I'd paid them," continued Anson.

"—seems to me that was at Mr. Trenholm's wedding."

"Don't know him," said Anson decisively. He was offended that a strange name should intrude upon his reminiscences; Nick perceived this.

"Naw—aw—" he admitted, "I ought to know that. It was one of *your* crowd—Brakins . . . . Baker—"

"Bicker Baker," said Anson responsively. "They put me in a hearse after it was over and covered me up with flowers and drove me away."

"Ha-ha-ha," said Nick. "Ha-ha-ha."

Nick's simulation of the old family servant paled presently and Anson went up-stairs to the lobby. He looked around—his eyes met the glance of an unfamiliar clerk at the desk, then fell upon a flower from the morning's marriage hesitating in the mouth of a brass cuspidor. He went out and walked slowly toward the blood-red sun over Columbus Circle. Suddenly he turned around and, retracing his steps to the Plaza, immured himself in a telephone-booth.

Later he said that he tried to get me three times that afternoon, that he tried every one who might be in New York—men and girls he had not seen for years, an artist's model of his college days whose faded number was still in his address book—Central told him that even the exchange existed no longer. At length his quest roved into the country, and he held brief disappointing conversations with emphatic butlers and maids. So-and-so was out, riding, swimming, playing golf, sailed to Europe last week. Who shall I say phoned?

It was intolerable that he should pass the evening alone—the private reckonings which one plans for a moment of leisure lose every charm when the solitude is enforced. There were always women of a sort, but the ones he knew had temporarily vanished, and to pass a New York evening in the hired company of a stranger never occurred to him—he would have considered that that was something shameful and secret, the diversion of a traveling salesman in a strange town.

Anson paid the telephone bill—the girl tried unsuccessfully to joke with him about its size —and for the second time that afternoon started to leave the Plaza and go he knew not where. Near the revolving door the figure of a woman, obviously with child, stood sideways to the light—a sheer beige cape fluttered at her shoulders when the door turned and, each time, she looked impatiently toward it as if she were weary of waiting. At the first sight of her a strong nervous thrill of familiarity went over him, but not until he was within five feet of her did he realize that it was Paula.

"Why, Anson Hunter!"

His heart turned over.

"Why, Paula—"

"Why, this is wonderful. I can't believe it, *Anson!*"

She took both his hands, and he saw in the freedom of the gesture that the memory of him had lost poignancy to her. But not to him—he felt that old mood that she evoked in him stealing over his brain, that gentleness with which he had always met her optimism as if afraid to mar its surface.

"We're at Rye for the summer. Pete had to come East on business—you know of course I'm Mrs. Peter Hagerty now—so we brought the children and took a house. You've got to come out and see us."

"Can I?" he asked directly. "When?"

"When you like. Here's Pete." The revolving door functioned, giving up a fine tall man of thirty with a tanned face and a trim mustache. His immaculate fitness made a sharp contrast with Anson's increasing bulk, which was obvious under the faintly tight cutaway coat.

"You oughtn't to be standing," said Hagerty to his wife. "Let's sit down here." He indicated lobby chairs, but Paula hesitated.

"I've got to go right home," she said. "Anson, why don't you—why don't you come out and have dinner with us to-night? We're just getting settled, but if you can stand that—"

Hagerty confirmed the invitation cordially.

"Come out for the night."

Their car waited in front of the hotel, and

Paula with a tired gesture sank back against silk cushions in the corner.

"There's so much I want to talk to you about," she said, "it seems hopeless."

"I want to hear about you."

"Well"—she smiled at Hagerty—"that would take a long time too. I have three children—by my first marriage. The oldest is five, then four, then three." She smiled again. "I didn't waste much time having them, did I?"

"Boys?"

"A boy and two girls. Then—oh, a lot of things happened, and I got a divorce in Paris a year ago and married Pete. That's all—except that I'm awfully happy."

In Rye they drove up to a large house near the Beach Club, from which there issued presently three dark, slim children who broke from an English governess and approached them with an esoteric cry. Abstractedly and with difficulty Paula took each one into her arms, a caress which they accepted stiffly, as they had evidently been told not to bump into Mummy. Even against their fresh faces Paula's skin showed scarcely any weariness—for all her physical languor she seemed younger than when he had last seen her at Palm Beach seven years ago.

At dinner she was preoccupied, and afterward, during the homage to the radio, she lay with closed eyes on the sofa, until Anson wondered if his presence at this time were not an intrusion. But at nine o'clock, when Hagerty rose and said pleasantly that he was going to leave them by themselves for a while, she began to talk slowly about herself and the past.

"My first baby," she said—"the one we call Darling, the biggest little girl—I wanted to die when I knew I was going to have her, because Lowell was like a stranger to me. It didn't seem as though she could be my own. I wrote you a letter and tore it up. Oh, you were *so* bad to me, Anson."

It was the dialogue again, rising and falling. Anson felt a sudden quickening of memory.

"Weren't you engaged once?" she asked— "a girl named Dolly something?"

"I wasn't ever engaged. I tried to be engaged, but I never loved anybody but you, Paula."

"Oh," she said. Then after a moment: "This baby is the first one I ever really wanted. You see, I'm in love now—at last."

He didn't answer, shocked at the treachery of her remembrance. She must have seen that the "at last" bruised him, for she continued:

"I was infatuated with you, Anson—you could make me do anything you liked. But we wouldn't have been happy. I'm not smart enough for you. I don't like things to be complicated like you do." She paused. "You'll never settle down," she said.

The phrase struck at him from behind—it was an accusation that of all accusations he had never merited.

"I could settle down if women were different," he said. "If I didn't understand so much about them, if women didn't spoil you for other women, if they had only a little pride. If I could go to sleep for a while and wake up into a home that was really mine—why, that's what I'm made for, Paula, that's what women have seen in me and liked in me. It's only that I can't get through the preliminaries any more.

Hagerty came in a little before eleven; after a whiskey Paula stood up and announced that she was going to bed. She went over and stood by her husband.

"Where did you go, dearest?" she demanded.

"I had a drink with Ed Saunders."

"I was worried. I thought maybe you'd run away."

She rested her head against his coat.

"He's sweet, isn't he, Anson?" she demanded.

"Absolutely," said Anson, laughing.

She raised her face to her husband.

"Well, I'm ready," she said. She turned to Anson: "Do you want to see our family gymnastic stunt?"

"Yes," he said in an interested voice.

"All right. Here we go!"

Hagerty picked her up easily in his arms.

"This is called the family acrobatic stunt," said Paula. "He carries me upstairs. Isn't it sweet of him?"

"Yes," said Anson.

Hagerty bent his head slightly until his face touched Paula's.

"And I love him," she said. "I've just been telling you, haven't I, Anson?"

"Yes," he said.

"He's the dearest thing that ever lived in this world; aren't you, darling? . . . Well, good night. Here we go. Isn't he strong?"

"Yes," Anson said.

"You'll find a pair of Pete's pajamas laid out for you. Sweet dreams—see you at breakfast."

"Yes," Anson said.

VIII

The older members of the firm insisted that Anson should go abroad for the summer. He had scarcely had a vacation in seven years, they said. He was stale and needed a change. Anson resisted.

"If I go," he declared, "I won't come back any more."

"That's absurd, old man. You'll be back in three months with all this depression gone. Fit as ever."

"No." He shook his head stubbornly. "If I stop, I won't go back to work. If I stop, that means I've given up—I'm through."

"We'll take a chance on that. Stay six months if you like—we're not afraid you'll leave us. Why, you'd be miserable if you didn't work."

They arranged his passage for him. They liked Anson—every one liked Anson—and the change that had been coming over him cast a sort of pall over the office. The enthusiasm that had invariably signalled up business, the consideration toward his equals and his inferiors, the lift of his vital presence—within the past four months his intense nervousness had melted down these qualities into the fussy pessimism of a man of forty. On every transaction in which he was involved he acted as a drag and a strain.

"If I go I'll never come back," he said.

Three days before he sailed Paula Legendre Hagerty died in childbirth. I was with him a great deal then, for we were crossing together, but for the first time in our friendship he told me not a word of how he felt, nor did I see the slightest sign of emotion. His chief preoccupation was with the fact that he was thirty years old—he would turn the conversation to the point where he could remind you of it and then fall silent, as if he assumed that the statement would start a chain of thought sufficient to itself. Like his partners, I was amazed at the change in him, and I was glad when the *Paris* moved off into the wet space between the worlds, leaving his principality behind.

"How about a drink?" he suggested.

We walked into the bar with that defiant feeling that characterizes the day of departure and ordered four Martinis. After one cocktail a change came over him—he suddenly reached across and slapped my knee with the first joviality I had seen him exhibit for months.

"Did you see that girl in the red tam?" he demanded, "the one with the high color who had the two police dogs down to bid her good-by."

"She's pretty," I agreed.

"I looked her up in the purser's office and found out that she's alone. I'm going down to see the steward in a few minutes. We'll have dinner with her to-night."

After a while he left me, and within an hour he was walking up and down the deck with her, talking to her in his strong, clear voice. Her red tam was a bright spot of color against the steel-green sea, and from time to time she looked up with a flashing bob of her head, and smiled with amusement and interest, and anticipation. At dinner we had champagne, and were very joyous—afterward Anson ran the pool with infectious gusto, and several people who had seen me with him asked me his name. He and the girl were talking and laughing together on a lounge in the bar when I went to bed.

I saw less of him on the trip than I had hoped. He wanted to arrange a foursome, but there was no one available, so I saw him only at meals. Sometimes, though, he would have a cocktail in the bar, and he told me about the girl in the red tam, and his adventures with her, making them all bizarre and amusing, as he had a way of doing, and I was glad that he was himself again, or at least the self that I knew, and with which I felt at home. I don't think he was ever happy unless some one was in love with him, responding to him like filings to a magnet, helping him to explain himself, promising him something. What it was I do not know. Perhaps they promised that there would always be women in the world who would spend their brightest, freshest, rarest hours to nurse and protect that superiority he cherished in his heart.

1926

JOHN STEINBECK

1902–

"I AM COMPLETELY partisan," Steinbeck once wrote. "Every effort I can bring to bear is and has been at the call of the common working-people to the end that they may eat what they raise, wear what they weave, use what they produce." As a novelist and short-story writer who rose to eminence in the period of the great depression of the 1930's, Steinbeck provides a memorable instance of the educated man who drew strength and purpose from a sympathetic involvement with an uprooted, downtrodden, and often desperate proletariat. He did not lack for examples in the region where he spent his early years and began his literary work: the brown hills and fertile valleys of Monterey County, south of San Francisco, California. Near his birthplace in Salinas is the sea-and-hill town of Monterey, scene of his humorous peasant-trilogy, *Tortilla Flat* (1935), *Cannery Row* (1945), and *Sweet Thursday* (1954). Southward lies Soledad and the fields where George and Lennie labored in *Of Mice and Men* (1937). To the north is the Pajaro (Torgas) Valley of *In Dubious Battle* (1936), the moving story of a Communist-inspired strike among itinerant fruit-pickers during the depression. The Promised Land of the Joad family, who flee the ruined dustbowl of their native state in *The Grapes of Wrath* (1939), is the San Joaquin Valley, due east of Salinas and the locale also of Frank Norris's novel of beleaguered farmers, *The Octopus*. Many of the stories in *The Long Valley* (1938) use the same background. In this region Steinbeck grew up, as notably recorded in the autobiographical portions of *East of Eden* (1952); there also he attended classes at Stanford University; and there he followed the fortunes of the "working-stiffs" who pick California's rich crops.

In the years since *The Grapes of Wrath*, Steinbeck's proletarian partisanship has become less apparent, somewhat to the detriment of his more recent work. As it receded in prominence, another long-standing interest of Steinbeck's—the literary possibilities of fables and parables— has come to dominance in its place. One example is *The Moon is Down* (1942), a socio-philo-sophical parable of the successful Norwegian resistance to German occupation during the early years of the second World War. *The Pearl* (1947) is a stylized re-telling of a Mexican folk-tale based on Jesus's parable in the thirteenth chapter of Matthew. In *The Wayward Bus* (1947) an assorted group of naturalistic malcontents gather in a battered vehicle for a danger-ous journey through a landscape strewn with metaphysical suggestions. *East of Eden* (1952), the most ambitious of Steinbeck's later novels, is a chronicle of psychological evil centering on an elaborate modernization of the Biblical story of Cain and Abel. Other late works include *A Russian Journal* (1948), *Burning Bright* (1950), *The Short Reign of Pippin IV* (1957), and *Once There Was a War* (1958).

L. C. Powell, "Towards a Bibliography of John Steinbeck," *Colophon*, III (Autumn, 1938), 558–568.

Robert Bennett, *The Wrath of John Steinbeck*, Los Angeles, 1939.

Lewis Gannett, *John Steinbeck: Personal and Bibliographical Notes* (pamphlet), New York, 1939.

Maxwell Geismar, "John Steinbeck: Of Wrath or Joy," in *Writers in Crisis*, Boston, 1942, pp. 237–270.

C. E. Jones, "Proletarian Writing and John Steinbeck," *Sewanee Review*, XLVIII (October–December, 1940), 445–456.

Peter Lisca, *The Wide World of John Steinbeck*, New Brunswick, 1958.

H. T. Moore, *The Novels of John Steinbeck*, Chicago, 1939.

E. W. Tedlock, *Steinbeck and His Critics, a Record of Twenty-five Years*, Albuquerque, 1957.

» » *From:* THE LONG VALLEY « «

THE RAID

It was dark in the little California town when the two men stepped from the lunch car and strode arrogantly through the back streets. The air was full of the sweet smell of fermenting fruit from the packing plants. High over the corners, blue arc lights swung in the wind and put moving shadows of telephone wires on the ground. The old wooden buildings were silent and resting. The dirty windows dismally re-
10 flected the street lights.

The two men were about the same size, but one was much older than the other. Their hair was cropped, they wore blue jeans. The older man had on a peajacket, while the younger wore a blue turtle-neck sweater. As they swung down the dark street, footsteps echoed back loudly from the wooden buildings. The younger man began to whistle *Come to Me My Melancholy Baby.* He stopped abruptly. "I
20 wish that damn tune would get out of my head. It's been going all day. It's an old tune, too."

His companion turned toward him. "You're scared, Root. Tell the truth. You're scared as hell."

They were passing under one of the blue street lights. Root's face put on its toughest look, the eyes squinted, the mouth went crooked and bitter. "No, I ain't scared." They
30 were out of the light. His face relaxed again. "I wish I knew the ropes better. You been out before, Dick. You know what to expect. But I ain't ever been out."

"The way to learn is to do," Dick quoted sententiously. "You never really learn nothing from books."

They crossed a railroad track. A block tower up the line a little was starred with green lights. "It's awful dark," said Root. "I wonder
40 if the moon will come up later. Usually does when it's so dark. You going to make the first speech, Dick?"

"No, you make it. I had more experience than you. I'll watch them while you talk and then I can smack them where I know they bite. Know what you're going to say?"

"Sure I do. I got it all in my head, every word. I wrote it out and learned it. I heard guys tell how they got up and couldn't think of

a thing to say, and then all of a sudden they just started in like it was somebody else, and the words came out like water out of a hydrant. Big Mike Sheane said it was like that with him. But I wasn't taking no chances, so I wrote it out."

A train hooted mournfully, and in a moment it rounded a bend and pushed its terrible light down the track. The lighted coaches rattled past. Dick turned to watch it go by. "Not many people on that one," he said with satisfaction. "Didn't you say your old man worked on the railroad?"

Root tried to keep the bitterness out of his voice. "Sure, he works on the road. He's a brakeman. He kicked me out when he found out what I was doing. He was scared he'd lose his job. He couldn't see. I talked to him, but he just couldn't see. He kicked me right out." Root's voice was lonely. Suddenly he realized how he had weakened and how he sounded homesick. "That's the trouble with them," he went on harshly. "They can't see beyond their jobs. They can't see what's happening to them. They hang on to their chains."

"Save it," said Dick. "That's good stuff. Is that part of your speech?"

"No, but I guess I'll put it in if you say it's good."

The street lights were fewer now. A line of locust trees grew along the road, for the town was beginning to thin and the country took control. Along the unpaved road there were a few little houses with ill-kept gardens.

"Jesus! it's dark," Root said again. "I wonder if there'll be any trouble. It's a good night to get away if anything happens."

Dick snorted into the collar of his peajacket. They walked along in silence for a while.

"Do you think you'd try to get away, Dick?" Root asked.

"No, by God! It's against orders. If anything happens we got to stick. You're just a kid. I guess you'd run if I let you."

Root blustered: "You think you're hell on wheels just because you been out a few times. You'd think you was a hundred to hear you talk."

"I'm dry behind the ears, anyway," said Dick.

Root walked with his head down. He said softly, "Dick, are you sure you wouldn't run?

Are you sure you could just stand there and take it?"

"Of course I'm sure. I've done it before. It's the orders, ain't it? Why, it's good publicity." He peered through the darkness at Root. "What makes you ask, kid? You scared you'll run? If you're scared you got no business here."

Root shivered. "Listen, Dick, you're a good guy. You won't tell nobody what I say, will you? I never been tried. How do I know what I'll do if somebody smacks me in the face with a club? How can anybody tell what he'd do? I don't think I'd run. I'd try not to run."

"All right, kid. Let it go at that. But you try running, and I'll turn your name in. We got no place for yellow bastards. You remember that, kid."

"Oh, lay off that kid stuff. You're running that in the ground."

The locust trees grew closer together as they went. The wind rustled gently in the leaves. A dog growled in one of the yards as the men went by. A light fog began to drift down through the air, and the stars were swallowed in it. "You sure you got everything ready?" Dick asked. "Got the lamps? Got the lit'ature? I left all that to you."

"I did it all this afternoon," said Root. "I didn't put the posters up yet, but I got them in a box out there."

"Got oil in the lamps?"

"They had plenty in. Say, Dick, I guess some bastard has squealed, don't you?"

"Sure. Somebody always squeals."

"Well, you didn't hear nothing about no raid, did you?"

"How the hell would I hear? You think they'd come and tell me they was going to knock my can off? Get hold of yourself, Root. You got the pants scared off you. You're going to make me nervous if you don't cut it out."

II

They approached a low, square building, black and heavy in the darkness. Their feet pounded on a wooden sidewalk. "Nobody here, yet," said Dick. "Let's open her up and get some light." They had come to a deserted store. The old show-windows were opaque with dirt. A Lucky Strike poster was stuck to the glass on one side while a big cardboard Coca-Cola lady stood like a ghost in the other. Dick threw open the double doors and walked in. He struck a match and lighted a kerosene

lamp, got the chimney back in place, and set the lamp on an up-ended apple box. "Come on, Root, we got to get things ready."

The walls of the building were scabrous with streaked whitewash. A pile of dusty newspapers had been kicked into a corner. The two back windows were laced with cobwebs. Except for three apple boxes, there was nothing at all in the store.

Root walked to one of the boxes and took out a large poster bearing a portrait of a man done in harsh reds and blacks. He tacked the portrait to the whitewashed wall behind the lamp. Then he tacked another poster beside it, a large red symbol on a white background. Last he up-ended another apple box and piled leaflets and little paper-bound books on it. His footsteps were loud on the bare wooden floor. "Light the other lamp, Dick! It's too damned dark in here."

"Scared of the dark, too, kid?"

"No. The men will be here pretty soon. We want to have more light when they come. What time is it?"

Dick looked at his watch. "Quarter to eight. Some of the guys ought to be here pretty soon now." He put his hands in the breast pockets of his peajacket and stood loosely by the box of pamphlets. There was nothing to sit on. The black and red portrait stared harshly out at the room. Root leaned against the wall.

The light from one of the lamps yellowed, and the flame slowly sank down. Dick stepped over to it. "I thought you said there was plenty of oil. This one's dry."

"I thought there was plenty. Look! The other one's nearly full. We can pour some of that oil in this lamp."

"How we going to do that? We got to put them both out to pour the oil. You got any matches?"

Root felt through his pockets. "Only two."

"Now, you see? We got to hold this meeting with only one lamp. I should've looked things over this afternoon. I was busy in town, though. I thought I could leave it to you."

"Maybe we could quick pour some of this oil in a can and then pour it into the other lamp."

"Yeah, and then set the joint on fire. You're a hell of a helper."

Root leaned back against the wall again. "I wish they'd come. What time is it, Dick?"

"Five after eight."

"Well, what's keeping them? What are they waiting for? Did you tell them eight o'clock?"

"Oh! Shut up, kid. You'll get my goat pretty soon. I don't know what's keeping them. Maybe they got cold feet. Now shut up for a little while." He dug his hands into the pockets of his jacket again. "Got a cigarette, Root?"

"No."

It was very still. Nearer the center of the town, automobiles were moving; the mutter of their engines and an occasional horn sounded. A dog barked unexcitedly at one of the houses nearby. The wind ruffled the locust trees in whishing gusts.

"Listen, Dick! Do you hear voices? I think they're coming." They turned their heads and strained to listen.

"I don't hear nothing. You just thought you heard it."

Root walked to one of the dirty windows and looked out. Coming back, he paused at the pile of pamphlets and straightened them neatly. "What time is it now, Dick?"

"Keep still, will you? You'll drive me nuts. You gots to have guts for this job. For God's sake show some guts."

"Well, I never been out before, Dick."

"Do you think anybody couldn't tell that? You sure make it plain enough."

The wind gusted sharply in the locust trees. The front doors clicked and one of them opened slowly, squeaking a little at the hinges. The breeze came in, ruffled the pile of dusty newspapers in the corner and sailed the posters out from the wall like curtains.

"Shut that door, Root. . . . No, leave it open. Then we can hear them coming better." He looked at his watch. "It's nearly half-past eight."

"Do you think they'll come? How long we going to wait, if they don't show up?"

The older man stared at the open door. "We ain't going to leave here before nine-thirty at the earliest. We got orders to hold this meeting."

The night sounds came in more clearly through the open door—the dance of dry locust leaves on the road, the slow steady barking of the dog. On the wall the red and black portrait was menacing in the dim light. It floated out at the bottom again. Dick looked around at it. "Listen, kid," he said quietly. "I know you're scared. When you're scared, just take a look at him." He indicated the picture with his thumb. "He wasn't scared. Just remember about what he did."

The boy considered the portrait. "You suppose he wasn't ever scared?"

Dick reprimanded him sharply. "If he was, nobody ever found out about it. You take that for a lesson and don't go opening up for everybody to show them how you feel."

"You're a good guy, Dick. I don't know what I'll do when I get sent out alone."

"You'll be all right, kid. You got stuff in you. I can tell that. You never been under fire."

Root glanced quickly at the door. "Listen! You hear somebody coming?"

"Lay off that stuff! When they get here, they'll get here."

"Well—let's close the door. It's kind of cold in here. Listen! There *is* somebody coming."

Quick footsteps sounded on the road, broke into a run and crossed the wooden sidewalk. A man in overalls and a painter's cap ran into the room. He was panting and winded. "You guys better scram," he said. "There's a raiding party coming. None of the boys is coming to the meeting. They was going to let you take it, but I wouldn't do that. Come on! Get your stuff together and get out. That party's on the way."

Root's face was pale and tight. He looked nervously at Dick. The older man shivered. He thrust his hands into his breast pockets and slumped his shoulders. "Thanks," he said. "Thanks for telling us. You run along. We'll be all right."

"The others was just going to leave you take it," the man said.

Dick nodded. "Sure, they can't see the future. They can't see beyond their nose. Run along now before you get caught."

"Well, ain't you guys coming? I'll help carry some of your stuff."

"We're going to stay," Dick said woodenly. "We got orders to stay. We got to take it."

The man was moving toward the door. He turned back. "Want me to stay with you?"

"No, you're a good guy. No need for you to stay. We could maybe use you some other time."

"Well, I did what I could."

III

Dick and Root heard him cross the wooden sidewalk and trot off into the darkness. The night resumed its sounds. The dead leaves scraped along the ground. The motors hummed from the centre of the town.

Root looked at Dick. He could see that the

man's fists were doubled up in his breast pockets. The face muscles were stiff, but he smiled at the boy. The posters drifted out from the wall and settled back again.

"Scared, kid?"

Root bristled to deny it, and then gave it up. "Yes, I'm scared. Maybe I won't be no good at this."

"Take hold, kid!" Dick said fiercely. "You take hold!"

Dick quoted to him, " 'The men of little spirit must have an example of stead—steadfastness. The people at large must have an example of injustice.' There it is, Root. That's orders." He relapsed into silence. The barking dog increased his tempo.

"I guess that's them," said Root. "Will they kill us, do you think?"

"No, they don't very often kill anybody."

"But they'll hit us and kick us, won't they? They'll hit us in the face with sticks and break our nose. Big Mike, they broke his jaw in three places."

"Take hold, kid! You take hold! And listen to me; if some one busts you, it isn't him that's doing it, it's the System. And it isn't you he's busting. He's taking a crack at the Principle. Can you remember that?"

"I don't want to run, Dick. Honest to God I don't. If I start to run, you hold me, will you?"

Dick walked near and touched him on the shoulder. "You'll be all right. I can tell a guy that will stick."

"Well, hadn't we better tie the lit'ature so it won't all get burned?"

"No—somebody might put a book in his pocket and read it later. Then it would be doing some good. Leave the books there. And shut up now! Talking only makes it worse."

The dog had gone back to his slow, spiritless barking. A rush of wind brought a scurry of dead leaves in the open door. The portrait poster blew out and came loose at one corner. Root walked over and pinned it back. Somewhere in the town, an automobile squealed its brakes.

"Hear anything, Dick? Hear them coming yet?"

"No."

"Listen. Dick. Big Mike lay two days with his jaw broke before anybody'd help him."

The older man turned angrily on him. One doubled fist came out of his peajacket pocket. His eyes narrowed as he looked at the boy. He walked close and put an arm about his shoulders. "Listen to me close, kid," he said. "I don't know much, but I been through this mill before. I can tell you this for sure. When it comes —it won't hurt. I don't know why, but it won't. Even if they kill you it won't hurt." He dropped his arm and moved toward the front door. He looked out and listened in two directions before he came back into the room.

"Hear anything?"

"No. Not a thing."

"What—do you think is keeping them?"

"How do you suppose I'd know?"

Root swallowed thickly. "Maybe they won't come. Maybe it was all a lie that fella told us, just a joke."

"Maybe."

"Well, are—we going to wait all night to get our cans knocked off?"

Dick mimicked him. "Yes, we're going to wait all night to get our cans knocked off."

The wind sounded in one big fierce gust and then dropped away completely. The dog stopped barking. A train screamed for the crossing and went crashing by, leaving the night more silent than before. In a house nearby, an alarm clock went off. Dick said, "Somebody goes to work early. Night watchman, maybe." His voice was too loud in the stillness. The front door squeaked slowly shut.

"What time is it now, Dick?"

"Quarter-past nine."

"Jesus! Only that? I thought it was about morning. . . . Don't you wish they'd come and get it over, Dick? Listen, Dick!—I thought I heard voices."

They stood stiffly, listening. Their heads were bent forward. "You hear voices, Dick?"

"I think so. Like they're talking low."

The dog barked again, fiercely this time. A little quiet murmur of voices could be heard. "Look, Dick! I thought I saw somebody out the back window."

The older man chuckled uneasily. "That's so we can't get away. They got the place surrounded. Take hold, kid! They're coming now. Remember that it's not them, it's the System."

There came a rushing clatter of footsteps. The doors burst open. A crowd of men thronged in, roughly dressed men, wearing black hats. They carried clubs and sticks in their hands. Dick and Root stood erect, their chins out, their eyes dropped and nearly closed.

Once inside, the raiders were uneasy. They

stood in a half-circle about the two men, scowling, waiting for some one to move.

Young Root glanced sidewise at Dick and saw that the older man was looking at him coldly, critically, as though he judged his deportment. Root shoved his trembling hands in his pockets. He forced himself forward. His voice was shrill with fright. "Comrades," he shouted, "you're just men like we are. We're all brothers—" A piece of two-by-four lashed out and struck him on the side of the head with a fleshy thump. Root went down to his knees and steadied himself with his hands.

The men stood still, glaring.

Root climbed slowly to his feet. His split ear spilled a red stream down his neck. The side of his face was mushy and purple. He got himself erect again. His breath burst passionately. His hands were steady now, his voice sure and strong. His eyes were hot with an ecstasy. "Can't you see?" he shouted. "It's all for you. We're doing it for you. All of it. You don't know what you're doing."

"Kill the red rats!"

Some one giggled hysterically. And then the wave came. As he went down, Root caught a moment's glimpse of Dick's face smiling a tight, hard smile.

IV

He came near the surface several times, but didn't quite make it into consciousness. At last he opened his eyes and knew things. His face and head were heavy with bandages. He could only see a line of light between his puffed eyelids. For a time he lay, trying to think his way out. Then he heard Dick's voice near to him.

"You awake, kid?"

Root tried his voice and found that it croaked pretty badly. "I guess so."

"What'd they do to you, Dick?"

"Oh, they bust my arm and a couple of ribs. You got to learn to turn your face down to the ground. That saves your eyes." He paused and drew a careful breath. "Hurts some to breathe when you get a rib bust. We are lucky. The cops picked us up and took us in."

"Are we in jail, Dick?"

"Yeah! Hospital cell."

"What they got on the books?"

He heard Dick try to chuckle, and gasp when it hurt him. "Inciting to riot. We'll get six months, I guess. The cops got the lit'ature."

"You won't tell them I'm under age, will you, Dick?"

"No. I won't. You better shut up. Your voice don't sound so hot. Take it easy."

Root lay silent, muffled in a coat of dull pain. But in a moment he spoke again. "It didn't hurt, Dick. It was funny. I felt all full up—and good."

"You done fine, kid. You done as good as anybody I ever seen. I'll give you a blow to the committee. You just done fine."

Root struggled to get something straight in his head. "When they was busting me I wanted to tell them I didn't care."

"Sure, kid. That's what I told you. It wasn't them. It was the System. You don't want to hate them. They don't know no better."

Root spoke drowsily. The pain was muffling him under. "You remember in the Bible, Dick, how it says something like 'Forgive them because they don't know what they're doing'?"

Dick's reply was stern. "You lay off that religion stuff, kid." He quoted, " 'Religion is the opium of the people.' "

"Sure, I know," said Root. "But there wasn't no religion to it. It was just—I felt like saying that. It was just kind of the way I felt."

1934

KATHERINE ANNE PORTER

1894–

THOUGH MISS PORTER is often discussed as a member of the contemporary school of Southern writers, much of her life has been lived outside her native Texas. As journalist and teacher she has spent years in Mexico, Europe, New York City, and in other parts of the United States. In consequence her stories are as likely to be set in Mexico or Berlin or Greenwich Village as New Orleans or Texas. People more than places count with her. As she has said, in commenting on her aims as a writer: "My whole attempt has been to discover and understand human motives, human feelings." As to her method, she has told us this: "The constant exercise of memory seems to be the chief occupation of my mind, and all my experience seems to be simply memory, with continuity, marginal notes, constant revision, and comparison of one thing with another. Now and again thousands of memories converge, harmonize, arrange themselves around a central idea in a coherent form, and I write a story."

When the memories do converge around a central idea, the story which results is perfect in every respect. Though the body of her writing is small—her stories are contained in three volumes, *Flowering Judas and Other Stories* (1930, 1935), *Pale Horse, Pale Rider* (1939), *The Leaning Tower and Other Stories* (1944)—she is a master craftsman and is widely recognized as such. By their example her twenty-two stories have helped to remake the genre. She discovered the path which would be followed by Kay Boyle, Eudora Welty, Robert Penn Warren, and Flannery O'Connor.

The story printed here, "The Grave," is a fine example of her method. We are taken quickly into the secret lives of two children, brother and sister. We learn what they are learning about: death and birth and their relatedness. The details are vivid and explicit as well as symbolic, but they are used with the utmost economy. The story widens out as it goes deeper.

Possibly Miss Porter's ability to evoke life from a single central episode explains why she has not finished the novel on which she has worked for years. There must be moments of let-down and repose in a novel. The evidence of these superb stories suggests that she cannot, as a writer of fiction, lower the pitch of excitement.

Edward Schwartz, *Katherine Anne Porter, A Critical Bibliography*, New York, 1953.
Lodwick Hartley, "The Lady and the Temple: The Critical Theories of Katherine Anne Porter," *College English*, XIV (April, 1953), 386–391.
Edward Schwartz, "The Way of Dissent: Katherine Anne Porter's Critical Position," *Western Humanities Review*, VIII (Spring, 1954), 119–130.
R. P. Warren, "Katherine Anne Porter (Irony with a Center)," *Kenyon Review*, IV (Winter, 1942), 29–42.
R. B. West, Jr., "Katherine Anne Porter and 'Histrionic Memory,'" *Hudson Review*, VI (Fall, 1952), 16–27.
V. A. Young, "The Art of Katherine Anne Porter," *New Mexico Quarterly Review*, XV (August, 1945), 326–341.

» » THE GRAVE « «

The grandfather, dead for more than thirty years, had been twice disturbed in his long repose by the constancy and possessiveness of his widow. She removed his bones first to Louisiana and then to Texas as if she had set out to find her own burial place, knowing well she would never return to the places she had left. In Texas she set up a small cemetery in a corner of her first farm, and as the family connection grew, and oddments of relations came over from Kentucky to settle, it contained at last about twenty graves. After the grandmother's death, part of her land was to be sold for the benefit of certain of her children, and the cemetery happened to lie in the part set aside for sale. It was necessary to take up the bodies and bury them again in the family plot in the big new public cemetery, where the grandmother had been buried. At last her husband was to lie beside her for eternity, as she had planned.

The family cemetery had been a pleasant small neglected garden of tangled rose bushes and ragged cedar trees and cypress, the simple flat stones rising out of uncropped sweet-smelling wild grass. The graves were lying open and empty one burning day when Miranda and her brother Paul, who often went together to hunt rabbits and doves, propped their twenty-two Winchester rifles carefully against the rail fence, climbed over and explored among the graves. She was nine years old and he was twelve.

They peered into the pits all shaped alike with such purposeful accuracy, and looking at each other with pleased adventurous eyes, they said in solemn tones: "These were graves!" trying by words to shape a special, suitable emotion in their minds, but they felt nothing except an agreeable thrill of wonder: they were seeing a new sight, doing something they had not done before. In them both there was also a small disappointment at the entire commonplaceness of the actual spectacle. Even if it had once contained a coffin for years upon years, when the coffin was gone a grave was just a hole in the ground. Miranda leaped into the pit that had held her grandfather's bones. Scratching around aimlessly and pleasurably as any young animal, she scooped up a lump of earth and weighed it in her palm. It had a pleasantly sweet, corrupt smell, being mixed with cedar needles and small leaves, and as the crumbs fell apart, she saw a silver dove no larger than a hazel nut, with spread wings and a neat fan-shaped tail. The breast had a deep round hollow in it. Turning it up to the fierce sunlight, she saw that the inside of the hollow was cut in little whorls. She scrambled out, over the pile of loose earth that had fallen back into one end of the grave, calling to Paul that she had found something, he must guess what . . . His head appeared smiling over the rim of another grave. He waved a closed hand at her. "I've got something too!" They ran to compare treasures, making a game of it, so many guesses each, all wrong, and a final showdown with opened palms. Paul had found a thin wide gold ring carved with intricate flowers and leaves. Miranda was smitten at sight of the ring and wished to have it. Paul seemed more impressed by the dove. They made a trade, with some little bickering. After he had got the dove in his hand, Paul said, "Don't you know what this is? This is a screw head for a *coffin!* . . . I'll bet nobody else in the world has one like this!"

Miranda glanced at it without covetousness. She had the gold ring on her thumb; it fitted perfectly. "Maybe we ought to go now," she said, "maybe one of the niggers 'll see us and tell somebody." They knew the land had been sold, the cemetery was no longer theirs, and they felt like trespassers. They climbed back over the fence, slung their rifles loosely under their arms—they had been shooting at targets with various kinds of firearms since they were seven years old—and set out to look for the rabbits and doves or whatever small game might happen along. On these expeditions Miranda always followed at Paul's heels along the path, obeying instructions about handling her gun when going through fences; learning how to stand it up properly so it would not slip and fire unexpectedly; how to wait her time for a shot and not just bang away in the air without looking, spoiling shots for Paul, who really could hit things if given a chance. Now and then, in her excitement at seeing birds whizz up suddenly before her face, or a rabbit leap across her very toes, she lost her head, and almost without sighting she flung her rifle up and pulled the trigger. She hardly ever hit any sort of mark. She had no proper sense of hunting at all. Her brother would be often completely disgusted with her. "You don't care whether you get your bird or not," he said. "That's no way to hunt." Miranda could not understand his indignation. She had seen him smash his hat and yell with fury when he had missed his aim. "What I like about shooting," said Miranda, with exasperating inconsequence, "is pulling the trigger and hearing the noise."

"Then, by golly," said Paul, "whyn't you go back to the range and shoot at bulls-eyes?"

"I'd just as soon," said Miranda, "only like this, we walk around more."

"Well, you just stay behind and stop spoiling my shots," said Paul, who, when he made a kill, wanted to be certain he had made it. Miranda, who alone brought down a bird once in twenty rounds, always claimed as her own any game they got when they fired at the same moment. It was tiresome and unfair and her brother was sick of it.

"Now, the first dove we see, or the first rabbit, is mine," he told her. "And the next will be yours. Remember that and don't get smarty."

"What about snakes?" asked Miranda idly. "Can I have the first snake?"

Waving her thumb gently and watching her gold ring glitter, Miranda lost interest in shooting. She was wearing her summer roughing outfit: dark blue overalls, a light blue shirt, a hired-man's straw hat, and thick brown sandals. Her brother had the same outfit except his was a sober hickorynut color. Ordinarily Miranda preferred her overalls to any other dress, though it was making rather a scandal in the countryside, for the year was 1903, and in the back country the law of female decorum had teeth in it. Her father had been criticized for letting his girls dress like boys and go careening around astride barebacked horses. Big sister Maria, the really independent and fearless one, in spite of her rather affected ways, rode at a dead run with only a rope knotted around her horse's nose. It was said the motherless family was running down, with the Grandmother no longer there to hold it together. It was known that she had discriminated against her son Harry in her will, and that he was in straits about money. Some of his old neighbors reflected with vicious satisfaction that now he would probably not be so stiffnecked, nor have any more high-stepping horses either. Miranda knew this, though she could not say how. She had met along the road old women of the kind who smoked corn-cob pipes, who had treated her grandmother with most sincere respect. They slanted their gummy old eyes side-ways at the granddaughter and said, "Ain't you ashamed of yoself, Missy? It's aginst the Scriptures to dress like that. Whut yo Pappy thinkin about?" Miranda, with her powerful social sense, which was like a fine set of antennae radiating from every pore of her skin, would feel ashamed because she knew well it was rude and ill-bred to shock anybody, even bad-tempered old crones, though she had faith in her father's judgment and was perfectly comfortable in the clothes. Her father had said, "They're just what you need, and they'll save your dresses for school . . ." This sounded quite simple and natural to her. She had been brought up in rigorous economy. Wastefulness was vulgar. It was also a sin. These were truths; she had heard them repeated many times and never once disputed.

Now the ring, shining with the serene purity of fine gold on her rather grubby thumb, turned her feelings against her overalls and sockless feet, toes sticking through the thick brown leather straps. She wanted to go back to the farmhouse, take a good cold bath, dust herself with plenty of Maria's violet talcum powder—provided Maria was not present to object, of course—put on the thinnest, most becoming dress she owned, with a big sash, and sit in a wicker chair under the trees . . . These things were not all she wanted, of course; she had vague stirrings of desire for luxury and a grand way of living which could not take precise form in her imagination but were founded on family legend of past wealth and leisure. These immediate comforts were

what she could have, and she wanted them at once. She lagged rather far behind Paul, and once she thought of just turning back without a word and going home. She stopped, thinking that Paul would never do that to her, and so she would have to tell him. When a rabbit leaped, she let Paul have it without dispute. He killed it with one shot.

When she came up with him, he was already kneeling, examining the wound, the rabbit trailing from his hands. "Right through the head," he said complacently, as if he had aimed for it. He took out his sharp, competent bowie knife and started to skin the body. He did it very cleanly and quickly. Uncle Jimbilly knew how to prepare the skins so that Miranda always had fur coats for her dolls, for though she never cared much for her dolls she liked seeing them in fur coats. The children knelt facing each other over the dead animal. Miranda watched admiringly while her brother stripped the skin away as if he were taking off a glove. The flayed flesh emerged dark scarlet, sleek, firm; Miranda with thumb and finger felt the long fine muscles with the silvery flat strips binding them to the joints. Brother lifted the oddly bloated belly. "Look," he said, in a low amazed voice. "It was going to have young ones."

Very carefully he slit the thin flesh from the center ribs to the flanks, and a scarlet bag appeared. He slit again and pulled the bag open, and there lay a bundle of tiny rabbits, each wrapped in a thin scarlet veil. The brother pulled these off and there they were, dark gray, their sleek wet down lying in minute even ripples, like a baby's head just washed, their unbelievably small delicate ears folded close, their little blind faces almost featureless.

Miranda said, "Oh, I want to *see*," under her breath. She looked and looked—excited but not frightened, for she was accustomed to the sight of animals killed in hunting—filled with pity and astonishment and a kind of shocked delight in the wonderful little creatures for their own sakes, they were so pretty. She touched one of them ever so carefully, "Ah, there's blood running over them," she said and began to tremble without knowing why. Yet she wanted most deeply to see and to know. Having seen, she felt at once as if she had known all along. The very memory of her former ignorance faded, she had always known just this. No one had ever told her anything outright, she had been rather unobservant of

the animal life around her because she was so accustomed to animals. They seemed simply disorderly and unaccountably rude in their habits, but altogether natural and not very interesting. Her brother had spoken as if he had known about everything all along. He may have seen all this before. He had never said a word to her, but she knew now a part at least of what he knew. She understood a little of the
10 secret, formless intuitions in her own mind and body, which had been clearing up, taking form, so gradually and so steadily she had not realized that she was learning what she had to know. Paul said cautiously, as if he were talking about something forbidden: "They were just about ready to be born." His voice dropped on the last word. "I know," said Miranda, "like kittens. I know, like babies." She was quietly and terribly agitated, standing
20 again with her rifle under her arm, looking down at the bloody heap. "I don't want the skin," she said, "I won't have it." Paul buried the young rabbits again in their mother's body, wrapped the skin around her, carried her to a clump of sage bushes, and hid her away. He came out again at once and said to Miranda, with an eager friendliness, a confidential tone quite unusual in him, as if he were taking her into an important secret on equal terms: "Lis-
30 ten now. Now you listen to me, and don't ever forget. Don't you ever tell a living soul that you saw this. Don't tell a soul. Don't tell Dad because I'll get into trouble. He'll say I'm leading you into things you ought not to do. He's always saying that. So now don't you go and forget and blab out sometime the way you're always doing . . . Now, that's a secret. Don't you tell."

Miranda never told, she did not even wish to tell anybody. She thought about the whole worrisome affair with confused unhappiness for a few days. Then it sank quietly into her mind and was heaped over by accumulated thousands of impressions, for nearly twenty years. One day she was picking her path among the puddles and crushed refuse of a market street in a strange city of a strange country, when without warning, plain and clear in its true colors as if she looked through a frame upon a scene that had not stirred nor changed since the moment it happened, the episode of that far-off day leaped from its burial place before her mind's eye. She was so reasonlessly horrified she halted suddenly staring, the scene before her eyes dimmed by the vision back of them. An Indian vendor had held up before her a tray of dyed sugar sweets, in the shapes of all kinds of small creatures: birds, baby chicks, baby rabbits, lambs, baby pigs. They were in gay colors and smelled of vanilla, maybe. . . . It was a very hot day and the smell in the market, with its piles of raw flesh and wilting flowers, was like the mingled sweetness and corruption she had smelled that other day in the empty cemetery at home: the day she had remembered always until now vaguely as the time she and her brother had found treasure in the opened graves. Instantly upon this thought the dreadful vision faded, and she saw clearly her brother, whose childhood face she had forgotten, standing again in the blazing sunshine, again twelve years old, a pleased sober smile in his eyes, turning the silver dove over and over in his hands.

1944

FLANNERY O'CONNOR

1925–

THE PUBLICATION of her first two novels and a distinguished collection of short stories established Flannery O'Connor as an extremely gifted newcomer to a circle of Southern-born women-writers which already included Elizabeth Madox Roberts, Katherine Anne Porter, Caroline Gordon, Carson McCullers, Eudora Welty, and Elizabeth Spencer. Born in Savannah, Georgia, and educated at first in convent schools, she was graduated from Georgia State College for Women; spent two years in the writing-classes of Paul Engle at the State University of Iowa; and upon returning to her native state, took up residence with her widowed mother on the 2,000-acre "Andalusia Farms" near Milledgeville, raising both cattle and (as a hobby) peacocks. In the following years she collected a large personal library, painted in oils, and labored intently over the stories by which her reputation was made.

The first novel, *Wise Blood* (1952), at once proved her power and originality, predicting also the directions her work would take in the ten short stories which make up *A Good Man Is Hard to Find* (1955) and in her second novel, *The Violent Bear It Away* (1960). Her own devout Catholicism, together with her more than avocational interest in theological problems, equipped her to examine with humor, pathos, terror, and irony the manifestations of religious fundamentalism and other forms of ignorance and superstition among the country people of Georgia and Tennessee. Both novels deal with fanatical religious obsessions in the Bible Belt of the Deep South. In *Wise Blood*, a young war veteran named Haze Motes attempts to establish a new religious cult, "The Church Without Christ." *The Violent Bear It Away*, whose title is from Matthew 11:12, centers on the rite of baptism and the struggle of an adolescent boy named Tarwater to carry out an obligation inherited from his fiercely fundamentalist great-uncle.

Although both novels earned Miss O'Connor immediate if not universal critical praise, it was held in some quarters that her true genius lay in the genre of the short story, where structural problems may be more easily solved, and where intensity of effect counts far more heavily than prolonged development in sequences of time. The title story of *A Good Man Is Hard to Fund*, which is here reprinted, well represents the qualities, both of humor and of horror, with which her name is associated.

G. F. Wedge, "Two Bibliographies: Flannery O'Connor, J. F. Powers," *Criterion*, II (Fall, 1958), 59–70.

Caroline Gordon, "Flannery O'Connor's *Wise Blood*," *Criterion*, II (Fall, 1958), 3–10.

Jane Hart, "Strange Earth, the Stories of Flannery O'Connor," *Georgia Review*, XII (Summer, 1958), 215–222.

Granville Hicks, *The Living Novel*, New York, 1957.

Robert McCown, "Flannery O'Connor and the Reality of Sin," *Catholic World*, CLXXXVIII (January, 1959), 285–291.

Sister M. B. Quinn, "View from a Rock: The Fiction of Flannery O'Connor and J. F. Powers," *Criterion* II (Fall, 1958), 19–27.

L. D. Rubin, Jr., "Flannery O'Connor: A Note on Literary Fashions," *Criterion*, II (Fall, 1958), 11–18.

———, "Two Ladies of the South," *Sewanee Review*, LXIII (Autumn, 1955), 671–681.

» » A GOOD MAN IS HARD TO FIND « «

The grandmother didn't want to go to Florida. She wanted to visit some of her connections in east Tennessee and she was seizing at every chance to change Bailey's mind. Bailey was the son she lived with, her only boy. He was sitting on the edge of his chair at the table, bent over the orange sports section of the *Journal.* "Now look here, Bailey," she said, "see here, read this," and she stood with one hand on her thin hip and the other rattling the newspaper at his bald head. "Here this fellow that calls himself The Misfit is aloose from the Federal Pen and headed toward Florida and you read here what it says he did to these people. Just you read it. I wouldn't take my children in any direction with a criminal like that aloose in it. I couldn't answer to my conscience if I did."

Bailey didn't look up from his reading so she wheeled around then and faced the children's mother, a young woman in slacks, whose face was as broad and innocent as a cabbage and was tied around with a green head-kerchief that had two points on the top like rabbit's ears. She was sitting on the sofa, feeding the baby his apricots out of a jar. "The children have been to Florida before," the old lady said. "You all ought to take them somewhere else for a change so they would see different parts of the world and be broad. They never have been to east Tennessee."

The children's mother didn't seem to hear her but the eight-year-old boy, John Wesley, a stocky child with glasses, said, "If you don't want to go to Florida, why dontcha stay at home?" He and the little girl, June Star, were reading the funny papers on the floor.

"She wouldn't stay at home to be queen for a day," June Star said without raising her yellow head.

"Yes and what would you do if this fellow, The Misfit, caught you?" the grandmother asked.

"I'd smack his face," John Wesley said.

"She wouldn't stay at home for a million bucks," June Star said. "Afraid she'd miss something. She has to go everywhere we go."

"All right, Miss," the grandmother said. "Just remember that the next time you want me to curl your hair."

June Star said her hair was naturally curly.

The next morning the grandmother was the first one in the car, ready to go. She had her big black valise that looked like the head of a hippopotamus in one corner, and underneath it she was hiding a basket with Pitty Sing, the cat, in it. She didn't intend for the cat to be left alone in the house for three days because he would miss her too much and she was afraid he might brush against one of the gas burners and accidentally asphyxiate himself. Her son, Bailey, didn't like to arrive at a motel with a cat.

She sat in the middle of the back seat with John Wesley and June Star on either side of her. Bailey and the children's mother and the baby sat in front and they left Atlanta at eight forty-five with the mileage on the car at 55890. The grandmother wrote this down because she thought it would be interesting to say how many miles they had been when they got back. It took them twenty minutes to reach the outskirts of the city.

The old lady settled herself comfortably, removing her white cotton gloves and putting them up with her purse on the shelf in front of the back window. The children's mother still had on slacks and still had her head tied up in a green kerchief, but the grandmother had on a navy blue straw sailor hat with a bunch of white violets on the brim and a navy blue dress

with a small white dot in the print. Her collars and cuffs were white organdy trimmed with lace and at her neckline she had pinned a purple spray of cloth violets containing a sachet. In case of an accident, anyone seeing her dead on the highway would know at once that she was a lady.

She said she thought it was going to be a good day for driving, neither too hot nor too cold, and she cautioned Bailey that the speed limit was fifty-five miles an hour and that the patrolmen hid themselves behind billboards and small clumps of trees and sped out after you before you had a chance to slow down. She pointed out interesting details of the scenery: Stone Mountain; the blue granite that in some places came up to both sides of the highway; the brilliant red clay banks slightly streaked with purple; and the various crops that made rows of green lace-work on the ground. The trees were full of silver-white sunlight and the meanest of them sparkled. The children were reading comic magazines and their mother had gone back to sleep.

"Let's go through Georgia fast so we won't have to look at it much," John Wesley said.

"If I were a little boy," said the grandmother, "I wouldn't talk about my native state that way. Tennessee has the mountains and Georgia has the hills."

"Tennessee is just a hillbilly dumping ground," John Wesley said, "and Georgia is a lousy state too."

"You said it," June Star said.

"In my time," said the grandmother, folding her thin veined fingers, "children were more respectful of their native states and their parents and everything else. People did right then. Oh look at the cute little pickaninny!" she said and pointed to a Negro child standing in the door of a shack. "Wouldn't that make a picture, now?" she asked and they all turned and looked at the little Negro out of the back window. He waved.

"He didn't have any britches on," June Star said.

"He probably didn't have any," the grandmother explained. "Little niggers in the country don't have things like we do. If I could paint, I'd paint that picture," she said.

The children exchanged comic books.

The grandmother offered to hold the baby and the children's mother passed him over the front seat to her. She set him on her knee and bounced him and told him about the things they were passing. She rolled her eyes and screwed up her mouth and stuck her leathery thin face into his smooth bland one. Occasionally he gave her a faraway smile. They passed a large cotton field with five or six graves fenced in the middle of it, like a small island. "Look at the graveyard!" the grandmother said, pointing it out. "That was the old family burying ground. That belonged to the plantation."

"Where's the plantation?" John Wesley asked.

"Gone With the Wind," said the grandmother. "Ha. Ha."

When the children finished all the comic books they had brought, they opened the lunch and ate it. The grandmother ate a peanut butter sandwich and an olive and would not let the children throw the box and the paper napkins out the window. When there was nothing else to do they played a game by choosing a cloud and making the other two guess what shape it suggested. John Wesley took one the shape of a cow and June Star guessed a cow and John Wesley said, no, an automobile, and June Star said he didn't play fair, and they began to slap each other over the grandmother.

The grandmother said she would tell them a story if they would keep quiet. When she told a story, she rolled her eyes and waved her head and was very dramatic. She said once when she was a maiden lady she had been courted by a Mr. Edgar Atkins Teagarden from Jasper, Georgia. She said he was a very good-looking man and a gentleman and that he brought her a watermelon every Saturday afternoon with his initials cut in it, E. A. T. Well, one Saturday, she said, Mr. Teagarden brought the watermelon and there was nobody at home and he left it on the front porch and returned in his buggy to Jasper, but she never got the watermelon, she said, because a nigger boy ate it when he saw the initials, E. A. T.! This story tickled John Wesley's funny bone and he giggled and giggled but June Star didn't think it was any good. She said she wouldn't marry a man that just brought her a watermelon on Saturday. The grandmother said she would have done well to marry Mr. Teagarden because he was a gentleman and had bought Coca-Cola stock when it first came out and that he had died only a few years ago, a very wealthy man.

They stopped at The Tower for barbecued sandwiches. The Tower was a part stucco and part wood filling station and dance hall set in a clearing outside of Timothy. A fat man named Red Sammy Butts ran it and there were signs stuck here and there on the building and for miles up and down the highway saying, TRY RED SAMMY'S FAMOUS BARBECUE. NONE LIKE FAMOUS RED SAMMY'S! RED SAM! THE FAT BOY WITH THE HAPPY LAUGH. A VETERAN! RED SAMMY'S YOUR MAN!

Red Sammy was lying on the bare ground outside The Tower with his head under a truck while a gray monkey about a foot high, chained to a small chinaberry tree, chattered nearby. The monkey sprang back into the tree and got on the highest limb as soon as he saw the children jump out of the car and run toward him.

Inside, The Tower was a long dark room with a counter at one end and tables at the other and dancing space in the middle. They all sat down at a board table next to the nickelodeon and Red Sam's wife, a tall burnt-brown woman with hair and eyes lighter than her skin, came and took their order. The children's mother put a dime in the machine and played "The Tennessee Waltz," and the grandmother said that tune always made her want to dance. She asked Bailey if he would like to dance but he only glared at her. He didn't have a naturally sunny disposition like she did and trips made him nervous. The grandmother's brown eyes were very bright. She swayed her head from side to side and pretended she was dancing in her chair. June Star said play something she could tap to so the children's mother put in another dime and played a fast number and June Star stepped out onto the dance floor and did her tap routine.

"Ain't she cute?" Red Sam's wife said, leaning over the counter. "Would you like to come be my little girl?"

"No I certainly wouldn't," June Star said. "I wouldn't live in a broken-down place like this for a million bucks!" and she ran back to the table.

"Ain't she cute?" the woman repeated, stretching her mouth politely.

"Arn't you ashamed?" hissed the grandmother.

Red Sam came in and told his wife to quit lounging on the counter and hurry up with these people's order. His khaki trousers reached just to his hip bones and his stomach hung over them like a sack of meal swaying under his shirt. He came over and sat down at a table

nearby and let out a combination sigh and yodel. "You can't win," he said. "You can't win,"
and he wiped his sweating red face off with a
gray handkerchief. "These days you don't
know who to trust," he said. "Ain't that the
truth?"

"People are certainly not nice like they used
to be," said the grandmother.

"Two fellers come in here last week," Red
Sammy said, "driving a Chrysler. It was a old
beat-up car but it was a good one and these
boys looked all right to me. Said they worked
at the mill and you know I let them fellers
charge the gas they bought? Now why did I
do that?"

"Because you're a good man!" the grandmother said at once.

"Yes'm, I suppose so," Red Sam said as if he
were struck with this answer.

His wife brought the orders, carrying the
five plates all at once without a tray, two in
each hand and one balanced on her arm. "It
isn't a soul in this green world of God's that
you can trust," she said. "And I don't count nobody out of that, not nobody," she repeated,
looking at Red Sammy.

"Did you read about that criminal, The Misfit, that's escaped?" asked the grandmother.

"I wouldn't be a bit surprised if he didn't at-
tact this place right here," said the woman. "If
he hears about it being here, I wouldn't be
none surprised to see him. If he hears it's two
cent in the cash register, I wouldn't be a tall
surprised if he . . ."

"That'll do," Red Sam said. "Go bring these
people their Co'-Colas," and the woman went
off to get the rest of the order.

"A good man is hard to find," Red Sammy
said. "Everything is getting terrible. I remember the day you could go off and leave your
screen door unlatched. Not no more."

He and the grandmother discussed better
times. The old lady said that in her opinion Europe was entirely to blame for the way things
were now. She said the way Europe acted you
would think we were made of money and Red
Sam said it was no use talking about it, she was
exactly right. The children ran outside into the
white sunlight and looked at the monkey in
the lacy chinaberry tree. He was busy catching fleas on himself and biting each one
carefully between his teeth as if it were a delicacy.

They drove off again into the hot afternoon.
The grandmother took cat naps and woke up

every few minutes with her own snoring. Outside of Toombsboro she woke up and recalled
an old plantation that she had visited in this
neighborhood once when she was a young
lady. She said the house had six white columns
across the front and that there was an avenue
of oaks leading up to it and two little wooden
trellis arbors on either side in front where you
sat down with your suitor after a stroll in the
garden. She recalled exactly which road to
turn off to get to it. She knew that Bailey
would not be willing to lose any time looking at
an old house, but the more she talked about it,
the more she wanted to see it once again and
find out if the little twin arbors were still standing. "There was a secret panel in this house,"
she said craftily, not telling the truth but wishing that she were, "and the story went that all
the family silver was hidden in it when Sherman came through but it was never
found . . ."

"Hey!" John Wesley said. "Let's go see it!
We'll find it! We'll poke all the woodwork and
find it! Who lives there? Where do you turn off
at? Hey Pop, can't we turn off there?"

"We never have seen a house with a secret
panel!" June Star shrieked. "Let's go to the
house with the secret panel! Hey Pop, can't we
go see the house with the secret panel!"

"It's not far from here, I know," the grandmother said. "It wouldn't take over twenty minutes."

Bailey was looking straight ahead. His jaw
was as rigid as a horseshoe. "No," he said.

The children began to yell and scream that
they wanted to see the house with the secret
panel. John Wesley kicked the back of the front
seat and June Star hung over her mother's
shoulder and whined desperately into her ear
that they never had any fun even on their vacation, that they could never do what THEY
wanted to do. The baby began to scream and
John Wesley kicked the back of the seat so
hard that his father could feel the blows in
his kidney.

"All right!" he shouted and drew the car to a
stop at the side of the road. "Will you all shut
up? Will you all just shut up for one second? If
you don't shut up, we won't go anywhere."

"It would be very educational for them," the
grandmother murmured.

"All right," Bailey said, "but get this: this is
the only time we're going to stop for anything
like this. This is the one and only time."

"The dirt road that you have to turn down is

about a mile back," the grandmother directed. "I marked it when we passed."

"A dirt road," Bailey groaned.

After they had turned around and were headed toward the dirt road, the grandmother recalled other points about the house, the beautiful glass over the front doorway and the candle-lamp in the hall. John Wesley said that the secret panel was probably in the fireplace.

"You can't go inside this house," Bailey said. "You don't know who lives there."

"While you all talk to the people in front, I'll run around behind and get in a window," John Wesley suggested.

"We'll all stay in the car," his mother said.

They turned onto the dirt road and the car raced roughly along in a swirl of pink dust. The grandmother recalled the times when there were no paved roads and thirty miles was a day's journey. The dirt road was hilly and there were sudden washes in it and sharp curves on dangerous embankments. All at once they would be on a hill, looking down over the blue tops of trees for miles around, then the next minute, they would be in a red depression with the dust-coated trees looking down on them.

"This place had better turn up in a minute," Bailey said, "or I'm going to turn around."

The road looked as if no one had traveled on it in months.

"It's not much farther," the grandmother said and just as she said it, a horrible thought came to her. The thought was so embarrassing that she turned red in the face and her eyes dilated and her feet jumped up, upsetting her valise in the corner. The instant the valise moved, the newspaper top she had over the basket under it rose with a snarl and Pitty Sing, the cat, sprang onto Bailey's shoulder.

The children were thrown to the floor and their mother, clutching the baby, was thrown out the door onto the ground; the old lady was thrown into the front seat. The car turned over once and landed right-side-up in a gulch off the side of the road. Bailey remained in the driver's seat with the cat—gray-striped with a broad white face and an orange nose—clinging to his neck like a caterpillar.

As soon as the children saw they could move their arms and legs, they scrambled out of the car, shouting, "We've had an ACCIDENT!" The grandmother was curled up under the dashboard, hoping she was injured so that Bailey's wrath would not come down on her all at once. The horrible thought she had had before the accident was that the house she had remembered so vividly was not in Georgia but in Tennessee.

Bailey removed the cat from his neck with both hands and flung it out the window against the side of a pine tree. Then he got out of the car and started looking for the children's mother. She was sitting against the side of the red gutted ditch, holding the screaming baby, but she only had a cut down her face and a broken shoulder. "We've had an ACCIDENT!" the children screamed in a frenzy of delight.

"But nobody's killed," June Star said with disappointment as the grandmother limped out of the car, her hat still pinned to her head but the broken front brim standing up at a jaunty angle and the violet spray hanging off the side. They all sat down in the ditch, except the children, to recover from the shock. They were all shaking.

"Maybe a car will come along," said the children's mother hoarsely.

"I believe I have injured an organ," said the grandmother, pressing her side, but no one answered her. Bailey's teeth were clattering. He had on a yellow sport shirt with bright blue parrots designed in it and his face was as yellow as the shirt. The grandmother decided that she would not mention that the house was in Tennessee.

The road was about ten feet above and they could see only the tops of the trees on the other side of it. Behind the ditch they were sitting in there were more woods, tall and dark and deep. In a few minutes they saw a car some distance away on top of a hill, coming slowly as if the occupants were watching them. The grandmother stood up and waved both arms dramatically to attract their attention. The car continued to come on slowly, disappeared around a bend and appeared again, moving even slower, on top of the hill they had gone over. It was a big black battered hearse-like automobile. There were three men in it.

It came to a stop just over them and for some minutes, the driver looked down with a steady expressionless gaze to where they were sitting, and didn't speak. Then he turned his head and muttered something to the other two and they got out. One was a fat boy in black trousers and a red sweat shirt with a silver stallion embossed on the front of it. He moved around on the right side of them and stood staring, his mouth partly open in a kind of loose grin. The other had on khaki pants and a blue striped coat and a gray hat pulled down very low, hiding most of his face. He came around slowly on the left side. Neither spoke.

The driver got out of the car and stood by the side of it, looking down at them. He was an older man than the other two. His hair was just beginning to gray and he wore silver-rimmed spectacles that gave him a scholarly look. He had a long creased face and didn't have on any shirt or undershirt. He had on blue jeans that were too tight for him and was holding a black hat and a gun. The two boys also had guns.

"We've had an ACCIDENT!" the children screamed.

The grandmother had the peculiar feeling that the bespectacled man was someone she knew. His face was as familiar to her as if she had known him all her life but she could not recall who he was. He moved away from the car and began to come down the embankment, placing his feet carefully so that he wouldn't slip. He had on tan and white shoes and no socks, and his ankles were red and thin. "Good afternoon," he said. "I see you all had you a little spill."

"We turned over twice!" said the grandmother.

"Oncet," he corrected. "We seen it happen. Try their car and see will it run, Hiram," he said quietly to the boy with the gray hat.

"What you got that gun for?" John Wesley asked. "Whatcha gonna do with that gun?"

"Lady," the man said to the children's mother, "would you mind calling them children to sit down by you? Children make me nervous. I want all you all to sit down right together there where you're at."

"What are you telling US what to do for?" June Star asked.

Behind them the line of woods gaped like a dark open mouth. "Come here," said their mother.

"Look here now," Bailey began suddenly, "we're in a predicament! We're in . . ."

The grandmother shrieked. She scrambled to her feet and stood staring. "You're The Misfit!" she said. "I recognized you at once!"

"Yes'm," the man said, smiling slightly as if he were pleased in spite of himself to be known, "but it would have been better for all of you, lady, if you hadn't of reckernized me."

Bailey turned his head sharply and said something to his mother that shocked even the

children. The old lady began to cry and The Misfit reddened.

"Lady," he said, "don't you get upset. Sometimes a man says things he don't mean. I don't reckon he meant to talk to you thataway."

"You wouldn't shoot a lady, would you?" the grandmother said and removed a clean handkerchief from her cuff and began to slap at her eyes with it.

The Misfit pointed the toe of his shoe into the ground and made a little hole and then covered it up again. "I would hate to have to," he said.

"Listen," the grandmother almost screamed, "I know you're a good man. You don't look a bit like you have common blood. I know you must come from nice people!"

"Yes mam," he said, "finest people in the world." When he smiled he showed a row of strong white teeth. "God never made a finer woman than my mother and my daddy's heart was pure gold," he said. The boy with the red sweat shirt had come around behind them and was standing with his gun at his hip. The Misfit squatted down on the ground. "Watch them children, Bobby Lee," he said. "You know they make me nervous." He looked at the six of them huddled together in front of him and he seemed to be embarrassed as if he couldn't think of anything to say. "Ain't a cloud in the sky," he remarked, looking up at it. "Don't see no sun but don't see no cloud neither."

"Yes, it's a beautiful day," said the grandmother. "Listen," she said, "you shouldn't call yourself The Misfit because I know you're a good man at heart. I can just look at you and tell."

"Hush!" Bailey yelled. "Hush! Everybody shut up and let me handle this!" He was squatting in the position of a runner about to sprint forward but he didn't move.

"I pre-chate that, lady," The Misfit said and drew a little circle in the ground with the butt of his gun.

"It'll take a half a hour to fix this here car," Hiram called, looking over the raised hood of it.

"Well, first you and Bobby Lee get him and that little boy to step over yonder with you," The Misfit said, pointing to Bailey and John Wesley. "The boys want to ast you something," he said to Bailey. "Would you mind stepping back in them woods there with them?"

"Listen," Bailey began, "we're in a terrible predicament! Nobody realizes what this is," and his voice cracked. His eyes were as blue and intense as the parrots in his shirt and he remained perfectly still.

The grandmother reached up to adjust her hat brim as if she were going to the woods with him but it came off in her hand. She stood staring at it and after a second she let it fall on the ground. Hiram pulled Bailey up by the arm as if he were assisting an old man. John Wesley caught hold of his father's hand and Bobby Lee followed. They went off toward the woods and just as they reached the dark edge, Bailey turned and supporting himself against a gray naked pine trunk, he shouted, "I'll be back in a minute, Mamma, wait on me!"

"Come back this instant!" his mother shrilled but they all disappeared into the woods.

"Bailey Boy!" the grandmother called in a tragic voice but she found she was looking at The Misfit squatting on the ground in front of her. "I just know you're a good man," she said desperately. "You're not a bit common!"

"Nome, I ain't a good man," The Misfit said after a second as if he had considered her statement carefully, "but I ain't the worst in the world neither. My daddy said I was a different breed of dog from my brothers and sisters. 'You know,' Daddy said, 'it's some that can live their whole life out without asking about it and it's others has to know why it is, and this boy is one of the latters. He's going to be into everything!' " He put on his black hat and looked up suddenly and then away deep into the woods as if he were embarrassed again. "I'm sorry I don't have on a shirt before you ladies," he said, hunching his shoulders slightly. "We buried our clothes that we had on when we escaped and we're just making do until we can get better. We borrowed these from some folks we met," he explained.

"That's perfectly all right," the grandmother said. "Maybe Bailey has an extra shirt in his suitcase."

"I'll look and see terrectly," The Misfit said.

"Where are they taking him?" the children's mother screamed.

"Daddy was a card himself," The Misfit said. "You couldn't put anything over on him. He never got in trouble with the Authorities though. Just had the knack of handling them."

"You could be honest too if you'd only try," said the grandmother. "Think how wonderful it would be to settle down and live a comfortable life and not have to think about somebody chasing you all the time."

The Misfit kept scratching in the ground with the butt of his gun as if he were thinking about it. "Yes'm, somebody is always after you," he murmured.

The grandmother noticed how thin his shoulder blades were just behind his hat because she was standing up looking down on him. "Do you ever pray?" she asked.

He shook his head. All she saw was the black hat wiggle between his shoulder blades. "Nome," he said. 10

There was a pistol shot from the woods, followed closely by another. Then silence. The old lady's head jerked around. She could hear the wind move through the tree tops like a long satisfied insuck of breath. "Bailey Boy!" she called.

"I was a gospel singer for a while," The Misfit said. "I been most everything. Been in the arm service, both land and sea, at home and 20 abroad, been twict married, been an undertaker, been with the railroads, plowed Mother Earth, been in a tornado, seen a man burnt alive oncet," and he looked up at the children's mother and the little girl who were sitting close together, their faces white and their eyes glassy; "I even seen a woman flogged," he said.

"Pray, pray," the grandmother began, "pray, pray . . ."

"I never was a bad boy that I remember of," 30 The Misfit said in an almost dreamy voice, "but somewheres along the line I done something wrong and got sent to the penitentiary. I was buried alive," and he looked up and held her attention to him by a steady stare.

"That's when you should have started to pray," she said. "What did you do to get sent to the penitentiary that first time?"

"Turn to the right, it was a wall," The Misfit said, looking up again at the cloudless sky. 40 "Turn to the left, it was a wall. Look up it was a ceiling, look down it was a floor. I forget what I done, lady. I set there and set there, trying to remember what it was I done and I ain't recalled it to this day. Oncet in a while, I would think it was coming to me, but it never come."

"Maybe they put you in by mistake," the old lady said vaguely.

"Nome," he said. "It wasn't no mistake. They had the papers on me." 50

"You must have stolen something," she said.

The Misfit sneered slightly. "Nobody had nothing I wanted," he said. "It was a head-doctor at the penitentiary said what I had done was kill my daddy but I known that for a lie. My daddy died in nineteen ought nineteen of the epidemic flu and I never had a thing to do with it. He was buried in the Mount Hopewell Baptist churchyard and you can go there and see for yourself."

"If you would pray," the old lady said, "Jesus would help you."

"That's right," The Misfit said.

"Well then, why don't you pray?" she asked trembling with delight suddenly.

"I don't want no hep," he said. "I'm doing all right by myself."

Bobby Lee and Hiram came ambling back from the woods. Bobby Lee was dragging a yellow shirt with bright blue parrots in it.

"Thow me that shirt, Bobby Lee," The Misfit said. The shirt came flying at him and landed on his shoulder and he put it on. The grandmother couldn't name what the shirt reminded her of. "No, lady," The Misfit said while he was buttoning it up, "I found out the crime don't matter. You can do one thing or you can do another, kill a man or take a tire off his car, because sooner or later you're going to forget what it was you done and just be punished for it."

The children's mother had begun to make heaving noises as if she couldn't get her breath. "Lady," he asked, "would you and that little girl like to step off yonder with Bobby Lee and Hiram and join your husband?"

"Yes, thank you," the mother said faintly. Her left arm dangled helplessly and she was holding the baby, who had gone to sleep, in the other. "Hep that lady up, Hiram," The Misfit said as she struggled to climb out of the ditch, "and Bobby Lee, you hold onto that little girl's hand."

"I don't want to hold hands with him," June Star said. "He reminds me of a pig."

The fat boy blushed and laughed and caught her by the arm and pulled her off into the woods after Hiram and her mother.

Alone with The Misfit, the grandmother found that she had lost her voice. There was not a cloud in the sky nor any sun. There was nothing around her but woods. She wanted to tell him that he must pray. She opened and closed her mouth several times before anything came out. Finally she found herself saying, "Jesus, Jesus," meaning, Jesus will help you, but the way she was saying it, it sounded as if she might be cursing.

"Yes'm," The Misfit said as if he agreed. "Jesus thown everything off balance. It was the same case with Him as with me except He hadn't committed any crime and they could prove I had committed one because they had the papers on me. Of course," he said, "they never shown me my papers. That's why I sign myself now. I said long ago, you get you a signature and sign everything you do and keep a copy of it. Then you'll know what you done and you can hold up the crime to the punishment and see do they match and in the end you'll have something to prove you ain't been treated right. I call myself The Misfit," he said, "because I can't make what all I done wrong fit what all I gone through in punishment."

There was a piercing scream from the woods, followed closely by a pistol report. "Does it seem right to you, lady, that one is punished a heap and another ain't punished at all?"

"Jesus!" the old lady cried. "You've got good blood! I know you wouldn't shoot a lady! I know you come from nice people! Pray! Jesus, you ought not to shoot a lady. I'll give you all the money I've got!"

"Lady," The Misfit said, looking beyond her far into the woods, "there never was a body that give the undertaker a tip."

There were two more pistol reports and the grandmother raised her head like a parched old turkey hen crying for water and called, "Bailey Boy, Bailey Boy!" as if her heart would break.

"Jesus was the only One that ever raised the dead," The Misfit continued, "and He shouldn't have done it. He thown everything off balance. If He did what He said, then it's nothing for you to do but thow away everything and follow Him, and if He didn't, then it's nothing for you to do but enjoy the few minutes you got left the best way you can—by killing somebody or burning down his house or doing some other meanness to him. No pleasure but meanness," he said and his voice had become almost a snarl.

"Maybe He didn't raise the dead," the old lady mumbled, not knowing what she was saying and feeling so dizzy that she sank down in the ditch with her legs twisted under her.

"I wasn't there so I can't say He didn't," The Misfit said. "I wisht I had of been there," he said, hitting the ground with his fist. "It ain't right I wasn't there because if I had of been there I would of known. Listen lady," he said in a high voice, "if I had of been there I would of known and I wouldn't be like I am now."

His voice seemed about to crack and the grandmother's head cleared for an instant. She saw the man's face twisted close to her own as if he were going to cry and she murmured, "Why you're one of my babies. You're one of my own children!" She reached out and touched him on the shoulder. The Misfit sprang back as if a snake had bitten him and shot her three times through the chest. Then he put his gun down on the ground and took off his glasses and began to clean them.

Hiram and Bobby Lee returned from the woods and stood over the ditch, looking down at the grandmother who half sat and half lay in a puddle of blood with her legs crossed under her like a child's and her face smiling up at the cloudless sky.

Without his glasses, The Misfit's eyes were red-rimmed and pale and defenseless-looking. "Take her off and thow her where you thown the others," he said, picking up the cat that was rubbing itself against his leg.

"She was a talker, wasn't she?" Bobby Lee said, sliding down the ditch with a yodel.

"She would of been a good woman," The Misfit said, "if it had been somebody there to shoot her every minute of her life." 10

"Some fun!" Bobby Lee said.

"Shut up, Bobby Lee," The Misfit said. "it's no real pleasure in life."   1955

EDMUND WILSON

1895–

BORN IN Red Bank, New Jersey, educated at the Hill School and Princeton, where he enjoyed the company of two other fledgling writers, F. Scott Fitzgerald and John Peale Bishop, Edmund Wilson entered, after graduation, on his long career as a journalist. During 1916–1917 he was a reporter on the New York *Evening Sun*. Returning from war service, he became managing-editor of *Vanity Fair* (1920–1921) and from 1926–1931 he was an associate editor of the *New Republic*. Later (1944–1948) he was the leading book reviewer for the *New Yorker*.

Although he has written poetry, plays, short stories (*Memoirs of Hecate County*, 1946), and travel books (*Travels in Two Democracies*, 1936; *Europe Without Baedeker*, 1947), Wilson's reputation rests largely on his criticism. He stands apart from other critics of his generation, most of whom have been intensely preoccupied with close analysis of particular literary works or refinements of literary theory or discussions of critical terminology. He belongs to no school and has no disciples.

In his "Thoughts on Being Bibliographed" (first published in the *Princeton University Library Chronicle*, February 1944) Wilson speaks of himself as primarily a journalist; as a critic, that is, who persuades editors to let him write about authors and books that interest him. His "strategy" has been "first to get books for review or reporting assignments to cover on subjects in which I happen to be interested; then, later, to use the scattered articles for writing general studies of these subjects; then, finally, to bring out a book in which groups of these essays were revised and combined." A new book by Wilson is therefore likely to be such a collection of essays as *The Triple Thinkers* (1938), *The Wound and the Bow* (1941), *Classics and Commercials* (1950), or *The Shores of Light* (1952).

But Wilson is no pedestrian reviewer, turning out his daily or weekly piece on whatever book the editor sends him. He is a journalistic critic in the now sadly decayed tradition which includes such heroes of his as Poe, De Quincey, and the young Bernard Shaw. Wilson is widely read in the Greek and Latin classics, and in French, Italian, and Russian literature.

He can bring to bear in his criticism his knowledge of historical movements, particularly the rise of Socialism and Communism (*To the Finland Station*, 1940), and his understanding of Freudian psychology and its possible applications to literature.

In the essay printed here, "The Historical Interpretation of Literature," Wilson sets forth the positions appropriated by the critics of his generation and indicates the preferences which have determined his career as a critic. By his training he was equipped to write the kind of non-historical comparative criticism which first brought T. S. Eliot fame as a critic. Like George Saintsbury or J. G. Huneker he might have become a connoisseur of literary vintages. Fascinated for a time, in the 1930's, with Marxist theories of literature, he was fortunately prevented from following that line by the effects of the Stalinist dictatorship on Russian literature. He has preferred, in the main, to study a writer's ideas in the light of the conditions, personal and social, which helped to form them. Having little use for the constraints of theory, as this essay shows, he has kept his mind open and attentive to new writing as it came along, and he can name with justifiable pride several modern authors whom he has "discovered."

Critics who object to Wilson's eclecticism are likely to say that his first, book-length, critical essay, *Axel's Castle: A Study in the Imaginative Literature of 1870-1930* (1931), contains his best work. In these influential studies of Yeats, Eliot, Proust, Joyce, and other writers, such critics say, Wilson had a thesis and a theme—the varieties of symbolism to be found in the work of these authors. But they fail to notice that even in this early book Wilson was studying origins, the why of the emergence of a particular style. He was bent on discovering why Symbolism was a necessary movement and what its relations were to Romanticism and to Naturalism.

Arthur Mizener, "Edmund Wilson: A Checklist," *Princeton University Library Chronicle*, V (February, 1944), 62–78.

Edmund Wilson, *Axel's Castle: A Study in the Imaginative Literature of 1870-1930*, New York, 1931.

———, *A Piece of My Mind: Reflections at Sixty*, New York, 1956.

———, *The Triple Thinkers: Ten Essays on Literature*, New York, 1938.

———, *To the Finland Station*, New York, 1940.

———, *The Wound and the Bow: Seven Studies in Literature*, Boston, 1941.

The Shock of Recognition: The Development of Literature in the United States Recorded by the Men Who Made It, Edmund Wilson, ed., New York, 1943.

R. Adams, "Masks and Delays: Edmund Wilson as Critic," *Sewanee Review*, LVI (April–June, 1948), 272–286.

J. P. Pritchard, *Criticism in America*, Norman, Oklahoma, 1956, pp. 269–276.

Delmore Schwartz, "The Writing of Edmund Wilson," *Accent*, II (Spring, 1942), 177–186.

George Snell, "An Examination of Modern Critics, II: Edmund Wilson, 'The Historical Critic,' " *Rocky Mountain Review*, VIII (Winter, 1944), 36–44.

» » THE HISTORICAL INTERPRETATION
OF LITERATURE [1] « «

I want to talk about the historical interpretation of literature—that is, about the interpretation of literature in its social, economic and political aspects.

To begin with, it will be worth while to say something about the kind of criticism which seems to be furthest removed from this. There is a kind of comparative criticism which tends to be non-historical. The essays of T. S. Eliot, which have had such an immense influence in our time, are, for example, fundamentally non-historical. Eliot sees, or tries to see, the whole of literature, so far as he is acquainted with it, spread out before him under the aspect of eter-

[1] A lecture delivered at Princeton University, October 23, 1940.

nity. He then compares the work of different periods and countries, and tries to draw from it general conclusions about what literature ought to be. He understands, of course, that our point of view in connection with literature changes, and he has what seems to me a very sound conception of the whole body of writing of the past as something to which new works are continually being added, and which is not thereby merely increased in bulk but modified as a whole—so that Sophocles is no longer precisely what he was for Aristotle, or Shakespeare what he was for Ben Jonson or for Dryden or for Dr. Johnson, on account of all the later literature that has intervened between them and us. Yet at every point of this continual accretion, the whole field may be surveyed, as it were, spread out before the critic. The critic tries to see it as God might; he calls the books to a Day of Judgment. And, looking at things in this way, he may arrive at interesting and valuable conclusions which could hardly be reached by approaching them in any other way. Eliot was able to see, for example—what I believe had never been noticed before—that the French Symbolist poetry of the nineteenth century had certain fundamental resemblances to the English poetry of the age of Donne. Another kind of critic would draw certain historical conclusions from these purely esthetic findings, as the Russian D. S. Mirsky did; but Eliot does not draw them.

Another example of this kind of non-historical criticism, in a somewhat different way and on a somewhat different plane, is the work of the late George Saintsbury. Saintsbury was a connoisseur of wines; he wrote an entertaining book on the subject. And his attitude toward literature, too, was that of the connoisseur. He tastes the authors and tells you about the vintages; he distinguishes the qualities of the various wines. His palate was as fine as could be, and he possessed the great qualification that he knew how to take each book on its own terms without expecting it to be some other book and was thus in a position to appreciate a great variety of kinds of writing. He was a man of strong social prejudices and peculiarly intransigent political views, but, so far as it is humanly possible, he kept them out of his literary criticism. The result is one of the most agreeable and most comprehensive commentaries on literature that have ever been written in English. Most scholars who have read as much as Saintsbury do not have Saintsbury's discriminating taste. Here is a critic who has covered the whole ground like any academic historian, yet whose account of it is not merely a chronology but a record of fastidious enjoyment. Since enjoyment is the only thing he is looking for, he does not need to know the causes of things, and the historical background of literature does not interest him very much.

There is, however, another tradition of criticism which dates from the beginning of the eighteenth century. In the year 1725, the Neapolitan philosopher Vico published *La Scienza Nuova*, a revolutionary work on the philosophy of history, in which he asserted for the first time that the social world was certainly the work of man, and attempted what is, so far as I know, the first social interpretation of a work of literature. This is what Vico says about Homer: "Homer composed the *Iliad* when Greece was young and consequently burning with sublime passions such as pride, anger and vengeance— passions which cannot allow dissimulation and which consort with generosity; so that she then admired Achilles, the hero of force. But, grown old, he composed the *Odyssey*, at a time when the passions of Greece were already somewhat cooled by reflection, which is the mother of prudence—so that she now admired Ulysses, the hero of wisdom. Thus also, in Homer's youth, the Greek people liked cruelty, vituperation, savagery, fierceness, ferocity; whereas, when Homer was old, they were already enjoying the luxuries of Alcinoüs, the delights of Calypso, the pleasures of Circe, the songs of the sirens and the pastimes of the suitors, who went no further in aggression and combat than laying siege to the chaste Penelope—all of which practices would appear incompatible with the spirit of the earlier time. The divine Plato is so struck by this difficulty that, in order to solve it, he tells us that Homer had foreseen in inspired vision these dissolute, sickly and disgusting customs. But in this way he makes Homer out to have been but a foolish instructor for Greek civilization, since, however much he may condemn them, he is displaying for imitation these corrupt and decadent habits which were not to be adopted till long after the foundation of the nations of Greece, and accelerating the natural course which human events would take by spurring the Greeks on to corruption. Thus it is plain that the Homer of the *Iliad* must have preceded by many years the Homer who wrote the *Odyssey;* and it is plain that the former must belong to the northeastern part of Greece, since he celebrates the Trojan War, which took place in his part of the country, whereas the latter belongs to the southeastern part, since he celebrates Ulysses, who reigned there."

You see that Vico has here explained Homer in terms both of historical period and of geographical origin. The idea that human arts and institutions were to be studied and elucidated as the products of the geographical and climatic conditions in which the people who created them lived, and of the phase of their social development through which they were passing at the moment, made great progress during the eighteenth century. There are traces of it even in Dr. Johnson, that most orthodox and classical of critics—as, for example, when he accounts for certain characteristics of Shakespeare by the relative barbarity of the age in which he lived, pointing out, just as Vico had done, that 'nations, like individuals, have their infancy.' And by the eighties of the eighteenth century Herder, in his *Ideas on the Philosophy of History*, was writing of poetry that it was a kind of 'Proteus among the people, which is always changing its form in response to the languages, manners, and habits, to the temperaments and climates, nay even to the accents of different nations.' He said—what could still seem startling even so late as that—that 'language was not a divine communication, but something men had produced themselves.' In the lectures on the philosophy of history that Hegel delivered in Berlin in 1822–23, he discussed the national literatures as expressions of the societies which had produced them—societies which he conceived as great organisms continually transforming themselves under the influence of a succession of dominant ideas.

In the field of literary criticism, this historical point of view came to its first complete flower in the work of the French critic Taine, in the middle of the nineteenth century. The whole school of historian-critics to which Taine belonged—Michelet, Renan, Sainte-Beuve—had been occupied in interpreting books in terms of their historical origins. But Taine was the first of these to attempt to apply such principles systematically and on a large scale in a work devoted exclusively to literature. In the Introduction to his *History of English Literature*, published in 1863, he made his famous pronouncement that works of literature were to be understood as the upshot of three interfusing

factors: *the moment, the race, and the milieu*. Taine thought he was a scientist and a mechanist, who was examining works of literature from the same point of view as the chemist's in experimenting with chemical compounds. But the difference between the critic and the chemist is that the critic cannot first combine his elements and then watch to see what they will do: he can only examine phenomena which have already taken place. The procedure that Taine actually follows is to pretend to set the stage for the experiment by describing the moment, the race and the milieu, and then to say: 'Such a situation demands such and such a kind of writer.' He now goes on to describe the kind of writer that the situation demands, and the reader finds himself at the end confronted with Shakespeare or Milton or Byron or whoever the great figure is —who turns out to prove the accuracy of Taine's prognosis by precisely living up to this description.

There was thus a certain element of imposture in Taine; but it was the rabbits he pulled out that saved him. If he had really been the mechanist that he thought he was, his work on literature would have had little value. The truth was that Taine loved literature for its own sake—he was at his best himself a brilliant artist—and he had very strong moral convictions which give his writing emotional power. His mind, to be sure, was an analytic one, and his analysis, though terribly oversimplified, does have an explanatory value. Yet his work was what we call creative. Whatever he may say about chemical experiments, it is evident when he writes of a great writer that the moment, the race and the milieu have combined, like the three sounds of the chord in Browning's poem about Abt Vogler, to produce not a fourth sound but a star.

To Taine's set of elements was added, dating from the middle of the century, a new element, the economic, which was introduced into the discussion of historical phenomena mainly by Marx and Engels. The non-Marxist critics themselves were at the time already taking into account the influence of the social classes. In his chapters on the Norman conquest of England, Taine shows that the difference between the literatures produced respectively by the Normans and by the Saxons was partly the difference between a ruling class, on the one hand, and a vanquished and repressed class, on the other. And Michelet, in his volume on the Regency, which was finished the same year that the *History of English Literature* appeared, studies the *Manon Lescaut* of the Abbé Prévost as a document representing the point of view of the small gentry before the French Revolution. But Marx and Engels derived the social classes from the way that people made or got their livings—from what they called the *methods of production;* and they tended to regard these economic processes as fundamental to civilization.

The Dialectical Materialism of Marx and Engels was not really so materialistic as it sounds. There was in it a large element of the Hegelian idealism that Marx and Engels thought they had got rid of. At no time did these two famous materialists take so mechanistic a view of things as Taine began by professing; and their theory of the relation of works of literature to what they called the *economic base* was a good deal less simple than Taine's theory of the moment, the race and the milieu. They thought that art, politics, religion, philosophy and literature belonged to what they called the *superstructure* of human activity; but they saw that the practitioners of these various professions tended also to constitute social groups, and that they were always pulling away from the kind of solidarity based on economic classes in order to establish a professional solidarity of their own. Furthermore, the activities of the superstructure could influence one another, and they could influence the economic base. It may be said of Marx and Engels in general that, contrary to the popular impression, they were tentative, confused and modest when it came down to philosophical first principles, where a materialist like Taine was cocksure. Marx once made an attempt to explain why the poems of Homer were so good when the society that produced them was from his point of view—that is, from the point of view of its industrial development—so primitive; and this gave him a good deal of trouble. If we compare his discussion of this problem with Vico's discussion of Homer, we see that the explanation of literature in terms of a philosophy of social history is becoming, instead of simpler and easier, more difficult and more complex.

Marx and Engels were deeply imbued, moreover, with the German admiration for literature, which they had learned from the age of Goethe. It would never have occurred to either

of them that *der Dichter* was not one of the noblest and most beneficent of humankind. When Engels writes about Goethe, he presents him as a man equipped for 'practical life,' whose career was frustrated by the 'misery' of the historical situation in Germany in his time, and reproaches him for allowing himself to lapse into the 'cautious, smug and narrow' philistinism of the class from which he came; but Engels regrets this, because it interfered with the development of the 'mocking, defiant, world-despising genius,' 'der geniale Dichter,' 'der gewaltige Poet,' of whom Engels would not even, he says, have asked that he should have been a political liberal if Goethe had not sacrificed to his bourgeois shrinkings his truer esthetic sense. And the great critics who were trained on Marx—Franz Mehring and Bernard Shaw—had all this reverence for the priesthood of literature. Shaw deplores the absence of political philosophy and what he regards as the middle-class snobbery in Shakespeare; but he celebrates Shakespeare's poetry and his dramatic imagination almost as enthusiastically as Swinburne does, describing even those potboiling comedies, *Twelfth Night* and *As You Like It*—the themes of which seem to him most trashy—as 'the Crown Jewels of English dramatic poetry.' Such a critic may do more for a writer by showing him as a real man dealing with a real world at a definite moment of time than the impressionist critic of Swinburne's type who flourished in the same period of the late nineteenth century. The purely impressionist critic approaches the whole of literature as an exhibit of belletristic jewels, and he can only write a rhapsodic catalogue. But when Shaw turned his spotlight on Shakespeare as a figure in the Shavian drama of history, he invested him with a new interest as no other English critic had done.

The insistence that the man of letters should play a political role, the disparagement of works of art in comparison with political action, were thus originally no part of Marxism. They only became associated with it later. This happened by way of Russia, and it was due to special tendencies in that country that date from long before the Revolution or the promulgation of Marxism itself. In Russia there have been very good reasons why the political implications of literature should particularly occupy the critics. The art of Pushkin itself, with its marvelous power of implication, had cer-

tainly been partly created by the censorship of
Nicholas I, and Pushkin set the tradition for
most of the great Russian writers that followed
him. Every play, every poem, every story, must
be a parable of which the moral is *implied*. If
it were stated, the censor would suppress the
book as he tried to do with Pushkin's *Bronze
Horseman*, where it was merely a question of
the packed implications protruding a little too
10 plainly. Right down through the writings of
Chekhov and up almost to the Revolution, the
imaginative literature of Russia presents the
peculiar paradox of an art that is technically
objective and yet charged with social messages.
In Russia under the Tsar, it was inevitable that
social criticism should lead to political conclusions, because the most urgent need from the
point of view of any kind of improvement was
to get rid of the tsarist regime. Even the neo-
20 Christian moralist Tolstoy, who pretended to
be non-political, was to exert a subversive influence, because his independent preaching
was bound to embroil him with the Church,
and the Church was an integral part of the
tsardom. Tolstoy's pamphlet called *What Is
Art?*, in which he throws overboard Shakespeare and a large part of modern literature,
including his own novels, in the interest of his
intransigent morality, is the example which is
30 most familiar to us of the moralizing Russian
criticism; but it was only the most sensational
expression of a kind of approach which had
been prevalent since Belinsky and Chernyshev-
sky in the early part of the century. The critics,
who were usually journalists writing in exile or
in a contraband press, were always tending to
demand of the imaginative writers that they
should dramatize bolder morals.

Even after the Revolution had destroyed the
40 tsarist government, this state of things did not
change. The old habits of censorship persisted
in the new socialist society of the Soviets, which
was necessarily made up of people who had
been stamped by the die of the despotism. We
meet here the peculiar phenomenon of a series
of literary groups that attempt, one after the
other, to obtain official recognition or make
themselves sufficiently powerful to establish
themselves as arbiters of literature. Lenin and
50 Trotsky and Lunacharsky had the sense to oppose these attempts: the comrade-dictators of
Proletcult or Lev or Rapp would certainly have
been just as bad as the Count Benckendorff
who made Pushkin miserable, and when the
Stalin bureaucracy, after the death of Gorky,

got control of this department as of everything
else, they instituted a system of repression that
made Benckendorff and Nicholas I look like
Lorenzo de' Medici. In the meantime, Trotsky,
who was Commissar of War but himself a great
political writer with an interest in belles-lettres,
attempted, in 1924, apropos of one of these
movements, to clarify the situation. He wrote a
brilliant and valuable book called *Literature
and Revolution*, in which he explained the aims
of the government, analyzed the work of the
Russian writers, and praised or rebuked the latter as they seemed to him in harmony or at
odds with the former. Trotsky is intelligent,
sympathetic; it is evident that he is really fond
of literature and that he knows that a work of
art does not fulfill its function in terms of the
formulas of party propaganda. But Mayakov-
sky, the Soviet poet, whom Trotsky had
praised with reservations, expressed himself in
a famous joke when he was asked what he
thought of Trotsky's book—a pun which implied that a Commissar turned critic was inevitably a Commissar still *; and what a foreigner
cannot accept in Trotsky is his assumption that
it is the duty of the government to take a hand
in the direction of literature.

This point of view, indigenous to Russia, has
been imported to other countries through the
permeation of Communist influence. The Communist press and its literary followers have reflected the control of the Kremlin in all the
phases through which it has passed, down to
the wholesale imprisonment of Soviet writers
which has been taking place since 1935. But
it has never been a part of the American system
that our Republican or Democratic administration should lay down a political line for the
guidance of the national literature. A recent
gesture in this direction on the part of Archibald MacLeish, who seems a little carried away
by his position as Librarian of Congress, was
anything but cordially received by serious
American writers. So long as the United States
remains happily a non-totalitarian country, we
can very well do without this aspect of the historical criticism of literature.

Another element of a different order has,
however, since Marx's time been added to the
historical study of the origins of works of literature. I mean the psychoanalysis of Freud. This
appears as an extension of something which

---

* Первый блин лег наркомом, *The first pancake lies
like a narkom* (people's commissar)—a parody of the Russian saying,
Первый блин лег комом, *The first pancake lies like a lump.*

had already got well started before, which had figured even in Johnson's *Lives of the Poets,* and of which the great exponent had been Sainte-Beuve: the interpretation of works of literature in the light of the personalities behind them. But the Freudians made this interpretation more exact and more systematic. The great example of the psychoanalysis of an artist is Freud's own essay on Leonardo da Vinci; but this has little critical interest: it is an attempt to construct a case history. One of the best examples I know of the application of Freudian analysis to literature is in Van Wyck Brooks's book, *The Ordeal of Mark Twain,* in which Mr. Brooks uses an incident of Mark Twain's boyhood as a key to his whole career. Mr. Brooks has since repudiated the method he resorted to here, on the ground that no one but an analyst can ever know enough about a writer to make a valid psychoanalytic diagnosis. This is true, and it is true of the method that it has led to bad results where the critic has built a Freudian mechanism out of very slender evidence, and then given us what is really merely a romance exploiting the supposed working of this mechanism, in place of an actual study that sticks close to the facts and the documents of the writer's life and work. But I believe that Van Wyck Brooks really had hold of something important when he fixed upon that childhood incident of which Mark Twain gave so vivid an account to his biographer—that scene at the deathbed of his father when his mother had made him promise that he would not break her heart. If it was not one of those crucial happenings that are supposed to determine the complexes of Freud, it has certainly a typical significance in relation to Mark Twain's whole psychology. The stories that people tell about their childhood are likely to be profoundly symbolic even when they have been partly or wholly made up in the light of later experience. And the attitudes, the compulsions, the emotional 'patterns' that recur in the work of a writer are of great interest to the historical critic.

These attitudes and patterns are embedded in the community and the historical moment, and they may indicate its ideals and its diseases as the cell shows the condition of the tissue. The recent scientific experimentation in the combining of Freudian with Marxist method, and of psychoanalysis with anthropology, has had its parallel development in criticism. And there is thus another element added to our equipment for analyzing literary works, and the problem grows still more complex.

The analyst, however, is of course not concerned with the comparative values of his patients any more than the surgeon is. He cannot tell you why the neurotic Dostoevsky produces work of immense value to his fellows while another man with the same neurotic pattern would become a public menace. Freud himself emphatically states in his study of Leonardo that his method can make no attempt to account for Leonardo's genius. The problems of comparative artistic value still remain after we have given attention to the Freudian psychological factor just as they do after we have given attention to the Marxist economic factor and to the racial and geographical factors. No matter how thoroughly and searchingly we may have scrutinized works of literature from the historical and biographical points of view, we must be ready to attempt to estimate, in some such way as Saintsbury and Eliot do, the relative degrees of success attained by the products of the various periods and the various personalities. We must be able to tell good from bad, the first-rate from the second-rate. We shall not otherwise write literary criticism at all, but merely social or political history as reflected in literary texts, or psychological case histories from past eras, or, to take the historical point of view in its simplest and most academic form, merely chronologies of books that have been published.

And now how, in these matters of literary art, do we tell the good art from the bad? Norman Kemp Smith, the Kantian philosopher, whose courses I was fortunate enough to take at Princeton twenty-five years ago, used to tell us that this recognition was based primarily on an emotional reaction. For purposes of practical criticism this is a safe assumption on which to proceed. It is possible to discriminate in a variety of ways the elements that in any given department go to make a successful work of literature. Different schools have at different times demanded different things of literature: *unity, symmetry, universality, originality, vision, inspiration, strangeness, suggestiveness, improving morality, socialist realism,* etc. But you could have any set of these qualities that any school of writing has called for and still not have a good play, a good novel, a good poem, a good history. If you identify the essence of good literature with any one of these elements or with any combination of them, you simply shift the emotional reaction to the recognition of the element or elements. Or if you add to your other demands the demand that the writer must have *talent,* you simply shift this recognition to the talent. Once people find some grounds of agreement in the coincidence of their emotional reactions to books, they may be able to discuss these elements profitably; but if they do not have this basic agreement, the discussion will make no sense.

But how, you may ask, can we identify this élite who know what they are talking about? Well, it can only be said of them that they are self-appointed and self-perpetuating, and that they will compel you to accept their authority. Impostors may try to put themselves over, but these quacks will not last. The implied position of the people who know about literature (as is also the case in every other art) is simply that they know what they know, and that they are determined to impose their opinions by main force of eloquence or assertion on the people who do not know. This is not a question, of course, of professional workers in literature— such as editors, professors and critics, who very often have no real understanding of the products with which they deal—but of readers of all kinds in all walks of life. There are moments when a first-rate writer, unrecognized or out of fashion with the official chalkers-up for the market, may find his support in the demand for his work of an appreciative cultivated public.

But what is the cause of this emotional reaction which is the critic's divining rod? This question has long been a subject of study by the branch of philosophy called esthetics, and it has recently been made a subject of scientific experimentation. Both these lines of inquiry are likely to be prejudiced in the eyes of the literary critic by the fact that the inquiries are sometimes conducted by persons who are obviously deficient in literary feeling or taste. Yet one should not deny the possibility that something of value might result from the speculations and explorations of men of acute minds who take as their given data the esthetic emotions of other men.

Almost everybody interested in literature has tried to explain to himself the nature of these emotions that register our approval of artistic works; and I of course have my own explanation.

In my view, all our intellectual activity, in whatever field it takes place, is an attempt to give a meaning to our experience—that is, to make life more practicable; for by understanding things we make it easier to survive and get around among them. The mathematician Euclid, working in a convention of abstractions, shows us relations between the distances of our unwieldy and cluttered-up environment upon which we are able to count. A drama of Sophocles also indicates relations between the various human impulses, which appear so confused and dangerous, and it brings out a certain justice of Fate—that is to say, of the way in which the interaction of these impulses is seen in the long run to work out—upon which we can also depend. The kinship, from this point of view, of the purposes of science and art appears very clearly in the case of the Greeks, because not only do both Euclid and Sophocles satisfy us by making patterns, but they make much the same kind of patterns. Euclid's *Elements* takes simple theorems and by a series of logical operations builds them up to a climax in the square on the hypotenuse. A typical drama of Sophocles develops in a similar way.

Some writers (as well as some scientists) have a different kind of explicit message beyond the reassurance implicit in the mere feat of understanding life or of molding the harmony of artistic form. Not content with such an achievement as that of Sophocles—who has one of his choruses tell us that it is better not to be born, but who, by representing life as noble and based on law, makes its tragedy easier to bear—such writers attempt, like Plato, to think out and recommend a procedure for turning it into something better. But other departments of literature—lyric poetry such as Sappho's, for example—have *less* philosophical content than Sophocles. A lyric gives us nothing but a pattern imposed on the expression of a feeling; but this pattern of metrical quantities and of consonants and vowels that balance has the effect of reducing the feeling, however unruly or painful it may seem when we experience it in the course of our lives, to something orderly, symmetrical and pleasing; and it also relates this feeling to the more impressive scheme, works it into the larger texture, of the body of poetic art. The discord has been resolved, the anomaly subjected to discipline. And this control of his emotion by the poet has the effect at second-hand of making it easier for the reader to manage his own emotions. (Why certain sounds and rhythms gratify us more than others, and how they are connected with the themes and ideas that they are chosen as appropriate for conveying, are questions that may be passed on to the scientist.)

And this brings us back again to the historical point of view. The experience of mankind on the earth is always changing as man develops and has to deal with new combinations of elements; and the writer who is to be anything more than an echo of his predecessors must always find expression for something which has never yet been expressed, must master a new set of phenomena which has never yet been mastered. With each such victory of the human intellect, whether in history, in philosophy or in poetry, we experience a deep satisfaction: we have been cured of some ache of disorder, relieved of some oppressive burden of uncomprehended events.

This relief that brings the sense of power, and, with the sense of power, joy, is the positive emotion which tells us that we have encountered a first-rate piece of literature. But stay! you may at this point warn: are not people often solaced and exhilarated by literature of the trashiest kind? They are: crude and limited people do certainly feel some such emotion in connection with work that is limited and crude. The man who is more highly organized and has a wider intellectual range will feel it in connection with work that is finer and more complex. The difference between the emotion of the more highly organized man and the emotion of the less highly organized one is a matter of mere gradation. You sometimes discover books—the novels of John Steinbeck, for example—that seem to mark precisely the borderline between work that is definitely superior and work that is definitely bad. When I was speaking a little while back of the genuine connoisseurs who establish the standards of taste, I meant, of course, the people who can distinguish Grade A and who prefer it to the other grades. 1948

H. L. MENCKEN

1880-1956

MOST OF HIS working life H. L. Mencken was a newspaperman. The oldest son of a prosperous Baltimore tobacco merchant, he smelled printer's ink, while still a boy, in the offices of the Baltimore *Morning Herald*. During his years at the Polytechnic Institute he was just as determined to be a journalist as his father was that he should carry on the family's tobacco business. When August Mencken died three years after Henry Louis's graduation from school, the young man—now the head of the family—was free to follow his bent. He was soon the Sunday editor of the *Herald*, but, always a prodigious worker, he found time to turn out many kinds of writing, including poetry and short stories, which he sold to other papers. In 1906 Mencken went over to the Baltimore *Sun*, with which he would thereafter be associated as reporter, columnist, or editor. His famous column, "The Free Lance," in which he took off after every person, idea, and institution he disliked, was stopped in 1915 because of his outspoken pro-German sentiments.

Meanwhile (1908) he had met the drama critic George Jean Nathan and had collaborated with him in writing reviews for *The Smart Set*. In 1914 they took over the editorship. Mencken commuted to New York when he had to be in the office of the magazine, but most of his writing was done in his Hollins Street home in Baltimore, soon to become one of the most famous addresses in America. In 1923, with the backing of Alfred A. Knopf, Nathan and Mencken laid plans for a new magazine, *The American Mercury*, the first issue of which appeared in January 1924. Under their editorship it became the liveliest magazine in America. It printed the work of excellent new writers. In its columns Mencken and Nathan waged war against the inanities and imbecilities of American life. The magazine with its brilliant green cover was vituperated by the respectable, but the young in heart displayed it as a talisman.

During the early years Mencken wrote hundreds of reviews and thought of himself, despite his newspaper work, as primarily a literary critic. In 1919 Knopf began collecting his reviews in a series called *Prejudices.* There were six of these volumes between 1919 and 1927. But when *Prejudices: Fourth Series* appeared in 1924, only one of the seventeen essays dealt with literature. Mencken the polemicist was crowding out Mencken the critic.

In no sense was Mencken a systematic critic. The essay presented here is the fullest statement of his critical principles, but it does little more than affirm the right of the critic to be creative, to put his own personality and beliefs into his criticism. His greatest service to American letters was his lampooning of the Harold Bell Wrights, Hamilton Wright Mabies, and other insipid writers and his championing of the new writers whom he admired. Among those he encouraged were Dreiser, Joseph Hergesheimer, Sinclair Lewis, James Branch Cabell, O'Neill, F. Scott Fitzgerald, and Edmund Wilson.

At the height of his fame as editor of *The American Mercury* Mencken was rightly called by the *New York Times* "the most powerful private citizen in America." When the Depression arrived, Mencken's invective lost the power to please. He wisely turned to two projects which proved to be his best creative efforts: the elaboration of his *The American Language* (1919) in a series of revisions and the addition of two *Supplements;* and the writing of his three-volume autobiography: *Happy Days, 1880–1892* (1940); *Newspaper Days, 1899–1906* (1941); and *Heathen Days, 1890–1936* (1943).

Carrol Frey, *A Bibliography of the Writings of H. L. Mencken,* Philadelphia, 1924.
Charles Angoff, *H. L. Mencken: A Portrait from Memory,* New York, 1956.
Isaac Goldberg, *The Man Mencken: A Biographical and Critical Survey,* New York, 1925.
Edgar Kemler, *The Irreverent Mr. Mencken,* Boston, 1950.
William Manchester, *Disturber of the Peace: The Life of H. L. Mencken,* New York, 1951.

» » FOOTNOTE ON CRITICISM « «

Nearly all the discussions of criticism that I am acquainted with start off with a false assumption, to wit, that the primary motive of the critic, the impulse which makes a critic of him instead of, say, a politician, or a stockbroker, is pedagogical—that he writes because he is possessed by a passion to advance the enlightenment, to put down error and wrong, to disseminate some specific doctrine: psychological, epistemological, historical, or æsthetic. This is true, it seems to me, only of bad critics, and its degree of truth increases in direct ratio to their badness. The motive of the critic who is really worth reading—the only critic of whom, indeed, it may be said truthfully that it is at all possible to read him, save as an act of mental discipline—is something quite different.

That motive is not the motive of the pedagogue, but the motive of the artist. It is no more and no less than the simple desire to function freely and beautifully, to give outward and objective form to ideas that bubble inwardly and have a fascinating lure in them, to get rid of them dramatically and make an articulate noise in the world. It was for this reason that Plato wrote the "Republic," and for this reason that Beethoven wrote the Ninth Symphony, and it is for this reason, to drop a million miles, that I am writing the present essay. Everything else is after-thought, mock-modesty, messianic delusion—in brief, affectation and folly. Is the contrary conception of criticism widely cherished? Is it almost universally held that the thing is a brother to jurisprudence, advertising,

10

laparotomy, chautauqua lecturing and the art of the schoolmarm? Then certainly the fact that it is so held should be sufficient to set up an overwhelming probability of its lack of truth and sense. If I speak with some heat, it is as one who has suffered. When, years ago, I devoted myself diligently to critical pieces upon the writings of Theodore Dreiser, I found that practically every one who took any notice of my proceedings at all fell into either one or two assumptions about my underlying purpose: (*a*) that I had a fanatical devotion for Mr. Dreiser's ideas and desired to propagate them, or (*b*) that I was an ardent patriot, and yearned to lift up American literature. Both assumptions were false. I had then, and I have now, very little interest in many of Mr. Dreiser's main ideas; when we meet, in fact, we usually quarrel about them. And I am wholly devoid of public spirit, and haven't the least lust to improve American literature; if it ever came to what I regard as perfection my job would be gone. What, then, was my motive in writing about Mr. Dreiser so copiously? My motive, well known to Mr. Dreiser himself and to every one else who knew me as intimately as he did, was simply and solely to sort out and give coherence to the ideas of Mr. Mencken, and to put them into suave and ingratiating terms, and to discharge them with a flourish, and maybe with a phrase of pretty song, into the dense fog that blanketed the Republic.

The critic's choice of criticism rather than of what is called creative writing is chiefly a matter of temperament—perhaps, more accurately of hormones—with accidents of education and environment to help. The feelings that happen to be dominant in him at the moment the scribbling frenzy seizes him are feelings inspired, not directly by life itself, but by books, pictures, music, sculpture, architecture, religion, philosophy—in brief, by some other man's feelings about life. They are thus, in a sense, secondhand, and it is no wonder that creative artists so easily fall into the theory that they are also second-rate. Perhaps they usually are. If, indeed, the critic continues on this plane—if he lacks the intellectual agility and enterprise needed to make the leap from the work of art to the vast and mysterious complex of phenomena behind it—then they *always* are, and he remains no more than a fugelman or policeman to his betters. But if a genuine artist is concealed within him—if his feelings are in any sense profound and original, and his capacity

for self-expression is above the average of educated men—then he moves inevitably from the work of art to life itself, and begins to take on a dignity that he formerly lacked. It is impossible to think of a man of any actual force and originality, universally recognized as having those qualities, who spent his whole life appraising and describing the work of other men. Did Goethe, or Carlyle, or Matthew Arnold, or Sainte-Beuve, or Macaulay, or even, to come 10 down a few pegs, Lewes, or Lowell, or Hazlitt? Certainly not. The thing that becomes most obvious about the writings of all such men, once they are examined carefully, is that the critic is always being swallowed up by the creative artist—that what starts out as the review of a book, or a play, or other work of art, usually develops very quickly into an independent essay upon the theme of that work of art, or upon some theme that it suggests—in a word, that it 20 becomes a fresh work of art, and only indirectly related to the one that suggested it. This fact, indeed, is so plain that it scarcely needs statement. What the pedagogues always object to in, for example, the *Quarterly* reviewers is that they forgot the books they were supposed to review, and wrote long papers—often, in fact, small books—expounding ideas suggested (or not suggested) by the books under review. Every critic who is worth reading falls inevitably into the same habit. He cannot stick to 30 his task: what is before him is always infinitely less interesting to him than what is within him. If he is genuinely first-rate—if what is within him stands the test of type, and wins an audience, and produces the reactions that every artist craves—then he usually ends by abandoning the criticism of specific works of art altogether, and setting up shop as a general merchant in general ideas, *i.e.*, as an artist working 40 in the materials of life itself.

Mere reviewing, however conscientiously and competently it is done, is plainly a much inferior business. Like writing poetry, it is chiefly a function of intellectual immaturity. The young literatus just out of the university, having as yet no capacity for grappling with the fundamental mysteries of existence, is put into writing reviews of books, or plays, or music, or painting. Very often he does it extremely well; it is, in 50 fact, not hard to do well, for even decayed pedagogues often do it, as such graves of the intellect as the New York *Times* bear witness. But if he continues to do it, whether well or ill, it is a sign to all the world that his growth ceased

when they made him *Artium Baccalaureus.*
Gradually he becomes, whether in or out of
the academic grove, a professor, which is to
say, a man devoted to diluting and retailing the
ideas of his superiors—not an artist, not even
a bad artist, but almost the antithesis of an
artist. He is learned, he is sober, he is painstaking and accurate—but he is as hollow as a
jug. Nothing is in him save the ghostly echoes
of other men's thoughts and feelings. If he were
a genuine artist he would have thoughts and
feelings of his own, and the impulse to give
them objective form would be irresistible. An
artist can no more withstand that impulse than
a politician can withstand the temptations of a
job. There are no mute, inglorious Miltons, save
in the hallucinations of poets. The one sound
test of a Milton is that he functions as a Milton.
His difference from other men lies precisely in
the superior vigor of his impulse to self-expression, not in the superior beauty and loftiness of
his ideas. Other men, in point of fact, often
have the same ideas, or perhaps even loftier
ones, but they are able to suppress them,
usually on grounds of decorum, and so they escape being artists, and are respected by right-
thinking persons, and die with money in the
bank, and are forgotten in two weeks.

Obviously, the critic whose performance we
are commonly called upon to investigate is a
man standing somewhere along the path leading from the beginning that I have described to
the goal. He has got beyond being a mere cata-
loguer and valuer of other men's ideas, but he
has not yet become an autonomous artist—he
is not yet ready to challenge attention with his
own ideas alone. But it is plain that his motion,
in so far as he is moving at all, must be in the
direction of that autonomy—that is, unless one
imagines him sliding backward into senile in-
fantilism: a spectacle not unknown to literary
pathology, but too pathetic to be discussed
here. Bear this motion in mind, and the true
nature of his aims and purposes becomes clear;
more, the incurable falsity of the aims and purposes usually credited to him becomes equally
clear. He is not actually trying to perform an
impossible act of arctic justice upon the artist
whose work gives him a text. He is not trying
with mathematical passion to find out exactly
what was in that artist's mind at the moment of
creation, and to display it precisely and in an
ecstasy of appreciation. He is not trying to
bring the work discussed into accord with some
transient theory of aesthetics, or ethics, or

truth, or to determine its degree of departure
from that theory. He is not trying to lift up the
fine arts, or to defend democracy against sense,
or to promote happiness at the domestic hearth,
or to convert sophomores into right-thinkers,
or to serve God. He is not trying to fit a group
of novel phenomena into the orderly process of
history. He is not even trying to discharge the
catalytic office that I myself, in a romantic moment, once sought to force upon him. He is,
first and last, simply trying to express himself.
He is trying to arrest and challenge a sufficient
body of readers, to make them pay attention to
him, to impress them with the charm and novelty of his ideas, to provoke them into an agreeable (or shocked) awareness of him, and he
is trying to achieve thereby for his own inner
ego the grateful feeling of a function performed, a tension relieved, a *katharsis* attained
which Wagner achieved when he wrote "Die
Walküre," and a hen achieves every time she
lays an egg.

Joseph Conrad is moved by that necessity to
write romances; Bach was moved to write
music; poets are moved to write poetry; critics
are moved to write criticism. The form is nothing; the only important thing is the motive
power, and it is the same in all cases. It is the
pressing yearning of every man who has ideas
in him to empty them upon the world, to
hammer them into plausible and ingratiating
shapes, to compel the attention and respect of
his equals, to lord it over his inferiors. So seen,
the critic becomes a far more transparent and
agreeable fellow than ever he was in the discourses of the psychologists who sought to
make him a mere appraiser in an intellectual
customs house, a gauger in a distillery of the
spirit, a just and infallible judge upon the cosmic bench. Such offices, in point of fact, never
fit him. He always bulges over their confines.
So labelled and estimated, it inevitably turns
out that the specific critic under examination
is a very bad one, or no critic at all. But when
he is thought of, not as a pedagogue, but as
artist, then he begins to take on reality, and,
what is more, dignity. Carlyle was surely no
just and infallible judge; on the contrary, he
was full of prejudices, biles, naïvetés, humors.
Yet he is read, consulted, attended to. Macaulay was unfair, inaccurate, fanciful, lyrical—
yet his essays live. Arnold had his faults too,
and so did Sainte-Beuve, and so did Goethe,
and so did many another of that line—and yet
they are remembered to-day, and all the

learned and conscientious critics of their time, laboriously concerned with the precise intent of the artists under review, and passionately determined to set it forth with god-like care and to relate it exactly to this or that great stream of ideas—all these pedants are forgotten. What saved Carlyle, Macaulay and company is as plain as day. They were first-rate artists. They could make the thing charming, and that is always a million times more important than making it true.

Truth, indeed, is something that is believed in completely only by persons who have never tried personally to pursue it to its fastnesses and grab it by the tail. It is the adoration of second-rate men—men who always receive it at second-hand. Pedagogues believe in immutable truths and spend their lives trying to determine them and propagate them; the intellectual progress of man consists largely of a concerted effort to block and destroy their enterprise. Nine times out of ten, in the arts as in life, there is actually no truth to be discovered; there is only error to be exposed. In whole departments of human inquiry it seems to me quite unlikely that the truth ever *will* be discovered. Nevertheless, the rubber-stamp thinking of the world always makes the assumption that the exposure of an error is identical with the discovery of the truth—that error and truth are simple opposites. They are nothing of the sort. What the world turns to, when it has been cured of one error, is usually simply another error, and maybe one worse than the first one. This is the whole history of the intellect in brief. The average man of to-day does not believe in precisely the same imbecilities that the Greek of the fourth century before Christ believed in, but the things that he *does* believe in are often quite as idiotic. Perhaps this statement is a bit too sweeping. There is, year by year, a gradual accumulation of what may be called, provisionally, truths—there is a slow accretion of ideas that somehow manage to meet all practicable human tests, and so survive. But even so, it is risky to call them absolute truths. All that one may safely say of them is that no one, as yet, has demonstrated that they are errors. Soon or late, if experience teaches us anything, they are likely to succumb too. The profoundest truths of the Middle Ages are now laughed at by schoolboys. The profoundest truths of democracy will be laughed at, a few centuries hence, even by schoolteachers.

In the department of aesthetics, wherein critics mainly disport themselves, it is almost impossible to think of a so-called truth that shows any sign of being permanently true. The most profound of principles begins to fade and quiver almost as soon as it is stated. But the work of art, as opposed to the theory behind it, has a longer life, particularly if that theory be obscure and questionable, and so cannot be determined accurately. "Hamlet," the Mona Lisa, "Faust," "Dixie," "Parsifal," "Mother Goose," "Annabel Lee," "Huckleberry Finn"— these things, so baffling to pedagogy, so contumacious to the categories, so mysterious in purpose and utility—these things live. And why? Because there is in them the flavor of salient, novel and attractive personality, because the quality that shines from them is not that of correct demeanor but that of creative passion, because they pulse and breathe and speak, because they are genuine works of art. So with criticism. Let us forget all the heavy effort to make a science of it; it is a fine art, or nothing. If the critic, retiring to his cell to concoct his treatise upon a book or play or what-not, produces a piece of writing that shows sound structure, and brilliant color, and the flash of new and persuasive ideas, and civilized manners, and the charm of an uncommon personality in free function, then he has given something to the world that is worth having, and sufficiently justified his existence. Is Carlyle's "Frederick" true? Who cares? As well as if the Parthenon is true, or the C Minor Symphony, or "Wiener Blut." Let the critic who is an artist leave such necropsies to professors of æsthetics, who can no more determine the truth than he can, and will infallibly make it unpleasant and a bore.

It is, of course, not easy to practice this abstention. Two forces, one within and one without, tend to bring even a Hazlitt or a Huneker under the campus pump. One is the almost universal human susceptibility to messianic delusions—the irresistible tendency of practically every man, once he finds a crowd in front of him, to strut and roll his eyes. The other is the public demand, born of such long familiarity with pedagogical criticism that no other kind is readily conceivable, that the critic teach something as well as say something—in the popular phrase, that he be constructive. Both operate powerfully against his free functioning, and especially the former. He finds it hard to resist the flattery of his customers, however lit-

tle he may actually esteem it. If he knows anything at all, he knows that his following, like
that of every other artist in ideas, is chiefly
made up of the congenitally subaltern type of
man and woman—natural converts, lodge join-
ers, me-toos, stragglers after circus parades. It
is precious seldom that he ever gets a positive
idea out of them; what he usually gets is mere
unintelligent ratification. But this troop, despite
10 its obvious failings, corrupts him in various
ways. For one thing, it enormously reënforces
his belief in his own ideas, and so tends to make
him stiff and dogmatic—in brief, precisely
everything that he ought not to be. And for another thing, it tends to make him (by a curious contradiction) a bit pliant and politic: he
begins to estimate new ideas, not in proportion
as they are amusing or beautiful, but in proportion as they are likely to please. So beset,
20 front and rear, he sometimes sinks supinely to
the level of a professor, and his subsequent
proceedings are interesting no more. The true
aim of a critic is certainly not to make converts.
He must know that very few of the persons
who are susceptible to conversion are worth
converting. Their minds are intrinsically flabby
and parasitical, and it is certainly not sound
sport to agitate minds of that sort. Moreover,
the critic must always harbor a grave doubt
30 about most of the ideas that they lap up so
greedily—it must occur to him not infrequently, in the silent watches of the night, that
much that he writes is sheer buncombe. As I
have said, I can't imagine any idea—that is, in
the domain of æsthetics—that is palpably and
incontrovertibly sound. All that I am familiar
with, and in particular all that I announce most
vociferously, seem to me to contain a core of
quite obvious nonsense. I thus try to avoid cher-
40 ishing them too lovingly, and it always gives
me a shiver to see any one else gobble them at
one gulp. Criticism, at bottom, is indistinguishable from skepticism. Both launch themselves,
the one by aesthetic presentations and the
other by logical presentations, at the common
human tendency to accept whatever is approved, to take in ideas ready-made, to be responsive to mere rhetoric and gesticulation. A
critic who believes in anything absolutely is
50 bound to that something quite as helplessly as
a Christian is bound to the Freudian garbage
in the Book of Revelation. To that extent, at all
events, he is unfree and unintelligent, and
hence a bad critic.

The demand for "constructive" criticism is
based upon the same false assumption that immutable truths exist in the arts, and that the
artist will be improved by being made aware
of them. This notion, whatever the form it
takes, is always absurd—as much so, indeed,
as its brother delusion that the critic, to be
competent, must be a practitioner of the specific art he ventures to deal with, *i.e.*, that a
doctor, to cure a belly-ache, must have a belly-
ache. As practically encountered, it is disingen-
uous as well as absurd, for it comes chiefly from
bad artists who tire of serving as performing
monkeys, and crave the greater ease and safety
of sophomores in class. They demand to be
taught in order to avoid being knocked about.
In their demand is the theory that instruction,
if they could get it, would profit them—that
they are capable of doing better work than
they do. As a practical matter, I doubt that this
is ever true. Bad poets never actually grow any
better; they invariably grow worse and worse.
In all history there has never been, to my
knowledge, a single practitioner of any art who,
as a result of "constructive" criticism, improved
his work. The curse of all the arts, indeed, is
the fact that they are constantly invaded by
persons who are not artists at all—persons
whose yearning to express their ideas and feelings is unaccompanied by the slightest capacity
for charming expression—in brief, persons with
absolutely nothing to say. This is particularly
true of the art of letters, which interposes very
few technical obstacles to the vanity and gar-
rulity of such invaders. Any effort to teach
them to write better is an effort wasted, as
every editor discovers for himself; they are as
incapable of it as they are of jumping over the
moon. The only sort of criticism that can deal
with them to any profit is the sort that employs
them frankly as laboratory animals. It cannot
cure them, but it can at least make an amusing
and perhaps edifying show of them. It is idle
to argue that the good in them is thus destroyed with the bad. The simple answer is that
there *is* no good in them. Suppose Poe had
wasted his time trying to dredge good work out
of Rufus Dawes, author of "Geraldine." He
would have failed miserably—and spoiled a
capital essay, still diverting after three-quarters
of a century. Suppose Beethoven, dealing with
Gottfried Weber, had tried laboriously to make
an intelligent music critic of him. How much
more apt, useful and durable the simple note:
"Arch-ass! Double-barrelled ass!" Here was absolutely sound criticism. Here was a judgment

wholly beyond challenge. Moreover, here was a small but perfect work of art.

Upon the low practical value of so-called constructive criticism I can offer testimony out of my own experience. My books are commonly reviewed at great length, and many critics devote themselves to pointing out what they conceive to be my errors, both of fact and of taste. Well, I cannot recall a case in which any suggestion offered by a constructive critic has helped me in the slightest, or even actively interested me. Every such wet-nurse of letters has sought fatuously to make me write in a way differing from that in which the Lord God Almighty, in His infinite wisdom, impels me to write—that is, to make me write stuff which, coming from me, would be as false as an appearance of decency in a Congressman. All the benefits I have ever got from the critics of my work have come from the destructive variety. A hearty slating always does me good, particularly if it be well written. It begins by enlisting my professional respect; it ends by making me examine my ideas coldly in the privacy of my chamber. Not, of course, that I usually revise them, but I at least examine them. If I decide to hold fast to them, they are all the dearer to me thereafter, and I expound them with a new passion and plausibility. If, on the contrary, I discern holes in them, I shelve them in a *pianissimo* manner, and set about hatching new ones to take their place. But constructive criticism irritates me. I do not object to being denounced, but I can't abide being school-mastered, especially by men I regard as imbeciles.

I find, as a practicing critic, that very few men who write books are even as tolerant as I am—that most of them, soon or late, show signs of extreme discomfort under criticism, however polite its terms. Perhaps this is why enduring friendships between authors and critics are so rare. All artists, of course, dislike one another more or less, but that dislike seldom rises to implacable enmity, save between opera singer and opera singer, and creative author and critic. Even when the latter two keep up an outward show of good-will, there is always bitter antagonism under the surface. Part of it, I daresay, arises out of the impossible demands of the critic, particularly if he be tinged with the constructive madness. Having favored an author with his good opinion, he expects the poor fellow to live up to that good opinion without the slightest compromise or faltering, and this is commonly beyond human power.

He feels that any let-down compromises *him* —that his hero is stabbing him in the back, and making him ridiculous—and this feeling rasps his vanity. The most bitter of all literary quarrels are those between critics and creative artists, and most of them arise in just this way. As for the creative artist, he on his part naturally resents the critic's air of pedagogical superiority and he resents it especially when he has an uneasy feeling that he has fallen short of his best work, and that the discontent of the critic is thus justified. Injustice is relatively easy to bear; what stings is justice. Under it all, of course, lurks the fact that I began with: the fact that the critic is himself an artist, and that his creative impulse, soon or late, is bound to make him neglect the punctilio. When he sits down to compose his criticism, his artist ceases to be a friend, and becomes mere raw material for his work of art. It is my experience that artists invariably resent this cavalier use of them. They are pleased so long as the critic confines himself to the modest business of interpreting them—preferably in terms of their own estimate of themselves—but the moment he proceeds to adorn their theme with variations of his own, the moment he brings new ideas to the enterprise and begins contrasting them with their ideas, that moment they grow restive. It is precisely at this point, of course, that criticism becomes genuine criticism; before that it was mere reviewing. When a critic passes it he loses his friends. By becoming an artist, he becomes the foe of all other artists.

But the transformation, I believe, has good effects upon him: it makes him a better critic. Too much *Gemütlichkeit* is as fatal to criticism as it would be to surgery or politics. When it rages unimpeded it leads inevitably either to a dull professorial sticking on of meaningless labels or to log-rolling, and often it leads to both. One of the most hopeful symptoms of the new *Aufklärung* in the Republic is the revival of acrimony in criticism—the renaissance of the doctrine that aesthetic matters are important, and that it is worth the while of a healthy male to take them seriously, as he takes business, sport and amour. In the days when American literature was showing its first vigorous growth, the native criticism was extraordinarily violent and even vicious; in the days when American literature swooned upon the tomb of the Puritan *Kultur* it became flaccid and childish. The typical critic of the first era was Poe, as the typical critic of the second was Howells. Poe carried on his critical jehads with such ferocity that he often got into lawsuits, and sometimes ran no little risk of having his head cracked. He regarded literary questions as exigent and momentous. The lofty aloofness of the don was simply not in him. When he encountered a book that seemed to him to be bad, he attacked it almost as sharply as a Chamber of Commerce would attack a fanatic preaching free speech, or the corporation of Trinity Church would attack Christ. His opponents replied in the same Berserker manner. Much of Poe's surviving ill-fame, as a drunkard and dead-beat, is due to their inordinate denunciations of him. They were not content to refute him; they constantly tried to dispose of him altogether. The very ferocity of that ancient row shows that the native literature, in those days, was in a healthy state. Books of genuine value were produced. Literature always thrives best, in fact, in an atmosphere of hearty strife. Poe, surrounded by admiring professors, never challenged, never aroused to the emotions of revolt, would probably have written poetry indistinguishable from the hollow stuff of, say, Prof. Dr. George E. Woodberry. It took the persistent (and often grossly unfair and dishonorable) opposition of Griswold *et al.* to stimulate him to his highest

endeavors. He needed friends, true enough, but he also needed enemies.

To-day, for the first time in years, there is strife in American criticism, and the Paul Elmer Mores and Hamilton Wright Mabies are no longer able to purr in peace. The instant they fall into stiff professorial attitudes they are challenged, and often with anything but urbanity. The *ex cathedra* manner thus passes out, and free discussion comes in. Heretics lay on boldly, and the professors are forced to make some defense. Often, going further, they attempt counter-attacks. Ears are bitten off. Noses are bloodied. There are wallops both above and below the belt. I am, I need not say, no believer in any magical merit in debate, no matter how free it may be. It certainly does not necessarily establish the truth; both sides, in fact, may be wrong, and they often are. But it at least accomplishes two important effects. On the one hand, it exposes all the cruder fallacies to hostile examination, and so disposes of many of them. And on the other hand, it melodramatizes the business of the critic, and so convinces thousands of bystanders, otherwise quite inert, that criticism is an amusing and instructive art, and that the problems it deals with are important. What men will fight for seems to be worth looking into.   1922

R. P. BLACKMUR

1904–

A NATIVE OF Massachusetts, where he was born in Springfield and raised in Cambridge, Blackmur began in his twenties a lengthy and hard-working apprenticeship as free-lance poet and critic. His emergence as poet was marked by the superb collection, *From Jordan's Delight* (1937), and his mastery of the gnomic lyric was further proved with *The Second World* (1942) and *The Good European* (1947). He also edited, with a valuable introduction, the critical prefaces which Henry James prepared for the New York Edition of his prose fiction.

Although he had long contributed critical essays and reviews to a wide variety of magazines, Blackmur's critical reputation may be said to have begun with the publication of *The Double Agent* (1935). Like *The Expense of Greatness* (1940), *Language as Gesture* (1952), and *The Lion and The Honeycomb* (1955), the first critical volume is a collection of essays organized loosely around a common theme. His association with Princeton University began in 1940, and his appointment as Professor of English there dates from 1951.

Joseph Frank has referred to the "sybilline quality" of much of Blackmur's prose, and there can be no doubt of its occasional difficulty. Yet it is clear that one whole side of his critical enterprise is summed up in the subtitle of an early collection: *Essays in Craft and Elucidation.* The terms refer to the technical niceties and virtuosities of the writer's craft and to the light which the critic is able to shed upon the formal and textural achievement of the artist. Such a program, rigorously pursued, is commonly associated with the so-called New Criticism. Yet Blackmur has sturdily resisted this tag, preferring to follow his imagination into whatever involvement with a given work the internal laws of that work may dictate. A second characteristic of his critical method is essentially dialectical; he moves between ideas of unity, orthodoxy, and order on the one hand and of diversity, heterodoxy, and chaos on the other. Depending upon the internal literary situation, these opposing ideas may be found to clash, coalesce, or remain disparate. As Blackmur defines it in the following essay, the enabling act of criticism is that act of submission by the critic to everything he can discover of clash, coalescence, or disparateness in any given work. Once this act is complete, the task of judgment may begin.

Carlos Baker, "R. P. Blackmur: A Checklist," *Princeton University Library Chronicle,* III (April, 1942), 99–106.
R. P. Blackmur, *The Double Agent,* New York, 1935.
———, *The Expense of Greatness,* New York, 1940.
———, *Language as Gesture,* New York, 1952.
———, *The Lion and the Honeycomb,* New York, 1955.
Joseph Frank, "Ideas of Order," (Review of *The Lion and the Honeycomb*) *Partisan Review,* XXIII (Spring, 1956), 265–273.
C. H. Grattan, ed., *Critique of Humanism,* New York, 1930, pp. 237–254.
S. E. Hyman, *The Armed Vision,* New York, 1948, pp. 239–271.
R. W. B. Lewis, "Casella as Critic: A Note on R. P. Blackmur," *Kenyon Review,* XIII (Summer, 1951), 458–474.
Delmore Schwartz, "The Critical Method of R. P. Blackmur," *Poetry,* LIII (October, 1938), 28–39.
Allen Tate, "R. P. Blackmur and Others," *Southern Review,* III (Summer, 1937), 183–198.

» » THE ENABLING ACT OF CRITICISM « «

There is a kind of resolute candor necessary to a full approach to literature which is impossible to any particular approach. The best that the individual can do positively is to insist that his particular work aims in the general direction of that candor, and the least that he can do negatively is not only to admit but to insist that other particular approaches also aim in that direction. Failure to make either insistence leads to irrelevance and arrogance of judgment, and if persisted in at the level of practice—whether in book-reviewing or in major criticism—tends to complete the separation of the literary critic from his proper subject-matter. Instead of practicing literary criticism he will find himself practicing self-expression or casual philosophy, practices which will be deceptive in the degree that they were not candidly undertaken. Thus when the critic takes Criticism itself as his subject—when he faces his own practice, when he confronts

other critics with their own practice—he must concern himself sooner or later with the relative stage of candor or deception which that practice discloses. And the sooner he does this the better, because for the life of me I cannot see how the critic judging of Criticism can do much more. Further, if he takes his job seriously, I cannot see how he can content himself with attempting less. Surely it is a tenable view that criticism must in the end come back to the task of saying what its objects are in terms of themselves; as surely, then, it is of first importance to distinguish in the work of a critic what is criticism from what is something else.

To put the matter quite practically, on the level where we actually use criticism, which is to say in our efforts towards a better understanding of literature, let us set up a series of questions designed to show the distinctions we want. We have a critic before us. What, when he is all done, does he tell us about the works he says he is examining? Is what he tells us everywhere subordinated to what we may call the interests of the works themselves: precisely, what it is within the work that interests us or defeats its own interest? Or, on the contrary, is what he tells us subordinated to some interest, no doubt worthy in itself, independent of the work in hand? If so, which interest predominates? And, if the extra-literary interest does predominate, can it yet be said that it nevertheless enlightens the literary interest, by situating it, say, among all the interests that go to make up a culture? This last, if we rephrase it, makes up the crucial question; for does it not ask, really, whether we can accept or reject a literary work by the application of literary standards alone? That is, to make one more rephrasing, do we in fact ever understand literature only by literary means?

If we can answer these questions as it were backwards, it is possible that we may come out somewhere near right in the end. At least we should have a beginning not merely provisional or wayward but with an end already and firmly in view: namely, a focus for literary experience, and a vantage for looking. We can think of the whole backward process as the enabling act of criticism.

Well, then, it is plain that we never do in fact understand literature solely by literary means any more than we understand water solely by drinking it, solely by chemical analysis, solely by looking at it, or solely by damming it up. It is the unified mind and sensibility that is engaged in the act of understanding; the act is imaginative; and to try to compartmentalize the act so as to emphasize one faculty over another is to invalidate the imagination and abort the act. Looked at in this way, the question of the final understanding of literature becomes either an artificial or an irrelevant question. If we do not use the whole mind we shall understand nothing; if we do use it, we do so as it were inarticulately, as the product of our whole culture: that is, we take it for granted.

But what is taken for granted must be attended just the same, like breathing; and in this case especially; for the unified, imaginative character of the understanding was not brought up here for nothing but indifferent acceptance. It was brought up in order to emphasize the fact that at the other end of the rod from criticism—in the act of the composition of literature itself—the process is the

same. Serious writing is done under the full tolerable weight of mind and sensibility. Imagination is in that sense absolute. All that can be made to bear, bears. That is why the critic must bring his full tolerable imagination to bear before judgment is possible.

In the word tolerable we introduce a consideration which brings us to the next question in our backwards moving series; the question whether, really, we can accept or reject a literary work by the application of literary standards alone. Here the answer is double; partly yes and partly no, only good sense—the taste of practice—determining which. T. S. Eliot's remark is initially in order, that while we can only tell that a work is literature by literary standards, we cannot tell whether it is great literature except by other than literary standards. A first qualifying reflection is that there is not very much great literature; and a second is that, even when a critic is concerned with great literature, most of the problems he handles will not directly affect his estimate of its greatness. Greatness is come up to, felt, discovered; not handled. A critic who tried to handle merely the greatness of Shakespeare or Dante would see it disappear before his eyes. And a critic who attempted to establish the greatness of Joyce or Eliot or Yeats would be largely wasting his time; for greatness is established by custom, by time, by the apprehension in the minds of many men of inexhaustibility, and even so greatness is transitory and variable. Milton is not so great to-day as a century ago. Dante is greater. And I use the copulative deliberately, for greatness is an act of estimation not an assertion of fact, and hence may be expected to vary, but not, once estimated, ever to disappear irrecoverably. It would be intolerable as well as impossible for us today to look at Milton either with our own full mind and sensibility or with those of his own generation, or with those of the eighteenth century. We use of our own what will bear, of the others only what will elucidate—and then only putatively. On the other hand—and this is the aspect of critical activity to which we shall return—it would be intolerable if we did not bring the full force of our literary standards to bear in order to determine what of Milton is literature and what is not. Equally, the other way round, we should bring as much as possible of Milton's literary achievement to bear on the products of our own time; and the extent to which this can be done will constitute a literary judgment on both Milton and our own time. Those other, extra-literary standards, the standards of the convictions of our whole culture, will thus tend to disappear or be transformed into the literary standards.

A very different thing happens—at this time; though it may not be at another—in the example of Dante, whose greatness has grown so in our estimation that the force of his work seems almost a quality of the air that poets must breathe to invigorate their own verse. Dante, said Yeats, was the chief imagination of Christendom; and I think it may be hazarded that his greatness lies in the fact that he showed the highest and fullest unity the Christian order ever reached actually at work in light and air and earth. As Eliot says, the Divine Comedy is a vast ordering of actual human feelings and emotions; which are our own feelings and emotions, and as we apprehend them expose us, as little in our own poetry is able to do, to the conviction of our own fate. This is to say, perhaps, that no matter how much of our extra-literary standards we bring to bear on Dante, it is not enough; it is rather that Dante's standards enlighten ours; so that, as far as actually accepting or rejecting Dante goes, we have only our literary standards to resort to. (I suggest that it is not our Christianity that brings us to Dante, but our desperate lack of it.) If this statement of present affairs is provisionally correct it constitutes a profound judgment of defect in our culture, established, in the fact, by literary means alone. Thus, in effect, we witness literary standards operating the Christian order as a "mere" principle of composition. This is not offered with approval or disapproval, but hazarded as a possible mode of approaching the problem of judging literature: namely, by the transformation of literary standards to the level of general conviction. It should be added that there does not seem to be any other poet—certainly not Shakespeare, who dramatized inertia rather than order—where such a possibility shows itself. Dante is alone in achievement.

You would not think so from a quick re-reading of the principal literary critics since the middle of the nineteenth century—since, that is, the specific decay of the Christian order began to be felt as a shifting towards disorder, towards dismay, towards corruption, in the general order of culture. In Taine and Sainte Beuve; in Arnold and Pater; in Babbitt and More; in the psychologists, the aestheticians, and the Marxists; in the critics associated with the *Action Française,* and in the secular neo-Thomists as well; indeed almost everywhere that men have taken literature seriously, you will find the tendency prevalent, at varying intensities, to estimate the value of writers in the degree that their *literary* standards did or did not operate in the place of other standards. Writers have been generally judged, along the lines of the critic's particular interest, as to whether or not they were able to effect deliberately such a transformation of standards as we have just been suggesting that Dante effected as it were inadvertently. There is not a writer of the last century of any stature who has not been condemned, or at least run down, for his failure in this direction by one or more of these our most eminent and best trained critics.

Now it may be that these critics are right in their preoccupation. It may be that the vast task of ordering human feelings and emotions has been imposed upon the arts and especially upon literature by the present lack of any authority otherwise derived. It may be that we are committed—I will not say condemned—to a wholly secular culture. Faced with the immediate alternatives in the wave, as Mrs. Lindbergh calls it, of fascist and soviet culture, we may even hope for a secular culture. But if assent is given to that idea, it does not follow that the literary critic in emphasizing the Dantesque aspect of literature can escape his obligation to explore and to master the primary aspect of literature: that aspect in which it represents the experience of the actual which is beneath and beyond merely moral experience, and which alone grounds or situates moral experience. Eliot's remark holds true that as morals are only a primary consideration for the saint, so they are only a secondary consideration for the artist.

This brings us up sharp on our next question, as to whether the extra-literary interest, if it predominates in the critic's mind, enlightens the literary interest. With regard to the general mass of critics to whom we referred above, the answer is plainly negative, and may be drawn from two approximate facts about their work. They seem, in the mass, seldom to have enjoyed literature, and they seem as individuals, and especially when concerned with the literature of their own times, to have been concerned with what a given work did not do to the virtual exclusion of what it did do. In short, and this is what makes one most suspicious of their candor, they not only made their criticism autonomous, which is a sin of pride, but they also made criticism appear to do the work of literature, which is the sin of putting God in second place. They defiled their literary knowledge to the point where it hardly seems recognisable as knowledge of literature at all; with the curious but natural result that their morals or politics or sociology or theology seemed second-rate, vitiated by isolation from the actual world which lay before them in the literature which was their declared subject-matter. That the literature has survived in spite of its criticism and continues to arouse the same sort of attention suggests that it was not that the intent of the critics was mistaken but that their method was inefficient and their attention inadequate.

It is not the business of this paper to decide to what uses literature may be put, and it is not the predilection if this writer to see literature made into a kind of Pandora's box of panaceas, or even into the source of a merely moral order; but if there is a demand for that sort of thing, and there is, then it had better be done along lines that admit the possibility of success at the beginning. Those lines exist, are available, and may be taught; they are indicated in the frame of questions around which these paragraphs have been laid down. Assuming that literature, being imaginative, is understood if at all by the whole imagination before it is understood or used in any other way, acknowledging that many interests not literary but moral, political, spiritual, are nevertheless imaginatively present in literature, and even insisting that it is in the light of those interests that literature shows its stature (thereby adding to our own) and must be judged, it remains necessary to approach those other interests through the interests of the works themselves: through what is told, shown, expressed. It is there, in the interest of the actual, shaped and composed by what Santayana calls the enormous burden of perception—all that the intellect ignores or merely schematises—it is there, straight in front of you, in the words and

the motions of the words, that the artist has focussed, or failed to focus, those interests you want. It could not be otherwise.

If you think otherwise, there is a primary defect in your contact with literature such as you would not permit yourself, say, in your contact with philosophy where it is a commonplace that the words are important and often difficult: where a universe is heaped in a phrase. If you think it is so but easy, you are rash and inexperienced. In the very degree that the work of literature does focus the interests you want it will be difficult—indeed an inexhaustible labor—to grasp the text. And until you have grasped the text you cannot paraphrase it; and to paraphrase in intellectual terms an imaginative experience is I suppose a generalized description of what you mean to do. But if you can grasp the text the rest will either come naturally, though arduously, or will seem irrelevant or superfluous. You will have either the labor of articulating your judgment of interest, or you will see that, so far as literature is concerned, it does not count.

The real difficulty lies further back, and is double in character. It consists, first, in being willing to concentrate your maximum attention upon the work which the words and the motions of the words—and by motions I mean all the technical devices of literature—perform upon each other. Secondly, it consists in submitting, at least provisionally, to whatever authority your attention brings to light in the words. In doing this you will be following in pretty close parallel the procedure which the writer followed. Whether your submission is permanent or must be withdrawn will be determined by the judgment of all the standards and all the interests you can bring to bear. These will differ with the work in hand. But the act of submission must be made before you can tell; it is an act of imagination, not of will; and it is the enabling act of criticism. If it does not provide you with another Dante, it will at least provide you with an interest in literature; and without that you would not know a Dante if he appeared.   1941

LIONEL TRILLING

1905–

ORN IN New York City on Independence Day in 1905, Trilling has since pursued a course suited to the day of his birth, belonging to no school of criticism and refusing to stay within the boundaries of any cultural or geographical unit save his critical integrity and the city of New York. Educated at Columbia University, he taught at Hunter College for three years before joining the faculty of Columbia, where he has been a professor of English since 1948. He is the author of two excellent critical studies, *Matthew Arnold* (1939) and *E. M. Forster* (1943); a distinguished novel, *The Middle of the Journey* (1947); and three collections of critical essays, *The Liberal Imagination* (1950), *The Opposing Self* (1955), and *A Gathering of Fugitives* (1956).

On the basis of a remark by Harry Levin, it is often said that Trilling has had the courage to be a moralist. Yet to this one should add at once that his moral concerns, though of central importance, have neither limited his imaginative range and depth nor driven him into the error of judging literature solely on the basis of its ethical content. One dominant image of his thought, indeed, is that of the artist or thinker as the free agent, building his formal structures in virtual defiance of a constricting world of necessity. In the brilliant essay here reprinted, that image is well exemplified in the person of Sigmund Freud, as Trilling examines the impact of literature upon Freud and the impact of Freud's teachings upon the literature of his own and later times.

Lionel Trilling, *A Gathering of Fugitives* (essays), Boston, 1956.
————, *The Liberal Imagination; Essays on Literature and Society*, New York, 1950.
————, *The Opposing Self; Nine Essays in Criticism*, New York, 1955.
C. E. Eisinger, "Trilling and the Crisis in Our Culture," *University of Kansas City Review*, XXV (Autumn, 1958), 27–35.
Joseph Frank, "Lionel Trilling and the Conservative Imagination," *Sewanee Review*, LXIV (Spring, 1956), 296–309.
R. W. B. Lewis, "Lionel Trilling and the New Stoicism," *Hudson Review*, III (Summer, 1950), 313–320.
Paul West, "Romantic Identity in the Open Society," *Queen's Quarterly*, LXV (Winter, 1959), 578–585.

» » *From:* THE LIBERAL IMAGINATION « «

FREUD AND LITERATURE

I

The Freudian psychology is the only systematic account of the human mind which, in point of subtlety and complexity, of interest and tragic power, deserves to stand beside the chaotic mass of psychological insights which literature has accumulated through the centuries. To pass from the reading of a great literary work to a treatise of academic psychology is to pass from one order of perception to another, but the human nature of the Freudian psychology is exactly the stuff upon which the poet has always exercised his art. It is therefore not surprising that the psychoanalytical theory has had a great effect upon literature. Yet the relationship is reciprocal, and the effect of Freud upon literature has been no greater than the effect of literature upon Freud. When, on the occasion of the celebration of his seventieth birthday, Freud was greeted as the "discoverer of the unconscious," he corrected the speaker and disclaimed the title.

10

"The poets and philosophers before me discovered the unconscious," he said. "What I discovered was the scientific method by which the unconscious can be studied."

A lack of specific evidence prevents us from considering the particular literary "influences" upon the founder of psychoanalysis; and, besides, when we think of the men who so clearly anticipated many of Freud's own ideas—Schopenhauer and Nietzsche, for example—and then learn that he did not read their works until after he had formulated his own theories, we must see that particular influences cannot be in question here but that what we must deal with is nothing less than a whole *Zeitgeist,* a direction of thought. For psychoanalysis is one of the culminations of the Romanticist literature of the nineteenth century. If there is perhaps a contradiction in the idea of a science standing upon the shoulders of a literature which avows itself inimical to science in so many ways, the contradiction will be resolved if we remember that this literature, despite its avowals, was itself scientific in at least the sense of being passionately devoted to a research into the self.

In showing the connection between Freud and this Romanticist tradition, it is difficult to know where to begin, but there might be a certain aptness in starting even back of the tradition, as far back as 1762 with Diderot's *Rameau's Nephew.* At any rate, certain men at the heart of nineteenth-century thought were agreed in finding a peculiar importance in this brilliant little work: Goethe translated it, Marx admired it, Hegel—as Marx reminded Engels in the letter which announced that he was sending the book as a gift—praised and expounded it at length. Shaw was impressed by it, and Freud himself, as we know from a quotation in his *Introductory Lectures,* read it with the pleasure of agreement.

The dialogue takes place between Diderot himself and a nephew of the famous composer. The protagonist, the younger Rameau, is a despised, outcast, shameless fellow; Hegel calls him the "disintegrated consciousness" and credits him with great wit, for it is he who breaks down all the normal social values and makes new combinations with the pieces. As for Diderot, the deuteragonist, he is what Hegel calls the "honest consciousness," and Hegel considers him reasonable, decent, and dull. It is quite clear that the author does not despise his Rameau and does not mean us to.

Rameau is lustful and greedy, arrogant yet self-abasing, perceptive yet "wrong," like a child. Still, Diderot seems actually to be giving the fellow a kind of superiority over himself, as though Rameau represents the elements which, dangerous but wholly necessary, lie beneath the reasonable decorum of social life. It would perhaps be pressing too far to find in Rameau Freud's id and in Diderot Freud's ego; yet the connection does suggest itself; and at least we have here the perception which is to be the common characteristic of both Freud and Romanticism, the perception of the hidden element of human nature and of the opposition between the hidden and the visible. We have too the bold perception of just what lies hidden: "If the little savage [i.e., the child] were left to himself, if he preserved all his foolishness and combined the violent passions of a man of thirty with the lack of reason of a child in the cradle, he'd wring his father's neck and go to bed with his mother."

From the self-exposure of Rameau to Rousseau's account of his own childhood is no great step; society might ignore or reject the idea of the "immorality" which lies concealed in the beginning of the career of the "good" man, just as it might turn away from Blake struggling to expound a psychology which would include the forces beneath the propriety of social man in general, but the idea of the hidden thing went forward to become one of the dominant notions of the age. The hidden element takes many forms and it is not necessarily "dark" and "bad"; for Blake the "bad" was the good, while for Wordsworth and Burke what was hidden and unconscious was wisdom and power, which work in despite of the conscious intellect.

The mind has become far less simple; the devotion to the various forms of autobiography —itself an important fact in the tradition— provides abundant examples of the change that has taken place. Poets, making poetry by what seems to them almost a freshly discovered faculty, find that this new power may be conspired against by other agencies of the mind and even deprived of its freedom; the names of Wordsworth, Coleridge, and Arnold at once occur to us again, and Freud quotes Schiller on the danger to the poet that lies in the merely analytical reason. And it is not only the poets who are threatened; educated and sensitive people throughout Europe become aware of the depredations that reason might make upon the affective life, as in the classic instance of John Stuart Mill.

We must also take into account the preoccupation—it began in the eighteenth century, or even in the seventeenth—with children, women, peasants, and savages, whose mental life, it is felt, is less overlaid than that of the educated adult male by the proprieties of social habit. With this preoccupation goes a concern with education and personal development, so consonant with the historical and evolutionary bias of the time. And we must certainly note the revolution in morals which took place at the instance (we might almost say) of the *Bildungsroman,* for in the novels fathered by *Wilhelm Meister* we get the almost complete identification of author and hero and of the reader with both, and this identification almost inevitably suggests a leniency of moral judgment. The autobiographical novel has a further influence upon the moral sensibility by its exploitation of all the modulations of motive and by its hinting that we may not judge a man by any single moment in his life without taking into account the determining past and the expiating and fulfilling future.

It is difficult to know how to go on, for the further we look the more literary affinities to Freud we find, and even if we limit ourselves to bibliography we can at best be incomplete. Yet we must mention the sexual revolution that was being demanded—by Shelley, for example, by the Schlegel of *Lucinde,* by George Sand, and later and more critically by Ibsen; the belief in the sexual origin of art, baldly stated by Tieck, more subtly by Schopenhauer; the investigation of sexual maladjustment by Stendhal, whose observations on erotic feeling seem to us distinctly Freudian. Again and again we see the effective, utilitarian ego being relegated to an inferior position and a plea being made on behalf of the anarchic and self-indulgent id. We find the energetic exploitation of the idea of the mind as a divisible thing, one part of which can contemplate and mock the other. It is not a far remove from this to Dostoevski's brilliant instances of ambivalent feeling. Novalis brings in the preoccupation with the death wish, and this is linked on the one hand with sleep and on the other hand with the perception of the perverse, self-destroying impulses, which in turn leads us to that fascination by the horrible which we find in Shelley, Poe, and Baudelaire. And always there is the profound interest in the dream—"Our dreams,"

said Gerard de Nerval, "are a second life"—and in the nature of metaphor, which reaches its climax in Rimbaud and the later symbolists, metaphor becoming less and less communicative as it approaches the relative autonomy of the dream life.

But perhaps we must stop to ask, since these are the components of the *Zeitgeist* from which Freud himself developed, whether it can be said that Freud did indeed produce a wide literary effect. What is it that Freud added that the tendency of literature itself would not have developed without him? If we were looking for a writer who showed the Freudian influence, Proust would perhaps come to mind as readily as anyone else; the very title of his novel, in French more than in English, suggests an enterprise of psychoanalysis and scarcely less so does his method—the investigation of sleep, of sexual deviation, of the way of association, the almost obsessive interest in metaphor; at these and at many other points the "influence" might be shown. Yet I believe it is true that Proust did not read Freud. Or again, exegesis of *The Waste Land* often reads remarkably like the psychoanalytic interpretation of a dream, yet we know that Eliot's methods were prepared for him not by Freud but by other poets.

Nevertheless, it is of course true that Freud's influence on literature has been very great. Much of it is so pervasive that its extent is scarcely to be determined; in one form or another, frequently in perversions or absurd simplifications, it has been infused into our life and become a component of our culture of which it is now hard to be specifically aware. In biography its first effect was sensational but not fortunate. The early Freudian biographers were for the most part Guildensterns who seemed to know the pipes but could not pluck out the heart of the mystery, and the same condemnation applies to the early Freudian critics. But in recent years, with the acclimatization of psychoanalysis and the increased sense of its refinements and complexity, criticism has derived from the Freudian system much that is of great value, most notably the license and the injunction to read the work of literature with a lively sense of its latent and ambiguous meanings, as if it were, as indeed it is, a being no less alive and contradictory than the man who created it. And this new response to the literary work has had a corrective effect upon our conception of literary biography. The literary critic or biographer who makes use of the Freudian theory is no less threatened by the dangers of theoretical systematization than he was in the early days, but he is likely to be more aware of these dangers; and I think it is true to say that now the motive of his interpretation is not that of exposing the secret shame of the writer and limiting the meaning of his work, but, on the contrary, that of finding grounds for sympathy with the writer and for increasing the possible significances of the work.

The names of the creative writers who have been more or less Freudian in tone or assumption would of course be legion. Only a relatively small number, however, have made serious use of the Freudian ideas. Freud himself seems to have thought this was as it should be: he is said to have expected very little of the works that were sent to him by writers with inscriptions of gratitude for all they had learned from him. The Surrealists have, with a certain inconsistency, depended upon Freud for the "scientific" sanction of their program. Kafka, with an apparent awareness of what he was doing, has explored the Freudian conceptions of guilt and punishment, of the dream, and of the fear of the father. Thomas Mann, whose tendency, as he himself says, was always in the direction of Freud's interests, has been most susceptible to the Freudian anthropology, finding a special charm in the theories of myths and magical practices. James Joyce, with his interest in the numerous states of receding consciousness, with his use of words as things and of words which point to more than one thing, with his pervading sense of the interrelation and interpenetration of all things, and, not least important, his treatment of familial themes, has perhaps most thoroughly and consciously exploited Freud's ideas.

II

It will be clear enough how much of Freud's thought has significant affinity with the anti-rationalist element of the Romanticist tradition. But we must see with no less distinctness how much of his system is militantly rationalistic. Thomas Mann is at fault when, in his first essay on Freud, he makes it seem that the "Apollonian," the rationalistic, side of psychoanalysis is, while certainly important and wholly admirable, somehow secondary and even accidental. He gives us a Freud who is committed to the "night side" of life. Not at all: the rationalistic element of Freud is foremost; before everything else he is positivistic. If the interpreter of dreams came to medical science through Goethe, as he tells us he did, he entered not by way of the *Walpurgisnacht* but by the essay which played so important a part in the lives of so many scientists of the nineteenth century, the famous disquisition on Nature.

This correction is needed not only for accuracy but also for any understanding of Freud's attitude to art. And for that understanding we must see how intense is the passion with which Freud believes that positivistic rationalism, in its golden-age pre-Revolutionary purity, is the very form and pattern of intellectual virtue. The aim of psychoanalysis, he says, is the control of the night side of life. It is "to strengthen the ego, to make it more independent of the super-ego, to widen its field of vision, and so to extend the organization of the id." "Where id was,"—that is, where all the irrational, non-logical, pleasure-seeking dark forces were—"there shall ego be,"—that is, intelligence and control. "It is," he concludes, with a reminiscence of Faust, "reclamation work, like the draining of the Zuyder Zee." This passage is quoted by Mann when, in taking up the subject of Freud a second time, he does indeed speak of Freud's positivistic program; but even here the bias induced by Mann's artistic interest in the "night side" prevents him from giving the other aspect of Freud its due emphasis. Freud would never have accepted the role which Mann seems to give him as the legitimizer of the myth and the dark irrational ways of the mind. If Freud discovered the darkness for science he never endorsed it. On the contrary, his rationalism supports all the ideas of the Enlightenment that deny validity to myth or religion; he holds to a simple materialism, to a simple determinism, to a rather limited sort of epistemology. No great scientist of our day has thundered so articulately and so fiercely against all those who would sophisticate with metaphysics the scientific principles that were good enough for the nineteenth century. Conceptualism or pragmatism is anathema to him through the greater part of his intellectual career, and this, when we consider the nature of his own brilliant scientific methods, has surely an element of paradox in it.

From his rationalistic positivism comes much of Freud's strength and what weakness he has. The strength is the fine, clear tenacity of his positive aims, the goal of therapy, the desire to bring to men a decent measure of earthly happiness. But upon the rationalism must also be placed the blame for the often naïve scientific principles which characterize his early thought —they are later much modified—and which consist largely of claiming for his theories a perfect correspondence with an external reality, a position which, for those who admire Freud and especially for those who take seriously his views on art, is troublesome in the extreme.

Now Freud has, I believe, much to tell us about art, but whatever is suggestive in him is not likely to be found in those of his works in which he deals expressly with art itself. Freud is not insensitive to art—on the contrary—nor does he ever intend to speak of it with contempt. Indeed, he speaks of it with a real tenderness and counts it one of the true charms of the good life. Of artists, especially of writers, he speaks with admiration and even a kind of awe, though perhaps what he most appreciates in literature are specific emotional insights and observations; as we have noted, he speaks of literary men, because they have understood the part played in life by the hidden motives, as the precursors and coadjutors of his own science.

And yet eventually Freud speaks of art with what we must indeed call contempt. Art, he tells us, is a "substitute gratification," and as such is "an illusion in contrast to reality." Unlike most illusions, however, art is "almost always harmless and beneficent" for the reason that "it does not seek to be anything but an illusion. Save in the case of a few people who are, one might say, obsessed by Art, it never dares make any attack on the realm of reality." One of its chief functions is to serve as a "narcotic." It shares the characteristics of the dream, whose element of distortion Freud calls a "sort of inner dishonesty." As for the artist, he is virtually in the same category with the neurotic. "By such separation of imagination and intellectual capacity," Freud says of the hero of a novel, "he is destined to be a poet or a neurotic, and he belongs to that race of beings whose realm is not of this world."

Now there is nothing in the logic of psychoanalytical thought which requires Freud to have these opinions. But there is a great deal in the practice of the psychoanalytical therapy which makes it understandable that Freud, unprotected by an adequate philosophy, should be tempted to take the line he does. The analytical therapy deals with illusion. The patient comes to the physician to be cured, let us say, of a fear of walking in the street. The fear is real enough, there is no illusion on that score, and it produces all the physical symptoms of a more rational fear, the sweating palms, pounding heart, and shortened breath. But the patient knows that there is no cause for the fear, or rather that there is, as he says, no "real cause": there are no machine guns, man traps, or tigers in the street. The physician knows, however, that there is indeed a "real" cause for the fear, though it has nothing at all to do with what is or is not in the street; the cause is within the patient, and the process of the therapy will be to discover, by gradual steps, what this real cause is and so free the patient from its effects.

Now the patient in coming to the physician, and the physician in accepting the patient, make a tacit compact about reality; for their purpose they agree to the limited reality by which we get our living, win our loves, catch our trains and our colds. The therapy will undertake to train the patient in proper ways of coping with this reality. The patient, of course, has been dealing with this reality all along, but in the wrong way. For Freud there are two ways of dealing with external reality. One is practical, effective, positive; this is the way of the conscious self, of the ego which must be made independent of the super-ego and extend its organization over the id, and it is the right way. The antithetical way may be called, for our purpose now, the "fictional" way. Instead of doing something about, or to, external reality, the individual who uses this way does something to, or about, his affective states. The most common and "normal" example of this is daydreaming, in which we give ourselves a certain pleasure by imagining our difficulties solved or our desires gratified. Then, too, as Freud discovered, sleeping dreams are, in much more complicated ways, and even though quite unpleasant, at the service of this same "fictional" activity. And in ways yet more complicated and yet more unpleasant, the actual neurosis from which our patient suffers deals with an external reality which the mind considers still more unpleasant than the painful neurosis itself.

For Freud as psychoanalytic practitioner there are, we may say, the polar extremes of reality and illusion. Reality is an honorific word, and it means what is *there*; illusion is a pejorative word, and it means a response to

what is *not there*. The didactic nature of a course of psychoanalysis no doubt requires a certain firm crudeness in making the distinction; it is after all aimed not at theoretical refinement but at practical effectiveness. The polar extremes are practical reality and neurotic illusion, the latter judged by the former. This, no doubt, is as it should be; the patient is not being trained in metaphysics and episte-
10 mology.

This practical assumption is not Freud's only view of the mind in its relation to reality. Indeed what may be called the essentially Freudian view assumes that the mind, for good as well as bad, helps create its reality by selection and evaluation. In this view, reality is malleable and subject to creation; it is not static but is rather a series of situations which are dealt with in their own terms. But beside this con-
20 ception of the mind stands the conception which arises from Freud's therapeutic-practical assumptions; in this view, the mind deals with a reality which is quite fixed and static, a reality that is wholly "given" and not (to use a phrase of Dewey's) "taken." In his epistemological utterances, Freud insists on this second view, although it is not easy to see why he should do so. For the reality to which he wishes to reconcile the neurotic patient is, after
30 all, a "taken" and not a "given" reality. It is the reality of social life and of value, conceived and maintained by the human mind and will. Love, morality, honor, esteem—these are the components of a created reality. If we are to call art an illusion then we must call most of the activities and satisfactions of the ego illusions; Freud, of course, has no desire to call them that.

What, then, is the difference between, on the
40 one hand, the dream and the neurosis, and, on the other hand, art? That they have certain common elements is of course clear; that unconscious processes are at work in both would be denied by no poet or critic; they share too, though in different degrees, the element of fantasy. But there is a vital difference between them which Charles Lamb saw so clearly in his defense of the sanity of true genius: "The . . . poet dreams being awake. He is not possessed
50 by his subject but he has dominion over it."

That is the whole difference: the poet is in command of his fantasy, while it is exactly the mark of the neurotic that he is possessed by his fantasy. And there is a further difference which Lamb states; speaking of the poet's relation to

reality (he calls it Nature), he says, "He is beautifully loyal to that sovereign directress, even when he appears most to betray her"; the illusions of art are made to serve the purpose of a closer and truer relation with reality. Jacques Barzun, in an acute and sympathetic discussion of Freud, puts the matter well: "A good analogy between art and *dreaming* has led him to a false one between art and *sleeping*. But the difference between a work of art and a dream is precisely this, that the work of art *leads us back to the outer reality by taking account of it*." Freud's assumption of the almost exclusively hedonistic nature and purpose of art bar him from the perception of this.

Of the distinction that must be made between the artist and the neurotic Freud is of course aware; he tells us that the artist is not like the neurotic in that he knows how to find a way back from the world of imagination and "once more get a firm foothold in reality." This however seems to mean no more than that reality is to be dealt with when the artist suspends the practice of his art; and at least once when Freud speaks of art dealing with reality he actually means the rewards that a successful artist can win. He does not deny to art its function and its usefulness; it has a therapeutic effect in releasing mental tension; it serves the cultural purpose of acting as a "substitute gratification" to reconcile men to the sacrifices they have made for culture's sake; it promotes the social sharing of highly valued emotional experiences; and it recalls men to their cultural ideals. This is not everything that some of us would find that art does, yet even this is a good deal for a "narcotic" to do.

III

I started by saying that Freud's ideas could tell us something about art, but so far I have done little more than try to show that Freud's very conception of art is inadequate. Perhaps, then, the suggestiveness lies in the application of the analytic method to specific works of art or to the artist himself? I do not think so, and it is only fair to say that Freud himself was aware both of the limits and the limitations of psychoanalysis in art, even though he does not always in practice submit to the former or admit the latter.

Freud has, for example, no desire to encroach upon the artist's autonomy; he does not wish us to read his monograph on Leonardo and then say of the "Madonna of the Rocks" that it is a fine example of homosexual, autoerotic painting. If he asserts that in investigation the "psychiatrist cannot yield to the author," he immediately insists that the "author cannot yield to the psychiatrist," and he warns the latter not to "coarsen everything" by using for all human manifestations the "substantially useless and awkward terms" of clinical procedure. He admits, even while asserting that the sense of beauty probably derives from sexual feeling, that psychoanalysis "has less to say about beauty than about most other things." He confesses to a theoretical indifference to the form of art and restricts himself to its content. Tone, feeling, style, and the modification that part makes upon part he does not consider. "The layman," he says, "may expect perhaps too much from analysis . . . for it must be admitted that it throws no light upon the two problems which probably interest him the most. It can do nothing toward elucidating the nature of the artistic gift, nor can it explain the means by which the artist works—artistic technique."

What, then, does Freud believe that the analytical method can do? Two things: explain the "inner meanings" of the work of art and explain the temperament of the artist as man.

A famous example of the method is the attempt to solve the "problem" of *Hamlet* as suggested by Freud and as carried out by Dr. Ernest Jones, his early and distinguished follower. Dr. Jones's monograph is a work of painstaking scholarship and of really masterly ingenuity. The research undertakes not only the clearing up of the mystery of Hamlet's character, but also the discovery of "the clue to much of the deeper workings of Shakespeare's mind." Part of the mystery in question is of course why Hamlet, after he had so definitely resolved to do so, did not avenge upon his hated uncle his father's death. But there is another mystery to the play—what Freud calls "the mystery of its effect," its magical appeal that draws so much interest toward it. Recalling the many failures to solve the riddle of the play's charm, he wonders if we are to be driven to the conclusion "that its magical appeal rests solely upon the impressive thoughts in it and the splendor of its language." Freud believes that we can find a source of power beyond this.

We remember that Freud has told us that the meaning of a dream is its intention, and we may assume that the meaning of a drama is its intention, too. The Jones research undertakes to discover what it was that Shakespeare intended to say about Hamlet. It finds that the intention was wrapped by the author in a dreamlike obscurity because it touched so deeply both his personal life and the moral life of the world; what Shakespeare intended to say is that Hamlet cannot act because he is incapacitated by the guilt he feels at his unconscious attachment to his mother. There is, I think, nothing to be quarreled with in the statement that there is an Oedipus situation in *Hamlet*; and if psychoanalysis has indeed added a new point of interest to the play, that is to its credit.[1] And, just so, there is no reason to quarrel with Freud's conclusion when he undertakes to give us the meaning of *King Lear* by a tortuous tracing of the mythological implications of the theme of the three caskets, of the relation of the caskets to the Norns, the Fates, and the Graces, of the connection of these triadic females with Lear's daughters, of the transmogrification of the death goddess into the love goddess and the identification of Cordelia with both, all to the conclusion that the meaning of *King Lear* is to be found in the tragic refusal of an old man to "renounce love, choose death, and make friends with the necessity of dying." There is something both beautiful and suggestive in this, but it is not *the* meaning of *King Lear* any more than the Oedipus motive is *the* meaning of *Hamlet*.

It is not here a question of the validity of the evidence, though that is of course important. We must rather object to the conclusions of Freud and Dr. Jones on the ground that their proponents do not have an adequate conception of what an artistic meaning is. There is no single meaning to any work of art; this is true not merely because it is better that it should be true, that is, because it makes art a richer thing, but because historical and personal experience show it to be true. Changes in historical context and in personal mood change the meaning of a work and indicate to us that artistic understanding is not a question of fact but of value. Even if the author's intention were, as it cannot be, precisely determinable, the meaning of a work cannot lie in the

[1] However, A. C. Bradley, in his discussion of Hamlet (*Shakespearean Tragedy*), states clearly the intense sexual disgust which Hamlet feels and which, for Bradley, helps account for his uncertain purpose; and Bradley was anticipated in this view by Löning. It is well known, and Dover Wilson has lately emphasized the point, that to an Elizabethan audience Hamlet's mother was not merely tasteless, as to a modern audience she seems, in hurrying to marry Claudius, but actually adulterous in marrying him at all because he was, as her brother-in-law, within the forbidden degrees.

author's intention alone. It must also lie in its effect. We can say of a volcanic eruption on an inhabited island that it "means terrible suffering," but if the island is uninhabited or easily evacuated it means something else. In short, the audience partly determines the meaning of the work. But although Freud sees something of this when he says that in addition to the author's intention we must take into account the mystery of *Hamlet's* effect, he nevertheless goes on to speak as if, historically, *Hamlet's* effect had been single and brought about solely by the "magical" power of the Oedipus motive to which, unconsciously, we so violently respond. Yet there was, we know, a period when *Hamlet* was relatively in eclipse, and it has always been scandalously true of the French, a people not without filial feeling, that they have been somewhat indifferent to the "magical appeal" of *Hamlet*.

I do not think that anything I have said about the inadequacies of the Freudian method of interpretation limits the number of ways we can deal with a work of art. Bacon remarked that experiment may twist nature on the rack to wring out its secrets, and criticism may use any instruments upon a work of art to find its meanings. The elements of art are not limited to the world of art. They reach into life, and whatever extraneous knowledge of them we gain—for example, by research into the historical context of the work—may quicken our feelings for the work itself and even enter legitimately into those feelings. Then, too, anything we may learn about the artist himself may be enriching and legitimate. But one research into the mind of the artist is simply not practicable, however legitimate it may theoretically be. That is, the investigation of his unconscious intention as it exists apart from the work itself. Criticism understands that the artist's statement of his conscious intention, though it is sometimes useful, cannot finally determine meaning. How much less can we know from his unconscious intention considered as something apart from the whole work? Surely very little that can be called conclusive or scientific. For, as Freud himself points out, we are not in a position to question the artist; we must apply the technique of dream analysis to his symbols, but, as Freud says with some heat, those people do not understand his theory who think that a dream may be interpreted without the dreamer's free association with the multitudinous details of his dream.

We have so far ignored the aspect of the method which finds the solution to the "mystery" of such a play as *Hamlet* in the temperament of Shakespeare himself and then illuminates the mystery of Shakespeare's temperament by means of the solved mystery of the play. Here it will be amusing to remember that by 1935 Freud had become converted to the theory that it was not Shakespeare of Stratford but the Earl of Oxford who wrote the plays, thus invalidating the important bit of evidence that Shakespeare's father died shortly before the composition of *Hamlet*. This is destructive enough to Dr. Jones's argument, but the evidence from which Dr. Jones draws conclusions about literature fails on grounds more relevant to literature itself. For when Dr. Jones, by means of his analysis of *Hamlet*, takes us into "the deeper workings of Shakespeare's mind," he does so with a perfect confidence that he knows what *Hamlet* is and what its relation to Shakespeare is. It is, he tells us, Shakespeare's "chief masterpiece," so far superior to all his other works that it may be placed on "an entirely separate level." And then, having established his ground on an entirely subjective literary judgment, Dr. Jones goes on to tell us that *Hamlet* "probably expresses the core of Shakespeare's philosophy and outlook as no other work of his does." That is, all the contradictory or complicating or modifying testimony of the other plays is dismissed on the basis of Dr. Jones's acceptance of the peculiar position which, he believes, *Hamlet* occupies in the Shakespeare canon. And it is upon this quite inadmissible judgment that Dr. Jones bases his argument: "It may be expected *therefore* that anything which will give us the key to the inner meaning of the play will *necessarily* give us the clue to much of the deeper workings of Shakespeare's mind." (The italics are mine.)

I should be sorry if it appeared that I am trying to say that psychoanalysis can have nothing to do with literature. I am sure that the opposite is so. For example, the whole notion of rich ambiguity in literature, of the interplay between the apparent meaning and the latent—not "hidden"—meaning, has been reinforced by the Freudian concepts, perhaps even received its first impetus from them. Of late years, the more perceptive psychoanalysts have surrendered the early pretensions of their teachers to deal "scientifically" with literature. That is all to the good, and when a study as modest and precise as Dr. Franz Alexander's essay on *Henry IV* comes along, an essay which pretends not to "solve" but only to illuminate the subject, we have something worth having. Dr. Alexander undertakes nothing more than to say that in the development of Prince Hal we see the classic struggle of the ego to come to normal adjustment, beginning with the rebellion against the father, going on to the conquest of the super-ego (Hotspur, with his rigid notions of honor and glory), then to the conquests of the *id* (Falstaff, with his anarchic self-indulgence), then to the identification with the father (the crown scene) and the assumption of mature responsibility. An analysis of this sort is not momentous and not exclusive of other meanings; perhaps it does no more than point up and formulate what we all have already seen. It has the tact to *accept* the play and does not, like Dr. Jones's study of *Hamlet,* search for a "hidden motive" and a "deeper working," which implies that there is a reality to which the play stands in the relation that a dream stands to the wish that generates it and from which it is separable; it is this reality, this "deeper working," which, according to Dr. Jones, produced the play. But *Hamlet* is not merely the product of Shakespeare's thought, it is the very instrument of his thought, and if meaning is intention, Shakespeare did not intend the Oedipus motive or anything less than *Hamlet;* if meaning is effect then it is *Hamlet* which affects us, not the Oedipus motive. *Coriolanus* also deals, and very terribly, with the Oedipus motive, but the effect of the one drama is very different from the effect of the other.

IV

If, then, we can accept neither Freud's conception of the place of art in life nor his application of the analytical method, what is it that he contributes to our understanding of art or to its practice? In my opinion, what he contributes outweighs his errors; it is of the greatest importance, and it lies in no specific statement that he makes about art but is, rather, implicit in his whole conception of the mind.

For, of all mental systems, the Freudian psychology is the one which makes poetry indigenous to the very constitution of the mind. Indeed, the mind, as Freud sees it, is in the greater part of its tendency exactly a poetry-making organ. This puts the case too strongly, no doubt, for it seems to make the working of the unconscious mind equivalent to poetry itself, forgetting that between the unconscious mind and the finished poem there supervene the social intention and the formal control of the conscious mind. Yet the statement has at least the virtue of counterbalancing the belief, so commonly expressed or implied, that the very opposite is true, and that poetry is a kind of beneficent aberration of the mind's right course.

Freud has not merely naturalized poetry; he has discovered its status as a pioneer settler, and he sees it as a method of thought. Often enough he tries to show how, as a method of thought, it is unreliable and ineffective for conquering reality; yet he himself is forced to use it in the very shaping of his own science, as when he speaks of the topography of the mind and tells us with a kind of defiant apology that the metaphors of space relationship which he is using are really most inexact since the mind is not a thing of space at all, but that there is no other way of conceiving the difficult idea except by metaphor. In the eighteenth century Vico spoke of the metaphorical, imagistic language of the early stages of culture; it was left to Freud to discover how, in a scientific age, we still feel and think in figurative formations, and to create, what psychoanalysis is, a science of tropes, of metaphor and its variants, synecdoche and metonomy.

Freud showed, too, how the mind, in one of its parts, could work without logic, yet not without that directing purpose, that control of intent from which, perhaps it might be said, logic springs. For the unconscious mind works without the syntactical conjunctions which are logic's essence. It recognizes no *because,* no *therefore,* no *but;* such ideas as similarity, agreement, and community are expressed in dreams imagistically by compressing the elements into a unity. The unconscious mind in its struggle with the conscious always turns from the general to the concrete and finds the tangible trifle more congenial than the large abstraction. Freud discovered in the very organization of the mind those mechanisms by which art makes its effects, such devices as the condensations of meanings and the displacement of accent.

All this is perhaps obvious enough and, though I should like to develop it in proportion both to its importance and to the space I have given to disagreement with Freud, I will not press it further. For there are two other elements in Freud's thought which, in conclusion, I should like to introduce as of great weight in their bearing on art.

Of these, one is a specific idea which, in the middle of his career (1920), Freud put forward in his essay *Beyond the Pleasure Principle*. The essay itself is a speculative attempt to solve a perplexing problem in clinical analysis, but its relevance to literature is inescapable, as Freud sees well enough, even though his perception of its critical importance is not sufficiently strong to make him revise his earlier views of the nature and function of art. The idea is one which stands besides Aristotle's notion of the catharsis, in part to supplement, in part to modify it.

Freud has come upon certain facts which are not to be reconciled with his earlier theory of the dream. According to this theory, all dreams, even the unpleasant ones, could be understood upon analysis to have the intention of fulfilling the dreamer's wishes. They are in the service of what Freud calls the pleasure principle, which is opposed to the reality principle. It is, of course, this explanation of the dream which had so largely conditioned Freud's theory of art. But now there is thrust upon him the necessity for reconsidering the theory of the dream, for it was found that in cases of war neurosis—what we once called shellshock—the patient, with the utmost anguish, recurred in his dreams to the very situation, distressing as it was, which had precipitated his neurosis. It seemed impossible to interpret these dreams by any assumption of a hedonistic intent. Nor did there seem to be the usual amount of distortion in them: the patient recurred to the terrible initiatory situation with great literalness. And the same pattern of psychic behavior could be observed in the play of children; there were some games which, far from fulfilling wishes, seemed to concentrate upon the representation of those aspects of the child's life which were most unpleasant and threatening to his happiness.

To explain such mental activities Freud evolved a theory for which he at first refused to claim much but to which, with the years, he attached an increasing importance. He first makes the assumption that there is indeed in the psychic life a repetition-compulsion which goes beyond the pleasure principle. Such a compulsion cannot be meaningless, it must have an intent. And that intent, Freud comes

to believe, is exactly and literally the developing of fear. "These dreams," he says, "are attempts at restoring control of the stimuli by developing apprehension, the pretermission of which caused the traumatic neurosis." The dream, that is, is the effort to reconstruct the bad situation in order that the failure to meet it may be recouped; in these dreams there is no obscured intent to evade but only an attempt to meet the situation, to make a new effort of control. And in the play of children it seems to be that "the child repeats even the unpleasant experiences because through his own activity he gains a far more thorough mastery of the strong impression than was possible by mere passive experience."

Freud, at this point, can scarcely help being put in mind of tragic drama; nevertheless, he does not wish to believe that this effort to come to mental grips with a situation is involved in the attraction of tragedy. He is, we might say, under the influence of the Aristotelian tragic theory which emphasizes a qualified hedonism through suffering. But the pleasure involved in tragedy is perhaps an ambiguous one; and sometimes we must feel that the famous sense of cathartic resolution is perhaps the result of glossing over terror with beautiful language rather than an evacuation of it. And sometimes the terror even bursts through the language to stand stark and isolated from the play, as does Oedipus's sightless and bleeding face. At any rate, the Aristotelian theory does not deny another function for tragedy (and for comedy, too) which is suggested by Freud's theory of the traumatic neurosis—what might be called the mithridatic function, by which tragedy is used as the homeopathic administration of pain to inure ourselves to the greater pain which life will force upon us. There is in the cathartic theory of tragedy, as it is usually understood, a conception of tragedy's function which is too negative and which inadequately suggests the sense of active mastery which tragedy can give.

In the same essay in which he sets forth the conception of the mind embracing its own pain for some vital purpose, Freud also expresses a provisional assent to the idea (earlier stated, as he reminds us, by Schopenhauer) that there is perhaps a human drive which makes of death the final and desired goal. The death instinct is a conception that is rejected by many of even the most thoroughgoing Freudian theorists (as, in his last book, Freud mildly noted); the late Otto Fenichel in his authoritative work on the neurosis argues cogently against it. Yet even if we reject the theory as not fitting the facts in any operatively useful way, we still cannot miss its grandeur, its ultimate tragic courage in acquiescence to fate. The idea of the reality principle and the idea of the death instinct form the crown of Freud's broader speculation on the life of man. Their quality of grim poetry is characteristic of Freud's system and the ideas it generates for him.

And as much as anything else that Freud gives to literature, this quality of his thought is important. Although the artist is never finally determined in his work by the intellectual systems about him, he cannot avoid their influence; and it can be said of various competing systems that some hold more promise for the artist than others. When, for example, we think of the simple humanitarian optimism which, for two decades, has been so pervasive, we must see that not only has it been politically and philosophically inadequate, but also that it implies, by the smallness of its view of the varieties of human possibility, a kind of check on the creative faculties. In Freud's view of life no such limitation is implied. To be sure, certain elements of his system seem hostile to the usual notions of man's dignity. Like every great critic of human nature—and Freud is that—he finds in human pride the ultimate cause of human wretchedness, and he takes pleasure in knowing that his ideas stand with those of Copernicus and Darwin in making pride more difficult to maintain. Yet the Freudian man is, I venture to think, a creature of far more dignity and far more interest than the man which any other modern system has been able to conceive. Despite popular belief to the contrary, man, as Freud conceives him, is not to be understood by any simple formula (such as sex) but is rather an inextricable tangle of culture and biology. And not being simple, he is not simply good; he has, as Freud says somewhere, a kind of hell within him from which rise everlastingly the impulses which threaten his civilization. He has the faculty of imagining for himself more in the way of pleasure and satisfaction than he can possibly achieve. Everything that he gains he pays for in more than equal coin; compromise and the compounding with defeat constitute his best way of getting through the world. His best qualities are the result of a struggle whose outcome is tragic. Yet he is a creature of love; it is Freud's sharpest criticism of the Adlerian psychology that to aggression it gives everything and to love nothing at all.

One is always aware in reading Freud how little cynicism there is in his thought. His desire for man is only that he should be human, and to this end his science is devoted. No view of life to which the artist responds can insure the quality of his work, but the poetic qualities of Freud's own principles, which are so clearly in the line of the classic tragic realism, suggest that this is a view which does not narrow and simplify the human world for the artist but on the contrary opens and complicates it.

1950

WALLACE STEVENS

1879–1955

POETRY is the supreme fiction, madame," wrote Stevens in one of his early poems. His later work proved many times over that the intensity and concentration of effect which are possible in a poem of the first order can lift poetry to a level well beyond the reach of most prose fiction. For half a century, this supreme fiction was Stevens's happiest, though not his only, avocation. Using a remarkable combination of wit, humor, irony, linguistic pyrotechnics, and a veritable magician's bag of wonderfully eccentric insights, Stevens left behind him a distinguished body of poetic fiction—the record, as he simply said, "of what [he] felt at what [he] saw."

Born in Reading, Pennsylvania, Stevens began writing poetry at Harvard, where he served in 1898–1900 successively as Board Editor and President of *The Harvard Advocate*, to which he contributed, often pseudonymously, a number of mannered lyrics. Throughout his subsequent career in law and business, beginning in 1904 with his admission to the New York Bar, and continuing through his accession in 1934 to the vice-presidency of the Hartford (Connecticut) Accident and Indemnity Company, Stevens quietly went on writing poetry. Fourteen years after his departure from Harvard, his verse began to appear in such little magazines as *Poetry*, *Rogue*, *Others*, *Soil*, *The Little Review*, *Contact*, *Broom*, *Measure*, *Hound & Horn*, and *The Dial*. During and immediately after the first World War, his growing reputation owed much to these avant-garde journals, and his work was already widely known and admired among the literati for some years before the publication of his first book, *Harmonium*, in 1923, when Stevens was well past forty. In the next quarter-century both his productivity and his fame steadily accelerated. Besides *Harmonium*, the *Collected Poems* of 1954 contains *Ideas of Order* (1936); *The Man with the Blue Guitar* (1937); *Parts of a World* and *Notes Toward a Supreme Fiction* (1942); *Transport to Summer* (1947); and *The Auroras of Autumn* and *The Rock* (1950). His original and perceptive essays on the art of poetry were collected in *The Necessary Angel* (1951).

Stevens interested himself in all the arts and in the powers of mind which compel the art process. Marianne Moore once described him as a "delicate apothecary of savors and precipitates," noting his delight also in the strong, natural colors—the bold pinks and yellows of the tropics, the Aztec hennas and greens of the bantams in the pines, the indigo glass in the grass, the "avocado and Kuniyoshi cabuchon emerald greens, the blent but violent excellence of ailanthus silk-moths and metallic breast-feathers." A devoted collector of art, particularly paintings, Stevens often writes as if he bore a palette in hand, intent to startle us free from the black-white-gray vision of reality. He quotes admiringly Henry James's assertion that art "makes life, makes interest, makes importance," and believes with James that no substitute exists for the "force and beauty" of the artistic process. The world outside us, he said, "would be desolate except for the world within us," and he observes with pleasure the operations of that "fictive covering" which "weaves always glistening from the heart and mind." Accordingly, like the English romantic poets to whom he owes much, he apotheosizes the imagination and "the miraculous kind of reason that the imagination sometimes promotes." Yet he never retreats from his healthy respect for reality, the "ABC of being, . . . the vital, arrogant, fatal, dominant X"—the violence from outside ourselves against which both our fancies and our imaginations must exert their counterpressures if we are not to be overcome with what Keats called the multitudinousness of things.

S. F. Morse, *Wallace Stevens; A Preliminary Checklist of His Published Writings: 1898–1954*, New Haven, 1954.

R. P. Blackmur, "Examples of Wallace Stevens," in *The Double Agent*, New York, 1935, pp. 68–102.

Richard Ellmann, "Wallace Stevens' 'Ice Cream,'" *Kenyon Review*, XIX (Winter, 1957), 89–105.

Northrop Frye, "The Realistic Oriole: A Study of Wallace Stevens," *Hudson Review*, X (Autumn, 1957), 353–370.

Harvard Advocate, Wallace Stevens number, December, 1940.

L. L. Martz, "Wallace Stevens: The World as Meditation," *Yale Review*, XLVII (Summer, 1958), 517–536.

Marianne Moore, "Unanimity and Fortitude," *Poetry*, XLIX (February, 1937), 268–272.

W. V. O'Connor, *The Shaping Spirit: A Study of Wallace Stevens*, Chicago, 1950.

Robert Pack, *Wallace Stevens, An Approach to His Poetry and Thought*, New Brunswick, 1958.

Wylie Sypher, "Connoisseur in Chaos: Wallace Stevens," *Partisan Review*, XIII (Winter, 1946), 83–94.

BANTAMS IN PINE-WOODS

Chieftain Iffucan of Azcan in caftan
Of tan with henna hackles, halt!

Damned universal cock, as if the sun
Was blackamoor to bear your blazing tail.

Fat! Fat! Fat! Fat! I am the personal.
Your world is you. I am my world.

You ten-foot poet among inchlings. Fat!
Begone! An inchling bristles in these pines,

Bristles, and points their Appalachian tangs,
And fears not portly Azcan nor his hoos.   10
                                          1923

THE EMPEROR OF ICE-CREAM

Call the roller of big cigars,
The muscular one, and bid him whip
In kitchen cups concupiscent curds.
Let the wenches dawdle in such dress
As they are used to wear, and let the boys
Bring flowers in last month's newspapers.
Let be be finale of seem.
The only emperor is the emperor of ice-cream.

Take from the dresser of deal,
Lacking the three glass knobs, that sheet   10
On which she embroidered fantails once
And spread it so as to cover her face.
If her horny feet protrude, they come
To show how cold she is, and dumb.
Let the lamp affix its beam.
The only emperor is the emperor of ice-cream.
                                          1923

ANGLAIS MORT À FLORENCE

A little less returned for him each spring.
Music began to fail him. Brahms, although
His dark familiar, often walked apart.

His spirit grew uncertain of delight,
Certain of its uncertainty, in which
That dark companion left him unconsoled

For a self returning mostly memory.
Only last year he said that the naked moon
Was not the moon he used to see, to feel

(In the pale coherences of moon and mood   10
When he was young), naked and alien,
More leanly shining from a lankier sky.

Its ruddy pallor had grown cadaverous.
He used his reason, exercised his will,
Turning in time to Brahms as alternate

In speech. He has that music and himself.
They were particles of order, a single majesty:
But he remembered the time when he stood
    alone.

He stood at last by God's help and the police;
But he remembered the time when he stood
    alone.   20
He yielded himself to that single majesty;

But he remembered the time when he stood
    alone,
When to be and delight to be seemed to be
    one,
Before the colors deepened and grew small.
                                          1936

A POSTCARD FROM THE VOLCANO

Children picking up our bones
Will never know that these were once
As quick as foxes on the hill;

And that in autumn, when the grapes
Made sharp air sharper by their smell
These had a being, breathing frost;

And least will guess that with our bones
We left much more, left what still is
The look of things, left what we felt

At what we saw. The spring clouds blow   10
Above the shuttered mansion-house,
Beyond our gate and the windy sky

Cries out a literate despair.
We knew for long the mansion's look
And what we said of it became

A part of what it is . . . Children,
Still weaving budded aureoles,
Will speak our speech and never know,

Will say of the mansion that it seems
As if he that lived there left behind   20
A spirit storming in blank walls,

A dirty house in a gutted world,
A tatter of shadows peaked to white,
Smeared with the gold of the opulent sun.

                                          1936

GIRL IN A NIGHTGOWN

Lights out. Shades up.
A look at the weather.
There has been a booming all the spring,
A refrain from the end of the boulevards.

This is the silence of night,
This is what could not be shaken,
Full of stars and the images of stars—
And that booming wintry and dull,

Like a tottering, a falling and an end,
Again and again, always there,   10
Massive drums and leaden trumpets,
Perceived by feeling instead of sense,

A revolution of things colliding.
Phrases! But of fear and of fate.
The night should be warm and fluters' fortune
Should play in the trees when morning comes.

Once it was, the repose of night,
Was a place, strong place, in which to sleep.
It is shaken now. It will burst into flames,
Either now or tomorrow or the day after   20
    that.

                                          1942

STUDY OF TWO PEARS

I

Opusculum paedagogum.
The pears are not viols,
Nudes or bottles.
They resemble nothing else.

II

They are yellow forms
Composed of curves
Bulging toward the base.
They are touched red.

III

They are not flat surfaces
Having curved outlines.
They are round
Tapering toward the top.

IV

In the way they are modelled
There are bits of blue.
A hard dry leaf hangs
From the stem.

V

The yellow glistens.
It glistens with various yellows,
Citrons, oranges and greens
Flowering over the skin.

VI

The shadows of the pears
Are blobs on the green cloth.
The pears are not seen
As the observer wills.

                                          1942

OF HARTFORD
IN A PURPLE LIGHT

A long time you have been making the trip
From Havre to Hartford, Master Soleil,
Bringing the lights of Norway and all that.

A long time the ocean has come with you,
Shaking the water off, like a poodle,
That splatters incessant thousands of drops,

Each drop a petty tricolor. For this,
The aunts in Pasadena, remembering,
Abhor the plaster of the western horses,

Souvenirs of museums. But, Master, there   10
    are
Lights masculine and lights feminine.
What is this purple, this parasol,

This stage-light of the Opera?
It is like a region full of intonings.
It is Hartford seen in a purple light.

A moment ago, light masculine,
Working, with big hands, on the town,
Arranged its heroic attitudes.

But now as in an amour of women
Purple sets purple round. Look, Master,   20
See the river, the railroad, the cathedral . . .

When male light fell on the naked back
Of the town, the river, the railroad were clear.
Now, every muscle slops away.

Hi! Whisk it, poodle, flick the spray
Of the ocean, ever-freshening,
On the irised hunks, the stone bouquet.
                                        1942

"ON HER TRIP AROUND THE WORLD"

On her trip around the world, Nanzia Nunzio
Confronted Ozymandias. She went
Alone and like a vestal long-prepared.

I am the spouse. She took her necklace off
And laid it in the sand. As I am, I am
The spouse. She opened her stone-studded belt.

I am the spouse, divested of bright gold,
The spouse beyond emerald or amethyst,
Beyond the burning body that I bear.

I am the woman stripped more nakedly   10
Than nakedness, standing before an inflexible
Order, saying I am the contemplated spouse.

Speak to me that, which spoken, will array me
In its own only precious ornament.
Set on me the spirit's diamond coronal.

Clothe me entire in the final filament,
So that I tremble with such love so known
And myself am precious for your perfecting.

Then Ozymandias said the spouse, the bride
Is never naked. A fictive covering   20
Weaves always glistening from the heart and
   mind.   1942

"THE POEM GOES FROM THE POET'S GIBBERISH"

The poem goes from the poet's gibberish to
The gibberish of the vulgate and back again.
Does it move to and fro or is it of both

At once? Is it a luminous flittering
Or the concentration of a cloudy day?
Is there a poem that never reaches words

And one that chaffers the time away?
Is the poem both peculiar and general?
There's a meditation there, in which there
   seems

To be an evasion, a thing not apprehended or
Not apprehended well. Does the poet
Evade us, as in a senseless element?

Evade, this hot, dependent orator,
The spokesman at our bluntest barriers,
Exponent by a form of speech, the speaker

Of a speech only a little of the tongue?
It is the gibberish of the vulgate that he seeks.
He tries by a peculiar speech to speak

The peculiar potency of the general,   10
To compound the imagination's Latin with
The lingua franca et jocundissima.   1942

MRS. ALFRED URUGUAY

So what said the others and the sun went down
And, in the brown blues of evening, the lady
   said,
In the donkey's ear, "I fear that elegance
Must struggle like the rest." She climbed until
The moonlight in her lap, mewing her velvet,
And her dress were one and she said, "I have
   said no
To everything, in order to get at myself.
I have wiped away moonlight like mud. Your
   innocent ear
And I, if I rode naked, are what remain."

The moonlight crumbled to degenerate forms,
While she approached the real, upon her
   mountain,   11
With lofty darkness. The donkey was there to
   ride,
To hold by the ear, even though it wished for
   a bell,
Wished faithfully for a falsifying bell.
Neither the moonlight could change it. And
   for her,
To be, regardless of velvet, could never be
   more
Than to be, she could never differently be,
Her no and no made yes impossible.

Who was it passed her there on a horse all will,
What figure of capable imagination?   20
Whose horse clattered on the road on which
   she rose,
As it descended, blind to her velvet and
The moonlight? Was it a rider intent on the
   sun,
A youth, a lover with phosphorescent hair,

Dressed poorly, arrogant of his streaming
   forces,
Lost in an integration of the martyrs' bones,
Rushing from what was real; and capable?

The villages slept as the capable man went
   down,
Time swished on the village clocks and dreams
   were alive,
The enormous gongs gave edges to their
   sounds,   10
As the rider, no chevalere and poorly dressed,
Impatient of the bells and midnight forms,
Rode over the picket rocks, rode down the
   road,
And, capable, created in his mind,
Eventual victor, out of the martyrs' bones,
The ultimate elegance: the imagined land.
                         1942

THE RIVERS OF RIVERS
IN CONNECTICUT

There is a great river this side of Stygia,
Before one comes to the first black cataracts
And trees that lack the intelligence of trees.

In that river, far this side of Stygia,
The mere flowing of the water is a gayety,
Flashing and flashing in the sun. On its banks,

No shadow walks. The river is fateful,
Like the last one. But there is no ferryman.
He could not bend against its propelling force.

It is not to be seen beneath the appearances
That tell of it. The steeple at Farmington 11
Stands glistening and Haddam shines and
   sways.

It is the third commonness with light and air,
A curriculum, a vigor, a local abstraction . . .
Call it, once more, a river, an unnamed flowing,

Space-filled, reflecting the seasons, the folk-lore
Of each of the senses; call it, again and again,
The river that flows nowhere, like a sea.
                         1950

THIS SOLITUDE OF CATARACTS

He never felt twice the same about the flecked
   river,
Which kept flowing and never the same way
   twice, flowing

Through many places, as if it stood still in one,
Fixed like a lake on which the wild ducks
   fluttered,

Ruffling its common reflections, thought-like
   Monadnocks.
There seemed to be an apostrophe that was not
   spoken.   11

There was so much that was real that was not
   real at all.
He wanted to feel the same way over and over.

He wanted the river to go on flowing the same
   way,
To keep on flowing. He wanted to walk beside
   it,

Under the buttonwoods, beneath a moon nailed
   fast.   20
He wanted his heart to stop beating and his
   mind to rest

In a permanent realization, without any wild
   ducks
Or mountains that were not mountains, just to
   know how it would be,

Just to know how it would feel, released from
   destruction,
To be a bronze man breathing under archaic
   lapis,   30

Without the oscillations of planetary pass-pass,
Breathing his bronzen breath at the azury
   centre of time.   1950

JOHN CROWE RANSOM

1888–

BORN IN Pulaski, Tennessee, in 1888, Mr. Ransom went from Vanderbilt University as a Rhodes Scholar to Oxford, and served during the first World War as an officer in the Field Artillery. His first volume of verse, *Poems About God* (1919), was dated from France in May, 1918. After the war he returned to Vanderbilt to teach and to participate in the activities of that brilliant group of militant southerners who called themselves "The Fugitives." In 1922, their influential little magazine, *The Fugitive*, commenced publication. In 1937 he moved to Kenyon College, where he combined teaching and the writing of criticism with editing the distinguished quarterly, the *Kenyon Review*.

By comparison with the work of Wallace Stevens, Mr. Ransom's poems are narrower in scope, lower in intensity, and more studiedly casual, except in a few instances like "Judith of Bethulia." Some of the best are about women and girl-children—tender, sympathetically observant, humorous, but twisted by an ironic awareness of what may lie in wait for innocence and delicacy. Many of them unobtrusively suggest a southern locale, where gentility has not surrendered to decadence or sweetness to reason, though all are present. His most characteristic work appears in two volumes, *Chills and Fever* (1924) and *Two Gentlemen in Bonds* (1927), while his *Selected Poems* (1945) supplements a choice from the earlier volumes with a few more recent compositions. Through many of the poems runs a deep religious strain, a serious but not solemn preoccupation with problems of sin and judgment. The subtitle of his early critical study, *God Without Thunder: An unorthodox defence of orthodoxy* (1930), fairly describes this internal aspect of his thinking. The subject of the book, the function of myths in civilization, suggests by contrast the degree to which Mr. Ransom has been willing to emerge into modern society. Without having come far enough to evolve a system of myths, he has shown himself a very able hand at the construction of wry and memorable human fables.

John Crowe Ransom, *Selected Poems*, New York, 1945.
———, *The New Criticism*, Norfolk, Connecticut, 1941.
———, *The World's Body*, New York, 1938.
———, *Sewanee Review*, LVI (Summer, 1948). Homage to John Crowe Ransom.
Louis D. Rubin, Jr., "John Ransom's Cruell Battle," *Shenandoah*, IX (Winter, 1958), pp. 23–35.

DEAD BOY

The little cousin is dead, by foul subtraction,
A green bough from Virginia's aged tree,
And none of the county kin like the transaction,
Nor some of the world of outer dark, like me.

A boy not beautiful, nor good, nor clever,
A black cloud full of storms too hot for keeping,
A sword beneath his mother's heart—yet never
Woman bewept her babe as this is weeping.

A pig with a pasty face, so I had said,
Squealing for cookies, kinned by poor pretense
With a noble house. But the little man quite dead,
I see the forebears' antique lineaments.

The elder men have strode by the box of death
To the wide flag porch, and muttering low send round
The bruit of the day. O friendly waste of breath!

Their hearts are hurt with a deep dynastic
    wound.

He was pale and little, the foolish neighbors
    say;
The first-fruits, saith the Preacher, the Lord
    hath taken;
But this was the old tree's late branch
    wrenched away,
Grieving the sapless limbs, the shorn and
    shaken,   20
                                        1927

JUDITH OF BETHULIA

Beautiful as the flying legend of some leopard
She had not yet chosen her great captain or
    prince
Depositary to her flesh, and our defense;
And a wandering beauty is a blade out of its
    scabbard.
You know how dangerous, gentlemen of three-
    score?
May you know it yet ten more.

Nor by process of veiling she grew the less
    fabulous.
Grey or blue veils, we were desperate to study
The invincible emanations of her white body,
And the winds at her ordered raiment were
    ominous.   10
Might she walk in the market, sit in the council
    of soldiers?
Only of the extreme elders.

But a rare chance was the girl's then, when the
    Invader
Trumpeted from the south, and rumbled from
    the north,
Beleaguered the city from four quarters of the
    earth,
Our soldiery too craven and sick to aid her—
Where were the arms could countervail this
    horde?
Her beauty was the sword.

She sat with the elders, and proved on their
    blear visage
How bright was the weapon unrusted in her
    keeping,   20
While he lay surfeiting on their harvest heap-
    ing,
Wasting the husbandry of their rarest vin-
    tage—

And dreaming of the broad-breasted dames for
    concubine?
These floated on his wine.

He was lapped with bay-leaves, and grass and
    fumiter weed,
And from under the wine-film encountered his
    mortal vision,
For even within his tent she accomplished his
    derision;
She loosed one veil and another, standing un-
    afraid;
And he perished. Nor brushed her with even
    so much as a daisy?
She found his destruction easy.   30

The heathen are all perished. The victory was
    furnished,
We smote them hiding in our vineyards, barns,
    annexes,
And now their white bones clutter the holes of
    foxes,
And the chieftain's head, with grinning sockets,
    and varnished—
Is it hung on the sky with a hideous epitaphy?
No, the woman keeps the trophy.

May God send unto our virtuous lady her
    prince.
It is stated she went reluctant to that orgy,
Yet a madness fevers our young men, and not
    the clergy
Nor the elders have turned them unto modesty
    since,   40
Inflamed by the thought of her naked beauty
    with desire?
Yes, and chilled with fear and despair.   1924

TWO IN AUGUST

Two that could not have lived their single
    lives
As can some husbands and wives
Did something strange: they tensed their vocal
    cords
And attacked each other with silences and
    words
Like catapulted stones and arrowed knives.

Dawn was not yet; night is for loving or sleep-
    ing,
Sweet dreams or safekeeping;
Yet he of the wide brows that were used to
    laurel

And she, the famed for gentleness, must quarrel,
Furious both of them, and scared, and weep-
ing.   10

How sleepers groan, twitch, wake to such a
mood
Is not well understood,
Nor why two entities grown almost one
Should rend and murder trying to get undone,
With individual tigers in their blood.

She in terror fled from the marriage chamber
Circuiting the dark rooms like a string of amber
Round and round and back,
And would not light one lamp against the
black,
And heard the clock that clanged: Remember,
Remember.   20

And he must tread barefooted the dim lawn,
Soon he was up and gone;
High in the trees the night-mastered birds were
crying
With fear upon their tongues, no singing nor
flying
Which are their lovely attitudes by dawn.

Whether those bird-cries were of heaven or
hell
There is no way to tell;
In the long ditch of darkness the man walked
Under the hackberry trees where the birds
talked   29
With words too sad and strange to syllable.
                                                    1927

MAN WITHOUT SENSE OF DIRECTION

Tell this to ladies: how a hero man
Assail a thick and scandalous giant
Who casts true shadow in the sun,
And die, but play no truant.

This is more horrible: that the darling egg
Of the chosen people hatch a creature
Of noblest mind and powerful leg
Who cannot fathom nor perform his nature.

The larks' tongues are never stilled
Where the pale spread straw of sunlight lies.
Then what invidious gods have willed   11
Him to be seized so otherwise?

Birds of the field and beasts of the stable
Are swollen with rapture and make uncouth
Demonstration of joy, which is a babble
Offending the ear of the fervorless youth.

Love—is it the cause? the proud shamed spirit?
Love has slain some whom it possessed,
But his was requited beyond his merit
And won him in bridal the loveliest.   20

Yet scarcely he issues from the warm chamber,
Flushed with her passion, when cold as dead
Once more he walks where waves past number
Of sorrow buffet his curse-hung head.

Whether by street, or in field full of honey,
Attended by clouds of the creatures of air
Or shouldering the city's companioning many,
His doom is on him; and how can he care

For the shapes that would fiddle upon his
senses,
Wings and faces and mists that move,   30
Words, sunlight, the blue air which rinses
The pure pale head which he must love?

And he writhes like an antique man of bronze
That is beaten by furies visible,
Yet he is punished not knowing his sins
And for his innocence walks in hell.

He flails his arms, he moves his lips:
"Rage have I none, cause, time, nor country—
Yet I have traveled land and ships
And knelt my seasons in the chantry."   40

So he stands muttering; and rushes
Back to the tender thing in his charge
With clamoring tongue and taste of ashes
And a small passion to feign large.

But let his cold lips be her omen,
She shall not kiss that harried one
To peace, as men are served by women
Who comfort them in darkness and in sun.
                                                    1927

ALLEN TATE

1899–

WHEN ALLEN TATE, a graduate of Vanderbilt University in 1922, joined in the formation of the Fugitives, John Crowe Ransom, who had taught him as an undergraduate, became one of his first masters in the art of poetry. Others from whom he learned were W. B. Yeats and T. S. Eliot. But Tate is no man's disciple. Few modern poets have so distinctive an idiom.

On first reading, many of Tate's poems seem difficult because his metaphors, though precise, are unexpected and because his allusions are often recondite. Difficulties gradually disappear when one knows something about the basic themes of his verse. A literary critic, novelist, and writer on political matters, Tate has given much thought to the particular frustrations to which modern man is subject. In much of his verse his theme is the dehumanization of society in our time. Though he has written affectionately about the South of his ancestors, he is not a romantic traditionalist. He knows that one cannot go back—either to ancient Greece and Rome or to the Confederacy.

The modern "sensibilist" must cope with the modern world as best he can. What he has to cope with Tate has stated succinctly in an essay ("Narcissus as Narcissus") written in explanation of his "Ode to the Confederate Dead." This poem, the best known of his works, is about the "failure of the human personality to function objectively in nature and society. Society (and 'nature' as modern society constructs it) appear to offer limited fields for the exercise of the whole man, who wastes his energy piecemeal over separate functions that ought to come under a unity of being. . . . Without unity we get the remarkable self-consciousness of our age."

Most of Tate's poems can be related to the ideas set forth in this passage: they display the self-consciousness of which he speaks. The early ones attack with a sharp wit the scientism and positivism which have driven the human personality into a corner. The later ones—notably the fine sequence entitled "Seasons of the Soul"—explore the tragedy of the moderns, who are maimed and do not bear "the living wound of love."

Willard Thorp, "Allen Tate: A Check List," *Princeton University Library Chronicle*, III (April, 1942), 85–98.
Allen Tate, *Poems, 1922–1947*, New York, 1948.
———, *Reactionary Essays on Poetry and Ideas*, New York, 1936.
———, *Reason in Madness: Critical Essays*, New York, 1941.
———, *The Forlorn Demon: Didactic and Critical Essays*, Chicago, 1953.
———, *Collected Essays*, Denver, 1959.
W. B. Arnold, *The Social Ideas of Allen Tate*, Boston, 1955.
Louise Cowan, *The Fugitive Group; a Literary History*, Baton Rouge, La., 1959.
Vivienne Koch, "The Poetry of Allen Tate," *Kenyon Review*, XI (Summer, 1949), 355–394.
Howard Nemerov, "The Current of the Frozen Stream: An Essay on the Poetry of Allen Tate," *Furioso*, III (Fall, 1948), 50–61.
Sewanee Review, LXVII (Autumn, 1959). Homage to Allen Tate issue.

THE MEDITERRANEAN

Quem das finem, rex magne, dolorum?

Where we went in the boat was a long bay
A slingshot wide, walled in by towering
  stone—
Peaked margin of antiquity's delay,
And we went there out of time's monotone:

Where we went in the black hull no light
  moved
But a gull white-winged along the feckless
  wave,
The breeze, unseen but fierce as a body loved,
That boat drove onward like a willing slave:

Where we went in the small ship the seaweed
Parted and gave to us the murmuring shore 10
And we made feast and in our secret need
Devoured the very plates Æneas bore:

Where derelict you see through the low twi-
  light
The green coast that you, thunder-tossed,
  would win,
Drop sail, and hastening to drink all night
Eat dish and bowl—to take that sweet land in!

Where we feasted and caroused on the sand-
  less
Pebbles, affecting our day of piracy,
What prophecy of eaten plates could landless
Wanderers fulfil by the ancient sea?   20

We for that time might taste the famous age
Eternal here yet hidden from our eyes
When lust of power undid its stuffless rage;
They, in a wineskin, bore earth's paradise.

Let us lie down once more by the breathing
  side
Of Ocean, where our live forefathers sleep
As if the Known Sea still were a month wide—
Atlantis howls but is no longer steep!

What country shall we conquer, what fair land
Unman our conquest and locate our blood? 30
We've cracked the hemispheres with careless
  hand!
Now, from the Gates of Hercules we flood

Westward, westward till the barbarous brine
Whelms us to the tired land where tasseling
  corn,

Fat beans, grapes sweeter than muscadine
Rot on the vine: in that land were we born.
                                    1936

TO THE LACEDEMONIANS

*An old soldier on the night before the vet-
erans' reunion talks partly to himself, partly to
imaginary comrades:*

The people—people of my kind, my own
People but strange with a white light
In the face: and the streets hard with motion
And the hard eyes that look one way.
Listen! the high whining tone
Of the motors, I hear the dull commotion:
I am come, a child in an old play.

I am here with a secret in the night;
Because I am here the dead wear gray.

It is a privilege to be dead; for you   10
Cannot know what absence is nor seize
The odor of pure distance until
From you slowly dying in the head
All sights and sounds of the moment, all
The life of sweet intimacy shall fall
Like a swift at dusk.

                    Sheer time!

                            Stroke of the heart
Towards retirement. . . .

                    Gentlemen, my secret is
Damnation: where have they, the citizens,
  all   21
Come from? They were not born in my father's
House nor in their fathers': on a street corner
By motion sired, not born; by rest dismayed.
The tempest will unwind—the hurricane
Consider, knowing its end, the headlong pace?
I have watched it and endured it, I have de-
  layed
Judgment: it warn't in my time, by God, so
That the mere breed absorbed the generation!

Yet I, hollow head, do see but little;   30
Old man: no memory: aimless distractions.

I was a boy, I never knew cessation
Of the bright course of blood along the vein;
Moved, an old dog by me, to field and stream
In the speaking ease of the fall rain;
When I was a boy the light on the hills
Was there because I could see it, not because
Some special gift of God had put it there.

Men expect too much, do too little,
Put the contraption before the accomplish-
   ment,   40
Lack skill of the interior mind
To fashion dignity with shapes of air.
Luxury, yes—but not elegance!
Where have they come from?

                       Go you tell them
That we their servants, well-trained, gray-
   coated
And haired (both foot and horse) or in
The grave, them obey . . . obey them,
What commands?

                 My father said   50
That everything but kin was less than kind.
The young men like swine argue for a rind,
A flimsy shell to put their weakness in;
Will-less, ruled by what they cannot see;
Hunched like savages in a rotten tree
They wait for the thunder to speak: Union!
That joins their separate fear.

              I fought
But did not care; a leg shot off at Bethel,
Given up for dead; but knew neither shell-
   shock   60
Nor any self-indulgence. Well may war be
Terrible to those who have nothing to gain
For the illumination of the sense:
When the peace is a trade route, figures
For the budget, reduction of population,
Life grown sullen and immense
Lusts after immunity to pain.

There is no civilization without death;
There is now the wind for breath.

Waken, lords and ladies gay, we cried,   70
And marched to Cedar Run and Malvern Hill,
Kinsmen and friends from Texas to the Tide—
Vain chivalry of the personal will!

Waken, we shouted, lords and ladies gay,
We go to win the precincts of the light,
Unshadowing restriction of our day. . . .
Regard now, in the seventy years of night,

Them, the young men who watch us from the
   curbs:
They hold the glaze of wonder in their stare—
Our crooked backs, hands fetid as old herbs, 80
The tallow eyes, wax face, our foreign hair!

Soldiers, march! we shall not fight again
The Yankees with our guns well-aimed and
   rammed—
All are born Yankees of the race of men
And this, too, now the country of the damned:

Poor bodies crowding round us! The white face
Eyeless with eyesight only, the modern
   power—
Huddled sublimities of time and space,
They are the echoes of a raging tower

That reared its moment upon a gone land,   90
Pouring a long cold wrath into the mind—
Damned souls, running the way of sand
Into the destination of the wind!   1936

SEASONS OF THE SOUL

To the memory of John Peale Bishop,
1892–1944

Allor porsi la mano un poco avante,
e colsi un ramicel da un gran pruno;
e il tronco suo gridò: Perchè mi schiante?

I. SUMMER

Summer, this is our flesh,
The body you let mature;
If now while the body is fresh
You take it, shall we give
The heart, lest heart endure
The mind's tattering
Blow of greedy claws?
Shall mind itself still live
If like a hunting king
It falls to the lion's jaws?   10

Under the summer's blast
The soul cannot endure
Unless by sleight or fast
It seize or deny its day
To make the eye secure.
Brothers-in-arms, remember
The hot wind dries and draws
With circular delay
The flesh, ash from the ember,
Into the summer's jaws.   20

It was a gentle sun
When, at the June solstice
Green France was overrun
With caterpillar feet.
No head knows where its rest is

Or may lie down with reason
When war's usurping claws
Shall take the heart escheat—
Green field in burning season
To stain the weevil's jaws.   30

The southern summer dies
Evenly in the fall:
We raise our tired eyes
Into a sky of glass,
Blue, empty, and tall
Without tail or head
Where burn the equal laws
For Balaam and his ass
Above the invalid dead,
Who cannot lift their jaws.   40

When was is that the summer
(Daylong a liquid light)
And a child, the new-comer,
Bathed in the same green spray,
Could neither guess the night?
The summer had no reason;
Then, like a primal cause
It had its timeless day
Before it kept the season
Of time's engaging jaws.   50

Two men of our summer world
Descended winding hell
And when their shadows curled
They fearfully confounded
The vast concluding shell:
Stopping, they saw in the narrow
Light a centaur pause
And gaze, then his astounded
Beard, with a notched arrow,
Part back upon his jaws.   60

II. Autumn

It had an autumn smell
And that was how I knew
That I was down a well:
I was no longer young;
My lips were numb and blue,
The air was like fine sand
In a butcher's stall
Or pumice to the tongue:
And when I raised my hand
I stood in the empty hall.   70

The round ceiling was high
And the gray light like shale
Thin, crumbling, and dry:

No rug on the bare floor
Nor any carved detail
To which the eye could glide;
I counted along the wall
Door after closed door
Through which a shade might slide
To the cold and empty hall.   80

I will leave this house, I said,
There is the autumn weather—
Here, nor living nor dead;
The lights burn in the town
Where men fear together.
Then on the bare floor,
But tiptoe lest I fall,
I walked years down
Towards the front door
At the end of the empty hall.   90

The door was false—no key
Or lock, and I was caught
In the house; yet I could see
I had been born to it
For miles of running brought
Me back where I began.
I saw now in the wall
A door open a slit
And a fat grizzled man
Come out into the hall: 100

As in a moonlit street
Men meeting are too shy
To check their hurried feet
But raise their eyes and squint
As through a needle's eye
Into the faceless gloom,—
My father in a gray shawl
Gave me an unseeing glint
And entered another room!
I stood in the empty hall   110

And watched them come and go
From one room to another,
Old men, old women—slow,
Familiar; girls, boys;
I saw my downcast mother
Clad in her street-clothes,
Her blue eyes long and small,
Who had no look or voice
For him whose vision froze
Him in the empty hall.   120

III. Winter

Goddess sea-born and bright,
Return into the sea

Where eddying twilight
Gathers upon your people—
Cold goddess, hear our plea!
Leave the burnt earth, Venus,
For the drying God above,
Hanged in his windy steeple,
No longer bears for us
The living wound of love.　　　130

All the sea-gods are dead.
You, Venus, come home
To your salt maidenhead,
The tossed anonymous sea
Under shuddering foam—
Shade for lovers, where
A shark swift as your dove
Shall pace our company
All night to nudge and tear
The livid wound of love.　　　140

And now the winter sea:
Within her hollow rind
What sleek facility
Of sea-conceited scop
To plumb the nether mind!
Eternal winters blow
Shivering flakes, and shove
Bodies that wheel and drop—
Cold soot upon the snow
Their livid wound of love.　　　150

Beyond the undertow
The gray sea-foliage
Transpires a phosphor glow
Into the circular miles:
In the centre of his cage
The pacing animal
Surveys the jungle cove
And slicks his slithering wiles
To turn the venereal awl
In the livid wound of love.　　　160

Beyond the undertow
The rigid madrepore
Resists the winter's flow—
Headless, unageing oak
That gives the leaf no more.
Wilfully as I stood
Within the thickest grove
I seized a branch, which broke;
I heard the speaking blood
(From the livid wound of love)　　　170

Drip down upon my toe:
"We are the men who died

Of self-inflicted woe,
Lovers whose stratagem
Led to their suicide."
I touched my sanguine hair
And felt it drip above
Their brother who, like them,
Was maimed and did not bear
The living wound of love.　　　180

IV. SPRING

Irritable spring, infuse
Into the burning breast
Your combustible juice
That as a liquid soul
Shall be the body's guest
Who lights, but cannot stay
To comfort this unease
Which, like a dying coal,
Hastens the cooler day
Of the mother of silences.　　　190

Back in my native prime
I saw the orient corn
All space but no time,
Reaching for the sun
Of the land where I was born:
It was a pleasant land
Where even death could please
Us with an ancient pun—
All dying for the hand
Of the mother of silences.　　　200

In time of bloody war
Who will know the time?
Is it a new spring star
Within the timing chill,
Talking, or just a mime,
That rises in the blood—
Thin Jack-and-Jilling seas
Without the human will?
Its light is at the flood,
Mother of silences!　　　210

It burns us each alone
Whose burning arrogance
Burns up the rolling stone,
This earth—Platonic cave
Of vertiginous chance!
Come, tired Sisyphus,
Cover the cave's egress
Where light reveals the slave,
Who rests when sleeps with us
The mother of silences.　　　220

Come, old woman, save
Your sons who have gone down
Into the burning cave:
Come, mother, and lean
At the window with your son
And gaze through its light frame
These fifteen centuries
Upon the shirking scene
Where men, blind, go lame:
Then, mother of silences,   230

Speak, that we may hear;
Listen, while we confess
That we conceal our fear;
Regard us, while the eye
Discerns by sight or guess
Whether, as sheep foregather
Upon their crooked knees,
We have begun to die;
Whether your kindness, mother,
Is mother of silences.   240

1944

» » *From:* REASON IN MADNESS « «

TENSION IN POETRY

I

Many poems that we ordinarily think of as good poetry—and some besides, that we neglect—have certain common features that will allow us to invent, for their sharper apprehension, the name of a single quality. I shall call that quality tension. In abstract language, a poetic work has distinct quality as the ultimate effect of the whole, and that whole is the "result" of a configuration of meaning which it is the duty of the critic to examine and evaluate. In setting forth this duty as my present procedure I am trying to amplify a critical approach that I have used on other occasions, without wholly giving up the earlier method, which I should describe as the analysis of the general ideas implicit in the poetic work.

Towards the end of this essay I shall cite examples of "tension" but I shall not say that they exemplify tension only, or that other qualities must be ignored. There are all kinds of poetry, as many as there are good poets, as many even as there are good poems, for poets may be expected to write more than one kind of poetry; and no single critical insight may impute an exclusive validity to any one kind. In all ages there are schools demanding that one sort only be written—their sort: political poetry for the sake of the cause; picturesque poetry for the sake of the home-town; didactic poetry for the sake of the parish; even a generalized personal poetry for the sake of the reassurance and safety of numbers. This last I suppose is the most common variety, the anonymous lyricism in which the common personality exhibits its commonness, its obscure and standard eccentricity, in a language that seems always to be deteriorating; so that many poets are driven to inventing private languages, or very narrow ones, because public speech has become heavily tainted with mass-feeling.

Mass language is the medium of "communication," and its users are less interested in bringing to formal order what is today called the "affective state" than in arousing that state.

Once you have said that everything is One it is 10
obvious that literature is the same as propaganda; once you have said that no truth can be known apart from the immediate dialectical process of history it is obvious that all contemporary artists must prepare the same fashionplate. It is clear too that the One is limited in space as well as time, and the no less Hegelian Fascists are right in saying that all art is patriotic.

What Mr. William Empson calls patriotic poetry sings not merely in behalf of the State; you 20
will find it equally in a lady-like lyric and in much of the political poetry of our time. It is the poetry of the mass language, very different from the "language of the people" which interested the late W. B. Yeats. For example:

What from the splendid dead
We have inherited—
Furrows sweet to the grain, and the weed subdued—
See now the slug and the mildew plunder.   30
Evil does overwhelm
The larkspur and the corn;
We have seen them go under.

From this stanza by Miss Millay we infer that her splendid ancestors made the earth a good place that has somehow gone bad—and you get the reason from the title: *Justice Denied in Massachusetts.* How Massachusetts could 40 cause a general desiccation, why (as we are told in a footnote to the poem) the execution of Sacco and Vanzetti should have anything to do with the rotting of the crops, it is never made clear. These lines are mass language: they arouse an affective state in one set of terms, and suddenly an object quite unrelated to those terms gets the benefit of it; and this effect, which is usually achieved, as I think it is here, without conscious effort, is sentimentality. Miss Millay's poem was admired when it first appeared about ten years ago, and it is no doubt still admired, by persons to whom it communicates certain feelings about social justice, by persons for whom the lines are the occasion of feelings shared by them and the poet. But if you do not share those feelings, as I happen not to share them in the image of desiccated nature, the lines and even the entire poem are impenetrably obscure.

I am attacking here the fallacy of communication in poetry. (I am not attacking social justice.) It is no less a fallacy in the writing of poetry than of critical theory. The critical doctrine fares ill the further back you apply it; I suppose one may say—if one wants a landmark—that it began to prosper after 1798; for on the whole nineteenth-century English verse is a poetry of communication. The poets were trying to use verse to convey ideas and feelings that they secretly thought could be better conveyed by science (consult Shelley's *Defense*), or by what today we call, in a significantly bad poetic phrase, the Social Sciences. Yet possibly because the poets believed the scientists to be tough, and the poets joined the scientists in thinking the poets tender, the poets stuck to verse. It may hardly be said that we change this tradition of poetic futility by giving it a new name, Social Poetry. May a poet hope to deal more adequately with sociology than with physics? If he seizes upon either at the level of scientific procedure, has he not abdicated his position as poet?

. . .

I have referred to a certain kind of poetry as the embodiment of the fallacy of communication: it is a poetry that communicates the affective state, which (in terms of language) results from the irresponsible denotations of words. There is a vague grasp of the "real" world. The history of this fallacy, which is as old as poetry but which towards the end of the eighteenth century began to dominate not only poetry, but other arts as well—its history would probably show that the poets gave up the language of denotation to the scientists, and kept for themselves a continually thinning flux of peripheral connotations. The companion fallacy, to which I can give only the literal name, the fallacy of mere denotation, I have also illustrated from Cowley: [1] this is the poetry which contradicts our most developed human insights in so far as it fails to use and direct the rich connotation with which language has been informed by experience.

II

We return to the enquiry set for this discussion: to find out whether there is not a more central achievement in poetry than that represented by either of the extreme examples that we have been considering. I proposed as descriptive of that achievement, the term *tension*. I am using the term not as a general metaphor, but as a special one, derived from lopping the prefixes off the logical terms *extension* and *intension*. What I am saying, of course, is that the meaning of poetry is its tension, the full organized body of all the extension and intension that we can find in it. The remotest figurative significance that we can derive does not invalidate the extensions of the literal statement. Or we may begin with the literal statement and by stages develop the complications of metaphor: at every stage we may pause to state the meaning so far apprehended, and at every stage the meaning will be coherent.

The meanings that we select at different points along the infinite line between extreme intension and extreme extension will vary with our personal "drive," or "interest," or "approach": the Platonist will tend to stay pretty close to the end of the line where extension, and simple abstraction of the object into a universal, is easiest, for he will be a fanatic in morals or some kind of works, and will insist upon the shortest way with what will ever appear to him the dissenting ambiguities at the intensive end of the scale. The Platonist (I do not say that his opponent is the Aristotelian) might decide that Marvel's "To His Coy Mistress" recommends immoral behavior to the young men, in whose behalf he would try to suppress the poem. That, of course, would be one "true" meaning of "To His Coy Mistress," but it is a

[1] In the omitted portion of his essay, Tate discusses Cowley's "Hymn: to light" as involving the fallacy of mere denotation.

meaning that the full tension of the poem will not allow us to entertain exclusively. For we are compelled, since it is there, to give equal weight to an intensive meaning so rich that, without contradicting the literal statement of the lover-mistress convention, it lifts that convention into an insight into one phase of the human predicament—the conflict of sensuality and asceticism.

I should like to quote now, not from Marvel, but a stanza from Donne that I hope will reinforce a little what I have just said and connect it with some earlier remarks.

> Our two soules therefore, which are one,
>   Though I must goe, endure not yet
> A breach, but an expansion,
>   Like gold to aiery thinnesse beate.

Here Donne brings together the developing imagery of twenty lines under the implicit proposition: the unity of two lovers' souls is a nonspatial entity, and is therefore indivisible. That, I believe, is what Mr. John Crowe Ransom would call the logic of the passage; it is the abstract form of its extensive meaning. Now the interesting feature here is the logical contradiction of embodying the unitary, nonspatial soul in a spatial image: the malleable gold is a plane whose surface can always be extended mathematically by one-half, towards infinity; the souls are this infinity. The spatial image of the gold, in extension, logically contradicts the intensive meaning (infinity) which it conveys; but it does not invalidate that meaning. We have seen that Cowley compelled us to ignore the denoted diaper in order that we might take seriously the violet which it pretended to swathe. But in Donne's "Valedictory: forbidding mourning" the clear denotation of the gold contains, by intension, the full meaning of the passage. If we reject the gold, we reject the meaning, for the meaning is wholly absorbed into the image of the gold. Intension and extension are here one, and they enrich each other.

Before I leave this beautiful object, I should like to notice two incidental features in further proof of Donne's mastery. "Expansion"—a term denoting an abstract property common to many objects, perhaps here one property of a gas: it expands visibly the quality of the beaten gold. "Endure not *yet*/A breach"—but if the lovers' souls are the formidable, inhuman entity that we have seen, are they not superior to the contingency of a breach? Yes and no: both answers are true answers; for by means of the sly "yet" Donne subtly guards himself against our irony, which would otherwise be quick to scrutinize the extreme metaphor. The lovers have not endured a breach, but they are simple, miserable human beings, and they may quarrel tomorrow.

Now all this meaning and more, and it is all one meaning, is embedded in that stanza: I say more because I have not exhausted the small fraction of significance that my limited powers have permitted me to see. For example, I have not discussed the rhythm, which is of the essential meaning; I have violently isolated four lines from the meaning of the whole poem. Yet fine as it is, I do not think the poem the greatest poetry; perhaps only very little of Donne makes that grade, or of anybody else. Donne offers many examples of tension in imagery, easier for the expositor than greater passages in Shakespeare.

But convenience of elucidation is not a canon of criticism. . . . I do not know what bearing my comment has had . . . upon the larger effects of poetry, or upon long poems. The long poem is partly a different problem. I have of necessity confined both commentary and illustration to the slighter effects that seemed to me commensurate with certain immediate qualities of language. For, in the long run, whatever the poet's "philosophy," however wide may be the extension of his meaning—like Milton's Ptolemaic universe in which he didn't believe—by his language shall you know him; the quality of his language is the valid limit of what he has to say. . . .

1938   1941

MARIANNE MOORE

1887–

IN THE PREFACE he wrote for her *Selected Poems* (1935), Marianne Moore's fellow-townsman, T. S. Eliot, said that her poems "form part of the small body of durable poetry written in our time; of that small body of writings, among what passes for poetry, in which an original sensibility and alert intelligence and deep feeling have been engaged in maintaining the life of the English language." One mark of Miss Moore's poetry since that time has been the notable infrequency with which it has appeared. The *Selected Poems* numbered forty-eight. The *Collected Poems* of 1951 included only seventy-one titles. Yet to the judges of that year the durability and distinction were perfectly apparent, and the slim volume earned Miss Moore a Pulitzer Prize, the National Book Award for Poetry, and the Bollingen Prize.

Born in St. Louis the year before Eliot, Miss Moore was graduated from Bryn Mawr in 1909. Twelve years later her first volume of verse appeared and she began a four-year association with the New York Public Library. This was followed by four more years as Acting Editor of *The Dial*. A long-time resident of Brooklyn, New York, where she was a faithful adherent of the Dodgers as long as they were faithful to Brooklyn, she has supplemented her work in poetry with some lecturing and teaching. Among her publications since the *Collected Poems* are the translation of *The Fables of La Fontaine* (1954), eleven new poems in *Like A Bulwark* (1956), and fifteen more in *O To Be a Dragon* (1959).

A quarter-century of essays, reviews, and sharp appreciations were gathered in her *Predilections* (1955) which, along with her habitual notes to the poems, offer an insight into that original sensibility and alert intelligence of which Eliot spoke. The prose volume includes commentaries on Henry James, Eliot, Stevens, Pound, Auden, Cummings, and William Carlos Williams, together with a charming retrospective account of Miss Moore's years on *The Dial*. The book likewise reveals many aspects of her personal aesthetic, including a devotion to precision of statement and to a "diction that is virile because galvanized against inertia." She speaks also of "the gusto of invention, with climax proceeding out of climax, which is the mark of feeling," of the desirability of stylistic plainness, and of "doing what idiosyncrasy" dictates. "The thing is to see the vision and not deny it," she says; "to care and admit that we do." Both vision and devotion are everywhere evident in the small body of her poetry.

E. P. Sheahy and K. A. Lohf, *The Achievement of Marianne Moore: A Bibliography*, New York, 1958.
Marianne Moore, *Selected Poems*, New York, 1935.
———, *Nevertheless*, New York, 1944.
———, *What Are Years*, New York, 1941.
Marie Borroff, "Dramatic Structure in the Poetry of Marianne Moore," *Literary Review*, II (Autumn, 1958), 112–123.
Kenneth Burke, "Motives and Motifs in the Poetry of Marianne Moore," *Accent*, II (Spring, 1942), 157–169.
Quarterly Review of Literature, IV, no. 2. Marianne Moore issue.

BLACK EARTH

Openly, yes,
with the naturalness
    of the hippopotamus or the alligator
    when it climbs out on the bank to experi-
      ence the

sun, I do these
things which I do, which please
    no one but myself. Now I breathe and
      now I am sub-
    merged; the blemishes stand up and shout
      when the object

in view was a
renaissance; shall I say   10
    the contrary? The sediment of the river
      which
    encrusts my joints, makes me very gray
      but I am used
to it, it may
remain there; do away
    with it and I am myself done away with,
      for the
    patina of circumstance can but enrich
      what was

there to begin
with. This elephant-skin
    which I inhabit, fibred over like the shell
      of
    the cocoanut, this piece of black glass
      through which no light   20

can filter—cut
into checkers by rut
    upon rut of unpreventable experience—
    it is a manual for the peanut-tongued and
      the

hairy-toed. Black
but beautiful, my back
    is full of the history of power. Of power?
      What
    is powerful and what is not? My soul shall
      never

be cut into
by a wooden spear; through-   30
    out childhood to the present time, the
      unity of
    life and death has been expressed by the
      circumference

described by my
trunk; nevertheless I
    perceive feats of strength to be inexplica-
      ble after
    all; and I am on my guard; external poise,
      it

has its centre
well nurtured—we know
    where—in pride; but spiritual poise, it has
      its centre where?
    My ears are sensitized to more than the
      sound of   40

the wind. I see
and I hear, unlike the
    wandlike body of which one hears so
      much, which was made
    to see and not to see; to hear and not to
      hear;

that tree-trunk without
roots, accustomed to shout
    its own thoughts to itself like a shell, main-
      tained intact
    by who knows that strange pressure of the
      atmosphere; that

spiritual
brother to the coral-   50
    plant, absorbed into which, the equable
      sapphire light
    becomes a nebulous green. The I of each
      is to

the I of each
a kind of fretful speech
    which sets a limit on itself; the elephant is
    black earth preceded by a tendril? Com-
      pared with those

phenomena
which vacillate like a
    translucence of the atmosphere, the ele-
      phant is
    that on which darts cannot strike deci-
      sively the first   60

time, a substance
needful as an instance
    of the indestructibility of matter; it
    has looked at the electricity and at the
      earth-

quake and is still
here; the name means thick. Will
    depth be depth, thick skin be thick, to one
      who can see no
beautiful element of unreason under it?
                       1921

PART OF A NOVEL, PART OF A POEM, PART OF A PLAY

THE STEEPLE-JACK

Dürer would have seen a reason for living
    in a town like this, with eight stranded
      whales
to look at; with the sweet sea air coming into
      your house
on a fine day, from water etched
    with waves as formal as the scales
on a fish.

One by one, in two's, in three's, the seagulls
    keep
    flying back and forth over the town clock,
or sailing around the lighthouse without mov-
      ing the wings—
rising steadily with a slight   10
    quiver of the body—or flock
mewing where

a sea the purple of the peacock's neck is
    paled to greenish azure as Dürer changed
the pine green of the Tyrol to peacock blue and
      guinea
grey. You can see a twenty-five-
    pound lobster; and fishnets arranged
to dry. The

whirlwind fife-and-drum of the storm bends
    the salt
    marsh grass, disturbs stars in the sky and
      the   20
star on the steeple; it is a privilege to see so
much confusion. Disguised by what
    might seem austerity, the sea-
side flowers and

trees are favoured by the fog so that you have
    the tropics at first hand: the trumpet-vine,
fox-glove, giant snap-dragon, a salpiglossis that
    has
spots and stripes; morning-glories, gourds,
    or moon-vines trained on fishing-twine
at the back   30

door. There are no banyans, frangipani, nor
    jack-fruit trees; nor an exotic serpent
life. Ring lizard and snake-skin for the foot, or
    crocodile;
but here they've cats, not cobras, to
    keep down the rats. The diffident
little newt

with white pin-dots on black horizontal spaced
    out bands lives here; yet there is nothing
      that
ambition can buy or take away. The college
    student
named Ambrose sits on the hill-side   40
    with his not-native books and hat
and sees boats

at sea progress white and rigid as if in
    a groove. Liking an elegance of which
the source is not bravado, he knows by heart
      the antique
sugar-bowl-shaped summer-house of
    interlacing slats, and the pitch
of the church

spire, not true, from which a man in scarlet lets
    down a rope as a spider spins a thread; 50
he might be part of a novel, but on the side-
    walk a
sign says C. J. Poole, Steeple Jack,
    in black and white; and one in red
and white says

Danger. The church portico has four fluted
    columns, each a single piece of stone,
      made
modester by white-wash. This would be a fit
      haven for
waifs, children, animals, prisoners,
    and presidents who have repaid   60
sin-driven

senators by not thinking about them. There
    are a school-house, a post-office in a
store, fish-houses, hen-houses, a three-masted
      schooner on
the stocks. The hero, the student,
    the steeple-jack, each in his way,
is at home.

It could not be dangerous to be living
    in a town like this, of simple people,
who have a steeple-jack placing danger signs
    by the church   70

while he is gilding the solid-
    pointed star, which on a steeple
stands for hope.

THE HERO

Where there is personal liking we go.
    Where the ground is sour; where there are
    weeds of beanstalk height,
    snakes' hypodermic teeth, or
    the wind brings the 'scarebabe voice'
    from the neglected yew set with
    the semi-precious cat's eyes of the owl—
awake, asleep, 'raised ears extended to fine
      points,' and so
on—love won't grow   80

We do not like some things, and the hero
    doesn't; deviating head-stones
    and uncertainty;
    going where one does not wish
    to go; suffering and not
    saying so; standing and listening where
      something
    is hiding. The hero shrinks
as what it is flies out on muffled wings, with
      twin yellow
eyes—to and fro—

with quavering water-whistle note, low,   90
    high, in basso-falsetto chirps
    until the skin creeps.
    Jacob when a-dying, asked
    Joseph: Who are these? and blessed
    both sons, the younger most, vexing Jo-
      seph. And
    Joseph was vexing to some.
Cincinnatus was; Regulus; and some of our fel-
      low
men have been, though

devout, like Pilgrim having to go slow
    to find his roll; tired but hopeful—   100
    hope not being hope
    until all ground for hope has
    vanished; and lenient, looking
    upon a fellow creature's error with the
    feelings of a mother—a
woman or a cat. The decorous frock-coated
      Negro
by the grotto

answers the fearless sightseeing hobo
    who asks the man she's with, what's this,
    what's that, where's Martha   110

buried, 'Gen-ral Washington
    there; his lady, here'; speaking
    as if in a play—not seeing her; with a
    sense of human dignity
and reverence for mystery, standing like the
      shadow
of the willow.

Moses would not be grandson to Pharaoh.
    It is not what I eat that is
    my natural meat,   120
    the hero says. He's not out
    seeing a sight but the rock
    crystal thing to see—the startling El Greco
    brimming with inner light—that
covets nothing that it has let go. This then you
      may know
as the hero.   1935

WHAT ARE YEARS?

    What is our innocence,
what is our guilt? All are
    naked, none is safe. And whence
is courage: the unanswered question,
the resolute doubt,—
dumbly calling, deafly listening—that
in misfortune, even death,
    encourages others
    and in its defeat, stirs

    the soul to be strong? He   10
sees deep and is glad, who
    accedes to mortality
and in his imprisonment, rises
upon himself as
the sea in a chasm, struggling to be
free and unable to be,
    in its surrendering
    finds its continuing.

    So he who strongly feels,
behaves. The very bird,   20
    grown taller as he sings, steels
his form straight up. Though he is captive,
his mighty singing
says, satisfaction is a lowly
thing, how pure a thing is joy.
    This is mortality,
    this is eternity.   1941

IN DISTRUST OF MERITS

Strengthened to live, strengthened to die for
    medals and position victories?

They're fighting, fighting, fighting the blind
    man who thinks he sees,—
who cannot see that the enslaver is
enslaved; the hater, harmed. O shining O
    firm star, O tumultuous
        ocean lashed till small things go
as they will, the mountainous
        wave makes us who look, know

depth. Lost at sea before they fought! O
    star of David, star of Bethlehem,
O black imperial lion
    of the Lord—emblem
of a risen world—be joined at last, be
joined. There is hate's crown beneath which
    all is
        death; there's love's without which
        none
        is king; the blessed deeds bless
    the halo. As contagion
        of sickness makes sickness,   20

contagion of trust can make trust. They're
    fighting in deserts and caves, one by
one, in battalions and squadrons;
    they're fighting that I
may yet recover from the disease. My
Self; some have it lightly, some will die. "Man's
    wolf to man" and we devour
        ourselves. The enemy could not
    have made a greater breach in our
        defenses. One pilot-   30

ing a blind man can escape him, but
    Job disheartened by false comfort knew
that nothing can be so defeating
    as a blind man who
can see. O alive who are dead, who are
proud not to see, O small dust of the earth
    that walks so arrogantly,
        trust begets power and faith is
    an affectionate thing. We
        vow, we make this promise   40

to the fighting—it's a promise—"We'll
    never hate black, white, red, yellow, Jew,

Gentile, Untouchable." We are
    not competent to
make our vows. With set jaw they are fighting,
fighting, fighting,—some we love whom we
    know,
    some we love but know not—that
        hearts may feel and not be numb.
    It cures me; or am I what
        I can't believe in? Some   50

in snow, some on crags, some in quicksands,
    little by little, much by much, they
are fighting fighting fighting that where
    there was death there may
be life. "When a man is prey to anger,
he is moved by outside things; when he holds
    his ground in patience patience
        patience, that is action or
    beauty," the soldier's defense
        and hardest armor for   60

the fight. The world's an orphans' home. Shall
    we never have peace without sorrow?
without pleas of the dying for
    help that won't come? O
quiet form upon the dust, I cannot
look and yet I must. If these great patient
    dyings—all these agonies
        and woundbearings and blood-
        shed—
    can teach us how to live, these
        dyings were not wasted.   70

Hate-hardened heart, O heart of iron,
    iron is iron till it is rust.
There never was a war that was
    not inward; I must
fight till I have conquered in myself what
causes war, but I would not believe it.
    I inwardly did nothing.
        O Iscariotlike crime!
    Beauty is everlasting
        and dust is for a time.   80
                1944

KARL SHAPIRO

1913–

ORN IN BALTIMORE, Karl Shapiro represents the new poetic generation. His first "public" book of verse, *Person, Place and Thing* (1942), appeared when he was on active duty "somewhere in the Pacific." With a few exceptions the poems in *V-Letter* (1944) were written "under the peculiarly enlivening circumstances of soldiering." His next book, *Essay on Rime* (1945), a tour de force which discusses the confusions in prosody, language, and belief to be found in modern poetry, was completed in the Netherlands East Indies, in November, 1944. Even his *Trial of a Poet* (1947) contains a group of poems which were inspired by his experience of the war.

And yet, though Shapiro matured as a poet during the war years, he was on his guard lest he become a "war poet." His vigilance was rewarded. His verse, at its best strong and controlled, is lyrical but not subjective. He views himself, as he views the things and events which he uses for symbols, quite objectively. Thus it was that in his war poems he was able, as he tried to do, "to see the great configuration abstractly, with oneself at the center reduced in size but not in meaning, like a V-letter."

Shapiro has surmounted other obstacles besides war. It has not been easy for any member of his poetic generation to escape the influence of the immediate masters of verse in their time. In his case the magnetism of Auden was powerful and to be resisted. There was also the weight of the new criticism which has so expertly analyzed both poetry and the poet's function that a young poet might be hobbled by it—as several have been.

The critics, indeed, have had to puff a little to keep pace with Shapiro's virtuosity and change of direction. Few modern poets can render the "thing" so well as he can (see "Drug Store" in the selections below). His object is sometimes simple, stark description. Sometimes he has satire in mind, and he can use his merciless wit to hurt those who deserve to be hurt. But his aim most often is the traditional aim of the poet:

> the miracle of water and wine,
> Stones to fishes, leaves to loaves,
> And common clay to prayer and pleasure domes.

Even when his aim is not clear or is not reached, his poems have the value, as one critic has said, of *études*. For Shapiro has the magician's sleight-of-hand. The topicality of his verse, its modern idiom, the suavity of its form conceal the art of an accomplished prosodist. It is a pleasure just to watch him work.

In 1946 Mr. Shapiro was appointed Consultant in Poetry at the Library of Congress. In 1947 he joined the faculty of Johns Hopkins University, where he taught writing until his appointment to the editorship of *Poetry* in 1950. After five years in that post he became Professor of English at the University of Nebraska. Among his recent publications are *Beyond Criticism* (essays, 1953) and *Poems of a Jew* (1958).

Louise Quesnel, ed., *A Bibliography of the Work of Karl Jay Shapiro, 1935–June, 1945*, Baltimore, 1945.
Conrad Aiken, "Karl Shapiro," in *A Reviewer's ABC: Collected Criticism of Conrad Aiken from 1916 to the Present*, New York, 1958, pp. 358–364. (Reprints of two earlier articles in the *New Republic*, 1945).

David Daiches, "The Poetry of Karl Shapiro," *Poetry*, LXVI (August, 1945), 266–273.

Dayton Kohler, "Karl Shapiro: Poet in Uniform," *College English*, VII (Fall, 1946), 243–249; *English Journal*, XXXV (Fall, 1948), 63–68.

W. V. O'Connor, "Karl Shapiro: The Development of a Talent," *College English*, X (November, 1948), 71–75.

Morton Seif, "Poet's Journey: The Struggle in the Soul of Karl Shapiro," *Menorah Journal*, XXXVII (Winter, 1949), 51–58.

MY GRANDMOTHER

My Grandmother moves to my mind in context
　　of sorrow
And, as if apprehensive of near death, in black;
Whether erect in chair, her dry and corded
　　throat harangued by grief,
Or at ragged book bent in Hebrew prayer,
Or gentle, submissive, and in tears to strangers;
Whether in sunny parlor or back of drawn
　　blinds.

Though time and tongue made any love dispa-
　　rate,
On daguerreotype with classic perspective
Beauty I sigh and soften at is hers.　　　　9
I pity her life of deaths, the agony of her own,
But most that history moved her through
Strangers lands and many houses,
Taking her exile for granted, confusing
The tongues and tasks of her children's chil-
　　dren.　　　　　　　　　　　1942

DRUG STORE

I do remember an apothecary,
　　And hereabouts 'a dwells
It baffles the foreigner like an idiom,
And he is right to adopt it as a form
Less serious than the living-room or bar;
　　For it disestablishes the cafe,
Is a collective, and on basic country.

Not that it praises hygiene and corrupts
The ice-cream parlor and the tobacconist's
Is it a center; but that the attractive symbols
　　Watch over puberty and leer
Like rubber bottles waiting for sick-use.　　10

Youth comes to jingle nickels and crack wise;
The baseball scores are his, the magazines
Devoted to lust, the jazz, the coca-cola,
　　The lending-library of love's latest.
He is the customer; he is heroized.

And every nook and cranny of the flesh
Is spoken to by packages with wiles.

'Buy me, buy me,' they whimper and cajole;
　　The hectic range of lipsticks pouts,
Revealing the wicked and the simple mouth.

With scarcely any evasion in their eye　　21
They smoke, undress their girls, exact a stance;
But only for a moment. The clock goes round;
　　Crude fellowships are made and lost;
They slump in booths like rags, not even drunk.
　　　　　　　　　　　　　　　1942

POET

Il arrive que l'esprit demande la poesie

Left leg flung out, head cocked to the right,
Tweed coat or army uniform, with book,
Beautiful eyes, who is this walking down?
Who, glancing at the pane of glass looks sharp
And thinks it is not he—as when a poet
Comes swiftly on some half-forgotten poem
And loosely holds the page, steady of mind,
　　Thinking it is not his?

And when will *you* exist?—Oh, it is I,
Incredibly skinny, stooped, and neat as pie,
Ignorant as dirt, erotic as an ape,　　11
Dreamy as puberty—with dirty hair!
Into the room like kangaroo he bounds,
Ears flopping like the most expensive hound's;
His chin received all questions as he bows
　　Mouthing a green bon-bon.

Has no more memory than rubber. Stands
Waist-deep in heavy mud of thought and
　　broods
At his own wetness. When he would get out,
To his own surprise he lifts in air a phrase　　20
As whole and clean and silvery as a fish.
Which jumps and dangles on his damned
　　hooked grin,
But like a name-card on a man's lapel
　　Calls him a conscious fool.

And childlike he remembers all his life
And cannily constructs it, fact by fact,
As boys paste postage stamps in careful books,
Denoting pence and legends and profiles,

Nothing more valuable.—And like a thief,
His eyes glassed over and concealed with guilt,
Fondles his secrets like a case of tools,⁣   31
      And waits in empty doors.

By men despised for knowing what he is,
And by himself. But he exists for women.
As dolls to girls, as perfect wives to men,
So he to women. And to himself a thing,
All ages, epicene, without a trade.
To girls and wives always alive and fated;
To men and scholars always dead like Greek
      And always mistranslated.⁣   40

Towards exile and towards shame he lures him-
    self,
Tongue winding on his arm, and thinks like Eve
By biting apple will become most wise.
Sentio ergo sum: he feels his way
And words themselves stand up for him like
    Braille
And punch and perforate his parchment ear.
All language falls like Chinese on his soul,
      Image of song unsounded.

This is the coward's coward that in his dreams
Sees shapes of pain grow tall. Awake at night
He peers at sounds and stumbles at a breeze.
And none holds life less dear. For as a youth
Who by some accident observes his love⁣   53
Naked and in some natural ugly act,
He turns with loathing and with flaming hands,
      Seared and betrayed by sight.

He is the business man, on beauty trades,
Dealer in arts and thoughts who, like the Jew,
Shall rise from slums and hated dialects⁣   59
A tower of bitterness. Shall be always strange,
Hunted and then sought after. Shall be sat
Like an ambassador from another race
At tables rich with music. He shall eat flowers,
Chew honey and spit out gall. They shall all
    smile
      And love and pity him.

His death shall be by drowning. In that hour
When the last bubble of pure heaven's air
Hovers within his throat, safe on his bed,
A small eternal figurehead in terror,
He shall cry out and clutch his days of straw
Before the blackest wave. Lastly, his tomb   70
Shall list and founder in the troughs of grass.
      And none shall speak his name.
                1942

TROOP TRAIN

It stops the town we come through. Workers
    raise
Their oily arms in good salute and grin.
Kids scream as at a circus. Business men
Glance hopefully and go their measured way.
And women standing at their dumbstruck door
More slowly wave and seem to warn us back,
As if a tear blinding the course of war
Might once dissolve our iron in their sweet
    wish.

Fruit of the world, O clustered on ourselves
We hang as from a cornucopia⁣   10
In total friendliness, with faces bunched
To spray the streets with catcalls and with
    leers.
A bottle smashes on the moving ties
And eyes fixed on a lady smiling pink
Stretch like a rubber-band and snap and sting
The mouth that wants the drink-of-water kiss.

And on through crummy continents and days,
Deliberate, grimy, slightly drunk we crawl,
The good-bad boys of circumstance and
    chance,⁣   19
Whose bucket-helmets bang the empty wall
Where twist the murdered bodies of our packs
Next to the guns that only seem themselves.
And distance like a strap adjusted shrinks,
Tightens across the shoulder and holds firm.

Here is a deck of cards; out of this hand
Dealer, deal me my luck, a pair of bulls,
The right draw to a flush, the one-eyed jack.
Diamonds and hearts are red but spades are
    black,
And spades are spades and clubs are clovers—
    black.
But deal me winners, souvenirs of peace.⁣   30
This stands to reason and arithmetic,
Luck also travels and not all come back.

Trains lead to ships and ships to death or trains,
And trains to death or trucks, and trucks to
    death,
Or trucks lead to the march, the march to
    death,
Or that survival which is all our hope;
And death leads back to trucks and trains and
    ships,
But life leads to the march, O flag! at last   38
The place of life found after trains and death
—Nightfall of nations brilliant after war.   1944

» » *The American Character* « «

DE CRÈVECOEUR, ADAMS, AND SANTAYANA

MUCH HAS been written, not all of it complimentary, about the American national character. Yet it is possible that no such thing has ever existed—only travesties or misrepresentations of it, or visions of a potential which has never become actual. It has in fact been held that we do not have an American character. Instead we have characters—of individuals or groups, parties or factions, races or creeds—which are so far apart in geography or in belief, so disparate in habit or attitude, that there is little hope of anyone's being able to summarize the American genius.

From time to time, nonetheless, certain hardy thinkers have sought to analyze our diversities in order to discover whatever unanimity of opinion and point of view exists beneath the American surface. One of the first to try was a Frenchman by birth, Michel-Guillaume Jean de Crèvecoeur (1735–1813). As a young man he explored the region of the Great Lakes, fought under General Montcalm in the French and Indian Wars, and then settled down as a naturalized American citizen to farm a small estate in Orange County, New York. Though he later became French consul in New York City, and at last returned to France to spend his old age, he had lived long enough among the American colonials in both war and peace to develop a clear conception of eighteenth-century America and Americans. His *Letters From an American Farmer* (1782), written while his experience in and on the land was still fresh in his mind, has since become a classic of its kind and its epoch.

More than a century later, Henry Adams (1838–1918) tried his hand at a summary of the American character. A native of Massachusetts and a member of the distinguished family which traced its American roots back into the time of Crèvecoeur, Adams was educated at Harvard, where he later taught history for a short time. Afterwards he was secretary to his father who was minister to the Court of St. James. He came home to crown a long life of observation and reading with a series of distinguished books. Among them are *Mont Saint-Michel and Chartres* (1905) and his famous autobiography, *The Education of Henry Adams* (1906, 1907, 1918). In his early fifties he wrote his memorable *History of the United States of America, 1801–1817* (1889–1891) in the conclusion to which he establishes the thesis that by the end of the War of 1812, the American character was formed, if not actually fixed. From historical evidence, he shows that Americans tended to dislike war as an instrument of national policy, though they fought well when it was required; that they governed with some success, though they were politically immature; that they gave promise of developing from a loose society of agrarians to a nation of scientific engineers; that they believed in the popular intelligence and wished

974

to provide a universal education to develop the people's potential to the utmost; and that they liked rapid change better than slow evolution. In much that he wrote, the historian Adams had the advantage of hindsight over the first century of the American republic. Such is the shrewdness of his appraisal, however, that what he wrote in 1890 may well continue to be applicable in 1990.

One generation after Adams's *History*, George Santayana (1863–1952) contributed a brilliant characterization of the United States from the point of view of a Spanish-born, Harvard-educated professional philosopher. A genuine cosmopolite, like Crèvecoeur and Adams, he was able to gain that perspective on things American which is possible to one who has lived for long periods outside the borders of the United States. A member of the philosophy department at Harvard from 1889 to 1912, he retired to Europe to live out the second half of his life. His philosophical novel, *The Last Puritan*, published when he was seventy-two, offers an amusing analysis of the Boston-Brahmin aspect of American culture in the twentieth century. Besides his five-volume *Life of Reason* (1905–1935), the four-volume *Realms of Being* (1927–1940) and other distinguished books in aesthetics and ethics and literary criticism, he also wrote a three-volume memoir, *Persons and Places* (1944–1953). The essay here reprinted is from his *Character and Opinion in the United States* (1920). Santayana persuasively argues that the inward temper of the composite American is a working union of materialism and idealism. Americans are "extreme idealists in the region of hope," being optimistically imaginative about their own and the nation's future. In the realm of morals, they tend towards materialism, and the habitual reduction of moral values to "the common denominator of quantity."

Michel-Guillaume Jean de Crèvecoeur
> *Letters from an American Farmer*, William P. Trent, ed., New York, 1925.
> Julia P. Mitchell, *St. Jean de Crèvecoeur*, New York, 1916.
> H. C. Rice, *Le Cultivateur Americain: Etude sur l'Oeuvre de Saint Jean de Crèvecoeur*, Paris, 1933 (contains bibliography).

Henry Adams
> *The Selected Letters of Henry Adams*, Newton Arvin, ed., New York, 1951.
> J. T. Adams, *Henry Adams*, New York, 1933.
> R. A. Hume, *Runaway Star: An Appreciation of Henry Adams*, Ithaca, New York, 1951.
> W. H. Jordy, *Henry Adams: Scientific Historian*, New Haven, 1952.
> J. C. Levenson, *The Mind and Art of Henry Adams*, Boston, 1957.
> Ernest Samuels, *The Young Henry Adams*, Cambridge, 1948.
> ———, *Henry Adams: The Middle Years, 1877–1891*, Cambridge, 1958.

George Santayana
> *The Works of George Santayana*, 14 vols., New York, 1936–1937.
> *The Philosophy of George Santayana; Selections*, Irwin Edman, ed., New York (1936), 1953.
> *Santayana's Essays in Literary Criticism*, Irving Singer, ed., New York, 1956.
> W. E. Arnett, *Santayana and the Sense of Beauty*, Bloomington, Indiana, 1955.
> Richard Butler, *The Mind of Santayana*, London, 1956.
> G. W. Howgate, *George Santayana*, Philadelphia, 1938.
> P. A. Schilpp, ed., *The Philosophy of George Santayana*, Chicago, 1940.
> Irving Singer, *Santayana's Aesthetics: A Critical Introduction*, Cambridge, 1957.

MICHEL-GUILLAUME JEAN DE CRÈVECOEUR

1735–1813

» » *From:* LETTERS FROM AN AMERICAN
FARMER « «

LETTER III

WHAT IS AN AMERICAN?

I wish I could be acquainted with the feelings and thoughts which must agitate the heart and present themselves to the mind of an enlightened Englishman, when he first lands on this continent. He must greatly rejoice, that he
10 lived at a time to see this fair country discovered and settled; he must necessarily feel a share of national pride, when he views the chain of settlements which embellishes these extended shores. When he says to himself, this is the work of my countrymen, who, when convulsed by factions, afflicted by a variety of miseries and wants, restless and impatient, took refuge here. They brought along with them their national genius, to which they principally
20 owe what liberty they enjoy, and what substance they possess. Here he sees the industry of his native country, displayed in a new manner, and traces in their works the embrios of all the arts, sciences, and ingenuity which flourish in Europe. Here he beholds fair cities, substantial villages, extensive fields, an immense country filled with decent houses, good roads, orchards, meadows, and bridges, where an hundred years ago all was wild, woody, and
30 uncultivated!

What a train of pleasing ideas this fair spectacle must suggest! it is a prospect which must inspire a good citizen with the most heartfelt pleasure. The difficulty consists in the manner of viewing so extensive a scene. He is arrived on a new continent; a modern society offers itself to his contemplation, different from what he had hitherto seen. It is not composed, as in Europe, of great lords who possess every thing,
40 and of a herd of people who have nothing. Here are no aristocratical families, no courts, no kings, no bishops, no ecclesiastical dominion, no invisible power giving to a few a very visible one; no great manufacturers employing thousands, no great refinements of luxury. The rich and the poor are not so far removed from each other as they are in Europe.

Some few towns excepted, we are all tillers of the earth, from Nova Scotia to West Florida. We are a people of cultivators, scattered over an immense territory, communicating with each other by means of good roads and navigable rivers, united by the silken bands of mild government, all respecting the laws without dreading their power, because they are equitable. We are all animated with the spirit of industry, which is unfettered, and unrestrained, because each person works for himself. If he travels through our rural districts, he views not the hostile castle, and the haughty mansion, contrasted with the clay-built hut and miserable cabbin, where cattle and men help to keep each other warm, and dwell in meanness, smoke, and indigence. A pleasing uniformity of decent competence appears throughout our habitations. The meanest of our log-houses is a dry and comfortable habitation. Lawyer or merchant are the fairest titles our towns afford; that of a farmer is the only appellation of the rural inhabitants of our country. It must take some time ere he can reconcile himself to our dictionary, which is but short in words of dignity, and names of honour. There, on a Sunday, he sees a congregation of respectable farmers and their wives, all clad in neat homespun, well mounted, or riding in their own humble waggons. There is not among them an esquire, saving the unlettered magistrate. There he sees a parson as simple as his flock, a farmer who does not riot on the labour of others. We have no princes, for whom we toil, starve, and bleed: we are the most perfect society now existing in the world. Here man is free as he ought to be; nor is this pleasing equality so transitory as many others are. Many ages will not see the shores of our great lakes replenished with inland nations, nor the unknown bounds of North America entirely peopled. Who can tell how far it extends? Who can tell the millions of men whom it will feed and contain? for no European foot has as yet travelled half the extent of this mighty continent!

The next wish of this traveller will be to know whence came all these people? they are a mixture of English, Scotch, Irish, French, Dutch, Germans, and Swedes. From this promiscuous breed, that race now called Americans have arisen. The eastern provinces must indeed be excepted, as being the unmixed descendants of Englishmen. I have heard many wish they had been more intermixed also; for my part, I am no wisher; and think it much better as it has happened. They exhibit a most conspicuous figure in this great and variegated picture; they too enter for a great share in the pleasing perspective displayed in these thirteen provinces. I know it is fashionable to reflect on them; but I respect them for what they have done; for the accuracy and wisdom with which they have settled their territory; for the decency of their manners; for their early love of letters; their ancient college, the first in this hemisphere; for their industry, which to me, who am but a farmer, is the criterion of every thing. There never was a people, situated as they are, who, with so ungrateful a soil, have done more in so short a time. Do you think that the monarchial ingredients which are more prevalent in other governments, have purged them from all foul stains? Their histories assert the contrary.

In this great American asylum, the poor of Europe have by some means met together, and in consequence of various causes; to what purpose should they ask one another, what countrymen they are? Alas, two thirds of them had no country. Can a wretch who wanders about, who works and starves, whose life is a continual scene of sore affliction or pinching penury; can that man call England or any other kindgom his country? A country that had no bread for him, whose fields procured him no harvest, who met with nothing but the frowns of the rich, the severity of the laws, with jails and punishments; who owned not a single foot of the extensive surface of this planet? No! urged by a variety of motives, here they came. Every thing has tended to regenerate them; new laws, a new mode of living, a new social system; here they are become men: in Europe they were as so many useless plants, wanting vegetative mould,

and refreshing showers; they withered, and were mowed down by want, hunger, and war; but now, by the power of transplantation, like all other plants, they have taken root and flourished! Formerly they were not numbered in any civil list of their country, except in those of the poor; here they rank as citizens. By what invisible power has this surprizing metamorphosis been performed? By that of the laws and that of their industry. The laws, the indulgent laws, protect them as they arrive, stamping on them the symbol of adoption; they receive ample rewards for their labours; these accumulated rewards procure them lands; those lands confer on them the title of freemen; and to that title every benefit is affixed which men can possibly require. This is the great operation daily performed by our laws. From whence proceed these laws? From our government. Whence that government? It is derived from the original genius and strong desire of the people, ratified and confirmed by government. This is the great chain which links us all, this is the picture which every province exhibits, Nova Scotia excepted. There the crown has done all; either there were no people who had genius, or it was not much attended to: the consequence is, that the province is very thinly inhabited indeed; the power of the crown, in conjunction with the musketos, has prevented men from settling there. Yet some part of it flourished once, and it contained a mild harmless set of people. But for the fault of a few leaders the whole were banished. The greatest political error the crown ever committed in America, was to cut off men from a country which wanted nothing but men.

What attachment can a poor European emigrant have for a country where he had nothing? The knowledge of the language, the love of a few kindred as poor as himself, were the only cords that tied him: his country is now that which gives him land, bread, protection, and consequence: *Ubi panis ibi patria*,[1] is the motto of all emigrants. What then is the American, this new man? He is either an European, or the descendant of an European; hence that strange mixture of blood, which you will find in no other country. I could point out to you a man, whose grandfather was an Englishman, whose wife was Dutch, whose son married a French woman, and whose present four sons have now four wives of different nations. *He* is an American, who, leaving behind him all his ancient

---

[1] *Where my bread is earned, there is my country.*

prejudices and manners, receives new ones from the new mode of life he has embraced, the new government he obeys, and the new rank he holds. He becomes an American by being received in the broad lap of our great *Alma Mater*.

Here individuals of all nations are melted into a new race of men, whose labours and posterity will one day cause great change in the world. Americans are the western pilgrims, who are carrying along with them that great mass of arts, sciences, vigour and industry, which began long since in the east; they will finish the great circle. The Americans were once scattered all over Europe: here they are incorporated into one of the finest systems of population which has ever appeared, and which will hereafter become distinct by the power of the different climates they inhabit. The American ought, therefore, to love this country much better than that wherein either he or his forefathers were born. Here the rewards of his industry follow with equal steps the progress of his labour; his labour is founded on the basis of nature, *self-interest;* can it want a stronger allurement? Wives and children, who before in vain demanded of him a morsel of bread, now, fat and frolicsome, gladly help their father to clear those fields whence exuberant crops are to arise to feed and to clothe them all; without any part being claimed, either by a despotic prince, a rich abbot, or a mighty lord. Here religion demands but little of him; a small voluntary salary to the minister, and gratitude to God; can he refuse these? The American is a new man, who acts upon new principles; he must therefore entertain new ideas, and form new opinions. From involuntary idleness, servile dependance, penury, and useless labour, he has passed to toils of a very different nature, rewarded by ample subsistence.—This is an American.

North America is divided into many provinces, forming a large association, scattered along a coast 1,500 miles extent and about 200 wide. This society I would fain examine, at least such as it appears in the middle provinces; if it does not afford that variety of tinges and gradations which may be observed in Europe, we have colours peculiar to ourselves. For instance, it is natural to conceive that those who live near the sea, must be very different from those who live in the woods; the intermediate space will afford a separate and distinct class. Men are like plants; the goodness and flavour of the fruit proceed from the peculiar soil and exposition in which they grow. We are nothing but what we derive from the air we breathe, the climate we inhabit, the government we obey, the system of religion we profess, and the nature of our employment. Here you will find but few crimes; these have acquired as yet no root among us. I wish I were able to trace all my ideas; if my ignorance prevents me from describing them properly, I hope I shall be able to delineate a few of the outlines, which are all I propose.

Those who live near the sea, feed more on fish than on flesh, and often encounter that boisterous element. This renders them more bold and enterprising; this leads them to neglect the confined occupations of the land. They see and converse with a variety of people; their intercourse with mankind becomes extensive. The sea inspires them with a love of traffic, a desire of transporting produce from one place to another; leads them to a variety of resources, which supply the place of labour. Those who inhabit the middle settlements, by far the most numerous, must be very different; the simple cultivation of the earth purifies them; but the indulgences of the government, the soft remonstrances of religion, the rank of independent free-holders, must necessarily inspire them with sentiments, very little known in Europe among people of the same class. What do I say? Europe has no such class of man; the early knowledge they acquire, the early bargains they make, give them a great degree of sagacity. As freemen, they will be litigious; pride and obstinacy are often the cause of law suits; the nature of our laws and governments may be another. As citizens, it is easy to imagine, that they will carefully read the newspapers, enter into every political disquisition, freely blame or censure governors and others. As farmers, they will be careful and anxious to get as much as they can, because what they get is their own. As northern men, they will love the chearful cup. As christians, religion curbs them not in their opinions; the general indulgence, leaves every one to think for himself in spiritual matters; the laws inspect our actions; our thoughts are left to God. Industry, good living, selfishness, litigiousness, country politics, the pride of freemen, religious indifference, are their characteristics. If you recede still farther from the sea, you will come into more modern settlements; they exhibit the same strong lineaments, in a ruder appearance. Religion seems to have still less influence, and their manners are less improved.

Now we arrive near the great woods, near the last inhabited districts; there men seem to be placed still farther beyond the reach of government, which in some measure leaves them to themselves. How can it pervade every corner? as they were driven there by misfortunes, necessity of beginnings, desire of acquiring large tracts of land, idleness, frequent want of economy, ancient debts; the reunion of such people does not afford a very pleasing spectacle. When discord, want of unity and friendship—when either drunkenness or idleness prevail in such remote districts—contention, inactivity, and wretchedness must ensue. There are not the same remedies to these evils as in a long established community. The few magistrates they have, are in general little better than the rest; they are often in a perfect state of war; that of man against man, sometimes decided by blows, sometimes by means of the law; that of man against every wild inhabitant of these venerable woods, of which they are come to dispossess them. There men appear to be no better than carnivorous animals of a superior rank, living on the flesh of wild animals when they can catch them; and when they are not able, they subsist on the grain.

He who would wish to see America in its proper light, and have a true idea of its feeble beginnings and barbarous rudiments, must visit our extended line of frontiers where the last settlers dwell, and where he may see the first labours of settlement, the mode of clearing the earth, in all their different appearances; where men are wholly left dependent on their native tempers, and on the spur of uncertain industry, which often fails, when not sanctified by the efficacy of a few moral rules. There, remote from the power of example, and check of shame, many families exhibit the most hideous parts of our society. They are a kind of forlorn hope, preceding by ten or twelve years the most respectable army of veterans which come after them. In that space, prosperity will polish some, vice and the law will drive off the rest, who uniting again with others like themselves will recede still farther; making room for more industrious people, who will finish their improvements, convert the log-house into a convenient habitation, and rejoicing that the first heavy labours are finished, will change in a few years that hitherto barbarous country into a fine, fertile, well regulated district.

Such is our progress, such is the march of the Europeans toward the interior parts of this continent. In all societies there are off-casts; this unpure part serves as our precursors or pioneers, my father himself was one of that class; but he came upon honest principles, and was therefore one of the few who held fast; by good conduct and temperance, he transmitted to me his fair inheritance, when not above one in fourteen of his contemporaries had the same 10 good fortune.

Forty years ago, this smiling country was thus inhabited, it is now purged, a general decency of manners prevails throughout; and such has been the fate of our best countries.

Exclusive of those general characteristics, each province has its own, founded on the government, climate, mode of husbandry, customs and peculiarity of circumstances. Europeans submit insensibly to these great powers, and 20 become in the course of a few generations, not only Americans in general, but either Pennsylvanians, Virginians, or provincials under some other name. Whoever traverses the continent, must easily observe those strong differences, which will grow more evident in time. The inhabitants of Canada, Massachusetts, the middle provinces, the southern ones will be as different as their climates; their only points of unity will be those of religion and language. 30

. . . Europe contains hardly any other distinctions but lords and tenants; this fair country alone is settled by freeholders, the possessors of the soil they cultivate, members of the government they obey, and the framers of their own laws, by means of their representatives. This is a thought which you have taught me to cherish; our distance from Europe, far from diminishing, rather adds to our usefulness and consequence as men and subjects. Had our fore- 40 fathers remained there, they would only have crouded it, and perhaps prolonged those convulsions which had shook it so long. Every industrious European who transports himself here, may be compared to a sprout growing at the foot of a great tree; it enjoys and draws but a little portion of sap; wrench it from the parent roots, transplant it, and it will become a tree bearing fruit also. Colonists are therefore intitled to the consideration due to the most 50 useful subjects; a hundred families barely existing in some parts of Scotland, will here in six years, cause an annual exportation of 10,000 bushels of wheat: 100 bushels being but a common quantity for an industrious family to sell, if they cultivate good land. It is here, then, that the idle may be employed, the useless become useful, and the poor become rich: but by riches I do not mean gold and silver; we have but little of those metals; I mean a better sort of wealth, cleared lands, cattle, good houses, good clothes, and an increase of people to enjoy them.

There is no wonder that this country has so many charms, and presents to Europeans so many temptations to remain in it. A traveller in Europe becomes a stranger as soon as he quits his own kingdom; but it is otherwise here. We know, properly speaking, no strangers; this is every person's country; the variety of our soils, situations, climates, governments, and produce, hath something which must please every body. No sooner does an European arrive, no matter of what condition, than his eyes are opened upon the fair prospects; he hears his language spoke, he retraces many of his own country manners, he perpetually hears the names of families and towns with which he is acquainted; he sees happiness and prosperity in all places disseminated; he meets with hospitality, kindness, and plenty every where: he beholds hardly any poor, he seldom hears of punishments and executions; and he wonders at the elegance of our towns, those miracles of industry and freedom. He cannot admire enough our rural districts, our convenient roads, good taverns, and our many accommodations; he involuntarily loves a country where every thing is so lovely. When in England, he was a mere Englishman; here he stands on a larger portion of the globe, not less than its fourth part, and may see the productions of the north, in iron and naval stores; the provisions of Ireland, the grain of Egypt, the indigo, the rice of China. He does not find, as in Europe, a crouded society, where every place is over-stocked; he does not feel that perpetual collision of parties, that difficulty of beginning, that contention which oversets so many.

There is room for every body in America: has he any particular talent, or industry? he exerts it in order to procure a livelihood, and it succeeds. Is he a merchant? the avenues of trade are infinite; is he eminent in any respect? he will be employed and respected. Does he love a country life? pleasant farms present themselves; he may purchase what he wants, and thereby become an American farmer. Is he a labourer, sober and industrious; he need not go many miles, nor receive many informations

before he will be hired, well fed at the table of his employer, and paid four or five times more than he can get in Europe. Does he want uncultivated lands? thousands of acres present themselves, which he may purchase cheap. Whatever be his talents or inclinations, if they are moderate, he may satisfy them. I do not mean, that every one who comes will grow rich in a little time; no, but he may procure an easy, decent maintenance, by his industry. Instead of starving, he will be fed; instead of being idle, he will have employment; and these are riches enough for such men as come over here. The rich stay in Europe; it is only the middling and poor that emigrate. Would you wish to travel in independent idleness, from north to south, you will find easy access, and the most chearful reception at every house; society without ostentation, good cheer without pride, and every decent diversion which the country affords, with little expense. It is no wonder that the European who has lived here a few years, is desirous to remain; Europe with all its pomp, is not to be compared to this continent, for men of middle stations or labourers.

An European, when he first arrives, seems limited in his intentions, as well as in his views; but he very suddenly alters his scale; two hundred miles formerly appeared a very great distance; it is now but a trifle; he no sooner breathes our air than he forms schemes, and embarks in designs he never would have thought of in his own country. There the plenitude of society confines many useful ideas, and often extinguishes the most laudable schemes which here ripen into maturity. Thus Europeans become Americans.

But how is this accomplished in that croud of low, indigent people, who flock here every year from all parts of Europe? I will tell you; they no sooner arrive than they immediately feel the good effects of that plenty of provisions we possess: they fare on our best food, and are kindly entertained; their talents, character, and peculiar industry are immediately enquired into; they find countrymen every where disseminated, let them come from whatever part of Europe.

Let me select one as an epitome of the rest; he is hired, he goes to work, and works moderately; instead of being employed by a haughty person, he finds himself with his equal, placed at the substantial table of the farmer, or else at an inferior one as good; his wages are high, his bed is not like that bed of sorrow on which he used to lie: if he behaves with propriety, and is faithful, he is caressed, and becomes, as it were, a member of the family. He begins to feel the effects of a sort of resurrection; hitherto he had not lived, but simply vegetated; he now feels himself a man, because he is treated as such; the laws of his own country had overlooked him in his insignificancy; the laws of this cover him with their mantle. Judge what an alteration there must arise in the mind and thoughts of this man; he begins to forget his former servitude and dependence; his heart involuntarily swells and glows; this first swell inspires him with those new thoughts which constitute an American. What love can he entertain for a country where his existence was a burden to him! if he is a generous good man, the love of his new adoptive parent, will sink deep into his heart. He looks around, and sees many a prosperous person, who but a few years before was as poor as himself. This encourages him much; he begins to form some little scheme, the first, alas, he ever formed in his life. If he is wise, he thus spends two or three years, in which time he acquires knowledge, the use of tools, the modes of working the lands, felling trees, &c. This prepares the foundation of a good name, the most useful acquisition he can make. He is encouraged; he has gained friends; he is advised and directed; he feels bold; he purchases some land; he gives all the money he has brought over, as well as what he has earned, and trusts to the God of harvests for the discharge of the rest. His good name procures him credit; he is now possessed of the deed, conveying to him and his posterity the fee simple, and absolute property of two hundred acres of land, situated on such a river. What an epocha in this man's life! He is become a free-holder, from perhaps a German boor—he is now an American, a Pennsylvanian. He is naturalized; his name is enrolled with those of the other citizens of the province. Instead of being a vagrant, he has a place of residence; he is called the inhabitant of such a county, or of such a district, and for the first time in his life counts for something; for hitherto he had been a cypher. I only repeat what I have heard many say, and no wonder their hearts should glow, and be agitated with a multitude of feelings, not easy to describe. From nothing to start into being; from a servant to the rank of master; from being the slave of some despotic prince, to become a free man, invested with lands, to which every municipal

blessing is annexed! What a change indeed! It is in consequence of that change, that he becomes an American.

This great metamorphosis has a double effect; it extinguishes all his European prejudices; he forgets that mechanism of subordination, that servility of disposition which poverty had taught him; and sometimes he is apt to forget it too much, often passing from one extreme to the other. If he is a good man, he forms schemes of future prosperity; he proposes to educate his children better than he has been educated himself; he thinks of future modes of conduct, feels an ardour to labour he never felt before. Pride steps in, and leads him to every thing that the laws do not forbid: he respects them; with a heart-felt gratitude he looks toward that government from whose wisdom all his new felicity is derived, and under whose wings and protection he now lives. These reflexions constitute him the good man and the good subject.

Ye poor Europeans, ye, who sweat and work for the great—ye, who are obliged to give so many sheaves to the church, so many to your lords, so many to your government, and have hardly any left for yourselves—ye, who are held in less estimation than favourite hunters or useless lap-dogs—ye, who only breathe the air of nature, because it cannot be withheld from you; it is here that ye can conceive the possibility of those feelings I have been describing; it is here the laws of naturalization invite every one to partake of our great labours and felicity, to till unrented, untaxed lands!

Many, corrupted beyond the power of amendment, have brought with them all their vices, and, disregarding the advantages held out to them, have gone on in their former career of iniquity, until they have been overtaken and punished by our laws. It is not every emigrant who succeeds; no, it is only the sober, the honest, and industrious: happy those to whom this transition has served as a powerful spur to labour, to prosperity, and to the good establishment of children, born in the days of their poverty: and who had no other portion to expect, but the rags of their parents, had it not been for their happy emigration. Others again, have been led astray by this enchanting scene; their new pride, instead of leading them to the fields, has kept them in idleness; the idea of possessing lands is all that satisfies them— though surrounded with fertility, they have mouldered away their time in inactivity, mis-

informed husbandry, and ineffectual endeavours. How much wiser, in general, the honest Germans than almost all other Europeans, they hire themselves to some of their wealthy landsmen, and in that apprenticeship learn every thing that is necessary. They attentively consider the prosperous industry of others, which imprints on their minds a strong desire of possessing the same advantages. This forci-
10 ble idea never quits them; they launch forth, and by dint of sobriety, rigid parsimony, and the most persevering industry, they commonly succeed. Their astonishment at their first arrival from Germany is very great; it is to them a dream; the contrast must be very powerful indeed; they observe their countrymen flourishing in every place; they travel through whole counties where not a word of English is spoken; and in the names and the language of
20 the people they retrace Germany. They have been an useful acquisition to this continent, and to Pennsylvania in particular; to them it owes some share of its prosperity; to their mechanical knowledge and patience, it owes the finest mills in all America, the best teams of horses, and many other advantages. The recollection of their former poverty and slavery never quits them as long as they live.

The Scotch and the Irish might have lived in
30 their own country perhaps as poor; but enjoying more civil advantages, the effects of their new situation do not strike them so forcibly, nor has it so lasting an effect. From whence the difference arises, I know not; but out of twelve families of emigrants of each country, generally seven Scotch will succeed, nine German, and four Irish. The Scotch are frugal and laborious; but their wives cannot work so hard as the German women, who, on the contrary, vie with
40 their husbands, and often share with them the most severe toils of the field, which they understand better. They have therefore nothing to struggle against, but the common casualties of nature. The Irish do not prosper so well; they love to drink and to quarrel, they are litigious, and soon take to the gun, which is the ruin of every thing; they seem, beside, to labour under a greater degree of ignorance in husbandry than the others; perhaps it is that their industry
50 had less scope, and was less exercised at home. I have heard many relate, how the land was parcelled out in that kingdom; their ancient conquest has been a great detriment to them, by over-setting their landed property. The

lands, possessed by a few, are leased down *ad infinitum;* and the occupiers often pay five guineas an acre. The poor are worse lodged there than any where else in Europe; their potatoes, which are easily raised, are perhaps an inducement to laziness: their wages are too low, and their whiskey too cheap.

There is no tracing observations of this kind, without making at the same time very great allowances; as there are everywhere to be found a great many exceptions. The Irish themselves, from different parts of that kingdom, are very different. It is difficult to account for this surprising locality; one would think on so small an island all Irishmen must be alike; yet it is not so; they are different in their aptitude to, and in their love of labour.

The Scotch, on the contrary, are all industrious and saving; they want nothing more than a field to exert themselves in; and they are commonly sure of succeeding. The only difficulty they labour under is, that technical American knowledge, which requires some time to obtain; it is not easy for those who seldom saw a tree, to conceive how it is to be felled, cut up, and split into rails and posts.

. . . After a foreigner from any part of Europe is arrived, and become a citizen; let him devoutly listen to the voice of our great parent, which says to him, "Welcome to my shores, distressed European; bless the hour in which thou didst see my verdant fields, my fair navigable rivers, and my green mountains!—If thou wilt work, I have bread for thee; if thou wilt be honest, sober and industrious, I have greater rewards to confer on thee—ease and independence. I will give thee fields to feed and clothe thee; a comfortable fire-side to sit by, and tell thy children by what means thou hast prospered; and a decent bed to repose on. I shall endow thee, beside, with the immunities of a freeman. If thou wilt carefully educate thy children, teach them gratitude to God, and reverence to that government, that philanthropic government, which has collected here so many men and made them happy, I will also provide for thy progeny: and to every good man this ought to be the most holy, the most powerful, the most earnest wish he can possibly form, as well as the most consolatory prospect when he dies. Go thou, and work and till; thou shalt prosper, provided thou be just, grateful and industrious."

1782

HENRY ADAMS

1838–1918

» » *From:* HISTORY OF THE UNITED STATES
OF AMERICA « «

THE AMERICAN CHARACTER

Until 1815 nothing in the future of the American Union was regarded as settled. As late as January, 1815, division into several nationalities was still thought to be possible. Such a destiny, repeating the usual experience of history, was not necessarily more unfortunate than the career of a single nationality wholly American; for if the effects of divided nationality were certain to be unhappy, those of a single society with equal certainty defied experience or sound speculation. One uniform and harmonious system appealed to the imagination as a triumph of human progress, offering prospects of peace and ease, contentment and philanthropy, such as the world had not seen; but it invited dangers, formidable because unusual or altogether unknown. The corruption of such a system might prove to be proportionate with its dimensions, and uniformity might lead to evils as serious as were commonly ascribed to diversity.

The laws of human progress were matter not for dogmatic faith, but for study; and although society instinctively regarded small States, with their clashing interests and incessant wars, as the chief obstacle to improvement, such progress as the world knew had been coupled with those drawbacks. The few examples offered by history of great political societies, relieved from external competition or rivalry, were not commonly thought encouraging. War had been the severest test of political and social character, laying bare whatever was feeble, and calling out whatever was strong; and the effect of removing such a test was an untried problem.

In 1815 for the first time Americans ceased to doubt the path they were about to follow. Not only was the unity of their nation established, but its probable divergence from older societies was also well defined. Already in 1817 the difference between Europe and America was decided. In politics the distinction was more evident than in social, religious, literary, or scientific directions; and the result was singular. For a time the aggressions of England and France forced the United States into a path that seemed to lead toward European methods of government; but the popular resistance, or inertia, was so great that the most popular party leaders failed to overcome it, and no sooner did foreign dangers disappear than the system began to revert to American practices; the national government tried to lay aside its assumed powers. When Madison vetoed the bill for internal improvements he could have had no other motive than that of restoring to the government, as far as possible, its original American character.

The result was not easy to understand in theory or to make efficient in practice; but while the drift of public opinion, and still more of practical necessity, drew the government slowly toward the European standard of true political sovereignty, nothing showed that the compromise, which must probably serve the public purpose, was to be European in form or feeling. As far as politics supplied a test, the national character had already diverged from any foreign type. Opinions might differ whether the political movement was progressive or retrograde, but in any case the American, in his political character, was a new variety of man.

The social movement was also decided. The war gave a severe shock to the Anglican sympathies of society, and peace seemed to widen the breach between European and American tastes. Interest in Europe languished after Napoleon's overthrow. France ceased to affect American opinion. England became an object of less alarm. Peace produced in the United States a social and economical revolution which greatly curtailed the influence of New England, and with it the social authority of Great Britain. The invention of the steamboat counterbalanced ocean commerce. The South and West gave to society a character more aggressively American than had been known before. That Europe, within certain limits, might tend toward American ideas was possible, but that America should under any circumstances follow the experiences of European development might thenceforward be reckoned as improbable. American character was formed, if not fixed.

The scientific interest of American history centred in national character, and in the workings of a society destined to become vast, in which individuals were important chiefly as types. Although this kind of interest was different from that of European history, it was at least as important to the world. Should history ever become a true science, it must expect to establish its laws, not from the complicated story of rival European nationalities, but from the economical evolution of a great democracy. North America was the most favorable field on the globe for the spread of a society so large, uniform, and isolated as to answer the purposes of science. There a single homogeneous society could easily attain proportions of three or four hundred million persons, under conditions of undisturbed growth.

In Europe or Asia, except perhaps in China, undisturbed social evolution had been unknown. Without disturbance, evolution seemed to cease. Wherever disturbance occurred, permanence was impossible. Every people in turn adapted itself to the law of necessity. Such a system as that of the United States could hardly have existed for half a century in Europe except under the protection of another power. In the fierce struggle characteristic of European society, systems were permanent in nothing except in the general law, that, whatever other character they might possess, they must always be chiefly military.

The want of permanence was not the only or the most confusing obstacle to the treatment of European history as a science. The intensity of the struggle gave prominence to the individual, until the hero seemed all, society nothing; and what was worse for science, the men were far more interesting than the societies. In the dramatic view of history, the hero deserved more to be studied than the community to which he belonged; in truth, he was the society, which existed only to produce him and to perish with him. Against such a view historians were among the last to protest, and protested but faintly when they did so at all. They felt as strongly as their audiences that the highest achievements were alone worth remembering either in history or in art, and that a reiteration of commonplaces was commonplace. With all the advantages of European movement and color, few historians succeeded in enlivening or dignifying the lack of motive, intelligence. and morality, the helplessness characteristic of many long periods in the face of crushing problems, and the futility of human efforts to escape from difficulties religious, political, and social. In a period extending over four or five thousand years, more or less capable of historical treatment, historians were content to illustrate here and there the most dramatic moments of the most striking communities. The hero was their favorite. War was the chief field of heroic action, and even the history of England was chiefly the story of war.

The history of the United States promised to be free from such disturbances. War counted for little, the hero for less; on the people alone the eye could permanently rest. The steady growth of a vast population without the social distinctions that confused other histories,— without kings, nobles, or armies; without church, traditions, and prejudices,—seemed a subject for the man of science rather than for dramatists or poets. To scientific treatment only one great obstacle existed. Americans, like Europeans, were not disposed to make of their history a mechanical evolution. They felt that they even more than other nations needed the heroic element, because they breathed an atmosphere of peace and industry where heroism could seldom be displayed; and in unconscious protest against their own social conditions they adorned with imaginary qualities scores of supposed leaders, whose only merit was their faculty of reflecting a popular trait. Instinctively they clung to ancient history as though conscious that of all misfortunes that could befall the national character, the greatest would be the loss of the established ideals which alone ennobled human weakness. Without heroes, the national character of the United States had few charms of imagination even to Americans.

Historians and readers maintained Old World standards. No historian cared to hasten the coming of an epoch when man should study his own history in the same spirit and by the same methods with which he studied the formation of a crystal. Yet history had its scientific as well as its human side, and in American history the scientific interest was greater than the human. Elsewhere the student could study under better conditions the evolution of the individual, but nowhere could he study so well the evolution of a race. The interest of such a subject exceeded that of any other branch of science, for it brought mankind within sight of its own end.

Travellers in Switzerland who stepped across the Rhine where it flowed from its glacier could follow its course among mediaeval towns and feudal ruins, until it became a highway for modern industry, and at last arrived at a permanent equilibrium in the ocean. American history followed the same course. With prehistoric glaciers and mediaeval feudalism the story had little to do; but from the moment it came within sight of the ocean it acquired interest almost painful. A child could find his way in a river-valley, and a hoy could float on the waters of Holland; but science alone could sound the depths of the ocean, measure its currents, foretell its storms, or fix its relations to the system of Nature. In a democratic ocean science could see something ultimate. Man could go no further. The atom might move, but the general equilibrium could not change.

Whether the scientific or the heroic view were taken, in either case the starting-point was the same, and the chief object of interest was to define national character. Whether the figures of history were treated as heroes or as types, they must be taken to represent the people. American types were especially worth study if they were to represent the greatest democratic evolution the world could know. Readers might judge for themselves what share the individual possessed in creating or shaping the nation; but whether it was small or great, the nation could be understood only by studying the individual. For that reason, in the story of Jefferson and Madison individuals retained their old interest as types of character, if not as sources of power.

In the American character antipathy to war ranked first among political traits. The majority of Americans regarded war in a peculiar light, the consequence of comparative security. No European nation could have conducted a war, as the people of America conducted the War of 1812. The possibility of doing so without destruction explained the existence of the national trait, and assured its continuance. In politics, the divergence of America from Europe perpetuated itself in the popular instinct for peaceable methods. The Union took shape originally on the general lines that divided the civil from the military elements of the British constitution. The party of Jefferson and Gallatin was founded on dislike of every function of government necessary in a military system. Although Jefferson carried his pacific theories to an extreme, and brought about a military reaction, the reactionary movement was neither universal, violent, nor lasting; and society showed no sign of changing its convictions. With greater strength the country might acquire greater familiarity with warlike methods, but in the same degree was less likely to suffer any general change of habits. Nothing but prolonged intestine contests could convert the population of an entire continent into a race of warriors.

A people whose chief trait was antipathy to war, and to any system organized with military energy, could scarcely develop great results in national administration; yet the Americans prided themselves chiefly on their political capacity. Even the war did not undeceive them, although the incapacity brought into evidence by the war was undisputed, and was most remarkable among the communities which believed themselves to be most gifted with political sagacity. Virginia and Massachusetts by turns admitted failure in dealing with issues so simple that the newest societies, like Tennessee and Ohio, understood them by instinct. That incapacity in national politics should appear as a leading trait in American character was unexpected by Americans, but might naturally result from their conditions. The better test of American character was not political but social, and was to be found not in the government but in the people.

The sixteen years of Jefferson's and Madison's rule furnished international tests of popular intelligence upon which Americans could depend. The ocean was the only open field for competition among nations. Americans enjoyed there no natural or artificial advantages over Englishmen, Frenchmen, or Spaniards; indeed, all these countries possessed navies, resources, and experience greater than were to be found in the United States. Yet the Americans developed, in the course of twenty years, a surprising degree of skill in naval affairs. The evidence of their success was to be found nowhere so complete as in the avowals of Englishmen who knew best the history of naval progress. The American invention of the fast-sailing schooner or clipper was the more remarkable because, of all American inventions, this alone sprang from direct competition with Europe. During ten centuries of struggle the nations of Europe had labored to obtain superiority over each other in ship-construction, yet Americans instantly made improvements which gave them superiority, and which Europeans were unable immediately to imitate even after seeing them. Not only were American vessels better in model, faster in sailing, easier and quicker in handling, and more economical in working than the European, but they were also better equipped. The English complained as a grievance that the Americans adopted new and unwarranted devices in naval warfare; that their vessels were heavier and better constructed, and their missiles of unusual shape and improper use. The Americans resorted to expedients that had not been tried before, and excited a mixture of irritation and respect in the English service, until Yankee smartness became a national misdemeanor.

The English admitted themselves to be slow to change their habits, but the French were both quick and scientific; yet Americans did on the ocean what the French, under stronger inducements, failed to do. The French privateer preyed upon British commerce for twenty years without seriously injuring it; but no sooner did the American privateer sail from French ports, than the rates of insurance doubled in London, and an outcry for protection arose among English shippers which the Admiralty could not calm. The British newspapers were filled with assertions that the American cruiser was the superior of any vessel of its class, and threatened to overthrow England's supremacy on the ocean.

Another test of relative intelligence was furnished by the battles at sea. Instantly after the loss of the "Guerriere" the English discovered and complained that American gunnery was superior to their own. They explained their inferiority by the length of time that had elapsed since their navy had found on the ocean an enemy to fight. Every vestige of hostile fleets had been swept away, until, after the battle of Trafalgar, British frigates ceased practice with their guns. Doubtless the British navy had become somewhat careless in the absence of a dangerous enemy, but Englishmen were themselves aware that some other cause must have affected their losses. Nothing showed that Nelson's line-of-battle ships, frigates, or sloops were as a rule better fought than the "Macedonia" and "Java," the "Avon" and "Reindeer." Sir Howard Douglas, the chief authority on the

subject, attempted in vain to explain British reverses by the deterioration of British gunnery. His analysis showed only that American gunnery was extraordinarily good. Of all vessels, the sloop-of-war,—on account of its smallness, its quick motion, and its more accurate armament of thirty-two-pound carronades,—offered the best test of relative gunnery, and Sir Howard Douglas in commenting upon the destruction of the "Peacock" and "Avon" could only say,—

"In these two actions it is clear that the fire of the British vessels was thrown too high, and that the ordnance of their opponents were expressly and carefully aimed at and took effect chiefly in the hull."

The battle of the "Hornet" and "Penguin" as well as those of the "Reindeer" and "Avon," showed that the excellence of American gunnery continued till the close of the war. Whether at point-blank range or at long-distance practice, the Americans used guns as they had never been used at sea before.

None of the reports of former British victories showed that the British fire had been more destructive at any previous time than in 1812, and no report of any commander since the British navy existed showed so much damage inflicted on an opponent in so short a time as was proved to have been inflicted on themselves by the reports of British commanders in the American war. The strongest proof of American superiority was given by the best British officers, like Broke, who strained every nerve to maintain an equality with American gunnery. So instantaneous and energetic was the effort that, according to the British historian of the war, "a British forty-six-gun frigate of 1813 was half as effective again as a British forty-six-gun frigate of 1812"; and, as he justly said, "the slaughtered crews and the shattered hulks" of the captured British ships proved that no want of their old fighting qualities accounted for their repeated and almost habitual mortifications.

Unwilling as the English were to admit the superior skill of Americans on the ocean, they did not hesitate to admit it, in certain respects, on land. The American rifle in American hands was affirmed to have no equal in the world. This admission could scarcely be withheld after the lists of killed and wounded which followed almost every battle; but the admission served to check a wider inquiry. In truth, the rifle played but a small part in the war. Winchester's men at the river Raisin may have owed their over-confidence, as the British Forty-first owed its losses, to that weapon, and at New Orleans five or six hundred of Coffee's men, who were out of range, were armed with the rifle; but the surprising losses of the British were commonly due to artillery and musketry fire. At New Orleans the artillery was chiefly engaged. The artillery battle of January 1, according to British accounts, amply proved the superiority of American gunnery on that occasion, which was probably the fairest test during the war. The battle of January 8 was also chiefly an artillery battle; the main British column never arrived within fair musket range; Pakenham was killed by a grapeshot, and the main column of his troops halted more than one hundred yards from the parapet.

The best test of British and American military qualities, both for men and weapons, was Scott's battle of Chippewa. Nothing intervened to throw a doubt over the fairness of the trial. Two parallel lines of regular soldiers, practically equal in numbers, armed with similar weapons, moved in close order toward each other, across a wide open plain, without cover or advantage of position, stopping at intervals to load and fire, until one line broke and retired. At the same time two three-gun batteries, the British being the heavier, maintained a steady fire from positions opposite each other. According to the reports, the two infantry lines in the centre never came nearer than eighty yards. Major-General Riall reported that then, owing to severe losses, his troops broke and could not be rallied. Comparison of the official reports showed that the British lost in killed and wounded four hundred and sixty-nine men; the Americans, two hundred and ninety-six. Some doubts always affect the returns of wounded, because the severity of the wound cannot be known; but dead men tell their own tale. Riall reported one hundred and forty-eight killed; Scott reported sixty-one. The severity of the losses showed that the battle was sharply contested, and proved the personal bravery of both armies. Marksmanship decided the result, and the returns proved that the American fire was superior to that of the British in the proportion of more than fifty per cent if estimated by the entire loss, and of two hundred and forty-two to one hundred if estimated by the deaths alone.

The conclusion seemed incredible, but it was supported by the results of the naval battles.

The Americans showed superiority amounting in some cases to twice the efficiency of their enemies in the use of weapons. The best French critic of the naval war, Jurien de la Gravière, said: "An enormous superiority in the rapidity and precision of their fire can alone explain the difference in the losses sustained by the combatants." So far from denying this conclusion the British press constantly alleged it, and the British officers complained of it. The discovery caused great surprise, and in both British services much attention was at once directed to improvement in artillery and musketry. Nothing could exceed the frankness with which Englishmen avowed their inferiority. According to Sir Francis Head, "gunnery was in naval warfare in the extraordinary state of ignorance we have just described, when our lean children, the American people, taught us, rod in hand, our first lesson in the art." The English textbook on Naval Gunnery, written by Major-General Sir Howard Douglas immediately after the peace, devoted more attention to the short American war than to all the battles of Napoleon, and began by admitting that Great Britain had "entered with too great confidence on war with a marine much more expert than that of any of our European enemies." The admission appeared "objectionable" even to the author; but he did not add, what was equally true, that it applied as well to the land as to the sea service.

No one questioned the bravery of the British forces, or the ease with which they often routed larger bodies of militia; but the losses they inflicted were rarely as great as those they suffered. Even at Bladensburg, where they met little resistance, their loss was several times greater than that of the Americans. At Plattsburg, where the intelligence and quickness of Macdonough and his men alone won the victory, his ships were in effect stationary batteries, and enjoyed the same superiority in gunnery. "The 'Saratoga,'" said his official report, "had fifty-five round-shot in her hull; the 'Confiance,' one hundred and five. The enemy's shot passed principally just over our heads, as there were not twenty whole hammocks in the nettings at the close of the action."

The greater skill of the Americans was not due to special training, for the British service was better trained in gunnery, as in everything else, than the motley armies and fleets that fought at New Orleans and on the Lakes. Critics constantly said that every American had learned from his childhood the use of the rifle, but he certainly had not learned to use the cannon in shooting birds or hunting deer, and he knew less than the Englishman about the handling of artillery and muskets. As if to add unnecessary evidence, the battle of Chrysler's Farm proved only too well that this American efficiency was not confined to citizens of the United States.

Another significant result of the war was the sudden development of scientific engineering in the United States. This branch of the military service owed its efficiency and almost its existence to the military school at West Point, established in 1802. The school was at first much neglected by the government. The number of graduates before the year 1812 was very small; but at the outbreak of the war the corps of engineers was already efficient. Its chief was Colonel Joseph Gardner Swift, of Massachusetts, the first graduate of the academy: Colonel Swift planned the defences of New York harbor. The lieutenant-colonel in 1812 was Walker Keith Armistead, of Virginia,—the third graduate, who planned the defences of Norfolk. Major William McRee, of North Carolina, became chief engineer to General Brown, and constructed the fortifications at Fort Erie, which cost the British General Gordon Drummond the loss of half his army, besides the mortification of defeat. Captain Eleazer Derby Wood, of New York, constructed Fort Meigs, which enabled Harrison to defeat the attack of Proctor in May, 1813. Captain Joseph Gilbert Totten, of New York, was chief engineer to General Izard at Plattsburg, where he directed the fortifications that stopped the advance of Prevost's great army. None of the works constructed by a graduate of West Point was captured by the enemy; and had an engineer been employed at Washington by Armstrong and Winder, the city would have been easily saved.

Perhaps without exaggeration the West Point Academy might be said to have decided, next to the navy, the result of the war. The works at New Orleans were simple in character, and as far as they were due to engineering skill were directed by Major Latour, a Frenchman; but the war was already ended when the battle of New Orleans was fought. During the critical campaign of 1814, the West Point engineers doubled the capacity of the little American army for resistance, and introduced a new and scientific character into American life.

In the application of science the steamboat was the most striking success; but Fulton's invention, however useful, was neither the most original nor the most ingenious of American efforts, nor did it offer the best example of popular characteristics. Perhaps Fulton's torpedo and Stevens's screw-propeller showed more originality than was proved by the "Clermont." The fast-sailing schooner with its pivot-gun—an invention that grew out of the common stock of nautical intelligence—best illustrated the character of the people.

That the individual should rise to a higher order either of intelligence or morality than had existed in former ages was not to be expected, for the United States offered less field for the development of individuality than had been offered by older and smaller societies. The chief function of the American Union was to raise the average standard of popular intelligence and well-being, and at the close of the War of 1812 the superior average intelligence of Americans was so far admitted that Yankee acuteness, or smartness, became a national reproach; but much doubt remained whether the intelligence belonged to a high order, or proved a high morality. From the earliest ages, shrewdness was associated with unscrupulousness; and Americans were freely charged with wanting honesty. The charge could neither be proved nor disproved. American morality was such as suited a people so endowed, and was high when compared with the morality of many older societies; but, like American intelligence, it discouraged excess. Probably the political morality shown by the government and by public men during the first sixteen years of the century offered a fair gauge of social morality. Like the character of the popular inventions, the character of the morals corresponded to the wants of a growing democratic society; but time alone could decide whether it would result in a high or a low national ideal.

Finer analysis showed other signs of divergence from ordinary standards. If Englishmen took pride in one trait more than in another, it was in the steady uniformity of their progress. The innovating and revolutionary quality of the French mind irritated them. America showed an un-English rapidity in movement. In politics, the American people between 1787 and 1817 accepted greater changes than had been known in England since 1688. In religion, the Unitarian movement of Boston and Harvard College would never have been possible in England, where the defection of Oxford or

Cambridge, and the best educated society in the United Kingdom, would have shaken Church and State to their foundations. In literature the American school was chiefly remarkable for the rapidity with which it matured. The first book of Irving was a successful burlesque of his own ancestral history; the first poem of Bryant sang of the earth only as a universal tomb; the first preaching of Channing assumed to overthrow the Trinity; and the first paintings of Allston aspired to recover the ideal perfection of Raphael and Titian. In all these directions the American mind showed tendencies that surprised Englishmen more than they struck Americans. Allston defended himself from the criticism of friends who made complaint of his return to America. He found there, as he maintained, not only a growing taste for art, but "a quicker appreciation" of artistic effort than in any European land. If the highest intelligence of American society were to move with such rapidity, the time could not be far distant when it would pass into regions which England never liked to contemplate.

Another intellectual trait, as has been already noticed, was the disposition to relax severity. Between the theology of Jonathan Edwards and that of William Ellery Channing was an enormous gap, not only in doctrines but also in methods. Whatever might be thought of the conclusions reached by Edwards and Hopkins, the force of their reasoning commanded respect. Not often had a more strenuous effort than theirs been made to ascertain God's will, and to follow it without regard to weaknesses of the flesh. The idea that the nature of God's attributes was to be preached only as subordinate to the improvement of man, agreed little with the spirit of their religion. The Unitarian and Universalist movements marked the beginning of an epoch when ethical and humanitarian ideas took the place of metaphysics, and even New England turned from contemplating the omnipotence of the Deity in order to praise the perfections of his creatures.

The spread of great popular sects like the Universalists and Campbellites, founded on assumptions such as no orthodox theology could tolerate, showed a growing tendency to relaxation of thought in that direction. The struggle for existence was already mitigated, and the first effect of the change was seen in the increasing cheerfulness of religion. Only when men found their actual world almost a heaven, could they lose overpowering anxiety about the world to come. Life had taken a softer aspect, and as a consequence God was no longer terrible. Even the wicked became less mischievous in an atmosphere where virtue was easier than vice. Punishments seemed mild in a society where every offender could cast off his past, and create a new career. For the first time in history, great bodies of men turned away from their old religion, giving no better reason than that it required them to believe in a cruel Deity, and rejected necessary conclusions of theology because they were inconsistent with human self-esteem.

The same optimism marked the political movement. Society was weary of strife, and settled gladly into a political system which left every disputed point undetermined. The public seemed obstinate only in believing that all was for the best, as far as the United States were concerned, in the affairs of mankind. The contrast was great between this temper of mind and that in which the Constitution had been framed; but it was no greater than the contrast in the religious opinions of the two periods, while the same reaction against severity marked the new literature. The rapid accumulation of wealth and increase in physical comfort told the same story from the standpoint of economy. On every side society showed that ease was for a time to take the place of severity, and enjoyment was to have its full share in the future national existence.

The traits of intelligence, rapidity, and mildness seemed fixed in the national character as early as 1817, and were likely to become more marked as time should pass. A vast amount of conservatism still lingered among the people; but the future spirit of society could hardly fail to be intelligent, rapid in movement, and mild in method. Only in the distant future could serious change occur, and even then no return to European characteristics seemed likely. The American continent was happier in its conditions and easier in its resources than the regions of Europe and Asia, where Nature revelled in diversity and conflict. If at any time American character should change, it might as probably become sluggish as revert to the violence and extravagances of Old World development. The inertia of several hundred million people, all formed in a similar social mould, was as likely to stifle energy as to stimulate evolution.

With the establishment of these conclusions, a new episode in American history began in 1815. New subjects demanded new treatment, no longer dramatic but steadily tending to becoming scientific. The traits of American character were fixed; the rate of physical and economical growth was established; and history, certain that at a given distance of time the Union would contain so many millions of people, with wealth valued at so many millions of dollars, became thenceforward chiefly concerned to know what kind of people these millions were to be. They were intelligent, but what paths would their intelligence select? They were quick, but what solution of insoluble problems would quickness hurry? They were scientific, and what control would their science exercise over their destiny? They were mild, but what corruptions would their relaxations bring? They were peaceful, but by what machinery were their corruptions to be purged?

1890

GEORGE SANTAYANA

1863–1952

» » *From:* CHARACTER AND OPINION
IN THE UNITED STATES « «

MATERIALISM AND IDEALISM
IN THE UNITED STATES

The language and traditions common to England and America are like other family bonds: they draw kindred together at the greater crises in life, but they also occasion at times a little friction and faultfinding. The groundwork of the two societies is so similar, that each nation, feeling almost at home with the other, and almost able to understand its speech, may instinctively resent what hinders it from feeling at home altogether. Differences will tend to seem anomalies that have slipped in by mistake and through somebody's fault. Each will judge the other by his own standards, not feeling, as in the presence of complete foreigners, that he must make an effort of imagination and put himself in another man's shoes.

In matters of morals, manners, and art, the danger of comparisons is not merely that they may prove invidious, by ranging qualities in an order of merit which might wound somebody's vanity; the danger is rather that comparisons may distort comprehension, because in truth good qualities are all different in kind, and free lives are different in spirit. Comparison is the expedient of those who cannot reach the heart of the things compared; and no philosophy is more external and egotistical than that which places the essence of a thing in its relation to something else. In reality, at the centre of every natural being there is something individual and incommensurable, a seed with its native impulses and aspirations, shaping themselves as best they can in their given environment. Variation is a consequence of freedom, and the slight but radical diversity of souls in turn makes freedom requisite. Instead of instituting in his mind any comparisons between the United States and other nations, I would accordingly urge the reader to forget himself and, in so far as such a thing may be possible for him or for me, to transport himself ideally with me into the outer circumstances of American life, the better to feel its inner temper, and to see how inevitably the American shapes his feelings and judgments, honestly reporting all things as they appear from his new and unobstructed station.

I speak of the American in the singular, as if there were not millions of them, north and south, east and west, of both sexes, of all ages, and of various races, professions, and religions. Of course the one American I speak of is mythical; but to speak in parables is inevitable in such a subject, and it is perhaps as well to do so frankly. There is a sort of poetic ineptitude in all human discourse when it tries to deal with natural and existing things. Practical men may not notice it, but in fact human discourse is intrinsically addressed not to natural existing things but to ideal essences, poetic or logical terms which thought may define and play with. When fortune or necessity diverts our attention from this congenial ideal sport to crude facts and pressing issues, we turn our frail poetic ideas into symbols for those terrible irruptive things. In that paper money of our own stamping, the legal tender of the mind, we are obliged to reckon all the movements and values of the world. The universal American I speak of is one of these symbols; and I should be still speaking in symbols and creating moral units and a false simplicity, if I spoke of classes pedantically subdivided, or individuals ideally integrated and defined. As it happens, the symbolic American can be made largely adequate to the facts; because, if there are immense differences between individual Americans—for some Americans are black—yet there is a great uniformity in their environment, customs, temper, and thoughts. They have all been uprooted from their several soils and ancestries and plunged together into one vortex, whirling irresistibly in a space otherwise quite empty. To be an American is of itself almost a moral condition, an education, and a career. Hence a single ideal figment can cover a large part of what each American is in his character, and almost the whole of what most Americans are in their social outlook and political judgements.

The discovery of the new world exercised a sort of selection among the inhabitants of Europe. All the colonists, except the Negroes, were voluntary exiles. The fortunate, the deeply rooted, and the lazy remained at home; the wilder instincts or dissatisfaction of others tempted them beyond the horizon. The American is accordingly the most adventurous, or the descendant of the most adventurous, of Europeans. It is in his blood to be socially a radical, though perhaps not intellectually. What has existed in the past, especially in the remote past, seems to him not only not authoritative, but irrelevant, inferior, and outworn. He finds it rather a sorry waste of time to think about the past at all. But his enthusiasm for the future is profound; he can conceive of no more decisive way of recommending an opinion or a practice than to say that it is what everybody is coming to adopt. This expectation of what he approves, or approval of what he expects, makes up his optimism. It is the necessary faith of the pioneer.

Such a temperament is, of course, not maintained in the nation merely by inheritance. Inheritance notoriously tends to restore the average of a race, and plays incidentally many a trick of atavism. What maintains this temperament and makes it national is social contagion

or pressure—something immensely strong in democracies. The luckless American who is born a conservative, or who is drawn to poetic subtlety, pious retreats, or gay passions, nevertheless has the categorical excellence of work, growth, enterprise, reform, and prosperity dinned into his ears: every door is open in this direction and shut in the other; so that he either folds up his heart and withers in a corner —in remote places you sometimes find such a solitary gaunt idealist—or else he flies to Oxford or Florence or Montmartre to save his soul —or perhaps not to save it.

The optimism of the pioneer is not limited to his view of himself and his own future: it starts from that; but feeling assured, safe, and cheery within, he looks with smiling and most kindly eyes on everything and everybody about him. Individualism, roughness, and self-trust are supposed to go with selfishness and a cold heart; but I suspect that is a prejudice. It is rather dependence, insecurity, and mutual jostling that poison our placid gregarious brotherhood; and fanciful passionate demands upon people's affections, when they are disappointed, as they soon must be, breed ill-will and a final meanness. The milk of human kindness is less apt to turn sour if the vessel that holds it stands steady, cool, and separate, and is not too often uncorked. In his affections the American is seldom passionate, often deep, and always kindly. If it were given me to look into the depths of a man's heart, and I did not find goodwill at the bottom, I should say without any hesitation, You are not an American. But as the American is an individualist his goodwill is not officious. His instinct is to think well of everybody, and to wish everybody well, but in a spirit of rough comradeship, expecting every man to stand on his own legs and to be helpful in his turn. When he has given his neighbour a chance he thinks he has done enough for him; but he feels it is an absolute duty to do that. It will take some hammering to drive a coddling socialism into America.

As self-trust may pass into self-sufficiency, so optimism, kindness, and goodwill may grow into a habit of doting on everything. To the good American many subjects are sacred: sex is sacred, women are sacred, children are sacred, business is sacred, America is sacred, Masonic lodges and college clubs are sacred. This feeling grows out of the good opinion he wishes to have of these things, and serves to maintain it. If he did not regard all these things as sacred he might come to doubt sometimes if they were wholly good. Of this kind, too, is the idealism of single ladies in reduced circumstances who can see the soul of beauty in ugly things, and are perfectly happy because their old dog has such pathetic eyes, their minister is so eloquent, their garden with its three sunflowers is so pleasant, their dead friends were so devoted, and their distant relations are so rich.

10 Consider now the great emptiness of America: not merely the primitive physical emptiness, surviving in some regions, and the continental spacing of the chief natural features, but also the moral emptiness of a settlement where men and even houses are easily moved about, and no one, almost, lives where he was born or believes what he has been taught. Not that the American has jettisoned these impedimenta in anger; they have simply slipped from him as

20 he moves. Great empty spaces bring a sort of freedom to both soul and body. You may pitch your tent where you will; or if ever you decide to build anything, it can be in a style of your own devising. You have room, fresh materials, few models, and no critics. You trust your own experience, not only because you must, but because you find you may do so safely and prosperously; the forces that determine fortune are not yet too complicated for one man to explore.

30 Your detachable condition makes you lavish with money and cheerfully experimental; you lose little if you lose all, since you remain completely yourself. At the same time your absolute initiative gives you practice in coping with novel situations, and in being original; it teaches you shrewd management. Your life and mind will become dry and direct, with few decorative flourishes. In your works everything will be stark and pragmatic; you will not un-

40 derstand why anybody should make those little sacrifices to instinct or custom which we call grace. The fine arts will seem to you academic luxuries, fit to amuse the ladies, like Greek and Sanskrit; for while you will perfectly appreciate generosity in men's purposes, you will not admit that the execution of these purposes can be anything but business. Unfortunately the essence of the fine arts is that the execution should be generous too, and delightful in itself;

50 therefore the fine arts will suffer, not so much in their express professional pursuit—for then they become practical tasks and a kind of business—as in that diffused charm which qualifies all human action when men are artists by nature. Elaboration, which is something to ac-

complish, will be preferred to simplicity, which is something to rest in; manners will suffer somewhat; speech will suffer horribly. For the American the urgency of his novel attack upon matter, his zeal in gathering its fruits, precludes meanderings in primrose paths; devices must be short cuts, and symbols must be mere symbols. If his wife wants luxuries, of course she may have them; and if he has vices, that can be provided for too; but they must all be set down under those headings in his ledgers.

At the same time, the American is imaginative; for where life is intense, imagination is intense also. Were he not imaginative he would not live so much in the future. But his imagination is practical, and the future it forecasts is immediate; it works with the clearest and least ambiguous terms known to his experience, in terms of number, measure, contrivance, economy, and speed. He is an idealist working on matter. Understanding as he does the material potentialities of things, he is successful in invention, conservative in reform, and quick in emergencies. All his life he jumps into the train after it has started and jumps out before it has stopped; and he never once gets left behind, or breaks a leg. There is an enthusiasm in his sympathetic handling of material forces which goes far to cancel the illiberal character which it might otherwise assume. The good workman hardly distinguishes his artistic intention from the potency in himself and in things which are about to realise that intention. Accordingly his ideals fall into the form of premonitions and prophecies; and his studious prophecies often come true. So do the happy workmanlike ideals of the American. When a poor boy, perhaps, he dreams of an education, and presently he gets an education, or at least a degree; he dreams of growing rich, and he grows rich— only more slowly and modestly, perhaps, than he expected; he dreams of marrying his Rebecca and, even if he marries a Leah instead, he ultimately finds in Leah his Rebecca after all. He dreams of helping to carry on and to accelerate the movement of a vast, seething, progressive society, and he actually does so. Ideals clinging so close to nature are almost sure of fulfilment; the American beams with a certain self-confidence and sense of mastery; he feels that God and nature are working with him.

Idealism in the American accordingly goes hand in hand with present contentment and with foresight of what the future very likely will actually bring. He is not a revolutionist; he believes he is already on the right track and moving towards an excellent destiny. In revolutionists, on the contrary, idealism is founded on dissatisfaction and expresses it. What exists seems to them an absurd jumble of irrational accidents and bad habits, and they want the future to be based on reason and to be the pellucid embodiment of all their maxims. All their zeal is for something radically different from the actual and (if they only knew it) from the possible; it is ideally simple, and they love it and believe in it because their nature craves it. They think life would be set free by the destruction of all its organs. They are therefore extreme idealists in the region of hope, but not at all, as poets and artists are, in the region of perception and memory. In the atmosphere of civilised life they miss all the refraction and all the fragrance; so that in their conception of actual things they are apt to be crude realists; and their ignorance and inexperience of the moral world, unless it comes of ill-luck, indicates their incapacity for education. Now incapacity for education, when united with great inner vitality, is one root of idealism. It is what condemns us all, in the region of sense, to substitute perpetually what we are capable of imagining for what things may be in themselves; it is what condemns us, wherever it extends, to think *a priori;* it is what keeps us bravely and incorrigibly pursuing what we call the good—that is, what would fulfil the demands of our nature—however little provision the fates may have made for it. But the want of insight on the part of revolutionists touching the past and the present infects in an important particular their idealism about the future; it renders their dreams of the future unrealisable. For in human beings—this may not be true of other animals, more perfectly preformed—experience is necessary to pertinent and concrete thinking; even our primitive instincts are blind until they stumble upon some occasion that solicits them; and they can be much transformed or deranged by their first partial satisfactions. Therefore a man who does not idealise his experience, but idealises *a priori*, is incapable of true prophecy; when he dreams he raves, and the more he criticises the less he helps. American idealism, on the contrary, is nothing if not helpful, nothing if not pertinent to practicable transformations; and when the American frets, it is because whatever is useless and impertinent, be it idealism or inertia, irri-

tates him; for it frustrates the good results which he sees might so easily have been obtained.

The American is wonderfully alive; and his vitality, not having often found a suitable outlet, makes him appear agitated on the surface; he is always letting off an unnecessarily loud blast of incidental steam. Yet his vitality is not superficial; it is inwardly prompted, and as sensitive and quick as a magnetic needle. He is inquisitive, and ready with an answer to any question that he may put to himself of his own accord; but if you try to pour instruction into him, on matters that do not touch his own spontaneous life, he shows the most extraordinary powers of resistance and oblivescence; so that he often is remarkably expert in some directions and surprisingly obtuse in others. He seems to bear lightly the sorrowful burden of human knowledge. In a word, he is young.

What sense is there in this feeling, which we all have, that the American is young? His country is blessed with as many elderly people as any other, and his descent from Adam, or from the Darwinian rival of Adam, cannot be shorter than that of his European cousins. Nor are his ideas always very fresh. Trite and rigid bits of morality and religion, with much seemly and antique political lore, remain axiomatic in him, as in the mind of a child; he may carry all this about with an unquestioning familiarity which does not comport understanding. To keep traditional sentiments in this way insulated and uncriticised is itself a sign of youth. A good young man is naturally conservative and loyal on all those subjects which his experience has not brought to a test; advanced opinions on politics, marriage, or literature are comparatively rare in America; they are left for the ladies to discuss, and usually to condemn, while the men get on with their work. In spite of what is old-fashioned in his more general ideas, the American is unmistakably young; and this, I should say, for two reasons: one, that he is chiefly occupied with his immediate environment, and the other, that his reactions upon it are inwardly prompted, spontaneous, and full of vivacity and self-trust. His views are not yet lengthened; his will is not yet broken or transformed. The present moment, however, in this, as in other things, may mark a great change in him; he is perhaps now reaching his majority, and all I say may hardly apply today, and may not apply at all tomorrow. I speak of him as I have known him; and whatever moral strength may accrue to him later, I am not sorry to have known him in his youth. The charm of youth, even when it is a little boisterous, lies in nearness to the impulses of nature, in a quicker and more obvious obedience to that pure, seminal principle which, having formed the body and its organs, always directs their movements, unless it is forced by vice or necessity to make them crooked, or to suspend them. Even under the inevitable crust of age the soul remains young, and, wherever it is able to break through, sprouts into something green and tender. We are all as young at heart as the most youthful American, but the seed in his case has fallen upon virgin soil, where it may spring up more bravely and with less respect for the giants of the wood. Peoples seem older when their perennial natural youth is encumbered with more possessions and pre-possessions, and they are mindful of the many things they have lost or missed. The American is not mindful of them. . . .

The circumstances of his life hitherto have necessarily driven the American into moral materialism; for in his dealings with material things he can hardly stop to enjoy their sensible aspects, which are ideal, nor proceed at once to their ultimate uses, which are ideal too. He is practical as against the poet, and worldly as against the clear philosopher or the saint. The most striking expression of this materialism is usually supposed to be his love of the almighty dollar; but that is a foreign and unintelligent view. The American talks about money, because that is the symbol and measure he has at hand for success, intelligence, and power; but as to money itself he makes, loses, spends, and gives it away with a very light heart. To my mind the most striking expression of his materialism is his singular preoccupation with quantity. If, for instance, you visit Niagara Falls, you may expect to hear how many cubic feet or metric tons of water are precipitated per second over the cataract; how many cities and towns (with the number of their inhabitants) derive light and motive power from it; and the annual value of the further industries that might very well be carried on by the same means, without visibly depleting the world's greatest wonder or injuring the tourist trade. That is what I confidently expected to hear on arriving at the adjoining town of Buffalo; but I was deceived. The first thing I heard instead was that there are more miles of asphalt pavement in Buffalo than in any city in the world.

Nor is this insistence on quantity confined to men of business. The President of Harvard College, seeing me once by chance soon after the beginning of a term, inquired how my classes were getting on; and when I replied that I thought they were getting on well, that my men seemed to be keen and intelligent, he stopped me as if I was about to waste his time. "I meant," said he, "*what is the number* of students in your classes."

Here I think we may perceive that this love of quantity often has a silent partner, which is diffidence as to quality. The democratic conscience recoils before anything that savours of privilege; and lest it should concede an unmerited privilege to any pursuit or person, it reduces all things as far as possible to the common denominator of quantity. Numbers cannot lie: but if it came to comparing the ideal beauties of philosophy with those of Anglo-Saxon, who should decide? All studies are good—why else have universities?—but those must be most encouraged which attract the greatest number of students. Hence the President's question. Democratic faith, in its diffidence about quality, throws the reins of education upon the pupil's neck, as Don Quixote threw the reins on the neck of Rocinante, and bids his divine instinct choose its own way.

The American has never yet had to face the trials of Job. Great crises, like the Civil War, he has known how to surmount victoriously; and now that he has surmounted a second great crisis victoriously, it is possible that he may relapse, as he did in the other case, into an apparently complete absorption in material enterprise and prosperity. But if serious and irremediable tribulation ever overtook him, what would his attitude be? It is then that we should be able to discover whether materialism or idealism lies at the base of his character. Meantime his working mind is not without its holiday. He spreads humour pretty thick and even over the surface of conversation, and humour is one form of moral emancipation. He loves landscape, he loves mankind, and he loves knowledge; and in music at least he finds an art which he unfeignedly enjoys. In music and landscape, in humour and kindness, he touches the ideal more truly, perhaps, than in his ponderous academic idealisms and busy religions; for it is astonishing how much even religion in America (can it possibly be so in England?) is a matter of meetings, building-funds, schools, charities, clubs, and picnics. To be poor in order to be simple, to produce less in order that the product may be more choice and beautiful, and may leave us less burdened with unnecessary duties and useless possessions —that is an ideal not articulate in the American mind; yet here and there I seem to have heard a sigh after it, a groan at the perpetual incubus of business and shrill society. Significant witness to such aspirations is borne by those new forms of popular religion, not mere variations on tradition, which have sprung up from the soil—revivalism, spiritualism, Christian Science, the New Thought. Whether or no we can tap, through these or other channels, some cosmic or inner energy not hitherto at the disposal of man (and there is nothing incredible in that), we certainly may try to remove friction and waste in the mere process of living; we may relax morbid strains, loosen suppressed instincts, iron out the creases of the soul, discipline ourselves into simplicity, sweetness, and peace. These religious movements are efforts toward such physiological economy and hygiene; and while they are thoroughly plebeian, with no great lights, and no idea of raising men from the most vulgar and humdrum worldly existence, yet they see the possibility of physical and moral health on that common plane, and pursue it. That is true morality. The dignities of various types of life or mind, like the gifts of various animals, are relative. The snob adores one type only, and the creatures supposed by him to illustrate it perfectly; or envies and hates them, which is just as snobbish. Veritable lovers of life, on the contrary, like Saint Francis or like Dickens, know that in every tenement of clay, with no matter what endowment or station, happiness and perfection are possible to the soul. There must be no brow-beating, with shouts of work or progress or revolution, any more than with threats of hell-fire. What does it profit a man to free the whole world if his soul is not free? Moral freedom is not an artificial condition, because the ideal is the mother tongue of both the heart and the senses. All that is requisite is that we should pause in living to enjoy life, and should lift up our hearts to things that are pure goods in themselves, so that once to have found and loved them, whatever else may betide, may remain a happiness that nothing can sully. This natural idealism does not imply that we are immaterial, but only that we are animate and truly alive. When the senses are sharp, as they are in the American, they are already half liberated, already a joy in themselves; and when the heart is warm, like his, and eager to be just, its ideal destiny can hardly be doubtful. It will not be always merely pumping and working; time and its own pulses will lend it wings.

1920

» » *Supplementary Reading List* « «

THE FOLLOWING reading list does not pretend to be an exhaustive compilation of all the worthwhile books about American Literature. It is strictly a supplementary listing, aimed at the student who is interested in reading more deeply in some general areas of scholarly investigation. The student interested in a more thorough study of particular aspects of American Literature should consult the *Literary History of the United States*, ed. R. E. Spiller, *et al.*, New York, 1948, especially Vol. III, *Bibliography*, and the *Bibliography Supplement* to the above, ed. R. M. Ludwig, New York, 1960.

Beer, Thomas, *The Mauve Decade, American Life at the End of the Nineteenth Century*, New York (1926), 1937.
Bewley, Marius, *The Eccentric Design*, New York, 1959.
Boas, R. P., *Social Backgrounds of American Literature*, Boston, 1933.
Bogan, Louise, *Achievement in American Poetry, 1900–1950*, Chicago, 1951.
Bowers, D. F., ed., *Foreign Influences in American Life: Essays and Critical Bibliographies*, New York (1944), 1952.
Bradbury, J. M., *The Fugitives; A Critical Account*, Chapel Hill, 1958.
Brooks, Van Wyck, *The Confident Years: 1885–1915*, New York, 1952.
———, *America's Coming-of-Age*, New York, 1915.
———, *The Flowering of New England, 1815–1865*, New York, 1936.
———, *New England: Indian Summer, 1865–1915*, New York, 1940.
Chase, Richard, *The American Novel and Its Tradition*, New York, 1957.
Cowie, Alexander, *The Rise of the American Novel*, New York, 1948.
Cowley, Malcolm, *After the Genteel Tradition; American Writers Since 1910*, New York, 1937.
———, *Exile's Return; A Literary Odyssey of the 1920's*, New York (1934), 1951.
———, *The Literary Situation*, New York, 1954.
Cunliffe, Marcus, *The Literature of the United States*, Baltimore, 1954.
Downer, A. S., *Fifty Years of American Drama, 1900–1950*, Chicago, 1951.
Feidelson, Charles, *Symbolism and American Literature*, Chicago, 1953.
Fiedler, Leslie, *Love and Death in the American Novel*, New York, 1960.
Frohock, W. M., *The Novel of Violence in America: 1920–1950*, Dallas, 1950.
Gelfant, B. H., *The American City Novel*, Norman, Oklahoma, 1954.
Granger, B. I., *Political Satire in the American Revolution, 1763–1783*, Ithaca, New York, 1960.
Gregory, Horace, and Zaturenska, Marya, *A History of American Poetry, 1900–1940*, New York, 1942.
Hart, J. D., *The Popular Book: A History of America's Literary Taste*, New York, 1950.
Hicks, Granville, *The Great Tradition: An Interpretation of American Literature Since the Civil War*, New York, 1935.
Hoffman, F. J., *Freudianism and the Literary Mind*, Baton Rouge, La., 1957.
Hoffman, F. J., Allen, Charles and Ulrich, Carolyn F., *The Little Magazine; A History and a Bibliography*, Princeton, 1946.
Howard, Leon, *Literature and the American Tradition*, New York, 1960.
Hubbell, Jay B., *The South in American Literature, 1607–1900*, Durham, N. C., 1954.

Hughes, Glenn, *Imagism and the Imagists: A Study in Modern Poetry*, Stanford, California, 1931.

Jones, H. M., *The Theory of American Literature*, Ithaca, New York, 1948.

Kazin, Alfred, *On Native Grounds*, New York (1942), 1956.

Krutch, J. W., *The American Drama Since 1918; An Informal History*, New York (1939), 1957.

Lawrence, D. H., *Studies in Classic American Literature*, New York, 1923.

Levin, Harry, *The Power of Blackness: Hawthorne, Poe, Melville*, New York, 1958.

Lewis, R. W. B., *The American Adam; Innocence, Tragedy, and Tradition in the Nineteenth Century*, Chicago, 1955.

Lynn, Kenneth, *The Dream of Success; A Study of the Modern American Imagination*, Boston, 1955.

Matthiessen, F. O., *American Renaissance; Art and Expression in the Age of Emerson and Whitman*, London and New York (1941), 1954.

May, H. F., *The End of American Innocence: A Study of the First Years of Our Own Time, 1912–1917*, New York, 1959.

Miller, Perry, *Errand Into the Wilderness*, Cambridge, Mass., 1956.

——, *The New England Mind: From Colony to Province*, Cambridge, 1953.

——, *The New England Mind: The Seventeenth Century*, New York, 1939.

——, *The Raven and the Whale: The War of Words and Wits in the Era of Poe and Melville*, New York, 1956.

Murdock, Kenneth B., *Literature & Theology in Colonial New England*, Cambridge, Mass., 1949.

Parrington, V. L., *Main Currents in American Thought*, 3 volumes, New York, 1927–1930.

Pattee, F. L., *The Development of the American Short Story*, New York, 1923.

Persons, Stow, ed., *Evolutionary Thought in America*, New Haven, 1950.

Persons, Stow and Egbert, D. D., eds., *Socialism and American Life*, 2 volumes, Princeton, 1952.

Pritchard, J. P., *Criticism in America*, Norman, Oklahoma, 1956.

Quinn, A. H., *A History of the American Drama, From the Beginning to the Civil War*, New York (1923), 1943.

Rideout, W. D., *The Radical Novel in the United States, 1900–1954*, Cambridge, Mass., 1957.

Rourke, Constance, *American Humor: A Study of the National Character*, New York, 1935.

Smith, H. N., *Virgin Land; The American West as Symbol and Myth*, Cambridge, Mass., 1950.

Smith, J. W. and Jamison, Leland, eds., *Religion in American Life*, 4 vols., Princeton, 1961–1962.

Spiller, R. E., *The Cycle of American Literature; An Essay in Historical Criticism*, New York, 1955.

Taylor, W. F., *The Economic Novel in America, 1870–1900*, Chapel Hill, N. C., 1942.

Thorp, Willard, *American Writing in the Twentieth Century*, Cambridge, Mass., 1960.

Van Doren, Carl, *The American Novel, 1789–1939*, New York, 1940.

Wagenknecht, Edward, *Cavalcade of the American Novel*, New York, 1952.

Walcutt, C. C., *American Literary Naturalism, A Divided Stream*, Minneapolis, 1956.

Warfel, H. R., *American Novelists of Today*, New York, 1951.

Winters, Yvor, *Maule's Curse: Seven Studies in the History of American Obscurantism*, Norfolk, Conn., 1938.

» » *Index* « «

» »　　« «

INDEX